CONTENTS

How to Read a Map — i	**Traveling with Pets** — xii
Interstate Directory — iv	**USA Map** — xvii
Road and Weather Conditions — vi	**Driving Distances Between Major U. S. Cities** — xviii
Area Codes by State — vii	**Focus on Festivals** — xvi
Useful Telephone Numbers — vii	**Low Clearances** — xxiv
State Towing Laws — viii	

HOW TO READ A MAP

Map Legend

- **311** - Exit Number
- **W-294** - Rest Area/Parking Area/Welcome Center/Service Plaza
- - Inspection Station/Weigh Station

Rest Area Westbound mile marker 294

Rest Area Both Directions mile marker 336

Inspection Station Mile marker 329 (see listings)

Black and white interstate shield for crossing interstates

Color interstate shield for the interstate you are on

Exit Number

Exit numbers on maps shown as numbers only (no letters A B C D...)

EXIT NOW

Copyright © 2009 by Affinity Media,
2575 Vista Del Mar Drive, Ventura, California 93001-2575
www.trailerlifedirectory.com

All rights reserved. No part of the *Exit Now* directory may be reproduced in any form without prior permission in writing from the publisher. While the publisher takes every precaution to ensure accuracy of listing information, ratings, and ad contents, no responsibility is assumed for inadvertent errors or changes that may occur before or after publication.

If you would like to provide us with updated information, or would like to be included in this publication, please email us at:
   info@exitnowdirectory.com

To make comments, ask questions, or to place an order please call:
   (800)766-1674

Distributed to the book trade by:
   Publishers Group West,
   1700 Fourth Street, Berkeley, CA 94710
   (800) 788-3123

ISBN 0-934798-92-3

Published in the United States of America.

PRIVACY PROMISE

We recognize that your privacy is very important to you and we're committed to helping you protect it. You should know that we will never intentionally share your name, address, and other personal information with anyone for their use if you have asked us not to do so. When you subscribe to our magazines, join our clubs or otherwise do business with us, please tell us if you don't want your name and address shared with other reputable companies or if you don't want to receive our marketing offers. We'll mark your account for a three-year period so that it will not be selected for products and/or services offers which you've told us you are not interested in receiving. If you change your mind, just get in touch with us and ask that we include you in future offerings. Obviously, you can ask to not be included in future offerings at any time and it'll be taken care of promptly. Please contact us at AGI Mail Preference Service, P.O. Box 6888, Englewood, CO 80155-6888 or telephone us at 1-800-766-1674.

Please note that this policy does not apply to e-mail marketing. We will not send you commercial emails unless you have authorized us to do so.

EXIT NOW:
Interstate Exit Directory

**PRESIDENT AFFINITY CLUBS
SR. VP AFFINITY MEDIA**
Joe Daquino

ASSOCIATE PUBLISHER
Cindy Halley

PRODUCTION

SENIOR DIRECTOR OF PRODUCTION & EDITORIAL
Christine Bucher

PRODUCTION MANAGER
Carol Sankman

EDITORIAL MANAGER
Ronny Wood

FEATURE DESIGN
Robert S. Tinnon

COVER DESIGN
Doug Paulin

SALES AND MARKETING

DIRECTOR OF SALES
Marsha Monico

NATIONAL SALES MANAGERS
Jack & Loretta Pressley

BULK SALES SPECIALIST
Debbie Brown

SENIOR DIRECTOR OF MARKETING
Kim Souza

DIRECT MARKETING MANAGER
Ellen Tyson

INTERNET MARKETING MANAGER
Samantha Price

Published by Affinity Media
2575 Vista del Mar Dr., Ventura, CA 93001
(800) 234-3450

HOW TO USE *EXIT NOW*

SERVICE LEGEND

TStop	Diesel/Gas Centers, Travel Centers with services available: Large vehicle access, parking, restaurants and/or fast food, services
FStop	Diesel/Gas location: Large vehicle access, fast food, other services may be available
Gas	Gas stations (locations listed in red may be large vehicle [RV] accessible)
Food	Restaurants and fast food
Lodg	Lodging services: Hotel, motel, and B&B (bed & breakfast)
AServ	Automotive services, tires
TServ	Diesel engine service, commercial vehicle services, tires
TWash	Large vehicle wash, trailer wash
Med	Hospitals, emergency service, other medical services
Other	Services and attractions near the exit, including but not limited to auto services, attractions, airports, banking, campgrounds, carwashes, colleges, convention centers, entertainment, golf courses, malls, RV parks, RV sales and services, racetracks, shopping, stadiums, and universities

EXIT NUMBERS

GREEN	Exit numbers
RED	Rest areas
BLUE	Inspection/weigh stations
BLACK	Interstate junctions, toll roads

LISTINGS

BOLD RED	Rest areas, Med: + medical services
RED	Large vehicle parking on site or nearby, pharmacies TStop/FStop: Diesel/gas for all size vehicles
BOLD BLUE	Inspection/weigh stations, highway patrol, police stations, and border crossings
BOLD GREEN	Casinos
BOLD BROWN	Campgrounds/RV parks/RV resorts, RV sales and services, RV dumps, and propane/LP

SYMBOL	LOCATION	MEANING
◇ (orange)	Next to gas station	Diesel available (Large vehicle parking and/or maneuvering large vehicles may not be possible)
◇ (green)	Next to gas station	Bio-diesel and/or ethanol available
♥	Next to listing	Pet services, pet friendly lodging
▲ (brown)	Next to RV parks/campgrounds	RV park and/or campground
▲ (blue)	Wal-Mart or business	RV parking permitted overnight
✈	Next to airports	Airport
DAD	Next to TStop/FStop	Difficult access diesel vehicles (RVers)
DAND	Next to TStop/FStop	Difficult access non-diesel vehicles (RVers)
MIL	Before campground listing	RV parks/campgrounds accessible to military personnel
COE	Before campground listing	Corps of Engineers campground
BLM	Before campground listing	Bureau of Land Management campground

REST AREA AND WELCOME CENTER ABBREVIATIONS

RR—Rest rooms
Phone—Pay phone
Pic—Designated picnic area
Playgr—Playground
Vend—Vending machines on site
WiFi—Wireless internet
Info—Traveler information
RVDump—Sanitary waste dump
RVWater—RV water

WB, EB, NB and SB—direction of rest area/welcome center (Westbound, Eastbound, Northbound, Southbound)
(Both dir)—Services available on both sides of interstate

INTERSTATE DIRECTORY

Interstate	State	Page
I-4	FL	1-4
I-5	WA	5-11
	OR	11-16
	CA	16-27
I-8	CA	28-30
	AZ	30-31
I-10	CA	31-36
	AZ	36-41
	NM	41-43
	TX	43-54
	LA	54-58
	MS	58-60
	AL	60-61
	FL	61-64
I-12	LA	64-65
I-15	MT	66-68
	ID	68-69
	UT	69-75
	AZ	75-76
	NV	76-78
	CA	78-82
I-16	GA	82-83
I-17	AZ	84-86
I-19	AZ	87
I-20	TX	88-95
	LA	95-98
	MS	98-100
	AL	100-103
	GA	103-107
	SC	107-108
	IL	109
	KY	109-110
	TN	110-113
	WY	113-115
	CO	115-121
	NM	121-124
	TN	124-125
	NC	125-126
	SC	126-129
	TX	130-131
	ND	131-133
	SD	133-135
	IA	135-136
	MO	136-137
I-30	TX	138-142
	AR	142-143
I-35	MN	144-148
	IA	148-150
	MO	150-152
	KS	152-154
	OK	154-157
	TX	157-170
I-37	TX	171-172
I-39	WI	173-175
	IL	175-176
I-40	CA	177
	AZ	177-180
	NM	180-183
	TX	183-185
	OK	185-189
	AR	189-193
	TN	193-200

Interstate	State	Page
I-40	NC	200-205
I-43	WI	206-208
I-44	TX	209
	OK	209-212
	MO	212-215
I-45	TX	216-221
I-49	LA	222-223
I-55	IL	224-227
	MO	227-229
	AR	229-230
	TN	230
	MS	230-234
	LA	234
I-57	IL	235-238
	MO	238
I-59	GA	238
	AL	238-241
	MS	241-243
	LA	243
I-64	MO	243-245
	IL	245-246
	IN	246
	KY	247-249
	WV	249-251
	VA	251-255
I-65	IN	255-259
	KY	259-261
	TN	261-263
	AL	263-268
I-66	VA	269-270
I 68	WV	271
	MD	271-272
I-69	MI	272-275
	IN	275-277
I-70	UT	278-279
	CO	279-284
	KS	284-288
	MO	288-292
	IL	292-294
	IN	294-295
	OH	295-299
	WV	299
	PA	299-301
	MD	301-302
I-71	OH	302-306
	KY	306-307
I-72	MO	308
	IL	308-309
I-74	IA	309
	IL	310-312
	IN	312-314
	OH	314
I-75	MI	314-316
	OH	316-321
	KY	321-326
	TN	326-328
	GA	328-331
	FL	338-343
I-76	CO	344-345
	OH	345-346
	PA	346-350
	NJ	350

Interstate	State	Page
I-77	OH	350-353
	WV	353-354
	VA	354-355
	NC	355-357
	SC	357-358
I-78	PA	359-360
	NJ	360
I-79	PA	361-363
	WV	363-364
I-80	CA	365-369
	NV	369-371
	UT	371-373
	WY	373-375
	NE	375-379
	IA	379-382
	IL	382-384
	IN	384-385
	OH	386-388
	PA	388-391
	NJ	391-392
I-81	NY	393-395
	PA	395-398
	MD	398
	WV	398-399
	VA	399-402
	TN	402-403
I-82	WA	404-405
	OR	405
I-83	PA	405-407
	MD	407
I-84	OR	407-411
	ID	411-414
	UT	414-415
	PA	415-416
	NY	416
	CT	416-419
	MA	419
I-85	VA	420
	NC	420-425
	SC	425-427
	GA	427-430
	AL	430-431
I-86	ID	432
	PA	433
	NY	433-437
I-87	NY	437-441
I-88	IL	442-443
	NY	443-444
I-89	VT	445-446
	NH	446
I-90	WA	447-450
	ID	450-451
	MT	451-455
	WY	455-456
	SD	456-459
	MN	459-461
	WI	461-463
	IL	463-465
	IN	465-467
	OH	467-469
	PA	469-470
	NY	470-473

Interstate	State	Page
I-90	MA	473-474
I-91	VT	475-476
	MA	476-477
	CT	477-478
I-93	VT	479
	NH	479-481
	MA	481-482
I-94	MT	483-484
	ND	484-486
	MN	486-489
	WI	489-494
	IL	494-495
	IN	496
	MI	496-501
I-95	ME	501-504
	NH	504
	MA	504-506
	RI	506-507
	CT	507-510
	NY	510
	NJ	510-511
	PA	511-512
	DE	512-513
	MD	513-515
	VA	515-518
	NC	518-520
	SC	520-522
	GA	522-524
	FL	524-531
I-96	MI	531-533
I-97	MD	534
I-99	PA	534-535
I-105	CA	535
I-110	CA	536
I-135	KS	537
I-196	MI	538
I-275	FL	539
	MI	540
I-276	PA	540-541
I-285	GA	541-542
I-294	IL	543
I-295	MA	544
	RI	544
	ME	544
	DE	544-545
	NJ	546
	VA	546
	FL	547
I-405	OR	547
	WA	548
	CA	549-551
I-459	AL	551
I-465	IN	552-553
I-476	PA	553
I-525	SC	555
I-605	CA	556
I-640	TN	556
I-680	CA	557-558
I-694	MN	559
I-710	CA	560

Join Us.

Having a great time. Wish you were here.

Saturday. Got to the campground early. Found a great site with a great view. And thanks to Good Sam, a great price, too. Same with our fuel. In fact, between the two, our Good Sam discounts saved us more than enough to pay for the burgers. And let me tell you, John can eat a lot of burgers. No wonder the Good Sam Club has more than a million members. You get so many benefits and discounts you can't afford not to join. And that doesn't even count all the fun, friendships and great information. So why not sign up right now? Come on, it just isn't the same without you. **Good Sam Club**

For more information or to join call 1-800-508-0393 or visit www.GoodSamClub.com

Go RVing
©2008 AGI

Good Service   Good Savings   Good Friends   Good Info

EXIT NOW

U. S. POSTAL SERVICE ABBREVIATIONS

Alabama	AL
Alaska	AK
American Samoa	AS
Arizona	AZ
Arkansas	AK
California	CA
Colorado	CO
Connecticut	CT
Delaware	DE
District of Columbia	DC
Federated States of Micronesia*	DC
Florida	FL
Georgia	GA
Guam	GU
Hawaii	HI
Idaho	ID
Illinois	IL
Indiana	IN
Iowa	IA
Kansas	KS
Kentucky	KY
Louisiana	LA
Maine	ME
Marshall Islands*	MH
Maryland	MD
Massachusetts	MA
Michigan	MI
Minnesota	MN
Mississippi	MS
Missouri	MO
Montana	MT
Nebraska	NE
Nevada	NV
New Hampshire	NH
New Jersey	NJ
New Mexico	NM
New York	NY
North Carolina	NC
North Dakota	ND
Northern Mariana Islands	MP
Ohio	OH
Oklahoma	OK
Oregon	OR
Palau*	PW
Pennsylvania	PA
Puerto Rico	PR
Rhode Island	RI
South Carolina	SC
South Dakota	SD
Tennessee	TN
Texas	TX
Utah	UT
Vermont	VT
Virginia	VA
Virgin Islands	VI
Washington	WA
West Virginia	WV
Wisconsin	WI
Wyoming	WY

*Although Palau, the Federated States of Micronesia, and the Marshall Islands are independent countries, each is still served by the United States Postal Service.

ROAD AND WEATHER CONDITION PHONE NUMBERS

State	Road Conditions	Weather Conditions
Alabama	205-945-7000	
Alaska	907-273-6037	907-936-2525
Arizona	888-411-7623	602-265-5550
Arkansas	800-245-1672	501-376-4400
California	916-445-7623	661-393-2340
Colorado	303-639-1111	303-337-2500
Connecticut	800-443-6817	508-822-0634
Delaware	800-652-5600	866-492-6299
Florida	800-475-0044	305-229-4522
Georgia	404-635-6800	770-455-7141
Idaho	888-432-7623	208-342-6569
Illinois	800-452-4368	312-976-1212
Indiana	317-232-8298	317-635-5959
Iowa	800-288-1047	515-244-5611
Kansas	800-585-7623	316-838-2222
Kentucky	866-737-3768	606-666-8000
Louisiana	225-379-1541	504-522-7330
Maine	800-698-7747	207-942-9480
Maryland	800-327-3125	410-936-1212
Massachusetts	616-374-1234	617-936-1234
Michigan	800-641-6368	313-976-3636
Minnesota	800-542-0220	218-732-8340
Mississippi	601-359-7017	601-354-3333
Missouri	800-222-6400	816-540-6021
Montana	800-652-7623	406-652-1916
Nebraska	800-906-9069	308-384-1907
Nevada	877-687-6237	702-248-4800
New Hampshire	800-918-9993	800-918-9993
New Jersey	800-336-5875	973-976-1212
New Mexico	800-432-4269	505-821-1111
New York	800-847-8929	716-844-4444
North Carolina	919-715-5525	919-515-8225
North Dakota	866-696-3511	701-235-2600
Ohio	614-466-7170	330-454-5454
Oklahoma	405-425-2385	405-478-3377
Oregon	800-977-6368	541-276-0103
Pennsylvania	888-783-6783	215-936-1212
Rhode Island	800-354-9595	401-976-5555
South Carolina	800-768-1501	843-744-3207
South Dakota	866-697-3511	605-341-2531
Tennessee	800-848-6349	615-244-9393
Texas	800-452-9292	713-529-4444
Utah	800-492-2400	801-524-5133
Vermont	802-828-2648	802-862-2475
Virginia	800-367-7623	540-982-2303
Washington	800-695-7623	206-526-6087
West Virginia	304-558-2889	304-345-2121
Wisconsin	800-762-3947	608-784-9180
Wyoming	800-442-2565	307-635-9901

EXIT NOW

AREA CODES BY STATE

States are listed in alphabetical order, and are followed by the area codes listed in numerical order.

Alabama	205, 251, 256, 334
Alaska	907
Arizona	480, 520, 602, 623, 928
Arkansas	479, 501, 870
California	209, 213, 310, 323, 408, 415, 424, 510, 530, 559, 562, 619, 626, 650, 661, 707, 714, 760, 805, 818, 831, 858, 909
Colorado	303, 719, 720, 970
Connecticut	203, 475, 860, 959
Delaware	302
Florida	239, 305, 321, 352, 386, 407, 561, 727, 754, 772, 786, 813, 850, 863, 904, 941, 954
Georgia	229, 404, 470, 478, 678, 706, 770, 912
Hawaii	808
Idaho	208
Illinois	217, 224, 309, 312, 331, 464, 618, 630, 708, 773, 815, 847, 872
Indiana	219, 260, 317, 574, 765, 812
Iowa	319, 515, 563, 641, 712
Kansas	316, 620, 785, 913
Kentucky	270, 502, 606, 859
Louisiana	225, 318, 337, 504, 985
Maine	207
Maryland	227, 240, 301, 410, 443, 667
Massachusetts	339, 351, 413, 508, 617, 774, 781, 857, 978
Michigan	231, 248, 269, 313, 517, 586, 616, 734, 810, 906, 947, 989
Minnesota	218, 320, 507, 612, 651, 763, 952
Mississippi	228, 601, 662
Missouri	314, 417, 557, 573, 636, 660, 816, 975
Montana	406
Nebraska	308, 402
Nevada	702, 775
New Hampshire	603
New Jersey	201, 551, 609, 732, 848, 856, 862, 908, 973
New Mexico	505
New York	212, 315, 347, 516, 518, 585, 607, 631, 646, 716, 718, 845, 914, 917
North Carolina	252, 336, 704, 828, 910, 919, 980, 984
North Dakota	701
Ohio	216, 234, 283, 330, 419, 440, 513, 567, 614, 740, 937
Oklahoma	405, 580, 918
Oregon	503, 541, 971
Pennsylvania	215, 267, 412, 445, 484, 570, 610, 717, 724, 814, 835, 878
Rhode Island	401
South Carolina	803, 843, 864
South Dakota	605
Tennessee	423, 615, 731, 865, 901, 931
Texas	210, 214, 254, 281, 361, 409, 469, 512, 682, 713, 737, 806, 817, 830, 832, 903, 915, 936, 940, 956, 972, 979
Utah	435, 801
Vermont	802
Virginia	276, 434, 540, 571, 703, 757, 804
Washington	206, 253, 360, 425, 509, 564
Washington, DC	202
West Virginia	304
Wisconsin	262, 414, 608, 715, 920
Wyoming	307

USEFUL PHONE NUMBERS

Airlines
American	800-433-7300
Continental	800-525-0280
Delta	800-221-1212
United	800-241-6522
US Air	800-428-4322

Auto Rentals
Alamo	800-462-5266
Avis	800-331-1212
Budget	800-527-0700
	800-468-8343
Dollar	800-800-4000
Enterprise	800-325-8007
Hertz	800-654-3131
	800-999-5500
National	800-227-7368
Rent-A-Wreck	800-421-7253
Thrifty	800-367-2277
Penske	888-996-5415
U-Haul	800-468-4285

Credit Cards
American Express	800-528-4000
Capital One	800-955-7070
Chase	800-935-9915
Citi Bank	800-374-9700
Discover	800-347-2683
Mastercard	800-626-8372
Visa	800-847-2911

Insurance
Allstate	866-621-6900
Geico	800-861-8380
Mercury	877-263-7287
Progressive	800-776-4737

Hotels/Motels
Adams Mark Hotels	800-444-2326
Baymont Inns & Suites	877-229-6668
Best Western	800-528-1234
Clarion Hotels	800-424-6423
Comfort Inns	800-424-6423
Country Inns & Suites	888-201-1746
Days Inns	800-329-7466
Doubletree Hotels	800-222-8733
Econolodge	877-424-6423
Embassy Suites	800-362-2779
Extended Stay America	800-804-3724
Fairfield Inn	800-228-2800
Fairmont Hotels	800-527-4727
Four Seasons	800-332-3442
Hilton Hotels	800-445-8667
Holiday Inns	800-465-4329
Howard Johnson	800-654-2000
Hyatt Hotels	800-233-1234
Jameson Inns	800-526-3766
La Quinta Inns	800-531-5900
Marriott Hotels	800-228-9290
Microtel	800-222-2142
Quality Inns	800-228-5151
Radisson Hotels	800-333-3333
Ramada Inns	800-228-2828
Red Roof Inns	800-733-7663
Sheraton	800-325-3535
Signature Inns	800-526-3766
Super 8	800-800-8000
Travelodge	800-578-7878
Westin	800-228-3000
Wingate	800-228-1000

TOWING LAWS BY STATE

STATE	Height	Width	Combined Length	Trailer Length	Trailer Width	Trailer Height	2-Vehicle Length	Triple Tow	Safety Chains	Breakaway
Alabama	13½'	8'6"	65'	57'0"[41]	8'0"	13'6"	65'	no	yes	yes[2]
Alaska	14'	8'6"	75'	40'0"	8'6"	14'0"	75'	yes	yes	yes[2]
Arizona	13½'	8'0"	65'	40'0"	8'0"	13'6"	65'	yes[43]	N/S	yes[2]
Arkansas	13½'	8'6"	65'	43'6"	8'6"	13'6"	2-unit limit, no max	L	yes	yes
California	14'	8'6"	65'	N/S	8'6"	14'0"	65'	yes[4]	yes	yes
Colorado	13'0"	8'6"	70'	N/S[42]	8'6"	13'0"	70'	yes[4]	yes	yes
Connecticut	13'6"	8'6"	60' max[1] >48'	53'0"[19]	8'6"	13'6"	60'[1, 13]	yes	yes	yes
Delaware	13'6"	8'6"	60'	N/S[19]	8'6"	13'6"	65'	no	N/S	N/S
DC	13'6"	8'6"	60'	N/S	8'0"	13'0"	55'	no	yes	yes
Florida	13'6"	8'6"	65'	40'0"	8'6"	13'6"	65'	no	yes	yes
Georgia	13'6"	8'6"	60'0"	N/S[19]	8'0"	13'6"	none	no	yes	N/S
Hawaii	14'0"	9'0"	65'0"	40'0"	9'0"	13'6"	65'	no	yes	yes[2]
Idaho	14'0"	8'6"	75'0"	48'0"	8'6"	14'0"	75'	yes[41]	N/S	yes
Illinois	13'6"	8'6"	60'0"	53'0"[19]	8'0"	13'6"	60'	yes[1]	yes[1]	yes[5]
Indiana	13'6"	8'6"	60'0"	40'0"	8'0"	13'6"	60'	yes[4]	yes	yes
Iowa	13'6"	8'6"	60'0"	N/S[19]	8'6"	13'6"	65'	yes	yes	yes
Kansas	14'6"	8'6"	65'0"	N/S[41]	9'0"	14'0"	65'	yes[4]	yes[37]	yes
Kentucky	13'6"	8'0"	65'0"	N/S[41]	8'0"	13'6"	65'	yes[4]	yes	yes
Lousiana	14'0"	8'6"	65'0"	30'0"	8'0"	13'6"	70'	yes[4]	yes[7]	yes
Maine	13'6"	8'6"	65'0"	48'0"	8'6"	13'6"	65'	no	yes	N/S
Maryland	13'6"	8'0"	55'0"	N/S	8'0"	13'6"	60'	yes	yes	yes[6]
Mass	13'6"	8'6"	60'0"	33'0"	8'6"	13'6"	60'	no	yes	N/S
Michigan	13'6"	8'0"	9'0"	53'0"[45]	8'0"	13'6"	65'	yes[4]	yes	yes
Minnesota	13'6"	8'6"	75'0"	45'0"	8'6"	13'6"	75'	yes[4]	yes	yes[7]
Mississippi	13'6"	8'6"	none	N/S	8'6"	13'6"	99'	yes	yes	yes
Missouri	14'0"	8'6"	65'0"	N/S[41]	8'6"	13'6"	65'	yes[4]	yes[37]	N/S
Montana	14'0"	8'6"	75'0"	N/S[40]	8'6"	13'6"	75'	yes[4]	yes	yes
Nebraska	14'6"	8'6"	65'0"	40'0"	8'6"	14'6"	65'	yes[4]	yes	yes
Nevada	14'0"	8'6"	70'0"	N/S	8'6"	43'0"	N/S	yes[4]	yes	yes
New Hamp	13½'	8'0"	none	48'0"	8'0"	13'6"	45'	no	yes	N/S
New Jersey	13'6"	8'0"	62'0"	40'0"	8'0"	13'6"	53'	no	yes	yes
New Mexico	14'6"[1]	8'6"	65'0"	N/S[41]	8'0"	14'0"	65'	yes	yes	N/S
New York	13'6"''	8'6" (w/some exceptions)	65'0"	N/S[41]	8'6"	13'6"	65'	no	yes	N/S
N Carolina	13½'	8'6"[25]	60'0"	N/S[19]	8'6"	13'6"	60'	no	yes	N/S
N Dakota	14'0"	8'6"	75'	53'0"	8'6"	14'0"		yes[40]	yes	yes
Ohio	13½'s	8'6"	65'	N/S[41]	8'6"	13'6"	65'[19]	yes[41]	yes	yes

EXIT NOW

TOWING LAWS BY STATE

Fire Exting	Flares Signs	Brake Laws Trailers	Brake Laws Towed Cars	O'night Parking	Max Tow Speed	Ride in 5th Wheel	Ride in Trailer	Axle	License Required
yes[36]	N/S	3000	Not required	P	70			20,000	Class D
N/S	yes	5000	Hook-up required if towed object > 3000 lbs	yes	55			N/A	Class D
N/S	N/S	3000[17]	Not required	yes[3]	75	yes	yes	20,000	Class D
N/S	yes	3000	N/L	yes	70			20,000	Class D
yes	yes	1500[17]	Must be sufficient to stop within a specified distance according to weight at 20 MPH	P	55	yes [10, 20]		20,000	< 40 ft class C < 40 ft > 40 ft- non-Class C > comm class B non-comm w/medical questionaire
N/S	N/S	3000[17]	N/L	N/S	75	yes		20,000	Class R
yes	yes	3000[17]	N/L	N/S	65			18,000	Class 2
N/S	yes	4000	If towed vehicle > 4000 lbs, brakes must be connected to those of towing vehicle	P	55			20,000	Class D
N/S	N/S	3000[17]	N/L	N/S	55			20,000	Class C
yes	yes	3000[17]	If towed vehicle > 3000 lbs, brake hook-ups as well as a breakaway system is required	P	70			20,000	Class D
yes	yes	1500	N/L	N/S	55			20,340	Class C
N/S	N/S	3000[17]	Hook-up required	N/S	55			22,500	Type 4 (Non-CDL)
N/S	N/S	1500	N/L	P	65			20,000	Class D
N/S	yes	3000[17]	Hook-up required	N/S	55	20,000			Class D
N/S	yes	3000[17]	N/L	yes	65	yes	yes	20,000	Class C
N/S	yes	3000	N/L	N/S	65	yes	yes	20,000	Class C
yes[36]	yes	yes[24]	N/L	yes	70	yes[33]	yes[33]	20,000	Class C 26,000 lbs Class B >= 26,000 lbs
yes		3000[6]	N/L	N/S	65			20,000	Class D
N/S	yes	3000	N/L	P	70			20,000	Class E
N/S	N/S	3000	N/L	P	55			22,400	Class C
yes	yes	3000[17]	N/L	P	65	yes	yes	22,400	Non-comm B>=
N/S	N/S	10,000	N/L	P	65			22,400	Class D
N/S	N/S	3000	N/L	P	55	yes	yes	18,000	Class B
N/S	yes	3000[17]	Hook-up required	P	70	yes	yes	20,000	Class D
N/S	yes	2000[17]	Hook-up required	N/S	55			20,000	Class R
N/S	N/S	N/S	Hook-up required	yes	70	yes	yes	20,000	Non-comm F
N/S	yes	3000	N/L	P	65	yes		20,000	Class D
N/S	yes	3000	N/L	N/S	75	yes	yes	20,000	Class O
N/S	N/S	1500	Braking system	yes[21]	75			20,000	Class A or B
N/S	N/S	3000	N/S	N/L	N/S	55		18,000	Class D
N/S	yes	3000	Hook-up required	P	65	yes		22,400	Class D
N/S	yes	3000[17]	Hook-up required	P	75	21,600			Class D
N/S	N/S	1000[9]	N/L	P	65			22,400	Non-CDL C may tow vehicles w/ a GVWR of 10,000
N/S	N/S	1000	N/L	N/S	55	yes	yes	20,000	Class A traveling w/ >= 10,001 lbs Class B traveling w/ >=26,001 lbs non-towing
N/S	yes	3000	N/L	yes	70	yes		20,000	Class D non-CDL
yes	yes	2000[17]	N/L	N/S	55			20,000	Class D

TOWING LAWS BY STATE

STATE	Height	Width	Combined Length	Trailer Length	Trailer Width	Trailer Height	2-Vehicle Length	Triple Tow	Safety Chains	Breakaway
Rhode Island	13'6"	8'6"	60'	NS	8'6"	13'6"	60'	no	N/S	yes
S Carolina	13'6"	8'6"	none	35'0"	8'6"	13'6"	N/A	no	yes	yes
S Dakota	14'0"	8'6"	75'0"	53'0"	8'6"	14'0"	80'0"	yes[40]	yes	yes
Tennessee	13'6"	8'6"	65'0"	40'0"[41]	8'0"	13'6"	65'0"	yes[41]	yes	yes[2]
Texas	14'0"	8'6"	65'0"	N/S[41]	8'6"	14'0"	65'0"	yes[41]	yes	yes[2]
Utah	14'0"	8'6"	65'0"	N/S[41]	8'6"	14'0"	65'0"	yes[41]	yes	yes[2]
Vermont	13'6"	8'6"	65'0"	N/S	8'6"	13'6"	68'0"	no	yes	yes[2]
Virginia	13'6"	8'0"	60'0"	NS[41]	8'6"	13'6"	65'0"	no	yes	yes[34]
Washington	14'0"	8'6"	75'0"	N/S[40]	8'6"	14'0"	75'0"	no	yes	yes[2]
W Virginia	13'6"	8'6"	55' max=60'	48'0"	8'0"	13'6"	55'0"[19]	no	yes	yes
Wisconsin	13'6"	8'6"	65'0"	45'0"	8'6"	13'6"	65'0"	yes[43]	yes	N/S
Wyoming	14'0"	8'6"	85'0"	60'0"	8'6"	14'0"	85'0"	yes	yes	N/S

THE RV REPAIR & MAINTENANCE MANUAL, 4th EDITION

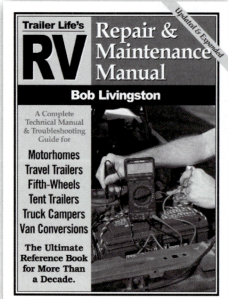

AN IDEA...

That Will Save You A Bundle Of Money On Maintenance You Can Do Yourself!

- Learn how to do Routine Maintenance and Small Repairs
- Step-by-Step, Easy to Follow Instructions
- Generously Filled with Detailed Illustrations
- Information on Systems and Accessories
- Better Than Ever Troubleshooting Guides & Checklists

SAVE OVER 40% OFF THE RETAIL PRICE
ONLY $20.97
plus $3.95 shipping & handling

TO ORDER

Call toll free: **1-877-209-6659 ext. 702**
Or visit us at: **www.TrailerLifeDirectory.com**
Or mail to: **RV Repair & Maintenance Manual
P.O. Box 22, Boulder, CO 80329-0022**

TOWING LAWS BY STATE

Fire Exting	Flares Signs	Brake Laws Trailers	Brake Laws Towed Cars	O'night Parking	Max Tow Speed	Ride in 5th Wheel	Ride in Trailer	Axle	License Required
N/S	yes	4000	N/L		yes	65		22,400	Class B>26,000; reg. operators <26,000 lbs; air brake endorsement required if >26,000 lbs w/air brakes
yes	yes	3000[17]	Required if combined exceeds 3,000 lbs	P	55			20,000	Class E >= vehicle weight 26,000 lbs Class F if towing
yes	yes	3000	Brakes, turn signals, and rear lights required	P	75	yes[10]		20,000	Non-comm Class 1
yes	yes	1500	Hookup required	yes	70			20,000	Class D <= 26,000 lbs
N/S	yes	4500	N/L	P[11]	70			20,000	Class B non-CDL >= 26,000 lbs
yes	yes	2000	N/L	P[23]	75			20,000	Class D
yes	yes	3000	N/L	N/S	65			20,000	Class B
N/S	N/S	3000	N/L	P	55			20,000	Class B
yes	yes	3000	N/L	yes[14]	65			20,000	Regular Operator's License
N/S	yes	3000[6, 17]	N/L	N/S	65		yes	20,000	Class E
N/S	N/S	3000[17]	Hook-up required if vehicle over 3,000 lbs	N/S	65	yes[27]		20,000	Class D
N/S	N/S	N/S	N/L		yes	75		20,000	Class B if GVWR>26,000 lbs; Class C if GVWR<26,000 lbs

SUPERSCRIPT LEGEND

1. On designated rural interstates; some exceptions
2. Required on trailers over 3000 lbs
3. Prohibited where posted
4. Required on trailers over 3000 lbs or if gross weight of trailer exceeds empty weight of tow vehicle
5. Required on trucks over 3700 kgs
6. Required if weight of trailer exceeds 40% of tow-vehicle weight
7. Required on trailers over 6000 lbs
8. Required if gross weight is over 2500 kgs
9. Required on trailers over 1000 lbs unloaded, 3000 lbs loaded
10. Riding in fifth-wheel with audible or visual device with tow vehicle and safety glass
11. 24-hour limit
12. Required if trailer exceeds 50% of tow-vehicle weight
13. Trailer limited to 48 ft in a 60 ft combination
14. 8-hour limit
15. Only if required by GSA at time of manufacture
16. 8.5 ft on certain federal road systems
17. Gross weight requiring brakes
18. Must have free access to drive compartment
19. Maximum combined length 60 ft on selected highways. Special permit needed in Oregon and Wisconsin
20. At least one exit must be opened from outside and inside
21. Not to exceed 18 hours in any two-week park
22. Headlights or daytime running lights required at all times
23. 12-hour limit
24. Must be able to stop in 40 ft at 20 mph
25. On interstate highways; secondary roads still 8 ft
26. 8.5 ft on all state routes. On some other roads 8 ft limits are posted
27. Some exceptions or restrictions
28. Special wide-body regulations
29. Two safety chains or a breakaway switch required on trailers
30. Required if RV is wider than 2 meters
31. Not recommended
32. Seats must be equipped with safety belts
33. 14 years of age and older
34. Required on trailers 3000 lbs and over
35. If passenger can communicate with driver, an exit can be opened from both interior and exterior
36. Suggested, but not required
37. Required on bumper hitches only
38. Required if gross weight is more than 1350 k
39. Headlights must be used when visibility is less than 500 ft
40. Total maximum combined length of 75 ft
41. Total maximum combined length of 65 ft California: third vehicle must be a boat
42. Total maximum combined length of 70 ft
43. With certain qualifications. Only with fifth-wheel trailer in Arizona, Illinois, Michigan, and Minnesota
44. Total maximum length of 72 ft
45. See state and provincial regulations
47-46. Total maximum combined length of 80 ft
48-47. Total maximum combined length of 21m
49-48. Total maximum combined length of 23m
50-49. Total maximum combined length of 20m
- **P** Indicates "as posted." Information is based on latest available data; laws may have changed since press time
- • Indicates "yes," item is permitted or required
- **N/L** Indicates "no law"
- **N/S** Indicates "not specified"

TRAVELING WITH PETS
By Joseph and Carol Berke

It's obvious that we Americans are in love with our pets. According to the 2007–2008 National Pet Owners Survey, 63 percent of U.S. households own a pet. That's more than 71 million homes! And who among us hasn't wanted to take our "furry" family members along on our RV trips with us? According to one study, more than 60 percent of all RVers travel with pets, so what's stopping the rest of you?

There are many good reasons for including Fido or Fluffy on your RV travels as long they are comfortable with traveling and as long as you plan to include them in activities. Having them along on trips can enhance your enjoyment as much as theirs, as they explore a whole new world they've never seen before—you know the feeling. They won't experience separation anxiety from being left home alone, with strangers, or in boarding kennels. Having your pets with you relieves your own worries about whether your pet

is properly cared for, happy, and in good health. But you don't need a reason; if you just plain want to take your pets along—go for it!

Our golden retriever, Barney, was an avid RVer and camper. We only needed to begin getting the rig ready and he'd go nuts, jumping in and out of the rig, encouraging us to hurry up and get on the road. Before setting off on any trip you always give your RV a checkup to make sure that all parts of the vehicle are in working order. Likewise, pets should also receive checkups from their veterinarian to ensure that they are also healthy enough for travel. But let's not get ahead of ourselves. . . .

Getting Ready to Depart

To any casual observer, it looked as if we just put our dog Barney in the rig and take off on our camping adventures. Traveling with pets takes a lot of preparation of both the animal and the supplies needed to keep it well and comfortable during the outing. If you have any questions, contact your pet's veterinarian for more complete information. Providing supplies for the RV also includes all the items required for your pet. A checklist will assist you with your packing (see the sidebar at the end of this article).

On the Road

It is best not to let a pet have free run of the RV while you are in motion.

Eric and Carol Anderson from Pine Grove, California, travel in their fifth-wheel with two boxers and an Australian shepherd. "The most important thing is to take the pets out with some frequency. If you take your pets out once a year they are not as comfortable and are anxious about the trip. We also take our dogs around town in our cars to keep up their travel experiences. On the road, our dogs travel in the back seat of our crew cab. We do not let them travel in the trailer; we want them near us so we can keep an eye on them," says Eric. Janene Butler and her family, of Citrus Heights, California, used to travel with cats. "We turned the top bunk in our triple-bunk fifth-wheel into a cat station where they had food, water, and a litter box. We had solid kennels to put them in while traveling. We even tried cat harnesses for walking them, which they hated," says Janene. The Butlers currently travel with two small dogs in a Class A motorhome. Julie and Chino Yap of Pine Island, Min-

nesota, travel in a motorhome with two terriers and a small poodle and they soon hope to add a cat. "When the RV is in motion, the dogs have their spots so they are not moving around," says Chino. The terriers also help keep the RV free of vermin. "One time," states Julie, "we were camping in the middle of nowhere in Utah and our terrier went nuts during the night. She was scratching at the cupboards, whining, and generally driving us crazy. She would not give up. I finally got her to calm down and go back to bed. The next morning, I got up to make coffee, opened a drawer, and found a big fat mouse staring up at me. The dog knew it was there. We dumped out the mouse and the contents of the drawer on the picnic table and cleaned it all out." Sarah and Nick Miccio of Palmdale, California, take their two golden retrievers and two Boston terriers along in their 40-foot fifth-wheel trailer pulled by a Chevy dually. "The back seat folds flat in the truck to make a big bed for the dogs to travel comfortably," says Sarah.

Keeping Your Pet Healthy

Pet wellness on the road should be a primary objective. Steve Thomasson, D.V.M. of the Cochise Animal Hospital in Scottsdale, Arizona, suggests a thorough vet check of your pet before the trip. He adds, "You will also need to have in the RV an up-to-date record of vaccinations that include parvovirus, hepatitis, and distemper. This record of vaccinations may be required in RV parks or when crossing state lines or international boundaries. Include records of significant health issues such as heart or kidney problems, allergies, or any illnesses that a veterinarian along the road may want to be aware of. If your pet is taking special medications, you will want to have a supply with you, along with information regarding why those meds are being given, and the dosages," says Thomasson. "You may also want to take along prescriptions for any medications you may need to fill at a pharmacy along the way."

Continued on page xiv

RV PET CHECKLIST

- Leashes, muzzles, harnesses
- Seatbelts, car seats or dividers for the vehicle
- Traveling crates or cages
- Bedding
- Bowls, food, water, and pet treats
- Sweaters or blankets for cold-sensitive pets
- Dog or cat booties or foot pads
- Combs, brushes, mat splitters
- Soaps, shampoos, flea and tick spray
- Towels and rags for cleaning the pet
- Floatation devices for water-loving dogs
- Ramps or steps for small dogs to climb in or out of the RV

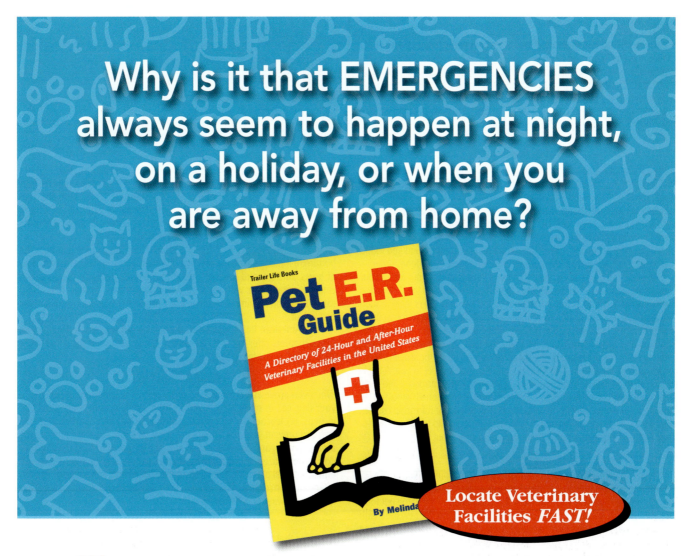

We know how much you love your pet, that's why Trailer Life Books provides the *Pet E.R. Guide*. When an accident or illness threatens the health of your pet, every moment counts. The *Pet E.R. Guide* helps you **locate 24-Hour or After Hour veterinary facilities** throughout the United States. The 200 page *Pet E.R. Guide* provides information to help you plan ahead and care for your pet in the event of an emergency at home or on the road.

Order your copy today and SAVE 10%
Order online at TrailerLifeDirectory.com/PetERGuide
or call toll free at 1-800-766-1674 ext. 409

TRAVELING WITH PETS, *continued from page xii*

your pets will just lounge around the RV and not participate in physical activities, it is still important to be vigilant about their condition. Learn to recognize illness or injuries. The predominant causes of illness are parasites, fleas, and ticks. Fleas are perhaps the most ubiquitous of the insects that may attack your pet. Although there are many different ways to control or get rid of fleas, the most common ways are bathing, spraying, dipping, or using a flea medication suitable for the animal.

Lost or Missing Pets

It may sound like a no-brainer, but when packing up to leave a site, be sure to check that your pet is with you in the RV. John and Jackie King of Elfrida, Arizona, travel with an eight-year-old female Lhasa Apso named Mattie. "One time we left a campground and got about five miles down the road and my wife looked in the cage and—NO MATTIE! It was at this point that I remembered tying the pup to the picnic table while I was draining the tanks and disconnecting the hoses and power. We returned to the campground and found her waiting for us. She just knew we were coming back," says John.

What do you do if you discover your pet is missing during your trip? If your pet gets out at home, and it has a sturdy collar and identification tag, it can often be recovered in the local area if someone finds it wandering. Pet identification is critical when you're hundreds of miles, or more, away from home in unfamiliar territory. I.D. tags are the best way to help you get your pet back. Microchips and identification tags for dogs and cats are also very important, although they're not foolproof. The chip is embedded under the skin and is encoded with all the information needed to return your lost pet to you. A tag is placed on the pet collar to let people know your pet has a microchip. The chips work only if the person finding your lost pet takes it to be scanned; almost all vet hospitals and animal shelters have scanners. The two major microchip companies are the AVID FriendChip and the HomeAgain Microchip Identification System. Both companies operate 24/7 to respond to calls about lost pets.

Pet Food

The fewer changes you make to your pet's diet, the happier it will be. If possible, bring enough food to last the whole trip, or buy the same brand of food if you need to replenish your supplies. If you cannot find the same pet food at your location, substitute a similar type of food, and mix the new food with some of the pet's regular food to reduce the shock of a new menu. The same applies to water. Bringing water from home will ensure that the pet does not drink bad water from puddles, streams, ponds, or even from faucets in the new location. Again, blending the new water with water you bring from home will help reduce the shock to the animal's system. This should reduce the onset of diarrhea, or other stomach or digestive ills.

After the recent pet food contamination scare and product recalls, many pet owners are starting to cook homemade meals for their dogs and cats. Although such meals made with fresh, high-quality ingredients often taste better than prepared foods, we need to be careful what we actually cook for our pets. There are numerous books on the subject of cooking for pets. Some examples are listed in the sidebar.

Pet First Aid

A first aid kit is an important addition to your pet's travel gear. Dr. Thomasson suggests that many of the items used in a human first aid kit will also work for your pet. Carol Anderson, a veterinary technician, made up her dog's first aid kit using a tool bag. First aid kits for pets can also be purchased on the Internet or at your pet supply store. Dr. Thomasson also suggests that, for the most part, you can use the same external salves and ointments on the pets that you use on yourself, especially if you are using them temporarily or until you can see a vet.

If you have a long-haired dog, you should trim some of the hair from the bottom of the dog's feet and between the toes. This will reduce the chances of burrs, stickers, and foxtails sticking in the hairs between the pads and causing irritation, or working their way into the pads or legs. Medicated salves are good for almost anything that hurts and should be included in the first aid kit.

The American Red Cross offers a book on pet first aid and many Red Cross chapters offer pet first aid classes. Check with your local Red Cross chapter for available classes.

Good Citizen Fido

When you arrive at a campground or RV park, it is important to make sure your dog, cat, or other pet is a good citizen. While outside, pets should be in pens, on leashes, or otherwise controlled. Common courtesy requires that you prevent your pet from being noisy, and not allow them to soil the area. Often, a good obedience class will go a long way toward making your dog a good citizen, socialized toward other people and their pets. Your veterinarian, local pet store, animal shelter, or breed club can suggest—or even offer—obedience classes for you and your dog to attend. Cats, on the other hand, are always well-behaved—right?

Medical Insurance:

A service that has become increasingly popular is pet medical insurance. There are many insurance companies which can be found on the Internet or as a recommendation from your veterinarian. Pet insurance is especially useful when traveling and away from your local vet. The insurance can reduce some of your anxiety when taking a sick or injured pet to a vet in a different part of the country.

Traveling with pets can be extremely enjoyable if no crisis arises during the trip. Making sure all the pet's needs are included in your trip planning will ensure a safe and happy trip. Having your pets with you can be stress reducing, and may help you meet new people as you walk around the campground, or hike through the woods. Bringing your pets along on your RV adventures allows them to be included in the family fun, and provide you a great deal of pleasure for years to come.

Visit www.trailerlifedirectory.com for more information.

PET IDENTIFICATION

The three major pet identifications services are:
- AVID FriendChip (www.avidmircochip.com).
- HomeAgain Microchip Identification System (www.HomeAgainID.com)
- Dog Registry (for dogs and other pets) 914-679-2335

PET FOOD COOKBOOKS

- *Best Ever RV Recipes,* Published by Trailer Life Books
- Dr. Pitcarin's New *Complete Guide to Natural Health for Dogs and Cats*
- *Real Food for Dogs: 50 Vet Approved Recipes to Please the Canine Gastronome,* by Arden Moore and Ann Davis
- *Crazy Kids Guide to Cooking for Your Pet,* by Barbara Denzer
- *Barkers Grub: Easy, Wholesome Home Cooking for Dogs,* by Rudy Edalati

---

SOURCES

- Steve Thomasson, D.V.M., sthomasson2@cox.net, (480) 991-2858
- Julie Yap, Julie@randomroadtrip.com, (507) 356-4377 or cell (612) 810-6522
- Janene Butler, endurhorse@hotmail.com
- Sarah Miccio, sarahdove03@yahoo.com, (661) 272-1530
- Eric and Carol Anderson, theandersons@volcano.net, 209-296-1278

WHATEVER IT COSTS, WE'LL PICK UP THE TAB!

EVEN IF your RV needs to be towed hundreds of miles to the nearest RV service center, WE'LL PICK UP THE TAB!

EVEN IF you need a flat tire changed, a battery jumped, or fuel delivered, WE'LL PICK UP THE TAB!

EVEN IF your truck, car, motorcycle or any other vehicle you own breaks down, WE'LL PICK UP THE TAB!

EVEN IF your spouse or other family driver is behind the wheel, WE'LL PICK UP THE TAB!

NEW! EVEN IF you break down in Mexico, Puerto Rico or the U.S. Virgin Islands, WE'LL PICK UP THE TAB!

NEW! EVEN IF you need directions or advice, OUR FREE RV CONCIERGE SERVICE PICKS UP THE TAB!

SPECIAL OFFER FOR EXIT NOW DIRECTORY USERS

We'll pick up the tab for **$30.00 OFF** your first year!

REGULAR ANNUAL RATE:	NEW MEMBER RATE FOR DIRECTORY USERS:
$~~109.95~~	$79.95

CALL TOLL-FREE: 1-800-510-3330
(Mention Code EXIT)

OR ENROLL ONLINE:
www.GoodSamERS.com

Good Sam RV EMERGENCY ROAD SERVICE
Affinity Road & Travel Club, Inc.

Note: All program benefits are subject to limitations set forth in the current Member Benefits Brochure which will be sent to you upon approval of your Membership and is accessible at www.GoodSamERS.com/pdf/ERS_nonMBB.pdf Benefits and services provided by Affinity Road & Travel Club, Inc.

5R-EXIT-192

FOCUS ON FESTIVALS*
Fairs, Frolics, and Fiestas
By Maxie Henry

Include some of these RV-friendly gatherings in your 2009 travel itineraries! Be sure to take along a camera (and film), comfortable shoes, a hat, lip balm, and sunscreen—and a cell phone in case your group gets separated.

PACIFIC REGION

The Rally, Albuquerque, New Mexico, April 17–20: It'll be a kick on Route 66! Plan to RV west in April 2009 and get your kicks at the tenth anniversary of the Greatest RV Rally in the World! It's the industry's biggest event of the year—celebrate and explore RV travel through seminars, exhibits, activities, entertainment, fellowship and a whole lot of fun. Come see the newest RV technologies, the latest RV gadgets and the most creative RV tech tips as The Rally hosts the "First Annual GO Green Ideas Contest!" Entertainment will be provided by Neil Sedaka, one of rock 'n' roll's legendary singer-songwriters. Albuquerque is an enchanting land rooted in centuries of history and rich in southwest style and high-desert beauty. (877) 749-7122, therally.com

Winter Break, Laughlin, Nevada, January 9–15: Celebrates life for those 50+ with all types of dancing, bingo and slot tournaments, cooking and exercise classes, seminars, a trade show and entertainment. (480) 926-5547, winterbreak.us

Lavender Festival, Sequim, Washington, July 17–19: Lavender's aroma and flavor readily blend into oils and fats, especially dairy fats—which makes it a good choice for ice cream and baked goods made with milk or butter. Sample lavender salad dressing, lavender lemonade and lavender chocolate-chip cookies. The festival features lavender farm tours, arts and crafts and how-to demonstrations. (877) 681-3035, lavenderfestival.com

Tour of Historic Homes, Albany, Oregon, July 25: Homes and buildings in Albany's Nationally Registered Historic Districts will be open for visitors during the annual tour. Costumed entertainers and townsfolk will delight visitors along the way. (800) 526-2256, albanyvisitors.com

Discovery Days and Yukon Riverside Art Festival, Dawson City, Yukon, August 12–17: Gold discovered in 1896 caused the Klondike Gold Rush, and turned this native summer fish camp into the "Paris of the North." Two years later, Dawson had telephone service, running water and steam heat, elaborate hotels, theatres, and dance halls, plus 22 saloons. Discovery Days features art, street performances, and the Gaslight Follies. (867) 993-5575, dawsoncity.ca

MOUNTAIN REGION

Little Big Horn Days and Custer's Last Stand Reenactment, Hardin, Montana, June 24–28: Using a script written from notes by Crow Tribal Historian Joe Medicine Crow, the reenactment tells the tale of the golden-haired general; row after row of Cavalry soldiers riding in formation over the rolling hills; war-painted Indians on horseback, fighting to keep what is theirs; and the bloody battle on Last Stand Hill. Many of the reenactors are descendants of the Indian scouts who rode with Custer or the homesteaders who came later and scratched out a living among the unforgiving hills and plains. Interact with cavalrymen in their camp; watch as they make bullets, clean weapons and get ready for the coming battle. Attend the Grand March and the Grand Ball. (888) 450-3577. custerslaststand.org.

River City Rod Run, Post Falls, Idaho, July 12–14: A three-day celebration of more than 900 hot rods, featuring a spectacular fireworks show, vendor alley, Miss Hot Rod Contest, burn outs, show and shine, kids games, Sunday demolition derby and recording artists. Other special events include fireworks, burn outs, wheel stander, a flame-throwing contest and the Sunday demolition derby. (208) 777-1712, hotrodcafe.com

Cheyenne Frontier Days, Cheyenne, Wyoming, July 17–26: Billed as the "World's Largest Rodeo & Western Celebration" established in 1897, it has nine PRCA rodeos, concerts, four parades, three free pancake breakfasts, the Wild Horse Carnival Midway, an Indian Village with Native American dancing and storytelling, a USAF Thunderbird aerial demonstration and a military air show. (800) 227-6336, cfdrodeo.com

Buffalo Roundup, Arts Festival and Buffalo Wallow Chili Cook-off, Custer State Park, South Dakota, September 26–28: Custer State Park in the beautiful Black Hills is full of lush forests, quiet and serene meadows and

majestic mountains. This 71,000-acre park is also home to one of the world's largest publicly owned bison herds, 1,500 strong. The ground rumbles and the dust flies as cowboys, cowgirls and park crews saddle up to bring in the thundering herd. Following the actual roundup, stay and watch as park staff sort, brand, and vaccinate the herd in preparation for the fall Buffalo Sale. (800) S-DAKOTA, travelsd.com

Norsk Hostfest, Minot, North Dakota, September 29–October 3: Tens of thousands of people attend this event to celebrate North America's largest Scandinavian Festival. More than 200 internationally recognized artisans, craftsmen and chefs participate. The cuisine as well as the clothing, art and jewelry are authentically Nordic. (701) 852-2268, hostfest.com.

Continued on page xxi

*Dates and details are subject to change, so be sure to verify before planning to attend.

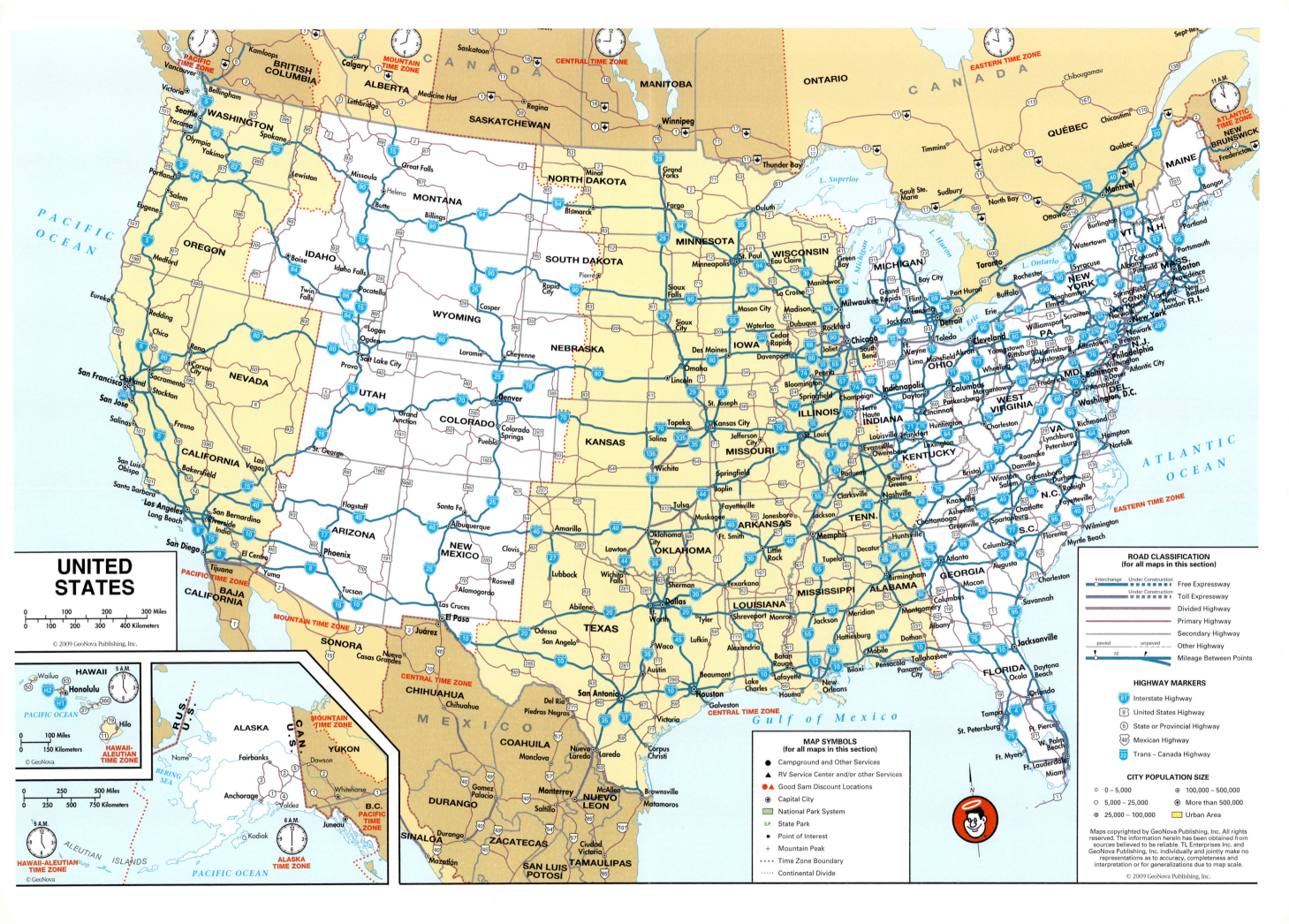

DRIVING DISTANCES BETWEEN MAJOR U.S. CITIES

	Albany NY	Albuquerque NM	Atlanta GA	Baltimore MD	Birmingham AL	Boston MA	Buffalo NY	Charlotte NC	Chicago IL	Cleveland OH	Dallas TX	Denver CO	Des Moines IA	Detroit MI	El Paso TX	Houston TX	Indianapolis IN	Kansas City MO	Las Vegas NV	Little Rock AR	Los Angeles CA	Memphis TN	Nashville TN	New Orleans LA	New York City NY	Norfolk VA	Oklahoma City OK	Orlando FL	Philadelphia PA	Phoenix AZ	Pittsburgh PA	Portland OR	St. Louis MO	San Antonio TX	San Diego CA	Salt Lake City UT	San Francisco CA	Seattle WN	Washington DC	Wichita KS	
Albany NY	**000**	2081	1016	331	1099	166	295	777	820	480	1680	1814	1138	648	2228	1770	791	1287	2560	1367	2833	1230	1020	1440	153	501	1536	1208	238	2544	472	2927	1040	1965-	2898	2206	2953	2899	365	1477	**Albany NY**
Albuquerque NM	2081	**000**	1406	1882	1259	2247	1792	1629	1341	1606	644	439	977	1591	267	890	1290	783	576	886	1290	1014	1223	1170	2019	1930	544	1739	1939	463	1649	2348	1041	715	817	626	1097	1456	1886	539	**Albuquerque NM**
Atlanta GA	1014	1406	**000**	673	148	1100	896	243	712	715	791	1415	961	723	1426	797	529	810	1982	531	2205	393	242	468	896	557	862	440	816	1862	686	2604	556	992	2154	1883	2503	2675	635	972	**Atlanta GA**
Baltimore MD	331	1882	673	**000**	783	407	373	436	704	379	1366	1693	1022	532	1999	1454	592	1088	2441	1051	2681	914	704	1125	203	234	1337	881	102	2345	251	2811	841	1649	2699	2070	2837	2783	38	1278	**Baltimore MD**
Birmingham AL	1099	1259	148	783	**000**	2673	905	391	1598	730	647	1364	910	727	1282	671	478	759	1835	384	2058	246	189	342	981	705	715	562	901	870	753	2553	505	866	2010	1832	2356	2624	743	825	**Birmingham AL**
Boston MA	166	2247	1100	407	1230	**000**	461	863	986	644	1768	1980	1304	814	2394	1896	957	1453	2726	1453	2999	1316	1106	1527	211	577	1702	1284	313	2710	586	3093	1206	2051	3064	2372	3119	3065	441	1643	**Boston MA**
Buffalo NY	295	1792	896	436	905	461	**000**	659	531	189	1376	1525	849	359	1939	1495	502	998	2271	1061	2554	924	1243	417	370	574	1247	1182	412	360	216	2638	751	1653	2609	1917	2664	2610	388	1188	**Buffalo NY**
Charlotte NC	777	1629	243	420	391	863	659	**000**	770	516	1034	1580	1067	645	1669	1040	589	975	2205	754	2428	617	407	711	659	320	10850	2255	530	510	2030	525	960	1235	2397	2048	2726	2840	398	1165	**Charlotte NC**
Chicago IL	820	1341	704	718	661	986	531	770	**000**	342	933	1009	333	278	1488	1089	179	529	1755	655	2028	536	472	927	811	891	1386	1152	761	1804	460	480	300	1210	2088	1401	2148	2070	705	719	**Chicago IL**
Cleveland OH	478	1606	715	379	719	644	189	516	350	**000**	1190	1336	660	170	1753	1309	316	812	2082	875	2355	738	530	1057	486	566	1061	1039	436	2069	2449	130	565	2423	2260	1728	2475	2421	380	1002	**Cleveland OH**
Dallas TX	1682	644	791	1366	640	1768	1376	1034	933	1190	**000**	882	746	1198	633	247	882	552	1220	315	1440	454	663	526	1564	1348	208	1096	1484	1069	1228	2124	633	1361	1670	1260	1741	2195	1326	365	**Dallas TX**
Denver CO	1814	439	1415	1693	1364	1980	1525	1580	1009	1336	882	**000**	674	1272	623	1129	1101	605	749	966	1022	1097	1175	1407	1805	1781	674	1855	1750	809	1460	1250	858	936	1082	530	1276	1321	1694	517	**Denver CO**
Des Moines IA	1138	977	961	1022	910	1304	849	1067	333	660	746	674	**000**	596	1124	926	483	194	1420	581	1693	623	721	1084	1129	1191	538	1401	1079	1440	778	1787	350	1011	1600	1070	1813	1820	1023	384	**Des Moines IA**
Detroit MI	648	1591	723	532	727	814	359	645	278	170	1198	1272	596	**000**	1738	1317	310	792	2018	883	2291	746	540	1070	639	719	1046	1163	589	2054	288	2385	550	1475	2351	1670	2411	2357	533	955	**Detroit MI**
El Paso TX	2228	267	1426	1999	1282	2394	1939	1669	1488	1753	633	623	1124	1738	**000**	753	1437	930	726	948	807	1087	1296	1100	2197	1983	691	1718	2117	436	1796	1627	1188	558	728	868	1188	1698	1959	740	**El Paso TX**
Houston TX	1770	890	797	1454	671	1856	1495	1040	1089	1309	247	1129	926	1317	753	**000**	1025	732	1466	434	1560	573	782	351	1652	1384	455	969	1572	1189	1347	2371	837	2240	1481	1650	1941	2442	1414	612	**Houston TX**
Indianapolis IN	791	1290	529	592	478	957	502	589	179	316	882	101	483	310	1420	1037	**000**	496	1849	591	2089	472	289	816	729	713	745	969	649	1753	359	2272	249	1159	2107	15510	2298	2256	593	686	**Indianapolis IN**
Kansas City MO	1287	783	820	1088	759	1453	998	975	529	812	552	605	194	792	980	732	496	**000**	1353	389	1626	526	570	917	1225	1176	344	1250	11145	1246	855	1792	253	817	1600	1071	1818	1863	1089	190	**Kansas City KS**
Las Vegas NV	2560	576	1984	2441	1837	2726	2271	2207	1755	2082	1222	749	1420	2018	726	1468	1849	1353	**000**	1461	275	1592	1801	1748	2551	2508	1120	2317	2498	290	2208	1021	1606	1286	335	416	569	1122	2464	1265	**Las Vegas NV**
Little Rock AR	1367	883	531	1051	384	1453	1061	754	655	875	315	966	581	883	948	434	591	420	1459	**000**	1682	1139	348	441	1249	1055	339	944	1169	1346	913	2208	403	592	1700	580	1980	2279	1011	449	**Little Rock AR**
Los Angeles CA	2833	799	2205	2680	2058	3000	2544	2428	2028	2355	1440	1022	1690	2291	807	1560	2089	1626	270	1680	**000**	1810	2020	1905	2825	2730	1343	2525	2740	370	2448	987	1840	3140	960	689	381	1140	2685	1392	**Los Angeles CA**
Memphis TN	1230	1014	393	914	246	1316	924	617	536	738	454	1097	623	746	1087	573	472	526	1590	139	1813	**000**	211	392	1112	918	470	806	1032	1477	776	2320	284	2310	1831	1599	2111	2391	874	580	**Memphis TN**
Nashville TN	1020	1223	242	704	189	1106	716	407	472	530	663	1175	721	538	1296	782	289	570	1799	348	2022	211	**000**	527	902	708	679	682	822	2686	568	2364	316	940	2040	1643	2320	2435	664	760	**Nashville TN**
New Orleans LA	1441	11700	468	1125	342	1527	1243	711	927	1057	526	1407	1014	1065	1100	351	816	917	1746	441	1907	392	527	**000**	1323	1040	733	640	1243	15360	1095	2649	675	546	1828	1780	2267	2720	1085	890	**New Orleans LA**
New York City NY	153	2019	896	203	981	211	417	659	811	486	1564	1805	1129	639	2197	1652	729	1225	2551	1249	2824	1112	902	1323	**000**	373	1474	1080	109	2482	388	2918	978	1847	2836	2197	2944	2890	237	1415	**New York City NY**
Norfolk VA	501	1930	557	234	705	577	574	320	891	566	1350	1781	1191	719	1983	1384	713	1176	2506	1055	2729	918	708	1055	373	**000**	1386	749	276	2393	438	2970	922	1579	2747	2249	2996	3041	196	1366	**Norfolk VA**
Oklahoma City OK	1536	544	830	1337	715	1702	1247	1100	796	1030	1061	674	538	1046	691	455	745	344	1110	339	1343	470	679	733	1474	1386	**000**	1275	1394	1007	1104	1916	496	473	15361	1100	1641	1987	1342	157	**Oklahoma City OK**
Orlando FL	1208	1739	440	881	562	1284	1182	525	1152	1039	1095	1855	1401	1163	1718	969	969	1250	2315	944	2525	806	682	640	1080	749	1275	**000**	979	2154	972	3044	996	1164	2446	2340	2836	3115	843	1385	**Orlando FL**
Philadelphia PA	238	1939	816	102	901	313	412	534	761	436	1484	1750	1079	589	2117	1572	649	1145	2498	1169	2738	1032	822	1243	109	276	1394	979	**000**	2402	308	2868	898	1767	2756	2150	2894	2840	136	1335	**Philadelphia PA**
Phoenix AZ	2490	460	1830	2310	1680	2670	2220	2030	1740	2030	1000	810	1430	2010	440	1180	1730	1240	290	1330	390	1470	1670	1500	2450	2350	980	2080	2370	**000**	2090	1270	1480	1000	350	650	760	1470	2300	1040	**Phoenix AZ1846**
Pittsburgh PA	450	1630	680	250	790	570	220	500	480	130	1210	1430	780	300	1780	1370	360	870	2210	900	2430	760	570	1140	380	420	1110	980	310	2090	**000**	2550	610	1480	2440	1846	2610	2520	250	1050	**Pittsburgh PA**
Portland OR	2920	1370	2660	2800	2590	3140	2670	2780	2120	2430	2040	1260	1820	2380	1630	2240	2240	1820	1000	1140	960	2310	2370	2540	2910	2970	1870	3070	2860	1270	2550	**000**	2060	2100	1090	760	640	170	2780	1750	**Portland OR**
St. Louis MO	1750	1040	570	830	510	1210	750	730	290	580	660	860	370	530	1180	780	240	260	1620	1440	1840	280	320	700	980	900	500	1000	900	1480	610	1280	**000**	950	1830	1360	2120	2140	860	460	**St. Louis MO**
San Antonio TX	1970	730	1000	1630	860	2020	1630	1240	1210	1450	270	950	980	1450	558	200	1190	780	1290	1670	1390	730	930	550	1820	1550	480	1170	1740	1000	1480	2100	950	**000**	1300	1330	1740	2180	1590	640	**San Antonio TX**
San Diego CA	2850	810	2150	2680	1990	2880	2530	2410	2090	2390	1350	1100	1770	2370	730	1490	2080	1590	340	1990	130	1810	2000	1840	2800	2680	1330	2410	2770	350	2440	1090	1830	1300	**000**	760	510	1260	2600	1400	**San Diego CA**
Salt Lake City UT	2250	600	1930	2070	1790	2380	1940	2080	1420	1760	1260	530	1070	1670	870	1440	1551	1570	420	580	690	1550	1700	1780	2190	2220	1100	2340	2150	650	1920	760	1360	1330	760	**000**	750	850	2050	1020	**Salt Lake City UT**
San Francisco CA	2980	1110	2480	2480	2370	3130	2670	2720	2170	2480	1750	1260	1830	2400	1200	1910	2290	1860	570	2250	390	2120	2330	2280	2930	3000	1660	2870	2900	760	26103	640	2120	1740	510	750	**000**	810	2840	1700	**San Francisco CA**
Seattle WN	2490	1450	2630	2710	2540	3020	2580	2740	2050	2390	2130	1340	1800	2330	1720	2370	2250	1860	1180	1010	1130	2320	2440	2590	2840	2890	1990	3090	2820	1470	2520	170	2140	2180	1260	829	810	**000**	2720	1860	**Seattle WN**
Washington DC	400	1850	620	40	740	450	410	380	710	360	1310	1620	1060	520	1930	1370	580	1040	2420	440	2650	850	660	1100	240	190	1330	850	130	2300	250	2780	860	1590	2600	2050	2840	2720	**000**	1280	**Washington DC**
Wichita KS	1490	590	950	1280	830	1630	1200	11090	730	1010	370	517	384	955	840	620	690	200	1180	449	1390	580	740	850	1420	1370	157	1390	1360	1040	1050	1750	460	640	1400	1020	1700	1860	1280	**000**	**Wichita KS**

Emma Crawford Festival, Coffin Race and Parade, Manitou Springs, Colorado, October 25: Emma Crawford came to the springs around the turn of the century seeking a cure for her tuberculosis, and believed she saw her Indian guide waiting on Red Mountain. Sadly, Emma died young and was laid to rest there. But Red Mountain is granite that eventually gave way and what remained of Emma's coffin washed down the side of the mountain. Come watch the coffin race, or recruit a team of your own! (800) 642-2567, manitousprings.org

Christmas Parade and Courthouse Lighting, Prescott, Arizona, December 5: Santa visits Arizona's Christmas City in this festive and elaborate parade through downtown. The celebration continues with caroling as the courthouse comes ablaze at the lighting ceremony. (800) 266-7534, prescott.org

CENTRAL REGION

Abraham Lincoln Bicentennial, Illinois, Kentucky and Nationwide, Year-long: A Bicentennial Birthday Gala will be held February 2 in Washington, D.C. with a world-class concert and entertainment special. Nineteenth-century popular and patriotic music will be performed by outstanding military bands. Abraham Lincoln was born in Kentucky, spent his youth in Indiana, and made Illinois his home. The State of Illinois captured this special relationship with Lincoln with its slogan "Land of Lincoln" Other events will be held across the country. Visit lincolnbicentennial.gov for links to participating states, or go directly to sites for Kentucky, kylincoln.org; Indiana, in.gov/Lincoln; or Illinois, lincoln200.net

St. Paul Winter Carnival, St. Paul, Minnesota, January 22–February 1: In 1885 a New York reporter wrote that Saint Paul was "another Siberia, unfit for human habitation" in winter. Offended by his attack on their city, the Chamber of Commerce decided to prove that its citizens were very much alive during winter. In 1886 the festival featured an ice castle, which has evolved into an icon for the event. (651) 223-4700, wintercarnivalfanclub.com

Shreveport-Bossier Krewe of Centaur Mardi Gras Parade, Shreveport, Louisiana, February 14: One of the largest parading Mardi Gras Krewes in north Louisiana. (318) 221-0505; kreweofcentaur.org

Charro Days Fiesta, Brownsville, Texas, February 22–March 1: With music and dancing, food and folklorico, Brownsville celebrates its connections with Mexico. The fiesta features taco-eating contests and a tortilla cook-off, costume displays, a Hands Across the Border ceremony and entertainment, an international parade and a golf tournament. (956) 542-4245; brownsville.org

Columbus Pilgrimage, Columbus, Mississippi, March 30–April 11: Tour antebellum mansions; many will feature re-created activities of the 1800s with period-costumed reenactors, adding even more authenticity. (662) 329-3533, historic-columbus.org

Chase County Prairie Fire Festival, Cottonwood Falls, Kansas, April 6–11: Tallgrass prairie lands were first fire-managed by Mother Nature with fires caused by lightning. Native Americans likely noticed that the bison returned to graze on freshly burned prairie, creating an ideal hunting situation; it is probable that they began to set the prairie ablaze as a management tool. European settlers learned the prairie-fire principal from them and incorporated the practice into the management of cattle-grazing lands. Watch managed fires, attend seminars and hear local musicians. (620) 273-6020, prairiefirefestival.com

Kewpiesta, Branson, Missouri, April 22–26, 2009: Take a tour of Rose O'Neill's home, Bonniebrook, during this celebration of her famous Kewpie dolls and related memorabilia. (800) 296-0463, explorebranson.com.

Country Music Association Music Festival, Nashville, Tennessee, June 11–14: The world's biggest country music festival features more than 400 artists appearing in concert and at downtown clubs during late-night performances. Other highlights are autograph and photo sessions, an acoustic corner where new artists perform and fun zones for all ages. (800) CMA-FEST; cmafest.com

NEBRASKAland Days, North Platte, Nebraska, June 11–21: The celebration hosts the Buffalo Bill Rodeo, with western decoration, real cowboys and cowgirls, parades and pageantry, festivity and western hospitality. (308) 532-7939, nebraskalanddays.com

World's Largest Catsup Bottle Summerfest Birthday Party and Car Show, Collinsville, Illinois, July dates to be determined: The World's Largest Catsup Bottle stands proudly next to Route 159. It's a 170-foot-tall water tower built in 1949 for the G.S. Suppiger catsup-bottling plant, bottlers of Brooks Old Original Rich & Tangy Catsup. In 1995, due to the efforts of the Catsup Bottle Preservation Group, the landmark roadside attraction was saved from demolition and beautifully restored to its original appearance. Festival highlights include the Hot Dog Smothered-in-Catsup Eating Contest. (618) 345-5598, catsupbottle.com

Lumberjack World Championships, Hayward, Wisconsin, July 24–26: The competition showcases more than 21 events ranging from men's and women's logrolling and chopping to the exciting 90-foot pole climb. 100+ competitors vie for more than $50,000 in prize money. (715) 634-2484, lumberjackworldchampionships.com

Gene Autry Oklahoma Film & Music Festival, Gene Autry, Oklahoma, September 23–27: Relive, revive and remember the music and memories of the singing cowboys. The local Gene Autry Oklahoma Museum boasts a large collection of memorabilia of stars from the musical Western movies of the 1930s and 1940s. (580) 294-3047; cow-boy.com

Wiederkehr Wine Festival, Wiederkehr Village, Arkansas, September 26: The Tyrolean-style village celebrates the annual harvest and its Swiss heritage. Tour historic wine cellars, visit the wine-tasting room, and catch a ride on a tram through the vineyards to a tower with a panoramic view of the Arkansas River Valley. Join in the Stein Stemmen (stone-toss) contest, the Baum Stossen (log-toss) contest, and the Grape-Stomping contest! Bring

your dancing shoes for the polka dancing to authentic German music. With sing-alongs in German and English, Alpine dancers, strolling musicians and a conga line through the cellars, there's plenty of fun! (800) 622-9463; wiederkehrwines.com

Madison County Covered Bridge Festival, Iowa, October 10–11: Residents and visitors gather amid the brilliant hues of autumn to celebrate historic bridges. The festival features old-time craft demonstrations, food, antiques and crafts vendors, music, a spelling bee, an antique and classic auto show and an antique vehicle parade complete with bands. (515) 462-1185 madisoncounty.com

Eastern Region

National Cherry Blossom Festival, Washington, D.C., March 28–April 12: The celebration of Japan's 1912 gift of 3,000 cherry trees culminates with a parade and the Sakura Matsuri Japanese Street Festival. Other events include The Smithsonian Kite Festival, performances at the Tidal Basin, fireworks, the International Drumming Festival, A Grand Sushi and Sake Tasting, and a visit by the Freedom Schooner Amistad. (202) 661-7584 nationalcherryblossomfestival.org

Virginia International Tattoo, Norfolk, Virginia, May 1–3: An exhibition of marching bands, massed pipes and drums, drill teams, gymnasts, Scottish dancers and choirs creates an unforgettable spectacle. (757) 282-2822 virginiaartsfest.com

Old Dover Days, Dover, Delaware, May 2: Throughout the Historic District of Colonial and Victorian homes, Dover celebrates its history as the Capitol of the First State. The past comes alive with maypole dancing, Colonial craft demonstrations, a house and garden tour and tea party, a civil war encampment and the Grand Ball. (800) 233-KENT, visitdover.com

(Photo Credit: Lou & Maxye Henry)

York County Made-In-America Days, York, Pennsylvania, June 17–21: Get a behind-the-scenes look at how some of your favorite products are made in "The Factory Tour Capital of the World!" You're invited onto the production floors at companies like Harley-Davidson, Pfaltzgraff, and Utz. Sample warm potato chips at Martin's or follow the York County wine trail to watch grapes transformed into fine wines. Plus, factory outlets offer unbeatable bargains by the bagful. (888) 858-YORK, factorytours.org

Vermont Quilt Festival, Colchester and Essex Junction, Vermont, June 19–20: See breathtaking new and antique quilts; enjoy lectures, gallery talks, classes and workshops with noted quilt artists. Shop more than 65 vendor booths full of quilts, fabrics, books, patterns, specialty tools, supplies, country crafts, antiques, jewelry, and wearable art. Have your antique or contemporary quilt appraised. (802) 485-7092, vqf.org

Charleston Harborfest, Charleston, South Carolina, June 26–28: A true harbor-wide celebration of the sea, with the USS Yorktown, tours of tall ships, an authentic pirate camp, wooden boats, a children's village, family boat building, a military interaction and educational village, a static boat display, helicopter harbor tours, a kids' zone, food and music. Water and bus shuttles provide transportation between locations.

Summer Redneck Games, East Dublin, Georgia, July dates to be determined: These "games" are an outrageous, politically incorrect spoof of the real Atlanta Olympics. Events include the Hubcap Hurl, the Bobbin' for Pig's Feet Fest, and Redneck Horseshoes—in which toilet seats are the objects thrown. People still talk about the 12-year-old boy who played Dixie with his underarm and palm a few years back. summerredneckgames.com

Annual Bristol Civic, Military and Fireman's Parade, Bristol, Rhode Island, July 3–4: The nation's oldest 4th of July parade, a tradition dating back to 1785, features marchers, dozens of floats, bands, patriotic pageantry, a drum-and-bugle corps competition and fireworks. (401) 253-0445, july4thbristolri.com

National Baseball Hall of Fame Induction Weekend, Cooperstown, New York, July 26: Who will be this year's honorees? Several new or improved exhibits include a multimedia show, an interactive children's play area, the Bullpen Theater, a World Series exhibit, an early baseball exhibit, an education gallery and an exhibit dedicated to baseball today, a pictorial history of the Hall of Fame, the Steele/Donruss Art Gallery of paintings and sculptures and Sacred Ground, an exhibit about ballparks. (888) 425-5633 baseballhalloffame.org

Maine Lobster Festival, Rockland, Maine, July 29–August 2: The focus of this festival is, of course, fresh hot Maine lobster and butter. As much as 12 tons of lobsters go into the world's largest lobster cooker. Other seafoods are on the menu—clams, Maine shrimp, mussels and scallops—plus coleslaw, corn on the cob and strawberry shortcake. And who would want to miss the crowning of the Maine Sea Goddess? (800) LOB-CLAW mainelobsterfestival.com

Weird Contest Week, Ocean City, New Jersey, August 17–21: Taffy sculpting, french-fry sculpting, artistic pie eating, wet T-shirt tossing (record: 165 feet), putrid puns and celebrity super-hero impersonations. The grand finale is the highly fashionable Miss Miscellaneous Contest. (609) 525-9300, oceancityvacation.com

D-Day Re-enactment, Conneaut, Ohio, August 22: History enthusiasts gather to recreate an amphibious assault such as that carried out against Nazi Germany in the Normandy region of France on June 6, 1944. Real U.S. Navy landing craft pick up hundreds of World War II reenactors dressed in period uniforms who carry the rifles and equipment of the day. These reenactors are then put ashore on a barricade-strewn beach in front of the blank-firing guns of German reenactors, who do their best to repel the invaders.

Behind the bluff is an array of military displays, vehicles, and encampments from both sides of the war. (800) 337-6746, conneautchamber.com

Auburn Cord Duesenberg Festival, Auburn, Indiana, September 3–7: These three great automobiles were designed, built and sold in this "Home of the Classics." Besides 5,000 collector cars, there are an auction, a swap meet, and the Parade of Classics, plus fine arts, arts-and-crafts and quilt shows, antiques and entertainment. The Auburn Cord Duesenberg Museum is housed in the art deco buildings of the Auburn Automobile Company, and the National Automobile and Truck Museum, the new World War II Victory Museum and the Kruse Automotive Museum are nearby. (260) 5-3600, acdfestival.org

Hampton Beach Seafood Festival, Hampton Beach, New Hampshire, September 5–6: Fifty top restaurants serve a "Taste of New England"—fried clams, crab cakes, sautéed calamari, New England clam chowder, and lobster that's steamed, fried, or on a roll—booths with locally made products; sidewalk sales; Kiddie Land; chef demonstrations; two music stages with the U.S. Air Force Band of Liberty, a fireworks display, and a sky-diving extravaganza. (603) 926-8718, hamptonbeachseafoodfestival.com

Great Lakes Lighthouse Festival, Alpena, Michigan, October dates to be determined: Great fall colors and this festival combine for a smashing celebration of these beacons that symbolize maritime history. Tours, displays, entertainment and educational programs highlight this popular program. (586) 566-1603, lighthousefestival.org.

Salem Haunted Happenings, Salem, Massachusetts, October 8–November 1: Grand Parade, Haunted City storytelling, tours of The Gables by lantern light, The Legacy of the Hanging Judge, costume contests and parties. (877) SALEM-MA, hauntedhappenings.org

Chowderfest, Mystic Seaport, Connecticut, October 9–11: Cool sea air, a warm autumn sun and piping-hot "chowda!" Taste seafood, desserts and beer, wine, and apple cider. Stroll through the village and enjoy live music; bring the kids for a "clammy" art project and story time in the Children's Museum. Learn about late-summer stars and mariners' navigation under the Planetarium dome. Or climb aboard the steamboat Sabino for a closer look at the colorful foliage. (888) 973-2767, mysticseaport.org

Woolly Worm Festival, Banner Elk, North Carolina, October 17–18: Fuzzy caterpillars with names like Merryweather, Patsy Climb, and Dale Wormhardt shimmy up a 3-foot length of string. Based on the color of his fuzz, the champion—who wins $1,000—is declared the official forecaster of how cold the upcoming winter will be. The festival also features crafts, food, and entertainment. (828) 898-5605, averycounty.com

New River Bridge Day, Fayetteville, West Virginia, October 17: Parachutists jump off the longest single-arch bridge in the world, plunging almost 900 feet to the gorge below. Enjoy a Taste of the Bridge Day, arts and crafts, and the once-a-year walk across the famous bridge. (828) 927-0263, officialbridgeday.com

Winterfest of Lights, Ocean City, Maryland, December 1–January 2, 2010: Take a ride on the Winterfest Express and ride past spectacular lighted displays—more 1,000,000 holiday than lights sparkle throughout the town. Visit Winterfest village for entertainment, caroling and hot cocoa. (800) OC-OCEAN. ococean.com

LOW CLEARANCES

Highway No.	Location	Height
Alabama		
AL 1/US 31	Seale	13'0"
AL 2/ US 43/72	Florence–5 miles east at Shoals Creek bridge	12'0"
AL 10	Greenville	10'0"
US 31 SB	Montgomery–at Coosa River	13'4"
AL 51	Opelika–south of jct I-85	13'4"
AL 53	Ardmore–West, east of jct I-65	10'8"
US 90	Mobile–Bankhead tunnel	12'0"
US 98 WB	Spanish Fort–0.3 mile west	13'6"
AL 111	Wetumpka at Coosa River bridge	12'6"
AL 251	Ardmore	11'0"
Swan Bridge Rd	Cleveland–1 mile west at Locust Fork River bridge	13'0"
Local Road	Nectar–1 mile east, Locust Fork River covered bridge	9'0"
Arizona		
AZ 80	Douglas–Mile Point 366.10	12'10"
AZ 84 EB	Casa Grande–Mile Point 177.66	13'6"
AZ 188	4 miles north of jct AZ 88 at Salt River–Mile Point 262.44	12'3"
US 191	Morenci tunnel at Mile Point 169.90	12'10"
6th Ave	Tucson–Mile Point 66.73	10'11"
Arkansas		
AR 7	Camden–north–0.8 mile northwest of US 79	13'1"
AR 42	Turrell–0.01 mile east of AR 77	11'9"
AR 43	Siloam Springs–jct US 12	13'6"
AR 51	Arkadelphia–0.59 mile east of US 67	12'6"
AR 69	Moorefield	12'6"
AR 69	Trumann–0.82 mile east of US 63	9'0"
AR 69	Trumann–0.19 mile northeast of US 63	12'0"
AR 75	Parkin	12'1"
AR 106	Batesville–west, 2.43 miles west of AR 69	10'6"
AR 127	Beavertown–between US Hwy 62 and AR Hwy 23, the Beaver Bridge at White River/Tablerock Lake	11'6"
AR 134	Garland–jct US 82	13'5"
AR 247	Pottsville–0.11 mile south of US 64	11'1"
AR 282	Mountainburg–approx 4.5 miles southwest	13'1"
AR 296	Mandeville–approx 0.5 mile southwest	11'0"
AR 307	Briggsville–2.5 miles south of Fourche LaFave river	13'0"
AR 365	North Little Rock–0.4 mile west of US 70	13'0"
California		
CA 2	Angeles National Forest west of CA 39 at Angeles Crest tunnel	13'6"
CA 33 NB, SB	Ventura–Matilija tunnel	13'0"
CA 41	Atascadero–1.3 miles northeast of US 101	13'2"
CA 70 WB	Belden–east of North Fork at Feather Ridge bridge	13'3"
CA 70	Marysville–0.7 mile north of CA 20	14'0"
CA 70 EB, WB	Spanish Creek tunnel south of Camp Alexander at Milepost 35.5	13'0"
I–80	San Francisco–San Francisco Oakland Bay tunnel	13'10"
I–80	San Francisco–San Francisco Oakland Bay tunnel	13'10"
CA 48NB, SB	Rio Vista–12 miles northwest of Yolo County line.	13'1"
US 101	Thousand Oaks–3.9 miles west of CA 23	14'0"
CA 110 NB	Los Angeles–College St overpass	13'6"
CA 110 NB	Los Angeles–Hill St overpass	14'0"
CA 110 NB	Los Angeles–tunnel 0.5 mile southwest of I-5	13'0"
CA 110 SB	Los Angeles–I-5 overpass	14'0"
CA 110 SB	Los Angeles–0.2 mile northeast of I-5	14'0"
CA 129 WB	River Oaks–2.8 miles west of US 101	14'0"
CA 151 EB, WB	Summit City–Coram overpass	13'9"
CA 160 NB (16th St)	Sacramento–0.6 mile south of American River	13'10"
CA 238 SB	Fremont–2.2 miles north of I-680	14'0"
Colorado		
US 6 EB (6th Ave)	Denver–0.4 mile west of CO 88 (Federal Ave) at Knox Ct Milepost 283.58	14'4"
US 6 WB (6th Ave)	Denver–0.4 mile west of CO 88 (Federal Ave) at Knox Ct Milepost 283.58	14'6"
US 6 EB (6th Ave)	Denver–CO 88 (Federal Blvd) overpass, Milepost 283.66	14'3"
US 6 WB (6th Ave)	Denver–CO 88 (Federal Blvd) overpass, Milepost 283.66	14'2"
US 6	Eagle–0.67 mile east of Eagle River, Milepost 150.24	14'4"
CO 14	Poudre Park tunnel 4.7 miles west, Milepost 107.25	14'5"
Bus CO 24	Manitou Springs–Milepost 3.14	13'10"
US 36	Westminster–West 80 Ave overpass, Milepost 53.93	14'4"
US 40/I-70	Deer Trail–4.92 miles west at Milepost 346.25	14'3"
US 287 WB BR US 50 EB	Pueblo–just south of I-25/US 85/87 at Arkansas River (Santa Fe Ave)	13'10"
I-70 EB	Idaho Springs–Milepost 238.689	14'4"
I-70 EB	Palisade-Beaver tunnel, Milepost 50.38	14'1"
CO 95 NB (Sheridan Blvd)	Denver–at I-70, Milepost 9.013	14'1"
CO 95 SB (Sheridan Blvd)	Denver–at I-70, Milepost 9.013	14'1"
CO 144	Fort Morgan–at I-76 overpass–Milepost 0.01	13'5"
CO 265 (Brighton Blvd)	Denver–1.2 miles north of I-70, Milepost 1.198	11'7"
US 550/CO 789	Ouray–tunnel 1.17 miles south at Milepost 90.86	13'9"
Connecticut		
US 1 (Boston Post Rd)	Branford–west between CT 142 and Branford Connector to I-95	13'1"
US 1	Darien–0.1 mile southwest of CT 124	11'1"
US 1	Madison–2.1 miles west of CT 79	12'7"
US 1 SB	Milford–Milford Parkway overpass	13'6"
US 1	Stamford–1.2 miles east of CT 137	13'1"
US 5	Wallingford–CT 15 overpass	13'5"
US 6	Bristol–0.5 mile west of CT 69	13'6"

Highway No.	Location	Height
US 6	Newtown–0.3 mile southwest of I-84	12'7"
CT 8	Derby–1 mile north of CT 34	13'6"
CT 10	Farmington–US 6 overpass	13'4"
CT 10	Hamden	13'6"
CT 10	Hamden–CT 15 overpass	13'6"
CT 12	Groton–CT 184 overpass	12'2"
CT 53	Bethel–1.3 miles south of CT 302	11'1"
CT 53	Norwalk–CT 15 overpass	12'0"
CT 58	Fairfield–CT 15 overpass	11'8"
CT 67	Seymour	12'6"
CT 71	Wallingford	10'0"
CT 72	Pequabuck–1 mile southeast of US 6	13'3"
CT 81	Clinton–0.1 mile north of US 1	11'10"
I-95	Darien–1.1 miles northeast of Exit 9	13'6"
I-95	Milford–0.2 mile west of Exit 38	13'6"
CT 104	Stamford–CT 15 overpass	11'10"
CT 106	New Canaan–0.4 mile north of CT 15	11'7"
CT 110	Stratford–0.2 mile north of I-95	11'2"
CT 113	Stratford–0.1 mile north of I-95	13'4"
CT 115	Seymour–0.2 mile east of CT 8	12'8"
CT 123 (Merritt Pkwy)	Norwalk–northwest at CT 15	12'4"
CT 130	Bridgeport–I-95 overpass	13'6"
CT 130	Bridgeport–0.1 mile north of I-95	11'1"
CT 133	Brookfield–0.2 mile east of US 1	12'1"
CT 135	Fairfield–0.1 mile south of I-95	10'4"
CT 136	Westport–0.1 mile south of I-95	10'8"
CT 137	Stamford–CT 15 overpass	12'3"
CT 138	Lisbon–southwest, 1 mile west of CT 12	12'2"
CT 146	Branford	9'6"
CT 146	Branford	9'9"
CT 146	Guilford–1.25 miles southwest	11'3"
CT 146	Leetes Island	13'6"
CT 159	Windsor–0.1 mile northeast of CT 305	12'9"
CT 190	Stafford Springs–1.4 miles northwest	13'6"
CT 243	New Haven–CT 15 overpass	12'8"
CT 275	Eagleville–0.2 mile west of CT 33	12'0"
CT 322	Milldale–CT 10 overpass	12'7"
CT 372	Berlin–1.5 miles west of US 5	11'2"
CT 533	Vernon	12'7"
CT 598	Hartford–Main Streeet overpass	12'1"
CT 598	Hartford–Columbus Blvd overpass	13'6"
CT 649	Groton–1.2 miles east of CT 349	10'6"
CT 719	Norwalk–CT 15 overpass	13'4"
CT 796 (Milford Pkwy)	Milford–0.2 mile north of I-95	13'6"
CT 847	Waterbury	12'8"
CT 847	Waterbury Lake Ave	12'10"
	Danbury–railroad bridge just off I-84 WB on Lake Ave	10'0"

Delaware

Highway No.	Location	Height
US 13A	Laurel	12'11"
DE 100 (Mountchannin Rd)	Guyencourt	13'0"
	Local Rd 018C Ogletown	10'8"
Local Rd 258	Ashland–covered bridge at Red Clay Creek	7'6"
Local Rd 35 A	Kirkwood–0.75 mile north, west of DE 71	11'4"
Local Rd 356 D (North Chapel St)	Newark–at Paper Mill Rd	12'3"
Casho Mill Rd	Newark–between DE 2 and DE 273, west of jct	8'11"
James St	Newport–0.1 mile south of jct DE 4	13'2"
Local Rd 336D	Stanton–1 mile south	11'1"
Local Rd 338 (Telegraph Rd)	Stanton–0.5 mile west	10'10"
18th St	Wilmington–just south of Augustine cutoff	13'0"
Rising Sun Rd	Wilmington–between DE 52 (Pennsylvania Ave) and DE 141 (New Bridge Rd) east of the junction	12'4"
Rising Sun Rd Wilmington	Wilmington between DE 52 (Pennsylvania Ave) and DE 141 (New Bridge Rd) at Brandywine River bridge	13'6"
Local Rd 263A	Wooddale–between DE 48 (Lancaster Pike) and Barley Mill Rd, west of Centerville Rd at Red Clay Creek bridge	9'6"

District of Columbia

Highway No.	Location	Height
3rd St	I-395 Mall tunnel	13'0"
Connecticut Ave	Q St underpass, near jct of Connecticut and New Hampshire Aves	13'5"
Massachusetts Ave	Underpass at Thomas Circle–jct of 14 St, M St, and Vermont	12'6"
Potomac R Fwy	US 50 (Theodore Roosevelt Memorial Bridge) overpass–	12'6"
Potomac R Fwy	between 27th St underpass	12'11"
Potomac R Fwy	Whitehurst Fwy ramp overpass	12'6"
8th St	Franklin St viaduct, north of US 1	13'0"
Florida Ave	block south of US 50 (New York Ave)	13'0"
L St	East of 1st St, under Washington Terminal Yards	13'6"
M St	East of 1st St, under Washington Terminal Yards	13'5"
2rd Sreet	underpass at Virginia Ave	13'6"
7th St	underpass at Virginia Ave	13'6"
Anacostia Dr	South Capital St overpass	13'4"
Canal St	overpass near I-395	13'3"
South Capital St	underpass north of I-395	13'4"
Suitland Pkwy	Anacostia Freeway overpass	12'6"

Florida

Highway No.	Location	Height
US 92 W	Lakeland–1.5 miles east of Wabash Ave	12'6"
Alton Road (FL 945)	Miami Beach–FL A1A/US 41 overpass	11'11"
Barth Road	Jacksonville–US 1/23 overpass	12'4"
Bloxam St	Tallahassee–FL 61 overpass	12'6"
College St	Jacksonville–I-95 overpass	12'8"
Gadsden St	Tallahassee–US 27 overpass	13'0"
Palm Ave	Jacksonville–I-95 overpass	8'6"
Sea World Dr	Orlando–southwest, I-4 overpass	13'1"
Washington St	Lake City–US 41 overpass	12'9"

Idaho

Highway No.	Location	Height
US 26 SB	Idaho Falls–Milepost 333.48	13'10"
US 30	Pocatello–Milepost 334.14	13'6"
US 30 B	Pocatello–Milepost 0.16	13'6"
US 30 B	Pocatello–Milepost 0.24	13'11"
I-84 B (11th Ave)	Nampa–Milepost 58.89	13'10"
I-84 B (11th Ave)	Nampa–Front St overpass, Milepost 58.88	13'9"
US 95 Spur SB	Weiser–Milepost 0.15	13'11"

Illinois

Highway No.	Location	Height
IL 1 NB, SB	Crete–4.78 miles north of jct IL 394	13'5"
US 6 EB, WB	Joliet–0.5 mile north of IL 53	12'2"
IL 7, NB, SB (Southwest Hwy)	Palos Park–86 Ave overpass	13'2"

EXIT NOW

Highway No.	Location	Height
IL 7 NB, SB (Southwest Hwy)	Palos Park–123 St overpass	13'2"
US 12/20 (95th St) EB, WB	Chicago–1.7 to 3.4 miles east of I-94	13'1"
US 12/20 EB, WB (95th St)	Chicago–just east of Chicago Skyway	13'5"
US 14/41 EB, WB (Foster Ave)	Chicago–just east of Broadway	11'11"
US 14 EB, WB (Peterson Ave)	Chicago–0.75 mile east of Western Ave	13'0"
IL 19 EB, WB	Chicago–0.25 mile west of Ashland Ave, 1800 West Irving Park Rd	13'5"
IL 19 EB, WB	Chicago–just west of I-90/94, 4200 west	13'0"
IL 25 SB (Broadway)	Aurora–0.3 miles south of New York St	13'0"
IL 25 NB OS 30 EB	Montgomery–0.5 mile south of US 30	13'0"
(Jefferson St)	Joliet–at Broadway, west of Des Plaines R	12'7"
US 30 EB	Joliet–0.6 mile east of IL 53	13'6"
US 30 WB	Joliet–0.6 mile east of IL 53	13'4"
US 41 EB, WB (Foster Ave)	Chicago–0.25 west of Ashland Ave	11'10"
IL 43 NB (Harlem Ave)	East Forest–0.5 mile north of Madison St	13'0"
IL 43 SB (Harlem Ave)	River Forest–0.5 mile south of Madison St	13'1"
US 45/150 NB (Springfield Ave)	Champaign–0.1 mile east of Neil St	12'8"
US 45/150 SB (Springfield Ave)	Champaign–0.1 mile east of Neil St	12'7"
US 45/52 NB, SB (Water St)	Kankakee–0.1 mile east of Washington Ave	12'9"
IL 50 NB, SB (Cicero Ave)	Chicago–just south of I-90	13'2"
US 52 EB, WB	Kankakee–0.1 mile east of Il 115	12'8"
IL 53 NB, SB (Chicago St)	Joliet–just south of Washington St	13'2"
IL 64 EB, WB (North Ave)	Chicago–0.3 mile east of Pulaski Rd	13'2"
IL 64 EB, WB (North Ave)	Chicago–just east of I-90/94	12'10"
IL 64 EB, WB (North Ave)	Chicago–east of I-94 at Chicago River	11'6"
IL 62 NB, SB	Geneseo–0.5 mile north of US 6	10'0"
US 150 (Springfield Ave)	Champaign–US 45/150 entry	12'7"

Indiana

Highway No.	Location	Height
IN 1	Connersville–0.47 mile north of IN 44	11'2"
IN 17	Plymouth–1.7 miles south of US 30	11'0"
IN 43 NB	Solsberry–4.13 miles north of IN 54	11'2"
IN 43 SB	Solsberry–4.13 miles north of IN 54	11'3"
US 136 EB	Clermont–1.5 miles west of IN 134	12'5"
US 136 EB	Clermont–1.5 miles west of IN 134	12'4"
US 150	Ferguson Hill–1.94 miles north of US 40	13'0"
US 231	Lake City–0.23 mile south of jct US 41	13'6"
IN 450 EB, WB	Williams–8.3 miles west of IN 158	12'11"

Iowa

Highway No.	Location	Height
IA 14	Corydon–north	13'6"
US 61 NB (Brady St)	Davenport–0.1 mile north of 4th St	12'2"
US 61 SB (Harrison Ave)	Davenport–0.3 mile north of US 61/67 (River Dr)	12'1"
IA 83	Atlantic–0.5 mile west	14'6"
IA 146	Grinnell–2 miles north	13'9"
IA 415 NB (2nd Ave)	Des Moines–0.9 miles outh of I–35/80	13'7"
IA 415 SB (2nd Ave)	Des Moines–0.9 mile south of I–35/80	13'6"

Kansas

Highway No.	Location	Height
KS 31/ US 59	Garnett–1.0 mile south	14'0"
KS 34	Bucklin–0.1 mile north of jct US 54	13'9"
US 40/59	Lawrence–1 mile south of jct I-70	14'0"
KS 53	Mulvane–0.3 mile west of KS 15	14'0"
US 56	Herington–3.3 miles east of US 77	13'6"
US 59	Garnett–at KS 31/US 59 entry	
US 147	Spillway at Cedars Bluff Reservoir	14'0"
US 166	Arkansas City–0.3 mile east of US 77	13'6"
Turner Diagonal EB	Kansas City–0.3 mile south of I-70 exit 415, Riverview Ave	14'0"

Kentucky

Highway No.	Location	Height
KY 7	Colson–3 miles east	12'10"
KY 7	Garrett–at KY 80 overpass	12'2"
KY 8 (4th St)	Newport–Covington-Licking River Bridge	13'6"
KY 8 (Elm St)	Ludlow	13'6"
KY 9	Newport–south of 12th St	13'2"
KY 17 (Scott St)	Covington–17th St	12'3"
KY 17 (Greenup St)	Covington–near 17th St	13'6"
US 25 (W 12th St)	Covington–I-71/75 overpass, 0.3 mile north of Jefferson St	13'5"
US 25 (Dixie Hwy)	Erlanger–0.1 mile northeast at jct KY 236	13'6"
US 25 W	Corbin–0.5 mile north of KY 312	12'0"
KY 26	Woodbine–3 miles southwest	13'6"
US 27 (Manmouth St)	Newport–south of 11th St	13'6"
US 27 (Broadway)	Lexington–0.1 mile southeast of KY 4, northern intersection	13'2"
US 31 W (Main St)	Louisville–at 14th St	13'0"
US 31 W (22nd St)	Louisville–0.25 miles south of Woodland	12'6"
KY 40	Paintsville–0.75 mile east of US 23/460	13'5"
US 45	Paducak–Ohio River bridge	13'1"
Bus US 45	Fulton	13'6"
KY 52	Beattyville–0.3 mile west of KY 11	13'4"
KY 57	2.3 miles west of KY 627	13'4"
US 60	Owensboro–0.5 mile east of US 431	13'0"
US 60	at US 231 Ohio River bridge underpass east of Paducah at Tennessee River	12'11"
Alt. US 60 (3rd St)	Louisville–at Eastern Parkway	12'2"
Alt. US 60 (3rd St)	Louisville–0.2 mile south of Eastern Parkway	12'2"
KY 70	Eubank–1.2 mile west of US 27	11'0"
KY 94	Fulton–north, 0.1 mile west of KY 307	11'6"
KY 139 & KY 293	Princeton–0.1 mile west of KY 91	12'1"
KY 177	Butler–1.1 mile west of US 27	10'3"
KY 254	Madisonville–0.2 mile south of KY 892	13'3"
KY 282	Kentucky Dam Village State Resort Park	13'2"
KY 307	Fulton–0.3 mile north of Tennessee state line	10'0"
KY 307	Fulton–1.1 miles north of Fulton County line	12'9"

Highway No.	Location	Height
US 421	Fayette County–1 mile east of Scott County line	13'6"
US 431	Central City–0.1 mile south of KY 70	11'9"
KY 867 EB	Royalton–1.5 miles west	8'0"
KY 867 WB	Royalton–1.5 miles west	13'3"
KY 1120 (W. 12th St)	Covington–I-71/75 overpass, 0.3 mile north of Jefferson ramp	13'5"
KY 2513 (2nd St)	Maysville–100 feet east of KY 8	12'4"

Louisiana

Highway No.	Location	Height
Bus. LA 1	Natchitoches	13'1"
LA 8	Sabine River bridge	12'1"
LA 15	Alto–Boeuf River bridge (curb)	13'1"
LA 23	Belle Chase–1 mile north of Belle Chase tunnel	13'4"
LA 48 SB	Norco–2 miles north of LA 627	13'2"
US 71	Alexandria–Allen bridge	13'6"
US 90	New Orleans–0.2 mile south of I-610	13'4"
Bus. US 165	Pineville	11'10"
US 171 NB	Leesville	13'0"
LA 385	Lake Charles–under I-10 Calcasieu River bridge	12'6"
LA 538	Mooringsport–4.75 miles southeast	13'1"
LA 546	Cheniere–0.5 mile south of I-20	12'6"
LA 729	Lafayette–just west of US 90, near Lafayette Regional Airport	12'7"

Maine

Highway No.	Location	Height
ME 9	Saco–Mile Marker 39.9	12'6"
ME 24	Richmond–Mile Marker 34.9	12'6"
ME 197	Richmond–at Kennebec River, Mile Marker 16.5	15'4"

Maryland

Highway No.	Location	Height
MD 7	North East	12'0"
MD 7	Perryville	13'0"
MD 7	Parryville	13'0"
MD 36	Frostburg	10'4"
MD 51	Northwest of Paw Paw, WV	13'4"
MD 75	Monrovia	12'6"
MD 109	Barnesville	13'0"
MD 117	Boyds	12'0"
MD 117	Bucklodge–1.5 miles northwest of Boyds	13'0"
MD 135	Cumberland–south of US 220 overpass	12'0"
MD 269	Colora	11'0"
MD 303	Cardova–northeast at MD 309	12'6"
MD 831A	Homewood–bypasses jct of US 40 and MD 36	11'3"

Massachusetts

Highway No.	Location	Height
US 1 (Lafayette Rd)	Salisbury–0.75 mile north of MA 110	13'3"
MA 1A (Dodge St)	Beverly–at jct MA 128	13'5"
MA 1A NB	Boston–at jct of road to Logan Int'l Airport	12'2"
MA 1A	Boston–at Porter St, west of airport	13'5"
MA 2 (Commonwealth Ave)	Boston–express underpass at jct MA 2A1	13'1"
MA 2/US 3 (Memorial Dr)	Cambridge–0.4 mile south of River St	11'10"
MA 3 NB	Boston–0.4 mile south of jct MA 28	11'6"
MA 3 (Memorial Dr)	Cambridge–express underpass at jct MA 2A	9'2"
MA 3A/113 (Kendall Rd)	Tyngsboro–at Merrimack River bridge	12'11"
US 5/ MA 10	Greenfield–0.2 mile south of MA 2A, Main St	12'10"
US 6 WB	West Barnstable–0.7 mile southwest at MA 149 overpass	13'4"
MA 6A (Main St)	Barnstable–approx 1 mile west	12'2"
MA 9 (Huntington Ave)	Boston–MA 2A (Massachusetts Ave) overpass	13'4"
MA 9 (Main St)	Northampton–just east of US 5	12'3"
MA 10/ US 202 (Elm St)	Westfield–0.25 mile south of Westfield River	13'5"
MA 13 (Main St)	Leonminster	13'6"
MA 10/ US 202 (N Elm St)	Westfield–just north of Westfield River	11'5"
MA 19 (Maple St)	Warren–just south of MA 67	13'0"
MA 21 (Parker St)	Springfield	12'5"
MA 27 (Crescent St)	Brockton–just east of MA 28	12'8"
MA 28 (McGrath Hwy)	Somerville–0.4 mile south of I-93	13'4"
MA 31 (Depot St)	Fitchburg–0.2 mile north of MA12	12'6"
MA 31 (Princeton Rd)	Fitchburg–1.6 miles north of MA 2	13'2"
MA 32A (Barre Rd/ Old MA 32)	Hardwick–0.2 mile west of MA 32	12'0"
MA 35 (High St)	Danvers	13'5"
MA 62/70 (Main St)	Clinton	11'0"
MA 62 (Main St)	Concord	12'2"
MA 68 (Gardner St)	Baldwinville–just east of US 202	13'6"
MA 85 (River St)	Cordaville–0.8 mile south of I-90	11'0"
I-93/ MA 3	Boston–1.5 mile south of I-90	13'6"
MA 101 (Parker St)	Gardner–0.75 mile west of MA 68	13'3"
MA 116 (Cabot St)	Holyoke	12'0"
MA 116 (Lyman St)	Holyoke–at Lyman and Main Sts	11'5"
MA 117 (Lancaster St)	Leominster–0.3 mile east of MA 12	13'3"
MA 122A	Holden	13'6"
MA 122 (Madison St)	Worcester–0.4 mile west of I-290	12'0"
MA 146	Uxbridge	13'6"
MA 202A (Union Ave)	Westfield	13'4"
MA 203 (Morton St)	Boston–American Legion Highway overpass	12'11"
Belmont	Belmont–Train Bridge at Common St/ Concord Ave and Leonard St	10'3"

Michigan

Highway No.	Location	Height
MI 1 EB (Woodward Ave)	Highland Park–Davidson Ave	13'1"
MI 1 WB (Woodward Ave)	Highland Park–Davidson Ave	13'3"

Minnesota

Highway No.	Location	Height
Bus US 2	East Grand Forks–Red River bridge at North Dakota state line–Mile Point 0.00	13'0"
MN 36	Stillwater–St Croix River bridge at Wisconsin state line Mile Point 205.25	13'2"
MN 39	Duluth–0.9 mile east of MN 23, St Louis River bridge, mile	11'0"
MN 70	Pine City–4.5 miles south at Mile Point 20.06	13'6"
MN 72	Baudette-Rainey River bridge, Mile Point 76.90	11'8"
MN 93	0.7 mile east of jct US 169, Mile Point 0.05	12'8"

EXIT NOW

Highway No.	Location	Height
Mississippi		
MS 12	Columbus–approx. 3.8 miles north of US 82	12'9"
Missouri		
MO 5	Laclede–0.5 mile north of US 36	13'10"
MO 5	Marceline–2.4 miles south of US 36	13'11"
MO 5	Syracuse–0.1 mile north of US 50	13'9"
MO 12 EB (Truman Rd)	Independence–0.4 mile west of Sterling Ave	13'11"
MO 12 WB (Truman Ave)	Independence–0.4 mile west of Sterling Ave	13'5"
MO 13	Higginsville–0.5 mile south of US 24	13'8"
MO 13	Polo–0.3 mile south of MO 116	13'8"
MO 19	Cuba–0.7 mile north of I-44	13'10"
MO 19	New Florence–2 miles north of I-70	13'9"
MO 21	Paulina Hills–east of Meramec River bridge	13'9"
US 24	Kansas City–0.2 mile west of jct I-435	12'3"
US 24 EB	West Quincy–at Mississippi River	13'10"
MO 28	Dixon–0.2 mile south of County Road C	13'10"
MO 30	Affton–0.3 mile east of jct MO 21	13'9"
US 36 EB	Bucklin–0.8 mile west of MO 129	13'9"
US 40	Kansas City–just south of I-70 at Blue Ridge Blvd overpass	13'4"
US 40	Kansas City–Topping Ave overpass	13'6"
US 50	Sedalia–1.3 miles east of US 65	13'9"
US 61 NB	Frontenac–at I-64 overpass	13'10"
US 61/67	Arnold–north at Meramec River bridge	13'9"
US 63	Clark–0.3 mile south of Bus US 63	13'11"
US 63B SB	Moberly–1.5 miles south of US 24	13'10"
US 69 NB	Claycomo	13'8"
US 69B	Excelsior Springs–0.5 mile west of jct County Road H	13'6"
I-70 BL	Columbia–at Paris Rd overpass	14'0"
MO 94	West Alton–0.1 mile west of US 67	12'9"
MO 94	West Alton–0.5 mile west of US 67	12'7"
MO 100	Gasconade–Gasconade River bridge	13'10"
US 159	Missouri River bridge	12'10"
MO 168	Palmyra–1.1 miles west of jct County Road C at North River	13'9"
MO Spur 180	Pagedale–0.2 mile north of jct Rte D (Page Ave)	13'8"
MO 350 EB	Raytown–1.7 miles southeast of I-435 at Blue Ridge Blvd overpass	13'7"
Highway No.	Location	Height
MO 350 WB	Raytown–1.7 miles southeast of I-435 at Blue Ridge Blvd overpass	14'0"
Montana		
MT 7	Wibaux–Milepost 79.9	13'6"
MT 13W	Wolf Point–Milepost 52.7	14'0"
MT 49	East Glacier Park–just west of US 2 at Milepost 209.3	13'6"
US 87 SB	Black Eagle–15th St–Milepost 3.70	14'0"
US 87	Great Falls–Smelter Ave–Milepost 3.77	14'0"
US 191	Big Timber–Milepost 0.79	13'8"
US 191	Malta–just south of US 2 at Milepost 157.5	13'5"
US 212/310	Laurel–0.5 mile north of I-90 at Milepost 54.5	13'3"
Nebraska		
NE 2/US 385	Alliance	13'11"
US 6/NE 31	Elkhorn–1 mile south, Link 28B	14'4"
US 6	Emerald	14'5"
US 6	Lincoln–2 miles west	13'10"
US 30 SB	Columbus–1 mile south at Loup River bridge	14'4"
NE 31	Gretna–at US 6 and Dodge St	14'4"
NE 71	Kimball–0.2 mile north of US 30	13'6"
US 81 SB	Columbus–Loup River bridge, 1 mile south	14'4"
US 81	York–at 14th St and 15th St	13'11"
NE 133 (90th St)	Omaha–0.2 mile south of NE 64 (Maple St) at Lake St	13'7"
US 275	at jct US 6 and NE 31	14'0"
Nevada		
US 50	Cave Rock tunnel–Lake Tahoe	12'4"
US 50	Cave Rock tunnel–Lake Tahoe	13'7"
NV 738	Las Vegas–south, Jean underpass	14'0"
NV 794 (Winnemucca Blvd)	Winnemucca	14'0"
Bonanza Rd (F.A.U. 579)	Las Vegas–Bonanza underpass	14'0"
2nd St and Kuenzil Lane (F.A.U. 648)	Reno–2nd St underpass	14'0"
Wells Ave (F.A.U. 663)	Reno–0.2 mile north of E 2nd St	13'10"
New Hampshire		
NH 9	Chesterfield–Connecticut River bridge	13'6"
NH 16A	Jackson–Ellis River bridge	12'3"
NH 16B	Rochester	12'2"
NH 25	Piermont–1.7 miles west, Conecticut River bridge	12'0"
NH 63	Hinsdale–2.3 miles south	12'8"
NH 85	Exeter	11'8"
NH 110	Berlin	10'4"
NH 110A	Milan	13'6"
NH 119	Hinsdale–7.3 miles north, Connecticut River bridge	12'0"
NH 135	Dalton	10'3"
NH 135	Woodsville–just north of US 302	10'11"
New Jersey		
US 1/9	Elizabeth–Mile Marker 44.6	13'3"
US 1/9 (Elizabeth St)	Elizabeth–Elizabeth River viaduct,	12'10"
US 1/9/46	Palisades Park–Oakdene Ave overpass–Mile Marker 63.86	13'5"
NJ 4	Englewood–Jones Rd overpass, Mile Marker 9.62	13'4"
NJ 5	Cliffside Park–Delia Blvd overpass, Mile Marker 0.5	10'6"
NJ 24 WB	Madison–Mile Marker 4.81	13'0"
NJ 28	Plainfield–Mile Marker 14.42	11'11"
US 30	Camden–Baird Blvd overpass, Mile Marker 2.49	13'4"
NJ 53	Denville–Mile Marker 4.2	13'2"
I-80	Columbia–Mile Marker 3.62	12'3"
I-80	Columbia–Decatur St overpass, Mile Marker 4.18	13'2"
NJ 93 (Grand Ave)	Palisades Park–US 46 overpass, Mile Marker 0.61	13'5"
NJ 94	Hainesburg–Scranton Branch overpass–Mile Marker 2.20	13'6"
US 130	Brooklawn (south of Gloucester City) Mile Marker 25.61	13'6"

Highway No.	Location	Height
NJ 173	Bloomsbury–Mile Marker 4.35	12'4"
US 202	Morris Plains–Mile Marker 46.96	13'6"
I-278	Linden–Mile Marker 0.66	12'0"
NJ 439	Elizabeth–Mile Marker 1.93	12'1"
I-495	Union City–Hudson Ave overpass, Mile Marker 1.85	13'3"
Access Road	Elmwood Park–I-80 underpass, Mile Marker 60.59	10'10"
Main St	Ft. Lee–US 1/9/46 overpass, Mile Marker 64.51	13'4"
Cemetary Road	River Edge–NJ 4 overpass, Mile Marker 5.5	13'0"
Bordentown Ave	South Amboy–NJ 35 overpass, Mile Marker 49.1	13'5"

New Mexico

Highway No.	Location	Height
US 54	Logan–0.4 mile east of jct NM 39	14'0"
US 56	Springer–0.1 mile east of jct I-25	13'8"
US 70	Lordsburg–29.6 miles east of Arizona state line	14'0"
US 84	Fort Sumner–0.4 mile north of jct US 60	13'11"
NM 118	Gallup–12.7 miles east of Arizona state line at I-40	14'0"
NM 118	Mentmore–8.4 miles east of Arizona state line at I-40	13'11"
NM 124	Grants–1.2 miles east of NM 117/124 at I-40	13'6"
NM 152	Kingston–1.2 miles east	12'8"
NM 152	Kingston–3.2 miles east	12'5"
NM 161	Watrous–at I-25 overpass at Exit 364	13'11"
NM 320 NB	Dona Ana–3.7 miles north of US 70	13'10"
NM 395	Hondo–0.2 mile south of jct US 70/380 at Rio Hondo	12'9"
NM 423	Albuquerque–0.8 mile west of jct 2nd St	13'11"
Paseo del Norte		
NM 423	Albuquerque–jct Rio Grande Blvd	13'11"
NM 567	Pilar–6.1 miles north of jct NM 68 at Rio Grande	12'10"
FR 4184	Aztec–0.1 mile east of US 550	11'3"
Highway No.	Location	Height
FR 4221	Belen–0.5 mile east of Loop 13/NM 309	13'6"
Central Ave	Albuquerque–0.1 mile east of 1st St	13'11"

New York

Highway No.	Location	Height
US 1	Pelham Manor–at Hutchinson River Pkwy overpass	13'8"
US 1	Port Chester	12'11"
US 1	Port Chester	12'8"
NY 3/26	Carthage–0.4 mile north of jct NY 3 and NY 26	12'6"
US 4	Fort Edward–0.5 mile north of NY 197	13'11"
US 4	Schuylerville–0.2 mile north of NY 32	12'10"
NY 5/US 20	Canandaigua–0.1 mile southwest of NY 332	11'7"
NY 5	Scotia–2.5 miles west of NY 147	13'11"
NY 5	Syracuse–1.4 miles west of US 11	12'2"
US 6	Port Jervis–0.5 mile north of I-84 at Neversink River bridge	13'4"
US 6	Shrub Oak–at jct US 6 and Taconic State Pkwy	13'0"
NY 7	Binghampton–0.1 mile north of US 11	12'4"
NY 7	Cobleskill	13'10"
NY 7	Cobleskill	13'9"
NY 7	Rotterdam–1.7 miles northwest of NY 146	13'9"
NY 7	Sanitaria Springs 5.5 miles east of NY 369	13'7"
US 9 SB	Albany–ramp to EB I-90	13'5"
US 9 NB	Albany–at ramp to I-90 WB	13'9"
US 9	New York City–2.3 miles north of I-95 at Harlem River	13'6"
US 9	Peekskill–at US 6 overpass	11'1"
US 9	South Glens Falls–at Hudson River bridge	12'10"
US 9	Underwood–at I-87 overpass, Exit 30	13'9"
US 9A	New York City–at Harlem River	12'8"
NY 9A	Ossining–0.2 miles north of NY 133	12'6"
NY 9A	Ossining–1.4 miles north of NY 133	11'9"
NY 9A/100	Briarcliffe Manor–1.5 miles north of jct NY 117	12'2"
NY 9A/100	Hawthorne–north, at NY 117 overpass	13'3"
NY 9J	Rensselaer–at jct with US 9/20	13'10"
NY 9J	Stuyvesant–1.6 miles north	13'9"
NY 9L	Lake George–0.3 mile northeast of US 9	13'5"
US 9W	Cementon–1.1 mile north	13'4"
US 9W	West Camp	13'1"
US 11	Binghamton–6 miles north at I-81 overpass	13'11"
US 11	Binghamton–0.4 mile north of NY 17C	13'11"
US 11	Binghamton–0.25 mile south of jct NY 7	13'2"
US 11	Champlain–2.5 miles east	13'10"
US 11	Evans Mills–0.8 mile south of NY 342	13'8"
US 11 (Wolf St)	Syracuse–0.4 mile south of I-90	12'11"
NY 11A	Cardiff–US 20 overpass	13'6"
NY 12	Waterville–0.5 mile north of US 20	13'9"
NY 12E	Watertown	13'9"
NY 13	Chittenango	13'11"
NY 14A	Reading Center–0.7 mile northwest of NY 14	13'10"
NY 15	Lakeville–2 miles north of Alt US 20	13'8"
NY 16 WB	Buffalo–0.5 mile west of Fillmore Ave	12'7"
NY 16	East Aurora	13'10"
NY 16	Machias–0.1 mile north of NY 242	13'11"
NY 16	West Seneca–at I-90 overpass	13'11"
NY 17	Corning–1.2 mile northwest of jct US 15	13'11"
NY 17	Harriman–0.9 mile west of I087	13'11"
NY 19	Brockport–0.5 mile south of New York State Barge Canal	11'8"
NY 19	Rock Glen–0.7 mile south	13'6"
NY 19A	Silver Springs–1.6 mile southeast of NY 19	13'0"
US 20	Border City–0.2 mile west of NY 96A	13'10"
US 20	Cherry Valley–0.2 miles east of NY 166	13'10"
US 20	Duanesburg–0.7 mile northwest of NY 7	13'9"
US 20	McCormack Corners–0.2 mile northwest of NY 146	13'11"
US 20	Sangerfield–0.2 miles west of NY 12	13'8"
US 20/NY 78	West Seneca–0.25 mile north of NY 400	13'6"
Alt. US 20	Warsaw–0.3 miles east of NY 19	13'6"
NY 22	North Hoosick–0.1 miles south of NY 67	13'11"
NY 22 SB	Petersburg–at jct NY 2 and NY 22	13'1"
NY 22A	Granville–2.6 miles northeast of NY 22	11'10"
NY 23	Catskill–0.5 mile east of NY 385	12'11"
NY 25	Mineola–at Northern State Pkwy overpass	13'5"
NY 25	New York City–Queensboro Bridge over East River	8'5"
NY 25	New York City–0.1 mile east of I-278	13'10"
NY 25	New York City–0.1 mile east of I-495	13'8"

EXIT NOW   xxix

Highway No.	Location	Height
NY 25	Smithtown—0.5 mile west	13'10"
NY 25	Smithtown—1 mile west	13'8"
NY 25A	New York City—1.5 mile west of I-295	13'6"
NY 25A	St James—1.5 miles northeast of NY 25	13'9"
NY 26	Endicott—0.2 mile north of NY 17C	13'0"
NY 27	Amityville—at NY 110 overpass	13'10"
NY 27	Freeport—Meadowbrook State Pkwy overpass	13'3"
NY 27	Lynbrook	13'5"
NY 27	Lynbrook—1.5 mile west	13'6"
NY 27	New York City—0.5 mile east of Rockaway Pkwy	12'4"
NY 28	Kingston	13'10"
NY 28	Thendara—1 mile northeast	13'5"
NY 30	Esperance—1.2 miles south of US 20	13'10"
NY 30A	Central Bridge—0.5 mile north of NY 7	13'11"
NY 31	Niagra Falls—0.4 miles east of NY 104	13'7"
NY 31	Rochester—0.7 miles northwest of I-490	12'9"
NY 31F	Macedon—0.9 mile north of NY 31	13'7"
NY 32	Albany—1.4 mile north of I-90	13'11"
NY 32	Albany—0.6 mile south of I-90	11'4"
NY 33	Rochester—1 mile east of New York State Barge Canal	12'0"
NY 33A	Rochester—0.1 mile east of New York State Barge Canal	13'0"
NY 33B	Buffalo—0.4 mile west of US 62	13'8"
NY 34	Spencer—4.3 miles north	12'6"
NY 37	Malone—0.5 mile north of US 11	13'7"
NY 38	Owego	13'7"
NY 38/96	Owego—south at NY 17 overpass	9'6"
NY 41	Afton	13'11"
NY 42	Lexington	12'3"
NY 46	Oneida—0.2 mile north of NY 5	13'8"

Highway No.	Location	Height
NY 49	Utica—1 mile west of NY 12	13'11"
NY 55	Billings—1.3 miles west at Taconic St Pkwy overpass	13'9"
NY 59	Nanuet—at NY 304 overpass	13'10"
US 62	Buffalo—0.6 mile north of NY 354	13'7"
US 62	Eden—1.5 mile south	13'9"
US 62	Lackawanna—2.9 mile north of NY 179	13'7"
NY 63	Griegsville—0.2 mile west of NY 36	13'10"
I-78	New York City—Holland tunnel	12'6"
Co. 80 (Mantauk Hwy)	East Port	11'11"
Co. 80 (Montauk Hwy)	Hampton Bays—1 mile west	13'9"
Co 80 (Montauk Hwy)	Moriches	12'6"
NY 85	New Scotland—0.7 mile west of NY 85A	13'9"
Co 85 (Montauk Hwy)	Sayville	13'7"
NY 85	Slingerlands—0.7 miles southwest of NY 140	12'2"
NY 85A	Voorheesville—0.2 mile west of NY 155	12'1"
I-90	Albany—at US 9 overpass	13'5"
I-90	Clifton—8.8 miles east of I-490, Exit 47	13'11"
I-95	New York City—0.7 mile east of I-87	13'10"
NY 102	East Meadow at Meadowbrook State Park overpass	13'11"
NY 104	Niagra Falls—0.1 mile north of NY 182	12'1"

Highway No.	Location	Height
NY 104	Rochester—0.1 mile east of St Paul Blvd	13'10"
NY 107	Massapequa—north at Southern State Pkwy	13'3"
NY 110	Huntington Station 1.3 miles north of NY 25	13'10"
NY 110	Melville at Northern State Pkwy overpass	13'4"
NY 112	Medford—0.5 mile south of I-495	13'9"
NY 114	East Hampton—1 mile northwest	12'0"
NY 115	Poughkeepsie—1.1 miles northeast	11'0"
NY 120	Rye—just south of I-95	11'9"
NY 120A	Port Chester	11'2"
NY 120A	Port Chester—0.1 mile north of US 1	12'0"
NY 129	Croton on Hudson—4.6 miles northeast	12'4"
NY 130	Depew—1.4 miles west of US 20	13'11"
NY 146	Schenectady—3.5 miles north of NY 7	13'11"
NY 158	Rotterdam—0.7 mile south of NY 7	13'8"
NY 164	Towners	12'5"
NY 164	Towners	12'4"
NY 164	Towners	12'0"
NY 173	Syracuse—3 miles south of I-81 overpass	13'11"
NY 182	Niagara Falls—at Niagara River	13'10"
I-190	Buffalo—0.8 mile east of NY 5	12'6"
I-190	Tonawanda—2 miles north of I-290	13'10"
NY 198	Buffalo—1.7 miles east of I-190	13'11"
NY 201	Johnson City 0.7 mile south of Exit 70 on NY 17	11'11"
US 202	Suffern—0.4 mile north of NY 59	12'3"
NY 208	Washingtonville—2.5 miles north	9'2"
NY 211	Otisville	12'6"
NY 237	Holley—0.4 mile southwest of NY 31	12'11"
NY 249	Farnham—0.3 mile east of NY 5	11'0"
NY 251	Scottsville	13'9"
NY 253	East Rochester	13'11"
NY 259	Spencerport—0.2 mile south of New York State Barge Canal	12'6"
NY 265	Buffalo—2.7 miles south of NY 324	13'8"
NY 266	Buffalo—0.3 mile north of NY 198	12'4"
NY 266	Tonawanda—0.5 mile north of NY 325	13'11"
I-278	New York City Brooklyn Bridge overpass	13'2"
I-278 WB	New York City—0.1 mile east of Brooklyn Bridge	13'4"
I-278	New York City—2.4 miles southwest of I-495	13'11"
I-278	New York City at 31st St overpass	13'8"
I-278	New York City at NY 25 overpass	13'7"
I-278	New York City—0.2 mile north of NY 25	13'10"
I-278	New York City—0.6 mile north of NY 25	13'10"
I-278	New York City—0.3 mile north of NY 25A	13'4"
I-278	New York City—0.2 mile south of NY 25A	13'10"
I-278	New York City—0.2 mile north of Exit 25, 26	13'10"
I-278	New York City—0.2 mile south of Exit 32	13'11"
I-278	New York City—1.9 mile west of jct I-95 and I-678	13'9"
NY 286	Macedon—0.75 mile north of NY 31	13'4"
NY 291	Stittsville—2 miles south of NY 365	13'11"
I-295	New York City 0.6 miles southeast of I-95	13'7"
NY 308	Rhineback—1.8 miles east at

Highway No.	Location	Height
	NY 9G overpass	13'11"
NY 311	Lake Carmel–0.34 mile north of NY 164	11'9"
NY 329	Watkins Glen–2 miles southwest	12'5"
NY 334	Fonda–0.6 mile northwest of NY 5	13'0"
NY 335	Elsmere	13'6"
NY 352 WB	Elmira–east of NY 14	13'6"
NY 354	Buffalo–0.7 mile west of US 62	12'3"
NY 354	Buffalo–1 mile west of US 62	13'6"
NY 354	Buffalo–1.4 miles west of US 62	12'10"
NY 356	Tonawanda–0.3 mile east of NY 384	13'0"
NY 362	Bliss–0.4 mile north of jct NY 39	13'5"
NY 366	Varna	13'8"
NY 370	Liverpool–1.3 miles northwest of I-81	10'9"
NY 370	Syracuse–at jct I-81	10'6"
NY 370	Syracuse–0.5 mile northwest of US 11	12'3"
NY 372	Greenwich	11'11"
NY 383	Scottsville–1 mile west	13'10"
NY 384	Buffalo–at jct NY 198	13'3"
NY 384	Niagra Falls–0.6 mile east of NY 61	13'7"
NY 385	Coxsackie–0.8 mile east of US 9W	13'5"
NY 417	Portville–0.4 mile east of NY 305	13'3"
NY 443	Delmar–2.4 miles southwest	13'6"
NY 443	Elsmere	13'6"
NY 470	Cohoes–0.8 mile southwest of NY 32	10'10"
I-478	New York City–Brooklyn Battery tunnel	12'9"
I-490	Rochester–0.2 mile northwest of NY 33	13'8"
I-495	Locust Grove–at NY 135 overpass	13'10"
NY 495	New York City–Queens Midtown tunnel	12'9"
NY 495	New York City–east end of Lincoln tunnel access	13'11"
NY 495	New York City–Lincoln tunnel	13'0"
I-678	New York City–at 14th Ave overpass	13'7"
I-678	New York City–at NY 25 overpass	13'8"
I-678	New York City 0.8 mile south of NY 25	11'0"
I-678	New York City–0.1 mile north of Exit 5 and Atlantic Ave	11'1"
I-678	New York City–at Kennedy Int'l Airport	13'8"
I-678	New York City–at Cross Island Pkwy	13'7"
I-787	Albany–on ramp to northbound I-787 over Hudson River	13'7"
Rte 951R	Vandalia–0.3 mile southeast at Allegheny River	11'3"
Brooklyn Battery Terminal	New York City–Exit 25 NB to I-278	13'8"
Brooklyn–Queens Expwy NB	New York City–at Astoria Blvd overpass	13'6"
F.D. Roosevelt Dr	New York City–at Battery Pl overpass	13'9"
F.D. Roosevelt Dr Ramp SB	New York City–60th St overpass	12'10"
F.D. Roosevelt Dr	New York City–at Williamsburg Bridge	10'6"
F.D. Roosevelt Dr	New York City–0.25 mile south of Williamsburg Bridge	13'8"
F.D. Roosevelt Dr	New York City–just north of NY 25	13'0"
F.D. Roosevelt Dr	New York City–0.2 mile northeast of NY 25	13'8"
F.D. Roosevelt Dr	New York City–0.9 miles northeast of NY 25	13'8"
F.D. Roosevelt Dr	New York City 1.3 miles northeast of NY 25	12'8"
F.D. Roosevelt Dr	New York City 0.5 miles south of Triborough bridge	12'6"

Highway No.	Location	Height
F.D. Roosevelt Dr	New York City at 78th St, 0.9 mile northeast of NY 25 Access Rd	13'0"
Harlem River Dr	New York City–at Willis Ave overpass	11'4"
Harlem River Dr	New York City–at 3rd Ave overpass	13'8"
Harlem River Dr	New York City–at 145th St overpass	13'7"
Harlem River Dr	New York City–0.75 mile south of I-95	13'9"

North Carolina

Highway No.	Location	Height
Bus US 15/501 EB (Chapel Hill Blvd)	Durham–at NC 1127 (Chapel Hill Road) and Cornwallis overpass	13'1"
Bus US/ 15/70/501 (Roxboro St)	Durham–0.25 mile north of NC 147	12'0"
Bypass	Chapel Hill–2.8 miles northeast of NC 86, Bus US 15/501/ 15/501 overpass	13'2"
NC 16	Crumpler–southwest, before jct US 221	13'1"
NC 54	Durham–0.1 mile west of NC 1959 (Miami Blvd)	13'6"
(Nelson Chapel Hill Hwy)	Durham–0.1 mile north of jct NC 147 NC 55	13'6"
NC 55 (Alston Ave)	Durham–0.2 mile north of NC 147	13'2"
NC 94	Fairfield–3.6 miles north at the Intracoastal Waterway	13'6"
Bus I-95/US 301	Fayetteville–Bus I-95/US 301 underpass before jct I-95	11'10"
US 157 (Guess Rd)	Durham–I-85 underpass 0.6 mile north of jct I-85 & NC 1321	13'6"
US 155 EB	Welden–0.5 mile west of jct US 301	13'6"
NC 215	Beach Gap–Blue Ridge Pkwy underpass	13'0"
NC 1603	Stoneville–1 mile north of NC 770	13'5"
NC 1603	Stoneville–0.8 mile south of NC 770	13'6"
NC 581	just south of Alt US 264	9'0"
SR 3841 (East Market St)	Greensboro–just west of Alt US 29	8'0"

North Dakota

Highway No.	Location	Height
Bus US 2 (Demers Ave)	Grand Forks–at Red River Bridge	13'0"
ND 8	Stanley–0.9 mile north of US 2	14'0"
ND 14	Towner–0.4 mile north of US 2	13'7"
ND 22	Dickinson–1.2 miles south of I-94	13'10"
US 10/52/I-94	Casselton–0.5 mile west of ND 18	13'9"
Bus US 81 (Main Ave)	Fargo	13'9"
Bus US 81 NB (10th St)	Fargo–0.1 mile north of Main Ave	14'0"
BUS 81 SB (University Dr)	Fargo–0.1 mile north of Main Ave	13'7"
Bus US 83 SB (7th St)	Bismarck–0.1 mile south of Main Ave	13'9"
Bus 83 NB (9th St)	Bismarck–0.1 mile south of Main Ave	13'11"

Ohio

Highway No.	Location	Height
OH 7	Bellaire–0.4 mile north of OH 147	12'6"
OH 7	Bellaire–0.5 mile north of jct OH 149	13'2"
OH 14	2.5 miles southeast of OH 165	13'6"
OH 17	In Brook Park and Cleveland .054 mile west of I-71	13'6"
OH 18	Hicksville–0.5 mile northwest of jct OH 2 and OH 49	12'6"
OH 19	Republic–0.6 mile south of jct OH 162	11'7"
US 20		

EXIT NOW

Highway No.	Location	Height
(Euclid Ave)	Cleveland—0.4 miles east of jct US 322 (Mayfield Rd)	13'6"
US 33 WB	Columbus—0.6 mile east of Olentangy River on Spring St	13'3"
US 36	Piqua—0.5 mile west of OH 185	13'0"
OH 37	Delaware—1 mile west of US 23	12'8"
OH 39	Mansfield—0.3 mile west of US 42	13'2"
US 42	Delaware—1.2 miles northeast of US 36	13'6"
US 42	Mansfield—0.2 mile east of OH 430	12'1"
OH 48	Covington—0.1 mile north of US 36	12'9"
OH 61	New Haven—0.2 mile north of OH 103	10'10"
US 62 (Rich St)	Columbus—0.1 mile west of Scioto River	12'10"
US 62	Columbus—0.4 mile southwest of I-71	13'6"
OH 66	Defiance—0.5 mile south of OH 15/18	13'0"
OH 82	Macedonia—0.2 mile east of I-271	13'6"
OH 100	Tiffin—0.3 mile north of OH 18	11'7"
OH 103	Willard—1.4 miles north of US 224	13'4"
OH 111 NB	Defiance—0.7 mile south of OH 424	11'11"
OH 111 SB	Defiance—0.7 mile south of OH 424	11'10"
OH 126	The Village of Indian Hills 1.7 miles east of US 22	12'9"
OH 148	Armstrong Mills—Captina Creek bridge—0.1 mile west of OH 9	13'5"
OH 175 (Richmond Rd)	Solon—0.6 mile north of jct OH 43 (Aurora Rd)	10'0"
OH 183	Alliance—1.5 miles north of US 62	11'8"
OH 212	Bolivar—0.3 mile west	12'6"
OH 245	West Liberty—0.8 mile west of US 68	13'0"
OH 303	Hudson—0.2 mile west of OH 91	13'5"
US 322 (Mayfield Rd)	Cleveland—0.3 mile east of US 20 (Euclid Ave)	12'8"
OH 335	Omega—approx 2.7 miles east	12'0"
OH 335	Portsmouth—3.8 miles north of US 52	12'8"
OH 508	DeGraff—0.3 mile south of OH 235	12'7"
OH 521	Delaware—1.4 miles northeast of US 36	12'9"
OH 558	East Fairfield—1.5 miles west of OH 517	13'0"
OH 611	Lorain—2.1 miles east of OH 58	13'4"
OH 646	Germano—0.8 mile east of OH 9	12'11"
OH 666	Zanesville—0.8 mile north	10'7"
OH 762	Orient—1 mile southeast of US 62	13'3"

Oklahoma

Highway No.	Location	Height
US 51 (Broken Arrow Expressway)	Tulsa, 31st, as it goes under the expressway	13'4"
US 70	Mead	13'6"
Alt US 75	Beggs—0.9 mile north of OK 16	13'6"

Oregon

Highway No.	Location	Height
OR 99W NB	Corvallis—0.6 mile south of US 20 at Mary's River bridge	12'9"
OR 180 (Eddyville–Blodgett Hwy)	Eddyville—approx 6 mile east of jct US 20	12'5"
OR 260	Merlin—approx 4 miles southwest of Robertson Bridge (Rogue River Loop Hwy)	12'6"

Pennsylvania

Highway No.	Location	Height
US 6	Mill Village—west at French Creek bridge	13'6"
PA 8 (Washington Blvd)	Pittsburg—0.3 mile north of PA 380	13'4"
PA 8 NB	Wilkinsburg—at I-376	13'2"
PA 8 NB	Wilkinsburg—at I-376	13'2"
US 13 (Highland Ave)	Chester—0.7 mile west of US 322	13'0"
US 13	Norwood—0.5 mile north at South Ave	12'9"
US 13	Philadelphia—0.15 mile south of Wissahickon Ave	13'4"
US 13 NB (Chester Pike)	Ridley Park—0.35 mile east of Fairview Rd	13'5"
US 19	Fairview—2 miles south	13'5"
US 19	Mercer—2.6 miles south of I-80	12'6"
PA 27	Pittsfield—0.2 mile west of jct 6	12'9"
US 29	Phoenixville—1.1 miles northeast of PA 23	13'6"
US 30 (Girard Ave)	Philadelphia—just west of Belmont Ave	13'2"
US 30	Stoystown—PA 281 overpass	13'5"
US 30 WB	Chambersburg—0.35 mile east of US 11	13'5"
PA 36	Altoona—0.2 mile northwest of PA 764 (7th Ave)	13'6"
PA 36	Punxsutawney—0.5 mile west of US 119	13'4"
PA 38	Hooker—0.3 mile south	13'6"
PA 45	Spruce Creek—just south of Little Juniata River	8'2"
PA 50	Woodrow—0.5 mile east	12'8"
PA 51 SB (Carson St)	Pittsburgh—just northwest of jct PA 51/US 19	13'5"
PA 53	Jamestown	13'1"
PA 53	Wilmore—0.4 mile west of PA 160	13'0"
PA 54	Danville—at Susquehanna River bridge	13'2"
PA 56/711	Seward—just north of Conemaugh River	13'4"
PA 58	Jamestown—just southwest of jct PA 56 and US 322	210'8"
PA 59	Ornsby—1.5 miles west of jct PA 646	13'3"
PA 61	Sunbury—east at Shamokin Creek bridge	13'6"
US 62	Mercer—1.5 miles northeast of jct US 19	12'3"
US 62	Tionesta—3 miles southwest at Allegheny River bridge	13'1"
PA 87	Mehoopany—0.5 mile south	12'6"
PA 89	Northeast—0.4 mile south of US 20	13'4"
PA 98	Fairview—0.8 mile north of US 20	13'3"
PA 100	Chadds Ford—0.3 mile south of US 1	10'10"
PA 108	New Castle—at Mahoning River bridge	11'6"
PA 168	Moravia—between PA 18 and Beaver River	12'6"
PA 173	Cochranton—west at French Creek Bridge	13'6"
PA 183	Cressona—1 mile west of PA 61	11'11"
PA 214	Seven Valleys	11'3"
PA 217	Blairsville—0.4 mile south of US 22/119	13'3"
PA 220	Hughesville—northeast at Muncy Creek bridge	13'4"
US 220 BUS	Tyrone	12'9"
PA 221	Taylorstown—0.9 mile north of US 40	13'2"
US 222	Quarryville—0.5 mile north of PA 372	10'0"
PA 225	Dornsife—at Mahanoy Creek bridge	12'8"
PA 249	Cowanesque—at Cowanesque River bridge	12'10"
PA 259	Bolivar	9'4"
PA 284	English Center—2.1 miles east of PA 287	11'1"

Highway No.	Location	Height
PA 288	Chewton	11'1"
PA 288	Wampum	13'4"
US 322	Downingtown–0.25 mile south of BR 20	10'3"
PA 324	Martic Forge–0.8 mile east of Pequea Creek	12'0"
PA 329	Northampton–at Lehigh River bridge	12'10"
PA 339	Mahanoy City–just north of PA 54	11'6"
PA 340	Bird in Hand–west of town	13'5"
PA 352	Frazer–0.25 mile south of US 30	10'3"
PA 372	Atglen–1.2 miles west of PA 41	11'2"
PA 412	Bethlehem–1.5 miles east of PA 378	13'3"
PA 413	West Bristol–just south of US 13 (Bristol Pike)	13'4"
PA 420	Prospect Park–0.4 mile north of US 13	12'8"
PA 438	La Plume–0.5 mile east of US 6/11	12'1"
Highway No.	Location	Height
PA 441	Middletown–0.45 mile south of jct PA 320	11'3"
PA 488	Ellport–1.3 mile east of PA 65	12'2"
PA 488	Wurtemburg–1.6 mile north of Slippery Rock Creek	11'3"
PA 501	Myerstown–1 mile south of jct US 422	13'6"
PA 532 NB	Holland–0.2 mile south	9'8"
PA 532 SB	Holland–0.2 mile south	9'11"
PA 532 SB	Newtown–2.2 miles south	13'5"
PA 568	Gibralter–just south of PA 724	13'6"
PA 611 NB	Easton–0.2 mile south	12'11"
PA 616	Railroad–0.4 mile north of PA 851	8'1"
PA 616	Seitzland	10'0"
PA 641	Carlisle–just west of US 11	12'10"
PA 690 EB	Moscow–just east of PA 435	12'10"
PA 690 WB	Moscow–just east of PA 435	12'5"
PA 849	Duncannon–just west of Juniata River	13'6"
PA 866	Ganister–1.7 mile east of US 22	12'4"
PA 885 (2nd Ave)	Pittsburg–0.2 mile south of I–376	12'1"
PA 981	Latrobe	9'10"

Rhode Island

High St	Central Falls–approx. 0.75 mile south of RI 123 and 0.1 mile east of RI 114 (Broad St)	11'3"
High St	Central Falls–approx. 1.5 miles south of RI 123 and 0.25 mile east of RI 114 (Broad St)	9'9"
Lincoln Ave	Lincoln Park–0.3 mile south of RI 37, between I-95 and US1 (Boston Post Rd)	10'3"
Blackstone Ave	Pawtucket	9'3"
Church St	Valley Falls	12'7"
West St	Westerly	11'5"
Main St	Woonsocket	12'7"

South Carolina

SC 10	McCormick–2 miles northwest	10'6"
US 25	Edgefield–0.6 mile south of SC 23	13'6"
SC 86	Piedmont–0.09 mile east of jct SC 20	11'6"
SC 86	Piedmont–0.13 mile east of jct SC 20	11'8"
SC 146 (Woodruff Rd)	Greenville–0.25 mile east of US 276	13'6"
SC 177	5 miles north of SC 9, north of Cheraw	13'6"
SC 183 NB (Cedar Lane)	Greenville–1 mile west of Bus US 25	13'4"
SC 823	Little River bridge–approx 3 miles north of Mt Carmel	12'7"

South Dakota

US 14	Pierre–downtown	11'1"
Alt. US 16	Keystone–2.8 miles southeast at Mile Marker 54.09	9'7"
Alt. US 16	Keystone–tunnel 3.3 miles southeast at Mile Marker 53.68	12'7"
Alt. US 16	Keystone–tunnel 4 miles southeast at Mile Marker 53.00	12'4"
Alt. US 16	Keystone–4 miles southeast at Mile Marker 53.02	12'6"
Alt. US 16	Keystone–tunnel 6.5 miles southeast at Mile Marker 50.49	12'1"
SD 53	White River bridge 13.8 miles south at I-90 at Mile Marker	11'7"
SD 79 NB	Rapid City–west of I-90 Interchange 51 at Mile Marker 87.08	13'10"
US 81	Yankton–12 miles north at James River Bridge at Mile Marker	12'4"
SD 87	Sylvan Lake tunnel–1 mile southeast in Custer State Park at Mile Marker 74.65	10'7"
SD 87	Sylvan Lake tunnel –2 mile southeast in Custer State Park at Mile Marker 72.85	11'9"
SD 87	Sylvan Lake-tunnel 6 mile southeast in Custer State Park at Mile Marker 66.85	12'5"
SD 248	Reliance–I-90 underpass at Interchange 248	13'5"
SD 271	Java–1.1 miles northeast of SD 130 at Mile Marker 167.65	12'1"

Tennessee

TN 17	Chattanooga–near Lookout Mountain, Mile Marker 2.05	8'6"
US 25 W/TN 9	Clinton–0.15 mile north of TN 61, Mile Marker 9.94	13'5"
US 27	Chattanooga–southeast of jct I-124 at McCallie tunnel	12'4"
US 31/ TN 6 (8th Ave S)	Nashville–0.2 miles north of I-40, Mile Marker 8.24	12'10"
TN 33 (Maryville Pike)	Knoxville–0.8 miles southwest of US 441, Mile Marker 4.76	10'2"
TN 33 (Maryville Pike)	Mt. Olive–0.3 miles north, Mile Marker 3.00	12'9"
TN 39	Riceville–0.2 mile east of US 11, Mile Marker 1.77	13'3"
TN 40/ US 64	Cleveland–0.9 mile east of Bypass US 11, Mile Marker 0.93	11'1"
US 41/64/ 72	Chattanooga–west of I-24, Mile Marker 5.75	13'6"
US 41/64/ 72	Chattanooga–1.2 mile west of I-24, Mile Marker 3.33	12'7"
US 41/76/ TN 8 NB	Chattanooga–Bachman Tubes (tunnel), Mile Marker 5.04	12'7"
US 41/ 76/ TN 8 SB	Chattanooga–Bachman Tubes (tunnel), Mile Marker 5.04	12'7"
TN 47	White Bluff–2 miles south of US 70, Mile Marker 8.57	11'10"

EXIT NOW

Highway No.	Location	Height
TN 58	Chattanooga—1 mile south of I-24, Mile Marker 3.25	10'11"
TN 87	Henning—0.5 mile east of TN 209, Mile Marker 20.7	9'0"
TN 116	Disney—1.27 miles north of I-75, Mile Marker 0.97	13'5"
TN 131	Ball Camp—1.1 mile north, Mile Marker 5.93	10'7"
TN 241	Center—6.9 miles north, Natchez Trace Pkwy overpass, mile	11'6"
TN 246	Columbia—3.4 miles north of jct US 31 and TN 99, Mile Marker	11'1"
TN 252	Clovercroft—1.7 miles southeast, Mile Marker 3.59	10'7"
TN 252	Clovercroft—Mile Marker 5.26	10'9"
TN 252	Clovercroft—2 miles north, Mile Marker 7.37	10'5"
TN 299	Oakdale—1.0 mile west of TN 328, Mile Marker 9.89	10'6"
TN 346	Church Hill—0.3 mile north of US 11W, Mile Marker 8.21	10'2"
US 441	Great Smokey Mountains National Park—1 mile north of North Carolina state line, Mile Marker 1.07	11'4"
US 441	Great Smokey Mountains National Park tunnel north of North Carolina state line at Mile Marker 6.40	11'0"

Texas

Highway No.	Location	Height
US 283	.75 miles south of B 120, Baird	14'0"
FM 2047	at IH 20, Baird	14'0"
FM 604	at IH 20, Clyde	14'0"
FM 18	1 mile west of B 120, Baird	14'0"
FM 821	IH 20, east of Coahoma	13'0"
FM 820	at IH 20, Coahoma	13'6"
FM 818	at IH 20, west of Big Spring	13'6"
FM 700 SB	at IH 20, Big Spring	14'0"
EB 120	at East IH 20, Westbrook	13'6"
WB 120	at IH 20, Loraine	13'6"
B 120	between West IH 20 and FM 644, Loraine	14'0"
East SH 208	at IH 20, Colorado City	14'0"
SH 163	.125 mile south of B 120, Colorado City	14'0"
FM 3525	at IH20, Colorado City	14'0"
FM 2836	at IH20, west of Colorado City	13'6"
FM 1899	at IH20, Colorado City	13'6"
FM 1229	at IH20, west of Colorado City	13'6"
West FM 670	at IH20, Westbrook	14'0"
West FM 644	at IH20, Loraine	13'6"
West B 120	at IH20, Roscoe	14'0"
BS 70	between B 120 and south SH 70, Sweetwater	14'0"
FM 608	at IH 20, Roscoe	14'0"
LP 170	at IH 20, Sweetwater	13'0"
US 84	FM 1673, Snyder, WB NFR, EB SFR, WB ML	14'0"
US 84 WB	at US180, Snyder	14'0"
North B 84	.25 mile south of North US 84, Snyder	14'0"
FM1673	at US 84, Snyder	14'0"
East B 120 WB	at IH 20, Trent	13'6"
West B 120 WB	at IH 20, Merkel	13'6"
B 120/FM 1235	at East IH 20, Merkel	13'0"
US 83	at IH 20, Abilene	14'0"
BU 83 SB	SB, at B 120, Abilene	14'0"
FM 3438	at B 120, Abilene	14'0"
FM 1085	at IH 20, Trent	13'6"
FM 126	at IH 20, Merkel	13'6"
SH 207	.10 mile north of US 60, Panhandle	13'6"
US 87	SB, between US 54 and N US 385, Dalhart	13'0"
US 87	NB, between US 54 and N.US 385, Dalhart	13'6"
US 385	.25 mile south of US 60, Hereford	14'0"
SH 70	between US 60 and N SH 152, Pampa at IH 40, Wildorado	14'0"
FM 809	between SH136 and E. LP335, Amarillo	14'0"
B 140/US 60	between SP279 and B 140, US 60 Amarillo	14'0"
US 287/US 87/ SP 279	1 mile west of US 287/US 87/US 60, Amarillo	13'6"
US 87 NB to WB	at South US 60, Canyon	13'6"
US 87 SB to WB,	at South US 60, Canyon	14'0"
SH 217	.25 mile south of US 60, Canyon	14'0"
FM 1541	at IH 27, Amarillo	14'0"
IH 30 NFR	between FM 559 and FM 1397, Texarkana	14'0"
US 82	between SH 93 and SP 14, Texarkana	14'0"
US 67	between SH 93 and US 82, Texarkana	13'6"
FM 1997	.125 mile north of US 80, Marshall	11'0"
SH 49	.5 mile north of FM 1969, Lassater	14'0"
SH 49	.5 mile east of FM 134, Jefferson	13'6"
US 259/SH 49/ SH 11	between East SH11 and West SH 11, Daingerfield	13'6"
BU 271	.125 mile north of SH 49, Mount Pleasant	14'0"
FM 12/SH 80 WB	at IH 35, San Marcos	14'0"
FM 12/SH 80 EB	at IH 35, San Marcos	13'6"
N LP 82 EB	at IH 35, San Marcos	13'6"
IH 35 SB	at Ceasar Chavez, Austin	14'0"
IH 35 Lower Level	at Manor, Austin	13'6"
IH 35 Lower Level	at 32nd, Austin	13'6"
IH 35 Lower Level	at 38 1/2, Austin	13'6"
US 290 SFR	EB on-ramp from Industrial Oaks, Austin	13'6"
SH 71 WB	at US 183, Austin	14'0"
N FM 487	at IH35, Jarrell	13'6"
SH 61	at IH10, Hankamer	14'0"
FM 563	at IH10, Hankamer	14'0"
US 287/US 96/ US 69	.25 mile north of SH87, Port Arthur	14'0"
US 287/US 96/ SH 347 SB SB,	US69 SB at West IH10, Beaumont at SH 73, Groves	14'0"
SH63	at Sabine River Truss Bridge, east of Burkeville	12'3"
SH 87 SB	at IH 10, Orange	14'0"
US I83/U S84	between FM2126 and FM1467, Brownwood	14'0"
US 377/US 67	between FM 3100 and FM 1467, Blanket	14'0"
SH 206	.5 mile north of West SH 153, Coleman	13'0"
US 377/US 67	.33 mile west of West SH 36, Comanche	14'0"
US 183	between FM 574 and US 84, Goldthwaite	14'0"
SH 16	.25 mile north of US 190, San Saba	13'6"
SH 16	at Colorado River Truss Bridge, north of San Saba	13'9"
SH 6 FR's	1 mile north of FM 974, Bryan	14'0"
SH 36	.75 mile south of FM 166, Caldwell	14'0"
FM 166	.33 mile east of SH 36, Caldwell	11'6"
FM 60	.25 mile north of FM 111, Deanville	13'0"
SH 75	.125 mile east of West LP 262, Streetman	14'0"
SH 75	at IH 45, north of Madisonville	14'0"
US 190/US 77/SH 36	.5mile east of FM1600, Cameron	13'0'

Highway No.	Location	Height
SH36	.1 mile south of East US 190/US 79, Milano	13'6"
IH45 NB	at South SH 75, Huntsville	14'0"
PR40	at IH 45, south of Huntsville	14'0"
FM390	1 mile west of SH 36, Gay Hill	10'6"
US83 NB	at Salt Fork of the Red River Truss Bridge, north of Welling	13'0"
SH203	at Salt Fork of the Red River Truss Bridge east of Wellington	13'6"
SH 6	at Brazos River Truss Bridge, north of Knox City	13'0"
IH 37 WFR	at RR and SH 234, south of Mathis	13'0"
US 181	NB to SB turnaround at south FM 2986, Portland	13'6"
SH 358	NB to SB turnaround at BS 286, Corpus Christi	13'6"
SH 359	between SP 459 and FM 666, Mathis	14'0"
US 380	EB to NB and WB to NB, at SH 78, Farmersville	13'6"
US 380	.75 mile east of SH 78, Farmersville	13'6"
SH 121 WB	WB and WB to SB at SH 5, Melissa	14'0"
SH 5	or less, .25 mile south of FM1378, Allen	12'0"
SH 78	NB/SB, SB to WB, SB to EB, at US 380, Farmersville	13'6"
SP 339	WB , WB to US 75 SB, McKinney	14'0"
IH 30	at NW 19th, Grand Prairie	14'0"
IH 30 EB	.25 mile east of West LP 12, Dallas	14'0"
IH 30 WB	at N Hampton Road, Dallas	14'0"
IH 30 WB	at Fort Worth Avenue, Dallas	14'0"
IH 30/IH 35E	between West IH 30 and E IH 30, Dallas	14'0"
IH 30	between E IH 35E and IH 45, Dallas	14'0"
IH 30 EB	at Dolphin Road, Dallas	14'0"
IH 30	at Jim Miller Road, Dallas	14'0"
IH 30	at St Francis Avenue, Dallas	14'0"
IH 35E SB	SB to SP 354, Carrollton	14'0"
IH 35E	between SH 356 and SH 183, Dallas	14'0"
IH 35E SB	at SH 180, Dallas	14'0"
IH 35 E	between South Marsalis Ave and South Beckley Ave, Dallas	14'0"
IH 635 EB	at MacArthur Blvd, Irving	14'0"
IH 635 EB	EB to SB, at SH 78, Garland	14'0"
IH 635 SB	SB to WB	
US 80,	Dallas	14'0"
US 175 SB	at Martin Luther King Blvd, Dallas	13'6"
US 175 FR's	at South Prairie Creek Rd, Dallas	14'0"
US 80 EB	at Big Town Blvd, Mesquite	14'0"
US 80	at Town East Blvd, Mesquite	14'0"
US 80	at IH 635, Mesquite	14'0"
SH 352	at US 80, Mesquite	13'6"
SH 352	at East LP 12, Dallas	14'0"
SH 183 EB	EB to NB at West LP 12, Irving	14'0"
SH 114 FR	EB, between SH 161 and SP 348, Irving	14'0"
SH 78	SB at IH 30, Dallas	14'0"
SH 78	NB at IH 30, Dallas	13'0"
SH 78	between SP 244 and IH 635, Dallas	14'0"
SH 78	SB to EB, NB to EB, at IH 635, Dallas	14'0"
BS 66	.25 mile south of West SH 66, Rowlett	12'0"
West LP 12 NB	NB at Old Irving Blvd, Irving	14'0"
West LP 12 FR	FR NB south of SH 356, Irving Blvd, Dallas	14'0"
West LP 12 NB	at NB exit ramp to SH 356, Irving	14'0"
North LP 12	at Skillman St, Dallas	14'0"
North LP 12	.25 mile east of SP 354, Dallas	14'0"
FM 1382	at IH 35E, Dallas	14'0"

Highway No.	Location	Height
SP 366 WB	WB on-ramp from Maple and Routh, Dallas	13'6"
US 380	.125 mile west of IH 35, Denton	14'0"
US 377	.5 mile south of IH 35E, Denton	14'0"
Highway No.	Location	Height
SH 114	EB/WB, WB to SB, and WB to NB, at FM 156, Justin	13'6"
BS 114	85 feet west of US 377, Roanoke	13'6"
BS 114	at US 377, Roanoke	13'6"
FM 3524	.125 mile south of US377, Aubrey	13'6"
FM 156	NB to EB and SB to EB, at SH 114, Justin	13'6"
IH 35E WFR	at Red Oak Road, Red Oak	14'0"
BU 287	.5 mile south of North IH 35E, Waxahachie	14'0"
US 80	3.3 miles east of East FM 429, east of Terrell	13'6"
SH 34	NB, at US 175, Kaufman	14'0"
FM 1641/FM 548	at US 80, Forney	14'0"
IH 45 NB	NB to South IH45 NB, Corsicana	14'0"
SH 14	2.5 miles south of Richland	14'0"
IH 30 NFR	EB/WB, WB to SB, WB to NB, at FM 549, Rockwall	13'0"
IH 30 NFR	EB/WB, EB to SB, EB to NB, at FM 551, Fate	13'6"
US 90/US 67	.3 mile west of FM 1703, Alpine	13'6"
US 90	7 miles south of IH 10, Van Horn	14'0"
SH 20 SB	at Mesa St/IH 10, El Paso	14'0"
East BI 10	.75 mile west of east IH 10, Sierra Blanca	13'0"
US 377	.5 mile north of North FM 56, Tolar	14'0"
IH 35W WFR	at Bethesda Road, Burleson	14'0"
North BI 35 SB	at North IH 35W, Alvarado	13'6"
BI35	at BS 67, Alvarado	13'6"
SP50	at IH 35W, Burleson	14'0"
US281	4.5 miles north of IH 20, Brazos	13'6"
US281	at Brazos River Truss bridge, Brazos	12'0"
IH 35W NB	NB and NB to WB, at North IH 820, Fort Worth	14'0"
IH 35W	.25 mile south of SH 180, Fort Worth	14'0"
IH 30/US 377	EB, at Merrick St, Fort Worth	14'0"
IH 30	at Ridgmar Road/Ridgle Ave, Fort Worth	14'0"
IH 30	EB to NB, and WB to SB, at SH 183, Fort Worth	14'0"
IH 30 EB	.25 mile east of SH360, Arlington	13'6"
IH 30 EB	at Fielder, Arlington	13'6"
East IH 820	NB to EB, NB to WB, and WB to EB at SH 180, Fort Worth	14'0"
East IH 820 FR's	SB/13'6" NB at SH 180, Fort Worth	14'0"
East IH 820 FR's	between SH 180 and SP 303, Fort Worth	14'0"
SH 360	at SH 180, Arlington	14'0"
SH 360	less than 600' south of SH 180, Arlington	14'0"
SH 183	between BU 287 and IH 35W, Fort Worth	13'6"
SH 183	SB to EB/13'6" NB to WB, at IH 30, Fort Worth	14'0"
SH 183 EB	EB to NB, at Southeast IH820, Fort Worth	14'0"
SH 180	EB to NB, at East IH 820, Fort Worth	13'6"
SH 180	WB to SB and EB to SB/	14'0"
SH 121	at Sylvania, Fort Worth	13'6"
SH 10 WB	WB to SB, at East IH 820, Fort Worth	14'0"
FM 157	at IH 30, Arlington	14'0"

EXIT NOW

Highway No.	Location	Height
FM 156 SB	at US 287/US 81, Fort Worth	14'0"
SP 465 NB	NB to WB, at SH 183, Fort Worth	14'0"
SP 341	SB, .25 mile south of state maint, Fort Worth	13'6"
SP 341	NB, .25 of a mile south of state maint., Fort Worth	14'0"
LP 303 WB	WB and WB to NB, at East IH 820, Fort Worth	14'0"
SH 332	350 feet east of FM 521, Brazoria	14'0"
SH 332	at FM 521, Brazoria	14'0"
SH 6	at SH 35, Alvin	14'0"
US 90A	at West SH 36, Rosenberg	13'6"
US 90A	.25 mile west of FM 3155, Richmond	14'0"
SH 36	200 feet north of West US 90A, Rosenberg	13'6"
IH 45 NB	NB to NB, at SH 6, Texas City	14'0"
SH 146 SB	SB to SB, at IH 45, Texas City	13'0"
SH 146/SH3 SB	SB, .25 mile north of IH 45, Texas City	14'0"
SH 146/SH3 SB	SB to NB, at SH 6, Texas City	14'0"
IH 45	SB to WB and NB to WB, at North IH 610, Houston	14'0"
IH 45	at West Dallas St, Houston	14'0"
IH 45	at Quitman St, Houston	13'0"
IH 45	NB, at North Main St, Houston	14'0"
IH 45	SB, at North Main St, Houston	13'6"
IH 45	at Cottage St, Houston	14'0"
IH 45/IH 10	between East IH 10 and West IH 10, Houston	13'6"
IH 10	at East IH 610, Houston	14'0"
IH 10 EB	EB to NB, at US 59, Houston	14'0"
IH 10 WB	at Southeast IH 45, Houston	14'0"
IH 10 WB	at Northwest IH 45, Houston	14'0"
IH 10	at Sawyer St, Houston	14'0"
IH 10	at West IH 610, Houston	14'0"
North IH 610	WB to SB, at North IH 45, Houston	14'0"
West IH 610 SB	WB to EB, at West IH 10, Houston	14'0"
US 90A	1.33 miles northwest of IH 45, Houston	14'0"
US 90A	1.25 miles southwest of IH 45, Houston	14'0"
US 59 SB	SB to SB, at southwest IH 610, Houston	14'0"
SH 225 EB	EB to NB, at southeast IH 610, Houston	14'0"
SH 225 FR	WB to SB, at SH 146, La Porte	14'0"
SH 146 FR	.25 mile south of SH 225, La Porte	14'0"
SH 146 FR	NB to WB, at SH 225, La Porte	14'0"
SH 35 SB	at South IH 610, Houston	14'0"
SH 225 FR	EB to SB, at SH 46, La Porte	14'0"
SH 6	at IH 10, Houston	13'6"
SP 261	at North IH 610, Houston	14'0"
SH 75	.25 mile south of FM 2854, Conroe	13'6"
FM 1572	4 miles west of US 90, Brackettville	13'0"
FM 469	at IH 35, Millet	14'0"
IH 35	1 mile north of North US 83, Webb	14'0"
FM 1472	at IH 35, Laredo	14'0"
SP 369	at IH 27, Abernathy	14'0"
IH 27 FR's	at North LP 289, Lubbock	14'0"
US 82	.5 mile west of IH 27, Lubbock	14'0"
US 62	.25 mile east of BU 87, Lubbock	14'0"
BU 87	.50 mile north of US 62, Lubbock	14'0"
PR 18	at US 82, Lubbock	13'6"
FM 597	power lines at SP 369, Abernathy	14'0"
SP 369	power lines north side of FM 579, Abernathy	14'0"
SH 86	between US 60 and West FM 173, Bovina	14'0"
FM 145	.1 mile east of US 84/US 70, Farwell	12'0"
US 87	at South SH 86, Tulia	14'0"

Highway No.	Location	Height
US 87/SH 86	between South SH 86 and North SH 86, railroad, Tulia	14'0"
US 59	between FM 3439 and FM 3521, Lufkin	13'6"
BU 69/S 103	WB .125 mile west of North BU 59, Lufkin	13'6"
BU 69/S 103	EB .125 mile west of North BU 59, Lufkin	14'0"
North BU 59	.25 mile south of US 69, Lufkin	13'6"
SH 94	.125 mile west of SP 266, Lufkin	13'6"
SH 21/7	between SH 19 and FM 229, Crockett	13'6"
FM 1	1 mile north of North FM 83, Magasco	13'6"
US 59	.1 mile south of South LP 424, Shepherd	13'6"
SH 7	.5 mile north of SH 87, Center	13'6"
SH 349	at BI 20, Midland	14'0"
US 75 FR	NB to SB turnaround at SH 56, Sherman	13'6"
US 69	.125 mile north of SH 56, Bells	13'6"
US 69	at Spruce St, Whitewright	14'0"
US 69	.25 mile south of FM 898, Whitewright	14'0"
BU 377	.1 mile north of South US 377, Whitesboro	13'0"
SH 91	to/from SP 503, Denison	14'0"
SH 91	at SH 75, Sherman	14'0"
SH 56	at US 377, Whitesboro	13'0"
SH 56	.125 mile east of US 69, Bells	14'0"
SP 503	at SH 91, Denison	14'0"
SP 503	to/from SH 91, Denison	14'0"
BU 271 NB	at North LP 286, Paris	14'0"
US 82/North LP 286	.25 mile west of N.US 271, Paris	14'0"
FM 499	.125 mile north of East IH 30, Cumby	14'0"
IH 30 EB	at SH 34, Greenville	13'6"
SH 11	at SH 224, Commerce	14'0"
FM 2642	at IH 30, west of Greenville	13'6"
FM 1903	at IH 30, west of Greenville	13'6"
FM 1570	at IH 30, Greenville	13'6"
East FM1565	at IH 30, west of Greenville	13'6"
West FM 36	at IH30, 8.5 miles west of Greenville	14'0"
South BU 77	SB, at US 83/US 77, San Benito	13'6"
FM 801	at US 83/US 77, Harlingen	14'0"
FM 1479	at US 83/US 77, Harlingen	14'0"
SP 486	at US 83/US 77, San Benito	14'0"
US 281	at US 83, Pharr	14'0"
SH 336	at US 83, McAllen	14'0"
IH10 NFR	at Johnson Fork Creek Truss Bridge, Segovia	14'0"
LP 481	at South Llano River Truss Bridge, Junction	10'0"
BU 67	between E.LP306 and US277, San Angelo	14'0"
South LP 306	EB to WB and WB to EB turnarounds at Ben Ficklin, San Angelo	13'6"
IH 35	SB, .5 mile north of SP 422, San Antonio	14'0"
IH 37/US 281	NB at Hot Wells Blvd, San Antonio	14'0"
IH 37/US 281	at New Braunfels Avenue, San Antonio	13'6"
IH 10	at New Braunfels Avenue, San Antonio	14'0"
IH 10	at Gevers, San Antonio	14'0"
IH 10 WB	at Walters St, San Antonio	14'0"
North IH 410 WB	at NW IH 10, San Antonio	14'0"
North IH 410 EB	at Airport Blvd, San Antonio	14'0"
North IH 410	at Starcrest Drive, San Antonio	14'0"
US 281 SB	at South IH 410, San Antonio	14'0"
West US 90	.75 mile west of West LP13, detourable, San Antonio	14'0"
SH 218	EB, at East LP 1604, Converse	14'0"
SH 16	NB, at West IH 410, San Antonio	14'0"
FM 2790	.25 mile south of South LP 1604, Somerset	13'6"
FM 2790	at South IH 410, San Antonio	13'6"

FREE CAMPING • FREE GAS • CASH BACK
FREE GOOD SAM MEMBERSHIPS & SERVICES

GET THIS...

AND GET REWARDED FOR
DOING WHAT YOU LOVE

Apply Today!
1-866-599-1275
www.goodsamcard.com/GS17

PLUS FREE GIFT CARDS AT CAMPING WORLD, LEADING MERCHANTS & RESTAURANTS AND MORE!

*The Good Sam VISA Card is issued by Barclays Bank Delaware. Important terms and conditions apply. Complete details on the rewards program will be described in the enrollment materials. If at the time of your application you do not meet the credit or income criteria previously established for this offer we may be unable to open an account for you. Please review the materials provided with your Cardmember Agreement for more details.

Highway No.	Location	Height
FM 2252 SB	SB to EB, at North IH 410, San Antonio	14'0"
FM 1346	at East IH 410, San Antonio	14'0"
SP 537	at North IH 410, San Antonio	13'6"
SP 371	1 mile south of US 90, San Antonio	14'0"
SP 368	at IH 35, San Antonio	14'0"
SP 117	at East IH 410, San Antonio	13'6"
LP 13 EB	at IH 37, San Antonio	14'0"
IH 35 FR's	NB/SB and SB to WB at FM 1102, Hunter	14'0"
IH 35 WFR	at Kohlenberg Road–Conrads Lane, New Braunfels	13'6"
IH 35 FR's	SB to NB and NB to SB turnarounds, at Guadalupe River, New B	14'0"
BS 46	.5 mile west of IH 35, New Braunfels	14'0"
BS 46	1.25 mile north of BI 35, New Braunfels	12'0"
North BI 35	.5 mile south of North IH 35, Pearsall	14'0"
FM 775	at IH 10, Seguin	14'0"
FM 725	.25 mile north of FM 78, McQueeney	14'0"
LP 534	at IH 10, Kerrville	14'0"
SH 132	1 mile north of SH 173, Devine	14'0"
SH 294	.1 mile east of US 84/US 79, Tucker	14'0"
SH135	NB, .75 mile south of SH 31, Kilgore	13'6"
SH135	SB, .75 mile south of SH 31, Kilgore	14'0"
SP 63 SB	.1 mile south of US 80, Longview	14'0"
SH 323	.5 mile south of SH 135, Overton	13'6"
FM 1513	.5 mile east of SH 42, New London	14'0"
US 69/SH 110/H 64	.125 mile south of SH 31, Tyler	14'0"
SH 135	at SH 64, Arp	13'6"
SH 31	EB, .125 mile east of US 69/SH 110/SH 64, Tyler	14'0"
SH 31	WB, .125 mile east of US 69/SH 110/SH 64, Tyler	13'6"
West LP 323	NB, .25 miles south of SH31, Tyler	14'0"
West LP 323	SB, .25miles south of SH31, Tyler	13'6"
IH 35	at FM 935, Troy	13'6"
IH 35	at US 190/SH 36/South LP 363, Temple	14'0"
IH 35 NB	at Stagecoach Rd, Salado	14'0"
FM 817	1.5 miles south of IH 35, Belton	13'6"
FM 817	.33 mile north of FM 93, Belton	14'0"
US 190/SH3 6/South LP 3631	.25 mile west of East LP 363, Temple	14'0"
FM 56	.1 mile southeast of FM1859, Kopperl	13'6"
BS 6	1 mile south of SH7, Marlin	14'0"
BS 6	.75 mile north of SH7, Marlin	13'6"
IH 35 SB	at County Line Rd, south of Abbott	14'0"
SH 81	1 mile south of SP579, Hillsboro	14'0"
US 77/SP 579 SB	at IH 35, Hillsboro	14'0"
IH35 NB	at Old Dallas Rd, Elm Mott	14'0"
IH35 NB	NB, at FM 3148, Lorena at FM 2063, south of Waco	14'0"
IH35	at North FM 2837, Lorena	14'0"
IH35	at South FM 2837, Lorena	14'0"
IH35 NB FR	NB to SB turnaround at BU 77/SP 299, Waco	14'0"
IH35 FR's	.75 mile south of FM 3149, north of Elm Mott	14'0"
BU 77	at US 84, Waco	14'0"
BU 77	NB to SB and SB to NB turnarounds at IH 35/SP 299, Waco	13'6"
SH 6	at SP 412, Woodway	14'0"
FM 2114	WB at IH 35, West	13'6
FM 2114	EB at IH 35, West	14'0"
FM 2417	at IH 35, north of Waco	14'0"
FM 308	at IH 35, Elm Mott	14'0"
LP 2	at IH 35, Waco	14'0"

Highway No.	Location	Height
SP 484 NB	NB to BU 77 SB, Waco	14'0"
SP 510	.125 mile north of US 287, Henrietta	14'0"
FM 922	at IH 35, Valley View	14'0"
FM 372	at IH 35, Gainesville	14'0"
FM 51	at IH 35, Gainesville	14'0"
US 82	.75 mile west of US 81, Ringgold	13'6"
FM 1125	.1 mile south of US 81, Bowie	14'0"
US 287	at Rifle Range Road, Iowa Park	14'0"
US 287 NB	at SP 11, Wichita Falls	13'6"
US 287	SB, at Wellington Lane, Wichita Falls	14'0"
US 287	NB, at Wellington Lane, Wichita Falls	13'6"
US 287	at Huntington Lane, Wichita Falls	13'6"
BU 287	.5 mile north of SH 240, Wichita Falls	13'6"
FM 369	at US 287, Wichita Falls	14'0"
FM 171	between BU 287 and South SH 240, Wichita Falls	14'0"
SP 325	SE to N, at US 287, Wichita Falls	13'0"
SP 325 WB	WB to US 287 SB, Wichita Falls	14'0"
US 183/S LP 145	at South US 287, Oklaunion	14'0"
SH 36	at US 90, Sealy	14'0"
US 90	3.3 miles east of E FM 155, Weimar	14'0"
BS 71	.1 mile north of US90, Columbus	13'6"
SH 111	.25 mile east of S BU 77, Yoakum	14'0"
US 90	between FM 2762 and West SH 95, Flatonia	14'0"
US 77	between US 90 and SP 222, Schulenburg	13'6"
West US 90	1.5 miles west of FM 794, Harwood	13'6"
FM 1686	at US 59, Victoria	14'0"

Vermont

Highway No.	Location	Height
US 2	Bolton–6.5 miles west of VT 100N	13'9"
US 2	Danville–4 miles east, 3.5 miles west of US 5	13'3"
US 2	Waterbury–0.2 miles west of VT 100 at Winooski River	11'0"
US 4	Hartford–0.1 mile east of jct US 4, US 5 and VT 14	13'8"
Bus US 7	Bennington–0.2 miles north of VT 67 A	12'6"
VT 12 NB	Berlin–2.7 miles south of US 2	13'2"
Alt VT 12	Roxbury–4 miles south	13'6"
VT 14	Royalton–northwest to jct VT 107	12'2"
VT 15	Walden–5.7 miles northwest of US 2	13'6"
Alt VT 22	Vergennes–north 0.3 miles south of US 7	13'6"
VT 102	Bloomfield–0.1 mile south of VT 105	12'9"
Alt VT 105	Stevens Mill–0.1 mile north of VT 105	12'8"
VT 123	Westminster–0.1 mile east of US 5	12'2"
VT 346	North Pownal–4.7 miles west of US 7 at Hoosick River, New York state line	11'8"

Virginia

Highway No.	Location	Height
US 1	Alberta–0.7 mile northwest of VA 46	13'6"
US 1	Woodbridge–4.5 mile north	13'3"
VA 2/ Bus	Fredericksburg–0.5 mile south of VA 3	13'6"
US 17 NB, SB, VA 5	Richmond–0.8 mile south of US 80	12'11"
VA 7	Alexandria–0.6 mile west of US 1	13'0"
US 11 SB	Staunton–0.5 mile south of jct VA 254	9'9"
US 13	Chesapeake Bay Bridge tunnel 7 miles north of US 60	13'3"
US 13	Kiptopeke	13'3"
US 13	Kiptopeke–1 mile south	13'3"
US 15	Orange	13'6"
Bus. US 23	Appalachia–0.4 mile southwest	13'3"

Highway No.	Location	Height
VA 24 WB	Vinton—east of Blueridge Pkwy overpass	13'0"
VA 27 WB	Arlington—at US 50 (Arlington Blvd)	13'0"
Bus. US 29	Charlottesville—0.4 mile south of Bus US 250	12'7"
Bus. US 29	Charlottesville—0.1 mile north of Bus US 250	13'3"
VA 31	Scotland—at James River Ferry, both banks	12'3"
VA 39	Goshen—0.1 mile south of VA 42	11'10"
VA 57	Martinsville—0.9 mile west of Bus. US 220	9'9"
US 58/VA 337	Portsmouth—Midtown Toll tunnel, both ends	13'3"
US 60	Covington—0.8 mile west of jct US 220	13'5"
US 60/I-64	WBHampton Roads Bridge tunnel	13'3"
VA 102	Bluefield—0.2 mile north of US 19	8'9"
VA 110	Arlington—0.5 mile southeast of US 50	13'4"
VA 113	Bristol	12'9"
VA 130	Glasgow—east at Blue Ridge Pkwy overpass	13'6"
VA 166	Chesapeake—at jct US 13/460	13'5"
VA 218	Ferry Farms—0.6 mile east of VA 3	13'5"
VA 240	Crozet	11'6"
US 250	Yancey Mills—7.3 miles east of jct I-64	13'3"
Bus US 250	Charlottesville—0.6 mile east of Bus US 29	10'8"
VA 254	Staunton—just east of US 11 overpass	13'1"
I-264 Alt US 460 WB	Portsmouth—Norfolk Downtown tunnel, both ends	13'3"
VA 311 SB	Crows—3.5 miles north	12'11"
VA 360	Danville—1.7 miles north of US 58/360	12'3"
US 501	Rustburg—0.2 mile north of VA 24	13'3"

Washington

Highway No.	Location	Height
US 2	Skykomish—tunnel 2.7 miles northwest, Milepost 45.98	19'6"
US 2/395 NB (Browne St)	Spokane—0.2 miles north of I-90, US 2 Milepost 287.18	14'6"
US 2/395 SB (Division St)	Spokane—0.2 miles north of I-90, US 2 Milepost 287.18	14'0"
I-5 NB	Seattle—ramp NB on I-5 to WA 522 (Lake City Way)	13'8"
I-5 NB	Vader—ramp northbound on I-5 to WB on WA 506	13'8"
WA 14 EB	five tunnels between Cook and Underwood, Mileposts 58.08, 58.45, 58.92, 59.61, & 60.23	14'6"
WA 14 EB	Lyle—two tunnels approx. 1 mile east, Mileposts 76.77 and 76.86	13'10"
WA 24 NB	Othello—1 mile south of WA 26 underpass, Milepost 79.63	13'10"
WA 99 SB, NB	Seattle—pedestrian overpass, 0.4 miles south of N 45 St	16'9"
WA 99 SB	Seattle—at Columbia St entrance ramp SB	14'0"
WA 99 SB (Alaskan Way Viaduct)	Seattle—3.8 miles north of jct WA 509, Milepost 29.84	14'3"
WA 125 NB (Pine St)	Walla Walla—north of Oregon state line, Milepost 5.93	14'3"
WA 167 NB	Renton—0.6 miles north of I-405, Milepost 26.90	13'9"
US 395 SB (Lewis St)	Pasco—WB on Lewis St to SB on US 395	14'5"
WA 506 WB	Vader—ramp WB on WA 506 to NB I-5	12'9"
WA 509 SB (East 11th St)	Tacoma—1.6 miles north of I-5 over City Waterway, Milepost 0.22	17'9"
WA 513 SB	Seattle—0.6 mile north of WA 520 at Univ of WA, Milepost 0.61	15'2"
WA 536	Mt Vernon—2nd St underpass, Milepost 4.98	14'0"
WA 538 EB	Mt Vernon—east of jct I-5	15'0"

West Virginia

Highway No.	Location	Height
Alt WV 10	Huntington—between 7th Ave and 8th Ave	13'4"
WV 16	War—approximately 1 mile north	13'5"
WV 16	Welch—0.27 mile south of WV 7	10'6"
WV 17	Logan—0.02 mile north of WV 10	9'4"
US 19	Kegley—0.5 mile south of WV 10	12'9"
County 21	0.2 miles south of US 50	13'4"
WV 28	0.16 miles south of Maryland state line	12'8"
Alt. WV 37	Wayne—0.15 mile south of US 52 at Twelvepole Creek	13'4"
US 40	Wheeling—just north of I-70	11'0"
WV 49	Matewan	11'8"
WV 63	Caldwell—0.23 mile south of US 60	9'11"
Wv 88	Bethany—0.9 miles south of WV 67 at Buffalo Creek bridge	11'9"
Alt. US 119	Mitchell Heights—0.64 miles north of US 119	12'0"
US 119	Williamson—0.02 miles south of US 52	13'5"
US 250	Philippi—south of US 119 at Tygart Valley River bridge	12'0"

Wisconsin

Highway No.	Location	Height
WI 32 NB (Kinnickinnic Rd)	Milwaukee—1 mile south of jct WI 15/59 (National Ave)	13'0"
WI 32 SB (Kinnickinnic Rd)	Milwaukee—1 mile south of jct WI 15/59 (National Ave)	13'3"
WI 32 NB (Kinnickinnic Rd)	Milwaukee—2.1 miles north of WI 62	13'5"
WI 32 SB (Kinnickinnic Rd)	Milwaukee—2.1 miles north of jct WI 62	13'3"
WI 32 SB (Kinnickinnic Rd)	Milwaukee—1.2 miles south of jct WI 15/59 (National Ave)	13'3"
WI 32 NB, SB	Milwaukee—0.3 miles north of jct WI 15/59 (National Ave)	13'6"
WI 32 NB (S 1st St)	Milwaukee—0.3 miles north of jct WI 15/59 (National Ave)	13'6"
WI 32 SB (S 1st St)	Milwaukee—0.3 miles north of jct WI 15/59 (National Ave)	11'0"
WI 32 NB, SB	South Milwaukee—2.6 miles north of jct WI 100	13'1"
WI 51 NB, SB	Plover—4.5 miles north of jct WI 54	13'6"
WI 64 EB, WB	Houlton—St Croix River bridge, 0.7 mile west of WI 95 at Minn state line	13'2"
WI 73 NB, SB	0.3 mile south of southern jct WI 64	13'1"
WI 105 EB	Oliver—St Louis River bridge at Minn state line	1'9"
WI 145 NB, SB (Fond Du Lac Ave)	Milwaukee—1.1 miles northwest of WI 57 at West Locust	13'6"
WI 145 NB (Fond Du Lac Ave)	Milwaukee—0.2 mile northwest of jct I-43 at 12th St	13'6"

Wyoming

Highway No.	Location	Height
Bus I-25	Casper—0.2 mile south of I-25 Center St Int at Milepost 0.44	13'5"
WY 96	La Prelle Int jct I-25, 5 miles west of Douglas at Milepost 3.11	13'10"
XR I-25	at Milepost 131.59	13'8"
XR I-25	Barber Int at Milepost 154.24	13'7"
XR I-25	Powder River Int at Milepost 246.56	14'0"
XR I-80	Coal Int at Milepost 21.75	13'9"
XR I-80	Bar Hat Int at Milepost 23.12	13'11"
XR I-80	French Int—at Milepost 28.71	13'8"
XR I-80	Union Int—at Milepost 33.18	13'8"

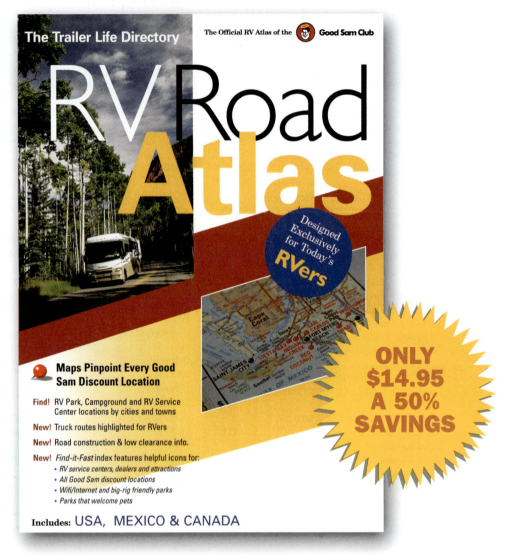

10 times better than other atlases... because this one's for RVers!

The Only Atlas that:

- Is made specifically by RVers, for RVers
- Provides an Index of All Campgrounds found in the Trailer Life Directory
- Indentifies All the Good Sam Locations
- Includes RV Service Centers, Tourist Attractions, and State Parks
- Highlights routes that are accessible to oversized vehicles

We Make Ordering Easy!
Call toll free to 1-877-209-6658 Ext. 702
Or Visit us at www.TrailerLifeDirectory.com

Or Mail to:
The Official Good Sam RV Road Atlas
PO Box 24
Boulder, CO 80329-0024

Please Include $4.95 for shipping and handling.
(CA residents, please include sales tax.)

EXIT		FLORIDA
	Begin Eastbound I-4 from Tampa, FL to Daytona Beach, FL	

⊙ FLORIDA

(I-4 begins/ends on I-95, Exit #260B)
(I-4 begins/ends on I-275, Exit #45B)
(EASTERN TIME ZONE)

(0)		Jct I-275S, Tampa Airport, St Petersburg, Gulf Beaches Jct I-275N, to I-75N, Ocala
1		FL 585, 21st St, 22nd St, Port of Tampa, Ybor City
	Gas	S: BP
	Food	S: Burger King, McDonald's
	Lodg	S: Hilton Garden Inn
	Other	S: Ybor City Shops, Brewery, Cigar Shops
3		US 41, 50th St, Columbus Dr
	TStop	S: Sunoco #2595
	Gas	N: Shell, Chevron
		S: BP, Speedway
	Food	S: Burger King, McDonald's, Pizza Hut, Subway, Waffle House
	Lodg	N: Days Inn♥, USA Inn♥
		S: Best Value Inn, Howard Johnson
5		FL 574, FL 583, ML King Jr Blvd
	Gas	S: BP, Shell, Sunoco
	Food	N: McDonald's, Sunshine Cafe
		S: Subway/Shell, Wendy's
	Lodg	S: Inns of America, Masters Inn
	TServ	N: Tampa Bay Truck Repairs & Wash
		S: Great Dane Trailers, Kenworth
6		Orient Rd (EB)
	Other	N: Seminole Hard Rock Casino & Hotel
		S: Holiday RV Superstore
7		US 92, to US 301, Hillsborough Ave (WB), US 301, US 92E, Riverview, Zephyrhills Ave (EB)
	FStop	S: Petro Mart #627/Marathon
	TStop	N: Citgo (Scales)
	Gas	N: Chevron, Circle K
		S: BP, Citgo, RaceTrac
	Food	N: Waffle House
		S: Denny's, Kettle Restaurant
	Lodg	N: Motel 6♥
		S: Baymont Inn, Holiday Inn Express, La Quinta Inn, Red Roof Inn♥
	Other	N: FL St Fairground, Vandenburg Airport✈,
		S: Holiday RV Superstore, Foretravel of Florida
(9)		Jct I-75, N - Ocala, S - Naples
NOTE:		EB/WB: New In Motion Weigh Station Due late 09/early 10 to be located Between Exits #10 and #14, #19 to be Removed then.

Personal Notes

EXIT		FLORIDA
10		CR 579, Seffner, Tampa, Mango, Thonotosassa
	TStop	N: Flying J Travel Plaza #5081 (Scales), Travel Center of America #158/BP (Scales)
	Gas	N: Marathon
		S: Shell
	Food	N: Rest/FastFood/FJ TP, Arby's/Popeye's/TA TC, Bob Evans, Cracker Barrel
		S: Hardee's, Wendy's
	Lodg	N: Hampton Inn
		S: Masters Inn, Quality Motel
	TServ	N: TA TC/Tires
	Other	N: Laundry/WiFi/RVDump/LP/FJ TP, Laundry/WiFi TA TC, Lazy Days RV Center/Rally RV Park▲, McCormick Lakes RV Park▲, Auto Dealer, Camping World, U-Haul

EXIT		FLORIDA
14		McIntosh Rd, Dover
	Gas	N: BP◊
		S: 7-11, BP, Hess, RaceWay
	Food	S: Burger King, McDonald's
	Other	N: Windward Knoll RV Park▲, Longview Motorhomes & RV Superstore
		S: Encore RV Park▲, Green Acres RV Travel Park▲, Tampa East RV Resort▲, Bates RV
17		Branch Forbes Rd, Plant City
	Gas	N: Shell
		S: Chevron, Citgo
	Food	S: Subway
	Other	N: Dinosaur World, Keel Farms Winery
(19)		Inspection Station (Both dir)
19		FL 566, Thonotosassa Rd
	Gas	N: BP
		S: RaceTrac
	Food	S: Applebee's, Carrabba's, McDonald's, Outback Steak House, Waffle House
	Med	S: + Hospital
	Other	S: Publix, Dollar General
21		FL 39, Alexander St, Buchman Hwy, Zephyrhills, Plant City (EB)
	Gas	S: BP◊, Shell
	Food	S: Tony's Pizza, Rest/Ramada Inn
	Lodg	S: Days Inn, Ramada Inn
	Med	S: + Hospital
	Other	N: Sundial RV Park▲
21AB		FL 39, Buchman Hwy, Alexander St, Zephyrhills, Plant City (WB)
22		FL 553, Park Rd, Plant City
	Gas	S: Shell, Texaco
	Food	N: Chancy's
		S: Arby's, Burger King, Denny's, Taco Bell/Subway/Shell
	Lodg	S: Comfort Inn, Days Inn, Holiday Inn Exp
	Other	S: Turning Wheel RV Center, Plant City Stadium, Hillsborough Community College, Strawberry Festival Fairgrounds
25		County Line Rd, Lakeland
	FStop	S: Speedlane Citgo
	Gas	S: Citgo◊, Shell
	Food	S: McDonald's, Wendy's
	Other	N: FL Air Museum, Lakeland Linder Reg'l Airport✈
		S: Florida RV World & Rentals
27		US 92, FL 570E (TOLL), Polk Pkwy, Lakeland, Winter Haven, Bartow
28		Memorial Blvd, FL 546, to US 92, N Galloway Rd, Lakeland (EB)
	TServ	S: to Truck PM Plus

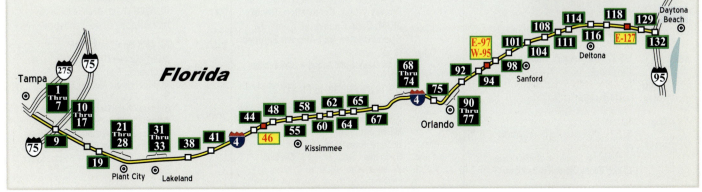

◊ = Regular Gas Stations with Diesel   ▲ = RV Friendly Locations   ♥ = Pet Friendly Locations

RED PRINT SHOWS LARGE VEHICLE PARKING/ACCESS ON SITE OR NEARBY   BROWN PRINT SHOWS CAMPGROUNDS/RV PARKS

Page 1

INTERSTATE 4 W–E

EXIT	FLORIDA
31	FL 539, Kathleen Rd, Lakeland
32	US 98, Lakeland, Dade City
Gas	**N:** Chevron◆, Shell, Sam's **S:** 7-11, BP, RaceTrac, Sunoco
Food	**N:** Denny's, Don Pablo, Golden Corral, Hooters, IHOP, KFC, McDonald's, Olive Garden, Red Lobster, Steak 'n Shake, Taco Bell, TGI Friday, Zaxby's
Food	**S:** Bob Evans, Burger King, Denny's, Long John Silver, Roadhouse Grill, Waffle House, Wendy's
Lodg	**N:** Comfort Inn, La Quinta Inn♥, Royalty Inn **S:** Best Western, Crossroads Motor Lodge, Days Inn, Holiday Inn, Motel 6♥, Ramada Inn
Med	**S:** + Hospital
Other	**N:** Best Buy, Dollar General, Goodyear, Kash n Karry, Lowe's, Publix, Sam's Club, Staples, Target, Walgreen's, Wal-Mart▲, Lazy Dazy Retreat, RV World of Lakeland, Tiki Village Resort▲, to Scenic View RV Park▲, to Gator Creek Campground▲ **S:** Auto Zone, Home Depot, Office Depot, U-Haul, Winn Dixie, Sanlan Ranch Campground▲, Bramble Ridge Golf Course
33	FL 33, Lakeland (EB), CR 582, to FL 33, Lakeland (WB)
Gas	**N:** 7-11, Exxon **S:** BP
Food	**N:** Applebee's, Cracker Barrel, Wendy's **S:** Waffle House
Lodg	**N:** Hampton Inn, Jameson Inn♥, Quality Inn, Sleep Inn **S:** Howard Johnson, Relax Inn
Med	**S:** + Hospital
Other	**S:** Harley Davidson Lakeland, Veterinary Emergency Care♥, to Lakeland RV Resort▲
38	FL 33, USA Int'l Speedway, Lakeland, Polk City
Other	**N:** USA Speedway, Ken Robertson RV Center
41	FL 570W (TOLL), Polk Pkwy, Lakeland (EB), FL 570W, Polk Pkwy, Auburndale, Lakeland (WB)
44	FL 559, Polk City, Auburndale
TStop	**S:** Love's Travel Stop #228 (Scales), MTC Petro/Petrol Mart #107 (Scales)
Food	**S:** Arby's/TJCinn/Love's TS
Other	**N:** WiFi/RVDump/Love's TS, Le Lynn RV Resort▲ **S:** Fantasy of Flight
(46)	Rest Area (Both dir) (RR, Phone, Picnic, Vend, Sec24/7)
48	CR 557, Lake Alfred, Winter Haven
Gas	**S:** BP◆
55	US 27, Davenport, Haines City, Clermont
FStop	**N:** Kangaroo Express #2125
TStop	**S:** (10 mi to US17/92) Commercial Truck Terminal/Citgo (Scales)
Gas	**N:** 7-11, Sunoco **S:** BP◆, Marathon, Raceway, Shell◆
Food	**N:** Cracker Barrel, Denny's, McDonald's, Shoney's, Waffle House **S:** Bob Evans, Hardee's, Perkins

Personal Notes
_____

EXIT	FLORIDA
Lodg	**N:** Comfort Inn, Hampton Inn, Florida Southgate **S:** Best Western, Days Inn, Quality Inn
TServ	**S:** CTT/Tires
TWash	**S:** CTT
Med	**S:** + Hospital
Other	**S:** Laundry/CTT **S:** Deer Creek RV Golf Resort▲, Fort Summit KOA Camping Resort▲, Theme World Campground▲
58	FL 532, Osceola Polk Line Rd, Davenport, Kissimmee, Poinciana
Gas	**N:** 7-11, BP
Food	**S:** China One, McDonald's, Subway
Other	**S:** Lakewood RV Resort▲, Mouse Mountain RV & MH Resort▲, 21 Palms RV Resort▲, Rainbow Chase RV Resort▲
60	FL 429 (TOLL), Apopka
62	FL 417N (TOLL) (EB), World Dr, Disney World, Celebration, Epcot, MGM, Cape Canaveral, Kennedy Space Center, Int'l Airport, Sanford
Other	**N:** to Disney World **S:** to Orlando Int'l Airport✈, Celebration Station
64A	US 192E, FL 536, to FL 417 (TOLL), Kissimmee, Celebration Station, Magic Kingdom, Disney, MGM Studios
Gas	**S:** Mobil, RaceTrac
Food	**S:** Charlie's Steak House & Seafood, Cracker Barrel, IHOP, KFC, Kobe Japanese, Joe's Crab Shack, McDonald's,

EXIT	FLORIDA
Food	**S:** Red Lobster, Shoney's, Subway, Wendy's, Waffle House, Western Sizzlin
Lodg	**S:** Best Western, Days Inn, Hampton Inn, Holiday Inn, Homewood Suites, Howard Johnson, Hyatt Hotel, Knights Inn, Quality Suites, Radisson, Rodeway Inn, Red Roof Inn♥, Suites at Ole Town, Super 8, Travelodge♥
Med	**S:** + Med-Plus Family Medical Center
Other	**S:** Walgreen's, Factory Outlet Stores Mall, US Post Office, 21 Palms RV Resort▲, Kissimmee KOA▲, Paradise RV Resort▲, Tropical Palms Resort & Campground▲, Sherwood Forest RV Resort, Disney's Fort Wilderness Resort & CG▲, Camping World
64B	US 192W, FL 536, Kissimmee, Celebration, Magic Kingdom, Disney, MGM Studios
Other	**N:** Orlando Harley Davidson South
65	Osceola Pkwy, Animal Kingdom, Kingdom, Wide World of Sports, Disney World, to International Dr.
67	FL 536, to FL 417 (TOLL), World Center Pkwy, to Epcot, Disney, International Dr
Gas	**S:** 7-11/Citgo
Food	**S:** Restaurant, Starbucks
Lodg	**S:** Holiday Inn, Marriott, Radisson
Other	**S:** CVS, Prime Outlet, Arabian Nights
68	FL 535, S Apopka Vineland Rd, Lake Buena Vista, Kissimmee
Gas	**N:** Chevron, Shell◆ **S:** 7-11, Chevron
Food	**N:** Black Angus Steaks, Chili's, China Buffet, Denny's, Dunkin Donuts, IHOP, Joe's Crab Shack, Kobe, McDonald's, Olive Garden, Perkins, Red Lobster, Shoney's, Steak 'n Shake, Subway, Taco Bell, TGI Friday, Waffle House **S:** Golden Corral, Landry's Seafood, Lonestar Steakhouse, Wendy's
Lodg	**N:** Best Western, Comfort Inn, Days Inn, DoubleTree, Fairfield Inn, Holiday Inn, Radisson, Springhill Suites, Wyndham **S:** Country Inn, Crowne Plaza, Fairfield Inn, Holiday Inn, Marriott, Sheraton
Other	**N:** Walgreen's **S:** Premium Outlets Mall, to Aloha RV Park▲, Kissimmee/Orlando KOA▲
71	Central Florida Pkwy, Sea World International Dr (EB, no EB rentry)
Gas	**S:** Chevron
Food	**S:** Wendy's
Lodg	**S:** Hilton Garden Inn, Marriott, Residence Inn, Westgate Leisure Resort
72	FL 528E (TOLL-Beeline Expwy), Int'l Airport, Cape Canaveral
74A	FL 482, Sand Lake Rd, International Drive
Gas	**N:** Chevron, 7-11 **S:** BP, Chevron, Mobil◆, Shell
Food	**N:** ChickFilA, McDonald's, Wendy's **S:** Burger King, Denny's, Fishbones, Golden Corral, IHOP, McDonald's, Perkins, Sizzler, Starbucks, Tony Roma
Lodg	**N:** Comfort Suites, Courtyard, Days Inn, Hampton Inn, Hawthorne Suites, Quality Suites

Page 2   ◆ = Regular Gas Stations with Diesel   ▲ = RV Friendly Locations   ♥ = Pet Friendly Locations
RED PRINT SHOWS LARGE VEHICLE PARKING/ACCESS ON SITE OR NEARBY   BROWN PRINT SHOWS CAMPGROUNDS/RV PARKS

INTERSTATE 4 W-E

EXIT		FLORIDA
	Lodg	**S:** Best Western, Comfort Inn, Crowne Plaza, Embassy Suites, Days Inn, Fairfield Inn, Hilton Garden Inn, Holiday Inn**X2**, Howard Johnson, Knights Inn, La Quinta Inn ♥, Masters Inn, Microtel, Quality Inn, Radisson, Red Roof Inn ♥, Residence Inn, Springhill Suites
	Med	**N:** + Hospital **S:** + Walk-In Family Medical Center
	Other	**N:** Publix **S:** Walgreen's, Convention & Civic Center, Tourist Info, Pirates Cove Adventure Golf, Wonderworks, International World RV Park▲
74B		**Universal Blvd, Universal Studios, Hollywood Way (WB)**
75A		**FL 435S (WB), Universal, International Dr, to FL 435S (WB)**
	Gas	**S:** 7-11, Chevron
	Food	**S:** Bill Wong's, Burger King, China Café, El Patio, IHOP, Red Lobster, Starbucks, Sweet Tomatoes, Rest/Bass Pro Shop
	Lodg	**S:** Best Western, Clarion, Days Inn, Econo Lodge, Hampton Inn, Hilton Garden Inn, Howard Johnson, Homewood Suites, Motel 6 ♥, Orlando Grand Plaza, Ramada Inn, Rodeway Inn, Sheraton, Super 8, Travelodge
	Other	**S:** Bass Pro Shop, Festival Bay Mall
75B		**FL 435N, Kirkman Rd (Left exit)**
	Gas	**N:** Chevron, Mobil
	Food	**N:** Cracker Barrel, Denny's, Hard Rock Cafe, McDonald's, Waffle House
	Lodg	**N:** AmeriSuites, Best Western, Days Inn, Fairfield Inn, Hard Rock Hotel, Holiday Inn, Motel 6 ♥, Quality Inn
(77)		**Jct FL Turnpike (TOLL), N - Ocala, S - Miami**
78		**Conroy Rd**
	Gas	**N:** Citgo **S:** Chevron, Shell
	Food	**N:** IHOP **S:** ChickFilA, Chinatown, Kelly's Cajun Grill, McDonald's, Mimi's, Olive Garden, Seafood Rest, Starbucks, TGI Friday, Tuscan Bistro, Wendy's
	Other	**N:** Orlando Harley Davidson, Holy Land Experience, Historic District, Golf Course **S:** BJ's, Home Depot, Petco ♥, Publix, Super Target, Mall at Millenia, Golf Course
79		**FL 423, John Young Pkwy, 33rd St, Orlando**
	Gas	**N:** Citgo, Chevron **S:** 7-11, RaceTrac, Shell◊
	Food	**N:** McDonald's **S:** Burger King, IHOP, KFC, McDonald's, Rest/Days Inn
	Lodg	**N:** Extended Stay America, Ramada Inn **S:** Days Inn ♥, Super 8
	Other	**N:** Harley Davidson **S:** Cedars RV Park▲, El Monte RV Rentals & Sales
80		**US 441, US 17, US 92 (WB)**
	Gas	**N:** 7-11 **S:** BP, Chevron, Mobil, RaceTrac, Texaco
	Food	**N:** China Palace **S:** Denny's, Krystal, McDonald's, Waffle House, Wendy's
	Lodg	**N:** Super 8, Sands Motel **S:** Days Inn, Melody Motel, Regency Inn

Personal Notes

EXIT		FLORIDA
	Other	**N:** Auto & Tire Services, Orlando Int'l Airport✈ **S:** Auto Services & Repairs, Gator Tire Store, Food Lion
80AB		**US 441S, US 17, US 92, Orlando International Airport (EB) US 441N, US 17, US 92 (EB)**
81A		**Michigan St (WB)**
	Gas	**N:** Citgo◊
	Lodg	**N:** Budget Motel, Sands Motel
81B		**Kaley Ave East (WB)**
81C		**Kaley Ave West (WB)**
81BC		**Kaley Ave East/West (EB)**
	Gas	**S:** Citgo, Marathon, Mobil, Sunoco
	Food	**S:** Burger King, Starbucks, Wendy's
	Med	**S:** + Hospital
	Other	**S:** Amtrak
82A		**FL 408, Jct East – West Expy (TOLL), to FL 526**
82C		**Anderson St. East, Downtown, Church St Station (diff reacc)**
83		**South St, to Church St Station, to Downtown (WB)**
83B		**FL 50, Colonial Dr, US 17, US 92, Amelia St (EB)**
84		**FL 50, Colonial Dr (WB), Ivanhoe Blvd, Orlando**
	Gas	**S:** Chevron, Citgo, Marathon
	Food	**S:** IHOP

EXIT		FLORIDA
	Lodg	**N:** Holiday Inn, Howard Vernon Motel **S:** Courtyard, Knights Inn, Sheraton
85		**Princeton St, Orlando**
	Gas	**N:** Hesss **S:** Chevron
	Food	**N:** Godfather's **S:** Giant Subs, Wendy's, White Wolf Cafe
	Lodg	**S:** Comfort Suites
	Med	**S:** + Hospital
86		**Par Ave (EB, No Rentry)**
	Gas	**S:** Shell
87		**FL 426, Fairbanks Ave, Winter Park**
	Gas	**S:** Chevron, Shell
	Food	**S:** Burger King, Poco's Mex Rest, Popeye's, Subway, Wendy's, Winter Park Diner
88		**FL 423, Lee Rd, Winter Park**
	Gas	**N:** Citgo, Texaco, 5-Star **S:** Chevron◊, Mobil◊
	Food	**N:** Arby's, Burger King, IHOP, McDonald's, Shoney's, Subway, Waffle House **S:** Denny's, Little Caesar's Pizza
	Lodg	**N:** Comfort Inn, InTown Suites, La Quinta Inn ♥, Motel 6 ♥, Travelers Inn **S:** Fairfield Inn, Park Inn, Ramada
	Med	**S:** + Hospital
	Other	**N:** Home Depot
90A		**FL 414, Maitland Blvd East (EB)**
90B		**FL 414, Maitland Blvd West (EB)**
90		**FL 414, Maitland Blvd (WB)**
	Gas	**N:** 7-11
	Food	**N:** Applebee's
	Lodg	**N:** Courtyard, Extended Stay America, Homewood Suites, Sheraton, Studio + **S:** Best Value Inn
	Other	**N:** Sportsplex **S:** Art Center, Jai Alai, Seminole Harley Davidson, Green Acres RV Park of Orlando▲
92		**FL 436, Altamonte Springs, Semoran Blvd, Apopka**
	Gas	**N:** 7-11, Shell, Shell◊ **S:** BP, Citgo, Hess, Shell
	Food	**N:** Cracker Barrel, Chuck E Cheese, Longhorn Steakhouse, McDonald's, Olive Garden, Perkins, Pizza Hut, Red Lobster, TGI Friday, Waffle House **S:** A&W, Chili's, Denny's, Steak 'n Shake
	Lodg	**N:** Best Western, Days Inn ♥, La Quinta Inn ♥, Holiday Inn ♥, Hampton Inn, Quality Inn, Residence Inn, Remington Inn, Springhill Suites, Travelodge **S:** Embassy Suites, Hilton, Marriott
	Med	**S:** + Florida Hospital
	Other	**S:** Altamonte Mall, Weikiwa Springs State Park▲
94		**FL 434, Longwood, Winter Springs**
	Gas	**N:** Mobil, Hess◊ **S:** 7-11, Chevron, Maverick, Mobil◊, Shell
	Food	**N:** Burger King, Denny's, Kobe Japanese Rest, Miami Subs, Pizza Hut, Roadhouse Grill, Starbucks, Wendy's **S:** Arby's, Bonefish Grill, Boston Market, Calypso Grill, Taco Bell
	Lodg	**N:** Comfort Inn ♥, Rodeway Inn
(95)		**Richey Green Rest Area (WB) (RR, Phone, Picnic, Vend, Sec 24/7)**

◊ = Regular Gas Stations with Diesel ▲ = RV Friendly Locations ♥ = Pet Friendly Locations
RED PRINT SHOWS LARGE VEHICLE PARKING/ACCESS ON SITE OR NEARBY BROWN PRINT SHOWS CAMPGROUNDS/RV PARKS

Page 3

W I-4

EXIT	FLORIDA
(97)	**Rest Area (EB)** (Last Rest Area I-4) (RR, Phone, Picnic, Vend, Sec 24/7)
98	**Lake Mary Blvd, Lake Mary, Heathrow**
Gas	N: Citgo, Exxon, Kangaroo, Shell S: 7-11, BP, Chevron, Citgo, Mobil◇
Food	N: Luigino's Pasta & Steakhouse, Wendy's S: Arby's, Bob Evans, Boston Market, Chili's, Chick-Fil-A, Checkers, KFC, McDonald's, Quiznos, Romano's Macaroni Grill, Steak 'n Shake, Starbucks, Taco Bell, TGI Friday, Wendy's
Lodg	N: Courtyard, Omni One S: Candlewood Suites, Extended Stay America, Hilton Garden Inn, Homewood Studio Suites, La Quinta Inn♥
Other	N: Walgreen's, Winn Dixie S: Albertson's, Pharmacy, Goodyear, Home Depot, Gander Mountain, Kmart, Publix, Staples, Target, Mall, US Post Office
101A	**CR 46A, Lake Mary, Sanford, Heathrow, Mt Dora (EB)**
101BC	**FL 417, CR 46, Central FL Greenway (TOLL), Int'l Airport (EB)**
101AB	**CR 46A, FL 417 (TOLL) (WB)**
101C	**FL 46, W 1st St, Sanford, Mt Dora (WB)**
Gas	N: 7-11, BP S: Chevron, Mobil, RaceTrac, Sunoco
Food	S: Bennigan's, Cracker Barrel, Don Pablo's, Denny's, IHOP, Grill & Bar, McDonald's, Olive Garden, Outback Steakhouse, Red Lobster, Ruby Tuesday, Steak 'n Shake, Waffle House, Wendy's
Lodg	S: Comfort Inn, Days Inn, Holiday Inn, Marriott, Springhill Suites, Super 8
Other	S: Seminole Towne Center Mall, Stores, Seminole Harley Davidson, Twelve Oaks RV Resort▲, CVS, Publix
104	**Orange Blvd, Zoological Park, Sanford (EB)** **US 17, US 92, Sanford (WB)**
Gas	S: Citgo
Food	S: Subway/Citgo
Med	S: + Hospital
Other	N: Featherlite Luxury Coaches S: Bates Motorhomes & Rentals
108	**Dirksen Dr, DeBary Dr, DeBary, Deltona, Enterprise**
Gas	N: Chevron, Citgo

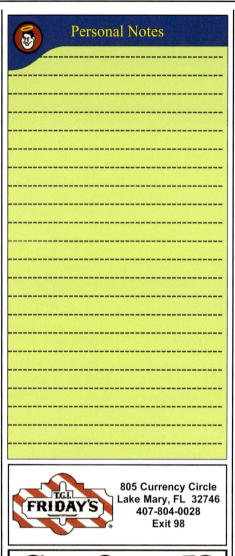

805 Currency Circle
Lake Mary, FL 32746
407-804-0028
Exit 98

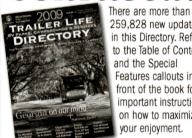

Confused? There are more than 259,828 new updates in this Directory. Refer to the Table of Contents and the Special Features callouts in the front of the book for important instructions on how to maximize your enjoyment.

EXIT	FLORIDA
Gas	S: Shell, Kangaroo
Food	N: Burger King, IHOP S: McDonald's, Subway, Waffle House
Lodg	N: Hampton Inn S: Best Western
Other	N: Publix, to Highbanks Marina & Camp Resort▲
111	**Saxon Blvd, Deltona, Orange City (WB)**
Gas	N: Circle K, Hess◇, RaceTrac, Shell S: Chevron
Food	N: Bob Evans, Chili's, Denny's, McDonald's, Perkins, Ruby Tuesday, Sonny's BBQ, Steak 'n Shake S: Wendy's
Lodg	N: Country Inn, Holiday Inn Express
Other	N: Walgreen's, Lowe's, Office Depot, to Highbanks Marina & Camp Resort▲ S: Albertson's, Publix
111A	**Saxon Blvd East (EB)**
Other	S: Deltona Hills Golf & Country Club
111B	**Saxon Blvd West (EB)**
Med	N: + Hospital
114	**FL 472, Deltona, Orange City, Deland, Cassadaga**
Other	N: DeLand/Orange City KOA▲, Sunburst RV Park▲, Village Park RV Resort▲, Orange City RV Resort▲, Blue Spring State Park
116	**W Main St, Lake Helen, Orange Camp Rd, Deland**
118	**FL 44, E New York Ave, Deland, New Smyrna Beach**
Gas	N: Shell◇
Food	N: Howard Johnson
Lodg	N: Howard Johnson Express
Med	N: + Hospital
Other	E: Lakeside Village RV Park▲
(127)	**Picnic Area (EB)**
129	**US 92E, Daytona Beach (EB, Left exit)**
Other	E: Int'l RV Park & Campground▲, Town & Country RV Park▲, Daytona Beach Int'l Airport✈, Daytona Int'l Speedway, Daytona Flea Market
(132)	**Jct I-95, N-Jacksonville, S-Miami, FL 400E, Daytona Beach (EB)**
Other	E: FL 400E to DB Int'l Airport

(I-4 begins/ends on I-275, Exit #45B)
(I-4 begins/ends on I-95, Exit #260B)

🎧 FLORIDA

Above lists Westbound I-4 from Daytona Beach, FL to Tampa, FL

◇ = Regular Gas Stations with Diesel   ▲ = RV Friendly Locations   ♥ = Pet Friendly Locations
RED PRINT SHOWS LARGE VEHICLE PARKING/ACCESS ON SITE OR NEARBY   BROWN PRINT SHOWS CAMPGROUNDS/RV PARKS

EXIT		WASHINGTON
		Below lists Southbound I-5 from US/Canada border to US/Mexico border.
⊙	**CANADA**	
⊙	**WASHINGTON**	
		(PACIFIC TIME ZONE)
		(I-5 begins/ends Ca/Mx Border)
(277)		US Customs & Immigration Port of Entry, USA/Canada Border
276		WA 548S, D St, Peace Portal Dr, Blaine
	Gas	E: MP◇, Shell◇, Topline, USA◇, Amex Border Fuel Stop
		W: Chevron
	Food	E: Denny's
		W: Cafe/ Motel International, Paso Del Norte Mexican, Pizza Factory, Subway
	Lodg	E: Northwoods Motel
		W: Anchor Inn Motel, Bayside Motor Inn, Motel International
	AServ	W: Chevron
	Other	E: Peace Arch State Park, Amex DutyFree Shopping
		W: Coast Hardware, NAPA, Visitor Info Center
275		WA 543N, Blaine, Port of Entry Truck Customs (NB, No Rentry) (All Comm'l Vehicles MUST Exit)
	TStop	E: Yorky's Market #7/Exxon (Scales)
	Gas	E: Chevron, Shell
	Food	E: Deli/Yorky's, Burger King
	TServ	E: Yorky's TS
	Other	E: Laundry/LP/Yorky's, Rite Aid, Blaine Muni Airport✈, Greyhound
274		Peace Portal Dr, Portal Way, to Blaine (NB, No Rentry)
	Gas	W: Star Power
	Food	W: Niki's Diner
	Other	W: Semiahmoo Resort Camping▲
270		Birch Bay-Lynden Rd, to Birch Bay, Lynden, Blaine
	Gas	W: Shell
	Food	W: Subway/Shell
	Lodg	W: Semiahmoo Resort
	Other	W: Lighthouse by the Bay RV Resort▲, Grandview Golf Course, to Beachside RV Park▲, Birch Bay Outlet Mall
(269)		Welcome Center (SB) (RR, Phone, Picnic, Vend)
(267)		Custer Rest Area (NB) (RR, Phone, Picnic, Vend, Info)
266		WA 548N, Custer, Grandview Rd
	Gas	W: ArcoAmPm
	Other	W: Birch Bay State Park
263		Portal Way, Ferndale
	Gas	E: Shell
	Other	E: The Cedars RV Resort▲
262		Main St, Ferndale, Bellingham
	FStop	E: Starvin' Sam's #4/76
	TStop	E: Ferndale Truck Stop/AmBest/Tesoro (Scales)
	Gas	W: 76, Citgo, Exxon, Shell
	Food	E: Denny's, McDonald's
		W: Bob's Burgers, DQ, Papa Murphy's Take 'n Bake, Thai Garden
	Lodg	E: Motel/Ferndale TS, Super 8♥
		W: Scottish Lodge Motel

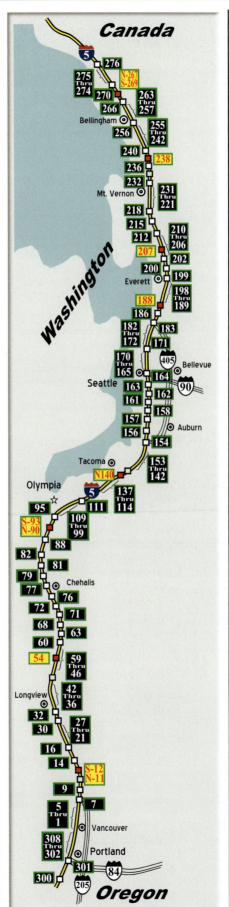

EXIT		WASHINGTON
	Other	E: Laundry/Ferndale TS, LP/76, U-Haul, Norwest RV Park▲
		W: Grocery, NAPA, Schwab Tire, Riverside Golf Course, Walgreen's
260		Slater Rd, Bellingham, to Lummi Island
	Gas	E: ArcoAmPm
		W: 76, Shell
	Other	E: El Monte RV Sales
		W: to Eagle Haven RV Park▲, Lummi Indian Reservation
258		Maplewood Ave, Bakerview Rd, Bellingham Int'l Airport
	FStop	W: Yorky's Market #6/Exxon (Scales)
	Gas	W: 76, ArcoAmPm
	Food	E: Papa Murphys Take n Bake, Starbucks
		W: Rest/Hampton Inn, Cruisin Coffee Airport 24hr, Mykonos Greek Rest
	Lodg	W: Hampton Inn, Shamrock Motel
	Other	E: to Whatcom Comm College, UPS Store, Bellis Fair Mall
		W: Bellingham RV Park▲, Bellingham Int'l Airport✈, LP/RVDump/Yorky's, WA State Hwy Patrol Post
257		Northwest Ave, Bellingham, to Lynden
	Gas	W: Shell
256		Meridian Rd (SB)
256B		Bellis Fair-Mall Pkwy, WA 539N, Meridian Rd (NB)
	FStop	E: (5mi on 539N) Pacific Pride
	Other	E: Bellis Fair Mall, Target
256A		WA 539N, Meridian St (NB)
	Gas	E: Exxon, Chevron, Shell, Costco
	Food	E: Arby's, Burger King, DQ, Denny's, Godfather's, McDonald's, Olive Garden, Pizza Hut, Shari's, Starbucks, Taco Time
		W: Eleni's Family Rest
	Lodg	E: Best Western, Comfort Inn, Days Inn, Holiday Inn Express♥, Quality Inn
		W: Rodeway Inn
	Med	E: + Hospital
	Other	E: Bellis Fair Mall, Best Buy, Costco, Home Depot, Office Depot, Petco♥, Safeway, Walgreen's, Wal-Mart, U-Haul, WA State Hwy Patrol Post RVDump/Carwash/Shell
255		WA 542E, to Mt Baker (SB), Sunset Dr, Bellingham (NB)
	Gas	E: Chevron◇, Exxon, Shell◇
	Food	E: Subway/Shell, Applebee's, Jack in the Box, Round Table Pizza, Taco Bell
	Med	W: + St Joseph Hospital
	Other	E: Grocery, Kmart, Lowe's, US Post Office, Walgreen's
254		Ohio St, State St, to City Center, Iowa St, Bellingham
	FStop	W: Pacific Pride
	Gas	E: Starvin Sam's/Conoco
		W: 76, Chevron, Shell
	Food	W: DQ, McDonald's, Skipper's Seafood, Subway
	AServ	W: Chevron
	Other	E: Vacationland RV Sales, Auto Dealers
		W: Auto Dealers, NAPA, Schwab Tire, RVDump/Chevron
253		Lakeway Dr, Bellingham (W Services same as Ex #252)
	Gas	E: USA
		W: Chevron

◇ = Regular Gas Stations with Diesel   ▲ = RV Friendly Locations   ♥ = Pet Friendly Locations

RED PRINT SHOWS LARGE VEHICLE PARKING/ACCESS ON SITE OR NEARBY   BROWN PRINT SHOWS CAMPGROUNDS/RV PARKS

Page 5

Interstate 5 — Washington

EXIT		WASHINGTON
	Food	E: Lakeway Teriyaki, Little Caesar's, Subway
	Lodg	E: Best Western, ValuInn Motel, A Secret Garden B&B
	Other	E: Grocery, Laundromat
252		Samish Way, Bellingham, West Washington University (E Services same as Ex #253)
	Gas	W: 76, Chevron, Mobil, Shell◆, Tesoro◆
	Food	W: Arby's, Black Angus Steakhouse, Burger King, Boomer's Drive In, IHOP, Denny's, Kyoto's, McDonald's, Pizza Hut, Starbucks, Subway
	Lodg	W: Aloha Motel, Bay City Motor Inn, Coachman Inn, Mac's Motel, Motel 6 ♥, Ramada Inn, Travelodge, Villa Inn
	Other	W: Grocery, to W WA Univ
250		WA 11, Old Fairhaven Pkwy, S Bellingham, to Chuckanut Dr
	Gas	W: ArcoAmPm, Chevron
	Food	W: Dos Padres Mexican, Tony's Cafe
	AServ	W: Chevron
	Other	W: Albertson's
246		Samish Way, North Lake Samish
	Gas	W: Shell◆
	Other	W: Lake Samish Terrace Park▲
242		Nulle Rd, South Lake Samish
240		Lake Samish Rd, to Alger
	FStop	E: Alger Food Mart/Shell
	Food	E: Alger Grille
	Lodg	E: Whispering Firs Motel & RV Park▲
	Other	E: RVDump/LP/Shell, Wildwood Resort▲
(238)		Bow Hill Rest Area (Both dir) (RR, Phone, Picnic, Vend, WiFi, Info)
236		Bow Hill Rd, Bow, Belfast, Edison
	Gas	E: Chevron
	Food	E: Rest/Skagit Resort
	Lodg	E: Skagit Valley Casino Resort
	Other	E: Burlington KOA▲, 1000 Trails Mt Vernon▲
(235)		Inspection Station (SB)
232		Cook Rd, Burlington, to Sedro Woolley
	FStop	E: Cook Rd Shell, Pacific Pride
	Gas	E: 76◆, Gas 'n Go, Shell◆
	Food	E: Bob's Burgers, DQ, Iron Skillet
	Med	E: + Hospital
	Other	E: Burlington KOA▲, Foley's RV/LP, RVDump/Shell
		W: Action RV Service
231		WA 11N, Chuckanut Dr, to Burlington, to Bow, Edison, Larrabee
	Other	E: Foley's RV & Marina/ RVDump▲
		W: WA State Hwy Patrol Post
230		WA 20, Anacortes, Burlington
	FStop	W: Pacific Pride
	Gas	E: Exxon, Shell, Tesoro
		W: ArcomPm◆, Chevron◆
	Food	E: Berry Patch Rest, Burger King, Jack in the Box, Pizza Factory, Outback Steak house, Subway
		W: McDonald's
	Lodg	E: Cocusa Motel
		W: Holiday Inn Express, Mark II Motel
	Med	E: + Hospital

EXIT		WASHINGTON
	Other	E: Grocery, Mall, Pharmacy, Target, Schwab Tire, to RV Parts Outlet, to JR's RV Repair
		W: Skagit Harley Davidson
229		George Hopper Rd
	Gas	E: ArcoAmPm, Chevron, USA◆, Costco
	Food	E: Olive Garden, Pizza Hut, Shari's, Taco Bell, Subway, Wendy's
	Lodg	E: Hampton Inn
	Other	E: Costco, Home Depot, Kmart, PetSmart ♥
		W: NAPA, Prime Outlets/Famous Brands Auto Dealers
227		WA 538E, College Way, Mt Vernon
	Gas	E: 76, Safeway
		W: Gas Express, Shell◆
	Food	E: Big Scoop, Denny's, Jack in the Box, KFC, McDonald's, Skipper's Seafood, Starbucks, Subway, Taco bell
		W: Arby's, Burger King, Buzz In Steak House, Cranberry Tree, Drummond's, Mitzel's Kitchen, Royal Fork Buffet, Taco Time, Rest/BW
	Lodg	E: Best Western ♥, Days Inn
		W: Best Western, Comfort Inn, Quality Inn, Travelodge
	Other	E: Albertson's, Auto Repair, Goodyear, Office Depot, Safeway, Wal-Mart▲
		W: Firestone, Lowe's, Riverbend RV Park▲, Valley RV
226		WA 536W, Kincaid St, Broad St, City Center, Mt. Vernon
	FStop	W: Pacific Pride
	Food	W: Old Towne Grainery, Skagit River Brewing Co
	Med	E: + Hospital
225		Anderson Road
	FStop	W: Gasco Truck Stop
	Gas	E: 76◆
		W: Chevron
	TServ	W: Freightliner
	Other	E: Lifestyle RV Center
		W: Poulsbo RV
224		Cedardale Rd, Old Hwy 99S, Hickox Rd, Mt Vernon (NB, no reacc) (NB Use #224, SB Use#225)
	TStop	W: Truck City Truck Stop (Scales)
	Food	W: Rest/Truck City TS
	TWash	W: Truck City TS
	TServ	W: Truck City TS
	Other	W: Laundry/Truck City TS
221		WA 534E, Pioneer Hwy, to Lake McMurray, to Conway, Stanwood
	Gas	E: Shell◆
		W: 76◆, Shell◆
	Food	W: Channel Lodge, Conway Deli
	Lodg	W: Ridgway B&B, Wild Iris B&B
	Other	W: Blake's RV Park & Marina▲
218		Starbird Road, Milltown Rd
	Gas	W: Foodmart
	Lodg	W: Hillside Motel
215		300th Ave NW
(214)		Inspection Station (NB)
212		WA 532W, 268th St NE, Bryant, Stanwood, Camano Island
	Gas	W: 76◆, Shell, Shell◆
	Food	W: Burger King, McDonald's

EXIT		WASHINGTON
210		236th St NE
208		WA 530, Pioneer Hwy, Silvana, to Arlington, to Stanwood
	FStop	E: Island Crossing Tesoro
		W: Arlington Fuel Stop/76
	Gas	E: 76, Chevron, Shell
	Food	E: Denny's, O'Brien's Turkey House, Wallers Family Rest
	Lodg	E: Arlington Motor Inn
	Med	E: + Hospital
(207)		Smokey Pt Rest Area (Both dir) (RR, Phone, Picnic, Vend, WiFi, Coffee, Info, RVDump)
206		WA 531, Smokey Point, 172nd St NE, to Lakewood
	Gas	E: 7-11, 76◆, ArcoAmPm, Mobil, Shell
		W: Chevron, Costco
	Food	E: Alfy's Pizza, Buzz Inn Steakhouse, Jack in the Box, KFC, McDonald's, Starbucks
		W: Nick's, Porky's, Village Inn
	Lodg	E: Crossroads Inn ♥, Hawthorn Inn & Suites, Quality Inn
		W: Smokey Point Motor Inn
	Other	E: LP/RVDump/76, Grocery, Lowe's, Harley Davidson, Arlington Muni Airport✈
		W: Cedar Grove Shores RV Park▲, Lake KI RV Resort▲, Costco
202		116th St NE, Tulalip, Marysville
	TStop	W: PTP/Donna's Truck Plaza/Chev (Scales)
	Gas	E: Shell, Texaco
	Food	E: Papa John's, Starbucks, Taco Bell
		W: FastFood/Donna's TS, McDonald's, Starbucks, Subway, Rest/Tulalip Resort
	Lodg	W: Tulalip Resort
	Other	W: Seattle Premium Outlets Mall, WA State Hwy Patrol Post, Albertson's, Tulalip Resort Casino/RV Park▲
200		88th St NE, Marysville
	Gas	E: 7-11, 76, Shell◆
		W: Miirastar, Murphy
	Food	E: Applebee's, Quiznos, Starbucks
	Lodg	E: Holiday Inn Express
	Other	E: LP/Shell, Grocery
		W: Home Depot, Wal-Mart▲
199		WA 528E, 66th St. NE, to Marysville, to Tulalip
	Gas	E: 76, ArcoAmPm, Chevron, Shell◆
		W: 76
	Food	E: Burger King, DQ, Don's, Jack in the Box, Starbucks, Subway/Shell, Village Inn
		W: Rest/Best Western, Arby's, Golden Corral, McDonald's, Wendy's
	Lodg	E: Village Motor Inn
		W: Best Western, Comfort Inn, Holiday Inn Express, Tulalip Inn
	Other	E: Albertson's, Costco, RiteAid, Schwab Tire, Staples, Marysville Towne Center Mall, All RV Repair, RV & Marine Supply
		W: RV Super Mall▲, Tulalip Indian Res
198		WA 529S, Pacific Hwy, Everett, N Broadway, Port of Everett, to Marysville (SB)
	Other	W: WA State Hwy Patrol Post
195		E Grand Ave, Port of Everett, Marine View Dr (NB)
	Med	W: + Hospital
194		US 2E, to WA 529W, Everett Ave
	Gas	W: 76, Shell◆

◆ = Regular Gas Stations with Diesel   ▲ = RV Friendly Locations   ♥ = Pet Friendly Locations
RED PRINT SHOWS LARGE VEHICLE PARKING/ACCESS ON SITE OR NEARBY   BROWN PRINT SHOWS CAMPGROUNDS/RV PARKS

EXIT	WASHINGTON
Food	W: Denny's, Best BBQ
Lodg	W: Best Western, Holiday Inn
TServ	W: Schwab Tires
193	**WA 529, Pacific Ave, Everett (NB) (Access to Ex #194 Serv)**
Gas	W: 76, Chevron, Shell
Food	W: Denny's, Grand Roaster, Hardee's
Lodg	W: Best Western, Howard Johnson ♥
Med	W: + Hospital
192	**Broadway (NB Left exit), City Center, Naval Station, Port of Everett**
Gas	W: 76, ArcoAmPm, Chevron, Exxon, Shell
Food	W: Alfy's Pizza, Jack in the Box, Taco Bell, McDonald's, Kings Table
Lodg	W: Days Inn, Super 8, Travelodge
189	**WA 526W, Everett, WA 99, to Lynnwood, WA 527, Mill Creek**
Gas	E: ArcoAmPm, Exxon, Shell◊ W: 7-11, Chevron, Shell
Food	E: Buzz Inn Steakhouse, McDonald's, Wendy's W: Denny's, Jack in the Box, Olive Garden, Red Robin, Starbucks, Taco Bell, Village Inn
Lodg	E: Travelodge W: Best Western, Comfort Inn, Days Inn, Extended Stay America, Motel 6 ♥, Rodeway Inn
Other	E: Costco W: Kmart, Everett Mall, Animal Hospital ♥, Boeing Co
(188)	**Inspection Station (Both dir)**
(188)	**Silver Lake Rest Area (SB) (RR, Phone, Picnic, Vend, WiFi, Info, Info, Coffee, RVDump)**
186	**WA 96E, 128th St**
Gas	E: 76, Chevron, Shell◊ W: 7-11, ArcoAmPm, Chevron, Shell, Texaco
Food	W: Alfy's Pizza, Burger King, Denny's, McDonald's, Miitzel's Kitchen, Pizza Hut, KFC, Skipper's Seafood, Starbucks, Subway, Taco Bell, Taco Time
Lodg	E: Comfort Inn, Holiday Inn, Quality Inn W: Best Western, Cypress Inn, Everett Inn, Holiday Inn Express La Quinta Inn & Suites ♥, Motel 6 ♥
Other	E: Lakeside RV Park▲, Silver Lake RV Park▲, McCollum Co Park W: Albertson's, Goodyear, Maple Grove RV Resort▲, Great American Casino, to Snohomish Co Airport✈
183	**164th St, to Mill Creek**
Gas	E: ArcoAmPm, Shell◊ W: Shell
Food	E: Jack in the Box, Panda Express, Taco Time, Shari's, Starbucks, Subway
Other	E: Wal-Mart, Walgreen's, Martha Lake Co Park W: Airport✈, Lakeside RV Park▲, Silver Lake RV Park▲
(182)	**Jct I-405S, to Bellevue, to I-90, WA 525, to WA99, Mukilteo, Alderwood Mall Blvd**
Other	W: to Maple Grove RV Resort▲
181	**196th St SW (SB), Lynnwood, to WA 524, 44th Ave W (NB)**
Gas	E: 76, ArcoAmPm, Shell, Texaco W: 7-11, 76, Chevron, Shell

Personal Notes

La Quinta Inn Everett #6187
12619 4th Ave W
Everett, WA 98204
(425) 347-9099
I-5 Exit 186
LAQUINTA INNS & SUITES
wake up on the bright side®

EXIT	WASHINGTON
Food	E: McDonald's W: Applebee's, Arby's, Black Angus Steakhouse, Burger King, Chuck E Cheese, Country Harvest, Denny's, IHOP, Hooters, Jack in the Box, McDonald's, Olive Garden, Red Lobster, Starbucks, Taco Bell, Tony Roma's
Lodg	E: Embassy Suites, Extended Stay America, Hampton Inn W: Best Western, Comfort Inn, Courtyard, Holiday Inn Express, La Quinta Inn ♥
Med	W: + Chec Medical Clinic
Other	E: Albertson's, Lowe's, Staples, PetCo ♥, Carwash/76 W: Alderwood Mall, Convention Center, US Post Office, Target
181B	**196th St SW, Poplar Way (NB)**
181A	**44th Ave W (NB), Lynnwood**
179	**220th St SW, Mountlake Terrace**
Gas	W: 7-11, Shell, Shell◊
Food	W: Azteca Mex Rest, Starbucks, Subway, Teriyaki Bowl
Lodg	W: Andy's Motel, Travelers Inn
Med	W: + Hospital, + Mt Lake Medical Immediate Care
Other	W: Fantasia Family Fun Park, Silver Dollar Casino

EXIT	WASHINGTON
178	**236th St SW, Mountlake Terr (NB)**
Gas	E: Shell
177	**(SB) Lakeview Dr, 236th St, 205th St (NB) 244th St SW, WA 104, to Edmonds, Lake Forest Park (Most West Serv on WA 99)**
Gas	E: Arco AmPm, Chevron**x2**, Shell◊ W: 76**x2**◊, Shell
Food	E: McDonald's, Starbucks, Subway W: Arby's, Denny's, Godfather Piz
Lodg	E: Motel 6 W: Days Inn, Golden West Motel, Harbor Inn, K&E Motor Inn, St Frances Motel, Travelodge
Med	E: + Ballinger Clinic
Other	E: RiteAid, Office Depot W: Costco, PetCo ♥, Home Depot, Les Schwab Tire, Auto Dealers
176	**NE 175th St, Seattle, to Shoreline**
Other	W: Evergreen RV Supply/ RVDump
175	**WA 523, NE 145th, 5th Ave NE (Serv W to WA 99)**
Lodg	W: Extended Stay America
Other	W: Golden Nugget Casino, Goldie's Shoreline Casino
174	**NE 125th, N 130th St, Roosevelt Way, to WA 99, Seattle (NB) (Serv W to WA 99)**
Gas	W: Texaco
Food	W: Burger King, Outback Steakhouse
Lodg	W: Best Western, Rodeside Lodge
173	**NE Northgate Way, 1st Ave NE**
Gas	E: 76, ArcoAmPm W: 7-11, 76, Chevron, Shell◊
Food	E: Ivar's Seafood Bar, Olive Garden, Red Robin, Romano's Macaroni Grill, Starbucks, Subway, Tony Roma's, Taco del Mar W: Arby's, Berkshire Grill, McDonald's
Lodg	W: Ramada Inn
Med	W: + Northwest Hospital
Other	E: Best Buy, FedEx Kinko's, Office Depot, Target, Northgate Mall
172	**N 85th St, N 80th St, Banner Way NE, Seattle**
171	**NE 71st St, NE 70th St, WA 522, Lake City Way, Bothell**
170	**NE Ravenna Blvd, Seattle (NB)**
169	**NE 50th St (SB), NE 45th St (NB)**
Gas	E: 76, Shell W: 7-11/Citgo
Food	E: Burger King, Subway, Godfather's W: Café, Dino's Pizza
Lodg	E: University Inn, Watertown Hotel W: University Plaza Hotel
Med	E: + University of Washington Medical Center
Other	E: to Univ of WA W: RiteAid, to Zoo
168B	**WA 520E, Boylston Ave, Roanoke St, to Bellevue, Kirkland**
168A	**Lakeview Blvd, Downtown Seattle**
Food	W: Sam's Steakhouse
167	**Eastlake Ave, Mercer St, Fairview Ave, Downtown Seattle (NB, Left exit)**
Gas	W: 76, Shell
Food	W: Chandler Crab House, Hooters
Lodg	W: Residence Inn, Silver Cloud Inn

◊= Regular Gas Stations with Diesel   ▲ = RV Friendly Locations   ♥ = Pet Friendly Locations

RED PRINT SHOWS LARGE VEHICLE PARKING/ACCESS ON SITE OR NEARBY   BROWN PRINT SHOWS CAMPGROUNDS/RV PARKS

EXIT	WASHINGTON
166	**Denny Way, Olive Way (NB), Stewart St (SB), Seattle**
Food	E: Starbucks, Timberline Rest
Lodg	E: Capitol Hill Inn, Garden Hotel
	W: SpringHill Suites
Other	W: Greyhound, Key Arena, Visitor Center
165C	**Union St (SB)**
Food	W: Ruth Chris Steakhouse
Lodg	W: Sheraton ♥
165B	**Seneca St, Madison St, 6th Ave, Ave, Downtown Seattle (SB)**
Food	W: Ruth Chris Steakhouse
Lodg	E: Wyndham Hotel
Med	E: + Swedish Medical
	W: Sheraton ♥
Other	W: Convention Center
165A	**University St, Seneca St, Down town (SB)**
Lodg	W: Crowne Plaza, Hilton
Med	E: + Virginia Medical Center
Other	E: to Seattle Univ
	W: Harlequin Cellar, Market Cellar Winery
165	**Seneca St, Downtown (NB, Left Exit)**
164	**Spring St, Madison St, 6th Ave (SB)**
164B	**4th Ave S, 8th Ave S, Dearborn St, to Kingdome**
Other	W: to Qwest Field, Safeco Field
(164A)	**Jct I-90E, to Spokane**
163B	**6th Ave S, S Forest St, Airport Way S (SB)**
Other	W: Rainier Brewery Tour
163A	**W Seattle Fwy, S Spokane St, S Columbian Way (SB)**
TServ	W: Cummins NW
Med	E: + Hospital
163	**S Spokane St, S Columbian Way, W Seattle Fwy (NB)**
162	**Corson Ave, Michigan St (NB Left Exit)**
Gas	W: Shell
Lodg	W: Georgetown Inn
161	**S Albro Place, Swift Ave S**
Gas	W: Shell
Other	W: Boeing Field/King Co Int'l Airport ✈
158	**Boeing Access Rd, MLK Jr Way S, E Marginal Way, Pacific Hwy S**
Gas	W: Chevron
Food	W: Randy's
Lodg	W: Hilton
TServ	E: Sea-Tac Ford, TEC of Seattle
	W: GMC Trucks, Kenworth
Other	W: Boeing Field/King Co Int'l Airport ✈
157	**M L King Jr Way, WA 900**
156	**Interurban Ave S, to WA 599N, Tukwila (SB, diff reacc)**
FStop	E: Pacific Express #160
	W: Tukwila Shell
Gas	W: 76◊
Food	E: Gordy's Steak & BBQ Smokehouse
	W: Denny's, Jack in the Box, Quiznos
Lodg	W: Days Inn, Quality Inn
Other	E: Golden Nugget Casino, Silver Dollar Casino, Grand Central Casino, Great American Casino
	W: Downtown Harley Davidson

EXIT	WASHINGTON
154B	**154th St, Southcenter Blvd, to WA 518 to Burien (SB)**
Gas	E: Arco AmPm
Food	E: Denny's
Other	E: Westfield Southcenter Mall
154A	**Southcenter Pkwy, to I-405N, to I-90, to Bellevue**
Lodg	W: Extended Stay America
TServ	E: Cummins NW
(154)	**Jct I-405N, WA 518 (NB)**
153	**Southcenter Pkwy, Seattle (NB) (Addt'l Serv E to Valley Hwy)**
Gas	E: ArcoAmPm, Chevron◊
	W: ArcoAmPm
Food	E: Applebee's, Azteca Mexican, Claim Jumper, Azteca Mexican, Denny's, Godfather's, Jack in the Box, McDonald's, Olive Garden, Red Robin, Outback Steakhouse, Starbucks, Subway, Taco Bell, Taco del Mar, Wendy's
Lodg	E: Doubletree Inn
Med	E: + Hospital
Other	E: RiteAid, Best Buy, PetSmart ♥, Target, Westfield Southcenter Mall
152	**S 188th St, Orillia Rd S, Airport**
Gas	W: 76◊
Food	W: Dave's Diner, Denny's, Jack in the Box, Spencer's Steak & Chops, Taco Bell
Lodg	W: Comfort Inn, Days Inn, Doubletree Hotel, Econo Lodge, Hampton Inn, La Quinta Inn ♥, Motel 6 ♥, Quality Inn, Red Lion Hotel, Super 8 ♥, Sea Tac Inn, Travelodge
Other	W: Seattle Tacoma Int'l Airport ✈, Silver Dollar Casino, Seattle/Tacoma KOA▲
151	**S 200th St, Military Road S, Kent**
Gas	E: Shell◊
	W: 7-11, 76, Chevron
Food	W: Bob's Burgers, Godfather's Pizza, IHOP
Lodg	E: Motel 6 ♥
	W: Best Value Inn, Best Western, Econo Lodge, Fairfield Inn, Hampton Inn, Howard Johnson, Holiday Inn ♥, Sleep Inn, Seatac Skyway Inn
TServ	W: Kenworth NW
149	**WA 516, Kent-Des Moines Rd, to Des Moines, Kent (SB)**
Gas	W: 7-11, 76, ArcoAmPm, Shell, Shell◊
Food	W: Burger King, Dunkin Donuts, Subway, McDonald's, Pizza Hut, Wendy's
Lodg	E: Century Motel
	W: Best Western, Garden Suites, Kings Arms Motel
Other	E: Poulsbo RV, Golf Course
	W: Albertson's, Walgreen's
149AB	**WA 516, Kent-DesMoines Rd, to Des Moines, to Kent (NB)**
147	**272nd St, Kent (Serv on Pacific Hwy)**
Gas	E: 76
	W: 7-11, Arco, Shell◊
Food	W: Jack in the Box, McDonald's, Papa Murphy's Take 'n Bake, Quiznos, Subway, Taco Bell
Lodg	W: Travel Inn
Other	W: Firestone, RiteAid, Safeway
143	**320th St, Federal Way**
Gas	W: 76, ArcoAmPm, BP, Shell◊

EXIT	WASHINGTON
Food	W: Applebee's, Azteca Mexican, KFC, Black Angus Steakhouse, Burger King, Coco's, Denny's, Ivar's Seafood Bar, McDonald's, Old Country Buffet, Outback Steakhouse, Pizza Hut, Red Lobster, Red Robin, Starbucks, Subway, Taco Bell
Lodg	W: Best Western, Comfort Inn, Courtyard, East Wind Motel, Extended Stay America, La Quinta Inn ♥, Ridgecrest Motel, Stevenson Motel
Other	W: Best Buy, FedEx Kinko's, Firestone, Goodyear, Kmart, Office Max, PetSmart ♥, RiteAid, Safeway, Target, Wal-Mart sc, Seatac Mall, Golf Course
142A	**WA 18E, Federal Way, to Auburn**
142B	**S 348th St, to WA 161**
142AB	**WA 18E, to Auburn, S 348th St, Enchanted Pkwy, Pacific Hwy S, Federal Way**
TStop	W: Ernie's Federal Way Fuel Stop #3/76
Gas	W: Chevron, Shell, Costco
Food	W: Burger King, DQ, Denny's, Jack in the Box, Olive Garden, McDonald's, Popeye's, Shari's, Taco Bell
Lodg	W: Days Inn, Holiday Inn Express, Quality Inn, Super 8
Med	W: + St Francis Hospital, + Sound Medical
Other	E: SuperMall, Wild Waves & Enchanted Village
	W: Laundry/Ernie's FS, Costco, Home Depot, Office Depot, Wal-Mart sc, Vets For Less ♥
(140)	**SeaTac Rest Area (NB) (RR, Phone, Picnic, Vend, WiFi, Info, RVDump)**
(140)	**Inspection Station (Both dir)**
137	**54th Ave E, Fife, WA 99N, Pacific Hwy, Tacoma, Milton**
TStop	W: Pacific Xpress/Gulf
Gas	E: ArcoAmPm, Chevron◊, Shell
	W: 76, ArcoAmPm
Food	E: BBQ, DQ, Johnny's
	W: Arby's, Burger King, Denny's, Los Cabos, KFC, McDonald's, Mitzel's, Pizza Experience, Pizza Hut/TacoBell, Subway, Starbucks, Taco Bell, Wendy's, FastFood/Pac Xpr
Lodg	E: Motel 6 ♥
	W: Best Value Inn, Best Western, Comfort Inn, Fife Motel, Kings Motor Inn, Quality Inn, Royal Coachman Inn
Other	E: Baydo's RV, Tacoma RV, Auto Dlrs
	W: Costco, Camping World, Great American RV Center, Pharmacy, Emerald Queen Casino
136	**20th St E, Port of Tacoma Rd (SB)**
136AB	**20th St E, Port of Tacoma Rd (NB)**
TStop	W: Flying J Travel Plaza #5060 (Scales)
Gas	W: Shell◊
Food	W: Rest/Fast Food/FJ TP, Jack in the Box
Lodg	W: Days Inn, Econo Lodge, Extended Stay America, Hometel Inn, Howard Johnson, Ramada Ltd, Travelodge
TServ	E: Western Peterbilt
	W: Flying J TP
Other	W: Laundry/WiFi/LP/FJ TP, Auto Dealers, Destination Harley Davidson, Wescraft RV, to Port of Tacoma

EXIT	WASHINGTON		EXIT	WASHINGTON		EXIT	WASHINGTON
135	E 28th, Bay St, WA 167S, Tacoma, to Puyallup		Med	W: + Hospital		Food	W: Burger King, Denny's, IHOP, Jack in the Box, Red Lobster, Shari's, Subway
Gas	E: Shell		Other	W: Auto Services, Great American Casino		Lodg	W: Ameritel Inn, Comfort Inn, Days Inn, Holiday Inn Express, La Quinta Inn♥, Quality Inn, Super 8
	W: 76, ArcoAmPm		**125**	Bridgeport Way, Lakewood, Pacific Hwy, McChord AFB, Tacoma			
Food	W: Café/LQ, Ports of Call Rest		FStop	W: 76		Med	W: + Hospital
Lodg	W: Bay Motel, La Quinta Inn♥		Gas	E: Exxon		Other	E: Grocery, Discount Tire
Other	E: River Lane RV Park▲			W: Chevron, Shell◆			W: Firestone, NAPA, Safeway
	W: Amtrak, to Tacoma Dome		Food	W: Black Angus Steakhouse, Denny's, KFC, Pizza Hut, Wendy's		**108**	Sleater-Kinney Rd, S College St, Lacey, Olympia
134	E "L" St, E 27th, Portland Ave (NB)		Lodg	W: Best Western, Fort Lewis Motel, Home Motel, Lakewood Lodge, Madison Motel, Rose Garden Motel		Gas	E: Shell◆
Gas	E: Shell						W: ArcoAmPm
	W: ArcoAmPm		Med	W: + St Clare Hospital		Food	E: Applebee's, Arby's, Jack in the Box, McDonald's, Starbucks, Subway
Food	W: Pegasus Rest		Other	E: MIL/McChord AFB/RV Park▲		Lodg	W: Quality Inn, Super 8
Lodg	W: La Quinta Inn♥			W: LP/76, Auto Services, Goodyear, Laundromat, Mall, U-Haul		Med	W: + Providence St Peter Hospital
Other	W: Button Vet Hospital♥		**124**	Gravelly Lake Dr, Nyanza Rd SW		Other	E: Firestone, Kmart, PetSmart♥, Safeway, Target
(133)	Jct I-705N, Ruston, WA 7S, Mt. Rainier, Tacoma		Gas	W: 76, ArcoAmPm		**107**	Pacific Ave, Olympia
Lodg	E: Corporate Suites		Food	W: El Toro, Pizza Casa		Gas	E: Shell◆
	W: Ramada Inn, Travel Inn		Lodg	W: Ft Clarke Motel, La Casa Motel		Food	E: Izzy's Café, Shari's, Sizzler, Skipper's Seafood, Taco Time
Other	W: Tacoma Dome/Civic Center, to Univ of WA/Tacoma		AServ	W: Arco			
			Med	W: + to American Lake Vets Hospital		Med	E: + Hospital
132	S 38th St, WA 16W, to Bremerton		**123**	Thorn Lane, Tillicum, Fort Lewis		Other	E: Albertson's, Home Depot
Gas	E: Shell, Safeway		**122**	Jackson Ave, Berkeley St SW, Blaine Ave, Madigan Hospital, Camp Murray		**105**	14th Ave, Henderson Blvd, E Bay Dr, State Capitol, City Center, Port of Olympia
	W: Tesoro, Circle K, Costco						
Food	W: Arby's, Burger King, McDonald's, Outback Steakhouse, Red Robin, Starbucks, TGI Friday's, Taco del Mar, Wendy's		Gas	W: 7-11, Chevron		Gas	W: Chevron, Shell◆
			Food	W: BBQ, McDonald's, Pizza Hut, Subway, Taco Bell, Wok Inn Express		Food	W: Casa Miia, Jack in the Box, McDonald's
			AServ	W: Chevron		Lodg	W: Best Western, Carriage Inn Motel, Econo Lodge, Quality Inn, Ramada Inn, Swantown Inn
Med	W: + Medical Center		Other	W: AutoZone, Laundromat, Grocery, Camp Murray National Guard			
Other	E: Safeway		**120**	41st Division Dr, Fort Lewis		Other	E: Grocery, Mall, RV Center
	W: Tacoma Mall, Best Buy, Costco, Dollar Tree, PetCo♥, Car Wash		Other	E: Ft Lewis Military Museum		**105AB**	Plum St, E Bay Dr (SB)
				W: Travel Campground▲		**104**	Deschutes Pkwy, W Olympia, US 101N, to Aberdeen
130	56th St, Tacoma Mall Blvd, Tacoma		**119**	Steilacoom-Dupont Rd, Clark Rd, Barksdale Ave, Fort Lewis, Dupont, to Steilacoom			
Gas	W: Shell					FStop	W: (to US 101, 1st Ex R) Pacific Pride
Food	W: Chuck E Cheese, El Torito, Pizza Hut, Subway, Tony Roma's, Wendy's		Gas	E: 76		Gas	W: 7-11, ArcoAmPm, Chevron, Shell◆
			Food	E: Happy Teriyaki, Subway, Starbucks		Food	W: Jack in the Box
Lodg	W: Extended Stay America		**118**	Center Dr, DuPont		Lodg	W: Extended Stay America, Red Lion Hotel
Other	W: Home Depot, to S Tacoma Univ Place		Lodg	W: GuestHouse Inn, Liberty Inn			
129	74th St, 72nd St, to Steilacoom		**(117)**	Inspection Station (NB)		**103**	2nd Ave, Custer Way, Capitol Blvd, Olympia, Tumwater
Gas	E: Chevron, Exxon		**116**	Mounts Rd, to Nisqually			
	W: Arco		**114**	Martin Way, Olympia, Nisqually		**102**	Trosper Rd, Black Lake, Olympia
Food	E: Applebee's, Burger King, DQ, Elmer's, IHOP, Jack in the Box, Mitzel's Kitchen, Olive Garden, Red Lobster, Shari's, Starbucks, Taco Bell		Gas	E: Chevron, Exxon, Shell◆		Gas	E: Shell◆
			Food	E: Nisqually Grill, Norma's Burgers			W: 76, Chevron, Albertsons, Costco
			AServ	E: Chevron		Food	E: Arby's, Burger King, Cattin's, Jack in the Box, KFC, Mexican, McDonald's, Pizza Hut, Subway, Taco Bell
	W: Hooter's, Quizno's, Yankee Diner		Other	E: Lost Lake RV Resort▲, Nisqually Plaza RV Park▲			
Lodg	E: Best Western, Howard Johnson, Motel 6♥, Shilo Inn, Travelodge		**111**	Marvin Rd NE, WA 510E, Olympia, to Yelm, to Mt Rainer			W: Panda Express, Papa Murphy's Take 'n Bake, Quiznos
	W: Days Inn						
Other	W: Auto & RV Country Store, Qwest Auto Service		FStop	E: Hawks Prairie Grocery & Deli		Lodg	E: Best Western♥, Motel 6♥
				W: Pacific Pride		Med	E: + Hospital
128	84th St, Hosmer St, Tacoma (NB)		Gas	E: 76, Chevron, Shell◆, Tesoro, Safeway		Other	E: Goodyear, Laundromat, Pharmacy
Gas	E: 76, Shell◆		Food	E: Burger King, DQ, Godfather's Pizza, Hawk's Prairie, McDonald's, Papa Murphy's Take 'n Bake, Ruby Tuesday, Starbucks, Subway, Taco Time			W: Albertson's, Costco, Home Depot, Olympia Campground▲
	W: Tesoro						
Food	E: Rest/BW, Denny's, Subway					**101**	Tumwater Blvd, Olympia Airport
	W: Ruby Tuesday					Gas	E: Chevron, Shell
Lodg	E: Best Western, Comfort Inn, Econo Lodge, Holiday Inn Express, Motel 6♥, Sherwood Inn			W: Country Junction, Mayan Mexican		Food	E: Quiznos
			Lodg	E: King Oscar Motel		Lodg	E: Best Western, Comfort Inn, Guesthouse Int'l, Super 8
Other	E: Casino		Other	E: Costco, Home Depot, Wal-Mart sc, Safeway, Walgreen's, Northwest Harley Davidson, Hawks Prairie Casino		Other	E: Olympia Muni Airport✈
	W: Cinema, Discount Tire, Casino					**99**	93rd Ave SW, WA 121S, Olympia, Tumwater, to Tenino, Scott Lake
127	S Tacoma Way, Lakewood, WA 512E, to Puyallup, Mt Rainier						
				W: Cabela's		TStop	E: Pilot Travel Center #151 (Scales)
Gas	W: 7-11, 76, ArcoAmPm, Chevron, Shell◆		**109**	Martin Way, Olympia, Lacey			W: Restover Truck Stop/Shell (Scales)
Food	W: Burger King, DQ, Denny's, IHOP, Ivar's Seafood, McDonald's, Sizzler, Subway, Starbucks, Wendy's		Gas	W: 76, ArcoAmPm, Exxon◆, Shell◆, Safeway		Gas	W: Exxon◆
						Food	E: McDonald's/Subway/Pilot TC
			Food	E: Chinese Buffet, Pizza Hut/Taco Bell			W: Rest/Restover TS
Lodg	W: Budget Inn, Econo Lodge, Knights Inn, Quality Inn, Ramada Inn, Vagabond Motel, Victory Motel, Western Inn					TServ	W: Restover TS

◆ = **Regular Gas Stations with Diesel**   ▲ = **RV Friendly Locations**   ♥ = **Pet Friendly Locations**

RED PRINT SHOWS LARGE VEHICLE PARKING/ACCESS ON SITE OR NEARBY   BROWN PRINT SHOWS CAMPGROUNDS/RV PARKS

EXIT	WASHINGTON
Other	E: Laundry/WiFi/Pilot TC, American Heritage Campground▲, Millersylvania State Park
	W: Laundry/LP/RVDump/Restover TS
95	Maytown Rd SW, WA 121N, to Littlerock Rd, to Tenino
(93)	Maytown Rest Area (SB) (RR, Phone, Picnic, Vend, WiFi, Info)
(90)	Scatter Creek Rest Area (NB) (RR, Phone, Picnic, Vend, WiFi, Info)
88	US 12W, Aberdeen, Rochester, Tenino, Old Hwy 99 SW (SB)
TStop	W: Pacific Pride
Gas	W: ArcoAmPm, Shell◊
Food	W: DQ, McDonald's, Little Red Barn, Rest/PacPride
Lodg	W: Grand Mtound Motel
Other	W: Outback RV Park▲, Harrison RV Park▲, to Lucky Eagle Casino/Rest/Hotel/RVParking
88AB	US 12W, Aberdeen, Rochester, Tenino, Old Hwy 99 SW (NB)
82	Harrison Ave, Centralia
Gas	E: ArcoAm/Pm, Shell◊
	W: Chevron, Circle K, Texaco, Safeway
Food	E: Burger King, Burgerville USA, Casa Ramos, DQ, Godfather's Pizza, Pizza Hut, Panda Inn, Quiznos, Shari's, Wendy's
	W: Arby's, Country Cousin, Denny's, Jack in the Box, McDonald's, Quiznos, Starbucks, Taco Bell
Lodg	E: Ferryman's Inn, King Oscar Motel, Econo Lodge, Riverside Motel
	W: Motel 6 ♥
Other	E: Pharmacy, Jiffy Lube, Auto & Diesel Repair
	W: Centralia Factory Outlet Mall, Centralia Tire, Safeway, Schwab Tire, Harrison RV Park▲, Mid-Way RV Park▲
81	WA 507N, Mellen St, Centralia
Gas	E: Shell
Food	E: The Oasis Rest, Subway
Lodg	E: Holiday Inn Express, Peppertree West Motor Inn & RV Park▲, Travel Inn Express
Med	W: + Providence Centralia Hospital
79	Chamber Way, Chehalis
Gas	E: Shell◊
	W: Airport Depot 76◊
Food	W: Burger King/76, Applebee's, Buckaroos Pizza, McDonald's, Starbucks, Subway, Taco del Mar, Wendy's
TServ	W: Cummins NW
Other	W: Home Depot, Kmart, Wal-Mart sc, Chehalis Centralia Airport✈, Riverside Golf Club
77	WA 6W, Main St, Chehalis
Gas	E: Cenex◊, Shell
Food	E: Dairy Bar
	W: McDonald's, Sowerby's
Other	W: WA State Hwy Patrol Post
76	13th St, Chehalis
Gas	E: Chevron
Food	E: Jack in the Box, Kit Carson, Subway
Lodg	E: Best Western, Chehalis Inn, Relax Inn
Other	E: Baydo's RV
72	Rush Road, Chehalis, Napavine
FStop	W: Rush Road Travel Center/Chevron, Pacific Pride

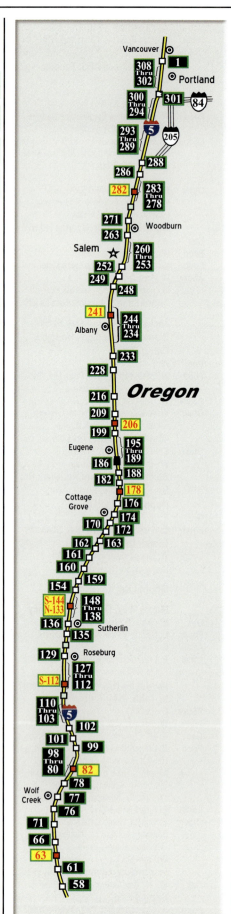

EXIT	WASHINGTON
TStop	E: Now Truck Stop/Shell (Scales)
Gas	W: Shell◊
Food	E: FastFood/Now TS, McDonald's, Beck's Rib Eye, Burger King, Subway
	W: Hot Stuff Pizza/RR TC
Other	E: LP/Shell, Country Canopy & RV Center
	W: J&D RV Sales, Uhlmann RV
71	Forest-Napavine Rd, WA 508E, Napavine, Onalaska
FStop	E: Eagle Truck Plaza/76 (Scales)
Food	E: FastFood/Eagle TP
68	Avery Rd, US 12E, Chehalis, to Morton, Yakima
Gas	E: ArcoAmPm, Shell
	W: Shell
Food	E: Spiffy's Rest
	W: Mustard Seed Rest
Other	E: Chehalis/Hwy 12E KOA▲, Lewis & Clark State Park▲
63	WA 505, Winlock, Toledo
Gas	W: Shell◊
Other	E: LP/Shell, to Mt St Helens Nat'l Volcanic Monument
60	WA 506, Toledo Vader Rd, Toledo, Vader
59	WA 506W, to Vader, Ryderwood
Gas	E: Shell◊
	W: Chevron
Food	E: Mrs Beesley's Burgers
	W: Subway/Chevron, Country House, Riverside Rest, Rick's Place
Other	W: River Oaks RV Park & CG▲
57	Jackson Hwy, Barnes Dr, Toledo
TStop	W: Gee Cee's Truck Stop (Scales)
Food	W: Rest/FastFood/Gee Cee's TS
TServ	W: Gee Cee's TS/Tires, Western Star Trucks
Other	W: Laundry/Gee Cee's TS
(54)	Toutle River Rest Area (Both dir) (RR, Phone, Picnic, WiFi, Info)
52	Barnes Dr, Old Pacific Hwy, Castle Rock
Other	E: Paradise Resort & RV Park▲
	W: Toutle River RV Park Resort▲
49	WA 411S, WA 504E, Castle Rock
TStop	E: Pacific Pride
Gas	E: 76, Chevron, Shell◊, Texaco◊
Food	E: Rest/PacPride TS, Burger King, El Compadre Rest, Peper's 49er Diner, Papa Pete's Pizza, Rose Tree, Subway
Lodg	E: Mt St Helens Motel, Motel 7 West, Timberland Motor Inn
Other	E: to Appr 2mi Mt St Helens RV Park▲, to Mt St Helens Nat'l Volcanic Monument
48	Huntington Ave, Castle Rock
Other	W: RVDump/City Park
46	Headquarters Rd, Pleasant Hill Rd, Pacific Ave N
Other	E: Cedars RV Park▲
(44)	Inspection Station (SB)
42	Ostrander Road, Kelso
40	N Kelso Ave, WA 431, to WA 4
FStop	W: Pacific Pride
Gas	W: 76, Texaco
Lodg	W: Best Western, Budget Inn, Best Value Inn, Econo Lodge
Med	W: + Hospital

◊ = Regular Gas Stations with Diesel   ▲ = RV Friendly Locations   ♥ = Pet Friendly Locations
RED PRINT SHOWS LARGE VEHICLE PARKING/ACCESS ON SITE OR NEARBY   BROWN PRINT SHOWS CAMPGROUNDS/RV PARKS

EXIT		WASHINGTON
39		WA 4, Allen St, Kelso, Longview
	Gas	E: ArcoAmPm, Shell
		W: Chevron
	Food	E: Denny's, McDonald's, Shari's
		W: Azteca Mex Rest, Burger King, DQ, Izzy's Pizza, Red Lobster, Starbucks, Taco Bell
	Lodg	E: Motel 6 ♥, Red Lion, Super 8 ♥
		W: Best Western, Comfort Inn
	AServ	W: Chevron
	Med	W: + Hospital
	Other	E: Grocery, Tourist Info, RiteAid
		W: Mall, Safeway, Target, Amtrak, to Long Beach, Ocean Beaches
36B		WA 432, Tennant Way (SB)
36A		WA 432, Old Hwy 99S (SB)
36		Old Hwy 99S, WA 432W, Tennant Way, to WA 4, Kelso, Longview (NB)
	FStop	E: Industrial Way Chevron
		W: Pacific Pride
	Gas	W: 76◇, ArcoAmPm
	Food	W: Rest/FastFood/I W Chevron
	Lodg	W: Budget Inn, Ramada Inn
	Med	W: + Hospital
	TServ	W: Peterbilt
	Other	W: Home Depot, Kelso Longview Airport✈, WA State Hwy Patrol Post, Longview RV Center
32		Kalama River Rd, Kelso
	Food	E: Fireside Cafe
	Other	E: Camp Kalama CG▲
30		Oak St (SB), Elm St (NB), Kalama
	Gas	E: 76, Chevron
		W: Spirit
	Food	E: Rest/Colum Inn, Burger Bar, Burger King Subway
	Lodg	E: Columbia Inn, Kalama River Inn
27		Robb Rd, Hwy 99, Old Pacific Hwy, Port of Kalama, Kalama
	TStop	E: Pacific Pride/ Rebel Truck Stop/Shell
	Food	E: Rest/Rebel Truck Stop
	Other	E: LP/Rebel TS
		W: to Port of Kalama
22		Dike Access Rd, Woodland
	FStop	W: CFN/Wilson Oil
	Food	W: McDonald's
	Other	E: to Woodland Shores RV Park▲
		W: to Columbia Riverfront RV Park▲
21		WA 503E, Scott Ave, Lewis River Rd, Woodland, Cougar
	FStop	E: Pacific Pride
	Gas	E: ArcoAmPm, Chevron, Shell◇
		W: Shell, Astro, Safeway
	Food	E: Burgerville USA, Casa Maria's, DQ, Rosie's, Quiznos, Subway
		W: McDonald's, Quiznos, Whimpy's
	Lodg	E: Best Western, Econo Lodge, Lewis River Inn, Woodlander Inn
		W: Lakeside Motel, Scandia Motel
	Other	E: Car Quest, Laundromat, U-Haul, Pharmacy, Woodland Shores RV Park▲, Lewis River RV Park▲, Woodland State Airport✈
		W: Safeway, NAPA
16		NW 319th St, NW La Center Rd, Ridgefield, to La Center
	FStop	E: Paradise Truck Stop/Shell
	Other	E: LP/Paradise TS, Paradise Point State Park▲

Personal Notes

EXIT		WASHINGTON
(15)		Inspection Station / Port of Entry (NB)
14		WA 501W, Pioneer St, NW 269th Ridgefield, to City Center
	Gas	E: ArcoAmPm, Circle K
		W: Chevron◇
	Food	E: Country Café, Subway
	Other	E: Tri-Mountain RV Park▲, Big Fir RV Park▲, to Battleground Lake State Park▲
(12)		Gee Creek Rest Area (SB) (RR, Phone, Picnic, Vend, WiFi, Info, RVDump)
(11)		Gee Creek Rest Area (NB) (RR, Phone, Picnic, Vend, WiFi, Info, RVDump)
9		WA 502E, NE 179th St, Ridgefield, to Battle Ground
	Gas	W: Chevron◇
	Food	E: Jollie's Restaurant
	Other	E: Poulsbo RV
		W: Clark Co Fairgounds
7		NE Tenney Rd, NE 134th St, to Jct I-205S, to I-84, WA-14, Portland Airport, Vancouver
	Gas	E: 7-11, 76, ArcoAmPm, Safeway,

MMMM...TOASTY!® I-5 Exit
Quiznos 1421 Pacific N & S
Woodland, WA 98674 # 21
Phone: 360/225-1923
Next to OIL CAN HENRY'S

EXIT		WA / OR
	Gas	E: Trail Mart◇
		W: Mobil
	Food	E: Burger King, Burgerville USA, Jack in the Box, McDonald's, Round Table Pizza, Subway, Taco Bell
	Food	W: Bamboo Hut, El Tapatio, Starbucks
	Lodg	E: Comfort Inn ♥, Holiday Inn Express, Shilo Inn
		W: Red Lion Hotel, University Inn
	Med	E: + Salmon Creek Hospital
	Other	E: Auto Services, Albertson's/Pharmacy, Safeway, 99 RV Park▲
5		NE 99th St, Vancouver
	Gas	E: 7-11, 76, ArcoAmPm, Foodmart, Miirastar, Murphy
		W: ArcoAmPm, Chevron
	Food	E: Burgerville, Carl's Jr, Del Taco, Domino's Pizza, Quiznos
		W: Applebee's, McDonald's
	Other	E: Auto Center, Grocery, Harley Davidson, Walgreen's, Wal-Mart
		W: Albertson's, Office Depot, PetCo ♥, Target
4		78th St, Vancouver, Hazel Dell
	Gas	E: 7-11, Exxon
		W: Shell◇
	Food	E: Burger King, Izzy's Pizza, KFC, McDonald's, Pizza Hut, Skipper's Seafood, Starbucks, Subway, Taco Bell
		W: Wendy's
	Lodg	E: Best Inn, Quality Inn
		W: Best Western
	Other	E: Car Quest, Firestone, Hazel Dell Car Wash, U-Haul, Vanover RV Park▲
		W: Safeway, RiteAid
3		NE Hwy 99, Main St, Vancouver
	Gas	W: ArcoAmPm
	Med	E: + Hospital
2		39th St, WA 500E, Vancouver
	FStop	W: Pacific Pride
1D		Fourth Plain Blvd, Mill Plain Blvd, McLoughlin Blvd, Vancouver, Port of Vancouver
1C		WA 501, Mill Plain Blvd, 15th St, 14th St, Downtown Vancouver
	Gas	W: Chevron
	Food	W: Burgerville USA, Black Angus Steak House, Denny's
	Lodg	W: Shilo Inn
	Other	E: Pearson Airpark✈
		W: Grocery, Auto Services, WA State Hwy Patrol Post
1B		6th St, C St, Downtown Vancouver
1A		WA 14E, to Camas
	Med	E: + Hospital

⋂ **WASHINGTON**
⋃ **OREGON** (PACIFIC TIME ZONE)

308		Hayden Island, Jantzen Beach
	Gas	E: Chevron
		W: 76◇, ArcoAmPm
	Food	E: Burger King, Hayden Island Steak house/DblTree, Starbucks, Taco Bell
		W: BJ's, Denny's, Original Joe's Café, Hooters, Homestead Rest, McDonald's, Newport Bay Seafood, Subway
	Lodg	E: Doubletree Hotel, Oxford Suites
		W: Holiday Inn Express
	Other	E: Safeway/Pharmacy

◇= Regular Gas Stations with Diesel   ▲ = RV Friendly Locations   ♥ = Pet Friendly Locations
RED PRINT SHOWS LARGE VEHICLE PARKING/ACCESS ON SITE OR NEARBY   BROWN PRINT SHOWS CAMPGROUNDS/RV PARKS

EXIT		OREGON
	Othe	W: Firestone, Home Depot, Kmart, Office Depot, Target, Jantzen Beach Mall, **Jantzen Beach RV Park**▲
307		OR 99E S, Martin Luther King Jr Blvd, Marine Dr, N Vancouver Wy
	TStop	E: Jubitz Travel Center/PacPr/AmBest (Scales), TEC Equipment
	Food	E: Rest/FastFood/Jubitz TC, Chompers Burgers, Pizza Mia
	Lodg	E: Portland Inn/Jubitz TC, Residence Inn
	TServ	E: Jubitz TC/Tires, Selectrucks of Portland, Portland Freightliner, Diesel Repair
	TWash	E: Blue Beacon TW/Jubitz TC
	Other	E: Laundry/Cinema/Chiro/Jacuzzi/BarbBtySh/**RVDump**/Jubitz TC, Laundry/TEC, **Columbia River RV Park**▲, Portland Meadows Racetrack, Portland Int'l Airport✈, Harley Davidson W: Expo Center
306B		US 30 ByP, Lombard St, Interstate Ave (SB), Delta Park (NB)
	Gas	E: 76
	Food	E: Burger King, Elmer's, Shari's
	Lodg	E: Best Western, Days Inn, Delta Inn
	Other	E: PetCo♥, Pet Clinic♥, Portland Meadows Golf Course, Lowe's, Portland Meadows Racetrack W: Portland Int'l Raceway
306A		Columbia Blvd (NB)
	FStop	E: (E to MLK Jr Blvd, Left) Pacific Pride
	Gas	E: 7-11, 76, Shell
	Food	W: Wendy's
305B		US 30 ByP, Lombard St W (NB)
305A		US 30 ByP, Lombard St E (NB)
304		Portland Blvd, Univ of Portland
	Gas	W: ArcoAmPm
	Food	W: Nite Hawk Café
303		Alberta St, Going St, Portland
	FStop	W: Pacific Pride
	Gas	W: 76
	Food	E: Big City Burritos, Golden Chopsticks, Cascade Café House, Vinny's Pizza W: Taco Bell, Taco Time, Subway
	Lodg	W: Budget Motel, Economy Inn, Monticello Motel, Palms Motor Hotel, Westerner Motel
	TServ	W: Cummins NW, Peterbilt/GMC
	Med	E: + Legacy Emanuel Hospital
302C		Greeley Ave (NB)
(302B)		Jct I-405, US 30W, Beaverton, St. Helens
	FStop	W: (Ex #3) Pacific Pride
302A		Coliseum, Broadway, Weidler St
	Gas	E: Circle K◊, Shell◊
	Food	E: McDonald's, Starbucks, Wendy's
	Lodg	E: Holiday Inn, Red Lion Inn
	Med	E: + Emmanuel Hospital
	Other	E: Coliseum, Rose Garden Arena
(301)		Jct I-84E (SB)
(300B)		Jct I-84E, US 30E, Portland Airport
300		Water Ave, Morrison St (NB), OR 99ES, US 26E, ML King Jr Blvd, Morrison St, Downtown (SB)
(299B)		Jct I-405W, Portland
299A		OR 43S, Macadam Ave (SB), US 26E, Ross Island Bridge, Powell Blvd (NB)

EXIT		OREGON
298		Corbett Ave (NB)
	FStop	E: (approx 10 blks) Pacific Pride
297		Terwilliger Blvd (NB), to OR 10, Bertha Blvd, Terwilliger Blvd (SB)
	Food	W: Burger King, KFC, Starbucks
	Med	W: + VA Hospital
296B		Multnomah Blvd (SB)
296A		OR 99W S, Barbur Blvd (SB)
	Gas	W: 7-11, 76◊, Chevron, Shell
	Food	W: Indian Cuisine, Old Barn, Original Pancake House, Subway, Wendy's
	Lodg	W: Capitol Hill Motel, King's Row Motel, Portland Rose Motel
295		Capitol Hwy (SB), Taylors Ferry Rd (NB)
	FStop	E: Pacific Pride (DAD)
	Gas	E: Shell◊
	Food	E: Dunkin Donuts, McDonald's, Round Table Pizza, Starbucks
	Lodg	E: Hospitality Motel, Ranch Inn Motel
294		OR 99W, Barbur Blvd (NB) OR 99W, Tigard, Newburg (SB)
	FStop	E: Pacific Pride (DAD)
	Gas	W: BP, Texaco
	Food	W: Arby's, Burger King, Buster's Texas BBQ, Carrow's, KFC, Newport Bay, Subway, Starbucks, Taco Bell
	Lodg	E: Comfort Suites W: Days Inn, Howard Johnson, Value Inn
	Other	W: Laundromat, Costco, PetCo♥, Les Schwab Tire, PetSmart♥
293		Dartmouth St, Haines St (SB), Haines St (NB)
292B		Kruse Way, Lake Oswego (NB)
	Gas	E: Shell
	Food	E: Rest/Residence Inn, Rest/Crowne Pl, Applebee's, Chili's, Classic Café, Olive Garden, Taco Bell, Starbucks
	Lodg	E: Crowne Plaza, Fairfield Inn, Hilton, Garden Inn, Phoenix Inn, Residence Inn
	Other	E: Grocery
292A		Jct OR 217W, Tigard, Beaverton
291		Carman Dr, Lake Oswego
	Gas	W: Chevron, Shell
	Food	W: Burgerville USA, Starbucks, Sweet Tomatoes, Subway
	Lodg	W: Courtyard, Travelodge
	Other	W: Home Depot
290		Lower Boones Ferry Rd, Lake Oswego (NB), Durham (SB)
	Gas	E: 76 W: 76, Chevron
	Food	E: Baha Fresh Mex Grill, Burger King, Carl's Jr, Skipper's Seafood, Taco Bell W: Fuddrucker's, Romano's Macaroni Grill, Village Inn
	Lodg	E: Motel 6♥, Red Roof Inn♥ W: Best Western, Bridgeport Value Inn, Quality Inn
	Other	E: Safeway, Walgreen's W: CarQuest
289		Nyberg St, Tualatin-Sherwood Rd
	Gas	E: Shell W: Arco, Chevron, Shell
	Food	E: The Sweetbrier Inn W: Jack in the Box, McDonald's, Wendy's
	Lodg	E: The Sweetbrier Inn W: Century Hotel

EXIT		OREGON
	Med	E: + Hospital
	Other	E: **RV Park of Portland**▲ W: Kmart, Grocery
(288)		Jct I-205, Oregon City
286		Elligsen Rd, Wilsonville, Stafford
	Gas	E: 76◊, Costco W: Exxon
	Food	E: Burger King, Moe's S/W Grill, Panda Express, Starbucks, Subway W: Rest/Hol Inn
	Lodg	E: La Quinta Inn♥, Super 8 W: Holiday Inn
	Other	E: Costco, PetSmart♥, Office Depot, **Pheasant Ridge RV Park**▲, **Camping World**
283		Wilsonville Rd, Wilsonville
	Gas	E: 76◊ W: 7-11, Chevron
	Food	E: Applebee's, Arby's, Bullwinkle's, DQ, Denny's, Izzy's Pizza, McDonald's, Shari's, Subway, Taco Bell, Wendy's W: Burger King, Chili's, Hunan Kitchen
	Lodg	E: Best Western, Comfort Inn, Snooz Inn W: Phoenix Inn
	Med	E: + Wilsonville Medical Clinic
	Other	E: NAPA, RiteAid, Schwab Tire, US Post Office, **Camping World** W: Albertson's, Walgreen's
282B		Miley Rd (SB)
282A		Canby, Hubbard (SB)
282		Miley Rd (NB)
(282)		Rest Area (Both dir) (RR, Phone, Picnic, Vend, Info)
278		Ehlen Rd, Aurora, Donald
	FStop	E: Pacific Pride/Fuel 'n' Mart
	TStop	W: Travel Center of America/Shell(Scales), Leathers Truck Stop/Shell, Flying J Travel Plaza (Scales)
	Food	W: Rest/Popeyes/TA TC/Deli/Leathers, Rest/FastFood/FJ TP
	TServ	W: TA TC/Tires, Speedco
	Other	E: FuelnMart/**RVPark**▲, **Aurora Acres RV Resort**▲, to Aurora State Airport✈ W: Laundry/WiFi/TA TC, LP/Leathers, Laundry/WiFi/FJ TP
(275)		Inspection Station (SB)
(274)		Inspection Station (NB)
271		OR 214, Woodburn
	Gas	E: 76, ArcoAmPm, Chevron, Exxon◊ W: Shell
	Food	E: Burger King, DQ, Denny's, KFC, McDonald's, Shari's, Subway, Taco Bell W: Arby's, Elmer's, Jack in the Box, Quiznos, Starbucks
	Lodg	E: Best Western, Fairway Inn & **RV Park**▲, Super 8 W: La Quinta Inn♥
	AServ	E: 76
	Other	E: Pharmacy, Wal-Mart sc W: Woodburn Co Stores/Famous Brands Outlet, **Portland- Woodburn RV Park**▲
263		Brooklake Rd, Salem, Brooks
	TStop	W: Pilot Travel Center #386 (Scales)
	Food	W: Subway/Taco Bell/Pilot TC
	Other	W: Laundry/WiFi/LP/Pilot TC
260B		Lockhaven Dr, Keizer (SB)
260A		OR 99E, Salem Pkwy, Salem (SB)

◊ = Regular Gas Stations with Diesel ▲ = RV Friendly Locations ♥ = Pet Friendly Locations
RED PRINT SHOWS LARGE VEHICLE PARKING/ACCESS ON SITE OR NEARBY   BROWN PRINT SHOWS CAMPGROUNDS/RV PARKS

EXIT		OREGON
260		**Lockhaven Dr, Keizer (NB)**
	Note	MM 259. 45th Parallel - Halfway between Equator & North Pole
258		**Portland Rd (SB), OR 99E, Salem, Pacific Hwy E (NB)**
	FStop	W: Pacific Pride
	Gas	E: 76
		W: 76, Chevron, Shell◆
	Food	E: Guesthouse, Italian, McDonald's, The Original Pancake House
		W: Jack in the Box
	Lodg	E: Best Western, Best Value, Days Inn
	Med	W: + Hospital
	Other	E: Auto Repair, Flea Market, Grocery, Highway RV Center
		W: OR State Hwy Patrol Post
256		**OR 213, Market St, State Capitol**
	FStop	W: Pacific Pride
	Gas	E: Shell
		W: ArcoAmPm, Chevron, Shell◆
	Food	E: Carl's Jr, Denny's, Elmer's, Italian, Mexican, Jack in the Box, Olive Garden, Skipper's Seafood, Taco Bell
		W: Almost Home, DQ, McDonald's, Newport Bay Seafood, Roger's 50's Diner, Tony Roma's, Village Inn
	Lodg	E: Best Western, Crossland Economy Inn, Tiki Lodge
		W: Holiday Lodge, Motel 6♥, Quality Inn, Shilo Inn, Super 8
	TServ	W: Brattain International
	Med	W: + Hospital
	Other	E: Albertson's, Goodyear, Mall, NAPA, Les Schwab Tires, Target, Walgreen's, Salem RV Park▲, Salem RV Sales, Phoenix RV Park▲, Salem Harley Davidson
		W: Grocery, Auto Dealers
253		**OR 22, OR 99E, Salem, Stayton**
	FStop	W: Pacific Pride
	Gas	E: Chevron, Shell
		W: Shell, Costco
	Food	E: Burger King, Carl's Jr, McDonald's, Shari's, Subway
		W: DQ, Denny's, Teriyaki Diner
	Lodg	W: Best Western, Comfort Suites, Motel 6♥, Holiday Inn Express♥, Howard Johnson, Residence Inn
	AServ	E: Chevron
	Med	W: + Salem Hospital
	Other	E: Grocery, Home Depot, Meadowlawn Golf Course
		W: AAA, Auto Dealers, Costco, Kmart, Lowe's, Les Schwab Tires, Roberson RV Center, McNaray Field Airport✈, OR State Hwy Patrol Post
252		**Kuebler Blvd, Salem**
	FStop	W: (3.5 mi Rt on Comm St) Pacific Pride
	Gas	W: 76, ArcoAmPm
	Food	W: Burger King, Jack in the Box, McDonald's, Shari's
	Lodg	W: Phoenix Inn
	Med	W: + Salem Hospital
	Other	W: Roberson RV Center
249		**Commercial St, Salem (NB)**
	FStop	W: (3.5 mi) Pacific Pride
248		**Sunnyside**
	FStop	W: Pacific Pride
	Other	E: Forest Glen Resort▲, Enchanted Forest Theme Park, Thrillville Fun Park

Personal Notes

EXIT		OREGON
244		Jefferson Hwy
243		Ankeny Hill Rd
242		Talbot Rd
(241)		**Rest Area (Both dir) (RR, Phone, Picnic, Vend, Info, RVDump)**
240		Hoefer Dr
239		Dever-Conner Rd
238		OR 99E, Jefferson (NB)
	Other	E: McKay Truck & RV Center/RVDump
237		Viewcrest, Century Dr, Albany (SB)
235		Millersburg (SB), Viewcrest (NB)
	Other	E: AMC Harley Davidson
234 B		OR 99E S, Albany (SB)
234A		Knox Butte Rd (SB)
234		OR 99E, Knox Butte Dr, Albany (NB)
	Gas	W: 76, ArcoAmPm, Shell◆, Costco
	Food	W: Rest/BW, Arby's, Burger King, DQ, China Buffet, McDonald's, Pizza Hut, Skippers Seafood, Subway, Taco Bell
	Lodg	E: Comfort Suites, Holiday Inn Express
		W: Best Western, Budget Inn, Days Inn, La Quinta Inn, Motel 6♥
	TServ	W: Lee's Diesel & Mobile Repair
	Med	W: + Hospital
	Other	E: Knox Butte RV Park▲, Albany Muni Airport✈
		W: Kmart, Costco, Auto Dealers

EXIT		OREGON
233		**US 20, Albany, Bend**
	FStop	E: (4175 Santiam Hwy SE) Carson Chevron Food Mart
	TStop	E: Jack's Truck Stop/76 (Scales)
	Gas	E: 76
		W: ArcoAmPm, Shell, Leathers
	Food	E: FastFood/Jacks TS, FastFood/Carson, Burgundy's, Chinese
		W: AppleTree, Burgerville USA, Carl's Jr, Elmer's, McDonald's, Mexican, Skipper's Seafood
	Lodg	E: Best Inn Suites, Econo Lodge♥, Motel Orleans, Relax Inn, Phoenix Inn
		W: Valu Inn
	Med	W: + Hospital
	Other	E: LP/Carson's, OR State Hwy Patrol Post, Home Depot, Albany Muni Airport✈, Lassen RV Center, Blue Ox RV Park▲
		W: Albertson's, Goodyear, RiteAid, Les Schwab Tires, Staples, Auto Dealers
228		**OR 34, Lebanon, Corvallis**
	FStop	E: I-5 76 Food Mart
		W: CFN/Younger Oil Co/Chevron
	Gas	W: ArcoAmPm, Shell
	Food	E: Pine Cone Café
	TServ	W: 24hr Towing & Auto/Truck Repair
	Other	W: Albany/Corvallis KOA▲, Benton Oaks RV & Camp▲, to Oregon St Univ
216		**OR 228, Brownsville, Halsey**
	TStop	E: Pioneer Villa Truck Plaza/76
	Gas	W: Shell◆
	Food	E: Rest/FastFood/Pioneer TP, Rest/BW
		W: Subway/Taco Bell/Shell
	Lodg	E: Best Western
	TServ	E: Pioneer Villa TP/Tires
	TWash	E: Pioneer Villa TP
	Other	E: Laundry/BarberSh/Pioneer Villa TP
209		**Harrisburg, Junction City**
	Food	W: The Hungry Farmer Cafe
	TServ	W: Diamond Hill Trailer Repair
	Other	W: Diamond Hill RV Park▲
(206)		**Rest Area (Both dir) (RR, Phone, Picnic, Vend, Info)**
199		**Coburg**
	TStop	E: Fuel n Go
		W: Travel Center of America/Truck n Travel
	Gas	W: Shell, Star Mart
	Food	E: Rest/Fuel n Go, Rest/Country Squire Inn
		W: Rest/FastFood/TA TC, The Hillside Grill
	Lodg	E: Country Squire Inn, Motel/FnG TS
		W: Motel/TA TC
	TServ	W: TA TC, Cummins NW, Farwest Truck Center, Pacific Detroit Diesel, Freightliner/GMC
	TWash	W: TA TC
	Other	E: Laundry/LP/FuelnGo, Premier RV Resort▲
		W: Laundry/WiFi/LP/RVDump/TA TC, La Mesa RV Center, Guaranty RV Center, Marathon Coach, Paradise RV
195B		Beltline Hwy W, Eugene (SB)
195A		Beltline Hwy E, N Springfield (SB)
195AB		Beltline Hwy E, N Springfield
	Gas	E: 76, ArcoAmPm, Chevron

◆ = Regular Gas Stations with Diesel   ▲ = RV Friendly Locations   ♥ = Pet Friendly Locations

RED PRINT SHOWS LARGE VEHICLE PARKING/ACCESS ON SITE OR NEARBY   BROWN PRINT SHOWS CAMPGROUNDS/RV PARKS

Page 13

EXIT		OREGON
	Food	E: Rest/Gateway Inn, Rest/Doubletree Hotel, Rest/Shilo Inn, Applebee's, Denny's, Elmer's, IHOP, Jack in the Box, KFC, McDonald's, Outback Steakhouse, Shari's, Sizzler, Taco Bell
	Lodg	E: Best Western, Comfort Suites, Double tree Hotel, Gateway Inn, Holiday Inn Express, Motel 6 ♥, Rodeway Inn, Shilo Inn, Super 8
	TServ	E: Stalick International Trucks
	Other	E: Best Buy, Target, US Post Office, OR State Hwy Patrol Post W: Costco
(194B)		Jct I-105W, Eugene
	Lodg	W: Best Value Inn ♥, Campus Inn, Red Lion Hotel
(194A)		Jct I-105E, OR 126, Springfield
192		OR 99N, Franklin Blvd, Eugene, Univ of Oregon (NB)
	Food	W: Burger King, McDonald's, Wendy's
	Lodg	W: Best Western, Days Inn, Quality Inn
	Med	W: + Hospital
	Other	W: Pharmacy
191		Glenwood Blvd
	Gas	W: 76◊, Shell
	Food	W: Denny's
	Lodg	W: Motel 6 ♥
	Other	E: Cat
190		30th Ave (SB)
189		30th Ave (NB)
	Gas	E: Shell◊ W: Exxon, SeQuential◊◊
	Other	E: Doyle's Harley Davidson, Doris Ranch Living History Farm W: Shamrock Village RV Park▲, Eugene RV Center
188		OR 58E, Oakridge, Klamath Falls, OR 99S, Goshen (SB)
188B		Franklin Blvd, Goshen (NB)
188A		OR 58E, Oakridge (NB)
	FStop	W: Pacific Pride
	Food	W: Café/PacPr
	TServ	W: PacPr, Superior Tire Truck & Service
	Other	E: Deerwood RV Park▲ W: Big Boy's RV Center
186		Dillard Rd, Goshen (NB)
182		Creswell
	Gas	W: 76◊, ArcoAmPm, Shell
	Food	W: Creswell Café, Pizza, TJ's
	Lodg	W: Best Western, Creswell Inn
	Other	W: Pharmacy, Grocery, Sherwood Forest KOA▲, Airport ✈
(178)		Rest Area (Both dir) (RR, Phone, Picnic, Vend, Info)
176		Saginaw
174		Cottage Grove, Dorena Lake
	FStop	E: Market Express/Chevron (Scales), Pacific Pride
	Gas	E: Shell W: 76◊, Shell◊
	Food	E: FastFood/MktExpress, Rest/B W, Subway, Taco Bell W: Arby's, Burger King, Carl's Jr, KFC, McDonald's, Subway, Vintage Inn
	Lodg	E: Best Western, Village Green Resort ♥ W: Comfort Inn, Holiday Inn Express, Relax Inn

EXIT		OREGON
	Med	E: + Hospital
	Other	E: Laundry/Mkt Expr, Wal-Mart, Auto Dealers, Cottage Grove State Airport ✈ W: Village Green RV Park▲, Safeway
172		6th St, Cottage Grove Lake (SB)
170		OR 99N, Cottage Grove (NB)
	Other	E: Cottage Grove RV Park▲
163		Curtin
	Gas	W: 76
	Lodg	E: Stardust Motel
	Other	E: US Post Office, Lucky Duck RV Park▲, Pass Creek RV Park▲
162		OR 99S, to OR 38, Drain, Reedsport
161		Buck Creek Rd, Anlauf (NB)
160		Salt Springs Rd
159		Elk Creek, Cox Rd
154		Scotts Valley Rd, Yoncalla (SB), Elkhead Rd (NB)
150		Yoncalla, Red Hill (SB) OR 99, Yoncalla, Drain (NB)
	Other	W: Trees of Oregon RV Park▲
148		Rice Hill
	TStop	E: Pilot Travel Center #233/CFN (Scales), Rice Hill Truck Plaza/Pacific Pr (Scales)
	Gas	E: Chevron
	Food	E: Rest/FastFood/Pilot TC, Homestead, Peggy's, Rest/Ranch Motel W: K-R Drive In
	Lodg	E: Best Western ♥, Ranch Motel
	TServ	E: Bridgestone Tire & Auto, Pro Fleet Diesel Service, NW Diesel Service
	Other	E: Laundry/WiFi/Pilot TC, Rice Hill RV Park▲, Economy Truck, Auto & RV Towing & Repair, Cat, Tires
146		Rice Valley
(143)		Rest Area (Both dir) (RR, Phone, Picnic, Vend)
142		Metz Hill Rd
140		OR 99S, Oakland (SB)
138		Oakland (NB)
136		OR 138W, Elkton, Sutherlin
	Gas	E: 76◊ Chevron◊, Shell◊, BP W: Mobil
	Food	E: Burger King, McDonald's, Papa Murphy's, Italian, Subway/76 W: DQ, Taco Bell, Subway
	Lodg	E: Sutherlin Inn, Town & Country Motel, Regency Inn ♥, Relax Inn W: Budget Inn
	TServ	W: Mobile Diesel Repair & Towing
	Other	E: Info Center, RVDump/BP, I-5 RV Center, RVDump/Shell, Sutherlin Muni Airport ✈ W: Hi-Way Haven RV Camping▲, Oak Hills Golf Club & RV Resort▲, U-Haul, Henry Winery
135		Sutherlin, Wilbur
	FStop	E: CFN
	Gas	E: Shell◊/LP
(130)		Inspection Station (SB)
129		Del Rio Rd, Winchester, N Roseburg
	Other	E: Kamper Korner RV Center/RVDump

EXIT		OREGON
127		Edenbower Blvd, N Roseburg
	Gas	W: Taco Maker/Texaco◊, Albertson's
	Food	W: Applebee's, Carl's Jr, IHOP, Subway, McDonald's, Taco Bell
	Lodg	E: Motel 6 ♥, Super 8 W: Sleep Inn ♥
	Med	W: + Mercy Medical Center
	Other	E: Home Depot, Lowe's, Mt Nebo RV Park▲ W: Albertson's, Kmart, Wal-Mart, Harley Davidson, Staples, Pharmacy
125		Garden Valley Blvd
	Gas	E: Chevron, Shell◊ W: 76, Chevron◊, Shell
	Food	E: Rest/Windmill Inn, Elmer's, Jack in the Box, KFC, Taco Bell, McDonald's, Wagon Wheel W: Arby's Burger King, Carl's Jr, IHOP, Izzy's Pizza, La Hacienda, Rodeo Steaks
	Lodg	E: Comfort Inn, Quality Inn, Windmill Inn ♥ W: Best Western, Econo Lodge, Howard Johnson Express
	Med	W: + Mercy Urgent Care, Roseburg Oregon Medical Center, VA Hospital
	Other	E: Albertson's, Car Quest, NAPA, RiteAid, OR State Hwy Patrol Post W: Mall, Auto Repair
124		OR 138E, Roseburg, Crater Lake NP
	Gas	E: 76◊, Mobil◊ W: Chevron, Shell
	Food	E: Denny's, HiHo W: Subway/Shell, Gay 90's Deli, KFC, Taco Time
	Lodg	E: Best Western, Dunes Motel, Holiday Inn Express, Holiday Motel, Travelodge
	Med	W: + Douglas Community Hospital
	Other	W: Safeway, RiteAid
123		Douglas Co Fairgrounds
	Other	W: Fairgrounds/RVDump/RVPark▲
121		McLain Ave
120		OR 99N, Green, S Roseburg
	Lodg	E: Shady Oaks Motel W: Best Western
119		OR 99S, to OR 42, Roseburg, Winston, Coos Bay
	TStop	W: Love's Travel Stop #312 (Scales), Pacific Pride/Chevron
	Gas	W: Shell◊
	Food	W: Arby's/TJCinn/Love's TS, Rest/PacPr, McDonald's, Papa Murphy's, Subway
	Other	W: WiFi/RVDump/Love's TS, Western Star RV Park▲
NOTE:		MM 116.5 SB: 6% Steep Grade
113		Clarks Branch Rd
	Lodge	W: Quikstop Motel/Market
	TServ	W: Diesel Repair
	Other	W: On the River Golf & RV Resort▲
112		Dillard (SB), OR 99N, to OR 42, Winston, Coos Bay (NB)
	Other	E: Rivers West RV Park▲
(112)		Rest Area (Both dir) (RR, Phone, Picnic)
(111)		Inspection Station (NB)
110		Boomer Hill Rd

◊= Regular Gas Stations with Diesel ▲ = RV Friendly Locations ♥ = Pet Friendly Locations
RED PRINT SHOWS LARGE VEHICLE PARKING/ACCESS ON SITE OR NEARBY BROWN PRINT SHOWS CAMPGROUNDS/RV PARKS

EXIT	OREGON
108	OR 99S, Myrtle Creek
Other	E: Myrtle Creek RV Park▲, City Park/RVDump
106	Weaver
103	Tri-City, Riddle (SB), Myrtle Creek, OR 99N, Tri City (NB) (Addt'l serv 3 mi E in Tri City)
FStop	W: Pacific Pride/Chevron
Gas	W: Chevron
Food	E: Diner
	W: McDonald's
Other	E: Tri City RV Park▲, South Country RV Center/LP, Bowling
102	Gazley Rd, Surprise Valley
Other	E: Surprise Valley RV Park▲
101	OR 99S, Riddle, Stanton Park (SB), Riddle (NB)
99	North Canyonville
TStop	W: 7 Feathers Travel Plaza (Scales)
Food	E: Burger King, Cow Creek Café
	W: Rest/FastFood/7 Feathers TP
Lodg	E: Riverside Motel, Valley View Motel, 7 Feathers Casino & Hotel
	W: Best Western
TServ	W: 7 Feathers TP/Tires
Other	W: 7 Feathers RV Resort▲/LP, Stanton Co Park/RVDump
98	OR 99N, Canyonville, to OR 227, Days Creek
Gas	E: 76◊, Shell◊
Food	E: Bob's Country Junction
Lodg	E: Leisure Inn
Med	E: + Pioneer Healthcare Clinic
	W: + Mercy Health Clinic
Other	E: Laundromat, Grocery, NAPA
	W: Bill's Tire & Auto Repair
95	Canyon Creek
NOTE:	MM 90 SB: 4% Steep Grade for 2 mi
88	Azalea
86	Quines Creek Rd, Barton Rd
Gas	E: Shell◊
Food	E: Heaven On Earth Rest & RVCamping
Other	E: Meadow Wood RV Park▲/RVDump
83	Barton Rd
(82)	Rest Area (Both dir) (RR, Phone, Picnic, Vend)
80	Glendale
Gas	W: Country Junction/LP
Food	W: Village Inn
NOTE:	MM 79.5 SB: 5% Steep Grade, Next 3 mi
78	Speaker Rd, Glendale
77	Speaker Rd (SB)
76	Wolf Creek (NB Diff reaccess)
TStop	W: Pacific Pride/Wolf Creek Bio◊
Gas	W: 76◊, Exxon◊
Food	W: Hungry Wolf Rest
Lodg	W: Wolf Creek Historic Inn
Other	W: Creekside RV Park▲
NOTE:	MM 73.5 SB: 6% Steep Grade next 2 mi
71	Sunny Valley Lp, Wolf Creek
Gas	E: Covered Bridge Gas & Country Store
Lodg	E: Sunny Valley Motel & RVParking▲
Other	W: Grants Pass/Sunny Valley KOA▲

EXIT	OREGON
NOTE:	MM 69: 6% Steep Grade next 3 mi
66	Hugo
Other	W: Joe Creek Waterfalls RV CG▲
(63)	Rest Area (Both dir) (RR, Phone, Picnic, Vend, Info)
61	Merlin Rd, Grants Pass
Gas	W: Shell◊
Other	E: Beaver Creek RV Resort▲, Twin Pines RV Park▲
	W: Rogue Valley RV Center & Repair, OR RV Outlet, Grants Pass Airport✈
58	OR 99, to OR 199, Grants Pass
Gas	W: 76◊, ArcoAmPm, BP, Chevron, Shell◊
Food	W: Angela's Mexican, Burger King, China Hut, Della's, Denny's, Pizza Hut, McDonald's, Sizzler, Subway, Skipper's Seafood, Taco Bell, Wendy's
Lodg	W: Best Way Inn, Comfort Inn♥, Hawk's Inn, Hawthorne Suites, La Quinta Inn♥, Royal Vue Motor Lodge, Shilo Inn, Super 8♥, Sunset Inn♥, Travelodge♥
Med	W: + Hospital
Other	W: 76/RVDump, AutoZone, Auto Dealers, OR State Hwy Patrol Post, Rogue Valley Overniter RV Park▲, Jack's Landing RV Resort▲
55	OR 199, Grants Pass, Crescent City, Siskiyou, Jason
Gas	W: ArcoAmPm, Exxon◊
Food	W: Applebee's, Arby's, Burger King, Carl's Jr, Elmer's, McDonald's, JJ North's Grand Buffet, Shari's, Subway, Taco Bell
Lodg	W: Best Western, Holiday Inn Express
Med	W: + Hospital
Other	W: Wal-Mart sc, Albertson's, Big O Tires, Big Lots, Dollar Tree, RiteAid, Staples, Visitor Info, Fairgrounds, Rogue College, Siskiyou RV World, Moon Mountain RV Resort▲, Riverfront RV Park▲, Caveman RV
48	Rogue River, Savage
Gas	E: Chevron◊, Exxon, Shell◊
Food	E: Abby's Pizza Inn
	W: Aunt Betty's Family Kitchen, Karen's Kitchen, Mexican Rest
Lodg	W: Best Western, Bella Rosa Inn, Rogue River Inn
Other	W: Chinook Winds RV Park▲, Bridgeview RV Resort▲, Grocery, Info Center, Savage Rapids Dams
45B	Valley of the Rogue State Park
	Rest Area (Both dir) (RR, Phone, Picnic, RVDump)
Other	W: to State Park▲
45A	Rogue River Hwy (SB), OR 99, Rogue River Hwy (NB)
Other	E: Cypress Grove RV Park▲
43	OR 99, OR 234, Gold Hill (SB), OR 99, Rogue River Hwy (NB)
Food	E: Café
Lodg	E: Rock Point Motel & RV Park▲
40	Gold Hill (SB), OR 99, OR 234, Gold Hill (NB)
Other	E: Medford/Gold Hill KOA/RVDump▲, Lazy Acres Motel & RV Park▲
	W: Dardanell's Trailer & RV Park▲
35	OR 99S, Central Point (SB), OR 99S, Blackwell Rd (NB)

◊ = Regular Gas Stations with Diesel   ▲ = RV Friendly Locations   ♥ = Pet Friendly Locations

RED PRINT SHOWS LARGE VEHICLE PARKING/ACCESS ON SITE OR NEARBY   BROWN PRINT SHOWS CAMPGROUNDS/RV PARKS

Page 15

EXIT		OREGON
33		Pine St, Central Point
	FStop	E: Pilot Travel Center #391 (Scales)
	Gas	E: Chevron W: 76, Shell◊, Texaco
	Food	E: Subway/Taco Bell/Pilot TC, Burger King, KFC, Shari's W: Bee Gee's, Pappy's Pizza, Mazaltan Grill, McDonald's
	Lodg	E: Fairfield Inn, Holiday Inn Express W: Courtyard, Grand Hotel, Super 8
	Other	E: Laundry/WiFi/Pilot TC, Fairgrounds Expo Park, Rogue Valley Int'l Airport✈, Fun Park, RV Camping, Triple A RV Center▲ W: RVDump/76, Albertson's, Central Point RV Center, RV Camping▲
30		OR 62, Crater Lake Hwy, Medford, Crater Lake Nat'l Park
	TStop	E: Witham Truck Stop/Chevron (Scales)
	Gas	E: 76, ArcoAmPm◊, Shell◊, Gas4Less W: Chevron◊, Shell◊
	Food	E: Rest/Witham TS, Arby's, Applebee's, Asian Grill, Denny's, DQ, Elmers, IHOP, Pizza Hut, Olive Garden, Red Robin, Starbucks, Subway, Taco Delight W: Burger King, KFC, Red Lobster, King Wah Chinese, Skipper's Seafood, Starbucks, Wendy's
	Lodg	E: Best Western, Cedar Lodge, Comfort Inn, Hampton Inn, Medford North, Motel 6♥, Quality Inn, Rogue Regency Inn, Ramada, Shilo Inn, Windmill Inn♥ W: Shilo Inn♥, Tiki Lodge Motel
	TServ	E: Witham TS/Tires, CAT Truck Engines Parts & Service, Cummins NW, Oregon Tire, Freightliner, Western Star Trucks
	Med	E: + Providence Medford Medical Ctr W: + Rogue Valley Manor Medical Hospital
	Other	E: LP/Witham TS, US Post Office, OR State Hwy Patrol Post, Aamco Repair, Ace, Albertsons, FedEx Kinko's, NAPA, Tires, Bowling, to Wal-Mart, Rogue Valley Int'l Medford Airport✈, Mike's RV Service, Ferrell Gas Propane/LP, Medford Oaks RV Park▲, River City RV Center, Southern OR RV, RV Consignment W: Rogue Valley Mall, Target, Tires, U-Haul
27		Barnett Rd, Medford
	FStop	W: Pacific Pride
	Gas	E: Exxon◊, Shell◊ W: 76, Chevron, Exxon, Shell◊
	Food	E: Black Bear Diner, DQ, Kopper Kitchen, Rest/Days Inn W: Abby's Pizza, Apple Annie's, Burger King, Jack in the Box, KFC, McDonald's, Hometown Buffet, Pizza Hut, Senor Sam, Shari's, Starbucks, Subway, Taco Bell, Wendy's
	Lodg	E: Best Western, Days Inn, Motel 6♥, Travelodge♥ W: Best Inn, Budget Inn, Cedar Lodge Motel, City Center Motel, Comfort Inn, Holiday Inn Express, Knights Inn, Red Carpet Inn, Red Lion Hotel
	Med	E: + Rogue Valley Manor Medical Hospital, Walk in Medical Center
	Other	W: Grocery, Kmart, Les Schwab Tire, Staples, Walgreen's

EXIT		OREGON
24		Fern Valley Rd, Phoenix
	TStop	E: Petro Stopping Center #24 (Scales)
	Gas	E: Texaco◊ W: Exxon, 76◊
	Food	E: IronSkillet/Petro SC, Rest/Super 8 W: Angelo's Pizza, Courtyard Café, Luigi's Cafe, McDonald's, Randy's Café, Subway
	Lodg	E: Super 8, RV Park▲ W: Bavarian Inn Motel, Phoenix Motel
	TServ	E: Petro SC/Tires, Pear Tree Center, Peterbilt/GMC, Cummins
	Other	E: Laundry/BarbSh/WiFi/RVDump/LP/Petro SC W: Holiday RV Park▲, Pear Tree Factory Outlet Stores, Car Quest, Grocery, Home Depot, Visitor Info, Roxy Ann Winery, Affordable Truck & RV, Jackson RV Parts & Service
(22)		Rest Area (SB) (RR, Phone, Picnic, Vend)
21		Talent
	TStop	W: Talent Truck Stop
	Gas	W: Gas 4 Less, Shell◊
	Food	E: Figaro's Pizza W: Rest/Talent TS, Expresso Café, Italian, Senor Sam's Mexican
	Lodg	W: Good Nite Inn
	TServ	E: T&T Repair
	Other	W: Wal-Mart, OR RV Round Up, American RV Resort▲, Paschal Winery
19		Valley View Rd, Ashland
	FStop	W: Pacific Pride
	Gas	W: 76◊, Shell
	Food	W: Burger King
	Lodg	W: Best Western, Econo Lodge, La Quinta Inn♥ & RV Park▲
	Med	W: + Hospital
	Other	W: U-Haul, Dick's Towing, to Jackson Wellsprings▲
(18)		Inspection Station (Both dir)
14		OR 66, Ashland St, Ashland, Klamath Falls
	Gas	E: 76◊, Chevron, Shell◊ W: 76, ArcoAmPm, Mobil, Texaco
	Food	E: Rest/Ashland Hills Inn, Denny's, KFC, Oak Tree Rest W: Rest/Knights Inn, McDonald's, DQ, Pizza Hut, Taco Bell, Wendy's
	Lodg	E: Ashland Hills Inn, Best Western, Holiday Inn Express, Relax Inn, Rodeway Inn, Windmill Inn♥ W: Knights Inn, Super 8
	Med	W: + Hospital
	Other	E: RVDump/Shell, Ashland Muni Airport✈, Klamath Falls KOA▲, to Emigrant Lake Rec Area▲, Glenyan RV Park & Campground▲, to Howard Prairie Lake Rec Area & Resort▲ W: Albertson's, RiteAid
NOTE:		MM 13.8 SB: Chain-Up Area
11		OR 99, Siskiyou Blvd, Ashland (NB)
	Gas	W: Shell
	Food	W: Italian, Little Caesar's Pizza, Senor Sam's, Subway, Wendy's
	Lodg	W: Best Western, Hillside Inn, Rodeway Inn, Stratford Inn
	Other	E: Ashland Muni Airport✈ W: Weisinger Brewery

EXIT		OR / CA
(9)		RunAway Truck Ramp (NB)
(7)		RunAway Truck Ramp (NB)
6		OR 273, Mount Ashland (fyi—Sadly Callahan's was lost to fire, not sure if rebuild,)
	Other	E: Ski Area
NOTE:		MM 4.5: 6% Steep Grade next 7 mi
(4)		Brake Inspection (Both dir) Siskiyou Summit
NOTE:		Elev 4310 Highest Elevation on I-5
1		OR 273, Windemar Rd, Siskiyou Summit (NB)

(PACIFIC TIME ZONE)

⓿OREGON
⓿CALIFORNIA

(PACIFIC TIME ZONE)

NOTE:		SB: 4% Steep Grade next 2 mi
796		Hilt Rd, Hornbrook
	Gas	W: Shell
	Food	W: Café/Shell
793		Bailey Hill Rd
(791)		Agricultural Insp Station (SB)
790		Hornbrook Hwy, Ditch Creek Rd
789		CR A-28, Henley, Hornbrook
	Gas	E: Chevron◊
	Other	W: Blue Heron RV Park▲, Robert Johnson Trailer & RV
786		CA 96, Klamath River Rd
	W:	Siskiyou Rest Area (Both dir) (RR, Phone, Picnic, Vend)
NOTE:		MM 781: SB: 5% Steep Grade next 3 mi
(780)		Vista Point (SB)
776		CA 3, Montague Rd, Yreka, Montague
	Gas	W: USA◊ Gasoline
	Food	W: Casa Ramos Mex Rest, Grandma's House Rest, Ma & Pa's, KFC
	Lodg	W: Mountain View Inn, Super 8♥
	Other	W: AmeriGas Propane/LP, Yreka RV Park▲, Laundromat, Grocery
775		Center St, Central Yreka
	FStop	E: Pacific Pride
	Gas	W: 76, Chevron, Miner St Station/Shell◊, Texaco◊, Valero◊
	Food	W: Classic 50's Diner, Denny's, Grandma's House Rest, Purple Plum, Nature's Kitchen
	Lodg	W: Best Western, Budget Inn, Comfort Inn, Econo Lodge, Relax Inn, Yreka Motel
	Med	W: + Siskiyou Gen'l Hospital
	Other	E: Vet♥ W: Car Quest, Grocery, RiteAid, US Post Office, Tire Service, Littrell's Auto & RV Service
773		CA 3, Yreka, Fort Jones, Etna
	FStop	E: CFN
	Gas	W: Exxon, Shell◊
	Food	W: Black Bear Diner, Burger King, Carl's Jr, KFC, McDonald's, Pizza Hut, Subway, Taco Bell

◊ = Regular Gas Stations with Diesel ▲ = RV Friendly Locations ♥ = Pet Friendly Locations
RED PRINT SHOWS LARGE VEHICLE PARKING/ACCESS ON SITE OR NEARBY BROWN PRINT SHOWS CAMPGROUNDS/RV PARKS

EXIT		CALIFORNIA
	Lodg	W: Amerihost Inn, Comfort Inn, Days Inn, Motel 6♥
	Med	W: + Hospital
	Other	W: Carwash, Grocery, NAPA, RiteAid, Wal-Mart, CA State Hwy Patrol Post
770		Shamrock Rd, Easy St, Yreka
	Gas	W: Easy Mart Fuel 24/7
766		CR A12, Grenada, Montague, Gazelle
	Gas	W: Fergie's Qwik Stop/Shell, Texaco
759		Louie Rd, Weed
753		Weed Airport Rd
	W:	Weed Rest Area (Both dir) (RR, Phone, Picnic)
	Other	E: Weed Airport✈
751		Stewart Springs Rd, Weed, Edgewood, Gazelle
	Other	E: RV Camping▲ W: to Stewart Mineral Springs Resort
748		CA 265, to US 97, Central Weed, Klamath Falls, N Weed Blvd
	Gas	E: Chevron, Shell, Spirit◊
	Food	E: Rest/Summit Inn
	Lodg	E: Motel 6♥, Summit Inn
747		Weed Blvd, Central Weed, College of Siskiyous (SB), US 97, Klamath Falls (NB)
	Gas	E: 76, Chevron, Shell◊, Spirit◊
	Food	E: Expresso Bakery, Café/Hi-Lo Motel, Pizza Factory, Rest/Summit Inn
	Lodg	E: Hi-Lo Motel & RV Park▲, Motel 6♥, Summit Inn, Townhouse Motel
	Other	E: NAPA, Laundromat, Grocery, Auto Repair
745		S Weed Blvd, Weed
	TStop	E: Travelers Travel Plaza/PacPr (Scales)
	Gas	E: Chevron◊, Shell
	Food	E: Subway/Trav TP, McDonald's, Silva's Family Rest, Burger King, Taco Bell
	Lodg	E: Best Inn, Comfort Inn, Quality Inn♥, Sis-Q-Inn Motel
	TServ	E: Trav TP
	Other	E: Laundry/LP/TravTP, Friendly RV Park▲
743		Summit Dr, Truck Village Dr
	FStop	E: CFN
741		Abrams Lake Rd, Mt Shasta
	Other	W: Abrams Lake RV Park▲
740		Mt Shasta City (SB) (NO reaccess, reacc via Ex #738)
	Gas	E: Pacific Pride
	Lodg	E: Cold Creek Inn
	Other	E: Mt Shasta City KOA▲
738		Central Mt Shasta
	Gas	E: 76◊, Chevron, Shell◊, Spirit◊
	Food	E: Rest/Best Western, Burger King, KFC/Taco Bell, Round Table Pizza, Subway W: Rest/Mt Shasta Resort
	Lodg	E: Best Western, Choice Inn, Travel Inn W: Mt Shasta Resort
	Med	E: + Hospital
	Other	E: Laundromat, Grocery, RiteAid, Mt Shasta City KOA/RVDump/LP▲ W: Lake Siskiyou RV Park▲
737		Mt Shasta City (NB) (Same Serv as Exit #738)
	Lodg	E: Swiss Holiday Lodge
736		CA 89, McCloud, Lassen NP
	Other	E: to appr 9mi McCloud Dance Country RV Resort▲

EXIT		CALIFORNIA
(735)		Inspection Station (SB)
	NOTE:	MM 734: 5% Steep Grade next 3 mi
734		Mott Rd, Mt Shasta, to Dunsmuir
732		Dunsmuir Ave, Siskiyou Ave, Dunsmuir
	Gas	W: Chevron◊, Shell◊
	Food	E: House of Glass Rest, Penny's Diner
	Lodg	E: Best Choice Inn W: Acorn Inn, Cedar Lodge
730		Dunsmuir Ave, Central Dunsmuir
	Gas	W: Chevron, Shell
	Food	W: Hitching Post, Micki's Better Burger
	Lodg	E: Dunsmuir Inn, Travelodge W: Cave Springs Resort
	Other	E: Grocery, Amtrak, US Post Office
729		Dunsmuir Ave, Hist District
728		Crag View Dr, Railroad Park Rd Castella (SB), Castle Crags Dr (NB)
	Gas	E: Manfredi's
	Food	E: Burger Barn, Pizza Factory, River Café, Salt H20 Cafe
	Lodg	E: Dunsmuir Lodge, Railroad Park Resort RV Park▲ & Caboose Motel, Rustic Trailer Park▲
727		Crag View Dr (NB)
726		Soda Creek Rd, Castella
724		Castle Creek Rd, Castella
	Gas	W: Chevron◊
	Other	W: to Castle Crags State Park▲

EXIT		CALIFORNIA
(723)		Vista Point (NB)
723		Sweetbrier Ave, Castella
721		Conant Rd
720		Flume Creek Rd
718		Sims Rd, Castella
714		Gibson Rd
712		Pollard Flat, Lakehead
	FStop	E: Pollard Flat USA/Exxon
	Food	E: Rest/PF USA
710		La Moine Rd, Slate Creek Rd, Lakehead
707		Vollmers, Dog Creek Rd, Delta Rd
	Lodg	E: to Delta Lodge
(705)		Lakehead Rest Area (SB) (RR, Phone, Picnic)
704		Riverview Dr, Lakehead
702		Lakeshore Dr, Antlers Rd
	Gas	E: Shell◊ W: 76
	Food	E: Brewster's, Subway, Top Hat Café, Café/New Lodge Motel W: Bar & Grill, Canyon Kettle
	Lodg	E: New Lodge Motel W: Lakeshore Inn & RV Park▲, Shasta Lake Motel
	Aserv	E: Auto Repair, Towing
	Other	E: US Post Office, Antlers RV Park & CG▲, Lakehead RV Park & CG▲ W: Lakeshore Villa RV Park▲, Shasta Lake RV Resort & CG▲, Rancheria RV Park▲, Whiskeytown Shasta Trinity Nat'l Rec Area
	NOTE:	MM 698: 5% Steep Grade next 2 mi
698		Salt Creek Rd, Gilman Rd
	Other	W: Salt Creek Resort▲, Trail In RV CG▲
695		Shasta Caverns Rd, Lakehead, to O'Brien
(694)		O'Brien Rest Area (NB) (RR, Phone, Picnic)
693		Packers Bay Rd (SB, no NB reacc)
692		Turntable Bay Rd, Lakehead
	Other	Whiskeytown Shasta Trinity Nat'l Rec Area
690		Bridge Bay Rd, Redding
	Food	W: Tail O'the Whale/Br Bay Resort
	Lodg	W: Bridge Bay Resort
	Other	W: Boat Rentals/BrBayResort
689		Fawndale Rd, Wonderland Blvd
	Lodg	E: Fawndale Lodge & RV Resort▲
	Other	E: Fawndale Oaks RV Park▲ W: Wonderland RV Park▲
687		Mountain Gate, Wonderland Blvd
	FStop	E: CFN/Chevron
	Gas	W: Shell◊
	Other	E: Mountain Gate RV Park▲, Bear Mountain RV Resort▲, Lake Shasta Info, Visitor Info
685		CA 151, Shasta Dam Blvd, Shasta Dam, Shasta Lake, Central Valley
	Gas	W: Circle K, Chevron, Valero
	Food	W: Burger King, Latinos Rest, McDonald's, Pizza Factory, Taco Shop

◊ = Regular Gas Stations with Diesel   ▲ = RV Friendly Locations   ♥ = Pet Friendly Locations

RED PRINT SHOWS LARGE VEHICLE PARKING/ACCESS ON SITE OR NEARBY   BROWN PRINT SHOWS CAMPGROUNDS/RV PARKS

EXIT	CALIFORNIA	EXIT	CALIFORNIA	EXIT	CALIFORNIA
Lodg	W: Shasta Dam Motel	Lodg	E: Amerihost, Best Western, Comfort Inn, Hilltop Lodge, Holiday Inn Express, La Quinta Inn♥, Quality Inn, Red Lion Hotel	653	Jellys Ferry Rd, Red Bluff
Med	W: + Shasta Dam Medical Clinic			Other	E: Bend RV Park▲
684	Pine Grove Ave, Shasta Lake			652	Wilcox Golf Rd
Gas	W: 76◆, Chevron		W: Best Value Inn, Howard Johnson Express, Motel 6♥, Vagabond Inn	651	Red Bluff, CA 36W, Fortuna (SB, no re-entry)
Food	W: Giant Orange Café, RC's BBQ & Steakhouse	Med	W: + Mercy Medical Center	650	Adobe Rd, Red Bluff
Other	E: Safari RV Parts & Service, Cousin Gary RV Supermart	Other	E: Costco, FedEx Kinko's, PetSmart♥, Walgreen's, Wal-Mart, Mt Shasta Mall, Les Schwab Tires	Gas	W: Chevron
682	Oasis Rd, Redding			Lodg	E: Econo Lodge♥, Hampton Inn
Gas	W: ArcoAmPm, QT		W: America's Tire, Big O Tire, Auto Dealers, Grocery, Office Depot, U-Haul, Cousin Gary's RV Center, to appr 4mi Green Acres RV Park▲, Redding RV Center	Other	W: Home Depot
Food	W: McDonald's			649	CA 36E Chico, CA 99, Lassen NP, CA 36W Red Bluff
TServ	W: Truck Repair			Gas	E: Exxon, Gas 4 Less, Shell◆
Other	W: Redding RV Center & Repair, CA RV Center, Myers Marine & RV Center, Shasta Lake RV, CA State Hwy Patrol Post				W: USA◆
		675	S Bonnyview Rd, Churn Creek Rd (SB), Bechelli Lane (NB), Redding	Food	E: Burger King, KFC, McDonald's
					W: Carl's Jr, Denny's, Egg Roll King, Pizza, Shari's, Subway
681B	CA 273, to Market St, Lake Blvd (SB, No re-entry)	Gas	E: Chevron◆, Valero	Lodg	E: Best Inn, Best Western♥, Comfort Inn, Motel 6♥, Super 8, Travelodge
FStop	W: CFN/SST Oil #893		W: Shell◆		W: Best Value Inn, Cinderella Riverview Motel
Gas	W: Exxon	Food	E: Taco Bell		
Med	W: + Hospital		W: Burger King/Shell	Other	E: CA State Hwy Patrol Post, to Red Bluff RV Park▲
TServ	E: Redding Freightliner	Lodg	E: Hilton Garden Inn, Super 8		W: Laundromat, Grocery, Pharmacy, Idle Wheels RV Park▲, O'Nite RV Park▲
	W: Redding Truck Center, Shasta Valley Ford Truck, Towing & Repair	TServ	E: Redding Kenworth		
		673	Knighton Rd, Redding Airport		
681A	Twin View Blvd, Redding (SB)	FStop	E: CFN/SST Oil #345	647B	Diamond Ave (SB)
FStop	W: Pacific Pride	TStop	E: Travel Center of America #57/76 (Scales)	647A	S Main St (SB)
Gas	E: 76	Food	E: CountryPr/PHut/Popeye's/TA TC	647	Red Bluff, Diamond Ave (NB)
Lodg	E: Motel 6♥, Ramada Ltd	TServ	E: TA TC	Gas	E: 76◆, Valero
	W: Holiday Inn Express♥	Other	E: Laundry/WiFi/TA TC, Redding Muni Airport✈		W: ArcoAmPm◆, Chevron
Other	E: Redding Harley Davidson			Food	E: Mexican Rest
681	Twin View Blvd, Redding (NB)		W: JGW RV Park▲, Sacramento River RV Park▲		W: Arby's, Jack in the Box, Italian, Pizza Hut, Starbucks, Taco Bell, Yogurt Alley
680	CA 299, Lake Blvd	670	Riverside Ave, Anderson	Lodg	E: Days Inn
Gas	W: ArcoAmPm, Chevron	668	Central Anderson, Lassen NP		W: Sky Terrace Motel, Triangle Motel
Food	W: Arby's, Carl's Jr, Cattleman's Steak House, Giant Burger, KFC, Giant Burger, McDonald's, Starbucks, Subway, Rest/River Inn Motel	Gas	E: 76◆, Beacon, USA	Med	E: + Hospital
			W: Anderson, Chevron, Sarco, Shell	Other	W: Grocery, Kmart, Staples, Walgreen's, Wal-Mart, Red Bluff Muni Airport✈
		Food	E: Burger King, McDonald's, Round Table Pizza, Subway, Taco Bell		
Lodg	W: River Inn Motel, Travelodge		W: Giant Burger, KFC, Pizza	642	Flores Ave, Proberta, Gerber
Other	E: to Shasta College	Lodg	E: Best Western, Valley Inn		NOTE: Trucks & RV's NOT ADVISED
	W: Grocery, Walgreen's, Waterworks Park, Premier RV Resort▲, Redding RV Park▲, to appr 34mi Mt Lassen/Shingletown KOA▲	Med	E: + Anderson Walk-In Medical Clinic	636	CR A11, Gyle Rd, Gerber, to Tehama, Los Molinos
		Other	E: Safeway, RiteAid, Ace, NAPA	Other	E: to Los Molinos RV Camping▲
		667	Deschutes Rd, Factory Outlet Blvd, Anderson, Cottonwood	633	Finnell Ave, Corning, Richfield
678B	CA 44W (SB)	Gas	E: Shell◆	(633)	Lt JC Herwick Rest Area (Both dir) (RR, Phone, Picnic, Vend)
678A	CA 44, Hilltop Dr, Lassen NP (SB)		W: Tower Mart		
678	CA 44, Eureka, Lassen NP (NB)	Food	W: Arby's, Cascade Beef, Jack in the Box, Ca Expresso, Long John Silver	631	Corning Rd, Corning
FStop	W: CFN/SST Oil #1472	Lodg	W: AmeriHost	Gas	E: 76◆, 7-11, Chevron, Shell◆
Gas	E: Chevron, Shell	Other	W: Prime Outlets, Wal-Martsc	Food	E: Burger King, Marco's Pizza, Olive Pit, Quiznos, Starbucks, Taco Bell
Food	E: Applebee's, Carl's Jr, Chevy's Mexican, Italian Cottage, Jack in the Box, Pizza Hut, Logan's Roadhouse, Pasta Pronto, McDonald's, Olive Garden, Outback Steakhouse, Quiznos, Red Lobster, Starbucks, Waters Seafood Grill	665	Cottonwood (SB, NB re-entry)		W: Bartell's Giant Burger
		Lodg	E: Alamo Motel & RV Park▲	Lodge	E: 7 Inn, American Inn, Best Western, Economy Inn
		664	Balls Ferry Rd, Gas Point Rd		
		FStop	W: CFN/SST/CircleB/Beacon	Other	E: Bob's Tires, Laundromat, NAPA, RiteAid, Safeway, Les Schwab Tire, to Corning Muni Airport✈, Heritage RV Park▲, to Woodson Bridge State Rec Area/RV Park▲
		Gas	E: Payless, Gas 4 Less		
			W: Holiday◆, Valero◆		
Food	W: Ca Cattle Co	Lodg	E: Travelers Motel, Alamo Motel & RV Park▲		
Lodg	E: Holiday Inn, Hilton, Motel 6♥	Other	E: Pharmacy, Grocery		W: Corning RV Park▲
	W: River Inn Motor Hotel		W: Laundromat	630	South Ave, Corning
Other	E: Albertson's, Best Buy, Costco, Home Depot, Office Depot, PetCo♥, Target, Wal-Mart, Mall, Laundromat	662	Bowman Rd, Cottonwood	TStop	E: Petro Stopping Center #9 (Scales), Travel Center of America #40/Arco (Scales) Flying J Travel Plaza (Scales)
		FStop	E: Cross Country Travel Center/Shell, Pacific Pride/Texaco		
Other	W: to Benton Field Airport✈, Amtrak	Food	E: Rest/PacPr		
677	Cypress Ave, Hilltop Dr, Redding	(660)	Inspection Station (Both dir)	Food	E: Buckhorn/Arby/Subw/TA TC, Rest/Petro SC, Rest/FastFood/FJ TP, McDonald's, Jack in the Box
FStop	E: CFN/Hilltop Circle K/76	659	Sunset Hills Dr, Auction Yard Rd		
	W: CFN/SST Oil #555	657	Auction Yard Rd, Hooker Creek Rd		
Gas	E: Chevron, Exxon, Shell, Spirit	Other	E: Truck & Trailer Repair		
	W: 76, Shell, USA◆	(656)	HJ Miles Rest Area (Both dir) (RR, Phone, Picnic)	Gas	E: Chevron, Spirit
Food	E: Applebee's, Carl's Jr, KFC, Little Caesar's Pizza, McDonald's, Taco Bell				
	W: Big Red's BBQ, CA Cattle Co, Denny's, Jack in the Box, Subway				

Page 18   ◆ = Regular Gas Stations with Diesel   ▲ = RV Friendly Locations   ♥ = Pet Friendly Locations
RED PRINT SHOWS LARGE VEHICLE PARKING/ACCESS ON SITE OR NEARBY   BROWN PRINT SHOWS CAMPGROUNDS/RV PARKS

EXIT		CALIFORNIA
	Lodg	E: Days Inn ♥, Holiday Inn Express
	TServ	E: TA TC, Petro SC/Tires, Speedco, Corning Truck & Radiator Service
	TWash	E: Blue Beacon TW/Petro SC, Royal Truck Wash
	Other	E: Laundry/WiFi/RVDump/TA TC, Laundry/WiFi/Petro SC, LP/RVDump/Flying J TP, U-Haul, Corning Truck & RV Center
628		CA 99W (NB), Liberal Ave (SB)
	FStop	E: Pacific Pride
	Gas	W: CFN/Chevron◊
	Food	W: Rest/PacPr, Rest/Ramada Inn/RHC
	Lodg	W: The Lodge/Ramada Inn/RHC
	Other	W: Rolling Hills Casino/RV Parking
621		CR 7, Orland
619		CA 32E, Orland, Chico
	Gas	E: Gas 4 Less, Orland Gas W: USA◊
	Food	E: Berry Patch, Burger King, Subway W: Taco Bell
	Lodg	E: Orlanda Inn
	Other	E: Walgreen's W: Old Orchard RV Park▲, The Parkway RV Resort & CG▲
618		CR 16, Orland
	FStop	E: USA Fuel Stop, CFN
	Food	E: Pizza Factory
	Lodg	E: Orland Inn
	Other	E: Laundromat, Grocery, Pharmacy, Orland MH & RV Park▲
614		CR 27
610		CR 33, Artois
(608)		Willows Rest Area (Both dir) (RR, Phone, Picnic, Vend)
607		CR 39, Willows
603		CA 162, Wood St, Willows, Oroville
	FStop	E: Pacific Pride
	Gas	E: ArcoAmPm, Chevron, Shell◊ W: 76
	Food	E: Rest/Best Western, Black Bear Diner, Burger King, Denny's, KFC, McDonald's, Round Table Pizza, Starbucks, Subway W: Nancy's 24hr Airport Café
	Lodg	E: AmeriHost, Baymont Inn, Best Western ♥, Days Inn, Economy Inn ♥, Motel 6, Super 8 ♥
	Med	E: + Glynn Medical Center
	Other	E: CA State Hwy Patrol Post W: Carwash, Radio Shack, US Post Office, Wal-Mart, Willow Glenn Co Airport✈, Willow Glenn RV Park▲
601		CR 57, Willows
	FStop	E: to CA99W, N: CFN/ValleyPetro
595		Norman Rd, Rd 68, Princeton
	Other	E: Sacramento Wildlife Refuge
591		Delevan Rd
588		Maxwell Rd (SB)
586		Maxwell Rd
	Gas	W: CFN/Chevron
	Other	E: to Colusa Casino
(583)		Maxwell Rest Area (Both dir) (RR, Phone, Picnic)
578		CA 20, Colusa, Clear Lake
	Gas	W: Orv's Cnty Store & Deli/Shell

EXIT		CALIFORNIA
	Lodg	W: Capri Williams, Travelers Motel
	Med	W: + Urgent Care Med Center
	Other	E: Williams Airport✈ W: CA Hwy Patrol Post
577		Williams
	FStop	E: Pacific Pride
	Gas	E: Shell W: 76, ArcoAmPm◊, Chevron, Shell◊
	Food	E: Subway, Taco Bell W: Burger King, Casa Lupe, Denny's, Granzella's Bakery & Rest, McDonald's, Subway, Wendy's
	Lodg	E: Holiday Inn Express W: Comfort Inn, Granzella's Inn, Motel 6, Stage Stop Inn
	Med	W: + Hospital
	Other	W: Pharmacy, NAPA, US Post Office, U-Haul, CA State Hwy Patrol Post, I-5 RV Park▲
575		Husted Rd, to Williams
569		Hahn Rd, Grimes
567		Putnam Lateral, Arbuckle
	FStop	E: Pacific Pride
	Gas	E: Exxon W: CFN
566		Arbuckle, College City
	FStop	E: Pacific Pride
	Gas	E: Shell
	NOTE:	MM 559: SB: Begin Call Boxes
559		County Line Rd
(557)		Dunnigan Rest Area (Both dir) (RR, Phone, Picnic)
556		CR E4, CR 6, Dunnigan
	Gas	E: BP, Chevron◊, Valero◊ W: 76, Shell
	Food	E: Bill & Kathy's, BBQ, Jack in the Box
	Lodg	E: Best Value Inn
	Other	W: Campers Inn & RV Golf Resort▲
554		CR 8, Chula Vista, Dunnigan
	TStop	E: Pilot Travel Center #168 (Scales) W: United (Scales)
	Food	E: Wendy's/Pilot TC, Oasis Grill W: FastFood/United
	Lodg	E: Budget 8, Horizon Motel, Sands Motel
	TWash	E: Pilot TC
	TServ	E: Bob's Truck Repair W: United
	Other	E: Laundry/WiFi/Pilot TC, Happy Time RV Park▲ W: Laundry/Wifi/United
(553)		Jct I-505S, Winters, to San Francisco (SB)
548		CR 13, CR E10, Zamora
	FStop	E: Pacific Pride
	Gas	E: Shell◊
	Food	E: Rest/PacPr, Zamora Mini Mart & Deli
	TServ	W: Peterson Power Systems
542		Yolo
541		CR E7, to CA 16, Woodland
	Med	W: + Hospital
540		CR 99, West St
	Food	W: Denny's
	Lodg	W: Cache Creek Lodge

◊ = Regular Gas Stations with Diesel   ▲ = RV Friendly Locations   ♥ = Pet Friendly Locations

RED PRINT SHOWS LARGE VEHICLE PARKING/ACCESS ON SITE OR NEARBY   BROWN PRINT SHOWS CAMPGROUNDS/RV PARKS

EXIT	CALIFORNIA
538	**CA 113N, East St, to Yuba City**
FStop	W: Pacific Pride
Gas	W: Chevron◇, Shell
Food	W: Denny's
Lodg	E: Valley Oaks Inn
	W: Best Western
537	**Main St, CA 113S, Davis**
FStop	W: Valero Food Stop, Pacific Pride
Gas	W: 76
Food	W: Burger King, Denny's, McDonald's, Taco Bell, Wendy's
Lodg	W: Comfort Inn, Days Inn, Motel 6♥
Other	E: CA State Hwy Patrol Post
536	**CR 102, Woodland**
Gas	E: ArcoAmPm, Shell, Murphy
	W: Chevron
Food	E: Burger King, Jack in the Box, McDonald's, Quiznos, Subway
Lodg	E: Hampton Inn, Holiday Inn Express
Other	E: Costco, Home Depot, Staples, Target, Wal-Mart
	W: CA State Hwy Patrol Post
531	**CR 22, Sacramento, Elkhorn**
(529)	**Elkhorn Rest Area (SB)** **(RR, Phone, Picnic)**
528	**Airport Blvd, Sacramento**
Gas	E: ArcoAmPm
Food	E: Foods/Airport, Jim's Tacos
Lodg	E: Host Airport Hotel
Other	E: Sacramento Metro Airport✈
525B	**CA 99N, Yuba City, CA 70, Marysville (diff reacc)** (begin run w/I-99)
525A	**Del Paso Rd**
Gas	E: ArcoAmPm, Chevron
Food	E: Jack in the Box, Starbucks, Teriyaki to Go
Lodg	E: Holiday Inn Express
Other	E: Arco Arena, RiteAid, Safeway
524	**Arena Blvd**
Other	E: Arco Arena, Natomas Field
(522)	**Jct I-80, E-Reno, W-San Francisco**
TServ	W: Cummins West
521	**Garden Hwy (SB)**
521B	**W El Camino Ave (NB)**
Food	E: Carl's Jr, Jack in the Box
Lodg	W: Residence Inn
521A	**Garden Hwy (NB)**
520	**Richards Blvd, Sacramento**
FStop	E: Pacific Pride
Gas	E: Chevron
	W: ArcoAmPm, Shell◇
Food	E: Burger King, Carl's Jr, Hungry Hunter, Lyon's, Memphis BBQ, McDonald's, Monterrey Bay
	W: Best Western, Restaurants
Lodg	E: Governors Inn, Hawthorne Inn, Ramada Inn, Super 8
	W: Best Western, Days Inn, La Quinta Inn♥, Motel 6♥, Super 8
Other	E: Convention Center, State Capitol
519B	**J St, Old Sacramento**
Food	E: Denny's
Lodg	E: Holiday Inn, Quality Inn
	W: Embassy Suites, Econo Lodge, Travelodge

EXIT	CALIFORNIA
519A	**Q St, Downtown Sacramento**
518	**to US 50, I-80W Bus, San Francisco, CA 99S, Fresno (NB)** (End run w/I-99)
516	**Sutterville Rd**
Other	E: Sacramento Zoo
515/B	**Fruitridge Rd, Seamas Ave**
514	**43rd Ave, Sacramento (SB)**
Gas	E: 76
Other	E: Sacramento Exec Airport✈
513	**Florin Rd**
Gas	E: ArcoAmPm, Chevron, Shell
Food	E: Rosalinda's Mexican, Round Table Pizza
	W: Panda Garden, Starbucks, Subway, Wendy's
AServ	E: Shell
Other	E: Grocery, Pharmacy
	W: Grocery, RiteAid
512	**Pocket Rd, Meadowview Rd, Sacramento, Freeport**
Gas	E: Shell, United◇
Food	E: IHOP, McDonald's
Other	E: Home Depot, Staples
508	**Laguna Blvd, Elk Grove**
Gas	E: 76◇, Chevron, Shell
506	**Elk Grove Blvd**
Gas	E: Chevron
Lodg	E: Comfort Suites
504	**Hood-Franklin Rd**
NOTE:	**SB: Gusty Wind Area next 3 mi**
498	**Twin Cities Rd, Walnut Grove**
Other	E: Franklin Field
493	**Walnut Grove Rd, Lodi**
Gas	E: 76◇, CFN, Chevron
Food	E: Subway/Chevron
490	**Peltier Rd**
487	**Turner Rd**
485	**CA 12, S-Lodi, N-Fairfield**
FStop	E: Chevron, Pacific Pride
TStop	E: 3 B's Truck & Auto Plaza/76, Flying J Travel Plaza (Scales)
Gas	E: ArcoAmPm
Food	E: Rest/3B's, CountryMkt/FastFood/FJ TP, Subway/Chevron, Rest/PacPr, Burger King, Carl's Jr, McDonald's, Starbucks, Taco Bell
Lodg	E: Best Western, Microtel
TServ	E: 3 B's TP/Tires
TWash	E: Blue Beacon TW/FJ TP
Other	E: Laundry/WiFi/LP/RVDump/FJ TP, Flag City RV Resort/LP▲
	W: CarWash/Chevron, Tower Park Resort▲, Stockton/Delta KOA▲
481	**Eight Mile Rd, Stockton**
Gas	W: Chevron, Valero
Food	W: Hawaiian BBQ, Jack in the Box, Italian Café, Panera Bread, Panda Express, Starbucks, Subway, Taco Bell, Wing Stop
Lodg	W: Vagabond Inn
Other	W: Lowe's, Office Depot, PetSmart♥, Sports Authority, Target
478	**Hammer Lane, Stockton (NO Trucks)**
Gas	E: ArcoAmPm, 76◇
	W: Exxon, Quik Stop

EXIT	CALIFORNIA
Food	E: KFC, McDonald's, Little Caesar's Pizza, Subway
	W: Burger King, Jack in the Box, Subway, Taco Bell
Lodg	W: Vagabond Inn
Other	E: Laundromat, Grocery/Pharmacy
477	**Benjamin Holt Dr, Stockton (NO Trucks)**
Gas	E: ArcoAmPm, Chevron
	W: Shell◇
Food	E: Pizza
	W: Lyon's, McDonald's, Subway
Lodg	E: Motel 6♥
Other	W: Ace Hardware
476	**March Lane, Stockton**
Gas	E: 7-11/Citgo
	W: 76◇, 7-11
Food	E: Applebee's, Black Angus, Carl's Jr, Denny's, Jack in the Box, McDonald's, Red Lobster, Taco Bell, Tony Roma, Wendy's
	W: Carrow's, Wong's Chinese
Lodg	E: Comfort Inn, Radisson
	W: La Quinta Inn♥, Super 8
Med	E: + Medical Center
Other	E: Grocery, Pharmacy, Stores, Malls
	W: Home Depot, Office Max
475	**Alpine Ave, Country Club Blvd**
474B	**Country Club Blvd, Alpine Ave**
Gas	E: Shell
	W: 7-11, USA
Food	W: Round Table Pizza, Subway
Other	W: Big Lots, Safeway, Pharmacy, Univ of the Pacific
474A	**Monte Diablo**
473	**Pershing Ave**
Gas	E: ArcoAmPm
Food	E: Catfish Café
Lodg	W: Best Value Inn, Red Roof Inn
Med	E: + Dameron Hospital, + SOS Medical Clinic
Other	E: Laundromat, CalState Univ
472	**CA 4E, Fresno Ave, Downtown Stockton**
471	**CA 4E, Charter Way**
TStop	W: PacPr/Vanco Truck & Auto Plaza/76 (Scales)
Gas	E: Chevron, Shell, United
	W: ArcoAmPm◇, Valero
Food	E: Burger King, Denny's, McDonald's, Jack in the Box, Taco Bell
Lodg	E: Best Western, Days Inn
	W: Motel 6♥
TWash	W: Truck Tub Truck Wash
TServ	W: Holt Bros, International Trucks, Peterbilt, Vanco TP
Other	E: Grocery, Amtrak, Pharmacy
	W: Laundry/Vanco TP
470	**8th St, Stockton**
Gas	W: Shell
Food	W: Subway/Shell
Lodg	W: Econo Lodge
469	**Downing Ave**
468	**French Camp Turnpike**
FStop	E: PacPr/Togo's/TigerExpr/76
Food	E: FastFood/Rest/PacPr/TigerExp
Med	W: + San Joaquin Hospital
Other	W: Pan Pacific RV Center

◇ = Regular Gas Stations with Diesel   ▲ = RV Friendly Locations   ♥ = Pet Friendly Locations
RED PRINT SHOWS LARGE VEHICLE PARKING/ACCESS ON SITE OR NEARBY   BROWN PRINT SHOWS CAMPGROUNDS/RV PARKS

EXIT		CALIFORNIA	EXIT		CALIFORNIA	EXIT		CALIFORNIA
467B		Mathews Rd, French Camp	**434**		Sperry Ave, Diablo Grand Pkwy, Patterson, Modesto	**365**		Manning Ave, San Joaquin
	FStop	E: CFN/Exxon		Gas	E: 76◊, ArcoAmPm	**357**		Kamm Ave, Mendota
	Med	W: + San Joaquin Hospital		Food	E: Subway/76, Carl's Jr, Denny's, Del Lago Steakhouse, Jack in the Box, KFC, Quiznos, Starbucks, Wendy's	**349**		CA 33N, Derrick Ave
	Other	E: to Stockton Metro Airport✈, to French Camp RV Park Resort & Golf Course▲				**337**		CA 33S, CA 145N, Coalinga
				Lodg	E: Best Western♥	**334**		CA 198, Doris Ave, Coalinga, Lemoore, Hanford, Huron
467A		El Dorado St, French Camp (NB)		Other	E: Kit Fox RV Park▲, CarWash, Grocery		FStop	E: Harris Ranch Shell, CFN/WHillsOil
	Other	E: Bennett's RV Sales & Service	**(430)**		Vista Point (NB)		Gas	W: 76/Circle K, Chevron, Mobil◊
465		Roth Rd, Lathrop	**428**		Fink Rd, Crows Landing		Food	E: Rest/Subway/Harris Ranch Inn
	TServ	E: Arrow Truck Sales, Peterbilt, Kenworth, Freightliner, Repairs		Other	E: Naval Aux Landing Field✈			W: Burger King, Carls Jr, Denny's, McDonald's, Oriental Express, Red Robin, Taco Bell
	Other	E: MIL/Sharp RV Park▲	**423**		Stuhr Rd, Newman			
463		Lathrop Rd, to CA 99, Lathrop		Med	E: + Hospital		Lodg	E: Harris Ranch Inn
	FStop	E: Joe's Travel Plaza (Scales)	**(422)**		Vista Point (SB)			W: Best Western♥, Motel 6♥, Travelodge♥
	Gas	E: Chevron, Valero, Tower Mart, United Food & Fuel/Citgo	**418**		CA 140E, Gustine, Merced		Med	W: + Coalinga Reg'l Med Center
	Food	E: Subway/Joe's TP, Applebee's, Carl's Jr, Country Kitchen/Days Inn, Denny's, Isadores Rest, Jack in the Box, Little Caesars Pizza, Subway		Gas	E: 76◊, Shell		Other	E: Harris Ranch Airport✈
			(417)		Picnic Area	**325**		Jayne Ave, Huron
			(409)		Inspection Station (Both dir)		Gas	W: ArcoAmPm
			407		CA 33, Gilroy, Santa Nell Blvd Santa Nella, Gustine		Med	W: + Coalinga State Hospital
	Lodg	E: Best Western, Comfort Inn, Days Inn♥					Other	W: CA Hwy Patrol Post, State Prison, Almond Tree RV Park▲, Sommerville RV Park▲
	Other	E: ATM's, Banks, to Best RV Center		TStop	E: Travel Center of America #163/76 (Scales), Pilot Travel Center #139 (Scales)			
462		Louise Ave, Lathrop				**(320)**		Coalinga Rest Area (Both dir) (RR, Phone, Picnic, Vend, RVWater)
	Gas	E: 76, ArcoAmPm, Circle K			W: Pac Pr/Rotten Robbie #59 Truck & Auto Plaza (Scales)			
	Food	E: Carl's Jr, Jack in the Box, McDonald's, Quiznos, Taco Bell		Gas	E: ArcoAmPm, Chevron, Shell◊	**319**		CA 269, Lassen Ave
					W: Shell◊, Valero◊		FStop	E: Valero
	Lodg	E: Holiday Inn Express		Food	E: Rest/FastFood/TA TC, FastFood/Pilot TC, Anderson's Pea Soup Rest, Burger King, Carl's Jr, Del Taco, Jack in the Box/Shell	**309**		CA 41, Avenal, Kettleman City
461		CA 120E, S - Manteca, N - Sonora					FStop	E: Valero Truck Stop (Scales), CFN/W Hills
	Other	E: to Oakwood Lake Resort Camping▲, to Yosemite					Gas	E: Chevron, Exxon, Mobil◊, Texaco◊
460		Manthey Rd (SB), Mossdale Rd (NB)			W: Denny's, McDonald's, Quiznos, Starbucks, Taco Bell		Food	E: Burger King, Carl's Jr, In 'n Out Burger, Jack in the Box, McDonald's, Mike's Roadhouse Café, Quiznos, PizzaHut/Taco Bell, Subway/Exxon
	Gas	E: ArcoAmPm◊						
(458B)		Jct I-205W, to I-580 (SB)		Lodg	E: Best Western, Holiday Inn Express♥			
458A		11th St, Tracy (SB)			W: Motel 6♥, Ramada Inn		Lodg	E: Best Western, Super 8
	FStop	W: Pacific Pride		TServ	E: TA TC		TServ	E: Kettleman City Tire & Repair Service
	Other	W: to Tracy Defense Depot, The Orchard Campground▲		TWash	E: TA TC		Med	W: + Hospital
				Other	E: Laundry/WiFi/RVDump/TA TC, WiFi/Pilot TC		Other	E: Travelers RV Park▲
457		Kasson Rd, Tracy				**305**		Utica Ave
	FStop	W: CFN/Valley Pacific #151			W: Santa Nella RV Park▲, Golf Course, Los Banos Muni Airport✈	**288**		Twissleman Rd, Lost Hills
452		CA 33S, S Ahern Rd, Patterson, Vernalis	**403B**		CA 152W, Monterey, Hollister Gustine, San Jose, Gilroy	**278**		CA 46, Lost Hills, Wasco
							FStop	W: Lost Hills Travel Center/Shell
449B		CA 132W, W Vernalis Rd, to San Francisco		TStop	W: Petro 2 #46 (Scales)		TStop	W: Pilot Travel Center #154 (Scales), Love's Travel Stop #230 (Scales)
				Food	W: PetroDiner/Petro2			
	Other	W: to The Orchard Campground▲		TServ	W: Petro2 SC/Tires		Gas	E: Texaco
449A		CA 132E, W Vernalis Rd, Modesto		Other	W: Laundry/WiFi/Petro SC, to San Luis RV Resort▲			W: 76◊, Beacon, Chevron◊, Mobil◊, Shell◊
(446)		Jct I-580W, Tracy, San Francisco (NB, Left Exit)	**403A**		CA 152E, Los Banos (SB), CA 33S (NB)		Food	E: Subway/Texaco
								W: Wendy's/Pilot TC, Arby's/Love's TS, Rest/Lost Hills TC, Carl's Jr, Denny's, Jack in the Box
(445)		Westley Rest Area (Both dir) (RR, Phone, Picnic, Vend, RVWater/Dump NB)		FStop	W: (5 mi on CA 152E) Pacific Pride			
				Med	E: + Hospital			
			391		CA 165N, Mercy Springs Rd		Lodg	W: Days Inn, Motel 6♥
441		Howard Rd, Ingram Creek, Westley		Gas	W: Shell		TServ	W: Lost Hills TC
	TStop	E: Westley Triangle Travel Plaza (Scales), Joe's Travel Plaza	**(386)**		Rest Area (Both dir) (RR, Phone, Picnic, RVDump/Wtr NB)		Other	W: Laundry/WiFi/Pilot TC, Laundry/WiFi/RVDump/Love's, to Lost Hills RV Park▲
	Gas	E: 76◊, Chevron◊	**385**		Nees Ave, Firebaugh	**268**		Lerdo Hwy
		W: Shell◊, Valero◊		FStop	W: MBP Travel Plaza (Scales)	**263**		Buttonwillow, McKittrick (SB)
	Food	E: Quiznos/Joe TP, McDonald's, Carls Jr		Food	W: FastFood/MBP TP		Lodg	W: Buena Vista Motel
		W: Ingram Creek Rest	**379**		Shields Ave, Mendota	**262**		7th Standard Rd (NB)
	Lodg	E: America's Best Value Inn♥, Days Inn, Econo Lodge, Holiday Inn Express	**372**		Russell Ave	**(259)**		Buttonwillow Rest Area (Both dir) (RR, Phone, Picnic, Vend)
			368		Panoche Rd, Mendota			
	TServ	W: Westley TP/Tires, Joes TP/Tires, Cummins West		FStop	W: Shell	**257**		CA 58, to Bakersfield (SB), Buttonwillow, McKittrick (NB)
				Gas	W: 76◊, Chevron, Mobil			
	TWash	E: Westley TP, Joes TP, A-1 Quality Truck Wash, G & S Truck Wash		Food	W: Rest/BW, McDonald's/Chevron, TacoBell/Mobil, Apricot Tree Rest		FStop	E: Chevron (Scales), Mobil
	Other	E: Laundry/WiFi/Joes TP, Laundry/Westley TP		Lodg	W: Best Western			
				Other	E: Cardella Winery			

◊ = Regular Gas Stations with Diesel ▲ = RV Friendly Locations ♥ = Pet Friendly Locations
RED PRINT SHOWS LARGE VEHICLE PARKING/ACCESS ON SITE OR NEARBY BROWN PRINT SHOWS CAMPGROUNDS/RV PARKS

Page 21

EXIT		CALIFORNIA
	TStop	E: Travel Center of America #160/76 (Scales)
	Gas	E: Texaco
	Food	E: CntryPr/PHut/TBell/TA TC, Carl's Jr, Denny's, McDonald's, Starbucks, Taste of India, Subway/Mobil FS
	Lodg	E: Homeland Inn, Motel 6♥, Red Roof Inn, Super 8
	TServ	E: TA TC/Tires, Cummins West
	TWash	E: TA TC, Chevron FS
	Other	E: Laundry/Med/WiFi/RVDump/TA TC
253		Stockdale Hwy
	TStop	E: EZ Trip
	Gas	E: 76, Shell◆
	Food	E: IHOP, Jack in the Box, Rest/EZ Trip
	Lodg	E: Best Inn, Best Western, Econo Lodge
	Other	E: CA State Hwy Patrol Post
246		CA 43, Taft, Maricopa
244		CA 119, Taft Hwy, Bakersfield, Pumpkin Center, Lamont
	Gas	E: Shell
239		CA 223, Bear Mountain Blvd
234		Old River Rd
228		Copus Rd, Bakersfield
225		CA 166, Maricopa Hwy, Mettler, Maricopa (Services approx 5mi E in Mettler)
221		CA 99N, Bakersfield, Fresno (NB, Left Exit)
219B		Laval Rd West
	TStop	W: Petro Stopping Center #27/Mobil (Scales)
	Food	W: IronSkillet/PHut/Subw/Wend/BskRob/Petro SC, McDonald's, Starbucks
	Lodg	W: Best Western
	TServ	W: Petro SC/Tires
	TWash	W: Blue Beacon TW/Petro SC
	Other	W: BarbrSh/Laundry/WiFi/Petro SC
219A		Laval Rd East, Wheeler Ridge
	TStop	E: Travel Center of America #38/Chevron (Scales)
	Gas	E: BP
	Food	E: BKing/PHut/Subw/TBell/TA TC,
	TServ	E: TA TC
	Other	E: Laundry/WiFi/RVDump/TA TC,
(218)		Inspection Station (SB)
215		Grapevine Rd, Bakersfield
	FStop	W: Shell
	Gas	E: Mobil W: 76◆
	Food	E: Denny's, Jack in the Box, Ranch House W: Taco Bell/Shell
210		Fort Tejon Rd
	TServ	W: B & J Heavy Duty Towing
(209)		Brake Inspection (Both dir)
(208)		Rest Area (SB) (RR, Phone, Picnic, Vend, RVDump/Water)
207		Lebec Rd, Lebec
	Other	E: CA State Hwy Patrol Post W: US Post Office
(206)		Rest Area (NB) (RR, Phone, Picnic, Vend, RVDump/Water)

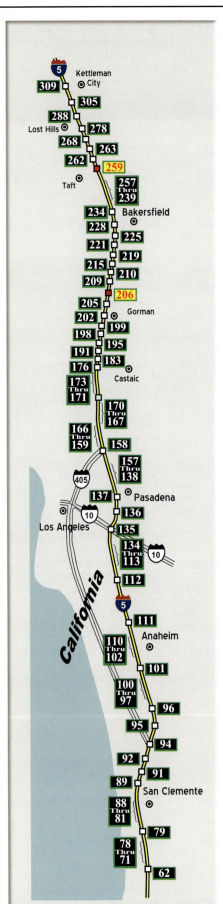

EXIT		CALIFORNIA
205		Frazier Mountain Park Rd, Lebec
	FStop	W: Frazier Park Chevron
	TStop	W: Flying J Travel Plaza #5055
	Gas	W: ArcoAmPm, Exxon, Shell, Texaco
	Food	W: Rest/FJ TP, Subway/Chevron, Jack in the Box, Okie Girl, San Remo Pizzeria & Coffee
	Lodg	W: Motel/FJ TP
	TServ	W: Bell Automotive & Diesel Repair, FJ TP
	Other	W: Laundry/BarbSh/WiFi/LP/RVDump/FJ TP, CA State Hwy Patrol Post
(204)		Truck Break Off Ramp (SB)
202		Gorman Rd, to Hungry Valley
	Gas	E: Chevron◆ W: Mobil
	Food	E: Brian's Diner, Carl's Jr, Sizzler W: McDonald's
	Lodg	E: Brian's Diner Motor Inn, Econo Lodge
199		CA 138E, Lancaster Rd, Lancaster, Palmdale (SB)
198		Quail Lake Rd, Coalinga (SB)
198B		Quail Lake Rd (NB)
198A		CA 138E (NB)
195		Smoky Bear Rd, Pyramid Lake
	Other	W: Pyramid Lake RV Park▲
191		Vista Del Lago Rd
(186)		Brake Inspection (SB)
NOTE:		SB: Begin Motorist Call Boxes
(185)		Truck Break Off Ramp (SB)
183		Templin Hwy
176		Lake Hughes Rd, Castaic (SB)
	TStop	E: NB Access via Ex #176B: Pilot Travel Center #372 (Scales), NB Access via Ex #176A: Village Truck Stop
	Gas	E: 7-11, ArcoAmPm W: 76, Mobil
	Food	E: Wendy's/Pilot TC, Burger King, Domino's Pizza, Del Taco, McDonald's W: Jack in the Box
	Lodg	E: Castaic Inn, Comfort Inn, Days Inn, Econo Lodge W: Comfort Suites
	TServ	E: Benny's Tire Service, Canyon Comm'l Tire & Towing, Castaic Truck Repair
	TWash	E: Castaic TW
	Other	E: Laundry/WiFi/Pilot TC, Grocery, RiteAid, US Post Office W: Auto Repair
176B		Lake Hughes Rd (NB)
	TStop	E: Pilot Travel Center #372 (Scales)
176A		Parker Rd, Castaic (NB)
	TStop	E: Village Truck Stop
173		Hasley Canyon Rd
172		CA 126W, Ventura
171		Rye Canyon Rd (SB)
	FStop	W: Rye Canyon Starmart/Shell
	Food	W: Del Taco, Jack in the Box
	Other	W: Fun Park
(171)		Inspection Station (NB)
170		CA 126, Magic Mountain Pkwy
	Gas	W: Chevron
	Food	E: Rest/Best Western, Denny's, Wendy's

◆ = Regular Gas Stations with Diesel ▲ = RV Friendly Locations ♥ = Pet Friendly Locations
RED PRINT SHOWS LARGE VEHICLE PARKING/ACCESS ON SITE OR NEARBY BROWN PRINT SHOWS CAMPGROUNDS/RV PARKS

EXIT		CALIFORNIA
	Food	W: El Torito Mexican, Red Lobster, Wendy's
	Lodg	E: Best Western, Holiday Inn Express W: Hilton Garden Inn
	Other	W: CA State Hwy Patrol Post, Six Flags of California
169		Valencia Blvd
168		McBean Pkwy
	Gas	E: Shell
	Food	W: Chili's, Chuck E Cheese, Claim Jumper, Starbucks, Subway, Wood Ranch BBQ
	Med	E: + Hospital
	Other	E: Staples
167		Lyons Ave, Pico Canyon Rd
	Gas	E: 76, Chevron, Exxon, Shell◇ W: ArcoAmPm, Mobil, Shell
	Food	E: Pizza, Burger King W: Chuys, CoCo's, Denny's, El Pollo Loco, IHOP, Jack in the Box, Subway, McDonald's, Yamato Japanese
	Lodg	W: Comfort Inn, Fairfield Inn, Hampton Inn, Residence Inn
	Other	W: Grocery, Wal-Mart, RV Service▲, Camping World
166		Calgrove Blvd, Stevenson Ranch
163		CA 14, Truck Route (SB)
162		CA 14N, Palmdale, Lancaster
161B		Balboa Blvd (SB), Jct I-210, Pasadena, San Fernando (NB)
(161A)		Jct I-210, Pasadena (SB), Truck Lane Off Ramp (NB)
(160A)		Jct I-210, San Francisco, Pasadena
159		Roxford St (SB)
	Gas	E: Chevron◇, Mobil◇
	Food	E: Denny's, McDonald's
	Lodg	E: Motel 6♥
159B		Roxford St West (NB)
159A		Roxford St East (NB)
(158)		Jct I-405S, San Diego Freeway (SB) Truck Lane Off Ramp (NB)
157		San Fernando Mission Blvd (SB)
157A		Brand Blvd (NB)
157B		SF Mission Blvd (NB)
	Gas	E: 76, Chevron, Mobil
	Food	E: Ameci Pizza, Carl's Jr, Popeye's
	Med	E: + Hospital, Mission Park Medical Center
	Other	E: Laundromat, Auto Zone, Kmart, RiteAid
156B		CA 118E (SB), Paxton St (NB)
156A		Paxton St (SB), CA 118 (NB)
155B		Van Nuys Blvd (NB, diff reaccess)
	Gas	E: 76, Mobil
	Food	E: KFC, McDonald's, Pizza Hut
	Other	E: Auto Zone
155A		Terra Bella St (NB)
	Gas	E: ArcoAmPm, Citgo
154		Osborne St, Arleta
	Gas	E: 76, ArcoAmPm W: 7-11, ArcoAmPm, Exxon, Mobil
	Food	W: CA Deli Mart, NY Giant Pizza

Personal Notes

EXIT		CALIFORNIA
	Other	E: Grocery, Target W: Laundry, Pharmacy, US Post Office
153B		CA 170, Hollywood Freeway (SB), Branford St (NB)
153A		Sheldon St
	Med	W: + Hospital
152		Lankershim Blvd
	FStop	W: Super Fine Truck Stop/Texaco
	Food	W: FastFood/Superfine TS
151		Penrose St
150		Sunland Blvd (SB)
150B		Sunland Blvd (NB)
	Gas	E: 7-11, 76, Mobil W: Shell
	Food	E: Acapulco Mexican, El Pollo Loco, Golden Wok Chinese W: Dimion's, Domino's, McDonald's
	Lodg	E: Scottish Inns
	Med	W: + Med-Cal Clinic
	Other	W: Laundromat
150A		Glen Oaks Blvd (NB)
	Gas	E: ArcoAmPm
149		Hollywood Way
	Gas	W: Shell◇
	Other	W: U-Haul
148		Buena Vista St
	Gas	E: Arco W: Exxon◇, World Gas
	Food	W: Jack in the Box
	Lodg	E: Bel Vista Motel W: Quality Inn, Ramada Inn

EXIT		CALIFORNIA
147C		San Fernando, Empire Ave (NB)
147B		San Fernando Blvd, Empire Ave (SB), Lincoln St (NB)
147A		Scott Rd
146B		Burbank Blvd
	Gas	E: 76 W: Chevron
	Food	E: Carl's Jr, Chuck E Cheese Pizza, Great Wall Buffet, El Pollo Loco, McDonald's, Popeye's, IHOP, Subway, Taco Bell W: Subway
	Lodg	E: Holiday Inn
	AServ	E: 76
	TServ	W: Fitzpatrick Trailer
	Other	E: Office Depot, Kmart, Grocery, Pharmacy
146A		Verdugo Ave (SB), Olive Ave (NB) Downtown Burbank
	Food	E: Black Angus Steakhouse, Fuddrucker's
	Lodg	E: Holiday Inn
	Med	E: + Hospital
145B		Alameda Ave
	Gas	E: Chevron W: Mobil, Shell
	Food	W: Sandwich Shop
	Lodg	W: Burbank Inn
145A		Western Ave
	Other	W: Gene Autry Museum
144		CA 134, Ventura Freeway (SB)
144B		CA 134W, Ventura Fwy (NB)
144A		CA 134E, Ventura Fwy (NB)
142		Colorado St, Glendale
141		Los Feliz Blvd, Griffith Park Dr (SB)
141B		Griffith Park Dr (NB)
141A		Los Feliz Blvd (NB)
	Gas	E: 76, Arco, Shell
	Food	E: Del Taco, Kathy's Kitchen
	Lodg	E: Los Feliz Motel
	Med	E: + Hospital
	Other	W: Griffith Park, Zoo
140B		Glendale Blvd (SB)
140A		Fletcher Dr (SB)
140		Glendale Blvd (NB)
	Gas	E: 76, Shell W: ArcoAmPm, Chevron
	Food	E: McDonald's W: KFC
139		CA 2, Glendale Freeway (SB)
139B		CA 2W, Echo Park (NB)
139A		CA 2, Glendale Freeway E (NB)
138		Stadium Way Connections
	Other	E: Home Depot W: Dodger Stadium
137B		CA-110, Pasadena Freeway S (SB) CA-110, Pasadena Frwy N (NB)
137A		CA-110, Pasadena Frwy N (SB), Figueroa St (NB)
136		Main St (SB)
136B		Broadway (NB)

◇ = Regular Gas Stations with Diesel ▲ = RV Friendly Locations ♥ = Pet Friendly Locations
RED PRINT SHOWS LARGE VEHICLE PARKING/ACCESS ON SITE OR NEARBY   BROWN PRINT SHOWS CAMPGROUNDS/RV PARKS

Page 23

EXIT	CALIFORNIA
136A	**Main St (NB)**
Gas	E: 76, Chevron
Food	E: McDonald's, Mr Pizza
135C	**Mission Rd (SB), Jct I-10E, San Bernardino Fwy (NB, end run w/I-10)**
Gas	E: 76, Chevron
Food	E: McDonald's, Jack in the Box
Lodg	E: Howard Johnson
Med	E: + Hospital
(135B)	**Jct I-10E, San Bernardino Freeway, (SB), Caesar Chavez Ave (NB)**
Med	W: + Hospital
135A	**4th St (SB, Begin run with I-10WB)**
134E	**CA 60E, Pomona, Golden State Freeway (SB)**
134D	**CA 60E, Soto St (SB)**
134C	**Soto St (SB), 7th St (NB Left Exit)**
134B	**CA 60E (SB, End with I-10WB) Soto St (NB, Begin run with I-10WB)**
134A	**Soto St (SB), CA 60W, Santa Monica Freeway (NB)**
133	**Euclid Ave (SB), Grand Vista Ave (NB), Los Angeles**
FStop	E: Speedy Fuel
Gas	E: ArcoAmPm
	W: Mobil, Shell
Med	W: + Hospital
132	**Indiana St (SB), Calzona St**
Gas	E: ArcoAmPm
131B	**Ditman Ave (SB)**
131A	**Olympic Blvd (SB)**
131	**Indiana St (NB)**
(130C)	**Jct I-710N, Pasadena (NB, Left Exit)**
(130B)	**Jct I-710, Long Beach Freeway (SB), Eastern Ave (NB)**
130A	**Triggs St (SB), Atlantic Blvd S (NB)**
Gas	W: 76
Food	W: Denny's
129	**Atlantic Blvd (NB), Eastern Ave**
Gas	W: Chevron
Food	W: Denny's, Steven's Steakhouse
Other	E: Outlet Mall
128B	**Washington Blvd, Commerce**
FStop	E: Unified Gas
	E: Commerce Truck Stop (Scales)
Gas	E: Chevron
Food	E: Gibbs Coffee Shop, McDonald's
Lodg	E: Commerce Hotel, Radisson
Aserv	E: Chevron
TServ	E: Westrux Int'l
	W: CA Transport Refrigeration
Other	E: Mall, Commerce Casino, Firestone, Office Depot
128A	**Garfield Ave (NB), Bandini Blvd**
Other	E: Home Depot, Office Depot
	W: Staples
126B	**Slauson Ave, Montebello**
FStop	E: AMF Chevron (Scales)
Gas	E: Mobil, Shell◊
	W: ArcoAmPm
Food	E: Burger King
	W: Denny's
Lodg	E: Best Western, Howard Johnson, Super 8

EXIT	CALIFORNIA
Lodg	W: Best Value Inn, Ramada Inn
TServ	E: ENGS Motor Truck
	W: Cummins Cal Pacific
Twash	E: AMF Chevron FS
126A	**Paramount Blvd, Downey**
Gas	E: Circle K, Shell
Food	E: Pizza, China Kitchen
Lodg	E: Super 8
125	**Lakewood Blvd, Rosemead Blvd CA 19, Downey**
Gas	E: ArcoAmPm, Mobil
	W: 76
Food	E: Taco Bell
	W: Jack in the Box, Little Caesar's Pizza, McDonald's, Golden Wok, Chris & Pitts BBQ, Subway
Lodg	E: Econo Lodge, GuestHouse Inn
Med	E: + Hospital
(124)	**Jct I-605, San Gabriel River Frwy**
123	**Florence Ave**
122	**Imperial Hwy, Pioneer Blvd**
Gas	E: Chevron
	W: Shell
Food	E: IHOP, Red Lobster, Subway, Wendy's
	W: Denny's, Pizza Hut, Sizzler
Lodg	E: Best Western
	W: Comfort Inn
Other	E: Grocery, Target
	W: Wal-Mart
121	**Norwalk Blvd, San Antonio Dr**
Gas	E: Chevron, Shell
	W: 76
Food	E: Jack in the Box, KFC, McDonald's
Lodg	E: Sheraton
	W: Marriott
120	**Rosecrans Ave, La Mirada (SB)**
120B	**Firestone Blvd, CA 42 (NB Left Exit)**
120A	**Rosecrans Ave, La Mirada (NB)**
Gas	E: 76, ArcoAmPm, Mobil◊, Shell◊
	W: ArcoAmPm
Food	E: Burger King, KFC, Pizza Hut/TBell
	W: El Pollo Loco
Other	W: El Monte RV Center
119	**Carmenita Rd, Buena Park**
Gas	E: 76, ArcoAmPm
	W: ArcoAmPm, Mobil
Food	E: Burger King, Carrow's, Jack in the Box
	W: Carl's Jr, China Express
Lodg	E: Motel 6♥
	W: Best Western, Super 8
TServ	E: Carmenita Truck Service
	W: Ryan's Truck Collision Repair Center
Other	E: Lowe's
118	**Valley View Blvd, La Mirada**
Gas	E: ArcoAmPm
	W: Chevron, Shell◊
Food	E: Carl's Jr, Red Robin
	W: Denny's, El Pollo Loco, Taco Tio
Lodg	E: Holiday Inn, Residence Inn
	W: Residence Inn
Other	E: Staples
	W: Thompson's RV Center, Camping World
117	**Artesia Blvd (NB), Knott Ave**
Gas	E: 76, Shell
116	**CA 39 (SB), Beach Blvd (NB)**
Gas	E: ArcoAmPm, Chevron
	W: Chevron, Mobil
Food	E: McDonald's

EXIT	CALIFORNIA
Food	W: Arby's, Black Angus Steakhouse, Denny's, KFC, Pizza Hut, Subway
Lodg	W: Hampton Inn, Red Roof Inn♥
Med	E: + Hospital
Other	E: Auto Dealers
	W: Laundromat, to Knotts Berry Farm
115	**Manchester Blvd, Auto Ctr Dr (NB)**
114B	**CA 91E, Riverside Hwy, to Airport (SB)**
114A	**Magnolia (SB)**
114	**Magnolia Ave, CA 91E (NB)**
Gas	E: Mobil
	W: 76
Food	E: Taco Bell
	W: Del Taco
Other	E: Laundromat, Harley Davidson
113	**Brookhurst St, La Palma Ave (SB)**
113C	**CA 91W (NB)**
113B	**La Palma Ave East (NB)**
113A	**Brookhurst St, La Palma Ave (NB)**
Gas	E: Chevron
	W: ArcoAmPm, Shell
Food	E: Donut Shop, Subway
	W: Mexican
Other	W: Staples
112	**Euclid St, Anaheim**
Gas	E: 7-11, Mobil
	W: 76, ArcoAmPm
Food	E: Chris & Pitts BBQ, McDonald's, Subway
	W: Arby's, Burger King, Denny's
Other	E: Wal-Mart
	W: Laundromat
111	**Lincoln Ave, Downtown Anaheim**
FStop	E: (E to Manchester) Buena Park Mart/Shell
Gas	E: 76
Food	E: FastFood/Shell
110B	**Disneyland Dr, Ball Rd (SB)**
110A	**Harbor Blvd (SB)**
110	**Harbor Blvd, Ball Rd (NB)**
Gas	E: 7-11, Chevron, Shell
	W: ArcoAmPm, Shell
Food	E: Burger King, El Pollo Loco, KFC, McDonald's, Subway, Taco Bell
	W: IHOP, McDonald's, Spaghetti Station
Lodg	E: Days Inn, Econo Lodge, Holiday Inn
	W: Best Western, Fairfield Inn, Holiday Inn, Ramada Inn, Sheraton, Super 8
Other	W: Convention Center, Camping World, to DisneyLand
109B	**Disney Way, Anaheim Blvd (SB)**
109A	**Katella Ave, Orangewood Ave (SB)**
109	**Katella Ave, Disney Way (NB), Disneyland Resort**
Gas	E: 76, ArcoAmPm
	W: 7-11
Food	E: Denny's, El Torito, McDonald's
	W: Café, CoCo's, Country Kitchen, Del Taco, Tony Roma
Lodg	E: Ramada Inn, Travelodge
	W: Best Western, Comfort Inn, Hampton Inn, Hilton, Howard Johnson, Marriott, Radisson, Red Roof Inn♥, Super 8
AServ	E: 76

Page 24   ◊ = Regular Gas Stations with Diesel   ▲ = RV Friendly Locations   ♥ = Pet Friendly Locations
RED PRINT SHOWS LARGE VEHICLE PARKING/ACCESS ON SITE OR NEARBY   BROWN PRINT SHOWS CAMPGROUNDS/RV PARKS

EXIT		CALIFORNIA
107C		State College Blvd, The City Drive
	Lodg	E: Hilton Suites, Motel 6 ♥
		W: Doubletree Hotel
	Med	W: + Hospital
107B		CA 22W, Bristol St, LaVeta Ave, Long Beach (SB), Chapman Ave (NB)
	Food	E: Burger King, Del Taco
		W: El Torito, Krispy Kreme
107A		CA 22E, Orange, La Veta Ave, Bristol St (SB), CA 57N, Pomona (NB)
106		CA 22W, Long Beach (NB)
105B		Main St, Broadway
	Gas	E: 76
	Food	E: Carl's Jr, Polly's Café, Starbucks
	Lodg	E: Red Roof Inn ♥
	Other	E: Mall, Pharmacy
105A		17th St, Santa Ana College
	Gas	E: 76◊
		W: Chevron
	Food	E: IHOP, McDonald's
		W: Ruby Tuesday
104B		Santa Ana Blvd, Grand Ave, Downtown (SB)
104A		1st St, 4th St (SB)
104		Grand Ave, Santa Ana Blvd (NB)
103		CA 55S, Newport Beach (SB)
103C		1st St, 4th St (NB)
	Gas	W: Chevron, Gas Right, Shell
	Food	W: Del Taco, Pizza
	Other	W: Laundromat, Santa Anna Zoo
103B		CA 55S, Newport Beach (NB)
103A		CA 55N, Riverside (NB)
102		Newport Ave (SB)
101B		Red Hill Ave, Tustin
	Gas	E: 76, ArcoAmPm, Mobil◊, Shell
		W: 76, Chevron
	Food	E: BBQ Buffet, Del Taco, Denny's, Wendy's
		W: Taco Bell
	Lodg	E: Key Inn
	AServ	E: Arco, Shell
	Other	E: Laundromat, Grocery, Pharmacy
101A		Tustin Ranch Rd
	Other	E: Auto Dealers, Costco, Kmart
100		Jamboree Rd
	Gas	E: 76, Shell
	Food	E: Black Angus Steakhouse, Burger King, El Pollo Loco, Red Robin, On the Border, Taco Bell
	Other	E: Costco, Lowe's, Target
99		Culver Dr
	Gas	E: Shell
	Food	E: Starbucks
		W: Denny's, Sizzler, Wendy's
	Other	E: Best Buy
		W: Police, Pharmacy
97		Jeffrey Rd
	Gas	W: 76
	Food	W: China Express
	Other	W: Albertson's, Grocery, Laundromat, Irvine Valley College
96B		CA 133N, Santa Margarita (SB)
96A		Sand Canyon Ave (SB)

Personal Notes
_____

EXIT		CALIFORNIA
96		Sand Canyon Ave (NB)
	Gas	W: 76
	Food	W: Burrell's BBQ, Denny's, Steakhouse
	Lodg	W: La Quinta Inn ♥
	TServ	W: CAT Truck Service
	Other	W: Traveland USA RV Park▲, Irvine RV Center
95		CA 133S, Laguna Beach (SB), CA 133N, Riverside (NB)
94		Alton Pkwy (SB)
94B		Alton Pkwy (NB)
	Gas	E: Shell
	Food	E: Carl's Jr, Taco Bell
	Lodg	W: Doubletree Hotel
	Other	E: Costco
(94A)		Jct I-405N, Santa Ana Fwy (NB)
92		Bake Pkwy, I-5 Truck Bypass, Lake Forest Dr (SB)
92B		Bake Pkwy (NB), I-5 Truck Bypass
92A		Lake Forest Dr (NB)
	Gas	E: Chevron, Shell◊
		W: Chevron, Shell
	Food	E: Black Angus, Burger King, Chinese, IHOP, Mimi's Cafe, Subway, Taco Bell
		W: Carl's Jr, Coco's, Del Taco, McDonald's
	Lodg	E: Best Western, Travelodge
		W: Comfort Inn, Courtyard, Quality Suites, Travelodge
	Other	E: Staples
91		El Toro Rd, Laguna Hills, Lk Forest
	Gas	E: ArcoAmPm, Chevron, Mobil, Shell◊, USA

EXIT		CALIFORNIA
	Gas	W: Chevron◊, Shell◊
	Food	E: Arby's, Jack in the Box, McDonald's
		W: Carrow's, Coco's, CA Pizza, Monterey Seafood
	Med	W: + Hospital
	Other	E: Office Depot, Grocery, Pharmacy
		W: Circuit City, Firestone, Mall, Walgreen's, Trader Joe's
90		Alicia Pkwy, Mission Viejo
	Gas	W: 76◊, Chevron
	Food	E: Denny's, Del Taco, Subway
		W: Togo's, Wendy's
	Other	E: Albertson's, Firestone, Target
89		La Paz Rd, Mission Viejo
	Gas	E: ArcoAmPm, Mobil
		W: 76, Chevron
	Food	E: Deli, KFC, Pizza Hut, Taco Bell
		W: Claim Jumper, Jack in the Box, Italian Rest, McDonald's, Outback Steakhouse
	Lodg	W: Holiday Inn
	Other	W: Best Buy, Goodyear
88		Oso Pkwy, Pacific Park Dr
	Gas	E: 76, Chevron
	Food	E: Carl's Jr
	Lodg	E: Fairfield Inn
86		Crown Valley Pkwy
	Gas	E: 76, ArcoAmPm, Chevron
		W: Chevron◊
	Food	E: Coco's, TJ's
	Med	E: + Hospital
	Other	E: Mall
85		Avery Pkwy (SB)
85B		Avery Pkwy (NB)
	Gas	E: Shell◊
		W: Shell◊, ArcoAmPm
	Food	E: Alberto's Mexican, Billy's Pizza, Del Taco, Carrow's, Jack in the Box, Sheesh Kabob, McDonald's
		W: Buffy's, In 'n Out Burger
	Lodg	W: Travelodge
	Other	E: Goodyear, Staples
		W: Firestone, Costco
85A		CA 73N (TOLL), Long Beach (NB)
83		Junipero Serra Rd
	Gas	W: Shell
82		CA 74, Ortega Hwy E, San Juan Capistrano
	Gas	E: 76, Chevron◊, Shell
		W: ArcoAmPm, Chevron
	Food	E: Denny's
		W: Del Taco, Jack in the Box, McDonald's
	Lodg	E: Best Western
		W: Mission Inn
81		San Juan Creek Rd, Valle Rd, Camino Capistrano
	Gas	W: Chevron
	Food	W: KFC, Starbucks
	Other	W: Goodyear, Grocery, Harley Davidson, RiteAid
79		CA 1, Pacific Coast Hwy, Camino Las Ramblas, Beach Cities
	Gas	W: ArcoAmPm, Shell
	Food	W: Carl's Jr, Del Taco, Denny's, McDonald's
	Lodg	W: Hilton, Ramada Inn
	Other	W: US Post Office
78		Camino Estrella (SB), Camino de Estrella (NB), San Clemente
	Gas	E: 76◊, Mobil
		W: ArcoAmPm

◊ = Regular Gas Stations with Diesel   ▲ = RV Friendly Locations   ♥ = Pet Friendly Locations
RED PRINT SHOWS LARGE VEHICLE PARKING/ACCESS ON SITE OR NEARBY   BROWN PRINT SHOWS CAMPGROUNDS/RV PARKS

Interstate 5 N/S

EXIT	CALIFORNIA
Food	E: Carl's Jr, China Well, Subway
	W: Little Caesar's Pizza, Taco Bell
Lodg	E: Budget Lodge, San Clemente Motel
Med	E: + Hospital
Other	E: Laundry, Grocery, Pharmacy
	W: Grocery, Kmart
77	**Avenida Vista Hermosa**
Gas	E: Mobil
	W: Chevron, Texaco
Food	E: Carrow's, McDonald's
	W: Burger Stop, Del Taco, Denny's
Other	W: Grocery, Pharmacy, US Post Office
76	**Avenida Pico**
Gas	E: Mobil
	W: Chevron, Exxon, Shell
Food	E: Carrow's, McDonald's
	W: Denny's, Pizza Hut, Subway
Other	E: Albertson's
	W: Staples, Pharmacy, US Post Office
75	**Avenida Palizada (SB), Avenida Presedio, San Clemente (NB)**
Gas	W: 7-11, ArcoAmPm, Valero
Food	W: KFC, Starbucks, Subway
Lodg	W: Holiday Inn
Other	W: Albertson's
74	**El Camino Real**
Gas	E: Chevron
	W: 7-11, 76, Mobil
Food	E: Burrito Basket, Wild Flower Café, San Clemente Café
	W: KFC, Little Caesar's Pizza, Taco Bell, Tommy's
Lodg	E: Budget Lodge♥, San Clemente Motel
	W: Motel del Mar
Other	E: Laundromat
	W: Grocery
73	**Ave Calafia (SB), Avenida Magdelena (NB)**
Gas	E: 7-11, 76, Shell
Food	E: Bob's Big Boy, Coco's, Jack in the Box, Pedro's Tacos, Beef Cutter
Lodg	E: Quality Suites, Travelodge
	W: San Clemente Inn
72	**Cristianitos Rd**
Food	E: Carl's Jr
Lodg	E: Comfort Suites, Quality Hotel
Other	E: San Mateo RV Park▲
71	**Basilone Rd, San Onofre**
Other	E: Mil/San Onofre Rec Beach RV
	W: San Clemente State Park
(69)	**Border Patrol Check Point**
(67)	**Inspection Station (Both dir)**
(63)	**Vista Point (SB)**
62	**Las Pulgas Rd**
(60)	**Rest Area (SB)**
	(RR, Phone, Picnic, Vend, RVDump)
(59)	**Rest Area (NB)**
	(RR, Phone, Picnic, Vend, RVDump)
54C	**Oceanside Harbor Dr, Camp Pendleton**
Gas	W: Chevron, Mobil
Food	W: Burger King, Del Taco, Denny's
Lodg	W: Comfort Inn, Sandman Motel, Travelodge
54B	**Coast Hwy, Oceanside (SB), Camp Pendleton (NB)**
Gas	E: Arco, Shell, Texaco
	W: Mobil

EXIT	CALIFORNIA
Food	E: Angelo's, Hamburger Heaven
	W: Carrow's, Flying Bridge
Lodg	W: Comfort Inn
54A	**CA 76E (SB), Coast Hwy (NB)**
53	**Mission Ave, Downtown Oceanside**
Gas	E: 76, ArcoAmPm, Mobil◊
Food	E: Burger King, Jack in the Box, Taco Shop, Jimmy's, McDonald's, Mission Donut House
	W: Carrow's, El Pollo Loco, Long John Silver's, Wendy's
Lodg	E: Comfort Inn, Econo Lodge, Motel 6♥, Ramada Ltd
Other	W: Auto Zone, Grocery, Office Depot, RiteAid
52	**Oceanside Blvd**
Gas	E: ArcoAmPm
	W: 76, Shell
Food	E: Bakers Square, IHOP, McDonald's, Pizza Hut, Subway, Taco Bell
Lodg	W: Best Western
Other	E: Laundromat, Pharmacy, Grocery
51C	**Cassidy St (SB), Oceanside, Vista Way (NB)**
Gas	W: 7-11, Mobil
51B	**CA 78E, Vista Way, Escondido**
Gas	E: 76, Chevron
Food	E: Applebee's, McDonald's, Mimi's Café, Olive Garden, Starbucks
Other	E: Best Buy, Staples, Target, Wal-Mart
51A	**Las Flores Dr**
50	**Carlsbad Village Dr, Elm Ave (SB), Downtown Carlsbad (NB)**
Gas	E: Shell
	W: 76, ArcoAmPm, Chevron
Food	E: Shari's
	W: Carl's Jr, Denny's, Jack in the Box, Mikko Japanese
Lodg	W: Motel 6♥
Other	E: Laundromat
	W: Albertson's, Pharmacy
49	**Tamarack Ave**
Gas	E: Chevron, Exxon◊
	W: 76
Food	E: Village Kitchen
	W: Koko Palms
Lodg	E: Carlsbad Lodge, Super 8
Other	E: Laundromat, Grocery, Pharmacy
48	**Cannon Rd, Legoland**
Other	E: Auto Dealers
47	**Palomar Airport Rd, Carlsbad Blvd**
FStop	W: Palomar Shell
Gas	E: 7-11, Chevron, Mobil◊
	W: Shell◊
Food	E: Carl's Jr, Denny's, TGI Friday, Taco Bell Subway, Anderson's Dutch Cooking
	W: Claim Jumper, McDonald's
Lodg	E: Best Western, Holiday Inn, Motel 6♥
Other	E: LP/Shell, Costco
45	**Poinsettia Lane, Aviara Pkwy**
Food	W: Chinese Cuisine, El Pollo Loco, Jack in the Box, Panda Buffet, Subway
Lodg	W: Inns of America, Motel 6♥, Ramada
Other	W: RiteAid
44	**La Costa Ave**
Gas	W: Chevron◊
43	**Leucadia Blvd**
Gas	W: Shell, Texaco
Lodg	E: Holiday Inn Express

EXIT	CALIFORNIA
41B	**Encinitas Blvd**
Gas	E: Chevron, Exxon, Mobil
	W: Shell
Food	E: Coco's, Del Taco, Hungry Hunter
	W: Rest/Best Western, Denny's, Wendy's
Lodg	W: Best Western, Days, Inn, Radisson
Med	W: + Hospital
Other	E: Grocery, Pharmacy, Quail Botanical Gardens
	W: Laundromat
41A	**Santa Fe Dr, to Encinitas (NB)**
Gas	E: 7-11, Shell
	W: 76
Food	E: Carl's Jr, Pizza, Hideaway Café, Encinitas Donuts
	W: Burger King/76, California Yogurt, NY Pizza
Med	W: + Hospital
Other	E: Laundromat, RiteAid
40	**Birmingham Dr**
Gas	E: Chevron, Mobil, Shell
	W: ArcoAmPm
Food	E: Glenn's, Taco Bell
Lodg	E: Countryside Inn
(39B)	**Vista Point (SB)**
39A	**Manchester Ave (SB)**
39	**Manchester Ave**
Gas	E: 76
Food	E: Kava Coffee Shop
Other	E: Miira Costa College
37	**Lomas Santa Fe Dr, Solana Beach**
Gas	W: Mobil, Shell◊
Food	E: Jolly Roger, Round Table Pizza
	W: Carl's Jr, Chinese, Starbucks
Other	W: Staples
36	**Via De La Valle, Del Mar**
Gas	E: 76, Chevron, Mobil
	W: ArcoAmPm, Shell◊
Food	E: Burger King, Chevy's, McDonald's, Milton's
	W: Denny's, The Fish Market
Lodg	W: Hilton
Other	E: Albertson's, Pharmacy
	W: Racetrack
34	**Del Mar Heights Rd**
Gas	E: Shell◊
	W: 7-11
Food	W: Jack in the Box
Other	W: Grocery, Pharmacy
33	**Carmel Valley Rd, CA 56E (SB)**
33B	**Carmel Valley Rd (NB)**
Gas	E: ArcoAmPm, Chevron, Shell
Food	E: Bakers Square, Taco Bell
Lodg	E: Doubletree Hotel, Hampton Inn
33A	**CA 56E (NB)**
32	**Carmel Mountain Rd**
(31)	**Jct I-805S, National City, Chula Vista (SB, Left Exit)**
30	**Sorrento Valley Rd (NB)**
29	**Genesee Ave**
Med	E: + Scripps Memorial Hospital
28	**La Jolla Village Dr (SB)**
28B	**La Jolla Village Dr (NB)**
Gas	W: Mobil◊
Food	E: Café, Grill, Italian

◊ = Regular Gas Stations with Diesel   ▲ = RV Friendly Locations   ♥ = Pet Friendly Locations
RED PRINT SHOWS LARGE VEHICLE PARKING/ACCESS ON SITE OR NEARBY   BROWN PRINT SHOWS CAMPGROUNDS/RV PARKS

N I-5 — CALIFORNIA

EXIT		CALIFORNIA
	Food	W: BJ's Grill, CA Pizza, El Torito, Pasta Bravo, Radisson
	Lodg	E: Embassy Suites, Hyatt
		W: Radisson
	Med	W: + VA Hospital
	Other	W: Grocery, Trader Joe's, Pharmacy
28A		Nobel Dr (NB)
27		Gilman Dr, La Jolla Colony Dr
26		CA 52E, Santee (SB)
26B		CA 52E (NB)
26A		W La Jolla Pkwy (NB) (Former Ardath Rd)
23		Balboa Ave, Garnet Ave (SB)
23B		Balboa Ave E (NB)
	Gas	E: Shell
		W: 76, 7-11, Mobil
	Food	E: Del Taco
		W: Arby's, In 'n Out Burger
	Lodg	W: Comfort Inn, Super 8
	Med	W: + Hospital
23A		Grand Ave, Garnet Ave (NB)
22		Clairemont Dr, Mission Bay Dr
	Gas	E: 76, Shell
	Food	E: Jack in the Box, McDonald's, Subway
	Lodg	E: Best Western, Days Inn
21		Sea World Dr, Tecolote Rd
	Gas	E: ArcoAmPm, Shell
	Lodg	W: Hilton Resort
	Other	W: CA Hwy Patrol Post
(20)		Jct I-8, E - El Centro, W - Beaches, CA 209S, Rosecrans St, Beaches
19		Old Town Ave
	Gas	E: ArcoAmPm, Shell
	Food	E: Old Town Deli
	Lodg	E: Courtyard, La Quinta Inn ♥, Ramada Inn, Travelodge
18B		Washington St
	Lodg	E: Comfort Inn
18A		Kettner St, S Diego Airport, Vine UC, Sassafras St (SB), Pacific Hwy Viaduct (NB)
17		Front St, Civic Center (SB)
17B		India St, Sassafras St (NB)
	Gas	E: 76, Mobil
		W: Exxon
	Lodg	W: Holiday Inn Express, Super 8
17A		Hawthorne St, SD Airport (NB)
	Gas	W: Exxon
	Lodg	W: Holiday Inn Express, Super 8
	Med	W: + Hospital
16		CA 163N, Escondido, 10th Ave (SB)
16B		6th Ave, Downtown San Diego (NB)
16A		CA 163N, Escondido (NB)
	Gas	W: Shell
	Lodg	W: Holiday Inn, Super 8
	Med	W: + Hospital
	Other	E: Aerospace Museum
15C		Pershing Dr, B St (SB)
15B		CA 94E, ML King Jr Fwy (SB), Civic Center, Pershing Dr (NB)
15A		Imperial Ave (SB), CA 94E, J St (NB)

EXIT		CALIFORNIA
14B		Cesar E Chavez Pkwy (Formerly Crosby St)
14A		CA 75S, (TOLL), Coronado
13B		National Ave, 28th St
	Gas	W: Shell
	Food	W: Alberto's Mexican, Burger King, El Pollo Loco, Long John Silver's, McDonald's
13A		CA 15N, Riverside, Wabash Blvd
12		Main St, National City Blvd (SB), Division St (NB)
	Gas	E: Mobil, Shell
	Food	E: Keith's
	Lodg	E: Suncoast Inn
11B		8th St, National City (SB), Plaza Blvd, Downtown (NB)
	Gas	E: ArcoAmPm, Shell
		W: Chevron ◊
	Lodg	E: Holiday Inn, Howard Johnson, Radisson, Ramada Inn, Super 8
11A		Civic Center Dr (SB), Harbor Dr
10		Bay Marina Dr, Mile of Cars (Formerly 24th St)
	TStop	W: So Cal Truck Stop
	Food	W: In 'n Out Burger
	Other	W: LP/SC TS
9		CA 54E, Lemon Grove
8B		E St, Chula Vista
	Gas	E: 76, Arco, Mobil, Shell
	Food	E: Aunt Emma's, Black Angus Steak House, Mary Kaye's, McDonald's, Pizza, Taco Bell, Wendy's
		W: Anthony's Fish Grotto

EXIT		CALIFORNIA
	Lodg	E: Best Western, Motel 6 ♥
		W: Days Inn, Good Nite Inn
	Other	E: Grocery, Laundromat
8A		H St
	Gas	E: 7-11, Arco, Chevron
	Food	E: Alberto's Mexican, El Pollo Loco
	Lodg	E: Early CA Motel
	Med	E: + Hospital
	Other	E: Goodyear
7B		J St, Marina Pkwy, to Chula Vista Harbor
7A		L St
	Gas	E: 7-11, 76, Shell ◊
	Food	E: Golden Pagoda
	Lodg	E: Best Western
	Other	E: AutoZone, Grocery, Office Depot
6		Palomar St
	Gas	E: ArcoAmPm
	Food	E: Del Taco, Home Town Buffet, KFC, McDonald's, Subway
	Lodg	E: Palomar Inn
	Other	E: Costco, Target, Grocery
5B		Main St, Imperial Beach
	Gas	E: ArcoAmPm
5A		CA 75, Palm Ave, Imperial Beach
	Gas	E: ArcoAmPm
		W: ArcoAmPm, Mobil, Shell
	Food	W: Burger King, Carl's Jr, Carrow's, \ Chinese, El Pollo Loco, McDonald's, Roberto's
	Lodg	W: Super 8
	Other	W: Grocery, Pharmacy, Auto Zone, Home Depot, Shops
4		Coronado Ave
	Gas	E: 7-11, Chevron, Shell
		W: ArcoAmPm, Shell, Texaco
	Food	E: Bakery, Denny's, Dos Panchos
	Lodg	E: Travelers Motel, Eazy 8 Motel
		W: Days Inn
3		CA 905, Tocayo Ave
2		Dairy Mart Rd, San Ysidro Blvd
	Gas	E: ArcoAmPm, Circle K
	Food	E: Burger King, Carl's Jr, CoCo's, Maty's Seafood, McDonald's
	Lodg	E: Americana Inn, Motel 6 ♥, Super 8
	Other	E: Pacifica RV Resort ▲ , CarQuest
1B		Via de San Ysidro
	Gas	E: 76, Exxon, Mobil
		W: Chevron
	Food	E: Santa Fe Chinese
		W: Denny's, KFC, Outback Steakhouse
	Lodg	W: Economy Inn, Motel 6 ♥, Motel 8 & RV Park ▲, Old Mill Hotel
	Other	W: International Inn & RV Park ▲
(1A)		Jct I-805N, San Ysidro Blvd (NB), Camino de la Plaza (SB)
	Food	E: Burger King, El Pollo Loco, KFC, IHOP, Jack in the Box, McDonald's, Subway
	Lodg	E: Flamingo Motel, Holiday Lodge, Travelodge
	Other	E: Greyhound, Customs Station
		W: Tourist Info, Kmart, Factory Outlets
(0)		US/Mexico Border, CA State Line, Mexican Customs

CALIFORNIA   Pacific Time Zone
MEXICO

Above lists Northbound I-5 from US / Mexico border to US / Canada border.

◊ = Regular Gas Stations with Diesel   ▲ = RV Friendly Locations   ♥ = Pet Friendly Locations

RED PRINT SHOWS LARGE VEHICLE PARKING/ACCESS ON SITE OR NEARBY   BROWN PRINT SHOWS CAMPGROUNDS/RV PARKS

 E

EXIT	CALIFORNIA
	Begin Eastbound I-8 from Jct I-5 in San Diego, CA to Jct I-10 in AZ.

CALIFORNIA
(PACIFIC TIME ZONE)
(I-8 begins/ends Jct I-10, Ex #199 AZ)

(0)	Sunset Cliffs Blvd, Nimitz Blvd, San Diego
Gas	N: Shell
Food	N: Deli, Jack in the Box
1	W Mission Bay Blvd, (WB) Sports Arena Blvd
Gas	S: 76, ArcoAmPm, Shell, Shell
Food	S: Arby's, Coco's, Denny's, Jack in the Box, Kobe, McDonald's, Red Lobster
Lodg	S: EZ 8 Motel, Holiday Inn Express, Holiday Inn, Marriott, Ramada Ltd
Other	N: to Sea World
	S: Home Depot, Ralph's, Von's
(2)	Jct I-5S, Downtown (EB)
(2A)	Jct I-5N, Los Angeles (WB)
Gas	S: Chevron
Food	S: Burger King, Denny's, Jack in the Box, McDonald's, Perry's Cafe
Lodg	S: Best Western, Days Inn, Holiday Inn, Howard Johnson, Quality Inn, Super 8
Other	S: Grocery, Goodyear, Staples, Pharmacy
(2B)	Jct I-5, N - LA, S - San Diego (EB) Rosecrans St (WB)
2C	Morena Blvd (WB)
3	Taylor St, Hotel Circle
Gas	N: Chevron
	S: Chevron
Food	N: DW Ranch, Hunter Steaks
	S: Rest/Kings Inn, Albie's, Valley Kitchen
Lodg	N: Best Western, Comfort Inn, Motel 6♥, Premier Inn, Red Lion Hotel, Town & Country Suites
	S: Best Western, Comfort Inn, Doubletree Hotel, Econo Lodge, Extended Stay America, Hawthorne Suites, Holiday Inn Express, Howard Johnson, Kings Inn, Ramada Plaza, Residence Inn, Travelodge
Other	N: Cinema, Golf Course
4A	Hotel Circle Dr (EB), CA 163S, Downtown (WB)
Lodg	S: Best Western, Days Inn, Extended Stay America, Hotel Circle Inn, Quality Inn, Ramada Plaza, Super 8, Vagabond Inn
4B	CA 163S, Downtown (EB) CA 163N, Hotel Circle (WB)

EXIT	CALIFORNIA
4C	CA 163N, Escondido (EB)
5	Mission Center Rd
Gas	N: Chevron, Mobil, Shell
	S: ArcoAmPm
Food	N: Applebee's, Hooters, Outback Steakhouse, Quiznos, Taco Bell
	S: Benihana, Denny's, TGI Friday, Wendy's
Lodg	N: Marriott
	S: Comfort Inn, Fairfield Inn, Hilton, Radisson, Sheraton
Other	N: Mall, Best Buy, Staples
	S: Auto Dealers
6A	Texas St, Qualcomm Way
Gas	N: Chevron
	S: Valero
(6B)	Jct I-805, N - LA, S - Chula Vista
7	CA 15S, to 40th St, Fairmont Ave, Mission Gorge Rd (EB)
FStop	N: CFN/Cosby Oil #7
7A	CA 15S (WB)
(7B)	Jct I-15N, to Riverside (WB)
(8)	Jct I-15, Mission Gorge Rd, San Diego (EB), Fairmont Ave (WB)
Gas	N: 7-11, ArcoAmPm, Mobil◊, Shell, Valero◊
Food	N: Arby's, Burger King, Chili's, Coco's, El Pollo Loco, Jack in the Box, KFC, McDonald's, Starbucks, Subway, Taco Bell
Lodg	N: Super 8, Travelodge
Med	N: + Hospital
Other	N: Home Depot, NAPA, Von's, RiteAid
9	Waring Rd, San Diego
Gas	N: 76, Shell
Food	N: Italian
Lodg	N: Good Nite Inn, Days Inn, Quality Inn
Other	N: Albertson's
10	College Ave
Gas	N: Chevron◊
	S: ArcoAmPm
Food	S: Jack in the Box, McDonald's, Pita Pit
Med	S: + Alvarado Hospital
Other	N: US Post Office
	S: San Diego St Univ
11	70th St, Lake Murray Blvd, Alvarado Rd, La Mesa
Gas	N: Shell

Best Western InnSuites Hotel & Suites
1450 Castle Dome Ave
Yuma, AZ 85365
(928) 783-8341 Ext 309
Exit 2A

EXIT	CALIFORNIA
	S: 7-11, Shell◊
Food	N: Mexican, Subway
	S: Deli, Denny's, Marie Callendar's, Mexican Rest
AServ	N: Chevron
	S: Shell
Med	S: + Hospital
Other	S: San Diego RV Resort▲
12	Fletcher Pkwy, La Mesa
Gas	N: 7-11, Shell
Food	N: Bakers Square, Boston Market, Carl's Jr, Chili's, McDonald's, Red Oak Steak House, Starbucks
	S: Mexican
Lodg	N: EZ 8 Motel, Comfort Inn
	S: Motel 6♥
Other	N: Albertson's, Costco
13A	Spring St (EB), El Cajon Blvd (WB)
Lodg	S: Travelodge
13B	Jackson Dr, Grossmont Blvd
Gas	N: 7-11, ArcoAmPm, Chevron, Mobil, Shell
Food	N: Arby's, Burger King, Chili's, Chuck E Cheese Pizza, Fuddrucker's, KFC, Olive Garden, Red Lobster, Starbucks, Taco Bell
	S: Jack in the Box
Other	N: Mall, Staples, Target, US Post Office
	S: Firestone, Ralph's, Wal-Mart, B&N
14A	CA 125(EB), Grossmont Ctr Dr (WB)
14B	La Mesa Blvd (EB), CA 125 (WB)
14C	Severin Dr, Fuerte Dr
Gas	N: 7-11, ArcoAmPm, Mobil
Food	N: Anthony's Fish, Charcoal House
	S: Seafood Rest
Lodg	N: Holiday Inn Express
15	El Cajon Blvd (EB)
Gas	S: Mobil, Shell
Food	S: BBQ
Lodg	N: Days Inn, Quality Inn
	S: Cottage Motel, Villa Serena Motel
16	Main St
Gas	N: 7-11, ArcoAmPm
	S: 76, Chevron
Food	N: Denny's, Papa's Pizza, Sombrero's
Lodg	N: Relax Inn, Thriftlodge
Other	S: Greyhound Terminal
17A	Johnson Ave, El Cajon (EB)
Food	N: Applebee's, Boston Market, Burger King, Carl's Jr, Coco's, KFC, Long John Silver's, Panda Express, Sizzler, Starbucks, Subway
Other	N: Albertson's, Home Depot, Kmart, RiteAid, Wal-Mart, Mall
	S: Cummins Cal Pacific

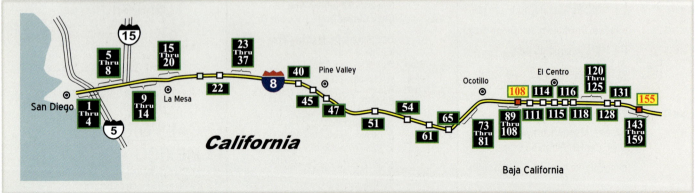

Page 28   ◊ = Regular Gas Stations with Diesel   ▲ = RV Friendly Locations   ♥ = Pet Friendly Locations
RED PRINT SHOWS LARGE VEHICLE PARKING/ACCESS ON SITE OR NEARBY   BROWN PRINT SHOWS CAMPGROUNDS/RV PARKS

EXIT		CALIFORNIA
17B	**CA 67N (EB)**	
	Other	N: Mall, Stores
17C	**Magnolia Ave (EB)**	
	Gas	N: ArcoAmPm
		S: Shell
	Food	N: Applebee's, China King, Jack in the Box, Long John Silver's, On the Border, Panda Express
	Food	S: Mexican, Perry's Café
	Lodg	S: El Cajon Inn, Motel 6♥, Travelodge
	Other	N: Best Buy, Kmart, Mall, Shopping
17	**Magnolia Ave, CA 67N (WB)**	
18	**Mollison Ave**	
	Gas	N: ArcoAmPm, Chevron, Citgo, Exxon
		S: ArcoAmPm, QT
	Food	N: Arby's, Denny's, Starbucks, Wendy's
		S: Taco Bell
	Lodg	N: Best Western, Plaza Int'l Inn
		S: Super 8, Valley Motel
19	**2nd St, El Cajon**	
	Gas	N: ArcoAmPm, Chevron, Exxon
		S: 76, Gas Depot, Shell**x2**
	Food	N: Taco Shop
		S: Arby's, Burger King, Carl's Jr, Jack in the Box, Golden Corral, IHOP, Pizza Hut, McDonald's, Subway, Taco Bell
	Lodg	S: Parkside Inn, Royal Inn
	Other	N: Grocery
		S: Firestone, Grocery, Walgreen's
20	**Greenfield Dr (EB)**	
20A	**E Main St (WB)** (Diff reaccess)	
	Gas	S: ArcoAmPm
	Food	N: Buffy's, Coco's, Italian Rest, Main St Grill, Starbucks
	Lodg	N: Best Western, Budget Inn, Fabulous 7 Motel
	Other	N: Vacationer RV Resort▲
20B	**Greenfield Dr, to Crest (WB)**	
	Gas	N: 7-11, Chevron◊, Exxon◊, Shell
		S: Mobil
	Food	N: Janet's Café, McDonald's
	Med	**N: + Hospital**
	Other	N: Albertson's, AutoZone, O'Reilly, Von's, Circle RV Resort▲, CA State Highway Patrol Post, Auto Repair
22	**Los Coches Rd Interchange (EB) Camino Canada, Lakeside**	
	Gas	N: 7-11, Mobil, Valero
		S: Shell◊
	Food	N: Mexican, Pizza
		S: Denny's, McDonald's, Subway, Taco Bell
	Other	N: Pharmacy, Rancho Los Coches RV Park▲
		S: Grocery, Midas, Wal-Mart
23	**Lake Jennings Park Rd**	
	Gas	N: ArcoAmPm◊
		S: 7-11
	Food	N: Jack in the Box/Arco
		S: Burger King, Marechiaro's
27	**Harbison Canyon Ln, Dunbar Ln**	
	Other	N: Oak Creek RV Resort▲
30	**Tavern Rd, to Alpine**	
	FStop	N: Alpine Valero, Tavern Rd Alliance
	Gas	S: 76, Shell
	Food	N: Breadbasket, Carl's Jr, La Carretta, Long John Silver's, Ramos BBQ
	Lodg	S: Country Inn, Harris Inn
	Other	N: LP/Tav Rd Alliance
		S: Grocery, RiteAid

EXIT		CALIFORNIA
33	**W Willows Rd, Alpine Blvd**	
	Other	N: Viejas Casino & Outlet Center, Lodge & Restaurants, Alpine Springs RV Resort▲
36	**E Willows Rd**	
	Other	N: Alpine Springs RV Park▲, Viejas Casino/Lodge/Rest/Outlet Center
(38)	**Vista Point (EB)**	
40	**CA 79N, Japatul Valley Rd, Alpine, to Descanso**	
	Other	N: to KQ Ranch RV Resort▲
45	**Pine Valley Rd, Campo, Pine Valley, Julian**	
	Food	N: Diner, Frosty Burger, Major's Coffee Shop, Pine Valley House Rest & Store
	Lodg	N: Pine Valley Inn Motel
	Other	N: Cuyamaca Ranch State Park
47	**Sunrise Hwy, Campo, CR S1**	
(48)	**Inspection Station (WB)**	
(51)	**Buckman Springs Rd, CR S1, to Lake Morena Buckman Springs Rest Area (Both dir) (RR, Phone, Picnic, RVDump)**	
	Other	S: to RV Camping▲
54	**Cameron Stn, Kitchen Creek Rd**	
61	**Crestwood Rd, Boulevard, Live Oak Springs, Campo**	
	TStop	S: Golden Acorn Casino & Travel Center
	Food	S: Rest/FastFood/Golden Acorn TC
	Lodg	S: Live Oak Springs Country Inn
	Other	S: Laundry/Casino/GA TC, Outdoor World RV Park▲,

EXIT		CALIFORNIA
	Other	S: Campo Indian Reservation
65	**CA 94S, Boulevard, Campo**	
	Gas	S: Mountain Top◊
	Food	S: Burning Tree
	Lodg	S: Buena Vista Motel, Lux Inn
		S: Grocery, Outdoor World Retreat▲
73	**Carrizo Gorge Rd, Jacumba**	
	Gas	S: Shell◊, Valero
	Food	S: Subway/Shell
	AServ	S: Towing/Shell
	Other	N: DeAnza Springs Nudist Resort▲
		S: NAPA, RV Camping▲
(75)	**Brake Inspection Area (EB)**	
77	**In-Ko-Pah Park Rd**	
	Other	N: Towing Service, Phone
80	**Mountain Springs Rd**	
(81)	**Runaway Truck Ramp (EB)**	
87	**CA 98, Calexico (EB)**	
89	**Imperial Hwy, CA 98, Ocotillco**	
	FStop	N: OTU Fuel Mart
		S: Desert Fuel Stop/76
	Gas	N: Shell
	Food	S: Desert Kitchen/Desert FS
	Lodg	N: Ocotillo Motel & RV Park▲
	TServ	S: 76
	Other	S: RV Camping▲, US Post Office
101	**Dunaway Rd, Imperial Valley**	
107	**Drew Rd, El Centro, Seeley**	
	Other	N: Sunbeam Lake RV Resort▲, El Centro Naval Air Facility
		S: Rio Bend RV Golf Resort▲
(108)	**Sunbeam Rest Area (Both dir) (RR, Phone, Picnic, RVDump)**	
111	**Forrester Rd, to Westmorland**	
114	**Imperial Ave, El Centro, Imperial**	
	Gas	N: 7-11, ArcoAmPm, Chevron, Shell, USA◊
	Food	N: 4 Seasons Buffet, Applebee's, Burger King, Carrow's, Del Taco, Denny's, Golden Corral, Jack in the Box, KFC, McDonald's, Sizzler, Taco Bell, Wendy's
	Lodg	N: Days Inn, Howard Johnson, Laguana Inn, Ramada Inn, Super 8, Vacation Inn
	Other	N: Albertson's, Costco, Goodyear, Kmart, Lowe's, Pep Boys, Staples, Target, Wal-Mart, Walgreen's, Vacation Inn RV Park▲, Ca State Hwy Patrol Post, Imperial Co Airport✈
115	**CA 86, 4th St, El Centro**	
	TStop	N: 7-11 Food Store
		S: Imperial 8 Travel Center/Mobil (Scales)
	Gas	N: ArcoAmPm, Chevron, Shell◊, USA
	Food	N: Carl's Jr, Chiba Express, Jack in the Box, McDonald's
		S: Subway/Pizza Hut/Rest/Imp 8 TC, Chili's, IHOP, Starbucks, Taco Bell
	Lodg	N: Holiday Inn Express, Motel 6♥
		S: Best Western, Comfort Inn, EZ 8 Motel, Rodeway Inn♥, Value Inn
	TServ	N: Kennedy's for Tires
	Other	N: Auto Dealers, Goodyear, Grocery,
		S: Laundry/LP/Imp 8 TC, Auto Dealers, Home Depot, Desert Trails RV Park & Golf Course▲
116	**Dogwood Rd**	
	FStop	N: Pacific Pride
	Food	S: Carino's, Chili's, Starbucks
	Other	N: RV Camping▲

◊ = Regular Gas Stations with Diesel   ▲ = RV Friendly Locations   ♥ = Pet Friendly Locations

RED PRINT SHOWS LARGE VEHICLE PARKING/ACCESS ON SITE OR NEARBY   BROWN PRINT SHOWS CAMPGROUNDS/RV PARKS

EXIT	CA/AZ
118A	CA 111S, Calexico (EB)
118B	CA 111N, Brawley (EB)
Other	N: Country Life RV Park▲
120	Bowker Rd
125	Orchard Rd, CR S32, Holtville (Serv 5 mi N in Holtville)
128	Bonds Corner Rd (Serv 5 mi N)
131	CA 115N, Vanderlinden Rd, Holtville (Serv 5 mi N)
143	CA 98W, to Calexico
146	Brock Center Rd, Winterhaven
151	Gordons Well Rd
Other	N: Gordons Well RV Park▲
(155)	Sand Hills Rest Area (Left Exit, Both dir) (RR, Picnic)
156	Grays Well Rd
159	Ogilby Rd, to Blythe
164	Sidewinder Rd
Gas	S: Shell
Other	N: CA State Hwy Patrol Post S: Pilot Knob RV Park▲
(165)	Inspection Station (WB)
166	CA 186S (EB), Algondones Rd
Other	Fort Yuma-Quechan Indian Reservation, S to Mexico
170	Winterhaven Dr, Winterhaven
Other	S: Rivers Edge RV Park▲
172	4th Ave, Yuma, Winterhaven
Gas	S: 76, Chevron, Shell
Food	S: Domino's Pizza, Jack in the Box, Mexican, Yuma Landing
Lodg	S: Best Western, Desert Sands Motel, Yuma Inn
Other	N: Fort Yuma Paradise Casino S: Rivers Edge RV Resort▲, Yuma State Park
NOTE:	MM# 178.5: Arizona State Line

⊙ CALIFORNIA (Pacific Time Zone)
⊙ ARIZONA (Mountain Time Zone)
(AZ does NOT observe D S T)

1	Giss Pkwy, 4th Ave, Redondo Center Dr, Yuma (Serv S on 4th Ave)
Gas	S: 76, Circle K, Chevron, Shell
Food	S: Jack in the Box
Lodg	S: Best Western, Lee Hotel, Yuma Inn
Other	N: Yuma Territorial Prison State Historical Park S: Amtrak, Auto Services, Grocery
(1)	Inspection Station (Both dir)
2	US 95, 16th St, Yuma, Yuma Proving Grounds, Quartzite (Addt'l Services-Gas, Food, Lodging, Shopping on 4th Ave S, Pacific Ave S)
Gas	N: 76, Murphy, Sam's S: ArcoAmPm, Mobil, Shell
Food	N: Rest/Shilo Inn, Chili's, Cracker Barrel, Denny's, Penny's Diner, Musick's, Taylor's Taste of TX S: Applebee's, Burger King, Carl's Jr, Carino's, IHOP, Jack in the Box,

Personal Notes

EXIT	ARIZONA
Food	S: Golden Corral, McDonald's, Outback Steakhouse, Red Lobster, Wendy's
Lodg	N: Best Western, Days Inn, Fairfield Inn, Hampton Inn, Motel 6♥, Oak Tree Inn, Shilo Inn, Springhill Suites S: Best Value Inn, Comfort Inn, Motel 6, Super 8, Travelodge
Other	N: Auto/Tire Repair, Sam's Club, Target, Wal-Mart sc S: Grocery, Home Depot, Staples, U-Haul, Towing, Yuma Int'l Airport✈
3	AZ 280S, Ave 3E, Yuma, Int'l Airport, Marine Corps Air Station
Tstop	S: Love's Travel Stop #349 (Scales)
Food	N: Burger King S: Chesters/Subway/Love's TS, KFC, Pizza Hut
TServ	S: Diesel Injection Service
Other	S: WiFi/RVDump/Love's TS, Purcell Tires, US Marine Corps Air Station, Yuma Co Fairgrounds, Az West RV Park▲, Sun Vista RV Resort▲, Del Pueblo RV Park & Tennis Resort▲, Araby Acres RV Resort▲
7	Araby Rd, 32nd St
FStop	S: Circle K Truxtop #1948/Unocal 76
TServ	S: Yuma Diesel Service
Other	S: Windhaven RV Park▲, Westwind RV & Golf Resort▲, La Mesa RV, AZ Sands RV Park▲, RV World, to Villa Alameda RV Resort▲, Northern AZ Univ, AZ Western College
9	I-8 Bus Lp, 32nd St, 4th Ave, Ave 8½ E, to Yuma (WB, diff reaccess)
Gas	S: 76, Chevron, Circle K

EXIT	ARIZONA
Food	S: Carl's Jr, Carrow's, Domino's Pizza, Jack in the Box, Pizza Hut, Taco Bell
Lodg	S: Holiday Inn Express, Quality Inn, Ramada Inn, Travelodge
Other	N: Sun Vista RV Park▲, Desert Paradise RV Resort▲ S: Albertson's, Auto Dealers, Lowe's, Pep Boys, Target, Walgreen's, Bonita Mesa RV Park▲
12	Fortuna Rd, to US 95N
FStop	S: Shell
TStop	N: Barney's Auto Truck Plaza/Shamrock (Scales)
Gas	N: Chevron, Shell S: 76
Food	N: Jack in the Box, Pizza Hut, Tyler's S: Burger King/Shell, DQ, Subway
Lodg	N: Courtesy Inn S: Microtel
TServ	N: Barney's TP/Tires
Other	N: Caravan RV Park▲, Oasis RV Park▲, Shangri La RV Park▲, Las Quintas Oasis RV Park▲, Cactus Gardens RV Resort▲ MIL/Lake Martinez Rec Facility, MIL/Desert Breeze Travel Camp▲ S: Fry's, Blue Sky RV Park▲
14	Foothills Blvd, Yuma
Food	S: Domino's, Foothills Rest, Kountry Kitchen Café, Mi Fajita
Other	N: Sundance RV Resort▲, Yuma Proving Ground, National Guard Rifle Range S: Sun Ridge RV Park▲, Foothills Village RV Park▲, Gila Mtn RV Park▲, Barry M Goldwater Air Force Base
(17)	Inspection Station/Border Patrol (EB)
21	Los Angeles Ave, Welton, Dome Valley Rd, Dome Valley
Food	N: Café
Other	N: Coach Stop RV Park▲
(22)	Parking Area (Both dir)
30	Ave 29E, Wellton
Gas	N: 76, Circle K
Other	N: Tier Drop RV Park▲
37	Ave 36E, Welton, to Roll
Other	S: Wellton Airport✈
42	Ave 40E, Welton, to Tacna
Gas	N: Chevron◇
Lodg	N: Chaparral Motel
Other	S: Colfred Airport✈
54	Ave 52E, Roll, Mt Mohawk Valley
(56)	Mohawk Rest Area (Both dir) (RR, Phone, Picnic, Vend)
67	Ave 64E, Roll, Dateland
Gas	S: Exxon
Other	S: Oasis RV Park▲, Dateland Palms Village & RV Park▲ N: Dateland Airfield✈
73	Aztec Rd
78	Spot Rd, Ave 75E, Dateland
(84)	Rest Area (EB) (RR, Phone, Picnic, Vend)

Page 30 ◇ = Regular Gas Stations with Diesel ▲ = RV Friendly Locations ♥ = Pet Friendly Locations
RED PRINT SHOWS LARGE VEHICLE PARKING/ACCESS ON SITE OR NEARBY BROWN PRINT SHOWS CAMPGROUNDS/RV PARKS

EXIT	ARIZONA
(85)	Rest Area (WB) (RR, Phone, Picnic, Vend)
87	Sentinel, Hyder, Aqua Caliente
102	Painted Rock Rd, Gila Bend
106	Paloma Rd, Gila Bend
111	Citrus Valley Rd
115	AZ 85, Ajo, (EB-Left) Bus Loop 8, Gila Bend, Phoenix, Ajo, Mexico
TStop	N: Love's Travel Stop #296, Bill Henry's Food Mart/Shell
Gas	N: 76, Chevron, Shell
Food	N: Taco Bell/Love's, Burger King, McDonald's
Lodg	N: Best Western, Yucca Motel
TServ	N: Bill's Texaco FS
Med	N: + Hospital
Other	N: WiFi/RVDump/Love's TS, RVDump/LP/Bill Henry's Shell, NAPA, Goodyear, Gila Bend Muni Airport✈, A Wheel Inn RV Park▲, Desert Trails RV Park▲

EXIT	ARIZONA
119	Bus 8, Gila Bend, Butterfield Trail, (EB), AZ 85N, to I-10, Gila Bend
TStop	N: Holt's Interstate Services/Shell (Scales)
Gas	N: Chevron
Food	N: Rest/BW, Rest/Holt's TS, Amer/Mex Café, DQ, Exit West Café
Lodg	N: Best Western, Super 8, America's ChoiceInn/Holt's TS
Other	N: RV Dump/RVPark/Holts Shell, Augie's Quail Trail RV Park▲, Gila Bend Muni Airport✈
140	Freeman Rd, Gila Bend
144	Vekol Rd
(149)	Picnic Area (Both dir)
151	AZ 84E, Maricopa Rd, to AZ 347N, Stanfield
Other	N: John Wayne RV Ranch▲, Harrah's Casino Resort S: Saguaro RV Park▲
161	Stanfield Rd, Stanfield
Gas	N: Circle K

EXIT	ARIZONA
167	Montgomery Rd, Casa Grande
Lodg	N: Francisco Grand Hotel & Golf Resort
Other	N: Sierra Vista RV Park▲, Casa Grande Golf & RV Resort▲
169	Bianco Rd
172	Thornton Rd, Casa Grande
Food	N: Sizzler
Lodg	N: Best Western, Holiday Inn, Super 8
Other	N: Sundance RV Resort▲, Casa Grande Muni Airport✈, to Arizona Motel & RV Park▲
174	Trekell Rd, Casa Grande
Med	N: + Hospital
Other	S: Casa Grande Military Reservation
(178A)	Jct I-10, E - Tucson
(178B)	Jct I-10, W - Phoenix (EB, Left exit)
Other	N: Buena Tierra Family CG & RV Park▲ (MOUNTAIN TIME ZONE) (AZ does not observe DST)

⊙ ARIZONA

Begin Westbound I-8 from Jct I-10 in AZ to Jct I-5 in San Diego, CA.

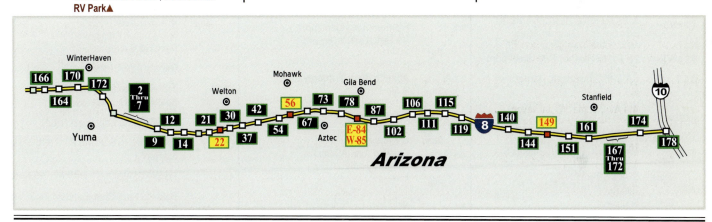

EXIT	CALIFORNIA
	Below lists Eastbound I-10 from Santa Monica, CA to Jct I-95 in Jacksonville, FL.

⊙ CALIFORNIA
(PACIFIC TIME ZONE)
(I-10 begins/ends in FL on I-95, Exit #351B)

EXIT	CALIFORNIA
(0)	CA 1N, Oxnard, Santa Monica Blvd, to Beaches
1A	4th St, 5th St
1B	20th St (EB), CA 1S, Lincoln Blvd (WB)
Gas	S: Chevron, Exxon, Shell
Food	N: Denny's, El Pollo Loco, Norm's Rest, Subway S: Jack in the Box
Lodg	N: Holiday Inn
Other	N: Mall, Auto Repair

EXIT	CALIFORNIA
1C	Cloverfield Blvd (WB)
Gas	N: ArcoAmPm, Shell
AServ	N: Shell
Med	N: + Hospital
2	Centinela Ave (EB)
2A	Centinela Ave, Pico Blvd (WB)
Food	N: Mexican, Taco Bell S: McDonald's, KFC
Lodg	S: Santa Monica Hotel
Other	S: Trader Joe's
2B	Bundy Dr S (WB)
Food	S: Taco Bell
Other	S: Santa Monica Airport✈
2C	Bundy Dr N (WB)
Gas	N: 76, Chevron, Shell
Food	N: Taco Bell
(3A)	Jct I-405N, to Sacramento
(3B)	Jct I-405S, to Long Beach

EXIT	CALIFORNIA
4	Overland Ave (WB), National Blvd
Gas	S: Mobil, Shell
Other	S: Jiffy Lube
5	National Blvd (WB)
Gas	N: 76 S: ArcoAmPm
Food	N: Papa John's, Subway, Starbucks S: KFC
6	Robertson Blvd, Culver City
Gas	N: Chevron, Mobil, Valero
Food	N: Del Taco, Starbucks, Taco Bell, Wendy's
Other	S: Albertson's
7A	La Cienega Blvd (EB), Venice Blvd
Gas	N: Chevron, Mobil S: ArcoAmPm, Mobil
Food	S: Carl's Jr, McDonald's, Subway
Med	S: + Kaiser Permanente Hospital
Other	S: Auto Services
7B	Fairfax Ave (EB), Washington Blvd

◆ = Regular Gas Stations with Diesel ▲ = RV Friendly Locations ♥ = Pet Friendly Locations

RED PRINT SHOWS LARGE VEHICLE PARKING/ACCESS ON SITE OR NEARBY   BROWN PRINT SHOWS CAMPGROUNDS/RV PARKS

Page 31

EXIT	CALIFORNIA
8	La Brea Ave, Englewood
Gas	N: Chevron, Shell
	S: Chevron
AServ	N: Shell
Other	N: Walgreen's
	S: Auto Zone, Ralph's, Auto Services
9	Crenshaw Blvd, Englewood
Gas	N: Mobil
	S: Chevron, Mobil, Shell, Thrifty
Food	N: Jack in the Box
	S: El Pollo Loco, McDonald's, Taco Bell
Other	S: U-Haul
10	Arlington Ave, Los Angeles
Gas	N: 76, Chevron, Mobil
Other	N: Auto & Tire Services
11	Western Ave, Normandie Ave
Gas	N: Chevron, Mobil
	S: Chevron, Texaco
Food	N: McDonald's
Other	N: Auto Zone, Food 4 Less, Pharmacy
	S: Auto Repair
12	Vermont Ave (EB), Hoover St
Gas	N: Mobil, Texaco
	S: ArcoAmPm, Chevron, Valero◊
Food	N: Burger King
	S: Jack in the Box
Other	N: Auto Services
	S: Staples, Office Depot, Univ of S Cal, Expo Center, LA Memorial Sports Arena, LA Memorial Coliseum
(13A)	Jct I-110S, Harbor Fwy, San Pedro
13B	CA 110N, Pasadena, Harbor Fwy (EB, Left Exit)
Other	N: Staples Center/Conv Center
(13)	Jct I-110, CA 110, Harbor Fwy, Downtown, San Pedro
14A	Maple Ave (EB), Los Angeles St
Gas	S: 76
Other	S: Auto Services
14B	San Pedro St
Gas	S: Chevron
Other	S: Auto & Tire Services
15A	Central Ave, Los Angeles
Gas	S: Shell
Lodg	S: Eastside Motel
AServ	N: Shell
15B	Alameda St, Downtown
FStop	S: Pacific Pride
TStop	N: Superfine Texaco II (Scales)
TServ	N: Superfine Texaco TS
TWash	N: Superfine Texaco TS
16A	Santa Fe Ave
Gas	S: Shell

EXIT	CALIFORNIA
16B	CA 60E, Pomona, I-5S, Santa Ana (WB Left Exit)
(17)	Jct I-5N
19	State St, Soto St (EB)
19A	State St (WB, Left exit)
Gas	N: Shell
Med	N: + USC Medical Center
19B	US 101, Los Angeles, I-5N, Sacramento (WB, Left exit)
19C	Soto St (WB)
Gas	N: Shell
	S: Mobil, Pronto, Shell
Lodg	S: Vista Motel
Med	N: + USC Medical Center
Other	S: Auto Services
20A	City Terrace Dr, Herbert Ave (EB)
20B	Eastern Ave (EB)
20	Eastern Ave, City Terrace Dr
Gas	S: Chevron, Mobil
Food	S: Burger King, McDonald's
TServ	N: L&S Diesel Service
(21)	Jct I-710, Long Beach Fwy (EB), Eastern Ave (WB)
22	Fremont Ave, Alahambra (All Serv N to N Valley Blvd)
Gas	S: 7-11
Med	N: + Hospital
23A	Atlantic Blvd, Monterey Park
Gas	N: Mobil
Food	N: Del Taco, Pizza Hut, Popeye's
Lodg	S: Best Western
Med	N: + Hospital
Other	S: Firestone, Ralph's
23B	Garfield Ave, Alhambra, Monterey Park
Gas	S: Shell◊
Med	N: + Garfield Medical Center
24	New Ave, to Monterey Park
Gas	N: Mobil
25A	Del Mar Ave, to San Gabriel
Gas	N: 76
	S: Arco, Chevron◊
Lodg	S: Best Value Inn
AServ	N: Auto Repair
25B	San Gabriel Blvd, San Gabriel
Gas	N: Arco, Mobil Shell
	S: Arco
Food	N: Carl's Jr, Popeye's, Taco Bell
	S: Burger King
Lodg	N: Budget Inn
AServ	N: Shell

EXIT	CALIFORNIA
26A	Walnut Grove Ave, Rosemead
26B	CA 164, Rosemead Blvd (EB), CA 19 (WB)
Food	N: Denny's, IHOP
	S: Jack in the Box, Starbucks
Lodg	N: Ramada Inn, Rosemead Inn, Vagabond Inn
Other	S: Office Depot, Target, U-Haul
27B	Temple City Blvd, Rosemead
27	Baldwin Ave (EB), Temple City Blvd, Rosemead
Gas	S: ArcoAmPm, USA
Food	S: Denny's, Edwards Steakhouse
28	Santa Anita Ave, El Monte
Gas	N: Shell
	S: 76
Other	N: El Monte Airport
29A	Peck Rd S, El Monte
29B	Peck Rd N (EB), Valley Blvd, El Monte
Gas	N: Chevron
	S: Mobil, Shell
Food	N: Carl's Jr, Denny's, KFC
	S: Del Taco, McDonald's
Lodg	N: Motel 6 ♥
Other	N: Auto Dealers
	S: El Monte RV Rentals & Sales
29C	Peck Rd N (WB)
30	Garvey Ave, El Monte (WB)
(31)	Jct I-605S, to Long Beach, N to Baldwin Park (WB)
(31A)	Jct I-605S, to Long Beach (EB)
(31B)	Jct I-605N, to Baldwin Park (EB) Frazier St (WB)
31C	Frazier St (EB)
32A	Baldwin Park Blvd, Baldwin Park
Gas	N: ArcoAmPm, Chevron, Shell
Food	N: Burger King, IHOP, In 'n Out Burger, Jack in the Box
Lodg	N: Angel Motel, Aristocrat Motel
Med	N: + Hospital
Other	N: CVS, Office Max, Target, Food 4 Less, CA RV
	S: Altman Winnebago
32B	Francisquito Ave, La Puente
Gas	S: Chevron
Food	N: In 'n Out
	S: Carl's Jr
Lodg	S: Grand Park Inn
Other	N: CA State Hwy Patrol Post

◊ = Regular Gas Stations with Diesel ▲ = RV Friendly Locations ♥ = Pet Friendly Locations
RED PRINT SHOWS LARGE VEHICLE PARKING/ACCESS ON SITE OR NEARBY BROWN PRINT SHOWS CAMPGROUNDS/RV PARKS

EXIT		CALIFORNIA
33		**Puente Ave, Baldwin Park**
	Gas	N: Chevron
		S: Valero◊
	Food	N: China Palace, Denny's, McDonald's, Panda Express, Sizzler, Starbucks
		S: Jack in the Box
	Lodg	N: Courtyard, Motel 6♥, Plaza Motel, Radisson
		S: Baldwin Motor Lodge, Regency Inn
	Other	N: Home Depot, Staples, **Wal-Mart sc**
		S: Laidlaw's Harley Davidson, U-Haul
34		**Pacific Ave, Covina Pkwy (EB)**
	Gas	S: Mobil, Shell
	Food	S: Chevy's Mex Rest
	Lodg	N: Covina Motel
	Med	S: + Dr's Hospital of W Covina
	Other	N: Laundromat, Grocery
		S: Goodyear, Kmart, Westfield Mall
34B		**Sunset Ave, West Covina (WB)**
	Lodg	N: Wayside Motel
34A		**Pacific Ave, W Covina Pkwy (WB)**
35		**Vincent Ave, Glendora Ave**
	Gas	N: Chevron, Mobil
		S: 76
	Food	N: KFC, Pizza Hut
		S: Applebees, CA Steak & Fries, Chevy's Mexican, Red Robin, Starbucks, Subway
	Other	S: Mall, Best Buy, B&N, Cinema, Greyhound
36		**CA 39, Azusa Ave, West Covina**
	Gas	N: 76, ArcoAmPm, Chevron
		S: Mobil, Shell
	Food	N: Black Angus Steakhouse, Subway, McDonald's, Red Lobster, Steak Corral
		S: Carrow's
	Lodg	N: El Dorado Motor Inn, Ramada
	Other	N: Auto Dealers
		S: Auto Dealers, Hertz RAC
37A		**Citrus St, W Covina**
	Gas	N: Chevron, Shell
		S: 76, Valero
	Food	N: Burger King, IHOP, TGI Friday
	Lodg	S: Comfort Inn, Courtyard, Five Star Inn
	Med	S: + Hospital
	Other	N: Grocery, Target, Office Depot
		S: Trader Joe's
37B		**Barranca St**
	Gas	N: Shell
	Food	N: Coco's, El Torito, Monterrey
		S: McDonald's, In 'n Out Burger
	Lodg	N: Best Western, Hampton Inn, Holiday Inn
		S: Comfort Inn
38A		**Grand Ave, W Covina**
	Gas	N: Arco
	Food	N: Chinese, Denny's
		S: McDonald's
	Lodg	N: Best Western
		S: Holiday Inn
38B		**Holt Ave, Garvey Ave**
	Lodg	N: Embassy Suites, Radisson
40		**Via Verde, Covina**
41		**Kellogg Dr, Cal Poly University**
42		**CA 57, Santa Ana, I-210W (WB)**
42A		**CA 57, Santa Ana, I-210W**
42B		**CA 71S, Corona**
43		**Fairplex Dr, La Verne (EB)**

Personal Notes
_____

EXIT		CALIFORNIA
44		**Dudley St (EB), Fairplex Dr (WB), Pomona, La Verne**
	Gas	N: 76, ArcoAmPm◊
		S: Chevron, Mobil
	Food	N: Denny's
		S: McDonald's, Jack in the Box
	Lodg	N: Lemon Tree Motel, Fairplex Sheraton
45		**Garey Ave, Pomona (WB)**
45A		**White Ave, Pomona (EB)**
45B		**Garey Ave, Pomona (EB)**
	Gas	S: Chevron, Shell◊ **(DAD)**
	Other	S: Carwash/Shell
46		**Towne Ave, Pomona**
	Gas	N: 7-11
	Food	N: Jack in the Box, Subway
47		**Indian Hill Blvd, Claremont**
	Gas	N: Mobil
		S: 76, Chevron, Shell
	Food	N: Baker's Square, Tony Roma
		S: Burger King, Carl's Jr, Denny's
	Lodg	N: Howard Johnson, Travelodge♥
		S: Ramada Inn♥
	Other	S: Albertson's, AutoZone, Greyhound
48		**Monte Vista Ave, Montclair**
	Gas	N: Shell
	Food	N: Applebee's, Black Angus Steakhouse, Olive Garden, Red Lobster
	Med	S: + Dr's Hospital of Montclair
	Other	N: Mall
49		**Central Ave, Montclair**
	Gas	N: 7-11, Mobil, Shell
		S: 76

EXIT		CALIFORNIA
	Food	N: El Pollo Loco, McDonald's
		S: Jack in the Box, Long John Silver's
	Other	N: Best Buy, Firestone, Goodyear, Harbor Freight Tools, Office Depot, PetSmart♥, Mall, **to Cable Airport**✈
		S: Costco, Kmart, Giant RV
50		**Mountain Ave, Upland, Ontario**
	Gas	N: ArcoAmPm, Chevron, Mobil, Shell◊
		S: 76◊
	Food	N: BBQ, Carrow's, Denny's, El Torito, Happy Wok, Mimi's Café, Subway, Wendy's
		S: Carl's Jr, Starbucks
	Lodg	N: Super 8
		S: Comfort Inn♥, Motel 6♥
	Other	N: Home Depot, Staples, Pharmacy, Trader Joe's
		S: Albertson's, RiteAid, Target, US Post Office, UPS Store
51		**CA 83, Euclid Ave**
	Food	N: Coco's
53		**4th St, to Ontario**
	Gas	N: ArcoAmPm, Chevron, Shell
		S: 76, ArcoAmPm, Exxon
	Food	N: Carl's Jr, Jack in the Box, Sizzler
		S: Denny's, KFC, Mexican, Pizza Hut
	Lodg	N: Motel 6♥, Quality Inn
		S: CA Inn, Days Inn, Travelodge
	Other	N: Grocery, Kmart, Radio Shack, Pharmacy
54		**Vineyard Ave, Ontario**
	Gas	N: Shell
		S: ArcoAmPm, Mobil, Shell, USA
	Food	N: Del Taco, Sizzler, Taco Bell
		S: Denny's, In 'n Out Burger, Indian Rest, Japanese Rest, Mexican Rest
	Lodg	S: Best Western, Country Suites, Red Roof Inn♥, Sheraton**x2**, Super 8
	Other	N: Grocery, AutoZone, RiteAid
55		**Archibald Ave, Ontario Airport**
55A		**Holt Blvd, Ontario (WB)**
	Gas	N: Mobil◊
	Food	N: Subway
	Med	N: + Family Urgent Care
	Other	S: Auto Dealers, Convention Center
55B		**Archibald Ave, Ontario Int'l Airport**
	Other	S: Ontario Int'l Airport✈
56		**Haven Ave, Rancho Cucamonga**
	Gas	N: Mobil
	Food	N: Black Angus Steakhouse, El Torito, Benihana, Tony Roma
		S: Panda Chinese, TGI Friday
	Lodg	N: Hilton, Holiday Inn, La Quinta Inn♥
		S: Fairfield Inn
	Other	N: Best Buy, Target
57		**Milliken Ave, Ontario**
	TStop	N: Travel Center of America #162/76 (Scales)
		S: Travel Center of America #26 (Scales)
	Gas	N: ArcoAmPm, Chevron, Mobil, Shell
	Food	N: Rest/PHut/Subw/TB/TA TC, Burger King, Coco's, McDonald's, Wendy's
		S: Rest/BKing/TB/ChesterFrChkn/TA TC
	Lodg	N: Country Suites, Extended Stay America
		S: Kings Lodge
	TWash	N: TA TC
	TServ	N: TA TC
		S: TA TC
	Other	N: Laundry/BarbSh/WiFi/TA TC, Ontario Mills Mall, Sam's Club
		S: Affordable RV Center▲, Laundry/WiFi/TA TC

◊ = Regular Gas Stations with Diesel   ▲ = RV Friendly Locations   ♥ = Pet Friendly Locations

RED PRINT SHOWS LARGE VEHICLE PARKING/ACCESS ON SITE OR NEARBY   BROWN PRINT SHOWS CAMPGROUNDS/RV PARKS

EXIT		CALIFORNIA
(58)		Jct I-15N, to Barstow, Las Vegas
		Jct I-15S, to San Diego (WB)
(58A)		Jct I-15N, to Barstow, Las Vegas
(58B)		Jct I-15S, to San Diego (EB)
59		Etiwanda Ave, Ontario, Fontana
	FStop	N: Pacific Pride
	Tstop	N: Flying J Travel Plaza (Scales)
	Food	N: Rest/FastFood/FJ TP
	Other	N: Laundry/WiFi/FJ TP, CA Speedway
61		Cherry Ave, Fontana
	FStop	N: A-Z Fuel Stop, Fontana Chevron
		S: BTE Gas Stop (Scales)
	TStop	N: Truck Town Truck & Travel Plaza (Scales)
		S: Three Sisters Truck Stop (Scales), North American Truck Stop
	Gas	N: ArcoAmPm, Valero
		S: 76/Circle K
	Food	N: Rest/TT TS, FastFood/Fontana Chev, Cozy Corner Café, Carl's Jr, Jack in the Box
		S: Farmer Boys Rest
	Lodg	N: Circle Inn Motel
	TWash	S: 3S TS
	TServ	N: TT TP, Big Rig Truck Repair, NA TS, Peterbilt
		S: 3S TS
	Other	N: Laundry/TT TP, Ford, CA Speedway
		S: Laundry/3S TS, California RV Sales
63		Citrus Ave, Fontana
	FStop	N: EZ Truck Stop/76
	Gas	N: ArcoAmPm
	Food	N: Bakers D/T, Mexican Rest
	Other	N: LP/EZ TS
64		Sierra Ave, Fontana
	Gas	N: ArcoAmPm, Mobil, Shell
		S: Circle K
	Food	N: Applebee's, Arby's, Burger King, DQ, Chuck E Cheese, Del Taco, Jack in the Box, Denny's, Millie's Kitchen, Sizzler, McDonald's, Popeye's, Taco Bell
		S: Old Country Buffet, Mexican
	Lodg	N: Comfort Inn, Econo Lodge, Motel 6♥
	Med	N: + Hospital
	Other	N: Albertson's, Cinema, Goodyear, Kmart, RiteAid
		S: Target
66		Cedar Ave, Bloomington
	Gas	N: ArcoAmPm, Mobil
		S: 7-11
	Food	N: Baker's D/T, Burger King
	Lodg	N: Sierra Crossing Motel
	Other	N: Auto Services
68		Riverside Ave, Bloomington, to Rialto, Colton
	FStop	S: Pacific Pride/Poma
	TStop	N: I-10 Truck Stop (Scales)
	Gas	N: Chevron
		S: 76/Circle K
	Food	N: Rest/I-10 TS, Burger King, China Place, Coco's, Hometown Buffet, Jack in the Box, McDonald's, Starbucks, Taco Joe's, Subway
	Lodg	N: American Inn, Best Western, Empire Inn, Rialto Motel, Rodeway Inn, Valley View Inn
	TWash	N: I-10 TS
	TServ	N: I-10 TS
	Other	N: Laundry/I-10 TS, Wal-Mart

EXIT		CALIFORNIA
69		Pepper Ave, Colton
	Gas	N: Valero
	Food	N: Baker's D/T
	Lodg	N: Lido Motel
	Med	N: + Arrowhead Reg'l Medical Ctr
	Other	N: California RV Sales
70A		Rancho Ave, Colton
	Food	N: Del Taco, El Rancho, Jack in the Box, KFC/TacoBell
70B		9th St, La Cadena Dr, Downtown, Colton
	Gas	N: Mobil
	Food	N: Burger King, Denny's, McDonald's, Mexican Rest
	Lodg	N: Hampton Inn
	Other	N: Carwash/Mobil
71		Mt Vernon Ave, Sperry Dr, Colton
	FStop	N: Pacific Pride
		S: CFN/Poma #26
	TStop	N: Valley Colton Truck Stop (Scales)
	Gas	N: Arco
	Food	N: Rest/Valley Colton TS, Pepito's
	Lodg	N: Colony Inn, Colton Motel
	TWash	N: Valley Colton TS
	TServ	N: Valley Colton TS
	Other	N: Laundry/LP/Valley Colton TS
(72)		Jct I-215, N - San Bernardino, S - Riverside
	TServ	S: Cummins Cal Pacific
73A		Waterman Ave S (EB)
73B		Waterman Ave N (EB)

EXIT		CALIFORNIA
73		Waterman Ave (WB)
	FStop	N: CFN/Ultramar Food 'n Fuel
		S: CFN/Ultramar Food 'n Fuel
	TStop	S: Beacon Truck Stop (Scales)
	Gas	N: 76, Shell◊
		S: ArcoAmPm
	Food	N: Black Angus Steakhouse, Bobby McGee's, Chili's, Coco's, IHOP, Olive Garden, Red Lobster, Starbucks, TGI Friday, Tony Roma
		S: Rest/Beacon TS, Burger King, Carl's Jr, Del Taco, Donut Factory, Hometown Buffet, KFC, Popeye's, Taco Bell
	Lodg	N: Comfort Inn, Hilton, La Quinta Inn♥ Super 8♥, Travelodge
		S: Days Inn, Motel 6♥
	TServ	S: Beacon TS
	Other	N: Best Buy, Home Depot, Office Depot, Office Max, PetSmart♥, Sam's Club
		S: Laundry/Beacon TS, Staples, La Mesa RV Center, Camping World
74		Tippecanoe Ave, Anderson St
	Gas	N: ArcoAmPm, Thrifty
		S: 76◊
	Food	N: Denny's, Jack in the Box, Wendy's
		S: Baker's, Del Taco, Hometown Buffet, KFC, Taco Bell
	Lodg	N: American Inn, Fairfield Inn, Loma Linda Lodge
	Other	N: Best Buy, Costco, Home Depot, PetSmart♥, Office Depot, Sam's Club, Staples, Sports Authority
		S: Harley Davidson, to Loma Linda Univ
75		Mountain View Ave, Loma Linda
	Gas	N: Mobil, Valero◊
	Food	S: Farmer's Boy, Lupe's, Subway
76		California St, Redlands
	Gas	S: ArcoAmPm, Shell
	Food	S: Applebee's, Jack in the Box, Mexican Rest, Subway, Wendy's
	Other	S: Grocery, Wal-Mart▲, El Monte RV, Mission RV Park▲
77A		Alabama St (reaccess via 77C)
	Gas	N: Chevron
		S: ArcoAmPm, Chevron, Shell
	Food	N: Denny's, Chili's, Red Robin
		S: IHOP, McDonald's, Starbucks
	Lodg	N: Motel 6♥, Motel 7, Redlands Motor Lodge, Super 8
		S: Comfort Suites, Country Inn, Good Night Inn
	Other	N: B&N, Target, U-Haul, Petco♥, RV Center
		S: Grocery, Home Depot, Kmart, Pharmacy, RV Center
77B		CA 210 W to CA 330 N, Pasadena, Running Springs
77C		Tennessee St (EB), CA 30, Highland (WB)
	Gas	S: Shell
	Food	S: Arby's, Burger King, Coco's, El Pollo Loco, Pizza, Subway, Taco Bell
	Lodg	S: Best Western
	Other	N: Home Depot, Mall
79		CA 38, 6th St, Redlands (WB)
	Gas	N: Chevron
		S: 76, Shell
	Food	N: Redlands
		S: Boston Market
	Lodg	N: Budget Inn, Stardust Motel

◊ = Regular Gas Stations with Diesel   ▲ = RV Friendly Locations   ♥ = Pet Friendly Locations
RED PRINT SHOWS LARGE VEHICLE PARKING/ACCESS ON SITE OR NEARBY   BROWN PRINT SHOWS CAMPGROUNDS/RV PARKS

EXIT	CALIFORNIA	EXIT	CALIFORNIA	EXIT	CALIFORNIA
	Other N: America's Tire S: Wal-Mart sc		Other S: ATMs, Banks, Albertson's, Best Buy, Home Depot, Kmart, WalMart SC, CA Hwy Patrol Post	120	Indian Ave, N Palm Springs FStop S: Pilot Travel Center #307 (Scales) Gas N: 76, Shell S: Chevron Food N: Denny's S: DQ/Wendy's/Pilot TC Lodg N: Motel 6 ♥ Med S: + Hospital Other S: WiFi/Pilot TC, Amtrak
79AB	CA 38, Orange St (EB)	98	Sunset Ave, Banning Gas N: Chevron◆ Food N: Domino's Pizza, Donut Factory, Gramma's Country Kitchen, Roman's Chicken Palace & Mexican Food Lodg N: Banning Suites, Sunset Motel Other N: Auto Zone, Grocery, RiteAid, RV Ctr S: Camper Corral		
80	University St (EB), Cypress Ave, Citrus Ave (WB) Med N: + Hospital				
81	Ford St (EB), Redlands Blvd Gas S: 76				
82	Wabash Ave (WB)			123	Palm Dr, Gene Autry Trail, to Desert Hot Springs Gas N: ArcoAmPm, Chevron Food N: Jack in the Box/Chevron Other N: Sands RV Resort & Golf▲, to Caliente Springs RV Resort▲, Sky Valley Resort▲, Desert Pools RV Resort▲ S: Palm Springs Int'l Airport✈, to Gene Autry Trail
83	Yucaipa Blvd, Redlands, Yucaipa FStop N: appr 2mi CFN/Valero #1611 Gas N: ArcoAmPm◆, Chevron S: Conv Store/Gas Lodg S: Vincent St George Motel	99	22nd St, Downtown, Banning Gas N: ArcoAmPm, Mobil, Shell Food N: BJ's BBQ, Carl's Jr, Carrow's, KFC, McDonald's, Sizzler, Starbucks, Subway, Taco Bell, Wendy's Lodg N: Days Inn, Super 8, Sunset Motel, Travelodge Other N: Auto Dealer, Goodyear, Banning Discount RV Center		
85	Live Oak Canyon Rd, Oak Glen Rd				
(86)	Rest Area (EB) (RR, Phone, Picnic)			126	Date Palm Dr, Cathedral City to Palm Springs, Rancho Mirage Gas S: ArcoAmPm, Mobil, Shell Food S: McDonald's/Shell, Round Table Pizza, Taco Bell Other S: Wal-Mart sc, to Desert Shadows RV Resort▲, Palm Springs Oasis RV Resort▲, Cathedral Palms RV Resort▲
87	County Line Rd, Calimesa Gas N: Shell Food N: Del Taco Lodg N: America's Best Value Inn Other N: Laundromat, Auto & Tire Services	100	CA 243S, 8th St, Banning Gas N: Chevron Food N: IHOP, Jack in the Box, Rest/SG Inn Lodg N: PeachTree Motel, Hacienda Inn, San Gorgonio Inn Other N: Visitor Info Center, Airport✈ S: Stagecoach RV Park▲		
88	Calimesa Blvd, Calimesa Gas N: ArcoAmPm, Chevron, Shell Food N: Jack in the Box, McDonald's, Subway, Taco Bell Lodg N: Calimesa Motor Inn	101	Hargrave St, Banning Gas N: 76, Shell, Valero Food N: Consuelo's Mexican Rest Lodg N: Country Inn Other N: LP/Valero, Carwash/Shell, Towing, Tires S: Banning Muni Airport✈	130	Ramon Rd, Varner Rd, Bob Hope Dr, Thousand Palms, Rancho Mirage, to Palm Springs, Cathedral City TStop N: Flying J Travel Plaza #5020 (Scales) (DAND) Gas N: Chevron, Ultramar, Valero Food N: Carl's Jr, Del Taco, Denny's, In 'n Out Burger, McDonald's Lodg N: Red Roof Inn ♥ S: Westin Hotel TServ N: Flying J TP, Parkhouse Tire, Little Sister Truck Wash Other N: Laundry/WiFi/LP/RVDump/Flying J TP S: Desert Shadows RV Resort▲, Agua Caliente Indian Reservation & Casino Resort & Spa
89	Singleton Rd, Calimesa (WB)	102	Ramsey St (WB) Lodg N: 5 Star Motel, Stagecoach Motor Inn Other N: Morongo Indian Res		
90	Cherry Valley Blvd, Desert Lawn Dr	(102)	Inspection Station/Truck Scales (Both dir)		
(91)	Rest Area (WB) (RR, Phone, Picnic)	103	Fields Rd, Ramsey St, Banning Gas N: Chevron Food N: McDonald's Other N: Desert Hills Factory Stores, Cabazon Outlets		
92	San Timoteo Canyon Rd, Oak Valley Parkway, Beaumont Lodg N: Holiday Inn Express Other N: Premium Outlet Mall	104	Apache Trail, Cabazon FStop N: Morongo Travel Center Gas N: Shell Food N: A&W, Coco's, Hadley's, Ruby's Diner TServ N: Charles Truck Repair Other N: RVDump/LP/Morongo TC, Morongo Indian Res Hotel & Casino/RVParking, Bowling, Desert Hills Factory Stores, Cabazon Outlets	131	Monterey Ave, Thousand Palms, Palm Desert, Rancho Mirage Gas N: ArcoAmPm, Chevron S: Costco Food N: Jack in the Box/Chevron S: IHOP, McDonald's, Panda Express, Subway, Taco Bell Other S: Costco, Home Depot, Sam's Club, Wal-Mart sc
93	CA 60W, Sixth St, Riverside (WB Left exit) Other S: Banning RV Discount Center				
94	CA 79S, Beaumont Ave, Beaumont Gas N: 76, ArcoAmPm Food N: Baker's, McDonald's, El Rancho Steaks S: Denny's, Del Taco Lodg N: Best Western ♥, Best Value Inn, Budget Host Inn, El Rancho Motel Other S: Country Hills RV Park▲, Golden Village Palms RV Resort▲	106	Main St, Cabazon TStop N: Cabazon Truck & Auto Stop/Shell Gas S: ArcoAmPm◆ Food N: Rest/Cabazon TS, Burger King, Spanky's BBQ, Wheel Inn Rest	134	Cook St, to Indian Wells Gas S: ArcoAmPm, Mobil Food S: Applebee's, Jack in the Box, Starbucks Lodg S: Courtyard, Hampton Inn, Residence Inn Med S: + Hospital Other S: Emerald Desert Golf & RV Resort▲, CA State Univ, Animal Clinic ♥
		110	Haugen Lehmann Way		
		111	Verbenia Ave, Haugen-Lehmann Way, Whitewater		
95	Pennsylvania Ave, Beaumont (WB) Gas N: 76/Circle K Food N: ABC, Rusty Lantern Lodg N: Hampton Inn, Mountain Vista Hotel, Windsor Motel Other N: Home Depot, Tom's RV & Trailer Sales S: Country Hills RV Park▲	112	CA 111, to Palm Springs (EB)	137	Washington St, Country Club Dr, Varner Rd, to Indian Wells Gas N: ArcoAmPm, Chevron S: 76, Mobil Food N: Burger King, Coco's, Del Taco, Starbucks S: Carl's Jr, Subway Lodg N: Comfort Suites, Motel 6 ♥ Other N: Auto Dealers, Mailbox Etc, Walgreen's, Thousand Trails RV Park▲, Sky Valley Resort▲, Giant RV
		(113)	Rest Area (Both dir) (RR, Phone, Picnic)		
		114	Whitewater		
96	Highland Springs Ave TStop N: Banning Truck Stop Gas N: ArcoAmPm, Chevron, Valero◆ S: Mobil Food N: Applebee's, Burger King, Denny's, Farmhouse Rest, Jack in the Box, Little Caesar's Pizza, Subway, Wendy's S: Carl's Jr, Chili's, McDonald's Lodg N: Hampton Inn, Super 8 TWash N: Banning TS TServ N: Banning TS Med N: + San Gorgonio Memorial Hospital Other N: Grocery, Walgreen's, Ray's RV	117	CA 62N, TwentyNine Palms, Yucca Valley, to Joshua Tree, NM		

◆ = Regular Gas Stations with Diesel ▲ = RV Friendly Locations ♥ = Pet Friendly Locations

RED PRINT SHOWS LARGE VEHICLE PARKING/ACCESS ON SITE OR NEARBY BROWN PRINT SHOWS CAMPGROUNDS/RV PARKS

Page 35

EXIT		CALIFORNIA
139		Jefferson St, Indio Blvd, Indio (Addt'l Serv appr 3mi S)
	TStop	N: Clark's Truck Stop/PacPride
	Food	N: Rest/Clark's TS
	TWash	N: Clark's TS
	Other	N: CarWash/Laundry/Clark's TS, CA State Hwy Patrol Post, Shadow Hills RV Resort▲, Sunnyside RV Park▲
		S: Bermuda Dunes Airport✈, to County Fairgrounds, Augustine Casino
142		Monroe St, Central Indio
	Gas	S: 76, Shell◆
	Food	S: Carrow's, Denny's
	Lodg	S: Best Western, Comfort Inn, Motel 6♥, Quality Inn, to Super 8
	Med	S: + Hospital
	Other	N: Bob's RV Roundup▲
		S: Target, Indian Waters RV Resort▲, to Augustine Casino
143		Jackson St, Indio
	Gas	S: Circle K
	Food	N: McDonald's
	Other	N: CVS, Home Depot, Super Target, Bob's RV Roundup▲
		S: Amtrak, to Augustine Casino
144		CA 111N, Auto Center Dr, Golf Center Pkwy, Indio
	Food	N: Big America Home Cooking, Mexican Restaurant
	Lodg	N: Holiday Inn Express
	Other	N: Classis RV Park▲, Rancho Casa Blanca Resort▲, Fantasy Springs Casino/Hotel/Rest
		S: Auto Dealers, Fairgrounds, US Post Office
145		CA 86S, Brawley, El Centro (EB)
146		Dillon Rd, to CA 86 Expy, to CA 111S, Coachella
	TStop	N: Love's Travel Stop #207 (Scales)
		S: Travel Center of America #41/Arco (Scales)
	Gas	N: Chevron, Valley Gas
	Food	N: Carl's Jr/Love's TS, Del Taco
		S: Rest/Arby/TB/ChestFrChkn/TA TC
	TServ	S: TA TC
	TWash	S: Eagle TW/TA TC
	Other	N: Laundry/WiFi/RVDump/Love TS, to appr 19 mi Sky Valley Resort▲, Caliente Springs Resort▲
		S: Laundry/BarbSh/WiFi/LP/TA TC, Spotlight 20 Casino, B&K RV Sales, Coachella Valley RV Rentals
	NOTE:	MM 158: WB: Steep Grade
(159)		Rest Area (Both dir) (RR, Phone, Picnic, RVDump/Water)
162		Frontage Rd
168		Cottonwood Springs Rd, Desert Center, to Mecca, Twenty Nine Palms
	Other	N: 29 Palms Resort▲, Joshua Tree National Park
173		Summit Rd, Chiriaco Summit
	FStop	N: Chevron
	Food	N: Café, Chiriaco Summit Coffee Shop
	Other	N: Truck & Tire Repair, Airport
177		Hayfield Rd, Desert Center
182		Red Cloud Mine Rd

Personal Notes

EXIT		CALIFORNIA
189		Eagle Mountain Rd
192		CA 177N, Desert Center Rice Rd, Desert Center, to Lake Tamarisk
	Gas	N: Stanco
	Food	N: Family Café
201		Chuckwalla Valley, Corn Springs Rd, Desert Center
217		Ford Dry Lake Rd
(222)		Wileys Well Rd, State Prison, Desert Center
	N:	Rest Area (Both dir) (RR, Phone, Picnic)
(231)		Inspection Station (WB)
232		Mesa Dr, Airport, Blythe
	FStop	S: Valero
	TStop	N: BB Travel Center/76 (Scales)
	Food	N: Rest/FastFood/BB TC
	TServ	N: BB TC
	TWash	N: BB TC
	Other	N: Laundry/BB TC, Blythe Airport✈
236		CA 78S, Neighbors Blvd, Blythe, to Ripley, Brawley
	FStop	N: CFN/COPA #1373
	Gas	N: Shell, Valero
239		Lovekin Blvd, Blythe
	FStop	N: CFN/COPA #590, Pacific Pride
	Gas	N: ArcoAmPm, Mobil, Shell
		S: 76◆, ArcoAmPm, Chevron, Shell◆
	Food	N: Carl's Jr, Del Taco, Jack in the Box, McDonald's, Pizza Hut, Popeye's, Sizzler, Starbucks

EXIT		CA / AZ
	Food	S: Burger King, Denny's, KFC, Towne Square Café, Taco Bell
	Lodg	N: Best Value Inn, Best Western, Comfort Inn, Days Inn, EZ 8 Motel, Hampton Inn, Willard Inn
		S: Holiday Inn Express, Motel 6♥, Super 8
	TServ	S: Triple A Refrigeration
	Med	N: + Hospital
	Other	N: Ace Hardware, Goodyear, Kmart, Ca Hwy Patrol Post
		S: RVDump/Water/City Park
240		7th St, Blythe
	Gas	N: Chevron
	Food	N: Blimpie, Subway
	Lodg	N: Blue Line Motel, Blythe Inn, Budget Inn, Comfort Suites, Dunes Motel, Paradise Inn
	Med	N: + Hospital
	Other	N: Albertson's/Starbucks/Pharmacy, AutoZone, Laundromat, Carwash, Dollar Tree, RiteAid, LP, RV Repair, Auto Repair, Hwy Patrol Post, Fairgrounds, to Banks, Kmart
241		US 95N, Intake Blvd, Blythe, Needles
	FStop	N: CFN/QuikChek Mobil COPA #2989
	Gas	N: Shell
	Food	N: Steaks & Cakes
	Lodg	N: Best Western, Travelers Inn Express, Willow Inn
	TServ	N: Ramsey Int'l/CAT/Cummins, Detroit Diesel Truck & Trailer Repair
	Other	N: Burton's MH & RV Park▲, Valley Palms RV Park▲
243		Riveria Dr, Blythe, Hobsonway
	Gas	N: Mobil, Shell
	Lodge	N: Desert Inn, Dunes Motel, Economy Inn Express
	Other	N: Fairgrounds
		S: Riviera RV Campground▲, to Destiny McIntyre Campground▲
(244)		Inspection Station (WB)

(PACIFIC TIME ZONE)

⊙ CALIFORNIA

⊙ ARIZONA

(MOUNTAIN TIME ZONE)
(AZ does not observe DST)

1		Posten Rd, Cibola, to Ehrenberg, Parker
	TStop	S: Flying J Travel Plaza #5250 (Scales)
	Food	S: Cookery/Wendy's/FJ TP
	Lodg	S: Best Western/FJ TP
	TWash	S: Flying J TP
	TServ	S: Flying J TP, Two Way CB Shop
	Other	N: Villa Verde RV & MH Park▲, River Breeze RV Park▲
		S: Laundry/CB/WiFi/RVDump/LP/FJ TP
(2)		Port of Entry/Insp Station (EB)
(3)		Inspection Station (WB)
(4)		Rest Area (Both dir) (RR, Phone, Picnic, Vend)
5		Tom Wells Rd, Cibola
	TStop	N: Ultramar/Beacon Truck Stop/Texaco
	Food	N: Quiznos/Texaco

◆ = Regular Gas Stations with Diesel   ▲ = RV Friendly Locations   ♥ = Pet Friendly Locations
RED PRINT SHOWS LARGE VEHICLE PARKING/ACCESS ON SITE OR NEARBY   BROWN PRINT SHOWS CAMPGROUNDS/RV PARKS

EXIT	ARIZONA
11	Dome Rock Rd, Parker
17	I-10 Bus, Quartzsite, US 95S to Yuma, AZ 95N to Parker
TStop	N: Pilot Travel Center #328 (Scales)
	S: Love's Travel Store #286 (Scales), QuikChek Shell
Gas	N: Mobil◇
Food	N: Subway/DQ/Pilot TS, Burger King/Mobil, Carl's Jr, McDonald's, Best Chinese Rest, BBQ, Taco Mio Mexican Rest
	S: ChestersChkn/Subway/Loves TS
Lodg	N: Best Western
	S: Super 8
TServ	N: Amer Custom Tire Truck/Auto/RV
Med	N: + Medical Center
Other	N: WiFi/Pilot TC, Big Market, US Post Office, LP/Mobil, NAPA, Auto & RV Service & Tires, Radio Shack, Hardware Store, Desert Oasis RV Park▲, 88 Shades RV Park▲, B-10 CGA, Holiday Palms RV Park▲, La Mirage RV Park▲, Hasslers RV Park▲
	S: WiFi/RVDump/Love's TS, Laundromat, Tyson Wells RV Park▲, Desert Sands RV Park▲, Paul Everts RV Sales, Guaranty RV Center, RV Lifestyles
19	Bus 10, Quartzsite, to US 95S to Yuma, AZ 95N to Parker
FStop	S: QuikChek Shell
TStop	N: Park Place Travel Center
Gas	N: Chevron◇, Shell
Food	N: Rest/Park Place TC, Taco Miio, Bakery
Other	N: Grocery, Family $, Laundromat, US Post Office, LP, La Mirage RV Park▲, Welcome Friends RV Park▲, La Mesa RV Center, RV Lifestyles, RV Pit Stop/RVDump, RV Corral, Park Plaza RV Resort▲
26	Gold Nugget Rd, Parker
31	US 60E, to Wickenburg, Prescott
45	Vicksburg Rd, to AZ 72N, Parker
TStop	N: Zip's Travel Plaza (Scales)
	S: PTP/Tomahawk AutoTruck Plaza/Valero (Scales)
Food	S: Rest/FastFood/Tomahawk TP
TServ	S: Jobski's Diesel Repair & Towing, C&S Tires
Other	N: LP/Zip's TP, to Black Rock RV Village▲
	S: Laundry/LP/RVDump/TomahawkTP, RV Park▲

EXIT	ARIZONA
(52)	Rest Area (Both dir) (RR, Phone, Picnic, Vend)
53	Hovatter Rd, Roll
69	Ave 75E, Roll
81	Salome Rd, Tonopah, Harquahala Valley Rd
(86)	Rest Area (Both dir) (RR, Phone, Picnic, Vend)
94	411th Ave, Tonopah, El Dorado Hot Springs
TStop	S: Miinute Mart #42/Shell
Gas	S: Chevron◇, Mobil◇
Food	S: Tonapah Family Rest, Subw/NRPizza/Chester's/Shell
Lodg	S: Miineral Wells Motel
Other	S: Laundry/LP/MM TS, US Post Office, El Dorado Hot Springs/RVDump, Saddle Mountain RV Park▲
98	Wintersburg Rd
103	339th Ave, Tonopah
TStop	S: Travel Center of America/Shell (Scales)
Food	S: CountryFare/PHut/Subw/TB/TA TC
TWash	S: TA TC
TServ	S: TA TC
Other	S: Laundry/WiFi/TA TC
109	Sun Valley Pkwy, Palo Verde Rd Buckeye
Other	S: Buckeye Muni Airport✈
112	AZ 85, to I-8, Gila Bend, Phoenix ByPass, I-10E Alt (EB), Yuma, to San Diego, Mexico (WB)
114	Miller Rd, Buckeye
TStop	S: Love's Travel Stop #280 (Scales)
Food	S: Subway/ChestFrChkn/Love's TS, Burger King
Lodg	S: Days Inn
Other	N: Buckeye Military Reservation
	S: Laundry/WiFi/RVDump/Love's TS, Leaf Verde RV Resort▲
117	Watson Rd, Buckeye (EB)
Food	S: Cracker Barrel
Other	S: ATM's, Banks, Fry's, Lowe's, Office Max, Wal-Mart
120	Verrado Way (EB)
121	Jackrabbit Trail, N 195th Ave
Gas	N: Chevron, Phillips 66◇
	S: Circle K
124	Cotton Lane, to Lp 303, Goodyear
Other	N: State Prison

EXIT	ARIZONA
Other	S: DestinyPhoenix RV Resort▲, Cotton Lane RV Resort▲
126	Pebblecreek Pkwy, Estrella Pkwy, to Estrella Park, Goodyear
Gas	S: Safeway
Food	S: Jack in the Box, McDonald's, Panda Express, Subway
Other	S: Safeway, Wal-Mart sc
128	Litchfield Rd, Litchfield Park, Goodyear, Luke Air Force Base
Gas	N: Mobil◇
	S: Chevron, Mobil
Food	N: Applebee's, Arby's, Bennett's BBQ, Chili's, Cracker Barrel, Denny's, McDonald's, TGI Friday, Wendy's
	S: Arby's, Burger King, Taco Bell
Lodg	N: Hampton Inn, Holiday Inn Express
	S: Best Western
Med	S: + Samaritan W Valley Health Center
Other	N: Best Buy, Target, Wildlife World Zoo, to Luke Air Force Base
	S: Albertson's, Osco, Phoenix Goodyear Muni Airport✈, CarWash
129	Dysart Rd, Goodyear, Avondale
Gas	N: Chevron, Shell
	S: Sam's Club
Food	N: Carino's, Jack in the Box, Mimi's, Panda Express, Taco Bell
	S: IHOP, KFC, McDonald's, Waffle House
Lodg	N: Wingate Inn
	S: Best Value Inn, Comfort Inn, Super 8, Ramada
Other	N: Lowe's, Fry's, PetSmart♥, Wal-Mart sc
	S: Walgreen's, Home Depot, Sam's Club
131	115th Ave, Avondale Blvd, Phoenix Int'l Raceway, to Cashion
Gas	N: Mobil
Lodg	S: Hilton Garden Inn
Other	S: Phoenix Int'l Raceway
132	107th Ave (EB)
Other	S: Auto Dealers
133A	99th Ave (EB), 107th Ave, Avondale
TStop	S: Pilot Travel Center #459 (Scales)
Gas	N: Chevron
	S: Costco
Food	N: Carrabba's, McDonald's
	S: Subway/Wendys/Pilot TC
TServ	S: Freightliner
Other	N: Costco, PetCo♥, + West Valley Naturopathic Canter, Walgreen's
	S: Laundry/WiFi/Pilot TC, Earnhardt's RV Center, Auto Dealers
133B	AZ 101N Loop
134	91st Ave, Tolleson

◇ = Regular Gas Stations with Diesel ▲ = RV Friendly Locations ♥ = Pet Friendly Locations

RED PRINT SHOWS LARGE VEHICLE PARKING/ACCESS ON SITE OR NEARBY   BROWN PRINT SHOWS CAMPGROUNDS/RV PARKS

INTERSTATE 10 W/E

EXIT	ARIZONA
NOTE:	MM 134: Begin HOV Lane (EB) End (WB)
135	**83rd Ave, Phoenix**
Gas	N: Circle K
Food	N: Arby's, Jack in the Box, Waffle House
Lodg	N: Comfort Suites, Econo Lodge
Other	N: Sam's Club
(136A)	**HOV Exit-79th Ave (WB)**
136B	**75th Ave, Phoenix**
Gas	N: Circle K, Chevron
	S: ArcoAmPm
Food	N: Denny's, Starbucks, PizzaHut/Taco Bell, Whataburger
Other	N: Lowe's, Wal-Mart sc, Home Depot, Staples, PetSmart♥, CarWash, Desert Sky Mall
137	**67th Ave, Phoenix**
TStop	S: Flying J Travel Plaza #5006 (Scales)
Gas	N: QT, 76/Circle K, Shell
Food	N: Church's Chicken
	S: CountryMarket/FastFood/FJ TP
Other	S: Laundry/WiFi/BarbSh/LP/RVDump/FJ TP
138	**59th Ave, Phoenix**
TStop	S: PTP/Liberty Fuel (Scales)
Gas	N: 7-11, Circle K
Food	N: Mexican
	S: Waffle House, Whataburger
TWash	S: Liberty Fuel/Tires
Other	N: Auto Zone, Walgreen's
	S: Laundry/WiFi/Liberty Fuel
139	**51st Ave, Phoenix**
Gas	N: Circle K, Chevron◊
Food	N: Burger King, El Pollo Loco, Chinese, McDonald's, Waffle House
	S: Carl's Jr, IHOP, Taco Bell
Lodg	N: Budget Inn, Days Inn, Holiday Inn, Motel 6♥, Red Roof Inn♥, Travelodge
	S: Fairfield Inn, Hampton Inn, Super 8
Other	N: 7-11, Auto Services, Laundromat, Discount Tire, Food City
140	**43rd Ave**
Gas	N: 7-11, Circle K, Mobil
	S: 7-11, Chevron, Circle K
Food	N: KFC, Subway, Wendy's
Med	N: + Priority Medical Center
Other	N: Walgreen's, Fry's, AutoZone
141	**35th Ave, Phoenix**
FStop	N: Bair's Gas Stop
Gas	N: Circle K
	S: Shell
Food	N: Jack in the Box
142	**27th Ave, State Capitol (EB)**
FStop	N: AFCO Gas
Gas	N: 7-11, Circle K
	S: Pacific Pride
Lodg	N: Comfort Inn
(143A)	**Jct I-17N, to Flagstaff**
(143B)	**Jct I-17S, US 60E, I-10 Trk Rte (EB)**
	Jct I-17S (WB), Phoenix
143C	**19th Ave, State Capitol, Fair grounds, Coliseum (WB)**
144	**7th Ave (WB)**
Other	S: Downtown Cultural, Sports Facilities
144A	**7th Ave (EB)** (HazMat MUST Exit)
Other	S: Downtwn Cultural, Sports Facilities
(144B)	**HOV Exit - 5th Ave, 3rd Ave (EB)**

Personal Notes
_____
_____
_____
_____
_____
_____
_____
_____
_____
_____
_____
_____
_____
_____
_____
_____
_____
_____

EXIT	ARIZONA
145	**7th St, Downtown**
	HOV Exit-3rd St (WB)
Gas	S: Circle K, Chevron, Shell
Food	N: McDonald's
Med	S: + Hospital
Other	S: Walgreen's
146	**16th St (EB)**
Gas	N: Circle K
	S: Circle K
Food	N: KFC
	S: Church's Chicken, Jack in the Box
Other	S: Kmart
147A	**AZ 202E Loop, to Mesa**
	HOV Exit - 202E (EB), HOV Exit- AZ 51N (WB)
147B	**AZ 51N, to Paradise Valley**
148	**Washington St, Jefferson St**
Gas	N: Chevron, Exxon
	S: Circle K
Food	N: Carl's Jr, McDonald's, Rally's
Lodg	N: Motel 6♥, Rodeway Inn
Med	S: + Hospital
Other	N: Airport Rental Car Return
149	**Sky Harbor Int'l Airport (EB), Buckeye Rd, Sky Harbor Center, Int'l Airport (WB)**
Lodg	N: Howard Johnson, Motel 6♥
Other	N: Airport, Greyhound
(150)	**Jct I-17N, to Flagstaff (EB)**
(150A)	**Jct I-17N to Flagstaff, US 60W to Wickenburg, I-10 Truck Rte (WB)**

EXIT	ARIZONA
150B	**24th St E (WB)**
Gas	N: Exxon
Food	N: Durados, Rest/Golden 9
	S: Rest/BW
Lodg	N: Golden 9 Motel, Knights Inn, Motel 6♥, Rodeway Inn
	S: Best Western
TServ	N: Purcell Western States Tire
151	**32nd St, University Dr (EB)**
151AB	**32nd St, University Dr, AZ State University**
Gas	S: Circle K
Lodg	N: Extended Stay America, La Quinta Inn♥, Radisson
Other	N: Univ of Phoenix
152	**40th St, Univ of Phoenix**
Gas	N: Shell◊
	S: Circle K
Food	S: Burger King
153	**AZ 143, 48th St, Broadway Rd (EB)**
Gas	S: Shell
Food	N: Denny's
Lodg	N: Comfort Suites, Courtyard, Fairfield Inn, Hilton, La Quinta Inn♥, Red Roof Inn♥, Sheraton
	S: Hampton Inn
TServ	N: Purcell Western States Tire
Other	N: Tempe Diablo Stadium
153A	**AZ 143N, Hohokam Expy, 48th St, to Sky Harbor Int'l Airport (WB)**
153B	**Broadway Rd, 52nd St (WB)**
	HOV Exit - US 60E (EB)
154	**US 60E, AZ 360, Superstition Fwy, to Tempe, Mesa, Apache Junction**
Other	N: to Mesa Spirit Resort▲
155	**Baseline Rd, Guadalupe**
Gas	N: 76, Mobil, Shell◊
Food	N: Carl's Jr, Jack in the Box, Shoney's, Waffle House
	S: Aunt Chilada's, Denny's
Lodg	N: AmeriSuites, Candlewood Suites, Holiday Inn, Ramada Inn, Residence Inn, Towneplace Suites
	S: Motel 6♥
Other	N: AZ Mills, Tourist Info
157	**Elliot Rd, Guadalupe, Tempe**
Gas	N: Circle K, Chevron
	S: 76, Mobil◊
Food	N: Applebee's, Arby's, Black Eyed Pea, Burger King, Chili's, Coco's, Kyoto's, Olive Garden, Red Robin, Taco Bell, Subway, Wendy's
	S: KFC, McDonald's, Pizza Hut
Lodg	N: Country Suites
	S: Best Western, Clarion, Quality Inn
Other	N: Costco, PetSmart♥, Staples, U-Haul, Wal-Mart
	S: Walgreen's, Auto Dealers
158	**Warner Rd, Tempe**
Gas	N: 76, Circle K
	S: ArcoAmPm
	S: Burger King, Chuck E Cheese, DQ, Quizno's, McDonald's, Taco Bell
Other	S: Osco, U-Haul, Tempe Auto Plex
159	**Ray Rd, Phoenix, Chandler**
Gas	N: 76, Shell◊
	S: Circle K, Exxon

◊ = Regular Gas Stations with Diesel ▲ = RV Friendly Locations ♥ = Pet Friendly Locations
RED PRINT SHOWS LARGE VEHICLE PARKING/ACCESS ON SITE OR NEARBY BROWN PRINT SHOWS CAMPGROUNDS/RV PARKS

EXIT		ARIZONA
	Food	N: Carraba's, McDonald's, Outback Steakhouse, Red Lobster S: BBQ, IHOP, Jack in the Box, Mimi's Café, Romano's Macaroni Grill, Sweet Tomatoes, Wendy's
	Lodg	N: Courtyard S: Extended Stay America
	Other	N: Home Depot, Lowe's, Sam's Club S: Albertson's, Best Buy, PetSmart♥, Target, Osco, Auto Dealers
	Med	S: + Thomas Davis Medical Center
160		Chandler Blvd, Pecos Rd, Phoenix, Chandler
	Gas	N: Circle K, Exxon, Mobil S: 7-11, Chevron, Phillips 66
	Food	N: Burger King, Damon's, Denny's, Perkins, Sizzler, Whataburger S: Cracker Barrel, Del Taco,
	Lodg	N: Fairfield Inn, Hampton Inn, Red Roof Inn♥, Super 8, Wyndham Garden Hotel S: Extended Stay America, La Quinta Inn♥, Holiday Inn Express, Intown Suites
	Med	S: + Hospital, + Awhatukee Foothills Medical Center
	NOTE:	MM 160: HOV Lane Ends EB, Begin WB
161		Loop 202E, Pecos Rd, Chandler
162		Wild Horse Pass Blvd, Sundust Rd, Firebird Sports Park (SB)
	TStop	N: Love's Travel Stop #328 (Scales)
	Food	N: Arby's/TJCinn/Love's TS
	Lodg	S: Wild Horse Pass Resort & Spa
	TServ	N: Freightliner
	Other	N: WiFi/Love's TS, Beaudry RV Center S: Firebird Sports Park, Firebird Int'l Raceway, Gila Bend Casino, Lone Butte Casino, Wild Horse Pass Casino, Gila River Indian Reservation
162A		Wild Horse Pass Blvd, Maricopa Rd, Chandler (EB)
162B		S Maricopa Rd, Chandler (EB)
164		Queen Creek Rd , AZ 347S, Maricopa, Ak-Chin Indian Comm
	Other	N: to Harrah's Casino S: Ak Chin Indian Comm
167		Riggs Rd, Sun Lakes
	FStop	N: Chevron
175		AZ 587, Casa Blanca Rd, Sacaton, Chandler, Gilbert
	Gas	S: Shell◆
	Other	S: Casa Blanca RV Park▲, Gila Indian Center
(181)		Rest Area (EB) (RR, Phone, Picnic, Vend, Info)
(183)		Rest Area (WB) (RR, Phone, Picnic, Vend)
185		AZ 187, AZ 387, Bus Loop 10, to Casa Grande, Sacaton, Florence
	Lodg	S: Francisco Grand Hotel & Golf Resort
	Other	S: Val Vista RV Village▲, Foothills RV Resort▲, Leisure Valley RV Resort▲, AZ State Hwy Patrol, Casa Grande Muni Airport✈
190		McCartney Rd, Central AZ Coll
	Other	N: to Central AZ College S: Casita Verde RV Resort▲, Desert Shadows RV Resort▲, Casa Grande Airport✈

EXIT		ARIZONA
194		AZ 287, Florence Blvd, Coolidge, Bus 10, Casa Grande
	Gas	S: ArcoAmPm◆, Chevron
	Food	S: Burger King, Cracker Barrel, Del Taco, Denny's, DQ/Chevron, Golden Corral, IHOP, JB's Rest
	Lodg	S: Best Western♥, Comfort Inn, Francisco Grand Hotel & Golf Resort, Mainstay Suites, Super 8
	Med	S: + Hospital
	Other	N: to appr 7mi Sunscape RV Resort▲, Pinal Co Fairgrounds, Mall S: Wal-Mart sc, Fry's, Albertson's, Walgreen's, to Palm Creek Golf & RV Resort▲, Fiesta Grande RV Resort▲
198		Jimmie Kerr Blvd, AZ 84, AZ 93, Casa Grande, to Eloy
	Food	S: Wendy's
	Other	S: Buena Tierra RV Park & CG▲, Outlets at Casa Grande, Dobson Ranch Golf Course
(199)		Jct I-8W, to Yuma, San Diego (Phoenix ByPass)
200		Sunland Gin Rd, Arizona City
	TStop	N: Petro Stopping Center #6 (Scales), Pride Travel Center S: Love's Travel Stop #265
	Food	N: Rest/Sunland Inn, Subway/Pride TC, Rest/Petro SC, Burger King, Mex Rest S: Golden 9 Family Rest, Arby's/Love's TS, Starbucks
	Lodg	N: Days Inn, Sunland Inn S: Motel 6♥

EXIT		ARIZONA
	TServ	N: Petro SC, Southwest Towing, Rocha's Truck Tire & Diesel Service S: Speedco
	TWash	N: Blue Beacon TW/Petro SC, Eagle Truck Wash
	Other	N: Laundry/Petro SC, Las Colinas RV Park▲ S: WiFi/Love's TS, High Chaparral RV Park▲, Quail Run RV Resort▲, AZ City Golf Course, Eddie's Auto & RV Service
203		Toltec Rd, to Eloy
	TStop	S: Travel Center of America/Exxon (Scales)
	FStop	S: Circle K Truxtop #2947
	Gas	N: Chevron
	Food	N: Carl's Jr, Mexican, Waffle House, McDonald's/Chevron S: Rest/TBell/TA TC, Pizza Hut
	Lodg	N: Best Value Inn, Knights Inn, Red Roof Inn♥, Super 8, Toltec Inn
	TWash	S: TA TC, Blue Beacon TW/Circle K TS
	TServ	N: West's I-10 Diesel S: TA TC/Tires
	Other	N: Golden Corridor RV Park▲, Desert Valley RV Resort▲ S: Laundry/WiFi/RVDump/TA TC
208		Sunshine Blvd, Eloy
	TStop	N: Pilot Travel Center #458 (Scales) (DAD) (DAND) S: Flying J Travel Plaza #5310/Conoco (Scales)
	Food	N: DQ/Subway/Pilot TC S: Cookery/FastFood/FJ TP
	TWash	S: Blue Beacon TW/FJ TP
	TServ	N: Diesel Service, M&M Truck Polishing
	Other	N: Laundry/WiFi/Pilot TC S: Laundry/WiFi/LP/RVDump/FJ TP
211A		Picacho, State Prison (EB)
	Other	S: Picacho RV Park▲, State Prison
211B		AZ 87N, to Coolidge
212		Picacho (WB)
	Other	S: State Prison
219		Picacho Peak Rd, Picacho
	Gas	N: Picacho Plaza/Citgo, Mobil
	Food	N: DQ/PP, Eddie's Bar & Grill
	Other	S: Picacho Peak RV Resort▲, Picacho Peak State Park▲, Ostrich Ranch
226		Sasco Rd, Red Rock
(228)		WB pull off, to Frontage Rd, APS Power Plant
232		Pinal Air Park Rd, Army National Guard Aviation Training Site
	Other	S: Pinal Airpark✈
236		Marana Rd, Marana
	Gas	S: 76, Circle K, Chevron◆
	Other	S: Valley of the Sun RV Park▲
240		Tangerine Rd, Oro Valley, Marana, to Rillito
	Other	N: A Bar A Campground▲
242		Avra Valley Rd, Marana
	Other	S: Avra Valley Airport✈
246		Cortaro Rd, Tucson
	Gas	N: Circle K, Chevron◆ S: Shell◆
	Food	N: Arby's, IHOP, Wendy's S: Burger King, Chili's, Cracker Barrel, KFC, McDonald's, Starbucks, Texas Roadhouse

◆ = Regular Gas Stations with Diesel   ▲ = RV Friendly Locations   ♥ = Pet Friendly Locations
RED PRINT SHOWS LARGE VEHICLE PARKING/ACCESS ON SITE OR NEARBY   BROWN PRINT SHOWS CAMPGROUNDS/RV PARKS

Page 39

EXIT		ARIZONA
	Lodg	S: Best Western, Days Inn, Holiday Inn Express, La Quinta Inn♥, Quality Inn, Super 8
	Other	S: Wal-Mart sc▲, to Saguaro Nat'l Park, RVCamping▲
248		Ina Rd, Tucson, Marana
	Gas	N: Circle K, Chevron◊
		S: Circle K, Exxon
	Food	N: Arby's, Burger King, Carl's Jr, DQ, Hooters, Jack in the Box, McDonald's, Pizza Hut, Taco Bell, Waffle House
		S: Denny's
	Lodg	N: Motel 6♥
		S: Comfort Inn♥, Park Inn, Red Roof Inn♥, Travelodge
	Other	N: Fry's, Lowe's, Office Depot, Target
		S: LP/Circle K, Sports Parks of America, Purcell Tire Center
250		Orange Grove Rd, Marana
	Gas	N: ArcoAmPm, Circle K
	Food	N: Wendy's
	Other	N: Costco, Home Depot, PetSmart♥, National RV Central
251		Sunset Rd, Frontage Rd, Tucson El Camino Del Cerro (EB)
	Other	N: National RV Central
252		El Camino Del Cerro, Ruthrauff Rd, Frontage Rd, Tucson (WB)
	Gas	N: ArcoAmPm
		S: Chevron
	Food	S: Jack in the Box/Chevron
	Other	S: Big Tex Trailers
254		Prince Rd, Tucson
	Gas	N: Circle K, Diamond Shamrock
	Lodg	S: Best Western
	TServ	N: Cummins SW, Thermo King Service
		S: Inland Kenwoth
	Other	N: U-Haul
		S: Prince of Tucson RV Park▲, Silverbell Golf Course
255		AZ 77N, Miracle Mile
256		Grant Rd, Tucson
	Gas	S: 76, Circle K, Exxon, Shell, Shamrock
	Food	N: Sonic
		S: IHOP, Subway, Waffle House
	Lodg	S: Hampton Inn, Holiday Inn Express, La Quinta Inn♥, Quality Inn, Super 8
	Other	S: Office Max, Walgreen's
257		Speedway Blvd, St Mary's Rd, Univ of AZ, Pima Comm College
	Gas	N: 7-11
		S: ArcoAmPm◊
	Lodg	S: Best Western
	Med	N: + Hospital
	Other	N: Office Depot, AZ Victory, to Univ of AZ
257A		St. Mary's Rd
	Gas	N: 76◊
		S: Shell
	Food	S: Burger King, Denny's, Jack in the Box
	Lodg	N: Inn Suites
		S: La Quinta Inn♥, Ramada
	Med	N: + Hospital
	Other	S: U-Haul
258		Congress St, Broadway Blvd, Conv Center, Downtown Tucson
	Gas	N: Circle K
	Food	N: Mexican, Sizzler
		S: Bennigan's, Carl's Jr
	Lodg	N: Holiday Inn, Motel 6♥, Ramada Inn
		S: Days Inn, Riverpark Inn
	Other	S: Amtrak

Arizona Legends RV Resort

PURCHASE YOUR SPOT!
AVAILABLE NOW!
Lots for You To Customize
Park Models to Purchase
More New Developments

Come, park your wagon where Geronimo and Cochise roamed, the Butterfield Stage was the main means of traveling, and Wyatt Earp, "Doc" Holliday, and other famous lawmen tamed the west.

1915 Casa Del Rio Drive
Benson, AZ 85602
(520) 586-1504
arizonalegendsrv.com
Exit #302 S. 1/2 Mile On 90

EXIT		ARIZONA
259		22nd St, 20th St, Starr Pass Blvd
	Gas	N: Circle K◊
		S: 76
	Food	S: Kettle, Waffle House
	Lodg	S: Comfort Inn, Holiday Inn Express, Howard Johnson, La Quinta♥, Motel 6♥, Super 8, Travel Inn
(260)		Jct I-19S, to Nogales
261		Bus Loop 19, 4th Ave-6th Ave
	Gas	N: Chevron
	Food	S: Burger King, Silver Saddle Steakhouse
	Lodg	N: Budget Inn, Econo Lodge, Star Motel, Quality Inn, Super Inn Motel
		S: Economy Inn, Lazy 8 Motel, Rodeway Inn
	TServ	S: Peterbilt
	Other	N: Food City
262		Bus Lp 10, Benson Hwy, Park Ave
	Gas	S: ArcoAmPm, Chevron, Shell
	Food	S: McDonald's, Waffle House, Rest/QI
	Lodg	S: Best Value Inn, Howard Johnson, Motel 6♥, Quality Inn, Rodeway Inn, Western Inn
	TServ	S: Peterbilt
263		Ajo Way, Kino Pkwy (WB)
	Gas	N: Chevron
	Med	N: + University Physicians Hospital
	Other	S: Oasis RV Center, Tucson Int'l Airport✈
263A		Kino Pkwy S (EB)
263B		Kino Pkwy N, Ajo Way (EB)
264		Irvington Rd, Palo Verde Rd (WB)
	Gas	N: Chevron◊

EXIT		ARIZONA
	Gas	S: Quik Mart
	Food	N: Carl's Jr, Denny's, Waffle House, Wendy's/Chevron
		S: Arby's, McDonald's
	Lodg	N: Days Inn, Fairfield Inn, Holiday Inn, Red Roof Inn♥
		S: Motel 6♥, Ramada Inn♥
	Med	N: + University Physicians Hospital
	Other	N: Freedom RV, Ed Hannon RV Center, Tucson Expo Center
		S: Fry's, Food City, Factory Outlet Mall, Beaudry RV, Camping World, La Mesa RV Center, Pedata RV & Rentals, Beaudry RV Resort▲ / RVDump
264A		Palo Verde Rd S (EB)
	Other	S: to Apollo RV Park▲
264B		Palo Verde Rd N, Irvington Rd (EB)
	Other	S: Kino Sports Complex
265		Alvernon Way, Davis-Monthan Air Force Base
	Other	N: Freedom RV
267		Valencia Rd, Tucson International Airport (EB), Valencia Rd, I-10 Bus Lp, Benson Hwy, Airport (WB)
	Gas	N: ArcoAmPm
	Food	N: Jack in the Box/Arco
	Lodg	S: Apache Tears Motel
	Other	N: Davis-Monthan Air Force Base
		S: Tucson Int'l Airport✈
268		Craycroft Rd, Tucson
	TStop	N: Triple T/Tucson Truck Terminal, Mr T's Conoco (Scales)
	Gas	N: 76/Circle K
	Food	N: Rest/FastFood/Triple T TS
	Lodg	N: Motel/Triple T TS
	TWash	N: Tucson Truck & RV Wash/Triple T TS
	TServ	N: Triple T TS
		S: Interstate Diesel Service
	Other	N: Laundry/CB/PostOffice/RVDump/LP/Triple T TS, Crazy Horse Campground & RV Park/LP▲
269		Wilmot Rd, Tucson
	Gas	N: Chevron◊
		S: Shell
	Food	N: A&W/Chevron
		S: Quiznos/Shell
	Lodg	N: Travel Inn
	Other	N: to Pima Air Museum
270		Kolb Rd, Tucson
	FStop	N: Gas City
	Gas	N: Chevron
	Other	N: RVDump/Carwash/Gas City, to 6mi Rincon Country East RV Resort▲
		S: Voyager RV Resort & Rentals▲
273		Rita Rd
	FStop	N: Rita Ranch Fuels
	Gas	N: Shell
	Other	S: Pima Co Fairgrounds
275		Houghton Rd, Tucson
	Other	N: ABTucson/Cactus Country RV Resort▲, to Saguaro Natl Park
279		Vail Rd, Wentworth Rd, Vail
	Other	N: to Colossal Caves
281		AZ 83S, to Sonoita, Patagonia
289		Marsh Station Rd, Mt Lemmon
292		Empirita Rd
297		Mescal Rd, J-Six Ranch Rd
	Gas	N: Quick Pic◊

◊ = Regular Gas Stations with Diesel   ▲ = RV Friendly Locations   ♥ = Pet Friendly Locations
RED PRINT SHOWS LARGE VEHICLE PARKING/ACCESS ON SITE OR NEARBY   BROWN PRINT SHOWS CAMPGROUNDS/RV PARKS

EXIT		ARIZONA
	Food	N: Deli/QP
299		Skyline Rd, Benson
302		AZ 90S, Benson, to Ft. Huachuca, Sierra Vista
	TStop	S: AmBest/Gas City #90/Coastal
	Gas	S: Shell
	Food	S: KFC/Taco Bell, McDonald's, Subway/Shell, Pizza Hut/Gas City TS
	Lodg	S: Holiday Inn Express, Motel 6 ♥
	TWash	S: Gas City TS
	Other	S: Cochise Terrace RV Resort▲, LP/RVDump/Gas City TS, RV/Car Wash, Arizona Legends RV Resort▲ (See AD Page 40) to Karchner Caverns, to Fort Huachuca Nat'l Historic Site
303		W 4th St, Benson, Bus 10, AZ 80, to Bisbee, Tombstone (EB)
	Gas	S: Mobil◊, Shell◊
	Food	S: Chinese, Mexican, Wendy's
	Lodg	S: Cavern Garden Motel, Quarter Horse RV Park▲ & Motel
	Other	S: Pardner's RV Park▲, Butterfield RV Resort & Observatory▲, Safeway, NAPA, Wal-Mart sc
304		Ocotillo St, Benson
	Gas	S: Chevron, Texaco
	Food	N: Denny's, Jack in the Box S: Apple Farm Rest, Burger King, Country Folks, Wendy's
	Lodg	N: Baymont Inn, Days Inn, Motel 6 ♥, Super 8 ♥ S: Best Western, Quail Hollow Inn
	Med	S: + Hospital
	Other	N: Benson KOA▲, Benson I-10 RV Park▲, Red Barn Campground▲, S: Pardner's RV Park▲, Dillons RV Sales, Family Dollar, Laundry, Safeway, US Post Office
306		Pomerene Rd, Benson (EB), AZ 80, Bus Loop 10 (WB)
	Gas	S: Mobil◊
	Food	S: Pizza
	Other	S: San Pedro RV Park▲, Pata Blanco Lakes RV Park▲, Amtrak
312		Sibyl Rd, Benson
318		Dragoon Rd, Benson
	Other	S: to Camping▲
(320)		Rest Area (Both dir) (RR, Phone, Picnic, Vend)
322		Johnson Rd, Benson
	FStop	S: Citgo◊
	Food	S: DQ/Citgo
331		US 191S, Sun Sites, Douglas

EXIT		ARIZONA
336		Bus Loop 10, Willcox
	FStop	S: Freeway Chevron
	Food	S: KFC
	Lodge	S: Desert Inn Motel
	Other	N: Cochise Co Airport✈ S: LP/Frwy Chevron, Ft Willcox RV Park▲, Lifestyle RV Resort▲
340		AZ 186, Rex Allen Dr, S Fort Grant Rd, Willcox
	FStop	S: Mobil
	TStop	N: Travel Center of America/Shell (Scales) S: Wilcox Travel Plaza/Chevron
	Gas	S: 76/Circle K
	Food	N: CountryFare/Subway/Popeye/TA TC S: Rest/Wilcox TC, Burger King, KFC, Mexican, Pizza Hut, McDonald's
	Lodg	N: Holiday Inn Express, Super 8 S: Best Western, Days Inn, Motel 6
	TWash	N: 340 Truck Wash
	TServ	N: TA TC, Freightliner
	Med	S: + N Cochise Comm Hospital
	Other	N: Laundry/WiFi/LP/RVDump/TA TC, Magic Circle RV Park▲, Crop Circle Winery S: Laundry/Wilcox TC, AutoZone, Big O Tire, Family Dollar, Food City, IGA, Safeway, Dicks Tire & Auto, RV & Truck, Chiricahua Nat'l Monument, Grande Vista RV Park▲, Lifestyle RV Resort▲
344		I-10 Bus Lp, Wilcox
	Gas	S: Chevron◊
	TServ	S: Wilcox Diesel Service
	Other	S: LP/Chevron, Coronado Vineyards, Lifestyle RV Resort▲
352		US 191N, to Safford
	Other	N: Roper Lake St Park
355		US 191N, to Safford
362		I-10 Bus Lp, Bowie
366		I-10 Bus Lp, Bowie
	FStop	N: Shell
	Food	N: Subway/BaskinRobbins/Shell
	Other	N: Alaskan RV Park▲, Ft Bowie Nat'l Historic Site
378		I-10 Bus Loop, San Simon
	TStop	N: 4K Truck Stop/Chevron (Scales)
	Gas	N: Shell
	Food	N: Rest/Chester Fr Chicken/4K TS, Kactus Kafe/Shell
	TServ	N: 4K TS/Tires, Car/Diesel/RV Repair, CAT
	Other	N: LP/4K TS
382		I-10 Bus Lp, Portal Rd, San Simon (access to Ex #378 Serv)

EXIT		AZ / NM
(383)		Weigh Station (EB) Inspection Station (WB)
(389)		Rest Area (Both dir) (RR, Phone, Picnic, Vend)
390		Cavot Rd, San Simon
	NOTE:	MM 391: NM State Line

(MOUNTAIN TIME ZONE, NO DST)

◐ **ARIZONA**
◓ **NEW MEXICO**

(MOUNTAIN TIME ZONE)

3		CR A12, Steins Rd, Steins, Lordsburg
5		NM 80S, Lordsburg, to Road Forks, Douglas, AZ, Agua Prieta, MX
	TStop	S: USA Travel Plaza #802 (Scales)
	Food	S: Rest/USA TP
	TServ	S: USA TP, CAT Service
	Other	S: Laundry/USA TP
11		NM 338S, to Animas
15		to Gary
20A		W Motel Dr, Lordsburg (EB)
20B		W Motel Dr, Lordsburg (EB)
20		W Motel Dr, Lordsburg
	S:	NM Welcome Center (EB) (RR, Phone, Picnic, WiFi, Info)
	FStop	S: Chevron
	TStop	N: Love's Travel Stop #276 (Scales)
	Food	N: Subway/Pizza/Love's TS S: GreenChiliGrill/Chevron
	Lodg	N: Days Inn
	Other	N: WiFi/RVDump/Love's TS
22		NM 494, US 70, Main St, Lordsburg, Silver City, Globe Az
	Gas	N: Save Gas, Snappy, Shamrock S: Chevron
	Food	N: DQ, McDonald's S: KFC, Taco Bell, Kranberry's Rest
	Lodg	N: Comfort Inn, Economy Inn, Holiday Motel, Days Inn S: Best Western, Holiday Inn Express, Motel 10, Super 8
	TServ	N: Oscar's Truck Service
	Other	N: Family Dollar S: Lordsburg KOA▲, Lordsburg Muni Airport✈, Amtrak, Laundromat
(23)		Weigh Station (Both dir)

◊ = Regular Gas Stations with Diesel ▲ = RV Friendly Locations ♥ = Pet Friendly Locations

RED PRINT SHOWS LARGE VEHICLE PARKING/ACCESS ON SITE OR NEARBY BROWN PRINT SHOWS CAMPGROUNDS/RV PARKS

Page 41

EXIT		NEW MEXICO
24		US 70W, I-10 Bus Loop, E Motel Dr, Lordsburg (acc to Ex #22 Serv)
	TStop	N: Pilot Travel Center #163 (Scales), Flying J Travel Plaza (Scales)
	Gas	N: Chevron
	Food	N: Arby's/TJCinn/Pilot TC, Rest/Fast Food/FJ TP
	Lodg	N: Budget Motel, Days Inn
	TServ	N: Great Western Truck Service, Towing, Tires
	Other	N: Laundry/WiFi/Pilot TC, Laundry/WiFi/RVDump/LP/FJ TP, Range RV Park▲, Amtrak
		S: Lordsburg Muni Airport✈
29		Ulmoris, Turbin
34		NM 113, Hurley, Playas, Muir, Lisbon
42		Separ Rd, Hurley, Separ
	Food	S: Continental Divide
	Other	N: Truck & Tire Repair
49		NM 146, Hachita, Antelope Wells
(51)		Continental Divide
(53)		Rest Area (EB) (RR, Picnic, Vend)
55		Frontage Rd, Deming, Quincy
(61)		Rest Area (WB) (RR, Picnic, Vend)
62		CR D094, to Gage
	FStop	S: Butterfield Station/Exxon
	Food	S: DQ/Exxon
	Other	S: Butterfield Station RV Park▲
68		NM 418, CR D006, Deming
	TStop	S: PTP/Savoy Travel Center
	Food	S: Rest/Savoy TC
	TWash	S: Savoy TC
	TServ	S: Savoy TC/Tires
	Other	S: Laundry/Savoy TC
81		I-10 Bus, Pine St, W Motel Dr, Deming
	TStop	S: Deming Truck Stop/Fina
	Gas	S: Chevron, Conoco◆, Shell, Shamrock◆
	Food	S: Rest/Deming TT, Rest/Grand Hotel, Rest/Western Motel, Arby's, Burger King, McDonald's, Sonic, Taco Bell
	Lodg	S: Balboa Motel, Best Western, Grand Hotel, Comfort Inn, Deluxe Inn, Deming Motel, Exel Inn, Super 8, Western Motel
	Tires	S: Deming TS
	TWash	S: Truck & RV Wash/Deming TS
	Med	S: + Hospital
	Other	N: City of Rocks State Park
		S: Laundry/LP/Deming TS, 81 Palms RV Park▲, Pancho Villa St Park, Rock Hound State Park
82A		US 180, NM 26, Deming, Silver City (Shortcut to I-25)
	Gas	N: Fina
		S: Chevron, Exxon, Shell
	Food	N: Blake's, Burger King, Lotaburger
		S: Burger King, Cactus Café, Denny's, K-Bob's Steakhouse, KFC, Long John Silver's, McDonald's, Pizza Hut, Subway
	Lodg	S: Grand Motel, Starlight Village Motel & RV Park▲
	TServ	S: Great Western Truck Service, Truck & Tire Repair

Personal Notes
_____

EXIT		NEW MEXICO
	Other	N: Silver City KOA▲, Amtrak
		S: AutoZone, Grocery, Kmart, Wal-Mart sc, Propane/LP, to Pancho Villa State Park, Rock Hound State Park
82B		Cedar St, Pearl St, Deming
	Gas	S: Chevron, Fina, Texaco
	Food	S: DQ, KFC, Rancher's Rest
	Lodg	S: Best Western, Days Inn, Holiday Inn, Grand Motor Inn, Motel 6♥
	Other	S: Auto Dealers, Goodyear, Little RV Park▲, Roadrunner RV Park▲, Wagon Wheel RV Park▲
85		I-10 Bus Lp, US 70, E Motel Dr, E Deming
	Gas	S: Chevron, Shell
	Lodg	S: Days Inn, Holiday Inn, La Quinta Inn♥, Motel 6♥
	Other	S: NM St Hwy Patrol, Deming Muni Airport✈
102		CR B049, Akela
	Gas	N: Bowlin's Exxon
(111)		Parking Area (WB)
116		NM 549, Las Cruces
(120)		US Border Patrol Checkpoint Inspection Station (WB) Parking Area (EB)
127		Corralones Rd, Las Cruces
	Gas	N: Bowlin's Old West Trading Post/Exxon
	Other	S: Fairgrounds, NM Corr Facility
132		Las Cruces Int'l Airport
	TStop	S: Love's Travel Stop #259 (Scales)
	Food	S: Subway/Love's TS

EXIT		NEW MEXICO
	Other	N: Airport✈
		S: WiFi/Love's TS
135		I-10 Bus, US 70E, Las Cruces, Alamo Gordo, Roswell
	Other	N: Las Cruces KOA▲
		S: Best View RV Park▲
(135)		Rest Area (EB) (RR, Phone, Picnic, RVDump)
139		NM 292, Motel Blvd, Las Cruces Amador Ave, Mesilla
	Fstop	S: Pacific Pride/Porter Oil Co
	TStop	N: Pilot Travel Center #226 (Scales), Travel Center of America #14/Shell (Scales)
	Food	N: Subway/Pilot TC, Rest/BKing/PHut/TBell/TA TC, Pit Stop Cafe
		S: Mexican Rest
	Lodg	S: Coach Light Innwar & RV Park▲
	TWash	S: TA TC
	TServ	N: Peterbilt
		S: TA TC
	Other	N: WiFi/Pilot TC, Sunny Acres RV Park▲, Fun City RV's
		S: Laundry/WiFi/RVDump/TA TC
140		NM 28, Avenida de Mesilla, Historic Mesilla Plaza, Las Cruces
	Gas	N: Phillips 66◆, Shell◆
		S: Shell
	Food	N: Applebee's, Blake's, Burger Time, Cracker Barrel, McDonald's, Santa Fe Grill
		S: DQ, Domino's Pizza, Old Town
	Lodg	N: Best Western, Comfort Inn, Hampton Inn, La Quinta Inn♥, Mesilla Valley Inn, Springhill Suites
	TServ	N: International
	Other	N: Wal-Mart sc▲, Sunny Acres RV Park▲, Hacienda RV Resort▲
		S: Barnett Harley Davidson, RV Doc's RV Park & Service▲, Siesta RV Park▲, Sunland RV Center, Leasburg Dam State Park
142		NM 478, Main St, Las Cruces, University Ave, NM St Univ
	Gas	N: Chevron◆
		S: Fina
	Food	N: Denny's, Taco Bell, Village Inn, Whataburger
	Lodg	N: Best Western, Comfort Inn, Days Inn, Holiday Inn Express, Motel 6♥, Plaza Suites, Ramada, Sands Motel, Super 8, Teakwood Inn & Suites
	Med	N: + Hospital
	Other	N: NM St Univ, Dalmonts RV Park▲
		S: US Post Office
(144)		Jct I-25N, to Albuquerque
151		NM 228, Mesquite, San Miguel
155		NM 227, Vado Dr, Vado, Berino
	TStop	S: National Truck Stop #305/Fina, Vado Travel City/Texaco
	Food	S: Rest/FastFood/Vado TC, Rest/FastFood/National TS, Ernesto's, Golden West, Your Place, Simon's Café
	TServ	S: National TS/Tires
	Other	N: Vado RV Park▲, Aguirre Springs Nat'l Rec Area
		S: Laundry/BarbSh/Vado TC, Laundry/WiFi/RVDump/National TS

Page 42   ◆= Regular Gas Stations with Diesel   ▲ = RV Friendly Locations   ♥= Pet Friendly Locations
RED PRINT SHOWS LARGE VEHICLE PARKING/ACCESS ON SITE OR NEARBY   BROWN PRINT SHOWS CAMPGROUNDS/RV PARKS

I-10 W/E

NM / TX

EXIT	
(159)	Weigh / Inspection Station (EB)
(160)	Weigh / Inspection Station (WB)
162	NM 404, O'Hara Rd, Anthony, Chaparral
Other	S: El Paso West RV Park▲
(164)	**NM Welcome Center (WB)** (RR, Phone, Picnic, WiFi, Info, Coffee)

(MOUNTAIN TIME ZONE)

◐ NEW MEXICO
◑ TEXAS
(MOUNTAIN TIME ZONE)

EXIT	
(0)	New Mexico Border, FM 1905, Anthony
N:	**Rest Area (WB)** (RR, Phone, Picnic)
TStop	N: Flying J Travel Plaza #5460/Conoco (Scales)
	S: Pilot Travel Center #435 (Scales)
Gas	S: 7-11, Chevron♦, Exxon♦, 7-11/Fina
Food	N: Cookery/FastFood/FJ TP
	S: Wendy's/Subway/Pilot TC, Burger King/Exxon
Lodg	N: Super 8
	S: Holiday Inn Express
TWash	S: Horizon Truck Wash
TServ	N: Southwest Refrigeration, TLC Trucks/ Great Dane Trailers
	S: Pilot TC/Tires
Other	N: Laundry/Wifi/RVDump/LP/FJ TP, American RV & Marine Resort▲ / Camping World
	S: Laundry/RVDump/Pilot TC, Anthony RV Center, Grocery, Dollar General, Wet & Wild Waterworld, Sun Country RV & Marine
(1)	**Welcome Center (EB)** (RR, Phone, Picnic, Info, Sec) **Inspection Station (WB)**
2	Vinton Rd, Canutillo, Westway, Vinton, El Paso
TStop	N: Petro 2 #50/Mobil (Scales) (DAND)
Gas	S: Piggy Bank, Circle N
Food	N: FastFood/Petro SC, Maria's, El Taco Rico, Natalie's Kitchen El Rincon Mexican Cafe
	S: Burger King/Piggy Bank, Great American Land & Cattle Steakhouse
TServ	N: Petro SC/Tires
	S: Westside Trucks/Tires
Other	N: Laundry/WiFi/Petro SC, Camping World/American RV Park▲
(5)	Inspection Station (EB)
NOTE:	8% Steep Grade
6	Lp 375, Trans Mountain Rd, Canutillo Rd
Gas	N: Shell♦
	S: Shell♦
Food	N: Taco Bell/DQ/Shell
	S: Subway/Shell
Other	N: Hoover Co, Franklin Mountain State Park▲
	S: Outlet Shops of El Paso, El Paso Comm College
8	TX 178, Artcraft Rd, Port of Entry
Gas	S: Howdy's, Shell
Food	S: Carl's Jr, Rusty's BBQ, Subway

TEXAS

EXIT	
	Lodg S: Microtel
	Other S: to Santa Teresa Airport✈, War Eagles Air Museum
9	Redd Rd, El Paso
Gas	N: Valero, Albertson's
	S: Circle K, Phillips 66♦, Albertson's
Food	S: Applebee's, Burger King, Double Dave's Pizzaworks, Pizza Hut, Starbucks
Lodg	S: Microtel
Other	N: Auto Dealers, Albertson's, Lowe's
	S: Auto Dealers, Budget RAC, Enterprise RAC
11	TX 20, Mesa St, El Paso
Gas	N: Chevron♦, Circle K, Shamrock♦, Sam's
	S: Chevron♦, Shamrock♦
Food	N: Carrow's, Chili's, CiCi's Pizza, **Cracker Barrel**, Denny's, Famous Dave's BBQ, Golden Corral, Long John Silver's, K-Bob's Steakhouse, Popeye's, Red Lobster, Taco Bell, Subway, Wendy's, Whataburger
	S: Burger King, Golden China, KFC, Luby's, McDonald's, Pizza Hut, Village Inn, Starbucks, Subway
Lodg	N: Baymont Inn, Comfort Inn, Econo Lodge, La Quinta Inn♥, Red Roof Inn♥
	S: Best Value Inn, Days Inn, Motel 6♥, Super 8, Travelodge
Other	N: Albertson's, Firestone, Goodyear, Home Depot, **Wal-Mart sc**, Sam's Club, Cinema
	S: AutoZone, Grocery, Walgreen's
12	Resler Dr, Mesa St (WB)
13	US 85, Sunland Park Dr, Paisano Dr, El Paso
Gas	N: Shamrock
	S: Shamrock♦, Shell
Food	N: Chuck E Cheese, Grand China, Great American Land & Cattle, IHOP, Olive Garden, Red Lobster
	S: McDonald's, Sonic, Subway
Lodg	N: Best Western, Comfort Suites, Holiday Inn♥, Sleep Inn, Studio Plus
Other	N: Sunland Park Mall, Best Buy, Office Depot, PetSmart♥, Target, Banks
	S: Sunland Park Race Track & **Casino**
16	Executive Center Blvd, El Paso
Gas	N: Shamrock
Food	N: Burger King
Lodg	N: Howard Johnson, Mesa Inn, Ramada Inn, Rio **Casino** & Suites
18A	Shuster Ave, UT El Paso
Med	N: + Providence Memorial Hospital, + Las Palmas Medical Center
Other	N: Sun Bowl
	S: Univ of Texas El Paso
18B	Porfirio Diaz St, Franklin Ave
19	TX 20, Downtown El Paso, to Conv Center, to Juarez MX (EB)
Gas	N: Chevron
	S: Texaco
Lodg	N: Holiday Inn
	S: Holiday Inn Express, International Hotel, Travel Lodge
Med	N: + Hospital
Other	S: Amtrak
19A	Mesa St, TX 20 (WB)
19B	TX 20, Mesa St, Downtown El Paso, to Conv Center, Juarez MX

TEXAS

EXIT	
20	Dallas St, Cotton St, Gatway Blvd, El Paso
Gas	N: Exxon
Lodg	N: Ramada
21	Piedras St
Gas	N: Exxon
Food	N: Burger King, McDonald's
Other	N: Family Dollar, Palms Mexican Insurance
22A	Lp 478, Copia St
Gas	N: Fina, Shamrock
Food	N: KFC
22B	US 54, to I-110, Patriot Fwy, Ft Bliss, to Juarez, Mexico
Gas	N: Diamond Shamrock
Food	N: KFC
Other	N: Coliseum, Mil/Fort Bliss RV Park▲
23A	Reynolds St, El Paso
Food	S: Arby's
Lodg	S: Motel 6♥, Super 8
Med	S: + Thomason Hospital, + Texas Tech Medical Center
23B	US 62, US 180, Paisano Dr, El Paso, Carlsbad
Food	N: Jack in the Box, McDonald's
Lodg	N: Budget Inn
Other	N: U-Haul, El Paso Int'l Airport✈, Ft Bliss Military Reservation
	S: El Paso Zoo
24A	Trowbridge Dr, El Paso
Gas	N: Fina
Food	N: Luby's, Steak & Ale, McDonald's
Lodg	N: Budget Inn
	S: Embassy Suites, La Quinta Inn♥
Med	S: + Gateway Medical Clinic
24B	Geronimo Dr, Surety Dr
Gas	N: Chevron
	S: 7-11, Phillips 66
Food	N: Seafood Galley, Steak & Ale
	S: Denny's, Rest/Travelodge
Lodg	N: El Rancho, Quality Inn, Residence Inn, Wingate Inn
	S: AmeriSuites, Embassy Suites, La Quinta Inn♥, Travelodge
Other	N: Mall, Banks, Target, Walgreen's, to El Paso Int'l Airport✈, Ft Bliss Mil Res
24	Geronimo Dr, Trowbridge Dr (WB)
25	Airway Blvd, El Paso Airport (access to Exit #26 Serv)
TStop	S: El Paso Truck Terminal/Chevron
Gas	N: Exxon, Shell♦
Food	N: Hooters, Jack in the Box, Landry's Seafood, Starbucks
	S: Rest/El Paso TT
Lodg	N: Courtyard, Hampton Inn, Holiday Inn, Radisson
TServ	S: El Paso TT, WhiteGMC
Other	S: Goodyear, El Paso Saddle Blanket
26	Hawkins Blvd, El Paso
Gas	N: Chevron, Shamrock, Shell, Sam's
	S: Shamrock
Food	N: Arby's, Burger King, Chili's, Country Kitchen, IHOP, Golden Corral, Landry's Seafood, Luby's, Olive Garden, Wyatt's
	S: China King, McDonald's, Village Inn
Lodg	N: Holiday Inn, Howard Johnson
	S: Best Western
TServ	N: Kenworth
Med	S: + Rio Grande Medical Center
Other	N: B&N, Cinema, Office Depot, Sam's Club, Pennzoil, **Wal-Mart sc**, Cielo Vista Mall, Ft Bliss Mil Rest, Int'l Airport✈

♦ = Regular Gas Stations with Diesel   ▲ = RV Friendly Locations   ♥ = Pet Friendly Locations
RED PRINT SHOWS LARGE VEHICLE PARKING/ACCESS ON SITE OR NEARBY   BROWN PRINT SHOWS CAMPGROUNDS/RV PARKS

Interstate 10 W/E

EXIT		TEXAS
27		Hunter Dr, Viscount Blvd (EB)
	Gas	N: 7-11, Shamrock
		S: Exxon◊, Shell
	Food	N: Carrow's, Red Lobster, Taco Bell
		S: Whataburger, Subway/Exxon
	Lodg	N: La Quinta Inn♥
	Other	N: Best Buy, Firestone, Fort Bliss
		S: Food City, El Paso Comm College
28A		McRae Blvd, FM 2316, Viscount Blvd
	Gas	N: Chevron
		S: 7-11, Chevron, Phillips 66
	Food	N: Chico's Tacos, Jack in the Box, KFC
		S: Gabriel's
	Lodg	N: InTown Suites
	Med	N: + Hospital
	Other	N: ATMs, Best Buy, Big Lots, Big O Tire, Firestone, Goodyear, Kmart, Office Depot, Walgreen's
28B		Yarbrough Dr, Sumac Dr
	Gas	N: Chevron, Murphy
		S: Shamrock, Shell
	Food	N: Burger King, Long John Silver's, McDonald's, Subway, Wendy's
		S: Applebee's, Fuddrucker's, Pizza Hut
	Lodg	N: Days Inn
		S: Baymont Inn, Comfort Inn
	Med	N: + Columbia Medical Center
	Other	N: Wal-Mart sc, PetSmart♥, Pharmacy
		S: Roadrunner RV Park▲
29		Lomaland Dr (EB)
	Gas	N: Exxon
		S: 7-11
	Food	N: Denny's, Whataburger
		S: Dot's BBQ, Café, Tony Roma
	Lodg	N: La Quinta Inn♥, Motel 6♥, Studio 6
		S: Ramada
	TServ	N: Kenworth
	Other	N: Auto Dealers, Discount Tire
		S: Barnett Harley Davidson
30		Lee Trevino Dr, Lomand Dr
	Gas	N: Exxon
		S: Shamrock
	Food	N: TGI Friday
	Lodg	N: Motel 6, Ramada Inn♥, Red Roof Inn♥, Studio 6
	Med	N: + Hospital
	Other	N: Firestone, Home Depot, Mall
32		FM 659, Zaragosa Rd, George Dieter Rd, El Paso
	Gas	N: 7-11/Fina, Chevron◊, Phillips 66
		S: Chevron, Fina, Shamrock◊
	Food	N: Famous Dave's BBQ, Furr's, IHOP, Logan's Roadhouse, Macaroni Grill, McDonald's, Outback Steakhouse, Whataburger, Village Inn

EXIT		TEXAS
	Lodg	N: Holiday Inn Express, Microtel
	TServ	N: Border Int'l Truck Service
	Med	N: + Hospital
	Other	N: Circuit City, Lowe's, Office Depot
34		Lp 375, Americas Ave, Joe Battle Blvd, El Paso
	Gas	N: Chevron◊, Shamrock◊, Texaco
	Lodg	N: Microtel, ValuePlace
	TServ	N: Western Star Trucks, Rush GMC Commercial Truck Center/Peterbilt
	Other	S: El Paso Museum of History, Mission RV Park▲
35		Eastlake Blvd
37		FM 1281, Horizon Blvd, El Paso
	TStop	N: Flying J Travel Plaza (Scales), Love's Travel Stop #214 (Scales)
		S: Petro Stopping Center #1/Mobil (Scales)
	Gas	N: Exxon
	Food	N: Rest/FastFood/FJ TP, Subway/Chesters/Love's TS
		S: IronSkillet/Blimpie/Petro SC, McDonald's
	Lodg	N: Americana Inn
		S: Deluxe Inn
	TServ	N: Flying J TP, Cummins SW, El Paso Thermo King, Truck Center of El Paso
		S: Petro SC, El Paso Freightliner, Speedco, Peterbilt, Expert Trailer Repair
	TWash	S: Blue Beacon TW/Petro SC, Texas TW
	Other	N: WiFi/Love's TS, Laundry/WiFi/LP/FJ TP, Vet♥, El Paso Connection
		S: Laundry/CB/BarbSh/WiFi/Petro SC, Laundry/El Paso TP, Samson RV Park▲
42		FM 1110, Clint, San Elizario
	Gas	S: Exxon◊
	Food	S: Rest/Cotton Valley Motel
	Lodg	S: Cotton Valley Motel & RV Park▲
49		FM 793, Clint, Fabens
	TStop	S: Texas 49 Truck Stop
	Gas	S: Phillips 66◊
	Food	S: Rest/TX 49 TS, Church's Chicken, McDonald's, Lower Valley Café, Subway
	Lodg	S: Fabens Inn
	TServ	S: Faben's Tire Co
	Other	S: Fabens Airport✈
(51)		Rest Area (Both dir) (RR, Picnic) (EB: Next Rest Area 95 mi)
55		Tornillo
68		Acala Rd
72		Spur 148, Knox Ave, Fort Hancock
	Gas	S: Shell◊
	Food	S: Rest/Shell
	Lodge	S: Ft Hancock Motel

EXIT		TEXAS
(77)		TRUCK Parking Area (WB)
78		TX 20W, McNary
81		FM 2217, Ft Hancock
85		Esperanza Rd
87		FM 34, Esperanza
	TStop	S: Tiger Travel Plaza/Drivers Travel Mart (Diesel Available ONLY)
	Food	S: Rest/FastFood/Tiger TP
	TServ	S: Tiger TP/Tires
	Other	S: Laundry/RVDump/Tiger TP
95		Frontage Rd (EB)
(98)		Picnic Area (EB)
99		Lasca Rd, Ft Hancock
	N:	Picnic Area (Both dir)
(102)		Inspection Station (EB)
105		I-10 Bus Lp, Sierra Blanca (EB)
106		I-10 Bus Lp, Sierra Blanca (WB)
107		RM 1111, Sierra Blanca Ave
	FStop	N: Exxon
	Gas	S: Chevron
	Food	N: Café, Michael's Rest
		S: Cafe
	Lodg	N: Sierra Motel
	TServ	N: Truck Tire Repair
	Other	N: Sierra Blanca RV Park▲
108		I-10 Bus, Sierra Blanca
129		Old Hwy 80, Allamore, Hot Wells
133		Frontage Rd (WB)
	NOTE:	MM 135: Mountain / Central Time Zone
(136)		Weigh Station (EB)
(136)		Scenic Overlook (Both dir)
138		Golf Course Dr, Lp 10, Van Horn
	TStop	S: Chevron Truck Stop
	Gas	N: Shell◊
	Food	N: Cattle Co Steakhouse, Chuey's, DQ, Pizza Hut
		S: CountryGrill/Chevron TS, McDonald's
	Lodg	N: Best Western♥, Budget Inn, Comfort Inn, Days Inn, Econo Lodge, Motel 6♥, Ramada Ltd
		S: Holiday Inn Express, Ramada, Super 8
	TServ	S: Bud's Diesel
	Other	N: Goodyear, Grocery, US Post Office, Municipal Golf Course
		Country Inn RV Park▲, Eagles Nest RV Park▲, LP
		S: Mountain View Golf Course

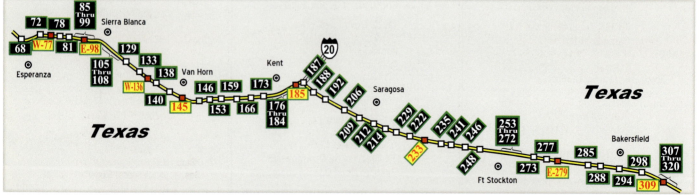

◊ = Regular Gas Stations with Diesel   ▲ = RV Friendly Locations   ♥ = Pet Friendly Locations
RED PRINT SHOWS LARGE VEHICLE PARKING/ACCESS ON SITE OR NEARBY   BROWN PRINT SHOWS CAMPGROUNDS/RV PARKS

Page 44

EXIT		TEXAS
140A		US 90, TX 54, Van Horn St, Harfa
	TStop	S: Pilot Travel Center #209 (Scales) (DAND)
	Gas	N: Phillips 66◊, Shell◊
		S: Exxon
	Food	N: Leslie's BBQ
		S: Papa's Café, Wendy's/Pilot TC
	Lodg	N: Days Inn, Desert Inn, Village Inn Motel
	Med	N: + Hospital
	Other	N: NAPA, US Post Office, Mike's Tire Service, El Campo RV Park▲
		S: WiFi/Pilot TC, Van Horn KOA▲, Mountain View RV Park▲, McDonald Observatory, Visitor Center
140B		I-10 Bus, Ross Dr, Van Horn
	TStop	N: Love's Travel Stop #256
	Gas	N: Chevron, Exxon◊
	Food	N: Pizza Palace, Subway/Love's TS, Rest/Days Inn, Rest/Sands Motel
	Lodg	N: Bells Motel, Days Inn, Motel 6♥, Sands Motel
	Other	N: WiFi/Love's TS, El Campo RV Park▲, Pharmacy, Auto/Truck Repair, Culberson Co Airport✈
		S: Mountain View RV Park▲
(145)		Rest Area (Both dir) (RR, Picnic)
(146)		Weigh Station (WB)
146		Wild Horse Rd, Van Horn
153		Evergreen Rd, Salt Flat, Michigan Flat
159		Moon Rd, Salt Flat, Plateau
	TStop	N: Plateau Truck & Auto Center/Fina
	Food	N: Rest/FastFood/Plateau TAC
	TServ	N: Plateau TAC
	Other	N: Laundry/Plateau TAC
166		Boracho Rd, Salt Flat
173		Hurds Draw Rd
176		TX 118, FM 2424, Kent, Ft Davis
	Gas	N: Chevron◊
	Other	S: to Davis Mountains State Park
181		Cherry Creek Rd, Fort Davis
	FStop	S: Chevron
184		Springhills
(185)		Picnic Area (Both dir)
(186)		Jct I-20E, to Dallas, Ft Worth (WB, Left exit)
(187)		Jct I-20E, to Pecos (WB)
188		Griffin Rd, Balmorhea
192		FM 3078E, to Toyahvale
206		FM 2903, Balmorhea, Toyah
209		I-10W Bus, TX 17S, Balmorhea
	Other	S: to Davis Mountains State Park
212		TX 17, Balmorhea, to Saragosa, Pecos
	FStop	S: I-10 Travel Stop/Fina
	Food	S: Rest/Fina FS
	Other	S: RVDump/Fina
214		FM 2448 (WB)
222		Hoefs Rd
229		Hovey Rd, Fort Stockton

EXIT		TEXAS
(233)		Rest Area (Both dir) (RR, Phone, Picnic, Vend)
235		Mendel Rd, Ft Stockton
241		Kennedy Rd
246		Firestone Rd, Fort Stockton
248		US 67S, FM 1776, to Alpine, Big Bend National Park
253		FM 2037, to Belding
256		I-10 Bus, Dickinson Blvd, US 285, Fort Stockton
	Gas	S: Shamrock◊, Shell◊
	Food	S: China Inn, DQ, K-Bob's Steak House, KFC, Pizza, Subway
	Lodg	S: Best Western, Comfort Inn, Econo Lodge, Motel 6♥, Sleep Inn, Super 8
	Med	S: + Hospital
	Other	S: SW Vet Clinic♥, Animal Medical Clinic♥, Pharmacy, Wal-Mart▲
257		US 285, Fort Stockton, to Pecos, Sanderson
	FStop	S: Town & Country #113/Chevron
	TStop	S: Comanche Springs Truck Terminal/Exxon
	Gas	S: Shamrock◊
	Food	S: Rest/Comanche Springs TT, BBQ, KFC, IHOP, Taco Bell, McDonald's, Pizza Hut, Sonic, Subway
	Lodg	S: Best Western, Comfort Inn, Days Inn, Hampton Inn, Holiday Inn Express, La Quinta Inn♥, Motel 6♥

EXIT		TEXAS
	TServ	N: I-10 Garage
		S: Comanche Sp TT
	TWash	S: Chaparral Truck Wash
	Other	N: Comanche Land RV Park▲, Fort Stockton-Pecos Co Airport✈, Desert Pines Golf Course, Fort Stockton Golf Course
		S: Laundry/WiFi/Comanche Sp TT, Wal-Mart▲, AutoZone, Goodyear
259B		TX 18, Ft Stockton, Monahans (WB)
259A		FM 1053 (WB)
259		TX 18, Monahan's, FM 1053 (EB)
	FStop	N: Oasis Travel /Shell
	TStop	N: Johnny's Circle n Food Store/Fina
	Gas	N: Apache Liquors & Fuel Center
	Food	N: Burger King/Shell, FastFood/Johnny's
	TServ	N: Johnny's TS/Tires
	Med	S: + Pecos Co Memorial Hospital
	Other	N: I-10 RV Park▲, Laundry/Johnny's
261		US 10, US 385, Marathon, Fort Stockton
	FStop	S: 7-D Exxon
	Lodg	S: Best Value Inn, Econo Lodge
	Med	S: + Pecos Co Memorial Hospital
264		Warnock Rd
	Other	N: Fort Stockton KOA▲
272		University Rd, Fort Stockton
273		US 67, US 385, Fort Stockton, to McCamey, San Angelo
	N:	Picnic Area (WB)
277		FM 2023, Fort Stockton
(279)		Picnic Area (EB)
285		McKenzie Rd
288		Ligon Rd, Fort Stockton
294		FM 11, Bakersfield
	Gas	N: Exxon
		S: Chevron◊
	Food	S: Café/Chevron
298		RM 2886
307		US 190, Iraan, to FM 305, to McCamey, Sheffield
(309)		Rest Area (Both directions) (RR, Phone, Picnic)
314		Frontage Rd
320		Frontage Rd, Iraan
325		TX 290, TX 349, Iraan, Sheffield
	Med	N: + Iraan General Hospital
328		River Rd, Ozona, to Sheffield
337		Live Oak Rd, Ozona
343		TX 290W, Sheffield
(346)		Parking Area (EB)
(349)		Parking Area (WB)
350		RM 2398, Howard Draw Rd
361		RM 2083, Pandale Rd, Ozona
363		Loop 466, RM 2398, Ozona
365		TX 163, Ozona, Sterling City, Comstock
	FStop	N: Town & Country #219
	Gas	N: Chevron◊, Exxon

◊ = Regular Gas Stations with Diesel   ▲ = RV Friendly Locations   ♥ = Pet Friendly Locations

RED PRINT SHOWS LARGE VEHICLE PARKING/ACCESS ON SITE OR NEARBY   BROWN PRINT SHOWS CAMPGROUNDS/RV PARKS

EXIT		TEXAS
	Gas	S: Chevron, Shell
	Food	N: Café/Texaco, FastFood/T&C, DQ, Burger King, Café Next Door, Subway
	Lodg	N: Best Western, Economy Inn ♥ & RV Park▲, Super 8, Travelodge
	Med	N: + Crockett Co Care Center
368		Loop 466, Ozona
	Med	N: + Crockett Co Care Center
372		Taylor Box Rd, Ozona
	TStop	N: AmBest/Circle Bar Auto & Truck Plaza/Chevron (Scales)
	Food	N: Deli/Rest/Circle Bar TP
	Lodg	N: Super 8
	TWash	N: Circle Bar TP
	TServ	N: Circle Bar TP/Tires
	Other	N: Laundry/RVDump/Circle Bar TP, Circle Bar RV Park▲, Auto Museum
381		FM 1312 (EB)
388		FM 1312 (WB)
392		FM 1312, RM 1989, Caverns of Sonora Rd, Sonora
(394)		Rest Area (Both dir) (EB Next RA 119 mi) (RR, Phone, Picnic, WiFi, RVDump)
399		Lp 467, Sonora (EB)
	Gas	S: Chevron, Exxon◊, Fina, Phillips 66, T & C
	Food	S: Subway
	Lodg	S: Days Inn
	Med	S: + Hospital
400		US 277, Sonora, San Angelo, Del Rio
	FStop	S: Skinny's Conv Store/Fina
	Gas	S: Shell◊ S: T&C◊, Exxon◊, Shell
	Food	N: Sutton County Steak House S: Country Cookin Café, DQ, Sonic La Mexicana, Pizza Hut
	Lodg	N: Days Inn S: Best Value Inn, Best Western, Comfort Inn ♥, Twin Oaks Motel
	Other	N: Sonora Muni Airport✈, Sonora Golf Club S: LP, Busters RV Park▲
404		Lp 467, RM 864, RM 3130, Sonora
	Med	S: + Hudspeth Memorial Hospital
412		RM 3130, Allison Rd
420		RM 3130, Baker Rd
(423)		Parking Area (Both dir)
429		RM 3130, Harrell Rd
437		Lp 291, Roosevelt (EB, Diff reacc)

EXIT		TEXAS
438		Lp 291, Roosevelt (WB)
442		Lp 291, RM 1674, Ft. McKavatt
445		FM 1674, Roosevelt (EB)
451		FM 2291, Cleo Rd
456		US 83N, US 377, Junction, London, Rocksprings, Menard, Mason
	FStop	N: Joy's Conoco S: Harold's Food Mart/Shell, Junction Country Store/Valero
	TStop	N: Gene's Go Truck Stop Chevron
	Gas	S: Exxon
	Food	N: FastFood/Gene's TS, BBQ, JR's, S: McDonald's/Valero, Junction Rest, DQ, Git-It, Rest/Slumber Inn
	Lodg	N: Comfort Inn S: Days Inn ♥, Lazy T Motel, Hills Motel, Legends Inn, Slumber Inn, Sun Valley Motel
	Med	S: + Kimble Hospital
	Other	N: Laundry/Gene's TS, Kimble Co Airport✈ S: WiFi/Jct CS, Lakeview RV Park▲, Lazy Daze RV Park▲, Junction KOA▲, Morgan Shady Park▲, to S Llano River State Park▲, TX Tech Univ
457		RM 2169, Junction, Martinez St
	FStop	N: Grandad's Corner Store/Shell
	Food	S: Rest/Days Inn
	Lodg	S: Days Inn
	Other	S: S Llano River State Park▲
(459)		Picnic Area (WB)
460		Bus Loop, Junction (WB)
(461)		Picnic Area (EB)
462		US 83S, to Uvalde
465		FM 2169, Junction, Segovia
	TStop	S: Segovia Truck Stop/P66
	Food	S: Rest/Segovia TS
	Lodg	S: Econo Lodge/Segovia TS
	TServ	S: Segovia TS/Tires
	Other	S: Laundry/Segovia TS, Pecan Valley RV Park▲
472		Old Segovia Rd, CR 450, FM 479, FM 2169, Junction
477		US 290E, to Fredericksburg
484		Midway Rd
488		TX 27, Mountain Home, Ingram
	Other	N: to 9mi Johnson Creek RV Resort▲

EXIT		TEXAS
490		TX 41, Mountain Home, Rock Springs
492		FM 479, Mountain Home
(497)		Picnic Area (Both dir)
NOTE:		MM 501: EB: 7% Steep Grade
501		FM 1338, Goat Creek Rd, Kerrville
	Other	N: Buckhorn Lake RV Resort▲ S: Kerrville KOA▲
(503)		Scenic View (Both dir)
NOTE:		MM 504: 7% Steep Grade
505		TX 783, Harper Rd, Kerrville, to Harper, Ingram (Serv S to TX 27)
	Gas	S: Exxon◊
	Lodg	S: Inn of the Hills
	Food	S: Chili's, CiCi's, McDonald's, Pizza Hut, Starbucks, Wendy's
	Other	S: Wal-Mart sc▲, Take It Easy Adult RV Park▲, Guadalupe River RV Resort▲, Classic Car Museum
508		TX 16, Kerrville
	Gas	N: Exxon◊ S: Chevron◊, Valero◊, Shell◊
	Food	S: Subway/Chevron, McDonald's/Shell, Burger King, Cracker Barrel, Denny's, IHOP, Jack in the Box, Luby's, Sonic
	Lodg	S: Best Western, Comfort Inn, Days Inn, Hampton Inn, Holiday Inn Express, Motel 6 ♥, La Quinta Inn ♥, Super 8
	Med	S: + Hospital
	Other	N: Johnson Creek RV Resort▲ S: AutoZone, Home Depot, Lowe's, Grocery, Walgreen's, Kerrville RV Center, Kerrville Schreiner State Park
NOTE:		MM 514: EB: 7% Steep Grade
(514)		Rest Area (Both dir) (RR, Phone, Picnic, Vend, WiFi, RVDump)
520		FM 1341, Cypress Creek Rd, Kerrville
523		US 87, Comfort, to San Angelo, Fredericksburg
	Gas	N: Chevron S: Exxon◊, Texaco
	Food	N: McDonald's/Chevron S: DQ
	Lodg	S: Executive Inn
	Other	N: Golf Course S: USA RV Park/LP▲

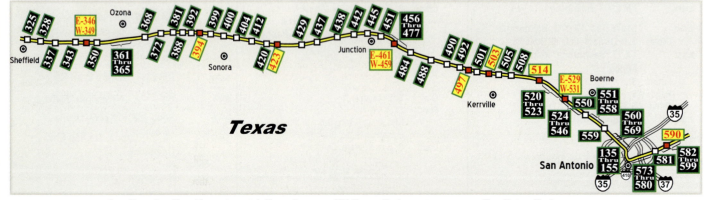

♦ = Regular Gas Stations with Diesel ▲ = RV Friendly Locations ♥ = Pet Friendly Locations
RED PRINT SHOWS LARGE VEHICLE PARKING/ACCESS ON SITE OR NEARBY   BROWN PRINT SHOWS CAMPGROUNDS/RV PARKS

EXIT		TEXAS
524		**US 87 Bus, FM 1621, Comfort, Waring**
	Gas	S: Chevron◆, Shell
	Food	S: Double D Family Rest
527		**FM 1621, Comfort, Waring (WB)**
(529)		**Picnic Area (EB)**
(531)		**Picnic Area (WB)**
533		**FM 289, Boerne, Welfare**
	Food	N: PoPo Family Rest
	Other	N: Top of the Hill RV Park▲
537		**US 87 Bus, Ranger Creek Rd, Boerne**
	Gas	N: Chevron, Shamrock
	Food	N: La Hacienda, Pete's Place, Subway
	Lodg	N: Best Western, Holiday Inn, Key to the Hills Motel
538		**Ranger Creek Rd, Boerne (WB)**
539		**Johns Rd, Boerne**
	Gas	S: Valero◆
	Lodg	N: La Quinta Inn ♥
	Other	S: LP/Valero, Boerne RV Service
540		**TX 46, New Braunfels, Bandera**
	Gas	N: Exxon, Shamrock, Shell◆, Murphy, HEB
	Food	N: Burger King, DQ, Denny's, Wendy's, Margarita's Café, Pizza Hut, Sonic, Starbucks
		S: Chili's, Whataburger
	Lodg	N: Best Western, Holiday Inn Express
		S: Hampton Inn
	Other	N: Auto Services, Grocery, Walgreen's, to Bus 87: Wal-Mart sc▲, ExploreUSA RV Sales
		S: Home Depot
542		**Bus 87, Boerne (WB)**
	Food	N: Wendy's
	Other	N: Tires
543		**Boerne Stage Rd, Cascade Cavern Rd, Scenic Loop Rd**
	FStop	N: Kwik Pantry/Citgo
	Gas	N: Chevron, Exxon, Valero
	Food	N: Café/Chevron, Café/Exxon, Copeland's Seafood & Steaks, Rest/Cavern Inn
	Lodg	N: Cavern Inn
	Other	N: Auto Dealers, Enterprise RAC, Lester's Auto Center Cars/Trucks/RV, Wal-Mart sc, Alamo Fiesta RV Park▲, American Dream Vacations RV Center, Cascade Caverns
546		**Fair Oaks Pkwy, Tarpon Dr, Fair Oaks Ranch**
	Gas	S: Chevron◆, Exxon◆
	Food	S: Café/Chevron, Café/Exxon
	Other	N: Javalina Harley Davidson, Vet♥, American Dream RV Sales & Rentals
		S: Auto Services, Ancira Auto & RV Center, Ron Hoover RV & Marine Centers, C & S RV Center, Boerne Stage Airport✈, Explore USA RV Center, to Tejas Valley RV Park▲
550		**FM 3351, Ralph Fair Rd, Boerne Stage Rd, Camp Stanley**
	FStop	N: Pico #10/Valero Travel Center
	Gas	N: Exxon
		S: Shell◆
	Food	N: FastFood/Pico, Mexican, Macaroni Grill, McDonald's/Exxon, Starbucks
		S: Domino's/Shell
	Other	N: Bank, Camp Stanley Military Res
		S: HEB

EXIT		TEXAS
551		**Boerne Stage Rd, San Antonio, to Leon Springs (WB)**
	Gas	S: HEB
	Other	S: HEB
554		**Camp Bullis Rd (WB)**
	Gas	N: Citgo
		S: Shell
	Food	N: ChickFilA, Habaneros Grill, Mimi's Cafe, Quiznos, Red Robin, TGI Friday
	Lodg	N: Motel 6 ♥
		S: Rodeway Inn
	Other	N: Bass Pro Shop, Best Buy, Palladium IMAX, Lowe's, Staples, Auto Services
555		**La Cantera Pkwy, Fiesta**
	Other	S: Univ of Texas San Antonio
556A		**Lp 1604, Anderson Loop**
	Lodg	S: Comfort Inn, La Quinta Inn ♥, Motel 6 ♥
	Other	S: to Sea World
556B		**Frontage Rd, San Antonio**
	Lodg	S: Motel 6 ♥
	Other	S: Best Buy, Bass Pro Shop, Lowe's, Palladium, Target
557		**Spur 53, Univ of Texas SA**
	Gas	S: Costco
	Lodg	N: Best Western, Econo Lodge, Howard Johnson, Super 8
	Other	N: Auto Dealers
		S: Auto Dealers, Costco, Discount Tire, Sam's Club
558		**De Zavala Rd, San Antonio**
	Gas	N: Chevron, Exxon◆, Shell
	Food	N: BBQ, Carrabba's, Chili's, Joe's Crab Shack, Jim's Rest, Logan's, McDonald's, Outback Steakhouse, Subway
		S: IHOP, TGI Friday, Whataburger

EXIT		TEXAS
	Lodg	N: Best Western, Econo Lodge, Howard Johnson, Holiday Inn Express, Super 8
		S: Days Inn
	Other	N: Bank, Home Depot, HEB, Office Max, PetSmart ♥, Target
		S: Sam's Club, Wal-Mart sc, Bowling
559		**Loop 335, Fredericksburg Rd, US 87, Woodstone Dr**
	Gas	S: Texaco
	Food	N: Barnacle Bill's Seafood, Carrabba's, Joe's Crab Shack, Outback Steakhouse, Starbucks
	Lodg	S: Econo Lodge, Studio 6
	Other	N: FedEx Kinko's
560A		**Huebner Rd, San Antonio (EB)**
	Gas	N: Chevron, Valero
		S: Exxon, Shell
	Food	N: BBQ, Golden Corral, On the Border, Romano's Macaroni Grill, Saltgrass Steakhouse
		S: Burger King, Cracker Barrel, Jim's Rest, McDonald's
	Lodg	S: AmeriSuites, Days Inn, Hampton Inn
	Other	N: AMC24 Cinema, Borders
560B		**Frontage Rd (EB)**
560C		**Medical Dr, Callaghan Rd**
561		**Huebner Rd, Wurzbach Rd**
	Gas	N: Mobil◆, Phillips 66
		S: Shell
	Food	N: Fuddruckers, Golden Corral, Jason's Deli, Popeye's, Sea Island Shrimphouse, Pappasito's, TX Land & Cattle
		S: Alamo Café, Benihana, Co Line BBQ, Denny's, Jack in the Box, IHOP, Luby's, McDonald's, Pizza Hut, Sombrero Rosa Cafe, Taco Bell, Wendy's, Village Inn
	Lodg	N: AmeriSuites, Ramada, Wyndham
		S: Best Western, Drury Inn, Holiday Inn Express, La Quinta Inn ♥, Motel 6 ♥, Residence Inn, Sleep Inn
	Med	S: + Hospital
	Other	N: Albertson's
562		**Frontage Rd, Wurzbach Rd (EB)**
563		**Callaghan Rd, San Antonio**
	Gas	N: Mobil
		S: Exxon
	Food	N: Las Palapas, Subway
		S: Mama's
	Lodg	N: Embassy Suites, Marriott
	Other	N: Auto Dealers
		S: Lowe's
(564AB)		**Jct I-410, to Airport, Connally Lp**
565A		**Crossroads Blvd, Dewhurst Rd, Balcones Heights Rd**
	Gas	N: Exxon, Shell
	Food	N: Denny's, WhataBurger
		S: El Pollo Loco, McDonald's
	Lodg	N: Comfort Suites, Rodeway Inn
		S: La Quinta Inn ♥, Super 8
	Other	N: Animal Hospital ♥
		S: Firestone, Mall, Super Target
565B		**Vance Jackson Rd, West Ave (EB), First Park Ten Blvd (WB)**
	Gas	S: Exxon, Shell
	Food	N: Bill Miller BBQ
	Lodg	N: Econo Lodge, Quality Inn
		S: La Quinta Inn ♥
	Other	N: Wal-Mart sc▲

◆ = Regular Gas Stations with Diesel   ▲ = RV Friendly Locations   ♥ = Pet Friendly Locations

RED PRINT SHOWS LARGE VEHICLE PARKING/ACCESS ON SITE OR NEARBY   BROWN PRINT SHOWS CAMPGROUNDS/RV PARKS

INTERSTATE 10 W/E

TEXAS

EXIT		
565C		Vance Jackson Rd (WB)
	Lodg	N: Quality Inn
		S: La Quinta Inn ♥
566A		Fresno Dr (EB), West Ave (WB)
	Gas	N: Exxon, Shamrock
566B		Fresno Dr, Hildebrand Ave, Fulton Ave, San Antonio
	Gas	S: 7-11, Exxon
567		Loop 345, Fredericksburg Rd, Woodlawn Ave (EB) (EB-Upper Level-to I-35S, I-10E, US 87S) (Lower Level to I-35N)
567A		Fulton Ave, Hildebrand Ave (WB)
567B		Loop 345, Woodlawn Ave (WB)
568		Spur 421, Culebra, Bandera (EB)
	Other	S: to St Mary's Univ
568A		Cincinnati Ave (WB)
568B		Spur 421, Culebra Rd
569		Santa Rosa St, Downtown (EB), Colorado St (WB)
569 A		N Colorado St (EB)
569B		N Frio St (EB)
NOTE:		I-10 & I-35 run together below for 3 mi. Exit #'s follow I-35.
(570/156)		Jct I-35N, to Austin
155C		W Houston St, Commerce St, Market Square (EB)
155B		Frio St, Durango Blvd (EB), Durango Blvd, Downtown (WB)
	Food	E: Jim Miller BBQ
	Lodg	E: Holiday Inn
		W: Radisson
155A		Spur 536, Alamo St (EB)
	Lodg	E: Microtel
154B		S Laredo St, Cevallos St
	FStop	E: Conoco (Scales)
	Gas	E: Exxon, Shell
	Food	E: McDonald's, Wendy's
	Lodg	E: Days Inn
154A		San Marcos St, Nogalios St (EB), Loop 353, Nogalitos St (WB)
	Gas	E: Conoco
	Lodg	E: Scottish Inn
(572/153)		Jct I-10E, US 90W, I-35S to Laredo, US 87, to I-37
NOTE:		I-10 follows I-35 Above for next 3 mi. Exit #'s follow I-35.
573		Probandt St, TX 536, Roosevelt Ave, Steves Ave, San Antonio
	Gas	S: Conoco, Valero
	Food	N: Bill Miller BBQ
(574)		Jct I-37, US 281, S - Corpus Christi, N - Johnson City
575		Pine St, Hackberry St
	Food	S: Little Red Barn Steakhouse
576		New Braunfels Ave, Gevers St
	Gas	S: Valero
	Food	S: McDonald's
577		US 87S, Roland Ave, Victoria
	Food	S: Whataburger
	Lodg	S: Super 8

Personal Notes

EXIT		TEXAS
578		Pecan Valley Dr, M L King Dr
	Gas	N: Phillips 66
579		Houston St, Commerce St
	Gas	N: Valero
		S: Chevron
	Lodg	N: Best Value Inn, Ramada, Travelodge
		S: Days Inn, Passport Inn
	Other	N: Coliseum
580		Lp 13, WW White Rd, San Antonio
	Gas	N: Chevron, Fina
		S: Exxon
	Food	N: Wendy's, Rest/Comfort Inn
		S: Bill Miller BBQ, McDonald's, Pizza Hut
	Lodg	N: Comfort Inn, Motel 6 ♥, Red Roof Inn, Rodeway Inn
		S: Econo Lodge, Quality Inn, Super 8, Spur Motel
	TServ	N: Bonanza Tire Sales
		S: Sterling, Grande Truck Sales, Davis Truck Service, Ford, WhiteGMC, Freightliner
	Other	N: Dixie Campground▲, San Antonio KOA▲
(581)		Jct I-410, Connally Loop
582		Ackerman Rd, Kirby
	TStop	N: Pilot Travel Center #306 (Scales)
		S: Petro Stopping Center #5/Mobil (Scales)
	Food	N: Wendys/PHut/Pilot TC
		S: IronSkillet/Petro SC, KFC/TacoBell
	Lodg	N: Bonita Inn Motel
		S: Rest Inn

EXIT		TEXAS
	TWash	S: Blue Beacon TW/Petro SC
	TServ	N: Petro SC, Fruehauf, International, Thermo King Service
		S: Petro SC
	Other	N: WiFi/Pilot TC
		S: Laundry/CB/WiFi/Petro SC, Martindale Army Air Field✈
583		Foster Rd, San Antonio
	TStop	N: Flying J Travel Plaza #5410/Conoco (Scales)
		S: Travel Center of America/Chevron (Scales)
	Gas	N: Valero◆
	Food	N: Rest/FastFood/FJ TP, Jack in the Box
		S: Rest/BKing/PHut/Popeye/TA TC
	Lodg	N: Holiday Inn Express, La Quinta Inn ♥
	TServ	N: Charlie's Truck Wash
		S: TA TC/Tires
	Other	N: Laundry/BarbSh/WiFi/RVDump/FJ TP
		S: Laundry/WiFi/RVDump/TA TC
585		FM 1516, Converse
	TStop	N: San Antonio Travel Center/Shell (Scales)
	Food	N: FastFood/SA TC, Rest/Windfield's
	Lodg	N: La Quinta Inn ♥, Rest Inn, Ramada, Windfield's Motel
	TServ	N: Arrow Truck Sales, Rush Truck Center
		S: Peterbilt/Freightliner, Kenworth, CB Sales & Svc, Werts Welding & Tank Svc
	Other	N: Laundry/San Antonio TC, Alamo City RV Center
587		Loop 1604, Anderson Loop, Randolph AFB, Universal City
	Other	N: to appr 13mi: Blazing Star Luxury RV Resort▲
589		Graytown Rd, Pfeil Rd
(590)		Rest Area (Both dir) (RR, Phone, Picnic, RVDump)
591		FM 1518, Converse, Schertz
	Other	S: to appr 9mi: Easy Acres RV Park▲
593		FM 2538, Trainer Hale Rd
	FStop	N: Citgo
	Food	N: DQ/Citgo, Mexican Rest
	AServ	N: Auto Repair
		S: Auto Repair
595		Zuehl Rd, Marion
597		Santa Clara Rd, Seguin
	Other	N: Rivercity Raceway
599		FM 465, Linne Rd, to Marion
600		Schwab Rd
601		FM 775, Seguin, New Berlin, La Vernia
	TStop	N: Sunmart/Chevron (Scales)
	Food	N: Subway/Sunmart
603		US 90E, Alt 90, Seguin (EB)
604		FM 725, Seguin, to Lake McQueeney
	Other	N: D & A RV Resort▲, Twin Palms RV Park▲, America Go RV Sales, Explore USA RV Center
		S: to Brian's Country RV Park▲
605		FM 464, Seguin
	Other	N: Twin Pines RV Park▲
		S: On the River RV Park▲, ABC RV Park▲

◆ = Regular Gas Stations with Diesel   ▲ = RV Friendly Locations   ♥ = Pet Friendly Locations
RED PRINT SHOWS LARGE VEHICLE PARKING/ACCESS ON SITE OR NEARBY   BROWN PRINT SHOWS CAMPGROUNDS/RV PARKS

EXIT		TEXAS
607		TX 46, FM 78, New Braunfels, to Lake McQueeney
	FStop	S: Pacific Pride
	Gas	N: Texaco
		S: Chevron, Exxon◇
	Food	N: Jack in the Box/Texaco, Huddle House
		S: Bill Miller BBQ, Chili's, IHOP, McDonald's, Kettle Rest, Mexican Rest
	Lodg	N: Alamo Country Inn
		S: Best Western, La Quinta Inn♥, Super 8♥
	Other	N: Geronimo Field, Texas Lutheran Univ
609		TX 123 Bus, Austin St, Seguin
	Gas	S: Mobil◇
	TServ	S: Seguin Diesel Service
	Other	S: Home Depot, Ryder
610		TX 123, Seguin, San Marcos, Stockdale
	TStop	N: Jud's Food & Fuel #5/Chevron
	Gas	N: Exxon
		S: Valero◇
	Food	N: FastFood/Jud's F&F, IHOP, K&G Steak House, Chili's, Mexican Rest, Luby's
		S: Taco Cabana
	Lodg	N: Comfort Inn, Hampton Inn, Holiday Inn
	Med	S: + Guadalupe Valley Hospital
	Other	N: D&D Trailer Sales, Tires, Dusty Oaks RV Park & Campground▲
		S: River Shade RV Park▲
612		US 90, Seguin
(615)		Weigh Station (EB)
(616)		Weigh Station (WB)
617		FM 2438, to Kingsbury
(619)		Rest Area (Both dir) (RR, Picnic, Vend)
620		FM 1104, Kingsbury
625		CR 217, Darst Field Rd
628		TX 80, Luling, Nixon, San Marcos
	TStop	N: to Luling Mini Mart/Shamrock
	Gas	N: Valero
	Food	N: FastFood/Luling Mini Mart
	Lodg	N: to Luling Inn, Coachway Inn
	Med	N: + Hospital
	Other	N: River Bend RV Park▲
		S: Rivershade RV Park▲
632		US 90, US 183, Gonzales, Luling, Cuero, Lockhart
	FStop	S: Buc-ee's (NO TRUCKS)
	TStop	N: Love's Travel Stop #264 (DAND)

EXIT		TEXAS
	Gas	S: Shell
	Food	N: Subway/Love's TS
	AServ	N: G&K Auto Repair
	TServ	N: Ballard Diesel Service
	Other	N: WiFi/RVDump/Love's TS
		S: to Palmetto State Park
637		FM 794, Harwood
642		TX 304, Bastrop, Gonzales
	Other	N: Kactus Korral RV Park▲
		S: to Palmetto State Park
649		TX 97, Waelder, Gonzales
653		US 90, Waelder
	Gas	N: Shell◇
(657)		Picnic Area (Both dir)
661		TX 95, FM 409, Flatonia, Moulton, Smithville, Shiner
	FStop	N: Joel's/Conoco
		S: CJ's Country Junction
	TStop	S: Stockman's Travel Center/Exxon, Flatonia Country Store/Shell
		S: Valero
	Food	N: Joel's BBQ
		S: FastFood/Flatonia CS, DQ, Jamie's Café, McDonald's/Shell, Thumper's Road House Grill, Two Sisters Rest
	Lodg	S: Carefree Inn, Grumpy's Motor Inn
	TServ	S: Tire & Lube
	Other	N: Flatonia RV Ranch, Flatonia Airfield✈
		S: Laundry/Flatonia CS, CarWash
668		FM 2238, Schulenburg, to Engle
674		US 77, Kessler Ave, Schulenburg, La Grange, Halletsville
	FStop	N: Speedy Stop #68/Exxon
		S: Andy's Food Mart/P66
	Gas	N: Chevron◇
		S: Citgo◇, Exxon◇, Shell◇, Valero
	Food	N: FastFood/Speedy Stop, Oakridge Smokehouse, McDonald's
		S: FastFood/Andy's FM, Burger King, DQ, Sonic, Whataburger
	Lodg	N: Oak Ridge Motor Inn, Executive Inn
		S: Best Western
	TServ	N: Auto & Diesel Repair
		S: International Cummins Truck Service
	Other	N: Potter's Country Store/Pecans, to Sun Catchers RV Park▲
		S: to Schulenburg RV Park▲
677		US 90, Schulenburg
682		FM 155, Eagle St, Weimar
	FStop	N: Fishbeck Shell
	Gas	N: Chevron, Exxon◇
	Food	N: Fishbeck BBQ, Subway, Tx Burger
	Lodg	N: Czech Inn, Super 8

EXIT		TEXAS
	Med	N: + Hospital
	Other	N: LP/Shell
689		US 90, CR 210, CR 219, Columbus, Hattermann Lane
	Other	N: Columbus KOA▲
(692)		Rest Area (Both dir) (RR, Phone, Picnic, Vend, WiFi, RVDump)
693		FM 2434, Columbus, Glidden
695		TX 71W, LaGrange, Austin (WB)
696		TX 71S, Bus TX 71E, Columbus, El Campo
	Gas	N: Chevron◇, Shell◇
		S: Citgo, Shell, Valero◇
	Food	N: Burger King, Denny's, Jack in the Box, Pizza Hut/TacoBell
		S: Church's/Citgo, Subway/Mobil, Nancy's Steak House, McDonalds, Sonic, Whataburger
	Lodg	N: Columbus Inn, Holiday Inn Express
		S: Country Hearth Inn
	Med	N: + Columbus Comm Hospital
	Other	N: HEB, Wal-Mart
		S: Columbus RV Park & CG▲
698		US 90, Alleyton Rd, Columbus
	FStop	S: Columbus Travel Center/Shell
	Food	S: Jerry Mikeska BBQ
		S: Taco Bell/Col TC
	Lodg	N: Passport Inn
699		FM 102, Eagle Lake
	Other	N: Yamaha, Happy Oaks RV Park▲
		S: to Eagle Lake St Park
(701)		Picnic Area (WB)
704		FM 949
709		FM 2761, Bernardo Rd
713		Beckendorff Rd
716		Pyka Rd, Mound Rd, Sealy
	TStop	N: Sealy Truck Stop/Exxon
	Food	N: Rest/Sealy TS
	Lodg	N: Ranch Motel
		S: Holiday Inn Express, Sealy Inn
	TServ	N: Sealy TS/Tires
	Other	N: Laundry/Sealy TS
718		US 90, Sealy, FM 3538, Rosenberg (EB)
720		TX 36, Meyer St, Sealy, to Bellville, Wallace
	FStop	S: Sunmart #123/Mobil
	Gas	N: Shell◇
		S: Chevron◇, Shell◇, Valero◇

◇ = Regular Gas Stations with Diesel   ▲ = RV Friendly Locations   ♥ = Pet Friendly Locations

RED PRINT SHOWS LARGE VEHICLE PARKING/ACCESS ON SITE OR NEARBY   BROWN PRINT SHOWS CAMPGROUNDS/RV PARKS

Page 49

EXIT		TEXAS
	Food	N: DQ, McDonald's, Sonic, Tony's S: China Buffet, Hinze's BBQ, Pizza Hut, KFC/TBell, Subway, Whataburger
	Lodg	N: Austin Motel, Ranch Motel S: Best Western ♥, Holiday Inn Express ♥, Rodeway Inn
	Other	N: Walgreen's, Jones RV Center ▲ S: Grocery, Wal-Mart ▲
720A		**Outlet Center Dr**
	Other	S: Outlet Center
721		**US 90, Outlet Center Dr (WB)**
	Gas	N: Shell
	Other	S: to Outlet Center
723		**FM 1458, Sealy, to San Felipe, Frydek**
	TStop	N: Sunmart #121/Exxon (Scales)
	Food	N: FastFood/Sunmart
	TServ	N: Peterbilt, Brown Bros Discount Truck Tire Center
	Other	N: Goodyear Riverside Tire Center, Stephen F Austin State Park
725		**Micak Rd (WB)**
726		**Chew Rd**
729		**Peach Ridge Rd (EB)**
(729)		**Weigh Station (EB)**
730		**Donigan Rd (WB)**
(731)		**Picnic Area (Both dir, Left Exit)**
731		**FM 1489, Koomey Rd, Simonton**
	Gas	N: Exxon♦, Shell
	Food	N: Mexican, Pizza West
	Lodg	N: Brookshire Motel, Carefree Inn, Travelers Inn
	TServ	S: Bayou City Ford Truck Sales
	Other	N: Houston West KOA▲
732		**FM 359, Brookshire**
	FStop	N: US Truxtop/Exxon
	TStop	N: Flying J Travel Plaza (Scales) (DAND) S: Houston West Ambest Travel Center/P66 (Scales)
	Gas	N: Shell S: Chevron♦
	Food	N: Chesters/Exxon, CountryMkt/Fast Food/FJ TP BBQ, Pizza Buffet S: Rest/Houston WTC, Jack in the Box, Charlie's
	Lodg	N: Executive Inn, Travelers Inn S: Super 8
	TServ	S: Houston W TC/Tires, Brookshire Truck & Trailer Service, Diesel Chaser
	TWash	S: 10 Star TW
	Other	N: Laundry/LP/RVDump/FJ TP, Houston West KOA▲, CarQuest S: Laundry/Houston WTC, LP
735		**Igloo Rd**
	Other	N: Igloo
737		**Pederson Rd, Katy**
	TStop	N: Love's Travel Stop #234 (Scales)
	Food	N: Arby's/Love's TS
	TServ	N: Bridgestone Tire & Auto
	Other	N: WiFi/Love's TS, RV World of TX S: Southwest RV Center, Holiday World RV Center, Cliff Jones RV, Camping World RV Supercenter
740		**FM 1463 (EB), Pin Oak Rd (WB)**
	Gas	S: Chevron
	Food	N: McDonald's, Sonic S: Café

Personal Notes

EXIT		TEXAS
Med		N: + Hospital
	Other	N: Adventure Yamaha & Marine S: Pyne RV Sales & Center
741		**US 90W, Katy, Pin Oak Rd (EB)**
	Gas	S: Chevron
	Food	S: Chuck E Cheese, Fuddrucker's, Jack in the Box, Red Lobster
	Lodg	S: SpringHill Suites
	Med	S: + Hospital
	Other	S: Bass Pro Shop, Katy Mills Outlet Mall, Discount Tire, AMC 20, Wal-Mart sc ▲
742		**US 90W, Katy (WB)**
	TStop	S: Sunmart #131/Mobil
	Food	S: FastFood/SunMart
	Other	S: Cinema, Shopping S: Auto Dealers
743		**TX 99, Grand Pkwy**
	Gas	S: Exxon, Shell♦
	Food	S: Chili's, Hooters, McDonald's, Popeye's, On the Bayou, Swampy's Cajun Shack
	Lodg	S: Best Western, Comfort Inn, Hampton Inn, Holiday Inn Express, Super 8
	Med	N: + Hospital
	Other	S: Kroger
745		**Mason Rd, Katy**
	Gas	S: Chevron, Exxon, Diamond Shamrock, Shell
	Food	S: Black Eyed Pea, Burger King, Chili's, Carrabba's, CiCi's, DQ, KFC, Landry's Seafood, Luby's, McDonald's, Monterey Pizza Hut, Salt Grass Steak House, Subway, Taco Bell
	Lodg	S: Comfort Inn, Hampton Inn, Holiday Inn Express, Super 8, Sleep Inn

EXIT		TEXAS
	Other	S: Auto Dealers, Car Quest, Discount Tire, Firestone, Goodyear, Kmart, Kroger, PetCo, Walgreen's
746		**West Gran Blvd**
747AB		**Fry Rd, Katy, Houston**
	Gas	N: Chevron, Phillips 66, Shamrock, Shell S: Chevron, Citgo, Shell
	Food	N: Applebee's, Bennigan's, Burger King, Church's, DQ, Denny's, McDonald's, Pizza Hut, Panda Express, SouperSalad, Subway, Taco Bell, Whataburger S: Capt Tom's Seafood, Jack in the Box, IHOP, Omar's Mexican, Outback Steakhouse, Quiznos, Wendy's
	Med	S: + Christus St Catherine Hospital
	Other	N: Best Buy, Home Depot, Wal-Mart sc, Sam's Club, Walgreen's, Vet ♥ S: Albertson's, Lowe's, PetSmart ♥, Target, U-Haul
748		**Barker Cypress Rd, W Houston**
	Food	N: Applebee's, Ruby Tuesday S: Cracker Barrel
	Lodg	S: Fairfield Inn
	Other	N: Garden Ridge S: Enterprise RAC, Lowe's, Hoover RV Center ▲
750		**Park Ten Blvd (EB)**
	Other	S: Auto Dealers, Hertz
751		**TX 6, FM 1960, to Addicks**
	Gas	N: Shell, Sam's Club S: Chevron, Conoco♦, Exxon, Texaco
	Food	N: Cattle Guard, Waffle House S: Blimpie, Denny's, El Yucatan, Jack in the Box, Wendy's
	Lodg	N: Crowne Plaza, Drury Inn, Holiday Inn, Red Roof Inn ♥ S: AmeriHost, Extended Stay, Fairfield Inn, La Quinta Inn ♥, Motel 6 ♥, Super 8
	Other	N: Sam's Club, Greyhound, to West Houston Airport ✈ S: Bank, US Post Office, Auto Dealers, Enterprise RAC, Ron Hoover RV & Marine Center
753A		**Eldridge Pkwy, Houston**
	Gas	N: Conoco♦ S: Valero
	Lodg	N: Omni Hotel S: Marriott
	Other	S: Pennzoil
753B		**Dairy-Ashford Rd**
	Gas	S: Exxon, Shamrock
	Food	S: Beck's, Shoney's, TX Land & Cattle Steakhouse, Whataburger
	Lodg	S: Courtyard, Guesthouse Inn, Holiday Inn Express, Shoney's Inn
	Other	N: Auto Dealers S: Auto Dealers, Discount Tire, FedEx/Kinko's, Hertz RAC
754		**Kirkwood Rd, Houston**
	Gas	S: Chevron♦, Shell
	Food	N: Taco Bell S: Carrabba's, IHOP, Subway
	Lodg	S: Extended Stay America, Hampton Inn
	Other	N: Auto Dealers S: Auto Dealers
755		**Beltway 8, Wilcrest Dr, Houston**
	FStop	S: Citgo Gas Stop
	Gas	S: Exxon, Thrifty
	Food	S: Denny's, IHOP, McDonald's/Exxon, Steak & Ale
	Lodg	S: La Quinta Inn ♥

♦ = Regular Gas Stations with Diesel   ▲ = RV Friendly Locations   ♥ = Pet Friendly Locations
RED PRINT SHOWS LARGE VEHICLE PARKING/ACCESS ON SITE OR NEARBY   BROWN PRINT SHOWS CAMPGROUNDS/RV PARKS

EXIT		TEXAS
756A		Beltway 8, Frontage Roads
756B		Sam Houston Toll Way
757		Gessner Rd
	Gas	N: Exxon
		S: Shell, Texaco
	Food	N: BBQ, Bennigan's, Chili's, CiCi's, McDonald's, Wendy's, Whataburger
		S: Fuddrucker's, Jack in the Box, Jason's Deli, Olive Garden, Pappadeaux Seafood, Pappasito's, Romano's Macaroni Grill
	Lodg	S: Radisson, Sheraton ♥
	Med	S: + Memorial City Hospital
	Other	N: Best Buy, Home Depot, Kroger, NAPA, PetSmart ♥, Radio Shack, Sam's Club, Wal-Mart, U-Haul
		S: Firestone, Goodyear, Office Depot, Office Max, Target, Mall
758A		Bunker Hill Rd
	Gas	N: Exxon, Costco
		S: Texaco
	Food	N: CiCi's
		S: Charlie's Burger, Mexican Rest, Subway, Texas BBQ
	Lodg	S: Days Inn, Howard Johnson, Super 8
	Other	N: Bank, Lowe's, Costco, PepBoys
		S: Firestone, Goodyear, Target
758B		Blalock Rd, Echo Lane
	Gas	N: Phillips 66
		S: Chevron◇
	Food	N: Sonic, McDonald's
	Other	S: Kroger, Target, Walgreen's
759		Campbell Rd (WB)
	Gas	S: Chevron, Exxon, Texaco
	Food	N: Ciro's Italian, Fiesta Foods
	Med	S: + Hospital
	Other	N: Bank, Costco
		S: Kroger, Walgreen's
760		Bingle Rd, Voss Rd
	Gas	S: Citgo, Exxon, Mobil◇
	Food	S: Café, Mason Jar, Pappy's Café, Sweet Tomatoes, Salt Grass Steak House, Starbucks, Subway, Texas BBQ
	Med	S: + Hospital
	Other	N: Home Depot
		S: CVS
761A		Chimney Rock Rd, Wirt Rd
	Gas	S: Chevron, Exxon, Shell
	Food	N: Capt Benny's Oyster Bar, Starbucks
		S: 59 Diner, Denny's, Dixie's Roadhouse, McDonald's, Mexican Rest, Steak & Ale
	Lodg	S: La Quinta Inn ♥
	Other	N: Home Depot
761B		Antoine Dr (EB)
	Gas	S: Exxon, Shell
	Food	N: Country Harvest Buffet, Chinese Rest
		S: Blue Oyster Bar, McDonald's
	Lodg	S: La Quinta Inn ♥, Wellesley Inn
	Other	S: Cingular, UPS Store, CVS
762		Silber Rd, Antoine Dr, Houston
	Gas	S: Shell
	Food	N: Aubrey's Ribs
		S: Jack in the Box
	Lodg	S: Best Western, Holiday Inn ♥, Ramada ♥
	Other	N: US Post Office
(763)		Jct I-610
764		Westcott St, Washington Ave
	Gas	S: Chevron
	Food	N: Denny's
		S: McDonald's, IHOP

EXIT		TEXAS
	Lodg	N: Comfort Inn, Rodeway Inn
		S: Scottish Inn
	Other	S: Memorial Park Muni Golf Course
765A		TC Jester Blvd, Houston
	Gas	S: Exxon, Texaco
765B		N Shepherd Dr, Patterson St, N Durham Dr
	Gas	N: Shamrock
		S: Valero
	Food	N: Wendy's
	Lodg	N: Howard Johnson Express
	Other	N: Vet ♥
766		Studemont St, Heights Blvd, Yale St (WB)
	Gas	N: Chevron
		S: Exxon
	Food	S: Chili's
	Other	S: Target
767A		Yale St, Heights Blvd, Studemont St (EB)
	Gas	S: Shell
767B		Taylor St
	Food	S: Chili's
	Other	S: Bank, Target
(768A)		Jct I-45, S to Galveston
(768B)		Jct I-45, N to Dallas
769A		Downtown, Smith St (EB)
769B		San Jacinto St, Main St
769C		McKee St, Hardy St, Nance St
770A		US 59S, Downtown, to Victoria
770C		US 59N, Cleveland
770B		Jensen Dr, Gregg St, Meadow St (EB Left Exit)
771A		Waco St
	Food	N: Frenchy's Fried Chicken
	Lodg	N: Waco Motel
771B		Lockwood Dr
	Gas	N: Chevron
		S: Phillips 66, Shell◇
	Food	N: McDonald's, Subway/Chevron
	Other	N: Family Dollar
772		Kress St, Lathrop St
	Gas	N: Conoco
	Food	S: Burger King
773A		US 90 Alt, N Wayside Dr
	FStop	S: Sunmart #314/Mobil
	TStop	S: Horseshoe Truck Stop
	Gas	N: Chevron◇, Exxon
		S: Shell
	Food	N: Jack in the Box, Whataburger
		S: BBQ, Church's Chicken/Shell
	TServ	N: Wayside Truck Service
	Other	S: NAPA
773B		McCarty Dr
	FStop	N: Conners Gas & Diesel, Fleet Fuel Management/Citgo
	Gas	N: Mobil, Shell
	Food	N: Don Chile Mexican
	TServ	N: Stewart & Stevenson Truck & Trailer Service
		S: Nick's Diesel Service
774		Gellhorn Dr, Houston (EB)
	FStop	S: Texas Truck Stop
	Food	S: FastFood/Texas TS
	Other	S: Anheuser Busch Brewery

EXIT		TEXAS
(775AB)		Jct I-610
	TServ	N: Lone Star White GMC, Cummins Southern Plains
776A		Mercury Dr, Jacinto City, Galena Park
	Gas	N: Conoco, Shamrock◇, Texaco
		S: Shamrock, Shell
	Food	N: Burger King, McDonald's, Pizza Inn
		S: Steak & Ale, Tony's Seafood
	Lodg	N: Best Western, Days Inn, Fairfield Inn, Hampton Inn, Quality Inn
	TServ	N: WhiteGMC, Volvo
	Other	N: Family Dollar, Kroger, NTB
		S: Banks
776B		John Ralston Rd, Holland Ave, Jacinto City, Galena Park
	Gas	N: Citgo, Mobil
	Food	N: Checker's, Long John Silver's, Luby's
	Lodg	N: Best Western, Comfort Inn
	Other	N: Kroger, Walgreen's
778A		FM 526, Federal Rd, Normandy St, Houston, Pasadena
	FStop	N: Sunmart #150/Mobil
	Gas	N: Chevron, Shell
		S: Shell, Valero
	Food	N: BBQ, Blimpie, Denny's, Jack in the Box, KFC, Pizza Hut, Popeye's, Taco Bell, Wendy's
		S: Chili's, Joe's Crab Shack, McDonald's, Mexican, Pappas Seafood
	Lodg	N: La Quinta Inn ♥
		S: Holiday Inn Express
	Other	N: Kroger, Target
		S: Auto Zone
778B		Normandy St (EB)
	FStop	N: Normandy Truck Stop
	Gas	N: Shell
		S: Citgo
	Food	N: Golden Corral, Jack in the Box
	Lodg	S: Bayou Motel, Mainstay Suites, Scottish Inn ♥
778		Normandy St (EB)
779A		Westmont Dr (WB, EB U-Turn Req)
	Lodg	N: Interstate Motor Lodge
779B		Uvalde Rd, Freeport St, Market St (WB, EB U-Turn Req'd)
	Gas	N: Chevron◇, Texaco
	Food	N: Cracker Barrel, IHOP, Jack in the Box, KFC, Taco Cabana, Subway, Sonic
	Lodg	N: Interstate Motor Lodge
	TServ	S: Diesel Repair
	Med	N: + Sunbelt Regional Medical Center
	Other	S: Wal-Mart
780		Market St, Uvalde Rd, Freeport St, Frances
	Gas	N: Chevron, Mobil, Texaco
		S: Mobil
	Food	N: Cracker Barrel, IHOP, Jack in the Box, KFC, Mexican, Subway, Taco Bell
		S: BlackEyed Pea, Thomas Steak & BBQ
	Med	N: + Hospital
	Other	N: FedEx Kinko's, Office Depot
		S: Circuit City, Home Depot, Sam's Club, Wal-Mart
781A		Redmond St, Beltway 8
	TStop	S: Sunmart #149/Mobil
	Food	S: FastFood/SunMart
781B		Beltway 8, Houston
	Lodg	N: Holiday Inn
	Med	N: + Hospital

◇ = Regular Gas Stations with Diesel   ▲ = RV Friendly Locations   ♥ = Pet Friendly Locations
RED PRINT SHOWS LARGE VEHICLE PARKING/ACCESS ON SITE OR NEARBY   BROWN PRINT SHOWS CAMPGROUNDS/RV PARKS

Page 51

EXIT	TEXAS
782	Dell Dale Ave, Grand Ave
Gas	N: Exxon
	S: Conoco
Lodg	N: Best Value Inn, Days Inn, Dell Dale Motel, I-10 Motel, Super 8
	S: Glen Shady Motel
Med	S: + Hospital
783	Sheldon Rd, Channelview
FStop	N: Texaco Mart
Gas	N: Coastal, Exxon, Shell
Food	N: Burger King, Jack in the Box, KFC, Pizza Hut, Taco Bell, Whataburger
	S: Captain D's, McDonald's, Wendy's
Lodg	N: Best Western, Days Inn, Super 8
	S: Scottish Inn
Other	N: Advance Auto Parts, Auto Zone, Goodyear, Pharmacy
784	Cedar Lane, Market St (EB) River Rd, Bayou Dr (WB)
FStop	N: Texaco Mart
Gas	N: Citgo
Lodg	N: Budget Lodge, Magnolia Motel, Ramada Ltd
785	River Rd (EB), Magnolia Ave (WB), Channelview
FStop	S: USA Truck Stop
TStop	N: Cobra Truck Stop/Shell (Scales)
	S: Key Truck Stop/P66 (Scales)
Food	N: FastFood/Cobra TS
	S: Rest/FastFood/Key TS, FastFood/USA TS
Lodg	N: Budget Lodge, Magnolia Motel, Ramada Inn
TServ	S: Key TS, Trak-ta Lube, Southern Truck Sales
TWash	S: Key TS
Other	N: Pharmacy
	S: Laundry/Key TS
786	Monmouth Dr
787	Spur 330, Crosby-Lynchburg Rd, FM 2100, Baytown, Highlands
FStop	N: Sunmart #136/Mobil
Gas	N: Texaco
	S: Phillips 66
Food	N: 4 Corners BBQ, Domino's, Jack in the Box, Subway
Other	N: Houston Leisure RV Resort▲
788	Spur 330, Baytown (EB)
(789)	Rest Area (Both dir) (RR, Phone, Picnic)
789	Thompson Rd, Baytown, McNair
TStop	N: Pilot Travel Center #86 (Scales), Baytown Express Travel Plaza (Scales)

EXIT	TEXAS
TStop	S: Flying J Travel Plaza (Scales), Travel Center of America #17 (Scales)
Gas	N: Shamrock, Valero
Food	N: McDonald's/Pilot TC
	S: Rest/FastFood/FJ TP, Rest/FastFood/TA TC
Lodg	S: Super 8
TServ	S: TA TC/Tires, Speedco, Truck King Lube
TWash	S: TA TC
Other	N: Laundry/WiFi/Pilot TC, Laundry/CB/Baytown TP
	S: Laundry/WiFi/TA TC, Laundry/WiFi/LP/RVDump/FJ TP
790	Ellis School Rd (WB), John Martin Rd, Baytown (EB)
Lodg	N: Super 8
791	John Martin Rd, Wade Rd (EB)
Other	N/S: Auto Dealers
792	Garth Rd, Baytown
Gas	N: Chevron
	S: RaceTrac, Shell◊
Food	N: Burger King, Cracker Barrel, Jack in the Box, Red Lobster, Shoney's, Waffle House, Whataburger
	S: McDonald's, Outback Steakhouse, Pancho's Mexican, Seafood Corner, Taco Bell, Wendy's
Lodg	N: Best Western, Baymont Inn, La Quinta Inn♥, Hampton Inn♥
	S: Holiday Inn Express
Med	S: + Hospital
Other	N: Auto Dealers
	S: Vaughn RV Center▲, Mall
793	N Main St, Baytown
TStop	S: Baytown Citgo Travel Center (Scales)
Gas	N: Shell
Food	S: FastFood/Citgo TC
Other	S: Laundry/Citgo, Baytown Airport✈
795	Sjolander Rd (WB) (Services at exit #797)
TStop	N: Pappa Truck Stop
796AB	Frontage Rd, Baytown (WB)
796	Frontage Rd, Baytown (EB)
797	TX 146, Mont Belviu, Baytown, Dayton
TStop	N: Conoco Travel Center (Scales)
	S: Sunmart Truck Stop #400 (Scales)
Gas	N: Chevron, Shell◊
	S: Exxon, RaceTrac◊
Food	N: DQ, IHOP, McDonald's, Pizza Inn, Waffle House, FastFood/Conoco TC
	S: Jack in the Box, FastFood/Sunmart

EXIT	TEXAS
Lodg	N: Crystal Inn, Motel 6♥, Super 8
TServ	S: Sunmart TS/Tires
Med	S: + Hospital
Other	N: Laundry/Conoco TC, L&R RV Park▲, A & J RV Park▲
	S: Houston East/Baytown KOA▲, Pinelakes RV Resort▲, Shady Oaks RV Park▲
800	FM 3180, Eagle Dr
Gas	N: Exxon◊
Other	N: Baytown KOA▲
803	FM 565, Baytown (EB)
Gas	S: Valero
Other	N: Lost River RV Park▲
806	Frontage Rd, Anahuac
807	Wallisville Liberty Rd, Anahuac, Wallisville
810	FM 563, TX 73, Anahuac, Liberty
Gas	S: Chevron, Shell◊
Food	S: Blimpie/Chevron, JackintheBox/Shell
811	Turtle Bayou TurnAround (EB)
Gas	S: Gator Jct
Food	S: Grandma's Diner, Gator Jct BBQ
Other	S: Turtle Bayou RV Park▲, Auto Dealers
(812)	Inspection Station (Both dir) (Commercial Vehicles Only MUST Exit)
812A	Frontage Rd, Indian Trail (WB)
812	TX 61, Anahuac. Hankamer (EB)
FStop	N: Country Boys Country Store/Shell
Gas	S: Exxon
Food	N: FastFood/Country Boys CS
	S: DJ's Diner, McDonald's
813	TX 61, Hankamer, Anahuac (WB)
FStop	N: Country Boys Country Store/Shell
Gas	S: Exxon
Food	N: FastFood/Country Boys CS
	S: McDonald's
Lodg	N: Best Value Inn
(815)	Weigh Station (Both dir)
817	FM 1724, Anahuac
819	Jenkins Rd
Gas	S: Texaco
Food	S: Stuckey's
822	FM 1410, Oak Island Rd
Other	S: Winnie Comm Airport✈
827	FM 1406, Winnie
828	TX 73, TX124, Winnie, Port Arthur (EB)

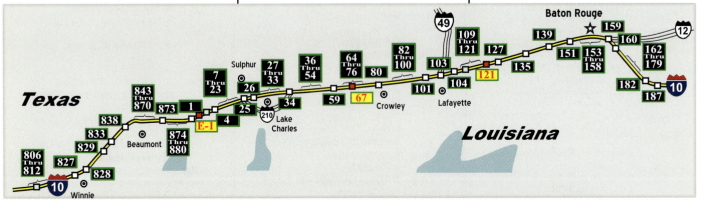

Page 52 ◊ = Regular Gas Stations with Diesel ▲ = RV Friendly Locations ♥ = Pet Friendly Locations
RED PRINT SHOWS LARGE VEHICLE PARKING/ACCESS ON SITE OR NEARBY   BROWN PRINT SHOWS CAMPGROUNDS/RV PARKS

EXIT	TEXAS
829	FM 1663, Anahuac, Winnie, TX 73, TX 124, Galveston, Beaches
FStop	S: Speedy Stop #15
TStop	S: Bingo Truck Stop/Chevron, Sunmart #111/Mobil (Scales)
Gas	N: Exxon◆, Mobil, Texaco
Food	N: McDonald's, Taco Bell, Whataburger S: Rest/Bingo TS, FastFood/Sunmart, Jack in the Box, Pizza Inn, R&W Seafood, Waffle House, Rest/Riceland Motel
Lodg	N: Holiday Inn Express S: Best Western, Ricelands Motel, Sands Motel, Studio 6, Winnie Inn & RV Park▲
Med	S: + Winnie Community Hospital
Other	S: Laundry/Bingo TS, Auto Dealers, Clinic/Vet♥, Flea Market, to Beaches
833	Hamshire Rd, Hamshire
(837)	Picnic Area (Both dir)
838	FM 365, Beaumont, Hamshire
Gas	N: Country Store/Gas
843	Smith Rd
845	FM 364, Major Dr, Beaumont
Other	S: Ford Park, Ford Arena, Gulf Coast RV Resort▲
846	Brooks Rd, Major Dr (EB)
847	to TX 364, Major Dr (WB)
Other	S: Gulf Coast RV Resort▲, Visitor Center, Baseball Fields
848	Walden Rd, Beaumont
TStop	S: Petro Stopping Center #4/Mobil (Scales)
Gas	N: Shell S: Chevron
Food	N: Pappadeaux, Rest/Holiday Inn S: Iron Skillet/Petro SC, Subway/Chevron, Carino's, Cracker Barrel, Jack in the Box, Joe's Crab Shack, Waffle House
Lodg	N: Holiday Inn, La Quinta Inn♥ S: Candlewood Suites, Hampton Inn, Hilton Garden Inn, Knights Inn, Ramada Ltd, Super 8
TWash	S: Blue Beacon TW/Petro SC
TServ	N: Kenworth, Mack S: Petro SC
Other	S: Laundry/CB/WiFi/Petro SC, Tinseltown USA
849	US 69S, Washington Blvd, Port Arthur, Airport, Beaumont
850	Washington Blvd (WB) (Access to Ex #851 Serv)
851	US 90, College St
Gas	N: Exxon, RaceWay S: Exxon, Mobil, Shell, Texaco, Sam's
Food	N: Burger King, Carrabba's, China Border, Golden Corral, Japanese Rest, Outback Steakhouse, Waffle House S: Rest/Hilton, IHOP, Jason's Deli, KFC, Pizza Hut, Taco Bell, Wendy's
Lodg	N: Best Western, Comfort Inn S: Econo Lodge, Fairfield Inn, Hilton, Motel 6♥, Premier Inn, Travelodge
TServ	N: Smart GM Trucks, GMC, Volvo S: Kinsel Ford
Med	S: + Hospital
Other	N: Auto Zone, Pennzoil, O'Reilly Auto Parts, Harley Davidson

EXIT	TEXAS
Other	S: Auto Dealers, Firestone, Office Depot, Sam's Club, Walgreen's
852A	Laurel St (EB)
Gas	N: Chevron◆, Shell, Valero S: Chevron
Food	N: Willy Ray's BBQ, Bennigan's, Chili's, Olive Garden, Steak & Ale S: McDonald's
Lodg	S: Castle Motel, Days Inn, Econo Lodge, La Quinta Inn♥
Med	S: + Stat Care
852B	Calder Ave, Harrison Ave, Gladys Ave (WB)
853A	US 69N, US 287, Beaumont, to Lufkin
853B	11th St
Gas	S: Texaco
Food	N: Ninfa's Mexican, Red Lobster, Waffle House, Rest/HI S: Jack in the Box, Luby's
Lodg	N: Best Value Inn, Best Western, Holiday Inn, Ramada Inn, Red Carpet Inn, Travelodge S: Best Western, Howard Johnson, Motel 6♥, Quality Inn, Rodeway Inn, Super 8
Med	S: + Hospital
Other	S: Bank, Staples
853C	8th St, 7th St (EB)
Gas	N: Fina
Food	N: Burger King, McDonald's, Mexican Rest, Red Lobster, Waffle House S: Rest/MCM
Lodg	N: Holiday Inn, Scottish Inn, Super 8 S: MCM Elegante

EXIT	TEXAS
854	Spur 380, Gulf St, ML King Pkwy, Magnolia Ave, Beaumont
Gas	S: Exxon, Shamrock, Russell's Service Center
Food	N: Burger King, Carrabba's S: Café Del Rio, McDonald's
Lodg	N: Super 8 S: Comfort Inn
855A	US 90, Downtown, Civic Center, Port of Beaumont (EB)
855B	US 90, Pine St, Magnolia Ave (WB)
856	Old Hwy 90, Rose City (EB)
857A	Rose City West (EB)
FStop	S: EZ Mart
857B	Workman Turn Around (WB)
858A	Rose City East (EB)
FStop	S: I-10 Fuel Mart (Scales)
858B	Asher Turn Around, Beaumont, Vidor (WB)
TStop	S: Gateway Truck Plaza/Chevron (Scales)
Food	S: Rest/FastFood/Gateway TP, Denny's
TServ	S: Gateway TP/Tires
Other	N: Boomtown RV Park▲ S: Laundry/Gateway TP
859	Bonner Turn Around, Dewitt Rd (EB)
860A	Dewitt Rd (WB)
860B	West Vidor (WB)
861A	FM 105, N Main St, Vidor
Gas	N: Chevron◆, Diamond Shamrock S: Exxon, Texaco
Food	N: DQ, Domino's Pizza, McDonald's, Waffle House S: Burger King, KFC, Pizza Hut, Sonic, Taco Bell, Whataburger
Lodg	S: La Quinta Inn♥
Med	S: + Vidor Family Medical Center
Other	N: Pharmacy, Grocery S: Laundromat
861B	Lamar St (WB)
Gas	N: Conoco◆
861C	Denver St (EB)
Gas	N: Conoco◆
861D	TX 12, Deweyville (WB)
862A	Railroad Ave (EB)
862B	Old Hwy 90, Vidor (WB)
862C	Lexington Dr, Timberlane Dr (EB)
864	FM 1132, FM 1135
Food	N: Burr's BBQ
Lodg	N: Budget Inn
865	Doty Rd, Frontage Rd (WB)
867	Frontage Rd (EB)
(867)	Rest Area (Both dir) (RR, Picnic, Vend, WiFi)
869	FM 1442, Orange, Bridge City
Other	S: Lloyd's RV Center
870	FM 1136
873	TX 62, TX 73, Orange, Bridge City, Port Arthur
TStop	N: Flying J Travel Plaza #5026/Conoco (Scales) (DAD) S: Pilot Travel Center #431 (Scales)

◆ = Regular Gas Stations with Diesel   ▲ = RV Friendly Locations   ♥ = Pet Friendly Locations
RED PRINT SHOWS LARGE VEHICLE PARKING/ACCESS ON SITE OR NEARBY   BROWN PRINT SHOWS CAMPGROUNDS/RV PARKS

EXIT	TX / LA	EXIT	LOUISIANA	EXIT	LOUISIANA
Gas	N: Exxon◊ S: Shell◊, Valero◊	Food	S: Rest/Delta Town TS, Rest/Delta Truck Plaza, FastFood/Tobacco Plus, Pelican Palace	Food Lodg	S: Cracker Barrel, Waffle House N: Comfort Suites, Days Inn S: Best Western, Fairfield Inn, Holiday Inn Express, Quality Inn, Super 8
Food	N: Rest/FastFood/FJ TP S: Wendy's/Subway/Pilot TC, Burger King, Church's/Shell, Jack in the Box, McDonald's, Sonic, Waffle House, Whataburger	Lodg	N: Motel/Longhorn TCP S: Cash Magic Casino & Hotel, Delta Down Motor Inn	Other	N: Dollar General, Lowe's, Wal-Mart SC
Other	N: Laundry/BarbSh/WiFi/RVDump/LP/FJ TP S: WiFi/Pilot TC	TServ Other	N: Longhorn TCP/Tires, State Line Truck S\ N: Laundry/Bayou Gold TS, Laundry/Casino/Longhorn TCP, Laundry/Cash Magic TS, Delta Downs Racetrack, Casino & Hotel S: Laundry/Delta Down TS, Laundry/Delta TP, Laundry/Tobacco Plus, Vinton KOA▲, Texas Pelican RV Park▲, Starz Casino, Pelican Palace	(25)	Jct I-210E, Lake Charles Loop
874A	US 90 Bus, to Orange (EB)			26	US 90W, Columbia Southern Rd, PPG Dr, Sulphur, to Westlake
Med	S: + Hospital			Gas	N: Circle K
Other	N: Oak Leaf Park RV Park▲			27	LA 378, LA 379, Westlake (Difficult reaccess)
874B	Womack Rd (WB)			Gas	N: Circle K, Fina, Shell S: Conoco
875	FM 3247, ML King Jr Dr	7	LA 3063, West St, Vinton	Food	N: Burger King, DQ, Pizza Hut
876	Frontage Rd, Adams Bayou	TStop	N: CFN/Delta Fuel Stop/Exxon S: Love's Travel Stop #362 (Scales)	Lodg	S: Isle of Capri Hotel & Casino
Gas	N: Exxon S: Chevron◊	Food	N: Lucky Delta Café/Delta FS, Burger King, Sonic, Subway S: Arby's/Love's TS	Other	N: to Big Oaks RV Park▲, Tall Pines RV Park▲, Whispering Meadow RV Park▲, to Sam Houston Jones State Park▲ S: Riverboat Casinos, to Westlake Casino Area
Food	N: Cafe, Luby's, Richard's Cafeteria & Grill, Waffle House	Other	N: Goodrich, Lucky Delta Casino S: WiFi/Love's TS		
Lodg	N: Best Western, Best Value Inn, Days Inn, Motel 6♥, Ramada Inn, Super 8	8	LA 108, Vinton	29	LA 385, Broad St, Lakeshore Dr, Business Dist, Civic Ctr (EB)
877	TX 87, 16th St, Port Arthur, Pinehurst, Orange, Newton	FStop	N: Tiger EZ Mart/Exxon	Gas	N: Exxon S: Citgo
FStop	N: Diamond Shamrock	Gas	N: Chevron, Citgo	Food	N: Waffle House S: LA Café, Renee's
Gas	N: Chevron◊, Exxon S: Shell◊	Food	N: Pizza Inn	Lodg	N: Days Inn, Lakeview Inn, Players Island Hotel & Casino S: Best Suites, Harrah's Casino & Hotel
Food	N: California Rib Hut, Cajun Cookery, Pizza Hut, Subway, Waffle House S: Burger King, Church's, DQ, Jack in the Box, McDonald's, Sonic, Taco Bell	Lodg	N: to Vinton Motel	Other	S: Tourist Info
		Other	N: Vinton RV Park▲	30A	LA 385, Broad St, Lakeshore Dr, Business Dist, Civic Center (WB)
Lodg	N: Best Value Inn, Best Western, Days Inn, Motel 6♥, Quality Inn, Super 8♥ S: Holiday Inn Express	20	to LA 27, Ruth St, LA 1256, Sulphur, Cameron	Gas	N: Exxon S: Citgo
Other	N: Grocery, CVS S: Kroger	TStop	S: Pilot Travel Center #85	Food	N: Waffle House S: Popeye's, Steamboat Bill's
(878)	Livestock Inspection Station	Gas	N: Circle K, Chevron, Exxon, Shell S: Shell	Lodg	N: Players Island Hotel & Casino, Days Inn S: America's Best Inn, Harrah's Casino & Hotel
878	US 90 Bus, Simmons Dr, Orange	Food	N: Rest/Hol Inn, Burger King, Bonanza, Cajun Charlie's Seafood, Checkers, Hong Kong, McDonald's, Pitt Grill, Subway, Taco Bell, Wendy's S: Pizza Hut, Sonic, Waffle House	Other	S: Tourist Info
TStop	N: Sunmart #363/Mobil			30B	Ryan St, Bus District (WB)
Food	N: FastFood/SunMart	Lodg	N: Best Value Inn, Econo Lodge, Hampton Inn, Holiday Inn S: Fairfield Inn, Microtel, La Quinta Inn♥, Wingate Inn	Food	S: Barolo's, Cajun Café, Montana's Smokehouse
(879)	TX Welcome Center (WB) Rest Area (Both dir) (RR, Phone, Picnic, Vend Info)			Lodg	S: Holiday Inn, Lakeview Motel
		Med Other	N: + W Calcasieu Cameron Hospital N: Pro Tire Care, Family Dollar, Grocery, Historical Museum S: WiFi/RVDump/Pilot TC, to Grand Acadian RV Resort & Campground▲	Other	N: Amtrak
(880)	Sabine River Turn Around (EB)			31A	US 90 Bus, Enterprise Blvd Lake Charles (Serv S to Broad St)
Note	MM 880.5 LA State Line			Gas	S: BP◊, Exxon
		21	LA 3077, LA 27, Arizona St, DeQuincy	Food	S: Captain Seafood, Jim's Seafood, Popeye's Chicken
ⓞ	**TEXAS**	FStop	N: Super Saver Express/Chevron	Lodg	S: Howard Johnson
ⓞ	**LOUISIANA** (CENTRAL TIME ZONE)	Gas	N: Conoco, Citgo, Exxon S: USA Super Shop/Citgo◊	31B	Prater St, Shattuck St, US 90E, to US 171, LA 14, Lake Charles (Difficult reaccess)
(1)	Sabine River Turn Around (WB)	Food	N: FastFood/Super Saver Exp, Boiling Point, China Taste, Papa John's S: Cajun Deli/USA	TStop	N: Road King Truck Stop/Shell (Scales) S: Coastal
(1)	LA Welcome Center (EB) Rest Area (RR, Phone, Vend, Sec)	Med Other	N: + W Calcasieu Cameron Hospital N: CVS, $ General, Kroger, NAPA, Walgreen's, to Royal Palace Casino S: Wagin Cajun$, to Hidden Ponds RV Park▲	Food	N: Rest/Road King TS S: McDonald's
(2)	Port of Entry/Weigh Station (Both dir)			Lodg	S: Econo Lodge, Motel 6♥, Sunrise Inn
				TServ	N: Road King TS/Tires
4	US 90E, LA 109, Toomey Rd, Vinton, to Toomey, Starks	23	LA 108, S Cities Service Hwy, Sulphur. Industries	32	Opelousas St, Lake Charles
TStop	N: Bayou Gold Truck Stop #3120/Exxon, Longhorn Truck & Car Plaza/Chevron (Scales), Cash Magic Truck Stop S: Delta Town Truck Stop/Shell, Delta Truck Plaza, Tobacco Plus #5/Exxon	TStop	N: CFN/Winners Choice Truck Stop/Citgo	Gas	N: Exxon
		Gas	N: Exxon, Murphy S: Circle K, Citgo, Conoco◊	Lodg	N: Motel 6♥ S: Treasure Inn
Food	N: Rest/Bayou Gold TS, Rest/FastFood/Longhorn TCP, Rest/FastFood/Cash Magic, Texas Longhorn, Waffle Shoppe	Food	N: Rest/FastFood/Winners Choice TS, Subway/Exxon, Blimpie, Chili's, China Wok, Little Caesar's Pizza, McDonald's/WalMart, Sonic, Taco Bell	33	US 171N, to LA 14, DeRidder
				Gas	N: Chevron, RaceWay, Shamrock
				Food	N: Burger King, McDonald's, Taco Bell

◊ = Regular Gas Stations with Diesel   ▲ = RV Friendly Locations   ♥ = Pet Friendly Locations
RED PRINT SHOWS LARGE VEHICLE PARKING/ACCESS ON SITE OR NEARBY   BROWN PRINT SHOWS CAMPGROUNDS/RV PARKS

EXIT		LOUISIANA
	Lodg	N: Baymont Inn, Best Western, Comfort Inn, Days Inn, La Quinta Inn♥, S: Holiday Inn Express, Motel 6♥
	Other	N: AutoZone, CVS, Wal-Mart sc, Walgreen's, Sam Houston Jones State Park, Yogi Bear's Jellystone Camp▲
(34)		Jct I-210W, Lake Charles Loop
	Other	N: Pine Shadows Golf Course S: Chennault Int'l Airport✈
36		LA 397, Ward Line Rd, Lk Charles to Creole, Cameron
	TStop	N: Fuel Stop 36/Conoco (Scales) S: Chardele Auto & Truck Plaza/Chevron
	Food	S: FastFood/Chardele ATP, J Wesley
	Lodg	S: Sunrise Inn
	TServ	N: FS 36/Tires
	TWash	N: FS 36
	Other	N: Jean LaFitte RV Park▲, to Yogi Bear's Jellystone Park▲ S: Laundry/RVDump/Chardele ATP, Casino, to Chennault Int'l Airport✈, Mallard Cove Golf Course
43		LA 383, Thompson Ave, Lake Charles, Iowa
	TStop	N: Love's Travel Stop #243 (Scales), King's Travel Plaza/Exxon (Scales) S: Speedy Stop/Conoco
	Gas	S: Citgo◆, Shell, Valero
	Food	N: Burger King, Hardee's/Love's TS, Rest/FF/King's TP S: McDonald's/Speedy Stop, Big Daddy's Cajun Seafood & Steaks, Fausto's Rest, Subway
	Lodg	N: Howard Johnson Express S: Deluxe Inn, Sunrise Inn
	TServ	N: King's TP/Tires
	Other	N: Laundry/Casino/WiFi/RVDump/Love's TS, Laundry/Casino/RVDump/King's TP, Jean Lafitte RV Park▲ S: Laundry/Speedy Stop, Factory Outlet Stores, Cypress Bend RV Park▲
44		LA 165, Iowa, Alexandria, Kinder
	Lodg	N: Scottish Inn
	Other	N: to 12mi: Quiet Oaks RV Park▲, to Coushatta Casino and Resort
48		LA 101, Iowa, Lacassine, Kinder
	Gas	S: Exxon
54		LA 99, Adams St, Welsh
	Gas	S: Chevron, Conoco◆, Exxon◆
	Food	S: Cajun Tales, DQ, Subway
59		LA 395, Roanoke
64		LA 26, Lake Arthur Ave, Jennings, to Elton, Lake Arthur
	TStop	S: Jennings Travel Center/Shell (Scales)
	Gas	S: Citgo, Chevron, Exxon, Fina, Valero, Murphy◆
	Food	N: Mike's Seafood Rest S: Rest/Jennings TC, Burger King, DQ, Denny's, General Wok, McDonald's, Pizza Hut, Shoney's, Taco Bell, Waffle House, Walker's Cajun Dining, Wendy's
	Lodg	N: Boudreax Inn, Budget Inn S: Holiday Inn, Quality Inn
	Med	S: + Jennings Hospital
	Other	S: Laundry/RVDump/Jennings TP, AutoZone, Auto Dealers, Dollar Tree, Bank, Goodyear, RiteAid, Wal-Mart sc▲, Tourist Info, Jennings Airport✈, La Maison RV Park▲

EXIT		LOUISIANA
65		LA 97, Evangeline Rd, Jennings
	FStop	S: Gottson Oi/Spur
	TStop	S: CFN/Road Master Travel Plaza/P66
	Food	S: Rest/FF/Road Master TP
	Lodg	S: Days Inn
	Other	S: Laundry/Casino/Road Master TP
72		Egan Hwy, Trumps Rd, Egan
	Other	S: Cajun Haven RV Park▲
76		LA 91, Crowley, Iota, Estherwood
	TStop	S: I-10 Auto/Truck Stop/Mobil, Petro 2 Exxon (Scales)
	Food	S: Rest/FF/I-10 ATS, PetroDiner/Subway/Petro 2
	TServ	S: I-10 ATS
	Other	S: Laundry/I-20 ATS, Laundry/Petro 2
80		LA 13, Parkerson Ave, Crowley
	TStop	N: Exit 80 Travel Plaza/Conoco (Scales)
	Gas	N: Texaco S: Chevron◆, Exxon◆, RaceWay
	Food	N: Rest/Ex 80 TP, Rest/BW, Rest/La Quinta, Fezzo's Seafood & Steakhouse, Rice Palace S: Burger King, Eldorado Mex, KFC, Lucky Wok, McDonald's, Mr Gatti's, PJ's Grill, Sonic, Subway, Taco Bell
	Lodg	N: Best Western, Crowley Inn, Days Inn, La Quinta Inn♥ S: Carriage House
	TServ	N: Dubus Engine Co S: Lee's Auto & Truck Repair
	Other	N: Laundry/Casino/Ex 80 TP, Muscrat Haven Campground▲ S: Auto Dealers, O'Reilly Auto, RiteAid, Winn Dixie, U-Haul
82		LA 1111, Tower Rd, E Crowley
	Gas	S: Murphy
	Food	S: Chili's, Subway, Wendy's
	Med	S: + American Legion Hospital
	Other	S: Wal-Mart sc▲
87		LA 35, LA 98, Rayne
	FStop	S: Econo-Mart/Mobil
	TStop	S: Frog City AmBest Travel Plaza/Citgo (Scales) (DAND)
	Gas	N: Chevron, Exxon S: Valero
	Food	N: Burger King, Chef Roy's Frog City Café, McDonald's, Subway/Exxpm S: Rest/FastFood/Frog City TP, Gabe's Cajun, Great Wall Chinese, Popeye's, DQ, McDonald's, Subway
	Lodg	N: Days Inn S: Best Western
	TServ	S: Frog City TP, Young's Trucking Svc, Raymond's Truck & Trailer Repair
	TWash	S: Frog City TP
	Med	S: + Hospital
	Other	N: Casino/Days Inn, Casino/Exxon S: Casino/Laundry/CB/LP/RVDump/Frog City TP, Advance Auto Parts, CVS, NAPA, Winn Dixie
92		LA 95, Rayne, to Duson
	TStop	N: Studebaker Texaco Travel Plaza (Scales) S: I-10/Duson Travel Center/Chevron, Big D Truck Stop/BP, Four Deuces Truck Stop/Exxon
	Food	N: Rest/FastFood/Studebaker TP S: FastFood/Duson TC, FastFood/Big D TS, Rest/Four Deuces TS, Thibodeaux's

EXIT		LOUISIANA
	Lodg	S: Super 8
	Other	N: Laundry/Casino/WiFi/RVDump/Studebaker Texaco TP S: Laundry/Duson TC, Laundry/4 Deuces TS, Laundry/Big D TS, Frog City RV Park▲
97		LA 93, LA 3168, Scott, Cankton
	Gas	S: Chevron, Cracker Barrel Convenience, Shell◆
	Food	S: Fezzo's Seafood & Steakhouse III, McDonald's/Chevron, Subway
	Lodg	N: Howard Johnson Express S: Holiday Inn Express
	Other	S: Lafayette KOA▲, Cajun Harley Davidson
100		LA 3184, Ambassador Caffery Pkwy, Scott
	Gas	N: Chevron◆, Exxon S: BP, Chevron, Exxon, RaceTrac, Shell◆
	Food	N: Subway/Exxon S: Burger King, Cracker Barrel, Taco Bell, Waffle House
	Lodg	N: Ambassador Inn S: Hampton Inn, Microtel, Sleep Inn
	TServ	S: Peterbilt
	Med	S: + University Medical Center, + Southwest Medical Center
	Other	N: Gauthier RV Center S: Family $, to Cajun Dome
101		LA 182, University Ave, Lafayette
	FStop	N: Jubilee Express #4627/Ride USA
	TStop	N: Travel Center of America #161 (Scales)
	Gas	N: Chevron S: Chevron, RaceTrac, Shell◆
	Food	N: CountryPride/Arby's/PizzaHut/TA TC, McDonald's/Chevron, Burger King, Waffle House, Whataburger S: Cracker Barrel, McDonald's, Subway, Taco Torro, Toddle House Diner
	Lodg	N: Red Roof Inn♥ S: Best Value Inn, Best Western, Days Inn, Drury Inn, Hilton Garden Inn, St Francis Motel
	TServ	N: TA TC
	Med	N: + Vermilion Hospital S: + Our Lady of Lourdes Med Ctr
	Other	N: Laundry/WiFi/RVDump/TA TC, Wetlands Golf Course S: Auto Service, Tires, O'Reilly Auto, to Univ of La/Lafayette
103A		US 167S, Lafayette, to US 90
	Gas	S: Chevron, Shell, Murphy
	Food	S: Checker's, KFC, McDonald's, Pizza Hut, Popeye's, Shoney's, Subway, Taco Bell, Waffle House
	Lodg	S: Best Western, Fairfield Inn, Holiday Inn, Jameson Inn, La Quinta Inn♥, Quality Inn, Shoney's Inn, Super 8
	Med	S: + Hospital
	Other	S: Albertson's, CVS, Firestone, Home Depot, Wal-Mart sc▲, to Lafayette Reg'l Airport✈, Visitor Center
(103B)		Jct I-49N, US 167, to Opelousas
	Gas	N: Shell
	Food	N: Church's Chicken
	Lodg	N: Motel 6♥, Ramada Inn, Rodeway Inn
	Other	N: to Flea Market, RV Center
104		Louisiana Ave, to Johnston St, to US 167, Lafayette (Services N to Moss St)
	Gas	N: Diamond Shamrock

◆ = Regular Gas Stations with Diesel   ▲ = RV Friendly Locations   ♥ = Pet Friendly Locations

RED PRINT SHOWS LARGE VEHICLE PARKING/ACCESS ON SITE OR NEARBY   BROWN PRINT SHOWS CAMPGROUNDS/RV PARKS

Page 55

EXIT	LOUISIANA
Food	N: Burger King, Mimi's Kitchen, Pizza
Other	N: Family Dollar
	S: Office Depot, Target, Shopping Center
(108)	Weigh Station (Both dir)
109	LA 328, Breaux Bridge
TStop	N: Silver's Travel Center/Texaco
	S: Pilot Travel Center #274 (Scales)
Gas	S: Chevron, Mobil, Shell
Food	N: Hardee's/Silver's TC, Crawdaddy's Seafood Boilers
	S: Arby's/TJCinn/Pilot TC, Burger King/Mobil, Popeye's/Chevron, Domino's, McDonald's, Waffle House, Wendy's
Lodg	S: Best Western, Sona Inn
Other	N: Laundry/BarbSh/Silver's TC, Tourist Info, Poche's Fish-N-Camp▲
	S: Laundry/Casino/WiFi/Pilot TC, Wal-Mart sc, Auto Dealers, Walgreen's, Pioneer Campground▲
115	LA 347, Grandpoint Hwy. Breaux Bridge, Henderson, Cecilia
FStop	N: Little Capital Exxon
	S: I-10 Travel Center/Valero
TStop	N: Diesi's Lucky Capital/BP
	S: PTP/Bayou Belle Truck Stop & Casino, Henderson Travel Plaza/Citgo (Scales)
Gas	N: Texaco◊
	S: Chevron◊, Shell
Food	N: FastFood/Little Capital Exxon, Rest/FastFood/Diesi's BP, Boudin's
	S: FastFood/Bayou Belle TS, FastFood/Henderson TP, FastFood/I-10 TC, Crawfish Town USA, Landry's Seafood, McDonald's/Shell, Subway, Waffle House
Lodg	N: Cajun Country Cottages
	S: Best Western, Holiday Inn Express
Other	S: Laundry/WiFi/Bayou Belle TS, Laundry/Casino/Henderson TP, to Pioneer Campground▲, Cajun Palms RV Resort▲
NOTE:	MM 115: Begin EB, End WB Call Boxes
121	LA 3177, Butte La Rose
Other	N: to Frenchmens Wilderness CG▲
	LA Welcome Center (Both dir) (RR, Vend, Sec, WiFi, RVDump)
127	LA 975, Grosse Tete, Whiskey Bay
135	LA 3000, Ramah, Maringouin
NOTE:	MM 136: Begin WB, End EB Call Boxes
139	LA 77, Bayou Rd, Grosse Tete, Rosedale, Maringouin
TStop	N: Bayou Shell Truck Stop
	S: Tiger Truck Stop/Conoco
Food	N: Subway/Shell
	S: Rest/FastFood/Tiger TS
TServ	N: Bayou TS/Tires
	S: Tiger TS/Tires
Other	N: Laundry/Casino/Bayou TS
	S: Laundry/LiveTigerExhibit/Tiger TS
151	LA 415, Lobdell Hwy, to US 190, Port Allen, Alexandria, Westport, Opelousas
TStop	N: Pilot Travel Center #426 (Scales), Port Allen Truck Stop & Casino, Cash's Truck Plaza (Scales), H&R Truck Stop, Minnow's II Truck Stop
	6mi W on US 190: Cajun Circus Truck Stop

EXIT	LOUISIANA
TStop	S: River Port Truck Stop/Shell, Love's Travel Stop #240 (Scales),
Gas	N: Chevron, RaceTrac
	S: Shell
Food	N: FastFood/Pilot TC, Rest/FastFood/Cash's TP, Rest/H&R TS, Rest/Port Allen TS, Rest/Cajun Circus TS, Burger King, Domino's, McDonald's, Kajun BBQ & Tamales, Popeye's, Shoney's, Waffle House, Wendy's
	S: Rest/FastFood/River Port TS, Arby's/Love's TS, KFC/TacoBell
Lodg	N: Best Western, Comfort Suites, Days Inn, Holiday Inn Express, Shoney's Inn
	S: Audubon Inn, Motel 6♥, Super 8
Other	N: Laundry/Casino/Cash's TP, Laundry/Casino/Cajun Circus TS, Goldmine Casino, Cajun Country Campground▲ Wal-Mart
	S: Laundry/WiFi/RVDump/Casino/Love's TS
153	LA 1, Port Allen, Plaquemine, Port of Baton Rouge
TStop	N: N to US 190: Lucky Louie's Truck Stop, TMI Fuel Stop (Scales)
	S: LA 1 South Truck Stop/BP
Gas	N: Amoco, Chevron, Shell, Spirit
	S: RaceTrac
Food	N: FastFood/Louie's TS, Rest/TMI FS, Best Lil PoBoy House, PicAPac Fried Chicken, River Queen Drive In
	S: FastFood/LA 1S TS, Waffle House
Lodg	N: Ed's Motel
	S: Days Inn, Port Allen Inn, Super 8
Other	N: Laundry/TMI FS, IGA, to Southern Univ, A&M College
	S: Laundry/LA 1S TS
155A	LA 30, Nicholson Dr, Highland Rd, Baton Rouge, Downtown
Gas	S: Mobil, Shell
Food	S: Chinese Inn
Lodg	N: Sheraton
Med	N: + Baton Rouge Medical Center
Other	N: FedEx/Kinkos, UPS Store, Belle of Baton Rouge Casino, Conv Center
	S: to Louisiana State Univ
(155B)	Jct I-110N, to Baton Rouge Bus District, Airport (EB-Left Exit)
Other	N: to Southern Univ, A&M College, Memorial Stadium, Baton Rouge Metro Airport✈
155C	Louise St, Baton Rouge (WB)
156A	Washington St (EB ex, WB reacc)
156B	Dalrymple Dr
Other	S: to LA State Univ
157A	Perkins Rd (Ebex, WB reacc)
Gas	S: Shell
Other	N: City Park Golf Course
	S: Wal-Mart
157B	Acadian Thruway, Stanford Ave
Gas	N: Chevron, Citgo, Shell
	S: Exxon, Shell
Food	N: Denny's, Rib's Rest
	S: Lone Star Steak House, Outback Steakhouse
Lodg	N: Comfort Inn, La Quinta Inn♥ Marriott
	S: Courtyard
Other	S: Wal-Mart

EXIT	LOUISIANA
158	College Dr, Baton Rouge
Gas	N: Jubilee Express/RideUSA
	S: Chevron, Shell
Food	N: CiCi's, Damon's, Fuddrucker's, Hooters, Jason's Deli, Macaroni Grill, Ruby Tuesday, Starbucks, Subway, Waffle House
	S: Burger King, Chili's, IHOP, Gino's Italian, McDonald's, Ruth Chris Steak House, Starbucks, Taco Bell
Lodg	N: Best Western, Chase Suites, Extended Stay, Homewood Suites, Marriott
	S: Comfort Inn, Crown Suites, Embassy Suites, Hampton Inn, Holiday Inn Express, Radisson
Med	N: + US Vets Outpatient Clinic, + Synergy Hospital
Other	N: B&N, Cinema, UPS Store
	S: Albertson's, Dollar Tree, RiteAid, Office Depot, Walgreen's, Wal-Mart sc ▲
(159)	Jct I-12E, to Hammond (EB, Left exit)
TServ	N: N US 61/US 190: Timmons Int'l
160	LA 3064, Essen Lane
Gas	S: Chevron, Exxon
Food	S: Burger King, Copeland's, McDonald's
Lodg	S: Fairfield Inn, SpringHill Suites
Med	S: + Our Lady of the Lake Regional Medical Center
Other	S: Albertson's, Walgreen's
162	Bluebonnet Blvd, Baton Rouge
Gas	N: Chevron◊
	S: RaceWay
Food	S: Boutin's Rest, Burger King, Copeland's, Logan's Roadhouse, Ralph & Kacoo's
Lodg	N: Quality Suites
	S: AmeriSuites
Med	S: + Health Center
Other	S: Mall of Louisiana, Best Buy
163	Siegen Lane
Gas	N: Chevron, RaceTrac, Shell
	S: Sam's
Food	N: Burger King, McDonald's, IHOP, Olive Garden, Shoney's, Smoky Bones BBQ, Subway, Taco Bell, Waffle House
	S: Chili's, Joe's Crab Shack, Subway, Wendy's
Lodg	N: Baymont Inn, Hampton Inn, Holiday Inn, Microtel, Motel 6♥
	S: Courtyard, Residence Inn
Other	N: PetCo♥, Office Depot, Target
	S: Lowe's, Sam's Club, Wal-Mart
166	LA 42, LA 427, Highland Rd
Gas	N: Chevron
	S: Shell, Texaco
Food	N: Cracker Barrel, Mexican, Popeye's, Sonic, Waffle House
	S: Subway
Other	N: Home Depot, Fun Park
173	LA 73, Geismar, Prairieville
Gas	N: Shell◊
	S: Exxon◊, Mobil◊
Food	S: Burger King, Sonic, Subway
Other	S: Twin Lakes RV Park▲
177	LA 30, Gonzalez, St Gabriel
TStop	N: USA Auto Truck Plaza/Citgo (Scales)
Gas	N: Shell
	S: Chevron, Shell
Food	N: Rest/USA ATP, Burger King, McDonald's, Jack in the Box, Shoney's, Taco Bell, Waffle House
	S: Chili's, Cracker Barrel, Wendy's

◊ = Regular Gas Stations with Diesel　▲ = RV Friendly Locations　♥ = Pet Friendly Locations
RED PRINT SHOWS LARGE VEHICLE PARKING/ACCESS ON SITE OR NEARBY　BROWN PRINT SHOWS CAMPGROUNDS/RV PARKS

W 10 E — INTERSTATE

EXIT		LOUISIANA
	Lodg	N: Motel/USA TP, Best Western, Days Inn, Budget Inn, Holiday Inn, Quality Inn S: Comfort Inn
	TWash	N: USA TP
	TServ	N: USA TP, Robert Tire Service
	Other	N: Laundry/USA TP, Auto Dealer, Cabela's S: Vesta RV Park▲, Tanger Outlet Mall
179		LA 44, Gonzales, Burnside
	FStop	N: Popingo's #202/Mobil
	Gas	N: Circle K
182		LA 22, Sorrento, Donaldsonville
	FStop	S: Speedy Junction
	TStop	S: Sorrento Super Stop/Chevron (Scales)
	Gas	N: Chevron
	Food	S: FastFood/Sorrento SS, Huddle House, McDonald's, Waffle House
	Other	S: Laundry/Sorrento SS
187		US 61, S - Gramercy, N - Sorrento
194		LA 641S, Gramercy, Lutcher
206		LA 3188S, Belle Terre Blvd, LaPlace, Reserve
	TStop	S: S to US 61W: Riverbend Truck Stop
	Gas	S: Shell
	Food	S: McDonald's
	Lodg	S: Millett Motel
(207)		Weigh Station (Both dir)
209		US 51 to I-55N (EB), La Place, Hammond, to Jackson
	FStop	S: Speedway
	TStop	S: Pilot Travel Center #82 (Scales), LaPlace Travel Center/Texaco (Scales)
	Gas	S: Chevron, Shell
	Food	S: Subway/Pilot TC, Rest/LaPlace TC, Basile's, McDonald's, Pier 51 Seafood Rest, Shoney's, Waffle House, Wendy's
	Lodg	S: Best Western, Days Inn, Holiday Inn, Hampton Inn
	TServ	S: LaPlace TC/Tires
	Other	S: Laundry/WiFi/RVDump/Pilot TC, Laundry/LaPlace TC, LaPlace Trailer Park & Camp▲, R&S MH & RV Park▲, Uncle Sam's RV & Trailer Park▲, Cruise America RV Rentals
(210)		Jct I-55N, Hammond (WB)
(220)		Jct 310S, Boutte, to Houma
221		Loyola Dr, Veterans Memorial Hwy, Kenner
	Gas	N: Circle K, Exxon◊, Shell◊, Spur, Sam's S: Amoco, Circle K
	Food	N: McDonald's, Popeye's, Rally's, Taco Bell S: Rick's Famous Café, Wendy's
	Lodg	S: Days Inn, Motel 6♥, Wingate Inn
	Med	N: + Kenner Regional Medical Center
	Other	N: Pharmacy, Sam's Club, Wal-Mart sc S: NO Int'l Airport✈
223AB		LA 49, Williams Blvd, NO Intl (EB)
223B		New Orleans Int'l Airport (WB)
223A		LA 49, Williams Blvd, 32nd St (WB)
	Gas	N: Exxon, Shell S: Exxon, Shell
	Food	N: Burger King, El Patio, Fisherman's Cove, Jade Palace, Pizza Hut, Taco Bell S: Denny's, McDonald's, Subway

Personal Notes

EXIT		LOUISIANA
	Lodg	N: Fairfield Inn S: Best Western, Comfort Inn, Days Inn, Extended Stay, Holiday Inn, La Quinta Inn♥, Radisson, Wingate Inn
	Other	N: AutoZone, Office Depot, PetCo♥, RiteAid, Wal-Mart S: Goodyear, NAPA, Mall, PetSmart♥, Wal-Mart, New Orleans West KOA▲
224		Power Blvd (WB)
225		Veterans Blvd, Metairie
	Gas	N: Chevron, Shell, Spur S: Shell, Speedway
	Food	N: Celebration Station, Denny's, Donut Den, McDonald's, Subway, Taco Bell S: Godfather's Pizza, Popeye's Chicken, Wendy's, New Orleans Seafood
	Lodg	N: La Quinta Inn♥ S: Holiday Inn
	Med	N: + Hospital
	Other	N: Mall, Lafreniere Park, RiteAid S: Best Buy, Home Depot, Kmart, Office Depot, Wal-Mart, Walgreen's, Celebration Station, to Sam's Club
226		LA 3152, Clearview Pky, Huey Long Bridge, Metairie
	Gas	N: Chevron, Exxon S: Chevron, Circle K
	Food	N: Café East, Ruby Tuesday, Webster's S: Burger King, Piccadilly's, Shoney's, Subway, Wing Zone
	Lodg	N: Sleep Inn S: Guest House, Shoney's Inn, SunSuites
	AServ	S: Green Acres Towing & Repair

EXIT		LOUISIANA
	Med	N: + E Jefferson General Hospital
	Other	N: Target, Clearview Mall, AMC 12
228		Causeway Blvd, Downtown Metairie, Mandeville
	Gas	N: Exxon, Shell S: BP, Exxon, Phillips 66
	Food	N: Acme Oysterhouse, Bravo Cucina Italian, Burger King, Causeway Grill, ChicFilA, Cuco's Mexican, Outback Steakhouse, Steak Escape S: Rest/Days Hotel, Rest/Wyndham, Cajun Grill & Bar, Café Fresca, Denny's, IHOP, NO Hamburger & Seafood, Subway
	Lodg	N: Best Western, Hampton Inn, Ramada Inn S: Courtyard, Days Hotel, Extended Stay, Holiday Inn, La Quinta Inn♥, Plaza Suite, Quality Inn, Sheraton, Wyndham
	Med	N: + Omega Hospital
	Other	N: Kmart, Grocery, Shopping Center S: to Sam's Club
229		Bonnabel Blvd, Metairie
(230)		Jct I-610E, to Slidell (EB)
(231B)		Jct I-610E, Florida Blvd, W End Blvd (WB)
231A		LA 611, Metairie Rd, City Park Ave, New Orleans
	Other	N: Degado Comm College, Tad Gormley Stadium S: New Orleans Museum of Art
232		US 61, Airline Hwy, Tulane Ave, Howard Ave, Carrollton Ave
	Gas	N: Amoco S: Exxon
	Food	N: Burger King S: McDonald's, Piccadilly
	Lodg	N: Crystal Inn, Quality Inn S: Keystone Motel
	Other	N: Fairgrounds Race Course S: Xavier Univ of LA
234A		US 90W, Claiborne Ave, Poydras St, Superdome (EB)
234B		Poydras St, Claiborne Ave, Superdome (EB, Left exit)
	Lodg	S: Hyatt, Holiday Inn, Ramada Inn
	Med	N: + Medical Center of LA West
	Other	N: Best Western S: Downtown, Superdome, NO Arena, Amtrak, Greyhound, LA State Univ, NO Centre
234C		Poydras St, Howard Ave, US 90 Bus, LA 3139, Claiborne Ave, Earhart Blvd (WB, Left exit)
	Med	S: + Tulane Univ Medical Center
	Other	S: Greyhound, Amtrak, Tulane Univ
235C		Poydras St, Superdome (WB)
235B		Canal St, Superdome (WB)
	Food	S: Rest/Days Inn
	Lodg	N: NO Grand Palace Hotel, Ramada, Rodeway Inn S: Clarion, Days Inn, Radisson, Warwick Hotel
235A		Orleans Ave, Vieux Carre French Quarter, Superdome
	Gas	S: Chevron
	Food	S: Café, Mama Rosa's

◊ = Regular Gas Stations with Diesel   ▲ = RV Friendly Locations   ♥ = Pet Friendly Locations

RED PRINT SHOWS LARGE VEHICLE PARKING/ACCESS ON SITE OR NEARBY   BROWN PRINT SHOWS CAMPGROUNDS/RV PARKS

EXIT	LOUISIANA
Lodg	N: Rainbow Inn Hotel
	S: Creole House, Maison Dupry Hotel
Other	S: French Quarter RV Resort▲
236A	**Esplanade Ave, Downtown (EB)**
Gas	S: Gas
236B	**LA 39, N Claiborne Ave (EB)**
TStop	N: PTP/Mardi Gras Truck Stop (Scales)
Food	N: Burger King, McDonald's
Other	N: Laundry/RVdump/Mardi Gras TS
236C	**St Bernard Ave, Downtown (WB)**
237	**LA 3021, Elysian Fields Ave**
TStop	N: Mardi Gras Truck Stop (Scales)
Gas	S: Chevron
Other	N: Laundry/RVdump/Mardi Gras TS, Dillard Univ, Univ of New Orleans
(238A)	**Jct I-610W, Baton Rouge, New Orleans Int'l Airport→ (WB)**
238A	**Franklin Ave (WB)**
(238B)	**Jct I-610W (WB)**
239	**Louisa St, Almonaster Blvd (WB)**
239AB	**Louisa St, Almonaster Blvd (EB)**
TStop	N: PTP/Big Easy Travel Plaza (Scales)
Gas	N: Chevron, Exxon
Food	N: Rest/FastFood/Big Easy TP, Burger King, McDonald's, Pizza Hut, Popeye's, Sonic, Wendy's
Lodg	N: Econo Lodge, Friendly Inn, Howard Johnson, Knights Inn, Royal Inn
TServ	N: Big Easy TP
Other	N: Laundry/RVdump/Big Easy TP, Goodyear, Kmart, Walgreen's, Winn Dixie, Mall
	Mardi Gras RV Park▲, Riverboat Travel Park▲
240A	**Jourdan Rd, Downman Rd, US 90 LA 3021, New Orleans (EB)**
Gas	N: Shell, Spur
	S: Chevron
Food	N: Church's, McDonald's, Popeye's
Lodg	N: Red Carpet Inn
Other	N: Mardi Gras RV Park▲, Riverboat Travel Park▲
240B	**US 90, Chef Hwy**
Gas	N: Chevron, Exxon, Shell
Food	N: Church's Chicken, Pizza Hut, Subway
Lodg	N: Econo Lodge, Howard Johnson, Monte Carlo Hotel, Knights Inn, Red Carpet Inn, Royal Inn, Super 8
241	**LA 3021, Morrison Rd**
Gas	N: Shell
Food	N: Burger King
AServ	N: Shell
Other	N: NO Lakefront Airport→

EXIT	LOUISIANA
242	**Crowder Blvd**
Gas	S: Exxon, Shell
Food	S: Denny's, Rally, Shoney's, Wendy's
Lodg	S: La Quinta Inn♥
244	**Read Blvd, New Orleans**
Gas	N: Shell
	S: Spur◊
Food	N: Lama Seafood, McDonald's, Subway
	S: Lamar's Creole, Popeye's, Pizza Palace
Lodg	S: Best Western, Days Inn, Holiday Inn Express, Studio 6
Med	S: + East Lake Hospital
Other	N: Sam's Club, Walgreen's, Wal-Mart
	S: Goodyear, Mall, Walgreen's
245	**Bullard Ave**
Gas	N: Chevron, Shell
	S: Exxon, Shell
Food	N: IHOP, James Seafood, Pizza Hut, Sonic
	S: Burger King, Shoney's, Subway, Taco Bell
Lodg	N: Comfort Suites, Fairfield Inn, La Quinta Inn♥
	S: Best Western, Studio 6
Med	S: + Hospital
Other	N: Home Depot, Pep Boys
(246AB)	**Jct I-510S, LA 47, S to Chalmette, Michoud (EB), N to Little Woods**
TStop	S: to EX 2C: The Palace Truckstop, Paradise Truck Stop
Other	S: to Six Flags of New Orleans, NASA Michoud Assembly Factory
248	**LA 68, Michoud Blvd**
251	**LA 72, Bayou Sauvage National Wildlife Refuge**
254	**US 11, Irish Bayou, N Shore Dr**
TStop	S: Irish Bayou Travel Center/BP
Food	S: FastFood/Irish Bayou TS
Other	S: Laundry/Irish Bayou TS
261	**Oak Harbor Blvd, Eden Isles**
Gas	N: Exxon
	S: BP
Food	N: Café
Lodg	S: Sleep Inn
263	**LA 433, Slidell**
FStop	S: Interstate Station #17/Texaco
TStop	S: Fleet Travel Center #601 (Scales)
Gas	S: BP, Exxon
Food	N: China Buffet, Waffle House
	S: Subway/Fleet TC, Rest/Holiday Inn, McDonald's, Wendy's
Lodg	N: Hampton Inn
	S: Holiday Inn Hotel

EXIT	LA / MS
Other	S: Factory Outlet Mall, New Orleans East KOA▲, Pinecrest RV Park
(265)	**Weigh Station (Both dir)**
266	**US 190, Slidell**
TStop	N: Travel Center of America #180 (Scales)
Gas	N: Exxon◊
	S: Chevron
Food	N: Rest/TA TC, Burger King, Denny's, KFC, McDonald's, Pizza Hut, Shoney's, Taco Bell, Wendy's
	S: Applebee's, Cracker Barrel, Osaka, Grill, Outback Steakhouse, Waffle House
Lodg	N: Best Western, Days Inn, Deluxe Inn, Motel 6♥, Super 8
	S: Guest Lodge, La Quinta Inn♥, Plaza Inn, Ramada Inn
TServ	N: TA TC
Med	S: + Northshore Reg'l Med Center
Other	N: Laundry/WiFi/RVdump/TA TC, Cinema 8, Harley Davidson, Office Depot, Grocery, U-Haul
	S: Casino, Lowe's, Wal-Mart▲
(267A)	**Jct I-59N, to Meridian**
(267B)	**Jct I-12W, to Baton Rouge**
(270)	**LA Welcome Center (WB) (CLOSED) Rest Area (RR, Vend, Sec, RVdump)**

(CENTRAL TIME ZONE)

ⓄLOUISIANA
ⓄMISSISSIPPI

(CENTRAL TIME ZONE)

(1)	**Weigh Station (Both dir)**
2	**MS 607, Bay St Louis, to Waveland, NASA Stennis Space Center**
S:	MS Welcome Center (Both dir) (RR, Phone, Picnic, RVdump, Sec247) (NO Trucks/Buses)
Other	S: John C Stennis Space Center
	S: Buccaneer State Park/Closed, Bay St Louis/Gulfport KOA▲
(10)	**Parking Area (EB)**
13	**MS 43, MS 603, Kiln Rd, Bay St Louis, Kiln, Picayune, Waveland (4-5 mi S to US 90)**
FStop	S: Todd's Chevron
Gas	S: Circle K, Exxon, Murphy
Food	S: FastFood/Todd's, Café Reef, Chester's Fried Chicken, Nick's House of Catfish, Subway

◊ = Regular Gas Stations with Diesel   ▲ = RV Friendly Locations   ♥ = Pet Friendly Locations
RED PRINT SHOWS LARGE VEHICLE PARKING/ACCESS ON SITE OR NEARBY   BROWN PRINT SHOWS CAMPGROUNDS/RV PARKS

INTERSTATE 10 W / E

EXIT		MISSISSIPPI
	Lodg	S: Hotel, Budget Inn, Casino Magic Inn, Holiday Inn, Texan Motel, Travel Express Inn, Waffles Rainbow Motel
	Med	S: + Hancock Medical Center
	Other	N: McLeod State Park/Closed, Stennis Int'l Airport✈, Nella's RV Park▲ S: Bay St Louis/Gulfport KOA▲, Bay Marina RV Park▲, Hollywood RV Park▲, U-Haul, Wal-Mart, Casino Magic, Amtrak, Auto Dealers
16		Interchange St, Diamondhead
	Gas	N: BP, Kangaroo Express #3752 S: Chevron
	Food	N: Burger King, Chipolte Mex Grill, DQ, Domino's, Subway, Waffle House
	Lodg	N: Ramada Inn S: Comfort Inn
	Med	N: + Hancock Medical Center
	Other	S: Diamondhead Airport✈
20		Kiln DeLisle Rd, Pass Christian
	Gas	N: Spur
24		Menge Ave, Pass Christian
	TStop	N: MS Fuel Center #17/Chevron (Scales)
	Gas	S: I-10 Quick Stop/Texaco
	Food	N: FastFood/MS FC
	TServ	N: MS FC
	TWash	N: MS FC
	Other	N: Laundry/RVDump/MS FC S: Flea Market & RV Park▲, Oaks Golf Club, to Beaches
28		County Farm Rd, Gulfport, to Long Beach, Pass Christian
	Gas	S: Chevron
	Other	S: to Magic River Resort▲, Plantation Pines Park▲
31		Canal Rd, Gulfport
	TStop	N: Love's Travel Stop #212 (Scales)(DAND) S: Flying J Travel Plaza #5065/Conoco (Scales)
	Gas	S: Shell
	Food	N: Arby's/Love's TS, McDonald's S: Rest/FastFood/FJ TP, Waffle House, Wendy's
	Lodg	S: CrystalInn/Flying J TP, Econo Lodge
	TServ	N: Dee's 24 Hr Tire Service
	Other	N: Laundry/WiFi/RVDump/Love's TS, BayBerry RV Park▲, RV Repair S: Laundry/BarbSh/WiFi/LP/RVDump/FJ TP, Plantation Pines RV Park▲, Univ of S MS Reg'l Campus, US Naval Reserve Station
34A		US 49S, Gulfport, Hattiesburg
	FStop	S: Hwy 49 Shell
	Gas	S: Chevron, Shell, RaceWay
	Food	S: Applebee's, Arby's, China Garden Express, Great Steak & Potato, Hooters, IHOP, McDonald's, Shoney's, Sonic, Subway, Waffle House, Wendy's
	Lodg	S: Best Value Inn, Best Western, Comfort Inn, Days Inn, Fairfield Inn, Hampton Inn, Holiday Inn Express, Holiday Inn, Motel 6♥, Quality Inn, Studio Inn, Shoney's Inn
	TServ	S: Empire Truck Sales
	Med	S: + Memorial Hospital Gulfport
	Other	S: Home Depot, Wal-Mart sc, Navy Seabee Center, Prime Outlets Mall, Sam's Club, Gulfport-Biloxi Regional Airport✈, Amtrak, US Naval Reserve Station, to South Wind Motel & RV Park▲, Gulfport Biloxi Int'l Airport✈

Personal Notes

EXIT		MISSISSIPPI
34B		US 49N, Gulfport, to Hattiesburg
	FStop	N: Interstate 49/Chevron
	Gas	N: Kangaroo Express, Texaco
	Food	N: Burger King, Chili's, Cracker Barrel, Hardee's, McDonald's, O'Charley's, Pizza Hut, TGI Friday, Starbucks, Waffle House
	Lodg	N: Deer Run Resort
	Med	N: + Garden Park Medical Center
	Other	N: Auto Dealers, Albertson's, B&N, CVS, Circuit City, Kroger, Office Depot, PetSmart♥, Winn Dixie, Crossroads Outlet Mall, Tinseltown Movie Theater, Waterpark, Southern Oaks MH & RV Community▲, Campgrounds of the South RV Park▲, RV Park▲
38		MS 605, Lorraine Rd
	Gas	N: Exxon, Fina, Kangaroo Express S: Pure Country
	Food	N: Captain Al's, McDonald's, Subway
	Lodg	S: Ramada Ltd
	Other	S: to William Carey College, Gulf Coast Comm College, Beaches, Sand Beach RV Park▲, appr 3mi ; Baywood Campground & RV Park▲, Fox's RV Park▲
41		MS 67N, Biloxi, Woolmarket
	Gas	N: BP, Chevron
	Other	S: Parker's Landing Campground▲, Mazalea Travel Park▲, Reliable RV Sales & Service Center
44		Cedar Lake Rd, Coast Coliseum, Biloxi
	FStop	S: Interstate Shell
	TStop	N: Pilot Travel Center #451 (Scales)

EXIT		MISSISSIPPI
	Gas	S: BP, Chevron
	Food	N: Wendy's/Subway/Pilot TC S: FastFood/Interstate Shell, Waffle House, McDonald's, Sonic
	Lodg	S: La Quinta Inn♥
	Med	S: + Gulf Coast Medical Center
	Other	N: Laundry/WiFi/RVDump/Pilot TC S: RVDump/Shell, Motorhome & Truck Service, Biloxi National Cemetery, Harley Davidson, Home Depot
(46AB)		Jct 110S, MS 15N, D'Iberville, Biloxi, Keesler AFB (South Serv on I-110, Exit #2)
	Gas	N: Chevron, Kangaroo
	Food	N: Chili's, McDonald's, Ruby Tuesday, Subway, Sonic, Waffle House, Wendy's
	Lodg	N: Wingate Inn
	Other	N: Lowe's, Wal-Mart sc, to Southern Comfort Camping Resort▲, Lakeview RV Resort▲ S: to Beaches, Keesler AFB, Boomtown Casinos, Majextic Oaks RV Resort▲, Fox RV Park▲
50		MS 609S, Tucker Rd, Biloxi, Ocean Springs
	TStop	S: Fleet Travel Center #504 (Scales)
	Gas	N: Shell S: BP
	Food	N: Domino's/Shell, Rest/Super 8 S: FastFood/Fleet TC, Denny's, McDonald's, Waffle House, Wendy's
	Lodg	N: Best Western, Comfort Inn, Ramada, Super 8 S: Country Inn, Days Inn, Hampton Inn, Holiday Inn Express, Howard Johnson, Sleep Inn
	Other	N: Martin's Lake Resort▲ S: RV Center
57		MS 57, Ocean Springs, Gautier, Fontainbleau, Vancleve
	Gas	N: Shell S: Exxon, Kangaroo
	Food	N: Shed BBQ
	Lodg	N: Suburban Inn
	Med	S: + Hospital
	Other	N: Camp Journey's End RV Park & Campground▲, Bluff Creek Camping▲ S: Gulf Island National Seashore, Naval Facilities
61		Vancleve Rd, Gautier, Vancleve
	Gas	S: BP
	Food	N: McDonald's, Pizza Hut, Wendy's
	Lodg	N: Best Western, Suburban Lodge
	Other	N: Bluff Creek Camping▲ S: to Indian Pt RV Resort▲, Gulf Coast Comm College, Jackson Co Campus, Sand Hill Crane Wildlife Refuge Area/CLOSED
(64)		Moss Point Rest Area (Both dir) (CLOSED) (RR, Phone, Picnic, RVDump, Sec24/7)
68		MS 613, Main St, Moss Point, Pascagoula, Escatawpa
	Gas	N: BP, Chevron S: BP
	Lodg	N: Super 8
	Med	S: + Hospital
	Other	N: Riverbend Park Resort▲

◆ = Regular Gas Stations with Diesel   ▲ = RV Friendly Locations   ♥ = Pet Friendly Locations

RED PRINT SHOWS LARGE VEHICLE PARKING/ACCESS ON SITE OR NEARBY   BROWN PRINT SHOWS CAMPGROUNDS/RV PARKS

EXIT	MS / AL
69	MS 63, E Moss Point, Escatawpa, E Pascagoula, Lucedale
FStop	S: Moss Point Chevron #2
TStop	S: Cone Auto/Truck Plaza #230 (Scales)
Gas	N: Texaco
	S: Exxon
Food	S: Rest/Cone ATP, Rest/BW, Cracker Barrel, Hardee's, McDonald's, Waffle House, Wendy's, Subway/Exxon
Lodg	N: Deluxe Inn, Econo Lodge, La Quinta Inn ♥, Super 8
	S: Best Western, Comfort Inn, Days Inn, Hampton Inn, Holiday Inn Express, Quality Inn, Ramada, Shular Inn
TServ	S: Chevron
Med	S: + Hospital
Other	N: Airport ✈
	S: Laundry/Cone ATP, Ingalls Ship Building
(75)	Weigh Station (Both dir)
(75)	MS Welcome Center (WB) (RR, Phone, Picnic, RVDump)
75	Franklin Creek Rd, to US 90
(77)	Weigh Station (WB)
	(CENTRAL TIME ZONE)
⭕ **MISSISSIPPI**	
⭕ **ALABAMA**	
	(CENTRAL TIME ZONE)
(1)	AL Welcome Center (EB) (RR, Phone, Picnic, Sec24/7, Vend, RVDump)
4	AL 188E, CR 11, Grand Bay, Dauphin Island
TStop	N: Travel Center of America #54/BP(Scales)
Gas	N: Citgo, Shell
	S: Chevron
Food	N: Rest/TA TC, DQ/Stuckey's/Shell, Sam's Super Burger, Waffle House
	S: Carole's Chicken, Hardee's
TServ	N: TA TC, Kenworth
Other	N: Laundry/Clinic/WiFi/TA TC
	S: Trav-L-Kamp
10	CR 39, McDonald Rd
Other	S: St Elmo Airport ✈
13	CR 30, Theodore Dawes Rd, Theodore, Irvington (Gas/Food/Lodg S to US 90)
TStop	N: Pilot Travel Center #302 (Scales)
Gas	N: Conoco, Shell, Texaco
Food	N: Wendy's/Pilot TC, McDonald's, Subway, Waffle House
Lodg	N: Spanish Oak Inn
Other	N: Laundry/WiFi/Pilot TC, Mobile Greyhound Park, Azalea RV Park▲
	S: I-10 Kampground▲, Shady Grove Campground▲, Bellingrath RV Park▲, Payne's RV Park▲
15AB	US 90, AL 16, Theodore, Historic Mobile Pkwy, Tillman's Corner
TStop	S: Shell
Gas	N: BP, Raceway, Shell
	S: BP, Conoco, Texaco
Food	N: Arby's, Burger King, Checkers, CiCi's, Dick Russell's BBQ, El Toro Mexican, Hooters, IHOP, KFC, McDonald's, Pizza Hut, Popeye's, Shoney's, Subway, Waffle House

EXIT	ALABAMA
Food	S: McDonald's, Hardee's, Waffle House
Lodg	N: Best Western, Comfort Inn, Days Inn, Econo Lodge, Hampton Inn, Holiday Inn, Motel 6♥, Red Roof Inn♥, Rodeway Inn, Ramada Inn, Super 8, Suite One, Travelodge
	S: Knights Inn♥, Red Roof Inn♥
TServ	S: Peterbilt
Other	N: AutoZone, Firestone, Goodyear, Grocery, Kmart, Walgreen's, Winn Dixie, S AL Bus Sales, Dog Track, Azalea RV Park▲
	S: Nestled Away RV Park▲, Cruise America RV Rentals, Johnny's RV Ctr
17AB	AL 193, Rangeline Rd, Higgins Rd, Mobile, to Tillman's Corner, Dauphin Island
FStop	S: Stop N Shop #2/Shell
Gas	N: Chevron, Citgo
Food	N: Boiling Pot, Burger King, CiCi's, Dick's BBQ, McDonald's, IHOP, Ruby Tuesday, Sonny's BBQ
	S: FastFood/StopNShop
Med	N: + Hospital
Other	N: Big Lots, Family Dollar, Lowe's, Wal-Mart sc▲, Christmas Town & Village
(20)	Jct I-65N, Montgomery (EB, Left exit)
TServ	N: Empire Truck Sales
22	AL 163, Dauphin Island Pkwy (EB)
22AB	AL 163, Dauphin Island Pkwy (WB)
Gas	N: BP
	S: Exxon, Shell

EXIT	ALABAMA
Food	S: Checker's, Waffle House
Lodg	N: Villager Lodge
	S: Heritage Inn
TServ	S: Volvo Kenworth
23	Michigan Ave, Ladd Stadium
Gas	N: Exxon
Other	S: Mobile Downtown Airport ✈
24	Broad St, Duval St, Mobile
Gas	N: Chevron, Citgo
25A	Virginia St (EB), Texas St (WB)
25B	Virginia St (WB)
Gas	N: Shell ♦
26A	Canal St, Civic Center, Cruise Terminal (EB)
26B	Water St, Downtown, Mobile Conv Center, Historic District
Food	N: Restaurants, Sports Bar
Lodg	N: Holiday Inn Express, Radisson
Note:	MM 27 George C Wallace Tunnel
	(runs under Mobile River)
27	US 90, US 98, Government St, Battleship Pkwy, Mobile (HAZMAT, Trucks Use US 90/98)
Food	S: Captains Table Seafood
Lodg	S: Best Western, Ramada Inn
TServ	N: Dixie Nationwide Truck Service
Other	S: to USS Alabama, Meaher State Park
Note:	MM 27-35 8 mi bridge over Mobile Bay
30	US 90, US 98, Battleship Pkwy, Battleship Park, Spanish Fort
Gas	S: Shell
Food	S: Oysterella's
35A	US 98, 90W, Daphne, Fairhope, Spanish Fort (EB)
35B	US 90E (EB)
35	US 98, 90, Daphne, Fairhope (WB)
Gas	N: BP
	S: Exxon, Shell, Oil
Food	S: Arby's, Burger King, Checkers, Hooters, IHOP, Mexican Rest, McDonald's, Krystal, O'Charley's, Shoney's, Subway, Taco Bell, Waffle House, Wendy's
Lodg	S: Comfort Inn, Eastern Shore Motel, Hampton Inn, Hilton Garden Inn, Quality Inn, Microtel
Med	S: + Hospital
Other	N: Bass Pro Shop, US Post Office
	S: Home Depot, Blakely State Park, Office Depot, US Sports Academy
38	AL 181, Daphne, Malbis
Gas	N: BP
	S: Chevron, Shell
Food	N: David's Catfish House, Cracker Barrel, Logan's, McDonald's, Olive Garden, Ryan's Grill, Wendy's
	S: Plantation Restaurant
Lodg	N: Holiday Inn Express, La Quinta Inn♥
	S: Malbis Motor Inn
TServ	N: CAT
Other	N: Best Buy, PetSmart♥, Walgreen's
	S: Lowe's, Sam's Club
44	AL 59, Loxley, Bay Minette, to Gulf Shores, Beaches
FStop	N: Love's Travel Stop #206 (Scales)
	S: Khan Food Mart
TStop	N: Econ Travel Center/Shell (Scales)

♦ = Regular Gas Stations with Diesel   ▲ = RV Friendly Locations   ♥ = Pet Friendly Locations
RED PRINT SHOWS LARGE VEHICLE PARKING/ACCESS ON SITE OR NEARBY   BROWN PRINT SHOWS CAMPGROUNDS/RV PARKS

EXIT		AL / FL
	Gas	S: Chevron, RaceTrac
	Food	N: Arby's/Love's TS, Rest/Econ TC
		S: Rest/Wind Chase Inn, Firehouse Café, Hardee's, McDonald's, Waffle Hous
	Lodg	S: Wind Chase Inn, Days Inn
	Other	N: Laundry, WiFi, RVDump/Love's TS, RVDump/Econ TC
		S: Auto & Truck Repair, Gulf Shore Beaches, Gulf Breeze RV Resort▲, Gulf State Park
53		CR 64, Wilcox Rd, Robertsdale
	TStop	N: AmBest/Oasis Travel Center/BP (Scales)
	Gas	S: Chevron, Outpost
	Food	N: Rest/FastFood/Oasis TC
		S: Café 64
	Lodg	N: Styx River Resort
	TWash	N: Oasis TC
	TServ	N: Oasis TC
	Other	N: Laundry/CB/RVDump/LP/Oasis TC
		S: Hilltop RV Park▲, Wilderness RV Park▲
(66)		Weigh Station (WB)
(66)		AL Welcome Center (WB) (RR, Phone, Picnic, Vend)
		(CENTRAL TIME ZONE)

⏾ ALABAMA
⏿ FLORIDA
(CENTRAL TIME ZONE)

(1)		Inspection Station (EB)
(3)		Weigh Station (Both dir)
(4)		FL Welcome Center (EB) (RR, Phone, Picnic, Vend, Info, Sec247)
5		US 90 Alt, Pensacola
	TStop	N: Fleet Travel Center #320/Shell (Scales)
	Food	N: Subway/Fleet TC
	TServ	N: CAT
	Other	N: Albertson's
		S: Leisure Lakes RV Park▲
7		FL 297, Pine Forest Rd, Pensacola Naval Air Station (WB)
	Gas	N: Exxon
		S: BP, Texaco
	Food	S: Burger King, Cracker Barrel, Hardee's, McDonald's, Ruby Tuesday, Subway, Sonny's BBQ, Waffle House
	Lodg	N: Comfort Inn, Rodeway Inn
		S: Holiday Inn Express. Microtel, Quality Inn, Sleep Inn
	Med	S: + Hospital
	Other	N: Tall Oaks Campground RV & MH Park▲

EXIT		FLORIDA
	Other	S: Grocery, Fun Station USA, US Naval Air Base, to MIL/Blue Angel Naval Rec Area▲, MIL/Oak Grove Park & Cottages▲, Leisure Lakes RV Park▲
7AB		FL 297S (EB)
7AB		FL 297N (EB)
10AB		US 29, FL 95, Pensacola
	TStop	N: Fleet Travel Center #319 (Scales)
	Gas	N: Williams
		S: RaceTrac
	Food	N: Hardee's, Waffle House
		S: Burger King, Denny's, McDonald's, Subway, Waffle House, Wendy's, IHOP
	Lodg	S: Best Value Inn, Comfort Inn, Days Inn, Econo Lodge, Holiday Inn Express, Howard Johnson Express, Quality Inn, Ramada Inn, Red Roof Inn♥, Super 8, Travelodge Inn
	Med	S: + Pensacola Blvd Family Care Center, + US Vets Outpatient Clinic
	Other	N: Cruise America RV Rentals, Drifters RV Park▲, Wal-Mart sc▲
		S: Lazy Days RV Campground▲, Hill Kelly RV Center, Turning Wheel RV Center, Leisure Time RV, Harley Davidson of Pensacola
(12)		Jct I-110, Pensacola
	Other	S: Gulf Islands Nat'l Seashore▲, to MIL/Mid Bay Shores Maxwell/Gunter Recreation Area▲
13		FL 291, N Davis Hwy, to US 90, Pensacola, Univ of West Florida
	Gas	N: Happy Store, Shell◊
	Food	N: Arby's, Barnhill's Buffet, Burger King, Captain D's, Denny's, McDonald's, La Hacienda, Montana's BBQ, Subway, Taco Bell, Waffle House
		S: Bennigan's, Steak & Ale, Waffle House
	Lodg	N: Best Western, Comfort Inn, La Quinta Inn♥, Motel 6♥, Shoney's Inn, Super 8
		S: Extended Stay, Fairfield Inn, Hampton Inn, Holiday Inn Express, Motel 6♥, Red Roof Inn♥, Residence Inn, Super 8
	Med	N: + West Florida Hospital, + Medical Center Clinic
	Other	N: Albertson's, CVS, Brookhaven RV Park▲
		S: Big 10 Tire, Firestone, Grand Slam Food & Fun, Time Out Family Rec Center, University Mall, University Mall Cinema, Pensacola Reg'l Airport →

EXIT		FLORIDA
17		US 90, FL 10A, Pensacola
	Gas	N: BP
		S: Exxon
	Food	S: DQ/Exxon, Rest/Ramada Inn
	Lodg	S: Ramada Inn
	Med	N: + Scenic Hwy Family Med Center
22		FL 281, Avalon Blvd, Milton
	Gas	N: Tom Thumb Food Store
		S: Circle K
	Food	N: McDonald's, Subway, Waffle House
	Lodg	N: Red Roof Inn♥
	Med	N: + Hospital
	Other	S: Avalon Landing RV Park▲, By the Bay RV Park▲
26		CR 191, Garcon Pt Rd, Milton
	FStop	S: Mike's
	Gas	N: Circle K
		S: Chevron, Shell
	Food	S: DQ
	Tires	S: Mike's
	Med	N: + Hospital
	Other	N: Pelican Palms RV Park▲
28		CR 89, Ward Basin Rd, Milton
	Med	N: + Hospital
	Other	S: Cedar Lakes RV Park & CG▲
(29)		Rest Area (Both dir) (RR, Phone, Picnic, Vend, Sec24/7)
31		FL 87, Milton, Navarre, Ft Walton Beach
	TStop	S: Rolling Thunder Truck Stop
	Gas	N: Exxon
		S: Shell
	Food	N: Rest/HI Expr, Quizno's, Waffle House
		S: Rest/FastFood/RT TS
	Lodg	N: Holiday Inn Express
		S: Comfort Inn, Red Carpet Inn
	Other	N: Gulf Pines/Milton KOA/RVDump▲
		S: Laundry/WiFi/Rolling Thunder TS
45		CR 189, Log Lake Rd, Holt
	FStop	N: Exprezit #743/Amoco
	Other	N: Eagle's Landing RV Park▲, Blackwater River State Park
		S: Rivers Edge RV Campground▲
56		FL 85, Crestview, Niceville
	FStop	N: CJ Food Mart #2 Chevron
	Gas	N: BP◊, Mobil, Shell
		S: Citgo, Exxon
	Food	N: Applebee's, Asian Garden, Burger King, McDonald's, Ryan's Grill, Sonny's BBQ, Starbucks, Taco Bell
		S: Arby's, Cracker Barrel, Hardee's, Hooters, Shoney's, Subway, Waffle House, Wendy's, Whataburger

◊ = Regular Gas Stations with Diesel   ▲ = RV Friendly Locations   ♥ = Pet Friendly Locations

RED PRINT SHOWS LARGE VEHICLE PARKING/ACCESS ON SITE OR NEARBY   BROWN PRINT SHOWS CAMPGROUNDS/RV PARKS

EXIT		FLORIDA
	Lodg	N: Econo Lodge, Quality Inn S: Comfort Inn, Days Inn, Hampton Inn, Holiday Inn, Jameson Inn, Super 8
	Med	N: + Gateway Medical Clinic
	Other	N: Advance Auto, Auto Zone, ATMs, Banks Days Tire & Service, Lowe's, Publix, Wal-Mart sc, Walgreen's S: to MIL/Eglin AFB/FamCamp▲
(58)		Rest Area (EB) (RR, Phone, Picnic, Vend, Sec24/7)
(61)		Rest Area (WB) (RR, Phone, Picnic, Vend Sec24/7)
70		FL 285, Mossy Head, DeFuniak, to Ft Walton Beach, Niceville, Eglin Air Force Base
	TStop	S: Lucky 13 Truck Stop & Auto Plaza/Citgo (Scales)
	Gas	N: Raceway
	Food	S: Rest/Subway/Lucky 13 TSAP
	Lodg	S: RodewayInn/Lucky 13 TSAP, Ramada Inn
	TWash	S: Lucky 13 TSAP
	TServ	S: Lucky 13 TSAP
	Other	S: Laundry/BarbSh/LP/Lucky 13 TSAP
85		US 331, DeFuniak Springs, Freeport
	FStop	S: Emerald Express #515
	Gas	N: Chevron, Texaco, Murphy S: Exprezit, Shell
	Food	N: Arby's, Burger King, McLain Family Steak House, Waffle House S: Hardee's, KFC, McDonald's
	Lodg	N: Best Value Inn, Sundown Inn, Super 8 S: Best Western
	AServ	N: Rockman's Auto Service
	Med	N: + Hospital, Gateway Medical Clinic
	Other	N: Walgreen's, Wal-Mart sc▲, Winn Dixie, DeFuniak Springs Airport✈, to 8 mi: Sunset Lake Resort, to Juniper Lake RV Campground▲ S: Longleaf RV Park▲, to Lazy Days RV Park▲, to Red Bay RV Park▲
96		FL 81, Ponce de Leon
	S:	Rest Area (take FL 81, 1st L) (Both dir) (RR, Phone, Picnic, Vend, Sec24/7)
	FStop	S: Exprezit #604
	Gas	N: Exxon S: BP
	Food	N: Sally's Seafood Kitchen S: FastFood/Exprezit
	Lodg	N: Ponce De Leon Motor Lodge & RV Park▲
	Other	N: Dollar General S: Ponce De Leon Springs St Rec Area
104		CR 279, Caryville
112		FL 79, Bonifay, Panama City Beach
	Gas	N: Chevron, Citgo, Exxon◊, Tom Thumb
	Food	N: Burger King, Hardee's, McDonald's, Pizza Hut, Subway, Waffle House
	Lodg	N: Bonifay Inn, Economy Lodge, Tivoli Inn
	Med	N: + Dr's Memorial Hospital
	Other	N: Florida Springs RV Resort▲
120		FL 77, Chipley, to Panama City
	Gas	N: Exxon, Exprezit, Murphy◊ S: Exprezit, Shell
	Food	N: Rest/Days Inn, Arby's, Burger King, KFC, McDonald's, Taco Bell, Wendy's, Waffle House

Personal Notes
_____
_____
_____
_____
_____
_____
_____
_____
_____
_____
_____
_____
_____
_____
_____
_____
_____

EXIT		FLORIDA
	Lodg	N: Comfort Inn, Days Inn, Executive Inn, Super 8
	Med	N: + Hospital
	Other	N: NW Florida Campground▲, Wal-Mart sc▲ S: Falling Waters State Park▲
130		US 231, FL 75, Cottondale, Panama City
	FStop	N: Exprezit #702/BP
	Gas	N: Chevron S: BP, Raceway
	Food	N: Hardee's, Pam's Diner, Subway
	Other	S: Sunny Oaks RV Park▲, to Pine Lake RV Park▲
(133)		Rest Area (Both dir) (RR, Phone, Picnic, Vend, Sec24/7)
136		FL 276, CR 167, Marianna
	Gas	N: Exprezit◊
	Lodg	N: Days Inn, Executive Inn
	Med	N: + Hospital
	Other	N: to Fort Caverns State Park S: Sunny Oaks RV Park▲
142		FL 71, Marianna, Blountstown
	FStop	S: Waco #18/Sunoco, Exprezit #601
	TStop	N: Pilot Travel Center #374 (Scales) S: Travel Center of America #178/BP (Scales)
	Gas	N: Murphy◊ S: Chevron◊
	Food	N: Arby's/TJCinn/Pilot TC, Firehouse Subs, Ruby Tuesday, Waffle House S: Rest/TA TC, FastFood/Waco, FastFood/Exprezit, Burger King, KFC, Po Folks, Shoney's, Sonny's BBQ, Waffle House

EXIT		FLORIDA
	Lodg	N: Comfort Inn, Country Inn, Fairfield Inn, Holiday Inn, Microtel, Quality Inn, Super 8 S: Amer Best Value Inn, Best Western, Hampton Inn, Holiday Inn Express
	TServ	S: TA TC/Tires
	Other	N: WiFi/Pilot TC, Wal-Mart sc▲, Winn Dixie, Greyhound, Marianna Muni Airport✈, Caverns State Park▲, to Arrowhead Campsites & RV Sales S: Laundry/WiFi/TA TC, Dove Rest RV & MH Park▲
152		FL 69, Grand Ridge, Blountstown
	FStop	N: Golden Lariat, 5miN: Blondie's Food & Fuel
	Food	N: Rest/Golden Lariat
(155)		Weigh Station (Both dir)
158		CR 286, Blueberry Dr, Sneads
	Note:	MM 160: Central / Eastern Time Zone
(162)		Rest Area (Both dir) (RR, Phone, Picnic, Vend, Sec247)
166		CR 270A, Chattahoochee
	Gas	S: Shell
	Other	S: Chattahoochee KOA▲
174		FL 12, Quincy, Greensboro
	FStop	N: Johnson & Johnson #18/Shell
	Food	N: Rest/J&J
	Other	N: Beaver Lake Campground▲
181		FL 267, Robert St, Quincy, to Tallahassee
	Gas	N: Exprezit, Murphy S: BP
	Lodg	S: Hampton Inn, Holiday Inn Express
	Med	N: + Hospital
	Other	N: Wal-Mart sc▲ S: to Bear Creek State Park
192		US 90, Havana, to Quincy, Tallahassee
	TStop	N: Flying J Travel Plaza #5054/Conoco (Scales) S: Pilot Travel Center #425 (Scales)
	Gas	N: BP
	Food	N: Rest/FastFood/Flying J TP, S: Subway/Pilot TC, Waffle House
	Lodg	N: Comfort Suites, Howard Johnson
	Other	N: Laundry/BarbSh/WiFi/LP/RVDump/FJ TP, Emerald Coast RV Center S: Laundry/WiFi/RVDump/Pilot TC, Midway Tire, Lakeside RV Park▲, Coe Landing RV Park▲, Eagles Nest MH & RV Park▲, Williams Landing CG▲
(194)		Rest Area (Both dir) (RR, Phone, Picnic, Vend, Sec24/7)
196		FL 263, Capital Circle, Tallahassee
	Gas	S: Chevron◊, Shell◊, Stop N Save
	Food	S: Firehouse Subs, Sonic, Steak 'n Shake, Subway, Waffle House, Wendy's
	Lodg	S: Sleep Inn
	TServ	S: Seminole Truck & RV Service
	Other	S: Capital City Harley Davidson, Home Depot, Lowe's, Museum, Winn Dixie, Zoo, Auto Dealers Tallahassee Regional Airport✈, S to 90: Wal-Mart sc
199		US 27, FL 63, Tallahassee
	Gas	N: Chevron, McKenzie Market S: BP, Chevron◊, Circle K, Shell, USA

◊ = Regular Gas Stations with Diesel ▲ = RV Friendly Locations ♥ = Pet Friendly Locations
RED PRINT SHOWS LARGE VEHICLE PARKING/ACCESS ON SITE OR NEARBY   BROWN PRINT SHOWS CAMPGROUNDS/RV PARKS

EXIT		FLORIDA
	Food	N: Burger King, Marie Livingston's Steak House, Taco Bell, Waffle House S: Rest/DI, Rest/La QI, Rest/Ramada, **Cracker Barrel**, Crystal River Seafood, Long John Silver, Longhorn Steaks, Red Lobster, Shoney's, Sonny's BBQ, Steak & Ale, Subway, Village Inn
	Lodg	N: Best Inn, Comfort Inn, Fairfield Inn, Hampton Inn, Holiday Inn, Microtel, Quality Inn, Villager Inn S: Days Inn, Econo Lodge, Hilton Garden, Inn, Howard Johnson, La Quinta Inn♥, Motel 6♥, Ramada Inn, Red Roof Inn♥, Shoney's Inn, Super 8, Wingate Inn
	Other	N: Food Lion, Sam's Club, Winn Dixie, appr 3 mi: **Big Oak RV Park**▲ S: Albertson's, AutoZone, Big O Tire, Fairgrounds & Civic Center, Firestone, Northwood Animal Hospital♥, Publix, Petland♥, Tallahassee Mall, Movies 8, Capital Cinemas, AMC 20/Tall Mall, Sun Tire, **Walgreen's**
203		**US 319, FL 61, FL 261, Thomasville Rd, Tallahassee, Thomasville**
	Gas	N: BP, Chevron, Circle K/Shell, USA S: Gas, Hogly Wogly
	Food	N: Applebee's, Bonefish Grill, Sonny's BBQ, McDonald's, Pizza Hut, Popeye's, Starbucks, Taco Bell, Wendy's, Waffle House S: Boston Market, Carrabba's, Outback Steakhouse, Osaka Japanese Steakhouse, Steak 'n Shake, TGI Friday's
	Lodg	N: Motel 6♥ S: Cabot Lodge, Courtyard by Marriott, Hilton Garden Inn, Residence Inn, Studio Plus
	Med	S: + Tallahassee Memorial Hospital
	Other	N: **CVS**, FedEx Kinko's, Kmart, Publix, **Walgreen's**, **Wal-Mart** sc ▲, Winn Dixie S: Home Depot, Office Depot, UPS Store
209AB		**US 90, Tallahassee, Monticello**
	Gas	S: Citgo, Shell
	Food	S: Cross Creek Creekside Grill, Waffle House, Wendy's
	Lodg	S: Best Western
	Other	S: Publix, Cross Creek Driving Range & Par 3 Golf, **Tallahassee RV Park**▲, **Pepco RV Center**
217		**FL 59, Lloyd**
	TStop	S: **PTP**/**Capital City Travel Center**/**BP** (Scales)
	Food	S: **Rest**/**Capital City TC**
	Lodg	S: **Motel**/**Capital City TC**
	TServ	S: **Capital City TC**
	Other	S: **Laundry**/**BarbSh**/**Capital City TC**, **Lloyd CB Sales & Service**
225		**US 19, FL 57, Monticello** (Addt'l serv 5 mi N in Monticello)
	TStop	S: **Fast Track #427**/**Shell**
	Gas	N: Amoco, Exxon/Wendy's S: Exprezit
	Food	N: Arby's S: **FastFood**/**FT**, Huddle House, Wendy's
	Lodge	N: **Days Inn**, Super 8
	TServ	S: **Interstate Towing & Repair**
	Other	N: **A Camper's World**▲ S: **Tallahassee East**/**Monticello KOA** ▲
233		**CR 257, Lamont, Aucilla**
	Gas	N: Citgo, Shell◊

Personal Notes

EXIT		FLORIDA
(233)		**Rest Area** (Both dir) (RR, Phone, Picnic, Vend, Sec24/7)
241		**US 221, Greenville, Perry**
	Gas	N: Mobil S: BP
251		**FL 14, Madison, Perry**
	Gas	N: Mobil
	Med	N: + Hospital
258		**FL 53, Madison**
	TStop	N: **Jimmie's Truck Stop**/**Citgo** S: **Johnson & Johnson #5**/**Shell**
	Food	N: **Rest**/**Jimmie's TS** S: **FastFood**/**J&J**
	Lodg	N: Days Inn, Holiday Inn Express, Super 8 S: Deer Wood Inn
	TServ	N: **Jimmie's Firestone & Service Center** S: **J&J**
	Med	N: + Madison Co Memorial Hospital
	Other	N: **Laundry**/**BarbSh**/**Jimmie's TS**, Wild Adventure Theme Park, Amtrak, Vet♥ S: **Laundry**/**J&J**, **Deadwood Madison Campground**▲, **Yogi Bear's Jellystone Park & RV Resort**/**RVDump**▲
262		**CR 255, Lee**
	TStop	S: **Jimmie's Auto & Truck Plaza**/**Citgo**
	Gas	N: Exxon S: Texaco
	Food	S: **Rest**/**Jimmie's ATP**, Kountry Kitchen, Red Onion Grill
	Lodg	S: Microtel
	TServ	S: **Jimmie's ATP**
	Other	N: to Suwannee River State Park
(264)		**Weigh Station** (Both dir)

EXIT		FLORIDA
(265)		**Rest Area** (Both dir) (RR, Phone, Picnic, Vend, Sec247)
(271)		**Weigh Station/Agricultural Inspection** (Both dir)
275		**US 90, Live Oak, Lee**
	Med	S: + Hospital
	Other	N: **Suwannee State Park**▲
283		**US 129, Live Oak, Jasper**
	FStop	N: **Penn Oil Co**, **Johnson & Johnson #25**
	Gas	S: Chevron, Shell
	Food	S: Huddle House, McDonald's, Subway, Waffle House, Wendy's
	Lodg	S: Best Western, Econo Lodge, Holiday Inn Express, Suwannee River Inn
	Med	S: + Hospital
	Other	N: **Spirit of the Suwannee Campground**▲ S: **Wal-Mart** sc ▲
292		**CR 137, Live Oak, to Wellborn**
(294)		**Rest Area** (EB) (RR, Phone, Picnic, Vend, Sec24/7)
(295)		**Rest Area** (WB) (RR, Phone, Picnic, Vend, Sec24/7)
(296AB)		**Jct I-75, N - Valdosta, S - Tampa**
301		**US 41, FL 100, Lake City, White Springs**
	FStop	N: **Exxon**
	Gas	N: BP S: Shell
	Med	S: + Hospital
	Other	N: **Kelly's RV Park**▲
303		**US 441, Lake City, Fargo**
	FStop	S: **S&S Food Store #37**/**Shell**
	Gas	S: Chevron◊, Citgo, Exxon
	Lodg	S: Days Inn♥
	Med	S: + Hospital
	Other	N: **Oak & Pine RV Campground**▲, **Lake City KOA**/**RVDump**▲
(318)		**Rest Area** (Both dir) (RR, Phone, Picnic, Vend, Sec24/7)
324		**US 90, Sanderson, Olustee**
	Gas	S: Citgo
327		**CR 229, Sanderson, Raiford**
333		**CR 125, Glen St Mary**
	FStop	N: **Glen Citgo**
335		**FL 121, MacClenny, Lake Butler**
	FStop	N: **S&S Food Store #34**/**BP** S: **Exxon #454**
	Gas	N: Citgo, Shell S: Raceway
	Food	N: KFC, Hardee's, McDonald's, Pizza Hut, Subway, Taco Bell, Waffle House, Woody's BBQ S: Burger King, China Garden
	Lodg	N: American Inn S: Econo Lodge, Travelodge
	Med	N: + **MacClenny Family Care Center**, S: + **Northeast FL Hospital**
	Other	N: Advance Auto, Food Lion, Jiffy Lube, Winn Dixie, Laundromat
336		**FL 228, MacClenny, Maxville**
	Med	N: + Hospital
	Other	N: **Wal-Mart** sc ▲, Fireworks
343		**US 301, Baldwin, to Starke**
	TStop	S: **Travel Center of America #125**/**BP** (Scales), **Pilot Travel Center #87** (Scales)

◊ = Regular Gas Stations with Diesel ▲ = RV Friendly Locations ♥ = Pet Friendly Locations

RED PRINT SHOWS LARGE VEHICLE PARKING/ACCESS ON SITE OR NEARBY BROWN PRINT SHOWS CAMPGROUNDS/RV PARKS

EXIT		FLORIDA
	Gas	S: Chevron, Citgo, Exxon
	Food	N: BBQ
		S: Rest/Arby's/TA TC, Subway/Pilot TC, Rest/Best Western, McDonald's, Waffle House
(345)		FUTURE - Branfield-Chaffee Expy
(349)		Rest Area (WB) (CLOSED) (RR, Phone, Picnic, Vend, Sec24/7)
(350)		Rest Area (EB) (RR, Phone, Picnic, Vend, Sec24/7)
351		FL 115C, Chaffee Rd, to Cecil Fields
	FStop	N: Kangaroo #6032
	Gas	S: Chevron, Shell
	Food	N: FastFood/Kangaroo #6032
		S: Cracker Barrel, King Wok Chinese, McDonald's, Quiznos, Wendy's
	Lodg	S: Hampton Inn
	Other	N: Rivers RV Service & Park▲
	NOTE:	MM 355: WB: Begin Call Boxes
355		Marietta
	Gas	N: Exxon, Gate◊
	Gas	S: Amoco, Lil Champ, Shell◊
	Food	S: Bill's Diner, Godfather Pizza
(356)		Jct I-295, N to Savannah, GA; S to St Augustine
357		FL 103, Lane Ave, Jacksonville
	Gas	N: Fuel Mart, Hess, Speedway
		S: BP, Chevron, Shell◊
	Food	N: Andy's, Rest/Days Inn
		S: Applebee's, Burger King, Denny's, Cross Creek BBQ & Steaks, Hardee's, KFC, McDonald's, Piccadilly, Shoney's
	Lodg	N: Days Inn♥, Ramada Ltd♥
		S: Budget Inn, Executive Inn, Super 8
	Other	S: CVS, Firestone, Home Depot, Winn Dixie, Office Depot
358		FL 111, Cassat Ave, Edgewood
	FStop	N: First Coast Energy/Amoco
	Gas	N: BP/Lil Champ, Chevron, Hess, Shell
		S: RaceTrac, Sunoco
	Food	N: Burger King, Blimpie's, McDonald's, Popeye's
		S: Dunkin Donuts, Krispy Kreme, Taco Bell
	Other	N: AutoZone
		S: Lowe's, Walgreen's, Winn Dixie
359		Lenox Ave, Edgewood Ave (WB, difficult reaccess)
360		FL 129, McDuff Ave, Waller St
	Gas	S: BP, Chevron
	Food	S: Popeye's Chicken
361		US 17S, Roosevelt Blvd (WB)
362		Stockton St, Riverside, Russell St
	Gas	S: BP, Gate◊
	Med	S: + Hospital
(363)		I-10 Begins/Ends on I-95, Ex #351B
(364)		Jct I-95N, to Savannah GA, Jct I-95S, to St Augustine FL

○ **FLORIDA**
Begin Westbound I-10 from Jct I-95 in Jacksonville, FL to Santa Monica, CA.

EXIT		LOUISIANA
		Begin Eastbound I-12 from Baton Rouge, LA to Jct I-10 near New Orleans, LA.

○ **LOUISIANA**
(CENTRAL TIME ZONE)
(I-12 Begins/Ends on I-10, Exit #159)

EXIT		LOUISIANA
(1A)		Jct I-10E, New Orleans (WB)
1B		LA 3064, Essen Ln, Baton Rouge (EB, no immed WB re-entry)
	Gas	S: RaceTrac
	Food	N: McDonald's, Subway
		S: Copelands, Fast Track Hamburgers, Vincent's Italian
	Med	N: + Hospital, + E-Med Walk-in Clinic
		S: + Our Lady of the Lake Med Center, LSU Medical Center
	Other	N: Family Dollar
		S: Grocery, Walgreen's
1B		to LA 73, Jefferson Hwy, Drusilla Lane (WB)
	Gas	N: Shell
	Food	N: Drusilla Seafood Rest, McDonald's
		S: Mr Gatti's
	Med	N: + Lake After Hours Clinic
	Other	S: Grocery, CVS
2A		US 61S, Airline Hwy
	FStop	S: S on US 61: Express 1 Stop/Shell
	Gas	S: Chevron, Circle K
	Food	S: McDonald's, Waffle House
	Lodg	S: Days Inn, Plantation Inn
	Other	S: Home Depot, Winn Dixie, Harley Davidson of Baton Rouge
2B		US 61N, Airline Hwy, Baton Rouge
	FStop	N: N on US 190: Mobil Truck Stop
	Gas	N: Amoco, Chevron, Exxon, Shell
	Food	N: Cracker Barrel, McDonald's, Pizza Hut/TacoBell, Shoney's, Subway, Wendy
	Lodg	N: Hampton Inn, Holiday Inn, Motel 6♥, Microtel, Shoney's Inn, Sleep Inn
	Other	N: Auto Dealers, Albertson's, Pep Boys, Walgreen's
4		Sherwood Forest Blvd
	Gas	N: Exxon, Shell◊
		S: Chevron, Shell
	Food	N: Bamboo House, Burger King, Chuck E Cheese, Denny's, KFC, McDonald's, Subway, Waffle House
		S: Bayou Cajun Seafood, Pasta Garden, Taco Bell
	Lodg	N: Crossland Inn, Red Roof Inn♥, Super 8
		S: Calloway Inn, Quality Inn
	Other	N: Grocery, RiteAid
		S: Harley Davidson of Baton Rouge
6		Millerville Rd
	Gas	N: Chevron
	Food	N: ChickFilA
7		LA 3245, O'Neal Ln, Baton Rouge
	Gas	N: Mobil
		S: BP◊, Chevron, RaceTrac, Texaco
	Food	S: Subway/BP, Burger King, China King, Las Palmas Mexican, Lone Star Steak house, McDonald's, Popeye's, Taco Bell, Waffle House, Wendy's
	Lodg	N: Comfort Suites
	TServ	N: Peterbilt
	Med	S: + Ochsner Summit Hospital, + Med Center, + Urgent Care
	Other	N: Night RV Park▲, Best Buy, Lowe's, Office Depot, Target, Auto Dealers
		S: Grocery, Wal-Mart, Walgreen's
10		LA 3002, S Range Ave, LA 1034, LA 16, Denham Springs
	TStop	N: Magnolia Plaza
		S: Pilot Travel Center #79 (Scales)

◊ = Regular Gas Stations with Diesel   ▲ = RV Friendly Locations   ♥ = Pet Friendly Locations
RED PRINT SHOWS LARGE VEHICLE PARKING/ACCESS ON SITE OR NEARBY   BROWN PRINT SHOWS CAMPGROUNDS/RV PARKS

EXIT	LOUISIANA	EXIT	LOUISIANA	EXIT	LOUISIANA
Gas	N: Chevron, Circle K, RaceTrac, Shell◊, Murphy◊ S: Shell	40	US 51 Bus, Hammond, Ponchatoula	Food	N: Applebee's, Burger King, IHOP, KFC, Outback Steakhouse, Piccadilly, Starbucks, Subway, Waffle House
Food	N: Arby's, Burger King, Cactus Café, IHOP, KFC, McDonald's, Popeye's, Ryan's Grill, Waffle House, Wendy's S: Subway/Pilot TC, Piccadilly's, Shoney's	TStop	S: Petro Stopping Center #19/Mobil (Scales), Pilot Travel Center #300 (Scales)	Lodg	N: Best Western, Comfort Inn, Hampton Inn, Holiday Inn, Super 8
		Gas	N: RaceTrac◊, Shell S: Shell	Med	N: + Hospital
Lodg	N: Best Western, Holiday Inn Express, Homegate Inn S: Days Inn, Highland Inn	Food	N: Burger King, China Garden, Border Café, IHOP, McDonald's, Pizza Hut, Ryan's Grill, Taco Bell, Wendy's S: Rest/Petro SC, Arby's/Pilot TC, Waffle House	Other	N: Albertson's, Home Depot, Lowe's, Office Depot, Wal-Mart sc▲ S: LA State Hwy Patrol Post
Other	N: Dollar General, Firestone, Family Dollar, Grocery, Home Depot, RiteAid, Wal-Mart, Gulf Coast RV Rentals & Repairs, RV Center S: Bass Pro Shop, Baton Rouge KOA▲			65	LA 59, Mandeville, Abita Springs
		Lodg	N: Best Western, Comfort Inn, Econo Lodge, Supreme Inn S: Colonial Inn, Days Inn	Gas	N: Chevron◊, Shell S: Kangaroo, Texaco
15	LA 447, Walker South Rd, Walker, Port Vincent	TServ	S: Petro SC, Speedco	Food	N: Waffle House S: FastFood/Kangaroo
FStop	N: Express One Stop S: Swifty's #16/Chevron, Pel State Oil	TWash	S: Blue Beacon Truck Wash/Petro SC	Other	N: Tourist Info S: Fontainebleau State Park▲
Gas	N: Citgo, Chevron, Shell, Texaco◊	Med	S: + Hospital	74	LA 434, Lacombe, St Tammany
Food	N: Burger King, Jack in the Box, McDonald's, Popeye's, Sonic, Subway, Waffle House, Wendy's	Other	N: Sandy Springs Campground▲, Mall, Walgreen's, U-Haul, Amtrak, Indian Creek Campground▲, SE LA Univ S: Laundry/Petro SC, Laundry/WiFi/Pilot TC, CB Radio Service, CarWash/Shell, New Orleans/Hammond KOA▲	Gas	S: Chevron
				Food	S: Subway
Lodg	N: La Quinta Inn♥			Med	N: + Hospital
Med	N: + Med Walk In Clinic			80	Airport Dr, North Shore Blvd
Other	N: Wal-Mart sc▲, Winn Dixie			Gas	S: Chevron, Kangaroo, Shell◊, Sam's
19	Satsuma Rd, Livingston, Satsuma	42	LA 3158, Airport, Hammond	Food	N: IHOP, Sonic S: Burger King, Chili's, McDonald's, Starbucks, Subway, Taco Bell, Wendy's
22	LA 63, Livingston, Frost	FStop	N: PT Self Service Auto Truck Stop/Chevron		
Gas	N: Chevron, Conoco, Mobil	Lodg	N: Friendly Inn	Lodg	N: Hotel
Food	N: Wayne's BBQ, Subway	TWash	N: Truck Wash	Med	M: + Hospital
Other	N: Lakeside RV Park▲	Other	S: Berryland Campers/LP	Other	N: Circuit City, PetSmart♥, Target S: Best Buy, Grocery, Goodyear, Home Depot, Office Depot, Sam's Club, Wal-Mart sc, North Shore Square Mall
(28)	Rest Area (Both dir) (RR, Phone, Picnic)	47	LA 445, Ponchatoula, Roberts		
		Other	N: Zemmurray Gardens, Hidden Oaks Family Campground▲, Yogi Bear Jellystone Campground▲		
29	LA 441, Holden			83	US 11, Pearl River, Slidell
Gas	N: L&W One Stop/Coastal	57	LA 1077, Covington, Goodbee, Madisonville	FStop	N: Interstate Station #23/Chevron S: Jubilee Express #4815/Marathon
32	LA 43, Hammond, to Albany, Springfield	Other	S: T Family Campground, Fairview Riverside State Park▲	Gas	N: Exxon◊ S: Shell
Gas	N: Chevron S: Citgo, Exxon	59	LA 21, Covington, Madisonville	Food	N: Burger King, CiCi's, McDonald's, Waffle House
Food	N: Subway	Gas	N: Chevron, Conoco, Shell S: Shell	Lodg	N: Best Western
Other	S: Tickfaw State Park▲	Food	N: Burger King/Conoco, Church's/Chevron, McDonald's S: Domino's/Shell	Med	S: + Hospital
35	Baptist Pumpkin Center, LA 1249, Hammond			Other	N: Grocery
Gas	N: Chevron, Exxon◊	Med	N: + Hospital	(85A)	Jct I-10W, to New Orleans
Other	N: Punkin Patch RV Park▲, J&W Campground▲, Dixie RV Superstore/Family RV Factory Outlet/Camping World S: Grocery	Other	S: Best Buy, Cinema, Target	(85B)	Jct I-59N, to Hattiesburg
		(60)	Rest Area (Both dir) (RR, Phone, Picnic)	(85C)	Jct I-10E, to Bay St Louis (Left Exit)
		63A	New Orleans via Causeway Toll Bridge, US 190, Covington, Mandeville, Bogalusa		(I-12 Begins/Ends on I-10, Exit #267) (CENTRAL TIME ZONE)
(37)	Weigh Station (Both dir)				
(38A)	Jct I-55, S to New Orleans	63B	US 190 Fwy/Expwy, Covington, Mandeville, Bogalusa		🎧 **LOUISIANA**
(38B)	Jct I-55, N to Jackson	Gas	N: Exxon, RaceTrac, Shell		Begin Westbound I-12 from Jct I-10 in Slidell, LA to Jct I-10, in Baton Rouge, LA.

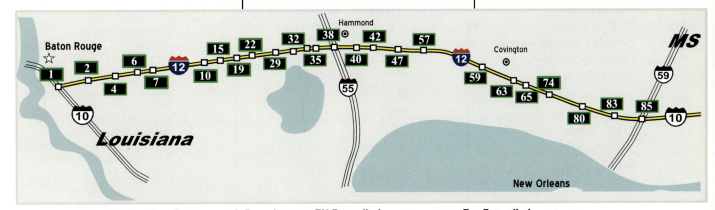

◊ = Regular Gas Stations with Diesel   ▲ = RV Friendly Locations   ♥ = Pet Friendly Locations
RED PRINT SHOWS LARGE VEHICLE PARKING/ACCESS ON SITE OR NEARBY   BROWN PRINT SHOWS CAMPGROUNDS/RV PARKS

INTERSTATE 15 S

EXIT	MONTANA
	Begin Southbound I-15 from the Canada / MT border, to Jct I-8 in San Diego, CA.

CANADA

(1)	in Canada, MT Weigh Station (Both dir)

MONTANA
(MOUNTAIN TIME ZONE)

(398)	MT / US / CANADA BORDER
397	**Sweetgrass**
W:	Rest Area (SB) (Open All Yr) (RR, Phone, Picnic, RVDump)
Gas	W: Sinclair
Food	W: Rest/Glocca Morro Motel
Lodg	W: Glocca Morra Motel
Other	W: Ross Int'l Airport✈, Duty Free Shops
394	McVey Rd, Ranch Acc, Sunburst
389	MT 552, Sunburst
Gas	W: Gas
Food	W: Kelly's Kitchen
Other	W: Sunburst RV Park▲
385	Swayze Rd, Sunburst
379	MT 215, MT 343, Kevin, Oilmont
Food	W: 4 Corner's Café
373	Potter Rd, Kevin
369	Bronken Rd, Shelby
(367)	Weigh Station (SB)
364	Bus Loop 15, Shelby
Lodg	E: Shelby Motel, Totem Motel
Other	E: Lewis & Clark RV Park/RVDump▲ Lake Shel-Oole Park/RVDump▲
	W: Shelby Airport✈
363	US 2, I-15 Bus, Shelby, Cut Bank, Port of Shelby
TStop	E: Town Pump Travel Plaza/Pilot #909/Exxon (Scales)
Gas	E: Conoco, Main St Conv, Noon's
Food	E: Subway/CountrySkillet/Deli/Town Pump, Dixie Inn, Dash Inn, Pizza Hut, South of the Border Café, The Griddle
	W: McDonald's
Lodg	E: Comfort Inn, Crossroads Inn, Glacier Motel, Sherlock Motel
Med	E: + Marias Heathcare Clinic
Other	E: Laundry/WiFi/Casino/RVDump/Town Pump TP, Marias Museum of History & Art, Albertson's, Amtrak, Williamson Park Campground▲, Lake Shel-Oole Park/ RVDump▲, Glacier RV Park/RVDump▲
	W: Shelby Airport✈, to Glacier Natl'l Park, to appr 20mi Riverview RV Park▲
(361)	Parking Area (NB)
358	Lincoln Rd, to Marias Valley Rd, Golf Course Rd, Shelby
352	Bullhead Rd, Conrad
348	MT 44, Valier Hwy, Conrad
345	MT 366, Ledger Rd, to US 91, Conrad, to Tiber Dam
339	I-15 Bus Lp, US 91, MT 218, Solid Rd, Conrad
TStop	W: Town Pump #8929/Exxon

EXIT	MONTANA
Gas	W: Cenex, Conoco, Exxon
Food	W: Deli/Subway/Town Pump, Arby's, A&W, Home Café, House of Pizza, Keg Family Rest
Lodg	W: Super 8/Town Pump, Conrad Motel, Northgate Motel
TWash	W: Robo TW
Med	W: + Hospital
Other	W: Laundry/Casino/Town Pump, IGA, U-Haul, Conrad Airport✈, Pondera Golf Club, Pharmacy, Pondera RV Park▲
335	Midway Rd, to Bus Lp 15, US 91, Conrad (Use 15Bus to access serv for Exit #339, approx 5 mi)
328	MT 365, Brady
321	Collins Rd, Dutton
(319)	Rest Area (Both dir) (Open All Yr) (RR, Phone, Picnic)
313	MT 221, MT 379, Main St, Dutton, to Choteau
Gas	W: Johnson's Conoco & Conv Store
Food	W: Café Dutton
Other	W: to 20mi: Choteau KOA▲
305	Bozeman
302	MT 431, Power
297	Anderson Rd, Vaugh S Frontage Rd, Power, Gordon
290	US 89N, MT 200W, Power, Vaugh, Vaugh S Frontage Rd, to Missoula, Choteau
Gas	W: Exxon◆, Valley Country Store/Sinclair◆
Other	W: RVDump/Valley CS
(288)	Parking Area (Both dir)
286	Manchester Rd, Vaughn Frontage Rd, Power
Food	W: Cattlemen's Cut Supper Club, Mary's Midway Casino & Rest
282	NW ByP, to US 87N, Great Falls (SB, No rentry)
Gas	E: Holiday Station Store, On Your Way, Town Pump, Sam's Club
Food	E: McDonald's, Pizza Hut, Subway
Lodg	E: Days Inn
TServ	E: Bouma Truck Sales, I State Truck Serv
Twash	E: Big Sky TW
Other	E: Kmart, Sam's Club, Staples, Albertson's, Wal-Mart, Westgate Mall
280	Central Ave W, I-15Bus, to US 87N, Great Falls
Gas	E: Conoco, Mini Mart
Food	E: Double Barrel Cafe, Ford's Drive In, Hardee's, KFC, Papa John's
Lodg	E: Alberta Motel, Best Western, Central Motel, Days Inn, Starlit Motel
Other	E: Bridgestone Tire, NAPA, Auto Dealers, U-Haul, Formula Fun Raceway, Great Falls Vet Service♥, to Electric City Speedway, Malmstrom AFB
278	US 89S, MT 200E, I-15 Bus, 10th Ave S, Great Falls (Loads over 12' wide not permitted)
Gas	E: Cenex, Conoco, Exxon, Holiday Station, Sinclair
Food	E: Rest/BW, Applebee's, Arby's, China Town, Country Kitchen, DQ,

◆ = Regular Gas Stations with Diesel ▲ = RV Friendly Locations ♥ = Pet Friendly Locations
RED PRINT SHOWS LARGE VEHICLE PARKING/ACCESS ON SITE OR NEARBY BROWN PRINT SHOWS CAMPGROUNDS/RV PARKS

Page 66

EXIT	MONTANA
Food	E: Elmer's Pancake & Steak House, Classic 50's Diner, Fuddrucker's, Golden Corral, McDonald's, Starbucks, Subway, Taco Bell, Tony Roma's, Willow Creek Steakhouse
Lodg	E: Best Western, Budget Inn, Comfort Inn, Fairfield Inn, Hampton Inn, Holiday Inn Express, La Quinta Inn♥, Super 8
Med	E: + Hospital
Other	E: Albertson's, Auto Dealers, Kmart, Home Depot, PetCo♥, Smith Food & Drug, Target, US Post Office, Holiday Village Mall, College of Great Falls, Dick's RV Park▲, Great Falls KOA▲, Travel Time RV Center, McCollum Modern RV's, RVDump/Sinclair, RVDump/Holiday, to MIL/Gateway FamCamp/Malmstrom AFB▲
	W: Great Falls Int'l Airport✈
277	31st St, Great Falls Int'l Airport Great Falls
TStop	E: Flying J Travel Plaza #5003 (Scales), Town Pump/Pilot #917 (Scales)
Food	E: Rest/FJ TP, Subway/TP
Lodg	E: Motel/FJ TP, Crystal Inn
TWash	E: Flying J TP
Other	E: Laundry/Casino/WiFi/LP/RVDump/FJ TP
	W: Great Falls Int'l Airport✈
(275)	Weigh Station (NB)
270	Center St, MT 330, Cascade, Ulm
Gas	E: Exxon◆
Lodg	W: Village Inn
Other	E: US Post Office
256	MT 68, Simms Cascade Rd, 1st St N, Cascade
Gas	E: Sinclair
Food	E: Pizza, Café/Badger Motel
Lodg	E: A&C Motel, Badger Motel
254	MT 68, 1st St S, Cascade (E-access Exit #256 Services)
250	Local Access
247	Old US 91, Frontage Rd, Hardy Creek, Cascade
(245)	Scenic View (SB)
244	Old US 91, Frontage Rd, Canyon Access, Cascade
Other	W: Rosie's Missouri Inn RV Park▲
240	Bald Eagle Dr, Cascade, Dearborn
Food	W: Dearborn Country Inn
Lodg	W: Dearborn Country Inn & Resort & RV Park▲
(240)	Rest Area (Both dir) (Open All Yr) (RR, Phone, Picnic)
234	Bridge St, Wolf Creek, Craig
Gas	E: O'Connell's Store
Food	E: Izaak's, Trout Shop Cafe
Lodg	E: Flyway Ranch, Trout Shop Lodge
Other	E: Choteau Dinosaur Museum
228	US 287N, Wolf Creek, to Augusta, Choteau
Lodg	W: Bungalow Bed & Breakfast
226	MT 434, Frontage Rd, Wolf Creek
Gas	E: Exxon◆
Food	E: Oasis Cafe
	W: Frenchman Café & Saloon

EXIT	MONTANA
Lodg	E: Frenchy's Motel & Trailer/RV
Other	E: Montana River Outfitters/FishTrips/Tours/FlyShop/Lodging/RVSites▲
(222)	Parking Area (Both dir)
219	Recreation Rd, Canyon Creek, Spring Creek (NB, no re-entry)
216	Chevallier Dr, Canyon Cr, Sieben
209	Gates of the Mountains Rd, Wolf Creek, Gates of the Mtn Rec Area
(205)	Turn Out (SB)
(202)	Weigh Station (SB)
200	MT 279, MT 453, Lincoln Rd, Helena
Gas	W: Sinclair◆
Food	W: Grub Stake
Other	W: to Lincoln Rd RV Park/RVDump▲, to Helena Campground & RV Park▲
193	I-15 Bus, Cedar St, to Washington St, Custer Ave, Helena
Gas	W: Conoco, Exxon, Sinclair
Food	W: Applebee's, Arby's, Godfather's, Jade Garden, McDonald's, Perkins, Pizza Hut, Subway, Taco Bell
Lodg	W: Howard Johnson Inn, Quality Inn, Wingate Inn
Other	E: Home Depot, Avis, Helena Reg'l Airport✈
	W: Albertson's, CarQuest, Jiffy Lube, Kmart, Target, US Post Office
(192AB)	Jct I-15, US 12, US 287, Townsend, Helena, Capitol Area
TStop	E: High Country Travel Plaza/Conoco
Gas	W: Exxon◆, Sinclair, Albertson's
Food	E: Rest/High Country TP, Burger King, Golden Corral, Subway
	W: DQ, KFC, JB's Rest, McDonald's, Overland Express, Starbucks, Village Inn, Wendy's, Rest/Jorgensen's Inn
Lodg	E: Hampton Inn
	W: Comfort Inn, Days Inn, Fairfield Inn, Holiday Inn Express, Jorgensen's Inn, Motel 6♥, Red Lion Hotel, Shilo Inn, Super 8
TWash	E: High Country TP
TServ	E: J&D Truck & Auto Repair & Service/RVDump
Med	W: + Hospital
Other	E: Laundry/RVDump/LP/High Country TP, Auto Dealers, Home Depot, Staples, Wal-Mart sc, Montana RV Center, D&D RV Center, Buzz Inn RV Park & Campground▲, to Kim's Marina & RV Resort, MT State Hwy Patrol Post, Keno King Casino
	W: Albertson's, Safeway, Goodyear, Osco, Capital Hill Mall, U-Haul, Last Chance Gulch Tour, State Capitol, Capital RV Center, to Fort William Henry Harrison
187	MT 518, Frontage Rd, Clancy, Montana City
Food	E: Hugo's Pizza, Montana City Grill & Saloon
Lodg	W: Elk Horn Mountain Inn
182	Legal Tender Ln, Clancy
Food	W: Legal Tender Restaurant
Other	E: Alhambra RV Park▲

EXIT	MONTANA
(178)	Rest Area (Both dir) (Open 4/15-11/15) (RR, Phone, Picnic)
176	Main St, Clancy, Jefferson City
(174)	Chain Up Area (Both dir)
(168)	Chain Up Area (Both dir)
164	MT 69, Main St, Boulder
FStop	E: Town Pump #310/Exxon
Food	E: Deli/Town Pump, Elkhorn Café & Supper Club, Bear Claw, DQ, Mountain Good Rest, Gator's Pizza
Lodg	E: Castoria Inn, O-Z Motel
Other	E: Lucky Lil's Casino/TP, RC RV Park▲, RVDump/Boulder City Park, Ace Hardware, Grocery
(161)	Parking Area (NB)
160	Galena Gulch Rd, Boulder
156	Basin, Cataract Creek Rd, Clancy
151	Boulder River Rd, Boulder, Bernice, Bear Gulch Access
(148)	Chain Up Area (Both dir)
(143)	Chain Up Area (Both dir)
138	Lowland Rd, Boulder, Elk Park
134	Woodville
(130)	Scenic Overlook (SB)
NOTE:	I-15N below runs with I-90 for 8m. Exit #'s Follow I-15.
(129)	Jct I-90E to Billings, Jct I-15S/I-90W to Butte
127AB	I-15 Bus, Harrison Ave, Butte (NB)
127	I-15 Bus, Harrison Ave, Butte (SB)
Gas	E: Conoco, Exxon, Sinclair, Town Pump
	W: Conoco, Town Pump
Food	E: 4 B's Rest, Arbys, Burger King, DQ, Godfather's, KFC, McDonald's, Perkins, Taco Bell, Wendy's
	W: Rest/Red Lion Hotel, Denny's, Hanging Five Family Rest, Papa John's, Papa Murphy's, Quiznos
Lodg	E: Best Western, Hampton Inn, Super 8
	W: Comfort Inn, Days Inn, Holiday Inn Express, Red Lion Hotel
Other	E: Casinos, Auto Dealers, Grocery, Kmart, Wal-Mart sc, Our Lady of the Rockies, Butte Plaza Mall, Bert Mooney Airport✈, Rocky Mtn RV Sales & Srv, Al's RV Center
	W: RVDump/Town Pump, Casino, Grocery, Laundromat, NAPA, Animal Hospital♥
126	Montana St, Butte
Gas	E: Thriftway, Town Pump◆
	W: Cenex, Kum & Go
Food	W: Jokers Wild Casino & Restaurant
Lodg	W: Budget Motel, Eddy's Motel
Med	W: + St James Healthcare
Other	W: Butte KOA/RVDump▲, Grocery
(124)	Jct I-115, Butte City Center, Harrison Ave, Montana St (NB)
122	MT 276, Butte, Rocker
TStop	E: Flying J Travel Plaza #5130 (Scales)
	W: Town Pump Travel Plaza/Pilot/Exxon

◆ = Regular Gas Stations with Diesel   ▲ = RV Friendly Locations   ♥ = Pet Friendly Locations

RED PRINT SHOWS LARGE VEHICLE PARKING/ACCESS ON SITE OR NEARBY   BROWN PRINT SHOWS CAMPGROUNDS/RV PARKS

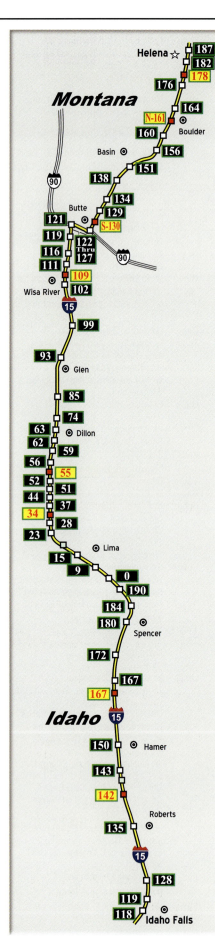

EXIT		MONTANA
	Food	E: Rest/FJ TP
		W: Arby's/Subway/TP TP, McDonald's
	Lodg	E: Rocker Inn
		W: Motel 6 ♥
	TServ	E: Rocker Repair
	Other	E: Casino/Laundry/WiFi/FJ TP
		W: Laundry/Casino/LP/WiFi/TP TP
(122)		Weigh Station (Both dir)
(121)		Jct I-90W to Missoula, I-15S to Idaho Falls, I-15N/I-90E to Butte
NOTE:		I-15N above runs with I-90 for 8 mi. Exit #'s Follow I-15.
119		German Gulch Rd, Butte, Silver Bow, Port of MT Hub Access
116		Buxton Rd, Butte, Buxton
111		Divide Creek Rd, Divide, Feely
(109)		Rest Area (Both dir) (Open All Year) (RR, Phone, Picnic)
102		MT 43, Divide, Wisdom
	Gas	W: Sinclair
99		Moose Creek Rd, Divide
93		Frontage Rd, Twin Bridges, to MT 361, Melrose
	Gas	W: Gas
	Food	W: Hitching Post, Melrose Bar & Café
	Lodg	W: Sportman Motel, Cabins & RV Park▲
85		Rock Creek Rd, Dillon, Glen
74		Birch Creek Rd, Dillon, Apex
63		MT 41, I-15 Bus, US 91, Dillon, Twin Bridges
	FStop	E: Cenex
	TStop	E: Town Pump #360/Exxon
	Gas	E: Phillips 66
	Food	E: FastFood/TP, Rest/BW, McDonald's, Pizza Hut, Subway
	Lodg	E: Best Western, Comfort Inn, Guest House Inn, Sundowner Motel, Super 8
	Med	E: + Hospital
	Other	E: Grocery, Pharmacy, Dillon KOA/RVDump▲, RVDump/Cenex
62		Bus Loop 15, Dillon
	Gas	E: Exxon
	Food	E: Rest/Crosswinds Motel, Artic Circle, Sparky's, Taco John
	Lodg	E: Crosswinds Motel, Creston Motel, Quality Inn, Rusty Duck
	Med	E: + Hospital
	Other	E: Southside RV Park/RVDump▲
59		MT 278, Dillon, Jackson, Wisdom
	Other	W: Countryside RV Park/RVDump▲
56		Rebich Lane, Dillon, Barretts
	TStop	W: Big Sky Truck Stop
	Food	W: Rest/Big Sky TS
	Other	W: Laundry/Big Sky TS
(55)		Parking Area (SB)
52		Grasshopper Creek
51		Dalys (SB)
44		MT 324, Dillon, Clark Canyon Reservoir
	Other	E: to (20mi) Armstead RV Park/RVDump▲, Beaverhead Marina & RV Park/RVDump▲

EXIT		MT / ID
	Other	W: Clark Canyon Reservoir Rec Area
37		Red Rock Rd, Dillon
(34)		Parking Area (Both dir) (RR)
29		Kidd
23		Old US 91, Main St, Lima, Dell
	Gas	E: Cenex, Exxon◆
		E: Stockyard Inn
(16)		Weigh Station (Both dir)
15		Bailey St, Lima
	Gas	E: Exxon◆
	Food	E: Jan's Cafe
	Lodg	E: Mountain View Motel & RV Park▲
	Med	E: + Ambulance Service
	Other	E: Auto Repair, Tire Repair, US Post Office
9		Snowline
0		MT 509, Lima, Monida
(MOUNTAIN TIME ZONE)		

⦿ MONTANA

⦿ IDAHO

(MOUNTAIN TIME ZONE)

190		Old Hwy 91, Spencer, Humphrey
184		W Camas Creek Rd, Spencer, Stoddard Creek Area, Old Beaver
	Other	E: Camping▲
		W: Stoddard Creek Camping▲
180		Old Hwy 91, Spencer
	Food	E: Cafe
		W: Spencer Bar & Grill
	Lodg	W: Spencer Camping Cabins
	Other	W: Spencer RV Park▲
172		Modoc Rd, US Sheep Experiment Station, Dubois
167		ID 22, CR A2, Dubois, Arco
		Rest Area (Both dir) (CLOSED in Winter) (RR, Phones, Picnic)
	FStop	E: Clark Co True Value/P66, Ike's 66
	TStop	E: Scoggins Exxon
	Food	E: Opal Mine Café, Tacos Tamazula
	Lodg	E: Crossroads Motel, Hernandez Motel
	TServ	E: Scoggins
	Other	E: LP/Exxon, LP/P66, Scoggins RV Park/RVDump▲, US Post Office, Dubois Muni Airport ✈
150		2100 North Rd, Hamer, Camas
	Food	E: Corner Bar & Cafe
143		ID 33, ID 28N, Terreton, to Mud Lake, to US 20, Rexburg
		Weigh Station (Both dir)
(142)		Parking Area / Historical Site
135		ID 48E, Roberts
	TStop	E: Teton Truck Stop/Tesoro
	Food	E: Rest/Teton TS
	Other	E: Western Wings RV Park▲
128		County Line Rd, Osgood Area
	Gas	E: Sinclair◆
119		US 20E, Idaho Falls, Rigby, W Yellowstone, Rexburg, Yellowstone National Park
	FStop	E: Gas N Grub/Sinclair (Scales)

Page 68

◆= Regular Gas Stations with Diesel   ▲= RV Friendly Locations   ♥= Pet Friendly Locations
RED PRINT SHOWS LARGE VEHICLE PARKING/ACCESS ON SITE OR NEARBY   BROWN PRINT SHOWS CAMPGROUNDS/RV PARKS

EXIT		IDAHO
	Gas	W: Shell
	Food	E: Rest/QI, Rest/Shilo Inn, Applebee's, Chili's, Denny's, JB's Family Rest, Outback Steakhouse
	Lodg	E: Best Western (2), Comfort Inn, Days Inn, Guest House Inn, Motel 6 ♥, Quality Inn, Shilo Inn, Super 8
	TServ	E: Rumble's Diesel
	Other	E: LP/GasNGrub, Idaho Falls KOA▲, Snake River RV Park & Campground/KOA▲, ID State Hwy Patrol Post
		W: Fanning Field, Idaho Falls Reg'l Airport ✈
118		US 20W, Broadway St, Idaho Falls Arco, Mountain Home, US 91S
	TStop	E: KJ's/P66
	Gas	W: Chevron♦, Exxon
	Food	E: FastFood/KJ's, Artic Circle, Chili's, Applebee's, Hometown Kitchen, Jack in the Box, Smitty's Pancake & Steak House, Wendy's
		W: Rest/Motel West, Burger King, DQ, Jack in the Box, McDonald's, Pizza Hut, Subway
	Lodg	E: Fairfield Inn
		W: Comfort Inn, Motel West
	Med	E: + Hospital
	Other	E: American RV & Marine, Harley Davidson, Wal-Mart sc, Idaho Falls KOA/RVDump▲
		W: Albertson's, Pharmacy
113		US 26E, Idaho Falls, Shelley, Grand Teton National Park
	TStop	E: Yellowstone Truck Stop/Exxon (Scales), Dad's Travel Center #113/Sinclair (Scales)
	Food	E: Rest/FastFood/Yellowstone TS, Rest/FastFood/Dad's TC
	Lodg	E: Motel/Yellowstone TS
	TServ	E: Yellowstone TS/Tires, Lake City Int'l, Lindsay Truck & Automotive, Peterbilt
	TWash	E: Dad's TC
	Med	E: + Hospital
	Other	E: Laundry/LP/RVDump/Yellowstone TS, Laundry/WiFi/RVDump/Dad's TC, Sunnyside Acres Park/RVDump▲, Targhee RV Park/RVDump▲
108		1250 North Rd, Shelley
	Gas	E: Chevron, Stop N Go
	Other	W: N Bingham Rec Site/RVDump
(101)		Rest Area (Both dir) (RR, Phones, Picnic, Vend)
98		River Rd, Rose-Firth Area
93		US 26W, W Blackfoot, Arco (NB), Snoshone, I-15 Bus, Blackfoot (SB)
	TStop	E: Flying J Travel Plaza #11182 (Scales)
	Gas	E: Chevron, Maverik
		W: Phillips 66
	Food	E: FastFood/FJ TP, Artic Circle, Domino's, Little Caesar's, McDonald's, Pizza Hut, Subway, Taco Bell, Wendys
	Lodg	E: Best Western, Super 8
	Med	E: + Hospital
	Other	E: WiFi/LP/RVDump/FJ TP, RVDump/Chevron, Albertson's, AutoZone, RiteAid, Schwab Tire, Wal-Mart sc ▲
89		US 91, I-15 Bus, S Blackfoot
80		Ross Fork Rd, Fort Hall
	TStop	W: TP Truck Stop/Sinclair
	Food	W: FastFood/TP TS

EXIT		IDAHO
	Other	W: Casino/TP TS, Shoshone Tribal Museum
74		Siphon Rd
(72)		Jct I-86W, to Twin Falls, Boise
	TServ	W: Cummins Intermountain, Western States Equipment
71		Pocatella Creek Rd, Pocatello
	Gas	E: Chevron, Jacksons Food, Shell
		W: Exxon, Common Cents
	Food	E: Rest/Qual Inn, Rest/RLionHotel, Rest/Hol Inn, Burger King, Hardee's, Jack in the Box, Perkins, Subway
		W: Sizzler, Pier 49 SF Pizza
	Lodg	E: Best Western ♥, Comfort Inn, Holiday Inn, Quality Inn, Red Lion Hotel ♥, Super 8 ♥
	Med	E: + Hospital
	Other	E: Pocatello KOA/RVDump▲, Bannock Co Fairgrounds/RVDump
		W: Albertson's, Walgreen's, Vet ♥
69		Center St, Clark St, Pocatello (NO Trucks)
	Gas	W: Shell
	Food	W: Artic Circle, Blimpie
	Med	E: + Pocatello Reg'l Medical Center, + US Vets Outpatient Clinic
		W: + Bannock Regional Medical Center, Portneuf Medical Center
	Other	W: to ID State Univ
67		US 30W, US 91N, I-15 Bus (NB), S 5th Ave (SB), Pocatello
	TStop	W: Forde Johnson Truck Service/P66 (Scales)

EXIT		ID / UT
	Gas	E: Common Cents Exxon
		W: Shell, Sinclair
	Food	W: Rest/Forde TS, Elmer's, McDonald's, Pizza Hut, Subway, Taco Bell
	Lodg	W: Best Western, Econo Lodge, Executive Inn, Sundial Inn, Thunderbird Motel
	Med	W: + Hospital
	Other	E: ID State Hwy Patrol Post
		W: Laundry/Forde TS, Cowboy RV Park/RVDump▲, Sullivans MH & RV Park/RVDump▲, Grocery
63		Portneuf Rd, Mink Creek Recreation Area
(59)		Rest Area (Both dir) (RR, Phones, Picnic, Vend)
(59)		Weigh Station (Both dir)
58		I-15 Bus, Inkom (SB)
	Gas	W: Sinclair
	Food	W: El Rancho Café
	Other	W: to Pebble Creek Ski Area
57		Inkom (NB)
47		US 30E, McCammon, Montpelier Lava Hot Springs, Soda Springs, to Jackson, WY
	TStop	E: Flying J Travel Plaza #50023/Conoco (Scales), McCammon Chevron
	Food	E: Rest/FJ TP, Taco Time/Chevron
	Other	E: Laundry/WiFi/LP/RVDump/FJ TP, Laundry/RVDump/McCammon Chevron, McCammon RV Park▲
44		I-15 Bus, Jensen Rd, McCammon
40		Arimo
	Gas	E: Sinclair
	Food	E: Cafe
36		US 91S, Virginia, Preston
31		ID 40E, to US 91S, Downey, Preston
	TStop	E: PTP/Flags West Truck Stop/Shell
	Food	E: Rest/FW TS
	Lodg	E: Motel/FW TS
	Other	E: Laundry/LP/RVDump/FW TS, Hot Springs RV Campground▲
(25)		Rest Area (SB) (RR, Phones, Picnic, Vend)
22		Malad Valley Rd, Devils Creek Rd, Devil Creek Reservoir
17		ID 36E, Weston, Preston
	Food	W: Jim's Deep Creek Inn
13		ID 38, Malad City
	Gas	W: Chevron, Phillips 66
	Food	W: Burger King/Chevron, Café/Taco Time/P66, Pizza, Restaurant
	Lodg	W: Village Inn Motel
	TServ	W: 3 R's Country Tire
	Med	W: + Hospital
	Other	W: Grocery, Auto Repair
(7)		ID Welcome Center (NB) (RR, Picnic, Vend, Info)
3		Woodruff, to Samaria
		(MOUNTAIN TIME ZONE)

⋂ **IDAHO**

⋃ **UTAH**

(MOUNTAIN TIME ZONE)

NOTE: MM 403: Idaho State Line

♦ = Regular Gas Stations with Diesel   ▲ = RV Friendly Locations   ♥ = Pet Friendly Locations
RED PRINT SHOWS LARGE VEHICLE PARKING/ACCESS ON SITE OR NEARBY   BROWN PRINT SHOWS CAMPGROUNDS/RV PARKS

EXIT	UTAH
398	Portage
392	20800 Rd N, to UT 13S, Portage, Plymouth
TStop	E: Fast-Stop/Chevron
Food	E: Subway/Fast Stop
Other	E: Camperworld Hot Springs▲, Camperworld Hot Springs Golf Course
385	15200 Rd N, UT 30E, Garland, Riverside, Logan, Fielding
Gas	E: Sinclair
Food	E: Riverside Grill/Sinclair
Lodg	E: Jay's Motel
381	1000N, to UT 102, Tremonton, Garland (Serv S to Main St)
Gas	E: Amoco, Chevron, Sinclair
Food	E: Coachman Café, Crossroads Family Rest, Mack's Family D/I Rest, Pizza Plus, Subway, Taco Time
Lodg	E: Marble Motel, Sandman Motel W: Western Inn♥
Med	E: + Bear River Valley Hospital
Other	E: Police Dept, Tremonton Muni Airport✈, Grocery, Family Dollar, Bear River Animal Hospital♥, Pharmacy, AmeriGas LP W: Archibald Propane LP
NOTE:	I-15N below runs with I-84 for 39mi. Exit #'s Follow I-15.
(379)	Jct I-84W, to Boise, Tremonton (NB, Left exit)
376	UT 13, N 5200 St W, Tremonton, to UT 102, Garland, Bear River (lodging N to UT 102W)
FStop	E: Exxon Travel Center
Gas	E: Conoco
Food	E: Arby's/Exxon TC, JC's Country Diner
Lodg	E: Marble Motel, Sandman Motel W: Western Inn♥
372	UT 240, Honeyville, to UT 13, UT 38, Bear River
(369)	UT Welcome Center (SB) (RR, Phones, Picnic, Vend, Info, WiFi)
365	UT 13, I-15 Bus, I-84 Bus, 900 North St, Brigham City, Corinne
Other	E: Brigham City Airport✈
363	Forest St, Brigham City
Other	E: Parson's Service Center, Auto & Truck Repair, Towing, U-Haul
362	US 91, to US 89, 1100 South St, Brigham City, Logan
FStop	E: Flying J Travel Plaza #1188
Gas	E: 7-11, Chevron, Sinclair
Food	E: Rest/FJ TP, Arby's, Aspen Grill, Burger King, KFC, McDonald's, Subway
Lodg	E: Crystal Inn, Galaxie Motel, Howard Johnson
TServ	E: Willard Auto & Diesel Service W: S&M Diesel Service
Med	E: + Brigham City Comm Hospital
Other	E: WiFi/LP/RVDump/FJ TP, Golden Spike RV Park▲, Walker Cinema, Auto Dealers, Auto Zone, Checkers Auto, Wal-Mart sc, Eagle Mtn Golf Course
(363)	Perry Rest Area (NB) (RR, Phones, Picnic, Vend, Info)
(361)	Port of Entry / Weigh Station (Both dir)

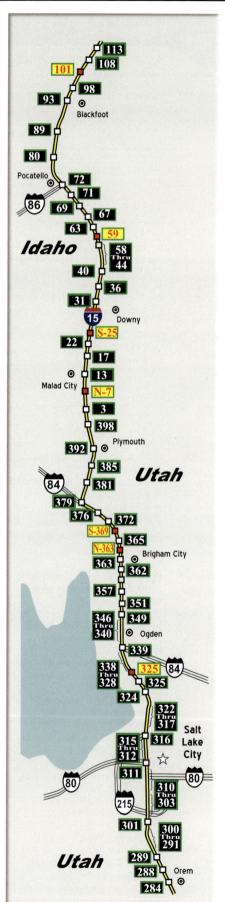

EXIT	UTAH
357	750N, UT 360, UT 15, N Willard, Perry, Willard Bay
TStop	E: Flying J Travel Plaza #1125 (Scales)
Food	E: Rest/FastFood/FJ TP
Other	E: Laundry/WiFi/RVDump/LP/FJ TP, Brigham City/Perry South KOA▲, Police Dept W: Willard Bay State Park▲
351	UT 126, to US 89, S Willard, Pleasant View, Willard Bay
Other	W: Willard Bay State Park▲
349	2700 N, UT 134, Ogden, Farr West, Pleasant View
Gas	E: 7-11, Chevron, Maverik, Phillips 66 W: Conoco◊
Food	E: Arby's, McDonald's, Melinas Mex Rest, Subway, Wendy's
Other	E: Auto Repair, Fort Carson Army Res Center
346	Pioneer Rd, Ogden, Harrisville, Defense Depot
Gas	W: Excel Conv Store
TServ	W: Diesel Service
Other	E: Mulligan's Golf Course, Fort Carson Army Res Center
344	UT 39, 1200S, 12th St, Ogden
TStop	W: Pilot Travel Center #294 (Scales)
Gas	E: Chevron, Phillips 66, Shell◊
Food	E: Rest/BW, Jeremiah's, Hogi Yogi W: DQ/Subway/TacoBell/Pilot TC, CJ's Rest & Bakery
Lodg	E: Best Western W: Holiday Inn Express, Sleep Inn
TServ	W: General Diesel Services
Other	E: Steve's Car Care W: WiFi/Pilot TC
343	UT 104, 21st St, Wilson Lane
FStop	W: Super Stop/Shell
TStop	E: Flying J Travel Plaza #50001/Conoco (Scales), Wilson Lane/Chevron
Gas	W: Phillips 66
Food	E: Rest/FastFood/FJ TP, Arby's/Wilson Lane, Cactus Red's, McDonald's, Mi Rancho Rest, Rest/ComfSts, Rest/HI W: FastFood/Texaco, Café/Super 8, Blimpie
Lodg	E: Flying J Inn/FJ TP, Big Z Motel, Best Rest Inn♥, Comfort Suites, Holiday Inn Express W: Super 8♥
Tires	E: Flying J TP, Wilson Lane
TWash	E: Wilson Lane Service
TServ	E: Ogden Diesel Sales & Service
Other	E: Laundry/CB/WiFi/RVDump/LP/FJ TP, RVDump/Wilson Lane, Century M/H & RV Park▲ W: Auto Repair, Diesel Services
342	UT 53, Pennsylvania Ave, 24th St, Ogden (NB Only)
FStop	E: Sinclair
Food	W: Sunrise Cafe
Other	E: Animal Hospital♥, Auto Repair, Fort Buenaventura State Park
341B	UT 79W, 31st St WB, Ogden
Other	W: Ogden Hinckley Airport✈, U-Haul
341A	UT 79W, 31st St EB, Hinckley, to UT 204, US 89, Ogden (Serv E to Wall St/UT204/US89)
Gas	E: 7-11
Food	E: Arby's, Golden Corral, Skippers
Lodg	E: Days Inn♥

◊ = Regular Gas Stations with Diesel   ▲ = RV Friendly Locations   ♥ = Pet Friendly Locations
RED PRINT SHOWS LARGE VEHICLE PARKING/ACCESS ON SITE OR NEARBY   BROWN PRINT SHOWS CAMPGROUNDS/RV PARKS

EXIT		UTAH
	Med	E: + Hospital
	Other	E: Newgate Mall, to Weber St Univ
(340)		Jct I-84E, to Cheyenne (SB)
	NOTE:	I-15N above runs with I-84 for 39mi. Exit #'s Follow I-15.
339		Riverdale Rd, UT 241, UT 26, to I-84E, Riverdale (NB)
	Gas	E: Conoco◊, Sinclair
	Food	E: Applebee's, Carl's Jr, Chili's, IHOP, Mexican Rest, McDonald's
	Lodg	E: Motel 6♥, Red Roof Inn♥
		W: Circle R Motel
	Other	E: Auto Dealers, Harley Davidson, Home Depot, Wal-Mart sc, Banks, Museum
		W: Auto Repair, Big O Tires, Police Dept
338		UT 97, 5600S, Roy, Sunset, Hill Air Force Base
	Gas	W: 7-11, Exxon, Phillips 66, Sinclair
	Food	W: Arby's, Artic Circle, Blimpie's, KFC, Burger King, DQ, Denny's, McDonald's, Pizza Hut, Taco Bell, Village Inn
	Lodg	W: Quality Inn, Motel 6♥
	Med	E: + Now Care Immediate Medical
	Other	E: Museums, MIL/Hill AFB FamCamp▲
		W: Albertson's, Auto Zone, Banks, Goodyear, Tires, Walgreen's
335		UT 103, 650N, N Clearfield, Sunset, Hill Air Force Base
	Gas	W: 7-11, Chevron, Conoco, Petro Mart, Texaco
	Food	W: Arby's, Carl's Jr, KFC, McDonald's, Skipper's, Subway, Taco Bell
	Lodg	W: Crystal Cottage Inn, Super 8
	Other	E: Hill AFB
		W: Big O Tires, RV Dealer
334		UT 193, Bernard Fisher Hwy, S Clearfield, Hill Air Force Base
	Gas	E: Circle K, Maverik, Tesoro
		W: Chevron
	Other	E: American Car Care Ctr
		W: Banks, Smith's Food & Drug, Banks
332		UT 108, Antelope Dr, Layton, Freeport, Antelope Island, Syracuse
	FStop	E: Phillips 66
	Gas	E: Chevron, Circle K
		W: 7-11, Conoco
	Food	E: Applebee's, Carl's Jr, Cracker Barrel, Chili's, Golden Corral, JB's Rest, Outback Steakhouse, Pier 49 SF Pizza, Sonic, Timberlodge Steaks, Tony Roma's
		W: Arby's, Burger King, McDonald's, Quiznos, Outback Steakhouse
	Lodg	E: Courtyard, Fairfield Inn, Hampton Inn, Holiday Inn Express, La Quinta Inn♥, Towneplace Suites
		W: Marriott
	Med	E: + IHC Healthcare
		W: + Davis Hospital & Med Center
	Other	E: Lowe's, Banks, Anderson's Auto & Tire Service, Layton Hills Mall, Tires, Tinseltown USA, Cinema
		W: Albertson's, Auto Repair, Banks, Univ of Utah, RV Dealer
331		UT 232, Hill Field Rd, to UT 126, N Layton
	Gas	E: Phillips 66

EXIT		UTAH
	Food	E: Denny's, Garcia's, McDonald's, Olive Garden, Red Lobster, Sizzler, Tony Roma
		W: Arizona Big Salad, Blimpie's, Burger King, China Buffet, Einstein Bros Bagel, Fuddrucker's, IHOP, KFC, Lone Star Steakhouse, Taco Bell
	Lodg	E: Comfort Inn
	Med	W: + Hospital
	Other	E: Layton Hills Mall, Tinseltown USA, Cinema, Hill AFB, Banks
		W: Discount Tire, Home Depot, NTB, Sam's Club, Staples, Wal-Mart sc, Weber St Univ, Banks, Auto Dealer, RV Dealer
330		to UT 126, Main St, to UT 109, S Layton (NB)
	Gas	W: Texaco
	Food	E: Little Orient Chinese
		W: Doug & Emmy's Fam Rest, Sills Cafe
	Other	E: American Car Care Center, Banks
		W: Auto Repair, Banks
328		UT 273, 200 North, Kaysville
	Gas	E: Chevron, Citgo, Phillips 66◊, Sinclair
	Food	E: Cutler's Sandwiches, Joanie's, KFC, Subway, Taco Time, Wendy's
	Lodg	W: West Motel
	Other	E: Auto Repair, Banks, Police Dept
		W: Albertson's, Blaine Jensen & Sons RV Center/RVDump, Auto Repair
(325)		Parking Area (Both dir)
325		UT 225, US 89, to UT 106, Lagoon Dr, Farmington (SB)
	Gas	E: Maverick
	Food	E: Arby's, Burger King, Pizza Hut
	Other	E: Pioneer Village, Banks
324		UT 225, US 89, to UT 106, Lagoon Dr, Farmington (NB)
	Gas	E: Maverick
	Food	E: Arby's, Burger King, Pizza Hut
	Other	E: Pioneer Village, Lagoon RV Park & Campground▲, Cherry Hill Camping Resort▲
322		UT 227, 200W, Lagoon Dr, Farmington (NB, NO reaccess)
	Other	E: Banks, Pioneer Village, Lagoon RV Park & Campground▲, Police Dept
319		UT 105, Parrish Ln, Centerville
	Gas	E: Chevron◊, Phillips 66◊
	Food	E: Arby's, Artic Circle, Carl's Jr, DQ, Hardee's, IHOP, Lone Star Steakhouse, McDonald's, Subway, Taco Bell, Wendy's
	Other	E: Albertson's, Big O Tires, Banks, Home Depot, Target, Police Dept
		W: Auto Repairs
317		UT 131, 400 North (NB) Bountiful, US 89S, 500W (SB, Left exit) Woods Cross (Reaccess both dir via US 89)
	Gas	E: Chevron, Conoco, Exxon, Texaco
	Food	E: Café Alicia
	Lodg	E: Country Inn
	Other	E: Auto, Truck & Marine Repair, Banks
		W: Police Dept
316		UT 68, 500S, Woods Cross
	TStop	W: RB's One Stop/P66
	Gas	E: Exxon, Tesoro
		W: Chevron

EXIT		UTAH
	Food	E: Burger King, Carl's Jr, Christopher's Seafood & Steakhouse, JB's Rest, KFC, Hogi Yogi, McDonald's, Mexican Rest, Sizzler, Subway, Taco Bell
		W: FastFood/RB's
	Lodg	E: Bear River Lodge, Country Inn Suites
	Med	E: + Benchmark Regional Hospital
	Other	E: Albertson's, Auto Zone, Auto Repair, Banks, Big O Tires, Costco, Firestone, Walgreen's, Univ of Utah, RV Service Center, Police Dept
		W: Laundry/RVDump/RB's, Diesel Service, Auto Repair, Skypark Airport✈
315		1100N, to US 89, Woods Cross
	FStop	E: Slim Olson's #2/Chevron
	Gas	E: Chevron◊, Sinclair, Texaco
		W: Conoco
	Food	E: Arby's, Apollo Burger, Burger King, Empire Chinese, KFC, McDonald's, Mexican, Pappas Steak House, Skipper's, Village Inn, Wendy's
		W: Denny's, Lorena's Rest
	Lodg	E: Best Western, Comfort Inn
		W: Hampton Inn, Motel 6♥
	Other	E: RVDump/LP/Slim Olson's, BF Goodrich Tires, Cinema, Banks, Hertz RAC, Enterprise RAC, Grocery Stores
		W: Colonial Woods RV & MH Park▲, Skypark Airport✈
314		Center St, N Salt Lake (SB no reacc)
	Tstop	W: (I-215, 1st Exit) Flying J Travel Plaza/Scales/FastFood/LP/RVDump
	Gas	E: Walker's
		W: Maverick
	Food	E: Quiznos, Puerto Vallarta
	Other	E: Diesel Repair & Service, Police Dept
		W: I-215, 1st Exit Pony Express RV Resort▲
(313)		Jct I-215W, Belt Route, to Salt Lake City Int'l Airport (SB)
312		US 89, Center St, N Salt Lake (NB), US 89, Beck St (SB) (NB access Exit #314 services)
311		2200N, to UT 68, Redwood Rd, Warm Springs Rd
310		900W, 1000N (SB)
	Lodg	W: Salt City Inn
309		UT 268, 600N, Salt Lake City (Addt'l Serv E to US 89) (Many Serv S on 900W to UT 186)
	Gas	W: Neil's Pro Service/Conoco
	Food	W: Papa John's
	Med	E: + Hospital
	Other	E: Univ of UT
		W: Smith's Food & Drug, Bank
	NOTE:	I-15N below runs with I-80 for 5 mi Exit #'s Follow I-15
(308)		Jct I-80W, SL Int'l Airport, Reno
307		400 South, UT 186 (SB), 400 South HOV Exit (NB)
	Gas	E: Chevron, Food Mart
	Food	E: Various
	Lodg	E: Courtyard, Hampton Inn, Rio Grande Hotel, Renaissance Suites, Residence Inn
	Other	E: Amtrak, Enterprise RAC, Aquarium, Museum, Auto Repair, Grocery, Banks
		W: Grocery

◊= Regular Gas Stations with Diesel   ▲ = RV Friendly Locations   ♥= Pet Friendly Locations

RED PRINT SHOWS LARGE VEHICLE PARKING/ACCESS ON SITE OR NEARBY   BROWN PRINT SHOWS CAMPGROUNDS/RV PARKS

EXIT	UTAH
306	**600 South, UT 269 (NB)**
Gas	E: Chevron, Maverick, Sinclair
Food	E: Denny's, McDonald's, Rest/Hilton, Salty Dogs, Rest/Quality Inn, Rest/Ramada, Rest/Travelodge
Lodg	E: Ameritel Inn, Best Western, Embassy Suites, Hilton, Motel 6♥, Quality Inn, Ramada, Red Lion Hotel, Super 8, Travelodge♥
Other	E: Amtrak, Enterprise RAC, Aquarium, Museum, Auto Repair, Grocery, Banks
305C-A	**Exit to SB Collector (SB)**
305D	**900 South (NB)**
Gas	E: Chevron, Sinclair
Food	E: Artic Circle, Chinese Rest, Mexican Rest
Lodg	E: Best Inns, Holiday Inn
Other	E: Auto Repairs, Tires
305C	**1300S, Salt Lake City**
Gas	E: Maverik
Food	E: Various
Other	E: Auto Repairs, Tires, Banks
305B	**2100S, UT 201, Salt Lake City (Addt'l Serv W to UT 68)**
FStop	E: Premium Oil/Chevron
Gas	E: 7-11, Petro Mart, Costco
Food	E: FastFood/Prem Oil, Burger King, Carl Jr's, IHOP, McDonald's, Subway
Lodg	E: Marriott
Other	E: LP/Prem Oil, Costco, Home Depot, Pep Boys, PetSmart♥, Bank, U-Haul
305A	**UT 201W, 900W, Salt Lake City (Addt'l Serv W to UT 68)**
TStop	W: Flying J Travel Plaza #50007 (Scales)
Food	W: Rest/FJ TP, Wendy's
TServ	W: Diesel Repair
TWash	W: Blue Beacon/FJ TP
Other	W: Laundry/WiFi/RVDump/LP/FJ TP, Goodyear, NAPA, Banks, Repair
305A-D	**Exit to NB Collector (NB)**
(304)	**Jct I-80E, to Cheyenne, Denver (Gas & Lodging at 1st Exit on I-80E)**
TServ	E: Cummins Intermountain
NOTE:	I-15N above runs with I-80 for 5 mi Exit #'s Follow I-15
303	**UT 171, 3300S, S Salt Lake**
Gas	E: 7-11
	W: Maverick
Food	E: Burger King, McDonald's
Lodg	E: Days Inn♥, InTown Suites, Marriott
Other	E: Banks, Cinema, Safeway, Repairs
	W: Sam's Club, Salt Valley GMC Trucks
301	**UT 266, 4500S, Murray, Kearns**
Gas	E: Chevron, Oil
	W: Chevron, Conoco, Shell, Sinclair, Texaco
Food	E: McDonald's
	W: Burger King, Denny's, Wendy's
Lodg	E: Skyline Mtn Resort
	W: Fairfield Inn, Hampton Inn, Marriott, Quality Inn
Other	E: Banks, Auto Repairs
	W: Lowe's, Bank
300	**UT 173, 5300S, Murray, Kearns**
Gas	W: 7-11, Chevron, Conoco
Food	E: Café Delights, Pizza Hut
	W: KFC, Hogi Yogi
Lodg	W: Reston Hotel
Med	E: + Hospital

EXIT	UTAH
Other	E: UT State Hwy Patrol Post
	W: Banks, Smith Food & Drug
(298)	**Jct I-215, Belt Route**
297	**UT 48, 7200S, Midvale**
Gas	E: Chevron, Conoco, Sinclair, Texaco
	W: BP, Maverik
Food	E: Chili's, Denny's, Furr's, KFC, Hooters, McDonald's, Midvale Mining Café, Sizzler, Taco Bell, Village Inn
Lodg	E: Best Western, Days Inn, Discovery Inn, La Quinta Inn♥, Motel 6♥
Other	E: Hertz RAC, Enterprise RAC
295	**UT 209, 9000S, Sandy, W Jordan**
Gas	E: Chevron, Sinclair
	W: Maverik, Texaco
Food	E: Arby's, Burger King, Hardee's, Sweet Tomatoes, Subway, Sizzler
	W: Village Inn
Lodg	E: Comfort Inn
Med	E: + Hospital
Other	E: Lowe's, to Alta & Snowbird Ski Areas
	W: Grocery
293	**UT 151, 10600S, Sandy, S Jordan**
Gas	E: BP, Conoco, Phillips 66, Tesoro
Food	E: Bennett's BBQ, Black Angus, Chili's, Shoney's, Starbucks, Subway, TGI Friday, Taco Bell, Village Inn, Wendy's
	W: Denny's
Lodg	E: Best Western, Courtyard, Extended Stay American, Hampton Inn, Quality Inn
	W: Country Inn, Sleep Inn, Super 8
Other	E: Costco, Auto Dealers, Mall, Target, Banks, Wal-Mart
	W: Auto Dealers

EXIT	UTAH
291	**UT 71, 12300S, Draper, Riverton**
Gas	E: Texaco
	W: Chevron, Conoco
Food	E: Artic Circle, Carl's Jr, Café Rio Mex, Fazoli's, Guadalahonky's, KFC, Quiznos, McDonald's, Panda Express, Ruby Tuesday, Wendy's, Wingers
Lodg	E: Country Side Motel, Fairfield Inn, Holiday Inn Express, Ramada Inn, Travelodge
TServ	E: Jake's Auto & Truck Repair
Other	E: Camping World▲, Outlet Mall, Goodyear, Bank, Smith's Food & Drug, Mountain Shadows RV Park▲
289	**UT 154, 10600 S, Bangerter Hwy**
Other	E: Mountain Shadows RV Park▲
288	**UT 140, 14600S, Higland Dr, Draper, Bluffdale, State Prison**
Gas	W: 7-11
Other	W: State Prison
284	**UT 92, 11000 N Lehi, Highland, Alpine**
Gas	W: Phillips 66
Food	W: Iceberg Drive In
TServ	W: Lane Peak Trailer Service
Other	E: to Timpanogos Cave National Monument, Cabela's Outfitters/RVDump
282	**US 89S, 1200W, Lehi**
Gas	E: Chevron
Food	W: Huckleberry's Rest
279	**UT 73, Main St, Lehi**
Gas	E: Conoco
	W: Chevron, Phillips 66
Food	E: One Man Band Diner
	W: Artic Circle, McDonald's, Subway, Wendy's, Wingers
Lodg	E: Motel 6♥
	W: Best Western, Comfort Inn, Days Inn, Super 8
TServ	E: Rex's Diesel Service
Other	W: Albertson's, Big O Tire, US Post Office, Banks, Repairs, Police Dept
278	**UT 145, Main St, American Fork**
FStop	E: Harts Fuel Stop/P66
Gas	E: Chevron
Food	E: FastFood/Harts, Arby's, China Isle, Del Taco, Hogi Yogi, McDonald's, Skipper Seafood, Subway
Lodg	E: Quality Inn
TServ	E: Rex Diesel, Vern's Towing
Other	E: Auto Dealers, Kmart, Home Depot, Target, Wal-Mart sc, Albertson's, Banks, Cinema, Police Dept
276	**UT 180, 500E, American Fork, Pleasant Grove**
Gas	E: Conoco, Phillips 66, Texaco
Food	E: Arby's, Carl's Jr, Denny's, Golden Corral, McDonald's, Subway, Wendy's
Lodg	E: Quality Inn
Med	E: + Glass Hospital
Other	E: American Campground▲, RV Dealer
275	**S Pleasant Grove Blvd, Pleasant Grove, American Fork, Lindon**
273	**UT 241, Lindon, Pleasant Grove**
FStop	E: Pirate Petroleum/Sinclair
Gas	E: Conoco, Express 66. Mobil
Food	E: Quiznos
TServ	W: Mickelson Diesel Service, Utah Diesel Center
Med	E: + Glass Hospital

◇ = Regular Gas Stations with Diesel   ▲ = RV Friendly Locations   ♥ = Pet Friendly Locations
RED PRINT SHOWS LARGE VEHICLE PARKING/ACCESS ON SITE OR NEARBY   BROWN PRINT SHOWS CAMPGROUNDS/RV PARKS

EXIT	UTAH
Other	E: Home Depot, Les Schwab Tire
272	**UT 52, 800N, to US 89, Orem** (Addt'l Serv E to US 89)
Gas	E: Phillips 66
Food	E: Arby's, Denny's, Sonic
Lodg	E: La Quinta Inn ♥
Other	E: All Coach RV Repair
271	**Center St, Orem**
Gas	E: 7-11, Conoco, GasNGo W: Tesoro
Food	E: Artic Circle, Burger King, Hardee's, Panda Express, Taco Bell
Lodg	W: Econo Lodge
Med	E: + Hospital
269	**UT 265, University Pkwy, BYU, 1200S, Orem**
Gas	E: Phillips 66◊, Sinclair W: Chevron, Express
Food	E: Applebee's, Black Angus, Carrabba's, Chili's, Fuddrucker's, Golden Corral, IHOP, McDonald's, Outback Steakhouse, Red Lobster, Subway, Village Inn W: Hogi Yogi
Lodg	E: Best Western, Fairfield Inn, Hampton Inn, La Quinta Inn ♥
Other	E: Lowe's, Mall, Wal-Mart, UT Valley State College, Office Depot
265	**UT 114W, Center St, Provo (SB)**
Gas	E: 7-11, Conoco, Shell, Sinclair W: Chevron, Conoco
Food	E: Lotus Garden, Osaka Japanese W: Taco Bell
Lodg	E: Marriott, Travelers Inn, Travelodge W: Econo Lodge
Other	E: Albertson's, UT Co Visitor Info Ctr W: Provo KOA▲, Utah Lake State Park, Lakeside Campground▲
265B	**UT 114W, Center St, Airport (NB)**
Other	W: Provo KOA▲, Utah Lake State Park, Lakeside Campground▲, Provo Municipal Airport✈, Grocery
265A	**UT 114, Center St, Provo (NB)**
263	**US 189N, University Ave, 1860S, Provo**
Gas	E: Chevron, Conoco◊, P66, Maverick
Food	E: Arby's, Blimpie's, Burger King, KFC, McDonald's, Red Robin, Ruby River Steakhouse, Shoney's, Sizzler, Taco Bell, Village Inn, Wendy's
Lodg	E: Best Western, Colony Inn, Fairfield Inn, Hampton Inn, Holiday Inn, Motel 6♥, Sleep Inn, Super 8
Other	E: Home Depot, Kmart, NAPA, Banks, Mall, Sam's Club, Staples, East Bay Golf Course, Amtrak, Repairs, to Brigham Young University, Visitor Info, Silver Fox Campground▲ W: Provo KOA▲, Lakeside Campground▲, UT Lake State Park
261	**UT 75, 1500N, N Springville, Provo**
TStop	E: Flying J Travel Plaza #11105 (Scales) (Springville Rest Stop - Both dir)
Gas	E: Maverick, Chevron
Food	E: CountryMarket/FJ TP, McDonald's
Lodg	E: Best Western
Other	E: Laundry/WiFi/LP/FJ TP, East Bay RV Park▲, Suntana Raceway W: Spanish Fork-Springville Airport✈, Sheriff's Dept, Canyon View RV Park▲/RVDump, Quality RV

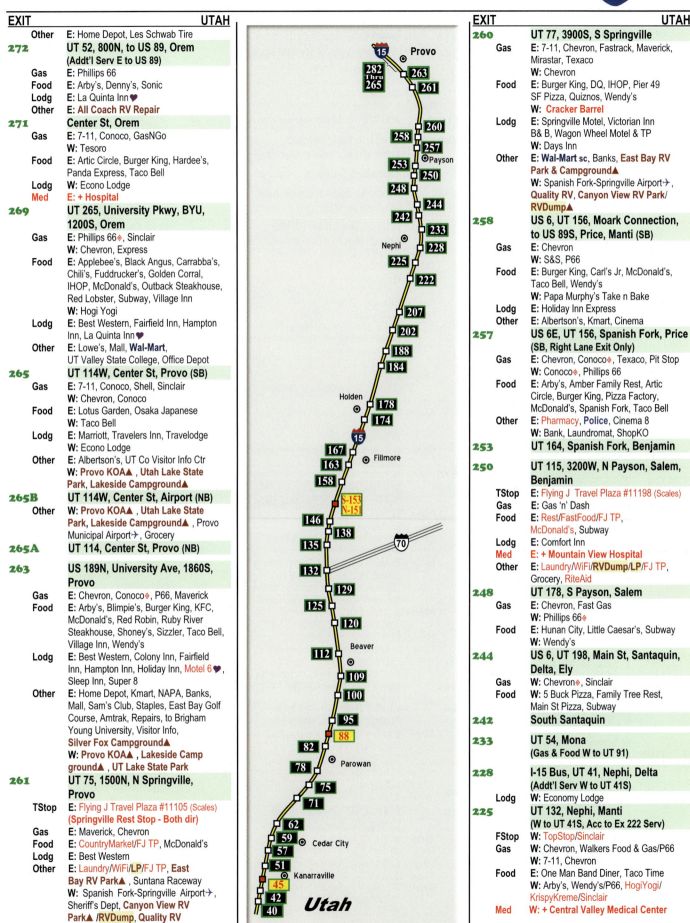

EXIT	UTAH
260	**UT 77, 3900S, S Springville**
Gas	E: 7-11, Chevron, Fastrack, Maverick, Mirastar, Texaco W: Chevron
Food	E: Burger King, DQ, IHOP, Pier 49 SF Pizza, Quiznos, Wendy's W: Cracker Barrel
Lodg	E: Springville Motel, Victorian Inn B&B, Wagon Wheel Motel & TP W: Days Inn
Other	E: Wal-Mart sc, Banks, East Bay RV Park & Campground▲ W: Spanish Fork-Springville Airport✈, Quality RV, Canyon View RV Park/RVDump▲
258	**US 6, UT 156, Moark Connection, to US 89S, Price, Manti (SB)**
Gas	E: Chevron W: S&S, P66
Food	E: Burger King, Carl's Jr, McDonald's, Taco Bell, Wendy's W: Papa Murphy's Take n Bake
Lodg	E: Holiday Inn Express
Other	E: Albertson's, Kmart, Cinema
257	**US 6E, UT 156, Spanish Fork, Price (SB, Right Lane Exit Only)**
Gas	E: Chevron, Conoco◊, Texaco, Pit Stop W: Conoco◊, Phillips 66
Food	E: Arby's, Amber Family Rest, Artic Circle, Burger King, Pizza Factory, McDonald's, Spanish Fork, Taco Bell
Other	E: Pharmacy, Police, Cinema 8 W: Bank, Laundromat, ShopKO
253	**UT 164, Spanish Fork, Benjamin**
250	**UT 115, 3200W, N Payson, Salem, Benjamin**
TStop	E: Flying J Travel Plaza #11198 (Scales)
Gas	E: Gas 'n' Dash
Food	E: Rest/FastFood/FJ TP, McDonald's, Subway
Lodg	E: Comfort Inn
Med	E: + Mountain View Hospital
Other	E: Laundry/WiFi/RVDump/LP/FJ TP, Grocery, RiteAid
248	**UT 178, S Payson, Salem**
Gas	E: Chevron, Fast Gas W: Phillips 66◊
Food	E: Hunan City, Little Caesar's, Subway W: Wendy's
244	**US 6, UT 198, Main St, Santaquin, Delta, Ely**
Gas	W: Chevron◊, Sinclair
Food	W: 5 Buck Pizza, Family Tree Rest, Main St Pizza, Subway
242	**South Santaquin**
233	**UT 54, Mona** (Gas & Food W to UT 91)
228	**I-15 Bus, UT 41, Nephi, Delta** (Addt'l Serv W to UT 41S)
Lodg	W: Economy Lodge
225	**UT 132, Nephi, Manti** (W to UT 41S, Acc to Ex 222 Serv)
FStop	W: TopStop/Sinclair
Gas	W: Chevron, Walkers Food & Gas/P66 W: 7-11, Chevron
Food	E: One Man Band Diner, Taco Time W: Arby's, Wendy's/P66, HogiYogi/KrispyKreme/Sinclair
Med	W: + Central Valley Medical Center

◊ = Regular Gas Stations with Diesel   ▲ = RV Friendly Locations   ♥ = Pet Friendly Locations

RED PRINT SHOWS LARGE VEHICLE PARKING/ACCESS ON SITE OR NEARBY   BROWN PRINT SHOWS CAMPGROUNDS/RV PARKS

EXIT		UTAH
	Other	W: Auto Repair & Towing, Big O Tires, Bank, Laundry/CarWash/Sinclair, High Country RV Camp▲
222		UT 28, I-15 Bus Loop, Nephi, UT 41, to I-70, Salina, Richfield
	FStop	W: Sunmart #903/Texaco
	TStop	W: Top Stop Truck Plaza/AmBest/ Sinclair (Scales), Flying J Travel Plaza #11196/Conoco (Scales)
	Food	W: HogiYogi/Top Stop TP, FastFood/ Sunmart, Burger King, Denny's, JC Mickelson's, Lisa's Country Kitchen, Subway, Rest/FastFood/Flying J TP
	Lodg	W: Best Western, Motel 6 ♥, Super 8, Roberta's Cove Motor Inn
	TServ	W: Circle C TS, Doyle's Diesel
	Other	W: Laundry/RVDump/Circle C, RVDump/Sunmart, Laundry/RVDump/ LP/WiFi/Flying J TP, High Country RV Camp▲
207		UT 78, Nephi, Mills, Levan
202		Old US 90, Nephi, Yuba Lake State Park
	Other	E: Yuba Lake State Park▲
188		US 50E, to I-70, Scipio, Fillmore, Salina
	Fstop	E: Eagles Landing Chevron (Scipio Rest Stop-Both dir)
	Gas	E: Phillips 66
	Food	E: Rest/FastFood/Eagles Landing
	Lodg	E: Super 8
184		Ranch Exit, Fillmore
178		US 50W, to Delta, Holden
	Other	W: to Great Basin Nat'l Park
174		UT 64, to US 50W, Ely, Holden, Delta
	Other	W: to Great Basin Nat'l Park
167		Bus Loop I-15, Fillmore
	W:	Fillmore Rest Stop (Both dir)
	FStop	E: Steve's Tire & Oil/Sinclair, Fillmore Shell, Miller Chevron
	Gas	E: Chevron (2)
		W: Texaco
	Food	E: Rest/Best Western, Burger King, Garden of Eat'n, 5 Buck Pizza
		W: Subway
	Lodg	E: Best Western
	TServ	E: Steve's Tire
	Med	E: + Fillmore Comm Medical Center
	Other	E: LP/Steve's, Wagons West RV Park & Campground▲, Paradise Golf Resort, Auto Repair, Grocery, Bank
		W: Territorial Statehouse State Park
163		I-15 Bus Loop, to UT 100, UT 99, Fillmore
	FStop	E: First Capital Chevron
		W: Sunmart #807/Texaco
	TStop	E: Sinclair #43041
	Food	E: FastFood/Sinclair, Arby's/Chevron, Rest/Best Western
	Lodg	E: Best Western, Country Garden Inn B&B, Spinning Wheel Motel
	Other	E: Fillmore KOA▲, Bank, Grocery
		W: Fillmore Airport ✈
158		UT 133, Main St, Fillmore, Meadow, Kanosh, Green River
	FStop	E: Meadow Chevron & Food Mart
	Gas	E: Shell, Sinclair
	Food	E: FastFood/Chevron
146		UT 133, Fillmore, Kanosh (Access same serv E as Ex #158)

EXIT		UTAH
138		Ranch Exit
135		Historic Cove Fort, UT 161, Paiute Indian Res, to I-70E
	FStop	E: Cove Fort Chevron (Rest Stop - Both dir)
	Food	E: Rest/FastFood/Cove Fort Chevron
(132)		Jct I-70E, Richfield, Denver
129		UT 161, to I-70E, Beaver, Sulphurdale, Chain Up Area NB
125		Ranch Exit, Beaver
120		Old US 91, Beaver, Manderfield (NB Chain Up Area)
112		to UT 21, Bus Lp 15, UT 153, Beaver, Milford (acc to #109 Serv)
	FStop	E: High Country Shell
	TStop	E: Ernie's Truck Plaza/Sinclair
		W: Eagles Landing Truck Plaza/Texaco (Beaver Rest Stop - Both dir)
	Gas	E: Conoco, Phillips 66
	Food	E: FastFood/Ernie's TP, Rest/BW, Arby's, El Bambi Cafe, Hunan Garden Chinese, McDonald's, Sportman Paradise Steakhouse, Subway
		W: Wendy's/Eagles L TP
	Lodg	E: Best Western ♥, Country Inn Motel ♥/Sinclair, Days Inn, De Lano Motel & RV
	ATServ	E: Anytime Road Svc & Repair, Southcreek Beaver Towing & Tire/ RVDump
	Other	E: Beaver KOA▲, Beaver Canyon Campground▲
		W: Laundry/Eagles Landing TP
109		to UT 21, I-15 Bus Loop, UT 160, Beaver, Milford (acc to #112 Serv)
	FStop	E: Southcreek Shell
	Gas	E: Chevron, Phillips 66
	Food	E: Burger King/Shell, Cindy's Pizza, Mel's Drive In, Rest/Best Western
	Lodg	E: Aspen Lodge Motel, Best Western ♥, Comfort Inn, De Lano Motel & RV, Eagles Roost Inn, Elk Meadows Resort, Mansfield Motel, Sleepy Lagoon Motel
	ATServ	E: Anytime Road Svc & Repair, Southcreek Beaver Towing & Tire/
	Med	E: + Beaver Valley Hospital
	Other	E: Beaver Canyon Campground▲, Evan's Garage, Anytime Road Svc & Repair, United Beaver Camperland▲
100		Ranch Exit, Freemont Rd
95		UT 20, Paragonah, to US 89, Panguitch, Kanab, Circleville
	Other	E: to Bryce Canyon National Park, Lake Powell
(88)		Lunt Park Rest Area (Both dir) (RR, Phones, Picnic, Vend, Info)
82		UT 271, Paragonah
78		I-15 Bus, UT 271, Main St, to UT 143, Parowan, Paragonah
	TStop	W: Travel Center of America #186
	Food	W: Subway/Taco Bell/TA TC
	Lodg	W: Ace Motel, Days Inn
	TServ	W: TA TC
	Other	E: Banks, Auto Service, to Brian Head & Cedar Breaks Ski Resorts
		W: WiFi/RVDump/LP/TA TC

EXIT		UTAH
75		I-15 Loop, UT 143, Parowan (Access to Ex #178 Serv E to UT 143N)
	Food	E: Pizza, Mexican
	Lodg	E: Days Inn
	Other	E: to Brian Head, Cedar Breaks Ski Resorts
71		Old US 91, Main St, Summit, Cedar City, Paraowan, Enoch (Acc to Ex #62 via Old US 91S)
	TStop	E: Sunshine Truck Stop
	Food	E: Rest/Sunshine TS
	Tires	E: Sunshine TS
	Other	E: Laundry/Sunshine TS
		W: to Riverside Motel & RV Park▲
62		I-15 Bus Loop, Cedar City, UT 130, to UT 14, Enoch, Minersville
	TStop	E: Love's Travel Stop #335 (Scales), JR's Truck Stop/Texaco (Scales)
	Gas	E: Phillips 66
		W: Sinclair
	Food	E: Carl's Jr/Subway/Love's TS, Fast Food/JR's TS, La Villa Mexican
		W: Steaks n Stuff
	Lodg	E: Best Western, Holiday Inn
		W: Travelodge, to Riverside Motel & RV Park▲
	TServ	W: JR's TS
	Other	E: WiFi/RVDump/Love's TS, Country Aire RV Park▲, Cedar City KOA/RVDump▲, State Hwy Patrol Post
59		UT 56, 200N, Cedar City
	Gas	E: Maverick, Phillips 66, Texaco
		W: Sinclair◆
	Food	E: Arby's, Denny's, Burger King, KFC, McDonald's, Shoney's, Taco Bell, Wendy's
		W: Subway, Rest/HolidayInn
	Lodg	E: Abbey Inn, Best Western, Comfort Inn, Econo Lodge, Rodeway Inn
		W: Holiday Inn, Motel 6 ♥, Super 8
	Other	E: Cedar City KOA/RVDump▲, S UT Univ, Coliseum, Auto Repairs
		W: Cedar City Muni Airport ✈
57		I-15 Bus Lp, UT 130, to UT 14, Cedar City
	Gas	E: Chevron, Phillips 66, Sinclair, Texaco
		W: Chevron◆, Mirastar, Murphy
	Food	E: DQ, Hunan Chinese, JB's, Subway
		W: Applebee's, Del Taco, McDonald's, Panda Express, Starbucks
	Lodg	E: Best Value Inn, Days Inn, Holiday Inn Express, Rodeway Inn
		W: Hampton Inn
	Med	E: + Hospital
	Other	E: Cedar City KOA/RVDump▲, Town & Country RV Park▲, Albertson's, AutoZone, Banks, Big O Tire, Smith's Food & Drug
		W: Cinema, Home Depot, Wal-Mart sc
51		5300W, 4000S, UT 130, Cedar City, Hamilton Fort, Kanarraville
(45)		Kanarraville Rest Area (Both dir) (RR, Phones, Picnic, Vend, Info) (SB - Next Rest Aea 196 mi)
42		UT 144, Cedar City, Kanarraville, New Harmony
40		Kolob Carqua Rd, Hurricane, Kolob Canyons, Zion Nat'l Park (Info / Scenic Drive)
	Other	E: Zion National Park

EXIT	UTAH
36	Ranch Exit, Hurricane
33	Ranch Exit
31	Pintura
30	Browse
27	UT 17, Hurricane, Tocquerville, Zion National Park
Other	E: Willowind RV Park▲, to US Air Force Proving Grounds, Silver Springs RV Resort▲, Virgin Territories RV Park▲
23	Silver Reef Rd, Hurricane, Leeds, Silver Reef (SB)
Lodg	E: Cottam's Leeds Motel & RV Park▲
22	UT 228, UT 212, Red Cliff Rd, Hurricane, Leeds, Silver Reef (NB)
Lodg	E: Cottam's Leeds Motel & RV Park▲
Other	E: Zion West RV Park▲, St George RV Resort▲
	W: BLM/Red Cliffs Campground▲
16	UT 9, Hurricane, Kanab, Grand Canyon, Zion Nat'l Park, Lk Powell
Gas	E: Shell
Food	E: Blimpie's, DQ, Ernesto's Mexican, McDonald's, Wendy's
Lodg	E: Best Western, Days Inn, Motel 6♥, Super 8, Travelodge
Other	E: Brentwood RV Resort▲, The Canyons RV Resort▲, Harrisburg RV Resort▲, Silver Springs RV Resort▲, Willowind RV Park▲, Quail Creek State Park Campground▲, Zions Gate RV Resort▲, To Zion Nat'l Park
13	Washington
10	UT 212, Middleton Dr, Green Springs Rd, Washington
TStop	W: Freeway Chevron
Gas	E: Phillips 66◊, Sinclair
	W: Shell
Food	E: FastFood/Frwy Chevron, Arby's, Artic Circle, Burger King, IHOP, Jack in the Box, St Helens of Washington, Wendy's
Lodg	E: Red Cliffs Inn
Tires	W: Freeway Chevron
Other	E: Albertson's, Banks, Best Buy, Costco, Home Depot, PetCo♥, Wal-Mart sc, Auto Repairs, Redlands RV Park▲, Valley View Trailer Park▲
	W: Tri City Auto & RV Repair, St George Campground▲
8	UT 100N, UT 34, St George Blvd, Bus 15, to UT 18, St George
FStop	W: Premium Oil/Sinclair
Gas	E: Texaco
	W: Chevron, Texaco, Maverick
Food	E: Applebee's, Arby's, Bodacious Rib & BBQ, Carl's Jr, Chili's, Chuck-A-Rama Buffet, Durango's Mex Grill, Outback Steakhouse, Panda Express, Quiznos, Red Lobster, Shoney's, Starbucks, Village Inn, Winger's
	W: Burger King, Denny's, McDonald's, KFC, Pizza Hut, Taco Bell, Wendy's
Lodg	E: Best Inn, Hampton Inn, Ramada Inn, Shoney's
	W: Chalet Motel, Comfort Inn, Days Inn, Econo Lodge, Howard Johnson, Motel 6♥, Park Inn, Sunbird Inn, Travelodge

EXIT	UT / AZ
TServ	W: Dixie Diesel Service
Med	E: + Dixie Reg'l Medical Center
	W: + VA Outpatient Clinic
Other	E: Auto Repair, Banks, Grocery, Lowe's, Staples, Target, Factory Outlet Stores, St George Campground & RV Park▲
	W: RVDump/LP/Premium Oil, Canyonland RV Rentals, Hillside Palms RV & MH Park, Grocery, NAPA, Banks, Auto Repairs Pharmacy, Animal Hospital♥, St George Muni Airport✈
6	UT 18, Bus 15, Bluff St, St George
Gas	E: Chevron, Sunmart, Texaco
	W: Chevron, Maverick, Texaco
Food	E: Cracker Barrel, Jack in the Box
	W: Burger King, Claimjumper Rest, DQ, Denny's, JB's Rest, McDonald's, Pizza Hut, Tony Roma, Wendy's
Lodg	E: Ambassador Inn, Fairfield Inn, Hilton Garden Inn
	W: Best Western, Budget Inn, Crystal Inn, Comfort Suites, Holiday Inn, Quality Inn, Ridgeview Inn, Super 8
TServ	E: Transport Tire Service
	W: Zion Motors Truck Service
Med	W: + Dixie Reg'l Medical Center
Other	E: Firestone, U-Haul, Auto Dealers, to Rio Virgin RV Park▲
	W: Albertson's, Auto Zone, Kmart, Auto Dealers, St George Muni Airport✈, Animal Hospital/Vet♥, Vacation World RV Center, Sun Country RV Center, Desert Coach RV, McArthur's Temple View RV Resort▲, St George Resort▲, Snow Canyon State Park Campground▲
4	Brigham Rd, St George, Bloomington
TStop	E: Flying J Travel Plaza #5101 (Scales) (DAD)
Gas	W: Bloomington Market, Mirastar
Food	E: FastFood/Flying J TP
	W: 2 Fat Guys Pizza, Arby's, Hunan City, Subway, Taco Bell, Wendy's
Other	E: WiFi/LP/Flying J TP
	W: Wal-Mart sc
(3)	UT Welcome Center (NB)
	(RR, Phone, Picnic, RVDump)
(0)	Port of Entry/Weigh Station (Both dir)
	(MOUNTAIN TIME ZONE)

○ UTAH
○ ARIZONA

(MOUNTAIN TIME ZONE, NO DST)

	NOTE: MM 29: Utah State Line
27	Black Rock Rd, Littlefield
(21)	TurnOut (SB)
(16)	TurnOut (Truck Parking)
(15)	TurnOut (Truck Parking) (NB)
(14)	TurnOut (Truck Parking) (NB)
18	Cedar Pocket Rd, Littlefield
Other	S: BLM/Virgin River Campground▲, Virgin River Gorge
(10)	TurnOut (Truck Parking) (NB)
9	Farm Rd, Littlefield

◊ = Regular Gas Stations with Diesel   ▲ = RV Friendly Locations   ♥ = Pet Friendly Locations

RED PRINT SHOWS LARGE VEHICLE PARKING/ACCESS ON SITE OR NEARBY   BROWN PRINT SHOWS CAMPGROUNDS/RV PARKS

Page 75

Interstate 15 N/S

EXIT	AZ / NV
8	CR 91, Cane Beds Rd, Littlefield, Beaver Dam
Other	E: Chief Sleep Easy RV Park▲
	W: Beaver Dam Resort & RV Park▲
	(M T Z -AZ does not observe DST)

◯ ARIZONA
◯ NEVADA
(PACIFIC TIME ZONE)

EXIT	
122	NV 144, I-15 Bus, Pioneer Blvd, Mesquite, to Bunkerville
E:	NV Welcome Center (Both dir)
FStop	W: Virgin River Food Mart/76
Gas	E: Chevron◆, Maverick, Shell, Texaco
	W: Food Mart
Food	E: Subway/Chevron, Burger King, Chinese Buffet, Golden West Rest & Casino, Jack in the Box, KFC, Taco Time
	W: McDonald's, Rest/Eureka Hotel, Arby's/Sinclair, Rest/Virgin River Hotel
Lodg	E: Budget Inn, Desert Palms Motel, Executive Suites, MV Motel
	W: Eureka Casino Hotel, Virgin River Hotel & Casino & RV Park▲, Mesquite Springs Suites
Other	E: Auto Parts, Banks, Cinema, Museum, US Post Office, Diesel & Auto Repair, Smith's Food & Drug, Police, Desert Skies RV Resort & Park▲
	W: LP/Virgin River FM, Int'l Sports Hall of Fame, Golf Courses, Mesquite Airport✈
120	Mesquite Blvd, to Pioneer Blvd, UT 170, Mesquite, to Bunkerville
Gas	E: C-Mart, Shell◆, Terrible Herbst◆
Food	E: McDonald's, Rest/Casablanca Resort, Rest/Oasis Resort, Rest/Stateline Motel
Lodg	E: Casablanca Resort & Casino & RV Park/RVDump▲, Oasis Resort Golf Spa Casino & RV Park▲, Stateline Motel & Casino, Valley Inn Motel
	W: Best Western, Falcon Ridge Hotel
Other	E: Desert Skies RV Resort▲, Auto Repair, Auto Parts, Banks, Mesquite Casino
112	NV 170, Mesquite, to Riverside, Bunkerville
(110)	Parking Area (Both dir)
100	Carp Elgin Rd, Bunkerville
(96)	Parking Area (NB)
93	NV 169, Moapa Valley Blvd, Logandale, Overton
Other	E: to gas, Clark Co Fairgrounds, Lost City Museum, Overton Muni Airport✈
91	NV 168, Glendale Blvd, Moapa, Glendale
Gas	W: Chevron
Food	W: Glendale Café/Chevron
Lodg	W: Glendale Motel/Chevron
Other	E: Fun N Sun Trailer/RV Park▲
	W: Palm Creek RV Park▲, Moapa Indian Reservation, Grocery
90	NV 168, Glendale, Moapa (NB) (Access to same serv as Ex #91)
88	NV 78, Hidden Valley Rd, to NV 168, Moapa

EXIT	NEVADA
84	Byron
80	Ute, Moapa River Indian Res
75	NV 169E, Valley of Fire State Park, Lake Mead
TStop	E: Moapa Paiute Travel Center/Sinclair/Rest/Casino/Laundry/Fireworks
Other	E: Valley of Fire State Park C
64	US 93N, NV 604, Great Basin Hwy, Moapa, Pioche, Ely
(61)	Check Station (SB)
58	NV 604, US 93, N Las Vegas, Nellis Air Force Base
Other	E: American Campgrounds▲, to Hitchin Post RV Park▲, Las Vegas Speedway, Nellis AFB/FamCamp▲
54	Speedway Blvd, Hollywood Blvd
TStop	E: Petro Stopping Center #31/Mobil (Scales)
Food	E: Rest/Petro SC, Fast Lane Cafe
TServ	E: Petro SC/Tires
Other	E: Laundry/RVDump/Petro SC, Las Vegas Speedway, Richard Petty Driving Experience
(52)	Jct I-215W, Las Vegas Beltway
50	Lamb Blvd, NV 610 (SB)
48	NV 573, Craig Rd, N Las Vegas
TStop	E: Pilot Travel Center #341 (Scales)
Gas	E: ArcoAMPM, Chevron, Mobil, Shell
	W: 7-11
Food	E: Burger King, DQ/KFC/PH/Pilot TC, Subway/Chevron, Speedway Grill

EXIT	NEVADA
Lodg	E: Barcelona Motel & Casino, Best Western, Hampton Inn, La Quinta Inn♥
	W: Cannery Casino Hotel, Holiday Inn Express
TWash	E: Fleet Wash
TServ	E: Diesel Specialist
	W: Truck Parts & Equipment, Cashman Equipment Co, Ford Trucks, McCandless International, Peterbilt, Freightliner
Other	E: Laundry/Pilot TC, to Nellis AFB, Grocery, Tire & Auto Ctr, Wal-Mart sc to Hitchin Post RV Park▲, American Campground▲
	W: Grocery, Auto Repair
46	Cheyenne Ave, NV 574, LV
TStop	E: (E to NV604) Maverick Truck Stop/76
	W: Hallmark Truck Center/Sinclair (Scales), Flying J Travel Plaza #10010 (Scale)
Gas	E: 7-11, ArcoAmPm, Exxon
	W: 7-11
Food	E: Rest/Ramada Inn, Popeye's, Rest/Maverick TS
	W: Rest/Hallmark TC, Rest/FJ TP, Denny's, McDonald's, Jack in the Box
Lodg	E: Ramada Inn & Casino
	W: Comfort Inn
TWash	W: ADC Truck Wash, Hallmark TC, Blue Beacon/FJ TP
TServ	W: Hallmark TC, FJ TP/Tires, SpeedCo, Tires, Kenworth
Other	E: LP/Maverick TP, NAPA, Auto Repair, Comm College of S Nevada, Hitchin Post RV Park▲
	W: Laundry/WiFi/RVDump/FJ TP, RVDump/Hallmark TC, N Las Vegas Air Terminal✈, N Las Vegas Golf Course
45	NV 147, Lake Mead Blvd (SB) (Addt'l Serv E to NV 604)
Gas	E: 7-11, Terrible Herbst
	W: Chevron, Terrible Herbst
Food	E: Carl's Jr, McDonald's, Wendy's
	W: Domino's, Long John Silver
Med	E: + Lake Mead Hospital Med Center
Other	E: NLV Police Dept, Banks
	W: Auto Repairs
45B	Lake Mead Blvd W (NB)
45A	NV 147E, Lake Mead Blvd E (NB)
44	Washington Ave, D St (SB)
Food	E: Rest/Best Western
Lodg	E: Best Western
Other	E: Casinos $, Shopping, Convention Center, Cashman Field, Museum, Visitor Center
43	D St, F St, to NV 579, Washington Ave (NB)
Gas	E: Gas
Food	E: Rest/Best Western
Lodg	E: Best Western♥
	W: Moulin Rouge Hotel & Casino
Other	E: Main St RV Park▲, Bank, Museum
(42)	Jct I-515S, US 93S, US 95, Phoenix, US 95N to Reno, MLK Jr Blvd (SB)
Gas	E: 76
	W: ArcoAmPm, Shell
TServ	W: Cummins Intermountain
Other	E: Casinos $
(42B)	Jct I-515. US 93, US 95 (NB)
42A	LV Expwy, US 95 (NB)

Page 76   ◆= Regular Gas Stations with Diesel   ▲ = RV Friendly Locations   ♥= Pet Friendly Locations
RED PRINT SHOWS LARGE VEHICLE PARKING/ACCESS ON SITE OR NEARBY   BROWN PRINT SHOWS CAMPGROUNDS/RV PARKS

EXIT	NEVADA
41	**NV 159, Charleston Blvd, MLK King Blvd, Las Vegas (SB)**
Gas	E: 7-11, ArcoAmPm◊
	W: 76, Shell, Rebel
Food	W: Carl's Jr, Del Taco, McDonald's
Med	W: + University Medical Center, + Valley Hospital Medical Center
Lodg	W: Marriott
Other	E: Las Vegas Premium Outlets, Ca Hotel Casino & RV Park▲, Western RV Park▲
	W: Banks, Univ of NV/Reno, Repairs
41B	**NV 159, Charleston Blvd W, Grand Central Pkwy, Las Vegas**
Gas	W: 76, Shell
Food	W: Carl's Jr, Del Taco, McDonald's
Med	W: + University Medical Center
41A	**NV 159, Charleston Blvd E, to NV 604, Main St, (NB) (Addt'l Serv E to Main St, NV 604)**
Gas	E: 7-11, ArcoAmPm
Lodg	E: Bridger Inn Hotel, Travel Inn
40	**Sahara Ave, Las Vegas**
TStop	E: Maverick Truck Stop/76
Gas	E: 76, Texaco
	W: 7-11, Texaco
Food	E: Rest/Maverick TS, Arby's, Golden Steer, Lunch Stop, Steak House, Southern Seafood, Vegas Pizza
Food	W: Blimpie, Denny's, In N Out Burger, McDonald's, Rest/Palace Station Hotel, Landry's Seafood, Romano's Macaroni Grill, Starbuck's
Lodg	E: Artesian Hotel & Spa, Bluemoon Resort, Las Vegas Inn & Casino, Sahara Hotel & Casino, Stratosphere Hotel & Casino & Tower, Travelodge
	W: Palace Station Hotel & Casino, Town Palms Hotel
TServ	E: Nevada RV & Truck Service
Other	E: to The Strip, Las Vegas Convention Center, Goodyear, AdventureDome, Wet 'N Wild, Banks, CircusCircus KOA/RVDump▲, Sahara RV Center
	W: Banks, Auto Repairs, Food
39	**Desert Inn Rd, Spring Mountain Rd (SB), Flamingo Rd, Twain Ave, Spring Mountain Rd (NB)**
Gas	W: ArcoAmPm, Circle K, Shell
Food	E: Deli, Port of Subs, Hawaiian BBQ,
	W: Deli
Lodg	E: Budget Suites, New Frontier Hotel & Casino, Stardust Hotel & Casino, Treasure Island Hotel & Casino, Mirage Hotel & Casino, Harrah's LV Hotel & Casino
Other	E: Fashion Show Mall, Budget, Banks, Auto Repairs, Hotels, Casinos, Food
	W: Auto Repair, Firestone, Goodyear
38A	**W Flamingo Rd (SB)**
Gas	W: ArcoAmPm, Texaco
Food	W: Burger King, Outback Steakhouse, Rest/Gold Coast Hotel, Rest/Rio Hotel
Lodg	W: Gold Coast Hotel & Casino, Rio Hotel & Casino, Palms Hotel & Casino
Other	W: Banks, Cinema, Food
38B	**E Flamingo Rd (SB)**
Gas	E: ArcoAmPm
Food	E: Bally's, Barbary Coast, Bellagio, Caesars Palace, Hilton, McDonald's

Personal Notes

EXIT	NEVADA
Lodg	E: Atrium Suites Hotel, Bally Hotel & Casino, Barbary Hotel & Casino, Bellagio Hotel & Casino, Caesars Palace Hotel & Casino, Crest Budget Motel, Days Inn, Flamingo Hilton Hotel & Casino, Holiday Inn, Paris Resort & Casino, Residence Inn, Super 8
38	**Flamingo Rd (NB)**
37	**Tropicana Ave, NV 593**
TStop	W: Wild Wild West Travel Plaza/King 8 Truck Plaza (Scales)
FStop	E: 76/The Bus Stop
Gas	W: 76, ArcoAmPm, Chevron, Shell
Food	E: Excalibur Hotel, Luxor Hotel, MGM Grand Hotel, Mandalay Bay, Motel 6♥, Tropicana Hotel, CoCo's
	W: Harley Davidson Cafe, Howard Johnson Hotel, IHOP, In-N-Out Burgers, Jack in the Box, KFC, King 8 Hotel, McDonald's, Pizza Hut, Taco Bell, Wendy's
Lodg	E: America's Best Value Inn♥, Comfort Inn, Excalibur Hotel & Casino, Hawthorn Suites, Luxor Resort & Casino, La Quinta Inn♥, MGM Grand Hotel & Casino, Motel 6♥, Monte Carlo Resort & Casino, New York New York Hotel & Casino, Tropicana Resort & Casino, Tropicana Inn, Travelodge
	W: American 5, Best Western, Budget Suites, Motel 6, Hampton Inn, Howard Johnson Hotel & Casino, King 8 Hotel/WildWildWest & Casino, Motel 6♥
Other	E: Cinema, Casinos $, Airport✈
	W: Cinema, Casinos $

EXIT	NEVADA
36	**Russell Rd, Las Vegas**
Gas	E: Shell
	W: Terrible Herbst/Chevron
Food	E: McDonald's, Panda Express
Lodg	E: Diamond Inn Motel, Four Seasons Hotel, Klondike Hotel & Casino, Royal Oasis Motel, Mandalay Bay Resort & Casino
	W: Interstate Hotel, Holiday Inn Express
Other	E: McCarran Int'l Airport✈
	W: Tourist Info
(34)	**Jct I-215E to Henderson, NV 604 Las Vegas Blvd, LV Beltway**
33	**NV 160, Blue Diamond Rd, to NV 604, Las Vegas, Pahrump, to Blue Diamond, Death Valley**
TStop	W: Travel Center of America /76 (Scales)
Gas	E: 7-11◊, ArcoAmPm, Terrible Herbst/ Chevron, Mobil◊
	W: Chevron
Food	W: BK/Subway/TacoTime/TA TC, Jack in the Box
Lodg	E: Budget Suites, Emerald Suites, Malibu Bay Suites, Residence Inn
	W: Firebird Motel/TA TC, Silverton Hotel & Casino & RV Parking▲
TServ	W: TA TC, D&D Tire
TWash	W: Truck Wash, TA TC
Other	E: Oasis LV RV Resort/RVDump▲ U-Haul, CVS, Cancun Casino Resort
	W: Bass Pro Shop, Factory Outlet Mall, Laundry/RVDump/HealthCl/TA TC, LP, Outdoor Resorts LV Motorcoach Resort▲
27	**NV 146, Lake Mead Dr, NV 604, St Rose Pkwy, Southern Highlands Pkwy, Henderson, to Lake Mead, Hoover Dam**
TStop	E: Vegas Valley Travel Center
Food	E: Rest/FastFood/VV TC
Other	E: Laundry/RVDump/LP/VV TC, Factory Outlet Stores, LV-Henderson Sky Harbor Airport✈, Wheelers LV RV, Las Vegas RV/Camping World
25	**Sloan Rd, Las Vegas**
Other	E: Wheeler's LV RV/LP
(24)	**Check Station (NB)**
12	**NV 161, Jean, to Goodsprings**
Other	NV Welcome Center (NB) (RR, Phone, Picnic, Vend, Info)
TStop	E: Gold Strike Auto Truck Plaza/Mobil
Gas	W: Shell/Nevada Landing Hotel & Casino
Food	E: Burger King/Gold Strike Hotel
Lodg	E: Gold Strike Hotel & Casino
Other	E: Jean Airport✈, Visitor Center, US Post Office
1	**Primm Blvd, Jean, Stateline**
Tstop	W: Whiskey Pete's Casino Truck Stop/ Shell (Scales)
Gas	E: 76, Chevron
Food	E: Carl's Jr, Denny's, McDonald's, Starbucks
	W: Rest/Whiskey Pete's TS
Lodg	E: Buffalo Bill's Resort & Casino & RV▲, Primm Valley Resort & Casino & RV▲
	W: Whiskey Pete's Hotel & Casino

◊ = Regular Gas Stations with Diesel   ▲ = RV Friendly Locations   ♥ = Pet Friendly Locations
RED PRINT SHOWS LARGE VEHICLE PARKING/ACCESS ON SITE OR NEARBY   BROWN PRINT SHOWS CAMPGROUNDS/RV PARKS

EXIT		NV / CA
	Other	E: Fashion Outlet of LV, Prima Donna RV Park▲, Laundry/Whiskey Pete's
		(PACIFIC TIME ZONE)

◯ NEVADA
◯ CALIFORNIA
(PACIFIC TIME ZONE)

EXIT		
291		Yates Well Rd, Nipton
286		Nipton Rd, Nipton
	Other	E: Mojave Nat'l Preserve
281		Bailey Rd, Nipton
	Gas	E: Gas
	Food	E: Food
	Other	E: Mojave Nat'l Preserve
(276)		Brake Inspection Area (NB)
272		Cima Rd, Nipton
	Other	E: Mojave Nat'l Preserve
(270)		Valley Wells Rest Area (Both dir) (RR, Phones, Picnic, Vend)
	NOTE:	MM 265: SB: Steep downgrade 17mi
265		Halloran Summit Rd, Baker
259		Halloran Springs Rd, Baker
248		Baker Blvd (SB) (Access to Exit #246 Serv)
246		CA 127, Kelbaker Rd, Baker, Death Valley
	FStop	W: Bandit Valero
	Gas	W: ArcoAmPm, Chevron, Mobil, Ultra
	Food	W: Arby's, Bob's Big Boy, Bun Boy, Burger King, Coco's Rest, Del Taco, Denny's, Jack in the Box, Starbucks, The Mad Greek, Taco Bell/Chevron, Subway/Valero
	Lodg	W: Bun Boy Motel, Royal Hawaiian Motel, Motel Wills Fargo, Microtel
	Other	W: NAPA, Auto Repair, ATM/Bank, Ken's Towing & Tire Car/Truck/RV, RVDump/Valero, A-1 LP
245		Baker Blvd (NB) (Access Ex #246 Serv)
239		Zzyzx Rd, Baker
233		Rasor Rd, Arrowhead Tr, Baker
	FStop	E: Rasor Road Services
	TServ	E: Rasor Rd Svc
230		Basin Rd, Cronese Lake Rd, Ludlow, Cronese Valley
221		Afton Rd, Ludlow, Dunn
	Other	W: Mini Market
(217)		Clyde Kane Rest Area (Both dir) (RR, Phones, Picnic)
213		Field Rd, Ludlow
206		Harvard Rd, Newberry Springs
	Gas	W: Gas
	Other	E: Twin Lakes RV Park▲, to I-40 W: Tires
198		Minneola Rd, Newberry Springs
	Gas	W: Valero
	Other	E: to Barstow-Daggett Airport✈, to I-40
(197)		Agricultural Insp Station (SB)
196		Yermo Rd, Newberry Springs

EXIT		CALIFORNIA
194		Calico Rd, Newberry Springs, Yermo, Bismarck
	Other	E: Barstow/Calico KOA▲
191		Ghost Town Rd, Daggett Yermo Rd, Yermo Rd, Newberry Springs, Daggett, to I-40
	TStop	E: Vegas Truck Stop/Mohsen Oil Truck & Travel W: Ghost Town Mini Mart/Shell
	Gas	E: ArcoAmPm W: 76
	Food	E: FastFood/Mohsen, Jack in the Box, Peggy Sue's 50's Diner, Penny's Diner W: Jenny Rose Rest, Jack in the Box, Old Miners Cafe
	Lodg	E: Calico Motel, Oak Tree Inn
	Other	E: Desert Springs RV Park▲, Shady Lane RV Camp▲ W: Barstow/Calico KOA▲, Calico Ghost Town Campground▲
189		Fort Irwin Rd, Meridian Rd, Yermo Rd, Barstow
186		Old Hwy 58, Barstow
	Other	W: Shady Lane RV Camp▲
184B		I-15 Bus, E Main St, to I-40E (NB)
	Gas	E: Gas, Texaco W: 76, Terrible Herbst/Chevron, Shell
	Food	E: Deli, Donut Star, Mexican Rest, McDonald's, Pizza, Popeye's, W: Burger King, Carl's Jr, CoCo's, IHOP, Jack in the Box, Long John Silver, Sizzler, Mexican Rest
	Lodg	E: Best Western, Gateway Motel W: Comfort Inn, Days Inn, Economy Inn, Econo Lodge, Executive Inn, Quality Inn, Ramada Inn, Super 8, Travelodge
	Other	E: Auto Repairs W: Auto Dealers, Amtrak, BJ's Natural Foods, Banks, Cinema
184		E Main St, to I-40E, Needles (SB)
	Gas	E: Chevron, Mobil◊, Shell W: 76, ArcoAmPm, Chevron, Shell◊
	Food	E: Burger King, McDonald's, Pizza, Popeye's, Mexican Rest W: Arby's, Carl's Jr, China Gourmet, CoCo's, Denny's, IHOP, Italian, KFC, Long John Silver's, Sizzler, Taco Bell
	Lodg	E: Best Western, Gateway Motel W: Comfort Inn, Days Inn, Econo Lodge, Quality Inn, Ramada Inn♥, Super 8
	AServ	E: Shell
	Other	E: Barstow Mall W: AutoZone, Laundromat, Grocery
(184A)		Jct I-40E, Needles (NB) (Begin/End I-40)
183		CA 247S, Barstow Rd, Barstow (Addt'l Serv W/N to I-15 Bus)
	Gas	E: 76, UltraMar/Beacon, Valero W: Chevron
	Food	E: Pizza Hut W: Little Caesar's, Steak Your Way
	Med	W: + Barstow Comm Hospital
	Other	W: Auto Repair, Auto Dealers, Amtrak, ATM's, Banks, Food 4 Less, Food Depot
181		L St, W Main St, Barstow (F/Tstops W Main/L St)
	FStop	W: Heartland Truck Stop (Scales)
	TStop	W: American Travel Center
	Gas	W: ArcoAmPm, Thrifty

EXIT		CALIFORNIA
	Food	W: Rest/ATC, Rest/HTS, Bun Boy, Pizza Palace, Mexican Rest
	Lodg	W: Holiday Inn Express, Motel 7, Red Roof Inn♥, Sunset Inn
	TWash	W: Heartland TS
	TServ	W: CB Service, Truck Ser/Heartland TS
	Other	W: Auto Repairs, Banks, Firestone, Grocery, Home Depot, Towing
179		CA 58W, to Bakersfield
178		Lenwood Rd, Barstow
	TStop	E: Flying J Travel Plaza #5090 (Scales), W: Pilot Travel Center #282 (Scales), Travel Center of America/Shell (Scales)
	Gas	E: Chevron◊, Shell, Valero W: Mobil
	Food	E: CountryMkt/Pizza/Chinese/FJ TP, Burger King, Bob's Big Boy, Del Taco, Jack in the Box, Taco Bell, Tommy's Hamburgers W: Subway/Pilot TC, CountryFare/ Subway/TA TC, Arby's, Baja Fresh, Carl's Jr, El Pollo Loco, KFC, Denny's, McDonald's, Panda Express, Starbucks, Wendy's
	Lodg	E: Hampton Inn, Holiday Inn Express♥ W: Good Nite Inn, Red Roof Inn
	TWash	E: Blue Beacon Truck Wash W: Truck Wash AmPm, Little Sisters Truck Wash
	TServ	W: TA TC
	Other	E: Laundry/BarbSh/WiFi/RVDump/LP/ FJ TP, Tanger Outlet Mall, Factory Merchants Barstow Outlets W: Laundry/WiFi/Pilot TC, Laundry/WiFi/ RVDump/TA TC
175		Outlet Center Dr, Sidewinder Rd
169		Hodge Rd, Stoddard Mtn Rd
165		Wild Wash Rd, Sorrel Trail, Helendale
161		Dale Evans Pkwy, Apple Valley
157		Stoddard Wells Rd, Bell Mountain Rd, Apple Valley, Victorville
154		Stoddard Wells Rd, Victorville
	Gas	W: 76, Mobil
	Food	E: Peggy Sue's 50's Diner W: Denny's, Rest/HJ
	Lodg	W: Howard Johnson, Motel 6♥
	Med	E: + St Mary Hospital
	Other	E: Victorville/Inland Empire KOA▲ W: Towing, Thrifty RAC, Repairs, Airport✈
153B		E Street, Victorville, Oroville
	Other	E: Amtrak
153A		CA 18E, D St, I-15 Bus, Victorville, to Apple Valley, Oro Grande, Silver Lakes
	Gas	E: 76 W: ArcoAmPm
	Med	E: + Victor Valley Comm Hospital
	Other	E: Amtrak, Museum, Auto Repair, Tires, to Mohave Narrows Regional Park▲ W: to Southern CA Int'l Airp
151B		Mojave Dr, to I-15 Bus, Victorville
	Gas	E: 76 W: Qwik Stop, Valero
	Food	E: Mama Rosa's W: Molly Brown's Country Cafe

◊= Regular Gas Stations with Diesel   ▲ = RV Friendly Locations   ♥ = Pet Friendly Locations
RED PRINT SHOWS LARGE VEHICLE PARKING/ACCESS ON SITE OR NEARBY   BROWN PRINT SHOWS CAMPGROUNDS/RV PARKS

EXIT		CALIFORNIA
	Lodg	E: Budget Inn W: Economy Inn, Mohave Village Motel, Sunset Inn
	Other	E: to I-15 Bus, Banks, ATM's, Food, San Bernardino Co Fairgrounds W: Auto Repair, Transmission, Tires
151A		**Roy Rogers Dr, La Paz Dr**
	Gas	E: Chevron, Mini Mart, Shell, USA, Costco W: ArcoAmPm
	Food	E: Carl's Jr, Hometown Buffet, IHOP, Jack in the Box, McDonald's, Wendy's
	Lodg	E: New Corral Motel
	Other	E: to I-15 Bus, ATM's, Banks, Budget RAC, Costco, Food 4 Less, Goodyear, Harley Davidson, RiteAid, Fairgrounds
150		**CA 18W, Palmdale Rd, 7th St, Victorville, Palmdale**
	TStop	W: to US 395N High Desert Travel Center
	Gas	E: ArcoAmPm, Chevron, Shell, Texaco W: ArcoAmPm, Chevron, Mobil, Shell, Valero
	Food	E: Rest/Best Western, Burger King, Carls Jr, Denny's, KFC, Richie's Diner W: Coco's, Del Taco, Long John Silver, McDonald's, Subway, Taco Bell, Rest/High Desert TC
	Lodg	E: Best Western, Quality Inn, Red Roof Inn W: Ambassador Hotel, Budget Inn, EZ 8 Motel, Ramada Inn
	Other	E: Auto Dealers, Golf Courses W: Auto Dealers, Auto Zone, Park Center Shopping Center, Target, Mall of Victor Valley, Police Dept, CA Hwy Patrol Post, Cruise America RV Rentals, Victor Valley RV Discount Center/El Monte RV Rentals & Sales
147		**Bear Valley Rd, Victorville, Lucerne Valley, Apple Valley**
	Gas	E: 76, 7-11, ArcoAmPm, Mobil, Shell W: Chevron, Valero
	Food	E: Burger King, Carl's Jr, Del Taco, KFC, Long John Silver's, McDonald's, Panda Express, Quiznos, Red Robin, Stein & Steer, TNT Cafe W: Applebee's, California Fresh, El Tio Pepe, El Pollo Loco, Carino's, Jack in the Box, Olive Garden, On the Border, Outback Steakhouse, Red Lobster, Roadhouse Grill, Starbucks, Subway, Tony Roma, Wendy's
	Lodg	E: Comfort Suites, Days Inn, Econo Lodge, Extended Stay, Hampton Inn, Hilton Garden Inn, La Quinta Inn♥, Super 8, Travelodge
	Med	E: + Desert Valley Hospital
	Other	E: AutoZone, Cinema, Firestone, Home Depot, Range RV Rentals, Staples, Tires, Wal-Mart, Budget RAC, Hertz RAC W: Albertson's, Avis RAC, Banks, Best Buy, Cinemark Bear Valley 10, Lowe's, Mall of Victor Valley, PetSmart♥, Tires
143		**Main St, to US 395, Hesperia**
	Gas	E: ArcoAmPm, Chevron, Shell, Texaco, Valero W: ArcoAmPm
	Food	E: Burger King, DQ, Denny's, In 'N Out, Main St Grill & Bakery, Pizza
	Lodg	E: Maple Motel, Thrifty Motel W: Holiday Inn Express, Springhill Suites

EXIT		CALIFORNIA
	Other	E: to Hesperia Airport✈, Hesperia Lake Park & Campground▲, Police Dept W: to US 395, Desert Willow RV Resort▲
141		**US 395N (NB), Joshua St, Palm Ave, US 395N (SB)**
	TStop	W: Pilot Travel Center #381 (Scales) Newton's Outpost Café & Truck N Travel
	Food	W: Wendy's/Pilot TC
	TWash	W: Newton's Outpost Café & Truck N Travel, Little Sisters Truck Wash
	TServ	W: CAT/Cummins
	Other	W: Laundry/WiFi/Pilot TC, RVDump/Newton's Outpost Café & Truck N Travel, Adelanto RV Park▲
138		**Oak Hill Rd, Hesperia**
	Gas	E: Shell
	Food	E: Café
	Other	W: Oak Hills RV Village▲
	NOTE:	MM 137: SB: 6% Steep Grade next 12mi
(133)		**RunAWay Truck Ramp (SB)**
131		**CA 138, San Bernardino, Palmdale, Silverwood Lake**
	Other	E: to Silverwood Lake, Silverwood Lake State Rec Area
(131)		**Weigh Station (Both dir)**
129		**Cajon Blvd, Cleghorn Rd**
	Other	W: to San Bernardino Nat'l Forest▲
124		**Kenwood Ave, Historic Rte 66, San Bernardino**
(123)		**Jct I-215S, San Bernardino Riverside (SB Exit Left)**
122		**Devore Rd, Glen Helen Pkwy**
	Gas	E: Devore Mini Mart
	Other	E: RVDump/Glen Helen Reg'l Park, Glen Helen Off Hwy Vehicle Park, Bank, Hyundai Pavilion
119		**Sierra Ave, Riverside Ave, Lytle Creek Rd, Fontana, Rialto**
	TStop	E: (S Riverside Ave) Rialto Shell Travel Center (Scales)
	Gas	W: ArcoAmPm, Shell
	Food	E: FastFood/Rialto TC W: Blimpie, Del Taco/Shell, Jack in the Box/Arco, McDonald's
	Other	E: Laundry/LP/RVDump/Rialto TC
116		**Beech Ave, Summit Ave**
	Gas	E: Chevron
115B		**CA 210E, to San Bernardino (SB), CA 210W, to Pasadena (NB)**
115A		**CA 210W, to Pasadena (SB), CA 210E, to San Bernardino (NB)**
113		**Baseline Rd, Fontana**
	Gas	E: Shell, USA W: Chevron, Speedway
	Food	E: Denny's, Jack in the Box, KFC, Rosa Maria's, Logan's Roadhouse, Pizza Hut, Starbucks, Wendy's W: Pizza
	Lodg	E: Comfort Inn
	Other	E: ATM, Grocery, Rialto Muni Airport✈ W: Winery, to PetCo♥
112		**CA 66, Foothill Blvd, Fontana, Rancho Cucaomonga, Hist Rte 66**
	Gas	E: Circle K, Chevron

◆ = Regular Gas Stations with Diesel   ▲ = RV Friendly Locations   ♥ = Pet Friendly Locations
RED PRINT SHOWS LARGE VEHICLE PARKING/ACCESS ON SITE OR NEARBY   BROWN PRINT SHOWS CAMPGROUNDS/RV PARKS

EXIT	CALIFORNIA
	W: ArcoAmPm, Mobil
Food	E: Arby's, Claim Jumper, Coco's, Hungry Howie's, In-N-Out Burger, McDonald's, Panda Express, Subway, Stuffed Bagel, Taco Bell
	W: Carl's Jr, Denny's, Farmer Boys
Lodg	W: Best Western
Med	W: + Rancho San Antonio Med Ctr
Other	E: Auto Repairs, ATM, Grocery, Costco, Food 4 Less, Office Depot, Target, Wal-Mart, U-Haul, J & J Diesel Repair
	W: AutoZone, ATM's, Banks, Best Buy, Lowe's, Globe Theatres, Home Depot, Police Station, Tires, PetSmart ♥, U-Haul
110	**4th St, Ontario**
Gas	W: ArcoAmPm, Mobil, Costco
Food	W: Baja Fresh, Carl's Jr, Coco's, Del Taco, Denny's, IHOP, KFC, McDonald's, Japanese Rest, Olive Garden, Outback Steakhouse, Panda Express, Red Lobster, Rainforest Café, Starbucks
Lodg	W: Amerisuites, Country Suites, Hilton, Extended Stay America, Holiday Inn, La Quinta Inn ♥
Other	E: California Speedway, Fontana Diesel Service, Auto Repairs
	W: AMC 30, Costco, IMAX, Ontario Mills Mall, Sam's Club, Empire Lakes Golf Course, Plaza Continental Factory Stores, Banks, ATM's, Tires
(109B)	**Jct I-10E, to San Bernardino (SB)**
(109A)	**Jct I-10W, to Los Angeles (SB)**
Other	W: to Ontario Int'l Airport ✈
(109)	**Jct I-10 (NB)**
108	**Jurupa Ave, Ontario, Fontana**
Gas	W: ArcoAmPm
Food	W: Carl's Jr
Other	E: Auto Dealers, U-Haul
	W: Auto Dealers, Auto Repairs, Ontario Int'l Airport ✈, Rental Car Companies, Scandia Amusement Park
106	**CA 60, W - LA, E - Riverside (SB)**
106B	**CA 60W, to Los Angeles (NB)**
106A	**CA 60E, to Riverside (NB)**
103	**Limonite Ave, Mira Loma (Gas & Food E in Riverside)**
100	**Sixth St, Norco Dr, Bus 15, Norco**
Gas	E: ArcoAmPm, Chevron
	W: Valero
Food	E: Jack in the Box, McDonald's
	W: Country Junction Rest
Other	W: Auto Service, Diesel Service, Banks
98	**2nd St, Bus 15 Norco, Corona**
Gas	W: 7-11, Shell, Shell
Food	W: Burger King, Denny's, Domino's, In N Out Burgers, Sizzler
Lodg	W: Howard Johnson Express
Other	W: Auto Dealers, Auto Service, Diesel Service, Banks, Truck Repair, Riverside Comm College
97	**Mountain Ave, Hidden Valley Pkwy, Norco**
Gas	W: 76, Chevron, Shell ◆
Food	W: Arby's, Carl's Jr, Chipolte Mexican Grill, DQ, Denny's, Fazoli's, Hong Kong Express, McDonald's, Papa John's, Quiznos, Starbucks, Taco Bell

EXIT	CALIFORNIA
Other	W: Albertson's, Big Lots, Target, UPS Store, to Corona Muni Airport ✈
96B	**CA 91W, Corona, Beach Cities, to Anaheim, Long Beach (SB)**
Other	W: to Corona Muni Airport ✈
96A	**CA 91E, to Riverside (SB)**
96	**CA 91, Beach Cities, Riverside (NB)**
95	**Magnolia Ave, Corona**
Gas	W: Mobil, Shell
Food	W: Burger King, Carl's Jr, Chinese Rest, CoCo's, Donut Star, Little Caesar's, Pizza Hut, McDonald's, Sizzler, Subway
Lodg	W: Gallery Inn
Med	W: + Corona Reg'l Medical Center
Other	E: Office Depot, Auto Repair
	W: Banks, Auto Repair, Grocery, CVS
93	**Ontario Ave, Corona**
Gas	E: Shell
	W: Chevron, Sam's
Food	W: Denny's, Jack in the Box, KFC, McDonald's, Quiznos, Tommy's Orig'l WF Hamburgers
Other	E: Auto Repair, Diesel Repair
	W: Albertson's, Home Depot, Sam's Club, Wal-Mart, US Post Office, Banks
92	**El Cerrito Rd, Corona, El Cerrito**
Gas	E: Circle K
91	**Cajalco Rd, Corona**
Food	E: Chili's, ChickFilA, On the Border Mexican Rest, Romano's Macaroni Grill
Other	E: Staples, Target
90	**Weirick Rd, Corona**
88	**Temescal Canyon Rd, Corona, Glen Ivy**
Gas	W: ArcoAmPm
Food	W: Carl's Jr
Other	W: to Glen Ivy RV Park ▲, Glen Ivy Hot Springs
85	**Indian Truck Trail, Corona**
81	**Lake St, Lake Elsinore, Alberthill**
78	**Nichols Rd**
Gas	W: ArcoAmPm
Food	W: Carl's Jr
Other	W: Lake Elsinore Outlet Center
77	**CA 74, Central Ave, Perris, San Juan Capistrano, Lake Elsinore**
Gas	E: ArcoAmPm, Chevron, Mobil
Food	E: Burger King, Douglas Burgers, Off-Ramp Cafe
	W: Farmer Boys
Lodg	W: to Bedrock Motel & Campground
Other	E: Costco, Elsinore Hills RV Park ▲
	W: Albertson's, Auto Repair, Lake Elsinore West Marina & RV Resort ▲, Weekend Paradise ▲, Lake Elsinore Campground ▲
75	**Main St, Lake Elsinore**
Gas	W: 76, Circle K
Food	W: Family Basket Rest
Lodg	W: Lake Elsinore Hot Spring Motel
Other	W: Lake Elsinore Tire & Auto
73	**Diamond Dr, Railroad Canyon Rd**
Gas	W: Mobil ◆
Food	E: El Pollo Loco, Denny's, In n Out Burger, KFC, McDonald's, Latte Express, Quiznos
	W: Burger King, Carl's Jr, Coco's, Pizza Hut, Sizzler, Subway, Taco Bell

EXIT	CALIFORNIA
Lodg	E: Lake Elsinore Inn
	W: Lake Elsinore Resort & Casino, Lake View Inn, Travel Inn
Other	E: Wal-Mart sc, Banks, Grocery, Jiffy Lube, , to Pepper Tree RV Park ▲
	W: Albertson's, AutoZone, Big Lots, Auto Dealers, Goodyear
71	**Bundy Canyon Rd, Wildomar**
Gas	W: ArcoAmPm
Food	W: Jack in the Box
Other	W: to Pepper Tree RV Park ▲, to Skylark Airport ✈, Casa De Mobile RV Park ▲
69	**Baxter Rd**
68	**Clinton Keith Rd, Wildomar**
Food	E: Starbucks
Med	E: + Inland Valley Reg Med Center
65	**California Oaks Rd, Kalmia St, Murietta**
Gas	E: 76, Chevron, Mobil, Shell
	W: ArcoAmPm, Chevron
Food	E: Burger King, Carl's Jr, DQ, KFC, McDonald's
	W: Carrow's, Farmer Boys, Jack in the Box
Other	E: Albertson's, Target, Police Dept
64	**Murrieta Hot Springs Rd, to I-215, Murrieta (Addtl Serv E past I-215)**
Gas	W: 7-11, Shell
Food	W: Arby's, Bella's Pizza, China Inn, IHOP, McDonald's
Med	E: + Rancho Springs Medical Center
Other	E: Temecula Valley RV/RVDump
	W: Big Lots, Grocery, Home Depot, PetSmart ♥, Wal-Mart sc, El Monte RV Sales & Rentals, RV Anywhere
(63)	**Jct I-215N, to San Bernardino, Riverside (NB)**
61	**CA 79N, Winchester Ave, Hemet, Temecula**
FStop	E: Jefferson Chevron
Gas	E: Costco
	W: ArcoAmPm, Chevron, Mobil
Food	E: Burger King, Carl's Jr, Coco's, Great Steak & Potato Co, McDonald's, Mimi's Café, On the Border, Panda Express, Roadhouse Grill, Quiznos, Starbucks, TGI Friday, Taco Bell
	W: Arby's, CA Grill, DQ, El Pollo Loco, Hungry Hunter Steakhouse, Jack in the Box, Richie's Diner, Sizzler, Tecate Grill, Taco Factory, Tony Roma's
Lodg	W: Best Western ♥, Comfort Inn ♥, Extended Stay America
Other	E: Auto Dealers, ATM's, Banks, Big O Tire, Costco, FedEx Kinko's, Food 4 Less, Office Depot, Stadium Cinemas 15, The Promenade
	W: ATM's, Auto Dealers, Banks, NAPA, Hertz, RV Supercenter, CA State Hwy Patrol Post, Richardson's RV Center
59	**Rancho California Rd, Temecula**
FStop	W: Temecula 76/Bill's Unocal 76
Gas	E: Mobil, Shell ◆
	W: Chevron
Food	E: Aloha Joe's, Black Angus, Chili's, Claim Jumper, Panda Express, Rockin Baja Lobster, Oscar's Rest, Round Table Pizza, Starbucks, Rest/Embassy Suites

◆ = Regular Gas Stations with Diesel   ▲ = RV Friendly Locations   ♥ = Pet Friendly Locations
RED PRINT SHOWS LARGE VEHICLE PARKING/ACCESS ON SITE OR NEARBY   BROWN PRINT SHOWS CAMPGROUNDS/RV PARKS

Interstate 15 N/S — California

EXIT		CALIFORNIA
	Food	W: Denny's, Domino's, KFC, Penfold's Café, Rosa's Cantina, Steak Ranch Rest, Taco Grill, Texas Lil's Rest
	Lodg	E: Embassy Suites W: Motel 6 ♥
	AServ	W: Chevron
	Other	E: Albertson's, ATM's, Banks, Kroger, Target, Auto Repair W: US Post Office, CA Hwy Patrol Post
58		CA 79S, Old Town Front Rd, Temecula, Indio
	Gas	E: 7-11, Mobil W: Shell
	Food	E: Carl's Jr, Italian Rest, Molina's, Pizza, Pedro's Tacos
	Lodg	E: Temecula Creek Inn & Golf Resort W: Hans Motel, Ramada Inn
	Other	E: Harley Davidson, Pechanga Indian Reservation, Pechanga RV Resort▲, to Woodchuck Campground & RV Park▲ W: Goodyear, RV Service
(55)		Inspection Station (NB)
54		Rainbow Valley Blvd, to US 395, Fallbrook
	Other	E: Phillips Diesel Repair W: CA Inspection Station
51		Mission Rd, US 395, Fallbrook
	Med	W: + Hospital
	Other	E: Rancho Corrido Campground▲
46		CA 76, Pala Rd, Pala, Oceanside
	Gas	W: Mobil
	Lodg	W: La Estancia Inn, Pala Mesa Resort
	Other	E: La Jolla Band of Indians Camping▲, to 5mi: Pala Casino Resort Spa
43		Old Hwy 395, US 95, W Lilac Rd, Escondido
41		Gopher Canyon Rd, US 395, Old Castle Rd, Escondido
	Gas	E: Texaco
	Lodg	E: Castle Creek Inn Resort & Spa
	Other	E: Lilac Oaks Campground▲, All Seasons RV Park & Campground▲, Champagne Lakes RV Resort▲, Deer Park Auto Museum, Lawrence Welk Museum, Lawrence Welk Resort▲
37		Deer Springs Rd, Mtn Meadow Rd, Escondido, San Marcos
	Gas	W: ArcoAmPm
34		Centre City Pkwy, Escondido (SB)
33		El Norte Pkwy, Escondido
	Gas	E: ArcoAmPm, Shell, Texaco W: 76, Circle K
	Food	E: Arby's, IHOP, Taco Bell W: Jack in the Box, Wendy's
	Lodg	E: Best Western
	Other	E: Escondido RV Resort▲ W: Grocery, Bank, ATM
32		CA 78, W to San Marcos, E to Ramona, to Oceanside (Serv E to Centre City Pkwy & Mission Ave)
	Other	E: Freeway Trailer Sales/RVDump
31		Valley Pkwy, Downtown Escondido (Addt'l Serv E to Centre City Pkwy)
	Gas	E: ArcoAmPm W: 7-11

EXIT		CALIFORNIA
	Food	E: Chili's, McDonald's, Olive Garden W: Applebee's, Burger King, Carl's Jr, Coco's, Del Taco, La Salsa, Starbucks, Wendy's
	Lodg	W: Comfort Inn, Holiday Inn Express ♥
	Med	E: + Palomar Medical Center
	Other	E: Police Dept, CA State Hwy Patrol Post, Winery, Grocery, Rental cars W: Albertson's, Hertz RAC, Home Depot, Carwash, Mall
30		9th Ave, Auto Park Way (Access to Ex #31 via Auto Park Way)
	Gas	W: Shell
	Food	W: Applebee's, Subway, Taco Bell
	Other	W: Target, Home Depot
29		Felicita Rd, Citricado Pkwy
28		Centre City Pkwy (NB)
27		Via Rancho Parkway
	Gas	E: Chevron, Shell W: Shell, Texaco
	Food	E: Big Jim's Old South BBQ, DQ, La Salsa, McDonald's, Red Lobster, Red Robin, Starbucks, Taco Bell W: McDonald's, Panda King, Tony's Spunky Steer Rest
	Other	E: Zoo, Shopping, Mall, Vineyard & Winery
26		W Bernardo Dr, Pomerado Rd, Highlands Valley Rd, San Diego, Escondido

EXIT		CALIFORNIA
24		Rancho Bernardo Rd, San Diego (Addt'l Serv E to Bernardo Ctr Dr)
	Gas	E: ArcoAmPm, Mobil W: 76, Shell
	Food	E: Roberto's Taco Shop W: Elephant Bar & Rest, Denny's, Wendy's
	Lodg	W: Best Western, Holiday Inn, Radisson, Travelodge
	AServ	W: Shell
	Other	E: Grocery, Banks, ATM's
23		Bernardo Center Dr, San Diego
	Gas	E: 7-11, Chevron
	Food	E: Burger King, Denny's, Hunan Chinese Jack in the Box, Quizno's, Taco Bell
	Other	E: ATM's, Banks, Avis RAC, Firestone
22		Camino del Norte
	Med	E: + Hospital
21		Carmel Mountain Rd, San Diego
	Gas	E: Chevron, Shell, Texaco W: 7-11, Chevron
	Food	E: CA Pizza, Chevy's Mexican, Claim Jumper, El Pollo Loco, McDonald's, Olive Garden, Subway, Taco Bell, TGI Friday
	Lodg	E: Residence Inn W: Doubletree Golf Resort
	Other	E: Banks, Costco, Grocery, Home Depot, Kmart, Staples, US Post Office W: Albertson's
19		Ted Williams Pkwy, CA 56W
18		Poway Rd, Rancho Penasquitos Blvd, San Diego
	Gas	E: ArcoAmPm W: 7-11, 76, Exxon, Mobil♦
	Food	E: Deli W: Burger King, IHOP, Little Caesar's Pizza, McDonald's, Starbucks, Subway, Sushi USA, Taco Bell
	Lodg	W: La Quinta Inn ♥
17		Scripps Poway Pkwy, Mercy Rd
	FStop	W: Pacific Pride
	Food	E: Carl's Jr, El Pollo Loco, Jack in the Box, Panda Express, Taco Bell
	Other	E: ATM, Auto Service, Bank, Carwash, Grocery
16		Mira Mesa Blvd, San Diego
	Gas	W: Shell
	Food	E: Chuck E Cheese, Denny's, Pizza Hut, Golden Crown Chinese W: Applebee's, Arby's, DQ, Jack in the Box, Mimi's Café, Rubio's, Starbucks, Subway, Taco Bell, Togo's, Wendy's
	Lodg	E: Quality Suites
	Other	E: ATMs, Banks, US Post Office W: Albertson's, Bank, Home Depot, US Post Office, Grocery, Pharmacy, Stadium 18, to Mira Mesa Mall
15		Carroll Canyon Rd
	Food	E: Carl Jr's
	Other	E: Bank, ATM, Grocery
14		Pomerado Rd, Miramar Rd
	Gas	W: Arco, Chevron, Mobil, Shell, Texaco
	Food	W: Carl's Jr, Keith's Family Rest, Pizza Hut, Subway, Indian, Mexican Rest
	Lodg	E: Marriott W: Best Western, Budget Inn, Hampton Inn, Holiday Inn
	Other	W: RVDump/Texaco, Auto Service, Banks, ATMs, Miramar Marine Corps Air Station, Alliant Int'l Univ

♦ = Regular Gas Stations with Diesel   ▲ = RV Friendly Locations   ♥ = Pet Friendly Locations
RED PRINT SHOWS LARGE VEHICLE PARKING/ACCESS ON SITE OR NEARBY   BROWN PRINT SHOWS CAMPGROUNDS/RV PARKS

 **N** INTERSTATE 15

 INTERSTATE 16 **E**

EXIT	CALIFORNIA
13	Miramar Way, US Naval Air Station, San Diego
12	CA 163, Downtown San Diego (SB)
11	Jct CA 52, Clairemont Mesa Blvd, W to La Jolla, E to Santee
10	Clairemont Mesa Blvd (NB)
9	CA 274, Balboa Ave, Tierrasanta Blvd, San Diego
8	Aero Dr, San Diego
Gas	W: ArcoAmPm, Shell
Food	W: Baja Fresh, Chinese, Jack in the Box, McDonalds, Sizzler, Starbucks, Taco Bell
Lodg	W: Extended Stay America, Holiday Inn
Other	W: Wal-Mart, Grocery, Montgomery Field Airport✈, Bank, ATM
7B	Friars Rd W, San Diego (NB)
7A	Friars Rd E, San Diego (NB)
7	Friars Rd, San Diego Stadium (SB)
Other	W: Qualcomm Stadium, Bank, ATM
(6B)	Jct I-8, W to Beaches, E to El Centro
6A	Adams Ave, Camino del Rio
Gas	E: Chevron
Food	E: KFC, Mexican Rest, Starbucks
Other	E: Diesel Service
	W: Bank, ATM
5B	El Cajon Blvd
Gas	W: Mobil
Food	E: Pizza Hut
Other	E: Bank, ATM
5A	University Ave, San Diego
Other	Both: Restaurants, Auto Repair, Grocery
3	to CA 94E (SB)
(3)	Jct I-805, to Chula Vista
2C	CA 94, ML King Jr Fwy, Dwtn (SB)
2B	CA 94W, MLK Jr Fwy, Dwtn (SB) CA 94E, ML King Jr Frwy, Home Ave (NB)
2A	Market St, San Diego
1D	National Ave, Ocean View Blvd (SB)
Gas	E: Save
(1C)	Jct I-5S, National City, Chula Vista (SB, Left Exit)
(1B)	Jct I-5N, to Downtown (SB)
1A	Main St, Wabash Blvd (SB)
Other	W: US Naval Station
1	Ocean View Blvd (NB)
(1)	CA Welcome Center (NB) (RR, Phones, Vend)

(PACIFIC TIME ZONE)

CALIFORNIA
Begin Northbound I-15 from Jct I-5 in San Diego, CA to Canada / MT border.

Personal Notes

Best Ever RV Recipes
Good Sam Members Favorite Recipes

Good Sam Members Share Their Favorite Road Recipes

Get 175 new recipes for your RV galley all in one place! For only $10.95 plus $4.25 shipping and handling, you can have *Best Ever RV Recipes: Good Sam Members Favorite Recipes*.

To Order:
- Call toll free 1-877-209-6659 ext. 702
- Or visit www.TrailerLifeDirectory.com

EXIT	GEORGIA
	Begin Eastbound I-16 from Jct I-75 at Macon, GA to Savannah, GA.

GEORGIA   Eastern Time Zone

(1)	Jct I-75, N - Atlanta, S - Valdosta (NB Exits Left)
1A	Spring St, US 23, US 129, GA 49, Macon, Milledgeville (EB)
Gas	N: BP, Citgo, Marathon, Speedway
	S: Conoco, Exxon, Spectrum
Food	N: Arby's, Burger King, El Sombrero, DQ, Golden Corral, Hong Kong Express, Huddle House, McDonalds, Pizza Hut, Subway, Taco Bell
	S: Burger King, Checkers, KFC, Krystal, Pizza Hut, Waffle House, Wendy's, Zaxby's, Rest/Crowne Plaza
Lodg	S: Crowne Plaza, Macon Inn
Med	S: + Medical Center of Central GA
Other	N: ATM, Banks, Jiffy Lube, Kroger, Midas, Wal-Mart, Walgreen's
	S: ATM, Banks, Greyhound Terminal, Grocery, Olson Tires, Tires +
1B	2nd St, GA 22, Macon, to US 129, to GA 49 (WB) (Acc Ex 1A Serv N&S)
Med	N: + Coliseum Medical Center
Other	S: ATM, Banks, Police Dept
2	US 80, GA 87, ML King Jr Blvd, Coliseum Dr
Gas	S: Oil
Med	N: + Coliseum Medical Center
Other	N: Auto Repair, Convention Center, Macon Coliseum
	S: Theatres, Museums, Truck Repair, Tourist Info, Auto Repair, Banks, ATM, to Robins AFB
6	US 23, Alt 129, Golden Isles Hwy, Ocmulgee East Blvd, Macon
TStop	S: Ocmulgee Chevron #419
Gas	N: BP, Spectrum
Food	N: DQ/Spectrum
	S: Rest/Ocmulgee TS, Huddle House, Subway
Lodg	S: Days Inn
TServ	S: Ocmulgee TS
Other	N: Herbert Smart Downtown Airport✈
	S: to appr 35mi Hillside Bluegrass RV Park▲
12	CR 193, Sgoda Rd, Dry Branch, Huber, to US 23, US 129, Macon
FStop	N: Quick Way Foods/Marathon
18	Alton White Blvd, Dry Branch, CR 189, Bullard, Jeffersonville
24	GA 96, Jeffersonville, Tarversville
FStop	N: Citgo Food Mart #16
TStop	S: 96 Truck Plaza/BP
Food	S: 96 TP, Huddle House
Lodg	S: Best Value Inn
Other	S: Laundry/96 TP, to Robins AFB
27	GA 358, Homer Chance Hwy, Danville, to US 80, to US 129
32	GA 112, Montrose, Allentown
Gas	S: Chevron
39	GA 26, Montrose, Cochran
42	GA 338, CR 348, Dudley, Dexter
Other	N: to 6mi: T&T Farms U-Pick
(44)	Rest Area (EB) (RR, Phone, Picnic, Vend, RVDump)

Page 82   ◆ = Regular Gas Stations with Diesel   ▲ = RV Friendly Locations   ♥ = Pet Friendly Locations
RED PRINT SHOWS LARGE VEHICLE PARKING/ACCESS ON SITE OR NEARBY   BROWN PRINT SHOWS CAMPGROUNDS/RV PARKS

EXIT		GEORGIA
(46)		Rest Area (WB) (RR, Phone, Picnic, Vend, RVDump)
49		GA 257, Dublin, Dexter
	TStop	S: Dublin 257 Truck Plaza, Love's Travel Stop #320 (Scales)
	Gas	S: Chevron
	Food	S: 257 TP, Chesters/Subway/Love's TS
	TServ	S: 257 Truck Tire Service
	Med	N: + Hospital
	Other	N: to Barron Airport✈ S: Laundry/257 TS, WiFi/RVDump/ Love's TS
51		US 319, US 441, Dublin, McRae
	FStop	N: Pilot Travel Center #68 (Scales), Neighbor's Express/Exxon, Jet Food Store #73/Shell
	Gas	S: Chevron
	Food	N: Arby's, Buffalo's Café, Burger King, KFC, McDonald's, Ruby Tuesday, Taco Bell, Waffle House, Wendy's S: Cracker Barrel
	Lodg	N: Best Western, Comfort Inn, Days Inn, Econo Lodge, Hampton Inn, Holiday Inn Express, Jameson Inn, Super 8 S: La Quinta Inn♥
	Med	N: + Hospital
	Other	N: GA State Patrol Post S: Little Ocmulgee State Park▲, to Little Ocmulgee State Golf Course, to Piney Woods Lakes Campground▲
54		GA 19, Dublin
	TStop	N: Friendly Gus #23/Chevron (Scales)
	Food	N: FastFood/Friendly Gus
	Other	N: Laundry/Friendly Gus
58		GA 199, Old River Rd, E Dublin
67		GA 29, Soperton
	Gas	S: Chevron◊, Citgo◊
	Food	S: Huddle House
71		GA 15, GA 78, Soperton, Adrian
	Gas	N: Chevron◊
78		US 221, GA 56, Soperton, Swainsboro
	Gas	N: BP◊
84		GA 297, Vidalia
	TServ	N: I-16 Truck Sales & Equip, Towing
90		US 1, GA 4, Oak Park, Swainsboro, Lyons
	TStop	N: Ed's Truck Stop/Pure, Red Roof Express/Citgo
	Gas	N: BP
	Food	N: Rest/Ed's TS, FastFood/Red Roof
	Lodg	N: Days Inn
	TServ	N: Red Roof Express TS
	Other	N: LP/Red Roof Express

EXIT		GEORGIA
98		GA 57, GA 46, Metter, Swainsboro, Stillmore, Altamaha State Park
	Gas	S: BP◊, Chevron◊
	Other	S: to Gordonia Altamaha State Park▲
104		GA 23, GA 121, Metter, Reidsville
	TStop	N: Jay's Fuel Stop/BP
	Gas	N: Chevron◊, Exxon, Shell◊ S: Citgo◊, Phillips 66
	Food	N: Burger King, Hardee's, Huddle House, Jomax BBQ, KFC, McDonald's, Subway, Waffle House, Wendy's
	Lodg	N: Comfort Inn, Days Inn, Econo Lodge, Holiday Inn Express, Metter Inn, Scottish Inn
	Med	N: + Hospital
	Other	N: ATM's, Banks, Randy's Wrecker & Service Center, Tires, to George Smith State Park▲ S: Auto Dealer, Metter Muni Airport✈, to Gordonia Altamaha State Park▲, to Altamaha State Golf Course
111		CR 49, Pulaski Excelsior Rd, Pulaski
	TStop	S: PTP/Grady's Truck Stop/Citgo
	Food	S: Grady's Grill
	Lodg	S: Motel/Grady's
	TServ	S: Grady's TS
	Other	S: Laundry/Grady's, Brookwood Parrish RV Park▲, Beaver Run RV Park▲
116		GA 73, US 25, US 301, Statesboro, Claxton, Register
	TStop	N: Po Jo's Gas 'N Go/Chevron (Scales), El Cheapo#89/Sunoco
	Food	N: El Cheapo TS, Po Jo's TS S: Huddle House
	Lodg	S: Red Carpet Inn, Scottish Inn
	Other	N: Laundry/Po Jo's, to Parkwood RV Park▲, to Statesboro Muni Airport✈, to Magnolia Springs State Park▲
127		GA 67/46, Brooklet, Statesboro, Pembroke, Fort Stewart
	FStop	N: Time Saver
	Gas	N: Shell◊ S: Chevron◊
	Food	N: Barnard's BBQ, Morgan's Creek
	Other	S: 24th Infantry Museum
132		Arcola Rd, Ash Branch Church Rd, CR 582, Pembroke
	Other	S: to Fort Stewart Military Reservation
137		GA 119, Pembroke, Ft Stewart
	Other	N: Historic Guyton
143		US 280, GA 30, to US 80, GA 26, Ellabell, Pembroke
	Gas	S: BP, El Cheapo
	Food	S: Subs/BP
	Other	S: Black Creek Golf Course

EXIT		GEORGIA
(144)		Weigh Station (Both dir)
148		CR 310, Old River Rd, to US 80
	Other	S: to Fort Stewart Military Reservation, to Bellaire Woods Campground▲
152		GA 17, Bloomingdale Rd, Bloomingdale
155		Pooler Pkwy, Savannah, Pooler
	Other	N: to Savannah Hilton Head Intl Airport✈
(157A)		Jct I-95, S to Brunswick, Jacksonville, FL
(157B)		Jct I-95, N to Florence
	Other	N: to Savannah Hilton Head Intl Airport✈
160		GA 307, Dean Forest Rd, N to US 80, S to US 17, Savannah
	FStop	N: Pilot Travel Center #72 (Scales)
	Gas	N: Chevron, Shell
	Food	N: Subway/Pilot TC, Ronnie's, Waffle House, Rest/Days Inn
	Lodg	N: Days Inn, Quality Lodge S: Quality Inn
	TServ	N: Truck & Tire Repair, Mack Trucks, Lil Truck Center
	Other	N: BarbSh/Pilot TC, Auto Repair & Towing, to Savannah Int'l Airport✈, Transmissions S: GA State Hwy Patrol Post, to Waterway RV Park▲
162		Chatham Pkwy, Savannah, N to US 80, I-516, S to US 17, GA 25
	Gas	S: Shell
	Other	N: Chatham Truck Center S: Bank, to Biltmore Gardens RV Park▲
(164AB)		Jct I-516, Lynes Pkwy, US 80, US 17, GA 21
165		GA 204, 37th St (EB)
166		US 17 Alt, GA 25, Gwinnett St, Louisville Rd, Savannah
167AB		ML King Jr Blvd, Gaston St, Montgomery St, Savannah
	Gas	N: BP◊, Enmark
	Food	N: Just Cuzzin's, Teaser's Café, Asst'd S: Burger King, KFC, Popeye's
	Lodg	N: Best Western, Comfort Suites, Days Inn, Courtyard, Howard Johnson, Hyatt, Quality Inn, Radisson S: Garden Inn, Paradise Inn, B&B's
	Other	N: Savannah Visitor Center, Carriage Tours of Atlanta, Gallery, Museums, Riverboat Cruises, Greyhound, Tourist Info, Assorted Tours, to Conv Center S: Amtrak, Auto Repairs, CarWash

GEORGIA

◊ = Regular Gas Stations with Diesel ▲ = RV Friendly Locations ♥ = Pet Friendly Locations
RED PRINT SHOWS LARGE VEHICLE PARKING/ACCESS ON SITE OR NEARBY BROWN PRINT SHOWS CAMPGROUNDS/RV PARKS

Interstate 17 S

EXIT	ARIZONA
	Begin Southbound I-17 at Jct I-40 near Flagstaff, AZ to Phoenix, AZ.

ARIZONA
(MOUNTAIN TIME ZONE, NO DST)
(Begins/Ends Jct I-40, exit #195)

341 McConnell Dr, Milton Rd, to US 180, to I-40 Bus, I-40, US 66, Flagstaff, Grand Canyon
- Gas: W: 76, Chevron, Circle K, Conoco, Exxon, Mobil, Shell
- Food: W: Arby's, Burger King, Carl's Jr, DQ, Denny's, Fazoli's, Fuddrucker's, IHOP, KFC, McDonald's, Olive Garden, Pizza Hut, Red Lobster, Sizzler, Village Inn
- Lodg: W: Amerisuites, Comfort Inn, Days Inn, Econo Lodge, Embassy Suites, Fairfield Inn, Hampton Inn, Hilton Garden Inn, La Quinta Inn ♥, Quality Inn, Ramada Ltd, Rodeway Inn, Sleep Inn, Travelodge
- Med: W: + Flagstaff Comm Hospital
- Other: W: ATM's, Banks, Cinema, Discount Tire, Kmart, Safeway, Staples, Target, New Frontiers Nat'l Foods, Wal-Mart, Walgreen's, Lowell Observatory, to US 66: Woody Mountain Campground & RV Park▲, Rt 66 RV & Auto Serv Center

(340B) Jct I-40, W to Kingman, to LA

(340A) Jct I-40, E to Albuquerque

339 Lake Mary Rd, Mormon Lake (NB)
- Gas: E: Mobil◇
- Food: E: Belgium Bistro
- Lodg: E: AZ Mtn Inn-Cabin Rentals

337 AZ 89A S, Flagstaff Airport, Pulliam Airport, Sedona, Oak Creek Canyon
- Other: E: Flagstaff Pulliam Airport✈
- W: Fort Tuthill/Coconino Co Park/RVDump, MIL/Fort Tuthill Rec Area/Luke Air Force Base

333 Kachina Blvd, Mountainaire Rd
- Gas: W: Pic-N-Run
- Food: W: Subway

331 Kelly Canyon Rd, Flagstaff

328 Newman Park Rd

326 Willard Springs Rd, Flagstaff

322 Pinewood Rd, Mormon Lake Rd, Frontage Rd, Munds Park
- FStop: E: Woody's/Chevron
- Gas: E: Chevron, Exxon◇
- Food: E: Lone Pines Restaurant
- Lodg: E: Motel in the Pines
- Other: E: Pines RV Camping▲
- W: Munds RV Resort/RVDump▲

320 Schnebly Hill Rd, Sedona

EXIT	ARIZONA

317 Fox Ranch Rd, Sedona

315 Rocky Park Rd

(313) Scenic View/Safety Pullout (SB)

306 Stoneman Lake Rd, Sedona

(300) Runaway Truck Ramp (SB)

298 AZ 179, Rimrock, Sedona, Oak Creek Canyon (Serv NW in Sedona)

(296) Rest Area (Both dir) (RR, Phone, Picnic, Vend)

293 CR 30, Cornville Rd, Cornville, Rimrock, Lake Montezuma
- Gas: E: Xpress Gas
- W: 76
- Food: E: McGuireville Café
- Other: E: Rimrock Airport✈, Montezuma Well National Monument, Auto Service Center

289 Middle Verde Rd, Camp Verde
- FStop: E: Texaco Star Mart
- Gas: E: Mobil◇, Shell
- Food: E: Café, Sonic
- Lodg: E: Cliff Castle Lodge & Casino
- Other: E: Montezuma Castle Nat'l Monument, Krazy K RV Park▲, RVDump/Texaco
- W: Camp Verde RV Resort▲, Distant Drums RV Resort▲, Camp Verde Indian Reservation

287 AZ 260, AZ 279, to AZ 89A, Camp Verde, to Cottonwood, Payson, Jerome, Clarkdale
- TStop: E: Camp Verde Shell #48
- Gas: E: ArcoAmPm, Chevron
- W: Chevron
- Food: E: Burger King, Denny's, McDonald's, Taco Bell, Subway/Shell
- W: Wendy's/Chevron
- Lodg: E: Comfort Inn, Days Inn, Territorial Town Inn, Microtel
- Other: E: Basha's, Banks, LP/RVDump/Shell, Trails End RV Park▲, Clear Creek RV Park▲, to Zane Grey RV Park▲
- W: Dead Horse Ranch State Park▲, Slide Rock State Park, Camp Verde RV Resort▲, Out of Africa Wildlife Park

285 General Crook Trail, Camp Verde
- Other: E: Fort Verde State Park▲, Trail End RV Park▲, to Zane Grey RV Park▲

(280) Safety Pullout (NB)

278 AZ 169, Cherry Rd, Mayer, to Prescott, Dewey

268 Dugas Rd, Orme Rd, Mayer
- Other: E: Agua Fria Nat'l Monument

262 AZ 69N, Mayer, Cordes Junction, Cordes Lake Rd, Prescott (NB)

262AB AZ 69N, Cordes Junction, Cordes Lake Rd, Arcosanti, Prescott (SB)
- FStop: E: Shell Travel Center #323

◇ = Regular Gas Stations with Diesel ▲ = RV Friendly Locations ♥ = Pet Friendly Locations
RED PRINT SHOWS LARGE VEHICLE PARKING/ACCESS ON SITE OR NEARBY BROWN PRINT SHOWS CAMPGROUNDS/RV PARKS

INTERSTATE 17 N/S

EXIT		ARIZONA
	Gas	E: Chevron
	Food	E: CJ Diner, McDonald's, Papa's Place, Subway/Shell
		W: Blondie's Kitchen
	Lodg	E: Cordes Junction Motel & RV Park▲
		W: Teskey's T Tumble 7 Motel
259		Bloody Basin Rd, Crown King
	Other	W: Horse Thief Basin Rec Area
256		Badger Springs Rd, Mayer
(252)		Rest Area (Both dir) (RR, Phone, Picnic, Vend, Scenic View)
248		Bumble Bee Rd, Crown King Rd, Black Canyon City
244		AZ 17 Bus, Black Canyon City, Clearwater Canyon Rd
	Gas	E: Chevron◊, Shell
	Food	E: Medicine Horse Café, School Peak Steak House
	Other	W: Bradshaw Mountain RV Resort▲
242		AZ 17 Bus, Rock Springs Rd, Black Canyon City
	Gas	W: Chevron◊
	Food	W: Rock Springs Café
	Other	E: Black Canyon City KOA▲
		W: Bradshaw Mountain RV Resort▲
236		Table Mesa Rd, New River
232		New River Rd, New River
229		Anthem Way, Phoenix
	Gas	E: Mobil◊
		W: Chevron, Mobil
	Food	E: McDonald's, Pizza Hut, Quiznos, Starbucks, Subway, Taco del Mar
		W: Burger King, Blimpie, Denny's, Del Taco, Fresca's Mex Grill, Papa John's, Taco Bell, Villa Pizza
	Lodg	W: Comfort Suites, Hampton Inn
	Other	E: Banks, Safeway, Osco, Walgreen's
		W: Anthem Outlets Mall, U-Haul, Tires, Wal-Mart sc, ATM, Bank, Ace
227		Daisy Mountain Dr, Phoenix
225		Pioneer Rd, Phoenix
	Other	W: Pioneer Living History Museum, Pioneer RV Park▲
223		AZ 74, Carefree Hwy, Phoenix, to Carefree, Wickenburg
	Gas	E: Chevron
	Food	E: McDonald's
	Other	E: Albertson's, Banks, to Cave Creek Rec Area/Maricopa Co Park▲,
		W: to Pleasant Harbor RV Resort▲, to Lake Pleasant Regional Park/Maricopa Co Park▲
218		Happy Valley Rd, Phoenix
	Food	E: Jack in the Box, Panda Express, Red Robin, Starbucks, TGI Friday
	Other	E: Lowe's, Staples, Wal-Mart sc
217		Pinnacle Peak Rd, Phoenix
	Food	W: Blimpie, KFC, McDonald's, Subway
	Other	W: Banks, ATM's, Adobe Dam Rec Area, Gray Mobile Tire Service, Thunderbird Park, Golf Course

Personal Notes

EXIT		ARIZONA
217B		Deer Valley Rd, Rose Garden Ln, Phoenix, Deer Valley Airport
	Gas	E: Circle K, Exxon, Texaco
		W: ArcoAmPm, Circle K, Texaco
	Food	E: Burger King, Jack in the Box, McDonald's, Sonic, Taco Bell, Wendy's
		W: Cracker Barrel, Denny's, Waffle House
	Lodg	W: Days Inn, Extended Stay America
	Other	E: Deserts Edge RV Village▲, Phoenix Metro RV Park▲, Phoenix Deer Valley Muni Airport✈, Auto Repair Services
		W: Ace, Auto Repairs, AutoZone, Walgreen's, Desert Sands RV Park▲, N Phoenix RV Park▲
217A		Rose Garden Lane (NB)
	Food	W: Baskin Robbins, Black Angus, 5 & Diner, Wendy's
	Lodg	E: Sea Castle Resort
		W: Country Inn, Extended Stay America
	Med	W: + John Lincoln Hospital
	Other	W: ATM, Bank
215		AZ 101
214		Yorkshire Dr (SB), Union Hills Dr (NB), Phoenix
	Gas	E: 7-11, Circle K/Shell, Shamrock
	Gas	W: Circle K, Mobil
	Food	E: Four Bros Pizza, KFC, Subway, Taco Bell
		W: 19th Hole, Bamboo Grill, Charley's, Chili's, Jack in the Box, Panda Express, McDonald's, Souper Salad, Subway

EXIT		ARIZONA
	Lodg	W: Best Western, Budget Suites, Country Inn, Days Inn, Marriott, Sleep Inn, Wyndham
	Med	W: + John C Lincoln Hospital
	Other	E: Frye's, Safeway
		W: AMC Theatres Deer Valley 30, Univ of Phoenix, Costco, NAPA, PetSmart♥, Target, Walgreen's, Desert Shadows RV Resort▲
212		W Bell Rd, Phoenix, Glendale, Scottsdale, to Sun City
	Gas	E: Chevron◊, Exxon, Mobil
		W: 76, Chevron◊, Mobil
	Food	E: Black Bear Diner, Burger Mania, Coco's, Jack in the Box, Long John Silver, McDonalds, Quiznos, Waffle House, Wendy's
		W: Applebee's, Burger King, Carl's Jr, Denny's, Good Egg, Garden of Eden, Hooters, Hometown Buffet, Pizza Hut, Kyoto Bowl, Native New Yorker, Thai, Sizzler, Subway, Village Inn
	Lodg	E: Best Western, Comfort Inn, Fairfield Inn, Motel 6♥
		W: Red Roof Inn♥, Studio 6
	Other	E: Auto Dealers, Checker Auto Parts, Osco, U-Haul, Wal-Mart sc, Sam's Club, Turf Paradise Racetrack, Rental Cars
	Other	W: Fry's, Cinema 8, Banks, ATM's, Rental Cars, Bell Canyon Pavilions, Albertson's, Firestone
211		Greenway Rd
	Gas	E: Circle K
		W: FastGas
	Food	E: Domino's, Rest/LQ Inn
		W: Cousins Subs, Famous Sam's Rest, Deli, Wendy's
	Lodg	E: Embassy Suites, La Quinta Inn♥
	Other	E: Cave Creek Muni Golf Course, Turf Paradise Race Track
		W: AZ State Univ W, Univ of Phx, Penske Auto Center, Grocery
210		Thunderbird Rd (SB)
	Gas	E: Circle K, Exxon
		W: QT
	Food	E: Jack in the Box, Pizza Hut, Wendy's
		W: Fazoli's, McDonald's
	Lodg	W: Hawthorne Suites
	Other	E: Home Depot, Jiffy Lube, Safeway, Walgreen's
		W: Lowe's, Best Buy, Banks, ATM, Fry's, Diesel Express
209		Cactus Rd, Phoenix
	Gas	W: 7-11, Chevron
	Food	W: Denny's, Stackers, Rest/RL Hotel
	Lodg	W: Ramada Plaza, Red Lion Hotel
	Other	W: Basha's, Food City, Bank, ATM
208		Peoria Ave
	Gas	W: 76, Chevron, Exxon, Mobil
	Food	E: Fajita's, Garden Fresh Rest, Lone Star Steakhouse, Pappadeaux, Outback Steakhouse, TGI Friday
		W: Burger King, Black Angus Steakhouse, Chipolte Mexican Grill, Coco's, El Torito, Olive Garden, Red Lobster, Sizzler, Starbucks, Souper Salad, Wendy's, Rest/Prem Inn

◊ = Regular Gas Stations with Diesel ▲ = RV Friendly Locations ♥ = Pet Friendly Locations
RED PRINT SHOWS LARGE VEHICLE PARKING/ACCESS ON SITE OR NEARBY BROWN PRINT SHOWS CAMPGROUNDS/RV PARKS

Page 85

N I-17

EXIT	ARIZONA
	Lodg E: AmeriSuites, Candlewood Suites, Comfort Suites, Homewood, Crowne Plaza, Extended Stay, Wellesley Inn
	W: Premier Inn, Sheraton
	Other W: Castles N' Coasters Theme Park, Firestone, Metro Center Mall, Devry Univ, Enterprise RAC, Staples, Banks, ATMs, Trader Joe's
207	**Dunlap Ave, Black Canyon Hwy**
	Gas E: 76, Shell◊
	W: Circle K, Exxon, Chevron
	Food E: Fuddrucker's, Outback Steakhouse, Lone Star Steakhouse, Sweet Tomato
	W: Denny's, Subway
	Lodg E: Courtyard, Mainstay Suites, Parkway Inn
	W: Sheraton
	Med E: + Hospital
	Other E: ATM, Bank, Auto Repair, Firestone, Mall, Conference Center, Royal Palm Campground▲
	W: Office Max, U-Haul, ATM, Banks
206	**Northern Ave**
	Gas E: Circle K, Mobil, Shell◊
	W: ArcoAmPm, Circle K
	Food E: Burger King, Denny's, El Pollo Loco, McDonald's, Mr Sushi, Pizza Hut, Subway, Starbucks, Yesterday's
	W: Bobby Q BBQ, Furr's Cafeteria, DQ, Village Inn
	Lodg E: Best Western, Hampton Inn
	W: Motel 6♥, Residence Inn, Super 8
	Other E: Albertson's, Walgreen's, US Post Office, Sun City RV
	Other W: Kmart, Dinner Theatre, Vet♥
205	**Glendale Ave, Phoenix**
	Gas W: Circle K, Exxon, Grand Serv Stn
	Food W: Jack in the Box, Pancho Villa, Lenny's
	Med E: + Community Hospital Med Center
	Other W: Greyhound, Auto Repairs, Bank, Covered Wagon RV Park▲, RVDump/Giant Grand Serv Stn
204	**Bethany Home Rd**
	Gas E: ArcoAmPm, Circle K, Shell
	W: Chevron◊, Exxon
	Food E: McDonald's, Subway, Whataburger
	Med E: + Community Hospital Med Center, + Phoenix Baptist Hospital
	Other E: Big Lots, Banks, ATMs, Chris Town Mall, Cinemas
	W: Food City, Bank, ATM, Jiffy Lube, Auto Repair, Welcome Home RV Park▲
203	**Camelback Rd, Phoenix**
	Gas E: ArcoAmPm, Circle K
	W: Mobil, QT
	Food E: Burger King, Country Boys, Denny's, Pizza Hut
	W: Bistro, Denny's, Jack in the Box, Taco Bell, Steakhouse, McDonald's
	Lodg W: Comfort Inn♥
	Other E: Auto Dealers, Auto Repairs, ATMs, Banks, Discount Tire, Grand Canyon Univ, Firestone, Walgreen's, Budget Car & Truck
	W: ATM, Flea Market, Enterprise RAC, Northwest Village

EXIT	ARIZONA
202	**Indian School Rd**
	Gas E: ArcoAmPm
	W: Circle K, Exxon, Shell
	Food E: Filiberto's, Jimmy's, Pizza Hut
	W: JB's, Wendy's
	Lodg W: Motel 6♥, Super 8
	Med E: + VA Hospital
	Other E: Albertson's, ATM, Banks
	W: ATM, Banks, Grocery, Desert Shadows Travel Trailer Resort▲
201	**US 60, Thomas Rd, Grand Ave**
	Gas E: Circle K
	W: QT
	Food E: Arby's, Denny's, Jack in the Box, Taco Bell, McDonald's
	W: Burger King
	Med E: + St Joseph's Hospital
	Lodg E: Days Inn, La Quinta Inn♥
	Other E: Coliseum, Municipal Golf Course, Ryder, State Fairgrounds, to Park Central Mall
	W: CarWash, Hertz RAC, Bank, Auto Repairs
200B	**McDowell Rd, Van Buren St**
	Gas W: Circle K, ArcoAmPm
	Food W: Subs
	Lodg W: Travelodge
	Other W: Truck & Trailer Repair, Diesel Service
(200A)	**Jct I-10, E-Tucson, W-Los Angeles**
199B	**Adams St, Van Buren St (NB) Jefferson St, State Capitol (SB)**
	Gas E: Circle K
	W: Circle K
	Food E: Jack in the Box, McDonald's
	W: Mexican Rest
	Lodg E: Sandman Motel
199A	**Grant St, Buckeye Rd**
	Gas E: Circle K
198	**Buckeye Rd (NB)**
197	**US 60, 19th Ave, Durango St**
	Gas E: Circle K
	Food E: Whataburger
196	**7th St, Central Ave, Phoenix**
	Med E: + Phoenix Memorial Hospital
	Other E: Amtrak Station
195B	**7th St, Central Ave**
	Gas E: Circle K, Exxon, Trailside Gas◊
	W: Total
	Food E: McDonald's, Lebanese Rest, Taco Bell, Rest/EZ8
	Lodg E: EZ 8 Motel
	Med E: + Phoenix Memorial Hospital
195A	**16th St (SB, diff reaccess)**
(194)	**Jct I-10 W, to Sky Harbor Int'l Airport, E to Globe, Tucson**

(I-17 Begins/Ends Jct I-10, exit #150A)
(MOUNTAIN TIME ZONE, NO DST)

🎧 ARIZONA

Begin Northbound I-17 at Phoenix, AZ to Jct I-40 near Flagstaff, AZ.

Page 86   ◊ = Regular Gas Stations with Diesel   ▲ = RV Friendly Locations   ♥ = Pet Friendly Locations
RED PRINT SHOWS LARGE VEHICLE PARKING/ACCESS ON SITE OR NEARBY   BROWN PRINT SHOWS CAMPGROUNDS/RV PARKS

EXIT	ARIZONA
	Begin Southbound I-19 at Jct I-10 in Tucson, AZ to Nogales @ AZ/MX Border

ARIZONA

(MOUNTAIN TIME ZONE, NO DST)
(Begins/Ends Jct I-10, Exit #260)

NOTE: I-19 mileposts signed in km

(101B)		Jct I-10W, Phoenix (NB)
(101A)		Jct I-10E, El Paso (NB)
99		AZ 86, Ajo Way, Old Tucson, Desert Museum, Tucson
	FStop	W: (7 mi) Superstop #619/Mobil
	Gas	E: Circle K, Star Mart W: Circle K, Chevron, Whiting
	Food	E: Buffalo Bell, Long John Silver, La Bella China, Pizza Hut, Subway, Taco Bell, Weinerschnitzel W: Bamboo Terrace, Burger King, Church's Chicken
	Med	E: + Pueblo Medical Clinic, + US Vets Hospital, + Golden West Med Center, + Madera Med Center
	Other	E: ATMs, Banks, Auto Repairs, IGA W: ATMs, Auto Repairs, Banks, Fry's, Desert Pueblo MH Park▲, Tucson Mountain RV Park▲, Rincon Country West RV Resort▲
98		Irvington Rd, Tucson
	Gas	E: Circle K, Chevron W: Chevron
	Food	E: Little Mexico Rest, Vida Rock Cafe W: China Olive Buffet, El Presidente Family Rest, McDonald's
	Med	E: + El Rio Health Center
	Other	E: Bus Station, ATM, Auto Repairs, Bank, Grocery, Rodeo Grounds, Tires, to Oasis RV Center W: Auto Repairs
95		Valencia Rd, Tucson Airport, Pascula Yaqui Pueblo
	Gas	E: Whiting W: Chevron
	Food	E: China Bay, DQ, Diego's, Jack in the Box, McDonald's, Whataburger W: Arby's, Denny's, McDonald's, Pizza Hut, Taco Bell, Wendy's
	Other	E: Cinema, Auto Service, Checker Auto, Bank, Grocery, Jiffy Lube, to Tucson Int'l Airport→ W: ATMs, Banks, Auto Repairs, Big O Tires, Enterprise RAC, Grocery, Tohono O'odham Indian Reservation, Wal-Mart sc
92		San Xavier Rd, San Xavier Mission, Tucson
	Other	E: to Mission View RV Resort▲, to Desert Diamond Casino W: San Xavier Indian Reservation, San Xavier Del Bac Mission
87		Papago Rd, Sahuarita
80		Pima Mine Rd, Sahuarita
	Other	E: Desert Diamond Casino
75		Helmut Peak Rd, Sahuarita Rd, Sahuarita, to I-19 Bus
69		Bus 19N (NB), Duval Mine Rd, US 89N, Green Valley
	Gas	W: Circle K

EXIT	ARIZONA
	Food	E: Pizza Hut
		W: Manuel's Mex Rest
	Lodg	W: Horizons
	Other	E: Bank, Grocery, Wal-Mart sc W: Auto Repairs, Big O Tires, Cinema, CarWash, Green Valley RV Resort▲, Titan Missile Silo-Natl Historic Landmark & Museum
65		Esperanza Blvd, Green Valley
	Gas	E: Texaco W: Exxon
	Food	W: AZ Family Rest, Diner, Rest/BW
	Lodg	W: Best Western
	Other	W: ATM, Banks, Green Valley Mall
63		Continental Rd, Madera Canyon Rec Area, Green Valley
	Gas	W: Super Center
	Food	W: Mama's Kitchen, McDonald's, Mesquite Willy's Rib & Steakhouse, KFC, Taco Bell
	Other	W: Auto Repairs, ATMs, Banks, Firestone, Safeway
56		Canoa Rd, Green Valley
(53)		Canoa Rest Area (Both dir) (RR, Phone, Picnic, Vend)
48		Arivaca Rd, Frontage Rd, Amado
	Other	E: De Anza Trails RV Resort▲, Mountain View RV Ranch▲

EXIT	ARIZONA
42		Agua Linda Rd, Frontage Rd
	Other	E: De Anza Trails RV Resort▲, Mountain View RV Ranch▲
40		Chavez Siding Rd, Amado, to Tubac
	Other	E: Tubac Golf Resort
34		Tubac, Tubac Presidio State Park
	Other	E: Tubac Presidio Hist State Park
29		Tumacacori, Carmen
	Other	E: Tumacacori National Hist Park
25		Palo Parado Rd, Rio Rico
22		Peck Canyon Rd Border Patrol Check Point (NB)
17		Rio Rico Dr, Yavapi Dr, Rio Rico
	Gas	W: Chevron
	Other	W: IGA, US Post Office, Rio Rico Resort & Country Club
12		AZ 289, Ruby Rd, Nogales Ranger Station, Rio Rico, Pena Blanca Lake Rec Area
	TStop	E: Pilot Travel Center #279 (Scales)
	Food	E: Wendy's/Pilot TC
	Other	E: Laundry/WiFi/Pilot TC W: to Pena Blanca Rec Area
8		Bus 19, Grand Ave, to AZ 82E, Patagonia (SB, Left Exit)
	TStop	E: Nogales Truck Stop (Scales)
	Gas	E: Circle K
	Food	E: Pizza, Mexican Rest
	TServ	E: 51 Diesel Truck Repair
	Other	E: Auto Service Center, Tires, Mi Casa RV Travel Park▲
4		AZ 189S, Mariposa Rd (SB, Border Truck Route)
	TStop	E: Nogales Truck Stop (Scales)
	Gas	E: Chevron
	Food	E: Rest/Nogales TS, Chinese, DQ, KFC, McDonald's, Rooster's Grill, Taco Bell, Yokohama Rice Bowl W: Carl's Jr, Famous Sam's Rest
	Lodg	E: Motel 6♥, Super 8
	TServ	E: Nogales TS/Tires
	Other	E: Laundry/Nogales TS, Auto Repairs, ATMs, Auto Dealers, Banks, Kmart, Walgreen's, Wal-Mart sc W: Auto Dealers
1B		Western Ave, Nogales (Services E to Bus 19, US 89)
	Gas	E: Circle K
	Med	W: + Holy Cross Hospital
	Other	E: Galen's Auto & Truck Repair
1A		International St (SB)
(0)		Bus I-19, US 89, Downtown, Int'l Border, Frwy Ends, to US 82 (SB)
	Gas	E: Circle K, Shell
	Food	E: Jack in the Box, McDonald's
	Lodg	E: Dos Marias
	Other	E: ATMs, Auto Repairs, Banks, Grocery, Museum, Walgreen's, Vet♥, to Patagonia RV Park▲

NOTE: I-19 mileposts signed in km

(I-19 Begins/Ends in Nogales, AZ/MX Border)
(MOUNTAIN TIME ZONE, NO DST)

ARIZONA

Begin Northbound I-19 @ AZ/MX Border to Jct I-10, Exit #260 in Tucson, AZ

◆ = Regular Gas Stations with Diesel   ▲ = RV Friendly Locations   ♥ = Pet Friendly Locations
RED PRINT SHOWS LARGE VEHICLE PARKING/ACCESS ON SITE OR NEARBY   BROWN PRINT SHOWS CAMPGROUNDS/RV PARKS

Page 87

INTERSTATE 20 E

Begin Eastbound I-20 from Jct I-10 near Van Horn, TX to Jct I-55 in Jackson, MS.

TEXAS
(Begins/Ends I-10, Exit #186)
(Recommendation—Keep Fueled Up!)

EXIT		TEXAS
3		Stocks Rd, Pecos
7		Johnson Rd, Pecos
13		McAlpine Rd, Pecos
22		FM 2903, Centre St, Pecos, Toyah
(25)		Picnic Area (EB), Parking Area (WB)
29		CR 211, Shaw Rd, Pecos
33		FM 869, Pecos
37		I-20E Bus, US 80, Pecos
	Lodg	N: Budget Inn
39		TX 17, Bickley Ave, Pecos, Fort Davis, Balmorhea
	Food	S: DQ
	Lodg	S: Best Western
40		Country Club Dr, Pecos
	Gas	S: Chevron
	Food	S: Subway/Chevron, Rest/BW
	Lodg	S: Best Western, Swiss Clock Inn
	Other	N: TX State Hwy Patrol
		S: Auto Dealers, Pecos Muni Airport, Trapark RV Park▲
42		US 285, Pecos, to Bus 20, Carlsbad, Ft Stockton, Pecos
	TStop	N: Flying J Travel Plaza #5260/Conoco (Scales)
	Gas	N: Chevron, Shell
	Food	N: Cookery/FastFood/FJ TP, McDonald's, Rest/QI
	Lodg	N: Motel 6♥, Oak Tree Inn, Quality Inn
	Other	N: Wal-Mart, Laundry/BarbSh/WiFi/LP/RVDump/FJ TP
44		Collie Rd, Pecos
49		FM 516, Barstow
52		20 Bus, Barstow (WB)
58		Frontage Rd, Barstow
66		FM 1927, TX 115, Barstow, to Pyote, Kermit
(69)		Ward Co Rest Area (Both dir) (RR, Phone, Picnic, WiFi) (EB: Next Rest Area 122 mi)
70		Spur 65, CR 415, Monahans

EXIT		TEXAS
73		FM 1219, Monahans, Wickett
	FStop	N: Allsup's #283/Shell
	TStop	S: SunMart #112/Mobil
	Gas	N: Chevron
	Food	S: Subway/SunMart
	Other	S: RVDump/SunMart
76		20E Bus, Spur 57, Monahans
	Other	N: Million Barrel Museum
79		Loop 464
	Gas	N: Exxon
	Other	N: Ray Hurd Memorial Airport
80		TX 18, Stockton Ave, Monahans, to Kermit, Fort Stockton
	TStop	S: Town & Country #82/Fina
	Gas	N: Chevron◊, Exxon
		S: Kent Kwik
	Food	N: Bar H Steaks, DQ, McDonald's
		S: FastFood/T&C, Taco Bell
	Lodg	N: Sunset Motel & RV Park▲
		S: Best Value Inn
	Other	N: ATMs, Banks, Grocery, Country Club RV Resort▲
		S: Auto Dealers
83		20W Bus, Monahans
86		TX 41, Monahans
	Other	N: Monahans Sandhills State Park▲
93		FM 1053, Odessa, Fort Stockton
101		FM 1601, Odessa, Penwell
(103)		Parking Area (Both dir)
(104)		Weigh Station (EB)
104		FM 866, FM 1936, Meteor Crater Rd, Odessa, Goldsmith
108		Moss Ave, Meteor Crater
	Other	S: Meteor Crater, Meteor & Crater Museum
112		FM 1936, Odessa
	TStop	N: Odessa Truck Stop/Drivers Travel Mart #405/Citgo (Scales)
	Food	N: FastFood/Drivers TM
	Tires	N: Driver TM
	Tserv	S: Kenworth
	Other	N: Laundry/Driver TM, Auto Repairs, Grocery
113		TX 302, Lp 338, Odessa, Kermit, Meteor Crater Rd
115		FM 1882, County Rd W, Frontage Rd, Odessa
	TStop	N: Town & Country #105
		S: Love's Travel Stop #339 (Scales)
	Food	N: Country Cookin'/T&C
		S: McDonald's/Subway/Love's TS

EXIT		TEXAS
	Med	N: + Tx Tech Univ Health Center
	Other	S: Laundry/WiFi/RVDump/Love's TS
116		US 385, Andrews, Crane
	Gas	N: Town & Country
		S: Fina, Shell
	Food	N: DQ
	Lodg	N: Best Western, Delux Inn, Villa West Inn
		S: Motel 6♥
	TServ	N: Diesel Services
	Med	N: + Hospital
	Other	N: Billy Sims Trailer Town
118		FM 3503, Grandview Ave
	Gas	N: Fina◊
	TServ	N: Cummins Southern Plains, Goodyear Truck Tire Center, Freightliner/Peterbilt, W TX Volvo, Mack, Warren CAT
		S: Diesel Service, Truck & Tire Repair
120		JBS Pkwy (WB)
121		Lp 338, Odessa
	Gas	N: 7-11
	Food	N: Denny's, McDonald's
	Lodg	N: Days Inn, Elegante Hotel, Holiday Inn Express, La Quinta Inn♥, Motel 6♥, Super 8
	Other	N: Presidential Museum, Univ of Tx/Permian Basin
		(Services on TX 191—3 mi W)
	Food	Chili's, Logan's, On the Border, Quiznos
	Lodg	Fairfield Inn, Hampton Inn
	Other	Albertson's, Home Depot, Sam's Club, Wal-Mart sc
126		FM 1788, Midland Int'l Airport, Warfield
	TStop	N: Pilot Travel Center #257 (Scales), Warfield Truck Terminal/SunMart #109/Mobil (Scales)
	Food	N: McDonald's/Pilot TC, Rest/Subway/SunMart
	Lodg	N: Ramada Inn
	TWash	N: SunMart
	TServ	N: SunMart/Tires, Warren CAT
	Other	N: Laundry/Pilot TC, Laundry/BarbSh/SunMart, Western Auto, Midland Airport, Museum, Rental Cars, Water Wonderland, Midessa Oil Patch RV Park▲
131		TX 158, Lp 250, Midland
	FStop	N: Flying J Cardlock
	Lodg	N: Travelodge
	Other	N: Auto Repairs, Sports Complex, Midland RV Campground▲, Pecan Grove RV Park▲
134		Midkiff Rd, Midland
	FStop	N: Town & Country #122/Chevron
	Food	N: Subway/T&C

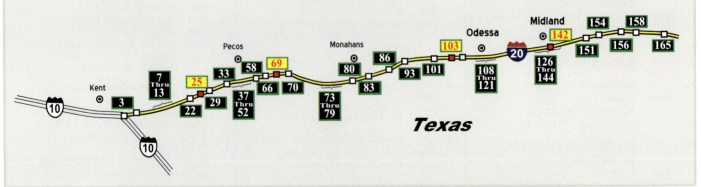

◊ = Regular Gas Stations with Diesel   ▲ = RV Friendly Locations   ♥ = Pet Friendly Locations
RED PRINT SHOWS LARGE VEHICLE PARKING/ACCESS ON SITE OR NEARBY   BROWN PRINT SHOWS CAMPGROUNDS/RV PARKS

EXIT		TEXAS
	Lodg	N: Days Inn, Executive Inn, La Quinta Inn♥, Sleep Inn
	Med	N: + Midland Memorial Hospital
	Other	N: Auto Dealers, Bo's RV Center
136		TX 349, Midland, Rankin, Lamesa
	TStop	S: Travel Mart #10/Exxon
	Gas	N: Phillips 66◆, NAPA Gas, Murphy◆
		S: Exxon, Texaco, Town & Country◆
	Food	N: McDonald's, IHOP, Sonic, Starbucks
		S: Burger King/Exxon
	Lodg	N: Comfort Inn, Howard Johnson, Super 8
	AServ	N: Harold Logan Auto Service
	Other	N: Auto & Tire Services, Advance Auto, CarWash, Convention Center, Discount Tire, Dollar Tree, Family Dollar, IGA, Museum, Wal-Mart sc
		S: Laundry/Travel Mart
137		Old Lamesa Rd
138		TX 158, FM 715, Midland, Greenwood, Garden City
	FStop	S: Town & Country #107
	Gas	N: Shell◆
	Food	N: KD's BBQ, Whataburger
		S: Subway/T&C
(142)		Picnic Area (Both dir)
143		Frontage Rd (EB)
144		20 Bus, TX 250 Lp, Midland
151		FM 829
154		20E Bus, US 80, Stanton
156		TX 137, Stanton, Lamesa
	TStop	S: Town & Country #209/P66 (DAND)
	Food	S: DQ, Sonic, CountryCookin/Subway/TC
158		Bus 20W, Lp 154, Stanton
165		FM 818, Big Spring
(168)		Picnic Area (Both dir)
169		FM 2599, Big Spring
171		Moore Field Rd
172		Cauble Rd, Big Spring
174		20E Bus, US 80, Big Spring
	Gas	S: Shell◆
	Food	S: IHOP
	Med	S: + Scenic Mountain Medical Center
	Other	S: Big Spring McMahon-Wrinkle Airport✈, to Big Spring State Park▲
176		Andrews Hwy, TX 176, Big Spring (Access to Ex #177 Services)
	FStop	S: Town & Country #103/Chevron
	Food	S: FastFood/T&C
	Lodg	N: Advantage Inn, Whitten Inn
	Other	S: RVDump/T&C
177		US 87, San Angelo, Lamesa
	FStop	S: Town & Country #103/Chevron
	TStop	N: Travel Center of America/P66 (Scales)
	Gas	N: Exxon
		S: Fina, HEB
	Food	N: CountryFare/Popeye's/Subway/TA TC
		S: Country Kitchen, DQ, McDonald's, Wendy's
	Lodg	N: Econo Lodge♥, Motel 6♥
		S: Days Inn, Holiday Inn Express
	TServ	N: TA TC/Tires
		S: Tx Truck Tire
	Med	N: + Big Spring State Hospital

EXIT		TEXAS
	Other	N: Laundry/WiFi/TA TC
		S: Big Spring Harley Davidson, Banks, Grocery, Museum, to appr 4 mi: Texas RV Park of Big Spring▲
178		TX 350, Snyder
	Gas	N: Shell◆
	Other	N: Don's Truck & Tire Service
179		20 Bus, US 80, Big Spring
	Gas	S: Fina, Texaco
	Food	S: DQ, Denny's, Café, TNT BBQ
	Lodg	S: Comfort Inn, Inn at Big Spring, Quality Inn
	Other	S: Bowling Alley
181A		FM 700, Airport, Big Spring
	Med	S: + Hospital
	Other	S: Big Spring State Park▲
181B		Refinery Rd
182		Midway Rd, Big Spring
	Other	S: Suburban East RV & Mobile Park▲
184		Moss Lake Rd, Sand Springs
	Gas	N: Phillips 66, Fina◆
	Other	N: Pioneer RV Park▲
		S: Whip In RV Park▲, Suburban East RV & Mobile Park▲, Big Spring Mall
186		Salem Rd, Sand Spring
188		FM 820, Coahoma Rd, Coahoma
	Gas	N: Town & Country
	Food	N: DQ, Country Cookin'
189		McGregor Rd
190		Snyder Field Rd
(191)		Howard Co Rest Area (EB) (RR, Phone, Picnic, WiFi)

EXIT		TEXAS
192		FM 821
194		E Howard Field Rd
194A		E Howard Field Rd
194B		Frontage Rd, Coahoma
195		Frontage Rd
199		Latan Rd, Westbrook
200		Conway Rd, CR 270
(204)		Mitchell Co Rest Area (WB) (RR, Phone, Picnic, WiFi)
206		FM 670, 20 Bus, Westbrook
	FStop	N: Citgo
207		20 Bus, Westbrook
209		Dorn Rd
210		FM 2836
	Gas	S: T & C/Fina◆
212		FM 1229, Westbrook
213		20E Bus, CR 204, Enderly Rd, Colorado City (Serv S 3-4 mi)
215		FM 3525, Rogers Rd
	Med	N: + Hospital
216		TX 208, Hickory St, Colorado City, Snyder
	FStop	N: T & C/Chevron
	Food	N: DQ, Subway
		S: Pizza Hut, Sonic
	Lodg	N: Days Inn♥
		S: American Inn♥
	Med	N: + Hospital
217		TX 208S, San Angelo
219		20 Bus, Colorado City (EB)
219A		Country Club Rd (WB)
219B		20 Bus W, Colorado City (WB)
220		FM 1899
221		Lasky Rd
223		Lucas Rd
224		20 Bus, TX 316 Spur, Loraine
225		FM 644S
226A		FM 644N
226B		CR 438, Loraine
227		Narrell Rd, Loraine
(228)		Picnic Area (Both dir)
230		FM 1230, Roscoe
235		20 Bus, Roscoe
	TStop	S: 235 Travel Stop
	Food	S: Rest/235 TS
236		FM 608, Roscoe
	FStop	N: Town & Country #226
	Gas	N: Shell
	Food	N: FastFood/T&C
		S: DQ
	Other	S: CB Shop
237		Cemetery Rd
238A		US 84W, Roscoe, Lubbock, Snyders

◆ = Regular Gas Stations with Diesel   ▲ = RV Friendly Locations   ♥ = Pet Friendly Locations
RED PRINT SHOWS LARGE VEHICLE PARKING/ACCESS ON SITE OR NEARBY   BROWN PRINT SHOWS CAMPGROUNDS/RV PARKS

Page 89

INTERSTATE 20 W/E

EXIT	TEXAS
238B	Blackland Rd
238C	Frontage Rd
239	May Rd, CR 256
240	TX 170, Lp 170, City Airport
Other	N: Avenger Field Airport✈
	S: Sweetwater RV Park▲
241	20 Bus, TX 432 Lp, Sweetwater
Other	S: Chaparrel RV Park▲, Rolling Plains RV Park▲
242	Hopkins Rd, Sweetwater
TStop	S: Travel Center of America/Conoco (Scales)(DAND)
Food	S: Rest/Popeye's/PHut/TA TC
TServ	S: TA TC/Tires
Other	S: Laundry/ChromeSh/WiFi/TA TC
243	Robert Lee St, Hillsdale Rd
Other	N: Family RV Center
244	TX 70S, TX 70 Bus, Lamar St, Sweetwater
Gas	N: Chevron◇, Fina◇, Murphy◇
	S: Chevron, Shell
Food	N: DQ, McDonald's, Wendy's
	S: Bud's BBQ, Jack's Family Steakhouse, Taco Bell
Lodg	N: Holiday Inn, Motel 6♥, La Quinta Inn♥, Super 8
	S: Best Western, Comfort Inn, Days Inn, Executive Inn, Holiday Inn Express, Quality Inn, Ranch House Motel, Super 8
Med	N: + Hospital
Other	N: A-1 Auto Parts, Lowe's, Pharmacy, Wal-Mart sc▲ Family RV Center
	S: Grocery, Kmart, Rolling Plains RV Park▲, Sweetwater RV Park▲
245	Arizona Ave
Med	N: + Hospital
Other	N: Family RV Center
246	Alabama Ave, CR 304
247	20 Bus, TX 70N, Sweetwater, Roby
249	FM 1856, Sweetwater
251	Eskota Rd, CR 277
255	Adrian Rd
256	Stink Creek Rd
(256)	Nolan Co Rest Area (Both dir) (RR, Phone, Picnic, Vend, WiFi)
258	White Flat Rd, Sweetwater
259	Sylvester Rd
261	20 Bus, Trent

EXIT	TEXAS
262	FM 1085
FStop	S: Fina/7-11
263	20 Bus, Trent
Other	N: Roadrunner RV Resort▲
264	Noodle Dome Rd
266	Derstine Rd
267	20 Bus, N 1st St, Merkel
269	FM 126, Kent St, Merkel
FStop	S: Skinny's Fina
Food	N: Subway
	S: DQ, Rest/Merkel Motel, Mesquite Bean BBQ, Pizza Pro
Lodg	N: Scottish Inn♥
	S: Merkel Motel
270	20 Bus, FM 1235, Merkel
TStop	S: Big Country Truck Stop/Shell
Gas	S: Conoco
Food	S: Rest/Big Country TS
	S: Holliday's Kitchen
Other	S: Laundry/Big Country TS
272	Wimberley Rd
274	Wells Lane
277	FM 707, I-20 Bus, Scott St, Abilene, Tye
TStop	N: Flying J Travel Plaza #5064/Shell (Scales)
Gas	S: Fina
Food	N: Country Market/FastFood/FJ TP
TServ	N: Peterbilt, Big Rig Lube
Other	N: Tye RV Park▲
	N: Laundry/BarbSh/WiFi/RVDump/LP/FJ TP
278	20 Bus, Spinks Rd, Market St, Tye
FStop	S: Top #18/Conoco
TStop	S: AmBest/Wes-T-Go Truck Stop/Conoco (Scales)
Food	S: Rest/FastFood/Wes-T-Go TS
Tires	S: Wes-T-Go TS
TServ	N: Volvo Mack
Other	N: Trailer Sales & Service
	S: Laundry/Wes-T-Go TS, Tye RV Park▲
280	Fulwiler Rd
282	FM 3438, Shirley Rd, Dyess AFB
Lodg	S: Motel 6♥
Other	S: Abilene KOA/RVDump▲, Kent's Harley Davidson
283A	US 83, 277S, Ballinger, San Angelo (WB Exit Left, Diff reaccess)
283B	US 83, 277N, Anson

EXIT	TEXAS
285	Old Anson Rd, Impact
Gas	N: Texaco◇
	S: Texaco◇
Lodg	N: Travel Inn
	S: Econo Lodge
286A	83 Bus, Abilene, Pine St
Gas	S: Diamond Shamrock, Fina
Lodg	S: Budget Host, Civil Plaza Hotel
Med	S: + Hendrick Medical Center
Other	N: Hardin Simmons Univ
286B	Abilene
286C	FM 600, W Lake Rd, Abilene
FStop	N: Allsup's #331/Exxon, Skinny's #77/Fina/7-11
Gas	S: Chevron◇
Food	N: FastFood/Skinny's, Denny's
Lodg	N: Best Western, La Quinta Inn♥, Super 8
288	TX 351, Abilene, Albany
Gas	N: Allsup's, Chevron, Murphy, Skinny's Fina
Food	N: Cracker Barrel, DQ, Oscar's, Skillets, Subway
Lodg	N: Comfort Inn, Days Inn, Executive Inn, Holiday Inn Express, Whitten Inn
Med	S: + Hendrick Medical Center
Other	N: Wal-Mart
	S: Abilene Christian College
290	TX 36, to Loop 322, Cross Plains, to Abilene Regional Airport
Other	S: Abilene Reg'l Airport✈, Zoo, Taylor Co Expo Center
292A	20 Bus, Abilene (WB Left Exit)
TServ	S: Young's Truck Service
292B	Elmdale Rd
Other	N: Big Country RV/RVDump
	S: Abilene RV Park▲, W TX RV, Duke's RV Repair
294	Buck Creek Rd, Clyde
Other	N: Buck Creek RV Park▲/RVDump
(296)	Callahan Co Rest Area (Both dir) (RR, Phone, Picnic, WiFi)
297	FM 603
299	FM 1707, S Hays Rd, CR 112N
300	FM 604N, Spur 189N, Clyde
Gas	S: Conoco, Shell
Food	S: Little Pit BBQ
Other	S: Laundromat, Arrowhead Campground▲, White's RV Park▲
301	FM 604S, Spur 189S, Clyde, Cherry Lane
Gas	N: Exxon
	S: Fina, Shell

◇ = Regular Gas Stations with Diesel   ▲ = RV Friendly Locations   ♥ = Pet Friendly Locations
RED PRINT SHOWS LARGE VEHICLE PARKING/ACCESS ON SITE OR NEARBY   BROWN PRINT SHOWS CAMPGROUNDS/RV PARKS

INTERSTATE 20 W/E — TEXAS

EXIT		
	Food	N: DQ, Little Pit BBQ, Sonic S: Pizza House, Subway, Whataburger
	TWash	S: 301 TW
	Other	N: U-Haul S: Auto Repairs, Bank, Family Dollar, Golf Course, IGA, Franklin RV Center
303		Union Hill Rd, CR 279, Clyde
306		20 Bus, FM 2047, Baird
	Other	N: Auto Dealers
307		US 283, Albany, Coleman
	Gas	S: Conoco
	Food	N: DQ
	Lodg	N: Baird Motor Inn & RV Park▲
	Other	N: Hanner RV
308		Bus 20, Baird
310		Finley Rd
313		FM 2228
316		Brushy Creek Rd, Baird
319		FM 880S, Putnam, Cross Plains
320		FM 880N, FM 2945N, Moran
322		Cooper Creek Rd
324		Scranton Rd
(327)		Picnic Area (EB)
(329)		Picnic Area (WB)
330		TX 206, Cross Plains, Cisco
	FStop	N: Chevron
	Food	N: White Elephant
	Lodg	N: Best Western, Best Value Inn
	Med	N: + Hospital
332		US 183, Cisco, Brownwood, Breckenridge, Albany
	FStop	S: Texas Express #10/Exxon
	Gas	N: Citgo
	Food	N: DQ, Sonic, Subway, Rest/Cisco MI S: FastFood/Tx Expr
	Lodg	N: Cisco Motor Inn♥, Days Inn
	TServ	N: Lee's Truck Service
	Other	N: Everett's RV Park▲
337		Spur 490, Cisco
	Other	N: Wild Country RV Resort▲
340		TX 6, Eastland, Gorman, Breckenridge
	TStop	S: Red Star Truck Terminal/Shell
	Gas	N: Chevron◆
	Food	S: Red Star Café/Red Star TS
	Med	N: + Hospital
	Other	N: Eastland Muni Airport✈
343		TX 112, FM 570, Eastland, Lake Leon
	Gas	N: Conoco, Fina, Shell S: Exxon
	Food	N: DQ, McDonald's, Rafter BBQ, Taco Bell, Sonic, Starbucks, Subway/Fina S: Pulido's Mexican, Burger King/Exxon
	Lodg	N: La Quinta Inn♥, Super 8 & RV Park▲ S: Budget Host Inn, Ramada Inn
	Med	N: + Hospital
	Other	N: Auto Dealers, Wal-Mart sc S: Auto Dealers
345		FM 3363, Olden (EB)
347		FM 3363, Olden (WB)

Personal Notes

EXIT		
349		FM 2461, Lp 254, US 80, Ranger College, Lake Leon
	TStop	N: Love's Travel Stop #270 (Scales)(DAND)
	Gas	S: Shell
	Food	N: Cattle Barron Rest, DQ, Godfather's/Subway/Godfathers/Love's TS S: Diner
	Lodg	N: Best Value Inn, Days Inn, Relax Inn
	Other	N: WiFi/Love's TS, RL RV Park▲, Ranger Muni Airport✈, ATMs, Banks, Auto Repairs, Grocery S: to appr 5mi: North Shore RV Park▲
351		Desdemona Blvd (EB)
352		Blundell St (WB)
354		Lp 254W, Ranger
358		Frontage Rd
361		TX 16, Ranger, Strawn, DeLeon
(362)		Parking Area (Both dir)
363		Tudor Rd Picnic Area (Both dir)
367		TX 108, FM 919, Mingus, Gordon, Bluff Dale, Stephenville
	Food	N: Smoke Stack S: New York Hill
370		TX 108, FM 919, Gordon, Stephenville
	FStop	N: Bar-B Travel Plaza/Citgo
	Gas	S: Exxon
	Food	N: Rest/FastFood/Bar-B TP
	Lodg	N: Longhorn Inn Motel

EXIT		
	TServ	N: Bar-B TP/Tires
373		TX 193, Gordon
376		Panama Rd, Blue Flat Rd
380		FM 4, Palo Pinto, Lipan-Santo
	Food	S: Sunday Creek Rest
	Other	S: Windmill Acres RV Park & Cafe▲
386		US 281, Stephenville, Mineral Wells
	FStop	N: Shell
	Gas	N: Fina
	Food	N: Subway/Shell
(390)		Palo Pinto Co Rest Area (Both dir) (RR, Phone, Picnic, Vend, WiFi)
391		Gilbert Pit Rd
394		FM 113, Millsap
	Other	N: Hillbilly Haven Campground▲, to 13mi Back Acre RV Park/RVDump▲
397		FM 1189, MillsapBrock
	Other	S: Oak Creek RV Park▲
402		Spur 312E, Weatherford (EB)
	Other	S: Buxton's Diamond B RV Park▲
403		Dennis Rd (WB)
	Other	N: Auto, Truck & Trailer Repair S: Buxton's Diamond B RV Park▲
406		Old Dennis Rd, S Bowie Dr, Weatherford
	TStop	N: Truck & Travel/Conoco (Scales) S: Pilot Travel Center #206 (Scales)
	Food	N: Rest/FastFood/Truck & Travel, Rest/Days Inn S: Wendy's/Pilot TC
	Lodg	N: QualityOne/Truck & Travel, Days Inn
	TServ	N: Truck & Travel/Tires S: Pilot TC/Tires
	Other	N: CB/RVDump/Truck&Travel S: Laundry/WiFi/Pilot TC
407		TX 171, FM 1884, Tin Top Rd (EB) (Access Ex #408 Services)
408		TX 171, FM 51, FM 1884, Tin Top Rd, Weatherford, Granbury, Cleburne
	Gas	N: Exxon◆, Mobil, Murphy S: Exxon, Shell◆
	Food	N: Applebee's, Bakers Ribs, Cracker Barrel, CiCi's, Golden Corral, IHOP, McDonald's, Subway, Starbucks, Taco Bueno, Taco Bell S: Burger King/Shell, Waffle House
	Lodg	N: La Quinta Inn♥, Super 8♥ S: Best Value Inn, Comfort Suites, Hampton Inn, Holiday Inn Express, Motel 6♥
	Med	N: + Campbell Memorial Hospital
	Other	N: Albertson's, ATMs, Banks, Discount Tire, Greyhound, Home Depot, Kroger, Museum, Wal-Mart sc, Winn Dixie, Weatherford College S: Lowe's, Office Depot, PetSmart♥, Target, Weatherford Fort Worth Kamp▲, Serenity Ranch RV Park▲, Hooves 'N Wheels RV Park▲
409		FM 2552, Clear Lake Rd, Santa Fe Rd, Weatherford
	TStop	N: Petro Stopping Center #2/Mobil (Scales)
	Gas	S: Chevron◆, Shell
	Food	N: IronSkillet/Petro SC, Jack in the Box, Catfish O'Charlie's

◆ = Regular Gas Stations with Diesel ▲ = RV Friendly Locations ♥ = Pet Friendly Locations
RED PRINT SHOWS LARGE VEHICLE PARKING/ACCESS ON SITE OR NEARBY BROWN PRINT SHOWS CAMPGROUNDS/RV PARKS

EXIT		TEXAS
	Lodg	N: Best Western/Petro SC
	TServ	N: Petro SC/Tires/Twash (Beacon)
	Med	N: + Campbell Memorial Hospital
	Other	N: CB/BarbSh/Laundry/WiFi/Petro SC
410		Bankhead Hwy, Weatherford
	TStop	S: Love's Travel Stop #273 (Scales)(DAND)
	Food	S: Subway/Love's TS
	Other	S: WiFi/Love's TS
413		Lakeshore Dr (EB)wal
	Gas	N: Texaco
	Food	N: Sonic, Steaks Plus
414		US 180, Weatherford, Mineral Wells, Hudson Oaks (WB)
	Gas	N: RaceTrac, Texaco◊
		S: Chevron◊
	Food	N: DQ, Jack's Family Rest, R&K Café, Sonic, Steaks Plus
	Other	N: Auto Dealers
415		Mikus Rd, Annetta Rd
	Gas	S: Shell
	Other	S: Exit 415 RV Center, Parker Co Airport✈
(417)		Weigh Station (WB)
418		Ranch House Rd, Willow Park
	FStop	N: Sprint #103/Gateway Shell
	Gas	N: Exxon
		S: Shell
	Food	N: FastFood/Gateway, Burger King, Pizza Hut, Subway, Taco Casa
		S: McDonald's, FastFood/Shell
	Lodg	S: Ramada Inn
	Other	N: Bank, ATM
		S: Fun Time RV Outlet
(419)		Weigh Station (EB)
420		FM 1187, Aledo, Farmer Rd
	Other	S: Cowtown RV Park▲
(421)		Jct I-30E, Downtown Ft Worth (EB, Left Exit)
425		Markham Ranch Rd, Ft Worth
426		FM 2871, Chapin School Rd
(428)		Jct I-820N, Ft Worth ByPass
429A		US 377, Granbury
	Gas	N: Conoco, Exxon, Phillips 66
		S: Chevron, Exxon, RaceTrac
	Food	N: Cracker Barrel
		S: McDonald's, Waffle House
	Lodg	N: Best Western
429B		Winscott Rd, Benbrook
431		Bryant-Irving Rd
	Food	N: Mimi's Café, Sushi, Keg Steakhouse
	Other	N: Best Buy, FedEx Kinko's, Lowe's, NTB, Sam's Club

EXIT		TEXAS
432		TX 183, Southwest Blvd
	Gas	S: Chevron, Exxon, Shell, QT
	Food	N: Deli, Hooters, Pizza Hut, Plaza Cafe
		S: Black Eyed Pea, Cajun Café, IHOP, Fuddrucker's, Italian Rest, Outback Steakhouse, Quiznos, Salt Grass Steak House, Starbucks, Subway
	Lodg	N: Towneplace Suites
		S: Amerisuites, Holiday Inn Express, La Quinta Inn♥, StudioPlus
	Med	S: + Hospital
	Other	N: ATMs, Banks
		S: ATMs, Banks, CarWash, Costco, Discount Tire, Goodyear, Grocery, Staples, Theatre, Target, Walgreen's
433		Hulen St, Fort Worth
	Gas	N: Star Mart
	Food	N: Chuck E Cheese, Grady's, Hooters, Olive Garden, Red Lobster, Starbucks
		S: Applebee's, Colter's BBQ, Denny's, McDonald's, Red Lobster
	Lodg	N: Town Place Suites
		S: Hampton Inn
	Med	N: + Hulen Medical Clinic
	Other	N: Albertson's, Circuit City, Home Depot, Office Depot
		S: ATMs, Banks, FedEx Kinko's, Hulen Mall, Hulen 10
434A		Granbury Dr, South Dr
	Gas	N: Phillips 66
	Food	S: DQ, Pancho's
	Other	S: Auto Service, Firestone, Goodyear, Wedgewood Tire & Auto Center
434B		Trail Lake Dr
	Gas	S: Citgo, Exxon, Shell
	Other	N: ATMs, Bank, Auto Services
		S: Auto Repairs
435		McCart Ave, West Creek Dr
	Gas	N: Conoco, Fina
		S: Shell
436A		FM 731, Crowley Rd, James Ave
	Gas	N: Star Mart
		S: Chevron, Conoco
	Food	S: DQ, Pizza Hut, Taco Bell
436B		Hemphill St
	Gas	N: Conoco, Shell
	Other	N: SaveALot
(437)		Jct I-35W, N to Fort Worth, S to Waco (Serv at 1st Exits N&S)
438		Oak Grove Rd, Fort Worth
	Gas	N: Shell
		S: Conoco
	Food	N: Burger King, Denny's, McDonald's
	Lodg	N: Days Inn
	Other	N: Enterprise RAC

EXIT		TEXAS
439		Campus Dr
	Gas	S: Sam's Club
	Other	S: Sam's Club
440A		Wichita St, Fort Worth
	Gas	N: Chevron
		S: Conoco, Fina
	Food	N: Taco Bell, McDonald's, Wendy's
		S: Bavarian Bakery, McDonald's, Pizza Hut, Whataburger, ChknExp/Conoco
	Other	N: Bank
440B		Forest Hill Dr
	Gas	S: Chevron, Conoco, Shell
	Food	S: Captain D's, CiCi's, DQ, Jack in the Box, Luby's Cafeteria, Sonic, Subway
	Lodg	S: Comfort Inn
	Other	S: Walgreen's
441		Anglin Dr, Hartman Lane
	Gas	N: Star Mart
		S: Conoco
	Lodg	N: Super 8
442A		287 Bus, Mansfield Hwy, Kennedale
(442B)		Jct I-820, 287N, Downtown Fort Worth
443		Bowman Springs Rd (WB)
444		US 287S, to Waxahachie
445		Green Oaks Blvd, Little Rd, Kennedale
	Gas	N: Conoco, Shell
		S: Chevron, Citgo
	Food	N: Arby's, Burger King, Colter's BBQ, Grandys, KFC, Pizza Hut, Taco Bell, Mac's Steak & Seafood, Whataburger
		S: IHOP, McDonald's, Pancho's Mex Buffet, Steak & Ale, Sake Japanese Steak House, Taco Bueno, Waffle House
	Other	N: Albertson's, Theatre
		S: ATMs, Bank, Auto Zone, Laundromat, Jiffy Lube, Winn Dixie
447		Park Springs Rd, Kelly-Elliott Rd
	Gas	N: Citgo
		S: Exxon, Fina
	Food	N: Church's Chicken
		S: Blimpie's/Fina
448		Bowen Rd, Arlington
	Gas	N: Shell
		S: Texaco
	Food	N: Cracker Barrel, Cafe
	Other	N: Grocery, Bowen 8 Theatre
449		FM 157, Cooper St, Arlington (WB)
	Gas	N: 7-11, Fina, Mobil, Shell
		S: Chevron, Citgo, Conoco

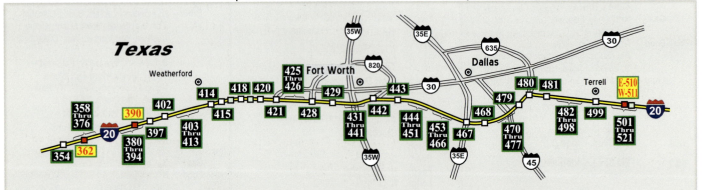

Page 92   ◊ = Regular Gas Stations with Diesel   ▲ = RV Friendly Locations   ♥ = Pet Friendly Locations
RED PRINT SHOWS LARGE VEHICLE PARKING/ACCESS ON SITE OR NEARBY   BROWN PRINT SHOWS CAMPGROUNDS/RV PARKS

INTERSTATE 20 W E

EXIT		TEXAS
	Food	N: BlackEyed Pea, CiCi's, Don Pablo, Golden Corral, Grady's, McDonald's, Red Lobster, Starbucks, Souper Salad, Subway S: Applebee's, Arby's, Burger King, Denny's, Long John Silver's, Old Country Buffet, Olive Garden, Shoney's
	Lodg	N: Best Western, Comfort Inn, Days Inn, Holiday Inn Express, La Quinta Inn ♥, Studio 6, Super 8
	Other	N: AMC 18, ATMs, Banks, Best Buy, Discount Tire, Office Depot, Super Target, Parks at Arlington Mall, Dick's Sporting Goods, Enterprise RAC, Treetops RV Village▲, Dallas Metro KOA▲ S: Albertson's, Home Depot, Kroger, Wal-Mart sc, Winn Dixie, Harold Patterson Sports Center
449A		FM 157S, Cooper St, Arlington (EB)
449B		FM 157N, Cooper St, Arlington (EB)
450		Matlock Rd
	Gas	N: Citgo, Fina S: Citgo, Diamond Shamrock, Shell
	Food	N: IHOP, Salt Grass Steakhouse, Steak 'n Shake, Taco Bell, Tony Roma, Wendy's S: Joe's Pizza, Pasta & Subs
	Lodg	N: Comfort Inn, Hampton Inn, La Quinta Inn ♥
	Med	N: + Columbia Medical Center
	Other	N: Lowe's, ATMs, Banks S: O'Reilly, Arlington Muni Airport ✈
451		Collins St, New York Ave
	Gas	N: Exxon, Mobil, RaceTrac S: Diamond Shamrock, Shell
	Food	N: IHOP, Jack in the Box S: McDonald's, Romano's Macaroni Grill
	Other	N: Traders Village Flea Market, Traders Village RV Park▲ S: Arlington Muni Airport ✈
453AB		TX 360, Dallas-Ft Worth Airport, Watson Rd (Serv at first exits)
454		Great Southwest Pkwy, Grand Prairie
	FStop	N: Golden Express #2/Conoco
	Gas	N: Chevron S: Exxon, Shell, Shamrock
	Food	N: McDonald's, Taco Bell, Texas Road House, Waffle House, Wendy's S: Burger King/Shamrock, Subway/Shell Applebee's, Arby's
	Lodg	N: Days Inn, Quality Inn S: Comfort Inn
	Med	N: + Hospital
	Other	N: Harley Davidson, Grand Prairie Muni Airport ✈ S: ATMs, Banks, Discount Tire, Kroger, Office Depot, Sam's Club, Wal-Mart sc
456		Carrier Pkwy, Grand Prairie
	Gas	S: Fina
	Food	N: Don Pablo, Starbucks, Whataburger S: Chili's, Denny's, IHOP, McDonald's, Soulman's BBQ, Mongolian BBQ, Cafe
	Other	N: ATM, Banks, Home Depot, Target S: Albertson's, ATM, Cinemark 16, Grand Prairie 10, Walgreen's
457		FM 1382, Grand Prairie, Cedar Hill
	Gas	N: Diamond Shamrock, Shell ◊ S: RaceTrac

Personal Notes

EXIT		TEXAS
	Food	N: Taco Bell, Waffle House S: Jack in the Box
	Other	N: Bank, Mtn Creek Lake State Park S: to Cedar Hill State Park▲
458		Mountain Creek Pkwy, Dallas
460		Spur 408 (diff reaccess)
461		Cedar Ridge Dr, Duncanville
	Gas	S: RaceTrac, Shamrock
462A		N Duncanville Rd (EB)
	Gas	S: Exxon
	Food	S: Arby's, Whataburger
	Lodg	S: Motel 6 ♥
	Other	N: Auto Service, Museum S: ATMs, Banks, Kroger
462B		N Main St (WB)
	Gas	S: Citgo, Exxon, Shell, Total
	Food	S: Arby's, Church's, KFC, Whataburger
	Lodg	S: Motel 6 ♥
	Other	S: ATM, Banks, Laundromat, Kroger
463		Cockrell Hill Rd, Camp Wisdom Rd, Duncanville, Dallas
	Gas	N: Chevron, Exxon S: Fina, Texaco
	Food	N: Catfish King, Denny's, Taco Cabana S: Blimpie's, Burger King, Red Lobster, Olive Garden, Subway, Wendy's
	Lodg	S: Hampton Inn, Holiday Inn, Motel 6 ♥, Ramada Inn
	Other	N: Auto Dealers, ATMs, Banks, Midas, Southwest Center Mall S: Best Buy, Enterprise RAC, Kmart, Target

EXIT		TEXAS
464AB		US 67, Dallas, Cleburne
465		Hampton Rd, Wheatland Rd
	Gas	N: Shell ◊ S: Chevron, RaceTrac
	Food	S: Arby's, Jack in the Box, Sonic, Taco Bell, Wendy's
	Lodg	S: Comfort Inn
	Med	S: + Hospital
	Other	S: Auto Dealers, Hertz RAC, Home Depot, Lowe's, PetSmart ♥, Sam's Club, Wal-Mart sc
466		S Polk St, Dallas
	TStop	S: Love's Travel Stop #294 (Scales)
	Gas	N: Citgo, Conoco ◊
	Food	N: DQ, Dean Seafood, Western BBQ S: Carl'sJr/Love's TS
	Tires	S: Love's TS
	Other	N: ATM, Bank S: WiFi/RV Dump/Love's TS
(467AB)		Jct I-35E, N to Dallas, S to Waco
468		Houston School Rd, Lancaster
	Gas	S: Tiger Mart/Exxon ◊
	Food	S: Whataburger
470		TX 342, Lancaster Rd, Dallas
	TStop	N: USA Travel Center/Texaco (Scales) S: Pilot Travel Center #433 (Scales)
	Gas	N: Chevron
	Food	N: CountryKitchen/Subway/USA TC, Big Bruce's BBQ, Wendy's, Soulman's BBQ S: DQ/Wendy's/Pilot TC, McDonald's, Sonic, Subway, Taco Bell, Whataburger
	Lodg	S: Days Inn, Quest Inn
	TWash	S: Galaxy TW, Dallas Super TW
	Other	N: ATM, Bank, Univ of N Tx/Dallas S: Chrome Shop, Laundry/WiFi/Pilot TC, CarQuest, Goodyear, Cedar Valley College
472		Bonnie View Rd, Dallas
	TStop	N: Flying J Travel Plaza #5520/Conoco (Scales) S: Travel Center of America/Exxon (Scales)
	Gas	N: Shell
	Food	N: Cookery/FastFood/FJ TP, Jack in the Box/Shell S: BK/TBell/PHut/TA TC
	Lodg	N: Ramada Ltd
	TServ	N: Flying J TP/Tires, Speedco, Kenworth S: TA TC/Tires
	TWash	N: Blue Beacon TW/FJ JTP, Eagle Truck Wash
	Other	N: Laundry/BarbSh/WiFi/RVDump/LP/FJ TP S: Laundry/WiFi/RVDump/TA TC
473A		JJ Lemmon Rd, Dallas (EB)
(473A)		Jct 45N, to Dallas (WB)
(473B)		Jct 45N, to Dallas
(473C)		Jct 45S, to Houston
474		TX 310N, S Central Expy (WB)
476		Dowdy Ferry Rd, Dallas
	Other	S: Carl's Auto & Truck Repair
477		St Augustine Rd
479AB		US 175, Kaufman, Dallas
	FStop	S: Marlow's Fuel Center/Shell
	Food	S: FastFood/Marlow's, Fat Bean BBQ
(480)		Jct I-635N, ByPass, to Mesquite
	TServ	N: Cummins Southern Plains

◊= Regular Gas Stations with Diesel ▲ = RV Friendly Locations ♥= Pet Friendly Locations

RED PRINT SHOWS LARGE VEHICLE PARKING/ACCESS ON SITE OR NEARBY BROWN PRINT SHOWS CAMPGROUNDS/RV PARKS

Interstate 20 W/E — TEXAS

EXIT		
481		Seagoville Rd, Dallas
	Gas	N: Fina, Valero
	Food	N: Taco Bell
		S: Lindy's Rest, Kiss My Ribs BBQ
	Lodg	N: Howard Johnson
482		Belt Line Rd
	Gas	S: Shell
483		Lawson Rd, Lasater Rd, Mesquite
487		FM 740, Forney
	Other	S: Lakeside RV Park▲
490		FM 741, Forney
491		FM 2932, Helms Trail Rd
493		FM 1641
	Gas	S: Exxon
498		TX 148, Terrell
	FStop	N: Terrell Travel Plaza/Exxon
	Gas	N: Shell
	Food	N: Rest/FastFood/Terrell TP, Denny's, Subway
	Other	S: Terrell RV Park▲
499A		to US 80W, to Dallas, Forney, Mesquite (No reaccess)
499B		Rose Hill Rd
501		TX 34, Terrell, Kaufman
	TStop	S: Valero #4532
		S: Total
	Gas	N: Chevron, Exxon
		S: Circle K, Phillips 66
	Food	N: DQ, Sonic, Waffle House
		S: McDonald's, IHOP, Wendy's, FastFood/Valero
	Lodg	N: Best Western, Comfort Inn, Days Inn, Holiday Inn Express, Motel 6♥
		S: Best Value Inn, Super 8
	Med	N: + Hospital
	Other	N: Home Depot, Terrell Muni Airport✈
		S: Tanger Outlet Mall
503		Wilson Rd, Terrell
	TStop	S: Travel Center of America/Shell (Scales)
	Food	S: Rest/PHut/Subway/TA TC
	TServ	S: TA TC/Tires
	Other	S: Laundry/WiFi/RVDump/LP/TA TC
506		FM 429, FM 2728, College Mound Rd, Terrell
	Other	N: Bluebonnet Ridge RV Park▲
509		Hiram Rd, Terrell
	TStop	S: McDonald's Phillips 66
	Food	S: FastFood/P66
(510)		Rest Area (EB) (RR, Phone, Picnic)
(511)		Rest Area (WB) (RR, Phone, Picnic)
(512)		Weigh Station (Both dir)
512		FM 2965, Hiram-Wills Point Rd
516		FM 47, Lake Tawakoni, Wills Pt
	Gas	S: Diamond Shamrock
	Food	S: Robertson's Cafe
	Lodg	S: Interstate Motel
519		Turner-Hayden Rd
	Other	S: Canton I-20 RV Park▲
521		Myrtle Cemetery Rd (WB), Myrtle Springs Rd (EB), Canton
523		TX 64, Canton, Wills Point
	Other	N: Canton CG/RV & Horse Park▲ ,

EXIT		
	Other	N: Sundown Trailers
526		FM 859, Edgewood
527		TX 19, Emory, Canton, Athens
	FStop	S: Kick 66/Circle K/P66
	Gas	N: Exxon, Texaco
		S: Chevron, Shell
	Food	N: Little Jewel's, Ranchero Rest, Subway, Whataburger
		S: DQ, Jerry's Pizza, McDonald's, KFC, Taco Bell
	Lodg	N: Comfort Inn, Holiday Inn Express, Super 8
		S: Best Western & RV Park▲ , Days Inn
	Other	N: Fish & Jog RV Park▲
		S: Hide-A-Way RV Ranch▲ , Ford RV Sales & Service
528		FM 17, Canton
530		FM 1255, Canton
533		Colfax Oakland Rd, Canton
	TStop	S: Canton Travel Plaza/Shamrock
	Food	S: Rest/Canton TP
	TServ	S: Canton TP
	Other	S: Laundry/WiFi/Canton TP
536		Tank Farm Rd
537		FM 773, FM 16, Ben Wheeler, Van
(538)		Van Zandt Co Rest Area (Both dir) (RR, Phone, Picnic, Vend, WiFi, RVDump)
540		FM 314, Van
	TStop	N: Love's Travel Stop #287 (Scales)
	Food	N: DQ, Carl's Jr/Love's TS
	Lodg	N: Van Inn
	Other	N: RVDump/WiFi/Love's TS, CB, Tires
544		Willow Branch Rd, Van
	TStop	N: Running W Truck Stop/Conoco
	Food	N: Rest/Running W TS
	TServ	N: Running W TS/Tires
	Other	N: Willow Branch RV Park▲
(546)		Inspection Station (Both dir)
548		TX 110, Grand Saline, Carol, Van, Lindale
	FStop	S: Oasis/Valero
	Gas	N: Exxon
552		FM 849, Lindale
	Gas	N: Chevron
554		Harvey Rd
556		US 69, Lindale, Tyler, Mineola
	FStop	N: Tyler Fuel Plaza/Shamrock
	Gas	N: RaceTrac, Murphy
		S: Chevron, Texaco
	Food	N: Burger King, Juanita's, McDonald's, Pizza Inn, Subway, Taco Bell
		S: Cracker Barrel, Wendy's
	Lodg	N: Best Western, Comfort Inn, Days Inn, Hampton Inn
		S: Best Value Inn♥
	Med	S: + Hospital
	Other	N: Lowe's, Wal-Mart sc
557		Jim Hogg Rd, Tyler
	Gas	N: Shell
	Other	N: Santa Land Amusement Park
560		Lavender Rd
	Other	N: Tyler State Park▲
		S: 5 Star RV Park/RVDump▲
562		TX 14, Tyler, State Park, Hawkins
	Food	N: Bodacious BBQ

EXIT		
	Other	N: Tyler State Park▲ , Northgate RV Park▲ , to appr 6mi:Whispering Pines Resort & Campground▲
565		FM 2015, Driskill, Lake Rd
567		TX 155, E Texas Center, Tyler, Gilmer, Winona, Big Sandy
	FStop	N: Wilco Travel Stop/Citgo
	Food	N: FastFood/Wilco TS
	Lodg	S: Days Inn
	Med	S: + E TX TB Hospital
	Other	N: Laundry/Wilco TS
		S: CB Shop
571A		US 271, Tyler, Gladewater
	Gas	S: Chevron
	Med	S: + E TX TB Hospital
571B		FM 757, Starrville, Oman Rd
(573)		Picnic Area (Both dir)
575		Barber Rd, Winona
579		CR 3111, Joy-Wright Mountain Rd, Gladewater
582		FM 3053, Liberty City, Overton
	Gas	N: Exxon, Chevron, Fina
	Food	N: DQ, Java Shop, Subway/Exxon
	Lodg	S: Thrifty Inn
583		TX 135, Kilgore, Gladewater, Overton, to US 271
	Gas	N: EZ Mart
		S: Exxon
	Other	N: Shallow Creek RV Resort▲
587		TX 42, Kilgore, White Oak
	Gas	N: Diamond Shamrock, Exxon
	Food	N: Bodacious BBQ, Country Kitchen
	Med	S: + Hospital
	Other	S: Wal-Mart sc, Museum
589A		US 259, TX 31, Kilgore, Longview, Henderson (EB)
589B		US 259, TX 31, Kilgore (EB Left Exit)
589		US 259, TX 31, Kilgore (WB Left Exit)
	FStop	S: Rudy's #3/Exxon
	Food	S: Rudy's #3/Exxon
	Lodg	N: Holiday Inn, Ramada
	Other	S: Kilgore College
591		FM 2087, FM 2011
	Other	S: Kilgore Airport✈
595AB		TX 322, FM 1845, Lp 281, Estes Parkway, Longview (EB)
595		TX 322, FM 1845, Lp 281, Estes Parkway, Longview (WB)
	Gas	N: Chevron♦, Shamrock, Texaco♦
		S: Chevron, Fina
	Food	N: DQ, Lupe's, McDonald's, Pizza Hut, Waffle House, Subway/Chevron
		S: Shoney's, KFC/Taco Bell
	Lodg	N: Best Western, Days Inn, Econo Lodge, Guest Inn
		S: Hampton Inn, La Quinta Inn♥, Motel 6♥
596		US 259N, TX 149, Eastman Rd, Carthidge
	FStop	N: Fastop Foods/Exxon, Howie's Get & Go #22/Shell
	Gas	S: Valero♦
	Food	N: Burger King, Whataburger
		S: Arby's
	Lodg	N: Comfort Suites, Microtel, Super 8
		S: Holiday Inn Express

♦ = Regular Gas Stations with Diesel   ▲ = RV Friendly Locations   ♥ = Pet Friendly Locations
RED PRINT SHOWS LARGE VEHICLE PARKING/ACCESS ON SITE OR NEARBY   BROWN PRINT SHOWS CAMPGROUNDS/RV PARKS

EXIT		TEXAS
599		Loop 281, FM 968, Longview
	TStop	S: PTP/ National Truck Stop/ Fina (Scales)
	Gas	S: Exxon
	Food	S: Rest/National TS
	Lodg	N: Best Western, Comfort Inn, Fairfield Inn, Wingate Inn
	TServ	S: National TS, Bridgestone Tire & Auto, Detroit Diesel, E Texas Truck Equip, TX Kenworth, Truck Parts World
604		FM 450, Hallsville
	Gas	N: Shamrock
	Other	N: 450 Hitching Post RV Park▲
(608)		Harrison Co Rest Area (Both dir) (RR, Phone, Picnic, Vend, WiFi)
610		FM 3251, Marshall
614		TX 43, Marshall, Kado Lake, Henderson
	Other	S: Martin Creek Lake State Park
617		US 59, Marshall, Carthage
	FStop	S: Pump & Pantry #15/Shamrock
	TStop	S: Pony Express Travel Center/Conoco (Scales)
	Gas	N: Exxon, Texaco S: Chevron, Exxon, Total
	Food	N: Applebee's, Catfish Express, Golden Corral, IHOP, McDonald's, Waffle House, Subway, Wendy's S: Rest/Pony Express TC, The Hungry Maverick
	Lodg	N: Best Western, Fairfield Inn, Holiday Inn, Hampton Inn, Executive Inn, La Quinta Inn♥ S: Days Inn, Econo Lodge, Holiday Inn Express, Motel 6♥, Super 8
	TServ	S: Pony Express TC/Tires
	Other	N: Country Pines RV Park▲ Holiday Springs RV, Auto Dealers, Auto Repairs S: Laundry/Pony Express TC
620		FM 31, Marshall, Elysian Fields
624		FM 2199, Scottsville
628		to US 80, Frontage Rd, Waskom
633		FM 9, FM 134, Caddo Lake
	Gas	N: Texaco
	Food	N: Catfish Village
	Other	S: Miss Ellie's RV Park▲
635		TX 156, TX 9, Spur 156, Waskom
	Gas	N: Chevron♦, Exxon♦
	Food	N: Burger King, DQ, Jim's BBQ, Sub Express
(636)		TX Welcome Center (WB) (RR, Phone, Picnic, WiFi) Parking Area (EB)

EXIT		TX / LA
		(CENTRAL TIME ZONE)
		ⓞ TEXAS
		ⓤ LOUISIANA
		(CENTRAL TIME ZONE)
(1)		Weigh Station (Both dir)
(2)		LA Welcome Center (EB) (RR, Vend, Sec, RV Water/RVDump)
3		US 79S, LA 169, Greenwood, to Shreveport
	TStop	S: Flying J Travel Plaza #5048/Conoco (Scales) (DAND), Love's Travel Stop #209 (Scales)
	Food	S: Rest/FF/FJ TP, Arby's/Love's TS, Sonic
	Lodg	S: to Country Suites, MidContinent Inn
	TServ	S: Flying J TP, Speedco
	Other	S: Laundry/BarbSh/Casino/RVDump/ LP/WiFi/FJ TP, Laundry/RVDump/WiFi/Casino/Love's TS, Zoo
5		US 79N, US 80, Greenwood
	FStop	S: Derrick Truck Stop
	TStop	N: Travel Center of America #237 (Scales)
	Food	N: FamilyRest/Subway/TA TC S: Angelina's Italian Rest
	Lodg	N: Country Inn S: Mid Continent Inn
	TWash	N: TA TC
	TServ	N: TA TC/Tires
	Other	N: Laundry/BarbSh/WiFi/RVDump/TA TC, Greenwood Flea Market S: Campers RV Center, B&D Truck & Gear, Auto Repairs, Rose Cottage Animal Hotel & Holistic Pet Care Center♥, Greenwood Flea Market, Watertown USA
8		US 80, LA 526E, Industrial Loop
	TStop	S: Petro Stopping Center #8/Mobil (Scales), J&S Citgo, Pilot Travel Center
	Gas	S: Chevron♦
	Food	N: Greenwood Rd Smoke House S: IronSkillet/Wendy's/Petro SC, Fast Food/Pilot TC, Jan's River Rest
	Lodg	N: Motel 6♥, Red Roof Inn♥ S: Motel California
	TServ	N: Detroit Diesel, Shreveport Truck Center, United Engines, Auto & Diesel Repair, Freightliner S: Petro SC
	TWash	S: Blue Beacon TW/Petro SC
	Other	S: Laundry/WiFi/Petro SC, Shreveport/Bossier KOA▲
10		Pines Rd, Shreveport
	Gas	N: BP♦ S: Chevron, Exxon♦, Shell, Murphy

EXIT		LOUISIANA
	Food	N: DQ, Pizza Hut, Popeye's, Subway, Western Sizzlin S: Burrito Stand, Burger King, Cracker Barrel, IHOP, Taco Bell, Waffle House
	Lodg	S: Comfort Suites, Courtyard, Fairfield Inn, Holiday Inn, La Quinta Inn♥, Jameson Inn
	Other	N: Grocery, Auto Repairs, Kroger S: Shreveport/Bossier KOA▲, Home Depot, Kroger, Walgreen's, CVS Wal-Mart sc, ATM, Bank, US Post Office, Diesel Service, Auto Dealers, American RV Parts & Service
(11)		Jct I-220E, LA 3132E, to I-49S, Inner Loop Expwy
13		Monkhouse Dr, Shreveport
	Gas	S: Chevron, Exxon, Texaco
	Food	N: Denny's, Kettle, Leona's Smokehouse S: Kings BBQ, Waffle House
	Lodg	N: Best Value Inn, Days Inn, Holiday Inn Express, Residence Inn S: Best Western, Hampton Inn, Ramada Inn, Super 8
	Other	N: Bank, Tires, Westwood Golf Course S: Airport✈ Casino, Rental Cars, Shreveport Reg'l Airport✈
14		Jewella Ave, Shreveport
	Gas	N: Texaco, Valero
	Food	N: Burger King, Church's Chicken, McDonald's, Subway, Taco Bell
	Other	N: Auto Zone, Walgreen's, Independence Stadium, ATM, Bank
16A		US 171, Hearne Ave
	Gas	N: Citgo S: Exxon, Fina, Raceway, Texaco
	Food	N: Subway S: KFC, Krystal's
	Lodg	S: Howard Johnson
	Med	N: + Hospital
	Other	N: Museum
16B		US 79, US 80, Greenwood Rd
	Gas	S: Citgo♦
	Food	S: Burger King, El Chico
	Lodg	S: Travelodge
	Med	N: + Medical Center
17A		Lakeshore Dr, Linwood Ave
	Gas	N: Circle K
	Lodg	N: Lakeshore Inn
	Med	N: + LSU Medical Center
(17B)		Jct I-49S, to Alexandria
18A		Common St, Line Ave (EB)
	Med	S: + Doctors Hospital
18C		Fairfield Ave (WB, diff reaccess)
	Gas	N: Circle K

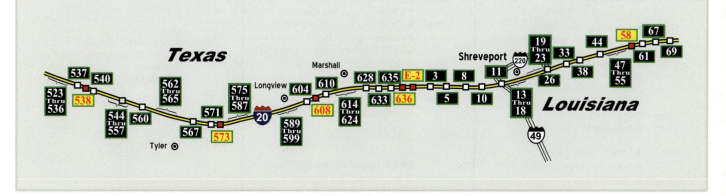

♦ = Regular Gas Stations with Diesel   ▲ = RV Friendly Locations   ♥ = Pet Friendly Locations

RED PRINT SHOWS LARGE VEHICLE PARKING/ACCESS ON SITE OR NEARBY   BROWN PRINT SHOWS CAMPGROUNDS/RV PARKS

Page 95

Interstate 20 W/E — LOUISIANA

EXIT	LOUISIANA
18D	Fairfield Ave, Louisiana Ave, Common St, Line Ave
19A	US 71N, LA 1, Spring St
Food	N: Rest/Holiday Inn
Lodg	N: Best Western, Holiday Inn
Other	N: Shreveport Riverfront Conv Center, Expo Hall, IMAX, Museums, Hollywood Casino, Harrah's Casino
19B	Traffic St, Riverside Dr
Gas	S: Exxon
Food	S: Circle B Ranch Steakhouse, Sundance Cantina, Cattleman's Buffet
Lodg	N: Horseshoe Casino$ & Hotel S: Boomtown Hotel & Casino$
Other	S: Bass Pro Shop
20A	Hamilton Rd, Isle of Capri Blvd
Gas	N: Circle K, Speedway, Texaco S: Chevron, Exxon
Food	N: Cobb Joe Bossier BBQ S: Calypso Buffet, Lucky Palace
Lodg	N: Comfort Inn S: Isle of Capri Casino$ Resort, Ramada
Other	N: Auto Repairs, Bank S: Isle of Capri RV Park▲
20B	LA 3, Benton Spur Rd (EB) (Access Same Serv as Ex #21 N)
20C	US 71S, Barksdale Blvd (EB)
21	LA 72, Old Minden Rd, to US 71S
Gas	N: Circle K, Exxon S: RaceTrac
Food	N: Burger King, Cowboys, El Chico, Kobe, McDonald's, Shoney's, Subway, Texas Roadhouse, Whataburger S: Waffle House, Wendy's
Lodg	N: Hampton Inn, Holiday Inn, La Quinta Inn♥, Residence Inn, Shoney's Inn S: Days Inn, Motel 6♥
Other	N: Bayou Outdoor Supercenter, Auto Repairs, Auto Dealers, AutoZone, Enterprise RAC, Dollar General S: Visitor Center
22	LA 3105, Airline Dr, Barksdale AFB, Bossier City
Gas	N: Chevron◊, Citgo, Exxon, Mobil, Valero S: Circle K, Kwik Trip, Texaco◊
Food	N: Applebee's, Arby's, Back Yard Burgers, Captain D's, Chili's, Chuck E Cheese, Grandy's Rest, Pizza, IHOP, Luby's Cafeteria, Pizza Hut, Red Lobster, Starbucks, Sonic, Taco Bell, Waffle House S: Catfish King, Darryl's Grill & Family Rest, Outback Steakhouse, Popeye's
Lodg	N: Best Western, Grand Isle Hotel, Rodeway Inn, Super 8 S: Baymont Inn, Microtel, Quality Inn, Red Carpet Inn
Med	N: + Hospital
Other	N: Albertson's, Firestone, Kmart, CVS, Pierre Bossier Mall, Cinema 9, Pep Boys, Office Depot, Wal-Mart, Walgreen's S: ATM, Auto Service, Bank, Grocery, Barksdale AFB, Air Force Museum
23	Industrial Dr, Barksdale AFB, to US 79, US 80, Bossier City
FStop	S: Industrial Dr Exxon
TStop	N: (I-220 Ex #17A) I-220 Travel Plaza/Chevron
Gas	N: Circle K, Exxon, Texaco S: Chevron◊
Food	N: Burger King, Country Kitchen, Great American Steak & Buffet, McDonald's, Popeye's, Taco Bell, Rest/I-220 TP S: Subway/Ind Dr Exxon
Lodg	N: Air View Motel, Capri Motel, Ramada, Town & Country Motel S: Quality Inn
Other	N: Laundry/I-220 TP S: Barksdale AFB, Southern RV Super Center, LA State Hwy Patrol Post
(26)	Jct I-220W ByPass
Other	N: to Exit #17A: I-220 Travel Plaza, Harrah's LA Downs/Rest/Hotel/Casino
33	LA 157, Haughton, Fillmore
TStop	S: Pilot Travel Center #199 (Scales)
Gas	N: Phillips 66 S: Exxon
Food	N: Mr Jim's Famous Chicken S: Arby's/TJCinn/Pilot TC, Waffle House
Other	N: Hilltop Campgrounds▲ S: Laundry/Casino/WiFi/RVDump/Pilot TC, Dollar General, Barksdale AFB, MIL/Barksdale AFB FamCamp▲
38	LA 117, Goodwill Rd, Minden
TStop	S: Fillmore Express/BP
Food	S: Rest/Fillmore Express, Tina's
Tires	S: BP
Other	N: Interstate RV Park▲ S: Lake Bistineau State Park▲, Green Park Resort▲, Circle T Trailers, LA Army Ammu Plant
44	US 371N, LA 7, to US 80, US 79, Minden, Cotton Valley (Addtl Serv E on US 80)
Gas	N: Exxon/Dixie Travel Center
Food	N: Crawfish Hole #2, Huddle House, Nicky's Mexican Rest
Lodg	S: Minden Motel
Other	N: Lakeside RV Park▲
47	US 371S, LA 159N, Sibley Rd, Minden, Sibley
Gas	N: Chevron◊, Citgo, Mobil◊, Texaco
Food	N: Domino's, Golden Biscuit Rest, Rest/Exacta Inn, Williams Chicken
Lodg	N: Best Western♥, Exacta Inn, Holiday Inn Express, Southern Inn
Med	N: + Hospital
Other	N: ATM, Bank, Auto Dealer, to Woods Ranch RV Park▲ S: to Lake Bistineau State Park▲, Madden Circle RV Park▲
49	LA 531, Industrial Dr, to US 79, US 80, Minden, Dubberly
TStop	N: Truckers Paradise/Shell, Love's Travel Stop #289 (Scales)
Gas	N: Wally's Fast Food, Murphy
Food	N: Rest/Truckers Paradise, Arby's/Love's TS, Wally's, Pepe's Mex Rest
Other	N: Casino/Truckers Paradise, WiFi/RVDump/Love's TS, Wal-Mart sc
52	LA 532, Minden, Dubberly, to US 80
TStop	N: Triple C Truck Travel Plaza & Casino/Exxon (Scales)
Food	N: Rest/Triple C
Other	N: Laundry/WiFi/Triple C
55	US 80, Gibsland, to Ada, Taylor
(58)	Rest Area (Both dir) (RR, Phone, Vend, Sec, RVDump)
61	LA 154, Gibsland, Athens
Other	N: to Lake Claiborne State Park▲
67	LA 9, Arcadia, Homer (Addtl Serv S on US 80 in Arcadia)
FStop	S: Rogers Shell
Other	N: to Lake Claiborne State Park▲ S: LP/Rogers
69	LA 151, Hazel St, Arcadia, Dubach
FStop	S: Fillmore Express #83/BP
Gas	S: Exxon, Shell
Food	S: Country Folks Kitchen, El Jarrito Mex Rest, McDonald's, Sonic, Subway
Lodg	S: Days Inn, Nob Hill Inn
Other	S: Auto Repairs, Diesel Repairs, Factory Outlet Mall, NAPA, Pharmacy, Bonnie & Clyde TradeDays & RV Park▲
77	LA 507, Simsboro
78	LA 563, Industry
Gas	S: Magnolia Corner Gen'l Store
81	LA 149, Grambling
Gas	S: Exxon
Other	S: to Grambling State Univ
(New)	Proposed-LA 818, Tarbutton Rd
84	LA 544, Cooktown Rd, Ruston, LA Tech, to Tarbutton Rd
Gas	N: Mobil◊ S: Chevron◊, Citgo, Exxon, Shell
Food	N: Dowling's Smokehouse S: DQ, Johnny's Pizza, Pizza Inn, Quiznos, Starbucks, Subway, Waffle House, Wendy
Lodg	S: Super 8
Med	S: + Lincoln General Hospital
85	US 167, LA 146, Ruston, Dubach
Gas	N: Chevron, Citgo, Exxon, Shell S: BP, Shell
Food	N: Applebee's, Burger King, Captain D's, Huddle House, McDonald's, Old Mexico Rest, Peking Rest, Shoney's, Subway, Wendy's S: Pizza Hut, Starbucks
Lodg	N: Econo Lodge, Hampton Inn, Holiday Inn, Howard Johnson, Ramada Inn, Relax Inn S: Best Value Inn, Best Western, Melody Hills Ranch, Sleep Inn
Med	S: + Lincoln General Hospital
Other	N: ATMs, Banks, Grocery, Office Depot, SpeeDee Oil S: ATMs, Banks, Jiffy Lube, UPS Store
86	LA 33, Farmerville Rd, Ruston, Farmerville
Gas	N: Citgo, RaceWay, Shell S: Texaco
Food	N: Cajun Café, Log Cabin Smokehouse, McDonald's, Ryan's Grill, Sonic
Lodg	N: Comfort Inn, Days Inn, Holiday Inn♥ S: Fairfield Inn, Holiday Inn Express♥, Lincoln Motel
Other	N: Auto Dealers, Wal-Mart, Tri Lake Marine & RV, to Lincoln Parish Park▲ S: Museums
93	LA 145, Elm St, Choudrant, Sibley
Gas	N: Oil S: Chevron, Mini Mart
Food	S: Doody's Diner
Other	S: Jimmie Davis State Park▲
(95)	Rest Area (EB) (RR, Phone, Vend, Sec, RVDump)

◊ = Regular Gas Stations with Diesel   ▲ = RV Friendly Locations   ♥ = Pet Friendly Locations
RED PRINT SHOWS LARGE VEHICLE PARKING/ACCESS ON SITE OR NEARBY   BROWN PRINT SHOWS CAMPGROUNDS/RV PARKS

EXIT	LOUISIANA
(97)	**Rest Area (WB)** (RR, Phone, Vend, Sec, RVDump)
101	**LA 151, Calhoun, Downsville**
Gas	N: Texaco
	S: Citgo, Exxon
Food	S: Huddle House
103	**US 80, Calhoun**
TStop	N: USA Auto/Truck Stop (Scales)
	S: 103 Truck Stop
Gas	N: Citgo
Food	N: Rest/USA TS, Subway, Johnny's Pizza
Lodge	N: Avant Motel West
TServ	N: USA ATS, Ogden's Tire & Diesel
107	**Camp Rd, Cheniere**
Other	N: Sunset Cove RV Park▲
108	**to US 80, LA 546, Cheniere**
Gas	N: Exxon◇, Shell
Other	N: Carter's Camping Center
112	**Well Rd, LA 3429, W Monroe**
TStop	S: Pilot Travel Center #428 (Scales)
Gas	N: Circle K, Shell◇, Texaco
Food	N: DQ, Flapjacks, McDonald's, Waffle House, Subway, Sonic
	S: Subway/Wendy's/Pilot TC
TServ	S: Frost Trailer Parts
Other	N: Auto & Tire Service, Dollar General
	S: Laundry/RVDump/Pilot TC, Pavilion RV Park▲
113	**Mane St, Downing Pines Rd (EB)**
114	**LA 617, Thomas Rd, W Monroe**
FStop	S: Harde Mart/Shell, Stop N Save #836/Exxon
Gas	N: RaceWay, Shell
	S: Citgo
Food	N: Bennigan's, Burger King, Captain D's, ChicFilA, El Chico, IHOP, KFC, McDonald's Pizza Hut, Popeye's, Shoney's, Subway, Taco Bell, Waffle House, Wendy's
	S: Chili's, Cracker Barrel, Hooters, Lone Star Steakhouse, Outback Steakhouse, Sonic, Waffle House, Western Sizzlin
Lodg	N: Shoney's Inn, Super 8, Wingate Inn
	S: Fairfield Inn, Holiday Inn Express♥
Other	N: ATMs, Banks, Walgreen's, Grocery, Office Depot, Wal-Mart sc, W Monroe Conv Center, Cinemark Tineseltown 17
	S: ATMs, Banks, LP/StopNSave, Clay's RV Center
115	**LA 34, Stella St, Mill St**
Gas	N: Citgo
TServ	S: Diesel Truck Repair Co
Other	N: Auto Repairs
	S: Auto Repairs, Clays RV Center
116A	**Fifth St, Coleman Ave**
Gas	N: Circle K, Phillips 66
Other	N: Museum
116B	**Jackson St, 2nd St, LA 15, to US 165 Bus, Monroe (EB)**
117A	**Hall St, Monroe (EB)**
Other	N: Civic Center
Med	N: + St Francis Medical Center
117B	**LA 594, Texas Ave**
117C	**US 165 Bus, LA 15 (WB)**
Med	N: + Hospital
117D	**Hall St, Catalpa St (WB)**

EXIT	LOUISIANA
118	**US 165, ML King Dr, N-Bastrop, S-Columbia (EB)**
Gas	S: Chevron, Citgo, Exxon, Shell
Food	S: Burger King, BBQ, KFC, McDonald's, Subway, Wendy's
Lodg	N: Holiday Inn, La Quinta Inn♥, Ramada Ltd
	S: Comfort Suites, Hampton Inn, Motel 6♥, Ramada Inn♥
Med	N: + St Francis Hospital
Other	N: Home Depot, Target, Monroe Reg'l Airport✈, to Univ of LA/Monroe
118A	**US 165S, Columbia (WB)**
118B	**US 165N, Bastrop (WB)**
120	**Garrett Rd, Pecanland Mall Dr**
Gas	N: Citgo, Shell
	S: Exxon
Food	N: Applebee's, Gators, IHOP, Zipps
	S: Olive Garden, Pizza Hut, Red Lobster
Lodg	N: Comfort Inn, Courtyard, Holiday Inn
	S: Best Western♥, Days Inn♥
Other	N: Cinema 10, Firestone, Pecanland Mall, Home Depot, Monroe Regional Airport✈, Target, Tilt, Best Buy
	S: Lowe's, Bleu Bayou Harley Davidson, Sam's Club, Hope's Camper Corner, Freightliner, Cooper Truck Center, Pecanland Estates & RV Park▲, Monroe Shilo RV & Travel Resort▲
124	**LA 594, Russell Sage Rd, Millhaven, R Sage Wildlife Area**
FStop	N: E-Z Mart #114
Other	N: LA State Hwy Patrol, Wildlife Area
	S: Shilo RV Resort▲

EXIT	LOUISIANA
132	**LA 133, to US 80, Rayville, to Columbia, Start**
Gas	N: Exxon◇
138	**LA 137, Rayville, Archibald**
FStop	S: Rayville Travel Center/Citgo
TStop	N: Pilot Travel Center #335 (Scales),
Gas	S: Exxon, Chevron
Food	N: Burger King, McDonald's, Quiznos, Huddle House, Wendy's/Pilot TC
	S: Big John's Steak & Seafood, Subway/Rayville TC, Popeye's, Waffle House
Lodg	N: Days Inn, Rayville Motel
	S: Ramada Ltd♥, Super 8
TServ	N: USA Truck Repair, Lee's Truck Srv
	S: Goodyear
Med	N: + Richland Parish Hospital, + Richardson Medical Center
Other	N: Firestone, Wal-Mart
	S: Cottonland RV Park▲
141	**LA 583, Bee Bayou Rd, Rayville**
TStop	N: Bee Bayou Truck Stop/BP
Food	N: Rest/Bee Bayou TS
TServ	N: Bee Bayou TS
Other	N: Laundry/Bee Bayou TS
145	**LA 183, Holly Ridge, Richland Parish 202**
148	**LA 609, Delhi, Dunn**
(150)	**Rest Area (Both dir)** (RR, Phone, Vend, Sec, RVWtr/RVDump)
153	**LA 17, Broadway St, Delhi, Winnsboro**
TStop	N: Jubilee Truck Stop #1201/Chevron
Gas	N: Exxon, Texaco
Food	N: DQ, Burger King, Hannah's Sideboard Rest, Taco Bell/Chevron, Subway
	S: Handy House Rest
Lodg	S: Best Western♥, Days Inn♥
TWash	N: The Truck Wash
Other	N: Grocery, Pharmacy, Carwash
157	**LA 577, Waverly**
TStop	N: Waverly Truck Stop
	S: Madison Auto Truck Plaza/Shell, Big Top Travel Center & Casino
Food	N: Rest/Waverly TS
	S: Rest/Madison TP, Subway
Other	N: Laundry/Waverly TS, Lucky's Casino
	S: Big Top Casino, Lucky Dollar Casino
171	**US 65, Tallulah, Vidalia, Newellton**
FStop	N: U-Pak-It/Chevron, Kangaroo #3450
TStop	S: Love's Travel Stop #237 (Scales), (DAND) Tallulah Truck Stop/Conoco (Scales), Travel Center of America #46/Mobil (Scales)
Gas	N: Citgo, Shell◇
	S: Texaco
Food	N: KFC, McDonald's, Subway
	S: Arby's/Love's TS, Rest/Tallulah TS, CountryPr/PHut/Popeye's/TA TC, Brushy Bayou
Lodg	N: Days Inn♥, Holiday Capri Motel
	Super 8♥
TServ	S: TA TC/Tires, Tallulah Truck & Tire Shop
Med	N: + Hospital
Other	S: Kings Treasure, Laundry/Casino/WiFi, RVDump/Love's TS, Laundry/Casino/Tallulah TS, Laundry/WiFi/TA TC

◇ = Regular Gas Stations with Diesel   ▲ = RV Friendly Locations   ♥ = Pet Friendly Locations
RED PRINT SHOWS LARGE VEHICLE PARKING/ACCESS ON SITE OR NEARBY   BROWN PRINT SHOWS CAMPGROUNDS/RV PARKS

EXIT		LA / MS
173		LA 602, to US 80, Tallulah, Richmond
182		LA 602, to US 80, Tallulah, Mound
(184)		**Mound Rest Area (Both dir)** (RR, Phone, Vend, Sec, RVDump)
186		US 80W, LA 193, Tallulah, Delta
	TStop	S: Interstate Station #7/Chevron
	Food	S: FastFood/Chevron
	Other	S: Laundry/Interstate Stn
(187)		Weigh Station (Both Dir)
	NOTE:	MM 189: Mississippi State Line
		(CENTRAL TIME ZONE)

○ **LOUISIANA**
◡ **MISSISSIPPI**
(CENTRAL TIME ZONE)

1A		Washington St, Warrenton Rd
		MS Welcome Center (Both dir) (RR, Phone, Picnic)
	Gas	N: Kangaroo Express◆, Shell◆
	Food	N: Ameristar Rest, Delta Point River, Goldie's Trail BBQ, Subway/Shell
		S: Waffle House
	Lodg	N: Delta Point Inn, Dixieana Motel
		S: La Quinta Inn♥, Ridgeland Suites
	Other	N: Auto Service, Tires, Towing, Isle of Capri RV Park▲, Isle of Capri Casino, Harrah's Casino, to (14mi N-Hwy 465) Sunset View RV Park▲
		S: Magnolia RV Park Resort▲, Rainbow Casino
1B		US 61S, to Pemberton Blvd, Vicksburg, Natchez (Access to #1-C via Pemberton Blvd)
	Gas	S: BP, Chevron, Kangaroo Express
	Food	S: McDonald's
	Other	S: Auto Service, Wal-Mart sc, to River Town Campground▲
1C		Halls Ferry Rd, Vicksburg
	Gas	N: Chevron, Exxon
		S: FastLane, Kangaroo Express
	Food	N: Burger King, Sonic
		S: Café Latte, Captain D's, DQ, Wok, El Sombrero Mex Rest, Hardee's, Pizza Hut, Ryan's Grill, Shoney's, Taco Bell, Wendy's
	Lodg	N: Econo Lodge, Travel Inn
		S: Days Inn, Fairfield Inn, Super 8
	Med	N: + Vicksburg Medical Center
	Other	N: Pharmacy

EXIT		MISSISSIPPI
	Other	S: ATMs, Auto Service, Tires, Cinema 4, Home Depot, Kroger, US Post Office, Mall, Banks, Walgreen's
3		Indiana Ave, Vicksburg
	Gas	N: Kangaroo Express, Texaco
		S: Kangaroo Express, Shell
	Food	N: Subway/Texaco, Krystal, McDonald's, Pizza Hut, Sun Garden, Waffle House
		S: KFC
	Lodg	N: Best Western, Delux Inn
		S: Best Inn
	Other	N: ATM, Bank, Grocery, IGA, RiteAid, Vicksburg Nat'l Military Park
		S: Auto Dealers
4		Clay St, Downtown Vicksburg, to US 80 (WB)
	Gas	N: Chevron, Kangaroo Express
		S: Shell
	Food	N: Cappes Steakhouse, KFC, Pizza Hut
		S: Billy's Italian Rest, China Buffet, Cracker Barrel, Pizza Inn, Dock Seafood, Waffle House
	Lodg	N: Hampton Inn, Motel 6♥, Park Inn, Vicksburg Inn
		S: Comfort Inn, Holiday Inn Express, Jameson Inn, Scottish Inn
	Other	N: Battlefield Campground▲, Museum
		S: Laundromat, Outlet Mall
4AB		Clay St, Downtown Vicksburg (EB)
5AB		US 61N, MS 27S, Rolling Fork, Utica, Yazoo City, Vicksburg
	FStop	N: Shell
	Gas	N: Kangaroo Express, Zips
		S: Kangaroo Express, Texaco
	Food	N: Cracker Barrel
		S: Domino's/Texaco, Bumpers, Rowdy's
	Lodg	S: Beechwood Inn, Comfort Inn, Jameson Inn, Scottish Inn
	Other	S: Laundromat
(6)		Parking Area (EB)
(8)		Weigh Station (EB)
(10)		Weigh Station (WB)
11		Tiffintown Rd, Bovina
	TStop	N: Bovina Truckstop
	Food	N: Bovina Café
	Other	N: RVDump/Bovina TS
15		Brabston Rd, Flowers
19		MS 22, to MS 467, Flora, Edwards
	Gas	S: Amoco
	Food	S: DQ
	Lodg	S: Relax Inn

EXIT		MISSISSIPPI
	Other	N: Askew Landing RV Camping▲, Petrified Forest
		S: Grocery, Police, Cactus Plantation
27		Bolton Brownsville Rd, Bolton
	Gas	N: BP, Chevron
31		Norrell Rd, Bolton
34		Natchez Trace Pkwy, Clinton
	Other	S: to Raymond Airport✈
35		US 80E, Clinton-Raymond Rd
	Gas	N: Chevron, Phillips 66, Shell
	Food	N: Backyard Burger, McAlister's Deli
	Other	N: MS College
		S: Eagle Ridge RV Park▲
36		Springridge Rd, Clinton
	Gas	N: Shell, Kroger, Murphy
		S: Exxon, Sprint, Orbit
	Food	N: Backyard Burger, Captain D's, DQ, McDonald's, Starbucks, Subway, Waffle House, Wendy's
		S: Applebee's, El Sombrero Mex, Pizza Hut, Shoney's, Taco Bell, Thai Garden, Waffle House
	Lodg	N: Clinton Inn, Days Inn
		S: Comfort Inn, Days Inn, Hampton Inn, Holiday Inn Express, Quality Inn, Ramada Inn, Ridgeland Inn
	Other	N: Mississippi College, Advance Auto, Enterprise RAC, Avis RAC, Home Depot, Kroger, Walgreen's, Wal-Mart sc▲, UPS Store, Police
		S: ATM, Bank, Clinton Center 10, Kroger, Springridge RV Park▲
40		MS 18W, Raymond, Robinson Rd, Jackson (EB)
	Gas	N: Phillips 66, Shell◆, Spur
		S: Conoco, Murphy
	Food	N: Arby's, El Chico, Krystal, Mazzio's Pizza, McDonald's, Piccadilly, Pizza Hut, Morrison's, Popeye's, Wendy's
		S: IHOP, Waffle House
	Lodg	N: Days Inn
		S: Comfort Inn
	Med	S: + Central MS Med Center
	Other	N: Bank, Home Depot, Metrocenter Mall, Office Depot, Hinds Comm College
		S: Wal-Mart sc
40B		MS 18E, Raymond, Robinson Rd
40A		MS 18W, Raymond, Robinson Rd
(41)		Jct I-220, US 49N, N Jackson, to Yazoo City (EB, Left exit & entrance)
42A		Ellis Ave S, Jackson
	Gas	S: Conoco, Exxon, Save
	Food	S: DQ, IHOP, Po Folks, Pizza Hut

Page 98   ◆= Regular Gas Stations with Diesel   ▲ = RV Friendly Locations   ♥ = Pet Friendly Locations
RED PRINT SHOWS LARGE VEHICLE PARKING/ACCESS ON SITE OR NEARBY   BROWN PRINT SHOWS CAMPGROUNDS/RV PARKS

INTERSTATE 20 W/E — MISSISSIPPI

EXIT		
	Med	S: + MEA Medical Clinic
	Other	S: Grocery, Big Lots
42B		**Ellis Ave N, Jackson**
	Gas	N: BP, Conoco, Shell
	Food	N: Burger King, Captain D's, Denny's, McDonald's, Waffle House
	Lodg	N: Best Western, Econo Lodge, Days Inn, Ramada Inn, Sleep Inn
	Other	N: AutoZone, Firestone, U-Haul, Zoo
43AB		**Terry Rd, to I-55, to Jackson. New Orleans**
	Gas	N: Shell S: Exxon
	Food	N: Bubba's BBQ, Kim's Seafood, Krystal, Southside Grill, West Family Grill
	Lodg	N: Tarrymore Hotel S: La Quinta Inn ♥
	Other	N: ATMs, Banks, Auto Repairs S: Grocery
	NOTE:	I-20 runs below with I-55 to Birmingham, AL. Exit #'s follow I-20
(44)		**Jct I-55S, to New Orleans, McComb** (WB, Left Exit)
45		**US 51N, State St, Gallatin St** (EB, Left exit)
45A		**Gallatin St** (WB)
	TStop	N: Petro Stopping Center #28/Mobil (Scales) S: Pilot Travel Center #77 (Scales)
	Gas	N: Chevron
	Food	N: IronSkillet/Petro SC S: McDonald's/Pilot TC
	Lodg	S: Knights Inn
	TWash	N: Blue Beacon TW/Petro SC
	TServ	N: Petro SC/Tires
	Other	N: Laundry/BarbSh/RVDump/Petro SC, Amtrak, Auto Repairs, Tires S: Laundry/WiFi/Pilot TC
45B		**US 51, State St** (WB)
	Gas	N: Chevron S: Speedway
	Other	N: Police
(46)		**Jct I-55N, to Grenada, Memphis** (EB, Left exit)
	NOTE:	I-20 runs above with I-55 to Birmingham, AL. Exit #'s follow I-20
47		**US 49S, Hattiesburg, Flowood** (WB)
47AB		**US 49, Hattiesburg, Flowood** (EB) (Serv N to US 80, S to US 49)
	FStop	S: Capital Fuel Center #2
	TStop	N: Flying J Travel Plaza #5072/Conoco (Scales), Pilot Travel Center #450 (Scales) S: Delta Travel Center (Scales)
	Food	N: Rest/FastFood/FJ TP, Subway/Pilot TC, Western Sizzlin' S: DQ, Waffle House
	Lodg	N: Airport Inn ♥, HOTEL S: Days Inn ♥, Super 8 ♥
	TServ	S: Empire Truck Sales, Freightliner, Kenworth
	Other	N: Laundry/WiFi/LP/RVDump/FJ TP, Laundry/WiFi/RVDump/Pilot TC, Bass Pro Shop, Auto Repairs, Tires, to Swinging Bridge RV Park▲ S: Wal-Mart sc, Truck-Man RV Center, Laundry/Delta TC

Personal Notes

EXIT		MISSISSIPPI
48		**MS 468, Pearson Rd, Pearl**
	FStop	N: Speedway S: Kangaroo Express
	Gas	N: Shell, BP, Super Saver S: Huff Texaco Food Shop
	Food	N: Arby's, Burger King, Cracker Barrel, KFC, McDonald's, O'Charleys, Ryan's Grill, Shoney's, Starbucks, Waffle House
	Lodg	N: Best Western, Comfort Inn, Fairfield Inn, Econo Lodge, Hampton Inn, Hilton Garden Inn, Holiday Inn Express, Motel 6 ♥, Jameson Inn S: Country Inn, Days Inn, La Quinta Inn ♥
	Other	N: Tinseltown USA, Travel America RV Center, Police, Kroger, ATM, Bank, Donald's Truck & Auto Repair, Jerry's Tire Service, Quality Trailer Service S: Dollar General
52		**MS 475, Airport Rd, Pearl, Int'l Airport, Whitfield**
	Gas	N: Chevron♦, Conoco♦, Texaco♦
	Food	N: Waffle House, Wendy's
	Lodg	N: Quality Inn, Ramada Ltd, Super 8
	TServ	N: Peterbilt, White/GMC Volvo, S: Buddy's Truck Repair
	Other	N: Jackson Int'l Airport✈, Rental Cars S: Central MS Correction Facility
54		**MS 18, Crossgates Blvd, US 80, Greenfield Rd, West Brandon**
	Gas	N: BP, Exxon, Phillips 66
	Food	N: Applebee's, Burger King, KFC, Mazios, McAlister's Deli, Pizza Hut, Popeye's, Subway, Waffle House, Wendy's
	Lodg	N: Ridgeland Inn

EXIT		MISSISSIPPI
	Med	N: + Rankin Medical Center
	Other	N: ATMs, Banks, Firestone, Kroger, Enterprise RAC, Tires, Wal-Mart S: Home Depot
56		**US 80, Government St, Downtown Brandon**
	Gas	N: Texaco S: Exxon, Shell
	Food	N: Burger King, CiCi's, Krystal, Sonny's BBQ, Taco Bell S: DQ, McDonald's, Sonic, Smoke House BBQ, Waffle House
	Lodg	N: Microtel S: Days Inn ♥, Red Roof Inn ♥
	Med	N: + Rankin Medical Center
	Other	N: AutoZone, ATM, Bank, Grocery, to Barnett Reservoir, Barnett Reservoir Campground▲ S: Police
59		**US 80, East Brandon (Serv 2 mi S)**
	Other	S: Police
68		**MS 43, to US 80, Pelahatchie, to Puckett**
	FStop	N: Chevron, Super Stop #21/Conoco S: BP Fuel Center
	Food	N: Subway/Chevron, Rest/Conoco
	Other	N: RV Dump/Conoco, Pelatchie Lake Campground▲, Police, to Vaiden Campground▲
(75)		**Rest Area** (WB) (RR, Phone, Picnic, Sec247, RVDump)
77		**MS 13, to US 80, Morton, Puckett**
	FStop	N: Phillips 66
	Med	N: + Hospital
	Other	N: Roosevelt State Park▲
80		**MS 481, Morton, Raleigh**
88		**MS 35, Forest, Raleigh**
	FStop	N: BP, to 1mi N: Forest Red Apple Texaco S: Chevron Express Line
	Gas	N: Shell, Murphy♦
	Food	N: Subway/BP, McDonald's, KFC, Wendy's S: Santa Fe Steak House & Grill
	Lodg	N: Apple Tree Inn, Best Value Inn, Comfort Inn ♥, Days Inn, Holiday Inn Express
	Med	N: + Hospital
	Other	N: Forest Muni Airport✈, J&J Tire, Auto Dealers, Grocery, Wal-Mart sc
(91)		**Rest Area** (EB) (RR, Phone, Picnic, Sec247, RVDump)
96		**Lake Norris Rd, to US 80, Lake** (Addtl Serv approx 3mi N)
	Food	N: Back Forty Seafood Rest
	Other	S: to Bienville National Forest▲
100		**US 80, Lake, Lawrence**
	TStop	S: 100 Travel Center/BP
	Food	S: Rest/100 TC
	Tires	S: 100 TC
109		**MS 15, to US 80, Newton, Union, Decatur, Philadelphia**
	FStop	N: Shell S: Conoco, Spanky's Food Mart
	Gas	S: Chevron♦
	Food	N: Boro Family Rest, Wendy's/Shell S: Hardee's, KFC, McDonald's, Pizza Hut, Sonic, Subway
	Lodg	N: Thrifty Inn S: Days Inn

♦ = Regular Gas Stations with Diesel   ▲ = RV Friendly Locations   ♥ = Pet Friendly Locations
RED PRINT SHOWS LARGE VEHICLE PARKING/ACCESS ON SITE OR NEARBY   BROWN PRINT SHOWS CAMPGROUNDS/RV PARKS

EXIT		MISSISSIPPI	EXIT		MS / AL	EXIT		ALABAMA
	Other	N: to Turkey Creek Water Park▲ S: Grocery, Wal-Mart sc		Food	S: CiCi's, McDonald's, O'Charley's, Outback Steakhouse, Ryan's Grill, Taco Bell	1		AL 8, to US 80E, Cuba, Demopolis
115		MS 503, Hickory, Decatur		Lodg	N: Days Inn, Economy Inn, Hampton Inn, Holiday Inn, Howard Johnson, Relax Inn, Super 8 S: Comfort Inn, Jameson Inn, Scottish Inn, Microtel		TStop	S: Rocking Chair/P66
121		Chunky					Gas	S: Chevron, Dixie
129		US 80W, Lost Gap, Meehan Jct					Food	S: Rest/Rocking Chair
	TStop	S: Spaceway Truck Stop/Conoco (Scales)				8		AL 17, York
	Food	S: Rest/Spaceway TS					TStop	S: PTP/York Truck Plaza/BP (Scales)
	Other	S: Laundry/WiFi/RVDump/Spaceway TS		Other	N: U-Haul, Auto Dealers S: Mall, Harley Davidson, Sam's Club		Lodg	S: Days Inn
	NOTE:	I-20 runs below with I-59 to Birmingham, AL. Exit #'s follow I-20.	154AB		MS19S, MS 39N, US 11N, US 80E, Butler AL, DeKalb, Naval Air Station (EB)		TServ	S: York TP/Tires
							TWash	S: York TP
							Med	S: + Hospital
(130/149)		Jct I-59S, to Laurel, New Orleans					Other	S: Bank, ATM
150		US 11S, MS 19N, Philadelphia, Meridian Airport	157AB		US 45, Macon, Quitman	17		AL 28, Livingston, Boyd
				Other	N: Benmark Coach & RV Park▲		FStop	S: Interstate BP
	FStop	S: Stuckey's Express #653/Chevron, SuperStop #10/Shell	160		Russell Mt Gilead Rd, Meridian		TStop	S: Noble Truck Stop/Citgo (Scales)
	TStop	N: Queen City Truck Stop (Scales)		TStop	N: Travel Center of America #47/BP (Scales) (DAND) S: Amoco		Gas	S: Chevron
	Food	N: Rest/Queen City TS					Food	S: Rest/Noble TS, Burger King, GM Steak Corral, Pizza Hut
		N: Subway/Stuckey's		Gas	S: Shell		Lodg	S: Comfort Inn
	Tires	N: QC TS		Food	N: CountryPride/TA TC		Med	S: + Hospital
	Other	N: Okitibbee Lake, Meridian Community College, LP/QC TS		TServ	N: TA TC/Tires		TServ	S: Noble TS/Tires, Bullocks Truck Service
				Other	N: Laundry/TA TC, Nanabe Creek Campground▲		Other	S: Laundry/Noble TS, Univ of W AL
		S: Key Field Airport✈	(164)		MS Welcome Center (WB) Lauderdale Co Rest Area (RR, Phone, Picnic, Vend, Sec24, RVDump)	23		CR 20, Main St, Epes, Gainesville
151		49th Ave, Valley Rd, Meridian				32		CR 20, Boligee
	FStop	S: Pilot Travel Center #388					TStop	N: Boligee Truck Stop/BP
	Food	S: Subway/Pilot TC					Gas	S: Chevron
152		29th Ave, MLK Jr Blvd, Meridian	165		Garrett Rd, Toomsuba		Food	N: Rest/Boligee TS
	Gas	N: Chevron◇		TStop	S: Love's Travel Stop #343 (Scales)			S: Subway/Chevron
	Lodg	N: Ramada S: Royal Inn		Gas	N: Shell, Texaco	(38)		Rest Area (EB) (RR, Phone, Picnic, Vend, RVDump)
					N: Subway/Shell, Chesters/Texaco			
153		MS 145S, 22nd Ave, Quitman, Downtown Meridian		Food	S: Arby's/Love's TS	(39)		Rest Area (WB) (RR, Phones, Picnic, Vend, RVDump)
	Gas	N: BP, Shell		Other	N: WiFi/Love's TS, Meridian East/ Toomsuba KOA▲	40		AL 14, Eutaw, Aliceville
		S: Chevron, Conoco, Exxon, Shell	169		Kewanee		Med	S: + Hospital
	Food	N: Arby's, Barnhill Buffet, Burger King, Captain D's, Chinese, Hardee's, KFC, McDonald's, Pizza Hut, Subway, Wendy's, Western Sizzlin S: Depot Rest, Waffle House		FStop	S: Kewanee One Stop		Other	N: Tom Bevil Lock & Dam
				Food	S: Rest/Kewanee One Stop	45		CR 208, to Union
			(170)		Weigh Station (Both dir)		TStop	S: Trackside BP
				NOTE:	I-20W & I-59S above run together to Meridian, MS. Exit #'s follow I-20.		Food	N: Cotton Patch Restaurant S: Hardee's, Southfork, Western Inn,
	Lodg	N: Relax Inn S: Astro Motel, Baymont Inn, Budget 8 Motel, Best Western, Econo Lodge, Holiday Inn♥, Motel 6♥, Sleep Inn					Lodg	S: Western Inn
					(CENTRAL TIME ZONE)		TServ	S: Trackside BP/Tires, Southfork Auto & Truck Center
	Med	N: + Hospital			⌒ MISSISSIPPI		Other	S: Greene Co Greyhound Park
	Other	N: ATMs, Banks, Amtrak, Goodyear, Grocery, Museums, Pharmacy S: Auto Dealers, Lowe's, Wal-Mart sc			⌒ ALABAMA (CENTRAL TIME ZONE)	52		US 11, US 43, Knoxville
							FStop	N: Speedmart Fuel Center/Exxon
154		MS 19S, MS 39N, US 11N, US 80E, Butler, DeKalb (WB)		NOTE:	I-20E & I-59N below run together from Meridian, MS to Birmingham, AL.		Food	N: FastFood/Speedmart FC
						62		CR10, CR 51, Holly Springs Ln, Fosters
	Gas	N: BP, Shell, Texaco S: Chevron, Conoco	(0)		AL Welcome Center (EB) (RR, Phone, Picnic, Vend, RVDump)		Gas	N: BP
	Food	N: Applebee's, Back Yard Burgers, Cracker Barrel, Krystal's, Waffle House				68		Tuscaloosa Western ByPass (Gas 2 mi N in Tuscaloosa)
						71A		AL 69S, to US 11, LA 7, Moundville
							Gas	N: Phillips 66

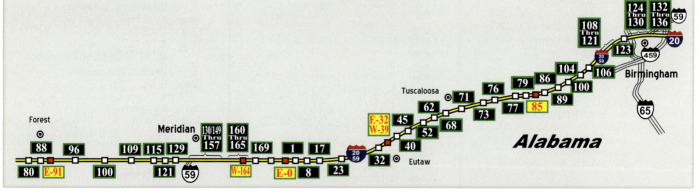

◇ = Regular Gas Stations with Diesel   ▲ = RV Friendly Locations   ♥ = Pet Friendly Locations
RED PRINT SHOWS LARGE VEHICLE PARKING/ACCESS ON SITE OR NEARBY   BROWN PRINT SHOWS CAMPGROUNDS/RV PARKS

Interstate 20 W/E — Alabama

EXIT		ALABAMA
	Gas	S: Chevron, Exxon◊, Shell
	Food	S: Arby's, Country Hic Café & BBQ, IHOP, Outback Steakhouse, Pizza Hut, Ryan's Grill, Waffle House, Wendy's
	Lodg	S: Courtyard, Fairfield Inn, Jameson Inn
	Other	S: Advance Auto, Firestone, Kmart, L&H Truck Service, Lowe's, Auto Svc, Police Dept
(71B)		Jct I-359, AL 69N, Tuscaloosa
	Other	N: Univ of AL, Amtrak, Bryant-Denny Stadium, Coleman Coliseum, Stillman College
73		US 82, AL 6, McFarland Blvd, Tuscaloosa, Centreville
	Gas	N: Chevron◊ x2, Exxon, RaceTrac, Shell◊
		S: Amoco, Exxon, Shell
	Food	N: Burger King, Captain D's, Krystal's, Long John Silver, Pizza Hut, Waffle House, Shoney's
		S: Chili's, Hardee's, Huddle House, KFC, Lone Star Steakhouse, McDonalds, Piccadilly, Subway, Taco Cabana, Taco Bell, Wendy's, Western Sizzlin, Waffle House
	Lodg	N: Best Western, Master's Inn, Shoney's
		S: Country Inn, Econo Lodge, Days Inn, La Quinta Inn♥, Motel 6♥, Quality Inn, Ramada Inn, Super 8
	Med	N: + DCH Reg'l Medical Center
	Other	N: ATMs, Banks, Firestone, Goodyear, U-Haul, Mall, CVS, Lake Lurleen State Park
		S: Winn Dixie, FoodWorld, NAPA, Sam's Club, Wal-Mart sc, McFarland Mall, Fox 12, ATMs, Banks, Enterprise, Office Depot, RiteAid, AL State Hwy Patrol Post
76		US 11, E Tuscaloosa, Cottondale
	TStop	S: Pilot Travel Center #76 (Scales)
	Gas	N: Citgo◊, Exxon, Shell◊
		S: Shell◊
	Food	N: Burger King, Cracker Barrel, Waffle House
		S: Subway/Pilot TC
	Lodg	N: Comfort Inn, Scottish Inn, Super Inn
		S: Sleep Inn
	TServ	S: Southland Int'l Trucks
	Med	N: to + US Vets Hospital
	Other	N: ATM, Bank, Sunset II Travel Park▲
		S: Laundry/WiFi/Pilot TC, Auto Service, Auto Dealers, AL State Hwy Patrol Post
77		CR 85, Buttermilk Rd, Cottondale
	TStop	N: Travel Center of America /BP (Scales) (DAND), WilcoHess Travel Plaza #5501 (Scales)
	Gas	N: Chevron
	Food	N: McDonald's/Chevron, CountryPride/Subway/Taco Bell, TA TC, Wendy's/WilcoHess TP, Captain Jim's Seafood & Steak, Pizza Hut, Ruby Tuesday
	Lodg	N: Hampton Inn, Microtel Inn
	TWash	N: Blue Beacon TW/TA TC
	TServ	N: TA TC/Tires, Speedco
	Other	N: Laundry/WiFi/RVDump/TA TC
		S: Laundry/WilcoHess TP
79		US 11, University Blvd, Coaling
	Gas	S: Chevron◊
(85)		Rest Area (Both dir) (RR, Phones, Picnic, RVDump)

EXIT		ALABAMA
86		CR 59, Covered Bridge Rd, Cottondale, Brookwood, Vance
	TStop	N: Brookwood Shell Truck Stop
	Food	N: Rest/Brookwood TS
89		Mercedes Dr, Vance, Tuscaloosa
	Lodg	N: Wellesley Inn
	Other	S: Mercedes Benz Auto Plant
100		AL 216, McCalla, Abernant, Bucksville
	TStop	S: Petro Stopping Center #19/ Chevron (Scales)
	Gas	N: Citgo
		S: BP, Exxon
	Food	S: Rest/Petro SC, Shenanigan's BBQ
	TServ	S: Petro SC/Tires
	Other	N: McCalla RV Park▲
		S: Laundry/WiFi/RVDump/Petro SC, Auto Repair, Sheriff Dept, Tannehill Nat'l Golf Course, Museum, Tannehill Ironworks Historic State Park▲
104		McAshen Dr, Rock Mountain Lakes, McCalla
	TStop	S: Flying J Travel Plaza #5042/Conoco (Scales)
	Food	S: Rest/FastFood/FJ TP
	Other	S: Laundry/BarbSh/WiFi/LP/RVDump/FJ TP
(106)		Jct I-459N, Montgomery, to Gadsden, Atlanta (South ByPass of Birmingham)
108		US 11, AL 5N, Academy Dr
	Gas	N: Exxon
		S: BP, Citgo

EXIT		ALABAMA
	Food	N: Applebee's, Cracker Barrel, Santa Fe Steakhouse, Waffle House
		S: Burger King, Cajun Landing Seafood, Milo's, McDonald's, Omelet Shop
	Lodg	N: Best Western, Comfort Inn, Jameson Inn, Holiday Inn Express, Motel 6♥, Travelodge
		S: Days Inn, Hampton Inn, Masters Economy Inn, Travelodge
	Med	S: + UAB West Medical Center
	Other	N: ATM, Bank, Civic Center, Visionland Theme Park, Watermark Place
		S: ATMs, Banks, Grocery, Mall, Wal-Mart sc, Winn Dixie, Frank House Muni Golf Course, West Lake Outlet Mall
110		Visionland Pkwy
112		18th St, 19th St, Bessemer
	Gas	N: Conoco, RaceTrac
		S: Chevron
	Food	N: Jack's Hamburgers
		S: Arby's, Burger King, Krystal's
	Other	N: Auto Repairs
		S: Bank, ATM, Auto & Tire Services, Grocery, Greyhound, Museum, Sheriff Dept, Police Dept
113		18th Ave, Brighton, Lipscomb
	FStop	S: I-20/59 Travel Center/Chevron
	Gas	S: Speedway
	Food	S: McDonald's
	Other	S: Police Dept
115		Jaybird Rd, 15th St, Pleasant Grove Rd, Birmingham, Allison Bonnett Memorial Dr
	Gas	N: Citgo, Phillips 66, RaceTrac, Shell◊
	Food	N: Hardee's, Subway
	Lodg	S: Best Western
	Other	N: Advance Auto
		S: to M&J RV Park▲
118		Valley Rd, Fairfield
	Lodg	S: Fairfield Inn, Villager Lodge
	Med	S: + Metro West Hospital
	Other	S: Home Depot, Winn Dixie, Auto & Tire Services, to Fairfield Civic Center, Western Hills Mall, Radio Museum, Police Dept
119A		RM Schrushy Pkwy, Ave F, Gary Ave, Lloyd Nolan Pkwy
	Gas	N: BP, Chevron◊
		S: Exxon, Mobil, Texaco
	Food	N: Burger King, Seafood Delite, Subway
		S: Omelete Shoppe
	TServ	N: Big Moe Spring & Alignment
	Med	S: + Metro West Hospital
	Other	S: Auto Repairs
119B		Ave I, 34th St (WB, reacc via #119A)
120		AL 269, 20th St, Ensley Ave, AL State Fair Complex (diff reaccess)
	Gas	N: BP, Crown
	Food	N: KFC, Taco Bell
	TServ	N: Wayne Gargus GMC
	Med	S: + Hospital
	Other	N: Police Dept
		S: AL State Fairgrounds, Birmingham International Raceway
121		19th St, Bush Blvd, Ave V, Ensley (WB, no re-entry)
	Gas	N: BP, Exxon
		S: Chevron
	Food	N: Fat Burger

◊ = Regular Gas Stations with Diesel   ▲ = RV Friendly Locations   ♥ = Pet Friendly Locations
RED PRINT SHOWS LARGE VEHICLE PARKING/ACCESS ON SITE OR NEARBY   BROWN PRINT SHOWS CAMPGROUNDS/RV PARKS

EXIT	ALABAMA
123	US 78, AL 4, Arkadelphia Rd, Birmingham, Jasper
TStop	N: Pilot Travel Center #369 (Scales)
Gas	N: BP, Chevron
Food	N: Wendy's/Pilot TC, Popeye's Chicken S: Pizza Hut
Lodg	N: Days Inn, La Quinta Inn ♥
Med	S: + Princeton Baptist Med Center
Other	N: Laundry/WiFi/Pilot TC, Birmingham Southern College S: Battle Coliseum, Legion Field
(124A)	Jct I-65S, Montgomery, Huntsville (WB, Left Exit)
(124B)	Jct I-65N, Nashville (EB, Left Exit)
125A	17th St, Dwntwn Birmingham (EB)
Other	S: Jazz Hall of Fame, Museum of Art
125B	22nd St, Dwtwn Birmingham (WB)
125	22nd St, Downtown Birmingham (WB, Left Exit)
Lodg	N: Best Western, Starwood Hotel, Sheraton
Other	N: B'ham Jefferson Conv Complex, Sports Hall of Fame, Sheriff's Dept
126A	US 31S, US 280E, Carraway Blvd
Med	S: + Cooper Green Hospital, + Children's Hospital of AL
126B	31st St, Sloss Furnaces
Gas	N: Circle K, Conoco, Shell
Food	S: McDonald's
TServ	S: Freightliner Trucks, Mack Trucks, K Diamond Truck Service
Med	N: + Carraway Methodist Med Center
Other	S: Laundromat, W AL Tire Service
128	AL 79, Tallapoosa St, Tarrant
TStop	N: Cowboys Food Mart #3672
Gas	N: Shell
Food	N: Subway/Cowboys FM
TServ	N: Cummins Alabama
129	Messer Airport Hwy, Birmingham
Gas	S: Texaco, Conoco, Shell
Food	N: Rest/Ramada Inn S: Huddle House, Rest/Holiday Inn
Lodg	N: Days Inn, Ramada Inn S: Holiday Inn
Other	N: Birmingham Int'l Airport ✈, Rental Cars
NOTE:	I-20 above runs with with I-59. Exit #'s follow I-20.
(130)	Jct I-20E, Atlanta, Jct I-59N, Gadsden, Chattanooga, Jct 20W, Jct 59S
130B	US 11S, 1st Ave (EB) (diff reacc) 1st Ave S (WB)
Gas	N: AmocoAmPm
Food	S: Mrs Winner's, McDonald's, Shoney's
Lodg	N: Bama Motel S: American Interstate Motel, Relax Inn, Sky Inn
Med	N: to + Hillcrest Hospital
Other	N: Grocery, Colonial RV Center S: Grocery, Bank, ATM
(130A)	Jct I-59N, to Gadsden, Chattanooga
132A	Oporto Rd, to US 78 (EB)
Gas	S: Crown, Shell
Food	S: Arby's, Burger King, Captain D's, Chili's, Denny's, Golden Palace, IHOP, KFC, Logan's Roadhouse, Mrs Winner's, McDonald's, O'Charley's,

Personal Notes

EXIT	ALABAMA
Food	S: Old Country Buffet, Olive Garden, Pizza Hut, Red Lobster, Ruby Tuesday, Steak & Ale, Shoney's, Taco Bell, Wendy's
Lodg	S: Motel Birmingham, Comfort Inn, Park Inn, USA Economy Lodge
Other	S: Grocery, Kmart, Century Plaza Mall, Eastwood Mall, Enterprise RAC, Firestone, Cobb Theatres, Penske Auto Center, ATMs, Banks
132B	to US 78, Montevallo Rd (EB)
Gas	N: Exxon
Food	N: Jack's Hamburgers, Krystal, Waffle House
Lodg	N: Eastwood Inn
Other	N: Lawson Field Stadium
132	to US 78, AL 4, Montevallo Rd, Oporto Rd (WB)
133	Kilgore Memorial Dr, to US 78, (EB), US 78, AL 4 (WB)
Gas	N: AmocoAmPm, Chevron, Exxon, Kangaroo S: BP
Food	N: Arby's, Golden Rule BBQ, Jack's, Krystal, Waffle House S: Arby's, McDonald's, Subway
Lodg	N: Comfort Inn, Super 8 S: Best Western ♥, Hampton Inn
Other	N: Banks, ATMs, Grocery S: Sam's Club, Dollar Tree, Wal-Mart
135	Old Leeds Rd, to US 78
Other	N: Birmingham Race Track
(136)	Jct I-459S, to Montgomery, Tuscaloosa, Gadsden

EXIT	ALABAMA
140	US 78, AL 4, Leeds
Gas	S: Chevron, Exxon
Other	S: Leeds Civic Center
144	US 411, Leeds, Moody (WB)
144AB	US 411, Leeds, Moody (EB)
FStop	S: Speedway #0119
Gas	N: BP, RaceTrac, Shell S: Exxon, RaceWay
Food	N: Arby's, Cracker Barrel, Pizza Hut, Milo's, Ruby Tuesday, Subway, Waffle House, Wendy's S: Burger King, Captain D's, KFC, Hardee's, McDonald's, Quincy's Steak House, Taco Bell
Lodg	N: Comfort Inn, Super 8 S: Days Inn
Other	N: Holiday Trav-L-Park▲, Winn Dixie, Auto Repairs S: AutoZone, Wal-Mart sc, Lowe's
147	Kelly Creek Rd, Pell City, to Brompton
Gas	N: Citgo S: Chevron
152	Cook Springs Rd, Pell City
153	US 78W, Chula Vista
156	US 78E, Pell City, Eden, Odenville
Gas	S: Chevron♦, Exxon, Shell
Other	S: to Gymno-Vita Nudist Park
158	US 231, Ashville, Pell City (EB)
FStop	S: Henson's Service
Gas	N: Exxon S: BP, Chevron, Citgo
Food	N: Arby's, Krystal, Western Sizzlin S: Burger King, Hardee's, KFC, Pizza Hut, McDonald's, Waffle House
Lodg	N: Hampton Inn S: Ramada
Med	S: + St Claire Reg'l Hospital
Other	N: Wal-Mart sc, Home Depot S: Auto Dealers, to Lakeside Landing RV Park & Marina▲
158AB	US 231, Ashville, Pell City (WB)
162	US 78, AL 4, Riverside, Pell City
Gas	S: BP, Chevron
Food	S: Pancake House
Lodg	S: Best Western
Other	N: Safe Harbor Camping▲
165	CR 207, Stemley Rd, Lincoln, Embry Cross Roads
TStop	S: I-20 Truck Stop/Shell (Scales), 165 Auto & Truck Plaza/Chevron
Food	S: HuddleHouse/165 TP, Rest/FastFood/I-20 TS, Old Hickory BBQ
Lodg	S: McCaig's Motel
TWash	S: TW
TServ	S: Bobby Orr Tire Shop & Garage, I-20 TS/Tires
Other	S: Laundry/WiFi/LP/I-20 TS, to Safe Harbor RV Park▲, Repair Services
168	AL 77, CR 5, Talladega, Lincoln
TStop	S: 77 Fuel Mart/Citgo N: Race City Travel Center/Shell
Gas	N: QV Gas, Chevron S: Shop n Fill
Food	N: Jack's Hamburger's, KFC, S: Rest/Race City TC, Burger King, Double E Family Rest, McDonald's, Pace Car Diner
Lodg	S: Days Inn ♥, McCaig's Motel

◆ = Regular Gas Stations with Diesel   ▲ = RV Friendly Locations   ♥ = Pet Friendly Locations
RED PRINT SHOWS LARGE VEHICLE PARKING/ACCESS ON SITE OR NEARBY   BROWN PRINT SHOWS CAMPGROUNDS/RV PARKS

Interstate 20 W/E

EXIT		ALABAMA
	TServ	N: 77 FM/Tires
	Other	N: Laundry/LP/77 FM
		S: Talladega Speedway, Int'l Motorsports Hall of Fame, Talladega Taz RV Park & Campground▲, Talladega Muni Airfield✈
173		AL 5, Lincoln, Eastaboga
	Gas	S: Shell, Texaco
	Food	S: Stuckey's/DQ/Texaco
	Lodg	S: Speedway Lodging
	Other	S: Talladega Speedway, Int'l Motor Sports Hall of Fame, Talladega Taz RV Park & Campground▲, Talladega Muni Airfield✈
179		CR 467, Oxford, to Munford, Coldwater (Addtl Serv N to US 78E)
	Other	N: Anniston Army Depot, G&J Truck Repair, Chevron (1 mi N)
185		AL 21, US 431N, Oxford, to Anniston
	FStop	S: Texaco Food Mart #155
	TStop	S: Cowboy's Food Mart #42 (Scales)
	Gas	N: BP◊, Chevron, Exxon, Shell◊
		S: RaceTrac, Mapco, Murphy
	Food	N: Arby's, Applebee's, Burger King, CiCi's, Hardee's, Krystal, McDonald's, Mex Rest, Pizza Hut, Red Lobster, Taco Bell, Shoney's, Starbucks, Waffle House
		S: ChickFilA, El Pablano Mexican Rest, Huddle House, Jazz Cajun Rest, Panda Chinese TakeOut, McDonald's, Outback Steakhouse, Pizza Express, Subway, Wendy's, FastFood/Texaco FS
	Lodg	N: Best Western, Days Inn, Howard Johnson Express, Red Carpet Inn, Travelers Inn
		S: Best Value Inn, Econo Lodge, Comfort Inn, Hampton Inn, Motel 6, Travelodge
	Med	N: + Stringfellow Memorial Hospital
	Other	N: Auto & Diesel Service, ATMs, Banks, Grocery, Firestone, RiteAid, Cinema 12, Quintard Mall, Office Max, Circuit City, Lowe's, Cheahea Harley Davidson, Auto Dealers, Anniston Museum of Natural History, to Amtrak, Fort McClellan Military Reservation
		S: Grocery, Home Depot, Dollar Tree, Best Buy, Wal-Mart sc, Auto & Tire Center, Auto Dealers, Vet♥, Target, Anniston Metro Airport✈
188		Morgan Rd, to US 78, Oxford, Anniston
	Gas	N: Exxon, Shell, Texaco
	Food	N: Brad's BBQ, Cracker Barrel, Huddle House, KFC, IHOP, Lone Star Steak House

EXIT		AL / GA
	Lodg	N: Holiday Inn Express, Budget Inn
	Other	N: Winn Dixie, U-Haul, Country Court RV Park▲
191		US 431, to US 78, Talladega Scenic Hwy
	Other	S: Cheaha State Park▲
199		AL 9, Heflin, Hollis
	FStop	N: Texaco Food Mart #185
		S: Super Mart #225/BP
	Gas	S: Chevron
	Food	N: Subway/TacoBell/Texaco FM, Hardee's, Pop's Burgers
		S: Huddle House
	Lodg	N: Howard Johnson
205		AL 46, Ranburne, to Heflin
	FStop	S: Adams Texaco, Spears Kwik Stop
	TStop	N: State Line Fuel Center/BP
	Food	N: FastFood/StateLine FC
	Tires	N: State Line FC
(208)		Weigh Station (WB)
210		AL 49, Abernathy
(214)		AL Welcome Center (WB) (RR, Phone, Picnic, Vend, Sec247, RVDump)

(CENTRAL / EASTERN TIME ZONE)

⊙ **ALABAMA**
⊙ **GEORGIA**

(EASTERN / CENTRAL TIME ZONE)

EXIT		
(1)		GA Welcome Center (EB) (RR, Phone, Picnic, Vend)
5		GA 100, Veterans Memorial Hwy, Tallapoosa, Bowdon
	FStop	N: Citgo Food Mart
	TStop	S: Noble Auto/Truck Plaza/Citgo (Scales), Pilot Travel Center #312 (Scales)
	Food	N: Waffle House
		S: Rest/DQ/Noble ATP, KFC/TacoBell/Pilot TC, Huddle House
	TWash	S: Noble ATP
	TServ	S: Noble ATP/Tires
	Other	S: Laundry/Noble ATP, Laundry/WiFi/Pilot TC
		N: Big Oak RV Park▲
9		Waco Rd, CR 348, Atlantic Ave
	TStop	N: Love's Travel Stop #311 (Scales)
	Food	N: Subway/Love's TS
	Other	N: Laundry/RVDump/Love's TS
11		GA 1, US 27, Martha Berry Hwy, Bremen, Carrollton
	FStop	N: Swifti Food Store #7/Texaco
		S: Cowboys Food Mart #69

EXIT		GEORGIA
	Gas	N: Murphy
		S: AmocoBP◊
	Food	N: Arby's, Cracker Barrel, McDonald's, Waffle House, Wendy's
		S: Waffle House
	Lodg	N: Days Inn, Hampton Inn, Travelodge
	Other	N: Ingles, Publix, Wal-Mart sc
		S: U-Haul
(15)		Weigh Station (WB)
19		GA 113, Temple-Carrollton Rd, Temple, Carrollton, W Atlanta
	TStop	N: Flying J Travel Plaza #5045/Conoco (Scales), Pilot Travel Center #417 (Scales)
	Gas	S: Shell
	Food	N: Rest/FastFood/FJ TP, Subway/Wendy's/Pilot TC, Hardee's, Waffle House
		S: Captain D's, Philly Connection, Waffle House
	TWash	N: Truckomat
	Other	N: Laundry/BarbSh/LP/FJ TP, Laundry/WiFi/Pilot TC
		S: to W GA Reg'l Airport✈
24		GA 61, Industrial Blvd, GA 101, Villa Rica, Carrollton
	FStop	N: Shell Mart
	Gas	N: BP, Exxon, RaceTrac
		S: Chevron, QT, Shell
	Food	N: Hardee's, KFC, McDonald's, Pizza Hut, Subway, Waffle House, Wendy's
	Lodg	N: Best Western Inn, Comfort Inn, Days Inn, Super 8
	Med	N: + Hospital
	Other	N: ATMs, Banks, CVS, Winn Dixie, GA State Hwy Patrol Post
		S: Wal-Mart sc, West GA College
26		CR 939, Liberty Rd, Villa Rica
	TStop	S: WilcoHess Travel Plaza #3010 (Scales)
	Gas	N: Shell◊
	Food	S: FastFood/Godfather Pizza/WilcoHess TP
	Lodg	S: American Inn
	TWash	S: WilcoHess TP
	TServ	S: WilcoHess TP/Tires
	Other	N: Auto Repairs
		S: Laundry/WilcoHess TP, Auto Repairs
30		CR 808, Post Rd, Winston
	Gas	S: Shell◊
34		GA 5, Bill Arp Rd, Douglasville
	Gas	N: RaceTrac, Shell
		S: Circle K, Chevron, Shell
	Food	N: China East, Hooters, Huddle House, Waffle House, Zaxby's
		S: Applebee's, Chili's, China King, IHOP, Krystal, Long John Silver,

◊ = Regular Gas Stations with Diesel   ▲ = RV Friendly Locations   ♥ = Pet Friendly Locations

RED PRINT SHOWS LARGE VEHICLE PARKING/ACCESS ON SITE OR NEARBY   BROWN PRINT SHOWS CAMPGROUNDS/RV PARKS

EXIT		GEORGIA
	Food	S: McDonald's, Pizza Hut, Red Lobster, Ruby Tuesday, Shoney's, Smoky Bones BBQ, Subway, Taco Bell, Waffle House, Wendy's
	Lodg	N: Holiday Inn, Lee's Motel, Sleep Inn
	Other	N: Auto Repair, Sam's Club, **Wal-Mart sc**, **Sheriff Dept** S: ATMs, Banks, Best Buy, Big 10 Tire, Goodyear, Home Depot, Kmart, Kroger, Lowe's, Office Depot, Publix, RiteAid, U-Haul, Walgreen's, US Post Office, Douglasville Crossings Shopping Center
36		CR 812WB, Chapel Hill Rd, Campbellton St N
	Gas	S: BP, Conoco, QT, Shell
	Food	S: Applebee's, Arby's, Asia Buffet, Hops Grill, Landry's, Logan's Roadhouse, O'Charley's, Olive Garden, Outback Steakhouse, Starbucks, Souper Salad, TGI Friday's, Waffle House
	Lodg	S: Hampton Inn, Super 8
	Med	N: + Promina Douglas Gen'l Hospital
	Other	N: Police Dept S: Circuit City, Firestone, Target, Arbor Place Mall, Arbor 18, **to** Seven Flags Speedway
37		GA 92, Fairburn Rd, Douglasville
	Gas	N: BP, Chevron, Citgo, RaceTrac S: RaceTrac, Shell
	Food	N: Arby's, Burger King, Cracker Barrel, Checkers, KFC, Krystal, McDonald's, Monterey Mex Rest, Mrs Winner's, Pagoda Express, Pizza Hut, Shoney's, Subway, Taco Bell, Waffle House, Wendy's S: Pizza, Mexican Rest
	Lodg	N: Comfort Inn, Days Inn. Holiday Inn Express, Ramada Inn, Royal Inn, Sun Suites, Super 8
	Med	N: + Promina Douglas Gen'l Hospital
	Other	N: ATMs, Banks, Advance Auto, Douglas Cinema 3, Auto Repairs, Big Lots, Kroger, **Super 1 RV Center** S: Ingles, Winn Dixie, Auto Repairs
41		CR 817, Lee Rd, Lithia Springs
	FStop	N: Econo Flash #5/Citgo S: Chevron Station
	Gas	S: BP, Shell
	Food	N: Hardee's, Courtni's Iron Skillet S: Waffle House
	Other	N: Auto Service, Tires, ATM, Banks S: Auto Service, Fleet Service, Grocery, **Sweetwater Creek State Park**▲
(42)		Weigh Station (EB)
44		GA 6, Thornton Rd, Austell, Atl Int'l Airport, Powder Springs, Lithia Springs
	Gas	N: Amoco, BP, Exxon, Phillips 66,
	Food	N: BBQ House, Burger King, ChicFilA, Cracker Barrel, Chilito's, Hardee's, KFC, IHOP, La Fiesta, McDonald's, New China, Olive Tree, Ruby Tuesday, Sonic, Subway, Shoney's, Taco Bell, Waffle House, Wendy's
	Lodg	N: Budget Inn, Extended Stay, Knights Inn, Shoney's Inn, Suite One S: Country Inn, Courtyard, Fairfield Inn, Knights Inn, Motel 6 ♥, SpringHill Suites
	Med	N: + Parkway Medical Center

Personal Notes

EXIT		GEORGIA
	Other	N: ATMs, Auto Dealers, Auto Repairs, Banks, CVS, Grocery, Kroger, Enterprise S: Auto Dealers, **Wal-Mart sc**
46		Riverside Pkwy S, CR 2623 (EB)
	Food	S: Wendy's, Waffle House
	Lodg	S: Days Inn, Sleep Inn, Wingate Inn
	Other	S: **to** Six Flags Over GA
46A		Riverside Pkwy SW, CR 2623, Six Flags Dr, Austell (WB) (Access Same as Exit #46)
46B		Six Flags Dr, CR 2633 (WB)
	Gas	N: Citgo, QT
	Food	N: Church's, Waffle House
	Lodg	N: La Quinta Inn ♥
47		Six Flags Pkwy, CR 4408, Six Flags Park (WB)
	Gas	N: BP
	Food	N: Waffle House S: McDonald's
	Lodg	N: La Quinta Inn ♥, Mark Inn S: Comfort Inn, Days Inn, Wingate Inn
	Other	S: Six Flags Over GA Amusement Park
49		GA 70, Fulton Industrial Blvd, Fulton Co Airport, Atlanta
	FStop	N: Citgo Truck Stop
	TStop	N: QT #777 (Scales)
	Gas	S: Amoco, Chevron, Conoco, Mapco
	Food	N: Checkers, EJ's Soul Food, Hardee's, DQ, Krystal, McDonald's, Mrs Winners, Shoney's, Subway, Waffle House, Wendy's, FastFood/QT, FastFood/Citgo S: Arby's, Blimpie, Burger King, Grand Buffet, Pizza Pizza, Waffle House

EXIT		GEORGIA
	Lodg	N: Days Inn, Efficiency Lodge, Masters Economy Inn, Ramada, Super 7 Inn S: Comfort Inn, Executive Inn, Parkview Inn, Red Roof Inn ♥, Super 8
	Other	N: ATMs, Banks, Greyhound, Fulton Co Brown Airport ✈ S: Grocery, U-Haul
(51A)		Jct I-285S, GA 407, to Macon, Montgomery (fr WB, left exit) (Serv at 1st Exits both dir)
(51B)		Jct I-285N, GA 407, to Chattanooga, Greenville
52		GA 280, Burton Rd, Holmes Dr, Hightower Rd, Atlanta (EB) (Gas & Food S to ML King Dr)
52AB		GA 280, HE Holmes Dr, Hightower Rd, Atlanta (WB)
53		to GA 139, M L King Jr Dr, Anderson Ave (Diff reaccess)
	Gas	N: Citgo, Shell S: BP
54		Langhorn St, Cascade Rd, Westview Dr, Sells Ave (WB)
55A		Lowery Blvd, Ashby St
	Gas	N: Chevron S: Exxon
	Food	S: Church's, Popeye's
	Other	S: Grocery, Mall, Bank, ATMs, Museums
55B		Lee St, Park St, to US 29 (WB) (Access to Ex #55A Services)
56A		McDaniel St, to US 19, US 29, US 41, Whitehall St (EB)
	Gas	N: Chevron
56B		Windsor St, Spring St, Turner Field, Central Ave, Pryor St,
	Other	N: GA State Univ, GA Dome, Philips Arena, The Omni, Underground Atlanta, CNN Studio Tour, GA World Congress Center, Greyhound, Loudermilk Conv Center S: Atlanta Fulton Co Stadium, Turner Field, Atlanta Braves
(57)		Jct I-75S, to Macon, I-85S to Montgomery, Jct I-75N to Chattanooga, I-85N, to Greenville
58A		Capitol Ave, Downtown (WB)
58B		Hill St, Turner Field (WB)
59A		Boulevard SE, to Confederate Ave
	Gas	S: BP
	Food	S: Factory BBQ
	Other	S: Youngblood Galleries, Art Exchange, Atl Zoo, Grant Pk, Cyclorama, Stockade
59B		GA 154 Conn, RR Ave, Glenwood Conn, Memorial Dr (EB)
60		US 23, GA 42, Moreland Ave (WB)
	Gas	N: Exxon, Texaco S: BP, Shell
	Food	S: Big Wok, Checker's, KFC, Krystal, Long John Silvers, Wendy's, McDonald's
	Lodg	N: Atlanta Motel

◇ = Regular Gas Stations with Diesel ▲ = RV Friendly Locations ♥ = Pet Friendly Locations
RED PRINT SHOWS LARGE VEHICLE PARKING/ACCESS ON SITE OR NEARBY BROWN PRINT SHOWS CAMPGROUNDS/RV PARKS

EXIT	GEORGIA	EXIT	GEORGIA	EXIT	GEORGIA
Other	N: Auto Services S: ATMs, Banks	Food	S: Burger King, DQ, McDonald's	Food	N: Outback Steakhouse, Red Lobster, Up the Creek Fish Camp & Grill, Subway S: Longhorn Steakhouse, McDonald's
60AB	**US 23, GA 42, Moreland Ave (EB)**	Lodg	N: Holiday Inn Express, Motel 6 ♥ S: Days Inn	Lodg	N: Holiday Inn, Richfield Lodge S: Comfort Inn
61A	**Maynard Terrace SE, to Memorial Dr, Atlanta (EB, No Re-Entry)**	Other	N: Laundromat, Grocery, Goodyear, Home Depot, Wal-Mart, Kroger, Ingles S: ATM, Bank, Auto Services, Truck Svc	Med	N: + Rockdale Hospital
Gas	N: BP	**71**	**Panola Rd, CR 5150, Lithonia**	Other	N: Carmike Cinemas, Rockdale Plaza, Auto Services S: Suncoast RV Center, Truck Repair, Laundromat, GA State Hwy Patrol Post
Food	N: Checkers, Wyatt's Diner	Gas	N: Exxon, Quik Trip, Shell		
61B	**GA 260, Glenwood Ave**		S: BP◊, Citgo, Exxon◊, Shell	**82**	**GA 20, GA 138, Stockbridge Hwy, Conyers, Monroe**
Gas	N: BP, Chevron	Food	N: Burger King, Checkers, Cajun, Cracker Barrel, KFC, McDonald's, Waffle House	FStop	N: Joy Food Mart
62	**Flat Shoals Rd SE (EB, No reaccess)**		S: IHOP, Popeye's, New China, Wendy's	Gas	N: BP, Speedway S: Chevron, QT, Shell◊
Gas	N: Citgo, Shell	Lodg	N: Holiday Inn Express, La Quinta Inn ♥, Super 8 S: Sleep Inn	Food	N: Cracker Barrel, Golden Corral, IHOP, McDonald's, Roadhouse Grill, Sonic, Waffle House, Woody's BBQ S: Arby's, Applebee's, Captain D's, DJ's Country Kitchen, Checker's, Chili's, CiCi's, Folks Rest, Hardee's, Hooters, KFC, Krystal, Long John Silver, Ruby Tuesday, Piccadilly, Shoney's, Taco Bell, Waffle House, Japanese Steak House
63	**Gresham Rd, CR 101, Flat Shoals Rd, CR 5194, Brannen Rd, Cook Rd (difficult reaccess)**	Other	N: 8 Cinemas S: Bank, Lowe's, Publix, NAPA, Tires +, Walgreen's, Wal-Mart sc		
Gas	N: Food Mart S: Amoco, Citgo, Phillips 66, Shell	**74**	**Evans Mills Rd, CR 6305, Lithonia, N to Stone Mountain**		
Food	S: G&G BBQ, Hot Spot, Church's	FStop	S: Citgo Truck Stop, Speedway		
Med	S: + Southside Healthcare Family Medical Clinic	Gas	N: BP, Chevron◊, Phillips 66, Shell◊		
65	**GA 155, Candler Rd, Decatur**	Food	N: KFC, McDonald's, Mamie's Kitchen, Shoney's, Waffle House, Wendy's S: DQ, Krystal, Waffle House, Rest/HJ	Lodg	N: Days Inn, La Quinta Inn ♥, Holiday Inn, Hampton Inn, Jameson Inn, Ramada S: Intown Suites, Suburban Lodge
Gas	N: Amoco, Citgo, Hess S: Amoco, Chevron, Conoco, Shell			Med	N: + Hospital
Food	N: Blimpie, Dundee's Café, Long John Silver, Pizza Hut, Red Lobster, Wendy's S: Arby's, Burger King, Checkers, DQ, Church's, KFC, McDonald's, Taco Bell	Lodg	S: Howard Johnson Express	Other	N: Auto Services, Shopping Plaza, ATM, Laundromat, Kmart, Staples, U-Haul, Wal-Mart sc, NAPA, Office Depot, Home Depot, Reid Stadium, Police Dept S: Firestone, Food Depot, Goodyear, Publix, RiteAid, Mall, Kroger, Shopping Center, Target, US Post Office
		Other	S: Grocery, CVS, to Stonecrest Mall		
		75	**GA 124, US 278, Turner Hill Rd**		
Lodg	N: Discover Inn, Econo Lodge, Howard Johnson S: Candler Inn, Sunset Lodge	FStop	N: Buddy's Fuel Stop #5/Citgo		
		Gas	N: BP, Citgo		
Other	N: CVS, U-Haul S: ATMs, Banks, Kroger, South Dekalb Mall, Winn Dixie, Firestone, Jiffy Lube, CarWash, Tires	Food	S: Applebee's, Bourbon St Café, Grand China, Great Steak & Potato, Kampai Sushi & Steak, McDonald's, La Costa, Olive Garden, Smokey Bones BBQ, Steak N Shake, Subway, This is it BBQ & Seafood, Zaxby's, Wendy's, Pizza	**(82)**	**Weigh Station (WB)**
				(83)	**Parking Area (WB)**
				84	**GA 162, Salem Rd**
66	**Columbia Dr, CR 5154, Decatur (EB, No Re-Entry)**			Gas	S: BP, Chevron, Liberty, RaceTrac
Gas	N: Texaco S: Fina			Food	S: Burger King, China Kitchen, Subway, Smokehouse BBQ, Waffle House
Other	N: Auto Repair	Lodg	S: AmeriSuites	Other	N: BJ's Club S: ATMs, Auto Service, Bank, Ingles, Golf Courses, Winn Dixie, Pharmacy, Crown RV, Super 1 RV Center
(67)	**I-285, S-Macon, N-Greenville (EB)**	Other	N: Rockdale Truck Repair S: Stonecrest Mall, Bank, ATM, Tires +		
(67A)	**Jct I-285S ByPass, to Atlanta Int'l Airport, Macon (WB)**	**78**	**Sigman Rd, CR 66, Conyers**		
		Gas	N: Circle K		
(67B)	**Jct I-285N ByPass, to Greenville, Chattanooga (WB)**	Food	N: Waffle House	**88**	**Almon Rd, CR 46, Crowell Rd, Covington, to Porterdale**
		Other	N: Auto Service, Tires, Diesel Service, Sheriff Dept S: Auto Dealers, GA State Hwy Patrol Post (Frontage Rd)		
68	**Wesley Chapel Rd, CR 5196, Snapfinger Woods Dr, Decatur**			Gas	N: Chevron S: BP
Gas	N: Conoco, Exxon, Shell S: BP, Chevron, Crown, Shell	**(79)**	**Parking Area (EB)**	Other	N: Riverside Estates RV Park ▲
Food	N: Blimpie, Captain D's, Checkers, Chick-Fil-A, Church's, Hardee's, Hong Kong Buffet, KFC, Long John Silvers, Popeye's, Subway, Taco Bell, 3 Dollar Café, Waffle House, Wendy's, Uncle Mack's BBQ	**80**	**West Ave, Klondike Rd, CR 437, Conyers**	**90**	**US 278E, GA 12, to GA 81, Turner Lk Rd NW, Covington, Oxford**
		Gas	N: Speedway◊, Exxon, Shell◊ S: Exxon◊	Gas	S: BP, Citgo, RaceTrac, Shell
		Food	N: Rest/Holiday Inn, Atl Bread Co, DQ, Don Pablo's, Golden Palace, IHOP, Mrs Winner's, O'Charley's, On the Border,	Food	S: Arby's, Checkers, Hardee's, Japanese Rib House, Shoney's, Taco Bell,

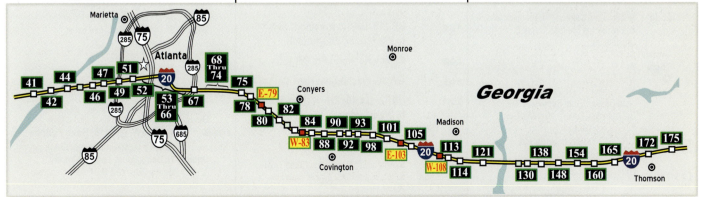

◊ = Regular Gas Stations with Diesel   ▲ = RV Friendly Locations   ♥ = Pet Friendly Locations

RED PRINT SHOWS LARGE VEHICLE PARKING/ACCESS ON SITE OR NEARBY   BROWN PRINT SHOWS CAMPGROUNDS/RV PARKS

Page 105

Interstate 20 W/E

EXIT		GEORGIA
	Food	S: Waffle House, Zaxby's
	Med	S: + Hospital
	Other	S: Auto Service, ATMs, Banks, Kroger, Kmart, Grocery, Tires
92		Alcovy Rd, CR 660, Covington (Addtl Serv S to US 278)
	FStop	N: Circle K #2284
	Gas	N: Chevron
	Food	N: Krystal's, McDonald's, Pippin's BBQ, Waffle House
	Lodg	N: Best Western, Days Inn, Econo Lodge, Holiday Inn, Cornerstone Lodge
	Med	S: + Hospital
	Other	N: Covington Muni Airport→
93		GA 142, John R Williams Hwy, Hazelbrand, Covington (Serv South to US 278)
	FStop	S: Flash Foods #259/Exxon
	Gas	S: Shell
	Food	S: Waffle House
	Lodg	S: Jameson Inn
98		GA 11, Social Circle, to Monroe, Monticello (Addtl Serv 4mi N in Soc Cir)
	Gas	S: BP, Chevron◊
	Food	S: Blimpie, Log Cabin BBQ
	Other	S: Fox Vineyards Winery
101		US 278, GA 12, Social Circle
(103)		Rest Area (EB) (RR, Phone, Picnic, Vend, RVDump)
105		Newborn Rd, CR 240, Rutledge
	Gas	N: BP
	Food	N: Carol's Wing Shack, Classic Rock Café, Yesterday's Cafe
	Other	N: Grocery, Bank, to Hard Labor Creek State Park▲
(108)		Rest Area (WB) (RR, Phone, Picnic, Vend, RVDump)
113		GA 83, Monticello Hwy, Madison
	Gas	S: BP
	Med	N: + Hospital
	Other	S: GA State Hwy Patrol Post
114		US 441, US 129, GA 24, Eatonton Hwy, Madison, Eatonton
	TStop	N: Pilot Travel Center #420 (Scales) S: Travel Center of America #45/BP (Scales), Fuel Mart #786
	Gas	N: Chevron, Citgo, RaceTrac S: Texaco
	Food	N: FastFood/Pilot TC, Arby's, Burger King, Cracker Barrel, KFC, Krystal, McDonald's, Open Air BBQ, Pizza Hut, Subway/Chevron, Taco Bell, Waffle House, Wendy's, Zaxby's, Rest/Days Inn S: Waffle House, CountryPride/Popeyes/TA TC
	Lodg	N: Days Inn, Comfort Inn, Hampton Inn, S: Holiday Inn Express, Super 8, Wingate Inn
	TWash	S: TA TC
	TServ	S: TA TC/Tires, Towing & Truck Repair
	Med	N: + Hospital
	Other	N: Laundry/WiFi/RVDump/Pilot TC, Auto Dealers, Auto Repairs, ATMs, Bi-Lo, Ingles, Lowe's, Wal-Mart sc S: Laundry/WiFi/TA TC
121		CR 251, Seven Islands Rd, Buckhead
(130)		Weigh Station (Both dir)

Personal Notes

EXIT		GEORGIA
130		GA 44, Eatonton Rd, Greensboro
	Gas	N: Exxon S: Chevron◊
	Food	N: McDonald's, Wendy's, Waffle House
	Lodg	N: Jameson Inn
	Other	S: Country Boy RV Park▲, to Parks Ferry Park/GA Power▲
138		GA 77, GA 15, Siloam, Union Point, Sparta
	TStop	N: Flying J Travel Plaza # (Scales)
	Gas	N: Amoco◊, Exxon
	Food	N: Rest/FastFood/FJ TP
	Med	S: + Hospital
	Other	N: Laundry/WiFi/LP/RVDump/FJ TP
148		GA 22, Crawfordville, Sparta
	TStop	S: Midway Truck Stop/Pure
	Gas	S: Amoco/BP◊
	Food	S: FastFood/Midway TS
	Tires	S: Midway TS
	Other	N: AH Stephens Hist Memorial State Park▲
154		US 278, GA 12, Norwood, to Warrenton, Washington
160		Cadley Norwood Rd, CR 185
165		GA 80, Washington Hwy, Camak
172		US 78, GA 10, GA 17, Thomson, to Washington
	TStop	N: Love's Travel Stop #354 (Scales) S: Circle K #5367 (Scales)
	Gas	N: BP◊, Chevron◊ S: AmocoBP, RaceTrac◊, Shell
	Food	N: ChestersGrill/Subway/Love's TS, Waffle House

EXIT		GEORGIA
		S: Amigos Rest, Burger King, Long John Silver, Krystal, McDonald's, Pizza Hut, Shoney's, Waffle House, Wendy's, Western Sizzlin', FastFood/Circle K
	Lodg	S: Best Western, Holiday Inn
	Med	S: + Hospital
	Other	N: WiFi/RVDump/Love's TS, GA State Patrol Post, Auto Dealers, Thomson McDuffie Co Airport→, to Big Hart Camp Area▲, Raysville Bridge Camp Area▲ S: AutoZone, Auto Repairs, ATMs, Banks, Food Lion, CVS, Kmart, Lowe's, Twin Cinema, Wal-Mart
175		GA 150, Cobbham Rd, Thomson
	TStop	N: USA Truck Stop/BP
	Food	N: Rest/USA TS
	Lodg	N: Days Inn
	TServ	N: USA TS
	Other	N: to Mistletoe State Park▲
(181)		Rest Areas (Both dir) (RR, Phone, Picnic, Vend, RVDump)
183		GA 47, US 221, Appling Harlem Rd, Harlem
	Gas	N: 76 S: BP◊
	Other	N: to MIL/Pointes West Rec Area▲, MIL/Fort Gordon Rec Area▲, to Ridge Road Camp Area▲, to Petersburg Camp Area▲
(187)		Weigh Station (Both dir)
190		GA 388, Lewiston Rd, Grovetown
	TStop	N: BP Pumping Station #8
	Gas	S: 76, Chevron
	Food	N: FastFood/BP PS, Waffle House S: McDonald's, Subway
	Other	S: Fort Gordon Military Res
194		GA 383, Belair Rd, Dyess Pkwy, Augusta, Evans
	FStop	N: Circle K #5382/76
	TStop	S: Pilot Travel Center #65 (Scales)
	Gas	N: Citgo, Phillips 66◊ S: AmocoBP◊
	Food	N: FastFood/Circle K, Burger King, Popeye's, Waffle House S: Subway/Pilot TC, Cracker Barrel, Huddle House, Waffle House
	Lodg	N: Georgia Inn, Villager Lodge S: America's Best Inn, Best Western, Hampton Inn, Quality Inn, Ramada Ltd
	Other	N: ATM, Banks, Food Lion, Funsville Amusement Park S: WiFi/Pilot TC, Goodyear
195		Wheeler Rd, CR 601, Augusta
	Gas	N: Chevron S: BP◊, Circle K◊, Shell◊
	Food	N: O'Charley's, Waffle House
	Lodg	S: Days Inn, Red Roof Inn♥, Ramada Inn
	Med	S: + Doctors Hospital
	Other	N: Auto Service, Tires S: ATMs, Banks, Auto Services
(196A)		Jct I-520E, GA 415, Bobby Jones Expwy (Access All Serv 1st Exit S)
	Other	S: Target, Best Buy, Office Depot
196B		GA 232W, GA 415, Bobby Jones Expwy (Access All Serv 1st Exit N)
	Other	N: Home Depot, Lowe's, Grocery, Sam's Club, Wal-Mart, Auto Services

Page 106
◊ = Regular Gas Stations with Diesel   ▲ = RV Friendly Locations   ♥ = Pet Friendly Locations
RED PRINT SHOWS LARGE VEHICLE PARKING/ACCESS ON SITE OR NEARBY   BROWN PRINT SHOWS CAMPGROUNDS/RV PARKS

EXIT		GA / SC
199		GA 28, Washington Rd, Augusta
	FStop	S: Circle K #5582/76
	Gas	N: BP, RaceTrac, Depot S: 76, Amoco, Crown
	Food	N: Applebee's, Burger King, Captain D's, Checkers, Damon's, Huddle House, Krystal, Pizza Hut, Japanese Steakhouse, McDonald's, Piccadilly, Sho Gun, Waffle House, Shoney's S: Bojangles, Carrabba's, Fat Tuesday, Hooter's, Long John Silver, Lone Star Steakhouse, McDonald's, Michael's, Malley's Bagel, Olive Garden, Outback Steakhouse, Red Lobster, Subway, TGI Fridays, Waffle House, Wendy's
	Lodg	N: Courtyard, Days Inn, Hampton Inn, Holiday Inn, Homewood Suites, Howard Johnson, Masters Inn, La Quinta Inn♥, Ramada Inn, Radisson Inn, Sunset Inn, Shoney's Inn, Travelodge S: Fairfield Inn, Guest House Inn, Knights Inn, Rodeway Inn, Westbank Inn
	TServ	S: Cummins South
	Med	S: + Hospital
	Other	N: ATM, Banks, Auto Service S: ATMs, Banks, Kroger, Pep Boys, Publix, Goodyear, Master 7 Cinema
200		GA 104, River Watch Pkwy, Augusta
	TStop	N: Pilot Travel Center #144 (Scales)
	Food	N: Wendy's/Pilot TC
	Lodg	N: Amerisuites, Quality Inn, Sleep Inn
	Other	N: Laundry/WiFi/Pilot TC
(201)		GA Welcome Center (WB) (RR, Phone, Picnic, Vend)

(EASTERN TIME ZONE)

⭕ GEORGIA
⭕ SOUTH CAROLINA

(EASTERN TIME ZONE)

(1)		SC Welcome Center (EB) (RR, Phone, Picnic, Vend)
1		SC 230, Martintown Rd, N Augusta (Addt'l Serv 4mi S in N Augusta)
	FStop	S: Circle K #5588/76
	Food	S: Blimpie/Circle K, Waffle House
5		US 25, SC 121, N Augusta Belvedere, Edgefield, Johnston
	FStop	S: Sunoco #2670
	TStop	N: S & S Truck Stop, Circle K #5350/76 (Scales)
	Gas	N: BP◆ S: Citgo◆, Phillips 66◆
	Food	N: Rest/Bojangles/S&S TS, FastFood/Circle K, DQ, Hardee's, Huddle House, Sonic S: Taco Bell, Waffle House
	Lodg	N: Sleep Inn
	Tires	N: S&S TS
	TWash	N: S&S TS
	Other	N: Laundry/S&S TS, Winn Dixie
11		SC 144, Graniteville
	TStop	N: Kent's Corner #24/BP (Scales)
	Food	N: Rest/Kent's
	TWash	N: Kent's
	Other	N: Laundry/Kent's

EXIT		SOUTH CAROLINA
18		SC 19, Aiken, Johnston
	FStop	S: Kent's Corner #15/BP
	Gas	S: Shell
	Food	S: FastFood/Kent's, Blimpie/Shell, Waffle House
	Lodg	S: Deluxe Inn, GuestHouse Inn
	Med	S: + Hospital
	Other	N: C&E Truck & Auto Repair, Auto & Cycle Shop
(20)		Parking Area (Both dir)
22		US 1, Columbia Hwy, Aiken, to Ridge Spring
	TStop	S: Circle K #5377
	Gas	S: 76, BP, RaceTrac, Shell
	Food	S: FastFood/Circle K, Baynham Family Rest, Hardee's, McDonald's, Waffle House
	Lodg	S: Days Inn, Inn of Aiken
	Other	S: Aiken RV Park▲, Pineacres Park, Aiken Muni Airport✈, Auto & Truck Serv
29		SC 49, Wire Rd, Aiken
33		SC 39, Batesburg, Wagener, Moneta
	TStop	S: Kent's Corner #18/BP
	Gas	N: Shell
	Food	N: Huddle House S: Rest/Kent's
(35)		Weigh Station (EB)
39		US 178, Orangeburg Rd, Batesburg, Leesville
	FStop	N: Mr B's Exxon
	TStop	S: Hill View Truck Stop/BP

EXIT		SOUTH CAROLINA
	Food	N: Mr B's Grill S: Rest/FastFood/Hill View TS
	TServ	S: Hill View TS/Tires
	Other	S: Cedar Pond Campground▲
44		SC 34, Gilbert
	TStop	N: 44 Truck Stop/Citgo
	Food	N: Rest/44 TS
	TServ	N: 44 TS/Tires
	Other	N: Laundry/44 TS
(48)		Parking Area (Both dir)
51		SC 204, Lexington, Gilbert
	FStop	S: Pitt Stop #38/Mobil
	TStop	N: Pitt Stop #15/Shell
	Gas	N: Exxon◆
	Food	N: FastFood/Pitt Stop S: Subway, Gertie's
(53)		Weigh Station (WB)
55		SC 6, Lexington, Swansea
	FStop	S: Kangaroo Express #3254/BP
	Gas	N: Shell S: Citgo, Kangaroo
	Food	N: Hardee's S: McDonald's, Subway, Waffle House
	Lodg	N: Comfort Inn, Hampton Inn S: Ramada Inn
	Other	S: CVS, ATM, Bank, Grocery, Day Star Truck & Trailer Repair, Auto Repairs, Ken's Bus Repair, Edmund RV Park▲, John's RV Sales & Service
58		US 1, Lexington, W Columbia
	TStop	N: Pitt Stop #6/Shell S: The 1 Truck Stop
	Gas	N: Exxon
	Food	N: FastFood/Pitt Stop, Waffle House S: Burger King, McDonald's, KFC
	Other	N: Auto Repairs, Police Dept, Sheriff Dept S: Barnyard RV Park▲, Auto Repair, Auto Rental, to Columbia Airport✈, Univ of SC
61		US 378, Sunset Blvd, Lexington, W Columbia
	Gas	S: 76, AmocoBP
	Food	S: Waffle House
	Med	S: + Lexington Medical Center
	Other	N: Rental Cars S: Lexington Automotive & Truck
63		SC 273, Bush River Rd, Columbia
	Gas	N: 76/Circle K S: Citgo, Raceway
	Food	N: Burger King, Cracker Barrel, Subway S: El Chico Mexican, Fuddrucker's, Waffle House
	Lodg	N: Sheraton, Travelodge S: Courtyard, Best Western, Knights Inn, Sleep Inn
	Other	N: Market Pointe Mall, CVS S: Rental Cars
(64A)		Jct I-26, US 76E, to Columbia
(64B)		Jct I-26, US 76W, to Greenville, Spartanburg
65		US 176, Broad River Rd, Columbia
	Gas	N: 76, Exxon S: Hess, RaceWay
	Food	N: Applebee's, Bojangles, Monterey Mex Rest, Subway, Waffle House S: Arby's, Church's, Cracker Jack's, Captain Tom's Seafood, Golden Corral,

◆ = Regular Gas Stations with Diesel   ▲ = RV Friendly Locations   ♥ = Pet Friendly Locations
RED PRINT SHOWS LARGE VEHICLE PARKING/ACCESS ON SITE OR NEARBY   BROWN PRINT SHOWS CAMPGROUNDS/RV PARKS

W I-20 — SOUTH CAROLINA

EXIT		SOUTH CAROLINA
	Food	S: Hooters, McDonald's, KFC, Touch of India, Wendy's
	Lodg	N: Best Inn
		S: American Inn, Econo Lodge, InTowne Suites, La Quinta Inn♥, Ramada
	Other	N: Auto & Tire Services
		S: CVS, Advance Auto, Food Lion, Jiffy Lube, Bank, ATMs
68		SC 215, Monticello Rd, Columbia, to Jenkinsville
	FStop	N: Pitt Stop #10/Shell
	Gas	N: Exxon
		S: Citgo
	Food	N: Sunrise Rest & Cafe
	Other	N: Diesel Repair, Auto Repair
70		US 321, Fairfield Rd, Columbia, Winnsboro
	TStop	S: Flying J Travel Plaza #5031/Conoco (Scales)
	Gas	S: Exxon
	Food	S: Rest/FastFood/FJ TP, Hardee's
	Lodg	S: Super 8
	Other	S: Laundry/BarbSh/WiFi/LP/RVDump/FJ TP
71		US 21, N Main St, Columbia
	TStop	N: AAW Travel Center/Exxon (Scales)
	Gas	N: BP
		S: Shell
	Food	N: FastFood/AAW TC, McDonald's
	Lodg	N: Days Inn
	TWash	N: AAW TC
	TServ	N: AAW TC
	Other	N: Laundry/LP/WiFi/AAW TC
72		SC 555, Farrow Rd
73A		SC 277S, Columbia
73B		SC 277N, to I-77N, Charlotte
74		US 1, Two Notch Rd, Ft Jackson
	Gas	N: 76, BP, Exxon◊
		S: Hess◊, Exxon, Shell◊
	Food	N: Arby's, Chili's, Denny's, IHOP, Outback Steakhouse, Waffle House
		S: Applebee's, Bojangles, Captain D's, Hardee's, McDonald's, O'Charley's, Roadhouse Grill, Santa Fe Mexican, Shoney's, Wendy's, Western Sizzlin'
	Lodg	N: Amerisuites, Baymont Inn, Comfort Inn, Best Western, Fairfield Inn, Holiday Inn, Microtel, Motel 6♥, Red Roof Inn♥, Ramada Plaza, Travelodge
		S: Days Inn♥
	Med	N: + Richland Memorial Hospital
	Other	N: ATMs, Banks, US Post Office, Home Depot, Bowling, to Sesquicentennial State Park▲

EXIT		SOUTH CAROLINA
	Other	S: ATMs, Banks, Auto Services, Best Buy, Firestone, NAPA, Lowe's, Staples, Columbia Place Mall, Theatres
(76)		Jct I-77, Charlotte, Charleston (EB)
(76A)		Jct I-77, N-Charlotte, S-Charleston
76B		SC 63, Alpine Rd, to Fort Jackson
	Other	N: Sesquicentennial State Park▲
		S: Little Pig BBQ, Fort Jackson Mil Res
80		Clemson Rd, Columbia
	Gas	N: 76, Exxon◊, Shell◊
		S: Circle K
	Food	N: McDonald's, Waffle House, Zaxby's
		S: Bojangles
	Lodg	N: Holiday Inn Express
	Other	N: CVS
82		SC 53, Pierce Rd, Elgin, Pontiac
	Gas	N: Shell
	Food	N: Piccadilly Pizza

EXIT		SOUTH CAROLINA
87		SC 47, White Pond Rd, Elgin
	FStop	N: BP
	Gas	N: Texaco◊
92		US 601, Lugoff, Camden
	TStop	N: Pilot Travel Center #346 (Scales)
	Gas	N: Shell
	Food	N: DQ/Subway/Pilot TC, Hardee's, Waffle House
	Lodg	N: Days Inn, Ramada, Travelodge
	Other	N: WiFi/Pilot TC, Camden RV Park▲
(93)		Rest Area (Both dir) (RR, Phone, Vend)
98		US 521, Camden, Sumter
	Gas	N: Citgo, Exxon, Shell
	Lodg	N: Fairfield Inn
	Med	N: + Hospital
101		SC 329, Camden
108		SC 31, to SC 34, Bishopville, to Manville, Jamestown
	Gas	N: Shell
		S: Citgo
116		US 15, Sumter Hwy, Bishopville, Sumter, to Hartsville
	TStop	N: Interstate Shell
		S: WilcoHess Travel Plaza #935 (Scales)
	Food	N: FastFood/Shell, McDonald's, Subway, Waffle House
		S: DQ/Wendy's/WilcoHess
	Lodg	N: Econo Lodge
	Other	N: Laundry/Interstate Shell
120		SC 341, Bishopville, Lynchburg, Lake City, Elliot
	Gas	S: Exxon◊
	Food	S: Restaurant
	Lodg	S: Howard Johnson
123		SC 22, Lamar, Lee State Park
	Gas	N: BP
	Other	N: Lee State Park▲
(129)		Parking Area (Both dir)
131		US 401, SC 403, Timmonsville, Darlington, Lamar
	Gas	S: BP, Exxon
	Food	S: Ronnie's Café, JJ's Drive In
	Other	N: to Darlington Int'l Raceway
137		SC 340, Darlington
(141AB)		Jct I-95, N-Fayetteville, S-Savannah

(I-20 starts/ends on I-95, Exit #160)

ⓘ SOUTH CAROLINA

Begin I-20 Westbound from Jct I-95 in Florence, SC to Jct I-55 at Jackson, MS.

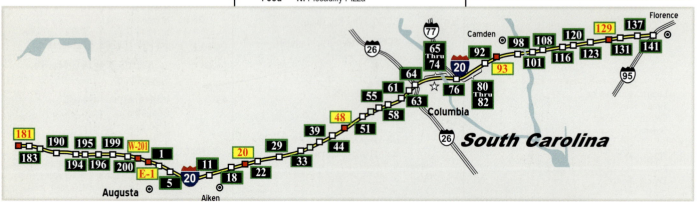

◊ = Regular Gas Stations with Diesel   ▲ = RV Friendly Locations   ♥ = Pet Friendly Locations
RED PRINT SHOWS LARGE VEHICLE PARKING/ACCESS ON SITE OR NEARBY   BROWN PRINT SHOWS CAMPGROUNDS/RV PARKS

EXIT		IL / KY
	Begin I-24 Eastbound at Jct I-57 near Marion, IL to Chattanooga, TN	

⊙ ILLINOIS
(CENTRAL TIME ZONE)
(I-24 begins/ends on I-57, Exit #44)

Exit		
(1)		Jct I-57, N-Chicago, S-Memphis
7		CR12, Goreville, Tunnel Hill
	FStop	N: Citgo
	Other	S: Ferne Clyffe State Park▲
14		US 45, Vienna, Harrisburg
	Gas	S: Citgo
	Other	N: Auto Repair
16		IL 146, Vienna, Golconda
	Gas	S: Citgo, Shell
	Food	N: Rest/Budget Inn
		S: DQ, McDonald's
	Lodg	N: Budget Inn
		S: Ramada Inn
27		CR 10, Metropolis, New Columbia, Big Bay
37		US 45, Metropolis, Brookport
	FStop	N: Veach Short Stop/Citgo
	TStop	S: Metropolis Truck & Travel Plaza/BP
	Food	S: Rest/Metropolis TTP, Pizza Hut, KFC, McDonald's, Waffle Hut, Rest/Days Inn
	Lodg	S: Best Inns of America, Best Western, Comfort Inn, Days Inn
	TServ	N: Veach SS
		S: Metropolis TTP
	Med	S: + Hospital
	Other	S: Auto Dealers, ATMs, Banks, CarWash, Metropolis Muni Airport✈, Players Casino, Fort Massac State Park▲
(37)		IL Welcome Center (Both dir) (RR, Phone, Picnic, Vend, Info)

(CENTRAL TIME ZONE)

◯ ILLINOIS
⊙ KENTUCKY
(CENTRAL TIME ZONE)

3		KY 305, Cairo Rd, Paducah
	TStop	N: Exit 3 Travel Plaza/BP (Scales)
		S: Pilot Travel Center #358 (Scales)
	Gas	S: BP
	Food	N: Rest/FastFood/Exit 3 TP, Huddle House, Rest/Comfort Inn
		S: Subway/Pilot TC, Waffle Hut
	Lodg	N: Comfort Inn, Ramada, Super 8
		S: Baymont Inn
	TServ	N: Exit 3 TP, A & K Truck Repair
		S: Whayne Power System
	TWash	N: Exit 3 TP

EXIT		KENTUCKY
	Other	N: Laundry/Exit 3 TP
		S: Fern Lake Campground▲
4		US 60, Bus Loop 24, Wickliffe, Paducah
	Gas	N: Shell, Star, Chevron
		S: Citgo, Shell, Murphy
	Food	N: Applebee's, Bob Evans, Burger King, Denny's, McDonald's, O'Charley's, Outback Steakhouse, Rest/Days Inn
		S: Backwoods BBQ, Captain D's, Chuck E Cheese, Cracker Barrel, Hardee's, Logan's, Olive Garden, Pizza Hut, Red Lobster, Ryan's Grill, Shoney's, Steak 'n Shake, Subway, Wendy's
	Lodg	N: Days Inn, El Rancho Inn, Holiday Inn
		S: Best Inns, Hampton Inn, Motel 6♥
	TServ	S: McBridge Mack Truck Sales
	Med	N: + Hospital
	Other	N: Auto Dealers, Auto Repairs, Kroger
		S: Advance Auto, Aldi, ATMs, Banks, Auto Services, Cinemark, Lowe's, Office Depot, Sam's, Wal-Mart sc, Mall, Mill springs Fun Park, Barkley Reg'l Airport✈
7		US 62, Blandville Rd, Paducah, US 45, Mayfield, Bardwell
	Gas	N: BP, Citgo, Petro2, Shell◊
		S: BP, Shell
	Food	N: Burger King, Subway, Taco Bell
		S: Arby's, Golden Corral, McDonald's, Sonic, Waffle House
	Lodg	N: Quality Inn
		S: Sunset Inn
	Med	N: + Hospital
	Other	S: Kmart, Grocery, Pharmacy
		KY Welcome Center (WB) (RR, Phones, Vend)
11		KY 1954, Husband Rd, Paducah
	TStop	N: Exit 11 Exxon
	Food	N: FastFood/Ex 11
	Lodg	N: Best Western
	TServ	N: Thurston Truck Parts
	Other	N: Laundry/Ex 11, Duck Creek RV Park▲
16		US 68, Paducah
	TStop	S: Southern Pride Auto/Truck Plaza/BP (Scales)
	Food	S: FastFood/Southern Pride TP
	TWash	S: Southern Pride ATP
	TServ	S: Southern Pride ATP
	Other	S: Laundry/SP ATP
25AB		Purchase Pkwy (TOLL), Fulton, Calvert City (Acc Serv 1mi N)
27		US 62, Calvert City, KY Dam
	TStop	S: Calvert City Travel Plaza (Scales)
	Gas	N: BP, Chevron, Shell

EXIT		KENTUCKY
	Food	N: Cracker Barrel, DQ, KFC, McDonald's, Waffle House
		S: Rest/Calvert City TP
	Lodg	N: Fox Fire Motor Inn, Super 8
		S: Ramada Inn Resort KY Dam
	TServ	N: Calvert City TP/Tires, Duckett Truck Center, Freightliner
	Other	N: Cypress Lakes RV Park▲, Paducah/I-24 Ky Lake KOA▲, to LazyDaz RV Park▲
		S: Ky Dam Village State Resort Park▲
31		KY 453, Grand Rivers, Smithland
	Gas	N: Amoco
		S: BP
	Food	S: Diana's Fam Rest, Miss Scarlett's
	Lodg	N: Microtel
		S: Best Western
	Other	S: Exit 31 RV Park▲, to Lake Barkley Canal Rec Area▲
(36)		Weigh Station (Both dir)
40		US 62, US 641, Kuttawa, to Eddyville
	FStop	S: BP
	TStop	S: AmBest/Huck's Travel Center (Scales)
	Gas	S: Shell
	Food	S: FastFood/Hucks TC, Wendy's/BP, Huddle House, Southwest Grill
	Lodg	N: Country Inn, Hampton Inn, Relax Inn
	Other	S: Laundry/Huck's TC
42		West KY Pkwy East, Eddyville, Princeton, Elizabethtown
45		KY 293, Eddyville, Princeton
	Gas	S: Chevron
	Lodg	S: Regency Inn
	Other	S: Lake Barkley RV Resort▲, Cedar Hill RV Park▲, Indian Point RV Park▲, Holiday Hills Resort▲
56		KY 139, Princeton, Cadiz
	FStop	S: Blue Spring Chevron
	Other	S: to Lake Barkley Hurricane Creek Rec Area▲, Goose Hollow Campground▲, to appr 9mi: Ky Lakes/Prizer Pt KOA▲
65		US 68, KY 80, Cadiz, Hopkinsville
	Gas	S: AmocoBP◊, Phillips 66◊, Shell
	Food	S: Cracker Barrel, Ky Smokehouse, McDonald's, Wendy's
	Lodg	S: Holiday Inn, Super 8
	Med	S: + Hospital
	Other	S: to Lake Barkley State Park Resort▲
73		KY 117, Hopkinsville, to Newstead, Gracey

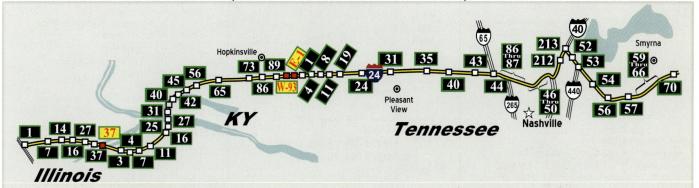

◊ = Regular Gas Stations with Diesel   ▲ = RV Friendly Locations   ♥ = Pet Friendly Locations   Page 109
RED PRINT SHOWS LARGE VEHICLE PARKING/ACCESS ON SITE OR NEARBY   BROWN PRINT SHOWS CAMPGROUNDS/RV PARKS

EXIT		KY / TN
86		US 41 Alt, Oak Grove, Hopkinsville, Fort Campbell
	TStop	N: I-24 Chevron Fuel Express (Scales)
		S: Flying J Travel Plaza #5058/Conoco (Scales), Pilot Travel Center #439
	Gas	S: BP
	Food	N: FastFood/I-24 Chevron FE
		S: Rest/FastFood/FJ TP, Subway/Wendy's/Pilot TC, Burger King, Great American Buffet, McDonald's, Waffle House
	Lodg	S: Baymont Inn, Best Western, Comfort Inn, Days Inn, Holiday Inn Express
	Med	S: + Hospital
	Other	S: Laundry/WiFi/LP/RVDump/FJ TP, Laundry/WiFi/Pilot TC, Tourist Info, ATMs, Banks, Ft Campbell Mil Res
89		KY 115, Pembroke, Oak Grove
	TStop	S: Pilot Travel Center #49/Speedway (Scales)
	Gas	S: Citgo
	Food	N: S&J Cafe
		S: McDonald's/Pilot TC
	TWash	S: Pilot TC
	Other	S: Laundry/WiFi/Pilot TC
(93)		KY Welcome Center (WB) (RR, Phone, Picnic, Vend)
		(CENTRAL TIME ZONE)

KENTUCKY
TENNESSEE
(CENTRAL TIME ZONE)

(1)		TN Welcome Center (EB) (RR, Phone, Picnic, Vend)
1		TN 48, Clarksville, Trenton
	Gas	N: Shell◆
		S: BP, Exxon
	Other	N: Clarksville RV Park & Campground▲
4		US 79, TN 13, Clarksville, Guthrie
	Gas	N: BP, Sam's
		S: BP, Citgo, Exxon, Texaco, Murphy
	Food	N: Cracker Barrel
		S: Applebee's, Arby's, Burger King, DQ, KFC, Golden Corral, Longhorn Steaks, McDonalds, Olive Garden, Ponderosa, Ryan's Grill, Red Lobster, Ruby Tuesday, Santa Fe Cattle Co, Shoney's, Sho Gun, Waffle House, Wendy's
	Lodg	S: Best Western, Comfort Inn, Days Inn, Econo Lodge, Fairfield Inn, Hampton Inn, Holiday Inn, Microtel, Ramada Ltd, Red Roof Inn♥, Shoney's Inn, Super 8, Wingate Inn
	Med	S: + Hospital
	Other	N: Sam's Club, Clarksville RV Super Center, Spring Creek Campground▲
		S: Advance Auto, Auto Dealers, Carmike Cinemas, Auto Services, ATMs, Banks, Kmart, Lowe's, Mall, Office Depot, PetSmart♥, Target, Wal-Mart sc, Winery, Truck Repair
8		TN 237, Rossview Rd
11		TN 76, Clarksville, Adams
	FStop	N: Sudden Service/Shell
		S: BP
	Gas	S: Citgo
	Food	S: McDonald's, Waffle House
	Lodge	S: Comfort Inn, Days Inn, Holiday Inn Express, Super 8

EXIT		TENNESSEE
	Med	S: + Hospital
	Other	S: Reliable Truck & Diesel, Red River Campground▲
19		TN 256, Maxey Rd, Springfield, to Adams
	Gas	N: BP
24		TN 49, US 41A, Pleasant View, to Springfield, Ashland City
	TStop	N: Mapco Express #1007
	Gas	N: BP, Williams
		S: Shell
	Food	S: BJ's Family Rest, Sonic, Subway
31		TN 249, New Hope Rd, Joelton
	FStop	S: Scot's Market/Citgo
	Gas	N: Shell
		S: BP
	Food	N: Taco Tico
		S: Buddy's Chop House, Italian Café
35		US 431, TN 65, Joelton, Springfield
	FStop	S: Chip's Quik Stop/BP
	Gas	S: Amoco
	Food	S: FastFood/Chips, Country Jct Rest, McDonald's, Mazatlan Mex, Subway
	Lodg	S: Days Inn
40		TN 45, Old Hickory Blvd, Whites Creek, Nashville
	Gas	N: Citgo◆, Shell, Phillips 66◆
	Food	N: Jack in the Box, Subway/Shell
	Lodg	N: Super 8
43		TN 155, Briley Pkwy, to Brick Church Pike, Nashville
	Gas	N: Citgo

EXIT		TENNESSEE
	Food	N: Little Barn BBQ
(44AB)		Jct I-65, to Nashville, Louisville
	NOTE:	I-24 below runs w/I-65 thru Nashville. Exit #'s follow I-65.
87		US 431, Trinity Lane
	TStop	E: Pilot Travel Center #292 (Scales)
	Gas	E: Circle K, Phillips 66
		W: BP, Chevron, Exxon, Shell, Texaco
	Food	E: Subway/Pilot TC, Arby's, Krystal, White Castle
		W: Burger King, Captain D's, Denny's, Jack in the Box, McDonald's, Shoney's, Taco Bell, Waffle House
	Lodg	E: Cumberland Inn, Deluxe Inn, Trinity Inn, Scottish Inn
		W: Best Value Inn, Days Inn, Hampton Inn, Holiday Inn, Knights Inn, Motel 6♥, Quality Inn, Ramada Inn, Regency Inn, Super 8
	Med	W: + FHC Nashville
	Other	E: WiFi/Pilot TC, Auto Service, Tires, Holiday Mobile Village▲
		W: Auto Services, American Baptist College
(86)		Jct I-24E, to I-40E, to Memphis
	NOTE:	I-24 above runs w/I-65 thru Nashville, Exit #'s follow I-65.
(46B)		Jct I-65S, Nashville (Left Exit)
47		Jefferson St, Spring St, US 41
	Gas	N: Express
		S: Conoco
	Lodg	S: Days Inn, Knights Inn
47A		US 41, US 431, Ellington Pkwy, Spring St
48		James Robertson Pkwy, Nashville
	TStop	S: Travel Center of America (Scales)
	Gas	N: Citgo, Shell
	Food	S: Buckhorn/TA TC, Shoney's
	Lodg	S: Ramada Inn, Stadium Inn
	TServ	S: TA TC/Tires
	Other	S: Laundry/WiFi/TA TC, ATM, Banks, State Capitol
49		Shelby Ave, Nashville
	Gas	S: Exxon
	Other	S: The Coliseum
(50B)		Jct I-40, E to Knoxville, W to Memphis, to I-65 Birmingham
	NOTE:	I-24 below runs w/I-40 thru Nashville, Exit #'s follow I-40.
212		Fesslers Lane (EB, No re-entry) TN 24, US 70 (WB, No re-entry)
	TStop	S: Daly's #604/Shell
	Food	N: Harley Davidson Grill
		S: Burger King, McDonald's, Wendy's
	Other	N: Harley Davidson
		S: Laundry/Daly's
213		US 41 (WB), Spence Lane
	Gas	N: Phillips 66◆
		S: Shell
	Food	S: Denny's, Red Lobster, Shoney's
(213A)		Jct I-24E, Jct I-440E
(213B)		Jct I-24W, Jct I-40W
	NOTE:	I-24 above runs w/I-40 thru Nashville, Exit #'s follow I-40.
(52AB)		Jct I-40, E-Knoxville, W-Memphis

◆ = Regular Gas Stations with Diesel ▲ = RV Friendly Locations ♥ = Pet Friendly Locations
RED PRINT SHOWS LARGE VEHICLE PARKING/ACCESS ON SITE OR NEARBY BROWN PRINT SHOWS CAMPGROUNDS/RV PARKS

INTERSTATE 24 W/E

EXIT	TENNESSEE
52	**US 41, Murfreesboro Rd**
Gas	N: BP, Shell, Texaco
Food	N: Bennigan's, Denny's, Golden Corral, Pizza Hut, Red Lobster, Waffle House
Lodg	N: Days Inn, Holiday Inn Express, Quality Inn, Ramada Inn, Scottish Inn
Other	N: ATM, Bank, State Fairgrounds S: Total Truck & Trailer Service, Auto Repairs, ATM, Bank
(53)	**Jct I-440W, to Memphis**
54	**TN 155, Briley Pkwy**
Other	N: Nashville Metro Airport✈, to Opryland
56	**TN 255, Harding Place**
Gas	N: Amoco, Mobil◆, Mapco Express S: Mapco Express, Shell◆
Food	N: Applebee's, Arby's, City Café, East Café, McDonald's, Japanese Rest, KFC, Subway, Taco Bell, Wendy's, Waffle House S: Burger King, Hooters, Jack in the Box, Waffle House
Lodg	N: Drury Inn, Executive Inn, Howard Johnson Express, Motel 6♥, Super 8 S: Best Value Inn, Economy Inn, Motel 6♥
Med	S: + Southern Hills Medical Center
Other	N: ATMs, Banks, Nashville Metro Airport✈ S: Repairs/Shell, Harding Mall
57	**Haywood Lane, Antioch (WB)**
Gas	N: Marathon, Speedway S: Phillips 66◆
Food	N: Hardee's, Pizza Hut, Waffle House, Whitts BBQ
Other	N: Auto Services, Food Lion, Walgreen's
57AB	**Haywood Lane, Antioch (EB)**
59	**TN 254, Bell Rd, Antioch Nashville**
Gas	N: Amoco, BP, Chevron, Mapco Express, Shell, Murphy S: Amoco, BP, Shell
Food	N: Applebee's, Arby's, Burger King, ChicFilA, Chuck E Cheese, **Cracker Barrel**, KFC, O'Charley's, Olive Garden, Pizza Hut, Panda Express, Red Lobster, TGI Friday, Taj Mahal Indian, Wendy's S: Casa Fiesta, Evergreen Rest, IHOP, Olive Garden, Shoney's, Steak 'n Shake, Waffle House
Lodg	N: Country Inn, Days Inn, Holiday Inn, Hampton Inn S: Economy Inn, Knights Inn, Super 8, Vista Inn
Other	N: ATMs, Auto Dealer, Auto Repairs, Banks, Carmike Cinemas, Enterprise, Firestone, Hickory Hollow Mall, Office Depot, Kroger, NTB, Wal-Mart sc S: Goodyear, Home Depot, IGA, Target
60	**Hickory Hollow Pkwy (Access to Exit #59 Services)**
62	**TN 171, Old Hickory Blvd**
FStop	N: Antioch Food Mart/Citgo
TStop	N: Travel Center of America/BP (Scales)
Gas	N: Chevron, Shell
Food	N: CountryPride/BurgerKing/Popeyes/TA TC, Mex Rest, Subway, Waffle House
Lodg	N: Best Western
TWash	N: TA TC
TServ	N: TA TC/Tires
Other	N: Laundry/WiFi/TA TC, **Music City Campground**▲
64	**Waldron Rd, La Vergne**
TStop	N: Pilot Travel Center #52 (Scales)

EXIT	TENNESSEE
Gas	N: Exxon, Kangaroo, Mapco, Speedway, Marathon S: Mapco Express◆
Food	N: Subway/Pilot TC, Arby's, Hardee's, Krystal, Las Canoas Mexican, McDonald's, Rice Bowl II, Waffle House
Lodg	N: Comfort Inn, Holiday Inn, Super 8 S: Driftwood Inn
Other	N: RVDump/WiFi/Pilot TC, **Music City Campground**▲, RV Sales & Service
66	**TN 266, Sam Ridley Pkwy, Smyrna**
Gas	N: Citgo◆, Shell, Scot Market, Kroger
Food	N: Chili's, Logan's, Sonic, Starbucks, Subway, Wendy's S: **Cracker Barrel**, Ruby Tuesday
Lodg	N: Days Inn S: Fairfield Inn, Hampton Inn, Sleep Inn
Med	N: + Hospital Medical Center
Other	N: **Nashville I-24 Campground**▲, Food Lion, Kroger, PetSmart♥, Staples, Target, Smyrna Airport✈ S: I-24 Expo Center
66AB	**TN 266, Sam Ridley Pkwy (EB)**
70	**TN 102, Lee Victory Pkwy, Smyrna**
Gas	N: Daly's/Shell S: BP, Kangaroo, Mapco Express
Food	S: McDonald's, Oishii Steak & Sushi, Sonic, Subway
Lodg	S: Deerfield Inn
Other	N: **Nashville I-24 Campground**▲, Nissan Plant, Kroger, Food Lion
74A	**TN 840W, Franklin**
74B	**TN 840E, Lebanon, Knoxville**
76	**Medical Center Pkwy, Manson Pike**
78A	**TN 96S, Old Fort Pkwy, Franklin**
Gas	S: AmocoBP◆, Chevron, Kangaroo Express◆, Mapco Express
Food	S: Captain D's, Hardee's, O'Charley's, Sonic, Subway, Taco Bell, Waffle House
Lodg	S: Value Place
Other	S: ATMs, Banks, Animal Medical Center♥, Kroger, Quality Tire & Auto, Sam's Club, UPS Store, Walgreen's, River Rock Outlet Mall
78B	**TN 96N, Old Fort Pkwy, Franklin Rd, Murfreesboro, Franklin**
Gas	N: Phillips 66◆, Shell◆, Texaco, Murphy
Food	N: Arby's, **Cracker Barrel**, Chic-Fil-A, IHOP, Jack in the Box/Shell, KFC, McDonald's, Outback Steakhouse, Ryan's Grill, Santa Fe Cattle Co, Steak 'n Shake, Starbucks, Subway, Waffle House, Wendy's, White Castle
Lodg	N: Best Western, Country Inn, Days Inn, DoubleTree Hotel, Econo Lodge, Fairfield Inn, Hampton Inn, Holiday Inn, Microtel, Motel 6♥, Red Roof Inn♥, Sleep Inn, Super 8, Wingate Inn
Med	N: + Hospital
Other	N: ATMs, Banks, Discount Tire, FedEx Kinko's, Home Depot, Lowe's, Petland♥, PetSmart♥, Office Depot, Staples, Target, **Wal-Mart sc**, Stones River Mall, Williams Animal Hospital♥, Old Fort Golf Course, Middle TN State Univ
81A	**US 231S, TN 10, Murfreesboro (EB)**
81B	**US 231N, TN 10, Murfreesboro (EB)**

EXIT	TENNESSEE
81	**US 231, TN 10, Murfreesboro, to Shelbyville (WB)**
FStop	N: Uncle Sandy's Auto Truck Plaza/BP
TStop	S: Pilot Travel Center (Scales) (DAND)
Gas	N: Exxon, RaceWay S: Citgo, Golden Gallon, Mapco Express
Food	N: Arby's, Burger King, **Cracker Barrel**, Krystal, Ponderosa, Parthenon Steak House, Shoney's, Waffle House, Wendy's S: Arby's/Pilot TC, La Siesta, Sonic McDonald's, Subway, Taco Bell, Waffle House
Lodg	N: Baymont Inn, Best Value Inn, Knights Inn, Quality Inn, Ramada Inn, Scottish Inn, Shoney's Inn S: Howard Johnson, Safari Inn, Vista Inn
TWash	S: Pilot TC
Tires	S: Pilot TC
Med	N: + Hospital
Other	N: Fireworks, U-Haul S: Laundry/Wifi/Pilot TC, Auto Services, Kroger, Food Lion, ATMs, Trailer Sales
84A	**Joe B Jackson Pkwy S (WB)**
84B	**Joe B Jackson Pkwy N (WB)**
84	**Joe B Jackson Pkwy (WB)**
89	**Epps Mill Rd, Christiana**
TStop	N: Love's Travel Stop #314 (Scales), Danny's Food & Fuel/Citgo
Gas	N: The Outpost General Store & Rest/Texaco
Food	N: McDonald's/Love's TS, Huddle House
Other	N: Laundry/WiFi/Love's TS S: I-24 Truck Repair, A & L RV Sales
97	**TN 64, Beechgrove Rd, Bell Buckle, Manchester, Shelbyville**
Gas	S: Beech Grove Market & Grill
105	**US 41, TN 2, Murfreesboro Hwy, Manchester, Beechgrove**
FStop	N: Busy Corner Travel Center/BP
Gas	N: Shell
Food	N: Busy Corner TC, Ranch House
Other	N: Auto Services S: Best Auto & Tire
110	**TN 53, Woodbury Hwy, Paradise St, Manchester, Woodbury**
FStop	S: Hullett Shell
Gas	N: BP, Kangaroo Express, Shell
Food	N: **Cracker Barrel**, Crockett's Roadhouse Rest, Floyd's Family Rest, Oak Rest, Waffle House S: Mexican Rest, Waffle House
Lodg	N: Ambassador Inn, Economy Inn, Hampton Inn S: Econo Lodge
Med	N: + Hospital
Other	N: Auto & Truck Repairs S: **Old Stone Fort State Park**▲
111	**TN 55, McMinnville Hwy, Manchester, to Tullahoma**
Gas	N: Chevron, Kangaroo Express S: BP
Food	S: Hardee's, J&G Pizza & Steakhouse
Med	N: + Hospital
Other	S: Tire & Repair Services, **Old Stone Fort Campground**▲, **Outback Kamping**▲

◆ = Regular Gas Stations with Diesel ▲ = RV Friendly Locations ♥ = Pet Friendly Locations
RED PRINT SHOWS LARGE VEHICLE PARKING/ACCESS ON SITE OR NEARBY BROWN PRINT SHOWS CAMPGROUNDS/RV PARKS

Page 111

INTERSTATE 24 W/E

EXIT	TENNESSEE
114	US 41, TN 2, Manchester
TStop	N: I-24 Truck Plaza/BP (Scales)
Gas	N: Marathon, Phillips 66, Shell◆, Murphy
	S: Cone, Golden Gallon, Raceway
Food	N: FastFood/I-24 TP, O'Charley's
	S: Arby's, Burger King, Krystal, KFC, McDonald's, Pizza Hut, Shoney's, Taco Bell, Subway, Waffle House, Wendy's
Lodg	N: Comfort Inn, Holiday Inn Express, Scottish Inn, Super 8, Truckers Inn
	S: Budget Motel, Best Value Inn, Country Inn, Days Inn, Knights Inn, Red Roof Inn♥, Ramada Inn, Royal Inn
TServ	N: I-24 TP
Other	N: Wal-Mart sc, Auto Dealers, Aerospace Museum, Manchester KOA▲, to TN Hills Campground▲
	S: ATMs, Banks, Advance Auto, Bi-Lo, Food Lion, Goodyear, Whispering Oaks Campground▲, to Old Stone Fort Campground▲
(116)	Weigh Station (Both dir)
117	US Air Force, Arnold Center, Tullahoma, UT Space Institute
(119)	TRUCK Parking Area (Both dir)
127	US 64, TN 50, Pelham, Winchester
Gas	N: AmocoBP, Phillips 66, Texaco
	S: Exxon◆
Food	N: Stuckey's/Texaco
Other	S: Fairview Devil Step Campground▲
(133)	Rest Area (Both dir)
	(RR, Phone, Picnic, Vend)
NOTE:	MM 134: WB: 5% Steep Grade next 4 mi
134	US 41 Alt, US 64, Monteagle, to Sewanee
Gas	N: Chevron, Fast Food & Fuel, Kangaroo Express, Mapco Express
	S: Citgo, Shell
Food	N: Depot Rest, High Point Rest, Jim Oliver's Smokehouse, Lockhart Diner, McDonald's, Subway, Waffle House
	S: Hardee's, Pizza Hut, Waffle House
Lodg	N: American Eagle Hotel, Budget Host Inn
	S: Best Western
Med	S: + Hospital
Other	N: CVS, The Cottages at Bear Hollow
	S: Firestone, Grocery, Monteagle Wine Cellars, Tims Ford State Park▲, Holiday Hills Campground▲
135	TN 2, Dixie Lee Hwy, to US 41, US 64, Monteagle, Tracy City
TStop	N: Monteagle Truck Plaza/P66 (Scales)
Gas	N: Pure Mystik

Personal Notes

EXIT	TENNESSEE
Food	N: Rest/Monteagle TP, Smokin B's BBQ
Lodg	N: Days Inn
TServ	N: Monteagle TP/Tires
TWash	N: Monteagle TP
Other	N: Laundry/Monteagle TP
143	TN 2, US 64, Martin Springs Rd
FStop	N: Chevron
152	US 72, TN 150, TN 27, US 64, S Pittsburg, Jasper, Kimball
Gas	N: BP, Phillips 66, RaceWay, Scot Market
Food	N: Arby's, Cracker Barrel, Hardee's, KFC, Krystal, Pizza Hut, McDonald's, Shoney's, Subway, Taco Bell, Waffle House, Wendy's
Lodg	N: Budget Host Inn, Comfort Inn, Days Inn, Holiday Inn Express♥
Med	N: + Hospital
Other	N: Lowe's, Wal-Mart sc

EXIT	TENNESSEE
155	TN 28, Jasper, Dunlap
FStop	N: Interstate Exxon
Gas	N: BP
Food	N: DQ, Hardee's, Western Sizzlin'
Lodg	N: Acuff County Inn
Med	S: + Grandview Medical Center
158	TN 27, to US 41, US 64, Dunlap
Gas	N: Shell
Other	S: TVA Shellmound Campground▲
(160)	TN Welcome Center (WB) Rest Area (EB) (RR, Phone, Picnic, Vend)
161	TN 156, Shellmound Rd, Guild, Haletown, New Hope
Gas	S: Chevron
Other	S: Camp on the Lake Campground▲
NOTE:	Exits #167 & #169 run thru GA
NOTE:	MM 167 Central/Eastern Time Zone
(167)	Jct I-59S, to Birmingham (WB, Left Exit)
169	GA 299, to US 11, Wildwood, GA
TStop	N: Fast Food & Fuel #166/Exxon
	S: Pilot Travel Center #254 (Scales), Fast Travel #190/BP (Scales)
Gas	S: RaceWay
Food	S: Subway/Pilot TC, Rest/FastTravel
Other	S: WiFi/Pilot TC
NOTE:	Exits #167 & #169 run thru GA MM 171: GA Border
(172)	TN Welcome Center (EB) (RR, Phone, Picnic, Vend)
174	US 64, US 11, US 41, Lookout Mountain, Chattanooga
FStop	S: Fast Food & Fuel/AmocoBP
Gas	S: Kangaroo Express
Food	N: Waffle House
	S: Circle C BBQ & Steak House, Cracker Barrel, Taco Bell, Waffle House
Lodg	S: Baymont Inn, Best Western, Comfort Inn, Country Inn, Days Inn, Hampton Inn, Holiday Inn Express, Quality Inn, Ramada Ltd, Super 8
Other	N: Chattanooga's Racoon Mountain Caverns & Campground▲
	S: Circle C Truck & Trailer Repair, ATM, Banks, Wal-Mart sc, TN State Hwy Patrol Post
175	Browns Ferry Rd, Lookout Mtn
FStop	S: Conoco Favorite Market
Gas	N: BP, Citgo, Exxon◆
	S: Shell◆

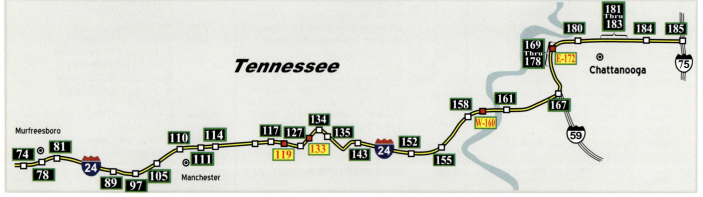

Page 112   ◆= Regular Gas Stations with Diesel   ▲ = RV Friendly Locations   ♥ = Pet Friendly Locations
RED PRINT SHOWS LARGE VEHICLE PARKING/ACCESS ON SITE OR NEARBY   BROWN PRINT SHOWS CAMPGROUNDS/RV PARKS

EXIT		TENNESSEE
	Food	S: Hardee's, McDonald's, Subway
	Lodg	N: Best Value Inn
		S: Comfort Inn, Econo Lodge, Quality Inn, Sleep Inn
	Other	N: CVS, Food Lion, Moccasin Bend Public Golf Course
		S: Bi-Lo, Ruby Falls, Lookout Mtn Attractions
178		US 27N, US 41, Market St, Lookout Mtn, Chattanooga (Difficult reaccess)
	FStop	N: Fast Food & Fuel #206/BP
	Gas	N: Citgo
	Food	N: Rest/Ramada, BBQ
		S: KFC
	Lodg	N: Days Inn, Knights Inn, Ramada Inn
		S: Comfort Inn, Hampton Inn, Motel 6♥
	Med	N: + Hospitals
	Other	N: Moccasin Bend Public Golf Course, Finley Stadium, Auto Repairs, Conv Center,

EXIT		TENNESSEE
	Other	N: Exhibit Hall, Prime Outlet Mall, U-Haul
		S: Enterprise RAC, Lookout Mtn Attractions Museum
180A		Rossville Blvd (diff reaccess)
180B		US 27S, Rossville Blvd
	FStop	S: Fast Food & Fuel #219/Exxon
	Gas	S: RaceTrac, Speedway
	Food	S: KFC, Long John Silver's
	Lodg	S: Hamilton Inn
181		Fourth Ave, Chattanooga
	Gas	N: Citgo◊, Conoco, Exxon◊
		S: Citgo
	Food	N: Bojangle's, Burger King, Captain D's, Hardee's, Krystal, Subway, Waffle House
		S: McDonald's, Wendy's
	Lodg	N: Villager Lodge
		S: Kings Lodge
	TServ	N: CAT Truck Service, Cummins South, Mack Trucks, Freightliner

EXIT		TENNESSEE
	Med	N: + Hospital
181A		US 41S, to US 76, East Ridge (EB-difficult reaccess)
	Gas	N: Citgo
	Food	S: Rest/Kings Lodge
	Lodg	S: Kings Lodge
	TServ	N: Doug Yates Diesel Repair
		S: Ace Truck & Trailer Repair
183		Germantown Rd (EB)
183A		Belvoir Avenue (WB)
184		Moore Rd, Chattanooga (All Serv N to US 11/64, S to US 76)
	Other	N: Eastgate Mall
(185AB)		Jct I-75, N-Knoxville, S-Atlanta (I-24 beings/ends on I-75, Exit #2) (EASTERN TIME ZONE)

Ⓞ **TENNESSEE**
Begin Westbound I-24 from Chattanooga, TN to Jct I-57 near Marion, IL.

EXIT		WYOMING
		Begin Southbound I-25 from Buffalo, WY to Jct I-10 in Las Cruces, NM.

Ⓞ **WYOMING**
(MOUNTAIN TIME ZONE)
(I-25 begins/ends on I-90, Exit #56)

EXIT		WYOMING
(300)		Jct I-90, E - Gillette, W - Billings
299		US 16, I-25 Bus, I-90 Bus, Buffalo
	TStop	W: Big Horn Travel Plaza, Kum & Go #943
	Gas	E: Cenex, Conoco, Exxon, Shell
	Food	W: Rest/Big Horn TP, Bozeman Trail Steak House, Dash Inn, Hardee's, Pizza Hut, McDonald's, Taco John's, Silver Dollar Steakhouse, Subway
	Lodg	E: Motel 6♥
		W: Best Western, Big Horn Motel, Comfort Inn, Crossroads Inn, Econo Lodge, Mansion House Inn, Mountain View Motel & Campground▲, Super 8 Occidental Hotel, Wyoming Motel
	Med	W: + Family Medical Center
	Other	E: NAPA, Deer Park Campground▲, Buffalo KOA▲
		W: Laundry/WiFi/RVDump/Big Horn TP, Jim's Auto & Tire, Auto Services, ATMs, Banks, Grocery, Carousel Park, Museum, Indian Campground▲, Big Horn Mountains Campground▲
298		25 Bus, US 87 Bus, Buffalo (Access to Exit #299 Services)
291		Trabing Rd, CR 13
280		Middle Fork Rd, Buffalo
(274)		Parking Area (Both dir)
265		Reno Rd, CR 208, Kaycee
254		WY 191, Kaycee
	W:	Rest Area (Both dir) (RR, Phone, Picnic, RVDump)

EXIT		WYOMING
	TStop	W: Kaycee Sinclair
	Gas	E: Exxon◊, Shell◊
	Food	E: Diner/Country Inn
		W: FastFood/Sinclair
	Lodg	E: Country Inn, Cassidy Inn
		W: Kaycee Bunkhouse
	Other	E: Powder River Campground▲
		W: LP/Sinclair, KC RV Park▲
249		TTT Rd, Lone Bear Rd
246		Powder River Rd, WY 196N
235		Tisdale Mountain Rd, CR 210S
227		WY 387E, CR 115, Midwest, to Edgerton
223		Ranch Access, to Kaycee
(219)		Parking Area (Both dir)
216		South Castle Creek Rd
210		WY 259, Horse Ranch Creek Rd
197		Ormsby Rd, CR 705, Casper
191		Wardwell Rd, to WY 254, Casper, to Bar Nunn
	Gas	W: MiniMart◊
	Other	W: Casper KOA▲
189		US 20, US 26, Salt Creek Hwy, to Shoshone, Airport, Port of Entry
	FStop	W: 5 mi SW: Ghost Town Fuel Stop/Conoco
188B		WY 220, Poplar St, Walnut St, to CY Ave, Casper
	Gas	E: Conoco, Shell
		W: Exxon
	Food	E: El Jarro Rest, JB's Family Rest
		W: Burger King, Caspers Good Cooking, DQ
	Lodg	E: Best Western, Econo Lodge, Hampton Inn, Holiday Inn, Radisson, Super 8

EXIT		WYOMING
	TServ	W: Casper Truck Center
	Other	W: Albertson's, Deluxe Harley Davidosn Buell, Safeway, Fort Casper Campground▲, to Alcova Dam RV & Trailer Park▲
188A		I-25 Bus, US 87 Bus, Center St, Central & Downtown Casper
	Gas	E: Conoco◊, Shell◊
		W: Cenex, Kum&Go
	Food	E: JB's, Taco John's
		W: Fish Factory, Poor Boy's Steakhouse, Platte River Rest
	Lodg	E: National 9 Inn, Holiday Inn
		W: Days Inn, Parkway Plaza Hotel
	Other	E: Auto Services
		W: Auto Services, ATMs, Banks, Visitor Info, Cinemas
187		McKinley St, to US 20/26, Casper
	Gas	E: Mini Mart
	Lodg	E: Ranch House Motel
	Med	W: + WY Medical Center
186		US 20, US 26, N Beverly St, Bryan Scott Stock Trail, Yellowstone Hwy, Casper
	Gas	W: Conoco
	Food	W: Highway Café Home Cooking, Plow's Diner, Rest/BW
	Lodg	W: Best Western
	TServ	E: Central Truck & Diesel
	Med	W: + WY Medical Center
	Other	E: Auto Dealers, Casper East RV Park & Campground▲
		W: Albertson's, Auto Dealers, Smith RV Sales & Service
185		WY 258, Curtis St, E Casper, Wyoming Blvd, to Evansville
	FStop	W: Loaf N Jug #127/Conoco, Mini Market/Conoco
	TStop	W: Flying J Travel Plaza #5029 (Scales)
	Gas	E: Kum&Go, Mini Mart
		W: Exxon◊

◊ = Regular Gas Stations with Diesel   ▲ = RV Friendly Locations   ♥ = Pet Friendly Locations
RED PRINT SHOWS LARGE VEHICLE PARKING/ACCESS ON SITE OR NEARBY   BROWN PRINT SHOWS CAMPGROUNDS/RV PARKS

Page 113

EXIT		WYOMING
	Food	E: Applebee's, Golden Dragon Chinese, IHOP, Kindler's Rest, Outback Steakhouse W: Cookery/FastFood/FJ TP, Arby's, Burger King, Flaming Wok, Hardee's, Hometown Buffet, McDonald's, Perkins, Red Lobster, Subway, Taco John's, Wendy's, Village Inn
	Lodg	E: Comfort Inn, Shiloh Inn, Super 8 W: Holiday Inn Express, Red Stone Motel
	Other	E: Sonny's RV W: Laundry/WiFi/RV Dump/LP/FJ TP, ATMs, Banks, Auto Dealers, Auto Repair, American Tire, AutoZone, Home Depot, Kmart, PetCo♥, Plains Tire, Sam's Club, Safeway, Target, Wal-Mart sc, Walgreen's, Vet♥, Eastridge Mall, Eastridge Theatre
182		WY 253, CR 606, Hat Six Rd, Cole Creek Rd, Evansville
	TStop	E: AmBest/Eastgate Travel Plaza/Sinclair (Scales)
	Food	E: Rest/FastFood/Eastgate TP W: Fire Rock Steak House
	Lodg	E: Sleep Inn
	Other	E: Laundry/RVDump/LP/Eastgate TP
(171)		Parking Area (Both dir)
165		WY 95, I-25 Bus, Deer Creek Rd, Glenrock
	Gas	E: General Store
	Food	E: Grandma's Kitchen, Noble Romans, Subway, Rest/Hotel Higgins
	Lodg	E: Glenrock Motel, Hotel Higgins
	Other	E: Deer Creek RV Park▲
160		US 87, US 20, US 26, Glenrock (Access to Ex #165 Services)
156		Bixby Rd, Glenrock
154		Barber Rd, Douglas
(153)		Parking Area (SB)
151		Natural Bridge Rd, CR 13
150		Inez Rd
146		WY 96, CR 30, La Prele Rd, to Cold Springs Rd
	Other	W: to Douglas KOA▲
140		WY 59, Douglas Esterbrook Rd, Douglas, Gillette
	Gas	E: Conoco◊, Maverick◊
	Food	E: Arby's, La Costa Mexican Rest, McDonald's, Subway/Conoco
	Lodg	E: Best Western, Holiday Inn Express, Super 8
	Med	E: + Memorial Hospital
	Other	E: LP, Auto Dealers, Pioneer Museum, State Fairgrounds, Converse Co Airport→, Vet♥, Lone Tree Village MH & RV Park▲ W: Douglas KOA▲
135		US 20, 26, 87, Douglas, to WY 59
	TStop	E: Broken Wheel Truck Stop/Sinclair (Scales)
	Food	E: Rest/Broken Wheel, Clementine's Cattle Co, KFC, Pizza Hut, Village Inn
	Lodg	E: Alpine Inn, First Interstate Inn
	TServ	E: Bud's Field Service & Truck Repair
	Med	E: + Memorial Hospital
	Other	E: Laundry/BW TS, Four Winds Campground▲, Auto Services, Towing, Auto Dealers, Douglas Int'l Raceway W: Douglas Comm Golf Course

EXIT		WYOMING
(129)		Parking Area (Both dir)
126		US 18, US 20, Douglas, Orin
	E:	Rest Area (RR, Phones, RVDump)
	TStop	E: Orin Junction Truck Stop/Sinclair
	Food	E: Rest/Orin Jct TS
	Other	E: Laundry/RVDump/Orin Jct TS
111		A St, CR 59, Horseshoe Creek Rd, Glendo
	FStop	E: Howard's General Store/Sinclair
	Food	E: FastFood/Howard's GS, Glendo Café, Rest/Howard's Motel
	Lodg	E: Lakeview Motel, Howard's Motel
	Other	E: Glendo State Park▲
104		Middle Bear Creek Rd
100		Cassa Rd, WY 319N
94		El Rancho Rd, Fish Creek Rd, Pepper Rd, Wheatland
92		US 26E, to WY 319, Wheatland, Guernsey, Torrington
	Other	E: to Guernsey State Park
(91)		Rest Area (Both dir) (RR, Picnic, RVDump)
87		Johnson Rd
84		Laramie River Rd, CR 47
80		I-25 Bus, US 87, to WY 320N, Wheatland
	TStop	E: Wheatland Travel Plaza/Sinclair
	Food	E: FastFood/Wheatland TP, Casey's Timber Haus, Pizza Hut
	Lodg	E: Best Western, Super 8, WY Motel
	Med	E: + Platte Co Memorial Hospital
	Other	E: Laundry/WiFi/LP/Wheatland TP, Auto Dealers, ATMs, Bank, Auto Repairs, Museum, Safeway, Arrowhead RV Campground▲
78		I-25 Bus, US 87, to WY 312S, Wheatland
	FStop	W: Common Cents/Exxon
	TStop	E: Wheatland Co-Op/Cenex (Scales) W: I-25 Conoco
	Gas	E: Cenex◊
	Food	E: Arby's, Burger King, China Garden, El Gringo's, Pizza Hut, Subway, Taco John's, Vimbo's Rest W: Motel West Winds
	Lodg	E: Best Western, Motel 6♥, Parkway Motel, Plains Motel
	Tires	E: Co-Op
	Med	E: + Platte Co Memorial Hospital
	Other	E: ATMs, Banks, Repairs, Cinema West, Grocery, Museum, Tires, Sheriff Dept W: Laundry/I-25, LP/Co-Op, Mountain View RV Park▲
73		WY 34W, Wheatland, to Laramie
70		Bordeaux Rd, WY 34, Wheatland
68		Antelope Rd, CR 264
66		Hunton Rd
(65)		Parking Area (Both dir)
65		WY 314E, Slater Rd, Wheatland
57		WY 321, Ty Basin Rd, Chugwater

◊ = Regular Gas Stations with Diesel ▲ = RV Friendly Locations ♥ = Pet Friendly Locations
RED PRINT SHOWS LARGE VEHICLE PARKING/ACCESS ON SITE OR NEARBY BROWN PRINT SHOWS CAMPGROUNDS/RV PARKS

EXIT	WYOMING
	NOTE: SB: Check Fuel!!
54	WY 211, Lp 25, Chugwater, to WY 322E, WY 321, WY 313
E:	Rest Area (Both dir) (RR, Phone, Picnic, RVDump)
FStop	E: Sinclair
Food	E: Buffalo Grill, Chugwater Soda Ftn
Lodg	E: Super 8
Other	W: Diamond Guest Ranch
47	Bear Creek Rd, to Little Bear Rd, CR 245, Chugwater
39	Little Bear Community Rd, CR 245, to Hirsig Rd, Moffett Rd, Dayton Rd, Cheyenne
34	Nimmo Rd, True Rd, to CR 232
29	CR 228, Whitaker Rd, Cheyenne
25	CR 224, Atlas Rd
21	Ridley Rd, CR 220, Little Bear Rd
17	US 85N, Yellowstone Rd, Cheyenne, to Torrington (SB L ex)
16	WY 211, Horse Creek Rd, Iron Mountain Rd, Cheyenne
Food	W: Little Bear Inn 2mi N via Service Rd
13	Vandehei Ave, Cheyenne
Gas	E: Loaf'n Jug W: Diamond Shamrock◊
12	US 87 Bus, US 85, Central Ave, Bus 25, WY 224, Cheyenne (Addtl Serv Yellowstone Rd, Dell Range Blvd)
Gas	E: Conoco, Exxon
Food	E: DQ, Double Eagle Diner, McDonald's
Lodg	E: Quality Inn♥
Med	E: + United Medical Center West
Other	E: ATMs, Bank, Albertson's, Cheyenne Muni Airport✈, Airport Golf Course, to Frontier Mall, Frontier Days Museum W: FE Warren AFB, Visitor Info, WY State Hwy Patrol Post
11	Randall Ave, Warren AFB-Gate 1
Other	E: to WY State Capitol, Museum W: MIL/FE Warren AFB Fam Camp▲
10B	Plant Rd, Missile Dr, Warren AFB-Gate 2
10D	Missile Dr, Happy Jack Rd Acc All Serv: E to US 30, I-80 Bus, Ex #9
Other	E: Police Dept, Sheriff Dept
9	US 30, I-80 Bus, W Lincolnway, Otto Rd, Cheyenne
TStop	W: AmBest/Little America Travel Plaza/Sinclair E: Big D Truck Stop/Conoco
Gas	E: Conoco
Food	E: Rest/FastFood/Big D TS, Denny's, Crossroads Café, Outback Steakhouse W: Rest/Little America
Lodg	E: Best Western♥, Days Inn, Econo Lodge, La Quinta Inn♥, Luxury Inn, Motel 6♥, Hampton Inn, Hitching Post Inn, Luxury Inn, Super 8, Village Inn W: Motel/Little America TP
TServ	E: Conoco FS, Wyoming Caterpillar W: Little America TP/Tires
	NOTE: NB: Check Fuel!!

EXIT	WY / CO
Other	E: Auto Dealers, Auto Services, ATMs, Banks, Convention Center, Home Depot, Museums, Train Station, Theatres, Laundry/LP/Big D TS W: LP/Little America, Little America Golf Course
(8B)	Jct I-80, W-Laramie
(8D)	Jct I-80, E-Omaha
7	US 87, Bus 25, WY 212, College Dr
W:	WY Welcome Center (Both dir) Rest Area/RR, Phone, Picnic
TStop	E: Love's Travel Stop #220 (Scales), Valero #4545 W: Flying J Travel Plaza #5018/Conoco (Scales)
Food	E: Wendy's/Love's TS, Subway/Valero W: Rest/FastFood/FJ TP, McDonald's
Lodg	E: Comfort Inn/FJ TP
Other	E: Laundry/WiFi/RVDump/Love's TS, Laundry/WiFi/Valero, AB RV Park & Campground▲, Art's Truck Repair W: Laundry/WiFi/LP/RVDump/FJ TP, Info Center
(6)	Weigh / Check Station WY Port of Entry (NB)
2	Terry Ranch Rd, WY 223E, to US 85, Cheyenne
Other	E: Terry Bison Ranch/Rest/Hotel, Wine Cellars, & RV Park▲
	(MOUNTAIN TIME ZONE)

⬆ **WYOMING**
⬇ **COLORADO**
(MOUNTAIN TIME ZONE)

(296)	Parking Area (Both dir)
293	CR 126, to Carr, Norfolk
288	CR 82, Buckeye Rd, Carr
281	CR 70, Wellington
Other	E: Ft Collins North/Wellington KOA/RVDump▲
278	CO 1S, Cleveland Ave, Wellington
Gas	W: Loaf 'n Jug, Shell
Food	W: Burger King, Subway
Lodg	W: Comfort Inn
Other	W: ATM, Bank, Auto Repair
271	CR 50, Mtn Vista Dr, Ft Collins
Other	W: Anheiser Busch Brewery
269B	CO 14W, Mulberry St, to US 287, Fort Collins, to Laramie
FStop	W: Phillips 66
Gas	W: Conoco
Food	W: BBQ, Burger King, Denny's, Italian, Sundance Steak House & Saloon, Waffle House
Lodg	W: Comfort Inn, Days Inn, Ft Collins Plaza Inn, Holiday Inn, Motel 6♥, Ramada Inn, Sleep Inn, Super 8
Med	W: + Poudre Valley Hospital
Other	W: Albertson's, Wal-Mart, Towing & Auto Service, to Colorado State Univ, Fort Collins Downtown Airpark✈, Fort Collins/Lakeside KOA▲
269A	CO 14E, to Ault, Sterling
Food	E: McDonald's
Lodg	E: Mulberry Inn

EXIT	COLORADO
268	CR 44, Prospect Rd, Fort Collins (Gas & Food W to Lemay Ave)
Med	W: + Poudre Valley Hospital
Other	E: Mannon Truck & Auto Repair W: Visitor Info, CO State Univ, Hughes Stadium, Welcome Center
(268)	Rest Area (Both dir) (RR, Picnic, Info)
(267)	Weigh / Check Station (Both dir)
265	CO 68W, Harmony Rd, Ft Collins (Serv approx 4 mi W)
Gas	W: Shell
Food	W: Carrabba's, Golden Corral, IHOP, Outback Steakhouse, Subway, Texas Roadhouse, Village Inn
Lodg	W: Courtyard, Comfort Suites, Hampton Inn, Marriott
Other	W: ATMs, Banks, Cinema, Grocery, Auto Services, Horsetooth Reservoir
262	CO 392E, CR 32, Windsor
Gas	E: Conoco, Phillips 66
Food	E: Arby's, McDonald's, Subway
Lodg	E: AmericInn, Super 8
259	CO 26, Crossroads Blvd
Other	W: Hertz RAC, Fort Collins-Loveland Airport✈, Thunder Mountain Harley Davidson, County Fairgrounds, Budweiser Events Center
257	US 34, Loveland, Greeley
257B	US 34W, Loveland, Rocky Mtn NP
Gas	W: Conoco◊
Food	W: Burger King, Chili's, DQ, Cracker Barrel, IHOP, Lone Star Steakhouse, McDonald's, Waffle House, Wendy's
Lodg	W: Best Western, Fairfield Inn, Hampton Inn, Holiday Inn, Marriott, Super 8
Med	W: + McKee Medical Center
Other	W: Prime Outlets at Loveland, Target, Visitor Center, Crystal Rapids Waterpark, Cloverleaf Kennel Club, Albertson's, Museum, Enterprise RAC, ATM, Bank, Police Station, Loveland RV Village Campground▲, to Boyd Lake State Park▲, Rocky Mountain National Park
257A	US 34E, Loveland, to Greeley
Gas	E: Diamond Shamrock
Lodg	E: Country Inn Suites
255	CO 402W, Loveland
Other	E: Loveland Station Campground▲
254	CR 16, to CO 60W, Campion (NB/SB reaccess via Ex #255)
TStop	E: AmBest/Johnson's Corner Truck Stop (Scales)
Food	E: Rest/Johnson's CTS
Lodg	E: Budget Host Inn
Other	E: Laundry/WiFi/LP/RVDump/Johnson's Corner TS, Johnson's Corner RV Retreat▲
252	CO 60E, CR 48, Berthoud, to Johnstown, Milliken
Other	W: Loaf 'n Jug
250	CO 56W, Berthoud, Carter Lake
245	CR 34, Mead
243	CO 66, CR 30, Longmont, Lyons, to Platteville
FStop	E: Shell
Gas	E: Conoco

◊ = Regular Gas Stations with Diesel   ▲ = RV Friendly Locations   ♥ = Pet Friendly Locations
RED PRINT SHOWS LARGE VEHICLE PARKING/ACCESS ON SITE OR NEARBY   BROWN PRINT SHOWS CAMPGROUNDS/RV PARKS

EXIT	COLORADO
Food	E: Blimpie/Shell, Scott's on 66, Pizza
Other	E: K&C RV Center, Big John's RV Center W: to Rocky Mountain Nat'l Park
240	**CO 119W, Longmont, Firestone**
FStop	E: Get on the Go/P66 W: Alpine Station #1/Conoco (Scales)
TStop	W: Shell Gas Stop (Scales)
Food	E: Carl's Jr, Morning Star Rest, Quiznos, Starbucks, Wendy's W: Subway/Conoco, Arby's, Burger King, McDonald's, Pizza Hut, Taco Bell, Waffle House
Lodg	E: Best Western W: Comfort Inn, Days Inn, Super 8, Travelodge
TWash	W: Del Camino TW
Med	W: + Hospital
Other	E: Del Camino RV Sales W: Laundry/Shell FS, Auto Repair, to Countrywood Inn & RV Park▲, St Vrain State Park, Barbour Ponds State Park, Valley RV Center
235	**CO 52, Dacono, Fort Lupton, Frederick, Firestone, Eldora**
TStop	W: 25-52 AutoTruck Plaza/Conoco
Food	W: Rest/25-52 ATP
Other	E: Grocery, Police Dept W: LP/RVDump/25-52 ATP
232	**CR 8, Erie, Dacono**
Other	E: CO Nat'l Speedway
229	**CO 7, Baseline Rd, Broomfield, to Lafayette, Brighton**
Other	W: Tri-County Airport✈, Vista Ridge Golf Course
(228)	**Jct E-470 TollWay S, to Limon, Colo Spgs, NW TollWay, Boulder**
226	**144th Ave, Broomfield**
225	**136th Ave, Denver**
223	**CO 128W, 120th Ave, Broomfield, Westminster, Northglenn**
Gas	E: Conoco, Sinclair, Valero W: Conoco, Valero
Food	E: Applebee's, Burger King, Chipolte Mex Grill, Café Mexico, Damon's, Fuddrucker's, Lone Star Steakhouse, McDonald's, Outback Steakhouse, Souper Salad W: Chili's, Cracker Barrel, Jade City, Perkins, Starbucks, Village Inn, Wendy's
Lodg	E: Days Inn, Hampton Inn, Holiday Inn, Radisson, Ramada Plaza, Sleep Inn W: Comfort Inn, Extended Stay, Fairfield Inn, La Quinta Inn♥, Super 8
Other	E: Albertson's, Budget RAC, Auto Repairs, Police Dept, PetCo♥, Tires, Walgreen's W: ATMs, Banks, FedEx Kinkos
221	**104th Ave, Denver, to Northglenn, Thornton**
Gas	E: Conoco, Phillips 66, Shamrock W: 7-11, Conoco, Shell◊
Food	E: Burger King, Denny's, IHOP, Texas Roadhouse, Subway, Taco Bell W: Applebee's, Atlanta Bread, Black Eyed Pea, CoCo's, Furr's, Hop's Grill, McDonald's, Red Lobster, Subway, Taco Bell
Lodg	W: La Quinta Inn♥, Ramada Ltd
Med	E: + North Suburban Medical Center

EXIT	COLORADO
Other	E: ATMs, Banks, AutoZone, Grocery, Home Depot, Target, Thornton Town Center 10 W: Albertson's, Firestone, Goodyear, Enterprise RAC, Lowe's, Auto Dealers, Northglenn Mall, Office Depot, RiteAid
220	**Thornton Pkwy, Denver**
Gas	W: Conoco, Valero
Food	E: Golden Corral, Starbucks
Med	E: + North Suburban Medical Center
Other	E: Sam's Club, Safeway, Wal-Mart sc, Police Dept W: Hyland Hills Water World
219	**84th Ave, Federal Heights**
Gas	E: Conoco, Valero W: Coastal, Valero
Food	E: Arby's, Bonanza Steakhouse, Taco Bell, Goodtimes Grill, Quiznos, Waffle House, Starbucks W: Burger King, DQ, Pizza Hut, Village Inn, Popeye's
Lodg	W: Motel 6♥, Hacienda Plaza Inn
Med	W: + St Anthony's Hospital
Other	E: North Valley Mall, Walgreen's W: CarQuest, Discount Tire, Hyland Hills Water World, Grocery
(217B)	**Jct I-270E, to Aurora, Limon, I-25S, to Denver (SB)**
Other	E: to Denver Int'l Airport✈
217A	**US 36W, Boulder, CO 224, Broadway (SB)**
217	**US 36W, to Boulder, I-25N, to Fort Collins (NB, Left exit)**
(216)	**Jct I-76W-Grand Junction, 76E-Fort Morgan, 70th Ave, CO 224 (NB)**
(216A)	**Jct I-76E, to Ft Morgan (SB)**
(216B)	**Jct I-76W, to Grand Junction (SB)**
215	**CO 53, 58th Ave, Denver**
Gas	W: Conoco, Shamrock
Food	E: Coffee World, McDonald's, Papa John's, Steak Escape, Wendy's W: Colorado Café
Lodg	E: Comfort Inn♥, Quality Inn W: Super 8
Other	E: Auto & Truck Repair
(214A)	**Jct I-70, E-Limon, Kansas City, W-Grand Junction (NB)**
Other	E: to Denver Int'l Airport✈
(214BA)	**Jct I-70, E-Limon, Kansas City, W-Grand Junction (SB)** **48th Ave, to Pecos St (SB)**
Food	W: Village Inn, Rest/BW, Rest/HI
Lodg	W: Best Western, Holiday Inn
Other	E: Airport, Coliseum
213	**38th Ave, Park Ave W, Fox St, Downtown, Coors Field**
Gas	E: BP, 7-11, Shell
Food	E: Burger King, Denny's, McDonald's
Lodg	E: La Quinta Inn♥ W: Regency Hotel, Town & Country Motel, Travelodge
212C	**20th St, Downtown Denver, Coors Field, Amtrak**
212B	**North Speer Blvd (NB)**
212A	**Speer Blvd, Downtown (NB)**
Gas	W: Conoco, Shell

Page 116   ◊= Regular Gas Stations with Diesel   ▲ = RV Friendly Locations   ♥= Pet Friendly Locations
RED PRINT SHOWS LARGE VEHICLE PARKING/ACCESS ON SITE OR NEARBY   BROWN PRINT SHOWS CAMPGROUNDS/RV PARKS

EXIT	COLORADO
Lodg	W: Continental Hotel, Residence Inn, Super 8
Other	E: Pepsi Center, Convention Center, Performing Arts Center, Six Flags, Elitch Garden, Ocean Journey, Amtrak, Union Station, Columbine Cellars
212	**Speer Blvd, Denver (SB)**
211	**23rd Ave, Water St, Denver**
Other	W: Invesco Field/Mile High Stadium
210C	**US 287, US 40, CO 33, 17th Ave, Denver (NB)**
Other	W: Mile High Stadium
210B	**US 40W, Colfax Ave, Auraria Pkwy, Aquarium Pkwy (NB)**
Food	W: Denny's, KFC, Rest/Ramada Inn, Rest/Red Lion
Lodg	W: Ramada Inn, Red Lion Hotel ♥
Other	E: Pepsi Center, Downtown W: Mile High Stadium
210A	**US 40, US 287, US 70 Bus, Colfax Ave, Downtown**
Med	W: + St Anthony's Hospital
Other	W: Invesco Field/Mile High Stadium, Downtown, Civic Center, State Capitol
209C	**8th Ave, Wyandot St (NB), Zuni St (SB), Downtown**
Lodg	E: Motel 7
Other	E: Auto Repair
209B	**US 6W, 6th Ave, Lakewood**
Lodg	W: Candlewood Suites ♥, Days Inn
209A	**6th Ave East, Downtown**
Med	E: + St Joseph Hospital
208	**CO 26W, Alameda Ave (SB)**
Gas	W: BP, Shamrock
Food	W: Burger King, Denny's
Lodg	W: Motel 5
Other	W: ATMs, Auto Repair, Shopping Ctr
207B	**US 85S, Santa Fe Dr, Edgewood, Littleton (SB), to CO 26W, US 85S, Alameda Ave (NB)**
Gas	E: BP, Shamrock W: Conoco
Food	E: Burger King, Denny's, Subway
Other	E: Albertson's, ATMs, Banks, Home Depot, Safeway W: Auto Services
207A	**Broadway (SB), Lincoln St (NB)**
Food	E: Griff's Burger Bar
Other	E: Amtrak, Auto Repairs
206	**Washington St, Emerson St, Louisiana Ave (SB), Downing St (NB)**
206B	**Washington St, Louisiana Ave (SB), Louisiana Ave (NB)**
206A	**Downing St (NB, reenter Buchtel Blvd)**
205	**University Blvd, Denver**
Gas	W: Conoco
Food	W: Domino's Pizza, Dunkin Donuts, Pita Jungle, Starbucks, Treehouse Cafe
Lodg	W: Comfort Inn, Days Inn ♥
Med	W: + University Park Medical Clinic
Other	E: Police Dept W: Univ of Denver
204	**CO 2, Colorado Blvd, Glendale**
Gas	E: 7-11, BP, Conoco
Food	E: Arby's, Black Eyed Pea, Grisanti Italian, Hooter's, Little Caesars, Quiznos, Starbucks, Subway, Village Inn

EXIT	COLORADO
	W: Crown Burgers, Denny's, KFC, Japanese Rest, Middle Eastern Rest, Perkins, Taco Stop, Wok USA
Lodg	E: Days Inn, Fairfield Inn, Ramada W: La Quinta Inn ♥, Metropolitan Suites
Other	E: ATMs, Banks, Best Buy, Enterprise RAC W: ATMs, Banks, Albertson's, Auto Repairs, Middle East Grocery, Colorado Center 9
203	**Evans Ave**
Gas	E: Shell
Food	E: Denny's, KFC, Rest/Holiday Inn
Lodg	E: Holiday Inn ♥, Ramada Ltd ♥, Rockies Inn W: Cameron Motel
Other	E: Auto Services, Hertz RAC W: W to CO 2, Access Exit #204 Serv
202	**Yale Ave, Denver, Englewood**
Gas	E: Sinclair, Valero W: Valero
201	**US 285S, CO 30E, Hampden Ave, Englewood, Aurora**
Gas	E: BP, Conoco, Phillips 66, Shell W: Conoco, Shell
Food	E: Bagel Deli, Benihana, BlackEyed Pea, Chili's, Domino's Pizza, Jason's Deli, McDonald's, On the Border, Skillet's Rest, Sushi Boat W: Burger King, Starbucks
Lodg	E: Embassy Suites, Marriott, Quality Inn, Towneplace Suites ♥
Med	E: + Rocky Mountain Health Center
Other	E: ATMs, Banks, Cinema 6, Grocery, Walgreen's, Tamarac Square Mall

EXIT	COLORADO
(200)	**Jct I-225N, Aurora, to I-70, Limon**
Other	E: to Denver Int'l Airport ✈
199	**CO 88W, Belleview Ave, Cherry Hills Village, Greenwood Village, Littleton**
Gas	E: BP, Phillips 66, Sinclair W: Conoco, Valero
Food	E: Garcia's, Harvest Grill, Sandwiches +, Original Pancake House, Wendy's W: McDonald's, Pizza Hut, Taco Bell
Lodg	E: Amerisuites, Marriott, Wyndham W: Days Inn, Holiday Inn Express, Homestead Suites, Wellesley Inn
Other	E: ATMs, Banks, Hertz RAC, National RAC W: Mtn View Golf Course
198	**Orchard Rd, Greenwood Village**
Gas	W: Shell
Food	E: Double Eagle Steak House, Mama Mia's Italian, Shepler's W: Quizno's, Le Peep's Café, Rest/Hilton
Lodg	W: Hilton
Other	W: Coors Amphitheater, Museum, Denver Tech Center, Police Dept
197	**CO 88E, Arapahoe Rd, Greenwood Village, Centennial**
Gas	E: BP, Conoco W: 7-11, Phillips 66, Valero
Food	E: Arby's, BlackJack Pizza, Brothers BBQ, Carrabba's, Denny's, IHOP, Landry's Seafood, Pizza Hut, Outback Steakhouse, Romano Macaroni Grill, Red Lobster, Subway, Sushi Wave, Taco Bell, Wendy's W: Arby's, Bakery, Boston Market, Black Eyed Pea, Chevy Fresh Mex, DQ, IHOP, KFC, La Monica's Steak & Chop House, Romano's Macaroni Grill, McDonald's, Quiznos, Red Robin, Ruby Tuesday, Souper Salad, Taco Bell
Lodg	E: Courtyard, Candlewood Suites ♥, Hampton Inn, Holiday Inn ♥, Sleep Inn, La Quinta Inn ♥, Radisson, Sheraton ♥ W: Executive Suites, Residence Inn
Other	E: Auto Dealers, Auto Repairs, Avis RAC, ATMs, Banks, Budget RAC, Lowe's, Target, Thrifty RAC, Wal-Mart sc, Centennial Airport ✈, Southshore Water Amusement Park W: Albertson's, District 9 Cinema, Big O Tire, Firestone, Coors Amphitheater, Goodyear, Greenwood Plaza 12, ATMs, Banks, Safeway, Office Depot
196	**Dry Creek Rd, Havana St, Centennial, Englewood**
Food	E: Big Bowl, IHOP, Landry's Seafood, Maggiano's, Trail Dust Steak House
Lodg	E: Best Western, Country Inn, Extended Stay American, Quality Suites ♥, Ramada W: Drury Inn, Marriott, Towneplace Suites
195	**County Line Rd, Centennial**
Gas	W: Conoco, Costco
Food	W: Burger King, J Alexander's, Champ's CA Pizza, DQ, High Tide Grill, Panda Express, McDonald's, PF Chang's, Red Robin, Starbucks, Steak Escape
Lodg	E: Courtyard, Residence Inn W: AmeriSuites, Towneplace Suites ♥
Other	W: Auto Services, Best Buy, Costco, Goodyear, Home Depot, PetCo ♥, Park Meadows Mall, Sam's Club, UPS Store

♦ = Regular Gas Stations with Diesel   ▲ = RV Friendly Locations   ♥ = Pet Friendly Locations
RED PRINT SHOWS LARGE VEHICLE PARKING/ACCESS ON SITE OR NEARBY   BROWN PRINT SHOWS CAMPGROUNDS/RV PARKS

EXIT	COLORADO
194AB	CO 470W, E470 N Toll Way, Limon, Grand Junction
194	CO 470 (TOLL), Grand Junction (Access Serv W to Quebec St)
Gas	W: Love's, Texaco, Murphy
Food	W: Arby's, ClaimJumper, Lone Star Steaks, On the Border, TGI Friday's
Lodg	W: Comfort Suites, Fairfield Inn
Other	W: Firestone, Home Depot, Wal-Mart sc
193	Lincoln Ave, Parker, Lone Tree, Highlands Ranch
Gas	W: Conoco
Food	E: Hacienda Colorado, Rest/Hilton GI W: Chili's, McDonald's, Pizza Hut
Lodg	E: Hilton Garden Inn W: Marriott
Med	W: + Sky Ridge Medical Center
Other	W: Safeway, Tire, Univ of Phoenix
191	Surrey Rd, Surrey Ridge, Schweiger Rd, Parker
189	Clydesdale Rd, Surrey Ridge
188	Castle Pines Pkwy, Castle Rock, Beverly Hills
Gas	W: BP, Conoco, Shell
Food	W: Subway, Starbucks, Wendy's, Wild Bean Cafe
187	Happy Canyon Rd, CR 33
184	US 85N, CO 86E, Meadows Pkwy, Founders Pkwy, Castle Rock, to Sedalia, Littleton, Franktown
Gas	E: Conoco, Texaco W: Conoco, Loaf 'n Jug
Food	E: Applebee's, Red Robin, Outback Steakhouse, Starbucks, Sonic, Taco Bell, Wendy's W: Arby's, BlackEyed Pea, Burger King, Chili's, Great Steak & Potato, IHOP, McDonald's, Subway, Taco Bell
Lodg	W: Best Western, Comfort Inn, Days Inn ♥, Hampton Inn
Other	E: ATMs, Banks, Grocery, Home Depot, Target, Walgreen's, Wal-Mart sc W: ATMs, Bank, Prime Outlets Castle Rock
182	Wolfensberger Rd, Wilcox St, Castle Rock, to CO 83E, CO 86
FStop	W: Shell Fuel Stop #1416
Gas	E: Conoco, Phillips 66, Save
Food	E: Mexicali Café, Nick & Willie's W: Burger King, KFC, McDonald's, Shari's, Taco Bell, Village Inn, Wendy's
Lodg	E: Castle Pines Motel W: Comfort Inn, Holiday Inn, Quality Inn, Super 8
Other	E: Museum, Greyhound, CO State Hwy Patrol Post, Police Dept W: Budget RAC, Auto Services
181	Wilcox St, Plum Creek Pkwy (SB), Castle Rock, to CO 86E (NB)
Gas	E: 7-11, BP, Shamrock
Food	E: New Rock Café, Pizza Hut, Subway
Lodg	E: Castle Rock Motel
Med	E: + Swedish Health Park
Other	E: Auto Dealers, Big O Tires, Douglas Co Fairgrounds, Safeway, Sheriff Dept
174	Bear Dance Dr, Tomah Rd
Other	W: Castle Rock Campground ▲

Personal Notes

EXIT	COLORADO
173	CR 53, Spruce Mountain Rd, Larkspur, Palmer Lake (SB, reaccess NB only)
Gas	W: Conoco
172	Upper Lake Gulch Rd, Larkspur
Gas	W: Conoco
(171)	Rest Area (Both dir) (RR, Picnic)
167	Greenland Rd, Larkspur
NOTE:	MM 163: Area Prone to Severe Weather
163	County Line Rd, Palmer Lake
(162)	Weigh Station (Both dir)
161	CO 105, Monument, Palmer Lake, Woodmoor Dr, Second St
TStop	W: Conoco Truck Stop #6507
Gas	E: BP W: 7-11, Texaco
Food	E: Rest/Falcon Inn W: Boston Market, Burger King, DQ, McDonald's, Pizza Hut, Rosie's Diner, Starbucks, Taco Bell, Village Inn
Lodg	E: Falcon Inn
Other	E: ATM, Bank, Colorado Heights Campground/RVDump ▲ W: ATMs, Banks, Auto Services, Tires, RiteAid, Safeway, Police Dept
158	Baptist Rd, Colorado Springs
FStop	W: Diamond Shamrock #4136 (Scales)
Gas	E: Shell ♦
Food	E: Chinese, Popeye's/Shell, Subway E: FastFood/DS

EXIT	COLORADO
Other	E: Grocery, Home Depot W: Laundry/DS
156B	North Gate Blvd West, US Air Force Academy, Visitor Center
Other	W: US Air Force Academy
156A	North Gate Road East (NB), Gleneagle Dr (SB)
153	Interquest Pkwy
(152)	Scenic View-Pikes Pike View (SB)
151	Briargate Pkwy, to CO 83, Black Forest, Colo Springs
Lodg	E: Hilton Garden Inn, Homewood Suites
Other	E: Focus on the Family Visitor Center
150AB	CO 83, Academy Blvd
150	CO 83, Academy Blvd
Gas	E: Diamond Shamrock, Shell
Food	E: Applebee's, Burger King, Captain D's Chevy's Mexican, Cracker Barrel, IHOP, Denny's, KFC, Joe's Crab Shack, Mimi's Café, McDonald's, Olive Garden, Pizza Hut, On the Border, Red Robin, Souper Salad, Starbucks, Wendy's, Village Inn
Lodg	E: Comfort Inn, Days Inn, Drury Inn, Marriott, Radisson, Red Roof Inn ♥, Sleep Inn, Super 8
Other	E: ATMs, Banks, Advance Auto, Big O Tire, Firestone, Home Depot, NAPA, Pharmacy, Carmike Cinema, Rental Cars Wal-Mart sc, Chapel Hills Mall, US Post Office, Auto Services W: South Entr - Air Force Academy
149	Woodmen Rd, Colo Springs, to CO 83, Academy Blvd
Gas	E: Conoco ♦, Loaf 'n Jug W: Shell
Food	E: Carrabba's, Carl's Jr W: Old Chicago Pasta & Pizza, TGI Friday's, Outback Steakhouse
Lodg	W: Comfort Inn, Embassy Suites, Fairfield Inn, Hampton Inn, Holiday Inn Express, Microtel ♥, Staybridge Suites
148B	Corporate Center Dr (SB)
Food	W: New South Wales Rest
Lodg	W: Comfort Inn, Hearthside, Extended Stay America
148A	Bus 25S, Nevada Ave, Colo Spgs (SB Exits Left)
Lodg	E: Howard Johnson Express
148	Bus 25S, Nevada Ave (NB)
147	Rockrimmon Blvd
Gas	W: Shell
Lodg	W: Bradford Home Suites, Wyndham
Other	W: Auto Repairs, Enterprise, Pro Rodeo Hall of Fame, Cowboy Museum, Safeway
146	Garden of the Gods Rd, Colo Spgs (Addt'l Serv East to US 85)
FStop	E: K&G #63/Shell
Gas	E: BP W: 7-11, Conoco, Phillips 66, Shamrock
Food	E: Carl's Jr, Denny's, McDonald's W: Applebee's, Arby's, BlackEyed Pea, Hungry Farmer Rest, Quiznos, Taco Bell, Subway, Village Inn, Wendy's
Lodg	E: Econo Lodge, La Quinta Inn ♥ W: Days Inn, Holiday Inn, Quality Inn, Towneplace Suites ♥

Page 118

♦ = Regular Gas Stations with Diesel   ▲ = RV Friendly Locations   ♥ = Pet Friendly Locations
RED PRINT SHOWS LARGE VEHICLE PARKING/ACCESS ON SITE OR NEARBY   BROWN PRINT SHOWS CAMPGROUNDS/RV PARKS

EXIT	COLORADO
Other	E: Rocky Mtn Greyhound Park, Auto Repair, High Country Truck Specialist, Hertz RAC, Enterprise RAC, Transmissions W: Albertson's, ATMs, Banks, Tire World, **to** Garden of the Gods
145	**CO 38E, Fillmore St** **(Addt'l Serv East to US 85)**
Gas	E: 7-11, Shamrock W: Conoco, Shell
Food	E: DQ W: County Line BBQ, Waffle House, Rest/BW
Lodg	E: Budget Host Inn, Ramada Inn W: Best Western ♥, Motel 6 ♥, Super 8
Med	E: + Penrose Hospital
Other	E: Auto Services, **to** Univ of Co W: Auto Repairs
144	**Fontanero St, Colo Springs**
143	**Uintah St**
Gas	E: 7-11
Other	E: CO College
142	**Bijou St, Kiowa St, Central Bus Distr, Dwntwn Colo Spgs**
Gas	W: Gas
Food	E: Rest/BW, Rest/Clarion W: Denny's
Lodg	E: Best Western, Clarion Hotel ♥, Doubletree Hotel W: Red Lion Hotel
Med	E: + Memorial Hospital
Other	E: ATMs, Banks, Museums, Monument Valley Park, Firestone, Auto Services, US Olympic Complex
141	**US 24W, Cimarron St, Manitou Spgs, Woodland Park** **(Addt'l Serv W to S 8th St)**
Gas	W: Conoco, Phillips 66
Food	W: Arby's, Burger King, Captain D's, McDonald's, Subway, Texas Roadhouse, Taco John's, Waffle House
Lodg	W: Express Inn, Holiday Inn Express
Other	E: Costco, Greyhound, Museum, Sheriff Dept W: AutoZone, Auto Dealers, Discount Tire, Office Depot, Wal-Mart sc, Ghost Town Museum, Auto Services, **to** Garden of the Gods Campground▲, Fountain Creek RV Park▲, Campground Goldfield /RVDump▲, Pike's Peak RV Park▲
140	**Bus 25N, US 85S, Nevada Ave, Tejon St (NB), Bus 25N, US 85S, to CO 115, Tejon St, Nevada Ave, Canon City (SB)**
Gas	W: Circle K, Conoco, Shamrock, Shell
Food	W: Burger King, El Miridor, KFC, McDonald's, Pizza Hut, Shogun, Subway, Taco Bell, Wendy's
Lodg	E: Chateau Motel, Economy Inn, Nevada Motel, Colorado Springs Motel, Howard Johnson W: American Inn, Chief Motel, Circle S Motel, Sun Springs Motel, Stagecoach Motel
Other	E: Auto & Truck Repair, Police Dept W: ATMs, Banks, Auto Dealers, Auto Repairs, Tires, Motorcycle Museum, Transmission, Cheyenne Mountain Zoo, Broadmoor, Royal Gorge

EXIT	COLORADO
139	**US 24E, E Fountain Blvd, Colorado Springs Airport, Limon**
Other	E: **to** Peterson AFB, Colo Spgs Airport✈
138	**CO 29, Circle Dr, Lake Ave**
Gas	E: Conoco, Texaco, Shell W: 7-11
Food	E: Days Inn, Sheraton W: Arby's, Burger King, Chili's, Carl's Jr, Carrabba's, Denny's, Olde World Bagel, Outback Steakhouse, Village Inn
Lodg	E: Days Inn, Sheraton, Super 8 W: Best Western, Budget Inn, Hampton Inn, DoubleTree Hotel, La Quinta Inn ♥, Quality Inn, Residence Inn
TServ	W: Colorado Kenworth
Other	E: Pikes Peaks Vineyards W: Auto Services, Colo Spgs World Arena, Tinseltown Movies, Cheyenne Mountain Zoo, Broadmoor
135	**CO 83, Academy Blvd, Colorado Springs Airport, Fort Carson**
132	**CO 16E, Mesa Ridge Pkwy, Magrath Ave, Fountain** **(Services E to US 85, 3 mi North)**
Gas	E: Love's Country Store #357
Food	E: Subway/Love's CS
Other	E: Colorado Springs South KOA▲ W: Fort Carson Military Res
128	**US 85N, Santa Fe Ave, Fountain**
TStop	W: PTP/ Tomahawk Auto Truck Plaza/ Shell (Scales)
Gas	E: Citgo, Conoco
Food	W: Rest/Tomahawk ATP
Lodg	W: Motel/Tomahawk ATP, Super 8
TWash	W: Tomahawk ATP
TServ	W: Tomahawk ATP, Ace Diesel Repair
Other	W: Laundry/WiFi/Tomahawk ATP
125	**Ray Nixon Rd**
123	**Midway Ranch Rd**
122	**Pikes Peak Int'l Raceway Buttes**
Other	W: Pikes Peak Int'l Raceway
119	**Rancho Colorado Blvd, Midway**
116	**County Line Rd, Henkel**
(115)	**Rest Area (NB)** **(RR, Picnic, RVDump)**
114	**Young Hollow Rd**
(111)	**Rest Area (SB)** **(RR, Picnic, RVDump)**
110	**Pinon**
TStop	W: AmBestRocky Mtn Travel Center/ Sinclair (Scales) **(10 mi N of Pueblo)**
Food	W: Rest/FastFood/Rocky Mtn TC
Lodg	W: Motel/Rocky Mtn TC, Pinon Tree Inn
TServ	W: Rocky Mtn TC/Tires
Other	W: Laundry/Rocky Mtn TC
108	**Purcell Blvd, Pueblo West**
Gas	E: RaceTrac
Other	E: Pueblo KOA▲
106	**Porter Draw (Frontage Rd Acc Only)**
104	**Dillon Dr W, N Elizabeth St, to Platteville Blvd, Pueblo West, Eden**
102	**Eagleridge Blvd, Pueblo** **(Frontage Rd Access to Ex #101)**

EXIT	COLORADO
Gas	E: Conoco◆, Sam's Club W: Shell◆, JR's Country Store
Food	E: Burger King, IHOP, Texas Roadhouse W: Cracker Barrel, DJ's Steakhouse, IHOP, Village Inn
Lodg	W: Comfort Inn, Days Inn, Hampton Inn, La Quinta Inn ♥, Wingate Inn
TServ	W: Kenworth Dealer
Other	E: Home Depot, Sam's Club
101	**US 50W, CO 47E, to US 50E Pueblo West, Canon City, Royal Gorge, La Junta**
FStop	W: Diamond Shamrock #4138
Gas	E: Conoco W: Conoco, Phillips 66
Food	E: Captain D's, Denny's, Ruby Tuesday, Souper Salad W: Applebee's, Arby's, Black Eyed Pea, Boston Market, Burger King, Country Kitchen, Golden Corral, McDonald's, Pizza Hut, Red Lobster, Santa Fe Café, Starbucks, Taco Bell
Lodg	E: Sleep Inn W: Holiday Inn, Motel 6 ♥, Quality Inn, Super 8, Villager Lodge
Med	W: + Emergicare Medical Clinic
Other	E: ATMs, Banks, Circuit City, U-Haul, Tinseltown USA, Wal-Mart sc, Pueblo Memorial Airport✈, Pueblo Mall, Colo State Univ/Pueblo W: Advance Auto, Albertson's, Lowe's, Goodyear, Kmart, Auto Services, ATMs, Banks, Auto Dealers, Pueblo Motor Sports Park, Pueblo West Campground & Horseman's Arena▲, Lake Pueblo State Park▲
100B	**29th St, Pueblo** **(E Frontage Rd Access to Ex #101)**
Gas	W: Amoco, Diamond Shamrock, Sinclair
Food	E: Country Buffet, KFC, Peter Piper Pizza, Panda Buffet W: BBQ, Gordo's, Pizza Hut, Sonic, Taco Casa
Lodg	W: USA Motel
Other	E: Bank, Grocery, Natural Grocery W: Safeway, MLK Jr Cultural Center
100A	**US 50E, to La Junta** **(E Frontage Rd Access to Ex #101)**
FStop	E: 1st Stop/P66
Gas	E: Conoco, Shamrock
Food	E: McDonald's, Pizza Hut, Wendy's
Lodg	E: Ramada Inn
Other	E: SavAlot, Pueblo Memorial Airport✈
99B	**US 50E Bus, 13th St, Santa Fe Ave**
Gas	W: Amoco
Food	W: Wendy's
Lodg	W: Best Western, Travelers Motel
Med	W: + Parkview Medical Center
99A	**6th St, to CO 96, Downtown Pueblo, State Fairgrounds (SB)** **(Access to Exit #99B Serv)**
98B	**1st St, Downtown Pueblo (SB), to CO 96 (NB)**
Gas	W: Conoco, Shell
Food	W: Carl's Jr, Outback Steakhouse
Lodg	W: Marriott
Other	W: Pueblo Zoo, Conv Center, Museums
98A	**US 50E Bus, La Junta (SB), US 50W Bus, Santa Fe Ave, Pueblo**
FStop	E: Cliff Brice Station/Sinclair W: Acorn Petroleum/P66

◆= Regular Gas Stations with Diesel   ▲= RV Friendly Locations   ♥= Pet Friendly Locations
RED PRINT SHOWS LARGE VEHICLE PARKING/ACCESS ON SITE OR NEARBY   BROWN PRINT SHOWS CAMPGROUNDS/RV PARKS

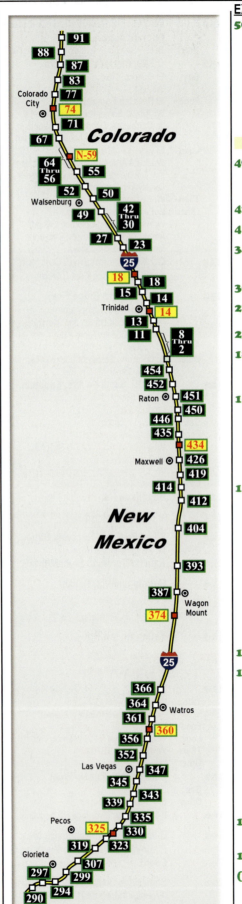

EXIT	COLORADO
	Food W: Sonic, Cucas
97B	**Abriendo Ave**
Gas	W: Texaco, Shamrock
Food	W: Wendy's
Lodg	W: Best Western
97A	**Central Ave, to Northern Ave**
Gas	W: Shamrock, Shell
Food	W: McDonald's, Mexican Restaurants
Other	W: Auto & Tire Services
96	**Minnequa Ave (SB, no reaccess), Indiana Ave (NB)**
Med	W: + St Mary Corwin Medical Center
95	**Illinois Ave (SB, no re-entry)**
94	**CO 45N, Pueblo Blvd, to US 50W, Pueblo, Canon City**
Gas	W: 7-11, Shamrock◆
Food	W: Pepper Coach Café, Pizza Hut, Taco Bell
Lodg	W: Hampton Inn, Microtel♥
Other	W: Fort's MH & RV Park▲, to Lake Pueblo State Park▲, Pueblo Zoo, Co State Fairgrounds, Pueblo Greyhound Park
91	**CR 308, Lime Rd, Stem Beach**
88	**CR 246, Burnt Mill Rd**
87	**CR 337, Verde Rd, Pueblo**
83	**Verde Rd, Brezell**
77	**CR 345, Abbey Rd, Beulah, to Cedarwood**
74	**CO 165W, Colorado City, Rye, San Isabel**
W:	Rest Area (Both dir) (RR, Picnic, RVDump)
FStop	E: Diamond Shamrock #4062
Gas	W: Shell◆
Food	E: FastFood/Shamrock
	W: Rest/Greenhorn Inn
Lodg	W: Greenhorn Inn
Other	E: Pueblo South/Colorado City KOA▲
71	**CR 344, Graneros Rd, Thacker Rd, Colorado City**
NOTE:	SB: Exits 67 - 50 High Wind Area
67	**CR 660, CR 670, Apache City**
64	**CR 110, CR 650, Lascar Rd**
60	**CR 104, Huerfano River Crossing**
(59)	**Scenic Area-Huerfano Butte (NB)**
59	**CR 103, Butte Rd**
56	**CR 610, Red Rock Rd, to CO 69W, Gardner**
55	**CR 101, Airport Rd**
Other	Johnson Field Airport✈
52	**Bus 25S, to CO 69W, Walsenburg, Gardner (NB), to US 160, CO 69, Alamosa (SB)**
TStop	W: Acorn Travel Plaza/P66
Gas	W: Loaf'n Jug
Food	W: Pizza Hut, Subway
Lodg	W: Alpha Motel, Hilltop Motel, Knights Inn♥, Country Host Motel & RV Park▲
Other	W: Laundry/Acorn TP, Auto Services, Dakota Campground▲

EXIT	COLORADO
50	**US 160W, Walsenburg, Alamosa, CO 10E, Hawley, La Junta**
Gas	W: Standard
Food	W: Alpine Rose Café, BJ's, Donuts & Deli, Carl's Jr, Fireside Cafe
Lodg	W: La Plaza Inn
Med	W: + Hospital
Other	W: Auto Services, Mining Museum, Safeway, to Lathrop State Park▲
NOTE:	NB: Exits 50 - 67 High Wind Area
49	**US 87, US 85, Bus 25N, to US 160W, Alamosa, Walsenburg (Access to Ex #50 Services)**
42	**CR 310, Rouse Rd, Pryor**
41	**CR 240, CR 310, Rugby Rd**
34	**Spur 25, CR 60, Aguilar**
TStop	E: Amato Truck Stop/BP
Food	E: Rest/Amato TS
30	**CR 63, Aguilar Rd**
27	**CR 44, Ludlow**
Other	W: Ludlow Monument
23	**CR 42, Hoehne Rd**
18	**CR 32, El Moro Rd**
W:	Rest Area (Both dir) (RR, Picnic)
15	**US 160E, to US 350, CO 239, Kit Carson Trail, La Junta**
Gas	W: Five Points Super Service, Texaco
Food	E: Burger King
	W: Frontier Café, Lee's DriveIn
Lodg	E: Super 8
	W: Frontier Motel
14	**Colorado Ave, Commercial St, Trinidad (NB)**
E:	CO Welcome Center (NB) (RR, Phone, Picnic, Info, Free Coffee)
Gas	E: BP, Shell, JR's
	W: Conoco, Phillips 66, Shamrock
Food	E: McDonald's, Pizza Hut, Subway
	W: DQ, Chinese Rest, Domino's Pizza, El Capitan Rest, McDonald's
Lodg	E: Inn on the Santa Fe Trail
	W: Prospect Plaza Motel
Other	E: Museums, Auto Repair, ATM, Bank
	W: Amtrak, Auto Repair, ATM
14B	**Colorado Ave, Trinidad (SB)**
13	**CO 12W, Main St, Trinidad (SB)**
Gas	E: Conoco◆
Food	E: Belle West Rest, McDonald's, Sonic
Lodg	E: Best Western, Blackjack's Saloon & Steakhouse Inn, Cawathon Motel & Campground▲, Downtown Motel, Royal Motel, Silver Dollar Inn, Villager Lodge
Med	E: + Mt San Rafael Hospital
Other	E: Fox Theatre, Safeway, ATM, Bank, Auto Services, Goodyear, Auto Dealers, Museums, Family Dollar
13B	**CO 12W, S 160E, Main St, US 350 Trinidad (NB)**
13A	**Country Club Dr, Trinidad (NB)**
(12)	**New Exit**

Page 120   ◆ = Regular Gas Stations with Diesel   ▲ = RV Friendly Locations   ♥ = Pet Friendly Locations
RED PRINT SHOWS LARGE VEHICLE PARKING/ACCESS ON SITE OR NEARBY   BROWN PRINT SHOWS CAMPGROUNDS/RV PARKS

Interstate 25 N/S

EXIT	CO / NM
11	**Santa Fe Trail, Trinidad, Starkville**
E:	Weigh/Check Station (NB)
TStop	E: Trinidad Fuel Stop/Shell
Food	E: Wendy's/Trinidad FS, 3 Margaritas
	W: Country Kitchen, Rest/Qual Inn
Lodg	E: Budget Host Derrick Motel & RV Park▲, Budget Summit Inn♥ & RV Park▲
	W: Quality Inn
Other	W: Auto Dealer, Wal-Mart sc, Tires, Auto Services, Trinidad Lake State Park▲
8	**Frontage Rd, Spring Creek**
6	**Frontage Rd, Gallinas**
2	**Morley, Wootton**
(0)	**Weigh Station (SB)** (MOUNTAIN TIME ZONE)

⬆ **COLORADO**
⬇ **NEW MEXICO** (MOUNTAIN TIME ZONE)

NOTE: MM 460: Raton Pass - Elev 7834 ft

(460)	**Port of Entry / Weigh Station (SB)**
Other	E: Cedar Rail Campground & RV Park▲
454	**I-25 Bus, Raton**
Gas	W: Shell
Lodg	W: Budget Host, Capri Motel, Robin Hood Motel, Pass Inn
Med	W: + Hospital
452	**NM 72, Cook Ave, Raton, Folsom**
Gas	W: Conoco
Lodg	W: Mesa Vista Motel
Other	W: Amtrak, ATMs, Banks, Auto Repairs, Auto Dealers, Museum
451	**US 64E, US 87, Raton, Clayton** (Addt'l serv W to Bus 25)
FStop	E: Raton Truck Stop/Shell
TStop	E: Hooter Brown Truck Stop/Total
Gas	E: Chevron♦
	W: Chevron♦, Conoco, Phillips 66, Shell
Food	E: Subway, Rest/Hooter Brown TS
	W: All Seasons Family, Arby's, DQ, Denny's, KFC, McDonald's
Lodg	W: Best Western, Comfort Inn, El Kapp Motel, Microtel♥, Super 8, Texan Motel, Travel Motel
TServ	W: Raton Auto & Truck Service
Med	W: + Hospital
Other	E: Laundry/Hooter Brown TS, Kickback RV Park▲
	W: Raton KOA▲, Raton RV Park▲, Summerlan RV Park▲, ATMs, Banks, Dollar General, Family Dollar, Kmart, NAPA
450	**I-25 Bus, US 64, S Raton**
FStop	W: Pendleton's 66
Gas	W: Conoco, Shamrock
Food	W: K-Bob's, Rainmaker Café, Sonic
Lodg	W: Holiday Inn Express, Maverick Motel
Med	W: + Hospital
Other	W: Raton KOA▲, LP/Pendleton's 66, Auto & Tire Services, La Mesa Airport✈, Grocery, Drive In Theatre, La Mesa Park Racetrack & Casino
446	**US 64W, Taos, Cimarron**
Other	W: Raton Muni Airport✈
435	**CR A9, Raton, to Tinaja**

EXIT	NEW MEXICO
(434)	**Rest Area (Both dir)** (RR, Picnic, Weather)
426	**NM 505, Maxwell Ave, Maxwell, Maxwell Lakes**
419	**NM 58, Springer, to Cimarron, Eagle Nest**
TStop	E: Russell Truck & Travel/Shell (Scales)
Food	E: Rest/Russell T&T
Tires	E: Russell T&T
TWash	E: Russell T&T
Other	E: Laundry/Russell T&T
414	**Lp 25, US 85, N Springer**
Gas	E: Phillips 66
Food	E: Dairy Delite
Lodg	E: Oasis Motel
412	**US 56, US 412, NM 21, NM 468 S Springer, Clayton**
Gas	E: Shamrock
404	**NM 569, Colmor, Charette Lakes**
393	**Levy, Wagon Mound**
387	**NM 120, Wagon Mound, to Roy, Ocate**
Gas	E: Chevron, Phillips 66
(375)	**Rest Area (SB)**
(374)	**Rest Area (NB)** (RR, Picnic, RVDump)
366	**NM 161, to NM 97, Fort Union, to Watrous, Valmora**
364	**NM 161, NM 97, Watrous**

EXIT	NEW MEXICO
361	**Warren Ranch Rd, Las Vegas**
(360)	**Parking Area (Both dir)**
356	**Onava**
352	**Airport, Las Vegas**
Other	E: Duke RV Park▲, Las Vegas Muni Airport✈
347	**Bus 25, to NM 518, N Las Vegas, to Taos**
FStop	W: Texaco
TStop	W: Pino's Travel Center/Fina
Gas	W: Phillips 66, SavOMat
Food	W: Rest/Pino's TS, Burger King, DQ, Great Wall Chinese, Mexican Kitchen, McDonald's, Taco Bell
Lodg	W: Budget Inn, Comfort Inn, Days Inn, El Camino Motel, Inn of Las Vegas, Inn on the Santa Fe Trail, Regal Motel, Town House Motel, Sunshine Motel
Med	W: + Las Vegas Medical Center
Other	W: LP/Pino's TC, ATMs, Banks, Big O Tire, Firestone, Pinos Wrecker Service, Kiva Theatre, Museums, Auto Dealers, Amtrak, Vegas Truck & Automotive, Vegas RV Park▲, Storrie Lake State Park▲
345	**NM 65, NM 104, University Ave**
Gas	W: Allsup's, Fina, Shell, SavOMat
Food	W: Arby's, DQ, Mexican Kitchen, KFC, Pizza Hut, Wendy's, Rest/El Camino Motel
Lodg	W: Budget Inn, El Fidel Motel
Med	W: + Las Vegas Medical Center
Other	W: ATMs, Banks, Museums, Theatre, Auto Services, Tires
343	**I-25 Bus, Grand Ave, to NM 518, S Las Vegas**
Gas	W: Chevron, Citgo, Fina, Phillips 66
Food	W: Burger King, McDonald's, Maryann's Famous Burrito Kitchen, Pizza Palace
Lodg	W: Plaza Motel, Thunderbird Lodge
339	**US 84, Las Vegas, to Romeroville, Santa Rosa, Historic Rte 66**
FStop	W: Tenorio's Travel Center/Texaco
Food	W: FastFood/Tesorio's TC
Other	E: Las Vegas/New Mexico KOA▲
335	**Tecolote, San Jose**
330	**Bernal**
(325)	**Parking Area (Both dir)**
323	**NM 3S, Ribera, Villanueva**
Gas	E: Shell
Other	E: to Pecos River Campground▲
319	**San Juan, San Jose, Sands**
307	**NM 63, Rowe, Pecos**
299	**NM 50, Glorieta, Pecos**
Other	E: Pecos National Hist Park
297	**Valencia**
294	**Canoncito at Apache Canyon**
Other	E: Santa Fe KOA▲, Pecos National Historic State Park
290	**US 285, Clines Corners, Lamy, Eldorado**
Other	E: Santa Fe KOA▲, Rancheros de Santa Fe Campground▲
284	**NM 466, Old Pecos Trail, Santa Fe**
Gas	W: Chevron♦, Fina

♦ = Regular Gas Stations with Diesel   ▲ = RV Friendly Locations   ♥ = Pet Friendly Locations

RED PRINT SHOWS LARGE VEHICLE PARKING/ACCESS ON SITE OR NEARBY   BROWN PRINT SHOWS CAMPGROUNDS/RV PARKS

Page 121

Interstate 25 N/S — NEW MEXICO

EXIT		
	Food	W: Bobcat Bite, India Palace, Italian Bisto, Rest/BW, Steaksmith
	Lodg	W: Bobcat Inn, Best Western, Pecos Trail Inn
	Med	W: + St Vincent Hospital
	Other	W: Quail Run Golf Course, Police Dept, Museums, Santa Fe Vineyards
282		**US 84, US 285, St Francis Dr, Santa Fe Plaza, Los Alamos, Taos (MANY Serv N 3mi)**
	FStop	W: Giant Travel Center #6046
	Gas	W: QuickStop/Conoco
	Food	W: Wendy's, Chicken, Mexican
	Lodg	W: to Cities of Gold Casino & Hotel, Camel Rock Casino & Suites, Ohkay Casino Resort
		W: Travelodge
	Med	W: + St Vincent Hospital
	Other	W: ATMs, Banks, Auto Service, Grocery
282		**US 84, US 285, St Francis Dr (SB)**
278		**I-25 Bus, NM 14, Cerrillos Rd, Santa Fe, Madrid**
	FStop	W: NM 14 3mi: Polk Oil/Shamrock
	Gas	W: Chevron◊, Conoco, Phillips 66◊, Shell◊
	Food	W: Applebee's, Arby's, Burger King, Blue Corn Café & Brewery, CiCi's, Bobby Rubino's Ribs, CoCo's, Denny's, IHOP, Horseman's Haven Café, KFC, Long John Silver, McDonald's, Olive Garden, Outback Steakhouse, Pizza Hut, Red Lobster, Village Inn
	Lodg	W: Cactus Lodge Motel, Comfort Inn, Comfort Suites, Days Inn, Fairfield Inn, Hampton Inn, Holiday Inn Express, La Quinta Inn♥, Luxury Inn, Park Inn♥, Ramada Inn, Red Roof Inn, Santa Fe Lodge, Sleep Inn, Super 8
	Other	E: Santa Fe Skies RV Park▲ W: Santa Fe Outlets, Villa Linda Mall, ATMs, Banks, Auto Dealers, Albertson's, Cinemas, Enterprise RAC, Firestone, Target, Walgreen's, Wal-Mart, Police Dept, Los Campos de Santa Fe RV Resort▲, Trailer Ranch RV Resort▲
278AB		**Cerillos Rd, Santa Fe (SB)**
276		**NM 599, NM 14, Madrid (SB)**
	Gas	E: Phillips 66◊ W: Conoco, Shell◊
	Lodg	W: Sunrise Springs Inn
	Other	E: Santa Fe Skies RV Park▲, National Guard Armory W: Downs at Santa Fe, Santa Fe County Muni Airport✈, Avis RAC, Hertz RAC
276AB		**NM 599, NM 14, Madrid (NB)**
271		**CR 50F, La Cienega**
	Other	W: Pinon RV Park▲
(268)		**Rest Area (NB) (RR)**
267		**Waldo Canyon Rd, Waldo**
264		**NM 16, Cochiti, Pueblo, Pena Blanco**
259		**NM 22, Santo Domingo Pueblo**
	FStop	W: Santo Domingo Tribal Gas Station/P66
257		**Budagher**
252		**San Felipe, Pueblo**
	TStop	E: San Felipe Travel Center/66

EXIT		NEW MEXICO
	Food	E: Rest/Grill/San Felipe TC
	Other	E: Laundry/RVDump/RVPark/Casino Hollywood/Speedway/San Felipe TC
248		**NM 474, Bernalillo, Algodones**
242		**NM 44, NM 165, US 550, Rio Rancho, Bernalillo, Placitas**
	Gas	W: Chevron, Conoco, Phillips 66, Shell◊
	Food	W: BurgerKing/Shell, Denny's, KFC, La Hacienda Express, Lota Burger, Pizza Hut, McDonald's, Subway, Taco Bell
	Lodg	W: Days Inn, Quality Inn, Super 8, Santa Ana Star Hotel & Casino
	Other	W: Albuquerque North KOA▲, Stagecoach Stop Resort RV Park▲, Coronado Campground▲, ATMs, Banks, Auto Services, Sheriff Dept
240		**NM 473, Bernalillo, Albuquerque**
	Gas	W: Allsups, Conoco◊
	Food	W: Range Café
	Other	W: Albuquerque N/Bernalillo KOA▲
234		**NM 556, Tramway Rd**
	Gas	E: Shamrock◊ W: Phillips 66◊
	Other	W: Casino Sandia
233		**Alameda Blvd, Albuquerque**
	Gas	E: Chevron W: Phillips 66◊
	Food	E: Burger King, Long John Silver W: Carl's Jr, Marlene's Mexican
	Lodg	E: Comfort Inn, Motel 6♥ W: Holiday Inn, Ramada Inn
	Other	E: Coronado Airport✈, Towing, Winery
232		**NM 423, Paseo del Norte NE**
	Gas	W: Texaco

EXIT		NEW MEXICO
	Food	W: Arby's
	Lodg	E: Country Inn, Motel 6♥ W: Courtyard, Embassy Suites
	Other	E: Lowe's W: Target
231		**San Antonia Ave, Ellison Rd**
	Food	E: Cracker Barrel, Kettle Rest
	Lodg	E: Country Inn, Howard Johnson Express, Homewood Suites, La Quinta Inn♥ W: Baymont Inn, Hampton Inn
	Med	E: + St Joseph's NE Heights Hospital
	Other	W: Auto Dealers, Century 10, Auto Serv
230		**San Mateo Blvd, Osuna Rd**
	Gas	E: Chevron, Conoco, Giant, Star Mart W: Chevron, Shamrock
	Food	E: Applebee's, Arby's, DQ, Burger King, KFC, McDonald's, Olive Garden, Sweet Tomato, Taco Cabana, Village Inn, Wendy's W: Cajun Kitchen, SW deli, Whataburger
	Lodg	E: Wyndham Garden Suites
	Other	E: ATMs, Bank, Auto Dealers, Firestone, Grocery, Cinema, Cliff's Amusement Park W: to Balloon View Homes & RV Park▲
229		**Jefferson St, Albuquerque**
	Food	E: Carrabba's, Landry's Seafood W: Fuddrucker's, Mimi's Café, Texas Land & Cattle, Rockfish Café
	Lodg	W: Residence Inn
	Med	E: + St Joseph's NE Heights Hospital
	Other	E: Cliff's Amusement Park
228		**Montgomery Blvd, Montano**
	Gas	E: Chevron, Shell
	Food	E: Blake's Lotaburger W: Arby's, IHOP, McDonald's, Subway, Starbucks, Wendy's
	Lodg	E: Best Western W: InTowne Suites
	Med	E: + St Joseph's NE Heights Hospital
	Other	W: Costco, Home Depot, Sam's Club
227B		**Comanche Blvd, Griegos**
227A		**Candelaria Rd, Menaul Blvd**
	TStop	E: Travel Center of America/Chevron (Scales) (NB Use Ex #225 to access TA TC)
	Gas	E: Circle K, Fina, Shell
	Food	E: Rest/TA TC, JB's Rest, IHOP, Subway, Village Inn W: Waffle House
	Lodg	E: Comfort Inn, Days Inn, Fairfield Inn, Hilton, Holiday Inn, Quality Inn♥, Super 8, Rodeway Inn W: Red Roof Inn♥, Travelodge
	TServ	E: TA TC/Tires
	Other	E: Laundry/WiFi/RVDump/TA TC
(226)		**Jct I-40, E-Amarillo, W-Flagstaff, Santa Rosa, Grants**
225		**Lomas Blvd, Albuquerque (NB Access to 227A)**
	Gas	E: Chevron
	Food	E: JB's Rest, Rest/Plaza Inn
	Lodg	E: Plaza Inn, Quality Inn♥, Rodeway Inn W: Embassy Suites
	Med	E: + Carrie Tingley Hospital
224B		**Dr Martin Luther King Jr Ave, Central Ave, Albuquerque**
	Gas	W: Chevron
	Food	W: Milton's, Rest/Econo Lodge
	Lodg	W: Crossroads Motel, Econo Lodge♥
	Med	E: + Presbyterian Hospital W: + St Joseph Medical Center

Page 122 — ◊ = Regular Gas Stations with Diesel   ▲ = RV Friendly Locations   ♥ = Pet Friendly Locations
RED PRINT SHOWS LARGE VEHICLE PARKING/ACCESS ON SITE OR NEARBY   BROWN PRINT SHOWS CAMPGROUNDS/RV PARKS

EXIT		NEW MEXICO
224A		Lead Ave, Coal Ave, Central Ave
	Gas	E: Texaco
	Lodg	E: Crossroads Motel, Econo Lodge
	Med	E: + Presbyterian Hospital
223		Avenida Caesar Chavez
	Gas	W: Chevron
	Lodg	E: Motel 6 ♥
	Other	E: Univ of NM Arena, Athletic Fields
222AB		Gibson Blvd, Kirtland AFB, Airport (SB)
222		Gibson Blvd, Kirtland AFB, Int'l Airport (NB)
	FStop	W: to NM 47: Duke City/CFN
	Gas	E: Phillips 66
		W: Fina
	Food	E: Applebee's, Burger King, Subway, Waffle House
		W: Blake's Lotaburger, Church's
	Lodg	E: Country Inn Suites, Comfort Inn, Fairfield Inn, Hampton Inn, Holiday Inn Express, La Quinta Inn ♥, Quality Suites, Radisson, Sleep Inn
	Med	E: + Lovelace Hospital & Med Ctr
	Other	E: Albuquerque Int'l Airport✈, Kirtland AFB, MIL: Kirtland AFB FamCamp▲
221		Sunport Blvd SE, Albuquerque
	Lodg	E: AmeriSuites, Holiday Inn Select, Wyndham
220		NM 500, Rio Bravo Blvd (Addtl Serv W to Isleta Blvd)
	Gas	W: Giant, Conoco
	Food	W: Burger King, McDonald's, Pizza Hut, Subway, Taco Bell
	Other	E: Albertson's, Auto Services, Diesel Service, Walgreen's, RVDump/Giant
215		NM 47, S Broadway
	Gas	E: Conoco
	Other	E: Isleta Gaming Palace & Casino Resort, Isleta Lakes & Rec Area▲, Isleta Eagle Golf Course
213		NM 314, Isleta Blvd
	Gas	W: Chevron◊
	Food	W: Subway/Chevron
209		NM 317, to NM 45, NM 314, Isleta Pueblo
203		NM 6, Main St, Los Lunas
	Gas	E: Chevron, Diamond Shamrock, Shell
		W: Phillips 66
	Food	E: Arby's, McDonald's, Ragin Cajun, Village Inn, Wendy's
		W: Carino's, Chili's
	Lodg	E: Comfort Inn, Days Inn
		W: Western Skies Inn
	Other	E: ATMs, Banks, Albertson's, Auto Serv, Police Dept
		W: Wal-Mart sc
195		Bus 25, Belen North, Los Chavez
	Gas	E: Murphy
	Food	E: McDonald's, Pizza Hut, Taco Bell
	Other	E: Wal-Mart sc
191		Camino del Llano Rd, Sosimo Padilla, Belen
	Gas	E: Conoco◊
	Food	E: Carlos Cantina & Grill, McDonald's, Deli, Golden Corral, Montano's, Pizza Hut, Subway, TJ's Mex Rest
		W: Rio Grande Diner
	Lodg	E: Best Western, Freeway Inn, Holiday Inn Express x2, La Mirada B&B & RV Park▲, Super 8

EXIT		NEW MEXICO
	Other	E: ATMs, Banks, Big O Tires, IGA
		W: Alexander Muni Airport✈
190		I-25 Bus, NM 314, S Belen
	Gas	E: Akins◊, Conoco◊, P66◊
	Food	E: A&W, Arby's, Casa de Pizza, Circle T Burger, KFC, McDonald's, Pizza Hut, TJ's Mexican Rest
	Lodg	E: Super 8
	Other	E: Tourist Info
175		US 60E, Bernardo, Mountainair
	Gas	E: Gas
	Other	W: Kiva RV Park & Horse Motel▲
169		La Joya State Game Refuge
	Other	W: Wildlife Refuge
(167)		Rest Area
		NB: (RR, Picnic, Vend, RVDump)
		SB: (RR, Picnic)
(165)		Weigh Station (NB)
163		Alamillo Rd, Magdalena, San Acacia, Polvadera
156		NM 408, Lemitar
	FStop	W: Roadrunner Travel Center/66
	Food	W: Café/Roadrunner TC
	Other	W: Laundry/RVDump/Roadrunner TC
152		Escondida
150		I-25 Bus, US 60W, N Socorro, Escondido Ln, Magdalena
	Gas	W: Chevron, Circle K, Exxon◊, Phillips 66◊, Shell, Valero
	Food	W: Denny's, KFC, McDonald's, Pizza Hut, Subway, Taco Bell
	Lodg	W: Best Western, Comfort Suites, Days Inn ♥, Econo Lodge, Economy Inn, El Camino Motel, Holiday Inn Express, Payless Inn, Rio Grande Motel, Super 8
	Other	W: ATMs, Banks, Auto Dealers, NAPA, Auto Services, Dollar General, Grocery, Wal-Mart sc, Auto Dealers, Ace Hdwr
147		I-25 Bus, US60W, US 85, S Socorro, Magdalena
	FStop	W: Chevron, Texaco
	Gas	W: Conoco, Shell◊
	Food	W: Arby's, Denny's, McDonald's, Pizza Hut
	Lodg	W: Best Inn, Econo Lodge, Economy Inn ♥, Holiday Inn Express ♥, Motel 6 ♥
	Med	W: + Socorro General Hospital
	Other	W: Socorro RV Park▲, Socorro Muni Airport✈
139		US 380E, San Antonio, Carrizozo
	Other	E: Bosque Bird Watchers RV Park▲
124		NM 178, Magdalena, to San Marcial
115		NM 107, Magdalena
	TStop	E: Santa Fe Diner & Truck Stop
	Food	E: Rest/FastFood/Santa Fe TS
	Tires	E: Santa Fe TS
	Other	E: Laundry/RVDump/Santa Fe TS
(114)		Rest Area (Both dir) (RR, Vend, Picnic)
100		Red Rock
92		Monticello Pt Rd, Mitchell Point
89		NM 181, US 85, NM 52, T or C, to Cuchillo, Monticello
	Other	E: Monticello RV Park▲, Elephant Butte State Park

◊ = Regular Gas Stations with Diesel ▲ = RV Friendly Locations ♥ = Pet Friendly Locations

RED PRINT SHOWS LARGE VEHICLE PARKING/ACCESS ON SITE OR NEARBY BROWN PRINT SHOWS CAMPGROUNDS/RV PARKS

Page 123

INTERSTATE 25 N

EXIT	NEW MEXICO
83	US 85, NM 181, NM 195, NM 52, Hot Springs Landing, Cuchillo, Monticello
Other	E: to appr 6mi: Cedar Cove RV Park▲, Enchanted View RV Park▲, Lakeside RV Park▲, Cozy Cove RV Park▲, Elephant Butte Lake State Park▲
	W: Truth or Consequences Airport✈
(82)	Inspection Station (NB)
79	I-25 Bus, N Truth or Consequences
FStop	E: Chevron
Gas	E: Circle K, Phillips 66◆
Food	E: DQ, K-Bobs Steakhouse, Sonic McDonald's, Pizza Hut, Subway
Lodg	E: Best Western, Comfort Inn, Days Inn, Holiday Inn, Ace Lodge, Super 8, Red Haven Motel♥
Other	E: T or C Golf Course, Auto Services, IGA, US Post Office
76	I-25 Bus, South Truth or Consequences, Williamsburg (SB)
(75)	Parking Area (Both dir)
75	US 85, S Broadway, I-25 Bus, Williamsburg, South Truth or Consequences (NB)
FStop	E: Fast Stop/Shell
Gas	E: Chevron, Conoco
Food	E: Café Rio, Hacienda, La Pinata
Lodg	E: Rio Grande Motel
Med	E: + NM Vets Center Hospital
Other	E: Laundry/FastStop, Cielo Vista RV Resort, RJ RV Park▲, Desert Skies RV Park▲, Cottonwood RV Park▲, Palmos RV Park▲, Hyde Ave/Public RVDump, Auto Repair & Service, ATMs, Banks, Auto Dealer, Museums, Grocery, Fairgrounds, Police Dept
71	Las Palomas
(67)	Parking Area (Both dir)
63	NM 152, Caballo, Hillsboro
Other	E: Lakeview RV Park▲/LP/Gas, US Post Office, U-Haul, Caballo Emergency Truck Repair, Lil Abner's Store & RV Park▲
59	NM 187, Arrey, Caballo-Percha State Parks, Caballo Lake
Other	E: Caballo Lake State Park▲ /RVDump
	W: to Percha Dam State Park▲, Arrey RV Park▲
51	NM 546, Arrey, Garfield, Derry
41	NM 26, Hatch, to Deming
Gas	W: Conoco
Food	W: DQ, B&E Burritos, Pepper Pot
Lodg	W: Village Plaza Motel
Other	E: Future Space Port
	W: ATMs, Banks, Hatch Muni Airport✈, Grocery, Happy Trails RV Park▲
35	NM 140W, Rincon
32	Upham
(27)	Scenic View (NB)
(26)	Inspection Station (NB)
(23)	Rest Area (Both dir) (RR, Picnic, Vend)
19	NM 157, Radium Springs
Other	W: Leasburg Dam State Park▲
9	NM 320, Dona Ana, Las Cruces
Gas	W: Chevron◆, Conoco◆
Food	W: Pizza Inn
Other	W: Auto Services
6AB	US 70, US 82E, Alamagordo, Las Cruces
Gas	E: Phillips 66◆, Texaco
	W: Chevron, Conoco, Shamrock, Shell
Food	E: Cattleman's Steakhouse, IHOP, Out back Steakhouse, Santa Fe Grill, Peter Piper Pizza
	W: Burger Time, DQ, KFC McDonald's, Sonic, Taco Bell
Lodg	E: Fairfield Inn, Motel 6♥, Super 8
Other	E: Kmart, Theatre
	W: Albertson's, AutoZone, Cinemas, IGA, Lowe's, Sunny Acres RV Park▲
3	NM 342, Lohman Ave, Las Cruces
Gas	E: Shamrock, Shell
	W: Conoco, Shell, Valero
Food	E: Burger King, Cattle Baron Steak & Seafood, Chili's, Carino's, KFC, Golden Corral, Hooters, Jack in the Box, Pizza Hut, Red Lobster, Starbucks, Village Inn
	W: Arby's, McDonald's, Quiznos, Texas Roadhouse, Wendy's
Lodg	E: Hilton Inn
Other	E: ATMs, Banks, Albertson's, Home Depot, PetCo♥, Target, Mall
	W: Big Lots, NAPA, PetSmart♥, Staples, Walgreen's, Wal-Mart sc, UPS Store
1	University Ave, Las Cruces (Access Ex #3 Serv E to Telshor Blvd)
Gas	W: Conoco
Food	W: DQ, McDonald's
Lodg	W: Comfort Suites
Med	E: + Memorial Medical Hospital
Other	W: FedEx Kinko's, NM State Univ
(0)	Jct I-10, E to El Paso, TX; W to Tucson, AZ
(0)	Weigh Station (NB)
	(I-25 begins/end on I-10, Exit #144)

○ NEW MEXICO

Begin Northbound I-25 from Jct I-10 in Las Cruces, NM to Jct I-90 in Buffalo, WY.

INTERSTATE 26 E

EXIT	TENNESSEE
	Begin Eastbound I-26 from VA Border to Jct I-17, near Charleston, SC

○ TENNESSEE
(EASTERN TIME ZONE)
(Former US 23, Last exit # remains)

EXIT	TENNESSEE
57	TN 36S, Lynn Garden Dr (WB exit, EB entr) (End US 23)
1	US 11W, TN 1, W Stone Dr, Kingsport
Gas	N: Exxon, Sunoco
	S: KenJo, Murphy, KarKorner
Food	N: Bamboo Garden, Little Caesar's, Paradise Café, Wendy's
	S: Burger King, McDonald's, Waffle House
Lodg	N: Days Inn, Kingsport Inn, Westside Inn
Med	N: + Wellmont Holston, + Valley Medical Center
Other	S: Auto Service, Towing, Stadium, Wal-Mart sc
	N: ATMs, Banks, Grocery
3	Meadow View Pkwy
4A	TN 93S, Kingsport
4B	TN 93N, Wilcox Dr
6	TN 347, Rock Spring Rd
Other	S: Eric's Truck & Trailer Repair
(8B)	Jct I-81, N to Bristol
(8A)	Jct I-81, S to Knoxville
10	Eastern Star Rd, Kingsport
13	TN 75, Suncrest Dr, Bobby Hicks Hwy, Johnson City
Gas	N: BP◆, Exxon◆
	S: BP◆
Food	N: Burger King, DQ, McDonald's, Pizza Hut, Japanese Rest, Subway, TCBY
Other	N: Grocery, RiteAid, Tri-Cities Airport✈
	TN 354, Boones Creek Rd, to Jonesborough
Gas	S: BP, Shell◆
Food	N: Bob Evans, Kemosabee's Roadhouse
	S: Burger King, Cracker Barrel, Waffle House, Wendy's
Lodg	S: Jameson Inn
19	TN 381, State of Franklin Rd, Oakland Ave, to US 321, Bristol
Gas	N: BP, Murphy
	S: Exxon
Food	N: McDonald's/BP, Dixie BBQ, Golden Corral, Logan's Roadhouse, Outback Steakhouse, Quiznos, Subway, Sonic
	S: Carrabba's, Fuddrucker's, IHOP
Lodg	N: Comfort Suites
	S: Hampton Inn
Other	N: Wal-Mart sc, Carwash, Auto Service
	S: Home Depot, Kmart, Lowe's, Natural Foods Market, Best Buy, Winn Dixie

◆ = Regular Gas Stations with Diesel ▲ = RV Friendly Locations ♥ = Pet Friendly Locations
RED PRINT SHOWS LARGE VEHICLE PARKING/ACCESS ON SITE OR NEARBY BROWN PRINT SHOWS CAMPGROUNDS/RV PARKS

EXIT		TENNESSEE
20		US 11E, US 19W, TN 34, N Roan St, Johnson City, Bluff City (EB)
	Gas	N: Citgo, Phillips 66
		S: BP, Sunoco
	Food	N: Arby's, Hardee's, Harbor House, Hardee's, Perkins, Sagebrush Steakhouse, Waffle House
		S: ChickFilA, McDonald's, Red Pig BBQ, Ryan's Grill, Shoney's, Subway
	Lodg	N: Best Western, Holiday Inn, Super 8
		S: Days Inn, Fairfield Inn
	Other	N: Auto Dealers, ATMs, Banks
		S: ATMs, Banks, Cinemas, Walgreen's
20A		US 11E, US 19W, TN 34, to Bluff City (WB)
20B		N Roan St, Johnson City (WB)
22		TN 400, Unaka Ave, Watauga Ave, Johnson City, Airport
23		TN 91, Market St, Main St, to 11E, Johnson City
	Gas	S: BP
	Food	N: DQ, McDonald's
	Other	S: Auto Services, Museum
24		US 321, TN 67, University Pkwy, to TN 381, to Elizabethton
	Gas	N: Shell◊
		S: BP◊
	Food	N: Deli
		S: Arby's, Burger King, Jerry's Café
	Lodg	S: Comfort Inn
	Med	S: + US Veterans Medical Center
	Other	S: Advance Auto, Food City, Roan Mountain State Park, E TN State Univ
27		TN 359N, Okolona Rd
	Gas	N: BP
	Lodg	N: Budget Inn
	Other	N: Milligan College
32		TN 173, Unicoi Rd
	Gas	N: Phillips 66
	Food	N: Maple Grove Cafe
	Lodg	N: Budget Inn
	Other	N: Grand View Campground▲
		S: Woodsmoke Campground▲
36		Main St, Erwin
	Gas	N: BP, Exxon
	Food	N: Backwood BBQ, Hardee's, KFC, Pizza Hut, Wendy's
37		TN 81, TN 107, Erwin, Jonesborough
	Gas	N: Shell◊
	Food	N: Huddle House, McDonald's, Sonic
		S: River's Edge

EXIT		TENNESSEE
	Lodg	S: Super 8
	Med	N: + Hospital
	Other	N: to Riverpark Campground▲, Cherokee Nat'l Forest▲
40		Jackson-Love Hwy, Erwin
	Gas	N: Apco, Exxon
	Food	N: Long John Silver/Apco, Pizza Plus
	Lodg	N: Holiday Inn Express
	Other	N: Nolichucky Gorge Campground▲
43		US 19W, TN 352, Temple Hill Rd
	Gas	N: Exxon
46		Clear Branch Rd, Flag Pond
	Other	N: Acorn Ridge RV Park▲
(48)		Scenic Overlook (WB) (NO Trucks)
50		Higgins Creek Rd, Flag Pond
(54)		Scenic Overlook (EB) (NO Trucks)

EXIT		TN / NC
(0)		Brake Check Area (EASTERN TIME ZONE)
		TENNESSEE
		NORTH CAROLINA (EASTERN TIME ZONE)
(2)		Runaway Truck Ramp (EB)
3		Mars Hill, US 23 Alt, Wolf Laurel
(5)		Runaway Truck Ramp (EB)
(6)		NC Welcome Center (EB) (RR, Phone, Picnic)
(7)		Runaway Truck Ramp (EB)
(8)		Scenic View (WB)
9		US 19N, Burnsville, Spruce Pine
11		NC 213, to Mars Hill, Marshall
	Gas	S: Chevron◊, Exxon◊, Shell◊
	Food	S: Hardee's, Waffle House
	Lodg	S: Comfort Inn
13		Forks of Ivy
	FStop	N: Payless Disc Beverage/BP
	Gas	S: Exxon◊
15		NC 197, Jupiter, Barnardsville
17		Flat Creek
18		US 19 Bus, Monticello Rd, Weaverville (Diff Reacc EB)
19AB		US 25N, US 70W, Marshall
	FStop	S: Mountain Energy/Shell, Mountain Energy/BP
	Gas	N: Shell◊
	Food	N: Arby's, Burger King, Waffle House
	Other	S: NAPA
21		New Stock Rd, Aiken Rd, Asheville to US 19 Bus, US 23 Bus
	Gas	N: Citgo
	Food	N: Pizza Hut
	Other	N: Ingles
23		Merrimon Ave, US 25, N Asheville, New Bridge, Weaverville Hwy
	Gas	N: Exxon◊, Phillips 66
	Food	N: Frank's Roman Pizza, Ilene's Café, New China Chinese Food
	Lodg	N: Days Inn, Mayflower Motel
	Other	N: Food Lion
24		Elk Mountain Rd, to Woodfin
25		NC 251, Broadway St, to UNC, Asheville

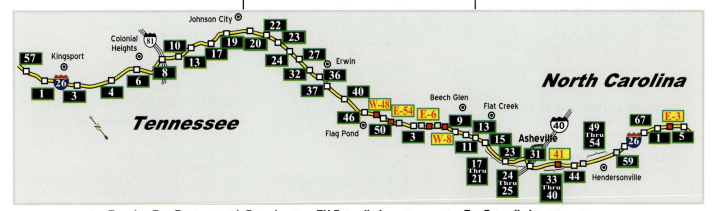

◊ = Regular Gas Stations with Diesel   ▲ = RV Friendly Locations   ♥ = Pet Friendly Locations

RED PRINT SHOWS LARGE VEHICLE PARKING/ACCESS ON SITE OR NEARBY   BROWN PRINT SHOWS CAMPGROUNDS/RV PARKS

EXIT	NORTH CAROLINA
(31B)	Jct I-40W, US 74W, to Canton, Knoxville, TN
(31A)	Jct I-40E, to Hickory (WB exit, EB entr)
33	NC 191, Brevard Rd, to Blue Ridge Parkway
Gas	N: Phillips 66
	S: Citgo, Phillips 66
Food	S: Garfield's, Harbor Inn Seafood, Long John Silver, Los Volcanos Mexican Rest, McDonald's, Original Prime Rib, Pacific Grill, Ryan's Grill, Souper Salad, Taco Bell, Texas Roadhouse, Waffle House
Lodg	S: Comfort Inn, Country Suites, Fairfield Inn, Hampton Inn, Holiday Inn Express, Super 8, Wingate Inn
Other	N: Ashville Bear Creek RV Park & Campground▲
	S: Grocery, Kmart, Biltmore Square Mall
37	NC 146, Long Shoals Rd, Arden, to Skyland
Gas	N: AmocoBP, Exxon, Shell◊
Food	N: Arby's, McDonald's, Shoney's, Waffle House
Lodg	N: Quality Inn
Other	N: CVS
	S: Vet♥
40	NC 280, Airport Rd, Fletcher, Arden, Asheville Reg'l Airport
Gas	N: Exxon◊, Shell◊
	S: BP◊
Food	N: Arby's, Carrabba's, Cracker Barrel, McDonald's, Pizza Hut, Ruby Tuesday, Waffle House, Rest/Holiday Inn
	S: Circle B Ranch BBQ, J & S Cafeteria
Lodg	N: Budget Inn, Days Inn, Econo Lodge, Hampton Inn, Holiday Inn Express
	S: Fairfield Inn
Other	N: Best Buy, Dollar Depot, Lowe's, Target, UPS Store
	S: Asheville Reg'l Airport✈, Rutledge Lake RV Park▲
(41)	Rest Area (Both dir) (RR, Phone, Picnic)
44	US 25, Hendersonville Rd, Fletcher, Mountain Home
TStop	S: Mountain Energy Travel Center/Shell (Scales)
Gas	N: Exxon◊
	S: Citgo◊
Food	N: Hardee's, Subway
	S: Mtn Energy TC, Burger King, Huddle House
TServ	S: Mountain Energy TC
Med	N: + Hospital
Other	S: Laundry/Mountain Energy TC, Todd's RV & Marine
(46)	Weigh Station (Both dir)
49A	US 64E, to Bat Cave
49B	US 64W, Hendersonville
49AB	US 64, Hendersonville, Bat Cave
Gas	N: Chevron, Shell◊, Texaco◊
	S: Chevron◊, Exxon◊, Shell◊
Food	N: Atlanta Bread Co, Sonic, Jack in the Box, Waffle House
	S: Applebee's, Arby's, Denny's, KFC, Hardee's, Long John Silver, McDonald's, Outback Steakhouse, Ryan's Grill,

Personal Notes
_____

EXIT	NORTH CAROLINA
Food	S: Shoney's, Taco Bell, Wendy's
Lodg	N: Best Western, Hampton Inn, Quality Inn, Ramada Inn
	S: Comfort Inn, Days Inn, Red Roof Inn♥
Med	N: + Park Ridge Hospital
Other	N: CarQuest, Staples, UPS Store, Wal-Mart sc, Sam's Club, Lazy Boy Travel Park▲, Apple Valley Travel Park▲, Red Gates RV Park▲, Phil & Ann's RV Sales & Service & RV Park▲
	S: ATMs, Banks, Aldi's, Auto Dealers, CVS, Home Depot, Kmart, Lowe's, Blue Ridge Mall, Four Seasons Cinema
53	Upward Rd, Hendersonville
Gas	N: Texaco
	S: Exxon◊, Shell◊
Food	N: Waffle House
	S: Pizza Inn/Shell, Burger King, Cracker Barrel, McDonald's
Lodg	S: Holiday Inn Express, Mountain Inn
Other	N: Lakewood RV Resort▲
	S: Auto Dealer, Park Place RV Park▲, Town Mountain Travel Park▲, Blue Ridge Comm College
54	US 25, to US 176, NC 225, to Greenville, E Flat Rock
NOTE:	MM 55: EB: 6% Steep Grade
59	Saluda
TStop	S: Saluda Truck Plaza/BP
Gas	S: Texaco
Food	S: Apple Mill Rest
Lodg	N: Heaven's View Motel, Saluda Mtn Motel

EXIT	NC / SC
Other	N: to appr 5.5 mi: Orchard Lake Campground▲
NOTE:	MM 62: EB: 6% Steep Grade
67	US 74E, NC 108, Columbus, Tryon, Rutherfordton, Shelby
Gas	N: BP◊
	S: Exxon, Shell
Food	N: Burger King, McDonald's, Subway, Waffle House, Wendy's
Lodg	S: Days Inn
Med	N: + Hospital
Other	N: Food Lion, CVS
(68)	NC Welcome Center (WB) (RR, Phone, Picnic)

(EASTERN TIME ZONE)
⬆ NORTH CAROLINA
⬇ SOUTH CAROLINA
(EASTERN TIME ZONE)

EXIT	
1	SC 14, Sc 128, Landrum
Gas	S: BP◊, Ingles
Food	S: BurgerKing/BP, Bojangles, Denny's, Pizza Hut, Subway
Other	S: Ingles
(3)	SC Welcome Center (EB) (RR, Phones, Picnic, Vend, Info)
5	SC 11, Foothills Scenic Hwy, Campobello, Chesnee
TStop	N: Kangaroo #3403 (Scales)
Gas	S: Phillips 66
Food	N: Aunt M's Café/Kangaroo
(9)	Parking Area (Both dir)
10	SC 292, Inman
TStop	N: Hot Spot Travel Center #2013/Shell (Scales)
Food	N: Subway/Hot Spot TC
Other	N: Laundry/Hot Spot TC
15	US 176, N Inman, Spartanburg
FStop	S: Corner Mart/Mystik
TStop	N: Circle K #5370/76 (Scales)
Gas	N: Fuel Stop, RaceTrac
Food	N: FastFood/Circle K, Waffle House
	S: FastFood/CornerMart, Burger King, Taco Bell
Med	N: + Hospital
16	John Dodd Rd, Wellford
FStop	N: Kangaroo Express #3415/Citgo
Food	N: FastFood/Kangaroo, Arby's
Other	N: Camping World/Holiday Kamper RV Center, Cunningham RV Park▲
17	New Cut Rd, Sigsbee
Gas	S: Chevron◊, Sunoco◊, Speedway
Food	S: Burger King, Fatz Café, McDonald's, Hardee's, Waffle House
Lodg	S: Comfort Inn, Days Inn, Relax Inn, Howard Johnson Express
Other	N: Spartanburg Tech College
	S: Spartanburg Cunningham RV Park▲, Spartanburg Expo Center
(18B)	Jct I-85, N-Charlotte
(18A)	Jct I-85, S-Greenville
19AB	I-85 Lp, Greenville, Spartanburg
Gas	N: Amoco, Phillips 66
Food	N: Cracker Barrel
Lodg	N: Budget Inn, Extended Stay America, Fairfield Inn, Ramada Inn, Radisson, Residence Inn

◊ = Regular Gas Stations with Diesel   ▲ = RV Friendly Locations   ♥ = Pet Friendly Locations
RED PRINT SHOWS LARGE VEHICLE PARKING/ACCESS ON SITE OR NEARBY   BROWN PRINT SHOWS CAMPGROUNDS/RV PARKS

Interstate 26 W/E — South Carolina

EXIT	SOUTH CAROLINA
Lodg	S: Brookwood Inn, USA Economy Lodge
Other	N: Goodyear
21AB	**US 29, Spartanburg, Greer**
Gas	N: BP, Crown, Exxon, Phillips 66, Kangaroo Express S: Citgo◊, Texaco◊, Sam's
Food	N: Burger King, CiCi's, Corona Mexican, Golden Corral, Hardee's, Jack in the Box, Lone Star Steakhouse, Monterey Mexican, O'Charley's, Red Lobster, Pizza Hut, Rock Ola Café, Souper Salad, Wendy's S: Applebee's, IHOP, McDonald's, Prime Sirloin, Shogun, Taco Bell, Waffle House
Lodg	N: Hilton Garden, Hampton Inn, Holiday Inn
Other	N: ATMs, Banks, Best Buy, Budget RAC, Circuit City, Cinema 8, Firestone, Home Depot, Goodyear, Office Depot, PetSmart♥, Wal-Mart sc, Westgate Mall S: Laundromat, Ingles, Lowe's, Target, RiteAid, Sam's Club
22	**SC 296, Reidville Rd, Spartanburg**
Gas	N: BP◊, Exxon S: BP◊
Food	N: Arby's, Carolina BBQ, Hong Kong Express, Outback Steakhouse, Ryan's Grill, Waffle House, Zaxby's S: Burger King, Denny's, Hardee's, TCBY, Subway, Waffle House
Lodg	S: Sleep Inn, Southern Suites, Super 8
Other	N: Carmike Cinemas, Grocery, U-Haul, ATMs, Banks, Spartanburg Downtown Memorial Airport✈ S: Auto Services, ATMs, CVS, Bi-Lo, Grocery, Walgreen's
28	**US 221, Roebuck, Spartanburg, Moore, Woodruff**
FStop	N: MiniMart Food Store #3416/Citgo
Gas	N: Shell◊
Food	N: Burger King, Hardee's, Waffle House, Walnut Grove Seafood Rest, Subway/Shell
Other	N: Pine Ridge Campground▲, to Walnut Grove Plantation, to approx 8 mi Croft State Park▲
35	**SC 50, Walnut Grove Rd, Woodruff**
FStop	S: Citgo
Food	S: Rest/Citgo
Med	S: + Hospital
38	**SC 146, Cross Anchor, Woodruff**
TStop	N: Hot Spot #6004/Shell
Food	N: Hardee's/Hot Spot, Big Country Rest
Other	N: Laundry/Hot Spot
41	**SC 92, Enoree**
Gas	N: Valero
44	**SC 49, Union Hwy, Laurens, Cross Anchor, Union**
(51)	**Jct I-385, Greenville, Laurens (WB exit, EB entr)**
52	**SC 56, Clinton, Cross Anchor**
TStop	N: Pilot Travel Center #61 (Scales)
Gas	S: Citgo, Phillips 66, Shell
Food	N: Subway/Pilot TC, McDonald's, Waffle House S: Hardee's, Waffle House, Wendy's
Lodg	N: Comfort Inn♥ S: Days Inn, Ramada Inn, Travelers Inn

EXIT	SOUTH CAROLINA
54	**SC 72, Clinton, Whitmire**
FStop	S: Corner Mart #49/Citgo
Gas	N: BP S: Exxon
Food	S: FastFood/Corner Mart
Other	N: to Cane Creek Resort▲
60	**SC 66, Joanna, Whitmire**
Gas	S: Chevron
Food	S: Joanna Cafe
Other	S: Magnolia Family Campground▲
(63)	**Rest Area (Both dir) (RR, Phone, Picnic, Vend)**
66	**SC 32, Jalapa Rd, Kinards**
72	**SC 121, Newberry, Whitmire, Union**
FStop	S: Corner Mart #44/Citgo
74	**SC 34, Newberry, Winnsboro**
FStop	S: I-26 Shell
Gas	N: BP, Shell
Food	N: Rest/Best Western S: Arby's, Captain D's, Hardee's, Waffle House, McDonald's
Lodg	N: Best Western S: Newberry Inn/I-26 Shell, Comfort Inn, Days Inn, Holiday Inn Express
Med	S: + Hospital
76	**SC 219, Pomaria, Newberry**
Gas	S: BP, Murphy
Food	S: Burger King, Wendy's
Lodg	S: Hampton Inn, Holiday Inn Express
Other	S: Wal-Mart sc
(81)	**Weigh Station (EB)**
82	**SC 773, Pomaria, Prosperity**
TStop	N: Kangaroo #3441/BP (Scales)
Food	N: Subway/Kangaroo
TServ	N: Kangaroo/Tires
85	**SC 202, Little Mountain**
Other	S: Dreher Island State Park▲
91	**SC 48, Columbia Ave, Chapin**
FStop	S: Pitt Stop #7/Shell, Rainbow Gas Garden #12/Exxon
Gas	S: BP◊
Food	S: Hardee's, McDonald's, Subway, Taco Bell, Waffle House
Other	S: Dreher Lake State Park▲
(94)	**Weigh Station (WB)**
97	**US 176, Ballentine, White Rock, Peak**
Gas	S: Exxon◊
Other	N: Woodsmoke Family Campground▲
101AB	**US 76, 176, Broad River Rd (WB)**
101	**US 76, US 176, Broad River Rd, Irmo, Ballentine, White Rock**
Gas	N: Exxon◊ S: 76, BP, Mobil
Food	N: Blimpie, Fatz Cafe S: Burger King, Crabs in the Pot Rest, Waffle House
Other	S: Discount Tire
102A	**SC 60S, Lake Murray Blvd**
Gas	S: 76, Exxon, Shell
Food	S: Arby's, Maurice's BBQ, Papa John's, McDonald's, Zaxby's
Med	S: + Lexington Medical Center
Other	S: ATMs, Banks, CVS, Grocery, Tires, Carolina RV, Police Dept

EXIT	SOUTH CAROLINA
102B	**SC 60N, Lake Murray Blvd**
Lodg	N: AmeriSuites, Extended Stay America, Wellesley Inn
103	**Harbison Blvd, Columbia**
Gas	S: Amoco, Exxon, Hess, Shell
Food	N: Applebee's, HOPS S: Bojangles, Chili's, Carrabba's, Cajun Café, Denny's, McDonald's, Monterey Mexican, Outback Steakhouse, Ruby Tuesday, Olive Garden, Smokey Bones BBQ, Sesame Inn Chinese Rest, Subway, Shoney's, Sonic, Texas Roadhouse, Taco Bell, Yamato Steakhouse
Lodg	N: Hampton Inn S: Comfort Inn, Country Inn, Fairfield Inn, Hilton Garden Inn, Holiday Inn, Suite 1, Towneplace Suites, Wingate Inn
Med	S: + Baptist Medical Center
Other	N: Auto Dealers, Home Depot, Lowe's, Frankie's Fun Park, Grocery S: ATMs, Banks, Best Buy, Carmike Cinemas, Grocery, Goodyear, Publix, RiteAid, Sam's Club, Staples, Target, Wal-Mart sc, Columbiana Centre Mall, Sheriff Dept
104	**Piney Grove Rd, W Columbia**
FStop	N: Sunoco #2634
Gas	S: Exxon◊, Shell
Food	N: Hardee's, McDonald's, Quincy's, Waffle House
Lodg	N: Comfort Inn, Fairview Inn, Knights Inn S: Comfort Inn, Microtel
Other	N: Conference Center
106AB	**SC 36, St Andrews Rd (WB)**
106	**St Andrews Rd, Columbia (EB)**
Gas	N: BP, Exxon◊ S: 76, Hess◊, Shell
Food	N: Blimpie's/Exxon, BB's Steak & Ribs, Burger King, ChicFilA, IHOP, Sonic S: Maurice's BBQ, Old Country Buffet, McDonald's, Pizza Hut, Ryan's Grill, Waffle House, Wendy's
Lodg	N: Motel 6♥ S: Red Roof Inn♥, Super 8
Other	N: Laundromat, CVS, Grocery, Kroger, Walgreen's, Holiday Kamper RV S: Food Lion
(107AB)	**Jct I-20, W to Augusta, GA, E to Florence**
108A	**Bush River Rd**
(108B)	**Jct I-126, Downtown Columbia**
(108)	**Jct I-126, Bush River Rd, Columbia**
Gas	N: Citgo, Shell◊ S: RaceWay, Sunoco
Food	N: Blimpie, Captain D's, Hardee's, KFC, Golden China, Piccadilly, Ruby Tuesday, Shoney's, Subway, Wendy's S: Cracker Barrel, El Chico Rest, Key West Grill, Waffle House
Lodg	N: Baymont Inn, Days Inn, La Quinta Inn♥, Scottish Inn, Western Inn S: Best Western, Courtyard, Days Inn, Howard Johnson, Knights Inn, Sleep Inn
Other	N: AMC Cinema, ATMs, Auto Services, Banks, Firestone, Kmart, Office Depot, Mall
110	**US 378, Lexington, W Columbia**
Gas	N: Conoco S: BP, 76

◊ = Regular Gas Stations with Diesel ▲ = RV Friendly Locations ♥ = Pet Friendly Locations
RED PRINT SHOWS LARGE VEHICLE PARKING/ACCESS ON SITE OR NEARBY BROWN PRINT SHOWS CAMPGROUNDS/RV PARKS

EXIT		SOUTH CAROLINA
	Food	N: Burger King, McDonald's, Subway, Pizza Hut, Waffle House, Western Sizzlin, Rest/Ramada S: Bojangles, Hardee's, Pizza Hut
	Lodg	N: Days Inn, Hampton Inn, Ramada Inn S: Executive Inn
	Med	S: + Lexington Medical Center
	Other	N: ATMs, Banks, Laundromat, CVS, Food Lion, U-Haul S: ATM, Bank
111A		US 1N, Augusta Rd, W Columbia
	Gas	S: Hess
	Food	S: Applebee's, Gilbert Rib, Wendy's
	Lodg	S: Super 8
	Other	S: CVS, Lowe's, Winn Dixie, U-Haul, Transmission, Auto Service
111B		US 1S, Augusta Rd, W Columbia
	Gas	N: 76, RaceTrac◊
	Food	N: #1 Chinese, Domino's, Dragon City Chinese, Hardee's, Maurice's BBQ, Ruby Tuesday, McDonald's, Subway, Waffle House, Sonic, Zaxby's
	Lodg	N: Delta Motel, Holiday Inn, Super 8
	TServ	N: Williams Truck Service
	Other	N: ATMs, Banks, Bi-Lo, Kroger, Oriental Grocery, Walgreen's, Wal-Mart sc
111AB		US 1, Augusta Rd, W Columbia, Lexington
113		SC 302, Columbia Airport, Cayce
	Gas	N: Pitt Stop/Exxon, Texaco S: 76, Exxon, RaceTrac
	Food	N: Waffle House, Rest/BW S: Burger King, Denny's, Don Pedro, Fat Boy, Shoney's, Subway, Waffle House, Wendy's
	Lodg	N: Best Western, Airport Inn, Knights Inn, Masters Inn S: Comfort Inn, Country Inn, Days Inn, Sleep Inn
	TServ	N: Cherokee Kenworth
	Other	N: Auto & Diesel Repair, Truck & Trailer Repair, S: ATM, Bank, Columbia Metro Airport✈
115		US 21, US 176, US 321, Gaston, Cayce, Columbia, Charleston Hwy
	TStop	S: Pilot Travel Center #338 (Scales), Corner Pantry #127/Shell
	Gas	N: RaceTrac
	Food	N: Waffle House S: DQ/Wendy's/Pilot TC, Bojangles, Hardee's, McDonald's, Subway
	Lodg	N: Palmetto Motel S: Ramada Inn
	Other	N: ATM, Bank, Bi-Lo, Farmers Market, Harley Davidson S: Grocery
(116)		Jct I-77N, to Charlotte, NC, to US 76, US 378, to Ft Jackson
119		US 21, US 176, W Columbia, to St Matthews, Dixiana
	FStop	N: The Pantry #3272/BP
	TStop	S: Pitt Stop #36/Exxon (Scales)
	Gas	N: 76 S: Shell
	Food	N: Rest/Pitt Stop S: Subway/Shell, Maggie Mae's Rest
	TServ	S: SC Truck & Trailer
(122)		Rest Area (Both dir) (RR, Phones, Picnic, Vend)

Personal Notes

EXIT		SOUTH CAROLINA
125		SC 31, Gaston
129		US 21, Swansea, Orangeburg
	Gas	N: Shell◊
136		SC 6, N Swansea, St Matthews
	TStop	N: Brakefield's Exxon
	Gas	N: BP
	Food	N: Rest/Brakefield's
	Tires	N: Brakefield's
	Other	N: LP/Brakefield's
139		SC 22, St Matthews
	TStop	S: WilcoHess Travel Plaza #933 (Scales)
	Gas	S: Phillips 66, Shell
	Food	S: Arby's/WilcoHess TP
	Other	N: Tire Country S: Sweetwater Lake Campground▲
145A		US 601S, to Orangeburg
145B		US 601N, to St Matthews
145AB		US 601, St Matthews, Orangeburg
	FStop	S: Sunoco #2679, Speedway #0284, Shell
	Gas	S: BP, Exxon
	Food	S: Burger King/Shell, Cracker Barrel, Fatz Café, Hardee's, KFC, McDonald's, Ruby Tuesday, Subway, Waffle House, Wendy's
	Lodg	S: Comfort Inn, Carolina Lodge, Days Inn, Fairfield Inn, Hampton Inn, Holiday Inn Express, Howard Johnson, Sleep Inn, Southern Lodge, Travelers Inn
	Med	S: + Hospital
	Other	S: SC State Univ
149		SC 33, Orangeburg, Cameron (All Serv 4-5mi S in Orangeburg)

EXIT		SOUTH CAROLINA
(150)		Rest Area (EB) (RR, Phones, Picnic, Vend)
(152)		Rest Area (WB) (RR, Phones, Picnic, Vend)
154B		US 301N, to Santee
154A		US 301S, to Orangeburg
154AB		US 301, Orangeburg, Santee
	TStop	S: Love's Travel Stop #326 (Scales)
	Gas	N: Exxon◊, Shell◊
	Food	N: Blimpie/Exxon, Rest/Days Inn S: Chesters/Subway/Love's TS
	Lodg	N: Days Inn
	Other	S: WiFi/Love's TS, Auto & Truck Service
159		SC 36, Bowman
	FStop	S: Phillips 66
	TStop	N: Pilot Travel Center #60 (Scales)
	Food	N: McDonald's/Pilot TC
	TServ	N: Pilot TC
	Other	N: Laundry/WiFi/Pilot TC
165		SC 210, Bowman, Vance
	FStop	S: Mac's Quick C/BP
	TStop	S: Bowman Shell Truck Stop (Scales), Flying J Travel Plaza # (Scales)
	Gas	S: Exxon
	Food	S: Rest/Mac's, Blimpie/Bowman TS Rest/FastFood/Flying J TP
	TServ	S: Bowman TS
(169A)		Jct I-95, S to Savannah, GA (All Serv Available at 1st Exit S)
(169B)		Jct I-95, N to Florence
(169AB)		Jct I-95, N-Florence, S-Savannah
172A		US 15S, to St George
172B		US 15N, to Holly Hill
172AB		US 15, Santee, to St George, Holly Hill
	TStop	S: EZ Shop Horizon Travel Center #27 (Scales)
	Food	S: Subway/EZ Shop
	Other	S: Laundry/EZ Shop
(173)		Weigh Station (EB)
(174)		Weigh Station (WB)
177		SC 453, Harleyville, Holly Hill
	FStop	S: Ronnie's Shell
	Food	S: Derrick's Country Kitchen
	Lodg	S: Ashley Inn RV Park & CG▲
	Other	S: LP/RVDump/Ronnie's
187		SC 27, Ridgeville, St George
	Gas	N: Phillips 66 S: BP◊
194		SC 16, Summerville, to Jedburg, Pinopolis
199A		Alt US 17S, to Summerville
199B		Alt US 17N, to Monck's Corner
199AB		Alt US 17, Monck's Corner, Summerville
	TStop	N: Pilot Travel Center #64 (Scales) S: Angler's Auto/Truck Plaza #3/Citgo (Scales)
	Gas	N: BP, Hess◊ S: 76, Enmark◊
	Food	N: McDonald's/Pilot TC, Boston Billy's, China Wok, Hardee's, KFC, Pizza Hut, Subway, Waffle House

Page 128 ◊ = Regular Gas Stations with Diesel ▲ = RV Friendly Locations ♥ = Pet Friendly Locations
RED PRINT SHOWS LARGE VEHICLE PARKING/ACCESS ON SITE OR NEARBY BROWN PRINT SHOWS CAMPGROUNDS/RV PARKS

EXIT	SOUTH CAROLINA
Food	S: Angler's/Citgo FS, Applebee's, Bojangles, Burger King, Hardee's, Huddle House, IHOP, Perkins, Quincy's, Ryan's Grill, Shoney's, Taco Bell, Waffle House, Wendy's
Lodg	S: Comfort Inn, Econo Lodge, Hampton Inn, Holiday Inn Express, Sleep Inn
TServ	N: Blanchard CAT
Other	N: Advance Auto, AutoZone, Auto Repairs, Diesel Service, CVS, Food Lion, Dollar General S: Laundry/Angler's, Home Depot, Lowe's, Staples, Target, Wal-Mart sc, Winn Dixie, Auto Dealers, Jiffy Lube, Tire, Auto & Truck Service, Meineke, ATMs, Banks, Ca Tire
(202)	Rest Area (WB) (RR, Phones, Picnic, Vend)
203	College Park Rd, Ladson, Goose Creek
FStop	N: Speedway
Gas	N: 76, GasMart S: Hess
Food	N: McDonald's, Waffle House, Wendy's S: Burger King, KFC
Lodg	N: Best Western, Days Inn
Other	N: Food Lion S: Grocery, Charleston/Mt Pleasant KOA▲
(204)	Rest Area (EB) (RR, Phones, Picnic, Vend)
205AB	US 78, to US 52, Goose Creek, Summerville
Gas	N: BP, Hess◊ S: Speedway◊
Food	N: Arby's, Chinese, Subway, Waffle House, Wendy's S: Ladson Seafood, KFC, Mama Mia's
Lodg	N: Fairfield Inn
Med	N: + Hospital
Other	S: Charleston/Mt Pleasant KOA▲
208	US 52W, US 78W, Moncks Corner, Kingstree (WB exit, EB entr)
209	Ashley Phosphate Rd, to US 52, N Charleston
Gas	N: Exxon, Kangaroo S: Citgo, Hess, RaceTrac
Food	N: Applebee's, ChikFilA, Chuck E Cheese, Denny's, Don Pablo, Hardee's, Hops, Hooter's, McDonald's, K&W Cafeteria, Olive Garden, Outback Steakhouse, Pizza Hut, Noisy Oyster, Perkins, Quincy's, Ryan's Grill, Subway, Taco Bell, Waffle House, Wendy's

EXIT	SOUTH CAROLINA
Food	S: Bojangles, Cracker Barrel, IHOP, Kobe, McDonald's, China Palace, Waffle House, Shoney's
Lodg	N: Clarion Inn, Holiday Inn Express, Red Roof Inn, Residence Inn, Super 8 S: Fairfield Inn, Hampton Inn, Howard Johnson, La Quinta Inn ♥, Motel 6 ♥, Relax Inn, Sleep Inn, Suburban Lodge
Other	N: ATMs, Banks, Auto Repair & Service, Best Buy, Kmart, Firestone, Home Depot, Lowe's, Target, Wal-Mart sc, Auto Dealers, Northwoods Mall, AMC
211A	Aviation Ave to Remont Rd, Air Force Base
211B	to US 52, US 78
211AB	Aviation Ave to Remont Rd, Air Force Base (Services N on US 52/78)
TStop	S: Charleston Travel Plaza/Citgo (Scales)
Gas	N: AmocoBP, Exxon
Food	N: Arby's, Burger King, Captain D's, Huddle House, McDonald's, Old Country Buffet, KFC, Shoney's, Sonic, Subway, Wendy's S: Rest/Charleston TP, Waffle House, Rest/Budget, Rest/BW
Lodg	S: Masters Inn S: Best Western, Budget Inn, Seagrass Inn, Travelodge
Other	N: Dollar General, Dollar Tee, Goodyear, Grocery, Sam's Club, ATMs, Banks, Auto Services & Repairs S: ATM, Bank, Charleston AFB, Laundry/Charleston TP
212A	Remount Rd, Hanahan (Serv North on US 52/78)
Gas	N: Exxon, Hess◊, Speedway
Food	N: Burger King, KFC, Taco Bell
Other	N: Office Depot
(212BC)	Jct I-526, W to Savannah, GA; E to Mount Pleasant
213A	Montague Ave
213B	Mall Dr
213	Montague Ave, Mall Dr (WB)
FStop	S: Kangaroo Express #3692/BP
Gas	N: Exxon S: Hess◊
Food	N: Piccadilly, Red Lobster S: Bojangles, Graby's Ribs, Waffle House
Lodg	N: Sheraton, Courtyard

EXIT	SOUTH CAROLINA
Lodg	S: Comfort Inn, Days Inn, Embassy Suites, Extended Stay America, Hampton Inn, Hilton Garden Inn, Homeplace Suites, Quality Inn, Ramada Inn, Super 8, Wingate Inn
TServ	S: Cummins
Other	N: ATM, Bank, Charles Towne Square, Cinema, Amtrak, Auto Serv, Police Dept S: ATMs, Banks, Auto Services
215	SC 642, Dorchester Rd
Gas	N: Hess◊ S: Amoco◊, Pantry
Food	N: Hardee's, Old Town Family Rest
Lodg	N: Howard Johnson S: Charleston Inn, Rest Inn
Other	S: Auto Services, ATM
216A	SC 7S, to US 17S, Naval Base
216B	SC 7N, Cosgrove Ave
Gas	N: Exxon
Food	S: Arby's, McDonald's
Med	N: + Hospital
217	N Meeting St, Charleston (EB ex, WB entr)
FStop	N: Kangaroo #3355
218	Spruill Ave, Naval Base (WB ex, EB entr)
Other	N: Bishops Towing, Jennings Towing, Jones Truck Service, Pressley's Gen'l Store & Rest, Tire Service
219A	Rutledge Ave, The Citadel (EB ex, WB entr)
Other	S: Diesel Service
219B	Mt Pleasant St to Morrison Dr, E Bay St (EB ex, WB entr) Meeting St (WB entr)
Other	S: Oaks Service Station
220	US 17N, Mt Pleasant, Georgetown (EB ex, WB entr) Cypress St, Brigade St (EB entr)
220A	Romney St (WB exit)
220B	US 17N, Mt Pleasant, Georgetown (WB exit, EB entr)
221B	Meeting St, Visitor Ctr (EB exit)
221A	US 17S, Savannah, GA (EB ex, WB entr) King St, Dwntown Charleston (EB exit)

⊙ SOUTH CAROLINA

Begin Westbound I-26 from Jct I-17 near Charleston to VA Border.

◊ = Regular Gas Stations with Diesel   ▲ = RV Friendly Locations   ♥ = Pet Friendly Locations
RED PRINT SHOWS LARGE VEHICLE PARKING/ACCESS ON SITE OR NEARBY   BROWN PRINT SHOWS CAMPGROUNDS/RV PARKS

EXIT	TEXAS
	Begin Southbound I-27 from Amarillo, TX to Lubbock, TX.

⊙ TEXAS
(CENTRAL TIME ZONE)
(I-27 begins/ends on I-40, Exit #70)

EXIT	
(123B)	**Jct I-40, US 287, US 87, Amarillo, Oklahoma City, Tucumcari**
123A	26th-29th Ave, Amarillo
Gas	E: Conoco
122B	32nd-34th Ave, Tyler St
122A	FM 1541, Washington St, 34th Ave
Gas	E: Shamrock,
	W: Texaco
Food	E: Sonic
	W: Taco Bell
121B	Hawthorne Dr, Austin St (SB)
Gas	W: Texaco
Lodg	E: Amarillo Motel
121A	Georgia St, Amarillo (SB)
Gas	E: Phillips 66
	W: Texaco
Lodg	W: Traveler Motel
TServ	W: Ford/Kenworth
Other	E: Sizemore RV, Wal-Mart sc
121	Georgia St (NB)
120B	45th Ave, Amarillo (SB)
Gas	E: Fina
	W: Shamrock
Food	E: Waffle House
	W: Burger King, Hardee's
120A	Republic Ave, Western St (SB)
120	45th Ave (NB)
119B	Western St, 58th Ave (SB)
Gas	W: Shamrock, Shell
Food	W: Arby's, Long John Silvers, Wendy's
119A	Hillside Rd (SB)
119	Hillside Rd, 58th Ave (NB)
117	Arden Rd (SB), Bell St (NB)
Gas	W: Fina, Shell
Food	W: Long John Silver, Sonic
Other	E: Auto/Repair Services
	W: Camper RoundUp RV
116	Lp 335, Hollywood Rd, Amarillo
TStop	E: Love's Travel Stop #261
Gas	E: Phillips 66◊
Food	E: Subway/Love's TS, McDonald's, Waffle House
Lodg	E: Days Inn
Other	E: WiFi/Love's TS
115	Sundown Lane
113	McCormick Rd, Amarillo
Gas	E: J's Country Corner
Other	W: Cinema 16, Family Camping RV▲
112	FM 2219, Lair Rd, Amarillo
111	Rockwell Rd, Canyon
110	US 87S, US 60W, Canyon, Hereford (SB)
Other	W: West TX State Univ
109	Buffalo Stadium Rd
108	FM 3331, Hunsley Rd, Canyon
106	TX 217, 4th Ave, Canyon
Gas	W: Pak-A-Sak

EXIT	TEXAS
Lodg	W: Holiday Inn Express
Other	E: Palo Duro Trailer & RV Park▲
103	FM 1541N, Washington St, Cemetery Rd, Canyon
99	Hungate Rd, Canyon
(98)	Parking Area (Both dir)
96	Dowlen Rd
94	FM 285, Wayside Dr, Canyon
92	Haley Rd
90	FM 1075, Happy Rd, to US 87, Canyon
Gas	W: Phillips 66
88	US 87, FM 1881 (SB)
88B	US 87N, Happy
88A	FM 1881, Happy
83	FM 2698
82	FM 214, Tulia
77	US 87, Tulia
75	NW 6th St (SB)
	(Gas & Food E in Tulia)
74	TX 86, to US 87, Tulia
TStop	W: Rip Griffin Travel Center (Scales)
Food	W: Rest/Subway/RipGriffin
Lodg	W: Select Inn
Other	W: Laundry/WiFi/Rip Griffin
(69)	Parking Area (Both dir)
68	FM 928, Tulia
63	FM 145, Kress
61	US 87, County Rd, Kress
56	FM 788, Plainview
54	FM 3183
53	Lp 27 Bus, Columbia St, Plainview
51	Quincy St, Industrial Blvd
50	TX 194, Dimmitt Rd, Plainview
Gas	E: Phillips 66
Food	W: Burger King, New China Buffet, Rice Steakhouse, Kettle Rest, Subway
Med	E: + Hospital
Other	W: Cinema 6
49	US 70, Olton Rd, Plainview
FStop	E: Uncles #82/Shamrock, Taylor's/Shell
Gas	E: Phillips 66
	W: Chevron, Phillips 66
Food	E: FastFood/Taylor's, Far East, KFC, Furr's, Kettle Rest, Long John Silver, Pizza Hut, Taco Bell
	W: Burger King, McDonald's, Monterey, Sonic, Subway, Taco Bell
Lodg	E: Best Western, Days Inn
	W: Holiday Inn
Other	E: Auto Dealers, Grocery, NAPA
	W: Wal-Mart sc
48	FM 3466 (NB)
45	I-27 Bus, Plainview
43	FM 2337, Plainview
41	CR-R, Hale Center

◊ = Regular Gas Stations with Diesel ▲ = RV Friendly Locations ♥ = Pet Friendly Locations
RED PRINT SHOWS LARGE VEHICLE PARKING/ACCESS ON SITE OR NEARBY   BROWN PRINT SHOWS CAMPGROUNDS/RV PARKS

EXIT	TEXAS
38	Ave E, Main St, Hale Center (SB)
37	FM 1914, 4th St, Cleveland St
Gas	E: Co-Op
Food	E: DQ
Med	W: + Hospital
36	FM 1424, Ave E, Hale Center
32	FM 37W, Abernathy
31	FM 37E
(28)	Rest Area (Both dir) (RR, Phone, Picnic)
27	CR 275, Abernathy
24	FM 54
22	Lp 369, 16th St, Abernathy
Gas	W: Phillips 66
Other	E: to Abernathy Muni Airport ✈
21	FM 597, FM 2060, Main St, Abernathy
Gas	W: Conoco, Co-Op
Food	W: DQ, Restaurant
20	FM 597, 1st (NB)
17	CR 54, CR 53, Lubbock
15	Lp 461, FM 1729, Main St, Lubbock, to New Deal
14	FM 1729, Main St, Lubbock
TStop	E: New Deal Truck Stop/Fina (Scales)
Food	E: Rest/FastFood/New Deal TS
Other	E: Laundry/WiFi/RVDump/New Deal TS
13	Lp 461, CR 57, Lubbock, New Deal
12	Access Rd, Auburn Ave (NB)
11	FM 1294, CR 6, Lubbock to Shallowater

EXIT	TEXAS
10	CR 6, Keuka St, Lubbock
9	Airport Rd, Lubbock Int'l Airport
Other	E: Lubbock Int'l Airport ✈
	W: Lubbock RV Park ▲
8	FM 2641, Regis St
7	Yucca Lane, Amarillo Rd, Ash Ave
6B	Loop 289 (SB)
6A	Spur 326, Ave Q, Amarillo Rd (SB)
Lodg	E: Texas Motel
Other	W: Pharr RV Park ▲
6	Loop 289, Amarillo Rd (NB)
Other	E: Pharr RV
5	Ave H, Municipal Dr, Buddy Holly Ave, to US 82, Lubbock (SB)
4	US 82, Bus 87, 4th St, Parkway Dr, Lubbock, to Crosbyton
TStop	W: Flying J Travel Plaza #5155
Food	W: Rest/FastFood/FJ TP
	Laundry/LP/RVDump/FJ TP
Other	E: MacKenzie State Park
	W: Auto Service, Texas Tech Univ
3	US 62, TX 114, 19th St, 23rd St, Floydada, Leveland, Depot Distr
Other	W: Auto Services, to Ann's RV Park ▲, Buffalo Lake Springs Campground ▲, I-27 Marine & RV, Bigham Auto & RV Service Center
3A	13th St, Buddy Holly Ave, to US 62, Broadway St (NB)
2	34th St, Ave H, to US 84, Bus 87
Gas	E: Phillips 66
Food	W: Mr Lee's Burgers, La Fiesta Rest
Lodg	E: Budget Motel

EXIT	TEXAS
Other	W: Auto Services, to Loop 289 RV Park ▲, Camelot Village RV & Campground ▲
1C	50th St, Ave H, Lubbock (SB)
TStop	E: (E to US 87N) PTP/Rip Griffin Travel Center
Gas	E: Fina
	W: Conoco, Fina, Shamrock
Food	E: Rest/RG TC, DQ, JoJo's, Café
	W: Bryan's Steaks, Burger King, China Star, Carrows Rest, DQ, KFC, Long John Silver, McDonald's, Pizza Hut, Subway, Whataburger
TServ	E: RG TC/Tires
Other	E: Laundry/WiFi/RG TC
	W: Auto & Tire Service, US Post Office, Walgreen's
1B	US 84E, Lp 289, US 87S, Slaton, Post, Tahoka (SB)
Gas	W: Skillet's
Food	W: 50th St Caboose Rest, Carrow's, Country Plate Diner, KFC, Long John Silver, Skillet's Burgers
Lodg	E: Days Inn
	W: Best Western, Comfort Inn, Econo Lodge, Holiday Inn Express
Other	W: Lubbock KOA ▲
1A	50th St (NB), Loop 289 (SB)
Lodg	W: Motel 6 ♥
Other	W: Sims RV Center ▲
1	82nd St (SB), Lp 289 (NB), Lubbock (Gas, Food, Serv W to University)
Other	E: Benson Auto, Truck & RV Repair
	W: Auto Services

⊙ **TEXAS** (CENTRAL TIME ZONE)

Begin Northbound I-27 from Lubbock, TX to Amarillo, TX.

EXIT	NORTH DAKOTA
	Begin Southbound I-29 from Canada Border Jct I-70, Kansas City, MO.
	⊙ **NORTH DAKOTA** (CENTRAL TIME ZONE)
(217)	US Customs (SB)
(215)	US Customs (NB)
215	ND 59, CR 55, Pembina, Neche
TStop	E: Gastrak (Scales)
Gas	E: Citgo ◊
Food	E: FastFood/Gastrak, The Depot Café, Subway
Lodg	E: Gateway Motel, Red Roost Motel
Other	E: LP/Gastrak, Duty Free Store
212	Pembina
208	CR 1, Pembina, to Bathgate
203	US 81, ND 5, Hamilton, Cavalier
TStop	W: Joliette Express Truck Stop (Scales)
Food	W: FastFood/JE TS
Other	W: WiFi/JE TS
(203)	Weigh Station / Port of Entry (Both dir)

EXIT	NORTH DAKOTA
200	93rd St NE, Pembina
196	CR 3, 89th St NE, Drayton
193	86th St NE
191	CR 11, Drayton, to St Thomas
187	ND 66, 80th St NE, Drayton
Gas	E: Cenex ◊
Food	E: Andy's Drive In, DQ, Rte 66 Cafe
Lodg	E: Motel 6 ♥, Red River Resort
184	160th Ave, SD 44, Drayton
180	CR 9, 73rd St NE, Grafton
(179)	Rest Area (Both dir, Left Exit) (RR, Phones, Picnic, Vend)
176	ND 17, Grafton (All Serv 10 mi W in Grafton)
Med	W: + Unity Medical Center
172	65th St, Minto
168	61st St, CR 15, Minto, Warsaw
164	57th St NE, Minto

EXIT	NORTH DAKOTA
161	ND 54, CR 19, to Oslo, Ardoch
157	CR 1, 32nd Ave NE, Manvel
152	CR 33, 28th Ave, US 81, Manvel
145	N Washington St, US 81 Bus, CR 11, Grand Forks
141	US 2, Gateway Dr, 18th Ave, Grand Forks, Emerado
FStop	E: Loaf'n Jug/Cenex
TStop	W: PTP/Simonson Travel Center (Scales), StaMart Travel Plaza #13/Tesoro (Scales)
Gas	E: Amoco, Conoco
Food	E: Burger King, Chuck House Ranch Rest, China Buffet, DQ, Hardee's, McDonald's, Rest/Holiday Inn
	W: Rest/Simonson TC, Rest/FastFood/StaMart TP, Emerald Grill, Perkins
Lodg	E: Budget Inn Express, Holiday Inn, Super 8, Westward Ho Motel
	W: Motel/Simonson TC, Prairie Inn
AServ	E: Gateway Amoco
TWash	W: Simonson TC

◊ = Regular Gas Stations with Diesel   ▲ = RV Friendly Locations   ♥ = Pet Friendly Locations

RED PRINT SHOWS LARGE VEHICLE PARKING/ACCESS ON SITE OR NEARBY   BROWN PRINT SHOWS CAMPGROUNDS/RV PARKS

EXIT	NORTH DAKOTA
TServ	E: Forks Freightliner, Dempsey Truck Service, Grand Forks Diesel Injection Service
	W: Simonson TC/Tires, StaMart TC/Tires, Cummins Scott's Express
Other	E: ATMs, Auto Dealers, Checker Auto Parts, Banks, Goodyear, Engelstad Arena, Museum, Randy's Repair & Towing, Univ of ND, U-Haul
	W: WiFi/Laundry/Simonson TC, Laundry/WiFi/RV Dump/LP/StaMart TP, Grand Forks Int'l Airport✈, to Grand Forks AFB, to 20 mi Turtle River State Park▲
140	**SD 297, CR 4, Demers Ave, City Center, Grand Forks**
Gas	E: BP, Conoco
Food	E: Subway
AServ	E: Demers Interstate Amoco
TServ	E: Interstate Detroit Diesel
Other	E: ATMs, Banks
	W: Amtrak
138	**US 81 Bus, 32nd Ave S**
TStop	W: AmBest/Big Sioux Travel Plaza/Conoco, SuperPumper
Gas	E: Amoco, Tesoro
Food	E: Applebee's, Burger King, Ground Round, China Garden, McDonald's, Quiznos, Red Lobster, Starbucks, Taco Bell, Village Inn, Wendy's
	W: Subway/Big Sioux TP
Lodg	E: Comfort Inn, Country Suites, C'Mon Inn, Days Inn, Fairfield Inn, Holiday Inn Express, Lakeview Inn, Road King Inn
TWash	W: Big Sioux TP
TServ	W: Big Sioux TP/Tires
Other	E: ATMs, Banks, Auto Dealers, Carmike Cinemas, Grocery, Lowe's, Sam's Club, Target, Mall, Wal-Mart, Grand Forks Campground & RV Park▲, Wagon Train RV Park▲
	W: Laundry/WiFi/LP/RVDump/Big Sioux TP, RVDump/SuperPumper
130	**US 81, ND 15, Thompson**
Gas	W: Tim's Quick Stop
Food	W: Fireside Grill
123	**CR 25, Reynolds**
(119)	**Inspection Station (Both dir)**
118	**CR 21, Hillsboro, to Buxton**
111	**ND 200W, Mayville, Cummings**
Other	W: Mayville State Univ
104	**CR 11, Hillsboro**
FStop	E: Cenex
Gas	E: Tesoro
Food	E: Burger King/Cenex, Country Hearth,
Lodg	E: Hillsboro Inn
Med	E: + Hillsboro Medical Center
Other	E: Hillsboro Campground & RV Park▲
100	**ND 200E, ND 200W Alt, Hillsboro, Halstead, Blanchard**
(99)	**Rest Area (Both dir) (RR, Phones, Picnic, Vend)**
92	**CR 11, Hillsboro, Grandin**
FStop	W: Nepstad's Stop N Shop/Citgo
Gas	E: Co-Op
Food	W: Rest/Deli/Nepstad's
86	**CR 26, Gardner**
79	**CR 4, 1st St, Argusville**

EXIT	NORTH DAKOTA
(74)	**Rest area (Both dir) (RR, Phones, Picnic)**
73	**CR 17, CR 22, Harwood**
TStop	E: Cenex
Food	E: Café/Cenex
69	**CR 20, Fargo**
67	**US 81 Bus, 19th Ave N**
Lodg	E: Days Inn
Med	E: + Vets Medical Center
Other	E: Hector Field Airport✈, FargoDome, The Coliseum, Dakotah Field, Bison Sports Arena
66	**12th Ave NW**
TStop	E: StaMart Travel Center #5/Tesoro (Scales) (BioDiesel)
Gas	E: Stop 'N Go
	W: Cenex◆
Food	E: Rest/FastFood/StaMart TC, North Town Grill
	W: Arby's, Freshway Cafe
Lodg	W: Microtel
TServ	W: Interstate Detroit Diesel, NW Truck & Trailer
Med	E: + MeritCare Medical Center
Other	E: Laundry/WiFi/RVDump/LP/StaMart, Auto Repairs, ND State Univ
65	**US 10, Main Ave, W Fargo**
TStop	E: StaMart Conv Ctr #14/Tesoro
Gas	E: Amoco, Simonson
	W: Cenex◆, Simonson◆
Food	E: Rest/FastFood/StaMart, Burger Time, China Buffet, Kroll's Café, Valley Kitchen
	W: Hardee's, Outback Steakhouse, Subway
Lodg	W: Best Western
TServ	W: Nelson International, Cummins
Med	E: + Dakota Heartland Hospital
Other	E: Civic Mem'l Auditorium, Grocery, Greyhound, Amtrak, NAPA, Auto Service, McLaughlin's RV & Marine
	W: CarQuest, Auto Dealers, Adventure RV Sales, ND State Hwy Patrol Post, Auto Services
64	**13th Ave SW, Downtown Fargo**
Gas	E: BP, Cenex, Conoco, StaMart◆
	W: BP, Cenex, Tesoro
Food	E: Applebee's, Arby's, Acapulco Mex, DQ, Ground Round, Hardee's, Mr Steak, Quiznos, Perkins, Subway, Wendy's
	W: Arby's, Chili's, Denny's, Hooters, McDonald's, Fuddrucker's, Lone Star Steakhouse, Olive Garden, Red Lobster, TGI Friday, Taco Bell, Timberlodge Steak House
Lodg	E: AmericInn, Best Western, Comfort Inn, Country Suites, Hampton Inn, Motel 6♥, Econo Lodge, Red Roof Inn, Super 8
	W: Comfort Inn, Days Inn, Fairfield Inn, Holiday Inn Express, Kelly Inn, Red Roof Inn♥, Long Term Stay Rooms & Suites, Ramada Plaza, Select Inn
TServ	W: Midwest Mack
Other	E: I-29 Amusement Park, Lindenwood Park Campground▲, Cactus Jack's Casino, ATMs, Banks, Auto Service, CarWash, Grocery, Goodyear, Tires +
	W: Best Buy, Grocery, Kmart, Lowe's, Office Depot, Sam's Club, Target, Wal-Mart sc, Walgreen's, West Acres Mall, Jail House Rock Casino, Brass Mint Casino,

Page 132 ◆= Regular Gas Stations with Diesel   ▲ = RV Friendly Locations   ♥ = Pet Friendly Locations
RED PRINT SHOWS LARGE VEHICLE PARKING/ACCESS ON SITE OR NEARBY   BROWN PRINT SHOWS CAMPGROUNDS/RV PARKS

Interstate 29 N/S

EXIT		ND / SD
	Other	W: Century 10 Cinema, West Acres 14, Baseball Museum, ATMs, Banks
(63AB)		Jct I-94, W-Bismarck, E-Minneapolis (Travel Ctrs & Serv loc 1st Ex E/W)
62		32nd Ave SW, Fargo
	TStop	W: Flying J Travel Plaza #5009/Conoco (Scales)
	Gas	E: AmocoBP, Tesoro
	Food	E: Country Kitchen
		W: Rest/FJ TP
	Lodg	W: Motel/FJ TP
	TServ	W: FJ TP/Tires, Goodyear, Peterbilt, Johnson Trailer, Isuzu Diesel
	TWash	W: FJ TP
	Other	W: Laundry/BarbSh/WiFi/LP/RVDump/FJ TP, Red River Valley Speedway, Red River Valley Campground▲, Pleasure Land RV
60		CR 6, 52nd Ave S, Frontier
56		CR 14, Horace, to Wild Rice
54		CR 16, to Oxbow, Davenport
50		CR 18, 52nd St SE, Hickson
48		ND 46, Walcott, to Kindred
44		US 81, Walcott, Christine
42		CR 2, 60th St SE, Walcott
(40)		Rest Area (Both dir) (RR, Phones, Picnic, Vend)
37		CR 4, 65th St SE, to Colfax
31		CR 8, Wahpeton, Galchutt
	Gas	E: Cenex
26		CR 10, 76th St SE, to Dwight
(24)		Weigh Station (Both dir)
23		ND 13, W-Mooreton, E-Wahpeton
23B		ND 13W, to Mooreton (SB)
23A		ND 13E, to Wahpeton (SB)
15		CR 16, Hankinson, to Great Bend, Mantador
8		ND 11, Hankinson, to Fairmount (Addt'l Serv 4mi W in Hankinson)
	TStop	E: MGS Oil/Mobil
	Food	E: FastFood/MGS
(3)		ND Welcome Center (NB) (RR, Phones, Vend, Info)
2		CR 22, 100th St SE, Hankinson
1		CR 1E, 102nd St SE
	Other	E: Dakota Magic Casino & Hotel/Gas/ConvStore/Restaurants/RVPark▲, Sisseton Indian Reservation

(CENTRAL TIME ZONE)
⬆ NORTH DAKOTA
⬇ SOUTH DAKOTA
(CENTRAL TIME ZONE)

(251)		SD Welcome Center (SB) (RR, Phone, Picnic, Info, RVDump)
246		SD 127, Rosholt, New Effington

Personal Notes

EXIT		SOUTH DAKOTA
242		CR 8, CR 23, Sisseton
(235)		Weigh Station / Port of Entry (SB)
232		SD 10, 119th St, Sisseton, Browns Valley (W Serv Approx 3.5 mi)
	TStop	E: Dakota Travel Center Connection Casino/Phillips 66
	Gas	W: BP, Cenex, Sinclair
	Food	W: American Hearth Rest, Country Kitchen, DQ, Dairy Freeze
	Lodg	W: I-29 Motel, Holiday Motel, Super 8
	Med	W: + Coteau des Prairies Hospital
	Other	E: Sisseton Indian Reservation, Dakota Connection Casino/Restaurants
		W: Camp Dakotah▲, Sisseton Muni Airport✈, to 20mi Roy Lake State Park▲
224		CR 5, 127th St, Peever
	Gas	E: Cenex
213		SD 15, SD 109, Summitt, to Wilmot
	E:	Rest Area (RR, Ph, Picnic, RVDump)
	Other	E: Servs 10mi, SD State Hwy Patrol
207		US 12, Summit, Aberdeen
	TStop	W: PTP/Coffee Cup Fuel Stop #1/Conoco (Scales)
	Food	E: High Plains Café, County Line
		W: Rest/Deli/CC FS
	Other	E: Bank, Grocery, Auto Service
201		CR 8, 149th St, Twin Brooks, to Milbank
193		SD 20, South Shore, Stockholm

EXIT		SOUTH DAKOTA
185		CR 6, 164th St, Watertown, Waverly
	Other	W: to 5mi: Dakota Sioux Casino & Hotel/Gas/ConvStore/Restaurant/RVPark▲, Sisseton Indian Reservation
180		US 81S, CR 10, 169th St, Bramble Park Zoo, Watertown
	Med	W: + Prairie Lakes Care Center
	Other	W: Zoo, Watertown Muni Airport✈
177		US 212, 172nd St, Watertown, to Kranzburg
	FStop	W: P&L Conv/Shell
	TStop	E: Stone's Truck Stop/Sinclair (Scales)
	Gas	W: Amoco, Cenex, Conoco, Sinclair
	Food	E: Rest/Subway/Stone's TS
		W: FastFood/P&L, Arby's, Hardee's, McDonald's, New Kitchen, Perkins, Pizza Hut, Kings Buffet, Coffeyville Cafe
	Lodg	E: Holiday Inn Express, Stone's Inn
		W: Comfort Inn, Days Inn, Drake Motor Inn, Budget Host Inn, Travelers Inn
	Med	W: + Prairie Lakes Care Center
	TServ	E: R&H Repairs & Service, Wheelco Brakes
	Other	E: RVDump/Stone's TS
		W: Advance Auto, Auto Dealers, Kmart, CarWash, Firestone, Grocery, Target, ShopKO, Vet♥, Wal-Mart sc, Mall, to Sandy Shores Rec Area▲
164		SD 22, Castlewood, Clear Lake (Gas/Food/Lodg/Hosp 10 mi E to ClearLake)
(160)		Rest Area (Both dir) (RR, Phone, Picnic, Vend, RVDump)
157		CR 313, Toronto, to Brandt
150		SD 15, SD 28, Toronto, Estelline (Serv 7-10 mi W)
	Other	W: to Lake Poinsett State Rec Area▲
140		SD 30, CR 6, White, Bruce (Gas, Food, Repairs 4mi E to White)
	Other	W: to Oakwood Lakes State Park▲
133		US 14 ByP, Brookings, Arlington
	Other	W: SD State Univ, Laura Ingalls Wilder Home
132		I-29 Bus, US 14, Brookings, Huron
	FStop	E: Kum & Go #623/Cenex
		W: Lloyd's Amoco
	Gas	W: Casey's Gen'l Store, Gas N More, Citgo, Shell
	Food	E: Burger King/Cenex.
		W: Burger King, Country Kitchen, DQ, Hardee's, KFC, McDonald's, Mad Jack's Brown Baggers, King Wok's Chinese, Pizza Ranch, Perkins, Subway, Rest/Qual Inn, Rest/Brookings Inn
	Lodg	E: Fairfield Inn, Super 8
		W: Brookings Inn, Comfort Inn, Quality Inn, Wayside Motel
	Med	W: + Brookings Health System
	Other	W: Auto Dealers, ATMs, Banks, Auto Services, Grocery, Brookings Muni Airport✈
127		SD 324, Brookings, to Elkton, Sinai
121		CR 4, Flandreau, Nunda, Ward
	E:	Rest Area (Both dir) (RR, Phones, Picnic, Vend, RVDump)
		E: SD Hwy Patrol Post
114		SD 32, Flandreau (All Serv 7-10 mi E in Flandreau)

◆ = Regular Gas Stations with Diesel   ▲ = RV Friendly Locations   ♥ = Pet Friendly Locations

RED PRINT SHOWS LARGE VEHICLE PARKING/ACCESS ON SITE OR NEARBY   BROWN PRINT SHOWS CAMPGROUNDS/RV PARKS

EXIT	SOUTH DAKOTA
109	SD 34, Madison, Colman, Egan
TStop	W: Crossroads Truck Stop/Shell, Prairie Junction Truck Stop/BP
Food	W: Rest/Crossroads TS, FastFood/Prairie Junction TS
Other	W: Eich Trucking Repair
104	CR 14, Trent, Chester
(103)	Parking Area (Both dir)
98	SD 115S, Dell Rapids, Chester (Serv 3-5mi E in Dell Rapids)
Gas	E: Mobil, Kum & Go
Food	E: DQ, Subway/TCBY, Pizza Ranch, Prairie View Steakhouse
TServ	E: Dell's Diesel Service
Med	E: + Dells Area Health Center
94	SD 114, Baltic, Lyons, Colton
Gas	E: Citgo
Other	E: ATM, Auto Repairs, Bank, EROS Data Center, Grocery
86	CR 130, Sioux Falls, to Renner, Crooks
(84AB)	Jct I-90, W-Pierre, E-Albert Lea
83	SD 38W, 60th St N, Sioux Falls, Airport (Addtl Serv E to N Cliff Ave)
TStop	E: Flying J Travel Plaza #5035/Conoco (Scales)
Food	E: Country Market/FastFood/FJ TP
Lodg	E: Quality Inn
TServ	E: Flying J TP, Holcomb Freightliner
Other	E: Laundry/WiFi/RVDump/LP//FJ TP, J & L Harley Davidson, Yogi Bear's Jellystone Campground▲, Sioux Falls KOA▲, Sioux Falls Reg'l Airport✈, ATM, Banks, Graham Tire, Catfish Bay Water Ski Park
82	Benson Rd, Sioux Falls
81	CR 140, SD 38E, Maple St, Russell St, Airport, Sioux Falls
Gas	E: BP, Gas Barrell
Food	E: Burger King, Country Kitchen, Roll'n Pin Rest, Front Porch Grill, Rest/Oaks Hotel
Lodg	E: Arena Motel, Best Western, Kelly Inn, Oaks Hotel, Motel 6♥, Ramada Inn, Sleep Inn, Sheraton, Super 8
TServ	E: Becks Truck Repair
Other	E: SD Hwy Patrol Post, Sioux Falls Convention Center, Sioux Falls Arena, Sioux Falls Stadium, Sioux Falls Reg'l Airport✈, Auto Services, Avis RAC, Budget RAC, Hertz RAC, National RAC, Schaap's RV Traveland
79	I-29 Bus, SD 42, 12th St
FStop	W: Kum & Go #619/Cenex
Gas	E: Amoco, Cenex W: Citgo, Phillips 66
Food	E: Burger King, Burger Time, Fryin Pan Family Rest, KFC, McDonald's, Golden Harvest Chinese, Pizza Hut, Taco Bell, Wendy's W: FastFood/K&G, Hardee's
Lodg	E: Ramada W: Pinecrest Motel, Westwick Motel
TServ	E: Graham Tire
Med	E: + Sioux Valley Hospital
Other	E: Kmart, Walgreen's, Auto Dealers, ATMs, Banks, Fairgrounds, Greyhound, Grocery, Museums, Great Plains Zoo, Thunder Road Amusement Park, USS SD Mem'l

Personal Notes

EXIT	SOUTH DAKOTA
Other	W: Tower Campground▲, Westwick RV Park▲, Jack's Campers, Kmart, Grocery, SF Tire, Auto Repairs
78	26th St, Sioux Falls
Gas	E: Phillips 66◆
Food	E: Bennigan's, Culver's, Rue 41, KFC, Cracker Barrel, Foley's Fish Chop & SteakHouse, Granite City Food & Brewery, Hibachi, Outback Steakhouse, Rio Bravo W: Dynasty Chinese, Papa John's, Quiznos, Spaghetti Shop, Westwinds
Lodg	E: Hampton Inn, Holiday Inn, Microtel W: Settle Inn
Other	E: Century Stadium 14, Grocery, Home Depot, Sam's Club
77	41st St, Sioux Falls
Gas	E: Amoco, Shell, Sinclair W: Citgo, Shell
Food	E: Applebee's, Arby's, Burger King, Chili's, China Buffet, Fryin Pan Family Rest, Inca Mexican Rest, KFC, Lone Star Steakhouse, McDonald's, Naps Southern BBQ, Olive Garden, Perkins, Starbucks, Red Lobster, Royal Fork Buffet, Subway, TGI Friday, Timber Lodge Steak House W: Burger King, Godfather's Pizza, Little Caesar's Pizza, IHOP, Perkins
Lodg	E: Best Western, Comfort Suites, Empire Inn, Fairfield Inn, Radisson, Residence Inn, Microtel, Super 8 W: AmericInn, Baymont Inn, Days Inn, Select Inn

EXIT	SOUTH DAKOTA
Other	E: ATMs, Banks, Auto Services, Empire Mall, CarWash, FedEx Kinko's, Grocery, PetCo♥, Sam's Club, Wal-Mart sc, Western Mall, Visitor Info W: Carmike Cinema, ATM, Banks
(75)	Jct I-229N, to I-90E
73	CR 106, Sioux Falls, Tea
TStop	E: Larry's I-29 Truck Plaza/Texaco
Food	E: Rest/Larry's TP, I-29 Bar & Grill
Other	W: Auto Services, Larson Truck Sales, Red Barn RV Park▲
71	CR 110, Harrisburg, Tea
Other	W: Red Barn RV Park▲
68	CR 116, Lennox, Parker
64	SD 44, Worthing, Lennox
Gas	E: Shell
Food	E: Old Towne Dinner Theatre
62	US 18E, Worthing, Canton
TStop	E: Countryside Convenience/Shell
Gas	E: Phillips 66
Food	E: FastFood/Countryside
Lodg	E: Charlie's Motel
59	US 18W, CR 134, to Davis, Hurley
56	CR 140, Beresford, Fairview
53	CR 146, Beresford, to Viborg
50	CR 152, to Centerville, Hudson
47	SD 46, W Cedar St, Beresford
TStop	E: Jet Truck Plaza/Sinclair W: Truck Towne/Cenex
Gas	E: Cenex, Casey's Gen'l Store
Food	E: Rest/FastFood/Jet TP, Burger King, Emily's, Good Times Pizza, Subway W: Rest/Truck Towne, Silver Dollar Rest
Lodg	E: Crossroads Motel, Super 8, Starlite Motel
TServ	E: Jet TP/Tires
Other	E: Grocery, Auto Services, ATMs, Bank, Windmill Campground▲ W: LP/Laundry/TT
42	CR 13, to Alcester, Wakonda
(40)	Parking Area (SB)
38	CR 15, Beresford, to Volin
Other	E: to Union Grove State Park▲
31	SD 48, Burbank, to Spink, Akron
26	SD 50, to Vermillion, Yankton (Addt'l serv 7 mi W)
E:	SD Welcome Center (Both dir) (RR, Phone, Picnic, Vend, RVDump)
TStop	W: PTP/Coffee Cup Fuel Stop #6/Conoco (Scales)
Food	W: Rest/Deli/Coffee Cup FS
Other	W: Laundry/CC FS
18	Bus Lp 29, Elk Point, Burbank
Gas	E: AmocoBP, Phillips 66
Food	E: Cody's Homestead, DQ
Lodg	E: Home Towne Inn, Sun Motel
Other	E: ATM, Bank, Grocery, Auto Repairs
15	29 Bus, Elk Point (Access Same Serv as Ex #18)
9	SD 105, Jefferson
FStop	E: Amoco
Food	E: Choice Cut/Amoco
4	CR 23, to SD 105, N Sioux City, to McCook
Other	W: Sioux City North KOA▲

Page 134 ◆ = Regular Gas Stations with Diesel ▲ = RV Friendly Locations ♥ = Pet Friendly Locations
RED PRINT SHOWS LARGE VEHICLE PARKING/ACCESS ON SITE OR NEARBY   BROWN PRINT SHOWS CAMPGROUNDS/RV PARKS

EXIT	SD / IA
(3)	Weigh Station / Port of Entry (NB)
2	SD 105N, N Sioux City
FStop	E: Connie's AmPride
Gas	E: Cenex
	W: Casey's Gen'l Store, Citgo
Food	E: Rest/AmPride, McDonald's, Taco John's, Razz's Pizza, Subway
Lodg	E: Comfort Inn, Super 8
	W: Hampton Inn♥, Red Carpet Inn
Other	E: to Stone State Park▲
	W: Sioux City North KOA▲
1	Dakota Dunes, N Sioux City
Gas	W: Dune's General Store
Food	W: Graham's Grill
Lodg	W: Country Inn
	(CENTRAL TIME ZONE)

⭕ SOUTH DAKOTA
⭕ IOWA
(CENTRAL TIME ZONE)

NOTE: WiFi Access in All Rest Areas

151	IA 12N, Riverside Blvd, Sioux City
Gas	E: Casey's Gen'l Store
149	Hamilton Blvd
W:	IA Welcome Center (SB) Rest Area (NB) (RR, Phone, Picnic, Vend, RVDump)
Gas	E: Conoco
Food	E: Rest/Qual Inn
Lodg	E: Quality Inn
Other	E: Jiffy Lube
	W: Museum, Belle of Sioux City Casino
148	US 77S, US 20 Bus, Wesley Way, to S Sioux City, NE
Gas	W: Conoco◆, Phillips 66
Food	W: McDonald's, Pizza Hut, Taco Bell
Lodg	W: Regency Inn
Other	W: to Scenic Park Campground▲
147B	US 20 Bus, IA 12S, Gordon Dr, Nebraska St, Bus District
Gas	E: Heritage Express
Food	E: Arby's, Burger King, Chili's, IHOP, Hardee's, Perkins, Rest/Hol Inn
Lodg	E: Best Western, Holiday Inn, Super 8♥
Med	E: + Hospital
Other	E: Walgreen's, Staples, US Post Office, Sioux City Auditorium
147A	Floyd Blvd, Stockyards, Sioux City
Gas	E: Ivy's EZ Stop
Other	W: Museum, to Riverboat Casino
144B	US 20W, US 75S, S Sioux City
144A	US 20E, US 75N, to Ft Dodge (Serv 1mi E on Lakeport St)
143	US 75, Industrial Rd, Singing Hills Blvd
TStop	E: Truck Haven/Shell (Scales)
	W: Sioux Harbor Travel Plaza/BP (Scales)
Gas	E: Cenex, Kum & Go, Murphy
Food	E: Rest/Truck Haven, McDonald's, Pizza Hut
	W: Rest/FastFood/SH TP, Wendy's
Lodg	E: Motel/TruckHaven, Baymont Inn, Days Inn
	W: Super 8
TServ	E: Truck Haven/Tires, Kenworth White GMC Volvo, Peterbilt

EXIT	IOWA
TServ	W: Sioux City Truck & Trailer
TWash	E: Truck Haven
Other	E: Laundry/WiFi/LP/Truck Haven, Sam's Club, Wal-Mart sc
	W: Laundry/WiFi/SH TP
141	CR D38, 1st St, Sioux Gateway Airport, Sergeant Bluff
Gas	E: Casey's Gen'l Store, Phillips 66◆, Shell◆
	W: Amoco
Food	E: China Taste, Pizza Ranch, Steak Block, Godfather's, Subway
	W: Jerry's Rib House
Lodg	E: Econo Lodge
	W: Motel 6♥
Other	W: Sioux Gateway Airport✈
(139)	Rest Area (Both dir) (RR, Phones, Picnic, RVDump)
135	CR D51, Port Neal Landing
134	CR K25, 275th St, Salix
Gas	E: Citgo, Total
Other	E: Grocery
	W: to Snyder Bend Park▲
(132)	Weigh Station (Both dir)
127	IA 141, 330th St, Sloan
Gas	E: Casey's Gen'l Store, Shell◆
Food	E: Italian Rest, Sloan Cafe
Lodg	E: Rip Van Winkle Motel
Other	E: Sloan Golf Course
	W: Winnavegas▲, to Winnebago Indian Reservation/Casino
120	CR E24, 160th St, Whiting
Other	W: Lighthouse Marina & CG▲
112	IA 175, Onawa, Decatur, Nebraska
FStop	E: Onawa 66
TStop	E: Dave's World/Conoco (Scales)
Food	E: Subway/Dave's, Oehler Bros Rest, Bamboo Village Chinese, Denise's Fam Rest, McDonald's, Pizza Hut
Lodg	E: Super 8
Med	E: + Burgess Hospital, + Family Medicine Clinic
Other	E: LP/Dave's, ATMs, Auto Dealer, Auto & Truck Repairs, On-Ur-Wa RV Park▲
	W: Onawa/Blue Lake KOA▲, Lewis & Clark State Park▲
(110)	Onawa Rest Area (Both dir) (RR, Phones, Picnic, Vend, RVDump)
105	E60, Blencoe
Gas	E: Foster's
95	IA 301, CR F20, Little Sioux
Gas	E: River Mart
Other	E: Auto Repairs
	W: Woodland RV Campground▲
(92)	Parking Area (Both dir)
89	IA 127, Mondamin
Gas	E: Jiffy Mart◆
82	CR F 50, Modale
Gas	W: Cenex
(80)	MO Valley Rest Area (SB)
(79)	MO Valley Rest Area (NB) (RR, Phones, Picnic, RVDump)
75	US 30, Missouri Valley, Blair, NE
FStop	E: Taylor Quick Pik/Shell
Gas	E: Casey's, Kum & Go
	W: BP, Conoco

EXIT	IOWA
Food	E: FastFood/T QP, Arby's, Mom's, Family Table Rest, McDonald's, Pizza Ranch, Subway
	W: Burger King, Oehler Bros, Kopper Kettle Rest
Lodg	E: Hill Side Motel, Sunnyside Motel
	W: Days Inn, Rath Traveler Inn, Super 8
Med	E: + Hospital
Other	E: ATMs, Bank, Grocery
	W: Auto Dealer
(74)	Weigh Station (SB)
(73)	Weigh Station (NB)
72	IA 362, Desota Ave, to Loveland
FStop	E: DeSoto Bend Mini Mart/Conoco
NOTE:	I-29 below runs with I-680 exits #71-61. Exit #'s follow I-29.
(71)	Jct I-680E, to Des Moines
66	Rosewood Rd, Crescent, to Honey Creek
FStop	W: IA Feed & Grain/Sinclair & Rest
(61B)	Jct I-680W, to North Omaha
NOTE:	I-29 above runs with I-680 exits 61-71. Exit #'s follow I-29.
61A	IA 988E, to Crescent
Gas	E: Phillips 66
Other	E: to Crescent Ski Area
56	IA 192S, Council Bluffs (SB, Left Exit)
55	N 25th St, Council Bluffs
Gas	E: Sinclair, Pump n Munch
Lodg	E: Ramada Inn
54B	N 35th St, G Ave (NB)
Gas	E: Texaco
54A	G Ave, Council Bluffs (SB)
Gas	W: WestEnd Service
(53B)	Jct I-480W, US 6W, to Omaha
53A	9th Ave, S 37th St, Harvey's Blvd
Gas	E: Conoco, Phillips 66, Shell, Shamrock
Food	E: Country Kitchen
Lodg	E: Days Inn
Other	W: Harrah's Casino & Hotel, Riverboat Casino
52	Nebraska Ave, Council Bluffs
Gas	E: Conoco◆
Lodg	E: Comfort Suites, Bluffs Run Casino, Hotel & RV Park▲
	W: AmeriStar Casino & Hotel, Hampton Inn, Holiday Inn, Harrah's Casino & Hotel & Rest
Other	E: Mid America Center
	W: Dodge Park Golf Course, Dog Track
NOTE:	I-29 & I-80 run together for 3 mi below. Exit #'s follows I-80.
(51/1A)	Jct I-80W, to Omaha
1B	S 24th St, Council Bluffs
TStop	N: Pilot Travel Center #329 (Scales), Sapp Bros Oasis/Shell (Scales)
Gas	N: Casey's, Conoco, Sinclair
Food	N: Arby's/Pilot TC, Rest/BK/Sapp Bros
Lodg	N: AmericInn, Best Western, Country Inn, Interstate Inn, Super 8
TWash	N: Sapp Bros/Blue Beacon TW
TServ	N: Sapps Bros/Tires, Goodyear, Peterbilt, Speedco, Boyers Diesel

◆ = Regular Gas Stations with Diesel   ▲ = RV Friendly Locations   ♥ = Pet Friendly Locations

RED PRINT SHOWS LARGE VEHICLE PARKING/ACCESS ON SITE OR NEARBY   BROWN PRINT SHOWS CAMPGROUNDS/RV PARKS

Page 135

EXIT		IOWA
	Other	N: Laundry/WiFi/Pilot TC, Laundry/WiFi/LP/RVDump/Sapp Bros, to Bluff's Run Casino Hotel & RV Park▲
3		IA 192, Council Bluffs
	TStop	S: Travel Center of America (Scales)
	Gas	N: Casey's Gen'l Store S: Phillips 66◊, Shell◊
	Food	S: CountryPride/Pizza Hut/TA TC, DQ, Applebee's, Burger King, Golden Corral, Cracker Barrel, Hardee's, McDonald's, Perkins, Red Lobster, Subway, Taco Bell
	Lodg	S: Comfort Inn, Days Inn, Fairfield Inn
	Tires	S: TA TC
	TServ	N: Whitehill Trailer Repair S: TA TC/Tires, Larry's Diesel Repair, CAT, Peterbilt, Cummins, V&Y Truck & Trailer
	Other	S: Laundry/WiFi/TA TC, Advance Auto, ATMs, Auto Dealers, Auto Repairs, Auto Rentals, Banks, Home Depot, Sam's Club, Wal-Mart sc, Grocery, U-Haul
(48/4)		Jct I-80E, to Des Moines (NB)
	NOTE:	I-29 & I-80 run together above for 3 mi. Exit #'s follow I-80.
47		US 275, IA 92, Lake Manawa
	Gas	E: Phillips 66 W: Gas Mart, Oil
	Other	W: Tomes Country Club Acres RV Park▲, Lake Manawa State Park▲, T & K Truck Repair
42		IA 370, Pacific Jct, to Bellevue, NE
	Food	W: K&B Steakhouse
	Other	W: to Offutt AFB, Haworth Park▲
(38)		Pacific Jct Rest Area (Both dir) (RR, Phone, Picnic, Vend, Weather, RVDump)
35		US 34E, Pacific Jct, to Glenwood, Red Oak (All Serv E 3-5mi in Glenwood)
	Gas	W: BP◊
	Food	W: Bluff View Cafe
	Lodg	W: Bluff View Motel
	Other	W: Walker's Harley Davidson
32		US 34W, Plattsmouth, Pacific Jct
24		CR L31, Thurman, Bartlett, Tabor
20		IA 145, CR J34, McPaul, Thurman
15		J26, Percival
	Gas	E: Percival Farm Service/BP◊
(11)		Weigh Station (NB)
10		IA 2, Percival to Sidney, Nebraska City, NE
	FStop	W: The Junction/Conoco
	TStop	W: Crossroads Travel Center/Shell (Scales), Sapp Bros/BP (Scales)
	Food	W: FastFood/The Jctn, FastFood/Cr Rds TC, Rest/FastFood/SappBros, Arby's, Burger King, McDonald's, Subway, Wendy's
	Lodg	W: Best Value Inn, Best Western, Days Inn, Super 8
	Other	E: to Waubonsie State Park▲ W: RVDump/CR TC, Laundry/WiFi/RVDump/SappBros, to Victorian Acres RV Park & Campground▲, Riverview Marina State Rec Area▲

EXIT		IA / MO
1		IA 333, CR J64, Hamburg
	Gas	E: Casey's Gen'l Store◊
	Food	E: Pizza Hut
	Lodg	E: Hamburg Motel
	Other	E: Auto Repairs, Grocery
	NOTE:	WiFi Access in All Rest Areas (CENTRAL TIME ZONE)

○ **IOWA**
○ **MISSOURI**
(CENTRAL TIME ZONE)

EXIT		
(121)		Weigh Station (Both dir)
116		CR A, CR B, to Watson
110		US 136, Rock Port, Phelps City
	FStop	E: Rockport Shell
	TStop	W: Trails End Truck Stop/P66, Rock Port Truck Plaza/BP (Scales)
	Gas	E: Speedys Conv 35/Conoco
	Food	E: Subway/Speedy's W: Rest/Tr End TS, FastFood/RP TP, McDonald's
	Lodg	E: Rockport Inn, White Rock Motel W: Motel/Trails End, Super 8
	TServ	W: Watson Auto & Truck Repair
	Other	E: Auto Services, Towing W: Laundry/RP TP, Rock Port KOA▲
(110)		Rest Area (SB) (RR, Phones, Vend, Picnic)
107		MO 111, Rock Port, Langdon
	TStop	Flying J Travel Plaza
	Lodg	W: Elk Inn/Cafe & RV Park▲
99		CR W, Fairfax, Corning
92		US 59, Craig, Fairfax
	Gas	W: Shell
84		MO 118, Mound City, Bigelow
	FStop	W: Mound City Shell
	Gas	E: Phillips 66, Sinclair W: King
	Food	E: Dick's Diner, Hardee's W: Taco Bell/Shell
	Lodg	E: Audrey's Motel, Super 8
(82)		Rest Area (Both dir) (RR, Phones, Vend, Picnic)
79		US 159, Mound City, to Rulo
75		US 59, Oregon
67		US 59N, Oregon
65		US 59, Amazonia, Fillmore
	FStop	E: Trip Stop/Conoco
	Food	E: FastFood/Trip Stop
60		MO CC, MO K, Amazonia
56A		Jct US 59N, US 71, Savannah
(56B)		Jct I-229S, St Joseph
53		I-71 Bus, Savannah, US 59S, I-29S Bus, St Joseph
	Gas	W: Phillips 66◊
	Other	E: Walnut Grove Campground▲, A-OK Overnite Campground▲
50		US 169, St Joseph, King City
	Gas	E: Conoco
	Food	W: Hardee's, McDonald's, Ryan's Grill

◊ = Regular Gas Stations with Diesel ▲ = RV Friendly Locations ♥ = Pet Friendly Locations
RED PRINT SHOWS LARGE VEHICLE PARKING/ACCESS ON SITE OR NEARBY BROWN PRINT SHOWS CAMPGROUNDS/RV PARKS

EXIT	MISSOURI
Other	W: Lowe's, Wal-Mart sc
47	**MO 6, Fredrick Blvd, St Joseph**
Gas	E: Conoco
	W: Sinclair, Phillips 66
Food	E: Bandana's BBQ, Country Kitchen
	W: Applebee'1, Cracker Barrel, Carlos O'Kelly's, Denny's, Hunan Rest, KFC, McDonald's, Perkins, Red Lobster, Rib Crib, Sonic, Subway, Taco Bell, Taste of China, Whiskey Creek Steakhouse
Lodg	E: Days Inn, Drury Inn, St Joe Inn
	W: Budget Inn, Comfort Suites, Hampton Inn, Motel 6♥, Ramada Inn, Super 8
Med	E: + Heartland Reg'l Medical Center
	W: + Heartland Health Hospital
Other	E: to MO Western State College
	W: Auto Dealers, ATMs, CVS, Food 4 Less, Banks, Museums, Office Depot, Walgreen's, Plaza 8 Cinema, UPS Store, Vet♥, Visitor Info, Beacon RV Park▲
46AB	**US 36, St. Joseph, Cameron**
	(Serv West to US 169 N&S)
Other	W: to Beacon RV Park▲
44	**I-29 Bus, US 169, St. Joseph**
TStop	E: Love's Travel Stop #235 (Scales)
	W: AmBest/ Wiedmaier Truck Stop/Shell (Scales)
Food	E: Subway/Love's TS, Mexican Rest
	W: Rest/Wiedmaier's TS, McDonald's, Taco Bell
Lodg	E: Best Western
TServ	E: Love's TS/Tires/TWash
	W: Wiedmaier TS/Tires
Other	E: Laundry/RVDump/Love's TS
	W: Laundry/WiFi/Wiedmaier's TS, Goodyear, Grocery, Wal-Mart
(43)	**Jct I-229N, Downtown St Joseph**
Other	W: River View Retreat & RV Park▲
35	**CR DD, Faucett**
TStop	W: Farris Truck Stop/66 (Scales)
Food	W: Rest/Subway/Farris TS
Lodg	W: Motel/Farris TS
TWash	W: Farris TS
TServ	W: Farris TS/Tires
Other	W: Laundry/Farris TS
30	**CR Z, CR H, Dearborn**
FStop	E: Trex Mart/Conoco
Food	E: Tank 'n Tummy
(27)	**Rest Area (Both dir)**
	(RR, Vending, Picnic)
25	**CR U, CR E, Camden Point**
Gas	E: Phillips 66
Food	E: Merle's Country Café
(24)	**Weigh Station (Both dir)**
20	**MO 92, MO 371N, Atchison, Weston, Leavenworth**
Gas	W: Phillips 66
Other	W: Vaughn Orchard & Store, Weston Red Barn Farm, to Weston Bend State Park▲
19	**CR HH, Platte City**
Gas	W: Amoco, Conoco, Phillips 66◊
Food	W: Branch St Café, DQ, Maria's Mex, Pizza Hut, Red Dragon Rest,
Lodg	W: Comfort Inn, Super 8, Travelodge Motel & RV Park▲

EXIT	MISSOURI
Other	W: ATMs, Auto Services, Grocery, Laundromat, Museum, Police Dept, Sheriff Dept, US Post Office
18	**MO 92, Platte City, Leavenworth, Weston**
FStop	W: QT #236 (Scales)
Gas	W: Conoco
Food	W: Burger King, McDonald's, Ma & Pa's Kettle Rest, Subway, Taco Bell, Waffle House, Wendy's, KFC/Conoco
Lodg	W: AmericInn, Comfort Inn, Super 8
Other	E: to Basswood Country Inn & RV Resort▲
(17)	**Jct I-435S, to Topeka**
15	**Mexico City Ave, Ks City**
Other	W: Auto Rentals/KC Int'l Airport✈
(14)	**Jct I-435E, to St Louis**
13	**CR D, to I-435E, KC Int'l Airport**
Lodg	E: Best Western, Clarion, Comfort Suites, Extended Stay America, Fairfield Inn, Hampton Inn, Holiday Inn, Microtel, Radisson
	W: Marriott
Other	E: KCI Expo Center
	W: KC Int'l Airport✈
12	**NW 112th St, Ks City**
Gas	E: BP, Conoco
Food	E: Allie's
Lodg	E: Days Inn, DoubleTree Hotel, Hampton Inn, Hilton
	W: Econo Lodge
Other	E: ATMs. Banks, Harley Davidson, Visitor Center
10	**Tiffany Springs Pkwy, Ks City**
Gas	E: Shell
Food	E: Del & More, Jade Garden Chinese, Smokebox BBQ Café, Tiffany Grill
	W: Cracker Barrel, Ruby Tuesday, Waffle House, Wendy's
Lodg	E: Embassy Suites, Homewood Suites
	W: AmeriSuites, Chase Suite, Courtyard, Drury Inn, MainStay Suites, Ramada Inn, Residence Inn, Sleep Inn
Other	W: US Post Office
9AB	**MO 152, to Liberty, Topeka**
8	**NW Barry Rd, Ks City**
Gas	E: Total
	W: Citgo, Phillips 66, QT
Food	E: Applebee's, Boston Market, Chili's, Bob Evans, China Wok, Einstein Bros, Golden Corral, Hooters, On the Border, Starbucks, Subway, Taco Bell, Wendy's
	W: Barry BBQ, Dirk's Bar & Grill, La Kitchen, Hardee's, Long John Silver, Outback Steakhouse, McDonald's, Taco John's, Mr Goodcents Subs
Lodg	W: Motel 6♥, Quality, Super 8
Med	E: + St Luke's Northland Hospital
Other	E: AMC, ATMs, Auto Services, Banks, Lowe's, Wal-Mart sc
	W: Auto Services, Tires +
6	**NW 72nd St, to Platte Woods**
Gas	E: Sinclair
	W: BP, QuikTrip
Food	W: DQ, KFC, Pizza Hut
Other	W: IGA, Police Dept

EXIT	MISSOURI
5	**MO 45N, NW 64th St, Ks City**
Gas	W: Texaco
Food	W: Blimpie's/Texaco, Colonial Bakery, Little Caesar's Pizza, McDonald's, Pizza Hut, Paradise Grill, Subway, Pete's Inn
4	**NW 56th St (NB)**
3C	**CR A, Gateway Ave, Riverside (SB)**
Food	W: Fisherman's Cove, Mean Gene's Deli & Pizza
Lodg	W: Riverside Motel
Other	W: Auto Services, Police Dept
(3B)	**Jct I-635S, to Kansas (NB, Left exit)**
3A	**CR AA, Waukomis Dr (NB)**
Other	E: Museum
2B	**US 169S, N Kansas City**
2A	**US 169N, Smithville**
1E	**US 69, Vivion Rd**
Gas	E: Shell◊
	W: QuikTrip
Food	E: Deli Depot, Steak n Shake
	W: McDonald's
Other	E: Auto Service, Auto Dealer, Grocery, Home Depot, Sam's Club
1D	**MO 283S, Oak Trafficway (SB)**
1C	**MO 283N, US 69, Gladstone**
(1B)	**Jct I-35N, Des Moines (SB)**
1A	**Davidson Rd**
Gas	E: Shell
NOTE:	I-29 & I-35 run together for 6 mi (End of I-29) Exit #'s follow I-35.
(8B)	**Jct I-35N, to Des Moines**
8A	**NE Parvin Rd, Kansas City**
Gas	E: Shell
Lodg	W: Super Inn
6AB	**MO 210, Armour Rd, N Ks City**
Gas	E: Phillips 66◊
	W: QT, Phillips 66, Texaco
Food	E: Arby's, Big Boy's, Captain D's
	W: Long John Silver, Pizza Hut, Taco Bell, Wendy's
Lodg	E: Baymont Inn, Days Inn
	W: American Inn, Country Hearth Inn
Med	E: + N KC Hospital
Other	E: ATMs, Banks, Harrah's Casino,
	W: Auto Services, ATMs, Banks, Conv Center, Police Dept
5B	**16th Ave (NB)**
5A	**Levee Rd, Bedford St**
4B	**Front St, Ks City (NB)**
Other	W: Isle of Capri Casino & Rest
4A	**US 24, Independence Ave (SB)**
Lodg	E: Capri Motel, Royale Inn Motel
Other	E: Auto Services, Grocery
(3)	**Jct I-70W, to Topeka**

(CENTRAL TIME ZONE)

MISSOURI

Begin Northbound I-29 from Jct I-70 in Kansas City, MO to Canada Border.

◊ = Regular Gas Stations with Diesel   ▲ = RV Friendly Locations   ♥ = Pet Friendly Locations

RED PRINT SHOWS LARGE VEHICLE PARKING/ACCESS ON SITE OR NEARBY   BROWN PRINT SHOWS CAMPGROUNDS/RV PARKS

Begin Eastbound I-30 from Ft Worth, TX to Jct I-40 in Little Rock, AR.

TEXAS
(CENTRAL TIME ZONE)
(I-30 begins/ends on I-20, Exit #421)

EXIT		TEXAS
(1A)		Jct I-20W, Weatherford, Abilene
1B		Linkcrest Dr, Aledo, Ft Worth
	FStop	S: SunMart #401/Mobil
	Gas	S: Chevron, Fina◆, Shamrock
2		Spur 580E
	Lodg	S: El Dorado Motel
	Other	S: Lost Creek Golf Course
3		RM 2871, Chapel Creek Blvd
5A		Alemeda St (EB, diff reaccess)
(5B)		Jct I-820N
(5C)		Jct I-820S
6		Las Vegas Trail, Ft Worth
	Gas	N: Chevron
		S: Citgo, Shell◆, Valero◆
	Food	N: McDonald's/Chevron, Waffle House
		S: Mex Rest, Pancake House, Wendy's
	Lodg	N: Best Western, Days Inn, Super 8
		S: Comfort Inn, Motel 6♥
	Other	N: Auto Dealer, Cinema
		S: AutoZone, Winn Dixie
7A		Cherry Lane, TX 183
	Gas	N: Conoco, Shell, Sam's
	Food	N: CiCi's, IHOP, Luby's, Popeye's, Ryan's Grill, Subway, Taco Bell, Wendy's
		S: Parton's Pizza, Whataburger
	Lodg	N: La Quinta Inn♥, Super 8
		S: Best Western, Hampton Inn, Holiday Inn Express, Quality Inn
	Other	N: Home Depot, Sam's Club, U-Haul Wal-Mart, Westridge Mall, Auto Services, White Settlement RV Park▲
		S: Target, Auto Dealers
7B		TX 183, Spur 341, Green Oaks Rd
	Gas	S: Diamond Shamrock
	Food	N: Don Pablo's, Jack in the Box, Olive Garden, Subway, Taco Bueno
	Lodg	S: American Inn, Green Oaks Hotel
	Other	N: Firestone, U-Haul, Ridgmar Mall, Naval Air Station Ft Worth
		S: Auto Services
8A		Green Oaks Rd (WB)
	Food	N: Applebee's, Chili's, Jack in the Box, Olive Garden, Old Country Buffet, Taco Bueno, Subway, TGI Friday
	Lodg	N: Hawthorne Suites

EXIT		TEXAS
	Other	N: ATMs, Banks, Albertson's, Best Buy, Firestone, Office Depot, NTB, Ridgmar Mall
8B		Ridgmar Blvd, Ridglea Ave (Access to #8A Serv)
	Gas	N: Citgo, Texaco, Valero
9A		Bryant-Irvin Rd, Ft Worth
	Gas	S: Shell
9B		US 377S, Camp Bowie Blvd
	Gas	N: Texaco
		S: 7-11, Exxon, Fina, Shell, Texaco
	Food	N: Tommy's Hamburgers, Uncle Julio's Mex Rest, Tokyo Café
		S: Burger King, Jack in the Box, Purple Cow Diner, Starbucks, Souper Salad, Subway, Wendy's, Whataburger
	Lodg	S: Embassy Suites
	Other	S: ATMs, Banks, Grocery, Auto Service, CarWash, UPS Store
10		Hulen St, Ft Worth
	Food	S: ChikFilA, Purple Cow Diner, Subway, Starbucks
11		Montgomery St
	Gas	S: Texaco
	Food	S: Whataburger
	Other	N: Ft Worth Botanic Gardens, Will Rogers Memorial Center
12		Montgomery St (WB)
12A		Montgomery St, University Dr (EB)
	Lodg	S: Ramada Inn
12B		Vickery Blvd, Rosedale St (EB)
12C		Forest Park Blvd, Ft Worth
	Food	N: Pappasito's, Pappadeaux
	Med	S: + Columbia Medical Center FW
13A		8th Ave, Downtown
13B		Summit Ave, Downtown
	Med	S: + Cooks Children's Medical Center
14		Summitt Ave, TX 199, Henderson St (EB)
(15)		Jct I-35W, US 81, N to Denton, S to Waco (EB)
15B		Jct US 287
(15A)		Jct I-35W, US 81 (WB)
16A		Riverside Dr S (WB)
	Food	S: Gladys Soul Food
	Lodg	S: Great Western Inn, Luxury Inn, Valley View Motel
	Other	S: Auto Services
16B		Riverside Dr N (WB)

EXIT		TEXAS
16C		Beach St, Ft Worth
	Gas	S: 7-11, Chevron
	Food	S: Ft Worth Cattle Drive Rest
	Lodg	S: Comfort Inn, Holiday Inn
	Other	S: ATM, Bank
18		Oakland Blvd
	Gas	N: Conoco, Phillips 66◆, Texaco
	Food	N: Burger King, Taco Bell, Waffle House
	Lodg	N: Motel 6♥
19		Brentwood Stair Rd, Woodhaven Blvd, Bridge St (EB)
	Gas	N: Chevron, Shell
		S: Citgo, Shell
	Food	N: Bennigan's, Italy Pasta & Pizza, Steak & Ale, Stroud's Rest
	Other	N: ATM, Bank, Kroger
		S: Auto Services, Meadowbrook Golf Course
(21A)		Jct I-820S (WB) (Serv at 1st Exit)
(21B)		Jct I-820N (WB) (Serv at 1st Exit)
21C		Bridgewood Dr, Ft Worth
	Gas	N: Mobil, Shell
		S: Fina, Shell◆
	Food	N: Dan's Seafood & Chicken, Luby's, KFC, Subway, Wendy's
		S: Burger King, McDonald's
	Other	N: Albertson's, Firestone, Home Depot, Kroger, U-Haul
23		Cooks Lane
	Gas	S: Mobil
24		Eastchase Pkwy, Ft Worth
	Gas	S: Chevron, Mobil, Shell, Shamrock
	Food	N: Jack in the Box
		S: Burger King, IHOP, McDonald's, Steak & More, Taco Bell, Wendy's, Whataburger
	Other	N: Sam's Club, Wal-Mart sc
		S: Cinema, Office Depot, Target
26		Fielder Rd, Arlington
27		Lamar Blvd, Cooper St
	Gas	N: Mobil
		S: 7-11, Shell
	Food	N: Hong Kong II, Jack in the Box, Subway
		S: Burger King, Denny's
	Med	S: + Arlington Memorial Hospital
	Other	N: Kroger, Pharmacy
		S: ATM, Banks, Cost Plus, Dallas Metro KOA▲, to Univ of TX/Arlington
28		FM 157, Collins St (WB)

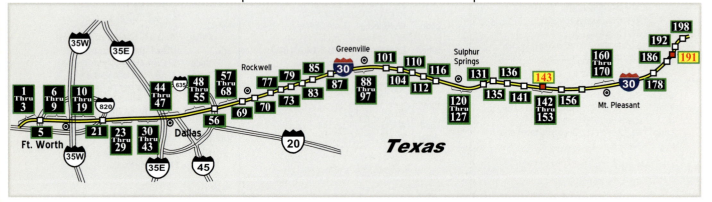

◆ = Regular Gas Stations with Diesel   ▲ = RV Friendly Locations   ♥ = Pet Friendly Locations
RED PRINT SHOWS LARGE VEHICLE PARKING/ACCESS ON SITE OR NEARBY   BROWN PRINT SHOWS CAMPGROUNDS/RV PARKS

INTERSTATE 30

EXIT	TEXAS
28A	**FM 157, Collins St (EB)**
Food	S: BlackEyed Pea, Chili's, ChicFilA, Country Kitchen, Colter's BBQ & Grill, Harrigan's, Hooters, Joe's Crab Shack, Landry Seafood, Olive Garden, Souper Salad, Red Hot & Blue Memphis BBQ, Pappadeaux Rest, TGI Friday, Taco Cabana, Tony Roma, Wendy's
Lodg	S: Courtyard, Days Inn, Howard Johnson Express, Wyndham
Other	S: Costco, FedEx Kinko's, Home Depot, Visitor Info Center, TX Stadium, Arlington Conv Center, Ameriquest Field, Baseball Museum, Six Flags Fun Park, to **Wal-Mart sc**
28B	**Nolan Ryan Expressway (EB)**
Gas	N: Mobil
Food	N: Waffle House, Whataburger
Lodg	N: Country Inn, Ramada Inn
29	**Ballpark Way**
Gas	N: Chevron, Citgo S: Fina
Food	N: Frijoles Café, Romano's Macaroni Grill, Manhattan's, Saltgrass Steakhouse, Trail Dust Steak House S: On the Border, Tx Land & Cattle
Lodg	N: Candlewood, Fairfield Inn, Hilton, Residence Inn, Springhill Suites, Studio Plus, Wingate Inn S: Howard Johnson, Marriott, Stadium Inn, Wyndham Hotel
Other	N: ATMs, Banks, S: Six Flags Fun Park, Arlington Conv Center, Ameriquest Field, Legends of the Game Baseball Museum, Visitor Center
30	**TX 360, Six Flags Dr, Airport**
Gas	N: Shell, Star Mart S: Conoco, Shell◆, Total
Food	N: Cracker Barrel, Grand Buffet, Salt Grass Steakhouse, McDonald's S: Denny's, Jack in the Box, Luby's, Ninfa's Mex Express, Pancho's Mexican Buffet, Steak & Ale, Subway
Lodg	N: Days Inn, Fairfield Inn, Flagship Inn, Homestead Studio, Park Inn, Studio Plus, Super 8, Travelodge, Wingate Inn S: Amerisuites, Baymont Inn, La Quinta Inn♥, Homewood Suites, Motel 6♥, Sleep Inn, Holiday Inn Express, Ranger Inn, Value Inn
Med	S: + Dallas FW Medical Center
Other	N: Great SW Golf Course, to Dallas FW Int'l Airport✈ S: ATMs, Banks, Cinemark Tinseltown 9, Auto Services & Repairs, Firestone, Greyhound, Kmart, Office Depot, Six Flags Mall, Six Flags Fun Park, General Motors Plant, U-Haul
32	**NW 19th St, Grand Prairie**
Gas	N: Exxon, Shamrock S: Fina, Mobil
Food	S: Denny's, Long John Silver, Taco Bell, McDonald's, Pizza Hut, Whataburger
Lodg	S: La Quinta Inn♥
Other	S: Banks, ATMs, Auto Service, U-Haul
34	**Belt Line Rd, NE 8th St**
Gas	N: Chevron S: Fina, RaceTrac, Shell, Shamrock
Food	S: Burger King, McDonald's, Subway
Lodg	N: Days Inn, Motel 6♥, Ramada Inn
Other	N: Ripley's Museum

Personal Notes

EXIT	TEXAS
36	**MacArthur Blvd, Grand Prairie**
Other	N: Starbuck Trucking & Auto S: to Dallas Millenium Airport✈
38	**Loop 12, Dallas**
Gas	N: Exxon
Food	N: Burger King
39	**Cockrell Hill Rd**
41	**Hampton Rd S, to Bus 180 (EB)**
Gas	S: Exxon, Star Mart
Food	S: Jack in the Box, Luby's, Wendy's
Other	S: Auto Services, Grocery, Goodyear, AutoZone, O'Reilly's
42	**Hampton Rd N, Westmoreland Rd**
43AB	**Sylvan Ave, to Beckley Ave (WB)**
Gas	N: Shell◆
Food	N: Pitt Grill
Lodg	N: Alamo Plaza Hotel, Budget Travel Inn
Med	S: + Methodist Medical Center
Other	N: ATMs, Banks, Auto Services, **Dallas West MH & RV Park**▲
(44A)	**to Beckley Ave, Jct I-35E N**
(44B)	**Jct I-35E S, Industrial Blvd**
(45)	**Jct I-35E N**
45B	**Lamar St, Griffin St**
Other	N: Amtrak, Downtown, Dallas Conv Center, Museums, Tourist & Visitor Info
46A	**Central Expressway (WB)**
Other	N: Dallas Farmers Market, Lodging, Restaurants, Museums, Galleries S: Restaurants, Lodging, Auto Services

EXIT	TEXAS
46B	**Central Expwy, to Jct I-45, US 75, to Houston (EB)**
47A	**1st Ave, Fair Pk (EB), 2nd Ave (WB)**
(47B)	**Jct I-45, US 75 (WB), Carroll Ave, Haskell Ave, Peak St (EB)**
Other	S: Cotton Bowl, Tx Vietnam Vets Mem'l, Aquarium, Science Place/IMAX, Planetarium, Various Museums
48A	**Barry Ave, to TX 78 (EB), Munger Blvd (WB)**
Gas	N: Shamrock S: Exxon
48B	**Winslow Ave, to Grand Ave, to TX 78, Dallas**
Gas	N: Saks Food & Gas, Texaco
Other	N: ATMs, Banks, Repairs, Samuell Grand Amphitheater, Restaurants, Grocery
48C	**Thorton Frwy, to Peak St, Haskell Ave (WB)**
49A	**Dolphin Rd, Samuell Blvd**
Gas	N: Fina, Phillips 66 S: Phillips 66, Shell
Food	N: Furr's, Chicken & Rice
Lodg	N: Welcome Inn, Eastern Hills Hotel
49B	**Lawnview Ave, Samuell Blvd (EB)**
Gas	N: Diamond Shamrock, Texaco
Lodg	S: Lawnview Motel
Other	S: **Woodshire MH & RV Park**▲
50	**Ferguson Rd, to Samuell Ave**
Gas	N: Shamrock, Phillips 66
Lodg	N: Howard Johnson Express
51	**Jim Miller Rd, to Highland Rd, to Samuell Blvd, Dallas**
Gas	N: Exxon S: Raceway, Shell◆
Food	N: Denny's, Luby's, McDonald's S: Burger King, Captain D's, Furr's, Grandy's, KFC, Sunny South BBQ, Subway, Wendy's
Lodg	N: La Quinta Inn♥ S: Holiday Inn Express, Super 7
Other	S: AutoZone
52A	**St Francis Ave, to Samuell Blvd**
Food	N: Luby's
Lodg	N: Dallas Park Motel, Lamplighter Motel, Super 8
Other	N: Enterprise RAC S: ATMs, Bank, Auto Services, Sam's Club, **Wal-Mart sc**
52B	**Loop 12, Buckner Blvd (EB)**
Gas	S: 7-11
Food	S: Whataburger
Other	S: Sam's Club
52C	**US 80E, to Terrell (EB)**
53	**Loop 12, Buckner Blvd (WB)**
Gas	N: RaceTrac, Exxon
Food	S: CiCi's, Whataburger
Lodg	S: Holiday Inn Express
Other	N: Auto Services, Grocery S: Kmart, Sam's Club, **Wal-Mart sc**, Staples, to Big Town Mall
54	**Big Town Blvd, Mesquite**
Gas	N: Shell, Shamrock
Lodg	N: Best Western S: Tejas Motel

◆ = Regular Gas Stations with Diesel ▲ = RV Friendly Locations ♥ = Pet Friendly Locations

RED PRINT SHOWS LARGE VEHICLE PARKING/ACCESS ON SITE OR NEARBY BROWN PRINT SHOWS CAMPGROUNDS/RV PARKS

EXIT	TEXAS
Other	**N:** Holiday World of Dallas RV Center, **to** Eastfield College **S:** Big Town Mall, Thrifty RAC
55	**Motley Dr, Mesquite**
Gas	**N:** Fina, Shell◊ **S:** Chevron
Lodg	**N:** Astro Inn, Ramada **S:** Microtel
Med	**S:** + Mesquite Community Hospital
56A	**Gus Thomasson Rd, Galloway Ave (EB), Jct I-635N (WB)**
Gas	**N:** Shamrock, Supertrac **S:** 7-11
Food	**N:** KFC, McDonald's, Sonic **S:** Arby's, Celebration Station, Checkers, Dickey's BBQ Pit, Hooters, Horny Toad Cantina, Luby's, Olive Garden, Outback Steakhouse, Red Lobster, Southern Maid Donut, Subway, Wendy's
Lodg	**S:** Delux Inn, Fairfield Inn
Other	**N:** Nichols RV & Trailer Ranch **S:** Auto Services, Grocery, **to** Town East Mall, NTB
(56B)	**Jct I-635N (EB), I-635S (WB)**
(56C)	**Jct I-635S (EB)**
57	**Galloway Ave, Mesquite (WB)**
Gas	**N:** Exxon, Mobil, Tetco **S:** Exxon
Food	**N:** Burger King, Cracker Barrel, TC's BBQ Express **S:** Slabs BBQ, **to** BlackEyed Pea, Boston Market, Chili's, Colter's BBQ, Denny's, Don Pueblo's, Grady's, Hogi Yogi, Long John Silver, McDonald's, Saltgrass Steak House, Spaghetti Warehouse, Souper Salad, Wing Zone, Whataburger
Other	**N:** Albertson's, Auto Repairs, Auto Dealer **S:** ATMs, Food Lion, **to** Town East Mall, Auto Services, Banks, Best Buy, Car Wash, Grocery
58	**Northwest Dr, Mesquite**
Gas	**N:** Exxon, Shamrock, Shell **S:** Fina
Food	**S:** Jack in the Box
Other	**N:** Mesquite Muni Golf Course **S:** Lowe's
59	**Broadway Blvd, N Belt Line Rd, Rowlett Rd, Garland**
Gas	**N:** 7-11, Conoco, Diamond Shamrock **S:** Exxon, Shell
Food	**N:** China City, Church's, KFC, Long John Silver, Whataburger **S:** Burger King, Waffle House
Lodg	**S:** Days Inn, Motel 6♥
Other	**N:** Auto Repairs, Grocery, Wal-Mart sc **S:** Kroger, Tx State Hwy Patrol Post
60A	**Rose Hill Rd, Garland**
Lodg	**S:** Garland Inn
60B	**Roan Rd, Bobtown Rd**
Gas	**N:** Pit Stop◊ **S:** EZ Mart
Food	**N:** Wendy's **S:** Catfish King, Jack in the Box, Kettle Rest, Subway
Other	**N:** Wal-Mart
61	**Zion Rd, Garland**
FStop	**N:** Golden Express Travel Center/Conoco
62	**Chaha Rd, Garland**
Gas	**S:** Shamrock, Texaco
Food	**N:** Mexican Rest

Personal Notes

EXIT	TEXAS
Lodg	**N:** Best Western
64	**Dalrock Rd, Rowlett**
Gas	**N:** Exxon, Diamond Shamrock◊
Food	**N:** Dickie's BBQ
Lodg	**N:** Comfort Suites
Med	**N:** + Hospital
Other	**N:** Dalrock Marina **S:** Tx Queen Riverboat, Bayview Marina
67A	**Horizon Rd, Village Dr, Rockwall (EB)**
Gas	**N:** Shamrock
Food	**N:** Saltgrass Steakhouse **S:** Jack in the Box, Linebackers, Oar House, Rockwall Coutry Café, Subway
Other	**S:** Cinema 8, Kroger, ATMs, Banks
67B	**FM 740, Ridge Rd (EB)**
Gas	**N:** Chevron, Mobil, Shell **S:** Chevron, Exxon, Shamrock
Food	**N:** Arby's, Burger King, Carrabba's, IHOP, Grandy's, McDonald's, Waffle House, Wendy's **S:** Applebee's, Black Eyed Pea, Carino's, Chili's, CiCi's, El Chico, Jack in the Box, McDonald's, Starbucks, Subway, Taco Bell, TCBY
Lodg	**S:** Country Inn Suites
Other	**N:** Goodyear, Wal-Mart sc **S:** Albertson's, Home Depot, Lowe's, Walgreen's, Target
67C	**Frontage Rd (EB)**
Food	**S:** Applebee's, Chili's, Chuck E Cheese, On the Border, Subway
Lodg	**S:** Country Inn

EXIT	TEXAS
67	**Frontage Rd, Ridge Rd, Village Dr (WB)**
Gas	**N:** Chevron
Food	**N:** Burger King, Grandy's, McDonald's, IHOP, Popeye's, Waffle House, Wendy's **S:** ChikFilA, Quiznos, Starbucks
Other	**N:** Auto Services, Goodyear, Wal-Mart sc **S:** Albertson's, Home Depot, Lowe's, Radio Shack, Walgreen's
68	**TX 205, Goliad St, Rockwall, to Terrell**
TStop	**S:** Travel Center of America #49/Exxon (Scales)
Gas	**N:** RaceTrac, Shell, Texaco
Food	**N:** Donna's Kitchen, DQ, Joe Willy's, KFC, Pizza Hut, Shirey's BBQ, Subway, Whataburger, Rest/Super 8 **S:** BKing/Starbucks/TA TC, Taco Bell
Lodg	**N:** Holiday Inn Express, Super 8
TServ	**S:** TA TC
Other	**N:** Enterprise RAC **S:** Laundry/WiFi/RVDump/TA TC
69	**Frontage Rd (WB)**
Other	**S:** Repair Services, All Season RV
70	**FM 549, Rockwall**
TStop	**S:** Love's Travel Stop #283 (Scales)
Food	**S:** Carl'sJr/Love's TS
Other	**N:** McClain's RV, Rockwall Muni Airport✈ **S:** Laundry/WiFi/RVDump/Love's TS
73	**FM 551, We Crawford Rd, Royse City, to Fate**
Other	**N:** McClain's RV
77A	**FM 548, Royse City**
Gas	**N:** Shell◊ **S:** Conoco, Exxon
Food	**N:** Jack in the Box, McDonald's
Lodg	**N:** Sun Royse Inn
Other	**N:** Johnson's Wrecker & Auto Service, Grocery, Police Dept
77B	**FM 35, CR 36, Royse City**
FStop	**N:** Exxon Prime Stop, Smart Stop
TStop	**N:** SunMart/Texaco (Scales)
Food	**N:** Richard's BBQ, Subway/Smart Stop
79	**FM 2642**
Other	**S:** N Texas Motor Speedway
83	**FM 1565**
Gas	**N:** Exxon◊
Other	**N:** Caddo Mills Muni Airport✈
85	**FM 36, Caddo Mills**
Other	**N:** Dallas NE/Caddo Mills KOA▲
87	**FM 1903 (EB)**
FStop	**S:** Greenville Exxon Truck Stop
Tstop	**N:** Pilot Travel Center #367 (Scales)
Gas	**N:** Chevron◊ **S:** Shell◊
Food	**N:** FastFood/Pilot TC, Pizza Inn/Chevron **S:** Pancake House/Greenville TS, Sonic/Shell
Other	**N:** Laundry/WiFi/Pilot TC
88	**FM 1903 (WB) (Access Ex #87 Serv)**
89	**FM 1570, Greenville**
Lodg	**S:** Luxury Inn
93A	**Bus 67S, TX 34S, Wesley St (EB)**
93B	**Bus 67N, TX 34N, Wesley St (EB)**
93	**Bus 67N, TX 34N, Wesley St (WB)**
NOTE:	Overpass Low Clearance 13' 10"

◊ = Regular Gas Stations with Diesel   ▲ = RV Friendly Locations   ♥ = Pet Friendly Locations
RED PRINT SHOWS LARGE VEHICLE PARKING/ACCESS ON SITE OR NEARBY   BROWN PRINT SHOWS CAMPGROUNDS/RV PARKS

INTERSTATE 30 W ↔ E

TEXAS

EXIT		
	Gas	N: Exxon, Mobil, Phillips 66 S: Chevron◊, Exxon◊
	Food	N: Applebee's, CiCi's, IHOP, Jack in the Box, KFC, Long John Silver, Pizza Hut, Ryan's Grill, Taco Bell, Wendy's
	Lodg	N: Hampton Inn
	Med	N: + Presbyterian Hospital
	Other	N: ATMs, Auto Services, Banks, Big Lots, Crossroads Mall, Rolling Hills Cinema 4, Lowe's, Staples, **Wal-Mart sc** S: Auto Services, Dollar Tree, Home Depot
94A		**US 69, US 380, Greenville, to Denison, McKinney**
94B		**Bus 69, Greenville, to Emory**
	Gas	N: Shamrock
	Food	N: Kettle, Mexican
	Lodg	N: American Inn, Royal Inn S: Economy Inn
95		**Division St**
	Med	S: + Glen Oaks Hospital
96		**Bus 67, Loop 302**
	Gas	S: Fina, Shamrock
	Lodg	N: Best Western S: Quality Inn
97		**Lamar St, Greenville**
	Gas	S: Exxon
	Lodg	N: Dream Lodge Motel S: Econo Lodge, Ramada Inn, Sunrise Motel
101		**TX 24, TX 50, Campbell, to Commerce**
	Gas	N: Phillips 66◊
	Other	N: to E Tx State Univ
104		**FM 513, FM 2649, Campbell**
110		**FM 275, S Mill St, Cumby**
	Gas	N: Phillips 66 S: Shell
112		**FM 499 (WB)**
116		**US 67, FM 2653, Brashear**
120		**US 67 Bus, Sulphur Springs**
122		**TX 19, Lp 301, to Emory**
	TStop	S: Crossroads Travel Center/66, Pilot Travel Center #157 (Scales)
	Gas	N: Chevron
	Food	S: Rest/Crossroads TC, Arby's/Pilot TC
	Med	N: + Hospital
	Other	N: Sulphur Springs Muni Airport✈ S: WiFi/Pilot TC, **Shady Lake RV Park**▲
123		**FM 2297, League St**
	Gas	N: Shell
124		**TX 11, TX 154, Sulphur Springs**
	Gas	N: Chevron◊, Exxon S: Exxon◊, Shell◊, Murphy
	Food	N: Catfish King, Domino's, Hal's Diner, KFC, Pitt Grill, Pizza Hut, Popeye's, Sonic, Subway S: Burger King, Chili's, Furr's Cafeteria, Grandy's, Jack in the Box, K-Bob's, Taco Bell, McDonald's, Pizza Inn, Wendy's, Whataburger
	Lodg	N: Royal Inn S: Holiday King Motel
	Med	N: + Hospital
	Other	N: AutoZone, Auto Dealers, Family $, Dollar General, Kroger, US Post Office S: **Wal-Mart sc**

EXIT		
125		**Frontage Rd**
	Lodg	N: Holiday Inn Express
126		**FM 1870, College St**
	Gas	S: Chevron, Exxon, Shell
127		**US 67 Bus, Loop 301**
	Gas	S: Chevron, Shell
	Food	S: Burton's Rest, Rest/Best Western
	Lodg	N: Budget Inn, Comfort Inn, Holiday Inn, Quality Inn S: Best Western
131		**FM 69, Sulphur Springs**
135		**US 67N, Como**
136		**FM 269, Weaver Rd, Como**
141		**FM 900, Saltillo Rd**
142		**County Line Rd, Mt Vernon (EB)**
(143)		**Rest Area (Both dir)** (**RR**, **Phones**, **Picnic**, **Vend**, **WiFi**)
146		**TX 37, Mt Vernon**
	TStop	S: Fina Food Fast #50
	Gas	N: Shell S: Chevron◊
	Food	S: FastFood/Fina, Burger King, DQ, Hubbard's Café, La Cabana, Sonic
	Lodg	S: Mt Vernon Motel, Super 8
	Med	N: + Hospital
147		**Spur 423, Service Rd, Mt Vernon**
	TStop	N: Love's Travel Stop #279 (Scales)
	Food	N: Subway/Chesters/Love's TS S: TX BBQ
	Lodg	S: Super 8
	Other	N: WiFi/Love's TS
150		**Ripley Rd**
153		**Spur 185, Winfield, Millers Cove**
	Gas	N: BP◊, Chevron, Citgo◊ S: Shamrock
	Food	N: Café/Citgo
	Other	N: **Paradise RV Park**▲
156		**Frontage Rd**
(157)		**Weigh Station (Both dir)**
160		**US 271, FM 1734, Mt Pleasant, Pittsburgh, Paris**
	FStop	S: Gateway #11/Shell
	Gas	N: BP S: Exxon◊
	Food	S: El Chico, Elmwood Café, Sally's Café, Western Sizzlin
	Lodg	S: Comfort Inn, Days Inn, Executive Inn, Knights Inn, Ramada Inn, Sands Motel
	Other	N: Lowe's, to appr 2mi: **Ramblin Fever RV Park**▲ S: to **Momentum Motorsports & RV**
162		**US 271, FM 1402, FM 2152, Mt. Pleasant**
	FStop	S: Gateway #11/Shell, Total Stop #2
	Gas	N: Exxon◊
	Food	N: Applebee's, Blalock BBQ, Pizza Hut, Pitt Grill, Subway S: Subway/Total, Burger King, DQ, McDonald's, Rest/BW
	Lodg	N: Best Western, Holiday Inn Express, Super 8 S: Best Western
	Med	S: + Titus Co Memorial Hospital
	Other	N: **Mt Pleasant KOA**▲ S: Family Dollar

EXIT		
165		**FM 1001, Cookville**
	FStop	S: Big Tex Fuel Stop/Exxon
	Food	S: FastFood/BT FS
170		**FM 1993, Cookville**
178		**US 259, Omaha, DeKalb**
	FStop	S: Armadillo's #23/Exxon
	Food	S: FastFood/Armadillo's
	Other	S: Laundry/Armadillo's
186		**FM 561**
(191)		**Rest Area (Both dir)** (**RR**, **Phones**, **Picnic**, **Vend**, **WiFi**)
192		**FM 990, DeKalb**
	TStop	N: Texas 192 Truck Stop
	Food	N: Rest/TX 192 TS
	TServ	N: TX 192 TS/Tires
198		**TX 98, New Boston, De Kalb**
	Gas	N: Shell
199		**US 82, New Boston, DeKalb**
	Gas	N: Shell
201		**TX 8, New Boston**
	FStop	S: Valero #4522, Circle K/Citgo
	Gas	N: Shell S: Chevron, Exxon, E-Z Mart, Phillips 66, Murphy◊
	Food	S: FastFood/DS, Catfish King, DQ, China Café, McDonald's, Pizza Hut, Subway, Taco Bell
	Lodg	N: Tex-Inn S: Best Western, Bostonian Motor Inn, Holiday Inn Express
	Med	S: + Hospital
	Other	N: Auto Dealers S: Auto Dealers, CVS, Grocery, **Wal-Mart sc**
206		**Spur 86, Red River Army Depot**
	Other	S: Red River Army Depot, to MIL/**Elliot Lake Rec Area**▲
208		**FM 560, Main St, Hooks**
	TStop	N: Quick Go S: SunMart #105 (Scales) (DAND)
	Food	N: TX BBQ S: Subway/SunMart, DQ, Granny's, Hooks Diner, Hooks Pizza, Sonic, Tastee House Rest
	Lodg	S: Ramada
	Other	N: Hooks Camper Center S: Cooper Tire
212		**Spur 74, Lone Star Army Ammo Plant**
	Gas	S: McDonald Shell & Grocery
213		**FM 2253, Leary Rd**
218		**FM 989, N Kings Hwy Nash**
	Gas	N: Citgo S: Exxon
	Food	S: Burger King/Exxon
	Other	N: McKinnon RV & Marine S: Barrett Trucks & Service, State Line Speedway
220A		**US 59S, Jarvis Pkwy, Texarkana**
	Gas	S: Exxon
	Food	S: Wendy's/Exxon, DQ
	Other	S: Mall, Lowe's, Sam's Club, Doolin's Harley Davidson, **Wal-Mart sc**, to **Palma Family RV Center**, to **Pratt's Truck Towing Services & RV**
220B		**FM 559, Richmond Rd, Texarkana**
	Gas	N: E-Z Mart, Exxon, Shell S: Chevron, Shamrock

◊= Regular Gas Stations with Diesel ▲= RV Friendly Locations ♥= Pet Friendly Locations

RED PRINT SHOWS LARGE VEHICLE PARKING/ACCESS ON SITE OR NEARBY BROWN PRINT SHOWS CAMPGROUNDS/RV PARKS

INTERSTATE 30 W/E

EXIT		TX / AR
	Food	N: Burger King, Carino's, **Cracker Barrel**, DQ, On the Border, Poncho's Mexican, Pizza Hut, Popeye's, Red Lobster, Sonic, Texas Roadhouse, Wendy's S: Arby's, Chili's, Chuck E Cheese, El Chico, Golden Corral, Luby's, Outback Steakhouse, McDonald's, Subway
	Med	N: + Christus St Michael Health
	Other	N: ATMs, Banks, Best Buy, Discount Tire, Gander Mountain, Grocery, Home Depot, Pc Net, Staples, Sam's Club, Target S: AutoZone, Albertson's, Office Depot, PetSmart♥, Office Depot, Central Mall, Walgreen's, to Texarkana College
222		TX 93, FM 1397, Summerhill Rd
	Gas	N: Shell, Total, Valero S: Chevron, Exxon, Shell
	Food	N: Applebee's, Kona Ranch Steaks & Seafood, McDonald's, Shogun Japanese, Waffle House S: Bryce's Cafeteria
	Lodg	N: Courtyard, Hampton Inn, Motel 6♥ S: Marriott, Ramada Inn, Towneplace Suites
	Med	N: + Christus St Michael Health
	Other	N: ATMs, Banks, Heintschel Auto & Lt Tire, Pharmacy S: Car Wash, Grocery
(223)		TX Welcome Center (WB) (RR, Phone, Picnic, Vend, Info)
223AB		US 59, US 71, State Line Ave
	TStop	S: 76 Auto/Truck Stop (Scales)
	Gas	N: Citgo◊, EZ Mart, Shell, Speedway S: Exxon, RaceTrac, Shell, Total
	Food	N: Denny's, IHOP, Pizza Inn, Red Lobster, Waffle House, Rest/Clarion S: Arby's, Burger King, El Chico, Cattleman's Steakhouse, KFC, La Carreta, Long John Silver, Popeye's, Taco Bell, Pizza Hut, Whataburger, Wendy's
	Lodg	N: Best Western, Budget Host Inn, Clarion, Hampton Inn, Holiday Inn, Holiday Inn Express, Quality Inn, Ramada, Super 8 S: Baymont Inn, Best Western, Best Value Inn, Comfort Inn, Days Inn, Econo Lodge, La Quinta Inn♥, Knights Inn, Motel 6♥, Texarkana Inn
	Other	N: Firestone, Texarkana KOA▲ S: AutoZone, Albertson's, Walgreen's, Wal-Mart sc, Auto Services, **Four States RV Sales**
		(CENTRAL TIME ZONE)
		⇧ TEXAS ⇩ ARKANSAS (CENTRAL TIME ZONE)
1		Jefferson Ave, Texarkana
	Lodg	S: Country Host Inn
	Other	N: Texarkana KOA▲
2		AR 245, US 67, Texarkana
	FStop	N: Circle K/Phillips 66 Fuel Stop, Roadrunner S: Camp I-30 Truck Stop/BP
	Food	S: Rest/Camp I-30 TS
	Other	S: Truck & Trailer Repair, Four States Fairgrounds & **RV Park**▲, Texarkana Reg'l Webb Airport✈

EXIT		ARKANSAS
7		AR 108, Texarkana, Mandeville
	TStop	N: Flying J Travel Plaza #5021/Conoco (Scales)
	Food	N: Cookery/FastFood/FJ TP, T-Town Diner
	TWash	N: TWA Truck Wash
	Other	N: Texarkana **RV Park**▲, Laundry/BarbSh/WiFi/RVDump/LP/FJ TP
(8)		AR Welcome Center (EB) Rest Area (WB) (RR, Phone, Picnic, Vend, Info)
12		AR 67, Fulton (EB)
18		Red Lake Rd, Fulton
	TStop	N: Red River Truck Stop
	Food	N: Red River TS
	TServ	N: Red River TS/Tires
(25)		Weigh Station (Both dir)
30		AR 4, US 278, Hope, to Nashville
	Gas	N: Phillips 66 S: Exxon, Shell, MurphyX
	Food	N: Western Sizzlin S: Burger King, McDonald's, Pizza Hut, Subway, Taco Bell, Waffle House, Wendy's
	Lodg	N: Best Western, Super 8 S: Days Inn, Holiday Inn Express
	Med	S: + Medical Park Hospital
	Other	N: to Hope Muni Airport✈ to Crater of Diamonds State Park▲ S: Advance Auto, Auto Dealer, Museum, Wal-Mart sc, RVDump/Hope City Park, to Fair City **RV Park**▲
31		AR 29, AR 32, Hope
	FStop	S: Triple J Fuel Stop #7/Shell
	Gas	S: Exxon, Shamrock
	Food	S: Catfish Den, KFC, Pitt Grill, Uncle Henry's Smokehouse BBQ
	Lodg	S: America's Best Value Inn, Hope Village Inn & **RV Park**▲, Relax Inn
36		AR 299, Hope, to Emmet
	Gas	S: Patriot
44		AR 24, US 371, Prescott
	TStop	N: Travel Center of America #224 (Scales) S: Exit 44 Truck Stop (Scales)
	Food	N: CountryFare/Subway/TacoBell/TA TC S: Rest/FastFood/Exit 44 TS, Sonic
	Lodg	S: Econo Lodge/Exit 44 TS
	Tires	S: Exit 44 TS
	TServ	N: TA TC/Tires
	TWash	S: Exit 44 TS
	Other	N: Laundry/WiFi/RVDump/LP/TA TC S: Laundry/Exit 44 TS
46		AR 19, Prescott, Magnolia
	TStop	N: J&J Fuels/Fina S: Love's Travel Stop #277 (Scales)
	Food	N: Deli/Fina S: Hardee's/Love's TS, Pizza Hut, Fly Wheel Pies
	TServ	N: Fina/Tires
	Other	S: Laundry/WiFi/RVDump/Love's TS, ByPass Diesel & Wrecker Service, Crater of Diamonds State Park▲
54		AR 51, Okolona, Gurdon
(56)		Rest Area (Both dir) (RR, Vend, Picnic)
63		AR 53, Gurdon
	TStop	N: Southfork Truck Stop/Citgo, Dillard's Shell Superstop
	Food	N: Rest/Southfork TS, Rest/Shell SS
	Lodg	N: Best Value Inn/Southfork TS

EXIT		ARKANSAS
	TServ	N: Southfork TS/Tires/CBShop
69		AR 26E, Arkadelphia, Gum Springs
73		AR 8, AR 26, AR 51, Arkadelphia
	Gas	N: Citgo◊, Shell, Valero S: Exxon◊, Fina◊, Shell
	Food	N: McDonald's, Western Sizzlin S: Ardy's, Burger King, Chile Peppers, Hamburger Barn, Italian Café, Kreg's, Subway, Taco Tico
	Med	S: + Baptist Medical Center
	Other	N: Wal-Mart sc, to Crater of Diamonds State Park▲ S: AutoZone, Auto Services, Amtrak, ATMs, Banks, Grocery, Pharmacy
78		AR 7, Caddo Valley, Arkadelphia, to Hot Springs
	FStop	S: Jordan's Kwik Stop/Valero
	TStop	S: Mid-Ark Auto/Truck Plaza #2/Fina (Scales), Superstop #81/Shell
	Gas	S: Exxon, Phillips 66
	Food	S: FastFood/Mid Ark TP, **Cracker Barrel**, Subway/Exxon, McDonald's, Pig Pit BBQ, Shoney's, Taco Bell, Waffle House, Wendy's
	Lodg	S: Best Western, Best Value Inn♥, Comfort Inn, Executive Inn, Hampton Inn, Holiday Inn, Motel 6♥, Quality Inn, Super 8
	TServ	N: Mid-Ark ATP/Tires
	Other	N: Arkadelphia KOA▲, to De Gray State Park▲
83		AR 283, Friendship
	Gas	S: Shell◊
91		AR 84, Old Military Rd, Malvern, Social Hill
(93)		Rest Area (Both dir, Exit Left) (RR, Phones, Vend, Picnic)
97		AR 84, AR 171, Malvern
	Other	N: to Lake Catherine State Park▲
98AB		US 270, AR 51, Malvern, to Hot Springs
	TStop	S: Winner's Circle/Fina, Superstop #80/Shell
	Gas	S: Phillips 66, Murphy◊
	Food	S: Burger King, Pizza Hut, Sonic, Taco Bell, Waffle House, Western Sizzlin
	Lodg	N: Super 8 S: Budget Inn, Economy Inn
	Med	S: + Hospital
	Other	N: to Pearson's Landing **RV Park**▲ S: AutoZone, Auto Dealers, Grocery, Wal-Mart sc, US Post Office
99		US 270S, Malvern
106		Old Military Rd, to US 67, Benton
	TStop	N: AmBest/JJ's Truck Stop/Fina (Scales)
	Food	N: Rest/JJ's TS
	Lodg	N: Motel 106
	TServ	N: JJ's TS/Tires
	Other	N: LP/JJ's, to Pathway Campground▲ S: JB's **RV Park & Campground**▲
111		US 70W, Hot Springs
	Other	N: to Cloud 9 **RV Park**▲
(112)		Inspection Station (Both dir)
114		US 67S, to W South St, Benton
116		Sevier St, W South St, Benton
	Gas	N: Bullock's SuperStop, Shell, Texaco S: BP, Shell, Star Mart
	Food	N: Ed & Kay's, Chinese

◊= Regular Gas Stations with Diesel   ▲= RV Friendly Locations   ♥= Pet Friendly Locations
RED PRINT SHOWS LARGE VEHICLE PARKING/ACCESS ON SITE OR NEARBY   BROWN PRINT SHOWS CAMPGROUNDS/RV PARKS

Page 142

EXIT		ARKANSAS
	S:	Arby's, El Cena Casa Rest, KFC, No Name Orig'l BBQ, Smokey Joe's
	Lodg N:	Trout Motel
	S:	Capri Motel, Days Inn
	Other S:	ATMs, Banks, Auto Services, Grocery, Museums
117		AR 35, AR 5, Benton (S Serv on Military Rd)
	Gas N:	Citgo, Shell
	Food N:	Bo's BBQ, Denny's, Firehouse Subs, Pizza Hut, Waffle House
	S:	Arby's, KFC, McDonald's, Smokey Joe's, Subway
	Lodg N:	America's Best Inn, Best Western, Cedarwood Motel, Econo Lodge, Ramada
	Med S:	+ Saline Memorial Hospital
	Other S:	ATMs, Banks, CarWash, Grocery, Auto Services
118		Congo Rd (EB)
	Gas N:	Big Red, Shell◆
	S:	Citgo, Exxon, Shell, Murphy
	Food N:	Benton Family Rest, CiCi's, Santa Fe Grill
	S:	Burger King, Colton's Steakhouse, Mexican, Shoney's, Sonic, Taco Bell, Waffle House, Western Sizzlin, Wendy's
	Lodg N:	Relax Inn
	S:	Best Western, Days Inn
	Other N:	Home Depot, Whitfield Tire,
	S:	Advance Auto, ATMs, Banks, Kroger, RV City II, Tire Town, US Post Office, Wal-Mart sc
121		Alcoa Rd, Benton
	TStop N:	Pilot Travel Center #118 (Scales)
	Gas S:	Texaco
	Food N:	Subway/Pilot TC, Pizza Hut, Sonic, Starbucks
	TWash N:	Superior Truck Wash & Lube
	Other N:	Laundry/WiFi/Pilot TC, Auto Dealers, Target
	S:	Auto Dealers, I-30 Travel Park▲
123		AR 183, Reynolds Rd, Bryant
	FStop S:	Speedzone/Conoco
	Gas N:	Phillips 66, Shell, Murphy
	S:	Exxon◆, Phillips 66
	Food N:	Arby's, Burger King, Catfish Barn, Cracker Barrel, KFC, Pizza Hut, Ruby Tuesday, Tamolly's, Waffle House
	S:	FastFood/Speedzone, McDonald's, Ole South Pancake House, Subway, Taco Bell, Wendy's
	Lodg N:	Best Value Inn, Comfort Inn, Holiday Inn Express
	S:	Super 8

EXIT		ARKANSAS
	Other N:	ATMs, Banks, Wal-Mart sc
	S:	ATMs, Banks, CarWash & Lube
126		AR 111, Alexander Rd, Alexander
	FStop S:	County Line Superstop/Shell
	Gas S:	Delta Express
	Food N:	KFC/Taco Bell
	Other N:	RVDump/Fred & Jack's Trailer Sales
128		Mabelvale West, Otter Creek Rd
	Gas S:	Phillips 66
	Food S:	Rest/La Quinta Inn♥
	Lodg S:	La Quinta Inn♥
	TServ S:	Purcell Tire/Goodyear
	Med S:	+ SW Regional Hospital
(129)		Jct I-430N, to Fort Smith
130		AR 338, Baseline Rd, Mabelvale Pike, Mabelvale
	Gas N:	Mapco Express
	S:	Phillips 66, Shell
	Food N:	The Hawg Diner, Frontier Diner
	S:	El Rancho Rest, Luby's, McDonald's, Pizza Hut, Popeye's, Sonic, Wendy's
	Lodg N:	Cimarron Inn, King Motel, Super 7 Inn
	Other N:	Jones Harley Davidson
	S:	Wal-Mart sc
131		Frontage Rd, Chicot Rd (EB)
	Gas S:	Shell, Sinclair
	Food S:	Popeye's/Shell, McDonald's, Ryan's Steakhouse, Waffle House
	Lodg S:	Knights Inn, Motel 6♥, Plantation Inn, Ramada, Super 7 Inn
	Other S:	ATMs, Auto Services, Firestone, Grocery, Wal-Mart sc
132		US 70B, University Ave (EB), Frontage Rd, W Baseline (WB)
133		Geyer Springs Rd, Little Rock
	Gas N:	Exxon, Hess
	S:	Conoco, Exxon, Phillips 66, Shell
	Food N:	Church's, Mama B's Big Burgers, Sim's BBQ, Subway, Whataburger
	S:	Arby's, Burger King, Dixie Cafe, El Chico, KFC, McDonald's, Pizza Inn, Taco Bell, Waffle House, Wendy's
	Lodg S:	Best Western, Comfort Inn, Hampton Inn, Rest Inn, Super 8
	TServ N:	Looney Truck & Tire Service
	Other S:	ATMs, Banks, Auto Services
134		Scott Hamilton Dr, Stanton Rd, Little Rock
	Gas S:	Exxon◆

EXIT		ARKANSAS
	Food S:	Waffle House
	Lodg S:	Best Value Inn, Motel 6, Red Roof Inn♥, Super 8
135		65th St, Little Rock
	Gas N:	Chevron, Exxon, Express, Shell
	Food S:	Denny's
	Lodg N:	Days Inn, Executive Inn♥
	S:	La Quinta Inn♥, Ramada Inn, Rodeway Inn
(138A)		Jct I-440E, Airport, Memphis (EB)
(138B)		Jct I-530S, US 167S, US 65S, Pine Bluff, El Dorado, LR Airport
(138)		Jct I-530S, US 167S, US 65S, Pine Bluff, El Dorado, LR Airport (WB, Left exit)
139A		AR 365, Roosevelt Rd
	Gas N:	Citgo, Exxon
	S:	Shell
	Other N:	Auto Zone
(139B)		Jct I-630W
140		9th St, 6th St, Little Rock (EB)
	Gas N:	Exxon, Shell
	S:	Phillips 66
	Food N:	Pizza Hut
	S:	Waffle House
	Lodg N:	Best Western
	S:	Comfort Inn, Masters Inn
140B		6th St (WB)
	Gas N:	Exxon
	Lodg N:	Holiday Inn
140A		9th St (WB)
	Gas N:	Shell
	Lodg S:	Comfort Suites
141A		E 2nd St, E 3rd St, to AR 10, Cantrell Rd, Markham St
141B		US 70E, US 67, Broadway
	Gas N:	Exxon
	S:	Citgo, Superstop
	Food N:	Burger King, Wendy's
	S:	Arby's, KFC, McDonald's, Popeye's, Taco Bell, Wendy's
	Other N:	Alltel Arena, Kroger
142		15th St, N Little Rock
	Gas S:	Phillips 66, Super Stop
(143AB)		Jct I-40, W-Ft Smith, E-Memphis

(I-30 begins/ends on I-40, Exit #153B)

☏ **ARKANSAS**

Begin Westbound I-30 from Jct I-40 in Little Rock, AR to Ft Worth, TX.

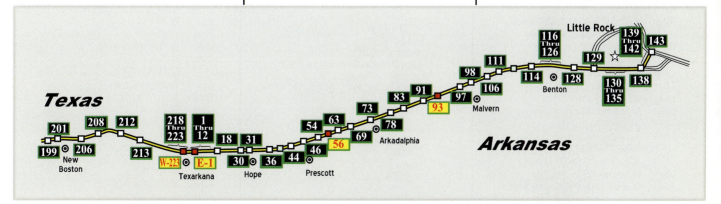

◆ = Regular Gas Stations with Diesel   ▲ = RV Friendly Locations   ♥ = Pet Friendly Locations
RED PRINT SHOWS LARGE VEHICLE PARKING/ACCESS ON SITE OR NEARBY   BROWN PRINT SHOWS CAMPGROUNDS/RV PARKS

INTERSTATE 35 S

EXIT	MINNESOTA
	Begin Southbound I-35 from Duluth, MN to Laredo, TX.

🛈 MINNESOTA
(I-35 begins/ends in Duluth, MN)
(CENTRAL TIME ZONE)

259 Jct MN 61, London Rd, 26th Ave, N Shore Dr, to Two Harbors
- Gas W: Holiday◇, ICO, Spur, Speedway
- Food W: Blackwood Grill, Burger King, KFC, McDonald's, Perkins, Pizza Hut, Taco John's Wendy's, Rest/BW
- Lodg W: Best Western, Edgewater Motel

NOTE: MM 258 - 256: Tunnel

258 21st Ave, Duluth (NB)
- Gas W: ICO
- Food W: Perkins
- Lodg W: Best Western
- Other E: to Univ of MN/Duluth

256B Lake Ave, 5th Ave, Mesaba Ave, Superior St
- Food E: Angie's Cantina & Grill, Burger King, DQ, Red Lobster
- Lodg E: Comfort Suites, Hampton Inn, Inn on Lake Superior, Park Inn, W: Holiday Inn, Radisson
- Other E: Omnimax Theater W: Grocery, Galleries, Museums

256A MN 194W, MN 23, Mesaba Ave, Michigan St, Superior St, Down town Duluth (NB)
- Med W: + Hospital

(255B) Jct I-535S, US 53, to Wisconsin (SB, Left Exit)

255A US 53N, Piedmont Ave, 21st Ave Duluth Intl Airport (NB, Left Exit)

254 27th Ave W, Truck Center Dr
- TStop W: (W to Truck Ctr Dr) Lincoln Park Travel Plaza (Scales)
- Gas W: BP, Holiday◇, Spur◇
- Food W: FastFood/Lincoln Park TP, Embers, Burger King, Quiznos, Subway
- Lodg W: Motel 6 ♥
- TServ W: Lincoln Park TP
- Other W: Laundry/Lincoln Park TP

253B 40th Ave
- TStop (to W 1st St) Lakehead Travel Plaza/BP
- Food W: FastFood/Lakehead TP, Perkins
- Lodg W: Comfort Inn, Super 8

253A 46th Ave, US 2E, Superior
- Gas W: ICO◇
- Food W: Grandma's Saloon, Taco John's

252 Central Ave, Duluth
- Gas W: Conoco, Holiday◇
- Food W: Giant Panda, KFC, McDonald's, Pizza Hut, Subway, Taco Bell
- Other W: Grocery, Walgreen's

251B MN 23S, Grand Ave (SB, Left exit)
- Other E: Zoo, to Indian Point Campground▲

251A Cody St (NB)
- Lodg W: Allyndale Motel
- Other E: Zoo, to Indian Point Campground▲

250 US 2W, Proctor (SB)
- MN Welcome Center (Both dir)
- Thompson Hill Rest Area
- (RR, Phone, Picnic, Vend, Info)
- Gas W: Holiday/Mobil
- Food W: Blackwoods Grill, Country Kitchen

EXIT	MINNESOTA
Lodg	W: AmericInn

249 CR 14, to US 2W (NB), Boundary Ave (SB), Duluth, to Proctor
- Gas E: Holiday◇ W: Phillips 66◇
- Food E: Country Kitchen, McDonald's/Holiday W: Blackwoods Grill
- Lodg E: Country Inn Suites, Sundown Motel W: Travelodge
- Other E: to Spirit Mountain Ski Resort & CGA▲

NOTE: MM 249 - 251: NB: 6% Steep Grade

246 CR 13, Midway Rd, Duluth
- Food W: Dry Dock Rest

245 CR 61, CR 3, Esko
- Food E: Buffalo House Rest
- Other E: Buffalo Valley Camping▲ W: Knife Island Campground▲

242 CR 1, Esko, to Thomson
- Gas E: BP
- Other E: to Jay Cook State Park▲

239 MN 45S, Cloquet, to CR 61, CR 16, Scanlon, Carlton
- Gas W: Conoco
- Food W: River Inn Bar & Grill, Wood City Grill
- Lodg W: Golden Gate Motel
- Med W: + Hospital
- Other E: to Cloquet/Duluth KOA▲, to Jay Cook State Park▲ W: Auto Dealers

237 MN 33, Cloquet
- Gas W: BP, Conoco, Spur, Murphy
- Food W: Country Kitchen, DQ, Hardee's, McDonald's, Perkins, Subway
- Lodg W: American Motel, Super 8
- Med W: + Fond du Lac Hospital
- Other W: Pharmacy, NAPA, Wal-Mart, Cloquet Carlton Co Airport ✈

(236) Weigh Station (SB)

235 MN 210, Carlton, Cromwell
- TStop E: Carlton Travel Center/BP, Junction Oasis #34/Spur (Scales)
- Food E: Rest/Carlton TC, Rest/Jct Oasis
- Lodg E: Royal Pines Motel, AmericInn W: Black Bear Casino, Hotel & Grill
- TWash E: Carlton TC
- TServ E: Junction Oasis
- Other E: Laundry/Carlton TC, LP/Jct Oasis W: Fond du Lac Indian Reservation

227 CR 4, Barnum, Mahtowa
- Gas W: Conoco
- Other E: Bent Trout Lake Campground▲

(226) Culkin Rest Area (NB)
(RR, Phones, Picnic, Vend, Playground)

220 CR 6, Main St, Barnum
- Gas W: BP◇
- Food W: Café/BP
- Lodg W: Northwoods Motel
- Other W: Auto Repairs

216 MN 27W, CR 8, Moose Lake (SB)
- Gas W: BP, Phillips 66
- Food W: Café, Wyndtree
- Lodg W: Moose Lake Motel
- Med W: + Hospital
- Other W: Moose Lake City Park▲

214 MN 73N, Moose Lake
- FStop W: Little Store/Conoco
- Gas W: BP, Holiday◇
- Food W: Subway/Little Store

Page 144

◇ = Regular Gas Stations with Diesel ▲ = RV Friendly Locations ♥ = Pet Friendly Locations
RED PRINT SHOWS LARGE VEHICLE PARKING/ACCESS ON SITE OR NEARBY BROWN PRINT SHOWS CAMPGROUNDS/RV PARKS

EXIT		MINNESOTA
Lodg	W:	AmericInn
Other	E:	Moose Lake State Park▲
	W:	Red Fox Campground & RV Park▲, to Moose Lake Carlton Co Airport✈, Museum, Theatre
209		CR 46, Sturgeon Lake
Gas	E:	Phillips 66
(208)		Gen'l Andrews Rest Area (SB) (RR, Phones, Picnic, Vend)
205		CR 43, Willow River
Gas	W:	Citgo◊
Other	W:	to Gen'l CC Andrews State Forest Willow River Campground▲
(198)		Kettle River Rest Area (NB) (RR, Phones, Picnic, Vend)
195		MN 23, MN 18W, Finlayson
Gas	E:	BP
Lodg	E:	Super 8
Other	E:	Banning State Park▲
191		MN 23E, to MN 123, Sandstone
Gas	E:	BP◊, Conoco◊
Other	E:	Sandstone Muni Airport✈
183		MN23W, MN 48E, Hinckley
FStop	W:	W to MN 61: Slim's Service/BP
Gas	E:	Conoco, Holiday
	W:	Mobil, Phillips 66
Food	E:	Burger King, Hardee's, Subway
	W:	Cassidy's
Lodg	E:	Days Inn
	W:	Gold Pine Inn
Other	E:	Grand Casino Hinckley RV Resort▲, Grand Casino Hinckley
	W:	LP/Slim's
180		MN 23, CR 61, Mora
175		CR 14, Beroun
Gas	E:	BP◊
171		CR 11, Pine City
FStop	E:	Speedway #4500
Food	E:	McDonald's
Other	E:	Auto Dealers, Pine City Muni Airport✈
169		MN 324, CR 7, Pine City
Gas	E:	BP◊, Holiday◊
Food	E:	DQ, Grizzly's Grill, KFC, Pizza Hut
Other	E:	Wal-Mart
165		MN 70, Rock Creek, Grantsburg
FStop	W:	Rock Creek Motor Stop/BP
Gas	E:	Citgo◊
Food	W:	Rest/Rock Creek MS
Lodg	E:	Chalet Motel
159		MN 361, CR 1, Rush City
TStop	E:	Holiday Travel Plaza
Food	E:	Burger King/Holiday TP
Med	E:	+ Hospital
Other	E:	Laundry/Holiday TP, Auto Service, to Rush City Muni Airport✈
	W:	to Rush Lake Resort & Campgrounds▲
(154)		Goose Creek Rest Area (NB) (RR, Phones, Picnic, Vend)
152		CR 10, Harris
147		MN 95, North Branch, Cambridge
FStop	E:	Gas Plus #8/Conoco
Gas	E:	BP, Holiday Station Store◊
Food	E:	DQ, KFC/Taco Bell, McDonald's, Perkins, Pizza Hut, Subway, Oak Inn
	W:	Burger King, Denny's, McDonald's
Lodg	E:	AmericInn, Super 8

EXIT		MINNESOTA
Other	E:	Grocery, NAPA, Golf Course
	W:	Tanger Outlet Mall
(143)		CR 17, New Exit
139		CR 19, Stacy Trail, Stacy
Gas	E:	BP, Phillips 66
	W:	Conoco◊
Food	E:	Rustic Restaurant
135		US 61S, CR 22, Wyoming
FStop	E:	Wyoming BP Food Shop
	W:	Wyoming Shell
Food	E:	FastFood/WY FS, Cornerstone Café, Pizza Zone, Subway
	W:	FastFood/WY Citgo, McDonald's, Village Inn, Rest/Exec Inn
Lodg	W:	Executive Inn♥
Med	E:	+ Hospital
Other	E:	IGA,
	W:	LP/WY Citgo
132		US 8E, to US 61, Forest Lake, Taylors Falls (NB)
131		CR 2, Broadway, Forest Lake
Gas	E:	Amoco, Holiday, Speedway
	W:	Holiday
Food	E:	Applebee's, Arby's, Perkins, Quack's
	W:	Famous Dave's BBQ, Quiznos
Lodg	E:	AmericInn
	W:	Country Inn Suites
Med	E:	+ Fairview Lakes Hospital
Other	E:	Checker Parts, Grocery, Target, Tires +, Wal-Mart
(131)		Forest Lake Rest Area (SB) (RR, Phone, Picnic, Vend)
129		MN 97, CR 23, Forest Lake
FStop	W:	Forest Lake BP
Food	W:	FastFood/FL BP
Other	E:	Auto & Truck Repair, to Forest Lake Airport✈
(128)		Weigh Station (SB)
		Listings below are for I-35E thru St Paul, MN.
(127)		Jct I-35W, to Minneapolis, I-35E to St Paul
123		CR 14, Main St, Centerville
Gas	W:	Citgo, Shell
Food	W:	Centerville Pizza & Subs, DQ, Embers, Kelly's Rest
Other	E:	Otter Lake RV Center
120		CR 81, CR J, Hugo (NB)
117		CR 96, St Paul
Gas	E:	Mobil, Super America
	W:	BP
Food	E:	Burger King
	W:	Applebee's, Arby's, Boston Market
Med	W:	+ Northeast Medical & Dental
Other	W:	Grocery, Walgreen's, Tires +
115		CR 15, CR E, St Paul
Gas	E:	BP, Conoco, Super America
Food	E:	Perkins
	W:	McDonald's, Quizno's, Wendy's
Lodg	E:	Holiday Inn
Other	W:	Target, Wal-Mart
(114)		Jct I-694E, Eau Claire (SB Left exit)
(113)		Jct I-694W, US 10W
112		CR 21, Little Canada Rd
Gas	E:	Citgo

EXIT		MINNESOTA
	W:	Sinclair
Food	W:	Porterhouse Steak & Seafood
111B		MN 36W, to Minneapolis
111A		MN 36E, to Stillwater
110B		Roselawn Ave, St Paul
110A		CR 30, Larpentur Ave, Wheelock Pkwy
Gas	E:	BP, Mobil
	W:	Sinclair
Food	W:	Subway
109		CR 31, Maryland Ave
Gas	E:	76, Super America
Other	W:	Kmart
108		CR 33, Pennsylvania Ave
107C		University Ave (SB)
Gas	E:	BP
Med	W:	+ Regions Hospital
Other	W:	to State Capitol
NOTE:		I-35E & I-94 run together below. Exit #'s follow I-35E.
(107B)		Jct I-94W, to Minneapolis
(107A)		Jct I-94E, to St Paul
Med	E:	+ St Joseph's Hospital
(106C)		Jct I-94E, 11th St, State Capitol (NB exit, SB reentry)
Lodg	E:	Holiday Inn
106B		Kellogg Blvd, to I-94W (NB exit, SB reentry)
106A		Grand Ave (NB exit, SB reentry)
Gas	E:	Mobil
Med	E:	+ United Hospital, + Children's Healthcare
Other	E:	SP Civic Center, Theatres, Museums
	W:	Theatres, Museums
105		St Clair Ave, St Paul (SB)
104C		Victoria St, Jefferson Ave (SB)
104B		Ayd Mill Rd (NB)
104A		CR 38, Randolph Ave
NOTE:		NB: All Trucks Over 9000# GVW MUST exit. Trucks over not allowed between MN 5 & I-94.
103B		MN 5, W 7th St, St Paul
Gas	E:	Mobil
	W:	Super America
Food	E:	Burger King
Lodg	W:	Crosby Lake Inn
103A		Shepard Rd (NB)
102		MN 13, Sibley Hwy
Gas	W:	BP, Holiday
101B		Mendota Rd W (SB)
101A		Mendota Rd E (SB)
101AB		MN 110, Mendota Rd (NB)
Gas	W:	Super America
Other	W:	Police Dept
(99B)		Jct I-494W, to Bloomington, Airport, Mall of America
(99A)		Jct I-494E, to Maplewood (SB)
99AB		MN 55, Jct I-494 (NB)

◊ = Regular Gas Stations with Diesel   ▲ = RV Friendly Locations   ♥ = Pet Friendly Locations

RED PRINT SHOWS LARGE VEHICLE PARKING/ACCESS ON SITE OR NEARBY   BROWN PRINT SHOWS CAMPGROUNDS/RV PARKS

Page 145

I-35 N/S

EXIT	MINNESOTA
98	**CR 26, Lone Oak Rd**
Gas	W: BP, Fina
Food	W: Joe's Grill, Thai Cafe
Lodg	E: Homestead Suites, Microtel
	W: Hampton Inn, Residence Inn
Other	E: Sam's Club
97AB	**CR 31, CR 28, Pilot Knob Rd, Yankee Doodle Rd (NB)**
Gas	E: Holiday, Phillips 66, Super America
	W: BP, Shell, Sinclair, Super America
Food	E: Applebee's, Arby's, Black Angus, Chili's, Don Pablo's, KFC, McDonald's, Hunan Rest, Houlihan's, Grand India, Perkins, Red Robin, Taco Bell, Wendy's
	W: Boston Market, Dragon Palace, El Loro Mex Rest, Chipolte, Steakhouse
Lodg	E: Marriott, Residence Inn, Towneplace Suites
	W: Best Western, Extended Stay
Med	E: + Eagan Medical Center
Other	E: ATMs, Banks, Cinema, Firestone, Grocery, Auto Services, Tires, **Wal-Mart sc**, Walgreen's, FedExKinko's, Mall, Office Depot
97A	**CR 28, Yankee Doodle Rd (SB)**
97B	**CR 31, Pilot Knob Rd (SB)**
94	**CR 30, Diffley Rd, St Paul**
Gas	W: Conoco
93	**CR 32, Cliff Rd**
Gas	E: Shell
	W: Holiday◊, Mobil, Total
Food	W: Burger King, Denny's, KFC, McDonald's, Subway, Taco Bell, Wendy's
Lodg	W: Hilton Garden Inn, Holiday Inn Express ♥, Sleep Inn, Staybridge Suites
Med	E: + Park Medical Center
	W: + Medical Center
Other	E: to Lebanon Hills Park▲
	W: ATMs, Banks, Cinema 16, Grocery, Target, Walgreen's
92	**MN 77, Cedar Ave, St Paul**
90	**CR 11, St Paul**
Gas	E: KwikTrip
	W: Freedom Valu Center
88B	**CR 42, Burnsville**
Gas	W: BP, Holiday, PDQ, Super America
Food	E: Ciatti's Italian Rest, Roadhouse Grill
	W: Arby's, Applebee's, Burger King, Chili's, Chipolte Mex Grill, KFC, TGI Friday, Fuddrucker's, McDonald's, Old Country Buffet, Outback Steakhouse, Panda Express, Romano's Macaroni Grill, Roadhouse Grill, Tin Alley Grill
Lodg	W: Country Inn, Fairfield Inn, Holiday Inn, Hampton Inn
Med	W: + Fairview Ridges Hospital
Other	E: Grocery, ATM, Bank
	W: ATMs, Banks, Auto Services, Home Depot, Circuit City, Goodyear, Target, Tires+, Cinemas, Burnsville Center
(88A)	**Jct I-35W (NB) to Minneapolis, Jct I-35, to Duluth**
NOTE:	I-35W begins/ends on I-35, Exit #127

Above listings are for I-35E thru St Paul.

EXIT	MINNESOTA
	Below listings are for I-35W thru Minneapolis, MN.
36	**MN 49, County 23, Circle Pines**
FStop	E: Oasis Market #557/BP
Gas	W: Phillips 66
Food	E: FastFood/Oasis
	W: McDonald's, Subway
Other	W: Target
33	**County 17, Lexington Ave**
Gas	E: BP
Food	E: Burger King, McDonald's
	W: Applebee's, Green Mill, Wendy's
Other	W: Home Depot, **Wal-Mart**, Walgreen's
32	**County 52, 95th Ave NE**
Other	W: Anoka Co Blaine Airport ✈
31B	**County 23, Lake Dr**
Gas	E: Shell◊
31A	**County 1, 85th Ave NE, County J (NB exit, diff reacc)**
30	**US 10W, to MN 65, Anoka**
29	**CR 3, County I**
Gas	W: Fina
28C	**CR 5, to Co 10W, CR H (SB)**
Gas	W: BP
Food	W: KFC, McDonald's, Perkins, Taco Bell, RJ Riches, Subway
Lodg	W: Days Inn
28B	**US 10E, St. Paul (SB), MN 10W, County H, Anoka (NB)**
Lodg	W: Skyline Motel
28A	**MN 96**
(27AB)	**Jct I-694, to St Cloud, Eau Claire**
26	**CR 73, County E2, 5th St NW**
Gas	W: Phillips 66◊
25B	**CR 88, New Brighton Blvd (SB, difficult reacc)**
Gas	E: Super America
	W: Mobil
Food	W: Jake's Cafe, Main Event, Perkins, McDonald's, Subway
Lodg	E: Courtyard, Fairfield Inn, Residence Inn
25A	**CR 19, County D, St Paul**
24	**CR 23, County C, St Paul**
FStop	W: Gas Discount
TStop	W: Cleanco Truck Wash & Fuel Stop
Food	E: Burger King
Lodg	E: Holiday Inn
	W: Comfort Inn
TWash	W: Cleanco TW & FS
TServ	W: Freightliner Trucks
Other	E: Enterprise RAC
	W: Auto Dealers
23B	**MN 36, Cleveland Ave, Stillwater (fr SB, Left Exit)**
Food	E: Burger King, India Palace
Lodg	E: Days Inn, Motel 6 ♥, Ramada
Other	E: to Rosedale Shopping Center
23A	**MN 280S, to Industrial Blvd (SB)**
22	**to MN 280 (NB), St Anthony Blvd, Industrial Blvd (SB)**
Lodg	E: Sheraton Inn
21A	**CR 88, Stinson Blvd (SB)**
Food	W: Country Kitchen, McDonald's, Pizza Hut/Taco Bell

EXIT	MINNESOTA
Other	W: Grocery, Home Depot, Target
21B	**Johnson St NE (NB)**
21A	**CR 88, Stinson Blvd, New Brighton Blvd**
Food	W: McDonald's
Other	W: to Lowry Grove Campground▲
19	**E Hennepin Ave (NB)**
Gas	W: EZ Stop
Other	E: Auto Services, Food, Museums
18	**4th St SE, University Ave**
Gas	E: BP
Food	E: Hardee's
	W: The Fish Basket
Lodg	E: Gopher Campus Motor Lodge
Other	E: Univ of MN
	W: Laundromat
17C	**CR 152, Washington Ave (SB)**
Other	W: to MetroDome
(17B)	**Jct I-94W, 11th Ave (SB)**
17A	**MN 55E, Hiawatha Ave (SB)**
17C	**Washington Ave, 3rd St, U of M**
Gas	W: Mobil
Lodg	E: Holiday Inn ♥
Med	W: + Hennepin Co Med Center
Other	E: Univ of MN
(16B)	**Jct I-94E, to St Paul (NB)**
Other	E: to + Fairview Riverside Med Center
16A	**MN 65N, I-94W, Downtown (NB, Left Exit)**
15	**CR 3, 31st St, Lake St (NB)**
Gas	W: Food 'n Fuel
Food	E: McDonald's, Taco Bell
	W: Subway, Wendy's
Med	E: + Abbott NW Hospital, + Childrens Healthcare
Other	E: Auto Services, ATMs, Bank, Grocery
	W: Grocery, Police Dept, Banks, ATMs
14	**35th St, 36th St**
13	**CR 46, 46th St, Minneapolis**
12B	**Diamond Lake Rd**
Food	W: Ja Mama's BBQ, Best Steak House
12A	**60th St (SB exit, NB reentry)**
Gas	W: Mobil
Other	W: Grocery, Auto Services
11B	**MN 62E, to Airport (SB, L ex)**
11A	**Lyndale Ave (SB)**
Gas	E: Shell
10B	**MN 62W (SB), MN 121N, 58th St, Lyndale Ave (NB, Left Exit)**
10A	**CR 53, 66th St**
Gas	E: SuperAmerica
9C	**76th St (SB exit, NB reentry)**
Other	W to Penn Ave: Food, Services at Southtown Center, Target, Best Buy
(9AB)	**Jct I-494, MN 5, to Airport**
Other	E: to Mall of America, MSP Intl Airport ✈
8	**82nd St**
Other	W to Penn Ave: Food, Services at Southtown Ctr, Target, Best Buy
7B	**90th St**
7A	**94th St (Addt'l Serv E to Lyndale Ave)**
Gas	E: BP
Lodg	W: Holiday Inn
Other	E: Auto Services, Goodyear

◊ = Regular Gas Stations with Diesel   ▲ = RV Friendly Locations   ♥ = Pet Friendly Locations
RED PRINT SHOWS LARGE VEHICLE PARKING/ACCESS ON SITE OR NEARBY   BROWN PRINT SHOWS CAMPGROUNDS/RV PARKS

MINNESOTA — I-35 S

EXIT		
6		**CR 1, 98th St**
	Gas	E: E-Z Stop
		W: Super America
	Food	E: Bakers Square, Deli, New China Buffet
		W: Burger King, Denny's, Subway
	Other	E: ATMs, Banks
		W: Auto Services
5		**106th St, Minnepolis**
4B		**Black Dog Rd**
4A		**CR 32, Cliff Rd**
	Other	E: Zoo
3AB		**MN 13, Shakopee, Mendota Hts**
2		**Burnsville Pkwy, Burnsville**
	Gas	E: Citgo
		W: BP
	Food	E: Denny's, Hardee's
		W: Perkins, Timber Lodge Steakhouse
	Lodg	W: Days Inn, Red Roof Inn ♥, Super 8
	Other	E: Mall
1/88B		**CR 42, Crystal Lake Blvd (SB)**
	Gas	E: BP, PDQ
		W: Amoco, Sinclair
	Food	E: Arby's, Burger King, McDonald's, Old Country Buffet
		W: Applebee's, Bakers Square, Chili's, Green Mill, Red Lobster
	Lodg	E: Country Inn, Holiday Inn
	Med	E: + Fairview Ridges Hospital
	Other	W: Target, UPS Store, Mystic Lake Casino & Hotel

Above listings are for I-35W thru Minneapolis, MN & I-35E thru St Paul, MN. I-35 SB listed below.

EXIT		
(88A)		**Jct I-35E to St Paul, Jct I-35W to Minneapolis**
87		**Crystal Lake Rd, Burnsville (NB)**
	Gas	W: KwikTrip
	Other	W: Auto Dealers, Auto Services, Buck Hill Ski Area
86		**CR 46, 162nd St, Lakeville, Apple Valley (NB)**
	Gas	E: KwikTrip, Super America
	Other	E: ATM, Bank, Auto Services, Twin Cities Harley Davidson
85		**CR 50, CR 5, Kenwood Trail, Lakeville**
	Gas	E: BP, Super America
		W: Holiday
	Food	E: Burger King, DQ, Lakeville Chinese, Pizza Hut, Taco Bell
		W: Cracker Barrel, Perkins
	Lodg	E: Comfort Inn, Lakeville Inn
		W: AmericInn
	Med	E: + Family Convenience Care
	Other	E: Goodyear, Grocery, Heartland Tire & Service, Pharmacy
		W: ATMs, Banks
84		**CR 60, 185th St W, Prior Lake**
	Other	W: Mystic Lake Casino & Hotel
81		**CR 70, Lakeville, Farmington**
	TStop	E: PTP/Mega Stop Holiday
	Food	E: Rest/FastFood/Mega Stop, Jordan's Steak House, McDonald's, Subway, Tacoville
	Lodg	E: Motel 6 ♥, Super 8
	TServ	E: Repairs, Towing

EXIT		
	Other	E: Laundry/BarbSh/Mega Stop, Airlake Airfield✈, Fairgrounds
76		**CR 2, 260th St, Elko, New Market**
	FStop	E: Phillips 66
	Other	W: Elko Speedway, to Sky Harbor Residential Airpark✈
(75)		**New Market Rest Area (SB)** **(RR, Phones, Picnic, Vend, Playground)**
69		**MN 19, Northfield, Little Chicago, Lonsdale, New Prague**
	FStop	W: PTP/Big Steer Travel Center/Conoco (Scales)
	Gas	E: Gas Mart
	Food	W: Rest/FastFood/Big Steer TC
	Other	E: to St Olaf College, Carlton College
		W: Laundry/RVDump/Big Steer TC
(68)		**Heath Creek Rest Area (NB)** **(RR, Phones, Picnic, Vend, Playground)**
66		**CR 1, Dundas, to Millersburg, Montgomery**
59		**MN 21, Bus 35, to MN 3, Faribault, Le Center**
	TStop	E: Truckers Inn #4/BP (Scales)
	Gas	E: Mobil, Super America
	Food	E: Rest/Truckers Inn, Burger King, Hardee's, Peppermill Grill, Pizza Hut
	Lodg	E: AmericInn, Days Inn, Super 8
	Other	E: Laundry/WiFi/Truckers Inn
		W: Faribault Muni Airport✈, Roberds Lake Resort & Campground▲
56		**MN 60, Faribault, Morristown**
	FStop	W: Petro Wash
	Gas	E: BP, Mobil

EXIT		
	Food	E: Burger King, Hardee's, Perkins
		W: DQ, Happy Chef
	Lodg	E: Galaxie Inn, Lyndale Motel
		W: Select Inn
	TServ	W: Cummins
	Med	E: + District One Hospital
	Other	E: Auto Dealers, Cinema 6, Goodyear, Grocery, Farbo West Mall, Tires +, Wal-Mart, Auto Services & Repairs
		W: Camp Faribo▲, to Sakatah Lake State Park▲, Camp Maiden Rock West▲
55		**CR 48, Faribault (NB, no re-entry)**
	Lodg	E: Budget Inn (Acc to Ex #56 Serv)
48		**CR 12, CR 23, Medford**
	Gas	E: Anhorn's Gas & Tire
	Food	W: McDonald's
	Other	W: Outlet Mall
45		**CR 9, CR 23, Owatonna, Clinton Falls**
	FStop	W: Kwik Trip #403
	Food	W: FastFood/KwikTrip, Green Mill, Timberlodge Steaks, Wendy's
	Lodg	E: Comfort Inn, Holiday Inn
43		**CR 34, 26th St, Airport Rd**
	Other	W: Owatonna Muni Airport✈
42B		**US 14W, Waseca (SB)**
42A		**CR 45, Owatonna (SB)**
42AB		**US 14W, CR 45, Owatonna, Waseca, Mankato (NB)**
	TStop	W: AmBest/Petrol Pumper #65/BP (Scales)
	Gas	E: Sinclair
		W: Murphy
	Food	E: Grace's Mex & Amer Rest, Kernel Rest
		W: FastFood/Petrol Pumper, Happy Chef, Culver's Family Rest, McDonald's, Perkins, Subway
	Lodg	E: AmericInn, Budget Host Inn
		W: Best Budget Inn, Super 8
	Other	E: Grocery, Auto Services, to Rice Lake State Park▲
		W: Laundry/LP/Petrol Pumper, Lowe's, Wal-Mart sc, Auto Dealers, Auto Service
41		**CR 25, Bridge St, Owatonna**
	Gas	E: Mobil◊
		W: Mobil◊
	Food	E: Arby's, Burger King, KFC, Quiznos, Subway, Starbucks, Taco Bell
	Lodg	E: Country Inn & Suites, AmericInn
		W: Microtel
	Med	E: + Hospital
	Other	W: Target
40		**US 218S, US 14E, Owatonna, to Rochester, Austin**
	Gas	E: Shell
	Food	E: Hardee's, Pizza Hut, Taco John
	Lodg	E: Oakdale Motel
	Med	E: + Hospital
	Other	E: Grocery, Pharmacy, Tires, to Rice Lake State Park▲
		W: Riverview Campground▲
(35)		**Straight River Rest Area (Both dir)** **(RR, Phone, Picnic, Vend, Playground)**
32		**CR 4, Owatonna, Hope**
	Other	E: Hope Oak Knoll Campground▲

◊ = Regular Gas Stations with Diesel   ▲ = RV Friendly Locations   ♥ = Pet Friendly Locations
RED PRINT SHOWS LARGE VEHICLE PARKING/ACCESS ON SITE OR NEARBY   BROWN PRINT SHOWS CAMPGROUNDS/RV PARKS

Interstate 35 N/S

EXIT	MN / IA
26	MN 30, Blooming Prairie, Ellendale, New Richland
TStop	W: Roki's/BP (Scales)
Gas	E: Cenex
Food	W: Rest/FastFood/Roki's, Rest/Cenex
22	CR 35, Geneva, Hartland
18	MN 251E, CR 31, Hollandale, Clarks Grove
FStop	W: Phillips 66
(13B)	Jct I-90W, Blue Earth, Sioux Falls
(13A)	Jct I-90E, Austin, La Crosse
12	US 65, Albert Lea (SB) (Access to Ex #11 Serv)
11	CR 46, Albert Lea, Hayward
FStop	W: Pump 'n Munch #5/Conoco
TStop	E: Travel Center of America #134/Shell (Scales)
	W: Flying J Travel Plaza (Scales), Love's Travel Stop #337 (Scales)
Gas	W: Phillips 66, Murphy
Food	E: TrailsRest/McDonald's/PHut/TA TC
	W: CountryMarket/FastFood/FJ TP, Chesters/Godfathers/Wendy's/Loves TS, Burger King, China Buffet, Golden Corral, Perkins, Subway, Wendy's
Lodg	E: Comfort Inn
	W: Country Inn, Countryside Motel, Days Inn♥, Guest House Inn, Super 8
TServ	E: TA TC/Tires
Med	W: + Hospital
Other	E: Laundry/WiFi/RV Dump/LP/TA TC, to appr 7mi Albert Lea/Austin KOA▲, to Myre Big Island State Park▲
	W: Laundry/WiFi/LP/FJ TP, WiFi/RV Dump/Love's TS, ATMs, AutoZone, Auto Dealers, Banks, Grocery, Home Depot, NAPA, Wal-Mart sc
8	I-35 Bus (NB), US 65, Albert Lea, Glenville (W to Access Ex #11 Serv)
Gas	W: Cenex, Citgo
Food	W: Hardee's, KFC
Lodg	W: Motel 65
5	CR 13, to Twin Lakes, Glenville
Other	W: to Hickory Hills Campground▲
2	CR 5, CR 18, Twin Lakes
(1)	MN Welcome Center (NB) Albert Lea Rest Area (RR, Phone, Picnic, Vend, Info)

(CENTRAL TIME ZONE)

⊙ MINNESOTA
⊙ IOWA
(CENTRAL TIME ZONE)

NOTE: WiFi Access Available at Rest Areas

214	CR 105, Northwood, Lake Mills
	IA Welcome Center (SB) (RR, Phone, Picnic, Vend, Info, RVDump)
FStop	W: Jo Stop/BP
Food	W: FastFood/BP
(212)	Weigh Station (Both dir)
208	CR A38, Hanlontown, to Joice, Kensett

EXIT	IOWA
203	IA 9, Hanlontown, to Manly, Forest City
FStop	W: Food-n-Fuel/BPAmoco
Med	W: + Hospital
Other	W: Pilot Knob State Park▲
197	CR B20, Clear Lake
(196)	Parking Area (Both dir)
194	US 18, Clear Lake, Mason City
FStop	W: Horizon Truck & Travel Plaza/Conoco (Scales)
TStop	W: Pilot Travel Center #407 (Scales)
Gas	W: Casey's, Shell◊
Food	E: Taco John's/Conoco, Wendy's/Shell
	W: Subway/Denny's/Pilot TC, Burger King, McDonald's, Perkins, Rest/Best Western
Lodg	W: AmericInn, Best Western, Budget Inn, Microtel, Lake Country Inn
Med	E: + Mercy Medical Center
Other	E: Laundry/Horizon TP, Mason City Muni Airport✈, Interstate Motor Trucks
	W: WiFi/Pilot TC, Meyer's Wrecker & Repair, to Clear Lake State Park▲, Oakwood RV Park▲, McIntosh Woods State Park▲
193	255th St, CR B35, Clear Lake, to Mason City
FStop	E: I-35 BP
Gas	W: Phillips 66
Food	E: Happy Chef
Lodg	E: Heartland Inn
Other	W: Clear Lake State Park▲
190	US 18, IA 27, to Mason City
188	CR B43, Rockwell, Burchinal
Other	W: to Twin Oaks Campgrounds▲, Clear Lake State Park▲, Oakwood RV Park▲, McIntosh Woods State Park▲
182	CR B60, Swaledale, to Rockwell
180	CR B65, 125th St, Thornton
Gas	E: Cenex
176	CR C13, Sheffield, Belmond
170	CR C25, Alexander
165	IA 3, Hampton, Clarion (All Serv 7-10 mi E in Hampton)
TStop	E: Dudley's Corner/Shell
Food	E: Rest/Dudley's Corner
Med	E: + Hospital
Other	E: to Beeds Lake State Park▲
159	CR C47, Dows
W:	IA Welcome Center (Both dir) (RR, Phone, Picnic, Vend, RVDump)
Other	W: Restored Railroad Depot, Historic Blacksmith Shop
151	CR R75, to C70, Woolstock
147	CR D20, to US 20E
144	220th St, CR R75, D25, CR 928, Williams
TStop	E: Boondocks USA Truck Stop/66
	W: Broadway Flying J Travel Plaza/Conoco (Scales)
Food	E: Rest/Boondocks TS
	W: Rest/Flying J TP
Lodg	E: Best Western/Boondocks TS
TServ	E: Boondocks TS/Tires
TWash	E: Boondocks TS

Page 148

◊ = Regular Gas Stations with Diesel   ▲ = RV Friendly Locations   ♥ = Pet Friendly Locations
RED PRINT SHOWS LARGE VEHICLE PARKING/ACCESS ON SITE OR NEARBY   BROWN PRINT SHOWS CAMPGROUNDS/RV PARKS

Interstate 35 N/S — IOWA

EXIT		IOWA
	Other	E: Laundry/Boondocks TS W: WiFi/BarbSh/LP/Flying J TP
142B		US 20W, to Fort Dodge
142A		US 20E, to Waterloo
139		CR D41, to Kamrar, Buckeye
133		IA 175, Ellsworth, to Jewell
	FStop	W: Cenex
	Gas	W: Kum&Go◊
	Other	W: to Little Wall Lake Campground▲
128		CR D65, to Randall, Stanhope
	Other	W: to Little Wall Lake Campground▲
124		115th St, CR E15, Story City
	FStop	W: Kum & Go #124
	Gas	W: Casey's, Texaco
	Food	W: DQ, Godfather's Pizza, McDonald's, Happy Chef, Subway, Valhalla Rest
	Lodg	W: Comfort Inn, Super 8, Viking Motor Inn
	Other	W: ATM, Bank, Auto Services, VF Factory Outlet Stores, Whispering Oaks RV Park▲, Gookin RV Center
123		IA 221, CR E18, to Roland, McCallsburg
(120)		Story City Rest Area (NB) (RR, Phone, Picnic, Vend, RVDump)
(119)		Story City Rest Area (SB) (RR, Phone, Vend, RVDump)
116		CR E29, Ames, to Story
	Other	W: Story Co Conservation Ctr
113		13th St, Ames
	Gas	W: BP, Kum & Go
	Food	W: Arby's/BP, Burger King/Kum&Go, Starlite Village Rest, Rest/Best Western
	Lodg	W: Best Western, Holiday Inn Express, Quality Inn
	Med	W: + Mary Greeley Medical Center
	Other	W: Towing, Zylstra Harley Davidson, IA State Univ
111B		US 30W, to Ames
	FStop	W: Fuel Right, Kum & Go #227
	TStop	W: Cyclone Truck Stop/Shell
	Food	W: Rest/FastFood/Cyclone TS, Happy Chef, El Azteca Rest
	Lodg	W: AmericInn, Comfort Inn, Hampton Inn, Heartland Inn, Super 8♥
	TWash	W: Cyclone TS
	TServ	W: Cyclone TS/Tires
	Other	W: Laundry/Cyclone TS, to IA State Univ, Ames Muni Airport✈
111A		US 30E, to Nevada
(106)		Weigh Station (Both dir)
102		IA 210, Maxwell, Slater
96		IA 87, NE 126th Ave, Elkhart, to Polk City
	Other	W: to Big Creek State Park, Saylorville Lake
(94)		Ankeny Rest Area (Both dir) (RR, Phones, Picnic, Vend)
92		1st St, IA 941, Ankeny
	Gas	W: BP, Casey's, Kum & Go, QT
	Food	W: Applebee's, Arby's, Burger King, Cazador, Golden Corral, Happy Chef, KFC, Long John Silver, McDonald's, Pizza Hut, Subway, Taco John's, Village Inn, Rest/BW

EXIT		IOWA
	Lodg	W: Best Western♥, Days Inn♥, Super 8 Fairfield Inn, Heartland Inn
	Other	W: Auto Services, Goodyear, Grocery, Museum, NAPA, O'Reilly Parts, Police Dept, Staples, Tires +, John Deere Assembly Plant, Cherry Glen Campground▲, Saylorville Lake
90		IA 160W, Oralabor Rd, Ankeny, to Bondurant
	Gas	W: Casey's◊, Phillips 66
	Food	E: Chip's Diner W: Amana Steaks & Chops, Burger King, Chili's, Culver's, IHOP, McDonald's, Panchero's Mex Grill, Starbucks
	Lodg	E: AmericInn, Country Inn, Holiday Inn Express W: Super 8
	Other	E: Ankeny Reg'l Airport✈ W: ATMs, Banks, Grocery, Home Depot, Springwood 9, Target, Wal-Mart sc
89		Corporate Woods Dr
(87BA)		Jct I-80W, to Council Bluffs, I-235W
(87A)		Jct I-80E, to Davenport
NOTE:		I-35 runs with I-80 below to bypass Des Moines. Exit #'s follow I-80.
136/85		US 69, NE 14th St, Des Moines
	TStop	S: QT #562 (Scales)
	Gas	N: BP, Phillips 66, Sinclair S: Casey's, Citgo
	Food	N: Bonanza Steak House, Country Kitchen, Rest/Best Western S: Burger King/QT, KFC, Long John Silver's, McDonald's, Pizza Hut
	Lodg	N: Best Western, Bavarian Inn, Red Roof Inn♥ S: 14th St Inn, Motel 6♥, Ramada
	TServ	N: GMC Trucks S: Mack Trucks, Auto & Truck Service
	Other	N: Sheriff Dept S: Advance Auto, Kmart, Auto Services, Hitch Service, Mid State RV Center
135/84		IA 415, NW 2nd St, to Polk City
	Gas	S: QT
	TServ	N: Interstate Detroit Diesel S: Freightliner Trucks
	Med	S: + Broadlawns Medical Center, + VA Medical Center
	Other	N: IA State Hwy Patrol Post S: ATMs, Auto Service, Banks, Park Fair Mall
131/79		IA 28, Merle Hay Rd, NW 58th St, Des Moines, Urbandale
	Gas	N: Casey's, QT S: BP◊, QT, Sinclair◊
	Food	N: North End Diner, Quiznos, Sonic S: Arby's, Burger King, Denny's, KFC, Famous Dave's BBQ, Ground Round, McDonald's, Perkins, Texas Cattle Co, Taco John's, Village Inn
	Lodg	N: Best Inn, Best Western♥, Ramada S: Comfort Inn♥, Days Inn, Holiday Inn, Quality Inn, Sheraton, Super 8
	Med	S: + VA Medical Center
	Other	N: Auto Dealer, Goodyear, Grocery S: Auto Dealers, Firestone, Goodyear, Grocery, Walgreen's, Merle Hay Mall,

EXIT		IOWA
	Other	S: Nova 10 Cinemas, ATMs, Banks, Best Buy, Office Depot, Enterprise
129/77		NW 86th St, Urbandale
	Gas	N: Kum & Go S: BP, Phillips 66
	Food	N: Burger King, McDonald's, Village Inn S: Arby's, Culver's, Embers, Pizza
	Lodg	N: Birchwood Creek Inn, Stoney Creek Inn S: Microtel♥
127/75		IA 141, Urbandale, Grimes, Perry
	FStop	N: Swift Stop/66
	Gas	N: BP
	Food	N: Subway/P66, Blimpie/BP
	Other	N: Vehicle Services S: Target
126/74		Douglas Ave, Urbandale
	TStop	N: Pilot Travel Center #373 (Scales)
	Gas	S: Kum & Go◊, QT
	Food	N: Rest/Pilot TC S: Blimpie, Dragon House, Happy Chef
	Lodg	S: Days Inn, Econo Lodge
	TWash	N: Pilot TC
	TServ	N: Pilot TC/Tires, Bar B Truck Repair
	Other	N: Laundry/WiFi/RVDump/Pilot TC S: Auto Repairs
125/73		US 6, Hickman Rd, to Clive
	TStop	N: Flying J Travel Plaza #5314/Conoco (Scales)
	Food	N: Rest/FastFood/FJ TP S: IA Machine Shed Rest
	Lodg	S: Comfort Suites, Clarion, Sleep Inn
	Other	N: Laundry/WiFi/LP/FJ TP S: Auto Dealers, Living History Farms, Metro Ice Sports Arena, Tire & Auto Center, Auto Services
124/72C		University Ave, W Des Moines
	FStop	N: Kum & Go #124
	Gas	N: BP, QT S: Phillips 66
	Food	N: Biaggi's Italian Rest, Burger King, Cracker Barrel, Mustard's Rest S: Applebee's, Bakers Square, Burger King, Chili's, Damon's, Don Pablo's, KFC, McDonald's, Outback Steakhouse, Ocean Grill, Romano's Macaroni Grill
	Lodg	N: Baymont Inn, Best Western, Country Inn, La Quinta Inn♥ S: Courtyard, Chase Suites, Fairfield Inn, Heartland Inn, Holiday Inn, Inn at University, Wildwood Lodge
	Med	S: + Mercy West Health Center, + Iowa Clinic
	Other	S: Valley West Mall, Best Buy, Lowe's, ATMs, Banks, Carmike Cinema, Grocery
(72B)		Jct I-80W
(72A)		Jct I-235E, to Des Moines
NOTE:		I-35 & I-80 above runs together around Des Moines. Exit #'s follow I-80. I-35 SB continues below.
70		Mills Civic Pkwy, W Des Moines
	Gas	E: Kum & Go
	Food	E: McDonald's
	Lodg	E: Residence Inn
	Other	W: Jordan Creek Town Center, Super Target
69AB		Grand Ave, W Des Moines
	Other	E: to Walnut Woods State Park▲
68		IA 5E, Des Moines Airport

◊ = Regular Gas Stations with Diesel   ▲ = RV Friendly Locations   ♥ = Pet Friendly Locations

RED PRINT SHOWS LARGE VEHICLE PARKING/ACCESS ON SITE OR NEARBY   BROWN PRINT SHOWS CAMPGROUNDS/RV PARKS

Interstate 35 N/S

EXIT		IOWA
65		CR G14, Cumming, to Norwalk
	Other	W: to John Wayne Birthplace
56		IA 92, Prole, to Indianola, Winterset
	FStop	W: Bussanmas Service/Shamrock, Kum & Go #56/Shell
	Food	W: Café, FastFood/K&G
	TServ	W: Bussanmas Service
	Other	W: Museum, Towing/Bussanmas
(53)		Parking Area (NB)
52		CR G50, St Mary's, St Charles
	Other	W: to John Wayne Birthplace, Madison Co Museum, Covered Bridges of Madison Co
(51)		Parking Area (SB)
47		CR G64, New Virginia, Truro
43		CR G76, IA 207, New Virginia
	Gas	E: Sinclair
		W: Total
36		IA 152, to US 69
34		Clay St, Osceola
	Gas	W: Kum & Go, Total
	Other	W: Terribles Lakeside Casino Resort & Campground▲
33		US 34, Osceola, Creston
	FStop	E: Osceola Travel Plaza/BP
	Gas	E: Casey's, Kum & Go
	Food	E: Family Table, Hardee's, McDonald's, Pizza Hut, Subway
		W: KFC/Taco Bell
	Lodg	E: Best Western, Days Inn, Super 8
		W: AmericInn, Blue Haven Motel
	Med	E: + Hospital
	Other	E: IA State Hwy Patrol Post, Tires, Auto Services, O'Reilly Parts, Pamida Shopping, Grocery
(32)		Osceola Rest Area (Both dir) (RR, Phones, Picnic, RVDump)
(31)		Weigh Station (Both dir)
29		CR H45, Elk St, Osceola
22		CR J14, to US 69, Van Wert
18		CR J20, Van Wert, to Grand River, Garden Grove
12		IA 2, Decatur City, to Leon, Kellerton, Mount Ayr
	TStop	E: Country Corner/Shell
	Gas	E: Phillips 66◆
	Food	E: Rest/Country Corner, 50's Diner
	Lodg	E: to Little River Motel
	Med	E: + Hospital
	Other	E: LP/CC
(7)		IA Welcome Center (NB) (RR, Phone, Picnic, Vend, RVDump)
4		US 69, Davis City, to Lamoni
	Gas	W: Casey's, Kum&Go/BP
	Food	W: Emu's Grill, Fastimes Rest, Outpost Café, Pizza Shack, Subway
	Lodg	W: Super 8, Chief Lamoni Motel
	Other	E: to Nine Eagles State Park▲
		W: ATMs, Auto Services, Banks, Cinema, Grocery
NOTE:		WiFi Access Available at Rest Areas

IOWA (CENTRAL TIME ZONE)

EXIT		MISSOURI
		MISSOURI (CENTRAL TIME ZONE)
114		to US 69, to Lamoni, IA
	FStop	W: Conoco State Line
	Food	W: FastFood/Conoco
	Other	W: RVDump/Walter Bros
(110)		Weigh Station (Both dir)
106		MO N, East St N, Eagleville, Blythedale
	TStop	E: Eagleville Travel Express/66 (Scales)
		W: Eagleville Texaco
	Gas	E: Conoco
	Food	E: Dinner Bell/Eagleville TE
		W: Square Meal Café
	Lodg	E: Eagles Landing Motel/Eagleville TE
	Tires	E: Eagleville TE/P66
		W: Hutton Tire Center
	TServ	E: Eagleville TE/P66
	Other	E: Laundry/WiFi/Eagleville TE
		W: I-35 RV Campground▲, Eagle Ridge RV Park▲
99		CR A, Ridgeway
	Other	W: to Eagle Ridge RV Park▲
93		US 69 Spur, Bethany
	Food	W: Big Boys BBQ, Dos Chiquita's
	Lodg	W: Sunset Motel
	Other	E: Bethany Memorial Airport✈
		W: Hillcrest Service Station, Bethany Tire & Auto
92		US 136, Miller St, Bethany, to Princeton
	FStop	E: Unlimited Convenience/Conoco
	Gas	W: Casey's, Kum & Go◆, Kwik Zone
	Food	W: Burger King, DQ, KFC, McDonald's, Pizza Hut, Taco Bell, Wendy's
	Lodg	W: Best Western♥, Family Budget Inn, Super 8
	Med	W: + Harrison Co Comm Hospital
	Other	W: Auto Dealer, Auto Repairs, ATMs, Banks, Grocery, Laundromat, Wal-Mart sc
88		MO 13, to US 69, Bethany, to Gallatin (W 3mi Acc to Ex #92 Serv)
84		CR H, CR AA, to Gilman City
	Other	E: to appr 20 mi Crowder State Park▲
(81)		Rest Area (Both dir) (RR, Phones, Vend, Picnic)
80		SR B, SR N, Coffey
78		SR C, Coffey, to Pattonsburg
72		SR DD
68		US 69, Altamont, to Pattonsburg
64		MO 6, to US 69, Altamont, to Gallatin, Weatherby, Maysville
	Other	W: to appr 11mi Pony Express RV Park & Campground▲
61		US 69, to US 6, Winston, to Altamont, Jamesport
	TStop	E: Winston Truck Stop/Shell
	Food	E: Rest/Winston TS
54		US 36, Bus 35, to US 69, Cameron
	FStop	E: Country Corner AmPride/Cenex
	TStop	E: PTP/Jones Travel Mart/BP
	Gas	W: Phillips 66, Shamrock

Page 150

◆ = Regular Gas Stations with Diesel   ▲ = RV Friendly Locations   ♥ = Pet Friendly Locations
RED PRINT SHOWS LARGE VEHICLE PARKING/ACCESS ON SITE OR NEARBY   BROWN PRINT SHOWS CAMPGROUNDS/RV PARKS

Interstate 35 N/S — Missouri

EXIT		MISSOURI
	Food	E: Rest/Jones TM, Wendy's/Shell W: Burger King, DQ, McDonald's, KFC Hardee's, Sonic, Taco Bell, Ma & Pa's Kettle Diner
	Lodg	E: Best Western ♥, Crossroads Inn & RV Park▲, Comfort Inn ♥ W: Days Inn, Econo Lodge ♥, Holiday Inn Express, Super 8
	TWash	E: Jones TM
	Other	E: Laundry/RVDump/Jones TM W: ATMs, Auto Services, Grocery, Kwik Lube & Car Wash, Wal-Mart sc, MO Correction Facility, to appr 14mi Pony Express RV Park & Campground▲
52		CR BB, Lp 35, Cameron (NB) (Gas & Food W to Bus 35, Acc to Ex #54)
	Med	E: + Cameron Regional Medical Center
	Other	W: to Cameron Memorial Airport ✈
48		US 69, Cameron
	Gas	W: R&B Whistle Stop
	Other	E: Wallace State Park▲ W: Down Under Camp Resort▲
40		MO 116, Lathrop, Polo, Plattsburg
	FStop	E: Trex Mart/66
	Food	E: Country Café/66
	Tires	E: Trex Mart/66
(35)		Rest Area (NB) (RR, Phones, Vend, Picnic)
(34)		Rest Area (SB) (RR, Phones, Vend, Picnic)
33		CR PP, Lathrop, to Lawson, Holt
	FStop	W: D&S Petroleum/Conoco, Phillips 66
	Food	W: Holt Cafe
	Other	E: JJ Campground▲
26		MO 92, 6th St Kearney, to Excelsior Springs
	TStop	W: Kearney Truck Plaza/Conoco (Scales), Pilot Travel Center #252 (Scales)
	Gas	E: Casey's, Conoco, PP66, Shell◆
	Food	E: Pizza Hut, McDonald's, Sonic W: Rest/Kearney TP, TacoBell/Pilot TC, Arby's, Burger King, Hardee's, Hunan Garden, Subway
	Lodg	E: Comfort Inn, Super 8 W: Country Hearth Inn ♥, Econo Lodge
	TServ	W: Kearney TP/Tires
	Other	E: Grocery, Interstate Auto & Towing Service, Police Dept, Clay Co Reg'l Airport ✈, to Watkins Mill State Park▲ W: Laundry/Kearney TP, Laundry/Love's TP, Grocery
(23)		Weigh Station (NB)
20		US 69, MO 33, Liberty, Excelsior Springs
	Med	E: + Liberty Hospital
17		MO 291, CR A, to I-435, Liberty
	Gas	W: Phillips 66◆
	Med	E: + Liberty Hospital
	Other	W: to Kansas City Int'l Airport ✈
16		MO 152, W Kansas St, NE Barry Rd, Kansas City, Liberty
	Gas	E: Conoco◆, Shell W: Phillips 66
	Food	E: Arby's, Carlito's Mex Food, CiCi's, Fuji Japanese Steakhouse, KFC, Long John Silver, Pizza Hut, Perkins, Taco Bell, Ponderosa, Village Inn, Wendy's
	Food	W: Applebee's, Bob Evans, Burger King, Back Yard Burgers, Country Kitchen, Cracker Barrel, Golden Corral,
	Food	W: Longhorn Steakhouse, McDonald's, Smokestack BBQ, Subway, Waffle House
	Lodg	E: Days Inn ♥, Super 8 ♥ W: Comfort Suites, Fairfield Inn, Hampton Inn, Holiday Inn Express
	Med	E: + Liberty Clinic
	Other	E: ATMs, Banks, Auto Repairs, Lowe's, Enterprise RAC, Firestone, Grocery, Kmart, Walgreen's, Miller's Kampark▲, Liberty RV, Museums W: ATM, Auto Services, Bank, Home Depot, NAPA, Office Depot, Super Target, Wal-Mart sc
14		US 69 (SB, Left exit), Pleasant Valley Rd, Liberty
	TStop	W: QT #179 (Scales) (NB Acc via Ex #13)
	Gas	E: Conoco◆, Sinclair
	Food	W: FastFood/QT, McDonald's
	AServ	E: Auto Services, Frank's Auto & Tow, Budget Auto Repair
	Other	E: I-35 RV Center, KC Ford Motor Plant W: Civic Center, Police Dept
13		US 69, to Liberty Dr, Pleasant Valley Rd, Liberty (NB) (Access to Ex #14 Services)
(12AB)		Jct I-435, St. Louis, St Joseph
11		US 69N, Vivion Rd
	Gas	W: QT, Total
	Food	W: Big Burger, Church's Chicken, Sonic, Smoke Shack, Stroud's Rest, Subway
	Other	W: to Antioch Shopping Center

EXIT		MISSOURI
10		N Brighton Ave, KC (NB) (Access to Ex #11 Serv US 69N)
9		MO 269, Chouteau Trafficway
	Gas	E: Phillips 66, Sinclair W: Amoco
	Food	E: IHOP, Outback Steakhouse, Subway W: Wendy's
	Other	E: to Harrah's Casino/Hotel/Restaurants W: to Antioch Shopping Center
8C		MO 1, NE Antioch Rd
	Gas	E: 7-11, Sinclair W: Phillips 66
	Food	E: Domino's W: Jumpin Catfish, Waffle House
	Lodg	E: Best Western, Inn Towne Lodge
	Other	W: to Antioch Shopping Center
	NOTE:	I-35 & I-29 below run together for next 6 exits, Exit #'s follow I-29SB.
(8B)		Jct I-29N, US 71N, to KCI Airport, St Joseph
8A		NE Parvin Rd, Ks City
	Gas	E: Shell
	Lodg	W: Super Inn
6AB		MO 210, Armour Rd, N Ks City
	Gas	E: Phillips 66◆ W: QT, Phillips 66, Texaco
	Food	E: Arby's, Big Boy's, Captain D's W: Long John Silver, Pizza Hut, Taco Bell, Wendy's, Rest/American Inn
	Lodg	E: Baymont Inn, Days Inn ♥ W: American Inn, Country Hearth Inn
	Med	E: + North KC Hospital
	Other	E: ATMs, Banks, Harrah's Casino W: Auto Services, ATMs, Banks, Conv Center, Police Dept
5B		16th Ave (NB)
5A		Levee Rd, Bedford St
4B		Front St, Ks City (NB)
	Other	W: Isle of Capri Casino & Rest
4A		US 24, Independence Ave (SB)
	Lodg	E: Capri Motel, Royale Inn Motel
	Other	E: Auto Services, Grocery
(3)		Jct I-70W, to Topeka
	NOTE:	I-35 & I-29 above run together for next 6 exits, Exit #'s follow I-29NB.
(2H)		Jct I-70E
2F		Oak St, Independence Ave, W 5th St, Kansas City (WB)
	Gas	W: Conoco
	Other	W: Restaurants, Auto Services
2D		Delaware St, Downtown
2C		US 169N, Broadway Blvd, Downtown Kansas City
2Y		W 6th St, US 169N, Broadway (NB)
2X		US 24W, US 169S, I-70/40W (NB, Left Exit)
2W		W 12th St, Kemper Arena, Conv Center, Downtown KC
2V		14th St, Downtown (NB)
(2U)		Jct I-70E, to St Louis (SB, Left exit) Broadway, I-670, Topeka (NB)

◆ = Regular Gas Stations with Diesel ▲ = RV Friendly Locations ♥ = Pet Friendly Locations
RED PRINT SHOWS LARGE VEHICLE PARKING/ACCESS ON SITE OR NEARBY BROWN PRINT SHOWS CAMPGROUNDS/RV PARKS

Page 151

Interstate 35 N/S

MO / KS

EXIT	
1D	W 20th St (SB)
1C	W 27th St, SW Blvd, W Pennway (NB exit, SB reaccess)
1B	27th St, Penn Valley Dr, Broadway St (SB, Left exit)
Lodg	E: Best Western ♥
Med	E: + Trinity Lutheran Hospital
1A	SW Trafficway (SB, Left exit)

(CENTRAL TIME ZONE)

⬆ MISSOURI
⬇ KANSAS
(CENTRAL TIME ZONE)

EXIT	
235	Eaton St, Cambridge Circle
Gas	E: QT
234	US 169, 7th St Trafficway, Ks City, Rainbow Blvd (SB)
Gas	E: Phillips 66
Food	E: Applebee's, Arby's, Burger King, McDonald's, Rosedale BBQ, Sol Azteca Mexican Grill, Wendy's, Rest/BW
Lodg	E: Best Western, Days Inn
Med	E: + Univ of KS Medical Center
234A	US 169S, Rainbow Blvd (NB)
234B	US 169N, 7th St Trafficway (NB)
233A	Mission Rd, SW Blvd
Food	E: Dagwood's Café, OK Joe's BBQ
Lodg	E: Days Inn, Redwood Inn
Other	E: Auto Repair, IGA
233B	37th Ave, SW Blvd (SB)
232B	US 69N, 18th St Expy, Ks City
Gas	E: QT, Phillips 66
Food	E: McDonald's
Lodg	W: Clark Motel
232A	Lamar Ave, S 24th St
Gas	E: QT
(231A)	Jct I-635N (fr NB, Left exit)
231B	US 69, Metcalf Ave (SB)
230	Antioch Rd, Mission
Gas	W: QT
Food	E: Bob Evans, Chili's, Quiznos
	W: Sonic
Other	E: Home Depot, Grocery, Cinemark 20
	W: Auto Services
229	Johnson Dr, Shawnee
Gas	E: Shell, Phillips 66
	W: Phillips 66◊
Food	E: Bob Evans, Chili's, Papa John's
	W: Café on Merriam
Other	E: Auto Services, Home Depot, Walgreen's
	W: Auto Services, Walnut Grove RV Park▲
228B	US 56E, US 69N, W 63rd St, Shawnee Mission Pkwy
Gas	E: Shell
Food	E: Checkers, Denny's, IHOP, Pizza Hut, Shoney's, Taco Bell, Winstead's
	W: Denny's, Long John Silver, Perkins
Lodg	E: Comfort Inn, Drury Inn, Homestead Suites
Other	E: Kmart, Pharmacy, Police Dept
228A	67th St, Mission
Gas	W: Phillips 66

KANSAS

EXIT	
Food	E: Burger King, Denny's
Lodg	E: Comfort Inn, Fairfield Inn, Quality Inn
Other	E: K-Mart
227	75h St, Overland Park
Gas	E: Circle K, Conoco, QT
	W: 7-11, QT◊, Shell
Food	E: McDonald's, Mexican Rest, Perkins
	W: Backyard Burgers, Big Burger, KC BBQ, Ryan's Grill, Sonic, Subway, Sakura Japanese, Taco Bell, Wendy's
Lodg	E: Wellesley Inn
	W: Hampton Inn
Med	E: + Shawnee Mission Medical Center
Other	E: Wal-Mart
	W: Cinema III, Jiffy Lube
225B	US 69, Overland Pkwy (SB)
225A	87th St, Overland Pkwy
Gas	E: Amoco
	W: Phillips 66, Shell
Food	E: Green Mill, Shoney's, Wendy's
	W: Arby's, DQ, El Caribe Mex, Holyland Café, Jalapenos Mex, KFC, Subway, Taco Bell, Zarda BBQ
Lodg	E: Holiday Inn, Microtel
Other	E: Grocery, Museum
	W: NTB, Police Dept, Auto Services, Grocery, ATMs, Banks, Museum
224	95th St, Lenexa
Gas	E: Phillips 66, Texaco
	W: Conoco, Costco
Food	E: Applebee's, Burger King, Denny's, Einstein Bros, McDonald's, MiMi's Café, Nature's Table, On the Border, Outback Steakhouse, Santa Fe Café, Shogun, TGI Friday, Taco Bell, Winstead's
	W: KC Burgers, LC's BBQ, Taboulay Café
Lodg	E: Days Inn, ExtendedStay, Holiday Inn, La Quinta Inn ♥, Motel 6 ♥, Radisson, Super 8
Med	E: + Overland Park Reg'l Med Ctr
Other	E: ATMs, AMC 6, Banks, Advance Auto, Best Buy, Enterprise, Firestone, Grocery, Oak Park Mall, Meineke, Jiffy Lube, Sam's Club
	W: Auto Services, Costco
(222B)	Jct I-435W
(222A)	Jct I-435E
220	119th St, Olathe
Gas	E: Conoco, Phillips 66, Shell
Food	E: Burger King, China Café, Chipolte Mex Grill, Cracker Barrel, IHOP, Joe's Crab Shack, Ks Machine Shed Rest, Long John Silver, McDonald's, Olive Garden, Rio Bravo, Ruby Tuesday, Steak n Shake, Souper Salad, Tres Hombres, Wendy's
Lodg	E: Comfort Suites, Fairfield Inn, Hampton Inn, Residence Inn
TServ	E: Mid West Kenworth
Other	E: AMC 30, ATMs, Auto Dealers, Banks, Best Buy, Barnes & Noble, Goodyear, Home Depot, PetSmart ♥, Super Target, U-Haul, Vet ♥
218	135th St, Santa Fe St, to US 169, to KS 150, Olathe
Gas	E: Amoco, Shell

◊ = Regular Gas Stations with Diesel   ▲ = RV Friendly Locations   ♥ = Pet Friendly Locations
RED PRINT SHOWS LARGE VEHICLE PARKING/ACCESS ON SITE OR NEARBY   BROWN PRINT SHOWS CAMPGROUNDS/RV PARKS

I-35 N/S — KANSAS

EXIT		KANSAS
	Gas	W: BP, Phillips 66, QT
	Food	E: Applebee's, Back Yard Burgers, Burger King, Gringo's, Guacamole Grill, Hardee's, Jose Peppers Grill, Perkins, McDonald's, Shoney's, Taco Bell
		W: Denny's, Gate's BBQ, Good Fortune Chinese, Ponderosa, Taco Bell, Waffle House, Wendy's
	Lodg	W: Days Inn, Villager Lodge
	Other	E: ATMs, Auto Repairs, Banks, Kmart, Firestone, Enterprise, Petland♥, Animal Hospital♥, Osco, FedEx Kinko's, Office Depot, Big Lots, $ General, Wal-Mart sc
		W: Auto Services, Museum, Grocery, Sheriff Dept
217		Old Hwy 56 (SB exit only, NB rentry, SB reaccess Exit #215)
	Gas	W: Conoco
	Lodg	W: Econo Lodge
	Med	W: + Olathe Medical Center
	Other	W: Great Mall of the Great Plains, Police Dept, Auto Services
215		151st St, US 169, KS 7, Olathe, to Paola, Spring Hill
	TStop	W: Star Fuel Center #101/Shell (Scales)
	Gas	E: Citgo, Phillips 66, QT, Shell
		W: Presto
	Food	E: Culver's, DQ, Jumpin Catfish, Sonic, McDonald's, Outback Steaks,
		W: FastFood/Star FC, Applebee's, Java Jive, Burger King, Blimpie, Chili's, Red Lobster, Country Kitchen, McDonald's, Taco Bell, Waffle House, Wendy's
	Lodg	W: Holiday Inn, Microtel, Sleep Inn
	Med	W: + Olathe Medical Center
	Other	E: Auto Repairs, Grocery, Home Depot, Target, Transmissions, Johnson Co Exec Airport✈, Happy Camper RV
		W: ATMs, Banks, Mall, Jungle Jim's Playland of KS
(213)		Weigh Station (Both dir)
210		US 56W, W 175th St, Gardner
	Gas	W: Phillips 66♦
	Food	W: McDonald's, Subway, Waffle House
	Lodg	W: Super 8
	Other	W: Towing, New Century Air Center and Business Park, Naval Air Museum
207		Gardner Rd
	Gas	W: Conoco♦, Shell♦
	Lodg	W: Santa Fe Trail Motel
	Other	E: Olathe Ford RV Center
202		Sunflower Rd, Edgerton
198		KS 33, Wellsville
	Gas	W: Conoco
193		Tennessee Rd, Wellsville
187		KS 68, Ottawa, Peoria
	FStop	W: I-35 Service
	Other	W: Museum, Auto Dealers
185		15th St, Marshall Rd, Ottawa (Gas/Food/Lodging 2mi W in Ottawa)
183B		US 59W, Ottawa (SB)
183B		US 59E, Ottawa (SB)
183		US 59, Ottawa, Lawrence, Garnett
	FStop	W: Jump Start #12/66
	Gas	W: BP, Citgo, Conoco♦
	Food	W: Applebee's, Burger King, Country Kitchen, China Palace, KFC,

EXIT		KANSAS
	Food	W: Long John Silver, McDonald's, Sirloin Stockade, Taco Bell, Wendy's, Rest/Travelodge
	Lodg	W: Best Western, Comfort Inn, Days Inn, Econo Lodge, Holiday Inn Express, Super 8, Travelodge, Village Inn Motel
	Other	W: Advance Auto, Auto Dealers, ATMs, Auto Services, Banks, Dollar General, Dollar Tree, Grocery, Wal-Mart sc
182AB		US 50, Eisenhower Rd, Ottawa
176		Idaho Rd, Williamsburg, Homewood
	Other	W: Homewood RV Park & Campground▲
(175)		Rest Area (Both dir) (RR, Phones, Vend, Picnic, RVDump)
170		KS 273, Williamsburg, Pomona
	Gas	W: Shell
	Food	W: Café/Shell
162		KS 31S, Waverly
160		KS 31N, Melvern
155		US 75, Lebo, Beto Junction
	TStop	E: Travel Center of America #70/Shell (Scales), BPAmoco Travel Center
	Food	E: CountryPride/Wendy's/TA TC, Subway/BPAmoco TC
	Lodg	E: Wyatt Earp Inn
	TServ	E: TA TC/Tires
	Other	E: Laundry/WiFi/RVDump/TA TC, Laundry/WiFi/BPAmoco TC
148		KS 131, Lebo
	FStop	E: S & S Lebo Plaza/66
	Gas	E: Casey's
	Food	E: FastFood/S&S, Lebo Grill, Wendy's
	Lodg	E: Universal Inn
	Other	W: to Melvern Lake
141		KS 130, Neosho Rapids, Hartford
138		CR U, Emporia
135		CR R1, Emporia, Thorndale
	Other	W: Dieker Trailer Sales & Service/ Overnite Camping▲
133		US 50, 6th Ave, Emporia
	Gas	E: Casey's
	Food	E: McDonald's, Pizza Hut
	Lodg	E: Budget Host Inn
131		Burlingame Rd, Emporia
	Gas	E: Conoco♦, Phillips 66
	Food	E: DQ, Hardee's, Mr Good Cents Subs
	Other	E: Grocery, Auto & Tire Service
130		KS 99, Merchant St
	Gas	E: Phillips 66♦
	Food	E: Godfather's, Domino's, Subway
128		Industrial Rd, Emporia
	TStop	W: Prairie Port Plaza/66 (Scales)
	Gas	E: Conoco
		W: Shell
	Food	E: Burger King, Coburn's Family Rest, Noah's, Pizza Hut, Subway
		W: Applebee's, Golden Corral, Taco Bell, McDonald's, Starbucks, Village Inn
	Lodg	E: Econo Lodge, Motel 6♥, Travelodge
		W: Comfort Inn, Candlewood Suites, Fairfield Inn, Holiday Inn Express♥
	Med	E: + Hospital
	Other	E: Cinema 8, Flinthills Mall, Grocery, Goodyear, Auto & Tire Services
		W: Wal-Mart sc

EXIT		KANSAS
127C		US 50W, KS 57N, Newton (SB, Left exit / LAST FREE Exit)
	TStop	E: Flying J Travel Plaza #5083/Conoco (Scales), S & S #13/P66 (Scales)
	Food	E: Rest/FastFood/FJ TP, FastFood/SS, Arby's, Chester's Fried Chicken, China Buffet, Hardee's, Wagon Wheel Grill, Rest/BW, Rest/Ranch House Motel
	Lodg	E: Best Western, Days Inn♥, Ranch House Motel, Super 8
	Other	E: Laundry/WiFi/RVDump/LP/FJ TP, Laundry/LP/S&S, Vet Hospital♥, Grocery, Auto & Truck Services
		W: Emporia RV Park▲
127B		US 50E, US 57S, Emporia (NB)
(127A)		Jct I-35S, KS Turnpike, Wichita
	Other	W: Emporia RV Park▲
	NOTE:	I-35 & Ks Tpk run together below. Exit #'s 19-92 follow KS Tpk.
(127)		TOLL PLAZA, Ks Turnpike
(111)		Cattle Pens
(97)		Matfield Green Service Area (Left Exit, Both dir)
	FStop	Phillips 66 #6368
	Food	McDonald's
92		KS 177, Cassoday, Salina
	TStop	E: Salina W TS, West Crawford 247
	Gas	E: Cassoday Country Store
76		US 77, El Dorado North (Gas/Food/Lodg approx 4mi E)
	Other	E: to El Dorado State Park▲
71		KS 254, KS 196, El Dorado
	Gas	E: Phillips 66
	Food	E: Burger King, Chinese Chef, Golden Corral, KFC, Long John Silver, Pizza Hut, McDonald's, Prime Cut Steak House, Subway, Taco Tico
	Lodg	E: Best Western, El Dorado Motel & Rest, Sunset Inn, Super 8
	Med	E: + Hospital
	Other	E: ATMs, Banks, Auto & Tire Services, Cinema, Grocery, Museum, Truck & Tire Service, Wal-Mart sc, Deer Grove RV Park▲
(65)		Towanda Service Area (Left Exit, Both dir)
	FStop	Phillips 66 #6369
	Food	McDonald's
57		21st St, Andover Rd, Andover
53		KS 96, Wichita
	Gas	W: Conoco
	Food	W: McDonald's, Two Bros BBQ, Subway, Wendy's
	Lodg	W: Courtyard, Cresthill Suites
	Other	W: Raytheon/Beech Factory/Airport✈, Lowe's, Wal-Mart sc, Cinema
50		US 54, US 400, Kellogg Ave
	Gas	E: Conoco
		W: Coastal
	Food	E: Burger King, IHOP
		W: Denny's, Green Mill, Hooters, KFC, KFC, McDonald's, Shoney's, Steak & Ale, Spangles, Taco Bell
	Lodg	E: Econo Lodge, Motel 6♥
		W: Best Western, Budget Inn, Comfort Inn, Days Inn, Fairfield Inn, Hampton Inn, Marriott, Residence Inn, Super 8, Wyndham Garden Hotel

♦ = Regular Gas Stations with Diesel   ▲ = RV Friendly Locations   ♥ = Pet Friendly Locations

RED PRINT SHOWS LARGE VEHICLE PARKING/ACCESS ON SITE OR NEARBY   BROWN PRINT SHOWS CAMPGROUNDS/RV PARKS

Interstate 35 — KS / OK

EXIT		KS / OK
	Other	E: McConnell Air Force Base, Lowe's, **Wal-Mart**, Auto Dealers
		W: Advance Auto, Firestone, Kmart, Pharmacy, Auto Dealers, Target, Towne East Square Mall
45		KS 15, Wichita
	Other	E: Boeing Factory, McConnell AFB
		W: K & R Travel RV Park▲, Emery Park BMX Track
(42)		Jct I-135, I-235, US 81, to 47th St (All Serv at 1st Exit)
39		US 81, Haysville, Derby
33		KS 53, Peck, Mulvane
	Other	W: Winery
(26)		Belle Plain Service Area (Left Exit, Both dir)
	FStop	Phillips 66 #6370
	Food	McDonald's
19		US 160E, Wellington (Services 3 mi West)
	TStop	W: Speedy Food N Fuel
	Gas	W: Conoco
	Food	W: KFC, DQ, Sonic
	Lodg	W: Sunshine Inn
	Other	W: Wheatland RV Park▲
(17)		TOLL Plaza
	NOTE:	I-35 & Ks Tpk run together above Exit #'s 19-92 follow KS Tpk
4		US 166, E 160th St S, to US 81, South Haven, Arkansas City
	TStop	E: Fleming Travel Plaza/66
	Food	E: FastFood/Fleming TP, Junction Café, Rest/Economy Inn
	Lodg	E: Economy Inn
	Other	W: Oasis RV Park▲, Strickland Road Service, Ks Badlands Off Road Park
(1)		Weigh Station (Both dir)
		(CENTRAL TIME ZONE)

⋂ KANSAS
⋃ OKLAHOMA
(CENTRAL TIME ZONE)

231		US 177, Braman
	TStop	E: Kanza Travel Plaza/Conoco (Scales)
	Food	E: Grab &' Dash/Kanza TP, Broadway Cafe
	Lodg	E: Kanza Motel
230		Braman Rd
(226)		OK Welcome Center (SB) Rest Area (NB) (RR, Phone, Picnic, Vend, RVDump)
222		OK 11, Blackwell, Medford, Alva, Newkirk
	TStop	E: Jiffy Trip Truck Stop #24/Conoco
	Gas	E: Phillips 66, Shell◊
	Food	E: KFC/Taco Bell, McDonald's, Subway
	Lodg	E: Best Value Inn♥, Comfort Inn, Days Inn, Super 8
	Med	E: + Hospital
218		Hubbard Rd, Tonkawa
(217)		Weigh Station (Both dir)
214		US 60, Tonkawa, to Lamont, Ponca City
	Gas	W: Cenex

Personal Notes
_____

EXIT		OKLAHOMA
	Food	W: Conestoga Restaurant
	Lodg	W: Western Motel
	Other	W: Woodland RV Park▲
211		Fountain Rd, Tonkawa
	TStop	W: Love's Travel Stop #213 (Scales)
	Food	W: Chesters/Subway/Love's TS
	Other	W: Laundry/WiFi/RVDump/Love's TS
(210)		Parking Area (Both dir)
203		OK 15, Billings, to Marland
	TStop	E: Cimarron Travel Plaza/Conoco (Scales)
	Food	E: DQ/FastFood/Cimarron TP
	Other	E: Laundry/Cimarron TP
(195)		Parking Area (Both dir)
194AB		US 64, US 412, Cimarron Tpk, Stillwater, Tulsa
193		to US 412, US 64W (NB)
186		US 64E, Fir St, Perry
	FStop	W: Sunmart #38
	Gas	E: Conoco, Gas Up
	Food	E: Subway, McDonald's, Pizza Hut
	Lodg	E: Super 8
		W: Days Inn
	Med	E: + Hospital
	Other	E: Auto Repairs, Grocery, Museum
185		US 77, OK 164, Perry, Covington
	TStop	W: Sooner's Corner/Conoco
	Gas	E: Sinclair
	Food	E: Rest/Best Western
		W: FastFood/Sooner's Corner
	Lodg	E: Best Western
		W: Sooner's Corner RV Park & Motel

EXIT		OKLAHOMA
	TServ	W: Sooner's Corner/Tires
	Other	W: Laundry/RVDump/Sooner's Corner
180		Orlando Rd, Perry
174		OK 51, Stillwater, Hennessey (Gas/Food/Lodg 12-14 mi E in Stillwater)
	Other	E: to Lake Carl Blackwell, OK State Univ, to Cedar Crest RV Park & Campsite▲, Wildwood Acres RV Park▲
(173)		Parking Area (Both dir)
170		Mulhall Rd, 56th St, Stillwater
157		OK 33, Guthrie, Cushing
	FStop	W: Love's Travel Stop #218
	Gas	W: Conoco◊, Shell, Valero
	Food	W: Subway/Love's TS, DQ, KFC, El Rodeo Mexican
	Lodg	W: Best Western♥ & RV Park▲, Interstate Motel
	Med	W: + Hospital
	Other	W: WiFi/Love's TS, Auto & Wrecker Service, Museums, Banks, ATMs, Grocery, Pharmacy, to Cedar Valley RV Park▲, Territorial Inn & RV Park▲
153		US 77, Guthrie, (NB, Left Exit) (Gas/Food/B&Bs - 3mi W)
	TServ	W: Coker's Auto & Truck Repair
	Other	W: Auto Dealers, Guthrie Muni Airport✈
151		Seward Rd, Guthrie
	Gas	E: Conoco, Shell◊
	Other	E: Pioneer RV Park▲
(149)		Weigh Station (Both dir)
146		Waterloo Rd, Edmond
	Gas	E: Edmond Travel Plaza, Shell
	Food	E: Catfish Ranch & Steakhouse, Pizza
	ATServ	W: Larry's Diesel Service, Auto repairs
143		Covell Rd, Edmond
142		Danforth Rd (NB)
141		US 77S, OK 66, 2nd St, Edmond
	Gas	W: Conoco, Phillips 66◊
	Food	W: Bennigan's, CiCi's, Coyote Café, Country Kitchen, Denny's, DQ, KFC/Taco Bell, IHOP, McDonald's, Marbo Chinese, Souper Salad, Western Sizzlin
	Lodg	W: Best Western♥, Fairfield Inn, Hampton Inn, Holiday Inn Express, Ramada Inn, Stafford Inn
	Med	W: + Columbia Edmond Med Center
	Other	W: Auto & Tire Services, Firestone, Banks, ATMs, Grocery, Police Dept, Univ of Central OK, Animal Clinic♥, PetCo♥
140		SE 15th St, Edmond
139		SE 33rd St, Frontage Rd
138D		Memorial Rd, Edmond
	Other	W: to Quail Springs Mall, AMC 24, Lions Fun Park
138C		Sooner Rd (SB)
(138B)		Jct Kilpatrick Turnpike
	NOTE:	I-35 & I-44 run together below for 8 miles, Exits #134-137, #'s follow I-35.
(138A)		Jct I-44E Tpk, to Tulsa

◊ = Regular Gas Stations with Diesel ▲ = RV Friendly Locations ♥ = Pet Friendly Locations
RED PRINT SHOWS LARGE VEHICLE PARKING/ACCESS ON SITE OR NEARBY   BROWN PRINT SHOWS CAMPGROUNDS/RV PARKS

EXIT	OKLAHOMA
137	**NE 122nd St, Service Rd, North OKC, Edmond**
TStop	E: Travel Stop #26/Shell
	W: Flying J Travel Plaza #5056 (Scales), Love's Travel Stop #205 (Scales)
Gas	E: Petro Plus 5
Food	E: FastFood/Travel Stop, Kettle Rest
	W: Rest/FastFood/FJ TP, Subway/TacoBell/Love's TS, Cracker Barrel, Chuck's BBQ, McDonald's, Sonic, Waffle House
Lodg	E: Sleep Inn, Travelodge
	W: Comfort Inn, Days Inn ♥, Economy Inn, Motel 6 ♥, Quality Inn ♥, Red Carpet Inn, Super 8
TWash	W: American Eagle TW
AServ	W: Interstate Auto Repair
Other	E: WiFi/TravelStop
	W: Laundry/WiFi/RVDump/LP/FJ TP, WiFi/RVDump/Love's TS, Abe's RV Park▲, OKC Welcome/Visitor Center, Frontier City Theme Park
136	**Hefner Rd, OKC**
	(Access to Ex #137 Serv)
Gas	W: Fuel at the Flag/Conoco◊
Food	W: Rest/Conoco
Other	W: Frontier City Theme Park
135	**Britton Rd, NE 93rd St, OKC**
134	**Wilshire Rd Blvd, NE 78th St**
Lodg	W: Executive Inn
Other	W: Blue Beacon TW, Tires
(133)	**Jct I-44W, Lawton, Amarillo**
Other	W: State Capitol, Cowboy Hall of Fame
NOTE:	I-35 & I-44 run together above for 8 mi. Exits #134-137, #'s follow I-35.
132B	**NE 63rd St (NB)**
Gas	E: Conoco◊, Fuel at the Flag
Food	E: Braum's
Lodge	E: Remington Inn
Other	W: Tinseltown 20, Museums, Zoo
132A	**NE 50th St, OKC**
Lodg	E: Red Stone Inn
Other	W: National Softball Hall of Fame, Oklahoma City Zoo, Omniplex, Air Space Museum, Firefighters Museum
131A	**NE 36th St, OKC**
Gas	W: Phillips 66◊
130	**US 62E, NE 23rd St, OKC**
Gas	E: Shell
Food	E: Burger King, Beef & Bun
	W: KFC, Krispy King, TJ's Seafood
Lodg	E: Deluxe Inn
	W: Relax Inn
Other	E: Auto Services
	W: Auto, Towing & Wrecker Services, 45th Infantry Div Museum, State Capitol
129	**NE 10th St**
FStop	E: Synergy Flash Mart #3/Conoco (Scales)
Gas	E: Total
Food	E: FastFood/FlashMart
	W: Tom's BBQ
Med	W: + VA Medical Center, + University Hospital, + Childrens Hospital of OK, + Presbyterian Hospital
Other	E: Wrecker Service
NOTE:	I-35 runs with I-40 below for 2 exits. Exit #'s follow I-35.
(128)	**Jct I-40E, to Fort Smith (SB, Left ex), Reno Ave, Eastern Ave, MLK Ave (SB)**

EXIT	OKLAHOMA
127	**Eastern Ave, Reno Ave (WB)**
TStop	W: JRS Travel Center (Scales), Stopping Center #16/Mobil (Scales)
Gas	W: Shell
Food	W: JRS Grill/Wendy's/JRS TC, IronSkillet/IronSkillet/Petro SC, Waffle House
Lodg	W: Bricktown Hotel, Econo Lodge, Quality Inn, Ramada Inn
TServ	W: Petro SC/Tires
TWash	W: Blue Beacon TW/Petro SC
Other	W: Laundry/JRS TC, Laundry/WiFi/Petro SC, Lewis RV Center
(126)	**Jct I-40, W-Amarillo (NB, Left Exit), E-Ft Smith, Jct I-235N, Edmond, Wichita, Jct I-35S, to Dallas (WB, Left exit)**
NOTE:	I-35 runs with I-40 above for 2 exits. Exit #'s follow I-35.
125D	**SE 15th St, Service Rd (SB)**
Gas	E: Conoco◊, Save
	W: 7-11
Food	E: El Sombrero Mexican, Skyline Rest.
Lodg	E: Green Carpet Inn
Other	W: Downtown Airpark✈
125B	**SE 15th St, Prospect Ave (NB)**
125A	**SE 25th St, SE 29th St (SB)**
Gas	W: Phillips 66
Food	E: Denny's, McDonald's, Taco Bell, Sonic, Waffle House
	W: IHOP, Mama Lou's Rest
Lodg	E: Plaza Inn, Royal Inn, Super 8
TServ	E: R & R Diesel Service
Other	E: Auto & Tire Service
	W: Auto Services
124B	**SE 29th St, SE 25th St (NB)**
Food	E: Days Inn, McDonald's, Waffle House
	W: IHOP, Mama Lou's Rest
Lodg	E: Days Inn, Plaza Inn, Super 8
Other	E: Auto Services
	W: Auto Services
124A	**Grand Blvd, OKC**
Lodg	E: Bricktown Guest Suites
	W: Drover's Inn, Executive Inn, Travelodge
TServ	E: Friday Truck Repair & Road Service
123B	**SE 44th St, OKC**
Gas	E: Conoco◊
Food	E: Chelio's Mex Rest, Domino's, Sonic
	W: DQ, Myrt's Diner, Pizza 44, Subway, Taco Mayo
Lodg	E: Best Value Inn, Courtesy Inn, Deluxe Inn
Med	W: + Integris SW Medical Center
Other	E: Auto Services, Roadrunner RV Park▲
	W: Auto Services, ATMs, Family Dollar, Grocery, US Post Office, Boat City Motor & RV Sales
123A	**SE 51st St, High Ave**
Gas	E: Conoco◊
Food	W: Rest/Southgate Inn, Las Chalupas
Lodg	E: Best Value Inn
	W: Southgate Inn
Other	E: Roadrunner RV Park▲
122B	**SE 59th St, Hillcrest St, OKC**
FStop	W: City Mart #4/Valero
Gas	W: EZ Mart
Food	E: Simple Simon's Pizza
	W: FastFood/City Mart

EXIT	OKLAHOMA
Other	E: Auto Services, Briscoes RV & Fun Park▲
	W: Repair Services
122A	**SE 66th St, Service Rd, OKC**
Gas	W: 7-11
Food	E: Burger King, Luby's, McDonald's, Subway, Texas Roadhouse
	W: Arby's
Lodg	E: Fairfield Inn, Ramada Inn, Residence Inn
Other	E: Best Buy, Firestone, Crossroads Mall, Cinema 8, Crossroads Mall 16
(121B)	**Jct I-240, OK 3, US 62W, Lawton**
121A	**SE 82nd St, Service Rd**
Food	W: Denny's
Lodg	W: La Quinta Inn ♥, Green Carpet Inn
120	**SE 89th St, OKC**
FStop	E: City Mart/Valero (Scales)
	W: Love's Travel Stop #211
Food	E: FastFood/City Mart
	W: Subway/Love's TS, Carl's Jr, Hardee's
Other	E: Laundry/City Mart
	W: WiFi/Love's TS, Repair Services
119B	**N 27th St, OKC**
Gas	E: Shell◊
Food	E: Rest/Luxury Inn
Lodg	E: Best Western, Luxury Inn
Other	E: Repair Services
	W: Repair Services, Lee's RV City South, Bryan Harley Davidson
119A	**Shields Blvd, Moore Ave (NB, L ex)**
Lodg	W: Days Inn, Greentree Inn
118	**N 12th St, Main St, Service Rd**
Gas	E: Sinclair, Total
	W: Phillips 66, Shell
Food	E: Pizza, Sonic
	W: Arby's, DQ, Grandy's, KFC, Long John Silver, McDonald's, Pizza Hut, Western Sizzlin, Wendy's
Lodg	E: Super 8
	W: Best Western ♥, Candlewood Suites, Comfort Inn, Days Inn, Motel 6 ♥
Other	E: Walker RV Center
117	**OK 37, S 4th St, Main St, N 5th St**
Gas	E: Shell
	W: Valero
Food	W: Mr Burger, Maria's Mexican Rest
Lodg	W: Ramada Inn
Med	W: + Moore Medical Center
Other	E: Auto Services
	W: Bank, Pharmacy, Wal-Mart
116	**S 19th St, OKC, Moore**
Gas	E: Conoco, Shell
	W: Murphy, Conoco
Food	E: BBQ House, Carl's Jr, McDonald's, Sonic, Taco Bell
	W: Burger King, McDonald's, Subway
Lodg	W: La Quinta Inn ♥
Other	E: Firestone, Goodyear
Other	W: Wal-Mart sc, Tire Center
114	**Indian Hills Rd, 179th St, Norman**
Food	E: Indian Hills Rest & Club
Other	E: I-35 RV Sales
113	**US 77S, Franklin Rd (SB, Left exit)**
112	**Tecumseh Rd, Norman**
Other	E: RV General Store, Max Westheimer Airport✈, Univ of OK
110A	**Interstate Dr, Robinson St (SB)**

◊ = Regular Gas Stations with Diesel ▲ = RV Friendly Locations ♥ = Pet Friendly Locations
RED PRINT SHOWS LARGE VEHICLE PARKING/ACCESS ON SITE OR NEARBY BROWN PRINT SHOWS CAMPGROUNDS/RV PARKS

Page 155

Interstate 35 N/S

EXIT	OKLAHOMA
110B	**Interstate Dr, Robinson St (SB)**
110	**Robinson St, Norman (NB)**
Gas	E: PetroStop
	W: 7-11, Conoco, Phillips 66
Food	E: Carl's Jr, Hardee's, Sonic, Taco Bell, Western Sizzlin
	W: Arby's, Braum's, BlackEyed Pea, Cracker Barrel, Danny's Steakhouse, House of Hunan, Joe's Crab Shack, Pizza Hut, Outback Steakhouse, Panda Garden, Rib Crib BBQ, Ryan's Grill, Santa Fe Cattle Co, Taste of China, Tulio's Mexican Rest, Waffle House
Lodg	E: Days Inn ♥
	W: Holiday Inn
Med	E: + Norman Regional Hospital, + Griffin Memorial Hospital
Other	E: Albertson's, Univ of Ok Westheimer Airpark✈, Auto Dealers, Tires, Griffin Park, Cruise America RV Rentals
	W: Cinemark 6, Carwash, Spotlight 14
109	**W Main St, Norman**
Gas	E: 7-11, Phillips 66, Shell, Murphy
	W: Conoco◊
Food	E: CiCi's, Denny's, Golden Corral, Panera Bread, Prairie Kitchen, Subway, Taco Cabana, Waffle House
	W: Applebee's, Burger King, Chili's, Don Pablo's, El Chico, Hooters, Olive Garden, McDonald's, On the Border, Pearls Oyster Bar, Pipers Coffee & Pastry, Piccadilly Cafeteria, Red Lobster, Souper Salad
Lodg	E: Days Inn, Econo Lodge, Guest Inn, Quality Inn, Super 8, Travelodge
	W: Fairfield Inn, Hampton Inn, La Quinta Inn ♥
Other	E: AutoZone, ATMs, Banks, Greyhound, Auto Dealers, Auto & Tire Services, Best Buy, Grocery, Lowe's, Target, Enterprise RAC, Wal-Mart sc, Amtrak, Hertz RAC
	W: ATMs, Banks, IGA, Sooner Fashion Mall, Barnes & Noble, Borders, Grocery
108AB	**OK 74A, Lindsey St, OK 9, Tecumseh, University of Oklahoma**
Gas	E: Citgo, Conoco, Shell, Texaco
Food	E: Arby's, McDonald's, Panda Buffet, Subway, Taco Bell
	W: IHOP
Lodg	E: Villager Lodge, Thunderbird Lodge
	W: Country Inn, La Quinta Inn ♥
Other	E: ATMs, Banks, Auto Services & Tires, Carwash, to Univ of Ok, OK Memorial Stadium, Owen Field✈
	W: Home Depot
108A	**OK 9E, to Tecumseh**
Food	E: Austin Bros, McDonald's
Lodg	E: Residence Inn
108B	**OK 74A, Lindsey St**
106	**OK 9W, Norman, to Chickasha, New Castle, Blanchard**
FStop	W: Love's Travel Stop #260
Food	W: TacoBell/Love's TS
Other	E: Floyd's Campers
	W: WiFi/Love's TS
104	**OK 74S, Main St, Washington, to Goldsby**
Gas	W: Shell, Sinclair

EXIT	OKLAHOMA
Other	E: Goldsby David J Perry Airport✈, Floyd's Campers
	W: Andrew Service Center
101	**Ladd Rd, Washington**
98	**Johnson Rd, CR N4040, Purcell**
Gas	E: Shamrock◊
95	**SR 74G, to US 77, Purcell, Lexington (SB exits Left)**
Gas	E: Conoco◊, Love's◊, Shell
Food	E: Carl's Jr, KFC, Pizza, Subway
Lodg	E: Best Western
Med	E: + Hospital
Other	E: Grocery
91	**OK 74, to US 77, OK 39, Purcell, Maysville, Lexington**
FStop	W: Star Travel Plaza/Shell
Gas	E: Conoco◊, Love's◊, Phillips 66◊
Food	E: Carl's Jr, McDonald's, Subway, Rest/Ruby's Inn
	W: FastFood/Star TP
Lodg	E: Econo Lodge, Horse Country Inn, Ruby's Inn, Uptown Motel
TServ	E: Diesel Dr, Precision Trailer Repair
Med	E: + Hospital
Other	E: Auto & Tire Services, Auto Dealers, Wal-Mart sc
86	**OK 59, Wayne, Payne, Rosedale**
Other	E: American RV Park ▲
79	**OK 145E, Paoli**
Gas	E: Phillips 66
74	**Kimberlin Rd, to OK 19, Pauls Valley**
72	**OK 19, Grant Ave, Pauls Valley, Lindsey, Maysville, Ada**
FStop	E: Pauls Valley Travel Center/66
	W: Love's Travel Stop #202
TStop	E: Travel Plaza/Shamrock (Scales)
Gas	E: Citgo
Food	E: Rest/Travel Plaza, FastFood/PV TC, Ballard's D/I, Carl's Jr, Denny's, KFC/Taco Bell, Pizza Hut, Sonic, Subway
	W: FastFood/Love's TS, Chaparral Steaks, McDonald's
Lodg	E: Days Inn, Relax Inn, Sands Inn
TWash	E: G&S TW
TServ	E: Travel Plaza, Tire & Service, Truck Repair
Other	E: Laundry/CB/Travel Plaza, Auto & Tire Services, ATMs, Banks, Auto Dealer, Grocery, Museum, Wal-Mart, Royal Twin Theatre
	W: WiFi/Love's TS
70	**Airport Rd, Pauls Valley**
Med	W: + Pauls Valley General Hospital
Other	E: Animal Hospital ♥, Pauls Valley Muni Airport✈
66	**OK 29, to US 77, Wynnewood, to Elmore City**
FStop	E: Kent's
Gas	W: Shell
Food	E: Rest/Kent's
Lodg	E: Motel/Kent's
64	**OK 17A, Wynnewood**
60	**Ruppe Rd, Wynnewood**
(58)	**Rest Area (Both dir) (RR, Phones, Picnic, RVDump)**

◊ = Regular Gas Stations with Diesel ▲ = RV Friendly Locations ♥ = Pet Friendly Locations
RED PRINT SHOWS LARGE VEHICLE PARKING/ACCESS ON SITE OR NEARBY BROWN PRINT SHOWS CAMPGROUNDS/RV PARKS

INTERSTATE 35 N/S

EXIT	OKLAHOMA
55	OK 7, Davis, to Duncan, Sulphur, Ada (All Serv 3-4 mi E in Davis)
FStop	E: Chickasaw Trading Post/Shamrock
Gas	W: Conoco
Other	W: Oak Hill RV Park▲
(53)	Weigh Station (Both dir)
51	US 77, Davis, Turner Falls Area
Gas	W: Sinclair
Food	W: Grill/Sinclair, Buffalo Gap BBQ
Lodg	E: Canyon Breeze Motel & RV Park▲
Other	E: to Chickasaw Nat'l Rec Area▲
	W: Turner Falls▲, Rose Grocery, RV Park & Canoe Rental▲
(49)	Scenic View (SB)
47	US 77, Turner Falls Area
Other	W: Turner Falls▲
(46)	Scenic View (NB)
42	OK 53W, Springer, Comanche
TStop	E: Sunmart #6/Exxon
Food	E: FastFood/Sunmart
40	US 77, OK 53E, Springer, Autrey, Ardmore, Airpark
TStop	E: Springer Shell
Food	E: FastFood/Springer
Other	E: Laundry/Springer, Melody Ranch▲
33	OK 142, Veterans Blvd, Ardmore
TStop	W: Flying J Travel Plaza (Scales)
Gas	E: Phillips 66◊
Food	E: Ryan's Grill
	W: CountryMarket/FastFood/FJ TP, McDonald's
Lodg	E: Guest Inn, Holiday Inn, La Quinta Inn♥, Regency Inn, Super 8
	W: Microtel♥
TServ	W: Truck Lube Plus
Other	E: ATMs, Banks, Wal-Mart
	W: Laundry/WiFi/RVDump/LP/FJ TP
32	12th Ave NW, Ardmore
FStop	E: Love's Travel Stop #266 (Scales)
Gas	E: Phillips 66
Food	E: Arby's, Burger King, Carl's Jr, Long John Silver, McDonald's, Ryan's Grill, Sirloin Stockade, Taco Bell
	W: Godfather's/Subway/Love's TS, McDonald's
Lodg	W: Microtel
Med	E: + Mercy Memorial Health Center
TServ	E: Priest Auto & Truck Repair
Other	E: ATMs, Banks, Grocery, Staples, Walgreen's, Wal-Mart sc
	W: Laundry/WiFi/Love's TS
31B	US 70W, W Broadway St, Ardmore, to Lone Grove, Waurika
FStop	W: Conoco
Other	W: Shady Cove RV Park▲, Auto Dealers
31A	OK 199E, Ardmore, to Dickson
Gas	E: Conoco, Shell, Sinclair◊
Food	E: Applebee's, Burger King, Broadway Café, BBQ Express, Cattle Rustler's Steakhouse, Denny's, El Chico, Golden China, Jack in the Box, KFC, Pizza Hut, McDonald's, Shoney's, Two Frogs Grill
Lodg	E: Best Western♥, Comfort Inn♥, Days Inn♥, Hampton Inn, Holiday Inn, Motel 6♥
Other	E: Grocery, AutoZone, Carmike Cinema,
29	US 70E, Ardmore
Other	E: Lake Murray State Park▲
	W: Hidden Lake RV Resort▲

EXIT	OK / TX
24	OK 77S, Ardmore
Gas	E: Sinclair
Other	E: Lake Murray State Park▲
21	Oswalt Rd, Marietta
Other	W: Ardmore/Marietta KOA▲
15	OK 32, Memorial Dr, Marietta, Ryan
TStop	E: Valero #4430
Gas	E: Phillips 66, Sinclair
	W: Phillips 66
Food	E: FastFood/Valero, Carl's Jr, Denim's Rest, Hardee's, Pizza Hut, Sonic
	W: Hickory House BBQ, Subway
Tires	E: Valero
Lodg	E: Lake Country Motel
Med	E: + Hospital
Other	E: Winn Dixie
5	OK 153, Thackerville
Other	E: Red River Ranch RV Resort▲
(3)	OK Welcome Center (NB) Rest Area (SB) (RR, Phone, Picnic, Vend)
1	US 77N, Thackerville
TStop	E: Thackerville Travel Plaza/Shamrock
Food	E: FastFood/Thackerville TP
Other	E: Laundry/Thackerville TP

(CENTRAL TIME ZONE)

⛁ OKLAHOMA
⛁ TEXAS

(CENTRAL TIME ZONE)

504	Frontage Rd, Gainesville
(503)	Parking Area (Both dir)
(502)	TX Welcome Center (SB) (RR, Phones, Picnic, Info)
501	FM 1202, Gainesville
Gas	W: Hilltop Conoco
Food	W: Hilltop Café, Applebee's, Cracker Barrel, Harper's Grill
Lodg	W: Hampton Inn
Other	E: Auto Dealer
	W: Gainesville Prime Outlets, CAMPING▲
500	FM 372, Service Rd, Gainesville
TStop	E: Hitchin Post AmBest Truck Stop/Shell (Scales), Gainesville Travel Stop/Citgo
Food	E: Rest/Hitchin Post TS, Rest/Gainesville/TS
TWash	E: Gainesville TS
TServ	E: Hitchin Post TS/Tires, Gainesville TS
Other	E: Laundry/Hitchin Post TS, Laundry/Gainesville TS
499	Frontage Rd, Service Rd (NB)
Gas	E: Exxon, Gainesville Fuel Stop
Food	E: Denny's
Lodg	E: Budget Host Inn, Bed & Bath Inn, Super 8
498A	US 82E, Summit Ave, Sherman, Wichita Falls
FStop	E: E&M Mini Market/66
TStop	E: (16mi) Whitesboro Truck Stop
Gas	E: Exxon, Shell, Valero, Murphy
Food	E: Catfish Louie's, Denny's, Golden Corral, KFC, Pizza Inn, Ranch House, Whataburger
Lodg	E: Twelve Oaks Inn, Trails Inn Motel, Wagon Inn Motel
Med	E: + Gainesville Memorial Hospital

EXIT	TEXAS
Other	E: ATMs, Banks, Auto & Tire Services, Big Lots, Dollar Tree, Enterprise RAC, Family Dollar, Grocery, Wal-Mart sc, to 14mi: Hwy 82 RV Park▲
498B	US 82W, W Summit Ave, Wichita Falls
Gas	W: Exxon◊
Lodg	W: Best Western♥, Days Inn♥, Texas Motel
Med	W: + N Texas Medical Center
Other	W: Auto Repairs, Auto Dealer, ATMs, Gainesville Muni Airport✈, Gainesville Muni Golf Course, David's RV & Trailer Park▲, 1st Choice RV's
497	Frontage Rd, Gainesville (NB access Ex #498 serv, SB access #496 serv)
496B	TX 51, California St, to Decatur
Gas	E: Chevron, Conoco, Mobil
	W: Texaco
Food	E: Burger King, Braum's, McDonald's, Starbucks, Taco Bell, Wendy's
	W: Chili's
Lodg	E: Holiday Inn, Quality Inn, Ramada Ltd
Other	E: ATMs, Banks, Auto Service, Grocery, Greyhound, Museum, Police Dept, City Park/RVDump/Camping▲
	W: Frank Buck Zoo, N Central Texas College
496A	Weaver St (NB)
495	Frontage Rd, Service Rd (SB)
494	to FM 1306, CR 218, Gainesville
(492)	Parking Area (SB)
491	Spring Creek Rd
(490)	Parking Area (NB)
489	Hockley Creek Rd (SB)
488	Frontage Rd, Hockley Crk Rd (NB)
487	FM 922, Obuch St, Valley View
FStop	W: Lucky Lady #14/Chevron
Food	W: FastFood/LuckyLady, DQ
Other	W: Auto Repairs, Bank, US Post Office
486	FM 1307, O'Brien St, Frontage Rd
485	Frontage Rd (SB ex, NB reacc)
483	FM 3002, Lone Oak Rd
Other	E: Lone Oak RV Park▲, to Ray Roberts State Park▲
482	Chisam Rd, Sanger
481	View Rd, Sanger
Other	W: Texas Sundown RV Resort▲
480	Lois Rd
479	Belz Rd, Sanger
Lodg	E: Sanger Inn
Other	E: Indian Village Campground▲
478	FM 455, Chapman Dr, Sanger, to Pilot Point, Bolivar
Gas	E: Phillips 66, Texaco
	W: Chevron
Food	E: DQ, Mexican Rest, Sonic
	W: Jack in the Box, Kirby's Rest, McDonald's, Subway
Lodg	E: Sanger Inn
Other	E: Grocery, Laundromat, Auto Repairs, Police Dept
	W: IGA, Wagon Master RV Park▲

◊ = Regular Gas Stations with Diesel   ▲ = RV Friendly Locations   ♥ = Pet Friendly Locations
RED PRINT SHOWS LARGE VEHICLE PARKING/ACCESS ON SITE OR NEARBY   BROWN PRINT SHOWS CAMPGROUNDS/RV PARKS

EXIT		TEXAS
477		Bus 35, 5th St, Keeton Rd, Sanger
	Gas	E: Phillips 66
		W: Shamrock◇
	Food	E: Mr Gatti's, No Frills Grill
	Other	E: Wal-Mart
		W: I-35 RV Center, Parkdale RV
475B		Rector Rd, Cowling Rd, Sanger
475A		FM 156, Denton, to Krum (SB)
474		Cowling TurnAround (NB)
473		FM 3163, Milam Rd, Denton
	FStop	E: Love's Travel Stop #217
	Food	E: Subway/Love's TS
	Other	E: WiFi/Love's TS
472		Ganzer Rd, Denton
471		US 77, N Elm St, to Loop 288, FM 1173, Denton, to Krum
	FStop	W: FMB/Fina
	TStop	E: Travel Center of America #104/ Conoco (Scales)
		W: Sunpower Travel Plaza (Scales)
	Food	E: Rest/FastFood/TA TC, Good Eats Grill, Red River Coffee & Bagel
		W: Rest/Sunpower TP
	Tires	E: Sunpower TS
	TWash	W: Sunpower TS
	TServ	E: TA TC/Tires
		W: Denton Truck Clinic, Sunpower TS
	Med	W: + Denton Regional Med Ctr
	Other	E: Laundry/WiFi/TA TC, Factory Stores, TX Instruments
		W: Laundry/CB/Sunpower TP, Funtime RV Sales/
470		Loop 288 (NB)
469		US 380, University Dr, Denton, to Decatur, McKinney
	FStop	W: Golden Express/Conoco
	Gas	E: Phillips 66, RaceTrac
		W: Diamond Shamrock, Shell◇
	Food	E: Catfish King, Cracker Barrel, China Town Café, McDonald's, Texas Espresso
		W: DQ, Denny's, Waffle House
	Lodg	E: Best Western
		W: Excel Inn, Howard Johnson, Motel 6♥
	Med	E: + Denton Community Hospital
		W: + Columbia Medical Center
	Other	E: Albertson's, Kmart, Auto Services, Tires, Towing
		W: to Denton Muni Airport✈
468		W Oak St, to FM 1515, Airport Rd Denton (SB)
		I-35 continues below as I-35E to Dallas
(467)		Jct I-35W, S to Ft Worth, Jct I-35E to Dallas (SB), Jct I-35N to OKC (NB)
466B		Ave D, Denton
	Gas	E: Citgo, Exxon◇
	Food	E: Burger King, IHOP, McDonald's, Pancho's Mexican Buffet
	Lodg	E: Comfort Suites
		W: Radisson
	Other	E: Univ of N TX
466A		McCormick St
	Gas	E: Phillips 66, Shell◇
		W: Citgo, Fina
	Lodg	E: Comfort Suites, Royal Hotel Suites
		W: Radisson

EXIT		TEXAS
	Med	E: + Denton Medical Clinic
	Other	W: Univ of N TX, Fouts Field
465B		US 377, Ft Worth Dr, Denton
	Gas	E: Citgo, RaceTrac, Shamrock
		W: Conoco, Phillips 66, Total
	Food	E: Kettle, Taco Bueno, Whataburger
		W: Frosty DriveN, Sonic, Taco Bell, Outback Steakhouse, Smokehouse
	Lodg	E: La Quinta Inn♥
		W: Days Inn
	Other	E: Auto Repair, Bank, Home Depot, U-Haul
		W: Grocery, RV Wurks, Post Oak Place RV Park▲
465A		FM 2181, Teasley Lane
	Gas	E: 7-11, Shell
		W: Exxon, Fina, Shell
	Food	E: Applebee's, KFC, Olive Branch Pizza, Pizza Hut
		W: Little Caesar's Pizza
	Lodg	E: Desert Sands Motor Inn, Hampton Inn
		W: Best Value Inn, Super 8
	Other	E: Grocery, N TX RV Repair
464		US 77, Dallas Dr, Denton
	Food	E: Burger King, Island Crab, Wendy's
	Lodg	E: Quality Inn
	Other	E: ATMs, Banks, Kroger, Office Depot, Wal-Mart, Golden Triangle Mall
463		Lp 288, Lillian Miller Pkwy, to McKinney
	Gas	E: Racetrac, Shell, Murphy
		W: Chevron

EXIT		TEXAS
	Food	E: Arby's, Burger King, Café China, CiCi's Pizza, Colters BBQ, Jason's Deli, Long John Silver, Wendy's
		W: Black Eyed Pea, Chili's, Jack in the Box, Luby's Cafeteria, Red Lobster, Red Pepper's Chinese, Tia's TexMex
	Other	E: ATMs, Enterprise RAC, Golden Triangle Mall, Goodyear, Kroger, Office Depot, PetCo♥, Target, Wal-Mart sc, River N Lakes RV Park▲
		W: Albertson's, FedEx Kinko's
462		State School Rd, Mayhill Rd
	Gas	E: Shell
		W: Exxon
	Food	W: Café/Exxon
	Med	E: + Denton Regional Medical Center, + N Texas Hospital
	Other	E: Explore USA RV Supercenter, U-Haul
		W: Auto Dealers, Grocery, Funtime RV Sales
461		Post Oak Dr, Shady Shores Rd
	Other	E: Auto Dealers
		W: Auto Dealers
460		Corinth St, Denton
	Gas	E: Chevron◇
	Other	E: McClains RV
459		Frontage Rd
	Food	W: Mr Brisket BBQ
	Other	W: Destiny Dallas RV Resort▲, American Eagle Harley Davidson
458		FM 2181, Swisher Rd, Teasley Ln, Frontage Rd, to Lake Dallas, Hickory Creek
	Gas	E: Circle K, Phillips 66
		W: Chevron, Exxon, Shell, Murphy
	Food	W: Burger King, ChikFilA, Jack in the Box, Mr Gatti's, McDonald's, Starbucks, Wendy's
	Lodg	E: Best Western
	Other	E: Grocery, O'Reilly Auto Parts, Rave Hickory Creek Cinemas 16, McClain's RV Superstore, to Lakeview Airport✈, Lakeview Marina
		W: Albertson's, Wal-Mart sc
457B		Denton Dr, Hundley Dr, Lake Dallas (NB)
	Gas	E: Chevron
		W: Tetco
	Food	E: Chubby Burgers, Subway
		W: Hickory Creek BBQ, McDonald's, Wendy's
457A		Frontage Rd, S Denton Dr, Hundley Dr, Lake Dallas (NB)
	Gas	E: Allsup's,
	Food	E: Papa's BBQ, Enrique's, Godfather's, Sonic, Salt & Peppers Smokehouse
	Other	E: Grocery, Police Dept
455		Garden Ridge Blvd (SB)
454B		Highland Village Rd (SB), Eagle Point Rd (NB), Garden Ridge Blvd, Lewisville
	Gas	W: Citgo
	Food	W: Wendy's
454A		FM 407, Justin Rd (SB), Jones St, Lake Park Rd (NB)
	Gas	E: Fina, Shamrock
		W: Exxon, Murphy
	Food	E: Al's Chuck Wagon
		W: McDonald's, Subway, Tx Hamburger Factory

Page 158

◇ = Regular Gas Stations with Diesel ▲ = RV Friendly Locations ♥ = Pet Friendly Locations
RED PRINT SHOWS LARGE VEHICLE PARKING/ACCESS ON SITE OR NEARBY BROWN PRINT SHOWS CAMPGROUNDS/RV PARKS

Interstate 35 N/S — TEXAS

EXIT		
	Other	E: Auto & Tire Service, Enterprise RAC, Lake Park Golf Course, **Lewisville Lake Park**▲
		W: ATMs, Auto Services, Banks, Car Wash, Grocery, **Wal-Mart**, Commercial Repair Service
453		**Service Rd, to Valley Ridge Blvd**
	Gas	W: Chevron
	Food	E: Subway
		W: Burger King
	Other	E: Enterprise RAC, Auto Dealer, **May's RVs, Buddy Gregg Motorhomes**
		W: Lowe's, Home Depot, Staples
452		**FM 1171, Main St, College Pkwy, Lewisville, to Flower Mound**
	Gas	E: Mobil, Shell
		W: Chevron, Exxon◆, Shell
	Food	E: IHOP, McDonald's, Taco Bueno
		W: ChikFilA, Golden Corral, Grandy's, McDonald's, Wendy's, Whataburger
	Lodg	E: Days Inn
		W: Baymont Inn
	Med	E: + Columbia Medical Center
	Other	E: Auto Services, ATMs, Banks, Vet♥, Pharmacy
		W: Grocery, Home Depot, Lowe's, Sam's Club, **Wal-Mart sc, Police Dept**, Auto Services, ATMs, Banks
451		**Fox Ave, Lewisville**
	Gas	E: Shell◆
		W: Chevron, Conoco◆, Shamrock
	Food	E: Braum's
		W: Black Eyed Pea, **Cracker Barrel**, El Chico
	Lodge	W: Hampton Inn, Microtel
	Other	W: Auto Services, Midas
450		**Tx Bus 121, Lakeland Plaza, to Grapevine, McKinney**
	FStop	W: **Whip n Stop**/Fina
	Gas	E: 7-11, RaceTrac
		W: Chevron, Citgo, QT, Texaco
	Food	E: BBQ, Mexican Rest
		W: Asian Seafood Buffet, Bonanza, Buddy Ray's, Burger King, Chili's, KFC, Long John Silver, McDonald's, Pancho's, Subway, Taco Bell, Waffle House
	Lodg	E: Ramada Inn, Pine Motel
		W: **Best Value Inn**, Crossroads Inn, J&J Motel, Super 8♥
	Other	E: Auto Services, Dollar General, Enterprise RAC, **Bob's RV Services**
		W: ATMs, Banks, Auto Repairs, Hertz RAC, Firestone, Kroger/**Pharmacy**, Towing
449		**Corporate Dr, Lewisville**
	Gas	E: Phillips 66
		W: Exxon
	Food	E: China Dragon, Dickeys BBQ, On the Border, Cajun Café, Hooter's
		W: Chili's, Jack in the Box, Kettle Rest
	Lodg	E: Extended Stay, Motel 6♥
		W: Best Western, InTown Suites, La Quinta Inn♥, **Sun Suites**
	Other	E: Auto & **Diesel** Repair, Cinema 10
448A		**FM 3040, Round Grove Rd, Hebron Pkwy, Lewisville**
	Gas	E: 7-11
		W: Exxon, RaceTrac, Murphy
	Food	E: ChikFilA, Chuck E Cheese, MiMi's Café, Japanese Rest, Olive Garden, Subway, Saltgrass Steak House, Souper Salad
	Food	W: Carino's, Don Pablo, IHOP, Luby's, Famous Dave's BBQ, Good Eats Grill, McDonald's, Outback Steakhouse, Panda Express, Red Lobster, Spring Creek BBQ, Romano's Macaroni Grill, TGI Friday, Tony Roma, Wendy's
	Lodg	E: Homewood Suites
		W: **Comfort Suites**, Fairfield Inn, Holiday Inn Express
	Other	E: ATMs, Banks, Auto & Tire Services, Best Buy, PetSmart♥, Target
		W: ATMs, Banks, Costco, Cinemark 12, Budget, Carwash, Circuit City, Target, Discount Tire, Office Depot, Petland♥, FedEx Kinko's, Vista Ridge Mall, **Wal-Mart sc**, Raytheon
448B		**Frontage Rd, to Spur 553. TX 121 (SB) (Access #448A Services)**
446		**Frankford Rd, Carrollton (SB)**
	Gas	E: RaceTrac, Texaco
	Food	E: Coltier's BBQ, Café, Ms Mary's Southern Cuisine
	Other	E: Auto Dealer, Auto Rental, Volvo, Indian Creek Golf Course
445B		**Pres Geo Bush Frwy/Tpke (SB)**
445		**Pres Geo Bush Frwy/Tpke (NB)**
444		**Whitlock Lane, Sandy Lake Rd, Serv Rd, Luna Rd, Old Denton Rd**
	Gas	E: Texaco
		W: Chevron
	Food	E: Taco Bell, Tommy's BBQ
		W: McDonald's
	Lodg	W: Delux Inn
	Other	E: Repair Services, Tires, Towing
		W: Sandy Lake Amusement Park, **Sandy Lake RV Park**/**RVDump**▲
443C		**Frontage Rd, Old Denton Rd, Whitlock Lane (NB) (Access #444 Serv)**
443B		**Belt Line Rd, Crosby Rd**
	Gas	E: Conoco, RaceTrac, Shell
	Food	E: Café on the Square, Chinese
	Other	E: ATMs, Banks, Albertson's, Firestone, Greyhound, NTB, Repair Services
		W: ATMs, Repair Services, **to Dr Pepper Star Center**
443A		**Service Rd, Crosby Rd (NB)**
442		**Valwood Pkwy, Dallas**
	Gas	E: Texaco
		W: Fina
	Food	E: DQ, Denny's, El Chico, Grandy's, Jack in the Box, Subway, Taco Bueno, Waffle House
	Lodg	E: Comfort Inn, Guest Inn, **Red Roof Inn**♥, Royal Inn
		W: Best Western, Days Inn
	Other	E: Auto Services, Kroger
441		**Valley View Ln, Serv Rd, Dallas**
	Gas	W: Exxon, Mobil
	Food	E: B&L Rest, Railroad China Rest
		W: Abuelo's, Michael's Cafe
	Lodg	W: Best Western, Days Inn, **Econo Lodge**, La Quinta Inn♥
(440B)		**Jct I-635E, to Garland**
(440C)		**Jct I-635W, to DFW Airport**
440A		**Forest Lane, to US 77 (NB)**
	Gas	E: Shell
	Food	E: Dickey's BBQ, Grandy's, IHOP
	Lodg	E: Courtyard, Motel 6♥
	Med	E: + RHD Memorial Medical Center
	Other	E: ATMs, Banks, Repair Services, Hertz, to Northtown Mall
439		**Royal Lane**
	Gas	E: Shell, Shamrock
		W: Chevron, Star Mart
	Food	E: Exit Café, McDonald's, Whataburger, Wendy's
		W: Cheers Diner, Jack in the Box
	Other	E: Auto Services & Repairs, Greyhound
		W: Auto Services & Repairs
438		**Walnut Hill Lane, Dallas**
	Gas	E: Fina, Mobil, Shell
		W: Chevron, Texaco◆
	Food	E: Burger King, Denny's, Chili's, Hunan Café, Old San Francisco Steak House, Steak & Ale, Porterhouse Steaks & Seafood, Taco Bell, TGI Friday, Trail Dust Steak House, Wendy's
	Lodg	E: **Comfort Inn**, Country Inn, Drury Inn, Garden Inn, Hampton Inn, Walnut Inn
	Other	E: ATMs, Banks, Auto Repairs
		W: Speed Zone
437		**Manana Dr (NB)**
436		**Lp 12, Spur 348, W Northwest Hwy, to DFW, Irving (NB ex, SB reacc)**
	Gas	E: Chevron, Exxon◆
		W: Exxon, RaceTrac
	Food	E: BlackEyed Pea, Bennigan's, Chili's, Bubba's 2, Don Pablo, IHOP, Joe's Crab Shack, Olive Garden, Outback Steak house, Papas BBQ, Pappadeaux Seafood, Pappas Bros Steakhouse, Pappasito's Cantina, Tx Land & Cattle, Waffle House
		W: Jack in the Box, McDonald's, Neno Pizza & Pasta, Thai Rice, Waffle House
	Lodg	E: **Baymont Inn**♥, Best Western, Days Inn, Comfort Suites, Hearthside Extended Stay, Quality Inn, **Radisson**
		W: Best Value Inn, Century Inn, Delux Inn
	Other	E: to Dallas Love Field✈
		W: ATMs, Auto Services, AMC 24, Grocery, Sam's Club, **to TX Stadium**
435		**Harry Hines Blvd, to W Northwest Hwy (NB ex, SB reaccess)**
	Gas	E: RaceTrac
	Food	E: Arby's
	Other	E: Repair Services, **to Dallas Love Field**✈
434B		**Regal Row, Dallas**
	Gas	E: Chevron, Fina
	Food	E: Denny's, Whataburger
	Lodg	E: **Econo Lodge**♥, La Quinta Inn♥
		W: Fairfield Inn
	Other	W: TBC Indoor Racing
434A		**Empire Central**
	Gas	E: Chevron, Tetco
		W: Exxon
	Food	E: McDonald's, Sonic, Tony's Mex Rest, Wendy's
		W: Burger King, Deli, Taco Bell
	Lodg	E: Budget Suites, Candlewood Suites, InTown Suites, **Radisson**♥, Red Roof Inn♥, Wingate Inn
	Other	E: Office Depot
433B		**Mocking Bird Lane, Dallas, Love Field Airport**
	Gas	E: Mobil, Tetco
		W: Chevron, Exxon, Shell

◆ = Regular Gas Stations with Diesel   ▲ = RV Friendly Locations   ♥ = Pet Friendly Locations

RED PRINT SHOWS LARGE VEHICLE PARKING/ACCESS ON SITE OR NEARBY   BROWN PRINT SHOWS CAMPGROUNDS/RV PARKS

INTERSTATE 35 N/S

EXIT		TEXAS
	Food	E: Jack in the Box
		W: Church's, McDonald's
	Lodg	E: Clarion Hotel, Crowne Plaza, Hawthorne Suites, Oak n Spruce Resort Club, Radisson, Residence Inn, Sheraton
	TServ	W: to Cummins Southern Plains
	Med	E: + Columbia Medical Arts Hospital, + St Paul Medical Center
	Other	E: to Dallas Love Field ✈
		W: Goodyear, Tires, U-Haul
432B		TX 356, Commonwealth Dr
	Gas	E: Texaco
	Lodg	E: Residence Inn
		W: Delux Inn
432A		Inwood Rd, Dallas
	Gas	E: Exxon
		W: Fina, Texaco
	Food	W: Whataburger
	Lodg	W: Hilton, Studio Plus
	Med	E: + SW Medical Center, + St Paul Medical Center
431		Motor St, Dallas
	Gas	E: Shell
		W: Shell
	Food	E: Denny's
		W: Ninfa's Mexican Rest
	Lodg	E: Stouffer Hotel
		W: Embassy Suites, Homewood Suites, Marriott, Wilson World Hotel
	Med	E: + Children's Medical Ctr of Dallas
	Other	E: Int'l Apparel Mart
		W: Auto Repairs & Services
430C		Wycliff Ave
	Food	E: T-Bones Steakhouse
	Lodg	E: Stouffer Hotel
		W: Hilton, Renaissance Hotel
	Other	E: Dallas Market Hall, Dallas Trade Mart, World Trade Center
430B		Market Center Blvd
	Food	W: Denny's
	Lodg	W: Quality Inn, Sheraton Suites, Wyndham Hotel
	Other	E: Dallas Trade Mart, World Trade Center
430A		Oak Lawn Ave
	Gas	E: Texaco
	Food	E: Rudy's Country Store & BBQ
429D		North Tollway (NB)
429C		Hi Line Dr, Victory Ave (NB)
	Lodg	W: Best Western
	Other	E: American Airlines Center
429B		Continental Ave
	Gas	W: Exxon
	Food	W: McDonald's, Popeye's
429A		Woodall Rogers Frwy, to I-45, to US 75, to Houston, Sherman
428E		Commerce St, Main St, Reunion Blvd, S Industrial Blvd (NB Left ex)
	Other	E: ATMs, Banks, Downtown, Museums, JFK Memorial, Greyhound, Restaurants, Hotels
		W: Dallas West MH & RV Park ▲
(428D)		Jct I-30W, Tom Landry Frwy, to Ft Worth (SB, Left exit)
428B		Industrial Blvd (SB), Jct I-30E (NB)
(428A)		Jct I-30E, to I-45S (SB, Left exit)
427C		Cadiz St, Industrial Blvd (NB)
	Other	W: to Dallas Convention Center

Personal Notes

EXIT		TEXAS
(427B)		Jct I-30E, Industrial Blvd
427A		Colorado Blvd, Dallas
426C		Jefferson Blvd
	Gas	E: Texaco
		W: Shell
426B		8th St, TX 180W
	Gas	E: Texaco
		W: Shell
	Lodg	E: Classic Motel
		W: Lasanta Motel, Sun Valley Motel
	Other	W: Auto Services
426A		Ewing Ave
	Food	E: McDonald's
	Lodg	W: Circle Inn
425C		Marsalis Ave, Ewing Ave
	Gas	E: Chevron
		W: Mobil
	Food	E: McDonald's
	Lodg	E: Dallas Inn Motel
	Other	E: Dallas Zoo & Aquarium
425B		Beckley Ave, 12th St
	Gas	W: 7-11, Exxon
425A		Zang Blvd, Beckley Ave
	Gas	W: Exxon, Shamrock, Texaco
425		W 12th St, Pembroke Ave (NB)
424		Illinois Ave, Dallas
	Gas	E: 7-11, Chevron, Shamrock
		W: Exxon
	Food	E: DQ, BBQ, KFC
		W: IHOP, Jack in the Box, Taco Bell
	Lodg	W: Oak Tree Inn
	Med	W: + Hospital

EXIT		TEXAS
	Other	W: Pharmacy, Kroger, Shopping Center
423B		Saner Ave
423A		US 67, Cleburne (SB)
422BA		Kiest Blvd, RL Thornton Fwy, to US 67 (SB)
	Gas	E: Shell
		W: Texaco
	Food	W: McDonald's
	Lodg	W: Dallas Inn
422B		Kiest Blvd, to US 67 (NB)
422A		Beckley Blvd, to Kiest Blvd, to US 67 (NB)
421B		Lp 12, W Ledbetter Dr
421A		Lp 12, E Ledbetter Dr, to Ann Arbor Ave
	Gas	E: RaceWay, Texaco
	Food	W: Luby's Cafeteria
	Lodg	E: Budget Inn, Howard Johnson, Motel 6 ♥
		W: Sunbelt Motel
420		Laureland Rd, Dallas
	Gas	W: Conoco, Mobil
	Lodg	E: Master Suite Hotel, Luxury Inn
		W: Embassy Inn, Linfield Inn
419		Camp Wisdom Rd
	Gas	E: Exxon
		W: Chevron, Shell
	Food	W: McDonald's
	Lodg	E: Oak Cliff Inn
		W: Sun Crest Inn
	Other	E: Auto Repairs & Services
(418B)		Jct I-20E, to Shreveport
(418A)		Jct I-20W, to Ft Worth
417		Wheatland Rd, Dallas (SB), Danieldale Rd, Lancaster (NB)
	Other	E: Auto Services, Truck Service
416		Wintergreen Rd, DeSoto
	Gas	W: 7-11
	Food	W: Cracker Barrel, Waffle House
	Lodg	W: Holiday Inn, Red Roof Inn ♥
	Other	E: Auto Care & Rental
		W: ATMs, Banks
415		Pleasant Run Rd, Lancaster, DeSoto
	Gas	E: Chevron, RaceTrac, Shell ◊
		W: Chevron, Exxon
	Food	E: Subway, Waffle House
		W: Burger King, El Chico, KFC, Long John Silver's, Luby's, McDonald's, Pizza Inn, On the Border, Outback Steakhouse
	Lodg	E: Great Western Inn, Royal Inn, Spanish Trails Motel
		W: Best Western
	Med	E: + Columbia Medical Center
	Other	E: Cinemark 14, CarMax, EnterpriseRAC
		W: ATMs, Banks, Enterprise RAC, Kmart, Kroger, Office Depot
414		FM 1382, Belt Line Rd, Lancaster
	Gas	W: One Stop
	Food	E: Whataburger
		W: McDonald's, Joe's Pizza
	Other	E: Wal-Mart sc
		W: Police Dept
413		Parkerville Rd, Lancaster
	Gas	W: Exxon, Total
	Food	W: Subway, Taco Bell

◊ = Regular Gas Stations with Diesel   ▲ = RV Friendly Locations   ♥ = Pet Friendly Locations
RED PRINT SHOWS LARGE VEHICLE PARKING/ACCESS ON SITE OR NEARBY   BROWN PRINT SHOWS CAMPGROUNDS/RV PARKS

EXIT		TEXAS
	Other	W: Auto Services, U-Haul
412		Bear Creek Rd, Red Oak to Glen Heights, Lancaster
	Gas	W: Shell◇
	Food	W: DQ, Jack in the Box
	Other	W: Police Dept, Dallas Hi Ho RV Park▲
411		FM 664, Ovilla Rd, Red Oak
	Gas	E: Exxon, RaceTrac
		W: Exxon, Texaco
	Food	E: Church's, McDonald's, Pizza Hut, Taco Bell, Whataburger
	Lodge	W: Howard Johnson
	Other	E: Grocery, Auto Service, Truck Service
410		Red Oak Rd, Red Oak
	TStop	E: NB Access Rd: Knox Super Stop/Shell (Scales)
	Food	E: FastFood/Knox SS, Denny's, Subway
	Lodg	E: Days Inn
	Other	W: Hilltop Travel Trailers/RVDump
408		US 77, to TX 342
406		Sterrett Rd, Waxahachie
405		FM 387, Butcher Rd, to US 77
	Gas	E: Chevron◇
404		Lofland Rd
403		US 287, to Corsicana, Ft Worth (Gas/Food/WalMart SC at 1st Exit East)
	Other	E: Auto Dealer, Civic Center
401B		US 287 Bus, FM 664, Ovilla Rd
	Food	E: Chisolm Trail Steakhouse
	Lodg	E: Best Western, Comfort Inn, Super 8
	Med	E: + Baylor Medical Center
401A		Brookside Rd, Waxahatchee
	Lodg	E: Best Value Inn, Ramada
	Other	E: TX State Hwy Patrol Post
399B		FM 1446 (SB)
399A		FM 66, Rogers St, to FM 876, FM 1446 (SB)
399		FM 66, Rogers St, to FM 876, FM 1446, Waxahachie (NB)
	Gas	E: Shamrock
		W: Chevron, Fina, Star Mart
	Lodg	E: Texas Inn Motel
	Other	E: Auto Services, Tires, Towing
		W: to Screams Amusement Park
397		US 77, Waxahachie
(392)		Ellis Co Rest Area (Both dir) (RR, Phones, Picnic, Vend, WiFi)
391		FM 329, Pecan Rd, to US 77, Forreston Rd
386		TX 34, Dale Evans Dr, Italy, Ennis
	FStop	W: Tiger Mart/Exxon (Scales)
	Gas	E: Shell◇
	Food	E: FastFood/Shell, DQ
		W: FastFood/TigerMart
	Lodg	W: Italy Inn
	Other	W: Laundry/TigerMart
384		Derrs Chapel Rd, Italy
381		FM 566, Water St, Crossmain St, Milford Rd, Milford
377		FM 934, Hillsboro
374		FM 2959, Carl's Corner
	TStop	W: Carl's Corner Truck Stop (Scales)
	Food	W: Rest/Carl's

EXIT		TEXAS
	Other	W: Laundry/Carl's
(371)		Jct I-35W, to Ft Worth, Jct I-35S, to Austin, Jct I-35E, to Dallas
(85A)		Jct I-35E, to Dallas, Jct I-35N, to OKC
		I-35E continues above thru Dallas
		I-35W continues below thru Ft Worth
84		FM 1515, Bonnie Brae St
	Med	E: + Denton Community Hospital
82		FM 2449, to Ponder
79		Crawford Rd
76		FM 407, Argyle, to Justin
	Gas	W: Phillips 66
	Other	W: Corral City RV Park▲
(75)		Parking Area (Both dir)
74		FM 1171, to Lewisville, Flower Mound
70		TX 114, to Dallas, Bridgeport
	Gas	E: Texaco
	Other	E: to Dallas/Ft Worth Airport✈, Northlake Village RV Park▲
		W: to Texas Motor Speedway
68		Eagle Pkwy
	Other	W: Airport✈
67		Alliance Blvd
66		Keller-Haslet Rd, Westport Pkwy, Haslet
	Gas	W: Mobil◇
	Food	W: Cactus Flower Café, Bryan's Smoke House, Subway
	Lodg	E: Hampton Inn
65		TX 170E, Ft Worth, Keller
	TStop	E: Pilot Travel Center #434 (Scales)
	Food	E: Rest/McDonald's/Subway/Pilot TC
	Other	E: Laundry/WiFi/RVDump/Pilot TC, Cabela's/RVDump
64		Golden Triangle Blvd, to Keller Hicks Rd
63		Park Glen Blvd, Heritage Trace
61		N Tarrant Pkwy
(60)		Jct US 287N, US 81N, to Decatur
(59)		Jct I-287S, I-35W, to Denton (fr SB)
58		Western Center Blvd
	Gas	E: 7-11, Texaco
	Food	E: BlackEyed Pea, Chili's, Denny's, Saltgrass Steakhouse, On the Border, Shady Oak BBQ, Wendy's
		W: Joe's Crab Shack, Starbucks
	Lodg	E: Best Western
(57B)		Jct I-820E
(57A)		Jct I-820W, Melody Hills Dr
(56B)		Jct I-820E (NB)
56A		Meacham Blvd, Ft Worth
	Gas	E: Shell
		W: Mobil
	Food	W: Cracker Barrel, McDonald's
	Lodg	E: Comfort Inn, La Quinta Inn♥

EXIT		TEXAS
	Lodg	W: Holiday Inn
	Other	E: McClains RV/
55		Pleasantdale Ave (NB)
54C		33rd St, Long Ave (NB)
	Gas	W: Circle K, Conoco◇, Valero
	Lodg	W: Motel 6
	TServ	E: Kenworth Cummins Southern Plains, Tarrant Truck Repair
		W: Ft Worth Gear & Axle
	Med	E: + Medical Clinic
54B		TX 183W, Papurt St
	Lodg	E: Motel 6
54A		TX 183E, NE 28th St, Ft Worth
	FStop	W: Super Lady #2/Fina (Scales)
54		TX 183, Ft Worth
	TStop	W: PTP/Drivers Travel Mart #412 (Scales)
	Food	W: FastFood/Drivers TM
53		North Side Dr, Yucca Ave
	Gas	E: Shell
52E		Carver St (NB)
52D		Carver St, Pharr St (NB)
52C		Pharr St
	Gas	W: Texaco
	TServ	W: Freightliner, Southwest Int'l, CAT, Cummins
52B		US 377N, Belknap St
52A		US 377N, TX 121, Belknap St
(51A)		I-30E to Abilene, (fr NB)
51		Spur 280, Downtown Ft Worth
(50CA)		Jct I-30, US 287S, US 377S, to Dallas, Abilene
	TServ	W: DARR Power Systems
50B		TX 180E (NB)
49B		Rosedale St
	Med	W: + Hospital
49A		Allen St, Rosedale St (NB)
	Gas	E: Shell
	Med	W: + Hospital
48B		Morning Side Dr (SB)
48A		Berry St
	Gas	E: Chevron, Citgo
		W: RaceTrac
	Food	E: McDonald's
	Other	E: Grocery
		W: U-Haul
47		Ripy St
	Lodg	W: Metro Inn South
46B		Seminary Dr
	Gas	E: RaceTrac
		W: Exxon, Texaco
	Food	E: Grandy's, Jack in the Box, Long John Silver's, Sonic, Taco Bell, Whataburger
		W: Denny's, IHOP, Wendy's
	Lodg	E: Days Inn, Delux Inn, Super 7 Inn
	Med	W: + Seminary South Medical Clinic
	Other	W: Firestone, Grocery, Pharmacy
46A		Felix St (NB)
	Gas	E: Mobil
	Food	E: Pulido's Mexican
		W: Burger King, McDonald's
	Lodg	E: South Oaks Motel
(45B)		Jct I-20E, to Dallas
(45A)		Jct I-20W, to Abilene

◇ = Regular Gas Stations with Diesel   ▲ = RV Friendly Locations   ♥ = Pet Friendly Locations

RED PRINT SHOWS LARGE VEHICLE PARKING/ACCESS ON SITE OR NEARBY   BROWN PRINT SHOWS CAMPGROUNDS/RV PARKS

EXIT		TEXAS
44		Altamesa Blvd
	Gas	W: Citgo
	Food	W: Waffle House
	Lodg	E: Holiday Inn
		W: Motel 6 ♥, South Loop Motel
43		Sycamore School Rd
	Gas	W: Exxon
	Food	W: Jack in the Box, Subway, Taco Bell
	Other	E: Miller Brewing Co
		W: Home Depot
42		Everman Pky, Sycamore Schl Rd
	FStop	E: QT #873 (Scales)
	Gas	E: Exxon
	Food	E: Deli/QT
41		Risinger Rd, Ft Worth
	Other	W: McClains RV/Camping World
40		Garden Acres Dr, Ft Worth
	TStop	E: Love's Travel Stop #281
	Food	E: Subway/Love's TS
	Lodg	E: Microtel
	Med	E: + Hospital
	Other	E: WiFi/RVDump/Love's TS, Happy Camper RV Center
		W: Fun Time RV Center
39		FM 1187, McAllister Rd, Rendon-Crowley Rd
	Gas	W: Citgo, Diamond Shamrock
	Food	W: Taco Bell, Waffle House
	Lodg	W: Howard Johnson
	Med	E: + Hospital
38		Alsbury Blvd, Burleson
	Gas	E: Chevron, Mobil◊
		W: Citgo, Racetrac
	Food	E: Chili's, Cracker Barrel, McDonald's, Old Country Steak House, On the Border
		W: Arby's, Applebee's, Burger King, Denny's, Donuts Plus, Pancho's, Olive Garden, Red Lobster, Taco Cabana
	Lodg	E: Holiday Inn Express, Super 8
	Med	W: + Medical Clinic
	Other	E: Lowe's
		W: Albertson's, Best Buy, Kmart, PetSmart ♥, Staples
37		TX 174, Wilshire Blvd, Cleburne (SB) (Access Ex #36 Serv)
	Gas	W: Exxon, Shell
	Other	W: Wal-Mart sc
36		Spur 50, FM 3391, TX 174S, Renfro St, Burleson
	Gas	E: Citgo, Mobil
		W: Chevron, Fina
	Food	E: Luby's, Sonic, Waffle House
	Lodg	E: Comfort Suites, Days Inn
	TServ	E: Prestige Trucks
34		Briaroaks Rd, Hidden Creek Pkwy (SB)
	Other	W: Mockingbird Hill RV Park▲
(33)		Johnson Co Rest Area (Both dir) (RR, Phones, Picnic, WiFi)
32		Bethesda Rd, Brier Oaks Rd
	Gas	E: Citgo, Valero
	Food	E: Rest/Five Star Inn
	Lodg	E: Five Star Inn
	Other	E: RV Ranch of S Ft Worth▲
		W: Elk Horn RV Lodge▲, Mockingbird Hill RV Park▲
30		FM 917, Joshua, Burleson, Mansfield
	FStop	E: KC Ranch House/Shell
	Gas	W: Fina

EXIT		TEXAS
	Food	W: Rest/KC Ranch House
	TServ	E: AAA Truck Parts & Service, Quality Truck Service & Supplies
	Other	W: Elk Horn RV Lodge▲, Smith's RV Center
27		FM707, FM 604
	Other	E: Ancira RV Center
26B		Bus 35W, Alvarado (SB)
26A		US 67, Cleburne, Dallas
	Gas	E: Citgo, Chevron, Exxon, Texaco
	Food	E: Pop's Honey Fried Chicken/Citgo
	Other	W: RV Ranch of Cleburne
24		FM 1706, FM 3136, Maple Ave, Alvarado
	TStop	E: Alvarado Shell Travel Plaza
	Gas	E: Chevron, Conoco
	Food	E: Rest/Alvarado TP, Alvarado House
21		FM 2258 Barnesville Rd, to Greenfield
17		FM 2258
16		TX 81S, FM 201, Grandview
15		FM 916, Grandview, Maypearl
	Gas	W: Mobil, Shamrock
12		FM 67
8		FM 66, Itasca
	W:	Parking Area
	FStop	E: Stars & Stripes/Shamrock
	TStop	W: Handy Plus/Citgo
	Food	E: Rest/Stars & Stripes

EXIT		TEXAS
7		FM 934
	E:	Parking Area
	Gas	W: Exxon
3		FM 2959, Hillsboro Airport
		I-35W above is thru Ft Worth.
	NOTE:	I-35SB continues below.
(371)		Jct I-35E, N to Dallas, Jct I-35S to Austin Jct I-35W, to Fort Worth
370		US 77N, Spur 579, Hillsboro
	Other	W: to Hillsboro Muni Airport ✈
368B		FM 286, Old Brandon Rd, Service Rd, TX 22 (SB)
	Gas	W: Exxon, Shamrock◊
	Food	E: Lone Star Steakhouse, Taco Bell, Wendy's
	Food	W: DQ, McDonald's, Pizza Hut
	Lodg	W: Best Western, Comfort Inn
	Med	W: + Hospital
	Other	E: Prime Outlets Mall
		W: Repair Services & Wrecker
368A		TX 22, TX 171, FM 286, Hillsboro, to Whitney, Corsicana
	FStop	W: Quix'n/Shell
	TStop	E: Love's Travel Stop #231 (Scales)
	Gas	E: 7-11
		W: Chevron, Exxon, Mobil
	Food	E: ChestersGr/Subway/Love's TS, Arby's, BlackEyed Pea, Burger King, Chinese Buffet, Golden Corral, Grandy's, IHOP, McDonald's, Starbucks
		W: DQ, Jack in the Box, KFC, Whataburger
	Lodg	E: Holiday Inn Express, Motel 6 ♥
		W: Best Western, Thunderbird Motel
	Other	E: Laundry/WiFi/Love's TS
		W: Wal-Mart sc, Auto Dealers
367		FM 3267, Old Bynum Rd
364B		TX 81N, Hillsboro (fr NB, Left ex)
364A		FM 310, Hillsboro
	FStop	W: Knox Fuel Stop (Scales)
	Gas	E: Conoco, Exxon◊
	Food	W: El Conquistador
362		Chatt Rd, Hillsboro
359		FM 1304, Hillsboro
	TStop	W: Sunmart #169/Mobil
	Food	W: FastFood/Sunmart
	Twash	W: Abbott Truck Wash
	Other	W: Laundry/Sunmart
t358		FM 1232, FM 1242E, CR 2341, Abbott
	Gas	E: Exxon
	Food	E: Cafe
356		CR 3102, Abest Rd
355		County Line Rd, Russels Dr, West
	Other	E: Waco North KOA▲
354		Marable St
	Other	E: Waco North KOA▲
353		FM 2114, Oak St, West
	Gas	E: Citgo, Fina, Shell
		W: Citgo◊, Exxon
	Food	E: DQ, Jerry's Chicken Shack, Pizza House, Subway

Page 162   ◊ = Regular Gas Stations with Diesel   ▲ = RV Friendly Locations   ♥ = Pet Friendly Locations
RED PRINT SHOWS LARGE VEHICLE PARKING/ACCESS ON SITE OR NEARBY   BROWN PRINT SHOWS CAMPGROUNDS/RV PARKS

EXIT		TEXAS
351		FM 1858, West
349		Wiggins Rd, West
347		FM 3149, Tours Rd
346		Ross Rd, Elm Mott, Ross
	TStop	E: Ross Truck Stop/Shell
		W: Will's Petro Stop/Exxon
	Food	E: Rest/FastFood/Ross TS
		W: Rest/Will's PS
	Other	E: Laundry/Ross TS
		W: I-35 RV Park▲
(345)		Parking Area (Both dir)
345		Old Dallas Rd, Hilltop St
	Other	W: I-35 RV Park▲ , Marek Truck Repair
343		FM 308, Elm Mott Dr, Elm Mott
	TStop	E: Ed's Truck Stop/Shell (Scales)
	Gas	E: Exxon, Fina◊
		W: Chevron◊
	Food	E: Rest/FastFood/Ed's TS, DQ/Exxon, Junction Café, Eddie Ray's Smokehouse
		W: Dee's Donut Shop
	TWash	E: Ed's TS
	TServ	E: Ed's TS
	Other	E: Laundry/Ed's TS
342B		US 77S Bus, Waco
	Other	W: North Crest RV Park▲
342A		FM 2417, Crest Dr, Waco
	Gas	W: Exxon, Shamrock
	Food	W: DQ
341		Craven Ave, to Lacy, Lakeview
	Gas	E: Chevron
		W: BP, Shell
	Lodg	W: Interstate North Motel
	Other	W: North Crest RV Park▲
340		Meyers Lane (NB)
339		Lp 340, Lake Shore Dr, Waco, to TX 6S, FM 3051, Lake Waco
	Gas	E: Shamrock◊, Valero
		W: Chevron, Citgo, Phillips 66
	Food	E: Domino's, Jack in the Box, Luby's, Pizza Hut, Sonic, Whataburger
		W: Burger King, Cracker Barrel, KFC, McDonald's, Papa John's, Starbucks
	Lodg	E: Country Inn Suites
		W: Hampton Inn, Kings Way, Knight's Inn
	Other	E: Auto Service, Dollar General, Sam's Club, Wal-Mart sc, to Concord RV Park▲
338		Behren's Cr, Waco (SB)
	FStop	E: K's Travel Center #3/Shell
338B		Behrens Circle, Bell Mead (NB)
	Gas	E: Shell
		W: Texaco◊
	Lodg	W: Days Inn, Knights Inn, Motel 6♥
338A		US 84, to TX 31, Waco Dr, Bell Mead , Waco
	Gas	E: Fina
		W: Shell
337		US 84, to TX 31, Waco Dr
	Other	W: to Shady Rest RV Park▲
337B		US 77N Bus (NB)
337A		US 77S Bus (NB)
336		Forrest St, Waco (NB)
335C		MLK Jr Blvd, Lake Brazos Dr
	Gas	E: Texaco
	Food	E: River Café, Mickey's

EXIT		TEXAS
	Lodg	E: River Place Inn, Holiday Inn
		W: Travel Inn
	Med	W: + Hospital
335B		FM 434, University Parks Dr, Fort Fischer
	Food	E: IHOP, Quiznos
		W: Arby's, Jack in the Box
	Lodg	E: Best Western
		W: Clarion, Lexington Inn
	Other	E: Baylor Univ, Museums
335A		4th St, 5th St
	Gas	E: Exxon, Texaco
		W: BP, Shamrock
	Food	E: Denny's, IHOP, Pizza Hut
		W: Fazoli's, McDonald's, Taco Bell
	Lodg	E: Best Western, La Quinta Inn♥
		W: Clarion Hotel
	Other	E: Baylor Univ
334B		8th St (NB) US 77S, 17th St, 18th St
	FStop	W: K's Travel Center/Shell
	Gas	E: Exxon
	Food	E: Denny's, Pizza Hut, Shoney's
		W: Long John Silver's, Pizza Inn, Sonic, Taco Bell, McDonald's
	Lodg	E: Best Western, La Quinta Inn♥
		W: Quality Inn
334		US 77S, 18th St, 17th St
	Gas	E: BP, Chevron, Mobil
		W: Phillips 66, Texaco
	Food	E: Burger King, Popeye's, Vitex
		W: DQ
	Lodg	E: Comfort Inn, Super 8
333A		US 77, Lp 396, La Salle Ave, Valley Mills Rd Dr, Waco
	Gas	E: Chevron
		W: RaceTrac, Valero
	Food	E: El Chico, Waco Elite Café, Texas Roadhouse, Oasis Cafe
		W: Burrito King, Catfish King, DQ, Jack in the Box, Sonic
	Lodg	E: Lone Star Motel, Motel 6♥
		W: Comfort Inn, Mardi Gras Motel
	TServ	W: Volvo, Freightliner
	Other	E: Auto Services
		W: Auto Services
331		New Rd, Waco
	TStop	W: Flying J Travel Plaza #5089 (Scales)
	Gas	E: Chevron
		W: Valero
	Food	W: Rest/FastFood/FJ TP
	Lodg	E: New Road Inn, Rodeway Inn
		W: Quality Inn
	Other	W: Laundry/WiFi/RVDump/LP/FJ TS, Harley Davidson
330		TX 6, TX 340, Meridian, Robinson
	FStop	W: 1miW Tx 6: CEFCO #41/Shell
	Gas	E: Chevron
		W: Citgo
	Food	W: FastFood/CEFCO, McDonald's, Outback Steakhouse
	Lodg	E: New Road Inn
		W: Fairfield Inn
	TServ	W: DARR Power Systems
	Other	W: Best Buy, Lowe's, Wal-Mart sc, to Quail Crossing RV Park▲
328		FM 2063, Sun Valley Dr, FM 2113, Moody, Hewitt, Robinson
	TStop	E: Pilot Travel Center #432 (Scales)
	Gas	W: Diamond Shamrock, Texaco
	Food	E: FastFood/Pilot TC, DQ, McDonald's, Pizza Hut
	Other	E: Laundry/WiFi/RVDump/Pilot TC

EXIT		TEXAS
325		FM 3148, Old Temple Rd, Robinson Rd, Hewitt
	TStop	W: TJ's Truck Stop, Ceejay/Shell
	Food	W: Rest/Ceejay
	Other	W: Walkabout RV Center
323		FM 2837W, Lorena (SB)
	Gas	W: Conoco
	Food	W: Pizza House
	Other	W: One Way Auto & Diesel Service
322		FM 2837E, Lorena
	Gas	E: Phillips 66◊
		W: Chevron◊
319		Woodlawn Rd, Bruceville
(318)		Parking Area (Both dir)
318B		Bruceville (SB)
318A		Frontage Rd, Bruceville
315		TX 7, FM 107, Eddy, to Moody, Chilton
	TStop	W: CEFCO #47/Shell
	Food	W: FastFood/CEFCO
	Other	W: Bruceville Eddy RV Park▲ , to Mother Neff State Park▲
314		Blevins Rd, Chilton
311		Big Elm Rd, Troy
	Other	W: All American RV Center
308		FM 935, Troy
	Gas	E: Shell
		W: Exxon
	Food	E: BBQ, Mexican Rest, Starbucks
	Other	W: All American RV Center
306		FM 1237, Troy, to Pendleton
	TStop	W: Love's Travel Stop #232
	Food	W: Subway/Love's TS
	TServ	W: All American Diesel & Tire
	Other	W: WiFi/RVDump/Love's TS, Temple RV Park & Sales▲
305		Berger Rd, Temple
	TStop	W: Truckers Heaven (Scales)
	Food	W: FastFood/Truckers Heaven
	Tires	W: Truckers Heaven
	TWash	W: Truckers Heaven
	Other	W: Laundry/Truckers Heaven, Temple RV Park & Sales▲
304		Lp 363, Dodgen Loop, Temple
	TStop	W: CEFCO #48/Shell (Scales)
	Gas	W: Diamond Shamrock◊
	Food	W: Wendy's/CEFCO
	Other	W: Laundry/CEFCO
303		Spur 290, N 3rd St, Temple (SB)
303B		Spur 290, Bellair N, Mayborn Civic & Conv Center (NB)
303A		Spur 290, FM 1143, Industrial Blvd, N 3rd St (NB)
	Gas	E: Diamond Shamrock
	Food	E: Fat Daddy's Rest, Jessie's Rest
	Lodg	E: Texas Inn
302		Nugent Ave, Frontage Rd, to TX 53, Temple
	Gas	E: EZ Way, Exxon◊, Texaco◊
		W: BP◊, Chevron
	Food	W: Denny's
	Lodg	E: Comfort Inn, Econo Lodge, Holiday Inn
		W: Days Inn, Motel 6♥, Stratford House
	Other	E: ATMs, Bank, Auto Services
		W: Auto Dealers

◊ = Regular Gas Stations with Diesel   ▲ = RV Friendly Locations   ♥ = Pet Friendly Locations

RED PRINT SHOWS LARGE VEHICLE PARKING/ACCESS ON SITE OR NEARBY   BROWN PRINT SHOWS CAMPGROUNDS/RV PARKS

INTERSTATE 35 N/S

EXIT	TEXAS
301	**TX 53, TX 36, FM 2305, Central Ave, Adams Ave, Temple**
Gas	E: Diamond Shamrock, Texaco
	W: Valero
Food	E: Arby's, KFC, Long John Silver, McDonald's, Starbucks, Subway, Taco Bell, Wendy's
	W: Catfish Shack
Lodg	E: La Quinta Inn ♥
	W: Best Western
Other	E: ATMs, Auto Services, Firestone, HEB, Museum, Amtrak
	W: ATMs, Auto Services, Albertson's, Auto Dealers, Bell Co Harley Davidson to Cedar Ridge Park▲/Belton Lake, to Draughon-Miller Central Tx Regl Airport✈
300	**Ave H, 49th - 57th Streets, Temple**
Gas	E: Shell, Texaco
	W: Shell
Food	E: Mexican Rest, TJ's Burgers
Lodg	E: Oasis Motel, Temple Inn
	W: Westerner Motel
Other	E: ATMs, Auto Services, CarWash, Nick's Camper Sales, U-Haul
299	**US 190E, TX 36, Loop 363, Gatesville, Cameron**
Gas	E: Shell, Texaco◊
	W: Exxon, Texaco
Food	E: Doyle Phillips Steak House, Jack in the Box, Mexican Rest, Oldies Cafe
	W: Burger King, Chili's, IHOP, Luby's
Lodg	E: Best Value Inn, Budget Inn
Med	E: + Scott & White Memorial Hospital
Other	E: Kmart
	W: Auto Dealers, Ancira Motorhomes, U-Haul
298	**Frontage Rd (NB)**
297	**FM 817, Midway Dr, Temple**
Gas	E: Citgo
	W: Shamrock
Food	E: Mexican Grill
Lodg	E: Classic Inn Motel, Super 8
Other	E: Family RV Sales, Animal Clinic ♥,
	W: Auto Dealer
294	**FM 93, 6th Ave, Belton**
294B	**FM 93, 6th Ave, Belton**
Gas	E: Texaco◊
Food	E: McDonald's
	W: Old Time Pit BBQ, Pizza Hut, Sonic, Southwinds Rest, Taco Bell, Whataburger
Lodg	W: Best Inns, River Forest Inn
TServ	E: Santana's Truck Shop, McGuire Truck & Auto Repair
Other	W: to DS Glory Summer Fun USA, Univ of Mary Hardin Baylor
294A	**Lp 253, Central Ave, Downtown**
Gas	W: Shell◊
Food	W: Burger King, Bobby's Burgers, Pizza Plus, Old Time Pit BBQ, Sonic
Lodg	W: Ramada Inn
Other	W: Auto Zone, Auto Services, Goodyear
293B	**TX 317, Main St, FM 436, US 190 (SB)**
293A	**US 190W, TX 317, FM 436, to Killeen, Fort Hood (NB)**
TStop	E: CEFCO #54/Shamrock
Gas	E: Fina
	W: Mobil

EXIT	TEXAS
Food	E: FastFood/CEFCO
	W: Blimpie/Mobil
Lodg	E: Budget Host
Other	W: Belton/Temple/Killeen KOA▲
292	**Loop 121, Belton (Access to Ex #293A Serv)**
Other	W: Belton/Temple/Killeen KOA▲
290	**Shanklin Rd, Belton**
Other	W: Belton/Temple/Killeen KOA▲, Picnic Area
289B	**Frontage Rd (NB)**
289A	**Tahuaya Rd, Salado**
287	**Amity Rd, Salado**
286	**FM 2484, FM 1670, Salado**
Other	W: to Union Grove Park▲/Stillhouse Hollow Lake
285	**FM 2268, Salado**
Gas	E: Conoco
	W: Chevron
Food	E: Subway
	W: Cowboys BBQ
284	**Thomas Arnold Rd**
Gas	E: Exxon
	W: Texaco
Food	E: Burger King/Exxon
	W: DQ
Lodg	E: Stagecoach Inn
	W: Super 8
283	**FM 2268, to FM 2843, Salado**
282	**FM 2115, FM 2843, Salado**
TStop	E: 2mi S: JD's Travel Center/Shamrock
Food	E: Rest/JD's TC
TServ	E: JD's TC/Tires,Lube&Oil
Other	E: Wagon Wheel RV Park▲
(282)	**Bell Co Rest Area (SB)** (RR, Phones, Picnic, Vend, WiFi)
(281)	**Bell Co Rest Area (NB)** (RR, Phones, Picnic, Vend, WiFi)
280	**Frontage Rd, Prairie Dell**
279	**Frontage Rd, Hill Rd, Salado**
277	**Yankee Rd**
275	**FM 487, Jarrell, to Florence, Bartlett**
TStop	E: PTP/Doc's One Stop/Shamrock (Scales)
Gas	E: Exxon◊
	W: Shell
Food	E: Rest/Doc's One Stop
Other	E: WiFi/Doc's OS, Riley's Wrecker Service
271	**Theon Rd, Jarrell**
FStop	W: Texas Star Station #166/Shell
Food	W: FastFood/Texas Star
Other	E: ExploreUSA RV Supercenter
268	**FM 972, Georgetown, Walburg**
Other	E: Crestview RV
266	**TX 195, Georgetown, to Florence, Killeen**
TStop	E: Sunmart #168/Mobil
Gas	W: Exxon
Food	E: FastFood/Sunmart
Other	E: Berry Springs RV Park▲, New Life RV Park▲
264	**Bus 35, TX 418, Lakeway Dr, Georgetown**
Other	E: Auto & Repair Services,

Page 164

◊ = Regular Gas Stations with Diesel ▲ = RV Friendly Locations ♥ = Pet Friendly Locations
RED PRINT SHOWS LARGE VEHICLE PARKING/ACCESS ON SITE OR NEARBY   BROWN PRINT SHOWS CAMPGROUNDS/RV PARKS

INTERSTATE 35 N/S — TEXAS

EXIT		Details
	Other	E: Berry Springs RV Park▲, New Life RV Park▲, San Gabriel River RV Camp Resort▲, East View RV Ranch▲ W: Georgetown Muni Airport✈
262		**RM 2338, Andice Rd, Georgetown Lake Georgetown**
	Gas	E: Shamrock W: Exxon, Phillips 66, RaceTrac
	Food	E: KFC, Luby's, McDonald's, Pizza Hut, NY Burrito Wraps, Sonic W: Chuck Wagon, DQ, Georgetown BBQ, Hardee's, Riverview Steakhouse, Taco Bueno, Wendy's, Whataburger
	Lodg	E: Comfort Suites, Holiday Inn Express W: Days Inn, La Quinta Inn ♥
	Other	E: Albertson's, ATMs, Auto Services, Enterprise RAC, Towing, UPS Store W: ATMs, Banks, Auto Services, Grocery, Wrecker Service
261A		**RM 2338, Williams Dr, Andice Rd, Lk Georgetown** (Acc to #262 Serv)
	Other	E: Crestview RV, San Gabriel River RV Camp Resort▲
261		**TX 29, W University Ave, Serv Rd Georgetown, to Taylor, Burnet**
	Gas	E: Chevron, Mobil, Shell W: Chevron
	Food	E: Applebee's, Burger King, Chili's, Harry's BBQ, Rio Bravo
	Lodg	E: Red Poppy Inn
	Med	E: + Georgetown Hospital
	Other	E: ATMs, Banks, Auto Services, Family Dollar, Golf Course, Grocery, Sheriff Dept, Wrecker Service, Southwestern University, Country Tyme RV Center, East View RV Ranch▲, to Shady River RV Resort▲ W: Best Buy, Home Depot, Office Depot, Target
260		**RM 2243, Leander Rd, to Bus 35, Georgetown to Leander**
	Gas	E: Jiffy Mart #2 W: Chevron, Tetco, Speedy Stop
	Food	W: Café, Jack in the Box, Pizza, Mexican
	Lodg	W: Holiday Inn, Quality Inn
	Med	E: + Georgetown Hospital
	Other	E: Auto Services, Georgetown Diesel & Auto Repair, Tires, Trailer Service W: to 8mi Sunshine RV Park▲
259		**Bus 35, Austin Ave, Georgetown**
	Other	E: East View RV Ranch▲ W: RV Outlet Mall, to Inter space Caverns
257		**Westinghouse Rd, Frontage Rd**
	Other	E: Auto Dealers W: Walkabout RV
(256)		**Rest Area (SB)** (RR, Phones, Picnic, Vend)
256		**FM 1431, CR 114, Chandler Rd, Round Rock**
(255)		**Rest Area (NB)** (RR, Phones, Picnic, Vend)
254		**Lp 35, FM 3406, Old Settlers Blvd, Round Rock**
	Gas	E: 7-11, Chevron, Texaco W: Phillips 66, Shell
	Food	E: Arby's, Castaways Seafood, Lone Star Café, McDonald's, Sonic, Subway W: Carino's, Cracker Barrel,
	Food	W: Denny's, Golden Corral, Good Eats Café, Kona Ranch Steak & Seafood, Rudy's Country Store, Saltgrass Steakhouse,
	Lodg	E: Best Western W: Courtyard, Hilton Garden Inn, La Quinta Inn ♥, Holiday Inn, Red Roof Inn ♥, Springhill Suites
	Med	E: + Round Rock Health Clinic
	Other	E: Auto Dealers, Cinemark 8, Firestone, Enterprise RAC, Fleetpride, Tires, Vet ♥ W: Albertson's, ATMs, Auto Dealer, Auto Services & Repairs
253		**US 79, Palm Valley Blvd, Sam Bass Rd, to Old Settlers Blvd, Round Rock to Austin, Taylor**
	Gas	E: Phillips 66◆, Shell, Shamrock W: Exxon◆, Shell◆
	Food	E: Arby's, DQ, Damon's, KFC, Lone Star Café, Lonesome Dove W: K-Bob's Steakhouse, Mexican & Seafood Grill, Joe's Smokehouse, Popeye's, Roadhouse Grill
	Lodg	E: Best Western, Wingate Inn W: Country Inn, Super 8
	Other	E: ATMs, Auto Services, Banks, Rental Cars, Police Dept, to Bullard's RV Park▲ W: Auto Services, US Post Office
252B		**RM 620, Frontage Rd**
	Gas	W: 7-11, BP
	Food	W: IHOP, Japanese Rest, McDonald's, Starbucks, Wendy's
	Other	W: Albertson's, Auto Services, Mall, Wholesale Tire
252A		**McNeil Rd, Frontage Rd**
	Gas	E: Shell◆ W: Fina, Phillips 66
	Food	E: Outback Steakhouse, Whataburger W: McDonald's, Wendy's
	Lodge	E: Days Inn, Candlewood Suites
	Other	E: ATMs, Banks, Auto Services, Tires W: Albertson's, Adventure Time RV Rentals
251		**Loop 35, Round Rock**
	Gas	W: Exxon, Texaco
	Food	E: Chili's, McDonald's, Outback Steak house, Souper Salad, Whataburger W: Burger King, Jack in the Box, Luby's
	Lodg	E: Residence Inn W: Country Inn, Days Inn
	Other	E: Big Lots, Auto Services W: Albertson's, NTB, Walgreen's
250		**FM 1325, L Henna Blvd, Austin**
	Gas	E: Chevron, Mobil W: Shell
	Food	E: Applebee's, Chili's, Jason's Deli, Joe's Crab Shack, McDonald's, Subway W: Chuck E Cheese, Hardee's, Hooters, Olive Garden
	Lodg	E: Hampton Inn W: Baymont Inn, Hilton, Pinnacle Suites
	Other	E: Best Buy, Discount Tire, Home Depot, FedEx Kinko's, Goodyear, Target, Wal-Mart sc W: ATMs, FedEx Kinko's, Lowe's, Office Depot, Sam's Club, Youngblood Tire & Auto, Austin RV Park North▲, Blessing MH & RV Park▲
248		**Grand Ave Pkwy, Pflugerville**
	FStop	E: 7701 N Gr Ave: Tex Con Oil/Shell FM 1825SE: Speedy Stop #248
	Gas	E: RaceTrac, Shamrock W: Chevron
	Food	E: FastFood/Speedy Stop W: McDonald's
	Lodg	W: Budget Suites
	Other	W: Auto Services, Fleet Service
247		**FM 1825, Pflugerville**
	FStop	E: FM 1825SE: Speedy Stop #248
	Gas	E: RaceTrac W: Exxon, Shell
	Food	E: Jack in the Box, Sonic, Wendy's W: KFC, Miller BBQ, Whataburger
	Lodg	W: Budget Suites, Quality Inn
	Other	E: Firestone, Cinema, HEB W: Diesel Tech, Goodyear
246		**Dessau Rd, Howard Lane, Austin**
	Gas	E: Shell◆, Texaco W: Diamond Shamrock
	Food	E: IHOP, Whataburger
	Other	E: Home Depot, AAA Truck & Trailer W: Auto Services, Wal-Mart sc, Smokey's RV Repair
245		**FM 734, Parmer Lane, Yager Ln**
	Gas	W: 7-11, Exxon
	Food	E: Bennigan's, Carino's, ChickFilA, Moe SW Grill, Panda Express, Subway
	Lodg	W: Residence Inn, Springhill Suites
	Other	E: Best Buy, Target
244		**Frontage Rd, Yager Lane, Austin**
243		**Braker Lane, Frontage Rd**
	Gas	E: Shamrock W: Texaco◆
	Food	E: Jack in the Box, Subway, Whataburger W: Sweetie Pies, Taste of Brazil
	Lodg	W: Austin Motor Inn, Walnut Forest Motel
	Other	E: Central TX Harley Davidson W: Albertson's, Auto Services, to IBM, Univ of TX/JJ Pickle Ctr
241		**Rundberg Lane**
	Gas	E: Exxon, Shamrock W: Chevron, Conoco, RaceTrac, Shell
	Food	E: Golden Corral, Jack in the Box, Pizza, Mr Catfish, Mexican Rest
	Lodg	E: Ramada Inn, Wellesley Inn W: Austin Village Motor Inn, Budget Inn, Budget Lodge, Economy Inn, Motel 6 ♥, Red Roof Inn ♥
	Other	E: Albertson's, Wal-Mart sc, U-Haul, TX Starter Service W: Auto Services, Grocery
240A		**US 183, Service Rd, Anderson Ln, to Lampasas, Lockhart**
	Gas	E: Exxon W: Chevron, Star Mart
	Food	E: Chili's, DQ, Jack in the Box, Old San Francisco Steak House W: Cancun Mexican Rest, McDonald's, Red Lobster
	Lodg	E: Days Inn, Hampton Inn, Wellesley Inn W: Best Western, Econo Lodge ♥, Red Roof Inn ♥, Sheraton, Super 8, Wingate Inn
	Other	E: Auto Services, Towing W: ATMs, Banks, Auto Services
240B		**US 183, Service Rd, Anderson Ln, to Lampasas, Lockhart (NB)**
	Gas	W: Star Mart
	Food	W: Burger Tex
	Lodg	W: Best Western, Sheraton
	Other	W: Daughters of the Republic of TX

◆ = Regular Gas Stations with Diesel   ▲ = RV Friendly Locations   ♥ = Pet Friendly Locations

RED PRINT SHOWS LARGE VEHICLE PARKING/ACCESS ON SITE OR NEARBY   BROWN PRINT SHOWS CAMPGROUNDS/RV PARKS

EXIT	TEXAS
239	**Service Rd, St Johns Ave, Anderson Ln, Austin**
Gas	E: Texaco W: Conoco◇, Exxon
Food	E: Chili's, Fuddrucker's, Pappadeaux Seafood, Shoney's, Steak & Egg W: Applebee's, Denny's, Souper Salad, Sushi House
Lodg	E: Best Value Inn, Days Inn, Doubletree Hotel, Drury Inn, Hampton Inn, Hawthorn Suites, Hearthside Suites, Studio 6 W: Amerisuites, American Inn, Comfort Inn, Country Inn, Holiday Inn Express, La Quinta Inn♥, Sheraton
Med	E: + Cornerstone Hospital
Other	E: Home Depot, Wal-Mart sc W: ATMs, Auto Services, FedEx Kinko's, Grocery, Greyhound, Highland Mall, Laser Quest, Office Depot
238BA	**US 290E, 51st St (SB)**
238B	**Frontage Rd, US 290E, FM 2222, Koenig Ln, 51st St, to Houston**
FStop	E: Conoco Fuel Mart
Gas	E: Exxon, Chevron, Phillips 66, Shell W: Texaco
Food	E: Burger King, Dixie's Roadhouse, El Torito, Fuddrucker's, Long John Silver, Pizza Hut, Tx Land & Cattle Steaks W: Bombay Bicycle Club, Captain's Seafood, Coco's, Carraba's, IHOP
Lodg	E: Doubletree Hotel, Embassy Suites, Econo Lodge, Holiday Inn, Red Lion Inn W: Country Inn, Courtyard, Drury Inn, Hilton, Quality Inn, Ramada
Other	E: Capitol Plaza, Auto Services, ATMs, Banks, Grocery W: Greyhound, Highland Mall, to Univ of Tx/Austin
238A	**Frontage Rd, Reinli St, Clayton Ln, 51st St (Access same as #238B)**
Food	E: CiCi's, Grandy's, McDonald's W: Captain's Seafood & Oyster Bar, Baby Acapulco, IHOP,
Lodg	W: Courtyard, Drury Inn, Fairfield Inn, La Quinta Inn♥, Motel 6♥, Quality Inn, Ramada, Super 8♥
237B	**51st St, Cameron Rd (NB)** (Access to Ex #238 Serv via Serv Rd)
237A	**Airport Blvd, 51st St, 38 1/2 St**
Food	E: Purple Sage BBQ W: Jack in the Box, Wendy's
Lodg	E: Best Western
Other	E: U-Haul W: Hancock Shopping Center, Univ of TX
NOTE:	Exits Below: Upper Level is Thru I-35, Lower Level is Downtown Access
236B	**38 1/2 St, Austin**
Gas	E: Chevron W: Texaco
Other	E: Planet Earth Adventures W: ATM, Bank, O'Reilly
236A	**26th—32nd Streets**
Food	E: Sonic
Lodg	E: Days Inn W: Rodeway Inn
Med	W: + St David's Medical Center
Other	W: LBJ Library & Museum, Museums, Tx Memorial Stadium, Galleries

EXIT	TEXAS
235B	**Manor Rd, 26th St**
Food	E: Denny's, Fuddruckers, Castaways W: Mexican Rest, Subway
Lodg	E: DoubleTree Hotel, Super 8, Wingate Inn W: Marriott, Ramada Inn
Other	E: Disch Falk Stadium W: State Capitol, Univ of TX
235A	**15th St, MLK Blvd**
Med	W: + Hospital
NOTE:	Exits Above: Upper Level is Thru I-35, Lower Level is Downtown Access
234C	**6th St—12th St, State Capitol**
Gas	E: Chevron, Exxon, Shell W: Exxon, Shell, Texaco
Food	E: Denny's W: Wendy's
Lodg	E: Doubletree Hotel, Super 8 W: Radisson, Sheraton
Med	W: + Breckenridge Hospital, + Children's Hospital of Austin
Other	E: Museums W: Fall Creek Vineyards, Frank Erwin Center, Museums, State Capitol
234B	**Cesar Chavez St, 8th-3rd Sts (SB)** **Cesar Chavez St, 2nd-4th Sts (NB)**
Gas	E: Chevron, Texaco W: Mobil
Other	W: Courthouses, Museums
234A	**1st St, Lp 343, Cesar Chavez St, Holly St, Downtown**
Food	E: Taco Bueno, Whataburger W: IHOP, Iron Works BBQ, Quiznos
Lodg	E: La Quinta Inn♥ W: Four Seasons Hotel
Other	E: Auto Services W: ATMs, Banks, Austin Conv Center, Visitor Center
233A	**1st—4th Streets**
233BC	**Festival Beach Rd (NB)**
Gas	E: Exxon, Shell W: Chevron
Lodg	W: Holiday Inn
233	**Riverside Dr, Town Lake**
Gas	E: Shell, Shamrock W: Chevron
Lodg	E: Riverside Quarters, Wellesley Inn W: Holiday Inn
232B	**Woodland Ave**
Gas	W: Shell
Lodg	E: Guest Inn
232A	**Oltorf St, Live Oak**
Gas	E: 7-11, Shell◇ W: Chevron, Exxon, Shell, Texaco
Food	E: Carrow's, Luby's Cafeteria W: Denny's, Marco Polo
Lodg	E: Exel Inn, La Quinta Inn♥, Motel 6♥, Park West Inn, Super 8 W: Clarion, Quality Inn
231	**Woodward St**
Gas	E: Shell◇
Food	E: Country Kitchen
Lodg	E: Holiday Inn, Motel 6♥, Super 8
Other	W: Home Depot
230A	**St Elmo Rd (SB)**
Food	W: Chili's, KFC, Tx Land & Cattle Steakhouse, Wendy's, Whataburger, Umi Sushi Bar & Grill

EXIT	TEXAS
Lodg	W: Candlewood Suites, Days Inn, La Quinta Inn♥
TServ	W: Hackney Auto & Truck Service
Other	W: Auto Dealers, Auto Services, National Tire, Metropolitan 14
230B	**Ben White Blvd, US 290W, TX 71 Burleson Rd, Austin (SB)**
FStop	E: Quick Mart #2/Conoco
Gas	W: Chevron, Shell
Food	W: Miller BBQ, Pizza Hut
Lodg	E: Best Western W: Hawthorne Suites
Other	W: Auto Services, Firestone
230	**US 290, TX 71, Ben White Blvd, St Elmo Rd, Austin (NB)**
FStop	E: Speedy Stop #216/Conoco 9105 US290E
Gas	E: Shell, Sam's
Food	E: Domino's Pizza, Jim's Rest, Subway, McDonald's, Western Steaks W: Furr's, IHOP
Lodg	E: Comfort Suites, Fairfield Inn, Hampton Inn, Homewood Suites, Holiday Inn, Marriott, Omni Hotel, Red Roof Inn♥, Residence Inn, Springhill Suites W: Candlewood Suites, Hawthorn Suites, Days Inn, La Quinta Inn♥
Med	W: + St David's South Hospital
Other	E: Sam's Club, Wal-Mart W: Auto Dealers, Auto Services
229	**Stassney Lane, Austin**
Gas	E: Exxon W: Shell, Albertson's
Food	E: Applebee's, McDonald's, Subway, Sonic, Taco Bell W: Burger King, Chili's, KFC, Long John Silver's, Whataburger
ATServ	W: Hackney Auto & Truck Service
Other	E: Cinemark Tinseltown, Wal-Mart, Austin Lone Star RV Resort▲, HEB, W: Albertson's, Auto Dealers, Lowe's, Firestone
228	**William Cannon Dr**
Gas	E: Exxon, Shamrock W: Texaco, RaceTrac
Food	E: Applebee's, McDonald's, Subway, Sonic, Taco Bell W: Burger King, Long John Silver, Whataburger, Wendy's
Other	E: Discount Tire, Grocery, Target, Austin Lone Star RV Resort▲ W: Auto Dealers, Firestone, Pharmacy
227	**Lp 275, Slaughter Ln, S Congress**
Gas	E: Shell◇ W: Shamrock, Tetco, Murphy
Food	W: Sonic
Other	E: Home Depot, Tires, Towing, Truck Service, U-Haul W: Albertson's, Wal-Mart sc
226	**FM 1626, Slaughter Creek**
Gas	E: Shell
225	**FM1626, Orion Creek Pkwy**
Gas	E: Shell
Other	E: Harley Davidson
223	**FM 1327, Buda**
221	**Loop 4, Buda**
TStop	E: Dorsett's 221 Truck Stop (Scales)
Gas	E: Chevron W: HEB
Food	E: Rest/221 TS, McDonald's W: Cracker Barrel, Jack in the Box, Subway

◇ = Regular Gas Stations with Diesel   ▲ = RV Friendly Locations   ♥ = Pet Friendly Locations
RED PRINT SHOWS LARGE VEHICLE PARKING/ACCESS ON SITE OR NEARBY   BROWN PRINT SHOWS CAMPGROUNDS/RV PARKS

EXIT		TEXAS
	Lodg	E: Best Value Inn
	TServ	E: 221 TS
	Other	E: Laundry/221 TS, All Star RV, Camper Clinic II
		W: HEB
220		FM 2001, Buda, to Niederwald
	Other	E: Marshall's Traveland
		W: Crestview RV Park & RV Center
217		Lp 4, CR 210, CR 131, Windy Hill Rd, Buda, Kyle
	FStop	E: Tex Best #3/Conoco
		W: Diamond Shamrock
	Gas	W: Exxon◊
	Food	W: Pizza Hut/Shamrock, Burger King
	Lodg	W: Best Western
	Other	E: Marshall's Traveland
		W: Evergreen RV Center, Beacon Lodge & RV Campground▲
215		Bunton Overpass
	Gas	E: Exxon
213		FM 150, W Center St, Kyle
	Gas	E: Diamond Shamrock◊, HEB
		W: Conoco
	Food	E: Restaurant
	Other	E: HEB
		W: Police Dept
(212)		Parking Area (NB)
(211)		Weigh Station (NB)
210		Yarrington Rd, Kyle
	Other	W: Plum Creek RV Resort▲
(209)		Weigh Station (SB)
208		Frontage Rd, San Marcos
206		US 81 Bus, Lp 82, Aquarena Springs Dr, San Marcos
	Gas	E: Conoco◊, Shamrock
		W: Exxon◊, Mobil◊, Payless, Phillips 66, Shell◊, Texaco
	Food	W: Mamacita's, Popeye's, Sonic
	Lodg	W: Comfort Inn, La Quinta Inn♥, Motel 6♥, Ramada, Super 8, University Inn
	Other	E: Auto Services, Sheriff Dept
		W: Office Depot, Tourist Info, to Tx State Univ/SanMarcos
205		TX 80, to TX 21, Hopkins St, TX 142, to Luling, Bastrop
	Gas	E: Chevron, Conoco, Mobil, Shell◊
		W: Circle K, Chevron, Shamrock
	Food	E: Arby's, DQ, Jason's Deli, Pit BBQ, McDonald's, Subway
		W: Applebee's, Burger King, CiCi's, Furr's, IHOP, Logan's, Long John Silver, McDonald's, Pizza Hut
	Lodg	W: Best Western, Days Inn, Microtel
	Other	E: ATMs, Auto Services, Banks, Dollar General, Grocery, Wal-Mart sc, San Marcos Muni Airport✈, Pharmacy Pecan RV Park▲, Riverbend Park▲, Wolf Creek Ranch & Resort▲, Leisure Resort▲
		W: Best Buy, Office Depot, Target, Walgreen's, Tourist Info, Vet♥
204B		Riverside Dr, CM Allen Pkwy (SB)
	Gas	W: Chevron, Conoco◊, Texaco◊
	Food	W: Chinese Buffet, KFC, Sonic
	Lodg	W: Best Western, Days Inn, Microtel, Parkside Inn, Red Roof Inn♥
	Other	W: Tourist Info, Auto Services

EXIT		TEXAS
204A		Lp 82W, TX 123E, San Marcos, to Seguin (SB)
	FStop	W: San Marcos Truck Stop/Texaco
	Food	W: FastFood/San Marcos TS, DQ
	Lodg	W: Econo Lodge
	Tires	W: San Marcos TS
	Other	W: Laundry/LP/San Marcos TS, Amtrak, FedEx Kinko's, Greyhound, Grocery
204		Lp 82E, TX 123E (NB)
	Gas	E: Conoco, Phillips 66, Shamrock
	Food	E: Golden Corral, Hardee's, Luby's Cafeteria, McDonald's, Whataburger
	Lodg	E: Best Western, Comfort Suites, Holiday Inn Express
	Med	E: + Hospital
	Other	E: Auto Dealers, Auto Service, Enterprise
202		FM 3407, Wonder World Dr
	Gas	E: Shell, Sac n Pack
		W: Shamrock
	Food	E: Jack in the Box
	Med	E: + Central Tx Medical Center
	Other	E: Auto Service, Discount Tire, Lowe's
		W: I-35 Tire & Service, Auto Services
201		McCarty Lane, CR 233
	Other	E: Auto Dealers
		W: Auto Dealers
200		Center Point Rd, San Marcos
	Gas	W: Diamond Shamrock
	Food	E: Branding Iron, Cracker Barrel, Lone Star Cafe, Subway, Taco Bell, Wendy's
		W: Kip's Tx BBQ, Starbucks, Whataburger
	Lodg	W: AmeriHost Inn

EXIT		TEXAS
	Other	E: Prime Outlets at San Marcos, Tanger Outlet Center
199		Posey Rd, CR 235 (SB)
	Other	W: Canyon Trail RV Resort▲
199A		Posey Rd (NB)
	Other	W: Canyon Trail RV Resort▲
196		FM 1102, York Creek Rd, New Braunfels, San Marcos
	Other	E: Southwest RV Center/Camping World, Roman Holiday Motorhomes
195		Watson Ln, Old Bastrop Rd
193		Conrads Rd, Kohlenberg Rd
	Gas	W: Travel Center of America #232/Shell (Scales)
	Food	W: CntryFare/Subway/Popeye's/TA TC
	TServ	W: TA TC
	Other	E: Camping World/Southwest RV Center, Roman Holiday Motorhomes
		W: Laundry/WiFi/RVDump/TA TC
191		FM 306, FM 483, New Braunfels, Canyon Lake
	FStop	W: Tex Best #5/Exxon
	Gas	E: Conoco, Texaco
		W: Chevron
	Food	E: Quizno's/Conoco
		W: FastFood/TexBest, Burger King
	Other	W: Guadalupe Valley Winery, Sundance Golf Course
190C		Post Rd, Bus 35 (SB)
190B		Lp 35S, N Elliot Knox Blvd, New Braunfels, to TX 46 (SB)
190A		Frontage Rd, to TX 46 (SB)
	Gas	E: Shell
	Food	W: McDonald's, Wendy's
	Lodg	W: Best Western, Comfort Suites, Quality Inn, Rodeway Inn
	Other	E: Home Depot
190		Frontage Rd, to Bus 35 (NB)
	Lodg	E: Howard Johnson
	Other	E: Evergreen RV Center
189		TX 46, TX 337, Seguin, Boerne
	Gas	E: Conoco, Exxon, Texaco
		W: Chevron, Diamond Shamrock
	Food	E: Luby's Cafeteria, Oma's
		W: Applebee's, IHOP, McDonald's, Taco Bell, Wendy's, New Braunfels Smoke House, Taco Cabana
	Lodg	E: Fountain Motel, Oakwood Inn, Super 8
		W: Days Inn, Hampton Inn, Holiday Inn, Motel 6♥, Rodeway Inn
	Med	W: + McKenna Memorial Hospital
	Other	E: Discount Tire, Home Depot, Kmart, Office Depot, Lakeside RV Park▲, New Braunfels Muni Airport✈
		W: New Braunfels Factory Stores, Walgreen's, Peformace Auto & Truck Repair, Auto Services, Museum, to Landa Park, Landa Falls, Waterpark
188		Frontage Rd, New Braunfels
187		FM 725, Seguin Ave
	Gas	E: Chevron
		W: Exxon◊
	Food	E: Arby's, Burger King, CiCi's, Cow Pies, Long John Silver, Mamacita's, Subway, Whataburger
		W: Adobe Café, China Kitchen, Jack in the Box, Peking Rest
	Lodg	W: Budget Inn
	Med	W: + Hospital

◊ = Regular Gas Stations with Diesel ▲ = RV Friendly Locations ♥ = Pet Friendly Locations

RED PRINT SHOWS LARGE VEHICLE PARKING/ACCESS ON SITE OR NEARBY BROWN PRINT SHOWS CAMPGROUNDS/RV PARKS

EXIT		TEXAS
	Other	E: Auto Dealers, Auto Services, Big Lots, Family Dollar, Grocery, Police Dept
		W: Enterprise RAC, NAPA, Navarro's Truck & Auto Repair, Auto Services
186		Walnut Ave, New Braunfels
	Gas	E: Exxon, Shamrock
		W: Conoco, Shamrock, Texaco
	Food	E: ChickFilA, Marina's Mexican Rest, McDonald's, Popeye's, Taco Bell
		W: KFC, Mr Gatti's, Papa John's
	Lodg	E: Executive Lodge, Red Roof Inn ♥
	Other	E: Wal-Mart
		W: AutoZone, Auto Services, Walnut 6, Target, Walgreen's, U-Haul
185		Bus 35, Bus 81, Spur St, FM 1044
184		Lp 337, FM 482, Ruekle Rd, New Braunfels
	TStop	E: Pilot Travel Center #330 (Scales)
	Gas	E: Shell
	Food	E: McDonald's/Pilot TC, Blimpie/Shell
	Other	E: Laundry/WiFi/Pilot TC, Auto Services, Auto Dealer, Hill Country RV Resort▲
183		Solms Rd, New Braunfels
	Gas	W: Exxon
182		Engel Rd
	Food	E: Pam's Country Kitchen
		W: Mesquite Pit BBQ
	Other	E: First RV of New Braunfels, Stahmann RV Sales
		W: Snake Farm, Noah RV Services
180		Schwab Rd
(180)		Comal Co Rest Area (Both dir) (RR, Phones, Picnic, WiFi, (NB) RVDump)
178		FM 1103, Cibolo, Hubertus Rd
	Gas	E: Shell◊
177		FM 482, FM 2252
	Other	W: Stone Creek MH & RV Park▲
176		Old Weiderstein Rd
175		FM 3009, Roy Richard Dr, Natural Bridge Caverns Rd, Schertz, to Garden Ridge
	Gas	E: Shamrock
		W: Shamrock, Texaco
	Food	E: McDonald's, Miller BBQ, Mexican Rest, Sonic, Taco Cabana
		W: Arby's, Burger King, Denny's, Jack in the Box, KFC, Wendy's
	Lodg	W: Country Inn
	Other	E: HEB
		W: Wal-Mart sc
174A		Frontage Rd, Schertz Pkwy
	Food	E: Rudy's Country Store
	Other	W: S Texas RV Superstore, to Crestview RV Superstore
174B		FM 1518, Selma, Schertz
	Other	W: Enterprise RAC, Retama Park Racetrack to Crestview RV Superstore
173		Olympia Pkwy, Old Austin Rd, Forum Blvd
	Food	E: Chili's, ChickFilA, IHOP, Romano's Macaroni Grill, Outback Steakhouse, Subway, TGI Friday
	Other	E: Home Depot, Target
		W: Retama Park Racetrack
172		Pat Booker Rd, Universal City, Randolph AFB, Toepperwein Rd, Live Oak (SB), Lp 1604, Anderson Loop, Forum Blvd (NB) TX 218
	Food	E: Mama's Rest, Mexican Rest

EXIT		TEXAS
	Lodg	E: Comfort Inn
	Other	E: ATM, Live Oak 18, to Randolph Air Force Base
		W: to Sea World
171		TX 218, Pat Booker Rd, Universal City, Randolph AFB (NB)
170		Judson Rd, to Converse (SB)
	Gas	W: Citgo, Exxon
	Food	E: Denny's, Kettle Rest, Subway, Whataburger
	Lodg	E: La Quinta Inn ♥
		W: Best Wester
	Med	E: + NE Methodist Hospital
	Other	E: Auto Dealers
		W: Enterprise RAC
170B		Toepperwein Rd (NB)
170A		Judson Rd, Converse (NB)
169		O'Connor Rd, Wurzbach Pkwy, San Antonio
	FStop	W: Timewise #10/Shell
	Gas	E: Exxon◊, Phillips 66
		W: RaceTrac, Shamrock
	Food	E: McDonald's, Taco Cabana
		W: Jack in the Box, Jim's Coffee Shop, Little Caesar's, Mi Casa
	Lodg	W: Best Western
	Other	E: El Monte RV Rentals, Iron Horse RV/LP/Rentals
		W: Greentree Village North Travel RV Park▲, Auto Services, Tires
168		Weidner Rd, Crosswinds Way
	Gas	E: Exxon, Shamrock
		W: Mobil
	Lodg	E: American Motel, Days Inn
		W: Ramada Inn, Super 8
	Other	E: Auto Services
		W: Auto Services
167B		Starlight Terrace, Thousand Oaks Dr (SB)
	Other	E: Auto & Truck Services
	Lodg	W: Best Western
167A		Randolph Blvd, Windcrest (SB)
	Lodg	W: Best Western, Days Inn, Classic Inn, Motel 6 ♥, Ruby Inn
	Other	E: RV Center
167		Starlight Terrace, Thousand Oaks Dr, San Antonio (NB)
(166)		Jct I-410W, Loop 368S
	Other	W: to Sea World
165		FM 1976, Walzem Rd, Windcrest
	Gas	E: Chevron, Shell, Shamrock, Texaco
		W: Mobil
	Food	E: Applebee's, Burger King, CiCi's, Chuck E Cheese, Ghengis Khan, IHOP, Jack in the Box, Jim's Coffee Shop, Luby's, Olive Garden, Red Lobster, Shoney's, Taco Cabana, Wendy's
		W: Mexican Rest, Sonic
	Lodg	E: Drury Inn, Hampton Inn
	Other	E: ATMs, Banks, Albertson's, AutoZone, Big Lots, Circuit City, Dollar General, Firestone, Home Depot, Office Depot, PetSmart ♥, Target, Wal-Mart sc, Windsor Park Mall, UPS Store
		W: Auto Services, National Tire, to TX RV Supply
164B		Eisenhauer Rd
	Gas	E: Exxon◊

Page 168   ◊ = Regular Gas Stations with Diesel   ▲ = RV Friendly Locations   ♥ = Pet Friendly Locations
RED PRINT SHOWS LARGE VEHICLE PARKING/ACCESS ON SITE OR NEARBY   BROWN PRINT SHOWS CAMPGROUNDS/RV PARKS

Interstate 35 N/S — Texas

EXIT	TEXAS
164A	**Rittiman Rd**
Gas	E: Conoco◊, Exxon, RaceTrac, Shell, Valero W: Chevron, Valero
Food	E: Burger King, Cracker Barrel, Denny's, Church's, Jack in the Box, McDonald's, Taco Cabana, Whataburger W: Miller BBQ, Popeye's, Sonic, Korean BBQ House, Wendy's
Lodg	E: Best Value Inn, Best Western, Comfort Suites, La Quinta Inn♥, Motel 6♥
Other	E: Auto Services, Towing
163C	**Holbrook Rd, Binz-Englemann Rd, Ft Sam Houston (SB)**
TServ	E: Cummins Southern Plains
163B	**Petroleum Dr**
(163A)	**Jct I-410S (SB, Left exit)**
(163)	**Jct I-410S, George Beach Ave (NB)**
Med	W: + Brooke Army Medical Center
(162)	**Jct I-410S, FM 78, Kirby, Lp 13, WW White Rd (NB), to FM 78, George Beach Ave, Binz-Englemann Rd (SB)**
Lodg	W: Holiday Inn, Microtel, Quality Inn
Other	E: Auto & Towing Services
161	**Binz-Englemann Rd (NB) (Access #162 Serv)**
160	**Splashtown Dr (NB), AT&T Center Pkwy, Freeman Coliseum Rd (SB)**
Gas	E: Exxon, Valero◊ W: Conoco, Shamrock
Food	W: Casey's BBQ, Mexican Rest, Rest/HI
Lodg	E: Delux Inn W: Days Inn, Holiday Inn, Microtel, Quality Inn, Super 8, Travelodge
Other	E: Auto Services, Fleet Service, Freeman, Coliseum, Willow Springs Muni Golf Course, Splashtown, San Antonio KOA▲ W: HEB, Ft Sam Houston
159B	**Walters Ave, Ft Sam Houston (SB), AT&T Center Pkwy, Freeman Coliseum (NB)**
Food	E: McDonald's
Lodg	W: Howard Johnson Express
Other	E: San Antonio KOA▲ W: to Fort Sam Houston
159A	**New Braunfels Ave**
Gas	E: Exxon, Star Mart W: Chevron, Shamrock
Food	W: Miller BBQ, Sonic
Lodg	W: Antonian Inn
Other	W: S Tx Diesel, to Fort Sam Houston
158C	**Alamo St, Austin St, Broadway (SB)**
(158B)	**Jct I-37S, US 281S, Corpus Christi (SB)**
158A	**US 281N, Johnson City (SB)**
(158)	**Jct I-37, US 281, Corpus Christi, Johnson City, Lp 368, Broadway (NB)**
157C	**St Mary's St, Quincy St, Lp 368, Broadway (NB)**
157B	**McCullough Ave, Brooklyn Ave**
Med	W: + Metropolitan Methodist Hospital

EXIT	TEXAS
157A	**San Pedro Ave, Main Ave, Lexington Ave**
Lodg	W: Travelodge♥
Med	E: + Baptist Medical Center
(156)	**Jct I-10W, US 87N, to El Paso**
155C	**W Commerce St, W Houston St, Market Square N Laredo St (SB)**
155B	**Durango Blvd, Downtown (NB), Frio St (SB)**
Food	E: Miller's BBQ W: McDonald's
Lodg	E: Best Western, Fairfield Inn, Courtyard, Holiday Inn, La Quinta Inn♥ W: Motel 6♥, Radisson Inn
Med	E: + Christus Santa Rosa Hospital
Other	E: Kmart, Univ of TX/San Antonio W: Court, Police Dept
155A	**Spur 536, S Alamo St, Frio St (SB), Spur 536, Guadalupe St (NB)**
Gas	E: Exxon, Shell W: Conoco
Food	E: Churchs, McDonald's, Pizza Hut, Wendy's
Lodg	E: Best Western, Comfort Inn, Mayfield Motel, Ramada Ltd W: Holiday Inn Express, Microtel, Riverside Lodging
Other	E: Auto Services, Museums
154B	**S Laredo St, Cevallos St**
Gas	E: Exxon, Texaco
Food	E: McDonald's, Pizza Hut, Wendy's
Lodg	E: Days Inn
154A	**San Marcos St, Nogalitos St, Loop 353S, Frontage Rd**
(153)	**Jct I-10E, US 90, US 87S, Del Rio, Houston, El Paso**
152B	**Malone Ave, Theo Ave**
Gas	W: Phillips 66, Texaco◊
Food	E: Taco Cabana
152A	**Division Ave, San Antonio**
Gas	E: Chevron W: Exxon, Phillips 66
Food	E: Miller BBQ, Whataburger
Lodg	E: Holiday Inn Express
Other	E: Auto Services, Tires
151	**Southcross Blvd**
Gas	E: Exxon, Shell W: Circle K, Texaco
150B	**Loop 13, Military Dr, Kelly AFB, Lackland AFB**
Gas	E: Chevron, Conoco, Texaco W: Exxon, Mobil, Shamrock
Food	E: Denny's, KFC, Taco Cabana W: Hungry Farmer, Jack in the Box, Long John Silver's, Luby's, Pizza Hut, McDonald's, Shoney's, Wendy's
Lodg	E: La Quinta Inn♥
Med	W: + Southwest General Hospital
Other	E: AutoZone, Century Plaza 8, Discount Tire, U-Haul, Auto Services, ATMs, Banks, Grocery W: Albertson's, Firestone, Pharmacy, Goodyear, Office Depot, Target, South Park Mall, ATMs, Banks, Police Dept
150A	**Zarzamora St (Access #150B Services)**
Lodg	E: Motel 6♥
Med	W: + Southwest General Hospital

EXIT	TEXAS
149	**Yarrow Blvd (SB) (Access #150B Services)**
Med	W: + Southwest General Hospital
148B	**Spur 422, Palo Alto Rd (fr NB, Left Exit)**
Gas	W: Phillips 66
Med	W: + Southwest General Hospital
148A	**Spur 422, TX 16S, to I-410 (fr SB, Exit Left)**
Gas	E: Chevron W: Phillips 66
Other	W: to Alamo Dragway
147	**Somerset Rd, Cassin Rd**
Gas	E: Texaco
146	**Cassin Rd, Somerset Rd (NB)**
Other	W: Leo's Truck & Trailer Repair
145B	**Loop 353N (fr NB, Left exit)**
(145A)	**Jct I-410, TX 16**
144	**Fischer Rd, Von Ormy, San Antonio**
TStop	E: Tetco #308/Valero (Scales) W: Love's Travel Stop #242 (Scales)
Food	E: Subway/Tetco W: Carl's Jr/Love's TS
Lodg	E: D&D Motel
TServ	E; to Sierra Diesel Truck Repair
Other	E: Hidden Valley RV Park▲ W: Laundry/WiFi/RVDump/Love's TS
142	**Medina River TurnAround (NB)**
141	**Benton City Rd, Von Ormy**
TStop	W: Timewise Landmark/Shell
Food	W: FastFood/Timewise, El Paradour Café
Other	E: Fort Retire RV Park▲ W: LP/Timewise
140	**FM 1604, Anderson Loop, to Somerset, Sea World**
FStop	E: Tex-Best #4/Exxon
TStop	W: AAA Travel Center/Valero (Scales)
Food	E: Burger King/TexBest W: FastFood/AAA TC
Other	E: to Fort Retire RV Park▲ W: Laundry/AAA TC, to Sea World
139	**Kinney Rd, Von Ormy**
137	**Shepherd Rd, Atascosa**
Other	E: Diesel Service W: Diesel Service
135	**Luckey Rd, Lytle**
133	**US 81, TX 132, Lytle (SB)**
131	**FM 3175, Benton City Rd, Lytle**
Gas	W: Conoco◊
Food	W: DQ, McDonald's, Pig Stand, Sonic
Lodg	W: Days Inn
Other	W: HEB
(130)	**Medina Co Rest Area (Both dir) (RR, Phones, Picnic, WiFi)**
127	**FM 471, Natalia**
124	**FM 463, Bigfoot Rd, Devine**
122	**TX 173, Hondo Ave, Devine, to Hondo, Jourdanton**
Gas	E: Exxon◊ W: Chevron
Food	E: Church's Chicken/Exxon W: Subway/Chevron, Triple C Steak House
Lodg	W: Devine Motel
TServ	W: M&W Truck & Auto Service

◊ = Regular Gas Stations with Diesel ▲ = RV Friendly Locations ♥ = Pet Friendly Locations

RED PRINT SHOWS LARGE VEHICLE PARKING/ACCESS ON SITE OR NEARBY BROWN PRINT SHOWS CAMPGROUNDS/RV PARKS

INTERSTATE 35 N — TEXAS

EXIT		
Other	W:	Devine Muni Airport ✈
121		TX 132N, Devine
Other	E:	Gusville RV Park ▲
(118)		Weigh Station (Both dir)
114		FM 462, Moore, Big Foot, Yancey
Gas	E:	Gas
111		US 57, Pearsall, to Eagle Pass
104		Bus 35, Pearsall (Acc #101 Serv-Approx 3 mi E)
101		FM 140, Pearsall, to Charlotte, Uvalde
FStop	W:	Valley Mart #12/Exxon
Gas	E:	Chevron
Food	E:	Cow Pokes BBQ
	W:	FastFood/Exxon
Lodg	E:	Royal Inn
	W:	Budget Inn
Med	W:	+ Hospital
99		US 35, FM 1581, Pearsall, Divot
(93)		Parking Area (Both dir)
91		FM 1583, Pearsall, Derby
Other	E:	McKinley Field Airport ✈
86		Loop 35, Dilley
85		FM 117, to Batesville, Garcia
Gas	W:	Exxon
Food	E:	Garcia Café
	W:	Café/Safari Motel
Lodg	E:	Garcia's Motel
	W:	Safari Motel
84		TX 85, Dilley, to Charlotte, Carrizo Springs
TStop	W:	Frio Self Serve/Shamrock, Cleo's Travel Center #3/Shell
Food	W:	FastFood/Frio SS, FastFood/Cleo's TC, Papa's
Lodg	W:	Executive Inn
Med	E:	+ Hospital
82		County Line Rd, Dilley
77		FM 469, Cotulla, to Millett
74		Gardendale
68		Bus #5, Main St, Cotulla (SB)
67		FM 468, Cotulla, to Big Wells
FStop	E:	Big's Travel Center/Shamrock
	W:	Tetco #70/Chevron (Scales)
Gas	E:	Conoco, Exxon
Food	E:	FastFood/Big's TC, Wendy's/Exxon, DQ, JJ's Café
	W:	McDonald's/Tetco
Lodg	E:	Executive Inn, Village Inn
TWash	E:	Cow Town Truck Wash
TServ	E:	Truck Tires
65		Lp 35, TX 3408, Main St, Cotulla
63		Elm Creek Interchange
(59)		Parking Area (Both dir)
56		FM 133, Artesia Wells
48		Caiman Creek Interchange

EXIT		
39		TX 44, Encinal, Laredo
FStop	E:	Love's Travel Stop #298 (Scales)
Food	E:	Chesters/Subway/Love's TS
Lodg	E:	Howard Johnson
Other	E:	Laundry/WiFi/Love's TS
38		TX 44, US 35, Encinal (NB)
32		San Roman Interchange
27		Callaghan Interchange
24		Camino Columbia TOLL Rd
22		Webb Interchange
18		US 83N, Laredo, to Carrizo Spgs, Uvalde, Eagle Path, Del Rio
Other	E:	TX Info Center/Rest Area
(15)		Parking Area (Both dir)
(15)		Inspection Area (NB)
13		Uniroyal Interchange, Laredo
TStop	E:	Pilot Travel Center #377 (Scales), Travel Center of America #153 (Scales)
	W:	Flying J Travel Plaza # (Scales)
Food	E:	Subway/Pilot TC, CtryPr/BKing/Subway/TB/TA TC
	W:	Rest/FJ TP
TWash	E:	Blue Beacon TW/Pilot TC
TServ	E:	TA TC
Other	E:	Laundry/Pilot TC, Laundry/WiFi/Chrome Sh/TA TC
	W:	Laundry/WiFi/RVDump/LP/FJ TP
10		Port Laredo, Carriers Dr (NB)
8B		Killam Ind Blvd, Lp 20, FM 3464, Bob Bullock Loop (SB)
8A		Lp 20, Bob Bullock Loop (NB)
8		Lp 20, FM 3464, Bob Bullock Loop
Lodg	E:	Best Western
Med	E:	+ Doctors Hospital of Laredo
Other	W:	to Costco, Deer Creek Village ▲
7		Shiloh Dr, Las Cruces Dr (SB)
Lodg	E:	Motel 9
4		FM 1472, Del Mar Blvd, Santa Maria Ave, Laredo
FStop	W:	FM1472&KillamBlvd: Laredo Fuel Ctr/Chevron, 8919 FM 1472: Mart/Shell, US 83S: La Noria Truck Stop, 11801 FM 1472: Speedy Stop#34/Exxon
TStop	W:	5301 Santa Maria: Gateway Truck Terminal (Scales), 4mi N Lp20: Discount Diesel (Scales)
Gas	E:	Exxon ◆, Chevron
Food	E:	Applebee's, Bennigan's, Burger King, Carino's, CiCi's, DQ, IHOP, Las Asadas, McDonald's, Shoney's, Whataburger
	W:	Rest/Gateway TT, Golden Corral
Lodg	E:	Days Inn, Extended Stay, Hampton Inn
	W:	Motel 6 ♥, Motel/Gateway TT
TServ	W:	Gateway TT/Tires
Other	E:	Albertson's, Lowe's, Petland ♥, HEB, Target, Northcreek 10
	W:	CB/Gateway TT, Laredo Harley Davidson, to Deer Creek Village ▲

EXIT		
3B		Mann Rd, Laredo
FStop	W:	5400 Santa Maria: Leyendecker Oil/Exxon
Gas	E:	Exxon
Food	E:	Cattlemen's Café, Logan's Roadhouse, Luby's
	W:	Subway, Taco Cabana
Lodg	E:	Fairfield Inn, Homewood Suites
	W:	Americana Inn, Family Garden Inn, Fiesta Inn, Motel 6 ♥, Springhill Suites
Med	E:	+ Dr's Hospital Health Center
Other	E:	Auto Dealers, Mall, UPS Store, Auto & Truck Service
	W:	Cinemark 12, Home Depot, Office Depot, Wal-Mart
3A		San Bernardo Ave, Calton Rd
Gas	E:	Texaco
	W:	Circle K, Chevron, Phillips 66
Food	E:	Chili's, Fuddrucker's, Luby's, Pizza
	W:	Bill Miller's BBQ, Burger King, Dunkin Donuts, El Pollo Loco, Julep's, McDonald's, Pizza Hut, Popeye's
Lodg	E:	Red Roof Inn ♥
	W:	Best Western, Gateway Inn, La Hacienda Hotel, Monterey Inn
Other	E:	ATMs, Banks, Carwash, Kmart, Mall Del Norte, Firestone, HEB, NAPA, Truck & Trailer Repair, Auto & Diesel Service
	W:	Auto Services, Grocery, Goodyear, PetCo ♥, Sam's Club, Towing
2		US 59, Lafayette St, Intl Airport, to Corpus Christi, Houston
Gas	E:	Conoco, Texaco
	W:	Chevron, Circle K, Exxon, Phillips 66
Food	E:	Jack in the Box
	W:	Church's, Denny's, Little Mexico, KFC, Raul's BBQ, Wendy's
Lodg	W:	Courtyard, Holiday Inn, La Quinta Inn ♥, Mayan Inn, Pan American Café & Motel
Med	E:	+ Laredo Medical Center
Other	E:	ATMs, Auto Services, to Laredo Int'l Airport ✈, Lake Casa Blanca State Park ▲
	W:	ATMs, AutoZone, Grocery, Mexican Insurance
1B		Park St, Frontage Rd
Gas	W:	Conoco, Fina
Food	W:	KFC, Pizza Hut, Popeye's
Lodg	W:	Holiday Inn
Other	W:	Auto Services, ATMs, Grocery
1A		Washington St, Frontage Rd
Gas	E:	Circle K, Exxon, Texaco
	W:	Exxon, Fina, Star Mart
Food	W:	KFC, McDonald's, Wendy's
Other	E:	Auto & Truck Repair
	W:	Auto Services, Firestone, Goodyear

(I-35 begins/ends on US 83 in Laredo, TX)
(CENTRAL TIME ZONE)

⛽ TEXAS

Begin Northbound I-35 from Laredo, TX to Duluth, MN.

◆ = Regular Gas Stations with Diesel   ▲ = RV Friendly Locations   ♥ = Pet Friendly Locations
RED PRINT SHOWS LARGE VEHICLE PARKING/ACCESS ON SITE OR NEARBY   BROWN PRINT SHOWS CAMPGROUNDS/RV PARKS

EXIT	TEXAS
	Begin Southbound I-37 from San Antonio, TX to Corpus Christi, TX.

TEXAS
(CENTRAL TIME ZONE)
(I-37 Begins/Ends on I-35, Exit # 158)

Exit	Description
(142B)	Jct I-35S, to Laredo (Left exit)
(142A)	Jct I-35N, to Austin
141C	Brooklyn Ave, McCullough Ave, Nolan St, Downtown (SB)
Gas	W: Fina
Food	W: Denny's
Lodg	W: Days Inn, La Quinta Inn♥, Marriott
141B	McCullough Ave, Houston St (SB)
Food	W: Denny's
Lodg	W: Days Inn, Hampton Inn, Red Roof Inn♥
Med	W: + Baptist Medical Center
Other	W: Auto Services, Greyhound, Municipal Auditorium, ATMs, Banks, Museums, Vietnam Vets Memorial, to Mall, the Alamo
141A	Commerce St, The Alamo, Downtown
Other	W: Alamo Museum, IMAX, Visitor Center, Rivercenter Mall
141	Commerce St, Downtown (NB)
Food	E: Exit 141 Hamburgers & Seafood, Ruth's Chris Steak House
	W: Big Easy Cajun, Casa Rio, DQ, Denny's Fig Tree Rest, Hooters, Morton's Steakhouse Planet Hollywood, Red Lobster, Starbucks, Steak Escape, Taco Bell, Tony Roma
Lodg	E: Holiday Inn
	W: AmeriSuites, Hilton, Homewood Suites, La Quinta Inn♥, Marriott, Riverwalk Vistas, Travelodge♥, Westin Hotel, Wyndham
Other	E: Amtrak, Grocery, SBC Center
	W: AMC 9, ATMs, Banks, Blum St Cellars Winery, Convention Center, Grocery, Hemisfair Arena, Hertz, IMAX, Museums, Rivercenter Mall, Tower of the Americas
140B	Market St, Durango Blvd, Frontage Rd, Alamodome (Acc to #141 Serv)
Food	E: Bill Miller BBQ
Other	E: Auto Services, Grocery, to the Alamodome
	W: Courts, Police Dept
140A	Florida St, Carolina St
Gas	E: Sunoco
Other	W: Enterprise
(139)	Jct I-10W, US 87, US 90, to Houston, El Paso, Del Rio, Victoria
Other	W: to Sea World
138C	Fair Ave (SB), Hackberry St (NB)
Gas	E: Chevron
	W: Exxon, Petro Pantry, Star Mart
Food	E: DQ, Jack in the Box, KFC, Taco Bell
Other	E: Family Dollar, Home Depot
138B	New Braunfels Ave, W Southcross Blvd (SB)
Gas	W: Exxon
Food	E: ChikFilA, Hong Kong Buffet, Jim's, McDonald's, Pizza Hut, Taco Cabana, Wendy's
	W: Burger King, Sonic
Other	E: ATMs, Banks, Cinemark 9, McCreless Mall

EXIT	TEXAS
138A	E Southcross Blvd (SB) (Acc to #138B Serv)
Med	E: + Methodist Family Health Center
138AB	Gevers St, Southcross Blvd (NB) (Acc to #138B Serv)
137	Hot Wells Blvd, San Antonio
Food	E: Popeye's
	W: IHOP
Lodg	W: Motel 6♥, Super 8
Other	W: Auto Service
136	Pecan Valley Dr
Gas	E: Citgo
Food	E: KFC, Taco Bell, Pizza Hut
Med	W: + San Antonio State Hospital
135	Lp 13, Military Dr, Brooks AFB
Gas	E: Chevron, Shell
	W: Valero
Food	E: Jack in the Box
	W: Burger King, Chili's, McDonald's, Subway, Village Inn, Wingstop, Whataburger
Lodg	E: Best Western
	W: Brookside Inn, La Quinta Inn♥
Other	E: Mission Trail RV Resort▲, Auto Parts
	W: Auto Repairs, HEB, Kmart, Office Depot PetCo♥, Target, Wal-Mart sc, Travelers World RV Resort▲, Museum, Brooks AFB, to Stinson Muni Airport✈
(133)	Jct I-410, US 281S, San Antonio
132	US 181S, to Floresville (SB), Presa St, Spur 122 (NB)
Gas	E: Food Mart, Shell, Valero
Food	E: Café, Mexican Rest
Other	E: Mission Gas/LP
130	Southton Rd, Donop Rd, Elmedorf, Lake Braunig, San Antonio
FStop	E: Tetco #303/Valero (Scales)
Food	E: FastFood/Tetco
Lodg	E: Comfort Inn
Other	E: RVDump/Tetco, I-37 RV Park▲, Braunig Lake RV Resort▲
127	San Antonio River TurnAround, Lake Braunig
125	Lp 1604, Anderson Loop, Elmedorf
FStop	E: Tex Best #101/Conoco
	W: EZ Mart #601/Citgo
Gas	W: Exxon◆
Food	E: Burger King/TexBest, Mi Reina Mexican
	W: FastFood/EZ Mart, Miller BBQ
Other	E: Riverside Ranch Nudist Resort▲
	W: Rustic Oaks Park▲
122	Priest Rd, Mathis Rd
120	Hardy Rd, San Antonio
117	FM 536, Pleasanton
113	FM 3006, Pleasanton
(112)	Parking Area (Both dir)
109	TX 97, Pleasanton, Floresville
FStop	E: ZS Super Stop/Chevron
Food	E: Rest/Super Stop
106	FM 1334, Coughran Rd
104	Spur 199, Leal Rd, to US 281(SB), Jim Brite Rd, Pleasanton (NB)
TStop	E: Kuntry Korner/Shamrock
Food	E: DQ, Rest/Kuntry Korner TS
Lodg	E: Kuntry Inn Motel/KK TS

◆ = Regular Gas Stations with Diesel   ▲ = RV Friendly Locations   ♥ = Pet Friendly Locations
RED PRINT SHOWS LARGE VEHICLE PARKING/ACCESS ON SITE OR NEARBY   BROWN PRINT SHOWS CAMPGROUNDS/RV PARKS

 **N I-37**

EXIT	TEXAS
103	US 281N, Leal Rd, Pleasanton (NB)
98	FM 541, to McCoy, Poth
92	US 281 Alt, Campbellton, Whitsett (SB)
88	FM 1099, to FM 791, Campbellton
83	FM 99, Campbellton, to Whitsett, Karnes City, Peggy
FStop	E: Shell
Gas	W: Chevron
(82)	Rest Area (SB) (RR, Phones, Picnic)
(78)	Rest Area (NB) (RR, Phones, Picnic)
76	US 281, FM 2049, Three Rivers, to Whitsett
(75)	Weigh Station (SB)
(74)	Weigh Station (NB)
72	US 281S, Three Rivers, Alice
Other	W: to Choke Canyon RV Park▲
69	TX 72, Three Rivers, Kennedy
TStop	W: Wolff's Travel Stop/Valero
Food	W: Rest/Wolff's TS
Tires	W: Wolff's TS
Other	W: to Choke Canyon RV Park▲
65	FM 1358, Oakville
Gas	W: Chevron
Food	E: Van's BBQ
59	FM 799, George West
(56)	Parking Area (SB)
56	US 59, to US 281, George West, to Beeville
FStop	E: Circle K
	W: Petro Pantry #17/Shell, Tetco
TStop	W: Stripes #2157, George West Truck Stop/Shell
Food	E: FastFood/Stripes
	W: FastFood/Petro Pantry, FastFood/GW TS
Other	W: LP/PetroPantry, to Smith Trailer & RV Park▲, Accurate Diesel Services
51	Hailey Ranch Rd
47	FM 3024, FM 534, to Swinney
Other	W: Lake Corpus Christi/Mathis KOA▲
(43)	Parking Area (SB)
(41)	Parking Area (NB)
40	FM 888, Mathis
Other	W: Lake Corpus Christi/Mathis KOA▲
36	TX 359E, to Skidmore
Gas	W: Shamrock
Lodg	W: Ranch Motel & Rest
Other	W: Mathis Motor Inn RV Park▲
34	TX 359W, Mathis
Gas	W: Shamrock, Shell
Food	W: Church's, DQ, Sonic, Van's BBQ
Other	W: Mathis Motor Inn RV Park▲, to Sunrise Beach RV Park▲, Wilderness Lakes RV Resort▲, Riverlake RV Park▲, ATMs, Banks, Grocery, Auto Services, Towing
31	TX 188, to Sinton, Rockport
22	TX 234, FM 796, to Edroy, Odem

EXIT	TEXAS
20B	CR 54, Cooper Rd, Mathis
(19)	Rest Area (Both dir) (RR, Phones, Vend, Picnic)
17	US 77N, Mathis, to Odem, Sinton
16	Access Rd, Nueces River Park
15	Access Rd, Sharpsburg Rd, Red Bird Lane, Corpus Christi
Gas	W: Whistle Stop
Food	E: Papa John's
	W: Burger King
14	US 77, Red Bird Lane, Kingsville (Serv in Northwest Blvd area & US 77)
Gas	W: Circle K, RaceTrac, Shell, Shamrock
Food	W: CiCi's, Denny's, K-Bob's Steakhouse, Pizza Hut, Popeye's, Quiznos, Sonic, TX A1 Steaks & Seafood, Whataburger
Lodg	W: Comfort Inn
Med	W: + Northwest Regional Hospital
Other	W: ATMs, Banks, Auto Services, Firestone, Dollar Tree, Home Depot, Wal-Mart sc(US 77)
13B	Sharpsburg Rd (NB)
13A	Leopard St, FM 1694, Callicoate Rd
Gas	W: Circle K
Other	W: Evelyn's MH & RV Park▲
11B	FM 24, Hart Rd, Violet Rd
Gas	E: Shell
	W: Circle K, Exxon
Food	E: Chicken Shack
	W: DQ, KFC, McDonald's, Sonic, Subway, Pizza, Whataburger
Lodg	E: Best Western, Hampton Inn
	W: La Quinta Inn ♥
Other	W: AutoZone, Family Dollar, Grocery
11A	FM 3386, McKinsey Rd
Gas	W: Circle K
Lodg	W: La Quinta Inn ♥
10	Carbon Plant Rd
9	Rand Morgan Rd, Up River Rd
Gas	W: Citgo, Valero
Food	W: Jim's Rest, Land & Sea Rest, Whataburger
Other	E: Koch Refinery
	W: Dollar General
7	Suntide Rd, Tuloso Rd, Clarkwood Rd
Other	E: Koch Refinery
	W: Bank, ATM, Gulley's MH & RV Park▲
6	Southern Minerals Rd
5	Corn Products Rd
Gas	E: Exxon
	W: PetroFleet
Food	W: Restaurant
Lodg	W: Eco Inn, Homegate Inn, Red Roof Inn ♥, Super 8, Travelodge
TServ	E: Ellison Truck Center/Kenworth
	W: Woody's Truck Center, Cummins Southern Plains
4B	Lantana St, McBride Lane (SB)
Lodg	W: Motel 6 ♥
4A	TX 358, to Padre Island (NB)
Gas	W: Shell◊
Lodg	W: Drury Inn, Deluxe Inn, Holiday Inn, Quality Inn, Gulf Way Motel, TV Inn
Other	W: Auto Services & Towing, Auto Rentals, Diesel Services, to Wal-Mart sc,

EXIT	TEXAS
Other	W: Corpus Christi Int'l Airport✈, Greyhound RV Park▲, Laguana Shores Village▲, to Marina Village Park▲, to Padre Palms RV Park▲, Pleasureland RV Center
4	TX 44, TX 358, CC Intl Airport, Padre Island (NB)
3B	McBride Lane, Lantana St (NB)
Gas	E: Circle K
	W: Valero, USA Food Mart
Lodg	W: Delux Inn, Rex Motel, Valley Motel
Other	W: Greyhound Racetrack, Greyhound RV Park▲
3A	Navigation Blvd, Corpus Christi
TStop	W: Corpus Christi Truck Stop (Scales)
Gas	W: Shell
	W: Exxon
Food	E: Rest/CC TS
	W: BBQ Man, Denny's, Miller BBQ, Las Milpas
Lodg	E: Clarion Inn
	W: Best Western, Days Inn, La Quinta Inn ♥, Ramada Ltd, Rodeway Inn ♥
TServ	W: CC TS/Tires
TWash	W: CC TS
Other	W: Laundry/RVDump/CC TS, Diesel Services, Auto & Truck Services, Convention Center, Commercial Coach Works
2	Up River Rd
Gas	E: Citgo
	W: Mobil
Food	W: KFC, Pizza Hut, Sonic
Lodg	W: Ramada Ltd
Other	W: Hatch RV Park▲
1E	Lawrence Dr, Nueces Bay Blvd
Gas	W: Circle K
Other	W: Auto & Truck Service, Firestone, HEB, US Post Office
1D	Port Ave, Brown Lee Blvd, Port of Corpus Christi (SB)
Gas	W: Citgo, Coastal
Food	E: Pitmaster BBQ, Ray's BBQ
Lodg	W: Howard Johnson
Other	E: Auto Service, Grocery
	W: Auto Services, Tire & Battery, Towing, Port of Corpus Christi
1C	TX 286, Crosstown Expressway
Med	W: + Christus Spohn Memorial Hospital, to + Christus Spohn Hospital Shoreline, + Doctors Regional Medical Center
1B	Brownlee Blvd, Port Ave (NB)
Gas	W: Chevron
1A	Buffalo St, City Hall (SB)
Other	W: Auto Services, Courts, Blucher Convention Center, Memorial Coliseum, Greyhound, Car & Truck Shop, Sheriff Dept
1	US 181, TX 35, to Portland
Other	E: Bayfront Plaza Conv Center, Museums, Tx State Aquarium, Visitor Info, to Puerto Del Sol RV Park▲, to Sea Breeze RV Park▲
	W: Convention Center, Coliseum

(Begin/End I-37 at Shoreline Blvd in Corpus Christi)
(CENTRAL TIME ZONE)

TEXAS

Begin Northbound I-37 from Corpus Christi to San Antonio, TX.

◊ = Regular Gas Stations with Diesel   ▲ = RV Friendly Locations   ♥ = Pet Friendly Locations
RED PRINT SHOWS LARGE VEHICLE PARKING/ACCESS ON SITE OR NEARBY   BROWN PRINT SHOWS CAMPGROUNDS/RV PARKS

EXIT		WISCONSIN
	Begin Southbound I-39 from Merrill, WI to Jct I-55 near Bloomington-Normal, IL.	

◐ WISCONSIN
(CENTRAL TIME ZONE)
(I-39 Begins/Ends on Bus 51 in Merrill)

211		US 51 Bus, CR K, Merrill
	Other	W: U-Haul, to Merrill Muni Airport✈
208		WI 64, WI 70, Merrill
	FStop	W: Pine Ridge Shell Travel Plaza
	Gas	W: BP◇, KwikTrip◇
	Food	W: Pine Ridge Rest/Shell, Burger King, China Inn, Diamond Dave's, Hardee's, McDonald's, Subway, Taco Bell, 3's Co
	Lodg	W: AmericInn, Pine Ridge Inn, Super 8
	Other	W: Auto Services, Auto Dealer, Piggly Wiggly, Museum, U-Haul, Wal-Mart, Jansen RV Sales & Service
205		US 51 Bus, CR Q, River Ave, Merrill
	TStop	E: Hwy 51 Truck Stop/Citgo
	Food	E: Rest/Hwy 51 TS
	Other	E: Laundry/WiFi/Hwy 51 TS
197		CR WW, US 51, Brokaw, Wausau
	FStop	W: Northside Citgo
194		US 51Bus, CR K (SB), CR U, Wausau
	Gas	E: KwikTrip, Mobil
	Food	E: McDonald's, Philly Subs
	Other	E: Auto Services, N Central Tech College
193		Bridge St
	Med	W: + Wausau Hospital
192		WI 52E, WI 29W, Stewart Ave, to Abbotsford
	Gas	E: Mobil, R-Store
	Food	E: Annie's American Café, Applebee's, Burger King, George's Rest, King Buffet, McDonald's, Noodles & Co, Pizza Chef, Starbucks, Subway
		W: 2510 Family Rest, Mandarin Chinese Rest
	Lodg	E: Exel Inn, Hampton Inn, La Quinta Inn ♥, Plaza Hotel, Super 8
	Med	W: + Wausau Hospital
	Other	E: ATMs, Auto Svcs, Banks, Crossroads Cinema, ShopKO/Pharmacy, UPS Store, Animal Hospital ♥, Marathon Co Park/RVDump
191		Sherman St, Wausau
		(Access #192 Serv via S 24th Ave N)
	FStop	E: 24th Ave to W Stewart: R-Store/BP
	Food	E: Applebee's, McDonald's,
		W: Burger King, Hardee's, Hereford & Hops
	Lodg	E: Hampton Inn, Super 8
	Med	W: + Wausau Hospital
	Other	E: Auto Services
		W: Auto Dealer, Home Depot
190		CR NN, N Mountain Rd, to Rib Mtn Dr, Rib Mountain State Park
	FStop	W: The Store #61/Citgo
	Gas	W: Mobil◇
	Food	E: Emma Krumbee's
		W: FastFood/The Store, Pizza, Subway
	Lodg	E: Howard Johnson
		W: Midway Hotel
	Other	E: to IGA
		W: Rib Mountain State Park▲, WI State Hwy Patrol Post, Ski Area
188		CR N, Rib Mountain Dr, US 51, Rib Mountain State Park
	TStop	E: Rib Mountain Travel Center/BP (Scales)
	Gas	E: Phillips 66◇

EXIT		WISCONSIN
	Food	E: Rest/RM TC, Country Kitchen, Fazoli's, Hong Kong Buffet, McDonald's, Pizza, Subway, Wendy's
	Lodg	E: Days Inn
	TServ	E: Peterbilt of WI
	Other	E: Laundry/WiFi/LP/RVDump/RM TC, Best Buy, Dollar Tree, PetCo ♥, PetSmart ♥, Sam's Club, Tires +, Wal-Mart SC, King's Campers, Kenmark RV Rental
(187)		I-39 Ends, US 51 continues NB
		(Exit #'s continue as I-39)
187		WI 29E, Wausau, to Green Bay
		(Gas/Food/Lodg Avail at 1st Ex #171)
	FStop	E: to 4005 Westview: The Store #60/Citgo (Scales)
	Food	E: FastFood/The Store
185		US 51 Bus, CR XX, Mosinee
	FStop	E: R Store #11/Mobil
	Gas	E: Mobil
	Food	E: Cedar Creek Café, Culver's Family Rest, Green Mill Rest, Denny's, Subway
	Lodg	E: Comfort Inn, Holiday Inn, Lodge at Cedar Creek, Rodeway Inn, Stoney Creek Inn
	Other	E: ATM, Auto Service, Bank, Visitor Center, Grocery, Cedar Creek Factory Stores, Harley Davidson
(183)		Rest Area (SB)
		(RR, Picnic)
181		Maple Ridge Rd, Mosinee
	TServ	W: WI Kenworth
	Other	W: Brookside Village▲
179		WI 153, East St, Mosinee
	Gas	W: BP◇, KwikTrip, Shell◇
	Food	W: Hardee's, McDonald's, Subway/BP
	Lodg	W: Amerihost Inn
	Other	E: Central WI Airport✈
(178)		Rest Area (NB)
		(RR, Picnic)
175		WI 34, Balsam Rd, Mosinee, Knowlton, to WI Rapids
	Gas	W: Cyran's du Bay Pit Stop
171		CR DB, Mosinee, to Knowlton
	Other	W: to Lakeview Log Cabin Resort
165		CR X, Saw Mill Rd, Stevens Point
	Other	E: to Rivers Edge Campground & Marina▲
161		US 51 Bus, Division St, Stevens Point
	Gas	W: BP, KwikTrip, R-Store
	Food	W: Country Kitchen, Cousin's Subs, Hardee's, KFC, McDonald's, Perkins
	Lodg	W: Comfort Suites, Country Suites, Holiday Inn, Point Motel
	Other	W: Museum, Golf Course, Univ of WI/StPt
159		WI 66, Stanley St, Stevens Point
	FStop	W: Kwik Trip #342
	Other	E: Stevens Pt Muni Airport✈, Jordan Co Park/▲ RVDump (1903 Co Hwy Y)
		W: Auto Dealer, Auto Services
158		US 10, Stevens Point (SB)
	Gas	E: Mobil◇
		W: BP
	Food	E: Applebee's, Arby's, Culver's Family Rest, Hong Kong Buffet, McDonald's, Shoney's, Taco Bell, Wendy's
		W: Hilltop Pub & Grill

◇ = Regular Gas Stations with Diesel   ▲ = RV Friendly Locations   ♥ = Pet Friendly Locations

RED PRINT SHOWS LARGE VEHICLE PARKING/ACCESS ON SITE OR NEARBY   BROWN PRINT SHOWS CAMPGROUNDS/RV PARKS

Interstate 39 N/S

EXIT	WISCONSIN		EXIT	WISCONSIN		EXIT	WISCONSIN
	Lodg	E: Fairfield Inn, Holiday Inn Express ♥, Holiday Inn W: La Quinta Inn ♥	106		WI 82W, WI 23E, Oxford		TServ Other	N: WI Kenworth N: Auto Services
	Other	E: ATMs, Banks, Grocery, Staples, Target W: Auto		FStop Food Lodg Other	W: Oxford Travel Center/Citgo W: FastFood/Oxford TC E: Crossroads Motel E: Auto Service & Towing, to Kilby Lake Campground▲, Buffalo Lake Camping Resort▲ W: to K&L Campground▲, Blue Lake Campground▲	132	TStop	US 51, De Forest, Madison N: Citgo Travel Center (Scales), Truckers Inn/Shell (Scales) S: Travel Center of America #50/Mobil (Scales)
156		CR HH, McDill Ave, Stevens Point, to Whiting					Food	N: Rest/Citgo TC, PineCone Rest/Truckers Inn S: CountryPride/Subway/TacoBell/TA TC
	Food Other	E: Cousin's Subs, Subway E: Best Buy, Lowe's, PetCo ♥, Wal-Mart sc					TWash	N: Truckers Inn S: TA TC
153		CR B, Plover Rd, Plover	104		RD D, to WI 23, Montello, Oxford, to Packwaukee (NB, Diff reaccess)		TServ	N: Truckers Inn/Tires S: TA TC/Tires, Peterbilt, Freightliner
	Gas Food	W: BP, Mobil W: Blake's Rest, Burger King, Cousin's Subs, IHOP, McDonald's, Subway	100	Gas Other	WI 23W, CR P, Endeavor E: BP◊ W: to Lake Mason Campground▲		Other	N: Laundry/Citgo TC, Laundry/BarbSh/CB/RVServ/Truckers Inn, Token Creek Co Park/RVDump▲ S: Laundry/WiFi/TA TC, Wisconsin RV World, RV Custom Service & Rentals, Dane Co Reg'l Airport✈, to Camperland RV
	Lodg Other	W: AmericInn, Hampton Inn, Sleep Inn W: Bank, Auto Services, Truck Services	92	FStop Gas Food	US 51S, Portage E: Kwik Trip #683 E: Mobil E: Big Mike's Super Subs, Culver's Family Rest, McDonald's, Subway, Taco Bell			
151		WI 54, US 51 Bus, Plover, to Waupaca		Lodg Other	E: Best Western, Ridge Motor Inn, Super 8 E: ATMs, Banks, AutoZone, Kmart, Staples, Piggly Wiggly, Walgreen's, Wal-Mart sc	135BA		US 151, Washington Ave, Madison, to Sun Prairie (EB)
	TStop Food Lodg Other	E: Super 39 Shell (Scales) E: FastFood/Super 39, Arby's W: 4 Star Family Rest E: Elizabeth Inn E: Laundry/CB/WiFi/Super 39, Craft's Trading Center				135ABC		US 151, High Crossing Blvd, Madison, Washington Ave, to Sun Prairie (WB) (C=High Crossing Blvd, B=N, A=S)
143		CR W, Main St, Bancroft, to WI Rapids	89BA	Gas Food Other	WI 16, to WI 127, Portage (SB) E: BP◊ E: Hitchin Post E: Portage Muni Airport✈, Auto Dealer, Auto Services, Tires, Towing, Amtrak		Gas Food	N: BP S: BP, Citgo, Shell, Sinclair N: KFC, Pizza, Subway S: Applebee's, Arby's, Country Kitchen, Cracker Barrel, Denny's, Hardee's, IHOP, KFC, Lotus Chinese, McDonald's, Mountain Jack's Steakhouse, Olive Garden, Pizza Hut, Pedro's Mex Rest, Red Lobster, TGI Friday, Steak n Shake, Tumbleweed Mex Rest, Wendy's
	Gas Food Other	E: Citgo◊ E: Cedarwood Family Rest E: Auto Service, Grocery, to Vista Royale Campground▲	89B		WI 16, Wisconsin St (NB)			
158B		US 10W, Stevens Point (NB)	89A		WI 16, Wisconsin St (NB)			
158A		US 10E, Stevens Point (NB)	87		WI 33, to I-90/94, Portage (All Serv 3mi E to WI 16, Wisconsin St)			
139		CR D, Plainfield, to Almond		Other	W: to Cascade Mtn Ski Area			
136		WI 73, Plainfield, to WI Rapids	85		Cascade Mountain Rd, Portage		Lodg	N: Courtyard, Staybridge Suites, Woodfield Suites S: Best Western, Comfort Inn, Crowne Plaza, East Towne Suites, Econo Lodge, Exel Inn, Fairfield Inn, Hampton Inn, Holiday Inn, Heritage Inn, Microtel, Motel 6 ♥, Red Roof Inn ♥, Select Inn
	FStop TStop Food Lodg Other	E: Plainfield AmocoBP E: Plainfield Truck Stop/Mobil (Scales) W: Plainfield 66 Travel Plaza E: Rest/FastFood/Plainfield TS W: FastFood/Plainfield TP E: Motel/Plainfield TS E: Laundry/Plainfield TS W: Laundry/Plainfield TP		NOTE:	I-39 runs with I-90 below. Exit #'s follow I-90.			
			(84/ 108AB)		Jct I-90, I-94 Jct I-39N, WI 78, to US 51N, Portage			
131		CR V, N Lake St, Hancock	(114)		Rest Area (Both dir) (RR, Phone, Picnic, Vend)		Med Other	S: + Meriter Hospital N: Auto Dealers, Auto Services, ATMs, Banks, Grocery, U-Haul S: Auto & Truck Repairs, East Towne Mall, Dane Co Reg'l Truax Field, ATMs, Grocery, Banks, Best Buy, Firestone, Goodyear, Home Depot, Midas, NTB, Office Depot, Penske, PetSmart ♥, AniMart ♥, ShopKO, Eastgate Cinema, Wal-Mart, Target, FedEx Kinko's
	Gas Food Lodg Other	E: Hancock Mini Mart E: Country Kettle Family Rest E: Motel 51 E: Hancock Village Park▲, Tomorrow Wood Campground▲, Nordic Mtn Ski Resort	115	FStop Food TServ Other	CR CS, CR J, Poynette, to Lake Wisconsin N: North Point Plaza/BP N: FastFood/BP N: Graham's Auto & Truck Clinic N: to Little Bluff Campground▲ S: to Smokey Hollow Campground▲			
(126)		Weigh Station (Both dir, Left Exit)	119		WI 60, Arlington, Lodi			
124		WI 21, E Follet Dr, Coloma		Gas Lodg Other	S: Mobil◊ S: Best Western S: Interstate RV Sales, Service & Rentals		NOTE:	I-90W & I-94W run together Exits #138-48, approx 92 mi. Exit #'s follow I-90.
	Gas Food Other	E: Mobil E: A&W, Lavore's on the Hill E: Auto Dealers, to Lake of the Woods▲ W: Coloma Camperland▲	126	Gas	CR V, De Forest, to Dane N: BP, Phillips 66◊ S: Exxon◊	(138A)		Jct I-94, E to Milwaukee (fr EB, Left Exit)
(120)		Rest Area (SB) (RR, Phone, Picnic, Vend)		Food Lodg Other	N: Culver's Family Rest, McDonald's, Subway N: Holiday Inn N: KOA/Madison/RVDump▲, WI State Hwy Patrol Post, Auto Services, Museum, Police Dept, Sheriff Dept	138B Other		WI 30, Madison, to US 151 (fr WB, Left Exit) S: Dane Co Airport✈, Access #135 Services
(118)		Rest Area (NB) (RR, Phone, Picnic, Vend)						
113		RD E, RD J, Westfield	131		WI 19, Windsor, to Waunakee, Sun Prairie (Acc #132 Serv E to US 51N)	142A		US 12, US 18, Madison, to US 151 (WB Exits Left)
	FStop Gas Food Lodg Other	W: Pioneer Mini Store/Mobil W: BP, Marathon W: Rest/FastFood/Pioneer MS, Point Pizza, McDonald's, Subway W: Pioneer Motor Inn W: Auto Services, Grocery		Gas Food Lodg	N: Mobil, KwikTrip, Speedway N: A&W, McDonald's N: Days Inn, Windsor Lodging	142B		US 12, US 18, Madison, to Cambridge

◊ = Regular Gas Stations with Diesel ▲ = RV Friendly Locations ♥ = Pet Friendly Locations
RED PRINT SHOWS LARGE VEHICLE PARKING/ACCESS ON SITE OR NEARBY BROWN PRINT SHOWS CAMPGROUNDS/RV PARKS

Page 174

INTERSTATE 39 N/S

EXIT	WISCONSIN
142AB	**US 12, US 18, Madison, to US 151, to Cambridge** (S Serv at 1st Exit/US 51)
Gas	N: Mobil
	S: Cenex◊, Shell◊
Food	N: McDonald's, Subway
Lodg	N: Knights Inn, Wingate Inn
Other	N: Golf Course
	S: to Dane Co Babcock Campground▲
(146)	**Weigh Station (EB)**
147	**CR N, Cottage Grove, to Stoughton**
TStop	S: Road Ranger Travel Center/Citgo
Gas	S: BP
Food	S: FastFood/RR TC, Arby's/BP
Other	S: to Lake Kegonsa State Park▲
(148)	**Weigh Station (WB)**
156	**US 51N, to Stoughton**
Other	S: Coachman Golf Resort, Inn & Rest, to Creekview Campground▲, Viking Village Campground & Resort▲
Med	S: + Stoughton Hospital
160	**US 51S, WI 73, WI 106, Edgerton, to Deerfield**
TStop	S: Edgerton AmBest Shell Oasis (Scales)
Gas	S: KwikTrip
Food	S: Rest/Edgerton Oasis
Lodg	S: Towne Edge Motel
TServ	S: Edgerton Oasis/Tires
Med	S: + Memorial Comm Hospital
Other	N: to Hickory Hills Campground▲, Lakeland Camping Resort▲
	S: Laundry/WiFi/LP/Edgerton Oasis, to Jana Airport✈, Auto Services, Grocery, Tires, Creekview Campground▲, Sugar Creek Camper Sales, Janesville RV Center
163	**WI 59, Edgerton, to Milton**
Gas	N: Mobil, Shell
Food	N: Red Apple Rest/Mobil, Burger King, Family Rest, McDonald's, Subs
Lodg	N: Comfort Inn
Other	N: Hidden Valley RV Resort & Campground▲, Rock River Marina, Sun Ray RV Services, to Lakeland RV Center, Lakeland Camping Resort▲, Blackhawk Campgrounds▲
(169)	**Rest Area (EB) (RR, Phone, Picnic, Vend)**
171AB	**WI 26, Milton Ave, Janesville (EB)**
171A	**WI 26, Janesville (WB)**
FStop	N: Mulligan's Truck Stop/66
TStop	S: Road Ranger Travel Center #107/Citgo
Gas	S: BP, KwikTrip
Food	N: Cracker Barrel
	S: Rest/RR TC, Arby's, Applebee's, Country Kitchen, Culver's, Famous Dave's BBQ, Ground Round, Hardee's, Prime Quarter Steak House, Perkins, Milwaukee Grill
Lodg	N: Best Western, Hampton Inn, Motel 6
	S: Ramada Inn, Select Inn, Super 8
Med	S: + Mercy Hospital
Other	N: Auto Dealer, Auto Services
	S: ATMs, Banks, Auto Services, Grocery, Firestone, Kmart, Target, Wal-Mart, Janesville Mall
171B	**US 14, Humes Rd, Janesville (WB)**
171C	**US 14E, Janesville, Milton**
TStop	N: Travel Center of America #71/Mobil (Scales)

EXIT	WISCONSIN
Food	N: Wendy's/TA TC, Damon's, Old Country Buffet, Steak n Shake
Lodg	N: Holiday Inn, Microtel
Med	S: + Mercy Hospital
Other	N: Laundry/WiFi/TA TC, Movies 10, Best Buy, Home Depot, Staples, Tires Plus
	S: Auto Dealers, ATMs, Banks, Kutter Harley Davidson
175A	**US 14 Bus, E Racine St**
Gas	S: BP
Food	S: DQ, Hardee's, Big Mike's Subs
Lodg	S: Lannon Stone Motel
Other	S: Black Hawk Golf Course, Auto Services
175B	**WI 11E, US 14 Bus, Janesville**
TStop	N: J & R Quick Mart/BP
Food	N: FastFood/J&R QM, Denny's, Subway
Lodg	N: Baymont Inn
177	**WI 11W, Avalon Rd, Janesville**
Other	S: Southern Wisconsin Reg'l Airport✈
183	**CR S, Shopiere Rd, Beloit**
TStop	S: Rollette Oil #4/Citgo
Food	S: FastFood/Rollette Oil
Med	S: + Beloit Memorial Hospital
Other	N: Turtle Creek Campground▲
185A	**WI 81, Milwaukee Rd, Beloit**
FStop	S: Speedway #4293
TStop	S: Pilot Travel Center #289 (Scales)
Gas	S: BP, Exxon, Shell
Food	S: TacoBell/Pilot TC, FastFood/Speedway, Applebee's, Arby's, Burger King, Country Kitchen, Culver's, Fazoli's, Hong Kong Buffet, McDonald's, Perkins, Wendy's
Lodg	S: Comfort Inn, Econo Lodge, Fairfield Inn, Holiday Inn Express, Super 8

EXIT	WI / IL
Other	S: WiFi/Pilot TC, Auto Dealers, ATMs, Banks, Luxury 10 Cinemas, Tires +, Staples, Wal-Mart sc
(185B)	**Jct I-43N, to Milwaukee**
(187)	**WI Welcome Center (NB) (RR, Phone, Picnic, Vend, Info)**
NOTE:	I-39 runs with I-90 above. Exit #'s follow I-90.

(CENTRAL TIME ZONE)

⏶ WISCONSIN
⏷ ILLINOIS

(CENTRAL TIME ZONE)

NOTE:	I-39 runs with I-90 below. Exit #'s follow I-90.
1	**US 51N, IL 75, S Beloit**
TStop	S: Flying J Travel Plaza #5097 (Scales), Road Ranger Travel Center #205 (Scales)
Food	S: Rest/FastFood/FJ TP, Subway/RR TC
Lodg	S: Knights Inn, Ramada Inn
TServ	S: FJ TP
Other	S: Laundry/WiFi/BarbSh/RVDump/LP/FJ TP, Auto Dealers, Auto Services, Pearl Lake Campground▲
(2)	**IL Welcome Center (EB) (RR, Phone, Picnic, Vend, Info, RVDump)**
3	**CR 9, Rockton Rd, Roscoe**
TStop	N: Love's Travel Stop #322 (Scales)
Food	N: Hardee's/Love's TS
Other	N: Laundry/WiFi/RVDump/Love's TS
	S: Auto Museum
(75.5)	**TOLL Plaza**
(66)	**CR 55, Riverside Blvd, Rockford**
TStop	S: Road Ranger Travel Center #211
Gas	S: BP, Phillips 66
Food	S: FastFood/RR TC, Arby's, Culver's, KFC, McDonald's, Subway, Wendy's
Lodg	S: Days Inn
Other	S: Auto Dealers, Auto Services, ATMs, Banks, Grocery
(63)	**US 20 Bus, E State St, Rockford**
Gas	N: Phillips 66◊
	S: BP, Mobil◊
Food	N: Cracker Barrel, Subway/Phillips 66
	S: Applebee's, Arby's, Burger King, Chili's, Country Kitchen, Denny's, Don Pablo, IHOP, Hooters, KFC, Lone Star Steakhouse, McDonald's, Machine Shed Rest, Olive Garden, Perkins, Ruby Tuesday, Steak n Shake, Tumbleweed Grill
Lodg	N: Baymont Inn, Exel Inn
	S: Alpine Inn, Best Western, Candlewood Suites, Comfort Inn, Courtyard, Fairfield Inn, Hampton Inn, Holiday Inn Express, Quality Suites, Ramada Inn, Red Roof Inn♥, Residence Inn, Sleep Inn, Super 8
Med	S: + St Anthony Medical Center
Other	N: Greyhound, Museum
	S: Amtrak, Auto Services, Best Buy, Home Depot, Kmart, Lowe's, Office Depot, Sam's Club, Target, Wal-Mart
(61)	**Jct I-39S, US 20, US 51, Cherry Valley, to Rockford**
Other	S: Magic Waters Theme Park
(123)	**Jct I-90E, TOLL, to Chicago**

◊ = Regular Gas Stations with Diesel   ▲ = RV Friendly Locations   ♥ = Pet Friendly Locations

RED PRINT SHOWS LARGE VEHICLE PARKING/ACCESS ON SITE OR NEARBY   BROWN PRINT SHOWS CAMPGROUNDS/RV PARKS

INTERSTATE 39

ILLINOIS

EXIT		
	NOTE:	I-39 runs with I-90 above (pg 175). Exit #'s follow I-90.
122AB		**US 20E, Harrison Ave, Cherry Valley** (NB: LAST FREE EXIT BEFORE TOLL)
	FStop	W: Oakview Diesel/Marathon
	Gas	W: Citgo
	Food	W: Rest/Oakview Diesel, Arby's, DQ, Burger King
	Other	W: Collier RV Center, Kegel Harley Davidson, Cherry Vale Mall, Cinema
119		**US 20W, to Freeport, Rockford**
	Gas	W: BP, Phillips 66, Shell, Speedway
	Food	W: BeefARoo, Burger King, Subway
	Other	W: Auto & Diesel Services, Tires, Quality Truck Repair, RC Truck & Auto Service
115		**CR 11, Baxter Rd, Rockford**
	TStop	E: I-39 Express Lane/Shell (Scales)
	Food	E: FastFood/I-39 Expr Ln
	TWash	E: I-39 Expr Ln
	TServ	E: I-39 Expr Ln/Tires
	Other	E: Laundry/CB/I-39 Expr Ln
		W: Black Hawk Valley Campground▲
111		**IL 72, Monroe Center**
	Gas	W: BP◆
104		**IL 64, Lindenwood, Esmond, to Oregon, Sycamore**
	Other	E: Cummins Northern IL
99		**IL 38, Rochelle, to De Kalb**
	FStop	W: Super Pantry #14/BP
	TStop	W: Petro Stopping Center #59/Mobil (Scales), Road Ranger Travel Center #310/Citgo (Scales)
	Gas	W: Shell
	Food	W: IronSkillet/FastFood/Petro SC, Subway/RR TC, Arby's, DQ, Hardee's, McDonald's, Wendy's
	Lodg	W: Amerihost, Holiday Inn Express, Super 8
	TWash	W: BlueBeacon/Petro SC
	TServ	W: Petro SC/Tires
	Other	W: Laundry/BarbSh/Med/RVDump/LP/Petro SC, Auto Services, ATMs, Banks, Grocery
97B		**IL 88W, TOLL, to Rock Falls**
97A		**IL 88E, TOLL, to Chicago**
93		**CR 2, Perry Rd, Steward**
87		**US 30, Lee, to Sterling, Rock Falls**
	Other	E: Shabbona Lake State Rec Area▲
		W: to O'Connell's Jellystone RV Park▲, Mendota Hills Campground▲, Green River Oaks Camping Resort▲
(85)		**Willow Creek Rest Area** (Both dir) (RR, Phone, Picnic, Vend, RVDump)
82		**CR 10, Chicago Rd, Paw Paw**
72		**US 34, N 43rd Rd, Mendota, to Earlville**
	FStop	W: Road Ranger Travel Center #140/Citgo
	TStop	W: Gromann I-39 Auto & Truck Plaza/BP (Scales)
	Food	W: Rest/Gromann ATP, McDonald's
	Lodg	W: Comfort Inn, Super 8
	Med	W: + Mendota Comm Hospital
	Other	W: Laundry/WiFi/Gromann ATP, Amtrak, Auto Services, Towing, Grocery, Grandpa's Farm Mendota Airport✈

EXIT		
66		**US 52, N 37th Rd, Mendota**
	Other	E: to KOA LaSalle/Peru▲
(59B)		**Jct I-80W, to Des Moines**
	Other	W: IL Valley Reg'l Airport✈
(59A)		**Jct I-80E, to Chicago**
	Other	E: to KOA LaSalle/Peru▲
57		**US 6, La Salle, to Peru**
	Gas	W: BP, Shell
54		**CR 23 Ext, Walnut St, Oglesby**
	Gas	E: BP, Phillips 66, Shell
	Food	E: Burger King, Hardee's, Subway
	Lodg	E: Holiday Inn Expres
	Other	E: to Starved Rock State Park▲, Matthiessen State Park
52		**IL 251, Oglesby, to La Salle, Peru**
51		**IL 71, N 23rd Rd, Oglesby, to IL 251, to Hennepin**
48		**IL 54, N 20th Rd, Tonica**
	FStop	E: Tonica Truck Stop/BP
	Gas	E: Casey's
	Food	E: FastFood/Tonica TS
41		**IL 18, N 13th Rd, Lostant, to Streator, Henry**
35		**IL 17, Wenona, to IL 251, to Lacon**
	TStop	E: Wenona Travel Mart/BP
	Gas	E: Casey's
	Food	E: FastFood/Wenona TM, Burger King, Pizza Hut
	Lodg	E: Super 8
27		**CR 2, Minonk, to IL 251**
	TStop	E: Fast Break Travel Center/Shell (Scales)
	Gas	E: Casey's
	Food	E: Rest/FastFood/Fast Break TC
	Lodg	E: Motel 6♥
	Other	E: ATMs, Banks, Auto Services
22		**IL 116, Minonk, to IL 251, to Peoria, Benson, Pontiac**
14		**US 24, to IL 251, El Paso, to Peoria**
	FStop	E: Fast Break/Shell, Freedom Oil #47
	Gas	E: Casey's
	Food	E: FastFood/Fast Break, DQ, Hardee's, McDonald's, Subway, Woody's Fam Rest
	Lodg	E: Days Inn
		W: Super 8
	Other	E: ATMs, IGA, El Paso RV Center
		W: Hickory Hills Campground▲
8		**IL 251, CR 8, Hudson, Kappa**
	Other	E: Lake Bloomington
		W: RV Camping▲, Lake, Park
5		**CR 12, Hudson**
2		**US 51 Bus, Normal, Bloomington**
(1)		**Jct I-55,** (Gas/Food/Lodg N to 1st Ex #165) (Pilot & TA S to 1st Ex #160A)

(CENTRAL TIME ZONE)

🎧 ILLINOIS
(I-39 Begins/Ends on I-55, Exit #164)

◆ = Regular Gas Stations with Diesel ▲ = RV Friendly Locations ♥ = Pet Friendly Locations
RED PRINT SHOWS LARGE VEHICLE PARKING/ACCESS ON SITE OR NEARBY   BROWN PRINT SHOWS CAMPGROUNDS/RV PARKS

INTERSTATE 40 E

EXIT	CALIFORNIA
	Begin Eastbound I-40 from Jct I-15 in Barstow, CA to US 17 in Wilmington, NC.
	CALIFORNIA
	(PACIFIC TIME ZONE)
	(I-40 begins/ends in Barstow on I-15)
1	Montaro Rd, E Main St
Gas	N: 76, Chevron, Mobil, Shell, Valero
	S: Mirastar
Food	N: Burger King, Carl's Jr, Carrow's, CoCo's, Del Taco, Denny's, IHOP, Jack in the Box, Long John Silver's, McDonald's, Popeye's, Sizzler, Straw Hat Pizza
	S: McDonald's
Lodg	N: Astro Budget, Best Motel, Best Western, California Inn, Days Inn, Motel 6♥, Oak Tree Inn, Pennywise Inn, Quality Inn, Ramada Inn, Red Roof Inn, Super 8, Travelodge
Other	N: ATMs, AutoZone, Auto Services, Amtrak, BJ's Natural Foods, Big Lots, Cinema, Grocery, U-Haul, to Shady Lane RV Camp▲
	S: Auto Service, Wal-Mart
3	Marine Corps Logistics Base
5	Nebo St, Daggett (EB)
7	A St, Daggett
FStop	N: DRS
Food	N: Rest/Daggett TS
Other	N: Barstow/Calico KOA▲, to Calico Ghost Town Campground▲
12	Hidden Springs Rd, Barstow-Daggett Airport
18	National Trails Hwy, Newberry Spgs
FStop	N: Calico Petroleum #2
	S: Kelly's Market
Other	N: to Twin Lakes RV Park▲
	S: Auto Repair & Towing
23	Fort Cady Rd, Newberry Springs
FStop	N: Wesco Fuel & Food Texaco
Food	N: Rest/Wesco TS
	S: Bagdad Café
Lodg	S: Newberry Mt RV Park▲ & Motel
Other	N: Laundry/Wesco TS
(28)	Desert Oasis Rest Area (Both dir) (RR, Phones, Picnic)
33	Hector Rd
50	Ludlow Rd, Crucero Rd, Amboy, 29 Palms, Historic Rte 66, Ludlow
FStop	S: Ludlow Truck Stop
Gas	N: to 76
Food	S: Ludlow Café, Roy's Cafe
Lodg	S: Ludlow Motel

EXIT	CALIFORNIA
TServ	S: Ludlow TS
78	Kelbaker Rd, to Amboy, Kelso
100	Essex Rd, Essex
Other	N: to Providence Mtn State Park, Mitchell Caverns
(106)	Fenner Rest Area (Both dir) (RR, Phones)
107	Goffs Rd, Essex
FStop	N: Hi Sahara Oasis
Other	S: to 29 Palms Golf & RV Resort▲, Knott Sky RV Park▲, Joshua Tree RV Lake▲
115	Mountain Spring Rd, Essex Amboy, 29 Palms
120	Water Rd
133	US 95N, to Searchlight, Las Vegas
139	W Park Rd, River Rd Cutoff (EB)
Gas	N: Gas Mart, Texaco
Food	N: Carl's Jr, China Garden, CA Pantry, Wagon Wheel Rest, Taco Bell
Lodg	N: Best Western Royal Inn♥, Best Western Colorado River Inn♥, Sunset Inn
AServ	N: Texaco
Other	N: Needles KOA▲, Fenders River Rd Resort & Motel, Rainbo Beach Resort▲, Desert View RV Resort▲, to Avi Resort Casino & RV Resort▲
141	W Broadway, Needles Hwy, River Rd, to AZ 95, Needles
FStop	N: Westside Chevron
Gas	S: ArcoAmPm, Mobil, Shell
Food	N: Hungry Bear Rest, KFC
	S: Carl's Jr, Wagon Wheel, Taco Bell
Lodg	N: Best Hotel, Desert Mirage Inn, River Valley Motor Lodge, Robinson's Motel, Sage Motel
	S: Best Western Royal Inn♥, Best Western♥, Budget Inn, Needles Inn, Relax Inn
TServ	N: A&A Diesel Service, Great West Truck & Auto
Other	N: Fort Mohave Indian Reservation, Needles Marina Park▲, to Spirit Mountain RV Park▲, Moon River RV Resort▲, Snowbird RV Resort▲
	S: Auto Service, Auto Dealers, Grocery, Transmissions
142	J St, Needles
Gas	N: 76
Food	N: Jack in the Box, McDonald's
	S: Denny's
Lodg	N: Traveler's Inn♥

EXIT	AZ / CA
	S: Days Inn♥, Motel 6
Med	S: + CO River Medical Center
Other	N: Auto & Truck Repair, ATMs, Banks, Big O Tires, Museum, Amtrak
	S: Courts, CA State Hwy Patrol Post
144	US 95S, E Broadway, to Blythe
FStop	N: Eastside Chevron
Gas	N: Mobil, Shell◆
Food	N: Burger King, Domino's Pizza, Roberto's Taco Shop
Lodg	N: Rte 66 Motel
	S: Best Value Inn♥
TServ	S: Big D Tire, Stout Comm'l Truck Tire Svc
Med	S: + Family Care Clinic
Other	N: ATMs, Banks, Basha's, Laundromat, RiteAid, U-Haul
	S: Needles Airport✈, to Calizona RV Park▲
147	Five Mile Rd US 95S, to Blythe
Other	S: Calizona RV Park▲, Needles Airport✈
(148)	Inspection Stop (Produce Trucks) (EB)
(149)	Inspection Stop (All Vehicles) (WB)
153	Park Moabi Rd
Other	N: Moabi Reg'l Park▲
NOTE:	MM 155: Arizona State Line
	(Pacific (CA) / Mountain (AZ) TIME ZONE)
	CALIFORNIA
	ARIZONA
	(MOUNTAIN TIME ZONE-NO DST)
1	Topock Rd, CR 10, AZ 95, Topock, to Bullhead City, Laughlin, NV (Gas approx 4 mi N)
2	Needle Mountain Rd
(3)	Weigh Station (Both dir)
9	AZ 95S, Rice Dr, Lake Havasu City, London Bridge Rd, to Parker
TStop	S: Pilot Travel Center #211 (Scales)
Food	S: Wendy's/Pilot TC
Other	S: Laundry/WiFi/Pilot TC, to Prospectors RV Resort▲, Lake Havasu Resort▲, Havasu Falls RV Resort▲, Havasu RV Resort▲, Lake Havasu City Airport✈
13	Franconia Rd
20	Gem Acres Rd, Bullhead City
(23)	Rest Area (EB) (RR, Phones, Picnic)

◆ = Regular Gas Stations with Diesel ▲ = RV Friendly Locations ♥ = Pet Friendly Locations

RED PRINT SHOWS LARGE VEHICLE PARKING/ACCESS ON SITE OR NEARBY BROWN PRINT SHOWS CAMPGROUNDS/RV PARKS

Page 177

INTERSTATE 40 W E

EXIT	ARIZONA
(24)	**Rest Area (WB)** (RR, Phones, Picnic)
25	Alamo Rd
Gas	N: GAS◊
26	Proving Ground Rd
28	Old Trails Rd
37	Griffith Rd
44	AZ 66, CR 10, Oatman Rd, Kingman
TStop	S: Crazy Fred's Truck Stop
Food	S: Café/Crazy Fred's, Burger Barn
TWash	S: Crazy Fred's TS
TServ	S: Crazy Fred's TS/Tires
Other	S: Laundry/WiFi/Crazy Fred's TS
48	US 93, to AZ 68, I-40 Bus, Beale St, Kingman, to Laughlin, Bullhead City Las Vegas
FStop	N: Hallum Fuel Mart/Shell
TStop	N: Travel Center of America #94/76 (Scales), USA AmBest Travel Center
Gas	N: Express Stop◊, Mobil, Woody's S: Chevron, Circle K
Food	N: Subway/USA TC, CountryPr/Popeye's/TA TC, House of Chan, Wendy's S: Quiznos/Chevron, Calico's, Carl Jr, Roadrunner Cafe
Lodg	N: Budget Inn, Frontier Motel, Knights Inn S: Arizona Inn♥, Motel 6♥, Beale Hotel, Hotel Brunswick, Quality Inn
AServ	N: Auto & RV Service, Best Tire & Auto S: Chevron, One Stop Automotive
TServ	N: TA TC/Tires, Great West Truck & Auto Service, Goodyear
Other	N: Laundry/WiFi/TA TC, RVDump/Mobil S: Ft Beale RV Park▲, Canyon West RV Park▲, ATM, Bank, Amtrak, Museum, to Adobe RV Park▲, Sir Albert's RV Park▲, Golden Valley RV Park▲, Desert Sunset Park▲
51	Stockton Hill Rd, CR 20, Kingman
Gas	N: ArcoAmPm, Chevron, Circle K S: Circle K, USA Fuel, Safeway
Food	N: Cracker Barrel, Domino's, Golden Corral, IHOP, KFC, Subway, Taco Bell, Whataburger S: DQ, Pizza Hut
Lodg	N: Travelodge
Med	N: + Kingman Regional Medical Center S: + Fastrax Urgent Care
Other	N: Albertson's, AutoZone, Auto Dealers ATMs, Banks, Brake Masters, Checkers, Holden's Auto & Truck Service, PetCo♥, Brake Masters, Office Depot, Safeway, Smith Food & Drug, Staples, Winston Tire, Wal-Mart sc▲, Walgreen's, Mohave Comm College, Trotter's RV, AZ NW RV, Kingman KOA▲, Circle S Campground▲ S: ATMs, Banks, CarQuest, Express Lube & Tires, Safeway, Kingman Muni Golf Course, Mohave Co Fairgrounds
53	AZ 66, I-40 Bus, Andy Devine Ave, Kingman
FStop	N: Shell
TStop	N: Flying J Travel Plaza/Conoco (Scales)
Gas	N: Chevron, Mobil S: 76, Shell, Shell, Sinclair
Food	N: Cookery/FastFood/FJ TP, Arby's, Burger King, Denny's, Jack in the Box, McDonald's, Maddog's Doghouse Sports Bar & Grill, Pizza Hut, Taco Bell

EXIT	ARIZONA
	S: ABC Buffet, Dambar Steak House, JB's Rest, Lo's Chinese, Oyster's Mexican & Seafood, Sonic
Lodg	N: Days Inn, Econo Lodge, First Value Inn, Motel 6♥, Silver Queen Motel♥, Super 8, Travelodge S: Best Value Inn, Best Western♥, Days Inn, Comfort Inn, Holiday Inn Express, High Desert Inn, Route 66 Motel Quality Inn, Rodeway Inn♥
TServ	N: Great West Commercial Tire, Goodyear
Other	N: Laundry/BarbSh/WiFi/RVDump/LP/ FJ TP, ATMs, Basha's, Laundromat, Kmart, Pharmacy, Mother Rd Harley Davidson, Russell's Auto & RV Service, Tire World, Trotter RV, Kingman Airport✈, Kingman KOA▲, Zuni Village RV Park▲ S: Economy Tire Service, NAPA, Penske, Sunrise RV Park▲, Police Dept
59	CR 259, DW Ranch Rd, Kingman
FStop	N: Love's Travel Stop #272
Food	N: Subway/Chesters/Love's TS
Other	N: Laundry/WiFi/RVDump/Love's TS
66	Blake Ranch Rd, Kingman
TStop	N: Petro Stopping Center #15/Mobil (Scales)
Food	N: IronSkllet/PizzaHut/Petro SC
TWash	N: Blue Beacon TW/Petro SC
TServ	N: Petro SC/Tires, Speedco
Other	N: Laundry/Petro SC, Blake Ranch RV Park & Horse Motel/RVDump▲
71	Jct US 93S, to Wickenburg, Phoenix
79	Silver Springs Rd
87	Willows Ranch Rd

EXIT	ARIZONA
91	Fort Rock Rd, Kingman
96	Cross Mountain Rd, Seligman
103	Jolly Rd
109	Anvil Rock Rd
121	AZ 66, I-40 Bus, Seligman
Gas	N: Chevron
123	AZ 66, I-40 Bus, CR 5, Seligman
FStop	N: Shell S: Johnsons Travel Center/Chevron
Food	S: Subway/Johnsons TC
Lodg	N: 66 Hotel, Canyon Lodge
Other	N: Seligman/Rte 66 KOA▲
(132)	Weigh Station (Both dir)
139	Crookton Rd, Ash Fork
144	I-40 Bus, Ash Fork
FStop	S: Texaco
Gas	S: Chevron
Other	N: Ash Fork/Grand Canyon KOA▲ S: Laundry/Exxon, Tourist Info, Museum, Hillside RV Park▲
146	AZ 89, Ash Fork, Prescott
Gas	N: Mobil◊
Food	N: Ranch House Café, Route 66 Grill
Lodg	N: Ash Fork Inn, Copperstate Motel
148	County Line Rd, Williams
149	Monte Carlo Rd
TStop	N: Monte Carlo Truck Stop
Food	N: Rest/Monte Carlo TS
TServ	N: Monte Carlo TS
151	Welch Rd (NO TRUCKS)
(156)	Safety Pullout (WB)
NOTE:	MM 156: 6% Steep Grade next 5 mi
157	Devil Dog Rd, Williams (NO TRUCKS)
161	I-40 Bus, Bill Williams Ave, Williams, Golf Course Dr, Grand Canyon
Gas	S: Chevron◊, Mobil, Shell◊
Food	S: Denny's, Parker House, Red's Steaks, Smokin Barrel
Lodg	S: Best Western, Comfort Inn, Days Inn, Motel 6, Norris Motel, Westerner Motel
Med	S: + Hospital
Other	N: Cataract Lake Co Park▲ S: NAPA
163	Grand Canyon Blvd, to AZ 73, Williams, Grand Canyon
Gas	N: Chevron◊ S: Conoco, Mobil, Shell◊
Food	N: Doc Holliday's Steakhouse, Subway S: Buckles, Jack in the Box, McDonald's, Pizza Hut, Rosa's Cantina
Lodg	N: Fairfield Inn, Holiday Inn S: Econo Lodge, Grand Canyon Hotel, Grand Motel, Knights Inn, Lodge on Rte 66, Rte 66 Inn
Other	N: to Canyon Gateway RV Park▲, to Williams Muni Airport✈ S: Amtrak, Auto & Truck Repair, Railside RV Ranch▲, to Bill Williams Ski Area
165	AZ 64, I-40 Bus, Red Lake, Williams, Grand Canyon
Gas	N: AJ's Mini Mart, Shell◊ (Serv approx 4.5 mi N)
Lodg	S: Econo Lodge, Motel 6, Super 8, Travelodge

◊ = Regular Gas Stations with Diesel   ▲ = RV Friendly Locations   ♥ = Pet Friendly Locations
RED PRINT SHOWS LARGE VEHICLE PARKING/ACCESS ON SITE OR NEARBY   BROWN PRINT SHOWS CAMPGROUNDS/RV PARKS

INTERSTATE 40 W/E — ARIZONA

EXIT		ARIZONA
	Other	N: Grand Canyon/Williams KOA▲ to Kaibab Natl Forest/Kaibab Lake Campground▲ S: Railroad RV Park▲
167		Garland Prairie Rd, Circle Pines Rd
	Other	N: Williams/Circle Pines KOA▲
171		Pittman Valley Rd, Deer Farm Rd
	Food	S: Rest/Quality Inn
	Lodg	S: Quality Inn
178		Parks Rd, Williams
	Gas	N: Mustang◊
	Other	N: Ponderosa Forest RV Park▲
(182)		Rest Area (EB) (RR, Phones, Vend, Weather)
(183)		Rest Area (WB) (RR, Phones, Vend, Weather)
185		Transwestern Rd, Bellemont
	TStop	N: Pilot Travel Center #180 (Scales)
	Food	N: McDonald's/Subway/Pilot TC S: 66 Roadhouse Grill
	Lodg	N: Microtel America's Best Value Inn
	TServ	N: Pilot TC
	Other	N: Laundry/WiFi/Pilot TC S: Navajo Army Depot, Nat'l Guard
190		A-1 Mountain Rd, Flagstaff
191		I-40 Bus, US 66, to Flagstaff, Grand Canyon (All Serv approx 5mi N)
	Other	N: Woody Mtn Campground & RV Park▲
192		Flagstaff Ranch Rd
	Other	N: Woody Mtn Campground & RV Park▲, Kit Carson RV Park▲
195		AZ 89S, to US 180, Flagstaff (WB)
195B		AZ 89N, to US 180, Flagstaff, to Grand Canyon
	Gas	N: 76, Chevron, Circle K, Conoco◊, Exxon◊, Mobil, Shell
	Food	N: Arby's, Burger King, Carl's Jr, DQ, CoCo's, Denny's, Fazoli's, Fuddrucker's, IHOP, KFC, McDonald's, Olive Garden, Pizza Hut, Red Lobster, Sizzler, Village Inn
	Lodg	N: Amerisuites, Comfort Inn, Days Inn, Econo Lodge, Embassy Suites, Fairfield Inn, Hampton Inn, Hilton Garden Inn, La Quinta Inn♥, Quality Inn, Ramada Ltd, Rodeway Inn, Sleep Inn, Travelodge
	Med	N: + Flagstaff Comm Hospital
	Other	N: ATM's, Banks, Cinema, Discount Tire, Kmart, Safeway, Staples, Target, New Frontiers Nat'l Foods, Wal-Mart, Walgreen's, Lowell Observatory, Northern AZ Univ, to US 66: Woody Mountain Campground & RV Park▲, Kit Carson RV Park▲, Rt 66 RV & Auto Serv Ctr

EXIT		ARIZONA
(195A)		Jct I-17S, AZ 89A, Sedona, Phoenix Northern Arizona University
	Other	S: to Flagstaff Pulliam Airport✈
198		Butler Ave, Flagstaff
	TStop	S: AmBest/Little America Travel Center/Sinclair (Scales)
	Gas	N: 76◊, Chevron, Conoco◊, Exxon◊, Giant◊, Shell S: Mobil
	Food	N: Burger King, Country Host, Cracker Barrel, Denny's, McDonald's, Outback Steaks, Taco Bell, Rest/Econo Lodge S: Black Bart's Steakhouse
	Lodg	N: Best Western, Econo Lodge, Flagstaff Inn, Holiday Inn, Howard Johnson, Motel 6, Quality Inn, Ramada Inn, Relax Inn, Super 8, Travelodge S: Little America Hotel
	TServ	S: Little America/Tires
	Other	N: AutoZone, Albertson's, Auto Dealers, Firestone, Fry's, RVDump/Conoco S: Laundry/WiFi/Little America TC, Black Bart's RV Park▲
201		US 89N, I-40 Bus, US 180W, Page, Grand Canyon, Flagstaff
	Gas	N: 76, Chevron, Conoco, Express Stop◊ S: Mobil
	Food	N: Arby's, Del Taco, Jack in the Box, Pizza Hut, Ruby Tuesday, Sizzler Steak House
	Lodg	N: Best Western, Days Inn, Hampton Inn, Super 8 S: Fairfield Resort, Residence Inn
	Med	N: + Hospital
	Other	N: ATMs, Banks, Auto Services, Flagstaff Mall, Cinemas, Discount Tire, Goodyear, Safeway, AT Stadium, Flagstaff RV Sales & Service, Flagstaff Grand Canyon KOA▲, J&H RV Park▲
204		Santa Fe Ave, to US 180, to US 89N, Walnut Canyon Rd
	Other	S: Walnut Canyon Nat'l Monument
207		Cosnino Rd
(208)		Weigh Station (Both dir)
211		CR 394, Flagstaff, Winona
	Gas	N: Shell◊
	Other	N: Winona Trading Post
219		NF 126, Twin Arrows
225		Buffalo Range Rd, Flagstaff
230		Old 66 Rd, Two Guns
233		Meteor Crater Rd, Flagstaff
	Gas	S: Mobil
	Food	S: Subway/Mobil
	Other	S: Meteor Crater RV Park▲

EXIT		ARIZONA
(235)		Rest Area (Both dir) (RR, Phones, Picnic, Info)
239		Meteor City Rd, Red Gap Ranch Rd
	Other	S: Meteor Crater Trading Post, to Meteor Crater
245		AZ 99, Flagstaff, to Leupp
252		AZ 87S, I-40 Bus, Winslow, Payson
	Gas	S: Shell◊
	Food	S: Burger King, Casa Blanca Café, Pizza Hut
	Lodg	S: Best Inn, Days Inn, Delta Motel, Rest Inn, Super 8, Travelodge
	Other	S: Auto Services, Glenn's RV Repair, Winslow Muni Airport✈
253		N Park Dr, Winslow
	TStop	N: Super American TS/USA Travel Center (Scales)
	Gas	N: Woody's S: Depot
	Food	N: Rest/Super Am TS, Arby's, Denny's, Captn Tony's Pizza, Pizza Hut, Subway S: KFC, McDonald's, Subway, Taco Bell
	Lodg	N: Best Western, Comfort Inn, Econo Lodge♥, Motel 6♥
	Med	S: + Winslow Memorial Hospital
	TWash	N: Super Am TS
	Other	N: RVDump/WiFi/Super Am TS, Big O Tire, Dollar General, Laundromat, Wal-Mart, Visitor Center, Santa Fe Station Golf Course S: ATMs, Banks, Basha's, Family Dollar, Safeway, NAPA, Laundromat, Winslow Muni Airport✈
255		Transcon Ln, to I-40 Bus, US 87S, Winslow, to Payson
	TStop	S: Flying J Travel Plaza #5041 (Scales)
	Food	S: CountryMkt/FJ TP, China Inn, DQ, Sonic, Triple R's Home Cooking
	Lodg	N: Holiday Inn Express
	TServ	S: High Chaparrel Truck Repair, Winslow Truck Repair
	Other	S: Laundry/BarbSh/WiFi/RVDump/LP/FJ TP, Amtrak
257		AZ 87N, AZ 66, to Second Mesa (Access to Ex #255 Serv S)
	Other	N: Homolovi Ruins State Park▲
264		Hibbard Rd, Winslow
269		Jackrabbit Rd
	Gas	S: Jack Rabbit Trading Post◊
274		I-40 Bus, to Joseph City
	Gas	N: Speedy's
	Food	N: Mr G's Pizza
	Other	N: Laundry, U-Haul, Dream Catcher RV Park▲, Norma's RV Park▲

◊ = Regular Gas Stations with Diesel   ▲ = RV Friendly Locations   ♥ = Pet Friendly Locations

RED PRINT SHOWS LARGE VEHICLE PARKING/ACCESS ON SITE OR NEARBY   BROWN PRINT SHOWS CAMPGROUNDS/RV PARKS

Page 179

Interstate 40 W/E

EXIT	ARIZONA	EXIT	AZ / NM	EXIT	NEW MEXICO
277	I-40 Bus, Winslow, Joseph City	339	US 191S, Sanders, St Johns		Food	N: Applebee's Arby's, Burger King, Cracker Barrel, Denny's, Furr's Cafeteria, Golden Corral, McDonald's, Pizza Hut, Sizzler, Sonic
TStop	N: Love's Travel Stop #278	Gas	S: Conoco		
Food	N: Subway/ChestersGr/Love's TS	Other	N: US Post Office		
Other	N: WiFi/Love's TS	(340)	Weigh Station / Inspection Station (Both dir)		S: Blake's Lotaburger, El Sombrero Rest, Garcia's Sunset Grill, Plaza Cafe
280	Hunt Rd, Geronimo Rd				
Other	N: Geronimo Trading Post	341	Cedar Point Rd, Ganado	Lodg	N: Hampton Inn, Quality Inn♥, Ramada Ltd
283	Perkins Valley Rd, Golf Course Rd	Gas	N: Amoco		
FStop	S: Fuel Express/Shell	343	Querino Rd, Ganado		S: Best Western, Days Inn♥, Economy Inn♥, Golden Desert Motel, Log Cabin Lodge, Super 8♥
Food	S: Rest/Fuel Express	346	Pine Springs Rd		
Other	S: Laundry/WiFi/Fuel Express	NOTE:	MM 347: Elevation 6000'	Med	S: + Gallup Indian Medical Center
285	I-40 Bus, US 180, Hopi Dr, to AZ 77, Holbrook	348	St Anselm Rd, Ganado, Houck	Other	N: AutoZone, Auto Dealers, ATMs, Big Lots, Firestone, Family Dollar, NAPA, Rio West Mall, Kmart, Laundromat, Safeway, Tires, UPS Store, Wal-Mart sc, Cinema, Cedar Animal Medical Center
Gas	S: Pacific Pride♦	Gas	N: Chevron		
Food	S: Butterfield Stage Co, BBQ, Pizza Hut, Wayside Café	Food	N: Pancake House Rest		
		351	Allentown Rd, Ganado		
Lodg	S: Best Inn♥, Budget Host Inn, Desert Inn, Holbrook Inn, Roseway Inn, Star Inn, Wigwam Motel	354	Hawthorne Rd		S: Amtrak, ATMs, Banks, Big O Tires, Firestone, Goodyear
		357	Indian Hwy 12N, St Michael's, Lupton, Window Rock	22	Ford Dr, Montoya Blvd
Other	S: Auto Services			N:	NM Welcome Center (Both dir)
286	AZ 77S, I-40 Bus, Navajo Blvd, US 180E, Holbrook, to Show Low	359	Grants Rd, Ganado, Lupton	Gas	S: 7-11, Armco, Chevron, Conoco, Giant, Shell
Gas	N: 76, Shamrock♦	TStop	N: Speedy's Truck Stop	Food	S: Burger King, Carl's Jr, Earl's, Long John Silver, McDonald's, Taco Bell
	S: Chevron♦, MiniMart, Woody"s	Food	N: Rest/Speedy's		
Food	N: KFC, McDonald's, Pizza Hut, Roadrunner Café, Taco Bell	TServ	N: Speedy's TS/Tires	Lodg	S: Best Western, Blue Spruce Lodge, El Rancho Hotel, El Capitan Motel, Lariat Lodge, Redwood Lodge
	S: DQ	Other	N: Laundry/LP/Speedy's TS		
Lodg	N: 66 Motel, Best Inn, Comfort Inn, Holiday Inn Express, BW Sahara Inn, Super 8, Travelodge	(359)	AZ Welcome Center (WB) Rest Area (EB) (RR, Picnic)	Other	S: Albertson's, ATMs, Auto Services, RV & Truck Service, Radio Shack, UPS Store, Walgreen's
	S: America's Best Value Inn, Budget Inn, Western Holiday Motel	NOTE:	MM 359: New Mexico State Line	26	I-40 Bus, NM 118, E Gallup
Med	S: + Petrified Forest Medical Center		(MOUNTAIN TIME ZONE-NO DST)	FStop	N: Chevron
Other	N: Cinema, Vet♥, OK RV Park▲		◐ ARIZONA	Gas	S: Conoco, Fina♦, Star Mart, Shell
	S: US Post Office		◐ NEW MEXICO	Food	N: Denny's
289	I-40 Bus, Holbrook		(MOUNTAIN TIME ZONE)	Lodg	N: La Quinta Inn♥, Sleep Inn
Gas	N: Chevron, Hatch's, Circle K, Mobil	(3)	Rest Area (Both dir) (RR, Phones, Picnic)		S: BW/Red Rock Inn, Super 8
Food	N: Denny's, Jerry's, McDonald's, KFC			Med	S: + Gallup Hospital
Lodg	N: Best Western, Comfort Inn, Days Inn, Econo Lodge, Motel 6♥, Ramada Inn	8	NM 118, Rte 66, to Manuelito	Other	N: Gallup KOA▲, Red Rock State Park▲
		(12)	Weigh / Inspection Station (EB)		S: NM State Hwy Patrol Post
Other	N: Holbrook Airport✈, Holbrook/ Petrified Forest KOA▲	16	I-40 Bus, NM 214, W Gallup	31	Fort Wingate Army Depot, Church Rock
292	AZ 77N, to Keems Canyon	TStop	N: Travel Center of America #8 (Scales), Texaco Travel Center	33	NM 400, McGaffey, Ft Wingate
TStop	N: AmBest/Hopi Travel Plaza/Conoco (Scales)		S: Love's Travel Stop #215	Other	N: to Red Rock State Park▲
Food	N: Rest/FastFood/Hopi TP	Gas	S: Chevron♦, Conoco, Shell	36	Iyanbito
Twash	N: Hopi TP	Food	N: CntryPr/Blimpie/TA TC, Rest/Texaco TC	39	Refinery, Jamestown
Other	N: Laundry/CB/Hopi TP		S: Subway/Chesters/Love's TS, Olympic Kitchen, NM Steak House, McDonald's, Rest/BW, Rest/HI, Westend Donut & Deli, Taco Bell	TStop	N: Pilot Travel Center #305 (Scales)
294	Sun Valley Rd			Food	N: GrandmaMax's/Subway/Pilot TC
Gas	S: Arizona Stage Stop			TWash	N: Pilot TC
Food	S: Arizona Stage Stop			TServ	N: Pilot TC/Boss Truck Shop/Tires
300	Goodwater Rd, Holbrook	Lodg	N: Howard Johnson/TA TC	Other	N: Laundry/BarbSh/RVDump/Pilot TC
303	Adamana Rd		S: Best Western, Budget Inn, Comfort Inn, Days Inn♥, Econo Lodge, Hampton Inn, Holiday Inn, Microtel, Red Roof Inn♥, Travelodge♥	(40)	Parking Area (EB)
Gas	S: Painted Desert Indian Center			44	Coolidge
311	Petrified Forest National Park			47	Continental Divide
Other	N: Petrified Forest Nat'l Park/Crystal Forest Gift Shop/RVParking▲	TWash	N: Blue Beacon TW/TA TC	Gas	N: Chevron
		TServ	N: TA TC/Tires, Texaco TC/Tires	Other	N: US Post Office
(316)	Parking Area (Both dir)		S: Mike's Auto, Truck & RV Repair & Tires, RG Truck & RV Services	53	NM 371, NM 612, Gallup, to Chaco Canyon, Thoreau
320	Pinta Rd, Chambers				
325	Pinta Rd, Navajo	Other	N: Laundry/WiFi/TA TC, Laundry/Tex TC, Kmart	63	NM 412, Prewitt, Bluewater St Park
FStop	S: Navajo Travel Center			72	Bluewater Village
Food	S: Subway/Navajo TC		S: WiFi/Love's TS, USA RV Park▲, Gallup Muni Airport✈, Arrow Automotive, UPS Store	Gas	N: Exxon♦
330	McCarrell Rd, Chambers			Food	N: DQ/Exxon
333	US 191N, Chambers, Ganado	20	US 491, NM 602S, Munoz Dr, to Shiprock, Zuni	79	NM 122, NM 605, Horizon Blvd, Milan, San Mateo
Gas	N: Chevron	Gas	N: 7-11, Giant, Phillips 66♦, Shell	TStop	N: Love's Travel Stop #257
	S: Mobil		S: Exxon, Shell♦		S: Petro Stopping Center #13/Mobil (Scales)
Food	S: Rest/Best Western			Food	N: Subway/ChestersGr/Love's TS
Lodg	S: Best Western				S: Iron Skillet/FastFood/Petro SC

♦ = Regular Gas Stations with Diesel   ▲ = RV Friendly Locations   ♥ = Pet Friendly Locations
RED PRINT SHOWS LARGE VEHICLE PARKING/ACCESS ON SITE OR NEARBY   BROWN PRINT SHOWS CAMPGROUNDS/RV PARKS

EXIT		NEW MEXICO
	Lodg	N: Crossroads Motel
	TServ	S: Petro SC/Tires, Speedco
	Other	N: Wifi/Love's TS, Bar S RV Park▲
		S: Laundry/Wifi/Petro SC, NM State Hwy Patrol Post, Grants-Milan Muni Airport✈
81A		NM 53S, San Rafael (EB)
81B		NM 53N, Grants (EB)
81		I-40 Bus, NM 53, Grants, San Rafael
	Gas	N: Chevron, Shell
	Food	N: Burger King, KFC, McDonald's
	Lodg	N: Sands Motel
	Med	N: + Cibola General Hospital
	Other	N: ATMs, Banks, Auto Services, Flea Market, Museum
		S: Grants/Cibola Sands KOA▲, Blue Spuce RV Park▲
85		I-40 Bus, NM 122, NM 547, Grants, Mt Taylor
	Gas	N: Chevron, Conoco, Shell
	Food	N: 4 B's Rest, Chona's Cafe, Denny's, NM Steakhouse, Pizza Hut, Subway, Taco Bell, Rest/BW
	Lodg	N: Best Western♥, Comfort Inn, Days Inn♥, Economy Inn, Holiday Inn Express♥, Motel 6♥, Super 8, Travelodge♥
	Med	N: + Cibola General Hospital
	Other	N: AutoZone, Wal-Mart sc, Golf Course, Lavaland RV Park▲
89		NM 117, Cubero, to Quernado
	Gas	N: Citgo, Conoco
	Food	N: Stuckey's/Citgo
(93)		Parking Area (EB)
96		NM 124, Cubero, McCartys
100		Acomita Rd, Cubero, to San Fidel
102		Sky City Rd, Casa Blanca, Acoma, Sky City
	S:	Rest Area (Both dir)
	TStop	N: AmBest/Sky City Travel Center
	Food	N: Rest/McDonald's/Sky City TC
	Lodg	N: Sky City Hotel/Sky City TC
	Med	N: + Hospital
	Other	N: Laundry/BarbSh/ChromeSh/Casino/RV Park▲/Sky City TC
		S: Sky City Culteral Museum
104		NM 124, to Cubero, Budville
108		NM 23, Paraje Dr, Casa Blanca
	TStop	N: PTP/Dancing Eagle Travel Center/Conoco
	Food	N: Rest/FastFood/DE TC

Personal Notes

EXIT		NEW MEXICO
	Other	N: Laundry/RVDump/RV Park▲/Casino/Grocery/DE TC
(113)		Parking Area/Scenic View (Both dir)
114		NM 124, Rte 66, to Laguna
	Gas	N: Conoco◊
117		Mesita Rd, Casa Blanca
126		NM 6, Laguna, to Los Lunas
131		Canoncito School Rd, Laguna
140		Rio Puerco, Laguna
	TStop	S: Route 66 Travel Center/Conoco
	Gas	N: Exxon
	Food	S: Rest/FastFood/Conoco
	Other	S: Laundry/Rte 66 TC, Route 66 Casino
149		Paseo Del Vulcan Rd, Central Ave, Albuquerque, Paseo, Del Volcan
	FStop	S: Nine Mile Hill Chevron, Hilltop Shamrock

EXIT		NEW MEXICO
	Food	S: Café, Hungry Cowboy Buffet, Tumbleweed Steakhouse
	Other	N: Enchanted Trails RV Park & Trading Post▲, American RV/Camping World, Double Eagle II Airport✈
		S: American RV Park▲, High Desert RV Park▲, Rte 66 RV & Auto Repair
153		98th St, Nolasco Rd
	TStop	S: Flying J Travel Plaza #5032/Conoco (Scales)
	Food	S: Rest/FastFood/FJ TP, Hungry Cowboy Buffet, Tumbleweed Steakhouse
	Lodg	S: Microtel
	Other	S: Laundry/BarbSh/WiFi/RVDump/LP/FJ TP, Palisades RV Park▲
154		Unser Blvd
	Gas	N: Shamrock
		S: U Pump It
	Food	S: Hungry Cowboy Buffet
	Lodg	S: JB's Rte 66 Motel
	Other	N: to Petroglyph Nat'l Monument
155		NM 448, Coors Rd, to Rio Rancho
	Gas	N: Chevron, Conoco◊, Shamrock◊
		S: Chevron, Phillips 66◊, Shell
	Food	N: Applebee's, Arby's, Chili's, Golden Corral, IHOP, McDonald's, Subway, Wendy's
		S: Denny's, Furr's, Pizza Hut, Taco Bell, Subway, Village Inn
	Lodg	N: Westside Inn
		S: Comfort Inn, Days Inn, Holiday Inn Express, La Quinta Inn♥, Motel 6♥, Super 8
	Other	N: Grocery, Goodyear, Home Depot, Staples, Walgreen's, Wal-Mart sc
		S: Albertson's, ATMs, Banks, CarWash, Discount Tire, Dalon RV Sales & Service
157A		Rio Grande Blvd
	Gas	N: Bubba's Conv Store
		S: Chevron, Shell
	Food	N: Burger King, Ned's
	Lodg	S: Best Western, Econo Lodge, Hotel Albuquerque, Sheraton
	Other	S: Museums
157B		12th St, Albuquerque (EB)
	Other	N: Walgreen's
158		8th St, 6th St, Albuquerque
	FStop	N: Love's Travel Stop #210
	Gas	N: Phillips 66
		S: Chevron
	Food	N: Subway/Love's TS
	Lodg	S: Interstate Inn, Travelers Inn
	TServ	N: Big West Trucks
	Other	N: WiFi/RVDump/Love's TS
159A		6th St, 4th St, 2nd St, Broadway, University Blvd (EB)
	FStop	N: 6th St NW: Love's Travel Stop #210

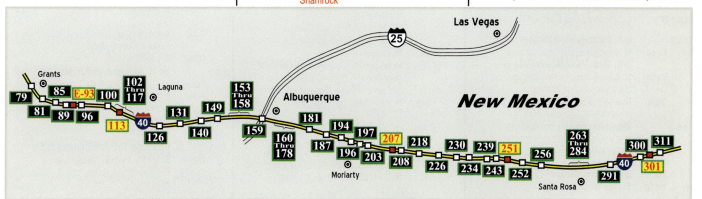

◊ = Regular Gas Stations with Diesel ▲ = RV Friendly Locations ♥ = Pet Friendly Locations

RED PRINT SHOWS LARGE VEHICLE PARKING/ACCESS ON SITE OR NEARBY BROWN PRINT SHOWS CAMPGROUNDS/RV PARKS

Page 181

INTERSTATE 40 W E

NEW MEXICO

EXIT		
	TStop	N: University Blvd NE: Travel Center of America #81/Chevron (Scales)
	Food	N: CountryPride/TA TC
	Gas	N: Chevron, Conoco
		S: Diamond Shamrock
	Food	N: Furr's, Whataburger
		S: Tony's Pizza, Village Inn
	Lodg	N: Comfort Inn, Fairfield Inn, La Quinta Inn ♥, Rodeway Inn
		S: Interstate Inn, Travelers Inn
	TServ	N: TA TC/Tires
		S: Great Basin Trucks
	Other	N: Laundry/WiFi/RVDump/TA TC
(159BC)		Jct I-25, S-Las Cruces, N-Santa Fe
159D		University Blvd (WB)
	TStop	N: Travel Center of America #81/Chevron (Scales)
	Food	N: CountryPride/TA TC
	Lodg	N: Candlewood Suites, Comfort Inn, Fairfield Inn, Holiday Inn Express, La Quinta Inn ♥, Rodeway Inn
	TServ	N: TA TC/Tires
	Med	S: + Carrie Tingley Hospital, + Univ Of NM Hospital
	Other	N: Laundry/WiFi/RVDump/TA TC
160		Carlisle Blvd, Albuquerque
	Gas	N: Circle K, Conoco, Shell
		S: Circle K, Shell
	Food	N: JB's, Pizza Hut, Rudy's Country Store & BBQ, Sonic, Village Inn
		S: Burger King, Whataburger
	Lodg	N: Candlewood Suites, Econo Lodge, Fairfield Inn, Hampton Inn, Holiday Inn Express, Motel 6 ♥, Radisson, Residence Inn, Super 8
	Med	S: + Univ of NM Hospital
	Other	N: ATMs, Banks, Grocery, Goodyear, Wal-Mart sc, Walgreen's, NM State Hwy Patrol Post
		S: Animal Clinic ♥, Laundromat, Kmart, Wild Oats Market, Auto Repair/Shell, Penske Auto Center
161B		San Mateo Blvd North (EB)
161A		San Mateo Blvd South (EB)
161		San Mateo Blvd (WB)
	Gas	N: Phillips 66◊, Shell
		S: Chevron
	Food	N: Burger King, Denny's, K-Bob's Seafood & Steaks, McDonald's, Starbucks, Subway
	Lodg	N: La Quinta Inn ♥
	Med	S: + Veteran's Medical Center
	Other	N: Auto Services, ATMs, Circuit City, FedEx Kinko's, Office Depot
		S: On the Road Again RV's
162A		Louisiana Blvd South (EB)
162B		Louisiana Blvd North (EB)
162		Louisiana Blvd, Albuquerque (WB)
	Food	N: Bennigan's, Le Peep, Macaroni Grill, Steak & Ale, Hickory Pit BBQ
	Lodg	N: AmeriSuites, Ambassador Inn, Homewood Suites, Marriott
	Other	N: ATMs, Banks, Cinema, FedEx Kinko's, Winrock Mall, Coronado Mall
164		Wyoming Blvd, Lomas Blvd
	Gas	N: Circle K, Don's, Phillips 66◊
	Food	N: Bumpers Bar & Grill
	Lodg	N: Best Western, Luxury Inn
	Med	N: + Kaseman Presbyterian Hospital

EXIT		
	Other	N: Auto Services, ATMs, Fresh Market, KC Auto & RV Repair
		S: Thrifty RAC, MIL/Kirtland AFB FamCamp▲, Desert RV Sales, Tom's RV Service, El Rancho MH & RV Park▲
165		Eubank Blvd
	Gas	N: Chevron, Phillips 66/Circle K
		S: Conoco, Sam's Club
	Food	N: JB's, Owl Café, Panda Express, Sonic
		S: Bob's Burgers, Burger King, Boston Market, Taco Bell, Wendy's
	Lodg	N: Days Inn ♥, Econo Lodge, Freeway Inn, GuestHouse Inn ♥, Holiday Inn Express, Howard Johnson, Quality Inn
	Other	N: ATMs, Banks, Auto Services, Best Buy, Carquest, Office Max, Petco ♥, Target, KC Auto & RV Repair
		S: ATMs, Banks, Auto Services, Costco, Office Depot, Sam's Club, Wal-Mart sc, MIL/Kirtland AFB FamCamp▲
166		Juan Tabo Blvd
	Gas	N: Chevron, Phillips 66
	Food	N: Burger King, Carrow's, McDonald's, Olive Garden, Pizza Hut, Village Inn
		S: Chin's Chinese, Whataburger
	Lodg	N: Best Value Inn, Super 8, TradeWinds Motel
	Other	N: Albertson's, Big O Tires, Discount Tire, Outdoor Adventures
		S: Auto Services, Grocery, Walgreen's, Albuquerque Central KOA▲, El Monte RV Rental

EXIT		
167		NM 556, Tramway Blvd, NM 333
	Gas	S: Chevron, Fina, Phillips 66, Shell
	Food	S: Einstein Bagels, KFC, McDonald's, Starbuck's, Waffle House
	Lodg	S: BW American Motor Inn & RV Park▲, Comfort Inn, Days Inn, Deluxe Inn, Econo Lodge ♥, Howard Johnson, Rodeway Inn
	Other	N: Laundromat
		S: ATMs, Auto Services, Banks, Cinemas, Goodyear, Grocery, Theatre, Towing, U-Haul, UPS Store, Chisolm Trail RV Repair & Service, Enchantment RV, Myers RV Center, Rocky Mtn RV & Marine Center, to Kirtland AFB
170		NM 333, Frontage Rd, Carnuel
175		NM 337, NM 14, Tijeras, Cedar Crest (Serv approx 2-3mi N)
	Gas	N: Chevron
	Food	N: Burger Boy, Cedar Point Grill, North 14 Diner, Ribs Hickory Smoked BBQ, Subway
	Other	N: to appr 5mi Turquoise Trail Campground & RV Park▲
		S: US Post Office, Mountain View Campground & RV▲
178		Zamora Rd, NM 333, Zuzax, Tijeras
	Gas	S: Chevron◊
	Other	S: Hidden Valley Camping Resort▲
181		NM 333, NM 217, Sedillo
187		NM 344, Edgewood
	Gas	N: Conoco◊
		S: Exxon, Phillips 66◊
	Food	N: DQ
		S: Home Run Pizza, McDonald's, Subway
	Other	N: to Sandia Airpark ✈
		S: AutoZone, Dollar General, Grocery, NAPA, Smith's Food & Drug, Walgreen's, US Post Office, Red Arrow Edgewood Campground▲
194		NM 41, I-40 Bus, Moriarty, Escancia
	TStop	S: Travel Center of America #229/Shell (Scales)
	Gas	S: Chevron, Phillips 66◊
	Food	S: CntryFare/BKing/PHut/TA TC, Arby's, McDonald's, Mama Rosa's Rest, Shorty's BBQ
	Lodg	S: Days Inn, Econo Lodge, Howard Johnson, Holiday Inn Express, Super 8
	TServ	S: TA TC/Tires
	Other	S: Auto Services, Auto Dealers, Laundry/BarbSh/WiFi/RVDump/LP/TA TC
196		NM 41, Howard Cavasos Blvd, Estancia, Santa Fe
	Gas	S: Circle K, Shell
	Food	S: Lotaburger, Super China Buffet, Village Grill
	Lodg	S: Comfort Inn, Lariat Motel, Motel 6 ♥, Super 8, Sunset Motel
	Other	S: Laundry, Pharmacy, Tires
197		Lp P, Abrahames Rd, Moriarty
	TStop	S: Lisa's Truck Center
	Food	S: Rest/Lisa's TC
	Lodg	S: Ponderosa Motel
	TServ	S: Lisa's TC/Tires
	Other	S: NAPA
203		Frontage Rd, Abrahames Rd
	Other	S: Zia RV Park & Campground▲
(207)		Rest Area (Both dir) (RR, Picnic)

◊ = Regular Gas Stations with Diesel   ▲ = RV Friendly Locations   ♥ = Pet Friendly Locations
RED PRINT SHOWS LARGE VEHICLE PARKING/ACCESS ON SITE OR NEARBY   BROWN PRINT SHOWS CAMPGROUNDS/RV PARKS

EXIT	NEW MEXICO
208	CR 60, Moriarty, Wagon Wheel
218	US 285, to Vaughn, Santa Fe (WB)
FStop	N: Cline's Corner Travel Center/Phillips 66
Food	N: Clines Corner Restaurant
218A	US 285, to Vaughn, Santa Fe (EB)
218B	US 285, to Vaughn, Santa Fe (EB)
(219)	Parking Area (WB)
(220)	Parking Area (EB)
226	Exit 226
230	NM 3, Encino, to Villaneuva
Other	S: to Villaneuva State Park
234AB	CR 054, Flying C Ranch (WB)
234	CR 054, Flying C Ranch (EB)
FStop	N: Bowlin's Flying C Travel Center/Exxon
Food	N: DQ/Bowlin's
239	Exit 239, CR 053, Encino
243AB	CR 4F, Milagro (WB)
243	CR 4F, Milagro (EB)
FStop	N: D&R Chevron
Food	N: Café/Chevron
(251)	Rest Area (Both dir) (RR, Phones, Picnic, RVDump)
252	Exit 252
256	US 84N, NM 219, Anton Chico, to Santa Rosa, Las Vegas, Pastura
263	CR 4B, Santa Rosa, San Ignacio
267	NM 379, CR 4H, to Colonias
FStop	N: Shell
Food	N: Stuckey's/Rest/Shell
273	US 84, I-40E Bus, Coronado St, to US 54S, Santa Rosa, to Vaughn
Gas	S: Chevron, Feed & Supply
Food	S: Mateo's Family Rest, KFC, Long John Silver, Joseph's Cantina
Lodg	S: Rancho Motor Lodge, Best Western, Comfort Inn, Days Inn, La Quinta Inn♥, Motel 6♥, Ramada Ltd
Other	N: to Santa Rosa Lake State Park▲ S: Ramblin Rose RV Park▲
275	I-40 Bus, US 54, Santa Rosa
Gas	N: Allsup's, Phillips 66, Shell S: Chevron, Fina, Shell◊
Food	N: Burger King, KFC, Long John Silver, McDonald's, Rte 66 Rest, TCBY S: Pizza Hut, Sun & Sand Rest
Lodg	N: Baymont Inn, Best Western Adobe Inn, Best Western Santa Rosa♥, Days Inn, La Quinta Inn♥, Travelodge S: American Inn, La Loma Lodge & RV Park▲, Sunset Motel, Sun n Sand Motel, Super 8, Tower Motel, Western Motel
Med	S: + Guadalupe Co Hospital
Other	N: Auto Services, Towing, Santa Rosa Campground & RV Park▲/LP, to Santa Rosa Lake State Park▲ S: Family Dollar, NM State Hwy Patrol Post
277	US 84, US 54, I-40 Bus, Santa Rosa, to Fort Sumner
TStop	S: Travel Center of America #23/Shell (Scales), Love's Travel Stop #285

EXIT	NEW MEXICO
Gas	N: Chevron
Food	N: DQ, Denny's, Golden Dragon Rest, Silver Moon Rest S: CountryPride/Subway/TA TC, Carl's Jr/Love's TS
Lodg	N: Baymont Inn, BW Santa Rosa♥, Comfort Inn, Holiday Inn Express, Motel 6♥
TServ	N: TA TC/Tires, Big Rig Truck Service
Other	N: Silver Moon Auto, Truck & RV Service, Santa Rosa Campground▲, Rt 66 Auto Museum, to Santa Rosa Lake State Park▲ S: Laundry/CB/WiFi/TA TC, RVDump/WiFi/Love's TS, Santa Rosa Muni Airport✈
284	Exit 284
291	Frontage Rd, Cuervo
Gas	N: GAS
Other	N: Wrecker Service
300	NM 129, to NM 104, Newkirk
Gas	N: Phillips 66◊
Other	N: to Conchas Lake State Park
(301)	Rest Area (Both dir) (CLOSED) (RR, Phones, Picnic, RVDump)
311	Quay Rd, Tucumcari, Montoya
321	Frontage Rd, Tucumcari, Palomas
FStop	S: Shell
Food	S: DQ/Stuckey's/Shell
329	US 54, I-40 Bus, Tucumcari (Access to #331/#332 Serv)
FStop	S: Tucumcari Travel Plaza
331	Camino del Coronado
Gas	N: Fina
Lodg	N: Paradise Motel, Tucumcari Inn, Tri Star Inn♥
TServ	N: Shipley Truck Service, John's Truck & RV Service
Other	N: Fairgrounds
332	NM 104, NM 209, 1st St, Tucumcari
TStop	N: MC Stop/Chevron
Gas	N: Phillips 66, Shell
Food	N: FastFood/MC Stop, Golden Dragon, KFC, McDonald's, Lotaburger, Pizza Hut, Sonic, Subway
Lodg	N: Americana Motel, Best Western, Buckaroo Motel, Days Inn, Friends Inn, Holiday Inn Express, Microtel, Payless Inn, PowWow Inn
TServ	N: John's Truck & RV Service
Med	N: + Memorial Hospital
Other	N: Laundry/MC Stop, NM State Hwy Patrol Post
333	US 54, Mountain Rd, Tucumcari
TStop	N: Love's Travel Stop #262 (Scales) Flying J Travel Plaza #5176 (Scales)
Gas	N: Circle K, Shell
Food	N: Arby's/Chester/Godfathers/Love's TS, CountryMarket/FastFood/FJ TP Pizza Hut, Sonic
Lodg	N: Best Western, Comfort Inn, Holiday Inn, Historic Rt 66 Motel, Relax Inn, Super 8, Travelodge
TServ	N: Jack's Truck Repair
Other	N: WiFi/Love's TS, Laundry/WiFiRVDump/LP/FJ TP, Auto Services, Kmart, Museum, Mountain Rd RV Park▲
335	Lp 40, Tucumcari Blvd
Gas	N: Chevron, Conoco, Shell
Food	N: Branding Iron Rest, Denny's, Del's Rest, Kix on 66, Mediterranean Café

EXIT	NM / TX
Lodg	N: Comfort Inn♥, Econo Lodge, Hampton Inn, Holiday Inn, Howard Johnson, Motel 6, Quality Inn, Super 8
Other	N: Auto Services, Tires, Towing, Empty Saddle RV Park▲, Kiva RV Park▲, Cactus RV Park▲, Tucumcari Gas/LP S: Tucumcari KOA▲
339	NM 286, NM 278, Tucumcari
Other	N: Tucumcari Muni Airport✈
343	Exit 343, Quay Rd AL
356	NM 469, San Jon
FStop	S: Fast Stop #24/P66
TStop	N: Drivers Travelmart #408/Citgo
Gas	S: Shell◊
Food	N: Diner/FastFood/Drivers TM
Lodg	S: San Jon Motel
TServ	N: Old Rte 66 Truck & Auto Service
Other	N: Laundry/WiFi/Drivers TM
(357)	Weigh Station (EB)
361	Quay Rd M, San Jon, Bard
369	NM 93S, NM 392N, to Endee
(373)	NM Welcome Center (WB) (RR, Phone, Picnic)
NOTE:	MM 374: Texas State Line

(MOUNTAIN / CENTRAL TIME ZONE)

🚻 **NEW MEXICO**
⛽ **TEXAS**

(MOUNTAIN / CENTRAL TIME ZONE)

EXIT	TEXAS
(0)	I-40 Bus, to Glenrio
(12)	Picnic Area (Both dir)
15	Ivy Rd, Adrian
18	FM 2858, CR 18, Gruhlkey Rd
Gas	S: Shell◊
Food	S: Stuckey's/Rest/Shell
22	TX 214, I-40 Bus, Adrian
Gas	S: Phillips 66◊
Food	N: Fabulous 40 Café
Lodg	N: Fabulous 40 Motel
TServ	N: Billy's Truck & Tire Service
Other	N: US Post Office
23	TX 290, TX 214 (EB)
23A	S Grand Ave, Old Rte 66 (WB)
23B	TX 290, TX 214 (WB)
28	CR 29, Vega, to Landergin
(31)	Parking Area (EB)
(32)	Parking Area (WB)
35	I-40 Bus, Vega, Old Rte 66
Food	N: Sand's Café/Best Western
Lodg	N: Best Western
Other	N: Oversized Vehicle Permit Station, Walnut RV Park▲
36	US 385, S Main St, Vega, to Dalhart, Hereford
FStop	N: Allsup's #304/Conoco
TStop	N: Texas Quick Stop/Texaco
Gas	N: Diamond Shamrock S: Shell
Food	N: FastFood/TX QS, DQ, Hickory Café, Old 66 Cafe

◊ = Regular Gas Stations with Diesel   ▲ = RV Friendly Locations   ♥ = Pet Friendly Locations
RED PRINT SHOWS LARGE VEHICLE PARKING/ACCESS ON SITE OR NEARBY   BROWN PRINT SHOWS CAMPGROUNDS/RV PARKS

Interstate 40 W/E — TEXAS

EXIT		
	Lodg	N: Bonanza Motel, Comfort Inn, Vega Motel
	TServ	N: Tx QS/Tires
	Other	N: RVDump/Tx QS, Oversized Vehicle Permit Station
37		I-40W Bus, Vega
	Other	S: Oldham Co Airport ✈
42		CR 42, Everett Rd, Vega
49		FM 809, N Locust St, Wildorado
	FStop	S: Wildorado Fuel Club/P66
	Food	S: Café, Rest/Royal Inn
	Lodg	S: Royal Inn
	Other	S: LP/P66
(53)		Parking Area (EB)
54		Adkisson Rd, Amarillo
(55)		Parking Area (WB)
57		RM 2381, Amarillo, to Bushland
	Gas	S: Shell◊
	Other	S: Longhorn Trailer Inn & RV Park▲
60		Arnot Rd, Amarillo, Bushland
	FStop	S: Love's Travel Stop #250 (Scales)
	Food	S: Subway/Love's TS
	Other	S: Laundry/WiFi/Love's TS, Oasis RV Resort▲
62A		Hope Rd, Helium Rd (EB)
	Other	S: Sundown Campgrounds▲, Amarillo West View RV Park▲
62B		I-40E Bus, Amarillo Blvd (EB)
	Other	N: Fort Amarillo RV Park▲
62		Old Rte 66, Hope Rd (WB)
64		Lp 335, Soncy Rd, Amarillo
	Gas	S: Shamrock
	Food	N: Carino's, Joe's Crab Shack, Logan's Roadhouse
		S: Applebee's, DQ, Hooters, McDonald's, On the Border, Ruby Tuesday, Subway
	Lodg	N: Comfort Inn, Drury Inn, Extended Stay America
	Other	N: Discount Tire, Gander Mountain
		S: Home Depot, K-Mart, PetSmart♥, Target, Westgate Mall, US Post Office
65		Coulter Dr, Amarillo
	Gas	N: BP, Phillips 66◊
		S: Chevron, Citgo, Shell
	Food	N: Arby's, Golden Corral, Luby's, Subway, Taco Bell, Waffle House
		S: Chuck E Cheese Pizza, CiCi's, Jason's Deli, McDonald's, Outback Steakhouse
	Lodg	N: Best Western, Comfort Inn, Days Inn, Fairfield Inn, La Quinta Inn♥, Quality Inn, Residence Inn
		S: Fifth Season Inn, Hampton Inn, Ramada Inn, Super 8

EXIT		
	Med	N: + Baptist St Anthony Hospital, + NW Tx Hospital
	Other	N: Discount Tire, Firestone
		S: Goodyear, IGA, Lowe's, Westgate Mall
66		Bell St, Avondale St, Wolffin Ave
	Gas	N: Citgo◊, Shamrock
		S: Chevron, Shell
	Food	S: Popeye's, Starbucks, Subway
	Lodg	N: Fairfield Inn, Motel 6♥, Quality Inn♥
	Other	S: Albertson's
67		Western St, Avondale, Amarillo
	Gas	N: Citgo, Shell
		S: Shamrock, Phillips 66
	Food	N: Beef Rigger Prime Rib, Black Eyed Pea, Burger King, Chili's, McDonald's, Pancho's, Rosa's Cafe, Sonic, Subway, Taco Bell
		S: Catfish Shack, IHOP, Olive Garden, Taco Cabana, Waffle House
	Lodg	S: Baymont Inn♥, Holiday Inn Express
	Other	S: Firestone, FedEx/Kinko's, NAPA
68A		Julian Blvd, Paramount Blvd
	Gas	N: Chevron, Shell
		S: Shamrock
	Food	N: Arby's, Chili's, Pancho's, Wendy's
		S: Cajun Magic, Calico Café, El Chico, Long John Silver, Pizza Hut, Red Lobster, Steak & Ale, TX Roadhouse
	Lodg	S: Holiday Inn Express, Travelodge
68B		Georgia St
	Gas	N: Shell
		S: Phillips 66
	Food	N: Subway/Shell, TGI Friday
		S: Burger King, Denny's, Furr's
	Lodg	N: Ambassador Hotel
		S: Econo Lodge, Quality Inn
	Med	S: + Hospital
	Other	S: Office Depot, K-Mart
69A		Crockett St
	Gas	N: Shell, Texaco
		S: Phillips 66
	Food	N: Subway/Shell, TGI Friday
		S: Burger King, Furr's, Domino's
	Lodg	N: Ambassador Hotel
		S: Howard Johnson
69B		Washington St, Amarillo College
	Gas	S: Phillips 66, Texaco
	Food	S: DQ, Subway
	Other	N: Albertson's
		S: Pharmacy
(70)		Jct I-27S, US 60W, US 87, US 287
71		Ross St, Osage St, Arthur St
	Gas	N: Conoco, Shamrock, Shell◊
		S: Shamrock, Sam's

EXIT		
	Food	N: Burger King, Long John Silver, McDonald's, Popeye's, Subway
		S: Arby's, Denny's, La Fiesta, Sonic, Taco Bell, Wendy's
	Lodg	N: Coach Light Inn, Comfort Inn, Days Inn, Holiday Inn, Microtel♥, Quality Inn
		S: Hampton Inn, Howard Johnson♥, La Quinta Inn♥, Ramada
	Other	N: Harbor Freight Tools
		S: Sam's Club, US Post Office, Auto Dealer
72A		Lp 395, Nelson St, Quarter Horse Dr, Tee Anchor Blvd
	Gas	S: Chevron, Shell◊
	Food	N: Cracker Barrel, KFC
	Lodg	N: Budget Host Inn, Econo Lodge, La Kiva Hotel, Luxury Inn, Ramada, Sleep Inn, Super 8, Value Inn
		S: Camelot Inn
	Other	N: American Quarterhorse Museum
72B		Grand St, Bolton St, Amarillo
	FStop	N: Pacific Pride
	Gas	N: Shell
		S: Exxon, Phillips 66, Murphy
	Food	N: Hank's BBQ, KFC
		S: Pizza Hut, Subway, Taco Villa
	Lodg	N: Red Roof Inn♥, Motel 6♥, Travelodge
		S: Motel 6
	TServ	S: Cummins
	Other	S: AutoZone, Grocery, Wal-Mart sc
73		Eastern St, Bolton St
	Gas	N: Shamrock◊, Shell◊
		S: Chevron◊, Citgo
	Food	N: Polly's
	Lodg	N: Motel 6♥
		S: Best Western
	TServ	S: Cummins Southern Plains
	Other	S: One Stop Auto & RV Service, Amarillo RV Ranch▲
74		Whitaker Rd, Amarillo
	TStop	S: Love's Travel Stop #200 (Scales), Travel Center of America #55/Exxon (Scales)
	Food	N: Big Texan Rest
		S: Subway/Godfathers/A&W/Love's TS, Buckhorn/BurgerKing/PizzaHut/Popeye's/TA TC
	Lodg	N: Big Texan Motel, Best Value Inn
		S: Budget Inn
	TWash	S: Blue Beacon TW/TA TC, Red Baron Eagle Truck Wash
	TServ	S: TA TC/Tires, Amarillo Truck Center, W Tx Peterbilt
	Other	N: Amarillo Ranch RV Park▲, Waterpark
		S: WiFi/RVDump/Love's TS, Laundry/WiFi/RVDump/TA TC

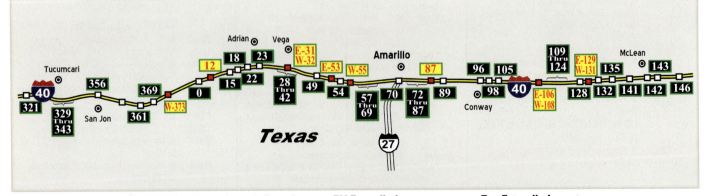

◊ = Regular Gas Stations with Diesel   ▲ = RV Friendly Locations   ♥ = Pet Friendly Locations
RED PRINT SHOWS LARGE VEHICLE PARKING/ACCESS ON SITE OR NEARBY   BROWN PRINT SHOWS CAMPGROUNDS/RV PARKS

EXIT		TEXAS	EXIT		TEXAS	EXIT		TX / OK
75		Lp 335, Lakeside Dr, Airport		Food	N: Subway/Love's TS, Café/Conway Inn	157		FM 1547, FM 2474, FM 3075, Lela
	TStop	N: Pilot Travel Center #436 (Scales)		Lodg	N: Conway Inn		Other	S: West 40 RV Park▲
		S: Petro Stopping Center #7/Mobil			S: Budget Host Inn	161		I-40 Bus, Shamrock
	Gas	N: Phillips 66, Shell		Other	N: WiFi/RVDump/Love's TS	163		US 83, Bus I-40, Shamrock, to
	Food	N: McDonald's/Subway/Pilot TC, Country	98		TX 207, Panhandle (WB)			Wheeler, Wellington (Addtl Serv S to 66)
		Barn, Waffle House	105		FM 2880, Groom		Fstop	S: Cantrell's Valero
		S: Iron Skillet/FastFood/Petro SC	(106)		Parking Area (EB)		TStop	S: Midway Truck & Travel/Taylor
	Lodg	N: Best Value Inn, Quality Inn, Ritz	(108)		Parking Area (WB)			Petroleum #6/66
		Carlton Airport Plaza, Super 8	109		FM 294, Groom		Gas	N: Chevron◊, Conoco
	TWash	S: Blue Beacon TW/Petro SC		Other	N: G&J Truck Sales		Food	N: Pizza Hut/Taco Bell
	TServ	S: Petro SC/Tires, Peterbilt	110		I-40E Bus, Groom, Old Rte 66			S: DQ, McDonald's, FastFood/Taylor's
	Other	N: Laundry/WiFi/RVDump/Pilot TC,	112		FM 295, Groom		Lodg	N: Best Western
		Overnite RV Park▲, Amarillo Int'l	113		FM 2300, Groom			S: Sleep Inn
		Airport✈, to KOA/Amarillo▲		Gas	S: Texaco◊		TServ	S: C&H Supply
		S: Laundry/WiFi/BarbSh/CB/Petro SC		Food	S: DQ		Other	S: LP/Cantrell's, Laundry/Taylor's, ATMs,
76		Spur 468, Int'l Airport, Amarillo		Lodg	S: Chalet Inn			Banks, Auto Services, Goodyear
		TEXAS TRAVEL INFO CENTER	114		Lp 40 Bus, Groom	164		Frontage Rd, I-40 Bus
	TStop	N: Flying J Travel Plaza #5350/Conoco	121		TX 70N, to Pampa	(164)		Weigh Station (EB)
		(Scales)	124		TX 70S, to Clarendon	167		FM 2168, Daberry Rd, Shamrock
	Gas	N: Shell	128		FM 2477, to Lake McClellan,		Fstop	N: Cantrell's Longhorn/Shamrock
	Food	N: Cookery/FastFood/FJ TP			Panhandle Training Natl Guard		Other	N: Shamrock Muni Airport✈
	Lodg	N: Holiday Inn Express	(129)		Rest Area (EB)	169		FM 1802, Carbon Black Rd
	TWash	N: Buster's TW			(RR, Phone, Picnic, Vend, WiFi, Shelter)	(173)		Picnic Area (EB)
	TServ	S: Speedco, Mack	(131)		Rest Area (WB)	(176)		Picnic Area (WB)
	Other	N: Laundry/WiFi/BarbSh/RVDump/LP/			(RR, Phone, Picnic, Vend, WiFi, Shelter)	(176)		Livestock Inspection Area (WB)
		FJ TP	132		Johnson Ranch Rd	176		Spur 30E, to Texola
		S: Custom RV Center	135		FM 291, Alanreed, Old Rte 66		NOTE:	MM 177: Oklahoma State Line
77		FM 1258, Pullman Rd		FStop	S: Alanreed Travel Center/Conoco			⋂ TEXAS
	TStop	N: USA Travel Plaza (Scales), Cee Teez		Food	S: Cafe			⋃ OKLAHOMA
		Truck Plaza		Lodg	S: Motel/Alanreed TC			(CENTRAL TIME ZONE)
	Food	N: FastFood/Arby's/USA TC, Rest/CTs TP		Other	S: US Post Office	1		E1240 Rd, Texola
	Tires	N: CTs TP	141		I-40E Bus, McClean		TStop	S: Double D Fuel Stop
	TWash	N: CTs TP			(Access to Ex #142 Serv)		Food	S: Rest/Double D FS
	TServ	N: Carrier Transporter Refrigeration,	142		TX 273, FM 3143, to McClean		Other	S: Laundry/RV Park/RVDump/Dbl D FS
		Stewart & Stevenson Truck Service		FStop	N: Country Corner Shell	5		I-40E Bus, Honeyfarm Rd, Erick,
	Other	N: Laundry/USA TC, Laundry/CT's TP		Food	N: FastFood/Country Corner, Red River			to Hollis
78		US 287S (EB), FM 1258			Steakhouse	7		OK 30, Sheb Wooley Ave, Main St,
80		Spur 228, to US 287		Lodg	N: Cactus Inn			Erick, to Sweetwater
	Gas	N: Texaco		Other	N: Country Corner RV Park▲		TStop	S: Love's Travel Stop #253 (Scales)
	Other	N: A OK Camper Park▲	143		McLean		Food	S: Subway/Love's TS, Cowboys Rest &
81		FM 1912, Amarillo	146		County Line Rd			Trading Post
	FStop	N: Fast Stop #25/66		Other	N: McLean'Gray Co Airport✈		Lodg	N: Comfort Inn♥
	TStop	S: Amarillo AmBest Travel Center (Scales)	148		FM 1443, Kellerville Rd, Kellerville			S: Days Inn♥
	Food	S: Rest/FastFood/AA TC	152		FM 453, Pakan Rd, Shamrock		Other	N: Laundry/WiFi/Love's TS
	TServ	S: AA TC/Tires		FStop	S: T&M Truck Stop	(9)		OK Welcome Center (EB)
	Other	S: Laundry/WiFi/AA TC		TServ	S: T&M TS/Tires			Rest Area (WB)
85		Amarillo Blvd, Durrett Rd						(RR, Phones, Picnic, RVDump)
(87)		Parking Area (Both dir)						
87		FM 2373, Panhandle						
89		FM 2161, to Old Rte 66						
96		TX 207, Claude, Conway, Panhandle						
	Fstop	N: Love's Travel Stop #229						

◆ = Regular Gas Stations with Diesel   ▲ = RV Friendly Locations   ♥ = Pet Friendly Locations

RED PRINT SHOWS LARGE VEHICLE PARKING/ACCESS ON SITE OR NEARBY   BROWN PRINT SHOWS CAMPGROUNDS/RV PARKS

Page 185

INTERSTATE 40 W/E

EXIT	OKLAHOMA
11	I-40W Bus, Erick (Access to #7 Serv S)
(13)	Weigh Station (Both dir)
14	Hext Rd, Erick
20	US 283, I-40E Bus, 4th St, Sayre, to Magnum (Acc #23/#25 Serv N)
TStop	N: Flying J Travel Plaza #5093/Conoco (Scales)
Food	N: CountryMarket/FastFood/FJ TP
Lodg	N: AmericInn
TWash	N: Industry TW
Other	N: Laundry/WiFi/RVDump/LP/FJ TP, Sayre Muni Golf Course, Superior Lube Cars,Truck & RV Service
23	OK 152, Madden Ave, to US 283, I-40 Bus, Sayre, to Cordell
FStop	S: Tosh Service Center/Shell
Food	N: Crazy Ladies Pastries & Bistro, Deb's Country Kitchen, River Bend Steakhouse S: Deli/Tosh SC
Lodg	N: AmericInn
TServ	S: Tosh SC/Tires
Other	N: ATMs, Banks, Museum
25	I-40W Bus, N 4th St, US 66, to US 283, Sayre
Gas	N: Shell
Lodg	N: Western Motel
Med	N: + Sayre Memorial Hospital
Other	N: Auto Dealer
26	Cemetery Rd, Sayre
TStop	S: Travel Center of America #152 (Scales)
Food	S: TacoBell/Subway/TA TC
TServ	S: TA TC/Tires
Other	N: Truck & Auto & Tire Repair, to Flying W Guest Ranch (also acc via #32 or #34) S: Laundry/WiFi/TA TC
32	OK 34S, I-40E Bus, OK 6, Elk City, to Mangum, Carter (EB Left exit)
34	Merritt Rd, to Bus 40, OK 6, Elk City (All Serv 5-7 mi NE on OK 6 in Elk City)
Other	N: to Gas, Food, Lodging, Steve's Diesel & Truck Service, Wal-Mart, Museum, Cinema, Elk City RV
38	OK 6, S Main St, Elk City, to Altus (Addtl Serv N to I-40 Bus)
FStop	N: Conoco
Gas	N: Shell◊ S: Phillips 66
Food	N: 20th St Diner, Arby's, Denny's, Long John Silver, McDonald's, Quiznos, Western Sizzlin, Hog Trough S: Old Glory Cafe
Lodg	N: Bedford Inn, Comfort Inn, Days Inn, Flamingo Inn, Ramada Inn S: Econo Lodge♥, Holiday Inn
Med	N: + Great Plains Reg'l Med Center
Other	N: Elk Creek RV Park▲, L&R Tire & Car Center, Adams Garage, Rolling Retreats RV Sales
40	Eastern Ave, to Bus 40, Elk City (Access to #41 Serv)
Food	N: Portobello Grill
41	OK 34N, I-40 Bus, to OK 66, Elk City (EB Exits Left) (Most Serv on OK 66)
FStop	N: Love's Travel Stop #201
Gas	N: Shell

EXIT	OKLAHOMA
Food	N: Subway/Love's TS, Braum's, Denny's, El Charro, Home Cooking Café
Lodg	N: Economy Express Inn, Howard Johnson, Motel 6♥, Super 8, Travel Inn, Travelodge♥
TServ	N: Great Plains Tire Service
Med	N: + Great Plains Reg'l Med Center
Other	N: WiFi/Love's TS, ATMs, Auto Dealers, Auto Services, Laundry, Pharmacy, Rte 66 Museum, Wal-Mart, Elk City Muni Airport✈, Elk Run RV Park▲, Lake Elk City
47	CR 2080, Canute
Gas	S: Shell
Lodg	S: Sunset Inn
50	Clinton Lake Rd, Canute
Other	N: Elk City/Clinton KOA▲, Clinton Lake
53	OK 44, Foss, to Altus, Burns Flat
FStop	S: Pendleton's Truck Stop/Shell
Food	S: FastFood/Shell
Tires	S: Pendleton's TS
Other	N: to appr 7mi Foss State Park▲
57	Stafford Rd, Clinton
61	Haggard Rd, Clinton
62	Parkersburg Rd, Commerce Rd
Other	S: Hargus RV Sales & Service/LP
65	I-40 Bus, Gary Blvd, Clinton (NO EB reaccess)
Gas	N: Conoco, Shell
Food	N: Carl's Jr, Country Kitchen, Del Rancho, Long John Silver, McDonald's, Taco Mayo, Mexican Rest
Lodg	N: Hampton Inn, Midtown Travel Inn♥, Ramada Inn, Red Roof Inn♥,

EXIT	OKLAHOMA
Lodg	N: BW/Trade Winds Motel, Travelodge♥ S: Clarion
Med	N: + Clinton Reg'l Hospital
Other	N: Dollar General, Family Dollar, Kmart, Museum
65A	10th St, Neptune Dr, Clinton
Gas	S: Phillips 66
Food	N: Braum's, Branding Iron, KFC, Pizza Hut, Subway
Lodg	N: Clinton Inn, Days Inn, Super 8
Other	N: Auto Services, Laundromat, Grocery, Winks RV Park▲ S: Challis Diesel Service, Parkers Truck Towing
66	US 183, S 4th St, to I-40 Bus, Clinton, Cordell
FStop	S: Fast Lane #300/66
TStop	S: Domino Food & Fuel/Shell (Scales)
Food	S: FastFood/Domino F&F
Tires	N: Great Plains Tire Service
TServ	S: Freightliner
Other	N: Auto Dealers, Auto Services, ATMs S: Auto Dealers
69	Lp 40W, Gary Blvd, Clinton (WB) (Access #66/#65 Serv)
71	Custer City Rd, Clinton
FStop	N: Love's Travel Stop #248
Food	N: Subway/Love's TS
Other	N: WiFi/Love's TS
80	OK 54, Weatherford, to Thomas
Gas	N: Shell
Food	N: Little Mexico
Lodg	N: Economy Inn
Other	N: Crowder Lake University Park
80A	I-40E Bus, W Main St (EB, No reacc) (Access to #82 Serv)
Other	N: Auto Services, Police Station
82	I-40W Bus, E Main St, Weatherford
Gas	N: Conoco, Shell, Shamrock, Sinclair
Food	N: Arby's, Braum's, Carl's Jr, Jerry's, McDonalds, KFC, Pizza Hut, Sonic, Taco Mayo, Mexican Rest
Lodg	N: Best Western, Comfort Inn, Days Inn, Scottish Inns, Travel Inn
Med	N: + Southwestern Memorial Hospital
Other	N: ATMs, Auto Services, Grocery, Vet♥, Wal-Mart, SW OK State Univ
84	Airport Rd, Weatherford
TStop	N: Fast Lane Travel Plaza #101/Texaco (Scales)
Gas	N: Phillips 66
Food	N: FastFood/Fast Lane TP
Lodg	N: Holiday Inn Express, Travel Inn
Other	N: Overnite Rte 66 RV Park▲, Thomas P Stafford Airport✈
88	OK 58, Hydro, Carnegie
(94)	Parking Area (WB)
95	Bethel Rd, Hydro
101	US 281, OK 8, Hinton, to Anardarko
FStop	S: Love's Travel Stop #385
TStop	S: Hinton AmBest Travel Plaza/Shell
Food	S: FastFood/Hinton TP, Chesters/Godfathers/Love's TX
Lodg	S: Microtel/Hinton TP
Other	S: Laundry/WiFi/Hinton TP, Red Rock Canyon State Park▲
104	Methodist Rd, Hinton

◊ = Regular Gas Stations with Diesel   ▲ = RV Friendly Locations   ♥ = Pet Friendly Locations
RED PRINT SHOWS LARGE VEHICLE PARKING/ACCESS ON SITE OR NEARBY   BROWN PRINT SHOWS CAMPGROUNDS/RV PARKS

EXIT	OKLAHOMA	EXIT	OKLAHOMA	EXIT	OKLAHOMA
108	Spur US 281N, Calumet, to Geary, Watonga	Lodg	N: Comfort Suites, Super 7 Motel S: Best Western, Super 8, HOTEL	Food	S: Arby's, Burger King, Chili's, Cracker Barrel, IHOP, Kona Ranch Steaks, Panera Bread, Santa Fe Grill, Steak & Ale, Tony Roma, Wendy's, Waffle House
FStop	N: Fast Lane Food Mart/66 S: Love's Travel Stop #251	Other	S: CVS, Food Lion		
TStop	N: Cherokee Travel Mart/Shell	**139**	John Kilpatrick Turnpike		
Food	N: FastFood/Fast Lane, Rest/FastFood/Cherokee TM S: Chesters/Godfathers/Love's TS	**140**	Morgan Rd, Okla City	Lodg	N: Best Western, Biltmore Hotel, Days Inn, Econo Lodge, Extended Stay America, Howard Johnson Express, Red Roof Inn♥, Residence Inn, Rodeway Inn, Super 8 S: AmeriSuites, Best Value Inn, Comfort Suites, Clarion, Courtyard, Embassy Suites, Hampton Inn, Hilton Garden Inn, Holiday Inn Express, La Quinta Inn♥, Lexington Hotel, Motel 6♥, Regency Inn, Sleep Inn
		TStop	N: Pilot Travel Center #460 (Scales), Travel Center of America #59/66 (Scales) S: Love's Travel Stop #203 (DAND), Flying J Travel Plaza #5027/Conoco (Scales) (DAND)		
TServ	N: Cherokee TM/Tires				
Other	N: to KOA Cherokee▲ S: WiFi/Love's TS, Tires	Food	N: McDonald's/Pilot TC, CountryPride/Popeye's/TA TC S: Subway/Love's TS, Cookery/FastFood/FJ TP, Ricky's Cafe, Sonic		
(111)	Parking Area (EB)				
115	US 270, Calumet Rd, Calumet			Other	N: Auto Services, ATMs, Enterprise RAC S: Celebration Station, Sooner Great Dane Peterbilt
Other	N: to Good Life RV Resort▲ S: KOA Calumet▲	TWash	S: Blue Beacon TW, G&S TW		
119	I-40 E Bus, OK 66, El Reno	TServ	N: TA TC/Tires S: Fleet Service, Speedco	**146**	Portland Ave (fr EB, no reaccess)
123	Country Club Rd, El Reno			Gas	N: Shell
FStop	S: Phillips 66	Other	N: Laundry/WiFi/Pilot TC, Laundry/CB, WiFi/TA TC, Double L Tire Co S: WiFi/Love's TS, Laundry/BarbSh/RVDump/LP/FJ TP	Food	N: Subway
Gas	N: Conoco, Shell♦, Valero, Murphy♦			Other	N: ATMs, Banks, White Water Bay WaterPark
Food	N: Arby's, Braum's, Carl's Jr, El Charro, KFC, Little Caesar's, McDonald's, Pizza Hut, Subway, Taco Bell S: Denny's, Rest/BW	**142**	Council Rd, OKC	**(147A)**	Jct I-44W, OK 3E, Dallas, Wichita (fr WB, Left exit)
		TStop	S: Travel Center of America #36 (Scales)		
		Gas	N: Shell, Sinclair	**(147B)**	Jct I-44E, OK 3W (fr EB, Left exit)
Lodg	N: Comfort Inn, Motel 6♥ S: Best Western♥ & Hensley's RV Park▲, Days Inn, Regency Inn	Food	N: Applebee's, Braum's, McDonald's, Subway, Taco Bell, Waffle House S: CountryPride/BurgerKing/TA TC		
				147C	May Ave, Okla City (fr WB)
Med	N: + Parkview Hospital	Lodg	N: Best Budget Inn S: Econo Lodge	Other	N: Auto Services, to AllSports Stadium, State Fair RV Park▲
Other	N: ATMs, Banks, Grocery, Greyhound, Wal-Mart sc, Lake El Reno S: to El Reno Muni Airport✈	TWash	S: TA TC, TruckOMat	**148A**	Agnew Ave, Villa Ave
		TServ	N: Turbo Diesel of OK, Fleet Pride S: TA TC/Tires	FStop	N: Roadway Ventures/66
125	US 81, Bus 40, El Reno			Gas	S: Conoco♦
Gas	N: Conoco, Love's Country Store♦	Other	N: Tires, Lyons Repair, Motley RV Repair S: Laundry/BarbSH/WiFi/RVDump/TA TC, Council Rd RV Park▲, Griffith RV Services	Food	S: Braum's, Real BBQ, Taco Bell
Food	N: China King Buffet, Serapio's Mex Rest, J & Kay Rest, Taco Mayo			TWash	N: Signal Tank Wash
Lodg	N: Economy Express, Western Sands			TServ	N: International Service, Fleet Services
Other	N: Animal Hospital♥, Convention Center, Auto Dealers, Auto Services, Towing, Phil's Cycle & ATV's, Lucky Star Casino▲ S: United Auto & Truck Service	**143**	Rockwell Ave, Okla City	Other	S: Harley Davidson World
		Gas	N: 7-11, Shell S: Interstate Gas	**148B**	Pennsylvania Ave (fr EB)
				Gas	N: Shamrock♦
		Food	N: Buffalo Wild Wings, Fire Mtn Grill, Pizza House Express	TServ	N: HD Copland Int'l
(130)	Weigh Station (Both dir)			Other	S: to Downtown Airport✈
130	Banner Rd, El Reno, to Union City	Lodg	N: Rockwell Inn, Rodeway Inn S: Sands Motel	**148C**	Virginia Ave (fr WB)
FStop	N: Shell Food Plaza	TServ	N: Quality Diesel Service, Truck Pro	**149A**	Western Ave, Reno Ave
Food	N: FastFood/Shell	Other	N: Best Buy, Harley Davidson World, Home Depot, PetCo♥, Tires +, McClain's RV Superstore/Camping World S: A OK Campgrounds▲, Rockwell RV Park▲, Price Auto & RV Repair	Gas	N: Total S: Conoco♦, Shell
132	Cimarron Rd, Yukon			Food	N: McDonald's, Sonic, Taco Bell S: Burger King, Popeye's
Other	S: Clarence Page Muni Airport✈			TServ	S: Jefferson Trailer Repair
136	OK 92, 11th St, Garth Brooks Blvd, Yukon, Mustang			Other	N: Auto Services S: Auto Services, Downtown Airpark✈
Gas	N: Star Mart, Shell, Murphy	**144**	MacArthur Blvd, OKC	**149B**	Classen Blvd (fr WB)
Food	N: Braum's, Carl's Jr, Harry's Grill, KFC, Great Wall Chinese, McDonald's, Primo's Italian Rest, Santa Fe Cattle Co, Starbucks, Taco Mayo, Waffle House, Wendy's S: Alfredo's Mexican Cafe, Chili's, Carino's, Pizza Hut, Quiznos, Rib Crib, Starbucks	Gas	N: Shell S: Conoco	**150A**	Walker Ave (fr EB)
		Food	N: Applebee's, Golden Corral, KFC, McDonald's, Sonic, Starbucks, Subway, Taco Cabana, Texas Roadhouse S: Ruby's, Signature Italian	Gas	S: Phillips 66
				Med	N: + St Anthony Hospital
				Other	N: Greyhound
		Lodg	N: Springhill Suites S: Econo Lodge, Green Carpet Inn, Microtel Inn, Quality Inn, Super 10 Motel, Travelodge	**150B**	Harvey Ave (No Reaccess)
Lodg	N: Hampton Inn S: Executive Suites			**150C**	Robinson Ave, Downtown (WB)
Med	N: + Canadian Valley Reg'l Hospital			Food	N: Zio's Italian
Other	N: AutoZone, ATMs, Banks, Big O Tires, Big Lots, Blockbuster, Movies 5, Wal-Mart sc, Walgreen's S: Lowe's, Staples	TServ	N: Cummins Southern Plains S: Oklahoma Kenworth, Peterbilt	Lodg	N: Courtyard, Renaissance Hotel, Sheraton Westin
		Other	N: Auto Rental, Best Buy, Office Depot, PetSmart♥, Wal-Mart sc▲ S: Garden Ridge, Sam's Club	Other	N: Convention Center, AP Murrah Bldg Memorial, Museums, Hertz, Ford Center, Amtrak, Civic Center, Theatres, Bass Pro Shop
137	Cornwell Dr, Czech Hall Rd				
Other	N: Albertson's	**145**	Meridian Ave, OKC		
138	OK 4, Mustang Rd, Yukon	Gas	N: Conoco, Shell S: Phillips 66/Circle K, Shell	**151A**	Byers Ave, Lincoln Blvd (EB)
Gas	S: Conoco♦, Shell			**(151B)**	Jct I-35S, to Dallas (EB)
Food	N: Denny's S: Arby's, Burger King, McDonald's, Sonic, Subway	Food	N: Denny's, McDonald's, On the Border, Outback Steakhouse	**(151C)**	Jct I-235N, State Capital, Edmond

♦ = Regular Gas Stations with Diesel ▲ = RV Friendly Locations ♥ = Pet Friendly Locations

RED PRINT SHOWS LARGE VEHICLE PARKING/ACCESS ON SITE OR NEARBY BROWN PRINT SHOWS CAMPGROUNDS/RV PARKS

Page 187

INTERSTATE 40

EXIT		OKLAHOMA
	NOTE:	I-40 below runs with I-35 for 1 exit, Exit #'s follows I-35.
127		**Eastern Ave, MLK Blvd (EB)**
	TStop	N: PTP/JRS Travel Center (Scales), Stopping Center #16/Mobil (Scales)
	Gas	N: Shell
	Food	N: FastFood/JRS TC, IronSkillet/Petro SC, Cholita's Mexican Rest, Dale's BBQ, Waffle House
	Lodg	N: Best Western, Bricktown Hotel, Quality Inn, Econo Lodge, Ramada Inn
	TServ	N: Petro SC/Tires
	TWash	N: BlueBeacon TW/Petro SC
	Other	N: Laundry/JRS TC, Laundry/WiFi/Petro SC, Lewis RV Center
(128/153)		**Jct I-35N, to Edmond, Wichita**
	NOTE:	I-40 above runs with I-35 for 2 exits, Exit #'s follows I-35.
154		**Scott St, Reno Ave, OKC**
	Gas	N: Sinclair S: 7-11◊, Phillips 66◊
	Lodg	N: Value Place Hotel
155A		**Sunnylane Rd, to Del City**
	Gas	N: Conoco S: Shell
	Food	S: Braum's, Dunkin Donuts, Pizza Hut, Subway
	Lodg	S: Value Place Hotel
	Med	S: + Midwest Reg'l Medical Center
155B		**SE 15th St, Del City, Midwest City**
	Gas	N: ArcoAmPm, Express, Shell S: Conoco
	Food	S: Ashley's Country Kitchen
	Other	N: Grocery/Pharmacy
156A		**Sooner Rd**
	Gas	N: Conoco
	Food	N: Kettle, Ray's Steakhouse, Waffle House
	Lodg	N: Comfort Inn, Hampton Inn, Holiday Inn Express, La Quinta Inn♥, Sheraton
	Other	N: Auto Dealers, Home Depot, Tires +
156B		**Hudibird Dr**
	Lodg	S: Motel 6♥
	Other	S: Auto Dealers
157A		**SE 29th St, to Midwest City**
	Gas	N: Conoco◊, Shell
	Food	N: IHOP, Pizza Inn, Santa Fe Cattle Co
	Lodg	N: Best Western, Planet Inn Motel, Super 8
	Med	S: + Midwest Reg'l Medical Center
	Other	N: Leisure Time RV S: Sam's Club
157B		**Air Depot Blvd**
	Gas	N: Conoco◊, Shell
	Food	N: Arby's, IHOP, Pizza Inn, Subway
	Lodg	N: Super 8
	Other	N: Firestone, Lowe's, O'Reilly Auto Parts, Walgreen's, OK Info Center S: Tinker AFB, Gate 1
157C		**Tinker Air Force Base, Eaker Gate**
159A		**Tinker AFB, Hruskocy Gate**
	Gas	N: Shell
	Food	N: China Grill
	Lodg	N: Executive Inn
	Other	N: Firestone, Eastland Hills RV Park▲ S: Tinker AFB, Gate 7
159B		**Douglas Blvd, OKC**
	Gas	N: Phillips 66, Total
	Food	N: Denny's, McDonald's, Taco Bell

EXIT		OKLAHOMA
	Med	N: + Hospital
	Other	N: Eastland Hills RV Park▲, Okie RV Park & Campground▲ S: Tinker AFB
162		**Anderson Rd**
	Other	N: Lundy's Propane/LP
(165)		**Jct I-240W, to Dallas (WB)**
166		**Choctaw Rd, Choctaw**
	TStop	N: Love's Travel Stop #241 (Scales) S: Anderson Travel Plaza/66 (Scales)
	Food	N: Subway/Love's TS S: Rest/FastFood/Anderson TP
	TServ	S: Billy's 24Hr Road Service, Truck & Trailer Repair
	Other	N: Laundry/WiFi/Love's TS, OKC East KOA▲ S: Laundry/BarbSh/WiFi/Anderson TP
169		**Peebly Rd, Newalla**
172		**Harrah Rd, Newalla**
	Gas	S: Shell
176		**OK 102N, McLoud Rd, McLoud**
	Gas	S: Love's Country Store #252
	Food	S: Subway/Love's, Curtis Watson's Rest
	Other	S: WiFi/Love's CS
178		**OK 102S, to Bethel Acres, Dale**
	Other	N: Firelake Grand Casino, Gas, Rest
181		**US 177, US 270, OK 3W, Shawnee to Stillwater, Tecumseh**
	FStop	S: Expo Stop/66
	Food	S: FastFood/Expo Stop
	Lodg	S: Budget Inn
	TWash	S: Expo Stop

EXIT		OKLAHOMA
	TServ	S: Days Diesel Service
	Other	S: Shawnee Expo Center, Shawnee Muni Airport✈, St Gregory's Univ, OK Baptist Univ
185		**OK 3E, Kickapoo St, Shawnee**
	Gas	N: Murphy S: Phillips 66
	Food	N: Braum's, Chili's, Garcia's, Red Lobster, Luby's Cafeteria, Taco Bueno S: Applebee's, CiCi's, Cracker Barrel, Garfield's, IHOP, McDonald's, Popeye's, Quiznos, Santa Fee Cattle Co, Shoney's, Starbucks, Taco Bell, Three Buddies BBQ & Burgers
	Lodg	N: Holiday Inn Express S: Hampton Inn♥, La Quinta Inn♥
	Med	S: + Shawnee Medical Center Clinic, + University Health Center
	Other	N: Wal-Mart sc▲, Shawnee Mall, Movie 6 S: Lowe's, Jones Theatres, Staples, Shawnee Muni Airport✈, St Gregory's Univ, OK Baptist Univ
186		**OK 18, Shawnee, to Meeker**
	Gas	N: Citgo◊, Shell
	Food	N: Denny's, Rest/Ramada S: Golden Corral, Sonic
	Lodg	N: Best Value Inn, Days Inn, Holiday Inn Express, La Quinta Inn♥, Motel 6♥, Ramada Inn, Super 8 S: Colonial Inn, Super 8♥
	Other	S: Cinema 8, Vet♥, Animal Hospital♥
192		**OK 9A, to Earlsboro**
	Gas	S: Shell◊
(197)		**Rest Area (Both dir) (RR, Phones, Picnic)**
200		**US 377, OK 99, Seminole, Prague**
	FStop	S: Love's Travel Stop #219, Seminole Food Mart/Citgo
	TStop	S: to Seminole Nation Travel Plaza
	Food	S: Subway/Love's TS, Rest/Sem TP, Catfish Round-Up, Pit Stop Rest
	Other	S: Laundry/WiFi/Love's, Laundry/Sem TP, Round-Up RV Park▲, to Seminole State College, Mystic Winds Casino
212		**OK 56, Wewoka, to Cromwell**
	Gas	N: Conoco S: Shell◊
	Food	N: BBQ S: Café/Shell
	Other	S: Museum
217		**OK 48, Okemah, to Bristow, Holdenville**
	FStop	S: Total
	Food	S: Café/Total FS
	Other	N: to 12mi Last Chance RV Park▲
221		**OK 27, US 62, Okemah, Wetumka**
	TStop	N: Okemah Travel Center/Shamrock S: Love's Travel Stop #274 (DAND)
	Gas	N: Conoco◊, Shell
	Food	N: FastFood/Okemah TC, Mazzio's Pizza, Sonic S: Chesters/A&W/Love's TS
	Lodg	N: Days Inn♥, OK Motel
	TServ	N: 24 Hr Truck Repair
	Med	N: + Creek Nation Comm Hospital
	Other	N: Laundry/Okemah TC, Auto & Tire Services, Okemah Flying Field✈ S: WiFi/RVDump/Love's TS

◊ = Regular Gas Stations with Diesel ▲ = RV Friendly Locations ♥ = Pet Friendly Locations
RED PRINT SHOWS LARGE VEHICLE PARKING/ACCESS ON SITE OR NEARBY BROWN PRINT SHOWS CAMPGROUNDS/RV PARKS

W 40 E

EXIT	OKLAHOMA	EXIT	OKLAHOMA	EXIT	OK / AR
227	Clearview Rd, Okemah	**270**	Texanna Rd, Porum Landing	**(313)**	OK Welcome Center (WB) (RR, Phone, Picnic, Info, RVDump)
Other	S: to Golden Pony Casino	Gas	S: Sinclair		
231	US 75S, Weleetka	**278**	US 266, OK 2, Warner, Muskogee	**(316)**	Rest Area (EB) (RR, Phone, Picnic, Vend, Info, RVDump)
FStop	S: Bernhardt's P66 Truck Stop	FStop	N: Jim Bob's Little Stores #21/66		
Food	S: Cow Pokes Café, Rest/Bernhardt's TS	Food	N: FastFood/JimBob's, Cowgirls D/I, McDonald's, Simple Simons, Subway	**321**	OK 64B N, to US 64, Muldrow
237	US 62, to US 75, Henryetta	Lodg	N: Sleepy Travel Motel	TStop	S: Arena Truck Stop/Shell
FStop	N: R&R Shell	**(283)**	Scenic Turnout (Both dir)	Food	N: Broadway Joe's Café, Dandee Café, Sonic, Shadow Mtn BBQ
TStop	N: Mobile Services/Citgo	**284**	Ross Rd, Webbers Falls		S: Rest/Arena TS, Hickory Pit, Wild Rose Ranch BBQ
Food	N: FastFood/Mobile Serv, Arby's, McDonald's, Pig Out Palace, Obee's Soup, Salad & Subs, KFC, Sheila's BBQ	**286**	Muskogee Turnpike, to Muskogee, Tulsa	Lodg	S: Economy Inn/Arena Truck Stop, Best Value Inn
	S: Hungry Traveler	**287**	OK 100N, Webbers Falls, Gore	AServ	S: Carl's Auto Repair, K&K Automotive
Lodg	N: Country Inn, Old Corral Motel	TStop	N: Love's Travel Stop #255	TServ	S: B&W Truck Repair
	S: Super 8	Food	N: Subway/Godfathers/Love's TS, Charlie's Chicken	TWash	S: B&W Truck Wash
TServ	N: Mobile Serv/Tires, Interstate Diesel	Lodg	N: Sleepy Traveler	**325**	US 64, Roland, Fort Smith
Med	N: + Family Care Clinic	TServ	S: Tire Shop	TStop	S: Pilot Travel Center #196 (Scales), Roland Truck Stop/Shell (Scales)
Other	N: Henryetta RV Park▲, Auto Services, ATMs, Carwash, Grocery, Museum, Towing	Other	N: WiFi/Love's TS, to MarVal Family Camping Resort▲, to Greenleaf State Park▲	Food	S: Wendy's/Pilot TC, FastFood/Roland's, McDonald's, Mazzio's Pizza
240A	Indian Nation Turnpike (TOLL)	**291**	OK 10N, Carlile Rd, Gore	Lodg	N: Days Inn/Cherokee Casino Inn
240B	US 62E, US 75N, to Okmulgee	Other	N: to Webbers Falls Lock & Dam▲		S: Interstate Inn
Other	N: to Okmulgee/Dripping Springs State Park▲	**297**	OK 82N, Vian, Talequah	Other	N: Cherokee Casino
247	Tiger Mt Rd, Checotah	Other	N: to 15mi: Tenkiller State Park▲		S: Laundry/WiFi/Pilot TC
(251)	Parking Area (EB)	**303**	Dwight Mission Rd, Sallisaw	**330**	OK 64D S, Roland, to Dora, Fort Smith (fr EB)
(252)	Parking Area (WB)	Other	N: Blue Ribbon Downs		
255	Pierce Rd, Service Rd	**308**	US 59, I-40 Bus, Sallisaw, Poteau	NOTE:	MM 331: Arkansas State Line
Other	N: Checotah/Lake Eufaula West KOA▲	FStop	N: Greg's Mini Mart/66		(CENTRAL TIME ZONE)
259	OK 150, Fountainhead Rd	TStop	S: Sallisaw Travel Center/Shell (Scales)		**◯ OKLAHOMA**
Gas	S: Shell	Gas	N: Citgo, Sinclair, Murphy		**◯ ARKANSAS**
Lodg	S: Lake Eufaula Inn	Food	N: Braum's, Dana's, McDonald's, Western Sizzlin, Wild Horse Mtn BBQ		(CENTRAL TIME ZONE)
Other	S: to Fountainhead State Park▲		S: Rest/FastFood/Sallisaw TC	**1**	to Ft Smith, Dora (WB)
262	Lotawatah Rd, to US 266	Lodg	N: Best Western, Days Inn, Golden Spur Inn, Microtel, Super 8	**(2)**	AR Welcome Center (EB) (RR, Phone, Picnic, Vend)
Gas	N: Phillips 66, Sinclair	TServ	S: Sallisaw TC/Tires	**3**	Lee Creek Rd, Van Buren
264A	US 69S, to Eufaula	Med	N: + Sequoyah Memorial Hospital	Other	N: Park Ridge Campground▲
264B	US 69N, to US 266, Muskogee	Other	N: Auto Services, Tires, Towing, Wal-Mart sc, to appr 10mi Brushy Lake State Park▲	**5**	AR 59, Fayetteville Rd, Van Buren, Siloam Springs (Addt'l serv 8mi S in Ft Smith)
FStop	N: H-Z Mart/Citgo		S: Laundry/Sallisaw TC, Auto Dealer, Sallisaw/Ft Smith W KOA▲, Sallisaw Muni Airport✈, to Lakeside RV Camp ground▲	TStop	S: Van Buren Travel Center (Scales)
TStop	N: Flying J Travel Plaza #5052/Conoco (Scales)			Gas	N: Citgo, Phillips 66, Murphy
Food	N: Rest/FastFood/FJ TP, Charlie's Chicken, McDonald's, Simple Simon's, Sooner Country Rest	**311**	US 64, Sallisaw, to Stillwell		S: Shell
		TStop	N: Ed's Truck Stop/66	Food	N: Arby's, Burger King, C&C Catfish, Chili's, Firehouse Subs, McDonald's, Popeye's, Santa Fe Café, Simple Simon's Pizza, Starbucks
Lodg	N: Best Value Inn, Executive Inn	Food	N: Rest/Ed's TS, Hardee's, Pizza Hut, Sonic, Subway, Taco Mayo		
Tires	N: M&J Tire, Checotah Tire & Lube	Lodg	N: Econo Lodge, Motel 6♥, Sallisaw Inn		S: Braum's, Big Jake's Cattle Co, KFC, Mazzio's Pizza, Rick's Ribhouse, Sonic, Subway, Taco Bell, Waffle House, Wendy's
TServ	N: Smith Diesel Repair	TServ	N: Ed's TS/Tires		
Other	N: Laundry/WiFi/LP/FJ TP, ATMs, Bank, Auto Services, Grocery, Wal-Mart	Med	N: + Sequoyah Memorial Hospital		
265	US 69 Bus, Checotah	Other	N: Laundry/Ed's TS, AutoZone, Wal-Mart sc		
TStop	N: Kwik N EZ Auto Truck Travel Plaza/Citgo				
Food	N: Kitchen Table Café, Pizza Hut, Sonic, FastFood/KwiknEZ				
Lodg	S: Budget Inn				

◆ = Regular Gas Stations with Diesel   ▲ = RV Friendly Locations   ♥ = Pet Friendly Locations
RED PRINT SHOWS LARGE VEHICLE PARKING/ACCESS ON SITE OR NEARBY   BROWN PRINT SHOWS CAMPGROUNDS/RV PARKS

INTERSTATE 40 W/E

EXIT		ARKANSAS
	Lodg	N: Best Western, Hampton Inn
		S: Motel 6♥, Super 8♥
	Tires	N: Cooley's Tires
	TServ	N: Arkansas Kenworth
		S: Carco International
	TWash	S: TWA Truck Wash
	Med	S: + Crawford Memorial Hospital
	Other	N: Wal-Mart sc, Auto Services, Dollar Tree, Dollar General, to Park Ridge Campground▲
		S: RVDump/Van Buren TC, ATMs, Banks, Auto Services, IGA, Walgreen's, Outdoor Living RV Center/ Overland RV Park▲
(7)		Jct I-540S, US 71S, Fort Smith (All Serv at 1st Ex #2)
(9)		Weigh Station (Both dir)
(12)		Jct I-540N, to Fayetteville
	Other	N: to Lake Ft Smith State Park▲
		S: Rick Yancey's RV
13		US 71, Alma, Fayetteville
	FStop	S: Alma Travel Mart/Citgo
	Gas	N: Phillips 66◊, Shell
		S: Shamrock, Murphy◊
	Food	N: Burger King, Cracker Barrel, DQ, KFC, Mazzio's, Subway, Taco Bell
		S: Braum's, McDonald's
	Lodg	N: Comfort Inn, Meadors Motor Inn
		S: Days Inn
	TServ	S: Long's Truck Service, Peterbilt
	Other	N: O'Reilly Auto Parts, to Univ of AR, Crabtree RV Center, Rentals & RV Park▲, Ft Smith/Alma KOA▲, to Lake Ft Smith State Park▲
		S: Grocery, NAPA, Wal-Mart, Rex Yancy's RV Superstore
20		US 64, Mulberry, Dyer
	TStop	S: Kountry Xpress/Shell
	Gas	N: Conoco◊
		S: Phillips 66
	Food	S: Rest/Kountry Xpress
	Lodg	S: Mill Creek Inn
	TServ	N: Freightliner
24		AR 215, Mulberry
35		AR 23, Ozark, to Huntsville
	Other	S: to Turner Bend Campground▲, Aux Ark Park/Ozark Lake▲
(35)		Rest Area (EB) (RR, Phones, Picnic)
(36)		Rest Area (WB) (RR, Phones, Picnic)
37		AR 219, Ozark
	TStop	S: Love's Travel Stop #271
	Gas	S: Shell
	Food	S: Subway/Love's FS, McDonald's/Shell, KFC/Taco Bell
	Lodg	S: Days Inn♥
	Med	S: + Mercy Hospital/Turner Memorial
	Other	S: WiFi/Love's TS, Ozark Airport✈
41		AR 186, Altus
	Other	S: Pine Ridge RV Park▲, Mt Bethel Winery
47		AR 164, Clarksville, to Coal Hill, Hartman
55		US 64, AR 109, Clarksville, Scranton
	TStop	S: Hwy 109 Truck Plaza/Conoco (on AR 109—2mi S), Exxon Tigermart Auto Truck Center

Personal Notes

_____

EXIT		ARKANSAS
	Gas	N: Citgo◊
	Food	N: Hardee's, Pizza Hut, Waffle Inn
		S: Rest/FastFood/Hwy 109 TP, FastFood/Exxon TM, Catfish House, Kountry Kitchen Grill, Western Sizzlin'
	Lodg	N: Hampton Inn
		S: Days Inn
	TServ	S: Hwy 109 TP/Tires
	Other	N: AR State Hwy Patrol Post
		S: Laundry/RVDump/Hwy 109TP
57		AR 109, Clarksville, Scranton
	TStop	S: Exit 57 Auto Truck Express/Shell
	Gas	N: Citgo, Conoco◊
	Food	N: Subway, Tastee Taco
		S: FastFood/Ex 57 TE
	Other	N: to Univ of the Ozarks
		S: Laundry/RVDump/Ex 57 TE, Towing
58		AR 103, AR 21, Clarksville
	TStop	S: South Park Truck Stop/Shell
	Gas	N: Phillips 66, Shell◊
		S: Murphy◊
	Food	N: KFC, McDonald's, Pizza Hut, Sonic, Waffle House, Wendy's, Woodward's
		S: Rest/S Park TS, Arby's
	Lodg	N: Comfort Inn, Economy Inn, Super 8
		S: Best Western♥
	TWash	S: S Park TS
	TServ	S: S Park TS/Tires
	Med	N: + Johnson Reg'l Medical Center
	Other	N: ATMs, Banks, to Clarksville Muni Airport✈
		S: Laundry/SP TS, Auto Dealers, Wal-Mart sc

EXIT		ARKANSAS
64		US 64, Lamar, Clarksville
	FStop	S: Valero
	Food	S: Rest/PizzaPro/Valero
	Other	S: RV Park▲
67		AR 315, Knoxville
(68)		Rest Area (EB) (RR, Phones, Picnic, Vend)
(70)		Scenic Overlook (WB)
(72)		Rest Area (WB) (RR, Phones, Picnic, Vend)
74		AR 333, London, Russellville
	Other	N: to Dardanelle Lake/Piney Bay▲
78		US 64, Russellville
	Gas	S: GAS
	Other	S: Lake Dardanelle State Park▲, Shadow Mountain RV Park▲
81		AR 7, Russellville
	Gas	N: SuperStop◊
		S: Exxon◊, Fina, Phillips 66◊, Shell
	Food	N: Captain Blys Pies & More, Seven Forty Supper Club
		S: Arby's, Burger King, Cracker Barrel, Colton's Steak House & Grill, Dixie Café, Pizza Inn, Ruby Tuesday, Santa Fe Café, Subway, Waffle House
	Lodg	N: Days Inn, Motel 6♥, Lakeside Resort Motel & RV Park▲
		S: Best Western, Best Value Inn, Economy Inn, Fairfield Inn, Hampton Inn, Holiday Inn♥, Super 8
	Med	S: + Dardanelle Hospital
	Other	N: Outdoor Living Center & RV Park/RVDump▲
		S: Goodyear, AR Tech Univ, Shadow Mountain RV Park▲, RV Center, to Lake Dardanelle State Park▲
83		AR 326, Weir Rd
84		US 64, AR 331, to AR 7, Russellville
	FStop	N: Hob Nob Shell (AR331N)
	TStop	N: Flying J Travel Plaza #5038/Conoco (Scales)
		S: Pilot Travel Center #430 (Scales)
	Gas	S: Phillips 66
	Food	N: Rest/FastFood/FJ TP
		S: Subway/Wendy's/Pilot TC, CiCi's, Country Joe's BBQ, Hardee's, Ryan's Grill, Shoney's, Waffle House
	Lodg	S: Comfort Inn
	TServ	N: Russellville Truck & Tire Repair
		S: Danny's Truck & Trailer Repair, Rick's Truck Repair International
	Other	N: Laundry/BarbSh/WiFi/RVDump/LP/FJ TP, Ivys Cove RV Retreat/RVDump▲
		S: Laundry/WiFi/RVDump/Pilot TC, AutoZone, ATMs, Auto Dealers, Banks, Grocery, Kmart, Lowe's, Staples, Tires, Towing, Wal-Mart sc, Valley Cinema, US Post Office, Russellville Muni Airport✈, Lake Dardanelle/Old Post Road Park▲
88		AR 363, Pottsville
	TServ	S: Gala Creek Truck Service, Tires, Exit 88 Truck Wash
94		AR 105, N Church St, Atkins
	Gas	N: BP◊, Exxon◊, Shell
	Food	N: McDonald's/BP, Subway/Exxon, KFC/Taco Bell, I-40 Grill, Jean's Country Kitchen, Sonic

Page 190   ◊ = Regular Gas Stations with Diesel   ▲ = RV Friendly Locations   ♥ = Pet Friendly Locations
RED PRINT SHOWS LARGE VEHICLE PARKING/ACCESS ON SITE OR NEARBY   BROWN PRINT SHOWS CAMPGROUNDS/RV PARKS

EXIT	ARKANSAS
101	**Fishlake Rd, Morrilton, Blackwell**
FStop	N: Valero
TStop	N: Blackwell Truck Stop (Scales)
Food	N: Diner/Deli/Blackwell TS
Other	N: Laundry/Blackwell TS
107	**AR 95, Oak Sts, Morrilton**
TStop	S: Love's Travel Stop #267
Gas	N: Shell◊
	S: Shell
Food	N: Morrilton Restaurant
	S: Subway/Love's TS, Wendy's
Lodg	N: Days Inn, Scottish Inn
Other	N: Morrilton/Conway KOA/RVDump▲
	S: WiFi/Love's TS
108	**AR 9, Bus 9, AR 287, Morrilton**
Gas	S: Phillips 66, Shell◊, Murphy
Food	S: Bonanza, KFC, McDonald's, Pizza Hut, Oretega's Mex Rest, Subway, Waffle House, Wendy's
Lodg	N: Super 8
	S: Days Inn, Super 8
Med	S: + St Anthony's Healthcare Center
Other	S: ATMs, Banks, Auto Dealers, Cinema, Goodyear, Kroger, Wal-Mart sc Auto Services, to Morrilton Muni Airport✈, to Lewisburg Bay MH & RV Park▲, to Petit Jean State Park▲
112	**AR 92, to US 64, Plumerville**
117	**to US 64, Menifee**
124	**AR 25, US 64, Conway (EB)**
Gas	S: Hess◊, Shell
125	**US 65N, US 65B, Conway, to Greenbrier, Harrison**
FStop	S: Garrett's Truck Stop
Gas	N: Conoco◊, Exxon◊, Phillips 66, Shell◊
	S: Citgo, Exxon◊
Food	N: Cracker Barrel, El Chico, Hardee's, McDonald's
	S: Burger King, CiCi's, IHOP, Outback Steakhouse, Ryan's Grill, Starbucks, Subway, Village Inn, Waffle House, Wendy's
Lodg	N: Comfort Inn
	S: Holiday Inn Express, Howard Johnson, Motel 6♥, Super 8
Med	S: + Conway Reg'l Medical Center
Other	N: Auto Services, Office Depot
	S: ATMs, Banks, Auto Dealers, Dollar General, Dollar Tree, Kelly Tire, Lowe's, Wal-Mart sc, Hendrix College
127	**US 64, Conway, Vilonia, Beebe**
Gas	N: BP, Exxon
	S: Raceway, Shell, Valero
Food	N: Annie's Fam Rest, Denny's, Waffle House

EXIT	ARKANSAS
Food	S: Burger King, Dillon's Steakhouse, Gringo's TexMex, Hardee's, McDonald's, Panda Café, Taco Bell, Wendy's
Lodg	N: Best Western, Comfort Inn, Days Inn, Hampton Inn
	S: Best Value Inn, Conway Inn, Economy Inn, Kings Inn
Med	S: + Conway Reg'l Medical Center
Other	N: Auto Dealers, Auto Services, Goodyear, Home Depot, Target, RV Center
	S: AutoZone, Auto Services, ATMs, Big Lots, Banks, Carmike Cinema, Kroger, Natural Way Health Foods, Walgreen's, Dennis F Cantrell Field✈, Univ of Central AR, Central Baptist College
129AB	**US 65B, AR 286, Conway (WB)**
129	**US 65B, AR 286, Conway (EB)**
FStop	S: Mapco Express #3059
Gas	S: Citgo, Exxon, Shell
Food	S: Arby's, Rio Grande Mexican, Subway, Taco Place, Wendy's
Lodg	S: Budget Inn, Continental Motel
Med	S: + Conway Reg'l Medical Center
Other	N: RV Center
	S: Midas, Wrecker & Repair services, to COE/Toad Suck Ferry Park▲, AR State Hwy Patrol Post
(133)	**Inspection Station** (Both dir)
135	**AR 89, AR 365, Mayflower**
Gas	N: Hess
	S: Exxon◊, Valero
Food	S: Sonic
Other	N: Mayflower RV Center, to Camp Joseph T Robinson
142	**AR 365, Morgan, Maumelle**
FStop	N: Morgan Valero (MacArthur Dr)
TStop	S: AmBest/Morgan Truck Stop/Shell (Scales)
Gas	S: Phillips 66
Food	S: FastFood/Morgan TS, I-40 Rest, KFC/Taco Bell, McDonald's, Waffle House
Lodg	N: Days Inn
	S: Comfort Suites, Quality Inn, Super 8
Other	N: Auto Services, Trails End RV Park▲
	S: Diesel Service & Parts
(147)	**Jct I-430S, to Texarkana**
Other	S: Little Rock North KOA▲
148	**AR 100, Crystal Hill Rd**
Gas	N: Shell
	S: Citgo
Other	N: Auto Services & Repairs
	S: Little Rock North KOA▲
150	**AR 176, Burns Park, Camp Pike, Camp Robinson**
Other	N: to MIL/Camp Robinson RV Park▲

EXIT	ARKANSAS
Other	S: Burns Park Golf Course, Burns City Park/RVDump▲
152	**AR 365, AR 176, 33rd St, to Levy**
Gas	N: Conoco, Shell
	S: Exxon, Phillips 66, Shell
Food	N: Burger King, McDonald's, Pizza Hut
	S: Church's Chicken
Med	S: + Hospital
Other	N: AutoZone, Kroger, Wal-Mart
	S: Grocery
153A	**AR 107, JFK Blvd, Main St**
Gas	N: Exxon, Mapco Express, Shell
	S: Exxon
Food	N: Deli
	S: Bonanza, Waffle House
Lodg	N: Travelodge
	S: Country Inn, Hampton Inn, Holiday Inn, Howard Johnson, Motel 6♥
Med	S: + Hospital
Other	N: Animal Clinic♥
(153B)	**Jct I-30W, US 65S, to Little Rock**
154	**N Hills Blvd, to Lakewood (EB)**
155	**US 67, US 167, Jacksonville** (ALL Serv on US 167N)
156	**Springhill Dr, N Little Rock**
Gas	N: Phillips 66
Food	N: Cracker Barrel, Paradise Grill & Seafood
Lodg	N: Fairfield Inn, Hampton Inn, Holiday Inn Express, La Quinta Inn♥, Residence Inn
Med	N: + Baptist Health Medical Center
157	**AR 161, to US 70, Prothro Rd, NLR**
FStop	S: Flash Market #123/Citgo
TStop	N: Mid-State Truck Plaza (Scales)
Gas	N: Exxon
	S: Phillips 66◊, Shell◊
Food	S: Burger King, McDonald's, Sonic, Subway, Taco Bell, Waffle House
Lodg	S: Best Value Inn, Comfort Inn, Days Inn, Masters Inn, Rest Inn, Red Roof Inn♥, Super 8
Other	S: Auto Services, Hills Mobile Truck & Trailer
(159)	**Jct I-440, River Port, Texarkana**
161	**AR 391, Galloway, NLR**
TStop	N: Love's Travel Stop #236
	S: TruckOMat (Scales), Petro Stopping Center #26/Mobil (Scales), Pilot Travel Center #332 (Scales) (DAND)
Food	N: Chesters/Love's TS
	S: IronSkillet/Petro SC, Subway/Pilot TC
Lodg	S: Days Inn, Galloway Inn
TWash	S: TruckOMat, Blue Beacon TW/Pilot TC
TServ	N: Trans America Tire, Freightliner

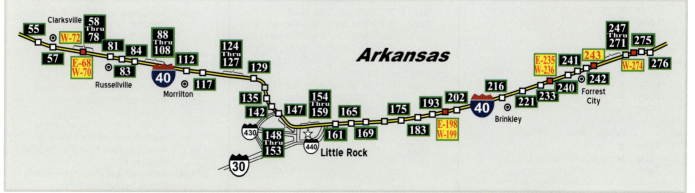

◊ = Regular Gas Stations with Diesel ▲ = RV Friendly Locations ♥ = Pet Friendly Locations
RED PRINT SHOWS LARGE VEHICLE PARKING/ACCESS ON SITE OR NEARBY   BROWN PRINT SHOWS CAMPGROUNDS/RV PARKS

Page 191

EXIT		ARKANSAS
	TServ	S: Petro SC/Tires, Speedco
	Other	N: WiFi/Love's TS
		S: Laundry/BarbSh/WiFi/Petro SC, Laundry/WiFi/Pilot TC, River City RV
165		Kerr Rd, Lonoke
169		AR 15, Remington Rd, to Cabot
(170)		Inspection Station (Both dir)
175		AR 31, Lonoke
	TStop	N: Crackerbox #35/Valero
	Gas	N: Exxon◆
		S: Shell
	Food	N: McDonald's, Rest/Economy Inn
		S: Pizza Hut, Sonic, Subway/Shell, Rest/Perry's Motel
	Lodg	N: Days Inn, Economy Inn, Super 8♥
		S: Holiday Inn Express, Perry's Motel
183		AR 13, Carlisle
	FStop	S: Conoco Truck Stop
	Gas	S: Exxon◆, Phillips 66, Citgo
	Food	S: Nick's Catfish & BBQ, Subway, Sonic
	Lodg	S: Best Value Inn♥, Carlisle Motel
193		US 63, AR 11, Hazen, Des Arc, Stuttgart, Clarendon
	FStop	S: Hazen Super Stop #88/Shell
	Gas	N: Exxon
		S: Citgo◆/T-Rick's
	Food	S: Outdoor Café, Subway
	Lodg	S: Super 8♥, Travel Inn
	Other	S: T Rick's RV Park/RVDump▲
(198)		Rest Area (EB)
		(RR, Picnic, Vend)
(199)		Rest Area (WB)
		(RR, Picnic, Vend)
202		AK 33, Biscoe
216		US 49, AR 17, Brinkley, Cotton Plant, Helena, Jonesboro
	FStop	N: Flash Market #49/Citgo
	TStop	N: Brinkley Travel Center
	Gas	N: Shell
		S: Express◆, Exxon◆, Phillips 66, Valero
	Food	N: FastFood/Brinkley TC, Western Sizzlin, Rest/Super 8
		S: Gene's BBQ, KFC, Laura's Diner, McDonald's, Pizza Hut, Taco Bell, Waffle House
	Lodg	N: Baymont Inn, Best Inn, Days Inn, Econo Lodge, Super 8 & RV Park▲
		S: Best Western, Budget Inn, Heritage Inn & RV Park▲
	Med	S: + Brinkley Medical Clinic
	Other	S: Auto Services, Firestone, Kroger, NAPA, Wal-Mart
221		AR 78, Wheatley, Marianna
	FStop	S: Mapco Express #3154
	TStop	N: Sweet Pea's Truck Stop #401/66, S: Fuel Mart #640
	Gas	S: BP
	Food	N: Rest/Sweet Pea's TS
		S: FastFood/Mapco, FastFood/FuelMart
	Lodg	N: Rest Inn, Super 8
	TServ	N: Sweet Peas TS/Tires
	Other	N: Laundry/Sweet Pea TS, Wheatley RV Park▲
233		AR 261, Main St, Palestine
	FStop	S: Kwik Stop/BP
	TStop	N: Love's Travel Stop #275 (Scales)
	Food	N: Subway/Chesters/Love's TS
		S: FastFood/Kwik Stop

EXIT		ARKANSAS
	Lodg	N: Rest Inn
	TServ	S: Tire Shop Truck Service
	Other	N: WiFi/RVDump/Love's TS
		S: B&E Tire Repair & Sales, White's Auto & Truck Repair
(235)		Rest Area (EB)
		(RR, Phones, Picnic, Vend)
239		AR 1, Wynne, Marianne, Wheatley
241B		AR 1B N, Forrest City, Wynne
	FStop	N: Forrest City AmocoBP
	Gas	N: Phillips 66◆
	Food	N: Denny's, HoHo Chinese, Popeye's, Wendy's
	Lodg	N: Best Value Inn, Days Inn, Econo Lodge, Hampton Inn, Holiday Inn, Luxury Inn, Super 8
	Other	N: Auto Dealers, AR State Hwy Patrol Post
241A		AR 1B S, Forrest City, Wynne
	Gas	S: Citgo, Exxon, Shell, Murphy
	Food	S: Bonanza, Burger King, Hardee's, KFC, Granny's Country Diner, McDonald's, Pizza Hut, Ponderosa, Ole Sawmill Cafe, Subway, Taco Bell, Waffle House
	Lodg	S: Best Western
	Other	S: Dollar General, Dollar Tree, Grocery, Fred's, SavALot, Wal-Mart
242		AR 284, Crowley's Ridge Rd, Forrest City
	Med	S: + Forrest City Medical Center
	Other	N: to Village Creek State Park▲
(243)		Rest Area (WB)
		(RR, Phones, Picnic, Vend)

EXIT		ARKANSAS
247		AR 38E, Widener, to Hughes
256		AR 75, AR 275, Heth, Parkin
	TStop	N: Mapco Express #3155
	Food	N: FastFood/Mapco Express
	Other	N: to 12 mi Parkin State Park
260		AR 149, Heth, to Earle
	FStop	N: Valero
	TStop	N: Travel Center of America #33/BP (Scales) (DAND)
	Gas	N: Citgo
		S: Shell
	Food	N: CountryPride/BurgerKing/TacoBell/PizzaHut/TA TC, Subway/Citgo
	Lodg	N: Super 8
	TWash	N: TA TC
	TServ	N: TA TC/Tires
	Other	N: Laundry/WiFi/RVDump/TA TC, Shell Lake Campground▲
		S: Carwash, Diesel Services
265		US 79, AR 218, Bings Store Rd, Crawfordsville, to Hughes
271		AR 147, Crawfordsville, Lehi
	TStop	S: PJ's/66 (W on US 70/79)
	Gas	S: Exxon, Shell
	Food	S: FastFood/PJ's
	Other	S: Frank's Auto & Tractor Service
(273)		Weigh Station (Both dir)
(274)		AR Welcome Center (WB)
		(RR, Phones, Info)
275		AR 118, Airport Rd, W Memphis
	Other	S: Tilden Rodgers Sports Complex, W Memphis Muni Airport✈
276		AR 76, Rich Rd (fr EB, diff reacc)
	Gas	S: Exxon, Mapco, Phillips 66, Shell
	Food	S: Bonanza, Burger King, Krystal, McDonald's, Shoney's
	Lodg	S: Ramada Ltd
	Other	S: ATMs, Banks, Wal-Mart sc Holiday Plaza Mall Shopping Center
NOTE:		I-40 runs with I-55 below, Exit #'s follow I-40.
(277)		Jct I-55N, Blytheville, St Louis
278		AR 77, 7th St, Missouri St, AR 191, W Memphis (Addt'l Serv S on Missouri St)
	FStop	S: Flash Market #11/Shell (S Serv Rd)
	Gas	N: Citgo
		S: Love's◆, RaceTrac, Exxon, Mapco
	Food	S: Cracker Barrel, KFC, Krystal, Mrs Winners, TCBY, McDonald's, Pizza Hut, Shoney's, Subway, Wendy's
	Lodg	S: Quality Inn, Ramada Inn
	Med	S: + Crittenden Memorial Hospital
	Other	S: RVDump/Flash Market, Auto Services, Goodyear,, Walgreen's, Wal-Mart sc, Kroger, Tom Sawyers Mississippi River RV Park/RVDump▲
279A		Ingram Blvd, W Memphis
	Gas	S: Citgo◆, Exxon, Shell
	Food	S: Perkins, Shoney's, Waffle House
	Lodg	N: Comfort Inn, Ramada, Red Roof Inn♥, Rodeway Inn
		S: Best Value Inn, Days Inn, Econo Lodge♥, Hampton Inn, Holiday Inn, Howard Johnson, Motel 6♥, Relax Inn, Rodeway Inn
	Other	N: U-Haul, Southland Greyhound Park
		S: Auto Dealers, Auto Services

Page 192 ◆ = Regular Gas Stations with Diesel ▲ = RV Friendly Locations ♥ = Pet Friendly Locations
RED PRINT SHOWS LARGE VEHICLE PARKING/ACCESS ON SITE OR NEARBY BROWN PRINT SHOWS CAMPGROUNDS/RV PARKS

EXIT	AR / TN	EXIT	TENNESSEE	EXIT	TENNESSEE
(279B)	Jct I-55S, to Memphis, TN, Jackson, MS (EB)	1C	US 51S, Danny Thomas Blvd (WB)	Other	S: Auto & Tire Services
		Gas	S: Exxon	12A	Summer Ave, US 64, US 70, US 79
NOTE:	I-40 runs with I-55 above, Exit #'s follow I-40.	Food	S: KFC	Gas	N: Star Mart, Mapco Express
		1D	US 51N, Danny Thomas Blvd (WB)		S: BP, Exxon, Star Mart
280/4	Club Rd, Southland Dr, Martin Luther King Jr Dr (I-55, Ex #4)	Med	N: + St Jude Research Center, + St Joseph Hospital	Food	N: Cracker Barrel, Luby's Cafeteria, Pappy & Jimmy's, Waffle House
TStop	N: Pilot Travel Center #429 (Scales), Harris Travel Center/Shamrock S: Petro Stopping Center #11 (Scales), Pilot Travel Center #272 (Scales), Flying J Travel Plaza #5333/Conoco (Scales)	(1E)	Jct I-240S, to Jackson, MS (Acc Hosp Via 1st 2 Exits)		S: Arby's, McDonald's, Pizza Hut, Wendy's, Western Sizzlin'
		Med	S: + Veteran's Medical Center, + Children's Medical Center, + Regional Medical Center, + Baptist Memorial Hospital, Univ of TN Hospital, + Methodist Hospital	Lodg	N: Baymont Inn, Holiday Inn Express, Ramada Inn S: Best Value Inn, Comfort Inn, Days Inn
Gas	N: BP◊			Other	N: Auto Dealer, Auto Rental, Cinema, Firestone, Goodyear, Greyhound, Kmart, U-Haul S: Auto Services, Firestone, Penske, Grocery, Tires
Food	N: Subway/Wendy's/Pilot TC, FastFood/ Harris TC S: Rest/FastFood/FJ TP, IronSkillet/ FastFood/Petro SC, Subway/Pilot TC, McDonald's, KFC/Taco Bell, Waffle House	1FG	TN 14, Jackson Ave, Memphis (WB Exit, EB entr)		
		Gas	S: Mapco Express, Exxon		
		Food	N: Jango's BBQ	12B	Sam Cooper Blvd (fr WB, Left Exit)
		Lodg	N: Rainbow Inn	(12C)	Jct I-240, W-Jackson, E-Nashville (fr EB, Left Exit)
Lodg	N: Express Inn S: Best Western, Budget Inn, Sunset Inn, Super 8 ♥	Other	N: Auto Services S: Auto Services, Laundromat, Memphis Zoo	12	Sycamore View Rd, to Bartlett
TWash	S: Blue Beacon TW/Petro SC	2	Chelsea Ave, Smith Ave	FStop	S: Mapco Express #3144
TServ	N: CAT, Chrome Shop, Goodyear S: Pilot TC/Tires, Petro SC/Tires, Speedco	Other	N: Auto Services, Grocery	Gas	N: Citgo◊, Phillips 66, Star Mart Texaco◊ S: Circle K◊/76, Citgo, Exxon
		2A	TN 300, to US 51, to Millington (fr EB, Left Exit) (Future I-69N)	Food	N: Burger King, Captain D's, Cracker Barrel, IHOP, KFC, McDonald's, Mrs Winner's, Perkins, Pizza Inn, Ruby Tuesday, Shoney's, Starbucks, Waffle House
Other	N: Laundry/WiFi/Pilot TC S: Laundry/BarbSh/WiFi/RVDump/LP/ FJ TP, WiFi/RVDump/Pilot TC, Laundry/CB/WiFi/Petro SC, Tom Sawyers Mississippi River RV Park/RVDump▲, Southland Greyhound Park	3	Watkins St, Memphis		
		Gas	N: BP, Mapco Express		S: China Buffet, Dunkin Donuts, Fortune Inn, Jimmy C's Café, Old Country Buffet, Subway, Tops BBQ, Wendy's
		Other	N: Auto Services, Laundromat		
		5	Hollywood St, Memphis		
		FStop	S: Mapco Express	Lodg	N: Baymont Inn, Drury Inn, Hampton Inn, Holiday Inn Express, Ramada Ltd, Red Roof Inn ♥, Value Place Hotel
281	AR 131, Mound City Rd, Mound City (WB)	Gas	N: BP		
		Food	N: Burger King, Hardee's, S: Fat Burger, Family BBQ		S: Best Value Inn, Days Inn, Fairfield Inn, La Quinta Inn ♥, Motel 6 ♥, Memphis Inn, Quality Inn, Super 8
(282)	Weigh Station (WB)	Other	N: ATMs, Carwash, Tires, Walgreen's S: Rhodes College		
NOTE:	MM #285: Tennessee State Line	6	Warford St, New Allen Rd		
	(CENTRAL TIME ZONE)	Other	N: Memphis Motorsports Park	Other	N: ATMs, AutoZone, Carwash, Dollar General, Laundromat, Piggly Wiggly, Walgreen's, Animal Clinic ♥, TN Hwy Patrol Post
⊙ ARKANSAS		8	TN 14, Jackson Ave (EB)		
⊙ TENNESSEE		Gas	N: 76, Citgo◊, Star Mart S: Citgo◊		
	(CENTRAL TIME ZONE)	Food	N: Sonic S: Central Park		S: Bass Pro Shop, SW TN Comm College
1	Riverside Dr, Front St (EB)	Lodg	N: Days Inn, Sleep Inn	14	Whitten Rd
S:	TN WELCOME CENTER (NO TRUCKS) (RR, Phone, Picnic, Vend, Info)	Med	N: + Methodist Hospital	Gas	N: 76, Mapco Express, Shell S: BP, Chevron
Lodg	S: Comfort Inn, Sleep Inn, Wyndham	Other	N: Auto Services S: AutoZone, Auto Services, Kelly Tire	Food	N: Quiznos, Sidecare Cafe S: Backyard Burger
Other	N: Pyramid Arena S: Riverfront, Convention Center, Museums	8A	TN 14N, Memphis (WB)	Lodg	S: Traveler's Inn
1A	Second St, Third St (WB ex, EB ent)	8B	TN 14S, Memphis (WB)	15	Appling Rd (WB)
Lodg	S: Marriott, Wyndham Garden Hotel	10	TN 204, Covington Pike, Memphis	15A	Appling Rd S (EB)
Med	N: + St Jude Research Center, + St Joseph Hospital	Gas	N: BP	15B	Appling Rd N (EB)
Other	N: C&L Bus Repair Service S: Convention Center, Courts, Museums	Food	N: McDonald's, Wendy's	16	TN 177, Germantown Blvd (EB)
		Other	N: Grocery, Auto Dealers, Auto Services, Auto Rental, Tires	Gas	N: 76, Shell S: Shell, Costco
1B	US 51, Danny Thomas Blvd (EB)				

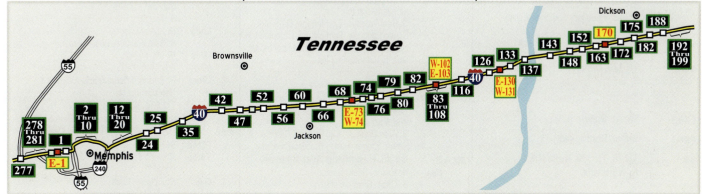

◊ = Regular Gas Stations with Diesel   ▲ = RV Friendly Locations   ♥ = Pet Friendly Locations

RED PRINT SHOWS LARGE VEHICLE PARKING/ACCESS ON SITE OR NEARBY   BROWN PRINT SHOWS CAMPGROUNDS/RV PARKS

Page 193

INTERSTATE 40 W-E

EXIT		TENNESSEE
	Food	N: Bahama Breeze, Burger King, Chili's, IHOP, Joe's Crab Shack, Logan's Road House, On the Border, Romano's Macaroni Grill, Red Lobster, McDonald's, Taco Bell, Wendy's S: Shogun, Waffle House
	Lodg	N: AmeriSuites, Hampton Suites S: Comfort Suites, Microtel, Wingate
	Other	N: Auto Dealers, Best Buy, Home Depot, Office Depot, Target, Walgreen's, Mall S: Costco
16AB		TN 177, Germantown (WB)
18		US 64, Somerville, Bolivar
	Gas	N: Shell S: 76, BP, Citgo
	Food	N: Bob Evans, Don Pablo, Hooter's, Luby's, Olive Garden, Steak n Shake, Smokey Bones, Waffle House S: Backyard Burger, KFC, Pizza Hut
	Lodg	N: Best Western, Fairfield Inn, Holiday Inn Express, Springhill Suites
	Other	N: Firestone, Goodyear, Lowe's, Sam's Club, Wal-Mart sc, Wolf Chase Mall S: Kroger, Walgreen's
20		Canada Rd, Lakeland
	FStop	N: Lakeland Shell
	Gas	N: 76 S: Exxon◊
	Food	N: FastFood/Lakeland Sh, Cracker Barrel, McDonald's, Waffle House, Rest/Days Inn S: Subway/Exxon, Cotton Cabin
	Lodg	N: Days Inn♥, Relax Inn, Super 8
	Other	S: Belz Factory Outlet Mall, Old Tyme Pottery, Memphis East KOA▲
24		TN 385, Millington, Collierville (Future I-269)
24A		TN 385W, Millington, Collierville
24B		TN 385E, Millington, Collierville
25		TN 205, Airline Rd, Arlington
	Gas	N: Chevron, Exxon◊, Shell◊ S: Horizon◊
	Food	N: Subway/Exxon, Chesters/Shell S: Backyard Burger/Horizon
	Other	S: Tourist Info
35		TN 59, US 70, Somerville, Covington
	FStop	S: Longtown Travel Center/BP (Scales)
	Food	S: Rest/Longtown TC
	Other	S: CB/Longtown TC
42		TN 222, Stanton Rd, Somerville
	TStop	S: Pilot Travel Center #149 (Scales) (DAND)
	Gas	S: Exxon◊
	Food	N: Bozo's Hot Pit BBQ, Shirley's Grill S: Chester's/Subway/Pilot TC, Café/Exxon,
	Lodg	N: Best Value Inn, Countryside Inn S: Deerfield Inn
	Other	N: Earl's Wrecker Service & Tires S: Laundry/WiFi/Pilot TC
47		TN 179, Darcyville Rd, Stanton
	TStop	S: Exit 47 Plaza (Scales)
	Food	S: Rest/Exit 47 Pl
	Tires	S: Exit 47 Pl
(49)		Weigh Station (EB)
(50)		Weigh Station (WB)
52		TN 76, TN 179, Koko Rd, to Whiteville

EXIT		TENNESSEE
56		TN 76, Anderson Ave, Brownsville, to Somerville
	FStop	N: Hopper Quik Stop #3/Exxon S: Bell's Truck Stop/Exxon
	Gas	N: BP, Citgo◊, Shell S: BP◊, Exxon◊
	Food	N: FastFood/Hooper QS, DQ, KFC, McDonald's, Pizza Hult, Subway/Citgo S: Huddle House/Exxon
	Lodg	N: Best Western, Comfort Inn, Days Inn, Econo Lodge, O'Bannon Inn♥
	Med	N: + Hospital
	Other	N: Tourist Info
60		TN 19, Mercer Rd, Brownsville
66		US 70, TN 1, Brownsville
	FStop	S: Gas Mart #628 (Scales)
	Food	S: FastFood/Gasl Mart
	Lodg	S: Motel 6♥
68		TN 138, Providence Rd, Denmark
	TStop	S: Travel Center of America/Wilhites/Citgo (Scales)
	Gas	N: BP, Valero
	Food	S: Rest/Subway/TA TC
	Lodg	S: Ole South Inn, Scottish Inn
	TServ	S: TA TC/Tires
	Other	N: Wrecker Service, Ft Pillow State Hist Park▲ S: Laundry/WiFi/TA TC, Joy-O RV Park▲
(73)		Madison Rest Area (Both dir) (RR, Phones, Picnic, Vend, Info)
74		Lower Brownsville Rd
76		TN 223S, Jackson
	Other	S: Whispering Pines RV Park▲, McKellar-Sipes Reg'l Airport✈
79		US 412, Jackson, Dyersburg
	FStop	N: Horizon Travel Plaza S: Ash's Citgo
	Gas	S: BP, Exxon, Mapco
	Food	S: FastFood/Ash's, GG's Rest, Reggi's BBQ
	Lodg	S: Days Inn♥
	Other	S: Jackson Mobile Village & RV Park▲, Auto Services, Galloway's Truck & Auto Repair, Union Univ
80AB		US 45ByP, Jackson, to Milan
	Gas	N: BP◊, Exxon, Sam's Club, WalMart S: BP, Citgo, Coastal◊, Phillips 66◊
	Food	N: Chili's, Corky's BBQ, IHOP, KFC, Lone Star Steakhouse, Perkins, Steak n Shake, Starbucks, TGI Friday's, Wendy's S: Applebee's, Arby's, Barnhill's Buffet, Burger King, Dunkin Donuts, El Chico, Logan's Roadhouse, O'Charley's, Sonic, McDonald's, Waffle House, Village Inn
	Lodg	N: AmeriHost Inn, Comfort Inn, Country Inn, Jameson Inn S: Best Western, Comfort Inn, Days Inn, Econo Lodge♥, Fairfield Inn, Hampton Inn, Holiday Inn, Motel 6♥, Old Hickory Inn♥, Quality Inn, Supertel Inn
	Med	S: + Jackson Madison Co Hospital, + Minor Medical Clinic
	Other	N: Best Buy, Cinema 12, Home Depot, Lowe's, PetSmart♥, Sam's Club, Wal-Mart sc S: Auto Dealers, Auto Repairs, Cinema 10, Kmart, Kroger, Harley Davidson, Penske
82AB		US 45, N Highland Ave, Jackson
	Gas	N: Exxon, Shell, Texaco S: Citgo, Exxon, RaceTrac

EXIT		TENNESSEE
	Food	N: Catfish Grill, Cracker Barrel, Western Sizzlin' S: Burger King, China Palace, Pizza Hut, Po Folks, Shoney's, Waffle House
	Lodg	N: Amerihost, Knight's Inn, Microtel S: Baymont Inn, Executive Inn, Old English Inn, La Quinta Inn♥, Quality Inn, Ramada Ltd, Super 8, Sheraton, Travelers Motel
	Other	N: Auto Repairs, Batteries Plus, Smallwoods RV, TN State Hwy Patrol S: AutoZone, Auto Repairs, Firestone, Goodyear, Grocery, Laundromat, Kroger, Office Depot, Radio Shack, Mall, Big Hill Pond State Park
83		Campbell St
	Gas	N: Exxon
	Lodg	S: Courtyard, Hampton Inn
85		Christmasville Rd, Jackson
	FStop	N: Express Food Mart & Deli/Exxon S: Pilot Travel Center #366 (Scales)
	Gas	N: BP◊ S: Shell
	Food	N: Subs/BP S: Denny's/Pilot TC
	Lodg	N: Howard Johnson Express
	Other	S: Laundry/Pilot TC
87		US 70, US 412, TN 1, Jackson, to Huntington, McKenzie
	FStop	S: BP Food Mart, Texaco Food Mart #3
	TStop	S: Love's Travel Stop #244 (Scales)
	Gas	N: Coastal◊ S: Exxon, Raceway
	Food	S: Hardee's/Love's TS, Waffle House
	Other	N: Auto & Truck Service S: Laundry/WiFi/RVDump/Love's TS, Freightliner, Bethel College
93		TN 152, Law Rd, to Lexington
	Gas	N: Phillips 66◊ S: Global Fuels
	Food	N: Deli/P66 S: Global Cafe
101		TN 104, Wildersville
	TStop	N: 101 Travel Center/Conoco
	Gas	N: Exxon
	Food	N: Rest/101 TC
	Other	N: WiFi/CB/101 TC
(102)		Parking Area (WB)
(103)		Parking Area (EB)
108		TN 22, Huntington, Lexington, Parkers Crossroads
	TStop	N: I-Mart #108/66, Bull Market #19/Citgo
	Gas	N: BP S: Exxon, Shell
	Food	N: BP/McDonald's, Bailey's Rest, DQ, Subway S: The Cotton Patch Rest
	Lodg	N: Knight's Inn S: Best Western, Best Value Inn
	Tires	N: Bull Market
	Med	S: + Hospital
	Other	N: Parker's Crossroads RV Park & Campground▲
116		TN 114, Westport
	Other	S: to Natchez Trace State Park▲
126		US 641, TN 69, Parsons, Camden
	FStop	S: Holladay Shell
	TStop	N: North Forty Truck Stop/66 (Scales), Sugar Tree Truck Stop
	Gas	N: Exxon◊, Shell

◊ = Regular Gas Stations with Diesel   ▲ = RV Friendly Locations   ♥ = Pet Friendly Locations
RED PRINT SHOWS LARGE VEHICLE PARKING/ACCESS ON SITE OR NEARBY   BROWN PRINT SHOWS CAMPGROUNDS/RV PARKS

EXIT		TENNESSEE
	Food	S: BP◊, Citgo
		N: Rest/FastFood/N 40 TS, Rest/Sugar Tree TS, Sandy's Burger Barn, Perry's Kountry BBQ & Fish, Rest/Days Inn
		S: DQ/Stuckey's/Citgo
	Lodg	N: Days Inn
		S: Apple Annie's Motel
	TServ	N: Sugar Tree TS, Wilson's Repair, Big John's Truck & Trailer Repair
	Other	N: Laundry/BarbSh/RVDump/N 40 TS, Northern Bedford Forrest State Park▲
		S: Mousetail Landing State Park▲
(130)		Benton Rest Area (EB)
		(RR, Phones, Picnic, Vend)
(131)		Benton Rest Area (WB)
		(RR, Phones, Vend)
133		TN 191, Birdsong Rd, Holladay
	Other	N: to Birdsong Resort, Marina & RV Park▲
		S: to Mousetail Landing State Park▲
137		Cuba Landing, Waverly
	Other	N: TN River Mountain Getaways Resort & Campground▲
143		TN 13, Hurricane Mills, to Linden, Waverly
	FStop	N: Pilot Travel Center # 53 (Scales)
	Gas	N: Phillips 66, Shell
		S: Exxon◊, Shell
	Food	N: Arby's/TJCinn/Pilot TC, Log Cabin, Loretta Lynn's Kitchen, McDonald's, Subway
	Lodg	N: Best Western, Days Inn♥, Holiday Inn Express, Knights Inn, Super 8
		S: Best Budget Motel
	TServ	N: I-40 Auto & Truck Center
	Other	N: Laundry/WiFi/Pilot TC, Greg's Tire & Repair, Buffalo KOA▲, 143 Off Road RV Park▲, to appr 7mi: Loretta Lynn's Ranch RV Park & Museum▲
		S: to Buffalo River Camping▲
148		TN 229, TN 50, Barren Hollow Rd, to Centerville
152		TN 230, Only, to Bucksnort
	Gas	N: Citgo
	Food	N: Rudy's Rest
	Lodg	N: Travel Inn
163		TN 48, Centerville, Dixon
	FStop	N: Phillips 66◊
	Gas	S: Shell
	Other	N: Truck & Tire Repair
		S: Tanbark Campground▲
(170)		Dickson Rest Area (Both dir)
		(RR, Phones, Picnic, Vend)
172		TN 46, Centerville, Dickson
	TStop	N: Pilot Travel Center #409 (Scales)
	Gas	N: BP◊, Citgo, Exxon, Shell
		S: Phillips 66, Shell◊
	Food	N: Wendy's/Pilot TC, Arby's, Burger King, Cracker Barrel, McDonald's, Subway, Ruby Tuesday, Waffle House
		S: O'Charley's, Sonic
	Lodg	N: Baymont Inn, Best Value Inn, Best Western, Comfort Inn, Econo Lodge, Hampton Inn, Knights Inn, Motel 6, Quality Inn, South Ave Inn, Super 8, I-40 Motel
		S: Budget Inn, Days Inn, Holiday Inn Express, Ramada Ltd♥
	Med	N: + Hospital

EXIT		TENNESSEE
	Other	N: Laundry/WiFi/RVDump/Pilot TC, Renaissance Center, Roadside Services, Dickson RV Park/LP◊
176		TN 840, Burns
182		TN 96, Dickson, Fairview, Franklin
	TStop	S: Flying J Travel Plaza #5051/Conoco (Scales), Horizon Family Travel Plaza
	Gas	N: BP, Citgo
	Food	S: CountryMarket/FastFood/FJ TP, Backyard Burger
	Lodg	N: Deerfield Inn, Fairview Inn
	Other	N: to Montgomery Bell State Park▲
		S: Laundry/WiFi/RVDump/LP/FJ TP
188		TN 249, Kingston Springs Rd, Ashland City, Pegram, Kingston Springs
	TStop	S: Petro 2 #49/Mobil (Scales)
	Gas	N: BP, Mapco Express◊, Shell
		S: Chevron
	Food	N: Blimpie/Express, Arby's/Shell, McDonald's, Pizza Pro, Sonic
		S: QuickSkillet/PizzaHut/Petro 2
	Lodg	N: Best Western, Econo Lodge, Motown Inn, Relax Inn
	TServ	S: Petro 2/Tires
	Other	S: Laundry/BarbSh/WiFi/Petro 2, Sundown Trailers
192		McCrory Lane, Pegram
	Other	N: 1 mi GAS
		S: Natchez Trace Parkway
196		US 70S, Bellevue, Newsom Station
	Gas	N: Mapco Express
		S: BP, Mapco Express◊, Shell

EXIT		TENNESSEE
	Food	N: Shoney's
		S: Applebee's, Jack in the Box, Quiznos, O'Charley's, Pizza Hut, Subway, Sonic, Taco Bell, Waffle House
	Lodg	S: Hampton Inn, Microtel
	Med	S: + Baptist Bellevue Med Center
	Other	N: Regal Cinema 12
		S: Firestone, Grocery, Home Depot, Publix, Staples, Walgreen's, Bellevue Center Mall
199		TN 251, Old Hickory Blvd
	Gas	S: BP, Mapco Express
	Food	S: Sonic, Waffle House
	Other	N: Wrecker Service
		S: PuttPutt Golf, Sam's Club, Wal-Mart
201A		US 70E, Charlotte Pike
201B		US 70W, Nashville
201		US 70, TN 24, Charlotte Pike (WB)
	Gas	N: Exxon, Shell
		S: Citgo, BP, Mapco, Costco
	Food	N: Cracker Barrel, Krystal, Waffle House
		S: Rest/Howard Johnson
	Lodg	N: Super 8
		S: Howard Johnson
	Other	N: Lowe's, Wal-Mart sc
		S: Auto Service, Costco, Food Lion, Firestone, PetSmart♥, U-Haul
204B		TN 155S, Briley Pkwy, Nashville Robertson Ave (WB)
204A		51st Ave N, Nashville (WB)
204		TN 155, Briley Pkwy, Nashville Robertson Ave, White Bridge Rd (Addtl Serv S to US 70/TN 24)
	Gas	N: Exxon, Shell◊
		S: Texaco
	Food	S: Burger King, Church's, KFC, Krystal, Shoney's, Uncle Bud's Catfish, Waffle House, White Castle
	Lodg	S: Baymont Inn, Best Western, Comfort Inn, Days Inn, Super 8
	Other	N: to John C Tune Airport ✈
		S: AutoZone, Auto Services, CVS, Enterprise, Goodyear, Walgreen's
205		46th Ave, 51st Ave, W Nashville
	Gas	S: BP, Mapco Express, Shell
	Food	S: McDonald's, Mrs Winner's
	Other	N: Harley Davidson
		S: Auto Services
(206)		Jct I-440E, to Knoxville, Huntsville, Chattanooga (WB Left Exit)
207		28th Ave, Jefferson St
	Med	S: + Metro Nashville Gen'l Hospital, + Meharry Medical College
	Other	N: Tn State Univ
		S: Fisk Univ
(208BA)		Jct I-65N, to Louisville (EB Left Exit)
(208)		Jct I-65N, to Louisville
209		US 70, TN 24, US 70S, US 431, Church St, Charlotte Ave (EB exit, WB entr)
	Gas	S: BP, Exxon
	Food	S: Burger King, Shoney's, White Castle
	Lodg	N: Holiday Inn
		S: Best Western, Comfort Inn, Shoney's Inn
	Med	S: + Baptist Hospital, + Columbia Centennial Medical Center

◊ = Regular Gas Stations with Diesel   ▲ = RV Friendly Locations   ♥ = Pet Friendly Locations

RED PRINT SHOWS LARGE VEHICLE PARKING/ACCESS ON SITE OR NEARBY   BROWN PRINT SHOWS CAMPGROUNDS/RV PARKS

EXIT	TENNESSEE
Other	N: Auto Services, Fleet Repair, Thrifty RAC Museums, State Capitol S: Auto & Tire Services, Budget, Museums
209A	US 70S, US 431, Broadway
209B	US 70S, US 431 Demonbreun St
Med	S: + Vanderbilt University Hospital
Other	N: Auto Services, Enterprise S: Music Row, Museums, Auto Services
(210)	Jct I-65S, to Birmingham (WB ex L)
(210AB)	Jct I-65S, to Birmingham
210C	US 31A, UA 41A, 2nd/4th Ave S
Food	S: Brown's BBQ
TServ	S: Bestway Truck & Tire Service
Other	N: Auto Services S: Auto Services, Museums
(211B)	Jct I-24W, Jct I-65N, Clarksville, Louisville (fr EB, Left exit)
(211A)	Jct I-65S, Birmingham, Jct I-40W, Memphis
212	Fesslers Lane
TStop	S: Dailey's #604/Shell
Food	N: Nashville Smokehouse S: Burger King, Krystal, McDonald's
Lodg	S: Drake Inn, Music City Motor Inn
TServ	N: Goodyear Tire & Auto, Neely Coble Sunbelt Truck Center, Tn Truck Sales S: PM Truck Service, Total Truck & Trailer Service
Med	S: + Hospital
Other	S: Laundry/Dailey's, Auto Services, Auto Dealers, Auto Rentals
(213A)	Jct I-24E, Jct I-40E, to Chattanooga
(213AB)	Jct I-24W, Jct I-440W
213	to US 41, Spence Lane
Gas	N: Shell S: BP
Food	S: Hunan Chinese, Piccadilly Cafeteria, Pizza Hut, Red Lobster, Taco Bell, Waffle House
Lodg	S: Days Inn, Econo Lodge, Holiday Inn Express, Hawthorne Inn, Quality Inn, Ramada Inn, Scottish Inn
TServ	N: Kenworth of TN S: Cummins Cumberland
215B	TN 155N, Briley Pkwy (EB)
Gas	N: Shell
Food	N: Denny's, Waffle House, Rest/Days Inn
Lodg	N: Days Inn, Embassy Suites, Holiday Inn, Hampton Inn, La Quinta Inn ♥, Quality Inn, Residence Inn

EXIT	TENNESSEE
215A	TN 155S, Briley Pkwy, (EB)
Gas	S: Shell
Food	S: Steak Out
Lodg	S: Marriott, Radisson Inn, Ramada, Royal Inn
215	TN 155, Briley Pkwy, Opryland
Other	N: to N Nashville KOA▲
216A	Nashville Int'l Airport (EB exit, WB entr) (NO TRUCKS)
Other	N: Auto Rentals
216B	Donelson Pike S, Airport (EB)
216C	TN 255, Donelson Pike N (EB)
216	TN 255, Donelson Pike, Nashville International Airport (WB)
Gas	N: BP, Citgo, RaceTrac, Shell
Food	N: Arby's, Backyard Burgers, Burger King, Chili's, KFC, Little Caesar's Pizza, Papa John's Pizza, McDonald's, Outback Steakhouse, Ruby Tuesday, Shoney's, Subway, Taco Bell, Waffle House, Wendy's
Lodg	N: AmeriSuites, Country Inn Suites, Fairfield Inn, Hampton Inn, Holiday Inn Express, La Quinta Inn ♥, Radisson Hotel, Red Roof Inn ♥, Springhill Suites, Super 8, Wingate Inn, Wyndham Garden Hotel
Other	N: Cruise America, Laundromat, Kmart, Walgreen's S: Auto Rentals
219	Stewarts Ferry Pike, Nashville
Gas	N: Mapco Express S: Mapco Express, Shell
Food	S: Cracker Barrel, La Hacienda Mex Rest, Subway, Waffle House
Lodg	S: Best Value Inn, Best Western, Country Inn, Days Inn, Family Inn, Howard Johnson, Sleep Inn
Other	S: Cook Campground▲
221A	TN 265, TN 45N, Central Pike, Old Hickory Blvd, Hermitage (EB)
Med	N: + Summit Medical Center
221B	TN 45S, Old Hickory Blvd (EB)
221	TN 45, Old Hickory Blvd
Gas	N: BP, Exxon, Mapco Express, RaceWay S: Phillips 66, Shell
Food	N: Applebee's, Hardee's, IHOP, Jack in the Box, Music City Café, Waffle House S: McDonald's, Po Folks, Shooters Sports Bar
Lodg	N: Comfort Inn, Holiday Inn Express, Motel 6, Quality Inn, Ramada Inn, Super 8, Vista Motel
Med	N: + Summit Medical Center
Other	N: CVS, Kroger, Walgreen's S: to the Hermitage Public Use Area

EXIT	TENNESSEE
(225)	Weigh Station (EB)
226A	TN 171S, Mt Juliet Rd, Mt Juliet, Nashville (EB)
226B	TN 171N, Mt Juliet Rd, Mt Juliet, Nashville (EB)
226	TN 171, Mt Juliet Rd, Mt Juliet, Nashville
Gas	N: BP, Exxon, Mapco Express◇, Shell◇ S: Mapco Express
Food	N: Arby's, Captain D's, McDonald's/BP S: Cracker Barrel, Ruby Tuesday, Waffle House
Lodg	S: Microtel, Quality Inn
Med	S: + Walk In Clinic
Other	N: to COE/Cedar Creek Campground▲ S: Laundromat
(228)	Weigh Station (WB)
229A	Beckwith Rd S (EB)
229 B	Beckwith Rd N (EB)
229	Beckwith Rd (WB)
232A	TN 109S, Lebanon, to Gallatin (EB)
232B	TN 109N, Lebanon, to Gallatin (EB)
232	TN 109, Lebanon, to Gallatin (WB)
Gas	N: Citgo, Mapco Express, Shell◇
Food	N: McDonald's, Subway, Waffle House S: Wendy's
Lodg	N: Best Western, Sleep Inn, HOTEL
Other	S: Countryside Resort RV Park▲
235	TN 840, to Chattanooga, Murfreesbo
236	Hartmann Dr
Gas	N: Mapco Mart, Shell
Food	N: Chili's, Outback Steakhouse
Med	N: + University Medical Center
Other	N: Home Depot, Lebanon Muni Airport✈
238	US 231, Lebanon, Murfreesboro
FStop	S: Scot Market #87/Citgo, Horizon Travel Plaza
TStop	S: Pilot Travel Center #411(Scales) (DAND)
Gas	N: BP, Exxon, Mapco Express, Shell◇
Food	N: Arby's, Cracker Barrel, Gondola Rest, Hardee's, Jack in the Box, McDonald's, Ponderosa, Waffle House, Wendy's S: FastFood/Scot Mkt, ChestersGr/McDonald's/Subway/Pilot TC, O'Charley's, Santa Fe Cattle Co, Sonic
Lodg	N: Best Value Inn, Comfort Inn, Executive Inn, Hampton Inn, Holiday Inn Express S: Country Inn, Comfort Suites, Days Inn, Knights Inn, Super 8
Med	N: + Hospital

◇ = Regular Gas Stations with Diesel   ▲ = RV Friendly Locations   ♥ = Pet Friendly Locations
RED PRINT SHOWS LARGE VEHICLE PARKING/ACCESS ON SITE OR NEARBY   BROWN PRINT SHOWS CAMPGROUNDS/RV PARKS

EXIT	TENNESSEE
Other	N: Wal-Mart sc, to Cumberland Univ S: Prime Outlets of Lebanon, Carwash, Laundry/WiFi/RVDump/Pilot TC, Cedars of Lebanon State Park▲, Shady Acres Campground▲, Timberline Campground▲, Family Campers▲, Bledsoe Creek State Park▲, RV Center
239A	US 70E, Watertown (EB)
TStop	S: Uncle Pete's Truck Stop/66 (Scales)
Food	N: Rest/FastFood/Uncle Pete's TS, Jalisco Mexican Rest
TServ	N: G&R Auto & Truck Repair S: Uncle Pete's TS/Tires
TWash	S: I-40 Repair & TW
Other	S: Laundry/WiFi/Uncle Pete's TS
239B	US 70W, Lebanon, Smithville (EB)
Gas	N: Citgo, RaceWay
Other	N: Auto Repairs
239	US 70, Lebanon, Watertown
245	Linwood Rd
Gas	N: BP◊
(252)	Parking Area (Both dir)
254	TN 141, to Alexandria
258	TN 53, Carthage, Gordonsville
Gas	N: BP, Exxon, Shell S: Citgo◊
Food	N: KFC/Taco Bell/Exxon, Connie's BBQ, McDonald's, Waffle House
Lodg	N: Comfort Inn
(267)	Rest Area (Both dir) (RR, Phones, Vend, Info)
268	TN 96, Buffalo Valley Rd, Center Hill Dam
Other	S: to Edgar Evans State Park▲
273	TN 56S, Smithville, McMinnville
Gas	S: BP◊, Phillips 66
Food	S: Rose Garden Restaurant
Lodg	S: Timber Ridge Inn
276	Old Baxter Rd
Gas:	N: Fuel Center S: Citgo◊
Other	N: Auto Service S: Jet Ski & Canoe Rental
280	TN 56N, Baxter, Gainesboro
TStop	N: Love's Travel Stop #330 (Scales)
Gas	N: Shell◊
Food	N: Subway/McDonald's/Love's TS
Other	N: WiFi/RVDump/Love's TS, Twin Lakes RV Park & Catfish Farm▲, TN Jaycee's Camp Discovery
286	TN 135, Burgess Falls Rd, S Willow Ave, Cookeville
Gas	N: BP, Exxon, RaceWay◊, Shell◊ S: BP◊, Citgo
Food	N: Applebee's, Hardee's, Waffle House S: Rest/Star Motor Inn
Lodg	N: Key West Inn S: Star Motor Inn♥
Med	N: + Hospital
Other	N: Auto Dealer, Grocery, Middle TN RV Center S: Auto Repairs, American Car & RV Wash, Burgess Falls State Park
287	TN 136, Cookeville, Sparta
FStop	S: Minit Mart #2293/Marathon
TStop	S: Pilot Travel Center #265 (Scales)
Gas	N: BP, Chevron◊, Exxon, Citgo, Shell◊
Food	N: Applebee's, Arby's, Burger King, Captain D's, ChickFilA, Chili's,

EXIT	TENNESSEE
Food	N: Cracker Barrel, DQ, Golden Corral, IHOP, Jack In the Box, Long John Silver's, Logan's Roadhouse, McDonald's, Pizza Hut, Ponderosa, Outback Steakhouse, Red Lobster, Ruby Tuesday, Ryan's Grill, Shoney's, Steak 'n Shake, Starbucks, Subway, Waffle House, Wendy's S: FastFood/MinitMart, Blimpie/Pilot TC, Gondola Pizza, KFC
Lodg	N: Best Value Inn, Best Western♥, Clarion Comfort Inn, Days Inn, Garden Hotel, Hampton Inn, Ramada, Super 8 S: Baymont Inn, Comfort Inn, Country Hearth, Country Inn, Econo Lodge
TServ	N: Walker Diesel Service S: Cumberland Tire & Truck
Other	N: TN Hwy Patrol Post, CVS, Firestone, Auto Services, Harley Davidson, Kroger, Kmart, Lowe's, Sam's Club, Tires, Wal-Mart, Mall S: WiFi/Pilot TC, Carmike 10 Cinema
288	TN 111, Livingston, Sparta
TStop	S: Middle TN Auto/Truck Plaza/66 (Scales)
Gas	S: Citgo
Food	S: Subway/Mid TN ATP, Huddle House,
Lodg	S: Knights Inn
Tires	S: I-40 Truck Tire & Repair
TWash	S: Middle TN ATP
TServ	S: Middle TN ATP/Tires, Don's Truck Service, King's Truck Repair
Other	S: Laundry/RVDump/LP/Mid TN ATP
290	US 70N, Cookeville
Gas	N: BP S: Citgo
Food	S: Restaurant
Lodg	S: Alpine Lodge & Suites
Other	N: Outdoor Junction
300	US 70N, TN 84, Monterey, Livingston
FStop	N: The Convenience Mart/Citgo
Food	N: FastFood/Conv Mart, Cup N' Saucer Rest, Hardee's, Subway
Lodg	S: Garden Inn
301	US 70N, TN 84, Monterey, Jamestown
Gas	N: Phillips 66, Shell
Food	N: Burger King, Subway
Other	N: Highland Manor Winery
(307)	Parking Area (WB)
311	Plateau Rd
Gas	N: Citgo◊ S: BP◊, Exxon
Other	N: Truck Sales & Parts
317	US 127, Crossville, Jamestown
Gas	N: BP◊, Chevron, Citgo, Exxon◊, Shell◊, Horizon Travel Plaza (NO TRUCKS) S: Citgo, Phillips 66, Murphy
Food	N: Huddle House, Rest/Ramada S: Cracker Barrel, Ponderosa, Ruby Tuesday, Ryan's Grill, Shoney's, Waffle House, Wendy's
Lodg	N: Best Value Inn, Best Western, La Quinta Inn♥, Ramada S: Days Inn, Heritage Inn, Scottish Inn
Med	S: + Hospital
Other	N: Auto Services, CAT, Flea Market, Wrecker Service S: Auto Dealers, Goodyear, Lowe's, Staples, Walgreen's, Wal-Mart sc, Cumberland Mountain Retreat Campground▲,

EXIT	TENNESSEE
Other	S: to Ballyhoo Family Campground▲, Geronimo Campground▲, Lake Tansi RV Park▲, Cumberland Mountain State Park▲
320	TN 298, Genesis Rd, Crossville
TStop	N: Pilot Travel Center #114 (Scales) S: Plateau Travel Plaza/BP (Scales)
Gas	S: Shell
Food	N: Wendy's/Pilot TC S: FastFood/Plateau TP, Catfish Cove, Krystal, Wendy's
TServ	S: Universal Tire
Med	S: + Hospital
Other	N: Laundry/WiFi/Pilot TC, Stonehaus Winery S: VT Outlet Mall
322	TN 101, Peavine Rd, Crossville
Gas	N: BP, Exxon, Phillips 66 S: Texaco
Food	N: Bean Pot/BP, Hardee's, McDonald's
Lodg	N: Holiday Inn Express S: Comfort Suites, Fairfield Glade Resort, Super 8
Med	S: + Hospital
Other	N: Bean Pot Campground▲, Ballyhoo RV Resort▲, to appr 4 mi: Spring Lake RV Resort▲, Deer Run RV Resort▲ S: Crossville/I-40 KOA▲, Lake's Rocky Top Retreat▲, TN Outdoors RV Center Sales & Service, Chestnut Hill Winery
(324)	Cumberland Rest Area (EB) (RR, Phones, Picnic, Vend)
(327)	Cumberland Rest Area (WB) (RR, Phones, Picnic, Vend)
329	US 70, Crab Orchard
FStop	N: Crab Orchard/BP
Gas	N: Exxon
Other	N: to Crossville KOA▲
(336)	Parking Area (EB)
338	TN 299S, Westel Rd, Rockwood
FStop	S: Shell◊
Gas	N: BP◊
NOTE:	MM340: Eastern/Central Time Zone
340	TN 299N, Airport Rd
NOTE:	MM #341: EB: 4% Steep Grade 2mi
347	US 27, Harriman, Rockwood
Gas	N: Phillips 66♥ S: BP, Exxon, Shell◊
Food:	N: Hardee's, KFC, Long John Silver, McDonalds, Pizza Hut, Taco Bell, Wendy's, Subway/Phillips 66 S: Cracker Barrel, Shoney's, Krystal/Shell, Captain D's, Mex Rest, Subway
Lodg	N: Best Western♥ S: Holiday Inn Express, Quality Inn, Super 8♥
Med	N: + Hospital
Other	N: Budget RAC, C & D Tire, Grocery, Hensley Tire, to Frozen Head State Park S: Advance Auto, Grocery, Kroger, to Appr 5mi: Wal-Mart sc
NOTE:	MM #350: EB: 7% Steep Grade
350	US 70, TN 29, Pine Ridge Rd, Harriman, Midtown
Lodg	S: Midtown Motel S: Midtown Discount Tire, Lowe's, Kroger, to Caney Creek RV Resort & Marina▲

◊ = Regular Gas Stations with Diesel ▲ = RV Friendly Locations ♥ = Pet Friendly Locations

RED PRINT SHOWS LARGE VEHICLE PARKING/ACCESS ON SITE OR NEARBY BROWN PRINT SHOWS CAMPGROUNDS/RV PARKS

INTERSTATE 40 W/E

EXIT	TENNESSEE
352	**TN 58S, Kingston**
Gas	S: Exxon, RaceWay, Shell
Food	N: Howard Johnson
	S: DQ, Hardee's, Jed's Family Steak House, McDonald's, Subway
Lodg	N: Knights Inn
	S: Comfort Inn
Other	N: Food Lion, NAPA
	S: to Watts Bar Lake, Four Seasons Campground▲, Watts Bar Lake Campground▲
355	**Lawnville Rd, Kingston**
TStop	N: Pilot Travel Center #132
Gas	N: Shell
Food	N: FastFood/Pilot TC
Other	N: WiFi/Pilot TC
	S: Heritage Propane/LP
356B	**TN 326, Gallaher Rd, Oak Ridge (WB)**
356A	**TN 58N, Gallaher Rd, Oak Ridge**
356	**TN 58, Gallaher Rd, to Oak Ridge**
Gas	N: BP, Weigel's◊
	S: Citgo
Food	N: Huddle House, Rest/Family Inns
Lodg	N: DoubleTree Inn, Family Inn, Kings Inn
	S: Days Inn♥
Other	N: Four Seasons Campground▲
360	**Buttermilk Rd, Lenoir City**
Other	N: Southeast RV Center, Soaring Eagle Campground & RV Park▲
(363)	**Parking Area (Both dir)**
364	**US 321, TN 95, to Oak Ridge**
Gas	N: Shell
Food	N: Outback Steakhouse
Lodg	N: Staybridge Suites
Other	N: to TVA/Melton Hill Dam▲
	S: to Crosseyed Cricket Campground▲
NOTE:	I-40 & I-75 below run together for 18 mi. Exit #'s follow I-40.
(368)	**Jct I-75S, to Chattanooga**
369	**Watt Rd, W Knoxville**
TStop	N: Flying J Travel Plaza #5034/Conoco (Scales)
	S: Petro Stopping Center #12/Mobil (Scales), Travel Center of America #107/BP (Scales)
Food	N: Rest/FastFood/FJ TP
	S: IronSkillet/Petro SC, Perkins/BKing/PizzaHut/TA TC
TWash	S: Blue Beacon TW/Petro SC
	N: Fast Point Truck Wash
TServ	N: Freightliner of Knoxville, Speedco
	S: Petro SC/Tires, TA TC /Tires, Knoxville Truck Sales
Other	N: Laundry/WiFi/RVDump/LP/FJ TP, Shadrack Watersport & RV's
	S: Laundry/WiFi/RVDump/Petro SC, Laundry/CB/WiFi/TA TC
(372)	**Weigh Station (Both dir)**
373	**Campbell Station Rd, Farragut**
FStop	S: Pilot Food Mart #221
Gas	N: Amoco, Marathon, Shell
	S: BP, Conoco, Wiegel's
Food	S: Cracker Barrel, Hardee's, Wendy's
Lodg	N: Comfort Suites, Country Inn, Super 8
	S: Baymont Inn, Holiday Inn Express
Other	N: Buddy Gregg Motorhomes
	S: Gander Mountain

EXIT	TENNESSEE
374	**TN 131, Lovell Rd, Knoxville**
TStop	N: Travel Center of America #13/BP (Scales)
	S: Pilot Travel Center #270 (Scales)
Gas	N: Texaco
	S: Citgo, Pilot Food Mart, Speedway
Food	N: CountryPride/FastFood/TA TC, McDonald's, Bojangles, Taco Bell, Waffle House
	S: Wendy's/Pilot TC, Arby's, Chili's, Krystal, Olive Garden, Shoney's, Tx Roadhouse, Wasabi Japanese, Rest/Days Inn
Lodg	N: Best Western, Knights Inn, La Quinta Inn♥, Travelodge/TA TC, Vista Inn
	S: Comfort Inn, Days Inn, Homewood Suites, Motel 6♥, Red Roof Inn
TServ	N: TA TC/Tires
Other	N: Laundry/CB/BarbSh/WiFi/TA TC, Harley Davidson, Buddy Gregg MH
	S: WiFi/Pilot TC, Auto Dealers, ATMs, Banks, Best Buy, Lowes, Staples, Super Target, Wal-Mart sc
376	**TN 162S, Maryville (EB)**
376A	**TN 162N, to Oakridge (WB)**
376B	**TN 162S, Maryville (EB)**
378AB	**Cedar Bluff Rd, Knoxville (WB)**
378	**Cedar Bluff Rd, Knoxville**
Gas	N: Amoco, Pilot Travel Center, Texaco
	S: Exxon
Food	N: Arby's, Burger King, Cracker Barrel, KFC, Long John Silver, McDonald's, Pizza Hut, Waffle House, Wendy's
	S: Applebee's, Bob Evans, Carraba's, Corky's Ribs & BBQ, Denny's, Fazoli's, Famous Dave's BBQ, Hops, IHOP, Outback Steakhouse
Lodg	N: Econo Lodge, Hampton Inn, Holiday Inn, Ramada
	S: Best Western, Courtyard, Comfort Inn, Extended Stay America, Jameson Inn, La Quinta Inn♥, Red Roof Inn♥, Sleep Inn
Med	N: + Hospital
Other	N: ATMs, Banks, Food Lion, Walgreen's
	S: ATMs, Banks, Auto Services, Best Buy, Carmike Cinema, Circuit City, Celebration Station, Lowe's, Staples, Walgreen's
379A	**Walker Springs Rd, Gallaher View,**
379	**Walker Springs Rd, Gallaher View, Bridgewater Rd (EB)**
Gas	N: Exxon, Pilot Food Mart, Shell
	S: BP, Pilot, Texaco
Food	N: McDonald's
	S: Bennett's Pit BBQ, Burger King, Chuck E Cheese, Don Pablo, Logan's, Old Country Buffet, Ryan's Grill, Shoney's
Lodg	N: Red Carpet Inn
	S: Holiday Inn, Scottish Inn
Other	N: Sam's Club, Wal-Mart sc
	S: AutoZone, Auto Services, Goodyear, Pharmacy
380	**US 11, US 70, West Hills**
Gas	S: BP, Citgo, Conoco, Pilot Food Mart, Shell, Weigel's
Food	S: Arby's, Applebee's, BlackEyed Pea, Chili's, KFC, Krystal, Little Caesar's, Olive Garden, Texas Roadhouse
Lodg	S: Howard Johnson, Quality Inn, Super 8

EXIT	TENNESSEE
Other	S: West Town Mall, Food Lion, Kmart, Office Depot, U-Haul, Walgreen's, TN State Hwy Patrol Post
383	**Papermill Dr, Knoxville**
Gas	S: Amoco, BP, Citgo, Pilot Food Mart
Food	S: Bombay Bicycle Club, Burger King, Captain D's, IHOP, McDonald's, Pizza Hut, Waffle House, Western Sizzlin'
Lodg	N: Budget Inn, Holiday Inn
	S: Econo Lodge, Super 8
(385)	**Jct I-75N, Jct I-640E, to Lexington**
NOTE:	I-40 & I-75 above run together for 18 mi. Exit #'s follow I-40.
386A	**University Ave, Middlebrook Pike, Henley St, Downtown, Conv Ctr (WB Exit Part of #386B)**
386B	**US 129, Alcoa Hwy, Airport, Great Smoky Mountains, Univ of TN**
387	**TN 62, 17th St, 21st St, Western Ave**
Med	S: + Children's Hospital
(387A)	**Jct I-275N, to Lexington**
NOTE:	EB: Exits 388-389 Closed for reconstr Thru 6/30/09. Use I-640.
388	**to US 441S, James White Pkwy, Univ of TN, Downtown (EB)**
388A	**James White Pkwy**
389	**Hall of Fame Dr**
389AB	**US 441N, Broadway, 5th Ave**
Gas	N: BP, Conoco
Food	N: Burger King, KFC, Krystal
Other	N: CVS, Firestone, Kroger, Walgreen's
NOTE:	EB: Exits 388-389 Closed for reconstr Thru 6/30/09. Use I-640.
390	**Cherry St**
FStop	N: Favorite Market #409/Shell
Gas	N: Marathon, Pilot Food Mart, Weigel's
	S: Amoco, Exxon
Food	N: Hardee's, Subway/Weigel's
	S: Arby's, KFC, Krystal, Wendy's
Lodg	N: Red Carpet Inn
	S: Regency Inn
TServ	N: Pemberton Truck Service, Truck Shop
Med	S: + Baptist Health System
Other	N: Advance Auto, AutoZone, Walgreen's
392AB	**US 11, Rutledge Pike**
392	**US 11W, Rutledge Pike**
Gas	S: Shell◊, BP
Food	S: Hardee's, Shoney's
Lodg	S: Family Inns
TServ	N: Cummins, International, Kenworth of Knoxville
Other	N: U-Haul
	S: Laundromat, Food City, Kroger
(393)	**Jct I-640W, Knoxville ByPass, to I-75N, to Lexington**
394	**US 11E, US 25W, US 70, Asheville Hwy**
Gas	N: BP, Mobil◊, RaceWay
	S: Exxon, Shell◊
Food	N: Subway, Wendy's
	S: Waffle House
Lodg	N: Best Value Inn, Gateway Inn
	S: Days Inn

◊ = Regular Gas Stations with Diesel ▲ = RV Friendly Locations ♥ = Pet Friendly Locations
RED PRINT SHOWS LARGE VEHICLE PARKING/ACCESS ON SITE OR NEARBY BROWN PRINT SHOWS CAMPGROUNDS/RV PARKS

EXIT		TENNESSEE
	Other	N: Food Lion, Kmart S: CVS, Kroger, Walgreen's
398		Strawberry Plains Pike
	FStop	N: Aztex BP S: Pilot Travel Center #219 (Scales)
	TStop	N: Kwik Fuel Center/Exxon
	Gas	N: Shell S: Citgo, Weigel's
	Food	N: FastFood/Kwik FC, McDonald's, Outback Steakhouse, Ruby Tuesday, Waffle House, Wendy's S: Subway/Pilot TC, Arby's, Burger King, Cracker Barrel, Krystal, Puleo's Grill
	Lodg	N: Baymont Inn, Country Inn, Courtyard, Comfort Suites, Econo Lodge, Hampton Inn, Quality Inn, Ramada Ltd, Super 8 S: Best Western, Fairfield Inn, La Quinta Inn♥, Motel 6, Quality Inn
	Other	N: TN RV Sales & Service/Camping World S: WiFi/Pilot
402		Midway Rd
	Other	N: River Island Golf Club
407		TN 66, Kodak, to Sevierville, Pigeon Forge, Gatlinburg
	Gas	N: Citgo S: BP, Exxon, Shell
	Food	N: Cracker Barrel, Huddle House/Citgo, McDonald's, Chop House, Rest/Bass Pro Shop S: Subway/Exxon, Wendy;s
	Lodg	N: Econo Lodge, Motel 6♥ S: Best Western♥, Comfort Suites, Days Inn, Holiday Inn Express, Quality Inn, Ramada Inn
	Other	N: Bass Pro Shop, Smokie's Baseball Stadium S: Auto Dealers, Fireworks Supermarket, 407 Great Smokey Flea Market, to Sevierville/PigeonForge/Gatlinburg attractions, gas, food, lodging, camping, malls, restaurants, shopping, Great Smoky Mountains National Park▲
412		Deep Springs Rd, Douglas Dam Dandridge
	TStop	N: Love's Travel Stop #306 (Scales) S: TR Truck/Auto Plaza/Chevron (Scales)
	Food	N: Subway/Chesters/Love's TS, Apple Valley Cafe S: Rest/TR TAP
	TServ	S: TR TAP/Tires
	Other	N: WiFi/RVDump/Love's TS S: Laundry/RVDump/TR TAP

Shauan's Riverside RV Park

Located in the Foothills of the Great Smoky Mountains

Right next to the roaring Big Pigeon River, Shauan's RV Park is the ideal place to bring the family. Our campground borders the Cherokee National Forest and is located near Martha Sundquist State Park as well as the Great Smoky Mountains National Park. All of our campsites have breathtaking views of the mountains and river.

Bass and Trout fishing river
Swimming
Lots of on property hiking
Food and beverage concessions
Great Ice Cream Parlor
Porch area on river with Jukebox

We're located at exit 447, right off I-40. Location:
3605 Trail Hollow Rd
Hartford, TN 37753
Phone: (423)487-4400
shauand@bellsouth.net

EXIT		TENNESSEE
415		US 25W, US 70, to Dandridge
	FStop	S: Shell
417		TN 92, Dandridge, to Jefferson City
	TStop	N: Pilot Travel Center #226 (Scales)
	Gas	N: BP S: Shell, Wiegel's
	Food	N: Subway/Pilot TC, Captain's Galley, Hardee's, McDonald's, Perkins, Ruby Tuesday S: KFC, Shoney's, Waffle House
	Lodg	N: Econo Lodge S: Comfort Inn, Holiday Inn, Jefferson Inn♥, Super 8
	TWash	N: Pilot TC
	TServ	N: Pilot TC/Tires
	Other	N: Laundry/WiFi/Pilot TC
(420)		Jefferson Rest Area (EB) (RR, Phones, Picnic, Vend)

EXIT		TENNESSEE
(421)		Jct I-81N, to Bristol (EB, Left Exit)
424		TN 113, Dandridge, White Pine
	FStop	N: FastTrax/BP
	Food	N: Grill/BP
	Other	S: Jack Benny RV Resort & Campground▲, Lake Cove Resort▲
(426)		Jefferson Rest Area (WB) (RR, Phones, Picnic, Vend)
432A		US 411, to Sevierville
	Gas	S: BP, Shell, Texaco
	Food	S: Rest/Family Inn
	Lodg	S: Family Inn
432B		US 25W, US 70, Newport, to Cosby (EB, Left Exit)
	TStop	N: PTP/Time Out Travel Center (Scales)
	Gas	N: Exxon
	Food	N: Huddle House/TimeOut TC, Lois's Family Rest, Grill/Exxon
	Lodg	N: Relax Inn, Comfort Inn
	TServ	N: Commercial Truck Center
	Other	N: Laundry/TimeOut TC, Auto Dealers, Newport Tire, Laundromat, CarWash, Bowling, TMC Campground▲, I-40/Newport/Smoky Mountain KOA▲
435		US 321, TN 32, Cosby Hwy, Newport to Gatlinburg, Cosby
	Gas	N: Exxon, Shell S: BP, Murphy
	Food	N: Arby's, Burger King, Hardee's, KFC, La Carreta, McDonald's, Sagebrush, Shoney's, Subway, Taco Bell S: Cracker Barrel, Ruby Tuesday, Waffle House, Wendy's, Rest/Holiday Inn
	Lodg	N: Motel 6♥ S: Best Western, Family Inn, Holiday Inn
	Med	N: + Hospital
	Other	N: CVS, Cinema 4, Mustard Seed Health Store S: Dollar Tree, Grocery, Lowe's▲, Wal-Mart sc▲
440		US 321S, TN 73, Wilton Springs Rd to Gatlinburg, Cosby
	TStop	N: Mtn View Truck Stop/Sunoco
	Gas	S: BP
	Food	N: Rest/MV TS
	Lodg	N: Mountain View Motel
	TServ	N: Mountain View Truck Service
	Other	S: to Adventure Bound Camping Resort/Gatlinburg▲, Arrow Creek Campground▲, Jellystone Campground▲
443		Foothills Pkwy, Great Smoky Mtns Nat'l Park, Gatlinburg (NO COMMERCIAL VEHICLES)

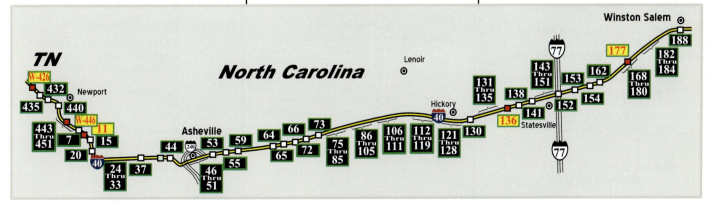

◊ = Regular Gas Stations with Diesel   ▲ = RV Friendly Locations   ♥ = Pet Friendly Locations

RED PRINT SHOWS LARGE VEHICLE PARKING/ACCESS ON SITE OR NEARBY   BROWN PRINT SHOWS CAMPGROUNDS/RV PARKS

Interstate 40 W/E

EXIT	TN / NC
(446)	**TN Welcome Center (WB)** (RR, Phones, Info) (NO Trucks)
447	Hartford Rd
Gas	N: Downtown Hartford Citgo / S: BP
Food	N: FastFood/DH Citgo, Pigeon River Smokehouse/BP, S: Shauan's Ice Cream & Coffee Shop, Beantree
Other	S: Shauan's RV Park▲ (See Ad on page 202), Whitewater Rafting Companies
451	Waterville Rd
NOTE:	MM 455: North Carolina State Line
	(EASTERN TIME ZONE)
⊙	**TENNESSEE**
⊙	**NORTH CAROLINA**
	(EASTERN TIME ZONE)
(4)	Tunnel (Both dir)
7	Harmon Den Rd
(8)	Tunnel (Both dir)
(11)	**NC Welcome Center (WB)** Rest Area (EB) (RR, Phones, Picnic, Vend)
15	Fines Creek
20	US 276, Jonathan Creek Rd, Waynesville, to Maggie Valley
Gas	S: BP◊, Citgo, Exxon◊
Food	S: J Creek Cafe
Lodg	S: Wynne's Creekside B&B
Other	S: to W Carolina Univ, Santa's Land, Great Smoky Mtn Nat'l Park, Creekwood Farm RV Park▲, Pride RV Resort▲, Winngray Family Campground▲, Stone Bridge Campground▲
24	NC 209, Crabtree Rd, Waynesville, to Lake Junaluska, Hot Springs
TStop	N: Pilot Travel Center #393 (Scales) S: Sam's Mart#45/Citgo
Gas	N: Texaco
Food	N: Subway/Pilot TC S: Rest/Sam's, Haywood Café
Lodg	N: Midway Motel
TServ	N: Pilot TC/Tires
Other	N: WiFi/Pilot TC S: Laundry/Sam's
27	to US 19, US 23, US 74W, Clyde, Waynesville, (WB: Truck US 64W)
Gas	S: Shell
Food	S: Shoney's, Subway, Taco Bell
Med	S: + Hospital
Other	S: Food Lion, Lowe's, Wal-Mart, to W NC State Univ
31	NC 215, Champion Dr, Canton
FStop	S: Sandy's Auto/Truck Plaza/BP
Gas	S: Chevron, Exxon, Shell
Food	N: Sagebrush Steakhouse S: Arby's/Shell, Burger King, McDonald's/Exxon, Subway, Taco Bell, Waffle House
Lodg	N: Econo Lodge S: Comfort Inn
TServ	S: Cummins, Western Star
Other	S: Grocery
33	Newfound Rd, to US 74
Other	N: Mt Pisgah Campgrounds▲

EXIT	NORTH CAROLINA
37	East Canton (WB), Candler (EB)
TStop	N: Travel Center of America #221/Citgo (Scales)
Gas	N: AmocoBP S: Exxon◊, Time Out
Food	N: Buckhorn/TA TC
Lodg	N: Quality Inn S: Days Inn, Owl's Nest Inn
TServ	N: TA TC/Tires S: Apollo Truck & Diesel Repair
Other	N: Laundry/WiFi/TA TC, S: Asheville West KOA▲, Laurel Bank Campground▲, Blue Ridge Motorcycle Campground▲, Riverside Campground▲, to appr 5 mi: Riverhouse Acres Campground▲
(41)	Weigh Station (Both dir)
44	US 74, W Asheville, US 19, US 23, Enka, Candler, W Asheville
FStop	N: Servco
Gas	N: BP, Chevron, Conoco, Exxon, Shell S: Shell, Hess
Food	N: Burger King, Cracker Barrel, Pizza Hut, Hardee's, Krystal, Po Folks, Chinese, Waffle House, Wendy's S: McDonald's, Shoney's, Subway
Lodg	N: Comfort Inn, Holiday Inn, Sleep Inn, Super 8 S: Ramada Inn
TServ	N: Freightliner
Med	N: + Reach Hospital
Other	N: Auto Services, CVS, Grocery, Lowe's S: Food Lion, Home Depot, Pharmacy, Biltmore Square 6 Cinemas, Mountain Retreat RV Park▲
(46A)	Jct I-26E, US 74E, Truck US 64E, Hendersonville, Spartanburg (EB) Asheville Airport (EB: Truck US 64E)
(46B)	Jct I-26W, I-240, Asheville (EB, Left Exit) (EB ex, WB entr)
47	Brevard Rd, NC 191, W Asheville Farmers Market
Gas	S: Phillips 66◊
Food	S: Moose Café, Subway
Lodg	S: Comfort Inn, Hampton Inn, Super 8
TServ	S: Carolina Engine
Other	N: Asheville Speedway, Farmers Mkt, Bear Creek RV Park▲ S: to Biltmore Square
50B	US 25N, Asheville (WB)
Other	N: Biltmore Estate, Biltmore Village
50A	US 25S (WB)
50	US 25, to NC 81, Hendersonville Rd, S Asheville (EB)
Gas	N: BP, Exxon◊, Shell◊ S: Hess, Phillips 66◊, Servco
Food	N: Arby's, Biltmore Dairy Bar & Grill, Hardee's, Long John Silver, McDonald's, Pizza Hut, Tx Roadhouse, TGI Friday S: Apollo Flame Pizza, Atlanta Bread, Huddle House, Quincy's
Lodg	N: Baymont Inn, Doubletree Suites, Holiday Inn Express, Howard Johnson, Sleep Inn S: Asheville Oaks Inn, Forest Manor Lodge, Holiday Inn Express
TServ	N: Baldwin Truck Service
Med	N: + Mission Memorial Hospital

EXIT	NORTH CAROLINA
Other	N: ATMs, Banks, Auto Services, Tires, Biltmore Estate, Biltmore Village S: Auto Services, Towing
51	US 25 Alt, Asheville
Other	N: to Biltmore Estate
53A	US 74E Alt, Blue Ridge Pkwy
Gas	S: BP, Phillips 66
(53B)	Jct I-240, US 74A, Asheville (Addt'l services 2-3 miles North)
Gas	N: BP, Exxon
Food	N: Burger King, IHOP, Little Caesar's, Olive Garden, Subway, Waffle House
Lodg	N: Comfort Inn, Days Inn, Econo Lodge
TServ	N: A Plus Truck Parts & Service
Other	N: Auto Services, Grocery
55	to US 70, E Asheville, Black Mtn, Hwy, Tunnel Rd
Gas	N: BP, Citgo, Conoco
Food	N: Arby's, Hardee's, Waffle House
Lodg	N: Best Inn, Days Inn, Econo Lodge, Holiday Inn, Motel 6♥, Travelodge
Med	N: + VA Hospital
Other	N: Mt Mitchell State Park▲, Top's RV Park▲, Grocery
59	Swannanoa, to US 70
TStop	N: Lee's Exxon
Gas	N: BP, Servco, Shell◊
Food	N: Rest/Lee's Exxon, Burger King, Firehouse Grill, Subway/BP
Med	N: + St Joseph's Urgent Care
Other	N: Laundry/Lee's Exxon, Asheville East KOA▲, Warren Wilson College, Miles RV Center & Campground▲ S: Mama Gertie's Hideaway Campground▲
64	NC 9, Black Mountain, Montreat Broadway St, Blue Ridge Rd
Gas	N: Exxon, Shell S: Phillips 66
Food	N: Pizza Hut, Subway/Shell S: Arby's, Black Mountain BBQ, Camp Fire Steak & Buffet, Denny's, Huddle House, KFC, McDonald's, Taco Bell
Lodg	N: Super 8 S: Comfort Inn
Other	N: Grocery S: Grocery, Pharmacy
65	US 70W, Black Mountain (WB ex, EB entr)
66	Ridgecrest
(67.5)	TRUCK Info Center (EB) (Trucks MUST Exit)
(70)	Truck RunAway Ramp (EB)
(70.5)	Truck RunAway Ramp (EB)
(70.8)	Truck RunAway Ramp (EB)
72	US 70E, Old Fort (EB ex, WB entr)
Other	N: to Tom Johnson Camping Center, to Mountain Stream RV Park▲, to Riverbreeze Campground▲
73	Old Fort
Gas	N: Citgo◊ S: Exxon
Food	N: Hardee's S: McDonald's
Other	N: Auto & Tire Service S: to Catawba Falls Campground▲

Page 200   ◊ = Regular Gas Stations with Diesel   ▲ = RV Friendly Locations   ♥ = Pet Friendly Locations
RED PRINT SHOWS LARGE VEHICLE PARKING/ACCESS ON SITE OR NEARBY   BROWN PRINT SHOWS CAMPGROUNDS/RV PARKS

W 40 E — NORTH CAROLINA

EXIT		NORTH CAROLINA
75		Parker Padgett Rd, Old Fort
	FStop	S: Stuckey's/Citgo
	Food	S: DQ/Stuckey's/Citgo
81		Sugar Hill Rd (WB), to Marion (EB)
	TStop	S: Marion Travel Plaza/Exxon (Scales)
	Gas	N: AmocoBP◆, Chevron, Citgo◆
	Food	N: Sugar Hill Rest, Burger King, McDonald's
		S: Rest/Marion TP
	Med	N: + McDowell Hospital
	Other	S: Laundry/Marion TP
(82)		Rest Area (Both dir) (RR, Phones, Picnic, Vend)
83		Ashworth Rd
85		US 221, Marion, Rutherfordton
	FStop	S: Dollar Mart #10/Shell
	Gas	S: BP
	Food	S: Sagebrush
	Lodg	S: Days Inn, Hampton Inn, Super 8
	Other	N: to Mountain Stream RV Park▲
86		NC 226, Marion, Shelby
	TStop	S: Love's Travel Stop #308 (Scales)
	Gas	N: Exxon
	Food	N: Hardee's, KFC
		S: Chesters/Subway/Love's TC
	Lodg	N: Carolina Motel
	Other	N: to Bear Den Campground▲, Jellystone Campground▲
		S: WiFi/Love's TS, NC Hwy Patrol Post
90		Nebo, Lake James
	FStop	S: Travel Store/AmocoBP
	TStop	N: Nebo Truck Stop/Exxon
	Food	N: Rest/Nebo TS
	Other	N: to Lake James State Park
		S: Springs Creek RV Center
94		Dysartsville Rd, Lake James
96		Kathy Rd
98		Causby Rd, Glen Alpine
100		Jamestown Rd, Glen Alpine
	Gas	N: BP
	Food	N: KFC/TacoBell/WaffleShop
	Lodg	N: Eagle Motel
	Other	N: Auto Services, Auto Dealer
103		US 64, Morganton, Rutherfordton
	Gas	N: Exxon◆, Shell
		S: Citgo, RaceWay
	Food	N: Mexican Rset
		S: Butch's BBQ, Denny's, Hardee's, KFC, Subway, Taco Bell
	Lodg	N: Super 8
		S: Comfort Suites
	TServ	S: Dale's Truck Repair
	Other	N: Auto Services, Food Lion, Tires
		S: Grocery, Goodyear, Lowe's, Wal-Mart
104		Enola Rd, Morganton
	Gas	S: Citgo
	Other	S: NC State Hwy Patrol Post
105		NC 18, Morganton, Shelby
	Gas	N: BP, Chevron
		S: Shell
	Food	N: Arby's, McDonald's, Harbor Inn Seafood, Peking Express, Pizza Inn, Shoney's, Wendy's, Western Sizzlin'
		S: El Paso Mexican, Sagebrush, Rest/Holiday Inn
	Lodg	N: Hampton Inn, Red Carpet Inn
		S: Days Inn, Holiday Inn, Sleep Inn
	Med	N: + Broughton Hospital

EXIT		NORTH CAROLINA
106		Bethel Rd, Morganton
	FStop	S: Exxon
	Lodg	S: Economy Inn
107		NC 114, Drexel Rd, Valdese
111		Valdese, Millstone Ave, Abees Grove Church Rd
	Food	N: McDonald's
112		Mineral Springs Mtn Rd, Valdese
113		Rutherford College, Connelly Springs
	FStop	N: Southern Convenience/66
	Gas	N: Citgo
	Med	N: + Hospital
	Other	N: CVS
116		Rhodhiss, Icard
	FStop	S: Jack B Quik #7/66
	Food	N: Frosty's Drive-in
		S: Burger King, Rest/Icard Inn
	Lodg	S: Icard Inn
118		Old NC 10
	Gas	N: Shell◆
119A		Henry River (EB)
119B		Hildebran, Longview (EB)
119		Hildebran, Henry River (WB)
	Gas	N: Shell◆
	Food	N: Hardee's, KFC, Subway/Shell
	Other	N: ATMs, Banks
121		Long View
123A		Gastonia
123B		Boone, Hickory Reg'l Airport

EXIT		NORTH CAROLINA
123		US 321, to US 70, to NC 127, Hickory, Lenoir, Lincolnton
	Other	N: to Hickory Reg'l Airport ✈
125		NC 127, Hickory (WB), Lenoir-Rhyne College (EB)
	Gas	N: Exxon, RaceTrac
		S: Hess, Servco◆, Shell◆
	Food	N: Bojangles, Golden Corral, Peddler, Rock-Ola Café, Western Steer
		S: Burger King, CiCi's, Cracker Barrel, El Sombrero, Fuddrucker's, Hardee's, Hooters, J&S Cafeteria, Kobe, Longhorn, Outback Steakhouse, Red Lobster, Ruby Tuesday, Sagebrush, Steak & Ale, Waffle House, Wendy's, Zaxby's
	Lodg	N: Red Roof Inn ♥
		S: Comfort Suites, Fairfield Inn, Hampton Inn, Holiday Inn, Jameson Inn, Sleep Inn
	Med	N: + Hospital
	Other	N: Auto Dealers
		S: Conv Center, Food Lion, Home Depot, Lowe's, Valley Hills Mall, Blue Ridge Harley Davidson, Hickory Furniture Mart, Lenoir Rhyne College
126		to US 70, Hickory, Newton
	FStop	S: The Pantry #170
	Gas	S: Citgo, Phillips 66, Shell
	Food	S: Applebee's, Bob Evans, IHOP, Libby Hill Seafood, McDonald's, O'Charley's
	Lodg	S: Holiday Inn Express
	Other	S: Kmart, Lowe's, Office Depot, Sam's Club, Wal-Mart sc, to Hickory Furniture Outlets
128		Fairgrove Church Rd, CR 1476
	FStop	N: Speedy Mart/Citgo
		S: Citgo Gas Center
	Gas	N: Shell
		S: Phillips 66
	Food	N: McDonald's, Waffle House
		S: Arby's, Bennett's Pit BBQ, Burger King, Harbor Inn Seafood, Mr Omelet, Shoney's, Wendy's, Rest/Days Inn
	Lodg	S: Best Western, Days Inn, Ramada Inn
	TServ	S: Carolina Engine, WhiteGMC Trucks, Newton Truck Service
	Med	N: + Hospital
	Other	S: NC Hwy Patrol Post, Catawba Valley College
130		Old US 70
	Gas	S: Citgo, Phillips 66
	Food	N: Domino's, Jack in the Box, Subway
	Other	N: Grocery, Kmart, NAPA
131		NC 16, Conover, Taylorsville (EB)
	Gas	N: BP◆, Shell
	Lodg	N: Holiday Inn Express
132		Mt Hope Church Rd, to NC 16, Conover, Taylorsville
	TStop	N: WilcoHess Travel Plaza #308
	Food	N: Wendy's/Wilco TP
		S: Subway, Pizza
	Lodg	N: Hampton Inn
133		US 70, to US 321, Rock Barn Rd
	TStop	S: WilcoHess Travel Plaza #351 (Scales)
	Gas	N: Exxon
	Food	S: Subway/TacoBell/WilcoHess TP
	Other	S: Laundry/WilcoHess TP, Big Tire Service
135		Claremont
	Gas	S: Shell
	Food	S: Burger King, Hardee's
	Lodg	S: Super 8

◆ = Regular Gas Stations with Diesel   ▲ = RV Friendly Locations   ♥ = Pet Friendly Locations
RED PRINT SHOWS LARGE VEHICLE PARKING/ACCESS ON SITE OR NEARBY   BROWN PRINT SHOWS CAMPGROUNDS/RV PARKS

EXIT	NORTH CAROLINA
Other	S: Carolina Coach & Camper
(136)	Rest Area (Both dir) (RR, Phones, Picnic, Vend)
138	NC 10, Oxford School Rd, to Catawba
FStop	N: Bunker Hill Exxon
141	Sharon School Rd
Gas	N: Citgo
(143)	Weigh Station (Both dir)
144	Old Mountain Rd
FStop	N: Chevron
Gas	S: BP◊, Shell◊
Food	N: Roger's BBQ
146	Stamey Farm Rd, Statesville
TStop	S: Homer's Truck Stop/Citgo (Scales)
Food	S: Rest/Homers TS
TServ	S: Homers TS/Tires, Pro Tow Truck & Repair
Other	S: Laundry/Homers TS
148	US 64, NC 90, W Statesville, Taylorsville
Gas	N: Citgo◊, Exxon, Quality Plus
Food	N: Arby's, Burger King, KFC, Prime Steakhouse, McDonald's, Subway
Lodg	N: Economy Inn
Other	N: CVS, Grocery S: Auto Services, Towing
150	NC 115, Statesville, N Wilkesboro
Gas	N: BP◊, Citgo, Shell
Food	N: Little Caesar's Pizza
Other	N: CVS, Food Lion, Family RV Center
151	US 21, Sullivan Rd, E Statesville, Harmony
Gas	N: Petro Express, Wilco Hess◊ S: Exxon
Food	N: JerseyMikesSubs/Petro Express, Applebee's, Bojangles, Burger King, Cracker Barrel, Golden Corral, K&W, KFC, Long John Silver, McDonald's, Red Lobster, Sagebrush Steakhouse, Sokora Japanese, Shoney's, Taco Bell, Wendy's, S: Hardee's, Huddle House, Lotus Pier, Waffle House, Rest/Hol Inn
Lodg	N: Days Inn, Sleep Inn S: Hampton, Holiday Inn, Super 8
Med	S: + Iredell Memorial Hospital
Other	N: Grocery, CVS, Home Depot, Lowe's, Tires, Wal-Mart sc, Cinema S: NC State Hwy Patrol Post
(152A)	Jct I-77S, to Charlotte
(152B)	Jct I-77N, to Elkin
153	US 64, Mocksville Hwy (EB ex, WB ent)
Gas	S: Citgo◊
Lodg	S: Hallmark Inn
154	to US 64 (WB), Old Mocksville Rd (EB)
Med	S: + Davis Community Hospital
162	US 64, to Cool Springs
Gas	S: Shell
Other	N: Lake Myers RV & Camp Resort▲ S: Midway Campground Resort▲
168	US 64, to Mocksville
Gas	N: Exxon◊ S: BP
Other	N: Lake Myers RV & Camp Resort▲
170	US 601, Mocksville, Yadkinville
FStop	S: BP
TStop	N: AmBest/Horn's Auto Truck Plaza/Pure (Scales)

EXIT	NORTH CAROLINA
Gas	N: Citgo S: BP◊, Exxon, Shell◊
Food	N: Country Kitchen/Horn's ATP, Prime Sirloin S: Arby's, Burger King, Pizza Hut, Pier 601 Seafood, Taco Bell/Shell, Wendy's, Western Steer
Lodg	S: Comfort Inn, Days Inn, Quality Inn
AServ	N: Horn's Garage, TLC Auto Svc.
TWash	N: Horn's ATP
TServ	N: Horn's ATP/Tires
Med	S: + Davie Co Hospital
Other	N: RV Superstore of Mocksville S: Advance Auto, CVS, Food Lion, Goodyear, Lowe's, Wal-Mart sc
174	Farmington Rd
FStop	N: Exxon
(177)	Rest Area (Both dir) (RR, Phones, Picnic, Vend)
180	NC 801 (WB), Tanglewood, Bermuda (EB)
Gas	S: Citgo◊, Exxon, Shell
Food	N: Captain's Galley S: McDonald's, Wendy's, Subway
Other	N: Grocery, Pharmacy S: CVS, Food Lion
182	Harper Rd, Tanglewood, Bermuda (WB ex, EB entr)
184	CR 113, Clemmons Rd, Lewisville
Gas	N: Shell, Texaco S: BP◊, Citgo, Exxon◊
Food	N: KFC, Quincy's Steakhouse S: Arby's, Burger King, Cracker Barrel, Dockside Seafood, Little Caesar's, Mandarin Chinese, McDonald's, Mi Pueblo Mexican Rest, Pizza Hut, Sagebrush Steakhouse, Taco Bell, Waffle House
Lodg	N: Holiday Inn S: Ramada Inn, Super 8
Other	S: CVS, Food Lion, Kmart, Staples, Walgreen's, US Post Office
188	Jct I-40E Bus, US 421, Winston-Salem (EB), Yadkinville (WB)
189	US 158, Stratford Rd
Gas	N: BP, Exxon S: BP, Shell, Costco
Food	N: Bojangles, Chili's, McDonald's, Olive Garden, Red Lobster, Sagebrush S: Applebee's, Corky's BBQ, Hooters, Longhorn Steakhouse, Romano's Macaroni Grill, Subway
Lodg	N: Best Western, Courtyard, Fairfield S: Hampton Inn, Sleep Inn
Med	S: + Forsyth Memorial Hospital
Other	N: Mall, Carmike 12 S: Best Buy, Costco, CVS, Food Lion, Home Depot, Lowe's, Sam's Club, Target
190	Hanes Mall Blvd, Silas Creek Pkwy (WB ex, EB entr)
Food	N: McDonald's, O'Charley's, Olive Garden, TGI Friday's S: Burger King, Little Caesar's, Lone Star Steakhouse, Outback Steakhouse, Oyster Bay Seafood, Souper Salad
Lodg	S: Comfort Inn, Microtel
Med	N: + Forsyth Memorial Hospital
Other	N: Mall, Shopping, AutoZone, Kroger, Office Depot S: CVS, Food Lion, Goodyear, Kmart

EXIT	NORTH CAROLINA
192	NC 150, Peters Creek Pkwy, Downtown Winston Salem
FStop	N: WilcoHess #102
Gas	N: Shell S: BP
Food	N: Arby's, Bojangles, Burger King, Checkers, IHOP, Little Caesar's, Monterey Mex, Old Country Buffet, Perkins, Pizza Hut, Quincy's, Red Lobster, Shoney's, Taco Bell S: McDonald's, Libby Hill Seafood
Lodg	N: Innkeeper, Knights Inn S: Holiday Inn Express
Med	N: + Crown Care Medical Center
Other	N: AutoZone, Kroger, NAPA S: CVS, Food Lion, Kmart
193C	Silas Creek Pkwy, S Main St (WB)
193A	US 52S, NC 8S, Lexington
193B	US 52N, US 311N, NC 8N, Mt Airy
FStop	S: Wilco Hess
Other	N: to Smith Reynolds Airport✈
193	US 52, NC 8, US 311N, Lexington, Mount Airy
195	NC 109, Clemmonsville Rd, Thomasville
FStop	S: WilcoHess #108
196	US 311S, High Point
201	Union Cross Rd
Gas	N: Exxon, Quality Plus
Food	N: Burger King
Other	N: Food Lion, CVS
203	NC 66, Kernersville, High Point
Gas	N: BP, Citgo, Exxon S: Shell
Food	N: Clark's BBQ, Suzie's Diner, Waffle House, Subway/Shell
Lodg	N: Quality Inn S: Holiday Inn Express
TServ	N: Bales & Truitt Truck Service
Other	S: Colfax RV Outlet
206	I-40 Bus N, US 421N, Kernersville, Downtown Winston-Salem (WB)
208	Sandy Ridge Rd, Colfax
FStop	N: WilcoHess #295 S: Neighbor's Fuel Center #9/Citgo
Other	N: Holiday Kamper, Colfax RV Outlet/RVDump S: Farmers Market
210	NC 68, High Point, PTI Airport
Gas	N: Phillips 66 S: Citgo, Exxon
Food	N: Arby's, Hardee's, Wendy's S: McDonald's/Citgo, Shoney's, Subway
Lodg	N: Days Inn, Holiday Inn S: Best Western, Hampton Inn, Motel 6♥, Ramada Inn, Red Roof Inn♥
TServ	N: Whites' International, Volvo, Cummins, CAT, Carolina Kenworth, Freightliner, Piedmont Ford, Piedmont Truck Tires
Other	N: Piedmont Triad Int'l Airport✈
211	Gallimore Dairy Rd, NC 1556
212	I-40E Bus, US 421S, to Bryan Blvd, Greensboro, PTI Airport
212A	Bryan Blvd (WB)
212B	I-40 Bus, US 421 (WB)

◊ = Regular Gas Stations with Diesel   ▲ = RV Friendly Locations   ♥ = Pet Friendly Locations
RED PRINT SHOWS LARGE VEHICLE PARKING/ACCESS ON SITE OR NEARBY   BROWN PRINT SHOWS CAMPGROUNDS/RV PARKS

EXIT	NORTH CAROLINA
212	Chimney Rock Rd
TServ	S: Carolina Engine, Carolina Diesel
213	Guilford College Rd, Jamestown
Gas	N: BP
	S: Exxon
Food	N: Damon's Ribs
Lodg	N: Clarion, Radisson
214A	Wendover Ave West (EB)
214B	Wendover Ave East (EB)
214	Wendover Ave, Greensboro (WB)
Gas	N: Citgo◆, Exxon◆, Shell◆
Food	N: Burger King, K&W Cafeteria, Ruby Tuesday, Waffle House
	S: Applebee's, Cracker Barrel, Golden Corral, IHOP, Logan's, McDonald's, Red Lobster, Shoney's, Subway
Lodg	N: Innkeeper, Holiday Inn Express, Microtel
	S: AmeriSuites, Courtyard, Shoney's Inn
Other	N: Auto Dealers, Goodyear
	S: Best Buy, Grocery, Home Depot, Kmart, Lowe's, Sam's Club, Target, Wal-Mart sc
216	NC 6W, Greensboro, Coliseum Area (fr EB, Left exit)
217	US 70A, US 29A, High Point Rd, Coliseum Area (EB) Koury Blvd (WB)
Gas	N: Exxon◆, Shell◆
	S: Crown, Exxon, Shell
Food	N: Arby's, Burger King, Chili's, Dunkin Donuts, Hooter's, Lone Star Steakhouse, McDonald's, Olive Garden, Osaka, Perkins, Po Folks, Subway
Food	S: Bojangles, Carraba's, Hardee's, Krispy Kreme, Kyoto, Nascar Café, Shoney's, Waffle House, Wendy's
Lodg	N: Howard Johnson, Red Roof Inn♥, Super 8, Travelodge
	S: Comfort Inn, Days Inn, Fairfield Inn, Hampton Inn, Residence Inn
Med	S: + Prime Care Medical Center
Other	S: AutoZone, Discount Tire, NAPA, Grocery, Office Depot, Mall
(218)	Jct I-85S, US 29, US 70W, High Point, Charlotte
218A	US 220S, to I-85S Bus, Asheboro (EB)
218B	Freeman Mill Rd (EB)
219	I-85S Bus, US 29S, US 70W, to US 220N, Greensboro (EB), to Charlotte (WB)

EXIT	NORTH CAROLINA
220	US 220S, Asheboro
NOTE:	I-40 below runs with I-85 Bus, Exit #'s 36-43. Exit numbers follow I-85 Bus.
(219)	Jct I-85S, to Charlotte, US 29S, US 70W, US 220 (WB)
(36A)	Jct I-85S, to Charlotte, US 29S, US 70W, US 220
36B	Randleman Rd
Gas	E: Exxon, Shell
	W: AmocoBP, Citgo, Crown, Shell
Food	E: Mayflower Seafood, Waffle House, Wendy's
	W: Arby's, Burger King, Captain D's, DQ, Hardee's, KFC, McDonald's, Pizza Hut, Shoney's, Taco Bell
Lodg	E: Cavalier Inn
	S: South Gate Motel
TServ	E: Cummins Diesel
Med	S: + Piedmont Carolina Medical Clinic
Other	N: Auto Services, Family Dollar, Food Lion, Harley Davidson
	S: Kmart
37	S Elm St, Eugene St
Gas	E: AmocoBP, Dairy Mart, Shell◆
	W: Chevron, Citgo◆
Food	W: Bojangles, Sonic
Lodg	E: Quality Inn, Super 8
	W: Homestead Lodge, Ramada
Other	E: Home Depot
	W: AutoZone, Food Lion
38	US 421S, to Sanford
Gas	E: Exxon
Food	E: Burger King, McDonald's, Old Hickory BBQ, Subway
Med	W: + Hospital
Other	E: CVS, Food Lion, Goodyear
39	US 29N, US 70, US 220, US 421, Reidsville, Danville (NB, No reaccess)
Other	N: KOA▲
41	NC 6, E Lee St
Gas	S: BP◆, Phillips 66
Food	N: FastFood/BP
Lodg	W: Holiday Inn Express
Other	W: to Coliseum, KOA▲
43	McConnell Rd
Gas	S: Shell
44	to I-85S, US 70
NOTE:	I-40 above runs with I-85 Bus, Exit #'s 36-43. Exit #'s follow I-85 Bus.

EXIT	NORTH CAROLINA
NOTE:	I-40 runs below with I-85N. Exit #'s follows I-85.
132	Mt Hope Church Rd, McLeansville
TStop	W: WilcoHess Travel Plaza
Gas	E: Citgo
Food	W: Wendy's/WilcoHess TP, Café America
Lodg	W: Hampton Inn
135	Rock Creek Dairy Rd
Gas	W: Citgo, Exxon
Food	W: Bojangles, Jersey Mike's, McDonald's
TServ	W: Battleground Tire & Wrecker
Other	W: CVS, Food Lion
138	NC 61, to Gibsonville, Greensboro
TStop	W: Travel Center of America #2/BP (Scales)
Gas	W: Shell◆
Food	W: CountryPride/BKing/Popeye's/TA TC
Lodg	W: Days Inn/TA TC
TWash	W: TA TC
TServ	W: TA TC/Tires
Other	W: Laundry/WiFi/TA TC, Hawley's Camping Center
(139)	Rest Area (Both dir) (RR, Phones, Picnic, Vend)
140	University Dr, Elon University
Other	W: Best Buy, Target
141	Huffman Mill Rd, to Burlington
Gas	E: BP, Shell, Kangaroo
	W: Phillips 66◆, Shell
Food	E: IHOP
	W: Applebee's, Arby's, Bojangles, Burger King, Cracker Barrel, Golden Corral, Hooters, KFC, McDonald's, Starbucks, Steak n Shake, Subway, Taco Bell
Lodg	E: Hampton Inn Comfort Inn
	W: Best Western, Country Suites, Courtyard, Super 8
Med	W: + Hospital
Other	W: Auto Dealers, Food Lion, Wal-Mart sc, Mall
143	NC 62, Burlington
Gas	E: Citgo
	W: 76, Exxon
Food	E: Wendy's/Citgo, Bob Evans, Hardee's Waffle House
	W: K&W, Libby Hill Seafood
Lodg	W: Ramada Inn
Other	W: Food Lion, Home Depot
145	NC 49, Burlington, Liberty
FStop	E: Interstate Shell
Gas	E: BP◆
	W: BP, Hess
Food	E: FastFood/Interstate Sh, Captain D's, Shoney's

◆ = Regular Gas Stations with Diesel ▲ = RV Friendly Locations ♥ = Pet Friendly Locations

RED PRINT SHOWS LARGE VEHICLE PARKING/ACCESS ON SITE OR NEARBY BROWN PRINT SHOWS CAMPGROUNDS/RV PARKS

Page 203

EXIT	NORTH CAROLINA
	W: Bojangles, Burger King, Hardee's, KFC, Subway, Waffle House
Lodg	E: Microtel, Red Roof Inn ♥
	W: Econo Lodge, Holiday Inn, La Quinta Inn ♥, Motel 6 ♥, Scottish Inn
Other	E: Davis Harley Davidson, NC State Hwy Patrol Post
	W: Dollar General, Food Lion
147	**NC 87, to Pittsboro, Graham**
Gas	E: BP, Servco
	W: Citgo, Exxon◊, Shell◊
Food	E: Arby's, Bojangles, Burger King, Great Wall, Harbor House Seafood, Sagebrush, Subway, Wendy's
	W: Biscuitville, Hardee's, McDonald's, Taco Bell
Med	W: + Hospital
Other	E: Food Lion, Winn Dixie, Laundromat, Goodyear, NC State Hwy Patrol Post
	W: CVS, Grocery, Walgreen's
148	**NC 54, Chapel Hill**
FStop	S: On the Run #70/Exxon
Gas	S: BP◊
Food	S: Waffle House
Lodg	S: Comfort Suites
	N: Travel Inn
150	**Haw River, to Roxboro, Graham**
TStop	N: Flying J Travel Plaza #5332/Conoco (Scales), WilcoHess Travel Plaza #165 (Scales)
Food	N: Rest/FJ TP, DQ/Wendy's/WH TP
Lodg	N: Best Western, Days Inn
TWash	N: Blue Beacon TW/FJ TP
TServ	N: Speedco
Other	N: Laundry/BarbSh/WiFi/RVDump/LP/FJ TP, Laundry/WilcoHess TP
152	**Jimmie Kerr Rd, Trollingwood Rd**
FStop	E: Pilot Travel Center #57 (Scales)
	W: Fuel City
Gas	W: AmocoBP
Food	E: McDonald's/Pilot TC
	W: Fuel City
TWash	E: Pilot TC
Other	E: Laundry/WiFi/Pilot TC
153	**NC 119, S 5th St, Mebane**
Gas	E: BP, Citgo
	W: Exxon
Food	E: Cracker Barrel, KFC, Taco Bell
	W: Burger King/Exxon, Subway
Lodg	E: Hampton Inn, Holiday Inn Express
Med	W: + Hospital
Other	E: Lowe's, Golf Course
	W: CVS, Food Lion
154	**Oaks Rd, Mebane**
FStop	W: Arrowhead Shell
Gas	E: Sheetz
	W: BP, Citgo, Exxon◊, Shelll
Food	E: Blimpie/Shell
	W: Biscuitville, Bojangles, McDonald's, Waffle House, Rest/Budget Inn
Lodg	W: Budget Inn
Med	W: + Mebane Clinic
Other	E: Wal-Mart sc
	W: Winn Dixie
157	**Buckhorn Rd, Mebane**
TStop	E: Petro Stopping Center #29/Mobil (Scales)
Gas	E: BP
	W: Citgo
Food	E: IronSkillet/FastFood/Petro SC
TServ	E: Petro SC/Tires
	W: Diesel Service

EXIT	NORTH CAROLINA
Other	E: Laundry/BarbSh/CB/WiFi/Petro SC
(158)	**Weigh Station (Both dir)**
160	**Efland**
Gas	W: BP◊, Exxon◊
161	**to US 70E, NC 86N**
(163/259)	**Jct I-40E, to Raleigh**
	Jct I-85N, to Durham (WB)
NOTE:	I-40 above runs with I-85. Exit #'s follow I-85.
261	**Hillsborough**
Gas	N: BP, Citgo, Shell
Food	N: Hardee's, McDonald's, Pizza Hut, Subway, Waffle House
Lodg	N: Holiday Inn, Microtel
Other	N: Visitor Info Center
263	**New Hope Church Rd**
266	**NC 86, to Chapel Hill**
Gas	S: BP, Citgo, Exxon, Hess
Food	S: Quiznos, Subway
Other	N: Birchwood RV Park▲
	S: ATMs, Cinema, Food Lion
270	**US 15, US 501, Chapel Hill, Durham**
Gas	S: BP, Exxon
Food	N: Bob Evans, Outback Steakhouse, Hardee's, Wendy's
Lodg	N: Comfort Inn
	S: Days Inn, Hampton Inn, Holiday Inn, Red Roof Inn ♥, Sheraton
Med	N: + Hospital
Other	N: Best Buy, Home Depot, Wal-Mart, to Duke Univ
	S: CVS, Lo
273B	**NC 54E, to Durham (WB)**
Other	S: Univ of NC-Chapel Hill
273A	**NC 54W, to Chapel Hill (WB)**
273	**NC 54, Chapel Hill, Durham (EB)**
Gas	N: Citgo, Shell◊
	S: BP◊
Food	S: Hardee's
Lodg	S: Hampton Inn, Holiday Inn Express
274	**NC 751, Hope Valley Rd, Durham, to Jordan Lake**
Gas	S: BP, Kangaroo
Food	N: Burger King, Waffle House
276	**Fayetteville Rd, Southpoint (End Motorist Assistance)**
Gas	N: Exxon◊, Phillips 66◊
Food	N: McDonald's, Ruby Tuesday, Souper Salad, Waffle House, Wendy's
Other	N: ATMs, Banks, Grocery, Mall, to NC Central Univ
278	**NC 55, to NC 54, Apex**
Gas	N: Citgo
	S: Exxon◊, Mobil◊, Phillips 66
Food	N: China One, Waffle House
	S: Arby's, Bojangles, Burger King, Golden Corral, KFC, McDonald's, Pizza Hut, Subway, Taco Bell, Wendy's
Lodg	N: Fairfield Inn, Innkeeper, La Quinta Inn ♥
	S: Candlewood Suites, Courtyard, Residence Inn
Other	N: ATMs, Banks
	S: ATMs, Auto Services, Food Lion, Pharmacy
279A	**NC 147S, Durham Freeway, to Alexander Dr**

EXIT	NORTH CAROLINA
279B	**NC 147N, Durham Frwy (EB), Downtown Durham (WB)**
280	**Davis Dr, Durham**
Lodg	S: Radisson
281	**Miami Blvd, Durham**
Gas	N: BP, Shell
Food	N: Wendy's
	S: Wok & Grille
Lodg	N: Best Western, Marriott, Studio Plus
	S: Clarion, Homewood Suites, Wellesley Inn
Med	N: + Park Medical Center
282	**Page Rd, Durham**
Food	S: McDonald's, Rest/Hilton, Rest/Sheraton
Lodg	N: Holiday Inn
	S: Comfort Inn, Hilton, Sheraton, Wingate
(283)	**Jct I-540N, to US 70, Apex (EB)**
(283B)	**Jct I-540N, to US 70 (WB)**
(283A)	**Jct I-540W, to US 70 (WB)**
284A	**Airport Blvd W, RDU Airport (EB)**
284B	**Airport Blvd E, Int'l Airport (EB)**
284	**Airport Blvd, RDU Int'l Airport (WB)**
Gas	S: BP◊, Citgo◊, Exxon◊, Shell◊
Food	S: Cracker Barrel, Quiznos, Waffle House, Wendy's
Lodg	S: Baymont Inn, Courtyard, Days Inn, Extended Stay America, Fairfield Inn, Hampton Inn, La Quinta Inn ♥, Residence Inn
Other	N: Auto Rentals
	S: Triangle Factory Shops
285	**Aviation Pkwy, Int'l Airport, Morrisville**
Lodg	N: Hilton Garden Inn
Other	S: Lake Crabtree Co Park
287	**Harrison Ave, Cary**
Gas	S: BP, Shell
Food	S: Arby's, McDonald's, Subway, Wendy's
Lodg	S: Embassy Suites, Studio Plus
Other	N: Wm B Umstead State Park▲
	S: Auto Services, Enterprise, Goodyear
289	**to I-440, US 1N, Wade Ave (WB) (diff reaccess)**
	to 440, to US 1N, Wade Ave (EB)
Med	N: + Hospital
Other	N: RBC Center, Carter Finley Stadium, Motorist Assistance Patrol
	S: Fairgrounds
290	**NC 54, Cary**
Gas	N: Shell
	S: Citgo
Food	N: Ole Time BBQ
	S: Carolina Chicken
Lodg	N: Comfort Suites
	N: Hampton Inn
Other	N: Amtrak
	S: State Fairgrounds
291	**Cary Towne Blvd, Cary**
Food	S: Burger King, McDonald's, Taco Bell
Other	S: Cary Town Center Shopping
(293)	**Jct I-440E, US 1, US 64W, Sanford, Asheboro, Wake Forest, Raleigh**
293	**US 1, US 64W, Sanford, Asheboro**
293A	**US 1S, US 64W, Sanford, Asheboro**
Gas	S: Citgo, Exxon, Shell

◊ = Regular Gas Stations with Diesel ▲ = RV Friendly Locations ♥ = Pet Friendly Locations
RED PRINT SHOWS LARGE VEHICLE PARKING/ACCESS ON SITE OR NEARBY BROWN PRINT SHOWS CAMPGROUNDS/RV PARKS

W 40

EXIT	NORTH CAROLINA
Food	S: Hardee's, Ruth's Chris Steakhouse, Kabuki Japanese, Shoney's, Waffle House
Lodg	S: Best Western, Fairfield Inn, Motel 6 ♥
Other	S: ATMs, Auto Services, Grocery
293B	Inner 440 Lp, US 1N, Raleigh, Wake Forest
295	Gorman St, Raleigh
Gas	N: Exxon, Kangaroo
Food	N: Hardee's, McDonald's
Other	N: NC State Univ, Coliseum
	S: Auto Services
297	Lake Wheeler Rd
Gas	N: Exxon
	S: Citgo
Food	N: Burger King
Med	N: + Hospital
Other	N: Farmers Market
298A	US 70E, US 401S, NC 50S, Fayetteville, Garner, S Sanders St S
Gas	S: BP, Hess, RaceWay, Servco
Food	S: Domino's, KFC, Shoney's
Lodg	S: Claremont Inn, Days Inn, Innkeeper
Other	S: Auto Services, Grocery, Sam's Club
298B	US 401N, US 70W, NC 50N, Raleigh, S Sanders St North
Gas	N: Exxon, Shell
Lodg	N: Red Roof Inn ♥
Other	N: Auto Services, Greyhound, Tires, Towing, Train Station
299	Person St, Hammond Rd (EB diff reaccess)
300	Rock Quarry Rd (EB)
300A	Rock Quarry Rd South (WB)
Gas	S: BP, Exxon
Food	S: Hardee's, Subway
Other	N: Kroger
	S: Food Lion, Laundromat, Winn Dixie
300B	Rock Quarry Rd North (WB)
(301)	Jct I-440W, US 64E, Rocky Mount (EB, Left Exit) (Exit Only)
303	Jones Sausage Rd
FStop	S: Country Cupboard #3/Shell
Gas	N: BP◊, Shell◊
Food	N: Burger King, Bojangles
	S: Smithfield BBQ
306	US 70, Smithfield, Garner, Clayton, Goldsboro (EB)
Other	S: Hawley's Camping Center/RVDump
306A	US 70W, Garner (WB)
Food	W: Chili's, McDonald's, Wendy's
Other	W: BJ's, Best Buy, Target
306B	US 70E, Smithfield, Clayton (WB)
Lodg	E: Suburban Lodge
Other	E: Auto & Tire Service, 70 East Mobile Acres Park▲, Hawley's Camping Center/RVDump
312	NC 42, Clayton, Fuquay-Varina, Garner
FStop	W: WilcoHess Travel Plaza #213
Gas	W: BP◊, Citgo◊, Shell◊
Food	E: DQ, Domino's, Huddle House, Ruby Tuesday, Waffle House
	W: Andy's, Burger King, Cracker Barrel, China King, Golden Corral, Smithfield Chicken & BBQ, McDonald's, Wendy's
Lodg	E: Best Western, Holiday Inn, Quality Inn, Super 8
	W: Hampton Inn, Sleep Inn

Personal Notes

EXIT	NORTH CAROLINA
Other	W: Auto Repairs, Carquest, Lowe's
	E: CVS, Food Lion
319	NC 210, Benson, Smithfield, Angier
Gas	E: Citgo, Shell
	W: Mobil
Food	E: FastFood/Citgo, McDonald's
	W: Café/Mobil, Subway, Waffle House, Wendy's
Other	W: Food Lion
(324)	Rest Area (Both dir) (RR, Phones, Picnic, Vend)
325	NC 242, to US 301, Benson
Gas	S: Citgo
(328A)	Jct I-95S, Benson, Fayetteville
(328B)	Jct I-95N, Smithfield, Rocky Mount
Other	N: to Smithfield KOA▲
334	NC 96, Benson, Meadow
341	NC 50, NC 55 (WB), to US 13 (EB), Newton Grove
Gas	N: Exxon◊
	S: BP, Shell
Food	N: Hardee's
	S: McDonald's/BP, Subway
343	US 701, Clinton (EB), to US 13, Newton Grove (WB)
Gas	N: Exxon
348	Suttontown Rd, Clinton
355	NC 403, to Faison, to US 117, to Goldsboro

EXIT	NORTH CAROLINA
364	NC 24W, Bus 24, to NC 50, Warsaw (EB), Clinton (WB)
	Rest Area (Both dir) (RR, Phones, Picnic, Vend)
FStop	S: BP, The Pantry #3130/Texaco Shell
TStop	N: WilcoHess Travel Plaza #225
Gas	S: Crown◊, Phillips 66◊
Food	N: Arby's/WilcoHess TP
	S: KFC, McDonald's, Smithfield's Chicken & BBQ, Subway, Waffle House, Wendy's, Bojangles/BP
Lodg	S: Days Inn, Holiday Inn Express
TServ	N: Joe's Truck Repair
Other	N: Auto Services
	S: Auto Services
369	US 117, Warsaw, Magnolia
373	NC 24E, NC 903, Magnolia, Kenansville
Gas	N: BP
Med	N: + Hospital
380	Brices Store Rd, Rose Hill (EB), to Greenevers (WB)
Gas	S: BP
384	NC 11, Teachey, Wallace
385	NC 41, Wallace, Chinquapin
Gas	N: Exxon
Lodg	N: Holiday Inn Express
Other	N: Hanchey's Auto & Truck Service
390	US 117, Wallace
398	NC 53, Burgaw, Jacksonville (All Serv Avail 3-4mi S in Burgaw)
Med	S: + Hospital
408	NC 210, Hampstead, Rocky Point, Moores Creek Nat'l Battlefield, Topsail Island
Gas	S: Exxon
Food	S: Café
TServ	S: Reeves Truck Repair
414	Castle Hayne, Hampstead, Brunswick Co Beaches
Gas	S: BP
Food	S: Hardee's
(416)	Jct I-140W, US 17, to Shallotte, Myrtle Beach, Topsail Island (EB)
(416A)	Jct I-140W, US 17S, to Shallotte, Myrtle Beach (WB)
Other	S: to USS NC Battleship Memorial
416B	US 17N, to Topsail Island, Jacksonville (WB)
420	US 117N, NC 132N, Gordon Rd (EB) (Addtl Serv Avail S on US 17)
Gas	N: Citgo◊
	S: BP◊
Food	N: McDonald's, Perkins
	S: Subway
Other	S: WAL★MARTsc, Howard RV Center, New Hanover Int'l Airport✈
420B	US 117, NC 132N (WB)
420A	Gordon Rd (WB)

(EASTERN TIME ZONE)

🎧 NORTH CAROLINA

Begin Eastbound I-40 from Wilmington, NC to I-5 in California.

◊ = Regular Gas Stations with Diesel ▲ = RV Friendly Locations ♥ = Pet Friendly Locations
RED PRINT SHOWS LARGE VEHICLE PARKING/ACCESS ON SITE OR NEARBY BROWN PRINT SHOWS CAMPGROUNDS/RV PARKS

Page 205

INTERSTATE 43 S

EXIT	WISCONSIN
	Begin Southbound I-43 from Green Bay, WI to Beloit, WI.

⊙ WISCONSIN
(CENTRAL TIME ZONE)
(I-43 begins/ends at Green Bay on US 41)

192B		US 41S, US 141S, Deerfield Ave, Velp Ave, Appleton, Green Bay (Serv South to Velp Ave)
	Gas	W: BP◇, KwikTrip, Mobil
	Food	W: Arby's, Burger King, McDonald's, Taco Bell
	Lodg	W: AmericInn
	Other	W: Auto Services, Towing, RV Dealers, to Austin Straubel Int'l Airport✈
192A		US 41N, US 141N, Appleton, Marinette, Iron Mountain
	TStop	E: 2mi N Lineville Travel Mart/Mobil
	Food	E: FastFood/Lineville TM, Barley's Deerfield Diner
	Other	E: Laundry/Lineville TM
		W: Auto & Truck Services & Repairs
189		Atkinson Dr, Velp Ave (SB) Port of Green Bay, Hurlbut St (NB)
187		Webster Ave, East Shore Dr
	Gas	W: Shell◇
	Food	W: McDonald's, Wendy's
	Lodg	W: Days Inn, Holiday Inn
	Med	W: + Hospital
	Other	E: RVDump/Bay Beach City Park
		W: Eagle Auto Repair
185		WI 54, WI 57, University Ave, to Algoma, Sturgeon Bay
	Gas	W: Citgo, Mobil, Shell
	Food	W: Cousin's Subs, Green Bay Pizza, Ponderosa, Subway, Taco Bell
	Lodg	W: Tower Motel
	Other	E: Univ of WI/GB
		W: Grocery, Walgreen's
183		CTH V, Mason St
	Gas	E: Shell◇
		W: BP, Citgo, Mobil◇
	Food	W: Applebee's, Burger King, Country Kitchen, Fazoli's, McDonald's, Perkins, Quiznos, Starbucks, Taco Bell
	Lodg	E: Amerihost Inn, Country Inn
		W: Candlewood Suites
	Med	E: + Aurora Baycare Medical Center
	Other	W: ATMs, Banks, Auto Services, Grocery, Goodyear, Dollar Tree, Kmart, Osco, Office Max, PetCo♥, ShopKO, Tires Plus, Wal-Mart, Walgreen's, East Town Mall
181		CTH JJ, Eaton Rd, Manitowoc Rd
	Gas	E: Citgo◇
		W: Express◇
	Food	E: Blimpie/Citgo, Hardee's, McDonald's
		W: Subway/Express
	Other	E: Home Depot, McCoy's Harley Davidson
		W: Grocery
180		WI 172, to US 41, Straubel Airport
	TStop	W: Country Express AutoTruck Stop/ Citgo (Scales) (W to WI 172 & GV)
	Gas	W: BP
	Food	W: Rest/Country Express ATS, Burger King, McDonald's
	Lodg	W: Best Western, Hampton Inn, Radisson
	TWash	W: Country Express A/S
	Med	W: + Hospital
	Other	W: Laundry/WiFi/Country Express ATS

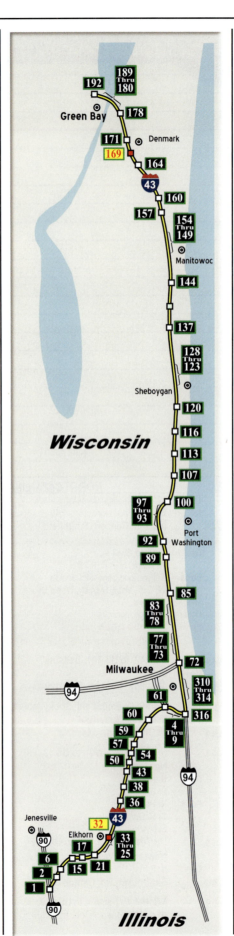

EXIT	WISCONSIN
178	US 141, to WI 29, CTH MM, Bellevue, Kewaunee
TStop	E: I-43 Shell
	W: Circle T Truck Stop (Scales)
Food	E: FastFood/Shell, Rest/Redwood Inn
Lodg	E: Redwood Inn
TServ	E: Glenn's 24Hr Towing
	W: Circle T TS/Tires
Other	W: Laundry/Circle T TS
171	WI 96, CTH KB, Greenleaf, Denmark
FStop	E: Village Mart/Citgo
Food	E: FastFood/Village Mart, Lorrie's Café, McDonald's, Subway
Other	E: LP/Village Mart, Towing, Auto Service
	W: Shady Acres Campground▲
(169)	Maribel Rest Area (Both dir) (RR, Phone, Vend, Picnic)
164	WI 147, CTH Z, Maribel, Mishicot WI 147, CTH Z, Maribel, Two Rivers
FStop	W: Maribel Express/Citgo
TStop	W: Fun n Fast Travel Center/Citgo, OCS Hotstop Travel Plaza/Marathon (Scales)
Food	W: FastFood/OCS TP, Cedar Ridge
TServ	W: Citgo
Other	E: Maribel Caves State Park
	W: Laundry/RVDump/FunNFast TC, Laundry/ OCS TP, Devils River Campground▲
160	CTH K, Kellnersville
157	CTH V, Hillcrest Rd, Manitowoc, to Mishicot, Francis Creek
FStop	E: Citgo
Food	E: Diner/Citgo
154	US 10W, WI 310, to Two Rivers, Appleton
Gas	E: Mobil
	W: Cenex
Med	E: + Holy Family Memorial Med Center
Other	E: Manitowoc Co Airport✈
	W: to Rainbows End Campground▲
152	US 10E, WI 42N, CTH JJ, Manitowoc
Med	E: + Holy Family Memorial Med Center
149	US 151, WI 42S, Manitowoc, Chilton
TStop	E: Manitowoc Shell
Gas	E: Mobil◇, Shell◇
	W: BP
Food	E: FastFood/Shell, Applebee's, Burger King, Country Kitchen, Culver's, Fazoli's, Perkins, Ponderosa
	W: McDonald's, Subway
Lodg	E: Birch Creek Inn, Comfort Inn, Holiday Inn, Super 8
	W: AmericInn
Med	E: + Holy Family Memorial
Other	E: LP/Shell, Auto Dealers, Lowe's, Tires, Wal-Mart sc
144	CTH C, St. Nazianz, Newton
Gas	E: Mobil◇
Other	E: Auto Repair
(142)	Weigh Station (SB)
137	CTH XX, North Ave, Cleveland, Kiel
FStop	E: Bonde's Quik Mart/Citgo
Food	E: FastFood/Bonde's QM, Cleveland Family Rest
Other	E: Wagner's RV Center
128	WI 42, Sheboygan, Howards Grove
FStop	E: Interstate Plaza/BP (Scales)
TStop	W: Citgo Oasis
Gas	E: Mobil

Page 206 ◇= Regular Gas Stations with Diesel ▲ = RV Friendly Locations ♥ = Pet Friendly Locations
RED PRINT SHOWS LARGE VEHICLE PARKING/ACCESS ON SITE OR NEARBY BROWN PRINT SHOWS CAMPGROUNDS/RV PARKS

EXIT		WISCONSIN
	Food	E: Hardee's
		W: Cousins Subs/Citgo
	Lodg	E: Comfort Inn
	Other	E: Laundry/Citgo, Gander Mountain
126		WI 32, Sheboygan, Kohler, Fond du Lac, Plymouth
	Gas	E: BP
	Food	E: Applebee's, Culver's, Hardee's, IHOP, McDonald's, Pizza Hut/Taco Bell
	Lodg	E: Baymont Inn, Ramada Inn, Super 8
	Med	E: + Hospital
	Other	E: Auto Dealers, Grocery, Firestone, ShopKO, Walgreen's, Wal-Mart, Mall
123		WI 28, Sheboygan, Sheboygan Falls
	FStop	E: Quality Q Mart/Citgo
	Gas	E: Mobil◊
	Food	E: McDonald's/Mobil, Perkins, Taco Bell, Wendy's
		W: Arby's, Chili's
	Lodg	E: AmericInn, Holiday Inn Express
	Other	E: Auto Centers, Thunder Truck & Auto Repair
		W: Home Depot, Radio Shack, Target
120		CTH V, CTH OK, Waldo, Sheboygan
	FStop	E: Western Shores/66
	Food	E: Judie's
	Lodg	E: Sleep Inn
	Other	E: Kohler Andrae State Park▲
		W: RV Center
116		CTH AA, Foster Rd, Oostburg
113		WI 32N, CR H, LL, Cedar Grove
	TStop	W: Hy-Way Service Center/Citgo
	Food	W: Country Grove Rest
	Other	W: Auto Repairs
107		CTH D, Belgium, Lake Church
	TStop	W: How-Dea Service Center/BP
	Gas	W: Mobil◊
	Food	W: Rest/FastFood/How-Dea SC, Hobos Korner Kitchen
	Lodg	W: AmericInn
	TWash	W: How-Dea SC
	TServ	W: How-Dea SC/Tires
	Other	W: Laundry/How-Dea SC Harrington Beach State Park
100		WI 32S, WI 84, CTH H, Fredonia, Port Washington
	Gas	E: Citgo◊
	Food	E: Arby's, Burger King, McDonald's
	Lodg	E: Best Western
97		WI 57N, Plymouth (NB ex, SB entr)
96		WI 33, Greeen Bay Dr, Saukville, Port Washington
	Gas	E: Mobil◊
		W: BP
	Food	E: Culver's Rest, Long John Silver/KFC
		W: Subway
	Lodg	W: Super 8
	Other	E: Auto Dealers, Grocery, Wal-Mart, Walgreen's
93		WI 32N, WI 57, CTH V, Grafton, Port Washington
	Food	E: Pied Piper Rest, Smith Bros Fish
	Lodg	E: Best Western

EXIT		WISCONSIN
92		WI 60, CTH Q, Grafton, Cedarburg
	Gas	W: Citgo◊
	Food	E: Ghost Town Rest, Quiznos, Starbucks, Subway
	Lodg	W: Baymont Inn
	Other	W: Home Depot, Target
89		CTH C, Cedarburg
	Gas	W: Mobil◊
	Lodg	W: Stage Coach Inn
	Med	W: + St Mary Hospital
85		WI 57S, WI 167, Mequon Rd, Thiensville
	Gas	W: Citgo◊, Mobil
	Food	W: Café 1505, Cousins Subs, Damon's Ribs, McDonald's, Subway, Wendy's
	Lodg	W: Best Western
	Other	W: ATMs, Banks, Cinema, Office Depot, Walgreen's
83		CTH W, Port Washington Rd (NB ex, SB entr at County Line Rd)
82BA		WI 32S, WI 100, Brown Deer Rd
	Gas	E: BP
	Food	E: Cousins Subs, McDonald's, Pizza Hut, Outback Steakhouse, Qdoba Mex Rest
	Lodg	E: Courtyard
		W: Sheraton
	Other	E: Best Buy, Cinema, Grocery, Walgreen's
82B		WI 100W, Brown Deer Rd

EXIT		WISCONSIN
82A		Brown Deer Rd E (NB) WI 32 S, Brown Deer Rd (SB)
80		Good Hope Rd
	Gas	E: BP, Mobil
	Lodg	E: Residence Inn
	Other	E: Grocery, Cardinal Stritch Univ
78		Silver Spring Dr, Milwaukee
	Gas	E: BP, Mobil
	Food	E: Applebee's, Burger King, Denny's, Little Caesars, Ground Round, Boston Market, Chinese, McDonald's, Perkins, Tumbleweed Grill, Wendy's, Taco Bell
	Lodg	E: Baymont Inn, Exel Inn, Woodfield Suites
	Med	W: + St Michael Hospital
	Other	E: ATMs, Banks, Firestone, Goodyear, Walgreen's, Bayshore Mall, B&N
77B		Hampton Ave W, Glendale (NB ex, SB entr)
77A		Hampton Ave E, Glendale (NB)
	Lodg	E: Hilton
76B		WI 57, WI 190W, Green Bay Ave, Capitol Dr (NB)
76A		WI 190E, Capitol Dr (NB)
76AB		WI 190, to WI 57, Green Bay Ave, Capitol Dr (SB)
	Gas	W: Citgo
	Food	W: Burger King
	Other	E: Home Depot
75		Atkinson Ave, Keefe Ave
	Gas	E: Mobil
		W: BP, Citgo◊
74		Locust St
	Other	E: Police Dept
73C		North Ave
73B		WI 145, Fond du Lac Ave
73A		4th St, Broadway
72C		Kilbourn Ave, Civic Ctr (NB) Highland Ave, Civic Ctr (SB)
	Med	E: + St Mary's Hospital
	Other	E: Civic Center, Bradley Center Arena
NOTE:		I-43 below runs with I-94 thru Milwaukee, WI. Exit #'s follow I-94.
(72B)		Jct I-94W, US 41N, to Madison
(72A)		Jct I-794, Lakefront, Port of Milw
310CAB		Downtown Milwaukee (fr SB, L exit)
311		WI 59, National Ave, 6th St
312AB		Becher St, Mitchell St, Lapham Blvd, Greenfield Ave (WB)
312B		Becher St, Lincoln Ave
312A		Lapham Blvd, Mitchell St

◊ = Regular Gas Stations with Diesel   ▲ = RV Friendly Locations   ♥ = Pet Friendly Locations

RED PRINT SHOWS LARGE VEHICLE PARKING/ACCESS ON SITE OR NEARBY   BROWN PRINT SHOWS CAMPGROUNDS/RV PARKS

Page 207

EXIT		WISCONSIN
314A		**Holt Ave**
	Gas	E: Citgo
	Med	W: + Hospital
314B		**Howard Ave**
	NOTE:	I-43 above runs with I-94 thru Milwaukee. Exit #'s follow I-94.
	NOTE:	Below exits run with I-894 around Milwaukee, Exit #'s follow I-894.
(316/10B)		**Jct I-43S, I-894W, to Beloit**
		Jct I-94E, US 41S, to Chicago
9AB		**WI 241, 27th St**
	Gas	E: BP, Citgo, Mobil
	Food	E: Arby's, Burger King, Cousins Subs, Dunkin Donuts, Pizza Hut, Rusty Skillet Rest
		W: Denny's, McDonald's, Taco Bell
	Lodg	E: Suburban Motel
	Med	W: + Hospital
	Other	E: AutoZone, Kmart, Target, Walgreen's
		W: Auto Dealers, Auto Services
8AB		**WI 36, Loomis Rd**
	Gas	E: BP
		W: Citgo
	Other	E: Walgreen's
7		**60th St**
	Gas	E: Speedway◇
		W: Speedway
	Other	W: Harley Davidson
5AB		**S 76th St, S 84th St (NB)**
5B		**76th St, 84th St (SB, diff reaccess)**
	Food	E: Applebee's, Burger King, Ground Round, Hooters, KFC, McDonald's, Olive Garden, Outback Steakhouse, Pizza Hut, Red Lobster, Wendy's
	Other	E: B&N, Best Buy, Borders, Circuit City, Firestone, Goodyear, Office Depot, Grocery, Southridge Mall
5A		**WI 24, Forest Home Ave (SB)**
	Gas	E: Citgo
(4/61)		**Jct I-43S, US 45S, to Beloit**
		Jct I-894W, US 45N, to Fond du Lac
	NOTE:	I-43 runs above with I-894 around Milwaukee. Exit #'s follow I-894.
60		**US 45S, WI 100, 108th St (fr SB, L ex)**
	Gas	E: BP, Citgo, Phillips 66
		W: Phillips 66
	Food	E: Amore Italian Rest, Charcoal Grill
		W: McDonald's
	Other	W: Grocery, Goodyear Tires, Walgreen's, Wal-Mart
59		**Layton Ave, Hales Corners (NB, Left Exit)**
57		**Moorland Rd, Muskego, Berlin**
	Gas	W: Mobil, Speedway◇
	Food	W: Applebee's, Atlanta Bread Co, McDonald's, Taco Bell, Tumbleweed, Texas Roadhouse
	Lodg	W: Baymont Inn, Best Western, Embassy Suites, Holiday Inn Express
	Other	W: Target
54		**CTH Y, Racine Ave, New Berlin**
	Gas	E: Citgo◇, KwikTrip
	Food	E: Cousins Subs, McDonald's
	Other	E: Kastle Kampground▲
50		**WI 164, Big Bend, Waukesha**
	Gas	W: Citgo
	Food	W: McDonald's

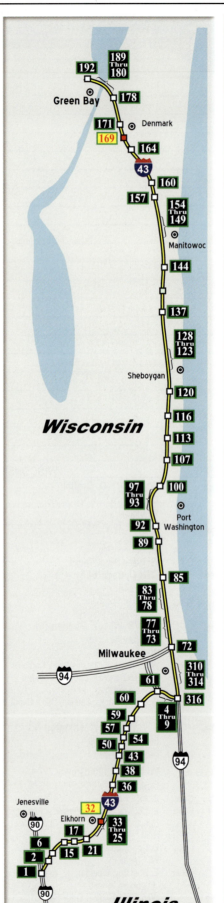

EXIT		WISCONSIN
43		**WI 83, Mukwonago, Waterford**
	FStop	E: BJ's BP
	Gas	W: Citgo, Shell
	Food	W: Burger King, Cousins Subs, Culver's, McDonald's, Subway, Taco Bell
	Lodg	W: Sleep Inn
	Other	E: to Country View Campground▲
		W: Cinema, Home Depot, Wal-Mart sc, Tire & Auto Services
38		**WI 20, East Troy, Waterford**
	TStop	W: Road Ranger #236
	Gas	W: BP, Clark, Shell
	Food	W: Subway/Road Ranger, Burger King
	Other	W: CarQuest, Auto Services, Towing
36		**WI 120, East Troy, Lake Geneva**
	TStop	W: Side View Travel Center/Citgo
	Lodg	E: Country Inn
33		**Bowers Rd, Elkhorn**
	Other	E: Apple Valley Resort & Golf Club
(32)		**Rest Area (Both dir)**
		(RR, Phones, Picnic, Vend)
29		**WI 11, Elkhorn, Burlington**
	Other	W: Fairgrounds
27AB		**US 12, Lake Geneva, Madison**
	Med	E: + Aurora Lakeland Medical Center
25		**WI 67, Elkhorn, Williams Bay**
	Gas	E: BP◇, Mobil
		W: Speedway◇
	Food	W: Burger King
	Lodg	E: AmericInn
		W: Lakeland Motel
	Other	E: Auto Dealers
		W: DeHaan Auto & RV Center
21		**WI 50, E Geneva St, Delavan, to Lake Geneva**
	Gas	E: Shell◇
		W: Mobil◇, Speedway◇
	Food	E: Chili's, Culver's, Quiznos
		W: Burger King, Hardee's, KFC, McDonald's, Subway, Taco Bell
	Lodg	W: Super 8
	Other	E: Grocery, Radio Shack, Wal-Mart sc, Greyhound Dog Track, Lake Lawn Resort
		W: ATMs, Auto Dealers, Auto Repairs, Kmart, Grocery, Shopko, Walgreen's
17		**CTH X, Delevan, Darien**
	Gas	W: BP
15		**US 14, CR C, Darien, to Janesville, Whitewater**
	Gas	E: Citgo◇
	Food	E: West Wind Diner
	Other	E: Auto Service, Tire Service, ATMs
6		**WI 140, Clinton, to Avalon**
	Gas	E: BP, Citgo
	Food	E: Subway
2		**CTH X, Hart Rd**
(1B)		**Jct I-90W, I-39N, to Madison**
(1A)		**Jct I-90E, I-39S, to Chicago**
		(Travel Ctrs & All Serv I-90, Ex #185A)
(0)		**WI 81, Beloit**

(I-43 begins/ends I-90, Exit #183)
(CENTRAL TIME ZONE)

⊙ WISCONSIN

Begin Northbound I-43 at Jct I-90 from Beloit to Green Bay.

◇ = Regular Gas Stations with Diesel   ▲ = RV Friendly Locations   ♥ = Pet Friendly Locations
RED PRINT SHOWS LARGE VEHICLE PARKING/ACCESS ON SITE OR NEARBY   BROWN PRINT SHOWS CAMPGROUNDS/RV PARKS

EXIT	TEXAS	EXIT	TX / OK	EXIT	OKLAHOMA
	Begin Eastbound I-44 from Wichita Falls, TX to near I-55 in St. Louis, MO.	6	Bacon Switch Rd, Wichita Falls	37	Gore Blvd, Lawton
	⛽ **TEXAS** (CENTRAL TIME ZONE)	7	East Rd	Gas	E: Phillips 66
	(I-44 begins/ends in Wichita Falls)	(9)	Picnic Area (Both dir)	Food	E: Sonic, Taco Mayo
1A	US 277S, 5th St, Central Freeway, Wichita Falls, to Abilene (SB)	11	FM 3429, Cropper Rd, Daniels Rd		W: Barry's Chicken Ranch, Cracker Barrel, Mike's Grill
FStop	E: Love's Travel Stop #269 (Scales) (on 287E)	12	TX 240, Sheppard Rd, Burkburnett	Lodg	E: Best Western
Gas	W: Conoco, Phillips 66	Gas	E: Chevron, Phillips 66		W: Fairfield Inn, Holiday Inn Express, Springhill Suites
Food	E: Subway/Love's TS		W: 7-11, Fina, Shamrock	Med	E: + Kiowa Indian Hospital
	W: Arby's, Burger King, IHOP, Papa John's, Popeye's, Subway, Whataburger	Food	W: Braum's, Hardee's, KFC, McDonald's		W: + Comanche Co Memorial Hospital
Lodg	E: Holiday Inn	Lodg	W: Ranchouse Motel	Other	W: ATMs, Banks, Central Mall, SavALot, Sheridan Mall, Cameron Univ, Office Depot, Harley Davidson
	W: Econo Lodge	Other	W: Auto Services, Auto Dealer		
Med	W: + Wichita Falls Gen'l Hospital	13	Glendale St, Burkburnett	39A	US 62, Cache Rd (NB, Left exit)
Other	W: Wichita Falls RV Park▲	Other	W: Family Dollar, SavALot, Wal-Mart	Gas	W: Phillips 66, Total◆
1B	N 3rd St, Scotland Park (NB)	14	TX 240, Lp 267, 3rd St	Food	W: Applebee's, Chili's, ChickFilA, Golden Corral, KFC, Ryan's Grill, Subway, Wendy's
Food	E: Johnnie's Chicken	Food	W: Circle H BBQ		
Lodg	E: Scotland Park Motel	Other	W: Burkburnett RV Park▲	Lodg	W: Baymont Inn, Days Inn, Economy Inn, Holiday Inn, Red Lion Hotel, Super 9
	W: Radisson	NOTE:	MM 15: Oklahoma State Line		
1C	Vermont St, Tx Travel Info Center		(CENTRAL TIME ZONE)	Other	W: U-Haul
Gas	E: Citgo		⛽ **TEXAS**	39B	US 281 Bus, NW 2nd St, Lawton (SB)
1D	US 287 Bus, Iowa Park Rd		⛽ **OKLAHOMA**	Lodg	W: Ramada Inn
Gas	W: Conoco◆		(CENTRAL TIME ZONE)	40A	US 62, Rogers Lane, Lawton
Food	W: El Chico, China Star, Whataburger	1	OK 36, Devol, to Grandfield	Gas	E: Fina
Lodge	W: Days Inn, Eagle Inn, River Oaks Hotel, Travelers Inn	5	US 277N, US 281, Randlett (Last FREE Exit NB)	Lodg	W: Super 8
Other	W: ATMs, Grocery, Auto Services	Gas	E: Shamrock◆	Other	W: Fort Sill Military Res
2	Maurine St, Wichita Falls	(19)	Begin TOLL, HE Bailey Turnpike	40B	US 62W, to Cache, Altus (SB)
Gas	E: 7-11◆, Texaco◆	20	US 277N, US 281, OK 5, Walters	Lodg	W: Super 8
	W: 7-11	(21)	Service Plaza/OK Welcome Center	Other	W: Fort Sill, Henry Post Army Air Field
Food	W: DQ, Denny's, Long John Silver	Gas	EZ Go Foods #44/66	40C	Post Rd, Gate Two, Fort Sill
Lodg	E: Best Value Inn, Comfort Inn, Motel 6♥, Quality Inn	Food	McDonald's	41	Sheridan Rd, Fort Sill Key Gate
	W: Best Western♥, Candlewood Hotel, Hampton Inn, La Quinta Inn♥, Super 8	(30)	End TOLL	45	OK 49, Medicine Park, to Carnegie
3A	US 287, to Vernon, Amarillo	30	OK 36, Geronimo, Faxon, Frederick	Gas	W: Love's Country Store #263
Gas	W: Shell	33	US 281 Bus, 11th St, Lawton	Food	W: Subway/Love's TS, Burger King
Food	W: Carl's Jr	Other	W: Plaza RV & Trailer Park▲, Lawton Muni Airport✈, Wrecker Service	Other	W: WiFi/Love's TS
Lodg	W: Ramada Ltd			46	US 62E, US 277N, US 281, Elgin, Apache, Anadarko (Last FREE Exit NB)
3B	Spur 325, to Sheppard AFB	36B	OK 7, Lee Blvd, to Duncan (SB)		
Other	E: Sheppard AFB, Wichita Falls Muni Airport✈	36A	OK 7, Lee Blvd, Lawton	53	US 277, 8th St, OK 17, Elgin, to Lake Ellsworth, Fletcher, Sterling
3C	FM 890, Municipal Airport	FStop	W: Expressway Fina, Kids #3		
Gas	W: Shamrock, Murphy	Gas	E: Phillips 66, Stripes	Gas	E: Conoco, Shamrock
Other	E: Wichita Falls Muni Airport✈	Food	W: Big Chef Rest, KFC, Leo & Ken's, Popeye's, Salas Mexican, Sonic		W: Phillips 66
	W: Wal-Mart sc, Wichita Falls RV Center	Lodg	W: Motel 6♥	(60)	Parking Area (EB)
4	City Loop	Tires	W: Expressway Fina	62	Whitfield Rd, Fletcher, to Elgin, Sterling (NB)
5	Access Rd	Med	W: + SW Medical Center	(63)	Parking Area (WB)
5A	FM 3492, Missile Rd, Reilly Rd	Other	W: Auto Services, Animal Hospital♥, Carwash, Towing, Fairgrounds	(79)	TOLL Plaza
Gas	W: Exxon◆			80	US 81, US 277, to OK 92, Grand Ave, Chickasha, Duncan
Other	E: Sheppard AFB, Towing			Gas	E: Conoco, Phillips 66◆, Shell◆
					W: Conoco, Love's, Star Mart◆

◆= Regular Gas Stations with Diesel ▲ = RV Friendly Locations ♥ = Pet Friendly Locations
RED PRINT SHOWS LARGE VEHICLE PARKING/ACCESS ON SITE OR NEARBY BROWN PRINT SHOWS CAMPGROUNDS/RV PARKS

INTERSTATE 44 W/E

EXIT	OKLAHOMA
Food	E: Burger King, Eduardo's, Western Sizzlin W: Arby's, Denny's, El Rancho, Hardee's, KFC, Little Caesar's Pizza, Long John Silver's, McDonald's, Pizza Hut, Subway, Sonic, Taco Bell, Taco Mayo
Lodg	E: Days Inn, Deluxe Inn W: Best Western, Ranch House Motel
Other	E: Auto Dealers, Dollar Tree, **Wal-Mart** W: Western Center RV Park▲, Auto Zone, Firestone, Grocery, CVS, Staples
83	US 62, US 277, OK 9, Chickasha
FStop	W: 62 Truck Stop/Shamrock
Gas	W: Conoco◆
Food	W: Subway
Other	W: Time Out RV Park▲
(85)	Service Plaza (Both dir, Left Exit)
FStop	EZ Go Foods #43/66
Food	McDonald's
(97)	Picnic Area (WB)
(98)	TOLL Plaza
(99)	Parking Area (EB) Rest Area
107	US 62W, US 277S, Newcastle (No reacc NB, NB reacc via Serv Rd Past Ex #108)
TStop	E: Chickasaw Travel Plaza/Shamrock
Food	E: KFC/Chickasaw TP, Pit Stop Grill, Sonic, Taco Mayo
Lodg	E: Newcastle Motel
Other	E: Laundry/Chickasaw TP, Police Dept
107A	Indian Hills Rd (SB)
108	OK 37W, NW 32nd to Tuttle, Minco
Gas	W: Phillips 66, Conoco◆
Food	W: Braum's, Carl's Jr, Little Caesar's, Mazzio's Pizza, McDonald's, Ribs n More
Other	E: A-AAA Adult RV Park▲ W: Dollar General, O'Reilly Auto Parts, **Wal-Mart sc**
108A	Frontage Rd (SB)
109	SW 149th St, Okla City
TServ	W: Southwest Diesel Service
Other	W: Auto Service
110	OK 37E, SW 134th St
Gas	E: Sinclair
TServ	W: Southwest Diesel Service
111	SW 119th St, OKC
Other	E: Walker RV Center
112	SW 104th St
FStop	W: Hi-Way Grill & Service Station/Shell
Gas	E: Shamrock
Food	W: Grill/Shell
113	SW 89th St, OKC
FStop	E: Love's Travel Stop #245
Gas	E: Valero◆
Food	E: Subway/Love's TS, McDonald's, Sonic, Taco Mayo
Other	E: WiFi/Love's TS W: Will Rogers World Airport✈
114	SW 74th St, OKC
Gas	E: Phillips 66, Sinclair
Food	E: Braum's, Burger King, Taco Bell
Lodg	E: Cambridge Inn W: Four Points Hotel
Other	E: Dollar General, RV & Truck Wash W: Will Rogers World Airport✈, Rental Cars, Women Pilots Museum
(115)	Jct I-240E, US 62E, OK 3E, Ft Smith

EXIT	OKLAHOMA
116A	SW 59th St
Gas	S: Conoco, Shell
Other	N: Will Rogers World Airport✈
116B	Airport Rd (fr NB, Left Exit)
Other	N: Will Rogers World Airport✈
117AB	SW 44th St
Gas	E: Shell
118	OK 152W, SW 29th St
Gas	S: 7-11, Conoco N: Phillips 66, Shell
Food	S: Burger King, Captain D's, KFC, Taco Bell, McDonald's, Taco Bueno
Lodg	N: Budget Inn, Bel-Aire Motel
Other	S: AutoZone, Walgreen's, Grocery, to Downtown Airpark✈
119	SW 15th St
(120A)	Jct I-40W, to Amarillo (NB, Left exit)
(120B)	Jct I-40E, to Ft Smith (SB, Left exit)
121 B	NW 10th St W, Fair Park
Gas	N: Shell
Other	N: Auto Services, Towing, McClain's RV Superstore/
121A	NW 10th St E, Fair Park
Gas	S: 7-11, Shell
Other	S: All Sports Stadium, Fairgrounds, State Fair Park▲
122	NW 23rd St, OKC
Gas	S: Conoco N: 7-11, Conoco
Food	S: Arby's, Sonic N: Church's, Long John Silver, Taco Mayo
Other	N: Tires Plus S: Big O Tire, Family Dollar
123A	NW 36th St, I-44, OK 66E
123B	OK 66W, NW 39th St, to Warr Acres, Bethany, Yukon
Food	N: Burger King, Carl's Jr, Meike's Rt 66, Quiznos, Taste of China
Lodg	N: Carlyle Motel, Comfort Lodge, Hollywood Hotel, Nuhoma Motel
Med	N: + First Med Urgent Care Clinic
Other	N: to Wiley Post Airport✈
124	North May Ave
Gas	N: Shell
Food	S: Wendy's, Whataburger N: Subway/Shell, Sonic
Lodg	N: Days Inn, Ramada, Super 8
125A	Penn Ave, to NW Expy, NW 36th
Gas	S: Shell N: Conoco◆
Food	N: Burger King/Conoco
Lodg	N: Habana Inn
125B	NW Expy, Classen Blvd, OKC (fr SB, Left exit)
Gas	N: Shell
Food	S: City Bites Subs, IHOP, McDonald's N: Cajun Café, Garcia's, Olive Garden
Lodg	S: AmeriSuites, Courtyard, Hawthorne Suites
Other	N: Penn Square Mall, **Wal-Mart sc**
125C	NW Expy (SB, Left Exit)
126	Western Ave, Grand Blvd
Lodg	S: Guest House Motel
(127)	Jct I-235S, US 77, OKC, Edmond
Gas	N: Conoco, Shell
Lodg	N: Best Western, Holiday Inn

EXIT	OKLAHOMA
128A	Lincoln Blvd, State Capitol
Lodg	S: Holiday Inn, Oxford Inn, Whitten Inn♥
128B	Kelly Ave
Gas	N: Conoco, Shamrock◆
Food	N: Sonic, Subway/Shamrock
Other	N: Cowboy Hall of Fame
129	M L King Ave
Food	N: County Line BBQ S: McDonald's
Lodg	N: Ramada
Other	S: Family Dollar, Remington Park Race Track, Tinseltown 20, Twin Fountains RV Park▲
(130)	Jct I-35S, to I-40, to Dallas
NOTE:	I-44 runs below with I-35, Exit 134-137. Exit #'s follow I-35.
133	NE 63rd St (NB, Fr I-35)
134	Wilshire Blvd, NE 78th St
Lodg	W: Executive Inn
Other	W: Blue Beacon TW
135	Britton Rd, NE 93rd St
136	Hefner Rd, OKC
Gas	W: Conoco◆, Gas at the Flag
Food	W: Rest/Conoco, DQ
Other	W: Frontier City Theme Park
137	NE 122nd St, to OKC
TStop	E: Travel Stop #26/Shell W: Flying J Travel Plaza #5036/Conoco (Scales), Love's Travel Stop #205 (Scales)
Gas	E: Petro Plus 5, Shamrock◆
Food	E: FastFood/Travel Stop, Charly's Rest W: CtryMarket/FastFood/FJ TP, Subway/Love's TS, Cracker Barrel, Sonic, McDonald's, Waffle House
Lodg	E: Motel 6♥, Sleep Inn, Travelodge W: Comfort Inn, Days Inn, Economy Inn, Motel 6, Quality Inn, Red Carpet Inn, Super 8
TWash	W: American Eagle TW
Other	E: WiFi/Travel Stop W: Laundry/WiFi/RVDump/LP/FJ TP, WiFi/Love's TS, Abe's RV Park▲
(138)	Jct I-35N, to Wichita
(138A)	Jct I-44E, Turner Turnpike (NB)
(138B)	Jct Kilpatrick Turnpike (NB)
NOTE:	I-44 runs above with I-35, Ex #'s134-137. Exit #'s follow I-35.
(153)	Parking Area (Both dir)
(157)	Service Area (WB)
FStop	Phillips 66
Food	McDonald's
158	OK 66, to Bus 66, US 177, Wellston
166	OK 18, Price Ave, Chandler, to Cushing
FStop	S: EZ Go Foods #51/66
Food	S: Little Caesar's, Marsha's Rest
Lodg	S: Econo Lodge♥, Lincoln Motel
Other	S: to Oak Glenn RV & MH Park▲, Chandler Tire, Chandler Muni Airport✈
(167)	Service Plaza (EB)
FStop	Phillips 66
(171)	Parking Area (EB)
(178)	Service Plaza (Both dir, Left exit)
FStop	EZ Go Foods #53/66
Food	McDonald's

◆ = Regular Gas Stations with Diesel   ▲ = RV Friendly Locations   ♥ = Pet Friendly Locations
RED PRINT SHOWS LARGE VEHICLE PARKING/ACCESS ON SITE OR NEARBY   BROWN PRINT SHOWS CAMPGROUNDS/RV PARKS

EXIT	OKLAHOMA
179	OK 99, Stroud, to Drumright
Gas	N: Citgo
	S: Phillips 66◆
Food	N: Subway, Wendy's, Rest/BW
	S: Mazzio's Pizza, Sonic, Taco Mayo
Lodg	N: Best Western
	S: Skyliner Motel, Sooner Motel
Med	S: + Stroud Regional Medical Center
Other	N: to Stroud Muni Airport ✈
(183)	TOLL Plaza
(189)	Parking Area (EB)
(192)	Parking Area (WB)
196	OK 48, OK 66, Bristow, Lake Keystone (Gas, Food, Lodg 2mi S in Bristow)
(197)	Service Plaza (EB)
FStop	Phillips 66
Food	McDonald's
(204)	Picnic Area (EB)
(205)	Picnic Area (WB)
(207)	Service Plaza (WB)
FStop	EZ Go Foods #52/66
211	OK 33, OK 66, Kellyville, Sapulpa
FStop	S: Fastop #135/Shell
215	OK 97, 9th St, Main St, Sapulpa, to Sand Springs
Gas	S: Kum & Go, Phillips 66◆
Food	S: Arby's
Lodg	N: Super 8
Med	S: + Hospital
218	Creek Turnpike, US 75A (NB)
Other	S: Rte 66 RV Park▲, 66 MH & RV Park▲
(221)	Turner Tpk Begins WB, Ends EB
221A	57th West Ave, Tulsa
221B	OK 66, US 75A, to Creek Tpke (SB, Left exit)
Other	S: Rte 66 RV Park▲, 66 MH & RV Park▲
222A	49th West Ave, Tulsa
TStop	S: QuikTrip #102 (Scales)
Gas	S: Git 'n Go
Food	N: Carl's Jr, Monterey Tex Mex
	S: Wendy's/QT, Arby's, Carl's Jr, McDonald's, Waffle House, Village Inn
Lodg	N: Interstate Inn, Motel 6♥
	S: Super 8
TServ	N: Mack
	S: Kenworth, Tulsa Freightliner, Volvo
222B	55th Pl S, Skelly Dr (NB)
Lodg	S: Days Inn, Economy Inn

EXIT	OKLAHOMA
222C	56th St, Skelly Dr (SB)
Lodg	N: Gateway Motor Inn, Interstate Inn, Super 9
(223A)	Jct I-244E, MLK Expwy, Downtown Tulsa (SB)
223B	Gilcrease Expwy, 51st St (SB)
223C	33rd West Ave, Tulsa
Gas	S: Phillips 66
Food	N: Braum's, Pizza
224	US 75, Elmblood Ave, Union Ave, to Okmulgee, Bartlesville
Gas	N: Citgo, QT◆
Food	N: KFC, Mazzio's Pizza, Subway
Lodg	S: Budget Inn, Royal Inn
TServ	S: FWF Truck Sales
Other	S: Dollar General, Laundromat
225	51st St, Elwood Ave (SB)
226A	Riverside Dr
Food	S: Village Inn
Lodg	N: Stratford House Inn
226B	Peoria Ave, Tulsa
Gas	N: Citgo, Conoco, Total
	S: QT, Shell
Food	N: China Wok, CiCi's Pizza, Egg Roll Express, Little Caesar's Pizza, Taco Bell, Pizza Hut, McDonald's, Waffle House
	S: Braum's, Burger King, Po Folks
Lodg	N: Super 8
Other	S: AutoZone, Grocery, Walgreen's
227	Lewis Ave, Oral Roberts University
Gas	S: Shell, Sinclair
Food	S: El Chico, Steak Stuffers, Wendy's
Other	S: Tires Plus, Walgreen's
228	Harvard Ave, Tulsa
Gas	N: Shell◆
	S: Citgo, Phillips 66
Food	N: Shoney's, Subway
	S: Blimpie's, Bodean Seafood Rest, Chili's, Lone Star Steakhouse, Long John Silver, McDonald's, Osaka, Piccadilly's
Lodg	N: Tradewinds East Inn, Towers Hotel, Trade Winds Central Inn
	S: Holiday Inn Express, Howard Johnson, Ramada Inn♥
Other	S: Albertson's, Dollar Tree, Kelly Tire
229	Yale Ave, St Francis Hospital
Gas	N: Shell
	S: Phillips 66◆, QuikTrip
Food	N: McDonald's
	S: Applebee's, Arby's, Braum's, Burger King, Carrabba's, Denny's, Don Pablo's, Outback Steakhouse, Red Lobster, Steak & Ale, Taco Bell, Village Inn

EXIT	OKLAHOMA
Lodg	S: Baymont Inn♥, Comfort Inn, Days Inn, Holiday Inn Select, Red Roof Inn♥, Travelodge
Med	S: + St. Francis Hospital, + Children's Medical Center
Other	N: Tulsa Promenade Mall, Firestone, PetCo♥
	S: Celebration Station
230	41st St, Sheridan Rd
Gas	N: Shell
Food	N: Carl's Jr, On the Border, Subway, TGI Friday, Whataburger
	S: Ramsey's Steakhouse
Lodg	N: La Quinta Inn♥
	S: Quality House
Other	N: Circuit City, B&N, Goodyear
	S: Best Buy, Home Depot, to Sam's Club
231	US 64, OK 51, Muskogee, E 31st St, Memorial Dr, Broken Arrow
Gas	N: Phillips 66
	S: Shell
Food	N: Whataburger
	S: Cracker Barrel, Cattleman's Steak House, IHOP, McDonald's, Village Inn
Lodg	N: Best Value Inn, Days Inn, Ramada Inn, Travelodge
	S: Best Western, Comfort Inn, Courtyard, Econo Lodge, Extended Stay America, Fairfield Inn, Hampton Inn, Holiday Inn Express, Quality Inn, Sleep Inn, Studio Plus, Super 8
Other	N: Police Dept
	S: Office Depot
232	Memorial Dr, 31st St (SB) (Access #231 Services)
233B	East 21st St (SB)
Gas	S: Citgo
Food	S: El Chico
Lodg	S: Comfort Suites
Other	S: Dean's RV Superstore
234A	US 169, Mingo Valley Expy, S to Broken Arrow, N to Owasso
234B	Garnett Rd (NB)
Gas	S: QT◆
Food	N: Denny's, Mazzio's Pizza, Sonic
	S: Braum's
Lodg	N: Econo Lodge, Motel 6♥
235	East 11th St, Garnett Rd
Gas	N: Phillips 66
Food	N: Carl's Jr, Denny's, Lotta Burger, Sonic, Waffle House
	S: Taco Bueno
Lodg	N: Executive Inn, Garnett Inn, Motel 6, Super 8
	S: Econo Lodge, National Inn

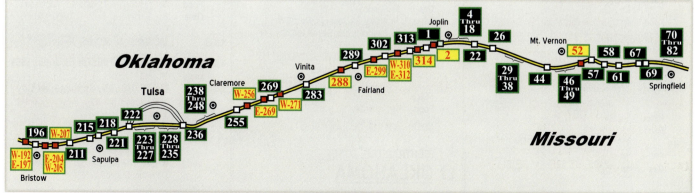

◆ = Regular Gas Stations with Diesel   ▲ = RV Friendly Locations   ♥ = Pet Friendly Locations

RED PRINT SHOWS LARGE VEHICLE PARKING/ACCESS ON SITE OR NEARBY   BROWN PRINT SHOWS CAMPGROUNDS/RV PARKS

Page 211

EXIT		OKLAHOMA
	Other	N: Dollar General, O'Reilly Auto Parts, Pharmacy
236A		129th East Ave, E Admiral Pl (SB)
	TStop	N: Flying J Travel Plaza #5008/Conoco (Scales)
	Food	N: Rest/FastFood/FJ TP, McDonald's
	Other	N: Laundry/WiFi/RVDump/LP/FJ TP, to Tulsa Raceway Park
(236B)		I-244W, Downtown Tulsa, Airport
	Other	N: Tulsa Int'l Airport✈, to Mingo RV Park▲
238		161st East Ave, Tulsa, Catoosa
	TStop	N: Shell (Scales), QuikTrip #71 (Scales)
	Food	N: Rest/Shell, FastFood/QT, Country Kettle S: Arby's, Burger King
	Lodg	S: Microtel
	TServ	N: Bridgestone Tire & Auto
	Other	S: Walker RV Center, Tulsa RV Sales & Service
240A		OK 167N, 193rd East Ave, Catoosa
	FStop	N: Johnny's Quick Stop/Shell (4 mi N), Speedy's #1/66
	TStop	N: SunMart #46
	Gas	S: QT, Shell◊
	Food	N: Rest/Speedy's, Rest/SunMart, KFC, McDonald's, Pizza Hut, Taco Mayo, Waffle House, Wendy's S: Mazzio's Pizza, Sonic, Subway
	Lodg	N: Super 8 S: Holiday Inn Express
	Other	N: KOA Tulsa▲, Ugly John's Custom Boats & RV S: Dollar General, Family Dollar, NAPA, Grocery, Auto & Tire Service
240B		US 412E, Choteau, Siloam Springs
241		OK 66E, to Catoosa, Claremore
(241)		Will Rogers Tpk Begins EB, Ends WB
248		OK 266, to OK 66, Claremore, to Catoosa
255		OK 20, Claremore, to Pryor
	Gas	N: Citgo, Kum & Go S: Phillips 66
	Food	N: Arby's, Carl's Jr, McDonald's
	Lodg	N: Best Western, Days Inn, Super 8
	Med	N: + Hospital
(256)		Parking Area (SB)
(269)		Parking Area (NB)
269		OK 28, Adair, to Chelsea (fr EB, No re-entry)
(271)		Picnic Area (SB)
283		US 69, Big Cabin
	TStop	N: AmBest/Big Cabin Travel Plaza/Shell (Scales)
	Food	N: Cherokee Rest/FastFood/Big Cabin TP
	Lodg	N: Super 8/Big Cabin TP
	TWash	N: Big Cabin TP
	TServ	N: Big Cabin TP/Tires
	Other	N: Laundry/Big Cabin TP
(286)		TOLL Plaza
(288)		Service Plaza (Both dir)
	FStop	EZ Go Foods #47/66
	Food	McDonald's
289		US 60, US 69, Vinita
	FStop	N: Phillips 66
	Gas	N: Citgo

Personal Notes

_____

EXIT		OKLAHOMA
	Food	N: Subway/66, Braum's, McDonald's, Carl's Jr, Pizza Hut
	Lodg	N: Holiday Inn Express
	Med	N: + Hospital
	Other	N: Auto Dealers, Auto Services, Tires, Dollar General, Grocery, WAL★MARTsc, OK State Hwy Patrol Post
(299)		Parking Area (NB)
302		US 59, US 69, US 60, Afton, to Fairland, Grove, Miami
	FStop	S: to Buffalo Ranch Travel Center/Citgo
	Food	S: FastFood/Buffalo Ranch TC
	Lodg	N: Shangri-La Inn
	Other	N: Bears Den Resort Campground▲
(310)		Parking Area (WB)
(312)		Parking Area (EB)
313		OK 10, to US 69, OK 66, Miami
	FStop	N: Eastern Shawnee Travel Center/Citgo
	Gas	N: Conoco◊
	Food	N: Arby's, McDonald's, Rest/BW
	Lodg	N: Best Western, Deluxe Inn, Super 8
	Med	N: + Hospital
	Other	N: ATMs, Auto Services, Towing, Miami RV & MH Park▲
(314)		Service Plaza/OK Welcome Ctr (WB)
	FStop	EZ Go Foods #48/66
	Food	McDonald's
	NOTE:	MM 329: Oklahoma State Line

(CENTRAL TIME ZONE)

OKLAHOMA

EXIT		MISSOURI

ⓞ MISSOURI
(CENTRAL TIME ZONE)

1		US 400, US 166, Joplin, to Baxter Springs, KS
(2)		MO Welcome Center (EB) Rest Area (WB) (RR, Phone, Picnic)
(3)		Weigh Station (Both dir)
4		MO 43S, Coyote Dr, Joplin, Seneca
	TStop	N: Love's Travel Stop #282 S: Petro Stopping Center #54/BP (Scales), Pilot Travel Center #317 (Scales)
	FStop	S: Rapid Robert's #122/Conoco
	Food	N: Hardee's/Love's TS S: IronSkillet/Blimpie/Petro, Wendy's/ Pilot TC, Subway/Conono, McDonald's
	Lodg	S: Motel/Petro SC, Sleep Inn
	TWash	S: TruckOMat/Petro SC
	TServ	N: Peterbilt S: Petro SC/Tires
	Other	N: WiFi/RVDump/Love's TS, Zan's Creek Side Campground▲ S: Laundry/BarbSh/WiFi/LP/Petro SC, WiFi/Pilot TC, WiFi/ Rapid Robert's, Joplin KOA▲
6		I-44 Bus, MO 43N, MO 86, Joplin, to Racine
	Gas	N: Citgo
	Food	N: Arby's, McDonald's, Pizza Hut
	Med	N: + Hospital
8BA		US 71 Bus, Range Line Rd, Joplin
	Gas	N: Citgo, Conoco, Kum & Go◊, Sam'sr S: Casey's, Citgo, Phillips 66
	Food	N: Applebee's, Arby's, Bob Evans, CiCi's, Country Kitchen, Denny's, Gringo's Grill, IHOP, KFC, Kyoto, McDonald's, Olive Garden, Outback Steakhouse, Steak 'n Shake, Subway, Waffle House, Wendy's S: Cracker Barrel
	Lodg	N: Baymont Inn, Best Value Inn, Best Western, Days Inn♥, Drury Inn, Hampton Inn, Fairfield Inn, Holiday Inn, Motel 6, Ramada, Residence Inn, Super 8♥ S: Microtel, Towneplace Suites
	TServ	N: Freightliner Trucks
	Other	N: ATMs, Auto Services, Grocery, Lowe's, Auto Dealers, NAPA, Office Depot, Sam's Club, Tires, Wal-Mart sc
11BA		US 71S, Neosho, Ft Smith (SB)
11A		US 71S, Neosho, Ft Smith
	TStop	S: Flying J Travel Plaza #5080/Conoco (Scales)
	Food	S: CtryMkt/FastFood/FJ TP, Applebee's
	Other	S: Laundry/BarbSh/WiFi/RVDump/LP/ FJ TP
11B		MO 249N, to MO 66, Joplin
15		I-44 Bus, MO 66, 7th St, Joplin (SB)
	Lodg	N: Tara Motel
18B		MO 59, US 71N, Carthage, Ks City
	FStop	N: Express Truck Stop, Flying W Conv Store
	Gas	N: Conoco, Phillips 66
	Food	N: Hardee's, Ranch House BBQ & Steaks, Taco Bell
	Lodg	N: Best Western, Budget Way Motel, Days Inn, Super 8

◊ = Regular Gas Stations with Diesel   ▲ = RV Friendly Locations   ♥ = Pet Friendly Locations
RED PRINT SHOWS LARGE VEHICLE PARKING/ACCESS ON SITE OR NEARBY   BROWN PRINT SHOWS CAMPGROUNDS/RV PARKS

EXIT		MISSOURI
	Other	N: Coachlight RV Center & Park▲, Big Red Barn RV Park▲, Precious Moments Cubby Bear's RV Park▲ S: Ballards Campground▲
18A		MO 59, Carthage, to Diamond
	Other	S: Ballard's Campground & Store▲
22		CR 10, 10th Rd, Carthage
	FStop	S: Express Truck Stop
	Food	S: FastFood/Express TS
26		MO 37, Bus 44, Sarcoxie, to Reeds
29		MO U, High St, Sarcoxie, La Russell
	FStop	S: Citgo
	Food	S: Rebel's Inn
	Lodg	S: Sarcoxie Motel
	Other	N: WAC RV Park▲
33		CR 1010, MO 97S, to Pierce City
	FStop	S: Zip Stop/Sinclair
	Food	S: Rest/Sinclair
38		MO 97, Stotts City, Pierce City
	Gas	N: Massie's Super Stop
44		MO H, Bus 44, Mt. Vernon, Monett
	Gas	N: Citgo
	Lodg	N: Walnuts Motel
46		MO 39, MO 265, Bus 44, Mt Vernon to Aurora
	TStop	N: Travel Center of America #72/Conoco (Scales)
	Gas	N: Phillips 66◊ S: BP◊
	Food	N: CountryPride/TA TC, Bamboo Garden, Country Kitchen, Hardee's, KFC/LJ Silver, McDonald's, Sonic, Subway, Taco Bell
	Lodg	N: Super 8, USA Inn S: Comfort Inn
	TWash	N: TA TC
	TServ	N: TA TC/Tires
	Other	N: Laundry/WiFi/TA TC, Dollar General, Family Dollar, O'Reilly Auto Parts
49		MO 174, CR CC, to Chesapeake
(52)		Rest Area (Both dir) (RR, Phones, Picnic, Vend)
57		MO 96, Bois d'Arc, to Halltown (SB)
58		MO Z, MO O, MO 96, Bois d'Arc
	Gas	S: Shell◊
61		MO K, MO PP, to MO 266
	TStop	N: Hood's Service Center/Cenex (Scales)
	Gas	N: AmocoBP
	Food	N: Rest/Hoods SC
	Lodg	N: Motel/Hoods SC
	Tires	N: Hoods SC
	Other	N: Laundry/LP/Hoods SC
67		MO T, MO N, Republic
	FStop	S: Citgo
69		MO 360, James River Expy, to US60
70		MO B, MO MM, Springfield
	Gas	S: Phillips 66
	Other	S: Springfield KOA▲
72		MO 266, Bus 44, Chestnut Expy
	FStop	S: Coastal Super Stop
	Gas	S: Casey's
	Food	S: Casey's C/O Pizza, Hardee's, Subway, Taco Bell, Waffle House
	Lodg	S: Best Budget Inn, Ramada Ltd
	Other	N: Travelers Park Campground▲
75		US 160, West ByPass, to Willard
	Gas	S: Conoco, Phillips 66
	Lodg	S: Courtyard, La Quinta Inn♥
	Other	N: Springfield Reg'l Airport✈

EXIT		MISSOURI
77		MO 13, Kansas Expy, to Bolivar
	FStop	N: (4 mi N) Crossroads Convenience Store/Conoco S: Phillips 66
	Gas	S: QT
	Food	S: Arby's, Braum's, CiCi's, Golden Corral, IHOP, McDonald's, Papa John's, Subway, Taco Bell, Waffle House, Wendy's
	Lodg	N: Interstate Inn S: Econo Lodge
	Med	S: + Springfield Clinic
	Other	N: Lowe's S: Mall, Big Lots, Dollar Tree, Grocery, Goodyear, O'Reilly Auto, Radio Shack, Staples, Wal-Mart sc, Walgreen's
80A		Bus 44, Glenstone Ave, Springfield
	FStop	S: to 2mi S Johnson One Stop/Conoco
	Gas	S: Phillips 66, QT, Shell
	Food	S: Bob Evans, Burger King, Captain D's, Cracker Barrel, Denny's, Hardee's, KFC, Long John Silver's, McDonald's, Pizza Hut, Rib Crib, Ruby Tuesday, Ryan's Grill, Steak n Shake, Subway, Taco Bell, Village Inn, Western Sizzlin
	Lodg	S: Best Western, Comfort Inn, Days Inn, Drury Inn, Econo Lodge, Hampton Inn, Lamplighter Inn, La Quinta Inn♥, Ozark Inn, Red Lion, Sheraton, Springfield Inn
	Med	S: + Doctors Hospital
	Other	S: LP/Johnson OS, AutoZone, Goodyear, Bass Pro Shop, Wal-Mart, Battlefield Mall, Fairgrounds, Zoo, S MO State Univ
80B		Glenstone Ave, MO H
	FStop	N: Rapid Robert's #123/Conoco (Scales)

EXIT		MISSOURI
	Gas	N: Phillips 66◊, Shell
	Food	N: Waffle House
	Lodg	N: Days Inn, Hotel 7, Motel 6, Quality Inn, Super 8
82A		US 65S, to Branson, Sedalia
	Gas	S: Phillips 66◊
	Food	S: McDonald's, Waffle House
	Lodg	S: American Inn, Days Inn, Super 8
	TServ	S: Cummins Ozark Kenworth, White GMC Volvo, Peterbilt of Springfield
	Other	S: MO State Hwy Patrol Post
82B		US 65N, to Branson, Sedalia
84		MO 744, Springfield
88		MO 125, Strafford, to Fair Grove
	FStop	N: Speedy's #5/66 (Scales)
	TStop	N: Travel Center of America #137/Amoco (Scales)
	Gas	S: Kum & Go, Conoco◊
	Food	N: CountryPride/Subway/TacoBell/TA TC, McDonald's S: Fox's Pizza Den, Grandaddy's BBQ
	Lodg	S: Super 8
	TWash	N: 18 Wheeler Truck Wash, Kearney Truck Wash & Lube
	TServ	N: TA TC/Tires
	Other	N: Laundry/RVDump/Speedy's, Laundry/WiFi/TA TC, Paradise in the Woods RV Park▲ S: Strafford RV Park▲
(89)		Weigh Station (Both dir)
96		MO B, Marshfield, Northview
	Other	N: Paradise in the Woods RV Park▲
100		MO 38, Spur Dr, Marshfield
	Gas	N: AmocoBP S: Conoco◊, Citgo◊, Kum & Go◊, Phillips 66◊, Shell
	Food	N: Tiny's Smokehouse BBQ S: Country Kitchen, El Charro, DQ, McDonald's, Pizza Hut, Sonic, Subway
	Lodg	N: Plaza Motel S: Holiday Inn Express
	Other	N: Goodyear, Fountain Plaza MH & RV Park▲ S: Grocery, Pharmacy, Wal-Mart▲, RV Express RV Park▲
107		Sampson Rd, Marshfield
(110)		Rest Area (Both dir) (RR, Phone, Picnic, Vend)
113		CR Y, CR J, MO M, Conway
	Gas	N: Phillips 66 S: Conoco
	Food	N: Cafe
	Lodg	N: Budget Inn
118		MO A, MO C, Phillipsburg
	Gas	N: Conoco◊ S: Phillips 66
123		Dove Rd, Phillipsburg
	Gas	S: EZ Mart
	Other	S: Happy Trails RV Center, Lebanon KOA▲
127		Bus Lp 44, Elm St, Lebanon
	TStop	N: Clayton's Conoco (Scales)
	Gas	N: Phillips 66◊, Sinclair S: Phillips 66◊
	Food	N: Rest/Clayton's TP, Ranch House, Waffle House
	Lodg	N: Days Inn, Econo Lodge, Hampton Inn, Holiday Inn, Super 8, Travelers Inn

◊ = Regular Gas Stations with Diesel ▲ = RV Friendly Locations ♥ = Pet Friendly Locations

RED PRINT SHOWS LARGE VEHICLE PARKING/ACCESS ON SITE OR NEARBY   BROWN PRINT SHOWS CAMPGROUNDS/RV PARKS

EXIT		MISSOURI	EXIT		MISSOURI	EXIT		MISSOURI
	TWash	N: Clayton's TP		Food	N: Cracker Barrel, Long John Silver, Pizza Hut, Popeye's, Ryan's Grill, Ruby Tuesday, Subway		Food	N: McDonald's, Pizza Hut, Subway
	TServ	N: Clayton's TP/Tires						S: Burger King
	Other	N: Laundry/LP/Clayton's TP, Auto Dealers, Firestone					Lodg	N: Comfort Inn, Economy Inn, Ozark Motel
					S: Arby's, Captain D's, Japanese Sushi, KFC, McDonald's, Subway, Taco Bell, Waffle House, Wendy's			S: Finn's Motel
		S: Auto Dealers					TServ	N: Rays Tire & Service Center
129		MO 5, MO 32, to Bus 44, MO 64, Lebanon, Hartville		Lodg	N: Baymont Inn, Candlewood Suites, Comfort Inn, Fairfield Inn, Hampton Inn, Red Roof Inn	203		MO F, MO ZZ, Cuba
							Other	N: Blue Moon RV & Horse Park▲
	Gas	N: Conoco, Kum & Go, Phillips 66◊				208		MO 19, Cuba, to Owensville
		S: AmocoBP, Conoco◊			S: Budget Inn, Econo Lodge, Holiday Inn Express, Microtel, Motel 6, Ramada Inn		TStop	N: Voss Truck Port (Scales)
	Food	N: Applebee's, Bamboo Garden, Burger King, Country Kitchen, DQ, Jay's Family Rest, KFC, Long John Silver, Pizza Hut, Papa John's, McDonald's, Shoney's, Sonic, Subway, Taco Bell, Western Sizzlin					Gas	N: Phillips 66
				Other	N: Dollar Tree, Wal-Mart sc			S: Casey's, Delano◊, Mobil, Phillips 66
					S: AutoZone, Firestone, Radio Shack		Food	N: Rest/FastFood/Voss TP, Country Kitchen, Huddle House, Pizza Hut, Rest/Best Western
			163		MO 28, St Robert, to Dixon			
				TStop	N: Road Ranger/Citgo (Scales)			
				Gas	S: Conoco			S: Burger King, Hardee's, Jack in the Box, McDonald's, Sonic, Subway
		S: Captain D's, Hardee's, Pizza Hut		Food	N: Cafe/Subway/Road Ranger			
	Lodg	N: Days Inn, Econo Lodge♥, Holiday Inn Express♥, Hampton Inn, Historic Rte 66 Inn, Super 8, Travelers Inn			S: Country Cafe, Sweetwater BBQ		Lodg	N: Best Western♥, Super 8
				Lodg	S: Best Western, Days Inn, Knights Inn, Super 8, Villager Lodge & RV Park▲			S: Holiday Inn Express
							TServ	N: Voss TP/Tires
	TServ	S: Johnson Service Center/Goodyear		Other	N: Laundry/Road Ranger, to appr 10 mi Boiling Spring Campground▲		Other	N: Laundry/BarbSh/WiFi/Voss TP
	Med	N: + St John's Hospital						S: Auto Dealer, O'Reilly Auto Parts, Wal-Mart, Onondaga Cave State Park▲, Huzzah Valley Resort▲
	Other	N: Auto Dealers, Advance Auto, Auto Zone, NAPA, O'Reilly Auto Parts, to appr 9 mi Oak Hill Campground▲	169		MO J, Newburg			
				Other	N: Boiling Spring Campground▲	210		MO UU, Cuba
			172		MO D, CR 242, Jerome		Other	N: Meramec Valley RV Campground▲
		S: Auto Dealers, Dollar General, Lowe's, Ozark Harley Davidson, Wal-Mart sc, to Floyd W Jones Lebanon Airport✈		Other	N: Arlington River Resort▲	214		CR H, CR 508, Leasburg
			176		CR 8490, CR 7300, Sugar Tree Rd, Newburg		Gas	N: Mobil◊
						218		CR C, CR J, CR N, Bourbon
130		Bus 44, CR MM, Lebanon					Gas	N: Citgo◊
	Gas	N: Conoco, Phillips 66	(178)		Rest Area (Both dir) (RR, Phone, Picnic, Vend)			S: Mobil
	Food	N: Rest/BW					Food	S: Henhouse Rest
	Lodg	N: Best Western♥, Holiday Motel					Lodg	N: Budget Inn
	TServ	Johnson Service Center/Goodyear	179		MO T, Truman St, Newburg		Other	S: Blue Springs Ranch Campground▲, Riverview Ranch Campground▲, Bourbon RV Center
	Med	N: + St John's Hospital		Gas	S: BP			
	Other	N: Forest Manor Motel & RV Park▲		Food	S: Cookin from Scratch/BP			
135		MO F, Lebanon, to Sleeper	184		Bus Lp 44, to US 63S, Rolla	225		MO 185, CR D, Sullivan
140		MO T, MO N, to Stoutland		Gas	S: Mobil, Phillips 66, Shell		TStop	S: Bobber Travel Center (Scales)
	FStop	S: Phillips 66		Food	S: Arby's, Burger King, Golden Corral, KFC, Long John Silver's, McDonald's, Pizza Hut, Shoney's, Sirloin Stockade, Subway, Waffle House, Wendy's, Zeno's Steakhouse, Rest/BW		Gas	N: Mobil, Phillips 66◊
	Food	S: Midway Chinese						S: Conoco
145		MO 133, Richland					Food	S: Domino's
	TStop	N: Oasis Truck Plaza/Conoco						S: Rest/Bobber TC, Cracker Barrel, Homer's BBQ, Jack in the Box, Pizza Hut, Sonic
	Food	N: Rest/Oasis TP						
	Tires	N: Oasis TP		Lodg	N: Comfort Suites		Lodg	N: Baymont Inn, Econo Lodge, Family Motor Inn, Super 8
150		MO 7, MO P, Richland, to Laquey			S: AmeriHost Inn, Best Western♥, Best Way Inn, Days Inn, Econo Lodge♥, Holiday Inn Express, Howard Johnson, Ramada Inn, Super 8, Travelodge, Western Inn, Zeno's Motel			
153		MO 17, Waynesville, to Buckhorn						S: Comfort Inn, Delta Motel
	FStop	N: Whitmore Farms/Cenex					Med	S: + Missouri Baptist Hospital
	Gas	S: Shell◊					Other	N: Vet♥, to Sullivan Reg'l Airport✈
	Food	N: Rest/Whitmore Farms		Med	S: + Hospital			S: Laundry/Bobber TC, Meramec Cinema I & II, Sullivan Memorial Airport✈
	Lodg	N: Ft Wood Inn		Other	S: Kroger, Wal-Mart			
	Other	S: Glen Oaks RV Park▲	185		MO E, Rolla	226		MO 185, Sullivan, to Oak Grove
156		Hwy H, Bus Loop 44, Waynesville		Gas	S: Phillips 66		TStop	S: Flying J Travel Plaza #5047/Conoco (Scales)
	Gas	N: Citgo◊, Smitty's		Food	S: Applebee's, DQ, Hardee's, Subway, Taco Bell			
	Food	N: Smitty's, McDonald's, Subway					Gas	S: Phillips 66
	Lodg	N: Star Motel		Other	S: MO State Hwy Patrol Post		Food	S: CtryMkt/FastFood/FJ TP, Denny's, Golden Corral, Hardee's, KFC, Pizza Hut, McDonald's, Steak 'n Shake, Subway
	Other	N: Dollar General, Grocery, Auto Dealers, Covered Wagon RV Park▲	186		US 63, Bus 44, N Bishop Ave, Rolla, Jefferson City			
				Gas	N: Sinclair			
		S: Fort Leonard Wood			S: AmocoBP, Mobil◊, Phillips 66		Other	S: Laundry/BarbSh/WiFi/RVDump/LP/FJ TP, Dollar General, O'Reilly Auto Parts, Wal-Mart sc, Cinema 6
159		MO 17, Bus Lp 44, St Robert		Food	N: Steak 'n Shake			
	Gas	N: Conoco			S: Denny's, Pizza Inn, Waffle House			
		S: BP◊, Phillips 66, Shell		Lodg	N: Drury Inn, Hampton Inn, Sooter Inn	230		MO JJ, MO W, Sullivan, to Stanton
	Food	N: DQ, Sonic			S: American Motor Inn		Gas	S: Phillips 66
		S: Oakwood Café, Pine Steakhouse		Med	S: + Hospital		Food	S: Roosters Steak House
	Lodg	N: Star Motel		Other	N: Lowe's		Lodg	N: Stanton Motel
		S: Microtel, Motel 6	189		MO V, Rolla, Dillon		Other	S: Stanton/Meramec KOA▲
	Med	S: + Mercy Medical Group		FStop	N: Love's Travel Stop # 341 (Scales)	(235)		Rest Area (Both dir, Left exit) (RR, Phones, Picnic, Vend)
	Other	N: Goodyear, Covered Wagon RV Park▲		Food	N: Subway/Love's TS			
161A		Bus 44S, Missouri Ave, St Robert, Ft Leonard Wood	195		US 68, MO 68, MO 8, St. James	(238)		Weigh Station (Both dir)
				Gas	N: Conoco◊, Mobil◊, Phillips 66◊	239		MO 30, CR AB, CR WW, St Clair
161B		MO Y, Bus 44N, St Robert			S: Phillips 66◊, Circle S Gas		Gas	S: AmocoBP
	FStop	S: St Robert Cenex						
	Gas	N: Mobil◊						
		S: Conoco, Cenex◊						

◊ = Regular Gas Stations with Diesel ▲ = RV Friendly Locations ♥ = Pet Friendly Locations
RED PRINT SHOWS LARGE VEHICLE PARKING/ACCESS ON SITE OR NEARBY   BROWN PRINT SHOWS CAMPGROUNDS/RV PARKS

INTERSTATE 44 W

EXIT	MISSOURI
240	**MO 47, Main St, St Clair, Union**
Gas	N: Phillips 66◊, Sinclair
	S: Mobil◊
Food	N: Burger King, Taco Bell/P66
	S: Hardee's, McDonald's, Subway
Lodg	S: Budget Lodge, Super 8
Other	N: Frank Reed RV Center
	S: Dollar General, 3 R RV Service Center
242	**Old Hwy 66, St Clair**
247	**US 50, Union (SB),**
	MO O, Villa Ridge (NB)
251	**MO 100, to Washington**
TStop	N: Fuel Mart #634 (Scales), Mr. Fuel #1/
	Conoco (Scales)
Food	N: FastFood/Fuel Mart, FastFood/Mr Fuel
253	**MO 100, Gray Summit, Eureka**
Gas	S: Phillips 66
Food	S: Rest/Best Western
Lodg	S: Best Western
257	**Bus Lp 44, Viaduct St, Pacific**
FStop	S: Pilot Travel Center #208
Gas	S: BP◊, Conoco, Mobil◊
Food	S: Subway/Pilot TC, Hardee's, KFC,
	McDonald's, Taco Bell
Lodg	N: Comfort Inn
	S: Holiday Inn Express, Quality Inn
261	**Lp 44, Six Flags Rd, to Allenton**
FStop	S: Shell #28
Gas	N: MotoMart◊
	S: Phillips 66◊
Food	N: Applebee's, Country Kitchen, KFC,
	Denny's, McDonald's, Lions Choice,
	Steak n Shake
Lodg	N: Econo Lodge, Ramada Inn, Red Carpet
	Inn, Super 8
Other	N: AutoZone, Wal-Mart sc, to Six Flags,
	Yogi Bears Jellystone Park Resort▲
	S: LP/Shell, St Louis West KOA▲
264	**MO 109, CR W, Eureka**
Gas	N: 7-11, Phillips 66
	S: QT◊, Shell
Food	N: Burger King, DQ, Domino's, KFC,
	McDonald's, Pizza Hut, Ponderosa,
	Smokers BBQ, Subway, Taco Bell,
	Wendy's, White Castle
Lodg	N: Days Inn
Other	N: Grocery, Firestone, NAPA, Byerly
	RV Center
	S: Walgreen's
265	**Williams Rd (NB)**
266	**Lewis Rd**

EXIT	MISSOURI
269	**Antire Rd, High Ridge, Beaumont**
272	**MO 141, Valley Park, Fenton**
FStop	S: MPC #23/66
Gas	N: MotoMart
	S: 7-11, QT, Shell
Food	S: Burger King, Culver's, McDonald's,
	Steak 'n Shake, Subway, Taco Bell
Lodg	S: Drury Inn, Hampton Inn
274	**Bowles Ave, Hwy Dr, Fenton**
Gas	N: Shell◊
	S: AmocoBP, Citgo◊, QT
Food	S: Cracker Barrel, Denny's, McDonald's,
	Quiznos, Souper Salad, White Castle
Lodg	S: Drury Inn, Econo Lodge, Fairfield Inn,
	Holiday Inn Express, Pear Tree Inn,
	Stratford Inn
TServ	S: Goodyear Truck Tire Center, Purcell
	Tire Co
Other	N: Daimler Chrysler Assembly Plant
275	**Soccer Park Rd, Yarnell Rd (SB)**
TStop	N: St Louis Truck Port/Shell (Scales)
Food	N: Rest/St Louis TP, Burger King
Lodg	S: Fairfield Inn, Towneplace Suites
TServ	N: St Louis TP/Tires, Kenworth
	S: Fabick Power Systems, Caterpillar
Other	N: Laundry/LP/St Louis TP
(276)	**Jct I-270, S - Memphis,**
	N - Chicago
277B	**US 61, US 67, US 50, Watson Rd,**
	Lindbergh Blvd, St Louis
Gas	N: Shell
	S: Citgo, Phillips 66, Shell
Food	N: Arby's, Chili's, Hardee's, Steak & Rice
	Chinese, Sunny China Int'l Buffet
	S: Bob Evans, Burger King, Denny's,
	House of Hunan, Longhorn Steakhouse,
	Steak n Shake
Lodg	N: Best Western
	S: Comfort Inn, Days Inn, Econo Lodge,
	Hampton Inn, Holiday Inn
Med	N: + St Joseph Hospital
	S: + Multi Medical Group
Other	N: Lowe's, Office Depot, Target,
	Wal-Mart sc, St Louis Comm College
	S: Home Depot, Sunset Hills Plaza
	Shopping Center,
	World Market
277A	**MO 366, Watson Rd (NB)**
Med	S: + Hospital
278	**Big Bend Blvd, St Louis**
Gas	N: Sam's
	S: Mobil◊, QT, Sinclair

EXIT	MISSOURI
Food	N: Hardee's, Sonic
	S: Denny's
Other	N: Sam's Club
279	**S Berry Rd, Big Bend Blvd (SB)**
280	**Elm Ave, St Louis**
Gas	N: AmocoBP
	S: Shell
282	**Murdoch Ave, Laclede Stn Rd (NB)**
Gas	N: Amoco, Mobil
Food	N: McDonald's, Starbucks, Subway
283	**Shrewsbury Ave (SB)**
284A	**Jamieson Ave (NB)**
284B	**Arsenal St (SB)**
285	**Southwest Ave**
	(fr SB, diff reacc)
286	**Hampton Ave, St Louis**
Gas	N: Mobil, Phillips 66, Shell
	S: Shell
Food	N: Denny's, Jack in the Box, McDonald's,
	Steak 'n Shake, Subway, Taco Bell
	S: Burger King, Hardee's, Village Inn
Lodg	S: Holiday Inn, Red Roof Inn ♥
Med	N: + Hospital
287A	**Kingshighway Blvd (NB)**
287B	**Vanderventer Ave**
288	**Grand Blvd.,**
	Downtown St. Louis
Gas	N: BP
Food	N: Jack in the Box
Med	N: + St Louis University Hospital,
	+ Incarnate Word Hospital
	S: + Hospital
289	**Jefferson Ave**
Gas	N: Citgo◊
	S: Conoco
Food	N: Subway
	S: McDonald's
Lodg	N: Holiday Inn Express
(290A)	**Jct I-55, S to Memphis (NB)**
290B	**18th St, Downtown St Louis (EB)**
290C/207	**S Tucker Blvd, Gravois Ave (SB)**

(I-44 begins/ends on I-55, Exit #207BC)
(CENTRAL TIME ZONE)

🎧 MISSOURI

Begin Westbound I-44 from St. Louis, MO to Wichita Falls, TX.

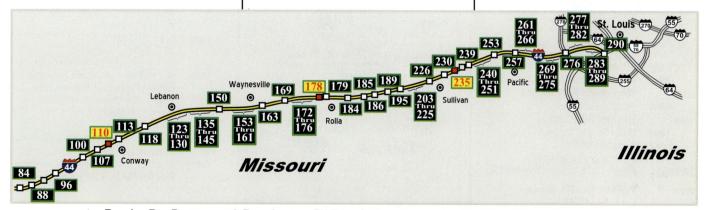

◊ = Regular Gas Stations with Diesel   ▲ = RV Friendly Locations   ♥ = Pet Friendly Locations
RED PRINT SHOWS LARGE VEHICLE PARKING/ACCESS ON SITE OR NEARBY   BROWN PRINT SHOWS CAMPGROUNDS/RV PARKS

INTERSTATE 45 S

EXIT	TEXAS
	Begin Southbound I-45 from Dallas to Galveston TX

○ TEXAS
(CENTRAL TIME ZONE)
(I-45 begins/ends in Dallas)

EXIT	
(286)	to I-35E, to Denton
285	US 75N, Bryan St
284C	Bryan St, Ross Ave, N Central Expy
Other	W: Westin City Center, Plaza of the Americas, Arts District
(284AB)	Jct I-30, W-Ft Worth, E-Texarkana
Med	E: + Baylor Univ Medical Center
283	US 175E, Kaufman
Gas	E: Shell
	W: Kwik Stop, Shamrock
Food	E: Captain D's, Hardeman's BBQ
	W: KFC/Taco Bell
Lodg	W: Colonial House Motel, Wayside Inn
Other	E: Tire & Service Center
283A	Lamar St
283B	Pennsylvania Ave, MLK Jr Blvd (SB)
281	Overton Rd, Dallas (SB)
Gas	E: Texaco
	W: Chevron
Lodg	E: Lamar Motel
Other	E: Auto Services
	W: Auto Services
280	Linfield Rd, Illinois Ave
Gas	W: Texaco
Lodg	E: Linfield Motel, Star Motel
	W: Luxury Inn Motel
Other	E: Auto Services
	W: Auto Services
279	Tx 12 Loop (SB)
279AB	Tx 12 Loop (NB)
Med	W: + Veterans Medical Center
277	Simpson Stuart Rd, Dallas
Gas	E: Conv Store
	W: Chevron
Food	W: Whitehouse BBQ
Lodg	E: ABC Motel
Other	W: Paul Quinn College
(276B)	Jct I-20E, to Shreveport
(276A)	Jct I-20W, to Ft Worth (Travel Center & All Serv 1st Exit W)
275	TX 310, S Central Expy, Dallas (NB, no reaccess)
274	Palestine St, Dowdy Ferry Rd, Hutchins
FStop	W: Tucker Oil (408 N Main)
Gas	E: Exxon, Texaco
Food	W: BBQ Express, DQ, Jack in the Box, Smith's Rest
Lodg	E: Gold Inn
Other	W: Auto Services, Grocery, Police Dept
273	Wintergreen Rd, Hutchins
Other	W: Hipps Bus Service
272	Fulgham Rd, Hutchins
TStop	W: Love's Travel Stop #331 (Scales)
Food	W: Carl's Jr/Love's TS
Other	W: Laundry/WiFi/RVDump/Love's TS
(272)	Weigh Station/Inspection Stn (SB)
271	Pleasant Run Rd, Wilmer

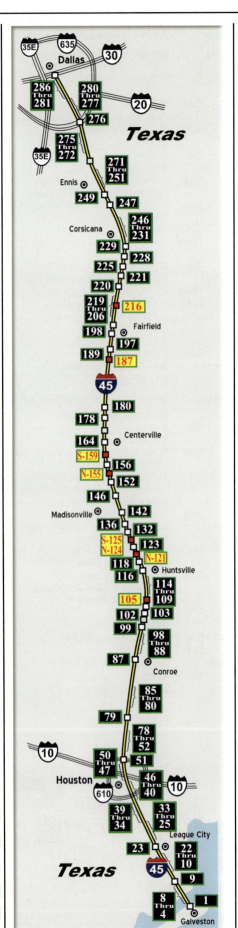

EXIT	TEXAS
270	Belt Line Rd, Wilmer
TStop	W: Citgo Fuel Stop
Gas	E: Shell◇, Texaco◇
	W: Exxon
Food	W: DQ, Sonic, Subway, Taco Bell
Other	W: Police Dept, Lancaster Airport✈
269	Mars Rd, Wilmer
268	US 45 Bus, Malloy Bridge Rd, to Ferris
267	Frontage Rd
266	5th St, FM 660, Ferris
Gas	E: Fina
	W: Shamrock
Food	W: DQ
Other	W: Auto Services, Police Dept
265	Lp 45, Ferris (NB)
264	Frontage Rd, Wester Rd
Other	W: Cortez Truck & Auto Repair
263A	Frontage Rd
263	Lp 561, to Trumbull
262	S Central St, Risinger Rd, Newton Rd
261	County Rd, Palmer (NB)
260	US 45 Bus, to FM 818, Hampel Rd
Other	W: Auto Services
259	FM 813, to FM 878, Palmer
258	Lp 45, US 75, Parker Hill Rd, Palmer
FStop	E: Exxon
TStop	W: Sunmart #170/Mobil (Scales)
Food	E: Subway/Exxon
	W: FastFood/Sunmart, Jenny's Café, Mexican Rest
Lodg	W: Palmer House Motel
TServ	W: Sunmart/Tires
Other	W: Laundry/Sunmart
255	FM 879, Ennis, to Garrett
Gas	E: Exxon◇
	W: Chevron◇
253	Lp 45, Ennis
Gas	W: Shell
251B	TX 34, Ennis Ave, to 35E, Ennis, to Kaufman, Italy
FStop	E: Tiger Mart #23/Exxon (2200 TX 34)
Gas	E: Fina, Texaco◇
	W: Chevron◇, Exxon◇
Food	E: Bubba's BBQ Steakhouse, McDonald's, Rest/Tiger Mart
	W: Arby's, AmeriMex Rest, Burger King, Braum's, Captain D's, Chili's, DQ, Golden Corral, Jack in the Box, McDonald's, KFC, Subway, Taco Bell, Waffle House, Wendy's, Whataburger
Lodg	E: Best Western, Holiday Inn Express
	W: Ennis Inn, Quality Inn
Med	W: + Ennis Regional Medical Center
Other	W: AutoZone, Auto Dealers, Enterprise, Grocery, Police Dept, Museum, Tires, Towing, Wal-Mart sc, to Ennis Muni Airport✈, Tx Motorplex, Jeff's RV Campgrounds▲
251A	FM 1181, Creechville Rd, to Bus 45, Ennis (Serv W to Bus 45)
Other	W: COE/Bardwell Lake/High View Park▲
249	Bus 45, FM 85, US 75, Ennis
FStop	W: Kwik Mart #6/Fina

Page 216

◇ = Regular Gas Stations with Diesel   ▲ = RV Friendly Locations   ♥ = Pet Friendly Locations
RED PRINT SHOWS LARGE VEHICLE PARKING/ACCESS ON SITE OR NEARBY   BROWN PRINT SHOWS CAMPGROUNDS/RV PARKS

Interstate 45 N/S — TEXAS

EXIT		
	Food	W: Ennis Family Rest
	Lodg	E: Budget Inn
	Twash	W: Blue Beacon TW
247		US 287N, to Waxahatchie
246		FM 1183, to Alma
	Gas	W: Chevron, Phillips 66
244		FM 1182, Ennis
243		Frontage Rd, Rice
242		Frontage Rd, Rice
239		FM 1126, Rice
	Gas	W: Phillips 66
238		FM 1603, Rice
	TStop	E: Interstate Travel Center/Fina
	Food	E: Rest/FastFood/Interstate TC
	Other	E: Laundry/Interstate TC, H&H Truck & Auto Repair
237		Frontage Rd, Rice
235B		Lp 45, to Corsicana (SB)
235A		Frontage Rd (SB)
235		Lp 45, to Corsicana (NB)
232		FM 3041, Roane Rd, Corsicana
231		TX 31, MLK Blvd, to Waco, Athens
	FStop	W: Tiger Tote/Exxon
	Gas	E: Texaco◊
		W: Chevron, Shell◊
	Food	E: Jack in the Box
		W: Subway/Exxon, DQ, McDonald's
	Lodg	E: Colonial Inn
		W: Comfort Inn
	Other	W: Auto Dealers, Auto Services, ATMs, to American RV Sales & Park▲
229		US 287S, Bus 287, to Palestine
	Gas	E: Exxon◊, Shell◊
		W: Chevron
	Food	E: Wendy's/Exxon
		W: Catfish King, DQ, Waffle House
	Lodg	W: Days Inn, Royal Inn, Travelers Inn
	Other	W: Home Depot
228B		Frontage Rd, Lp 45 (NB, Left exit)
228A		Frontage Rd, 15th St (NB)
	Gas	E: Phillips 66
225		FM 739, Corsicana, Angus, Mustang
	TStop	E: Lucky 7 Quick Stop
	Gas	E: Chevron, Exxon
		W: Citgo◊, Shell
	Food	E: FastFood/Lucky 7 QS
	Other	E: Corsicana Muni Airport✈
221		Frontage Rd, Corsicana
220		Frontage Rd, Richland
219B		Frontage Rd
219A		TX 14, Richland, to Mexia (SB)
	Gas	W: Richland Store
	Food	W: Dragon Palace
218		FM 1394, Richland (NB)
(216)		Navarro Co Rest Area (Both dir) (RR, Phones, Picnic, WiFi)
213		FM 246, Richland, to Wortham, Streetman
	Gas	E: Bonds Travel Shoppe
		W: Chevron, Texaco◊
	Food	W: Country Smoke House

EXIT		
211		FM 80, Spur 114, Streetman, Kirvin
206		FM 833, Streetman, Fairfield
198		FM 27, Fairfield, Wortham
	TStop	W: Love's Travel Stop #288
	Gas	E: Exxon, Shell
		W: Exxon
	Food	E: PJ's Café, BBQ/Shell
		W: FastFood/Love's TS, Gilberto's
	Lodg	W: Budget Inn, Super 8
	Med	E: + E Tx Medical Center
	Other	W: WiFi/RVDump/Love's TS, I-45 RV Park▲
197		US 84, Teague St, Fairfield, Teague
	FStop	W: Bond Texaco Truck Center
	TStop	W: I-45 Shell Truck Stop
	Gas	E: Chevron, Exxon, Fina
	Food	E: Jack in the Box/Exxon, Sam's BBQ/Fina, DQ, McDonald's, Pizza Hut, Sonic, Subway, Texas Burger
		W: Rest/I-45 Shell TS
	Lodg	E: Regency Inn, Holiday Inn Express, Sam's Motel
		W: Best Value Inn, Super 8
	TServ	W: I-45 Shell TS/Tires
	Other	E: Pharmacy
		W: Auto Repairs
189		TX 179, Teague, to Dew
	TStop	E: Jet Travel Plaza/Exxon
	Food	E: FastFood/Jet TP, Dew Café
	Tires	E: Jet TP
	Other	E: Laundry/Jet TP
(187)		Parking Area (Both dir)
180		TX 164, Buffalo, to Groesbeck
178		US 79, W Commerce, Buffalo
	TStop	W: Buffalo Truck Stop/Shamrock, Tiger Mart Travel Plaza/Exxon (Scales), Sunmart #115/Mobil
	Gas	E: Shell
		W: Chevron
	Food	E: Café, Subway, Texas Burger, Weathervane Restaurant
		W: FastFood/Buffalo TS, FastFood/Tiger Mart TP, FastFood/SunMart, DQ, Pitt Grill, Sonic, Rainbow Rest
	Lodg	E: Wayside Inn
		W: Best Western, Economy Inn
	TServ	W: Triangle Tire
	Other	W: Laundry/Buffalo TS, Laundry/Tiger Mart TP
(166)		Weigh Station (SB)
164		TX 7, Centerville
	TStop	W: Woody's Diesel Express/Shell
	Gas	E: Woody's Smokehouse Shell
		W: Exxon
	Food	E: Country Cousins, Texas Burger
		W: FastFood/Woody's, DQ
	Lodg	E: Days Inn, Fiesta Motel
	Other	E: ATMs, Banks, Auto Services
		W: Laundry/Woody's
(159)		Parking Area (SB)
156		FM 977, Leona
	Gas	W: Exxon◊
(155)		Parking Area (NB)
152		TX OSR, to Normangee
	Gas	W: Chevron◊
	Other	W: Yellow Rose RV Park▲

EXIT		
146		TX 75, Madisonville
142		US 190, TX 21, to Bryan, Crockett
	Gas	E: Exxon◊, Texaco◊
		W: Citgo, Shamrock◊, Shell
	Food	E: Church's, Corral Café
		W: Lakeside Rest, McDonald's, Pizza Hut, Sonic, Subway, Texas Burger
	Lodg	E: Best Western, Madisonville Inn
		W: Budget Motel, Western Lodge
	Other	W: Auto Services, Towing
136		Spur 67, Madisonville
	Other	W: Home on the Range RV Park▲
132		FM 2989, Huntsville
(125)		Walker Co Rest Area (SB) (RR, Phones, Picnic, Vend, WiFi)
(124)		Walker Co Rest Area (NB) (RR, Phones, Picnic, Vend, WiFi)
123		FM 1696, Huntsville
(121)		Parking Area (NB)
118		TX 75, Huntsville
	TStop	E: Hitchin Post AmBest Truck Terminal/Shell (Scales)
		W: Pilot Travel Center #234 (Scales)
	Food	E: Rest/Hitchin Post TT
		W: Wendy's/Pilot TC
	Lodg	E: Econo Lodge, Motel 6♥, La Quinta Inn♥
	TWash	E: Hitchin Post TT/Tires
	TServ	E: Hitchin Post TT
		W: Pilot TC/Tires
	Other	E: Laundry/Hitchin Post TT, Huntsville Muni Airport✈, Auto Dealers, Bowling Alley
		W: Laundry/WiFi/Pilot TC
116		TX 30, US 190E, Huntsville
	Gas	E: Citgo, Shamrock◊
		W: Chevron, Exxon, Shell
	Food	E: El Chico, Golden Corral, McDonald's
		W: Burger King, Chili's, CiCi's, IHOP, KFC, Pizza Hut, Subway, Taco Bell
	Lodg	E: Comfort Inn, Econo Lodge, Motel 6♥, La Quinta Inn♥
		W: Holiday Inn Express
	Other	E: Auto Dealers, to Sam Houston Teachers College
		W: Home Depot, Kroger, Office Depot, Wal-Mart sc, Walgreen's, W Hill Mall
114		FM 1374, Montgomery Rd, Huntsville
	Gas	E: Exxon◊, Shell
		W: Chevron, Shamrock◊
	Food	E: DQ
	Lodg	E: Gateway Inn, Super 8
		W: Quality Suites
	Med	W: + Huntsville Memorial Hospital
	Other	W: Auto Services
113		TX 19, Huntsville, Crockett (NB)
112		TX 75
	Gas	E: Citgo
	Other	E: to Sam Houston State Univ

◊ = Regular Gas Stations with Diesel   ▲ = RV Friendly Locations   ♥ = Pet Friendly Locations

RED PRINT SHOWS LARGE VEHICLE PARKING/ACCESS ON SITE OR NEARBY   BROWN PRINT SHOWS CAMPGROUNDS/RV PARKS

Page 217

Interstate 45 N/S

TEXAS

EXIT	
109	TX P40, Huntsville
Other	W: to Huntsville State Park▲
(105)	**Picnic Area (Both dir)**
103	TX 150, FM 1374, FM 1375, to New Waverly (SB)
Gas	W: Citgo
102	TX 150, FM 1374, FM 1375, to New Waverly (NB)
Gas	E: Shell
(101)	Weigh Station (NB)
99	Danville Rd, Shepard Hill Rd (SB)
98	Danville Rd, Shepard Hill Rd (NB)
Other	E: Convenience RV Park▲ , The Catfish Pond▲
95	Longstreet Rd, Willis
Other	W: to Castaways RV Park▲
94	FM 1097, Willis
Gas	E: Kroger W: Chevron, Exxon, Shell
Food	E: Jack in the Box, Sonic W: McDonald's, Subway
Lodg	W: Best Western
Other	E: Kroger, Lone Star/**LP** W: Auto & Diesel Service, Sunset Shores RV Park▲ , to Omega Farms RV Retreat▲
92	FM 830, Seven Coves Rd, Panorama Village, Willis
Lodg	W: to Seven Coves Resort
Other	W: Park on the Lake▲
91	League Line Rd, Conroe
Gas	E: Chevron W: Shell
Food	E: Subway, Wendy's W: Cracker Barrel
Lodg	E: Comfort Inn
Other	W: to Lake Conroe RV Resort & Marina▲
90	FM 3083, Texas Nursery Rd
Other	E: to Montgomery Co Airport✈
88	Lp 336, Wilson Rd, Conroe, to Cleveland, Navasota
FStop	E: 336 Shell
Gas	E: Mobil, Shamrock W: Chevron
Food	E: Arby's, McDonald's, Sonic, Subway W: KFC, Ryan's Grill
Other	E: Cinema, Goodyear, Kroger, Walgreen's W: Lowe's, Sam's Club, Wal-Mart sc to Lake Conroe RV & Camping Resort▲ to Havens Landing RV Resort▲
87	TX 105, FM 2854, Conroe
Gas	E: Shamrock W: Exxon, Texaco◊
Food	E: Burger King, CiCi's, Jack in the Box, Luther's BBQ, McDonald's, Outback Steak House, Village Inn W: Golden Corral, Luby's, Taco Bell
Other	E: ATMs, Auto Services, Kroger, Firestone, Museum, Sunset Truck & Auto, to Country Place RV Park▲ W: ATMs, Bank, Grocery, Home Depot, Kroger, Target, to Houston North KOA▲ (appr 13 mi)
85	Gladstell St, Conroe
Gas	E: Citgo◊

EXIT	
Gas	W: Shell◊
Lodg	W: Days Inn, Motel 6♥
Other	E: Auto Services
84	TX 75N, Lp 336, Frazier St
Gas	E: Conoco, Texaco W: Shell
Food	W: Pizza Hut, Taco Cabana
Lodg	E: Holiday Inn, Ramada Inn
Other	W: Albertson's, Kmart, Kroger, Tires
83	Creighton Rd, Camp Starke Rd
81	FM 1488, Conroe, to Magnolia, Hempstead
FStop	W: Valero #591
Gas	E: Citgo◊
Other	W: Camperland
80	Needham Rd (SB)
79	TX 242, College Park Dr, Needham
Gas	E: Texaco
Food	E: McDonald's/Texaco W: Popeye's, Willie's Grill
Lodg	W: Country Inn Suites
Other	E: Outdoors & More RV Rentals, Woodland Lakes RV Resort▲ W: Firestone, Wal-Mart sc
78	Tamina Rd, Research Forest Dr (SB)
Gas	E: Conoco, Texaco W: Shamrock
77	Woodland Pkwy, Robinson, Oak Ridge, Chateau Woods, Spring
Gas	E: Conoco◊, Texaco

EXIT	
Gas	W: Shamrock, Texaco
Food	E: Babin's Steakhouse, Hooters, Pancho's, Pappadeaux Seafood, Saltgrass Steak house W: Benihana, BlackEyed Pea, ChikFilA, Luby's, Romano's, Outback Steakhouse
Lodg	E: Budget Inn W: Comfort Inn, Days Inn, Hampton Inn, Homewood Suites, La Quinta Inn♥
Med	E: + Urgent Care W: + Memorial Hospital
Other	E: Home Depot, Sam's Club, Walgreen's, Office Depot, Police Dept W: Best Buy, Target, Woodlands Mall
76	Research Forest Dr, Tamina Rd (SB)
Gas	E: Chevron◊, Conoco, Coastal, Shamrock, Texaco W: Exxon, Shell, Texaco
Food	E: Long John Silver, Luther's BBQ, Pancho's Mex, Red Lobster W: Carrabba's, Chili's, El Chico, IHOP, Landry's Seafood, Kyoto, Olive Garden, Sweet Tomato, Starbucks, TGI Friday
Lodg	W: Courtyard, Drury Inn, Hilton Garden Inn, Marriott, Residence Inn
Med	W: + Memorial Hospital
Other	W: ATMs, Banks, Auto Services, Cinema 17, Woodlands Mall
76B	Woodlands Pkwy, Spring (NB)
Gas	E: Shamrock W: Shell
Other	E: Auto Services, Police Dept W: FedEx Kinko's, Goodyear, Woodlands Mall, Sunshare RV
76A	Oakwood Dr (NB)
73	Rayford Rd, Sawdust Rd, Spring
TStop	W: Sunmart #116/Mobil
Gas	E: Conoco, Shell W: Shell
Food	E: Golden China, Jack in the Box, Mario's Mex Rest, McDonald's, Sonic W: FastFood/Sunmart, Cajun, Grandy's, Sam's Café, Sweet Bella, Subway
Lodg	E: Hawthorn Suites, Holiday Inn Express W: Crossland Economy Studios, Red Roof Inn♥
Other	E: ATMs, AutoZone, Auto Services, Bank, Firestone, O'Reilly, UPS Store, Vet♥, to Rayford Crossing RV Resort▲ W: ATMs, Banks, FedEx Kinko's, HEB, Goodyear, Kroger, Auto Services
73A	Frontage Rd, Hardy Toll Rd (SB)
72	Frontage Rd, Spring
Other	W: Spring Oaks RV & MH Park▲
70B	Spring-Stuebner Rd, Spring
Other	W: Spring Oaks RV & MH Park▲
70A	Louetta Rd, Spring Cypress Rd, FM 2920, Spring, to Tomball
Gas	E: Exxon W: Chevron, Shell

Page 218 ◊ = Regular Gas Stations with Diesel ▲ = RV Friendly Locations ♥ = Pet Friendly Locations
RED PRINT SHOWS LARGE VEHICLE PARKING/ACCESS ON SITE OR NEARBY BROWN PRINT SHOWS CAMPGROUNDS/RV PARKS

EXIT		TEXAS
	Food	E: McDonald's, Pizza Hut, Wendy's W: Burger King, Taco Bell, Whataburger
	Other	E: Old Town Spring Shopping, **Wal-Mart sc**, Splashtown, Tourist Info, Walgreen's, **Bates Motorhomes**, **Vaughn's RV** W: to David Wayne Hooks Memorial Airport✈, to **Corral MH & RV Park of Tomball▲**, to **Burns RV Park▲**
68		Cypresswood Dr, Creekford Dr, Holzwarth Rd, Spring
	Gas	E: Texaco◆ W: Chevron
	Food	E: Burger King, Pizza Hut/Taco Bell W: Denny's, Jack in the Box, Popeye's
	Lodg	W: Motel 6♥
	Other	E: Albertson's, Kroger, WalMart SC W: Home Depot, Lowe's, Office Depot, PetCo♥, Target, Walgreen's, **Texan RV**, **Hornet Campers**
66		FM 1960, Houston, to Humble
	Gas	E: Chevron, RaceTrac, Shell W: Chevron, Exxon, Shell, Star Mart
	Food	E: Jack in the Box, Potato Patch Rest, Pancho's, Popeye's W: Bennigan's, Chili's, Grandy's, IHOP, Luby's, Luther's BBQ, McDonald's, Outback Steakhouse, Pizza Hut, Red Lobster, Steak & Ale, Subway
	Lodg	E: Days Inn W: Best Value Inn, Comfort Suites, Emerald Inn, La Quinta♥, Studio 6
	Med	W: + Houston Northwest Medical Center
	Other	E: Auto Dealers, **Lonestar RV Sales**, to George Bush Int'l Airport✈, PetSmart♥ W: Auto Dealers, ATMs, Banks, Kroger, Auto Services, NTB, Randall's, UPS Store
64		Richey Rd, Houston
	TStop	W: **Flying J Travel Plaza #5094/Conoco** (Scales)
	Gas	W: GasMart
	Food	E: Café, Pappasito's Cantina W: Rest/FastFood/FJ TP, Church's, **Cracker Barrel**, Jack in the Box, Joe's Crab Shack, Saltgrass Steakhouse, Whataburger
	Lodg	E: Holiday Inn, Lexington Hotel Suites W: Best Value Inn, La Quinta Inn♥
	Other	E: Sam's Club, Tires W: Laundry/WiFi/RVDump/LP/FJ TP, U-Haul, **Cliff Jones RV**
63		Airtex Blvd, Rankin Rd, Houston
	FStop	E: Sunmart #110/Mobil
	Gas	W: Chevron, RaceTrac
	Food	W: **Cracker Barrel**, Joe's Crab Shack, McDonald's, Saltgrass Steakhouse, Zio's Italian, Whataburger
	Lodg	W: Best Western, Guest House
	Other	E: **Lone Star RV** W: Celebration Station, **De Montrond RV**
62		Rankin Rd, Kuykendahl Rd
	FStop	E: Sunmart #190/Mobil
	Gas	W: Shell
	Food	W: Captain Seafood, Sonic
	Lodg	E: Executive Inn Express, Scottish Inn♥ W: Riata Inn, Sun Suites
	Other	W: Auto Dealers
61		Greens Rd, Houston
	Food	E: IHOP, Jack in the Box, McDonald's, Monterrey's W: Burger King, Luby's Cafeteria

EXIT		TEXAS
	Lodg	E: Days Inn, Wyndham W: Comfort Inn
	Other	E: Circuit City, Greenspoint Mall
60D		Beltway 8E, Houston (NB)
	Lodg	E: Travelodge
60C		Beltway 8E, Houston (SB)
60B		Beltway 8, Sam Houston Toll W (SB) TX 525, Aldine Bender Rd (NB)
	Other	E: Greenspoint Mall
60A		W Dyna Dr, Aldine Bender Rd, N Belt Dr E, Beltway 8 (NB)
	Other	E: **Red Dot RV Park▲**, **Central Houston KOA/LP/RVDump▲** W: Best Buy, Office Depot, WalMart SC
60		Bell Tollway 8, Intercontinental Airport, Sam Houston Tollway
59		West Rd, Blue Bell Rd
	Gas	E: Exxon, Shell W: Exxon
	Food	E: Burger King, Denny's, Long John Silver, McDonald's, Michoccan Mex Rest, Pappas Rest, Pizza Hut, Wendy's W: Chili's, Jalisco's, McDonald's, Starbucks Taco Bell, Whataburger
	Lodg	E: America's Best Value Inn Motel W: Best Western
	Other	E: Carwash/Shell, Firestone, NTB W: Best Buy, Discount Tire, Kmart, Office Depot, Pep Boys, Penske, Radio Shack, Walgreen's, **Wal-Mart sc**

EXIT		TEXAS
57B		TX 249, W Mt Houston Rd
	Gas	E: Conoco◆, Exxon◆ W: Shell
	Food	E: McDonald's W: Checker's, KFC, Pizza Inn, Sonic
	Lodg	W: Holiday Inn, La Quinta Inn, Ramada Inn
	Other	E: Auto Service, Kroger, Enterprise, Tires W: CVS, Auto Dealer, Auto Services, Family Dollar
57A		Gulf Bank Rd, Houston
	FStop	E: Sunmart #133/Mobil
	Lodg	E: HiWay Inn W: Days Inn
	Other	E: **Holiday World RV**, Discount Tire W: Enterprise RAC, Auto Dealers
56C		W Canino Rd (NB)
56B		Spur 261, Shepherd Dr, Little York Rd (SB)
	Gas	W: Shell
	Food	W: Denny's, Luby's, McDonald's
	Lodg	W: Gulf Wind Motel, Houston Motor Inn, Passport Inn
	Other	W: Auto Dealers, to Post Office
56A		Canino Rd, Houston (NB)
	Other	E: **Holiday World RV**, PJ Trailers, Big Tex Trailers W: Auto Dealers, Auto Services
55B		Rittenhouse St, W Little York Rd (NB)
	Gas	E: Chevron W: Shell
	Food	E: China Border, Sam's BBQ, Whataburger W: Captain D's, Denny's, KFC, Popeye's
	Lodg	W: Best Value Inn, Econo Lodge
	Other	W: Harley Davidson, US Post Office
55A		Rittenhouse St, Parker Rd, Yale St
	TStop	E: Sunmart #119/Mobil
	Gas	E: Texaco
	Food	E: McDonald's
	Lodg	E: Olympic Motel W: Guest Motel, Town Inn
	Med	E: + Columbia Medical Center
	Other	E: Auto Services, Advance Auto, Grocery, **Atlas Supply of TX** W: Auto Services, Walgreen's
54		Tidwell Rd, Houston
	Gas	E: Exxon, Mobil, Shell W: Shell, Chevron
	Food	E: Aunt Bea's, Pancho's, Taco Cabana W: Starbucks
	Lodg	W: Scottish Inn, Southwind Motel, Sundown Inn
	Other	E: Big Lots, Family Dollar, Propane/LP
53		Airline Dr, Victoria Dr
	Gas	E: Chevron, Texaco W: Conoco
	Lodg	W: Villa Provencial Motor Inn
	Other	E: Northline Shopping Center
52B		Crosstimbers St
	Gas	E: Shell, Texaco◆ W: Chevron, Exxon
	Food	E: Burger King, China Inn, Denny's, Hungry Farmer BBQ, Jack in the Box, KFC, Pizza Hut, McDonald's, Pappas BBQ, Sonic W: Monterey's, Wendy's, Whataburger
	Lodg	W: Econo Lodge, Luxury Inn, Palace Inn, Star Inn, Texan Inn
	TServ	W: **Davenport Trucking & Wrecker**
	Other	E: Northline Mall, Auto Services W: Auto Services, **Felton's RV Services**

◆ = Regular Gas Stations with Diesel   ▲ = RV Friendly Locations   ♥ = Pet Friendly Locations

RED PRINT SHOWS LARGE VEHICLE PARKING/ACCESS ON SITE OR NEARBY   BROWN PRINT SHOWS CAMPGROUNDS/RV PARKS

Interstate 45 N/S

EXIT		TEXAS
52A		**Frontage Rd**
	Lodg	W: Road Runner, Northline Inn
(51)		**Jct I-610**
50		**Cavalcade St, Patton St (SB)**
	TStop	E: Pilot Travel Center #383 (Scales)
	Gas	E: Exxon, Shamrock, Star Mart
	Lodg	W: Astro Inn
	Tserv	E: Alg Truck & Trailer Repair
	Other	E: Auto Services
		W: Auto Services
50B		**Cavalcade St (NB)**
50A		**Patton St, Houston (NB)**
	TStop	E: Pilot Travel Center #383 (Scales)
	Gas	E: Citgo
	Food	E: Wendy's/Pilot TC
	TWash	E: Pilot TC
	Other	E: Laundry/WiFi/Pilot TC
49B		**N Main St, Houston Ave, Pecore St**
	Gas	W: Exxon◊, Texaco
	Food	W: KFC, McDonald's, Subway
49A		**Quitman St, Houston Ave**
(48AB)		**Jct I-10, W-SanAntonio, E-Beaumont**
(48B)		**Jct I-10W, to San Antonio (NB, Left exit)**
(48A)		**Jct I-10E, to Beaumont (SB, Left exit)**
47D		**Heiner St, Houston Ave, Dallas St, Allen Pkwy, Pierce Ave**
	Other	W: Police Dept
47C		**McKinney St, Bagby St, Smith St (SB)**
47B		**Houston Ave, Allen Pkwy E**
	Other	E: City Hall
47A		**Allen Pkwy W (Both dir, Exit Left)**
46AB		**US 59, W- Lake Jackson, E-Freeport**
46B		**US 59W, to US 288, to Lake Jackson (NB, Left exit)**
	Med	W: + to Texas Medical Center
	Other	W: to Rice Univ & Stadium, Houston Zoo
46A		**US 59E, to Freeport (SB, Left ex)**
	Med	E: + St Joseph Hospital
	Other	E: to George Brown Convention Center
45A		**Scott St, Cullen Bvd, Spur 5 (SB)**
	Other	W: to TX Southern Univ
45		**Cullen Blvd, Scott St (NB)**
44C		**Cullen Blvd, Spur 5, Lockwood Dr, Elgin St (SB)**
	Other	W: Univ of Houston, Robertson Stadium, Hofheinz Pavilion
44B		**Calhoun St, Spur 5**
44A		**Lockwood Dr, Elgin St (NB)**
43A		**Telephone Rd, to US 90A**
43B		**Tellepsen St (NB)**
42		**US 90 Alt, Wayside Dr, Spanish Tr**
	Gas	E: Stop 'N Go
		W: Exxon
	Food	W: McDonald's
	Lodg	E: Days Inn, Gulf Freeway Inn
41B		**Griggs Rd, Broad St**
	Gas	W: Shamrock
	Lodg	E: Houtex Inn, Red Carpet Inn
	Other	W: Home Depot, Kmart, Office Depot, Mall, Lowe's, Auto Services

EXIT		TEXAS
41A		**Woodridge Dr**
	Gas	E: Shell
	Food	E: Denny's, McDonald's
		W: Brisket House, IHOP, Pappas BBQ
	Other	W: Auto Services, Home Depot, Mall
(40)		**Jct I-610**
(40C)		**Jct I-610W (NB, Left exit)**
(40B)		**Jct I-610E (fr SB, Left exit), TX 35 (SB)**
	Other	E: to Port of Houston Industrial Complex
40A		**Frontage Rd, Broadway St (NB)**
39		**Park Place Blvd, Broadway St**
	Gas	E: Valero
		W: Quick Mart
	Food	E: Jack in the Box, Taco House, Wendy's
38B		**Bellfort Ave, TX 3, Monroe Rd (Gas, food, Lodg W to Broadway St)**
38		**TX 3, Monroe Rd**
	Gas	E: Chevron◊, Shell
		W: Chevron, Shell, Texaco◊
	Food	E: Jack in the Box, Kip's, Lone Wolf Café, Luby's, Luther's BBQ, Wendy's
		W: Subway, Ninfa's Mexican
	Lodg	W: Best Western, Holiday Inn, Smile Inn, Super 8, Travel Inn
36		**College Ave, Airport Blvd**
	FStop	W: Airport Gas Mart
	Gas	E: Shell, Shamrock
		W: Exxon, Shell
	Food	E: Burger House, City Café, DQ, Smokey Joe's, Waffle House
		W: Damon's, Denny's, Taco Cabana

EXIT		TEXAS
	Lodg	E: Best Value Inn, Roadway Inn
		W: Baymont Inn, Comfort Inn, Country Suites, Drury Inn, Hampton Inn, Holiday Inn, Marriott, Motel 6♥, Red Roof Inn♥, Regency Inn, Springhill Suites
	Other	E: ATMs, Auto Services, Banks, Firestone, Food City, Walgreen's, RV Repair, to Just Passin Thru RV Park▲
		W: Auto Repairs, Auto Rentals, Lone Star RV Sales, Wm P Hobby Airport✈
35		**Clearwood Dr, Edgebrook Dr**
	Gas	E: Chevron, Exxon, RaceTrac
		W: Shell
	Food	E: Burger King, China One, Grandy's, Jack in the Box, Subway, Waffle House
		W: McDonald's, Pizza Hut
	Lodg	E: Airport Inn
		W: La Quinta Inn♥
34		**Almeda Genoa Rd, S Shaver Rd**
	Gas	E: Conoco
		W: Chevron, Murphy, Shamrock
	Food	W: Burger King, Wendy's
		W: McDonald's, Taco Bell, Wendy's
	Lodg	W: Post Oak Inn, Scottish Inn
	Other	E: Terry Vaughn RV's
		W: Almeda Mall, Best Buy, Dollar Tree, Kmart, NTB, Target, Holiday World RV
33		**Fuqua St, Houston**
	Food	E: Chili's, Luby's, Chili's, Mexico Lindo, Olive Garden, TGI Friday
		W: Brown Sugar BBQ, Casa Ole', BlackEyed Pea, Golden Corral, Joe's Crab Shack, Outback Steakhouse, Steak & Ale
	Other	E: Auto Dealers, Comedy Club, Cinema
		W: Almeda Mall, Sam's Club, Auto Services
(32)		**Sam Houston Tollway**
31		**FM 2553, Scarsdale Blvd**
	Gas	W: Exxon, Shell
	Food	W: DQ, McDonald's
	Med	W: + Memorial Hospital
	Other	W: San Jacinto College
30		**FM 1959, Dixie Farm Rd, Houston**
	Gas	E: Conoco◊, Shell◊
		W: RaceWay
	Food	E: Subway
	Lodg	E: Suburban Extended Stay
	Other	E: Ellington Field✈
		W: Lone Star RV Sales
29		**FM 2351, Choate Rd, Friendswood**
27		**El Dorado Blvd, Webster**
	Gas	E: Texaco, Shamrock, Valero
	Food	E: DQ, Jack in the Box
		W: Tx Roadhouse, Whataburger
	Other	E: Auto & Tire Services
		W: Sam's Club, Wal-Mart sc
26		**Bay Area Blvd, Webster**
	Gas	E: Exxon, Shell
		W: Chevron, Shell
	Food	E: Angelo's Pizza & Pasta, Kettle, Lake Garden Chinese, Outback Steak House, Pappasito's, Red Lobster, Ryan's Grill, Romano's Macaroni Grill, Starbucks
		W: Bennigan's, Burger King, Denny's, McDonald's, Olive Garden, On the Border Café, Rico's, Steak & Ale
	Lodg	E: Best Western, Comfort Suites, Hampton Inn, InTown Suites, La Quinta Inn♥,

◊ = Regular Gas Stations with Diesel   ▲ = RV Friendly Locations   ♥ = Pet Friendly Locations
RED PRINT SHOWS LARGE VEHICLE PARKING/ACCESS ON SITE OR NEARBY   BROWN PRINT SHOWS CAMPGROUNDS/RV PARKS

EXIT		TEXAS
	Med	E: + Columbia Medical Center, + Clear Lake Regional Medical Center
	Other	E: ATMs, Banks, Best Buy, FedEx Kinko's, Cinema, Lowe's, Univ of Houston/CL W: Baybrook Mall, ATMs, Banks, Office Depot, PetSmart♥, Target
25		FM 528, NASA Rd 1, Webster
	Gas	E: Express Mart, Texaco
	Food	E: Bayou Steak House, Chili's, CiCi's, Saltgrass Steak House, Waffle House, Indian Rest, Durango's Mexican Rest W: Cajun Seafood, DQ, Hooters, Subway
	Lodg	E: Days Inn, Howard Johnson Express, Motel 6♥
	Med	E: + St John Hospital
	Other	E: ATMs, Big Lots, Cinemark 18, Dollar 8 Cinema, Home Depot, Kmart, Lyndon B Johnson Space Center, Office Depot W: Challenger Seven Memorial Park, Wal-Mart, Bay RV Park▲
23		FM 518, W Main St, League City
	Gas	E: RaceTrac, Shell◆, Star Mart W: Exxon
	Food	E: Burger King, Jack in the Box, KFC, Grand Buffet, Kelley's Country Cookin, Pancho's Mex Buffet, Sonic, Subway W: Cracker Barrel, McDonald's, Taco Bell, Village Pizza, Waffle House, Wendy's
	Lodg	W: Super 8
	Other	E: Auto Services, Kroger, Eckerd W: Auto Services, ATMs, Banks, Space Center RV Resort▲
22		Calder Dr, Brittany Bay Blvd, TX 96 (Access #23 Serv via Caulder Dr N)
	Other	E: Houston Gulf Airport✈ W: Visitors Center, Safari MH Comm▲
20		FM 646, to FM 517, Santa Fe, Bacliff
	Gas	W: Shamrock◆, Chevron
	Other	E: to Green Caye RV Park▲ W: PetCo♥, UPS Store, Vet♥
19		FM 517, Main St, Pine Dr, Hughes Rd, Dickinson
	Gas	E: Shell W: Exxon, Star Mart
	Food	E: Pizza Inn, Mexican Rest, Village Pizza W: KFC, Kettle, McDonald's, Pizza Hut, Subway, Taco Bell, Wendy's
	Lodg	W: Days Inn
	Other	E: Enterprise, HEB, Bay Colony RV Resort▲, Dues RV Center, Adventure Out RV Park▲, to Via Bayou RV Park▲ W: Kroger, Auto Rental
17		Holland Rd, to FM 646, Dickinson
16		FM 1764, Texas City (SB)
	Other	E: Mall of the Mainland, (Access #15 Serv)
15		FM 1764, FM 2004, La Marque
	Gas	E: Shell W: Mobil, Shell
	Food	E: China One, Gringo's, Jack in the Box, Olive Garden W: Sonic, Subway, Waffle House, Whataburger, Wendy's
	Lodg	E: Fairfield Inn
	Other	E: Auto Dealers, Lowe's, Mall of the Mainlar De Montrond Motorhomes W: Gulf Greyhound Park, Wal-Mart sc
13		Delaney Rd, to FM 1764, FM 1765
	Gas	E: Chevron

EXIT		TEXAS
	Food	E: Kelley's Rest, Village Pizza
	Lodg	W: Grand Suites, Super 8
	Med	E: + Mainland Medical Center
	Other	E: Mall of the Mainland W: Gulf Greyhound Park, Destination Luna RV Campground▲
12		FM 1765, La Marque
	Gas	E: Circle T Quick Stop W: Shell
	Food	E: Domino's, Jack in the Box, Sonic
	Lodg	W: Travel Inn
	Other	W: U-Haul, Destination Luna RV Campground▲
11		Vauthier St, La Marque
10		FM 519, Main St, Lake Rd
	FStop	W: Shoppers Mart #5/Shell
	Gas	E: Valero
	Food	E: McDonald's, Rocky's
	Other	E: MCH Wrecker Service, Auto & Truck Repair, to TX City Industrial Complex W: Oasis Resort & RV Park▲, to Gulf Holiday RV Park▲, Sunset RV Park▲, Highland Bayou RV Park▲, Lily's by the Bay RV Resort▲, Bob's Mobile RV Service
9		Frontage Rd (SB)
8		Frontage Rd, Bayou Rd (NB)
7		TX 146, TX 6, TX 3, to Texas City, Hitchcock (SB)
7C		TX 146, TX 6, TX 3, to Texas City, Hitchcock (NB)
7B		TX 6, Hitchcock (NB, Left exit)
7A		TX 146, TX 3, Texas City (NB)
6		Frontage Rd (SB)
5		Frontage Rd
4		Tiki Dr, Village Tiki Island, Galveston
	Gas	E: Tiki Island Store/Conoco◆
1C		Ave J, Harborside Dr, Teichman Rd, 77th St, Port Industrial Rd, Galveston Island
	FStop	E: Island Food Mart/Shell
	TStop	E: Harborside Food Mart/Citgo
	Gas	E: Exxon
	Food	E: FastFood/RVDump/Harborside FM W: American Grill, Clary's Seafood Rest
	Lodg	E: Motel 6♥, Howard Johnson
1B		Ave J, 71st St, 61st St
1A		Spur 342, 61st St (Cont on TX 87 for serv)
	Gas	E: E-Z Mart W: Exxon, Shell, Racetrac
	Food	E: Denny's W: 61st St Diner, Leon's BBQ, Taco Bell
	Lodg	W: Days Inn
	Other	E: Enterprise, Home Depot, Target W: ATMs, Banks, Auto Services, Office Depot, Walgreen's, Scholes Field✈, to Bayou Haven RV Resort▲

(CENTRAL TIME ZONE)
(I-45 begins/ends on TX 87 in Galveston)

🕮 **TEXAS**

Begin Northbound I-45 from Galveston, TX to Dallas, TX.

◆ = Regular Gas Stations with Diesel   ▲ = RV Friendly Locations   ♥ = Pet Friendly Locations

RED PRINT SHOWS LARGE VEHICLE PARKING/ACCESS ON SITE OR NEARBY   BROWN PRINT SHOWS CAMPGROUNDS/RV PARKS

INTERSTATE 49 S

EXIT	LOUISIANA

Begin Southbound I-49 from Shreveport, LA to Lafayette, LA. (I-10, Exit #103 and I-20, Exit #17)

LOUISIANA
(CENTRAL TIME ZONE)

(206) Jct I-20, E - Monroe, W - Dallas

205 Kings Hwy, Shreveport
- Gas: W: Valero◊
- Food: E: McDonald's, Piccadilly's
  W: Burger King, Long John Silver, Subway, Taco Bell
- Med: W: + LSU Health Sciences Center
- Other: E: Mall St Vincent, ATMs, Banks

203 Hollywood Ave, Pierremont Rd (Gas/Food/Lodg 2mi W)
- Gas: W: Fina
- Other: W: to I-20, Shreveport Reg'l Airport✈

202 LA 511E, 70th St
- Gas: E: Raceway
  W: Circle K, Chevron
- Food: W: Sonic
- Other: W: Auto Services, Tires

201 LA 3132, to Dallas, Texarkana

199 LA 526, Bert Kouns Industrial Loop
- Gas: E: Chevron◊, Citgo, Exxon, RaceWay
  W: Express, Shell
- Food: E: Arby's/Chevron, Burger King, KFC, Taco Bell, Wendy's
  W: McDonald's
- Lodg: E: Comfort Inn
- Other: E: Home Depot

191 LA 16, LA 3276, Stonewall, Frierson

186 LA 175, to Frierson, Kingston
- TStop: E: Relay Station #3/Exxon (Scales)
- Food: E: Rest/Relay Stn
- Other: E: WiFi/Casino/Relay Stn

177 LA 509, Mansfield, Carmel
- TStop: E: Eagles Truck Stop/BP
- Food: E: Rest/Eagles TS
- Other: E: Laundry/Eagles TS

172 US 84, to Mansfield, Grand Bayou

169 Asseff Rd

162 US 371, LA 177, Mansfield, Pleasant Hill, Coushatta, Evelyn

155 LA 174, Robeline, Ajax, Lake End
- TStop: W: Spaulding Truck Stop
- Other: W: WiFi/Spaulding TS, Ajax Country Livin at I-49 RV Park▲

148 LA 485, to Allen, Powhatan

142 LA 547, Posey Rd

138 LA 6, Many, Natchitoches
- TStop: W: Shop-A-Lott #10/Chevron
- Gas: E: BP, Exxon, RaceWay
  W: Casey's, Texaco◊
- Food: E: Shoney's, Wendy's
  W: FastFood/ShopALot, Burger King, Huddle House, McDonald's
- Lodg: E: Best Western, Holiday Inn Express, Super 8
  W: Comfort Inn, Econo Lodge, Hampton Inn
- Med: E: + Hospital
- Other: E: to Wal-Mart sc, Albertson's, to NW State Univ, Natchitoches Reg'l Airport✈
  W: Laundry/RVDump/ShopAlott TS, Nakatosh RV Park▲, Dogwood Ridge Camper Park▲

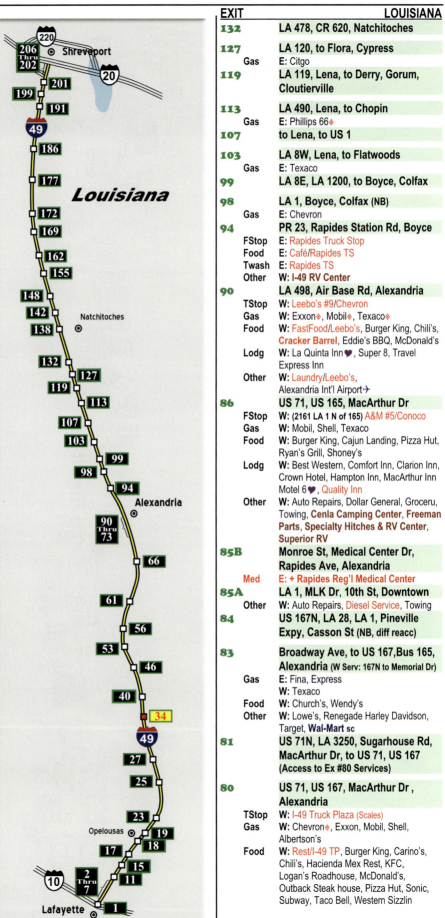

EXIT	LOUISIANA

132 LA 478, CR 620, Natchitoches

127 LA 120, to Flora, Cypress
- Gas: E: Citgo

119 LA 119, Lena, to Derry, Gorum, Cloutierville

113 LA 490, Lena, to Chopin
- Gas: E: Phillips 66◊

107 to Lena, to US 1

103 LA 8W, Lena, to Flatwoods
- Gas: E: Texaco

99 LA 8E, LA 1200, to Boyce, Colfax

98 LA 1, Boyce, Colfax (NB)
- Gas: E: Chevron

94 PR 23, Rapides Station Rd, Boyce
- FStop: E: Rapides Truck Stop
- Food: E: Café/Rapides TS
- Twash: E: Rapides TS
- Other: W: I-49 RV Center

90 LA 498, Air Base Rd, Alexandria
- TStop: W: Leebo's #9/Chevron
- Gas: W: Exxon◊, Mobil◊, Texaco◊
- Food: W: FastFood/Leebo's, Burger King, Chili's, Cracker Barrel, Eddie's BBQ, McDonald's
- Lodg: W: La Quinta Inn♥, Super 8, Travel Express Inn
- Other: W: Laundry/Leebo's, Alexandria Int'l Airport✈

86 US 71, US 165, MacArthur Dr
- FStop: W: (2161 LA 1 N of 165) A&M #5/Conoco
- Gas: W: Mobil, Shell, Texaco
- Food: W: Burger King, Cajun Landing, Pizza Hut, Ryan's Grill, Shoney's
- Lodg: W: Best Western, Comfort Inn, Clarion Inn, Crown Hotel, Hampton Inn, MacArthur Inn, Motel 6♥, Quality Inn
- Other: W: Auto Repairs, Dollar General, Grocery, Towing, Cenla Camping Center, Freeman Parts, Specialty Hitches & RV Center, Superior RV

85B Monroe St, Medical Center Dr, Rapides Ave, Alexandria
- Med: E: + Rapides Reg'l Medical Center

85A LA 1, MLK Dr, 10th St, Downtown
- Other: W: Auto Repairs, Diesel Service, Towing

84 US 167N, LA 28, LA 1, Pineville Expy, Casson St (NB, diff reacc)

83 Broadway Ave, to US 167, Bus 165, Alexandria (W Serv: 167N to Memorial Dr)
- Gas: E: Fina, Express
  W: Texaco
- Food: W: Church's, Wendy's
- Other: W: Lowe's, Renegade Harley Davidson, Target, Wal-Mart sc

81 US 71N, LA 3250, Sugarhouse Rd, MacArthur Dr, to US 71, US 167 (Access to Ex #80 Services)

80 US 71, US 167, MacArthur Dr, Alexandria
- TStop: W: I-49 Truck Plaza (Scales)
- Gas: W: Chevron◊, Exxon, Mobil, Shell, Albertson's
- Food: W: Rest/I-49 TP, Burger King, Carino's, Chili's, Hacienda Mex Rest, KFC, Logan's Roadhouse, McDonald's, Outback Steak house, Pizza Hut, Sonic, Subway, Taco Bell, Western Sizzlin

◊ = Regular Gas Stations with Diesel   ▲ = RV Friendly Locations   ♥ = Pet Friendly Locations
RED PRINT SHOWS LARGE VEHICLE PARKING/ACCESS ON SITE OR NEARBY   BROWN PRINT SHOWS CAMPGROUNDS/RV PARKS

N I-49 LOUISIANA

EXIT	LOUISIANA
	Lodg W: Best Western, Days Inn, Hampton Inn, Holiday Inn, Super 8
	TServ W: to Timmons Int'l
	Other W: Albertson's, ATMs, Banks, Cinema, Alexandria Mall, PetSmart♥, Sam's Club, U-Haul
73	**LA 3265, PR 22, Lecompte, to US 165, Woodworth**
	FStop W: Tiger Fuel Stop/Exxon
	Food W: FastFood/Tiger FS
	Other W: to Indian Creek Rec Area▲, to Claiborne Range Military Res
66	**LA 112, Forest Hill, Lecompte**
	Gas W: Leebo's/Chevron◊
	Food W: Burger King/Leebo's
61	**US 167, Cheneyville, to Turkey Creek, Meeker**
56	**LA 181, Cheneyville**
53	**LA 115, McArthur St, Bunkie** (Gas/Food/Lodg/Casinos/Etc 4mi+ E)
	TStop E: Sammy's Truck Auto Plaza/Chevron
	Food E: Rest/Sammy's TAP
	Other E: Laundry/Casino/WiFi/Sammy's TAP
46	**LA 106, Bunkie, to St Landry**
	Other W: to Chicot State Park▲
40	**LA 29, Ville Platte** (Addtl Serv 8mi W)
	TStop E: Tiger Trax #7/Exxon
	Food E: Rest/FastFood/Tiger Trax
	Other E: Laundry/Casino/Tiger Trax
(34)	**Grand Prairie Rest Area** (Both dir) (RR, Phones, Picnic, RVDump)
27	**LA 10, LA 182, Washington, Lebeau**
25	**LA 103, Washington, Port Barre**
	Gas W: Citgo, Mobil
23	**US 167, LA 744, Opelousas, to Ville Platte**
	TStop E: I-49 Truck Stop/Texaco, Quarters Travel Plaza/Chevron
	W: 167 Truck Stop/Exxon
	Food E: Rest/I-49 TS, Subway/Quarters TP
	W: Rest/FastFood/167 TS
	Lodg W: Best Value Inn, Days Inn
	Other E: Laundry/I-49 TS, Casino/Laundry/Quarters TP
	W: Casino/Laundry/167 TS
19	**US 190, Opelousas, Baton Rouge** (SB)
	TStop W: (12120 190W) Opelousas Truck Stop/Conoco
	Gas W: Exxon◊, Mobil
	Food W: Rest/Op TS
	Tires W: Tires/Op TS
	Med W: + Opelousas General Hospital
	Other W: Laundry/Op TS, Auto Repairs, Tires, ATMs, Banks, Lowe's, Museums, Tourist Info, St Landry Parrish Airport✈
19A	**US 190E, to Baton Rouge** (NB)
19B	**US 190W, Opelousas** (NB)
	Gas W: Mobil, Tiger Trax Exxon◊
	Food W: Blimpie
	Med W: + Hospital
18	**LA 31, Creswell Lane**
	FStop W: Valero
	Gas E: Murphy◊
	W: Chevron◊, Shell
	Food E: Casa Ole, Little Caesar's, Subway, Rest/Hol Inn

EXIT	LOUISIANA
	Food W: Burger King, McDonald's, Pizza Hut, Ryan's Grill, Subway, Taco Bell, Wendy's
	Lodg E: Holiday Inn
	W: Best Value Inn, Days Inn
	Other E: Auto Dealer, Evangeline Downs Racetrack & Casino, Dollar Tree, Home Depot, Wal-Mart sc
	W: Auto Dealer, Family Dollar, Firestone, CVS, Walgreen's, Opelousas City Park▲
17	**Judson Walsh Dr, Opelousas**
	Gas E: Texaco◊
	Other W: Goodyear
15	**Harry Guilbeau Rd, to LA 182**
	Lodg W: Best Value Inn
11	**LA 93, Sunset, Grand Coteau**
	TStop E: Beau Chere Truck Stop/Chevron, USA Speedtrac
	Gas E: Citgo◊, Exxon◊
	Food E: Rest/FastFood/Beau Chere TS, Gram's Country Kitchen, Fast-Food/USA
	W: Subway
	Lodg E: Sunset Motor Inn
	Other E: Laundry/Beau Chene TS, Laundry/USA, USA Raceway
	W: Dollar General, Family Dollar, Acadiana Wilderness Campground▲
7	**LA 182**
	Lodg W: Acadian Motor Inn
	Other W: Premier RV, Primeaux RV
4	**LA 726, Carencro**
	Gas E: Depot
	W: Chevron◊, Citgo, Texaco◊
	Food W: Burger King, McDonald's, Popeye's
	Lodg W: Economy Inn
	TServ W: Mack/Kenworth
	Other E: Auto & Engine Service
	W: ATMs, Banks, Auto Services, U-Haul, Foreman RV
2	**LA 98, Gloria Switch Rd**
	Gas E: Citgo, Chevron◊, Pit Stop
	W: Shell
	Food E: Blimpie/Citgo, Deli/Chevron, Chili's, IHOP, Wendy's
	W: Church's, Domino's, Mexican Rest
	Other E: Lowe's, Stevens RV Center, to Bayou Wilderness RV Resort▲, Poches Fish-n-Camp▲ (app 9mi)
	W: Prejeans Auto & Truck Repair
1B	**Point Des Mouton Rd, Lafayette**
	Gas E: Exxon◊, Star Mart Shell
	Food E: Subway/Shell, Burger King
	Lodg E: Motel 6♥, Plantation Motor Inn
	Other E: Winn Dixie
	W: Budget, Stelly's Auto & Truck Repair
(1A)	**Jct I-10, W to Lake Charles, E to Baton Rouge**
	Gas S: Chevron◊, RaceTrac, Shell, Albertson's, Murphy
	Food S: Checker's, Kajun Kitchen, KFC, McDonald's, Pizza Hut, Shoney's, Taco Bell, Waffle House, Wendy's, Western Sizzlin'
	Lodg S: Best Western, Comfort Suites, Fairfield Inn, Holiday Inn, Jameson Inn, La Quinta Inn♥, Quality Inn, Super 8
	Med S: + Hospital
	Other S: Albertson's, Dollar General, Firestone, Home Depot, RiteAid, Wal-Mart sc

ⓘ LOUISIANA

Begin Northbound I-49 from Lafayette, LA to Shreveport, LA. (I-10, Exit #103 and I-20, Exit #17)

◊ = Regular Gas Stations with Diesel   ▲ = RV Friendly Locations   ♥ = Pet Friendly Locations
RED PRINT SHOWS LARGE VEHICLE PARKING/ACCESS ON SITE OR NEARBY   BROWN PRINT SHOWS CAMPGROUNDS/RV PARKS

EXIT	ILLINOIS
	Begin Southbound I-55 from Chicago, IL to New Orleans, LA.

ILLINOIS
(CENTRAL TIME ZONE)
(I-55 begins/ends on Lakeshore Dr/US 41)

295	US 41, Lakeshore Dr, Chicago
293D	**Martin Luther King Dr (NB)**
Gas	E: BP
Food	E: McDonald's
Med	E: + Mercy Hospital
Other	W: to Soldier Field, Museums, Aquarium
293C	**S State St (SB)**
Gas	E: Amoco
Food	E: McDonald's
Med	E: + Mercy Hospital
(293B)	**Jct I-90/94E, to Indiana**
293A	**Wentworth Rd, 22nd St, Cermak Rd, Chinatown**
(292B)	**Jct I-90/94W, to Chicago**
(292A)	**Jct I-90/94E, to Indiana**
292	**Stewart Ave, Archer Ave, I-90/94N (SB)**
290	**Damen Ave, Ashland Ave, Western Ave**
Gas	E: Marathon
Food	E: Burger King, Popeye's, Subway
TServ	E: Chicago Truck Center, Tony's Truck Service
Other	E: Dollar Tree
	W: Auto Services, Fleet Service, Truck & Auto Service
289	**California Ave (NB)**
FStop	E: Speedway #8315
Food	E: Subway/Speedway
Med	W: + St Anthony Hospital
288	**Kedzie Ave (SB, NB reacc)**
Gas	E: Citgo, Speedway
Food	E: Subway
287	**Pulaski Rd**
Gas	E: Mobil◇, Shell
Food	E: Burger King, Quiznos, Subway
TServ	W: American Reefer Service, Mensik Fleet Service
Other	E: Auto Services, Repairs, Towing, Grocery Target, Walgreen's
286	**IL 50, Cicero Ave, Chicago, Cicero**
FStop	E: Mansoor Citgo (4759 IL 50)
	W: Tuxedo Jctn (2 blks N Cicero)
Gas	E: BP, Marathon, Phillips 66
Food	E: McDonald's, Subway, Starbucks
Lodg	E: Sportsman Inn Motel
TServ	W: Fast Action Truck & Trailer, South Side Truck Service
Other	E: Family Dollar, to Chicago Midway Airport ✈
	W: Hawthorne Race Course, Sportman's Park, Chicago Motor Speedway, Auto & Tire Services, ATMs, Grocery
285	**Central Ave, Chicago, Cicero**
FStop	E: BP Connect #2705
Gas	E: T&C
	W: Citgo
Food	E: Burger King, Steak & Egger
TServ	E: International Truck, BJ Truck & Trailer Repair, E&D Truck Repair
Other	E: Auto Services

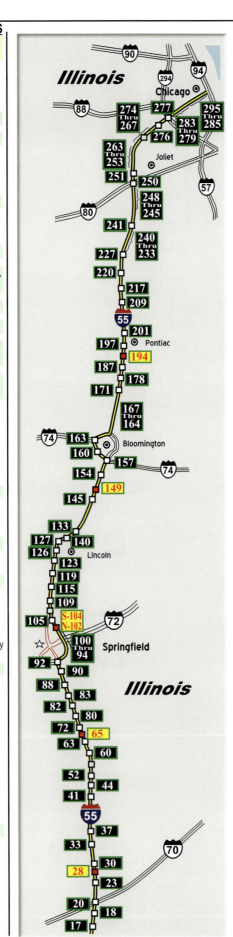

EXIT	ILLINOIS
283	**IL 43, Harlem Ave, Lyons**
Gas	E: Shell
	W: BP
Food	E: Arby's, Burger King, Subway
Other	W: Police Dept
282B	**IL 171W, Joliet Rd (NB)**
282A	**IL 171E, Archer Ave (NB)**
282	**IL 171, Archer Av, Joliet Rd (SB)**
FStop	E: JJ Peppers Marathon
Other	E: Amtrak
	W: General Motors ElectroMotive Plant, to Chicago Zoological Park
279B	**US 12N, US 20N, US 45N, LaGrange Rd, Joliet Rd**
Gas	W: BP, Mobil, Shell, Sam's
Food	W: Applebee's, Arby's, Boston Market, Burger King, KFC, Long John Silver, Lone Star Steakhouse, McDonald's, Pizza Hut, Popeye's, Subway, Taco Bell, Wendy's, White Castle
Lodg	W: Holiday Inn, Hampton Inn
Med	W: + to LaGrange Memorial Hospital
Other	W: Auto Services, Auto Dealer, ATMs, Banks, Best Buy, Circuit City, Grocery, Home Depot, Pep Boys, NTB, Rental Cars, Sam's Club, Target, Wal-Mart
279A	**US 12S, US 20S, to Archer Ave, to I-294 TOLL, S to Indiana**
(277B)	**Jct I-294 (TOLL), S-Indiana (NB)**
(277A)	**Jct I-294 (TOLL), N-Wisconsin**
276C	**Joliet Rd (NB, Left exit)**
276AB	**County Line Rd, Willowbrook**
Food	E: Max & Erma's, Subway
Lodg	E: Best Western, Extended Stay America, Marriott, Ramada Inn
	W: AmeriSuites
TServ	E: Freightliner of Chicago
Med	W: + Suburban Hospital
Other	E: Police Dept
274	**IL 83, Kingery Hwy**
Gas	E: Shell
	W: Mobil◇, Phillips 66, Shell
Food	W: Bakers Square, Burger King, Dunkin Donuts, Denny's, Little Caesar's
Lodg	E: Best Western
	W: Baymont Inn, Fairfield Inn, Holiday Inn, Red Roof Inn ♥
Other	W: Kmart, Target, Repairs, Towing, Tires, Police Dept
273AB	**Cass Ave, Darian**
Gas	W: Shell
Other	E: Argonne Nat'l Laboratory
271B	**Lemont Rd N, Downers Grove**
Gas	W: Shell
271A	**S Lemont Rd**
Lodg	E: Extended Stay America
(269)	**Jct I-355N (TOLL), Woodward Ave, West Suburbs**
(267)	**Weigh Station (NB)**
267	**IL 53, Bolingbrook, Romeoville**
TStop	E: PTP/Greater Chicago I-55 Auto Truck Plaza/BP (Scales)
Gas	E: AmocoBP, Citgo, Phillips 66
	W: Shell, Speedway◇
Food	E: Rest/I-55 ATP, Bob Evans, Bono's Rest, Escapades Rest, McDonald's

◇ = Regular Gas Stations with Diesel   ▲ = RV Friendly Locations   ♥ = Pet Friendly Locations
RED PRINT SHOWS LARGE VEHICLE PARKING/ACCESS ON SITE OR NEARBY   BROWN PRINT SHOWS CAMPGROUNDS/RV PARKS

EXIT		ILLINOIS
	Food	W: Arby's, Denny's, Family Square Rest, Golden Corral, Hardee's, IHOP, KFC, Pizza Hut, Popeye's, Subway, Wendy's, White Castle
	Lodg	E: La Quinta Inn ♥, Ramada Ltd, Super 8 W: AmericInn, Comfort Inn, Hampton Inn, Holiday Inn, Springhill Suites
	TWash	E: I-55 ATP
	TServ	E: NW Truck, I-55 ATP/Tires
	Med	W: + Hospital
	Other	E: Laundry/LP/I-55 ATP, Air Stream of Chicago, Home Depot, US Adventure RV W: Dollar General, Dollar Tree, Family Dollar, Goodyear, Grocery, Walgreen's, Wal-Mart, U-Haul, Camping World
263		Weber Rd, W Normantown Rd, W 127th St, Romeoville
	Gas	E: BP◊, Citgo, Gas City◊ W: Shell
	Food	E: Applebee's, Burger King, McDonald's, Popeye's, Quiznos, Subway, Starbucks W: Arby's, Cracker Barrel, Wendy's
	Lodg	E: Best Western W: Comfort Inn, Country Inn, Extended Stay America, Howard Johnson Express
	Other	E: Discount Tire, Grocery, Walgreen's W: CarWash/Shell, Home Depot, to Clow Int'l Airport✈
261		IL 126W, E Main St, Plainfield (SB exit, NB reaccess)
257		US 30, W Lincoln Hwy, Plainfield, Plainfield Rd, Joliet, Aurora
	TStop	W: Joliet I-55 Truck Stop/Clark (Scales)
	Gas	E: Citgo, Shell W: BP◊
	Food	E: Applebee's, Burger King, Hardee's, Lone Star Steakhouse, McDonald's, Pizza Hut, Red Lobster, Steak 'n Shake, Taco Bell, Texas Roadhouse, TGI Friday, Wendy's W: Rest/Subway/I-55 TS
	Lodg	E: Comfort Inn, Fairfield Inn, Hampton Inn, Holiday Inn Express, Motel 6 ♥, Super 8
	TWash	W: I-55 TS
	TServ	W: I-55 TS/Tires
	Other	E: ATMs, Banks, Best Buy, Circuit City, Discount Tire, Grocery, Home Depot, Kmart, Office Depot, PetSmart ♥, Pharmacy, Cinemark 10 & 8, Target, Westfield Louis Joliet Mall W: Laundry/WiFi/I-55 TS, Auto Services
253		US 52, W Jefferson St, Joliet, to Shorewood
	FStop	W: BP/Amoco Fuel Stop
	Gas	E: Citgo◊, Phillips 66, Shell
	Food	E: McDonald's, KFC, Pizza Hut, Wendy's W: Ali Baba's Rest, Burger King, Subway
	Lodg	E: Best Western, Best Value Inn, Wingate Inn
	Med	E: + Provena St Joseph Medical Center W: + Hospital
	Other	E: Rick's RV Center▲, Joliet Park District Airport✈, Joliet Memorial Stadium, Joliet Jr College
251		IL 59, Cottage St, Shorewood, Plainfield (NB exit, SB reacc)
(250AB)		Jct I-80, E-Toledo, W-Des Moines
248		US 6, W Eames St, Channahon Rd, Moriss, Joliet, Channahon

Personal Notes

EXIT		ILLINOIS
	TStop	E: Pilot Travel Center #473
	Gas	E: Citgo◊, Speedway W: BP
	Food	E: Subway/Pilot TC, Daylight Donuts, Quiznos W: McDonald's/BP
	Lodg	E: Manor House Motel
	Other	E: Radio Shack
247		CR 77, W Bluff Rd, Channahon
245		Arsenal Rd
	Other	E: Joliet Army Ammo Plant W: Mobil Oil Refinery, Dow Chemical
241		N River Rd, Wilmington
	Other	W: Des Plaines Fish & Wildlife Area/RVDump▲
240		CR 80, Lorenzo Rd, Wilmington
	FStop	E: Lorenzo Rd Fuel Stop/66
	TStop	W: River Truck Plaza/Citgo
	Food	W: Rest/FastFood/River TP
	Lodg	W: Motel 55/River TP
	Other	W: Laundry/River TP
238		IL 129S, Strip Mine Rd, Braidwood (SB Left exit, NO SB reaccess)
	Other	E: to Fossil Rock Rec Area▲
236		IL 113, Coal City Rd, Coal City, Kankakee
	Gas	W: BP, Citgo, Mobil◊
	Food	E: The Good Table Rest W: McDonald's, Subway
	Other	E: Auto Dealer
233		CR 37, Reed Rd, Kennedy Rd
	Gas	E: Marathon
	Lodg	E: Sands Motel, Sun Motel
	AServ	E: Repairs/Marathon

EXIT		ILLINOIS
227		IL 53, CR 49, Main St, Gardner Rd, Gardner
	Gas	E: Casey's W: BP◊
	Food	E: Gardner Haus Rest
220		Il 47, Union St, Morris, Dwight
	FStop	E: Circle K #1207
	Gas	E: BP◊, Clark
	Food	E: BurgerKing/BP, Arby's, McDonald's
	Lodg	E: Classic Inn Motel, Super 8
217		IL 17, Mazon Ave, Dwight, Streator
	TStop	E: Circle K #187/Shell
	Gas	E: Casey's, Phillips 66
	Food	E: Rest/Circle K, DQ, Old Rte 66 Family Rest, Pete's Family Rest & Pancake House
	Other	E: Laundry/Circle K
209		Prairie St, Odell
	Gas	E: BP
201		IL 23, O'Dell, to Pontiac, Streator
	Other	E: Pontiac RV, Airport✈
197		IL 116, Pontiac, Flanagan
	FStop	E: Pontiac BP Travel Mart
	Gas	E: Shell, Thornton's◊ W: Citgo
	Food	E: Subway/BP, Arby's, Burger King, Busters, Taco Bell, McDonald's, Wendy's
	Lodg	E: Comfort Inn, Holiday Inn Express, Super 8
	Med	E: + Hospital
	Other	E: AutoZone, Auto Dealers, Grocery, Wal-Mart, IL State Hwy Patrol Post, to Pontiac Muni Airport✈
(194)		Rest Area (Both dir) (RR, Phones, Picnic, Vend)
187		US 24, Cemetery Rd, Chenoa
	TStop	E: Chenoa Thrifty Mart/Shell
	Food	E: Casey's, Phillips 66 W: FastFood/Chenoa TM, Chenoa Family Rest, DQ, McDonald's/P66
	Lodg	E: Super 8
178		CR 8, Lexington
	Gas	E: BP◊, Freedom◊
	Food	E: McDonald's/BP
171		CR 29, Towanda
167		I-55 Bus, Veterans Pkwy, to Normal (SB, Left Exit)
	Lodg	E: Comfort Suites, Holiday Inn Express
	Other	E: to Sam's Club, Wal-Mart sc, to Bloomington Normal Airport✈
165		US 51 Bus, Bloomington (SB)
165AB		US 51 Bus, Bloomington, Normal
	Gas	E: BP, Mobil◊, Shell
	Food	E: Arby's/Mobil, Denny's, Pizza Hut, Steak 'n Shake
	Lodg	E: Best Western, Holiday Inn, Super 8
	TServ	W: McLean County Truck, Central Illinois Truck, Cummins, International Truck, White GMC Volvo/Kenworth
	Med	E: + Hospital
	Other	E: Dollar General, NAPA
(164)		Jct I-39, US 51, Rockford, to Peru
NOTE:		I-55 runs below with I-74. Exit #'s follow I-55.
(163)		Jct I-74W, to Champaign, Peoria
160A		US 150, IL 9, Market St, Bloomington
	FStop	E: Circle K/Citgo, Speedway #8326, Freedom Oil #39

◊ = Regular Gas Stations with Diesel   ▲ = RV Friendly Locations   ♥ = Pet Friendly Locations

RED PRINT SHOWS LARGE VEHICLE PARKING/ACCESS ON SITE OR NEARBY   BROWN PRINT SHOWS CAMPGROUNDS/RV PARKS

EXIT		ILLINOIS
	TStop	E: Pilot Travel Center #299 (Scales), Travel Center of America #92/BP (Scales)
	Gas	E: BP, Clark, Shell W: Citgo◆, WalMart
	Food	E: Wendy's, Pilot TC, CtryPride/Popeyes/PizzaHut/TA TC, Arby's, Burger King, Carl's Jr, Cracker Barrel, Hardee's, KFC, McDonald's, Subway, Taco Bell W: Bob Evans, Country Kitchen, Steak 'n Shake
	Lodg	E: Best Inn♥, Comfort Inn, Days Inn♥, Econo Lodge, Hawthorn Suites, Quality Inn W: Country Inn, Hampton Inn, Wingate
	TWash	E: Blue Beacon TW
	TServ	E: TA TC/Tires
	Med	E: + Hospital
	Other	E: Laundry/BarbSh/WiFi/Pilot TC, Laundry/WiFi/TA TC, Grocery, NAPA Factory Outlet Stores, Wal-Mart sc
160B		US 150, IL 9, Market St
	Gas	W: Citgo◆, WalMart
	Food	W: Country Kitchen, Steak 'n Shake
	Lodg	W: Country Inn♥, Hampton Inn, Ramada Inn♥, Wingate Inn
	Other	W: Factory Outlet Mall, Wal-Mart sc
	NOTE:	I-55 runs above with I-74. Exit #'s follow I-55.
157B		Bus 55, US 51, Veteran's Pkwy, Bloomington
	Gas	E: Shell
	Food	E: Rest/Parkway Inn, CJ's Rest
	Lodg	E: Parkway Inn, Sunset Inn
(157A)		Jct I-74E to Indianapolis, I-55, US 51 to Decatur
154		CR 34, McLean, to Shirley
(149)		Rest Area (Both dir) (RR, Phones, Picnic, Vend, Playground)
145		US 136, McLean, Heyworth
	TStop	W: Dixie Travel Plaza/Citgo (Scales)
	Gas	W: Shell
	Food	W: Rest/Dixie TP, McDonald's
	Lodg	W: Super 8
	TServ	W: Dixie TP/Tires
	Other	W: Laundry/BarbSh/WiFi/Dixie TP
140		CR 25, CR 6, Atlanta, Lawndale
	FStop	W: Ray's Fast Stop
	Food	W: Country Aire Restaurant
	Lodg	W: I-55 Motel
133		I-55 Bus, Lincoln
	Gas	E: Mini Mart
	Lodg	E: Budget Inn
	Med	E: + Hospital
	Other	E: McMillen's Camp-A-While▲, to Logan Co Airport✈, Amtrak, Lincoln College
(127)		Jct I-155N, to Peoria, Hartsburg
126		IL 10, IL 121, Lincoln, Mason City
	TStop	E: Thorton's Travel Plaza/P66 (Scales)
	Food	E: Rest/FastFood/Thorton's TP, Burger King, Cracker Barrel, Hardee's, Long John Silver, McDonald's, Pizza Hut, Steak n Shake, Wendy's
	Lodg	E: Comfort Inn, Holiday Inn Express, Super 8
	Med	E: + Abraham Lincoln Memorial Hospital
	TServ	E: TNT Truck & Trailer Service
	Other	E: Laundry/Thornton's TP, AutoZone, Auto Services, Dollar General, Grocery, Kroger, Radio Shack, Wal-Mart

EXIT		ILLINOIS
123		I-55 Bus Lp, to Lincoln
119		CR 12, Elkhart, to Broadwell
115		CR 10, Elkhart
	Gas	W: Shell
109		IL 123, CR 2, New Salem St, Williamsville, Petersburg
	TStop	E: Love's Travel Stop #249 (Scales)
	Food	E: McDonald's/Love's TS
	Other	E: WiFi/RVDump/Love's TS
(107)		Weigh Station (SB)
105		IL 124, I-55 Bus Lp, Peoria Ave, Sherman Blvd, Sherman
	Gas	W: BP, Casey's, Shell
	Food	W: DQ, Subway
(104)		Rest Area (SB) (RR, Phones, Picnic, Vend)
(102)		Rest Area (NB) (RR, Phone, Picnic, Vend)
100B		IL 54, Sangamon Ave, Clinton, Springfield
	Gas	W: BP, Shell, Speedway◆, WalMart
	Food	W: Arby's, Burger King, Culver's, Hickory River BBQ, McDonald's, Ryan's Gill, Sonic, Steak 'n Shake, Subway, Wendy's
	Lodg	W: Ramada Ltd
	Other	W: ATMs, Banks, Grocery, Lowe's, Wal-Mart sc, Harley Davidson, IL State Fairgrounds, to Capitol Airport✈
100A		IL 54, Springfield, Clinton
	TStop	E: Road Ranger Travel Center #118 (Scales)
	Rest	E: Rest/Road Ranger TC
	Tires	E: Road Ranger TC
	TServ	E: Kenworth/Volvo Trucks
(98B)		Jct I-72, IL 97W, Clear Lake Ave
	Gas	W: BP, Circle K, Shell◆
	Food	W: Hardee's, McDonald's, Subway, Taco Bell, Starbucks, Wendy's
	Lodg	W: Best Western, Best Rest Inn, Lincoln's Lodge, Parkview Motel, Shamrock Motel
	TServ	W: Ford Truck
	Med	W: + St John's Hospital
	Other	W: Bergen Public Golf Course, Kmart, Auto Services, Convention Center, Penske, Purcell Tire, Goodyear, Walgreen's
(98A)		Jct I-72, US 36E, to Decatur
96A		IL 29S, Taylorville, Springfield
96B		IL 29N, S Grand Ave
	Gas	W: BP, Citgo◆
	Food	W: Burger King, Godfather's Pizza
	Lodg	W: Quest Inn, Red Roof Inn♥, Super 8
	Other	W: Auto Dealers, AutoZone, AdvanceAuto, Grocery, Greyhound
94		Stevenson Dr, E Lake Shore Dr Springfield
	Gas	W: BP/Circle K, Mobil◆
	Food	W: Arby's, Bob Evans, Denny's, Hooters, Hardee's, Little Caesars, Long John Silver, Maverick Steak House, McDonald's, Outback Steakhouse, Pizza Hut, Red Lobster, Smokey Bones BBQ, Quiznos, Steak n Shake, Taco Bell, Wendy's
	Lodg	W: Best Western, Comfort Suites, Crowne Plaza Hotel, Days Inn, Drury Inn, Hampton Inn, Hilton Garden Inn, Pear Tree Inn
	Other	E: Springfield KOA▲ W: Big Lots, Cinema, Dollar General, Radio Shack, ShopKO, Walgreen's,

EXIT		ILLINOIS
	Other	W: to Univ of IL/Springfield, Lincoln Land Comm College, ▲ Mr Lincoln's Campground▲
92A		Bus Lp 55, 6th St, Springfield (SB)
(92B)		Jct I-72W, US 36W, Jacksonville (SB)
(92AB)		Jct I-72W, US 36W, Jacksonville (NB, Left exit)
	Gas	W: Citgo◆
	Food	W: Arby's, Burger King, KFC, McDonald's, Subway, Taco Bell
	Lodg	W: Super 8, Travelodge
	Other	W: Walgreen's
90		Toronto Rd, Springfield
	Gas	E: Qik-N-Ez◆, Shell
	Food	E: Burger King, China Express, Cracker Barrel, Hardee's, Hen House, McDonald's, Subway, Taco Bell
	Lodg	E: Baymont Inn, Ramada Ltd
	Med	E: + Doctors Hospital
	Other	E: to Univ of IL/Spgfld
88		East Lake Shore Dr, to Chatham
	Other	E: Springfield KOA▲, IL State Hwy Patrol Post W: to Double J Campground & RV Park▲
83		Old Rte 66, Glenarm
	Other	W: to Double J Campground & RV Park▲
82		IL 104, Divernon, Auburn, Pawnee
	FStop	W: Auburn Travel Center/Mobil (Scales)
	Food	W: FastFood/Auburn TC
	TServ	W: Homestead Garage
	Other	W: Laundry/WiFi/RVDump/Auburn TC
80		E Brown St, Divernon
	Gas	W: Phillips 66◆
	Food	W: Bearden's Rest
72		CR 17, Mine Ave, Farmersville
	FStop	W: Jumpin Jimmy's/66
	Gas	W: Shell
	Food	W: FastFood/Jumpin Jimmy's, Subway, Rest/Art's Motel
	Lodg	W: Art's Motel
(65)		Rest Area (Both dir) (RR, Phones, Picnic, Vend, Playgorund)
63		IL 48, IL 127, Waggoner, Raymond
60		IL 108, to Carlinville
	FStop	W: Shell
	Food	W: Café/Shell, Rest/Holiday Inn
	Lodg	W: Holiday Inn
	Other	E: Kamper Kompanion▲
(56)		Weigh Station (NB)
52		IL 16, Litchfield
	TStop	E: Fast Stop Travel Center/66 (Scales)
	Gas	E: AmocoBP, Casey's, Shell, WalMart
	Food	E: FastFood/Fast Stop TC, Ariston Café, Arby's, DQ, Hardee's, Long John Silver, Maverick Steak House, McDonald's, Pizza Hut, Ruby Tuesdau, Subway, Taco Bell, Wendy's
	Lodg	E: Baymont Inn, Best Value Inn, Comfort I Inn, Hampton Inn, Holiday Inn Express, Super 8
	TServ	E: Barny's Truck & Trailer, Den-Mar Truck Service
	Med	E: + Hospital
	Other	E: Laundry/Fast Stop TC, Cinema, Grocery, Dollar General, Dollar Tree, Goodyear, Kroger, Wal-Mart sc

Page 226   ◆= Regular Gas Stations with Diesel   ▲ = RV Friendly Locations   ♥ = Pet Friendly Locations
RED PRINT SHOWS LARGE VEHICLE PARKING/ACCESS ON SITE OR NEARBY   BROWN PRINT SHOWS CAMPGROUNDS/RV PARKS

EXIT		ILLINOIS
	Other	W: to Lankels Lazy Days Campground▲
		IL State Hwy Patrol Post
44		IL 138, Lakeview Dr, Mt Olive
	Gas	E: Mobil◇
	Food	E: Crossroads Rest
	Lodg	E: Budget 10 Motel
41		CR 12, Staunton Rd, to Staunton
	Gas	W: Casey's
	Food	W: DQ, Subway
	Lodg	W: Super 8
	Med	W: + Hospital
37		New Douglas Rd, Livingston
	FStop	W: Meyer's BP
	Food	W: Country Inn Café
	Lodg	W: Country Inn
33		IL 4, Worden, to Staunton, Lebanon
	Gas	W: Schlechtes Service Station
	Food	W: Deli, Diggers Dugout
30		IL 140, State St, Worden, Hamel
	Gas	W: Shell
	Food	E: Rest/Inn Keeper
	Lodg	E: Inn Keeper
(28)		Rest Area (Both dir)
		(RR, Phones, Picnic, Vend)
23		IL 143, Edwardsville, Highland, Marine
	Gas	E: Mobil◇
	TServ	E: Joe's Car & Tractor Service
	Other	W: to Red Barn Rendezvous RV Park▲
(20B)		Jct I-270W, to Kansas City
(20A)		Jct I-70E, to Indianapolis
	NOTE:	I-55 runs below with I-70E for 18 mi. Exit #'s follow I-55.
18		IL 162, Edwardsville Rd, Troy
	TStop	E: Pilot Travel Center #249 (Scales), Travel Center of America #199/BP (Scales)
	Gas	W: Mobil◇
	Food	E: Arby's/TJCinn/Pilot TC, Rest/TA TC, Burger King, DQ, Jack in the Box, KFC, Little Caesar's, McDonald's, Perkins, Pizza Hut, Subway
		W: China Garden, Cracker Barrel, Taco Bell
	Lodg	E: Relax Inn
		W: Holiday Inn Express♥, Red Roof Inn♥, Scottish Inns, Super 8
	TWash	E: 18 Wheeler's Truck Wash
	TServ	E: TA TC/Tires, Carron's Auto & Truck Repair
	Med	E: + Hospital
	Other	E: Laundry/WiFi/Pilot TC, Laundry/BarbSh /WiFi/TA TC, Grocery, Family Dollar
17		US 40E, Troy
	TServ	E: ADR Auto & Truck Repair, M&M Truck Repair
15AB		IL 159, Collinsville, Maryville
	Gas	E: Citgo, Phillips 66◇, Shell
		W: Conoco
	Lodg	W: Econo Lodge
	Other	E: Grocery, Dollar General, Auto Dealer
(14)		Weigh Station (SB)
11		IL 157, Bluff Rd, Collinsville, to Edwardsville
	FStop	W: Moto Mart
	Gas	E: BP, Casey's, Shell
	Food	E: Denny's, Hardee's, Long John Silver, McDonald's, Pizza Hut, Waffle House Wendy's

EXIT		IL / MO
	Food	W: Arby's, Bandanas BBQ, Bob Evans, Burger King, DQ, Ponderosa, Shoney's, Steak 'n Shake, White Castle
	Lodg	E: Best Western, Days Inn, Howard Johnson, Motel 6♥, Pear Tree Inn
		W: Drury Inn♥, Fairfield Inn, Hampton Inn, Holiday Inn, Ramada, Super 8
	Other	W: Auto Dealers, Visitor Center, IL State Hwy Patrol Post
(10)		Jct I-255, S to Memphis, N to I-270
9		Black Lane (NB, no reacc)
	Other	E: to Fairmount Park
6		IL 111, Great River Rd, Wood River, Fairmont City, Washington Park
	Gas	E: Phillips 66
	Lodg	E: Rainbow Court Motel
	Other	E: Grocery, Pharmacy
	NOTE:	MM 5: NB: Begin Call Boxes
4		IL 203, Collinsville Rd, Granite City, E St Louis (NB)
	TStop	W: Pilot Travel Center #313 (Scales)
	Gas	E: Phillips 66◇
	Food	W: Subway/TacoBell/Pilot TC
	Lodg	E: Western Inn
	TWash	W: Pilot TC
	TServ	W: Pilot TC/Tires
	Other	W: Laundry/WiFi/Pilot TC, Gateway Int'l Raceway
4B		IL 203W, E St Louis (SB)
	TStop	W: Pilot Travel Center #313 (Scales)
4A		IL 203E, Collinsville Rd (SB)
3		Exchange Ave, E St Louis
(2)		Jct I-64E, IL 3N, St Clair Ave
2B		3rd St (SB, left exit)
	Other	W: Casino Queen RV Park▲
2A		MLK Bridge, to St Louis Downtown (SB, Left exit)
1		IL 3, to Sauget (SB)
	NOTE:	I-55 runs above with I-70E for 18 mi. Exit #'s follow I-55.

(CENTRAL TIME ZONE)

O ILLINOIS
U MISSOURI

(CENTRAL TIME ZONE)

	NOTE:	MM 209: Illinois State Line
(209B)		Jct I-70W, to Kansas City
209A		to St Louis Arch, Busch Stadium
208		7th St, Park Ave, Downtown
	Gas	W: BP
	Food	E: Burger King, McDonald's
		W: Hardee's, Taco Bell
	Lodg	W: Drury Plaza, Marriott, Radisson. Park Ave B&B
	TServ	E: Broadway Ford Dealership
	Other	E: Haunted Theme Park
(207)		Jct I-44W, to Tulsa (fr SB)
(207B)		Jct I-44W, to Tulsa (fr NB, Left Exit)
207A		MO 30, Russell Blvd, Gravois Ave
	Gas	E: Citgo
	Food	E: Jack in the Box

◇ = Regular Gas Stations with Diesel ▲ = RV Friendly Locations ♥ = Pet Friendly Locations
RED PRINT SHOWS LARGE VEHICLE PARKING/ACCESS ON SITE OR NEARBY   BROWN PRINT SHOWS CAMPGROUNDS/RV PARKS

Page 227

Interstate 55 N/S

MISSOURI

EXIT		Details
206C		**Arsenal St, St Louis**
	Gas	W: Shell
	Other	E: Anheuser Busch Tour Center
206B		**S Broadway (NB, no reaccess)**
	Other	W: Auto & Truck Service
206A		**Potomac St (NB, no reaccess)**
205		**Gasconade St (SB ex, NB reaccess)**
	Med	W: + Alexian Bros Hospital
204		**Broadway, St Louis**
	Gas	E: Mobil
		W: Clark, Sinclair
	Food	W: Hardee's, McDonald's, Pizza Hut
	Med	W: + Alexian Bros Hospital
	Other	W: Radio Shack, Walgreen's
203		**Bates St, Virginia Ave**
	Gas	W: 7-11, BP
	Other	E: Auto Repair & Towing
202C		**Loughborough Ave, St Louis**
202B		**Germania Ave (SB exit, NB reacc)**
202A		**Carondelet Blvd (NB)**
201B		**Weber Rd (NB)**
201A		**Bayless Ave, St Louis**
	Gas	E: BP, QT, Shell
		W: 7-11, BP, Shell
	Food	E: McDonald's
		W: DQ, Jack in the Box, Subway, Taco Bell
	Other	W: Grocery, Goodyear, Pharmacy
200		**Union Rd (SB exit, NB reaccess)**
199		**Reavis Barracks Rd**
	Gas	E: BP, Shell
	Food	E: Steak n Shake
197		**US 61, US 50, Lindbergh Blvd**
	Gas	E: BP, Phillips 66
	Food	E: Applebee's, Arby's, Chuck E Cheese, Hooters, KFC, Long John Silver, McDonald's, Po Folks, Ruby Tuesday, Steak n Shake
		W: Bob Evans, Casa Gallerdo, Denny's, Pasta House, Ponderosa, Shoney's
	Lodg	E: Holiday Inn, Super 8
		W: Motel 6 ♥, Oak Grove Inn
	Other	E: Advance Auto, ATMs, Banks, Best Buy, Auto Dealers, Goodyear, NTB, S County Center Mall, Circuit City, Auto Services
		W: Grocery, Auto Dealers, Costco, Office Depot, Target
(196B)		**Jct I-270W, to Kansas City (SB)**
(196A)		**Jct I-255E, to Chicago (SB)**
(196)		**Jct I-255E, to Chicago, I-270W, to Kansas City (NB)**
195		**Butler Hill Rd, St Louis**
	Gas	E: Phillips 66
		W: Sinclair
	Food	W: Burger King, Hardee's, Subway, Taco Bell, Waffle House
	Lodg	E: Holiday Inn
		W: Econo Lodge
	Other	E: Walgreen's
193		**Meramec Bottom Rd**
	Gas	E: Mobil, QT
	Food	E: Cracker Barrel
	Lodg	E: Best Western ♥
	Other	E: Howard RV Supercenter
191		**MO 141, Arnold**
	Gas	E: Citgo, PetroMart, QT, Shell
		W: Mobil, Phillips 66 ♦

MISSOURI

EXIT		Details
	Food	E: Applebee's, Bandana's BBQ, CiCi's, China King, Denny's, Fazoli's, Hardee's, McDonald's, Steak n Shake
	Lodg	E: Drury Inn, Ramada Ltd
	Other	E: Grocery, K-Mart, Mall, Wal-Mart sc, Bowling Center, Auto Services, Pharmacy
190		**Richardson Rd, Arnold**
	Gas	E: Express Mart, QT, Shell ♦
		W: 7-11, Phillips 66 ♦, Shell ♦
	Food	E: DQ, Domino's, Ponderosa, Pizza Hut, Subway, Taco Bell, White Castle
		W: Burger King, McDonalds, Ruby Tuesday, Waffle House
	Lodg	W: Comfort Inn
	Other	E: Arnold Cinema 14, Grocery, Firestone
		W: Grocery, Home Depot, Target, Walgreen's
186		**Imperial Main St, Imperial, Kimmswick**
	Gas	E: Conv Food Mart/Shell
185		**MO M, Barnhart, to Antonia**
	FStop	W: Express Mart/Citgo
	Food	W: Café
	Other	W: LP/ExpressMart, Walgreen's, to St Louis South KOA▲
(184)		**Weigh Station (Both dir)**
180		**CR Z, Pevely, to Hillsboro**
	TStop	W: Mr Fuel #3, I-55 Motor Plaza/66 (Scales)
	Gas	E: Mobil
	Food	E: Burger King, Country Kitchen, Domino's, KFC
		W: FastFood/Mr Gas, McDonald's/I-55 MP
	Lodg	W: Super 8
	Other	E: IGA, Banks, ATMs, to I-55 Raceway
		W: Laundry/LP/I-55 MP
178		**Bus 55, McNutt St, Herculaneum**
	TStop	E: QuikTrip #611 (Scales)
	Gas	E: Shell
	Food	E: Wendy's/QT, Cracker Barrel, Jack in the Box, DQ, La Pachanga Mex Rest
	Other	E: to I-55 Raceway
		W: Auto Dealer
175		**Veterans Blvd, Festus, Crystal City**
	Gas	E: Phillips 66 ♦
		W: 7-11, Phillips 66 ♦
	Food	E: Arby's, Bob Evans, Captain D's, Fazoli's, McDonald's, Ryan's Grill, Steak n Shake, Subway, Taco Bell, Wendy's, White Castle
		W: Hardee's, Ruby Tuesday, Waffle House
	Lodg	E: Drury Inn, Holiday Inn Express
		W: Baymont Inn
	Other	E: Advance Auto, Grocery, Home Depot, Tires, Wal-Mart sc, ATMs, Banks
		W: Cinema, Lowe's
174A		**US 67E, US 61, S Truman Blvd (Access #175 Services)**
	Gas	E: Phillips 66, WalMart
	Food	E: Arby's, McDonald's, Ryan's Grill
	Med	E: + Jefferson Memorial Hospital
	Other	E: WalMart SC, Festus Memorial Airport ✈
174B		**US 67W, to Park Hills**
	Fstop	W: One Stop
	Other	W: Tires, Towing, RVDump/One Stop, Buff's RV
170		**US 61, Festus**
	FStop	W: BP
	Other	W: LP/BP
162		**MO DD, MO OO, to US 61, Bloomsdale**

MISSOURI

EXIT		Details
(160)		**Rest Area (Both dir) (RR, Phones, Picnic, Vend)**
157		**MO Y, to US 61, Bloomsdale**
	FStop	W: Bloomsdale Food Mart/Valero
	Gas	E: Phillips 66
154		**MO O, Ste Genevieve, Rocky Ridge**
150		**MO 32, MO B, MO A, Ste Genevieve**
	Gas	E: BP
		W: Phillips 66 ♦
	Food	E: DQ
	Med	E: + Hospital
	Lodg	W: Microtel
	Other	W: Auto Dealer
143		**MO M, MO N, MO J, St Mary, Ozora**
	TStop	W: AmBest/Ozora Truck & Travel Plaza/Valero (Scales)
	Gas	W: Sinclair
	Food	W: Rest/FastFood/Ozora TP
	Lodg	W: Family Budget Inn
	TWash	W: Ozora TP
	TServ	W: Ozora TP/Tires
	Other	W: Laundry/WiFi/Ozora TP
141		**MO Z, St Mary**
135		**MO M, Perryville, Brewer**
129		**MO 51, Perryville Blvd, Perryville**
	FStop	E: Rhodes 101 Stop/P66
	Gas	E: MotoMart ♦
		W: Rhodes 101 Stop Shell ♦
	Food	E: Burger King, KFC, McDonald's, Skinny's Diner, Ponderosa, Sonic, Taco Bell
	Lodg	W: Best Western, Comfort Inn, Super 8
	Med	E: + Perry Co Memorial Hospital
	Other	E: Wal-Mart sc, Auto Dealers, Perryville/Cape Girardeau KOA▲
123		**MO B, Perryville, to Biehle**
	FStop	W: Rhodes 101 Stop/66
	Food	W: Country Kettle Rest
117		**MO KK, Oak Ridge, to Appleton**
	Gas	E: Sewing's Travel Center
111		**MO E, Oak Ridge**
(110)		**Rest Area (Both dir) (RR, Phones, Picnic, Vend)**
105		**US 61, Jackson, Fruitland**
	Gas	E: BP ♦, Casey's, Rhodes 101 ♦
		W: D-Mart
	Food	E: Casey's C/O Pizza, Pie Bird Cafe
		W: DQ, Pizza Inn
	Lodg	W: Drury Inn
	Other	W: McDowell South Truck, RV & Trailer Sales
99		**Bus 55, US 61, MO 34, Cape Girardeau, Jackson,**
	Gas	W: Murphy
	Food	E: DQ, Fazoli's, Subway
	Lodg	E: Super 8
	Other	E: Cape Camping & RV Park/RVDump, Capetown RV Sales
		W: Wal-Mart sc
96		**MO K, William St, Cape Girardeau, Gordonville**
	Gas	E: BP, Citgo ♦, D-Mart
		W: Shell
	Food	E: Bob Evans, Blimpie, Burger King, Cracker Barrel, DQ, McDonald's, Logan's Roadhouse, Olive Garden, O'Charley's, Red Lobster, Ruby Tuesday, Ryan's Grill, Steak n Shake, Taco Bell, Sonic, Subway
		W: Outback Steakhouse, White Castle

♦ = Regular Gas Stations with Diesel   ▲ = RV Friendly Locations   ♥ = Pet Friendly Locations
RED PRINT SHOWS LARGE VEHICLE PARKING/ACCESS ON SITE OR NEARBY   BROWN PRINT SHOWS CAMPGROUNDS/RV PARKS

EXIT		MISSOURI
	Lodg	E: Drury Lodge ♥, Holiday Inn Express, Pear Tree Inn ♥, Victorian Inn W: Drury Inn, Hampton Inn
	TServ	E: Purcell Tire
	Med	E: + St Francis Medical Center
	Other	E: ATMs, Banks, B&N, Best Buy, Big Lots, Grocery, Walgreen's, W Park Mall W: Cinema, Circuit City, Dollar Tree, Lowe's, Sam's Club, Staples, Target, Wal-Mart sc
95		MO 74E, to US 61
93B		US 61, Cape Girardeau (NB)
93A		MO 74, Dutchtown (NB)
93		MO 74W, Cape Girardeau (SB)
91		CR AB, Nash Rd, Cape Girardeau, Scott City, Airport
	TStop	E: PTP/Rhodes Travel Center/66 (Scales)
	Food	E: Rest/FastFood/Rhodes TC
	TWash	E: Rhodes TC
	Tires	E: Rhodes TC, Raben Tire
	TServ	E: Sam's Service & Repair
	Other	E: Laundry/WiFi/RVDump/Rhodes TC, Minor's Harley Davidson W: Cape Girardeau Muni Airport→, Capetown RV Sales
89		US 61, MO M, MO K, Main St, Scott City
	Gas	E: Rhodes 101, Shell
	Food	E: Burger King, DQ, Sonic, Waffle Hut
	Other	E: Dollar General, NAPA
80		MO 77, Benton
	Gas	W: BP◊, Express◊
	Food	W: McDonald's/BP
	Other	E: Auto Service
69		MO HH, Sikeston, Miner
	TStop	W: Keller Truck Service (Scales)
67		US 62, Malone St, Sikeston, Miner
	TStop	E: Break Time #3147/MFA W: Keller Truck Service (Scales)
	Gas	W: Citgo, Larry's Pit Stop
	Food	E: Deli/Break Time, JD's Steakhouse W: Rest/Keller TS, Burger King, Frankie's Country Cooking, McDonald's, Mex Rest, Pizza Hut, Ruby Tuesday, Shoney's, Sonic, Skinny's Diner, Taco Bell, Wendy's
	Lodg	E: Best Western, Holiday Inn Express, Red Carpet Inn W: Country Hearth Inn, Days Inn, Drury Inn, Pear Tree Inn, Ramada Inn, Super 8
	TWash	W: Keller TS
	TServ	E: Raben Tire, White GMC Volvo W: Keller TS/Tires
	Med	W: + Hospital
	Other	E: Hinton Park Campground▲, Town & Country RV Resort▲, RV America W: Laundry/Keller TS, AutoZone, Auto Services, Family Dollar, Goodyear, Grocery, Walgreen's, Wal-Mart sc, Sikeston Memorial Muni Airport→
66B		US 60W, to Poplar Bluff
(66A)		Jct I-57E, to Chicago, US 60W
58		MO 80, Matthews, East Prairie
	TStop	E: Travel Center of America #51/Citgo (Scales) W: Flying J Travel Plaza #5074/Conoco (Scales), Love's Travel Stop #313 (Scales)
	Food	E: CountryPride/TacoBell/TA TC

Lambert's Cafe

EXIT		MISSOURI
	Food	W: Rest/FastFood/FJ TP, Subway/Chesters/Love's TS
	TWash	E: DJ's TW, Cranford's TW
	TServ	E: TA TC/Tires W: J & S Truck Repair
	Other	E: Laundry/WiFi/TA TC W: Laundry/BarbSh/WiFi/RVDump/FJ TP, WiFi/RVDump/Love's TS
52		MO P, New Madrid, Kewanee
	TStop	E: BJ's Travel Center/AmocoBP
	Food	E: FastFood/BJ's TC
49		US 61, US 62, Lp 55, New Madrid (Access #44 Serv S to New Madrid)
44		US 61, US 62, New Madrid
	Gas	E: Casey's, Express
	Food	E: Casey's Pizza, Kinsey's Family Rest, Pro Pizza, Rosie's Grill
	Lodg	E: Relax Inn & Kampgrounds▲
	Other	E: Auto Services, Tires, Towing
(42)		MO Welcome Center (NB) Rest Area (SB) (RR, Phones, Picnic, Vend)
40		MO Ee, St Jude Rd, Marston
	TStop	E: Pilot Travel Center #301 (Scales) W: Break Time #3149/MFA
	Food	E: Arby's/TJCinn/Pilot TC W: FastFood/BreakTime
	Lodg	E: Super 8 W: Budget Inn
	Other	E: Laundry/WiFi/Pilot TC
32		US 61, MO 162, Portageville
	FStop	W: Martin & Ivie Gas & Go/BP
	Gas	W: Casey's
	Food	W: FastFood/Martin&Ivie, McDonald's
27		MO K, MO A, MO BB, to Wardell
	Other	E: to Hayti/Portageville KOA▲
19		US 412, MO 84, Hayti
	FStop	E: Break Time #3153/MFA
	TStop	E: Pilot Travel Center #442 (Scales), Hayti Travel Center (Scales)
	Gas	W: BP, Conoco
	Food	E: Arbys/TJCinn/Pilot TC, Rest/Hayti TC, Chubby's BBQ, KFC, McDonald's, Pizza Hut, Wendy's W: BBQ, DQ, Pizza Inn
	Lodg	E: Comfort Inn, Executive Inn W: Budget Inn, Drury Inn
	AServ	W: D&H Tire & Auto Repair
	Tires	E: Raben Tire
	TServ	W: Tatum Repair, Ace Wrecker & Repair
	Med	W: + Medical Care
	Other	E: Laundry/WiFi/RVDump/Pilot TC, MidContinent Airport→, to Hayti/Portageville KOA▲ W: ATMs, Bank, Auto Services, Goodyear
(17A)		Jct I-155E, US 412, to Dyersburg, TN
14		MO J, MOR H, MO U, Caruthersville, Braggadocio
(10)		Weigh Station (Both dir)
8		MO 164, US 61, Steele
	TStop	W: AmBest/Deerfield Travel Plaza/BP (Scales)
	Gas	E: Flash Market
	Food	W: Subway/BP, Boss Hogg BBQ, Show Me Pizza
	Lodg	W: Deerfield Inn
	TWash	W: Deerfield TP
	Other	W: WiFi/Deerfield TP

EXIT		MO / AR
4		MO E, Steele, to Cooter, Holland
(3)		Weigh Station (SB)
(2)		Rest Area (Both dir) (RR, Phones, Picnic, Vend)
1		MO O, to US 61, Steele, to Holland
	Gas	E: RaceWay W: Coastal, Shell◊
		(CENTRAL TIME ZONE)
		⊙ **MISSOURI**
		⊙ **ARKANSAS**
		(CENTRAL TIME ZONE)
	NOTE:	MM 72: Missouri State Line
72		State Line Rd (NB)
(71)		Weigh Station (SB)
71		AR 150, Blytheville
	Gas	W: Citgo◊
(68)		AR Welcome Center (SB) (RR, Phones, Picnic)
67		AR 18, AR 151, Blytheville
	FStop	E: Hard Hat/Exxon W: Flash Market #177/Citgo
	TStop	E: Lone Wolf Truck Stop
	Gas	W: BP◊
	Food	E: Rest/Lone Wolf TS, Burger King, Chinese Buffet, Rest/Days Inn W: Arby's, Grecian Steak House, Hardee's, KFC, Mazzio's Pizza, McDonald's, Perkins, Pizza Inn, Poor Boys Café, Shoney's, Sonic, Subway, Wendy's
	Lodg	E: Days Inn W: Comfort Inn ♥, Hampton Inn, Travel Lodge Inn
	Med	W: + Baptist Memorial Hospital
	Other	E: Dollar Tree, Lowe's, WAL★MART sc, Blytheville Muni Airport→ W: Animal Hospital ♥, Auto Services, Family Dollar, Pharmacy, Blytheville AFB
63		US 61, Blytheville
	FStop	W: Shell
	Gas	W: Dodge' Store◊, Citgo, Exxon
	Food	W: McDonald's/Shell, Dodge's Chicken
	Lodg	W: Best Western, Relax Inn
	Tires	W: Raben Tire
57		AR 148, Burdette
53		AR 158, Osceola, to Luxora, Victoria
48		AR 140, Osceola (All Serv E in Osceola)
	TStop	E: Shell Truck Stop
	Gas	E: Mobil◊
	Food	E: Cotton Inn Rest, Huddle House
	Lodg	E: Best Western, Days Inn, Deerfield Inn, Plum Point Inn
	Med	E: + Baptist Memorial Hospital
	Other	E: Osceola Muni Airport→
(45)		Rest Area (NB) (RR, Picnic, Phones)
44		AR 181, to Wilson, Keiser
41		AR 14, Dyess, to Marie, Leparto
36		AR 181, Bassett, to Evandale
(35)		Rest Area (SB) (RR, Picnic, Phones)

◊ = Regular Gas Stations with Diesel   ▲ = RV Friendly Locations   ♥ = Pet Friendly Locations
RED PRINT SHOWS LARGE VEHICLE PARKING/ACCESS ON SITE OR NEARBY   BROWN PRINT SHOWS CAMPGROUNDS/RV PARKS

INTERSTATE 55 N/S

EXIT	ARKANSAS
34	AR 118, Bassett, Joiner, Tyronza
23AB	US 63N, AR 77S, Gilmore, Marked Tree, Jonesboro, Turrell
21	AR 4 2, Turrell
TStop	W: Fuel Mart #798 (Scales)
Food	W: FastFood/Fuel Mart
17	AR 50, Clarkedale Rd, to Jericho
14	CR 4, James Mill Rd, Marion, Crawfordsville, Jericho
TStop	E: Fast Market #36/Citgo (Scales)
Gas	W: Citgo◊
Food	W: Stuckey's/Citgo
Other	E: B&M Truck & Trailer Service
	W: Memphis KOA▲
10	US 64, Marion, Sunset, Wynne
FStop	E: Mapco Express #3058
Gas	E: BP, Citgo, Shell◊
	W: BP, Shell
Food	E: Sonic, Tops BBQ, McDonald's/Shell, Subway/Citgo
	W: Wendy's, Rest/Best Western
Lodg	E: Inn of America
	W: Best Western
Other	E: Grocery, Dollar General
(9)	Weigh Station (Both dir)
(8)	Jct I-40W, to Little Rock
7	AR 77, Missouri St (SB ex, NB entr)
Gas	E: Texaco, Exxon, Mapco
Food	E: Shoney's, Bonanza, Cracker Barrel, Krystal, Pizza Inn, Popeye's, Subway
Lodg	E: Ramada Inn
Other	E: ATMs, Banks
NOTE:	Next 4 Exits below run with I-40. Exit #'s follow I-40.
(277)	Jct I-55N, Blytheville, St Louis
278	AR 77, 7th St, Missouri St, AR 191, W Memphis (Addt'l Serv S on Missouri St)
FStop	S: Flash Market #11/Shell (S Serv Rd)
Gas	N: Citgo
	S: Love's◊, RaceTrac, Exxon, Mapco
Food	S: Cracker Barrel, KFC, KFC, Krystal, Mrs Winners, TCBY, McDonald's, Pizza Hut, Shoney's, Subway, Wendy's
Lodg	S: Quality Inn, Ramada Inn
Med	S: + Crittenden Memorial Hospital
Other	S: RVDump/Flash Market, Auto Services, Goodyear, Kroger, Walgreen's, Wal-Mart sc, Tom Sawyers Mississippi River RV Park/RVDump
279A	Ingram Blvd, W Memphis
Gas	S: Citgo◊, Exxon, Shell
Food	S: Perkins, Shoney's, Waffle House
Lodg	N: Comfort Inn, Ramada, Red Roof Inn♥, Rodeway Inn
	S: Days Inn, Econo Lodge♥, Hampton Inn, Holiday Inn, Howard Johnson, Motel 6♥, Relax Inn
Other	N: U-Haul, Southland Greyhound Park
	S: Auto Dealers, Auto Services
(279B)	Jct I-40E, to Memphis, Jackson
280/4	Club Rd, Southland Dr, Martin Luther King Dr (I-55, Ex #4)
TStop	N: Pilot Travel Center #429 (Scales), Harris Travel Center/Shamrock
	S: Petro Stopping Center #11 (Scales), Pilot Travel Center #272 (Scales),

EXIT	AR / TN
TStop	S: Flying J Travel Plaza #5333/Conoco (Scales)
Gas	N: BP◊
Food	N: Subway/Wendy's/Pilot TC, FastFood/Harris TC
	S: Rest/FastFood/FJ TP, IronSkillet/FastFood/Petro SC, Subway/Pilot TC, McDonald's, KFC/Taco Bell, Waffle House
Lodg	N: Express Inn
	S: Budget Inn, Sunset Inn, Super 8♥
TWash	S: Blue Beacon TW/Petro SC
TServ	S: Pilot TC/Tires, Petro SC/Tires, Speedco
Other	N: Laundry/WiFi/Pilot TC
	S: Laundry/BarbSh/WiFi/RVDump/LP/FJ TP, WiFi/RVDump/Pilot TC, Laundry/CB/WiFi/Petro SC, Tom Sawyers Mississippi River RV Park/RVDump, Southland Greyhound Park
NOTE:	Next 4 Exits above run with I-40. Exit #'s follow I-40.
3B	US 70, US 79, Club Rd, Broadway Blvd (NB, Left Exit)
3A	AR 131, Mound City Rd (NB exit, SB re-entry)
(2)	Weigh Station (NB)
1	Bridgeport Rd, W Memphis

(CENTRAL TIME ZONE)

⊙ ARKANSAS
⊙ TENNESSEE
(CENTRAL TIME ZONE)

NOTE:	MM 13: Arkansas State Line
12C	Delaware St, Metal Museum Dr
12B	Riverside Dr, Downtown
12A	East Crump Blvd, US 61, US 64 (NB)
TServ	E: G&W Diesel Service
11	McLemore Ave, Presidents Island
10	South Parkway W, Memphis
Gas	E: BP◊, Conoco
TServ	W: Haygood Truck & Trailer, TruckPro
9	Mallory Ave, Memphis
TServ	E: Fruehauf, Great Dane Sales & Service
8	Horn Lake Rd, Florida St (SB Exit, NB Ent)
7	US 61S, TN 14, 3rd St, to Vicksburg (difficult reaccess)
FStop	E: Mapco Express #3138 (E on Mallory Ave)
	W: Roadrunner Petro
Gas	E: AmocoBP, Exxon
	W: Citgo
Food	E: Interstate BBQ, Lotaburger, Taco Bell
	W: KFC, McDonald's, Subway
Lodg	W: Rest Inn, Starlite Inn
Other	E: Auto Services, Walgreen's
	W: Auto Services, Diesel Service, Towing
(6AB)	Jct I-240, to I-40, to Nashville
5B	US 51, Elvis Presley Blvd, South Brooks Rd, Graceland, Memphis
Gas	W: BP, Citgo◊, Exxon, Phillips 66
Food	W: Captain D's, KFC, Kettle, Taco Bel
Lodg	W: American Inn, Graceland Inn, Super 7 Inn, Heartbreak Hotel
Med	W: + Hospital

EXIT	TN / MS
TServ	W: Pinkston Diesel & Truck Repair, Stephens Truck Service, Roadway Diesel & Gas Repair
Other	W: Advance Auto, Auto Services, Vet♥, Goodyear, Bell Brook Industrial Park, D&N Camper Sales, Davis Motorhome Mart, Elvis Presley Blvd RV Park▲, Memphis Graceland RV Park & Campground▲
5A	South Brooks Rd, to US 51, Elvis Presley Blvd, Graceland (NB)
TStop	E: Mapco Express #3159
Gas	E: AmocoBP, Exxon
Food	E: Burger King, Crown Rest, Dad's Place, Mrs Winner's, Popeye's, Shoney's
Lodg	E: Airport Inn, Clarion Hotel, Days Inn, Quality Inn, Travelodge
TServ	E: Freightliner, Peterbilt of Memphis, Heavy Truck & Trailer Repair, Mid-America International, Cummins, Mid-South Diesel Service
Other	E: ATMs, Bank, Memphis Int'l Airport✈
(3)	TN Welcome Center (NB) (RR, Phones, Picnic, Vend)
2AB	TN 175, Shelby Dr, to White Haven
Gas	E: BP◊, Citgo, Conoco, Exxon
	W: BP, Citgo, Shell
Food	E: Cheyenne Country, Pollards BBQ, Subway/Citgo
	W: Burger King, CK's Coffee Shop, Pizza Inn, IHOP, Mrs Winner's
Lodg	E: Colonial Inn
Other	E: Auto Services, Laundromat
	W: Family Dollar, Grocery, Goodyear, Southland Mall, U-Haul, Pharmacy

(CENTRAL TIME ZONE)

⊙ TENNESSEE
⊙ MISSISSIPPI
(CENTRAL TIME ZONE)

NOTE:	MM 291.5: Tennessee State Line
291	State Line Rd, Main St, Southaven
Gas	E: Exxon, Horizon
	W: In n Out
Food	E: Burger King, Interstate BBQ, Little Caesars, McDonald's, Shoney's, Subway, Tops BBQ, Waffle House
	W: Capt D's, Checkers, Mrs Winner's, Sonic, Taco Bell, Wendy's
Lodg	E: Best Value Inn, Comfort Inn, Holiday Inn Express♥, Quality Inn, Southern Inn
	W: Budget Inn, Travelers Inn
Other	E: Firestone, Goodyear, Kmart, Kroger, Penske, Walgreen's, Southaven RV Park▲
	W: ATMs, Banks, Auto Services, Cinema, Big Lots, Tires, RiteAid, Walgreen's, US Post Office, Pharmacy, to Wal-Mart sc
289	MS 302, Goodman Rd, Horn Lake, Olive Branch, South Southaven
FStop	W: Goodman Rd Food Plaza/66
Gas	E: 76, Shell, Sam's, Murphy
	W: BP, Phillips 66◊, Shell◊
Food	E: Backyard Burgers, Burger King, Chick-Fil-A, Chili's, Fazoli's, IHOP, Krystal, McDonald's, Moe's SW Grill, Logan's Roadhouse, Lone Star Steakhouse, Outback Steakhouse, Smokey Bones BBQ, Steak n Shake, Starbucks, TGI Friday

◊ = Regular Gas Stations with Diesel ▲ = RV Friendly Locations ♥ = Pet Friendly Locations
RED PRINT SHOWS LARGE VEHICLE PARKING/ACCESS ON SITE OR NEARBY BROWN PRINT SHOWS CAMPGROUNDS/RV PARKS

INTERSTATE 55

MISSISSIPPI

EXIT		
	Food	W: Applebee's, Arby's, Bob Evans, Chuck E Cheese, **Cracker Barrel**, Hooters, KFC, Papa John's, Pizza Hut, Popeye's, Ryan's Grill, Texas Roadhouse, Waffle House, Wendy's, Zaxby's
	Lodg	E: **Comfort Suites**, Courtyard, Fairfield Inn, Hampton Inn, Residence Inn W: **Days Inn**, Drury Inn, Motel 6 ♥, Ramada Ltd, Sleep Inn
	TServ	E: E&W Auto/Truck Service W: **Gateway Tire & Truck Service**
	Med	E: + Baptist Memorial Hospital
	Other	E: Auto Dealers, Auto Services, ATMs, Circuit City, Dollar Tree, Grocery, Harley Davidson of DeSoto, Lowe's, NAPA, Office Depot, PetCo ♥, **Pharmacy**, Sam's Club, **Wal-Mart sc**, UPS Store W: Auto Services, Family Dollar, Home Depot, Kroger, Target, **Walgreen's**, Bruce Rossmeyer's Southern Thunder Harley Davidson, **Audubon Point RV Park▲**
(288)		**Future Exit**, Nail Rd
287		Church Rd, Southaven
	Gas	E: AmocoBP, Citgo◊ W: Shell◊
	Food	E: Chesters Fried Chicken/Texaco W: DQ/Shell, McDonald's, Quiznos, Subway, Waffle House
	Lodg	W: Country Hearth Inn, Magnolia Inn, Super 8
	Other	W: **Southaven RV Supercenter**, **EZ Daze RV Park▲**, **Audubon Point RV Park▲**
(285)		Weigh Station (Both dir)
(285)		**Future Exit**, Star Landing Rd
284		Nesbit Rd, to US 51, Pleasant Hill Rd, Nesbit
	Gas	E: Wayne's Quick Stop/BP
	Food	E: Happy Daze
(283)		Jct I-69S, MS 304S, to Tunica
	NOTE:	Begin NB I-55/I-69 concurrency, End SB
280		MS 304, US 51, Commerce St, Hernando
	FStop	W: **Chevron**
	Gas	E: Exxon, Murphy W: BP◊, Citgo◊, Shell◊, Kroger
	Food	E: Captain D's, Guadalara Mex Grill, Huddle House, Sonic W: **Subway**/**Chevron**, Coleman's, BBQ, McDonald's, Papa John's, Pizza Hut, Quiznos, Wendy's
	Lodg	E: Budget Inn, Days Inn, Hernando Inn W: Super 8
	Other	E: Auto Services, NAPA, **Wal-Mart sc** W: ATMs, Banks, Auto Services, Museum, Kroger, Piggly Wiggly, Tires, Visitor Center
(279)		**MS Welcome Center (SB)** **(RR, Phones, Picnic, Sec24/7, RVDump)**
(276)		**Hernando Rest Area (NB)** **(RR, Phones, Picnic, Sec24/7, RVDump)**
271		MS 306, Cemetery Rd, to US 51, Coldwater, Independence
	Gas	E: Coldwater Market & Deli W: AmocoBP, Citgo, Exxon
	Other	W: **Memphis South Campground & RV Park▲**, to COE/**Hernando Point**/**Arkabutla Lake**

EXIT		MISSISSIPPI
265		MS 4, Main St, Senatobia, to Holly Springs, Tunica
	TStop	W: **Fuel Mart #622**, **Kangaroo Express**
	Gas	W: Exxon
	Food	W: **Huddle House**/**Kangaroo Exp**, Coleman's BBQ, Domino's, Pizza Hut, Rio Lindo Mex Rest, Sonic, Subway, Taco Bell, Waffle House, Wendy's
	Lodg	W: **Days Inn**, Motel 6 ♥
	TServ	W: **Kangaroo Exp**/Tires
	Med	W: + N Oak Reg'l Medical Center
	Other	W: **Laundry**/**Kangaroo Exp**, ATMs, Bank, Auto Dealers, CarWash, Carquest, Grocery, **Pharmacy**, **Wal-Mart sc**, **Senatobia RV & Trailer Sales**, NW MS Comm College
263		MS 740, to US 51, S Senatobia
257		MS 310, Oak Ave, Como
	Gas	E: BP◊
	Other	E: to North Sardis Lake
252		MS 315, Lee St, Sardis
	FStop	W: **Chevron**
	Gas	E: Shell, Pure◊ W: BP, Shell
	Food	E: McDonald's, Nonnie & Pop's, BBQ, Sonic, Smokin Catfish
	Lodg	E: **Lake Inn**, Super 8 W: Knights Inn
	Med	E: + Hospital
	Other	E: to John Kyle State Park▲ W: Grocery, Dollar General, **Pharmacy**
246		MS 35, N Batesville
	TStop	W: Maggie T's/Shell
	Gas	W: Gas Mart Mobil
	Food	W: Rest/Maggie T's
	Other	E: to Sardis Dam
243B		MS 6W, Batesville, to Marks
	Gas	W: Chevron◊, Exxon◊, Phillips 66◊, Shell◊
	Food	W: Captain D's, **Cracker Barrel**, DQ, Hardee's, Huddle House, McDonald's, KFC, Pizza Hut, Sonic, Subway, Taco Bell, Wendy's, Western Sizzlin
	Lodg	W: AmeriHost Inn, **Comfort Inn**, **Days Inn**, Hampton Inn, Holiday Inn, Ramada Inn
	Other	W: ATMs, Banks, Advance Auto, Auto Dealers, Auto Services, Dollar General, **Diesel Services**, Family Dollar, Grocery, Kroger, Lowe's, O'Reilly, Radio Shack, Tires, UPS Store, Outlet Stores
243A		MS 6E, Batesville, to Oxford
	FStop	E: **Gas Mart Shell**
	Gas	E: BP◊, Murphy USA◊
	Food	E: Backyard Burgers, Subway
	Med	E: + Tri Lakes Medical Center
	Other	E: Wal-Mart sc, to S Sardis Lake
(239)		**Batesville Rest Area (Both dir)** **(RR, Phones, Picnic, Sec24/7, RVDump)**
237		Hentz Rd, to US 51, Courtland, Pope
	FStop	W: **Winters Travelstop**/Pure
233		CR 36, Oakland, Enid
	Gas	W: Benson's
	Other	E: to COE/**Wallace Creek**/Enid Lake▲
227		MS 32, Oakland, to Water Valley, Charleston
	FStop	W: **55-32 Gas Mart**/Exxon
	Gas	W: Shell
	Food	W: FastFood/55-32 GM
	Other	E: **George Payne Cossar St Park▲**, COE/**Water Valley Landing Campground**/Enid Lake▲

◊ = Regular Gas Stations with Diesel   ▲ = RV Friendly Locations   ♥ = Pet Friendly Locations
RED PRINT SHOWS LARGE VEHICLE PARKING/ACCESS ON SITE OR NEARBY   BROWN PRINT SHOWS CAMPGROUNDS/RV PARKS

Page 231

INTERSTATE 55 N/S

EXIT	MISSISSIPPI
220	MS 330, Tillatoba Rd, Tillatoba Oakland
TStop	E: Griffis Truck Stop
Food	E: Rest/Griffis TS
TServ	E: Griffis TS/Tires
Other	E: Laundry/LP/WiFi/CB/Griffis TS
211	MS 7, MS 333, Grenada, Coffeeville
FStop	W: 55-7 Gas Mart/Shell
Gas	W: BP◆
Food	W: FastFood/55-7 GasMart
Other	W: Frog Hollow Campground▲
208	Papermill Rd, Grenada
Other	E: Grenada Muni Airport✈
206	MS 7, MS 8, Grenada, Greenwood
FStop	W: Shell
Gas	E: Exxon◆, RaceWay W: Exxon
Food	E: Burger King, Huddle House, La Cabana, McDonald's, Pizza Hut, Shoney's, Subway, Taco Bell, Western Sizzlin, Rest/BW
Lodg	E: Best Value Inn, Best Western♥, Comfort Inn, Days Inn, Holiday Inn Express, Jameson Inn, Knights Inn, Quality Inn, Super 8 W: Country Inn, Econo Lodge
Med	E: + Grenada Family Medical Clinic
Other	E: AutoZone, Auto Dealers, Auto Services, Advance Auto, Auto Zone, Dollar General,
Other	E: Kroger, US Post Office, Wal-Mart sc, to Hugh White State Park▲
(203)	Parking Area (SB)
(202)	Parking Area (NB)
199	Trout Rd, Grenada, Elliott
Other	E: to Camp McCain Military Res
195	MS 404, McCarley, to Duck Hill
Gas	W: Conoco◆
185	US 82, Winona, to Greenwood
TStop	W: Pilot Travel Center #261 (Scales)
Gas	E: Exxon, Shell◆
Food	E: Huddle House, KFC, McDonald's, Pizza Hut, Subway W: TacoBell/Pilot TC
Lodg	E: Magnolia Lodge, Relax Inn, Western Inn
Med	E: + Tyler Holmes Memorial Hospital
Other	E: MS State Univ, Ms Univ for Women W: Laundry/WiFi/Pilot TC, MS Valley State Univ
174	MS 430, MS 35, Vaiden, Carrollton
FStop	E: Vaiden Shell
TStop	E: 35-55 Travel Center/Chevron (Scales)
Gas	W: Exxon◆
Food	E: Rest/35-55 TC W: Stuckey's/Exxon
Lodg	E: Motel/35-55 TC
TServ	E: 35-55 TC
Other	E: Laundry/WiFi/35-55 TC, Vaiden KOA/RVDump▲
(173)	Rest Area (SB) (RR, Phones, Picnic, Sec24/7, RVDump)
164	MS 19, West
FStop	W: West Pit Stop/Pure
TServ	W: West PS/Tires
Other	W: WiFi/West PS
(163)	Rest Area (NB) (RR, Phones, Picnic, Sec 24/7, RVDump)

EXIT	MISSISSIPPI
156	MS 12, Durant, Lexington
FStop	E: 55-12 Gas Mart/Shell
Food	E: FastFood/55-12 GM
Lodg	E: Super 8
Med	W: + University Hospital
150	State Park Rd, Georgeville Rd
Other	E: Holmes Co State Park▲
146	MS 14, Goodman, Ebenezer
Other	W: to Little Red Schoolhouse
144	MS 17, Pickens, Lexington
TStop	E: J's Truck Stop/Chevron W: Dickerson Petro #101/BP
Food	E: Rest/J's TS W: Rest/Dickerson BP
Other	E: WiFi/J's TS
139	MS 432, Vaughan, Pickens, Benton
133	Vaughan Rd, Vaughan
124	MS 16, N Canton, Yazoo City
(120)	Parking Area (SB)
119	MS 22, MS 16, to US 51, Canton
FStop	E: Nancy's Restaurant & Fuel Center
TStop	W: Love's Travel Stop #208 (Scales)
Gas	E: AmocoBP◆, Exxon, Shell W: Chevron, Super Saver Citgo◆
Food	E: Rest/Nancy's FC, McDonald's, Pizza Hut, Subway/BP, Sonic, Wendy's W: Arby's/Love's TS, Bumpers DriveIn, KFC, Two Rivers Rest, Western Sizzler
Lodg	E: Days Inn W: Best Western, Comfort Inn, Econo Lodge, Hampton Inn, Holiday Inn Express
Med	E: + Hospital
Other	E: Discount Auto Repair, Ross Barnett Reservoir Upper Lake W: WiFi/RVDump/Love's TS
118AB	Nissan Parkway, Canton
Other	E: Nissan North America Plant/Canton
(117)	Parking Area (NB)
114	Sowell Rd
112	Gluckstadt Rd, Madison
FStop	E: Kangaroo #3424, C Store #635/Exxon
Food	E: Subway/Kangaroo, Krystal/Exxon
Lodg	E: Super 8
Other	W: Camper Corral
108	MS 463, Main St, Madison
Gas	E: Shell◆, Texaco◆ W: Exxon◆
Food	E: Applebee's, Back Yard Burgers, ChickFilA, Chili's, Domino's/Texaco, Haute Pig Rest, Penn Station Subs W: KFC/Exxon, Bonefish Grill, Papito's Mex Grill, Pizza Inn, Wendy's
Lodg	W: Hilton Garden Inn
Other	E: Lowe's, Wal-Mart sc W: CVS, Home Depot
105B	Old Agency Rd, W Jackson St, Ridgeland
Gas	E: Chevron◆
105A	Natchez Trace Pkwy, Ridgeland
(104)	Jct I-220W, West Jackson
103	County Line Rd, Jackson
Gas	E: BP, Circle K, Exxon◆, Shell W: Speedway

EXIT	MISSISSIPPI
Food	E: Applebee's, Burger King, ChickFilA, Cuco's Mex Rest, Fuddruckers, Hardee's, KFC, Mazzio's, McDonald's, Moe's SW Grill, On the Border, Roadhouse Grill, Ruby Tuesday, Romano's Macaroni Grill, Santa Fe Grill, Shoney's, Starbucks, Subway, Taco Bell, Wendy's
Food	W: Logan Roadhouse, Olive Garden, Red Lobster
Lodg	E: Cabot Lodge, Courtyard, Days Inn, Econo Lodge, Hilton, Homewood Suites, Staybridge Suites, Studio Plus W: Comfort Suites, Drury Inn, Motel 6
Other	E: ATMs, Banks, B&N, Best Buy, Cinema 14, Circuit City, CompUSA, Northpark Mall, Goodyear, Office Depot, Sam's Club, Wal-Mart, Auto Services, Auto Dealers W: Home Depot, PetSmart♥, Pharmacy, Target, Tougaloo College
102	Beasley Rd, Briarwood Dr, Adkins Blvd, Jackson (SB)
102 B	Beasley Rd, Adkins Blvd (NB)
Gas	E: BP, Chevron, Shell W: Exxon
Food	E: Cracker Barrel, Fazoli's, Japanese Rest Mex Rest, Lone Star Steakhouse, Outback Steakhouse, Starbucks, Subway, Tony Roma W: McDonald's
Lodg	E: Ramada Inn W: Best Western, Extended Stay Hotel, Fairfield Inn, Hampton Inn, InTown Suites, Jameson Inn
Other	E: Auto Dealers, Enterprise RAC, Firestone, Office Depot, Kroger
102A	Briarwood Dr, Frontage Rd (NB Exit, SB Entr)
Gas	E: BP, Phillips 66
Food	W: Chili's, El Chico, Hops, McDonald's, Perkins, Red Lobster, Steak & Ale
Lodg	E: La Quinta Inn♥ W: Best Value Inn, Comfort Inn, Fairfield Inn, Hampton Inn
Other	W: Big Lots, Kmart, Office Depot
100	Northside Dr, Downtown Jackson
Gas	E: BP, Chevron, Shell, Sprint W: AmocoBP, Exxon, Kangaroo
Food	E: Burger King, Dunkin Donuts, Krystal, McDonald's, Papa John's, Piccadilly's, Shoney's, Subway, Wendy's, Western Sizzlin W: Bennigan's, Hooter's, IHOP, Pizza Hut, Shoney's, Waffle House
Lodg	E: Holiday Inn W: Knights Inn, Super 8
Other	E: ATMs, Auto Services, AutoZone, Firestone, Goodyear, Pharmacy, Kroger, Office Depot, Winn Dixie
99	Meadowbrook Rd (NB)
98CB	MS 25, Lakeland Dr, Carthage
Gas	E: Shell
Med	E: + to River Oaks Hospital W: + St. Dominic Memorial Hospital, Univ Ms Medical Center
Other	E: Smith Wills Stadium, LeFleur's Bluff State Park▲, to Antonelli College, Jackson Int'l Airport✈ W: Veterans Memorial Stadium

Page 232 ◆ = Regular Gas Stations with Diesel ▲ = RV Friendly Locations ♥ = Pet Friendly Locations
RED PRINT SHOWS LARGE VEHICLE PARKING/ACCESS ON SITE OR NEARBY BROWN PRINT SHOWS CAMPGROUNDS/RV PARKS

INTERSTATE 55 N/S

MISSISSIPPI

EXIT		
98A		Woodrow Wilson Dr, (NB Left exit) to State St (diff reaccess)
	Med	W: + University of Mississippi Medical Center, + VA Hospital
	Other	W: MS State Hwy Patrol Post
96C		Fortification St, Jackson
	Lodg	E: Residence Inn
	Med	W: + Ms Univ Medical Center
	Other	E: Bellhaven College, Hawkins Field ✈
96B		High St, Downtown Jackson
	Gas	W: Sprint Mart, Texaco◊
	Food	W: Burger King, DQ, Domino's Pizza, Dunkin Donuts, Popeye's, Shoney's, Taco Bell, Waffle House, Wendy's
	Lodg	E: Red Roof Inn ♥
		W: Best Western, Days Inn, Holiday Inn Express, Hampton Inn, Microtel, Red Roof Inn
	Other	W: MS State Capitol, Fairgrounds, MS Coliseum
96A		Pearl St, Downtown Jackson
	Lodg	W: Clarion, Quality Inn
	Other	W: MS Museum of Art, Natural Science Museum, State Fairgrounds
NOTE:		I-55 below runs with I-20. Exit #'s follow I-20.
(94/46)		Jct I-20E, to Meridian, Jct I-55N, to Grenada, Memphis, US 49S
45		US 51, State St, Gallatin St (EB, Left exit)
45B		US 51, State St (WB)
	Gas	N: Chevron
		S: Speedway
	Other	N: Police
45A		Gallatin St (WB)
	TStop	N: Petro Stopping Center #28/Mobil (Scales) (Exit 45 EB)
		S: Pilot Travel Center #77 (Scales)
	Gas	N: Chevron
	Food	N: IronSkillet/Petro SC
		S: McDonald's/Pilot TC
	Lodg	S: Knights Inn
	TWash	N: Blue Beacon TW/Petro SC
	TServ	N: Petro SC/Tires
	Other	N: Laundry/BarbSh/CB/RVDump/Petro SC, Amtrak, Auto Repairs, Tires
		S: Laundry/WiFi/Pilot TC
(44/92C)		Jct I-20W, to Vicksburg, US 49S, Jct I-55S, to New Orleans, McComb (WB, Left Exit)
		Jct I-20W, US 49N, to Vicksburg, Yazoo City (NB, Left exit)
NOTE:		I-55 above runs with I-20. Exit #'s follow I-20.
92B		US 51N, State St, Gallatin St (NB)
92A		McDowell Rd, Jackson
	Gas	W: Shell, Texaco◊
	Food	W: McDonald's, Smiley's BBQ, Thai House, Waffle House, Wendy's
	Lodg	W: Super 8
90B		Daniel Lake Blvd, Cooper Rd (SB)
	Gas	W: Shell
90A		Savanna St, Jackson
	Gas	W: AmocoBP
	Food	E: Charley's Steak & Seafood/Save Inn
		W: Bo Don's Catfish & Seafood
	Lodg	E: Save Inn
88		Elton Rd, Jackson
	Gas	W: Chevron, Exxon◊
	Food	W: Subway/Chester/Exxon
85		Siwell Rd, Byram
	Gas	E: BP◊
		W: Conoco◊, Spur, Texaco◊
	Food	E: Krystal, Mex Rest
		W: Captain D's, Dragon Garden Chinese, McDonald's, Pizza Hut, Popeye's, Sonic, Subway, Taco Bell, Waffle House, Wendys
	Lodg	W: Days Inn
	Other	E: Swinging Bridge RV Park ▲, Swinging Bridge Raceway
		W: ATMs, Banks, Auto Services, Grocery, Dollar General, Pharmacy, Tires, PawPaw's Camper City
81		Wynndale Rd, Terry
	FStop	W: Super Stop #44/Conoco
78		Cunningham St, Terry, to MS 473
	FStop	E: Red Apple/Texaco
	Gas	W: Circle K, Mac's #11
	Food	E: FastFood/Texaco
	Other	E: Auto Service, Police Dept
72		MS 27, North Crystal Springs, to Vicksburg
	FStop	E: 27-55 Gas Plaza/66
	Gas	E: Exxon◊
	Food	E: Louise's BBQ, McDonald's, Popeye's, Subway/Exxon
	Other	E: Auto Service, Auto Dealer
68		Pat Harrison Dr, to US 51, S Crystal Springs
	Other	E: Auto Service
65		Byrd Town Rd, Hazlehurst, Gallman
	Gas	E: Shell
	Food	E: Stuckey's/Shell
61		MS 28, Hazlehurst, Fayette
	Gas	E: Chevron, Exxon, Phillips 66, Texaco
	Food	E: Burger King, KFC, McDonald's, Pizza Hut, Wendy's, Western Sizzlin
	Lodg	E: Days Inn, Claridge Inn, Western Inn Express
	Med	E: + Hardy Wilson Memorial Hospital
	Other	E: ATMs, Banks, Amtrak, Auto Services, Dollar General, Family Dollar, Grocery, Pharmacy, Wal-Mart
59		County Farm Rd, S Hazlehurst (Access #61 Serv via US 51N)
56		Tower Rd, Hazlehurst, Martinsville
(54)		Hazlehurst Rest Area (Both dir) (RR, Phones, Picnic, Vend, Sec24/7, RVDump)
51		Sylvarena Rd, Wesson, Beauregard
	TStop	W: Country Junction Truck Stop/Chevron
	Food	W: Rest/Country Jct TS
	TWash	W: Country Jct TS
	TServ	W: Country Jct TS/Tires
	Other	E: Timberlands Campground & Ranch▲
		W: Laundry/RVDump/Country Jct
48		Mt Zion Rd, Wesson
42		Dunn Ratcliff Rd, N Brookhaven
	TStop	E: Brookhaven Truckstop/66
	Gas	E: Exxon, Shell◊
	Food	E: Rest/P66
	Lodg	W: Super 8
	Tires	E: Brookhaven TS
	TWash	E: Brookhaven TS
	Med	E: + Hospital
	Other	E: Auto Dealers
40		Brookway Blvd, to MS 550, Downtown Brookhaven
	Gas	E: AmocoBP, Exxon, Shell◊, Murphy
	Food	E: Burger King, DQ, Cracker Barrel, KFC, McDonald's, Pizza Hut, Shoney's, Taco Bell, Western Sizzlin, Wendy's
	Lodg	E: Best Inn, Budget Inn, Comfort Inn, Days Inn, Hampton Inn, Spanish Inn Motel
	Med	E: + Kings Daughters Medical Center
	Other	E: AutoZone, Amtrak, Auto Dealers, ATMs, Banks, Cinema, CarQuest, Dollar Tree, Grocery, Walgreen's, Wal-Mart sc
		W: Animal Medical Center ♥, Home Depot
38		US 84, S Brookhaven, Natchez, Monticello, Meadville
	FStop	W: 84 Chevron
	Gas	E: Exxon◊
	Tires	W: 84 Chevron
	Other	W: LP/84 Chevron
30		Bogue Chitto, Norfield
	TStop	E: Bogue Chitto Shell Auto/Truck Stop
	Food	E: Rest/FastFood/Bogue Chitto ATS
	Other	E: Laundry/WiFi/Bogue Chitto ATS
(26)		Parking Area (NB)
24		Freeman SW Rd, Summitt, Johnston Station, Lake Dixie Springs
(23)		Parking Area (SB)
20AB		US 98W, Summit, to Natchez
	FStop	W: Shawn Mart/66
	Gas	E: BP◊, Shell◊
		W: Exxon◊
	Other	E: SW Mississippi Comm College
18		MS 570, Smithdale Rd, N McComb
	FStop	W: Chevron
	Gas	E: BP
	Food	E: Burger King, McDonald's, Piccadilly's, Ruby Tuesday
		W: Arby's
	Med	E: + Hospital
	Lodg	W: Hawthorne Inn
	Other	E: Lowe's, Mall, Wal-Mart sc
17		Delaware Ave, Downtown McComb
	Gas	E: BP, Chevron◊, Exxon, Raceway, Shell◊
	Food	E: Burger King, China Palace, DQ, Golden Corral, Huddle House, McDonald's, Pizza Hut, Subway/BP, Taco Bell, Wendy's
	Lodg	E: Comfort Inn, Super 8
		W: Days Inn
	Med	E: + Hospital
	Other	E: AutoZone, ATMs, Banks, Amtrak, CVS, Family Dollar, Grocery, Kroger
		W: Auto Dealer
15AB		US 98E, MS 24W, Presley Blvd, Tylertown, Liberty, S McComb
	FStop	W: Hwy 24 BP
	Gas	E: Exxon, Shell
	Food	E: Hardee's, KFC, Subway/Exxon
	Lodg	E: Chameleon Motel, Economy Inn

◊ = Regular Gas Stations with Diesel ▲ = RV Friendly Locations ♥ = Pet Friendly Locations
RED PRINT SHOWS LARGE VEHICLE PARKING/ACCESS ON SITE OR NEARBY   BROWN PRINT SHOWS CAMPGROUNDS/RV PARKS

N I-55

EXIT		MS / LA
	TServ	E: Peterbilt of Mississippi
	Other	E: Auto Services
		W: to Percy Quin State Park▲
13		Fernwood Rd, McComb
	TStop	W: PTP/Fernwood Truck Stop/Conoco (Scal
	Food	W: Fernwood Family Rest/Fernwood TS
	Lodg	W: Fernwood Motel/Fernwood TS
	TWash	W: Fernwood TS
	TServ	E: Interstate Trucking
		W: Fernwood TS/Tires
	Other	W: Laundry/LP/Fernwood TS, Percy Quin State Park▲
10		MS 48, to US 51, Magnolia (All Serv E in Magnolia)
8		MS 568, Magnolia, to Gillsburg
4		Chatawa Rd, to US 51, Osyka
(3)		MS Welcome Center (NB) (RR, Phones, Picnic, Sec24/7, RVDump)
(2)		Weigh Station (Both dir)
1		MS 584, Osyka, to Gillsburg
	Other	E: Osyka Springs Campground▲

(CENTRAL TIME ZONE)

⊙ MISSISSIPPI
⊙ LOUISIANA

(CENTRAL TIME ZONE)

NOTE: MM 65: Mississippi State Line

(65)		LA Welcome Center (SB) (RR, Phone, Picnic, Sec, Info, RVDump)
(64)		Weigh Station (NB)
61		LA 38, Ave G, Kentwood, Liverpool
	FStop	W: Kangaroo #3467, Super Station/Exxon
	Gas	E: Chevron, Texaco
	Food	E: Jam Fried Chicken & Seafood, Pizza Shack, Sonic
	Other	E: Auto Dealer, Dollar General, Family Dollar
		W: to Great Discovery Inspiration Park▲
(59)		Weigh Station (SB)
57		LA 440, Kentwood, Tangipahoa
(54)		Rest Area (NB) (RR, Phones)
53		LA 10, Fluker, Greensburg
50		LA 1048, Arcola, Roseland
	FStop	E: Chevron
47		LA 16, Amite, Montpelier
	TStop	W: Amite Plaza, Forest Gold Truck Plaza & Casino
	Gas	E: Exxon◊, Racetrac
	Food	E: KFC, McDonald's, Mike's Catfish Inn, Popeye's, Sonic, Subway, Wendy's
		W: Amite Grill, Ardillo's
	Lodg	E: Comfort Inn
		W: Colonial Inn Motel
	TServ	W: Forest Gold TP
	Med	E: + Hood Memorial Hospital
	Other	E: Auto Services, AutoZone, Cinema, Grocery, Pharmacy, Tires, Wal-Mart sc
		W: to Natalabany Creek Campground▲, Sweetwater Campground▲

EXIT		LOUISIANA
41		LA 40, Independence
	Gas	E: Conoco
	Med	E: + Hospital
	Other	W: Indian Creek Campground & RV Park▲
36		LA 442, Tickfaw
	FStop	E: Tickfaw Pit Stop/Chevron
	Food	E: FastFood/Tickfaw PS
	Other	E: New Cherokee Beach Campground▲ Global Wildlife Center
32		LA 3234, Wardline Rd, Hammond
	Gas	E: Chevron, Kangaroo◊
		W: Chevron
	Food	E: Burger King, McDonald's, Sonic, Subway, Wendy's
	Lodg	E: Best Western
	Other	E: ATMs, Banks, to Southeastern LA Univ
31		US 190, Albany, Hammond
	Gas	E: Chevron◊, Citgo, Exxon◊
	Food	E: Applebee's, Burger King, Chili's, CiCi's, Cracker Barrel, Krystal, McDonald's, Pizza Hut, Shoney's, Shorty's Ribs & Seafood, Waffle House, Wendy's
	Lodg	E: Comfort Inn, Hampton Inn, Super 8
	AServ	E: Chevron
	TServ	E: Bridgestone Tire & Auto
	Med	E: + Hospital
	Other	E: AutoZone, Auto Dealers, ATMs, Banks, Albertson's, Big Lots, Dollar General, Grocery, Lowe's, Office Depot, Radio Shack, Walgreen's, Wal-Mart sc, Auto Services, Hidden Oaks Family Campground▲, Yogi Bear's Jellystone Campground▲
(29BA)		Jct I-12, W-Baton Rouge, E-Slidell (Travel Center, All Serv, 1st Exit E #40)
28		US 51N, Hammond
	Gas	E: RaceTrac
	Food	E: Catfish Charlie, CiCi's, Don's Seafood Rest, Rest /Holiday Inn
	Lodg	E: Days Inn, Holiday Inn, Ramada Inn
	TServ	E: Big Wheel Diesel Repair
	Med	E: + Hospital
	Other	W: New Orleans/Hammond KOA▲
26		LA 22, Ponchatoula, Springfield
	Gas	E: Chevron◊, Conoco, Exxon◊, Shell◊
	Food	E: Burger King, KFC, McDonald's, Popeye, Sonic, Waffle House, Wendy's
	Lodg	E: Microtel
	Med	E: + Hospital
	Other	E: AutoZone, Dollar General, Pharmacy, Walgreen's, Winn Dixie
23		US 51 Bus, Ponchatoula
22		Frontage Rd (SB)
15		Manchac
7		Ruddock
1		US 51S, to I-10, LaPlace, to Baton Rouge (Travel Center, All Serv, 1st Exit #209)

(I-55 begins/ends I-10, Exit #209)

⊙ LOUISIANA

Begin Northbound I-55 from New Orleans, LA to Chicago, IL.

◊ = Regular Gas Stations with Diesel   ▲ = RV Friendly Locations   ♥ = Pet Friendly Locations
RED PRINT SHOWS LARGE VEHICLE PARKING/ACCESS ON SITE OR NEARBY   BROWN PRINT SHOWS CAMPGROUNDS/RV PARKS

Page 234

EXIT	ILLINOIS
	Begin Southbound I-57 from Jct I-94 in Chicago, IL to Jct I-55 in St Louis, MO

ILLINOIS
(CENTRAL TIME ZONE)
(I-57 begins/ends on I-94, Exit #63)

(359) Jct I-94, E - Chicago, Indiana

357 IL 1, Halsted St, Chicago
- Gas: E: BP, Mobil
- W: Marathon, Phillips 66
- Food: E: Ruby's Restaurant
- W: I 57 Rib House, McDonald's, Shark Fish
- Lodg: E: Grand Motel
- Other: E: Auto Repairs

355 111th St, 112th St, Monterey Ave
- Gas: W: BP, Frye's

354 119th St

353 127th St, Burr Oak Ave, Riverdale
- Gas: E: Marathon, Shell
- W: BP, Gas City
- Food: E: Burger King, McDonald's, Wendy's
- Lodg: E: Best Western, Super 8
- Other: E: AZ Auto & Truck Service

350 IL 83, Sibley Blvd, 147th St, Posen
- Gas: E: Citgo, Marathon◆
- W: BP

348 US 6, 159th St, Markham
- Gas: E: Marathon
- W: Citgo◆, Mobil◆
- Food: E: Burger King, Taco Bell
- Lodg: E: Hi-Way Motel
- W: D-Lux Budget Motel
- Med: W: + Oak Forest Hospital

346 167th St, Cicero Ave, IL 50
- Gas: E: BP, Citgo
- W: Shell
- Lodg: E: Ramada Inn ♥
- Med: W: + Oak Forest Hospital
- Other: E: Peterson Towing, Auto & Truck Repair, Auto Services, Wal-Mart sc, AMC 16

(345B) Jct I-80W, to Iowa
- Other: W: to Windy City Campground & Beach▲

(345A) Jct I-80E, to Indiana, to I-294N, TriState Tollway, to Wisconsin

342B Vollmer Rd W (SB)

342A Vollmer Rd E (SB)
- Gas: E: Shell
- Med: E: + St James Hospital

342 Vollmer Rd, Matteson (NB)

340B US 30W, 211th St, Lincoln Hwy

340A US 30E, 211th St, Lincoln Hwy

340 US 30, Lincoln Hwy, Matteson
- Gas: E: BP, Citgo◆, Mobil, Shell, Sam's
- Food: E: Applebee's, Bob Evans, Chuck E Cheese Pizza, Cracker Barrel, Denny's, Fuddrucker's, IHOP, McDonald's, Olive Garden, Panera, Panda Express, Pizza Hut, Quiznos, Red Lobster, Starbucks, Subway, Taco Bell, Wendy's, Rest/Hol Inn
- Lodg: E: Country Inn, Days Inn, La Quinta Inn ♥, Holiday Inn, Matteson Motel
- Other: E: ATMs, Banks, Auto Services, Best Buy, Circuit City, Enterprise, FedEx Kinko's, Firestone, Grocery, Goodyear, Home Depot PetSmart ♥, Sam's Club, Target, UPS Store, U-Haul, Wal-Mart, Lincoln Mall

EXIT	ILLINOIS

- Other: W: Auto Dealers & Services, to Terry's RV Center

339 Sauk Trail, Richton Park
- Gas: E: Citgo
- Food: E: McDonald's
- Other: E: Grocery, Police Dept
- W: Bowling Alley

335 CR 6, Monee Manhattan Rd, Monee
- TStop: E: Petro Stopping Center #65/Mobil (Scales)
- W: Pilot Travel Center #39 (Scales)
- Gas: W: BP
- Food: E: IronSkillet/FastFood/Petro SC, Burger King, Lucky Burrito, Max's, Pizza Inn
- W: McDonald's/Pilot TC, FastFood/BP
- Lodg: E: Country Host Motel, Best Western, Holiday Inn Express, Super 8
- TWash: E: Petro SC, Blue Beacon TW
- TServ: E: Petro SC/Tires
- Other: E: Laundry/CB/WiFi/Petro SC, Governor's State Univ
- W: Laundry/WiFi/Pilot TC, Towing

(332) IL Welcome Center (Both dir)
(RR, Phones, Picnic, Vend, Info, RVDump)

(330) Weigh Station (Both dir)

327 Wilmington Rd, Peotone, Wilmington
- Gas: E: Casey's, Shell
- Food: E: Pizza/Casey's McDonald's, Taco Bell
- Other: E: Fairgrounds

322 CR 9, to US 45, US 52, Manteno, to Wilmington
- FStop: W: Gas City #9
- Gas: E: BP, Phillips 66
- Food: E: Hardee's, Pizza Hut, McDonald's/BP, Subway/P66
- W: FastFood/Gas City
- Lodg: E: Country Inn, Howard Johnson
- Med: E: + Manteno State Hospital
- Other: E: Land of Lincoln Harley Davidson

315 IL 50, to US 45, US 52, Bourbonnais
- Gas: W: BP
- Food: E: Cracker Barrel, Light House Pizza
- W: Applebee's, Arby's, Bakers Square, Checkers, Denny's, Hardee's, McDonald's, IHOP, Lone Star Steakhouse, Old Country Buffet, Steak n Shake, Starbucks, Subway, Taco Bell, Wendy's
- Lodg: E: Hampton Inn, Holiday Inn Express
- W: Motel 6 ♥, Northgate Motel, Quality Inn, Ramada Inn, Super 8
- Other: W: Auto Dealers, ATMs, Auto Services, Banks, B & N, Cinema 10, Grocery, Kmart, Lowe's, PetCo ♥, Wal-Mart, Olivet Nazarene Univ, Brown & Brown RV Center, Quality MH & RV Service

312 IL 17, E Court St, Kankakee, Momence
- Gas: W: BP, Shell
- Food: W: McDonald's, Subway, Wendy's, JJ's Fish & Chicken, Rest/Days Inn
- Lodg: W: Avis Motel, Days Inn
- TServ: W: International
- Med: W: + Provena St Mary's Hospital
- Other: W: ATMs, Banks, Auto Services, Laundromat, Walgreen's

308 US 45, US 52, Kankakee
- Gas: W: Gas Depot
- Food: W: JJ Ruffles
- Lodg: W: Fairview Motel

◆ = Regular Gas Stations with Diesel   ▲ = RV Friendly Locations   ♥ = Pet Friendly Locations
RED PRINT SHOWS LARGE VEHICLE PARKING/ACCESS ON SITE OR NEARBY   BROWN PRINT SHOWS CAMPGROUNDS/RV PARKS

INTERSTATE 57 N/S

EXIT		ILLINOIS
	Other	E: I-57 Truck & Trailer Services, County Fairgrounds, Greater Kankakee Airport✈, Kankakee South KOA▲ W: Kankakee Comm College
302		CR 37, CR 3400N, Chebanse
	Gas	W: BP
	TServ	W: Ken's Truck Repair
297		CR 4, Clifton
	Gas	W: Phillips 66
293		IL 116, to US 45, Ashkum
	Gas	E: BP
	Food	E: DQ W: The Loft
	TServ	E: Meier Bros Tire
	Other	E: IL State Hwy Patrol Post
283		US 24, CR 1700N, Gilman, Chatsworth
	TStop	E: K&H Truck Plaza/BP (Scales), Apollo Travel Center W: Gilman Truck Stop/P66
	Gas	E: Shell
	Food	E: Rest/K&H TP, Rest/FastFood/ApolloMart TP, Burger King, DQ, McDonald's W: Subway/Gilman TS
	Lodg	E: Budget Host Inn, Super 8, Travel Inn
	TServ	E: K&H TP/Tires
	Other	E: Amtrak, Laundry/WiFi/K&H TP, Laundry/ApolloMart TP, W: R&R RV Sales/RVDump
280		IL 54, CR 1450N, W Seminary Ave, to US 45, Onarga, Roberts
	Gas	E: Casey's, Marathon, Phillips 66
	Other	E: Auto Repairs, Truck Service W: Lake Arrowhead RV Campground▲
272		CR 9, CR 800N, Buckley, Roberts
(268)		Rest Area (Both dir) (RR, Phones, Picnic, Vend)
261		IL 9, W Ottawa Rd, Paxton, to Gibso City, Rankin
	Gas	E: Casey's, Citgo W: AmocoBP, Marathon
	Food	E: Hardee's, Pizza Hut, Subway W: Country Gardens Rest
	Lodg	W: Paxton Inn♥
	Other	E: Auto Dealer, Laundry, Auto Services W: Paxton Airport✈
250		US 136, Champaign Ave, Rantoul, Fisher
	Gas	E: BP, Circle K, Phillips 66
	Food	E: Arby's, Burger King, Domino's, Hardee's, Long John Silver's, McDonalds, Subway, Taco Bell, Rest/Days Inn
	Lodg	E: Best Western♥, Days Inn, Super 8♥
	Other	E: ATMs, Amtrak, Banks, Auto Services, to CityPark/Prairie Pines Campground▲, Rantoul Nat'l Aviation Center/Frank Elliott Field✈, Chanute Air Force Base
240		Market St, CR 20, Champaign
	TStop	E: Road Ranger #132/Citgo
	Food	E: Rest/Road Ranger
	TServ	E: Road Ranger/Tires
	Other	W: D&W Lake Camping & RV Park▲
238		Olympian Dr St, Champaign
	Gas	W: Mobil
	Food	W: DQ
	Lodg	W: Microtel
	Other	E: to Prospect Ave: Cinema, Circuit City, Target, Wal-Mart sc, Food, Lodging W: ATMs, Banks

EXIT		ILLINOIS
(237B)		Jct I-74W, to Peoria
(237A)		Jct I-74E, to Indianapolis (All Serv, E to 1st Ex # 181)
	Other	E: to Parkland College, Univ of IL
(235B)		Jct I-72W, to Decatur, Springfield
(235A)		Jct I-72E, to Champaign, Urbana
	Other	E: Serv Avail E to Mattis Ave, IL 10: Auto Services, Diesel Services, Food, to Univ of IL
229		CR 18, Monticello Rd, Champaign, to US 45, Monticello, Savoy, Tolono (Serv 2.5-4mi E, use US 45N)
	FStop	E: Speedway #5365
	Other	E: to Wal-Mart sc, Auto Services, Food, Univ of IL-Willard Airport✈
(222)		Rest Area (Both dir) (RR, Phones, Picnic, Vend)
220		US 45, Pesotum, Tolono
	Gas	W: Citgo
	Other	E: IL State Hwy Patrol Post
212		US 36, Southline Rd, Tuscola, Newman
	TStop	E: Fuel Mart #787 W: Road Ranger #139 (Scales)
	Gas	W: BP
	Food	E: FastFood/FuelMart W: FastFood/RoadRanger, Amishland Red Barn Buffet, Burger King, Denny's, Four Seasons Family Rest, McDonalds, Pizza Hut, Proud Mary's, Subway
	Lodg	W: AmeriHost Inn, Holiday Inn Express, Super 8, Tuscola Cooper Motel
	Other	E: LP/FuelMart W: ATMs, Auto Services, Banks, IGA, Firestone, Quality Truck & Trailer Repair, Visitor Center, to Tuscola Airport✈
203		IL 133, Springfield Rd, Arcola, Paris
	FStop	E: Gasland Food Mart/Citgo
	Gas	E: Sun Rise Gas, Shell
	Food	W: DQ, Hardee's, Hen House Family Rest, La Cazuelas Mex Rest, Monical's Pizza, Subway
	Lodg	W: Budget Inn♥, Comfort Inn♥
	Other	E: to Walnut Point State Park▲ W: ATMs, Auto Services, Banks, Grocery, IGA, Towing, Arcola Camper Stop▲
190AB		IL 16, Broadway Ave, Mattoon, Windsor, Charleston
	Gas	E: Citgo W: Phillips 66, Murphy
	Food	W: Arby's, Cracker Barrel, McDonald's, Steak n Shake, Taco Bell, Wendy's
	Lodg	W: Comfort Suites, Days Inn, Fairfield Inn, Hampton Inn, Ramada Inn, Super 8
	TServ	E: Raben Tire Co
	Med	E: + Sarah Bush Lincoln Health Center
	Other	E: Coles Co Memorial Airport✈, to E IL Univ, Happy Trails RV Rentals W: ATMs, Big Lots, Cross Country Mall, Banks, Grocery, Home Depot, Staples, Wal-Mart sc, Amtrak, to Cross Country RV Center, Wolf Creek State Park, Eagle Creek State Park, COE/Campgrounds▲/Lake Shelbyville
184		US 45, IL 121, Mattoon (Addt'l Serv 3-4 mi W in Mattoon)
	Gas	E: Citgo◊ W: Marathon◊, Shell

EXIT		ILLINOIS
177		US 45, Neoga
	TStop	E: Neoga Truck Stop/BP W: ASW Phillips 66 Truck Plaza
	Gas	E: Casey's
	Food	E: Rest/FastFood/Neoga TS W: Rest/ASW P66 TP, Casey's C/O Pizza, Villa Family Rest
	Other	E: WiFi/Neoga TS W: Auto Repair
(165)		Rest Area (Both dir) (RR, Phones, Picnic, Vend)
(163)		Jct I-70E, Indianapolis (SB, Left ex) Jct I-70W, to St Louis
	NOTE:	I-57 below runs with I-70W for 6 mi. Exit #'s follow I-57.
162		US 45, N 3rd St, Effingham
	TStop	W: Pilot Travel Center #165 (Scales)
	Gas	E: Moto Mart W: Citgo
	Food	W: McDonald's/Pilot TC
	TWash	W: Pilot TC
	Med	E: + St Anthony's Memorial Hospital
	Other	E: Legacy Harley Davidson W: Laundry/WiFi/LP/Pilot TC, Crossroads RV Center, Camp Lakewood RV Park▲
160		IL 32, IL 33, N Keller Dr, Effingham
	TStop	E: Flying J Travel Plaza #5107 (Scales) Travel Center of America #35/BP (Scales)
	Gas	E: BP, Shell W: Phillips 66, Murphy
	Food	E: KFC, Lone Star Steakhouse W: Rest/FastFood/FJ TP, CountryPride/Popeye's/Sbarro/TA TC, Arby's, Burger King, Cracker Barrel, Denny's, Long John Silver, McDonald's, Ponderosa, Ryan's Grill, Ruby Tuesday, Steak n Shake, Starbucks, Subway, Taco Bell, TGI Friday, Wendy's
	Lodg	E: Comfort Inn, Hampton Inn W: Hotel/FJ TP, Country Inn, Hilton Garden Inn, Holiday Inn Express♥, Motel 6, Ramada Ltd, Super 8♥, Travelodge
	TWash	W: Blue Beacon TW/FJ TP, TA TC
	TServ	W: TA TC/Tires, Speedco, Peterbilt, Clarke Power Services
	Med	E: + St Anthony's Memorial Hospital
	Other	E: ATMs, Banks, Dollar General, Grocery, Kmart, Kroger, Walgreen's W: ATMs, Towing, U-Haul, Wal-Mart sc, Laundry/WiFi/RVDump/LP/FJ TP, Laundry/BarbSh/WiFi/TA TC, Camp Lakewood RV Park▲
159		Fayette Ave, Effingham
	FStop	E: Econo Fuel Express/Citgo
	TStop	W: Petro Stopping Center #21/Mobil (Scales), Truck-O-Mat (Scales)
	Gas	E: BP, Phillips 66
	Food	E: China Buffet, Culver's, Hardee's, Neimerg's Steak House, Subway W: IronSkillet/Petro SC, Rest /BW
	Lodg	E: Abe Lincoln Motel, Comfort Suites♥, Econo Lodge, Howard Johnson Express♥, Lincoln Lodge♥, Paradise Inn, Rodeway Inn♥ W: Best Western♥
	TWash	W: Blue Beacon/Petro SC, TruckOMat
	TServ	E: Effingham Truck Sales W: Petro SC/Tires

Page 236   ◊ = Regular Gas Stations with Diesel   ▲ = RV Friendly Locations   ♥ = Pet Friendly Locations
RED PRINT SHOWS LARGE VEHICLE PARKING/ACCESS ON SITE OR NEARBY   BROWN PRINT SHOWS CAMPGROUNDS/RV PARKS

INTERSTATE 57 N/S — ILLINOIS

EXIT		ILLINOIS
	Other	E: ATMs, Auto Services, Amtrak, CarWash, to Village Square Mall
		W: Laundry/BarbSh/CB/WiFi/Petro SC
NOTE:		I-57 above runs with I-70W for 6 mi. Exit #'s follow I-57.
(157)		Jct I-70W, to St Louis (NB, Left exit)
151		to IL 37, to IL 45, Mason, Watson
	Other	E: to Percival Springs Airport & Campground▲, Effingham Co Memorial Airport✈, Scheid Diesel Service
145		CR 29, Edgewood
	Gas	E: Citgo
	Other	E: Laundry/Citgo
135		IL 185, Washington St, Farina, Vandalia
	FStop	E: Farina Super K #131/Shell
	Food	E: Rest/Farina Super K
127		CR 8, CR 1050, Kinoka Rd, Alma, to Patoka, Kinmundy
	Other	E: Kinmundy Truck & Auto Repair, to 7 mi Stephen A Forbes State Park▲
116		US 50, W Main St, Salem, to Odin, Sandoval, Flora
	Gas	E: Clark, MotoMart, Shell, Swifty
		W: Phillips 66, Murphy, Shell
	Food	E: Burger King, KFC, McDonalds, Pizza Hut, Subway, Taco Bell, Wendy's
		W: Applebee's, Arby's, Denny's
	Lodg	E: Budget Inn
		W: Comfort Inn, Holiday Inn, Salem Inn, Super 8
	TServ	E: Fabick Cat
		W: Salem Tire Center, Salem Truck & Diesel
	Med	E: + Hospital
	Other	E: AutoZone, Auto Dealers, ATMs, Banks, Pharmacy, Grocery, Salem-Leckrone Airport✈
		W: Auto Dealers, Wal-Mart sc
(114)		Rest Area (Both dir) (RR, Phones, Picnic, Vend)
109		IL 161, E McCord St, Centralia
	Gas	W: Marathon
	Food	W: Biggies Café/Marathon
	Other	W: Centralia Muni Airport✈
103		CR 39, W South St, Dix
	FStop	E: Illini Mart/66
	Food	E: Deli/Illini Mart
	Lodg	E: Scottish Inns
(96)		Jct I-64W, to St Louis
95		IL 15, Broadway St, Mt Vernon, Ashley
	TStop	W: Travel Center of America #43/Citgo (Scales), Ambest/Huck's Travel Center (Scales)
	Gas	E: BP◊, Marathon, Phillips 66
		W: Shell
	Food	E: Bonanza, Burger King, Fazoli's, Hardee's, KFC, McDonald's, Pizza Hut, Steak n Shake, Subway, Taco Bell, Wendy's, Western Sizzlin
		W: CountryPride/Popeyes/TA TC, Rest/FastFood/Huck's TC, Applebee's, Arby's, Burger King, Bob Evans, Cracker Barrel, Lone Star Steakhouse, McDonald's, Ryan's Grill, Sonic, Subway
	Lodg	E: Best Inn, Comfort Suites, Drury Inn, Motel 6♥, Super 8

EXIT		ILLINOIS
	Lodg	W: Comfort Inn, Days Inn, Fairfield Inn, Hampton Inn, Holiday Inn, Quality Inn
	TWash	W: TA TC, XVIII Wheelers Truck Wash
	TServ	W: TA TC/Tires, Freightliner
	Med	E: + Crossroads Comm Hospital
	Other	E: AutoZone, ATMs, Banks, CVS, Kmart, Kroger, Walgreen's, Mt Vernon Outland Airport✈, Animal Hospital♥
		W: Laundry/WiFi/TA TC, Laundry/Huck's TC, Lowe's, Outlet Mall, Staples, Wal-Mart sc, Mt Vernon Airport✈, Quality Times RV Park▲
(92)		I-64E, to Louisville (SB, Left exit)
83		North Ave, CR 42, Ina, Spring Garden
	FStop	E: Lakeview BP
	TStop	E: Love's Travel Stop #318 (Scales)
	Food	E: Deli/BP, McDonald's/Love's TS
	Other	E: RVDump/Love's TS, Sherwood Camping Resort▲
		W: Rend Lake, to Rend Lake College
(79)		Rest Area (SB) (RR, Phones, Picnic, Vend)
77		IL 154, Whittington, Sesser
	Gas	E: Shell
	Food	E: Burton Café, Gibby's Lounge & Grill
		W: Seasons Rest (@ Golf Course)
	Lodg	W: to Rend Lake Resort & Rest, Season Lodge & Condos
	Other	E: Benton Best Holiday Trav-L- Park Campground▲
		W: Wayne Fitzgerrell State Park▲, COE/Rend Lake/Gun Creek Rec Area▲, Rend Lake Golf Course
(74)		Rest Area (NB) (RR, Phones, Picnic, Vend)
71		IL 14, IL 34, Benton, Christopher
	FStop	W: West City Shell
	Gas	E: Citgo, Phillips 66
		W: BP
	Food	E: Hardee's, KFC, Long John Silver, Pizza Hut, Taco Bell, Wendy's
		W: FastFood/WC Shell, Applebee's, Burger King, McDonald's, Subway
	Lodg	E: Benton Gray Plaza Motel, Super 8
	Med	E: + Franklin Hospital
	Other	E: ATMs, Auto Services, Auto Dealers, Banks, Museum, SavALot, Tires
		W: ATMs, Bank, Auto Services, CVS, Wal-Mart sc, Benton Muni Airport✈, Benton KOA▲, to COE/Rend Lake/S Marcum Rec Area▲
65		IL 149, W Main St, W Frankfort
	Gas	E: BP, Citgo, Shell
		W: Casey's
	Food	E: Hardee's, KFC, Long John Silver
		W: Burger King, Casey's Pizza, McDonald's, Triple E Plus
	Lodg	E: Gray Plaza Motel
		W: Best Value Inn
	Med	E: + Hospital
	Other	E: Grocery
		W: Auto Services, CVS, Factory Outlet Stores of America, Kmart, Kroger
59		Herrin Rd, Broadway Blvd, Johnston City, Herrin
	Gas	E: BP◊, Shell
	Food	E: DQ, Hardee's, McDonald's, Subway
	Med	W: + Herrin Hospital
	Other	E: ATMs, Bank, Auto Services, to Arrowhead Lake Campground▲

◊ = Regular Gas Stations with Diesel ▲ = RV Friendly Locations ♥ = Pet Friendly Locations
RED PRINT SHOWS LARGE VEHICLE PARKING/ACCESS ON SITE OR NEARBY   BROWN PRINT SHOWS CAMPGROUNDS/RV PARKS

INTERSTATE 57 N

EXIT	ILLINOIS
Other	W: Golf Courses, to Four Seasons Campground▲
54B	**IL 13W, W Deyoung St, Marion, to Carbondale, Murphysboro**
TStop	W: Marion Truck Plaza/BP (Scales)
Gas	W: Phillips 66, Sam's Club
Food	W: Rest/Marion TP, Applebee's, Burger King, Bob Evans, McDonald's, O'Charley's, Ryan's Grill, Red Lobster, Steak n Shake, Sonic, Taco Bell
Lodg	W: Best Inn, Drury Inn, Fairfield Inn, Hampton Inn, Motel 6 ♥, Super 8
Other	W: WiFi/Marion TP, Auto Dealers, ATMs, Home Depot, Sam's Club, Wal-Mart sc, Target, IL Centre Mall, Campbell's Harley Davidson, Animal Hospital ♥, Williamson Co Airport ✈
54A	**IL 13E, E Deyoung St, Marion**
Gas	E: Phillips 66, Kroger
Food	E: Arby's, Fazoli's, Hardee's, KFC, Long John Silver, Pizza Hut, Quiznos, Subway, Wendy's, Western Sizzlin
Lodg	E: Days Inn, Econo Lodge, Marion Gray Plaza Motel
Med	E: + Heartland Regional Medical Center
Other	E: AutoZone, ATMs, Banks, Auto Services, Kroger, US Post Office, UPS Store
53	**Main St, Marion**
Gas	E: Shell
	W: MotoMart
Food	E: DQ, TCBY
	W: Cracker Barrel, 20s Hideout Steak House
Lodg	E: Motel Marion & Campground▲
	W: Comfort Inn ♥, Comfort Suites, Holiday Inn Express
TServ	E: Raben Tire Co
Med	E: + VA Medical Center, + First Priority Medical Center

EXIT	ILLINOIS
Other	E: ATMs, Auto Services, U-Haul, Marion Campground & RV Park▲
(46)	Weigh Station (Both dir)
45	IL 148, N Refuge Rd, to IL 37, Marion, to Herrin, Pulleys Mill
Gas	E: King Tut's◊
Food	E: Rameses
Other	E: to Lake of Egypt, Marina
(44)	Jct I-24E, to Nashville
(40)	TurnOut / Scenic View
40	Goreville Rd, Jenkins Rd, Goreville
Gas	W: Citgo◊
Other	E: Hilltop Campground▲, to Ferne Clyffe State Park▲
36	CR 4, Lick Creek Rd, Anna
(32)	Rest Area (Both dir) (RR, Phones, Picnic, Vend)
30	IL 146, Dongola, to Anna, Vienna Jonesboro, Mt Pleasant
Gas	W: Shell
Food	W: Rest/Shell
TServ	W: Linson's Service Center
Med	W: + Union Co Hospital
25	US 51N, Anna, to Carbondale (NB, Left exit)
24	CR 14, Cypress Rd, Dongola
Gas	W: Shell
18	Ullin Rd, Ullin
Gas	W: Citgo◊
Lodg	W: Best Western
8	Mounds Rd, to Mound City
FStop	E: K&K Auto Truck Stop
TServ	E: K&K ATS
1	IL 3, to US 51S, Cairo
FStop	E: Cairo Truck Plaza/BP
Gas	E: Phillips 66
Food	E: Rest/Cairo TP

EXIT	IL / MO
Lodg	E: Belvedere Motel, Days Inn
Other	W: Cairo Airport ✈
	(CENTRAL TIME ZONE)
⊙	**ILLINOIS**
⊙	**MISSOURI**
	(CENTRAL TIME ZONE)
NOTE:	MM 22 : Illinois State Line
(18)	Weigh Station (Both dir)
12	US 60, US 62, I-57 Bus, MO 77, Charleston, to Wyatt
TStop	E: Cheers Travel Center (Scales)
	W: Sunshine Travel Center (Scales)
Gas	E: Casey's, Sinclair
Food	E: FastFood/Cheers TC
	W: Casey's C/O Pizza, KFC
Lodg	W: Econo Lodge, Economy Motel
Other	W: ATMs, Banks, Auto Repairs, Grocery
10	MO 105, Bus 57, Charleston, Prairie
FStop	E: Pilot Travel Center #359 (Scales)
Gas	E: Charleston Boomland/AmocoBP
	W: Casey's
Food	E: Subway/Pilot TC, Rest/Boomland
	W: DQ, McDonald's, Pizza Hut
Lodg	W: Comfort Inn
Other	E: WiFi/Pilot TC, Boomland RV Park & Campground▲
4	IL B, to US 62, Bertrand
Other	W: Town & Country Camping▲
(1B)	Jct I-55N, to St Louis
	(Gas/Food/Lodg/CG - 1st Ex #67)
(1A)	Jct I-55S, to Memphis
	(I-57 begins/ends I-55, Exit #66AB)
⊙	**MISSOURI** (CENTRAL TIME ZONE)
	Begin I-57 Northbound from Jct I-55 in St Louis, MO to Jct I-94 in Chicago, IL

INTERSTATE 59 S

EXIT	GEORGIA
	Begin Southbound I-59 from Jct I-24 near Chattanooga, TN to Jct I-10 in LA.
⊙	**GEORGIA**
	(CENTRAL TIME ZONE)
	(I-59 begins/ends on I-24, Exit #157)
(19)	Jct I-24W, to Nashville, Jct I-24E, to I-75, Chattanooga, TN
17	Slygo Rd, Trenton, to New England
Gas	W: Citgo◊
Other	W: Lookout Mountain KOA▲
11	GA 136, White Oak Gap Rd, Trenton
Gas	E: Chevron◊, Exxon◊
	W: Kangaroo Express, Mapco Express
Food	E: Burger King, Hardee's, McDonald's, Pizza Hut, Subway
	W: Huddle House, Krystal, Taco Bell
Lodg	E: Days Inn
Other	E: CVS, to Cloudland Canyon State Park▲
	W: Bi-Lo, Food Lion, Auto Services

EXIT	GA / AL
4	Puddin Ridge Rd, Deer Head Cove Rd, to GA 58, US 11, Rising Fawn
TStop	W: Pilot Travel Center #415 (Scales)
Gas	E: Citgo
	W: Mapco Express
Food	E: Depot Diner, Rising Fawn Cafe
	W: Subway/Chesters/Pilot TC, Lazy Bones BBQ
Tires	W: Pilot TC
Other	W: Laundry/WiFi/Pilot TC
	(EASTERN/CENTRAL TIME ZONE)
⊙	**GEORGIA**
⊙	**ALABAMA**
(241)	AL Welcome Center (SB) (RR, Phone, Picnic, Vend, RVDump)
239	CR 140, Valley Head, to US 11, Sulphur Springs Rd
Other	E: to Sequoyah Caverns & Ellis Homestead▲

EXIT	ALABAMA
231	AL 40, AL 117, Valley Head, to US 11, Hammondville, Henagar
Other	E: to Sequoyah Caverns▲, Serenity Campground▲
222	US 11, AL 7, Fort Payne
Gas	E: Shell
	W: QuikStop, Citgo◊, Texaco
Food	E: Arby's, Krystal, KFC, Jack's Rest, Pizza Hut, Subway, Western Sizzlin
	W: Waffle King
Lodg	E: Travelodge
Other	E: Auto Dealer, ATMs, Banks, Cinema, Carwash, Foodland, SavALot
	W: Auto Repairs, Isbell Field ✈, Wills Creek RV Park▲
218	AL 35, Glenn Blvd, Fort Payne, Rainsville, Scottsboro
TStop	W: Kangaroo Express #3668
Gas	E: Conoco◊
	W: Chevron, Victory, WalMart
Food	E: Captain D's, China King, Golden Rule BBQ, McDonald's, Papa John's,

◊ = Regular Gas Stations with Diesel   ▲ = RV Friendly Locations   ♥ = Pet Friendly Locations
RED PRINT SHOWS LARGE VEHICLE PARKING/ACCESS ON SITE OR NEARBY   BROWN PRINT SHOWS CAMPGROUNDS/RV PARKS

EXIT	ALABAMA
Food	E: Pizza Hut, Quiznos, Taco Bell, Wendy's, Zaxby's
	W: Burger King, Cracker Barrel, Hardee's, Huddle House, Ryan's Grill, Ruby Tuesday, Subway, Waffle House
Lodg	W: Days Inn, Econo Lodge, Holiday Inn Express, Hampton Inn
Med	W: + DeKalb Regional Medical Center
Other	E: AutoZone, ATMs, Banks, Auto Services, Auto Dealer, Big Lots, Dollar General, Goodyear, to DeSoto State Park▲
	W: Auto Dealers, Dollar Tree, Kmart, Lowe's, Walgreen's, Wal-Mart sc
205	**AL 68, Collinsville, Crossville**
FStop	W: Conoco
Gas	E: Chevron
	W: Shell
Food	E: Jack's, Patrick's Big Valley Rest, Smokin Joe's
Lodg	E: Howard Johnson
Other	W: Auto Repairs
188	**AL 211, to US 11, Noccalula Pkwy, Noccalula Falls, Gadsden**
Gas	E: Chevron, Jet Pep
	W: BP, Jet Pep◊
Other	E: Noccalula Falls & Campground▲
183	**US 278, US 431, Cleveland Ave, Forrest Ave, Attalla, Gadsden**
Gas	E: Amoco, Jet Pep◊, Shell
	W: Chevron, Exxon, Texaco
Food	E: Hardee's, Magic Burger, Waffle House, Wendy's
	W: McDonald's, Pizza Hut, Krystal, Subway, KFC/Taco Bell
Lodg	E: Best Value Inn♥, Budget Inn, Days Inn♥, Rodeway Inn
	W: Econo Lodge
Med	E: + Riverview Regional Medical Center
(182)	**Jct I-759E, Attalla, to Gadsden**
181	**AL 77, Gilbert Ferry Rd SE, Gadsden, Attalla, Rainbow City**
FStop	E: Supermart Travel Center/BP (Scales)
TStop	E: Petro Stopping Center (Scales)
Gas	W: Citgo, Kangaroo♦, Pure♦
Food	E: FastFood/Supermart TC, Austin's Steak&Seafood/Pizza/Café/Petro SC
	W: Cracker Barrel, DQ, Domino's, Hardee's, Papa John's, Ruby Tuesday, Subway, Waffle House
Lodg	E: Days Inn
	W: Best Western, Comfort Suites, Holiday Inn Express
Other	E: Laundry/BarbSh/Chiro/CB/WiFi/ RVDump/LP/ Petro SC, Gadsden Muni Airport✈
	W: Dollar Tree, O'Reilly Auto Parts, Radio Shack, Wal-Mart sc
174	**Steele Station Rd, Steele**
TStop	W: Steele City Truck Stop/Jet
Gas	W: Chevron◊
Food	W: Rest/Steele City TS
TWash	W: Steele City TS
TServ	W: Steele City TS/Tires
Other	E: Alabama Int'l Dragway
	W: Laundry/CB/Steele City TS
(167)	**Rest Area (SB)**
	(RR, Phones, Picnic, Vend, RVDump)
166	**US 231, Oneonta, Ashville**
FStop	E: Bama Chevron
	W: Asheville Texaco

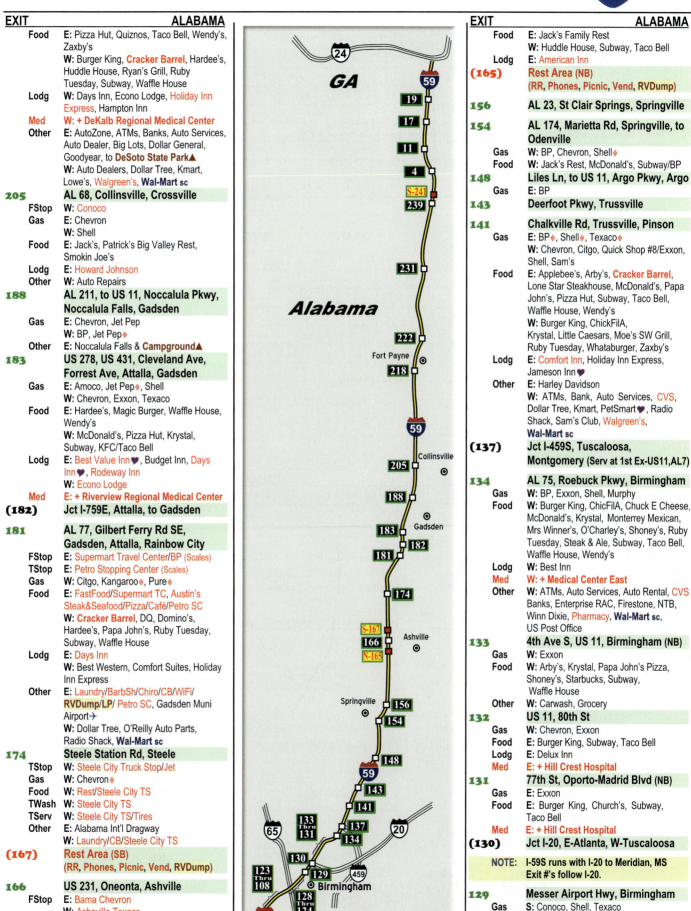

EXIT	ALABAMA
Food	E: Jack's Family Rest
	W: Huddle House, Subway, Taco Bell
Lodg	E: American Inn
(165)	**Rest Area (NB)**
	(RR, Phones, Picnic, Vend, RVDump)
156	**AL 23, St Clair Springs, Springville**
154	**AL 174, Marietta Rd, Springville, to Odenville**
Gas	W: BP, Chevron, Shell◊
Food	W: Jack's Rest, McDonald's, Subway/BP
148	**Liles Ln, to US 11, Argo Pkwy, Argo**
Gas	E: BP
143	**Deerfoot Pkwy, Trussville**
141	**Chalkville Rd, Trussville, Pinson**
Gas	E: BP◊, Shell◊, Texaco◊
	W: Chevron, Citgo, Quick Shop #8/Exxon, Shell, Sam's
Food	E: Applebee's, Arby's, Cracker Barrel, Lone Star Steakhouse, McDonald's, Papa John's, Pizza Hut, Subway, Taco Bell, Waffle House, Wendy's
	W: Burger King, ChickFilA, Krystal, Little Caesars, Moe's SW Grill, Ruby Tuesday, Whataburger, Zaxby's
Lodg	E: Comfort Inn, Holiday Inn Express, Jameson Inn♥
Other	E: Harley Davidson
	W: ATMs, Bank, Auto Services, CVS, Dollar Tree, Kmart, PetSmart♥, Radio Shack, Sam's Club, Walgreen's, Wal-Mart sc
(137)	**Jct I-459S, Tuscaloosa, Montgomery (Serv @ 1st Ex-US11,AL7)**
134	**AL 75, Roebuck Pkwy, Birmingham**
Gas	W: BP, Exxon, Shell, Murphy
Food	W: Burger King, ChicFilA, Chuck E Cheese, McDonald's, Krystal, Monterrey Mexican, Mrs Winner's, O'Charley's, Shoney's, Ruby Tuesday, Steak & Ale, Subway, Taco Bell, Waffle House, Wendy's
Lodg	W: Best Inn
Med	W: + Medical Center East
Other	W: ATMs, Auto Services, Auto Rental, CVS, Banks, Enterprise RAC, Firestone, NTB, Winn Dixie, Pharmacy, Wal-Mart sc, US Post Office
133	**4th Ave S, US 11, Birmingham (NB)**
Gas	W: Exxon
Food	W: Arby's, Krystal, Papa John's Pizza, Shoney's, Starbucks, Subway, Waffle House
Other	W: Carwash, Grocery
132	**US 11, 80th St**
Gas	W: Chevron, Exxon
Food	E: Burger King, Subway, Taco Bell
Lodg	E: Delux Inn
Med	E: + Hill Crest Hospital
131	**77th St, Oporto-Madrid Blvd (NB)**
Gas	E: Exxon
Food	E: Burger King, Church's, Subway, Taco Bell
Med	E: + Hill Crest Hospital
(130)	**Jct I-20, E-Atlanta, W-Tuscaloosa**
NOTE:	I-59S runs with I-20 to Meridian, MS Exit #'s follow I-20.
129	**Messer Airport Hwy, Birmingham**
Gas	S: Conoco, Shell, Texaco

◊= Regular Gas Stations with Diesel   ▲ = RV Friendly Locations   ♥= Pet Friendly Locations
RED PRINT SHOWS LARGE VEHICLE PARKING/ACCESS ON SITE OR NEARBY   BROWN PRINT SHOWS CAMPGROUNDS/RV PARKS

Page 239

INTERSTATE 59 N/S

EXIT		ALABAMA
	Food	N: Hardee's
		S: Huddle House, Holiday Inn
	Lodg	N: Best Inn, Sheraton
		S: Holiday Inn
	Other	N: Birmingham Int'l Airport ✈, Auto Rentals
128		**AL 79, Tallapoosa St, to Tarrant**
	TStop	N: Kangaroo #3672
	Gas	N: Shell
	Food	N: FastFood/Kangaroo
126B		**31st St, Sloss Furnaces, Civic Ctr**
	Gas	N: Conoco, Shell
	Food	N: McDonald's
	TServ	S: K Diamond Truck Service
	Med	N: + Carraway Methodist Medical Center
	Other	S: Laundromat, W AL Tire Service
126A		**US 31S, US 280E, Carraway Blvd**
	Med	S: + St Vincent Hospital
125		**22nd St, Downtown Birmingham (SB, Left exit)**
	Lodg	N: Best Western, Sheraton
	Other	N: AL Sports Hall of Fame, Civic Center
		S: Museum, Sheriff Dept
125B		**22nd St, Downtown Birmingham**
125A		**17th St, Downtown Birmingham (NB)**
	Other	S: Auto Services, Greyhound
(124B)		**Jct I-65N, to Nashville**
(124A)		**Jct I-65S, Montgomery, Huntsville**
123		**US 78, Arkadelphia Rd, to Jasper**
	TStop	N: Pilot Travel Center #369 (Scales)
	Gas	N: BP, Chevron, Shell
	Food	N: Wendy's/Pilot TC, Charlie's Café, Popeye's
	Lodg	N: Days Inn ♥
	Med	S: + Princeton Baptist Medical Center
	Other	N: Laundry/WiFi/Pilot TC, Auto Services
		S: Bill Battle Coliseum, Birmingham Southern College
121		**Bush Blvd, 19th St Ensley, Ave V (SB, no re-entry)**
	Gas	N: BP, Exxon
	Food	N: Fat Burger
120		**AL 269, 20th St Ensley, Ensley 5 Pts W Ave, Birmingham (diff reaccess)**
	Gas	N: Crown
		S: BP
	Food	N: KFC
	Med	S: + Hospital
	Other	N: Police Dept
		S: Auto Dealer, AL State Fairgrounds, Fairgrounds Speedway, Birmingham Int'l Raceway
119B		**Ave I, Birmingham (SB, diff reacc)**
119A		**Richard M Scrushy Pkwy, Gary Ave, Lloyd Nolan Pkwy, Fairfield**
	Gas	N: BP, Chevron
		S: Mobil
	Food	N: Burger King, Fairfield Seafood, Subway
		S: Omelet Shop, Mama's Kitchen, Wings & Stuff
	TServ	S: Big Moe Spring & Alignment
	Med	S: + HealthSouth Metro West Hospital
	Other	S: Auto Services, U-Haul
118		**Valley Rd, Fairfield**
	Lodg	S: Fairfield Inn
	Med	S: + HealthSouth Metro West Hospital
	Other	S: Auto Services, U-Haul, to Western Hills Mall, Gas, Grocery, Restaurants

Personal Notes

EXIT		ALABAMA
115		**15th St, Jaybird Rd, Allison Bonnett Memorial Dr, to US 11, Birmingham**
	Gas	N: Citgo, RaceTrac, Shell
	Food	N: Hardee's, Subway
	Other	S: to M&J RV Park▲
113		**18th Ave, Jaybird Rd, Birmingham, Brighton, Lipscomb, Bessemer**
	FStop	S: 20-59 Travel Center/Chevron
	Food	S: FastFood/20-59 TC
112		**18th St, 19th St, to US 11, Bessemer**
	Gas	N: Conoco, RaceTrac
		S: Chevron
	Food	N: Jack's Hamburgers
		S: Arby's, Burger King, Krystal
	Other	S: ATMs, Auto Services, Banks, Grocery, Greyhound, Tires, AL RV, General Auto & Truck Service
110		**Visionland Pkwy**
108		**US 11, AL 5N, Academy Dr**
	Gas	N: Exxon
		S: BP, Citgo
	Food	N: Applebee's, Cracker Barrel, Santa Fe Steakhouse, Waffle House
		S: Burger King, Cajun Landing Seafood, Milo's, McDonald's, Omelet Shop
	Lodg	N: Best Western, Comfort Inn, Jameson Inn, Holiday Inn Express, Motel 6 ♥, Travelodge
		S: Days Inn, Hampton Inn, Masters Economy Inn, Travelodge
	Med	S: + UAB West Medical Center

EXIT		ALABAMA
	Other	N: ATM, Bank, Civic Center, Visionland Theme Park, Watermark Place
		S: ATMs, Banks, Grocery, Wal-Mart sc, Winn Dixie, Frank House Muni Golf Course, West Lake Mall, Outlet Mall
(106)		**Jct I-459N, Gadsden, Atlanta (South ByPass of Birmingham)**
104		**McAshen Dr, Rock Mountain Lakes, McCalla**
	TStop	S: Flying J Travel Plaza #5042/Conoco (Scales)
	Food	S: Rest/FastFood/FJ TP
	Other	S: Laundry/BarbSh/WiFi/LP/RVDump/FJ TP
100		**AL 216, McCalla, Abernant, Bucksville**
	TStop	S: Petro Stopping Center #19 (Scales)
	Gas	N: Citgo
		S: BP, Exxon
	Food	S: IronSkillet/Petro SC, Shenanigan's BBQ
	TServ	S: Petro SC/Tires
	Other	N: McCalla RV Park▲
		S: Laundry/WiFi/RVDump/Petro SC, Auto Repair, Sheriff Dept, Tannehill Nat'l Golf Course, Museum, Tannehill Ironworks Historic State Park▲
97		**US 11S, AL 5S, West Blocton**
	FStop	S: Caffee Jct BP, Rajpari Shell
	Gas	S: Exxon◊
	Food	S: Dots, KFC, Jack's Family Rest
89		**Mercedes Dr, Vance, Tuscaloosa**
	Lodg	N: Baymont Inn, Wellesley Inn
	Other	S: Mercedes Benz Auto Plant
86		**CR 59, Covered Bridge Rd, Cottondale, Brookwood, Vance**
	TStop	N: Brookwood Shell Truck Stop
	Food	N: Rest/Brookwood TS
(85)		**Rest Area (Both dir) (RR, Phones, RV Dump)**
79		**US 11, University Blvd, Coaling**
	Gas	S: Chevron◊
77		**CR 85, Buttermilk Rd, Cottondale**
	TStop	N: Travel Center of America #16/BP (Scales)
		S: WilcoHess Travel Plaza #5501 (Scales)
	Gas	N: Chevron
	Food	N: McDonald's/Chevron, CountryPride/Subway/Taco Bell/TA TC, Captain Jim's Seafood & Steak, Pizza Hut, Ruby Tuesday
		S: Wendy's/WilcoHess TP
	Lodg	N: Hampton Inn, Microtel Inn
	TServ	N: TA TC/Tires, Speedco
	TWash	N: Blue Beacon TW/TA TC
	Other	N: Laundry/WiFi/RVDump/TA TC
		S: Laundry/WilcoHess TP
76		**US 11, E Tuscaloosa, Cottondale**
	TStop	S: Pilot Travel Center #76 (Scales)
	Gas	N: Citgo◊, Exxon, Shell◊
		S: Shell◊
	Food	N: Burger King, Cracker Barrel, Waffle House
		S: FastFood/Pilot TC
	Lodg	N: Comfort Inn, Scottish Inn, Super Inn
		S: Sleep Inn
	TServ	S: Southland Int'l Trucks
	Med	N: + US Vets Hospital
	Other	N: ATM, Bank, Sunset II Travel Park▲
		S: Laundry/WiFi/Pilot TC, Auto Service, Auto Dealers, AL State Hwy Patrol Post

◊ = Regular Gas Stations with Diesel   ▲ = RV Friendly Locations   ♥ = Pet Friendly Locations
RED PRINT SHOWS LARGE VEHICLE PARKING/ACCESS ON SITE OR NEARBY   BROWN PRINT SHOWS CAMPGROUNDS/RV PARKS

Interstate 59 N/S

ALABAMA

EXIT	
73	**US 82, AL 6, McFarland Blvd, Tuscaloosa, Centreville**
Gas	N: Chevron◆ x2, Exxon, RaceTrac, Shell◆ S: AmocoBP◆, Exxon, Shell, Sam's
Food	N: Burger King, Captain D's, Krystal's, Long John Silver, Pizza Hut, Waffle House, Shoney's S: Chili's, Hardee's, Huddle House, KFC, Lone Star Steakhouse, McDonalds, Taco Cabana, Subway, Taco Bell, Wendy's, Piccadilly, Western Sizzlin, Waffle House
Lodg	N: Best Value Inn, Best Western, Comfort Suites, Guest Lodge, Master's Inn, Shoney's Inn S: Country Inn, Econo Lodge, Days Inn, La Quinta Inn♥, Motel 6♥, Quality Inn, Ramada Inn, Super 8
Med	N: + DCH Reg'l Medical Center
Other	N: ATMs, Banks, Big 10 Tire, Firestone, Goodyear, U-Haul, Mall, CVS, Lake Lurleen State Park S: Winn Dixie, FoodWorld, NAPA, Sam's Club, Wal-Mart sc, McFarland Mall, Fox 12, ATMs, Banks, Enterprise RAC, Office Depot, RiteAid, AL State Hwy Patrol Post
(71B)	**Jct I-359, AL 69N, Tuscaloosa**
Other	N: Univ of AL, Amtrak, Bryant-Denny Stadium, Coleman Coliseum, Stillman College
71A	**AL 69S, to US 11, LA 7, Moundville**
Gas	N: Phillips 66 S: Chevron, Exxon◆, Shell
Food	S: Arby's, Country Hic Café & BBQ, IHOP, Outback Steakhouse, Pizza Hut, Ryan's Grill, Waffle House, Wendy's
Lodg	S: Courtyard, Fairfield Inn, Jameson Inn
Other	S: Advance Auto, Firestone, Kmart, L&H Truck Service, Lowe's, Auto Repairs, Police Dept
68	**Tuscaloosa Western ByPass** (Gas 2 mi N in Tuscaloosa)
62	**CR 10, CR 51, Holly Springs Lane, Fosters**
Gas	N: BP
52	**US 11, US 43, Knoxville**
FStop	N: Speedmart Fuel Center/Exxon, Kangaroo #3726
Food	N: FastFood/Speedmart FC
45	**CR 208, AL 37, Union Rd, Eutaw**
TStop	S: Trackside BP, Mott Oil #23
Food	N: Cotton Patch Restaurant S: Hardee's, Southfork, Rest/Western Inn
Lodg	S: Western Inn
TServ	S: Trackside BP/Tires, Southfork Auto & Truck Center
Other	S: Greene Co Greyhound Park
40	**AL 14, Eutaw, Aliceville**
Med	S: + Hospital
Other	N: Tom Bevil Lock & Dam
(39)	**Rest Area (SB)** (RR, Phones, RVDump)
(38)	**Rest Area (NB)** (RR, Phones, RVDump)
32	**CR 20, Boligee**
TStop	N: Boligee Truck Stop/BP
Gas	S: Chevron
Food	N: Rest/FastFood/Boligee TS

ALABAMA / MISSISSIPPI

EXIT	
23	**CR 20, Gainesville, Epes**
17	**AL 28, Livingston, Boyd**
TStop	S: 1st Stop Interstate Shell, Noble Truck Stop/Citgo (Scales)
Gas	S: Chevron
Food	S: Rest/FastFood/1st Stop, Rest/FastFood/Noble TS, Burger King, Pizza Hut
Lodg	S: Comfort Inn
TServ	S: Noble TS/Tires, Bullocks Truck Service
Med	S: + Hospital
Other	S: Laundry/Noble TS, Univ of W AL
8	**AL 17, York**
TStop	S: PTP/York Truck Plaza/BP (Scales)
Food	S: Deli/Rest/York TP
Lodg	S: Days Inn/York TP
TWash	S: York TP
TServ	S: York TP/Tires
Med	S: + Hospital
Other	S: Laundry/CB/York TP, Bank, ATM
1	**AL 8, to US 80E, Cuba, Demopolis**
TStop	S: Rocking Chair/P66
Gas	S: Chevron, Dixie
Food	S: Rest/Rocking Chair
(1)	**AL Welcome Center (NB)** (RR, Phones, RV Dump)
NOTE:	I-20E & I-59N run together from Meridian, MS to Birmingham, AL, Exit #'s follow I-20.

(CENTRAL TIME ZONE)

⊙ **ALABAMA**
⊙ **MISSISSIPPI**

(CENTRAL TIME ZONE)

NOTE:	I-20W & I-59S run together below to Meridian. Exit #'s follow I-20.
NOTE:	MM 172: Alabama State Line
(170)	**Weigh Station (Both dir)**
169	**US 11, US 80, Kewanee**
FStop	S: Kewanee One Stop
Food	S: Rest/Kewanee One Stop
165	**Garrett Rd, Toomsuba**
TStop	S: Fuel Mart #631 (Scales)
Gas	N: Shell, Texaco
Food	N: Subway/Shell, Chesters/Texaco S: Arby's/FuelMart
Other	S: Meridian East/Toomsuba KOA▲
(164)	**MS Welcome Center (SB)** (RR, Phones, Picnic, Sec24/7, RVDump)
160	**Russell Mt Gilead Rd, Meridian**
TStop	N: Travel Center of America #47/BP (Scales)
Food	N: CountryPride/TA TC
TServ	N: TA TC/Tires
Other	N: Laundry/TA TC, Nanabe Creek Campground▲
157AB	**US 45, Macon, Quitman**
Other	N: Benmark Coach & RV Park▲
154	**MS 19S, MS 39N, US 11N, US 80E, Butler, DeKalb (WB)**
Gas	N: BP◆, Shell, Texaco S: Chevron, Conoco◆
Food	N: Applebee's, Back Yard Burgers, Cracker Barrel, Krystal's, Waffle House

MISSISSIPPI

EXIT	
Food	S: CiCi's, McDonald's, O'Charley's, Outback Steakhouse, Ryan's Grill, Taco Bell
Lodg	N: Days Inn, Economy Inn, Hampton Inn, Holiday Inn, Howard Johnson, Relax Inn, Super 8 S: Comfort Inn, Jameson Inn, Scottish Inn, Microtel
Other	N: U-Haul, Auto Dealers S: Mall, Harley Davidson, Sam's Club, RV Center, RVDump/Conoco
154AB	**MS 19S, MS 39N, US 11N, US 80E, Butler AL DeKalb, Naval Air Stn (EB)**
153	**MS 145S, 22nd Ave, Quitman, Downtown Meridian**
Gas	N: BP, Shell S: Chevron◆, Conoco◆, Exxon◆, Shell, WalMart
Food	N: Arby's, Barnhill Buffet, Burger King, Captain D's, Chinese, Hardee's, KFC, McDonald's, Pizza Hut, Subway, Wendy's, Western Sizzlin S: Depot Rest, Waffle House
Lodg	N: Relax Inn S: Astro Motel, Baymont Inn, Budget 8 Motel, Best Western, Econo Lodge, Holiday Inn Express♥, Motel 6♥, Sleep Inn
Med	N: + Hospital
Other	N: ATMs, Banks, Amtrak, Goodyear, Grocery, Museums, RiteAid S: Auto Dealers, Lowe's, Wal-Mart sc
152	**29th Ave, MLK Jr Blvd, Meridian**
Gas	N: Chevron◆
Lodg	N: Ramada S: Royal Inn
151	**49th Ave, Valley Rd, Meridian**
TStop	S: Pilot Travel Center #388 (Scales)
Food	S: Subway/Pilot TC
Other	S: WiFi/Pilot TC
150	**US 11S, MS 19N, Philadelphia**
FStop	S: Stuckey's Express #653/Chevron, Super Stop #10/Shell
TStop	N: Queen City Truck Stop (Scales)
Food	N: Rest/Queen City TS S: FastFood/Stuckey's Exp
TServ	N: Mack's Truck Service
Other	N: LP/Queen City TS, Okitibbee Lake S: Meridian Airport/Key Field ✈
(149)	**Jct I-20W, to Jackson, Jct I-59S, to New Orleans**
NOTE:	I-20 above runs with I-59 to Birmingham, AL.
142	**Meehan Savoy Rd, Meridian, to Savoy, Dunn's Falls**
137	**CR 370, N Enterprise, to Stonewall**
134	**MS 513, S Enterprise, Rose Hill**
126	**MS 18, Pachuta, Quitman, Rose Hill**
FStop	E: Burns #6, BP Truck Plaza
Food	E: FastFood/Burns #6, FastFood/BP TP
118	**CR 119, Vossburg, to Paulding, Stafford Springs, Waulkaway Springs**
113	**MS 528, N Pine Ave, Heidelberg, to Bay Springs**
FStop	E: Stuckey's Express #619/Chevron
TStop	E: JR's I-59 Truck Stop/BP

◆ = Regular Gas Stations with Diesel   ▲ = RV Friendly Locations   ♥ = Pet Friendly Locations
RED PRINT SHOWS LARGE VEHICLE PARKING/ACCESS ON SITE OR NEARBY   BROWN PRINT SHOWS CAMPGROUNDS/RV PARKS

Interstate 59 N/S

EXIT		MISSISSIPPI
	Gas	E: Exxon, Shell
	Food	E: Rest/JR's TS, FastFood/Stuckey's, Subway/PizzaInn/Exxon
	Other	E: Laundry/RVDump/JR's TS
(109)		Parking Area (NB)
(106)		Parking Area (SB)
104		Main St, Sharon-Sandersville Rd, Laurel, to Sharon, Sandersville
99		US 11, N Laurel
	Gas	E: T&B◇
	Food	E: Pizza Hut/Magnolia Motor Lodge
	Lodg	E: Magnolia Motor Lodge
	Other	E: Laurel KOA▲
97		US 84E, Chantilly St, Meridian Ave, Waynesboro, Chantilly
	TStop	E: 84E Truck Stop/Exxon, Kangaroo
	FStop	W: Texaco
	Gas	W: BP◇
	Food	E: Rest/FastFood/84E TS, FastFood/Kangaroo, Hardee's
		W: KFC, Vic's
	Lodg	E: Hotel/84E Truck Stop
	Other	E: Laundry/CB/84 E TS
		W: Auto Services, B&W Towing, Keys Auto & Truck Repair
96B		MS 15S, Cooks Ave, to Richton
	TStop	E: Busy Bee Truck Stop
	Other	E: Ronnie's MH & RV Service
		W: Auto & Truck Services, Towing
96A		4th Ave, Masonite Rd
	Other	E: Auto Service, Diesel Power Service
95C		Beacon St, Downtown Laurel
	Gas	E: Texaco
		W: Chevron
	Food	W: Burger King, Church's, McDonald's, Catfish One, Old Mexico Rest, Popeye's, Rest/Town House Motel
	Lodge	W: Town House Motel
	Other	W: Family Dollar, Museum, Pharmacy, Tires, Winn Dixie, US Post Office
95AB		US 84W, MS 15N, 16th Ave, to Collins, Bay Springs
	Gas	W: Amoco, Exxon◇
	Food	W: DQ, KFC, McDonald's, Pizza Hut, Shoney's, Subway, Waffle House, Wendy's
	Lodg	W: Comfort Suites, Econo Lodge, Hampton Inn, Holiday Inn Express, Super 8
	Med	W: + S Central Regional Med Center
	Other	W: Advance Auto, Auto Services, ATMs, Banks, Dollar General, Grocery, Lowe's, Office Depot, Walgreen's, Wal-Mart sc
93		US 11, Ellisville Ave, S Laurel, Fairgrounds, Industrial Park
	FStop	W: Rapid Express/Shell
	TStop	W: American Foods Truck Stop/Citgo
	Gas	W: Exxon◇
	Food	W: FastFood/Rapid Exp, Rest/American Foods TS, Hardee's, Subway/Exxon
	Other	E: Auto Services, Tires
		W: Hesler Noble Field ✈
90		US 11, Palmer Rd, Ellisville
	FStop	W: Dixie Oil #93
88		MS 29, MS 588, Hill St, Ellisville
	FStop	E: Chevron
		W: Woody's Kwik Stop/Exxon
	Food	E: KFC, McDonald's, Pizza Hut, Subway
		W: Ellisville Rest, Fisherman's Choice Seafood Rest, Glenda's Diner

EXIT		MISSISSIPPI
	Lodg	W: Best Western
	Other	E: ATMs, Auto Services, Banks, Grocery, Family Dollar, NAPA, to Jones Co Comm College
85		MS 590, Eubanks Rd, Ellisville
80		Moselle-Seminary Rd, Moselle
78		Raymer Rd, Sanford Rd, Moselle
76		Terminal Dr, Moselle
	Other	W: Hattiesburg-Laurel Reg'l Airport ✈
73		Monroe Rd, Hattiesburg
69		Eatonville Rd, Glendale, Hattiesburg
	Other	W: Auto Repairs
67B		US 49N, Hattiesburg, to Jackson
	FStop	W: Dandy Dan #523, Maple Truck Stop, Dandy Dan's #512, Sid's Discount Fuel
	Gas	W: Chevron, Citgo, RaceTrac, Shell
	Food	W: Sonic, Subway/DandyDan's, Waffle House
	Lodg	W: Best Western, Econo Lodge, Hawthorne Suites, Holiday Inn
	Other	W: JD Tire & Truck Service, to appr 6 mi Country Creek RV Center, Camper City, Shady Cove RV Park▲
67A		US 49S, Hattiesburg, to Gulfport
	TStop	E: Kangaroo Express
	Gas	E: Exxon, Shell
	Food	E: FastFood/Kangaroo Exp, Arby's, Burger King, Cracker Barrel, Conestoga Steak House, KFC, McDonald's, Pizza Hut, Starbucks, Taco Bell, Three Pigs BBQ, Waffle House
	Lodg	E: Comfort Inn, Days Inn, Econo Lodge, Inn on the Hill, La Quinta Inn ♥, Motel 6 ♥, Scottish Inn, Super 8
		W: Budget Inn, Holiday Inn, University Inn
	Other	E: Laundry/Kangaroo Exp, ATMs, Auto Services, Big 10 Tire, Dollar General, Hattiesburg Cycles, Hattiesburg Conv & Visitors Bureau/RVDump
65		US 98W, Hardy St, to Columbia (SB)
	FStop	W: Kangaroo Express #3399/BP
	Gas	E: Dandy Dan's, Exxon, Shell◇, Texaco
		W: Dandy Dan's, Shell, Sam's
	Food	E: Applebee's, Burger King, CiCi's, KFC, Domino's, Front Porch BBQ, IHOP, Long John Silver, Krystal, McDonald's, Pizza Hut, Ponderosa, Quiznos, Starbucks, Subway, Taco Bell
		W: FastFood/Kangaroo Exp, Arby's, Backyard Burger, Burger King, ChickFilA, Chili's, Hardee's, Lone Star Steakhouse, McDonald's, Olive Garden, Outback Steakhouse, Pizza Hut, Red Lobster, Ryan's Grill, Taco Bell, Waffle House, Wendy's, Zaxby's
	Lodg	E: Best Western Inn, Days Inn, Fairfield Inn, Western Motel
		W: Baymont Inn, Comfort Suites, Hampton Inn, Microtel, Sun Suites
	Med	E: + Immediate Care Medical Center
		W: + Forrest Co Gen'l Hospital
	Other	E: Amtrak, ATMs, Auto Services, Banks, CVS, Deep South Cycles, Dollar General, Goodyear, Home Depot, Walgreen's, Univ of S MS, Vet ♥
		W: Advance Auto, ATMs, Best Buy, Auto Services, Firestone, FedEx Kinko's, Goodyear, Grocery, Lowe's, Office Depot, PetSmart ♥, Radio Shack, RiteAid, Sam's Club

Page 242 ◇ = Regular Gas Stations with Diesel ▲ = RV Friendly Locations ♥ = Pet Friendly Locations
RED PRINT SHOWS LARGE VEHICLE PARKING/ACCESS ON SITE OR NEARBY BROWN PRINT SHOWS CAMPGROUNDS/RV PARKS

Interstate 59 N

EXIT		MISSISSIPPI
	Other	W: Turtle Creek Mall, Target, UPS Store, Walgreen's, Wal-Mart sc, Ken Pickett RV Center, Cinema 9, ATMs, Banks
65AB		US 98W, Hardy St, Hattiesburg (NB)
60		US 11, S Hattiesburg
	TStop	W: Kangaroo Express #3395
	Gas	E: Shell◊
		W: AmocoBP◊
	Food	W: FastFood/Kangaroo Expr
	Other	E: to Wm Carey College
59		US 98E, Lucedale, Mobile, to US 49, to MS Gulf Coast
	FStop	E: to US 49N: Dan's Truck Stop/BP
	Other	E: Thomas Tire Repair, to Hattiesburg Muni Airport✈, to MIL/Camp Shelby Military Res/Camp Shelby/Lake Walker Family Campground▲, Paul B Johnson State Park▲
(56)		Parking Area (SB)
51		MS 589, Purvis
	Other	W: Dunn's Falls
41		MS 13, Main Ave, Lumberton
	Gas	W: Pure
	Other	W: to Little Black Creek Water Park▲
35		Hillsdale Rd, Lumberton
	FStop	E: Pure
	Lodg	E: Georgetowne Inn, Hillsdale Resort Inn
29		MS 26, Poplarville, Wiggins
	Gas	W: Kangaroo◊
	Food	W: Burger King
	Other	W: Pearl River Comm College
27		MS 53, Poplarville, Necaise
	Gas	W: Shell◊
	Other	E: Poplarville Pearl River Co Airport✈
19		Savannah-Millard Rd, Poplarville

EXIT		MISSISSIPPI
15		McNeill Steep Hollow Rd, Carriere
	TStop	W: McNeill Travel Center
	Food	W: Rest/McNeill TC
	TServ	W: McNeill TC/Tires
	Other	W: to Lacy RV Park Campground▲
(14)		Parking Area (SB)
10		W Union Rd, Carriere
	TStop	E: Keith's Super Store/Chevron
	Food	E: Rest/FastFood/Keith's SS
	TServ	E: Keith's Super Store/Tires
	Other	E: Laundry/Keith's SS, to appr 6 mi Clearwater RV Park & Campground▲
(8)		Parking Area (NB)
6		MS 43N, Sycamore Rd, N Picayune
	Gas	W: Chevron◊
	Lodg	W: Budget Host Inn
	Med	W: + Hospital
	Other	W: ATMs, Grocery, Winn Dixie
4		MS 43S, Memorial Blvd, Picayune, Kiln
	Gas	E: Murphy
		W: BP, Exxon◊, Shell◊, Spur
	Food	E: McDonald's, Ryan's Grill
		W: Burger King, Domino's, Golden China, Hardee's, KFC, McDonald's, Pizza Hut, Panda Palace, Popeye's, Shoney's, Taco Bell, Waffle House, Wendy's
	Lodg	W: Comfort Inn, Days Inn, Heritage Inn
	Med	W: + Crosby Memorial Hospital
	Other	E: Auto Dealers, Home Depot, Walgreen's, Wal-Mart sc, Sun Roamers RV Resort▲, Picayune Vet Clinic♥
		W: Advance Auto, Auto Dealers, Amtrak, Firestone, Fred's, RiteAid, Radio Shack, Tires, Winn Dixie, PawPaw's Camper City, Picayune Pearl River Airport✈, Animal Clinic♥

EXIT		MS / LA
(2)		MS Welcome Center (NB) (RR, Phones, Picnic, Vend, RVDump)
(1)		Weigh Station (Both dir)
1		US 11N, MS 607, Nicholson, NASA Nat'l Space Tech Lab, Stennis Space Center, Naval Oceanographic Office
	Gas	W: Chevron◊, BP, Spur
	Other	W: Auto & Truck Repairs, ATMs, Winn Dixie

○ **MISSISSIPPI** (CENTRAL TIME ZONE)
○ **LOUISIANA**

11		Pearl River TurnAround
NOTE:		SB: Begin Motorist Call Boxes
5B		Honey Island Swamp
5A		LA 41 Spur, Pearl River
	Gas	E: Chevron
	Food	W: Café, Mama's Kitchen
3		US 11S, LA 1090, Pearl River
(1)		Slidell Welcome Center (SB) (RR, Phones, Picnic, Info, RVDump)
1CB		Jct I-10, E to Bay St Louis, W to New Orleans
1A		Jct I-12W, to Hammond

(I-59 begins/ends I-12, Exit# 85AC)
(I-59 begins/ends I-10, Exit #267AB)

(CENTRAL TIME ZONE)

○ **LOUISIANA**
Begin I-59 Northbound from Jct I-10 in LA to Jct I-24 in Chattanooga, TN

Interstate 64 E

EXIT		MISSOURI
		Begin Eastbound I-64 from Jct I-70 in Wentzville, MO to Chesapeake, VA

○ **MISSOURI** (CENTRAL TIME ZONE)

NOTE: MO DOT is extending I-64 to I-70. Construction will continue thru 2009. Check with www.modot.org or 1-888-275-6636 for updates, etc.

(?)		FUTURE-US 61N, Hannibal (WB ex, EB entr)
(?)		FUTURE-Jct I-70W, US 40W, to Kansas City (WB exit, EB entr)
(?)		FUTURE-Jct I-70E, St Charles (WB exit only)
(?)		FUTURE-Lake St Louis Blvd
(4)		FUTURE-MO N
(?)		FUTURE-MO DD, Winghaven Blvd

EXIT		MISSOURI
9		MO K, St Charles, O'Fallon
	Gas	N: QT, Mobil
	Food	N: Cracker Barrel, Culpeppers, Culvers, J Bucks, Joey's Seafood & Grill, Ruby Tuesday, Timber Creek Grill
	Lodg	N: Country Inn, Staybridge Suites
10		MO 94, St Charles
	Gas	N: QT
	Food	N: Jack in the Box, McDonald's
	Med	N: + Center Pointe Hospital
	Other	N: ATMs, Bank, Auto Repairs, Tires, Walgreen's, Animal Hospital♥
11		Research Park Circle (WB ex, EB ent)
14		Chesterfield Airport Rd, to MO 109, Long Rd, Chesterfield (EB ex, WB ent)
	Gas	S: Phillips 66
	Lodg	S: Comfort Inn
	Other	S: ATMs, Bank, Auto Repairs, Budget RAC, Tires, Aviation Museum, Spirit of St Louis Airport✈, to appr 5 mi Babler State Park▲
16		Long Rd, Chesterfield (WB ex, EB ent)
	Gas	S: BP

EXIT		MISSOURI
	Food	S: Central MO Pizza, Lisa's TX BBQ, McDonald's, Mr Goodcents
	Other	S: Police Dept
17		Boones Crossing St, Frontage Rd, Long Rd, Chesterfield Airport Rd
	Gas	S: BP, Mobil, Phillips 66
	Food	S: Longhorn Steakhouse, NY Burrito Gourmet Wraps, O'Charley's, Old Country Buffet, Olive Garden, Quiznos, Red Lobster Sonic, Steak n Shake, Starbucks, Subway
	Lodg	S: Hampton Inn, Hilton Garden Inn
	Other	S: ATMs, Banks, Best Buy, Dollar Tree, Lowe's, Pharmacy, PetSmart♥, Sam's Club, Target, Wal-Mart sc, UPS Store
19A		Chesterfield Pkwy N
	Gas	S: Shell
	Food	N: Rest/DoubleTree
		S: Bahama Breeze, Keith's, Lettuce Leaf, Stoney River Rest
	Lodg	N: Doubletree Hotel
		S: Homewood Suites
	Other	N: Avis, ATM, Bank, Monsato Co, Pfizer Global R&D, to Arrowhead Airport✈, Creve Coeur Airport✈

◊ = Regular Gas Stations with Diesel ▲ = RV Friendly Locations ♥ = Pet Friendly Locations
RED PRINT SHOWS LARGE VEHICLE PARKING/ACCESS ON SITE OR NEARBY BROWN PRINT SHOWS CAMPGROUNDS/RV PARKS

EXIT		MISSOURI
	Other	S: Chesterfield Mall, ATMs, Auto Services, Bank, Tires
19B		**Clarkson Rd, Olive Blvd, MO 340**
	Gas	N: Amoco, Shell
		S: Mobil
	Food	N: Applebee's, Taco Bell, YiaYia's
		S: Aqua Vin, Crazy Bowls & Wraps, CA Pizza Kitchen, Chili's, Curry in a Hurry, Einstein Bros, Fuji Sushi, Hunan Express, KC Masterpiece, McDonald's, Pasta House, Panda Express, Quiznos, Romano's Macaroni Grill, Starbucks
	Lodg	N: Hampton Inn, Residence Inn ♥, Springhill Suites
		S: Drury Inn
	Other	N: ATMs, Banks, Goodyear, Grocery, Walgreen's
		S: ATMs, Banks, Clarkson 6 Cinema, FedEx Kinko's, Grocery, PetCo ♥, Trader Joe's, Wild Oats, UPS Store
20		**Chesterfield Pkwy, Frontage Rd (WB exit, EB entr) (Access to Ex #19B, #19A Serv)**
21		**Timberlake Manor Pkwy**
22		**MO 141, Woods Mill Rd, Chesterfield** (Addt'l Serv 2-3 mi S to Clayton Rd)
	Gas	N: 7-11, BP
	Food	N: Dock Café, McDonald', Wendy's
		S: Blimpie, Dave's World Famous Bar & Rest, Hot Wok Café
	Lodg	N: Courtyard, Marriott
	Med	N: + St Luke's Hospital
	Other	N: Maryville Univ
23		**Maryville Centre Rd (WB ex, EB entr)**
24		**S Mason Rd, St Louis (WB)** (Gas & Food S 1.5 mi to Clayton Rd)
	Other	N: MO State Hwy Patrol Post
(25)		**Jct I-270, N - Chicago, S -Tulsa**
26		**New Ballas Rd, MO JJ, Clayton Rd**
	Gas	S: BP, Shell
	Med	N: + St John's Mercy Medical Center
		S: + MO Baptist Medical Center
	Other	S: Auto Services, Police Dept
27		**S Spoede Rd, St Louis**
28A		**US 61S, US 67S, to Clayton Rd**
	Food	S: Bistro, Chef's Express, Italian Rest
	Lodg	S: Hilton
	Med	S: + Shriners Hospital/Crippled Children
	Other	S: ATMs, Bank, Grocery, Police Dept, Shopping Plaza
28B		**US 67, US 61, Lindbergh Blvd**
	Gas	N: Amoco

EXIT		MISSOURI
	Food	N: CoCo's, Grassi's Italian Rest
	Other	N: ATM, Auto Services, Towing
28C		**Clayton Rd, St Louis (WB ex, EB entr)**
	Gas	N: Texaco
	Food	N: Baskin Robbins, Carolyn's, Starbucks
	Other	N: ATMs, Banks
30		**McKnight Rd, St Louis**
	NOTE:	EB: For 2009: I-64 below will be closed. For detour info, contact www.modot.org Or 1-888-275-6636.
31		**Brentwood Blvd, to I-170, St Louis (EB)**
	Gas	S: BP, Mobil
	Food	S: Corwin's, Romano's Macaroni Grill, Subway
	Other	S: ATMs, Auto Services, Borders, Circuit City, Goodyear, Target, Whole Foods, Serra Mission Winery
31A		**Brentwood Blvd, to I-170 (WB)**
	Gas	N: Shell
	Food	N: Burger King, Cajun Café, IHOP, KFC, Fazoli's, Pasta House, Steak n Shake, St Louis Bread, Starbucks, TGI Friday
	Lodg	N: Residence Inn
	Other	N: AMC 6, Galleria Mall
(31B)		**Jct I-170N, to I-70, to Chicago (WB)**
32A		**Eager Rd S, Hanley Rd S**
32B		**Hanley Rd N, St Louis**
	Gas	S: Shell, QT
	Food	S: McDonald's, Lion's Choice
	Other	S: Home Depot, Police Dept
32C		**Laclede Station Rd, (WB ex, EB entr)**
	Other	S: Auto & Towing Service
33A		**S Big Bend Blvd (WB ex, EB entr)**
	Other	S: Auto Services, Tires, Police Dept
33B		**Big Bend Blvd (WB ex, EB entr)**
	Gas	N: Texaco
33C		**Bellevue Ave (EB ex, WB entr)**
	Med	N: + St Mary's Health Center
33D		**McCausland Ave S, St Louis (WB)**
	Gas	N: Amoco
	Food	N: Chinese Express, Del Taco
33E		**McCausland Ave N (WB)**
	Med	N: + St Mary's Health Center
34A		**Oakland Ave (EB ex, WB entr)**
34B		**Clayton Rd, Skinker Blvd (WB)**
34C		**Hampton Ave S, Oakland Ave**
	Gas	S: Mobil, Amoco
	Food	S: Courtesy Diner, Hardee's, Subway
	Med	S: + Forest Park Hospital
34D		**Concourse Dr, Forest Park**
	Other	N: Golf Courses

EXIT		MISSOURI
36A		**Kingshighway Blvd S, to I-44**
	Gas	S: Amoco
	Other	S: Auto Repairs
36B		**Kingshighway Blvd N**
	Lodg	N: Best Western, Chase Park Plaza, Marriott
	Med	N: + Barnes Jewish Hospital, + St Louis Children's Hospital
	NOTE:	WB: For 2009: I-64 above will be closed. For detour info, contact www.modot.org Or 1-888-275-6636.
36C		**Boyle Ave (WB ex, EB entr)**
36D		**Vandeventer Ave, Choteau Ave (EB ex, WB entr)**
	Gas	N: BP
		S: Oil
	Other	S: Auto Services
37A		**Market St, Bernard St (EB ex, WB ent)**
	Food	S: Shoney's
	Med	S: + St Louis University Hospital, + Cardinal Glennon Children's Hospital, + Bethesda General Hospital
37B		**N Grand Blvd (EB ex, WB entr)**
	Gas	N: Oil
	Food	N: Asst'd
	Lodg	N: Marriott
	Med	N: + John Cochrane VA Medical Center
	Other	N: Museums, Theatres
38A		**Forest Park Blvd, Grand Blvd (WB)**
	Other	N: Auto Services, Towing
38B		**Market St (WB ex, EB entr)**
38C		**Jefferson Ave, to I-44 (WB ex, EB ent)**
	Lodg	N: Courtyard
	Other	N: Auto Services, ATMs, Banks, Enterprise, Firestone, St Louis RV Park▲
38D		**Chestnut St, 20th St (EB ex, WB ent)**
39A		**Market St, 21st St (WB ex, EB ent)**
	Lodg	N: Courtyard, Drury Inn, Hampton Inn, Hyatt Regency
39B		**S 14th St, St Louis (EB ex, WB entr)**
	Lodg	N: Marriott, Sheraton
39C		**S 11th St, Stadium (EB ex, WB ent)**
	Lodg	N: Marriott, Sheraton
	Other	N: Courts, Sheriff Dept, Museums
40A		**9th St, Tucker Blvd, Stadium (WB Exit Only)**
40B		**Broadway, 7th St (EB ex, WB entr)**
	Gas	S: BP
	Food	Many Choices North & South
	Lodg	N: Drury Plaza, Marriott, Millennium Hotel, Westin Hotel

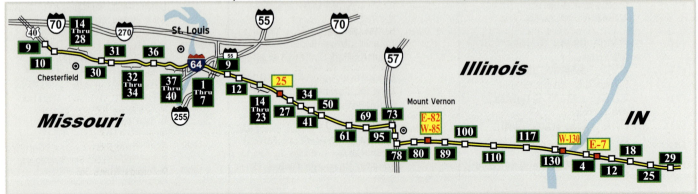

Page 244

◆ = Regular Gas Stations with Diesel   ▲ = RV Friendly Locations   ♥ = Pet Friendly Locations
RED PRINT SHOWS LARGE VEHICLE PARKING/ACCESS ON SITE OR NEARBY   BROWN PRINT SHOWS CAMPGROUNDS/RV PARKS

INTERSTATE 64 W/E

EXIT		MO / IL
	Other	N: Busch Memorial Stadium, Cardinals Hall of Fame Museum, Gateway Arch, to Convention Centers, Courts, Museums S: Auto Services, Museum, to Darkness Haunted Theme Park
(40C)		Jct I-55S to Memphis, Jct I-44W, to Tulsa (WB exit, EB entr)
	NOTE:	MM 41: Illinois State Line
	(CENTRAL TIME ZONE)	
	MISSOURI	
	ILLINOIS	
1		IL 3S, Cahokia, E St Louis
	Other	S: to St Louis Downtown Airport, Cahokia RV Parque▲
2A		MLK Memorial Bridge (WB, Left exit)
2B		3rd St, E St Louis (WB, Left exit)
	Med	S: + St Mary's Hospital
	Other	N: Casino Queen Hotel & RV Park▲ S: ATMs, Banks, Police Dept
2C		MLK Memorial Bridge, Missouri Ave, Downtown (WB)
3		IL 3N, St Clair Ave, I-55N, I-70E, to Chicago, Indianapolis, to Gateway Int'l Raceway
4		Baugh Ave, N 15th St, St Clair Ave
	Lodg	N: Blackmon's Motel
	Other	S: Auto Repair
5		N 25th St, East St Louis
6		IL 111, N Kingshighway
	Gas	N: BP, Mobil, Shell
	Food	N: Popeye's, China House S: Stoplight Restaurant
	Lodg	N: Econo Inn
(7)		Jct I-255, N-Chicago, S-Memphis
9		IL 157, N 88th St, Caseyville, to Centerville, Belleville
	Gas	N: BP, Phillips 66 S: BP◊
	Food	N: Hardee's, Wendy's, Subway/P66 S: Cracker Barrel, Domino's, DQ, Pizza Hut, McDonald's, Taco Bell
	Lodg	N: First Western Inn S: Best Inn, Days Inn, Econo Lodge♥, Motel 6♥, Quality Inn
	AServ	N: Phillips 66 S: BP
12		IL 159, N Illinois St, Fairview Heights, to Collinsville, Belleville
	Gas	N: Conv Food Mart◊ S: BP, Mobil, Moto Mart◊
	Food	N: Applebee's, Bob Evans, Carrabba's, Houlihan's, Joe's Crab Shack, Lotawata Creek, Olive Garden, Red Lobster, TGI Friday S: Boston Market, Burger King, Captain D's Chili's, Denny's, Hardee's, IHOP, Longhorn Steakhouse, Little Caesars Pizza, Long John Silver's, McDonald's, Ponderosa, Popeye's, Outback Steakhouse, Ruby Tuesday, Steak n Shake, Taco Bell
	Lodg	N: Best Western, Drury Inn, Fairfield Inn, Hampton Inn, Ramada Inn, Super 8♥

Personal Notes

EXIT		ILLINOIS
	Other	N: Circuit City S: ATMs, Auto Services, Banks, Best Buy, Borders, Firestone, FedEx Kinko's, Goodyear, Dobbs Tires, Kmart, NTB, PetCo♥, St Clair Square Mall, Natures Market, Craft Mall, Target, Walgreen's
14		W US 50, O'Fallon, to Shiloh
	Gas	N: QT, Shell S: Mobil, Conv Food Mart
	Food	N: IHOP, Japanese Garden, Steak n Shake S: Chevys Fresh Mex, DQ, Hardee's, Jack in the Box, KFC, Lone Star Steakhouse, McDonald's, O'Charley's, Quiznos, Taco Bell, Western Sizzlin'
	Lodg	N: Baymont Inn, Extended Stay America, Howard Johnson, Sleep Inn S: Candlewood Suites, Guest House Inn, Econo Lodge, Quality Inn
	Other	N: ATMs, Auto Dealers, Banks, CVS S: ATMs, Banks, Cinema 15, Grocery, Home Depot, PetSmart♥, Sam's Club, Wal-Mart
16		N Greenmount Rd, O'Fallon, Shiloh
	Food	N: Denny's, Sonic S: Applebee's, Cracker Barrel, Quiznos, Golden Corral, St Louis Bread
	Lodg	S: Holiday Inn Express
	Other	S: Grocery, Target, UPS Store
(18)		Weigh Station (EB)
19AB		US 50, IL 158, O'Fallon, Scott AFB, Air Mobility Dr, Scott Troy Rd
	Gas	N: Moto Mart S: Citgo◊

EXIT		ILLINOIS
	Food	N: Hero's Pizza/Subs S: Deli/Citgo, Ivory Chopsticks
	Lodg	N: Comfort Inn
	Other	S: Mid-America Airport, Scott AFB
23		IL 4, Mascoutah, Lebanon (Gas, Food, Lodg 4mi N in Lebanon)
	Other	S: Mid-America Airport, Scott AFB
(25)		Gateway Rest Area (Both dir) (RR, Phones, Picnic, Vend, Weather)
27		IL 161, New Baden
	Gas	N: Shell◊
	Food	N: McDonald's, Outside Inn, Subway
	Other	N: ATMs, Auto Services
34		to Albers
41		IL 177, Okawville
	FStop	S: Ron's One Stop #5/Phillips 66
	Gas	S: Gas Mart
	Food	S: Deli/Ron's P66, DQ, Hen House
	Lodg	S: Original Springs Hotel, Super 8
	TServ	S: Ex 41 Service Center, Obermeier Truck Service
50		IL 27, Nashville, to Carlyle
	FStop	S: Nashville Fuel Stop/Citgo
	TStop	S: Little Nashville Truck Stop/Conoco (Scales)
	Gas	S: BP, Shell◊
	Food	S: Rest/Little Nashville TS, Deli/Citgo, Hardee's, McDonald's, Subway
	Lodg	S: Best Western, Little Nashville Inn
	TServ	S: Little Nashville TS/Tires
	Med	S: + Hospital
	Other	N: to Carlyle Lake
61		US 51, Richview, Centralia
69		CR 9, Woodlawn Ln, Woodlawn
	NOTE:	I-64 below runs with I-57 for 5 mi. Exit #'s follow I-57.
(73)		Jct I-57, N - Chicago, S - Memphis
(78)		Jct I-57, S - Memphis, N - Chicago
	NOTE:	I-64 above runs with I-57 for 5 mi. Exit #'s follow I-57.
80		IL 37, Mt Vernon, Bakerville
	Gas	N: BP◊, Marathon
	Food	N: Burger King/BP
	Lodg	N: Royal Inn
	Other	N: Auto Services, Towing, to Mt Vernon Outland Airport
(82)		Rest Area (EB) (RR, Phones, Picnic, Vend)
(85)		Rest Area (WB) (RR, Phones, Picnic, Vend)
89		CR 17, Belle River, Bluford
95		IL 15, Broadway St, Mt Vernon
	TStop	W: Travel Center of America #43/Citgo (Scales), Huck's Travel Center (Scales)
	Gas	E: BP◊, Marathon, Phillips 66 W: Shell
	Food	E: Bonanza, Burger King, Fazoli's, Hardee's, KFC, McDonald's, Pizza Hut, Steak n Shake, Subway, Taco Bell, Wendy's, Western Sizzlin W: CountryPride/Popeyes/TA TC, Rest/Huck's TC, Applebee's, Arby's, Burger King, Cracker Barrel, Lone Star Steakhouse, McDonald's, Ryan's Grill

◊ = Regular Gas Stations with Diesel   ▲ = RV Friendly Locations   ♥ = Pet Friendly Locations

RED PRINT SHOWS LARGE VEHICLE PARKING/ACCESS ON SITE OR NEARBY   BROWN PRINT SHOWS CAMPGROUNDS/RV PARKS

INTERSTATE 64 W/E

EXIT	IL / IN
Lodg	E: Best Western, Comfort Suites, Drury Inn, Motel 6♥, South Gate Inn, Super 8 W: Comfort Inn, Days Inn, Fairfield Inn, Hampton Inn, Holiday Inn, Quality Inn
TWash	W: XVIII Wheelers TW
TServ	W: TA TC/Tires
Med	E: + Mt Vernon Hospital
Other	E: AutoZone, CVS, Kmart, Kroger, Walgreen's, Harley Davidson W: Laundry/WiFi/TA TC, Laundry/Huck's TC, Auto Dealers, Lowe's, Outlet Mall, Staples, Wal-Mart sc, Quality Times RV Park▲
100	IL 242, Wayne City, McLeansboro
Gas	N: Marathon◊
110	US 45, Barnhill, Norris City, Fairfield
FStop	N: Fuel Stop
117	CR 20, Burnt Prairie
FStop	S: Chuckwagon Charlie's/Marathon
Food	S: Cafe/Marathon
130	IL 1, Grayville, Carmi
FStop	N: Grayville Shell Plaza
Gas	S: Phillips 66◊
Food	N: Rest/BW, Subway
Lodg	N: Best Western, Super 8
Other	N: Auto Repairs
(130)	IL Welcome Center (WB) (RR, Phones, Picnic, Vend, Info, Weather)
NOTE:	MM 131.5: Indiana State Line

☐ ILLINOIS
☐ INDIANA (EASTERN TIME ZONE)

4	IN 69S, Griffin, to New Harmony
Gas	N: Depot
Food	N: Café/Depot
Other	S: to Harmony State Park
(7)	IN Welcome Center (EB) (RR, Phones, Picnic)
12	IN 165, Poseyville
18	IN 65, Evansville, Cynthiana
FStop	S: I-64 Moto Mart
25B	US 41N, Terre Haute
TStop	N: Flying J Travel Plaza #5098 (Scales), Pilot Travel Center #395 (Scales), Pilot Travel Center #447 (Scales)
Food	N: CountryMarket/FJ TP, Wendy's/Pilot TC, Rest/Pilot TC
Lodg	N: Quality Inn♥
Tires	N: Pilot TC #395
TWash	N: Blue Beacon TW/Pilot TC

EXIT	INDIANA
Other	N: Laundry/WiFi/RVDump/FJ TP, Laundry/WiFi/Pilot TC x2
25A	US 41S, Evansville, Haubstadt
FStop	S: Busler #102/Citgo
TStop	S: Busler Truck Stop I-64 (Scales)
Gas	S: BP
Food	S: Rest/Busler TS, Arby's, Denny's, McDonald's
Lodg	S: Best Western♥, Comfort Inn, Holiday Inn Express, Super 8♥
TWash	S: Busler TS
TServ	S: Busler TS/Tires
Other	S: Laundry/Busler TS, IN State Hwy Patrol Post
(29A)	Jct I-164, IN 57S, Evansville, to Henderson KY
TServ	S: Clarke Detroit Diesel
29B	IN 57N, Petersburg
FStop	N: Circle A Food Mart #109/Sunoco (Scales)
Food	N: Subway/Circle A FM
39	IN 61, Lynnville, to Boonville
Gas	N: Shell
Food	N: Pizza House, Rest/Old Fox Inn
Lodg	N: Old Fox Inn
54	IN 161, Tennyson, Holland
57	US 231, Dale, Jasper, Huntingburg
TStop	N: 231 AmBest Plaza (Scales)
Gas	S: Shell◊
Food	N: Rest/231 Plaza S: Denny's
Lodg	N: Scottish Inns S: Baymont Inn, Motel 6♥
TServ	N: 231 Plaza/Tires
Med	N: + Hospital
Other	N: Laundry/231 Plaza S: Abe Lincoln's Boyhood Home, to Lincoln State Park
(58)	Rest Area (Both dir) (RR, Phones, Picnic, Vend, Info)
63	IN 162, Santa Claus, Ferdinand
Gas	N: Sunoco◊
Food	N: Wendy's
Lodg	N: Comfort Inn, Harvest Moon Motel
Other	S: Lake Rudolph RV Campground▲, to appr 7 mi: Holiday World & Splashin Safari
72	IN 145, Bristow, Birdseye
79	IN 37S, Tell City, St Croix
(80)	Parking Area (EB)
(81)	Parking Area (WB)
86	IN 37N, Sulphur, English

EXIT	INDIANA
92	IN 66, Carefree, Leavenworth
TStop	S: Carefree Marathon, Country Style Plaza, Shell (Scales), Days Inn Truck Stop/BP, Pilot Travel Center #478 (Scales)
Food	S: Rest/Citgo, Rest/Country Style Plaza, Kathy'sKitchen/Days Inn TS, Subway/Pilot
Lodg	S: Days Inn, The Leavenworth Inn
Other	N: to Veringo Caves S: Laundry/WiFi/Shell, Laundry/WiFi/Pilot TC, to Wyandotte Caves
(97)	Parking Area (Both dir)
105	IN 135, Corydon, Palmyra
Gas	N: Citgo◊, Shell S: BP◊, Chevron
Food	N: Big Boy, KFC S: Arby's, Burger King, Cracker Barrel, China Best Buffet, DQ, Hardee's, Lee's Famous Recipe Chicken, Long John Silver, McDonald's, O'Charley's, Papa John's, Ryan's Grill, Subway, Taco Bell, Waffle House, Wendy's, White Castle
Lodg	N: Quality Inn, First Capitol Hotel♥ S: Baymont Inn, Hampton Inn, Holiday Inn Express, Super 8♥
Med	S: + Hospital
Other	S: AutoZone, Auto Dealers, Dollar General, Dollar Tree, Grocery, Radio Shack, Wal-Mart sc
113	to Lanesville
(115)	IN Welcome Center (WB) (RR, Phones, Picnic, Vend)
118	IN 62, IN 64W, Georgetown
FStop	N: Gas 'n Stuff/Marathon
Gas	N: Shell S: Marathon◊
Food	N: Korner Kitchen, McDonald's
Lodg	N: Days Inn, Motel 6♥
Other	N: LP, GasnStuff, Grocery
119	US 150W, to Greenville, Paoli
Gas	N: Citgo◊, Marathon
Food	N: Papa John's, Sam's Family Rest, Tumbleweed Grill
(121)	Jct I-265E, to I-65 (EB, Left Exit)
123	IN 62E, New Albany
Gas	N: BP, Bigfoot◊, Speedway S: BP, Marathon
Food	S: DQ, Freedom Waffle, Minny's Café, Waffle & Steak
Lodg	S: Hampton Inn, Hilton, Holiday Inn
Med	S: + Hospital
NOTE:	MM 124: Kentucky State Line

☐ INDIANA (EASTERN TIME ZONE)

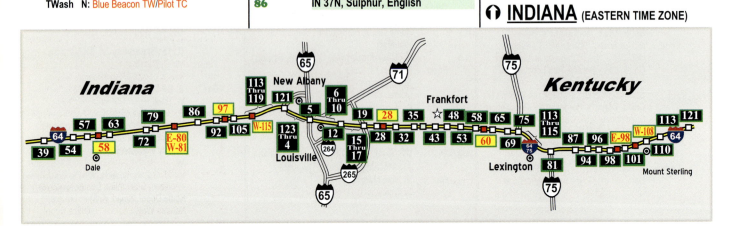

◊ = Regular Gas Stations with Diesel   ▲ = RV Friendly Locations   ♥ = Pet Friendly Locations
RED PRINT SHOWS LARGE VEHICLE PARKING/ACCESS ON SITE OR NEARBY   BROWN PRINT SHOWS CAMPGROUNDS/RV PARKS

KENTUCKY
(EASTERN TIME ZONE)

EXIT	KENTUCKY
(1)	Jct I-264, Louisville ByP, Shively
TServ	S: Whayne Power Systems
3	US 150E, 22nd St, Portland Ave
Gas	S: Chevron, Dairy Mart
Food	S: DQ, McDonald's, Subway
Other	S: Auto Repairs, to Simmons Bible College
4	9th St, Roy Wilkins Ave, Downtown
Food	S: Various Rest S to US 60
Other	S: Greyhound, Louisville Slugger Visitor Center, Museums, Science Center/IMAX, Courts, Police Dept
(5B)	Jct I-65N, to Indianapolis (EB), 3rd St, River Rd, Downtown (WB)
(5A)	Jct I-65S, to Nashville
Med	E: + Univ of Louisville Hospital, + Kosair Childrens Hospital, + Jewish Hospital, Louisville Medical Center
(6)	Jct I-71N, to Cincinnati (EB)
Med	E: + VA Medical Center (Ex #2)
7	Story Ave, US 42, US 60, N Spring St, Mellwood Ave, Louisville
Gas	N: Speedway S: BP
Food	S: Moby Dick Seafood Rest
Other	S: Auto Repairs
8	Grinstead Dr, Cherokee Pkwy (Gas/Food/Lodg S to US 150)
Gas	S: BP, Chevron, Swifty
Food	N: Beef O'Brady's S: Chinese Bistro, KT's Rest & Bar
Other	N: Southern Baptist Seminary S: to Expo Center, Presbyterian Seminary
10	KY 2048, Cannons Lane
Other	S: Bowman Field Airport ✈
(12A)	Jct I-264W, Watterson Expwy (EB)
Med	N: + Baptist Hospital East S: + Norton Suburban Hospital
(12B)	Jct I-264E, Watterson Expwy (EB) (All Serv at 1st Ex #20AB/US 60) (Gas/Food/Lodg/Malls/Repairs)
(12)	Jct I-264, Watterson Expwy, Airport, St Mathews, Churchill Downs (WB)
Other	W: to Freedom Hall, Fairgrounds
15	KY 1747, Hurstbourne Pkwy, Jeffersontown, Middletown (WB)
Gas	N: BP◇, Chevron◇, Shell◇ S: BP◇, Shell, Thornton's, Meijer◇
Food	N: Arby's, Bob Evans, Burger King, Carrabba's, Chili's, Don Pablo, Lone Star Steakhouse, McDonald's, Olive Garden, Papa John's, Perkins, Romano's Macaroni Grill, TGI Friday, Waffle House S: Applebee's, Chuck E Cheese, Damon's, O'Charley's, Piccadilly's, Shoney's, Shogun, Starbucks, Wendy's
Lodg	N: AmeriSuites, Baymont Inn♥, Courtyard, Days Inn, Drury Inn, Holiday Inn, Red Roof Inn, Travelodge S: Clarion Hotel, Days Inn, Extended Stay America, Hampton Inn, Marriott, Red Carpet Inn, Suburban Extended Stay
TServ	N: Cummins Cumberland S: Clarke Detroit Diesel

EXIT	KENTUCKY
	Other N: ATMs, B&N, CompUSA, FedEx Kinko's, Kroger, Lowe's, to Univ of Louisville/Shelby S: ATMs, Auto Dealers, Auto Repairs, Auto Services, Banks, Cinema, CVS, Home Depot, Kroger, Office Depot, PetSmart♥, Radio Shack, Staples, Target, UPS Store, Wal-Mart sc, Winn Dixie, Walgreen's
15A	KY 1747S, Hurstbourne Pkwy, Industrial Pkwy, Jeffersontown (EB)
15B	KY 1747S, Hurstbourne Pkwy (EB)
15C	KY 1747N, Hurstbourne Pkwy (EB)
17	Blankenbaker Pky, Industrial Park, Jeffersontown
Gas	N: Marathon, Dairy Mart◇ S: BP, Citgo, Chevron, Shell, Thornton's◇
Food	S: Arby's, Backyard Burger, Burger King, Cracker Barrel, Kingfish, Rest, King Buffet, McDonald's, Ruby Tuesday, Subway, Taco Bell, Waffle House, Wendy's
Lodg	N: Staybridge Suites S: Comfort Suites, Country Inn, Hampton Inn, Hilton Garden Inn, Holiday Inn Express Homestead Studio Suites♥, Jameson Inn, Microtel♥, Super 8, Wingate Inn
TServ	S: Clarke Detroit Diesel
Other	N: Bluegrass Harley Davidson S: Sam's Club, Outlet Stores, McKendree College
(19A)	Jct I-265S, KY 841S
(19B)	Jct I-265N, KY 841N
Other	N: to Tom Sawyer State Park

EXIT	KENTUCKY
28	Veechdale Rd, Simpsonville
TStop	N: Pilot Travel Center #354 (Scales) (DAND)
Gas	S: BP◇
Food	N: Wendy's/Pilot TC, Rest/Old Stone Inn, Brandon's BBQ S: JT's Pizza & Subs,
Lodg	N: Old Stone Inn
Other	N: Laundry/WiFi/Pilot TC
(28)	KY Welcome Center (EB) Rest Area (WB) (RR, Phone, Picnic, Vend, Info)
32A	KY 55S, Taylorsville, Finchville (EB)
32B	KY 55N, Shelbyville (EB)
32	KY 55, Taylorsville Rd, Shelbyville, to Taylorsville, Finchville (WB)
Gas	N: Shell◇, Murphy S: Shell
Food	N: Arby's, Burger King, McDonald's, Waffle House S: KFC, Subway, Wendy's
Lodg	N: Best Western, Country Hearth Inn, Days Inn, Ramada
Med	N: + Jewish Hospital
Other	N: ATMs, Auto Dealer, Auto Service, Lee's Tire Center, Wal-Mart sc, Lake Shelby Campground▲ S: ATMs, Bank, Auto Dealer, to Taylorsville Lake State Park▲
35	KY 53, Mt Eden Rd, Shelbyville
Gas	N: BP◇, Chevron◇, Kroger S: Shell◇
Food	N: BBQ, Cracker Barrel, McDonald's, Subway, Waffle House S: FastFood/Shell
Lodg	S: Holiday Inn Express
Other	N: Kroger
(38)	Weigh Station (Both dir)
43	KY 395, Waddy, Peytona, Shelbyville
TStop	N: Flying J Travel Plaza #5036/Conoco (Scales) S: PTP/Waddy Travel Center/Citgo (Scales)
Food	N: Rest/FastFood/FJ TP S: CountryMkt/FastFood/Waddy TC
TWash	S: Waddy TC
TServ	S: Tires/Waddy TC
Other	N: Laundry/WiFi/RVDump/LP/FJ TP S: Laundry/RVDump/Waddy TC
48	to KY 151, to US 60, Frankfort, to US 127S, Lawrenceburg
Gas	S: BP, Chevron, Shell
Food	S: Subway/Shell
Other	N: to Smith Diesel Service
53	US 127, to Lawrenceburg, Frankfort
Gas	N: Chevron, Shell◇, Marathon, Speedway, Kroger, Murphy S: BP, Marathon◇, Speedway
Food	N: Applebee's, Burger King, Chili's, Chuck E Cheese, Hardee's, Longhorn Steakhouse, McDonald's, O'Charley's, Panera Bread, Pizza Hut, Quiznos, Steak 'n Shake, Shoney's, Subway, Taco Bell
Lodg	N: Best Value Inn, Days Inn, Hampton Inn, Holiday Inn Express, Marriott, Super 8
Med	N: + Frankfort Regional Medical Center
Other	N: Advance Auto, Auto Services, ATMs, CarWash, Convention Center, Goodyear, Home Depot, Kmart, Kroger, Lowe's, Natures Way, Pharmacy, Office Depot

◇ = Regular Gas Stations with Diesel   ▲ = RV Friendly Locations   ♥ = Pet Friendly Locations
RED PRINT SHOWS LARGE VEHICLE PARKING/ACCESS ON SITE OR NEARBY   BROWN PRINT SHOWS CAMPGROUNDS/RV PARKS

Page 247

Interstate 64 W-E — KENTUCKY

EXIT	KENTUCKY
Other	N: Wal-Mart sc, UPS Store, Capital City Airport✈, KY State Univ, State Capitol, KY State Hwy Patrol Post S: Harrod's Diesel & Towing, Auto Service, Animal Hospital♥
53A	US 127S, to Lawrenceburg
53B	US 127N, to US 60, Frankfort
58	US 60, Versailles Rd, Frankfort, Versailles
Gas	N: BP◇, Chevron◇, Citgo◇, Shell, Marathon, Kroger
Food	N: Arby's, Captain D's, KFC, Market Café, McDonald's, Sandy's Steaks, White Castle
Lodg	N: Best Western, Bluegrass Inn, Fairfield Inn
Other	N: Auto Dealers, ATMs, Banks, Barker's Auto & Truck Service, Auto Repairs, Tires, Winn Dixie, KY State Univ, to appr 5 mi: Elkhorn Campground▲
(60)	Rest Area (Both dir) (RR, Phones, Vend)
65	KY 341, to US 421, US 62W, Midway, Versailles
FStop	S: Midway Travel Center/Citgo
Other	S: Midway College
69	US 62E, Paynes Depot Rd, Georgetown
Other	N: Georgetown College
NOTE	I-64 runs below with I-75 for 7mi. Exit #'s follows I-75.
(75)	Jct I-75N, to Cincinnati (EB)
Other	N: to Kentucky Horse Park▲
115	KY 922, Newtown Pike, Lexington
Gas	E: Exxon◇, Shell W: Chevron◇
Food	E: Cracker Barrel, McDonald's, Subway, Waffle House W: Denny's, JWS Steakhouse, Post Rest
Lodg	E: Knights Inn, La Quinta Inn♥, Starwood Hotel & Resort W: Embassy Suites, Holiday Inn, Marriott
TServ	S: Kentuckianna Truck & Trailer Repair, Whayne Power Systems, Volvo/GMC
Other	W: Auto Services S: Truck & Auto Repairs, Five Star RV Rental
113	US 27, US 68, Broadway, Paris Pike, Lexington, Paris
Gas	E: BP◇, Food Mart, Speedway, Thornton's W: Chevron◇, Shell
Food	E: Waffle House, Rest/Ramada W: Burger King, Fazoli's, Hardee's, Long John Silver, Penn Station E Coast Subs, Shoney's, Subway, Waffle House
Lodg	E: Ramada Inn W: Catalina Motel, Congress Inn Motel, Days Inn, Red Roof Inn♥
Med	E: + VA Hospital
Other	E: Auto Service, Bowling W: ATMs, Auto Dealer, Auto Services, CarWash, Greyhound, Kroger, Bluegrass RV/Cruise America, Northside RV, to Univ of KY, Rupp Arena
(81/111)	Jct I-75S, to Knoxville (WB) Jct I-64E, to Winchester, Ashland, Huntington, WV (Left Exit)
NOTE	I-64 runs above with I-75 for 7mi. Exit #'s follows I-75.

EXIT	KENTUCKY
87	KY 859, Bluegrass Station, Lexington Army Depot
94	KY 1958, Truck KY 627S, Van Meter Rd, Winchester
TStop	N: Shell Food Mart #4 (Scales) S: Speedway #8256/Marathon
Gas	N: Chevron◇ S: BP◇
Food	N: FastFood/Shell FM S: FastFood/Speedway, Applebee's, Arby's, Burger King, Captain D's, Cantuckee Diner, Domino's, El Rio Grande Rest, Fazoli's, Golden Corral, KFC, Hardee's, Little Caesars, Long John Silver, McDonald's, Pizza Hut, Popeye's, Sonic, Subway, Waffle House, Wendy's
Lodg	N: Best Value Inn, Holiday Inn Express S: Best Western, Budget Inn, Travelodge
TServ	S: Bob Rayburn Truck Repair
Med	S: + Hospital
Other	N: Codell Airport✈ S: AutoZone, Auto Repairs, Auto Dealer, ATMs, Banks, Laundromat, Kmart, Kroger, Lowe's, Office Depot, Radio Shack, Tires, Wal-Mart sc, to Fort Boonesborough State Park▲
96	KY 627, Truck KY 627N, to Winchester, Paris (EB)
TStop	N: L to Ind Park: 96 Truck Stop/Citgo (Scales)
Gas	N: BP◇ S: Marathon◇, Speedway
Food	N: Rest/96 TS
Lodg	S: Days Inn♥, Hampton Inn, Quality Inn
TWash	N: 96 TS
TServ	N: 96 TS/Tires, S&W Truck & Trailer Serv
Other	S: Auto Dealer, Auto Services, ATMs, Banks, Grocery, Tires
96A	KY 627S, Maple St, Winchester (WB)
96B	KY 627N, Paris Rd, to Paris (WB)
98	Bert T Combs Mountain Pkwy (EB)
(98)	Rest Area (EB) (RR, Phones, Picnic, Vend)
101	US 60, Winchester
(108)	Rest Area (WB) (RR, Phones, Picnic, Vend)
110	US 460, KY 11, Mt Sterling
Gas	N: Chevron, Shell◇ S: BP◇, Exxon, Marathon, Speedway
Food	N: Cracker Barrel, Krystal/Shell S: Applebee's, Arby's, Burger King, KFC, Golden Corral, Hardee's, Huddle House, Long John Silver, McDonald's, Taco Bell
Lodg	N: Fairfield Inn, Ramada Ltd S: Budget Inn, Days Inn♥
Med	S: + Mary Chiles Hospital
Other	S: Advance Auto, Auto Repairs, ATMs, Banks, Food Lion, Wal-Mart sc, to Mt Sterling Montgomery Co Airport✈
113	US 60, Midland Trail, Mt Sterling
FStop	N: Super Express Stop #5/Chevron
TStop	N: Pilot Travel Center #41 (Scales)
Food	N: McDonald's/Subway/Pilot TC, Deli/Spr Exp Stop
Other	N: Laundry/WiFi/Pilot TC
121	KY 36, Owingsville, Frenchburg
TStop	N: Appco/Marathon
Gas	N: BP◇, Citgo◇

EXIT	KENTUCKY
Food	N: DQ, McDonald's, Subway
Lodg	N: Best Western
Other	N: Dollar General, Laundromat, Pharmacy
123	US 60, Owingsville, to Salt Lick
Gas	N: Chevron◇
133	KY 801, Morehead, to Sharkey, Farmers
TStop	S: Eagle Travel Plaza (Scales)
Food	S: Diner/Eagle TP
Lodg	S: Comfort Inn
Other	S: to Outpost RV Park & Campground▲, Cave Run Lake RV Outlet, COE/Twin Knobs Rec Area▲, COE/Zilpo Rec Area▲
137	KY 32, Flemingsburg Rd, Morehead, to Flemingsburg
Gas	N: BP S: BP, Chevron◇, Exxon◇
Food	N: Cutter's Road House, DQ S: Burger King, China Star, Domino's, Hardee's, KFC, McDonald's, Papa John's, Jim Bo's Rest, Shoney's, Taco Bell
Lodg	S: Days Inn, Holiday Inn Express, Knights Inn, Quality Inn, Mountain Lodge, Super 8
Other	N: Big Lots, Kroger
Other	S: Dollar General, Food Lion, Goodyear, Radio Shack, Wal-Mart, KY State Patrol Post, Morehead St Univ
(141)	Rest Area (Both dir) (RR, Phones, Picnic, Vend)
(147)	Weigh Station (Both dir)
156	KY 2, KY 59, Olive Hill, Vanceburg
TStop	S: Smokey Valley Truck Stop
Food	S: Rest/Smokey Valley TS
161	US 60, KY 182, to Olive Hill
Tstop	N: Appco #80 (Scales)
Gas	S: Marathon◇
Other	N: Carter Caves State Resort Park▲
172	KY 1, KY 7, to AA Hwy, KY 9, Grayson, Maysville, Vanceburg
TStop	N: First Class Travel Center/Citgo, Super Quik 8 S: Pilot Travel Center #364 (Scales)
Gas	S: BP, Chevron, Exxon, Marathon, Speedway
Food	N: FastFood/First Class TC, Domino's, Huddle House, KFC, Long John Silver, Shoney's, Subway, Western Steer S: Wendy's/Pilot TC, Arby's, Burger King, China House, DQ, Hardee's, KFC, McDonald's, Pizza Hut, Subway
Lodg	N: American Inn, Country Squire Inn, Days Inn, Holiday Inn Express, Quality Inn S: Super 8
AServ	S: Service Garage
TServ	N: Clay's Tire, Grayson Tire & Svc Center, Grayson Truck Repair, CR Truck Sales, Interstate Truck Supply S: Halls Bros
TWash	S: Miller's TW
Other	N: LP/SuperQuik8, Dollar General, Dollar Tree, Grocery, Kmart, Valley Breeze RV Campground▲, to Greenbo Lake State Park Resort S: WiFi/Pilot TC, AutoZone, Dollar General, Dollar Tree, Family Dollar, RiteAid, to Grayson Lake State Park▲
(173)	KY Welcome Center (WB) Rest Area (EB) (RR, Phones, Picnic, Vend)

◇ = Regular Gas Stations with Diesel   ▲ = RV Friendly Locations   ♥ = Pet Friendly Locations
RED PRINT SHOWS LARGE VEHICLE PARKING/ACCESS ON SITE OR NEARBY   BROWN PRINT SHOWS CAMPGROUNDS/RV PARKS

I-64 W/E

EXIT	KY / WV
179	KY 67, Industrial Pkwy
181	US 60, Grayson, Princess, Rush
TStop	N: Exit 181 BP
Gas	S: Marathon
Food	N: Deli/Exit 181 TS
185	KY 180, Catlettsburg, to Ashland
FStop	N: Super Quick 9
TStop	S: Flying J Travel Plaza #5118 (Scales)
Gas	N: BP◆, Chevron
Food	N: Arby's, Burger King, Hardee's, Subway, Taco Bell, Wendy's S: CountryMarket/FastFood/FJ TP
Lodg	N: Budget Inn, Days Inn, Fairfield Inn, Hampton Inn, Knights Inn
TServ	N: Whayne Power Systems
Other	N: LP/SuperQuick9, KY State Hwy Patrol Post S: Laundry/WiFi/RVDump/LP/FJ TP
191	US 23, to Ashland, Louisa
Gas	N: Exxon, Marathon◆, Speedway
Food	N: Burger King, McDonald's, Subway
Lodg	N: Holiday Inn Express, Ramada Ltd
Med	N: + Hospital
Other	N: RiteAid
	NOTE: MM 192: West Virginia State Line
	(EASTERN TIME ZONE)

○ KENTUCKY
○ WEST VIRGINIA
(EASTERN TIME ZONE)

1	US 52S, WV 75, Kenova, Ceredo
Gas	N: Exxon
Food	N: Burger King, McDonald's, Pizza Hut
Lodg	N: Hollywood Motel
Other	N: Auto Repairs, Kenova RV & Auto Repair, ATM, Bank, SavALot, Getaway RV Rentals S: Tri-State Airport✈, Rental Cars: Avis, Budget, Hertz, National
6	US 52N, W Huntington, Ironton OH
Gas	N: GoMart, Marathon, Shell, Speedway
Food	N: DQ, Hardee's, Pizza Hut, Shoney's
Lodg	N: Coach's Inn
Med	N: + Hospital
Other	N: Auto & Truck Services, Radio Museum, Tires, to Lawrence Co Airpark✈
8	WV 152S, WV 527N, 5th St E
Gas	S: Speedway
Food	S: DQ, Laredo Steaks & Seafood
Med	N: + Family Urgent Care Clinic
Other	N: Huntington Museum of Art S: Grocery

EXIT	WEST VIRGINIA
(10)	WV Welcome Center (EB) (RR, Phones, Picnic, Vend)
(11)	Weigh Station (EB)
11	WV 10, Hal Greer Blvd, Downtown
Gas	N: BP, Chevron, Shell
Food	N: Arby's, Bob Evans, Hugo's Pizza, McDonald's, Wendy's
Lodg	N: Ramada Ltd, Super 8
Med	N: + Cabell Huntington Hospital
Other	N: to Marshall Univ, Civic Center S: Beech Fork State Park▲
15	US 60, 29th St E, Midland Trail, Huntington, Barboursville
FStop	N: Go Mart #59
Gas	N: Sunoco S: Exxon
Food	N: Arby's, Omelette Shoppe, Pizza Hut, Ponderosa, Wendy's, Rest/Econo Lodge S: Golden Corral, KFC, McDonald's, Shoney's, Taco Bell
Lodg	N: Colonial Inn Motel, Econo Lodge S: Days Inn, Red Roof Inn♥, Stone Lodge
Med	N: + Hospital
Other	S: Auto Dealers, CVS, Grocery, Pharmacy, UPS Store, Wal-Mart, Hidden Trails Campground▲, Setzers RV World of Camping
18	US 60, to WV 2, Merrick Creek Rd, Barboursville
Gas	S: Chevron
Food	S: Hardee's
Other	S: Home Depot, Kroger, Target
20	US 60, Mall Rd, Barboursville (WB)
Gas	N: Chevron, Exxon S: BP, Exxon
Food	N: Applebee's, Arby's, Bob Evans, Burger King, Chili's, CiCi's, China Max, Fiesta Bravo, Fuddrucker's, IHOP, Logan's Roadhouse, McDonald's, Olive Garden, Ruby Tuesday, Wendy's S: Cracker Barrel, Gino's, Ponderosa, Subway, TCBY, Taco Bell
Lodg	N: Comfort Inn, Holiday Inn, Ramada Inn S: Best Western, Hampton Inn
Med	N: + Emergi-Care Walk-In Med Ctr
Other	N: Best Buy, Borders, Firestone, Lowe's, Huntington Mall, Wal-Mart sc S: Auto Dealer
20A	US 60W, West Mall Rd (EB)
20B	US 60E, East Mall Rd (EB)
28	US 60, CR 13, Mason Rd, Milton
Gas	S: Chevron, Exxon, Go Mart, Shell

EXIT	WEST VIRGINIA
Food	S: DQ, Granny K's Rest, McDonald's, Pizza Hut, Subway, Wendy's
Other	S: Auto Services, Laundromat, Grocery, Pharmacy, Huntington/Fox Fire KOA▲
34	CR 19, Hurricane Creek Rd, Teays Valley Rd, Hurricane
Gas	N: Chevron S: Chevron, Exxon, Shell, Sunoco
Food	S: McDonald's, Pizza Hut, Subway
Lodg	S: Days Inn, Super 8, Smiley's Motel
Med	S: + Hospital
Other	S: Auto Services, ATMs, Banks
(37)	Rest Area (Both dir) (RR, Phones, Picnic, Vend, RVDump)
(38)	Weigh Station (Both dir)
39	WV 34, Hurricane, Scott Depot
FStop	N: Go Mart #43
TStop	S: Travel Center of America/76 (Scales)
Gas	S: Exxon, Go Mart
Food	N: Arby's/BP, Applebee's, Bob Evans, Hardee's, Rio Grande S: CountryPride/TA TC, Burger King, Captain D's, Creek Side Café, Fazoli's, KFC, McDonald's, Kobe, Papa John's, Shoney's, Subway, Taco Bell, TCBY, Wendy's
Lodg	N: Days Inn, Holiday Inn, Red Roof Inn♥ S: Hampton Inn
TServ	S: TA TC/Tires
Med	S: + Health Plus Walk-In Clinic
Other	N: Advance Auto, Laundromat, Grocery, US Post Office S: Laundry/WiFi/TA TC, Kmart, Kroger, Pharmacy, Auto & Truck Services
(40)	New Exit
44	US 35, Scott Depot, St Albans
Gas	S: Chevron◆
45	WV 25, 1st Ave, Nitro
TStop	N: Pilot Travel Center #243 (Scales)
Gas	S: BP, Exxon
Food	N: Arby's/TJCinn/Pilot TC, Hardee's S: Biscuit World, Checkers, Gino's Pizza, McDonald's, Subway, Wendy's
Lodg	N: Econo Lodge
Med	S: + Modern Medicine Walk-In Clinic
Other	N: Laundry/WiFi/Pilot TC
47	WV 622, Goff Mountain Rd, Charleston (WB)
Gas	N: Chevron, Exxon, Shell, Speedway
Food	N: Biscuit World, Bob Evans, Captain D's, Domino's, Hardee's, McDonald's, Pizza Hut, Taco Bell, Wendy's S: Arby's, Burger King, Cracker Barrel,

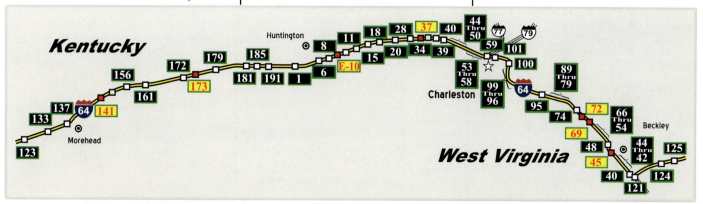

◆ = Regular Gas Stations with Diesel   ▲ = RV Friendly Locations   ♥ = Pet Friendly Locations
RED PRINT SHOWS LARGE VEHICLE PARKING/ACCESS ON SITE OR NEARBY   BROWN PRINT SHOWS CAMPGROUNDS/RV PARKS

Interstate 64 W/E — WEST VIRGINIA

EXIT		WEST VIRGINIA
	Food	S: CoCo's, DQ, Golden Corral, KFC, Shoney's, TGI Friday
	Lodg	N: Motel 6 ♥
		S: Comfort Inn, Sleep Inn
	TServ	S: Mountain International
	Med	N: + Health Plus Walk-In Clinic
	Other	N: Advance Auto, CVS, Kroger, Auto & Tire Services/Repairs
		S: Lowe's, Wal-Mart sc, Dog Racetrack
47A		WV 622S, Goff Mountain Rd (EB)
47B		WV 622N, Cross Lanes (EB)
50		WV 25, Fairlawn Ave, Institute
	Gas	S: Go Mart
	Other	S: WV State Univ
53		WV 25, 10th St, Dunbar
	Gas	S: Go Mart
	Food	S: Captain D's, McDonald's, Shoney's, Subway, Wendy's
	Lodg	S: Super 8 ♥, Travelodge
	Other	S: Advance Auto, CVS, Kroger, Police
54		US 60, to WV 601, MacCorkle Ave, Jefferson Rd, Charleston
	Gas	S: Chevron, Citgo
	Food	N: Subway, TCBY
		S: Bob Evans, KFC, Long John Silver, McDonald's, Taco Bell, Wendy's
	Lodg	N: Red Roof Inn ♥
		S: Days Inn
	TServ	S: Cummins Cumberland
	Med	N: + Health Plus Walk-In Clinic
		S: + Thomas Memorial Hospital
	Other	N: Auto Dealers, Kroger
		S: SavALot, Tires
55		to WV 601, Kanawha Turnpike (WB)
56		Montrose Dr, S Charleston
	Gas	N: Chevron, Exxon◊, SuperAmerica
	Food	N: Hardee's, Shoney's
	Lodg	N: Microtel, Ramada Plaza, Wingate Inn
		S: Holiday Inn Express
	Other	N: Advance Auto, Kmart, Pharmacy
58A		US 119S, Oakwood Rd, Logan
58B		US 119N, Virginia St, Civic Ctr (EB)
	Lodg	S: Hampton Inn, Holiday Inn
58C		US 60, Lee St, Civic Center (EB)
		US 60, Washington St (WB)
	Gas	N: BP, Exxon, GoMart
	Med	S: + Hospital
	NOTE:	I-64 below follows I-77 between Charleston and Beckley. Exit #'s follow I-77.
(59/101)		to Jct I-77N, Jct I-79N, Parkersburg, Clarksburg, Jct I-64W, to Huntington
100		Broad St, Capitol St
	Gas	E: Chevron
	Food	E: Ponderosa
	Lodg	E: Fairfield Inn, Holiday Inn, Super 8
	Med	W: + St Francis Hospital
	Other	W: Auto Services, ATMs, CVS, Kroger, Towing, Charles Town Center Mall
99		WV 114, Greenbrier St, State Capitol
	Gas	W: Citgo, Exxon
	Food	W: Domino's, Subway, Wendy's
	Other	W: Yeager Airport →, Laidley Field, State Museum

EXIT		WEST VIRGINIA
98		WV 61, 35th St Bridge (SB) (EB)
	Gas	W: Sunoco
	Food	W: McDonald's, Shoney's, Subway, TacoBell/KFC, Wendy's
	Med	W: + Hospital
	Other	W: Univ of Charleston, WVU Charleston
97		US 60W, Midland Trail, Kanawha Blvd, Charleston (NB) (WB)
(96)		WV Turnpike Begin/End
96		US 60E, Midland Trail, Belle
	Food	E: Gino's Pizza
	Lodg	E: Budget Host Inn
	TServ	E: Walker Machinery
95		WV 61, MacCorkle Ave
	FStop	E: Go-Mart #31
	Gas	E: BP
		W: Ashland, Chevron, Exxon, GoMart
	Food	E: Bob Evans, Burger King, IHOP, Lone Star Steakhouse, McDonalds
		W: Applebee's, Captain D's, Cracker Barrel, Hooters, La Carreta, Ponderosa, Shoney's, Southern Kitchen
	Lodg	E: Comfort Suites, Country Inn, Days Inn, Hawthorn Inn, Knights Inn, Motel 6 ♥, Red Roof Inn ♥
	Other	E: Advance Auto, Kmart
		W: Kroger, Lowe's, NAPA, Mall, WVU Charleston, Univ of Charleston
89		WV 61, WV 94, Marmet, Chesapeake
	FStop	E: Market Express #7/Exxon
	Gas	E: Go-Mart, Shell, Sunoco
	Food	E: Subway/Exxon, Biscuit World, Gino's Pizza, Hardee's, KFC, Subway, Wendy's

EXIT		WEST VIRGINIA
	Other	E: Kroger, Pharmacy, Marmet Locks & Dam, Kanawha River
85		US 60, WV 61, Chelyan, East Bank
	Gas	E: GoMart◊
	Food	E: McDonald's, Shoney's
	Other	E: Kroger
(82)		TOLL Plaza
79		CR 79/3, Cabin Creek Rd, Sharon
74		WV 83, Paint Creek Rd, Montgomery
(72)		Service Plaza (NB) (WB)
	FStop	N: Exxon
	Food	N: Burger King, Starbucks, TCBY
	Other	N: RVDump
(69)		Rest Area (SB) (EB) (RR, Phones, Picnic)
66		WV 15, Mahan
	Gas	E: Sunoco
60		WV 612, Mossy, Oak Hill
	Gas	E: Exxon
(55)		TOLL Plaza
54		CR 2, CR 23, Pax, Mt Hope
	Gas	W: BP
48		US 19N, N Beckley, Summersville (Addt'l Serv E US 19/WV 16)
	Gas	E: BP◊
	Food	E: Subway/BP
	Lodg	E: Ramada Inn
(45)		Service Plaza (Both dir)
	TStop	S: Exxon
	Food	S: Biscuit World, Starbucks, TCBY
44		WV 3, Harper Rd, Beckley
	TStop	W: Go-Mart #50
	Gas	E: Chevron◊, Exxon, Marathon, Shell
		W: BP
	Food	E: Applebee's, Burger King, Hibachi Japanese Steakhouse, McDonald's, Omelet Shoppe, Outback Steakhouse, Pizza Hut, Western Steer
		W: Bob Evans, Cracker Barrel, Wendy's
	Lodg	E: Best Western, Comfort Inn, Courtyard, Fairfield Inn, Holiday Inn, Howard Johnson, Quality Inn, Super 8
		W: Days Inn, Hampton Inn, Microtel, Park Inn
	Med	E: + Raleigh General Hospital
	Other	E: ATMs, Kroger, to Beckley Exhibition Coal Mine & Campground ▲
		W: Bob's Truck & Car Repairs, CVS, Kroger, College of WV
42		WV 16, WV 97, Robert C Byrd Dr, Beckley, Mabscott
	Gas	W: Amoco
	Food	W: Subway
	TServ	E: Walker Machinery
	Med	E: + VA Medical Center
	Other	W: to Twin Falls Resort State Park ▲
(40/121)		Jct I-64E, to Lewisburg Jct I-77S, Bluefield, Charleston (WB)
	NOTE:	I-64 above follows I-77 between Charleston and Beckley. Exit #'s follow I-77.
124		US 19, Eisenhower Dr, Beckley NOTE: Last FREE Exit WB
	Gas	N: Exxon, GoMart, Speedway
	Lodg	N: Honey Rock Motel, Pinecrest Motel

◊ = Regular Gas Stations with Diesel   ▲ = RV Friendly Locations   ♥ = Pet Friendly Locations
RED PRINT SHOWS LARGE VEHICLE PARKING/ACCESS ON SITE OR NEARBY   BROWN PRINT SHOWS CAMPGROUNDS/RV PARKS

EXIT	WEST VIRGINIA
125	WV 307, Airport Rd, Beaver (WB)
Gas	N: Shell
	S: Chevron, Exxon, GoMart
Food	S: Hardee's, McDonald's, Pizza Hut
Lodg	N: Sleep Inn
	S: Patriot Motel
Other	N: Raleigh Co Memorial Airport ✈
125A	WV 307, Beaver (EB)
125B	Airport Rd (EB)
129	CR 9, Grandview Rd, Beaver (WB)
Gas	S: Exxon, Shell
Other	N: Grandview State Park ▲
	S: Little Beaver State Park ▲
129A	CR 9S, Shady Spring (EB)
129B	CR 9N, Grandview Rd (EB)
133	CR 27, Pluto Rd, Bragg
NOTE:	ALL TRUCKS MUST STOP (EB)
139	CR 7, WV 20, Green Sulphur Springs, Sandstone, Hinton
Gas	S: Citgo
Other	S: to Bass Lake Park ▲, Bluestone State Park ▲, Pipestem State Park ▲, Rock Ridge Resort ▲
143	WV 20, Green Sulphur Springs, Meadow Bridge, Rainelle
Gas	N: Chevron
150	CR 29, WV4, Dawson
Lodg	S: Dawson Inn & Campground ▲
Other	N: Summer Wind RV Park & Campground ▲
156	US 60, Midland Trail, Sam Black Church, Crawley, Rupert, Rainelle
Gas	N: Citgo ◊, Exxon ◊, Shell ◊
161	WV 12, Asbury, Alta
FStop	S: 161 Truck Stop/Chevron
Food	S: Grandpa's Rest
Other	S: to Greenbrier River Campground ▲
169	US 219, Lewisburg, Ronceverte
FStop	S: Exxon
Gas	S: Shell
Food	S: Applebee's, Arby's, Bob Evans, Hardee's, Shoney's, Western Sizzlin'
Lodg	N: Days Inn
	S: Brier Inn, Econo Lodge, Hampton Inn, Rodeway Inn, Super 8
Med	S: + Hospital
Other	N: Greenbrier Valley Airport ✈
	S: ATMs, Auto Dealers, Cinema, Museums, Theatres, Lewisburg Fruit & Produce, Wal-Mart sc, State Fairgrounds

EXIT	WV / VA
175	US 60, WV 92, White Sulphur Springs, Caldwell
FStop	N: Dixon's Auto Truck Stop/Shell
Gas	N: Chevron, Exxon
Food	N: Rest/Dixon's ATS, McDonald's, Taco Bell, Wendy's
TServ	N: Dixon's ATS/Tires
Other	S: to Greenbrier Mountainaire Campground ▲, Greenbrier State Forest, Nat'l Radio Astronomy Observatory, Cass Scenic RR, Resort, Ski Areas
(179)	WV Welcome Center (WB) (RR, Phones, Picnic)
181	US 60, WV 92, White Sulphur Springs, Caldwell (WB, diff reaccess)
Gas	N: Amoco, Shell
Food	N: Hardee's, Pizza Hut, Taco Bell
Lodg	N: Budget Inn, Old White Motel
	S: Allstate Motel
Other	N: Food Lion, NAPA, Pharmacy,
	S: Twilight Overnite Campground ▲, to Ski Areas, Nat'l Radio Astronomy Observatory
183	VA 311, Crows (EB)
Other	S: to Moncove Lake State Park ▲
NOTE:	MM 184: Virginia State Line
	(EASTERN TIME ZONE)
⬆	WEST VIRGINIA
⬇	VIRGINIA
	(EASTERN TIME ZONE)
1	VA 198, Jerrys Runs Tr, Covington
(2)	VA Welcome Center (EB) (RR, Phones, Picnic)
7	VA 661, Midland Trail, Covington
10	US 60E, VA 159S, to VA 311, Covington, to Callahan
Gas	S: Marathon ◊
Other	S: LP/Marathon
14	VA 154, Durant Rd, Covington, to Hot Springs
Gas	N: Exxon, Sunoco
Food	N: Arby's/Exxon, Hardee's, KFC, Little Caesars Pizza, Subway, Wendy's
Lodg	N: Budget Motel, Town House Motel
Other	N: AutoZone, Auto Services, ATMs, CVS, Banks, Carwash, Family Dollar, Kroger
	S: Dollar Tree, Wal-Mart sc
16	US 60W, US 220N, Covington, to Hot Springs
Gas	N: Amoco, Exxon, Shell

EXIT	VIRGINIA
Food	N: Burger King/Exxon, Western Sizzlin'
	S: Long John Silver, McDonald's
Lodg	N: Best Value Inn, Best Western, Holiday Inn Express, Highland Motel, Pinehurst Motel
	S: Comfort Inn
Other	S: Dollar General, Kmart, Radio Shack
16B	US 60W, US 220N, Covington (WB)
21	VA 696, Covington, Lowmoor
Med	S: + Alleghany Regional Hospital
24	US 60E, US 220S, Clifton Forge
Gas	S: Shell ◊
Food	S: Hardee's, Taco Bell
Other	N: Lancaster Comm College
	S: Amtrak, Auto Repairs, ATMs
27	US 60W Bus, US 220S, VA 629 Clifton Forge
Gas	S: Citgo ◊, Exxon
Other	N: to Douthat State Park ▲
29	VA 269E, VA 42N, Clifton Forge
Gas	S: Exxon ◊
Food	S: Rest/Exxon
Other	S: Repairs/Exxon
(33)	Truck Parking Area (EB)
35	VA 269, VA 850, Clifton Forgde, Longdale Furnace
43	VA 780, Goshen
50	US 60, VA 623, Lexington (All Serv 3.5-5 mi S US 60 in Lexington)
55	US 11, to VA 39, Lexington, Goshen
Gas	N: Exxon ◊
	S: Citgo ◊, Texaco
Food	N: Burger King, Ruby Tuesday, Waffle House
	S: Subway/Citgo, Applebee's, DQ, Redwood Family Rest, Shoney's
Lodg	N: Best Western, Country Inn, Sleep Inn, Super 8 ♥, Wingate Inn
	S: Best Western, Comfort Inn, Country Inn, Econo Lodge, Holiday Inn Express
Med	S: + Stonewall Jackson Hospital
Other	N: ATMs, Auto Dealer, Banks, Dollar Tree, Blue Ridge Animal Clinic ♥, Radio Shack, Wal-Mart sc, to Long's Campground ▲
	S: ATMs, Auto Service, Bank, to VA Military Institute, Washington & Lee Univ
NOTE:	I-64 runs below with I-81. Exit #'s follow I-81.
(56/ 191)	Jct I-81S, Roanoke Jct I-64W, Lewisburg WV, Beckley, to US 60, Charleston (NB, Left Exit)

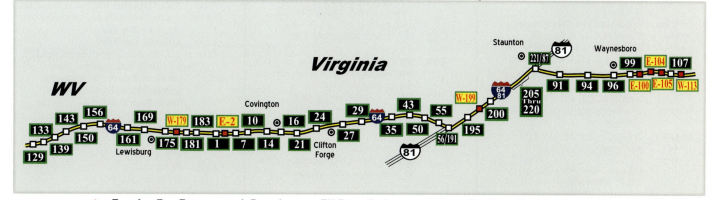

◊ = Regular Gas Stations with Diesel ▲ = RV Friendly Locations ♥ = Pet Friendly Locations
RED PRINT SHOWS LARGE VEHICLE PARKING/ACCESS ON SITE OR NEARBY   BROWN PRINT SHOWS CAMPGROUNDS/RV PARKS

Page 251

INTERSTATE W 64 E

EXIT	VIRGINIA
195	**US 11, Lee Hwy, Lexington**
TStop	W: Lee Hi Travel Plaza/Shell (Scales)
Gas	W: Citgo
Food	E: Maple Hall Lodging & Dining W: Rest/Lee TP, Rest/Howard Johnson
Lodg	E: Lexington Historic Inn, Maple Hall W: Days Inn, Howard Johnson, Ramada Inn
TServ	W: Lee Hi TP/Tires, VA Truck Center
Other	W: Laundry/WiFi/RVDump/RVPark/Lee Hi TP
(199)	**Rest Area (WB) (SB)** **(RR, Phones, Picnic, Vend)**
200	**VA 710, Fairfield**
FStop	W: Fairfield Exxon, Stop in Food Store #62/Shell
Gas	E: BP
Food	E: McDonald's/BP, Whistlestop Cafe W: Subway/Exxon
TServ	W: Smith's Garage
205	**VA 606, Raphine, Steeles Tavern**
FStop	E: Orchard Creek Auto RV Plaza/Exxon
TStop	E: Gas City, White's AmBest Truck Stop (Scales) W: WilcoHess Travel Plaza #735 (Scales)
Gas	E: Sunoco
Food	E: Rest/White's TS, Burger King/Orchard Creek W: Wendy's/WilcoHess TP, Rest/Days Inn
Lodg	E: Motel/White's TS W: Days Inn, Howard Johnson
TServ	E: White's TS/Tires/TWash W: Peterbilt
Other	E: Laundry/White's TS, Montebello Camping & Fish Resort▲, to Tye River Gap Campground▲, Crabtree Falls Campground▲
213	**US 11, to US 340N, Lee Jackson Memorial Hwy, Greenville, to Mint Spring, Waynesboro (NB)**
TStop	E: Pilot Travel Center #396 (Scales)
Gas	E: BP, Shell
Food	E: Arby's/Pilot TC, Subway/BP, German Rest
Lodg	E: Budget Host Inn
Other	E: Laundry/WiFi/Pilot TC, to Shenandoah Acres Resort▲
213A	**US 11S, Greenville (SB)**
213B	**US 11N, Greenville (SB)**
217	**VA 654, Mint Spring, Stuarts Draft**
TStop	W: Kangaroo Express/Citgo
Gas	E: BP, Exxon
Food	E: Subway/BP W: AuntM's/Kangaroo
Lodg	E: Days Inn W: Relax Inn
Other	E: to Walnut Hills Campground▲, Shenandoah Acres Resort▲
220	**VA 262, to US 11, Staunton**
Gas	W: BP, Citgo, Exxon
Food	W: Burger King, Hardee's, Hong Kong Buffet, McDonald's, Red Lobster
Lodg	W: Budget Inn, Hampton Inn, Microtel
Other	W: Advance Auto, Shenandoah Harley Davidson
(221/87)	**Jct I-64E, Charlottesville, Richmond Jct I-81N, to Winchester**
NOTE:	I-64 runs above with I-81. Exit #'s follow I-81.

EXIT	VIRGINIA
91	**VA 608, Tinkling Spring Rd, Fisherville, Stuarts Draft**
Gas	N: Shell S: Exxon, Sheetz
Food	S: McDonald's/Exxon
Lodg	N: Hampton Inn
Med	N: + Augusta Medical Center
94	**US 340, Waynesboro, Stuarts Draft**
Gas	N: 7-11, Exxon S: Shell
Food	N: Arby's, Burger King, Cracker Barrel, KFC, Japanese Steakhouse, McDonald's, Shoney's, Wendy's, Western Sizzlin
Lodg	N: Days Inn, Holiday Inn Express, Super 8
Med	N: + Hospital
Other	N: Waynesboro Muni Airport✈, Vet♥, Brooks Auto & Truck Repair Center S: Ladd Auto & Truck Repair, Museum
96	**VA 624, Mt Torry Rd, Waynesboro, to Lyndhurst** **(Trucks use lower gear on exit)**
Gas	N: Shell
Food	N: Quality Inn
99	**US 250, Blue Ridge Pky, Skyline Dr, Waynesboro, Afton**
Food	N: Colony House Motel
Lodg	N: Colony House Motel S: Afton Inn
(100)	**Parking Area (EB) (NO Trucks/Bus)**
(104)	**Parking Area (EB) (NO Trucks/Bus)**
(105)	**Rest Area (EB)** **(RR, Phones, Picnic, Vend)**
107	**US 250, Rockfish Gap Tpk, Crozet**
Gas	N: to Exxon
Other	S: Misty Mountain Camp Resort▲
(113)	**Rest Area (WB)** **(RR, Phones, Picnic, Vend)**
114	**VA 637, Dick Woods Rd, Charlottesville, Ivy**
118AB	**US 29, Charlottesville, Lynchburg (Future 785) (N Serv 2-4mi)**
Gas	N: AmocoBP, Citgo◊, Exxon, Shell S: Exxon◊
Food	N: Blimpie, Hardee's, Shoney's, Subway
Lodg	N: Best Western, Budget Inn, English Inn, Econo Lodge
Med	N: + Univ of VA Medical Center
Other	N: VA State Hwy Patrol Post, to Univ of VA S: Charlottesville KOA▲
120	**VA 631, 5th St, Charlottesville**
Gas	N: Exxon◊, Shell
Food	N: Amigos, Burger King, Domino's, Hardee's, Jade Garden, McDonald's, Taco Bell, Waffle House, Wendy's
Lodg	N: Affordable Suites, Holiday Inn, Sleep Inn
Other	N: Amtrak, CVS, Family Dollar, Food Lion, Greyhound, Laundromat, ATMs, Banks, Service Pro Auto & Truck Repair
121	**VA 20, Charlottesville (WB)**
Gas	N: Amoco◊ S: Exxon
Med	N: + Martha Jefferson Hospital
Other	N: Auto Repairs S: Visitor Center, Charlottesville KOA▲, to Monticello, Thomas Jefferson Home

EXIT	VIRGINIA
121AB	**VA 20, Charlottesville, Scottsville**
124	**US 250, Richmond Rd, Charlottesville Jefferson Hwy, Shadwell**
Gas	N: Amoco, Shell, WilcoHess
Food	N: Applebee's, Aunt Sarah's Pancake House, Burger King, McDonald's, Quiznos, Sticks Kebob Shop, Taco Bell, Tip Top Rest
Lodg	N: Hilton Garden Inn S: Comfort Inn, Ramada Inn
Med	N: + Hospital
129	**VA 616, Keswick, Boyd Tavern**
Gas	S: BP
Lodg	N: Keswick Hotel
Other	S: Auto Repairs
136	**US 15, James Madison Hwy, Zion Crossroad, Gordonsville, Palmyra**
FStop	S: Crossing Point Citgo
Gas	S: BP◊, Exxon◊, Shell◊
Food	S: Burger King/Exxon, Blimpie/Citgo, McDonald's/BP, Rest/Crescent Inn
Lodg	S: Crescent Inn, Zion Cross Roads Motel
Other	S: WiFi/Crossing Point, Auto Repairs
143	**VA 208, Louisa, Ferncliff**
Gas	S: Citgo◊, Exxon◊
Other	N: to 7mi Small Country Campground▲
148	**VA 605, Shannon Hill Rd, Louisa**
152	**Old Fredericksburg Rd, to US 250, Goochland, Hadensville**
159	**US 522, Cross Country Rd, Gum Spring, Goochland, Jackson**
Gas	N: Exxon◊
167	**VA 617, Oilville Rd, Oilville, Goochland**
Gas	N: Exxon◊ S: AmocoBP◊
(168)	**Rest Area (WB)** **(RR, Phones, Picnic, Vend)**
(169)	**Rest Area (EB)** **(RR, Phones, Picnic, Vend)**
173	**VA 623, Ashland Rd, Rockville**
Gas	N: Citgo S: BP◊, Exxon◊, Shell◊
Food	S: Bill's BBQ, Red Oak Café, Sattershwite Rest
Other	N: Auto Repairs, Towing S: ATMs, Banks, Dollar General
175	**VA 288, Broad St, Manakin Sabot**
(177)	**Jct I-295, to I-95, to Washington, Norfolk, VA Beach, Williamsburg**
178A	**US 250S, Broad St, Richmond**
Gas	S: 7-11, BP, Citgo
Food	S: Baja Fresh Mex Grill, Burger King, Casa Grande, Captain D's, McDonald's, Taco Bell, TGI Friday, Wendy's
Lodg	S: Candlewood Suites
Other	S: ATMs, Auto Services, Banks, Best Buy, B&N, Dollar Tree, Goodyear, Home Depot, Lowe's, PetSmart♥, Regal Cinemas, Richmond Harley Davidson, Staples, Target, Tires, Wal-Mart sc
178B	**US 250N, Broad St, Richmond**
Gas	N: BP◊, Citgo, Exxon◊, Shell◊, Texaco
Food	N: DQ, Great Taste Buffet, Starbucks, Thai Garden
Lodg	N: AmeriSuites, Comfort Suites, Hilton Garden Inn, Hampton Inn

Page 252   ◊ = Regular Gas Stations with Diesel   ▲ = RV Friendly Locations   ♥ = Pet Friendly Locations
RED PRINT SHOWS LARGE VEHICLE PARKING/ACCESS ON SITE OR NEARBY   BROWN PRINT SHOWS CAMPGROUNDS/RV PARKS

INTERSTATE 64 W ← → E

EXIT	VIRGINIA
Lodg	N: Homestead Suites ♥, Marriott, Towneplace Suites
Other	N: ATMs, Banks, Auto Services, Firestone, U-Haul
180	**Gaskins Rd, Richmond (EB)** (Addt'l Services N to Broad St)
Gas	N: BP, Shell◆
Food	N: DQ, Golden Corral, IHOP, O'Charley's, Ruby Tuesday
Lodg	N: Courtyard, Holiday Inn Express, Fairfield Inn, Residence Inn, Studio Plus
Med	N: + Universal Hospital
Other	N: ATMs, Banks, Circuit City, Costco, FedEx Kinko's, Goodyear, Lowe's, Office Depot, Sam's Club, UPS Store
180AB	**Gaskins Rd (WB)**
181	**Parham Rd (EB)** (Serv N to Broad St)
Med	N: + Henrico Doctors Hospital
181AB	**Parham Rd (WB)**
183	**US 250, Broad St, Glenside Dr (EB)** (Addt'l Services N to Broad St)
Gas	N: Chevron
Food	N: Bob Evans, McDonald's, Waffle House
Lodg	N: Best Western, Comfort Inn, Embassy Suites, Super 8
Med	S: + Henrico Doctors Hospital
Other	N: CVS, Grocery, Mall, Winn Dixie
183A	**US 250, Glenside Dr (WB)**
183B	**US 250, W Broad St (WB)**
183C	**Bethlehem Rd (WB)**
185	**US 33, Staples Mill Rd, Richmond** (Addt'l Serv S to Broad St)
Gas	N: Exxon, Fast Fare, Texaco
Lodg	S: Shell
Lodg	S: Holiday Inn
Other	N: Auto & Truck Service, Amtrak, Towing
185A	**US 33, Dickens Rd (EB)**
185B	**US 33, Staples Mill Rd (EB)**
(186)	**Jct I-195S, to Powhite Pkwy, Richmond (SB/WB, Left exit)**
NOTE:	I-64 below runs with I-95. Exit #'s follow I-95.
(187/79)	**Jct I-95N, to Washington (EB, Left ex) Jct I-64W, I-195S, Charlottesville**
78	**VA 161, N Boulevard, Hermitage Rd, Robin Hood Rd, Boulevard** (diff reacc)
Gas	E: Texaco
	W: BP, Citgo◆
Food	E: Café, Zippy's
	W: Bill's Va BBQ
Lodg	E: Holiday Inn
	W: Days Inn ♥, Red Carpet Inn
TServ	W: International, Lawrence Truck Service
Med	E: + Richland Memorial Hospital
Other	E: to Richmond Int'l Raceway
	W: Auto Services, U-Haul, Visitor Center, The Diamond, Parker Field
76B	**Gilmer St, W Leigh St, to US 1, US 301, Belvidere (SB)**
76A	**Chamberlayne Ave (NB)**
Other	E: Dorsey RV

EXIT	VIRGINIA
(75/190)	**Jct I-64E, VA Beach, Williamsburg, Norfolk, 7th St N 5th St, Jct I-95S, to Rocky Hill, Miami**
NOTE:	I-64 above runs with I-95. Exit #'s follow I-95.
192	**US 360, Mechanicsville Turnpike, Richmond, Mechanicsville**
Gas	N: Chevron, Citgo◆
	S: BP, Citgo
Food	N: McDonald's
	S: Church's, Hook Fish & Chips
Other	N: Auto Services, to Richmond Int'l Raceway
	S: Auto Repairs, Sheriff Dept
193AB	**VA 33, Nine Mile Rd, Richmond**
Gas	N: BP, Exxon
Food	N: Subway/Exxon, Burger King, Crab Lady, McDonald's
	S: Carolina BBQ
Med	S: + Richmond Community Hospital
Other	N: Auto Repairs
	S: Auto Repairs
195	**Laburnum Ave, to Williamsburg Rd, VA 33, US 60, VA 5, Richmond**
Gas	N: Chevron, Mobil, Shell
	S: BP, Exxon
Food	S: Applebee's, Burger King, China King, Hardee's, KFC, Little Caesar's, Popeye's, Shoney's, Subway, Taco Bell, Wendy's, Western Sizzlin'
Lodg	S: Airport Inn, Wyndham Garden Hotel
Other	N: Auto Repairs/Shell
	S: ATMs, Auto Services, Banks, CVS, Dollar General, Dollar Tree, Firestone, Grocery, Kroger, Radio Shack, RiteAid, Auto Rentals, Richmond Int'l Airport✈
197AB	**VA 156, S Airport Dr, E Nine Mile Rd, Williamsburg Rd, Sandston**
Gas	N: BP◆, Citgo, Shell◆
	S: BP, Shell◆
Food	N: Bojangles, Domino's, Hardee's, Pizza Hut, Subway
	S: Arby's, Burger King, Ma & Pa's Diner, Waffle House
Lodg	S: Best Western, Comfort Inn, Days Inn, Econo Lodge, Hampton Inn, Homewood Suites, Microtel, Motel 6 ♥, Wingate Inn
Other	N: Advance Auto, CVS, Winn Dixie
	S: ATMs, Auto Services, Tires, Richmond Int'l Airport✈
(200)	**Jct I-295, N-Washington, DC, S to Rocky Mount, NC, US 60, VA 156**
(203)	**Weigh Station (Both dir)**
205	**New Kent Hwy, VA 33E, VA 249W, to US 60, Quinton, Bottoms Bridge**
Gas	N: BP◆, Exxon◆
	S: Exxon, Shell◆
Food	N: Casa Pizza, Subway
	S: McDonald's
Other	N: Food Lion, US Post Office, Pharmacy
211	**VA 106, Emmaus Church Rd, Providence Forge, to Talleysville, Prince George, Hopewell**
TStop	N: Pilot Travel Center #159 (Scales)
Food	N: Subway/Pilot TC
Other	N: WiFi/Pilot TC
	S: Auto Service, Tires, New Kent Co Airport✈

EXIT	VIRGINIA
(213)	**Rest Area (Both dir)** (RR, Phones, Picnic, Vend)
214	**VA 155, N Courthouse Rd, New Kent, to US 60, Providence Forge, Lanexa**
Gas	S: Exxon◆
Lodg	S: Jasmine Plantation B&B
Other	S: Colonial Downs Racetrack, to Ed Allen's Campground▲, Rockahock Campground▲, Riverside Campground▲
220	**VA 33E, Eltham Rd, Lanexa, to West Point**
227	**VA 30, Old Stage Rd, Barhamsville Rd, to US 60, Toano, to West Point, Williamsburg**
FStop	S: Interstate Shell
Gas	S: Exxon◆
Food	S: McDonald's
231AB	**VA 607, to VA 30, Croaker Rd, Williamsburg, to Croaker, Norge**
Gas	N: 7-11
	S: Shell◆
Food	S: Candle Factory, KFC, Trader Café, Wendy's
Other	S: American Heritage RV Park▲, Outdoor World Williamsburg▲
234AB	**VA 199, VA 646, Newman Rd, to Colonial Williamsburg**
Gas	S: 7-11, Exxon, Mobil◆, Shell◆
Food	S: Burger King, Blue Plate Diner, ChickFilA, KFC, Hardee's, IHOP, Lightfoot Pancake & Steak House, McDonald's, Pierce's Pitt BBQ, Sonic, Subway, Top China
Lodg	S: Comfort Inn, Courtyard, Days Inn, Econo Lodge, Family Inn, Great Wolf Lodge Resort, Howard Johnson, Super 8, Ramada Inn
Other	N: Williamsburg KOA▲
	S: ATMs, Auto Services, Dollar General, Home Depot, Lowe's, Wal-Mart sc, Williamsburg Outlet Mall, Williamsburg Pottery Mall, Revolutionary Harley Davidson, Fair Oaks Family Campground▲, Scenic View RV Rentals, Williamsburg Pottery Campground▲
238	**VA 143, Merrimac Trail, to US 60, Colonial Williamsburg, Camp Peary**
Gas	S: 7-11, Shell
Food	S: Ben & Jerry's, Captain George's Seafood, Cracker Barrel, Golden Corral, Hardee's, McDonald's, Outback Steakhouse, Olive Garden, Rest/Best Western, Rest/Holiday Inn, Rest/Quality Inn
Lodg	S: Best Western, Comfort Inn, Country Inn, Days Inn, Econo Lodge, Hampton Inn, Holiday Inn, Howard Johnson, Marriott, Quality Inn, Ramada, Red Roof Inn ♥, Sleep Inn, Travelodge
Other	N: Camp Peary Naval Reservation
	S: to Anvil Campground▲, ATMs, Auto Services, Banks, Cinemas, Grocery, Rental Cars, Tires
242AB	**VA 199, Colonial Pkwy, Williamsburg**
Gas	N: BP
	S: 7-11, Crown, Shell

◆ = Regular Gas Stations with Diesel ▲ = RV Friendly Locations ♥ = Pet Friendly Locations
RED PRINT SHOWS LARGE VEHICLE PARKING/ACCESS ON SITE OR NEARBY BROWN PRINT SHOWS CAMPGROUNDS/RV PARKS

Page 253

INTERSTATE 64 W/E

EXIT	VIRGINIA
Food	N: Rest/Days Inn
	S: Burger King, McDonald's, Starbucks, Subway, Wendy's
Lodg	N: Days Inn
	S: Best Western, Clarion Hotel, Courtyard
Other	N: Cheatham Annex Naval Supply Center, US Naval Weapons Station
	S: William & Mary College, Colonial Nat'l Historic Park, Busch Gardens
243A	to US 60, VA 143W, Merrimac Trail, Pocahontas Trail, Busch Gardens, Williamsburg
243B	VA 143W, Merrimac Trail, Williamsburg (WB, Left exit)
247	VA 143, Merrimac Tr, Jefferson Ave (EB), VA 238, Yorktown Rd, Jefferson Ave (WB, diff reacc)
Gas	N: 7-11, BP
248	VA 238, Yorktown, Lee Hall (WB)
261AB	Hampton Roads Ctr Pky, Hampton
Gas	N: Exxon
	S: Citgo
Food	S: Chuck E Cheese, McDonald's, Peking, Roma Italian Rest, Subway, Taco Bell, Topeka Steakhouse
Lodg	N: Candlewood Suites, Suburban Lodge
Other	N: Thomas Nelson Comm College
	S: ATMs, Banks, AMC Cinema, Food Lion
262B	Hampton Roads Center Pkwy (EB)
262	VA 134, Magruder Blvd (WB)
Gas	N: Exxon
Lodg	N: Candlewood Suites, Suburban Lodge
Other	N: Thomas Nelson Comm College
263AB	US 258, VA 134, W Mercury Blvd, James River Bridge, Hampton
Gas	N: Exxon, Shell
	S: 7-11, BP, Exxon
Food	N: Applebee's, Burger King, Chili's, Denny's, Golden Corral, Hooters, IHOP, KFC, McDonald's, Olive Garden, Outback Steakhouse, Pizza Hut, Red Lobster, Waffle House, Wendy's
Food	S: Cracker Barrel, CiCi's, Lone Star Steakhouse, Old Country Buffet, Pizza Hut, Waffle House
Lodg	N: Comfort Inn, Courtyard, Days Inn ♥, Embassy Suites, Extended Stay America, Fairfield Inn ♥, Hampton Inn, Holiday Inn ♥, Quality Inn ♥, Red Roof Inn ♥, Sheraton
	S: Best Western, Econo Lodge, Hampton Bay Plaza, La Quinta Inn ♥
Other	N: ATMs, Auto Services, Banks, Firestone, Goodyear, Grocery, Office Depot, Target, Wal-Mart sc, Coliseum Mall, Hampton Coliseum
	S: Advance Auto, ATMs, Auto Services, Auto Rentals, Bass Pro Shop, Banks, Lowe's, Office Max, Pep Boys
(264)	Jct I-664S, Dwntwn Newport News, Pembrook Pkwy, Suffolk
265B	VA 167, N Armistead Ave (WB)
265A	VA 134, N Armistead Ave, VA 167, LaSalle Ave, Hampton
Gas	N: Citgo, RaceTrac
	S: BP
Food	S: McDonald's, Taco Bell/KFC
Lodg	N: Super 8
Med	S: + Hospital

Personal Notes

EXIT	VIRGINIA
265C	Armistead Ave, Langley AFB, Rip Rap Rd (EB)
Other	S: Tops Auto & Truck Repair, Towing
267	US 60, VA 143, W County St, Settlers Landing Rd, Woodland Rd
Food	S: Burger King
Med	S: + Sentara Hampton General Hospital
Other	S: Darling Memorial Stadium
268	VA 169, Mallory St, Franklin Blvd, Fort Monroe, Hampton
Food	N: Hardee's, McDonald's
(269)	Weigh / Inspection Station (EB)
272	W Ocean View Ave, Bayville St, Willoughby Beach, Norfolk
Food	S: Fisherman's Wharf Seafood Rest
Lodg	S: Days Inn
273	4th View St, W Ocean View Ave
Gas	N: BP◊
Lodg	N: Econo Lodge, Super 8
274	Bay Ave, Naval Air Station (WB)
(276)	Jct I-564, US 460E, Granby St (EB)
276A	US 460W, Granby St (EB)
Gas	S: AmocoBP, Exxon
Food	S: Amigos, Pancake House, Mediterranean Café, Subway
Other	S: ATMs, Banks, Kroger
(276B)	Jct I-564, US 460E, Granby St (WB)
276C	VA 165, E Little Creek Rd, to US 460, Norfolk (EB)
Gas	N: Shell
	S: AmocoBP, Exxon

EXIT	VIRGINIA
Food	S: McDonald's, KFC, Taco Bell, Wendy's
Other	S: ATMs, Banks, Grocery
277AB	VA 168, Tidewater Dr, Thole St
Gas	N: 7-11
	S: BP, Citgo
Food	N: Bamboo Hut, Hardee's
	S: Hunan Express, Seafood Rest
Med	S: + Hospital
Other	N: Food Lion, Grocery
	S: Auto Repairs
278	VA 194S, Chesapeake Blvd
Gas	S: Amoco, Exxon, Shell
Food	S: Burger King, KFC, McDonald's
279	VA 247, Norview Ave, Norfolk Int'l Airport, Chesapeake Blvd (EB)
Gas	N: Shell
	S: Shell
Food	N: Golden Corral, Pizza Hut, Wendy's
	S: KFC, McDonald's
Other	N: Norfolk Int'l Airport ✈, Kmart, Rental Cars, Auto Services, Food Lion
279A	Norview Ave S (WB)
279B	Norview Ave, Norfolk Int'l Airport
Other	N: Norfolk Int'l Airport ✈
281	VA 165, N. Military Hwy (WB) VA 165, N Robin Hood Rd (EB)
Gas	N: BP◊, Shell◊
	S: Citgo, Exxon, Shell
Food	N: Golden Corral, Pizza Hut, Wendy's
	S: DQ
Lodg	N: Econo Lodge
	S: Hampton Inn, Holiday Inn, Hilton
Other	N: Auto Dealers, Kmart
	S: Firestone, Target
281A	VA 165, Military Hwy, N Robin Hood Rd, Almeda Ave (EB)
282	US 13, VA 166, Northhampton Blvd, to Chesapeake Bay Bridge Tunnel
TStop	N: Big Charlie's Truck Plaza (Scales)
Gas	N: Amoco, Exxon, Texaco
Food	N: Rest/Big Charlie's TP, Burger King, McDonald's, Pizza Hut, Waffle House
Lodg	N: Quality Inn, Wingate Inn, Econo Lodge
TServ	N: Big Charlie's TP/Tires
Med	S: + Lake Taylor Hospital
Other	N: Laundry/Big Charlie's TP, VA Wesleyan College, Auto Services, to Chesapeake Bay Bridge Tunnel
	S: Auto Services, Tires
(284AB)	Jct I-264 Norfolk, VA 44, VA Beach (Serv: N to Newtown Rd: Gas, Food, Lodg S to Military Hwy: Gas, Food, Lodg, Mall)
Med	N: + Sentara Leigh Hospital
286AB	VA 407, Indian River Rd, Va Beach
Gas	N: BP◊, Hess◊, Shell
	S: Citgo, Exxon, Sunoco◊
Food	N: Hardee's
	S: Captain D's, Waffle House
Lodg	S: Founders Inn & Conf Ctr
289AB	Greenbrier Pkwy, Chesapeake
Gas	N: Citgo
Food	N: Burger King, Taco Bell, Wendy's
	S: Blimpie, Boston Market, Cheers Grill, Don Pablo, Flaming Wok, Joe's Crab Shack, Kyoto Japanese, Lone Star Steakhouse, Landry's Rest, McDonald's, Old Country Buffet, Olive Garden, Ruby Tuesday, Starbucks, Subway, Taco Bell
Lodg	N: Hampton Inn ♥ Holiday Inn ♥, Motel 6 ♥ Red Roof Inn ♥, Wellesley Inn

◊ = Regular Gas Stations with Diesel ▲ = RV Friendly Locations ♥ = Pet Friendly Locations
RED PRINT SHOWS LARGE VEHICLE PARKING/ACCESS ON SITE OR NEARBY   BROWN PRINT SHOWS CAMPGROUNDS/RV PARKS

EXIT	VIRGINIA
Lodg	S: Courtyard, Comfort Suites, Fairfield Inn, Extended Stay America
Other	N: Auto Dealers, ATMs, Banks, Food Lion, U-Haul
	S: Best Buy, Circuit City, Cinema 13, NTB, Dollar General, Pharmacy, Office Depot, Target, Greenbrier Mall
290AB	VA 168, Battlefield Blvd, Great Bridge
Gas	S: BP◊, Shell
Food	N: Applebee's, Burger King, Chuck E Cheese, Dunkin Donuts, Golden Corral, Hardee's, Ryan's Grill, Taco Bell, TGI Friday, Waffle House, Wendy's
Lodg	N: Days Inn, Super 8

EXIT	VIRGINIA
TServ	N: Tidewater Mack Trucks
Med	N: + Chesapeake General Hospital
Other	N: US Post Office, Home Depot, Lowe's, Sam's Club, Walgreen's, Wal-Mart sc
(291AB)	Jct I-464, US 17, VA 168, to Norfolk, Elizabeth City, Nags Head
292	VA 190, Great Bridge Blvd, VA 104, Dominion Blvd (WB)
296	US 17, Portsmouth, Elizabeth City, Chesapeake (WB)
Other	S: to Chesapeake Campground▲
296A	US 17N, Portsmouth (EB)
Lodg	N: Colonial Motel, Days Inn

EXIT	VIRGINIA
296B	US 17S, Chesapeake (EB)
297	US 13, US 460, Military Hwy
Gas	N: Exxon
TServ	N: Burton's Truck Repair, Carter Power Systems
Other	N: Auto Repairs
	S: Auto Repairs
(299AB)	Jct I-264 Portsmouth, I-664 Suffolk, US 13, US 58, US 460, Norfolk

(I-64 Begins/Ends on I-264)
(EASTERN TIME ZONE)

○ **VIRGINIA**
Begin Westbound I-64 from Chesapeake, VA to Jct I-70 in Wentzville, MO.

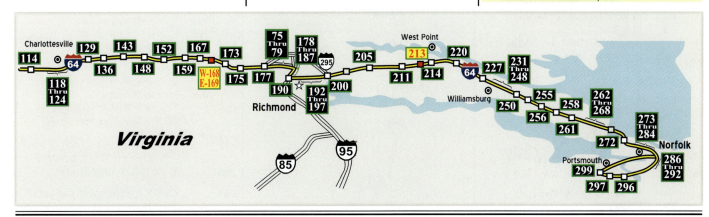

EXIT	INDIANA
	Begin Southbound I-65 from Jct I-80/90 at Gary, IN to Jct I-10 near Mobile, AL.

○ **INDIANA**
(EASTERN TIME ZONE)
(I-65 begins/ends on US12/US 20)

(262)	Jct I-90 (TOLL), W-Chicago, E-Ohio, US 20, US 12, 16th Ave, Gary (NB)
261	E 15th Ave, to 16th Ave, US 12, US 20, Gary
Gas	W: EZ Go Marathon
TServ	E: Pozzo Mack Sales & Service
	W: Cummins, Inland Detroit Diesel/ Allison, Lakeshore Truck Service
(259A)	Jct I-80/94W, to Chicago
(259B)	Jct I-80/94E, US 6, to Ohio
258	US 6 Bus, 37th Ave, Ridge Rd
Gas	E: Mobil, Speedway◊
	W: Citgo, Marathon, Phillips 66
Food	E: Diner's Choice, Subway
Other	E: Auto Services, Towing, IN Univ NW
255	61st St Ave, Merrillville, Hobart (Addt'l Serv W to Broadway)
TStop	E: Speedway #7575
Gas	E: Marathon, Thornton's
Food	E: FastFood/Speedway, Arby's, Cracker Barrel, McDonald's, Taco Bell, Wendy's
Lodg	E: Lee's Inn♥

EXIT	INDIANA
Med	E: + St Mary Medical Center
Other	E: Midwest Auto & Tire Repair
253B	US 30W, 81st Ave, Merrillville
Gas	W: Gas City, Shell, Speedway◊, Meijer◊
Food	W: Arby's, Applebee's, Blimpie, Celebration Station, Denny's, Dunkin Donuts, Hooter's, KFC, Lone Star Steakhouse, Outback Steakhouse, Pizza Hut, Rio Bravo, Shoney's, Smoky Bones BBQ, Steak n Shake, Subway, Starbucks, Texas Corral, Wendy's, White Castle
Lodg	W: Courtyard, Fairfield Inn, Hampton Inn, Holiday Inn Express, Radisson, Red Roof Inn♥, Residence Inn
Med	W: + Prompt Medical Care, + Methodist Hospital of Merrillville
Other	W: Auto Dealers, ATMs, Banks, Dollar Tree Discount Tire, Firestone, FedEx Kinko's, Grocery, Kmart, Meijer's, Staples, UPS Store, Walgreen's
253A	US 30E, 81st Ave, Merrillville
FStop	E: US 30 & IN 51: Gas City #51
Gas	E: BP◊, Speedway, Costco
Food	E: Bob Evans, Burger King, Casa Gallardo, Chili's, Chuck E Cheese, Don Pablo, Great China Buffet, McDonald's, Olive Garden, Red Lobster, Ruby Tuesday, Starbucks, Subway, TGI Friday, FastFood/Gas City
Lodg	E: Best Western, Comfort Suites,Economy Inn, Extended Stay America♥

EXIT	INDIANA
Lodg	E: Days Inn, Knights Inn, La Quinta Inn♥, Motel 6♥, Super 8
Other	E: Best Buy, Circuit City, Costco, Home Depot, Lowe's, Office Max, Office Depot, PetCo♥, Petland♥, Sam's Club, Target, Wal-Mart sc, Southlake Mall, Cinemas, LP/Gas City, Rose RV Sales
247	US 231, IN 8, Crown Point, Hebron
Gas	W: Mobil
Med	W: + Hospital
(241)	Lake Co Weigh Station (Both dir)
240	IN 2, 181st Ave, Lowell, Hebron
TStop	E: Flying J Travel Plaza #5119 (Scales) (DAND), Pilot Travel Center #448 (Scales)
Gas	E: Speedway
	W: Marathon, Mobil, Speedway
Food	E: Rest/FastFood/Flying J TP, McDonald's/Pilot TC
	W: Burger King/Mobil
Lodg	E: Super 8
TWash	W: Anchor TW, Truck Wash
TServ	E: Flying J TP/Tires
Med	E: + Hebron Medical Center
Other	E: Laundry/WiFi/RVDump/LP/FJ TP, Laundry/WiFi/Pilot TC
	W: IN State Hwy Patrol Post
(231)	Jasper Co Rest Area (Both dir) (RR, Phones, Picnic, Vend, Info)
230	IN 10, Roselawn, Demotte
TStop	E: Steel City Plaza 65

◊ = Regular Gas Stations with Diesel   ▲ = RV Friendly Locations   ♥ = Pet Friendly Locations
RED PRINT SHOWS LARGE VEHICLE PARKING/ACCESS ON SITE OR NEARBY   BROWN PRINT SHOWS CAMPGROUNDS/RV PARKS

Page 255

INTERSTATE 65 N/S

EXIT	INDIANA
Gas	E: Family Express, Holiday Shell, Marathon, Risner's Gas Stop, Zylstra's Service & Tire W: Marathon
Food	E: Rest/Steel City Plaza, China Wok, Holley's Rest, Subway W: Renfrow's, The Rodeo
Med	W: + Lake Holiday Medical Clinic
Other	E: Laundry/LP/Steel City Plaza W: IGA, CarQuest, Dollar General, CVS, Dr Bob's RV Repair, Lake Holiday Country Campground▲, Pioneer Family Campground▲
215	**IN 114, Morocco, Rensselaer**
FStop	E: Family Express #35
TStop	W: Grandma's Travel Center (Scales), Trail Tree Truck Stop/Shell
Gas	E: Kerr McGee, Phillips 66, Marathon
Food	E: Arby's, DQ, KFC, McDonald's W: Rest/FastFood/Grandma's TC, Rest/FastFood/Trail Tree TS, Burger King
Lodg	E: Holiday Inn Express, Knights Inn W: Economy Inn
TServ	E: Anderson's Service W: Coopers Tire & Service
Med	E: + Jasper Co. Hospital
Other	E: Auto Repair W: Laundry/Grandma's TC, Laundry/Trail Tree TS
205	**US 231, Remington, Rensselaer**
TStop	E: Crazy D's (Scales)
Gas	E: Phillips 66, Shell
Food	E: Rest/Crazy D's
Lodg	E: Carson Inn
Med	E: + Hospital
Other	E: Laundry/CB/Crazy D's
201	**US 24, US 231, Remington, Wolcott**
FStop	W: Family Express◆, Remington Mobil
TStop	W: Petro Stopping Center #75 (Scales), Pilot Travel Center #34 (Scales)
Food	W: IronSkillet/Petro SC, Subway/Pilot TC, Casey's C/O Pizza, KFC, McDonald's
Lodg	W: Days Inn, Super 8
TServ	W: Petro SC/Tires
Other	W: Laundry/Petro SC, WiFi/Pilot TC, Caboose Lake Campground▲
(196)	**White Co Rest Area (Both dir)** **(RR, Phones, Picnic, Vend)**
193	**US 231, Wolcott, Chalmers**
Gas	E: BP
Food	E: DQ, Wayfara Rest/BP
188	**IN 18, Brookston, Fowler**
178	**IN 43, W Lafayette, Delphi**
Gas	E: Phillips 66, Shell
Food	E: McDonald's, Subway
Lodg	E: Days Inn
Other	E: IN State Hwy Patrol Post W: to Purdue Univ
175	**IN 25, Lafayette, Delphi**
Gas	E: Marathon
Med	E: + Hospital
Other	E: Aretz Airport✈ W: Lafayette Travel Trailer Sales/RVDump, to Purdue Univ
172	**IN 26, Lafayette, Rossville**
Gas	E: Meijer W: BP◆, Shell, Speedway◆
Food	E: Cracker Barrel, El Rodeo, Starbucks, Steak n Shake, Waffle House, White Castle

EXIT	INDIANA
Food	W: Arby's, Bob Evans, Burger King, DQ, Country Café, Chili's, Damon's, Don Pablo, Denny's, IHOP, McDonald's, Olive Garden
Lodg	E: Baymont Inn, Budget Inn, Comfort Suites, Days Inn, Hawthorne Suites, Holiday Inn Express, Lee's Inn, La Quinta Inn♥, Microtel, Motel 6 W: Best Western, Dollar Inn, Fairfield Inn, Hampton Inn, Knight's Inn, Radisson, Red Roof Inn, Signature Inn, Super 8
TServ	W: Double D Truck Repair
Med	W: + Hospital
Other	E: Visitor Center W: CVS, CarWash, Dollar Tree, Lowe's, NAPA, Sam's Club, Target, Wal-Mart sc, Amtrak, Tippecanoe Mall, Auto Dealers, Auto Services, Museums, to Purdue Univ
168	**IN 38, Lafayette, Dayton**
FStop	E: Super Pantry Fuel Center #18/Mobil
Food	E: FastFood/Super Pantry FC
158	**IN 28, Attica, Frankfort**
FStop	E: to Good Oil/AmocoBP
Gas	E: Marathon
Med	E: + Hospital
Other	E: Harley Davidson
(149)	**Boone Co Rest Area (SB)** **(RR, Phones, Picnic, Vend)**
(148)	**Boone Co Rest Area (NB)** **(RR, Phones, Picnic, Vend)**
146	**IN 47, Thorntown, Sheridan**
141	**US 52N, Lafayette Ave, Lebanon, Thorntown**
Med	E: + Hospital
140	**IN 32, Lebanon, Crawfordsville**
TStop	W: McClure Oil #52
Gas	E: BP W: Shell
Food	E: Denny's, McDonald's, White Castle W: FastFood/McClure, Arby's, Burger King, KFC, Ponderosa, Subway, Taco Bell
Lodg	E: Comfort Inn, Econo Lodge W: Dollar Inn, Lee's Inn, Super 8
Med	E: + Hospital
Other	E: AutoZone, Goodyear, Laundromat
139	**IN 39, Lebanon St, Lebanon, Lizton**
FStop	E: Gas America
TStop	W: Flying J Travel Plaza #5069 (Scales)
Gas	W: Phillips 66
Food	E: Hardee's, Starbucks, Wendy's W: Rest/FastFood/FJ TP
Lodg	W: Quality Inn, Ramada Inn
TServ	W: to Jerry's Truck & Trailer Repair
Other	W: Laundry/WiFi/RVDump/LP/FJ TP, David's Chocolates
138	**CR 100, N 156th St, Indianapolis Ave, Lebanon**
Gas	E: Citgo◆
Other	E: Auto Repairs W: Boone Co Airport✈
133	**IN 267, N 126th Rd, Lebanon, Brownsburg, Whitestown**
130	**IN 334, to Zionsville, Whitestown**
TStop	E: Crystal Flash #34 W: Travel Center of America #173/BP (Scales)
Gas	E: Shell
Food	E: FastFood/Crystal Flash, Burger King, Starbucks W: CountryPride/Popeye's/TA TC

Page 256

◆ = Regular Gas Stations with Diesel   ▲ = RV Friendly Locations   ♥ = Pet Friendly Locations
RED PRINT SHOWS LARGE VEHICLE PARKING/ACCESS ON SITE OR NEARBY   BROWN PRINT SHOWS CAMPGROUNDS/RV PARKS

EXIT		INDIANA
	TServ	W: TA TC/Tires
	Other	W: Laundry/WiFi/TA TC
(129)		Jct I-865E, US 52E, to Ft Wayne, Columbus, OH (SB)
124		Delong Rd, 71st St, Indianapolis
	Gas	E: BP
	Food	E: Hardee's, Max & Erma's Rest, Quiznos, Wendy's
	Lodg	E: Courtyard, Residence Inn, Wingate Inn
	Other	W: Eagle Creek Park
(123)		Jct I-465S, Peoria, St Louis (SB), Jct I-465N, Ft Wayne, Columbus Peoria (NB)
	Other	S: to Eagle Creek Airpark ✈, Indianapolis Motor Speedway
121		Lafayette Rd, Indianapolis
	Gas	E: Gas America, Speedway◊ W: BP, Shell, Meijer
	Food	W: Applebee's, Papa John's, Subway, Sizzling Wok
	Lodg	E: Lee's Inn W: Travelodge
	Med	W: + Westview Hospital
	Other	W: ATMs, Banks, Auto Services, Auto Dealers, Borders, Batteries Plus, Cinema, Discount Tire, FedEx Kinko's, Grocery, PepBoys, Lafayette Square, Tires
119		38th St, N Kessler Blvd, Lafayette Rd, Fairgrounds (Acc to #121 Serv)
	Gas	W: Meijer's◊, Speedway
	Food	W: Arby's, KFC, Lone Star Steakhouse, New China Buffet, Red Lobster
	Lodg	W: Days Inn, Express Inn
	Med	W: + Westview Hospital
	Other	E: to IN State Fairgrounds W: ATMs, Auto Services, Cinema, Family Indoor Golf, Kmart, Mall, Office Depot, Staples, to Indianapolis Motor Speedway
117		ML King Jr Dr, St Michigan Rd (SB)
116		29th St, 30th St (NB)
115		21st St, Fall Creek Pkwy
	Gas	E: Shell
	Med	E: + Methodist Hospital of IN
114		W 11th St, ML King Jr St, to West St, to Downtown
	Med	W: + University Hospital, + IN Univ Medical Center, + Riley Hospital for Children, + Wishard Memorial Hospital
113		Illinois St, 11th St, Pennsylvania St, US 31, Meridian St, to Downtown
(112A)		Jct I-70E, to Columbus
111		Market St, Michigan St, Ohio St, Fletcher Ave, US 40, US 31
	Other	W: to Indianapolis Zoo, RCA Dome, Victory Field, Convention Center
(110B)		Jct I-70W, to St. Louis
110A		Morris St, Prospect St
109		Raymond St
	Gas	W: Speedway
	Med	E: + Hospital
	Other	E: CVS
107		Keystone Ave, Indianapolis
	Gas	E: Mystik Food Mart W: Citgo, Phillips 66◊, Speedway
	Food	W: Burger King, Denny's, McDonald's, Subway, Wendy's

EXIT		INDIANA
	Lodg	E: Days Inn W: Holiday Inn Express
	Med	E: + St Francis Hospital
	Other	E: Auto Repairs W: ATMs, Banks, Grocery, Univ of Indianapolis
(106)		Jct I-465, I-74, Columbus, St Louis (All Serv E to 1st Ex, #52)
103		Southport Rd, Indianapolis
	Gas	E: AmocoBP, Circle K, Meijer◊, Shell W: Circle K, Speedway◊, Super 7
	Food	E: Arby's, ChickFilA, McDonald's, Long Horn Steakhouse, O'Charley's, Pizza Hut, Starbucks, Sonic, Taco Bell W: Bob Evans, Burger King, Carrabba's, Cracker Barrel, KFC, McDonald's, Texas Roadhouse, Waffle Steak, Wendy's
	Lodg	W: Best Western, Country Inn, Courtyard, Fairfield Inn, Hampton Inn, Jameson Inn, Quality Inn, Signature Inn, Super 8
	Med	W: + St Francis Hospital
	Other	E: Firestone, Home Depot, Menard's, Staples, Target, Indianapolis Southside Harley Davidson W: ATMs, Auto & Tire Services, IN State Fairgrounds Campground▲, to Indy Lakes Campground▲
101		County Line Rd, Indianapolis
	Food	W: BW3, Blimpie, Subway
	Med	W: + St Francis Hospital
	Other	W: ATMs, Banks, Gander Mountain Store, Kmart, Kroger, Greenwood Park Mall, Office Max, Office Depot, Wal-Mart sc, Aaron RV Rental, Greenwood Muni Airport ✈
99		950N, Greenwood Rd, Greenwood
	TStop	E: Road Ranger #226/Citgo (Scales)
	Gas	W: 7-11, Amoco, Circle K, Shell
	Food	E: Subway/Road Ranger W: Arby's, Bob Evans, Denny's, KFC, McDonald's, Subway, Starbucks, Taco Bell, Waffle & Steak, White Castle
	Lodg	W: Comfort Inn, InTown Suites, Lee's Inn, Red Carpet Inn
	TServ	W: Road Ranger/Tires
	Med	W: + Hospital
	Other	E: Laundry/RVDump/Road Ranger W: Pharmacy, Sam's Club, Stout's RV Sales/Camping World, All Good Mobile RV Services
95		CR 500N, Whiteland Rd, Whiteland
	TStop	E: MT Travel Plaza #2774/Marathon Flying J Travel Plaza #5087/Shell (Scales) W: Pilot Travel Center #397 (Scales), Pilot Travel Center #37 (Scales)
	Food	E: Rest/FastFood/MT TP, Rest/FastFood/FJ TP W: Arby's/TJCinn/Pilot TC#397, McDonald's/Pilot TC #37
	TWash	W: Pilot TC #37
	TServ	E: MT Travel Plaza/Tires W: Pilot TC #37/Tires, Scott Truck Systems Whiteland Tire & Fleet
	Other	E: Laundry/Marathon TP, Laundry/WiFi RVDump/LP/FJ TP W: Laundry/WiFi/Pilot TC #397, Laundry/WiFi/Pilot TC #37, Auto Repairs, to Lee's RV Center
90		IN 44, King St, Franklin, Shelbyville
	Gas	W: BP, Circle K, Shell

◊ = Regular Gas Stations with Diesel   ▲ = RV Friendly Locations   ♥ = Pet Friendly Locations

RED PRINT SHOWS LARGE VEHICLE PARKING/ACCESS ON SITE OR NEARBY   BROWN PRINT SHOWS CAMPGROUNDS/RV PARKS

Page 257

INTERSTATE 65 N/S

EXIT		INDIANA
	Food	W: Burger King, McDonald's, Waffle & Steak, Subway, Rest/Days Inn
	Lodg	W: Carlton Lodge, Howard Johnson, Quality Inn, Super 7, Super 8
	Med	W: + Johnson Memorial Hospital
	Other	W: to Auto Services, ATMs, Banks, Museum, Franklin College
80		IN 252, Edinburgh, Flat Rock
	Gas	W: BP, Marathon, Shell◊
	Other	E: Adventure RV Rentals
		W: Camp Atterbury Mil Res, Johnson Co Park & Rec Area▲, Mobile RV Repair Service, Edmundson RV Sales
76A		US 31S, Taylorsville, Columbus
	FStop	E: Big Foot 65/Shell
	Gas	E: Speedway◊
	Food	E: Burger King, KFC, Waffle & Steak
	Lodg	E: Comfort Inn
	Other	E: to Columbus Bakalar Muni Airport✈
76B		US 31N, Edinburgh
	Gas	W: BP, Citgo◊, Thornton's◊
	Food	W: Arby's, Cracker Barrel, Hardee's, Max & Erma's, McDonald's, Ruby Tuesday, Subway
	Lodg	W: Best Western, Hampton Inn, Holiday Inn Express, Red Roof Inn♥
	TServ	W: White River Truck Repair, Greene's Truck Auto Service, Goodyear, Truck Wash
	Other	W: Premium Outlets at Edinburgh, Mann's Harley Davidson, Blue's Canoe Livery, Driftwood Camp RV Park▲, Camp Atterbury Military Res, Johnson Co Park & Rec Area▲, Mark's Mobile RV Repair Service, Edmundson RV Sales
(73)		Taylorsville Rest Area (SB)
		(RR, Phones, Picnic, Vend)
(71)		Taylorsville Rest Area (NB)
		(RR, Phones, Picnic, Vend)
68		IN 46, Columbus, to Nashville, Bloomington
	Gas	E: Big Foot, BP◊, Shell, Speedway◊
		W: Circle K, Marathon, Swifty
	Food	E: Burger King, McDonald's, Waffle House, Subway, Rest/Holiday Inn
		W: Bob Evans, Denny's, Subway, Taco Bell, Wendy's
	Lodg	E: Holiday Inn, Ramada Inn, Sleep Inn, Super 8
		W: Days Inn, Knights Inn, Travelodge
	Med	E: + Hospital
	Other	E: ATMs, Cinema, Museums
		W: ATMs, Banks, CVS, Dollar General, Grocery, U-Haul, to Westward Ho Campground▲, The Last Resort Campground & RV Park▲, Brown Co State Park▲
64		IN 58, to Ogilville, Walesboro
	Gas	E: Marathon◊
	Other	W: Woods n Waters Campground▲
55		IN 11, Seymour, to Jonesville
	Gas	E: BP
(51)		Weigh Station (Both dir)
50B		US 50W, Seymour, N Vernon
	Gas	W: BP, Shell, Speedway◊, Sunoco◊
	Food	W: Arby's, Bob Evans, Burger King, Cracker Barrel, Chili's, Denny's, Long John Silver, Max & Erma's, Ponderosa, Ryan's Grill, Santa Fe Mexican, Subway, Wendy's

Personal Notes

EXIT		INDIANA
	Lodg	W: Hampton Inn, Holiday Inn Express, Knights Inn, Lee's Inn
	TServ	W: Cummins, Mack Trucks, Towing
	Other	W: AutoZone, Auto Dealers, Auto Repairs, ATMs, Banks, Grocery, Home Depot, Staples, Tires, Wal-Mart sc
50A		US 50E, Seymour, Brownstown
	FStop	E: Seymour Marathon
	TStop	E: Travel Center of America #65/BP (Scales)
	Gas	E: Swifty
	Food	E: CountryPride/TA TC, Tokyo Japanese Sushi Bar, McDonald's, Waffle House
	Lodg	E: Allstate Inn, Days Inn, Econo Lodge, Motel 6♥, Super 8
	TWash	E: TA TC
	TServ	E: TA TC/Tires
	Other	E: Laundry/WiFi/TA TC, Tanger Outlets, Visitor Center, Jiffy Lube, Great Escape
41		IN 250, Crothersville, Uniontown
	FStop	W: Uniontown Fuel Stop
	Food	W: Uniontown Rest/Uniontown FS
	TServ	W: Uniontown Fuel Stop/Tires
36		US 31, Crothersville, Austin
	Gas	E: Shell
		W: Marathon
34B		IN 256W, W Main St, Austin (SB)
34A		IN 256, W Main St, Austin (SB)
34		IN 256, W Main St, Austin (NB)
	TStop	W: AmBest/Fuel Mart #783
	Gas	E: Big Foot
	Food	E: Main St Family Rest, Tammy's Dairy Bar
		W: A&W
	Other	E: Auto Services

EXIT		INDIANA
29B		IN 56W, W McClain Ave, Scottsburg
29A		IN 56E, Scottsburg, Salem (SB)
29		IN 56, Scottsburg, to Salem (NB)
	Gas	E: BP, MotoMart, Speedway◊
		W: Citgo◊, Shell, Murphy
	Food	E: Burger King, Cracker Barrel, KFC, Ponderosa, Subway, Rest/Mariann Motel
		W: Arby's, McDonald's, Waffle & Steak, Pizza Hut, Wendy's
	Lodg	E: Holiday Inn Express, Marianne Motel, Travel Inn
		W: Best Western, Hampton Inn, Super 8
	Med	E: + Hospital
	Other	E: ATMs, Banks, Auto Services, Auto Dealers, CVS
		W: Big O Tire, Wal-Mart sc, Yogi Bear Jellystone Raintree Campground▲
(22)		IN Welcome Center (NB) Henryville Rest Area (SB) (RR, Phones, Picnic, Vend)
19		IN 160, Henryville, Charlestown
	Gas	E: Bigfoot, Shell
16		Memphis-Blue Lick Rd, Crone Rd, Memphis Rd, Memphis, Sellersburg
	TStop	E: Love's Travel Stop #359 (Scales)
		W: Pilot Travel Center #152 (Scales)
	Gas	E: BP
	Food	E: Subway/McDonald's/Love's TS
		W: Arby's/TJCinn/Pilot TC
	Tires	W: Pilot TC
	TWash	W: Pilot TC
	Other	E: WiFi/Love's TS, Truck Sales, American Flea Market
		W: Laundry/WiFi/Pilot TC, Customers First RV Center
9		IN 311, Sellersburg, Speed
	Gas	E: BP, Chevron, Shell
		W: Dairy Mart
	Food	E: Arby's, Cracker Barrel, Waffle & Steak
		W: Burger King, McDonald's, Taco Bell
	Lodg	E: Ramada Inn
		W: Comfort Inn
	Other	E: ATMs, Auto Services, Banks, Laundry, Grocery, Pharmacy, IN State Hwy Patrol
7		IN 60, Sellersburg, Clarksville
	Gas	E: BP◊
		W: Citgo
	Food	W: KFC
	Lodg	W: Days Inn
	Other	E: Clark Co Airport✈
(6B)		Jct I-265W, to I-64W, to New Albany, St Louis
	Other	E: to IN Univ SE
(6A)		Jct I-265E, IN 62, to Jeffersonville
	Other	E: to US Military Res/IN Arsenal
5		Veterans Parkway, to US 31
	Gas	W: Dairy Mart
	Food	W: Asian Buffet, ChickFilA, Cheddar's Café, Famous Dave's, Ruben's Mex Rest, Ruby Tuesday, Subway, Taco Bell
	Other	W: Best Buy, Lowe's, PetSmart♥, Sam's Club, Target, Wal-Mart sc, RV Center, Wheatley Truck Services
4		US 31N, IN 131S, McCullough Pike, Clarksville, Jeffersonville
	Gas	E: Thornton's
		W: SavAStep, Speedway
	Food	E: Subworks/Thornton's, White Castle

Page 258

◊ = Regular Gas Stations with Diesel ▲ = RV Friendly Locations ♥ = Pet Friendly Locations
RED PRINT SHOWS LARGE VEHICLE PARKING/ACCESS ON SITE OR NEARBY   BROWN PRINT SHOWS CAMPGROUNDS/RV PARKS

Interstate 65 N/S

IN / KY

EXIT		
	Food	W: Arby's, Applebee's, Bob Evans, Burger King, Captain D's, Denny's, Don Pablo, Golden Corral, Hooters, Pizza Hut, Logan's, Outback Steakhouse, Rally's, Red Lobster, Steak n Shake, Starbucks, Taco Bell, Wendy's
	Lodg	E: Crest Motel W: Best Western ♥, Dollar Inn, Hampton Inn
	TServ	E: KY Truck Sales, Freightliner, S & R Truck Tires, Dan's Truck & Diesel Repair W: Goodyear
	Other	W: ATMs, Bank, AutoZone, Auto Dealers, Circuit City, Firestone, Home Depot, Kroger Office Depot, Target, Bass Pro Shop, River Fair Family Fun Park, Green Tree Mall, US Post Office Cracker Barrel
2		Eastern Blvd, to IN 131, Clarksville, Jeffersonville
	Gas	E: Thornton's W: Circle K, SavAStep, Swifty
	Food	W: Denny's, Hungry Pelican, Ryan's
	Lodg	E: Best Inn, Comfort Suites, Motel 6 ♥, Super 8 W: Days Inn ♥
	Med	E: + Hospital W: + Immediate Care Walk-In Clinic
	Other	W: ATMs, Auto Services, Banks, Tires
1A		W New Albany (NB)
1		US 31S, 4th St, IN 62, Stansifer Ave, W 14th St, Jeffersonville, Clarksville
	Food	W: Derby Dinner Playhouse
	Lodg	W: Holiday Inn
	Other	W: Cummins Cumberland, Louisville Metro KOA▲, Tom Stinnett RV Center/Camping World
0		US 31, Market St, 4th St, Court Ave, Jeffersonville
	Gas	E: BP, Thornton's, Tobacco Rd
	Food	E: Hardee's, McDonald's, Waffle & Steak W: Buckhead Mtn Grill, Kingfish, Rocky's Italian Grill
	Lodg	E: Alben Motel, River Falls Motel W: Fairfield Inn, Ramada Inn
	Med	E: + Hospital
	Other	E: ATMs, Banks, Auto Services, Museums, Tires

(EASTERN TIME ZONE)

⬆ INDIANA
⬇ KENTUCKY

NOTE: MM 138: Indiana State Line

(137)		Jct I-71N, Jct I-64W, I-64E (NB)
136C		Jefferson St, Brook St (SB) Muhammad Ali Blvd (NB)
	Gas	W: Chevron, Shell
	Food	W: McDonald's, Papa John's
	Lodg	W: Comfort Inn, Courtyard, Days Inn, Hampton Inn, Hyatt, Marriott
	Other	E: Walgreen's W: Louisville Galleria, Museums, Tires
136B		E Gray St, S Brook St, Chestnut St Broadway St (NB)
	Gas	W: Speedway, Thornton's
	Lodg	W: Hilton, Holiday Inn
	Med	E: + Jewish Hospital, + Norton Hospital, + Univ of Louisville Hospital, + Kosair Childrens Hospital

KENTUCKY

EXIT		
136A		College St, Jacob St, Brook St (NB)
	Lodg	W: Holiday Inn
	Other	E: Auto Services
135		St Catherine St, Kentucky St
	Gas	E: Big Foot, Circle K, Shell
	Lodg	W: Alexander House, Dupont Mansion, Victorian Secret B&B
134B		Woodbine Ave
	Gas	W: BP
	Lodg	W: Days Inn
134A		S Preston St, Woodbine Ave
133		Arthur St, Eastern Pkwy (SB)
133B		E Warnock St, Crittenden Dr (NB)
	Food	E: Denny's, Papa John's, Subway W: Cracker Barrel
133A		Alt US 60, Eastern Pkwy (NB)
	Gas	W: BP◊, Shell
	Food	E: Denny's, Papa John's, Subway W: McDonald's
	Other	W: Univ of Louisville, to Churchill Downs
132		Crittenden Dr, Louisville (SB)
	FStop	W: Crittendon Drive BP
	Food	E: Denny's W: Burger King, Cracker Barrel
	Lodg	E: Ramada Inn
	TServ	E: Huber Tire
	Other	E: Winn Dixie W: KY Fair & Expo Center
(131BA)		Jct I-264, Watterson Expy, Freedom Way, Phillips Lane
	Lodg	E: La Quinta Inn ♥, Red Roof, Super 8 W: Airport Inn, Comfort Inn, Courtyard, Executive Inn, Hampton Inn
	Other	W: KY Fair & Expo Center, Louisville Int'l Airport✈, Auto Rentals
130		KY 61, Preston Hwy, Grade Ln
	Gas	E: BP, Dairy Mart, Speedway, Thornton's
	Food	E: Bob Evans, Burger King, Domino's, KFC, McDonald's, Ponderosa, Subway, Taco Bell, Waffle House, Wendy's
	Lodg	E: Red Roof Inn ♥, Super 8
	Other	E: Auto Services, Auto Dealers, Big O Tire, Dollar General, O'Reilly Auto, Radio Shack, Staples, Tires +, Winn Dixie, U-Haul, Right Stop RV Center W: Louisville Int'l Airport✈, Warbirds Museum, Rental Cars
128		KY 1631, Fern Valley Rd
	Gas	E: BP, Big Foot, Chevron, Five Star, Thornton's
	Food	E: Arby's, Golden Wall Chinese, Hardee's, McDonald's, Outback Steakhouse, White Castle, Shoney's, Subway, Waffle House, Subworks/Thornton's
	Lodg	E: Comfort Suites, Holiday Inn, InTown Suites, Jameson Inn W: Holiday Inn
	Other	E: Auto Services, ATMs, Sam's Club, Walgreen's, Wrecker Service W: Ford Assembly Plant, Louisville Int'l Airport✈
127		KY 1065, Outer Loop
	Gas	W: Chevron, Marathon
	Food	E: Texas Roadhouse W: McDonald's
	Other	E: to Jefferson Mall, Kroger, Winn Dixie W: Louisville Motor Speedway, Louisville RV Center
(125)		Jct I-265E, KY 841 (SB)

◊ = Regular Gas Stations with Diesel ▲ = RV Friendly Locations ♥ = Pet Friendly Locations

RED PRINT SHOWS LARGE VEHICLE PARKING/ACCESS ON SITE OR NEARBY BROWN PRINT SHOWS CAMPGROUNDS/RV PARKS

EXIT	KENTUCKY
125B	Jct KY 841W
(125A)	Jct I-265E, KY 841E
121	KY 1526, Brooks Rd, Louisville, Brooks, Shepherdsville
TStop	W: Pilot Travel Center #356 (Scales)
Gas	E: BP, Chevron
	W: BP, Shell
Food	E: Arby's, Burger King, Cracker Barrel
	W: Subway/TacoBell/Pilot TC, Waffle House
Lodg	E: Fairfield Inn, Hearthstone Inn♥, Holiday Inn Express
	W: Comfort Inn, Econo Lodge, Hampton Inn, Quality Inn
Other	E: Scott's Auto & Truck Repair, Tinker's Toy Interstate RV
	W: WiFi/Pilot TC, Sunrise RV & Trailer Sales, Off Road Adventures
117	KY 44, Mt Washington Rd, 4th St, Shepherdsville
FStop	W: Five Star Food Mart
Gas	E: BP, 44 Shell
	W: Chevron◊, Speedway◊
Food	E: Denny's, Hardee's, Rest/BW
	W: Arby's, Burger King, Fazoli's, KFC, Long John Silver, McDonald's, Papa John's, Sonic, Subway, Taco Bell, Waffle House, Wendy's, White Castle
Lodg	E: Best Western, Days Inn♥
	W: Country Inn, Motel 6♥, Super 8
Other	E: Louisville South KOA▲
	W: Big O Tires, Dollar General, Family Dollar, Kroger, NAPA, Pharmacy
116	KY 480, to KY 61, Cedar Grove Rd, Shepherdsville
TStop	E: Love's Travel Stop #238 (Scales)
Gas	E: Shell◊
Food	E: Chester's/Subway/Love's TS
Other	E: Laundry/RVDump/WiFi/Love's TS
	W: Grandma's RV Park▲, Leisure Life RV Supercenter
(114)	Rest Area (Both dir)
	(RR, Phone, Picnic, Vend)
112	KY 245, to Clermont, Bardstown
Gas	E: Shell◊
105	KY 61, Preston Hwy, Lebanon Jct
FStop	W: 105 Quik Stop
TStop	W: Pilot Travel Center #399 (Scales)
Gas	W: Citgo
Food	W: Subway/McDonald's/Pilot TC, Back in Time Rest, Daddio's
TServ	W: Pilot TC/Tires
Other	W: Laundry/WiFi/Pilot TC, Fort Knox Military Res
102	KY 313, Joe Prather Highway, KY 434, Radcliff, Vine Grove
94	US 62, KY 61, Elizabethtown
Gas	E: Five Star Food Mart, Plaza 94 Food Mart, Marathon◊
	W: BP◊, Chevron◊, Speedway◊, Swifty
Food	E: Denny's, Golden Corral, KFC/Taco Bell, Waffle House, White Castle
	W: Arby's, Burger King, Black Angus Grill, Cracker Barrel, KFC, McDonald's, Pizza Hut, Ryan's Grill, Shoney's, Subway, Wendy's

EXIT	KENTUCKY
Lodg	E: Days Inn♥, Quality Inn♥, Super 8
	W: Best Western, Country Hearth Inn, Fairfield Inn, Hampton Inn, Howard Johnson, La Quinta Inn♥, Motel 6♥, Ramada Inn
Med	W: + Hardin Memorial Hospital
Other	E: Carwash/Plaza 94, Elizabethtown Crossroads Campground▲
	W: Advance Auto, CVS, Dollar Tree, Dollar General, Kroger, Skagg'sRV Country, KY State Hwy Patrol Post
93	to Bardstown, Bluegrass Pkwy
91	US 31W, KY 61, Western KY Pkwy, Elizabethtown, Paducah
Gas	E: Chevron, Shell
	W: Chevron
Food	E: Back Yard Burgers, Long John Silver, McDonald's, Omelette House
	W: Jerry's Rest
Lodg	E: Bluegrass Inn, Budget Holiday Motel, Common Wealth Lodge, Heritage Inn
	W: KY Cardinal Inn, E'Town Motel, Roadside Inn
Med	W: + Hardin Memorial Hospital
Other	E: Auto Repairs, Orville's Diesel Service, Diesel Doc's, Budget, Ryder, U-Haul
	W: Towing, Wayne's Tire Center
(90)	Weigh Station (Both dir)
86	KY 222, to US 31W, Glendale
TStop	E: Pilot Travel Center #48 (Scales)
	W: Petro Stopping Center #30/Mobil (Scales)
Food	E: McDonald's/Pilot TC
	W: IronSkillet/FastFood/Petro SC, Depot Rest, Whistle Stop Rest
Lodg	W: Glendale Economy Inn
TWash	W: Blue Beacon/Petro SC
TServ	W: Petro SC/Tires, Quality Diesel Service
Other	E: Laundry/WiFi/Pilot TC, Glendale Campground▲
	W: Laundry/BarbSh/WiFi/Petro SC
(82)	Rest Area (SB)
	(RR, Phones, Picnic, Vend)
(81)	Rest Area (NB)
	(RR, Phones, Picnic, Vend)
81	KY 84, Western Ave, Sonora
FStop	E: Sammy's Market (DAD / DAND)
TStop	E: Pilot Travel Center #392 (Scales)
Gas	E: Fast Way Food Mart
	W: Shell
Food	E: Rest/Sammy's, Subway/Pilot TC
TWash	E: Blue Beacon/Pilot TC
Other	E: Laundry/WiFi/RVDump/Pilot TC, to Abe Lincoln Birthplace
76	KY 224, Upton-Talley Rd, Upton
Gas	E: Upton Mini Mart, Marathon
	W: Hawke's Service Station
NOTE:	MM 75: Eastern / Central Time Zone
71	KY 728, Bonnieville
65	US 31W, Dixie Hwy, Munfordville
Gas	E: BP, Chevron, Shell
	W: BP, Citgo
Food	E: DQ, McDonald's, Pizza Hut
	W: Country Fixins, Sonic, Subway
Lodg	E: Super 8
(61)	Rest Area (Both dir)
	(RR, Phones, Picnic, Vend)

EXIT	KENTUCKY
58	KY 218, to KY 335, Horse Cave
TStop	E: Love's Travel Stop # (Scales)
	W: Drivers Travel Mart #400/Chevron
Gas	W: BP, Marathon◊
Food	E: Chesters/McDonald's/Love's TS
	W: FastFood/Drivers TM, Aunt B's Rest/Budget Host Inn
Lodg	W: Budget Host Inn, Hampton Inn
Med	E: + Caverna Memorial Hospital
Other	E: WiFi/Love's TS, KY Down Under
	W: Auto & Truck Repairs/Marathon, Horse Cave KOA/RVDump▲
(55)	Rest Area (SB)
	(RR, Phones, Picnic, Vend)
53	KY 70, KY 90, US 31W, Cave City
Gas	E: BP◊, Chevron, Marathon◊
	W: Shell, SuperAmerica
Food	E: Burger King, Cracker Barrel, DQ, Jerry's Rest, KFC, Long John Silver, McDonald's, Pizza Hut, Subway, Sahara Steakhouse, Taco Bell, Wendy's
	W: Bel-Air, Joe's Diner, KFC, Subway
Lodg	E: Best Western♥, Comfort Inn, Comfort Inn & Suites, Days Inn, Executive Inn, Knights Inn♥, Quality Inn, Super 8, WigWam Village
	W: Park View Motel, Oakes Motel & Campground
Other	E: Auto Services, ATM, Auto Dealer, Bank, Guntown Mtn, Museum, SavALot, Road & Field Diesel Service, Crystal Onyx Cave & Campground▲
	W: KY Action Park, Hillbilly Hound Fun Park, Mammoth Cave Jellystone Park Camp Resort▲, Singin Hills Campground & RV Park▲, Mammoth Cave Nat'l Park▲
48	KY 255, to US 31W, Park City
FStop	E: Park City Shell
Food	E: FastFood/Park City Shell
Lodg	E: Parkland Motel
Other	W: Diamond Caverns, Diamond Caverns Campground▲, Mammoth Cave Nat'l Park▲, Singin Hills Campground & RV Park▲
43	Cumberland Pkwy (TOLL), Glasgow, Somerset
Other	E: to Barren River Lake State Resort Park▲, COE/Barren River Lake/The Narrows▲/Tailwater Below Dam▲
(40)	Rest Area (NB)
	(RR, Phones, Picnic, Vend)
38	KY 101, S Main St, Smiths Grove
TStop	W: Smith Grove BP Travel Center (Scales)
Gas	W: Chevron, Shell
Food	W: Rest/FastFood/Smith Grove TC, McDonald's, Wendy's
Lodg	W: Bryce Motel
TServ	W: Smith Grove TC/Tires/TWash
Other	E: COE/Barren River Lake/Tailwater Below Dam▲
	W: BarbSh/Smith Grove TC
36	US 68, KY 80, Oakland (NB exit, SB reaccess only)
(30)	Rest Area (SB)
	(RR, Phones, Picnic, Vend)
28	KY 446, to US 31W, US 68, Bowling Green, Plum Springs
Gas	W: BP, Shell

Page 260

◊ = Regular Gas Stations with Diesel   ▲ = RV Friendly Locations   ♥ = Pet Friendly Locations
RED PRINT SHOWS LARGE VEHICLE PARKING/ACCESS ON SITE OR NEARBY   BROWN PRINT SHOWS CAMPGROUNDS/RV PARKS

KENTUCKY

EXIT		
	Food	W: Hardee's, Jerry's Rest, Smokey Pig BBQ, Wendy's
	Lodg	W: Best Western, Country Hearth Inn, Continental Inn, Value Lodge
	Other	W: ATMs, Bank, Auto Services, Corvette Museum, Tires, Towing, Beech Bend Family Campground▲, Camping World/RVDump, Bowling Green RV Sales
22		US 231, Scottsville Rd, Bowling Green
	Gas	E: Citgo◆, Shell W: BP, Chevron◆, Exxon, RaceWay, Shell◆, Speedway
	Food	E: Cracker Barrel, Culver's, DQ, Denny's, Domino's, Godfather's, Hardee's, Mancino Grinders & Pizza, Ryan's Grill, Sonic, Waffle House, Zaxby's W: Applebee's, Arby's, Bob Evans, Burger King, CiCi's, Captain D's, ChickFilA, KFC, Krystal, Longhorn Steakhouse, Lone Star Steakhouse, McDonald's, Moe's SW Grill, O'Charley's, Olive Garden, Pizza Hut, Santa Fe Steaks, Shoney's, Shogun of Japan, Smokey Bones BBQ, Starbucks, Taco Bell, TGI Friday, Waffle House, Wendy's, White Castle
	Lodg	E: Best Western, Comfort Inn, Days Inn, Econo Lodge, Fairfield Inn, Home-Towne Suites, Microtel, Quality Inn, Ramada Inn W: Baymont Inn, Courtyard, Drury Inn♥, Hampton Inn, Motel 6♥, Red Roof Inn♥
	TServ	W: Whayne Power Systems
	Med	W: + Hospital
	Other	E: ATMs, Banks, Harley Davidson BG, US Post Office W: Advance Auto, Auto Dealers, CVS, ATMs, AMC Cinema, Banks, Best Buy, Dollar General, FedEx Kinko's, Goodyear, Grocery, Home Depot, Kmart, Kroger, Office Depot, PetCo♥, Staples, Sam's Club, Trailer World, Target, UPS Store, U-Haul, Wal-Mart sc, Greenwood Mall, Bowling Green Warm Co Airport✈, Bowling Green KOA▲
20		Green River Pkwy (TOLL), Bowling Green, Owensboro
	Other	W: to W Ky Univ, KY State Police
6		KY 100, Franklin
	TStop	E: AmBest/Bluegrass Travel Plaza (Scales) W: Pilot Travel Center #46(Scales), Pilot Travel Center #438 (Scales)
	Gas	E: BP
	Food	E: FastFood/Bluegrass TP W: Subway/Pilot TC #46, Wendy's/Pilot TC #438
	Lodg	W: Days Inn, Super 8
	TWash	W: Pilot TW
	TServ	W: Speedco, Bluegrass Truck & Tire Repair, Petro Lube Service & Tires
	Med	W: + Hospital
	Other	W: WiFi/Pilot TC #46, Laundry/WiFi/Pilot TC #438, Bluegrass Music RV Park▲
(4)		Weigh Station (NB)
2		US 31W, Nashville Rd, Franklin
	TStop	E: Flying J Travel Plaza #5053/Conoco (Scales), Keystop Truck Stop/Marathon
	Gas	W: BP
	Food	E: FastFood/Keystop TS, Rest/FastFood/FJ TP

KY / TN

EXIT		
	Food	W: Cracker Barrel, Jim's BBQ, Shoney's, McDonald's, Waffle House, Subway/BP
	Lodg	W: Best Value, Comfort Inn, Econo Lodge, Hampton Inn, Super 8
	Med	W: + Hospital
	Other	W: Laundry/BarbSh/WiFi/RVDump/LP/FJ TP
(1)		KY Welcome Center (NB) (RR, Phones, Picnic, Vend)

(CENTRAL TIME ZONE)

⇧ **KENTUCKY**
⇩ **TENNESSEE**
(CENTRAL TIME ZONE)

	NOTE:	MM 121.5: Kentucky State Line
(121)		TN Welcome Center (SB) (RR, Phones, Picnic, Vend)
(119)		Weigh Station (Both dir)
117		TN 52, Orlinda, Portland (Addtl Serv 4-5mi E in Portland)
	Gas	E: Shell◆ W: AmocoBP◆
	Lodg	W: Budget Host Inn
	Med	E: + Hospital
112		TN 25, Cross Plains, Gallatin, Springfield
	TStop	W: Mapco Express #1028
	Gas	E: BP W: Exxon, Shell◆
	Food	W: FastFood/Mapco Exp, Diddles Café, Trues BBQ

TENNESSEE

EXIT		
	TServ	W: Mapco Exp
108		TN 76, Springfield Rd, White House, Springfield
	Gas	E: Keystop, Mapco Express W: AmocoBP
	Food	E: Cracker Barrel, DQ, Hardee's, KFC, McDonald's, Taco Bell, Waffle House W: Rest/Days Inn, Red Lantern
	Lodg	E: Holiday Inn Express W: Days Inn
	TServ	W: American Coach & Truck
	Med	W: + Hospital
104		TN 257, Bethel Rd, Goodlettsville, Ridgetop
	TStop	E: Ridgetop Auto Truck Center/66
	Gas	W: Shell
	Food	E: Rest/Ridgetop ATC
	Lodg	E: Ridgetop Motel
	TWash	E: Ridgetop ATC
	TServ	E: Ridgetop ATC/Tires
	Other	E: Laundry/Ridgetop ATC W: Owl's Roost Campground▲
98		US 31W, TN 41, TN 11, Goodlettsville, Millersville, Springfield
	Gas	E: Citgo◆, RaceWay, Shell W: AmocoBP◆
	Food	E: Subway, Waffle House
	Lodg	E: Economy Inn
	Other	E: Auto Services, Grocery, Blackwoods Truck Repair, Nashville Country RV Park▲ W: Auto Services, Nashville I-65N Campground▲
97		TN 174, Long Hollow Pike, Goodlettsville, Gallatin
	FStop	W: Dailey's Shell
	Gas	E: BP◆, Exxon, Mapco Express
	Food	E: Arby's, Captain D's, Cracker Barrel, China Express, KFC, McDonald's, Shoney's, Subway, Waffle House, Wendy's W: Bob Evans, Hardee's, Jack in the Box, Krystal, Little Caesar, Sonic
	Lodg	E: Comfort Inn, Econo Lodge, Hampton Inn, Holiday Inn Express♥, Red Roof Inn♥, Shoney's Inn W: Baymont Inn, Motel 6♥
	Other	E: ATMs, Banks, Kmart, Kroger W: ATMs, Banks, Walgreen's, to Nashville I-65N Campground▲
96		Rivergate Pkwy, Gallatin Pike, Two Mile Pkwy, Goodlettsville
	Gas	E: BP, Citgo◆, Phillips 66, Shell W: Chevron
	Food	E: Arby's, Burger King, Cracker Barrel, Checkers, ChickFilA, Chili's, Chuck E Cheese, El Chico, Hooters, IHOP, Krystal, Lone Star Steakhouse, Mrs Winners, McDonald's, Olive Garden, Outback Steakhouse, Pizza Hut, Red Lobster, Starbucks, Subway, Steak n Shake, Waffle House, Wendy's
	Lodg	E: Best Value Inn, Comfort Suites, Days Inn, Crestwood Suites, Quality Inn, Rodeway Inn, Red Roof Inn♥, Super 8
	Other	E: ATMs, Banks, Auto Services, CVS, Auto Dealers, Best Buy, Cinemas, Circuit City, Firestone, Circuit City, FedEx Kinko's, Goodyear, Boswell Harley Davidson, Home Depot, NTB, Office Depot, PepBoys, PetSmart♥, Sam's Club, Target, Walgreen's, Wal-Mart, UPS Store, Rivergate Mall

◆ = Regular Gas Stations with Diesel ▲ = RV Friendly Locations ♥ = Pet Friendly Locations
RED PRINT SHOWS LARGE VEHICLE PARKING/ACCESS ON SITE OR NEARBY BROWN PRINT SHOWS CAMPGROUNDS/RV PARKS

Interstate 65 N/S

EXIT	TENNESSEE
95	TN 386, Vietnam Vets Blvd, Hendersonville, Gallatin (NB)
92	TN 45, Old Hickory Blvd, Madison (Serv E&W to US 31E or US 31W)
Med	E: + Nashville Memorial Hospital
90	US 31W, US 41, TN 155E, Briley Pky, Dickerson Pike, Nashville (NB)
Other	E: to Opryland
90B	TN 155E, Briley Pkwy (SB)
Other	E: to Opryland, Nashville KOA▲
90A	TN 155E, Briley Pkwy (SB)
90A	US 41, US 31W, Dickerson Pk (NB)
Gas	E: Citgo, Mapco Expr◊, Phillips 66, Shell◊
Food	E: Arby's, Burger King, Captain D's, China King Buffet, Domino's, KFC, McDonald's, Mrs Winner's, Pizza Hut, Shoney's, Subway, Taco Bell, Waffle House, Wendy's
Lodg	E: Days Inn, Econo Lodge, Sleep Inn, Super 8
Med	W: + Skyline Medical Center
Other	E: Advance Auto, ATMs, Banks, CVS, Kroger, Walgreen's, Camping World
(88B)	Jct I-24W, to Clarksville
(88A)	Jct I-24E, to Nashville
87AB	US 431, TN 65, Trinity Ln, Nashville
TStop	E: Pilot Travel Center #292 (Scales)
Gas	E: Circle K, Phillips 66
	W: BP, Chevron, Exxon
Food	E: Subway/Pilot TC, Krystal, White Castle
	W: Burger King, Captain D's, Denny's, Jack in the Box, McDonald's, Ponderosa, , Subway, Taco Bell, Waffle House
Lodg	E: Cumberland Inn, Delux Inn
	W: Best Value Inn♥, Comfort Inn♥, Days Inn♥, Quality Inn, Regency Inn, Super 8, Travelodge
Med	W: + FHC Nashville
Other	E: Auto Services, Grocery, Tires, Holiday Mobile Village▲
	W: Auto Services, to Jackson Truck & Trailer Repair, American Baptist College
(86)	Jct I-24E, to I-40E, to Memphis
85	US 41A, TN 12, 8th Ave, Metrocenter Blvd
Gas	W: Exxon
Food	W: Arby's, Krystal, McDonald's, Pizza Hut, Subway, Taco Bell
Lodg	W: La Quinta Inn♥
NOTE:	I-65 below runs with I-40 for 2 exits. Exit #'s follow I-40.
(84AB/208)	Jct I-65N, I-40W, to Memphis; Jct I-65N, I-40E, to Knoxville
209	US 70, TN 24, US 70S, US 431, Church St, Charlotte Ave
Gas	S: BP, Exxon
Food	S: Burger King, Shoney's, White Castle
Lodg	N: Holiday Inn
	S: Comfort Inn, Shoney's Inn
Med	S: + Baptist Hospital, + Columbia Centennial Medical Center
Other	N: Auto Services, Fleet Repair, Thrifty RAC, Museums, State Capitol
	S: Auto & Tire Services, Budget RAC, Museums

EXIT	TENNESSEE
209A	US 70S, US 431, Broadway
Med	S: + Metro Nashville Gen'l Hospital
209B	US 70S, US 431 Demonbreun St
Med	S: + Vanderbilt University Hospital, + Columbia Centennial Medical Center, + Baptist Hospital
Other	N: Auto Services, ATMs, Banks, Courts, Enterprise RAC, Firestone, Goodyear, Country Music Hall of Fame & Museum, Gaylord Ent Center, Nashville Visitor Info, TN State Capitol, Ryman Auditorium, TN Convention Center, Nashville Muni Auditorium
	S: Auto Services, ATMs, Banks, Budget RAC, Music Row, Museums
(210/211)	Jct I-24E, I-40E, I-65S, Nashville, Chattanooga (SB) (WB, Left exit)
(82/83)	Jct I-65N, I-40W, to Memphis
(82B)	Jct I-40E, Knoxville (NB, Left Exit)
NOTE:	I-65 above runs with I-40 for 2 exits. Exit #'s follow I-40.
81	Wedgewood Ave, Nashville
Gas	W: BP, Exxon, Scot Market
Food	W: Burger King, McDonald's, Mrs Winners
Med	W: + Vanderbilt Univ Hospital, + Veterans Medical Center
Other	E: to TN State Fairgrounds, Trevecca Nazarene Univ, Greer Stadium, Science Museum, Nashville Speedway USA
	W: CVS, Dollar General, Dollar Tree, Kroger, Walgreen's, U-Haul, to Museums, Belmont Univ, Vanderbilt Univ
(80)	Jct I-440, W-Memphis, E-Knoxville (NB, Left Exit W) (SB, Left exit E)
79	Armory Dr, Powell Ave, Nashville
Gas	E: Scot Market, Shell
Food	E: Applebee's, Baja Border Café, Rice Bowl, Subway, Taco Bell, Wendy's
Other	E: ATMs, Banks, Auto Services, CarMax, Cinema, Goodyear, PetSmart♥, UPS Store, One Hundred Oaks Mall, TN National Guard, Police Dept
	W: to CVS, Kroger, Walgreen's
78	TN 255, Harding Place (Addtl Serv E to US 31/Nolensville Pk)
Gas	E: Mapco Express, Marathon, Shell
Food	E: Cracker Barrel, Santa Fe Cattle Co, Waffle House
Lodg	E: La Quinta Inn♥, Red Roof Inn♥
Med	E: to + Southern Hills Medical Center
Other	E: to Museum, Nashville Zoo, Harding Mall
74AB	TN 254, Old Hickory Blvd, Church St, Brentwood, Nashville
Gas	W: BP, Exxon, Mapco Exp, Shell, Texaco
Food	E: Captain D's, Shoney's, Waffle House
	W: Mrs Winners, O'Charley's, Papa John's Pizza, Ruby Tuesday, Starbucks, Wendy's
Lodg	E: AmeriSuites♥, Comfort Inn, Extended Stay America♥, Holiday Inn, Hilton, Steeple Chase Inn, Studio Plus
	W: Courtyard, Hampton Inn, Mainstay Suite
Med	E: + Hospital
Other	E: Target, Tires
	W: ATMs, Auto Services, Auto Dealers, Banks, CVS, Cinema, FedEx Kinko's, Harris Teeter, Kroger, Office Depot, Tires, Walgreen's, US Post Office

◊ = Regular Gas Stations with Diesel   ▲ = RV Friendly Locations   ♥ = Pet Friendly Locations
RED PRINT SHOWS LARGE VEHICLE PARKING/ACCESS ON SITE OR NEARBY   BROWN PRINT SHOWS CAMPGROUNDS/RV PARKS

EXIT		TENNESSEE
71		TN 253, Concord Rd, Brentwood
69		TN 441, Moores Lane, Franklin
	Gas	E: Mapco Express◆, Shell
		W: BP, Marathon, Shell◆
	Food	E: Applebee's, Cozymel's, Joe's Crab Shack, Japanese Rest, Krystal, Outback Steakhouse, Shogun, Sonic, Starbucks, Tony Roma's
		W: McDonald's, Red Lobster, Romano's Macaroni Grill, Ruby Tuesdays, Subway, TCBY, Taco Bell
	Lodg	E: AmeriSuites, Homestead Studio, Red Roof Inn♥, Wingate Inn
		W: Sleep Inn
	Other	E: Albertson's, ATMs, Banks, Home Depot, PetSmart♥, Publix
		W: Best Buy, Barnes & Noble, Carmike Cinemas, Costco, CVS, Goodyear, Harley Davidson Cool Springs, Target, Walgreen's, Waldenbooks, Galleria Mall
68AB		Cool Springs Blvd, Franklin
	Gas	W: Exxon, Shell
	Food	W: Carrabba's, Chili's, Jack in the Box, McDonald's, Ruby Tuesday, Starbucks, TGI Friday, Wendy's
	Lodg	E: Embassy Suites, Marriott
		W: Country Inn, Hampton Inn
	Other	W: ATMs, Banks, Borders, Auto Services, Cinema, FedEx Kinko's, Home Depot, Kroger, Lowe's, Office Depot, Staples, Sam's Club, Walgreen, Wal-Mart sc, UPS Store
65		TN 96, Murfreesboro Rd, Franklin, Murfreesboro
	Gas	E: Exxon, Mapco Expr, Shell◆
		W: BP◆, Mapco Expr◆, Shell◆
	Food	E: Cracker Barrel, Steak n Shake, Sonic
		W: Arby's, Hardee's, Famous Chinese Buffet, KFC, McDonald's, Shoney's, Taco Bell, Waffle House, Wendy's
	Lodg	E: Best Value Inn, Comfort Inn, Days Inn♥, Holiday Inn Express, La Quinta Inn♥, Ramada
		W: Best Western, Super 8
	Med	E: + Williamson Medical Center
	Other	E: Auto Dealer, Auto Services, Food Lion, Walgreen's
		W: Animal Hospital♥, Home Depot, Kmart, Kroger, Publix, UPS Store, Walgreen's
61		TN 248, Peytonsville Rd, Goose Creek ByPass, Franklin, Spring Hill
	FStop	E: Kwik Sak #610
	TStop	E: Travel Center of America # 157/BP (Scales)
	Gas	W: Mapco Express, Scot Market
	Food	E: ForkintheRoad/TA TC
		W: Rest/Goose Creek Inn
	Lodg	W: Goose Creek Inn
	TServ	E: TA TC/Tires
		W: RLS Sales & Service
	Other	E: Laundry/WiFi/TA TC
59		TN 840, E to Almaville
53		TN 396, Saturn Pkwy, Spring Hill (Gas, Food Lodg 3-4 mi W to US 31N)
(49)		Parking Area (NB)
46		US 412, TN 99, Bear Creek Pike, Columbia, Chapel Hill
	FStop	W: Stan's Rest & Country Store/Texaco, RP Williams Co

EXIT		TENNESSEE
	TStop	E: Love's Travel Stop #346 (Scales)
	Gas	E: Chevron
		W: BP
	Food	E: FastFood/Love's TS
		W: Stan's Rest, Burger King, Cracker Barrel, Waffle House, Wendy's
	Lodg	W: Best Value Inn, Comfort Inn, Holiday Inn, Relax Inn
	TWash	W: RP Williams Co
	Med	W: + Maury Regional Hospital, + Nashville Memorial Hospital
	Other	E: WiFi/Love's TS, Campers RV Family Campground▲, Travelers RV Park & Campground▲, to appr 13mi: Henry Horton State Park▲
37		TN 50, New Lewisburg Hwy, Columbia, Lewisburg
	Med	E: + Hospital
32		TN 373, Mooresville Hwy, Lewisburg, Columbia (Addt'l Serv 6-7 mi E in Lewisburg)
	Gas	E: Williams Interstate Market/Exxon◆
27		TN 129, Lynnville Rd, Cornersville (Addt'l Serv 4 mi E in Cornersville)
	Other	E: Texas T Campground▲
(25)		Parking Area (SB)
(24)		Parking Area (NB)
22		US 31A, TN 11, Cornersville
	TStop	E: The Tennessean Truck Stop/AmocoBP (Scales)
		W: Pilot Travel Center #406 (Scales)
	Gas	W: Serve & Go/Shell◆
	Food	E: Rest/FastFood/Tennessean TS, McDonald's, Subway

EXIT		TN / AL
	Food	W: Deli/Pilot TC
	Lodg	E: Econo Lodge
	TServ	E: Tennessean TS/Tires
	Other	E: Laundry/WiFi/Tennessean TS
		W: WiFi/Pilot TC
14		US 64, TN 15, Pulaski, Fayetteville
	Gas	E: BP◆, Shell◆
	Other	E: TN Valley RV Park▲
6		TN 273, Bryson Rd, Ardmore, Elkton
	TStop	E: Shady Lawn Truck Stop/66 (Scales)
	Food	E: Rest/Shady Lawn TS
	Lodg	E: Best Value Inn
	TServ	E: Shady Lawn TS/Tires
	Other	E: Laundry/Shady Lawn TS
(2)		TN Welcome Center (NB) (RR, Phones, Picnic, Vend, Info)
1		US 31, TN 7, Main St, Pleasant Hill Rd, Ardmore, Lawrenceburg
	Gas	E: Chevron◆, Exxon◆, Shell
	Food	E: Church's, DQ, Hardee's, Subway

(CENTRAL TIME ZONE)

⬆ TENNESSEE
⬇ ALABAMA

(CENTRAL TIME ZONE)

NOTE: MM 366: Tennessee State Line

365		AL 53, Elkmont, to Ardmore, TN
	Gas	E: Country Store
	Lodg	E: Budget Inn
(364)		AL Welcome Center (SB) (RR, Phones, Picnic, Vend, Info, RVDump)
361		Sandlin Rd, Thach Rd, Elkmont
	TStop	W: Pam's Truck Stop/Citgo
	Food	W: Rest/Pam's TS, Sonny G's BBQ
	TServ	W: Pam's TS/Tires
	Other	W: Morris Garage & Towing Service
354		US 31S, AL 3, AL 99, Athens (Acc to #351 Serv via US 31S)
	Gas	W: Chevron
	Food	W: Subway
	Med	W: + Hospital
	Other	W: ATMs, Banks, Auto Services & Repairs, Northgate RV Travel Park▲
351		US 72, AL 2, Athens, Huntsville
	Gas	E: BP, Exxon, RaceWay, Shell
		W: Chevron, J Mart, Texaco◆, Murphy
	Food	E: BBQ, Burger King, Cracker Barrel, McDonald's, Subway/Shell, Waffle House, Wendy's
		W: Applebee's, Arby's, Backyard Burger, Catfish Cabin, Hardee's, Krystal, Papa John's, McDonald's, Ruby Tuesday, Sonic, Shoney's, Starbucks, Subway
	Lodg	E: Comfort Inn, Country Hearth Inn, Hampton Inn
		W: Best Western♥, Bomar Inn, Days Inn♥, Super 8♥, Sleep Inn♥
	Med	W: + Hospital
	Other	E: to Bolton Service Center, Cagle's Motorhome Parts & Service, Limestone Flea Market
		W: ATMs, Auto Dealers, Auto Services, Banks, Big 10 Tire, Dollar General, Goodyear, Kroger, Lowe's, O'Reilly Auto, Staples, Wal-Mart sc, Athens State College, to Joe Wheeler State Park▲

◆ = Regular Gas Stations with Diesel   ▲ = RV Friendly Locations   ♥ = Pet Friendly Locations

RED PRINT SHOWS LARGE VEHICLE PARKING/ACCESS ON SITE OR NEARBY   BROWN PRINT SHOWS CAMPGROUNDS/RV PARKS

Interstate 65 N/S — Alabama

EXIT	ALABAMA
(340)	Jct I-565, AL 20, Alt US 72, Huntsville, Decatur (NB)
Other	E: Huntsville Madison Co Int'l Airport✈, Redstone Arsenal
340A	Alt US 72, AL 20, Huntsville-Decatur Hwy, to Decatur (SB)
(340B)	Jct I-565, Alt US 72, Huntsville (SB) (Services 7-10 mi W in Decatur)
Other	E: Huntsville-Madison Co Int'l Airport✈, NASA Space & Rocket Center
334	AL 67, Point Mallard Pky, Decatur, Priceville, Somerville
FStop	W: J-Mart #567/BP
TStop	W: Pilot Travel Center #441 (Scales)
Gas	E: AmocoBP, RaceTrac◊ W: Chevron, Texaco
Food	W: Subway/Wendy's/Pilot TC, Hardee's, BBQ Smokehouse, Krystal, McDonald's, Waffle House
Lodg	E: Days Inn, Super 8, Southeastern Motel W: Comfort Inn
Med	W: + North AL Reg'l Hospital
Other	E: Foodland W: Laundry/WiFi/RVDump/Pilot TC, Vet♥, American Truck Repair, Hood Tractor & RV Center, Andy's RV Services, Wheeler Nat'l Wildlife Refuge
328	AL 36, Main St, Hartselle
Gas	W: AmocoBP, Chevron◊, Cowboys◊, Shell
Food	W: Huddle House, Homestyle BBQ
Med	W: + Hospital, + Hartselle Medical Center
Other	W: ATMs, Banks, Auto Services, Kroger, Tires, Vet♥, N on US 31: Wal-Mart sc
325	Thompson Rd, Hartselle
322	Hwy 55E, Pike Rd, Falkville, Eva
TStop	E: J&J Oil/322 Truck Stop/BP
Gas	W: Chevron
Food	E: Rest/322 TS
318	US 31, AL 3, to Lacon, Vinemont
Gas	E: BP
Food	E: Stuckey's/DQ/BP
310	AL 157, Finis St John III Dr, Cullman, West Point, Fairview
FStop	E: Dowd Hwy 157 Shell
Gas	E: AmocoBP, Chevron, Conoco◊ W: BP◊, Exxon◊
Food	E: Arby's, Backyard Burger, Burger King, Cracker Barrel, Denny's, McDonald's, Ruby Tuesday, Taco Bell, Waffle House
Lodg	E: Best Western♥, Comfort Inn, Hampton Inn, Holiday Inn Express, Sleep Inn W: Super 8
Med	E: + Hospital
Other	E: Cullman Towing, Auto Dealers, Auto Services, ATMs W: Cullman Campground▲
308	US 278, AL 74, Cullman, Double Springs, Ave Maria Grotto
FStop	E: US 31: Westside Shell
Gas	W: Chevron
Food	E: FastFood/Westside Shell, Rest/Days Inn, BBQ, Omelette Shop W: Rest/Howard Johnson
Lodg	E: Days Inn♥ W: Howard Johnson
Med	E: + Hospital
Other	E: Carmike Town Square 3, C&M Truck & Trailer Repair W: Cullman Flea Market

EXIT	ALABAMA
304	AL 69N, CR 437, Cullman, Good Hope
TStop	E: Jack's Truck Stop/Shell (Scales), Good Hope Exxon
Gas	E: BP, Chevron, Texaco◊ W: JetPep◊
Food	E: Rest/Jack's TS, Hardee's, Waffle House
Lodg	E: Econo Lodge♥
TWash	E: Jack's TS, Good Hope Exxon
TServ	E: Jack's TS/Tires, Good Hope Exxon/Tires, Mark's Truck Service, C&M Truck & Trailer Repair, Truck Express Lube
Med	E: + Hospital
Other	E: Laundry/Good Hope Exxon, ATMs, Auto Repairs, Laundromat, Wal-Mart, Good Hope Campground▲ W: Speegles Marina & Campground▲, to Smith Lake
(302)	Cullman Co Rest Area (Both dir) (RR, Phones, Picnic, Vend, RVDump)
299	AL 69S, CR 490, Cullman, Dodge City, Jasper
FStop	W: 69 Chevron
TStop	W: Dodge City Travel Center (Scales)
Gas	E: Citgo W: BP◊, Shell◊, Texaco◊
Food	W: Dodge City BBQ, Jack's Rest, Roadhouse BBQ & Grill, Subway
TServ	E: Ray's Truck & Trailer Repair
Other	E: Millican RV W: Laundry/WiFi/Dodge City TC, Dollar General, CarQuest, Bremen Lake View Resort▲
291	AL 91, Hanceville, Arkadelphia, Colony
TStop	W: Parker's I-65 Truck Stop/Shell
Gas	E: Conoco
Food	E: AJ's BBQ W: Rest/Parker's TS
Lodg	W: Motel I-65/Parker's TS
Tires	W: Parker's TS
TWash	W: Parker's TS
Other	E: Country View RV Park▲ W: WiFi/Parkers TS
289	CR 5, Hayden, Empire
Gas	E: BP
Food	W: Stuckey's/BP
Other	W: Rickwood Caverns State Park▲
287	US 31N, AL 3, Bee Line Hwy, Hayden, Garden City, Blount Springs
Gas	E: Conoco◊, Citgo◊
284	US 31S, AL 160E, Warrior, Hayden
Gas	E: Phillips 66, Shell◊
Food	E: Bryant's Seafood, Perry's Catfish
Other	W: Rickwood Caverns State Park▲, Scenic Drive
282	CR 140, Warrior Jasper Rd, Cane Creek Rd, Warrior, Robbins
Gas	E: Chevron, Exxon, County Line Fuelz & Spirits◊
Food	E: Hardee's, McDonald's/Exxon, Pizza Hut, Taco Bell
Other	E: ATMs, Banks, Auto Services, Tires
281	Dana Rd, Warrior (Access to #282 Services)
280	to US 31, AL 3, Warrior, Kimberly
Other	E: Auto Dealer, Enterprise RAC
275	to US 31, AL 3, Mary Buckelew Pky, Gardendale, Morris, Kimberly
Other	E: Auto Service, Diesel Service

◊ = Regular Gas Stations with Diesel   ▲ = RV Friendly Locations   ♥ = Pet Friendly Locations

RED PRINT SHOWS LARGE VEHICLE PARKING/ACCESS ON SITE OR NEARBY   BROWN PRINT SHOWS CAMPGROUNDS/RV PARKS

Interstate 65 N/S — Alabama

EXIT		
272	**Mt Olive Rd, CR 112, Gardendale**	
Gas	E: BP, Chevron	
	W: Chevron, Shell◊	
271	**Fieldstown Rd, CR 118, Gardendale**	
Gas	E: Chevron, Circle K, RaceWay, Shell, Murphy	
	W: Shell	
Food	E: Arby's, ChickFilA, DQ, Fire Mountain Grill, Habanero's Mex Grill, Little Caesar's, McDonald's, Milo's Hamburgers, Pizza Hut, Ruby Tuesday, Shoney's, Subway, Taco Bell, Waffle House	
	W: Cracker Barrel	
Lodg	E: Microtel	
	W: Best Western	
Other	E: ATMs, Auto Services, AutoZone, Banks, Dollar Tree, Firestone, Wal-Mart sc, Walgreen's, Civic Center	
267	**Walker Chapel Rd, Fultondale**	
Gas	E: Chevron◊, Shell◊	
	W: BP, Chevron◊	
Food	E: Burger King, Domino's, Hardee's, O'Charley's, Outback Steakhouse, Waffle House	
Lodg	E: Comfort Suites, Fairfield Inn, Holiday Inn Express, Hampton Inn	
Other	E: ATMs, Banks, CVS, Dollar General, Grocery, Lowe's, RiteAid, Target, Police Dept	
266	**US 31, Fultondale, Birmingham**	
Gas	E: Chevron, Raceway	
Lodg	E: Days Inn♥, Super 8	
(265)	**Proposed Exit - US 78, Corridor X Freeway**	
264	**41st Ave, Birmingham**	
TStop	E: Flying J Travel Plaza #5091 (Scales)	
Food	E: CountryMarket/FastFood/FJ TP	
Other	E: Laundry/WiFi/RVDump/LP/FJ TP	
263	**33rd Ave (SB), 32nd Ave (NB)**	
Gas	E: Chevron◊, Shell	
	W: Exxon	
Food	E: Hardee's, Little Caesars	
Lodg	E: Apex Motel, Oak Mountain Lodge	
Other	W: Auto Repair, Colonial RV	
262B	**Finley Blvd, to US 78W, AL 4**	
TStop	E: South Star Fuel Center (Scales)	
	W: Food N Gas/Conoco (Scales)	
Gas	E: AmocoBP, Bama Gas◊	
	W: Chevron, Citgo	
Food	E: FastFood/South Star FC	
	W: FastFood/Food N Gas, Captain D's, McDonald's, Popeye's, Shoney's	
TServ	E: South Star FC	
Med	E: + to Carraway Methodist Medical Ctr	
262A	**16th St N, 18th St N (NB)**	
Other	E: to Civic Center	
(261A)	**Jct I-20/59, E to Gadsden (SB, Left exit)**	
(261B)	**Jct I-20/59, W to Tuscaloosa (NB, Left exit)**	
260	**US 11, 6th Ave N, Downtown (SB)**	
Gas	E: BP, Shell	
	W: Chevron	
Food	E: Church's, Hardee's, Mrs Winners	
Lodg	W: Adam's Inn	
Other	W: Auto Services, Diesel Services	
260B	**2nd Ave N, US 78, US 11 (NB)**	
259B	**4th Ave S, 11th St S (SB)**	
259A	**6th Ave S (SB, diff reacc)**	
Gas	E: BP	
Food	E: Waffle House	
Lodg	E: Best Western, Medical Center Inn	
TServ	E: Lynn Strickland Sales & Service	
Med	E: + Hospital	
259	**AL 149, 8th Ave S (NB, diff reacc)**	
258	**Green Springs Ave**	
Gas	E: BP, Chevron, Citgo	
Food	E: Irish Deli, Kebab & Curry	
256AB	**Oxmoor Rd, Homewood (SB)**	
256	**Oxmoor Rd, Homewood (NB)**	
Gas	E: Exxon◊, Mobil◊, Shell	
	W: BP, Chevron	
Food	E: Arby's, Burger King, KFC, Subway	
	W: McDonald's, Shoney's, Waffle House	
Lodge	E: Howard Johnson, Oxmoor Lodge Extended Stay	
	W: Alta Vista Hotel, Comfort Inn, Fairfield Inn, Holiday Inn, Microtel♥, Quality Inn, Ramada♥, Shoney's Inn, Super 8	
TServ	W: Southland International Trucks	
Med	E: + Homewood Medical Clinic	
Other	E: ATMs, Auto Services, Auto Zone, Banks, Big Lots, CVS, Dollar Tree, Firestone, Grocery, Goodyear, Office Depot	
	W: Auto Services, ATMs, Banks, Batteries Plus	
255	**Lakeshore Pkwy, Lakeshore Dr, Birmingham**	
Gas	E: BP, Circle K	
	W: Citgo, Chevron, Sam's Club	
Food	E: Sonic	
	W: Arby's, Captain D's, ChickFilA, Chili's, Dragon Chinese Rest, IHOP, Hooters, Landry's Seafood, Moe's SW Grill, Lone Star Steakhouse, McDonald's, O'Charley's, Taco Bell, Wendy's, BBQ	
Lodg	W: Best Western, Drury Inn, Hampton Inn, La Quinta Inn♥, Hilton Garden Inn, Residence Inn, Studio Plus, Sun Suites Extended Stay, Towneplace Suites	
Med	E: + Brookwood Medical Center	
Other	E: to Samford Univ, Brookwood Village Mal	
	W: ATMs, Banks, Cinemas, Dollar General, Dollar Tree, FedEx Kinko's, Lowe's, NTB, Office Max, Sam's Club, Wal-Mart sc, UPS Store	
254	**Alford Ave, CR 97, Birmingham**	
Gas	E: Chevron	
	W: BP, Citgo	
252	**US 31, AL 3, Montgomery Hwy, to Hoover, Vestavia Hills**	
Gas	E: BP, Chevron, Shell	
	W: BP, Chevron, Exxon, Shell	
Food	E: Arby's, Aladdin's, Back Yard Burgers, Captain D's, Chuck E Cheese, Hardee's, Ichiban Japanese, Piccadilly's, Pizza Hut, Ranch House Family Rest, Taco Bell, Waffle House	
	W: Burger King, Golden Corral, Krystal, McDonald's, Subway, Waffle House	
Lodg	E: Baymont Inn♥, Comfort Inn, Quality Inn, Premier Living Suites, Vestavia Motorlodge	
	W: Days Inn, Quality Inn	
Med	E: + Brookwood Medical Center	
Other	E: Animal Clinic♥, Auto Dealers, Auto Services, ATMs, Big 10 Tire, CVS, NAPA, Civic Center	
Other	W: Auto Dealers, ATMs, Auto Services, Advance Auto, Banks, Circuit City, Dollar Tree, Firestone, Goodyear, RiteAid, to Riverchase Galleria, Costco, Sam's Club
(250)	**Jct I-459, to US 280, Atlanta, Gadsden (All Serv at 1st Exit W, #13)**
247	**CR 17, Valleydale Rd, Birmingham, to Helena, Hoover**
Gas	E: Circle K, Spectrum
	W: Racetrac, Kangaroo Express
Food	E: Hardee's, Happy China, Popeye's, Tin Roof BBQ
	W: Arby's, IHOP, Papa Johns, Subway, Waffle House
Lodg	W: In Towne Suites, La Quinta Inn♥, Oak Mountain Lodge
Med	E: + Med Plex Care Center
Other	E: ATMs, Banks, Grocery
	W: Walgreen's
246	**AL 119, Cahaba Valley Rd, Pelham**
FStop	W: The Store #4/BP
TStop	W: Kangaroo Express #3682 (Scales)
Gas	W: RaceTrac, Shell, Murphy
Food	W: FastFood/Kangaroo Exp, Applebee's, Arby's, Cracker Barrel, ChickFilA, Golden Corral, Hooters, KFC, Krystal, McDonald's, O'Charley's, Pizza Hut, Ruby Tuesday, Shoney's, Sonic, Taco Bell, Texas Roadhouse, Waffle House, Wendy's
Lodg	W: Best Western♥, Hampton Inn, Holiday Inn Express, Quality Inn, Ramada Ltd, Sleep Inn, Travelodge♥
Med	W: + Hospital
Other	E: Vet♥, Country Sunshine RV Park▲, Oak Mountain State Park▲
	W: ATMs, Banks, Auto Services, CVS, Firestone, Grocery, Heart of Dixie Harley Davidson, AL Outdoors
242	**CR 52, Pelham, to Helena (Gas, Food, Serv W to US 31)**
FStop	E: Allen's Food Mart #74/Exxon
Gas	E: Chevron◊, Shell
Food	E: FastFood/Allen's FM
Lodg	W: Shelby Motel
Tires	E: Allen's FM
TServ	E: 242 Tire & Truck Service
Other	W: Staples, Birmingham South Campground▲
238	**US 31, AL 3, Alabaster**
Gas	E: Murphy◊
	W: Chevron◊, Shell◊, Cannon KwikStop
Food	E: ChickFilA, Habanero's, Moe's SW Grill, Ruby Tuesday, Subway, Taco Bell
	W: Waffle House
Lodg	W: Shelby Motor Lodge
Med	W: + Baptist Shelby Medical Center
Other	E: Best Buy, Lowe's, Target, Wal-Mart sc, Burton Campers
	W: Auto Services, CVS, Pharmacy, RiteAid, SavALot, Walgreen's
234	**CR 87, Calera**
Gas	E: BP
	W: Chevron◊, Shell◊
Food	E: Subway/BP
Other	E: Cahaba RV
	W: Shelby Co Airport✈, Univ of Montevallo, Cain's Auto & Truck Service
231	**US 31, AL 3, Montgomery Hwy, to CR 22, AL 70, Calera, Saginaw**
Gas	E: BP◊, Shell

◊ = Regular Gas Stations with Diesel   ▲ = RV Friendly Locations   ♥ = Pet Friendly Locations
RED PRINT SHOWS LARGE VEHICLE PARKING/ACCESS ON SITE OR NEARBY   BROWN PRINT SHOWS CAMPGROUNDS/RV PARKS

INTERSTATE 65 N/S

EXIT		ALABAMA
	Food	E: Captain D's, **Cracker Barrel**, Fish Market Rest, McDonald's, Mexican Rest, Subway
		W: **Donna's Café**
	Lodg	E: Holiday Inn Express
	Other	E: Dollar Tree, **Wal-Mart** sc, **Rolling Hills Campground**▲, **Burton Campers**
		W: **Camper Repair Center**
228		AL 25, Calera, Montevallo
	TStop	E: **Speed Track**/**Shell**
	Gas	E: **Citgo**◊
		W: **Chevron**◊
	Food	E: **FastFood**/**SpeedTrack**
		W: to US 31
	Lodg	E: **Best Value Inn** ♥, **Days Inn**
	Other	W: ATMs, Auto Repairs, Banks, Dollar General, Family Dollar, to **Brierfield Works State Park**
219		AL 42, Jemison, Thorsby
	TStop	E: **PTP**/**Speedways Exxon**
	Gas	E: **Chevron**◊
		W: **Shell**
	Food	E: **Subway**/**Speedways Exxon**
	TServ	E: **Speedways Exxon**/Tires
	Other	E: **Laundry**/**Speedways Exxon**, **Peach Queen Campground**▲
		W: **Chilton Camper Sales**/**Central AL RV Sales & Service**
(214)		**Clanton Rest Area** (Both dir) (RR, Phones, Picnic, Vend, RVDump)
212		AL 145, Lay Dam Rd, Clanton
	TStop	W: **Headco Truck Stop**
	Gas	E: **Chevron**◊
		W: **BP**
	Food	W: **FastFood**/**Headco**, Subway/BP
	Med	W: + Chilton Medical Center
	Other	E: Auto Repairs
		W: Gragg Field ✈
208		CR 28, Clanton, to Lake Mitchell
	FStop	W: **Allan's Food Mart #60**/**Exxon**
	TStop	E: **Love's Travel Stop #368** (Scales)
	Food	E: **Arby's**/**Love's TS**, Kountry Kitchen
		W: **Shoney's**
	Lodg	W: Guest House Inn
	Med	W: + Chilton Medical Center
	Other	E: **WiFi**/**Love's TS**
		W: **Dandy RV Sales**, Pecan Farm, Gragg Field ✈
205		US 31, AL 22, 7th St, Verbena, Clanton
	FStop	E: **Sunny Foods #6**/**Shell**
		W: **The Store #1**/**BP**
	Gas	E: I-65 Kountry Mart
		W: **Chevron**◊, Murphy
	Food	E: McDonald's, Waffle House
		W: Burger King, Captain D's, Pizza Hut **Hardee's**, KFC, Subway, Taco Bell
	Lodg	E: Best Western ♥, **Days Inn** ♥, Holiday Inn Express, Scottish Inn
		W: Key West Inn
	Other	W: Dollar General, Dollar Tree, **Wal-Mart** sc
200		CR 59, Verbena
	FStop	E: **Shop N Fill #24**/**BP**
	Gas	W: **Shell**◊
	Food	W: Stuckey's/DQ/Shell
186		US 31, AL 3, Prattville
	Gas	W: **BP**◊, Chevron, Citgo, Conoco◊
	Food	W: Country Diner, Vivian's Cafe
	Lodg	W: Pine Motel

Personal Notes

EXIT		ALABAMA
	Med	W: + Prattville Baptist Hospital
	Other	E: Confederate Memorial Park
181		AL 14, Fairview Ave, Millbrook, Prattville, Wetumpka, Coosada
	Gas	E: **Chevron**◊, **Entec**◊
		W: Exxon, Kangaroo, QV
	Food	W: **Cracker Barrel**, Ruby Tuesday, Subway, Waffle House, Wendy's
	Lodg	W: Best Western, Comfort Inn, Hometowne Suites, Super 8 ♥
	Med	W: + Prattville Baptist Hospital
179		US 82, AL 6, Cobbs Ford Rd, Prattville, Millbrook
	FStop	W: **Petro Kwik Sak**
	Gas	E: **Chevron**◊
		W: JetPep, RaceWay, Shell, USA◊
	Food	E: Asian Grill, Catfish House, Fantail
		W: **Hardee's**, Longhorn Steakhouse, Subway, O'Charley's, McDonald's, Steak n Shake, Shoney's, Subway, Waffle House
	Lodg	E: Country Inn, **Key West Inn** ♥
		W: Days Inn, Econo Lodge, Holiday Inn, Hampton Inn, Jameson Inn ♥, Marriott
	Other	E: Auto Services, **K&K Camping Center & Campground**/**LP**▲, **Clarks RV Center**
		W: ATMs, Auto Services, Banks, Food World, Kmart, Office Depot, Tires, **Wal-Mart** sc, UPS Store, Prattville Auto & **RV** Service, to Emerald Falls Adventure Park, to **Bakers RV Park**▲
176		AL 143N, Montgomery, to Millbrook, Coosada (NB, NO reaccess) (Access #179 Serv, N to Cobbs Ford Rd)

EXIT		ALABAMA
173		AL 152, North Blvd, to US 231 (diff reaccess, Both dir)
	Other	E: Montgomery Zoo
172AB		Bell St, Clay St, Herron St, Downtown Montgomery
	Gas	E: Amoco, KwikShop
		W: Chevron◊
	Lodg	E: Capitol Inn, Embassy Suites
	TServ	W: **Southland International Trucks**, **AL Diesel Service**
	Other	E: Auto Services, ATMs, Banks, Tires, Riverwalk Stadium, Troy Univ
		W: Auto Services, Maxwell AFB
(171)		Jct I-85N, to Atlanta, Day St (SB, Left exit)
	Food	W: Church's, Hardee's, McDonald's
	Other	E: to AL State Univ
		W: Auto Services, to Maxwell AFB
170		Fairview Ave, Montgomery
	Gas	E: Jack's Quick Mark, Citgo, Gas Depot
		W: Exxon
	Food	E: China King, Church's, Krystal, Pizza, McDonald's
		W: Hardee's, Seafood
	TServ	W: **Cummins Alabama**
	Other	E: Advance Auto, AutoZone, **CVS**, U-Haul, Tony's Tire Service, Huntington College
		W: Firestone, Family Dollar, Grocery
169		Edgemont Ave, Oak St (SB)
	Gas	E: BP, Citgo, Exxon
	Food	E: McDonald's, Krystal
168		US 80/82E, South Blvd, to US 31, US 231, US 331, Montgomery
	FStop	W: **Speedy #1**, to US 31: **Byrd's Pit Stop**/**66**
	TStop	E: **Travel Center of America #111**/**Citgo** (Scales)
	Gas	E: Kangaroo, Spectrum, Entec◊
		W: RaceTrac, Shell◊
	Food	E: **CountryPride**/**TA TC**, Arby's, Capt D's, Krystal, KFC, McDonald's, Shoney's, Taco Bell, Waffle House
		W: DQ, **Hardee's**, Quincy's, Wendy's, Subway/Shell
	Lodg	E: Best Inn, Best Western, Days Inn, Diplomat Inn, **Economy Inn** ♥, Quality Inn
		W: Airport Inn, **Econo Lodge**, Holiday Inn, Inn South, Peddler's Motor Inn, Ramada Ltd, **Super 8**
	TServ	E: **TA TC**/Tires
		W: **Curley's Tire & Auto**, **AL Spring & Brake**
	Med	E: + Hospital
	Other	E: Laundry/CB/WiFi/TA TC, Auto Services, Grocery, U-Haul, **The Woods RV Park & Campground**▲
		W: Auto & Tire Services, U-Haul
167		US 80W, Selma, to Meridian, MS
	Gas	W: Citgo, PaceCar
	Food	W: Subway, Church's Chicken
	Lodg	W: Executive Inn
	Other	W: Dannelly Field/Montgomery Reg'l Airport ✈, Winn Dixie, Hertz RAC, Auto Services
(165)		**Proposed Exit** - Montgomery Outer Loop
164		US 31, AL 3, Mobile Hwy, Hope Hull, Montgomery
	FStop	E: **Petro Plus**
	TStop	E: **Saveway Travel Center** (Scales)

◊ = Regular Gas Stations with Diesel   ▲ = RV Friendly Locations   ♥ = Pet Friendly Locations
RED PRINT SHOWS LARGE VEHICLE PARKING/ACCESS ON SITE OR NEARBY   BROWN PRINT SHOWS CAMPGROUNDS/RV PARKS

EXIT		ALABAMA
	Gas	E: AmocoBP
		W: BP, Chevron, Exxon, Liberty
	Food	E: FastFood/Saveway TC, Momma's House
		W: Burger King/BP, Subway/Liberty, Waffle House
	Lodg	E: Lakeside Hotel
		W: Best Western, Hampton Inn, Motel 6 ♥
	Other	E: Laundry/Saveway TC, Montgomery KOA▲, Auto & Tire Services
158		Tyson Rd, to US 31, Hope Hull, to Tyson, Hayneville
	TStop	W: Flying J Travel Plaza (Scales)
	Gas	E: BP
	Food	E: Stuckey's/DQ/BP
		W: CountryMarket/FastFood/FJ TP
	Other	W: Laundry/WiFi/RVDump/LP/FJ TP
151		AL 97, Hayneville, Letohatchee
	Gas	W: BP, PaceCar
142		AL 185, E Old Fort Rd, Fort Deposit, Logan
	Gas	E: BP♦, Shell♦, USA
		W: Chevron
	Food	E: Subway
		W: Interstate Cafe
	Other	W: Priester's Pecans
(133)		Greenville Rest Area (Both dir) (RR, Phones, Picnic, Vend, Weather, RVDump)
130		AL Truck 10E, AL 185E, Greenville
	Gas	E: BP♦, Chevron♦, Citgo, Shell
		W: Exxon, Glass 66, Texaco♦, Murphy
	Food	E: Arby's, Captain D's, Hardee's, KFC, McDonald's, Pizza Hut, Real Pit BBQ, Steak 'n Shake, Waffle House, Wendy's
		W: Burger King, Bates Turkey Rest, Cracker Barrel, Krystal, Ruby Tuesday, Shoney's, Subway, Taco Bell
	Lodg	E: Best Value Inn, Days Inn♥, Econo Lodge
		W: Best Western♥, Comfort Inn, Hampton Inn, Jameson Inn♥
	Other	E: AdvanceAuto, CVS, Carwash/Chevron, Dollar General, Greenville Muni Airport✈
		W: ATMs, Auto Dealer, Banks, Grocery, Wal-Mart sc, to appr 4mi Sherling Lake Campground▲
128		AL 10, Pineapple Hwy, Greenville, Pine Apple
	Gas	E: Shell♦
		W: BP
	Food	E: The Smokehouse Rest
	Med	E: + Stabler Memorial Hospital
114		AL 106, Georgiana, Starlington
	Med	E: + Georgiana Hospital
	Other	E: to Hank Williams Sr Museum
107		CR 7, Hank Williams Rd, Georgiana, to Grace, Garland
101		AL 29, CR 29/22, Evergreen, Owassa
	FStop	E: Owassa BP
		W: Owassa Food Store/Exxon
	Other	W: Owassa Lakeside RV Park▲
96		AL 83, Liberty Hill Dr, Evergreen
	TStop	W: PTP/McIntyre Travel Center/Citgo
	Gas	E: Chevron, Shell
		W: BP
	Food	E: Burger King, Hardee's, McDonald's, KFC/Taco Bell, Pizza Hut
		W: Subway/Chester/McIntyre TC, Waffle House

EXIT		ALABAMA
	Lodg	W: Comfort Inn, Days Inn
93		US 84, AL 12, to Monroeville
	FStop	E: Econ #12/Shell, USA Travel Center
		W: Diamond Gasoline #20/BP
	Food	W: FastFood/Diamond Gasoline
	Other	E: Greyhound, Overnite Park▲, Pine Crest Park/Campground▲
(89)		AL Welcome Center (SB) (RR, Phones, Picnic, Vend, Weather, RVDump)
(85)		Conecuh Rest Area (NB) (RR, Phones, Picnic, Vend, Weather, RVDump)
83		CR 6, Castleberry, Lenox
	Gas	E: Exxon♦, Texaco
	Food	E: Louise's Restaurant
	Other	E: Country Sunshine RV Park▲
77		AL 41, Lenox, to Brewton, Repton
	FStop	W: Range Shell #126, Econ #18/Citgo
	Gas	E: BP
		W: Shell
	Food	W: Old Timer's Rest, Ranch House Rest
69		AL 113, CR 17, Flomaton, Wallace
	TStop	E: Wallace Interstate Shell (Scales)
		W: Minute Stop #153/Conoco
	Gas	E: Chevron
	Food	E: Subway/Chevron
		W: Huddle House
	TServ	E: Wallace Interstate/Tires
	Other	E: Laundry/LP/Wallace Interstate
57		AL 21, Atmore, Uriah, Monroeville
	FStop	E: RJ's Exxon
	Gas	E: Shell♦
		W: BP♦
	Food	E: RJ's BBQ/RJ's
		W: Creek Family Rest/BW
	Lodg	E: Royal Oaks B&B
		W: Best Western
	TServ	E: Atmore Tire & Retreading
	Other	E: Creek Bingo Palace & Ent Center
		W: to Ponderosa RV Park▲, to appr 12 mi Little River State Forest/Claude D Kelley State Park▲
54		CR 1, Atmore
	FStop	E: Diamond Gasoline #21/BP
	Gas	E: Citgo♦
	Food	E: Subway/BP
45		CR 47, Rabun, Perdido
	FStop	W: Diamond Gasoline #18/BP
	Food	W: Subs&Pizza/Diamond Gas
37		AL 287, Rabun Rd, Gulf Shores Pky Rabun, Bay Minette
	Gas	E: BP
34		AL 59, Bay Minette, Stockton
	Med	E: + Hospital
31		AL 225, Bay Minette, Stockton, Spanish Fort
	FStop	W: Minute Stop #159/Shell
	Food	W: FastFood/Minute Stop
	Other	E: Historic Blakely State Park▲
		W: Live Oak Landing Campground▲
22		Sailor Rd, Creola
	Other	W: to Mark Reynolds N Mobile Co Airport✈, Dead Lake Marina & Campground▲
19		US 43, AL 13, Satsuma, Creola
	FStop	E: Satsuma Chevron
	TStop	E: Pilot Travel Center #75 (Scales) (DAND)
	Gas	W: BP, Shell

◆ = Regular Gas Stations with Diesel ▲ = RV Friendly Locations ♥ = Pet Friendly Locations
RED PRINT SHOWS LARGE VEHICLE PARKING/ACCESS ON SITE OR NEARBY   BROWN PRINT SHOWS CAMPGROUNDS/RV PARKS

EXIT	ALABAMA
Food	E: Arby's, TJCinn/Pilot TC, McDonald's, Waffle House
Other	E: Laundry, WiFi/RVDump/Pilot TC, Carwash/Chevron
	W: I-65 RV Campground▲
15	**CR 41, Celeste Rd, Saraland, Citronelle**
Gas	E: Chevron
	W: Shell
Food	W: Subway/Shell
13	**AL 158, AL 213, Industrial Pkwy, Saraland, Eight Mile, Citronelle**
Gas	E: BP◊, Shell◊, Starvin Marvin, Murphy
	W: Exxon
Food	E: McDonald's, Ruby Tuesday, Shoney's, Subway, Waffle House
	W: Pizza Inn, Subway
Lodg	E: Days Inn, Comfort Suites, Holiday Inn Express, Quality Inn
	W: Hampton Inn
TServ	E: On Site Truck & Trailer Repair
	W: Pitt & Son Truck Repair
Other	E: Wal-Mart sc, Auto & Diesel Services, Saraland RV Sales, Stevens RV Repairs
	W: Co Park/Chickasabogue Park & Campground▲, W AL Tire Service, to Univ of Mobile
10	**W Lee St, Chickasaw, Mobile**
Gas	E: Conoco, Shell
Food	E: Subway/Shell
Lodg	E: America's Best Inn
(9)	**Jct I-165S, to I-10, Prichard, Downtown Mobile**
8AB	**US 45, AL 17, Prichard, Citronelle to Meridian, MS**
TStop	W: Express Truck Wash & Fuel/Pride (Scales)
Gas	E: Conoco, Glenn's Shell◊
	W: Conoco◊, Exxon, RaceWay, Diamond
Food	E: Church's Chicken
	W: Burger King, McDonald's
Lodg	E: Star Motel
TWash	W: Express TW
TServ	E: Cummins Alabama, Peterbilt of Mobile, Cummins/Onan
	W: Empire Truck Sales/Freightliner
Other	E: Family Dollar
	W: Laundry/Express TW
5B	**US 98, AL 42, Moffett Rd, to Hattiesburg, MS**
FStop	W: Minute Stop
Gas	E: Exxon◊
Food	E: Burger King, DQ, McDonald's
	W: Hardee's
Lodg	W: Super 8
TServ	E: Taylor Truck Service, Cummins Mid South
	W: Empire Truck Sales, Goodyear Truck Alignment & Retreading, Reliable Diesel Service
Other	W: ATMs, Auto Services, Moffett Rd RV, Aces RV Park▲, Browns RV Park▲, JR's RV Park▲
5A	**Spring Hill Ave**
Gas	E: Chevron, Shell◊
	W: Chevron◊, Exxon, Shell◊
Food	E: Burger King, DQ, McDonald's
	W: Waffle House
Lodg	E: Crichton Lodging
	W: Extended Stay America, Wingate Inn
Med	E: + USA Medical Center

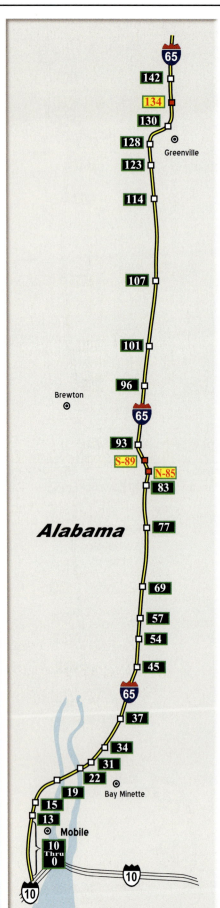

EXIT	ALABAMA
Other	E: AutoZone, Big 10 Tire, Grocery, Auto Services, Pharmacy, Tires
4	**Dauphin St, Mobile**
Gas	E: BP◊, Spectrum, Shell, Summit◊
Food	E: Checker's, ChickFilA, Cracker Barrel, Krystal, McDonald's, Popeye's, Subway, Taco Bell, Waffle House, Wendy's
Lodg	E: Comfort Inn, Red Roof Inn♥, Rodeway Inn
	W: Motel 6♥
Med	W: + Spring Hill Medical Center
Other	E: Auto Dealer, ATMs, Banks, Dollar General, Lowe's, RiteAid, Wal-Mart sc
	W: Spring Hill College, Mobile Museum of Art, to Univ of S AL, ATMs, Banks
3AB	**CR 56, Airport Blvd, Mobile**
FStop	W: Econ #21/Citgo
Gas	E: BP
	W: Exxon, Shell x2, Spur◊
Food	E: Burger King, ChickFilA, Golden China, Hooters, Deli, Mr Wok, Wendy's
	W: Arby's, Carrabba's, Chili's, Chuck E Cheese, Denny's, El Monterey Mex Rest, Lone Star Steakhouse, IHOP, O'Charley's, Olive Garden, Outback Steakhouse, Pizza Hut, Popeye's, Quiznos, Red Lobster, Shoney's, Starbucks, Tony Roma, Waffle House
Lodg	E: Marriott, Quality Inn
	W: Best Inn, Best Western, Courtyard, Days Inn, Drury Inn, Econo Lodge, Family Inn, Fairfield Inn, Hampton Inn, Holiday Inn, La Quinta Inn♥, Motel 6♥, Ramada Inn, Residence Inn, Towneplace Suites, Westmont Inn
Med	W: + Spring Hill Medical Center, + Providence Hospital
Other	E: ATMs, Banks, Best Buy, B&N, Firestone, Goodyear, Lowe's, Mobile Bay Harley Davidson, Sam's Club, Staples, Target, CarWash, Colonial Mall, Springdale Mall
	W: ATMs, Banks, Circuit City, Dollar Tree, FedEx Kinko's, Home Depot, Kmart, Office Depot, Pep Boys, PetSmart♥, Radio Shack, Sam's Club, U-Haul, UPS Store, Walgreen's, Vet♥, to Univ of Southern AL, Mobile Reg'l Airport✈, Crown Classic Coach
1AB	**US 90, AL 16, Government Blvd**
Gas	E: Chevron, BP
	W: Conoco, Shell
Food	E: Burger King, Deli, McDonald's, Steak n Shake
	W: China Garden, Subway, Waffle House
Lodg	E: Howard Johnson
	W: Bama Motel, Rest Inn
Other	E: Hank Aaron Stadium, Auto Dealers, ATMs, Banks, Family Dollar, Theatres, Harley Davidson
	W: Auto Services, ATMs, Big 10 Tires
(0)	**Jct I-10, W to New Orleans, LA, Mississippi; E to Pensacola, FL (SB, Left Exit E)**

(I-65 begins/ends on I-10, Exit #20)
(CENTRAL TIME ZONE)

🎧 **ALABAMA**

Begin Northbound I-65 from Jct I-10 near Mobile, AL to Jct I-80/90 near Gary, IN.

Page 268

◊ = Regular Gas Stations with Diesel   ▲ = RV Friendly Locations   ♥ = Pet Friendly Locations
RED PRINT SHOWS LARGE VEHICLE PARKING/ACCESS ON SITE OR NEARBY   BROWN PRINT SHOWS CAMPGROUNDS/RV PARKS

INTERSTATE 66 E

EXIT	VIRGINIA
	Begin Eastbound I-66 from Jct I-81 near Middletown, VA to Washington, DC

VIRGINIA
(EASTERN TIME ZONE)
(I-66 begins/ends on I-81, Exit #300)

(1B)	Jct I-81, N to Winchester
(1A)	Jct I-81, S to Roanoke (WB, Left exit)
6	US 340, US 522, Front Royal, Winchester, Linden
FStop	N: Quarles Food Store
Gas	S: 7-11, Exxon, East Coast, Shell
Food	N: FastFood/Quarles FS S: Arby's, Dunkin Donuts, Hardee's, Little Caesar's, McDonald's, Pizza Hut, Wendy's
Lodg	S: Hampton Inn, Cool Harbor Motel, Relax Inn, Bluemont Inn, Shenandoah Motel
Med	S: + Warren Memorial Hospital
Other	N: Auto Dealer, Target S: Auto Repairs, ATMs, Banks, Cinema, Grocery, Kmart, Big Lots, Family Dollar, Tires, Towing, Confederate Museum, to Front Royal Airport✈, Shenandoah National Park, Front Royal RV Campground▲, Poe's Southfork Campground▲, Gooney Creek Campground▲, Low Water Bridge Campground▲, Country Wave RV Resort▲, Skyline Caverns
13	VA 79, to VA 55, Linden, Front Royal (Access to #6 Serv via VA 55)
Gas	S: Exxon◆, Shell
Food	S: The Apple House Rest
Other	S: Fox Meadow Winery
18	VA 688, to VA 55, Markham
23	to VA 55, VA 729, US 17N (EB) US 17N, Delaplane, Winchester (WB)
27	Free State Rd, to VA 55, US 17, US 17 Bus, Marshall
Gas	N: Chevron◆, Exxon◆
Food	N: Marshall Diner, Old Salem Rest
Other	N: ATMs, Bank, Auto & Truck Repair, IGA, Vet♥
28	US 17, Winchester Rd, Marshall
Gas	N: BP◆
Food	N: McDonald's/BP, Subway

Personal Notes

EXIT	VIRGINIA
Other	N: Animal Clinic♥, Food Lion, Premier RV Repair, Small Country Campground▲
31	VA 245, Old Tavern Rd, The Plains, Great Meadow, Warrenton
40	US 15, Warrenton, Haymarket
FStop	S: to VA 55E: Q-Stop #616/Mobil
Gas	S: Shell◆, Sheetz
Food	N: Old Carolina Smokehouse S: McDonald's, Subway
Other	N: Greenville Farm Campground▲ S: ATM, Auto Repairs, Bank, Food Lion, Police Dept
43A	US 29S, Lee Hwy, Gainesville, to Warrenton
Gas	S: 7-11, RaceWay, Shell◆, WaWa

EXIT	VIRGINIA
Food	S: IHOP, McDonald's, Ruby Tuesday, Osaka Japanese, Subway, Wendy's
TServ	S: Patriot Truck
Other	S: ATM, Bank, Goodyear, Grocery, Lowe's, PetSmart♥, Target, Auto & Tire Services, UPS Store, Golf Courses, Nissan Pavilion
43B	US 29N, Lee Hwy, Gainesville
Other	N: Manassas Nat'l Battlefield Park
44	VA 234S, Prince William Parkway, Manassas
TServ	S: Elliot Wilson Capitol Trucks
Other	S: Manassas Reg'l Airport✈
47	VA 234 Bus, Sudley Rd, Manassas (EB)
Gas	N: Shell◆ S: AmocoBP◆, Exxon, Raceway◆, Shell, Sunoco
Food	N: Cracker Barrel, Golden Corral, Pizza, Uno Chicago Grill, Wendy's S: Arby's, Bob Evans, Burger King, Chili's, Chipotle Mex Grill, Damon's, Denny's, Domino's, Don Pablo, Hooters, Hunan Deli, KFC, Logan's Roadhouse, McDonald's, Olive Garden, Perfect Pita, Pizza Hut, Red Lobster, Red, White & Blue, Shoney's, Starbucks, TGI Friday, Taco Bell, Wendy's, Rest/BW
Lodg	N: Country Inn, Courtyard, Fairfield Inn S: Best Western, Comfort Suites, Hampton Inn, Quality Inn, Red Roof Inn♥, Residence Inn, Super 8
Med	S: + Prince William Hospital
Other	N: Manassas Nat'l Battlefield Park, Nova Comm College, Regal Cinema S: ATMs, Banks, Auto Services, Auto Dealers, Best Buy, Burlington Coat Factory, Budget RAC, Cinemas, Costco, Cruise America MH Rental, Circuit City, CVS, Enterprise RAC, FedEx Kinko's, Home Depot, Kmart, Lowe's, NTB, Office Depot, Pep Boys, PetCo♥, PetSmart♥, Penske, Staples, Reines RV Center/Camping World, Wal-Mart, U-Haul, UPS Store, Manassas Mall, to Patriot Harley Davidson, Ben Lomond Reg'l Park/Splash Down Water Park, Amtrak, Museums, Subway Stations, to Quantico US Marine Corps Res, Prince William Forest Park
47A	VA 234 Bus, Sudley Rd S (WB)
47B	VA 234 Bus, Sudley Rd N (WB)
(49)	Rest Area (Both dir) (RR, Phone, Picnic)

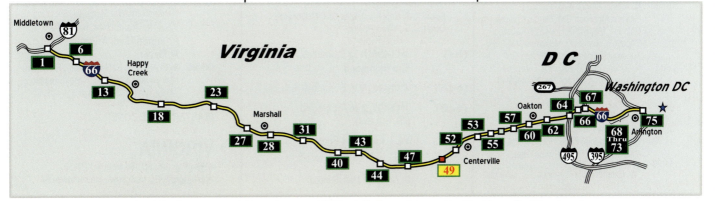

◆ = Regular Gas Stations with Diesel   ▲ = RV Friendly Locations   ♥ = Pet Friendly Locations

RED PRINT SHOWS LARGE VEHICLE PARKING/ACCESS ON SITE OR NEARBY   BROWN PRINT SHOWS CAMPGROUNDS/RV PARKS

Page 269

INTERSTATE W 66

EXIT	VIRGINIA
52	**US 29, Lee Hwy, Centreville**
Gas	N: Circle K
	S: 7-11, Exxon, Mobil◊
Food	S: BBQ Country, Carrabba's, McDonald's, Lone Star Steakhouse, Pizza Hut, Quiznos, Ruby Tuesday, Starbucks, Wendy's
Lodg	S: Springhill Suites
Med	S: + Centreville Urgent Care
Other	N: Bull Run Park▲, Manassas Nat'l Battlefield Par
Other	S: ATMs, Banks, Auto Services, CVS, Centreville Multiplex Cinemas, Nature Food Center, Radio Shack, Tires
53	**VA 28, Sully Rd, to Lee Hwy, Centreville, Chantilly**
Other	N: to Capitol Expo Center, Washington-Dulles Int'l Airport✈, Air & Space Museum
	S: Access to Exit #52 Services
55	**VA 7100, Fairfax Co Pky, Fairfax to US 50, to US 29**
Gas	N: Exxon, Mobil, Sunoco
	S: Exxon
Food	N: Applebee's, Burger King, Crab House, Logan's Roadhouse, Olive Garden, Red Robin, Pizza Hut, Starbucks, Wendy's
Lodg	N: Hyatt, Residence Inn
Med	N: + Fair Lakes Urgent Care Center, + Inova Fair Oaks Hospital
Other	N: Fair Lakes Shopping Center, Best Buy, BJ's Whls, Food Lion, PetSmart♥, Target, Wal-Mart, ATMs, Banks
	S: Costco, Office Depot, to George Mason Univ, Patriot Center
55A	**VA 7100, Fairfax Co Pky, Fairfax, to US 29, Springfield (WB)**
55B	**VA 7100, Fairfax Co Pky, Fairfax, to US 50, Reston, Herndon (EB)**
(56)	**Weigh Station (Both dir)**
57A	**US 50S, Lee Jackson Hwy, Fairfax, Winchester**
Gas	S: Amoco, Citgo, Shell
Food	S: Chipolte Mex Grill, CA Pizza, Italian Café, Subway
Lodg	S: Candlewood Suites, Courtyard
Other	S: ATMs, Banks, FedEx Kinko's, Firearms Museum, Greyhound, Kmart, Natural Foods, Office Depot, PetCo♥, UPS Store, Visitor Info, to George Mason Univ
57B	**US 50N, Lee Jackson Hwy, Fair Oaks, Winchester**
Food	N: Arby's, Burger King, French Bakery, Grady's American Grill, Hunan Chinese, Chinese, Moby Dick House of Kabab, Popeye's, Romano's Macaroni Grill, Ruby Tuesday, Subway, Uno Chicago Grill
Lodg	N: Extended Stay America, Extended Stay Deluxe, Hilton Garden Inn, Homestead Studio, Marriott
Med	N: + Fair Oaks Urgent Care, + Inova Fair Oaks Hospital
Other	N: Fair Oaks Shopping Center, ATMs, Banks, Cinema, FedEx Kinko's, PetCo♥, Safeway, UPS Store, Police Dept, to Washington-Dulles Int'l Airport✈

EXIT	VIRGINIA
60	**VA 123, Chain Bridge Rd, Fairfax, to Oakton, Vienna**
Gas	N: Exxon, Mobil
	S: Exxon, Shell, Sunoco
Food	N: McDonald's, Subway, Starbucks
	S: Bombay Bistro, Denny's, Fuddrucker's, Hooters, Minerva Indian Rest
Lodg	S: Best Western, Hampton Inn, Holiday Inn Express
Med	S: + Med First Urgent Care
Other	N: ATMs, Banks, Auto Services
	S: ATMs, Banks, Auto Services, CVS, Patriot Harley Davidson, RiteAid
62	**VA 243, Nutley St, Vienna, Fairfax (Gas & Food N to Maple St/Chain Bridge Rd) (Addt'l Serv S to Arlington Blvd)**
Gas	S: Exxon
Food	S: Baja Fresh Mex Grill, McDonald's
Other	S: ATMs, Banks, Auto Services
(64)	**Jct I-495, N to Baltimore, S to Richmond**
(64A)	**Jct I-495, N to Baltimore (EB)**
(64B)	**Jct I-495, S to Richmond (EB, Left Exit)**
66	**VA 7, Leesburg Pike, Falls Church**
Gas	N: Exxon
	S: 7-11, Xtra Mart, Sunoco

EXIT	VIRGINIA
Food	N: China King, Jerry's Subs, Starbucks
	S: Chicken Out, Indian Rest, Long John Silver, McDonald's, Pizza Hut
Lodg	N: Westin Inn
	S: Inns of VA
Other	N: to Tyson's Corner Shopping Center, ATMs, Banks, Gas, Food, Lodging
	S: ATMs, Banks, Auto Services, Subway
66B	**VA 7N, Leesburg Pike (WB)**
66A	**VA 7S, Leesburg Pike (WB)**
67	**VA 267N, Dulles Access Rd, I-495N, to Dulles Airport, Baltimore (WB)**
68AB	**Westmoreland St, Arlington (EB)**
69	**US 29, VA 237, Washington Blvd, Lee Hwy, Sycamore St, Arlington**
Gas	N: Exxon
Food	S: Various - .5 mi S to Broad St
Lodg	S: Econo Lodge
Other	N: ATMs, Banks, Addtl Serv N on Lee Hwy
	S: ATMs, Banks, Auto Services
71	**Glebe Rd, Fairfax Dr, VA 120, VA 337, Arlington (WB, diff reaccess, ReAcc via Fairfax Dr)**
Gas	S: Exxon
Food	S: Various-S on Glebe Rd
Lodg	S: Comfort Inn, Holiday Inn
Med	N: + Arlington Hospital
Other	N: Gas, Food, Serv N to Lee Hwy
	S: ATMs, Auto Services, Banks, Cinema, Grocery, Pharmacy
72	**US 29, Lee Hwy, Spout Run Pkwy, Arlington (EB, diff re-entry, Re-Enter via Lee Hwy/US 29)**
Gas	N: 7-11, Exxon
	S: 7-11, Exxon
Food	N: China Express, Pizza Hut
	S: Starbucks
Lodg	N: Inns of VA
Other	N: Auto Services, Grocery
	S: ATM, Bank, CVS, Courts, Grocery, Addtl Serv S to Wilson Blvd
73	**US 29, Lee Hwy, Fort Meyer Dr, N Lynn St, Arlington**
Gas	S: Chevron
Food	S: Burger King, McDonald's
Lodg	N: Marriott
	S: Best Western, Holiday Inn, Hyatt
Med	N: to + Georgetown Univ Hospital
Other	N: to Georgetown Univ, Georgetown
	S: to Museums, Arlington Nat'l Cemetery, Marine Corps War Memorial, Shopping
75	**VA 110, Davis Hwy, to US 50, Arlington Blvd, Arlington, Ft Meyer**
Other	S: to Arlington Nat'l Cemetery, Pentagon, Monuments, Shopping, Ronald Reagan Washington Nat'l Airport✈

(EASTERN TIME ZONE)

🎧 VIRGINIA

Begin Westbound I-66 from Jct US 50, Washington, DC to Jct I-81, Middletown, VA

Page 270

◊ = Regular Gas Stations with Diesel   ▲ = RV Friendly Locations   ♥ = Pet Friendly Locations
RED PRINT SHOWS LARGE VEHICLE PARKING/ACCESS ON SITE OR NEARBY   BROWN PRINT SHOWS CAMPGROUNDS/RV PARKS

EXIT		WEST VIRGINIA
	Begin Eastbound I-68 from Jct I-79, Morgantown, WV to Hagerstown, MD.	
	WEST VIRGINIA (EASTERN TIME ZONE)	
	(I-68 begins/ends on I-79, Exit #148)	
(0)	Jct I-79, N-Washington, S-Fairmont	
1	US 119, University Ave, Grafton Rd, Downtown Morgantown	
Gas	N:	Exxon◊
	S:	Chevron
Food	N:	Rest/Ramada Inn
	S:	Subway
Lodg	N:	Comfort Inn, Ramada Inn, Almost Heaven B&B
Other	S:	Wal-Mart sc, Auto Repairs, Towing
4	WV 7, Earl Core Rd, to Sabraton	
Gas	N:	BP, Exxon, Sheetz
	S:	Gas◊
Food	N:	Blimpie/KFC/Exxon, Arby's, Burger King, Hardee's, Long John Silver, McDonald's, Pizza Hut, Subway, Wendy's
Other	N:	ATMs, Banks, Auto Services, CVS, Dollar General, Family Dollar, Food Lion, Kroger, NAPA
7	CR 857, to US 119, Morgantown	
Gas	N:	BP, Exxon◊
Food	N:	Taco Bell/Exxon, Bob Evans, IHOP, Little Caesar's, Outback Steakhouse, Ruby Tuesday, Subway/BP, Wendy's
	S:	Tiberio's Pasta
Lodg	N:	Holiday Inn Express, Super 8
Med	N:	+ Hospital
Other	N:	Auto Services, Lowe's, Grocery, Tires, Triple S Harley Davidson, Morgantown Muni Airport✈, W Va Univ/Stadium
10	CR 857, Fairchance Rd, to Cheat Lake, Morgantown	
Gas	N:	BP◊, Exxon◊
Food	N:	Ruby's & Ketchy's, Subway
	S:	Burger King, Stone Crab Inn
Lodg	S:	Lakeview Resort & Conf Ctr
(12)	RunAway Truck Ramp (WB)	
NOTE:	WB: MM 15-10: Steep Grade	
15	CR 73/12, Bruceton Mills, Coopers Rock	
Other	S:	Coopers Rock State Forest▲
(16)	Weigh Station (WB)	
23	WV 26, Bruceton Mills	
TStop	N:	Little Sandy's Truck Stop/Mobil
FStop	N:	BFS Foods #10/BP
Food	N:	FastFood/BFS BP, Rest/Little Sandy's TS, Mill Place Rest, Pizza Pro, Twila's Res

EXIT		WV / MD
Lodg	N:	Maple Leaf Motel
Other	N:	LP/BFS BP, US Post Office, to Glade Farms Campground▲
29	CR 5, Hazelton Rd, Bruceton Mills	
Gas	N:	Mobil◊
Other	S:	to Pine Hill Campground▲, Big Bear Lake Campland▲
(30)	WV Welcome Center (WB) (RR, Phones, Picnic, Vend, Info)	
NOTE:	MM 32: Maryland State Line	
	(EASTERN TIME ZONE)	
	WEST VIRGINIA	
	MARYLAND	
	(EASTERN TIME ZONE)	
4	MD 42, Friendsville Rd, Maple St, to US 219, Friendsville	
Gas	N:	BP◊
	S:	Citgo
Food	N:	Jubilee Diner, Subs & Pizza
Lodg	N:	Riverside Hotel, Sunset Inn, Yough Valley Motel
Other	N:	ATM, Bank
	S:	to Wisp Ski Resort
(8)	MD Welcome Center (EB) (RR, Phones, Picnic, Vend, Info)	
14	Garrett Hwy (EB)	
14A	US 219S, Garrett Hwy S	
Other	S:	to Wisp Ski Resort, Deep Creek Lake State Park▲, Garrett Co Airport✈
14B	Garrett Hwy N, US 40, Nat'l Pike	
FStop	N:	Keysers Ridge Auto Truck Stop/BP
Gas	N:	Citgo◊
Food	N:	Rest/Keysers Ridge TS, McDonald's
Other	N:	Auto Repairs
19	MD 495, to US 40 Alt, Grantsville, to MD 669, Swanton, Bittinger	
Gas	N:	Exxon◊, Mobil
Food	N:	Hey Pizza, Rest/Casselman Motel, Penn Alps Rest & Craft Shop
Lodg	N:	Casselman Motel, Elliot House Victorian Inn
Other	N:	ATMs, Banks, US Post Office, Casselman River State Park
22	US 219N, to US 40 Alt, Chestnut Ridge Rd, to Meyersville, PA	
FStop	N:	Fuel City/BP (Scales)
TStop	S:	Pilot Travel Center #408 (Scales)
Gas	S:	AmocoBP, Exxon
Food	N:	Rest/Fuel City, Burger King, Subway
	S:	Arby's/Pilot TC

EXIT		MARYLAND
Lodg	N:	Little Meadows Motel
	S:	Holiday Inn
TServ	S:	Cummins
Other	N:	Laundry/Fuel City, Pharmacy, Penn Alps Artesian Village
	S:	Laundry/BarbSh/WiFi/Pilot TC, to New Germany State Park▲
24	to US 40 Alt, Meyersdale Rd, Lower New Germany Rd	
NOTE:	MM 26: Eastern Continental Divide	
NOTE:	EB: Area Prone to Low / No Visibility due to Fog	
29	MD 546, to US 40 Alt, Finzel Little Rd, Beall School Rd, Frostburg	
(31)	Weigh Station (EB)	
NOTE:	WB: Area Prone to Low / No Visibility due to Fog	
33	Midlothian Rd, Braddock Rd	
Other	N:	Frostburg State Univ
34	MD 36, Frostburg, Westernport	
Gas	N:	AmocoBP, Sheetz
Food	N:	Burger King, McDonald's, Pizza Hut, Subway
Lodg	N:	Days Inn, Hampton Inn
Med	N:	+ Hospital
Other	N:	Auto Dealer, Auto Repairs, ATMs, Dollar General, Food Lion, RiteAid
	S:	to Dans Mountain State Park
NOTE:	EB: 6% Steep Grade	
39	US 40 Alt, Nat'l Hwy, to MD 53, to US 220S, Cumberland (WB) (Access to Ex #40 Serv)	
Gas	N:	Citgo, Exxon
Food	N:	Burger King, Long John Silver, Pizza Hut, Subway, Rest/BW
Lodg	N:	Best Western, Slumberland Motel, Super 8
40	Vocke Rd, MD 53S, Winchester Rd, MD 49, Braddock Rd, Campground Rd, US 40 Alt, TRUCK US 220S	
Gas	N:	BP, Citgo◊, Exxon, Mobil
Food	N:	Arby's, Bob Evans, Burger King, DQ, Denny's, KFC, Long John Silver, McDonald's, Pizza Hut, Ruby Tuesday, Wendy's, Rest/BW
	S:	Applebee's, China Buffet, CiCi's
Lodg	N:	Best Western, Comfort Inn, Super 8, Slumber Land Motel
	S:	Red Roof Inn
Med	N:	+ Hospital

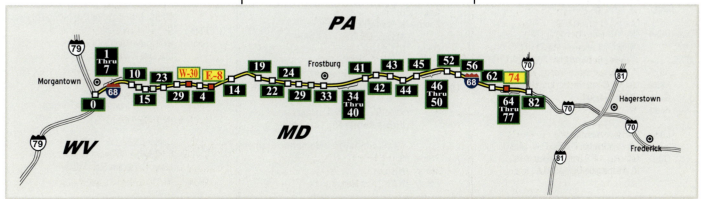

◊ = Regular Gas Stations with Diesel   ▲ = RV Friendly Locations   ♥ = Pet Friendly Locations
RED PRINT SHOWS LARGE VEHICLE PARKING/ACCESS ON SITE OR NEARBY   BROWN PRINT SHOWS CAMPGROUNDS/RV PARKS

Page 271

W I-68

EXIT		MARYLAND
	Other	N: AdvanceAuto, Budget RAC, CVS, Grocery, Lowe's, Staples, Highland Harley Davidson, U-Haul, MD State Hwy Patrol Post
		S: ATMs, Banks, Auto Services, Country Club Mall, Wal-Mart sc
41		to MD 49, Braddock Rd, Seton Rd (WB) (No Re-Entry to I-68)
	Med	N: + Sacred Heart Hospital
42		US 220S, McMullen Hwy (EB), Fletcher Dr, Greene St, US220S (WB)
	Other	S: to Allegany Co Fairgrounds
	NOTE:	EB: 6% Steep Grade
43A		Johnson St (EB), Beall St (WB), to Alt MD 28, to W Va
	Gas	N: Sheetz
	Other	N: ATMs, Banks, Court, Museums
43B		MD 51, Industrial Blvd
	Gas	S: AmocoBP, Citgo◊
	Food	N: McDonald's
		S: Dunkin Donuts, Taco Bell, Wendy's
	Lodg	N: Holiday Inn
	Other	S: Convention Center, to Mexico Farms Airport✈
43C		Queen City Dr, Downtown (EB) Harrison St, Liberty St (WB)
	Gas	S: Shell
	Food	N: McDonald's
	Other	N: Amtrak, Theatre, ATMs, Banks
43D		Maryland Ave, Cumberland
	Gas	N: Citgo
		S: Liberty◊
	Food	N: Wendy's
		S: ChickFilA, Subway

EXIT		MARYLAND
	Med	S: + Memorial Hospital of Cumberland
	Other	N: Amtrak, ATMs, Banks, Downtown
		S: Grocery
44		US 40 Alt, Baltimore Ave (WB) MD 639, Willow Brook Rd (EB)
	Other	S: Wal-Mart sc, to Allegany College
45		Hillcrest Dr, CR 952, Cumberland
	FStop	S: Fuel City/BP
46		Baltimore Pike NE, to US 220N (EB) Naves Cross Rd, MD 144, Mason Rd NE, to US 220N (WB)
	Food	N: Lindy's Rest, Rest/Maryland Motel
		S: JB's Steak House
	Lodg	N: Cumberland Motel, Maryland Motel
47		MD 144, Baltimore Pike NE, US 220N, Cumberland (WB)
50		Pleasant Valley Rd, to MD 144
	Lodg	N: Rocky Gap Lodge & Golf Resort♥
	Other	N: Rocky Gap State Park▲
52		MD 144E, National Pike, Flintstone (EB, No ReEntry)
56		MD 144, National Pike, Flintstone
	Gas	S: Sunoco
	Other	S: US Post Office, Repairs/Sunoco
62		Fifteen Mile Creek Rd, US 40 Scenic
64		MV Smith Rd, Flintstone
	Other	S: Scenic Overlook: Green Ridge State Forest (Picnic, Phone)
68		Orleans Rd, Little Orleans
	FStop	N: Belle Grove Auto Truck Stop/Exxon
	Food	N: Rest/FastFood/Belle Grove ATS

EXIT		MARYLAND
72		US 40 Scenic, High Germany Rd, Mann Rd, Little Orleans
	FStop	S: AmocoBP
(72)		RunAway Truck Ramp (WB)
74		US 40E Scenic, Mountain Rd, Hancock (EB, No Re-Entry)
(75)		Rest Area / Sideling Hill Exhibit (NO Trucks) (Both dir) (RR, Phones, Picnic, Vend, Info)
	NOTE:	Both dir: 6% Steep Grade
(75)		RunAway Truck Ramp (EB)
77		US 40W Scenic, MD 144E, Woodmont Rd, Hancock
		NOTE: NO Thru Trucks Over 13T on MD 144 in Hancock.
	Other	S: to Happy Hills Campground▲
(82C)		Jct I-70W, US 522N, to Breezewood (EB, Left exit)
(82B)		Jct I-70E, US 40E, to Hagerstown
82A		US 522S, Hancock
	Gas	S: Citgo, Sheetz
	Food	S: Hardee's, Pizza Hut, Weavers Rest
	Lodg	S: Best Value Inn, Super 8
	Other	S: ATMs, Banks, Dollar General, Grocery, Jimco Trailer Sales

(I-68 begins/ends on I-70, Exit #1)
(EASTERN TIME ZONE)

ⓘ MARYLAND

Begin Westbound I-68 from Hagerstown, MD to Jct I-79 in Morgantown, WV.

I-69 S

EXIT		MICHIGAN
		Begin Southbound I-69 from Port Huron, MI to Indianapolis, IN.

ⓘ MICHIGAN
(EASTERN TIME ZONE)
(I-69 begins/ends on MI 25, Pine Grove Ave)

	NOTE:	I-69 below runs with I-94. Exit #'s follow I-94.
275		MI 25, Pine Grove Ave, Port Huron
	Gas	N: BP, Marathon, Shell, Speedway
	Food	N: McDonald's, Wendy's
	Lodg	N: Days Inn, Holiday Inn
	Med	S: + Port Huron Hospital
	Other	N: ATMs, Banks, Family Dollar, Can-Am Duty Free, TOLL Bridge to CANADA
274		Water St, to Lapeer Ave, Port Huron
	N:	MI Welcome Center/Rest Area (WB)
	FStop	S: By-Lo Speedy Q #6
	Gas	S: Speedway◊
	Food	N: Cracker Barrel
		S: Bob Evans
	Lodg	N: Best Western
		S: Comfort Inn, Fairfield Inn, Hampton Inn
	Other	N: Gilbert's Harley Davidson, Pt Huron Twp Park Campground▲, to Lake Port State Park

EXIT		MICHIGAN
	NOTE:	I-69 above runs with I-94. Exit #'s follow I-94.
199		I-69 Bus, Port Huron
	Gas	S: Mobil◊, Sam's
	Med	S: + Mercy Hospital
	Other	S: ATMs, Auto Services, Banks, Kmart SC, Kroger, Sam's Club, Truck Services
(198)		Jct I-94, S - Detroit, N - Canada
196		Wadhams Rd, Lapeer Ave, Smiths Creek, Kimball
	FStop	N: Bi-Lo
	Gas	N: Shell◊
	Food	N: Burger King, Hungry Howie's Pizza & Subs, McDonald's, Subway
	Other	N: Grocery, Pharmacy, At Your Service Auto & Truck Repair, Pete's Camping Services, Port Huron KOA▲
194		Barth Rd, Taylor Dr, Smiths Creek
	Other	N: Fort Trodd Family Campground RV Resort▲, to Ruby Campground▲
189		Wales Center Rd, Goodells
184		MI 19, Kinney Rd, Memphis, Emmett
	FStop	S: Sunrise C-Store #29/Marathon
	TStop	N: Bisco's Truck Stop/Citgo (Scales)
	Food	N: Rest/FastFood/Bisco's TS

EXIT		MICHIGAN
	Food	S: FastFood/Sunrise
	TWash	N: Bisco's TS
	TServ	N: Bisco's TS/Tires
	Other	N: Laundry/RVDump/LP/Bisco's TS
180		Riley Center Rd, Memphis
	Other	N: Emmett KOA▲
176		Capac Rd, Capac
	FStop	N: Express Food Depot/BP (Scales)
	Food	N: McDonald's/Express BP
	Other	N: Auto & Truck Services
(174)		Rest Area (SB) (RR, Phones, Picnic, Vend)
168		MI 53, S Van Dyke Rd, Imlay City
	FStop	N: Speedway #8772, Spencer Oil/BP
	Food	N: Big Joe's Pizza & Chicken, Burger King, DQ, Little Caesars, Lucky's Steakhouse, McDonald's, New China Buffet, Taco Bell, Tim Horton's, Wendy's
	Lodg	N: Days Inn, M-53 Motel, Super 8
	Other	N: ATMs, AutoZone, Auto Services, Grocery, Tires, Pharmacy, E&A Auto, Truck & RV Repair, Imlay City Service Center-RV Repair
		S: Woodland Waters Campground▲
163		Lake Pleasant Rd, Attica
	Other	N: Industrial Diesel Service, Greg's Truck & Auto Repair

Page 272 ◊ = Regular Gas Stations with Diesel   ▲ = RV Friendly Locations   ♥ = Pet Friendly Locations
RED PRINT SHOWS LARGE VEHICLE PARKING/ACCESS ON SITE OR NEARBY   BROWN PRINT SHOWS CAMPGROUNDS/RV PARKS

INTERSTATE 69 N/S — MICHIGAN

EXIT	
(161)	**Rest Area (NB)** (RR, Phones, Picnic, Vend)
159	**Wilder Rd, Lapeer**
155	**MI 24, Lapeer Rd, Lapeer, Pontiac**
Gas	N: BP, Marathon◊, Meijer◊, Murphy S: Mobil◊
Food	N: Arby's, Burger King, DQ, KFC, Little Caesars, McDonald's, Nick's Rest, Subway, Taco Bell, Tim Horton's, Wendy's, Greek & Amer Rest
Lodg	N: Best Western, Fairfield Inn
Med	N: + Lapeer Regional Hospital
Other	N: ATMs, Banks, Auto Services, AutoZone, Dollar Tree, Grocery, Kmart, Kroger, Office Depot, Radio Shack, Tires, Vet♥, Amtrak, MI State Hwy Patrol Post, to Dupont Lapeer Airport✈, RVDump/City Park, Wal-Mart SC, Circle K RV's, Crystal Creek Campground▲ S: Auto Dealers, to Metamora Hadley State Rec Area▲
153	**Lake Nepessing Rd, Lapeer**
Other	N: CJ Auto & Truck Service S: Hilltop Campground▲
149	**Elba Rd, Lapeer**
Other	S: Cummings RV & Trailer
145	**MI 15, State Rd, Davison, Clarkston**
Gas	N: Shell◊, Speedway S: Mobil◊
Food	N: Applebee's, Arby's, Big John Steak & Onion, Burger King, Country Sun Rest, Dunkin Donuts, Hungry Howie's, KFC, Little Caesars, McDonald's, Subway, Taco Bell, Tim Horton's
Lodg	N: Comfort Inn
Other	N: ATMs, Auto Services, Auto Dealer, Banks, CarWash, CVS, Kroger, RiteAid, Radio Shack, U-Haul
143	**Irish Rd, Davison**
Gas	N: Shell◊ S: 7-11, Marathon, Shell
Food	S: Dunkin Donuts, McDonald's
Other	N: to Outdoor Adventures/Lakeshore Resort▲ appr 5mi Genesee Co Park/ Timber Wolf Campground▲
141	**Belsay Rd, Flint, Burton, Genesee**
Gas	N: BP, Shell◊ S: Road Runner Express◊
Food	N: Country Kitchen, McDonald's, Little Caesars, Subway, Taco Bell, Wendy's S: Long John Silver/A&W/Road Runner
Other	N: ATMs, Grocery, Home Depot, Kmart, Wal-Mart, Golf Course, American RV S: Bud's Trailer Center
139	**Center Rd, Burton, Flint**
Gas	N: Marathon, Speedway◊, Total S: Marathon, Meijer◊
Food	N: Applebee's, Boston Market, McDonald's, Old Country Buffet, Ponderosa, Quiznos, Starbucks, Subway, Tim Horton's, Wendy's S: Bob Evans, China 1, DQ, McDonald's, Walli's Rest
Lodg	S: America's Best Inn♥, Super 8
Other	N: ATMs, Auto Services, Banks, Cinema, Family Dollar, Grocery, Home Depot, Lowe's, Courtland Center Mall S: Office Depot, Staples, Target, IMA Sports Arena

EXIT	
138	**MI 54, Dort Hwy, Flint**
FStop	N: Speedway #8748
Gas	N: BP S: Marathon, 7-11
Food	N: Anna's Kitchen, Big John Steaks, Little Caesars, YaYa's Chicken S: Arby's, American Diner, Burger King, House of Hunan, KFC, McDonald's, Subway, Taco Bell
Lodg	S: Travel Inn
Med	N: + Genesys Regional Medical Center
Other	N: ATMs, AutoZone, RiteAid, Tires, Walgreen's, U-Haul, Golf Course S: ATMs, Auto Services, Campbells Auto & Truck Repair, Tri County Diesel
(137)	**Jct I-475, UAW Freeway, N to Saginaw, S to Detroit**
136	**Saginaw St, Downtown Flint**
Med	N: to + Hurley Medical Center
Other	N: ATMs, Banks, Courts, Greyhound, Convention Center, Police Dept, to Univ of MI/Flint S: Auto Services, Graff Truck Center
135	**Hammerberg Rd, Flint**
(133)	**Jct I-75, N - Saginaw, S - Detroit, US 23S to Ann Arbor** (Gas/Food/Lodg N to 1st Exit)
131	**MI 121, Bristol Rd, Miller Rd, American Veterans Hwy, Flint**
Gas	N: Speedway, Sunoco S: Mobil
Food	N: Arby's, Burger King, Chili's, Chuck E Cheese, Logan's, Long John Silver, Mongolian BBQ, Old Country Buffet, Outback Steakhouse, Ryan's Grill, Ruby Tuesday, Starbucks, Subway, Taco Bell
Other	N: ATMs, Auto Rentals, Auto Services, Banks, Best Buy, Borders, Circuit City, Dale's Natural Foods, Discount Tire, FedEx Kinko's, Firestone, Goodyear, Gander Mountain, NTB, Office Depot, Pep Boys, PetCo♥, PetSmart♥, Target, UPS Store, Mall S: Bishop Int'l Airport✈
129	**Miller Rd, Swartz Creek**
Gas	S: Speedway, Kroger
Food	S: Arby's, Burger King, DQ, McDonald's, Wendy's
Other	N: Auto Service, GM Serv Parts Oper S: Kroger, Vet♥
128	**Morrish Rd, Swartz Creek**
Gas	S: BP, Admiral
Food	S: China Wok, CJ's Café, Pizza, Subway
Other	S: ATMs, Banks, Auto Services, Kroger, Sports Creek Raceway
(126)	**Rest Area (NB)** (RR, Phones, Picnic)
123	**MI 13, County Line Rd, Lennon**
FStop	N: Speedway #8797
Other	S: Holiday Shores RV Resort & Golf Course▲, Jenkins Auto & Truck Repair
118	**MI 71, Lansing Rd, Durand, Vernon**
FStop	S: Monroe Point Shell
Gas	N: Mobil S: Marathon
Food	S: FastFood/Monroe Pt, Burger King, Hardee's, Hungry Howie's, McDonald's, Subway, Wendy's
Med	S: + Memorial Urgent Care

◊ = Regular Gas Stations with Diesel ▲ = RV Friendly Locations ♥ = Pet Friendly Locations
RED PRINT SHOWS LARGE VEHICLE PARKING/ACCESS ON SITE OR NEARBY   BROWN PRINT SHOWS CAMPGROUNDS/RV PARKS

Page 273

EXIT		MICHIGAN
	Other	S: Amtrak, Family Dollar, Grocery, Museum, Radio Shack, RiteAid, Rainbow RV Sales
113		Grand River Rd, Bancroft
	Gas	S: BP◊
	Other	S: to appr 6 mi Walnut Hills Family RV Resort & Campground▲
105		MI 52, Main St, Perry, Owosso
	TStop	S: Glitzy Ritz Auto Truck Plaza/Sunoco
	Gas	S: 7-11, Phillips 66◊
	Food	S: Rest/Subway/Glitzy Ritz ATP, Burger King, Hungry Howie's, McDonald's, Taco Bell/P66
	Lodg	S: Heb's Inn♥
	Other	S: ATMs, Auto Dealer, Auto Services, IGA, Family Dollar, Harts Auto & RV Repair, Police Dept, RiteAid
(101)		Rest Area (SB) (RR, Phones, Picnic)
98		Woodbury Rd, Haslett, to Laingsburg, Shaftsburg
89B		US 127, Jackson (NB)
89A		US 127, E Lansing (SB)
87		US 27, DeWitt, Lansing, to Clare
	FStop	N: Speedway #8740
	Gas	N: BP◊
		S: Speedway◊
	Food	N: FastFood/Speedway, Arby's, Burger King, Bob Evans, FlapJack's, Marco's, McDonald's, Little Caesars, Subway
	Lodg	N: Sleep Inn
		S: Amerihost Inn
	Med	N: + Delta Medical Center
	Other	N: ATMs, Auto Services, Annie Rae RV
		S: Auto Services, ATMs
85		DeWitt Rd, Lansing, to DeWitt
84		Airport Rd, to I-96/69 Bus, Lansing
	Other	S: to Capital City Airport✈, Dennis Trailer Sales
	NOTE:	I-69 below runs with I-96. Exit #'s follow I-96.
(81/90)		Francis Rd, Jct I-96W, Grand Ledge (SB), Grand River Ave, Bus 69/96
	TStop	W: Flying J Travel Plaza #5126 (Scales)
	Food	W: CountryMarket/FastFood/FJ TP
	Other	E: Capital City Airport✈
		W: Laundry/WiFi/RVDump/LP/FJ TP
(91)		Jct I-69N, US 27, to Flint, Clare
93A		I-69 Bus, MI 43W, W Saginaw Hwy to Grand Ledge
	Gas	W: BP, Shell, Speedway◊
	Food	W: Arby's, Bob Evans, Cracker Barrel, McDonald's, Steak n Shake, Subway
	Lodg	W: Springhill Suites
	Other	W: Discount Tire, Lowe's, PetSmart♥, Staples, Wal-Mart, FunTyme Park
93B		I-69 Bus, MI 43E, W Saginaw Hwy
	Gas	E: Shell, Speedway◊, Total, Meijer◊
	Food	E: Burger King, Carrabba's, Denny's, McDonald's, Mountain Jack's Steakhouse, Outback Steakhouse, Red Robin, TGI Friday

Personal Notes

EXIT		MICHIGAN
	Lodg	E: Best Western, Fairfield Inn, Hampton Inn, Holiday Inn, Motel 6♥, Quality Suites, Red Roof Inn♥, Residence Inn
	Med	E: + Delta Medical Center
	Other	E: AMC, ATMs, Auto Services, Auto Dealer Alamo RAC, Banks, Big Lots, Better Health Market, CarWash, Cinema, Enterprise RAC, FedEx Kinko's, Firestone, Goodyear, Kroger, Midas, Office Max, Target, UPS Store, Lansing Mall, GM Lansing Assembly
(95)		Jct I-496, Downtown Lansing
	Med	E: to + Ingham Reg'l Medical Center
	Other	E: to MI State Univ
(97/72)		Jct I-69S, US 27, to Charlotte, Ft Wayne, I-96E, to Detroit, W to Grand Rapids
	NOTE:	I-69 above runs with I-96. Exit #'s follow I-96.
70		Lansing Rd, to I-96, Charlotte
	TStop	E: Windmill AmBest Truck Stop/Citgo (Scales)
	Food	E: Rest/Windmill TS, Wendy's
	TWash	E: Windmill TS
	TServ	E: Windmill TS/Tires
	Other	E: Laundry/LP/Windmill TS, MI State Hwy Patrol Post
(68)		Rest Area (NB) (RR, Phones, Picnic, Vend)
66		MI 100, Hartel Rd, Charlotte, Potterville, Grand Ledge
	Gas	W: BP, Shell
	Food	W: McDonald's, Subway

EXIT		MICHIGAN
61		Lansing Rd, MI 79, Lansing St
	FStop	E: Marathon
	Gas	E: Mobil
		W: Speedway
	Food	E: Applebee's, Subway
		W: Arby's, Burger King, Hot n Now, KFC, Little Caesars, McDonald's, Pizza Hut, Taco Bell, Subway, Wendy's
	Lodg	E: Comfort Inn, Crestview Motel
	Med	W: + Hayes Green Beach Hospital
	Other	E: Auto Dealers, AutoZone, Grocery, Wal-Mart sc, Fitch H Beach Airport✈
		W: ATMs, Advance Auto, Auto Dealers, Auto Services, Banks, CarQuest, Cinema, Family Dollar, Grocery, Radio Shack, Police Dept
60		MI 50, E Shepherd St, E Clinton Tr, Charlotte, Eaton Rapids
	Gas	E: Meijer◊
	Lodg	E: Holiday Inn Express
		W: Super 8
	Med	W: + Hospital
	Other	E: Auto Services
		W: Auto Services, Acc to Ex #61 Serv
57		Cochran Rd, Loop 69, Marshall Rd, Charlotte
51		Ainger Rd, Olivet (Acc to Ex #51 Serv)
48		MI 78, Butterfield Hwy, Olivet, Bellevue, Lee Center
	Gas	E: Citgo
	Food	E: Subway, Taco Bell
	Other	E: ATMs, Banks, Auto Service, Police
42		N Drive North, Marshall
(41)		Rest Area (SB) (RR, Phones, Picnic)
(38)		Jct I-94, W to Chicago, E to Detroit
36		Michigan Ave, I-94 Bus, MI 96, Marshall, to I-94
	Gas	E: Citgo◊, Mobil, Shell
	Food	E: Applebee's, Arby's, Burger King, Little Caesars, McDonald's, Pizza Hut, Subway, Taco Bell, Wendy's
	Lodg	E: Amerihost Inn, National House Inn
		W: Arbor Inn, Howard's Motel, Imperial Motel
	Med	E: + Hospital
	Other	E: ATMs, Auto Services, AutoZone, Auto Dealers, Dollar Tree, Grocery, Kmart, Radio Shack, RiteAid, Brooks Field Airport✈, MI State Hwy Patrol Post
		W: Auto Services, Towing, Marshall RV
32		MI 227N, F Drive South, Marshall
	Gas	E: Shell
	Other	E: to Tri-Lake Trails Campground▲, Quality Camping▲
(28)		Rest Area (NB) (RR, Phones, Picnic)
25		MI 60, Tekonsha, to Three Rivers, Jackson
	FStop	E: Snappy Food Mart/BP, Tekonsha Sunoco
	TStop	E: Te-Kon AmBest Travel Plaza/Citgo (Scales)
	Food	E: FastFood/Snappy FM, Rest/Subway/Te-Kon TP, McDonald's
	TWash	E: Te-Kon TP

Page 274 ◊ = Regular Gas Stations with Diesel   ▲ = RV Friendly Locations   ♥ = Pet Friendly Locations
RED PRINT SHOWS LARGE VEHICLE PARKING/ACCESS ON SITE OR NEARBY   BROWN PRINT SHOWS CAMPGROUNDS/RV PARKS

EXIT		MI / IN
	TServ	E: Te-Kon TP/Tires, NAPA/Courtesy Car & Truck Parts & RV Repairs
	Other	E: Laundry/Te-Kon TP, to Quality Camping▲ W: to Turtle Lake Nudist Resort▲
23		Marshall Rd, Tekonsha
	Gas	E: Citgo
	Other	W: to Potawatomie Rec Area▲
16		Jonesville Rd, Coldwater
	Gas	W: AmocoBP
	Other	W: Waffle Farm Campground▲, Love's Lazy Lagoon▲, Narrows Resort & Campground▲
13		US 12, I-69 Bus, E Chicago St, Coldwater, to Quincy, Batavia
	Gas	E: Meijer◊, Speedway◊ W: BP, Citgo, Speedway◊, Sunoco
	Food	E: Applebee's, Bob Evans, Super Grand Buffet W: Arby's, Burger King, Chinese Rest, Cottage Inn Pizza, Coldwater Garden Rest, KFC, Little Caesars, KFC, McDonalds, Mr Gyros, Pizza Hut, Ponderosa, Subway, TCBY, Taco Bell, Wendy's
	Lodg	E: Red Roof Inn♥ W: Cadet Motor Inn, Econo Lodge, Holiday Inn Express, Super 8, Travelodge♥
	Med	W: + Hospital, + Family Medicine Clinic
	Other:	E: AutoZone, ATMs, Auto Services, Auto Dealer, Aldi's, Banks, Big Lots, Cinema, Dollar General, Dollar Tree, Grocery, Home Depot, Radio Shack, SavALot, Wal-Mart sc, Haylett's N Country Auto & RV Center, to Cottonwood Resort▲, to Historic Marble Springs Family Campground & Park▲, to appr 15 mi: Gateway Park Campground▲, Sugar Bush Park▲, Way-Back-In CG▲ W: ATMs, Auto Services, Auto Dealers, Banks, RiteAid, Walgreen's, MI State Hwy Patrol Post, to Branch Co Mem'l Airport✈
10		Fenn Rd, to I-69 Bus, Coldwater
(8)		Weigh Station (NB)
(6)		MI Welcome Center (NB) (RR, Phones, Picnic, Vend, Info)
3		Copeland Rd, Coldwater
	Other	E: to Coldwater Lake Campground▲, Butler Resort▲ W: to Green Acres Campground▲, Coldwater River Campground▲

(EASTERN TIME ZONE)
⊖ MICHIGAN
⊙ INDIANA
(EASTERN TIME ZONE)

	NOTE:	MM 158: Michigan State Line
157		Baker Rd, Lk George Rd, to IN 120, Angola, Fremont, Jamestown
	TStop	E: Petro2 Stopping Center #45/Mobil (Scales) W: Pilot Travel Center #29 (Scales), Pioneer Auto Truck Stop/Shell

EXIT		INDIANA
	Food	E: Rest/FastFood/Petro SC W: Wendy's/Pilot TC, Subway/Pioneer, McDonald's, Red Arrow Rest
	Lodg	E: Lake George Inn/Petro SC W: Holiday Inn Express, Redwood Motor Lodge
	Other	E: Laundry/WiFi/Petro SC W: Laundry/WiFi/Pilot TC, Prime Outlets at Fremont, to Barton Lake RV Sales & Service, Yogi Bear's Jellystone Camp▲, Manapogo Park▲
(156)		Jct I-80/90 (TOLL), W to Chicago, E to Toledo, Ohio
154		IN 127, to IN 727, IN 120, W 400 N, Angola
	Gas	W: Marathon◊
	Food	E: Applebee's, Ruby Tuesday, Scoops
	Lodg	E: Budgeteer Inn, Hampton Inn, Ramada Inn, Super 8, Travelers Inn W: Pokagon Motel
	Other	E: Oakhill Campground▲ W: Pokagon State Park▲, Prime Outlets, to Manapogo Park▲
150		CR 200W, Angola, Lake James
	Gas	E: BP◊ W: Shell
	Food	W: BB's Smokehouse, Caruso's Italian
	Lodg	W: to Lake James Family Resort
	Other	W: Fun Spot Amusement Park & Zoo
148		US 20, Angola, LaGrange (Addt'l Serv Serv E to IN 127N)
	FStop	E: Speedway #8336
	Gas	E: Citgo◊, Gas America
	Food	E: McDonald's, Subway, Hatchery, Rice Bowl, Timbers Rest, Wendy's W: Best Western
	Lodg	E: Redwood Motel W: Best Western, Sycamore Hill B&B
	TWash	E: Speedway
	Med	E: + Hospital
	Other	E: ATMs, Auto Services, Auto Dealers, Banks, Dollar General, Grocery, Towing, Golf Course, Happy Acres RV Park▲, Buck Lake Ranch▲, to Wal-Mart sc, Panterra Coach & RV W: Circle B Campground▲, to Gordon's Camping Resort▲, Tri State Steuben Co Airport✈
(144)		Steuben Co Rest Area (SB) (RR, Phones, Picnic, Vend, Info)
140		IN 4, State St, W 800S, Ashley, Hamilton, Hudson
	Gas	W: Ashley Deli, BP
	Food	W: Deli, Cones & Coney, Pizza
	Other	W: Auto Repairs, ATMs, Banks, Tires, to Story Lake Resort▲
134		US 6, Grand Army of the Republic, Waterloo, Kendallville (Addt'l Serv E to IN 427)
	TStop	W: Kaghann's Korner/Marathon, Morning Star Truck & Auto Plaza/ Citgo To open Fall 2008 Flying J Travel Plaza
	Food	W: Rest/Kaghann's Korner, Rest/Morning Star TAP, Rest/FastFood/FJ TP
	Lodg	E: Lighthouse Inn
	Other	E: Amtrak W: Laundry/WiFi/FJ TP

◊ = Regular Gas Stations with Diesel   ▲ = RV Friendly Locations   ♥ = Pet Friendly Locations
RED PRINT SHOWS LARGE VEHICLE PARKING/ACCESS ON SITE OR NEARBY   BROWN PRINT SHOWS CAMPGROUNDS/RV PARKS

INTERSTATE 69 N/S

INDIANA

EXIT		
129		**IN 8, 7th St, Garrett, Avilla, Auburn**
	Gas	E: BP◊, Clark, GasAmerica, Marathon◊, Shell, Speedway◊
	Food	E: Applebee's, Arby's, Bob Evans, Burger King, DQ, McDonald's, Ponderosa, Pizza Hut, Subway, Taco Bell, Wendy's
		W: Cracker Barrel
	Lodg	E: Best Western♥, Comfort Inn, Country Hearth Inn, Holiday Inn Express, La Quinta Inn♥
	Med	E: + DeKalb Memorial Hospital
	Other	E: AutoZone, ATMs, Auto Dealers, Auto Services, Banks, CVS, Cinema, Dollar General, Grocery, Kroger, Radio Shack, Staples, Wal-Mart sc, Golf Course
		W: Home Depot, to Indian Springs Resort Campground▲
126		**CR 11A, Garrett, Auburn**
	Other	E: Auburn Dekalb Airport✈
		W: Auburn/Ft Wayne North KOA▲ /RV Dump, to Indian Springs Resort Campground▲
(123)		**DeKalb Co Rest Area (Both dir)** (RR, Phones) (Closed for renovation)
116		**IN 1N, Dupont Rd, Ft Wayne, Cedarville-Leo, Huntertown**
	Gas	E: Citgo
		W: BP◊, Speedway◊
	Food	E: Burger King, Culver's
		W: Bob Evans, KFC, McDonald's, Mancino's Grinders & Pizza, Subway
	Lodg	E: Comfort Suites
		W: AmericInn, Sleep Inn
	Med	E: + Parkview North Hospital
		W: + Dupont Hospital
	Other	W: ATMs, Banks, Auto Services, Golf Courses, Kroger, Walgreen's
(115)		**Jct I-469S, US 30E, to New Haven, Van Wert, Ohio**
112AB		**IN 327, Coldwater Rd, Ft Wayne (SB)**
	Gas	E: BP◊, Marathon, Max Food Mart
	Food	E: Arby's, AAJ India Rest, Burger King, Cork 'n Cleaver, Don Hall's Factory Rest, Lone Star Steakhouse, Old Country Buffet, Red River Steaks & BBQ, Steak n Shake, Taco Bell, Wendy's, Yokohama Japanese
	Lodg	E: AmeriSuites, Marriott♥
	Other	E: ATMs, Auto Services, Banks, Best Buy, Cinema 8, Dollar Tree, Grocery, Office Depot, NAPA, PetCo♥, Radio Shack, Walgreen's, Wal-Mart sc, Glenbrook Square Mall, U Haul, to Concordia Unlv, IN Purdue Univ, Memorial Coliseum
		W: to appr 13 mi: Indian Springs Resort Campground▲
112A		**IN 327E, Coldwater Rd, Ft Wayne (NB)**
112B		**IN 327W, Coldwater Rd (NB)**
111B		**US 27S, IN 3N, Lima Rd, Ft Wayne, Kendalville**
	Gas	W: BP◊, Marathon, Meijer◊, Sam's
	Food	W: Applebee's, Burger King, Cracker Barrel, IHOP, KFC, Logan's Roadhouse, McDonald's, Mega Wraps, O'Charley's, Starbucks, Subway, Texas Roadhouse
	Lodg	W: AmeriHost Inn, Baymont Inn, Best Value Inn, Candlewood Suites, Courtyard, Days Inn, Dollar Inn, Fairfield Inn, GuestHouse Inn, Hampton Inn, Lee's Inn, Studio Plus

EXIT		
	Other	W: ATMs, Auto Services, Home Depot, Lowe's, Sam's Club, Coleman Camper Center
111A		**US 27S, IN 1S, Lima Rd, to IN 930, Ft Wayne**
	Gas	E: Shell, Speedway
	Food	E: Arby's, Chuck E Cheese, China Express, DQ, Don Pablo, Denny's, Fazoli's, Golden Corral, Hardee's, McDonald's, Starbucks, Subway, Wendy's
	Lodg	E: Residence Inn
	Other	E: ATMs, Auto Dealers, Auto Services, Banks, Discount Tire, Fedex Kinko's, Grocery, Target, Glenbrook Square Mall
109B		**US 30W, US 33N, Ft Wayne, to Columbia City, Elkhart**
	FStop	W: to US 33N, 1mi: Old Fort Travel Plaza/Marathon
	TStop	W: @ NA VanLines: Speed-Ease
	TServ	W: Speed-Ease/Tires
	Other	W: Laundry/Speed-Ease, Tires Plus, U-Haul, to Eel River Campground▲, Blue Lake Campground & Resort▲
109A		**IN 930E, Goshen Rd, Ft Wayne**
	FStop	E: Ray's Truck Wash/Sunoco (Scales)
	TStop	E: Ft Wayne Truck Plaza/Citgo (Scales)
	Gas	E: BP
	Food	E: Rest/McDonald's/Subway/Ft Wayne TP, Liberty Diner, Point Rest
	Lodg	E: Best Inn, Econo Lodge, Knights Inn, Motel 6♥, Quality Inn, Red Roof Inn♥
	TWash	E: Ft Wayne TP, Ray's TW, Blue Beacon
	TServ	E: Clarke Detroit Diesel/Allison, Cummins, Ft Wayne Truck Center/Kenworth, Wise International Trucks
	Med	E: + Hospital
	Other	E: Laundry/BarbSh/CB/WiFi/Ft Wayne TP, Goodyear, FW Childrens Zoo, U-Haul
105B		**IN 14W, Illinois Rd, Ft Wayne, South Whitley**
105A		**Illinois Rd, Ft Wayne**
	Gas	E: BP, Meijer◊, Shell◊, Speedway
	Food	E: Bob Evan's, O'Charley's, Steak 'n Shake, Smokey Bones BBQ, Subway
	Lodg	E: Klopfenstein Inn
	TServ	E: to Discover Volvo Trucks
	Med	E: + St Joseph Hospital
	Other	E: ATMs, Auto Dealers, Auto Services, Animal Hospital♥, Banks, B&N, Best Buy, Dollar Tree, FedEx Kinko's, Grocery, Lowe's, PetSmart♥, Staples, UPS Store, Wal-Mart sc, Jim Bailey's Harley Davidson, Univ of St Francis
102		**US 24W, W Jefferson Blvd, Ft Wayne, Huntington**
	Gas	W: BP, Marathon
	Food	E: Casa D'Angelo, Subway, Taco Bell
		W: Applebee's, Arby's, Bob Evans, Carlos O'Kelly's, Captain D's, McDonald's, Outback Steakhouse, Pizza Hut, Starbucks, Sara's Family Rest, Wendy's
	Lodg	E: Extended Stay America, Hampton Inn, Residence Inn
		W: Best Western, Comfort Suites, Holiday Inn Express, Hilton Garden Inn
	Med	E: + Lutheran Hospital of IN
	Other	W: ATMs, Auto Services, Banks, Grocery, Kroger, UPS Store, Walgreen's, IN State Hwy Patrol Post

EXIT		
99		**Lower Huntington Rd, Ft Wayne**
	Other	E: to Ft Wayne Int'l Airport✈, IN Nat'l Guard, General Mills
		W: GM Truck & Bus Group
96B		**Lafayette Center Rd, to US 24, Roanoke Station, Huntington**
	Other	W: GM Truck & Bus Group
96A		**IN 469N, US 24E, to US 33S, US 27, New Haven, Decatur**
	Other	E: to Ft Wayne Int'l Airport✈, IN Nat'l Guard, General Mills
(91)		**Wells Co Rest Area (SB)** (RR, Phones, Picnic, Vend)
(89)		**Huntington Co Rest Area (NB)** (RR, Phones, Picnic, Vend)
86		**US 224, Markle Rd, Logan Rd, Huntington, Markle**
	Gas	E: Phillips 66, Sunoco
	Food	E: DQ, Pizza, Subway
	Lodg	E: Super 8
	Med	E: + Markle Medical Center
	Other	W: Markle State Rec Area, Little Turtle State Rec Area, Kil-So-Quah State Rec Area
(80)		**Weigh Station (SB)**
78		**IN 5, Warren Rd, Warren**
	TStop	W: Crazy D's (Scales)
	Gas	E: Sunoco◊
	Food	E: Ugalde's Family Rest
		W: Rest/FastFood/Crazy D's, McDonald's
	Lodg	E: Huggy Bear Motel
		W: Comfort Inn, Super 8
	Med	W: + Huntington Memorial Hospital
	Other	E: to appr 13 mi Bluffton/Ft Wayne South KOA▲
		W: Laundry/WiFi/RVDump/Crazy D's
73		**IN 218, IN 5, Warren, La Fontaine**
64		**IN 18, Marion, Montpelier, Roll**
	TStop	E: Love's Travel Stop #323 (Scales)
	Gas	W: BP◊, Marathon
	Food	E: McDonald's/Love's TS
		W: Arby's, Subway
	Med	W: + Hospital
	Other	E: Laundry/WiFi/RVDump/Love's TS, Stone's Harley Davidson, to Ickes RV Surplus Supply, Wildwood Acres Campground
59		**US 35N, IN 22, Gas City, Upland** (Addt'l Serv 3-4mi W-Gas City, E-Upland)
	TStop	W: McClure Oil #59
	Gas	E: Gas City, Village Pantry
		W: Marathon◊, Shell◊
	Food	E: Burger King, Cracker Barrel, Subway
		W: FastFood/McClure Oil, Arby's, McDonald's, KFC/Taco Bell
	Lodg	E: to This Old Barn B&B
		W: Holiday Inn Express
	TServ	E: C&C Truck Service
	Other	E: Sports Lake Campground▲, to Mar-Brook Campground▲
55		**IN 26, Hartford City, Fairmount**
	Gas	W: Marathon
(51)		**Delaware Co Rest Area (Both dir)** (RR, Phones, Picnic, Vend)
45		**US 35S, IN 28, Alexandria, Muncie** (Addt'l Serv 4 mi W in Alexandria)
	TStop	E: Petro Stopping Center #74/Shell (Scales)

◊ = Regular Gas Stations with Diesel   ▲ = RV Friendly Locations   ♥ = Pet Friendly Locations

RED PRINT SHOWS LARGE VEHICLE PARKING/ACCESS ON SITE OR NEARBY   BROWN PRINT SHOWS CAMPGROUNDS/RV PARKS

Page 276

EXIT		INDIANA
	Food	E: IronSkillet/TacoBell/Petro SC
	TServ	E: Petro SC/Tires
	Other	E: Laundry/WiFi/Petro SC, Big Oak Park▲ W: to Hoosierland Park▲
41		IN 332E, Muncie, Frankton (Addt'l Serv 6-7mi E in Muncie)
	Gas	E: Citgo◆
	Med	E: + Ball Memorial Hospital
	Other	E: to Delaware Co Johnson Field✈, Ball State Univ
35		IN 32, Main St, Daleville, Muncie Chesterfield, Anderson
	Gas	E: AmocoBP
	Food	W: BBQ, Café, DQ, Pizza Hut
	Lodg	E: Hampton Inn
	TServ	W: Troy's Truck & Auto Service
	Other	E: Auto Repairs & Towing, Grocery W: to Timberline Campground▲, Mounds State Park▲, Anderson Muni Airport✈, Anderson Univ
34		IN 67N, Commerce Rd, to IN 32, Main St, Daleville, Muncie, Chesterfield
	FStop	W: Gas America #41
	TStop	E: Pilot Travel Center #28 (Scales) W: Pilot Travel Center #446 (Scales)
	Gas	E: Shell
	Food	E: Subway/Pilot TC, FastFood/Shell, Arby's, Burger King, Taco Bell W: Rest/Pilot TC, McDonald's, Wendy's
	Lodg	E: Budget Inn W: Super 8
	TServ	E: Clarke Power Services/Allison, Bigelow Trailer Sales & Service W: Keep it Moving Truck & Trailer
	Other	E: WiFi/Pilot TC W: Laundry/WiFi/Pilot TC, ATMs, Banks, Central IN Auto & RV, Anderson Muni Airport✈, Great American Flea Market, Timberline Family Campground▲, Mounds State Park▲
26		IN 9N, IN 109S, Scatterfield Rd, Anderson, Alliance
	Gas	E: Meijer◆ W: BP, Marathon, Petro Mart◆, Shell
	Food	W: Applebee's, Arby's, Bob Evans, Burger King, Cracker Barrel, Culver's, IHOP, McDonald's, Little Caesars, Lone Star Steakhouse, Perkins, Pizza Hut, Red Lobster, Ruby Tuesday, Steak 'n Shake, Taco Bell, Waffle & Steak, Wendy's
	Lodg	E: Hampton Inn, Quality Inn W: America's Best Inn♥, Baymont Inn, Comfort Inn, Days Inn, Econo Lodge, Fairfield Inn, Holiday Inn, Lee's Inn, Motel 6♥, Super 8
	TServ	W: Stoops Freightliner
	Med	W: + Community Hospital
	Other	W: ATMs, Auto Services, Auto Dealer, Grocery, Radio Shack, Target, Tires, Wal-Mart, to Mounds State Park▲
22		IN 67S, IN 9S, Pendleton Ave, Anderson, Pendleton
	Gas	W: Gas America
	Food	W: Red Brick Inn Rest, Yesterday DriveIn
	Lodg	W: Anderson Country Inn♥
	Other	W: Modern Trailer Sales
19		IN 38, Pendleton, Clarksville (Addtl Serv E to IN 67)
	Gas	E: Marathon
	Food	E: DQ, McDonald's, Subway

EXIT		INDIANA
	Other	W: to Pine Lake Camping & Fishing▲
14		IN 13, Pendleton, Lapel, Fortville
	TStop	W: Pilot Travel Center #362 (Scales)
	Food	W: Subway/Pilot TC
	Other	W: WiFi/Pilot TC, to Glo Wood Campground▲
10		IN 238, Greenfield Ave, Olio Rd, Noblesville, Fortville
	Med	E: + Hospital
6		IN 37N, Noblesville (NB)
	Gas	E: Shell
	Food	E: Blimpie, Chinese, Wendy's
5		IN 37N, 116th St, Fishers
	Gas	W: Shell, Speedway
	Food	W: BBQ, Hardee's, KFC, McDonald's, O'Charley's, Quiznos, Steak n Shake, Starbucks, Wendy's
	Lodg	W: Hampton Inn
	Other	W: ATMs, Auto Service, Target, Visitor Info, Police Dept, Cruise America RV Rental
3		96th St, Fishers, Indianapolis
	Gas	E: Meijer◆, Shell, Stop n Go, Murphy W: Marathon, Sam's
	Food	E: Applebee's, Blimpie, Cracker Barrel, Hardee's, McDonald's, Panera Bread, Qdoba Mex Rest, Ruby Tuesday, Steak 'n Shake, Starbucks, Wendy's W: Arby's, Bob Evans, Burger King, Culver's, Panda Express, Quiznos, Taco Bell
	Lodg	E: Hilton Garden Inn, Holiday Inn Express, Sleep Inn W: Comfort Suites♥, Residence Inn, Ramada Inn, Staybridge Suites, Studio 6
	Other	E: ATMs, Banks, Cinema, Grocery, Pep Boys, PetCo♥, Radio Shack, Staples, Wal-Mart sc W: Auto Services, Dollar Tree, Goodyear, Home Depot, NAPA, Sam's Club, PFM Car & Truck Care, Golf Course, Indianapolis Metro Airport✈
1		82nd St, Castleton, Indianapolis
	Gas	E: BP, Shell, Speedway
	Food	E: Golden Corral, Pizza Hut W: Arby's, Burger King, Checkers, Cancun Mexican, Denny's, KFC, Hooters, Max & Erma's, McDonald's, Olive Garden, On the Border, Outback Steakhouse, Pizza Hut, Perkins, Red Lobster, Skyline Chili, Steak n Shake, Starbucks, Taco Bell, Tony Roma, Tuscany Italian Grill, Wendy's
	Lodg	E: Country Inn, Dollar Inn, Hilton, Super 8 W: Best Western♥, Candlewood Suites, Days Inn, Fairfield Inn, Hampton Inn, Red Roof Inn
	Med	E: + Community Hospital North, + Urgent Care Center
	Other	E: CVS, Lowe's, Walgreen's W: AMC Cinema, ATMs, Auto Services, Avis RAC, Banks, Best Buy, Costco, Discount Tire, Firestone, Goodyear, Kroger, National RAC, PetSmart♥, Tires, Target, Vet♥, Castleton Square Mall, Convention Center, Golf Course
(0)		Jct I-465, Indianapolis ByPass, IN 37, Binford Dr, Lawrence (I-69 Begins/ends on I-465, Exits #37AB) (EASTERN TIME ZONE)

🎧 INDIANA

Begin Northbound I-69 from Indianapolis, IN
Port Huron, MI.

◆ = Regular Gas Stations with Diesel   ▲ = RV Friendly Locations   ♥ = Pet Friendly Locations
RED PRINT SHOWS LARGE VEHICLE PARKING/ACCESS ON SITE OR NEARBY   BROWN PRINT SHOWS CAMPGROUNDS/RV PARKS

Interstate 70 E

EXIT	UTAH
	Begin Eastbound I-70 at Jct I-15, near Cove Fort, UT to Baltimore, MD.
	UTAH (MOUNTAIN TIME ZONE) (I-70 Begins/Ends on I-15, Exit #132)
(0)	Jct I-15, N to Salt Lake City, S to St George, to AZ, to NV
1	UT 161, Fillmore, Historic Cove Fort (Chain-Up Area)
Other	N: Paiute Indian Reservation
8	Ranch Exit, Sevier
(13)	Brake Check Area (EB)
(16)	RunAway Truck Ramp (EB)
17	Kimberly Rd, Sevier, Fremont Indian State Park (Chain-Up Area)
Other	N: Fremont Indian Museum
23	US 89S, Sevier, to Marysvale, Panguitch, Kanab, Bryce Canyon
Other	S: to Lizzie & Charlie's RV/ATV Park▲, Bryce Canyon National Park
25	UT 118, to US 89, Joseph, Monroe
Gas	S: Flying U Country Store◆
Food	S: Rest/Flying U CS
Other	S: Flying U Country Store Campground & RV Park▲, to Mystic Hot Springs▲
31	UT 258, Monroe, Elsinore
37	I-70 Lp, UT 120, S Main St, Richfield
Gas	S: Phillips 66◆, JR Munchie's/Conoco◆, Tesoro◆
Food	S: Burger King, McDonald's, Wendy's/P66
Lodg	S: Budget Host Inn, Days Inn, Quality Inn, Travelodge
Other	S: Albertson's, Auto Service, Wal-Mart sc, Kmart, Vet♥, Richfield Muni Airport✈, Cove View Golf Course, Richfield KOA▲, JR Munchies Campground▲, UT State Hwy Patrol
40	I-70 Lp, UT 120, Main St, Richfield
FStop	S: Top Stop/Sinclair
TStop	S: Flying J Travel Plaza #11186
Gas	S: Chevron, Shell
Food	S: Rest/FJ TP, Arby's, Burger King, Garden Grill, R & R Frontier Village, Subway
Lodg	S: Apple Tree Inn, Best Western♥, Days Inn, Microtel, Super 8
Med	S: + Sevier Valley Hospital
Other	S: WiFi/RVDump/LP/FJ TP, Pearson Tire, ATMs, Albertson's, Auto Dealers, Auto Repairs, Big O Tires, Family Dollar, NAPA, UPS Store, Red Hills Truck & Auto Repair, Richfield KOA▲

EXIT	UTAH
48	UT 259, Old Hwy 89 to UT 24, to US 50, Richfield, Sigurd, Aurora
NOTE:	EB: Gas Check! Next Fuel x #160
56	State St, I-70 Bus, US 89N, to US 50, Salina, to Reno, Salt Lake City
FStop	N: Salina Express/Sinclair
TStop	N: Scenic Quik Stop/66
Gas	N: Conoco, Maverik, Sinclair◆
Food	N: Rest/Quik Stop, BurgerKing/Sinclair, Denny's, El Mexicano Rest, Subway,
Lodg	N: Best Western, Rodeway Inn, Ranch Motel, Super 8
Other	N: Laundry/QuikStop, Auto Repairs, CarQuest, Grocery, U-Haul, Butch Cassidy Campground▲, Salina Creek RV Campground▲
61	Gooseberry Rd, Salina
NOTE:	MM 69: Summit Elev 7076'
72	Ranch Exit
NOTE:	MM 83.5: Summit Elev 7923'
(84)	Ivie Creek Rest Area (WB) (RR, Picnic, Info)
86	UT 72, Loa, Capital Reef Nat'l Park
91	UT 72, UT 10, Salina, to Emery, Huntington
97	Ranch Exit
(102)	Salt Wash View Area (Both dir) (RR, Info)
108	Ranch Exit
(114)	Devil's Canyon View Area (EB) (RR) Eagle Canyon View Area (WB) (RR, Info)
116	Moore Cutoff, Moore
(120)	Ghost Rocks View Area (Both dir) (RR, Info)
131	Ranch Exit
(136)	Brake Check Area (EB)
(139)	RunAway Truck Ramp (EB)
(141)	Black Dragon View Area (EB) San Rafael View Area (WB) (RR, Info)
(141)	RunAway Truck Ramp (EB)

EXIT	UTAH
(144)	Spotted Wolf View Area (WB) (RR)
149	UT 24, Hanksville, Lake Powell, to Capital Reef Nat'l Park, Bryce Canyon Nat'l Park
157	US 6W, US 191N, to Price, Salt Lake
160	I-70 Bus (EB), UT 19, W Main St, Green River (Access to #164 Serv)
TStop	N: PTP/Gas n Go #13/Conoco
Gas	N: Chevron◆
Food	N: Arby's/Gas n Go, Burger King, Subway/Chevron, Ben's Café, Ray's Rest, Tamarisk Rest
Lodg	N: Budget Inn, Robbers Roost Motel, Rodeway Inn, Sleepy Hollow Motel
Other	N: Laundry/Gas n Go, Amtrak, Museum, Auto Service, US Post Office, Green River Golf Course, AmeriGas Propane/LP, Green River State Park, A OK RV Park▲, Shady Acres RV Park & Campground▲ /Silver Eagle Gas & Diesel/Blimpie
164	UT 19, I-70 Bus (WB), E Main St, Green River (Access to #160 Serv)
TStop	N: AmBest/West Winds Truck Stop/Sinclair (Scales)
Gas	N: Short Stop◆
Food	N: Rest/West Winds TS, Burger King, Rest/Book Cliff Lodge, Tamarisk Rest
Lodg	N: Motel/West Winds TS, Best Western, Book Cliff Lodge, Comfort Inn, Holiday Inn Express♥, Motel 6, Ramada Ltd♥, Super 8♥
TWash	N: West Winds TS
TServ	N: West Winds TS/Tires/RV Repair
Other	N: Laundry/RVDump/LP/West Winds TS, Green River KOA▲, Shady Acres RV Park & Campground▲ /Silver Eagle Gas & Diesel/Blimpie, Museum, Green River State Park
NOTE:	WB: GAS Check! Next Fuel x #56
175	Ranch Exit
(180)	Crescent Jct Rest Area (EB) (RR, Phone, Picnic)
182	US 191, Crescent Jct, to Moab
Other	S: to appr 30mi: Arches National Park, Canyonlands National Park, Dead Horse Point State Park, (Numerous Campgrounds & RV Parks)
187	Sego Canyon Rd, to UT 94, Thompson, to Thompson Springs
FStop	N: Outwest Food n Food #34/Shell

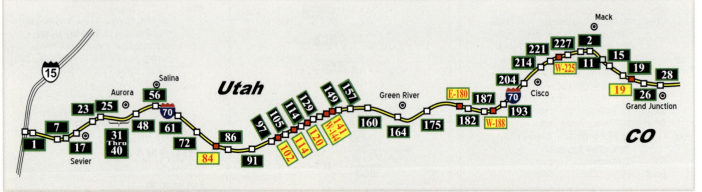

◆ = Regular Gas Stations with Diesel ▲ = RV Friendly Locations ♥ = Pet Friendly Locations
RED PRINT SHOWS LARGE VEHICLE PARKING/ACCESS ON SITE OR NEARBY   BROWN PRINT SHOWS CAMPGROUNDS/RV PARKS

EXIT		UT / CO
(188)		UT Thompson Welcome Center (WB) (RR, Phone, Picnic, Vending, Info)
193		Ranch Exit
204		UT 128, US 6 Bus, to Cisco
214		US 6 Bus, Thompson, to Cisco
221		Ranch Exit
(226)		Harley Dome View Area (WB) (RR)
227		Hay Canyon Rd, to US 6 Bus, Thompson, Westwater
	NOTE:	MM 232: Colorado State Line

(MOUNTAIN TIME ZONE)

⋂ UTAH
⋃ COLORADO
(MOUNTAIN TIME ZONE)

2		to Rabbit Valley Rd, Mack
11		US 6E, US 50, Loma, Mack
(14)		Loma Weigh Station (Both dir)
15		CO 139N, 13 Rd, Loma, Rangely
	Other	N: to James Hutton Truck Repair, Highline State Rec Area▲
19		CO 340, to US 6, US 50, Fruita
	S:	CO Welcome Center (Both dir) (RR, Phones, Picnic, Info, RVDump)
	TStop	S: Loco Travel Stop #17/Conoco
	Gas	N: BP, Conoco S: Shell◆
	Food	N: Burger King, Munchies Pizza, Mex Rest S: Rest/SubwayLoco TS, Wendy's/Shell, Chinese Rest, McDonald's, Pablo's Pizza Rib City Grill, Taco Bell
	Lodg	N: Balanced Rock Hotel S: Comfort Inn, La Quinta Inn♥, Super 8
	Med	S: + St Mary's Hospital
	Other	N: ATMs, Auto Services, Banks, CarQuest, Grocery, NAPA, US Post Office S: Laundry/LP/Loco TS, Dinosaur Journey, Adobe Creek Nat'l Golf Course, Monument RV Resort▲, to CO Nat'l Monument, CO River State Park
26		I-70 Bus, US 6, US 50E, 22 Road, Grand Junction, Delta, Montrose (Addt'l Serv 3- 5mi S in Grand Junction)
	TStop	S: Acorn Travel Plaza #2330/Conoco
	Food	S: FastFood/Acorn TP, Rest/Westgate Inn
	Lodg	S: West Gate Inn
	TServ	S: Transwest Trucks
	Other	N: Junction West RV Park▲ S: Laundry/WiFi/Acorn TP, Mobile City RV Park▲, to Auto Dealers, ATMs, Banks, Auto Services, Mesa Mall, Big J RV Park▲, Bob Scott RV's, Centennial RV, Gibson RV's, to Grand Junction KOA▲
28		24 Rd, Redlands Pkwy, Grand Jct
	Gas	S: Stop N Save
	Food	S: Black Bear Diner, IHOP, Olive Garden
	Lodg	S: Holiday Inn Express
	TServ	N: MHC Kenworth
	Other	S: ATMs, Auto Services, Banks, Mesa Mall, Museums, Rental Cars
31		Horizon Dr, Grand Junction
	Gas	N: Shamrock, Shell◆ S: Conoco◆, Phillips 66◆

Personal Notes

EXIT		COLORADO
	Food	N: CoCo's, Peppers, Shake, Rattle & Roll Diner, Wendy's S: Applebee's, Burger King, Denny's, Pizza Hut, Shanghai Garden Rest, Subway, Taco Bell, Rest/DblTree
	Lodg	N: Best Value Inn, Comfort Inn, Grand Vista Hotel, Holiday Inn, La Quinta Inn♥, Ramada Inn, Residence Inn S: Best Western, Budget Host, Country Inn, DoubleTree Hotel, Mesa Inn, Quality Inn, Super 8
	Med	S: + St Mary's Hospital, + VA Med Ctr
	Other	N: Avis RAC, Budget RAC, Hertz RAC, US Post Office, Walker Field✈, Grand Jct Harley Davidson S: ATMs, Auto Services, Banks, Safeway, Mesa State College, BLM/Nat'l Forest Info
37		I-70W Bus, to CO 141, US 6, US 50E, Clifton, Grand Junction, Delta
	Gas	S: Conoco◆, Shamrock, Phillips 66, Shell
	Food	S: Burger King, Captain D's, KFC, McDonald's, Pizza Hut, Subway, Taco Bell, Texas Roadhouse, Village Inn
	Lodg	S: Best Western
	Other	S: ATMs, Albertson's, Auto Services, Auto Zone, Big Lots, Banks, Discount Tire, Family Dollar, Grocery, Kmart, Walgreen's, Wal-Mart sc, A1 Truck Repair, RV Ranch @ Grand Junction▲, to Grand Junction KOA▲, Big J RV Park▲
42		37 3/10 Rd, to US 6, Palisade (Gas, Food, Lodg S to US 6/8th St)
44		I-70W Bus, US 6W, to Palisade (Access to Ex #42 Serv 3-4 mi S)

EXIT		COLORADO
46		Cameo
47		Island Acres, CO River State Park
	FStop	S: Diamond Shamrock #4062
	Food	S: Rest/Shamrock
	Other	N: CO River State Park S: Laundry/Shamrock
49		CO 65S, De Beque, to CO 330E, Grand Mesa, Collbran
	Other	S: to Sundance RV Camp▲, to Powderhorn Ski Area
(50)		Parking Area (EB)
62		45 1/2 Rd, De Beque
	Other	N: to Canyon Lake Campground▲
75		CR 300, CR 215, Parachute, Battlement Mesa
	N:	Parachute Rest Area (Both dir) (RR, Phones, Picnic, Info)
	FStop	N: Shell Food Mart
	Gas	N: Sinclair◆ S: Conoco◆
	Food	N: El Rio Café, Dragon Treasure Chinese, Hong's Garden, Outlaws Rest, Subway, Sunrise Scramble S: Wendy's/Conoco
	Lodg	N: Super 8 S: Holiday Inn Express
	Other	N: Laundry/Shell FM, NAPA, Radio Shack, US Post Office S: to Battlement Mesa RV Park▲
81		CR 323, Rulison Rd, Rulison
87		to CO 13N, US 6E, US 24, Meeker, to West Rifle (Acc #90 Serv/ Gas, Food, Lodg 2-3mi)
90		CO 13N, CR 346, Airport Rd, Rifle, Meeker
	N:	Rifle Rest Area (Both dir) (RR, Phones, Vend, Picnic, Info, RVDump)
	Gas	N: AmocoBP, Kum & Go, Phillips 66◆ S: Conoco◆, Phillips 66◆
	Food	N: Base Camp Café, Pam's Country Cooking, Outlaws Rest, Texas Mesquite BBQ, The HideOut S: Burger King, Domino's, McDonald's, Subway, Sonic, Rest/Red River Inn
	Lodg	N: Buckskin Inn♥, Winchester Motel S: Grand Timber Lodge, La Quinta Inn♥, Red River Inn, Rusty Cannon Motel
	Med	S: + Grand River Medical Center
	Other	N: ATMs, Banks, Advanced Auto & Truck Service, Auto Service/AmocoBP, Auto Services, Cinema, Grocery, Pharmacy, Towing, Towing/Conoco, to Rifle Gap State Park▲ S: Auto Services, Silver Spur Outfitters, Auto Repairs, Thrifty RAC, Garfield Co Reg'l Airport✈, Wal-Mart sc, Vet♥
94		CR 315, Mamm Creek Rd, Garfield Co Airport Rd (Acc to #90 Serv)
	Other	S: Garfield Co Reg'l Airport✈
97		9th St, I-70 Bus, US 24, US 6, Silt
	Gas	N: Conoco◆, Kum & Go, Phillips 66
	Food	N: Miners Claim Rest, Silt Cafe
	Lodg	N: Red River Inn
	Other	N: to Harvey Gap State Park S: Heron's Nest/Viking RV Park▲

◆ = Regular Gas Stations with Diesel   ▲ = RV Friendly Locations   ♥ = Pet Friendly Locations

RED PRINT SHOWS LARGE VEHICLE PARKING/ACCESS ON SITE OR NEARBY   BROWN PRINT SHOWS CAMPGROUNDS/RV PARKS

EXIT	COLORADO
105	CR 240, to US 6, US 24, Bruce Rd, New Castle
Gas	N: Conoco◊, Kum & Go, Sinclair S: Phillips 66
Food	N: Hong's Garden Chinese, New Castle Diner, Subway
Lodg	N: Rodeway Inn
Other	N: Grocery, Pharmacy, Bowling, Auto Service, to Elk Creek Campground▲
(107)	Parking Area (EB)
109	US 6W, US 24, New Castle, Canyon Creek, Chacra
111	CR 134, S Canyon Creek Rd, to US 6, US 24, Glenwood Springs
114	Mel Ray Rd, US 6, US 24, W Glenwood, Glenwood Springs
TStop	N: Tomahawk Auto Truck Plaza/Amoco
Gas	N: 7-11, Shell S: Conoco◊, Kum & Go◊
Food	N: Burger King, DQ, High Noon, Hombres Mexican, Fireside Family Steakhouse, Los Desperados, Marshall Dillons Steakhouse, Taco John's, Ocean Pearl Chinese
Lodg	N: Affordable Inn, Best Value Inn, Budget Host Motel, First Choice Inn, Red Mountain Inn S: Quality Inn
Other	N: Laundry/LP/Tomahawk ATP, ATMs, Auto Dealers, Auto Repairs, Banks, Big O Tire, Kmart, Radio Shack, Staples, Tires, Vet♥, Taylors Auto & RV Center, Glenwood Springs Mall, Glenwood Springs Golf Course, to Ami's Acres Campground▲
(115)	W Glenwood Spgs Rest Area (EB) (RR, Picnic)
116	River Dr, 6th St, CO 82E, Grand Ave, Glenwood Springs, Aspen
NOTE:	CO 82, Independence Pass, No Vehicles Over 35' / CLOSED each winter
Gas	N: BPAmoco, Conoco◊, Shell◊ S: 7-11, Conoco, Phillips 66◊, Sinclair
Food	N: KFC, Pizza Hut, Smoking Willie's BBQ, Subway, Village Inn S: Arby's, Glenwood Canyon Brewing Co, Glenwood Café, Juicy Lucy's Steakhouse, McDonald's, Ron's Rib Shack, Sushi Bar, Starbucks, Taco Bell, Wendy's
Lodg	N: Best Western, Glenwood Motor Inn, Hampton Inn, Holiday Inn Express, Hot Springs Lodge, Ramada Inn, Starlight Lodge Motel, Silver Spruce Motel♥

EXIT	COLORADO
Lodg	S: Best Value Inn, Hotel Denver, Western Hotel
Med	S: + Valley View Hospital
Other	N: Auto Dealers, ATMs, Greyhound, Glenwood Caverns, Glenwood Hot Springs, Yampah Spa & Vapor Caves, Yampa Hot Springs S: ATMs, Auto Services, Amtrak, Banks, Cinema, Grocery, Goodyear, Good Health Store, NAPA, Museum, RiteAid, Tires, Wal-Mart, Vet♥, Aspen Valley Harley Davidson, CO State Hwy Patrol Post, Sheriff Dept, Glenwood Springs Muni Airport✈, to Aspen, Snowmass, Buttermilk, Sunlight Mtn Ski Areas
(117)	No Name Tunnel
NOTE:	MM 117-129: Vehicles Over 10,000 lbs GVW: NO PASSING, Use Right Lane next 12 miles.
119	CR 129, No Name Exit, Glenwood Springs Rest Area (Both dir) (RR, Phones, Picnic, RVCamping)
Other	N: Glenwood Canyon Resort/Whitewater Rafting/Cabins/CO RV Park▲
121	Grizzly Creek, to Hanging Lake S: Grizzly Creek Rest Area (Both dir) (RR, Picnic)
123	Shoshone (EB, No EB reaccess)
Other	S: CO River Raft Access
125	Hanging Lake (No EB reaccess) Hanging Lk Rest Area (Both dir) (RR, Phones, Picnic)
(125)	Hanging Lake Tunnel
(127)	Reverse Curve Tunnel (WB)
(128)	Parking Area (EB)
129	Bair Ranch S: Bair Ranch Rest Area (Both dir) (NO Vehicles Over 35') (RR, Phones, Picnic)
NOTE:	MM 117-129: Vehicles Over 10,000 lbs GVW, NO PASSING, Use Right Lane Next 12 miles
133	CO River Rd, Dotsero, Gypsum
Other	N: to River Dance RV Resort▲, Deep Creek, BLM/Eagle River Rec Areas
140	US 6E, Trail Gulch Rd, Gypsum
Gas	S: Phillips 66◊
Food	S: Mexican Café, Pizza, Manuelito's
TServ	S: Jerry's Auto & Truck Repair
Other	S: Eagle Co Reg'l Airport✈, Rental Cars

EXIT	COLORADO
147	I-70 Bus, Eby Creek Rd, Eagle
S:	Rest Area (Both dir) (RR, Info)
FStop	S: AmocoBP
Gas	N: Shamrock◊ S: Conoco◊
Food	N: Burger King, McDonald's, Taco Bell/Shamrock S: Eagle Diner, Subway/BP, Wendy's
Lodg	N: AmericInn, Comfort Inn, Holiday Inn Express S: Best Western, Suburban Lodge
Other	S: ATMs, Auto Services, Banks, Grocery, Carwash, Museum, US Post Office, to Sylvan Lake State Park▲
157	CO 131N, Eagle, to Wolcott, Steamboat Springs
Other	N: to Steamboat Springs Ski Area
(160)	Parking Area (Both dir)
163	I-70 Bus, Edwards Access Rd, Edwards
S:	Edwards Rest Area (Both dir) (RR, Phones, Picnic, RVDump)
Gas	S: Conoco, Shell
Food	S: Fiesta's, Gashouse, Main St Grill, Subway, Starbucks, Wendy's
Lodg	S: Riverwalk Inn, Seven Lakes Lodge
Other	S: ATMs, Banks, Auto Service, to Arrowhead Ski Area
167	Avon Rd, Avon, Beaver Creek, Arrowhead, Nottingham Rd
Gas	N: Conoco, Phillips 66
Food	N: Pizza Hut S: Burger King, Coyote Café, Denny's, Domino's, Quizno's, Starbucks, Subway
Lodg	S: Beaver Creek West Condos, Comfort Inn, Christie Lodge, Sheraton, Seasons at Avon, Vail Beaver Creek Resort
Med	S: + Avon Medical Center
Other	N: Auto & Tire Service S: ATMs, Banks, Grocery, Pharmacy, Wal-Mart sc, Tourist Info, Beaver Creek Golf Course, Beaver Creek Ski Area
168	William J Post Blvd, Avon (Access to #167 Serv)
169	US 6, Eagle, Vail (WB) (Access to #167 Serv)
171	US 24E, US 6W, Minturn, Leadville (Gas, Food & Lodging 3mi+ S)
Other	S: to Leadville Corral RV Park▲
173	Frontage Rd, W Entrance, Vail
Gas	N: 7-11, Phillips 66, Shell◊ S: Conoco◊

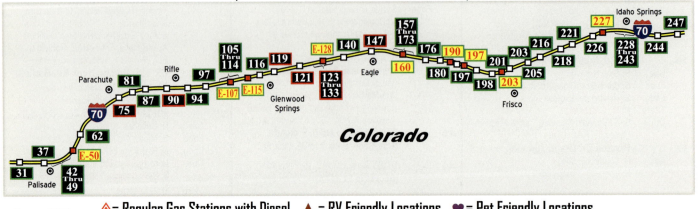

◊ = Regular Gas Stations with Diesel ▲ = RV Friendly Locations ♥ = Pet Friendly Locations
RED PRINT SHOWS LARGE VEHICLE PARKING/ACCESS ON SITE OR NEARBY   BROWN PRINT SHOWS CAMPGROUNDS/RV PARKS

INTERSTATE W 70 E — COLORADO

EXIT		COLORADO
	Food	N: McDonald's, Subway, Wendy's
	Lodg	N: Holiday Inn, Roost Lodge, West Vail Lodge, WildRidge Inn S: Marriott Streamside, Savory Inn, Vail Cascade Condos
	Other	N: Grocery, Pharmacy, Safeway S: Repairs/Conoco, Vet ♥
176		**Frontage Rd, Spraddlecreek Rd, Vail Rd, Vail, Lions Head**
	Gas	S: Amoco ◊, BP
	Food	S: La Cantina, Marble Slab Creamery, Mirabella Rest, Ore House Rest, Osaki Sushi Japanese Rest, Russell's Rest, Sweet Basil Rest, Terra Bistro
	Lodg	N: Wren Hotel S: Austria Haus Hotel, Evergreen Lodge, Holiday Inn, Lodge at Vail, Sitzmark Lodge, Vail Village Inn, Best Western
	Med	S: + Vail Valley Medical Center
	Other	S: ATMs, Grocery, Greyhound, Museums, Pharmacy, Tourist Info
180		**Bighorn Rd, Frontage Rd, East Entrance, Vail**
(183)		**RunAway Truck Ramp (WB)**
(186)		**RunAway Truck Ramp (WB)**
NOTE:		WB: MM 189-181: 7% STEEP GRADE next 8 mi. Trucks Over 30,000#: Speed Limit 45mph
(189)		**Truck Brake Check Area (Both dir)** **TRUCK Parking Area (Both dir)**
NOTE:		EB: MM 195-190: STEEP GRADE
(190)		**Vail Pass Rest Area (Both dir)** **(RR, Phones, Picnic)**
195		**CO 91S, Copper Rd, Wheeler Jct, Copper Mountain, Dillon, Frisco, to Leadville**
	Gas	S: Conoco ◊
	Food	S: Alexanders on the Creek, Blue Moose Pizza, Columbine Café, Creekside Café, Imperial Palace Chinese Rest
	Lodg	S: Copper Mtn Resort, Copper Springs Lodge, Foxpine Inn
	Other	S: to Ski Cooper, Copper Mtn Ski Area
(197)		**Parking Area (Both dir)**
198		**Officers Gulch, Dillon**
201		**Main St, to Summit Blvd, Frisco to CO 9S, Breckenridge (EB only)**
	Gas	S: Conoco
	Food	S: Backcountry Brewery, Claim Jumper Rest, Country Kitchen, Farley's Chop House, KFC, Log Cabin Café, Pizza Hut, Subway, TCBY, Woody's
	Lodg	S: 1899 B&B, Blue Spruce Inn, Cedar Lodge, Cross Creek Resort, Frisco Lodge, Hotel Frisco CO ♥, Sky-Vue Motel, Snowshoe Motel
	Other	S: Big O Tire, Grocery, NAPA, Wal-Mart, Alpine Natural Foods, to Frisco Nordic Rec Area, Peninsula Rec Area, Tiger Run RV Resort ▲
203		**CO 9S, Summit Blvd, Frisco, Breckenridge**
	Gas	S: 7-11, Conoco, Shamrock, Shell

Personal Notes

EXIT		COLORADO
	Food	S: Chili Parlor, Claim Jumper, KFC, Country Kitchen, Pizza Hut, Smoking Willie's BBQ, Starbucks, Subway, Taco Bell, Whiskey Creek, Rest/Hol Inn
	Lodg	S: Alpine Inn, Best Western, Holiday Inn ♥, Ramada Ltd ♥, Summit Inn
	Med	S: + Frisco Medical Center
	Other	S: ATMs, Auto Services, Banks, Big O Tire, Discount Tire, Laundromat, NAPA, Pharmacy, Radio Shack, Safeway, Wal-Mart, Towing/Shell, White Water Rafting, to Tiger Run RV Resort ▲
(203)		**Parking Area (Both dir)**
205		**CO 9N, US 6E, Blue River Pkwy, Silverthorne, Dillon**
NOTE:		EB: Haz-Mat-Mandatory Exit, NO Haz-Mat on EB I-70
	Gas	N: 7-11, Conoco, Shell ◊ S: Shamrock, Phillips 66, Tesoro
	Food	N: Burger King, Denny's, Old Chicago, Quiznos, Old Dillon Inn Mexican, Village Inn, Wendy's S: Arby's, DQ, Dragon Chinese, BBQ, Pizza Hut, Ruby Tuesday, Starbucks, Subway
	Lodg	N: Days Inn ♥, Hampton Inn, Howard Johnson, La Quinta Inn ♥, Luxury Inn ♥, Quality Inn, Sheraton, Alpine Hutte Lodge, Mountain Vista B&B, First Interstate Inn S: Comfort Suites, Dillon Inn, Super 8, Days Inn, Best Western ♥
	Other	N: Auto Dealers, Greyhound, to White River Nat'l Forest ▲

EXIT		COLORADO
	Other	S: ATMs, Laundromat, Grocery, Outlets at Silverthorne, to Keystone, Arapahoe Basin Ski Area
(209)		**RunAway Truck Ramp (WB)**
(212)		**RunAway Truck Ramp (WB)**
NOTE:		WB: MM 213-205: 7% Steep Grade next 8 mi, Trucks Over 30000# GVW, Speed Limit of 30mph.
(213)		**Truck Brake Check Area (Both dir)** **TRUCK Parking Area (Both dir)**
NOTE:		MM **213-215** Eisenhower / Johnson Memorial Tunnel (Elev 11158'- highest point along the interstate hwy system)
NOTE:		Haz-Mat & Vehicles Over 13'11, MUST Use Loveland Pass
NOTE:		MM **214** Pacific/Atlantic Continental Divide
(215)		**Truck Brake Check Area (Both dir)** **TRUCK Parking Area (Both dir)**
216		**US 6W, Loveland Pass**
NOTE:		WB: Haz-Mat-Mandatory Exit, NO Haz-Mat on EB I-70
	Other	S: to Loveland Valley, Loveland Basin, Arapahoe Basin, Keystone Ski Areas
218		**Herman Gulch Rd, Idaho Springs**
221		**CR 321, CR 302, Stevens Gulch Rd, Bakerville, Idaho Springs**
NOTE:		EB: MM 226-229: 6% STEEP GRADE next 3 mi. Trucks Over 25,000# GVW: Speed Limit 45mph, Must Use Right Ln
226		**Woodward Ave, Silver Plume**
	Gas	N: Buckley Bros
	Lodg	N: Brewery Inn
	Other	N: US Post Office
(227)		**Overlook Pull Out (Both dir)**
228		**15th St, Georgetown**
	Gas	S: Conoco, Phillips 66, Shamrock ◊
	Food	S: New Peking Garden, Mountainbuzz Café, Happy Cooker, Subway
	Lodg	S: All Aboard Inn, Georgetown Mountain Inn ♥, Super 8
	Other	S: US Post Office
232		**US 40W, to Empire, Granby (WB: to Salt Lake City via I-70 or US 40)**
	Other	N: to Rocky Mtn Nat'l Park, Winter Park/ Mary Jane, SolVista Ski Areas
233		**Alvarado Rd, Lawson (EB)**
234		**Stanley Rd, CR 308, Downieville, Dumont, Lawson** **Dumont Weigh Station (Both dir)**
	TStop	N: Downieville Fuel Stop/Conoco/LP
	Food	N: FastFood/Downieville FS, Burger King, Starbucks
235		**CR 308, Stanley Rd, Dumont (WB)**
238		**Fall River Rd, CR 275, St Mary's Glacier, Alice**
239		**Stanley Rd, to I-70E Bus, Idaho Springs**
	Gas	N: BP, Phillips 66
	Lodg	N: Blair Motel

◊ = Regular Gas Stations with Diesel ▲ = RV Friendly Locations ♥ = Pet Friendly Locations

RED PRINT SHOWS LARGE VEHICLE PARKING/ACCESS ON SITE OR NEARBY BROWN PRINT SHOWS CAMPGROUNDS/RV PARKS

Page 281

EXIT	COLORADO
240	CO 103, 13th Ave, Idaho Springs, Mount Evans, Golden
Gas	N: Shell, Sinclair
Food	N: Two Bros Deli, McDonald's, Main St Rest, Picci's Pizzeria, Skipper's Ice Cream
Lodg	N: Hanson Lodge, Miners Pick B&B S: Baxter's on the Creek, Indian Springs Resort, Inn at Chicago Creek
Other	N: ATMs, Laundromat S: to Mt Evans, Nat'l Forest Info, Scenic Byway to CO 5, Mt Evans Hwy-Highest US Auto Road
241AB	I-70W Bus, Colorado Blvd, Frontage Rd, CR 314, Idaho Springs
Gas	N: 7-11, BP, Phillips 66, Shell
Food	N: A&W, AJ's Mex Rest, Cherry Blossom Asian Rest, Grampa's Shack, Hilldaddy's Wildfire Rest, King's, McDonald's, Marion's, Subway, Taco Bell
Lodg	N: 6&40 National 9 Inn, Columbine Inn, H&H Motor Lodge, Heritage Inn, Idaho Springs Motel, JC Suites, Peoriana Motel
Other	N: ATMs, Auto Services, Pharmacy, Safeway, US Post Office
(242)	Twin Tunnels
243	Frontage Rd, Central City Pkwy, Hidden Valley, Central City
244	US 6E, US 40, Evergreen, to CO 119, to Golden (EB, Left exit)
NOTE:	WB: MM 246-244: 6% STEEP GRADE next 3 mi. Trucks Over 25,000# GVW: Speed Limit 45mph.
247	Beaver Brook, Floyd Hill (EB)
248	CR 65, Beaver Brook, Floyd Hill (WB)
251	El Rancho, to CO 74S, Evergreen Pkwy (EB)
252	CO 74S, Evergreen Pkwy, El Rancho, Bergen Park, Evergreen (WB)
Gas	S: Conoco
Food	S: Burger King, El Rancho Rest, McDonald's, Subway
Lodg	S: Quality Suites
Other	S: Big O Tire, Home Depot, Wal-Mart
253	Genesee Dr, Chief Hosa, Golden
Other	S: Chief Hosa Lodge & Campground▲
NOTE:	EB: MM 254-259: 6% STEEP GRADE next 6 mi. Trucks Over 30,000# GVW: Speed Limit 35 mph, Must Use Low Gear & Right Lane
(254)	Overlook Pull Out (Both dir)
254	Mt Vernon Country Club Rd, Genesee Park, Lookout Mountain
Gas	S: Conoco
Food	S: Chart House Rest, Genesee Town Café & Pizza
Other	S: LP/Conoco, US Post Office
256	CO 45, US 40, Lookout Mountain, Mother Cabrini Shrine Rd
Other	N: to William Buffalo Bill Cody Grave & Museum, Mother Cabrini Shrine
(257)	RunAway Truck Ramp (EB)
259	I-70E Bus, US 40, Colfax Ave, CO 26, CR 93, Golden, Morrison
Gas	N: Conoco

Personal Notes

EXIT	COLORADO
Food	N: Arby's, Garden Grill, Quiznos
Lodg	N: Hampton Inn
Other	N: Heritage Square Funpark, Dakota Ridge RV Park▲, to Golden Terrace South▲ S: to Red Rocks Amphitheater, Dinosaur Ridge
NOTE:	WB: MM 259-254: 6% STEEP UPHILL GRADE next 5 mi.
260A	CO 470E, Colorado Springs (EB)
260B	CO 470W, to US 6W, to CO 93, 6th Ave, Golden, Boulder (EB)
261	US 6E, 6th Ave (EB) (Addt'l Serv S to Union Blvd)
Lodg	S: Courtyard, Residence Inn, Sheraton
Other	S: Windish RV Center
262	I-70 Bus, US 40, Colfax Ave, to US 6, Golden, Lakewood
Gas	N: Sinclair S: Conoco, Shell
Food	S: Outback Steakhouse, Romano's Macaroni Grill, Wendy's, Rest/Days Inn
Lodg	S: Days Inn♥, Holiday Inn, Mountain View Motel, Ramada, Residence Inn
Other	N: PetCo♥, Five-R Trucks, K&C RV/Camping World, Dakota Ridge RV Park▲ S: Colorado Mills Mall, Office Max, Super Target, UPS Store, Jefferson Co Fairgrounds▲
263	Denver West Blvd, Golden
Lodg	N: Marriott♥
Other	N: Nat'l Renewable Energy Lab, Camp George West, Best Buy, Office Depot

EXIT	COLORADO
Other	S: Colorado Mills Mall
264	CR 181, 32nd Ave, Youngfield St, Wheat Ridge, W Denver
Gas	N: Conoco S: 7-11, BP, Conoco, Shamrock
Food	N: Country Café, Good Times S: Chili's, Chipolte MexGrill, McDonald's, Italian Rest, Noodles, Subway
Lodg	S: La Quinta Inn♥
Other	N: RV America S: PetSmart♥, Wal-Mart, Walgreen's, Vet♥, Camping World, Steve Casey's RV
265	CO 58W, Golden, Central City (WB)
Other	N: to Coors Brewery, CO Schools of Mines
266	CO 72W, Ward Rd, 44th Ave, Wheat Ridge, Arvada
TStop	S: Travel Center of America #174 (Scales)
Gas	N: Shell S: Shamrock
Food	S: Rest/TA TC
Lodg	S: Quality Inn
TWash	S: TA TC
TServ	S: TA TC/Tires
Other	S: Laundry/WiFi/TA TC, Prospect RV Park/RVDump▲
267	CO 391, Kipling St, Wheat Ridge
Gas	N: 7-11, Amoco, Shell◊ S: Conoco
Food	N: Burger King, Carl's Jr, Denny's, Furrs Family Rest, Subway S: Taco Bell, Village Inn
Lodg	N: American Inn, Holiday Inn Express, Motel 6♥ S: Comfort Inn, Interstate Inn, Ramada Inn
Med	S: + Lutheran Medical Center
Other	N: Auto Dealer, Target S: Ketelsen Campers of CO
269A	CO 121, Wadsworth Blvd (EB)
Gas	N: 7-11, Conoco◊, Phillips 66◊, Costco
Food	N: Applebee's, Bennigan's, Country Buffet, IHOP, Lone Star Steakhouse, McDonald's, Red Robin, Ruby Tuesday, Starbucks, Taco Bell S: China's Best, KFC, McDonald's, Red Lobster, Wendy's
Med	S: + Hospital
Other	N: Advance Auto, Costco, Home Depot, Lowe's, Office Depot, PetSmart♥, Sam's Club, Tires Plus, UPS Store S: Discount Tire, AAA Propane/LP, to Freedom Harley Davidson, Walgreen's
(269B)	Jct I-76E, to Ft Morgan, Ft Collins; Jct I-70E, to Denver (EB)
269	CO 121, Wadworth Blvd (WB)
Med	S: + Hospital
270	Harlan St, to CO 95, Sheridan Blvd, Wheat Ridge, Commerce City (Lodging appr 3m S to US 70)
FStop	S: Valero
Food	S: Arby's, El Paraiso, Cafe
Other	N: U-Haul S: Lakeside Center Mall, Target, Lakeside Amusement Park
271A	CO 95, Sheridan Blvd, Denver (WB)
271B	Lowell Blvd, Tennyson St (WB)
272	US 287, CO 88, Federal Blvd, to I-76, Denver
Gas	N: Amoco, Sinclair

Page 282

◊ = Regular Gas Stations with Diesel ▲ = RV Friendly Locations ♥ = Pet Friendly Locations
RED PRINT SHOWS LARGE VEHICLE PARKING/ACCESS ON SITE OR NEARBY BROWN PRINT SHOWS CAMPGROUNDS/RV PARKS

EXIT	COLORADO
Gas	S: 7-11, Conoco
Food	N: Burger King, Good Times, McCoy's, McDonald's, Pizza Hut, Subway, Taco Bell, Village Inn, Wendy's S: Rest/HJ, Popeye's
Lodg	N: Motel 6 ♥ S: Denver Inn, Howard Johnson ♥
Med	S: + to St Anthony's Hospital
Other	N: Kmart, Laundromat, Regis Univ S: to Invesco Field, Mile High Stadium
273	**Pecos St, W 48th St, Denver**
Gas	S: Conoco, Phillips 66
Food	N: Subs & Pizza
Lodg	N: Best Western
Other	N: Grocery, Ryder Propane/LP
(274)	**Jct I-25, N to Cheyenne, S to Colo Springs, Ft Collins**
Other	N: to I-76, I-270 S: to Amtrak, Greyhound, Coors Field, Invesco Field, Mile High Stadium, Denver Zoo, Six Flags
275A	**Washington St, Denver (WB)**
FStop	S: Conoco @ Brighton, Denver Sinclair Fuel Stop
Gas	N: Citgo
Food	N: Pizza Hut S: McDonald's, Subway
275B	**CO 265N, Brighton Blvd, Denver**
TServ	N: to Trans-West Freightliner
Other	N: Denver Coliseum, National Western Complex
275C	**York St, 45th Ave (EB)**
276A	**US 6E, US 85N, Steele St, Vasquez Blvd, Commerce City, Denver**
TStop	N: Pilot Travel Center #316 (Scales)
Gas	S: 7-11
Food	N: Wendy's/DQ/Pilot TC S: Burger King
Lodg	N: Colonial Manor, Western Motor Inn
TWash	N: Blue Beacon/Pilot TC
Other	N: Laundry/WiFi/Pilot TC, Mountain State Ford S: to Mile High Greyhound Racing
276B	**CO 2, Colorado Blvd, (EB), to US 6E, to US 85N, Commerce City**
Med	S: + Univ of CO Hospital
Other	S: Denver Zoo, Denver Museum of Nature & Science
277	**Stapleton Dr, Frontage Rd, to Dahlia St, Holly St, Monaco St**
278	**CO 35, Quebec St, Commerce City, Denver**
TStop	N: Sapp Bros. Truck Stop/Sinclair (Scales), Travel Center of America #148 (Scales)
Gas	N: Shamrock
Food	N: Rest/FastFood/Sapp Bros TS, CountryPride/PizzaHut/Popeyes/Quiznos/TA TC, Denny's, Del Taco, Subway, TGI Friday, Rest/Bass Pro Shop S: IHOP, McDonald's, Starbucks, Subway, Rest/HI
Lodg	N: Best Inn, Comfort Inn S: Courtyard, Guest House Hotel, Holiday Inn, Radisson, Ramada Inn, Red Lion Hotel
TWash	N: Sapp Bros TS
TServ	N: Sapp Bros TS/Tires, TA TC/Tires
Med	S: + Next Care Urgent Care
Other	N: Laundry/BarbSh/WiFi/Sapp Bros TS, Laundry/WiFi/HealthClinic/RVDump/TA TC, Circuit City, Super Target, Mall, Bass Pro Shop, Rocky Mountain Arsenal,

EXIT	COLORADO
Other	N: Denver Coliseum, Mile High Greyhound Racing S: Home Depot, Office Depot, PetSmart ♥, Radio Shack, Sam's Club, UPS Store, Wal-Mart sc▲, Walgreen's, Mall, B&B RV, Johnson & Wales Univ
(279)	**Jct I-270W, to I-25N, US 36W, to Boulder, Ft Collins (WB)**
280	**Havana St, Denver**
Lodg	N: Embassy Suites S: Marriott
Other	S: Rocky Mountain Arsenal
281	**Peoria St, Denver**
FStop	N: Conoco
Gas	N: 7-11, Phillips 66 S: Conoco, Cenex, Shamrock ♦
Food	N: Big Bubba's BBQ, Burger King, McDonald's, Subway, Village Inn S: Denny's, IHOP, KFC, La Carreta Mex Rest, Pizza Hut, Subway, Taco Bell, Waffle House, Wendy's
Lodg	N: Drury Hotel ♥, Timbers Hotel S: Motel 6 ♥, Quality Inn, Star Motel
Med	S: + Univ of CO Hospital
Other	N: Big O Tires S: Auto Repairs, Coast RV
(282)	**Jct I-225S, Aurora, Peoria St, to I-25S, Colorado Springs**
283	**Chambers Rd, Aurora**
Gas	N: Conoco, Shell S: Shamrock, Phillips 66, Valero
Food	N: Applebee's, Pizza Hut, Popeye's, Quiznos, Sonic, Wendy's S: Burger King, Hardee's, Taco Bell
Lodg	N: AmeriSuites, Country Inn, Hilton Garden Inn, Holiday Inn, Marriott, Residence Inn, Sleep Inn S: Extended Stay America
Other	N: Safeway, Tires, U-Haul S: Greyhound, Kmart SC, Mountain States RV
284	**Pena Blvd, to E-470, CO 32 (EB)**
Other	N: Denver Int'l Airport ✈
285	**Airport Blvd, Pena Blvd, to CO 32, Tower Rd, Aurora, Denver**
TStop	S: Flying J Travel Plaza #5061/Conoco (Scales)
Gas	S: Shell ♦
Food	S: CountryMarket/FastFood/FJ TP, McDonald's/Shell
Lodg	S: Comfort Inn, Crystal Inn
Other	N: to Denver Int'l Airport ✈ S: Laundry/WiFi/BarbSh/RVDump/LP/FJ TP, Mile High Harley Davidson, Grocery, to Buckley Air Nat'l Guard Base
286	**CO 32, Tower Rd, Aurora**
Food	N: Chipolte Mex Grill, Del Taco
Lodg	N: Comfort Suites, Country Inn, Hampton Inn, Microtel ♥
TServ	N: CAT
Other	N: Wal-Mart sc▲, to Denver Int'l Airport ✈ S: Albertson's, Best Buy
288	**I-70 Bus, US 40W, US 287N, Colfax Ave (fr WB, 2 Ln Left exit) (Serv W on I-70 Bus/US 287)**
Other	S: Buckley Air Nat'l Guard Base

EXIT	COLORADO
(289)	**E-470 TOLLway, Gun Club Rd, Colorado Springs, Ft Collins (NO Local Toll to Smith Rd, Colfax Ave, S Frontage, Gun Club Rd)**
(290.5)	**Aurora Weigh Station (Both dir)**
292	**CO 36E, Airpark Rd, Watkins**
Other	S: Aurora Airpark ✈
295	**CR 97, Lessig St, E Colfax Ave, I-70N Bus, to CO 36, Watkins**
TStop	N: PTP/Tomahawk Auto Truck Plaza/Shell ♦ (Scales)
Food	N: Rest/Tomahawk ATP
Lodg	N: Country Manor Motel
TServ	N: Tomahawk ATP/Tires
Other	N: Laundry/LP/Tomahawk ATP, to Front Range Airport ✈
299	**CR 113, Manila Rd, CR 28N, to CO 36, Bennett, Manila**
FStop	N: Diamond Shamrock #2
Food	N: FastFood/Diamond Shamrock
Other	N: Front Range Airport ✈
304	**1st St, CO 79N, CR 133, Bennett**
Gas	N: Bennett Travel Shoppe/Conoco ♦
Food	N: Bev's Kitchen, China Kitchen, Just Right Pizza, Country Rose Cafe
Lodg	N: Willow Tree Country Inn
Other	N: Auto/RV Repair
305	**CR 137, CR 34, Kiowa Bennett Rd, Kiowa (EB)**
306	**CO 36, Colfax Ave, Kiowa Bennett Rd, Kiowa, Bennett (WB) (NO EB Entry, Enter at Strasburg)**
N:	Bennett Rest Area (Both dir) (RR, Phone, Picnic)
310	**I-70 Bus, to CO 36, Wagner St, Frontage Rd, Strasburg**
Gas	N: Conoco ♦, Ray's Gas & Tire
Food	N: B&K Pizza, Old Town Diner, The Pizza Shop, Slackers Rest.
Lodg	N: Strasburg Inn
Other	N: Strasburg/Denver East KOA ▲, NAPA
316	**US 36E, CO 36W, Main St, Byers**
Gas	N: Sinclair S: Gas
Food	N: Rest/Budget Host Longhorn Motel S: Country Burger, The Golden Spike, Stagecoach Steakhouse
Lodg	N: Budget Host Longhorn Motel S: Lazy 8 Motel
322	**CR 201, Peoria Rd, Peoria**
328	**I-70 Bus, Cedar St, Deer Trail**
Gas	N: Phillips 66 ♦ S: Corner Gas
Food	S: Brown Derby, Deer Trail Café
(332)	**Deer Trail Rest Area (WB) (RR, Phones, Picnic, Vend)**
336	**CR 178, to Lowland**
340	**I-70 Bus, CR 166, Agate**
348	**CR 134, to Cedar Point**
352	**CO 86W, CR 142, to Kiowa**
354	**CR 118, Limon**

♦ = Regular Gas Stations with Diesel   ▲ = RV Friendly Locations   ♥ = Pet Friendly Locations

RED PRINT SHOWS LARGE VEHICLE PARKING/ACCESS ON SITE OR NEARBY   BROWN PRINT SHOWS CAMPGROUNDS/RV PARKS

EXIT		COLORADO
359		I-70E Bus, to US 24, Limon (EB), US 24W, Colorado Springs (WB), US 40E, US 287S, Limon
	FStop	S: Gottschalk Oil/Valero
	TStop	S: Travel Center of America #228/Shell (Scales)
	Gas	S: Phillips 66
	Food	S: CountryFare/Subway/TA TC, Arby's, Denny's, McDonald's, Oscar's Steak House
	Lodg	S: Best Western, Comfort Inn, Tyme Square Inn, Econo Lodge, Super 8
	TServ	S: TA TC/Tires
	Other	S: Laundry/WiFi/TA TC, CO State Hwy Patrol Post
(360)		Limon Weigh Station (Both dir)
361		to CO 71 (EB), I-70 Bus, US 24, US 40, US 287, Limon
	TStop	S: Flying J Travel Plaza #5011/Conoco (Scales)
	Gas	S: Phillips 66◊
	Food	S: Rest/FastFood/FJ TP, DQ, Pizza Hut, Wendy's
	Lodg	S: Econo Lodge, First Inn Gold, Limon Inn East, Preferred Motor Inn, Silver Spur Motel, Travel Inn
	Other	N: Limon Muni Airport✈ S: Laundry/WiFi/RVDump/LP/FJ TP, Limon KOA▲
363		US 40E, US 287S, I-70 Bus, US 24, Hugo, Kit Carson (EB), I-70W Bus, US 24W, to CO 71, Limon (WB) (Gas Food Lodg S in Hugo)
	Med	S: + Hospital (appr 12 mi)
	Other	N: Limon Muni Airport✈
371		CR 31, CR 109, Genoa, Hugo
	Med	S: in Hugo + Hospital
376		CR 36, Genoa, Bovina
383		CR 63, Arriba
	S:	Arriba Rest Area (Both dir) (RR, Phones, Picnic, RVCamping)
	Gas	N: DJ Food Store/P66◊
	Food	N: Café/DJ Food Store
	Lodg	N: DJ Motel
395		CR 5, Flagler
	FStop	S: Country Store/Cenex
	Gas	N: Loaf N Jug◊
	Food	N: Dairy King, JC's Bar & Grill S: Café/Country Store
	Lodg	N: Little England Motel & RV Park▲
	TServ	S: Country Store/Tires

EXIT		COLORADO
405		CO 59, US 24, Seibert
	FStop	S: Seibert Travel Plaza/Conoco
	Food	S: FastFood/Seibert TP
	Other	N: ATMs, Banks, Grocery, Post Office, Shady Grove Wi-Fi Campground/RVDump/RVService▲
412		I-70 Bus, CR 23, Vona
419		CO 57N, CR 30, Colorado Ave, Stratton
	FStop	N: AmPride/Cenex
	Gas	N: Conoco◊
	Food	N: Rest/BW, Dairy Treat
	Lodg	N: Best Western, Claremont Inn
	TServ	N: Plains Diesel Service
	Med	N: + Stratton Medical Clinic
	Other	N: Marshall Ash Village RV Park▲, Trail's End Campground▲, Bernie's RV Service & Repair
429		CR 40, Bethune
437		US 385, I-70E Bus, Lincoln St, Burlington, Wray, Cheyenne Wells
	FStop	N: Amacks BPAmoco
	TStop	N: Travel Shoppe #4/Conoco
	Gas	N: Phillips 66◊
	Food	N: Interstate House/Conoco, FastFood/P66, Burger King, DQ, McDonald's, Sonic, Subway, The Route Steakhouse, Rest/Western Motor Inn, Rest/Burlington Inn
	Lodg	N: Burlington Inn, Chaparral Motor Inn, Comfort Inn, Sloan's Motel, Super 8, Western Motor Inn
	TServ	N: D & J Diesel
	Med	N: + Hospital
	Other	N: Grocery, Goodyear S: Kit Carson Airport✈
(438)		CO Welcome Center (WB) Rest Area (EB) (RR, Phones, Picnic, Info, RVDump)
438		US 24, I-70W Bus, CR V, Rose Ave, Burlington
	FStop	N: Amacks BPAmoco
	Gas	N: Conoco, Sinclair
	Food	N: BJ's, Restaurant Panaderia
	Lodg	N: Comfort Inn, Hi-Lo Motel, Super 8
	Med	N: + Hospital
	Other	N: Auto Dealers, CarQuest, Goodyear, Grocery
NOTE:		MM 451: Kansas State Line

(MOUNTAIN TIME ZONE)

COLORADO

EXIT		KANSAS
		KANSAS (MOUNTAIN / CENTRAL TIME ZONE)
(0)		Weigh Station (EB)
1		KS 267, CR 3, Kanorado
(7)		KS Welcome Center (EB) Rest Area (Both dir) (RR, Phones, Picnic, Vend, WiFi, Info, RVDump)
9		CR 1, CR 64, Ruleton
12		CR 14, Caruso
17		Bus 24, KS 27, CR 19, Goodland, St Francis, Sharon Springs
	FStop	N: Frontier Equity Exchange/Conoco
	TStop	N: Presto #14/P66
	Gas	S: Valero
	Food	N: Buffalo Inn, El Reynaldo's Mexican, KFC, Pizza Hut, McDonald's, Subway, Taco John's, Wendy's, Rest/BW
	Lodg	N: Best Western♥, Comfort Inn, Economy 9 Motel, Howard Johnson♥, Super 8 S: Holiday Inn Express, Welcome Inn
	TWash	N: Car/Truck/RV Wash
	TServ	N: Truck & Trailer Repair
	Med	N: + Goodland Regional Medical Center
	Other	N: Pharmacy, Wal-Mart sc, Tourist Info, Mid America Campground▲
19		Bus 24, KS 27 Spur, Goodland
	Gas	N: Sinclair◊
	Food	N: Pizza
	Lodg	N: Best Value Inn
	Other	N: Museum, Goodland KOA▲
27		KS 253, CR 29, Edson
NOTE:		MM 35: Mountain / Central Time Zone
36		KS 184, CR 2, Brewster
	Gas	N: Fuel Depot◊
45		US 24, CR 11, CR 407, Levant
(48)		Rest Area (Both dir) (RR, Phone, Picnic, Vend, RVDump)
53		KS 25, CR 19, S Range Ave, Colby, Atwood, Leoti
	FStop	N: JJ Oil Co #8/Conoco
	TStop	N: Colby 24-7/BP S: Petro 2/Oasis Travel Plaza/P66
	Gas	N: Amoco, Phillips 66, Total
	Food	N: DQ/Conoco, McDonald's/BP, Arby's, Burger King, City Limits Grill, KFC, Long John Silver, Pizza Hut, Subway, Taco John S: Starbucks/Quiznos/Chesters/P66, Village Inn

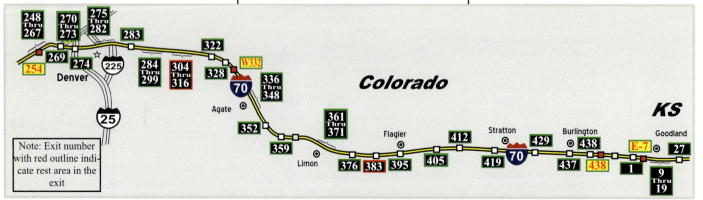

Page 284

◊ = Regular Gas Stations with Diesel   ▲ = RV Friendly Locations   ♥ = Pet Friendly Locations
RED PRINT SHOWS LARGE VEHICLE PARKING/ACCESS ON SITE OR NEARBY   BROWN PRINT SHOWS CAMPGROUNDS/RV PARKS

EXIT		KANSAS	EXIT		KANSAS	EXIT		KANSAS
	Lodg	N: Days Inn, Econo Lodge, Holiday Inn Express, Motel 6 ♥, Quality Inn, Super 8 S: Budget Inn, Crown Inn ♥		Gas Food	N: Sinclair◊ N: Rest/Budget Host Inn S: DQ		Gas Food	N: Mirastar S: BP, Holiday 66 Food Plaza N: Applebee's, Carlos O'Kelly's, Golden Corral, IHOP, Quiznos S: Arby's, China Garden, Country Kitchen, Hardee's, Imperial Garden, KFC, Long John Silver, McDonald's, Montana Mike's Steakhouse, Papa John's, Village Inn
	TWash TServ	N: Truck Town Truck, Trailer & RV Wash N: JJ Oil/Conoco, Central Power/ONAN Truck & Bus Service, Detroit Diesel Allison, Cummins Diesel, CAT		Lodg Med Other	N: Budget Host Inn N: + Hospital N: Sunflower RV Campground▲			
	Med Other	N: + Hospital N: AutoZone, Auto Dealers, Carwash, Dollar General, Goodyear, Grocery, Radio Shack, Wal-Mart sc, Tourist Info S: Laundry/RVDump/Petro2 Oasis TP, Factory Outlet Stores, Auto Dealers	115 120 127		KS 198N, Banner Rd, Collyer Voda Rd US 40 Bus, US 283, S 1st St, Wa Keeney, Ness City			
							Lodg	N: Fairfield Inn, Sleep Inn S: Best Western, Comfort Inn, Days Inn, Econo Lodge, Hampton Inn, Holiday Inn ♥, Motel 6 ♥, Super 8
54	Other	CR 20, Country Club Dr (Access to Ex #53 Serv) N: Bourquins RV Park▲		FStop TStop Gas Food	N: Town Pump/P66 S: WaKeeney 24/7 Travel Plaza/BP S: Conoco◊ N: McDonald's/P66, Jade Garden, Pizza Hut S: Real Country Café/BP, Subway/Conoco		AServ TServ	S: Davis Automotive, Dave's Auto Repair Mike's Automotive Tire Repair N: Detroit Diesel, I-70 Truck Repair S: Kansasland Tire, Hay's Mack
62 70	Gas	CR K, CR 24, Mingo N: AmPride◊ US 83, US 383, Rexford, Spica, Oakley					Med Other	S: + Hayes Medical Center N: ATMs, Auto Dealer, Home Depot, Radio Shack, Wal-Mart sc, KS State Hwy Patrol Post S: Advance Auto, Auto Dealers, ATMs, Firestone, Grocery, Walgreen's, Mall
	TStop Gas Food Lodg TServ Med Other	S: JJ Oil Co #6/P66 S: Sinclair◊ S: Colonial Steakhouse N: Free Breakfast Inn S: JJ Oil/P66 S: + Hospital S: Prairie Dog Town, Museum, High Plains Camping▲	128	Lodg TServ Other FStop	N: Best Western, Ks Kountry Inn S: Econo Lodge S: WaKeeney TP/Tires S: Laundry/WaKeeney TP, WaKeeney/ Hays KOA▲ US 40 Bus, to US 283N, S 13th St, Wa Keeney, Hill City N: Sinclair	161 163 168	Gas	270th Ave, Commerce Pkwy Toulon Ave KS 255, Cathedral Ave, Victoria S: AmPride◊
76	TStop Food Lodg TWash TServ Med Other	US 40W, Old Hwy 40, Oakley, Sharon Springs S: Travel Center of America/Shell (Scales) S: Buckhorn/Subway/TA TC S: Best Value Inn, First Interstate Inn, Econo Lodge, Ks Kountry Inn & RV Park▲ S: Blue Beacon/TA TC S: TA TC/Tires S: + Hospital N: Auto Dealer, John Deere S: Laundry/WiFi/TA TC	(131) (133) 135 140	Lodg Med Other Gas Other	N: Ks Kountry Inn, Super 8 N: + Hospital N: Always Christmas Shop Rest Area (EB) (RR, Picnic, RVDump) Rest Area (WB) (RR, Picnic, RVDump) KS 147, Ogallah Riga Rd, Ogallah, Riga N: Schreiner Fuels S: to Cedar Bluff State Park	172 175 180 184	FStop Gas Food Lodg	Walker Ave KS 257, Gorham Galatia Rd, 176th St, Gorham 181st St, Balta Rd, Balta US 281, US 40 Bus, Russell, Hoisington N: 24-7 Store/BP N: AmPride, Phillips 66◊ N: McDonald's, Meridy's, Pizza Hut, Subway N: AmericInn, Days Inn, Russell Inn, Super 8 Inn
79 85	Gas Food	Campus Rd KS 216, S Oak, Grinnell S: BP S: Stuckey's/DQ/BP	145	FStop Gas Food	KS 247, Ellis Ave, Washington St, Ellis S: Ellis Travel Plaza/P66 S: Casey's, Total S: DQ/Subway/Ellis TP, Alloway's, Bo's Landing, Casey's C/O Pizza, Matt's Rib Shack, Railroader Lanes & Dining Car, TJ's		TWash Med Other	N: RV & Truck Wash N: + Hospital N: Oil Patch Museum, Triple J RV Park▲, Fossil Creek RV Park▲
93 95 (97)	Gas Other	KS 23, Grainfield, Gove N: Sinclair◊ KS 23, Hoxie, Grainfield N: Betterbuilt Trailers Rest Area (Both dir) (RR, Picnic, Vend, RVDump)	153 157	Lodg Other Other	S: Ellis House Inn N: Museums, Lakeside Campground▲ Yocemento Ave US 183 South ByPass, 230th Ave, Hays, LaCrosse S: Fort Hays Historic Site, Tourist Info	(187) 189	Other	Rest Area (Both dir) (RR, Phones, Picnic, RVDump) US 40 Bus, 189th St, Pioneer Rd, Russell N: Airport✈
99 107	Gas FStop	KS 211, Park N: Sinclair◊ KS 212, Castle Rock Rd, Quinter S: RC Petroleum/Shell	159	FStop TStop	US 183, Vine St, Hays, Plainville S: Valero S: Golden Ox Truck Stop/Conoco	193	TStop Food Other	193rd St, Bunker Hill Rd N: Sunmart/Conoco N: Bear House Café/Conoco, Bunker Hill Café N: Wilson Wildlife Area

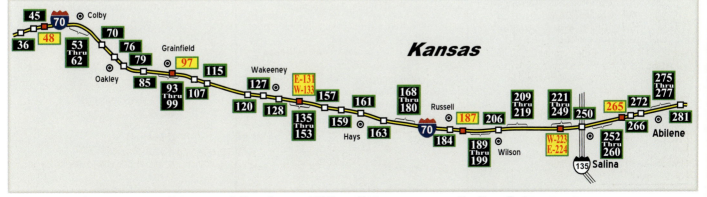

◊ = Regular Gas Stations with Diesel ▲ = RV Friendly Locations ♥ = Pet Friendly Locations

RED PRINT SHOWS LARGE VEHICLE PARKING/ACCESS ON SITE OR NEARBY BROWN PRINT SHOWS CAMPGROUNDS/RV PARKS

Page 285

EXIT		KANSAS
199		KS 231, 200th Blvd, Dorrance
	Gas	S: Kerr-McGee
206		KS 232, Wilson, Lucas
	Gas	N: Conoco Travel Shoppe
	Lodg	N: Pioneer Village Motel & Campground▲
	Other	N: to Lake Wilson▲
209		6th Rd, Wilson, Sylvan Grove
216		12th Rd, Vesper
	Gas	S: BP
	Food	S: DQ/Stuckey's/BP
219		KS 14S, Ellsworth
	FStop	S: Cliff's Service/Conoco
	Tires	S: Cliff's
221		KS 14N, to Lincoln
(223)		Rest Area (WB) (RR, Phones, Picnic, RVDump)
(224)		Rest Area (EB) (RR, Phones, Picnic, RVDump)
225		KS 156, Ellsworth, Great Bend
233		N 290th Rd, Beverly, Carneiro
238		N Brookville Rd, Brookville, Glendale, Tescott
244		N Hedville Rd, Hedville, Culver
	Gas	S: Cenex◇
	Food	S: Outpost Rest & Fun Center
	Other	N: Sundowner West RV Park▲
		S: Rolling Hills Wildlife Adventure, Glasco RV Park▲
249		N Halstead Rd, Trenton, Shipton
(250A)		Jct I-135S, US 81S, to Wichita, Lindsborg
250B		US 81N, to Concordia
252		KS 143, 9th St, Salina
	TStop	N: Petro 2 Truck Stop #81/Shell (Scales)
		S: Bosselman Travel Center/Pilot #903/Sinclair (Scales)◇, I-70 24-7/BP
	Gas	N: Valero◇
		S: Pump Mart, Total
	Food	N: PizzaHut/Wendy's/Petro2, DQ, IHOP, Rest/Salina Inn, Rest/Super 8
		S: Grandma Max's/Bosselman's TC, McDonald's, Ks Steak, Ponderosa
	Lodg	N: Best Inn, Days Inn, Holiday Inn Express, Motel 6♥, Salina Inn, Super 8
		S: Best Western, Econo Lodge
	TWash	S: Blue Beacon TW/Petro2
	TServ	N: Palmer Truck & Trailer Repair
		S: Bosselman TC/Tires, Inland Truck Parts, Central Detroit Diesel, Roberts Truck Center/Volvo
	Other	N: Laundry/Petro2, Smoky Hill Vineyards Winery, Salina KOA▲
		S: Laundry/Bosselman TC, Laund/WiFi/BP, Salina Arts Center
253		Ohio St, Bicentennial Ctr, Salina
	TStop	S: Flying J Travel Plaza/Conoco (Scales)
	Food	S: CountryMarket/FastFood/FJ TP
	TServ	S: Kenworth
	Med	S: + Hospital
	Other	S: Laundry/WiFi/RVDump/LP/FJ TP, Harley Davidson
260		Niles Rd, New Cambria
(265)		Rest Area (Both dir) (RR, Phones, Picnic)

Personal Notes

EXIT		KANSAS
266		KS 221, Solomon Rd, Solomon
	TStop	S: Solomon Travel Center/Total (Scales)
	Food	S: Rest/Solomon TC
272		CR 829, Fair Rd, Solomon, to Abilene, Talmage
275		KS 15, Abilene, Clay Center
	Gas	S: Phillips 66, Shell, Alco Fuel Ctr
	Food	N: DQ
		S: Burger King, La Fiesta, McDonald's, Pizza Hut, Subway
	Lodg	N: Brookville Hotel, Holiday Inn Express
		S: Best Value Inn, Days Inn, Super 8
	Med	S: + Hospital
	Other	S: AutoZone, Auto Dealers, Grocery, Tourist Info, Excursion Train, Museums, Eisenhower Museum, Greyhound Hall of Fame, CW Parker Carousel, Covered Wagon RV Resort▲
277		CR 841, Jeep Rd, Abilene
281		KS 43, CR 845, Mink Rd, Enterprise
	Gas	N: Four Seasons Shell
	Other	N: Four Seasons RV Acres/Dealer▲
286		KS 206, CR 857, Rain Rd, Chapman
	Gas	S: Casey's General Store
	Food	S: Casey's C/O Pizza
	Other	S: Ks Auto Racing Museum
290		Milford Lake Rd, Junction City
(294)		Rest Area (WB) (RR, Picnic, Phone, RVDump)

EXIT		KANSAS
295		US 77, KS 18, Junction City, Marysville, Herrington
	TStop	N: Sapp Bros/P66 (Scales)
	Food	N: Sapp Bros
	Lodg	N: Motel 6♥
	TServ	N: Sapp Bros/Tires
	TWash	N: Sapp Bros
		S: Champion Car & Truck Wash
	Med	N: + Hospital
	Other	N: Laundry/WiFi/Sapp Bros, Harley Davidson, Flagstop Resort & RV Park▲, Milford State Park▲
		S: Owl's Nest Campground▲, RV Center
296		US 40 Bus, Washington St
	FStop	N: GS Conv Store/Cenex
	Gas	N: BP, Phillips 66, Shell◇
	Food	N: Country Kitchen, DQ, Hardee's, KFC, Long John Silver, McDonald's, Peking Rest, Sirloin Stockade, Sonic, Subway
	Lodg	N: Budget Host & RV Park▲, Comfort Inn, Days Inn, Ramada Ltd
	Other	N: Grocery
298		East St, Chestnut St, Junction City
	FStop	N: Shell Travel Center (Scales)
	Food	N: Burger King/Shell TC, Cracker Barrel, Arby's, Taco Bell
	Lodg	N: Best Western, Courtyard, Holiday Inn
	Other	N: Laundry/Shell TC, ATMs, Dollar Tree, Dollar General, Grocery, Wal-Mart sc
299		US 40 Bus, KS 57, J Hill Rd, Flint Hills Blvd, Junction City
	Gas	N: Handy's BP◇
	Food	N: Stacy's Rest, Pizza/BP
	Lodg	N: Econo Lodge, Dream Land Motel, Great Western Inn, Red Carpet Inn, Super 8
	Other	N: Laundromat
300		US 40 Bus, KS 57, Council Grove
	Lodg	N: Dream Land Motel
301		Henry Rd, Fort Riley, Marshall Field
	Lodg	N: Dream Land Motel, Sunset Motel & RV Park▲
	Other	N: Ft Riley Military Reservation, Custer's House, Calvary Museum
303		KS 18, Clarks Creek Rd, Ft Riley, Ogden, Manhattan
304		Humboldt Creek Rd, Jct City NOTE: Low Clearance 13'9"
307		CR 901, McDowell Creek Rd
(309)		Rest Area (Both dir) (RR, Phones, Picnic, RVDump)
311		Moritz Rd
313		KS 177, Pillsbury Dr, Manhattan, Council Grove (Serv N in Manhattan)
316		CR 911, Deep Creek Rd
318		Frontage Rd, Manhattan
323		Frontage Rd, Tallgrass Rd, Alma
324		Wabaunsee Rd, Alma
	Other	N: Grandma Huerney Natural Foods
328		KS 99, Alma, Wamego
	Other	N: Oz Museum
		S: Museum
333		KS 138, Paxico
	Other	N: Auto Repairing & Towing, Wyldewood Cellars

◇ = Regular Gas Stations with Diesel   ▲ = RV Friendly Locations   ♥ = Pet Friendly Locations
RED PRINT SHOWS LARGE VEHICLE PARKING/ACCESS ON SITE OR NEARBY   BROWN PRINT SHOWS CAMPGROUNDS/RV PARKS

EXIT	KANSAS	EXIT	KANSAS	EXIT	KANSAS
335	Snokomo Rd, Skyline Scenic Dr, Paxico	358	US 75, KS 4, Gage Blvd (EB)	Lodg	S: Hampton Inn, Holiday Inn, Quality Inn, Ramada Inn, Super 8
Other	N: Paxico Shops, Mill Creek RV Park▲	Other	N: Topeka KOA▲	Med	S: + Hospital
(336)	Rest Area (Both dir, Left exit) (RR, Phones, Picnic, WiFi, RVDump)	358A	US 75N (WB)	Other	S: Firestone, to Univ of KS
		Other	N: Topeka KOA▲	204	US 24, US 59, E Lawrence
338	Vera Rd, McFarland, Vera	358B	Gage Blvd (WB)	Gas	S: Citgo
341	KS 30, Windy Hill Rd, Maple Hill, St Marys	Gas	S: Conoco	Food	S: Burger King
		Food	S: McDonald's, Subway, Wendy's	Lodg	S: Bismark Inn, Jayhawk Motel
FStop	S: 24-7 Maple Hill Truck Stop/BP	Aserv	S: Huntington Park Auto Center	Med	S: + Hospital
Food	S: Café/Maple Hill TS	Med	S: + Hospital	(209)	Lawrence Service Plaza (Both dir, Left exit)
Other	S: RVDump/Maple Hill TS	Other	S: Zoo, Rain Forest	FStop	EZ Go #70/Conoco
342	Eskridge Rd, Keene Blacktop Rd	359	MacVicar Ave, Topeka	Food	McDonald's
343	Frontage Rd, Ranch Rd, Maple Hill	Other	S: Hummer Sports Park	(217)	TOLL Plaza
346	Carlson Rd, Willard, Rossville, Dover	361A	1st Ave, Alt US 75, Topeka Blvd (EB, NO reaccess)	224	KS 7, S 130th St, to US 73, Bonner Springs, Leavenworth
		Other	S: Ryder		NOTE: (LAST FREE EXIT)
347	W Union Rd, Topeka	361B	3rd St, Monroe St (EB)	Gas	N: Shell
350	Valencia Rd, Topeka	362A	4th St, Madison St (WB)		S: Citgo
351	Frontage Rd, Patton Rd (EB)	Lodg	S: Ramada Inn	Food	N: KFC, Waffle House
353	KS 4, Auburn Rd, to Eskridge	362B	8th Ave, Downtown Topeka		S: McDonald's, Mr Goodcents Subs & Pasta, Ross's Steakhouse
(355)	Jct I-470S, US 75S	Lodg	S: Days Inn	Lodg	N: Holiday Inn Express, Super 8
Med	S: + Veteran's Medical Center	362C	10th Ave, Madison St	Other	N: Verizon Amphitheater
TServ	S: Martin Truck Service	Gas	N: BP		S: Wal-Mart sc
356	Wanamaker Rd, Topeka	Lodg	N: Ramada	NOTE:	I-70 above runs with KS Tpk. Exit #'s follow KS Tpk.
TStop	S: Topeka Travel Plaza (Scales)	Other	N: KS State Capitol Bldg		
Gas	S: BP, Phillips 66◆	363	Adams St, Branner Trafficway	410	110th St
Food	N: Sirloin Stockade	364A	California Ave, Topeka	Other	N: Ks Speedway
	S: Rest/Topeka TP, Applebee's, Boston Market, Burger King, Chili's, Chuck E Cheese, Cracker Barrel, Coyote Canyon, Denny's, Golden Corral, Hooters, IHOP, KFC, McDonald's, Old Country Buffet, Olive Garden, Panera Bread, Pizza Hut, Perkins, Red Lobster, Shoney's, Steak 'n Shake, Taco Bell, Timberline Steaks, Wendy's	Gas	S: BP◆, Conoco	(411A)	Jct I-435S, Overland Park
		Food	S: Burger King, McDonald's, Pizza Hut, Rosa's Mexican, Subway	(411B)	Jct I-435N, St Joseph
		Other	S: AutoZone, Walgreen's	Other	N: to Woodlands Race Track, KCI Int'l Airport✈
		364B	US 40, KS 4, Carnahan Ave, Deer Creek Trafficway	414	78th St, Kansas City
		365	21st St, Rice Rd, Topeka	Gas	N: QT
					S: Conoco
		NOTE:	I-70 below runs with KS Tpk. Exit #'s follow KS Tpk.	Food	N: Arby's, Burger King, Cracker Barrel, Hardy's, Sonic, Wendy's
Lodg	N: AmeriSuites			Lodg	N: Microtel
	S: Candlewood Suites, Clubhouse Inn, Comfort Inn, Country Inn, Days Inn, Econo Lodge, Fairfield Inn, Hampton Inn, Motel 6♥, Quality Inn, Sleep Inn, Super 8	(366)	Jct I-470W, to Wichita		S: American Inn, Comfort Inn
		(367)	TOLL Plaza	Med	N: + Hospital
		(183)	Jct I-70W, US 40, KS 4, Topeka, Salina	Other	N: Walgreen's
TServ	S: Topeka TP/Tires	(182)	Jct I-335, I-470, KS Tpk, Emporia, Wichita (Left exit)	(414)	Parking Area (Both dir)
Med	N: + Tallgrass Immediate Care Center			(415)	Inspection Station (Both dir)
Other	S: Laundry/Topeka TP, ATMs, Best Buy, Banks, Grocery, FedEx Kinko's, Home Depot, Kmart, Lowe's, Office Depot, Sam's Club, Wal-Mart sc, West Ridge Mall	(187)	Topeka Service Plaza (Both dir)	415A	US 40E, Riverview Ave, 65th St (EB)
		FStop	Conoco	415B	US 40W, State Ave (EB)
357A	Fairlawn Rd, SW 6th Ave, Topeka	Food	Hardee's	415	Riverview Ave, 65th St, US 40, State Ave (WB)
Gas	S: Phillips 66	197	KS 10, Lawrence, Lecompton		
Food	S: Rest/Holiday Inn	202	US 59, West Lawrence	417	57th St, Kansas City
Lodg	S: Holiday Inn, Motel 6♥	Gas	S: BP, Phillips 66		
357B	Danbury Lane, Topeka (WB)	Food	S: Mr Goodcents Subs & Pasta		

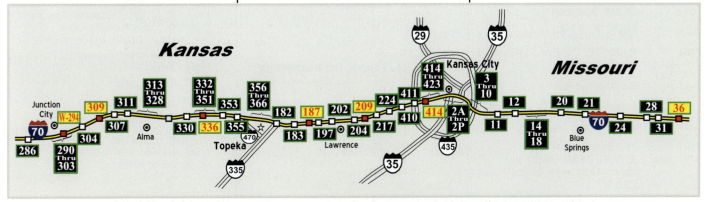

◆ = Regular Gas Stations with Diesel   ▲ = RV Friendly Locations   ♥ = Pet Friendly Locations

RED PRINT SHOWS LARGE VEHICLE PARKING/ACCESS ON SITE OR NEARBY   BROWN PRINT SHOWS CAMPGROUNDS/RV PARKS

Page 287

EXIT	KS / MO	EXIT	MISSOURI	EXIT	MISSOURI
(418A)	Jct I-635S, to Overland Park	5A	27th St, Mersington Ave (EB)	Food	N: Applebee's, Arby's, Bob Evans, Burger King, Chili's, Denny's, Hops, Lone Star Steakhouse, McDonald's, Starbucks, TGI Friday
TStop	S: I-635 SB, Exit 3: QT, Shamrock	5B	31st St, Myrtle Ave (EB)		
(418B)	Jct I-635N, to Missouri	5C	29th St, Jackson Ave (WB)		
419	Park Dr, 38th St, State Ave (Serv 3-5 mi N on State Ave)	6	Van Brunt Blvd	Lodg	N: Fairfield Inn, Residence Inn
		Gas	N: 7-11	Other	N: Albertson's, B&N, Best Buy, Circuit City, Sam's Club, Target, Wal-Mart sc, Mall
420A	Jct US 69S, 18th St Expy		S: BP		
420B	18th St, Kansas City	Food	S: McDonald's, Subway, Taco Bell	17	Little Blue Pkwy, 39th St, US 40, Memorial Pkwy, Blue Springs
Gas	N: Conoco	Med	S: + VA Hospital		
Lodg	N: Eagle Inn Motel	Other	S: Carwash, Family Dollar, NAPA	Gas	S: QT, Costco
Med	N: + Hospital	7A	31st S, US 40E	Food	N: Applebee's, Joe's Crab Shack, Romano's Macaroni Grill, O'Charley's, On the Border, Starbucks
421A	Service Rd, to Railroad Yard (WB)	7B	Manchester Trafficway		
(421B)	Jct I-670W	TServ	N: Arrow Truck Sales		
422A	US 69N, US 169S, 7th St TrWy (EB)	(8A)	Jct I-435S, to Wichita		S: Carrabba's, Hooters, IHOP, Kobe, Outback Steakhouse, Wendy's
422B	US 69, US 169, 7th St TrWy (WB)	(8B)	Jct I-435N, to Des Moines	Lodg	N: Comfort Suites, Hilton Garden Inn
422C	Service Road	9	Blue Ridge Cut-Off, Kansas City		S: Holiday Inn Express
422D	Central Ave (EB) 6th St, Reynolds Ave (WB)	Gas	N: Conoco	Med	N: + Hospital
			S: BP, Sinclair	Other	N: Mall
423A	5th St (EB)	Food	N: Denny's, Wendy's		S: Costco, CompUSA, Lowe's
423B	James St, 3rd St (EB)		S: Taco Bell	18	Woods Chapel Rd, NW Duncan Rd, Blue Springs, Independence, Lake Tapawingo, Fleming Park (Access to Ex #20 Services)
423C	US 24, US 169, Minnesota Ave, Washington Blvd	Lodg	N: Clarion Hotel, Drury Inn♥		
			S: Holiday Inn		
423D	Fairfax District	Med	N: + Hospital		
NOTE:	MM 424: Missouri State Line	Other	S: Royals, Arrowhead Stadium, Water Pk, KC Museum, Welcome Center/RVDump	Gas	N: Quik Stop/BP
	(CENTRAL TIME ZONE)				S: Conoco, QT, Phillips 66◊
	KANSAS	10	Sterling Ave (EB)	Food	N: King Dragon
	MISSOURI	11	US40, Blue Ridge Blvd, Sterling Ave		S: China Kitchen, KFC/Taco Bell, McDonald's, Pizza Hut, Waffle House
	(CENTRAL TIME ZONE)	Gas	N: QT, Conoco, Shell		
(2A)	Jct I-35S, to Wichita		S: 7-11, BP, GasMart, Sinclair	Lodg	N: American Inn, Best Value Inn, Interstate Inn, Microtel
2B	Beardsley Rd	Food	N: Burger King, Bob Evans, Gates & Son BBQ, McDonald's, Long John Silver, Rosie's Café, Sonic, Subway, V's Italian Rest		
2C	US 169N, Broadway, 5th St, Airport			AServ	N: Jefferson Service Center
2D	Main St, Delaware St, Downtown				S: Dave's Service Center
2E	MO 9, 6th St, Oak St			Other	N: CarWash, Blue Springs Harley Davidson
2F	Oak St, Independence Ave (WB)		S: Applebee's, Hong Kong Buffet, Old Country Buffet, Papa John's, Taco Bell		S: Laundromat
2H	US 24E, Independence Ave			20	MO 7, Lake Lotawana, Blue Springs
Lodg	N: Comfort Inn	Lodg	N: Budget Inn, Delux Inn, Sports Stadium Motel	Gas	N: Phillips 66◊, Sinclair, Valero
(2G)	I-29/35N, US 71N, to Des Moines				S: BP◊, QT, Shamrock, Shell
2J	10th St, 11th St, Charlotte St	Other	N: Stadium RV Park▲	Food	N: Backyard Burger, Bob Evans, Pizza Hut, Quiznos, Sonic
2L	US 71, I-70 Alt, I-670, to I-35S		S: Blue Ridge Mall, Family Dollar, O'Reilly Auto Parts, Wal-Mart sc		
2K	Harrison St, 12th St (WB)	12	Noland Rd, Independence, Ks City		S: Applebee's, Arby's, Burger King, China Buffet, Captain D's, Denny's, Einstein Bros, Golden Corral, KFC, Long John Silver, McDonald's, Starbucks, Subway, Wendy's, Village Inn
Med	N: + Hospital	Gas	N: QT, Shell◊		
2M	US 71S, Downtown		S: Phillips 66		
2P	13th St, Downtown (No re-entry)	Food	N: Chuck E Cheese, Denny's, Hardee's, Shoney's, Sonic		
3A	to US 71S, The Paseo, 14th St, Truman Rd			Lodg	N: Econo Lodge, Motel 6♥, Ramada, Sleep Inn, Super 8
			S: Arby's, Burger King, Country Kitchen, Fuddruckers, McDonald's, KFC/TBell, Old Country Buffet, Olive Garden, Pizza Hut, Red Lobster, Ruby Tuesday, Steak n Shake, Wendy's		
3B	Brooklyn Ave (EB)				S: Hampton Inn, Holiday Inn Express, Quality Inn
3C	Prospect Ave, 14th St			Other	N: ATMs, Ace Hardware, Auto Service, Dollar General, Grocery, Home Depot, O'Reilly Auto Parts, Walgreen's
4A	Benton Blvd, E Truman Rd (EB)	Lodg	N: Best Western, Shoney's Inn, Super 8		
4B	18th St, Askew Ave		S: American Inn, Quality Inn, Red Roof Inn♥		S: Advance Auto, Firestone, Goodyear, Grocery, NAPA, Office Depot, Radio Shack
Other	N: Pioneer College, American Jazz Museum. Negro League Baseball Museum	Other	N: Advance Auto, CVS, Dollar General, Firestone, Kmart, Office Depot, Osco, Walgreen's, U-Haul	21	Adams Dairy Pkwy
				Gas	S: Phillips 66◊, Murphy
				Food	S: Burger King/P66, Bob Evans
				Lodg	S: Courtyard, Rodeway Inn, Sleep Inn
4C	23rd St		S: Best Buy, Dollar Tree, Grocery, Tires, Museum	Other	S: Grocery, Home Depot, Wal-Mart sc
		14	Lee's Summit Rd, Independence	24	US 40, MO AA, MO BB, Main St, Grain Valley, Buckner
		Food	S: Cracker Barrel, Olive Garden, Steak n Shake	FStop	N: McLeroy Oil Co
				TStop	N: Apple Trail Travel Center/P66 (Scales)
		Other	S: Home Depot		S: Conoco Travel Center (Scales)
		(15AB)	Jct I-470, MO 291, Independence, Liberty, Lees Summit	Food	N: Rest/Apple Trail TC
					S: Subway/Conoco TC
				Lodg	N: Comfort Inn, Travelodge
		(15A)	Jct I-470S, MO 291S, Lees Summit		S: Kozy Inn Motel
		15B	MO 291N, Independence	Other	N: Laundry/WiFi/RVDump/Apple Trail TC, Country Campers & RV Center▲, Nationwide RV, Show Me Campers & Boats
		Gas	N: 7-11, QT, Phillips 66		

Page 288   ◊ = Regular Gas Stations with Diesel   ▲ = RV Friendly Locations   ♥ = Pet Friendly Locations
RED PRINT SHOWS LARGE VEHICLE PARKING/ACCESS ON SITE OR NEARBY   BROWN PRINT SHOWS CAMPGROUNDS/RV PARKS

W 70 E — MISSOURI

EXIT		
	Other	S: Trailside RV Center, Trailside RV Park▲
28		MO F, MO H, Broadway St, Oak Grove, Levasy
	TStop	N: Travel Center of America #52/Conoco (Scales) S: Petro Stopping Center #70/BP (Scales), Quik Trip #150 (Scales)
	Food	N: Rest/Popeye's/PizzaHut/TA TC S: Rest/Blimpie/DQ/Wendy's, Petro SC, Deli/QT, Hardee's, KFC, McDonald's, Subway, Waffle House
	Lodg	N: Days Inn S: Econo Lodge
	TWash	N: Blue Beacon TW/TA TC, Quality Truck Wash S: TruckOMat/Iowa80/Petro SC
	TServ	N: TA TC/Tires S: Petro SC/Tires, Speedco
	Other	N: Laundry/CB/WiFi/RVDump/TA TC, KsCityEast/Oak Grove KOA▲ S: Laundry/WiFi/RVDump/Petro SC, Laundry/QT, Wal-Mart sc
31		MO Z, 2nd St, MO D, Bates City
	TStop	S: open Fall 08 Flying J Travel Plaza (Scales)
	Gas	S: BP◆
	Food	S: Rest/FastFood/FJ TP, Bates City BBQ, Sonic, Taco John's
	Lodg	S: Bates City Motel & Campground▲
	TServ	S: Mid America Truck Center
	Other	S: Laundry/WiFi/FJ TP, Flea Market
(36)		Truck Parking (Both dir)
37A		MO 131, Odessa, Wellington
37		MO 131, Odessa, Wellington
	FStop	S: Odessa BP
	Gas	S: BP, Shell
	Food	N: Countryside Family Dining S: McDonald's, Pizza Hut, Taco John's
	Lodg	S: Odessa Inn, Parkside Inn
	Other	N: Country Gardens RV Park▲, New Oak Winery S: Auto Dealer, Grocery, O'Reilly, Prime Outlets of Odessa, Grand Junction KOA▲
38		MO 131S, Johnson Dr, Odessa (WB)
	FStop	S: Odessa BP
	Gas	S: Shell
	Food	S: McDonald's, Sonic, Subway, Wendy's
41		MO M, MO O, Lexington
	Other	N: I-70 Speedway
(43)		Weigh Station (Both dir)
45		MO H, to Mayview
49		MO 13, Higginsville, Warrensburg
	TStop	N: Pilot Travel Center #443 (Scales)
	Gas	N: BP

EXIT		
	Food	N: McDonald's/Subway/Pilot TC S: Rest/Super 8
	Lodg	N: Best Western, Best Value Inn S: Camelot Inn, Super 8
	Other	N: Laundry/RVDump/Pilot TC, U-Haul, R&S Towing S: Interstate RV Campground▲
52		MO T, Blue Jay Rd, Aullville
(57)		Rest Area (Both dir) (RR, Phones, Picnic, Vend) (LAST REST AREA WB IN MO)
58		MO 23, Main St, Concordia
	FStop	S: Fat Boyz/Conoco
	TStop	N: Travel Center of America #18 (Scales)
	Gas	N: Casey's S: Breaktime, Shell
	Food	N: CountryPride/PizzaHut/Subway/TA TC

EXIT		
	Food	S: Biffles Smokehouse BBQ, Hardee's, KFC, McDonald's, Topsy's Rest
	Lodg	S: Budget Inn, Days Inn, Fannie Lee B&B, Travelodge
	TServ	N: TA TC/Tires
	Other	N: Laundry/WiFi/TA TC, Dollar General S: NAPA, St Paul's College, RV Center
62		MO Y, MO W, Elm St, Concordia, Emma
66		MO 127, Locust St, Sweet Springs, Mt Leonard, Knob Noster
	Gas	S: Conoco, Phillips 66, Break Time, MFA
	Food	S: Aunt Bea's Bakery, Brownsville Station Rest, Sweet Water Rest, Sonic
	Lodg	S: Motel 6♥, Peoples Choice Motel, Super 8
71		MO K, MO EE, Marshall, Houstonia
74		MO YY, CR 329, Sweet Springs
	TStop	N: Betty's Truck Stop/Shell
	Food	N: Rest/Betty's TS
	Lodg	N: Betty's Motel
	TServ	N: Betty's TS/Tires
78A		US 65S, to Sedalia
	FStop	S: Break Time #3068/MFA
	Other	S: Lazy Days Camping▲, MO Valley College, Fairgrounds, Historic Sites
78B		US 65N, to Marshall
	FStop	N: Conoco
	Other	N: Fireworks, Whitman Air Force Base✈
84		MO J
	Gas	N: BP
	Food	N: Stuckey's/DQ/BP
89		MO K, MO Z, Bryant Bottom Rd, Blackwater, to Arrow Rock
98		MO 135, CR 41, Arrow Rock, Boonville, Lamine, Pilot Grove
	TStop	S: Dogwood Truck Stop/Conoco
	Gas	S: Shell◆
	Food	S: DogwoodRest/Dogwood TS
	TServ	S: Dogwood TS/Tires, Tony's Diesel Service
101		I-70 Bus, US 40, MO 5, Ashley, Boonville, Tipton
	TStop	N: Pilot Travel Center #44 (Scales) S: Love's Travel Stop #347
	Food	N: Arby's/Wendy's/Pilot TC, Burger King S: Hardee's/Love's TS
	Lodg	N: Comfort Inn♥, Holiday Inn Express
	TWash	N: Pilot TC
	TServ	N: Pilot TC
	Other	N: Laundry/WiFi/Pilot TC, Auto Dealers S: Auto Dealers

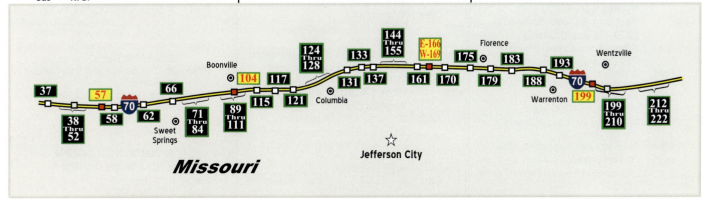

Missouri

◆ = Regular Gas Stations with Diesel ▲ = RV Friendly Locations ♥ = Pet Friendly Locations
RED PRINT SHOWS LARGE VEHICLE PARKING/ACCESS ON SITE OR NEARBY BROWN PRINT SHOWS CAMPGROUNDS/RV PARKS

Page 289

EXIT	MISSOURI
103	**MO B, Main St, Boonville**
TStop	S: Boonville Truck Stop/Conoco (Scales)
Gas	N: Break Time, Phillips 66◆, Speedy's Gas S: BP Cenex
Food	N: Cowboy Toad, Domino's, La Hacienda Mex Rest, Pizza Hut, McDonald's, Sonic, Subway, Taco Bell, KFC/Long John Silver S: Bobber Cafe/Boonville TS, Arby's, DQ, Mr Goodcents Subs
Lodg	N: Days Inn, Super 8
Med	S: + Cooper Co Memorial Hospital
Other	N: Dollar General, Radio Shack, Wal-Mart, RV Express Park▲ S: Laundry/RVDump/Boonville TS, Windmill Campground▲, Bobber Lake Campground▲, to Isle of Capri Casino & Hotel
(104)	**Rest Area (Both dir)** **(RR, Phones, Picnic, Vend)**
106	**Bus 70, MO 87, Boonville, Bingham Rd, Prairie Home**
Gas	N: Cenex, Conoco◆, Phillips 66◆
Food	N: Diner 87, Rest/Atlasta Motel
Lodg	N: Atlasta Motel
111	**MO 179, MO 98, Overton, Wooldridge**
Gas	S: Phillips 66◆
Other	S: Tires/Repair/P66
115	**MO BB, Roby Farm Rd, Rocheport**
Other	N: Les Bourgouis Winery, to State Park
117	**MO J, MO O, Harrisburg, Huntdale**
121	**US 40W, MO 240, MO UU, Columbia, Fayette**
TStop	N: PTP/Midway Truck Plaza/Conoco (Scales)
Gas	N: Phillips 66
Food	N: Rest/Midway TP
Lodg	N: Budget Inn
TServ	N: Midway TP, Goodyear, Truck & Tire Service
Other	N: Laundry/Midway TP, Central Methodist Univ, UMC Dairy Farm
124	**MO 740, MO E, Stadium Blvd**
Gas	N: Break Time S: Phillips 66, Shell
Food	S: Applebee's, Alexander's Steakhouse, Burger King, G&D Steak House, Great Wall Chinese Buffet, Hardee's, KFC, Pasta House, Red Lobster, Subway, Taco Bell, Rest/Holiday Inn
Lodg	N: Extended Stay America, Motel 6♥ S: Baymont Inn, Days Inn, Drury Inn, Holiday Inn
Other	S: Columbia Mall, Best Buy, Circuit City, Kmart, Radio Shack, Target, UPS Store, Wal-Mart, to Univ of MO
125	**West Blvd, N Creasy Springs Rd, Lp 70, I-70 Bus, Columbia**
Gas	S: Break Time◆, Conoco◆, Phillips 66◆, Shell
Food	S: Denny's, El Maguey, Hong Kong, Long John Silver, Olive Garden, Outback Steakhouse, Pizza Hut, Perkins, Red Lobster, Ryan's Grill, Wendy's
Lodg	S: Delux Inn, Econo Lodge, Howard Johnson, Scottish Inn
Other	S: Advance Auto, Auto Dealers, ATMs, Firestone, Grocery, U-Haul

EXIT	MISSOURI
126	**MO 163, Providence Rd, Columbia**
Gas	N: BP S: BP, Break Time◆
Food	N: Bandana's BBQ, Country Kitchen S: Burger King, McDonald's, Pizza Hut, Sonic, Subway, Taco Bell
Lodg	N: Best Value Inn, Quality Inn, Red Roof Inn
Med	S: + Hospital
Other	N: Auto Dealers S: AutoZone, Dollar General, Enterprise RAC, Grocery, O'Reilly Auto
127	**MO 763, Rangeline St, Columbia**
Gas	N: Break Time◆ S: Phillips 66◆
Food	N: McDonald's, Waffle House S: Burger King, DQ, Sonic, Taco Bell
Lodg	N: Budget Host, Ramada, Travelodge S: Super 7
Other	N: Auto Dealers, Dollar General, Harley Davidson S: Bass Pro Shops Outdoor World
128	**I-70 Bus, Columbia (WB, Left exit)**
Gas	S: Conoco◆
Med	S: + Hospital
Other	S: Stephens College
128A	**to US 63N, Jefferson City, Moberly**
Gas	N: BP, Casey's, QT S: Conoco
Food	N: Bob Evans, Burger King, Cracker Barrel, Golden Corral, Hooters, KFC, Lone Star Steakhouse, McDonald's, Ruby Tuesday, Steak n Shake, Taco Bell S: Applebee's, Chili's, CiCi's, IHOP, Longhorn Steakhouse, Quiznos, Subway
Lodg	N: Fairfield Inn, Hampton Inn, Hilton Garden Inn, Residence Inn, Super 8 S: Best Western, Candlewood Suites, Holiday Inn Express, La Quinta Inn♥, Motel 6♥, Wingate Inn
Other	N: Bass Pro Shop, Home Depot, Cottonwoods RV Park▲ S: ATM, Bank, Grocery, Lowe's, Sam's Club, Staples, Wal-Mart sc, Finger Lakes State Park▲, Pine Grove Village
131	**St Charles Rd, Lake of the Wood Rd**
Gas	N: BP, Phillips 66◆ S: Conoco◆
Food	S: Sonic, Subway/P66
Lodg	N: Super 8
Other	N: Mid-America Harley Davidson, Lakeview Mall, Tourist Info S: RV Park▲
133	**MO Z, Rangeline Rd, to Centralia**
TServ	N: Fabick Cat, Bobcat S: Kenworth
Other	N: Loveall's RV
137	**MO DD, MO J, Millersburg**
TServ	S: Freightliner
144	**MO M, MO HH, Cort 223, to Hatton**
Other	S: Shoemaker RV Center, Crooked Creek Campground▲
148	**US 54, CR 201, Gold Ave, CR 211, Kingdom City**
TStop	S: FastLane/P66, Gasper's Travel Center/Shell (Scales), Petro Stopping Center #18 / Mobil (Scales), Westland Travel Center / Conoco (Scales)
Gas	N: BP, Phillips 66◆
Food	N: Taco Bell

EXIT	MISSOURI
Food	S: McDonald's/FastLane, Arby's/Gasper's TC, Iron Skillet, FastFood/Petro SC, Subway/Westland TC
Lodg	N: Holiday Inn S: Comfort Inn, Days Inn, Red Carpet Inn, Super 8
TServ	S: Gasper's TC/Tires, Petro SC/Tires
Other	N: Nostalgia Village USA, Tourist Info, MO Military Academy, to Mark Twain Lake S: Laundry/Gasper's TC, Laundry/BarbSh/RVDump/Petro SC, Lake of the Ozarks
155	**MO A, MO Z, Fulton, Auxvasse**
161	**MO YY, MO D, Williamsburg, Old US 40, CR 177, Bachelor, Calwood**
TStop	S: Jump Stop Travel Center/Conoco
Gas	S: Ray's Garage
Food	S: Rest/Jump Stop TC
(166)	**Rest Area (EB)** **(RR, Phones, Picnic, Vend)**
(169)	**Rest Area (WB)** **(RR, Phones, Picnic, Vend)**
170	**MO 161, MO J, Danville, Montgomery City**
Gas	N: Citgo, Phillips 66
Other	N: Graham Cave State Park▲, Kan-Do Kampground▲ S: Lazy Day Campground▲
175	**MO 19, Boonslick Rd, New Florence, Hermann, Montgomery City**
FStop	N: Abel's Fuel Center #17/Shell, Junction Fuel & Grocery/BP
Gas	N: Phillips 66
Food	N: McDonald's/Shell, Maggie's Café, Pizza Cabin, Hardee's
Lodg	N: Best Inn, Super 8, Harbour Haus Inn
Other	N: Cuno RV, Stone Hill Winery, to Mark Twain Lake, Cannon Dam (appr 51 mi) S: Hermann Winery, Adam Punate Winery
179	**MO F, High Hill**
Lodg	S: I-70 Budget Motel, Colonial Inn
183	**MO Y, MO NN, MO E, N 1st St, CR 250, Jonesburg**
Gas	S: Fastlane/66, Shell
Other	N: Jonesburg Gardens Campground▲
188	**MO A, MO B, Warrenton**
TStop	S: Flying J Travel Plaza #5016/Conoco (Scales)
Food	S: Cookery/FastFood/FJ TP
Lodg	S: Budget Inn
Other	S: Laundry/WiFi/RVDump/LP/FJ TP
193	**MO 47, Warrenton, to Hawk Point, Marthasville**
Gas	N: 7-11, Phillips 66◆, ZX S: BP, Casey's, Phillips 66◆, Shell
Food	N: Burger King, DQ, Jack in the Box, Pizza Hut, McDonald's, Subway, Waffle House S: Denny's, Hardee's, KFC, Taco Bell
Lodg	N: Days Inn, Holiday Inn Express, Super 8 S: AmeriHost, Budget Host Inn
Other	N: ATMs, Banks, Family Dollar, Grocery, Wal-Mart sc S: Auto Dealers, AutoZone, Kelly Tires, NAPA, Outlet Mall
(199)	**Rest Area (Both dir)** **(RR, Phones, Picnic)**
199	**Wildcat Dr, MO H, to MO M to MO J, Wright City (WB)**
Gas	N: Shell
Food	N: McDonald's

◆ = Regular Gas Stations with Diesel ▲ = RV Friendly Locations ♥ = Pet Friendly Locations
RED PRINT SHOWS LARGE VEHICLE PARKING/ACCESS ON SITE OR NEARBY BROWN PRINT SHOWS CAMPGROUNDS/RV PARKS

EXIT		MISSOURI
	TServ	S: Porter Truck Sales, Volvo
200		MO J, MO F, Elm Ave, Wright City
	Gas	N: Citgo◊, Shell◊, MidWest Petro
		S: Phillips 66
	Food	N: Abilene's Rest, Mexican Rest
		S: Big Boy
	Lodg	S: Super 7 Inn
	TServ	N: Freightliner
	Other	N: Chiropractor
203		MO T, MO W, Foristell
	TStop	N: Travel Center of America #175/BP (Scales), Mr Fuel #4 (Scales)
		S: Foristell Truck Stop/P66
	Food	N: Rest/Popeye's/PizzaHut/TacoBell/TA TC FastFood/Mr Fuel
		S: Rest/Foristell TS
	Lodg	N: Best Western
	TServ	N: TA TC/Tires, Fabick CAT
	Other	N: Laundry/WiFi/TA TC
		S: Marlen Gas Co/LP
(205)		Weigh Station (Both dir)
208		Pearce Blvd, Wentzville Pkwy, Wentzville
	Gas	N: Citgo, QT◊
		S: BP, Shell, Phillips 66
	Food	N: McDonald's, Pizza Hut, Steak n Shake, Taco Bell, Wendy's, Waffle House
		S: Captain D's, Hardee's, Pizza
	Lodg	S: Super 8
	Med	N: + Hospital
	Other	N: ATMs, Banks, Best Buy, Grocery, Home Depot, Walgreen's, Bill Thomas Camper
		S: Wal-Mart, Pinewood RV Park▲
209		MO Z, Church St, to New Melle (WB)
	Gas	S: Phillips 66
	Food	N: DQ
210AB		US 40S, US 61, to I-64, Wentzville
	TStop	S: Wentzville P66
	Gas	S: Conoco, Shell
	Food	S: Rest/Wentzville P66
	Lodg	N: Budget Inn, Econo Lodge, Knights Inn
212		MO A, Freymuth Rd, Lake St Louis
	Gas	S: Citgo◊, Mobil
	Food	S: Arby's, Burger King, Willie's Steaks
	Lodg	N: Ramada Econo Lodge, Knights Inn
		S: Holiday Inn
	Other	N: General Motors Assembly Plant, Freedom RV
214		Lake St Louis Blvd, Lake St Louis
	Gas	S: Phillips 66◊, Shell
	Food	S: Denny's, Hardee's, Subway
	Lodg	S: Days Inn
	Med	S: + St Joseph Hospital West
	Other	N: Ryder, Marina
		S: Grocery
216		Bryan Rd, W Terra Ln, O'Fallon
	Gas	S: Casey's, Conoco, Phillips 66
	Lodg	S: Super 8
	TServ	N: Peterbilt
217		MO K, Veterans Memorial Pkwy, MO M, S Main St, O'Fallon
	Gas	N: BP, QT
		S: Citgo◊, Dirt Cheap, Fina, Shell, Phillips 66, ZX
	Food	N: Burger King, Hardee's, Jack in the Box, Ponderosa, Taco Bell, Waffle House
		S: Arby's, Bob Evans, IHOP, Lion's Choice, Longhorn Steakhouse, Pizza Hut, Papa John's, McDonald's, Steak 'n Shake, Stefanina's Pizza

EXIT		MISSOURI
	Lodg	S: O'Fallon Motel
	Other	N: Firestone, Radio Shack, Cherokee Camping▲
		S: AutoZone, Grocery, Lowe's, Midas, Walgreen's, RV Center
219		Belleau Creek Rd, TR Hughes Blvd, Cool Springs Rd, O'Fallon
	Gas	S: QT
	Lodg	S: Comfort Inn
220		MO 79, Salt Lick Rd, St Peters, to Elsberry
	Gas	S: 7-11, BP
	Food	S: Hardee's, McDonald's, Quiznos, Smokehouse Rest, Sonic, Subway
	Other	N: Cherokee Camping & Fishing▲
222		MO C, Mid Rivers Mall Dr, St Peters
	FStop	S: QuikTrip #608 (Scales)
	Gas	S: Citgo, Mobil
	Food	N: Burger King
		S: Arby's, Bob Evans, Chili's, Hardee's, Jack in the Box, Joe's Crab Shack, Olive Garden, McDonald's, Pizza Hut, Red Robin, Ruby Tuesday, Steak 'n Shake, Subway, Steak Escape, Taco Bell, Wendy's
	Lodg	S: Drury Inn, Extended Stay America
	Other	N: Auto Dealers, Daniel Boone Monument
		S: AutoZone, B&N, Best Buy, Big Lots, Costco, Circuit City, Discount Tire, Grocery, Walgreen's, U-Haul, Westfield Mall
224		MO 370E
	TServ	N: Kenworth
	Other	S: Auto Dealer
225		Cave Springs Rd, Harry Truman Rd, St Peters, St Charles
	Gas	N: BP, Citgo, Shell

EXIT		MISSOURI
		S: Conoco, Mobil, QT, ZX
	Food	N: Patty's Café, Taco Bell, Wendy's
		S: Burger King, Denny's, Ground Round, IHOP, Jack in the Box, Long John Silver, McDonald's, Pasta House, Pizza Hut, Ponderosa, Red Lobster, Steak n Shake, Subway
	Lodg	N: Hampton Inn, Knights Inn, Motel 6♥
		S: Holiday Inn Express, Budget Motel
	Med	S: + Hospital
	Other	N: Auto Dealers, U-Haul
		S: ATMs, Budget RAC, Firestone, Grocery, Home Depot, Kmart, Office Depot, Target
227		Zumbehl Rd, St Charles
	Gas	N: Shell, ZX
		S: BP, Mobil
	Food	N: Burger King, Culpepper's
		S: Applebee's, Black Eyed Pea, Boston Market, Bob Evans, Chevy's Mexican, CiCi's, Fratelli's, Golden Corral, Hardee's, Little Caesars, Lone Star Steakhouse, Old Country Buffet, Popeye's, Quiznos, Subway, Taco Bell
	Lodg	N: Econo Lodge, Super 8
		S: Best Western, Comfort Inn, Red Roof Inn♥, TownPlace Suites, Travelodge
	Other	N: Cinema, Grocery, Lowe's
		S: Big Lots, Dollar Tree, Grocery, Sam's Club, Wal-Mart, Glendale Christian Family Resort, Access to Ex #228
228		MO 94, First Capitol Dr, St Charles, to Weldon Springs
	Gas	N: Citgo, Phillips 66, Shell
		S: Mobil, Shell, QT
	Food	N: Arby's, DQ, Hardee's, Long John Silver, Papa John's, Pizza Hut, Steak 'n Shake, Wendy's
		S: Chuck E Cheese, Fazoli's
	Lodg	S: Best Western, Days Inn, InTowne Suites
	Other	N: Advance Auto, Auto Zone, Firestone, Grocery, Radio Shack, Walgreen's
		S: Kmart, Lynnwood Univ
229		5th St, River Rd, St Charles (EB)
	Gas	N: BP, Mobil◊
		S: Phillips 66, QT
	Food	N: Burger King, Denny's, Jack in the Box, McDonald's, Subway, Waffle House
		S: Cracker Barrel
	Lodg	N: Baymont Inn, Best Western, Comfort Suites, Quality Inn, St Charles Hotel
		S: Comfort Inn, Days Inn, Fairfield Inn, Ramada Inn, Suburban Lodge
	Other	N: Walgreen's, Bass Pro Shop, Casino
		S: Convention Center, Mall, RV Park▲
229A		S 5th St, S River Rd (WB)
229B		Bus 70N, 5th St (WB)
231AB		Earth City Expy, Maryland Hts Expy
	FStop	N: MPC #62/P66
	Gas	S: Mobil
	Food	N: JackintheBox/P66, McDonald's
		S: Burger King, Town Square Café
	Lodg	N: Candlewood Suites, Courtyard, Fairfield Inn, Residence Inn, Sheraton, Studio Plus
		S: Holiday Inn Express, Wingate Inn
	Other	S: Harrah's Riverport Casino, Riverport Amphitheatre, RV Park▲
(232)		Jct I-270, N-Chicago, S-Memphis

◊ = Regular Gas Stations with Diesel   ▲ = RV Friendly Locations   ♥ = Pet Friendly Locations
RED PRINT SHOWS LARGE VEHICLE PARKING/ACCESS ON SITE OR NEARBY   BROWN PRINT SHOWS CAMPGROUNDS/RV PARKS

EXIT	MISSOURI
234	MO 180, St. Charles Rock Rd, Bridgeton
Gas	N: Phillips 66, Shell
Food	N: Applebee's, Casa Gallardo's, Hatfield/McCoy Rest, Lone Star Steakhouse, Long John Silver, McDonald's, Old Country Buffet, Ponderosa, Red Lobster, Shoney's, Steak n Shake, Taco Bell
Lodg	N: Knights Inn
Med	N: + Hospital
Other	N: Best Buy, Circuit City, Kmart, Office Depot, Sam's Club, Target, Walgreen's
235AB	US 67, Lindberg Blvd (WB)
235A	US 67S, Lindberg Blvd
Gas	S: Shell
Food	S: Steak 'n Shake, TGI Friday
Lodg	S: Crown Plaza, Embassy Suites, Homestead Inn, Radisson
Other	S: Firestone, Mall
235B	US 67N, Lindberg Blvd
Gas	N: Shell
Food	N: Rest/Holiday Inn
Lodg	N: Econo Lodge, Holiday Inn, Howard Johnson
Other	N: St Louis Int'l Airport ✈
235C	MO B, Cypress Rd, Nat'l Bridge Rd
Other	N: St Louis Int'l Airport ✈
236	Lambert St Louis Int'l Airport
Gas	S: BP
Food	S: CoCo's, Hardee's, Rafferty's
Lodg	S: Best Western, Days Inn, Drury Inn, Hampton Inn, Holiday Inn, Hilton Garden Inn, Marriott, Motel 6 ♥
237	MO 115, Natural Bridge Rd (EB)
Gas	S: Phillips 66, Shell
Food	S: Arby's, Burger King, Denny's, Jack in the Box, Pizza Hut, Steak 'n Shake, Waffle House, Wendy's
Lodg	S: Best Western, Days Inn, DoubleTree Hotel, Travelodge
238A	Lambert St. Louis Airport (WB)
(238B)	Jct I-170S
(238C)	Jct I-170N
239	Hanley Rd
Gas	S: Mobil
Food	S: McDonald's
240	MO N, Florissant Rd
Gas	N: BP
Food	N: McDonald's, Taco Bell
241A	Stanwood Dr, Bermuda Ave
Gas	S: Shell, Sinclair
241B	MO U, Lucas-Hunt Rd
Gas	N: Shell

EXIT	MISSOURI
Gas	S: Citgo
242	Jennings Station Rd
Gas	N: Shell
243	Goodfellow Blvd
243A	Riverview Blvd
243B	Bircher Blvd, Riverview Blvd (WB)
243C	Bircher Blvd (EB)
244A	Riverview Blvd, Bircher Blvd (EB) Union Blvd (WB)
244B	N Kingshighway Blvd
245A	Shreve Ave, Bircher Ave
Gas	S: BP
245B	W Florissant Ave, Bircher Blvd
246A	Broadway (WB), E Carrie Ave (EB)
Gas	N: Mobil ◊
Other	N: Freightliner
246B	Adelaide Ave
247	Grand Blvd, St Louis
FStop	N: MPC #42/P66
Lodg	N: First Western Inn
248A	N 9th St, Salisbury St (WB) N 11th St, Salisbury St (EB)
Gas	S: BP, Mobil ◊
248B	Branch St, N 9th St (WB) N 11th St, St Louis Ave (EB)
249A	Madison St (WB), Howard St (EB)
Gas	N: Phillips 66 ◊
Other	N: Busch Stadium, Riverboat Gambling
249C	Cass Ave, N Broadway, 6th St (EB)
250A	Cole St, N Broadway
Lodg	N: Econo Lodge, Embassy Suites S: Drury Inn, Hampton Inn, Holiday Inn
Other	N: Convention Center
250B	Memorial Dr, Downtown
Gas	S: Shell
Food	S: McDonald's
Lodg	S: Adams Mark, Days Inn, Radisson
(251A)	Jct I-55S, to Memphis, to I-44, Downtown
251B	Memorial Dr (WB)
NOTE:	MM 252: Illinois State Line

(CENTRAL TIME ZONE)

🎧 **MISSOURI**

EXIT	ILLINOIS
	🎧 **ILLINOIS** (CENTRAL TIME ZONE)
NOTE:	I-70 runs below with I-55 for 18 mi. Exit #'s follow I-55.
1	IL 3, to Sauget (SB)
2A	MLK Bridge, to St Louis Downtown (SB, Left exit)
2B	3rd St (SB, Left exit)
Other	W: Casino Queen RV Park▲
2C	MLK Memorial Bridge (SB)
(2)	Jct I-64E, IL 3N, St Clair Ave
3	Exchange Ave, St Clair Ave, E St Louis
4A	IL 203E, Collinsville Rd (SB)
4B	IL 203W, E St Louis (SB)
4	IL 203, Collinsville Rd, Granite City, E St Louis (NB)
TStop	W: Pilot Travel Center #313 (Scales) (SB Access via Exit # 4B)
Gas	E: Phillips 66 ◊
Food	W: Subway/TacoBell/Pilot TC
Lodg	E: First Western Inn
TWash	W: Pilot TC
TServ	W: Pilot TC/Tires
Other	W: Laundry/WiFi/Pilot TC, Gateway Int'l Raceway
NOTE:	MM 5: EB: Begin Motorist Call Boxes
6	IL 111, Great River Rd, Wood River, Fairmont City, Washington Park
Gas	E: Phillips 66 ◊
Lodg	E: Royal Relax Inn, Royal Budget Inn, Indian Mound Motel
Other	E: Grocery, Pharmacy, Safari RV Park▲, Indian Mounds Golf Course, to Cahokia Mounds State Park W: to Horseshoe Lakes State Park, Lakeside Airport ✈
9	Fairmont Ave, Black Lane (NB exit, SB reaccess)
Other	E: to Fairmount Park, Cahokia Mounds State Park
(10)	Jct I-255, S-Memphis, N to I-270
11	IL 157, Bluff Rd, Collinsville, to Edwardsville
FStop	W: Moto Mart
Gas	E: BP, Casey's, Shell
Food	E: Denny's, Hardee's, Long John Silver, McDonald's, Waffle House, Wendy's

Page 292   ◊ = Regular Gas Stations with Diesel   ▲ = RV Friendly Locations   ♥ = Pet Friendly Locations
RED PRINT SHOWS LARGE VEHICLE PARKING/ACCESS ON SITE OR NEARBY   BROWN PRINT SHOWS CAMPGROUNDS/RV PARKS

EXIT		ILLINOIS
	Food	W: Arby's, Applebee's, Bandanas BBQ, Bob Evans, Burger King, DQ, Pizza Hut, Ruby Tuesday, Steak 'n Shake, White Castle, Rest/Hol Inn
	Lodg	E: Best Western, Howard Johnson, Motel 6♥ W: Comfort Inn, Days Inn, Drury Inn♥, Fairfield Inn, Holiday Inn, Super 8
	Other	E: Randy's Trailer Town W: Auto & Tire Service, Auto Dealers, Visitor Center, Convention Center, IL State Hwy Patrol Post
(14)		Weigh Station (SB)
15AB		IL 159, Vandalia St, Maryville Rd, Collinsville, Maryville
	Gas	E: Citgo, Phillips 66♦, Shell W: Conoco
	Lodg	W: Econo Lodge
17		US 40E, to Troy, St Jacob
	TServ	E: ADR Auto & Truck Repair, M&M Truck Repair
18		IL 162, Edwardsville Rd, Troy
	TStop	E: Pilot Travel Center #249 (Scales), Travel Center of America #199/BP (Scales)
	Gas	W: Phillips 66♦
	Food	E: Arby's/TJCinn/Pilot TC, Rest/TA TC, Burger King, DQ, Jack in the Box, KFC, Little Caesar's, McDonald's, Perkins, Pizza Hut, Subway W: China Garden, Cracker Barrel, Taco Bell
	Lodg	E: Relax Inn W: Holiday Inn Express♥, Red Roof Inn♥, Scottish Inns, Super 8
	TWash	E: 18 Wheeler's Truck Wash
	TServ	E: TA TC/Tires, Carron's Auto & Truck Repair
	Med	W: + Anderson Hospital
	Other	E: Laundry/WiFi/Pilot TC, Laundry/BarbSh/TA TC, Family Dollar, Grocery
(20A)		Jct I-70E, to Indianapolis
(20B)		Jct I-270W, to Kansas City
(15AB)		Jct I-55, N-Chicago, S-St Louis, I-270W, to Kansas City
	NOTE:	I-70 runs above with I-55 for 18 mi. Exit #'s follow I-55.
21		IL 4, Marine, to Lebanon, Staunton
	NOTE:	MM 23: WB:Begin Motorist Call Boxes
24		IL 143, Marine, Highland
	Med	S: + Hospital
(27)		IL Welcome Center (EB) Silver Lake Rest Area (WB) (RR, Phones, Picnic, Vend, Weather)
30		US 40, to IL 143, Steiner Rd, Highlan
	Gas	S: Shell♦
	Food	S: Blue Springs Restaurant
	Med	S: + Hospital
	Other	S: to Tomahawk Campground▲
36		US 40, CR 21, 475E, Pocahontas
	Gas	S: AmocoBP♦, Phillips 66♦
	Food	S: Rest/Powhatan Motel
	Lodg	S: Powhatan Motel, Tahoe Motel, Wikiup Motel
	ATServ	S: Auto Truck Tires & Service
41		US 40E, to Greenville, 970E

EXIT		ILLINOIS
45		IL 127, to US 40, Greenville, to Carlyle Lake, Carlyle
	Gas	N: Citgo♦, Phillips 66♦, Shell♦
	Food	N: KFC, McDonald's, Rest/BW S: Circle B Western Steakhouse
	Lodg	N: Best Western, Budget Host Inn, Super 8
	Med	N: + Greenville Regional Hospital
	Other	N: Auto Services, Towing S: to Greenville Airport✈
52		CR 10, Maple St, Mulberry Grove
	Gas	N: Citgo♦
	Other	S: Cedarbrook RV Park & Campground▲
61		US 40, Vandalia, Mulberry Grove
	Gas	S: Fastop♦, Phillips 66♦, Murphy♦
	Food	S: KFC/Taco Bell, Ponderosa
	Lodg	S: Ramada
	Other	N: Vandalia Muni Airport✈ S: Auto Services, Wal-Mart sc, NAPA
63		US 51, US 40, Vandalia, Pana
	Gas	S: BP, Marathon, Shell♦
	Food	N: Long John Silver S: DQ, Hardee's, KFC, McDonald's, Pizza Hut, Subway, Wendy's
	Lodg	N: Days Inn S: Jay's Inn♥, Travelodge
	Med	S: + Fayette Co Hospital
	Other	S: Grocery, Pharmacy
68		US 40, Brownstown, Bluff City
(71)		Weigh Station (EB)
76		US 40, CR 7, 2125E, St Elmo
82		IL 128, CR 25, 300th St, Altamont
	Gas	N: Casey's, Stuckey's/Citgo♦, Marathon, Speedway♦

EXIT		ILLINOIS
	Gas	S: Phillips 66
	Food	N: McDonald's, Subway, Rest/Altamont Motel
	Lodg	N: Altamont Motel, Knights Inn S: Super 8
(87)		Rest Area (Both dir) (RR, Phones, Picnic, Vend)
(92)		Jct I-57, N - Chicago, S - Memphis
	NOTE:	I-70 below runs with I-57 for 6 mi. Exit #'s follow I-57.
159		Fayette Ave, Effingham
	FStop	E: Econo Fuel Express/Citgo
	TStop	W: Petro Stopping Center #21/Mobil (Scales), Truck-O-Mat (Scales)
	Gas	E: BP, Phillips 66
	Food	E: China Buffet, Culver's, Hardee's, Neimerg's Steak House, Subway W: IronSkillet/Petro SC, Rest/BW
	Lodg	E: Abe Lincoln Motel, Comfort Suites♥, Econo Lodge, Howard Johnson Express♥, Lincoln Lodge♥, Paradise Inn, Rodeway Inn♥ W: Best Western♥
	TWash	W: Blue Beacon/Petro SC, TruckOMat
	TServ	E: Effingham Truck Sales/International W: Petro SC/Tires
	Other	E: ATMs, Auto Services, Amtrak, CarWash, to Village Square Mall, Effingham Co Memorial Airport✈ W: Laundry/BarbSh/CB/WiFi/Petro SC
160		IL 32, IL 33, N Keller Dr, Effingham
	TStop	W: Flying J Travel Plaza #5107 (Scales), Travel Center of America #35/BP (Scales)
	Gas	E: BP, Shell W: Phillips 66, Murphy♦
	Food	E: KFC, Lone Star Steakhouse W: Rest/FastFood/FJ TP, CountryPride/Popeye's/Sbarro/TA TC, Arby's, Burger King, Cracker Barrel, Denny's, Long John Silver, McDonald's, Ponderosa, Ryan's Grill, Ruby Tuesday, Steak n Shake, Starbucks, Subway, Taco Bell, TGI Friday, Wendy's
	Lodg	E: Comfort Inn, Hampton Inn W: Hotel/FJ TP, Country Inn, Hilton Garden Inn, Holiday Inn Express♥, Motel 6, Ramada Ltd, Super 8♥, Travelodge
	TWash	W: Blue Beacon TW/FJ TP, TA TC
	TServ	W: TA TC/Tires, Speedco, Peterbilt, Clarke Power Services
	Med	E: + St Anthony's Memorial Hospital
	Other	E: ATMs, Banks, Dollar General, Grocery, Kmart, Kroger, Walgreen's W: Laundry/WiFi/RVDump/LP/FJ TP, Laundry/BarbSh/WiFi/TA TC, ATMs, Towing, U-Haul, Wal-Mart sc, Camp Lakewood RV Park▲
162		US 45, N 3rd St, Effingham
	TStop	W: Pilot Travel Center #165 (Scales)
	Gas	E: Moto Mart W: Citgo
	Food	W: McDonald's/Pilot TC
	TWash	W: Pilot TC
	Med	E: + St Anthony's Memorial Hospital
	Other	E: Legacy Harley Davidson W: Laundry/WiFi/LP/Pilot TC, Crossroads RV Center, Camp Lakewood RV Park▲
	NOTE:	I-70 above runs with I-57 for 6 mi. Exit #'s follow I-57.

♦ = Regular Gas Stations with Diesel   ▲ = RV Friendly Locations   ♥ = Pet Friendly Locations

RED PRINT SHOWS LARGE VEHICLE PARKING/ACCESS ON SITE OR NEARBY   BROWN PRINT SHOWS CAMPGROUNDS/RV PARKS

EXIT		IL / IN
(98)		Jct I-57N, to Chicago
105		Montrose
	Gas	S: BP◊, Citgo◊, Shell
	Food	S: Rest/Montarosa Motel
	Lodg	S: Montarosa Motel
119		IL 130, Greenup, Charleston
	Gas	S: BP◊, Citgo◊, Phillips 66, Shell
	Food	S: DQ, Dutch Pan Restaurant
	Lodg	S: Budget Host Inn
129		IL 49, Casey, Kansas
	Gas	S: BP◊, Casey's, Citgo◊, Speedway
	Food	S: DQ, Hardee's, KFC, McDonald's, Pizza Hut
	Lodg	S: Comfort Inn
	Other	S: Casey Muni Airport✈
136		to Martinsville
	Gas	S: BP◊
147		IL 1, Marshall, Paris
	FStop	S: Marshall Junction 66
	Gas	S: Jiffy◊, Casey's
	Food	N: Hardee's, Jerry's Rest
		S: Burger King, McDonald's, Pizza Hut
	Lodg	S: Peak's Motor Inn, Super 8
(149)		IL Welcome Center (WB)
		(RR, Phones, Picnic, Vend, Weather)
(151)		Weigh Station (WB)
154		US 40W
	NOTE:	MM 157: Indiana State Line
		(CENTRAL TIME ZONE)

◎ **ILLINOIS**
◎ **INDIANA**
(CENTRAL TIME ZONE)

1		US 40E, W National Rd, W Terre Haute to Terre Haute
(2)		IN Welcome Center (EB)
		(RR, Phones, Picnic, Vend, Info)
3		Darwin Rd, W Terre Haute
7		US 41, US 150, Terre Haute
	Gas	N: BP◊, Marathon◊, Thornton's◊
		S: Jiffy, Shell, Speedway◊, Sunoco, Sam's
	Food	N: Arby's, Bob Evans, Cracker Barrel, Fazoli's, Hardee's, IHOP, Little Caesar's, Pizza Hut, Shoney's, Steak n Shake, Texas Roadhouse, Starbucks
		S: DQ, Damon's Ribs, Hardee's, Denny's, Long John Silver, McDonald's, Olive Garden, Outback Steakhouse, Red Lobster, Subway, Taco Bell, Wendy's

EXIT		INDIANA
	Lodg	N: Comfort Suites, Days Inn, Dollar Inn, Drury Inn, Econo Lodge, Fairfield Inn, Signature Inn, Super 8
		S: Hampton Inn, Holiday Inn, Motel 6♥
	TServ	N: GMC/Volvo
		S: McCord Tire & Auto Service
	Med	S: + Hospital
	Other	N: AutoZone, IN State Hwy Patrol Post
		S: ATMs, Auto Dealers, Big Lots, Gander Mountain, Harley Davidson, Kmart, Kroger, Sam's Club, Wal-Mart sc, Walgreen's
11		IN 46, Hulman Rd, Terre Haute
	TStop	N: Pilot Travel Center #297 (Scales)
	Gas	N: Thornton's
	Food	N: Arby's/TJCinn/Pilot TC, Burger King, McDonald's
	TServ	N: Russ Fisher Truck Parts
	Other	N: WiFi/Pilot TC, Hulman Reg'l Airport✈
		S: Terre Haute KOA▲
23		IN 59, Brazil, Linton
	TStop	N: Pilot Travel Center #444 (Scales)
		S: Brazil 70 AmBest Truck Stop/Shell (Scales), Road Ranger #141/Citgo (Scales)
	Gas	S: Sunoco
	Food	N: McDonald's/Subway/Pilot TC
		S: Rest/Brazil 70 TS, Subway/RoadRanger, Burger King, Ike's Great American Rest, Rally/Sunoco
	Lodg	S: Howard Johnson
	TServ	S: Brazil 70 TS
	Med	N: + Hospital
	Other	N: Laundry/WiFi/Pilot TC, to appr 20 mi Willow Rose RV Park▲, to appr 17 mi Fallen Rock Park Campground▲
		S: Laundry/Brazil70 TS, Ex 23 70 CB Shop
37		IN 243, Cloverdale, Putnamville
	FStop	S: Marathon #211
	Other	N: Dogwood Springs Campground▲
41		US 231, IN 43, Cloverdale, to Greencastle, Spencer
	TStop	S: PTP/Cloverdale Travel Plaza (Scales)
	Gas	S: BP◊, Shell
	Food	N: Long Branch Steakhouse
		S: Rest/FastFood/Cloverdale TP, Burger King, Arby's, KFC, McDonald's, Wendy's
	Lodg	N: Midway Motel
		S: Best Western, Budget Inn, Days Inn, Dollar Inn, Holiday Inn Express, Super 8
	TWash	S: Cloverdale TP
	TServ	S: Cloverdale TP/Tires
	Med	N: + Hospital
	Other	N: Cloverdale RV Park▲
		S: Laundry/Cloverdale TP, to appr 11 mi Hickory Hills Campground▲

EXIT		INDIANA
51		Little Point Rd, CR 1100W, IN 42, Stilesville
	Gas	S: Koger's Country Mart
	TServ	S: Curtin Garage & Wrecker Service, Koger's Garage
59		IN 39, Clayton, Belleville, Monrovia
	TStop	S: Travel Center of America #102/Citgo (Scales)
	Gas	N: Marathon
	Food	S: CountryPride/NobleRomans/TA TC
	TServ	S: TA TC/Tires
	Other	S: Laundry/WiFi/LP/TA TC
(64)		Rest Area (Both dir)
		(RR, Phones, Picnic, Vend, Info)
66		IN 267, Quaker Blvd, Plainfield, to Mooresville
	Gas	N: BP, Shell, Speedway◊, Thornton's◊
	Food	N: Arby's, Bob Evans, Cracker Barrel, Hog Heaven BBQ, McDonald's, Perkins, Quiznos, Subway, Wendy's
	Lodg	N: Amerihost Inn, Comfort Inn, Days Inn, Dollar Inn, Hampton Inn, Holiday Inn Express, Lee's Inn, Super 8
	Other	N: Harley Davidson, Winery
(73A)		Jct I-465S, I-74E
(73B)		Jct I-465N, I-74W
75		Airport Expwy, to Raymond St, to I-465, I-74 (WB)
	Gas	N: Marathon, Speedway
	Food	N: Denny's, Waffle & Steak
	Lodg	N: Adams Mark, AmeriSuites, Baymont Inn, Fairfield Inn, La Quinta Inn♥, Motel 6♥, Residence Inn, Wellesley Inn
	Other	N: Indianapolis Int'l Airport✈
77		Holt Rd, Indianapolis
	Gas	S: Shell
	Food	S: McDonald's
	TServ	S: Cummins, Discover Volvo Trucks, Ford, Fruehauf, Kenworth of Indianapolis
78		Harding St, to Downtown
79A		West St, S Capitol Ave (EB)
		Capitol Ave, S Missouri St (WB)
79B		Illinois St, W McCarty St
(80)		Jct I-65S, to Louisville
83A		Michigan St, Ohio St, Fletcher Ave, Indianapolis
(83B)		Jct I-65N, to Chicago
85AB		Rural St, Keystone Ave (WB)
	Gas	N: Amoco
		S: Marathon

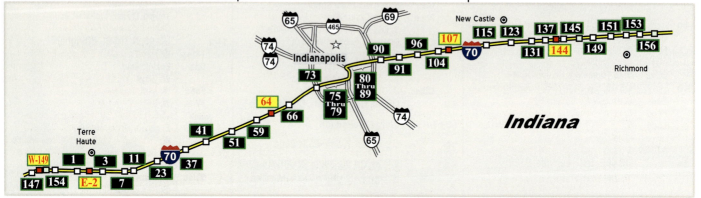

◊ = Regular Gas Stations with Diesel ▲ = RV Friendly Locations ♥ = Pet Friendly Locations
RED PRINT SHOWS LARGE VEHICLE PARKING/ACCESS ON SITE OR NEARBY BROWN PRINT SHOWS CAMPGROUNDS/RV PARKS

INTERSTATE 70 W / E

INDIANA

EXIT	
85A	Rural St (EB)
85B	Rural St, Keystone Way (EB)
87	Emerson Ave
Gas	N: BP, Speedway
Food	N: McDonald's/BP
89	Shadeland Ave, 21st St, Jct I-465, (fr EB)
Gas	S: Circle K, Shell, Speedway
Food	N: Bob Evans, Waffle House
	S: Black Angus, Burger King, Damon's, Red Lobster, Subway, Wendy's
Lodg	N: Comfort Inn, Hampton Inn, Motel 6
	S: Budget Inn, Fairfield Inn, Holiday Inn, Knights Inn, La Quinta Inn♥, Ramada Ltd
Other	S: CVS
(90)	Jct I-465, Louisville, Ft Wayne (WB)
91	Post Rd, E 21st, E 25th St
Gas	N: 7-11/Marathon
	S: BP, Shell
Food	N: Cracker Barrel, Denny's, Joe's Crab Shack, McDonald's, Outback, Wendy's
	S: Hardee's, Taco Bell, Waffle & Steak
Lodg	N: Baymont Inn, La Quinta Inn♥, Suburban Lodge
	S: Best Western, Days Inn, Dollar Inn, Quality Inn, Super 8
Other	N: IN State Hwy Patrol Post
	S: Grocery, CVS, Home Depot
96	600W, Greenfield, Mt Comfort
TStop	N: Pilot Travel Center #30 (Scales)
Gas	N: Gas America
	S: Shell
Food	N: PizzaHut/Pilot TC, Burger King, Wendy's
	S: McDonald's
Other	N: WiFi/Pilot TC, Heartland Resort▲
	S: Indianapolis KOA▲, RV Center, RV Park▲
104	IN 9, State St, Greenfield, Maxwell
Gas	N: Gas America
	S: Shell, Sunoco, Murphy
Food	S: Applebee's, Arby's, Bob Evans, Burger King, Cracker Barrel, Hardee's, KFC, McDonald's, Starbucks, Steak n Shake, Taco Bell, Waffle House, Wendy's
Lodg	S: Comfort Inn, Dollar Inn, Holiday Inn Express, Lee's Inn, Super 8
Other	S: Advance Auto, Big Lots, Big O Tire, CVS, Home Depot, Wal-Mart sc
(107)	Rest Area (Both dir) (RR, Phones, Picnic, Vend, RVDump)
115	IN 109, Knightstown, Wilkinson
TStop	N: Gas America #43 (Scales)
Food	N: Rest/GA, Burger King
Other	N: CB/Laundry/RVDump/GA
123	IN 3, Spiceland, New Castle
FStop	S: BP
TStop	S: Flying J Travel Plaza #5111 (Scales)
Gas	N: Shell, Speedway, Murphy
	S: Marathon, Phillips 66
Food	N: Denny's, McDonald's
	S: Rest/FastFood/FJ TP
Lodg	N: All American Inn, Days Inn, Holiday Inn Express
TServ	N: Hartley Truck Parts
	S: Hopkins Towing
Med	N: + Hospital
Other	N: CarQuest, Wal-Mart, RV Park▲
	S: Laundry/WiFi/RVDump/LP/FJ TP

EXIT	INDIANA
131	Wilbur Wright Rd, New Lisbon
TStop	S: Hoosier Heartland Travel Plaza/Marathon (Scales)
Food	S: KFC/TacoBell/Hoosier TP
TServ	S: Hoosier TP/Tires
Other	S: New Lisbon Family Campground▲
137	IN 1, Cambridge City, Connersville, Hagerstown
FStop	S: Crazy D's/Clark (Scales)
Gas	S: Gas America, Shell
Food	S: Rest/Crazy D's, Burger King, McDonald's
TServ	S: Crazy D's/Tires
Other	S: Laundry/Crazy D's, to appr 16mi Whitewater River Campground▲
(144)	Rest Area (Both dir) (RR, Phones, Picnic, Vend)
145	Centerville Rd, Centerville
Gas	N: BP
Food	N: DQ/Stuckey's/BP
Lodg	N: Super 8
TServ	N: Goodyear
(148)	Weigh Station (Both dir)
149A	IN 38S, Williamsburg Pike
Other	S: Tom Raper RV Center
149B	US 35N, IN 38N, Richmond
TStop	N: Love's Travel Stop #222 (Scales)
Food	N: Hardee's/Love's TS
Other	N: Laundry/WiFi/RVDump/Love's TS
	S: RV Center
151	US 27, Chester Blvd, Richmond, to Fountain City, Chester (WB)
Other	N: Richmond KOA▲, RV Center

EXIT	IN / OH
151AB	US 27, Chester Blvd, Richmond, to Fountain City, Chester (EB)
Gas	S: Meijer◊, Speedway, Shell, Sunoco
Food	N: Maverick Rest
	S: Bob Evans, Burger King, McDonald's, Pizza Hut, Subway, Wendy's
Lodg	S: Comfort Inn, Super 8
Other	N: Richmond KOA▲, RV Center
153	IN 227, Richmond, Whitewater
Other	N: Deer Ridge Camping Resort▲, Grandpa's Farm Campground RV Park▲
156A	US 40, National Rd, Richmond, Lewisburg, OH
Gas	S: Shell, Speedway, Murphy
Food	S: Applebee's, Bob Evans, Burger King, Cracker Barrel, Golden Corral, McDonald's, O'Charley's, Red Lobster, Ryan's Grill, Steak n Shake, Texas Roadhouse, White Castle
Lodg	S: Days Inn, Holiday Inn, Hampton Inn, Lee's Inn, Knights Inn
Other	S: Firestone, Goodyear, Kroger, Lowe's, Target, U-Haul, Wal-Mart sc
156B	US 40, National Rd, Richmond, Lewisburg, OH, New Paris, OH
FStop	N: Fuel Mart #604
TStop	N: Petro Stopping Center (Scales)
Gas	N: Highway Oil, Swifty
	N: Iron Skillet/PizzaHut/Petro SC
TWash	N: Blue Beacon TW/Petro SC
TServ	N: Petro SC/Tires
Other	N: Laundry/BarbSh/CB/WiFi/Petro SC
(156)	Weigh Station (WB)
NOTE:	MM 157: Ohio State Line
	(EASTERN TIME ZONE)

○ **INDIANA**
○ **OHIO**

(EASTERN TIME ZONE)

(1)	Weigh Station (EB)
1	OH 35E, Eaton (EB exit, WB reaccess)
(3)	OH Welcome Center (EB) Rest Area (WB) (RR, Phones, Picnic, Vend, Info-EB)
10	US 127, Eaton, Greenville
TStop	N: Travel Center of America #11/BP (Scales)
	S: Pilot Travel Center #286 (Scales)
Gas	N: Marathon
Food	N: CountryPride/BKing/Subway/TA TC
	S: Subway/Pilot TC
Lodg	S: Econo Lodge
TWash	N: TA TC
Other	N: Laundry/CB/WiFi/TA TC
	S: Laundry/WiFi/Pilot TC
14	OH 503, Lewisburg, W Alexandria
Gas	N: Sunoco◊
	S: Lewisburg Food Mart/Citgo◊
Food	N: Subway/Sunoco
Lodg	N: Super Inn Motel
Other	N: Grocery, ATM, Golf Course
21	CR 533, Arlington Rd, Brookville
FStop	S: Speedway #1219
Gas	N: Gas America
	S: BP◊
Food	N: Subway/GA
	S: Arby's, DQ, KFC/Taco Bell, McDonald's,

◊ = Regular Gas Stations with Diesel   ▲ = RV Friendly Locations   ♥ = Pet Friendly Locations
RED PRINT SHOWS LARGE VEHICLE PARKING/ACCESS ON SITE OR NEARBY   BROWN PRINT SHOWS CAMPGROUNDS/RV PARKS

INTERSTATE 70 W/E — OHIO

EXIT		
	Food	S: Waffle House, Wendy's
	Lodg	S: Days Inn, Holiday Inn Express
24		OH 49N, Brookville-Salem Pike, Brookville, Clayton, Greenville (EB, no EB reaccess)
	Gas	S: Sunoco
	Other	N: Dayton KOA▲
26		OH 49S, Salem Ave (EB), Hoke Rd, Clayton, Trotwood (WB)
	Gas	N: Shell, Murphy
	Food	N: Bob Evans, Subway, Wendy's
	Other	N: Wal-Mart sc, OH State Hwy Patrol Post, Hara Arena
29		OH 48, Main St, Dayton, Englewood
	Gas	N: BP, Speedway, Sunoco◊ S: Meijer◊
	Food	N: Arby's, Bob Evans, Perkins, Pizza Hut, Skyline Chilil, Taco Bell, Wendy's S: McDonald's, Steak n Shake, Tumbleweed SW Grill, Waffle House
	Lodg	N: Best Western, Hampton Inn, Holiday Inn, Motel 6♥, Super 8♥ S: Comfort Suites, Red Roof Inn♥
	TServ	N: Cummins Diesel Service
	Other	N: Advance Auto, Grocery, Pharmacy, McNulty RV Center S: Hara Arena
32		Dayton Int'l Airport, Vandalia
	Other	N: Dayton Int'l Airport✈
(33A)		Jct I-75S, to Dayton (All Serv at 1st Exit S, #60)
(33B)		Jct I-75N, to Toledo
36		OH 202, Old Troy Pike, Huber Hts
	Gas	N: Shell, Speedway S: BP◊, Sunoco◊, Kroger
	Food	N: Applebee's, El Toro, Pizza Hut, Ruby Tuesday, Steak n Shake, Subway, Taco Bell, Waffle House, Wendy's S: Arby's, Bob Evans, Long John Silver, McDonald's, White Castle
	Lodg	N: Super 8 S: Days Inn, Hampton Inn, Holiday Inn Express
	TServ	N: Ed's Truck & Trailer, CAT, Western Ohio Freightliner
	Other	N: Grocery, Gander Mountain, Lowe's, Radio Shack, Staples, Target, Vet♥, Cinema, Auto Services, ATM S: CVS, Kmart, Kroger, OH State Hwy Patrol
38		OH 201, Brandt Pike, Dayton
	Gas	S: Shell
	Food	S: Bob Evans, Denny's, McDonald's, Tim Hortons, Waffle House, Wendy's

EXIT		
	Lodg	S: Comfort Inn, Travelodge
	Other	S: ATM, Wal-Mart sc
41		OH 4, OH 235, Dayton Lakeview Rd, Dayton, New Carlisle
	Gas	N: BP◊, Sunoco◊
	Food	N: McDonald's, Subway, Wendy's
(44A)		Jct I-675S, to Cincinnati (EB)
44B		Medway (EB)
(44)		Jct I-675, to Cincinnati (WB)
47		OH 4N, to Springfield (EB exit, WB reaccess)
	Gas	N: Speedway
	Other	N: Enon Beach Campground▲
48		Enon-Xenia Rd, to OH 4, Enon, Donnelsville (WB exit, EB reaccess) (Access to Ex #47 Serv)
52A		OH 68S, Xenia
	Other	S: to Springfield Beckley Muni Airport✈, Antioch College, John Bryan State Park
52B		OH 68N, Urbana
54		OH 72, Limestone St, Springfield, Cedarville
	Gas	N: BP◊, Shell, Speedway, Sunoco◊ S: Swifty
	Food	N: Arby's, Bob Evans, China Gate, Cracker Barrel, Denny's, Hardee's, KFC, Long John Silver, Perkins, Pizza Hut, Rally's, Subway, Taco Bell, Wendy's
	Lodg	N: Comfort Inn, Days Inn, Hampton Inn, Holiday Inn, Ramada Ltd, Red Roof Inn, Super 8
	Other	N: ATM, Auto Services, Grocery, CVS, Kroger, Walgreen's, Wittenburg Univ
59		OH 41, S Charleston Pike
	TStop	S: Prime Fuel Center
	Gas	S: BP◊, Clark
	Med	N: + Hospital
	Other	N: Harley Davidson, Clark Co Fairgrounds/RVDump, OH Nat'l Guard, OH State Hwy Patrol Post
62		US 40, E National Rd, Springfield
	Gas	N: Rich
	Food	N: Pizza
	Lodg	N: Harmony Motel
	Other	N: Buck Creek State Park S: Tomorrow's Stars RV Resort▲, Beaver Valley Resort▲, Crawfords Market & Campground▲
66		OH 54, N Urbana St, to US 40, S Vienna, Catawba, S Charleston
	FStop	N: Fuel Mart #764
	Gas	S: Speedway◊

EXIT		
	Other	S: Crawford RV Park▲, Beaver Valley Campground▲, Golf Course
(71)		Rest Area (Both dir) (RR, Phones, Picnic, Vend)
72		OH 56, London, Mechanicsburg
	Gas	N: Marathon
	Med	S: + Hospital
	Other	S: Madison Co Airport✈, Auto Repair, Madison Co Fairgrounds
79		US 42, W Jefferson, London
	FStop	S: Speedway #5360
	TStop	N: Pilot Travel Center #454 (Scales) S: Travel Center of America/BP (Scales)
	Gas	S: Sunoco◊
	Food	N: Waffle House, Arby's/TJCinn/Pilot TC S: McDonald's, Wendy's, CountryPride/Popeye's/PizzaHut/TA TC
	Lodg	S: Holiday Inn Express, Knights Inn
	TWash	S: Red Baron TW/TA TC
	TServ	S: TA TC/Tires
	Med	S: + Hospital
	Other	N: Laundry/WiFi/Pilot TC S: Laundry/WiFi/TA TC, OH State Hwy Patrol Post
80		OH 29, Mechanicsburg, Urbana
	Other	S: OH State Hwy Patrol Post, Truck Repair
85		OH 142, CR 7, Georgesville Rd, W Jefferson, to Plain City
91		CR 3, Hilliard Rome Rd (EB)
91AB		CR 3, Hilliard Rome Rd, Columbus, Hilliard, New Rome
	Gas	N: Meijer◊, Shell, Speedway, Murphy S: BP◊, Marathon◊
	Food	N: Applebee's, Arby's, Big Boy, Burger King, Cracker Barrel, Fazoli's, KFC, McDonald's, Perkins, Taco Bell, Wendy's S: Bob Evans, Steak n Shake
	Lodg	N: Best Value Inn, Comfort Suites, Fairfield Inn, Hawthorn Inn, Hampton Inn, Motel 6♥, Red Roof Inn♥, Super 8 S: Best Western, Country Inn, Microtel
	Other	N: ATMs, Carwash, Cinema, Discount Tire, Firestone, Grocery, Sam's Club, Wal-Mart sc
NOTE:		Through trucks carrying haz-mat MUST use I-270 around Columbus.
(93A)		Jct I-270S, Col ByP, Cincinnati (EB)
(93B)		Jct I-270N, Col ByP, Cleveland (EB)
(93)		Jct I-270, Columbus ByPass, S - Cincinnati, N - Cleveland (WB)

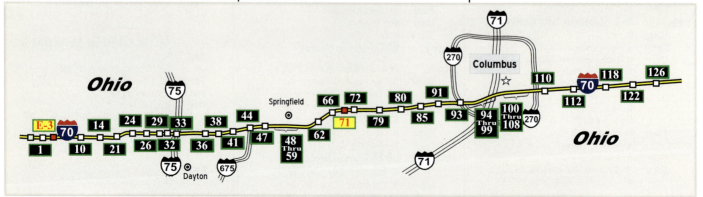

◊ = Regular Gas Stations with Diesel   ▲ = RV Friendly Locations   ♥ = Pet Friendly Locations
RED PRINT SHOWS LARGE VEHICLE PARKING/ACCESS ON SITE OR NEARBY   BROWN PRINT SHOWS CAMPGROUNDS/RV PARKS

EXIT		OHIO
94		Wilson Rd, Columbus
	TStop	S: Pilot Travel Center #213 (Scales)
	Gas	S: BP, Shell, Speedway, Marathon◊
	Food	S: Wendy's/Pilot TC, Waffle House, McDonald's, Subway, Taco Bell, Wendy's
	Lodg	S: Econo Lodge
	Other	S: Laundry/WiFi/Pilot TC
95		Hague Ave (WB)
	Gas	S: Sunoco
(96)		Jct I-670 (EB, Left exit)
97		US 40, W Broad St
	Gas	N: Valero
	Food	N: Arby's, Burger King, KFC, McDonald's, Pizza Hut, Subway, Taco Bell, Tim Hortons, Wendy's, White Castle
	Lodg	N: Knights Inn
	Other	N: ATM's, Auto Services, Convention Center, Cooper Stadium, Nationwide Arena US Post Office, U-Haul, Pharmacy
98A		US 62, OH 3, Central Ave, Sullivant Ave (WB)
98B		Mound St (WB, diff reaccess)
	Gas	N: Marathon
	Food	N: Long John Silver, McDonald's
	Other	N: Auto Repair, Cooper Stadium
(99A)		Jct I-71S, to Cincinnati
99B		OH 315N, Dwntwn, Worthington (EB)
99C		Rich St, Town St (WB)
100A		US 23S, Front St, High St
	Gas	S: Shell
	Food	S: BW3's, Ludlow's, Plank's Rest, Tommy's Tony's Italian Rest, Victory Bar & Grill
	Lodg	S: Best Western, Clarmont Inn
	Med	S: + Grant Hospital
	Other	S: ATMs, Brewery District, Convention Center, German Village, OH Statehouse
100B		US 23N, 4th St, Livingston Ave (EB) E Fulton St, US 23, US 33 (WB)
	Food	N: Brown Bag Deli, Cup O'Joe, Michael's Bistro, Max & Erma's, Roosters, Starbucks
(101A)		Jct I-71N, to Cleveland
101B		18th St (EB, No reaccess)
	Med	S: + Children's Hospital
102		Miller Ave, Kelton Ave
	Med	S: + Children's Hospital
103A		Main St, Bexley, US 40E (EB)
103B		Alum Creek Dr, Livingstone Dr (fr EB, diff reaccess)
	Gas	N: BP, Speedway◊, Thornton's, Kroger S: Shell
	Food	N: Domino's, Subway, Taco Bell S: McDonald's, White Castle, Wendy's
	Med	S: + Hospital
	Other	N: Family Dollar, Kroger
105A		US 33, College Ave, Lancaster (EB)
	Gas	S: 7-11/Citgo
105B		James Rd, Bexley (WB)
	Food	N: Great Wall Chinese, McDonald's
	Other	N: Port Columbus, Int'l Airport ✈
107		OH 317, Hamilton Rd (WB)
107A		OH 317S, Hamilton Rd S (EB)
	Gas	S: BP, Citgo◊, Sunoco◊
	Food	S: Arby's, Bob Evans, Burger King, McDonald's, Olive Garden, Red Lobster, Steak n Shake, Subway, Taco Bell
	Lodg	S: Hampton Inn, Holiday Inn, Knights Inn, Residence Inn
	Other	S: ATM, Auto Repair, Cinema, Eastland Mall, Fort Rapids Resort & Waterpark, Pharmacy
107B		OH 317N, Hamilton Rd, Whitehall (EB)
	Gas	N: BP, Marathon, Sunoco
	Other	N: Auto Repair, ATM
(108)		Jct I-270, N to Cleveland, S to Cincinnati (EB)
(108A)		Jct I-270S, to Cincinnati (WB)
(108B)		Jct I-270N, to Cleveland (WB)
NOTE:		Through trucks carrying haz-mat MUST use I-270 around Columbus.
110		CR 117, Brice Rd, Reynoldsburg (WB)
110A		CR 117, Brice Rd S (EB)
	Gas	S: BP, Meijer◊, Shell, Sunoco, Speedway, Kroger
	Food	S: Applebee's, Arby's, Boston Market, Burger King, Chipolte, El Chico, Genji Japanese, KFC, McDonald's, Perkins, Skyline Chili, Starbucks, Subway, Taco Bell, Wendy's, White Castle
	Lodg	S: Comfort Suites, Days Inn, Econo Lodge, Motel 6♥
	Other	S: CVS, Kroger, Magic Mtn Fun Center, Mall, Lowe's, Sam's Club, Target, Wal-Mart
110B		CR 117, Brice Rd N, Reynoldsburg (EB)
	Gas	N: BP, Shell, Speedway, Sunoco, Thornton's
	Food	N: Arby's, Bob Evans, Burger King, Pizza Hut, Popeye's, Japanese Steak House, Roadhouse Grill, Ryan's Grill, Waffle House
	Lodg	N: Best Western, Extended Stay America, La Quinta Inn♥, Red Roof Inn♥, Super 8
	Other	N: Grocery, Home Depot
112A		OH 256E, Reynoldsburg Baltimore Rd, Pickerington
	Gas	S: Exxon, Speedway
	Food	S: Arby's, Bob Evans, CiCi's, Cracker Barrel, Damon's, KFC, Mexican Grill, Longhorn Steakhouse, McDonald's, Long John Silver, Steak n Shake, Wendy's
	Lodg	S: Best Western, Hampton Inn, Hawthorne Suites, Holiday Inn Express
	Other	S: CVS, Motorcycle Museum & Hall of Fame
112B		OH 256W, Reynoldsburg Baltimore Rd, Reynoldsburg
	Gas	N: BP, Shell, Sunoco◊, Kroger, Sam's
	Food	N: Chipolte Mex Grill, KFC, McDonald's, O'Charley's, Panera Bread, Smokey Bones BBQ, TGI Friday
	Lodg	N: Country Suites, Fairfield Inn, Lenox Inn
	Other	N: Best Buy, Sam's Club, Tires, Wal-Mart sc, Walgreen's
112C		Blacklick-Eastern Rd
	Gas	N: BP, Exxon, Speedway, Kroger
118		OH 310, Hazelton Etna Rd
	Gas	N: Speedway◊, Sunoco S: Duke◊
	Food	N: Etna Pizza, Duchess Shop, McDonald's
	Other	N: Etna Towing, Candle Shop
122		OH 158, Baltimore Rd, 5th St, CR 40, Pataskala, Kirkersville, to Baltimore
	TStop	S: Flying J Travel Plaza #5030 (Scales)
	Food	S: CountryMarket/FastFood/FJ TP
	Lodg	N: Regal Inn
	Other	S: Laundry/BarbSh/WiFi/RVDump/LP/FJ TP
126		OH 37, Lancaster Rd, Hebron, Granville, Lancaster, Millersport
	FStop	N: Certified #423/Citgo
	TStop	N: Pilot Travel Center #285 (Scales) S: Travel Center of America #39/BP (Scales) Truck-O-Mat (Scales)
	Gas	N: Starfire Express◊ S: Sunoco
	Food	N: ChestersChicken/Subway/Pilot TC S: CountryPride/Popeye's/Sbarro/TA TC
	Lodg	S: Delux Inn, Red Roof Inn♥
	TWash	S: Truck-O-Mat
	TServ	S: TA TC/Tires, Eastern OH Truck & Trailer
	Other	N: WiFi/Pilot TC, LP/Certified S: Laundry/WiFi/CB/TA TC
129A		OH 79S, to Buckeye Lake
	TStop	S: Duke's Travel Plaza/BP (Scales)
	Gas	S: Citgo, Shell
	Food	S: Rest/Duke's TP, Burger King, Subway, McDonald's, Wendy's
	Lodg	S: Duke's Inn, Super 8
	AServ	S: Joe's Auto Service, A-1 Auto Parts
	TWash	S: Beechridge Truck Wash
	TServ	S: Duke's TP/Tires
	Other	S: Laundry/Duke's TP, Grocery, U-Haul, Tourist Info, State Park, Buckeye Lake/Columbus East KOA▲

◊ = Regular Gas Stations with Diesel   ▲ = RV Friendly Locations   ♥ = Pet Friendly Locations
RED PRINT SHOWS LARGE VEHICLE PARKING/ACCESS ON SITE OR NEARBY   BROWN PRINT SHOWS CAMPGROUNDS/RV PARKS

INTERSTATE 70 W/E — OHIO

EXIT		OHIO
129B		OH 79N, Hebron Rd, Buckeye Lake, Hebron, Heath
	FStop	N: Speedway #9385
	Gas	N: Kroger
	Other	N: Kroger, Buckeye Outdoors
(131)		Rest Area (Both dir) (RR, Phones, Picnic, Vend)
132		OH 13, Jacksontown Rd, Newark, Thornville, Somerset
	Gas	N: BP, Shell S: Marathon
141		OH 668, Brownsville Rd, Brownsville to Gratiot (EB exit, WB reacc)
142		US 40, Mt Perry Rd, Gratiot (WB exit, EB reaccess difficult)
	Other	N: Camping▲
152		US 40, National Rd, Zanesville
	Gas	N: BP, Exxon, Starfire
	Food	N: McDonald's, A&W
	Lodg	N: Super 8
	TServ	N: White GMC/Volvo/Cummins
153A		OH 146W, State St
	Gas	N: Speedway◊ S: BP
153B		Maple Ave, to OH 60N (WB, NO re-entry)
	Gas	N: BP, Moto Mart
	Food	N: DQ, KFC, Papa John's, Wendy's
	Med	N: + Hospital
	Other	N: Colony Square Mall
154		5th St, to US 40 (EB, NO re-entry)
155		OH 60, OH 146, Underwood St (WB), 7th St (EB)
	Gas	S: Exxon◊
	Food	N: Bob Evans, Red Lobster, Shoney's, Steak n Shake, Tumbleweed S: Cracker Barrel, Subway, Wendy's
	Lodg	N: Comfort Inn, Fairfield Inn, Hampton Inn S: AmeriHost Inn, Best Western, Econo Lodge, Travelodge
	Med	N: + Hospital
	Other	N: Camping▲
157		OH 93, to US 22, US 40, Zanesville
	Gas	N: BP, Duke S: Marathon, Shell◊
	Food	S: Blimpie's, Subs Express
	Other	S: OH State Hwy Patrol Post, KOA▲
160		OH 797, CR 52, US 40, Zanesville, Airport, East Pike, Sonora
	TStop	N: Love's Travel Stop #221 (Scales)
	Gas	S: BP, Exxon◊, Starfire Express
	Food	N: Arby's/Love's TS S: Denny's, McDonald's, Wendy's

EXIT		OHIO
	Lodg	S: Best Value Inn, Best Western, Days Inn, Holiday Inn, Red Roof Inn♥, Super 8
	Other	N: Laundry/WiFi/RVDump/Love's TS S: Flea Market, Zanesville Muni Airport✈, OH State Hwy Patrol Post
(163)		Rest Area (WB) (RR, Phones, Picnic, Vend)
164		US 22, US 40, National Rd, Norwich
	Gas	N: BP
	Lodg	N: Baker's Motel
	Other	N: Museum, Pottery Outlets, Shopping
169		OH 83, Friendship Dr, West Rd, New Concord, Cumberland
	FStop	N: 1mi N to US 40: Fuel Mart #706
	Gas	N: BP
	Food	N: Dairy Duchess, Domino's, Subway
(173)		Weigh Station (Both dir)
176		OH 723, US 22, US 40, to Cambridge
	Gas	N: Sunoco◊
	Lodg	N: Budget Inn
	Other	N: Civic Center, OH State Hwy Patrol
178		OH 209, Southgate Rd, Cambridge
	TStop	S: Pilot Travel Center #6 (Scales)
	Gas	N: BP◊, Shell, Kmart Express S: Speedway, Murphy USA
	Food	N: Bob Evans, Cracker Barrel, DQ, KFC, McDonald's, Taco Bell, USA Steak Buffet S: Subway/Pilot TC, Burger King
	Lodg	N: Best Western, Budget Host, Comfort Inn, Days Inn, Holiday Inn, Super 8 S: AmeriHost Inn
	Med	N: + Hospital
	Other	N: AutoZone, Kmart, Kroger, CVS, 84 Lumber, Auto Dealer, Dollar General S: WiFi/Pilot TC, Wal-Mart sc, Spring Valley Campground▲, Cambridge Airport✈, Cinema, Museum, Winery
(180A)		Jct I-77S, to Marietta, Charleston
(180B)		Jct I-77N, to Cleveland
186		US 40, OH 285, Wintergreen Rd, Old Washington, to Senecaville
	FStop	S: Go Mart #57
	Gas	S: BP, Fuel Mart
	Other	S: Fairgrounds, Camping▲, Seneca Lake
(189)		Rest Area (EB) (RR, Phones, Picnic, Vend)
193		OH 513, Batesville Rd, Quaker City
	TStop	N: Fuel Mart #727 (Scales)
	Gas	N: BP, Shell
	Food	N: Pizza/BP
	Other	N: R&R Auto/Truck Repair

EXIT		OHIO
198		CR 114, Barnesville, Fairview
	Other	N: Penny Royal Opera House, US Post Office
202		OH 800, Barnesville, Woodfield
	FStop	S: U-Save Fuel Mart
	Med	S: + Hospital
204		US 40E, National Rd, CR 100, Bethesda (EB exit, WB reaccess)
208		OH 149, Belmont Morristown Rd, Belmont, Morristown, Bethesda
	FStop	N: Two-O-Eight Fuel Plaza/BP
	Gas	S: Chevron, Marathon
	Food	N: Deli/208 FP, McDonald's, Quiznos, Schlepp's Family Rest
	Lodg	N: Arrowhead, Sunset Motel
	TServ	S: Terex Truck Service
	Med	N: + Morristown Clinic
	Other	N: LP/208 FP S: Valley Harley Davidson, Cannonball Motor Speedway, Golf Course
(210)		Rest Area (Both dir) (RR, Phones, Picnic, Vend, Info-WB)
213		OH 331, Airport Rd (WB), Flushing, US 40 (EB), St Clairsville
	Gas	S: BP, Marathon, Sunoco◊
	Food	S: Mi Ranchito, Subway
	Lodg	S: Twin Pines Motel
	TWash	S: Valley 1 Auto/Semi Coin Wash
	Other	S: Sheriff Dept, Alderman Airport✈
215		US 40, National Rd, St Clairsville
	Gas	N: Citgo
	Food	S: Burger King, Domino's, Subway
216		OH 9, St Clairsville
	Gas	N: BP S: Marathon
	Other	S: Fairgrounds
218		CR 28A, Mall Rd, Banfield Rd, to US 40, St Clairsville, to Blaine
	Gas	N: BP◊, Citgo, Exxon S: USA◊
	Food	N: Applebee's, Arby's, Burger King, Denny's, Eat 'n Park, Outback Steakhouse, Pizza Hut, Red Lobster, Steak n Shake, Taco Bell, W Texas Steaks S: Bob Evans, Bonanza, Cracker Barrel, Long John Silver, Longhorn Steakhouse, McDonald's, Undos Pizza
	Lodg	N: Best Value Inn, Econo Lodge, Hampton Inn, Holiday Inn Express♥, Knight's Inn, Red Roof Inn♥, Super 8 S: Fairfield Inn
	Med	N: + Urgent Care
	Other	N: AutoZone, Auto Dealers, Circuit City, Dollar Tree, Lowe's, Sam's Club, Staples,

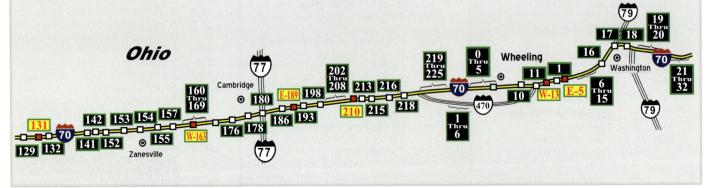

◊ = Regular Gas Stations with Diesel   ▲ = RV Friendly Locations   ♥ = Pet Friendly Locations
RED PRINT SHOWS LARGE VEHICLE PARKING/ACCESS ON SITE OR NEARBY   BROWN PRINT SHOWS CAMPGROUNDS/RV PARKS

INTERSTATE 70 W E

EXIT		OH / WV
	Other	N: Wal-Mart sc, RV Center, OH State Hwy Patrol Post
		S: Kroger, CVS, Cinema, OH Valley Mall
(219)		Jct I-470, to Washington, PA, Wheeling, WV
220		CR 214, National Rd, US 40, Bellaire-High Ridge Rd, Bridgeport
	Gas	N: Citgo, Chevron◆, Exxon
		S: Marathon, Sunoco◆
	Lodg	N: Holiday Inn Express
		S: Days Inn, Plaza Motel
225		Marion St, to US 40, to US 250W, OH 7, Bridgeport, Martins Ferry
	Gas	N: Marathon, Starfire Express, Sunoco
		S: Exxon, Gulf
	Food	N: KFC, Papa John's, Pizza Hut, Wendy's
		S: Domino's
	Med	N: + Hospital
	Other	N: AutoZone, ATMs, Family Dollar, Wheeling Downs
	NOTE:	MM 226: West Virginia State Line

(EASTERN TIME ZONE)

☝ OHIO
☟ WEST VIRGINIA

(EASTERN TIME ZONE)

0		US 250, US 40, Zane St, Wheeling
	Gas	N: Exxon◆
(1)		Tunnel
1A		US 40, WV 2, Main St, Wheeling
	Lodg	S: Best Western
1B		US 250S, WV 2, S Wheeling
2A		US 40, National Rd, to WV 88
	Gas	N: Exxon, Sheetz, Kroger
	Food	N: Bob Evans, Hardee's, Long John Silver, Perkins, Subway, TJ's
	Lodg	N: Hampton Inn
	Other	N: AdvanceAuto, CVS, Kroger, NTB
2B		Armory Dr, Washington Ave
	Gas	N: Exxon, Kroger
	Food	N: Subway
	Other	N: Kroger
(3)		Weigh Station (WB)
4		US 40, WV 88N (EB)
	Gas	S: BP, Exxon
(5A)		Jct I-470W, to Columbus (WB)
5		US 40, WV 88S, Wheeling, Elm Grove, Triadelphia
	Gas	N: Marathon
		S: Exxon◆, Mobil
	Food	N: Christopher's Cafe, Hoss's Steak & Seafood, Pizza Hut, Subway, Wendy's
		S: Arby's, DQ, McDonald's
	Lodg	N: Super 8
	Other	N: Pharmacy, Grocery, Family Dollar
		S: Advance Auto, Auto Dealers, ATMs, Laundromat, NAPA
10		CR 65, Cabela Dr
	Food	N: Applebee's, Bob Evans, Cracker Barrel, Eat 'n Park, McDonald's, Wendy's
	Other	N: Cabela's, Target, Wal-Mart sc
11		CR 41, Dallas Pike Rd, Triadelphia, Wheeling
	TStop	N: Travel Center of America (Scales)
		S: AmBest/Dallas Pike Fuel Center/Citgo (Scales)

EXIT		WV / PA
	Gas	S: Exxon, Mobil◆
	Food	N: Rest/TA TC
		S: Rest/FastFood/Dallas Pike FC
	Lodg	N: Comfort Inn, Days Inn
		S: Holiday Inn Express
	TServ	N: TA TC/Tires
	Other	N: Laundry/BarbSh/WiFi/TA TC
		S: Laundry/RVDump/Dallas Pike FC
(13)		WV Welcome Center (WB) (RR, Phones, Picnic, Vend, RVDump) Note: RVDump Closed in Winter Months
	NOTE:	MM 14.5: Pennsylvania State Line

(EASTERN TIME ZONE)

☝ WEST VIRGINIA
☟ PENNSYLVANIA

(EASTERN TIME ZONE)

1		Maple Ave, West Alexander
(5)		PA Welcome Center (EB) (RR, Phones, Picnic, Vend)
6		Old National Pike, US 40, PA 231, Claysville, West Alexander
	TStop	S: Petro 2 #83 (Scales)
	Gas	N: Exxon
	Food	S: Rest/Sbarro/Subway/Petro2
	TServ	S: Petro2/Tires
	Other	S: Laundry/WiFi/RVDump/Petro2

EXIT		PENNSYLVANIA
11		Jolly School Rd (EB), Buffalo Church Rd (WB), to PA 221, S Bridge Rd, Washington, Taylorstown
	Other	S: to Washington Co Airport✈
15		US 40, Chestnut St, Washington
	Gas	S: BP, Starfire, Sunoco◆
	Food	N: USA Steak Buffet
		S: Bob Evans, Denny's, Hardee's, Long John Silver, McDonald's, Pizza Hut, Wendy'
	Lodg	S: Days Inn, Econo Lodge, Interstate Motel, Ramada Inn ♥, Red Roof Inn ♥
	TServ	S: International
	Other	N: Laundry, Grocery
		S: Auto Repairs, ATMs, Banks, Dollar General, Tires, Franklin Mall, Gander Mountain, Vet ♥, Washington & Jefferson College, Washington Co Airport✈
16		Sheffield St, Jessop Pl, Wilmington St
	Other	S: Pat's Auto & Truck Repair
17		PA 18, Jefferson Ave, Washington
	Gas	N: Crossroads Food Mart
		S: Nick's Service Station
	Food	N: DQ, McDonald's
		S: Barry's, Burger King, Subway
	Other	N: Carwash, RiteAid
		S: AdvanceAuto, Grocery
	NOTE:	I-70 & I-79 run together below, Exits 19-21, Exit #'s follow I-70.
(18)		Jct I-79N, to Pittsburgh
19AB		US 19, Murtland Ave, Washington Rd
	Gas	N: BP
		S: AmocoBP, Exxon, Sunoco
	Food	N: Applebee's, Arby's, Cracker Barrel, McDonald's, Ponderosa, Red Robin, Red Lobster, Starbucks, Subway, TGI Friday
		S: Bob Evans, Burger King, Chinese Rest, CiCi's, KFC, Long John Silver, McDonald's, Pizza Hut, Shoney's, Taco Bell
	Lodg	N: Springhill Suites
		S: Hampton Inn, Motel 6 ♥
	Med	S: + Washington Hospital
	Other	N: Grocery, Lowe's, PetSmart ♥, Sam's Club, Target, Wal-Mart sc, ATMs, Auto Dealers
		S: Washington Mall, Firestone, Home Depot, Kmart, Staples, PA State Hwy Patrol
20		PA 136, Beau St, Washington
	Other	S: Washington/Pittsburg SW KOA▲
(21)		Jct I-79S, to Morgantown, Waynesburg
	NOTE:	I-70 & I-79 run together above, Exits #'s 19-21, Exit #'s follow I-70.
25		PA 519, Eighty Four, Glyde
	FStop	S: 7-11 #185/BP
	Gas	N: GetGo
		S: Sunoco
	Food	S: 7-11/Diner/BP
	Other:	S: CB Shop/BP
27		Brownlee Rd, Somerset Dr, Eighty Four, Dunningsville
	Lodg	S: Avalon Motor Inn
31		McIlvaine Rd, to PA 917, Sprowls Rd, Bentleyville, Kammerer
	Food	N: Carlton Kitchen

◆ = Regular Gas Stations with Diesel   ▲ = RV Friendly Locations   ♥ = Pet Friendly Locations
RED PRINT SHOWS LARGE VEHICLE PARKING/ACCESS ON SITE OR NEARBY   BROWN PRINT SHOWS CAMPGROUNDS/RV PARKS

INTERSTATE W 70 E

EXIT		PENNSYLVANIA
	Lodg	N: Carlton Motel
32A		PA 917, Pittsburgh Rd, Bentleyville (Trucks Use Exit #32B)
32B		Wilson Rd, to PA 917, Bentleyville
	TStop	S: Pilot Travel Center #348 (Scales)
	Gas	S: AmocoBP◆, Sheetz
	Food	S: DQ/Subway/Pilot TC, Burger King, McDonald's
	Lodg	S: Best Western
	TWash	S: Blue Beacon TW/Pilot TC
	Med	S: + Hospital
	Other	S: Laundry/WiFi/Pilot TC, AdvanceAuto, Grocery, RiteAid
35		PA 481, Charleroi, to Centerville
36		Twin Bridges Rd, Charleroi, Lover (WB exit, NO re-entry)
37AB		PA 43, Mon Fayette Expwy
39		Maple Dr, Charleroi, Speers
	Gas	S: Exxon
	Food	N: Lorraine's Family Rest
40		PA 88, Pennsylvania Ave, Belle Vernon, Charleroi, Dunlevy
	Gas	N: Amoco, Sunoco
41		PA 906, Main St, Belle Vernon
42		Fayette Ave, N Belle Vernon
	Gas	S: BP, Exxon, Pantry
	Food	S: DQ, McDonald's/BP
42A		Tyrol Blvd, to PA 906, Monessen
43		PA 201, Rostraver Rd (EB)
43AB		PA 201, Rostraver Rd, Belle Vernon, to Donora, Pricedale (WB)
	Gas	S: Exxon
	Food	S: Burger King, Denny's, Hoss's Steak & Seafood, KFC, Little Caesar, Long John Silver, McDonald's, Ponderosa, Starbucks, Subway, Wendy's
	Lodg	N: Hampton Inn
	Med	N: + Hospital
	Other	S: ATMs, CVS, Grocery, Kmart, Kelly Auto Parts, Lowe's, Staples, Wal-Mart sc
44		Indian Hill Rd, to PA 201, Arnold City
46AB		PA 51, to Pittsburgh, Uniontown
	Gas	N: Exxon, BP◆
		S: GetGo
	Food	N: Burger King
	Lodg	N: Sleeper Inn
		S: Holiday Inn, Relax Inn
	Other	N: Cerini Harley Davidson, Auto Dealers

EXIT		PENNSYLVANIA
49		Dutch Hollow Rd, Turkeytown Rd, to PA 981, Smithton
	TStop	N: Flying J Travel Plaza (Scales), Smithton Truck Stop/Citgo (Scales)
	Food	N: Rest/FJ TP, Rest/Smithton TS
	Lodg	N: Motel/Penn Stn TP, Motel/Smithton TS
	TWash	N: Smithton, Southwestern Star Trucks, Trucks of W Pa
	TServ	N:FJ TP
	Other	N: Laundry/WiFi/RVDump/LP/FJ TP, Laundry/WiFi/Smithton TS
51AB		PA 31, Mt Pleasant Rd, Ruffs Dale, West Newton, Mt Pleasant
53		PA 3010, Huntingdon St, Ruffs Dale, West Newton, to Yukon
54		Waltz Mill Rd, Ruffs Dale, Madison
	Gas	S: Rhodes Service Station
	Other	N: Madison/Pittsburgh SE KOA▲
57		Center Ave, New Stanton
	Gas	N: Exxon
		S: BP
	Food	N: Bob Evans, KFC, McDonald's, Pizza Hut, Quiznos, Subway, Wendy's
		S: Cracker Barrel
	Lodg	N: Budget Inn, Comfort Inn, Days Inn, Fairfield Inn, Quality Inn, Super 8
		S: New Stanton Motel
	TServ	N: Fox & James Freightliner
57A		New Stanton, Hunker (WB)
NOTE:		I-70 below runs with I-76/PA Turnpike, (TOLL), for 86 mi. Exit #'s follow I-76.
NOTE:		EB: Begin Call Box Area.
(58)		Jct I-76/PA Turnpike (TOLL)
(75)		Jct I-70W, US 119, to PA 66
(78)		New Stanton Service Plaza (WB)
	FStop	W: Sunoco
	Food	W: McDonald's, King's Family Rest
91		PA 711, Donegal
	Gas	S: BP, Exxon◆, Sunoco◆
	Food	S: DQ, Hardee's/Pizza Hut/BP
	Lodg	S: Days Inn, Donegal Motel
	TServ	N: Freightliner
	Other	N: Hidden Valley Ski Resort, Laurel Mtn Ski Resort, Seven Springs Ski Resort, Laurel Hill State Park
(94)		Parking Area (WB)
110		PA 601, to US 219, Somerset
	Gas	N: Sheetz
		S: Exxon, Shell◆
	Food	N: Hoss's Steak & Seafood, Pizza Hut

EXIT		PENNSYLVANIA
	Food	S: Arby's, China Garden, Dunkin Donuts KFC, Long John Silver, McDonald's
	Lodg	N: Dollar Inn, Economy Inn
		S: Best Western, Budget Host Inn, Days Inn, Holiday Inn, Hampton Inn, Knights Inn, Ramada Inn, Super 8
	Other	N: Auto Dealers, AdvanceAuto, Somerset Historical Center, Flight 93 Memorial
		S: Harley Davidson
(112)		Somerset Service Plaza (Both dir)
	FStop	Sunoco #7077/#7076
	Food	S: Big Boy, Cinnabon, Hot Dog City, Roy Rogers, Starbucks
		N: Burger King, Cinnabon, Hot Dog City, Hershey's Ice Cream
(123)		Allegheny Mountain Tunnel (Headlights on / Check Hazmat Restr)
(142)		Parking Area (WB)
146		US 220, to I-99, Bedford
	FStop	N: RG's Travel Plaza/BP, SAC Shop/BP
	Gas	N: Sheetz
	Food	N: China Inn, Denny's, Ed's, Hoss's Steak & Seafood, Pizza Hut, Wendy's
	Lodg	N: Best Western, Econo Lodge, Quality Inn, Super 8, Travelodge
		S: Hampton Inn
	TServ	N: Shaw Mack
	Other	N: Bedford Airport✈, to Shawnee State Park, Blue Knob State Park
(147)		Midway Service Plaza (Both dir)
	FStop	Sunoco #7078/#7079
	Food	S: Cinnabon, Hot Dog City, Sbarro
		N: Cinnabon, Hot Dog City, KFC, TCBY, Sbarro, Starbucks
147/161		US 30, Lincoln Hwy, to I-70E, Breezewood, Everett
	FStop	S: Breezewood BP
	TStop	S: Travel Center of America / Mobil (Scales), Petro 2 (Scales)
	Gas	S: BP◆, Exxon◆, Shell, Sunoco◆
	Food	S: Rest/DQ/Dominos/Subway/TA TC, Perkins/FastFood/Petro 2, Arby's, Big John's Steak & Buffet, Bob Evans, Bonanza, Burger King, Denny's, Hardee's, KFC, Pizza Hut, Taco Bell, Wendy's
	Lodg	N: Best Western, Econo Lodge
		S: Comfort Inn, Holiday Inn Express, Quality Inn, Ramada Inn
	TWash	S: Blue Beacon TW/Petro 2
	TServ	S: TA TC/Tires, Petro 2/Tires
	Other	S: Laundry/BarbSh/WiFi/TA TC, Laundry/CB/WiFi/Petro 2
NOTE:		I-70 above runs with I-76/PA Turnpike, (TOLL) for 86 mi. Exit #'s follow I-76.

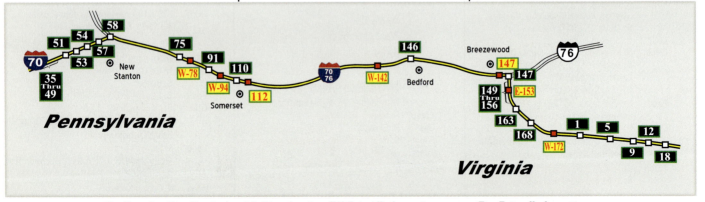

◆ = Regular Gas Stations with Diesel   ▲ = RV Friendly Locations   ♥ = Pet Friendly Locations
RED PRINT SHOWS LARGE VEHICLE PARKING/ACCESS ON SITE OR NEARBY   BROWN PRINT SHOWS CAMPGROUNDS/RV PARKS

INTERSTATE 70 W E

EXIT	PA / MD
149	Breezewood Rd (EB), Lighthouse Rd (WB), to US 30W, Everett, Breezewood (difficult reaccess WB)
Food	S: Blimpie, Denny's, McDonald's
Lodg	S: Redwood Motel, Wildwood Inn
Other	S: Brush Creek Campground▲
151	PA 915, Valley Rd, Crystal Spring
Food	N: Cornerstone Cafe
Other	N: Fischer's Garage
	S: Brush Creek Campground▲
(153)	Rest Area (EB) (RR, Phones, Picnic, Vend)
156	PA 643, Flickerville Rd, Old Rte 126, Crystal Spring, Town Hill
FStop	N: Town Hill Travel Plaza/Sunoco
Food	N: Rest/Town Hill TP
Lodg	N: Days Inn/Town Hill TP
163	PA 731S, Old Rte 126, Mill Hill Rd, Warfordsburg, Amaranth
168	US 522N, Great Cove Rd, PA 484, Buck Valley Rd, Warfordsburg
Gas	N: Exxon◇
(172)	PA Welcome Center (WB) (RR, Phones, Picnic, Vend, Info)
NOTE:	MM 172: Maryland State Line
	(EASTERN TIME ZONE)

○ PENNSYLVANIA
○ MARYLAND
(EASTERN TIME ZONE)

EXIT	
(1A)	Jct I-68W, US 40W, to Cumberland (WB, Left exit)
1B	US 522S, Hancock, Winchester, VA (WB, Left exit)
Gas	S: Citgo◇, Pit Stop Gas, Sheetz
Food	S: Hardee's, Pizza Hut, Weaver's Rest
Lodg	S: Best Value Inn, Super 8
Other	S: Auto Service, Auto Dealer, Dollar General, Grocery, Laundromat, Pharmacy, Fleetwood Travel Trailers of MD, Visitor Info
3	MD 144W, E Main St, Hancock (WB Left exit, diff reaccess WB)
TStop	S: Hancock Truck Stop/BP
Gas	S: AC&T◇
Food	S: Rest/Hancock TS, Hardee's, Pizza Hut
Lodg	S: Motel/Hancock TS
Tires	S: Hancock TS
Other	S: WiFi/Hancock TS, Auto Repair
5	MD 615, Millstone Rd (EB Left exit, NO immed EB reaccess)

EXIT	MARYLAND
9	US 40, National Pike, Big Pool, Indian Springs (EB, Left exit)
12	MD 56, Big Pool Rd, Indian Springs
FStop	S: Big Pool AC&T/Exxon
Other	S: Ft Frederick State Park
18	MD 68, Clear Spring Rd, Clear Spg
Gas	N: BP
	S: Exxon◇
Food	N: McDonald's
	S: Windy Hill Family Rest
Other	N: Ski Area
24	MD 63, Greencastle Pike, Hagerstown Williamsport, Huyett
TStop	N: Pilot Travel Center #150 (Scales)
Food	N: Subway/Pilot TC
Other	N: WiFi/Pilot TC
	S: Hagerstown/Antietam Battlefield KOA▲
(26AB)	Jct I-81, N - Harrisburg, S - Roanoke
Other	N: Hagerstown Reg'l Airport✈
28	MD 632, Downsville, Hagerstown
Gas	N: Shell
Food	N: Burger King, ChickFilA, Pizza Hut, Shoney's, Western Sizzlin
Lodg	N: Country Inn
Other	N: Auto Services, Grocery, Yogi Bear's Jellystone Campground▲
29	MD 65, Sharpsburg Pike (WB)
29AB	MD 65, Sharpsburg, Hagerstown
FStop	N: Sharpsburg Pike AC&T/Exxon
Gas	N: Sheetz, Sunoco◇
	S: Shell◇
Food	N: Longhorn Steakhouse, Pizza Hut, Starbucks, Subway
	S: Blimpie/Shell, Burger King, Cracker Barrel, McDonald's, Waffle House
Lodg	S: Sleep Inn♥
Med	N: + Hospital
Other	N: Auto Repair, Prime Outlets, MD State Hwy Patrol Post
	S: Greyhound, to Antieam Battlefield
32AB	US 40, Hagerstown
Gas	N: 7-11, BP, Exxon, Sunoco
Food	N: Bob Evans, Burger King, Denny's, McDonald's, Pizza Hut, Popeye's, Red Horse Steaks, Subway, Taco Bell, Texas Roadhouse
Lodg	N: Comfort Suites, Days Inn, Hampton Inn, Holiday Inn, Quality Inn, Sheraton, Super 8
Med	N: + Hospital
Other	N: Auto Dealers, CVS, Goodyear, Grocery, Outlet Mall
	S: Auto Dealers

EXIT	MARYLAND
35	MD 66, Mapleville Rd, Hagerstown, Beaver Creek, Boonsboro
Other	S: Greenbrier State Park, Washington Monument State Park
(39)	Rest Area (Both dir) (RR, Phones, Picnic, Vend, Info)
42	MD 17, Myersville Rd, Myersville
Gas	N: Exxon, Sunoco◇
	S: BP◇
Food	N: Burger King, McDonald's
Other	N: Greenbrier State Park, Gambrill State Park
48	US 40E, Frederick (EB, no reaccess) (Serv avail to WB via Exit #49, then N)
Gas	N: Chevron, Citgo◇, Exxon◇, Sunoco
Food	N: Arby's, Bob Evans, Burger King, Denny's, McDonald's, Outback Steakhouse, Pizza Hut, Red Lobster, Ruby Tuesday, Starbucks, Subway, Taco Bell, Wendy's
Lodg	N: Comfort Inn, Holiday Inn
Other	N: 7-11, Grocery, Auto Services, Tires, Home Depot, Kmart, CVS, to Fort Detrick Military Res
49	US 40W Alt, Braddock Hts, Middletown (WB, no reaccess)
Other	S: Washington Monument State Park, Ski Area
52	US 340W, US 15S (WB)
52A	US 340W, US 15S, Charlestown WV
52B	US 15N, US 40W, Gettysburg (EB)
(53)	US 15N, US 40W, Gettysburg (WB) Jct I-270S, to Washington (EB)
54	MD 355, Urbana Pike, to MD 85, Buckeystown Pike (EB), MD 355, to MD 85, to I-270 (WB), Frederick
Gas	N: Amoco, Costco
	S: Chevron, Exxon◇, Sheetz, Shell
Food	S: Bob Evans, Burger King, Cracker Barrel, El Paso, KFC, McDonald's, Papa John's, Popeye's, Subway, Wendy's
Lodg	S: Days Inn, Econo Lodge, Fairfield Inn, Hampton Inn, Holiday Inn Express
Other	S: Auto Dealers, Best Buy, Circuit City, Lowe's, Sam's Club, Wal-Mart, Mall
55	Reich's Ford Rd, Smiths Rd, South St, MD144, Frederick
Gas	N: Citgo, Sheetz
Other	N: Frederick Muni Airport✈
56	MD 144, Baltimore Nat'l Pike (EB), Patrick St (WB), Frederick (WB reaccess difficult)
Gas	N: Citgo, Sheetz

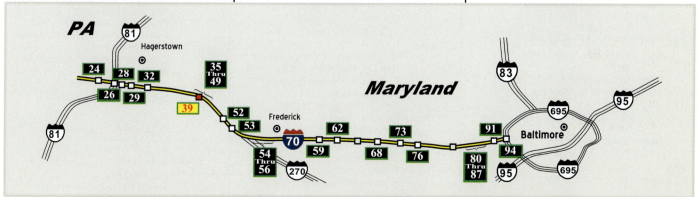

◇ = Regular Gas Stations with Diesel   ▲ = RV Friendly Locations   ♥ = Pet Friendly Locations
RED PRINT SHOWS LARGE VEHICLE PARKING/ACCESS ON SITE OR NEARBY   BROWN PRINT SHOWS CAMPGROUNDS/RV PARKS

EXIT		MARYLAND
	Food	N: Burger King, McDonald's, Taco Bell, Waffle House, Wendy's
	Other	N: Dollar General, Triangle RV Center
59		MD 144W, Old National Pike, Meadow Rd, Frederick (WB)
62		MD 75, Green Valley Rd, New Market, Libertytown, Hyattsville
	Gas	N: Mobil◊, Shell
	Food	N: McDonald's
(64)		Weigh / Inspection Station (EB)
68		MD 27, Ridge Rd, Mt Airy, Damascus
	Gas	N: 7-11, AmocoBP◊, Shell S: Exxon◊
	Food	N: Arby's, Burger King, KFC, Pizza Hut, Roy Rogers, TCBY
	Other	N: ATMs, Auto Dealers, Grocery Stores, RiteAid, Radio Shack, Safeway, Wal-Mart, US Post Office S: Patuxent River State Park

EXIT		MARYLAND
73		MD 94, Woodbine Rd, Woodbine
	Gas	N: Shell S: BP◊
	Food	N: McDonald's, Pizza Hut
	Other	N: RV Park▲ S: Patuxent River State Park
76		MD 97, Roxbury Mills Rd, Hoods Mills Rd, Cooksville, Westminster
(79)		Weigh / Inspection Station (WB)
80		MD 32, Sykesville Rd, W Friendship, Sykesville, Columbia
	Gas	S: Citgo
82		US 40E, Baltimore National Pike, Marriottsville, Ellicott City (EB)
83		Marriottsville Rd, to US 40E (WB exit, NO reaccess)

EXIT		MARYLAND
87AB		US 29, to MD 99, Columbia, Ellicott City, Columbia Pike (WB, Left Exit) (All Serv South to US 40)
	Gas	N: BP◊, Shell, Sunoco
	Food	N: Burger King, BBQ, McDonald's, Subway, Wendy's
	Other	N: ATMs, Auto Dealers, Advance Auto, Grocery, Goodyear, Home Depot, NAPA, Tires, RiteAid, Wal-Mart, Patapsco Valley State Park
(91AB)		Jct I-695, Baltimore Beltway, Towson, Glen Burnie
	Other	N: Gas/Food/Lodg, Best Buy, Staples, Firestone, Mall, Grocery S: to Baltimore-Washington Intl Airport✈
94		MD 122, Security Blvd, Woodlawn
		(I-70 begins/ends on Security Blvd/Baltimore) (EASTERN TIME ZONE)

⊙ **MARYLAND**

Begin Westbound I-70 from Baltimore, MD to Jct I-15, near Cove Fort, UT.

EXIT		OHIO
		Begin Southbound I-71 in Cleveland, OH to Jct I-65 in Louisville, KY

⊙ **OHIO**
(EASTERN TIME ZONE)
(I-71 starts/ends in OH: I-90, Exit #170B & on I-490, Exit #1A)

EXIT		OHIO
(247B)		Jct I-90W, Jct I-490E
247A		14th St, Clark Ave, Cleveland
246		OH 176, Jennings Fwy, Jennings Rd, Denison Ave, Cleveland (SB)
245		US 42, OH 3, Fulton Rd, Pearl Rd
	Gas	E: BP, Shell, Sunoco
	Food	E: China Town, McDonald's, Wendy's
	Med	E: + Metro Health Medical Center
	Other	E: CVS, Cleveland Zoo, U-Haul
244		Denison Ave, 65th St (NB, Left exit, diff reaccess)
242		W 130th St, Bellaire Rd
242AB		W 130th St, Bellaire Rd
	Gas	W: Citgo, Marathon, Sunoco
	Food	W: Burger King, Little Caesar's
	Other	E: Auto & RV Repair W: Auto Services, Discount Tire
240		W 150th St, Cleveland
	Gas	E: Marathon, Speedway◊ W: BP◊
	Food	E: Denny's, Deli, Rest/Marriott W: Burger King, Taco Bell, Rest/Hol Inn
	Lodg	E: Marriott♥ W: Baymont Inn, Holiday Inn, La Quinta Inn♥
	Other	E: ATMs, Banks, Tires W: Auto Services, ATM, Bank, Kmart
239		OH 237, Airport (SB)
	Other	W: Office Max, to Airport✈

EXIT		OHIO
(238)		Jct I-480, Toledo, Youngstown
	Other	W: to Cleveland Hopkins Int'l Airport✈, Ford Motor Co
237		Snow Rd, OH 291, Engle Rd, Brook Park, Parma (NB)
237AB		Snow Rd, OH 291, Engle Rd, Brook Park, Parma
	Gas	E: BP◊, Citgo, Shell
	Food	E: Bob Evans, Denny's, McDonald's, Ponderosa, Subway
	Lodg	E: Best Western, Holiday Inn Express, Howard Johnson W: Sheraton
	Med	E: + Parma Medical Center
	Other	E: Carwash/Shell, Auto Services W: Ford Motor Co, Cleveland Hopkins Int'l Airport✈
235		Bagley Rd, to US 42, Pearl Rd, US 291, Engle Rd, Berea, Middleburg Hts
	Gas	E: Speedway W: BP◊, Speedway, Shell
	Food	E: Bob Evans W: Arby's, Back Home Buffet, Burger King, Damon's, Denny's, Friendly's, McDonald's, Max & Erma's, Olive Garden, Perkins, Pizza Hut, Panera Bread, Taco Bell
	Lodg	E: Clarion W: Comfort Inn♥, Courtyard, Hampton Inn, Motel 6♥, Plaza Hotel, Red Roof Inn♥, Residence Inn, Ramada Inn, Studio Plus, Towneplace Suites♥
	Med	W: + SW General Health Center
	Other	W: Grocery, Kmart, Pharmacy, Baldwin-Wallace Univ, Fairgrounds
234		OH 42, Pearl Rd, Parma Heights Strongsville
	Gas	E: Shell, Sunoco◊
	Food	E: House of Hunan, Italian, Wendy's

EXIT		OHIO
	Lodg	W: A Slice Above, Jennifer's W: Days Inn♥, Kings Inn, La Siesta Motel, Metricks Motel, Village Motel
	Other	E: Laundromat W: Home Depot, Wal-Mart
(233)		Jct I-80, OH Turnpike (TOLL), to Toledo, Youngstown
231B		OH 82, N Royalton, Strongsville
	Gas	W: BP◊, Marathon◊, Sunoco◊
	Food	W: Applebee's, County Kitchen, Panera Bread, Longhorn Steakhouse, Romano's Macaroni Grill, Red Lobster
	Other	W: Grocery, Pharmacy, Target, South Park Center, Iceland USA, Mall
231A		OH 82, Royalton Rd, Strongsville
	Gas	E: Shell
	Food	E: Rest/Holiday Inn
	Lodg	E: Holiday Inn Select, Motel 6♥, Red Roof
231		OH 82, Strongsville (NB)
226		OH 303, Center Rd, Brunswick
	Gas	E: Shell◊ W: BP, Marathon◊, Sunoco◊, GetGo
	Food	E: Pizza Hut W: Arby's, Applebee's, Bob Evans, Burger King, CiCi's, Little Ceasar's, McDonald's, Pizza Hut, Starbucks, Subway, Steak n Shake, Taco Bell, Tony Roma's, Wendy's
	Lodg	W: Howard Johnson Express, Sleep Inn♥
	Other	E: Sirpilla RV Center/Camping World W: ATM, Dollar General, Grocery, Kmart
(225)		Rest Area (NB) (RR, Phones, Picnic)
(224)		Rest Area (SB) (RR, Phones, Picnic)
222		OH 3, Weymouth Rd, Medina
	Other	W: Medina Co Fairgrounds, OH State Hwy Patrol Post
(220)		Jct I-271N, to Erie, PA (NB)

◊ = Regular Gas Stations with Diesel   ▲ = RV Friendly Locations   ♥ = Pet Friendly Locations
RED PRINT SHOWS LARGE VEHICLE PARKING/ACCESS ON SITE OR NEARBY   BROWN PRINT SHOWS CAMPGROUNDS/RV PARKS

EXIT	OHIO
218	**OH 18, Medina Rd, Medina, Akron**
Gas	E: BP◊, Citgo◊, Shell◊, Sunoco◊
	W: SuperAmerica◊
Food	E: Blimpie's, Burger King, DQ, Cracker Barrel, McDonald's, Perkins
	W: Arby's, Bob Evans, Denny's, Pizza Hut, Wendy's, Waffle House
Lodg	E: Best Value Inn, Holiday Inn Express, Super 8♥, Travelers Choice
	W: Hampton Inn, Motel 6♥, Red Roof Inn♥
Med	W: + Immed Care Center
Other	E: Medina Muni Airport✈, Avalon RV & Marine, Bank, ATM
	W: ATM, Banks, Grocery, Pharmacy, Century Harley Davidson, Medina Co Fairgrounds, Walsh Univ
(209)	**Jct I-76, to Akron, US 224, Lodi, Seville**
TStop	W: Pilot Travel Center #13 (Scales), Travel Center of America #15/BP (Scales)
Food	W: CountryKitchen/Subway/Pilot TC, CountryPr/BKing/Popeye/Starbucks/TA TC
Lodg	W: Super 8♥
TWash	W: Blue Beacon TW/TA TC
TServ	W: TA TC/Tires
Other	E: Maple Lakes Campground▲
	W: Laundry/WiFi/Pilot TC, Laundry/WiFi/RVDump/TA TC
204	**OH 83, Avon Lake Rd, Burbank, Lodi, Wooster**
TStop	E: Love's Travel Stop #332 (Scales)
	W: Pilot Travel Center #287 (Scales)
Gas	E: BP, Duke
Food	E: Hardee's/Love's TS
	W: Wendy's/Pilot TC, Burger King, Bob Evans, McDonald's, Taco Bell
Lodg	E: Plaza Motel
Med	W: + Lodi Comm Hospital
Other	E: WiFi/Love's TS
	W: Laundry/WiFi/Pilot TC, Prime Outlets of Lodi, Auto Dealers
198	**OH 539, Congress Rd, W Salem**
(197)	**Rest Area** (Both dir) (RR, Phones, Picnic, Vend)
196	**OH 301, Elyria Rd, W Salem** (NB exit, NO NB re-entry)
(190)	**Weigh Station** (SB)
186	**US 250, Main St, Ashland, Wooster**
FStop	W: GoAsis Travel Plaza (NO SEMIS)
Gas	E: Marathon
Food	E: Perkins
	W: PHut/Starbucks/Taco Bell/GoAsis TP, Bob Evans, Denny's, Jake's, Java Hut Cafe, McDonald's, Starbucks, Wendy's
Lodg	W: AmeriHost Inn, Days Inn♥, Holiday Inn Express, Super 8♥
Med	W: + Samaritan Hospital
Other	E: to 7mi Hickory Lakes Campground▲
	W: ATMs, Dollar General, Home Depot, Wal-Mart sc, UPS Store, Grandpa's Village, OH State Hwy Patrol, to Ashland Univ, Ashland Co Airport✈
176	**US 30, Mansfield, Wooster** (Addtl Serv 3.5 mi W on US 30)
Lodg	E: Econo Lodge, Ohio Hilltop
	W: Best Value Inn/Mansfield Inn♥
Med	W: + Hospital

EXIT	OHIO
Other	E: COE/Charles Mill Lake Park▲, to Wooster College
	W: RV Centers, to Mansfield Muni Airport✈
173	**OH 39, Lucas Rd, to Mansfield**
169	**OH 13, Mansfield, Bellville, Mt Vernon**
Gas	E: Marathon◊, Murphy
	W: Marathon
Food	E: Applebee's, Cracker Barrel, Steak 'n Shake, Wendy's, Subway/WalMart
	W: Arby's, Bob Evans, Burger King, McDonald's, Taco Bell
Lodg	E: AmeriHost Inn, La Quinta Inn♥
	W: Hampton Inn, Super 8, Travelodge♥
Med	W: + Hospital
Other	E: Wal-Mart sc, to Mohican State Park, Malabar Farm State Park
	W: OH State Hwy Patrol Post
165	**OH 97, Bellville, Lexington**
Gas	E: BP, Shell◊, Speedway◊
Food	E: Burger King, Dutch Heritage Amish Rest, KC's Steak & Ribs, McDonald's, Subway
	W: Wendy's
Lodg	E: Days Inn, Comfort Inn, Economy Inn, Knights Inn, Quality Inn
	W: Mid Ohio Motel, Ramada
Other	E: to Mohican State Park, Ski Area, app 12mi KOA▲
	W: to Mid Ohio Race Track
151	**OH 95, Mt Gilead, Fredericktown**
TStop	E: Mt Gilead Truck Plaza/Duke
Gas	E: BP, Marathon
	W: Sunoco◊, Shell◊
Food	E: Gathering Inn Rest, McDonald's, Wendy's
Lodg	E: Best Western
	W: Knights Inn♥
Med	W: + Hospital
Tires	E: Mt Gilead TP
Other	E: Laundry/Mt Gilead TP, OH State Hwy Patrol Post, ODOT Facility
	W: to Mt Gilead State Park, Mid-OH Race Track
140	**OH 61, Marengo, to Mt Gilead, Cardington**
TStop	E: Pilot Travel Center #455 (Scales)
Gas	W: BP, Duke, Sunoco
Food	E: Arby's/TJCinn/Pilot TC
	W: Farmstead Rest, Subway/Sunoco, Taco Bell/BP
Other	E: Laundry/WiFi/Pilot TC, OH Country Music & RV Park▲
	W: 61&71 CB Shop, Cardinal Center Campground▲
131	**US 36, OH 37, Sunbury, Delaware**
TStop	E: Flying J Travel Plaza #5028/Conoco (Scales), Pilot Travel Center #14 (Scales)
Gas	W: BP, Shell
Food	E: Rest/FastFood/Flying J TP, Subway/Pilot TC, Burger King, McDonald's
	W: Arby's, Bob Evans, Cracker Barrel, KFC, Long John Silver, McDonald's, Wendy's, Waffle House, White Castle
Lodg	W: Days Inn, Hampton Inn, Holiday Inn Express
Med	W: + Hospital
Other	E: Laundry/WiFi/RVDump/LP/Flying J TP, WiFi/Pilot TC, Golf Course, to appr 7mi Autumn Lakes Family Campground▲
	W: Flea Market, Alum Creek State Park, Alum Creek RV & Marina Campground▲

◊ = Regular Gas Stations with Diesel ▲ = RV Friendly Locations ♥ = Pet Friendly Locations

RED PRINT SHOWS LARGE VEHICLE PARKING/ACCESS ON SITE OR NEARBY BROWN PRINT SHOWS CAMPGROUNDS/RV PARKS

INTERSTATE 71 N/S — OHIO

EXIT	
(129)	Weigh Station (NB)
(128)	Rest Area (Both dir) (RR, Phones, Picnic, Vend)
121	OH 750, Polaris Pkwy, Gemini Pl, Columbus
Gas	E: BP, Shell W: Marathon, Costco
Food	E: Buffalo Wild Wings, Dynasty Express, McDonald's, Polaris Grill, Quiznos, Skyline Chili, Steak n Shake W: Subway/Marathon, Arby's, Bob Evans, Carrabba's, Chipolte Mex Grill, Max & Erma's, O'Charley's, MiMi's Café, Olive Garden, Quaker Steak & Lube, Red Lobster, Smokey Bones BBQ, Starbucks, Texas Roadhouse, Tim Hortons, Waffle House, Wendy's
Lodg	E: Best Western, Hampton Inn, Wingate Inn W: Candlewood Suites, Comfort Inn, Extended Stay, Hilton Garden Inn
Med	E: + St Ann's Hospital
Other	E: Amphitheater W: ATMs, Banks, Best Buy, B&N, Costco, Kroger, Lowe's, Pharmacy, PetSmart ♥, Office Max, Target, Wal-Mart sc, Polaris Fashion Mall
NOTE:	Haz-Mat Trucks MUST use I-270 around Columbus.
(119B)	Jct I-270W, Col ByP, to Indianapolis
(119A)	Jct I-270E, Col ByP, to Wheeling
(119)	Jct I-270, Columbus ByPass, E to Wheeling, W to Indianapolis (NB)
NOTE:	Haz-Mat Trucks MUST use I-270 around Columbus.
117	OH 161, Dublin Granville Rd, Columbus, to Worthington
Gas	E: BP◊, Shell, Sunoco W: Shell, Speedway, Giant Eagle/GetGo
Food	E: Burger King, China Wok, Golden Corral, KFC, Lone Star Steakhouse, Max & Erma's, Pastabilities, Outback Steakhouse, Red Lobster, Shell's Seafood, Subway, Super Seafood Buffet W: Bob Evans, Casa Fiesta, Don Pablo's, Domino's, McDonald's, Olive Garden, Otani Japanese, Waffle House, Wendy's
Lodg	E: Comfort Inn, Days Inn, Holiday Inn Express, Knight's Inn, Motel 6 ♥ W: AmeriHost, Best Western, Clarion, Country Inn, Econo Lodge, Extended Stay America, Hampton Inn, Super 8
Other	E: AdvanceAuto, Firestone, Grocery, Staples W: ATM, Best Way Auto Care, Bowling, Cinema, Grocery, Laundromat, Pharmacy, Continent Mall, to OSU Airport ✈
116	US 23, Morse Rd, Sinclair Rd
Gas	E: BP, Shell, Speedway W: Sunoco
Food	E: Grandad's Pizza, Max & Erma's, McDonald's, Subway, Yogi's Hoagies W: La Hacienda
Lodg	E: Howard Johnson W: Best Value Inn, Motel 6 ♥
Med	E: + Urgent Care

Personal Notes

EXIT	OHIO
Other	E: ATM, Auto Repair, Grocery, CVS W: Ohio School for the Deaf, to Anheuser Busch Sports Park
115	Cooke Rd, to US 23, Columbus
Gas	E: Sunoco
Other	W: Auto Repair & Towing
114	North Broadway St, Columbus
Gas	E: Sunoco
Food	E: Subway
Med	W: + Riverside Methodist Hospital
113	Weber Rd, Columbus
Gas	E: Weber Rd Market/Auto Service W: Speedway◊
Other	W: Auto Services
112	Hudson St, Columbus
Gas	E: Shell, Marathon
Food	E: Wendy's
Lodg	E: Holiday Inn Express
Other	E: Auto Repair, Tires, Crew Stadium W: NTB, Grocery
111	17th Ave, to US 23, Summit St (Gas & Food approx 1mi W to Summit St)
Lodg	W: Comfort Suites, Days Inn
Other	W: Ohio Expo Center & State Fairgrounds, Crew Stadium
110B	11th Ave, Columbus
Med	W: + OSU Hospitals & Clinics
Other	W: Ohio Expo Center & State Fairgrounds
110A	5th Ave (SB)
Gas	E: Sunoco W: Citgo
Food	E: KFC, McDonald's, White Castle W: Wendy's

EXIT	OHIO
(109A)	Jct I-670W (SB)
(109B)	Jct I-670E, Leonard Ave, Cleveland Ave (NB) (difficult reaccess)
Med	W: + Veteran's Medical Center
Other	E: to Port Columbus Int'l Airport ✈ W: Fort Hays Army Res, Columbus St Comm College
109C	Spring St, Downtown (SB, Left exit)
Other	W: Columbus St Comm College
108B	US 40, US 62, Broad St, Oak St
Gas	E: BP, Marathon
Other	E: Franklin Park Observatory W: Pro Care Automotive Service, ATM, to State Capitol, Supreme Court
108A	Main St, Main-Rich St Connector, Columbus (SB)
Food	W: JP's BBQ, McDonald's
Other	W: ATM, Pharmacy, Downtown
NOTE:	I-71 below runs with I-70. Exit #'s follow I-70.
(107/ 101A)	Jct I-70E (SB) Jct I-71N, to Cleveland
100B	US 33, US 23, Fulton St (SB) US 33, US 23, Livingston Ave (NB)
100A	Fulton St, High St (NB)
99C/99B	OH 315N, Columbus, Downtown OH 315N, to Worthington
(99A/ 106A)	Jct I-70W, to Dayton Jct I-71S, to Cincinnati (I-71 NB, Left exit)
NOTE:	I-71 above runs with I-70. Exit #'s follow I-70.
105	Greenlawn Ave, Columbus
Gas	E: BP, SuperAmerica W: Marathon
Med	W: + Hospital
Other	W: ATM, Cooper Stadium, German Village
104	OH 104, Frank Rd, Columbus
Gas	W: Certified, Mobil
NOTE:	Haz-Mat Trucks MUST use I-270 around Columbus.
(101B)	Jct I-270W, to Indianapolis
(101A)	Jct I-270E, to Wheeling
NOTE:	Haz-Mat Trucks MUST use I-270 around Columbus.
100	CR 135, Stringtown Rd, Grove City
FStop	W: Speedway #1231
Gas	E: BP W: BP, GetGo, Sunoco
Food	E: Bob Evans, Chipolte Mexican Grill, DQ, Longhorn Steakhouse, Panda Express, O'Charley's, Roosters, Steak 'n Shake, Smokey Bones BBQ, Subway, White Castle W: Applebee's, Arby's, Burger King, Capt D's, CiCi's, Cracker Barrel, Damon's, KFC, McDonald's, Perkins, Ruby Tuesday, Starbucks, Tim Hortons, Taco Bell, Tee Jaye's, Waffle House, Wendy's
Lodg	E: Best Western, Drury Inn, Hampton Inn, Hilton Garden Inn, Holiday Inn, La Quinta Inn ♥, Motel 6, Red Roof Inn ♥, Super 8

Page 304   ◊ = Regular Gas Stations with Diesel   ▲ = RV Friendly Locations   ♥ = Pet Friendly Locations
RED PRINT SHOWS LARGE VEHICLE PARKING/ACCESS ON SITE OR NEARBY   BROWN PRINT SHOWS CAMPGROUNDS/RV PARKS

INTERSTATE 71 N/S — OHIO

EXIT		OHIO
	Lodg	W: Comfort Inn, Microtel, Saver Motel, Value Inn
	Med	W: + Urgent Medical Care, Urgent Dental Care
	Other	E: Best Buy, Discount Tire, PetSmart♥, Staples, TJ Maxx, Wal-Mart sc W: ATM, Big Lots, CVS, Goodyear, Grocery, Kmart, Kroger, Radio Shack, Walgreen's, UPS Store, Beulah Park Racetrack
97		**OH 665, London-Groveport Rd, Groveport**
	Gas	E: Marathon, Sunoco, Kroger
	Food	E: Arby's, McDonald's, Quiznos, Subway, Tim Hortons, Wendy's
	TServ	E: Peterbilt, ELW Co, RW Diesel Svc
	Med	E: + Urgent Care
	Other	W: ATM, Pharmacy, Eddie's Repair Service, Scioto Downs Racetrack
94		**US 62, OH 3, Harrisburg Rd, Grove City, Orient, Harrisburg**
	Gas	E: BP W: Sunoco◊
	Other	W: Beulah Park Track
84		**OH 56, Mt Sterling, London**
	Gas	E: BP, Circle K, Sunoco, Kroger W: Eddie's Super Service
	Food	E: Subway/BP
	Lodg	E: Royal Inn
	Other	E: Flea Market, Kroger, to COE/Deer Creek State Park, Deer Creek Camping Resort▲
75		**OH 38, Bloomingburg, Midway**
	Gas	W: Sunoco◊
69		**OH 41, OH 734, Jeffersonville, Solon**
	TStop	E: Flying J Travel Plaza #5046/Conoco (Scales)
	Gas	W: BP, Marathon, Shell◊
	Food	E: Rest/FastFood/FJ TP W: Subway/Shell, Arby's, Wendy's
	Lodg	W: AmeriHost Inn
	Med	E: + Fayette Co Memorial Hospital
	Other	E: Laundry/WiFi/RVDump/LP/FJ TP, Walnut Lake Campground▲, Barker's Towing, ATM, Flea Market, Home Works Outlet Mall
(67)		**Rest Area (Both dir) (RR, Phones, Picnic, Vend)**
65		**Old US 35 NW, to US 35, Jeffersonville, Washington CH**
	FStop	E: True North #757/Shell
	TStop	E: Travel Center of America #139/BP (Scales) W: Fuel Mart #643 (Scales), Love's Travel Stop #352 (Scales)
	Food	E: CountryPride/PizzaHut/Popeye/TA TC, Bob Evans, Burger King, McDonald's, Taco Bell, Waffle House, Wendy's, Werner's BBQ W: Hardee's/Love's TS
	Lodg	E: AmeriHost Inn, Hampton Inn, Super 8
	TServ	E: TA TC/Tires W: Fuel Mart
	Med	E: + Fayette Co Memorial Hospital
	Other	E: Laundry/WiFi/TA TC, Prime Outlets W: WiFi/RVDump/Love's TS
58		**OH 72, Sabina, Jamestown**
(54)		**Weigh Station (SB)**

EXIT		OHIO
50		**US 68, Wilmington, Xenia**
	FStop	W: Mt Pleasant Shell
	TStop	W: Pilot Travel Center #16
	Gas	W: BP◊
	Food	W: Subway/Pilot TC, DQ/BP, Max & Erma's, McDonald's, Subway, Wendy's
	Lodg	W: Budget Inn, Holiday Inn
	TServ	W: Goodyear
	Other	E: Clinton Field✈ W: WiFi/Pilot TC, Convention Center, Wilmington College, Auto & Truck Repair
(48)		**Weigh Station (NB)**
45		**OH 73, Wilmington, Waynesville**
	Gas	E: BP, Marathon◊
	Med	E: + Clinton Memorial Hospital
	Other	E: to Thousand Trails RV Park▲, Wilmington College, Airborne Airpark✈ W: Flea Market, to Caesar Creek State Park▲
36		**CR 7, Wilmington Rd, Oregonia**
	Other	E: to Olive Branch Campground▲, Fort Ancient State Memorial
(34)		**Rest Area (Both dir) (RR, Phones, Picnic, Vend, Info)**
32		**OH 123, Lebanon, Morrow**
	Gas	E: BP, Citgo, Marathon
	Food	E: Country Kitchen W: Bob Evans, Skyline Chili
	Other	E: Morgan's Riverside Campground▲, Warren Co Fairgrounds, Ft Ancient W: to Cedarbrook Campground▲, Lebanon Raceway
28		**OH 48, Lebanon, S Lebanon**
	Other	W: Lebanon Raceway, OH State Hwy Patrol Post, to Cedarbrook Campground▲
25AB		**OH 741, Kings Mill Rd, Mason**
	Gas	E: Shell, Speedway◊ W: BP, Exxon
	Food	E: El Toro, McDonald's, Popeye's, Ruby Tuesday, Taco Bell W: Arby's, Big Boy, Bob Evans, Burger King, GoldStar Chili, Outback Steakhouse, Perkins, Skyline Chili, Subway, Waffle House, Wendy's
	Lodg	E: Comfort Suites, Kings Island Resort W: Best Western, Hampton Inn, Microtel, Super 8
	Other	E: Cinema, Kings Island Amusement Park, Kings Island Campground▲ W: CVS, Kroger, Kings Golf Center, The Beach WaterPark
24		**Western Row Rd, Kings Island Dr (NB, Exit only)**
	Gas	E: Sunoco
	Lodg	E: Kings Island Resort, Great Wolf Lodge
	Other	E: Kings Island Amusement Park, Laser Kraze, Kings Island Campground▲
19		**Mason Montgomery Rd, Fields Ertel Rd, US 22, OH 3, Cincinnati**
	Gas	E: BP, Shell, Sunoco W: Ameristop, BP◊, Marathon◊, Shell
	Food	E: Arby's, Bob Evans, Cracker Barrel, Golden Corral, KFC, Little Caesars, McDonald's, Olive Garden, Pizza Hut, Taco Bell, TGI Friday, Wendy's, White Castle W: Amon Steak House, Applebee's, Burger King, Carrabba's, Chipolte Mexican Grill, Fuddrucker's, GoldStar Chili

◊ = Regular Gas Stations with Diesel   ▲ = RV Friendly Locations   ♥ = Pet Friendly Locations
RED PRINT SHOWS LARGE VEHICLE PARKING/ACCESS ON SITE OR NEARBY   BROWN PRINT SHOWS CAMPGROUNDS/RV PARKS

EXIT	OHIO	EXIT	OH / KY	EXIT	KENTUCKY
Food	W: Lone Star Steakhouse, Mimi's Cafe, O'Charley's, Qdoba Mexican Rest, Red Robin, Steak n Shake, Skyline Chili, Subway, Waffle House, Wendy's	Food	W: Denny's, Golden Corral, McDonald's, Pizza Hut, Subway, Taco Bell, Wendy's	Gas	W: Marathon◊, Speedway, Shell
		Lodg	W: Howard Johnson	Food	E: Little Caesars Pizza
Lodg	E: Comfort Inn, Quality Inn	Other	E: AutoZone, Sam's Club, Target		W: Indigo Cafe
	W: AmeriSuites, Days Inn, Kings Luxury Inn, La Quinta Inn♥, Marriott, Quality Inn, Ramada Ltd, Red Roof Inn♥		W: Goodyear, Grocery, Home Depot, Lowe's, Office Depot, Wal-Mart	Lodg	W: Holiday Inn
		8B	OH 562, Norwood Lateral Expy (NB)	186	KY 371, Buttermilk Pike, Covington, Ft Mitchell
Med	W: + Children's Medical Center, + Jewish Medical Center	8A	Ridge Ave S (NB)	Gas	E: BP◊, Citgo◊
		7	OH 562, Norwood Lateral (SB)		W: BP, Shell, Sunoco◊
Other	E: AutoZone, Auto Dealers, Auto Repairs, Best Buy, B&N, Costco, Firestone, Kroger, Office Max, PetSmart♥, Sam's Club, Radio Shack, Target, Walgreen's, Tires, Vet♥	6	OH 561, Williams Ave, Edwards Rd (SB), Edmondson Rd, to OH 561, Smith Rd (NB)	Food	E: Oriental Wok, Rest/Drawbridge Inn, Papa John's
		Gas	E: BP, Shell, Speedway		W: Arby's, Bob Evans, Burger King, Dominos, Goldstar Chili, Long John Silver, McDonald's, Outback Steakhouse, Pizza Hut, Subway
	W: ATM, Animal Hospital♥, Auto Repair, Grocery, Home Depot, Lowe's, NAPA, Staples, Wal-Mart sc, UPS Store, Wild Oats Market		W: Shell		
		Food	E: Bonefish Grill, Boston Market, BW3, China Bistro, Don Pablo, Gold Star Chili, J Alexander's, La Rose, Longhorn Steakhouse, Max & Erma's, Starbucks	Lodg	E: Cross Country Inn, Drawbridge Inn
					W: Best Western
NOTE:	Through trucks MUST take I-275 around Columbus, OH.			Other	W: Grocery, Walgreen's
(17B)	Jct I-275W, to I-75	Other	E: ATM, Auto Repair, Rockwood Commons and Pavilion	(185)	Jct I-275, W to Cincinnati Airport, I-275E, to I-471
(17A)	Jct I-275E, to OH 52		W: Midas	184	KY 236, Donaldson Rd, to Erlanger (NB)
NOTE:	Through trucks MUST take I-275 around Columbus, OH.	5	Dana Ave, Montgomery Rd	184AB	KY 236, Commonwealth Ave, Donaldson Hwy, Erlanger
		Other	W: Cincinnati Zoo, Xavier Univ	Gas	E: BP, Marathon
15	Pfeiffer Rd, Blue Ash, Montgomery	3	William Howard Taft Rd, to US 42, Reading Rd (SB)		W: Ron's Svc Ctr, Speedway
Gas	W: BP, Shell◊, Sunoco◊	Other	W: Cincinnati Zoo, Univ of Cinncinati	Food	E: Double Dragon, Rally's
Food	W: Ambo Japanese, Applebee's, Bob Evans, Brown Dog Café, Buffalo Wild Wings & Rings, Subway	2	US 42, Reading Rd, Gilbert Ave, Dorchester Ave, Eden Park Dr (NB, Left Exit)		W: Waffle House
Lodg	W: Clarion Inn, Courtyard, Embassy Suites, Hampton Inn, Red Roof Inn♥			Lodg	W: Comfort Inn, Days Inn, Econo Lodge, Howard Johnson
Med	E: + Bethesda North Hospital	(1J)	Jct I-471S, Newport, Ky (SB) Downtown, Riverfront, Third St (SB) Dwntwn, Riverfront, Second St (NB)	Med	W: + Doctors Urgent Care
Other	W: ATMs, Banks, Auto Services, Office Depot, Cincinnati Blue Ash Airport✈			Other	E: US Post Office, Police Dept
		Other	Cintas Center, Freedom Center, Paul Brown Stadium, Great American BallPark		W: Cincinnati-N Ky Int'l Airport✈
14	OH 126, Ronald Reagan Hwy, Cross County Hwy, to I-75	(1A)	US 50W, River Rd Jct I-75N, to Dayton (SB)	182	KY 1017, Turfway Rd, Florence
12	US 22, OH 3, Kenwood Rd, Montgomery Rd, Cincinnati, Madeira, Silverton	NOTE:	SB I-71 runs below with I-75 to Ex #173 in KY. Exit #'s follows I-75.	Gas	E: BP, Shell
					W: Meijer◊
			(EASTERN TIME ZONE)	Food	E: Big Boy, Lee's Chicken, New Wok, Ryan's Grill
Gas	E: BP◊, Shell, Sunoco		⊖ OHIO		W: Applebee's, Burger King, Cici's, Cracker Barrel, Famous Dave's BBQ, Fuddrucker's, Longhorn Steakhouse, O'Charley's, Rafferty's, Shell's Seafood, Steak 'n Shake, Subway, Wendy's
	W: Chevron		⊖ KENTUCKY		
Food	E: Arby's, Bob Evans, Burger King, KFC, Chipolte Mex Rest, Lone Star Steakhouse, Outback Steakhouse, Red Lobster, Subway, TGI Friday, Wendy's		(EASTERN TIME ZONE)		
		NOTE:	SB I-71 below runs with I-75 to Ex#173. Exit #'s follows I-75.	Lodg	E: Courtyard, Fairfield Inn, Howard Johnson Rodeway Inn, Signature Inn
	W: Burger King, IHOP, McDonald's, Max & Erma's, Potbelly's, Ruby Tuesday, Starbucks, Taco Bell	192	5th St, Crescent Ave, Covington(SB) US 25, US 127, 9th St, 5th St (NB)		W: Extended Stay, Hampton Inn, Hilton, La Quinta Inn♥, Studio Plus
Lodg	E: Best Western	Gas	E: BP, Speedway, Shell	Med	W: + St Luke Hospital West
	W: Hannerford Suites	Food	E: Burger King, Goldstar Chili, Hardee's, KFC, McDonald's, Subway, Waffle House, White Castle	Other	E: Office Depot, Big Lots, Grocery
Med	W: + Jewish Hospital				W: Best Buy, Grocery, Home Depot, Sam's Club, Lowe's, Target, Turfway Park Racing
Other	E: Auto Dealers, Firestone, Goodyear, Pep Boys	Lodg	E: Courtyard, Extended Stay America, Holiday Inn, Radisson	181	KY 18, Burlington Pike, Florence, Burlington
	W: ATM, Auto Repair, Kenwood Town Ctr, Mall & Cinema, B&N, Firestone, Staples		W: Hampton Inn	TStop	E: Travel Center of America/Sunoco (Scales)
11	Kenwood Rd (NB, diff reaccess) (Access Services at Exit #12)	Other	E: Riverboat Casino	Gas	E: Speedway, Swifty
		191	9th St, Pike St (SB), 12th St (NB)		W: BP◊, Chevron, Shell
Gas	W: Chevron	Med	E: + Hospital	Food	E: Arby's/PizzaHut/Popeye/Subway/TA TC, Waffle House
Med	W: + Hospital	189	KY 1072, Kyles Lane, Ft Wright		W: Applebee's, Chili's, Cracker Barrel, IHOP, Hooters, Lonestar Steakhouse, O'Charley's, Wendy's
10	Stewart Ave, Silverton (NB)	Gas	W: BP◊, Marathon◊, Shell◊, Speedway		
Gas	W: Marathon◊	Food	W: Hardee's, Pizza Hut	Lodg	E: Best Value Inn
9	Red Bank Expwy, Fairfax	Lodg	W: Days Inn, Lookout Motel, Ramada		W: Microtel
Gas	W: Mobil, Speedway	Other	W: Grocery, Walgreen's	TServ	E: Tires/TA TC
8	Highland Ave, Ridge Ave (SB)	188	US 25, US 127, Dixie Hwy, Fort Mitchell, Covington	Med	W: + Hospital
8C	Ridge Ave (NB)			Other	E: Laundry/WiFi/TA TC
Gas	E: BP, Meijer, Sam's	Gas	E: Sunoco		W: ATMs, Auto Services, Auto Dealers, Kmart, Staples, Wal-Mart sc, ProCare Automotive Service
	W: Marathon◊, Shell, Speedway				

◊ = Regular Gas Stations with Diesel ▲ = RV Friendly Locations ♥ = Pet Friendly Locations
RED PRINT SHOWS LARGE VEHICLE PARKING/ACCESS ON SITE OR NEARBY BROWN PRINT SHOWS CAMPGROUNDS/RV PARKS

I-71 N — KENTUCKY

EXIT	KENTUCKY
180A	**Steinberg Dr, Mall Rd (SB)**
Food	W: Cathay Kitchen, China Max, Hardee's, Olive Garden, Old Country Buffet, Subway
Other	W: Florence Mall, Kroger, Staples, Walgreen's
180	**US 42, US 127, Dixie Hwy, Mall Rd, Florence, Union**
Gas	E: BP◇, Speedway, Thornton's W: BP, Chevron◇, Shell◇, Speedway
Food	E: Bob Evans, Burger King, Captain D's, Dunkin Donuts, Long John Silver, McDonald's, Pizza Hut, Red Lobster, Smokey Bones BBQ, Starbucks, Subway, Wendy's W: Arby's, KFC, Perkins, Ponderosa, Waffle House, White Castle
Lodg	E: Budget Host Inn, Holiday Inn, Travelodge W: Knight's Inn, Motel 6♥, Ramada, Super 8
Other	W: AutoZone, CVS, NTB, Tires, Walgreen's
178	**KY 536, Mt Zion Rd, Florence**
Gas	E: BP◇, Mobil, Shell, Sunoco◇
Food	E: Goldstar Chili, Jersey Mike's Subs, Steak n Shake, Subway
Other	E: Grocery, Goodyear, Kroger, Pharmacy
(177)	**KY Welcome Center (SB)** **Rest Area (NB)** **(RR, Phones, Picnic, Vend, RVDump)**
175	**KY 338, Richwood Dr, Walton**
TStop	E: Travel Center of America/BP (Scales), Pilot Travel Center #278 (Scales) W: Pilot Travel Center #321 (Scales)
Gas	W: BP, Shell◇
Food	E: Rest/TacoBell/TA TC, Subway/Pilot, Arby's, Burger King, White Castle W: Subway/Pilot TC, McDonald's, Skyline Chili, Waffle House, Wendy's/BP
Lodg	E: Holiday Inn Express W: Econo Lodge
TServ	E: TA TC/Tires
Other	E: Laundry/WiFi/TA TC, WiFi/Pilot TC, RV Park▲ W: WiFi/Pilot TC, to Big Bone Lick State Park▲
(173/77)	Jct I-71S, to Louisville Jct I-75S, to Lexington
NOTE:	I-71 above runs with I-75 to OH. Exit #'s follow I-75.
(75)	**Weigh Station (SB)**
72	**KY 14, Verona Mudlick Rd, Verona**
Gas	E: BP◇, Chevron◇
Other	E: to appr 6mi: Oak Creek Campground▲
62	**US 127, Warsaw, to Glencoe**
FStop	W: Marathon
TStop	E: Exit 62 Fuel Stop & Restaurant
Food	E: Rest/Exit 62 FS W: Rest/Marathon
Lodg	W: 127 Motel
TServ	E: Exit 62 FS/Tires

EXIT	KENTUCKY
57	**KY 35, Sparta, Warsaw**
Gas	E: Marathon◇ W: BP◇
Other	E: Sparta Campground▲ W: KY Speedway
55	**KY 1130, Sparta**
Other	E: Sparta Campground▲ W: KY Speedway
43	**KY 389, Carrollton, to KY 55**
34	**US 421, Campbellsburg, Bedford**
Gas	W: Citgo◇, Marathon◇
28	**KY 153, Pendleton, KY 146, to US 42, Newcastle, Sulphur**
TStop	E: Pilot Travel Center #50 (Scales) W: Pilot Travel Center #440 (Scales)
Gas	E: Marathon◇
Food	E: Subway/Pilot TC W: McDonald's/Pilot TC
TServ	E: Dan's Truck & Diesel W: Pilot TC/Tires, SpeedCo
Other	E: Laundry/WiFi/Pilot TC, to Lake Jericho Rec Area▲ W: Laundry/WiFi/Pilot TC
22	**KY 53, S 1st St, La Grange**
Gas	E: Marathon, Super America, Kroger W: Chevron◇, Shell, Swifty
Food	E: Burger King, Papa John's, Ponderosa, Rally's, Waffle House, Wendy's W: Arby's, Cracker Barrel, DQ, Home town Pizza, KFC, Long John Silver, McDonald's, Subway, Taco Bell
Lodg	E: Best Western, Days Inn, Holiday Inn Express W: Comfort Suites, Super 8
Med	E: + First Stop Urgent Care, + Baptist Hospital Northeast
Other	E: Big O Tire, Kroger, Wal-Mart sc, CarWash W: Auto Services, Grocery, Pharmacy, US Post Office, Vet♥
18	**KY 393, La Grange, Buckner**
Gas	W: Marathon
17	**KY 146, Buckner, Crestwood, Pewee Valley**
Gas	W: Shell◇, Thornton's◇
Other	W: KY State Police
14	**KY 329 Crestwood, Pewee Valley**
Gas	E: Chevron, Shell
(13)	**Rest Area (Both dir)** **(RR, Phones, Picnic, Vend)**
(9AB)	Jct I-265, KY 841, to I-65
Other	E: to Sawyer State Park
(5)	Jct I-264, Watterson Expy (SB Left ex)
2	**Zorn Ave, Louisville**
Gas	W: BP, Chevron
Food	W: Kingfish Rest, Rest/Ramada Inn
Lodg	W: Ramada Inn
Med	E: + VA Hospital
(1B)	Jct I-65, N to Indianapolis, S to Nashville (Left Exit)
(1A)	Jct I-64W, to St Louis

(EASTERN TIME ZONE)

🎧 KENTUCKY

Begin Northbound I-71 from Louisville, KY to Cleveland, OH.

◇ = Regular Gas Stations with Diesel   ▲ = RV Friendly Locations   ♥ = Pet Friendly Locations
RED PRINT SHOWS LARGE VEHICLE PARKING/ACCESS ON SITE OR NEARBY   BROWN PRINT SHOWS CAMPGROUNDS/RV PARKS

INTERSTATE 72 E

EXIT	MO / IL
	Begin Eastbound I-72 from Hannibal, MO to near Jct I-57 in Champaign, IL.

⊙ MISSOURI
(CENTRAL TIME ZONE)
(I-72 begins/ends near I-57, Exit #235B in IL)

156	US 61, US 36 Bus, Hannibal, to New London, Palmyra
Gas	N: BP, Conoco◊
	S: Shell, Ayerco Conv Store
Food	N: Burger King, Country Kitchen, Golden Corral, Hardee's, McDonald's, Pizza Hut, Sonic, Subway, Taco Bell
	S: DQ, Gran Rio Mex, KFC, Wendy's
Lodg	S: Comfort Inn, Days Inn, Econo Lodge, Holiday Inn Express, Howard Johnson, Super 8♥
Other	N: ATMs, Banks, Big Lots, Dollar General, Kroger, Wal-Mart sc, to Bay View Campers Park▲
	S: AutoZone, ATMs, Banks, Family Dollar, Grocery, Pharmacy, Walgreen's, Injun Joe Campground▲
157	US 61 Bus, US 36 Bus, MO N, MO 79, Hannibal, Palmyra
Gas	N: BP, Conoco, Shell, Ayerco
Lodg	N: Super 7, Travelodge
Other	S: Pharmacy, to American RV Center

(CENTRAL TIME ZONE)

⌒ MISSOURI
⊙ ILLINOIS
(CENTRAL TIME ZONE)

1	IL 106, to Hull
(4AB)	Jct I-172N, to Quincy
10	IL 96, to IL 106, Kinderhook, to Hull, Payson
20	CR 4, to IL 106, Barry
FStop	S: Barry Travel Plaza/P66
Gas	S: Shell
Food	S: Wendy's
Other	S: Laundry/Barry TP, Golf Course
31	CR 2, CR 3, New Salem, Pittsfield (Serv appr 5 mi S in Pittsfield)
Med	S: + Hospital
35	US 54, IL 107, Pittsfield, Griggsville (Serv appr 4 mi N in Griggsville)
Med	S: + Hospital
Other	N: to Siloam Springs State Park▲
	S: Pine Lakes Resort▲, IL State Hwy Patrol Post, to Pittsfield Muni Airport✈

EXIT	ILLINOIS
46	IL 100, Meredosia, to Bluffs
52	Old Rte 36, to IL 106, Winchester
60AB	US 67N, Lp 72 Bus, Jacksonville, Alton (Serv N to I-72 Bus E)
64	US 67, Jacksonville, Greenfield
Gas	N: Gas, Circle K
	S: BP◊
Food	N: Subway, Chinese
	S: McDonald's, Subway
Lodg	N: Econo Lodge
Med	N: + Hospital
Other	N: Hopper RV Center, to Muni Airport✈
68	IL 104, Lp 72 Bus, Jacksonville
Gas	N: BP
Med	N: + Hospital
76	IL 123, to Ashland, Alexander
82	New Berlin
TStop	S: New Berlin Travel Plaza/P66
Food	S: FastFood/New Berlin TP
91	IL 54, Wabash Ave, Springfield
Other	S: Coleman's Country Campers
93	IL 4, Springfield, Chatham
Gas	N: Thornton's
	S: Meijer◊
Food	N: Applebee's, Arby's, Burger King, Chili's, Corky's BBQ, Damon's, Denny's, Lone Star Steakhouse, McDonald's, Olive Garden, Panera Bread, Perkins, Qdoba Mex Rest, Sonic, Starbucks, TGI Friday, Taco Bell, Wendy's
	S: Bob Evans, O'Charley's, Steak n Shake
Lodg	N: Comfort Inn, Fairfield Inn, Sleep Inn
	S: Hampton Inn, Staybridge Suites
Other	N: Best Buy, B&N, Batteries Plus, Circuit City, Discount Tire, Grocery, Kmart, Lowe's, Office Depot, Sam's Club, Staples, ShopKO, Target, Walgreen's, Wal-Mart, White Oaks Mall
	S: Auto Dealers
NOTE:	I-72 below runs with I-55. Exit #'s follow I-55.
(97AB)	Jct I-55S, Springfield, St Louis
Gas	N: Shell
Food	N: McDonald's
Lodg	N: Ramada, Super 8, Travelodge
(92)	Jct I-55S, Springfield, St Louis (SB)
94	Stevenson Dr, East Lake Dr
Gas	W: Circle K, BP, Mobil◊
Food	W: Arby's, Bob Evans, Denny's, Hardee's, Hooters, Long John Silver, Maverick Steakhouse, McDonald's,

EXIT	ILLINOIS
Food	W: Outback Steakhouse, Quiznos, Pizza Hut, Red Lobster, Smokey Bones BBQ, Steak n Shake, Subway, Taco Bell, Wendy's
Lodg	W: Comfort Suites, Days Inn, Drury Inn, Hampton Inn, Hilton Garden Inn, Holiday Inn Express, Microtel, Signature Inn
Other	E: to app 7mi KOA▲
	W: Auto Dealers, CVS, Dollar General, Radio Shack, Walgreen's, US Post Office, RV Center & Campground▲
96AB	IL 29N, Grand Ave, Springfield, Taylorville
TStop	W: RoadRanger/Citgo
Gas	W: BP
Food	W: Burger King
Lodg	W: Red Roof Inn, Super 8
Other	W: AutoZone, Auto Dealers, Grocery
(98AB/ 103AB)	Jct I-72, US 36E, to Decatur Jct I-55, N to Chicago, S to St Louis, IL 97W, to Springfield
NOTE:	I-72 above runs with I-55. Exit #'s follow I-55.
104	Mechanicsburg Rd
Food	N: Hardee's, McDonald's, Starbucks, Wendy's
Lodg	N: Best Western, Best Rest Inn
108	Riverton
114	Mechanicsburg, Buffalo
122	to Mt Auburn, Illiopolis
Gas	N: Citgo
128	Niantic
133AB	US 51S, US 36E, Pana, Decatur
Gas	S: Citgo◊, Phillips 66◊
Food	S: Subway/P66
Lodg	S: Days Inn, Holiday Inn Select
138	IL 121, Decatur, Lincoln
Med	S: + Hospital
141AB	US 51N, Decatur, Bloomington
Gas	N: Circle K/Shell
Food	N: Applebee's, Cracker Barrel, Country Kitchen, McDonald's, O'Charley's, Pizza Hut, Red Lobster, Steak n Shake, Subway, Taco Bell, Texas Roadhouse
	S: Arby's, Burger King, Quiznos
Lodg	N: Baymont Inn♥, Comfort Inn, Country Inn, Fairfield Inn, Hampton Inn, Ramada♥, Wingate Inn
Med	S: + Hospital
Other	N: Auto Dealers, AdvanceAuto, Best Buy, Harley Davidson, Lowe's, PetSmart♥, Staples, Hickory Pt Mall, Golf Course

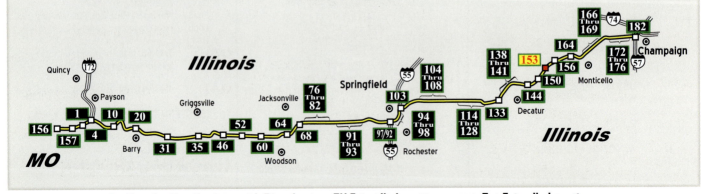

Page 308   ◊ = Regular Gas Stations with Diesel   ▲ = RV Friendly Locations   ♥ = Pet Friendly Locations
RED PRINT SHOWS LARGE VEHICLE PARKING/ACCESS ON SITE OR NEARBY   BROWN PRINT SHOWS CAMPGROUNDS/RV PARKS

EXIT		ILLINOIS
	S:	Circuit City, PetCo ♥, Radio Shack, Sam's Club, **Wal-Mart** sc, Walgreen's
144		IL 48, Decatur, Oreana
FStop	S:	RoadRanger #134
TStop	N:	Oasis Truck Stop/Marathon,
	S:	Pilot Travel Center #368 (Scales)
Food	S:	McDonald's/Subway/Pilot TC
Lodg	S:	Sleep Inn
Med	S:	+ Hospital
Other	S:	Laundry/Pilot TC, Auto Dealers
150		Argenta Rd, IL 25, to IL 48

EXIT		ILLINOIS
(153)		Rest Area (Both dir) (RR, Phone, Picnic, Vend)
156		IL 48, Cisco, Weldon
Other	N:	to Friends Creek Co Park ▲
164		IL 5, Bridge St, DeLand, Monticello
Food	S:	Hardee's, McDonald's, Pizza Hut
Med	S:	+ John & Mary Kirby Hospital
Other	S:	Platt Co Airport ✈
166		IL 105, Monticello
Gas	S:	Mobil ◊
Food	S:	Rest/BW
Lodg	S:	Best Western ♥

EXIT		ILLINOIS
Med	S:	+ John & Mary Kirby Hospital
Other	S:	Auto Dealers, Platt Co Airport ✈
169		Garfield Ave, White Heath
172		IL 10, Seymour, Lodge
176		IL 47, to Mahomet
(182AB)		Jct I-57, N - Chicago, S - Memphis, to I-74

(I-72 begins/ends on US 61, Exit #155 in Hannibal, MO.)

⊙ **ILLINOIS** (CENTRAL TIME ZONE)

Begin Westbound I-72 from Champaign, IL to Jct US-61 in Hannibal, MO.

EXIT		NORTH CAROLINA
		Begin Southbound I-73 from Virginia Border to to South Carolina Border.

⊙ **NORTH CAROLINA**

I-73 in NC is being constructed in segments. We have listed what is currently signed as I-73 or Future I-73. Other roads, mainly US Highways that are part of the Future I-73 Corridor will be noted without exit details. This will change as new parts of I-73 are open to traffic. We have tried to be as accurate as possible and List Exit #'s and Mile Markers where available.

(Segment 1)		US 220/Future I-73 Corridor, (Va Border/ US 220 to NC 68), (Current plans show construction to begin after 2015)
(Segment 2)		US 220, NC 68 to US 220/NC 68 Connector (Construction 2010-2013)
(Segment 3)		US 220/NC 68 Connector from Summerfield to NC 68, N of Greensboro (Construction to start 2013)
(Segment 4)		NC 68/Bryan Blvd (from US 220- NC 68 Conn to Greensboro Urban Loop (Future I-73/I-840)
109		NC 68S, High Point
(107)		FUTURE Exit - Piedmont-Triad Int'l Airport
3/105		Bryan Blvd, PTI Airport
2/104		W Friendly Ave
(Segment 5)		Greensboro Urban Lp Freeway (Bryan Blvd to US 220) Future I-73/I-840, I-73, US 421)
103B/80		US 421N, Winston-Salem
103A/80		US 421S, Greensboro
102/78		Wendover Ave
121A/ 73		Groometown Rd (fr I-85S Exit #120) (SB for I-85, Bus 85 are 97A & 97B)
(98)		FUTURE EXIT - High Point Rd
(97A)		Jct I-85, US 29S, US 70W, to High Point, Charlotte
97B		Bus Lp 85, US 29N, US 70E, to Greensboro
(97)		Jct I-85, Bus 85, US 29, US 70 (SB)
NOTE:		NB: joins US 421N on Greensboro Loop
NOTE:		SB: leaves US 421S onto US 220S

EXIT		NORTH CAROLINA
95		US 220, Asheboro, Rockingham
(79)		Jct I-85, US 29, US 70, Burlington, Charlotte (SB)
79B		Bus 85S, US 29S
79A		Bus 85N, US 29N
(78)		Jct I-85N, US 421S, to Durham, Raleigh (SB)
(78B)		Jct I-73N, US 421N, Winston-Salem, to Groometown Rd (NB) (Use 79B to access I-85S)
NOTE:		SB End Future I-73/74. Begin I-73/74
51		US 220 Bus N, NC 134S, Ulah, Troy
49		New Hope Church Rd, Asheboro
45		NC 705, Little River Rd, Seagrove, Robbins
Gas	E:	Quik Chek
Other	E:	Wheatley Truck Repair
41		Black Ankle Rd, Seagrove
39		Alt US 220, Star, Ether, Steeds
36		Spies Rd, Star, Robbins (Serv W to Alt US 220)
Other	W:	to Montgomery Co Airport ✈
77		Old Randleman Rd, Greensboro
Gas	W:	Summer Food Mart, BP
74		NC 62, Climax, High Point
71		US 220 Bus S, Level Cross
67		High Point St, Randleman
Gas	E:	Tank and Tummy
Food	E:	Bojangles, Hardee's, McDonald's, Soprano's Rest, Wendy's
Other	E:	Express Care
65 (Seg 7/8)		US 311, High Point, Randleman (US 220, Future I-73, Future I-74: 2013+) (Future I-74 starts SB, Ends NB) (Addt'l Serv E to Bus US 220N)
Gas		Quik N Easy, Exxon
63		Pineview St
62		Spero Rd
60		to US 220 Bus N, Fayetteville St, Vision Dr

EXIT		NORTH CAROLINA
59		NC 1462, Presnell St (Serv E to US 220 Bus)
59A		Presnell Dr
59B		to Bus US 220
58		NC 42, Salisbury St, Lexington Rd, Asheboro (Both dir, Left Exit) (Addt'l Services E to US 220 Bus)
Gas	E:	Amoco, Servco
56		US 64, NC 49, to Raleigh, Lexington, Charlotte
Gas	E:	BP, Gulf, Wilco
	W:	Exxon
Food	E:	Arby's, Bamboo Garden, Burger King, Dixie Express, Huddle House, McDonald's
	W:	Heritage Diner
Lodg	E:	Asheboro Inn, Days Inn
	W:	Super 8
Other	E:	Grocery
55		McDowell Rd
Gas	E:	Tank and Tummy, Oil
Food	W:	K&W Cafeteria
NOTE:		NB End I-73/74, Begin Future I-73/74
33		NC 24, NC 27, Biscoe
Gas	W:	Quik Chek
Food	W:	Chinese Rest
Lodg	W:	Days Inn
Other	W:	Food Lion
28		NC 211, Candor, Pinehurst
FStop	E:	WilcoHess Travel Center
Gas	W:	Quik Chek
Food	E:	Wendy's
	W:	Chinese Rest, Hardee's
24		Alt US 220N, Candor
22		Tabernacle Church Rd
18		Norman
16		NC 73
13		J Barwell Rd, Haywood Parker Rd
11		Millstone Rd, to NC 73W, Ellerbe
8		Bus US 220N, Ellerbe

⊙ **NORTH CAROLINA**

◊ = Regular Gas Stations with Diesel ▲ = RV Friendly Locations ♥ = Pet Friendly Locations

RED PRINT SHOWS LARGE VEHICLE PARKING/ACCESS ON SITE OR NEARBY BROWN PRINT SHOWS CAMPGROUNDS/RV PARKS

INTERSTATE 74 E

EXIT	IOWA
	Begin Eastbound I-74 from Jct I-80 in Davenport, IA to Jct I-75 in Cincinnati, OH.

IOWA
(CENTRAL TIME ZONE)
(I-74 begins/ends on I-80, Exit #298)

(0) Jct I-80, W to Des Moines, E to Chicago (WB, Left exit)

1 E 53rd St, Davenport
- Gas E: Phillips 66
  W: AmocoBP, Murphy
- Food E: Arby's, Bamboo Garden, Chili's, Golden Corral, IHOP, Texas Roadhouse, Wendy's
  W: Red Robin, Ruby Tuesday, Steak 'n Shake, Subway, Taco Bell
- Lodg E: Country Inn, Hampton Inn, Residence Inn, Staybridge Suites
  W: Sleep Inn
- Other E: Golf Course
  W: Best Buy, PetSmart♥, Staples, Target, Wal-Mart sc, Walgreen's, Hamilton Tech College, US Adventure RV Center

2 US 6W, Spruce Hill Dr, Kimberly Rd, Bettendorf, Davenport
- Gas E: Gary's Quik Service, Phillips 66
  W: AmocoBP◊, Citgo, Sam's
- Food E: Domino's, Mother Hubbard Cupboard, Old Chicago Pizza, Shoney's
  W: Applebee's, Bob Evans, Burger King, Panera, Red Lobster
- Lodg E: Courtyard, Heartland Inn♥, The Lodge Hotel♥, Ramada, Super 8
  W: Days Inn, Econo Lodge, Fairfield Inn, La Quinta Inn♥
- Other E: Auto Dealers, Auto Service, Golf Course, Lowe's, U-Haul
  W: Auto Services, ATM, Banks, PetCo♥, Sam's Club, Staples, Northpark Mall, Kaplan Univ, IA State Hwy Patrol Post

3 Middle Rd, Locust St, Kimberly Rd, Bettendorf, Davenport
- Gas W: One Stop Mart
- Food W: China Taste, McDonald's, Pizza Hut, Quiznos, Starbucks, Subway
- Lodg W: Holiday Inn
- Med W: + Genesis Medical Center
- Other W: Goodyear, Home Depot, Walgreen's, ShopKO, Golf Course, to Putnam Museum & IMAX

4 US 67, Grant St, State St, Riverfront
- Gas E: BP, Phillips 66◊, Shell
- Food E: Ross Restaurant
  W: Village Inn
- Lodg E: Abbey Hotel, Traveler Motel, Isle of Capri Casino & Hotel

EXIT	IA / IL
Lodg	W: City Center Motel
Other	E: Auto Services, CarQuest
	W: Dollar General, NAPA

(CENTRAL TIME ZONE)

IOWA
ILLINOIS
(CENTRAL TIME ZONE)

1 River Dr, Moline (EB)
- Other E: Visitor Info

2 7th Ave, to IL 92, Moline

3 23rd Ave, Ave of the Cities, Moline

4AB IL 5, John Deere Rd, Moline
- Gas N: BP, Citgo
  S: Citgo, Mobil
- Food N: Applebee's, Burger King, Old Country Buffet, Ryan's Grill, Starbucks, Steak 'n Shake, Wendy's
  S: Arby's, Burger King, Denny's, IHOP, Long John Silver, Pizza Hut, Subway, Taco Bell, Wendy's
- Lodg S: Best Western, Comfort Inn♥, Fairfield Inn, La Quinta Inn♥, Super 8
- Med S: + Trinity Medical Center
- Other N: Lowe's, Staples, Wal-Mart sc, Tires, Blackhawk College, John Deere Co World Hdqtrs
  S: Auto Dealers, Best Buy, Firestone, Grocery, FedEx Kinko's, Office Max, Pharmacy, PetCo♥, Southpark Mall, to Blackhawk State Park

NOTE: I-74 runs with I-280 to MM14, Jct I-80

(5A) Jct I-280W, US 6W, to Des Moines

5B US 6E, Quad City Airport, Moline
- Food S: Denny's, McDonald's, Montana Jack's
- Lodg S: Country Inn, First Choice Inn♥, Hampton Inn, Holiday Inn Express, La Quinta Inn♥, Quality Inn, The Fifth Season Hotel♥
- Other S: Quad City Int'l Airport✈, to Niabi Zoo

(6) Weigh Station (EB)

(8) Weigh Station (WB)

(14) Jct I-80, E-Chicago, I-80/280W, to Des Moines

NOTE: I-74 runs with I-280 to MM 14, Jct I-80

24 IL 81, Lynn Center, Andover
- Other S: to appr 15mi Gibson's RV Park & Campground▲

(28) Rest Area (EB)
(RR, Phones, Picnic, Vend, RVDump)

EXIT	ILLINOIS
(30)	Rest Area (WB) (RR, Phones, Picnic, Vend, RVDump)

32 IL 17, Woodhull, Alpha
- TStop S: Woodhull Truck Plaza/Mobil (Scales)
- Gas N: BP◊, Shell
- Food S: Rest/Woodhull TP, Homestead Rest, Subway
- Other N: to Shady Lakes Campground▲
  S: Laundry/Woodhull TP

46AB US 34, Galesburg, Monmouth, Kewanee (Serv 3.5mi S in Galesburg)
- FStop S: Mobil (1.75 mi E of US 34)
- Other S: Lake Storey Campground▲

48 Main St, E Galesburg (EB)

48AB Main St, Galesburg (WB)
- Gas S: Clark, Hy-Vee, Mobil, Phillips 66
- Food S: Hardee's, KFC, McDonald's, Jalisco's Mex Rest, Pizza Hut, Taco Bell
- Lodg N: Best Western♥
  S: Days Inn, Holiday Inn Express, Relax Inn, Super 8
- Other S: Galesburg Muni Airport✈

51 CR 9, Henderson St, CR 10, US 150, Galesburg, Knoxville
- FStop S: Knoxville Travel Mart/BP (CR 9S)
- TStop S: The Junction/66 (US 150)
- Gas S: Casey's General Store
- Food S: Hardee's, McDonald's, Subway
- Other S: Laundry/Junction, Fairgrounds

54 US 150, to IL 97, Knoxville, Gilson, Dahinda, Lewistown
- Other N: Golf Course, Dean's RV Service, Best Holiday Trav-L Park▲, Galesburg East Campground▲
  S: Whispering Oaks Campground▲

(62) Rest Area (Both dir) (RR, Phones, Picnic, Vend, Weather)

71 CR R18, to IL 78, US 150, Brimfield, Canton, Kewanee, Elmwood

75 CR R25, N Maher Rd, Brimfield, Oak Hill

82 CR 18, CR R40, Edwards, Kickapoo
- FStop S: Freedom Oil/Shell
- Gas N: Mobil◊
- Food S: SubExpress/Freedom Oil
- Other N: Jubilee College State Park, Wildlife Prairie State Park

(87A) Jct I-474E, to Indianapolis
- Other S: to Greater Peoria Reg'l Airport✈

87B Jct IL 6N, to Chillicothe

◊ = Regular Gas Stations with Diesel   ▲ = RV Friendly Locations   ♥ = Pet Friendly Locations
RED PRINT SHOWS LARGE VEHICLE PARKING/ACCESS ON SITE OR NEARBY   BROWN PRINT SHOWS CAMPGROUNDS/RV PARKS

EXIT		ILLINOIS
88		Sterling Ave, to US 150W, War Memorial Dr, Peoria
	Lodg	N: Springhill Suites
89		US 150E, War Memorial Dr
	Gas	N: BP, Clark
	Food	N: Bob Evans, Burger King, Denny's, IHOP, Ned Kelly's Steakhouse, Outback Steakhouse, Perkins, Pizza Hut, Red Lobster, Subway, Wendy's
	Lodg	N: Baymont Inn, Best Western♥, Comfort Suites♥, Extended Stay America, Red Roof Inn♥, Residence Inn♥, Sleep Inn♥, Super 8
	Med	N: + to Proctor Hospital
	Other	N: Circuit City, Lowe's, Target, Walgreen's, Tires, Northwoods Mall, Wal-Mart sc, to IL Central College
90		Gale Ave, Peoria
	Gas	N: Circle K
		S: Speedway
	Other	S: Kmart
91		University St, Peoria (EB)
91AB		University St, Peoria
	Gas	N: BP, Phillips 66
	Other	S: AutoZone, Walgreen's, Wal-Mart, to Bradley Univ, Shea Stadium, Museum, Expo Gardens, Fairgrounds
92A		IL 40N, IL 88, Knoxville Ave
92B		to IL 40S, Glen Oak Ave, Downtown
	Med	N: + St Francis Med Center, VA Hospital S: + Methodist Med Center
	Other	S: Peoria Civic Center, O'Brien Field
93		to US 24, IL 29, Washington St (EB), Adams St, Jefferson Ave (WB)
	Lodg	S: Mark Twain Hotel♥
	Other	S: Riverplex, Tourist Info, Greater Peoria Reg'l Airport✈, Riverfront, Downtown
94		IL 40N, Riverfront Dr, Downtown
	Gas	S: Citgo
	Food	S: Burger King/Citgo, Papa John's, Steak 'n Shake
	Other	S: Lowe's, Office Max, Radio Shack, Wal-Mart sc
95		US 150W, IL 116, N Main St (WB)
95A		US 150, IL 116, N Main St (EB)
	Gas	S: BP
	Food	S: Applebee's, Bob Evans, Hardee's, Long John Silver, Subway
	Lodg	S: Baymont Inn♥, Motel 6♥
	Other	S: AdvanceAuto, CVS, Dollar General, Grocery, Kroger, ShopKO, Walgreen's

EXIT		ILLINOIS
95B		US 150, IL 8E, Camp St (EB)
	Other	N: Par-A-Dice Riverboat Casino, IL Central College
96		to IL 8, Washington St (EB), to US 15
	Food	N: Subway, Wendy's
	Lodg	N: Super 8
	Other	N: Eastside Sports Complex
98		Pinecrest Dr, Peoria
(99)		Jct I-474 W, to Moline Rock Island, Pekin, Peoria Reg'l Airport
(101)		Jct I-155 S, IL 121, to Lincoln
102AB		IL 121, N Morton Ave, Morton (EB)
102		IL 121, N Morton Ave, to US 150, Jackson St, Morton (WB)
	TStop	N: Morton Travel Center/Mobil (Scales)
	Gas	N: BP, Casey's, Citgo◊ S: Clark, Shell◊
	Food	N: Arby's/Morton TC, Blimpie/Citgo, Burger King, Cracker Barrel, Country Kitchen, Morton Family Rest, Taco Bell, Wendy's S: Judy's Rest, KFC, McDonald's, Subway
	Lodg	N: Best Western, Comfort Inn, Days Inn, Holiday Inn Express, Townhouse Inn
	Other	N: Laundry/WiFi/Morton TC S: CVS, Kmart, Kroger
112		IL 117, Deer Creek, Goodfield
	FStop	N: Freedom Oil #77/Shell
	Food	N: Subway/Freedom Oil
(114)		Rest Area (Both dir) (RR, Phones, Picnic, Vend, Weather, RVDump)
120		CR 153, W Washington St, Carlock
(122)		Weigh Station (Both dir)
125		US 150, Mitsubishi Motorway, Normal, to Bloomington
NOTE:		I-74 runs below with I-55 for 6 mi. Exit #'s follow I-55.
(163/ 127)		Jct I-74W, to Champaign, Peoria Jct I-55N, US 51, to Chicago S to St Louis, I-74W, to Peoria
160A		US 150, IL 9, Market St, Bloomington, Pekin
	FStop	E: Circle K/Citgo, Speedway #8326, Freedom Oil #39
	TStop	E: Pilot Travel Center #299 (Scales), Travel Center of America #92/BP (Scales)
	Gas	E: BP, Clark, Shell

EXIT		ILLINOIS
	Food	E: Wendy's/Pilot TC, CountryPride/Popeyes PizzaHut/TA TC, Arby's, Burger King, Carl's Jr, Cracker Barrel, Hardee's, KFC, McDonald's, Subway, Taco Bell
	Lodg	E: Best Inn♥, Comfort Inn, Days Inn♥, Econo Lodge, Hawthorn Suites, Quality Inn
	TWash	E: Blue Beacon TW
	TServ	E: TA TC/Tires
	Med	E: + Hospital
	Other	E: Laundry/BarbSh/WiFi/Pilot TC, Laundry/WiFi/TA TC, Grocery, NAPA, Pharmacy, Wal-Mart
160B		US 150, IL 9, Market St
	Gas	W: Citgo◊
	Food	W: Country Kitchen, Steak 'n Shake
	Lodg	W: Country Inn♥, Hampton Inn, Ramada Inn♥, Wingate Inn
	Other	W: Factory Outlet, Wal-Mart
(157A/ 134A)		Jct I-74E, to Indianapolis, I-55 US 51, to Decatur Jct I-55, S to Memphis, N to Chicago
157B/ 134B		Bus 55, US 51, Veteran's Pkwy, Bloomington
	Gas	E: Shell◊
	Food	E: Rest/Parkway Inn, CJ's
	Lodg	E: Parkway Inn, Sunset Inn
NOTE:		I-74 runs above with I-55 for 6 mi. Exit #'s follow I-55.
135		US 51S, US 51N Bus, Bloomington
	Gas	N: Mobil◊ S: Shell◊
	Food	N: McDonald's
	Other	S: Budget Truck Rental
142		CR 27, CR 36, Downs
	Gas	N: BP◊
149		CR 21, Le Roy, Clinton Lake
	TStop	N: Love's Travel Stop #367 (Scales) S: Le Roy Truck Plaza/Shell (Scales)
	Gas	N: BP◊, Freedom Oil
	Food	N: Arby's/Love's TS, KFC, McDonald's, Subway S: Rest/LeRoy TP
	Lodg	S: Super 8
	Other	N: Grocery, Pharmacy, Moraine View State Park, Wildwood Campground▲
152		US 136, Le Roy, to Heyworth
(156)		Rest Area (Both dir) (RR, Phones, Picnic, Vend, Weather)
159		IL 54, Farmer City, Gibson City
	Gas	S: Casey's General Store
	Food	S: Farmer City Café, Peoples Cafe
	Lodg	S: Budget Motel, Days Inn

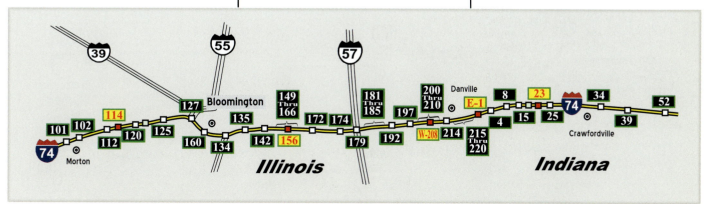

◊ = Regular Gas Stations with Diesel   ▲ = RV Friendly Locations   ♥ = Pet Friendly Locations
RED PRINT SHOWS LARGE VEHICLE PARKING/ACCESS ON SITE OR NEARBY   BROWN PRINT SHOWS CAMPGROUNDS/RV PARKS

Page 311

INTERSTATE 74 W/E

EXIT	ILLINOIS		EXIT	ILLINOIS		EXIT	INDIANA	
166	CR 2, Mansfield			TServ	S: Ron's Truck & Auto Repair		**INDIANA**	
	Gas	S: BP		Other	S: Laundromat, Firestone, Grocery		(EASTERN TIME ZONE)	
172	IL 47, Mahomet, Gibson City		185	US 150, IL 130, University Ave		(1)	IN Welcome Center (EB)	
	Gas	S: Mobil, Shell◊						(RR, Phones, Picnic, Vend, Info, RVDump)
	Food	S: Arby's, Hardee's, Subway	192	CR 12, N Main St, St Joseph				
	Lodg	S: Heritage Inn	197	IL 49S, 2700E, Ogden, Royal		4		IN 63, Covington, Perrysville, W Lebanon, Newport
	Other	S: Laundromat, Grocery, CVS, NAPA	200	IL 49N, Rankin, Fithian			TStop	N: Pilot Travel Center #339 (Scales)
174	Prairie View Rd, to CR 50, Lake of the Woods Rd, Mahomet			Other	N: Five Bridges RV Park▲		Gas	N: BP
	FStop	N: Super Pantry #42/Mobil	206	CR 10, Oakwood Rd, Oakwood, Potomac			Food	N: Arby's/TJCinn/Pilot TC, Beef House Rest, Wendy's
	Gas	N: Casey's, BP◊		TStop	N: I-74 Auto Truck Plaza/Marathon (Scales) Colonial Pantry Travel Plaza/66 (Scales) S: Oakwood Truck Plaza/Marathon (Scales)		Other	N: Laundry/WiFi/Pilot TC
	Food	N: Pickle Tree Farm Rest, Subway				8		S Stringtown Rd, Covington
	Other	N: Tincup RV Park▲, RV Center					Gas	N: Shell
(179AB)	Jct I-57, S - Memphis, N - Chicago			Gas	S: Casey's	15		US 41, US 136, Veedersburg
181	Prospect Ave, Champaign, Urbana			Food	N: Rest/I-74 ATP, FastFood/Colonial TP S: Oaks Grill/Oakwood TP, McDonald's		Gas	S: Marathon◊, Phillips 66
	Gas	N: Meijer◊, Murphy, Sam's				(19)	Weigh Station (EB)	
		S: Clark, Freedom Oil◊, Mobil		TServ	N: I-74 ATP/Tires, Truck & Trailer Repair	(23)		Rest Area (Both dir) (RR, Phones, Vend)
	Food	N: Applebee's, Burger King, Chili's, Culver's, Damon's, Hardee's, Lone Star Steakhouse, O'Charley's, Old Country Buffet, Outback Steakhouse, Red Lobster, Ryan's Grill, Steak 'n Shake, Subway, Wendy's		Other	N: Laundry/LP/Colonial Pantry TP S: Laundry/Oakwood TP	25		IN 25, Waynetown, Wingate
			(208)	IL Welcome Center (WB) Rest Area (EB) (RR, Phones, Picnic, Vend, Weather)			Other	S: Charlarose Lake & Campground▲
						34		US 231, IN 43, Crawfordsville
							TStop	S: Crawfordsville Travel Plaza/Marathon (Scales)
		S: Arby's, KFC, Long John Silver	210	US 150, W Main St, MLK Dr		Gas	S: BP, Gas America, Shell
	Lodg	N: Courtyard, Drury Inn, Extended Stay America, Fairfield Inn		Med	N: + Hospital		Food	S: Burger King, KFC, McDonald's
			214	G St, Tilton		Lodg	S: Comfort Inn, Days Inn, Holiday Inn, Ramada, Super 8
		S: Days Inn, Econo Lodge	215	US 150, IL 1, Gilbert St, Danville			
	Other	N: ATMs, Bank, Advance Auto, Best Buy, Circuit City, Dollar Tree, Lowe's, Staples, Sam's Club, Office Depot, Target, Tires, Wal-Mart sc, Auto Dealers, Auto Services, Market Place Mall		Gas	N: Speedway		TWash	S: Truck Wash of America
					S: Casey's, Clark, Speedway◊		TServ	S: D & B Truck Service
				Food	N: Arby's, Burger King, Hardee's, Long John Silver, McDonald's, Pizza Hut, Steak n Shake, Subway, Taco Bell S: Burger King, Family Restaurant		Med	S: + Hospital
							Other	S: Laundry/Crawfordsville TP, Crawfordsville KOA▲, Sugar Creek Campground▲
		S: Dollar General, Home Depot, Walgreen's		Lodg	N: Best Western, Days Inn S: Budget Motel	39		IN 32, Crawfordsville, to Lebanon
182	Neil St, Champaign						TStop	S: Pilot Travel Center #247 (Scales)
	Gas	S: Mobil		Med	N: + Hospital		Food	S: Subway/Pilot TC
	Food	N: Bob Evans, Chevy's Mex Rest, Denny's, McDonald's, Olive Garden, Smokey Bones BBQ, Subway, Taco Bell		Other	N: Grocery, Pharmacy S: AutoZone, Family Dollar, Grocery, Auto Dealers		Other	S: Laundry/WiFi/Pilot TC
						52		IN 75, Jamestown
			216	CR 6, Perrysville Rd, Bowman Ave	(57)		Rest Area (Both dir) (RR, Phones, Picnic, Vend)
	Lodg	N: Baymont Inn, Comfort Inn, La Quinta Inn♥, Red Roof Inn♥		Gas	N: Freedom Oil, Mobil◊			
		S: Howard Johnson	220	Lynch Rd, to US 136, Danville	58		IN 39, N State St, Lizton, Lebanon
183	Lincoln Ave, Urbana			TStop	N: Lynch Creek Plaza/Marathon (Scales)	61		CR 275E, Jeff Gordon Blvd, Pittsboro
	Gas	S: Mobil◊, Speedway		Gas	N: BP◊		TStop	S: Love's Travel Stop #319 (Scales)
	Food	S: Urbana's Garden Rest, Rest/Hol Inn		Food	N: Big Boy, What's Cooking Rest		Food	S: Godfathers/Subway/Love's TS
	Lodg	S: Holiday Inn, Holiday Inn Express, Ramada Ltd♥, Sleep Inn, Super 8		Lodg	N: Best Western♥, Comfort Inn, Fairfield Inn, Holiday Inn Express, Redwood Motor Inn, Super 8		Other	S: WiFi/RVDump/Love's TS
						66		IN 267, N Green St, Brownsburg
	Other	S: to Univ of IL/Urbana-Champaign		Other	N: Laundry/Tires/Lynch CP		Gas	N: Phillips 66, Shell
184	US 45, Cunningham Ave, Urbana		NOTE:	MM 221: Indiana State Line			S: BP◊, Speedway◊, Kroger
	Gas	S: Circle K, Freedom Oil◊, Super America		(CENTRAL TIME ZONE)				
	Food	S: Cracker Barrel, Dominos, Hickory River Smokehouse, Longhorn Steakhouse, Ned Kelly's Steakhouse, Steak 'n Shake		**ILLINOIS**				
	Lodg	N: Park Inn						
		S: Best Value Inn, Best Western, Eastland Suites, Motel 6♥						

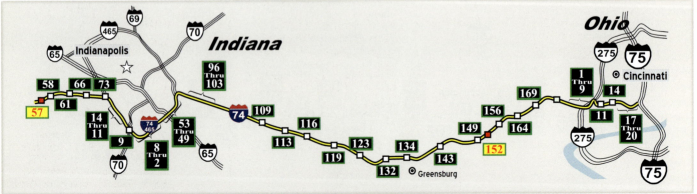

◊ = Regular Gas Stations with Diesel ▲ = RV Friendly Locations ♥ = Pet Friendly Locations
RED PRINT SHOWS LARGE VEHICLE PARKING/ACCESS ON SITE OR NEARBY BROWN PRINT SHOWS CAMPGROUNDS/RV PARKS

EXIT	INDIANA
Food	N: Hardee's, Steak n Shake, Subway S: Arby's, Bob Evans, Burger King, McDonald's, Taco Bell, Wendy's
Lodg	N: Dollar Inn, Holiday Inn Express S: Comfort Inn, Super 8
Med	S: + Family Medicine Immed Care
Other	N: Big O Tires S: CVS, Kmart, Kroger, Wal-Mart sc
NOTE:	I-74 runs below with I-465 for 21 mi. Exit #'s follow I-465.
(73A/16B)	Jct I-465S, Indianapolis ByPass, Jct I-74
(73B/16A)	Jct I-465N, to I-65, to I-865, Crawfordsville Rd, to Chicago, Ft Wayne, Jct I-74
14AB	W 10th St, Indianapolis
Gas	N: Marathon, Shell S: BP, Gas America, Speedway
Food	N: Pizza Hut, Wendy's S: Arby's, Hardee's, McDonald's, Noble Roman's Pizza, Taco Bell
Med	N: + Hospital
Other	N: Grocery, Lowe's S: CVS
13AB	US 36E, Rockville Rd, Danville
Gas	N: Citgo S: Speedway
Food	N: Burger King S: Bob Evans
Lodg	N: Comfort Inn, Sleep Inn, Wingate Inn S: Best Western
Other	N: Sam's Club
12AB	US 40E, Washington St, Plainfield
Gas	N: BP S: Phillips 66, Shell, Thornton's
Food	N: Burger King, Fazoli's, McDonald's, Taco Bell, White Castle S: Arby's, Burger King, Hardee's, KFC, Long John Silver, Omelet Shop, Pizza Hut, Steak 'n Shake, Subway, Wendy's
Lodg	S: Dollar Inn
Med	+ Hospital
Other	N: AutoZone, Dollar General, Kroger, Laundromat, Walgreen's, U-Haul S: Goodyear, Laundromat, Kmart, Target
11AB	Airport Expy, Indianapolis Int'l Airport
Gas	S: BP
Food	S: Burger King
Lodg	N: Adams Mark, Baymont Inn, Days Inn, Courtyard, Extended Stay America S: Holiday Inn, Hilton, La Quinta Inn ♥, Ramada, Residence Inn, Wellesley Inn
(9AB)	Jct I-70, E to Indianapolis, W to Terra Haute
8	IN 67S, Kentucky Ave
Gas	S: BP◊, Speedway, Shell
Food	S: Denny's, Hardee's, KFC
Med	S: + Hospital
7	Mann Rd (WB)
4	IN 37S, Harding St, Indianapolis, Martinsville, Bloomington
TStop	N: Mr Fuel #6 (Scales), Pilot Travel Center #318 (Scales) S: Flying J Travel Plaza #5440/Conoco (Scales)
Gas	S: Marathon

Personal Notes

EXIT	INDIANA
Food	N: FastFood/Pilot TC, FastFood/MrFuel, Omelet Shoppe S: Cookery/FastFood/FJ TP, Hardee's, McDonald's, Waffle & Steak, White Castle
Lodg	N: Best Value Inn, Super 8 S: Knights Inn
TWash	S: Blue Beacon TW/FJ TP
TServ	S: FJ TP/Tires, Stoop's Freightliner, Paul's Trailer Sales & Service
Other	N: Laundry/WiFi/MrFuel, WiFi/Pilot TC S: Laundry/BarbSh/CB/WiFi/RVDump/LP/FJ TP
2AB	US 31S, IN 37, East St, Indianapolis
Gas	N: BP, Speedway S: Shell, Sunoco
Food	N: Arby's, Burger King, DQ, Golden Wok, Hardee's, KFC, Long John Silver, Papa John's, McDonald's, Old Country Buffet, Pizza Hut, Ponderosa, Steak & Ale, Steak 'N Shake, Wendy's, White Castle S: Applebee's, Bob Evans, Denny's, Red Lobster
Lodg	S: Best Inn, Comfort Inn, Days Inn, Four Winds Resort & Marina, Holiday Inn Express, Ramada Inn, Ramada Ltd
Other	N: AutoZone, Auto Dealers, CVS, Dollar General, Family Dollar, Firestone, Kroger, Goodyear, Office Depot, Radio Shack, Target, U-Haul
(53AB)	Jct I-65, N to Indianapolis, S to Louisville
52	Emerson Ave, Beech Grove, Indianapolis
Gas	N: Shell, Speedway

EXIT	INDIANA
Gas	S: Shell, Speedway◊
Food	N: Burger King, Domino's Pizza, KFC, Subway, Taco Bell, Wendy's S: Arby's, DQ, Fazoli's, Hardee's, Pizza Hut, McDonald's, Steak 'n Shake, Subway, White Castle
Lodg	N: Motel 6 ♥ S: Holiday Inn, Red Roof Inn ♥, Super 8
Med	N: + Hospital
Other	N: CVS S: AutoZone, Kmart, Walgreen's
(49AB/94)	Jct I-74E, US 421S Jct I-465/I-74W, I-465N, I-421N Southwestern Ave, Columbus, OH; Ft Wayne
NOTE:	I-74 runs above with I-465 for 21 mi. Exit #'s follow I-465.
96	Post Rd, Indianapolis
Gas	N: Marathon◊ S: Shell◊
Food	N: McDonald's S: Wendy's
99	Acton Rd, Southeastern Ave
Other	N: Buck Creek Winery
101	Pleasant View Rd, Fairland
Gas	N: Marathon
103	N700W, London Rd, to Boggstown
109	W400N, Fairland Rd, Fairland
TStop	N: Pilot Travel Center #242 (Scales)
Food	N: FastFood/Pilot TC
Other	N: WiFi/Pilot TC, Indiana Downs, Shelbyville Muni Airport ✈ S: RV Park▲
113	IN 9, Shelbyville, Greenfield
FStop	S: Crystal Flash #10
Gas	N: Gas America S: BP, Shell
Food	N: Cracker Barrel, Santa Fe Cattle Co, Wendy's S: McDonald's, Waffle & Steak
Lodg	S: Best Western, Comfort Inn, Days Inn, Hampton Inn, Holiday Inn, Knights Inn ♥, Super 8
Med	S: + Hospital
116	IN 44, to IN 9, Shelbyville, Manilla
FStop	N: Big Foot #28/Shell
Gas	S: BP, Marathon, Shell, Kroger, Murphy
Food	S: Applebee's, Arby's, Burger King, Bob Evans, China Inn, Denny's, Dominos, Golden Corral, McDonald's, Pizza Hut, Starbucks, Subway, Taco Bell, Wendy's
Lodg	S: Lee's Inn
Med	S: + Hospital
Other	S: ATMs, Auto Dealers, CVS, Grocery, Kroger, NAPA, Pharmacy, Wal-Mart sc
119	IN 244, Waldron, Milroy, Andersonville
123	N CR 8W, St Paul, Middletown
Other	S: Hidden Paradise Campground▲, Thorntree Lake Campground▲
132	US 421S, Greensburg (EB)
134AB	IN 3, to US 421, Greensburg, Rushville, Columbus
Gas	S: Big Foot, BP◊, Shell, Speedway
Food	S: Arby's, Big Boy, Burger King, Chili's, Hardee's, Little Caesar's Pizza, KFC, McDonald's, Papa John's, Ponderosa, Subway, Taco Bell, Waffle House, Wendy's

EXIT		INDIANA
	Lodg	S: Best Western, Holiday Inn, Lee's Inn
	Other	S: AdvanceAuto, AutoZone, Big O Tire, CVS, Dollar General, Radio Shack, Staples, Wal-Mart sc
143		CR 850E, Greensburg, to New Point, St Maurice
	TStop	N: Petro Stopping Center #73 (Scales)
	Gas	S: Marathon
	Food	N: IronSkillet/FastFood/Petro SC
	TServ	N: Petro SC/Tires
	Other	N: Laundry/WiFi/Petro SC
149		IN 229, Walnut St, Batesville, to Oldenburg
	Gas	N: Shell◊, Sunoco S: BP
	Food	N: McDonald's, Subway, Wendy's S: Arby's, Skyline Chili, Waffle House
	Lodg	N: Hampton Inn S: Comfort Inn, Sherman House
	Med	S: + Hospital
	Other	N: Dollar General, Kroger S: Pharmacy
(152)		Rest Area (Both dir) (RR, Phones, Picnic, Vend)
156		IN 101, CR 875E, Sunman, Milan
	Gas	S: Exxon◊
164		IN 1, Woodbridge Ln, W Harrison, Lawrenceburg, St Leon
	Gas	N: Exxon, Shell◊ S: BP◊

EXIT		IN / OH
	Food	N: Christina's Family Rest
169		US 52W, West Harrison, Brookville
(171)		Weigh Station (WB)
	NOTE:	MM 171.5: Ohio State Line
		(EASTERN TIME ZONE)
		⌒ INDIANA
		⌒ OHIO
		(EASTERN TIME ZONE)
1		New Haven Rd, Harrison
	Gas	N: BP◊ S: Marathon, Shell, Speedway◊, Sunoco
	Food	N: Cracker Barrel, Gold Star Chili S: Arby's, Burger King, Hardee's, Pizza Hut, McDonald's, Shoney's, Waffle House, Wendy's, White Castle
	Lodg	N: Comfort Inn S: Holiday Inn, Quality Inn
	Other	N: Home Depot, Tires S: AutoZone, Big Lots, CVS, Firestone, Kmart, Kroger, Goodyear, Walgreen's
(2)		Weigh Station (EB)
3		Dry Fork Rd, Harrison
	FStop	S: 74 Fuel Stop/Shell
	Gas	N: Citgo
	Food	S: Burger King, McDonald's
	Other	N: Cincinnati West Airport✈
(5)		Jct I-275S, to Kentucky

EXIT		OHIO
7		OH 128, Cleves, to Hamilton
	Gas	N: BP◊, Marathon◊
	Food	N: Wendy's
(9)		Jct I-275N, to I-75, to Dayton (WB)
11		Rybolt Rd, Harrison Ave, Cincinnati
	Gas	S: BP
	Food	S: Rest/Imperial House
	Lodg	S: Imperial House
14		N Bend Rd, to Cheviot
	Gas	N: Citgo, Speeedway◊, Shell, Sam's S: BP
	Food	N: McDonald's, Pizza Hut, Perkins, Subway, Wendy's S: Bob Evans
	Lodg	S: Tri-Star Motel
	Med	N: + Hospital
	Other	N: Grocery, Sam's Club, Tire Discounters, Walgreen's
17		Montana Ave, W Fork Rd (WB)
18		US 27N, Colerain Ave, Beekman St
19		Elmore St, Colerain Ave, to Spring Grove Ave, William Dooley Byp (WB)
(20)		Jct I-75, N to Dayton, S to Cincinnati (EB)
		(I-74 begins/ends on I-75, Exit #4)
		(EASTERN TIME ZONE)
		⌒ OHIO
		Begin Westbound I-74 at Jct I-75 in Cincinnati, OH to Davenport, IA.

EXIT		NORTH CAROLINA
		Begin Eastbound I-74 from Virginia Border to to South Carolina Border.
		⌒ NORTH CAROLINA
		(EASTERN TIME ZONE)
		I-74 in NC is being constructed in segments. We have listed what is currently signed as I-74 or Future I-74. Other roads, mainly US Highways that are part of the Future I-74 Corridor will be noted without exit details. This will change as new parts of I-74 are open to traffic. We have tried to be as accurate as possible and List Exit #'s and Mile Markers where available.
	NOTE:	I-74 below runs with I-77 from VA Border to Exit #101/Jct I-74.
(105)		NC Welcome Center (SB) (RR, Phones, Picnic, Vend, Info)
(103)		Weigh Station (Both dir)
(101)		Jct I-74E, Mount Airy, to Winston-Salem (fr SB, Left Exit)
	NOTE:	I-74 above runs with I-77 to VA Border. I-74 begins below to Mt Airy.
(5)		Jct I -77, N to Wytheville, VA; S to Statesville

EXIT		NORTH CAROLINA
6		NC 89, to I-77, W Pine St, Mt Airy
	TStop	S: Brintle Travel Plaza/Citgo (Scales)
	Gas	N: Citgo S: Marathon◊
	Food	N: Subway S: Rest/Brintle TP, Subway, Wagon Wheel Rest
	Lodg	S: Best Western
	TServ	S: Brintle TP/Tires, Pooles 89 Truck Service & Car Repair
8		Red Brush Rd, Mount Airy
	Other	S: Pine Ridge Golf Course
11		US 601, Rockford Rd, Mt Airy, White Plains, Dobson (Serv 2 mi+ E on US 601)
	Gas	N: Citgo, Texaco
	Food	N: Arby's, Biscuitville, Burger King, Chinese Rest, Golden Corral, Hardee's, Little Caesars, Japanese Rest, Long John Silver, Mex Rest, Ruby Tuesday, Subway, Taco Bell, Waffle House, Wendy's
	Lodg	N: Hampton Inn, Quality Inn
	Med	N: + Northern Hospital of Surry Co
	Other	N: ATMs, Auto Services, Banks, Carolina Tire, Grocery, Pharmacy, Wal-Mart sc
13		Park Dr

EXIT		NORTH CAROLINA
(17/140)		US 52N, Mount Airy (EB) Jct I-74W, to I-77, to Wytheville, VA
	Other	N on US 52: to Downtown Mt Airy, Mt Airy/Surry Co Airport✈
	NOTE:	EB: End I-74, Begin US 52/Future I-74 Corridor. Exit #'s below follow US 52.
136		Cook School Rd, Pilot Mtn
	Gas	E: Shamrock
135		Pilot Mountain (EB, Left Exit)
134		NC 268, Pilot Mtn, Elkin
	Gas	N: Citgo, Exxon, Wilco
	Food	N: Cousin Gary's Family Rest, McDonald's, Mountain View Rest, Wendy's
	Lodg	N: Best Western
	Other	N: ATMs, Auto Services, Golf Course, Grocery
131		Pilot Mountain State Park
	Other	W: Pilot Mountain State Park
129		Perch Rd, Pinnacle
	Gas	N: BP
	Food	N: EJ's Rest, Trails End Grill
	Other	N: Auto Services
123		S Main St, King, Tobaccoville
122		Moore/RJR Dr
120		Westinghouse Rd

◊ = Regular Gas Stations with Diesel ▲ = RV Friendly Locations ♥ = Pet Friendly Locations
RED PRINT SHOWS LARGE VEHICLE PARKING/ACCESS ON SITE OR NEARBY BROWN PRINT SHOWS CAMPGROUNDS/RV PARKS

EXIT	NORTH CAROLINA
118	NC 65, Rural Hall, Bethania
NOTE:	(Construction to begin 2012) EB: Future I-74 to be routed onto Winston-Salem Northern Beltway. WB: to be routed onto US 52/Future I-74 from Winston-Salem Beltway.
NOTE:	Begin US 311/Future I-74 Corridor (Construction to begin by 2011)
(55)	I-40, US 311N, Winston-Salem
56	Ridgewood Rd
59/31	Union Cross Rd, Winston-Salem
Gas	N: Marathon
Other	N: Tire & Auto Services, to I-40 S: Golf Courses
60/30	High Point Rd, Kernersville
Gas	S: Little Cedar Groceries
63/27	NC 66, Kernersville
Other	S: Auto Services
65/25	Bus US 311S, N Main St, High Point (Serv available S on N Main)
66/24	Johnson St, High Point
Other	N: Golf Course, City Park/Oak Hollow Family Campground ▲
67/23	NC 68, Eastchester Dr, to I-40 PTI Airport
Gas	S: 76, Kelly C-Store, Marathon
Food	S: ChickFilA, Chu's Express, Garfield's, Juice n Java, La Hacienda Mex Rest, Sbarro, Wendy's
Lodg	S: Courtyard
Other	S: ATMs, Auto & Tire Services
69/21	Greensboro Rd
Gas	N: Amoco, BP S: Citgo, Oil
Food	N: Henry James BBQ S: Fortune Cookie Express, McDonald's
70/20	Kivett Dr, High Point
Other	N/S: Auto, Tire, Towing Services
71A/19B	E Green Dr
71B/19A	US 311S, Bus 85, US 29, US 70, Thomasville, Greensboro
71	US 311S, Bus 85, US 29, US 70, Thomasville, Greensboro
NOTE:	EB I-74 to continue under construction On US 311 Bypass to US 220. WB to be routed to under construction US 311 Bypass to current US 311.
(75AB)	Jct I-85, N to Greensboro, S to Charlotte
79	Cedar Square Rd
NOTE:	US 311/Future I-74 to be under Construction Thru 2012. US 311 Bypass from E of I-85, Archdale, to US 220, Sophia.
NOTE:	I-74 will join I-73 about 1mi S of Current Jct US 311/US 220. Road Is signed US 220/Future I-73/Future I-74. Expect construction. Future I-74 runs with Future I-73 below. Exit #'s follow Future I-73.

EXIT	NORTH CAROLINA
65 (Seg 7/8)	US 311, High Point, Randleman (US 220, Future I-73, Future I-74: 2013+) (Future I-74 starts SB, Ends NB) (Addt'l Serv E to Bus US 220N)
Gas	E: Quik N Easy W: Exxon
(Future)	Future - Jct I-74W, High Point, to Winston-Salem
63	Pineview St, Randleman
62	Spero Rd, Asheboro (Services E to US 220 Bus)
60	to US 220 Bus N, Fayetteville St, Vision Dr
59	NC 1462, Presnell St (Services E to US 220 Bus)
59B	to Bus US 220, Fayetteville St
59A	Presnell Dr
58	NC 42, Salisbury St, Lexington Rd, Asheboro (Both dir, Left Exit) (Addt'l Services E to US 220 Bus)
Gas	E: Amoco, Servco
56	US 64, NC 49, to Raleigh, Lexington, Charlotte
Gas	E: BP, Gulf, Wilco W: Exxon
Food	E: Arby's, Bamboo Garden, Burger King, Dixie Express, Huddle House, McDonald's W: Heritage Diner

EXIT	NORTH CAROLINA
Lodg	E: Asheboro Inn, Days Inn W: Super 8
Other	E: Grocery
56B	US 64W, NC 49S, to Lexington, Charlotte
56A	US 64E, NC 49N, to Siler City, Raleigh
55	McDowell Rd
Gas	E: Tank and Tummy, Oil
Food	W: K&W Cafeteria
NOTE:	NB End I-73/74, Begin Future I-73/74 SB End Future I-73/74, Begin I-73/74
51	US 220 Bus N, NC 134S, Ulah, Troy
49	New Hope Church Rd, Asheboro
45	NC 705, Little River Rd, Seagrove, Robbins
Gas	E: Quik Chek
Other	E: Wheatley Truck Repair
( )	Rest Area (Both dir) (To Open 12/09)
41	Black Ankle Rd, Seagrove
39	Alt US 220, Star, Ether, Steeds
36	Spies Rd, Star, Robbins (Serv W to Alt US 220)
Other	W: to Montgomery Co Airport ✈
33	NC 24, NC 27, Biscoe
Gas	W: Quik Chek
Food	W: Chinese Rest
Lodg	W: Days Inn
Other	W: Food Lion
28	NC 211, Candor, Pinehurst
FStop	E: WilcoHess Travel Center
Gas	W: Quik Chek
Food	E: Wendy's W: Chinese Rest, Hardee's
NOTE:	NB: Begin I-73/I-74, SB End, Begin US 220, Future I-73/I-74.
24	Alt US 220N, Candor
22	Tabernacle Church Rd
18	Norman
16	NC 73
13	J Barwell Rd, Haywood Parker Rd
11	Millstone Rd, to NC 73W, Ellerbe
8	Bus US 220N, Ellerbe
NOTE:	NB Begin Frwy, SB End
(22)	Future - Bus Lp I-73, Bus Lp I-74, Rockingham
NOTE:	(Construction to begin after 2015) NB I-73/74 to be routed onto Planned US 220 Bypass Fwy to current US 220 SB to be routed onto Planned US 220 Bypass to US 74 Bypass.
(15)	Future - US 74W, Monroe, Charlotte
NOTE:	Begin US 74, Future I-73, Future I-74, NB End, SB Begin. Exit #'s are US 74.
(12/311)	US 1, Rockingham, Southern Pines, Cheraw, to US 220, Ellerbe, Asheboro, Greensboro

◇ = Regular Gas Stations with Diesel ▲ = RV Friendly Locations ♥ = Pet Friendly Locations

RED PRINT SHOWS LARGE VEHICLE PARKING/ACCESS ON SITE OR NEARBY   BROWN PRINT SHOWS CAMPGROUNDS/RV PARKS

W I-74

EXIT	NORTH CAROLINA
(7/316)	NC 177, Hamlet
NOTE:	NB joins US 74 Rockingham Bypass from NC 38 Corridor from SC Border. SB leaves US 74 Rockingham Bypass along NC 38 Corridor to SC Border.
(168/319)	NC 38, Hamlet, Bennettsville
NOTE:	I-73 proposed to leave I-74/US 74 on future fwy at or near NC 38. Begin EB Future I-74 / US 74 .
(320)	NC 381, Hamlet, Gibson
(321)	Bus US 74, Hamlet (WB)
NOTE:	Begin US 74, I-74
207	Bus US 74, Lauringburg (EB)
208	NC 79, Gibson (WB)
209	US 15, US 401N, US 501, N to Fayetteville, S to Bennettsville
210	Bus US 15, US 401, Laurinburg
211	US 501S, Rowland, Myrtle Beach
212	to Bus 74, Laurinburg
213	Bus US 74, Maxton, E Laurinburg
216	Maxton-Laurinburg Airport Rd

EXIT	NORTH CAROLINA
217	NC 71, Maxton, Red Springs
220A	Bus US 74W, Maxton (EB)
220	Alt US 74, Bus US 74, Maxton (WB)
220B	Alt US 74E (EB)
223	Cabinet Shop Rd
226	NC 710, Pembroke, Red Springs
203	Dew Rd, Pembroke
207	Back Swamp Rd
(209)	Jct I-95, US 301, N to Fayetteville, S to Florence
(209B)	Jct I-95N, US 301N, to Lumberton, Fayetteville
(209A)	Jct I-95S, US 301S, to Florence
( )	Future - Rest Area (tbo in 2009)
210	Alt US 74
212	NC 41, Lumberton, Fairmont
NOTE:	EB End Fwy, WB Begin
(228)	NC 242, Evergreen
(234)	NC 410, Bus US 74, NC 130E, Chadbourn, Bladenboro

EXIT	NORTH CAROLINA
NOTE:	MM 236: EB: I-74 routed onto existing US 74/76 fwy around Whiteville, WB routed from existing fwy around.
NOTE:	EB Begin Fwy, EB End
(236)	US 76, I-20W, Chadbourn, FairBluff
(238)	Union Valley Rd
(239)	US 701 Bypass, Whiteville, Clarkton
(242)	Bus US 74/76, Whiteville
NOTE:	EB End Fwy, WB Begin
(260)	US 74, US 76, I-20E, Wilmington
(285)	US 17N, Supply, Wilmington
(294)	NC 904, Grissettown, Ocean Isle Beach
(298)	US 17S, to Myrtle Beach
NOTE:	MM 301: SC State Line

(EASTERN TIME ZONE)

NORTH CAROLINA
Begin Northbound I-74 from South Carolina border to Virginia Border.

S I-75

EXIT	MICHIGAN
	Begin Southbound I-75 from the Canada / Michigan border to Miami, FL.

☂ MICHIGAN
(EASTERN TIME ZONE)
(I-75 starts / ends at Int'l Toll Bridge)

EXIT	MICHIGAN
(0)	Canadian Customs (NB), US Customs (SB) (All Vehicles MUST Stop)
394	I-75 Bus, MI 129, Easterday Ave, W Portage Ave, Sault Ste Marie, to Toledo, OH
NOTE:	NB: LAST USA exit before TOLL
W:	MI Welcome Center (NB) (RR, Phone, Picnic, Info, Weather) (Addt'l serv on W Portage Ave/NE)
FStop	W: Holiday Station #262
Gas	E: Citgo◊
Food	E: Applebee's, Arby's, McDonald's W: Freighters Rest, Lakeside Pub, Subway
Lodg	E: Holiday Inn Express♥
Other	E: Sault Ste Marie Muni Airport✈, River of History Museum, Tower of History, Lake Superior State Univ
392	I-75 Bus, 3 Mile Rd, Sault Ste Marie
FStop	E: I-75 BP
TStop	E: Admiral Ship Store/Marathon
Gas	E: Mobil◊, Shell, USA◊
Food	E: FastFood/Admiral, Applebee's, Arby's, Burger King, Country Kitchen

EXIT	MICHIGAN
Food	E: Great Wall Chinese, Jeff's Fifties Cafe, La Senorita, McDonald's, Subway, Wendy's
Lodg	E: Best Value Inn, Best Western, Budget Host, Comfort Inn, Days Inn, Hampton Inn, Motel 6 ♥, Plaza Motor Motel, Super 8
Med	E: + Hospital
Other	E: LP/Admiral, ATM, Auto, Grocery, Kmart, NAPA, RiteAid, Wal-Mart, MI State Hwy Patrol Post, Sault Ste Marie Muni Airport✈ W: Varsity Cinemas
(389)	Sault Ste Marie Rest Area (NB) (RR, Phones, Picnic, Vend, Info)
386	MI 28, 9 Mile Rd, Dafter, Newberry
Food	E: Sharolyn Rest/Motel
Lodg	E: Sharolyn Motel, Sunset Motel
Other	W: to Brimley State Park, Minnow Lake Campground▲ , Bay Mills Resort & Casino
379	Gaines Hwy, Kincheloe
Other	E: to Barbeau Area, Clear Creek Campground▲
378	MI 80, Tone Rd, Kincheloe, Kinross
Other	E: Chippewa Co Int'l Airport✈
373	MI 48, W 19 Mile Rd, Rudyard
Gas	W: AmocoBP◊
359	MI 134, St Ignace, DeTour Village, Drummond Island
Other	E: to Loons Pt Campground▲, Cedarville RV Park & Campground▲
352	MI 123, Newberry, to Moran

EXIT	MICHIGAN
348	I-75 Bus Loop, St Ignace, Evergreen Shores, Castle Rock Rd, to Allentow
Gas	E: Shell
Food	E: Shore's Rest
Lodg	E: Comfort Inn, Days Inn, Great Lakes Motel, Harbor Pointe, Holiday Inn Express, Pines Motel, Quality Inn, Sands Motel
Other	E: Castle Rock Campark▲, Tiki Travel Park▲, MI State Hwy Patrol Post, Mackinac Co Airport✈
(346)	St Ignace Rest Area (SB) (RR, Phone, Picnic) (Closed Winter)
345	Portage St, to US 2, St Ignace (SB)
Gas	E: Marathon
Other	W: Lakeshore Park Campground▲
344A	I-75 Bus Loop, St Ignace (NB)
Gas	E: Shell
Food	E: Northern Lights Rest, Subway
Lodg	E: Comfort Inn, Quality Inn
Med	E: + Hospital
Other	E: US Post Office, MI State Hwy Patrol, Straits State Park
344B	US 2W, Manistique (NB)
TStop	W: St Ignace Truck Stop/BP
Gas	W: Holiday◊, Shell◊
Food	W: Big Boy, Burger King, Hardee's, McDonald's, Miller's Camp Rest, Seafood Palace, UpNorth Rest
Lodg	W: Quality Inn ♥, Super 8
Other	W: LP/St Ignace TS, St Ignace/Makinac Island KOA▲

Page 316 ◊= Regular Gas Stations with Diesel   ▲ = RV Friendly Locations   ♥= Pet Friendly Locations
RED PRINT SHOWS LARGE VEHICLE PARKING/ACCESS ON SITE OR NEARBY   BROWN PRINT SHOWS CAMPGROUNDS/RV PARKS

EXIT	MICHIGAN
344	I-75 Bus, US 2W, St Ignace (SB)
(344)	St Ignace Welcome Center (NB) (RR, Phones, Picnic, Info, Weather)
(343)	TOLL Booth, to TOLL Bridge
(341)	TOLL, Mackinac Bridge W-Lake Michigan, E-Lake Huron
339	Jamet St, Mackinaw City
Gas	E: AmocoBP W: Phillips 66, Shell
Food	E: Audie's Family Rest, Big Boy, DQ, KFC, McDonald's, Subway W: Darrow's Rest
Lodg	E: Budget Host Inn, Days Inn, Econo Lodge, Lighthouse View Motel, Super 8 W: Holiday Inn Express
338	US 23, Mackinaw Hwy (SB) MI 108, Mackinaw Hwy (NB)
E:	Mackinaw City Welcome Ctr (Both dir) (RR, Phones, Picnic, Info, Weather)
FStop	E: Next Door Store #17/Marathon
Gas	E: BP
Food	E: Anna's Country Buffet, Burger King, DQ, Mackinaw Pizza, Subway
Lodg	E: Baymont Inn, Courtyard
Other	E: Mackinaw City/Mackinac Island KOA▲
337	MI 108, Mackinaw Hwy, Cheboygan to US 23, Huron Ave (NB, diff reacc)
Gas	E: Citgo◆
Food	E: Rest/Embers Motel, Dockside Deli, Lighthouse Rest, Mario's
Lodg	E: Best Western♥, Embers Motel, Kings Inn, Starlite Budget Inn, Sundown Motel
Other	E: Mackinaw City/Mackinac Island KOA▲, Tee Pee Campground▲, Old Mill Creek State Park, Mackinaw Mill Creek Camping▲ W: Wilderness State Park
336	US 31S, Petoskey, Charlevoix (SB)
(328)	Hebron Rest Area (SB) (Closed Winter) (RR, Phones, Picnic, Info) (NO Truck/RV)
326	CR C66, Levering Rd, to Cheboygan
Gas	E: Marathon
Med	E: + Hospital
322	CR C64, Riggsville Rd, Cheboygan (Serv 8mi E in Cheboygan)
(317)	Topinabee Rest Area (NB) (Closed Winter) (RR, Phones, Picnic, Info, View)
313	MI 27N, Straits Hwy, Indian River, to Topinabee
Lodg	W: Navajo Motel, Topinabee Motel
Other	E: Indian River RV Resort & Camp▲, Indian River Country Cabins▲
310	MI 68, Indian River, Burt Lake, Afton
Gas	W: AmocoBP◆, Shell
Food	W: Burger King, Café, DQ, Indian River Steak House
Lodg	E: Holiday Inn Express W: Coach House Motel, Indian River Motel & Cottages
Other	E: Pigeon Bay Campground▲, Yogi Bear Jellystone Campground▲ W: Burt Lake State Park, Indian River Trading Post▲, Crooked River RV Park▲

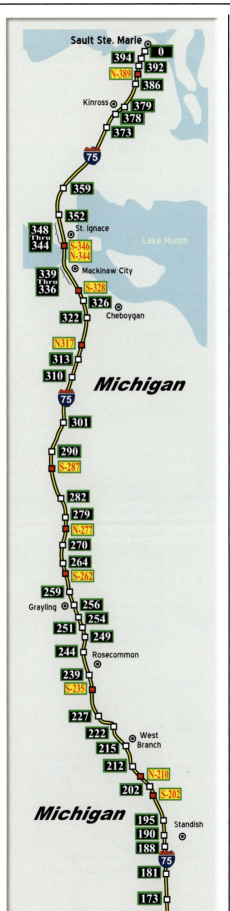

EXIT	MICHIGAN
301	CR C58, Afton Rd, Wolverine
Gas	E: Marathon
Other	E: Elkwood Campground▲ W: Sturgin River Campground▲
290	CR C48, N Old 27, Vanderbilt
Gas	E: BP W: Andy's Mobil
Food	E: Gateway Rest
Other	E: LP/BP W: RVDump/Mobil
(287)	Vanderbilt Rest Area (SB) (RR, Phones, Picnic, Vend, Info, View)
282	I-75 Bus, MI 32, Main St, Gaylord
FStop	E: Forward Shell Food Mart W: Chalet Marathon, Gaylord Fuel Stop
Gas	E: 7-11, BP◆, Clark, Holiday, Speedway◆ W: BP◆, Shell
Food	E: Arby's, Burger King, DQ, La Senorita, KFC, McDonald's, N MI Seafood, Quiznos, Red Rose Rest, Subway, Wendy's W: Applebee's, Big Boy, Bob Evans, China 1, Culver's, Mancino's Grinders & Pizza, Hut, Ponderosa, Ruby Tuesday, Red Rose Rest, Sweet Basil, Spicy Bob's Ital Express, Starbucks, Subway, Taco Bell
Lodg	E: Baymont Inn♥, Best Western♥, Best Value Inn, Downtown Motel, Quality Inn, Royal Crest Motel♥ W: Hampton Inn, Holiday Inn Express
Med	E: + Hospital
Other	E: Auto Dealer, Family Dollar, Grocery, Kmart, RiteAid, Golf Courses, Otsego Co Fairgrounds, MI Sheriff Office, MI State Hwy Patrol Post W: LP/Marathon, ATMs, Auto Dealer, Big Lots, Dollar Tree, Home Depot, Grocery, Lowe's, Wal-Mart sc, Golf Course, Otsego Co Airport✈, Gaylord Alpine RV Park & Campground▲, Burnside RV Center
NOTE:	MM 279: 45th Parallel—Halfway Point between the Equator & North Pole
279	I-75 Bus, Old US 27, Gaylord
FStop	E: South End Marathon
Gas	E: Mobil◆, Shell
Food	E: Burger King, Mama Leones Italian, Subway/Marathon
Lodg	E: Econo Lodge, Timberly Motel
Other	E: Auto Dealers, Gaylord KOA▲, MI Sheriff, MI State Hwy Patrol Post W: to Otsego Lake State Park, Beaver Creek Resort & RV Park▲, Golf Courses
(277)	Gaylord Rest Area (NB) (RR, Phones, Picnic, Vend, Info)
270	Marlette Rd, Gaylord, Waters
TStop	E: Hilltop BP Truck Stop
Food	E: Rest/Hilltop TS
Other	W: Grocery, to Otsego Lake State Park
264	CR 612, Frederic, Grayling
Other	E: Hartwick Pines St Park North Ent, Camp Grayling MI Nat'l Guard Military Res
(262)	Hartwick Pines Rest Area (SB) (RR, Phones, Picnic, Vend, Info)
259	I-75 Bus, MI 93, Hartwick Pines Rd, Downtown Grayling, Traverse City
Other	E: Hartwick Pines St Park South Ent, Camp Grayling MI Nat'l Guard Mil Res W: Grayling Army Air Field✈, Camp Grayling MI Nat'l Guard Miilitary Res

◆ = Regular Gas Stations with Diesel   ▲ = RV Friendly Locations   ♥ = Pet Friendly Locations

RED PRINT SHOWS LARGE VEHICLE PARKING/ACCESS ON SITE OR NEARBY   BROWN PRINT SHOWS CAMPGROUNDS/RV PARKS

EXIT		MICHIGAN
256		N Down River (SB), to I-75 Bus, IN 93, IN 72, Grayling
254		I-75 Bus, MI 72, Grayling (NB, L exit)
	Gas	W: Admiral, BP, Citgo, Phillips 66, Shell, Speedway
	Food	W: A&W, Burger King, DQ, Hardee's, KFC, Little Caesars, McDonald's, Pizza Hut, Subway, Taco Bell, Wendy's
	Lodg	W: Days Inn, Holiday Inn, Super 7 Inn
	TWash	W: Wagon Wheel Cleaning Center
	TServ	W: MI CAT
	Med	W: + Hospital
	Other	W: CarQuest, Grocery, Kmart, RiteAid
(252)		Grayling Rest Area (NB) (RR, Phones, Picnic, Vend, Info)
251		4 Mile Rd, Grayling
	TStop	W: Charlie's Country Corner/Marathon
	Food	W: FastFood/Charlie's CC
	Lodg	W: Super 8
	Other	E: Yogi Bear Jellystone RV Camp▲ W: Laundry/RVDump/LP/Charlie's CC, Camp Grayling MI Nat'l Guard Mil Res
249		US 127S, CR 301, Claire, Roscommon (SB, no reaccess)
	Other	W: to N Higgins Lake State Park
244		I-75 Bus, CR200, W Federal Hwy, Old MI 76, Roscommon
	FStop	W: Knight Enterprises/Sunoco
	Food	E: Tee Pee Rest
	Lodg	E: Tee Pee Motel
	Other	W: Higgins Hills RV Park▲, to N Higgins Lake State Park, Higgins Lake
239		MI 18, Roscommon Rd, I-75 Bus, Lake St, Houghton Lake, Gladwin
	Other	W: Higgins Lake State Park
(235)		Nine Mile Hill Rest Area (SB) (RR, Phones, Picnic, Vend)
227		MI 55W, W Branch Rd, St Helen (Serv 5mi W in Prudenville)
	Other	W: to Houghton Lake
222		MI 76, St Helen Rd, St Helen
215		I-75 Bus MI 55E, Old MI 76, West Branch, Tawas City
	Gas	E: Citgo◊
	Lodg	E: La Hacienda Motel
	Med	E: + Hospital
	TServ	E: West Branch Diesel Repair
	Other	E: Schmitt Tire, MI Sheriff, MI State Hwy Patrol Post, W Branch Comm Airport✈
212		I-75 Bus, Cook Rd, West Branch, to MI 76, Alger Rd, to MI 55
	FStop	E: 7-11/Marathon W: Jaxx Snaxx W Branch/BP
	Gas	E: Shell
	Food	E: Arby's, Burger King, McDonald's, Ponderosa, Taco Bell, Wendy's, Rest/QI, Subway/Shell
	Lodg	E: Quality Inn, Super 8
	Med	E: + Hospital
	Other	E: ATM, Home Depot, Wal-Mart sc, Tanger Outlet Mall, West Branch Comm Airport✈, MI State Hwy Patrol, to Outdoor Adventures/Lake of the North Resort▲
(210)		W Branch Rest Area (NB) (RR, Phone, Picnic, Vend)

Personal Notes

EXIT		MICHIGAN
202		MI 33, Brock Rd, Alger Rd, Alger
	FStop	E: Mobil
	Gas	E: BP, Shell
	Food	E: Subway/Pizza/Shell
	Other	E: Greenwood Campground▲
(202)		Alger Rest Area (SB) (RR, Phones, Picnic, Vend)
195		W Sterling Rd, Sterling, Omer
	Gas	E: Forward, Sunrise Side Towing
	Food	E: Dave & Kathie's, Iva's
	Other	E: River View Campground & Canoe▲, Crystal Creek Campground▲, Outdoor Adventures/Rifle River Resort▲
190		MI 61, Standish, to MI 76, US 23
	Gas	W: Mobil, Shell
	Food	E: A&W, Little Caesars, Moon Gate Chinese, N Forest Café, Subway, Wheeler's Rest, Taco Bell
	Lodg	E: Forward Lodging, In Town Motel
	Other	E: Big Bend Campground▲, Riverbend Campground▲
188		US 23, S Huron Rd, Standish
	Other	E: Standish Industrial Airport✈, to Big Bend Campground▲, Riverbend Camp ground▲, Outdoor Adventures/ Saginaw Bay Resort▲, Outdoor Adventures/Wildnerness Resort▲
181		Pinconning Rd, Pinconning
	TStop	W: Pinconning Express Stop/Sunoco
	Gas	E: Mobil, Shell◊, Speedway
	Food	E: McDonald's/Shell, Pizza, Subway W: FastFood/Pinconning ES
	Lodg	E: Pinconning Trail House Motel

EXIT		MICHIGAN
(175)		Linwood Rest Area (NB) (RR, Phone, Picnic, Vend)
173		Linwood Rd, Linwood
	Gas	E: BP◊, Mobil
	Other	E: Hoyle's Marina & Campground▲
168		Beaver Rd, Kawkawlin, to Willard
	Other	E: Bay City State Park
164		Wilder Rd, MI 13 Conn, Bay City
	Gas	E: Meijer◊
	Food	E: Cracker Barrel, McDonald's, Pizza
	Lodg	E: AmericInn
162		US 10W, MI 25, Midland, Bay City
162B		US 10W, Midland (NB)
	Other	W: to appr 12mi Valley Plaza Resort▲
162A		MI 25, Bay City (NB)
160		MI 84, Westside Saginaw Rd
	Gas	E: Mobil◊, Shell W: 7-11, Speedway
	Food	E: Dunkin Donuts/Shell, Subway/Mobil W: Berger Family Rest, Burger King, McDonald's
	Lodg	W: Bay Valley Hotel & Resort, Econo Lodge
	Other	E: to Finn Rd Campground▲ W: International RV World
(158)		Bay City Rest Area (SB) (RR, Phone, Picnic, Vend)
(155)		Jct I-675, Downtown Saginaw
154		Adam St, Saginaw, Zilwaukee
153		MI 13, Bay City Rd, Saginaw
151		MI 81, Washington Rd, Saginaw, Caro, Reese
	TStop	E: M-81 Express/Sunoco W: Flying J Travel Plaza (Scales)
	Food	E: BurgerKing/M-81 Express W: Wendy's/FJ TP
	TWash	W: Coty's Hi-Pressure Wash
	TServ	E: Upper Lakes Tire W: Fruehauf Parts & Service, MI CAT
	Other	E: Laundry/M-81 Express W: Laundry/WiFi/RVDump/LP/FJ TP
(150)		Jct I-675N, Saginaw
149AB		MI 46, Holland Ave, Saginaw
	Gas	W: Amoco, Circle K, Sunoco, Speedway◊
	Food	W: Arby's, Burger King, Big John Steak & Onion, McDonald's, Taco Bell, Wendy's
	Lodg	W: Best Western, Motel 6♥, Welcome Inn
	TServ	W: Scott Tire Sales
	Med	W: + Hospital
	Other	W: Grocery, Kmart
144		Dixie Hwy, Bridgeport, Frankenmuth
144A		Dixie Hwy, Bridgeport (NB)
	FStop	E: Speedway (Scales)
	TStop	E: North Star Travel Plaza/Marathon (Scales)
	Gas	E: Shell
	Food	E: Subway/Marathon, Blimpie/Shell
	Lodg	E: Heidelberg Inn Motel
	Other	E: to Yogi Bear's Jellystone RV Park Campground▲
144B		Dixie Hwy, Bridgeport, Frankenmuth
	TStop	W: Travel Center of America #198/Citgo (Scales)
	Gas	W: Mobil
	Food	W: CountryPride/TA TC, Arby's, Burger King, Cracker Barrel, McDonald's, Peking City, Subway, Taco Bell, Wendy's

◊ = Regular Gas Stations with Diesel   ▲ = RV Friendly Locations   ♥ = Pet Friendly Locations

Page 318   RED PRINT SHOWS LARGE VEHICLE PARKING/ACCESS ON SITE OR NEARBY   BROWN PRINT SHOWS CAMPGROUNDS/RV PARKS

INTERSTATE 75 N/S

MICHIGAN

EXIT		
	Lodg	W: Baymont Inn, Days Inn, Villager Lodge
	TServ	W: TA TC/Tires
	Other	W: Laundry/WiFi/RVDump/TA TC, IGA, Pharmacy, MI State Hwy Patrol Post
136		**MI 54, MI 83, Birch Run Rd, Birch Run**
	FStop	E: Conlee Travel Center #2/Mobil
		W: Birch Run Express Stop/Sunoco, Fast Pax/Marathon
	Gas	E: Shell
		W: 7-11, BP
	Food	E: Exit Rest, Little Caesars, KFC, Subway
		W: Arby's, Bob Evans, McDonald's, Quiznos, Starbucks, Taco Bell, Tony's Birch Run, Wendy's
	Lodg	E: Best Western, Comfort Inn, Holiday Inn Express♥, Super 8
		W: Country Inn
	Other	E: CarQuest, Laundry, Pine Ridge RV Campground▲, RV Center, Frankenmuth Jellystone Park▲
		W: Pharmacy, Prime Outlets, Auto Dealers
131		**MI 57, Vienna Rd, Clio, to Montrose, Thetford Center**
	Gas	E: Shell, Sunoco
		W: AmocoBP◊, Mobil◊
	Food	E: Arby's, Big John Steak & Onion, Burger King, KFC, McDonald's, Taco Bell, Subway
		W: Big Boy, Wendy's
	Other	E: AutoZone, Kmart
(130)		**Clio Rest Area (SB)** (RR, Phones, Picnic, Vend)
(129)		**Dodge Rd Rest Area (NB)** (RR, Phones, Picnic, Vend, Info)
126		**Mt Morris Rd, Mount Morris**
	FStop	E: Amir's Mini Mart
		W: I-75 BP #8
	TStop	E: Quick-Sav #7/BP (Scales)
	Food	E: FastFood/BP
	Other	W: I-75 Malls, ATMs, CarWash
(125)		**Jct I-475, UAW Freeway, Flint**
122		**Pierson Rd, Flint, Flushing**
	Gas	E: AmocoBP, Clark, Marathon
		W: Citgo, Shell, Meijer◊
	Food	E: KFC, McDonald's, Ponderosa, Subway
		W: Arby's, Bob Evans, Burger King, Cracker Barrel, Denny's, Long John Silver, Pizza Hut, Red Lobster, Taco Bell, Wendy's, YaYa's Chicken
	Lodg	E: Super 8
		W: Baymont Inn, Great Western Inn, Ramada Inn, Sheraton Inn
	Other	W: ATMs, Discount Tire, Home Depot
118		**MI 21, Corunna Rd, Flint, Owasso**
	Gas	E: Sunoco, Kroger
		W: AmocoBP, Citgo, Mobil, Shell
	Food	E: Badawest Lebanese Rest, Big John Steak & Onion, Burger King, Hardee's, Little Caesar's, Taco Bell
		W: Burger King, Domino's, Happy Valley Oriental
	Lodg	W: Economy Motel
	Med	E: + McLaren Reg'l Med Center
	Other	E: AdvanceAuto, Dollar General, Kroger, Pharmacy, RiteAid
		W: AutoZone, CarQuest. Home Depot, Lowe's, Pharmacy, Sam's Club, Wal-Mart, MI State Hwy Patrol Post

MICHIGAN

EXIT		
117		**Miller Rd, to I-69 (SB)**
117B		**Miller Rd, Flint (NB)**
	Gas	E: Speedway◊, Sunoco◊
		W: Amoco, Speedway
	Food	E: Applebee's, Arby's, Don Pablo, Fuddrucker's, KFC, McDonald's, Lone Star Steakhouse, Subway
		W: Bob Evans, Burger King, Chuck E Cheese, Hooters, Old Country Buffet, Olive Garden, Outback Steakhouse, Pizza Hut, Starbucks, Taco Bell, Wendy's
	Lodg	E: Comfort Inn, Motel 6♥, Sleep Inn
		W: Howard Johnson, Red Roof Inn♥, Super 8
	Other	E: Kmart, Grocery
		W: Best Buy, Goodyear, Office Depot, Target, U-Haul, Genesee Valley Center Mall
(117A)		**Jct I-69, E-Lansing, W-Pt Huron (NB)**
116B		**MI 121, Bristol Rd, Am Vets Hy (SB)**
116A		**MI 121, Amer Veterans Hwy (SB)**
116		**MI 121, American Veterans Hwy**
	FStop	W: Bristol Mobil (SB 116B)
	Gas	E: Amoco, Citgo, Speedway◊
	Food	E: KFC, McDonald's
	Lodg	E: Days Inn
		W: Econo Lodge
	TServ	E: Scott Tire Sales
	Other	E: AutoZone, GM Truck & Bus Assembly Plant, to I-475
		W: Bishop Int'l Airport✈
115		**US 23S, to Ann Arbor, MI (SB)** (Serv at Ex #90 on US 23, W Hill Rd)
(111)		**Jct I-475N, UAW Frwy (NB)**
109		**MI 54, Dort Hwy, Grand Blanc Rd** (Difficult reaccess SB)
	Gas	E: Marathon
	Food	E: Big Boy, Damon's, Wendy's
108		**Holly Rd, Grand Blanc**
	Gas	E: Marathon
		W: BP
	Food	E: Quiznos
		W: McDonald's
	Lodg	E: AmeriHost Inn
	Med	W: + Genesys Reg'l Medical Center
106		**MI 54, Dixie Hwy, S Saginaw Rd Holly** (SB, Left Exit, NO NB return)
101		**Grange Hall Rd, to Ortonville, Holly**
	Gas	E: Sunoco
	Other	E: Holly State Rec Area, Yogi Bear's Jellystone RV Campground/RVDump▲, Clear Water Campground▲
		W: Groveland Oaks County Park, Seven Lakes State Park
98		**E Holly Rd, Holly, Springfield**
	FStop	E: E Holly Truck Stop/Sunoco
(96)		**Davisburg Rest Area (NB)** (RR, Phones, Picnic, Vend, Info)
(94)		**Clarkston Rest Area (SB)** (RR, Phones, Picnic, Vend, WiFi)
	NOTE:	SB: Last Rest Area in MI
93		**US 24, Dixie Hwy, Clarkston, Springfield**
	Gas	E: BP◊, Kroger
		W: Speedway

◊ = Regular Gas Stations with Diesel   ▲ = RV Friendly Locations   ♥ = Pet Friendly Locations
RED PRINT SHOWS LARGE VEHICLE PARKING/ACCESS ON SITE OR NEARBY   BROWN PRINT SHOWS CAMPGROUNDS/RV PARKS

Page 319

EXIT		MICHIGAN
	Food	W: McDonald's, Subway, Wendy's
	Other	W: Pontiac Lake State Rec Area
91		MI 15, N Main St, Ortonville Rd, Clarkston, Ortonville, Waterford
	Gas	E: Marathon
		W: Shell◊
	Food	W: Clarkston Café, Mesquite Rest
	Lodg	W: Mill Pond Inn
89		Sashabaw Rd, Clarkston
	Gas	E: Shell◊
		W: AmocoBP
	Food	E: Ruby Tuesday
		W: McDonald's, Subway, Wendy's
(86)		Weigh Station (SB)
84		Baldwin Rd, Auburn Hills (SB)
	Gas	E: Shell, Sunoco◊
		W: Mobil
	Food	E: Arby', Big Boy, Joe's Crab Shack, Longhorn Steakhouse, Wendy's
		W: Chili's, McDonald's, Sbarro, Starbucks, Steak n Shake
	Lodg	W: Towne Suites
	Other	E: Best Buy, Costco, Discount Tire, Office Max, PetCo♥, Staples, Target, UPS Store Great Lakes Crossing Outlet Mall
		W: Circuit City, FedEx Kinko's
84AB		Baldwin Rd, Auburn Hills (NB)
83		Joslyn Rd, Auburn Hills
	Gas	E: Meijer◊, Sam's
	Food	E: Applebee's, McDonald's, Olive Garden
	Other	E: Foodtown, Kmart, Sam's Club, Tires
83AB		Joslyn Rd
81		I-75 Bus, Lapeer Rd, MI 24, Pontiac (difficult reaccess)
	Gas	E: AmocoBP
	Other	E: The Palace Arena
79		University Dr, Auburn Hills, Pontiac Rochester Hills, Rochester
	Gas	E: Amoco
		W: Speedway◊
	Food	E: Domino's, Dunkin Donuts, Subway
		W: Big Buck Brewery & Steakhouse, McDonald's, Mountain Jack's Steakhouse, Taco Bell, Tim Horton's, Wendy's
	Lodg	W: AmeriSuites, Comfort Inn, Courtyard Inn, Candlewood Suites, Fairfield Inn, Holiday Inn, Hampton Inn, Motel 6♥
	Med	W: + Hospital
	Other	W: A&S RV Center/RVDump
78		Chrysler Dr, Auburn Hills
	Other	E: Daimler Chrysler Tech Center
77AB		MI 59, Veterans Memorial Frwy, E to Utica, W to Pontiac
	Other	W: Pontiac Silverdome Stadium
75		Square Lake Rd (NB, Left Exit)
74		Adams Rd, Troy
72		Crooks Rd, Troy
	Food	W: Quiznos, Red Robin, Starbucks
	Lodg	W: Embassy Suites, Hilton Inn, Marriott
69		W Big Beaver Rd, Troy
	Gas	W: AmocoBP, Shell
	Food	W: Denny's, Ruth Chris Steakhouse
	Lodg	E: Drury Inn, Marriott
		W: Candlewood Hotel
67		Rochester Rd, E Big Beaver Rd
	Gas	E: Marathon, Mobil, Shell
	Food	E: Arby's, Burger King, Dunkin Donuts, KFC, Mr Pita, Popeye's Chicken

EXIT		MICHIGAN
	Food	W: Mountain Jack Steakhouse
	Lodg	W: Embassy Suites, Holiday Inn, Red Roof Inn♥
	Other	E: Discount Tire, Office Depot, Radio Shack
		W: Tires
65AB		14 Mile Rd, Troy, Madison Heights
	Gas	E: Mobil, Shell
		W: Mobil
	Food	E: Bob Evans, Burger King, Chili's, Denny's, Logan's Roadhouse, McDonald's, Panera Bread Co, Steak & Ale, Taco Bell, Wendy's
		W: Applebee's, Big Fish Seafood Rest, McDonald's, Outback Steakhouse, White Castle
	Lodg	E: Motel 6♥, Red Roof Inn♥
		W: Best Western, Econo Lodge, Extended Stay America, Fairfield Inn, Hampton Inn, Residence Inn
	Med	E: + Walk-In Clinic
	Other	E: ATMs, Banks, Circuit City, CompUSA, Firestone, Goodyear, FedEx Kinko's, Office Depot, Pharmacy, Target, Sam's Club, UPS Store, Oakland Mall
		W: ATMs, Banks, CVS, Discount Tire, Grocery
63		12 Mile Rd, Madison Heights
	Gas	E: Marathon, Speedway
		W: Mobil, Marathon, Costco
	Food	E: Blimpie, McDonald's, Red Lobster
		W: Denny's, Dunkin Donuts/Marathon
	Med	W: + Hospital
	Other	E: Kmart, Home Depot
		W: Pharmacy, Costco

EXIT		MICHIGAN
62		11 Mile Rd, 10 Mile Rd W
	Gas	E: Mobil
		W: BP, Mobil
	Food	E: Domino's Pizza
		W: Hardee's, KFC, Taco Bell
(61)		Jct I-696, E-Port Huron, W-Lansing
	Other	W: to Hazel Park Raceway
60		9 Mile Rd, Hazel Park
	Gas	E: Mobil◊
		W: Mobil, Shell
	Food	E: China One, DQ, McDonald's, Subway
		W: Big Boy, Wendy's
	Lodg	E: Guesthouse Inn
59		MI 102, 8 Mile Rd, Highland Park
	Gas	E: Amoco
		W: 76, Shell
	Food	E: Arby's, Burger King, Subway, Wendy's
	Lodg	E: Bali Motel
	Other	E: Family Dollar, Grocery, Pharmacy
		W: MI State Fairgrounds
58		7 Mile Rd, Highland Park, Detroit
	Gas	W: AmocoBP◊
57		McNichols Rd, Highland Park
	Gas	E: BP
56AB		MI 8, Davison Freeway
55		Caniff Ave, Holbrook St, Detroit
	Gas	E: Mobil
	Food	W: KFC, Taco Bell
	Other	W: Daimler Chrysler Gen'l Offices
54		Grand Blvd, Clay St, Detroit
	Gas	W: BP, Shell
	Food	W: Super Coney Island
(53B)		Jct I-94, Ford Fwy, to Port Huron, Chicago
53A		Warren Ave, Detroit
	Gas	E: Shell
		W: AmocoBP
	Food	E: Little Caesars, McDonald's
	Med	E: + Hospital
	Other	W: Detroit Institute of Arts
52		Mack Ave, Detroit
	Gas	E: Shell
	Food	E: McDonald's
	Med	W: + Children's Hospital of Michigan, Harper Hospital, + Detroit Receiving Hospital
(51C)		Jct I-375, Chrysler Freeway, Flint
	Other	E: Comerica Park, Ford Field, Civic Ctr, Tunnel to Canada, Greektown, Greektown Casino, Joe Louis Arena, Cobo Hall, MGM Grand Casino
51B		MI 3, Gratiot Ave (NB, Left exit)
51A		MI 1, Woodward Ave
50		Grand River Ave, Downtown
	Gas	W: AmocoBP
49B		MI 10, Lodge Freeway (SB)
49A		Rosa Parks Blvd
	Gas	W: Mobil
	Med	E: + Hospital
	Other	E: Tiger Stadium
49		Rosa Parks Blvd
(48)		Jct I-96, Jeffries Freeway, Lansing (I-96 begins/ends I-75 Ex# 48)
47B		Porter St, to Windsor Canada
	FStop	E: Ammex
	Other	E: Bridge to Canada, DutyFree 24/7

Page 320   ◊ = Regular Gas Stations with Diesel   ▲ = RV Friendly Locations   ♥ = Pet Friendly Locations
RED PRINT SHOWS LARGE VEHICLE PARKING/ACCESS ON SITE OR NEARBY   BROWN PRINT SHOWS CAMPGROUNDS/RV PARKS

EXIT	MICHIGAN	EXIT	MICHIGAN	EXIT	MI / OH
47A	MI 3, Clark St, Fort St, Detroit	34	Dix Toledo Hwy, Sibley Rd (NB)	11	Laplaisance Rd, Monroe
FStop	E: USA Fuel Mart/BP	FStop	W: Sunoco Plaza (SB: Access via 34B)	Gas	W: Amoco, Marathon, Speedway
46	Livernois Ave, Downtown Detroit	Gas	W: AmocoBP	Food	W: Burger King, McDonald's, Wendy's
TStop	E: Detroit Truck Stop/Marathon	Food	W: McDonald's, Subway	Lodg	W: AmeriHost Inn, Comfort Inn
Food	E: KFC	32	West Rd, Woodhaven, Trenton	Other	W: Harbortown RV Resort▲, Outlet Mall, MI State Hwy Patrol Post
45	Fort St, Springwells Ave	TStop	E: AmBest/Detroiter Travel Center/Citgo (Scales)	(10)	MI Welcome Center (NB) (RR, Phones, Picnic, Vend, Info, Playground)
Gas	E: BP◆	Gas	E: Meijer◆, Speedway◆		
	W: Mobil		W: AmocoBP, Shell		
Food	W: McDonald's, Wendy's	Food	E: Cafe/Deli/Detroiter TC, Applebee's, Bob Evans, Burger King, Dunkin Donuts, Long John Silver, Panera Bread, Pizza Hut, Taco Bell, White Castle	9	S Otter Creek Rd, to La Salle
44	Dearborn St (NB exit, NO NB re-entry)			(8)	Weigh Station (Both dir)
FStop	E: Dearborn Food Mart/Citgo			6	Luna Pier Rd, Erie, Luna Pier
43	MI 85, Fort St, Schaefer Hwy (NB)		W: Country Skillet, McDonald's	TStop	W: Luna Pier Fuel Center/Sunoco
TStop	W: Motor City Truck Plaza/Marathon, Fuel Mart of America/BP (SB 43B)	Lodg	E: Motel/Detroiter TC	Food	E: Gander's
			W: Best Western, Knight's Inn, Holiday Inn Express♥	Lodg	E: Super 8
Gas	E: AmocoBP, Sunoco	TWash	E: Detroiter TC	Other	W: Laundry/Luna Pier FC
TServ	W: Marathon Motor City TP/Tires	TServ	E: Detroiter TC	5	Erie Rd, Erie, to Temperance
Other	W: Ford Plant	Other	E: Laundry/BarbSh/RVDump/Detroiter TC, ATMs, Discount Tire, Firestone, Home Depot, Kroger, Office Depot, Target, Wal-Mart, Ford Woodhaven Stamping Plant	2	Summit St, Erie, Temperance
43B	MI 85, Fort St, Schaefer Hwy (SB)				
43A	MI 85, Fort St, Schaefer Hwy (SB)				(EASTERN TIME ZONE)
42	Outer Dr, Detroit				**◯ MICHIGAN**
Gas	W: BP◆, Mobil◆				**◯ OHIO**
Food	E: Coney Island		W: Pharmacy		(EASTERN TIME ZONE)
Med	E: + Oakwood Medical Center	29	Gibraltar Rd, Flat Rock (NB)		
41	MI 39, Southfield Rd, Lincoln Park	Gas	W: Marathon	NOTE:	MM 211: Michigan State Line
FStop	W: Marathon	Lodg	W: Sleep Inn	210	OH 184, E Alexis Rd, Toledo
Food	E: A&W, Tim Hortons	29AB	Gibraltar Rd, Flat Rock	TStop	W: Pilot Travel Center #15 (Scales)
	W: Dunkin Donuts	28	MI 85, Fort St (NB)	Gas	W: BP◆, Meijer◆
Lodg	E: Budget Inn	27	N Huron River Dr, Rockwood	Food	W: Subway/Pilot TC, Arby's, Bob Evans, Burger King, McDonald's, Taco Bell, Wendy's
	W: Sleep Inn	Gas	E: Marathon◆		
TServ	W: Speedy Muffler King		W: Speedway◆	Lodg	W: Comfort Inn, Hampton Inn, Raceway Motel, Sunset Motel
Other	W: Pharmacy	Food	E: Benito's Pizza, Huron River Rest, Ocean Chinese	TServ	W: Alexis Diesel & Truck Service, Ron's Diesel Service, John's Standard Diesel Service, Bi-State Ford Truck
40	Dix Hwy, to IN 85, Lincoln Park				
Gas	E: Citgo, Marathon, Speedway	Lodg	E: Huron River Inn		
	W: Mobil, Shell	26	S Huron River Dr, Rockwood	Other	W: WiFi/Pilot TC, Raceway Park, North Towne Square Mall, Tires Plus, Toledo Speedway
Food	E: Pizza, Ponderosa	Gas	E: Sunoco◆		
	W: Burger King, DQ, Dunkin Donuts, Long John Silver, McDonald's, Pizza Hut, Taco Bell	Food	E: Dixie Café	209	Ottawa River Rd (NB)
		21	Newport Rd, Swan Creek Rd, Newport	Gas	E: BP, Sunoco
Lodg	W: Holiday Motel			Food	E: Little Caesar's Pizza
TServ	E: Downriver	TStop	W: Newport Travel Center/Marathon	Other	E: Foodtown, RiteAid
Other	E: Pharmacy	Gas	E: AmocoBP	(208)	Jct I-280S, to I-80/90, to Cleveland
	W: CVS, Foodland, Firestone	Food	E: TacoBell/Amoco	207	La Grange St, (SB) Stickney Ave (NB)
37	Northline Rd, Allen Rd, Southgate		W: FastFood/Newport TC	Gas	E: BP, Citgo, Sunoco
FStop	W: Allen Rd Mini Mart/Citgo	Other	E: Newport Auto Repair, Jerry's Towing, US Post Office	Food	E: McDonald's, Wendy's
Gas	E: AmocoBP, Mobil, Speedway			Other	E: Kmart, Family Dollar, Grocery
Food	E: Pizza		W: Laundry/LP/Newport TC	206	Phillips Ave, to US 24
	W: Arby's, Burger King, McDonald's	(20)	Jct I-275N, to Flint	205B	Berdan Ave, to US24 (NB, No reacc)
Lodg	E: Holiday Inn	18	Nadeau Rd, Monroe	Other	E: Daimler Chrysler Toledo Assembly Plant
	W: Best Value, Comfort Suites, La Quinta Inn♥	TStop	W: Pilot Travel Center #284 (Scales)	205A	Willy's Pkwy, to Jeep Pkwy
		Food	W: Arby/TJCinn/Pilot TC	(204)	Jct I-475W, to US 23, Maumee, Sylvania, Ann Arbor
Other	E: Auto Repair Service, Sam's Club	Other	W: WiFi/Pilot TC, Shady Creek RV Park & Campground▲		
	W: Wayne Co Comm College	15	MI 50, N Dixie Hwy, Monroe	203B	US 24, OH 51, N Detroit Ave
36	Eureka Rd, Southgate, Taylor	TStop	W: Pilot Travel Center #24 (Scales), TravelCenter of America #69/BP (Scales)	Gas	W: BP, Shell
Gas	E: BP, Shell, Speedway			Food	W: KFC, McDonald's, Wendy's
	W: Meijer◆	Gas	E: Shell	Other	W: Pharmacy, Grocery, U-Haul, Museum
Food	E: Bob Evans, Denny's, Fire Mountain Grill	Food	E: Bob Evans, Burger King, Red Lobster	203A	Bancroft St, to OH 51, Dwntwn (NB)
	W: Baker's Square, Famous Dave's BBQ, Hooters, Mountain Jack's Steakhouse, Rio Bravo, Subway, Wendy's		W: Subway/Pilot TC, CountryPride/ PizzaHut/Popeye/Quiznos/TA TC, Denny's, Cracker Barrel, McDonald's, Wendy's	202B	Collingwood Blvd, to Dorr St (SB)
				202A	Dorr St, Indiana Ave, to Washington St, Downtown Toledo (SB)
Lodg	E: Ramada Inn, Super 8	Lodg	E: Best Value Inn, Best Western, Hampton		
	W: Red Roof Inn♥		W: Holiday Inn Express, Knights Inn	Gas	E: BP
Other	W: ATMs, Banks, Best Buy, CVS, Discount Tire, FedEx Kinko's, Home Depot, PetCo♥, Staples, Southland Center Mall	TWash	W: TA TC		
		TServ	W: TA TC/Tires		
35	US 24, Telegraph Rd (NB, Left exit)	Other	W: WiFi/Pilot TC, Laundry/WiFi/TA TC		
34B	Sibley Rd, Wyandotte (SB)	14	Elm Ave, to Monroe		
34A	Dix Toledo Hwy, Trenton (SB)	13	Front St, Monroe		

◆ = Regular Gas Stations with Diesel ▲ = RV Friendly Locations ♥ = Pet Friendly Locations

RED PRINT SHOWS LARGE VEHICLE PARKING/ACCESS ON SITE OR NEARBY BROWN PRINT SHOWS CAMPGROUNDS/RV PARKS

EXIT		OHIO
	Food	W: McDonald's
	Lodg	E: Radisson, Wyndham
	Med	E: + Hospital
	Other	E: Convention Center, Zoo
201A		OH 25S, Anthony Wayne Trail, Maumee, Toledo Zoo
201B		OH 25N, Downtown Toledo (NB)
	Food	E: Bronze Boar, Dirty Bird, Fricker's, Grumpy's, Spaghetti Warehouse
	Lodg	E: Radisoon, Riverfront Hotel, Seagate Hotel
	Other	E: Fifth Third Field, COSI, Conv Center
200		South Ave, Kuhlman Ave
199		OH 65, N-Miami St, S-Rossford
199AB		OH 65, N-Miami St, S-Rossford
	Gas	E: 76, Sunoco
	Lodg	E: Days Inn
198		Wales Rd, Oregon Rd, Rossford, Northwood
	FStop	E: Wales Rd Shell
	Food	E: Subway/Shell, Arby's, China Wok, Pizza Hut
	Lodg	E: AmeriHost Inn, Baymont Inn, Comfort Inn
197		Buck Rd, Perrysburg, to Rossford
	Gas	E: Shell◆
		W: BP, Sunoco◆
	Food	E: Tim Horton's, Wendy's
		W: Denny's, McDonald's
	Lodg	W: American Inn, Knights Inn♥
(195)		Jct I-80/90, OH Turnpike (TOLL) (SB) OH 795, Indiana Rd (NB)
	Gas	E: BP◆, Barney's◆
	Food	E: Subway
	Lodg	E: Courtyard
193		US 20, US 23S, Perrysburg, Fremont
	Gas	E: BP◆, Meijer, Sunoco, Kroger
		W: Speedway◆
	Food	E: Arby's, Big Boy, Bob Evans, Burger King Chili's, China City, Cracker Barrel, IHOP, McDonald's, Subway, Taco Bell, Wendy's
	Lodg	E: Best Western, Comfort Suites, Days Inn, Holiday Inn Express
		W: La Quinta Inn♥
	Other	E: ATMs, Banks, Kmart, Kroger, Lowe's, PetSmart♥, Target, Walgreen's, to appr 7 mi: Toledo East/Stony Ridge KOA▲
		W: AutoZone, Signature Harley Davidson
(192)		Jct I-475N, US 23N (NB, Left exit) to Maumee, Ann Arbor, MI
187		OH 582, Middleton Pike, Bowling Green, to Haskins, Luckey
181		OH 64, E Wooster St, OH 105, Bowling Green Rd, Bowling Green
	Gas	E: Meijer
		W: BP, Citgo◆, Speedway, Sunoco◆
	Food	W: Bob Evans, Big Boy, Burger King, Chipolte Mex Grill, Fricker;'s, Little Caesars, McDonald's, Ranch Steak & Seafood, Starbucks, Subway, Tim Horton's, Waffle House, Wendy's
	Lodg	E: Holiday Inn Express
		W: Best Western, Buckeye Inn, Days Inn, Hampton Inn, Quality Inn
	Med	W: + Wood Co Hospital
	Other	W: Wood Co Airport✈, Golf Course, to Bowling Green State Univ

EXIT		OHIO
179		US 6, Bowling Green, to Fremont
	Other	E: Cactus Flats Campground▲
		W: Fire Lake Camper Park▲
(178)		Rest Area (Both dir) (RR, Phones, Picnic, Vend)
(175)		Weigh Station (NB)
171		OH 25, Cygnet Rd, Cygnet
168		Eagleville Rd (SB), Quarry Rd (NB) North Baltimore
	FStop	E: Fuel Mart #714
167		OH 18, Deshler Rd, N Baltimore, to Fostoria
	TStop	E: Petro Stopping Center #25/Mobil (Scales)
		W: Love's Travel Stop #356 (Scales)
	Gas	W: Sunoco
	Food	E: IronSkillet/FastFood/Petro SC, McDonald's, Pizza Hut
		W: Arby's/Love's TS
	Lodg	W: Crown Inn
	TWash	E: Blue Beacon TW/Petro SC
	TServ	E: Petro SC/Tires, Buckeye Truck Repair, D & R Towing & Repair Service
	Other	E: Laundry/BarbSh/WiFi/Petro SC
		W: WiFi/Love's TS
164		OH 613, Market St, Van Buren, Fostoria, McComb
	TStop	W: Pilot Travel Center # 360 (Scales)
	Food	W: Subway/TacoBell/Pilot TC
	Other	E: Shady Lake Campground▲, Van Buren Lake State Park
		W: WiFi/Pilot TC
(162)		Weigh Station (SB)
161		CR 99, Findlay
	FStop	E: Speedway #8502
	Gas	E: Shell
	Food	E: Subway
	Lodg	E: Comfort Suites
	Med	E: + Physicians Plus Urgent Care
	Other	E: Quick Lane Repair & Tire, Shadylake Campground▲, OH State Hwy Patrol Post
159		US 224, OH 15, W Trenton Ave, Findlay, to Ottawa, Tiffin
	Gas	E: BP◆, Speedway◆, Swifty
		W: Shell◆, Murphy
	Food	E: Burger King, Dakota Grill, Domino's, McDonald's, Ponderosa, Subway, Taco Bell, Wendy's
		W: Bob Evans, Cracker Barrel, Denny's, Max & Erma's, Outback Steakhouse, Steak n Shake, Subway, Waffle House
	Lodg	E: Drury Inn, Red Roof Inn♥, Rodeway Inn♥, Super 8♥
		W: Country Inn, Hampton Inn, Holiday Inn Express, Quality Inn♥
	TServ	W: Easter Tire & ReTreading
		W: Peterbilt of NW Ohio
	Med	E: + Hospital
	Other	E: Cinema, Golf Course, Pharmacy, Univ Of Findlay
		W: Wal-Mart sc
157		OH 12, W Main Cross St, Findlay Columbus Grove
	TStop	W: Highway Travel Center
	Gas	E: GasAmerica◆, Marathon◆
	Food	E: Blimpie, Noble Roman's
		W: CountryGriddleRest/Highway TC, Big Boy, Fricker's, Pilgrim Family Rest

◆ = Regular Gas Stations with Diesel   ▲ = RV Friendly Locations   ♥ = Pet Friendly Locations

RED PRINT SHOWS LARGE VEHICLE PARKING/ACCESS ON SITE OR NEARBY   BROWN PRINT SHOWS CAMPGROUNDS/RV PARKS

EXIT		OHIO	EXIT		OHIO	EXIT		OHIO
	Lodg	E: Days Inn		Food	E: Pizza Hut, Red Lobster, Ryan's Grill, TCBY, Taco Bell, Texas Roadhouse, Wendy's	94		CR 25A, Sidney
		W: Best Value Inn, Econo Lodge				93		OH 29, St Mary's Ave, Sidney
	Tires	W: Cooper Tire				92		OH 47, W Michigan St, Sidney
	TServ	E: Sparks Comm'l Tire, Phillips Garage		Lodg	W: Damon's, Papa John's		Gas	E: Shell, Speedway◊
		W: Miami Industrial Trucks, Helton Ent,			E: Holiday Inn, Hampton Inn, Motel 6 ♥			W: BP, Citgo◊, Sunoco◊, Valero, Murphy
	Other	W: Laundry/WiFi/Highway TC		Med	W: Super 8, Travelodge		Food	E: Applebee's, Arby's, Subway, Taco Bell, Wendy's
156		US 23/68, OH 15E, Findlay, to Carey			W: + Hospital			
	TServ	E: Findlay Int'l		Other	E: Kmart, Pharmacy, Sam's Club, Wal-Mart sc, RV Center, Co Fairgrounds			W: BW3, Bob Evans, Burger King, China Garden Buffet, McDonald's, KFC, Perkins, Pizza Hut, Waffle House
	Med	E: + Hospital						
	Other	E: Findlay Airport✈			W: Laundromat, Grocery, RiteAid		Lodg	W: Comfort Inn, Days Inn, Econo Lodge, Holiday Inn, Travel Inn
(153)		Rest Area (Both dir) (RR, Phones, Picnic, Vend)	124		E 4th St, Lima			
				Other	E: OH State Hwy Patrol Post		Med	E: + Hospital
145		OH 235, Bluffton, Mt Cory, Ada	122		OH 65, St Johns Ave, Lima, Ottawa		Other	E: AutoZone, CVS, Dollar General, NAPA, Grocery, Walgreen's
	Gas	W: Gastown		FStop	W: Four Star Food Mart/Shell			
	Other	E: Twin Lakes Park		Gas	E: Speedway◊			W: Auto Dealers, ATMs, Big Lots, Lowe's, Kroger, Radio Shack, Staples, Wal-Mart sc
		W: Kirtland's Auto Repair Center		TServ	W: Buckeye Truck Center/International, S&S Volvo/GMC Truck Center, King Bros Truck Center, Stoops Freightliner			
142		OH 103, Bluffton, Arlington				90		Fair Rd, Sidney
	FStop	E: BP					Gas	W: Clark, Marathon◊
	Gas	E: Sterling◊, Sunoco◊	120		W Breese Rd, Lima, Ft Shawnee		Lodg	W: Hampton Inn
		W: Marathon, Shell		Other	W: Lima Harley Davidson	83		CR 25A, Piqua
	Food	E: Denny's, Eagles Nest Rest.	118		E Main St, National Rd, Lima, Wapakoneta, to Cridersville		Gas	W: Super Station/Marathon
		W: Arby's, Burger King, KFC, McDonald's, Subway, Taco Bell					Food	W: NobleRoman's/Café/SuperStation
	Lodg	E: Knights Inn		FStop	W: Fuel Mart		Lodg	W: Red Carpet Inn
		W: Comfort Inn		Gas	W: Speedway◊		Other	W: Auto Dealers, RV Center
	ATS	W: Ken's Auto & Truck Service		Food	W: Subway/FuelMart, Bears Den, Bella Mama, Village Café, Westside Pizza	82		OH 36, E Ash St, Piqua, to Urbana
	Med	W: + Blanchard Valley Reg'l Hospital					Gas	W: Citgo, Speedway, Valero, Murphy
	Other	E: CarWash, Bluffton College, Bluffton Airport✈	(114)		Rest Area (Both dir) (RR, Phones, Picnic, Vend)		Food	E: Arby's, China East, China Garden Buffet, El Sombrero, Great Steak & Potato, KFC, Long John Silver, Pizza Hut, Taco Bell, Waffle House, Wendy's
140		Bentley Rd, OH 103, Bluffton	113		OH 67, Wapakoneta, Uniopolis			
135		Lincoln Hwy, Main St, to OH 696, US 30, Beaverdam, Lima, Delphos	111		Bellefontaine St, Wapakoneta			
				TStop	E: Travel Center of America #82/Marathon (Scales)			W: Bob Evans, Burger King, Cracker Barrel, El Sombrero Mex Rest, McDonald's, Red Lobster
	TStop	E: Pilot Travel Center #457 (Scales)						
		W: Flying J Travel Plaza # (Scales)		Gas	W: BP◊, Citgo, Shell, Murphy		Lodg	W: Comfort Inn, Knights Inn, La Quinta Inn ♥, Ramada Inn
	Gas	E: Speedway		Food	E: CountryFare/TA TC			
	Food	E: McDonald's/Subway/Pilot TC			W: Arby's, Bob Evans, Burger King, Captain D's, El Azteca, McDonald's, Pizza Hut, Taco Bell, Waffle House, Wendy's		Med	W: + Hospital
		W: Cookery/FastFood/FJ TP					Other	E: Miami Valley Center Mall, Big Lots, Goodyear, Home Depot, Cinema, OH State Hwy Patrol Post
	TWash	W: Blue Beacon TW/FJ TP						
	TServ	E: Pilot TC/Bridgestone Tire & Auto		Lodg	E: Days Inn			
		W: Beaverdam Fleet Services			W: Holiday Inn Express, Super 8, Travelodge	(81)		Rest Area (Both dir) (RR, Phones, Picnic, Vend)
	Other	E: Laundry/WiFi/Pilot TC						
		W: Laundry/BarbSh/WiFi/RVDump/LP/FJ TP		TServ	E: TA TC/Tires, Sterling/Western Star	78		CR 25A, Troy
				Other	E: Laundry/WiFi/TA TC, Astro Lanes, Pay Sta Campground▲, Wapakoneta KOA▲, Lakewood Village Resort ▲		Med	E: + Upper Valley Medical Center
134		OH 696, Napoleon Rd, Beaverdam Upper Sandusky (NB, NO NB re-entry)					Other	E: Miami Co Fairgrounds
						74AB		OH 41, Main St, Troy, Covington
130		Blue Lick Rd, Lima			W: Advance Auto, Family Dollar, Pharmacy Wal-Mart sc, Neil Armstrong Air & Space Museum, OH State Hwy Patrol Post	74		OH 41, W Main St, Troy, Covington
	Gas	E: Citgo, Marathon◊					Gas	E: BP◊
	Food	E: Northside Pizza						W: Shell, Speedway◊, Meijer◊
	Lodg	E: Best Value Inn	110		US 33, to St Mary's, Bellefontaine		Food	E: China Garden, Little Caesar's, Long John Silver, McDonald's, Perkins, Pizza Hut, Subway
127		OH 81, Findlay Rd, Lima, to Ada (SB)		Other	E: OH State Hwy Patrol Post, Wapakoneta/Lima South KOA▲			
	Gas	W: BP, Clark, Marathon◊, Speedway						
	Food	W: Waffle House, Rest/Days Inn			W: Easy Campground ▲			W: Applebee's, BW3, Bob Evans, Burger King, DQ, El Rancho Mex Rest, Ruby Tuesday, Outback Steakhouse, Steak n Shake
	Lodg	W: Comfort Inn, Days Inn, Econo Lodge	104		OH 219, CR 22, Botkins Rd, Botkins			
	TServ	E: E&R Trailer		FStop	W: Botkins Sunoco			
		W: Easter Tire Truck Auto & RV, Whiteford Kenworth		Gas	W: Marathon, Shell			
				ood	W: Subway		Lodg	W: Best Value Inn ♥, Fairfield Inn, Hampton Inn, Holiday Inn Express, Knights Inn, Residence Inn
	Other	E: Northland Auto Service		Lodg	W: Budget Host Inn			
		W: Gilroy's Auto Service	102		OH 274, Botkins, to New Bremen, Jackson Center			
127AB		OH 81, Findlay Rd, Lima, to Ada					Med	E: + Upper Valley Medical Center
125AB		OH 309E, OH 117E, Lima	99		OH 119, Main St, Anna, to Minster		Other	E: Goodyear, Pharmacy, Miami Co Fairgrounds
125B		OH 309W, OH 117W, Lima		TStop	E: Sav-A-Ton/Citgo (Scales)			
125		OH 309, OH 117, Lima (NB)		Gas	W: Gas America, Marathon, Sunoco◊			W: AutoZone, CVS, Hobart Arena, Lowe's, Wal-Mart sc
	FStop	E: Speedway		Food	E: Café/SavATon			
		W: Shell			W: Subway, Wendy's	73		OH 55, Troy, to Ludlow Falls
	Gas	E: BP◊		TWash	W: Truck Wash		Gas	E: BP, Shell, Kroger
	Food	E: Arby's, Bob Evans, Big Boy, Burger King, Captain D's, Cracker Barrel, McDonald's, Olive Garden		TServ	E: L&O Tire Service		Food	E: Jersey Mike's Subs, Papa John's, Waffle House, Wendy's
					W: Truck Repair & Towing			
				Other	E: Auto Repair Unlimited			
					W: Movin On CB Sales			

◊ = Regular Gas Stations with Diesel ▲ = RV Friendly Locations ♥ = Pet Friendly Locations

RED PRINT SHOWS LARGE VEHICLE PARKING/ACCESS ON SITE OR NEARBY BROWN PRINT SHOWS CAMPGROUNDS/RV PARKS

Page 323

EXIT	OHIO
Lodg	E: Best Western, Econo Lodge, Super 8
Med	E: + Hospital
Other	E: Kroger
69	**CR 25A, Tipp City**
Gas	E: BP, Citgo, Starfire◇
Food	E: Subway
Other	E: Auto Dealers, RV Center
68	**OH 571, Main St, Tipp City, W Milton**
Gas	E: BP◇, Shell, Speedway
	W: Citgo◇, Speedway◇
Food	E: Burger King, McDonald's, Subway
	W: Arby's, Big Boy, Bob Evans, Hickory Rivers Smokehouse, Wendy's
Lodg	W: Holiday Inn Express, Travelodge
Other	E: CVS, Family Dollar, Grocery, Goodyear
64	**Northwoods Blvd, Vandalia**
Gas	E: Kroger
Food	E: El Toro Mex Rest, Family Garden Rest, Quzinos
Other	E: Kroger, Dollar Tree
63	**US 40, National Rd, Vandalia**
Gas	E: Speedway◇
	W: BP◇, Shell, Speedway
Food	W: Arby's, KFC, McDonald's, Pizza Hut, Subway, Taco Bell, Waffle House, Wendy's
Lodg	E: Crossroads Motel
	W: Super 8, Travelodge
Other	W: Grocery, Kroger, Pharmacy, Dayton Int'l Airport✈
NOTE:	SB: Ongoing construction thru 2011
(61B)	**Jct I-70W, to Indianapolis, to Dayton Int'l Airport✈**
(61A)	**Jct I-70E, to Columbus**
59	**Wyse Rd, Benchwood Rd, Dayton**
Gas	W: Sunoco, Speedway, Murphy, Sam's Club
Food	E: Azteca Grande
	W: Arby's, Bob Evans, Cracker Barrel, Don Pablo, El Rancho Grande, Golden Corral, Hooters, Joe's Crab Shack, Lone Star Steakhouse, Max & Erma's, Olive Garden, O'Charley's, Outback Steakhouse, Ryan's Grill, Ruby Tuesday, Smokey Bones BBQ, Skyline Chili, Steak 'N Shake, Tim Horton's, Wendy's
Lodg	E: Hawthorn Suites, Howard Johnson, Residence Inn
	W: Comfort Inn, Country Inn, Courtyard, Drury Inn, Extended Stay America, Fairfield Inn, Hampton Inn, Knights Inn, Motel 6♥, Ramada, Red Roof Inn♥
TServ	E: Miami Valley International
Other	E: ATM, Auto Service, Discount Tire, FedEx Kinko's, RV Center
	W: ATMs, Banks, Sam's Club, Wal-Mart sc, Walgreen's, RV Center, Brookville KOA▲, to Hara Arena Conf & Exhibition Center
58	**Needmore Rd, Wright Bros Pkwy**
Gas	E: BP◇, Shell, Thornton's
	W: Marathon◇, Speedway◇, Sunoco◇, Swifty, Kroger
Food	E: Hardee's
	W: Arby's, Burger King, Captain D's, Domino's, Frisch's, Long John Silver, McDonald's, Roosters, Waffle House, Wendy's
Lodg	E: Best Western, Dayton Executive Hotel
Other	E: Goodyear

EXIT	OHIO
Other	W: ATM, AdvanceAuto, Kroger, US Post Office
57B	**Wagner Ford Rd, Dixie Dr**
Gas	E: Sunoco
	W: Mobil, Speedway, UDF
Food	W: Little Caesars, Subway
Lodg	E: Holiday Inn
	W: Days Inn
TServ	W: Dayton-Evans Motor Truck
Other	W: Pharmacy, Kelly Tire
57A	**Neva Dr, Dayton (NB exit, SB reacc)**
56B	**Stanley Ave W, Dayton (SB)**
56A	**Stanley Ave E, Dayton (SB)**
56AB	**Stanley Ave, Dayton**
FStop	E: True North/Shell
Gas	W: Clark
Food	W: Dominos, GoldStar Chili, Great Steak Co, McDonald's, Taco Bell, Wendy's
Lodg	W: Dayton Motor Hotel, Plaza Motel, Royal Motel
55	**Keowee St, Dayton (SB)**
55B	**Keowee St N, Leo St (NB)**
Gas	W: BP
Other	E: Chrysler Corp Dayton Thermal Prod
55A	**Keowee St (NB)**
54C	**OH 4, Webster St, to Springfield**
Med	E: + Children's Medical Center
Other	E: to Wright Patterson AFB
54B	**OH 48, Main St, Dayton**
Gas	W: BP
Food	W: Benjamin's Burgers, Chicken Louie's
Med	W: + Grandview Medical Center
54A	**Grand Ave (SB Left exit, NB entr)**
Med	W: + Grandview Medical Center
53B	**OH 49, W 1st St, Salem Ave, Downtown Dayton**
Lodg	E: Days Inn
53A	**OH 49, 3rd St, 2nd St, Dayton**
Gas	E: Sunoco
Lodg	E: Crowne Plaza, DoubleTree Hotel
Med	W: + Grandview Medical Center
Other	E: Convention Center
52B	**OH 35, W to Eaton, E to Dayton**
52A	**Albany St, Stewart St (SB)**
51	**Nicholas Rd, Edwin C Moses Blvd**
Gas	W: BP◇
Food	W: McDonald's, Wendy's
Lodg	W: Courtyard, Econo Lodge
Med	E: + Dayton Heart Hospital, + Miami Valley Hospital
Other	E: Montgomery Co Fairgrounds
50B	**OH 741S, Springboro Rd (SB exit, NB entr)**
50A	**Dryden Rd, Dayton**
Gas	E: Citgo
	W: Sunoco
Food	W: Subway, TJ's Rest
Lodg	W: Holiday Inn, Super 8
Other	E: Auto Service, Vet♥
47	**Central Ave, Dixie Hwy, Dayton Moraine, Kettering, W Carrollton**
Gas	E: Marathon, Sunoco
	W: BP, Speedway
Food	E: Big Boy, Waffle House
	W: McDonald's, Pizza Hut, Taco Bell, Wendy's

EXIT	OHIO
Med	E: + Kettering Memorial Hospital
Other	W: US Post Office, Moraine Air Park✈
44	**OH 725, Miamisburg-Centerville Rd**
Gas	E: BP◇, Shell, Speedway
	W: BP, Marathon, Shell
Food	E: Applebee's, Blimpie's, Burger King, Captain D's, Chuck E Cheese Pizza, Denny's, Dunkin Donuts, Fuddrucker's, Friendly's, Golden Corral, Hardee's, KFC, McDonald's, Max & Erma's, O'Charley's, Olive Garden, Pizza Hut, Red Lobster, Roosters, Steak 'n Shake, Subway, Taco Bell, TGI Friday, Wendy's
	W: Bob Evans, Jersey Mike Subs, Perkins
Lodg	E: Comfort Suites, Courtyard, Holiday Inn, DoubleTree Hotel, Extended Stay America, Hilton, Homewood Suites, Motel 6♥, Residence Inn, Studio 6, Suburban Lodge
	W: Knights Inn, Ramada, Red Roof Inn♥, Signature Inn, Yankee Mill Inn
Med	E: + Southview Hospital, Budget Care Medical Walk-In Center
	W: + Sycamore Hospital Kettering, Medical Center
TServ	E: Clarke Detroit Diesel
Other	E: ATMs, Auto Services, Dayton Mall, Best Buy, B&N, Circuit City, CompUSA, Cinema, Discount Tire, Firestone, Goodyear, Home Depot, Lowe's, NTB, Office Depot, PetSmart♥, Pep Boys, Sam's Club, Target, Tire Discounters, Wal-Mart
	W: Dollar General, NAPA
(43)	**Jct I-675N, Dayton, to Columbus**
NOTE:	NB: Ongoing construction thru 2011
38	**OH 73, E 2nd St, W Central St, Springboro, to Franklin**
Gas	E: BP, Shell, Speedway, Sunoco
	W: DM, Exxon, Shell
Food	E: Applebee's, Arby's, Bob Evans, Long John Silver, Hardee's, McDonald's, Perkins, Pizza Hut, Skyline Chili, Subway, Taco Bell, Tim Horton's, Wendy's
Lodg	E: Hampton Inn, Holiday Inn Express
	W: Econo Lodge, Knights Inn
Other	E: Kmart, Kroger, Radio Shack, Tires
	W: AutoZone, Dollar General, Grocery
36	**OH 123, Franklin, to Lebanon**
TStop	E: Pilot Travel Center #9 (Scales)
Gas	E: Shell, Exxon◇
	W: BP, Marathon
Food	E: PizzaHut/Subway/Pilot TC, Wendy's/Exxon, McDonald's, Waffle House
	W: White Castle
Lodg	E: Quality Inn
TWash	E: Truck Wash Express
TServ	E: Truck Lube USA, Steve's Towing, Truck & Trailer Repair
Other	E: Laundry/WiFi/Pilot TC, U-Haul
32	**OH 122, Franklin, to Middletown**
Gas	E: BP, Duke
	W: Citgo, Meijer◇, Speedway. Murphy
Food	E: McDonald's, Waffle House
	W: Applebee's, Bob Evans, Cracker Barrel, Frisch's Big Boy, GoldStar Chili, Golden Corral, Hardee's, KFC, Lone Star Steakhouse, McDonald's, Olive Garden, Old Country Buffet, O'Charley's, Shell's, Steak 'n Shake, Wendy's
Lodg	E: Best Value Inn, Comfort Inn, Ramada Inn, Super 8

◇ = Regular Gas Stations with Diesel ▲ = RV Friendly Locations ♥ = Pet Friendly Locations
RED PRINT SHOWS LARGE VEHICLE PARKING/ACCESS ON SITE OR NEARBY BROWN PRINT SHOWS CAMPGROUNDS/RV PARKS

OHIO

EXIT		
	Lodg	W: Best Western, Drury Inn, Fairfield Inn, Hawthorne Inn, Holiday Inn Express ♥, Howard Johnson, Red Carpet Inn
	Med	W: + Doctor's Urgent Care Clinic, + Middletown Regional Hospital
	Other	W: ATMs, Auto Services, Kroger, Lowe's, Pharmacy, Target, Staples, Wal-Mart sc, Towne Mall
29		**OH 63, Hamilton Lebanon Rd, Lebanon, to Monroe, Hamilton**
	FStop	E: Marathon
	TStop	E: Stony Ridge Travel Center (Scales)
	Gas	E: Shell W: BP◊, Speedway◊, Sunoco◊
	Food	E: Rest/Stoney Ridge TC, WhiteCastle/Marathon, Burger King, GoldStar Chili, McDonald's, Popeye's, Waffle House, Wendy's W: McDonald's, Perkins
	Lodg	E: Motel/Stony Ridge TC, Days Inn, Howard Johnson W: Hampton Inn
	TWash	E: Interstate Truck Care
	TServ	E: Bishop Truck Care, S&C Towing & Recovery, CB Shoppe
	Other	E: Laundry/Stony Ridge TC W: Auto Technics, Flea Market
(28)		**Rest Area (Both dir) (RR, Phones, Picnic, Vend, Info)**
24		**OH 129W, Michael A Fox Hwy, Middletown, to Hamilton**
22		**Tylersville Rd, West Chester, to Hamilton, Mason**
	Gas	E: BP, Marathon, Sunoco W: Shell, Speedway◊, Thornton's, Meijer◊
	Food	E: Arby's, Bob Evans, Bonefish Grill, Burger King, Fazoli's, GoldStar Chili, KFC, Johnny Carino's, IHOP, Long John Silver, McDonald's, Perkins, Pizza Hut, Subway, Ruby Tuesday, Taco Bell, TGI Friday, Waffle House W: O'Charley's, Steak 'n Shake, Starbucks
	Lodg	E: Econo Lodge, Howard Johnson W: Wingate Inn
	Med	E: + Urgent Care
	Other	E: ATMs, Big Lots, Firestone, Home Depot, Kroger, Radio Shack, Target, Tires Plus, Walgreen's W: Car-X Auto Service, Tire Discounters, Wal-Mart
21		**Cincinnati-Dayton Rd**
	Gas	W: Mobil◊, Shell, Speedway◊
	Food	E: Arby's, Big Boy W: Papa John's, Subway, Waffle House
	Lodg	E: Holiday Inn Express W: Knights Inn
	Other	W: Wal-Mart sc, Vet ♥, Camperland RV Center
19		**Union Centre Blvd, West Chester, to Fairfield, Hamilton**
	Gas	W: BP, Marathon, Shell
	Food	W: Applebee's, Bob Evans, Burger King, Chipotle Mexican Grill, Dickey's BBQ, Don Pablo, Max & Erma's, Red Robin, Roadhouse Grill, Starbucks
	Lodg	W: Comfort Inn, Courtyard, Marriott, Sleep Inn, Staybridge Suites

OHIO

EXIT		
	NOTE:	Through trucks MUST take I-275 around Cincinnati.
(16)		**Jct I-275, to I-71, I-74, to Columbus, Indianapolis**
	Lodg	E: Red Roof Inn ♥ W: Econo Lodge, Extended Stay America, Residence Inn
	TServ	E: Peterbilt of NW Ohio
	NOTE:	Through trucks MUST take I-275 around Cincinnati.
15		**Sharon Rd, Chester Rd, Cincinnati, to Glendale, Sharonville**
	Gas	E: BP, Chevron, Marathon◊, Shell, Sunoco, Thornton's W: Speedway
	Food	E: Bob Evans, Cracker Barrel, Pizza Hut, Skyline Chili, Waffle House W: Arby's, Burger King, Captain D's, Chuck E Cheese Pizza, Jim Dandy's BBQ, Long John Silver, McDonald's, Pizza Hut, Ruby Tuesday, Subway, Texas Roadhouse, Taco Bell, Wendy's
	Lodg	E: Baymont Inn, Country Inn, Drury Inn, Fairfield Inn, Hampton Inn, Holiday Inn, Hilton Garden Inn, Motel 6 ♥, Ramada, Red Roof Inn ♥ W: Comfort Inn, Extended Stay America, Econo Lodge, Residence Inn, Signature Inn, Super 8, Sheraton, Travelodge
	TServ	E: Clarke Detroit Diesel, Kenworth of Cincinnati
	Other	E: Ford Plant W: Costco, Auto Repair, Convention Ctr
14		**Glendale Milford Rd, Cincinnati**
	Gas	W: Swifty
	Lodg	W: Best Value Inn, Quality Inn, Travelodge & RV Park▲, Wingate
13		**Shepherd Lane, Shepherd Ave**
12		**Cooper Ave (SB) to Wyoming Ave, Davis St to Jefferson Ave (NB)**
10		**Galbraith Rd, Arlington Hts (SB)**
	Gas	E: Shell, Speedway, Sunoco
	Other	E: Budget RAC, Pharmacy
10B		**Galbraith Rd, Arlington Hts (NB, Left Exit)**
10A		**Ronald Reagan Cross County Hwy**
9		**OH 4, Paddock Rd, Vine St, OH 561, Seymour Ave**
	Gas	E: Speedway
	Food	E: White Castle
	Other	E: Hamilton Co Fairgrounds
8		**Towne St, to Paddock Rd (NB)**
7		**OH 562, to I-71**
6		**Mitchell Ave, St Bernard**
	Gas	E: Marathon, Shell, Speedway W: BP◊
	Food	E: KFC, Wendy's, White Castle W: McDonald's
	Lodg	E: Holiday Inn Express
	Med	E: + VA Hospital
	Other	E: Kroger, Tires, CarWash W: Walgreen's, to Cincinnati Zoo
(4)		**Jct I-74W, US 52W, US 27N, to Indianapolis**

◊ = Regular Gas Stations with Diesel   ▲ = RV Friendly Locations   ♥ = Pet Friendly Locations

RED PRINT SHOWS LARGE VEHICLE PARKING/ACCESS ON SITE OR NEARBY   BROWN PRINT SHOWS CAMPGROUNDS/RV PARKS

Page 325

EXIT		OH / KY
3		Hopple St, to US 27S, US 127S (NB, Left Exit)
	Gas	E: Marathon
		W: BP, Shell
	Food	E: Big Boy, Subway, White Castle, Wendy's
	Lodg	E: Budget Host Inn, Days Inn, Interstate Motel, Rest Inn
	Med	W: + Hospital
2B		Western Hills Viaduct, to US 27, US 127, Cincinnati, Harrison Ave
	Gas	W: BP
	Food	W: McDonald's, Subway
2A		Western Ave, Liberty St (SB)
2		Harrison Ave, Cincinnati
1H		Western Ave, Ezzard Charles Dr (SB) (ReAccess from 8th St)
1G		Freeman Ave, Gest St, 8th St W, (SB) to US 50W, OH 264 (NB)
	FStop	W: Marathon
1F		7th St, Downtown Cincinnati (SB)
	Lodg	W: Holiday Inn
1E		5th St, US 127, I-71N, US 50
(1)		Jct I-71N, to I-471, to Cincinnati
		(EASTERN TIME ZONE)

OHIO
KENTUCKY
(EASTERN TIME ZONE)

	NOTE:	MM 193: Ohio State Line
	NOTE:	I-75 below runs with I-71 to Ex #173. Exit #'s follows I-75.
192		5th St, Crescent Ave, Covington (SB) US 25, US 127, W 9th, W 5th (NB)
	Gas	E: BP, Speedway
	Food	E: Burger King, Hardee's, KFC, McDonald's Riverview Revolving Rest, Skyline Chili, Subway, Waffle House
	Lodg	E: Courtyard, Extended Stay America, Holiday Inn, Radisson
		W: Hampton Inn
191		W 9th St, Pike St, W 12th St
	Med	E: + Hospital
189		KY 1072, Kyles Lane, Ft Wright
	Gas	W: Marathon, Speedway
	Lodg	W: Days Inn, Lookout Motel, Ramada
188		US 25, Dixie Hwy, Fort Mitchell
	Gas	E: Sunoco
		W: Marathon, Speedway
	Food	E: Little Caesar's Pizza
		W: Indigo Cafe
	Lodg	W: Holiday Inn
186		KY 371, Buttermilk Pike, Ft Mitchell
	Gas	E: BP◆, Citgo◆
		W: BP, Shell, Sunoco◆
	Food	E: Oriental Wok, Rest/Drawbridge Inn
		W: Bob Evans, Burger King, Long John Silver, McDonald's, Outback, Subway
	Lodg	E: Cross Country Inn, Drawbridge Inn
	Other	W: Grocery, Home Depot, Walgreen's
(185)		Jct I-275, W to Cincinnati Airport
184		KY 236, Erlanger
184AB		KY 236, Commonwealth Ave, Donaldson Hwy, Erlanger
	Gas	E: BP, Marathon

EXIT		KENTUCKY
	Gas	W: Ron's Svc Ctr, Speedway, Sunoco
	Food	E: Double Dragon Chinese
		W: Southern Kitchen, Waffle House
	Lodg	E: Days Inn, Chandler Inn
		W: Comfort Inn, Days Inn, Econo Lodge
	Med	W: + Doctors Urgent Care
	Other	E: US Post Office, Police Dept
		W: Cincinnati-N Ky Int'l Airport✈
182		KY 1017, Turfway Rd, Florence
	Gas	E: BP, Shell
		W: Meijer◆
	Food	E: Big Boy, Lee's Chicken, Ryan's Grill
		W: Applebee's, Cracker Barrel, Famous Dave's BBQ, Longhorn Steakhouse, Ming Gardern, Rafferty's, Shell's Seafood, Steak 'n Shake, Subway
	Lodg	E: Courtyard, Fairfield Inn, Signature Inn
		W: Extended Stay America, Hampton Inn, Hilton, La Quinta Inn ♥
	Med	W: + St Luke Hospital West
	Other	E: ATM, Big Lots, Office Depot
		W: Best Buy, Home Depot, Lowe's, Sam's Club, Target
181		KY 18, Burlington Pike, Florence, Burlington
	TStop	E: Travel Center of America/Sunoco (Scales)
	Gas	E: Speedway, Swifty
		W: ProCare Auto Service/BP, Chevron
	Food	E: Arby/PizzaHut/Popeye/Subway/TA TC, Waffle House
		W: Applebee's, Chili's, Cracker Barrel, Hooters, Lone Star Steakhouse, O'Charley's, Wendy's
	Lodg	E: Best Value Inn
		W: Microtel, Suburban Lodge
	TServ	E: TA TC/Tires
	Med	W: + Hospital
	Other	E: Laundry/WiFi/TA TC, ProCare Auto Service
		W: Kmart, Staples, Wal-Mart sc
180A		Steinberg Dr, Mall Rd (SB)
	Food	W: Cathay Kitchen, China Max, Olive Garden, Hardee's, Old Country Buffet, Subway, Taco Bell
	Other	W: Florence Mall, Kroger, Walgreen's
180		US 42, US 127, Florence, Union
	Gas	E: BP◆, Speedway, Thornton's
		W: BP, Chevron, Shell◆, Speedway
	Food	E: Bob Evans, Burger King, Captain D's, Dunkin Donuts, Long John Silver, McDonald's, Pizza Hut, Red Lobster, Subway, Wendy's
		W: Arby's, KFC, Perkins, Ponderosa, Waffle House, White Castle
	Lodg	E: Holiday Inn, Travelodge
		W: Knight's Inn, Motel 6 ♥, Ramada, Super 8, Wildwood Inn
	Other	W: AutoZone, CVS, NTB, Walgreen's
178		KY 536, Mt Zion Rd
	Gas	E: BP◆, Mobil, Shell◆, Sunoco
	Food	E: Goldstar Chili, Jersey Mike's Subs, Steak 'n Shake, Subway
	Other	E: Grocery, Goodyear
(177)		**KY Welcome Center (SB)** **Rest Area (NB)** **(RR, Phones, Picnic, Vend, RVDump)**
175		KY 338, Richwood Dr, Walton
	TStop	E: Travel Center of America/BP (Scales), Pilot Travel Center #278 (Scales)
		W: Pilot Travel Center #321 (Scales)
	Gas	W: BP, Shell◆

EXIT		KENTUCKY
	Food	E: Rest/TacoBell/TA TC, Subway/Pilot, Arby's, Burger King, White Castle
		W: Subway/Pilot TC, Wendy's/BP, McDonald's, Skyline Chili, Waffle House
	Lodg	E: Holiday Inn Express
		W: Econo Lodge
	TServ	E: TA TC/Tires
	Other	E: Laundry/WiFi/TA TC, WiFi/Pilot TC, Florence RV Park▲
		W: WiFi/Pilot TC
(173)		Jct I-71S, to Louisville
	NOTE:	I-75 above runs with I-71 to OH. Exit #'s follow I-75.
171		KY 14, KY 16, Walton
	TStop	W: Flying J Travel Plaza/Conoco (Scales) (DAD)
	Gas	E: BP, Citgo
	Food	E: Waffle House
		W: Rest/FastFood/FJ TP
	TWash	W: Blue Beacon TW/FJ TP
	TServ	W: Quick Lube Truck Center
	Other	W: Laundry/WiFi/RVDump/LP/FJ TP, Oak Creek Campground▲, RV Center
(168)		Weigh Station (SB)
166		KY 491, Violet Rd, Crittenden
	Gas	E: BP, Marathon◆
		W: Chevron, Shell◆
	Food	E: McDonald's, Taco Bell
		W: Burger King, Subway
159		KY 22, KY 467, Broadway St, Taft Hwy, Dry Ridge
	Gas	E: BP, Shell◆
		W: Marathon, Speedway◆, Sunoco◆
	Food	E: Arby's, Burger King, McDonald's, Lil Shrimp, Waffle House, Wendy's
		W: Cracker Barrel, Shoney's
	Lodg	E: Country Inn, Dry Ridge Motor Inn, Microtel, Super 8
		W: Hampton Inn, Holiday Inn
	Med	E: + Hospital
	Other	E: Wal-Mart, I-75 Camper Village▲
		W: Dry Ridge Outlet Mall, Tires
156		Barnes Rd
154		KY 36, US 25, Williamstown
	Gas	E: Citgo◆, Shell◆
		W: BP◆, Marathon◆
	Food	E: Chester's Fr Chicken, Rest/K Inn
		W: Williamstown Pizza
	Lodg	E: Fountain Inn, Knights Inn
		W: Best Value Inn, Cedar Valley Resort, Days Inn, Howard Johnson
	Med	E: + Hospital
144		KY 330, Corinth, to Owenton
	TStop	E: Noble's Fuel/Marathon
	Gas	W: BP
	Food	E: Rest/Noble's
		W: Donna's Diner, Peg's Pit Stop
	Lodg	W: Three Springs Suites
	TServ	E: Noble's Fuel/Tires
	Other	E: CBShop/Noble's
136		KY 32, to Sadieville
	Gas	W: Marathon
(131)		Weigh Station (NB)
129		KY 620, Cherry Blossom Way, Delaplain Rd, to US 25, Georgetown
	TStop	E: Pilot Travel Center #353 (Scales)
		W: Pilot Travel Center #47 (Scales)
	Gas	W: Shell

◆ = Regular Gas Stations with Diesel ▲ = RV Friendly Locations ♥ = Pet Friendly Locations
RED PRINT SHOWS LARGE VEHICLE PARKING/ACCESS ON SITE OR NEARBY BROWN PRINT SHOWS CAMPGROUNDS/RV PARKS

INTERSTATE 75 N/S — KENTUCKY

EXIT		KENTUCKY
	Food	E: Wendy's/Pilot TC, Waffle House W: McDonald's/Pilot TC
	Lodg	E: Days Inn, Motel 6♥
	Other	E: Laundry/WiFi/Pilot TC, Georgetown Toyota Plant W: Laundry/WiFi/Pilot TC
(127)		Rest Area (Both dir) (RR, Phones, Picnic, Vend)
126		US 62, to US 460, Cherry Blossom Way, Georgetown
	Gas	E: BP, Chevron, Marathon, Murphy W: BP, Shell, Speedway◆
	Food	E: Applebee's, McDonald's, O'Charley's, Steak 'n Shake W: Cracker Barrel, KFC, Waffle House
	Lodg	E: Econo Lodge W: Comfort Suites, Country Inn, Fairfield Inn, Hampton Inn, Holiday Inn Express, Hilton Garden Inn, Microtel, Super 8
	Med	W: + Hospital
	Other	E: Lowe's, Wal-Mart sc W: Kmart, Outlet Mall, Auto Dealer
125		US 460, Paris Pike, Georgetown (NB)
	Gas	E: BP◆, Shell W: Swifty
	Food	E: Rest/Flag Inn W: Arby's, DQ, Little Caesars, Long John Silver, Wendy's
	Lodg	E: Econo Lodge, Flag Inn, Super 8 W: Winner's Circle Motel
	Med	W: + Hospital
	Other	W: Advance Auto
120		KY 1973, Iron Works Pk, Lexington
	TStop	E: AmBest/Donerail Travel Plaza/Citgo (Scales)
	Food	W: Rest/Sunset Motel
	Lodg	W: Sunset Motel
	Other	E: KY State Horse Farm Park & Campground/RVDump▲
	Med	W: + Hospital
(118)		Jct I-64W, Frankfort, Louisville (SB)
115		KY 922, Newtown Pike, Bluegrass Pkwy, Lexington
	Gas	E: Exxon, Shell W: Chevron◆
	Food	E: Cracker Barrel, McDonald's, Waffle House W: Denny's
	Lodg	E: Knight's Inn, La Quinta Inn♥, Sheraton W: Embassy Suites, Holiday Inn, Marriott
113		US 27, US 68, Broadway, Paris Pike, Paris, Lexington
	Gas	E: BP◆, Speedway W: Chevron◆, Shell
	Food	E: Waffle House W: Burger King, Fazoli's, Hardee's, Long John Silver, Shoney's, Subway
	Lodg	E: Ramada Inn W: Days Inn, Econo Lodge, Red Roof Inn
	Other	E: Joyland Bowl & Park, KY Horse Center W: Car Wash, Kroger, RV Center
(111)		Jct I-64E, to Winchester, Ashland, Huntington, WV
110		US 60, Winchester Rd, Lexington
	FStop	W: Speedway #9393
	Gas	W: Shell, Thornton's
	Food	W: Arby's, Bob Evans, Bonefish Grill, Cracker Barrel, International Buffet, McDonald's, Shoney's, Waffle House

Personal Notes

EXIT		KENTUCKY
	Lodg	W: Baymont Inn, Best Western, Country Inn, Hampton Inn, Howard Johnson, Holiday Inn, Microtel, Motel 6♥, Super 8
	TServ	W: International Trucks, Mack
	Med	W: + Hospital
	Other	W: Lowe's
108		KY 1425, Man O'War Blvd
	Gas	W: BP◆, Citgo◆, Shell, Speedway, Meijer, Chevron
	Food	W: Applebee's, Arby's, Burger King, Carrabba's, ChickFilA, Chipotle Mex Rest, Damon's, Don Pablo, Fire Mtn Grill, Goldstar Chili, Logan's Roadhouse, Max & Erma's, Outback Steakhouse, Starbucks, Steak 'n Shake, Taco Bell, Waffle House, Wendy's
	Lodg	W: Courtyard, Hilton, Homestead Suites, Sleep Inn
	Med	W: + Hospital
	Other	W: Circuit City, Target, Walgreen's, Harley Davidson, Meijer
104		KY 418, Athens Boonesboro Rd, Lexington
	Gas	E: Exxon◆, Shell W: BP◆, Speedway
	Food	E: Wendy's/Exxon, Arby's, Hooters, Subway, Waffle House W: Arby's, Jerry's
	Lodg	E: Holiday Inn, Red Roof Inn♥ W: Comfort Inn, Days Inn, Econo Lodge
	TServ	W: Whayne Power Systems
	Med	W: + Hospital

EXIT		KENTUCKY
99		US 25N, US 421N, Lexington
97		US 25S, US 421S, Richmond, Clay's Ferry Landing
	TStop	E: Clays Ferry Travel Center/Exxon (Scales)
	Food	E: HuddleHouse/Clays Ferry TC, Blimpie's, McDonald's
	Other	E: Laundry/Clays Ferry TC, GI Joe's CB Radio, to Ft Boonesborough State Park
95		KY 627, KY 3055, Richmond, to Winchester, Boonesborough
	FStop	W: Dishman's Shell Food Mart
	TStop	E: Love's Travel Stop #291 (Scales)
	Food	E: Arby's/TJCinn/Love's TS W: Burger King/Dishman's
	Other	E: Laundry/WiFi/Love's TS, Fort Boonesborough State Park
90		US 25, US 421, Richmond, Irvine
	Gas	E: BP◆, Shell W: Citgo, Exxon, Shell
	Food	E: Cracker Barrel, Outback Steakhouse W: Arby's, Big Boy, Hardee's, Pizza Hut, Subway, Waffle House, Wendy's
	Lodg	E: Best Western, Knights Inn, La Quinta Inn♥, Red Roof Inn♥ W: Days Inn, Motel 6, Super 8
	Other	E: Richmond Flea Market W: NTB
87		KY 876, Barnes Hill Rd, Richmond, Lancaster, Richwood
	Gas	E: BP◆, Chevron, Citgo, Shell◆, Speedway W: BP◆
	Food	E: Arby's, Burger King, Denny's, Dunkin Donuts, Fazoli's, Hardee's, Hooters, KFC, Krystal, Long John Silver, McDonald's, Pizza Hut, Taco Bell, Waffle House W: Bob Evan's, Ryan's Grill, Steak 'n Shake, Sonny's BBQ, Starbucks
	Lodg	E: Best Western, Econo Lodge, Holiday Inn W: Comfort Suites, Hampton Inn, Jameson
	Med	E: + Hospital
	Other	E: ATM, Big Lots, Goodyear, Winn Dixie, Ky Univ
(83)		Rest Area (Both dir) (RR, Phones, Picnic, Vend)
77		KY 595, Walnut Meadow Rd, Berea
	Gas	W: BP, Shell
	Food	W: Subway/BP, Columbia Steak House, Huddle House
	Lodg	W: Days Inn, Holiday Inn Express♥
	Med	E: + Hospital
	Other	E: Berea College
76		KY 21, Chestnut St, Lancaster Rd, Berea
	TStop	W: 76 Truck Center/Spur
	Gas	E: BP, Citgo, Shell, Speedway◆ W: BP, Chevron, Marathon◆
	Food	E: Arby's, Burger King, Cracker Barrel, DQ, KFC, Long John Silver, Little Caesars, McDonald's, Subway, Taco Bell, Wendy's W: Lee's Chicken, Pantry Family Rest
	Lodg	E: Budget Inn, Holiday Motel, Howard Johnson, Knights Inn, Super 8 W: Comfort Inn, Econo Lodge, Fairfield Inn
	TServ	W: 76 TC/Tires
	Med	E: + Hospital
	Other	E: ATM, Auto Service, Dollar General, Radio Shack, Wal-Mart sc W: OH - KY Campground▲

◆ = Regular Gas Stations with Diesel   ▲ = RV Friendly Locations   ♥ = Pet Friendly Locations

RED PRINT SHOWS LARGE VEHICLE PARKING/ACCESS ON SITE OR NEARBY   BROWN PRINT SHOWS CAMPGROUNDS/RV PARKS

EXIT		KENTUCKY	EXIT		KY / TN	EXIT		TENNESSEE
62		US 25, to KY 461, Renfro Valley, Mt Vernon		Lodg	E: Quality Inn, Super 8 W: Baymont Inn, Comfort Inn, Fairfield Inn, Hampton Inn, Knights Inn		Gas Food	E: Shell E: Stuckey's/Shell, Perkins W: Subway/Pilot TC, Stuckey's/Shell
	TStop Gas	E: Derby City South Travel Plaza E: Shell W: BP, Chevron, Shell, Marathon		TWash TServ	E: Blue Beacon TW/Corbin TP E: Corbin TP/Tires W: Q-Fix		Lodg Other	W: Comfort Inn W: WiFi/Laundry/Pilot TC, Big South Fork NRA
	Food	E: Hardee's, KFC, Waffle House W: DQ, Denny's, McDonald's, Wendy's		Other	E: Laundry/WiFi/Pilot TC, Laundry/WiFi/Corbin TP, Wal-Mart sc, to Cumberland	134		US 25W, TN 63, Caryville, La Follette, Jacksboro
	Lodg	E: Country Hearth Inn, Heritage Inn, Renfro Valley Inn W: Days Inn, Econo Lodge			National Park, Pine Mountain State Park W: RVDump/WiFi/Love's TS, Corbin KOA▲, to Laurel River Lake Rec Area		Gas Food	E: Shell W: BP E: Waffle House
	Med	W: + Hospital	25		US 25W, Cumberland Falls Hwy, Corbin		Lodg	W: Shoney's E: Econo Lodge, Family Inn, Hampton Inn, Super 8
59		US 25, US 150, Mt Vernon, Livingston		Gas	E: Speedway◊ W: BP, Exxon◊, Shell		Med	W: Budget Host Inn E: + Hospital
	TStop Gas	E: Mt Vernon Fuel Center E: BP, Marathon◊, Shell◊ W: BP		Food	E: Burger King, Jerry's Rest, McDonald's W: Arby's, Waffle House		Other	E: to Cove Lake State Park▲
	Food Lodg TServ	E: Pizza Hut, Rest/Kastle Inn E: Kastle Inn E: Mt Vernon FC/Tires		Lodg	E: Country Inn, Days Inn, Holiday Inn Express W: Best Western, Regency Inn	(130) 129		Weigh Station (Both dir) US 25W S, TN 116, Lake City
49		KY 909, to US 25, Livingston		Med Other	E: + Hospital E: Auto Service & Repair		Gas	E: BP, Mystik, Sunoco W: Citgo, Exxon, Shell
	TStop Food Other	W: 49er Diesel Center/Shell W: 49er Diner/49er DC W: Laundry/49er DC	15		W: to Cumberland Falls State Park US 25W, Williamsburg		Food	W: Burger King, Cracker Barrel, KFC, McDonald's
41		KY 80, London, Somerset		Gas	W: Chevron◊, Shell		Lodg	W: Days Inn, Lambs Inn Motel
	TStop	W: Petrol Auto Truck Center/Citgo, London Auto Truck Center/BP (Scales)	11	TStop	KY 92, Williamsburg W: Pilot Travel Center #437 (Scales)	128	Gas	US 441, TN 71, to Lake City E: BP, Sunoco W: Exxon◊, Shell
	Gas	E: Chevron, Marathon, Speedway W: Chevron, Shell		Gas	E: BP◊, Exxon◊, Shell W: Shell		Lodg	W: Blue Haven Motel, Days Inn, Lake City Motel
	Food	E: Arby's, Burger King, DQ, McDonald's, KFC, Pizza Hut W: Cracker Barrel, Long John Silver, Taco Bell, Waffle House, Wendy's		Food	E: Arby's, DQ, Hardee's, McDonald's, Pizza Hut, Subway, Taco Bell W: Wendy's/Pilot TC, Burger King, Huddle House, Krystal, Long John Silver		TServ Other	E: Precision Truck & Trailer Repair W: Hicks Truck Service E: U-Haul, to Mtn Lake Marina & Campground▲
	Lodg	E: Best Western, Days Inn, Holiday Inn Express, Red Roof Inn♥, Sleep Inn, Super 8 W: Budget House Inn & RV Park▲, Westgate Inn Motel & RV Park▲		Lodg	E: Cumberland Inn, Super 8 W: Days Inn, Williamsburg Motel & RV Park▲	122	TStop Gas	TN 61, Andersonville Hwy, Norris, Andersonville, Clinton W: Kwik Fuel Center #122/P66 (Scales) E: Shell
	TWash Med Other	W: London ATC E: + Hospital E: ATMs, Auto Services, CVS, Dollar General, Kroger, Pharmacy, KY State Hwy Patrol, Tires, Tourist Info Center/RVDump W: Laundry/Petrol ATC, Laundry/WiFi/London ATC		Other	E: Auto Services, Dollar General, Firestone, Grocery, U-Haul, Ky Splash Waterpark W: Laundry/WiFi/RVDump/Pilot TC, Wal-Mart sc		Food	W: Exxon, Marathon◊ E: Shoney's W: Burger King, Hardee's, Krystal, McDonald's, Shoney's, Waffle House, Wendy's
38		KY 192, Somerset Rd, London, Daniel Boone Pkwy	(1)		KY Welcome Center (NB) (RR, Phones, Picnic, Vend)		Lodg Other	W: Best Western, Comfort Inn, Super 8 E: Fox Inn Campground▲, IGA, Museum of Appalachia
	FStop Gas	E: Expressway Shell Auto Truck Stop E: BP◊, Citgo◊, Speedway◊			(EASTERN TIME ZONE)			W: Laundry/Kwik FC, Food Lion, ATMs
	Food	E: Burger King, Captain D's, Domino's Pizza, Huddle House, Krystal, Perkins, McDonald's, Ponderosa, Taco Bell			# KENTUCKY # TENNESSEE	117	TStop	TN 170, W Raccoon Valley Rd, Heiskell, to Powell E: Pilot Travel Center #403 (Scales)
	Lodg	E: Comfort Suites, Country Inn, Days Inn, Hampton Inn, Holiday Inn, Ramada			(EASTERN TIME ZONE)		Gas Food	E: BP◊ E: BurgerKing/Subway/Pilot TC
	TServ Med Other	E: CAT Truck Service, Western Star E: + Hospital E: Laundry/Shell, AdvanceAuto, Kroger, Wal-Mart sc, US Post Office	(161)	NOTE:	MM 161.5: Kentucky State Line TN Welcome Center (SB) (RR, Phones, Picnic, Vend)		Lodg Other	W: Valley Inn Motel E: WiFi/Pilot TC W: Volunteer RV Park▲, Escapees Raccoon Valley RV Park▲
(34)		Weigh Station (Both dir)	160	FStop	US 25W, TN 9, Jellico W: Shell	112	Gas	TN 131, Emory Rd, Powell E: BP◊, Chevron
29		US 25, US 25E, Hwy 770, Corbin		Gas	E: BP, Citgo, Exxon◊, Marathon W: BP		Food	W: Exxon, Shell◊ E: Buddy's BBQ, Krystal, McDonald's, Starbucks, Wendy's
	TStop	E: Pilot Travel Center #231 (Scales) (DAND), Corbin Travel Plaza/Citgo (Scales) W: Love's Travel Stop #321 (Scales)		Food	E: KFC, Rest/Jellico Motel, Subway/Exxon W: Arby's/Shell, Hardee's, Wendy's		Lodg	W: Hardee's, Shoney's, Waffle House E: Country Inn, Holiday Inn Express W: Comfort Inn
	Gas	E: BP, Murphy W: BP◊, Chevron◊, Shell◊		Lodg Med	E: Jellico Motel, Best Value Inn W: Days Inn W: + Hospital	110	Other	E: CVS, Ingles Callahan Dr, Knoxville
	Food	E: Subway/Pilot TC, Rest/FastFood/Corbin TP, Burger King, Huddle House, Shoney's, Taco Bell		Other NOTE:	W: to Indian Mountain State Park▲ MM 156: Steep Grade Next 4 mi		Gas	E: Coastal, Weigels W: BP
		W: Hardee's/Love's TS, Cracker Barrel, Krystal/BP, Sonny's BBQ, Taco Bell	156 144		Rarity Mountain Rd Stinking Creek Rd, Jacksboro		Food Lodg	E: Rest/Quality Inn W: Burger King, Chili's, McDonald's E: Knights Inn, Quality Inn, Rodeway Inn W: Scottish Inn
			141	FStop	TN 63, H Baker Hwy, Jacksboro, La Follette, Huntsville, Oneida W: Pilot Travel Center #224 (Scales)			

Page 328 ◊ = Regular Gas Stations with Diesel ▲ = RV Friendly Locations ♥ = Pet Friendly Locations
RED PRINT SHOWS LARGE VEHICLE PARKING/ACCESS ON SITE OR NEARBY BROWN PRINT SHOWS CAMPGROUNDS/RV PARKS

INTERSTATE 75 N/S

TENNESSEE

EXIT	
108	**Merchant Dr, to 25W, Knoxville**
Gas	E: BP◊, Citgo, Pilot◊, Texaco, Weigels
	W: Pilot/Conoco, Shell
Food	E: Applebee's, Cracker Barrel, Denny's, Hooters, Logan's Roadhouse, O'Charley's, Olive Garden, Ryan's Grill, Pizza Hut, Sagebrush, Starbucks, Waffle House
	W: Arby's, Bob Evans, Burger King, Great American Steak & Buffet, IHOP, McDonald's, Outback Steakhouse, Red Lobster, Subway, Waffle House
Lodg	E: Best Western, Comfort Inn, Days Inn, Hampton Inn, Howard Johnson, Ramada, Sleep Inn
	W: Comfort Suites, Econo Lodge, Clarion Inn, Family Inn, La Quinta Inn♥, Red Roof Inn♥, Super 8
Other	E: CVS, Ingles
	W: AdvanceAuto, Kroger, Walgreen's
NOTE:	I-640 Knoxville ByPass runs with I-75 below. Exit #'s follow I-640.
(107)	**Jct I-640E, Knoxville ByPass**
3	**TN 25W, Clinton Hwy, Clinton**
Gas	N: BP, Texaco
Food	N: Hardee's, KFC, Krystal, Long John Silver, Pizza Hut, Taco Bell, Wendy's
Other	N: CVS, Kmart, Kroger
3B	**Gap Rd NW, Knoxville (NB)**
(3A)	**Jct I-75N, to Lexington, I-275S, to Knoxville**
1	**TN 62, Western Ave**
Gas	N: Exxon◊, Marathon, RaceTrac, Shell
	S: BP, Texaco
Food	N: Golden Corral, Hardee's, Krystal, Ruby Tuesday, Shoney's, Taco Bell, Wendy's
	S: Hardee's, Krystal, Subway
TServ	E: Cummins Cumberland
Other	N: CVS, Kroger, Walgreen's
	S: Auto Services, US Post Office
NOTE:	I-640 Knoxville ByPass runs with I-75 above. Exit #'s follow I-640.
NOTE:	I-40 & I-75 below run together for 18 mi. Exit #'s follow I-40.
(385)	**Jct I-75N, Jct I-640E, to Lexington**
383	**Papermill Rd, TN 372, Knoxville**
Gas	S: Amoco, BP, Citgo, Pilot
Food	S: Bombay Bicycle Club, Burger King, Captain D's, IHOP, McDonald's, Pizza Hut, Waffle House, Western Sizzlin'
Lodg	N: Budget Inn, Holiday Inn
	S: Econo Lodge, Super 8
380	**US 11, US 70, West Hills**
Gas	S: BP, Citgo, Conoco, Pilot, Shell, Weigel's
Food	S: Arby's, Applebee's, BlackEyed Pea, Chili's, KFC, Krystal, Little Caesar's, Olive Garden, Texas Roadhouse
Lodg	S: Howard Johnson, Quality Inn, Super 8
Other	S: West Town Mall, Food Lion, K-Mart, Office Depot, PetSmart♥, U-Haul, Walgreen's, TN State Hwy Patrol Post
379A	**Walker Springs Rd, Gallaher View,**
379	**Walker Springs Rd, Gallaher View, Bridgewater Rd**
Gas	N: Exxon, Pilot, Shell
	S: BP, Pilot, Texaco

EXIT	
Food	N: McDonald's/Pilot
	S: Bennett's Pit BBQ, Burger King, Chuck E Cheese, Don Pablo, Logan's Roadhouse, Old Country Buffet, Ryan's Grill, Shoney's
Lodg	N: Red Carpet Inn
	S: Holiday Inn, Scottish Inn
Other	N: Sam's Club, Wal-Mart sc
	S: AutoZone, Auto Services, Goodyear, Pharmacy, Auto Dealer
378AB	**Cedar Bluff Rd, Knoxville**
378	**Cedar Bluff Rd, Knoxville**
Gas	N: Amoco, Pilot, Texaco
	S: Exxon
Food	N: Arby's, Burger King, Cracker Barrel, KFC, Long John Silver, McDonald's, Pizza Hut, Waffle House, Wendy's
	S: Applebee's, Bob Evans, Carraba's, Corky's Ribs & BBQ, Denny's, Fazoli's, Hops, IHOP, Outback Steakhouse
Lodg	N: Econo Lodge, Hampton Inn, Holiday Inn, Ramada
	S: Best Western, Comfort Inn, Courtyard, Extended Stay America, Jameson Inn, La Quinta Inn♥, Red Roof Inn♥, Sleep Inn
Med	N: + Hospital
Other	N: ATMs, Banks, Food Lion, Walgreen's
	S: ATMs, Banks, Auto Services, Best Buy, Carmike Cinema, Circuit City, Celebration Station, Lowe's, Staples, Walgreen's
376B	**TN 162S, Maryville (EB)**
376A	**TN 162N, to Oakridge (WB)**
376	**TN 162S, Maryville (EB)**
374	**TN 131, Lovell Rd, Knoxville**
TStop	N: Travel Center of America #13/BP (Scales)
	S: Pilot Travel Center #270 (Scales)
Gas	N: Texaco
	S: Citgo, Pilot Food Mart, Speedway
Food	N: CountryPride/FastFood/TA TC, McDonald's, Taco Bell, Waffle House
	S: Wendy's/Pilot TC, Arby's, Chili's, Krystal, IHOP, Olive Garden, Shoney's, Texas Roadhouse, Wasabi Japanese, Rest/D Inn
Lodg	N: Best Western, Knights Inn, La Quinta Inn♥, Travelodge/TA TC, Vista Inn
	S: Days Inn, Homewood Suites, Motel 6♥, Springhill Suites
TServ	N: TA TC/Tires
Other	N: Laundry/CB/BarbSh/WiFi/TA TC, Buddy Gregg Motorhomes
	S: WiFi/Pilot TC, Auto Dealers, ATMs, Banks, Target, Wal-Mart sc
373	**Campbell Station Rd, Farragut**
FStop	S: Pilot Food Mart #221
Gas	N: Shell◊, Marathon
	S: BP
Food	S: Cracker Barrel, Hardee's, Wendy's/Pilot
Lodg	N: Comfort Suites, Country Inn, Super 8
	S: Baymont Inn, Holiday Inn Express
Other	N: Buddy Gregg Motorhomes▲
	S: Gander Mountain
(372)	**Weigh Station (Both dir)**
369	**Watt Rd, W Knoxville**
TStop	N: Flying J Travel Plaza #5034/Conoco (Scales)

◊ = Regular Gas Stations with Diesel   ▲ = RV Friendly Locations   ♥ = Pet Friendly Locations

RED PRINT SHOWS LARGE VEHICLE PARKING/ACCESS ON SITE OR NEARBY   BROWN PRINT SHOWS CAMPGROUNDS/RV PARKS

EXIT		TENNESSEE
	TStop	S: Petro Stopping Center (Scales), Travel Center of America #107/BP (Scales)
	Food	N: Cookery/FastFood/Flying J TP
		S: IronSkillet/Petro SC, Perkins/B King/PizzaHut/TA TC
	TWash	N: Fast Point Truck Wash
		S: Blue Beacon TW/Petro SC
	TServ	N: Freightliner of Knoxville, Speedco
		S: Petro SC/Tires, TA TC/Tires
	Other	N: Laundry/WiFi/RVDump/LP/FJ TP, Shadrack Watersport & RV's
		S: Laundry/WiFi/RVDump/Petro SC, Laundry/CB/WiFi/TA TC, Fireworks
(368/84A)		Jct I-75S, to Chattanooga
		Jct I-40E, I-75N, to Knoxville
(84B)		Jct I-40W, to Nashville (Left exit)
	NOTE:	I-40 & I-75 above run together for 18 mi. Exit #'s follow I-40.
81		US 321, TN 73, Lenoir City, Oak Ridge, Great Smoky Mtns Nat'l Park
	Gas	E: BP, Exxon, Mobil, Shell, Murphy
		W: Citgo◊, Shell◊, Mobil
	Food	E: Burger King, Buddy's BBQ, Chili's, Cracker Barrel, KFC, McDonald's, Shoney's, Waffle House, Wendy's, Zaxby's, Rest/KI, Subway/Exxon
		W: Ruby Tuesday
	Lodg	E: Days Inn, Hampton Inn, Holiday Inn Express, Inn of Lenoir, Kings Inn, Super 8
		W: Comfort Inn, Econo Lodge, Ramada Ltd
	Other	E: Home Depot, Wal-Mart sc, Radio Shack, to Ft Loudon Dam, Smoky Mtns Nat'l Park, to app 18 mi Smoky Mountain Harley Davidson
76		TN 324, Hotchkiss Valley Rd E, Sugar Limb Rd, Lenoir City
	Other	E: to Watts Bar Lake
		W: to TN Valley Winery
72		TN 72, Loudon
	Gas	E: BP, Shell◊
		W: Citgo
	Food	E: McDonald/BP, Wendy/Shell, Hardee's
	Lodg	E: Country Inn, Super 8 ♥
		W: Best Value Inn ♥
	Other	E: Express RV Park▲
68		TN 323, Pond Creek Rd, Loudon, to Philadelphia
	Gas	E: BP◊, Sunoco
	Other	E: Sweetwater Valley Cheese Farm
62		TN 322, Oakland Rd, Sweetwater
	Gas	E: Phillips 66
		W: 48's Fireworks
	Food	E: Dave's Rest, Dinner Bell Rest
	Other	W: Sweetwater KOA▲, Trailer Center
60		TN 68, Lost Sea Pike, Sweetwater, to Spring City, Lost Sea
	FStop	W: Kangaroo Express #3599/Citgo
	Gas	E: BP, Marathon, RaceWay, Shell
		W: BP◊, Conoco
	Food	E: Burger King, Huddle House, KFC, McDonald's, Bradley's Pit BBQ, Wendy's
		W: Aunt M's Fr Chicken/Kangaroo, Cracker Barrel, Hardee's
	Lodg	E: Best Value Inn, Comfort Inn, Days Inn, Knights Inn, Super 8
		W: Best Western, Magnuson Hotel, Quality Inn
	Other	E: to Lost Sea Underground Lake
		W: Flea Market, Tourist Info, Tellico Plains KOA▲

Personal Notes

EXIT		TENNESSEE
56		TN 309, Union Grove Rd, Niota
	TStop	E: PTP/Crazy Ed's/BP (Scales)
	Food	E: Rest/Crazy Ed's, Front Porch Rest
	TServ	E: Crazy Ed's/Tires
	Other	E: TN Country Campground▲
52		Hwy 305, Mt Verd Rd, Athens
	Gas	E: BP, Citgo
		W: BP, Exxon
	Food	E: Subway
	Lodg	E: Heritage Motel
		W: Ramada Inn ♥, Travelodge
	Other	E: Overniter RV Park▲, Mayfield Dairy Tour
49		TN 30, Athens, to Decatur
	Gas	E: BP, Conoco, Kangaroo, RaceWay, Shell◊
		W: Shell
	Food	E: Applebee's, Burger King, Hardee's, KFC, McDonald's, Krystal, Ruby Tuesday, Shoney's, Steak n Shake, Subway, Waffle House, Wendy's, Western Sizzlin
		W: Cracker Barrel
	Lodg	E: Days Inn, Econo Lodge, Hampton Inn, Holiday Inn Express, Homestead Inn, Knights Inn, Motel 6 ♥, Super 8
		W: Homestead Inn
	Med	E: + Hospital
	Other	E: Athens I-75 Campground & Park▲
(45)		Rest Area (Both dir) (CLOSED) (RR, Phone, Picnic, Vend, Info)
42		TN 39, Riceville Rd, Calhoun
	Gas	E: Citgo
	Lodg	E: Relax Inn, Rice Inn
	Other	E: Mouse Creek Campgound▲

EXIT		TENNESSEE
36		TN 163, Big Spring Calhoun Rd, Lamontville Rd, to Calhoun
33		TN 308, Lauderdale Memorial Hwy, Charleston
	TStop	W: Ponderosa Truck Plaza/Shell (Scales), Love's Travel Stop
	Gas	E: Citgo
	Food	W: Rest/Ponderosa TP, McDonald's/Subway/Love's TP
	TServ	W: Ponderosa TP/Tires
	Other	E: Exit 33 Campground▲
		W: Laundry/Ponderosa TP, WiFi/Love's TS
27		Sgt Paul Huff Pkwy, Cleveland
	FStop	W: BP
	Gas	E: Phillips 66, Murphy
		W: Exxon, Texaco
	Food	E: Applebee's, Chili's, CiCi's, Golden Corral, IHOP, McDonald's, O'Charley's, Outback Steakhouse, Panera Bread, Ryan's Grill, Steak 'n Shake, Taco Bell
		W: Denny's, Hardee's, Waffle House
	Lodg	E: Jameson Inn
		W: Comfort Inn, Hampton Inn, Quality Inn, Ramada, Royal Inn, Super 8
	TServ	E: Cleveland Tire Center
	Other	E: AutoZone, CVS, Dollar Tree, Food Lion, Goodyear, Home Depot, Lowe's, PetCo ♥, Staples, Wal-Mart sc, Grocery, Bradley Square Mall
		W: Target
25		TN 60, 25th St NW, Georgetown Rd, Cleveland, to Dayton
	FStop	E: Orbit Chevron
	Gas	E: BP, Citgo, RaceWay, Texaco◊
		W: Shell
	Food	W: Bojangles, Burger King, Cracker Barrel, Hardee's, McDonald's, Waffle House, Wendy's, Zaxby's
		W: Perkins, Uncle Bud's Catfish
	Lodg	E: Colonial Inn, Days Inn, Econo Lodge, Economy Inn, Fairfield Inn, Howard Johnson, Knights Inn, Quality Inn, Red Carpet Inn, Travel Inn
		W: Baymont Inn ♥, Economy Inn ♥, Holiday Inn, Wingate Inn
	Med	E: + Hospital
	Other	E: Tourist Info, Golf Course, CarWash, Lee Univ, Comm College
(23)		Weigh Station (NB)
20		US 74, TN 311 to US 64 ByPass E, to Cleveland
	Gas	E: Exxon, Shell
		W: Exxon◊, Horizon◊
	Food	E: Golden Corral, Hardee's, McDonald's, Subway, Taco Bell
	Other	W: Chattanooga N/Cleveland KOA▲
(16)		Scenic View (SB)
(13)		Weigh Station (SB)
11		US 11E N, US 64E, Ooltewah
	Gas	E: BP, Chevron, Citgo, RaceWay, Shell, Murphy
		W: BP◊, Kangaroo
	Food	E: Arby's, Burger King, Cracker Barrel, Hardee's, McDonald's, Subway, Taco Bell, Quiznos, Wendy's, Zaxby's
		W: Krystal, Waffle House
	Lodg	E: Hotel
		W: Super 8 ♥
	Med	E: + Family Walk-In Medical Center

◊ = Regular Gas Stations with Diesel ▲ = RV Friendly Locations ♥ = Pet Friendly Locations
RED PRINT SHOWS LARGE VEHICLE PARKING/ACCESS ON SITE OR NEARBY BROWN PRINT SHOWS CAMPGROUNDS/RV PARKS

INTERSTATE 75 N/S

EXIT	TENNESSEE
Other	E: Grocery, Publix, Wal-Mart sc W: to Harrison Bay State Park▲
9	Volunteer Ordinance Rd
7	Lee Hwy, to US 64W, US 11S, TN 317, to Chattanooga (SB)
Gas	E: Exxon W: Chevron, Shell
Food	W: Taco Bell, Waffle House
Lodg	W: AmeriSuites, Best Inn, Best Western, Comfort Inn, Days Inn, Econo Lodge, Motel 6♥
Other	W: Harley Davidson
7A	Lee Hwy, TN 317E, to Summit, Collegedale (NB)
7B	Bonny Oaks Dr, US 64, US 11, TN 317W, Chattanooga (NB)
5	Shallowford Rd, Hamilton Place Blvd, to US 11, US 64, Chattanooga
Gas	W: BP, Citgo, Exxon, Shell
Food	E: Arby's, CiCi's, Famous Dave's BBQ, Hops Grill, Krystal, Logan's Roadhouse, McDonald's, Old Country Buffet, Romano's Macaroni Grill, Red Lobster, Steak 'n Shake, Starbucks, Taco Bell W: Applebee's, Cracker Barrel, Golden Corral, KFC, Domino's, McDonald's, O'Charley's, Pizza Hut, Rio Bravo, Sonic, Shoney's, Subway, Waffle House, Wendy's
Lodg	E: Comfort Suites, Courtyard, Quality Inn, Wingate Inn W: Country Inn, Days Inn, Fairfield Inn, Guesthouse Inn, Hampton Inn, Hilton Garden Inn, Homewood Suites, Holiday Inn, Knights Inn, La Quinta Inn♥, Ramada Ltd, Red Roof Inn, Sleep Inn
Med	W: + Hospital
Other	E: ATMs, Auto Service, B&N, Best Buy, Circuit City, Firestone, Home Depot, Lowe's Office Depot, PetSmart♥, Staples, Walgreen's, Wal-Mart sc, Grocery W: ATMs, CVS, Grocery, Goodyear, Univ of TN/Chattanooga
4A	Hamilton Place Blvd (NB, diff reacc)
Food	E: Bonefish Grill, Carrabba's, DQ, Grady's, Hardee's, Outback Steakhouse, Olive Garden, Red Lobster, Ruby Tuesday, TGI Friday
Lodg	E: Courtyard
Med	E: + Physicians Walk-In Clinic
Other	E: ATMs, Firestone, Staples, World Market, Hamilton Place Mall, Tourist Info
4	TN 153N, to US 64, US 11
Other	W: to Lovell Field Airport✈
3B	TN 320W, E Brainerd Rd
3A	TN 320W, E Brainerd Rd
3	TN 320W, E Brainerd Rd (SB)
Gas	E: AmocoBP
Food	E: Baskin Robbins
Other	E: Concord Public Golf Course W: to Lovell Field Airport✈
(2)	Jct I-24W, to I-59, Lookout Mtn, Chattanooga, Nashville (NB, Left Ex)
(1)	TN Welcome Center (NB) (RR, Phones, Picnic, Vend)
1B	US 41W, US 46, Chattanooga

EXIT	TN / GA
1A	US 41, US 46, Chattanooga
1	US 41, US 46, Chattanooga
Gas	E: BP, Exxon, Texaco W: Chevron, Conoco◊, Shell◊
Food	E: Country Vittles Buffet, Trip's Seafood W: Arby's, Burger King, Cracker Barrel, Hardee's, Krystal, Long John Silver, McDonald's, Pizza Hut, Shoney's, Subway, Taco Bell, Waffle House
Lodg	E: Best Value Inn, Comfort Inn, Crown Inn, Econo Lodge, Hawthorne Suites, Howard Johnson, Knights Inn, Ramada Ltd W: Best Inn, Days Inn, Fairfield Inn, Holiday Inn Express, Super 8, Superior Creek Lodge, Waverly Hotel
Other	E: Grocery, CVS, Flea Market, Shipp's RV Center▲ / Camping World W: U-Haul, Best Holiday Trav-L Park▲

(EASTERN TIME ZONE)
⊙ TENNESSEE
⊙ GEORGIA
(EASTERN TIME ZONE)

NOTE:	MM 355: Tennessee State Line
353	GA 146, Cloud Springs Rd, Ringgold, to Rossville, Ft Oglethorpe
Gas	E: BP, Chevron W: BP◊, Shell
Food	W: Subway/Shell
Lodg	E: Knights Inn
TServ	E: Freightliner
Other	W: Island Joe's Food & Fun, Antique Mall
(352)	GA Welcome Center (SB) (RR, Phones, Picnic, Vend, RVDump)
350	GA 2, Battlefield Pkwy, Ringgold, to Fort Oglethorpe
Gas	E: BP◊, Kangaroo, W: Conoco◊, RaceTrac, Murphy
Med	E: + Hospital
Other	W: Wal-Mart sc, Chattanooga S KOA▲
348	GA 151, Alabama Hwy, Ringgold, to LaFayette
FStop	E: 10/20 Fuel Center #141 W: Shell Fuel Center #1027
Gas	E: Conoco W: Chevron, Exxon, Texaco
Food	E: Aunt Effie's, Cracker Barrel, KFC, McDonald's, Pizza Hut, Subway, Taco Bell, Waffle House W: Hardee's, Krystal, Ruby Tuesday, Wendy's
Lodg	E: Best Western, Days Inn, Holiday Inn Express, Super 8 W: Comfort Inn, Red Roof Inn
TServ	E: JTS Truck Sales W: Peterbilt of Lookout Mountain, Yates, Freightliner
Other	E: AdvanceAuto, CVS, Family Dollar, Grocery, N GA RV Country, All Aboard RV & Trailer Depot W: Playtime Amusement Park/Holcomb Rd, Northgate RV Center, Auto Dealers
345	US 41, US 76, GA 3, Ringgold, Tunnel Hill
TStop	E: AmBest/Choo Choo Truck Plaza, Cochran's Travel Center/Exxon (Scales)

◊ = Regular Gas Stations with Diesel ▲ = RV Friendly Locations ♥ = Pet Friendly Locations
RED PRINT SHOWS LARGE VEHICLE PARKING/ACCESS ON SITE OR NEARBY BROWN PRINT SHOWS CAMPGROUNDS/RV PARKS

EXIT	GEORGIA
Gas	E: BP
	W: Kangaroo
Food	E: Rest/Cochran's TC
	W: Subway/Kangaroo, Waffle House
Lodg	W: Friendship Inn
TWash	E: Choo Choo TW
TServ	E: Cochran's TC/Tires
Other	E: U-Haul
	W: Bell's Towing, Bell's Wrecker Svc
(343)	**Weigh Station (Both dir)**
341	**GA 201, N Varnell Rd, Tunnel Hill, Varnell**
Gas	W: Chevron, Shell
Other	W: Assorted Carpet Outlets
336	**US 41, US 76, GA 3, Chattanooga Rd, Dalton, Rocky Face**
FStop	E: Fast Food & Fuel/Conoco (GA 71N & US 76 N ByPass)
Gas	E: Chevron, RaceTrac, Shell, Murphy
	W: BP◊, Exxon
Food	E: Blimpie/Chevron, Mr Biscuit, Waffle House
	W: Denny's, Los Pablos, Wendy's, Rest/BW
Lodg	E: Econo Lodge, Howard Johnson
	W: Best Western, Motel 6♥, Royal Inn, Super 8
Med	E: + Hamilton Healthcare Hospital
Other	E: Home Depot, Wal-Mart sc
	W: GA State Hwy Patrol Post
333	**GA 52, GA 71, Walnut Ave, Dalton**
Gas	E: BP◊, Chevron, Exxon, RaceTrac◊, Kroger
	W: Shell
Food	E: Applebee's, Burger King, ChickFilA, CiCi's, Cracker Barrel, Fuddruckers, IHOP, Long John Silver, Longhorn Steakhouse, McDonald's, KFC, Outback Steakhouse, O'Charley's, Shoney's, Steak 'n Shake, Taco Bell, Waffle House, Wendy's
	W: Chili's, Red Lobster
Lodg	E: America's Best Inn, Days Inn, Hampton Inn, Travelodge
	W: Comfort Inn, Country Inn, Courtyard, Jameson Inn, La Quinta Inn, Ramada Inn, Wellesley Inn, Wingate Inn
Other	E: Kmart, Kroger, Walgreen's, Tanger Outlets, Harley Davidson
	W: NW Georgia Trade Center
328	**SR 3 Conn, to US 41, S Dalton ByPass, Dalton**
TStop	E: Pilot Travel Center #319 (Scales)
Gas	E: Food Mart/BP◊, Exxon
Food	E: Arby's/TJCinn/Pilot TC, Blimpie/BP, Country Kitchen, Waffle House, Wendy's
Lodg	E: Super 8♥
Other	E: WiFi/Pilot TC, Comm'l Driver License Facility
	W: Various Carpet Outlets
326	**Carbondale Rd, CR 665, to US 41N, GA 3, Carbondale, Dalton**
FStop	W: Fast Food & Fuel #175/66
TStop	E: Pilot Travel Center #421 (Scales)
Gas	E: Chevron◊
	W: BP, Exxon
Food	E: McDonald's/Subway/Pilot TC, BBQ, Pizza
Lodg	E: Country Boy Inn
TWash	E: Pilot TC

EXIT	GEORGIA
TServ	E: Pilot TC/Tires
	W: Cummins South
Other	E: Laundry/WiFi/RVDump/Pilot TC
320	**GA 136, Hill City Rd, Resaca, to LaFayette**
TStop	E: Flying J Travel Plaza #5470/Conoco (Scales)
Food	E: Rest/FastFood/FJ TP
Tires	E: A&J Tire Svc
TWash	E: Dependable TW
TServ	E: Reece Truck Service/Tires
Other	E: Laundry/BarbSh/WiFi/RVDump/LP/FJ TP, C&C Electronics/CB
(320)	**Rest Area (SB)**
	(RR, Phones, Picnic, Vend, RVDump)
318	**US 41, GA 3, Dixie Hwy, Calhoun**
TStop	E: WilcoHess Travel Plaza #3005 (Scales)
Gas	W: Shell◊
Food	E: DQ/Wendy's/WilcoHess TP, Hardee's, Huddle House
	W: Chuckwagon Rest, Rest/Duffy's Motel
Lodg	E: Best Western, Knights Inn
	W: Best Inn, Budget Inn, Duffy's Motel, Smith Motel, Super 8
Other	E: Laundry/WilcoHess TP
317	**GA 225, Chatsworth Hwy NE, Calhoun, Chatsworth**
Gas	W: BP
Lodg	W: Express Inn
315	**GA 156, Red Bud Rd, Calhoun**
Gas	E: BP, Citgo, Kangaroo
	W: BP◊, Liberty, Shell
Food	E: Shoney's, Subway, Waffle House
	W: Arby's
Lodg	E: Ramada Inn, Scottish Inn
	W: Days Inn, Oglethorpe Inn
Med	W: + Gordon Hospital
Other	E: ATM, Auto Service, Food Lion, Calhoun KOA▲
312	**GA 53, Fairmont Hwy, Calhoun to Fairmont, Rome**
Gas	E: BP, Shell
	W: Chevron◊, Kangaroo, RaceWay, Murphy, Kroger
Food	E: Cracker Barrel, Denny's, Rest/Budget Host Inn
	W: Arby's, Bojangle's, Burger King, Captain D's, Checkers, DQ, Golden Corral, Hickory House BBQ, Huddle House, IHOP, KFC, Krystal, Long John Silver, McDonald's Pizza Hut, Ruby Tuesday, Subway, Taco Bell, Waffle House, Wendy's
Lodg	E: Budget Host Inn, Country Inn, Quality Inn
	W: Comfort Inn, Days Inn, Hampton Inn, Holiday Inn Express, Jameson Inn, Royal Inn
Other	E: Prime Outlets, GA State Hwy Patrol
	W: ATMs, AutoZone, Auto Dealers, CVS, Dollar General, Goodyear, Home Depot, Kroger, Office Depot, Wal-Mart sc
(308)	**Rest Area (NB)**
	(RR, Phone, Picnic, Vend, RVDump)
306	**GA 140, Folsom Rd, Adairsville, to Summerville, Rome**
TStop	E: Patty's Truck Stop (Scales), QT #757 (Scales)
	W: All American Truck Stop (Scales)
Gas	E: Cowboys◊, Shell
	W: BP◊, Chevron, Exxon

EXIT	GEORGIA
Food	E: Rest/Patty's TS, Cracker Barrel, Wendy's
	W: Rest/All Amer TS, Bamboo Garden, Burger King, Hardee's, McDonald's, BBQ, Taco Bell, Subway, Waffle House, Wendy's, Zaxby's
Lodg	W: Best Western, Comfort Inn, Ramada, Relax Inn
TWash	E: Patty's TS
	W: All Amer TS
TServ	E: Patty's TS/Tires
Other	E: Laundry/Patty's TS, Adairsville Towing & Auto
	W: Harvest Moon RV Park▲
296	**CR 630, Cassville-White Rd, Cartersville, White**
TStop	E: Travel Center of America/Exxon (Scales), Pilot Travel Center #67 (Scales) (DAND)
Gas	E: Pure, Texaco
	W: Chevron, Citgo, Shell
Food	E: CountryPride/BurgerKing/Popeye/P Hut/T Bell/TA TC, McDonald's/Subway/Pilot TC, Country BBQ & Grill
	W: Waffle House
Lodg	E: Sleep Inn, Red Carpet Inn
	W: Best Value Inn, Budget Host Inn, Howard Johnson Express Inn♥, Travelodge
TWash	E: Pilot TC
TServ	E: TA TC/Tires
Other	E: Laundry/BarbSh/WiFi/Med/RVDump/TA TC, Laundry/WiFi/Pilot TC, CB Shop
	W: Cartersville/Cassville-White KOA▲
293	**US 411, GA 61, Chatsworth Hwy, Cartersville, to White**
Gas	E: Citgo, Chevron, Texaco
	W: Chevron◊, Citgo
Food	W: Cafe, Slopes BBQ, Waffle House
Lodg	E: Courtesy Inn, Holiday Inn, Scottish Inn
Other	W: GA State Hwy Patrol Post
290	**GA 20, Canton Hwy, Rome, Canton**
FStop	E: Kangaroo Express #3675
Gas	E: Chevron◊, Exxon
	W: BP, Shell
Food	E: Arby's, McDonald's, Wendy's
	W: Cracker Barrel, BBQ, Shoney's, Subway, Waffle House
Lodg	E: Best Western, Comfort Inn, Country Inn, Econo Lodge, Ramada, Super 8
	W: Days Inn, Hampton Inn, Motel 6♥
Med	W: + Hospital
Other	E: COE Camping
	W: CAMPING▲
288	**GA 113, Main St, Cartersville**
FStop	W: Cowboy's Food Mart #24/BP
Gas	W: Amoco, Exxon◊
Food	W: Applebee's, Blimpie, Burger King, ChickFilA, McDonald's, Mrs Winner's, Krystal, Pizza Hut, Subway, Waffle House
Lodg	W: Knights Inn, Quality Inn
Other	W: Kroger
285	**CR 633, Red Top Mountain Rd, Cartersville, Emerson**
Gas	E: Shell
Lodge	E: Red Top Mountain Lodge
Other	E: to appr 1,5 mi Red Top Mountain State Park▲
283	**CR 397, Emerson-Allatoona Rd**
Other	E: to appr 2 mi Allatoona Landing Campground▲

◊ = Regular Gas Stations with Diesel   ▲ = RV Friendly Locations   ♥ = Pet Friendly Locations
RED PRINT SHOWS LARGE VEHICLE PARKING/ACCESS ON SITE OR NEARBY   BROWN PRINT SHOWS CAMPGROUNDS/RV PARKS

EXIT		GEORGIA
278		**CR 633, Glade Rd, Acworth**
	Gas	E: BP, Shell
		W: Chevron, Citgo
	Food	E: Subway/BP
		W: Burger King, Country Club Café, KFC, Krystal, Pizza Hut, Subway, Taco Bell, Waffle House, Western Sizzlin
	Lodg	E: Guest House Inn
		W: Red Roof Inn ♥
	Other	E: Old 41 Campground▲, COE/Clark Creek North Campground▲, COE/McKinney Campground▲
		W: AutoZone, Big Lots, CVS, Grocery, Ingles, Kmart, NAPA, Radio Shack
277		**GA 92, Alabama Rd, Acworth**
	Gas	E: BP, Exxon◊, RaceTrac, Shell◊
		W: Chevron◊, Shell◊
	Food	E: Hardee's, Shoney's, Waffle House
		W: McDonald's, Mex Rest, Waffle House, Wendy's, Zaxby's
	Lodg	E: Comfort Suites, Holiday Inn Express, Ramada
		W: Best Western, Days Inn, Econo Lodge, Quality Inn
	Other	E: COE/Payne Campground▲
		W: CVS, Publix
273		**Wade Green Rd, to GA 92, Kennesaw**
	Gas	E: BP, Citgo◊, RaceTrac
		W: Conoco, Shell
	Food	E: Arby's, Burger King, China King, Mrs Winner, McDonald's, Subway, Waffle House
		W: Blimpie/Shell
	Lodg	E: Rodeway Inn, Travelodge
	Other	E: Publix, Pharmacy, Tires
271		**Chastain Rd, to I-575N**
	Gas	E: Pacer Fuel/Chevron
		W: Citgo, Shell◊
	Food	E: Cracker Barrel, O'Charley's, Panda Express
		W: Arby's, Waffle House, Wendy's
	Lodg	E: Best Western, Comfort Inn, Fairfield Inn, Extended Stay America, Residence Inn
		W: Country Inn, La Quinta Inn, Spring Hill Suites, Sun Suites
	Med	E: + Physician's Immed Med Clinic
	Other	E: Goodyear, Wal-Mart, Mall
		W: Cobb Co McCollum Field ✈
269		**GA 5, to US 41, Barrett Pkwy, Kennesaw, to Marietta**
	FStop	E: Shell Food Mart
	Gas	E: Chevron
		W: BP, Exxon
	Food	E: Applebee's, Atlanta Bread, Burger King, Fuddrucker's, McDonald's, Longhorn Steakhouse, Olive Garden, Piccadilly's, Red Lobster, Shoney's, Starbucks, Smokey Bones BBQ, Waffle House
		W: Chili's, Golden Corral, Joe's Crab Shack, Outback Steakhouse, Roadhouse Grill, TGI Friday, Starbucks, Steak 'n Shake
	Lodg	E: Econo Lodge, Holiday Inn Express, Red Roof Inn ♥, Super 8
		W: Comfort Inn, Days Inn, Hampton Inn, Hilton Garden Inn, Sleep Inn, Town Place Suites, Quality Inn, Wingate Inn
	Med	W: + Hospital
	Other	E: ATMs, Big 10 Tire, B&N, Firestone, Home Depot, Publix, Town Center at Cobb Mall

EXIT		GEORGIA
	Other	W: ATMs, Auto Dealers, Best Buy, Borders, Office Depot, Target, Cobb Place Shopping Center
(268)		**Jct I-575N, GA 5N, to Canton**
267A		**GA 5N, Canton Rd**
267B		**to US 41S, GA 5S, Marietta**
	Med	W: + Hospital
265		**GA 120 Lp, N Marietta Pkwy, Marietta, Roswell**
	Gas	W: Chevron, Shell◊
	Food	W: Arby's, Bojangles, Sonny's BBQ
	Lodg	W: Budget Inn, Crown Inn, Days Inn, Spinnaker Resort, Sun Inn, Travel Motel
	Med	W: + Hospital, + Medical Care Center
	Other	E: Nat'l Bus Sales
		W: to WhiteWater Park, American Adventure Amusement Park
263		**120W, Marietta, S Marietta Pkwy, 120E, Roswell, Southern Poly**
	Gas	E: Chevron◊, QT
		W: QT, Exxon◊, RaceTrac
	Food	W: Applebee's, Captain D's, China Kitchen, Chili's, DQ, Hardee's, Piccadilly's, Subway
	Lodg	W: Best Western, Fairfield Inn, Hampton Inn, Super 8, Ramada Ltd, Regency Inn, Wyndham
	Other	W: Brookwood RV Park▲, U-Haul
261		**GA 280, Delk Rd, Lockheed, to Dobbins AFB**
	Gas	E: Exxon◊, RaceTrac, Shell
		W: BP, Chevron, Shell
	Food	E: Denny's, Hardee's, McDonald's, KFC, Ruby Tuesday, Spaghetti Warehouse, Texas BBQ, Waffle House
		W: Cracker Barrel, China Chef, Mexican Rest, Waffle House
	Lodg	E: Budget Inn, Courtyard, Drury Inn, Motel 6 ♥, Scottish Inn, Sleep Inn, Super 8, Travelers Inn
		W: Best Inn, Comfort Inn, Days Inn, Fairfield Inn, Holiday Inn, La Quinta Inn ♥, Wingate Inn
	Other	E: ATM, Grocery
		W: RVs n Such
260		**CR 1720, Windy Hill Rd, Smyrna**
	Gas	E: BP, Shell
		W: Citgo, Shell, Texaco
	Food	E: Deli, Fuddrucker's, Mrs Winner, Pappasito Cantina, Pappadeaux Seafood, Starbucks, Subway, TGI Friday
		W: Arby's, ChickFilA, McDonald's, Popeye, Waffle House, Wendy's, $3 Cafe
	Lodg	E: Crown Plaza, Econo Lodge, Extended Stay, Hilton Garden Inn, Hyatt Regency ♥, Marriott
		W: Best Western, Country Inn, Days Inn, Courtyard, DoubleTree Hotel, Masters Inn, Radisson, Red Roof Inn ♥
	Med	W: + Kennestone Hospital
	Other	E: CVS, FedEx Kinko's
		W: Best Buy, FedEx Kinko's, Target
(259)		**Jct I-285, E-Augusta, W-Birmingham**
(259A)		**Jct I-285E, Atlanta ByPass, to Augusta, Greenville (SB)**
(259B)		**Jct I-285W, Atlanta ByPass, to Birmingham, Montgomery (SB)**
NOTE:		All through trucks MUST take I-285 around Atlanta. West ByPass is shorter.

EXIT		GEORGIA
258		**Akers Mill Rd, Cumberland Blvd**
	Food	W: Hooter's, Longhorn Steakhouse, Subway
	Lodg	W: Homewood Suites, Embassy Suites, Residence Hotel, Sheraton
	Other	W: Galleria Specialty Mall, AMC 15, Cumberland Mall, Cobb Co Conv & Visitor Center, Costco, Office Max, PetSmart ♥, UPS Store
256		**to US 41, Mt Paran Rd, CR 624, GA 3, US 41, Northside Pkwy**
	Med	W: + Hospital
255		**to US 41, West Paces Ferry Rd, Northside Pkwy**
	Gas	E: Chevron, Shell◊, BP
		W: Exxon
	Food	E: ChickFilA, China Moon, DQ, McDonald's Steak 'n Shake, Starbucks
	Med	W: + Hospital
	Other	E: Publix
254		**Moores Mill Rd**
252		**Howell Mill Rd, to US 41, GA 3**
252B		**Howell Mill Rd, to US 41, GA 3**
	Gas	E: Exxon, Shell◊
		W: Shell
	Food	E: ChickFilA, Domino's, Hardee's, McDonald's
		W: Arby's, Einstein Bros, KFC, Long John Silver, Piccadilly, Subway, Taco Bell, Waffle House, Wendy's, US BBQ
	Lodg	E: Budget Inn
		W: Castlegate Hotel, Holiday Inn
	Med	E: + Hospital
	Other	E: Grocery, Goodyear, Office Depot, Pharmacy, PetSmart ♥
		W: Kroger, Firestone, Wal-Mart sc
252A		**US 41, GA 3, Northside Dr, Ga Dome**
	Gas	W: BP, Shell
	Food	W: Hickory BBQ, Krystal, McDonald's, Waffle House
	Lodg	W: Days Inn
(251)		**Jct I-85N, Greeneville, to I-75N, to Chattanooga, TN (SB Left Exit)**
250		**Williams St, 10th St NW (NB) 17th St NW, Techwood Dr (SB)**
	Lodg	E: Hampton Inn, Residence Inn
		W: Courtyard, Sleep Inn, Travelodge
	Other	W: Ga Inst of Technology
249D		**US 29, US 278, Linden Ave, Spring St, 10th St, to US 19, 228**
	Gas	E: BP, Chevron
	Food	E: Checker's, Pizza Hut
		W: McDonald's
	Lodg	E: Fairfield Inn, Regency Suites, Residence Inn
		W: Comfort Inn, Courtyard, Holiday Inn Express
	Med	E: + Crawford Long Hospital
	Other	E: to Civic Center
249C		**Downtown Atlanta, Williams St, Ga Dome, Aquarium (SB)**
249B		**Pine St, Peachtree St NE, Atlanta Civic Center (NB)**
249A		**Courtland St, Baker St (SB)**
	Other	W: GA State Univ
248D		**Ellis St, Jesse Hill Dr, JW Dobbs Ave (SB)**

◊ = Regular Gas Stations with Diesel   ▲ = RV Friendly Locations   ♥ = Pet Friendly Locations

RED PRINT SHOWS LARGE VEHICLE PARKING/ACCESS ON SITE OR NEARBY   BROWN PRINT SHOWS CAMPGROUNDS/RV PARKS

EXIT	GEORGIA
248C	Freedom Pkwy, Carter Center, International Blvd (NB)
Med	E: + Atlanta Medical Center
248B	Edgewood Ave, Auburn Ave, Butler St, JW Dobbs Ave (NB)
Med	E: + Grady Memorial Hospital
248A	Martin Luther King Jr Dr, State Capitol, Stadium (SB)
(247)	Jct I-20, E-Augusta, W-Birmingham (SB-E Left Lane, NB-W-Left Lane)
246	Central Ave, Georgia Ave, Fulton St Abernathy Blvd, Turner Field
Gas	E: BP
Lodg	E: Hampton Inn, Holiday Inn
Other	E: to Stadium
	W: to Coliseum, GA State Univ
245	Washington St, Ormond St (NB)
Lodg	E: Comfort Inn, Country Inn, Holiday Inn, Hampton Inn
Other	W: State Capitol
244	University Ave, Pryor St
Gas	E: Chevron, Exxon
TServ	E: Cummins South, Southern Freight
	W: Brown Transport, Ford Trucks, Freight Direct, Great Dane Trailers
243	GA 166, Langford Pkwy
(242)	Jct I-85S, Atl Airport, Montgomery
241	Cleveland Ave
Gas	E: BP, Chevron
	W: Shell, Citgo, Marathon
Food	E: Checkers, Churchs Chicken, McDonald's
	W: Burger King, Krystal, Pizza Hut
Lodg	E: Palace Inn
	W: American Inn, Days Inn, Travelodge
Med	W: + Hospital
Other	E: ATM, Advance Auto, Kmart
	W: CVS, Kroger
239	US 19, US 41, Henry Ford II Ave, Central Ave, CW Grant Pkwy
Gas	E: Chevron◊
	W: BP, Citgo
Food	E: Checkers, Waffle House
	W: ChickFilA, Krystal, McDonald's
Lodg	W: Best Western
(238A)	Jct I-285E, 407E, to Augusta, Greenville
(238B)	Jct I-285W, 407W, Atlanta Airport, to Chattanooga
237A	to GA 85S, Riverdale (SB)
237	to GA 85, GA 331, Forest Pkwy, Fort Gillem
TStop	E: Happy Store (Scales), PTP/Patriot (Scales)
Gas	E: Chevron, Exxon
	W: BP
Food	E: FastFood/HS, Fast Food/Patriot, Burger King, McDonald's, Waffle House
	W: Subway
Lodg	E: Econo Lodge, Motel 6♥
	W: Days Inn, Ramada Ltd
TWash	E: Happy Store, Patriot
TServ	E: Happy Store/Tires, Patriot/Tires
	W: FStop Sales & Service
Other	E: Laundry/Happy Store, Laundry/CB/WiFi/LP/Patriot, Grocery

Personal Notes

EXIT	GEORGIA
235	US 19, US 41, Jonesboro, to Griffin (NB reacc on Westside of Hwy)
FStop	W: Fuel Mart #638
Gas	E: Chevron, Exxon◊, Phillips 66, Hess
	W: Racetrac, Shell
Food	E: Waffle House, Hardee's
	W: Shoney's, Waffle House, Burger King, KFC, Krystal, Red Lobster
Lodg	E: Travelodge, Super 8, Howard Johnson
	W: Best Value Inn, Comfort Inn, Days Inn, Econo Lodge, Holiday Inn Express, Super 8
TServ	E: Atlanta Freightliner, Stith Equipment
Med	W: + Southern Reg'l Medical Center
Other	E: Atlanta RV Center
	W: ATM, Dollar General, Office Depot
233	GA 54, Jonesboro Rd, Morrow, Jonesboro, Lake City
Gas	E: BP, Chevron, Citgo◊, Gulf, Murphy
	W: Circle K, Exxon, Food Mart
Food	E: RJ BBQ, Cracker Barrel, Krystal, Taco Bell, Mrs Winners, Waffle House, Wendy's
	W: Bennigan's, KFC, Pizza Hut, Long John Silver, McDonald's, Outback Steakhouse, Shoney's,
Lodg	E: Best Western, Days Inn, Drury Inn
	W: Hampton Inn, Quality Inn, Red Roof Inn♥
Med	W: + Immediate Medical Care
Other	E: ATMs, Banks, Wal-Mart sc, to Clayton State Univ
	W: ATMs, Auto Services, Banks, Best Buy, Clayton Co Harley Davidson, Costco, Firestone, Goodyear, Southlake Mall, Sam's Club

EXIT	GEORGIA
231	CR 28, Mt Zion Blvd, Morrow
Gas	E: QT, Citgo, Conoco, Exxon
	W: Chevron, Gas Xpress
Food	W: Arby's, Blimpie, Chili's, McDonald's, Longhorn Steakhouse, Steak 'n Shake, Waffle House, Wendy's
Lodg	W: Country Inn, Extended Stay America, Sun Suites, Sleep Inn
Other	W: ATMs, AMC 24, HH Gregg, Home Depot, NTB, Publix, Target
228	GA 138, GA 54, Stockbridge Hwy, Stockbridge
Gas	E: Exxon, RaceWay
	W: BP, Chevron, Sunoco
Food	E: Arby's, Burger King, CiCi's, Golden Corral, IHOP, Krystal, McDonald's, Long John Silver, Shoney's, Subway, Taco Bell, Waffle House, Wendy's
	W: Waffle House
Lodg	E: Best Western, Comfort Inn, Days Inn, Holiday Inn, La Quinta Inn♥, Motel 6, Red Roof Inn♥, Shoney's Inn
Other	E: Kmart, Kroger, Tires
	W: Auto Dealer, CVS
(227)	Jct I-675N, Atlanta ByPass, to I-285E, Augusta, Greenville (NB)
224	Hudson Bridge Rd, Eagle's Landing Parkway, Stockbridge
Gas	E: BP, Citgo, Phillips 66, Texaco◊
	W: QT, Murphy
Food	E: ChickFilA, Outback Steakhouse, KFC, McDonald's, Subway, Waffle House
	W: Arby's, Blimpie, China Café
Lodg	E: AmeriHost Inn♥, Microtel
	W: Baymont Inn, Super 8
Med	E: + Henry General Hospital
Other	E: ATMs, Banks, Publix, Walgreen's
	W: Wal-Mart sc, Kroger, Walgreen's
222	GA 351, Jodeco Rd, McDonough
Gas	E: Pantry, Citgo, Texaco
	W: BP, Chevron◊
Food	E: Waffle House, Hardee's
Other	W: Atlanta South RV Resort▲
221	Jonesboro Rd, McDonough, Lovejoy
TStop	E: Travel Center
Gas	E: BP, Williams
Food	E: FastFood/TC
	W: Burger King, Chili's, CiCi's, Golden Corral, Hong Kong Café, Logan Roadhouse, McDonald's, Wendy's, Yuki Japanese
Lodg	E: Days Inn
TServ	E: Stirling
Other	W: Home Depot, Sam's Club, Atlanta South RV Park ▲
218	GA 20, GA 81, Hampton McDonough
FStop	W: Fuel Stop #359
Gas	E: QT, RaceTrac Texaco, Murphy
	W: Speedway
Food	E: Applebee's, Arby's, Cracker Barrel, McDonald's, Mrs Winner, Subway, Wendy's
	W: Pizza, Subway, Waffle House
Lodg	E: Best Western, Hampton Inn, Super 8
	W: Comfort Inn, Econo Lodge, Masters Inn♥
Other	E: ATMs, Lowe's, Wal-Mart sc, McDonough RV Center, RV Sales
	W: RV Repairs

◊ = Regular Gas Stations with Diesel   ▲ = RV Friendly Locations   ♥ = Pet Friendly Locations
RED PRINT SHOWS LARGE VEHICLE PARKING/ACCESS ON SITE OR NEARBY   BROWN PRINT SHOWS CAMPGROUNDS/RV PARKS

EXIT	GEORGIA
216	**GA 155, McDonough**
FStop	E: Liberty Center Texaco
	W: Kangaroo #3333
Gas	E: Chevron◊, Shell◊
	W: BP, Citgo, RaceTrac
Food	E: Waffle House, BBQ
	W: Krystal, Shoney's, Waffle House
Lodg	E: Beset Value Inn, Days Inn, Microtel Inn
	W: Country Inn, Quality Inn, Sleep Inn
TServ	W: Kenworth
212	**Bill Gardner Pkwy, Locust Grove Rd, to US 23, Locust Grove, Hampton, Jackson**
Gas	E: BP◊, Chevron, Exxon, Liberty, Shell
	W: Chevron, Citgo◊, Exxon
Food	E: BurgerKing/Chevron, McDonald's/BP, Denny's, DQ, Hardee's, Huddle House, Taco Bell, Waffle House, Wendy's, Zaxby's
Lodg	E: Econo Lodge, Executive Inn, Ramada Ltd, Red Roof Inn
	W: Country Inn, Super 8, Scottish Inn
Other	E: Tanger Factory Outlet Mall, Atlanta Motor Speedway
205	**GA 16, Griffin, Jackson**
FStop	E: Jackson Super Mart/BP
Gas	E: Citgo◊
	W: BP, Chevron◊
Food	E: Simmons Smokehouse BBQ
Other	W: Forest Glen RV Park▲
201	**GA 36, Barnesville-Jackson Rd, Jackson, Barnesville**
FStop	W: Interstate BP
TStop	E: WilcoHess Travel Plaza #3030 (Scales), Travel Center of America/Citgo (Scales) (DAND), Love's Travel Stop #307 (Scales) (DAND)
	W: Flying J Travel Plaza #5280/Conoco (Scales)
Food	E: DQ/Wendy's/WilcoHess TP, Rest/Subw/ TBell/TA TC, McDonald's/Love's TS
	W: Rest/Hardee's/FJ TP, Fast Food/Interstate BP, O'Rudy's Rib Shack, Buckner's Family Rest
TWash	E: Blue Beacon TW/TA TC, Jason's TW
	W: Eagle TW/FJ TP
TServ	E: TA TC/Tires, GA Motor Truck, Hinkle Interstate Truck Tires
	W: Speedco, 201 Truck Service
Other	E: Laundry/WilcoHess TP, Laundry/WiFi/ TA TC, WiFi/Love's TS
	W: Laundry/WiFi/RVDump/LP/FJ TP, RV Connection, Sagon RV Supercenter
198	**CR 277, Highfalls Rd, Jackson**
Food	W: High Falls BBQ
Other	E: Buck Creek Campground▲, High Falls State Park
	W: High Falls Campground▲
193	**CR 275, Johnstonville Rd**
Gas	E: BP
(189)	**Weigh Station** (Both dir)
188	**GA 42, N Lee St, Forsyth**
Gas	E: Liberty◊, Shell
Food	E: Captain D's, Pizza Hut/TacoBell/KFC, Subway
Lodg	E: Best Value Inn, Best Western, Budget Inn
	W: Sundown Lodge
Other	E: Ingles, Pharmacy, Indian Springs State Park▲
187	**GA 83, Cabaniss Rd, Lee St, Forsyth**
Gas	W: BP, Citgo◊, Marathon, Texaco

EXIT	GEORGIA
Food	W: Burger King, Captain D's, Hardee's, McDonald's, Pizza Hut, Subway, Taco Bell, Waffle House, Wendy's
Lodg	E: Econo Lodge, Regency Inn
	W: Days Inn
Other	W: Grocery, CVS, Wal-Mart
186	**Juliette Rd, Tift College Dr**
Gas	W: BP◊, Minit Mart, Shell
Food	W: Waffle House, Hong Kong Café, DQ
Lodg	W: Hampton Inn, Holiday Inn Express, Super 8
Other	W: Forsyth KOA▲
185	**GA 18, Harold Clark Pkwy, Forsyth**
Gas	E: Shell
	W: BP, Shell◊
Food	E: Pippin's BBQ
	W: Shoney's
Lodg	E: Comfort Inn, Comfort Suites
Other	E: L&D Campground▲, GA State Hwy Patrol Post
181	**CR 34, Rumble Rd, Forsyth, to Smarr**
FStop	E: Rumble Road BP
Gas	E: Shell◊
Food	E: Stuckey's/BP
Other	E: Roy's Auto & 24hr Repair, Tires
(179)	**Rest Area (SB)** **(RR, Phones, Picnic, Vend, RVDump)**
(177)	**Jct I-475S, GA 408, Macon ByPass, to Valdosta (SB)**
175	**Pate Rd, to GA 19, to US 41** (NB, No Re-entry)
172	**to US 23, Dames Ferry, Bass Rd**
Gas	W: Citgo◊
Other	E: Bass Pro Shop
171	**Riverside Dr, US 23, Dames Ferry**
Gas	E: BP, Marathon◊
Food	E: Cracker Barrel, Huddle House
169	**to GA 19, to US 41, US 23, Arkwright Rd**
Gas	E: Shell, BP◊
	W: Chevron, Conoco◊
Food	E: Carrabba's, China Gourmet, Outback Steakhouse, Waffle House
	W: Applebee's, Arby's, Backyard Burger, Burger King, ChickFilA, Chili's, Chinese Rest, **Cracker Barrel**, Dunkin Donuts, El Azteca Mex, Hooters, KFC, Krystal, Longhorn Steakhouse, McDonald's, Papa John's, Popeye's, Ryan's Grill, Rio Bravo, Steak n Shake, Subway, Waffle House
Lodg	E: Comfort Inn, Courtyard, Fairfield Inn, La Quinta Inn♥, Residence Inn, Red Roof Inn♥, Red Roof Inn, Super 8
	W: Hampton Inn, Holiday Inn, Quality Inn, Ramada Inn, Wingate Inn
Med	W: + Hospital
Other	W: ATMs, Auto Dealers, Banks, B&N, FedEx Kinko's, Kmart, Kroger, Pharmacy, Publix, Radio Shack, RiteAid
167	**GA 247, N Pierce Ave, Macon**
Gas	W: BP◊, Chevron, Exxon, Marathon◊, Shell◊
Food	W: Applebee's, Arby's, Pizza Hut, Red Lobster, Texas Cattle Co, Waffle House, Wendy's
Lodg	W: Best Western, Budget Inn, Comfort Inn, Days Inn, Econo Lodge, Holiday Inn Express, Howard Johnson, Motel 6
Other	W: Goodyear, Pharmacy

◊ = Regular Gas Stations with Diesel ▲ = RV Friendly Locations ♥ = Pet Friendly Locations
RED PRINT SHOWS LARGE VEHICLE PARKING/ACCESS ON SITE OR NEARBY BROWN PRINT SHOWS CAMPGROUNDS/RV PARKS

EXIT	GEORGIA
(165)	Jct I-16E, to Savannah (SB, Left Ex)
164	US 41, GA 19, Georgia Ave, Macon
Med	E: + Medical Center of Central GA
163	GA 74, Mercer University Dr
Gas	W: Marathon◆
Lodg	W: Red Carpet Inn
Other	E: Mercer Univ
162	US 80, GA 22, Eisenhower Pkwy
Gas	W: Chevron, Flash
Food	W: Captain D's, IHOP, McDonald's, Mrs. Winners, Subway, Taco Bell, Wendy's
Other	W: ATMs, Goodyear, Home Depot, Office Depot, PetSmart♥, Walgreen's, Colonial Mall
160	US 41, GA 247, to GA 74 Spur, to Rocky Creek Rd, Houston Ave (NB)
Gas	E: RaceWay, Marathon, Mini Food Store W: BP, Chevron, Enmark◆
Food	E: Johnny V's, Waffle House W: Arby's, KFC, McDonald's, Subway, Waffle House
Lodg	E: Masters Inn, Magnolia Court Motel
Other	W: Auto Services, Dollar General, Grocery
160A	US 41, GA 247, to Houston Ave (SB)
160B	Rocky Creek Rd, to US 41 (SB)
NOTE:	Follow I-475 below to bypass Macon. Exit #'s follow I-475 for next 15 mi.
15	US 41, Bolingbroke
Gas	W: Exxon◆, Marathon◆
9	Zebulon Rd, Wesleyan College
Gas	E: Shell, Murphy◆ W: Citgo, Exxon, Marathon
Food	E: ChickFilA, Fuddruckers, Japanes Rest, Krystal, Margarita's Mex Grill, McDonald's, Pizza Hut, Popeye's, Sonic, Taco Bell, Waffle House, Wendy's
Lodg	E: Baymont Inn, Fairfield Inn, Sleep Inn
Med	W: + Hospital
Other	E: ATMs, Banks, Tires, Wal-Mart sc
(8)	Rest Area (NB) (Next RA on I-75 138mi) (RR, Phone, Picnic)
5	GA 74, Macon, Thomaston, Mercer University Dr
Food	E: Waffle House W: Grill Works, Church's Chicken
Lodg	W: Howard Johnson
3	US 80, GA 22, Macon, Roberta, Macon College
Gas	E: Oil, RaceTrac, Spectrum W: Shell
Food	E: Cracker Barrel, Chesterfield Cafe, Indian Rest, JL's Open Pit BBQ, McDonald's, Subway, Waffle House W: Burger King
Lodg	E: Days Inn, Hampton Inn, Knights Inn, Motel 6, Ramada, Rodeway Inn, Super 8, Travelodge W: Scottish Inn, Econo Lodge, Knights Inn
Other	E: to Colonial Mall, Best Buy, Staples, Central GA Tech College W: Macon State College
(156)	Jct I-475N, GA 408, Macon ByPass, to Atlanta (NB, Left exit)
NOTE:	Follow I-475 above to bypass Macon. Exit #'s follow I-475 for next 15 mi.

EXIT	GEORGIA
155	CR 740, Hartley Bridge Rd, Macon
Gas	E: BP◆, Shell, Kroger W: Citgo
Food	E: Hong Kong Garden, KFC, Wendy's W: McDonald's, Subway, Waffle House
Lodg	W: Amer Best Value Inn
Other	E: Kroger
149	GA 49, Byron, to Fort Valley
FStop	W: Marathon Fuel Stop #2, Byron Citgo, Flash Foods
Gas	E: Enmark, Shell W: BP, RaceWay
Food	E: Burger King, Denny's, McDonald's, Krystal, Shoney's, Subway, Waffle House, Wendy's, Zaxby's W: Country Cupboard, Huddle House, Mex Rest, Popeye's, Subway, Waffle House
Lodg	E: Best Western, Holiday Inn Express W: Comfort Inn, Days Inn, Econo Lodge, Passport Inn, Super 8
TServ	W: Tires/Citgo, Sterling Western, CAT
Other	E: Peach Outlet Shops, Various Outlet Stores, Mid State RV Center W: CarQuest, NAPA, Auto Dealers, Interstate RV Center, Sun Coast RV Center Camping World
146	GA 247, Centerville Rd, Byron, to Centerville
FStop	W: Raceway Food Mart #2502
TStop	W: Pilot Travel Center #267 (Scales)
Gas	E: Flash Foods, Exxon, Shell, Enmark◆
Food	E: Outback Steakhouse, Subway, Waffle House, River Bend Fish Camp & Grill W: Arby's/TJCinn/Pilot TC
Lodg	E: Budget Inn, Comfort Suites, Economy Inn, Hampton Inn W: Red Carpet Inn
Other	E: Robbins AFB W: Laundry/WiFi/Pilot TC, Mid Ga RV Service
144	Russell Pkwy, Fort Valley
142	GA 96, Housers Mill Rd, Ft Valley
Gas	E: Chevron◆, Shell
Other	E: Perry Ponderosa Park Campground▲
138	GA 11 Conn, N Perry Pkwy, Thompson Rd, Perry
FStop	E: Super Food Mart/Texaco
Food	E: FastFood/Super Food Mart
Other	W: Perry Ft Valley Airport✈
136	US 341, GA 7, Sam Nunn Blvd, Perry
FStop	E: Flash Foods #267
Gas	E: Amoco, Chevron, Speedway W: Chevron, RaceWay, Texaco
Food	E: Arby's, Burger King, Captain D's, ChickFilA, Jalisco Mex Grill, KFC, Krystal, Longhorn Steakhouse, McDonald's, Red Lobster, Sonny's BBQ, Subway, Waffle House, Wendy's, Zaxby's W: Applebee's, Angelina's Italian Garden Cafe
Lodg	E: Great Inn, Hampton Inn, Howard Johnson, Jameson Inn♥, Super 8♥ W: Comfort Inn, Econo Lodge, Holiday Inn♥, Knights Inn, Quality Inn♥
Med	E: + Hospital
Other	E: Advance Auto, Dollar Tree, Kroger, NAPA, Pharmacy, Radio Shack, Wal-Mart sc, Bolands RV Park▲ W: Crossroads of GA Campground▲

EXIT	GEORGIA
135	US 41, GA 127, Marshallville Rd, Perry, Fort Valley
Gas	E: BP◆, Exxon, Shell, Flash Foods
Food	E: Cracker Barrel, DQ, Huddle House, Subway, Waffle House
Lodg	E: Best Western♥, Crossroads Motel, Howard Johnson, Passport Inn, Red Carpet Inn, Relax Inn, Rodeway Inn♥, Travelodge
Med	E: + Hospital
Other	E: Kmart, Kroger, GA Fairgrounds, Welcome Center W: Fair Harbor RV Park & CG▲, GA State Hwy Patrol Post
134	to US 41, GA 7, S Perry Pkwy, Perry, Marshallville
Gas	E: Texaco◆
Lodg	E: HOTEL
Other	E: Ga Fairgrounds
127	GA 26, Montezuma, Hawkinsville
Gas	W: Chevron
Other	E: Twin Oaks RV Park▲
122	GA 230, 2nd St, Unadilla
Gas	E: Dixie◆
Lodg	E: Red Carpet Inn
121	US 41, GA 7, Pine Ave, Unadilla, to Pinehurst
FStop	W: All State Truck Stop (Scales)
Gas	E: BP, Flash Foods Shell/Stuckey's◆
Food	E: DQ/Stuckey's, Cotton Patch Rest, Don Ponchos W: Rest/All State TS
Lodg	E: Days Inn, Economy Inn, Scottish Inn W: Regency Inn
TServ	W: All State TS/Tires
Other	E: Grocery, Tires, Southern Trails RV Resort▲ W: Laundry/WiFi/LP/All State TS
(118)	Rest Area (SB) (RR, Phones, Picnic, RVDump)
117	to US 41, Pinehurst-Hawkinsville Rd, Pinehurst
TStop	W: Pinehurst Travel Center/BP (Scales)
Food	W: Rest/Pinehurst TC
Other	W: Laundry/Pinehurst TC
112	GA 27, Vienna, Hawkinsville
FStop	W: Rachel's BP
Gas	E: Pure W: Marathon
109	GA 215, Union St, Vienna, Pitts
TStop	E: Pilot Travel Center #398 (Scales)
Gas	W: BP◆, Citgo◆, Shell
Food	E: FastFood/Pilot TC W: Hardee's, Huddle House, Popeye's, Subway, Vienna Cafe
Lodg	W: Executive Inn
Med	E: + Hospital W: + Dooly Medical Center
Other	E: Laundry/WiFi/Pilot TC W: to Middle GA Tech College
(107)	Rest Area (NB) (RR, Phones, Picnic, Vend, RVDump)
104	Farmers Market Rd, Cordele
Gas	W: Conoco/P66
Lodg	W: Cordele Inn
102	GA 257, Cordele, Hawkinsville
Gas	E: Shell
Food	W: Smookies BBQ
Med	W: + Hospital

Page 336   ◆= Regular Gas Stations with Diesel   ▲ = RV Friendly Locations   ♥ = Pet Friendly Locations
RED PRINT SHOWS LARGE VEHICLE PARKING/ACCESS ON SITE OR NEARBY   BROWN PRINT SHOWS CAMPGROUNDS/RV PARKS

Interstate 75 — Georgia

EXIT		GEORGIA
101		**US 280, GA 90, GA 30, Cordele, Abbeville, Presidential Route**
	TStop	E: Pilot Travel Center #416 (Scales)
	Gas	E: Exxon◆, Shell
		W: BP◆, Chevron, Liberty, RaceWay
	Food	E: Arby's/TJCinn/Pilot TC, Denny's, Golden Corral, Marise's Country Cooking, Waffle House
		W: Burger King, Captain D's, DQ, Cracker Barrel, Farm House Rest, Hardee's, KFC, Krystal, McDonald's, Pizza Place, Shoney's, Wendy's, Zaxby's
	Lodg	E: Days Inn, Fairfield Inn, Ramada
		W: Ashburn Inn, Best Western, Comfort Inn Delux Inn, Econo Lodge, Hampton Inn, Holiday Inn, Super 8, Travelodge
	Other	E: GA State Hwy Patrol Post
		W: Laundry/WiFi/Pilot TC, CVS, Dollar General, CarWash, Family Dollar, Grocery, Radio Shack, Winn Dixie, Wal-Mart sc, to appr 9mi GA Veterans State Park▲
99		**GA 300, GA-FL Pkwy, Albany, Sylvester**
	Gas	W: BP
	Lodg	W: Country Inn
97		**GA 33, Rock House Rd, Cordele Wenona, Sylvester**
	TStop	W: Travel Center of America/BP (Scales)
	Food	W: CountryPride/PizzaHut/Popeyes/TA TC
	Lodg	E: Royal Inn
	TWash	W: TW
	TServ	W: TA TC/Tires, Carter Thermo King, Perlis
	Other	E: Cordele RV Campground▲
		W: Laundry/CB/WiFi/TA TC, Cordele KOA▲
92		**CR 357, Arabi Rd, Arabi**
	Gas	E: Chevron/Plantation House
		W: BP◆
	Other	W: Southern Gates RV Park▲
(85)		**Rest Area (NB)**
		(RR, Phones, Picnic, Vend, RVDump)
84		**GA 159, North St, Ashburn, Amboy**
	TStop	W: A-1 Truck Stop/Chevron
	Gas	E: Shell◆
	Food	W: DQ/Subway/A-1 TS
	Lodg	W: Ashburn Inn & RV Park▲
	Other	W: Laundry/A-1 TS
82		**GA 107, GA 112, Washington Ave, Sylvester, Ashburn, Fitzgerald**
	Gas	W: BP, Chevron, TC Gas
	Food	W: Huddle House, Krystal, McDonald's, Shoney's, Waffle House
	Lodg	W: Best Western, Days Inn, Super 8
	Other	W: Ashburn Tire Service, O'Reilly Auto Parts, RiteAid
80		**Bussey Rd, Sycamore**
	FStop	W: Shorty's 26 Chevron
	TStop	E: Exxon Truck Plaza
	Gas	E: Qwik Stop
	Food	E: Deli/Exxon TS
	Lodg	E: Budget Lakeview Inn
	TServ	E: Exxon TS
		E: S GA Diesel Services, Clark's Diesel Services, Allen's Tire & Auto Truck RV Service
	Other	E: Laundry/Exxon TP
78		**GA 32, Jefferson Davis Hwy, Sycamore, Ocilla**

EXIT		GEORGIA
(76)		**Rest Area (SB)**
		(RR, Phones, Picnic, Vend, RVDump)
75		**CR 252, Inaha Rd, Sycamore**
	Gas	E: Chevron
		W: BP/Stuckey's
	Food	W: DQ/Stuckey's/BP
71		**CR 11, Willis Still Rd, Sunsweet**
69		**CR 421, Chula-Brookfield Rd**
	Gas	E: Phillips 66◆
	Food	E: Rest/Red Carpet Inn
	Lodg	E: Red Carpet Inn
		W: to Shalom House B&B
66		**CR 410, Brighton Rd**
64		**I-75 Bus Loop, US 41, Tifton**
	Gas	E: BP◆
		W: Petro
	Med	E: + Hospital
63B		**Whiddon Mill Rd, 8th St, Tifton**
	Gas	E: AmocoBP, Exxon, Shell
	Food	E: Hardee's, KFC, Krystal, Subway
	Lodg	E: Budget Inn, Davis Bros Motor Lodge
	Med	E: + Hospital
	Other	E: Pharmacy, Winn Dixie
63A		**King Rd, 2nd St, Tifton**
	Gas	E: Chevron
		W: Citgo, Shell◆
	Food	E: Arby's, Burger King, McDonald's, Krystal, Taco Bell
		W: Waffle House
	Lodg	E: Econo Lodge, Super 8♥
		W: Quality Inn♥, Travelodge
	Other	E: Kmart
62		**to US 82, GA 520, to US 319, GA 35, Tifton, Sylvester, Moultrie**
	Gas	E: BP, Citgo, Exxon◆
		W: BP, RaceWay, Shell
	Food	E: Applebee's, Cracker Barrel, Golden Corral, Waffle House, Western Sizzlin'
		W: Burger King, Captain D's, Longhorn Steakhouse, Shoney's, Starbucks, Waffle House, Wendy's/Shell
	Lodg	E: Comfort Inn, Courtyard, Hampton Inn, Microtel
		W: Days Inn, Holiday Inn, Ramada Ltd
	Med	E: + Walk-In Medical Center
	Other	E: AdvanceAuto, Tires
		W: Auto Dealers, CarWash/Shell, Lowe's, Wal-Mart sc
61		**CR 299, Omega Rd, Tifton**
	TStop	W: Citgo Travel Plaza
	Food	W: Stuckey's/WaffleKing/Citgo TP
	Lodg	E: Days Inn, Motel 6
	TWash	W: Citgo TP
	TServ	W: Prince Truck Ctr/WhiteGMC Volvo
	Other	W: Laundry/Citgo TP, Little River Harley Davidson, The Pines Campground▲, RV Overnite▲
60		**CR 418, Central Ave, Tifton**
	TStop	W: Pilot Travel Center #192 (Scales)
	Gas	E: Circle K, Chevron
	Food	W: Rest/Subway/Pilot TC
	TWash	W: Blue Beacon TW/Pilot TC
	TServ	W: Pilot TC/Tires, Ten Speed Truck Service
	Other	W: Laundry/WiFi/RVDump/Pilot TC, Amy's S GA RV Park & RV Center▲
59		**CR 204, Southwell Blvd, Widdon Rd, to US 41, GA 7, Tifton**
	TStop	E: Love's Travel Stop #325 (Scales)

EXIT		GEORGIA
	Food	E: Hardee's/Love's TS
	Other	E: WiFi/RVDump/Love's TP, Lairsey's Auto Service Center, U-Haul, Henry Tift Myers Airport✈
55		**CR 418, Omega Eldorado Rd, Tifton**
49		**GA 547, Kinard Bridge Rd, Lenox**
	FStop	W: Lenox BP
	Gas	E: Chevron, Dixie◆
		W: Phillips 66◆
	Food	W: Stella's Diner
	Lodg	W: Knights Inn
	Other	W: Laundry/Lenox BP
(48)		**Rest Area (SB)**
		(RR, Phones, Picnic, RVDump)
(46)		**Rest Area (NB)**
		(RR, Phones, Picnic, RVDump)
45		**CR 253, Barneyville Rd**
41		**Roundtree Bridge Rd, Moultrie Rd, Sparks, to GA 37, US 41**
39		**GA 37, W 4th St, Adel, Moultrie, to Nashville, Lakeland**
	TStop	W: Adel Truck Plaza/Citgo (Scales)
	Gas	E: Shell◆, Dixie, Chevron
		W: BP
	Food	E: McDonald's/Shell, Hardee's, Subway, Waffle House, Wendy's
		W: HuddleHouse/Stuckeys/Adel TP, Burger King, Captain D's, China Buffet, Popeye's, Taco Bell, Western Sizzlin, IHOP/DaysInn
	Lodg	E: Budget Lodge, Scottish Inn♥, Super 8♥
		W: Days Inn♥, Hampton Inn
	TServ	W: Adel TP/Tires
	Med	E: + Memorial Hospital
	Other	E: RiteAid, Winn Dixie, ATMs, Auto Service
		W: Laundry/Adel TP, Cook Co Airport✈, Reed Bingham State Park
37		**CR 216, Old Quitman Rd, Adel**
32		**CR 240, Old Coffee Rd, Adel, Cecil**
	Gas	W: Chevron
	Other	W: Cecil Bay RV Park▲
29		**US 41, GA 122, GA 7, Sheriff's Boys Ranch, Hahira, to Lakeland**
	TStop	W: Big Foot Travel Center BP
	Gas	E: Jimmy's 66, Pure
	Food	E: City Café, Joyce's Fried Chicken
		W: Apple Valley Rest/BF TC, Blimpie/BP
	Lodg	W: Knights Inn, Super 8
	Other	E: Car Wash, Hahira Auto Service
(24)		**Weigh Station (Both dir)**
22		**I-75 Bus, US 41S, N Valdosta Rd, Moody AFB, Valdosta**
	Gas	E: BP, Shell◆
		W: Citgo◆
	Food	W: Burger King/DQ/Stuckeys/Citgo
	Lodg	W: Days Inn♥/Citgo
	Med	E: + Smith Northview Hospital
18		**GA 133, St Augustine Rd, Valdosta, Moultrie, Valdosta St University**
	Gas	E: BP, Citgo, Exxon, Shell◆
		W: BP, RaceWay, Shell◆
	Food	E: Applebee's, Arby's, Burger King, China Garden, ChickFilA, Cracker Barrel, Denny's, Hooters, KFC, McDonald's, Longhorn Steakhouse, Red Lobster, Outback Steakhouse, Sonic, Subway, Taco Bell, Waffle House, Wendy's

◆ = Regular Gas Stations with Diesel ▲ = RV Friendly Locations ♥ = Pet Friendly Locations
RED PRINT SHOWS LARGE VEHICLE PARKING/ACCESS ON SITE OR NEARBY   BROWN PRINT SHOWS CAMPGROUNDS/RV PARKS

Page 337

EXIT	GEORGIA
	Lodg E: Best Western◊, Country Inn, Comfort Suites, Courtyard, Days Inn, Fairfield Inn, Hampton Inn, Holiday Inn, Howard Johnson, La Quinta Inn♥, Quality Inn, Rodeway Inn, Scottish Inn
	W: Econo Lodge, Sleep Inn
	Other E: ATMs, Best Buy, Home Depot, Publix, Target, Walgreen's, Wal-Mart, Valdosta Mall
	W: River Park RV Park▲
16	US 84, US 221, GA 38, Valdosta
	FStop E: Big Foot Travel Stop Citgo, Jack Rabbit #4/BP
	TStop W: Buzz's Auto Truck Plaza/Shell (Scales)
	Gas E: Phillips 66, Fina, Sam's
	Food E: Blimpie/Citgo, Burger King, IHOP, Japanese Steak House, McDonald's, Pizza Hut, Sonic, Shoney's, Waffle House, Wendy's
	W: HuddleHouse/Buzz's ATP, Austin Cattle Co
	Lodg E: Days Inn♥/Citgo, Guest House Inn♥, Hampton Inn, Holiday Inn, Motel 6, Quality Inn♥, Ramada Ltd♥, Super 8♥
	W: Comfort Inn♥, Knights Inn
	TServ W: Buzz's ATP/Tires
	Med E: + Hospital
	Other E: Sam's Club, Wal-Mart sc, Convention Center
	W: Laundry/Buzz's ATP
13	CR 785, Old Clyattville Rd, Valdosta
	Other E: Valdosta Reg'l Airport✈
	W: to appr 4mi Wild Adventures Theme Park
11	GA 31, Colin P Kelly Jr Hwy, Valdosta, to Madison FL
	TStop E: Pilot Travel Center #73 (Scales), Wilco Hess Travel Plaza #3050 (Scales)
	Gas W: BP
	Food E: Subway/Pilot TC, Stuckey's/WilcoHess TP, Waffle House
	Lodg E: Travelers Inn
	TWash E: Blue Bird Truck Wash, TW/Pilot TC
	TServ E: Pilot TC/Tires, Hwy 31 Truck & Tire Repair
	W: All Star International, S&S Truck Repair
	Other E: WiFi/Pilot TC, Laundry/WiFi/RVDump/ WilcoHess TP, Valdosta Reg'l Airport✈
5	GA 376, Clyattville-Lake Park Rd, Lake Park, Madison
	TStop W: GA-FL Fuel Center/Shell, Citgo TP
	Gas E: Chevron, Phillips 66, RaceWay, Shell
	Food E: ChickFilA, China Garden, Farm House Rest, Hardee's, Krystal, Shoney's, Sonny BBQ, Subway, Waffle House
	W: FastFood/Citgo TP, Cracker Barrel, McDonald's, Pizza Hut, Taco Bell
	Lodg E: Holiday Inn, Guest House Inn, Quality Inn
	W: Days Inn, Hampton Inn, Super 8, Travelodge
	Other E: Preferred Outlets of Lake Park, Flea Market, NAPA, Winn Dixie, Valdosta/Lake Park KOA▲, Eagles Roost RV Resort▲, Travel Country RV Center
	W: Suncoast RV Center & CG▲
(3)	GA Welcome Center (NB) (RR, Phone, Picnic, Vend, RVDump)
2	Lake Park Rd, Lake Park, Bellville
	TStop E: Travel Center of America/BP #128 (Scales)

EXIT	GA / FL
	W: Flying J Travel Plaza #5044/Conoco (Scales)
	Gas E: Shell
	Food E: Rest/Arby's/TA TC, Lakeside Rest
	W: Rest/FastFood/FJ TP
	Lodg E: Best Western
	W: Lake Park Inn
	TWash W: Lake Park Truck & RV Wash
	TServ E: TA TC/Tires, Speedco, Great American Chrome Shop
	W: CB Shop
	Other E: Laundry/WiFi/TA TC
	W: Laundry/BarbSh/WiFi/RVDump/LP/ FJ TP
	(EASTERN TIME ZONE)
	ⓞ GEORGIA
	ⓤ FLORIDA
	(EASTERN TIME ZONE)
	NOTE: MM 471: Georgia State Line
	NOTE: MM 471: SB: Begin Motorist Call Boxes
(470)	FL Welcome Center (SB) (RR, Phone, Picnic, Vend, Info)
467	FL 143, Jennings
	FStop W: Johnson & Johnson #9/Exxon
	Gas E: Chevron, Texaco
	W: Amoco
	Food W: Burger King, Jennings House Rest.
	Lodg W: Budget Lodge, Econo Lodge, N Florida Inn
	Other W: Fireworks Super Center, Jennings Outdoor Resort & Campground▲
460	FL 6, Jennings, to Jasper, Madison
	TStop E: Johnson & Johnson #14/Exxon
	Gas E: RaceWay, Texaco
	W: BP, Shell, Texaco
	Food E: HuddleHouse/J&J, Sheffield's Country Kitchen
	Lodg E: Days Inn♥, Scottish Inns
	ATServ W: Dennis Garage
	Med E: + Hospital
	Other E: Laundry/BarbSh/J&J, Walker's Pecan House
451	US 129, FL 51, Jasper, Live Oak (Gas, Food, Lodging E to Jasper)
	Med E: + Madison Co Memorial Hospital
	Other W: Spirit of the Suwanee Music Park▲
(450)	Weigh Station / Agricultural Inspection (Both dir)
439	FL 136, White Springs, Live Oak
	Gas E: BP◊, Gate◊
	Food E: McDonald's, BB Ann's Country Cafe
	Lodg E: Scottish Inn
	W: Best Value Inn
	Other E: Suwannee Valley Campground▲, Lee's Country Campground▲, Stephen Foster State Folk Center▲, to Kelly's RV Park▲
	W: Powell's Auto Service, U-Haul
(435)	Jct I-10, E-Jacksonville, W to Tallahassee
427	US 90, Lake City, Live Oak
	NOTE: Low Clearance 14' 4"
	Gas E: BP, Chevron◊, Gas N Go, Exxon, Shell, Murphy
	W: BP, Shell

◊ = Regular Gas Stations with Diesel ▲ = RV Friendly Locations ♥ = Pet Friendly Locations
RED PRINT SHOWS LARGE VEHICLE PARKING/ACCESS ON SITE OR NEARBY BROWN PRINT SHOWS CAMPGROUNDS/RV PARKS

Page 338

INTERSTATE 75 N/S — FLORIDA

EXIT		FLORIDA
	Food	E: Applebee's, Arby's, Burger King, Cedar River Seafood, **Cracker Barrel**, DQ, Hardee's, IHOP, KFC, Krystal, Pizza Hut, McDonald's, Ryan's Grill, Red Lobster, Ruby Tuesday, Sonny's BBQ, Steak 'n Shake, Taco Bell, Texas Roadhouse, Waffle House, Wendy's
		W: Bob Evans, Shoney's, Waffle House
	Lodg	E: Best Inn, **Days Inn**, Driftwood Inn, **Howard Johnson**, Holiday Inn, Jameson Inn ♥, Knights Inn, Ramada Ltd, **Rodeway Inn**, Scottish Inns
		W: Best Western, Comfort Inn, **Country Inn**, Courtyard, **Econo Lodge**, Hampton Inn, **Motel 6** ♥, Quality Inn, Red Roof Inn
	Med	E: + Lake City Medical Center
	Other	E: ATMs, Auto Services, AutoZone, AdvanceAuto, **CVS**, CarWash, Kmart, Lowe's, NAPA, Office Max, Radio Shack, **Wal-Mart sc**, Tires, Tire Kingdom, True Value Hardware, UPS Store, Lake City Mall, **In & Out RV Park▲**, to **Oak N Pines RV Campground▲**, **Lake City KOA▲**
		W: Auto Dealers, **Wayne's RV Resort▲**, **Travel Country RV Center**
423		**FL 47, Lake City, to Fort White**
	Gas	E: Mobil, Shell◊
		W: BP◊, Chevron
	Food	W: Little Caesar's, Subway
	Lodg	E: Super 8
	TServ	E: **Ring Power**/CAT
		W: **Tom Nehl Truck Co**/**Freightliner**, **Mike's Truck & Auto**
	Other	E: to Lake City Muni Airport ✈
		W: **Casey Jones Campground▲**, **Neverdunn's Slow & Easy Living RV Park▲**
414		**US 41, US 441, Lake City, Ellisville**
	FStop	W: **S&S Food Store #38**/**Shell**, **B&B Food Store #32**/**BP**
	TStop	W: **Country Station Truck Plaza** (Scales)
	Gas	E: Chevron, Texaco
	Food	W: Huddle House, Subway
	Lodg	E: Travelers Inn
		W: Travelodge, **Motel**/**Country Station TP**
	TServ	W: **Country Station TP**/**Tires**
	Other	E: **October Bend RV Park▲**
		W: **Laundry**/**LP**/**Country Station TP**, **E-Z Stop RV Park▲**, **Turning Wheels RV Ctr O'Leno State Park▲**
(413)		**Rest Area** (Both dir) (RR, Phone, Picnic, Vend)
404		**CR 236, High Springs, Alachua, Lake Butler**
	Gas	E: Citgo, Shell◊
	Lodg	E: HOTEL
	Other	W: **High Springs Campground▲**
399		**US 441, ML King Blvd, Alachua, High Springs**
	Gas	E: BP◊, Exxon
		W: Chevron, Citgo◊, Exxon
	Food	E: McDonald's, Pizza Hut, Taco Bell, Sonny's BBQ, Subway, Waffle House
		W: **KFC**, Wendy's
	Lodg	E: Econo Lodge, Quality Inn
		W: **Days Inn**, Ramada Ltd
	Other	E: CarWash, **Travelers Campground▲**, **JD Sanders RV Center**
		W: Greyhound, to **River Rise Resort▲**

EXIT		FLORIDA
390		**FL 222, NW 39th Ave, Gainesville**
	Gas	E: Exxon◊, Kangaroo◊
		W: BP◊, Chevron◊
	Food	E: Burger King, McDonald's, Sonny's BBQ, Wendy's
		W: Cross Creek Café
	Lodg	W: Best Western
	Other	E: UPS Store, Publix, **Walgreen's**, Santa Fe Comm College
		W: Gainesville Harley Davidson, Auto Repair/BP
387		**FL 26, NW 8th Ave, Gainesville**
	Gas	E: BP, Citgo, Shell◊, Speedway, Texaco
		W: BP, Citgo, Chevron◊, Exxon◊, Gator
	Food	E: Burger King, Boston Market, Perkins, Japanese Steak & Sushi, New Century Buffet, Quincy's Steakhouse, Red Lobster, Ruby Tuesday, Rib City Grill, Starbucks, Subway, Wendy's
		W: Krystal, Hardee's, KFC, Shoney's, Taco Bell, Waffle House
	Lodg	E: La Quinta Inn ♥
		W: **Days Inn**, **Econo Lodge**, Fairfield Inn ♥, Holiday Inn
	Med	E: + Immediate Care Walk-In Clinic, + N Florida Reg'l Medical Center
	Other	E: ATMs, Bank, **Pharmacy**, Oaks Mall, Office Depot, PetCo ♥, Shell/Carwash, U-Haul, Vet ♥, Citgo Repair & Towing, to Univ of FL
		W: ATMs, Auto Services, Circuit City, Dollar Tree, Home Depot, Jiffy Lube, Kmart, Publix, **Walgreen's**, Tires
384		**FL 24, SW Archer Rd, Gainesville**
	Gas	E: BP, Chevron◊, Exxon◊, Shell, Speedway
		W: Chevron, Kangaroo Express, Mobil◊, Shell
	Food	E: Atlanta Bread, Bennigan's, Bob Evans, Burger King, ChickFilA, Chili's, Chipolte Mex Grill, Hops Grill, KFC, Lone Star Steakhouse, McDonald's, Olive Garden, On the Border, Papa John's, Pizza Hut, Shoney's, Sonny's BBQ, Steak & Ale, Steak 'n Shake, Taco Bell, TGI Friday, Texas Roadhouse, Waffle House
		W: **Cracker Barrel**
	Lodg	E: Best Value Inn, Cabot Lodge, Comfort Inn, Courtyard, Extended Stay America, Hampton Inn, **Motel 6** ♥, Ramada, Red Roof Inn ♥, Super 8
		W: Baymont Inn, Country Inn, Holiday Inn Express
	Med	E: + N FL Reg'l Medical Center
	Other	E: ATMs, Albertson's, B&N, Best Buy, CarQuest, **CVS**, Dollar Tree, Firestone, Lowe's, Publix, Radio Shack, Target, **Wal-Mart**, Winn Dixie, Oaks Mall, **Suburban LP**, Univ of FL
		W: Fred Bear Museum, **Sunshine MH & Over Nite Park▲**
(383)		**Rest Area** (Both dir) (RR, **Phones**, Picnic, Vend, Sec24/7)
382		**FL 121, Williston Rd, to FL 331 Gainesville**
	Gas	E: Citgo◊, Mobil◊
		W: BP◊, Chevron◊, Kangaroo
	Lodg	E: Gator Inn, Rest Inn
		W: Quality Inn, Travelodge
	Other	E: Publix
		W: Goodyear, to **Williston Crossings RV Resort▲**

EXIT		FLORIDA
374		**CR 234, Micanopy**
	Gas	E: BP, Chevron
		W: Citgo◊, Texaco
	Lodg	W: Knights Inn
	Other	E: **Antique Mall**
		W: Auto Repairs/Texaco
368		**CR 318, Reddick, Orange Lake**
	TStop	E: **Petro Stopping Center #23**/**Mobil** (Scales)
	Gas	E: Chevron
	Food	E: **IronSkillet**/**Wendy's**/**Petro SC**, Jim's BBQ
	TServ	E: **Petro SC**/**Tires**
	Other	E: **Laundry**/**BarbShop**/**RVDump**/**LP**/**Petro SC**, Dave's Towing, Pro Automotive, U-Haul, Midway Transmissions, **Water's Edge Oaks RV Park▲**, **Sportman's Cove▲**, **South Shore Fish Camp▲**
		W: **Grand Lake RV Resort▲**, **Ocala North RV Park▲**
358		**CR 326, Ocala**
	TStop	E: **Pilot Travel Center # 424** (Scales)
		W: **Pilot Travel Center #92** (Scales)
	Gas	E: BP◊, Mobil◊
		W: Chevron
	Food	E: Arby's/TJCinn/**Pilot TC**, Chuck & Von's BBQ To Go, McDonald's/Mobil
		W: Wendy's/**Pilot TC**, DQ, McDonald's
	TServ	E: **Ocala Freightliner**
		W: **American** Auto & Truck Repair, **326 Chrome Shop**, **10-4 CB Store**, **Trucker Svc Ctr Oil & Lube**, **I-75 Truck Sales**
	Other	E: **Laundry**/**WiFi**/**Pilot TC**, Harley Davidson, **Liberty RV & Marine Center**
		W: **Laundry**/**WiFi**/**Pilot TC**
354		**US 27, FL 500, Ocala, Williston**
	Gas	E: BP, RaceTrac
		W: BP◊, Chevron, Circle K, Shell, Texaco◊
	Food	E: Burger King, Krystal, Rascal's BBQ
		W: Huckle Berry Finn's Rest, Waffle House
	Lodg	E: Payless Inn
		W: Budget Host Inn, Comfort Suites, **Days Inn**, Howard Johnson, Ramada, Travelodge
	TServ	W: **American Diesel Service**, **Martin Truck & Tire**
	Other	E: **Wild Frontier Campground▲**
		W: ATM, Dollar General, Publix, Winn Dixie, **Walgreen's**, Super Flea Market, **Oak Tree Village Campground▲**, **Arrowhead Campsites▲**, **Williston Crossings RV Resort▲**, **Turning Wheel RV Center**
352		**FL 40, W Silver Springs Blvd, Ocala, to Silver Springs**
	Gas	E: BP◊, Citgo, RaceTrac
		W: Shell◊, Texaco
	Food	E: McDonald's, PizzaHut/Taco Bell, Wendy's, Whataburger
		W: Denny's, Dunkin Donuts, Waffle House
	Lodg	E: Days Inn, Economy Inn, Quality Inn, Motor Inns Motel & **RV Park▲**
		W: Comfort Inn, Hornes Motor Lodge, **Red Roof Inn** ♥, Super 8, Travelodge
	Other	E: to **Wilderness RV Park Estates▲**, **Silver River State Park**
		W: **Holiday Trav-L RV Park▲**, to Ocala Int'l Airport ✈, **Turning Wheel RV Center**
350		**FL 200, College Rd, Ocala, Silver Springs, to Hernando, Dunnellon**
	Gas	E: Chevron, Citgo, RaceTrac, Shell◊, Texaco◊
		W: BP, Chevron, Sam's

◊ = Regular Gas Stations with Diesel   ▲ = RV Friendly Locations   ♥ = Pet Friendly Locations

RED PRINT SHOWS LARGE VEHICLE PARKING/ACCESS ON SITE OR NEARBY   BROWN PRINT SHOWS CAMPGROUNDS/RV PARKS

Page 339

EXIT		FLORIDA
	Food	E: Applebee's, Arby's, Bob Evans, Burger King, Chili's, ChickFilA, Chuck E Cheese, Hooters, Hops, Krystal, McDonald's, Lone Star Steakhouse, Olive Garden, Outback Steakhouse, Papa John's, Perkins, Ruby Tuesday, Shoney's, Sonny's BBQ, Subway, Taco Bell, TGI Friday, Wendy's W: Burger King, Cracker Barrel, KFC, Steak 'n Shake, Waffle House
	Lodg	E: La Quinta Inn♥, Hampton Inn, Hilton W: Best Western, Courtyard, Country Inn, Fairfield Inn, Holiday Inn Express, Residence Inn
	Med	E: + Hospital
	Other	E: ATMs, Advance Auto, Auto Dealers, Best Buy, B&N, Circuit City, Dollar General, CVS, Goodyear, Home Depot, Lowe's, PetSmart♥, Publix, Pep Boys, Target, Tires, Walgreen's, Wal-Mart sc, UPS Store, Paddock Mall W: Sam's Club, Tires, Ocala KOA▲, Ocala RV Camp Resort▲
(346)		Rest Area (SB) (RR, Phones, Picnic, Vend, Sec24/7)
(345)		Rest Area (NB) (RR, Phones, Picnic, Vend, Sec24/7)
341		FL 484, Ocala, Belleview, Dunellon
	TStop	W: Pilot Travel Center #293 (Scales)
	Gas	E: Chevron, Citgo, Exxon◊, Shell W: BP
	Food	W: Arby's/DQ/TJCinn/Pilot TC, Cracker Barrel, Dunkin Donuts, McDonald's, Sonny's BBQ, Waffle House
	Lodg	E: Microtel, Sleep Inn W: Hampton Inn
	Other	W: WiFi/Pilot TC, BP/Auto & RV Repair, Ocala Ranch RV Park▲
(338)		Weigh Station (Both dir)
329		FL 44, Wildwood, Inverness
	TStop	E: Pilot Travel Center #95 (Scales), PTP/Gate #1142 (Scales) W: Travel Center of America/BP (Scales)
	Gas	E: Mobil◊
	Food	E: Steak n Shake/Gate, Burger King, Denny's, IHOP, McDonald's, Waffle House, Wendy's W: CountryPride/PizzaHut/Popeye/Subway/TA TC
	Lodg	E: Budget Suites, Days Inn, Economy Inn, Microtel, Super 8, Wildwood Inn
	Tires	E: Tommy's Tire Shop
	TWash	E: Wildwood TW W: TA TC
	TServ	E: 75 Truck Service Center, All Fleet Refrigeration, Wildwood CB Shop W: TA TC/Tires, 75 Chrome Shop
	Other	E: WiFi/Pilot TC, Laundry/Gate, Auto Svc, Wildwood KOA▲ W: Laundry/WiFi/TA TC
(328)		FL Tpk (TOLL), to Orlando, to Miami (fr SB, Left Exit)
321		CR 470, Lake Panasoffkee, Bushnell, Sumterville
	FStop	W: Lake Panasoffkee BP
	TStop	E: Spirit Travel Center (Scales)
	Food	E: Rest/Spirit TC W: Hardee's/Subway/BP
	Lodg	W: Motel USA

EXIT		FLORIDA
	TServ	W: BP/Tires
	Other	W: Countryside RV Park▲, Turtleback RV Resort▲
314		FL 48, Bushnell
	Gas	E: BP◊, Citgo, Murphy W: Shell◊, Sunoco◊
	Food	E: DQ/Citgo, Chinese, Dunkin Donuts, McDonald's, KFC, Pizza, Subway, Taco Bell, Wendy's W: Beef O'Brady's, McDonald's, Sonny's BBQ, Waffle House
	Lodg	E: Best Western, GuestHouse Inn W: Microtel
	Other	E: Wal-Mart sc, Webster Flea Market, Farmers Market, ATMs, Auto Services, Banks, Winn Dixie, Red Barn RV Resort & MH Park▲, Oaks RV Resort▲, Blueberry Hill RV Resort▲, Florilow Oaks Camp▲, Dade Battlefield State Park, to Sunshine Village MH Comm & RV Resort▲ W: Flagship RV Sales & Service
309		CR 476B, Bushnell, Webster
	Other	E: Breezy Oaks RV Park▲, Sumter Oaks RV Park▲
(308)		Rest Area (SB) (RR, Phones, Picnic, Vend)
(307)		Rest Area (NB) (RR, Phones, Picnic, Vend)
301		US 98, FL 50, Orlando, Brooksville
	Gas	E: BP, RaceTrac, Speedway, Murphy W: Hess◊, Chevron◊, Sunrise
	Food	E: Arby's, Cracker Barrel, Denny's, McDonald's, Waffle House, Wendy's W: Burger King, Subway
	Lodg	E: Days Inn W: Best Western, Hampton Inn
	Med	W: + Hospital
	Other	E: ATMs, Dollar General, Pharmacy, Winn Dixie, to Webster Travel Park▲, Sunshine Village MH & RV Resort▲
293		CR 41, Blanton Rd, Dade City
	Other	W: Travelers Rest Resort▲
285		FL 52, San Antonio, to Dade City, New Port Richey
	TStop	E: Flying J Travel Plaza #5037/Conoco (Scales) W: Four Star Fuel Mart/Citgo (Scales)
	Food	E: CountryMarket/FastFood/FJ TP W: Rest/Four Star FM, Waffle House
	Med	E: + Pasco Reg'l Medical Center
	Other	E: Laundry/BarbSh/WiFi/RVDump/LP/FJ TP, Costco, Marathon Coach W: Laundry/Four Star FM
279		FL 54, Zephyrhills, Land O' Lakes, Wesley Chapel
	Gas	E: Hess◊, RaceTrac, Shell W: 7-11, BP, Circle K◊
	Food	E: Applebee's, Burger King, Carino's, Sonny's BBQ, Subway, Waffle House, Wendy's W: Cracker Barrel, Denny's, KFC, McDonald's, Outback Steakhouse
	Lodg	W: Best Western, Comfort Inn, Holiday Inn Express, Sleep Inn
	Other	E: Advance Auto, Walgreen's, Winn Dixie, Publix, Leisure Days RV Resort▲, Ralph's Travel Park▲, Happy Days RV Park▲, to Jim's RV Park▲ W: Best Buy, Goodyear, PetSmart♥, Sweet Bay Grocery, Quail Run RV Park▲

◊ = Regular Gas Stations with Diesel   ▲ = RV Friendly Locations   ♥ = Pet Friendly Locations
RED PRINT SHOWS LARGE VEHICLE PARKING/ACCESS ON SITE OR NEARBY   BROWN PRINT SHOWS CAMPGROUNDS/RV PARKS

EXIT	FLORIDA
(278)	**Rest Area (Both dir)** **(RR, Phones, Picnic, Vend, Sec24/7)**
275	FL 56, to Zephyrhills
Gas	E: Shell
Lodg	E: Hampton Inn
(274)	Jct I-275S, Tampa, St Petersburg(SB)
270	CR 581, Bruce B Downs Blvd, Tampa
Gas	E: 7-11, Hess◆, Mobil, Shell◆ W: 7-11
Food	E: Boston Market, Burger King, ChickFilA, Golden China, Lee Roy Selmon's, Moe's SW Grill, Panera Bread, Papa John's, Ruby Tuesday, Subway, Steak 'n Shake, Starbucks, Taco Bell W: McDonald's, Olive Garden, Red Lobster
Lodg	E: Comfort Inn, Holiday Inn Express, Wingate Inn
Other	E: Circuit City, Publix, Home Depot, Tires, Walgreen's W: BJ's, Lowe's
266	CR 582A, CR 579, E Fletcher Ave, Morris Bridge Rd, Tampa
Gas	E: Circle K W: 7-11, Mobil, Shell◆
Food	W: Bob Evans, Great American Grill, Hooters, Starbucks, Wendy's
Lodg	W: Courtyard, Days Inn, Hampton Inn, Hilton Garden Inn, Residence Inn, Sleep Inn
Med	E: + Hospital, + Moffitt Cancer Center
265	FL 582, Fowler Ave, Temple Terrace
Gas	W: BP, Shell
Food	W: Burger King, Denny's, McDonald's, Perkins, Ryan's Grill
Lodg	W: Holiday Inn, La Quinta Inn♥, Ramada Inn, Wingate Inn
Other	E: Happy Traveler RV Park▲ W: to Busch Gardens, Universal Studios
(261)	Jct I-4, E-Orlando, W-Tampa, US 92, FL 600, to Brandon (NB)
Gas	E: BP, Citgo, Chevron
Food	E: Bob Evans, **Cracker Barrel**, Danny's All American Diner, Subway, Wendy's
Lodg	E: Camp Knox Motel, Hampton Inn, Masters Inn, Suites Motel
TServ	W: **Cummins SE** (W to exit 6C)
Other	E: **Lazydays RV Supercenter/Rally Park▲** W: **RV Mobile Service**, Vandenburg Airport✈
260	FL 574, ML King Blvd, Mango (SB)
260B	FL 574W, ML King Blvd, Mango
Gas	W: BP, Hess
Food	W: McDonald's, Subway
Lodg	W: AmeriSuites, Hilton Garden Inn, Radisson, Residence Inn
TServ	W: **Kenworth of Central FL**
Other	E: Grocery, **Walgreen's** W: Grocery, US Post Office, CitiBank Ctr, FL State Fairgrounds
260A	FL 574E, ML King Blvd, Mango
Gas	E: Chevron, Citgo, RaceTrac, Shell
Food	E: McDonald's, Quiznos, Waffle House
257	FL 60, Adamo Dr, Brandon Blvd, Causeway Blvd, Tampa, to Brandon
Gas	E: Circle K, Mobil, Shell W: Citgo, Circle K, Shell

EXIT	FLORIDA
Food	E: Chili's, Chuck E Cheese, Denny's, Don Pablo, Olive Garden, Moe's SW Grill, Outback Steakhouse, Panda Express, Papa John's, Red Lobster, Romano's Macaroni Grill, Sam Seltzer's Steakhouse, Smokey Bones BBQ, Steak 'N Shake, TGI Friday, Wings Gone Wild W: Bob Evans, Burger King, Hooters, McDonald's, Subway, Sonny's BBQ, Sweet Tomatoes, Wendy's
Lodg	E: La Quinta Inn♥, Holiday Inn W: Baymont Inn, Best Western, Comfort Inn, Days Inn, Fairfield Inn, Hampton Inn, Red Roof Inn♥
TServ	W: **Freightliner of Tampa**, **Tampa Mack Sales**
Med	E: + Brandon Reg'l Hospital
Other	E: ATMs, Auto Services, AMC 20, Banks, Best Buy, B&N, Firestone, Pep Boys, Petco♥, Sam's Club, Staples, Target, **Wal-Mart sc**, Brandon Towne Mall, Hillsborough Comm College, **Tom's RV**, **Adventure RV** W: Auto Dealers, Circuit City, Home Depot, Office Depot, **Bates RV**
(256)	FL 618W/Crosstown Expwy (TOLL), Causeway Blvd, Brandon, Tampa
254	US 301, Riverview, to FL 60, to Crosstown Expwy, Brandon, Tampa
Gas	E: Mobil W: 7-11◆, Chevron, Shell
Other	E: ATMs, Banks, Costco, CVS, FedEx Kinko's, Home Depot, PetSmart♥, Publix, **Walgreen's**, **Wal-Mart** W: **La Mesa RV**, **Freightliner**
250	Gibsonton Dr, Riverview
Gas	E: Racetrac, 7-11 W: BP, Murphy
Food	E: McDonald's, Pizza Hut, Quiznos, Ruby Tuesday, Taco Bell, Wendy's W: McDonald's
Other	E: Winn Dixie, **Alafia River RV Resort▲**, **Hidden River Travel Resort▲** W: **Wal-Mart sc**
246	CR 672, Big Bend Rd, Gibsonton, to Apollo Beach, Riverview
Gas	E: 7-11, Chevron W: 7-11
Other	E: **RV Anywhere Service**, to **Hidden River Travel Resort▲** W: **Holiday Palms RV Park▲**
240B	FL 674W, College Ave, Sun City Ctr Blvd, Ruskin, Sun City Center (SB)
Gas	W: Circle K, Hess, RaceTrac
Food	W: KFC, McDonald's, Subway
Lodg	W: Holiday Inn Express
Other	W: **Sun Lake RV Resort▲**, to **River Oaks RV Resort▲**, **Hide-A-Way RV Resort▲**, **Tampa South RV Resort▲**, **Hawaiian Isles RV Resort▲**, **Lone Pine Travel Trailer Park▲**
240A	FL 674E, College Ave, Sun City Ctr
E:	**Ruskin Welcome Center**
Gas	E: Chevron
Food	E: Beef O'Brady's, Bob Evans, Denny's, Hungry Howie's, King Buffet, Pizza Hut, Sonny's BBQ, Taco Bell, Wendy's
Lodg	E: Comfort Inn
Med	E: + South Bay Hospital

EXIT	FLORIDA
Other	E: ATMs, Banks, CVS, Home Depot, Kash & Karry, **Pharmacy**, Publix, NAPA, Radio Shack, Sweet Bay Grocery, **Walgreen's**, **Wal-Mart**, Winn Dixie
240	FL 674, Sun City Center (NB)
(238)	**Rest Area (SB)** **(RR, Phones, Picnic, Vend, Sec24/7)**
(237)	**Rest Area (NB)** **(RR, Phones, Picnic, Vend, Sec24/7**
229	CR 6, Moccasin Wallow Rd, to Parrish, Palmetto
Other	W: **Winterset Travel Trailer Park▲**, **Terra Ceia RV Resort▲**, **Fiesta Grove RV Resort▲**, **Frog Creek RV Campground▲**, **Fisherman's Cove RV Resort▲**
(228)	Jct I-275N, to St Petersburg
224	US 301, Ellenton, to Palmetto
TStop	W: **Pilot Travel Center #89** (DAND)
Gas	E: BP, Chevron, RaceTrac, Shell◆
Food	E: Applebee's, Checkers, Little Caesars, McDonald's, Ruby Tuesday, Wendy's W: **Subway/Pilot TC**, Denny's, Oyster Bar, Shoney's, Waffle House
Lodg	E: Hampton Inn, Sleep Inn W: GuestHouse Inn, Ramada Ltd
Other	E: Kmart, Publix, **Walgreen's**, US Post Office, Ellenton Outlet Mall/Prime Outlets, Ellenton Ice & Sports Complex, Darlene's Shell, Tourist Info, **Ellenton Gardens Campground▲** W: **WiFi/Pilot TC**
220B	FL 64W, Bradenton (NB)
FStop	W: **Circle K Truxtop #1686/76**
Gas	W: BP◆, Hess, RaceTrac, Shell
Food	W: Burger King, **Cracker Barrel**, Wendy's McDonald's, Sonny's BBQ, Waffle House
Lodg	W: Comfort Inn, Days Inn, Econo Lodge, Holiday Inn Express, Motel 6♥
Med	W: + Hospital
Other	W: ATMs, Banks, Manatee River Harley Davidson, Publix, Winn Dixie, **Wal-Mart sc**, Vet♥, **Dream RV Center**, **Encore RV Resort▲**
220A	FL 64E, Zolfo Springs (NB)
Other	E: **Lake Manatee State Rec Area▲**
220	FL 64, Bradenton, Zolfo Springs (SB)
Other	E: **Lake Manatee State Park▲**
217B	FL 70W, Bradenton, Myakka City
Gas	W: BP◆, Circle K, Exxon◆, Shell
Food	W: Arby's, Applebee's, Bob Evans, ChickFilA, McDonald's, Starbucks, Subway
Other	W: CVS, Publix, Lowe's, Tires, **Pleasant Lake RV Resort▲**, **Horseshoe Cove RV Resort▲**, to **Arbor Terrace RV Resort▲**, **Tropical Gardens Travel Park▲**, **Linger Lodge RV Resort▲**
217A	FL 70, Bradenton, Myakka City
Gas	E: Hess◆
Food	E: Wing Factory, Subs/Pizza/Hess
Other	E: ATMs, Banks, CarWash, Grocery
217	FL 70, Bradenton, Arcadia, Myakka City, Lakewood Ranch (SB)
213	University Pkwy, to Sarasota, to International Airport
Gas	E: Chevron◆ W: Chevron

◆= Regular Gas Stations with Diesel   ▲ = RV Friendly Locations   ♥ = Pet Friendly Locations

RED PRINT SHOWS LARGE VEHICLE PARKING/ACCESS ON SITE OR NEARBY   BROWN PRINT SHOWS CAMPGROUNDS/RV PARKS

Page 341

INTERSTATE 75 N/S

EXIT	FLORIDA
Food	E: Alamo Steakhouse Grill, Chili's, China Coast, Quiznos, Subway/Chevron W: Atlanta Bread, Bonefish Grill, Carrabbas, Ruby Tuesday, Wendy's
Lodg	E: Fairfield Inn, Holiday Inn W: Comfort Suites, Courtyard, Residence Inn, Springhill Suites
Other	E: Publix, Walgreen's W: BJ's, CVS, Staples, Target, Sarasota/Bradenton Int'l Airport✈, Sarasota Outlet Center, Ringling Museum, Sarasota Jungle Gardens, Sarasota Classic Car Museum, Sarasota Lakes RV Resort▲
210	**FL 780, Fruitville Rd, Sarasota**
Gas	W: BP◆, Chevron, Mobil◆
Food	W: Applebee's, Bob Evans, Burger King, ChickFilA, Don Pablo, KFC, Longhorn Steakhouse, McDonald's, Perkins, Subway, Taco Bell
Lodg	W: AmericInn
Med	W: + Hospital
Other	E: Sun N Fun RV Resort▲ W: ATMs, Advance Auto, Dollar Tree, Pharmacy, Publix, Radio Shack, Sam's Club, Target, Winn Dixie, Shopping at St Armand Circle, Campbell RV, Adventure RV
207	**Bee Ridge Rd, Sarasota**
Gas	W: BP, Mobil◆, Shell
Food	W: Arby's, Chili's, Checker's, McDonald's, Pizza Hut, Steak 'n Shake, Taco Bell, Woody's BBQ
Lodg	W: Hampton Inn
Med	W: + Dr's Hospital of Sarasota
Other	W: ATMs, Dollar Tree, Goodyear, Home Depot, Publix, Radio Shack, Sweet Bay Foods, Walgreen's, Wal-Mart
205	**FL 72, Clark Rd, Sarasota, Arcadia**
Gas	W: BP, Exxon◆, Mobil
Food	W: Applebee's, Arby's, Burger King, ChickFilA, McDonald's, Quiznos, Starbucks, Waffle House, Wendy's
Lodg	W: Comfort Inn, Country Inn, Ramada
Other	W: ATMs, CVS, Publix, Walgreen's, Beach Club RV Resort▲, Windward Isle RV Park▲, Sarasota RV Center
200	**FL 681S, Venice, Osprey (SB)**
Med	W: + Hospital
195	**Laurel Rd, Nokomis, Laurel** (Serv 3.5mi W in Nokomis & Laurel)
193	**Jacaranda Blvd, Venice**
Gas	W: Chevron, Citgo◆, Hess◆, RaceTrac
Food	W: Cracker Barrel, McDonald's, Waffle House
Lodg	W: Best Western, Holiday Inn Express
Med	W: + Hospital
Other	W: Caribbean Bay Club, Palm & Pines Mobile & RV Park▲
191	**River Rd, Venice, to North Port, Warm Mineral Springs, Englewood** (Serv 3mi W in Venice)
Other	W: Venice Airport✈, Buchanan Airport✈, Venice Campground▲, Ramblers Rest▲
182	**Sumter Blvd, North Port**
Other	W: Myakka River RV Park▲
179	**Toledo Blade Blvd, North Port**
170	**CR 769, Kings Hwy, Port Charlotte**
FStop	W: Kings Chevron

Personal Notes
_____

EXIT	FLORIDA
Gas	E: 7-11◆, RaceTrac W: BP, Hess◆, Mobil
Food	W: Denny's, McDonald's, Cracker Barrel, Pizza Hut, Waffle House, Wendy's
Lodg	E: Holiday Inn, Hampton Inn
Other	E: Wal-Mart sc W: Advance Auto, CVS, Dollar General, Grocery, Publix, Walgreen's, US Post Office
167	**CR 776, Harborview Rd**
164	**US 17, FL 35, Punta Gorda, Arcadia**
TStop	E: Duncan Rd Shell
Gas	E: Chevron◆, RaceWay W: Circle K
Food	W: McDonald's
Med	W: + Hospital
Other	E: Waters Edge RV Resort▲, Charlotte Harbor RV Park▲, Charlotte Co Airport✈, Lettuce Lake Travel Resort▲
161	**CR 768, Jones Lp Rd, Punta Gorda**
E:	Rest Area (Both dir) (RR, Phones, Picnic, Vend, Sec24/7)
TStop	W: Pilot Travel Center #94 (Scales)
Gas	W: BP◆
Food	W: Arby's/TJCinn/Pilot TC, Burger King, Pizza Hut, Taco Bell, Waffle House, Wendy's
Lodg	W: Motel 6♥, Days Inn, Super 8
Other	E: Charlotte Co Airport✈ W: WiFi/Pilot TC, Punta Gorda RV Resort▲, Encore RV Park▲, Golf Course
(160)	**Weigh Station (Both dir)**

EXIT	FLORIDA
158	**CR 762, Tuckers Grade**
Gas	W: Circle K
Other	E: Babcock-Webb Wildlife Area W: Pelican Perch RV Park▲, Our Family RV Center
143	**FL 78, Bay Shore Rd, N Ft Myers**
Gas	E: Citgo◆ W: RaceTrac
Other	E: Seminole Campground▲, Up River Campground▲ W: Pioneer Village Mobil & RV Park▲
141	**FL 80, Palm Beach Blvd, Ft Myers**
Gas	E: BP◆, Chevron, Exxon W: 7-11, RaceTrac, Hess◆
Food	E: Cracker Barrel, Waffle House W: Hardee's, Little Caesar's, Perkins, Pizza Hut, Sonny's BBQ, Subway, Taco Bell
Lodg	E: Comfort Inn
Other	E: Pharmacy, Publix, Orange Harbor RV Park▲ W: Big Lots, CVS, Dollar General, Publix, Radio Shack, North Trail RVCenter
139	**Luckett Rd, Ft Myers**
TStop	W: Pilot Travel Center #352 (Scales)
Food	W: Subway/Pilot TC, Grandma's Kitchen
TServ	W: Pilot TC/Tires
Other	E: Cypress Woods RV Park▲, RV Center W: Laundry/WiFi/Pilot TC, Camping World, RV Park▲
138	**FL 82, MLK Blvd, Ft Myers**
Gas	E: Hess◆ W: Citgo◆, Speedway
TServ	W: Cummins SE, Wallace Int'l
136	**FL 884, Colonial Blvd, Ft Myers**
Gas	W: 7-11, BP, Shell◆, Murphy
Food	W: Bob Evans, Steak 'n Shake
Lodg	W: Baymont Inn, Courtyard, Howard Johnson, La Quinta Inn♥, Super 8
Med	W: + Hospital
Other	E: Home Depot W: ATMs, Lowe's, Wal-Mart sc
131	**Daniels Pkwy, International Airport, Fort Myers, Cape Coral**
E:	Cape Coral Rest Areas (Both dir) (RR, Phones, Picnic, Vend, Sec24/7)
Gas	E: BP◆ W: Hess◆, RaceTrac, Shell
Food	E: Subway/BP W: Arby's, Bob Evans, Burger King, Cracker Barrel, Denny's, McDonald's, Waffle House, Wendy's
Lodg	W: Best Western, Country Inn, Hampton Inn, Sleep Inn, Springhill Suites
Med	W: + Hospital
Other	E: Southwest Florida Int'l Airport✈, to Golden Palms Motorcoach Estates▲ W: Tires, Publix
128	**Alico Rd, San Carlos Park**
Gas	E: Costco W: Hess◆
Food	W: Subway, Wendy's
Lodg	E: Hilton Garden Inn, Homewood Suites
Other	E: ATMs, Bass Pro Shop, Best Buy, Costco, Petco♥, Staples, Super Target W: to Woodsmoke Camping Resort▲
123	**CR 850, Corkscrew Rd, Estero**
Gas	E: BP◆ W: 7-11, Chevron, Hess◆

◆ = Regular Gas Stations with Diesel ▲ = RV Friendly Locations ♥ = Pet Friendly Locations
RED PRINT SHOWS LARGE VEHICLE PARKING/ACCESS ON SITE OR NEARBY BROWN PRINT SHOWS CAMPGROUNDS/RV PARKS

EXIT		FLORIDA
	Food	E: McDonald's, Perkins, Starbucks, Subway
	Other	E: CVS, Grocery, Publix W: Lowe's, Tires
116		**Bonita Beach Rd, Bonita Springs**
	Gas	E: Chevron◊ W: BP, Shell, Albertson's
	Food	W: Bob Evans, McDonald's, Waffle House
	Lodg	W: Baymont Inn, Hampton Inn, Holiday Inn Express
	Other	E: Publix W: Albertson's, CVS, Imperial RV Park▲
111		**CR 846, Immokalee Rd, Naples Park**
	Gas	E: 7-11, Mobil W: Shell◊
	Food	E: Bob Evans, Pizza Hut W: McDonald's
	Lodg	E: Hampton Inn
	Med	W: + Hospital
	Other	W: ATMs, Albertson's, CVS, Publix, Super Target, Wal-Mart sc
107		**CR 896, Pinebridge Rd, Naples**
	Gas	E: BP◊ W: Chevron◊, RaceTrac, Shell◊
	Food	E: McDonald's/BP W: Applebee's, Burger King, IHOP, Perkins, Waffle House
	Lodg	W: Best Western, Hilton Garden Inn
	Other	E: Publix, Walgreen's W: Tires, Harley Davidson
105		**CR 886, Golden Gate Pkwy**
101		**FL 84, CR 951, Naples**
	NOTE:	SB: LAST Free Exit before TOLL
	Gas	W: Mobil◊, Shell◊
	Food	W: Burger King, Checkers, Cracker Barrel, McDonald's, Subway, Waffle House
	Lodg	W: Baymont Inn, Comfort Inn, La Quinta Inn♥, Red Roof Inn♥, Super 8
	Other	W: RV Center, RV Park▲, Naples/Marco Island KOA▲
(100)		**TOLL Plaza (Both dir)**
80		**FL 29, to Everglades City**
(71)		**Big Cypress Nat'l Preserve**
(63)		**Rest Area (Both dir)** (RR, Phones, Picnic, Vend, Sec24/7)
49		**FL 833, Government Rd (NB)**
	TStop	E: Miccosukee Service Plaza/Mobil
	Other	E: Laundry/M SP
(41)		**Picnic Area (SB)**
(38)		**Picnic Area (NB)**
(35)		**Rest Area (Both dir)** (RR, Phones, Picnic, Vend, Sec24/7)
(32)		**Picnic Area (Both dir)**
(26)		**TOLL Plaza (WB)**
	NOTE:	Begin NB/End SB Callboxes
23		**US 27, FL 25, Miami, South Bay**
	NOTE:	Begin I-75N TOLL Road
22		**Glades Pkwy, Arvida Pkwy, Ft Lauderdale**
21		**FL 84W, Indian Trace (NB)**
	Gas	W: Citgo◊

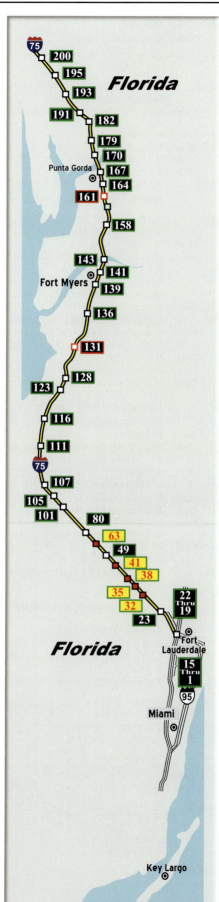

EXIT		FLORIDA
19		**I-595E, FL 869 (TOLL), Sawgrass Expwy, Ft Lauderdale**
15		**Royal Palm Blvd, Weston**
	Gas	W: Exxon
	Food	E: Pastability W: Subway, Wendy's
	Lodg	E: AmeriSuites, Courtyard W: Marriott, Residence Inn
	Other	W: Best Buy
13B		**FL 818, Griffin Rd W**
	Gas	W: 7-11
	Food	W: Chili's, McDonald's
	Other	W: Home Depot. Publix, Auto Dealers
13A		**FL 818, Griffin Rd E, SW 46th St**
	Gas	E: Shell◊
	Food	E: Burger King, Outback Steakhouse, Waffle House
	Med	E: + Hospital
	Other	E: Publix
11B		**Sheridan St W, SW 72nd St, Pembroke Pines**
	Gas	W: Shell
	Food	W: Cracker Barrel, McDonald's, Starbucks Subway, TGI Friday
	Other	W: Publix, Lowe's
11A		**SW 72nd St, Sheridan St E**
	Gas	E: Chevron
	Lodg	E: Hampton Inn, Holiday Inn
9B		**FL 820W, Pines Blvd**
	Gas	W: Mobil, 76, Shell
	Food	W: KFC/TacoBell, McDonald's, Sweet Tomatoes
	Lodg	W: Grand Palms Hotel Resort
	Other	W: ATMs, AdvanceAuto, Costco, Publix, Tires
9A		**FL 820E, Pines Blvd**
	Gas	E: Shell
	Food	E: Arby's, Chili's, Romano's Macaroni Grill, Shell's Seafood, Starbucks, Subway, Wendy's
	Other	E: Best Buy, B&N, BJ's, Circuit City, Home Depot, Target, Walgreen's
7B		**Miramar Pkwy West**
	Gas	W: Shell
	Food	W: Starbucks
7A		**Miramar Pkwy East**
	Gas	E: Chevron
	Food	E: McDonald's, Subway, Wendy's
	Lodg	E: Hilton Garden Inn, Wingate Inn
	Other	E: Publix, Home Depot, Walgreen's
5		**to FL 821S, FL Tpk (TOLL) (SB)**
4		**NW 186th St, Miami Gardens Dr**
	Gas	E: BP, Chevron
	Food	E: IHOP, McDonald's, Subway
	Other	E: CVS, Publix
2		**NW 138th St, Graham Dairy Rd**
	Gas	W: Mobil, Shell
	Food	W: McDonald's, Subway, Wendy's
	Other	W: Publix, Walgreen's
1B		**FL 826S, Palmetto Expwy**
1A		**FL 826N, Palmetto Expwy**

(EASTERN TIME ZONE)
(I-75 begins/ends on FL 826)

FLORIDA

Begin Northbound I-75 from Miami, FL to the MICHIGAN / CANADA border.

◊ = Regular Gas Stations with Diesel   ▲ = RV Friendly Locations   ♥ = Pet Friendly Locations
RED PRINT SHOWS LARGE VEHICLE PARKING/ACCESS ON SITE OR NEARBY   BROWN PRINT SHOWS CAMPGROUNDS/RV PARKS

INTERSTATE 76 E

EXIT	COLORADO
	Begin Eastbound I-76 from near Julesburg, CO To near Jct I-80 in Big Springs, NE.
	COLORADO (MOUNTAIN TIME ZONE) (I-76 begins/ends near I-80 Jct in Nebraska)
1A	CO 121, Wadsworth Blvd (WB)
Gas	N: 7-11, Conoco, Lucky Mart, Costco
Food	N: Applebee's, Bennigan's, Country Buffet, Lone Star Steakhouse, Subway, McDonald's, Ruby Tuesday, Starbucks, Texas Roadhouse, Taco Bell
Med	N: + Hospital
Other	N: ATMs, AdvanceAuto, Costco, Home Depot, Lowe's, Office Depot, Sam's Club, Tires, Mall, Arvada Center S: Discount Tire
1B	CO 95, Sheridan Blvd, Arvada
3	US 287, Federal Blvd, to I-70, Denver
Gas	N: Shamrock◊
Food	S: Taco House
Lodg	N: N Federal Valley Motel S: Joy Motor Hotel, Primrose Motel, White Rock Motel
Other	S: Regis Univ
4	Pecos St
(5)	Jct I-25, N to Ft Collins, Boulder, S to Denver, Colo Springs (EB)
(5AB)	Jct I-25, S-Denver, N to Ft Collins, Boulder (WB)
(6)	Jct I-270E, to I-70E, Limon, DIA (EB)
(6A)	I-270E, to I-70E, Limon, DIA (WB)
(6B)	I-270W, to I-25N Ft Collins, US 36W Boulder (WB)
8	CO 224, 74th Ave, to US 85, Commerce City, Welby (EB, diff reacc)
FStop	N: Shoco Oil◊ S: Shamrock◊
TWash	N: Shoco Oil
Other	S: to Wal-Mart sc
9	US 85S, US 6W, to CO 2S, Brighton Blvd, Commerce City (WB)
Gas	S: Shell
TServ	S: Freightliner
Other	S: Road Bear RV, CO State Hwy Patrol Post
10	88th Ave, Henderson
Gas	N: Conoco◊
Food	N: Blimpie/Conoco
Lodg	N: Holiday Inn Express, Super 8
Other	S: Mile High Flea Market

EXIT	COLORADO
11	96th Ave
Other	S: Diesel Repair Services
12	US 85N, Greeley, Brighton (fr EB, Left Exit)
16	CO 2W, Sable Blvd, 120th Ave, Brighton, Commerce City
TStop	N: PTP/Tomahawk Auto Truck Plaza/Shell (Scales)
Food	N: Rest/FastFood/Tomahawk ATP
TWash	N: Tomahawk ATP
TServ	N: Tomahawk ATP/Tires
Other	N: Laundry/Tomahawk ATP
(18)	Jct I-470E (TOLL), to DIA, Limon, Aurora, Colorado Springs (WB)
20	136th Ave, Barr Lake, Brighton (Access to Ex #22 Serv-N to US 85)
Food	N: Chili's
Other	N: ATMs, Target, Barr Lake RV Park▲ S: Barr Lake State Park▲
21	144th Ave, Brighton (Access to Ex #22 Serv-N to US 85)
Other	N: Home Depot, Wal-Mart sc,
22	152nd Ave, Bromley Lane, Brighton
Gas	N: Shamrock◊, Amer Pride, GasAMat
Food	N: Applebee's, Arby's, Starbucks, Wendy's
Lodg	N: Comfort Inn, Super 8
Med	N: + Platte Valley Medical Center
Other	N: ATMs, Albertson's, Kmart, Pharmacy, Lowe's, Wal-Mart sc, UPS Store
25	Frontage Rd, 160th Ave, CO 7W, Brighton, Lochbuie
Gas	N: Shell
Other	N: Big O Tires, Safeway, Walgreen's, Auto & Truck Services S: Staples
31	CO 52, Hudson, Prospect Valley
Tstop	N: Love's Travel Stop #377 (Scales)
Gas	S: Conoco◊, Phillips 66◊
Food	N: Carl'sJr/Subway/Love's TS S: El Faro, Pepper Pod Rest, Mex Rest
Other	N: WiFi/Love's TS S: Denver NE Pepper Pod CG▲
34	CR 49, Kersey Rd, Hudson, Greeley, Kersey
39	I-76 Bus, Market St, Keenesburg
Gas	S: Phillips 66◊
Food	S: Corner Kitchen, Coffee Bistro
Lodg	S: Keene Motel
48	CR 73, Roggen, to CO 79, Bennett
Gas	N: Shell
49	Painter Rd, CR 386 (WB)
57	CO 51, CR 91

EXIT	COLORADO
60	to CO 144, to Orchard
64	US 6E, Central Ave, CR 3, Wiggins
66A	CO 39, CO 52, Wiggins, Goodrich
S:	Rest Area (Both dir) (RR, Phone, Picnic, Vend)
FStop	N: Wiggins Junction Truck Stop S: Stub's Gas & Oil/Sinclair
Food	N: Rest/Wiggins Jct TS
TServ	N: Wiggins Jct/Tires/Towing
Other	S: LP/Stub's
66B	US 34W, CR R, Greeley (WB)
73	Long Bridge Rd, CR 12, Ft Morgan
(75)	Weigh Station (Both dir)
75	I-76 Bus, US 34, Ft Morgan
Gas	S: Loaf 'n Jug◊
Lodg	S: Motel
Other	S: I-76 Speedway
79	CO 144, Weldona, Log Lane Village (fr WB, no re-entry)
80	CO 52, Ft Morgan, Raymer
Gas	S: Conoco◊, Shell◊, Valero◊
Food	S: DQ, Arby's, KFC, McDonald's, Taco John's, A&W, Sonic, Subway
Lodg	S: Days Inn, Super 8
Med	S: + Hospital
Other	N: Ft Morgan Muni Airport✈ S: AutoZone, RiteAid
82	CR 20, Barlow Rd, Ft Morgan
FStop	N: Conoco Outpost
Gas	S: Phillips 66◊
Food	N: Maverick's Country Grill S: Burger King, Quiznos
Lodg	S: Comfort Inn, Rodeway Inn
Other	N: Wal-Mart sc
86	CR 24, Dodd Bridge Rd, Ft Morgan
89	CR 27, Hospital Rd, Brush
Med	S: + E Morgan Co Hospital
90A	CO 71S, to US 34, Colorado Ave, Brush, Limon, Akron
FStop	S: Acorn Food Store #2380/Conoco
TStop	N: PTP/Tomahawk Truck Plaza/Shell (Scales)
Food	N: Rest/Tomahawk TP, Pizza Hut, Peking China Buffet, Wendy's S: McDonald's, Subway
Lodg	N: Econo Lodge♥ S: Microtel
TServ	N: Tomahawk ATP/Tires
90B	CO 71N, Snyder

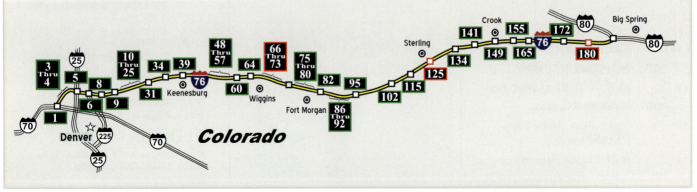

Page 344 ◊ = Regular Gas Stations with Diesel   ▲ = RV Friendly Locations   ♥ = Pet Friendly Locations
RED PRINT SHOWS LARGE VEHICLE PARKING/ACCESS ON SITE OR NEARBY   BROWN PRINT SHOWS CAMPGROUNDS/RV PARKS

EXIT		COLORADO
92AB		to US 6E, I-76 Bus, to US 34, CO 71, Brush, Limon
	Other	S: Brush Muni Airport✈
95		CR 33, Hillrose
102		CO Q, Akron, to Merino
115		CO 63, Merino, to Atwood, Akron
	FStop	N: Atwood Sinclair
	Gas	S: Interstate Standard Station◊
	Food	N: Café/Sinclair FS
		S: Atwood Steakhouse
125		I-76 Bus, US 6W, to CO 138, CO 14, CO 62S, Sterling, Otis, Atwood
	N:	Rest Area (Both dir) (RR, Phone, Picnic, Vend, RVDump)
	FStop	S: Phillips 66
	TStop	N: AmPride #2/Cenex
	Gas	N: Conoco, Sinclair, SavOMat

EXIT		COLORADO
	Food	N: Arby's, Burger King, McDonald's, Sonic, Taco John's, Wendy's
		S: FastFood/P66, McDonald's, Quiznos
	Lodg	N: Best Western♥, First Interstate Inn, Fountain Lodge, Sterling Motor Lodge
		S: Ramada Inn♥, Super 8, Travelodge
	TServ	N: Sterling Diesel Service
	Med	N: + Hospital
	Other	N: Laundry/AmPride, Big O Tires, Wal-Mart sc, Pharmacy, Grocery, Golf Course, Museum, Sterling RV, Sterling State Park
		S: Buffalo Hills Campground & RV Park▲
134		CR 55, Iliff
141		CR 67, CR 65, Crook, Proctor
149		CO 55, Crook, to Fleming
	TStop	S: Kuskie Interstate Svc & Café/Sinclair
155		CR 93, Red Lion Rd, Fleming

EXIT		COLORADO
165		CO 59, CR 15, Sedgwick, Haxtun
	Gas	N: Lucy's Place
172		CR 27, CR 29, Ovid
180		US 385, CR 45, Julesburg, Holyoke
	N:	CO Welcome Center (Both dir) (RR, Phone, Info, RVDump)
	FStop	N: Flying JTravel Plaza #5014/Conoco
	Gas	N: Texaco
		S: Conoco◊
	Food	N: Rest/FJ TP, Subway
	Lodg	N: Budget Host Inn, Grand Motel
	Med	N: + Sedgwick Co Memorial Hospital
	Other	N: WiFi/LP/FJ TP, Julesburg Muni Airport✈
NOTE:		MM 184: Nebraska State Line

(I-76 begins/ends on I-70, Ex #269B)
(MOUNTAIN TIME ZONE)

◯ COLORADO

EXIT		OHIO
		◯ OHIO
		(EASTERN TIME ZONE)
		(Begin/End I-76 on I-71, Exit #209)
(1)		Jct I-71, N-Cleveland, S-Columbus, US 224W, to Lodi
	TStop	W: Travel Center of America/BP, Pilot Travel Center #13
	Gas	W: 76, Citgo, Sunoco
	Food	W: CountryPride/B King/Popeye/Starbucks/TA TC, Subway/Pilot TC, McDonald's
	Lodg	W: Super 8♥
	Tires	W: TA TC
	Other	W: Laundry/WiFi/RVDump/TA TC, WiFi/Pilot TC, Chippewa Valley Campgrounds▲
2		OH 3, Wooster Pike Rd, Seville, Medina
	Gas	N: Circle K
		S: Citgo◊
	Food	N: DQ, Hardee's, Huddle House, Subway
	Lodg	N: Comfort Inn, Hawthorne Inn
	Other	N: Maple Lakes Campground▲
(6)		Weigh Station (Both dir)
7		OH 57, Wadsworth Rd, Wadsworth, to Rittman, Medina
	Gas	N: Marathon◊

EXIT		OHIO
	Med	S: + Hospital
	Other	S: Wadsworth Muni Airport✈, Akron Univ
9		OH 94, High St, Wadsworth, N Royalton
	Gas	N: Circle K
		S: BP◊, Citgo, Marathon, Shell, Sunoco
	Food	N: Arby's, Bob Evans, Burger King, DQ, McDonald's, Pizza Hut, Ponderosa, Subway, Taco Bell, Wendy's
		S: Casa Del Rio, Country Café, Denny's
	Lodg	N: Holiday Inn Express, Ramada
		S: Legacy Inn♥
	Other	N: Pharmacy, Grocery, Home Depot, Kmart, Wal-Mart sc
		S: Auto Zone, Auto Service
11		OH 261, Akron Rd, Wadsworth, Norton
	Gas	N: Speedway
	Other	S: Target
13AB		OH 21, S-Massillon, N-Cleveland
14		CR 17, Cleveland-Massillon Rd, Norton
	Gas	S: BP, Citgo, Marathon
	Food	S: Charlie's Rest
16		Barber Rd, Norton Ave, Barberton
	Gas	S: Sunoco
	Med	S: + Hospital

EXIT		OHIO
17		Wooster Rd, East Ave (WB)
	Gas	N: Duke
	Other	N: Auto Services
17A		State St (EB, No EB re-entry)
	Food	N: Arby's, Iguana's, Long John Silver, McDonald's, Subway, Wendy's
	Other	N: Rolling Acres Mall, Goodyear, NTB, Firestone
17B		OH 619, Wooster Rd, to Barberton, Wooster (EB)
	Gas	N: Marathon
	Food	N: Family Restaurant
	Med	S: + Hospital
	Other	S: Tires
(18)		Jct I-277, US 224E, to I-77, Canton, Mogadore, Barberton
19		Kenmore Blvd (EB), Battles Ave (WB)
(20)		Jct I-77, N-Cleveland, S-Akron (EB)
21A		East Ave (WB, no WB re-entry)
	Gas	N: 76
21B		Bowery St, Lakeshore Ave, Downtown (EB)
21C		OH 59E, MLK Frwy (EB), Dart Ave, (WB), Downtown Akron
	Med	N: + Akron General Med Center

◊ = Regular Gas Stations with Diesel   ▲ = RV Friendly Locations   ♥ = Pet Friendly Locations

RED PRINT SHOWS LARGE VEHICLE PARKING/ACCESS ON SITE OR NEARBY   BROWN PRINT SHOWS CAMPGROUNDS/RV PARKS

EXIT		OHIO
	Other	N: to Akron Zoo
22A		Main St, Broadway, Downtown
	Other	N: ATM, Amtrak, Convention Center
22B		Grant St, Wolf Ledges Blvd
	Gas	S: BP
	Food	S: McDonald's
	Lodg	N: Quaker Crown Plaza
	Other	N: ATM, Akron Univ, Quaker Square, Inventors Hall of Fame
(23A)		Jct I-77S, to Canton
23B		OH 8N, Buchtel Ave, to Cuyahoga Falls, Univ of Akron (fr EB Left Exit)
24A		Johnston St, Inman St (WB)
24		Arlington St, Kelly Ave (EB)
	Other	S: to Akron Fulton Int'l Airport ✈
24B		Arlington St, Kelly Ave (WB)
25A		Martha Ave, Seiberling St (EB)
25B		Englewood Ave, Seiberling St (EB)
25		Martha Ave, Market St (WB)
	Other	N: Goodyear Rubber Co
26		OH 18, E Market St, Brittain Rd, Mogadore, N Springfield
	FStop	N: Knacks Morgan's Truck Plaza/Marathon (EB: Access Via Exit #25B)
	Gas	N: Citgo◆, Shell S: Gas
	Food	S: Arby's, McDonald's, Subway, Wendy's
	Other	S: ATM, Auto Service, Akron Rubber Bowl
27		Gilchrist Rd, to OH 91, Akron
	Gas	S: Marathon◆, Sunoco
	Food	N: Bob Evans, S: Hardee's, Wendy's, Subway/Marathon
	Lodg	S: Best Western
	Other	N: Goodyear Metroparks S: Truck & Trailer Repair
29		OH 532, Southeast Ave, Tallmadge, Mogadore
	Gas	N: Duke S: Citgo
	Other	N: Summit Racing Parts Store
31		CR 18, Tallmadge Rd, to Kent
	Other	N: to Summit Co Fairgrounds
33		OH 43, Kent, Hartville
	Gas	N: BP◆ S: Speedway◆
	Food	N: Bob Evans, Burger King, Pizza Hut S: McDonald's, Subway, Wendy's
	Lodg	N: Alden Inn, Days Inn, Hampton Inn, Holiday Inn Express, Quality Inn, Relax Inn, Super 8
	Other	N: to Kent State Univ S: Cherokee Park Family Campground▲ Akron Mogadore Reservoir▲
38A		OH 44S, Ravenna Louisville Rd, Rootstown, Ravenna (EB)
38B		OH 44N, OH 5, Ravenna Louisville Rd, Rootstown, Rd (EB)
38		OH 44, to OH 5, Ravenna Louisville Rd, Ravenna, Rootstown (WB)
	Gas	N: BP, Speedway◆ S: Dairy Mart, Marathon
	Food	N: McDonald's, Taco Bell, Wendy's S: Burger King, Cracker Barrel, David's
	Med	N: + Regency Hospital

Personal Notes

EXIT		OHIO
	Other	S: Auto Repair, Grocery, Randolph Fairgrounds, NEO College of Medicine, Friendship Acres RV Park▲
43		OH 14, Rootstown, Ravenna, Alliance
	FStop	S: Certified Oil #410/Citgo
	Other	N: West Branch State Park▲ S: Truck Repair
(46)		Rest Area (Both dir) (RR, Phones, Picnic)
48		OH 225, Alliance, Diamond, Palmyra
	Other	N: Country Acres Campground▲, Leisure Lake Park/CtC/RPI S: to Berlin Lake
54		OH 534, Lake Milton, Newton Falls
	Gas	S: BP
	Other	N: Green Acres Lake Park▲, Lake Milton State Park
57		CR 65, Bailey Rd, to OH 45, Warren
	Other	N: to GM Lordstown Assembly Plant S: Leonard Truck & Trailer
	NOTE:	I-76 runs with I-80/OH Tpk Below. Exit #'s follow I-80
(61/218)		Jct I-80/76, OH Tpk (TOLL) (EB joins, WB Ends)
232		OH 7, Market St, North Lima, to Boardman, Youngstown
	TStop	S: Pilot Travel Center #011 (Scales)
	Gas	N: Shell, Sheetz S: Shell◆, Speedway◆
	Food	N: DQ S: FastFood/Pilot TC

EXIT		OH / PA
	Lodg	N: Budget Inn, Economy Inn, Holiday Inn Express, Quality Inn♥, Ramada S: Davis Motel, Rodeway Inn
	Med	N: + Hospital
	TWash	S: Pilot TC
	Other	S: WiFi/Pilot TC, to appr 10 mi Beaver Creek State Park, Ponderosa Park, Chaparral Family Campground▲
(234)		I-680N, Youngstown, Poland (WB)
(237)		Glacier Hills Service Plaza (EB) Mahoning Valley Service Plaza (WB)
	TStop	Valero
	Food	McDonald's
	Other	Picnic
(239)		TOLL Booth (EB End, WB Begin)
	NOTE:	I-76 runs with I-80/OH Tpk above. Exit #'s follow I-80.

(EASTERN TIME ZONE)

⏶ OHIO
⏷ PENNSYLVANIA

(EASTERN TIME ZONE)

(1.5)		TOLL Booth
	NOTE:	Begin EB/End WB Call Box Area EB for next 326 mi.
(2)		Parking Area (EB)
(6)		Parking Area (EB)
10		PA 60 (TOLL), James E Ross Hwy, to Pittsburgh, Newcastle
	Other	S: to Pittsburgh Int'l Airport ✈
13		PA 18, Big Beaver Blvd, Beaver Falls, Ellwood City
	Food	N: Rest/Holiday Inn S: Rest/Conley Inn, Giuseppe's Italian Rest
	Lodg	N: Alpine Inn, Beaver Valley Motel, Hilltop Motel, Holiday Inn♥ S: Conley Inn
(16)		Parking Area (Both dir)
(22)		Zelienople Travel Plaza (EB)
	E:	PA WELCOME CENTER
	FStop	Sunoco
	Food	Roy Rogers, Mrs Fields Cookies, Hershey's Ice Cream
(24)		Parking Area (EB)
(26)		Parking Area (EB)
(27)		Parking Area (EB)
28		US 19, Perry Hwy, to I-79, Cranberry, to Pittsburgh, Erie
	Gas	N: Amoco/BP◆, Exxon◆, Sheetz, Sunoco, Costco, GetGo S: BP◆
	Food	N: Arby's, Bob Evans, Burger King, CiCi's, Denny's, Dunkin Donuts, Hardee's, Long John Silver, Lone Star Steakhouse, Max & Erma's, McDonald's, Perkins, Primanti Bros, Pizza Hut, Subway, Wendy's S: China Garden, Quaker Steak & Lube
	Lodg	N: Comfort Inn, Fairfield Inn, Hampton Inn, Hyatt Place, Marriott, Motel 6♥, Red Roof Inn♥, Super 8, Sheraton S: Residence Inn
	Med	N: + UPMC Hospital

Page 346 ◆ = Regular Gas Stations with Diesel ▲ = RV Friendly Locations ♥ = Pet Friendly Locations
RED PRINT SHOWS LARGE VEHICLE PARKING/ACCESS ON SITE OR NEARBY BROWN PRINT SHOWS CAMPGROUNDS/RV PARKS

Interstate 76 W/E — PENNSYLVANIA

EXIT		PENNSYLVANIA
	Other	N: ATMs, Auto Services, Banks, Best Buy, CarQuest, Cinema, Costco, FedEx Kinko's, Goodyear, Home Depot, Office Max, PetCo♥, Pharmacy, RiteAid, Radio Shack, Staples, Target, **Wal-Mart sc**, Cranberry Mall, UPS Store, US Post Office, Grocery
(29)		**Parking Area (EB)**
(30)		**TOLL Plaza**
39		**PA 8, William Flynn Hwy, Gibsonia, to Pittsburgh, Butler, Butler Valley**
	Gas	N: Exxon◊, Sheetz S: BP, Sunoco◊
	Food	N: Eat 'n Park, Max & Erma's, McDonald's S: Arby's, Burger King, DQ, Dunkin Donuts, Panera Bread, Quiznos, Subway, Taco Bell, Wendy's
	Lodg	N: Comfort Inn, Richland Hotel S: Econo Lodge
	Other	N: Advance Auto, Auto Dealers, Dollar Tree Grocery, Pharmacy, Vet♥, **Wal-Mart**, Ross Park Mall S: AutoZone, CVS, Firestone, Goodyear, Tire Auto Services
48		**to PA 28, Pittsburgh, New Kensington**
	Gas	N: 76 S: Exxon◊
	Food	S: Bob Evans, Burger King, Eat 'n Park, KFC, Fuddrucker's, McDonald's, Subway, Ponderosa, Taco Bell, Wendy's
	Lodg	S: Comfort Inn, Days Inn, Holiday Inn, Holiday Inn Express, Super 8, Valley Motel
	TServ	S: Cummins Interstate Power
	Other	S: ATM, Grocery
(49)		**Oakmont Service Plaza (EB)**
	FStop	Sunoco
	Food	Burgers Etc, Hershey's Ice Cream, Nathan's Hot Dogs, Pizza
(57)		**Jct I-376, US 22, Penn-Lincoln Pkwy, Monroeville, to Pittsburgh**
	FStop	S: Stop #22/Citgo
	Gas	S: BP, Sheetz
	Food	S: Arby's, Burger King, Chinese, Dunkin Donuts, Damon's, Denny's, Eat 'n Park, Lone Star Steakhouse, Max & Erma's, McDonald's, Outback Steakhouse, Quiznos, Red Lobster, Starbucks, Taco Bell, Wendy's
	Lodg	N: East Exit Motel S: Days Inn♥, Extended Stay America, ExecuStay, Hampton Inn, Holiday Inn♥, Radisson, Red Roof Inn♥, Springhill Suites, Sunrise Inn
	Med	S: + Forbes Regional Hospital
	Other	N: CCAC Boyce Campus S: ATM, Auto Services, Auto Dealers, Banks, Grocery, FedEx Kinko's, NTB, Office Depot, Office Max, Pharmacy, Petco♥, PetSmart♥, Target, UPS Store, Monroeville Mall, ExpoMart, **to** Three Rivers Stadium, Kennywood Park, Mellon Arena
67		**US 30, Lincoln Hwy, Irwin, to Greensburg, McKeesport**
	FStop	S: Marathon (W on US 30)
	Gas	N: BP◊, Sheetz S: Gulf, Sunoco, Sunoco
	Food	N: Blimpie/BP, Pizza S: Bob Evans, Burger King, CiCi's, Denny's, Eat 'n Park, Long John Silver, Quiznos, McDonald's, Pizza Hut, Taco Bell

Personal Notes
_____

EXIT		PENNSYLVANIA
	Lodg	N: Motel 3 S: Holiday Inn Express, Penn Irwin Motel
	TServ	N: Fox & James
	Med	S: + Walk-In Medical Clinic, + Westmoreland Hospital
	Other	N: Auto Service, ATM, Bank, Laundromat RV Center, **to** St Vincent College, Seton Hill Univ S: Advance Auto, Auto Service, ATMs, Banks, Grocery, Dollar Tree, Target, **RV Center**
NOTE:		I-76/PA Tpk runs with I-70 below. Exit #'s follow I-76.
(75)		**Jct I-70W, to US 119, PA 66 (TOLL), New Stanton, Greensburg, Wheeling**
	Gas	N: Sunoco S: BP◊, Exxon, Sheetz, Sunoco
	Food	N: Cedar Steakhouse/Motel S: Bob Evans, Eat 'n Park, McDonald's X2, Chinese, Cracker Barrel, KFC, Pizza Hut, Quzinos, Subway, Wendy's
	Lodg	N: Cedar Motel S: Budget Inn, Comfort Inn, Days Inn, Fairfield Inn, Howard Johnson, Quality Inn, Super 8
	Other	N: to Univ of Pittsburgh/Greensburg S: to Madison KOA▲, Camping▲
(78)		**New Stanton Service Plaza (WB)**
	FStop	Sunoco #7089
	Food	Kings Family Rest, McDonald's
91		**PA 31, to PA 711, Donegal, to Ligonier, Uniontown (NO Trucks PA 31W)**
	Gas	S: BP, Exxon◊, Sunoco◊

EXIT		PENNSYLVANIA
	Food	S: Hardees/Pizza/BP, DQ
	Lodg	S: Days Inn
	Other	N: to St Vincent College S: Donegal Campground▲, Laurel Highlands Campland▲, Mountain Pines RV Resort▲, **to** Rivers Edge Campground▲, Kooser State Park, Laurel Hill State Park, Ohiopyle State Park, Seven Springs Ski Resort, Hidden Valley Ski Resort, Laurel Mtn Ski Resort
(94)		**Parking Area (WB)**
110		**PA 601, Center Ave, to US 219, to PA 31, Somerset, Johnstown** NOTE: Tunnel Restrictions for HazMat
	TStop	S: Jim's Auto Truck Stop
	Gas	N: KwikFill, Sheetz S: Exxon, Shell◊
	Food	N: Hoss's Steak & Sea House, Pizza Hut S: Arby's, Burger King, Subway, Wendy's
	Lodg	N: A1 Economy Inn, Inn at Georgian Place S: Best Western, Days Inn, Hampton Inn, Holiday Inn, Knights Inn, Quality Inn♥, Ramada Inn, Super 8♥
	TServ	N: Truck Service S: Beckwith Machinery, Jim's Auto & Truck Service
	Med	S: + Hospital
	Other	N: Auto Services, Auto Dealers, Ryder, U-Haul, Factory Shops at Georgian Place, **to** Somerset Co Airport✈, **to** Woodland Campsites▲, Flight 93 Memorial S: ATMs, Banks, Glades Court Mall, Greyhound, Penske, Pharmacy, Harley Davidson, **to** Hidden Valley Resort, Pioneer Park Campground▲, Scotty Camping Resort & RV Sales▲
(112)		**Somerset Service Plaza (Both dir)**
	FStop	Sunoco
	Food	E: Big Boy, Cinnabon, Hershey's Ice Cream, Roy Rogers, Starbucks W: Burger King, Cinnabon, Hot Dog City, Hershey's Ice Cream
(123)		**Allegheny Mtn Tunnel (Headlights on)**
146		**US 220 Bus, to I-99, to US 220, Bedford, to Altoona, Johnstown** NOTE: Tunnel Restrictions for HazMat
	FStop	N: RG's Travel Plaza/BP
	TStop	N: SAC Shop/BP (US 220)
	Gas	N: Sheetz
	Food	N: Arena Rest, Burger King, China Inn, Denny's, Ed's SteakHouse, Hoss's Steak & Sea House, Long John Silver, Pizza Hut, McDonald's, Wendy's
	Lodg	N: Best Western♥, Econo Lodge, Quality Inn♥, Super 8, Travelodge S: Hampton Inn, Janey Lynn Motel
	TServ	N: Truck Service & Parts S: Rte 220 Truck Repair
	Other	N: Laundry/WiFi/SAC BP, Bedford Airport✈, Bedford Co Airport✈, **to** Shawnee State Park, Blue Knob State Park S: Friendship Village Campground & RV Park▲
(147)		**Midway Service Plaza (Both dir)**
	FStop	Sunoco #7078/#7079
	Food	E: Cinnabon, Hershey's Ice Cream, Hot Dog City, Sbarro W: Cinnabon, Hershey's Ice Cream, KFC, Sbarro, Starbucks

◊ = Regular Gas Stations with Diesel   ▲ = RV Friendly Locations   ♥ = Pet Friendly Locations

RED PRINT SHOWS LARGE VEHICLE PARKING/ACCESS ON SITE OR NEARBY   BROWN PRINT SHOWS CAMPGROUNDS/RV PARKS

I-76 W/E

EXIT	PENNSYLVANIA
(161)	Jct I-70E, to US 30, Lincoln Hwy, Breezewood, Everett (Serv N to US 30)
FStop	N: Breezewood BP
TStop	N: Gateway Travel Plaza/Valero Travel Center of America #75 (Scales), Petro 2 #84/Shell (Scales)
Gas	N: Exxon◆, Mobil◆, Sunoco◆
Food	N: GatewayRest/DQ/Dominos/Subway/ TA TC, Perkins/Blimpie/HersheyIC/Petro 2, Café/Sunoco, Arby's, Big John's Steak & Buffet, Bob Evans, Bonanza Steakhouse, Burger King, Denny's, Hardee's, KFC, Pizza Hut, Subway, Taco Bell, Wendy's
Lodg	N: Gateway Travel Lodge/Holiday Inn Express/Gateway TC, Best Western, Comfort Inn, Econo Lodge, Heritage Inn, Howard Johnson, Penn Aire Motel, Quality Inn, Ramada Inn
TWash	N: Blue Beacon TW/Petro 2
TServ	N: TA TC/Tires, Petro 2/Tires
Other	N: Laundry/BarbSh/RadioShack/WiFi/ TA TC, Laundry/BarbSh/CB/WiFi/Petro 2, Breezewood Campground▲
NOTE:	I-76/PA Tpk runs with I-70 above. Exit #'s follow I-76.
(172)	Sideling Hill Service Plaza (Both dir)
FStop	Sunoco
Food	Big Boy, Burger King, Hershey's Ice Cream, Starbucks
180	US 522, Fort Littleton, Mount Union, McConnellsburg, Mercersburg Note: Tunnel Restrictions-HazMat
Gas	N: BP◆, Shell◆
Food	N: Fort Family Rest
Lodg	N: Downes Dixie Motel #2
Med	N: + Hospital
Other	N: PA State Hwy Patrol Post S: to Cowans Gap State Park▲
(187)	Tuscarora Mtn Tunnel (Headlights on)
189	PA 75, Ft Loudon, Willow Hill
Food	S: Rest/Willow Hill Motel
Lodg	S: Willow Hill Motel
(197)	Kittatinny Mtn Tunnel (Headlights on)
(199)	Blue Mtn Tunnel (Headlights on)
201	PA 997, Blue Mountain, Chambersburg, Shippensburg Note: Tunnel Restrictions-HazMat
Food	S: Rest/Johnnie's Motel
Lodg	S: Johnnie's Motel, Kenmar Motel
Other	S: to Letterkenny Ord Depot Area
(202)	Parking Area (EB)

EXIT	PENNSYLVANIA
(203)	Blue Mountain Service Plaza (WB)
FStop	Sunoco
Food	Hershey's Ice Cream, Nathan's, Roy Rogers
(204)	Parking Area (EB)
(214)	PA State Hwy Patrol Post (WB)
(215)	Parking Area (EB)
(219)	Plainfield Service Plaza (EB)
FStop	Sunoco
Food	Hershey's Ice Cream, Hot Dog City, Roy Rogers
(224)	Parking Area (EB)
226	US 11, Harrisburg Pike, to I-81, Carlisle, Harrisburg
FStop	N: I-81 Carlisle Fuel Stop/Citgo
TStop	N: Gables of Carlisle All American Plaza/ Shell(Scales), Petro Stopping Center (Scales), Flying J Travel Plaza #5200 (Scales), Pilot Travel Center #342 (Scales)
Gas	N: BP S: Exxon, Sheetz
Food	N: FastFood/GablesofCarlisle, IronSkillet/ NobleRoman/Petro SC, Rest/FastFood/ Flying J TP, Wendy's/Pilot TC, Arby's, Bob Evans, Eat 'n Park, McDonald's, Middlesex Diner, Subway, Waffle House S: Hoss's Steakhouse & Sea House
Lodg	N: Best Western, Hampton Inn, Howard Johnson, Quality Inn♥, Ramada, Rodeway Inn, Super 8 S: Best Western, Motel 6♥, Pike Motel
TWash	N: Blue Beacon TW/Petro SC, Gables
TServ	N: Petro SC/Tires, Gables/Tires
Med	S: + Carlisle Regional Medical Ctr
Other	N: Laundry/Gables, Laundry/BarbSh/CB/ WiFi/Petro SC, Laundry/WiFi/RVDump/LP/ Flying J TP, Laundry/WiFi/Pilot TC, ATM, Grocery, Greyhound, Dickerson College, Carlisle Campground▲ S: Auto Service, Budget, U-Haul, Animal Clinic♥, to US Army War Coll Carlisle Barracks, to Carlisle Airport✈
236	US 15, Gettysburg Pike, Mechanicsburg, to Gettysburg, Harrisburg
Gas	N: BP, Mobil, Shell S: Sheetz
Food	N: Brothers Pizza, Issac's Rest & Deli, Mary's Family Rest, Subway S: Burger King, Cracker Barrel, Hong Kong Chef, Hoss's Steak & Sea House, Quiznos, McDonald's, Wendy's

EXIT	PENNSYLVANIA
Lodg	N: Comfort Inn, Country Inn, Econo Lodge, Hampton Inn♥, Homewood Suites S: Best Western, Wingate Inn
Med	N: + Hospital
Other	N: Auto Service, Tires, U-Haul, to BJ's, Capital City Mall, State Capitol S: ATMs, Auto Services, Banks, Dollar General, Grocery, to Messiah College Gettysburg National Military Park
(237)	Parking Area (EB)
(242)	Jct I-83, Memorial Hwy, Harrisburg
Gas	N: BP, Hess, Mobil
Food	N: Bob Evans, Doc Holliday's Steakhouse, Eat 'n Park, McDonald's, Pizza Hut
Lodg	N: Best Western, Comfort Inn, Holiday Inn♥, Motel 6♥, Rodeway Inn, Travel Inn S: Days Inn, Highland Motel
Other	N: Animal Hospital♥, Capital City Airport✈ to State Capitol Complex
(247)	Jct I-283, to PA 283, Lancaster, Hershey, Harrisburg
Gas	N: Sunoco
Food	N: Taco Bell, Wendy's
Lodg	N: Best Western, Days Inn, Rodeway Inn
TServ	N: to Cummins Power Systems
Other	N: Harrisburg East Campground▲, to State Capitol S: Etnoyer's RV World & Mobile RV Repair, Penn State Univ, Harrisburg Int'l Airport✈
(250)	Highspire Service Plaza (EB)
FStop	Sunoco
Food	Nathan's, Cinnabon, Hershey's Ice Cream, Sbarro
(253)	Parking Area (EB)
(254)	Parking Area (WB)
(255)	Parking Area (WB)
(258)	Lawn Service Plaza (WB)
FStop	Sunoco
Food	Burger King, Cinnabon, Hot Dog City, Hershey's Ice Cream
Other	RV Dump
(263)	Parking Area (EB)
(264)	Parking Area (EB)
266	PA 72, Lebanon Rd, Manheim, Lebanon, Lancaster
FStop	N: Hess Express #38429
Gas	N: Mobil
Food	N: Café
Lodg	N: Red Carpet Inn, Rodeway Inn, Farmers Hope Inn♥ & Restaurant S: Hampton Inn

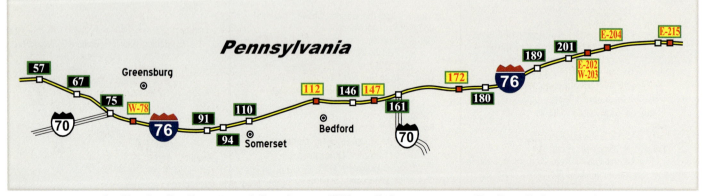

◆ = Regular Gas Stations with Diesel ▲ = RV Friendly Locations ♥ = Pet Friendly Locations
RED PRINT SHOWS LARGE VEHICLE PARKING/ACCESS ON SITE OR NEARBY BROWN PRINT SHOWS CAMPGROUNDS/RV PARKS

EXIT	PENNSYLVANIA
Med	N: + Hospital (in Lebanon)
Other	N: Auto Service, Pinch Pond Family Campground▲, to Starlite Camping Resort▲, Refreshing Mountain Camp▲ S: Auto Service, Winery, Gretna Oaks Campground▲
(268)	Parking Area (EB)
(269)	Parking Area (EB)
(270)	Parking Area (EB)
(280)	Truck Inspection Station (WB)
286	US 222, to PA 272, Denver, Reading, Lancaster
FStop	N: Al's Exxon
Gas	N: Citgo, Shell◆ S: Sunoco
Food	N: Park Place Diner & Rest, Zia Maria Ital Rest, Rest/Black Horse Lodge S: Casual's Neighborhood Café, Baskin Robbins/Dunkin Donuts
Lodg	N: Black Horse Lodge, PA Dutch Motel, Penn Amish Motel S: Comfort Inn♥, Econo Lodge, Holiday Inn, Red Carpet Inn
Other	N: Dutch Cousins Camping▲, Shady Grove Campground▲, to Hickory Run Family Campground▲, Lake in Wood Resort▲, Oak Creek Campground▲, Starlite Camping Resort▲, to Refreshing Mountain Camp▲, Cocalico Creek Campground▲, to Sun Valley Campground▲, Reading Outlet Center S: Red Run Campground▲, to Dutch Wonderland, Lancaster Outlet Center, Tanger Outlet Center, Rockvale Outlets
(289)	PA State Hwy Patrol Post (EB)
(290)	Bowmansville Service Plaza (EB)
FStop	Sunoco
Food	Chicken Express, Hershey's Ice Cream, Pizza Hut Express, Snack Bar, Starbucks
(291)	Parking Area (EB)
(294)	Parking Area (WB)
(295)	Parking Area (EB)
(297)	Parking Area (EB)
(298)	Jct I-176, PA 10, Morgantown Expy, Reading, Morgantown
Gas	S: Exxon, Sheetz
Food	N: Rest/Heritage Motel S: McDonald's, Rest/Holiday Inn
Lodg	N: Heritage Motel S: Holiday Inn♥, Red Carpet Inn

EXIT	PENNSYLVANIA
Med	N: + St Joseph Medical Center S: + Reading Hospital
Other	N: to Lake in Wood Resort▲, Sun Valley Campground▲, to VF Outlet Village, Maple Grove Raceway, to French Creek State Park S: ATMs, Banks, Animal Hospital♥, to Berry Patch Campground▲
(300)	Parking Area (WB)
(305)	Peter J Camiel Service Plaza (WB)
FStop	Sunoco
Food	Cinnabon, Hershey's Ice Cream, Nathan's, Roy Rogers, Sbarro, Starbucks
312	PA 100, Exton, Chester Springs, Pottstown, W Chester, Downington
Gas	S: Sunoco◆, WaWa
Food	S: Hoss's Steak & Sea House, Red Robin
Lodg	S: Best Western, Comfort Inn, Extended Stay America, Fairfield Inn, Hampton Inn, Holiday Inn Express, Residence Inn
Med	S: + Hospital
Other	N: Smaltz Harley Davidson S: ATMs, Banks, QVC Studio Park, to Mall, Target, Shady Acres Campground▲, Brandywine Creek Campground▲, Marsh Creek State Park
(325)	Valley Forge Service Plaza (EB)
FStop	Sunoco
Food	Burger King, Nathan's, Pizza Uno
NOTE:	I-76 WB above runs with PA Tpk. EB continues as I-276.
NOTE:	Begin WB TOLL, End EB on I-76
NOTE:	Begin WB, End EB Call Box Area WB for next 326 mi
(326)	Jct I-76, I-276E/PA Tpk, to US 202, Valley Forge, Bristol, New Jersey (fr EB, Left exit)
327	PA 363, Gulph Rd, Mall Blvd, King of Prussia, to Valley Forge
Gas	N: Exxon◆
Food	N: Ruth's Chris Steak House
Lodg	S: Holiday Inn Express, Homestead Suites, MainStay Suites, McIntosh Inn, Radisson, Sheraton, Sleep Inn, Scantico Valley Forge Motel
Other	N: King of Prussia Mall S: Valley Forge Convention Center, AmeriGas/LP
328A	US 202S, DeKalb Pike, to US 422, West Chester, Norristown
Other	S: PetSmart♥, Staples, Trader Joe's, UPS Store

EXIT	PENNSYLVANIA
328B	US 202N, DeKalb Pike, King of Prussia
Gas	N: Exxon◆, Lukoil, Mobil, Sunoco, WaWa
Food	N: Arby's, Burger King, CA Café, Chili's, ChikFilA, Friendly's, Lone Star Steakhouse, KFC, McDonald's, Morton's Steakhouse, Ruby King of Prussia Diner, Starbucks, Subway, Sullivan's Steakhouse, TGI Friday
Lodg	N: Best Western, Comfort Inn, Crowne Plaza, Fairfield Inn, Motel 6♥
Other	N: ATMs, Auto Services, Banks, Best Buy, Borders, Costco, King of Prussia Mall, Cinemas, IMAX, PetCo♥, Pharmacy, Staples, Tires, UPS Store
330	PA 320, Gulph Rd, Gulph Mills
Other	S: to Villanova Univ, Valley Forge Military Academy
(331A)	Jct I-476S, Veterans Memorial Hwy, Chester (fr WB, Left exit)
(331B)	Jct I-476N, Veterans Memorial Hwy, Plymouth Meeting, PA 23, Conshohocken (EB)
332	PA 23, Conshohocken (WB)
337	Hollow Rd, River Rd, Gladwyne (WB)
338	Belmont Ave, Green Lane, Philadelphia
Gas	S: Sunoco, WaWa
Med	N: + Roxborough Memorial Hospital
Other	N: Pharmacy
339	US 1S, City Line Ave (fr WB, Left exit)
Lodg	S: Holiday Inn, Homewood Suites, NA Motor Inn
Other	N: to Philadelphia Univ S: to St Joseph's Univ
340A	Kelly Dr, Lincoln Dr, to Germantown (fr EB, Left Exit)
Med	N: + Roxborough Memorial Hospital
Other	N: CVS
340B	US 1N, Roosevelt Blvd, Philadelphia (fr EB, Left Exit)
341	Montgomery Dr, W River Dr (NO Trucks Permitted)
342	US 13, US 30W, Girard Ave, Philadelphia
Gas	S: Sunoco
Other	N: Girard College S: Philadelphia Zoo
343	Spring Garden St, Haverford Ave (EB)

◆ = Regular Gas Stations with Diesel ▲ = RV Friendly Locations ♥ = Pet Friendly Locations

RED PRINT SHOWS LARGE VEHICLE PARKING/ACCESS ON SITE OR NEARBY BROWN PRINT SHOWS CAMPGROUNDS/RV PARKS

 W

EXIT	PENNSYLVANIA
(344)	Jct I-676E, US 30, Vine St, Central Philadelphia (fr EB, Left Exit, NO EB re-entry)
345	30th St, Market St (exit only)
Other	S: Amtrak, Drexel Univ
346A	South St, Philadelphia (Left exit)
Med	S: + Childrens Hospital, + Univ of PA Hospital
Other	S: Univ of PA
346B	Grays Ferry Ave, University Ave (fr WB, Exit only)
Other	S: Civic Center
346C	28th St (EB), Vare Ave (WB)
347	Passyunk Ave (WB)
Med	N: + Methodist Hospital
347A	Penrose Ave, to PA 291, to I-95S (EB, Left exit)
Other	S: to Philadelphia Int'l Airport, Sun Oil, Gulf Oil, Commanders Naval Base
347B	Passyunk Ave, Oregon Ave (fr EB, Left Exit)

EXIT	PENNSYLVANIA
348	PA 291W, Penrose Ave, to Chester (WB, Left Exit)
Lodg	S: America's Best Inn
Other	S: Philadelphia Int'l Airport
349	PA 611, Broad St, Sports Complex
Gas	N: Sunoco
Med	N: + Methodist Hospital
Other	S: Lincoln Financial Field, Citizens Bank Park, Wachovia Center, PA Naval Business Center
350	Packer Ave, 7th St, to I-95 (EB, Exit Only)
TStop	(3540 S Lawrence) S: Walt Whitman Truck Stop (Scales)
Food	S: Rest/WW TS
Lodg	S: Holiday Inn
TServ	S: WW TS/Tires
Other	S: Laundry/RVDump/WW TS, Ports
351	Vietnam Veterans Memorial Hwy, Front St, to I-95, N-Trenton, S to Chester (WB)
(352)	Neshaminy Service Plaza (WB)
FStop	Sunoco
Food	Burger King, Nathan's, Starbucks Breyers, McDonald's, Nathan's

EXIT	PA / NJ
358	US 13, Delaware
Gas	N: WaWa S: Getty, Mobil, Sunoco
Lodg	S: Comfort Inn

(EASTERN TIME ZONE)

PENNSYLVANIA

NEW JERSEY

(EASTERN TIME ZONE)

(2)	Jct I-676N, I-76WB
1D	US 130N, PA 168, to NJ Tpk, Camden Waterfront, Blackhorse Pike (WB)
1C	US 130S, Market St, Brooklawn, Westville
(1B)	Jct I-295N, to NJ Tpk, Trenton
(1A)	Jct I-295S, DE Memorial Bridge
(0)	NJ 42S, Atlantic City

NEW JERSEY

Begin Westbound I-76 from Jct I-295 in NJ to Jct I-71 near Cleveland, OH.

 S

EXIT	OHIO
	Begin Southboundl -77 from Jct I-90 in Cleveland, OH to Jct I-26 in Columbia, SC.

OHIO

(EASTERN TIME ZONE)
(I-77 Starts/Ends on I-26, Exit #116 in SC)

163C	E 9th St, Carnegie Ave, Cleveland
Other	W: ATMs, Jacobs Field, Gund Arena, to Cleveland Conv Center, Cleveland Browns Stadium, Rock & Roll Hall of Fame
(163AB)	Jct I-90, W-Toledo, E- Erie, PA (NB)
162B	E 22nd, E 14th (NB)
Med	E: + St Vincent Charity Hospital
162A	E 30th St, Woodland Ave, to US 422, OH 8, OH 43
(161B)	Jct I-490W, to I-71, E 55th St, Toledo to I-90W
161A	OH 14, Broadway Ave (NB)
160	Pershing Ave (NB)
Med	E: + St Michael Hospital
159B	Fleet Ave, Cleveland
Gas	E: BP
Food	E: Subway/BP
159A	Harvard Ave, Newburgh Heights
FStop	W: Speedway #3328
Gas	W: BP, Marathon
Food	W: Subway/BP
Other	W: WiFi/Speedway
158	Grant Ave, Cuyahoga Heights
157	OH 21, OH 17, E 71st St, Brecksville Rd, Granger Rd (SB)
Other	E: Tires W: Vet

EXIT	OHIO
(156)	Jct I-480, to Toledo, Youngstown
Other	W: to Cleveland Hopkins Int'l Airport, Cleveland Metroparks Zoo
155	Rockside Rd, Seven Hills, Independence
Gas	E: Shell, Sunoco W: BP
Food	E: Bob Evans, Bonefish Grill, Delmonico's, Denny's, McDonald's, Outback Steakhouse Shula Steak House, Wendy's, Rest/Hol Inn W: Applebee's, Damon's, Red Lobster, Longhorn Steakhouse, Rest/Clarion
Lodg	E: Baymont Inn, Comfort Inn, DoubleTree Hotel, Embassy Suites, Holiday Inn, Red Roof Inn W: Clarion, Courtyard, Hampton Inn, Hyatt Place, Residence Inn, Sheraton
Med	W: + Urgent Care
Other	E: ATMs, Banks, Auto Repair, NTB, Carwash/Shell, Walgreen's, to Garfield Mall Cuyahoga Valley Nat'l Park W: ATMs, Banks, to Shopping Center, Grocery, Office Max, Pharmacy
153	Pleasant Valley Rd, Seven Hills, Independence
151	Wallings Rd, Broadview Hts
149	OH 82, Broadview Hts (NB)
149AB	OH 82, E Royalton Rd, Brecksville, Broadview Heights (SB)
Gas	E: BP
Food	W: Boneyard Grill, CoCo's, Domino's
Lodg	W: Tally Ho
Other	E: Golf Course, Museum, Cuyahoga Valley National Park, Brecksville Reservation

EXIT	OHIO
147	Miller Rd, to OH 21 (SB)
Other	E: BF Goodrich Headquarters
(146)	I-80/OH Tpk (TOLL), to Toledo, Youngstown, OH 21, Brecksville Rd (Access #145 Serv before Toll)
145	OH 21, Brecksville Rd, Richfield (NB)
TStop	E: Pilot Travel Center #130 (Scales)
Food	E: Wendy's/Pilot TC, Burger King, DQ, Richfield Family Rest, Subway
Lodg	E: Hampton Inn, Quality Inn, Super 8
Other	E: Laundry/WiFi/Pilot TC, Furnace Run Metro Park, to Brandywine Ski Resort W: Brushwood Lake, Furnace Run Park
(144)	Jct I-271, N-Erie, PA, S-Columbus
143	OH 176, Wheatley Rd, to I-271S
Gas	W: BP, Sunoco
Food	W: McDonald's, Subway
Other	E: Cuyahoga Valley Nat'l Park, to Blossom Music Center
(141)	Rest Area (Both dir) (RR, Phones, Picnic, Vend)
138	Ghent Rd, Akron
Gas	W: Circle K
Food	W: Vaccaro's Italian Rest
Other	E: to Sand Run Metro Park W: to Bath Nature Preserve
137AB	OH 18, Medina Rd, Akron, Fairlawn, Medina
Gas	E: BP, Circle K, Marathon, Shell, Speedway W: Citgo
Food	E: Applebee's, Baja Fresh Mex Grill, Bob Evans, Chili's, Chipotle Mex Grill, Cracker Barrel, Friendly's, Golden Corral, Max & Erma's, Lonestar Steakhouse, McDonald's,

Page 350 ◆ = Regular Gas Stations with Diesel ▲ = RV Friendly Locations ♥ = Pet Friendly Locations
RED PRINT SHOWS LARGE VEHICLE PARKING/ACCESS ON SITE OR NEARBY   BROWN PRINT SHOWS CAMPGROUNDS/RV PARKS

Interstate 77 N/S — OHIO

EXIT		OHIO
	Food	E: Olive Garden, Red Lobster, Panera, Romano's Macaroni Grill, Ruby Tuesday, Steak 'n Shake, Starbucks, Taco Bell, Wendy's W: Burger King, Damon's, Don Pablo, Fuddrucker's, Mario's, Outback Steakhouse, TGI Friday
	Lodg	E: Courtyard, Holiday Inn, Hampton Inn, Motel 6, Quality Inn, Super 8, Hilton, Sheraton W: Best Western, Comfort Inn, Extended Stay America, Radisson, Residence Inn, Studio Plus
	Med	E: + Medical Clinic
	Other	E: ATMs, Auto Services, Bank, Best Buy, FedEx Kinko's, Firestone, Goodyear, NTB, Grocery, Home Depot, Lowe's, Office Max, PetSmart♥, Pharmacy, RiteAid, Sam's Club, Staples, Target, Wal-Mart, UPS Store, Summit Mall, to Univ of Akron, to Hale Farm & Village, to Blossom Music Center W: ATM, Bank, Medina Muni Airport✈, Avalon RV & Marine
136		OH 21S, to Massillon (fr NB, Left exit)
135		CR 17, Cleveland-Massillon Rd (NB)
133		Ridgewood Rd, Miller Rd, Akron
	Gas	E: Citgo◊
	Food	E: Wendy's
132		White Pond Rd Dr, Mull Ave
131		OH 162, Copley Rd, Akron
	Gas	E: Citgo W: BP◊, Marathon◊
	Food	E: China Star, Church's, Pizza W: McDonald's, Pizza Hut
	Other	E: Grocery, US Post Office, to Akron Zoo
130		OH 261, Wooster Ave, Vernon Odom Blvd, Akron
	Gas	E: BP, Circle K
	Food	E: Burger King, Church's, McDonald's, Pizza Hut Subway, White Castle W: KFC
	Med	E: + to Akron Gen'l Medical Center
	Other	E: AutoZone, Family Dollar, NAPA W: ATMs, Auto Services, Grocery, Tires, Target, U-Haul, to Rolling Acres Mall
	NOTE:	I-77 below runs with I-76. Exit #'s follow I-76.
(129)		Jct I-76W, to I-277, to Barberton
21A		East Ave, Akron (NB)
	Other	W: Amtrak
21B		W South St, Lakeshore Blvd (SB)
21C		Bowery St, Russell Ave, Dart Ave, to OH 59, Akron
22A		Main St, Broadway St
	Other	W: Zeigler Tire
22B		Wolf Ledges Pkwy, Grant St
	Other	E: Center Auto Machine Gas & Diesel Shop W: Greyhound Bus Lines
(23A/125B)		Jct I-76E, to Youngstown I-77S, to Canton
	NOTE:	I-77 above runs with I-76. Exit #'s follow I-76.
125A		OH 8N, to Cuyahoga

EXIT		OHIO
124B		Lovers Lane, Cole Ave, Akron
124A		Archwood Ave, Firestone Blvd
123B		OH 764, Wilbeth Rd, Waterloo Rd
	Other	E: Akron Fulton Int'l Airport✈
123A		Waterloo Rd
(122AB)		Jct I-277, US 224E, to I-76, Akron, Barberton, Mogadore
	Other	E: Akron Fulton Int'l Airport✈
120		CR 15, Arlington Rd, Akron, Green
	Gas	E: Speedway◊ W: BP, Speedway
	Food	E: Applebee's, Denny's, Friendly's, IHOP, Pizza Hut, Ryan's Grill, Waffle House, White Castle W: Bob Evans, Burger King, Blimpie, IHOP, McDonald's, Starbucks, Subway, Taco Bell, Wendy's, White Castle
	Lodg	E: Comfort Inn, Quality Inn, Red Roof Inn♥ W: Fairfield Inn, Hampton Inn
	Other	E: ATMs, Banks, Dollar General, Home Depot, Pharmacy, Wal-Mart W: ATMs, Auto Service, Auto Dealers, Goodyear, Grocery, Regal Cinema 18, Sirpilla RV Supercenter/Camping World, to Portage Lakes State Park▲
118		OH 241, Massillon Rd, to OH 619, Green, Uniontown
	Gas	E: Speedway◊ W: Circle K, GetGo
	Food	E: Pizza, Subway W: Arby's, Lucky Star Chinese, Lunch Box Deli, McDonald's, Menches Bros Rest, Quiznos
	Lodg	W: Cambria Suites, Super 8
	Other	W: ATMs, Banks, Grocery, to Portage Lakes State Park▲
113		Akron-Canton Reg'l Airport, Canton
	Lodg	W: Hilton Garden Inn
	Other	W: Akron Canton Reg'l Airport✈, Tourist Info, Clay's RV Center
111		Portage St, North Canton
	TStop	E: Travel Center of America #95/Marathon (Scales)
	Gas	E: Circle K, Sunoco◊ W: BP◊, Speedway, Sam's Club
	Food	E: CountryPride/TA TC, Burger King, KFC, Geisen Haus, Subway W: Carrabba's, Cracker Barrel, Don Pablo, Einstein Bros Bagels, IHOP, Longhorn Steakhouse, McDonald's, Panera, Pizza Hut, Quiznos, Red Robin, Starbucks, Taco Bell, Wendy's
	Lodg	W: Best Western, Microtel, Motel 6♥
	TWash	E: TA TC
	TServ	E: TA TC/Tires
	Other	E: Laundry/WiFi/TA TC, Auto Services, CarWash, Cinemark 10 W: ATMs, Banks, BJ's, Best Buy, Borders, Freedom Harley Davidson, Grocery, Grander Mountain, Home Depot, Lowes, Office Max, Sam's Club, Wal-Mart, Tinseltown, to Kent State Univ/Stark
109		Everhard Rd, Whipple Ave (SB)
	Food	W: Bob Evans, Boston Market, CiCi's, Chili's, ChikFilA, DQ, Friendly's, Hometown Buffet, Max & Erma's, Panera, Quiznos, Ruby Tuesday, Starbucks, Steak Escape, Taco Bell

◊ = Regular Gas Stations with Diesel ▲ = RV Friendly Locations ♥ = Pet Friendly Locations
RED PRINT SHOWS LARGE VEHICLE PARKING/ACCESS ON SITE OR NEARBY BROWN PRINT SHOWS CAMPGROUNDS/RV PARKS

EXIT		OHIO
	Lodg	W: Courtyard, Days Inn, Holiday Inn, Knights Inn♥, Parke Resident Suites, Red Roof Inn♥
	Other	W: ATMs, Auto Services, Banks, Belden Village Mall, NTB, PetSmart♥, Pharmacy, Tires, Target
109B		Everhard Ave (NB)
	Gas	E: Citgo, Speedway◊
	Food	E: Burger King, Denny's, Fazoli's, McDonald's, Subway, Taco Bell, Waffle House
	Lodg	E: Comfort Inn, Fairfield Inn, Hampton Inn♥, Residence Inn♥
	Other	E: Little Guy Teardrop Camper Sales
109A		Whipple Ave, Everhard Rd (NB)
	Gas	W: Marathon
	Food	W: Applebee's, Arby's, Bob Evans, Damon's, Eat 'n Park, Fuddrucker's, Lone Star Steakhouse, Mulligan's Pub, Outback Steakhouse, Olive Garden, Pizza Hut, Ponderosa, Romano's Macaroni Grill, Red Lobster, Subway, TGI Friday, Wendy's
	Lodg	W: Days Inn, Knights Inn, Sheraton
	Other	W: Best Buy, Circuit City, Firestone, FedEx Kinko's, PetCo♥, Office Max, Radio Shack, Target, UPS Store, Belden Village Mall, to Kent State Univ/Stark
107B		US 62, Canton, to Alliance
	Other	E: Malone College, to Mt Union College
107A		OH 687, Fulton Rd, Fulton Dr
	Gas	E: Marathon
		W: Circle K
	Food	E: Subway, Woody's Rootbeer Stand
	Other	W: Pro Football Hall of Fame
106		13th St NW, 12th St NW, Canton
	Med	E: + Mercy Medical Center
	Other	E: Pharmacy, Civic Center, McKinley Presidential Museum, Discovery World
105B		OH 172, Tuscarawas St (SB)
105A		6th St SW (SB, diff reaccess)
105		OH 172, W Tuscarawas St (NB)
	Gas	E: Stop n Go, Sunoco
		W: Citgo
	Food	E: McDonald's, Subway
		W: Hungry Howie's, KFC
	Med	W: + Aultman Hospital
	Other	E: Water Works Park, Discover World, McKinley Museum, Nationall First Ladies Museum
		W: Laundromat, Pharmacy, to Shopping Center, Perry Diesel Services, Stark Co Fairgrounds
104B		US 30, US 62W, East Liverpool, Massillon (NB)
104A		OH 30E, East Liverpool (NB)
104		US 30, US 62, East Liverpool, Downtown Canton, Massillon (SB)
103		OH 800S, Cleveland Ave, Canton
	Gas	E: Citgo, Speedway
	Food	E: Arby's, Burger King, McDonald's, Subway, Taco Bell, Waffle House
101		OH 627, Faircrest St, Canton
	TStop	E: Gulliver's 77 Travel Plaza/Citgo (Scales)
	Gas	E: Speedway, Shell
	Food	E: Rest/Gulliver's TP, Wendy's, McDonald's/Speedway
	Other	E: Laundry/CB/Gulliver's TP

Personal Notes

EXIT		OHIO
99		Fohl St SW, to Navarre
	Gas	W: Shell
	Other	E: to Bear Creek Resort Ranch/KOA▲
93		OH 212, Bolivar, to Zoar
	Gas	E: Speedway
		W: Citgo
	Food	E: McDonald's, Pizza Hut, Subway, Wendy'
		W: DQ/Citgo
	Lodg	E: Sleep Inn
	Other	E: Golf Course, Grocery, NAPA, Pharmacy, to Bear Creek Resort Ranch/KOA▲
(92)		Weigh Station (Both dir)
87		US 250, CR 74, Wooster Ave, to OH 21, Dover, Strasburg, Massillon, Wooster
	FStop	W: Sibley Fuel Mart
	Gas	W: Citgo◊
	Food	W: Lugnut Café, McDonald's, Quiznos, Rosalie's Rest, Subway
	Lodg	W: Ramada Ltd, Twins Motel
(85)		Rest Area (Both dir) (RR, Phones, Picnic)
83		OH 39, OH 211, Dover, Amish Country, to Sugarcreek, Dover
	Gas	E: BP, Speedway◊
		W: Marathon
	Food	E: Bob Evans, KFC, McDonald's, Shoney's, Subway, Wendy's
		W: DQ/Marathon
	Lodg	E: Hospitality Inn
		W: Comfort Inn
	Med	E: + Hospital
	Other	E: Auto Dealers, Vet♥, Ziegler Tire

EXIT		OHIO
81		US 250W, US 250 Bus, OH 39, W High Ave, CR 21, CR 52, Dover, New Philadelphia
	TStop	W: Eagle Auto Truck Plaza/BP
	Gas	E: Kwik Fill, Sheetz, Speedway
	Food	E: Rest/Eagle ATP, Burger King, Denny's, Hog Heaven BBQ, Hong Kong Chinese, Long John Silver, McDonald's, Pizza Hut, Taco Bell, Texas Roadhouse
	Lodg	E: Hampton Inn, Holiday Inn, Knights Inn♥ Motel 6♥, Schoenbrunn Inn, Super 8
	TServ	W: Peterbilt
	Med	E: + Hospital
	Other	E: Grocery, AdvanceAuto, Wal-Mart sc, U-Haul, Tourist Info, Schoenbrunn Village
		W: Adventure Harley Davidson, RV Park▲
73		OH 751, CR 21, Stone Creek
	Gas	W: Marathon
65		US 36, Newcomerstown, Coshocton, Port Washington
	TStop	W: Newcomerstown Truck Stop/Duke (Scales)
	Gas	W: BP, Marathon
	Food	W: Duke's Fam Rest, McDonald's, Wendy's
	Lodg	W: Hampton Inn, Super 8
	TServ	W: Duke TS/Tires
	Other	W: Laundry/Duke TS, to Tri City Airport✈
54		OH 541, CR 831, Plainfield Rd, Kimbolton
	Gas	W: BP
	Food	W: Jackie's Family Rest
	Other	E: to Salt Fork State Park
47		US 22, Cadiz Rd, Cambridge, Cadiz
	Gas	W: BP
	Med	W: + Hospital
	Other	E: Hillview Acres Campground▲, to Salt Fork State Park
46		US 40, Wheeling Ave, Cambridge, Old Washington (SB)
46B		US 40, Cambridge, Old Washington
	FStop	W: FuelMart #708/Ashland
	Gas	W: BP, Exxon◊, Speedway◊
	Food	W: Burger King, J&K Rest, McDonald's, Long John Silver, Exxon/Wendy's
	Lodg	W: Longs Motel
	Other	W: ATMs, Auto Repairs, Grocery
46A		US 40E, Old Washington (NB)
(44B)		Jct I-70W, Cambridge, to Columbus (fr NB, Left exit) (TStop, Gas, Food, Lodg avail @ 1st exit W, # 178 on I-70)
	Med	W: + Hospital
	Other	W: ATMs, Tourist Info, Winery, Shopping, Museum, Spring Valley Campground▲, Cambridge Muni Airport✈
(44A)		Jct I-70E, to Wheeling, WV
41		OH 209, OH 821, CR 35, Main St, Byesville
	Gas	W: BP◊, KwikFill, Starfire Express
	Food	W: McDonald's
	Other	W: Family Dollar, Grocery, Cambridge Muni Airport✈
(40)		Rest Area (NB) (RR, Phones, Picnic, Vend)
37		OH 313, Clay Pike Rd, Pleasant City, Senecaville, Buffalo City
	Gas	E: BP, Duke
	Food	E: Buffalo Grill, BBQ, Subway

Page 352   ◊ = Regular Gas Stations with Diesel   ▲ = RV Friendly Locations   ♥ = Pet Friendly Locations
RED PRINT SHOWS LARGE VEHICLE PARKING/ACCESS ON SITE OR NEARBY   BROWN PRINT SHOWS CAMPGROUNDS/RV PARKS

EXIT		OH / WV
	TServ	E: Truck Service
	Other	E: US Post Office, to approx 7mi Buffalo Hills Camping Resort▲, Senecaville Lake
(36)		Rest Area (SB) (RR, Phones, Picnic, Vend)
28		OH 821, Main St, Public Rd, Caldwell, Belle Valley
	Gas	E: Sunoco◆
	Food	E: Marianne's Rest
	Other	E: Grocery, US Post Office, Wolf Run State Park▲, Noble Co Airport✈
25		OH 78, Caldwell, Woodsfield
	TStop	E: Pilot Travel Center #309 (Scales)
	Gas	E: BP, Sunoco◆
	Food	E: Arby's/TJCinn/Pilot TC, Lori's Family Rest, McDonald's, Subway/Sunoco
	Lodg	E: Best Western
	Other	E: Laundry/WiFi/Pilot TC, ATM, Auto Repair, Tourist Info, US Post Office
16		OH 821, Macksburg, Dexter City
6		OH 821, Marietta, Lower Salem
	FStop	W: Miller's AmPm/BP
	Gas	E: Exxon
	Lodg	W: Best Western
	Med	W: + Hospital
(4)		OH Welcome Center (NB) (RR, Phones, Picnic, Vend, Info)
1		OH 7, Newport Pike, Marietta
	TStop	E: Go Mart #58
	Gas	W: BP◆, Duke◆, Speedway◆
	Food	E: China Gate, CiCi's, DQ, Ryan's Grill W: Applebee's, Arby's, Bob Evans, Burger King, Captain D's, KFC, McDonald's, Pizza Hut, Shoney's, Subway, Taco Bell, Wendy's
	Lodg	E: Comfort Inn♥, Economy Lodge, Holiday Inn, Lafayette Hotel W: Best Value Inn, Hampton Inn, Super 8
	Med	W: + Marietta Memorial Hospital
	Other	E: ATMs, Auto Dealers, Grocery, Lowe's, Harley Davidson, Wal-Mart sc, Landing's Family Campground▲, Marietta RV & Outdoor World W: ATMs, AutoZone, Big Lots, Carwash, CVS, Kmart, Kroger, Marietta College, OH State Hwy Patrol

⊙ OHIO
⊙ WEST VIRGINIA
(EASTERN TIME ZONE)

185		WV 14, WV 31, Highland Ave, Williamstown, Vienna WV Welcome Center/Rest Area
	Gas	W: 7-11, Gas n Goods
	Food	W: Family Rest, Subway
	Lodg	W: Days Inn
	Other	W: to Fenton Art Glass Factory Tour
179		WV 2N, WV 68, Emerson Ave, North Parkersburg, Vienna
	Gas	E: Exxon W: BP
	Lodg	W: Red Carpet Inn
	Med	W: + Camden Clark Memorial Hospital
	Other	E: Wood Co Airport/Mid OH Valley Reg'l Airport✈ W: to OH Valley College

EXIT		WEST VIRGINIA
176		US 50, 7th St, Downtown Parkersburg Clarksburg
	Gas	W: 7-11, GoMart, Speedway, Kroger
	Food	W: Bob Evans, Burger King, Long John Silver, McDonald's, Mountaineer Family Rest, Omelet Shoppe, Shoney's, Wendy's
	Lodg	W: Knights Inn, Motel 6♥, Parkersburg Inn, Red Roof Inn♥
	Other	E: to N Bend State Park
174		WV 47, Staunton Ave, Davisville
	Gas	E: Exxon◆ W: Citgo
	Other	E: WVU/Parkersburg W: to Oil & Gas Museum
173		WV 95, Camden Ave, Downtown Parkersburg
	Gas	E: Marathon◆ W: BP
	Food	W: Hardee's
	Med	W: + Hospital
170		WV 14, Mineral Wells
	FStop	E: Pifer's Service Center/BP
	TStop	E: PTP/Liberty Truck Stop (Scales), New Parkersburg Truck Stop (Scales)
	Gas	E: Chevron
	Food	E: Rest/Liberty TS, FastFood/NP TS, McDonald's, Subway, Taco Bell, Wendy's W: Cracker Barrel
	Lodg	E: Comfort Suites, Hampton W: AmeriHost, Microtel
	TWash	E: Liberty TS
	TServ	E: Liberty TS/Tires, NP TS/Tires
	Other	E: Laundry/CB/WiFi/Liberty TS, Laundry/WiFi/NP TS, US Post Office, WV Motor Speedway
(169)		Weigh Station (Both dir)
(167)		WV Welcome Center (SB) Rest Area (NB) (RR, Phones, Picnic, Vend, RVDump)
161		CR 21, CR 17, Rockport
154		CR 1, Medina Rd
146		WV 2S, US 33W, Ravenswood, to WV 68, Silverton
	Gas	W: BP◆, Exxon, Marathon◆
	Lodg	W: Scottish Inns
	Other	W: Camping▲
138		US 33E, WV 62S, Ripley
	Gas	E: BP◆, Exxon, Marathon W: Exxon◆
	Food	E: KFC, Long John Silver, McDonald's, Pizza Hut, Taco Bell, Wendy's, Rest/BW W: Ponderosa, Shoney's, Subway
	Lodg	E: Best Western, Super 8 W: Holiday Inn Express
	Med	W: + Hospital
	Other	E: Kroger, NAPA, Wal-Mart, Ruby Lake Campground▲
132		WV 21, Ripley, Fairplain
	FStop	E: Fairplain BP #5521, Go Mart #33
	Food	E: Burger King/BP
	Lodg	E: 77 Motor Inn
	TServ	E: International
	Other	E: RV Park▲
124		WV 34, CR 19, Kentuck Rd, Kenna
	Gas	E: Exxon
	Food	E: Family Rest
119		WV 21, Kenna, Goldtown

◆ = Regular Gas Stations with Diesel ▲ = RV Friendly Locations ♥ = Pet Friendly Locations
RED PRINT SHOWS LARGE VEHICLE PARKING/ACCESS ON SITE OR NEARBY BROWN PRINT SHOWS CAMPGROUNDS/RV PARKS

Page 353

INTERSTATE 77 N/S

EXIT		WEST VIRGINIA
116		CR 21, Haines Branch, Sissonville, Charleston
	Other	E: Ripplin Waters Campground▲
114		WV 622, Sissonville Dr, Charleston, Pocatalico, Sissonville
	Gas	E: Mountain Mart Gas & Grocery
111		CR 29, Tuppers Creek Rd
	Gas	W: BP◊
	Food	W: Subway/BP
106		CR 27, Edens Fork Rd
	Gas	W: Chevron◊
(104)		Jct I-79N, to Clarksburg
102		US 119, Westmoreland Rd, O'Dell Ave, Crescent Rd, Charleston
	Gas	E: 7-11, BP, Go Mart
	Food	E: China Garden, Hardee's
	Lodg	E: Paisley Motor Inn
	Other	E: Pharmacy, Grocery, Yeager Airport✈
	NOTE:	I-77 below follows I-64 between Charleston and Beckley. Exit #'s follow I-77.
(101/59)		Jct I-64, W-Huntington, E-Beckley
100		Broad St, Capitol St, Charleston
	Gas	W: Chevron
	Lodg	W: Fairfield Inn, Holiday Inn, Super 8, Embassy Suites, Marriott
	Med	W: + St Francis Hospital
	Other	W: CVS, Kroger, Charlestown Town Center Mall
99		WV 114, Greenbrier St, State Capitol
	Gas	W: Citgo, Exxon
	Food	W: Domino's, McDonald's, Wendy's
	Other	E: Yeager Airport✈ W: to State Capitol, Museum
98		WV 61, 35th St Bridge (SB)
	Gas	W: Sunoco
	Food	W: McDonald's, Shoney's, Subway, TacoBell/KFC, Wendy's
	Med	W: + Hospital
	Other	W: Univ of Charleston, WVU
97		US 60W, Midland Trail, Kanawha Blvd Charleston (NB)
96		US 60E, Midland Trail, Belle
	Food	E: Gino's Pizza
	Lodg	E: Budget Host Inn
	TServ	E: Walker Machinery
(96)		WV Turnpike Begins/Ends
95		WV 61, MacCorkle Ave, Charleston
	FStop	E: Go Mart #31
	Gas	E: BP◊ W: Ashland, Chevron, Exxon, Marathon
	Food	E: Bob Evans, IHOP, McDonald's, Wendy's W: Applebee's, Arby's, Captain D's, Cracker Barrel, Hooters, La Carreta, Pizza Hut, Shoney's
	Lodg	E: Comfort Suites, Country Inn, Dyas Inn, Knights Inn, Motel 6, Red Roof Inn W:
	Other	E: Advance Auto, Kmart W: Grocery, Lowe's, Mall, Vet♥, WVU, Univ of Charleston
89		WV 61, WV 94, Marmet, Chesapeake
	FStop	E: Market Express #7/Exxon
	Gas	E: Go-Mart, Shell, Sunoco
	Food	E: Subway/Exxon, Biscuit World, Gino's Pizza, Hardee's, KFC, Subway, Wendy's
	Other	E: Kroger, Pharmacy

EXIT		WEST VIRGINIA
85		US 60, WV 61, Chelyan, East Bank
	Gas	E: Go Mart◊
	Food	E: McDonald's, Shoney's
	Other	E: Kroger, Tires, WVU Inst of Tech
(82)		TOLL Plaza
79		CR 79/3, Cabin Creek Rd, Sharon
74		CR 83, Paint Creek Rd
	Other	E: WVU Inst of Tech
(72)		Morton Service Plaza (NB)
	FStop	Exxon
	Food	Burger King, Starbucks, TCBY
	Other	RVDump
(69)		Rest Area (SB) (RR, Phones, Picnic, Vend)
66		CR 15, to Mahan
	Gas	E: Sunoco◊
60		WV 612, Oak Hill, Mossy
	Gas	E: Exxon◊
(55)		TOLL Plaza
54		CR 2, CR 23, Pax, Mt Hope
	Gas	W: BP
48		US 19N, N Beckley, Summersville (E on US 19 for addt'l food, WalM, etc)
	Gas	E: BP◊
	Food	E: Subway/BP
	Lodg	E: Ramada Inn
	Other	E: Appalachian Bible College
(45)		Tamarack Travel Plaza (Both dir)
	TStop	Exxon
	Food	BiscuitWorld, Burger King, Sbarro's, Starbucks, TCBY
	Other	RVDump
44		WV 3, Harper Rd, Beckley
	TStop	W: Go-Mart #50
	Gas	E: Chevron◊, Exxon, Marathon, Shell W: BP
	Food	E: Applebee's, Burger King, Hibachi Japanese Steakhouse, McDonald's, Omelet Shoppe, Outback Steakhouse, Pizza Hut, Western Steer W: Bob Evans, Cracker Barrel, Wendy's
	Lodg	E: Best Western, Comfort Inn, Courtyard, Fairfield Inn, Holiday Inn, Howard Johnson, Quality Inn, Super 8 W: Days Inn, Hampton Inn, Microtel
	Med	W: + Raleigh General Hospitall
	Other	W: CVS, Kroger, Mountain State Univ, College of WV, Exhibition Coal Mine/RV Camping▲
42		WV 16, WV 97, Robert C Byrd Dr, to Mabscott
	Gas	W: AmocoBP◊
	Food	W: Subway
	TServ	E: Walker Machinery
	Med	E: + Hospital, VA Med Center
	Other	W: Wal-Mart sc, to Twin Falls Resort Park▲
(40)		Jct I-64E, to Lewisburg
	NOTE:	I-77 above follows I-64 between Charleston and Beckley. Exit #'s follow I-77.
(35)		Rest Area (Both dir) (RR, Phones, Picnic, RVDump)
(30)		TOLL Plaza
28		CR 48, Odd Rd, Ghent, Flat Top
	Gas	E: BP, Marathon◊

EXIT		WV / VA
	Lodg	E: Glade Springs Resort, to Appalachian Resort Inn W: Econo Lodge
	Other	E: US Post Office, to Ski Area
20		US 119, to Camp Creek
	FStop	E: Exxon◊
	Other	W: Camp Creek State Park▲
(17)		Bluestone Travel Plaza (NB) Weigh Station (NB), Parking (SB)
	FStop	Exxon
	Food	Roy Rogers, Starbucks, TCBY
	Other	RVDump
14		WV 20, CR 7, Athens Rd, Princeton
	Gas	E: Citgo
	Other	E: to Princeton/Pipestem KOA▲, Pipestem Resort Park▲, Lake Ridge RV Resort Family Campground▲, Concord College
(9)		WV Turnpike Begins/Ends
9		US 460, Veterans Memorial Hwy, Princeton; Pearisburg, VA
	E:	WV WELCOME CENTER (RR, Phone, Picnic, Vend)
	FStop	E: Blue Flash FoodMart #460
	TStop	E: I-77 Truck Stop
	Gas	W: BP◊, Chevron◊, Exxon, Marathon
	Food	E: Applebee's, Bob Evans, DQ, Cracker Barrel, Hardee's, McDonald's, Omelette Shoppe, Shoney's, Wendy's
	Lodg	W: Comfort Inn, Days Inn, Hampton Inn, Ramada, Sleep Inn, Super 8
	Med	W: + Hospital
	Other	E: Wal-Mart sc W: WV State Hwy Patrol Post
7		CR 27, Twelve Mile Rd, Ingleside (NB, Exit only, NO re-entry)
5		WV 112 (SB, Exit only, NO re-entry)
1		US 52N, US 460, CR 290, Bluefield (Serv 5mi W in Bluefield)
	Med	W: + Hospital
	Other	W: Ashland KOA▲, Bluefield State College

⬆ WEST VIRGINIA
⬇ VIRGINIA
(EASTERN TIME ZONE)

66		US 52, VA 598, to East River Mtn
64		US 52, VA 61, to Rocky Gap
62		VA 606, Bastian, to South Gap
(61)		VA Welcome Center (SB) (RR, Phone, Picnic, Vend, Info)
(59)		Rocky Gap Rest Area (NB) (RR, Phones, Picnic, Vend)
58		VA 666, to US 52, Bastian
	FStop	E: BP W: Kangaroo Express
	Gas	W: Exxon◊
(56)		RunAWay Ramp (NB)
52		US 52, VA 42, Bland
	FStop	W: Sentry Food Mart #28/Shell
	Gas	E: Citgo
	Food	W: Rest/Big Walker Motel
	Lodg	W: Big Walker Motel
	Other	E: Conv Store

◊= Regular Gas Stations with Diesel ▲ = RV Friendly Locations ♥ = Pet Friendly Locations
RED PRINT SHOWS LARGE VEHICLE PARKING/ACCESS ON SITE OR NEARBY BROWN PRINT SHOWS CAMPGROUNDS/RV PARKS

Page 354

INTERSTATE 77 N/S

EXIT	VIRGINIA
(52)	**Weigh Station** (Both dir)
47	VA 717, CR 601, Krenning Rd, Deer Trail, Wytheville, Max Meadows
Other	W: to Deer Trail Park & Campground▲
41	VA 610, Peppers Ferry Rd, Wytheville
TStop	W: Kangaroo Express, Travel Center of America #143/BP (Scales)
Food	E: Sagebrush Steakhouse W: FastFood/Kangaroo Express, Rest/Popeye/Subway/TacoBell/TA TC, Country Kitchen, Wendy's, Rest/Ramada
Lodg	W: Comfort Suites, Hampton Inn, Ramada
TServ	W: TA TC/Tires
Med	W: + Hospital
Other	W: Laundry/WiFi/RVDump/TA TC
NOTE:	I-77 below runs with I-81 next 9 mi. Exit #'s follow I-81.
(40/72)	Jct I-81S, to Bristol, US 52 I-77N, to Bluefield (Serv located at 1st exit on I-81)
73	US 11S, Wytheville
Gas	W: BP, Citgo, Kangaroo Express
Food	E: Sagebrush Steakhouse W: Applebee's, Bob Evans, Burger King, Cracker Barrel, Chinese, Hardee's, KFC, Pizza Hut, Ocean Bay Seafood, Shoney's, Waffle House
Lodg	E: Sleep Inn W: Budget Host Inn, Days Inn, Holiday Inn, Econo Lodge, Motel 6♥, Quality Inn, Red Carpet Inn, Red Roof Inn, Travelodge
Other	W: ATMs, Auto Services, CVS, Food Lion, Harley Davidson, Kmart, Pharmacy, Tires, Wytheville Comm College
77	Service Rd, Wytheville
FStop	E: WilcoHess C Store #605
TStop	E: Kangaroo Express/Citgo, Flying J Travel Plaza #5420 (Scales) W: WilcoHess Travel Plaza #606 (Scales)
Food	E: Subway/Kangaroo Express, Rest/FJ TP, Burger King W: Arby's/WilcoHess TP
TWash	W: TruckOMat/WilcoHess TP
Other	E: Laundry/BarbSh/WiFi/RVDump/LP/FJ TP, Wytheville KOA▲ W: Laundry/WilcoHess TP, VA State Hwy Patrol Post
80	US 52S, VA 121N, Max Meadows, Fort Chiswell
FStop	W: Sentry Food Mart #21
TStop	E: Flying J Travel Plaza #1123 (Scales)
Gas	E: BP♦ W: AmocoBP
Food	E: Cooker/Wendy's/FJ TP, BurgerKing/BP W: Family Rest, McDonald's
Lodg	E: Hampton Inn, Super 8 W: Comfort Inn♥
TWash	E: Blue Beacon TW/FJ TP
TServ	E: FJ TP/Tires W: Speedco
Other	E: Laundry/WiFi/LP/FJ TP, Ft Chiswell Outlet Mall, Ft Chiswell RV Park▲
(81/32)	Jct I-81N, US 11, Roanoke I-77S, to Charlotte
NOTE:	I-77 above runs with I-81 next 9 mi. Exit #'s follow I-81.

EXIT	VA / NC
24	VA 69, Lead Mine Rd, Austinville, to Poplar Camp
FStop	W: Citgo
Gas	E: Pure
TServ	E: Poplar Camp Truck Repair
19	VA 620, Coulson Church Rd, Hillsville
Other	W: Twin Co Airport✈
14	US 58, US 221, Hillsville, Galax
FStop	W: Cockerham Fuel Center #4/Chevron
Gas	E: Race In W: EZ Stop, On the Way
Food	E: Burger King, Pizza Hut W: DQ, McDonald's, Shoney's, Wendy's
Lodg	E: Comfort Inn, Red Carpet Inn W: Best Western, Comfort Inn, Hampton Inn, Holiday Inn Express, Quality Inn, Super 8
Med	E: + Hospital
Other	E: to Lake Ridge RV Resort Family Campground▲ W: Carrollwood Campground▲, to appr 19mi Deer Creek RV Resort▲
8	VA 148, VA 755, Chances Creek Rd, to US 52, Fancy Gap
FStop	W: Kangaroo Express #3367/Citgo
Gas	W: BP, Exxon
Lodg	W: Days Inn, Country View Inn
Other	E: Fancy Gap/Blue Ride KOA▲, Fancy Gap Cabins & Campgrounds▲, UTT's Campground▲
(6)	RunAWay Ramp (SB)
(4)	RunAWay Ramp (SB)
(3)	RunAWay Ramp (SB)
1	VA 620, Lambsburg Rd, Old Pipers Gap Rd, Lambsburg
(1)	VA Welcome Center (NB) (RR, Phones, Picnic, Info)

(EASTERN TIME ZONE)

⇑ VIRGINIA
⇓ NORTH CAROLINA

(EASTERN TIME ZONE)

(105)	NC Welcome Center (SB) (RR, Phones, Picnic, Vend, Info)
(103)	Weigh Station (Both dir)
(101)	Jct I-74E, Mt Airy, to Winston-Salem (fr SB, Left exit)
100	NC 89, Mount Airy, to Galax, Va
TStop	E: PTP/Brintle Travel Plaza/Citgo (Scales)
Gas	E: Exxon♦, Marathon♦, Shell
Food	E: Rest/Brintle TP, Subway/Marathon, Wagon Wheel Rest
Lodg	E: Best Western, Comfort Inn
TServ	E: Brintle TP/Tires
Other	E: Laundry/Brintle TP W: to appr 17mi Deer Creek RV Resort▲
93	Zephyr Rd, Dobson, Surry
FStop	E: Fast Track Shell #119
Gas	E: Citgo♦ W: On the Way Food Store
Food	E: FastFood/FT Shell, Diner
Lodg	E: Surry Inn
Other	E: Camping▲

♦ = Regular Gas Stations with Diesel ▲ = RV Friendly Locations ♥ = Pet Friendly Locations
RED PRINT SHOWS LARGE VEHICLE PARKING/ACCESS ON SITE OR NEARBY   BROWN PRINT SHOWS CAMPGROUNDS/RV PARKS

Page 355

INTERSTATE 77 N/S

N CAROLINA

EXIT		
85		CC Camp Rd, Elkin, to US 21 ByP
	Gas	W: Exxon◊, Shell
	Other	E: to Elkin Muni Airport✈
83		US 21 ByP, to Sparta (NB, Left exit)
82		NC 67, Jonesville, Elkin, Boonville
	FStop	E: Four Bros Food Store #300/BP
		W: G&B Food Mart #290/Exxon
	Gas	E: Chevron◊, Citgo
	Food	E: Arby's
		W: Bojangles, Cracker Barrel, Glenn's BBQ, Jordan's Country Rest, McDonald's, Waffle House, Wendy's
	Lodg	E: Holiday Inn Express
		W: Comfort Inn, Days Inn, Hampton Inn
	Other	E: Holly Ridge Family Campground▲
		W: Grocery, Pharmacy, Vet♥
79		US 21 Bus, US 21S, Jonesville, to Arlington
	Gas	E: Shell
		W: Shell◊
	Food	W: Sally Jo's Kitchen
	Lodg	E: Super 8
		W: Country Inn
73AB		US 421, Hamptonville, to Winston-Salem, Wilkesboro
	FStop	E: Fast Track Shell #143
	Food	E: FastFood/FT Shell
	Lodg	E: Welborn Motel, Yadkin Inn
(72)		Rest Area (NB)
		(RR, Phones, Picnic, Vend)
65		NC 901, Union Grove, Harmony
	FStop	W: Union Grove Quick Stop/BP, Fast Track Shell #137, Knight's BP
	Food	W: FastFood/FT Shell, Burger Barn
	Other	E: Van Hoy Farms Family Campground▲
		W: Fiddlers Grove Campground▲, New Hope Stables & Campgrounds▲
(62)		Rest Area (SB)
		(RR, Phones, Picnic, Vend)
59		NC 1890, Tomlin Mill Rd, Statesville
54		US 21, Statesville, to Turnersburg
	FStop	W: Fast Track Shell #130
	Gas	E: Citgo
	Other	W: Staples
(51B)		Jct I-40W, to Hickory
(51A)		Jct I-40E, to Winston Salem
50		E Broad St, Statesville
	Gas	E: BP, Citgo◊, Kangaroo◊, Shell
	Food	E: Arby's, Bojangles, Burger King, Domino's, Hardee's, IHOP, Long John Silver, McDonald's, Pizza Hut, Starbucks, Subway, Wendy's
	Lodg	E: Fairfield Inn, Red Roof Inn♥
	Med	W: + Iredell Memorial Hospital
	Other	E: ATMs, Banks, Dollar General, Dollar Tree, Grocery, Kmart, Pharmacy, Signal Hill Mall, UPS Store, US Post Office
		W: to Carolina Mountain Sports
49B		Salisbury Rd, to I-70, to Downtown
	Gas	E: USA Mart Chevron
		W: Amoco, Citgo, Exxon
	Food	E: KFC, Waffle House
	Lodg	W: Best Value Inn
	Other	W: Auto Services
49A		US 70E, Statesville
	FStop	E: Kangaroo Express #3195
	Gas	E: BP, Circle K, Shell

EXIT		
	Food	E: Waffle House
	Lodg	E: Comfort Inn, Holiday Inn, Motel 6♥, Super 8
	Other	E: Lane's Tire & Auto, Tilley Harley Davidson, Camping World/RVDump
45		Amity Hill Rd, Statesville, to Troutman, Barium Springs
	FStop	W: Chevron
	Other	E: Statesville KOA▲, Rent Me RV America
42		US 21, NC 115, Troutman
	TStop	E: WilcoHess Travel Plaza #357 (Scales)
	Food	E: Subway/TacoBell/WilcoHess TP
	Other	W: to Lake Norman State Park▲
(39)		Rest Area (Both dir)
		(RR, Phones, Picnic, Vend)
(38)		Weigh Station (Both dir)
36		NC 150, W Plaza Dr, Mooresville
	Gas	E: Exxon, Shell
		W: BP◊, Citgo, Shell◊, Servco, BJ's
	Food	E: Applebee's, Bob Evans, Burger King, Denny's, McDonald's, Pizza Hut, Taco Bell, Waffle House, Wendy's
		W: Arby's, Cracker Barrel, Golden Corral, Hardee's, Hooters, Kyoto's, Subway
	Lodg	E: Days Inn, Fairfield Inn, Holiday Inn
		W: Hampton Inn, Sleep Inn, Super 8
	Other	E: Kmart, Grocery, Staples, Wal-Mart sc
		W: Food Lion, Lowe's, Walgreen's
33		US 21N, Mooresville
	Gas	E: Phillips 66
		W: BP, Citgo◊
	Food	E: McDonald's, Subway
	Lodg	E: Springhill Suites
	Med	E: + Hospital
30		Griffith St, Davidson
	Gas	E: Exxon◊
28		Catawba Ave, to US 21, NC 73, to Lake Norman, Cornelius
	Gas	E: AmocoBP, Citgo
	Food	E: Bojangles, Subway, Rest/Hol Inn
		W: Burger King, Domino's, Jersey Mike's, KFC, Kobe, Little Caesars, Lone Star Steakhouse, McDonald's, Pizza Hut, Taco Bell, Wendy's
	Lodg	E: Hampton Inn, Holiday Inn
		W: Best Western, Comfort Inn, Quality Inn, Econo Lodge, Microtel
25		NC 73, Sam Furr Rd, Huntersville, to Concord, Lake Norman
	Gas	E: Shell◊
		W: Circle K◊
	Food	E: Burger King, Chili's, Fuddruckers, McDonald's, O'Charley's, Wendy's
		W: Arby's, Bob Evans, Bojangles, DQ, Carrabba's, Outback Steakhouse, Subway
	Lodg	E: Country Suites, Hawthorn Inn, Quality Inn
		W: Candlewood Suites, Courtyard, Residence Inn, Sleep Inn
	Other	E: ATMs, Banks, Home Depot, Lowe's, Target, Winn Dixie
		W: ATM, Food Lion
23		Gilead Rd, Huntersville
	Gas	E: BP, Citgo, Shell
		W: Sam's Mart
	Food	E: Captain's Galley, Hardee's, Subway, Waffle House, Wendy's

EXIT		
	Lodg	E: Holiday Inn Express, Red Roof Inn♥
	Med	W: + Presbyterian Hospital
	Other	E: ATM, Pharmacy, Food Lion, US Post Office
		W: ATM, CVS, Grocery
18		NC 24, to US 21, Charlotte Harris Blvd, Reames Rd
	Gas	E: BP, Phillips 66◊, Shell, Sam's Mart
	Food	E: Arby's, Bob Evans, Corner Deli & Grill, Jack in the Box, Quiznos, Waffle House
		W: ChikFilA, The Grape, Food Court
	Lodg	E: Comfort Suites, Fairfield Inn, Hilton Garden Inn, Suburban Extended Stay
	TServ	E: Carolina Engine
	Med	E: + Hospital
	Other	W: Northlake Mall, FedEx Kinko's
16AB		US 21, Sunset Rd, Charlotte
	TStop	W: AmBest/Charlotte Travel Plaza/Shell (Scales)
	Gas	E: Circle K
		W: Citgo, Circle K
	Food	E: Captain D's, Hardee's, KFC, McDonald's, Taco Bell, Wendy's
		W: FastFood/Charlotte TP, Bubba's BBQ, Bojangles, Denny's, Domino's, Jack in the Box, Waffle House
	Lodg	E: Days Inn, Super 8
		W: Microtel, Sleep Inn
	Other	E: AutoZone, CVS, Auto & Truck Services, Tires
		W: Laundry/Charlotte TP, CVS, Food Lion, Family Dollar, Charlotte Bus & RV Sales
(13AB)		Jct I-85, N to Greensboro, S to Spartanburg
12		LaSalle St, Charlotte
	Gas	W: Citgo◊, Shell◊
(11AB)		Jct I-277, NC 16, Brookshire Fwy
10C		Trade St, 5th St, Downtown (SB)
10B		Trade St, Downtown Charlotte (SB)
	Gas	W: Citgo
	Food	W: Bojangles
	Other	E: Greyhound Bus Lines
		W: Johnson C Smith Univ
10A		US 29, NC 27, Morehead St (SB)
	Med	E: + Hospital
	Other	E: Bank of America Stadium
10		Trade St, W 5th St (NB)
	Other	W: to Discovery Place
(9)		Jct I-277, US 74, Wilkinson Blvd
	Med	E: + Hospital
	Other	E: to Stadium
9C		US 74, Wilkinson Blvd, US 29, NC 27, Charlotte
(9B)		Jct I-277
9A		NC 160, West Blvd (SB)
8		Remount Rd (fr NB, exit only, NO reacc)
7		Clanton Rd, to NC 49, Charlotte
	FStop	E: Petro Express #10/Citgo
	Gas	W: BP, Shell
	Food	E: to South Blvd
	Lodg	E: Econo Lodge, Motel 6♥, Super 8
	Other	E: Tires, Auto Services
6A		US 521, Woodlawn Rd, Charlotte
	Gas	E: 76, BP, Citgo, Shell◊, Speedway◊
	Food	E: Arby's, Azteca, Bojangles, Burger King, Captain D's, Checkers, IHOP, KFC,

◊ = Regular Gas Stations with Diesel   ▲ = RV Friendly Locations   ♥ = Pet Friendly Locations

RED PRINT SHOWS LARGE VEHICLE PARKING/ACCESS ON SITE OR NEARBY   BROWN PRINT SHOWS CAMPGROUNDS/RV PARKS

INTERSTATE 77 N/S

EXIT	N CAROLINA
	Food E: Krispy Kreme, Mex Rest, McDonald's, Shoney's, Steak & Ale, Waffle House, Wendy's
	Lodg E: Best Western, Days Inn, Four Points Sheraton, Howard Johnson, Ramada
	Other E: CVS
6B	**NC 49, Tryon St, US 521, Woodlawn Rd, Billy Graham Pkwy**
	Gas W: Phillips 66, Petro Express
	Food W: McDonald's, Omaha Steak House, Wendy's
	Lodg W: Embassy Suites, Extended Stay Hotel, Holiday Inn, Homestead Studio, La Quinta Inn♥, InTown Suites, Summerfield Suites
	Other W: Charlotte Coliseum, to Charlotte Douglas Int'l Airport✈
5	**Tyvola Rd, to US 49, US 521, Charlotte**
	Gas E: Citgo◊, Petro Express, Texaco
	Food E: Black Eyed Pea, Chili's, China King, Carolina Country BBQ, Hooters, Lone Star Steakhouse, McDonald's, Sonny's BBQ, Subway
	Lodg E: Candlewood Suites, Comfort Inn, Hampton Inn, Marriott, Quality Inn, Residence Inn W: Extended Stay, Wingate Inn
	Other E: Grocery, Target W: to Charlotte Coliseum
4	**Nations Ford Rd, Charlotte**
	Gas E: AmocoBP, Circle K, Citgo W: Shell
	Food E: Caravel Seafood, Shoney's W: Burger King
	Lodg E: Best Inn, Knights Inn, Motel 6, Ramada
	Other E: Grocery
3	**Arrowood Rd, to I-485 (SB)**
	Gas E: Shell
	Food E: Bob Evans, Jack in the Box, Long John Silver, McDonald's, Sonic, Wendy's W: Bojangles, Café, Ruby Tuesday
	Lodg E: AmeriSuites, Courtyard, Fairfield Inn, Holiday Inn Express, Mainstay Suites, Staybridge Suites, TownePlace Suites W: Hampton Inn
	Other E: CVS, Family Dollar, Food Lion W: to Wal-Mart, Tires
2	**Arrowood Rd (NB), to I-485 (SB) (Access to Ex #3 Serv)**
(1)	**NC Welcome Center (NB) (RR, Phones, Picnic, Vend)**
1	**Westinghouse Blvd, to I-485**
	Gas E: BP◊, Shell◊ W: BP, Exxon, Shell◊, Petro Express
	Food E: Jack in the Box, Subway, Waffle House W: Burger King
	Lodg E: Super 8

(EASTERN TIME ZONE)

NORTH CAROLINA

EXIT	S CAROLINA
	SOUTH CAROLINA (EASTERN TIME ZONE)
90	**US 21, Carowinds Blvd, Ft Mill**
	Gas E: Petro Express, Shell W: 76, Circle K, Exxon, Petro, Shell
	Food E: Burger King, Denny's W: Cracker Barrel, KFC, Shoney's, Wendy's
	Lodg E: Days Inn, Super 8 W: Best Western, Comfort Inn, Holiday Inn Express, Motel 6♥, Plaza Hotel, Sleep Inn
	Other E: CAMP▲, National RV Rentals W: Carowinds Amusement Park, Outlet Mall, Carolina Pottery, Carowinds Camp Wilderness Resort▲
(89)	**SC Welcome Center (SB) (RR, Phones, Picnic, Vend, Info)**
(88)	**Weigh Station (NB)**
88	**SC 98, Gold Hill Rd, to Pineville**
	Gas W: Exxon◊, Gate◊, Shell◊
	Food W: Bojangles, John's Place, Logan Farms & Market Cafe
	Other W: Auto Dealers, Charlotte/Ft Mill KOA▲, Tracy's RV
85	**SC 160, Fort Mill**
	Gas E: Exxon W: BP◊, Circle K
	Food E: Subway W: Backyard Burger, Bojangles, Wendy's
(84)	**Weigh Station (SB)**
83	**SC 49, Sutton Rd, Fort Mill**
	TStop W: Love's Travel Stop #333 (Scales)
	Food W: Godfathers/ChesterFr/Love's TS
	Other W: WiFi/RVDump/Love's TS
82C	**SC 161, Celanese Rd, York**
	Gas W: Allsup's, Petro Express
	Food W: Chinese Bistro, Hooters, Outback Steakhouse, Sonic, Starbucks
	Lodg W: Courtyard
	Med W: + Piedmont Medical Center
	Other W: ATMs, CVS, Grocery, to Bryant Field✈
82B	**US 21, Cherry Rd, Rock Hill (SB)**
	Gas W: Exxon, Petro Express, RaceTrac◊
	Food W: Arby's, Burger King, Bojangles, Captain's Galley, ChickFilA, Denny's, Firebonz BBQ, McDonald's, Pizza Hut, Sake Express, Sakura Japanese, Subway, Taco Bell, Waffle House
	Lodg W: Best Western, Country Inn, Days Inn, Howard Johnson, Microtel, Regency Inn, Super 8♥
	Other W: ATMs, AdvanceAuto, Auto Dealers, Auto Services, Dollar General, Family Dollar, Firestone, Grocery, Kmart, Office Depot, Pep Boys, Pharmacy, Towing, U-Haul, Winthrop Univ, Winthrop Coliseum

EXIT	S CAROLINA
15B	**SC 12W, Percival Rd, Ft Jackson (NB)**
82A	**US 21, Cherry Rd (NB)**
	Gas E: Food Mart
	Food E: IHOP, Sonny's BBQ, Steak 'n Shake, Zaxby's
	Lodg E: Quality Inn, Ramada Inn
	Other E: ATM, Greyhound, Home Depot, PetSmart♥
79	**SC 122, Dave Lyle Blvd, Downtown**
	Gas E: BP W: Petro Express
	Food E: Applebee's, Charanda's Mex Rest, ChickFilA, Cracker Barrel, Hardee's, Longhorn Steakhouse, O'Charley's, Ryan's Grill, Ruby Tuesday W: Bob Evans, Chili's, McDonald's, Olive Garden, Moe's SW Grill, Panera, Quiznos, Sagebrush, Subway, Taco Bell, Wendy's
	Lodg E: Hampton Inn, Wingate Inn W: Hilton Garden Inn
	Med W: + Piedmont East Urgent Care Center
	Other E: ATMs, Banks, Food Lion, Cox Harley Davidson, Lowe's, Radio Shack, Staples, Discount Tire, Tire Kingdom, Rock Hill Galleria Mall, Rock Hill Truck Services, Wal-Mart sc▲ W: ATMs, Best Buy, Target, UPS Store, to York Tech College
77	**US 21, SC 5, Anderson Rd**
	FStop W: Pride Truck Stop (Scales) W: Cone Oil #220
	Gas E: BP◊, Citgo◊, Exxon◊ W: Exxon
	Food E: Subway W: Bojangles, KFC, McDonald's, Papa John's, Subway, Waffle House
	Other E: Cox Harley Davidson W: Laundry/Pride TS, Auto Service
75	**Porter Rd, Rock Hill**
	Gas E: Texaco
	Other E: Fireworks
73	**SC 901, Mt Holly Rd, Rock Hill**
	FStop E: Crenco Auto Truck Plaza #8/Exxon W: Citgo
	TStop E: Flying J Travel Plaza (Scales)
	Food E: CountryMarket/FastFood/FIJ TP
	Other E: Laundry/WiFi/RVDump/LP/FJ TP
(66)	**Rest Area (Both dir) (RR, Phones, Picnic, Vend)**
65	**SC 9, SC 901, Lancaster Hwy, Richburg, to Lancaster, Chester**
	FStop E: Shell W: Crenco Auto Truck Plaza #2/Exxon
	Gas E: BP
	Food E: Subway, Waffle House W: Burger King, Country Omelet, KFC, McDonald's
	Lodg E: Days Inn, Econo Lodge, Relax Inn W: Comfort Inn, Rodeway Inn, Super 8
	Other W: Laundry/Crenco ATP
62	**SC 56, Old Richburg Rd, Richburg, to SC 9, SC 901, Fort Lawn**
55	**SC 97, Great Falls Rd, to Chester**
	Gas E: Exxon◊

◊ = Regular Gas Stations with Diesel   ▲ = RV Friendly Locations   ♥ = Pet Friendly Locations

RED PRINT SHOWS LARGE VEHICLE PARKING/ACCESS ON SITE OR NEARBY   BROWN PRINT SHOWS CAMPGROUNDS/RV PARKS

Page 357

EXIT	S CAROLINA
48	SC 200, Winnsboro, to Great Falls
TStop	E: Grand Central Station/Shell (Scales)
	W: WilcoHess Travel Plaza #932 (Scales)
Food	E: Rest/Grand Central Station
	W: DQ/Wendy's/WH TP
TWash	E: Grand Central
TServ	E: Grand Central/Tires
Other	E: Laundry/Grand Central
	W: Laundry/RVDump/WH TP
46	SC 20-42, Camp Welfare Rd, White Oak, Winnsboro
41	SC 20-41, Old River Rd, Winnsboro
34	SC 34, Ridgeway, Camden
FStop	W: Sharp Shoppe #5/Exxon
TStop	E: AmPm Food Mart
Food	W: Blimpie/Exxon, Lois's, Waffle House
Lodg	E: Ridgeway Motel
	W: Ramada Ltd
Med	W: + Hospital
Other	E: Ridgeway Campground/RVDump▲
27	Blythewood Rd, to US 21, Blythewood
Gas	E: BP, Exxon◇
Food	E: KFC, McDonald's, Subway, Waffle House, Wendy's, Bojangles/Exxon
Lodg	E: Comfort Inn, Days Inn, Holiday Inn Express
Other	E: Pharmacy, Grocery
	W: Food Lion
24	US 21, Wilson Blvd, Blythewood, to Columbia
FStop	E: Pitt Stop #3/Shell
Gas	E: BP
Food	E: Subway/Shell, Myers BBQ
22	Killian Rd, to US 21, Columbia
19	SC 555, Farrow Rd, LeGrand Rd
Gas	E: BP, Exxon, Shell◇
	W: Shell◇
Food	E: Wendy's
	W: Waffle House
Lodg	E: Courtyard, Residence Inn
Med	E: + Hospital
Other	E: Pharmacy
18	US 277, to I-20W, Columbia (SB)
17	US 1, Two Notch Rd, to I-20
Gas	E: BP, Circle K, Kangaroo
Food	E: Burger King, Texas Roadhouse, Waffle House
	W: Chili's, IHOP, Outback Steakhouse, Waffle House
Lodg	E: Fairfield Inn, InTown Suites, Quality Inn, Columbia Plaza Hotel, Wingate Inn
	W: AmeriSuites, Baymont Inn♥, Comfort Inn, Hampton Inn, Holiday Inn, Microtel, Motel 6♥, Red Roof Inn♥, Travelodge
Other	E: ATMs, Banks, Grocery, Target, Wal-Mart▲, U-Haul, Royal Z Bowling Center, Sesquicentennial State Park
	W: ATMs, Banks, Home Depot, Kmart, Auto Services, Tires, Columbia Mall
(16B)	Jct I-20W, to Augusta
(16A)	Jct I-20E, to Florence
(16AB)	Jct I-20, W-Atlanta, E-Florence (fr NB, Left exit to WB)
15	SC 12, Percival Rd, Ft Jackson (SB)
Gas	W: Exxon, Shell

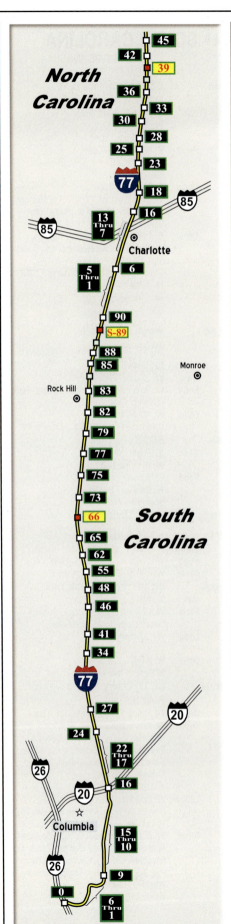

EXIT	S CAROLINA
15A	SC 12E, Percival Rd, Ft Jackson (NB)
Other	E: Ft Jackson Mill Res
13	Decker Blvd, to SC 12 (NB)
Other	W: Staples
12	Imboden St, to SC 12, Forest Dr, Strom Thurmond Blvd
Gas	W: BP◇, Shell◇
Food	W: Bojangles, Golden Corral, Hardee's, McDonald's, Steak & Ale, Subway
Lodg	W: Extended Stay America, Marlboro Inn, Super 8
Med	W: + Hospital
Other	E: Fort Jackson Military Res
	W: Sam's Club, Wal-Mart▲
10	SC 760, Fort Jackson Blvd, to US 76 US 378, SC 16
Gas	W: BP
Food	W: Applebee's, Bojangles, Ruby Tuesday, Subway
Lodg	W: Econo Lodge, Liberty Inn
Other	E: Ft Jackson Museum, Ft Jackson, MIL/ Weston Lake Rec Area▲
	W: Kmart
9B	SC 262, Leesburg Rd, Columbia, to US 76, US 378, Sumter (SB)
9A	US 76, US 378, Columbia, Sumter (SB)
9	US 76, US 378, to SC 262, Leesburg Rd, Columbia, to Sumter (NB)
Gas	E: BP, Citgo, Hess◇, Kangaroo◇
	W: Corner Pantry, Circle K
Food	E: Captain D's, KFC, McDonald's, Pizza Hut, Shoney's, Subway, Waffle House
	W: CiCi's, Hardee's, Starbucks, Wendy's
Lodg	E: Best Western, Comfort Inn, Days Inn, Country Inn, Holiday Inn Express, La Quinta Inn♥, Sleep Inn
	W: Howard Johnson
Med	W: + Hospital, VA Medical Center
Other	E: Advance Auto, Firestone, Lowe's, Grocery, Walgreen's, U-Haul, Wal-Mart▲, US Post Office
	W: ATMs, Grocery, Pharmacy, Target, Woodhill Mall, USC School of Med
6	SC 768, Shop Rd, Columbia (SB)
Other	W: to State Fairgrounds, Coliseum
6B	SC 768W, Shop Rd, Columbia (NB)
6A	SC 768E, Shop Rd, Columbia (NB)
5	SC 48, Bluff Rd, Gadsen
Gas	E: 76
	W: Shell
Food	W: Burger King/Shell
Other	W: to Columbia Owens Downtown Airport→
2	12th St Ext, to Cayce
1	US 21, US 176, SC 73, US 321 (Serv on US 176/US 21)
Other	W: to Cayce Speedway
(0)	Jct I-26, W-Spartanburg, E-Charleston (to EB, Left exit)

(I-77 begins/ends on I-90, Ex #172A)
(EASTERN TIME ZONE)

🎧 SOUTH CAROLINA

Begin Northbound I-77 from Jct I-26 in Columbia, SC to Jct I-90 in Cleveland, OH.

◇ = Regular Gas Stations with Diesel   ▲ = RV Friendly Locations   ♥ = Pet Friendly Locations
RED PRINT SHOWS LARGE VEHICLE PARKING/ACCESS ON SITE OR NEARBY   BROWN PRINT SHOWS CAMPGROUNDS/RV PARKS

EXIT	PENNSYLVANIA
	Begin Eastbound I-78 from Jct I-81 near Fredericksburg, PA to Jct I-95 in Newark, NJ.

⊙ PENNSYLVANIA
(EASTERN TIME ZONE)
(Begin/End I-78 on I-81, Ex #89)

Exit		Description
(1A)		Jct I-81S, to Harrisburg (Left exit)
(1B)		Jct I-81N, to Hazelton
6		PA 343, Legionaire Dr, to US 22, Fredricksburg, Lebanon (EB)
	FStop	S: Pacific Pride
	Other	S: Farmers Pride Airport✈, to appr 5mi: Jonestown KOA▲
8		US 22W, to PA 343, Fredericksburg, Lebanon (WB)
10		PA 645, Camp Swatara Rd, Myerstown, Frystown
	TStop	N: Gables of Frystown/Shell (Scales) S: Frystown All American Plaza (Scales)
	Food	N: Deli/Gables S: Rest/All Amer Pl
	Lodg	S: All American Motel/All Amer Pl
	TServ	S: All American Plaza/Tires/TWash
	Other	S: Laundry/CB/WiFi/LP/All Amer Pl
13		PA 501, Lancaster Ave, Bethel
	FStop	N: Shell
	TStop	S: I-78 Truck Stop/Exxon
	Food	S: Rest/I-78 TS
	TServ	S: Midway Truck Service, Towing
15		Court St, Frantz Rd Midway, Grimes (NO Trucks)
16		Midway Rd, Bethel, Midway
	FStop	N: Midway Exxon Travel Center, Midway Fuel & Truck Wash/Citgo
	Food	N: Midway Diner
	Lodg	N: Comfort Inn
	TWash	N: Midway Exxon TC
	Other	N: Auto & Truck Repair
17		PA 419, Four Point Rd, Bethel, to Rehrersburg
	Gas	N: Best◆
	Lodg	N: Lamplighter Motel
	Other	N: Truck Repair, Tires
19		PA 183, Bethel, to Strausstown
	Gas	S: Shell◆
	Other	S: to Bashore & Stoudt Country Winery, Calvaresi Winery, Clover Hill Winery
23		Mountain Rd, Shartlesville
	FStop	N: Sunoco
	Food	N: Stuckeys/DQ/Sunoco S: Blue Mountain Family Rest, Haag's PA Dutch Rest/Haags Motel, Riverboat Saloon
	Lodg	N: Dutch Motel

Exit		Description
	Lodg	S: Scottish Inn, Haag's Motel
	Other	N: PA Dutch Campsites▲, Martin's RV Center, Appalachian Campsites▲, Mountain Springs Camping Resort▲ S: to Blue Marsh Lake
29A		PA 61S, Hamburg, to Reading
	Food	S: Hamburg Diner
	Other	S: Grocery
29B		PA 61N, to Pottsville
	FStop	N: Square One Market/Shell
	Food	N: Burger King, Cracker Barrel, Italian Rest, Subway, Taco Bell, Wendy's
	Lodg	N: Microtel
	Other	N: Boat n RV Superstore, Cabela's/RVDump, RV Center, to Hawk Mountain, Blue Mtn Airport✈, to app 9mi Christmas Pines Campground▲
30		N 4th St, Hamburg
	Gas	S: Getty, Mobil
	Food	S: Subway, Rest/Amer Hse Htl
	Lodg	S: American House Hotel
	Other	S: ATMs, Banks, Hamburg Truck Service, Tom Schaeffer RV Superstore
35		PA 143, Lenhartsville
	Other	N: Blue Rocks Family Campground▲, Robin Hill Camping Resort▲ S: PA Dutch Folk Culture Center
40		PA 737, Krumsville, Kutztown
	Gas	S: Shell
	Food	S: Skyview Country Rest
	Lodg	S: Top Motel
	Other	N: Pine Hill RV Park▲, Robin Hill Camping Resort▲
45		PA 863, Kutztown, to Lynnport, New Smithville
	FStop	N: Bandit Truck Stop #1/Sunoco
	Gas	N: Exxon
	Food	N: FastFood/Bandit TS, DeMarco's Italian Rest, Subway/Exxon
	Lodg	N: Super 8
	Other	N: WiFi/Bandit TS
49AB		PA 100, Fogelsville, Trexlertown
49A		PA 100S, to Trexlertown
	Gas	S: Shell, Sunoco, WaWa
	Food	S: Burger King, Damons, Starlite Diner, Taco Bell, Yocco's Hot Dogs
	Lodg	S: Hampton Inn, Hilton Garden Inn, Holiday Inn, Sleep Inn, Staybridge Suites
	Other	S: ATMs, Grocery Store, Grover Hill Winery, PA State Hwy Patrol Post
49B		PA 100N, to Fogelsville
	Food	N: Arby's, Cracker Barrel, Long John Silver, Pizza Hut
	Lodg	N: Comfort Inn, Hawthorne Suites
	Other	N: ATM, Auto Services, Bank, Pharmacy,

Exit		Description
	Other	N: Purcell Tire, Tires, to Allentown KOA▲
51		US 22E, to I-476, Pa Tpk, to PA 309N PA 33N, Whitehall (EB, exit only)
	Other	to Lehigh Valley Int'l Airport✈
53		PA 309N, to I-476N, Pa Tpk (WB)
54		US 222, Hamilton Blvd (EB, Exit only)
	Gas	N: Hess S: Sunoco, WaWa
	Food	N: Boston Market, Burger King, Carrabba's, Dunkin Donuts, McDonald's, Mangos, Perkins, Subway, TGI Friday, Wendy's S: Hunan Chinese, Pizza Hut
	Lodg	N: Comfort Suites, Holiday Inn Express, Howard Johnson S: Days Inn, Wingate Inn
	Other	N: ATMs, FedEx Kinko's, Grocery, Cedar Crest College, Muhlenberg College, Wild Water King Park, Dorney Park, S: U-Haul, Tires
54A		US 222S, Hamilton Blvd (WB)
54B		US 222, Hamilton Blvd (WB)
55		PA 29s, Cedar Crest Blvd
	Gas	S: Post & Shell
	Food	S: Cafe
	Med	S: + Lehigh Valley Hospital
	Other	S: Indian Museum
57		Lehigh St, Allentown
	Gas	N: Hess◆ S: Turkey Hill, Getty
	Food	N: Arby's, IHOP S: Bennigan's, Burger King, Bob Evans, Dunkin Donuts, Friendly's, McDonald's, Perkins, Subway, Taco Bell, Wendy's
	Lodg	N: Days Inn
	Other	N: ATM, Big Lots, CVS, Family Dollar, Grocery, Home Depot, Queen City Muni Airport✈, Mack Truck WHQ S: ATMs, Banks, Auto Dealers, Grocery, PetCo♥, Staples, Tires, UPS Store, South Mall
58		Emmaus Ave, Allentown (WB)
	Gas	S: Gulf, Turkey Hill
	Other	N: Pharmacy S: ATMs, Banks, Grocery, Pharmacy
59		Rock Rd, to PA 145, Summit Lawn (EB)
60		PA 309S, Quakertown (EB)
	Other	N: DeSales Univ
60A		PA 309S, Quakertown (WB)
	Other	N: DeSales Univ
60B		PA 145N, S 4th St, Quakertown, Coopersburg (WB)

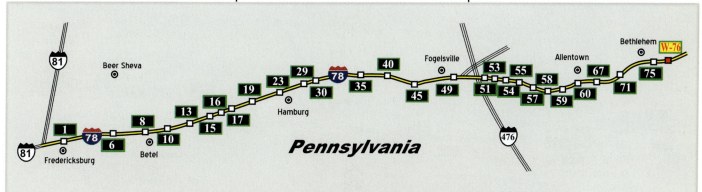

◆= Regular Gas Stations with Diesel ▲ = RV Friendly Locations ♥ = Pet Friendly Locations
RED PRINT SHOWS LARGE VEHICLE PARKING/ACCESS ON SITE OR NEARBY BROWN PRINT SHOWS CAMPGROUNDS/RV PARKS

W INTERSTATE 78

EXIT		PA / NJ
67		PA 412, Hellertown Rd, Hellertown, to Bethlehem
	Gas	N: Turkey Hill
		S: Citgo, Mobil◆, Sunoco
	Food	N: Wendy's
		S: Burger King, McDonald's, Waffle House
	Lodg	N: to Comfort Suites
		S: to Holiday Inn Express
	Med	N: + to St Luke's Hospital
	Other	N: to Lehigh Univ, Historic Bethlehem
71		PA 33N, to US 22, Bethlehem, to Easton, Stroudsburg, Pocono Mtns
	Other	N: Circuit City, Lowe's, Staples, to Lehigh Valley Int'l Airport ✈
75		Morgan Hill Rd, to PA 611, Easton, to Philadelphia
	Gas	N: Turkey Hill
	Food	N: McDonald's, Perkins
	Lodg	N: Best Western
	Other	N: to Lafayette College, Crayola Attractions
(75)		TOLL PLAZA (WB)
(76)		PA Welcome Center (WB) (RR, Phones, Picnic, Vend, Info)
	NOTE:	MM 77: New Jersey State Line

○ PENNSYLVANIA
○ NEW JERSEY (EASTERN TIME ZONE)

3		US 22, NJ 173, Phillipsburg
	FStop	N: PTP/US Gas, Michael Petroleum
	TStop	N: Penn-Jersey Truck Stop (US 22N)
	Gas	N: Citgo◆, Getty
	Food	N: Rest/PennJersey TS, Applebee's, Burger King, China Grill Buffet, McDonald's, Panera Bread, Ruby Tuesday
	Lodg	N: Clarion Hotel, Phillipsburg Inn
	Med	N: + Hospital
	Other	N: ATMs, Banks, Circuit City, Grocery, Home Depot, Lowe's, Pharmacy, Staples, Target, Wal-Mart sc
4		CR 637, Main St, Stewartsville (WB, Exit only)
	Lodg	N: Stewart Inn
(6)		Weigh Station (Both dir)
6		CR 632, Bloomsbury Rd, Asbury (EB, Exit Only)
7		NJ 173, Clinton St, Bloomsbury
	TStop	S: Travel Center of America #48/Mobil
	TStop	S: Pilot Travel Center #280 (Scales)
	Gas	S: Citgo◆
	Food	S: CountryPride/Burger King/TA TC, Subway/Pilot TC, Rest/KrispyKreme/Citgo
	TServ	S: TA TC/Tires/TWash

EXIT		NEW JERSEY
	Other	N: Jugtown RV Park▲
		S: Laundry/WiFi/TA TC, WiFi/Pilot TC
(8)		Picnic Area (Both dir)
11		NJ 173, West Portal, Pattenburg
	Gas	N: Coastal, Shell◆
	Other	N: Jugtown RV Park▲, NJ State Hwy Patrol Post
12		CR 625, Perryville Rd, CR 635, Charlestown Rd, NJ 173, Hampton, Clinton, to Jutland, Norton
	TStop	N: Johnny's Truck Stop/Citgo (Scales) Pilot Travel Center #190 (Scales)
	Gas	N: Exxon◆
		S: Shell◆
	Food	N: Rest/Johnny's TS, Rest/Pilot TC
	TServ	N: Johnny's TS/Tires
	Other	N: Laundry/BarbSh/Johnny's TS, Spruce Run State Park
13		Rupell Rd, to NJ 173W, Clinton
	TStop	N: Clinton Truck Stop
	Food	N: Clinton Diner
15		CR 513, NJ 173E, Clinton, Pittstown
	Gas	N: Citgo, Exxon, Shell◆
	Food	N: Subway
		S: Cracker Barrel, Hunan Wok
	Lodg	N: Holiday Inn Select
		S: Hampton Inn
	Other	N: Red Mill Museum Village
		S: Dollar Tree, Grocery, Wal-Mart
16		NJ 31, Center St, Clinton, to CR 513, to Washington (EB) (Acc to Ex #17)
17		NJ 31, Annandale, to CR 513, to Clinton, Flemington
	FStop	N: Hampton Mobil
	Gas	N: Exxon, Hess
	Food	N: King Buffet, McDonald's
18		CR 626, Beaver Ave, US 22, Annandale, to Lebanon
20		CR 639, Cokesbury, Lebanon (WB)
	Gas	S: Exxon, Shell
	Food	S: Deli, Dunkin Donuts, Diner
	Lodg	S: Courtyard, Fountain Motel
	Other	S: Lebanon Train Station, Round Valley State Park
24		CR 523, Oldwick Rd, to CR 517, to Oldwick, to US 22, Whitehouse
26		NJ 523 Spur, North Branch, CR 665
(29)		Jct I-287, to US 202, US 206, to I-80, to I-95, to Morristown, Somerset
(32)		Scenic Overlook (WB) (NO Trailers, Trucks)

EXIT		NEW JERSEY
33		CR 525, Liberty Corner Rd, Basking Ridge, Bernardsville, Martinsville
	Gas	S: Exxon, Sunoco
	Food	N: Rest/Somerset Hills Hotel
	Lodg	N: Courtyard, Somerset Hills Hotel
36		CR 651, King George Rd, Basking Ridge, Warrenville
	Gas	N: Exxon
40		CR 531, Hillcrest Rd, The Plainfields
	Gas	S: BP
	Med	S: + Hospital
41		Dale Rd, to CR 663, CR 44, Watchung, to Berkeley Heights, Scotch Plains
43		Oak Way, CR 39, CR 642, Diamond Hill Rd, Watchung, New Providence
	Other	N: Lucent Technologies
		S: Watchung Reservation
44		CR 527, Glenside Ave, Berkeley Hts (EB)
45		CR 36, CR 527, Glenside Ave (EB)
48		to NJ 24, NJ 124W, to I-287N, Springfield, to Morristown
	NOTE:	MM 48: I-78 divides to I-78 Expr & I-78
49AB		NJ 124, Springfield Ave, to NJ 82, to Vauxhall, Maplewood, Union (EB
50AB		CR 30, CR 630, Union, Millburn (WB)
	Gas	N: Exxon, Mobil
	Other	N: Home Depot, US Post Office
52		NJ Garden State Pkwy (NO Trucks)
54		Winans Ave, Fabyan Place, to CR 601, Newark, Irvington, Hillside (EB)
55		Leslie St, Fabyan Pl, Newark, to Hillside, Irvington (WB)
	Gas	N: BP, Getty, Hess
	Food	N: Wendy's
	Med	S: + Newark Beth Israel Med Ctr
56		Hillside Ave, Peddie St, Newark Clinton Ave (Fr EB, Left exit)
57		US 1S, US 9S, US 22, Newark International Airport
	Lodg	S: Best Western, Courtyard, Days Inn, Hilton, Hampton Inn, Holiday Inn, Marriott, Sheraton
58AB		US 1N, US 9N, NJ Tpk, Newark

○ NEW JERSEY (EASTERN TIME ZONE)

Begin Westbound I-78 from Jct I-95 in Newark, NJ to Jct I-81 near Fredericksburg, PA

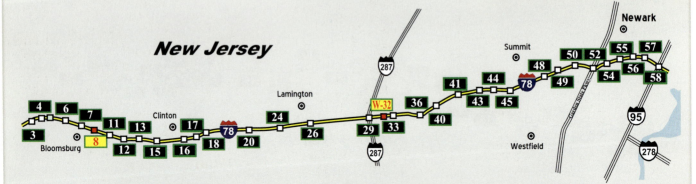

◆ = Regular Gas Stations with Diesel   ▲ = RV Friendly Locations   ♥ = Pet Friendly Locations
RED PRINT SHOWS LARGE VEHICLE PARKING/ACCESS ON SITE OR NEARBY   BROWN PRINT SHOWS CAMPGROUNDS/RV PARKS

INTERSTATE 79 S

EXIT	PENNSYLVANIA

Begin Southbound I-79 from Erie, PA to Jct I-77 in Charleston, WV.

PENNSYLVANIA
(EASTERN TIME ZONE)
(I-79 begins/ends on PA 5, Ex #183AB)

183B — PA 5W, 12th St, Erie (NB)
- Gas: W: Citgo, Sunoco
- Food: W: Applebee's, Bob Evans, Chinese, KFC, Italian Rest, McDonald's, Taco Bell
- Lodg: W: Comfort Inn, Thunderbird Motel
- Med: W: + Priority Care
- Other: W: ATMs, AdvanceAuto, Big Lots, CVS, Dollar General, Grocery, Pharmacy, Tires, U-Haul, Vet♥, Waldameer Amusement and Water Park, Golf Course, to Erie Int'l Airport✈, Presque Isle State Park, Sara's Campground▲

183A — PA 5E, PA 290, 12th St (NB, Exit only)
- FStop: E: Greengarden Shell
- Other: E: to Gannon Univ, Lampe Marina Campground▲

182 — US 20, 26th St, Erie (fr SB, Exit only)
- Gas: E: Citgo, KwikFill
  W: BP, Country Fair
- Food: E: Subway
  W: Arby's, Burger King, Hoss's Steak & Sea House, Little Caesars, McDonald's, Pizza Hut, Subway, Super China Buffet, Tim Hortons
- Lodg: W: Village Motel
- Med: E: + St Vincent Health Center
  W: + Hamot Medical Center
- Other: E: Auto Service, Family Dollar, Grocery, Commercial Truck Repair, to Erie Zoo
  W: ATMs, Auto Services, CVS, Grocery, Dollar General, Kmart, U-Haul, to Erie Int'l Airport✈

180 — Interchange Rd, to US 19, Erie, to Waterford
- Gas: W: Citgo◊
- Food: E: Arby's, Eat 'n Park, KFC, Lone Star Steakhouse, Max & Erma's, McDonald's, Outback Steakhouse, Olive Garden, Panda Express, Ponderosa, Red Lobster, Roadhouse Grill, Smokey Bones BBQ, Starbucks, Subway, Wendy's
- Lodg: E: Fairfield Inn, Homewood Suites♥
  (Addt'l lodg S on US 19)
- Med: E: + Millcreek Community Hospital
- Other: E: ATMs, Auto Dealers, Banks, Best Buy, B&N, Borders, FedEx Kinko's, Gander Mountain, Firestone, Goodyear, Office Depot, Office Max, PetCo♥, Mill Creek Mall, Home Depot, Lowe's, Pharmacy, Target, UPS Store, Wal-Mart, Sam's Club, Tinseltown, Family First Sports Park

(178B) — Jct I-90W, to Cleveland, OH

(178A) — Jct I-90E, to Buffalo, NY

74 — West Rd, McKean
- Other: W: Erie KOA▲

166 — US 6N, Edinboro, Albion, Washington
- Gas: E: Country Fare, Sheetz
- Food: E: Burger King, McDonald's, Perkins, Ital Rest, Subway, Taco Bell, Wendy's
- Lodg: E: Edinboro Inn
- Other: E: Wal-Mart sc, Golf Course, Campbell Pottery, Edinboro Univ, Wooden Nickel Buffalo Farm, Gift Shop & Rest

EXIT	PENNSYLVANIA

(163) — PA Welcome Center (SB) Rest Area (NB) (RR, Phones, Picnic, Vend, Info)

154 — PA 198, Saergertown, Conneautville

147B — US 6W, US 322W, US 19S, Conneaut Lake
- Gas: W: BP, Sheetz, Kwik Fill
- Food: W: Burger King, King's Rest, McDonald's, Ponderosa, Red Lobster
- Lodg: W: Quality Inn, Super 8
- Other: W: ATMs, AutoZone, Auto Dealers, Dollar General, Grocery, Goodyear, Kmart, Staples, Wal-Mart sc▲, Port Meadville Airport✈, PA State Hwy Patrol Post, to Conneaut Lake Park, Pymatuning Deer Park, Pymatuning State Park/Lake, to Pineview Camplands▲, Playland Camping Park▲

147A — US 6E, US 322, US 19N, Meadville
- Gas: E: Country Fair
- Food: E: Applebee's, Cracker Barrel, Chovy's Italian, Hoss's Steak & Sea House, Perkins, Super China Buffet
- Lodg: E: Days Inn♥, Holiday Inn Express, Motel 6♥
- Med: E: + Meadville Medical Center
- Other: E: Advance Auto, Grocery, Home Depot, Allegheny College, to appr 7mi Brookdale Family Campground▲

141 — PA 285, Meadville, to US 19, Custards, to Geneva, Cochranton
- TStop: W: Exit 141 Auto Truck Stop
- Food: W: Rest/Ex 141 ATS
- Other: E: to appr 6.5mi French Creek Campground▲
  W: LP/Ex 141 ATS

(135) — Rest Area (Both dir) (RR, Phones, Picnic, Vend)

130 — PA 358, Sandy Lake Greenville Rd, to Sandy Lake, Greenville
- Med: W: + Greenville Regional Hospital
- Other: E: Maurice Goddard State Park, to Goddard Park Vacationland▲
  W: to Thiel College, appr 7mi Farma Family Campground▲

121 — US 62, Franklin Rd, Jackson Center, to Mercer, Franklin
- FStop: W: Jiffy Mart/Sunoco
- Other: W: to RV Village Camping Resort▲, PA State Hwy Patrol Post

(116B) — Jct I-80W, to Sharon, Mercer

(116A) — Jct I-80E, to Clarion

113 — PA 208, Leesburg Grove City Rd, to PA 258, to Grove City, Leesburg
- Gas: E: BP, Citgo◊
  W: KwikFill, Sheetz
- Food: W: Eat 'n Park, Hoss's Steak & Sea House, McDonald's, Wendy's, Subway, Elephant & Castle Pub & Rest
- Lodg: W: Americana Inn, Comfort Inn, Hampton Inn, Holiday Inn Express, Super 8, E&C
- Med: E: + Hospital
- Other: E: to Grove City College
  W: Grove City Airport✈, Prime Outlets at Grove City, Mercer/Grove City KOA▲, to Westminster College

(110) — Rest Area (SB) (RR, Phones, Picnic)

◊ = Regular Gas Stations with Diesel ▲ = RV Friendly Locations ♥ = Pet Friendly Locations
RED PRINT SHOWS LARGE VEHICLE PARKING/ACCESS ON SITE OR NEARBY BROWN PRINT SHOWS CAMPGROUNDS/RV PARKS

EXIT	PENNSYLVANIA	EXIT	PENNSYLVANIA	EXIT	PENNSYLVANIA
(108)	**Rest Area (NB)** (RR, Phones, Picnic)	Other	W: ATMs, Auto Services, Banks, B&N, Best Buy, Cinema 8, Costco, Firestone, Grocery, Goodyear Comm'l, Goodyear, Home Depot, Office Max, PetCo♥, Pharmacy, Radio Shack, Wal-Mart sc▲, UPS Store, US Post Office, Vet♥, Cranberry Mall	**(59A)**	Jct I-279N, US 22E, US 30E, to Pittsburgh
105	PA 108, New Castle Rd, to Slippery Rock, New Castle (Addt'l Serv 3-5 mi E in Slippery Rock)			Other	E: to Heinz Field, Univ of Pittsburgh, Carnegie Mellon Univ
Food	E: Rest/Evening Star Motel	77	US 19, to I-76, PA Tpk (TOLL), to Harrisburg, Youngstown OH (fr SB, exit only) (Acc to #78/76 Serv)	57	Noblestown Rd, to I-279, Carnegie
Lodg	E: Evening Star Motel			55	PA 50, Washington Pike, Bridgeville, Heidelberg, Kirwan Hts
Other	E: Slippery Rock Campground▲, to Slippery Rock Univ	NOTE:	NO Trucks over 13'6" on I-76 / PA Tpk		
99	US 422, Benjamin Franklin Hwy, New Castle Rd, Portersville, to Prospect, New Castle, Butler	76	to US 19N, Perry Hwy, Cranberry (NB, Left Exit only) (Acc Ex #78 Serv)	Gas	E: Sunoco
				Food	E: Arby's, Bob Evans, CiCi's, DQ, Damons, Eat 'n Park, KFC, McDonald's, Pizza Hut, Starbucks, Subway, Taco Bell, Wendy's
TStop	W: Pilot Travel Center #81 (Scales)	Gas	W: BP◊, Exxon	Med	E: + Kane Memorial Hospital
Food	W: McDonald's/Subway/Pilot TC	Food	W: Arby's, Bob Evans, Burger King, Eat 'n Park, Lone Star Steakhouse, Max & Erma's, Perkins	Other	E: ATMs, Auto Services, Big Lot, Firestone, Goodyear, Home Depot, Kmart, Pharmacy, Wal-Mart▲, UPS Store, Mall, Laundromat, Shopping Centers
Other	E: Big Butler Fairgrounds, Moraine State Park, to Lake Arthur Family Campground▲	Lodg	W: Comfort Inn, Four Points Sheraton, Holiday Inn Express♥, Hyatt Place♥, Motel 6♥, Red Roof Inn♥, Super 8		
	W: Laundry/Pilot TC, New Castle Harley Davidson, Living Treasures Animal Park, Cooper's Lake Campground▲, Rose Point Park Campground▲	Med	W: + UPMC Hospital	54	PA 50, Millers Run Rd, Bridgeville (fr SB, Exit only)
		Other	W: ATMs, Auto Services, FedEx Kinko's	Gas	E: BP◊, Exxon◊ W: Sunoco
96	PA 488, Portersville Rd, to US 422, to US 19, to Prospect, Portersville	75	Warrandale Bayne Rd, to US 19S, Warrendale, Rte 8, OH River Blvd, Red Belt (NB, Exit only) (Acc to Ex # 76-78 Serv via US 19)	Food	E: Burger King, McDonald's, Wendy's
Other	E: Bear Run Campground▲, to Moraine State Park W: to McConnell Mill State Park			Lodg	E: Holiday Inn Express W: Knights Inn
				TServ	W: Firestone Tire & Auto
88	Little Creek Rd, Harmony, to US 19, PA 68, to Zelienople (SB Ex, NB reacc) (Access #87 Serv)	73	PA 910E, Wexford Bayne Rd, Orange Belt, Wexford	Med	E: + Hospital
		Gas	E: BP, UniMart, Gas/T-Bones Groc W: Exxon	Other	E: Grocery, Laundromat, Pharmacy
Other	W: Indian Brave Campground▲	Food	E: Eat 'n Park, King's Family Rest, Oriental Express, Pizza, Starbucks W: Carmody's Rest, Stone Mansion Rest	**(50.5)**	Weigh Station (Both dir)
87	PA 68, Evans City Rd, Harmony, to US 19, Zelienople (NB Ex, SB reacc)			**(49)**	Rest Area (Both dir) (RR, Phone, Picnic)
Gas	W: Exxon	Lodg	E: America's Best Inn♥	48	PA 1032, Southpointe Blvd, Canonsburg, to Southpointe, Hendersonville
Food	W: Burger King, Pizza Hut, Subway	Med	E: + Hospital		
Lodg	W: Zelienople Motel	Other	E: FedEx Kinko's, T-Bones Marketplace	Food	E: Big Jim's Roadhouse W: Jackson's Rest, Subway
Other	W: Greyhound, Indian Brave Campground▲	**(72)**	I-279S, to Pittsburgh (SB, Left exit)	Lodg	W: Hilton Garden Inn
85	US 19, PA 528, Evans City (NO Trucks) (SB Ex, diff NB reacc)	68	Blackburn Rd, Mount Nebo Rd North Park, Yellow Belt	45	McClelland Rd, to PA 980 (SB, NB reacc), Weavertown Rd, to PA 980, to US 19 (NB ex, SB ent), Canonsburg
83	PA 528, Lindsay Rd, to US 19, Evans City, Zelienople (NB Exit, SB reaccess) (NO Trucks)	66	PA 65, Ohio River Blvd, (NB) Glenfield Rd, to PA 65, (SB) to Emsworth, Sewickley		
		Med	W: + Hospital	Gas	E: Sheetz W: BP, Citgo
NOTE:	Trucks over 10,000# to Evans City, Use Exit #87	Other	W: to North Shore Areas: PA 65S	Food	W: Hoss's Steak & Sea House, KFC, Long John Silver, McDonald's, Pizza Hut, Quiznos, Starbucks, Subway, Taco Bell, Wendy's
Med	W: + Butler Memorial Hospital	65	Grand Ave, Neville Island (NB), to PA 51, Corapolis, Yellow Belt (fr SB, Exit Only)		
(81)	Picnic Area (Both dir) (Phones)			Lodg	W: Super 8
(80)	Truck Scales (SB)	64	PA 51, Coraopolis, McKees Rocks (NB)	Other	W: ATM, Auto Services
78	PA 228, Cranberry Twp, to US 19, Mars, Cranberry (fr NB, exit only)	NOTE:	NB: TRUCK ALERT—WINDING ROAD ROLL OVER AREA NEXT 2 1/4 mi	43	PA 519, Hill Church Houston Rd, to US 19, Canonsburg, Houston, Eighty Four
Gas	E: 7-11, Texaco W: Exxon◊, Sheetz, Sunoco, GetGo	60B	PA 60N, to US 22W, US 30W, Pittsburgh Intl Airport, Robinson (SB)	Gas	E: Amoco◊, Sunoco W: Sunoco
Food	E: Applebee's, Dunkin Donuts, Hereford & Hops Steakhouse, McDonald's, Moe's SW Grill, Olive Garden, On the Border, Quiznos, Red Robin, Smokey Bones BBQ, Starbucks, Subway W: Burger King, CiCi's, Denny's, Fatburger, Jersey Mike's, Long John Silver, Panera, Papa John's, Primanti Bros, Quaker Steak & Lube, Subway, Wendy's			Med	E: + Canonsburg General Hospital
		Food	W: McDonald's	Other	W: Auto Services, to Jones RV
		Lodg	W: AmeriSuites♥, Holiday Inn Express, Red Roof Inn	41	Racetrack Rd, to US 19, Washington Meadow Lands
		60A	PA 60S, Crafton (SB)	Gas	E: Exxon W: BP◊
		Gas	E: Exxon	Food	E: McDonald's, Waffle House, Wendy's
		Food	E: King's Family Rest, Primanti Bros	Lodg	E: Comfort Inn, Holiday Inn
Lodg	E: Marriott W: Fairfield Inn, Hampton Inn, Residence Inn	Lodg	E: Comfort Inn, Econo Lodge, Motel 6♥, Travel Inn	Other	E: The Meadows Race Track & Casino W: Washington Co Fairgrounds
		Med	E: + Hospital	40	Locust Ave, Pike St, Meadow Lands (NB, NO re-entry)
Med	W: + UPMC Hospital	59B	US 22W, US 30W (NB)		
Other	E: ATMs, Lowe's, PetSmart♥, Pharmacy, Staples, Target, Vet♥	Other	W: to Allegheny Co Settlers Cabin Park▲, Greater Pittsburgh Int'l Airport✈, PA Air National Guard	Other	W: Washington Co Fairgrounds, Museum

◊ = Regular Gas Stations with Diesel   ▲ = RV Friendly Locations   ♥ = Pet Friendly Locations
RED PRINT SHOWS LARGE VEHICLE PARKING/ACCESS ON SITE OR NEARBY   BROWN PRINT SHOWS CAMPGROUNDS/RV PARKS

EXIT	PENNSYLVANIA
NOTE:	I-79 below runs with I-70. Exit #'s follow I-70.
(38/18)	Jct I-70W, to Wheeling, WV (fr NB, Left exit) Jct I-79N, to Pittsburgh
19AB	US 19, Murtland Ave, Washington Rd
Gas	N: BP S: AmocoBP◆, Exxon, Sunoco
Food	N: Applebee's, Arby's, **Cracker Barrel**, McDonald's, Ponderosa, Red Robin, Red Lobster, Starbucks, Subway, TGI Friday S: Bob Evans, Burger King, Chinese Rest, CiCi's, KFC, Long John Silver, McDonald's, Pizza Hut, Shoney's, Taco Bell
Lodg	N: Springhill Suites S: Hampton Inn, Motel 6♥
Med	S: + Washington Hospital
Other	N: ATMs, Auto Dealers, Grocery, Lowe's, PetSmart♥, Sam's Club, Target S: Washington Mall, Firestone, Home Depot, Kmart, Staples, Wal-Mart sc▲, PA State Hwy Patrol Post
20	PA 136, Beau St, Washington
Other	S: Washington/Pittsburg SW KOA▲
(21)	Jct I-79S, to Morgantown, Waynesburg
(34)	I-70E, to New Stanton (fr SB, Left exit)
NOTE:	I-79 above runs with I-70. Exit #'s follow I-70.
33	US 40, Maiden St, Washington, to Laboratory
Gas	W: Amoco
Other	W: Washington/PittsburghSW KOA▲
(30.5)	Parking / Weigh Area (SB)
30	US 19, Waynesburg Rd, Amity Ridge Rd, Washington, Amity, Lone Pine
23	Ten Mile Rd, Amity, to Marianna, Prosperity
19	PA 221, to US 19, Ruff Creek, Jefferson
14	PA 21, Roy E Furman Hwy, Waynesburg, Masontown
FStop	E: Deputy Dawg Amoco
Gas	W: 7-11, Exxon, Sheetz, GetGo
Food	W: Deputy Dawg Sub Shop, Burger King, DQ, Golden Wok, KFC, Long John Silver, McDonald's, Subway, Wendy's
Lodg	E: Comfort Inn W: Econo Lodge, Holiday Motel, Super 8
Med	W: + Hospital
Other	E: Greene Co Airport✈ W: ATMs, Auto Dealers, Auto Service, Big Lots, CVS, Grocery, PA State Hwy Patrol,
7	Kirby-Garards Fort Rd, Waynesburg, to Kirby, Garards Fort
(6)	PA Welcome Center (NB) (RR, Phone, Picnic, Vend, Info)
1	Bald Hill Rd, Mount Morris
TStop	E: BFS Truck Auto Plaza/Citgo (Scales)
Gas	W: BP◆, Marathon
Food	E: Rest/BFS TAP
Other	E: Laundry/BFS TAP W: Mt Morris Campground▲

EXIT	PENNSYLVANIA / WEST VIRGINIA (EASTERN TIME ZONE)
NOTE:	MM 160: Pennsylvania State Line
(159)	WV Welcome Center (SB) (RR, Phones, Picnic, Vend, RVDump)
155	US 19, Osage Rd, to WV 7, Osage Granville, Morganton
Gas	E: Sheetz, GetGo
Food	E: Arby's, Burger King, ChikFilA, CiCi's, Golden Corral, Long John Silver, Longhorn Steakhouse, McDonald's, Olive Garden, Shoney's, Starbucks, Texas Roadhouse
Lodg	E: Best Western, Econo Lodge, Euro Suites, Hampton Inn, Holiday Inn, Quality Inn, Residence Inn
Med	E: + Ruby Hospital
Other	E: ATMs, Auto Service, Banks, B&N, Best Buy, CVS, PetCo♥, Sam's Club, Target, Tires, Wal-Mart sc▲, UPS Store, WV Univ
152	US 19, CR 49, Downtown Morgantown, Westover
Gas	E: BP◆, Exxon
Food	E: McDonald's, Pizza Hut, Subway, Taco Bell, Western Sizzlin' W: Bob Evans, Burger King
Lodg	E: Econo Lodge
Other	E: ATMs, Auto Services, Tires W: ATMs, Auto Services, K-Mart, Lowe's, Office Max, Mall, Tires
(148)	Jct I-68E, Morgantown, to US 119, Grafton, to Cumberland, MD
Gas	E: Exxon◆
Food	E: Rest/Ramada Inn
Lodg	E: Almost Heaven B&B, Comfort Inn, Ramada Inn
Other	E: WVU Football Stadium, Tygart Lake State Park
146	CR 77, Goshen Rd, to US 119
Other	W: Sport Rider Outdoors
(141)	Weigh Station (Both dir)
139	CR 33, Prickets Creek, E Fairmont
TStop	W: K & T Truck Stop/BP (Scales)
Gas	E: Chevron W: Exxon
Food	W: Rest/K&T TS
TServ	W: K & T TS/Tires
Other	W: Laundry/K&T TS
137	WV 310, Downtown Fairmont
Gas	E: BP, Exxon◆
Food	E: Subway W: KFC, McDonald's, Wendy's
Lodg	E: Holiday Inn
Med	W: + Hospital
Other	E: Grocery W: UPS Store, Fairmont State Univ
135	CR 64, Millersville Rd, to Pleasant Valley Rd, Fairmont
133	CR 64/1, Kingmont Rd, Fairmont
FStop	E: BFS Foods #39/BP
Gas	W: Chevron◆
Food	E: Subway/BP, Cracker Barrel
Lodg	E: Super 8 W: Comfort Inn, Days Inn, Red Roof Inn♥
Other	E: Mountain Man RV Center W: Fairmount Muni Airport✈

◆ = Regular Gas Stations with Diesel ▲ = RV Friendly Locations ♥ = Pet Friendly Locations
RED PRINT SHOWS LARGE VEHICLE PARKING/ACCESS ON SITE OR NEARBY BROWN PRINT SHOWS CAMPGROUNDS/RV PARKS

Page 363

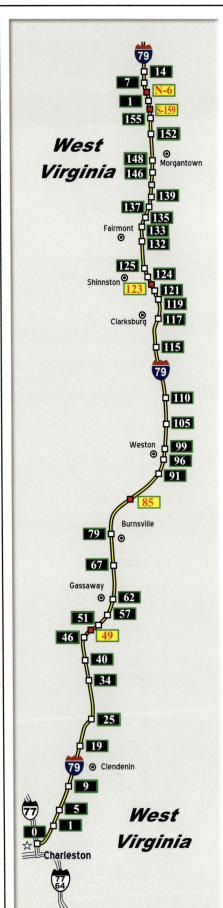

EXIT	WEST VIRGINIA
132	**US 250, Adams St, S Fairmont**
Gas	W: Exxon, Sunoco
Food	E: Arby's, Bob Evans, Hardee's, McDonald's, Subway, Taco Bell
Lodg	E: Days Inn, Red Roof Inn ♥
TServ	E: Cummins Cumberland
Med	W: + Hospital
Other	E: ATMs, Advance Auto, Harley Davidson, Grocery, Sam's Club, Wal-Mart sc▲, Middletown Mall
	W: Auto Dealers, Trailer City RV Center, Fairmont State Univ
125	**WV 131, Grande Meadow Rd, Saltwell Rd, Bridgeport**
Gas	W: Exxon◊
Lodg	W: Super 8
124	**WV 279, to US 50E, Bridgeport**
Other	E: to Benedum Airport✈
(123)	**Rest Area (Both dir)** (RR, Phones, Picnic, Vend, RVDump)
121	**CR 24, Meadowbrook Rd**
Gas	E: GoMart, Sheetz
	W: Exxon◊
Food	E: Bob Evans, Blimpie/GoMart
	W: Arby's, Burger King, Ponderosa
Lodg	E: Hampton Inn
	W: Econo Lodge, Super 8
Other	E: to Benedum Airport✈
	W: Pharmacy, Target, Mall
119	**US 50, W Main St, Clarksburg, Bridgeport**
Gas	E: Chevron◊, Exxon◊, GoMart, Speedway
Food	E: Denny's, Hardee's, KFC, Little Caesars Pizza, Long John Silver, McDonald's, Shoney's, Subway, TCBY, Taco Bell
Lodg	E: Comfort Inn, Days Inn, Holiday Inn, Knights Inn, Sleep Inn, Towne House Motor Lodge East
Med	E: + Hospital
Other	E: ATMs, Big Lots, Circuit City, Grocery, Home Depot, Kmart, Kroger, Lowe's, Sam's Club, Wal-Mart sc▲, Salem Int'l Univ, to Harrison Marion Regional Airport✈
117	**WV 58, Smithfield Ave, Anmoore**
FStop	W: 7-11 #5602/BP
Food	E: Arby's, Applebee's, Burger King, Ruby Tuesday, Ryan's Grill, Subway
Other	E: ATMs, Bank, Grocery, Staples, Wal-Mart sc▲
115	**WV 20, Mt Clare, to Stonewood**
Gas	E: BP, Chevron, Exxon
110	**WV 270, Milford Rd, Lost Creek Rd, Lost Creek**
105	**CR 7, to US 19, Jane Lew**
TStop	E: Jane Lew Truck Stop/Chevron (Scales)
Gas	W: Exxon
Food	E: Rest/Jane Lew TS
TServ	E: Jane Lew TS/TWash/Tires
Other	E: Laundry/Jane Lew TS
99	**US 33, US 119, Weston, Horner**
Gas	E: Exxon, Sheetz
	W: BP
Food	E: McDonald's, Subway
	W: Hardee's, Pizza Hut, Wendy's
Lodg	E: Comfort Inn, Days Inn, Super 8
Med	W: + Hospital
Other	E: Kroger, Wal-Mart, Pharmacy
	W: NAPA
96	**CR 30, CR 19/39, Weston**
Other	E: Stonewall Jackson State Park

EXIT	WEST VIRGINIA
91	**US 19, Weston, to Roanoke**
Other	E: Stonewall Jackson Lake State Park
(85)	**Rest Area (Both dir)** (RR, Phones, Picnic, Vend, RVDump)
79	**WV 5, 5th Ave, 5th St, Burnsville, Glenville**
Gas	E: Exxon
	W: GoMart, Shell
Food	E: Rest/Motel 79
Lodg	E: Motel 79
Other	E: Glenville State College, Burnsville Dam
67	**WV 15, US 19, Flatwoods**
FStop	E: Go Mart #44, Lloyd's Food Store/Chevron
TStop	E: John Skidmore Truck Stop/Ashland
Gas	E: Exxon◊
Food	E: Rest/John Skidmore TS, DQ, KFC, McDonald's, Waffle Hut
	W: Shoney's, Wendy's
Lodg	E: Days Inn
	W: John Skidmore Motel/Pennzoil
Tires	W: John Skidmore TS
Other	E: to Sutton Lake Rec Area
62	**WV 4, State St, Sutton, Gassaway**
Gas	W: GoMart
Food	W: Long John Silver, Pizza Hut
Med	W: + Hospital
Other	W: CVS, Kroger
57	**US 19S, Mountaineer Expwy, Beckley, Summersville**
51	**WV 4, to Frametown, Strangetown**
(49)	**Rest Area (Both dir)** (RR, Phone, Picnic, Vend, RVDump)
46	**CR 11, Servia Rd, Duck**
40	**WV 16, Big Otter, Nebo, Wallback**
FStop	E: GoMart #86
	W: Big Otter Food Mart/Exxon
34	**WV 36, Wallback, Clay, Newton**
25	**CR 29, Big Sandy Creek, Amma**
Gas	E: Exxon◊
19	**US 119, Bufflick Rd, Spencer Rd, to WV 4, to Clendenin**
Gas	E: BP◊
Food	E: BiscuitWorld
9	**CR 43, Frame Rd, Elkview**
Gas	E: GoMart
	W: Exxon◊, Speedway◊
Food	W: Bob Evans, McDonald's, Ponderosa, Subway, Arby's/Exxon
Other	W: AdvanceAuto, CVS, Kmart, Kroger
5	**WV 114, CR 41, Copper Creek Rd, Charleston, to Big Chimney**
Gas	E: Exxon
Food	E: Hardee's
1	**US 119, Pennsylvania Ave, Mink Shoals, to Charleston**
Food	E: Family Rest
Lodg	W: Sleep Inn
Other	E: Yeager Airport✈, Coonskin Park
(0)	**Jct I-77, S to Charleston, N to Parkersburg**
	(I-79 starts/ends on I-77, Ex #104)
	(EASTERN TIME ZONE)

◎ WEST VIRGINIA

Begin Northbound I-79 from Jct I-77 in Charleston, WV to Erie, PA.

Page 364

◊ = Regular Gas Stations with Diesel   ▲ = RV Friendly Locations   ♥ = Pet Friendly Locations
RED PRINT SHOWS LARGE VEHICLE PARKING/ACCESS ON SITE OR NEARBY   BROWN PRINT SHOWS CAMPGROUNDS/RV PARKS

EXIT	CALIFORNIA
	Begin Eastbound I-80 from San Francisco, CA to Jct I-95 in Englewood, NJ.

◯ CALIFORNIA
(PACIFIC TIME ZONE)
(I-80 begins/ends on 7th St, San Francisco)

EXIT		CALIFORNIA
1		7th St, 8th St, Harrison St, Bryant St, Downtown San Francisco (EB)
1C		9th St, Civic Center (WB)
1B		US 101N, Golden Gate Bridge (WB)
1A		US 101S (WB, Left exit)
2		4th St, Embarcadero (EB)
2C		Fremont St (WB)
2B		Harrison St (WB, Left exit)
2A		5th St (WB, Left exit)
4A		Treasure Island (EB, Left exit)
4B		Yerba Buena Island (EB)
4		Treasure Island Rd (WB, Left exit)
	TServ	S: Cummins West
	Other	S: US Coast Guard SF
(7)		TOLL Plaza (WB)
8A		Maritime St, W Grand Ave, to I-880, Harbor Terminals, Oakland
	Other	S: Oakland Army Base
(8B)		I-580E, Oakland, Hayward Stockton; I-880S (WB, Left exit) (end shared I-580)
9		Powell St, Emeryville (EB begins shared with I-580)
	Gas	N: Shell S: Beacon
	Food	N: Chevy's Mexican Rest S: Burger King, Denny's, Starbucks
	Lodg	N: Holiday Inn S: Courtyard, Sheraton, Wyndham
	Other	S: ATMs, Borders, Circuit City, Grocery, Trader Joe's
10		CA 13, Ashby Ave, Shellmound St, Berkeley
11		University Ave, Berkeley
	Gas	S: 76, Beacon
	Lodg	N: Doubletree Inn S: Holiday Inn Express, Marina Lodge Motel, University Inn
	Other	S: to Univ of CA/Berkeley, Amtrak, Berkeley Aquatic Park
12		Gilman St
	Other	N: Golden Gate Fields Racetrack

EXIT		CALIFORNIA
13		to I-580, Albany (WB) (Begin share I-580)
13A		Buchanan St, Albany (EB)
	Lodg	S: Meyer Motel
(13B)		Jct I-580W, Point Richmond
14A		Central Ave, Richmond, El Cerrito
	Gas	S: 76, Shell, Valero
	Food	S: Burger King, KFC
	Other	S: ATMs, Costco, Mall
	Other	N: Golden Gate Fields Racetrack
14B		Carlson Blvd, Richmond
	Gas	N: 76
	Lodg	N: Forty Flags Motel S: Super 8
15		Potrero Ave, Cutting Blvd, El Cerrito
	Gas	N: ArcoAmPm S: Chevron
	Lodg	S: Best Inn
16A		Mac Donald Ave (EB)
16B		San Pablo Ave (EB)
	Gas	N: 76 S: Chevron
16		San Pablo Ave, Richmond (WB)
17		Solano Ave (EB), McBryde Ave
	Gas	N: 7-11, ArcoAmPm S: Chevron
	Food	N: Burger King, KFC, Taco Bell S: Wendy's
	Med	N: + Dr's Medical Center
	Other	S: Albertson's, Safeway, B & L RV
18		San Pablo Dam Rd
	Gas	N: 76, 7-11, Shell S: Shell
	Food	N: Burger King, Denny's, McDonald's
	Lodg	N: Holiday Inn
	Med	N: + Hospital
	Other	N: Albertson's, Kmart, Pharmacy, UPS Store
19A		El Portal Dr, San Pablo, El Sobrante
	Gas	N: Shell
	Food	S: McDonald's
19B		Hilltop Dr, Richmond
	Gas	N: Chevron, Shell S: Hilltop Fuel◇
	Food	N: Olive Garden, Red Lobster, Subway S: BBQ
	Lodg	N: Courtyard, Extended Stay America
	Other	N: Albertson's, Firestone, Hilltop Mall Wal-Mart sc▲
20		Richmond Pkwy, to I-580, Fitzgerald Dr, Pinole, San Pablo
	Gas	N: Chevron S: Chevron, Shell

EXIT		CALIFORNIA
	Food	N: McDonald's, Red Lobster, Subway S: Applebee's, Outback Steakhouse, Starbucks
	Lodg	S: Motel 6♥
	Other	N: ATMs, Auto Dealers, B&N, B Dalton, Circuit City, Hilltop Mall, PetSmart♥, Greyhound S: FedEx Kinko's, Grocery, Staples, Target
21		Appian Way, Pinole
	Gas	N: Beacon S: Valero◇
	Food	N: McDonald's S: Burger King, Hometown Buffet, KFC, Panda Express, Sizzler, Subway, Starbucks, Taco Bell, Wendy's
	Lodg	S: Days Inn, Motel 6♥
	Other	N: Grocery, Pharmacy, Safeway S: Albertson's, AutoZone, Best Buy, Goodyear, Kmart, UPS Store
22		Pinole Valley Rd, Pinole
	Gas	S: 76, 7-11, Chevron◇, Shell
	Food	S: China House, Jack in the Box, Pizza, Subway, Waffle Shop
	Other	S: Albertson's
23		CA 4, John Muir Pkwy, Willow Ave, San Pablo Ave, Hercules, Stockton
	Gas	N: Shell
	Food	N: Starbucks
	Other	N: Albertson's, Pharmacy
24		Willow Ave, to CA 4, Rodeo, Hercules
	Gas	N: 76◇ S: Circle K◇
	Food	N: Pizza S: Burger King
	Other	N: Grocery, NAPA
26		Cummings Skyway, to CA 4, to San Pablo Ave, Martinez, Concord
27		Crockett Port Costa, Crockett
(28)		TOLL Plaza (EB)
29A		CA 29, Sonoma Blvd (EB), Maritime Academy Dr (WB)
	Gas	N: Chevron
	Food	N: Subway
	Lodg	N: Motel 6♥, Rodeway Inn
	Other	N: CarWash
29B		Sequoia Ave (EB), Magazine St (WB)
	Lodg	N: Budget Inn, El Rancho Inn
29C		Magazine St, Vallejo (EB)
	Gas	N: Shell S: 7-11
	Food	N: Hickory Pit S: McDonald's

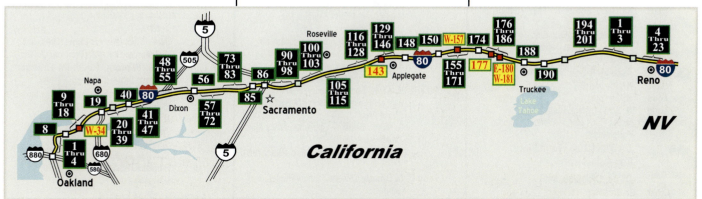

◇ = Regular Gas Stations with Diesel　▲ = RV Friendly Locations　♥ = Pet Friendly Locations

RED PRINT SHOWS LARGE VEHICLE PARKING/ACCESS ON SITE OR NEARBY　BROWN PRINT SHOWS CAMPGROUNDS/RV PARKS

Page 365

INTERSTATE 80 W/E — CALIFORNIA

EXIT		
Lodg	N: Budget Inn, Motel 7	
	S: Knights Inn	
Other	N: Tradewinds RV Park▲ , Twin Bridges MH Park▲	
(30A)	Jct I-780, Curtola Pkwy, Benecia, to Martinez	
Other	N: Greyhound	
30B	Benecia Rd (EB)	
	Georgia St, Central Vallejo (WB)	
Gas	S: Shell	
Lodg	S: Crest Motel	
30C	Georgia St, Central Vallejo	
Gas	N: Safeway	
	S: Shell◊	
Food	S: Mandarin Chinese, Starbucks/Shell	
Lodg	S: California Motel	
31A	Solano Ave, Springs Rd, Vallejo	
Gas	N: Chevron◊	
	S: Beacon, Chevron, QuikStop	
Food	N: Burger King, Church's	
	S: DQ, McDonald's, Pizza Hut, Subway	
Lodg	N: Best Value Inn, Travelodge	
	S: Islander Motel, Relax Inn	
Other	N: Albertson's, RiteAid, U-Haul	
	S: Walgreen's	
31B	Tennessee St, Vallejo, Mare Island	
Gas	S: 76, Valero	
Food	S: Jack in the Box	
Lodg	S: Great Western Inn, Quality Inn	
Other	N: CarQuest	
	S: Sunset Trailer Park▲	
32A	Redwood Pkwy (EB)	
Other	S: FedEx Kinko's	
32B	Redwood St (EB)	
32	Redwood St, Vallejo (WB)	
Gas	N: 76, Shell, Stop & Save	
	S: Shell	
Food	N: Denny's, Annie's Panda Garden	
	S: Indian Rest, Little Caesar's	
Lodg	N: Days Inn, Motel 6♥	
Med	N: + Hospital	
Other	N: Albertson's, Auto Services, Tires, Crane's RV Refrig Svc	
	S: Auto Dealers, AutoZone, Safeway, Target	
33	CA 37, Auto Mall Columbus Pkwy, Marine World Pkwy, Vallejo (EB)	
Gas	N: Chevron	
Food	N: Carl's Jr	
	S: Applebee's, Black Angus Steakhouse, IHOP, McDonald's, Mountain Mike's Pizza, Panda Express, Red Lobster, Subway, Taco Bell, Wendy's	
Lodg	N: Best Western, Courtyard	
	S: Comfort Inn, Ramada Inn♥	
Other	N: ATMs, Grocery, Six Flags Marine World, Co Fairgrounds	
	S: ATMs, Banks, Best Buy, Costco, Dollar Tree, Home Depot, Office Max, Pep Boys, PetCo♥	
33A	Auto Mall Columbus Pkwy (WB)	
Gas	N: Chevron	
Food	N: Carl's Jr,	
Lodg	N: Best Western, Courtyard	
Other	N: Six Flags Marine World, Solano Co Fairgrounds	
33B	CA 37, Marine World Pkwy, San Rafael (WB)	
Gas	N: Chevron	
Food	N: Carl's Jr,	

EXIT		
Lodg	N: Best Western, Courtyard	
Other	N: Six Flags Marine World, Solano Co Fairgrounds, to Sears Point Raceway	
(34)	Hunter Hill Rest Area (WB) (RR, Phones, Picnic, Info)	
36	American Canyon Rd, Vallejo	
39A	Red Top Rd, Fairfield (WB)	
Gas	N: 76	
39B	CA 12, Napa, Sonoma (WB)	
Food	N: Happy Garden Chinese, Subway	
Other	N: Costco, Pharmacy, Safeway	
39	Red Top Rd, Fairfield (EB)	
(40)	Jct I-680, Benecia, San Jose (WB)	
	I-680, Green Valley Rd, Benecia (EB)	
41	Suisun Valley Rd, Green Valley Rd, Fairfield	
Gas	S: 76◊, ArcoAmPm, Chevron, Flyers◊, Shell◊	
Food	S: Arby's, Burger King, Carl's Jr, Denny's, Jack in the Box, McDonald's, Starbucks, Subway, Taco Bell, Wendy's	
Lodg	S: Best Western, Comfort Inn, Days Inn, Econo Lodge, Fairfield Inn, Hampton Inn, Holiday Inn Express, Overniter Lodge	
Other	N: Solano Comm College	
	S: Ray's RV, Camping World/RVDump	
(42)	Weigh Station (Both dir)	
43	CA 12, Rio Vista, Chadbourne Rd (EB), Abernathy Rd, Suisun City (WB)	
Other	S: Pharmacy, Wal-Mart, Anheuser-Busch Brewery, Jelly Belly Factory Tour	
44A	Abernathy Rd (EB)	
44B	W Texas St, Fairfield (EB)	
44	W Texas St, Rockville Rd (WB)	
Gas	N: Shell	
	S: 76, Exxon, Valero	
Food	N: Chuck E Cheese, Denny's, In n Out Burger	
	S: DQ, Jack in the Box, McDonald's	
Lodg	N: Extended Stay America, Holiday Inn Select	
	S: Economy Inn, Sleepy Hollow Motel	
Other	N: ATMs, FedEx Kinko's, Target	
	S: ATMs, Circuit City, Home Depot, Target, Walgreen's	
45	Travis Blvd, Fairfield	
Gas	N: ArcoAmPm, Chevron, Shell	
	S: Shell	
Food	N: Burger King, Chuck E Cheese, Denny's, McDonald's, Starbucks, Subway, Taco Bell	
	S: Applebee's, Carino's, China Express, Mimi's Café, Panda Express, Red Lobster, Starbucks, Subway	
Lodg	N: Extended Stay America, Holiday Inn, Motel 6♥	
	S: Hilton Garden Inn	
Med	S: + Northbay Medical Center	
Other	N: ATMs, Banks, Grocery, PetCo♥, Fairfield Harley Davidson, CA State Hwy Patrol Post	
	S: ATMs, Best Buy, Firestone, Office Max, Trader Joe's, Westfield Mall	
47	Waterman Blvd, Air Base Pkwy (EB)	
Gas	S: 7-11	
Food	N: Dynasty Chinese, Hungry Hunter, Starbucks	

EXIT		
Med	S: + Hospital	
Other	N: Safeway, Village RV Center	
	S: to Travis Air Force Base	
47A	Air Base Pkwy, Travis AFB (WB)	
47B	Waterman Blvd (WB)	
48	N Texas St, Fairfield	
Gas	S: ArcoAmPm, Chevron, Shell	
Food	S: Burger King, Panda Express, Starbucks	
Lodg	S: EZ 8 Motel	
Other	S: Golf Course	
51A	Lagoon Valley Rd, Cherry Glen Rd, Fairfield, Vacaville	
51B	Pena-Adobe Rd	
Other	S: Lagoon Valley Regional Park	
52	Cherry Glen Rd (WB)	
53	Alamo Dr, Merchant St	
Gas	N: Chevron, Shell◊	
	S: 76	
Food	N: Bakers Square, Lyon's	
	S: Jack in the Box, KFC, McDonald's, Pizza Hut, Starbucks, Stir Fry Chinese	
Lodg	N: Alamo Inn	
54A	Davis St, Vacaville	
Gas	N: Chevron	
	S: QuikStop	
Food	N: McDonald's/Chevron, Outback Steakhouse	
Lodg	N: Hampton Inn	
Other	S: Grocery	
54B	Peabody Rd Elmira (EB), Mason St (WB)	
Gas	N: Chevron	
	S: 7-11, ArcoAmPm	
Food	S: Carl's Jr	
Lodg	N: Hampton Inn, Royal Motel, Super 8	
Other	N: Albertson's, ATMs, AutoZone, Big O Tire, Firestone, Goodyear, NAPA, Pharmacy	
	S: Auto Repair/Shell, Costco, Goodyear, Greyhound	
55	Monte Vista Ave, Allison Dr, Nut Tree Parkway	
Gas	N: 76, Citgo, Shell	
	S: ArcoAmPm, Chevron	
Food	N: Arby's, Burger King, Denny's, IHOP, McDonald's, Taco Bell, Wendy's	
	S: Applebee's, Baja Fresh Mexican, Carl's Jr, Chili's, HomeTown Buffet, Jack in the Box, McDonald's, KFC, Starbucks	
Lodg	N: Best Western, Super 8	
	S: Courtyard, Fairfield Inn, Holiday Inn Express, Motel 6, Residence Inn	
Med	S: + Vaca Valley Hospital	
Other	N: America's Tire, Firestone, Goodyear, U-Haul, Lee's MH & RV Park▲	
	S: ATMs, CompUSA, Pharmacy, Safeway, Sam's Club, Staples, Target, Tires, Wal-Mart▲, Vacaville Premium Outlets	
(56)	I-505, Winters, Redding, Orange Dr (EB), I-505N, Redding (WB)	
Lodg	S: Courtyard, Fairfield Inn, Holiday Inn, Motel 6♥, Residence Inn	
Other	N: Weslo's RV Center, Vacaville Nut Tree Airport✈, Vineyard RV Park▲	
	S: ATMs, FedEx Kinko's, Home Depot, Staples, UPS Store, Vacaville Harley Davidson	

◊ = Regular Gas Stations with Diesel   ▲ = RV Friendly Locations   ♥ = Pet Friendly Locations
RED PRINT SHOWS LARGE VEHICLE PARKING/ACCESS ON SITE OR NEARBY   BROWN PRINT SHOWS CAMPGROUNDS/RV PARKS

EXIT	CALIFORNIA	EXIT	CALIFORNIA	EXIT	CALIFORNIA
57	**Leisure Town Rd, Vaca Valley Pky**	**82**	**I-80 Bus Lp, US 50, S Lake Tahoe**	Food	S: Loco, IHOP, Jack in the Box, McDonald's, Starbucks, Subway, Taco Bell
Food	S: Jack in the Box, Kings Buffet		(EB, Left exit) US 50E, Bus Loop 80,		
Lodg	S: Extended Stay America		Sacramento (WB)	Lodg	N: Motel 6♥, Vagabond Inn
Other	N: Nelson's RV Parts & Service	**83**	**Reed Ave, W Sacramento**		S: Holiday Inn, La Quinta Inn♥
	S: Auto Dealers	Gas	N: 76	Other	N: McClellan AFB
59	**Meridian Rd, Weber Rd**		S: Shell◊		S: Auto Service, Goodyear, Target, U-Haul
60	**Midway Rd, Lewis Rd, Elmira**	Food	N: Jack in the Box, Panda Express, Subway, Starbucks	**98**	**Greenback Lane, Elkhorn Blvd**
Other	N: to appr 7mi) Vineyard RV Park▲		S: McDonald's/Shell	Gas	N: 76, Circle K
63	**CR 238, Dixon Ave, Grant Rd, Dixon**	Lodg	N: Extended Stay America	Food	N: Carl's Jr, McDonald's, Pizza Hut C/O, Subway, Taco Bell
Gas	N: Chevron	TServ	S: Cummins West		
	S: ArcoAmPm, Shell	**85**	**W El Camino Ave, El Centro Rd**	Med	N: + Intermediate Care Medical Clinic
Food	S: Carl's Jr, KFC/A&W	TStop	N: AmBest/Sacramenta 49er Travel Plaza/	Other	N: Pharmacy, Safeway
Lodg	S: Super 8		Shell (Scales)	**(100)**	**Weigh Station (Both dir)**
Other	N: RVDump/Chevron	Gas	N: Chevron◊	**100**	**Antelope Rd, Citrus Heights**
64	**CR 124, Pitt School Rd**	Food	N: SilverSkilletRest/49er TP, Burger King, Subway/Chevron	Gas	N: 76
Gas	S: Chevron, Valero			Food	N: Burger King, Carl's Jr, Giant Pizza, KFC, Little Caesar's, Long John Silver, McDonald's, Subway, Taco Bell
Food	S: Arby's, Burger King, Denny's, IHOP, McDonald's, Pizza Hut, Starbucks, Subway	Lodg	N: Motel/49er TP, Fairfield Inn, Super 8		
Lodg	S: Best Western, Microtel	TWash	N: 49er TP		
Other	S: Safeway	TServ	N: 49er TP/Tires	Other	N: Albertsons, Pharmacy, US Post Office
66	**CA 113S, Curry Rd, First St (EB)**	Other	N: Laundry/CB/Chiro/Med/WiFi/RVDump/ LP/49er TP	**102**	**Riverside Ave, Auburn Blvd,**
	(EB Begin Shared CA 113, WB End)				**Citrus Heights, Roseville**
66A	**CA 113S, Rio Vista, Dixon**	**(86)**	**Jct I-5, N-Redding, S-Sacramento,**	Gas	N: Arco, Valero◊
FStop	S: CFN/Ramos Oil/Shell		**Los Angeles, S to CA 99**		S: Flyers◊, Shell
Gas	S: 76◊, ArcoAmPm	**88**	**Truxel Rd, Sacramento**	Food	N: Starbucks, Subway
Food	S: Cattleman's Steakhouse, Jack in the Box	Gas	N: Shell◊		S: Jack in the Box
		Food	N: Applebee's, Chili's, Chipolte Mex Rest, Del Taco, Hooters, On the Border, Quiznos, Starbucks, TGI Friday	Other	S: AutoZone, Kmart, Tires
Other	S: Wal-Mart▲			**103AB**	**Douglas Blvd (WB)**
66B	**Milk Farm Rd, Dixon (WB)**			Gas	N: 76, ArcoAmPm, Beacon, Exxon
FStop	S: CFN/Ramos Oil	Other	N: ATMs, B&N, Best Buy, Home Depot, PetSmart♥, Staples, Target, Wal-Mart▲, Mall, to Arco Arena		S: ArcoAmPm, Chevron, Shell
67	**CR 104, Pedrick Rd**			Food	N: Burger King, Claim Jumper, DQ, Jack in the Box, KFC, McDonald's, Taco Bell
69	**Kidwell Rd**				
70	**CA 113N, Davis, to Woodland**	**89**	**Northgate Blvd, Sacramento**		S: Carl's Jr, Carrow's, Del Taco, Denny's
	(WB Begin Shared CA 113, EB End)	Fstop	N: CFN / Ramos Oil #3962	Lodg	N: Best Western, Extended Stay America, Heritage Inn
Other	N: Univ of CA/Davis Airport✈	Gas	S: Circle K, Shell◊, Valero◊		
71	**Old Davis Rd, UC Davis Off Ramp**	Food	S: Burger King, Carl's Jr, IHOP, KFC, Long John Silver, McDonald's, Taco Bell		S: Oxford Suites
72	**Richards Blvd, Davis (EB)**			Med	S: + Roseville Hospital
Gas	N: Shell	Lodg	S: Extended Stay America, Red Roof Inn♥ Quality Inn	Other	N: Big O Tires, Dollar Tree, Firestone, Grocery, Pharmacy, Radio Shack, Trader Joe's
	S: Chevron				
Food	N: Café Italia	Other	N: Arco Arena		
	S: Applebee's, IHOP, KFC, Wendy's		S: Goodyear, Grocery, Kmart, Tires		S: Albertson's, Laundromat, Pharmacy, Office Depot, PetCo♥, Target
Lodg	N: Aggie Inn, Best Western, Econo Lodge, Hallmark Inn, University Park Inn	**90**	**Norwood Ave**		
		Gas	N: ArcoAmPm, Valero	**103**	**Douglas Blvd, Sunrise Ave (WB)**
	S: Comfort Suites, Holiday Inn Express	Food	N: McDonald's, Starbucks, Subway	**105A**	**Atlantic St, Eureka Rd (EB)**
Other	N: ATMs, Auto Services, NAPA, Amtrak, Greyhound, Univ of CA/Davis	Other	N: RiteAid, Grocery		**Eureka Rd, Taylor Rd (WB)**
		91	**Raley Blvd, Marysville Blvd**	Gas	S: 76, Chevron, Pacific Pride, Shell
		Gas	N: ArcoAmPm, Chevron◊	Food	S: Brookfields, Black Angus, Carvers Steaks & Chops, Taco Bell, Wendy's
72A	**Richards Blvd South, Davis**	**92**	**Winters St**		
72B	**Richards Blvd, Davis (WB)**	Other	N: McClellan AF Base	Lodg	S: Marriott
73	**Olive Dr (WB)**	**93**	**Longview Dr, Light Rail Station**	Other	S: Auto Dealers, Home Depot, Sam's Club, Mall, RVDump/Chevron
75	**Mace Blvd, Chiles Rd, Davis**	**94A**	**Watt Ave (EB)**		
Gas	S: 76, Chevron, Shell, Valero◊	Gas	N: 7-11, 76, ArcoAmPm, Shell	**105B**	**Taylor Rd Rocklin (EB),**
Food	S: Burger King, Denny's, McDonald's, Subway, Taco Bell, Wendy's	Food	N: Carl's Jr, Carrow's, DQ, Jack in the Box, KFC, Pizza Hut, Taco Bell, The Golden Egg Café		**Atlantic St (WB), Roseville**
				Gas	S: 76
Lodg	S: Howard Johnson, Motel 6♥			Food	N: Cattlemen's
Other	S: Auto Dealers, La Mesa RV		S: Burger King, Denny's	Lodg	S: Courtyard, Fairfield Inn, Hilton Garden Inn, Residence Inn
78	**East Chiles Rd, CR 32A, CR 32B,**	Lodg	N: Days Inn, Motel 6♥		
	Frontage Rd	Other	N: McClellan AFB	Other	N: RV Center
81	**Enterprise Blvd, W Capital Ave,**	**94B**	**Auburn Blvd (EB)**	**106**	**CA 65, to Lincoln,**
	Industrial Blvd, W Sacramento	Med	S: + Heritage Oaks Hospital		**Marysville**
FStop	N: W Sacramento Truck Stop/Chevron	**94**	**Light Rail Stations (WB, Left exit)**	Gas	N: Shell
	S: CFN / Ramos Oil #1580	**95**	**to I-80 Bus, Capital City Frwy,**	Food	N: Applebee's, Carl's Jr, Jack in the Box
Gas	S: 76◊		**Sacramento, to CA 99S**	Lodg	N: Comfort Suites
Food	N: Eppie's Rest	**96**	**Madison Ave**	Other	N: ATMs, B&N, Costco, Grocery, Wal-Mart
	S: Denny's, Quiznos, Subway	Gas	N: Beacon, Shell		
Lodg	N: Granada Inn		S: 76, ArcoAmPm, Shell	**108**	**Rocklin Rd**
Other	S: Sacramento West/Old Town KOA▲	Food	N: Brookfield's, Denny's, Java Coffee	Gas	N: Exxon, Flyers
			S: Boston Market, Burger King, El Pollo		S: ArcoAmPm

◊ = Regular Gas Stations with Diesel ▲ = RV Friendly Locations ♥ = Pet Friendly Locations

RED PRINT SHOWS LARGE VEHICLE PARKING/ACCESS ON SITE OR NEARBY BROWN PRINT SHOWS CAMPGROUNDS/RV PARKS

Interstate 80 — California

EXIT		CALIFORNIA
	Food	N: Arby's, Burger King, Carl's Jr, China Gourmet, Denny's, Jack in the Box, KFC, Starbucks, Subway, Taco Bell
	Lodg	N: Days Inn, Howard Johnson, Microtel
		S: Marriott, Rocklin Park Hotel
	Med	N: + Medical Clinic
	Other	N: Camping World, Gamel RV Center, Pharmacy, CarQuest, Radio Shack, Safeway
109		Sierra College Blvd
	Gas	N: 76, Chevron◊
	Food	N: Carl's Jr.
	Lodg	N: Days Inn
	Other	N: Loomis RV Park/RVDump▲
110		Horseshoe Bar Rd, Loomis
112		Penryn Rd, Loomis
	Gas	N: 76, Gasco
	Food	S: Cattle Baron
115		Indian Hill Rd, Newcastle Rd, Hidden Trail Rd, Newcastle
	Gas	S: ArcoAmPm, Flyer's
	Food	S: Denny's
	Other	S: CA State Hwy Patrol Post
116		CA 193, Taylor Rd, Lincoln
	Other	S: Wagner's Truck Repair, RV Center
118		Ophir Rd (WB)
119A		Maple St (EB), Nevada St (WB), Auburn
	Gas	S: Shell
	Food	S: Shanghai Rest, Tio Pepe
119B		CA 49, CA 193, to Grass Valley, Placerville
	Gas	N: Shell
	Food	N: Granny's Café, Java Junction
	Lodg	N: Holiday Inn
	Med	N: + Hospital
	Other	N: Laundromat, Grocery, Pharmacy, Staples
119C		Elm Ave, Auburn
	Gas	N: 76, Shell
	Food	N: Blimpie, Taco Bell
	Lodg	N: Holiday Inn
	Other	N: Amtrak, Albertson's, Pharmacy, U-Haul
120		Lincoln Way (EB), Russell Rd (WB) (Access Ex #121 Serv)
	Gas	S: BP, Shell
121		Auburn Ravine Rd, Foresthill
	Gas	N: Flyers, Thrifty
		S: 76◊, ArcoAmPm, Chevron◊, Shell◊
	Food	N: Arby's, Denny's, Taco Bell
		S: Bakers Square, Burger King, Carl Jr, Country Waffles, DQ, Jack in the Box, KFC, McDonald's, Sizzler, Subway
	Lodg	N: Best Inn, Foothills Motel, Motel 6♥, Sleep Inn, Super 8
		S: Best Western, Country Squire Inn, Travelodge
	Other	S: Grocery, Auburn State Rec Area
122		Bowman Rd, Lincoln Way, Auburn (Access Ex #121 Serv)
123		Bell Rd, Auburn
	Med	N: + Hospital
	Other	N: Auburn RV Park▲
124		Dry Creek Rd
125		Clipper Gap Rd, Placier Hills Rd, Auburn, Meadow Vista
128		Orchard Rd, Applegate
	Gas	N: Applegate Gas◊

EXIT		CALIFORNIA
	Food	N: Cruise In
	Lodg	N: The Original Firehouse Motel
		S: Applegate Motel
129		Applegate Rd, Heather Glen
130		Paoli Lane, Applegate, Colfax
	Gas	S: Weimar Country Store◊
131		Weimar Crossroad, Canyon Way
133		S Auburn St, to Placer Hills Rd, Canyon Way, Colfax
135		CA 174, S Auburn Ave, Canyon Way, Colfax, Grass Valley
	Gas	N: 76◊, Chevron
		S: Chevron◊, Beacon
	Food	N: McDonald's, Pizza Factory, Rosy's Café, Starbucks, Taco Bell
		S: Subway
	Lodg	N: Colfax Motor Inn
	Other	N: Laundromat, Grocery, NAPA
		S: Sierra RV
139		Rollins Lake Rd, Magra Rd (WB)
140		Magra Rd, to Rollins Lake Rd, Secret Town Rd, Colfax
143		Magra Rd, Gold Run Rd, Dutch Flat
(143)		Gold Run Rest Area (Both dir) (RR, Phones, Picnic)
144		Gold Run Rd, Sawmill (WB)
145		Ridge Rd, Dutch Flat
	Gas	S: Tesoro◊
	Food	N: Monte Vista
	Other	N: CAMP▲

EXIT		CALIFORNIA
	Other	S: CA State Hwy Patrol Post
146		Alta Bonnynook Rd, Alta, Dutch Flat
148A		Crystal Springs Rd, Alta
148B		Baxter Rd, Alta
150		Drum Forebay Rd, Alta
155		Blue Canyon Rd, Putt Rd, Alta
	Other	S: Blue Canyon-Nyack Airport ✈
156		Nyack Rd, Alta
	FStop	S: Shell
	Food	S: Burger King/Shell FS, Nyack Cafe
(157)		Vista Point (WB)
158A		Emigrant Gap (EB)
	Gas	S: Shell◊
	Food	S: Café/Rancho Sierra Inn
	Lodg	S: Rancho Sierra Inn
158B		Laing Rd (EB)
158		Emigrant Gap, Laing Rd (WB)
160		Yuba Gap Rd, Crystal Lake Rd
161		CA 20, Soda Springs, Nevada City
164		Eagle Lakes Rd, Crystal Lake Rd
	Other	N: CAMP▲
165		Cisco Rd, Cisco Grove, Norden
	Gas	S: Mobil, Valero◊
	Other	N: RV CAMP/RVDump▲
166		Donner Pass Rd, Hampshire Rocks Rd, Norden, to Big Bend (EB)
168		Rainbow Rd, Big Bend
	Food	S: Rest/Rainbow Lodge
	Lodg	S: Rainbow Inn
171		Donner Pass Rd, Troy, Kingvale
	Gas	S: Shell
174		Donner Pass Rd, Soda Springs
	FStop	S: 76
	Food	S: Rest/Donner Summit Lodge
	Lodg	S: Donner Summit Lodge
176		Boreal Ridge Rd, Soda Springs, Castle Peak
	Food	S: Rest/Boreal Inn
	Lodg	S: Boreal Inn
(177)		Donner Summit Rest Area (Both dir) (RR, Phones, Picnic)
(180)		Vista Point (EB)
180		Donner Lake Rd, Truckee
	Lodg	S: Donner Lake Village Resort, Richards Motel
(181)		Vista Point (WB)
184		Donner Pass Rd, Truckee
	FStop	N: Shell
		S: Chevron
	Gas	S: 76
	Food	N: Mountain Grill
		S: Donner House Rest, Donner Lk Pizza
	Lodg	N: Sunset Inn
		S: Alpine Village Motel, Holiday Inn Express
	Other	S: Donner Memorial State Park, CAMP/RVDump▲
185		CA 89S, Truckee, to Lake Tahoe (EB Begin shared CA 89, WB end)
	Gas	N: Sierra Super Stop
		S: Shell

◊ = Regular Gas Stations with Diesel   ▲ = RV Friendly Locations   ♥ = Pet Friendly Locations
RED PRINT SHOWS LARGE VEHICLE PARKING/ACCESS ON SITE OR NEARBY   BROWN PRINT SHOWS CAMPGROUNDS/RV PARKS

I-80 W/E

EXIT		CA / NV
	Food	N: Burger King, DQ, La Bamba, Little Caesars, Panda Express, Pizza, Sizzler S: Burger King, China Garden, KFC, McDonald's, Subway
	Lodg	N: Sunset Inn S: Inn at Truckee, Super 8
	Med	N: + Tahoe Forest Hospital
	Other	N: CA Hwy Patrol Post, CarQuest, RiteAid, Safeway S: Albertson's, Long's Pharmacy, RV CAMP▲
186		Donner Pass Rd, Central Truckee (reaccess WB only)
	Gas	S: 76
	Food	S: Dragonfly, Ponderosa, Truckee Diner, Wagontrain Cafe
	Lodg	S: Alta Hotel, Cottage Hotel, Truckee Hotel
	Med	N: + Hospital
	Other	S: Amtrak
188A		Donner Pass Rd, to CA 89N, CA 267S, Truckee (EB)
188B		CA 89N, Sierraville, CA 267S, Kings Beach (EB) (EB End shared CA 89)
	Other	S: Truckee Tahoe Airport✈
188		CA 89N, Sierraville, CA 267S, Kings Beach, Truckee ByPass (WB) (WB begin Shared CA 89)
	Other	N: Coachland RV Park/RVDump▲
190		Prosser Village Rd, Truckee
(191)		Weigh Station (WB)
194		Hirschdale Rd
	Gas	S: United Trails Gen'l Store
	Other	S: RV CAMP▲
199		Floriston Way, Floriston
201		Farad
	NOTE:	MM 208: Nevada State Line
		(PACIFIC TIME ZONE)
○ CALIFORNIA		
○ NEVADA		
		(PACIFIC / MOUNTAIN TIME ZONE)
1		Gold Ranch Rd, Verdi (WB)
2		Gold Ranch Rd, I-80 Bus, 3rd St
	Gas	N: ArcoAmPm◊/Gold Ranch
	Food	N: Jack in the Box/Sierra Café/Gold Ranch
	Lodg	N: Gold Ranch Casino & RV Resort▲
3		Verdi Rd, Verdi (WB)
(4)		Weigh Station (EB)

EXIT		NEVADA
4		Boomtown-Garson Rd, Verdi
	TStop	N: AmBest/Boomtown Casino Truck Stop (Scales)
	Food	N: Cassidy's Steakhouse/Sundance Cantina SilverScreenBuffet/Starbucks/FastFood/Boomtown TS
	Lodg	N: Boomtown Hotel
	Other	N: Laundry/RVDump/Boomtown TS & Reno KOA/Boomtown RV Park▲
(4.5)		Scenic View (EB)
5		I-80 Bus, NV 425, to E Verdi (WB)
(6)		Parking Area (Both dir)
7		W 4th St, Reno, Mogul
8		W 4th St, US 40, NV 647 (EB)
9		Robb Dr, Reno
	Gas	N: 76◊
10		McCarran Blvd, Reno
	Gas	N: 7-11, ArcoAmPm, Tesoro S: 7-11
	Food	N: Arby's, Burger King, Carl's Jr, Chili's, El Pollo Loco, IHOP, Jack in the Box, McDonald's, Starbucks, Taco Bell S: Little Caesars/Kmart
	Lodg	S: Inn at Summit Ridge
	Other	N: Albertson's, Big O Tire, Dollar Tree, Grocery, ShopKO, Tires+, Walgreen's, Wal-Mart sc, to Bonanza Terrace RV Park▲ S: Home Depot, Kmart
12		Keystone Ave, Reno
	Gas	N: 7-11, ArcoAmPm S: 76◊, Chevron, Exxon
	Food	N: Pizza Hut S: Coffee Grinder Inn, Jack in the Box, KFC, McDonald's, Port of Subs, Ritz Café, Taco Bell, Wendy's
	Lodg	N: Gateway Inn, Motel 6♥ S: Carriage Inn, Courtyard, Crest Inn, Donner Inn, El Tavern Motel, Gold Dust West Casino & Motel, Travelodge
	Med	S: + Family & Urgent Medical Care, + Medina Medical Center
	Other	N: Grocery, Laundromat, Pharmacy S: Albertson's, Greyhound, Olsen Tire, Pharmacy, Shopping, Keystone RV Park▲, Chism Trailer Park▲, to Casinos
13		Sierra St, Center St, US 395 Bus, Virginia St, Reno
	Gas	N: Shell S: Chevron, Shell◊

EXIT		NEVADA
	Food	N: Breakaway, Carl's Jr, Giant Burger, Jimmy John's Gourmet Sandwiches, Jimboy's Tacos S: DQ, McDonald's, Sterling's Seafood Steakhouse
	Lodg	N: Capri Motel, Silver Dollar Motor Lodge, Sundance Motel S: Aspen Motel, Chalet Motel, Flamingo Hilton, Golden West Motor Lodge, Monte Carlo Motel, Silver Legacy Resort Casino, Sands Hotel & Casino, Savoy Motor Lodge, Showboat Inn
	Med	S: + St. Mary's Hospital
	Other	N: Fleischmann Planetarium, to Univ of NV, Bonanza Terrace RV Park▲, Shamrock RV Park▲ S: to Univ of NV/Reno, The Gambler Casino, Circus Circus Hotel & Casino, Eldorado Hotel & Casino, Harrah's, Silver Legacy Resort Casino, The Nugget, Various Casinos, Silver Sage RV Park▲, Reno RV Park▲
14		Wells Ave
	Gas	S: Chevron, Shell
	Food	S: Carrow's, Denny's
	Lodg	N: Motel 6♥ S: Days Inn, Econo Lodge, Holiday Inn Diamonds Casino, Motel 6, Reno Hotel & Casino
	Other	N: Washoe Co Fairgrounds
15		US 395, to Carson City, Susanville
	Gas	N: Chevron, Shell◊
	Food	N: Arby's, Burger King, Chinese, Del Taco, Sonic, Subway, Taco Bell S: Alejos Inn, Everybody's Inn Motel, Gold Coin Motel, HiWay 40 Motel
	Lodg	S: Alejos Inn, Everybody's Inn Motel, Gold Coin Motel, HiWay 40 Motel
	Other	N: Home Depot, Wal-Mart, Bonanza Terrace RV Park▲, Bonanza Casino, Shamrock RV Park▲, to appr 15mi: Bordertown Casino & RV Resort/Fuel/LP S: Reno Hilton KOA▲, to Reno Tahoe Int'l Airport✈
16		Prater Way, E 4th St, Sparks
	Gas	N: ArcoAmPm S: ArcoAmPm◊, Chevron, Pacific Pride◊
	Food	N: Jack's Coffee Shop, Plantation Station S: Gallett's Coney Island Bar
	Lodg	N: Motel 6♥, Pony Express Lodge S: Gold Coin Motel, Hilton
	Other	N: Rail City Casino
17		Rock Blvd, Nugget Ave, Sparks
	FStop	S: to Glendale & Intl Way CFN / Western Energetix
	Gas	N: ArcoAmPm, Exxon

◊ = Regular Gas Stations with Diesel   ▲ = RV Friendly Locations   ♥ = Pet Friendly Locations
RED PRINT SHOWS LARGE VEHICLE PARKING/ACCESS ON SITE OR NEARBY   BROWN PRINT SHOWS CAMPGROUNDS/RV PARKS

INTERSTATE 80 W/E

NEVADA

EXIT		
	Food	N: Jack's Coffee Shop
	Lodg	N: Craig Motel, Grand Sierra Resort, Casino, & RV Park▲, Nugget Hotel & Casino, Safari Motel, Victorian Inn, Wagon Train Motel
	Other	N: Laundromat, Rail City Casino
		S: Baldini's Sports Casino
18		**NV 445, Pyramid Way, Nugget Ave, Victorian Ave, Sparks**
	Food	N: Steak Buffet, Victoria's Steak House
		S: John's Oyster Bar, Steakhouse Grill
	Lodg	N: DeSoto Hotel, Lariat Motel, Nugget Courtyard, Sunrise Motel, Silver Club Hotel & Casino
		S: Nugget Hotel & Casino
	TServ	S: Cummins Intermountain
	Med	N: + Occu-Family Care
	Other	N: Victorian Mall, Casinos
19		**McCarran Blvd, Nugget Ave, Sparks**
	TStop	N: Travel Center of America #172/76 (Scales)
	Gas	N: Chevron◆
	Food	N: TruckersGrill/TA TC, Applebee's, Arby's, Black Bear Diner, Burger King, El Pollo Loco, IHOP, Jack in the Box, KFC, McDonald's, Sizzler, Subway, Wendy's
		S: Denny's, BJ's BBQ, Super Burrito
	Lodg	N: Aloha Inn, Western Village Inn & Casino
		S: Quality Inn, Motel 6
	TWash	N: TA TC
	TServ	N: TA TC/Tires
	Other	N: Laundry/WiFi/RVDump/LP/TA TC, Mall, Radio Shack, Safeway, Pharmacy, Victorian RV Park▲, Sparks Marina RV Park▲
20		**Sparks Blvd, E Greg St, Sparks**
	Gas	N: Shell◆
	Food	N: Carl's Jr, Outback Steakhouse
	Other	N: Factory Outlets of NV
21		**Vista Blvd, E Greg St, Sparks**
	TStop	S: Alamo Travel Center/Petro Stopping Center #38 (Scales)
	Gas	N: Chevron, KwikStop
	Food	N: Del Taco, McDonald's
		S: IronSkillet/FastFood/Petro SC
	Lodg	N: Fairfield Inn
		S: Super 8♥/Petro SC
	TWash	S: Petro SC
	TServ	S: Petro SC/Tires, Allison, International, Kenworth, Freightliner
	Med	N: + Hospital
	Other	N: Joe Gandolio Arena
		S: Laundry/BarbSh/CB/Chiro/Casino/Petro SC
22		**Canyon Rd, Lockwood Dr**
23		**Mustang Ranch Rd, Sparks**
	Gas	S: Chevron◆
	Food	N: Mustang Station Café
(25)		**Weigh Station (WB)**
(27)		**Scenic View (EB)**
28		**NV 655, to Waltham Way, Patrick**
32		**Clark Station Rd, Virginia City**
36		**Derby Dam**
38		**Orchard**
40		**NV 421, Painted Rock, Reno**
(41)		**Rest Area (WB)** (RR, Phones, Picnic, RVDump)

EXIT		
(42)		**Weigh Station (EB)**
43		**NV 427, Wadsworth, Pyramid Lake**
	Other	N: Pyramid Lake Indian Res/Gas◆/Camping▲
46		**NV 427, US 95 Alt, W Main St, W. Fernley, Silver Springs, Wadsworth**
	TStop	N: Love's Travel Stop #246 (Scales)
		S: Pilot Travel Center #340 (Scales)
	Gas	S: Chevron, Exxon
	Food	N: Arby's/Love's TS
		S: DQ/Wendy's/Pilot TC, China Chef, Jack in the Box, La Fiesta Mex Rest
	Lodg	S: Best Value Inn, BestWestern♥ and RV Park▲
	TWash	S: Blue Beacon TW/Pilot TC, Speedco
	Other	N: Laundry/WiFi/Love's TS
		S: Laundry/Casino/WiFi/Pilot TC, To appr 4mi: Desert Rose RV Park▲
48		**NV 343, US 50 Alt, E Fernley**
	FStop	N: Texaco
	TStop	N: Fernley Truck Inn (Scales)
		S: CFN/Winners Corner #50/76
	Gas	S: Chevron◆
	Food	N: Rest/FastFood/Fernley TI
		S: Domino's, Jack in the Box, McDonald's, Pizza Factory
	Lodg	N: Fernley Truck Inn/Seven Z's Motel
		S: Super 8
	TWash	N: Fernley TI
	TServ	N: Fernley TI/Tires
	Other	N: Laundry/Casino/RVDump/LP/Fernley Truck Inn
		S: Casinos, Goodyear, Grocery, Radio Shack, to appr 4mi Desert Rose RV Park▲
65		**Nightingale Rd, to Hot Springs**
78		**to Jessup**
83		**US 95S, to Fallon, Las Vegas**
	S:	Rest Area (Both dir) (RR, Phone, Picnic)
93		**Ragged Top Rd, Lovelock**
105		**80 Bus Lp, Lovelock, to Toulon**
	Gas	N: Shell◆
	Food	N: La Casita Rest
	Lodg	N: Brookwood Motel & MH RV Park▲
106		**Main St, Downtown Lovelock (Access from Exit #105 or #107)**
	FStop	N: Chevron
	Gas	N: 76, Shell◆
	Food	N: Longhorn Saloon, McDonald's, Pizza Factory, Ranch House Rest
	Lodg	N: Cadillac Motel, Covered Wagon Motel, Sage Motel
	Med	N: + Pershing General Hospital
	Other	S: Sturgeon's Restaurant/Casino/Inn, Laundromat, NAPA, Pharmacy
107		**Airport Rd, E Lovelock (WB)**
	Gas	N: Exxon
	Food	N: Rest/Lovelock Inn
	Lodg	N: Lovelock Inn
112		**Coal Canyon Rd, to US 395, NV 396**
119		**Etna Rd, Lovelock-Unionville Rd, to Rochester, to Oreana**
129		**NV 401, Rye Patch Reservoir Rd**
	FStop	S: Rye Patch Truck Stop
	Food	S: Café/Rye Patch TS
	Other	S: Rye Patch Reservoir, Rye Patch State Recreation Area▲

EXIT		
138		**Humboldt House Interchange Rd**
145		**NV 416, Imlay**
	Other	N: Village Store & Campground▲
149		**NV 400, Imlay, Mill City, to Unionville**
	TStop	N: Travel Center of America #181/Arco (Scales) (WB Access Via Ex #151)
	Food	N: ForkinRoad/Subway/TacoBell/TA TC
	Lodg	N: Knights Inn♥/TA TC
	TServ	N: TA TC/Tires
	Other	N: Laundry/WiFi/TA TC, I-80 Campground
		S: General Store & Camping▲
151		**NV 415, Mill City, Dun Glen (WB Access to Ex #149)**
158		**Cosgrave Rd, to Cosgrave**
	S:	Rest Area (SB) (RR, Phone, Picnic, RVDump)
168		**to Rose Creek**
173		**I-80 Bus, NV 289, Winnemucca**
	Other	S: to Winnemucca Muni Airport✈
176		**US 95N, I-80 Bus, NV 289, Winnemucca Blvd, Downtown**
	FStop	N: Pacific Pride
		S: CFN/Western Energetix 3245 W Potato Rd
	TStop	S: Flying J Travel Plaza #5025/Conoco (Scales), Pilot Travel Center #485 (Scales)
	Gas	S: Chevron◆, Shell◆
	Food	S: CrossRoadDeli/FJ TP, Subway/Pilot TC, Arby's, Burger King, Denny's, KFC, Pizza Hut, Round Table Pizza, Taco Time, Taco Bell
	Lodg	S: Best Western, Days Inn, Holiday Inn Express, Motel 6♥, Quality Inn, Ramada, Santa Fe Inn, Super 8, Winner's Hotel & Casino, Red Lion Inn & Casino
	TServ	S: Freightliner
	Med	S: + Humbolt General Hospital
	Other	S: Laundry/WiFi/RVDump/LP/FJ TP, Laundry/Casino/RVDump/Pilot TC, Auto Dealer, Auto Service, Grocery, Goodyear, Schwab Tire, Wal-Mart sc▲, Model T Casino & RV Park▲, Winnemucca Indian Colony
178		**I-80 Bus, E 2nd St, to US 40, NV289, US 95, Winnemucca Blvd.**
	Gas	S: Chevron, Exxon, Maverick, Shell
	Food	S: Burger King, China Gate, El Mirador Mexican, Pizza Hut, Subway
	Lodg	S: Best Western, Park Motel, Overland Hotel, Scottish Inn, Super 8, Thunderbird Hotel
	Med	S: + Humbolt General Hospital
	Other	S: Grocery, Pharmacy, Amtrak, Golf Course, Winnemucca KOA▲, Casinos
180		**I-80 Bus, US 40, Winnemucca Blvd**
	Other	S: High Desert RV Park▲
187		**to Button Point**
	S:	Rest Area (Both dir) (RR, Phones, Picnic, RVDump)
194		**NV 790, Golconda, Midas**
	Gas	N: Water Hole Gas & Store
	Food	N: Bar Z & Grill
	Lodg	N: Water Hole Motel
	Other	N: Grocery, US Post Office
(200)		**Parking Area (Both dir)**
203		**to Iron Point**

◆ = Regular Gas Stations with Diesel   ▲ = RV Friendly Locations   ♥ = Pet Friendly Locations
RED PRINT SHOWS LARGE VEHICLE PARKING/ACCESS ON SITE OR NEARBY   BROWN PRINT SHOWS CAMPGROUNDS/RV PARKS

EXIT	NEVADA
205	to Pumpernickel Valley
212	Stonehouse Hwy, Stonehouse
216	Valmy
S:	Rest Area (Both dir) (RR, Phones, Picnic, RVDump)
FStop	N: CFN/76
Food	N: Rest/Golden Motel
Lodg	N: Golden Motel
222	to Mote
229	I-80 Bus, NV 304, to NV 305, Downtown Battle Mountain
Gas	N: Shell◆
Lodg	N: Battle Mountain Inn, Big Chief Motel, Comfort Inn, Nevada Hotel
Med	N: + Hospital
Other	N: Grocery, Te-Moak Indian Res S: Te-Moak Indian Res, Mill Creek Rec Area▲
231	NV 305, S Broad St, Battle Mtn
FStop	N: to CFN/Western Energetix 345 N 1st St
TStop	N: Flying J Travel Plaza/Conoco (Scales)
Gas	N: Chevron◆
Food	N: ColtRest/Blimpie/FJ TP, Donna's Diner, Mama's Pizza S: HideAway Steakhouse
Lodg	N: Hotel/FJ TP, Comfort Inn, Nevada Hotel, Super 8
TServ	N: North Nevada Tire, Smith Detroit Diesel, Allison
Other	N: Laundry/WiFi/RVDump/LP/FJ TP S: Mill Creek Rec Area▲
233	NV 304, Hill Top Rd, Battle Mountain
Gas	N: Conoco◆, Exxon
Lodg	N: Big Chief Motel, Comfort Inn
Med	N: + Hospital
Other	N: Grocery, Auto & Truck Service S: Battle Mountain Airport✈
244	to Argenta
254	to Dunphy
(259)	Rest Area (Both dir) (RR, Picnic, RVDump)
261	NV 306, Crescent Valley, Beowawe
268	to Emigrant
(270)	Parking Area (Both dir)
271	Frenchie Rd, to Palisade
279	NV 278, NV 221, I-80 Bus, Carlin, Eureka (EB)
280	NV 766, Central Carlin, Eureka
FStop	S: to 424 Chestnut St CFN/Western Energetix
TStop	S: Pilot Travel Center #387 (Scales)
Gas	S: Shell, Sinclair
Food	S: Subway/Pilot TC, BurgerKing/Shell, Chin's Café, Pizza Factory, Whistle Stop Cafe, State Café
Lodg	S: Best Inn, Cavalier Motel
TServ	N: Anderson Diesel Repair
Other	N: WiFi/Casino/RVDump/Pilot TC, Grocery
282	to I-80 Bus, NV 221, Carlin, Eureka
292	Maggie Creek Ranch Rd, Hunter
298	80 Bus Loop, NV 535, West Elko
Other	S: Te-Moak Indian Reservation

EXIT	NEVADA
301	NV 225, Mountain City Hwy, Elko, I-80 Bus, NV 535
FStop	S: 920 Mtn City Hwy CFN/Western Energetix
Gas	N: Maverick S: Conoco◆, Phillips 66◆, Shell◆
Food	N: Arby's, McDonald's, Round Table Pizza S: KFC, New China Café, Taco Bell
Lodg	N: Oak Tree Inn, Shilo Inn S: American Inn, Key Motel, Manor Motor Lodge, Ruby Hill Motel, Stampede Motel
TServ	S: Cummins Intermountain, Western Tire Center
Med	S: + Hospital
Other	N: ATM, Grocery, Kmart, Laundromat, Home Depot, Wal-Mart sc S: CarQuest, Grocery, IGA, Pharmacy, Casinos, Elko Reg'l Muni Airport✈, RVDump/Phillips66/RVDump/Shell, Cimarron West RV Park/Gas/Rest▲
303	NV 535, I-80 Bus, East Elko
FStop	N: CFN/Chevron S: Bonus Star Mart #53/Sinclair
Gas	S: Chevron, Conoco◆, Shell, Tesoro◆
Food	S: Burger King, Coffee Mug, Cowboy Joe, Golden Corral, McDonald's, Pizza Hut, Subway, Taco Time, Wendy's
Lodg	S: Best Western♥/RVPark▲/Casino, Days Inn, Elko Motel, Hi Desert Inn, Hilton Garden Inn, Holiday Inn, Motel 6♥, Microtel, Park View Inn, Red Lion Inn & Casino, Super 8
TServ	S: CAT, Allison, Cummins InterMountain
Med	S: + Hospital
Other	N: Golf Course S: Albertson's, Auto Dealers, Pharmacy, Double Dice RV Park▲, Valley View RV Park▲, Iron Horse RV Resort▲, to Ryndon Campground RV Park▲
310	NF 421, E Idaho St, to Osino
(312)	Weigh Station (Both dir)
314	CR 721A, CR 742, Elko, to Ryndon, Devils Gate
Other	S: to Ryndon Campground RV Park▲
317	NF-423, CR 71, to Elburz
321	NV 229, Halleck, Ruby Valley
328	River Ranch
333	NV 230, Deeth, Starr Valley
343	NV 230, Deeth, to Welcome
Other	N: Welcome Station RV Park▲
348	6th St, Wells, Crested Acres
351	I-80 Bus, NV 223, Humboldt Ave
Gas	N: Tesoro◆
Lodg	N: Chinatown Motel
Other	N: Grocery, US Post Office, Mountain Shadows RV Park▲, to PL/Angel Lake Campground▲, Crossroads RV Park▲
352AB	US 93, Great Basin Hwy, 6th St, I-80 Bus, NV 223, Wells
FStop	N: CFN/Western Energetix 881 6th St
TStop	N: Flying J Travel Plaza S: Flying J Travel Plaza #5068/Conoco (Scales), Love's Travel Stop #365 (Scales)
Gas	N: Chevron, Shell
Food	N: FastFood/FJ TP, Burger King, Dee's, Old West Inn Casino & Café, Ranch House

EXIT	NEVADA
Food	S: Cookery/FastFood/FJ TP, McDonald's, Love's TS
Lodg	N: Best Western, Motel 6♥, Rest Inn, Super 8, Wagon Wheel Motel
TWash	N: Roadway Diesel
TServ	N: Intermountain Car & Truck Repair, Roadway Diesel, Goodyear
Other	S: Laundry/Casino/WiFi/RVDump/LP/FJ TP
(354)	Parking Area (EB)
360	Moor
365	Independence Valley
(373)	Rest Area (Both dir) (RR, Picnic)
376	Pequop
378	NV 233, to Oasis, Montello
FStop	N: Country Store & Gas
387	Shafter
398	Pilot Peak
407	Wendover Blvd, Wendover
410	US 80 Bus Loop, US 93 Alt, Wendover Blvd, Wendover
S:	NV Welcome Center (WB) (RR, Phone, Info)
TStop	S: Pilot Travel Center #147 (Scales)
Gas	S: Chevron, Shell◆
Food	S: Arby's/TJCinn/Pilot TC, Burger King, McDonald's, Pizza Hut, Subway
Lodg	S: Best Western, Days Inn, Motel 6♥, Nevada Crossing Hotel, Peppermill Inn & Casino/RVPark▲, Red Garter Hotel & Casino, Rainbow Hotel & Casino, Super 8, Stateline Hotel & Casino, Silver Smith Hotel & Casino
Other	S: Laundry/Casino/WiFi/Pilot TC, Grocery, Goodyear, Stateline RV Park▲, Silver Sage RV Park▲, Wendover KOA▲, Wendover Air Force Aux Field✈
NOTE:	MM 411: Utah State Line

(PACIFIC / MOUNTAIN TIME ZONE)

○ **NEVADA**
○ **UTAH**

(MOUNTAIN / PACIFIC TIME ZONE)

2	UT 58, Wendover Blvd, Wendover (EB reaccess only)(WB diff reaccess)
Gas	S: R Place #4/Shell◆
Food	S: Subway, Taco Poblano
Lodg	S: Best Western, Days Inn♥, Motel 6♥
Other	N: Danger Cave State Park S: ATM, Auto Services, Family Dollar, Grocery, US Post Office, Museum, Wendover Airport✈, to NV Casinos, RV Parking & Camping▲
(3)	Port of Entry/Weigh Station (Both dir)
NOTE:	EB: CHECK YOUR FUEL Next Ex #99
4	Salt Flats Rd, Bonneville Speedway
FStop	N: Bonus Star Mart/66 (Scales), Hardy Ent/Sinclair
Food	N: Café
Other	N: Bonneville Salt Flats State Park

◆ = Regular Gas Stations with Diesel   ▲ = RV Friendly Locations   ♥ = Pet Friendly Locations
RED PRINT SHOWS LARGE VEHICLE PARKING/ACCESS ON SITE OR NEARBY   BROWN PRINT SHOWS CAMPGROUNDS/RV PARKS

Interstate 80 W/E

EXIT	UTAH		EXIT	UTAH		EXIT	UTAH
(10)	Salt Flats Rest Area (Both dir) (RR, Phones, Picnic, Vend, Info)		(117)	Jct I-215, N-Ogden, S-Provo		Food	E: FastFood/Prem Oil, Burger King, Carl Jr's, IHOP, McDonald's, Subway
41	Knolls		118	UT 68, Redwood Rd, to Temple		Lodg	E: Marriott
49	to Clive		FStop	N: Pilot Travel Center #194 (Scales)		Other	E: LP/Prem Oil, Costco, Home Depot, Pep Boys, PetSmart♥, Bank, U-Haul
(54)	Grassy Mtn Rest Area (Both dir) (RR, Phones, Picnic, Vend)		Gas	N: 7-11, Chevron◇, Maverik, Tesoro S: 7-11		305A	UT 201W, 900W, Salt Lake City (Addt'l Serv W to UT 68)
56	to Aragonite		Food	N: Arby's/Pilot TC, Burger King, Carl's Jr, Denny's, KFC, Subway, Taco Bell,		TStop	W: Flying J Travel Plaza #50007
62	Military Area, Lakeside		Lodg	N: Airport Inn, Baymont Inn, Candlewood Suites, Comfort Suites, Days Inn, Dream Inn, Holiday Inn Express, Motel 6, Quality Inn, Radisson, Sheraton		Food	W: Rest/FJ TP, Wendy's
70	Delle					TWash	W: Blue Beacon/FJ TP
FStop	S: Delle Auto & Truck Plaza/Sinclair					TServ	W: Diesel Repair
Food	S: Café/Delle ATP		Med	N: + Hospital		Other	W: Laundry/WiFi/RVDump/LP/FJ TP, Goodyear, NAPA, Banks, Repair
Lodg	S: Motel/Delle ATP		Other	N: Laundry/Pilot TC, Salt Lake City KOA▲		(305A-D)	Exit to NB Collector (NB)
77	UT 196, Rowley, Dugway		(120)	Jct I-15N, to Ogden		(304)	Jct I-80E, to Cheyenne, Denver (Gas & Lodging at 1st Exit on I-80E)
84	UT 138, Grantsville, Tooele		121	W 600S, UT 269, Salt Lake City		TServ	E: Cummins Intermountain
88	to Grantsville		NOTE:	I-80 below runs with I-15. Exit #'s follow I-15.		NOTE:	I-80 above runs with I-15. Exit #'s follow I-15.
99	UT 36, Tooele, Stansbury		(308)	Jct I-80W, Airport, Reno		(123AB)	I-15, N to Ogden, S to Provo
TsSop	S: Flying J Travel Plaza #5015/Conoco (Scales), Travel Center of America #60/Tesoro (Scales)		307	400 South, UT 186 (SB), 400 South HOV Exit (NB)		122	2100S, UT 201, Salt Lake City
			Gas	E: Chevron, Food Mart		124	US 89, State St
Gas	S: Chevron, Shell◇		Food	E: Various		Gas	N: 7-11, Chevron S: Sinclair
Food	S: Rest/FastFood/FJ TP, CountryPride/ BurgerKing/TacoBell/TA TC, Subway/ Chevron, McDonald's		Lodg	E: Courtyard, Hampton Inn, Rio Grande Hotel, Renaissance Suites, Residence Inn		Food	N: Burger King, Central Park, Subway, Taco Bell, Wendy's S: KFC, Pizza Hut
Lodg	S: Oquirrh Motor Inn & RV Park▲		Other	E: Amtrak, Enterprise RAC, Aquarium, Museum, Auto Repair, Grocery, Banks W: Grocery		Lodg	S: Ramada Ltd
TWash	S: Blue Beacon TW/TA TC					Other	N: ATM, Auto Dealers, Discount Tire
TServ	S: TA TC/Tires		306	600 South, UT 269 (NB)		125	UT 71, 7th East
Other	S: Laundry/WiFi/RVDump/LP/FJ TP, Laundry/WiFi/RVDump/TA TC, Tooele Army Depot		Gas	E: Chevron, Maverick, Sinclair		126	UT 181, 13th East, Sugar House
			Food	E: Denny's, McDonald's, Rest/Hilton, Salty Dogs, Rest/Quality Inn, Rest/ Ramada, Rest/Travelodge		Gas	N: Chevron, Shell
NOTE:	WB: CHECK YOUR FUEL Next Ex #4		Lodg	E: Ameritel Inn, Best Western, Embassy Suites, Hilton, Motel 6♥, Quality Inn, Ramada, Red Lion Hotel, Super 8, Travelodge♥		Food	N: KFC, Olive Garden, Pizza Hut, Red Lobster, Sizzler, Taco Bell, Wendy's
102	UT 201, to Magna (EB)					127	UT 195, S2300E, to Holladay
Med	S: + Hospital					(128)	Jct I-215S (EB)
104	UT 202, Saltair Dr, Magna					129	UT 186W, Foothill Dr, Parleys Way
Other	N: Great Salt Lake State Park		Other	E: Amtrak, Enterprise RAC, Aquarium, Museum, Auto Repair, Grocery, Banks		Med	N: + Hospital
111	S7200W, Salt Lake City		(305C-A)	Exit to SB Collector (SB)		(130)	Jct I-215S (WB)
113	S5600W, UT 172, Salt Lake City		305D	900 South (NB)		131	Quarry
Gas	N: Phillips 66		Gas	E: Chevron, Sinclair		132	Ranch Exit
Food	N: Perkins, Pizza Hut, Pizza Palace, Subwa		Food	E: Artic Circle, Chinese, Mexican		133	Utility Exit (EB)
Lodg	N: Best Western, Comfort Inn, Fairfield Inn, Hampton Inn, Hilton, Holiday Inn, Holiday Inn Express, Super 8		Lodg	E: Best Inns, Holiday Inn		134	UT 65, Park City, Emigration & East Canyons
			Other	E: Auto Repairs, Tires			
114	Wright Bros Dr (WB) (Access to Ex #113 Serv)		305C	1300S, Salt Lake City		137	Lambs Canyon Rd, Lambs Canyon
			Gas	E: Maverik		140	Parleys Summit
Lodg	N: Courtyard, La Quinta Inn♥, Microtel, Residence Inn		Food	E: Various		Gas	S: Sinclair◇
			Other	E: Auto Repairs, Tires, Banks			
115	UT 154, Bangerter Hwy, Salt Lake City Airport		305B	2100S, UT 201, Salt Lake City (Addt'l Serv W to UT 68)			
Other	N: Salt Lake City KOA▲		FStop	E: Premium Oil/Chevron			
			Gas	E: 7-11, Petro Mart, Costco			

◇ = Regular Gas Stations with Diesel   ▲ = RV Friendly Locations   ♥ = Pet Friendly Locations
RED PRINT SHOWS LARGE VEHICLE PARKING/ACCESS ON SITE OR NEARBY   BROWN PRINT SHOWS CAMPGROUNDS/RV PARKS

EXIT		UTAH
	Food	S: Cafe
141		Homestead Rd, Jeremy Ranch
	Gas	N: Phillips 66
	Food	N: Blimpie/P66, Pizza Hut
(144)		Scenic View (EB)
145		UT 224, Kimball Junction, Park City
	Gas	S: 7-11, Chevron, Shell
	Food	S: Arby's, Denny's, JB's, Little Caesars, McDonalds, Panda Express, Quiznos, Ruby Tuesday, Subway, Taco Bell, Wendy's
	Lodg	S: Best Western, Hampton Inn, Holiday Inn Express
	Other	N: Park City RV Resort▲
		S: Grocery, Kmart, Wal-Mart, Tanger Outlet Center at Park City, US Post Office, Powderwood Resort▲, Ski Area
146		US 40, Silver Creek Rd, Park City, to Heber, Provo
	FStop	N: Sinclair
	Food	N: Blimpie's/Sinclair
150		Ranch Exit
155		UT 32, Main St, Wanship Rd, Peoa, Wanship, Kamas
	Gas	S: Sinclair
	Food	N: Café/Spring Chicken Inn
	Lodg	N: Spring Chicken Inn
	Other	S: Rockport State Park
162		W 100 St, UT 280, Coalville
	TStop	N: Holiday Hills/66
	Gas	S: Chevron◊, Sinclair, Shell
	Lodg	N: Best Western
		S: Moore Motel
	Other	N: LP/Holiday Hills, Holiday Hills Campground/RVDump▲
		S: Laundromat, Pharmacy, US Post Office, Echo Res Rec Area
(166)		Scenic Area (Both dir)
(168)		Jct I-84, W to Ogden, E to Cheyenne
169		Echo Dam Rd, Echo
(170)		Welcome Center (WB) REST AREA (EB) (RR, Phones, Picnic, Vend, Info, RVDump)
178		Emory (WB)
(180)		Port of Entry / Weigh Station (WB)
185		Castle Rock
187		Ranch Exit

EXIT		UT / WI
191		Wahsatch Rd, Coalville
	NOTE:	MM 197: Wyoming State Line
		(MOUNTAIN TIME ZONE)
		⊙ UTAH
		⊙ WYOMING
		(MOUNTAIN TIME ZONE)
(1)		Old Utah Port of Entry (EB), Weigh Station (WB)
3		US 189, 30, Harrison Dr, Evanston
	TStop	N: Flying J Travel Plaza #5180 (Scales)
	Gas	N: Chevron◊, Phillips 66, Sinclair, Tesoro
		S: Phillips 66◊
	Food	N: Cookery/FJ TP, Burger King, JB's, KFC, Lottie's, Rest/BW
		S: KFC, McDonald's
	Lodg	N: Best Western, Comfort Inn, Country Inn, Days Inn, Economy Inn♥, Holiday Inn Express, Howard Johnson
	Med	N: + Hospital
	Other	N: Laundry/WiFi/FJ TP, Golf Course
		S: Tires
5		WY 89N, WY 150S, Front St, Downtown Evanston
	Gas	N: Chevron◊, Maverik, Sinclair
	Food	N: Arby's, Dragon Wall Chinese, McDonald's, Sonic, Subway
	Lodg	N: Super 8
	Med	N: + Hospital
		S: + WY State Mental Hospital
	Other	N: AutoZone, CarWash, Family Dollar, NAPA, Wal-Mart sc▲
6		I-80 Bus, US 189, WY 89, Bear River Dr, Evanston
	S:	WY Welcome Center (SB) (RR, Phones, Picnic, Info, RVDump)
	TStop	N: Pilot Travel Center #141 (Scales), Sinclair Truck Stop
	Food	N: Subway/Pilot TC, Kelly's Roadhouse Grill, Mexican Rest
	Lodg	N: Best Value Inn, Evanston Inn, Holiday Inn Express, Prairie Inn, Motel 6♥
	Other	N: Laundry/WiFi/Pilot TC, Laundry/Sinclair, CarQuest, Goodyear, Grocery, Racetrack, Bear River State Park, Bear River RV Park▲, Philips RV Park▲
10		Painter Rd, CR 180
13		Divide Rd
(14)		Parking Area (Both dir)
15		Guild Rd (EB)

EXIT		WYOMING
18		US 189, CR 181, Kemmerer
21		Coal Rd
23		Bar Hat Rd
24		CR 141, CR 173, Leroy Rd
(28)		Parking Area (Both dir)
28		French Rd
30		Bigelow Rd, Fort Bridger
	TStop	N: Travel Center of America #188/ Tesoro (Scales)
	Food	N: ForkinRoad/BurgerKing/TacoBell/TA TC
	TServ	N: TA TC/Tires
	Other	N: Laundry/WiFi/TA TC
33		Union Rd
34		I-80 Bus Loop, to Fort Bridger
	Gas	S: Phillips 66
	Lodg	S: Wagon Wheel Café & Motel
	Other	S: Fort Bridger RV Campground▲
39		WY 412N WY 414S, Lyman, to Carter Mountain View
41		WY 413, Lyman
	S:	Rest Area (Both dir) (RR, Phones, Picnic)
	TStop	N: Gas n Go #15
	Food	N: Rest/FastFood/GasnGo, Cowboy Café, Taco Time
	Lodg	N: Gateway Inn
	TServ	N: GasNGo/Tires
	Other	S: Lyman KOA▲
48		I-80 Bus, Lyman, Fort Bridger
53		Church Butte Rd
(60)		Parking Area (Both dir)
61		WY 374, Cedar Mountain Rd, to Granger
66		US 30, Kemmerer, Pocatello
68		WY 374E, Little America
	FStop	N: AmBest/Little America Fuel Center/ Sinclair (Scales)
	Food	N: Rest/Little America TC
	Lodg	N: Motel/LA TC
	TServ	N: LA TC/Tires
	Other	N: Laundry/RVDump/LP/LA TC, Camp▲
(71)		Parking Area (Both dir)
72		Westvaco Rd, to WY 374, McKinnon
83		WY 372, LaBarge Rd
85		Covered Wagon Rd, Green River

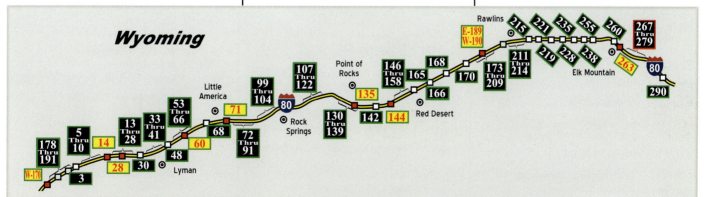

◊ = Regular Gas Stations with Diesel   ▲ = RV Friendly Locations   ♥ = Pet Friendly Locations

RED PRINT SHOWS LARGE VEHICLE PARKING/ACCESS ON SITE OR NEARBY   BROWN PRINT SHOWS CAMPGROUNDS/RV PARKS

Page 373

EXIT		WYOMING
89		US 30 Bus, Green River
	Gas	S: Sinclair
	Food	S: McDonald's, Pizza Hut, Ponderosa
	Lodg	S: Super 8, Walker Motel, Western Motel
	Other	S: RV Service
91		I-80 Bus, US 30, to WY 530 (Services same as Exit #89)
99		US 191, WY 373, East Flaming Gorge Rd, Rock Springs
	FStop	S: Cruel Jack's Travel Plaza/Conoco
	Food	S: Rest/Cruel Jack's TP
	Other	S: Laundry/Cruel Jack's TP
102		I-80 Bus, US 30 Bus, Dewar Dr, to WY 376, WY 430, Rock Springs
	Gas	N: Exxon, Sinclair◇
		S: Mobil◇
	Food	N: Applebee's, Denny's, Pam's BBQ, Sizzler
		S: Arby's, Burger King, IHOP, JB's, Pizza Hut, Quiznos, Sizzler, Subway, Village Inn, Wendy's
	Lodg	N: Best Value Inn, Motel 6♥, La Quinta Inn♥, Ramada Ltd, The Inn at Rock Springs
		S: Budget Inn, Comfort Inn, Hampton Inn, Motel 8, Quality Inn
	Med	S: + Hospital
	Other	N: Auto Dealers, Grocery, Home Depot, Harley Davidson, Kmart, RV Dealer,
		S: Albertson's, AutoZone, Wal-Mart sc, Walgreen's
103		College Dr, Rock Springs
	Gas	S: Conoco
	Med	S: + Hospital
	Other	S: Western WY Comm College
104		US 191N, Elk St, Rock Springs
	TStop	N: Flying J Travel Plaza #5017/Conoco (Scales), Outlaw Sinclair
	Gas	N: Exxon, Shell
		S: Exxon◇
	Food	N: Thad's/FastFood/FJ TP, McDonald's, BurgerKing/Sinclair, TacoTime
	Lodg	N: Best Western, Econo Lodge
		S: Days Inn
	TServ	N: Cummins Intermountain
	Other	N: Laundry/WiFi/RVDump/LP/FJ TP, Laundry/Sinclair, Auto Dealers, Grocery
107		I-80 Bus, US 30, WY 376, WY 430, Rock Springs, Pilot Butte Ave
	Gas	N: Mobil◇, Phillips 66◇
	Lodg	S: Springs Motel
111		Baxter Rd
	Other	S: Rock Springs Sweetwater Co Airport✈
122		WY 371, to Superior
130		Point of Rocks
	Gas	N: Conoco◇
	Food	N: Rest/Conoco
(135)		Parking Area (Both dir)
136		Black Butte Rd
139		Red Hill Rd
142		Bitter Creek Rd
(144)		Rest Area (Both dir) (RR, Phones, Picnic) (Next RA 102mi)
146		Patrick Draw Rd
150		Table Rock Rd, Wamsutter
	Gas	S: Major/Sinclair◇

Personal Notes

EXIT		WYOMING
152		Bar X Rd
154		B L M Rd
156		G L Rd
158		Tipton Rd
165		Red Desert
	Gas	S: Saveway Gen'l Store
166		Booster Rd
168		Frewen Rd, Wamsutter
170		Rasmussen Rd
173		Wamsutter Crooks Gap Rd, CR 23, Wamsutter
	FStop	S: Wamsutter Conoco
	TStop	N: Love's Travel Stop #310 (Scales), Sinclair Fuel Stop
		S: Phillips 66 Travel Center
	Food	N: Chester/Subway/Love's TS, FastFood/Sinclair TS
		S: Rest/FastFood/P66 TC
	Lodg	S: Sagebrush Motel
	TServ	N: Sinclair TS/Tires
		S: Wamsutter Conoco/Tires
	Other	N: WiFi/RVDump/Love's TS
		S: Laundry/P66 TC
184		Continental Divide Rd
187		WY 789S, Baggs Rd, Wamsutter
(189)		Parking Area (EB)
(190)		Parking Area (WB)
196		Riner Rd

EXIT		WYOMING
201		Daley Rd
204		Knobs Rd, Rawlins
206		Hadsell Rd
209		Johnson Rd, Rawlins
	TStop	N: Flying J Travel Plaza #5040/ (Scales)
	Food	N: Cookery/FastFood/FJ TP
	Other	N: Laundry/WiFi/RVDump/LP/FJ TP
(211)		Weigh Station (WB)
211		I-80 Bus, US 30 Bus, to WY 789N, Spruce St, Rawlins
	FStop	N: West End Sinclair
	Gas	N: Conoco◇, Exxon◇, Phillips 66
	Food	N: JB's, Rest/BW
	Lodg	N: Best Western, Golden West Motel, Rawlins Motel, Super 8, Sunset Motel
	Med	N: + Hospital
	Other	N: RV Center, Rawlins KOA▲
214		WY 78, Higley Blvd, Rawlins
	TStop	S: Travel Center of America #234/Shell (Scales)
	Food	S: CountryFare/Subway/TA TC
	Lodg	S: Motel/TA TC
	TServ	S: TA TC/Tires
	Other	S: Laundry/RVDump/TA TC
215		I-80 Bus, US 30 Bus, US 287 BypP, Cedar St, Rawlins
	Gas	N: Conoco◇, Phillips 66, Shell, Sinclair
	Food	N: McDonald's, Pizza Hut, Subway
	Lodg	N: Days Inn, First Choice Inn, Holiday Inn Express, Quality Inn
	TServ	N: Truck & Radiator Repair
	Other	N: Auto Dealers, CarQuest, Grocery, Rawlins KOA▲
219		Lincoln Ave, W Sinclair
221		WY 76, E Sinclair
	FStop	N: I-80 Travel Plaza/66
	Food	N: Rest/I-80 TP
228		Fort Steele Rd
	N:	Rest Area (Both dir) (RR, Phones, Picnic)
235		US 30E, US 287S, WY 130E, Hanna, Walcott, Saratoga
	FStop	N: Shell
	Food	N: Café/Shell
238		Peterson Rd
255		WY 72, Hanna, Elk Mountain
	Gas	N: Conoco
260		CR 402, Elk Mtn Medicine Bow Rd
(262)		Parking Area (Both dir)
267		Wagonhound Rd
	S:	Rest Area (Both dir) (RR, Phones, Picnic)
272		WY 13N, to Arlington
	Gas	N: Exxon
279		Cooper Cove Rd, Dutton Creek Rd
290		CR 59, Quealy Dome Rd, Laramie
	TStop	S: Sinclair
	Food	S: FastFood/Sinclair
	TServ	S: Sinclair
	Other	S: Laundry/Sinclair
297		WY 12, Herrick Lane

Page 374   ◇ = Regular Gas Stations with Diesel   ▲ = RV Friendly Locations   ♥ = Pet Friendly Locations
RED PRINT SHOWS LARGE VEHICLE PARKING/ACCESS ON SITE OR NEARBY   BROWN PRINT SHOWS CAMPGROUNDS/RV PARKS

EXIT	WYOMING	EXIT	WYOMING	EXIT	WY / NE
310	CR 322, Curtis St, N Laramie	335	Buford Rd, Laramie	Other	N: Laundry/RVDump/Cheyenne TP, Laundry/Pilot TC, Cheyenne KOA▲
TStop	N: Pilot Travel Center #308 (Scales), Valero #4552	FStop	S: 24 Hr Gas & Diesel	370	US 30, Field Station Rd, to Archer
	S: Petro Stopping Center #3 (Scales)	Food	S: Rest/24Hr G&D	TStop	N: Sapp Bros (Scales)
Food	N: Wendy's/Pilot SC, Café/Valero,	339	Remount Rd	Food	N: Rest/Sapp Bros TS
	S: IronSkillet/Petro SC	(341)	Parking Area (Both dir)	Lodg	N: Big G Motel/Sapp Bros TS
Lodg	N: Days Inn, Econo Lodge, Holiday Inn Express, Motel 8, Quality Inn, Super 8	342	Harriman Rd	TServ	N: Sapp Bros TS/Tires
	S: AmeriHost Inn	(344)	Parking Area (Both dir)	Other	N: Laundry/WiFi/Sapp Bros TS
TWash	N: Pilot TC	345	Warren Rd, Cheyenne	(371)	Port of Entry/Check Station (WB)
	S: Blue Beacon TW/Petro SC	348	Otto Rd	377	WY 217, Hillsdale Rd, Cheyenne, Hillsdale
TServ	N: Petro SC/Tires	358	I-80 Bus, US 30, WY 225, Otto Rd, W Lincolnway, Cheyenne	TStop	N: Travel Center of America #187/Amoco (Scales)
Med	N: + Hospital	TStop	N: AmBest/Little America Travel Center, Big D Truck Stop/Conoco	Food	N: Buckhorn/BurgerKing/TacoBell/TA TC
Other	N: Laundry/WiFi/Pilot TC, Grocery		(WB: Access via Ex #359)	Lodg	N: Motel/TA TC
	S: Laundry/WiFi/Petro SC, Laramie KOA▲	Food	N: Rest/Little America TC, Rest/FastFood	TServ	N: TA TC/Tires
311	WY 130, WY 230, Snowy Range Rd, Laramie, Snowy Range		Big D TS, Denny's, Outback Steakhouse, Pizza Inn, Village Inn	Other	N: Laundry/WiFi/TA TC, WY RV Park & Campground▲
FStop	S: High Country Sportsman/Sinclair	Lodg	N: Motel/Little America TC, Days Inn, Econo Lodge, Hampton Inn, La Quinta Inn♥, Luxury Inn, Motel 6♥, Super 8, Wyoming Motel	386	US 30, WY 213, WY 214, Burns, Carpenter
Gas	S: Conoco◊, Phillips 66◊			TStop	N: Antelope Truck Stop
Food	S: McDonald's, Subway			Food	N: Rest/Antelope TS
Lodg	S: Best Value Inn, Howard Johnson, Travel Inn	Med	N: + Hospital	Other	N: Laundry/Antelope TS
Other	S: Laundry/LP/RVDump/High Country Sportsman, RV Center, Ski Area, Univ of WY	Other	N: Laundry/WiFi/LP/Big D TS, Home Depot	391	Egbert South Rd, Burns
		(359A)	Jct I-25S, US 87S, to Denver	401	I-80 Bus, US 30 Bus, WY 215, Pine Bluffs
313	US 287, 3rd St, Laramie	(359C)	Jct I-25N, US 87N, to Casper	S:	WY Welcome Center (Both dir) (RR, Phones, Picnic, Info)
N:	Port of Entry	(362)	Jct I-180, US 85, Central Ave, Cheyenne, to Greeley, CO	TStop	N: AmPride/Cenex, RaceTrac
Gas	N: Conoco◊, Exxon, Phillips 66, Shell◊	FStop	S: Diamond Shamrock #4550	Gas	N: Sinclair
Food	N: Burger King, Denny's, Great Wall Chinese, McDonald's, Village Inn	Gas	S: Conoco◊, Safeway	Food	N: FastFood/AmPride, Rest/FastFood/RaceTrac
Lodg	N: First Inn Gold, Sunset Inn, Motel 8	Food	N: Arby's, Applebee's, Golden Corral, Hardee's	Lodg	N: Gater's Travel & Motel
	S: Holiday Inn, Motel 6♥, Ramada		S: Subway/Conoco, Burger King, Sonic, Taco John	TServ	N: AmPride TS
Med	N: + Ivinson Memorial Hospital	Lodg	N: Lariat Motel	Other	N: Auto Repair/Sinclair, US Post Office, Pine Bluff RV Park▲
316	I-80 Bus, US 30, Grand Ave, Laramie		S: Holiday Inn, Round Up Motel	NOTE:	MM 402: Nebraska State Line
Gas	N: Conoco◊, Albertson's	TServ	N: Cheyenne Truck Center		⊙ WYOMING
Food	N: Applebee's, Arby's, Burger King, Hong Kong Buffet, JB's, McDonald's, Taco Bell, Taco John's, Wendy's	Med	S: + Hospital		⊙ NEBRASKA
Lodg	N: Comfort Inn, Sleep Inn	Other	N: Greyhound		(MOUNTAIN TIME ZONE)
Med	N: + Ivinson Memorial Hospital		S: Safeway	1	NE 53B, State Line Rd, Bushnell
Other	N: Albertson's, Wal-Mart sc, Univ of WY	364	I-80 Bus, WY 212, S College Dr, E Lincolnway, Cheyenne	8	NE 53C, CR 17, to Bushnell
NOTE:	MM 317: EB: 5% Steep Grade for 6 mi	Gas	N: Shell	(10)	Kimball Rest Area (EB) (RR, Phones, Picnic, Info)
(322)	Chain-Up Area (Both dir)	Food	N: Burger King, Chili's, IHOP, McDonald's, Papa John's, Pizza Hut, Taco Bell	(18)	Weigh Station (EB)
323	WY 210, Happy Jack Rd, Laramie	Lodg	N: Cheyenne Motel, Fleetwood Motel	20	NE 71, S Chestnut St, Kimball
NOTE:	Highest Elev point on I-80	Med	N: + Hospital	FStop	N: Travel Shop/Sinclair
N:	Rest Area (Both dir) (RR, Phones, Picnic)	Other	N: AutoZone, Grocery	Food	N: Pizza Hut, Subway
329	Vedauwoo Rd	367	Campstool Rd, Cheyenne		S: Burger King
(333)	Parking Area (Both dir)	TStop	N: Cheyenne Travel Plaza/Sinclair, Pilot Travel Center #402 (Scales)		
		Food	N: Arby's/Sinclair, Subway/Pilot TC		

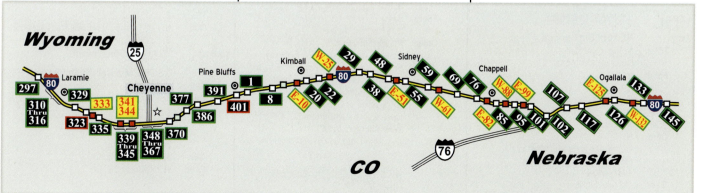

◊ = Regular Gas Stations with Diesel   ▲ = RV Friendly Locations   ♥ = Pet Friendly Locations
RED PRINT SHOWS LARGE VEHICLE PARKING/ACCESS ON SITE OR NEARBY   BROWN PRINT SHOWS CAMPGROUNDS/RV PARKS

INTERSTATE 80 W/E

EXIT		NEBRASKA
	Lodg	N: Best Value Inn, Days Inn, First Interstate Inn, Super 8
	Med	S: + Hospital
	Other	S: Twin Pines RV Park▲, Kimball Muni Airport✈
22		NE 53E, Kimball, East Entrance
	Other	N: Kimball KOA▲
(25)		Kimball Rest Area (WB) (RR, Phones, Picnic)
29		NE 53A, Dix
38		NE 17B, Potter
	Gas	N: Cenex◊, Shell
48		NE 17C, Sidney, to Brownson
(51)		Sidney Rest Area (EB) (RR, Phones, Picnic, Observation Area)
55		I-80 Bus, NE 19, Sidney (Serv 3mi N in Sidney)
59		I-80 Bus, NE 17J, to US 30, US 385, Sidney, Bridgeport
	TStop	N: Sapp Bros Travel Center/Shell US 385
	Gas	N: Conoco◊ S: BP◊, Phillips 66
	Food	N: FastFood/Sapp Bros, KFC/TacoBell/Conoco, Arby's, McDonald's, Perkins, Quiznos, Runza Rest, Taco John
	Lodg	N: AmericInn, Comfort Inn, Days Inn, Motel 6♥, Super 8 S: Holiday Inn
	TWash	S: Sauder
	TServ	S: Sauder
	Other	N: WiFi/Sapp Bros, ATMs, Wal-Mart sc, Bear Family RV Park▲, RV Center, Cabela's/RVDump S: Sidney Muni Airport✈
(61)		Sidney Rest Area (WB) (RR, Phones, Picnic)
69		NE 17E, to Sunol
76		NE 17F, to Lodgepole
(82)		Chappell Rest Area (EB) (RR, Phones, Picnic)
85		NE 25A, Chappell
	Gas	N: AmPride
	Other	N: US Post Office, Billy G Ray Field✈, Creekside RV Park▲
(88)		Chappell Rest Area (WB) (RR, Phones, Picnic)
95		NE 27, Julesburg, Oshkosh
(99)		Scenic View (EB)
101		US 138, Big Springs, Julesburg
(102)		Jct I-76S, to Denver
107		NE 25B, Big Springs
	TStop	N: Bosselman Travel Center/Pilot #904/Sinclair (Scales), Total #4419
	Food	N: GrandmaMax/LittleCaesars/Subway/Bosselman TC
	Lodg	N: Best Value Inn
	TWash	N: Bosselman TC
	TServ	N: Bosselman TC/Tires
	Other	N: Laundry/WiFi/Bosselman TC, Laundry/Total, to appr 25mi Lake McConaughy, Eagle Canyon Hideaway▲

EXIT		NEBRASKA
117		NE 51A, Brule
	TStop	N: Happy Jack/Sinclair
	Food	N: FastFood/Happy Jack
	Other	N: Laundry/RVDump/Park▲/HappyJack
(125)		Ogallah Rest Area (EB) (RR, Phones, Picnic, Info)
126		US 26, NE 61, Ogallala, Grant
	TStop	N: Sapp Bros Travel Center/Shell S: Travel Center of America #90/76 (Scales)
	Gas	N: BP, Phillips 66◊, Sinclair, Texaco S: Conoco◊, Phillips 66
	Food	N: Deli/Sapp Bros TC, Arby's, Burger King, Country Kitchen, McDonald's, Pizza Hut, Taco John, Valentino's S: CountryPride/TA TC, KFC, Panda Chinese, Wendy's
	Lodg	N: Best Western, Days Inn, Holiday Inn Express, Plaza Inn S: Comfort Inn, Econo Lodge♥, Super 8
	TServ	S: TA TC/Tires
	Med	N: + Hospital
	Other	N: WiFi/Sapp Bros TC, ATM, Dollar General, Greyhound, NAPA, Safeway, Scottsbluff/Chimney Rock KOA▲, to appr 25mi Lake McConaughy, Eagle Canyon Hideaway▲ S: Laundry/WiFi/RVDump/TA TC, Open Corral Campground▲, Country View Campground▲
(132)		Ogallala Rest Area (WB) (RR, Phones, Picnic, Info)
133		NE 51B, Ogallala, to Roscoe

EXIT		NEBRASKA
145		NE 51C, Paxton Elsie Rd S, Paxton
	Gas	N: Texaco◊/Ole's
	Food	N: Ole's Big Game Steakhouse & Lounge
	Lodg	N: Ole's Lodge/Paxton Days Inn/Ole's RV Park & Campground▲
	NOTE:	MM 149: Central / Mountain Time Zone
158		NE 25, Sutherland, Wallace
	Gas	N: Ozzie's General Store S: Sinclair
(160)		Sutherland Rest Area (Both dir) (RR, Phones, Picnic) (WB: Historical Site Oregon Trail)
164		NE 56C, Dickens Rd, Hershey
	TStop	N: Western Convenience Truck Stop (Scales)
	Gas	N: KwikStop
	Food	N: Rest/Western Conv TS
	Other	N: Laundry/RVDump/Western Conv TS
177		US 83, North Platte, McCook
	Gas	N: BP, Conoco◊, Shell◊, Sinclair◊ S: Phillips 66, Shell
	Food	N: Applebee's, Arby's, Burger King, DQ, McDonald's, Quiznos, Rogers Diner, Subway, Village Inn, Wendy's, Whiskey Creek Steakhouse S: Taco Bell/Conoco, Rest/Shell, Bud's Steakhouse, Country Kitchen, Mi Ranchito, Perkins
	Lodg	N: Best Western, Hampton Inn, Hospitality Inn, Motel 6♥, Oak Tree Inn, Quality Inn S: Comfort Inn, Days Inn, Holiday Inn Express, Ramada, Super 8
	TServ	N: High Plains Power Systems S: Mid America Diesel, Herbst Towing & Repair, Truck & Trailer Repair
	Med	N: + Great Plains Regional Medical
	Other	N: ATMs, AdvanceAuto, Auto Services, Banks, Goodyear, Grocery, Laundromat, Staples, Wal-Mart sc♥, UPS Store, Mall, Towing, Carmike Mall Cinemas, Budkes Harley Davidson, Mid Plains Tech College, Ft Cody Trading Post, Cody Go-Karts Rides & Games, Holiday Trav-L/Holiday RV Park & Campground▲, NE State Hwy Patrol Post, to Buffalo Bill's Ranch, Buffalo Bill State Rec Area, RV Repair S: Auto Dealers, Kmart, to Lake Maloney State Rec Area
179		NE 56G, to US 30, to N Platte
	TStop	S: Flying J Travel Plaza #5059/Conoco (Scales)
	Gas	N: Casey's, Sinclair
	Food	S: CountryMarket/FastFood/FJ TP
	Lodg	S: La Quinta Inn♥
	TWash	S: Red Arrow Truck & RV Wash
	TServ	S: Boss Truck Shop
	Other	N: Golf Course, to N Platte Reg'l Airport✈ S: Laundry/WiFi/RVDump/LP/FJ TP
(182)		Weigh Station (Both dir)
190		NE 56A, Maxwell, Ft McPherson
	FStop	N: Ranchland C-Store/Sinclair
	Other	S: Ft McPherson Campground/RVDump▲
(194)		Brady Rest Area (Both dir) (RR, Phones, Picnic, Info)
199		NE 56D, Brady
	Gas	N: Brady One Stop
	Food	N: DQ/Brady OS

◊ = Regular Gas Stations with Diesel ▲ = RV Friendly Locations ♥ = Pet Friendly Locations
RED PRINT SHOWS LARGE VEHICLE PARKING/ACCESS ON SITE OR NEARBY   BROWN PRINT SHOWS CAMPGROUNDS/RV PARKS

EXIT	NEBRASKA
211	NE 47, S Lake Ave, Gothenburg
FStop	N: Plaza Shell
TStop	N: I-80 Pit Stop/Sinclair
Gas	S: Sinclair/KOA
Food	N: Rest/FastFood/I-80 Pit Stop, McDonald's, Pizza Hut, Runza Rest
Lodg	N: Pony Express Inn, Super 8♥, Travel Inn
Med	N: + Gothenburg Memorial Hospital
Other	N: Auto Services, Auto Dealers, Museum, to Quinn Field✈
	S: Gothenburg KOA▲
222	NE 21, NE 22, S Meridian Ave, Cozad
FStop	N: Gas N Shop/66
Gas	N: BP, Sinclair
Food	N: Burger King, DQ, Pizza Hut, Subway
Lodg	N: Budget Host Circle S Motel
	S: Motel 6♥
Other	N: Cozad Muni Airport✈
(226)	Cozad Rest Area (EB) (RR, Phones, Picnic)
(227)	Cozad Rest Area (WB) (RR, Phones, Picnic)
231	NE 24A, Rd 428, Lexington
Other	S: Exit 231 Truck Wash
237	US 283, Plum Creek Pkwy, Lexington, Arapahoe, Elwood
FStop	N: AmPride
TStop	S: NebraskaLand Tire Truck Center/Sinclair
Gas	N: Conoco, Phillips 66◊
Food	N: Amigo's, Arby's, Burger King, KFC, McDonald's, Pizza Hut, Wendy's
	S: Rest/Nebraskaland
Lodg	N: Comfort Inn, Days Inn, First Interstate Inn, Holiday Inn Express, Minuteman Motel
	S: Super 8
TServ	S: NebraskaLand/Tires
Other	N: ATMs, AdvanceAuto, Dollar General, Goodyear, Grocery, Wal-Mart sc▲, to Jim Kelly Field✈
	S: Laundry/NebraskaLand
248	NE 24B, Rd 444, Overton
TStop	N: Mian Bros Travel Center/BPAmoco
Food	N: Rest/MB TC
Other	N: Laundry/MB TC
257	US 183, Elm Creek, Holdrege
TStop	N: Bosselman Travel Center/Pilot #901/Sinclair (Scales)
Food	N: LittleCaesars/Subway/TacoExpress/Bosselman TC
Lodg	N: First Interstate Inn
Other	N: Laundry/WiFi/Bosselman TC, Sunny Meadows Campground▲

EXIT	NEBRASKA
263	NE 10B, Odessa Rd, Odessa
TStop	N: Sapp Bros Travel Center/Shell
Food	N: Rest/Deli/Sapp Bros TC
Lodg	S: to Lakeside Motel & RV Park▲
TServ	N: Sapp Bros TC/Tires
Other	N: Laundry/WiFi/LP/Sapp Bros TC
	S: Union Pacific State Rec Area
(269)	Kearney Rest Area (EB) (RR, Phones, Picnic, Info, Fishing)
(271)	Kearney Rest Area (WB) (RR, Phones, Picnic, Info, Fishing)
272	NE 44, 2nd Ave, Kearney, Axtell
Gas	N: Phillips 66◊, Shamrock, Shell◊
	S: BP, Shamrock◊
Food	N: Amigo's, Arby's, Burger King, DQ, Country Kitchen, McDonald's, Perkins, Pizza Hut, Red Lobster, Runza Rest, Taco Bell, Valentino's, Wendy's, USA Steak Buffet, Whiskey Creek Wood Fire Grill, Rest/Hol Inn, Rest/Ramada
	S: Grandpa's Steakhouse, Skeeter's BBQ
Lodg	N: AmericInn, Best Western, Comfort Inn, Country Inn, Days Inn, Fairfield Inn, Hampton Inn, Holiday Inn, Ramada, Super 8, Western Inn, Wingate, Cranewood Country Inn & RV Park▲
	S: Fort Kearney Inn, Holiday Inn Express
Med	N: + Good Samaritan Hospital
TServ	N: Cummins Great Plains
Other	N: ATM, Auto Dealers, Banks, Goodyear, Grocery, Office Max, UPS Store, Vet♥, to Hilltop Mall, Wal-Mart sc▲, Fairgrounds, Univ of NE/Kearney, Clyde & Vi's Campground▲
	S: Fort Kearney Historical Park▲
279	NE 10, Gibbon, Minden
FStop	S: Ft Kearney Trading Post/Shell
Other	N: to Kearney Muni Airport✈
	S: to appr 12mi S: Pioneer Village Rest/Motel/Campground▲
285	NE 10C, Lowell Rd, Gibbon
Gas	N: Petro Oasis
Lodg	S: Country Inn
Other	N: Windmill State Park▲
291	NE 10D, Shelton
Other	N: War Axe State Park
300	NE 11, 40D Spur, Wood River
TStop	S: Bosselman Travel Center/Pilot #912/Sinclair (Scales)
Food	S: GrandmaMax/Subway/Bosselman FS
Lodg	S: Laundry/WiFi/Bosselman FS, Wood River Motel & Campground▲

EXIT	NEBRASKA
305	NE 40C, 80th Rd, CR 26, Alda Rd, Wood River, Alda, Junita
	Rest Area (WB) (RR, Phones, Picnic)
FStop	N: Gas N Shop #33/Sinclair
TStop	N: Travel Center of America #193 (Scales)
Food	N: CountryPride/TA TC
TServ	N: TA TC/Tires
Other	N: Laundry/WiFi/RVDump/TA TC, RVDump/GasNShop
312	US 34, US 281, Alda, to Grand Island, Hastings, Doniphan (N Serv are appr 5mi N)
TStop	N: Bosselman Travel Center/Pilot #902/Sinclair (Scales)
Gas	N: Phillips 66
	S: BP
Food	N: GrandmaMax/Subway/TacoExpress/Bosselman TC
	S: Rest/USA Inn, 9 Bridges Family Rest
Lodg	N: Holiday Inn Express, Holiday Inn
	S: USA Inn
TWash	N: Diamond TW
TServ	N: Graham Tire, Boss Truck Shop
	S: High Plains Power Systems, NE Truck Center, Peterbilt
Med	N: + Hospital
Other	N: Laundry/WiFi/RVDump/Bosselman TC, Morman Island State Rec Area, to Rich & Son's Camper Sales/RVDump, to Sam's Club, Central Reg'l NE Airport✈, to US 34E/Wal-Mart sc▲
	S: to appr 15mi Hastings Campground▲
314	Locust St, Grand Island
(315)	Grand Island Rest Area (EB) (RR, Phones, Picnic, Vend, Info, Fishing)
(317)	Grand Island Rest Area (WB) (RR, Phones, Picnic, Vend, Info)
318	NE 2, to US 34, Grand Island
Other	S: Grand Island KOA▲
324	NE 41B, Giltner Spur, to Giltner
332	NE 14, Aurora
TStop	S: Love's Travel Stop #309 (Scales), Fast Fuel #2/Sinclair
Gas	N: Casey's, Shell◊
Food	N: McDonald's, Pappy Jack's, Subway, Rest/Hamilton Motor Inn
	S: Arby's/Love's TS
Lodg	N: Hamilton Motor Inn
Other	N: City Park/Streeter Park/RVDump
	S: WiFi/RVDump/Love's TS, Laundry/FastFuel

◊ = Regular Gas Stations with Diesel   ▲ = RV Friendly Locations   ♥ = Pet Friendly Locations

RED PRINT SHOWS LARGE VEHICLE PARKING/ACCESS ON SITE OR NEARBY   BROWN PRINT SHOWS CAMPGROUNDS/RV PARKS

EXIT		NEBRASKA
338		NE 41D, Aurora, Hampton
342		NE 93A, Rd B, Henderson, Sulton
	TStop	S: Fuel Mart #791
	Food	S: FastFood/Fuel Mart
	Lodg	S: First Interstate Inn
	Other	N: Prairie Oasis RV Park & Campground▲
348		NE 93E, York, to Bradshaw
(350)		York Rest Area (EB) (RR, Phones, Picnic, Vend, Info)
353		US 81, York, Geneva
	TStop	N: Sapp Bros/Sinclair (Scales)
		S: Crossroads Fuel Stop/Shell, Petro Stopping Center #62/66 (Scales)
	Gas	N: BP◊, Shell◊
	Food	N: Subway/Sapp Bros, Amigo's, Arby's, Burger King, Country Kitchen, KFC, McDonald's, Wendy's
		S: Rest/FastFood/Crossroads FS, IronSkillet/PizzaHut/Petro SC, Applebee's, Chris's Steak House/USA Inns
	Lodg	N: Best Western, Comfort Inn, Days Inn, Quality Inn, Super 8, Y Motel & RV Park▲
		S: Holiday Inn Int'l, USA Inn
	TWash	S: Blue Beacon TW/Petro SC
	TServ	S: Petro SC/Tires
	Other	N: Laundry/WiFi/Sapp Bros, Auto Dealers, ATMs, Wal-Mart sc▲, to York Muni Airport✈
		S: WiFi/Crossroads FS, Laundry/WiFi/RVDump/LP/Petro SC
(355)		York Rest Area (WB) (RR, Picnic, Phone, Vend, Info)
360		NE 93B, York, to Waco, Exeter
	TStop	N: Fuel Mart #642
	Food	N: Rest/Fuel Mart
	Other	S: Double Nickel Campground▲
366		NE 80F, CR 462, Beaver Crossing, to Utica
369		NE 80E, CR 420, Beaver Crossing
373		NE 80G, CR 364, Goehner
	Gas	N: Sinclair
(376)		Goehner Rest Area (WB) (RR, Phones, Picnic, Vend)
379		NE 15, Seward, Fairbury
	Gas	N: Phillips 66
		S: Shell◊
	Food	N: McDonald's
	Lodg	N: Super 8
	Med	N: + Hospital
	Other	N: Wal-Mart sc▲
(381)		Blue River Rest Area (EB) (RR, Phones, Picnic, Vend)
382		Matzke Hwy, to US 34, Seward, to US 6, Milford
	Other	N: to Branched Oak Lake State Rec Area▲
388		NE 103, CR 154, Crete
	Other	N: Pawnee Lake State Rec Area▲
395		US 6, NW 48th St, Lincoln
	TStop	S: AmBest/Shoemaker'sTruck Station/Shell (Scales)
	Gas	N: Sinclair
	Food	N: Runza Rest
		S: Cafe/Shoemaker's TS

Personal Notes

EXIT		NEBRASKA
	Lodg	S: Motel/Shoemaker's TS, Cobbler Inn, Shoney's Inn, Super 8, Travelodge
	TWash	S: Shoemaker's TS
	TServ	S: Shoemaker's TS/Tires, Freightliner
	Other	N: NE State Hwy Patrol Post
		S: Laundry/Shoemaker's TS
396		US 6, W O St, Lincoln (EB)
	Gas	S: GasNShop◊
	Food	S: Blimpie, Mexican Rest,
	Lodg	S: Super 8, Travelodge
	TServ	S: High Plains Power Systems
397		US 77S, Lincoln, to Beatrice
	Gas	S: Conoco
	Lodg	S: Congress Inn Motel, Red Carpet Inn, Super 8, Travelodge
399		W Adams St, NW 12th St, Cornhusker Hwy, to I-180, Lincoln
	Gas	N: BP◊, Phillips 66
		S: Cenex
	Food	N: Denny's, McDonald's, Perkins, Quiznos
	Lodg	N: Best Western, Best Value Inn♥, Comfort Inn, Days Inn, Hampton Inn, Holiday Inn Express, Motel 6♥, Sleep Inn
		S: Econo Lodge, Inn 4 Less Motel
	TServ	S: Cornhusker International
	Other	N: Lincoln Muni Airport✈
		S: to Lincoln State Fairgrounds▲
(401)		I-180, US 34, to 9th St, Lincoln (EB)
	Other	S: Campaway RV Resort & Campground▲
(401A)		I-180, US 34E, to 9th St, Lincoln
401B		US 34W
403		27th St, Lincoln
	Gas	S: Conoco◊, Mobil, Phillips 66◊, Shell

EXIT		NEBRASKA
	Food	S: Wendy's/Conoco, Subway/P66, Applebee's, Arby's, Burger King, CiCi's, Cracker Barrel, DQ, Golden Corral, IHOP, McDonald's, Popeye's, Ruby Tuesday, Valentino's, Village Inn
	Lodg	S: AmericInn, Best Western♥, Baymont Inn, Comfort Suites, Country Inn, Fairfield Inn, Lincoln SettleInn♥, Microtel♥, Ramada Ltd, Red Roof Inn♥, Super 8
	Other	S: ATMs, Auto Dealers, Grocery, Home Depot, Sam's Club, Wal-Mart sc, to State Fairgrounds▲, Univ of NE East, Leach Camper Sales/RVDump
405		US 77, 56th St, Lincoln
	Gas	S: Conoco, Phillips 66
	Food	S: Misty's
	Lodg	S: Howard Johnson, Motel 6♥
409		US 6, Waverly, East Lincoln
(416)		Weigh Station (Both dir)
420		NE 63, 238th St, Greenwood, Ashland
	FStop	N: Speedy Mart/Shell
	TStop	N: Cubby's Greenwood Travel Plaza/Conoco (Scales)
	Food	N: Rest/Greenwood TP
		S: Corner Rest
	Lodg	S: Big Inn
	Other	N: Laundry/Greenwood TP, Pine Grove Campgrounds▲
(425)		Platte River Rest Area (EB) (RR, Phones, Picnic, Vend, Info)
426		Ashland, Mahoney State Park
	Other	N: to Eugene T Mahoney State Park/Lodge/Rest/Campground▲/Family Aquatic Center/Other Activities
(432)		Melia Hill Rest Area (WB) (RR, Phones, Picnic, Info)
432		US 6, NE 31, Gretna, Ashland
	TStop	S: Flying J Travel Plaza #5012/Conoco (Scales)
	Gas	N: Sinclair
	Food	N: McDonald's
		S: Cookery/FastFood/FJ TP
	Lodg	N: Super 8
	Other	N: Laundry/BarbSh/WiFi/RVDump/LP/FJ TP, NE Crossing Factory Outlet Stores, to appr 12 mi : W Omaha KOA▲
439		NE 370, Omaha, to Gretna, Bellevue
	Gas	N: Phillips 66◊
	Food	N: Blimpie, The Happy Chef
	Lodg	N: Days Inn, Suburban Inn
	Med	S: + Hospital
440		NE 50, S 144th St, Omaha, to Springfield, Louisville
	FStop	N: Wally's Place/Conoco
	TStop	N: Sapp Bros Travel Center/Shell (Scales)
	Gas	S: BP◊
	Food	N: Rest/Subway/Deli/Sapp Bros TC, Cracker Barrel, Hardee's, McDonald's, Subway
	Lodg	N: Ben Franklin Motel, Budget Inn, Comfort Inn♥, Days Inn, Quality Inn
	TWash	N: Classic TW
	TServ	N: Sapp Bros TC/Tires
	Med	N: + Hospital
	Other	N: Laundry/BarbSh/Massg/WiFi/Sapp Bros TC

◊ = Regular Gas Stations with Diesel ▲ = RV Friendly Locations ♥ = Pet Friendly Locations
RED PRINT SHOWS LARGE VEHICLE PARKING/ACCESS ON SITE OR NEARBY BROWN PRINT SHOWS CAMPGROUNDS/RV PARKS

EXIT	NEBRASKA
442	126th St, Harrison St, Omaha
Lodg	S: Hampton Inn
Other	N: Millard Airport✈
444	Q St, L St, Omaha
	(Access to Ex #445 Serv)
445	US 275, NE 92, I/L/Q St, Center Rd
Gas	N: Cenex◇
	S: Conoco◇, QT, Sinclair
Food	N: Austin's Steakhouse, NE Steak & Grill, Perkins, Village Inn
	S: Arby's, Burger King, Hardee's, Hong Kong Café, McDonald's, Long John Silver, Valentino's, Wendy's
Lodg	N: Clarion, Residence Inn, Sheraton
	S: Comfort Inn, Days Inn, Econo Lodge♥, Hampton Inn, Holiday Inn Express, Hawthorne Suites, Motel 6♥, La Quinta Inn♥, Super 8
Med	N: + Hospital
Other	N: Sam's Club, Wal-Mart sc, Lucent Tech, AC Nelsen RV World
	S: Albertson's, Goodyear
(446)	Jct I-680N, Downtown, to Boystown, Irvington
448	84th St, Papillion
Gas	N: BP, Shell
	S: Phillips 66◇, QT, Shell
Food	N: Arby's, Denny's, McDonald's, Subway, Taco Bell
	S: Wendy's
Lodg	N: Econo Lodge
Other	N: Goodyear, Grocery, NAPA
	S: Auto Dealers, CarQuest, Grocery, Tires, U-Haul
449	72nd St, La Vista, Ralston
Gas	N: BP
	S: Phillips 66◇
Food	N: Burger King, Perkins, Rest/Hol Inn
Lodg	N: Baymont Inn, Comfort Inn, DoubleTree, Hampton Inn, Holiday Inn, Homewood Suites, Howard Johnson, Quality Inn, Super 8, Travelodge
Med	N: + Hospital
TServ	S: Kenworth of Omaha
Other	N: College of St Mary, Golf Course
450	60th St, Omaha
Gas	N: Conoco, Phillips 66◇, Shell
	S: Phillips 66◇
Food	S: Country Kitchen
Lodg	S: Microtel, Relax Inn
TServ	S: Cummins Allison
Other	N: Univ of NE/Omaha
451	42nd St, Omaha
Gas	N: 76, Phillips 66, Texaco
	S: Phillips 66

EXIT	NE / IA
Food	S: Burger King, McDonald's, Taco Bell
Med	N: + Douglas Co Hospital
(452)	Jct I-480N, US 75N, US 75S
453	24th St (EB)
454	13th St, Omaha
Gas	N: BP◇, Shamrock
	S: Phillips 66◇
Food	N: Burger King, KFC, McDonald's
Lodg	N: Comfort Inn
Med	N: + St Joseph's Hospital
Other	N: to Omaha Botanical Gardens
	S: to IMAX, Rosenblatt Stadium, Zoo
NOTE:	MM 455: Iowa State Line
	(CENTRAL TIME ZONE)
	⊙ NEBRASKA
	⊙ IOWA
	(CENTRAL TIME ZONE)
(1A)	Jct I-29N, to Sioux City (EB, Left exit)
NOTE:	I-80 below runs with I-29. Exit #'s follow I-80.
1B	24th St, Council Bluffs
TStop	N: Pilot Travel Center #329 (Scales), Sapp Bros Travel Center/Shell (Scales)
Gas	N: Conoco, Sinclair
Food	N: Arby's/TJCinn/Pilot TC, Rest/BurgerKing/Sapp Bros TC
Lodg	N: American Inn, Best Western, Super 8
TWash	N: Blue Beacon TW/Sapp Bros TC
TServ	N: Sapp Bros/Tires, Peterbilt, Speedco
Other	N: Laundry/WiFi/Pilot TC, Laundry/WiFi/LP/Sapp Bros TC, Dog Track, Bluffs Run Casino, Mid America Center
3	IA 192N, S 4th St, S Expressway St, Council Bluffs, Lake Manawa
TStop	S: Travel Center of America #66 (Scales), Phillips 66
Gas	N: Casey's
Food	S: CountryPride/PizzaHut/TA TC, Applebee's, Burger King, Cracker Barrel, DQ, Golden Corral, Long John Silver, McDonald's, Perkins, Red Lobster, Subway, Taco Bell
Lodg	S: Days Inn, Fairfield Inn, Motel 6♥, Settle Inn
TWash	S: TruckOMat
TServ	S: TA TC/Tires
Other	S: Laundry/WiFi/TA TC, AdvanceAuto, Auto Dealers, Sam's Club, U-Haul, Wal-Mart▲, Lake Manawa State Park

EXIT	IOWA
(4)	Jct I-29S, to Kansas City (WB, Left ex)
NOTE:	I-80 above runs with I-29. Exit #'s follow I-80.
5	Madison Ave, Council Bluffs
Gas	N: AmocoBP
	S: Conoco, Shell
Food	N: Burger King, KFC, McDonald's, Pizza Hut, Subway
	S: DQ, Valentino's, Village Inn
Lodg	N: Heartland Inn
	S: Western Inn Motor Lodge♥
Other	N: ATMs, Grocery, Target, Walgreen's, Mall of the Bluffs
8	US 6, Kanesville Blvd, Council Bluffs, Oakland
Gas	N: Coastal, Fill & Food, Phillips 66
Other	N: IA Western Comm College
	S: IA State Hwy Patrol Post, to Council Bluffs Muni Airport✈
17	G30, Magnolia Rd, Underwood
TStop	N: Underwood Truck Stop/66
Food	N: Rest/Underwood TS, Rest/I-80 Inn
Lodg	N: I-80 Inn, Underwood Motel
TServ	N: A 1 Truck Repair
(19)	IA Welcome Center (EB) Rest Area (WB) (RR, Phone, Picnic, Vend, RVDump, WiFi, Weather)
23	IA 244, L55, 298th St, Neola
FStop	S: Kum & Go #23
Other	S: Arrowhead Park▲
(27)	Jct I-680W, to N Omaha, Sioux City (fr EB, Left exit)
29	L66, 335th St, Minden
Gas	S: Phillips 66◇
(32)	Parking Area (Both dir)
34	M16, 385th St, Avoca, Shelby
FStop	N: Taylor Quick-Pik/Shell
Food	N: Country Pizza, DQ/Shell
Lodg	N: Shelby Country Inn & RV Park▲
40	US 59, Avoca Ln, Avoca, Harlan
TStop	N: Wings America Travel Center/Conoco (Scales)
Gas	S: Shell◇
Food	N: Rest/FastFood/Wings Amer TC
	S: Embers, Parkway Café & Campground▲
Lodg	N: Motel 6♥
	S: Avoca Motel
TWash	N: Wings Amer TC

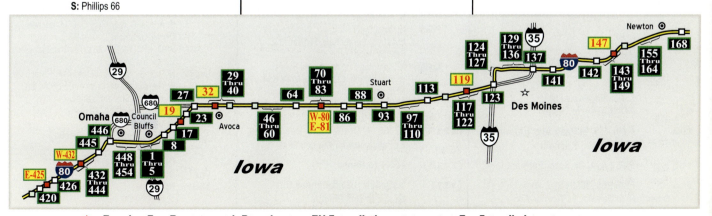

◇ = Regular Gas Stations with Diesel   ▲ = RV Friendly Locations   ♥ = Pet Friendly Locations
RED PRINT SHOWS LARGE VEHICLE PARKING/ACCESS ON SITE OR NEARBY   BROWN PRINT SHOWS CAMPGROUNDS/RV PARKS

EXIT		IOWA
	Med	N: + Hospital
	Other	N: Laundry/BarbSh/RVDump/LP/Wings Amer TC
		S: Parkway Café & Campground▲, Pottawattamie Co Fairgrounds▲
(44)		Weigh Station (Both dir)
46		M47, 505th St, Walnut Antique City Dr, Walnut
	FStop	S: Kum & Go #46
	Gas	S: BP
	Food	S: The Villager Rest, McDonald's
	Lodg	S: Red Carpet Inn & RV Park▲, Super 8, Antique City Inn B&B
	Other	N: to Prairie Rose State Park▲
51		M56, Marne
54		IA 173, Mame, Atlantic, Elk Horn, Kimballton (Serv appr 6mi N)
	Other	N: to Danish Windmill, Danish Museum
57		N16, Atlantic
	Med	S: + to Hospital
60		US 6W, US 71W, Atlantic, Villisca, Audubon
	TStop	S: Valley Oil Co/66
	Gas	S: Shamrock
	Food	S: Rest/P66
	Lodg	S: Days Inn
	TServ	S: Valley Oil/Tires
64		N28, Anita, to Wiota
70		IA 148, Anita, to Exira
	Other	S: to Lake Anita State Park▲
75		G30, Anita Adair Rd, Adair
76		N54, 5th St, Adair
	FStop	N: Kum & Go #76
	Gas	N: Amoco BP, Casey's◊
	Food	N: Happy Chef, Subway/Kum & Go
	Lodg	N: Budget Inn, Super 8
	Other	N: Auto Repair
(80)		Rest Area (WB) (RR, Phone, Picnic, Vend, RVDump, WiFi)
(81)		Rest Area (EB) (RR, Phone, Picnic, Vend, RVDump, WiFi)
83		N77, Antique County Dr, Casey
86		IA 25, to Guthrie Center, Greenfield
	Other	S: to Springbrook State Park▲
88		P20, Redwood Ave, Pinewood Ave, Casey, to Menlo
93		P28, Division St, to Stuart, Panora
	TStop	N: Prairie Dog Truck Travel Center/Conoco (Scales)
		S: Stuart 66 Truck Stop
	Gas	N: BP◊
	Food	N: FastFood/Prairie Dog TTC, Burger King, McDonald's, Subway
		S: Rest/Stuart TS, Country Kitchen
	Lodg	N: AmericInn♥, Super 8
		S: New Edgetowner Motel
97		P48, Casey, to Dexter
100		F 60, P53, El Paso Ave, Eldorado Ave, Dexter, Redfield
104		P57, I Ave, De Soto, Earlham
106		F90, P58, 360th St, L Ave
	Other	N: to Des Moines West KOA▲

Personal Notes

EXIT		IOWA
110		US 169, US 6, Desoto, Adel, Winterset
	Gas	S: Casey's, Kum & Go
	Lodg	S: De Soto Motor Inn, Edgetowner Motel
	Other	S: John Wayne Birthplace, Tourist Info, Covered Bridges of Madison Co
113		R16, Van Meter
(114)		Weigh Station (EB)
117		R2, Waukee, Booneville
	Gas	S: Kum & Go
	Food	S: Rube's Steakhouse
	Other	N: Timberline Campground▲
(119)		Rest Area (Both dir) (RR, Phone, Picnic, Vend, WiFi, RVDump)
121		74th St, Jordan Creek Pkwy, Waukee, W Des Moines
	Gas	N: BP, Hy-Vee
		S: Kum & Go
	Food	N: West Diner
		S: Arby's, Burger King, McDonald's, Perkins, Taco John
	Lodg	N: Hampton Inn, Hawthorne Suites
		S: Fairfield Inn, Quality Inn, Motel 6♥
	Other	N: Grocery, Home Depot, Target
122		60th St, W Des Moines (EB)
	Gas	S: Kum & Go
(123A)		I-235E, W Des Moines, Des Moines St Fairgrounds (EB, Left Exit)
(123B)		I-35S, to Kansas City
(123)		I-35/I-80N, I-35 S-Kansas City, I-235E to Des Moines

EXIT		IOWA
	NOTE:	I-80 below runs with I-35 for 14mi. Exit #'s follow I-80.
124/72C		University Ave, Clive
	Gas	N: BP, Kum & Go, QT
		S: Phillips 66
	Food	N: Cracker Barrel
		S: Applebee's, Bakers Square, Chili's, Colton's Steakhouse, Don Pablo, KFC, McDonald's, Outback Steakhouse, Romano's Macaroni Grill
	Lodg	N: Baymont Inn, Best Western, Country Inn, La Quinta Inn♥, Ramada
		S: Chase Suites, Courtyard, Fairfield Inn, Heartland Inn, Holiday Inn, Marriott, Residence Inn, Wildwood Lodge
	Med	N: + Hospital
		S: + Mercy West Health Center
	Other	S: ATMs, Banks, B&N, Best Buy, CompUSA, Kmart, Lowe's, World Market
125		US 6, Hickman Rd, W Des Moines, Clive, Adel
	TStop	N: Flying J Travel Plaza #5314/Conoco (Scales)
	Food	N: Cookery/FastFood/FJ TP
	Lodg	S: Clarion, Comfort Suites, Sleep Inn
	Other	N: Laundry/WiFi/LP/FJ TP
		S: Goodyear, to Living History Farms
126		Douglas Ave, Urbandale, Des Moines
	TStop	N: Pilot Travel Center #373 (Scales)
	Gas	S: Kum & Go◊
	Food	N: GrandmaMax/Pilot TC
		S: Dragon House
	Lodg	S: Days Inn, Econo Lodge
	TWash	N: Pilot TC
	TServ	N: Pilot TC/Tires
	Other	N: Laundry/WiFi/RVDump/Pilot TC
127		IA 141, Urbandale, Grimes, Perry
	FStop	N: Swift Stop/66
	Food	N: Subway/66
		S: Quiznos
	Other	S: Target
129		NW 86th St, Urbandale, Camp Dodge
	Gas	N: Kum & Go
		S: BP, Phillips 66
	Food	N: Burger King, McDonald's
		S: Arby's, Culver's, Ember's
	Lodg	N: Hilton Garden Inn, Stoney Creek Inn
		S: Microtel
131		IA 28S, NW 58th St, Merle Hay Rd, Urbandale, Des Moines
	Gas	N: Casey's, QT
		S: BP◊, QT, Sinclair◊
	Food	N: North End Diner, Quiznos, Shoney's, Rest/BW
		S: Arby's, Burger King, Country Kitchen, Denny's, Famous Dave's BBQ, Hostetler's BBQ, KFC, McDonald's, Perkins, Pizza Hut, Village Inn, Wendy's
	Lodg	N: Best Inn♥, Best Western♥, Ramada♥
		S: Comfort Inn, Days Inn, Holiday Inn, Quality Inn, Sheraton, Super 8
	Med	S: + VA Hospital
	Other	N: Grocery, Goodyear
		S: ATMs, Auto Dealers, Best Buy, Firestone, Office Depot, Walgreen's, Mall
135		IA 415, 2nd Ave, Polk City
	Gas	S: Coastal, QT
	TServ	N: Interstate Detroit Diesel
		S: Freightliner

◊ = Regular Gas Stations with Diesel ▲ = RV Friendly Locations ♥ = Pet Friendly Locations
RED PRINT SHOWS LARGE VEHICLE PARKING/ACCESS ON SITE OR NEARBY BROWN PRINT SHOWS CAMPGROUNDS/RV PARKS

EXIT		IOWA
	Med	S: + Hospital
	Other	N: IA State Hwy Patrol Post, Easter Seals Camp
136		US 69, E 14th St, Ankeny
	FStop	S: QT #562 (Scales)
	Gas	N: BP◊, Phillips 66, Sinclair
		S: Casey's, Citgo◊
	Food	N: Bonanza Steak House, Country Kitchen, Rest/BW
		S: Burger King/QT FS, KFC, Kin Folks BBQ, Long John Silver, McDonald's, Pizza Hut, Village Inn, Wendy's
	Lodg	N: Best Western, Motel 6 ♥
		S: 14th Street Inn, Ramada, Red Roof Inn
	TServ	N: Cummins Great Plains, White Volvo/GMC of Des Moines
		S: Mack Trucks, Midstates Ford Truck
	Other	S: Advance Auto, Goodyear, RV Center, Easter Seals Camp
(137A/87)		Jct I-235W, to Des Moines
(137B/87)		Jct I-35N, to Minneapolis (fr NB, Left Exit)
	NOTE:	I-80 above runs with I-35 for 14mi. Exit #'s follow I-80.
141		US 65S, Altoona, Des Moines (EB) Pleasant Hill, Des Moines (WB)
	Other	WB: IA State Fairgrounds
142A		US 6W, Altoona (EB)
142B		US 65N, Bondurant, Marshalltown (EB, Left exit)
142		US 6W, US 65N, Altoona, Bondurant
	TStop	S: Bosselman Travel Center/Pilot #913/Sinclair (Scales)
	Food	S: GrandmaMax/FastFood/Bosselman TC, Big Steer Rest, Burger King, McDonald's, Pizza Hut, Subway, Taco John
	Lodg	S: Adventureland Inn, Country Inn, Holiday Inn, Howard Johnson, Motel 6 ♥ Settle Inn & Suites ♥
	TWash	S: Blue Beacon TW/Bosselman TC
	TServ	S: Bosselman TC/Tires, International
	Other	N: to Plaza RV Center, Griff's Valley View RV Park▲
		S: Laundry/WiFi/Bosselman TC, Wal-Mart sc, Williamsburg Outlet Mall, Prairie Meadows Horse Racing & Casino, Adventureland Resort, Adventureland RV Park▲
143		1st Ave N, CR S14, Altoona, Bondurant
	Gas	S: Casey's
	Food	S: Settle Inn

EXIT		IOWA
(147)		Rest Area (Both dir) (RR, Phone, Picnic, Vend, WiFi)
149		S27, NE 112th St, Mitchellville (DO NOT PICK UP HITCHIKERS)
(151)		Weigh Station (WB)
155		IA 117, Colfax, Mingo, Prairie City
	FStop	S: Kum & Go #32
	TStop	N: PTP/Colfax Valley Travel Center/BP (Scales)
	Gas	S: Casey's
	Food	N: McDonald's/Colfax Valley TC
	Lodg	S: Comfort Inn
	TServ	N: Colfax Valley TC/Tires
	Other	N: Laundry/Colfax Valley TC
159		F48, to S52, Newton, Baxter
164		US 6, IA 14, Newton, Monroe
	Gas	N: BP, Kum & Go, Phillips 66◊
	Food	N: Country Kitchen, KFC, Perkins
		S: Rest/Best Western, Newton Inn
	Lodg	N: Days Inn ♥, Ramada ♥, Super 8
		S: Best Western
	Med	N: + Hospital
	Other	S: to Lake Red Rock, Central College Casinos, Horse Racing
168		IA Speedway Dr, Newton
	TStop	S: Love's Travel Stop #361 (Scales)
	Gas	N: Casey's◊
	Food	N: Arby's, Taco John
		S: McDonald's/Chesters/Love's TS
	Other	N: Wal-Mart sc, Best Holiday Trav-L-Park/Rolling Acres RV Park▲, IOWA Speedway
		S: Newton Muni Airport ✈
173		IA 224N, T22S, Kellogg, Sully
	Gas	N: Phillips 66◊
	Food	N: IA Best Burger Café/P66 & Kellogg RV Park▲
	Other	N: to Rock Creek State Park▲
		S: Chk for open dates: Camp Lake Pla-Mor Campground▲
179		T38, Grinnell, to Lynnville, Oakland Acres
(180)		Rest Area (Both dir) (RR, Phone, Picnic, Vend, WiFi, RVDump/EB)
182		IA 146, Grinnell, New Sharon
	Gas	N: Casey's
	Food	N: AJ's Steakhouse, Country Kitchen, KFC, Taco Bell
	Lodg	N: Budget Inn, Country Inn, Days Inn, Econo Lodge, Super 8
	Other	N: Grocery, Wal-Mart, Grinnell College, Grinnell Reg'l Airport ✈
		S: Fun Valley Ski Area

EXIT		IOWA
191		US 63, Montezuma St, Malcolm, Tama, Montezuma
	TStop	S: Fuel Mart #794
	Food	S: Rest/Fuel Mart
	Other	S: Fun Valley Ski Area
197		V18, Brooklyn
	FStop	N: Randhawa's Travel Center/BP
	Food	N: Rest/Randhawa's TC
	Other	N: LP/Randhawa's TC
201		IA 21, Brooklyn, to Belle Plaine, Deep River
	TStop	N: AmBest/Shortstop Travel Plaza/66
		S: KwikStar #303 (Scales)
	Food	N: QtrPostCare/Subs/Shortstop TP
		S: Rest/FastFood/KwikStar
	Lodg	N: Motel/Shortstop TP
	TServ	S: KwikStar/Tires
	Other	N: Laundry/Shortstop TP
		S: Laundry/WiFi/KwikStar
205		V38, B Ave, Victor
(208)		Rest Area (Both dir) (RR, Phone, Picnic, WiFi, RVDump/EB)
211		V52, H Ave, Ladora, Millersburg
	Other	N: Lake Iowa Park
216		V66, M Ave, Williamsburg, to Marengo, North English
	FStop	N: Kum & Go #443/Shell
220		IA 149S, V77N, Highland St, to US 6, Williamsburg, Parnell (NEXT 2 EXITS—Amana Colonies)
	FStop	N: Landmark Handymart/66
	Gas	N: BP, Casey's
	Food	N: McDonald's, Pizza Hut, Subway
	Lodg	N: Crest Motel, Super 8
		S: Days Inn, Ramada
	Other	N: Outlet Mall
225		US 151N, W21S, U Ave, Homestead, Cedar Rapids, Amana Colonies
	Gas	S: BP, Phillips 66
	Food	S: Colony Haus, Colony Village, Little Amana Rest, Maid-Rite, Rest/DI
	Lodg	N: Comfort Inn
		S: Days Inn, Holiday Inn, My Little Inn, Econo Lodge, Super 8
	Other	N: to Amana Colonies, Amana Colonies RV Park▲
230		W38, Black Hawk Ave, Oxford
	Other	N: Sleepy Hollow Campground▲, FW Kent Park, Kalona Village Museum
(237)		Rest Area (Both dir) (RR, Phone, Picnic, Vend, WiFi, RVDump)
237		Ireland Ave, Tiffin
	Other	N: FW Kent Park

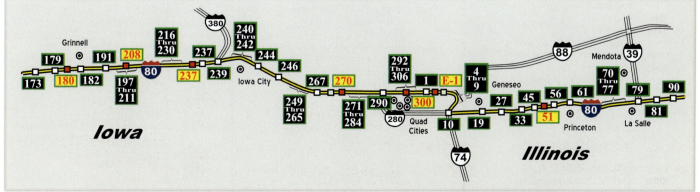

◊ = Regular Gas Stations with Diesel ▲ = RV Friendly Locations ♥ = Pet Friendly Locations
RED PRINT SHOWS LARGE VEHICLE PARKING/ACCESS ON SITE OR NEARBY BROWN PRINT SHOWS CAMPGROUNDS/RV PARKS

Page 381

EXIT	IOWA
239A	US 218S, IA 27, Mount Pleasant, Keokuk
(239B)	I-380, US 218N, Cedar Rapids, Waterloo
240	Coral Ridge Ave, 27th Ave, to US 6, Coralville, North Liberty
Gas	N: Phillips 66 S: BP, Conoco, Phillips 66
Food	N: McDonald's, Steak n Shake, Village Inn, Wendy's S: Applebee's, Chili's, Olive Garden, Outback Steakhouse, Red Lobster
Lodg	N: AmericInn, Country Inn, Ramada Inn S: Days Inn♥, Holiday Inn Express
Other	N: Wal-Mart sc, Harley Davidson, Colony Country Campground▲ S: ATMs, B&N, Grocery, Best Buy, Lowe's, Target, Tires, U-Haul, Coral Ridge Mall, Univ of IA/Oakdale, to IA City Muni Airport✈
242	1st Ave, Coralville, Iowa City
FStop	S: Kum & Go #201
Gas	S: BP, Conoco
Food	S: Arby's, Burger King, Country Kitchen, McDonald's, KFC, Lone Star Steakhouse, Perkins, Pizza Hut, Subway, Taco Bell
Lodg	N: Hampton Inn, Holiday Inn S: Baymont Inn, Best Western, Comfort Inn, Days Inn, Fairfield Inn, Motel 6♥, Red Roof Inn♥, Super 8♥
Med	S: + VA Hospital, + Univ of IA Hospital
Other	S: Walgreen's, Visitor Info, Firefighters Memorial, Univ of IA, Carver Hawkeye Arena
244	W66, Dubuque St, Downtown, Iowa City
Med	S: + Hospital
Other	N: Coralville Lake
246	IA 1, Dodge St, Iowa City, to Mt Vernon
Gas	N: BP◊, Phillips 66 S: Sinclair
Lodg	N: Highlander Inn, Quality Inn S: Country Suites, Travelodge♥
249	F44, Herbert Hoover Hwy, Iowa City
254	X30, Baker Ave, Downey St, West Branch, to Buchanan, West Liberty
Gas	N: BP◊, Casey's S: Kum & Go, Phillips 66
Food	S: McDonald's
Lodg	S: Best Value Inn, Presidential Inn
Other	N: Herbert Hoover Historical Site & Presidential Museum
259	X40, Garfield Ave, West Liberty
FStop	S: J&M Oil/BP
Food	S: FastFood/J&M Oil
Lodg	S: Econo Lodge
Other	N: Herbert Hoover National Library & Museum S: RVDump/J&M Oil, West Liberty KOA▲
265	X46, Atalissa Rd, Atalissa
TStop	S: AmBest/Diesel Depot/66 (Scales)
Food	S: Birdie's/Chesters/AustinBluesBBQ/Diesel Depot
267	IA 38N, X54S, Moscow Rd, Tipton, Moscow
Food	S: The Cove Café
Other	N: Cedar River Campground▲

EXIT	IOWA
(268)	Weigh Station (WB)
(270)	IA Welcome Center (WB) Rest Area (EB) (RR, Phone, Picnic, Vend, WiFi, RVDump)
271	US 6W, IA 38S, Wilton, Muscatine
277	Y26, Yankee Ave, Durant, Bennett
280	Y30, 20th Ave, Durant, Stockton, New Liberty
Other	S: IA State Hwy Patrol Post
284	Y40, 60th Ave, Walcott, Plain View
TStop	N: IA 80 Travel Center of America #77/BP (Scales), Pilot Travel Center #43 (Scales) S: Pilot Travel Center #268 (Scales)
Gas	N: Phillips 66
Food	N: IA 80Kitchen/Blimpie/DQ/Wendys/IA 80 TA TC/Arby's/TJCinn/Pilot TC, Gramma's Kitchen S: Subway/Pilot TC, McDonald's
Lodg	N: Comfort Inn, Super 8 S: Days Inn
TWash	N: Blue Beacon TW/IA 80 TA TC
TServ	N: IA 80 TA TC/Tires, Speedco
Other	N: Laundry/BarbSh/CB/WiFi/IA 80 TA TC, Laundry/WiFi/Pilot TC S: WiFi/Pilot TC, Cheyenne Camping Center
(290)	Jct I-280E, US 6E, to Rock Island, Moline (fr WB, Left Exit)
TServ	S: Cummins Great Plains, Peterbilt
Other	S: Quad City Airport✈
292	IA 130W, Northwest Blvd, Davenport, Maysville
TStop	N: Flying J Travel Plaza #5071/Conoco (Scales)
Gas	S: BP, Sinclair
Food	N: Cookery/FastFood/FJ TP S: Machine Shed Rest
Lodg	N: Hotel/FJ TP S: Comfort Inn
Other	N: Laundry/BarbSh/WiFi/RVDump/LP/FJ TP, Interstate RV Park & Campground▲, Water Park, IMAX, Putnam Museum S: Hidden Lake Campground▲
295A	US 61S, Brady St, Davenport, Downtown, Riverfront
295B	US 61N, Eldridge, De Witt
295	US 61, Brady St, Davenport
Gas	N: BP S: BP◊, Shell
Food	S: Burger King, Country Kitchen, Cracker Barrel, Hardee's, Hooters, McDonald's, Steak 'n Shake, Village Inn
Lodg	S: Baymont Inn, Best Western, Days Inn, Heartland Inn, Motel 6, Residence Inn
Other	N: Davenport Muni Airport✈, Scott Co Park, Terry Frazer RV Center S: ATMs, AutoZone, Auto Dealers, Northpark Mall, US Adventure RV
(298)	I-74E, to Bettendorf, Davenport, to Peoria
(300)	Rest Area (Both dir) (RR, Phone, Picnic, Vend, WiFi)
301	Middle Rd, Bettendorf

EXIT	IA / IL
306	US 67, Cody Rd, Le Claire, Bettendorf, Clinton
N:	IA Welcome Center (WB) (RR, Phone, Picnic) (NO Trucks)
Gas	N: BP, Phillips 66◊ S: BP◊
Food	N: Subway, Cowboy Steaks
Lodg	N: Comfort Inn, Super 8
Other	N: Buffalo Bill Museum
NOTE:	MM 307: Illinois State Line

(CENTRAL TIME ZONE)

ⓘ IOWA
ⓘ ILLINOIS
(CENTRAL TIME ZONE)

EXIT	ILLINOIS
1	IL 84, 20th St, Great River Rd, E Moline, Savanna
Gas	N: BP S: Citgo
(1)	IL Welcome Center (EB) (RR, Phone, Picnic, Info)
(2)	Weigh Station (Both dir)
4A	IL 92S, IL 5S, Silvis
Other	S: to Quad City Downs, Lundeen Campground▲
(4B)	I-88, IL 92E, Sterling, Rock Falls
7	Cleveland Rd, Colona, Green Rock
Gas	N: Shell◊
9	US 6, Colona, to Geneseo
Other	N: Niabi Zoo, Winery
(10)	From EB:
AHEAD	Jct I-74E, to Peoria (EB) to Galesburg, Western IL Univ
1st Rt	Jct I-280W, I-74W, to Moline, Rock Island (EB) to Quad City Airport✈
2nd Rt	Jct I-80E, to Chicago (EB)
	From WB:
AHEAD	Jct I-280W, I-74, Moline, Rock Island
1st Rt	Jct I-80W, to Davenport
2nd Rt	Jct I-74E, to Peoria
19	IL 82, Geneseo, Cambridge
FStop	N: Beck Oil/P66
Gas	N: BP, Shell
Food	N: Hardee's, McDonald's, Subway S: KFC
Lodg	N: Deck Plaza, Oakwood Motel
Med	N: + Hospital
Other	N: Wal-Mart, Geneseo Campground▲, RV Center
27	CR 5, Atkinson, to Galva
TStop	N: Atkinson Plaza #93/Mobil
Gas	N: Casey's
Food	N: Rest/Atkinson Plz
Twash	N: Atkinson Plz
Other	N: LP/Atkinson Plz
33	IL 78, Annawan, Kewanee, to Prophetstown
Gas	S: Mobil◊, Phillips 66◊
Food	S: The Loft, Olympic Flame
Lodg	S: Holiday Inn Express
Other	S: Johnson Sauk Trail State Park
45	IL 40, 900 St E, Peoria, Sterling
Gas	N: Marathon◊
Food	N: Rest/Marathon, Rest/Days Inn
Lodg	N: Days Inn

◊ = Regular Gas Stations with Diesel ▲ = RV Friendly Locations ♥ = Pet Friendly Locations
RED PRINT SHOWS LARGE VEHICLE PARKING/ACCESS ON SITE OR NEARBY BROWN PRINT SHOWS CAMPGROUNDS/RV PARKS

EXIT		ILLINOIS
	Other	N: to President Ronald Reagan birthplace S: Hennepin Canal State Park▲
(51)		**Great Sauk Trail Rest Area (Both dir)** **(RR, Phone, Picnic, Vend, RVDump,** **Weather)**
56		IL 26, N Main St, Princeton, Dixon
	TStop	N: Road Ranger #225/Citgo (Scales)
	Gas	S: BP, Phillips 66, Shell
	Food	N: Rest/FastFood/Road Ranger S: Burger King, Country Kitchen, KFC, McDonald's, Taco Bell, Wendy's
	Lodg	N: Super 8 S: Comfort Inn, Days Inn, Princeton Motel
	TWash	N: Road Ranger
	TServ	N: Road Ranger/Tires
	Other	N: Laundry/Road Ranger S: ATMs, Auto Services, Auto Dealers, Dollar General, Grocery, Wal-Mart sc, Amtrak Station
(61)		Jct I-180S, to Hennepin
70		IL 89, S Main Ave, Ladd, to Spring Valley
73		CR 76, Plank Rd, Peru
	TStop	N: Sapp Bros Travel Center◊◊ (Scales)
	Food	N: Rest/FastFood/Sapp Bros TC
	TServ	N: Sapp Bros TC/Tires
	Other	N: Laundry/WiFi/LP/Sapp Bros TC, S: IL Valley Reg'l Airport✈
75		IL 251, Peru, Mendota
	FStop	N: Clocktower Shell
	TStop	N: Crazy D's (Scales)
	Gas	N: BP S: BP
	Food	N: Arby's, McDonald's, Taco Bell, Rest/Tiki Inn S: Applebee's, Bob Evans, Culver's, Red Lobster, Steak 'n Shake, Subway, Wendy's
	Lodg	N: Baymont Inn, Econo Lodge, Kings Inn, Motel 6♥, Super 8, Tiki Inn & RV Park▲ S: Fairfield Inn, La Quinta Inn♥
	Med	S: + Hospital
	Other	N: Laundry/Crazy D's S: Auto Dealers, AutoZone, Grocery, Goodyear, Home Depot, Kmart, Midas, Staples, Target, Walgreen's, Wal-Mart, Peru Mall, IL Valley Comm College
77		IL 351, St Vincent Ave, La Salle
	TStop	S: Flying J Travel Plaza #5076 (Scales)
	Food	S: CountryMarket/FastFood/FJ TP
	Lodg	S: Daniels Motel
	TWash	S: FJ TP
	Other	S: Laundry/BarbSh/WiFi/RVDump/LP/ FJ TP, IL State Hwy Patrol Post

EXIT		ILLINOIS
(79)		Jct I-39N, US 51, N to Rockford, S to Bloomington
(79A)		I-39S, US 51, Bloomington, Normal
(79B)		I-39N, US 51, to Rockford
81		IL 178, CR 43, E 8th Rd, Utica
	TStop	N: Love's Travel Stop #351 (Scales)
	Gas	S: BP, Shell◊
	Food	N: McDonald's/Subway/Love's TS
	Other	N: WiFi/RVDump/Love's TS, La Salle/Peru KOA▲ S: Hickory Hollow Campground▲, Starved Rock State Park▲
90		IL 23, Ottawa, De Kalb
	Gas	N: BP S: BP◊, Shell
	Food	N: Cracker Barrel, Taco Bell, Subway/BP S: China Inn, Country Kitchen, Dunkin Donuts, McDonald's, KFC, Ponderosa
	Lodg	N: Hampton Inn, Holiday Inn Express S: Comfort Inn, Super 8, Travelodge
	Med	N: + Hospital
	Other	N: Auto Dealers S: Kroger, Kmart, Harley Davidson, Pharmacy, Wal-Mart, US Post Office, Ace RV Center
93		IL 71, Ottawa, Oswego
	FStop	N: JMP Oil #76/Mobil
	TStop	N: Oasis Clocktower Shell
	Food	N: Rest/Oasis CS
	TServ	N: Oasis CS/Tires
	Other	N: Skydive Chicago RV Park▲
97		CR 15, E 24th Rd, Marseilles
	Other	S: Glenwood RV Resort▲, Troll Hollow Campground▲, Illini State Park▲
105		Seneca Rd, Morris, Seneca
	Other	S: Whispering Pines RV Sales
112		IL 47, US 6, Division St, Morris, to Yorkville
	FStop	N: Northside Fuel/Citgo
	TStop	N: Travel Center of America #236/BP (Scales)
	Gas	S: BP, Mobil, Shell
	Food	N: Rest/Quiznos/Romines, Chili's S: Burger King, KFC, McDonald's, Maria's, Morris Diner, Pizza Hut, Subway, Taco Bell, Wendy's
	Lodg	N: Comfort Inn, Days Inn♥, Holiday Inn Express S: Morris Motel, Park Motel, Super 8♥
	TServ	N: TA TC/Tires
	Med	S: + Morris Hospital
	Other	N: Laundry/WiFi/Romines TC, Grundy Co Fairgrounds

EXIT		ILLINOIS
	Other	S: ATMs, Auto Services, Grocery, Radio Shack, Walgreen's, Wal-Mart sc, Pro Source Motorsports
(117)		**Rest Area (EB)** **(RR, Phone, Picnic, Weather)**
(118)		**Rest Area (WB)** **(RR, Phone, Picnic, Weather)**
122		CR 11, Ridge Rd, Minooka
	FStop	N: McCoy's Citgo
	TStop	S: Pilot Travel Center #236 (Scales)
	Gas	S: BP
	Food	S: Arby's/TJCinn/Pilot TC, DQ, McDonald's, Subway, Wendy's,
	Other	S: Laundry/WiFi/Pilot TC, Grocery
(126AB)		Jct I-55, N-Chicago, S-St Louis
127		Houbolt Rd, Empress Rd, Joliet
	Gas	N: 7-11, BP
	Food	N: Burger King, Cracker Barrel, McDonald's
	Lodg	N: Fairfield Inn, Hampton Inn, Ramada
	Other	N: Harley Davidson, Joliet Park District Airport✈ S: Empress River Casino
130AB		IL 7, Larkin Ave, Joliet
	Gas	N: Citgo, Clark, Marathon, Speedway, Shell, Thornton◊
	Food	N: Bob Evans, Burger King, Dunkin Donuts, KFC, Pizza Hut, Steak 'n Shake, Subway, Taco Bell, Wendy's, White Castle
	Lodg	N: Comfort Inn, Holiday Inn Express, Microtel, Motel 6♥, Red Roof Inn♥, Super 8
	TServ	N: International
	Med	N: + Hospital
	Other	N: Grocery, Goodyear, Kmart, Sam's Club, Wal-Mart
131		Center St, US 6, Railroad St, S Raynor Ave
	Other	N: to Riverboat Casino
132AB		US 52E, IL 53, Chicago St
	Other	N: Harrah's Joliet Casino, Amtrak
133		Richards St, Joliet
134		CR 54, Briggs Rd
	Gas	N: Speedway S: 7-11◊
	Other	N: Martin Campground▲ S: Starting Line Campground▲, Chicago Land Speedway, Rte 66 Speedway
137		US 30, Maple St, Lincoln Hwy, New Lenox
	Gas	S: Speedway◊
	Food	N: Rest

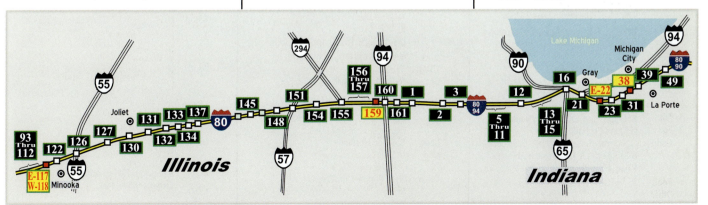

◊ = Regular Gas Stations with Diesel   ▲ = RV Friendly Locations   ♥ = Pet Friendly Locations

RED PRINT SHOWS LARGE VEHICLE PARKING/ACCESS ON SITE OR NEARBY   BROWN PRINT SHOWS CAMPGROUNDS/RV PARKS

INTERSTATE 80 W E

EXIT		ILLINOIS
	Food	S: Burger King, KFC, McDonald's, Pizza Hut, Taco Bell
	Other	N: Kmart
		S: Grocery, Walgreen's
(143)		Weigh Station (EB)
145AB		US 45, 96th Ave, Mokena
	FStop	S: Shell Food Mart
	Gas	N: Gas City
		S: BP, Gas City
	Food	N: Subway/Gas City
		S: Burger King, DQ, Denny's, Subway, Wendy's, White Castle
	Lodg	S: Super 8
(147)		Weigh Station (WB)
148AB		IL 43, Harlem Ave, Tinley Park
	FStop	N: Speedway
	Food	N: Subway/Speedway, Burger King, Chicago Café, Cracker Barrel, Wendy's
	Lodg	N: Baymont Inn, Comfort Suites, Fairfield Inn, Holiday Inn Select, Sleep Inn
	Other	S: Windy City Campground & Beach▲
(151AB)		Jct I-57, S-Memphis, N-Chicago (Left Exits)
154		Kedzie Ave, Hazel Crest (EB)
(155)		I-294N (TOLL), Tri State Tollway, to Wisconsin
	NOTE:	I-80 below runs with I-294. Exit #'s follow I-80.
156		Dixie Hwy (EB)
157		IL 1, Halsted St, Hazel Crest
	Gas	N: Citgo◊, Marathon◊
		S: Shell, Speedway
	Food	N: Burger King
		S: Applebee's, Arby's, Dunkin Donuts, KFC, Popeye's, McDonald's, Subway, Taco Bell, Wendy's
	Lodg	N: Best Western, Comfort Inn, Hilton Garden Inn, Hampton Inn, Holiday Inn, Motel 6♥, Sleep Inn
		S: Days Inn, Rodeway Inn, Super 8
	TServ	N: K&J Truck Tire Repair
	Other	S: ATMs, Auto Services, Firestone, Goodyear, Home Depot, Kmart, Pharmacy, Target
(159)		Lincoln Oasis (Both dir)
	FStop	Mobil
	Food	Burger King, TCBY
160A		IL 394S, to Danville
(160B)		Jct I-94W, to Chicago
	NOTE:	EB End TOLL, WB Begin TOLL Road I-80 above runs with I-294. Exit #'s follow I-80.
161		US 6, IL 83, Torrence Ave, Lansing
	FStop	S: Park Service/Mobil
	Gas	N: BP
		S: Gas City, Marathon
	Food	N: Arby's, Bob Evans, Checkers, Chili's, Hooters, IHOP, Olive Garden, On the Border, Wendy's
		S: Burger King, DQ, Dunkin Donuts, McDonald's, Pappy's Gyros
	Lodg	N: Comfort Suites, Days Inn, Extended Stay America, Fairfield Inn, Red Roof Inn♥, Ramada Inn, Sleep Inn, Super 8
	Med	N: + Ingalls Urgent Aid Walk-In Clinic

Personal Notes

EXIT		IL / IN
	Other	N: ATMs, Auto Services, Auto Dealers, Best Buy, Grocery, Home Depot, Kmart
		S: ATMs, Grocery, Sam's Club, Walgreen's
	NOTE:	MM 163: Indiana State Line

(CENTRAL TIME ZONE)

⊙ ILLINOIS
⊙ INDIANA (CENTRAL TIME ZONE)

	NOTE:	I-80 runs with I-94 below. Exit #'s follow I-94.
1		US 41N, Calumet Ave, Hamilton
	Gas	N: BP◊, Gas City
		S: BP, Gas City, Marathon, Shell
	Food	N: Dunkin Donuts, Subway/BP
		S: Arby's, Burger King, Starbucks, Taco Bell, Wendy's
	Other	N: ATM, Firestone, Laundromat, Walgreen's
		S: CVS, Grocery
2AB		US 41S, IN 152N, Indianapolis Blvd, Hamilton, Hammond
	TStop	S: Pilot Travel Center #31 (Scales)
	Gas	N: SavAStop, Shell
		S: Thorntons
	Food	N: Arby's, Domino's, Dunkin Donuts
		S: Subway/Pilot TC, Burger King, Little Caesar's, Taco Bell
	Lodg	S: Ameri Host Inn
	Med	N: + Hospital
		S: + Hospital
	Other	N: to Purdue Univ/Calumet
		S: WiFi/Pilot TC, Grocery, Kmart

EXIT		INDIANA
3AB		Kennedy Ave, Hammond
	Gas	N: Clark, Speedway
		S: Citgo, Speedway
	Food	N: Burger King, Dominos, McDonald's
		S: Cracker Barrel, Subway, Wendy's
	Lodg	S: Courtyard, Fairfield Inn, Residence Inn
	Other	N: Walgreen's, NAPA
5AB		IN 912, Cline Ave, Gary, Hammond
	Gas	S: BP, Clark, Shell, Speedway
	Food	S: Arby's, Bob Evans, Burger King, DQ, McDonald's, Pizza Hut, White Castle
	Lodg	S: Best Western, Motel 6♥
6		Burr St, Gary
	TStop	N: Travel Center of America #10/BP (Scales), Pilot Travel Center #271 (Scales)
	Gas	N: BP
		S: Shell◊
	Food	N: CountryPride/Chester/PizzaHut/TacoBell TA TC, Subway/Pilot TC
	TWash	N: Pilot TC
	TServ	N: TA TC/Tires
	Other	N: Laundry/CB/WiFi/TA TC, WiFi/Pilot TC
9AB		Grant St, Gary
	TStop	S: Flying J Travel Plaza #5024 (Scales), Steel City AmBest Truck Plaza (Scales)
	Food	N: Chicago Hot Dogs
		S: Cookery/FastFood/FJ TP, Rest/Fast Food/Steel City TP, Burger King, DQ, KFC, McDonald's, Subway
	TWash	S: FJ TP
	TServ	S: FJ TP/Tires
	Other	N: Laundromat, Walgreen's
		S: Laundry/WiFi/RVDump/LP/FJ TP, ATMs, AutoZone, Grocery, Firestone, Outlet Mall
10AB		IL 53, Broadway, Gary
	Gas	N: Citgo, Marathon
		S: BP, Citgo
	Food	N: Broadway BBQ
		S: DQ, Rally's
(11)		Jct I-65S, Indianapolis (EB)
(12A)		Jct I-65S, to Indianapolis (WB)
(12B)		Jct I-65N, to Gary, IN
13		Central Ave (EB, No re-entry)
15A		US 6E, IN 51S, to US 20, Lake Station
	TStop	S: Road Ranger Travel Center #240/ Citgo (Scales)
	Gas	S: Mobil◊, Shell
	Food	S: Subway/RoadRanger, Burger King, DQ, Papa John's, Long John Silver, Wendy's
	Other	S: Walgreen's
15B		US 6W, IN 51N, Ripley St, Melton Rd, Central Ave, Gary, Lake Station
	TStop	N: Road Ranger Travel Center #239/Citgo (Scales), Flying J Travel Plaza #5085 (Scales), Travel Center of America #219/BP (Scales), Dunes Center Truck Stop (Scales)
	Food	N: Subway/Road Ranger TC, Rest/ FastFood/FJ TP, Buckhorn/Popeyes/ Subway/TA TC, McDonald's, Ponderosa
	TWash	N: Road Ranger, FJ TP, TA TC
	TServ	N: FJ TP/Tires, TA TC/Tires, Dunes Center TS/Tires
	Other	N: Laundry/BarbSh/CB/WiFi/FJ TP, Laundry/WiFi/TA TC
	NOTE:	I-80 runs with I-94 above. Exit #'s follow I-94.

◊ = Regular Gas Stations with Diesel   ▲ = RV Friendly Locations   ♥ = Pet Friendly Locations
RED PRINT SHOWS LARGE VEHICLE PARKING/ACCESS ON SITE OR NEARBY   BROWN PRINT SHOWS CAMPGROUNDS/RV PARKS

EXIT		INDIANA
	NOTE:	I-80 below runs with I-90 to Elyria OH. Exit #'s follow I-90. I-94 continues East to Detroit.
(16/21)		Jct I-90W, Jct I-94E, IN Toll Road
(22)		George Ade Service Area (EB) John McCutcheon Service Area (EB)
	FStop	BP #70512/#70511 (Scales)
	Food	Hardee's, Hershey's Ice Cream
23		600W, Portage, Port of Indiana
	Gas	N: Marathon, Shell S: AmocoBP, Marathon
	Food	S: Burger King, Dunkin Donuts, KFC, Jimmy John Subs, First Wok, McDonald's, Starbucks, Subway, Wendy's
	Lodg	N: Comfort Inn, Holiday Inn Express
	Other	N: Yogi Bear's Jellystone Park▲ S: Grocery, Walgreen's, US Post Office
(24)		TOLL Plaza
31		IN 49, Chesterton, Valparaiso
	Lodg	N: Hilton Garden Inn
	Other	N: Sand Creek RV Park▲
(38)		Truck Rest Area (Both dir)
39		US 421, Westville, Michigan City (Serv Appr 5mi N)
	Other	N: Michigan City Campground▲
49		IN 39, La Porte (Gas, Food, Lodg appr 4 mi S)
	Lodg	S: Cassidy Motel & RV Park▲
	Other	N: to Sand Creek Campground▲
(56)		Knute Rockne Service Area (EB) Wilbur Shaw Service Area (WB)
	FStop	BP #70510/#70509
	Food	McDonald's, DQ
	Other	RVDump
	NOTE:	MM 62: Central / Eastern Time Zone
72		US 31, St Joseph Valley Pky, South Bend, to Plymouth, Niles
	FStop	N: Speedway #6674 (Scales)
	TStop	N: Pilot Travel Center #35 (Scales)
	Food	N: Subway/Pilot TC S: McDonald's, Ponderosa, Taco Bell
	Lodg	N: Super 8 S: Days Inn, Quality Inn
	TServ	S: Whiteford Kenworth
	Other	N: WiFi/Speedway, WiFi/Pilot TC S: Amtrak, Michiana Reg'l Transportation Center Airport✈, South Bend Reg'l Airport✈, IN State Hwy Patrol Post
77		IN 933, US 31 Bus, South Bend, to Notre Dame University
	Gas	N: Meijer◊, Mobil, Phillips 66 S: Marathon, Phillips 66◊

EXIT		INDIANA
	Food	N: Arby's, Burger King, DQ, Damon's, Fazoli's, McDonald's, Papa John's, Pizza Hut, Ponderosa, Steak & Ale, Subway S: Bob Evans, Denny's, Perkins, Taco Bell, Wendy's
	Lodg	N: Comfort Suites, Days Inn, Hampton Inn, Motel 6♥, Ramada Inn, Super 8 S: Best Inn, Howard Johnson, Holiday Inn, Knights Inn, Inn at St. Mary's, Signature Inn, Wingate Inn
	Other	N: Walgreen's S: to Notre Dame Univ
83		IN 331, Capital Ave, Granger, to Mishawaka
	Gas	N: BP◊, Citgo, Phillips 66◊ S: Meijer
	Food	N: Applebee's, Arby's, Olive Garden, Panda Express, Pizza Hut, Taco Bell, Wendy's S: Arby's, Burger King, Carrabba's, Chili's, Lone Star Steakhouse, McDonald's, Outback Steakhouse, Ryan's Grill, Steak 'n Shake, Subway, TGI Friday
	Lodg	N: Carlton Lodge, Fairfield Inn, Hampton Inn, Holiday Inn, Super 8 S: Best Western, Courtyard, Extended Stay America, Studio Plus
	Other	N: Best Buy, CVS, Kroger, Office Depot, Target, Walgreen's, Mall, South Bend East KOA▲ S: Auto Dealers, Discount Tire, Lowe's, Sam's Club, Wal-Mart sc
(90)		George Craig Service Area (EB) Henry Schricker Service Area (WB)
	TStop	BP #70508/#70507
	Food	Burger King, Pizza Hut, Starbucks
	Other	RVDump
92		IN 19, Cassopolis St, Elkhart
	Gas	N: 7-11, Phillips 66◊ S: Marathon◊, Shell, Speedway
	Food	N: Applebee's, Cracker Barrel, Perkins, Steak 'n Shake, Starbucks S: Arby's, Bob Evans, Burger King, KFC, Long John Silver, McDonald's, Olive Garden, Red Lobster, Ryan's Grill, Taco Bell, Texas Roadhouse, Wendy's
	Lodg	N: Best Western, Comfort Suites, Country Inn, Econo Lodge, Hampton Inn, Holiday Inn Express, Knights Inn, Quality Inn, Sleep Inn S: Budget Inn, Days Inn, Jameson Inn, Ramada, Red Roof Inn♥, Super 8
	Med	S: + Hospital
	Other	N: Grocery, CVS, Kmart, RV Repair, Tiara RV Center, Elkhart Campground▲

EXIT		INDIANA
		S: ATMs, AutoZone, Walgreen's, Wal-Mart sc, Elkhard City Airport✈, Holiday World RV Center, Michiana RV, Cruise America, to Camping World/RVDump
96		CR 17, Elkhart
101		IN 15, Bristol, to Goshen
	Gas	S: 7-11, Speedway◊
107		US 131, IN 13, Middlebury, Constantine (Addt'l Serv 5 mi S in Middlebury)
	FStop	N: Marathon S: Snappy Food Mart/BP
	Lodg	N: Plaza Motel
	Other	S: Elkhart Co/Middlebury KOA▲, Eby's Pines Campground▲
(108)		Truck Rest Area (Both dir)
121		IN 9, Howe, Sturgis, LaGrange
	Food	N: Applebee's, Golden Corral, Wendy's
	Lodg	N: Hampton Inn, Travel Inn Motel, Comfort Inn, Knights Inn S: Holiday Inn, Super 8
	Med	N: + Hospital S: + Hospital
	Other	N: Wal-Mart S: to Grand View Bend RV Park/RVDump
(126)		Gene Porter Service Area (EB) Ernie Pyle Service Area (EB)
	FStop	Mobil #70572
	Food	Hardee's
	Other	RVDump
(144)		Jct I-69, US 27, Fremon, Angola, Fort Wayne, Lansing
	TStop	N: Petro 2 #45/Mobil (Scales), Pilot Travel Center #29 (Scales), Pioneer Auto Truck Stop/Shell (At Exit #157 on I-69)
	Gas	S: Marathon◊
	Food	N: Rest/FastFood/Petro2, Wendy's/Pilot TC
	Lodg	N: Redwood Lodge S: Hampton Inn, Holiday Inn Express, Super 8, Travelers Inn
	TServ	S: Cummins, Discover Volvo Trucks
	Other	N: Laundry/WiFi/LP/Petro2, Laundry/WiFi/Pilot TC S: Outlet Mall, U-Haul
(146)		JR Riley Service Area (EB) Booth Tarkenton Service Area (WB)
	FStop	Mobil #70580/#70580
	Food	McDonald's
(153)		IN TOLL Plaza
	NOTE:	MM 157: Ohio State Line

🎧 **INDIANA**(EASTERN TIME ZONE)

◊ = Regular Gas Stations with Diesel ▲ = RV Friendly Locations ♥ = Pet Friendly Locations
RED PRINT SHOWS LARGE VEHICLE PARKING/ACCESS ON SITE OR NEARBY BROWN PRINT SHOWS CAMPGROUNDS/RV PARKS

EXIT		OHIO
	OHIO I-80/OH TPK (EASTERN TIME ZONE)	
	NOTE:	I-80 / OH TPK runs below with I-90. Exit #'s follow I-80.
		Begin TOLL EB, End WB
(2.7)		TOLL Plaza Westgate
2		OH 49, Edon, Edgerton, to US 20, Allen MI
	Gas	N: Mobil
	Food	N: Burger King, Subway
13		OH 15, US 20 Alt, Holiday City, Montpelier, Bryan
	FStop	S: Holiday City Stop N Go/Sunoco, Hutch's Karry Out/Marathon
	Food	S: Subway/Marathon, Country Fair Rest
	Lodg	S: Econo Lodge♥, Holiday Inn Express, Ramada Inn
	TServ	S: Hutch's Marathon/Tires
	Other	N: Lazy River Resort Campground▲, to appr 7 mi Loveberry's Funny Farm Campground▲
(21)		**Tiffin River Service Plaza (EB)** **Indian Meadow Service Plaza (WB)**
	TStop	Sunoco #7106/#7105
	Food	Hardee's
	Other	Picnic, RVDump/Overnite▲
25		OH 66, Archbold-Fayette, Burlington
	Lodg	S: to Sauder Heritage Inn
	Other	N: to Harrison Lake State Park▲, S: to Hidden Valley Campground▲
34		OH 108, Wauseon, Napoleon
	TStop	S: Turnpike Shell
	Gas	S: Circle K, DM, Mobil
	Food	S: Subway/Shell, Burger King, Pizza Hut, McDonald's, Smith's Rest, Taco Bell, Wendy's
	Lodg	S: Arrowhead Motel♥, Best Western, Holiday Inn Express, Super 8
	TServ	S: Turnpike Shell, Wood Truck Service
	Med	S: + Hospital
	Other	N: Fulton Co Fairgrounds/RVDump▲, appr 5mi Sunny's Shady Rec Area▲, to appr 18mi Lake Hudson Rec Area▲ S: ATMs, Auto Service, Family Dollar, Wal-Mart
39		OH 109, Delta, Lyons
	TStop	S: Country Corral/Citgo
	Food	S: Rest/Country Corral
	Other	S: Delta Wings Airport✈, Maumee State Forest
(49)		**Fallen Timbers Service Plaza (EB)** **Oak Openings Service Plaza (WB)**
	TStop	Valero
	Food	Nathan's, Cinnabon, Pizza Uno, Great American Bagel
	Other	Picnic
52		OH 2, Swanton, Toledo Airport
	Lodg	S: Days Inn, Quality Inn
	Other	N: CFS Truck & Fleet Repair S: Grocery, Budget, U-Haul, Express Auto & Truck Service, Toledo Express Airport✈, RV Center, to Big Sandy Campground▲ Twin Acres Campground▲, Bluegrass Campground▲, Hidden Lake Campground▲, Betty's Country Campground▲

EXIT		OHIO
59		US 20, Reynolds Rd, to I-475, to US 23, Maumee, Toledo
	Gas	N: BP◊, Shell, Speedway◊ S: Meijer◊, Speedway
	Food	N: Arby's, Bob Evans, Damon's, Dragon Buffet, Little Caesars, McDonald's, Olive Garden, Pizza Hut, Steak n Shake, Waffle House S: Fazoli's, Outback Steakhouse, Red Lobster, Taco Bell
	Lodg	N: Clarion, Econo Lodge, Holiday Inn, Motel 6♥, Quality Inn S: Baymont Inn, Courtyard, Country Inn, Comfort Inn, Days Inn, Econo Lodge, Fairfield Inn, Hampton Inn, Homewood Suites, Red Roof Inn♥, Super 8
	Med	N: + to Medical Univ of OH/Toledo S: + St Luke's Hospital
	Other	N: ATMs, Advance Auto, Banks, FedEx Kinko's, Grocery, Goodyear, Kmart, RiteAid, Walgreen's, Southwyck Mall, Auto & RV Repair, to Toledo Stadium S: Auto Dealers, UPS Store
(64)		Jct I-75N, Perrysburg, Toledo
	Other	to Bowling Green State Univ, Toledo Zoo, Fifth Third Field
71		I-280, OH 420, Perrysburg, Stony Ridge, Toledo, to I-75N, Detroit
	TStop	N: I-280/1B: Petro Stopping Center #17/ Mobil (Scales), Flying J Travel Plaza #5450/Conoco (Scales) S: Travel Center of America #87/BP (Scales), Fuel Mart #641 (Scales), Pilot Travel Center #12 (Scales)
	Food	N: IronSkillet/PizzaHut/Petro SC, Cookery/ FastFood/Flying J TP S: CountryPride/BurgerKing/TacoBell/ TA TC, Rest/Fuel Mart, McDonalds/Pilot TC, Wendy's
	Lodg	N: Motel/Petro SC, Howard Johnson, Crown Inn, Ramada Ltd, Stony Ridge Inn, Super 8, Vista Inn Express
	TWash	N: Blue Beacon TW/Petro SC S: Fuel Mart
	TServ	N: Petro SC/Tires S: TA TC/Tires, Fuel Mart/Tires, 795 Tire Service, Williams Detroit Diesel
	Other	N: Laundry/BarbSh/WiFi/Petro SC, Laundry BarbSh/WiFi/RVDump/LP/FJ TP, to Metcalf Field✈ S: Laundry/WiFi/TA TC, Laundry/Fuel Mart, WiFi/Pilot TC, Toledo East/Stony Ridge KOA▲
(77)		**Wyandot Service Plaza (EB)** **Blue Heron Service Plaza (WB)**
	TStop	Valero
	Food	Hardee's, Gloria Jeans Coffees, Mancino's Italian Eatery
	Other	WiFi, Picnic Area, RVDump/OverNite▲
81		OH 51, Elmore, Gibsonburg, Woodville
	Other	S: Wooded Acres Campground▲, to Eagle Lake Camping Resort▲
91		OH 53, Fremont, Port Clinton, to US 6, US 20, US 2, Sandusky
	FStop	S: BP #137
	Lodg	N: Days Inn S: Comfort Inn, Fremont Turnpike Motel, Hampton Inn, Holiday Inn

EXIT		OHIO
	Med	S: + Hospital
	Other	N: to Lake Erie Islands, Rutherford B Hayes Presidential Center, to RV Dealer, Shade Acres Campground▲, Erie Islands Resort & Marina▲ S: Wooded Acres Campground▲, RV Dealer, Fremont Airport✈, to Cactus Flats Campground▲
(100)		**Comm Perry Service Plaza (EB)** **Erie Islands Service Plaza (WB)**
	TStop	Valero
	Food	Burger King, Carvel, Cinnabon, Einstein Bros, Starbucks, Sbarro
	Other	WiFi, Picnic Area
110		OH 4, Bellevue, Sandusky, Attica
	Other	N: to Cedar Point, Lazy J RV Resort▲
118		US 250, Sandusky, Norwalk, Milan
	Gas	N: Marathon, Speedway
	Food	N: McDonald's, Subway S: Homestead Rest
	Lodg	N: Comfort Inn, Colonial Inn South & Milan Travel Park▲, Days Inn, Fairfield Inn, Great Wolf Lodge, Hampton Inn, Holiday Inn Express, Motel 6♥, Super 8
	Other	N: Wal-Mart sc, to Cedar Point, Lake Erie S: OH State Hwy Patrol Post, to Milan Thomas Edison Museum, Wilcart RV, Pin Oak RV, Norwalk Raceway Park
135		Baumhart Rd, to OH 2, Amherst, Vermilion, Huron, Sandusky
	Other	N: to Swift Hollow RV Resort▲, Neff Bros RV/RVDump
(139)		**Vermilion Valley Service Plaza (EB)** **Middle Ridge Service Plaza (WB)**
	TStop	Valero
	Food	Burger King, Great Steak, Manchu Wok, Panera, Popeye's, Starbucks, TCBY
	Other	Picnic, WiFi, RVDump/OverNite▲
140		OH 58, Leavitt Rd, Amherst, Oberlin
	Gas	N: Sunoco◊
	Food	N: Subway/Sunoco
	Other	S: to Lorain Co Reg'l Airport✈
(142)		I-90E, to OH 2, W Cleveland (EB)
	Other	to Cleveland, Erie PA, Buffalo NY
	NOTE:	I-80/OH TPK runs above with I-90. Exit #'s follow I-80.
	NOTE:	I-80/OH TPK below continues EB. To Exit #218. Exit #'s follow I-80.
145		OH 57, Lorain Blvd, to I-90, Elyria, Lorain
	Gas	N: BP◊, Shell, Speedway S: Shell, Speedway
	Food	N: McDonalds/BP, Applebee's, Arby's, Bob Evans, Burger King, Country Kitchen, Denny's, Fazoli's, Lone Star Steakhouse, Pizza Hut, Red Lobster, Smokey Bones BBQ, Subway, Wendy's
	Lodg	N: Best Western, Comfort Inn, Country Inn, Days Inn♥, Econo Lodge, Holiday Inn, Red Carpet Inn, Red Roof Inn♥ S: Howard Johnson Express♥, Super 8
	Med	S: + to Elyria Memorial Hospital
	Other	N: ATMs, Auto Services, Best Buy, Family Dollar, Firestone, Grocery, Goodyear, Home Depot, Lowe's, NTB, Pharmacy, PetSmart♥, Staples, Sam's Club, Target, Wal-Mart, Elyria Midway Mall S: Laundromat, OH State Hwy Patrol Post, to Cascade Park

◊ = Regular Gas Stations with Diesel ▲ = RV Friendly Locations ♥ = Pet Friendly Locations
RED PRINT SHOWS LARGE VEHICLE PARKING/ACCESS ON SITE OR NEARBY BROWN PRINT SHOWS CAMPGROUNDS/RV PARKS

EXIT	OHIO
(151)	I-480E, to N Ridgeville, Cleveland, Cleveland Hopkins Int'l Airport (EB)
152	OH 10, Lorain Rd, North Olmstead, Cleveland
Gas	N: BP, Marathon, Sheetz, Speedway◊ S: BP
Food	N: McDonald's
Lodg	N: Motel 6, Super 8
Other	N: Grocery, U-Haul, Crystal Springs Campground▲, Moore's RV Sales & Service
(161)	I-71, to US 42, Pearl Rd, to I-480, Cleveland, to US 82, Strongsville (Gas, Food, Lodg on US 42)
Gas	N: Circle K
Food	N: Mad Cactus, Pizza Hut, Subway
Lodg	N: Days Inn
Med	N: + Hospital
Other	N: Home Depot, to Cleveland Hopkins Int'l Airport✈, Browns Stadium, Rock & Roll Hall of Fame & Museum, Jacobs Field
(170)	Towpath Service Plaza (EB) Great Lakes Service Plaza (WB)
TStop	Valero
Food	Burger King, Panera Bread, Pizza Hut/KFC, Starbucks
Other	Picnic Area, WiFi
173	OH 21, Brecksville Rd, Richfield, to I-77, to I-271, Cleveland, Akron
TStop	N: I-77 X146: Pilot Travel Center #130 (Scales)
Gas	N: BP
Food	N: Wendy's/Pilot TC S: DQ, Subway
Lodg	N: Howard Johnson, Lake Motel S: Hampton Inn, Quality Inn, Super 8
Tires	N: Pilot TC
TServ	S: Richfield Radiator Repair
Other	N: Laundry/WiFi/Pilot TC, BF Goodrich Hdqtrs, to Jacobs Field/Gund Arena, Cleveland Browns Stadium, Rock & Roll Hall of Fame/Museum, Great Lakes Science Center, Brandywine Ski Area
180	OH 8, to 271N, to I-90E, Akron
Gas	N: Marathon S: BP◊, Starfire Express
Lodg	N: Comfort Inn, Country Inn, Days Inn, Hampton Inn, Holiday Inn, Hudson Inn, Knights Inn, La Quinta Inn♥, Motel 6♥
Other	S: Kamper City/RVDump, Cuyahoga Valley National Park
(187)	I-480, OH 14, Streetsboro
Gas	S: BP, DM, Shell, Sheetz
Food	S: Arby's, Bob Evans, Burger King, DQ, Denny's, KFC, Long John Silver, Perkins, Ruby Tuesday, Subway, Taco Bell

EXIT	OHIO
Lodg	S: Comfort Inn, Econo Lodge, Fairfield Inn, Hampton Inn, Holiday Inn Express, Microtel, Super 8, Towneplace Suites♥, Wingate Inn
Other	N: Woodside Lake Park▲, to Tinker's Creek State Park, to Geauga Lake & Wildwater KingdomCG S: ATMs, Auto Services, CVS, Firestone, Grocery, Home Depot, Kmart, Staples, Wal-Mart, Mall, to Kent State Univ, Mar-Lyn Lake Park/Streetsboro KOA▲, Hudson Springs Park, Valley View Lake Park▲
193	OH 44, Ravenna
Other	S: Mills Airport✈, Portage Co Airport✈
(197)	Brady's Leap Service Plaza (EB) Portage Service Plaza (WB)
TStop	Valero
Food	McDonald's, Krispy Kreme, Popeye's, Sbarro, Starbucks
Other	OH Marketplace, Picnic, WiFi, RVDump/OverNite▲
209	OH 5, Newton Falls, Warren
TStop	N: PTP/Short Stop Travel Plaza/Marathon (Scales)
Food	N: KountryKubboardRest/Short Stop TP
Lodg	N: Budget Lodge S: Econo Lodge, Holiday Inn Express
TServ	N: Short Stop TP/Tires, Youngstown Warren Reg'l Airport✈
Other	N: Laundry/Short Stop TP S: to appr 5mi Country Acres Campground▲, Ravenna Ordinance Plant
215	Ellsworth Bailey Rd, Lordstown (EB)
Other	N: GM Plant
216	Hallock Young Rd, to OH 45, Lordstown (WB)
NOTE:	I-80/OH TPK continues above Exit #'s follow I-80.
NOTE:	OH TPK continues below to PA. (OH TPK below runs with I-76 EB to exit #237)
218	CR 18, Mahoning Ave, I-76W to Akron, I-80E, to I-680, to OH 11, Youngstown, Pittsburgh, NY City
232	OH 7, Market St, N Lima, to Youngstown
TStop	S: Pilot Travel Center #011 (Scales)
Gas	N: Shell, Sheetz S: Shell◊, Speedway◊
Food	N: DQ S: FastFood/Pilot TC

EXIT	OH / PA
Lodg	N: Budget Inn, Economy Inn, Holiday Inn Express, Quality Inn♥, Ramada S: Davis Motel, Rodeway Inn
Med	N: + Hospital
TWash	S: Pilot TC
Other	S: WiFi/Pilot TC, to appr10 mi Beaver Creek State Park, Ponderosa Park, Chaparral Family Campground▲
(234)	I-680N, Youngstown, Poland (WB)
(237)	Glacier Hills Service Plaza (EB) Mahoning Valley Service Plaza (WB)
TStop	Valero
Food	McDonald's
(239)	TOLL Plaza Eastgate
NOTE:	End TOLL EB, Begin WB

OH / PA Border

NOTE:	OH I-80 continues EB End TOLL, WB Begin TOLL
223B	OH 46N, Niles, Warren (WB)
223A	OH 46S, Austintown, Canfield (WB)
223	OH 46, Austintown, Canfield, Youngstown, Niles (EB)
TStop	N: Pilot Travel Center #3 (Scales) S: AmBest Fuel Mart #730 (Scales), Travel Center of America #58 (Scales)
Gas	N: Citgo◊ S: BP◊, Sunoco
Food	N: McDonald's/Pilot TC, Bob Evans, Burger King S: CountryPride/TA TC, Arby's, Cracker Barrel, McDonald's, Perkins, Starbucks, Taco Bell, Wendy's
Lodg	N: Best Value Inn, Comfort Inn S: Super 8/TA TC, Best Western♥, Country Inn, Econo Lodge, Hampton Inn, Knights Inn, Sleep Inn, Super 8
TWash	S: Blue Beacon TW/TA TC
TServ	S: TA TC/Tires, Freightliner Trucks, White/GMC Volvo
Other	N: Laundry/WiFi/Pilot TC S: Laundry/CB/WiFi/RVDump/TA TC
224	OH 11S, to Canfield (WB)
224A	OH 11S, to Canfield (EB)
(224B)	I-680S, Youngstown (EB)
226	Salt Springs Rd, to I-680S, Girard, to McDonald, Youngstown
TStop	S: Mr Fuel #5 (Scales), Petro Stopping Center #20/Mobil (Scales), Pilot Travel Center #281 (Scales)

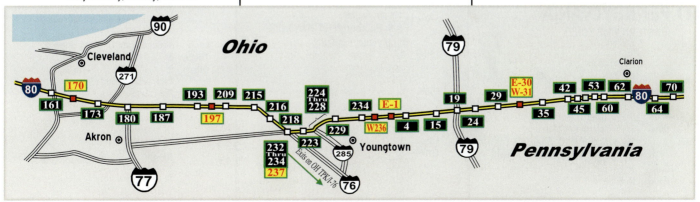

◊ = Regular Gas Stations with Diesel   ▲ = RV Friendly Locations   ♥ = Pet Friendly Locations

RED PRINT SHOWS LARGE VEHICLE PARKING/ACCESS ON SITE OR NEARBY   BROWN PRINT SHOWS CAMPGROUNDS/RV PARKS

OH / PA

EXIT		
	Gas	N: BP◊, Sheetz
	Food	N: Subway/BP, McDonald's, Waffle House
		S: Rest/Mr Fuel, Iron Skillet/Petro SC, Arby's/TJCinn/Pilot TC
	TWash	S: Blue Beacon TW/Petro SC, Eagle Truck Wash, Frank's Truck Wash
	TServ	S: Petro SC/Tires, Speedco, OH Cat
	Other	S: Laundry/CB/BarbSh/Med/Massg/WiFi/Petro SC, WiFi/Pilot TC
227		US 422, State St, Girard, Niles, Youngstown
	Gas	N: Shell◊
	Food	N: Burger King, Subway
228		OH 11N, Ashtabula (fr EB, Left exit)
229		OH 193, Belmont Ave, Youngstown
	Gas	N: Speedway◊
		S: Shell
	Food	S: Arby's, Bob Evans, Burger King, KFC, Denny's, Long John Silver, McDonald's, Perkins, Pizza Hut, Subway, Taco Bell, Wendy's, Western Sizzlin'
	Lodg	N: American Inn, Days Inn, Hampton Inn, Holiday Inn, Super 8
		S: Days Inn, Econo Lodge, Quality Inn
	Med	N: + Hospital
	Other	S: ATMs, Advance Auto, AutoZone, Big Lots, Firestone, Grocery, Goodyear
234AB		US 62, OH 7, Main St, Hubbard (EB)
234		US 62, OH 7, Main St, Hubbard, Youngstown, to Sharon, PA (WB)
	TStop	N: EB Access via Ex #234B: PTP/Truck World/Shell (Scales), Flying J Travel Plaza #5112 (Scales), Love's Travel Stop #370 (Scales)
	Food	N: GlobeRest/Truck World, CountryMarket/FastFood/FJ TP, Chesters/Subway/Love's TS, Arby's, Burger King, McDonald's, Waffle House
	Lodg	N: Motel/Truck World, Motel/FJ TP, Best Western
	TWash	N: Blue Beacon TW/Truck World
	TServ	N: Truck World/Tires
		S: Youngstown Kenworth
	Other	N: Laundry/CB/BarbSh/Truck World, Laundry/WiFi/RVDump/LP/FJ TP, Homestead RV Center, Hubbard's Heaven Family Campground▲, Chestnut Ridge Park & Campground▲
(236)		OH Welcome Center (WB) (RR, Phones, Picnic, Vend, Info)
NOTE:		MM 237: Pennsylvania State Line

(EASTERN TIME ZONE)

◠ OHIO I-80/OH TPK
◡ PENNSYLVANIA

(EASTERN TIME ZONE)

(1)		PA Welcome Center (EB) (RR, Phone, Picnic, Vend, Info)
4A		PA 60S, New Castle
	Gas	N: Sunoco
		S: DM
	Food	S: DQ, Diner
	Other	S: PA Motor Sports Museum
4B		PA 60N, to PA 18, Sharon, Hermitage, W Middlesex, Farrell
	Gas	N: BP, Sunoco
	Food	N: Subway

PENNSYLVANIA

EXIT		
	Lodg	N: Comfort Inn, Holiday Inn, Radisson
	Other	N: Rocky Springs Campground▲, to appr 14mi Shenango Valley RV Park▲
15		US 19, Perry Hwy, Mercer
	Gas	N: BP
	Food	N: Burger King, McDonald's, Rest/HJ
	Lodg	N: Howard Johnson
	Other	N: PA State Hwy Patrol Post, to RV Village Camping Resort▲, Rocky Springs Campground▲
		S: Jct 19-80 Campground▲
(19A)		Jct I-79S, to Pittsburgh
	Other	S: to Grove City Airport✈, Mercer/Grove City KOA▲
(19B)		Jct I-79N, to Erie
24		PA 173, Sandy Lake Rd, Grove City, Sandy Lake
	Med	S: + Hospital
	Other	N: to Goddard Park Vacationland Campground▲
29		PA 8, Pittsburgh Rd, Harrisville, Barkeyville, Franklin
	TStop	S: Kwik Fill Auto Truck Plaza #229 (Scales), Exit 29 Fuel Stop/Citgo, Travel Center of America #67/BP (Scales)
	Food	N: Arby's, Burger King
		S: Rest/KwikFill ATP, FastFood/Exit 29, CountryPr/Subway/TA TC
	Lodg	N: Comfort Inn, Days Inn, Super 8
	TServ	S: TA TC/Tires
	Other	S: Laundry/WiFi/TA TC, to Slippery Rock Univ, Venango Regional Airport✈
(30)		Rest Area (EB) (RR, Phone, Picnic, Vend)

PENNSYLVANIA

EXIT		
(31)		Rest Area (WB) (RR, Phone, Picnic, Vend)
35		PA 308, Butler St, Clintonville
	FStop	N: Phoenix Quik Stop
42		PA 38, Emlenton
	TStop	N: Emlenton Travel Center/Citgo (Scales)
	Gas	N: Exxon
	Food	N: Rest/Emlenton TC, Subway/Exxon
	Lodg	N: Motel/Emlenton TC
	TServ	N: Emlenton TC/Tires
	Other	N: Laundry/WiFi/Emlenton TC, Gaslight Campground▲
45		PA 478, Emlenton, St Petersburg
53		Canoe Ripple Rd, to PA 338, Knox
	Gas	N: Exit 7 Gulf
	Food	N: BJ's Eatery, Wolf's Den Rest
	TServ	S: Good Tire Service
	Other	N: Wolf's Camping Resort▲, to Colwell's Campground▲
(57)		Weigh Station (Both dir)
60		PA 66N, to Shippenville
	Gas	N: QuikStop
	Other	N: PA State Hwy Patrol Post, to appr 3mi Clarion Co Airport✈, Rustic Acres Campground▲
62		PA 68, Clarion
	Gas	N: 7-11, BP
		S: KwikFill◊
	Food	N: Arby's, Burger King, Cozumel, Eat 'n Park, Long John Silver, McDonald's, Perkins, Pizza Hut, Subway, Taco Bell
	Lodg	N: Comfort Inn, Hampton Inn, Holiday Inn, Microtel, Quality Inn, Super 8
	Med	N: + Clarion Hospital
	Other	N: AdvanceAuto, ATMs, Bank, Kmart, Grocery, Staples, Wal-Mart sc, Mall, Clarion Univ, to appr 11mi Kalyumet Campground▲, Cook Forest State Park▲
64		PA 66S, Clarion, New Bethlehem
	Other	N: to Clarion Univ
		S: to Piney Meadows Park▲, Penn Wood Campground▲
70		US 322, Strattanville
	TStop	N: Keystone All American Plaza/Shell (Scales)
	Food	N: Rest/Keystone Plz
	TServ	N: Keystone Plz/Tires
	Other	N: Laundry/Keystone Plz
29		PA 8, Pittsburgh Rd, Harrisville, Barkeyville, Franklin
	TStop	S: Kwik Fill Auto Truck Plaza #229 (Scales), Exit 29 Fuel Stop/Citgo, Travel Center of America #67/BP (Scales)
	Food	N: Arby's, Burger King
		S: Rest/KwikFill ATP, FastFood/Exit 29, CountryPr/Subway/TA TC
	Lodg	N: Comfort Inn, Days Inn, Super 8
	TServ	S: TA TC/Tires
	Other	S: Laundry/WiFi/TA TC, to Slippery Rock Univ, Venango Regional Airport✈
(30)		Rest Area (EB) (RR, Phone, Picnic, Vend)
(31)		Rest Area (WB) (RR, Phone, Picnic, Vend)
35		PA 308, Butler St, Clintonville
	FStop	N: Phoenix Quik Stop

◊ = Regular Gas Stations with Diesel ▲ = RV Friendly Locations ♥ = Pet Friendly Locations
RED PRINT SHOWS LARGE VEHICLE PARKING/ACCESS ON SITE OR NEARBY BROWN PRINT SHOWS CAMPGROUNDS/RV PARKS

EXIT		PENNSYLVANIA
42		PA 38, Emlenton
	TStop	N: Emlenton Travel Center/Citgo (Scales)
	Gas	N: Exxon◆
	Food	N: Rest/Emlenton TC, Subway/Exxon
	Lodg	N: Motel/Emlenton TC
	TServ	N: Emlenton TC/Tires
	Other	N: Laundry/WiFi/Emlenton TC, Gaslight Campground▲
45		PA 478, Emlenton, St Petersburg
53		Canoe Ripple Rd, to PA 338, Knox
	Gas	N: Exit 7 Gulf
	Food	N: BJ's Eatery, Wolf's Den Rest
	TServ	S: Good Tire Service
	Other	N: Wolf's Camping Resort▲, to Colwell's Campground▲
(57)		Weigh Station (Both dir)
60		PA 66N, to Shippenville
	Gas	N: QuikStop
	Other	N: PA State Hwy Patrol Post, to appr 3mi Clarion Co Airport✈, Rustic Acres Campground▲
62		PA 68, Clarion
	Gas	N: 7-11, BP
		S: KwikFill◆
	Food	N: Arby's, Burger King, Cozumel, Eat 'n Park, Long John Silver, McDonald's, Perkins, Pizza Hut, Subway, Taco Bell
	Lodg	N: Comfort Inn, Hampton Inn, Holiday Inn, Microtel, Quality Inn, Super 8
	Med	N: + Clarion Hospital
	Other	N: AdvanceAuto, ATMs, Bank, Kmart, Grocery, Staples, Wal-Mart sc, Mall, Clarion Univ, to appr 11mi Kalyumet Campground▲, Cook Forest State Park▲
64		PA 66S, Clarion, New Bethlehem
	Other	N: to Clarion Univ
		S: to Piney Meadows Park▲, Penn Wood Campground▲
70		US 322, Strattanville
	TStop	N: Keystone All American Plaza/Shell (Scales)
	Food	N: Rest/Keystone Plz
	TServ	N: Keystone Plz/Tires
	Other	N: Laundry/Keystone Plz
73		PA 949, Corsica
	Other	N: to Clear Creek State Park, Cook Forest State Park▲, Campers Paradise Campground▲
78		PA 36, Brookville, Sigel
	TStop	N: Travel Center of America #3/BP (Scales), Flying J Travel Plaza #5092 (Scales)
	Gas	S: Citgo, Sheetz, Sunoco

EXIT		PENNSYLVANIA
	Food	N: Country Pr/TacoBell/TA TC, Country Market/FastFood/FJ TP, McDonald's, Pizza Hut
		S: Arby's, Burger King, Plyer's Pizza & Family Rest, Subway
	Lodg	N: Howard Johnson/TA TC, Super 8♥
		S: Days Inn♥, Gold Eagle Inn, Holiday Inn Express
	TServ	N: TA TC/Tires, FJ TP/Tires
	Other	N: Laundry/WiFi/RVDump/TA TC, Laundry/WiFi/RVDump/LP/FJ TP, RV Dealer, to Clear Creek State Park, Cook Forest State Park▲, Campers Paradise Campground▲
81		PA 28, Brookville, to Hazen
	Med	S: + Hospital
86		PA 830, PA 810, Reynoldsville
(88)		Rest Area (Both dir) (RR, Phones, Picnic)
90		PA 830E, DuBois Reg'l Airport
97		US 219, Buffalo-Pittsburgh Hwy, Falls Creek, Du Bois, Brockway
	TStop	S: Sheetz Travel Center #194 (Scales), Pilot Travel Center #336 (Scales)
	Food	S: FastFood/Sheetz TC, Arby's/TJCinn/Pilot TC, Dutch Pantry Rest
	Lodg	S: Best Western, Holiday Inn Express
	Med	S: + DuBois Reg'l Medical Hospital
	Other	N: PA State Hwy Patrol Post
		S: Laundry/Sheetz TC, Laundry/WiFi/Pilot TC, DuBois Harley Davidson, Kmart, Penn State/DuBois
101		PA 255, Du Bois, Penfield
	Gas	N: BP
		S: Citgo, Sheetz
	Food	S: Arby's, Burger King, Domino's, Eat 'n Park, Hoss's Steak & Sea House, Italian Oven, McDonald's, Perkins, Ponderosa, Red Lobster, Ruby Tuesday, Subway, Taco Bell, Wendy's
	Lodg	N: Best Western, Hampton Inn
		S: Clarion, Ramada Inn
	Med	S: + DuBois Reg'l Medical Hospital
	Other	N: to appr 10mi Parker Dam State Park▲
		S: ATMs, Banks, Auto Services, Grocery, Kmart, Lowe's, Staples, Wal-Mart, DuBois Mall, PA State Hwy Patrol Post
111		PA 153, Penfield, Clearfield
		NOTE: Trucks over 5 Tons, Use Ex #120 Highest Pt on I-80 E of the Mississippi
	Med	S: + Hospital
	Other	N: SB Elliott State Park, to Parker Dam State Park▲
		S: Curwensville Lake Rec Area▲

EXIT		PENNSYLVANIA
120		PA 879, Clearfield, Shawville
	TStop	N: Sapp Bros Travel Center/Shell (Scales)
	Gas	S: BP, Sheetz, Snappy's
	Food	N: Cafe/Deli/FastFood/Sapp Bros TC
		S: Arby's, Burger King, Dutch Pantry, McDonald's, KFC/PizzaHut/TacoBell, Tacamba's Mex Rest
	Lodg	S: Days Inn, Comfort Inn, Econo Lodge, Holiday Inn Express, Super 8
	TServ	N: Sapp Bros/Tires, Cumberland Truck Parts
		S: Cummins, Purcell Tire
	Med	S: + Clearfield Hospital
	Other	N: Laundry/BarbSh/WiFi/Sapp Bros TC
		S: ATM, Kmart, Lowe's, Wal-Mart sc Pharmacy, Clearfield Co Fairgrounds, to Curwensville Lake Rec Area▲
123		PA 970, Woodland, Shawville
	FStop	S: Pacific Pride
	Other	N: Woodland Campground▲
		S: PA State Hwy Patrol Post
133		PA 53, Winburne, Grassflat, to Kylertown, Phillipsburg
	TStop	N: Kwik Fill Auto Truck Plaza #226 (Scales)
	Gas	N: Sunoco
	Food	N: Rest/Kwik Fill ATP
	Lodg	N: Motel/Kwik Fill ATP
	TServ	N: Kwik Fill ATP/Tires
	Med	S: + Hospital
	Other	S: to Mid State Reg'l Airport✈, Black Moshannon State Park
(146)		Rest Area (Both dir) (RR, Phone, Picnic)
147		Beech Creek Rd, PA 144, Snow Shoe
	TStop	N: Snow Shoe Auto Truck Plaza/Citgo, Reese Truck Stop/Exxon
	Food	N: Rest/Snow Shoe ATP, Rest/Reese TS
	TServ	N: Reese TS/Tires
	Other	N: Laundry/Reese TS, Grocery
158		US 220S Alt, to I-99, PA 150, Bellafonte, Altoona, Milesburg
		NOTE: Steep grade on exit, Use low gear
	TStop	N: Bestway Travel Center/Shell (Scales), Travel Center of America #214/Amoco (Scales)
	Gas	N: Citgo
	Food	N: Rest/FastFood/Bestway TC, Buckhorn/TA TC
	Lodg	N: Motel/Bestway TC, Holiday Inn
	TServ	N: Best Way TC/Tires, TA TC/Tires
	Other	N: Laundry/CB/WiFi/Bestway TC, Laundry/WiFi/TA TC, to Bald Eagle State Park
		S: PA State Hwy Patrol Post, to Beaver Stadium

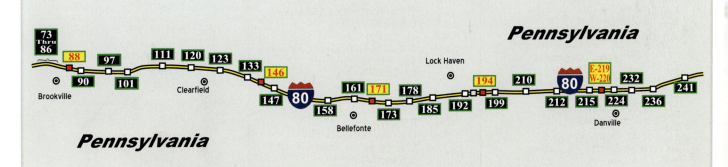

◆ = Regular Gas Stations with Diesel   ▲ = RV Friendly Locations   ♥ = Pet Friendly Locations

RED PRINT SHOWS LARGE VEHICLE PARKING/ACCESS ON SITE OR NEARBY   BROWN PRINT SHOWS CAMPGROUNDS/RV PARKS

Page 389

INTERSTATE 80 W/E

EXIT	PENNSYLVANIA
161	US 220S, PA 26, Bellefonte, Howard (Future I-99S)
Gas	S: Kwik Fill, Shell
Other	N: Fort Bellafonte Campground▲, Bellefonte/State College KOA▲, to Bald Eagle State Park S: Centre RV Dealer, to Penn State Univ, to Woodward Cave▲, Lake Raystown Resort & Lodge▲
(171)	Parking Area (Both dir)
173	PA 64, Nittany Valley Dr, Hall, Lamar, to Mill Hall
TStop	N: Pilot Travel Center #1 (Scales) S: Travel Center of America #68/Mobil (Scales), Flying J Travel Plaza #5113 (Scales)
Gas	S: Citgo
Food	N: Subway/Pilot TC, McDonald's, Perkins, Rest/Comfort Inn S: CountryPride/Subway/TA TC, Country Market/FastFood/FJ TP
Lodg	N: Comfort Inn
TServ	S: TA TC/Tires
Other	N: Laundry/WiFi/Pilot TC, PA State Hwy Patrol Post S: Laundry/WiFi/TA TC, Laundry/WiFi/RVDump/LP/FJ TP
178	US 220, Frank O'Reilly Hwy, Mill Hall, to Lock Haven (Addt'l Serv 5mi N in Mill Hall)
Gas	S: Citgo◊
Food	N: Belle Springs Family Rest
Other	N: Clinton Co Fairgrounds/Speedway, to Bald Eagle State Park, Lock Haven Univ
185	PA 477, Long Run Rd, Loganton
Gas	N: Mobil S: Valley Service
Other	N: Holiday Pines Campground▲ S: to Raymond B Winter State Park
192	Valley Rd, PA 880, Ranchtown Rd, Carroll, Loganton, Jersey Shore
TStop	N: Pit Stop Travel Center/Citgo
Food	N: Pit Stop Rest/Pit Stop TC
Med	S: + Hospital
Other	N: Laundry/Pit Stop TC, to Ravensburg State Park, McCall Dam State Park
(194)	Rest Area (Both dir) (RR, Phone, Picnic)
(194)	Weigh Station (Both dir)
199	Mile Run Rd, Lewisburg
210A	US 15S, to Lewisburg (Exit only)
Gas	S: Citgo
Food	S: Bonanza/Comfort Inn
Lodg	S: Comfort Inn, Holiday Inn Express
Other	S: Sunbury Bucknell Univ, Lewisburg Federal Penitentiary, to appr 6 mi Williamsport South/Nittany Mtn KOA▲, to appr 13mi River Edge RV Camp & Marina▲, Little Mexico Campground▲, Penn's Creek Campground▲, Hidden Valley Camping Resort▲
210B	US 15N, to Williamsport (Exit only)
Other	N: to Reptiland Zoo, Little League Hall of Fame/Museum, Int'l HQ
212A	PA 147S, to Milton
(212B)	I-180W, to Williamsport

EXIT	PENNSYLVANIA
215	PA 254, Milton, Limestoneville
TStop	N: Milton 32 Truck Plaza (Scales) S: Petro Stopping Center/Shell (Scales)
Food	N: Rest/Milton TP S: Iron Skillet/Subway/Petro SC
TWash	S: Eagle TW/Petro SC
TServ	N: Milton TP/Tires S: Petro SC/Tires
Other	N: Laundry/Milton TP S: Laundry/CB/WiFi/RVDump/Petro SC
(219)	Rest Area (EB) (RR, Phones, Picnic)
(220)	Rest Area (WB) (RR, Phones, Picnic)
224	PA 54, Continental Blvd, to Danville
Gas	N: BP, Mobil◊ S: Shell◊
Food	N: Country Kitchen, Subway S: Dutch Kitchen, McDonald's
Lodg	N: Quality Inn S: Days Inn, Hampton Inn, Red Roof Inn♥, Travelodge
Med	S: + Hospital
Other	S: to appr 8mi Splash Magic Campground & RV Resort▲
232	PA 42, Mall Blvd, Bloomsburg, Buckhorn
TStop	N: Travel Center of America #212/BP (Scales)
Gas	N: Shell◊
Food	N: Buckhorn/Subway/TA TC, Cracker Barrel, KFC, Perkins, Ruby Tuesday, Wendy's
Lodg	N: Econo Lodge, Holiday Inn Express

EXIT	PENNSYLVANIA
TServ	N: TA TC/Tires
Other	N: Laundry/WiFi/TA TC, Home Depot, Columbia Mall, Turner's High View Campground▲ S: Lowe's, Wal-Mart sc, Knoebel's Amusement Park, to appr 4-6mi Indian Head Campground▲, Shady Rest Campground▲, Mt Zion Family Campground▲
236A	PA 487S, to Bloomsburg (WB)
236B	PA 487N, Light St (WB)
236	PA 487, Light St, Bloomsburg
Gas	S: Sunoco, UniMart
Food	S: Denny's
Lodg	S: Hampton Inn, Inn at Turkey Hill
Med	S: + Bloomsburg Hospital
Other	N: to appr 4mi Deihl's Camping Resort▲ S: Cinema Center, Bloomsburg Univ, Bloomsburg Muni Airport✈
241A	US 11S, to Lime Ridge
Gas	S: Coastal, Shell, Sheetz◊
Food	S: Applebee's, Arby's, Burger King, China Queen, Long John Silver, McDonald's, Pizza Hut, Subway, Wendy's
Lodg	S: Budget Host Inn, Tennytown Motel
Other	S: ATMs, Auto Dealers, Advance Auto, Big Lots, CVS, Grocery, Staples, U-Haul, Wal-Mart sc, Bloomsburg Muni Airport✈, PA State Hwy Patrol Post
241B	US 11N, to Berwick
Lodg	N: Red Maple Inn, Super 8
Med	N: + Hospital
242	PA 339, Nescopeck to Mifflinville, Mainville
TStop	N: Brennan's Auto Truck Plaza/Shell (Scales), Love's Travel Stop #324 (Scales) S: Kreiser Truck Stop/Citgo
Food	N: Rest/Brennan's ATP, Arby's/Love's TS, McDonald's S: FastFood/Kreiser TS
Lodg	N: Super 8
TServ	N: Brennan's ATP/Tires
Other	N: Laundry/CB/Brennan's ATP, WiFi/RVDump/Love's TS
(246)	Rest Area (Both dir) (RR, Phones, Picnic)
(246)	Weigh Station (Both dir)
256	PA 93, Berwick Hazelton Hwy, Drums, Conyngham, Nescopeck
TStop	N: Pilot Travel Center #298 (Scales)
Gas	N: Sunoco S: Shell◊
Food	N: Subway/Pilot TC S: Brass Buckle, Tom's Kitchen, Stewarts
Lodg	N: Lookout Motor Lodge S: Best Value Inn, Days Inn, Hampton Inn
Med	S: + Hospital
Other	N: WiFi/Pilot TC, Penn State Univ/Hazelton, to appr 7mi Moyers Grover Campground & Country RV▲, to Jim Thorpe Camping Resort▲
(260A)	Jct I-81S, to Harrisburg
(260B)	Jct I-81N, to Wilkes-Barre (Fr EB, Left Exit)
262	PA 309, N Hunter Hwy, Drums, to Mountain Top, Hazleton
Gas	N: BP, Shell
Food	N: Mountain View Rest, Wendy's

◊ = Regular Gas Stations with Diesel ▲ = RV Friendly Locations ♥ = Pet Friendly Locations
RED PRINT SHOWS LARGE VEHICLE PARKING/ACCESS ON SITE OR NEARBY BROWN PRINT SHOWS CAMPGROUNDS/RV PARKS

INTERSTATE 80 W/E

EXIT		PENNSYLVANIA
	Lodg	N: Econo Lodge, Holiday Inn Express, Mountain View Motel
	Other	S: PA State Hwy Patrol Post
(270)		Rest Area (EB) (RR, Phones, Picnic, Vend)
273		PA 940, to PA 437, Church St, Whitehaven, Freeland
		NOTE: NO Trucks with Underclearance less than 15' on PA 940E
	Gas	N: BP, Mobil
274		PA 534, Hickory Run State Park
	TStop	N: Bandit Truck Stop/Sunoco #2, AmBest/Hickory Run Travel Plaza/Exxon (Scales)
	Food	N: FastFood/Bandit TS, Rest/Hickory Run TP
	TServ	N: Hickory Run TP/Tires
	Other	N: WiFi/Hickory Run TP, to Hickory Run State Park, Lehigh Gorge Campground & RV Center/LP▲
277		PA 940, Lake Harmony, to I-476, PA Tpk (TOLL), Wilkes-Barre, Allentown
	Gas	N: BP, Shell, WaWa
	Food	N: Arby's, Burger King, Denny's, Gino's, McDonald's, Rest/Howard Johnson
	Lodg	N: Comfort Inn, Days Inn, Econo Lodge, Howard Johnson, Mountain Laurel Resort
284		PA 115, Blakeslee, to Ski Areas
	Gas	N: WaWa S: Exxon◊
	Food	N: Rest/Blakeslee Inn
	Lodg	N: Best Western, Blakeslee Inn S: Tudor Inn
	Other	N: PA State Hwy Patrol Post S: to appr 5mi WT Family Campground RV Sales & Service▲, to Pocono Int'l Raceway, Wilkes Barre Ski Area, Jack Frost Ski Area, Big Boulder Ski Area
(293)		I-380N, to Scranton (fr EB, Left Exit) NOTE: Trucks to WilkesBarre: Use I-380N
(295)		Rest Area (EB) (RR, Phones, Picnic, Vend)
298		PA 611, to Scotrun, Mt Pocono
	Gas	N: Shell, Sunoco◊
	Food	N: Plaza Deli, Anthony's Steakhouse, Scotrun Diner
	Lodg	N: Scotrun Motel
	Other	N: Four Seasons Campground▲, PA State Hwy Patrol Post, to Mt Pocono, Camel Back Ski Area
299		PA 715, Singer Ave, Tannersville
	Gas	N: BP, Mobil S: Sunoco
	Food	N: Deli, Friendly's, Rest/Chateau Inn S: Tannersville Diner
	Lodg	N: Ramada, Chateau Inn, Great Wolf Lodge S: Days Inn, Summit Resort
	Other	N: Four Seasons Campground▲, The Crossings Factory Outlet Mall S: to Big Pocono State Park, Camelback Ski Area
302A		PA 33S, to US 209S, Snydersville
302B		PA 611N, Bartonsville
	TStop	N: AmBest/Crossroads Travel Center (Scales), Bartonsville Travel Center
	Food	N: Rest/Subway/TBell/PHut/Crossroads TC
	Lodg	N: Comfort Inn, Howard Johnson, Knights Inn
	TWash	N: Bartonsville TC

EXIT		PA / NJ
	TServ	N: Crossroads TC/Tires
	Other	N: Laundry/CB/Crossroads TC, Lowe's S: Pocono Vacation Park▲
302		PA 611, Bartonsville
	Other	S: to appr 6mi Silver Valley Campsites▲
303		9th St, Stroudsburg (EB)
	Gas	N: BP
	Food	N: Arby's, Boston Market, Pizza Hut
	Other	N: Stroud Mall, ATMs, Cinemas, CVS
304		US 209S, to PA 33S, Stroudsburg to Snydersville (WB)
	Other	S: to appr 6mi Silver Valley Campsites▲
305		US 209 Bus, Main St, Stroudsburg
	Gas	N: Mobil S: Exxon
	Food	N: Perkins S: Damon's
	Lodge	N: Quality Inn S: Alpine Motel
	Other	N: to Stroud Mall
306		Dreher Ave (WB)
307		PA 611, Park Ave, to PA 191 (EB), PA 191, Broad St (WB)
	Gas	N: Gulf
	Food	N: Chinese, KFC, McDonald's, Mex Rest
	Lodg	N: Best Western, Hampton Inn, Hillside Inn S: Days Inn
308		Prospect St, E Stroudsburg
	Gas	N: Shell, WaWa
	Food	N: Arby's, Burger King, McDonald's
	Lodg	S: Budget Motel, Super 8
	Med	N: + Pocono Medical Center
	Other	N: ATMs, Auto Service, Grocery, Goodyear, Kmart, NAPA, Tires, Wal-Mart sc, Univ
309		US 209, PA 447, Seven Bridge Rd, Stroudsburg, Marshalls Creek
	Gas	N: Exxon◊
	Food	N: Rest/Pocono Grand Hotel
	Lodg	N: Shannon Inn, Pocono Grand Hotel S: Super 8
	Med	N: + Pocono Medical Center
	Other	N: Grocery, RiteAid, Pocono Flea Market, The Christmas Factory, to appr 7mi Otter Lake Camp Resort▲, Delaware Water Gap KOA▲, Cranberry Run CGA , Mountain Vista Campground▲
310		Foxtown Hill Rd, Broad St, to PA 611, DE Water Gap
	S:	PA Welcome Center (WB) (RR, Phone, Picnic, Vend, Info)
	Gas	S: BP, Gulf
	Food	S: Water Gap Diner
	Lodg	S: Deer Head Inn, Pocono Inn
	Other	N: to appr 6mi Delaware Water Gap KOA▲, Foxwood Family Campground▲ S: to Driftstone on the Delaware Campground▲
		NOTE: MM 311: New Jersey State Line

(EASTERN TIME ZONE)

Ⓞ PENNSYLVANIA
Ⓞ NEW JERSEY

(EASTERN TIME ZONE)

1		NJ 606, River Rd (WB)
(2)		Weigh Station (EB)
3		Hainesburg River Rd, Columbia

EXIT		NEW JERSEY
4A		Decatur St, to US 611 Alt, US 46E, NJ 94, Portland, Columbia (EB)
4B		NJ 94, US 46E, US 611 Alt (EB)
	FStop	S: Columbia Fuel Stop/Shell
4C		NJ 94N, Columbia (EB)
4		NJ 94, US 46, Columbia, Portland (WB)
	FStop	S: Columbia Fuel Stop/Shell
	TStop	N: Travel Center of America #6/Mobil (Scales)
	Food	N: McDonald's, CountryPride/Pizza Hut/TacoBell/TA TC
	Lodg	N: Days Inn
	TServ	N: TA TC/Tires
	Other	N: Laundry/WiFi/TA TC, Worthington State Forest, to appr 7mi Camp Taylor Campground▲ S: Delaware River Family Campground▲
(6)		Scenic Overlook (WB) (Autos only)
(7)		NJ Welcome Center (EB) (RR, Phone, Picnic, Vend)
12		CR 521, Hope Blairstown Rd, Hope, Blairstown, Great Meadows
	Gas	S: Shell
	Other	N: to appr 5mi TripleBrook Family Camping Resort▲
19		CR 517, Hackettstown, Andover
	Gas	S: Shell
	Food	S: Rest/Panther Valley Inn
	Lodg	S: Panther Valley Inn
	Med	S: + Hospital
	Other	N: Panther Lake Camping Resort▲
(21)		Scenic Overlook (Both dir)
25		US 206, Newton, Stanhope
	Gas	N: Exxon S: Shell
	Food	N: McDonald's, Subway
	Lodg	N: Extended Stay American, Residence Inn, Wyndham Garden
	Other	N: to Green Valley Beach Family Campground▲, appr 4mi Columbia Valley Campground▲, Panther Lake Camping Resort▲, Windy Acres Campground▲ S: Sam's Club
26		US 46, Main St, Netcong, to Budd Lake, Hackettstown (WB)
	Gas	N: Exxon, Mobil S: Shell
	Food	N: Cattleman's Steakhouse S: Golden Bowl
	Lodg	N: Days Inn S: Best Western, Comfort Suites, Kennedy's Bud Lake Motel
	Other	N: to Goodland Nudist Country Club▲ S: ATMs, CVS, Lowe's, Staples, Sam's Club, Wal-Mart, Delaware River Family Campground▲, Fla-Net Park▲
27		US 206S, NJ 183, Netcong, Flanders, Sommerville
	Gas	N: Mobil◊ S: B&S Auto Repair, Exxon, Shell
	Food	N: Circle Grill, El Coyote, Perkins S: Chili's, Longhorn Steakhouse, Wendy's Mandarin House, McDonald's, Romano's Macaroni Grill
	Other	N: Auto services S: ATMs, Auto service, Wal-Mart, Fla-Net Park▲

◊ = Regular Gas Stations with Diesel   ▲ = RV Friendly Locations   ♥ = Pet Friendly Locations

RED PRINT SHOWS LARGE VEHICLE PARKING/ACCESS ON SITE OR NEARBY   BROWN PRINT SHOWS CAMPGROUNDS/RV PARKS

W I-80

EXIT	NEW JERSEY
28	CR 631, US 46, to NJ 10, Landing, Ledgewood, Lake Hopatcong
Gas	S: GasNGo, Gulf, Hess, Shell
Food	S: Burger King, Deli, Diner, Domino's, KFC, McDonald's, Pizza Hut, Outback Steakhouse, Red Lobster, Ruby Tuesday, Subway, TGI Friday, Tom's Diner, Wendy's
Lodg	S: Days Inn, Kingstown Motel, Roxbury Circle Motel
Other	S: ATMs, Auto Services, BJ's, CVS, Roxbury Mall, Grocery, Tires, Wal-Mart, Walgreen's
30	CR 615, Howard Blvd, Ledgewood, to Mount Arlington
Gas	N: CF, Exxon◇
Food	N: China City, Cracker Barrel, IHOP
Lodg	N: Courtyard, Holiday Inn Express
(32)	TRUCK Rest Area (WB)
34	CR 634, Main St, to NJ 15, Wharton, to Sparta, Randolph
Gas	N: Exxon, Gulf
Food	N: Deli, Ming Court Buffet, Subway
	S: Hot Rod's BBQ, Maria's Pizzeria, Ming's Kitchen, Pancho Villa
Med	S: + St Clares Hospital
Other	N: Grocery, Laundromat, RiteAid, to Valley Beach Family Campground▲
34A	NJ 15S, Wharton, to Dover (WB)
34B	NJ 15N, Wharton, to Sparta (WB)
Other	N: to Picatinny Arsenal, appr 14mi Beaver Hill Campground▲, to Cedar Ridge Campground▲, Kymer's Camping Resort▲
35AB	CR 661, Mt Hope Ave, Dover
35	CR 661, Mt Hope Ave, Dover
Gas	S: Exxon
Food	S: Olive Garden, Steak Escape, Subway, Starbucks, Wendy's
Lodg	S: Hilton Garden Inn
Med	S: + Urgent Medical Care
Other	S: ATMs, Best Buy, PetSmart♥, Wal-Mart, Rockaway Townsquare Mall
37	CR 513, Hibernia Ave, Rockaway
Gas	N: Exxon, Shell
Food	N: Damon's, Hibernia Diner
	S: Sherwood's Deli
Lodg	N: Best Western, Hampton Inn
Med	S: + Hospital
38	US 46E, to NJ 53, Denville (EB)
Gas	N: Exxon, Sunoco
	S: Shell
Food	N: Burger King, Wendy's
Med	N: + Hospital

EXIT	NEW JERSEY
39	US 46, to NJ 53, Denville (WB)
Gas	N: Exxon, Getty, Shell, Sunoco
Food	N: Banzai Steak House, Denville Diner, Ichiban's, King's Palace, Starbucks, Sushi
Med	N: + St Clare's Hospital
42	NJ 46, NJ 202, Parsippany, Morris Plains
42ABC	US 202, Cherry Hill Rd, to US 46, Parsippany, US 202, to NJ 10, Morris Plains (Serv N to US 46)
(43)	Jct I-287, to US 46, Morristown, Boonton, Mahwah
(43A)	Jct I-287, to US 46, Morristown, Boonton, Mahwah
45	CR 637, Beverwyck Rd, to US 46, to Lake Hiawatha, Whippany (EB)
Gas	N: BP, Gulf
Food	N: Bennigan's, Burger King, Chili's, IHOP, Outback Steakhouse, Taco Bell, Wendy's, Stockyard Steakhouse/Hol Inn
Lodg	N: Holiday Inn, Howard Johnson, Ramada Inn, Red Roof Inn♥
Other	N: ATMs, Best Buy, Grocery, Kmart, Pharmacy, Staples
(47A)	Jct I-280E, Newark (EB)
47B	US 46, Parsippany (EB)
47	US 46W, Parsippany (WB)
48	Hook Mtn Rd, to US 46, Pine Brook, The Caldwells, Lincoln Park, Montville, Pinebrook (WB)
Gas	S: Coastal, Getty
Food	S: Don Pepe II Rest, Wendy's
Lodg	S: Holiday Inn, Sunset Motel
52	Two Bridges Rd, to US 46, Fairfield, Lincoln Park, Caldwells
Other	S: to Essex Co Airport✈
53	US 46E, NJ 23, Wayne, Butler, Verona
Gas	S: Exxon, Mobil, Sunoco
Food	S: Applebee's, Burger King, McDonald's, Hooters, Red Lobster, Ruby Tuesday, Steak & Ale, TGI Friday, Wendy's
Lodg	S: Holiday Inn, Ramada Inn
Other	S: ATMs, Auto Services, Costco, Firestone, Home Depot, Staples, Target, Willowbrook Mall
54	CR 642, Minnisink Rd, Totowa, Little Falls
Gas	S: BP
Other	S: Best Buy, Office Depot, Staples

EXIT	NEW JERSEY
55AB	CR 646, Union Blvd, Totowa, Little Falls
56	CR 636, McBridge Ave (WB)
56AB	CR 636, Squirrelwood Rd, Little Falls, W Paterson, Paterson
Gas	S: Mobil
57AB	NJ 19, Main St, Downtown Paterson, Clifton
57C	Main St, Paterson (WB)
58AB	Madison Ave, Patterson, Clifton
Gas	N: Exxon
Med	S: + St Joseph's Reg'l Medical Center
59	Market St (WB)
60	NJ 20, to US 46, Hawthorne
61	NJ 507, Garfield, Elmwood Park
Gas	S: Sunoco
62	Garden State Pkwy (WB)
62A	to Garden State Pkwy, Saddlebrook
Gas	N: Shell
Lodg	N: Howard Johnson, Marriott
	S: Holiday Inn
62B	Saddle River Rd (EB)
63	to NJ 4, NJ 17N, Rochelle Park, Paramus, Lodi, Fairlawn
Gas	N: BP, Citgo, Hessd
64AB	to NJ 4, NJ 17, to US 46E, Newark, Rochelle Park, Paramus
Gas	S: BP, Exxon
Lodg	S: Hilton
Med	N: + Hackensack Univ Med Center
65	Green St, Teterboro, S Hackensack
Gas	S: Exxon
Lodg	S: Airport Motel, Marriott
Other	S: to Wal-Mart, Teterboro Airport✈
66	Hudson St, Hackensack, Little Ferry
Other	N: Costco
67	Bogota, Ridgefield Park (EB)
(68A)	Jct I-95S, NJ 46, NJ Tpk (TOLL)
(68B)	Jct I-95N, George Washington Bridge, New York

NOTE: NJ TPK / I-95 continues into NY

(EASTERN TIME ZONE)

🎧 NEW JERSEY

Begin Westbound I-80 from Jct I-95 in Englewood, NJ to San Francisco, CA

◇ = Regular Gas Stations with Diesel ▲ = RV Friendly Locations ♥ = Pet Friendly Locations
RED PRINT SHOWS LARGE VEHICLE PARKING/ACCESS ON SITE OR NEARBY   BROWN PRINT SHOWS CAMPGROUNDS/RV PARKS

INTERSTATE 81 S

EXIT	NEW YORK
	Begin Southbound I-81 from Canada/New York border to Jct I-40 near Knoxville, TN.

ⓘ NEW YORK
(EASTERN TIME ZONE)
(I-81 begins/ends at NY/CANADA border)

NOTE: NYS is NOT mileage based exits. Listed is Mile Marker/Exit #.

Exit	Description
(183)	**US/CANADA Border, Customs, AmEx Duty Free Be Prepared to STOP**
182/52	CR 191, Island Rd, De Wolf Point
NOTE:	NB: LAST US EXIT
179/51	Island Rd, Island State Parks
Gas	E: Citgo
Food	E: South of the Border Café
Lodg	E: Torchlite Lodge & Motel
(178)	**1000 Islands Bridge (NB: TOLL)**
177/50	NY 12, Alexandria Bay, Clayton
	NOTE: NB: Last FREE Exit Before TOLL
	NY Welcome Center (SB) (RR, Phone, Picnic, Info) **Rest Area (NB)** (RR, Phone, Picnic, NY State Police)
Gas	W: Citgo, Mobil
Food	E: Beefers Diner & Steakhouse, Kountry Kottage, Subway
Lodg	E: Bridgeview Motel, Rock Ledge Motel
Med	E: + Hospital
Other	E: Keewaydin State Park▲, Pine Tree Point Resort▲ W: Captain Clayton Campground▲, Thousand Island Campground▲
(174)	**Rest Area (NB)** (RR, Phone, Picnic, Info, NY St Police)
167/49	NY 411, Plank Rd, Theresa
(166)	**Parking Area (SB)**
(162)	**Parking Area (NB)**
160/48	NY 342, Fort Drum, Black River (SB) to US 11, to NY 37 (NB), Watertown
FStop	E: Nice n Easy Grocery #36/Citgo
TStop	E: Longways Truck Stop/Mobil, Sugar Creek Store #590/Sunoco
Food	E: FastFood/Nice n Easy, Rest/Longways TS, FastFood/Sugar Creek
Lodg	E: Allen's Budget Motel, Microtel, Royal Inn
Other	E: Laundry/WiFi/LP/Sugar Creek, Fort Drum Military Res
(159)	**Parking Area (Both dir)**
157/47	NY 12, Bradley St, Watertown, Clayton
FStop	E: Nice n Easy Grocery/Mobil
Other	E: PetCo♥, RV Center
156/46	NY 12F, Coffeen St, Watertown
Gas	E: Mobil W: Citgo
Food	E: Cracker Barrel, Diner
Med	E: + Urgent Care
Other	E: ATM, Home Depot W: FedEx Kinko's, Jefferson Comm College, Watertown Muni Airport✈, to appr 6mi Black River Bay Campground▲
155/45	NY 3, Arsenal St, Watertown
Gas	E: Citgo, Mobil

EXIT	NEW YORK
Food	E: Applebee's, Burger King, China Café, Denny's, Dunkin Donuts, McDonald's, KFC, Pizza Hut, Panda Buffet, Ponderosa, Taco Bell, Wendy's W: Bob Evans, Red Lobster
Lodg	E: Days Inn, Econo Lodge, Holiday Inn Express W: Ramada
Med	E: + Hospital
Other	E: ATMs, Banks, Auto Zone, Big Lots, Grocery, Laundromat, Pharmacy, Staples, UPS Store, US Post Office W: ATMs, Gander Mountain, Kmart, Sam's Club, Target, Wal-Mart sc, Salmon Run Mall, Cinemas, to Bedford Creek Marina & Campground▲, Westcott State Park▲
(151)	**Parking Area (NB)**
150/44	NY 232, Watertown Center (Serv 4 mi E in Watertown)
Med	E: + Hospital
(150)	**Rest Area (SB)** (RR, Phone, Picnic, NY St Police)
148/43	to US 11, Kellogg Hill
146/42	NY 177, Smithville, Adams Center
Gas	E: Mobil, Sunoco
141/41	NY 178, Church St, Adams, Henderson
Gas	E: Citgo◆
Food	E: McDonald's
135/40	NY 193, Ellisburg, Pierrepont Manor
Other	W: Southwick Beach State Park
(134)	**Parking Area (Both dir)**
133/39	CR 90/94, Lilac Park Dr, Mannsville
131/38	US 11, Mannsville
128/37	CR 15 (NB), CR 22A (SB), Sandy Creek, Lacona, Boylston
Gas	W: Gas Mart, Sunoco◆
Food	E: J&R Diner W: Subway
Lodg	E: Harris Lodge
Other	W: Laundromat, Oswego Co Fairgrounds, Sandy Island Beach State Park
121/36	CR 2, Richland Rd, Pulaski (SB, No reaccess) NY 13, Rome St, to US 11, Pulaski (NB, No reaccess)
Gas	E: Citgo W: KwikFill, Mobil
Food	E: Ponderosa W: Arby's, Burger King, McDonald's, Stefano's Pizza, Waffleworks
Lodg	E: Redwood Motel W: Super 8
Other	E: Stoney's Pineville Campground▲, Fox Hollow Salmon River Lodge▲ W: ATMs, Auto Dealer, Grocery, Pharmacy, NAPA, Fish Hatchery, Selkirk Shores State Park, NY State Police
119/35	to US 11, Tinker Cavern Rd
115/34	NY 104, to Mexico, Oswego
TStop	E: Sun-Up Auto Truck Plaza/Sunoco, Ezze Auto Truck Stop (Scales)
Food	E: Rest/SunUp ATP, Rest/Ezze ATS
Lodg	W: La Siesta Motel
Other	E: WiFi/BarbSh/LP/SunUp ATP, Laundry/Ezze ATS, Steamside Campground▲

◆ = Regular Gas Stations with Diesel   ▲ = RV Friendly Locations   ♥ = Pet Friendly Locations
RED PRINT SHOWS LARGE VEHICLE PARKING/ACCESS ON SITE OR NEARBY   BROWN PRINT SHOWS CAMPGROUNDS/RV PARKS

Page 393

Interstate 81 N/S

NEW YORK

EXIT		
	Other	W: to J & J Campground▲, Salmon Country Marina & Campground▲, Yogi Bear Jellystone Campground▲
111/33		NY 69, E Main St, Parish
	FStop	E: Sunoco/Grist Mill Rest
	Gas	W: Kwik Fill, Mobil◆
	Food	E: Grist Mill Rest
	Lodg	E: Parish Motel
	Other	E: to appr 4mi Bass Lake Resort▲, appr 8mi Up Country Family Campground▲
104/32		NY 49, Central Square
	TStop	E: Penn Can Truck Stop/Mobil
	Gas	W: Fastrac
	Food	E: FastFood/Penn Can TS
		W: Burger King, Hardee's, McDonald's
	TWash	E: Penn Can TS
	Other	E: WiFi/LP/Penn Can TS
		W: Grocery
(101)		Inspection Station (SB)
(101)		Rest Area (SB) (RR, Phones, Picnic) (Next RA 73 mi)
100/31		Bartel Rd, to US 11, Brewerton
	Gas	W: Mobil, Sunoco
	Food	E: Good Golly Rest
		W: Burger King, Dunkin Donuts, McDonald's, Subway
	Lodg	W: Holiday Inn Express
	Other	E: Oneida Shores Co Park▲
		W: Laundromat, Pharmacy, Wal-Mart
95/30		NY 31, Cicero, Bridgeport
	Gas	E: Hess, Mobil, Sunoco
		W: Kwik Fuel
(93/29)		Jct I-481, NY 481, S to Syracuse, DeWitt, N to DeWitt, Oswego (SB: Use I-481 to ByPass) (Serv @ 1st Ex, Ex #10)
92/28		Taft Rd, N Syracuse (SB)
91/27/28		Syracuse Airport, Taft Rd, N Syracuse (NB)
	Gas	E: Mobil
		W: KwikFill
	Food	W: Burger King, Ponderosa, Taco Bell, Wendy's
	Lodg	E: Ledge Inn
		W: Traveler's Motel
	Other	E: Pharmacy, Kmart, USMC Reserve Training Center, NY Army Natl Guard, Hancock Field USAF Base, NY State Police
92/27/26		US 11, Syracuse Airport, Mattydale, Syracuse (SB)
	Gas	E: Mobil, Sunoco
		W: Hess◆, Kwik Fill, Mobil
	Lodg	W: Econo Lodge, Rest Inn
	Other	E: ATMs, Big Lots, Kmart, Staples
		W: Auto Dealers, Auto Services, US Post Office, NY State Police
90/26		US 11, Brewerton Rd, Mattydale (NB)
	Gas	E: Citgo, Mobil
		W: Hess, KwikFill
	Food	E: Asian 98 Buffet, China Road, Café, Friendly's, Pizza Hut
		W: Beneventos Italian, Burger King, McDonald's, Ponderosa, Sal's Seafood, Taco Bell, Wendy's
	Lodg	E: Red Carpet Inn
		W: Candlewood Suites, Rest Inn

EXIT		
	Other	E: Pharmacy, Kmart, USMC Reserve Training Center, NY Army Natl Guard, Hancock Field USAF Base
(89/25A)		I-90, NY ThruWay, Rochester, Buffalo, Albany
88/25		7th North St, Liverpool
	TStop	E: Pilot Travel Center #380 (Scales)
	Gas	W: Mobil
	Food	E: McDonald's/Pilot TC
		W: Bob Evans, Colorado Mine Co Steak house, Denny's, Friendly's, Tully's Good Times, Rest/Ramada Inn
	Lodg	W: Days Inn, Econo Lodge, Quality Inn, Ramada Inn, Super 8
	TWash	E: Express Wash/Pilot TC
	TServ	E: Valerino Auto & Truck Repair, Syracuse Crank & Machine
	Other	E: Laundry/WiFi/Pilot TC, Auto Services
87/23AB, 22		NY 298, to I-690W, Hiawatha Blvd, Bear St, Carousel Center Dr (SB)
	Gas	W: Hess
	Food	E: Market Diner, Wendy's
	Other	E: Alliance Bank Stadium, Amtrak, Greyhound, Carousel Center
87/24AB/23		NY 370, Hiawatha Blvd, Park St, Old Liverpool Rd, Onandaga Lake Pkwy, Liverpool (NB) NOTE: Trucks / Vehicles 9'+ MUST use Old Liverpool Rd to Liverpool
	Gas	W: Hess
	Food	E: Market Diner, Wendy's
	Other	E: Alliance Bank Stadium, Amtrak, Greyhound, Carousel Center
		W: Mall
86/22		NY 298, Sunset Ave, Court St (NB)
85/21		Spencer St, Catawba St (SB)
84/20		Franklin St, West St, Downtown Syracuse (SB)
84/19		Clinton St, Salina St (SB)
(84)		I-690, E Syracuse, Baldwinsville, Fairgrounds (NB), I-690E (SB)
83/18		Adams St, Harrison St
	Lodg	E: Genesee Inn, Marriott, Marx Hotel, Sheraton
		W: Hotel Syracuse, Harbor Inn
	Med	E: + Hospital
	Other	E: CVS, to Syracuse Univ
82/17		S Salina St, Brighton Ave, State St
(81/16A)		I-481N, to De Witt (fr SB, L exit) (NB: Use 481N to ByPass)
77/16		US 11, Nedrow, Onondaga Nation Territory
	Gas	W: Hess, Daniels Car Care/Mobil
	Food	W: McDonald's, Nedrow Diner, Pizza Hut
	Other	W: Onandaga Indian Res
73/15		US 20 (SB), to US 11 (NB), La Fayette
	FStop	E: Nice n Easy Grocery #7/Sunoco
	Food	E: Deli, Pizza
		W: McDonald's
	Other	E: Grocery, NAPA, US Post Office, NY State Police
(70)		Inspection Station (Both dir)
66/14		NY 80, US 11, Tully
	FStop	E: Nice n Easy Grocery #12/Sunoco
	Food	E: Deli/Nice n Easy

EXIT		
	Food	W: Burger King
	Lodg	W: Best Western
	Other	E: Highland Forest Co Park
62/13		NY 281, Tully, to Preble
(60)		Inspection Station (NB)
(60)		Rest Area (NB) (RR, Phones, Picnic, Info, NY St Police)
54/12		US 11, NY 41, NY 281, Cortland, Homer, Ithaca
	FStop	W: Express Mart #323/Mobil
	Gas	W: KwikFill
	Food	W: Applebee's, Burger King, Fabio's Italian, Pizzeria
	Lodg	W: Budget Inn, Country Inn
	Other	W: to Fillmore Glen State Park
52/11		NY 13, Clinton Rd, Cortland, Ithaca
	Gas	W: Mobil
	Food	E: Denny's
		W: Arby's, Bob Evans, Friendly's, Little Caesars, McDonald's, Subway, Taco Bell, Wendy's, Rest/Holiday Inn
	Lodg	E: Comfort Inn, Super 8
		W: Holiday Inn
	TServ	W: Cortland Tire Service
	Other	E: Yellow Lantern Kampground▲
		W: Pharmacy, Grocery, AdvanceAuto, Courtland Co Chase Field✈, Fillmore Glen State Park
49/10		US 11, NY 41, Cortland, McGraw
	FStop	W: Express Mart #308/Mobil
	TStop	W: Pit Stop Travel Center/Citgo
	Gas	W: Sunoco
	Food	W: Subway/Expr Mart, BurgerKing/PizzaHut Pit Stop TC, Diner, Pizza Express
	Lodg	W: Cortland Motel, Days Inn♥
	Other	W: LP/Express Mart, Laundry/WiFi/LP/ Pit Stop TC
38/9		NY 221, Main St, Marathon
	Gas	W: Citgo, XtraMart
	Food	W: Kathy's Diner, NY Pizzeria, Reilly's Café, Rest/3 Bear Inn
	Lodg	W: Three Bear Inn
	Other	W: Grocery, Yogi's Campground▲, Country Hills Campground▲, Bowman Lake State Park
(33)		Inspection Station (SB)
(33)		Rest Area (SB) (RR, Phones, Picnic, NY St Police)
30/8		NY 79, to US 11, to NY 26, to NY 206, Whitney Point (SB)
	Gas	E: Hess, Mobil
	Food	E: McDonald's, Subway
	Lodg	E: Point Motel
28/8		NY 26, to US 11, to NY 79, to NY 206, Whitney Point (NB)
21/7		US 11, Castle Creek
16/6		US 11, NY 12, to I-88E (SB), US 11, NY 12, Chenango Bridge (NB)
	Gas	E: Exxon, Hess◆, Mobil
		W: Kwik Fill, Mobil
	Food	E: Burger King, Denny's, Pizza Hut, McDonald's, Ponderosa, TCBY, Wendy's
	Lodg	W: Days Inn, Comfort Inn, Motel 6♥
	Other	E: CVS, Grocery, Lowe's, Staples, Northgate Speedway, Broome Co Comm College Norwich Binghamton Reg'l Airport✈

◆ = Regular Gas Stations with Diesel   ▲ = RV Friendly Locations   ♥ = Pet Friendly Locations
RED PRINT SHOWS LARGE VEHICLE PARKING/ACCESS ON SITE OR NEARBY   BROWN PRINT SHOWS CAMPGROUNDS/RV PARKS

EXIT	NY / PA
(15)	I-88E, to Albany (NB)
14/5	US 11, Front St NB), to I-88 (SB)
Gas	E: Mobil, Valero
Food	E: Great Wall Chinese W: Applebee's, Cracker Barrel, Quiznos, Starbucks
Lodg	E: Howard Johnson, Riverfront B&B, Super 8 W: Days Inn, Fairfield Inn, Motel 6 ♥, Super 8
Other	E: Broome Co Comm College
13	NY 17W, Owego, Elmira (fr NB, Left exit)
12/4	NY 7, Binghamton, Hillcrest
Gas	W: Express Mart, Mobil
Food	W: Subway
Lodg	W: Howard Johnson, Super 8
Other	W: ATM, CVS, Grocery
12/3	Broad Ave, Downtown (NB)
Gas	W: Exxon
9/3	Colesville Rd, Industrial Park, Binghamton (SB)
TStop	W: NB: Acc Via Ex #2 Travel Center of America #207 (Scales), Pilot Travel Center #170 (Scales)
Gas	W: Exxon
Food	W: Buckhorn/TA TC/Wendy's/Pilot TC, KFC, McDonald's
Lodg	W: Del Motel, Holiday Inn, Super 8, Wright Motel
Other	W: Laundry/WiFi/TA TC, Laundry/WiFi/Pilot TC, CVS, Grocery
(7)	NY 17, New York, I-86E (SB, Left Exit)
7/2	US 11, Five Mile Pt (SB) I-86E, NY 17, US 11, New York, Industrial Park (NB)
4/1	Cedarhurst St, to US 11, NY 7, Kirkwood, Conklin
Gas	W: Mobil
Lodg	W: Kirkwood Motel, Larrabee B&B
(1)	NY Welcome Center (NB) (RR, Phone, Picnic, Vend, NY St Police)
(1)	Inspection Station (NB)
NOTE:	NYS is NOT mileage based exits. Listed is Mile Marker/Exit #.

⬆ NEW YORK
⬇ PENNSYLVANIA
(EASTERN TIME ZONE)

NOTE:	MM 233: New York State Line
(232)	PA Welcome Center (SB) (RR, Phone, Picnic, Info)
(232)	Truck Scales (SB)
230	PA 171, to US 11, Great Bend, Susquehanna
Gas	E: Mobil W: Exxon◆, Sunoco◆
Food	W: Burger King, Country Kitchen, McDonald's, Subway, Rest/Colonial Motel
Lodg	W: Colonial Brick Motel
223	PA 492, New Milford, Lakeside
Gas	W: Gulf◆, Mobil
Other	W: Montrose Campsites▲, East Lake Campground▲

EXIT	PENNSYLVANIA
219	PA 848, Harford Rd, PA 2081, New Milford, to Gibson
TStop	W: Flying J Travel Plaza #5062/Shell (Scales), Gibson Travel Plaza/Exxon
Food	W: CountryMarket/FastFood/FJ TP, McDonald's/Gibson TP
Lodg	W: Holiday Inn Express
TServ	W: Gibson Truck & Tire Service
Other	E: April Valley Campsites▲, PA State Hwy Patrol Post W: Laundry/WiFi/RVDump/LP/FJ TP
217	PA 547, Harford
TStop	E: PTP/Liberty Travel Plaza/Exxon, Penn Can Travel Plaza/Getty
Food	E: Subway/Liberty TP, Rest/Penn Can TP
TServ	E: Penn Can TS/Tires
Other	E: CB/Liberty TP
211	PA 92 (SB), PA 106 (NB), Lenox
Gas	W: Mobil◆, Shell◆
Food	W: Lenox Rest
Other	W: to appr 6mi Shore Forest Campground▲
(208)	PA Welcome Center (SB) (RR, Phones, Picnic, Info)
206	PA 374, Lenoxville, to Glenwood
Other	E: to ELK Mountain Ski Resort
(203)	Rest Area (NB) (RR, Phones, Picnic)
202	PA 107, Fleetville, Tompkinsville
201	PA 438, East Benton
Gas	W: Mobil◆
199	PA 524, Scott
TStop	E: Scott 60 Truck & Travel Plaza/Gulf, BP 60
Gas	W: Exxon
Food	E: Rest/FastFood/Scott 60 TTP
Lodg	W: Motel 81
TWash	E: Scott 60 TTP
Tires	E: Scott 60 TTP
Other	E: Laundry/Scott 60 TTP
197	PA 632, Clarks Summit, Waverly
Gas	W: Sunoco
Food	W: Deli
Other	E: Food Mart, RiteAid
194	US 6W, US 11, to I-476S, PA Tpk, Clarks Summit
Gas	W: Shell◆, Sheetz, Sunoco◆
Food	W: Burger King, Damon's, Garlic Jim's, McDonald's, Pizza Hut, Subway, Starbucks, Taco Bell, Wendy's
Lodg	W: Comfort Inn, Econo Lodge, Hampton Inn, Nichols Village Inn, Ramada
Other	W: AdvanceAuto, Grocery, Pharmacy, Tires, UPS Store, to appr 8 mi Highland Campground▲, appr 14 mi Yogi Bear Jellystone Park Camp Resort▲
191B	to US 11, Scranton Expwy, Scranton NOTE: Trucks Over 10.5 Tons, Use Ex #185
Other	W: to Lackawanna Coal Mine Tour, Anthracite Museum
191A	US 6E Bus, Dickson City, Carbondale
Gas	E: Shell, Sheetz
Food	E: Applebee's, Arby's, Burger King, China Buffet, Denny's, Lone Star Steak House, McDonald's, Olive Garden, Pizza Hut, Perkins, Red Lobster, Subway, TGI Friday, Wendy's

◆ = Regular Gas Stations with Diesel   ▲ = RV Friendly Locations   ♥ = Pet Friendly Locations

RED PRINT SHOWS LARGE VEHICLE PARKING/ACCESS ON SITE OR NEARBY   BROWN PRINT SHOWS CAMPGROUNDS/RV PARKS

Page 395

EXIT	PENNSYLVANIA
Lodg	E: Days Inn, Fairfield Inn, Residence Inn
Other	E: ATMs, Borders, Circuit City, Firestone, Grocery, Home Depot, PetSmart♥, Target, **Wal-Mart sc**, Viewmont Mall, Electric City Harley Davidson
190	**Main Ave, Dickson City**
Food	E: Arby's, Charlie Brown's Steakhouse, Golden Corral, Old Country Buffet, Pizza Hut, Uno Chicago Grill, Wendy's
Lodg	E: Fairfield Inn, Residence Inn
Other	E: Viewmont Mall, Gander Mountain, Lowe's, Sam's Club, Staples, Endless Mountain Theater
	W: Auto & Truck Repairs, **Royal RV Center**
188	**PA 347, Blakely St, Scranton, to Throop, Dunmore**
Gas	E: Sunoco, Sheetz
	W: Mobil
Food	E: China World Buffet, McDonald's, Quiznos, Wendy's
	W: Burger King, Pizza, Subway
Lodg	E: Days Inn, Dunmore Inn, Sleep Inn, Super 8♥
TServ	E: Motor Truck Equipment Co, Freightliner
Other	E: CVS, Grocery, PA State Hwy Patrol Post, Penn State Scranton Campus
	W: to Marywood Univ
(187)	**Jct I-84E, I-380S, US 6E, to Milford, Mt Pocono, Carbondale**
Other	E: to appr 20mi Keen Lake Camping & Cottage Resort▲
186	**Drinker St, Dunmore (NB)**
Gas	E: Mobil
	W: Citgo
185	**Central Scranton Expressway (NB Left Exit, SB Exit Only)**
Other	W: UPS Store, to Scranton Memorial Stadium, Univ of Scranton
184	**PA 307, Moosic St (SB), River St, to PA 307 (NB), Scranton**
Gas	W: Citgo, Exxon
Food	W: Dunkin Donuts, Pizza
Lodg	W: Clarion
Med	W: + Hospital
Other	W: CVS, Dollar Tree, Grocery
182	**Montage Mountain Rd, Davis St (NB)**
Gas	E: Exxon
	W: Mobil
Food	E: Ruby Tuesday
	W: McDonald's, Wendy's
Lodg	E: Comfort Inn, Courtyard, Hampton Inn
	W: Econo Lodge
Other	W: US Post Office
182B	**Davis St (SB)**
182A	**Montage Mountain Rd (SB)**
180	**US 11, Birney Ave, to PA 502 Moosic (fr NB, Left Exit)**
Gas	W: BP◊
Food	W: Subway/BP
178B	**PA 315S, to Avoca**
TStop	W: Petro Stopping Center #63 (Scales)
Food	W: IronSkillet/PizzaHut/Petro SC
TServ	W: Petro SC/Tires
Other	W: Laundry/BarbSh/Massg/WiFi/RVDump/Petro SC
178A	**PA 315N, to Wilkes Barre, Scranton Int'l Airport**
Food	E: Damon's
Lodg	E: Holiday Inn Express
Other	E: Wilkes-Barre Scranton Intl Airport✈

EXIT	PENNSYLVANIA
175B	**PA 315N, to Dupont (SB)**
175A	**PA 315S, to I-476/PA TPK to Pittston (SB)**
175	**PA 315N, to I-476/PA TPK, Dupont, Pittston (NB)**
FStop	W: Hi-Way Auto & Truck Plaza/Getty
TStop	W: Pilot Travel Center #370 (Scales)
	(SB Access via Ex# 175B)
Gas	E: Mobil◊, Sunoco
Food	E: Arby's, BBQ Express, Dunkin Donuts, McDonald's, Perkins
	W: Wendy's/Pilot TC
Lodg	E: Knights Inn♥, Quality Inn, Super 8
TServ	W: Hi-Way ATP/Tires, Pilot TC/Tires
Other	W: Laundry/WiFi/Pilot TC, Wal-Mart
170B	**PA 309N, Wilkes-Barre**
Gas	W: Exxon◊, Sunoco◊
	W: Sunoco◊
Food	W: McDonald's, Perkins, Pizza Hut, Lone Star Steakhouse, TGI Friday
Lodg	E: Best Western
	W: Days Inn, Hampton Inn, Holiday Inn, Red Roof Inn♥, Woodlands Inn
Med	W: + US Veterans Hospital, + Mercy Family Health Center
Other	W: Wyoming Valley Mall, Kings College, Wilkes Univ
170A	**PA 115S, Bear Creek**
Gas	E: Exxon◊, Sunoco◊
Lodg	E: Best Western, East Mountain Inn
Med	E: + Wyoming Valley Medical Center
Other	E: to Pocono Downs Racetrack
168	**Highland Park Blvd, Wilkes-Barre**
Gas	W: Sheetz
Food	W: Applebee's, Bob Evans, Burger King, Chili's, **Cracker Barrel**, Ground Round, McDonald's, Olive Garden, Panera, Outback Steakhouse, Red Robin, Smokey Bones BBQ, Starbucks, Wendy's
Lodg	W: Best Western, Hilton Garden Inn, Ramada Inn, Travelodge
Other	W: Wyoming Valley Mall, ATMs, Best Buy, B&N, Circuit City, FedEx Kinko's, Lowe's, Office Depot, PetCo♥, Sam's Club, Target, **Wal-Mart sc**, Wachovia Arena, Arena Hub Plaza
165B	**PA 309 Bus, Wilkes-Barre (NB, Left ex)**
Gas	W: BP◊
Food	W: McDonald's, Perkins, Taco Bell
Lodg	W: Comfort Inn, Econo Lodge
Other	W: ATM, Auto Services, Kmart
165A	**PA 309S, Mountain Top (NB)**
165	**PA 309S, PA 309 Bus, Mountain Top, Wilkes-Barre (SB)**
164	**PA 29N, Ashley, Nanticoke**
159	**Church St, Mountain Top, Nuangola**
Gas	W: BP
NOTE:	MM 158: Begin Call Box SB, End NB
(158)	**Rest Area (SB)**
	(RR, Phones, Picnic)
(157)	**Truck Scales (SB)**
(156)	**Rest Area (NB)**
	(RR, Phones, Picnic)
(155)	**Truck Scales (NB)**

EXIT	PENNSYLVANIA
155	**Blue Ridge Trail, Mountain Top, to Dorrance, Drums**
TStop	E: Blue Ridge Plaza
Gas	E: Sunoco
(151B)	**Jct I-80W, to Bloomsburg**
(151)	**Jct I-80E, to Stroudsburg**
145	**PA 93, Berwick Hazelton Hwy, Susquehanna Blvd, W Hazelton**
Gas	E: Shell, Sunoco◊, Shell, Turkey Hill
Food	E: Friendly's, Ground Round, Long John Silver, McDonald's, Perkins, Pizza Hut, Taco Bell, Wendy's
Lodg	E: Comfort Inn, Fairfield Inn, Ramada Inn
	W: Hampton Inn
Med	E: + Hospital
Other	E: Hazelton Muni Airport✈, Penn St Univ/Hazelton
	W: PA State Hwy Patrol Post
143	**PA 924, Hazelton**
FStop	W: Uni-Mart/Exxon
Other	W: to appr 8mi Red Ridge Lake Campground▲
141	**PA 424E, to PA 309, Hazelton**
138	**PA 309, McAdoo, Tamaqua**
134	**Grier Ave, Delano**
(132)	**Parking Area (Both dir)**
131B	**PA 54W, to Mahanoy City**
Gas	W: Exxon, Shell
131A	**PA 54E, to Hometown**
Other	E: to Bendinsky Airport✈, Locust Lake State Park▲, Tuscarora State Park
124B	**PA 61N, to Frackville**
FStop	W: Central Hwy Oil Co/Gulf
Gas	W: Hess, Mobil
Food	W: Dutch Kitchen Rest, Pizza, Subway, Taco Bell
Lodg	W: Econo Lodge, Inn 81
Med	W: + Good Samaritan Reg Med Center
Other	W: RiteAid, PA State Hwy Patrol Post
124A	**PA 61S, to St Clair**
Food	E: Cracker Barrel, Granny's, McDonald's
Lodg	E: Holiday Inn Express, Granny's Motel
TServ	E: Cleveland Bros CAT
Other	E: ATMs, Kmart, Laundromat, Schuylkill Mall, Pioneer Coal Mine Tunnel, Anthracite Coal Museum, 3 mi **Wal-Mart sc**
119	**Highridge Park Rd, Gordon Mtn Rd Pottsville, Ashland, Gordon**
Lodg	E: Country Inn
Med	E: + Hospital
116	**PA 901, Sunbury Rd, Pottsville, to Minersville, Hegins**
Other	W: Schuylkill Co Airport✈
112	**PA 25, E Main St, Tremont, Hegins**
Other	W: Camp-A-While Campground▲
NOTE:	MM 108: Begin Call Box NB, End SB
107	**US 209, Tremont, Tower City**
Food	E: Carter Mtn Girls Cafe, Family Rest, Pizza
104	**TR 634, to Tremount Rd, PA 125, Tremont, Ravine**
TStop	W: PTP/Raceway Truck Stop/Exxon
Food	W: Rest/Raceway TS, Rachel's Country Kitchen
TServ	W: Raceway TS/Tires

Page 396 ◊ = Regular Gas Stations with Diesel ▲ = RV Friendly Locations ♥ = Pet Friendly Locations
RED PRINT SHOWS LARGE VEHICLE PARKING/ACCESS ON SITE OR NEARBY   BROWN PRINT SHOWS CAMPGROUNDS/RV PARKS

INTERSTATE 81 N/S

PENNSYLVANIA

EXIT		
	Other	E: Echo Valley Campground▲
		W: Laundry/Raceway TS
100		**PA 443, Pine Grove**
	FStop	W: Empire Fuel Stop/Sunoco
	TStop	W: Gooseberry Farms Travel Plaza (Scales)
	Gas	E: Exxon◆
	Food	E: McDonald's
		W: Rest/Gooseberry Farm, Arby's, Subway
	Lodg	E: Comfort Inn
		W: Econo Lodge, Hampton Inn
	TServ	W: Gooseberry Farms TC/Tires
	Other	W: to appr 5mi Twin Grove Park & Campground▲, Swatara State Park▲
90		**PA 7, Old Forge Rd, to US 22, Jonestown, Annville, Lebanon**
	TStop	E: Love's Travel Stop #366 (Scales)
	Gas	E: Hess, Shell
		W: Exxon
	Food	E: Chesters/McDonald's/Love's TS, Subway, Wendy's
	Lodg	E: Days Inn
		W: Best Western, Quality Inn
	Other	E: WiFi/Love's TS, PA State Hwy Patrol Post, Lickdale Campground▲, to appr 5 mi Jonestown/I-81/I-78 KOA▲
		W: Fort Indiantown Gap Military Res
(89)		**Jct I-78E, to Allentown (fr SB, L exit)**
85B		**Fort Indiantown Gap (NB)**
	Gas	W: Mobil
	Food	W: Family Rest
	Other	W: PA National Guard Res, Memorial Lake State Park
85A		**PA 934S, Fisher Ave, Annville (NB)**
	TStop	E: Ono Truck Center/Shell
	Other	E: Laundry/Ono TC, Auto Services, Tires, Lebanon Valley College
85		**PA 934S, to US 22, Annville, Ono Ft Indiantown Gap (SB)**
80		**to PA 743, Grantville, Hershey (fr NB, Exit only)**
	Gas	E: Mobil◆
		W: Exxon, Shell
	Lodg	E: Econo Lodge, Hampton Inn
		W: Comfort Inn, Holiday Inn
	Med	E: + Greater Hanover Medical Center
	Other	E: to appr 16mi Hershey Attractions, Hershey Highmeadow Campground▲
		W: Penn National Racetrack
(79)		**Weigh Station (Both dir)**
(78)		**Rest Area (Both dir) (RR, Phones, Picnic)**
77		**PA 39, Linglestown Rd, Harrisburg, to Hershey, Manada Hill**
	FStop	W: Gables of Harrisburg/Shell (Scales)
	TStop	E: Pilot Travel Center #245 (Scales)
		W: Travel Center of America #12 (Scales), WilcoHess Travel Plaza #7001 (Scales)
	Gas	E: Exxon◆, Mobil◆
	Food	E: PizzaHut/Pilot TC, Café/Mobil
		W: CountryPride/TA TC, Perkins/WH TP, Subway/Gables
	Lodg	E: Country Hearth, Country Inn, Howard Johnson, Scottish Inn
		W: Daystop Inn/TA TC, Comfort Inn
	TServ	W: TA TC/Tires, WH TP/Tires, Diesel Injection & Turbo Service
	Other	E: WiFi/Pilot TC, PA State Hwy Patrol, West Hanover Winery, to Hershey Attr

PENNSYLVANIA

EXIT		
	Other	W: Laundry/CB/WiFi/TA TC, Laundry/WiFi/WH TP
72B		**Linglestown (NB)**
72A		**to US 22, Paxtonia (NB)**
72		**Mountain Rd, Harrisburg, Paxtonia, Linglestown (SB)**
	Gas	E: Citgo◆, Hess◆, Shell, Sunoco◆
	Food	E: Applebee's, Burger King, Great Wall, McDonald's, Red Robin, Wendy's
	Lodg	E: Holiday Inn Express, Quality Inn
		W: Baymont Inn, Best Western
	Med	E: + Penn State Hershey Medical Center
	Other	E: CVS, Grocery, U-Haul
(70)		**Jct I-83S, US 322E, PA Tpk, to Hershey, York (fr SB, Left exit)**
	Other	E: to Harrisburg Int'l Airport✈
69		**Progress Ave, Harrisburg**
	Gas	E: 7-11, Gulf
	Food	E: Cracker Barrel, Moe's SW Grill, Romano's Macaroni Grill
		W: Arby's, China Chef, Damon's, Nature's Table, Middle Eastern Rest, Western Sizzlin
	Lodg	W: Best Western♥, Red Roof Inn♥
	Other	E: National Civil War Museum, PA State Hwy Patrol Post
		W: Widener Univ
67B		**US 22W, US 322, Lewistown**
67A		**US 22E, to PA 230, Cameron St**
66		**Front St, Downtown Harrisburg (fr SB, Exit Only)**
	Gas	W: Exxon
	Food	W: McDonald's, Pizza Hut, Wendy's
	Lodg	W: Days Inn, Super 8
	Med	E: + Hospital
	Other	E: US Navy Marine Reserve, Amtrak, Bus Terminal
65B		**US 11N, US 15, Marysville (SB)**
65A		**US 11S, US 15, Enola (SB)**
	Gas	E: Mobil, Sunoco◆
	Food	E: DQ, Eat 'n Park, KFC, McDonald's, Subway, Wendy's
	Lodg	E: Quality Inn
	Other	E: Kmart, Radio Shack, RiteAid, to Central PA College
65		**US 11, US 15, Enola, Marysville (NB)**
61		**PA 944, Wertzville Rd, Enola**
	Med	E: + Hospital
59		**PA 581E, US 11 (SB), to I-83 (NB), Camp Hill (fr SB, Left exit)**
		Trucks to Gettysburg, Use PA 581E
57		**PA 114, New Willow Mill Rd, to PA 944, US 11, Mechanicsburg**
	Other	W: to Paradise Stream Family Campground▲
52B		**US 11S, Middlesex, to I-76, Pa Tpk, Pittsburgh, Philadelphia (NB)**
52A		**US 11N, New Kingstown (NB)**
52		**US 11, Harrisburg Pike, to I-76, PA Tpk, New Kingstown, Pittsburgh**
	FStop	E: I-81 Carlisle Fuel Stop/Citgo
		W: Gables of Carlisle/Shell (Scales)
	TStop	E: Flying J Travel Plaza #5200 (Scales)
		W: Petro Stopping Center #36 (Scales), Pilot Travel Center #342 (Scales)

PENNSYLVANIA

EXIT		
	Food	E: CountryMarket/FastFood/FJ TP, Bob Evans, Duffy's, Middlesex Diner
		W: IronSkillet/FastFood/Petro SC, Wendy's/Pilot TC, Arby's, Dunkin Donuts, Hoss's Steak & Sea House, Subway, McDonald's, Waffle House, Rest/HJ,
	Lodg	E: America's Best Inn, Econo Lodge, Holiday Inn, Hotel Carlisle, Super 8
		W: Hampton Inn, Howard Johnson, Quality Inn♥, Ramada Inn
	TWash	W: Blue Beacon TW/Petro SC, Gables of Carlisle TW
	TServ	E: FJ TP/Tires
		W: Petro SC/Tires
	Other	E: Laundry/WiFi/RVDump/LP/FJ TP,
		W: Laundry/BarbSh/CB/WiFi/Petro SC, Laundry/WiFi/Pilot TC, Eddie's Tire & Auto Service, Greyhound, Carlisle Fairgrounds, Carlisle Campground▲
49		**PA 641, High St (SB, diff reaccess)**
	Gas	W: Hess
	Food	E: Red Robin, Starbucks
		W: Burger King, McDonald's, Pizza Hut
	Other	E: Carlisle Airport✈
		W: Carlisle Plaza Mall, Office Max, Target, Dickinson College
48		**PA 74, York Rd (NB, diff reaccess)**
	Gas	W: Gulf, Hess, Kwik-Fill
	Food	W: Blue Mountain Krinkles, Burger King, Farmer's Market Rest, Rillo's
	Other	E: Carlisle Airport✈
		W: CVS, Lowes, Carlisle Plaza Mall
47B		**PA 34N, Hanover St (SB)**
	Gas	W: Mobil
	Food	W: Applebee's, Chili's, Panera, Subway
	Other	W: ATMs, Grocery, Pharmacy, Wal-Mart sc, Carlisle Mall, Greyhound, US Army War College, Carlisle Fairgrounds
47A		**PA 34S, Hanover St (SB)**
	Food	E: Cracker Barrel
	Lodg	E: Sleep Inn
	Other	E: Carlisle Airport✈
47		**PA 34, Hanover St, Carlisle (NB)**
45		**College St, Walnut Bottom Rd**
	Gas	E: BP◆, Mobil, Shell
	Food	E: Bonanza Steakhouse, Dunkin Donuts, Great Wall Buffet, McDonald's, Shoney's
	Lodg	E: Days Inn, Holiday Inn, Super 8
	Med	W: + Hospital
	Other	E: Grocery, Staples, Target, UPS Store, Western Village RV Park▲
44		**PA 465, Allen Rd, to Plainfield**
	Gas	W: Sheetz
	Food	W: Subway
	Other	E: PA State Hwy Patrol Post
		W: Carlisle Fairgrounds
(39)		**Rest Area (SB) (RR, Phones, Picnic)**
(38)		**Rest Area (NB) (RR, Phones, Picnic)**
37		**PA 233, Centerville Rd, Newville**
	Other	E: Pine Grove Furnace State Park
		W: to Col Denning State Park
29		**PA 174, King St, Walnut Bottom Rd, Shippensburg, Walnut Bottom**
	TStop	E: Pharo's Truck Stop (Scales)
	Gas	E: Sunoco
	Food	E: Rest/Pharo's TS
		W: Chinatown, Subway, Wendy's

◆ = Regular Gas Stations with Diesel   ▲ = RV Friendly Locations   ♥ = Pet Friendly Locations

RED PRINT SHOWS LARGE VEHICLE PARKING/ACCESS ON SITE OR NEARBY   BROWN PRINT SHOWS CAMPGROUNDS/RV PARKS

Page 397

INTERSTATE 81 N/S

PENNSYLVANIA

EXIT		
	Lodg	E: Budget Host Inn
		W: AmeriHost Inn, Best Western
	TServ	E: Pharo's TS/Tires
	Med	W: + Seavers Medical Center
	Other	E: Laundry/CB/Pharo's TS
		W: Shippensburg Univ, Shippensburg Airport ✈
24		PA 696, Fayette St, Old Scotland Rd
20		PA 997, Black Gap Rd, to PA 696, Chambersburg, Scotland
	FStop	W: RGS Food Shop #9/BP
	Gas	E: Exxon◆
		W: Sunoco
	Food	E: Flamers Burger, McDonald's, Subway
	Lodg	E: Comfort Inn, Super 8
		W: Sleep Inn
	Other	E: ATMs, Gander Mountain, Chambersburg Mall, to Caledonia State Park, Mont Alto State Park
		W: to Chambersburg Muni Airport✈, Letterkenny Army Depot
17		Walker Rd (fr NB, Exit only)
16		US 30, Lincoln Hwy, Chambersburg, Gettysburg (fr SB, Exit only)
	Gas	E: Exxon, Sheetz
		W: Hess◆
	Food	E: Arby's, KFC, Hong Kong Rest, Perkins, Popeye's, Shoney's, Waffle House
		W: Burger King, Dunkin Donuts, Long John Silver's, McDonald's, Pizza Hut, Starbucks, Taco Bell
	Lodg	E: Days Inn, Four Points Hotel
		W: Best Western, Travelodge
	Med	W: + Hospital
	Other	E: ATMs, Food Lion, Grocery, Lowe's, Radio Shack, WalMart SC, PA State Hwy Patrol Post
		W: Advance Auto, Grocery, to Wilson College
14		PA 316, Wayne Ave, Chambersburg
	Gas	W: Exxon, KwikFill, Sheetz, Shell
	Food	E: Bob Evans, Cracker Barrel
		W: Applebee's, Arby's, China Buffet, Denny's, Dunkin Donuts, Red Lobster, Little Caesar's, Subway, Wendy's
	Lodg	E: Hampton Inn
		W: Fairfield Inn, Econo Lodge, Holiday Inn, Quality Inn
	Other	W: CVS, Grocery, Kmart, Staples
(11)		Truck Scales (SB)
10		PA 914, Marion
(7)		Truck Scales (NB)
5		PA 16, Buchanan Tr, Greencastle, Waynesboro
	FStop	E: t Greencastle Food Mart/Sunoco
	TStop	E: Travel Center of America #213/BP (Scales)
	Gas	W: Exxon◆
	Food	E: Buckhorn/TA TC, Arby's, McDonald's, Subway
		W: Hardee's, Rest/Greencastle Motel
	Lodg	E: RodewayInn/TA TC, Econo Lodge ♥
		W: Castle Green Motel
	TServ	E: TA TC/Tires
	Med	W: + John L Grove Medical Center
	Other	E: Laundry/CB/WiFi/TA TC, to White Tail Ski Resort
3		US 11, Molly Pitcher Hwy
	Gas	E: Molly Pitcher Mini Mart/Exxon

Personal Notes

	Food	E: Rest/Pizza
	Lodg	E: Comfort Inn
(1)		PA Welcome Center (NB) (RR, Phones, Picnic, Vend, Info)
1		PA 163, Mason-Dixon Rd
	Food	W: Mason-Dixon Rest
	Lodg	W: Best Value Inn, State Line Motel
	Other	E: Washington Co Reg'l Airport✈
		W: Keystone RV Center

⊙ PENNSYLVANIA
⊙ MARYLAND (EASTERN TIME ZONE)

NOTE: MM 12: Pennsylvania State Line

10AB		Showalter Rd, to US 11, Hagerstown, Maugansville
9		Maugans Ave, Maugansville, Hagerstown (NB)
	Gas	E: Sheetz, Shell
	Food	E: McDonald's, Taco Bell, Waffle House
		W: Burger King
	Lodg	E: Hampton Inn
		W: Microtel
	TServ	W: Martin WhiteGMC, Mack Trucks
	Other	E: Washington Co Reg'l Airport✈
8		Maugansville Rd (SB exit, NB reacc)
7AB		PA 58, Cearfoss Pike, to US 11, to US 40, Hagerstown
6AB		US 40, E to Hagerstown, W to Huyett
	Gas	E: Exxon◆, Shell

MD / WV

EXIT		
	Food	E: Golden Crown Chinese, Steak-Out, Perkins, Wendy's
		W: Arby's, IHOP, KFC, McDonald's, Ryan's Grill, Subway, TGI Friday
	Lodg	E: Comfort Suites, Days Inn, Holiday Motel, Quality Inn, Super 8
	Med	E: + Hospital
	Other	W: ATMs, Circuit City, Grocery, Home Depot, Wal-Mart sc
5B		Halfway Blvd N, tHagerstown (NB)
5A		Halfway Blvd S, Hagerstown (SB)
5		Halfway Blvd, to US 11, Hagerstown
	TStop	E: Pilot Travel Center #179 (Scales)
		W: AC&T Fuel Center (Scales)
	Gas	E: Sheetz, Shell
		W: Exxon
	Food	E: McDonald's/Subway/Pilot TC, Burger King, CiCi's, Chinatown, Crazy Horse Steakhouse, McDonald's, Olive Garden, Outback Steakhouse, Pizza Hut, Red Lobster, Shoney's, Western Sizzlin
		W: Rest/AC&T FC
	Lodg	E: Country Inn, Holiday Inn Express, Motel 6 ♥, Plaza Hotel
		W: AC&T FC, Super 8
	TServ	E: Massey Ford Trucks
		W: AC&T FC/Tires, C Earl Brown Freightline
	Other	E: Laundry/WiFi/Pilot TC, ATMs, Auto Services, Auto Dealers, CVS, Firestone, Grocery, Kmart, Lowe's, Office Depot, PetCo ♥, Sam's Club, Staples, Target, Valley Mall
		W: Laundry/WiFi/RVDump/AC&T FC
(4)		I-70E, to Frederick, Washington, Baltimore, I-70W, to Hancock, to I-68, Cumberland
2		US 11, Williamsport
	FStop	W: Williamsport Sunoco
	Gas	E: Chevron
		W: Exxon, Shell
	Food	W: McDonald's, Waffle House, Rest/RRI
	Lodg	W: Red Roof Inn ♥
	Other	E: Woodman of the World Campground ▲
		W: Hagerstown/Antietam Battlefield KOA▲
1		MD 63, MD 68, Williamsport
	Gas	W: Citgo
	Lodg	W: State Line Motel
	Other	E: Yogi Bear's Jellystone Park Camp Resort ▲

⊙ MARYLAND (EASTERN TIME ZONE)
⊙ WEST VIRGINIA

NOTE: MM 26: Maryland State Line

(25)		WV Welcome Center (SB) (RR, Phone, Picnic, Info)
23		US 11, Marlowe, Falling Waters
	Gas	W: 7-11, Shell
	Other	E: Falling Waters Campground ▲
		W: RV Center
20		WV 901, Spring Mills Rd, Martinsburg
	Gas	W: Shell ◆
	Lodg	E: Econo Lodge
		W: Holiday Inn Express

Page 398

◆ = Regular Gas Stations with Diesel   ▲ = RV Friendly Locations   ♥ = Pet Friendly Locations
RED PRINT SHOWS LARGE VEHICLE PARKING/ACCESS ON SITE OR NEARBY   BROWN PRINT SHOWS CAMPGROUNDS/RV PARKS

EXIT — WA / VA

16 — WV 9E, N Queen St, Shepherdstown, WV 9W, Berkeley Springs
- Gas: E: Citgo, Exxon◊, Sheetz W: Shell◊
- Food: E: China King, Denny's, Hoss's Steak & Sea House, KFC, Long John Silver, McDonald's, Waffle House
- Lodg: E: Comfort Inn, Knight's Inn, Super 8, Travelodge
- Med: W: + Hospital

14 — CR 13, Dry Run Rd, Martinsburg

13 — CR 15, King St, Downtown
- Gas: E: BP◊, Sheetz
- Food: E: Applebee's, Burger King, **Cracker Barrel**, Outback Steakhouse, Pizza Hut, Kobe, Shoney's, Wendy's
- Lodg: E: Hampton Inn, Holiday Inn, Relax Inn, Scottish Inn
- Med: E: + Hospital
- Other: E: Wal-Mart sc, Amtrak, Tanger Outlet Mall

12 — WV 45, Winchester Ave
- Gas: E: Citgo◊, Sheetz, Shell◊
- Food: E: Arby's, Bob Evans, ChickFilA, **Hardee's**, McDonald's, Papa John's, Ryan's Grill, Ruby Tuesday, Taco Bell, Waffle House, Wendy's
- Lodg: E: Comfort Suites, Economy Inn, Relax Inn, Scottish Inn
- Med: E: + VA Medical Center
- Other: E: ATMs, AutoZone, Auto Services, Grocery, Kmart, Lowe's, Mall

8 — CR 32, Tablers Station Rd, Inwood

5 — WV 51, Inwood, Charlestown
- Gas: E: 7-11, Exxon, Sheetz, Shell◊
- Food: E: Burger King, McDonald's, Pizza Hut, Subway, Waffle House
- Lodg: E: Hampton Inn
- Other: E: ATMs, Food Lion W: to Lazy A Campground▲

(2) — WV Welcome Center (NB)
(RR, Phone, Picnic, Vend, Info)

◯ WEST VIRGINIA
◯ VIRGINIA
(EASTERN TIME ZONE)

NOTE: MM 324: West Virginia State Line

323 — VA 669, US 11, Clear Brook, Whitehall, Winchester
- TStop: W: Flying J Travel Plaza #5073 (Scales)
- Gas: E: Exxon
- Food: W: CountryMarket/FastFood/FJ TP
- Other: W: Laundry/BarbSh/WiFi/RVDump/LP/FJ TP

321 — VA 672, to US 11, Hopewell Rd, Brucetown Rd, Clearbrook
- FStop: E: Old Stone Truck Stop/Citgo
- Food: E: Old Stone Rest

(320) — VA Welcome Center (SB)
(RR, Phones, Picnic, Vend, Info)

317 — US 11, VA 37, Martinsburg Pike, Winchester, Stephenson
- Gas: W: Citgo◊, Exxon◊, Liberty◊, Sheetz◊
- Food: W: Burger King, Denny's, McDonald's
- Lodg: W: Comfort Inn, Econo Lodge, Holiday Inn Express
- Med: W: + Hospital

EXIT — VIRGINIA

Other: E: Mountain Lake Campground▲ W: Various Museums, to 3mi Candy Hill Campground▲, appr 12mi The Cove Campground▲

315 — VA 7, Berryville Pike, Winchester, to Berryville
- Gas: E: Exxon, Sheetz W: Chevron◊, Exxon, Liberty◊, Shell◊
- Food: E: 220 Seafood Rest, Quiznos, Starbucks W: Arby's, Burrough's Steak & Seafood, Captain D's, Hardee's, Little Caesar's, McDonald's, Shoney's, Subway, Wendy's
- Lodg: W: Hampton Inn, Shoney's Inn
- Med: W: + Winchester Hospital
- Other: E: Veramar Vineyard, to appr 9.5mi Watermelon Park▲ W: AutoZone, Food Lion, CVS, Greyhound

313AB — US 17, US 50, US 522, Winchester

313 — US 17, US 50, US 522, Winchester
- Gas: E: BP◊, Exxon, Shell◊ W: Sheetz
- Food: E: **Cracker Barrel**, Golden Corral, Hoss's Steak & Sea House, Hardee's, IHOP, Texas Roadhouse, Waffle House W: Bob Evans, Buffalo Wild Wings, Chili's, CiCi's, KFC, McDonald's, Olive Garden, Perkins, Ruby Tuesday, Subway, Wendy's
- Lodg: E: Comfort Inn, Fairfield Inn, Holiday Inn♥, Red Roof Inn♥, Sleep Inn, Super 8, Travelodge♥ W: Best Western, Hampton Inn, Holiday Inn Express, Quality Inn, Wingate Inn
- Med: W: + Winchester Medical Center
- Other: E: ATMs, Big Lots, Food Lion, Costco, Apple Blossom Mall, Winchester Harley Davidson, to Winchester Reg'l Airport✈ W: ATM, Apple Blossom Mall, Borders, Grocery, Home Depot, Kmart, Kroger, Lowe's, Office Max, **Pharmacy**, Staples, Target, UPS Store, **Wal-Mart** sc, Shenandoah Univ, to The Log Cabin Campground▲

310 — VA 37, to US 11, to US 50W, to US 522, Winchester
- Food: W: Dragon Garden, McDonald's, Outback Steakhouse
- Lodg: W: Best Value Inn, Country Inn, Echo Village Budget Motel, Days Inn, Relax Inn, Royal Inn
- Med: W: + Hospital
- Other: W: ATM, Auto Services, CarQuest, to appr 6mi Candy Hill Campground▲

307 — VA 277, Fairfax St, Fairfax Pike, Stephens City, Greenway Court
- Gas: E: 7-11, Chevron, Shell W: Exxon, Sheetz
- Food: E: Burger King, KFC/Taco Bell, McDonald's, Subway, Waffle House, Wendy's, Western Steer
- Lodg: E: Comfort Inn♥, Holiday Inn Express
- Other: E: ATMs, Food Lion, RiteAid

(304) — Weigh Station (Both dir)

302 — Reliance Rd, VA 627, Middletown
- Gas: E: Exxon◊ W: 7-11, Liberty◊
- Food: W: Rest/Wayside Inn
- Lodg: W: Super 8♥, Wayside Inn
- Other: W: Rte 11 Potato Chip Factory, Camping World, Battle of Cedar Creek Campground▲

◊ = Regular Gas Stations with Diesel   ▲ = RV Friendly Locations   ♥ = Pet Friendly Locations
RED PRINT SHOWS LARGE VEHICLE PARKING/ACCESS ON SITE OR NEARBY   BROWN PRINT SHOWS CAMPGROUNDS/RV PARKS

INTERSTATE 81 N/S

EXIT	VIRGINIA
(300)	Jct I-66E, to Washington, DC, Skyline Dr, Shenandoah Natl Park (SB, Left Exit)
298	US 11, Strasburg
Gas	E: BP◇, Exxon◇
Food	E: Arby's, Burger King, McDonald's
Lodg	E: Hotel Strasburg, Ramada Inn
Other	E: ATM, Family Dollar, Grocery, RiteAid, Battle of Cedar Creek Campground▲
296	VA 55, US 48, John Marshall Hwy, Strasburg
291	VA 651, Mt Olive Rd, Toms Brook
TStop	W: Love's Travel Stop #305 (Scales), WilcoHess Travel Plaza #705 (Scales)
Food	W: Arby's/TJCinn/Love's TP, Milestone Rest/DQ/WH TP
Lodg	E: Budget Inn
TWash	W: WilcoHess TP
TServ	W: Love's TP/Tires
Other	W: WiFi/Love's TP
283	VA 42, Reservoir Rd, Woodstock
Gas	E: BP, Chevron, Liberty, Shell W: Exxon◇, Sunoco
Food	E: Arby's, Dunkin Donuts, Hardee's, KFC, McDonald's, Pizza Hut, Ponderosa, Taco Bell, Wendy's W: Cracker Barrel, Subway
Lodg	E: Budget Host Inn♥, Comfort Inn, Holiday Inn Express
Med	E: + Hospital
Other	E: RiteAid, Massanutten Military Academy W: ATMs, Dollar Tree, Lowe's, Wal-Mart sc
279	VA 185, Stoney Creek Blvd, to US 11, Edinburg
Gas	E: BP◇, Exxon◇, Shell◇
Food	E: Edinburg Mill Rest, Subway
Other	E: Creekside Campground▲, to appr 11mi Luray Country Waye RV Resort▲, Fort Valley Horse & Mule Campgr▲
277	VA 614, Bowmans Crossing
273	VA 292, VA 703, Mt Jackson
TStop	E: Shenandoah Truck Center/Liberty (Scales), Sheetz Travel Center #701 (Scales)
Gas	E: 7-11, Exxon◇
Food	E: Blimpie's/Liberty TC, Wendy's/Sheetz TC Burger King, China King, Denny's
Lodg	E: Best Western, Shenandoah Valley Inn
Other	E: Laundry/WiFi/LP/Shenandoah TC, Laundry/Sheetz TC, Food Lion, US Post Office, to Ski Area
269	VA 730, Caverns Rd, to US 11, Mt Jackson, Shenandoah Caverns
Gas	E: Chevron◇
264	US 211, New Market, Timberville, Luray
Gas	E: BP◇, Chevron◇, Exxon◇, Shell◇ W: 7-11
Food	E: Burger King, McDonald's, Pizza Hut, Southern Kitchen, Taco Bell
Lodg	E: Budget Inn, Quality Inn W: Days Inn♥
Other	E: to Shenandoah Nat'l Park
(262)	New Market Rest Area (Both dir) (RR, Phones, Picnic, Vend, Info)
257	US 11, Lee Jackson Memorial Hwy, to VA 259, N Valley Pike, Broadway
Gas	E: Liberty

Personal Notes

EXIT	VIRGINIA
Food	E: BK/Godfathers/Liberty
Other	E: Harrisonburg/New Market KOA▲, Endless Caverns & RV Resort▲
251	US 11, N Valley Pike, Harrisonburg
Gas	W: Exxon◇
Lodg	W: Economy Inn
247B	US 33W, to US 11, Harrisonburg
247A	US 33E, Harrisonburg
247	US 33, E Market St, Harrisonburg
Gas	E: BP◇, Royal, Shell W: Exxon◇, Sheetz, Texaco
Food	E: Applebee's, Bob Evans, Captain D's, Chili's, CiCi's, Golden Corral, IHOP, Long John Silver, Mex Rest, O'Charley's, Outback Steakhouse, Ponderosa, Red Lobster, Ruby Tuesday, Shoney's, Starbucks, Taco Bell, Texas Steakhouse, Waffle House, Wendy's W: Arby's, Golden China, Hardee's, KFC, Kyoto, McDonald's, Pizza Hut, Subway
Lodg	E: Best Western, Candlewood Suites, Comfort Inn, Courtyard, Econo Lodge, Hampton Inn, Holiday Inn, Jameson Inn♥, Motel 6, Shoney's Inn, Sleep Inn
Med	W: + Hospital
Other	E: ATMs, Auto Services, B&N, Banks, Circuit City, Costco, Firestone, Food Lion, Home Depot, K-Mart, Kroger, Lowe's, Office Depot, PetSmart♥, PetCo♥, Staples, Target, UPS Store, Wal-Mart sc, Valley Mall W: CVS, AdvanceAuto, Food Lion, James Madison Univ, Memorial Stadium

EXIT	VIRGINIA
245	VA 659, Port Republic Rd, to US 11, Harrisonburg
Gas	E: Exxon◇, Liberty◇, Texaco
Food	E: Blimpie/Liberty, Subway/Exxon, China Express, Little Caesar's, McDonald's W: Starbucks
Lodg	E: Days Inn, Howard Johnson
Med	W: + Hospital
Other	W: FedEx Kinko's, James Madison Univ
243	US 11, S Main St, Harrisonburg
TStop	W: Harrisonburg Travel Center (Scales)
Gas	W: 7-11, Exxon◇, Liberty
Food	W: Rest/Harrisonburg TC, Burger King, Cracker Barrel, McDonald's, Pizza Hut, Taco Bell, Waffle House
Lodg	E: Country Inn, W: Holiday Inn Express♥, Ramada Inn, Red Carpet Inn, Super 8
TWash	W: Harrisonburg TC
TServ	W: Mack, Kenworth, ThermoKing, Trailers, Southside Auto Truck & RV Service
Other	W: Laundry/WiFi/Harrisonburg TC,
240	VA 257, VA 682, Mt Crawford
Gas	W: Exxon◇
Food	W: Burger King, Country Buffet, Village Inn
Other	W: Bridgewater Air Park✈, Vet♥, to appr 10 mi Natural Chimneys Campground▲
235	VA 256, US 11, Weyers Cave Rd, Weyers Cave, Grottoes
FStop	W: Deno's Food Mart #10/BP
Gas	E: Texaco W: Exxon
Food	E: Subway
TServ	W: Freightliner
Other	E: Grand Caverns, Shenandoah Valley Reg'l Airport✈
(232)	Mt Sydney Rest Area (Both dir) (RR, Phones, Picnic, Vend, Info)
227	VA 612, Laurel Hill Rd, Verona
FStop	E: BP
Gas	W: Citgo◇, Exxon, Shell
Food	E: Waffle Inn W: Arby's, Burger King, Chili's, Hardee's, McDonald's, Wendy's
Lodg	W: Knights Inn
TServ	E: Interstate Auto & Truck Repair
Other	E: Food Lion, to Waynesboro North 340 Campground▲ W: CVS, RiteAid, Carwash/Shell, Food Lion, to Staunton/Verona KOA▲
225	VA 275, Woodrow Wilson Pkwy, VA 262, Staunton, Waynesboro
Food	E: Rest/Q I W: Rest/H I
Lodg	E: Quality Inn W: Days Inn, Holiday Inn♥
222	US 250, Jefferson Hwy, Staunton, Fisherville
Gas	E: Citgo, Exxon, Texaco W: Sheetz
Food	E: Cracker Barrel, McDonald's, Shoney's, Texas Steakhouse, Wendy's W: Burger King, Chili's, Ryan's Grill, Waffle House
Lodg	E: Best Western, Guesthouse Inn, Sleep Inn♥, Shoney's Inn W: Comfort Inn, Econo Lodge, Microtel, Super 8
Other	W: AutoZone, Lowe's, Wal-Mart sc, VA State Hwy Patrol Post, Amtrak

◇ = Regular Gas Stations with Diesel ▲ = RV Friendly Locations ♥ = Pet Friendly Locations
RED PRINT SHOWS LARGE VEHICLE PARKING/ACCESS ON SITE OR NEARBY BROWN PRINT SHOWS CAMPGROUNDS/RV PARKS

EXIT	VIRGINIA
(221)	Jct I-64E, Skyline Dr, Shenandoah Nat'l Park, to Charlottesville, Richmond, Blue Ridge Pkwy
220	VA 262, to US 11, Staunton
Gas	W: BP, Citgo, Exxon
Food	W: Arby's, Burger King, Hardee's, KFC, McDonald's, Red Lobster
Lodg	W: Budget Inn, Hampton Inn, Microtel
Other	W: Shenandoah Harley Davidson, RV Center
217	VA 654, White Hill Rd, Stuarts Draft, Mint Spring
FStop	W: Kangaroo Express/Citgo
Gas	E: BP◊, Exxon◊
Food	E: Subway/BP
	W: Aunt M's/Kangaroo
Lodg	E: Days Inn♥
	W: Relax Inn
Other	E: to appr 8mi Shenandoah Acres Resort▲
	W: appr 4mi Walnut Hills Campground & RV Park▲
213B	US 11W, VA 340, Greenville (SB)
213A	US 11E, VA 340, Greenville (SB)
213	US 11, Staunton, Greenville
TStop	E: Pilot Travel Center #396 (Scales)
Gas	E: BP, Shell
Food	E: Arby's/TJCinn/Pilot TC, Subway/BP, German Rest
Lodg	E: Budget Host Inn
Other	E: Laundry/WiFi/Pilot TC, to Walnut Hills Campground & RV Park▲
205	VA 606, Raphine Rd, Raphine, Steeles Tavern, Vesuvius
TStop	E: AmBest White's Truck Stop (Scales), Smiley's Fuel City, Orchard Creek Auto & RV Plaza/Exxon
	W: WilcoHess Travel Plaza #735 (Scales)
Food	E: Rest/Subway/Starbucks/White's TS, BurgerKing/Orchard Plaza
	W: Wendy's/WH TP, Rest/D I
Lodg	E: Motel/White's TS
	W: Days Inn
TServ	E: White's TS/Tires/TWash
	W: Peterbilt
Other	E: Laundry/CB/WiFi/White's TS, to Crabtree Falls Campground▲, Tye River Gap Campground▲
	W: RV Center
200	VA 710, Sterrett Rd, Fairfield
FStop	W: Stop In Food Store #62/Shell, Fairfield Exxon
Gas	E: BP◊, Texaco
Food	E: Fairfield Diner, McDonald's/BP
	W: Subway/Exxon, Whistlestop Cafe
TServ	W: Smith's Garage
(195)	Fairfield Rest Area (SB) (RR, Phones, Picnic, Vend, Info)
195	US 11, Lee Hwy, Lexington
TStop	W: PTP/Lee-Hi Travel Plaza/Shell (Scales)
Gas	W: Citgo◊
Food	E: Rest/Maple Hall Country Inn
	W: Berky's Rest/Lee Hi TP, Aunt Sarah's Pancake House
Lodg	E: Maple Hall Country Inn, Lexington Historic Inn
	W: Days Inn, Howard Johnson, Ramada Inn
TServ	W: Lee-Hi TP/Tires/VA Truck Center
Other	W: Laundry/BarbSh/WiFi/LP/Lee Hi TP/Campground▲, Auto Repair

BAILEYTON RV PARK
Baileyton, Tennessee
423-234-4992

CAMPGROUND
HORTON HWY
172 ● BAILEYTON
81 EXIT 36
⇐ to Knoxville 65 Miles   to BRISTOL 42 Miles ⇒

GPS Co-ord Latitude 36.33910 N Longitude 82.82332 W

www.BaileytonRVPark.com
1-888-296-2267
7485 Horton Hwy
Baileyton, TN. 37745
I-81 Exit 36

Good Sam Park

EXIT	VIRGINIA
(191)	Jct I-64W, Charleston (fr NB, Left Ex)
188B	US 60W, to Lexington
188A	US 60E, to Buena Vista
188	US 60, E-Buena Vista, W-Lexington (Serv 3-5mi E)
Gas	E: Exxon
	W: Exxon
Food	E: Hardee's, KFC, Long John Silver, Taco Bell, McDonald's, Pizza Hut, Wendy's
Lodg	E: Budget Inn, Comfort Inn, Days Inn
	W: Days Inn, Hampton Inn, Holiday Inn
Other	E: to Stonewall Jackson Home, Museum
	W: Auto Dealers, to VA Military Institute, Washington & Lee Univ
180	US 11, S Lee Hwy, Natural Bridge Glasglow (fr SB, Left Exit)
Gas	E: Shell◊
	W: Shell◊
Food	E: Fancy Hill Rest
	W: Diner
Lodg	E: Relax Inn, Red Carpet Inn
	W: Budget Inn
Other	W: to Natural Bridge/Lexington KOA▲
175	US 11, Natural Bridge, Glasgow
Gas	E: Exxon
Other	E: to Natural Bridge Hotel, Attractions
	W: Yogi Bear's Jellystone Park Resort▲ Speedway, Zoo, Museum
168	VA 614, Arcadia Rd, Buchanan
Gas	E: Shell
Food	E: Burger King, Rest/Wattstull Motel
Lodg	E: Wattstull Motel
Other	E: to appr 6mi Middle Creek CG▲

EXIT	VIRGINIA
167	US 11, Buchanan (SB)
162	US 11, Lee Hwy N, Buchanan
Gas	E: Exxon◊
	W: Texaco
Food	W: Subway/Texaco
(158)	Troutville Rest Area (SB) (RR, Phones, Picnic, Vend, Info)
156	Brughs Mill Rd, VA640, to US 11, to US 220, Fincastle, Troutville
Gas	E: Exxon◊
150B	US 220N, Daleville
150A	US 220S, to 460E, Cloverdale
150	US 220, Roanoke Rd, Lee Hwy, Troutville, Roanoke, Cloverdale
FStop	E: Kangaroo Express/Citgo
TStop	E: Travel Center of America #21/BP(Scales), Pilot Travel Center #258 (Scales)
Gas	W: BP◊, Exxon◊
Food	E: CountryPride/TA TC, Subway/Pilot TC, Burger King, Cracker Barrel, Hardee's, McDonald's, Shoney's, Taco Bell, Waffle House, Wendy's
	W: Bojangles, Pizza Hut
Lodg	E: Days Inn/TA TC, Comfort Inn♥, Holiday Inn Express, Red Roof Inn♥, Travelodge
	W: Econo Lodge, Howard Johnson
TWash	E: Truckwash
TServ	E: TA TC/Tires, Carter Power Systems, Montvale Truck Service VA Truck Center/GMC
Other	E: Laundry/WiFi/TA TC, WiFi/Pilot TC, CVS, Winn Dixie, Berglund RVCenter, McFarland RV Park▲
(149)	Weigh Station (Both dir)
146	VA 115, Plantation Rd, Roanoke, to Hollins, Cloverdale
Gas	E: Exxon, Shell◊
Food	E: Burger King, Hardee's, Harbor Inn Seafood, McDonald's, Subway
Lodg	E: Country Inn, Fairfield Inn, Hampton Inn, Knights Inn
	W: Days Inn
Other	E: Hollins Univ
(143)	Jct I-581, US 220, Roanoke (fr SB, Left Exit) (Serv at 1st 2 exits) (Addt'l Services on Hershberger Rd)
Gas	E: BP, Exxon, Shell
Food	E: Chinese, Mex Rest, Pizza, Waffle House
Lodg	E: Hampton Inn, Holiday Inn, Knights Inn, Quality Inn, Ramada Inn, Super 8
TServ	E: Highway Motors, Wood's Fleet & Truck Service
Other	E: ATMs, Staples, Target, Wal-Mart sc, Mall, Harley Davidson, Roanoke Reg'l Airport✈
141	VA 419, N Electric Rd, to VA 31, Roanoke, to Salem
Gas	E: BP, Liberty, Texaco
	W: BP◊, Citgo
Food	E: Burger King, Hardee's, McDonald's
	W: Fuddrucker's
Lodg	E: Baymont Inn, Quality Inn
Med	E: + Hospital
140	VA 311, Thompson Memorial Dr, Salem, Newcastle
Other	S: to Roanoke College

◊ = Regular Gas Stations with Diesel   ▲ = RV Friendly Locations   ♥ = Pet Friendly Locations
RED PRINT SHOWS LARGE VEHICLE PARKING/ACCESS ON SITE OR NEARBY   BROWN PRINT SHOWS CAMPGROUNDS/RV PARKS

Page 401

Interstate 81 N/S

EXIT	VIRGINIA
137	**VA 112, Wildwood Rd, Salem**
Gas	E: BP, Exxon, GoMart, Sheetz, Shell◊
Food	E: Applebee's, Arby's, Burger King, Denny's, Hardee's, KFC, Long John Silver, McDonald's, Omelette Shoppe, Shoney's, Taco Bell
Lodg	E: Comfort Inn, Econo Lodge, Knights Inn, Super 8
	W: Best Value Inn, Holiday Inn, Howard Johnson Express
Other	E: ATMs, AutoZone, Big Lots, Food Lion, Goodyear, Kmart, Kroger, **Wal-Mart sc**, Walgreen's, **Snyder's RV**
	W: Havens State Game Refuge
132	**VA 647, Dow Hollow Rd, to US 11, US 460, Salem, Dixie Cavern**
Gas	E: Citgo, Shell
Lodg	E: Budget Host Inn
Other	E: Dixie Caverns & Pottery Shop/**Campground▲**, VA State Hwy Patrol Post
(129)	**Ironto Rest Area (NB)** (RR, Phones, Picnic, Vend, Info)
128	**US 11, VA 603, N Fork Rd, Elliston**
TStop	W: Stop In Food Store #144/Citgo
Gas	W: Texaco
Food	W: Subway/Stop In FS
118ABC	**US 11, US 460, Christiansburg, Blacksburg**
FStop	E: Stop In Food Store #40/Shell (118C)
	W: Charlie's Market/Crown
Gas	W: BP, Exxon, RaceWay, Shell
Food	E: Denny's, Cracker Barrel
	W: McDonald's, Hardee's, Pizza Hut, Ruby Tuesday, Shoney's, Waffle House, Wendy's, Western Sizzlin
Lodg	E: Days Inn, Fairfield Inn, Holiday Inn, Quality Inn, Super 8♥ (118C)
	W: Econo Lodge♥, Howard Johnson, Knights Inn♥ (118C)
Med	W: + Hospital
Other	E: **Interstate Overnight Park▲** (118C)
	W: Auto Dealers, ATMs, Banks, Advance Auto, U-Haul, 84 Lumber, to VA Tech, to **New River Junction Campground▲**
114	**VA 8, W Main St, Christiansburg**
Gas	W: Citgo
Food	W: Burger King, Hardee's
Lodg	W: Budget Inn
109	**VA 177, Tyler Rd, VA 600, Radford**
TStop	W: Radford Travel Center/BP
Lodg	W: appr 4 mi Best Western, Comfort Inn, La Quinta Inn♥, Super 8
Med	W: + Hospital
(108)	**Radford Rest Area (Both dir)** (RR, Phones, Picnic, Vend, Info)
105	**VA 232, VA 605, 1st St, Quarry Rd, Little River Rd, Radford**
Gas	E: Marathon
Other	E: **Sportsman Campground▲**
101	**VA 660, State Park Rd, Dublin**
TStop	W: Lancer Travel Plaza/Shell #142 (Scales)
Gas	W: Citgo◊
Food	W: Omelette Shop/Taco Bell/Lancer TP
Lodg	E: Claytor Lake Inn, Sleep Inn
TServ	W: Lancer TP/Tires
Other	E: to Claytor Lake State Park
	W: Laundry/Lancer TP, Radford Army Ammunition Plant

Personal Notes

EXIT	VIRGINIA
17	**US 58 Alt, VA 75, Abingdon**
Gas	E: Valero
	W: Chevron, Citgo, Exxon
Food	E: Domino's, Long John Silver
	W: Arby's, Hardee's, KFC, Pizza Hut, McDonald's, Shoney's, Taco Bell
Lodg	E: Hampton Inn
	W: Martha Washington Inn, Super 8
Med	W: + Hospital
Other	E: to appr 8.5 mi **Wolf Lair Village Campground▲**, **Lake Front Family Campground▲**, **Lake Shore Campground▲**
	W: Advance Auto, CVS, Dollar General, Food City, Kmart, Kroger
14	**US 19N, VA 140, Jonesboro Rd**
Gas	W: Chevron◊, Exxon, Shell◊
Food	W: McDonald's, DQ, Subway
Lodg	E: Maxwell Manor B&B
	W: Comfort Inn
Other	W: to appr 7mi **Riverside Campground▲**
(13)	**Abingdon TRUCK Rest Area (NB)** (RR, Phone, Picnic, Vend, Info)
13	**Spring Creek Rd, US 611, to US 11, US 19, Abingdon**
Gas	W: Shell◊
TServ	W: Blue Ridge Kenworth, Peterbilt
Other	W: VA Highlands Airport ✈
10	**US 11, US 19, Lee Hwy, Bristol**
FStop	W: Exit 10 Quick Stop/BP
Gas	W: Chevron, Marathon

EXIT	VA / TN
Lodg	W: Beacon Motel, Evergreen Motel, Red Carpet Inn, Skyland Inn
7	**Old Airport Rd, Bristol**
Gas	E: Citgo, Shell◊
	W: BP◊, Conoco◊
Food	E: Bob Evans, Cracker Barrel
	W: Chili's, Damon's, Golden Corral, IHOP, Kobe, McDonald's, Logan's Roadhouse, Outback Steakhouse, Perkins, Prime Sirloin Buffet, Ruby Tuesday, Subway, Starbucks, Sagebrush Steakhouse
Lodg	E: La Quinta Inn♥, Quality Inn
	W: Courtyard, Holiday Inn, Microtel, Motel 6♥
Med	W: + Lee Urgent Medical Care
TServ	W: Goodpasture White/GMC
Other	W: ATMs, Advance Auto, Auto Services, Bowling, Cinemas, Food City, Grocery, Home Depot, Lowe's, Office Depot, Pharmacy, UPS Store, **Wal-Mart sc**
5	**US 11, US 19, Lee Hwy, Bristol**
Gas	E: Chevron, Shell
	W: Exxon◊
Food	E: Arby's, Burger King, Hardee's, KFC, Long John Silver, McDonald's, Shoney's
Lodg	E: Budget Inn, Crest Motel, Super 8
	W: Comfort Inn
Other	E: CVS, Walgreen's, US Post Office
	W: Kelly Tire, **Lee Hwy Campground▲**
(3)	**Jct I-381S, to Bristol**
Gas	E: Chevron, Citgo◊, Conoco, Exxon
Food	E: Applebee's, Pizza Hut, Ryan's Grill
Lodg	E: Enchanted Lodge, Days Inn, Econo Lodge
1	**US 58, US 421, Bristol, Gate City**
Gas	E: Chevron, Citgo
Food	E: Burger King, KFC, Krispy Kreme, Long John Silver, McDonald's, Wendy's
Lodg	E: Budget Host Inn, Howard Johnson, Knights Inn
Med	E: + Hospital
Other	E: ATMs, Auto Dealers, CVS, Food Lion, Kroger, Walgreen's, **Wal-Mart**, Mall
(0)	**VA Welcome Center (NB) (NO Trucks)** (RR, Phone, Picnic, Vend, Info)

⌒ **VIRGINIA** (EASTERN TIME ZONE)
⌣ **TENNESSEE**

NOTE:	MM 75: Virginia State Line
(75)	**TN Welcome Center (SB)** (RR, Phones, Picnic, Vend, Info)
74B	**US 11W, Lee Hwy, Bristol, Kingsport**
Gas	W: Exxon
Food	W: Rest/Bristol Lodge
Lodg	W: Bristol Lodge
TServ	W: WE Truck & Diesel Repair
Other	W: Towing
74A	**TN 1, State St, to US 11E, US 421, Bristol, Kingsport** (Addtl Serv 2-3 mi E in VA)
Gas	E: appr 2 mi E Shell, Roadrunner/BP
Food	E: appr 2 mi E in VA Usual Brand Fast Food
Lodg	E: Days Inn♥, Hampton Inn
Med	E: + Wellmont Reg'l Medical Center
Other	E: appr 2 mi ATMs, Auto Services, CVS, K-Mart, Kroger, Walgreen's, **Wal-Mart**, U-Haul

◊ = Regular Gas Stations with Diesel ▲ = RV Friendly Locations ♥ = Pet Friendly Locations
RED PRINT SHOWS LARGE VEHICLE PARKING/ACCESS ON SITE OR NEARBY BROWN PRINT SHOWS CAMPGROUNDS/RV PARKS

N I-81 — TENNESSEE

EXIT	TENNESSEE
69	TN 394, TN 37, to US 11E, Blountville
Gas	E: Roadrunner/BP
Food	E: Subway/BP, Arby's, Burger King, Domino's, McDonald's
Other	E: Advance Auto, to appr 4-5mi Appalachian Caverns, Bristol Motor Speedway, Blue Ox Campground/BMS▲, Earhart Campground▲, Thunder Valley Campground▲, Red Barn Campground▲, Farmer Bob's Campground▲, Raceway Cove Campground▲, Lakeview RV Park▲, All American Campground▲, Twin City Drive-In Campground▲, Camp at the Lake Campground▲, to Cherokee Trails Campground & Stables▲
66	TN 126, Memorial Blvd, Blountville, to Kingsport
Gas	E: Roadrunner/BP◊, W: Chevron◊
Food	W: McDonald's
Other	W: Factory Stores, Carolina Pottery
63	TN 357, to TN 75, Airport Pkwy, Kingsport
TStop	W: Appco #23/Citgo
Gas	E: Roadrunner/BP◊, Shell◊ W: Roadrunner/BP
Food	E: Cracker Barrel, Wendy's, TacoBell/Krystal/Exxon, Subway/Shell
Lodg	E: La Quinta Inn♥, Sleep Inn♥ W: Red Carpet Inn♥
TServ	W: Stowers Machinery CAT
Other	E: Tri City Reg'l Airport✈ W: Dollar General, Sam's Club, Marsh/LP, Rocky Top Campground & RV Park▲, Bristol/Kingsport KOA/RVDump▲, Countryside Winery
59	TN 36, Ft Henry Dr, Kingsport, to Johnson City
Gas	E: Speedy Mart/Citgo◊ W: Roadrunner/BP, Citgo, Sunoco
Food	W: Burger King, Hardee's, Huddle House, Little Caesars, La Carreta, McDonald's, Perkins, Piccadilly, Subway, Wendy's
Lodg	E: Super 8 W: Comfort Inn, Best Western
Other	W: CVS, Grocery, Firestone, Wal-Mart, Ft Henry Mall, to Warrior's Path State Park▲
(57AB)	Jct I-26, US 23 S-Johnson City, I-181, US 23N to Kingsport
56	Fordtown Rd, Kingsport
TServ	E: Smokey Mountain Truck Center
50	TN 93, to TN 81, Fall Branch, Jonesborough
Other	W: TN State Hwy Patrol Post
44	Jearoldstown Rd, Chuckey
Gas	E: Exit 44 Market
Other	E: I-81 Motorsports Park/Camp▲
(41)	Rest Area (SB) (RR, Phones, Picnic, Vend)
(38)	Rest Area (NB) (RR, Phones, Picnic, Vend)
36	TN 172, Baileyton Rd, Baileyton, Greeneville
TStop	E: Pilot Travel Center #51 (Scales)(DAND)

EXIT	TENNESSEE
TStop	W: Travel Center of America / GOASIS Travel Center (Scales), Roadrunner #119/Shell
Gas	W: BP◊
Food	E: Subway/Pilot TC W: Rest/GOASIS TA TC, Subway/Shell, Pizza Plus
Lodg	W: 36 Motel
TServ	W: GOASIS TA TC/Tires, Looney's Truck & Trailer
Med	W: + Medical Center
TWash	E: McAmis Truck Wash
Other	E: WiFi/Pilot TC W: Laundry/GOASIS TA TC, Family Dollar, Around Pond RV & Campground▲, Baileyton RV Park(See ad on page 401)▲
30	TN 70, to TN 66, Lonesome Pine Trail, Bulls Gap, to Greeneville, Rogersville
Gas	E: Exxon◊
Food	E: DQ/Stuckey's/Exxon
23	US 11E, TN 24, Bulls Gap, Greeneville
TStop	W: Kwik Fuel #23/66 (Scales)
Gas	E: BP, Mobil, Quick Stop W: Quick Shop/Exxon
Food	E: Subway, Wendy's W: McDonald's, TacoBell
Lodg	W: Best Western, Super 8
Other	E: to Davy Crockett State Park▲ W: Bulls Gap Racetrack, Tony's Wrecker Service & Repair
(21)	Weigh Station (SB)
15	TN 340, Fish Hatchery Rd
12	TN 160, Morristown, Lowland
Gas	E: Phillips 66 W: Shell◊
8	US 25E, TN 32, Morristown, to White Pine, Dandridge (Addt'l Serv 5mi N on US 25E) NOTE: 25E: NO Trucks in Cumberland Gap Tunnel
Gas	W: Shell◊, BP◊
Food	W: Cracker Barrel, Hardee's, Rest/HI
Lodg	W: Holiday Inn, Parkway Inn, Super 8
Other	W: to Wal-Mart sc, Dollar Tree, Auto & Truck Services, Food, Lodging, Colboch Harley Davidson
4	TN 341, Roy J Messer Hwy, White Pine Rd, White Pine
TStop	E: Pilot Travel Center #412 (Scales)(DAND) W: WilcoHess Travel Plaza #4001 (Scales)
Food	E: McDonald's/Pilot TC W: Huddle House, Wendy's/WilcoHess TP
Lodg	W: Days Inn
Other	E: Laundry/WiFi/RVDump/Pilot TC W: Laundry/WilcoHess TP
(2)	Rest Area (SB) (RR, Phones, Picnic, Vend)
(1B)	Jct I-40E, to Asheville, NC (fr SB, Left Exit)
(1A)	Jct I-40W, to Knoxville, to I-75

(I-81 starts/ends on I-40, Exit #421)
(EASTERN TIME ZONE)

ⓘ TENNESSEE

Begin Northbound I-81 from Jct I-40 near Dandridge TN to NY/Canada border.

◊ = Regular Gas Stations with Diesel   ▲ = RV Friendly Locations   ♥ = Pet Friendly Locations
RED PRINT SHOWS LARGE VEHICLE PARKING/ACCESS ON SITE OR NEARBY   BROWN PRINT SHOWS CAMPGROUNDS/RV PARKS

EXIT	WASHINGTON	EXIT	WASHINGTON	EXIT	WASHINGTON
	Begin Eastbound I-82 at Jct I-90 near Ellensburg, WA to Jct I-84 near Hermiston, OR.	Food	N: Chesters/Shell, Burger King, DQ, McDonald's S: DQ, Domino's, Libby's Rest, Sub Shop, Taco Bell	38	Main St, US 97, Yakima (WB, Left exit) (Acc to #x #36 Serv)
	WASHINGTON (PACIFIC TIME ZONE) (I-82 begins/ends Exit #110, I-90)	Lodg	N: Oxford Inn, Oxford Suites S: Cedar Suites♥, Fairfield Inn, Hilton Garden Inn, Holiday Inn Express♥, Red Lion Hotel♥	40	Thorp Rd, Parker Rd, Yakima Valley Highway, Wapato
3	WA 821S, Thrall Rd	Med	S: + Yakima Reg'l Medical Center	44	Wapato Rd, Yakima Valley Hwy
Other	S: Yakima River RV Park▲	Other	N: Auto Dealer, Wal-Mart sc, Auto & RV Service	Gas	N: Shell◊
(8)	Manastash Ridge Viewpoint (Both dir)		S: ATMs, Albertson's, Cinema, Firestone Les Schwab Tires, Office Max, PetCo♥, Safeway, Target, Tires, UPS Store, Yakima Conv Center, Yakima Sundome	50	WA 22E, Buena Rd, to US 97S, Zillah, to Toppenish (Serv appr 3mi S)
11	Military Rd, Ellensburg	34	WA 24E, Nob Hill Blvd, Yakima, to Moxee City	Food	S: Dad's Rest, KFC, McDonald's, Pizza, Subway, Taco Bell
Other	N: US Military Res Yakima Training Ctr	Gas	S: 7-11, ArcoAmPm, Chevron◊	Lodg	S: Best Western, El Corral Motel
(22)	Selah Creek Rest Area (WB) (RR, Phones, Picnic, RVDump)	Food	S: Arby's, McDonald's, Mex Rest	Med	S: + Hospital
(24)	Selah Creek Rest Area (EB) (RR, Phones, Picnic, Info, RVDump)	TServ	S: Cummins NW, Kenworth NW, Mobil Fleet Service	Other	S: ATMs, Safeway, to Yakama Nation RV Resort▲, Yakima Nation Legends Casino
26	Firing Center Rd, WA 821S, WA 823S, Harrison Rd, Selah	Other	N: Auto Dealer, Yakima KOA▲, Yakima Sportman State Park▲ S: ATMs, Auto Services, Kmart, UPS Store, Valley Mall, State Fair Park, Yakima Speedway, Casino Caribbean, Circle H RV Ranch▲, Aubrey's RV Center, to Nob Hill Casino	52	Zillah Rd, Meyers Rd, Zillah
Gas	S: 7-11, Shell			Gas	N: Chevron, Cherry Patch Mini Mart, Shell
Other	S: to appr 16mi Stagecoach RV Park▲			Food	N: El Porton, McDonald's, Subway
29	E Selah Rd			Lodg	N: Comfort Inn
30A	WA 823S (WB)			Other	S: to Yakama Indian Res
30B	Rest Haven Rd, Selah (WB)			54	Yakima Valley Hwy, Division Rd, Zillah, (National Historic Site)
30	WA 823, Rest Haven Rd, Selah (EB)	36	US 82, Valley Mall Blvd, Old Town Rd, Union Gap, Yakima	Other	S: Grocery, RVDump, Teapot Dome Service Station
31B	US 12, Yakima, Naches (EB)	FStop	S: PacPr/Rainier Place/ArcoAmPm	58	WA 223S, Van Belle Rd, Granger
31	US 12, Yakima, Naches, to Chinook Pass, White Pass (fr WB, Left exit)	TStop	S: AmBest/GearJammer Travel Plaza/Shell (Scales)	Gas	S: Conoco◊
FStop	S: to 1408 N 1st Pacific Pride	Gas	S: BJ's Get N Go	Other	S: to Yakama Indian Reservation
Gas	S: ArcoAmPm◊, Exxon, Shell, Roadrunner	Food	S: Rest/GearJammer TP, Applebee's, Burger King, Denny's, Jack in the Box, IHOP, Miner's D/I Rest, McDonald's, Old Country Buffet, Outback Steakhouse, Shari's, Skippers Seafood, Starbucks, Subway	63	Sunnyside Rd, Yakima Valley Hwy, Outlook, Sunnyside, Granger (Acc to Ex #67 Serv 3mi N)
Food	S: Amer Mex Rest, Artic Circle, Black Angus, Gasperetti's, Golden Moon Chinese, Jack in the Box, Ital Rest, Olive Garden, Red Lobster, Waffles Cafe, Wendy's			Lodg	N: Country Inn♥, Travel Inn
Lodg	S: All Star Motel, Best Western, Clarion♥, Days Inn♥, Motel 6♥, Ramada Ltd♥, Yakima Inn	Lodg	S: Motel/GearJammer TP, Best Western, Pioneer Motel, Quality Inn, Super 8	Other	N: Sunnyside RV Park▲
		TWash	S: GearJammer TP	67	Midvale Rd, 1st St, Sunnyside
Med	S: + Yakima Reg'l Medical Center	TServ	S: GearJammer TP/Tires, Western Peterbilt	Gas	N: CFN/Chevron◊
Other	S: ATMs, Albertson's, Woodland Park▲, Trailer Inns RV Park▲, North Acres MH Park▲, Trailer Village MH & RV Park▲, to Sun Tides Golf Course & RV Park▲	Med	S: + Valley Medi-Center	Food	N: Jack in the Box
		Other	S: Laundry/WiFi/RVDump/LP/Gear Jammer TP, ATMs, Best Buy, Borders, Costco, Cinemas, FedEx Kinko's, Tires, Goodyear, Home Depot, Lowe's, Office Depot, PetCo♥, PetSmart♥, RiteAid, Safeway, ShopKO, Valley Mall, Yakima Air Terminal✈, Canopy Country RV Center	Med	N: + Hospital
				Other	N: Bi-Mart, Pharmacy, Safeway
33A	Fair Ave, Terrace Hts Dr (EB)			69	WA 241, Waneta Rd, to WA 24, Sunnyside, to Mabton
33B	Terrace Hts Dr, Yakima (EB)			FStop	N: PacPride/The Outpost/Shell
33	Yakima Ave, Terrace Hts Dr, Fair Ave, Yakima (WB)			Gas	N: ArcoAmPm◊, Texaco◊
Gas	N: Chevron, Shell◊ S: 7-11, ArcoAmPm	37	US 97S, Main St, Union Gap, Yakima, Wapato (EB)	Food	N: Arby's, Burger King, China Grove, DQ, KFC, McDonald's, Pizza Hut, Subway, Taco Bell
				Lodg	N: Best Western, Rodeway Inn♥, Country Inn♥, Travel Inn
				Med	N: + Sunnyside Comm Hospital
				Other	N: LP/The Outpost, ATMs, Auto Repairs, Banks, Dollar Tree, Grocery, Les Schwab Tires, Kmart, RiteAid, Radio Shack, Tires, Staples, Wal-Mart sc, Vet♥, Mid Valley Mall, Sunnyside Muni Airport✈

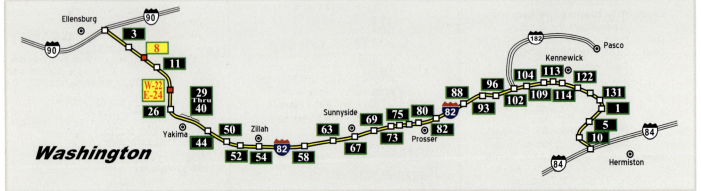

◊ = Regular Gas Stations with Diesel   ▲ = RV Friendly Locations   ♥ = Pet Friendly Locations
RED PRINT SHOWS LARGE VEHICLE PARKING/ACCESS ON SITE OR NEARBY   BROWN PRINT SHOWS CAMPGROUNDS/RV PARKS

INTERSTATE 82 W

EXIT	WASHINGTON
73	W Wine Country Rd, Yakima Valley Hwy, Grandview
Gas	S: Grandview Market/Exxon, Smitty's Conoco◆ & Car Wash
Food	S: Eli & Kathy's Family Rest, New Hong Kong Rest, Subway
Lodg	S: Apple Valley Motel
Other	S: ATMs, Auto Repairs, Les Schwab Tires, Laundromat, Pharmacy, Safeway, Smitty's RV Overniter▲
75	E Wine Country Rd, Grandview (Access to Ex #73 Serv)
FStop	S: Pacific Pride 501 E Wine Country Rd
(76)	Weigh Station (EB)
80	Gap Rd, Wine Country Rd, Prosser
S:	Prosser Rest Area (Both dir) (RR, Phone, Picnic, Info, RVDump)
TStop	S: Horse Heaven Hills Travel Plaza/Shell (Scales)
Food	S: Blue Goose Rest, KFC, McDonald's, Speedway Café, Subway
Lodg	S: Best Western♥, Barn Motor Inn/Rest/RV▲
Med	S: + Prosser Memorial Hospital
Other	S: WiFi/RVDump/LP/Horse Heaven Hills TP, Wine Country RV Park▲, Auto Dealers, Hinzerling Winery, Prosser Airport✈
82	Wine Country Rd, E Meade Ave, Prosser, to WA 22, to Mabton, to WA 221, to Paterson (Access to Ex #80 Serv)
88	Gibbon Rd
93	Yakitat Rd, to Benton City, 1st St, WA 225, to WA 240, Benton City, to Richland, Kennewick, Pasco, to WA 224E, W Richland
Other	N: Beach RV Park▲, Elm Grove RV Park▲, to appr 6mi RV Village Resort▲

EXIT	WASHINGTON
(102)	Jct I-182, US 12E, to US 395, Richland, to Pasco
Other	N: to Richland Airport✈, to App 6mi Horn Rapids RV Resort▲, Sandy Heights RV Resort▲
104	Dallas Rd, Goose Gap Rd, Richland, Kennewick
Gas	N: Conoco◆
109	Badger Rd, Clearwater Ave
Gas	N: SunMart, Shell
Other	N: to appr 3 mi+ Food, Lodging, Columbia Center Mall, Tri-Cities RV Park▲, Wrights Desert Gold Motel & RV Park▲, Vista Field Airport✈
113	Jct US 395, to I-182, to Kennewick, Pasco (Serv 3-5mi N)
FStop	N: Tesoro Truck Stop (S Ely & W 4th)
Gas	N: Exxon, Murphy
Food	N: Rest/Tesoro TS, Burger King, Café, Carl Jr's, Fiesta Mexican, Jack in the Box, McDonald's, Starbucks, Subway
Lodg	N: Best Western, Econo Lodge, Holiday Inn Express, La Quinta Inn♥
TServ	N: Eagle Freightliner, Freedom Truck Ctr
Med	N: + Greater Columbia Regional
Other	N: RVDump/Tesoro TS, ATMs, Grocery, Home Depot, Radio Shack, Walgreen's, Wal-Mart sc, to Tri-Cities Airport✈, to Franklin Co RV Park at TRAC▲
114	WA 397, Locust Grove Rd
122	Coffin Rd
(130)	Port of Entry / Weigh Station (WB)

EXIT	WA / OR
131	WA 14W, McNary Rd, Plymouth Rd, Kennewick, Plymouth, Vancouver
NOTE:	MM 132: Oregon State Line
(PACIFIC TIME ZONE)	
⋂ WASHINGTON	
⋃ OREGON	
(PACIFIC TIME ZONE)	
1	US 395S, US 730, Columbia River Hwy, Umatilla, Hermiston
	OR Welcome Center (SB)
	WEIGH STATION (SB)
FStop	W: Tesoro #62180
TStop	W: CFN/Crossroads Truck Stop/Shell
Food	W: Rest/Crossroads TS, Subway/Tesoro
Lodge:	E: Desert River Inn
	W: Lamplighter Motel, Umatilla Inn
Med	W: + Umatilla Urgent Care
TServ	W: Krome Diesel Repair/Tires/Crsrds TS
Other	E: Comm'l Tire Center, Wildood RV Park▲, RV Repair, RV Center, to appr 5mi Wal-Mart sc
	W: NAPA, Pharmacy, OR State Hwy Patrol Post, Shady Rest MH & RV, to Oasis RV Park
5	Power Line Rd
10	CR 1232, Walker Rd, Westland
Med	E: + Good Shepherd Comm Hospital
Other	E: to Pioneer RV Park▲, to Hermiston Muni Airport✈
	W: Umatilla Ordinance Depot
(I-82 begins/ends at Exit #179, on I-84)	
(PACIFIC TIME ZONE)	
⋂ OREGON	
Begin Westbound I-82 at Jct I-84 near Hermiston, OR to Jct I-90 Ellensburg, WA.	

INTERSTATE 83 S

EXIT	PENNSYLVANIA
Begin Southbound I-83 in Harrisburg, PA to Fayette St, Exit #1 in MD.	
⋃ PENNSYLVANIA	
(EASTERN TIME ZONE)	
(51B)	Jct -81N, to Hazelton
(51A)	Jct I-81S, US 322W, Carlisle, Chambersburg (Left Exit Only)
50B	US 22W, Harrisburg, Progress
50A	US 22E, Jonestown Rd, Colonial Park, Harrisburg,
Gas	E: Shell, Sunoco
Food	E: Applebee's, Arby's, Colonial Park Diner, McDonald's, Long John Silver, Olive Garden, Red Lobster, Red Robin, Subway, Taco Bell
	W: Friendly's, KFC, Roberto's Pizza
Other	E: ATMs, Colonial Park Mall, Best Buy, CVS, Circuit City, Costco, Goodyear, Home Depot, NTB, Target, Tires

EXIT	PENNSYLVANIA
48	Union Deposit Rd, Harrisburg
Gas	E: Sunoco
	W: BP
Food	E: Arby's, Burger King, Denny's, Hong Kong Chef, Lone Star Steakhouse, Panera Bread, Wendy's
	W: Hardee's, McDonald's, Outback Steakhouse, Starbucks, Subway, Waffle House
Lodg	E: Sheraton
	W: Comfort Inn, Fairfield Inn
Med	E: + Comm General Hospital
Other	E: Grocery, Pharmacy, Staples
	W: Lowe's, Office Depot, Office Max, UPS Store, State Farm Complex
47	US 322E, Derry St, Paxton St, Eisenhower Blvd, Hershey (3B, Exit Only)
Other	E: Home Depot, to Hershey Park & Attractions, Milton Hershey Medical Center, Hershey Highmeadow Campground▲

EXIT	PENNSYLVANIA
46B	US 322E, to Hershey (NB)
FStop	E: Hess Express
Other	E: Home Depot, PetSmart♥, Cummins
(46A)	Jct-283S, to I-76, PA Tpk (SB) (Services Accessible I-283)
Other	S: to Harrisburg Int'l Airport✈, to Harrisburg East Campground▲
45	Paxton St, Harrisburg
Gas	E: Sheetz
Food	E: Applebee's, Burger King, ChickFilA, Fuddrucker's, Pizza Hut, Wendy's
Other	E: ATMs, Bass Pro Shop, Harrisburg Mall, Radio Shack, Auto Dealers, Auto Services
44B	17th St (SB), 19th St (NB)
Gas	E: Pacific Pride, Hess, Sunoco
Food	E: Benihana, Hardee's
Other	E: Auto Dealers, Auto Services, Firestone, Tires, Advance Auto, CarQuest
44A	13th St, to PA 441, Harrisburg
Gas	W: Chevron
Other	W: DMV

◆ = Regular Gas Stations with Diesel ▲ = RV Friendly Locations ♥ = Pet Friendly Locations
RED PRINT SHOWS LARGE VEHICLE PARKING/ACCESS ON SITE OR NEARBY BROWN PRINT SHOWS CAMPGROUNDS/RV PARKS

Page 405

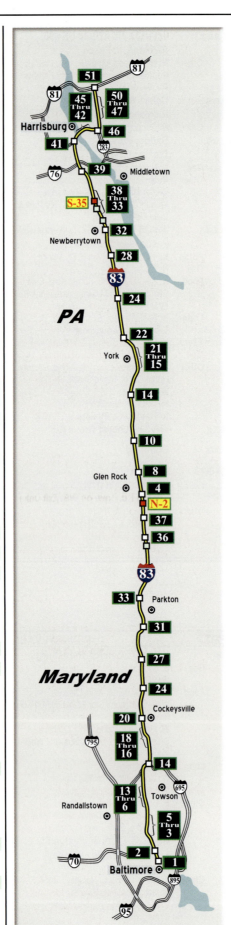

EXIT	PENNSYLVANIA
43	**2nd St, to State Capitol**
Lodg	W: Crowne Plaza
Med	W: + Hospital
Other	W: Amtrak, Greyhound, State Capitol
42	**3rd St, Lemoyne**
41B	**Louther St, Highland Park (NB)**
Gas	W: Mobil
Food	W: KFC, Subs
41A	**PA 581W, Camp Hill (Both, Left Exit)**
40B	**Simpson Ferry Rd, New Cumberland**
Gas	W: BP◇, Shell
Food	W: McDonald's, Subway
40A	**Limekiln Rd, New Cumberland**
Gas	E: BP, Mobil
	W: Hess
Food	E: Bob Evans, McDonald's, Pizza Hut
Lodg	E: Comfort Inn, Fairfield Inn, Holiday Inn, Rodeway Inn, Travelodge
	W: Best Western, Motel 6♥, Travel Inn
(39B)	**Jct I-76, PA TPK (TOLL), to Philadelphia, Pittsburgh**
Other	E: to Harrisburg Int'l Airport✈
39A	**PA 114, Lewisberry Rd**
Lodg	E: Days Inn
Other	E: Capitol City Airport✈
38	**Evergreen Rd, Pleasant View Rd, Reesers Summit, New Cumberland**
36	**PA 262, Fishing Creek**
Gas	E: Hess
	W: Citgo, Shell
35	**PA 177, Lewisberry**
Gas	W: Mobil
Food	E: Hillside Cafe
Lodg	W: Alpine Inn
Other	W: Gifford Pinchot State Park, Ski Roundtop
(35)	**Parking Area (SB)**
(35)	**Weigh Station (SB)**
34	**Valley Green (NB)**
FStop	E: Hess Express #38422
Food	E: Blimpie/Hess
Lodg	E: Super 8
Other	E: UPS Store, Parks Away Parks Campground▲
(33)	**Weigh Station (NB)**
33	**PA 392, Yocumtown**
FStop	E: Hess Express
TStop	E: Henry's Truck Stop
Food	E: Rest/Henry's TS, Burger King, McDonald's
Lodg	E: Super 8
TServ	E: Henry's TS/Tires
Other	E: Laundry/Henry's TS
32	**PA 382, Newberrytown**
FStop	E: Rutter's Farm Stores #53
Gas	E: Sunoco, Exxon◇
Food	E: Pizza Hut/Rutters
Other	W: Gifford Pinchot State Park, Ski Roundtop
28	**PA 295, Strinestown, Zions View**
FStop	W: Rutters/Exxon
Food	W: Wendy's
24	**PA 238, Emigsville**
Gas	W: Mobil
Food	W: Steakhouse
Other	W: US Weightlifting Hall of Fame

EXIT	PENNSYLVANIA
22	**US 83S, PA 181, to US 30W (SB), PA 181N, N George St (NB)** (Access to Ex #21B Serv)
Gas	E: Rutter's
	W: Rutter's
21	**US 30, to Gettysburg (SB)**
21B	**US 30W, York, to Gettysburg (NB)**
Gas	W: BP, Exxon, Mobil
Food	W: Burger King, China Kitchen, Dunkin Donuts, Damon's, Hardee's, Hooters, KFC, Lone Star Steakhouse, McDonald's, Olive Garden, Pizza Hut, Ruby Tuesday, Subway, Smokey Bones BBQ, Taco Bell, TGI Friday, Wendy's
Lodg	W: Motel 6♥, Super 8
Other	W: West Manchester Mall, York Expo Center, CVS, Grocery, Auto Dealers, Harley Davidson, Staples, Wal-Mart sc, Ben Franklin Campground RV Park▲, to Conewago Isle Campground▲
21A	**US 30E, Arsenal Rd, York (NB)**
Gas	E: Rutter's
Food	E: Bob Evans, Round the Clock Diner, San Carlos
Lodg	E: Days Inn, Holiday Inn, Motel 6♥, Sheraton
Med	E: + Hospital
Other	E: Harley Davidson Plant & Museum
19B	**PA 462W, Market St (SB)**
19A	**PA 462E, Market St (SB)**
Gas	E: Hess, Mobil
Food	E: Perkins, Outback Steakhouse, Taco Bell, Wendy's
Lodg	E: Quality Inn
Med	E: + Hospital
Other	E: York Mall, ATMs, Advance Auto, Dollar General, Grocery, NTB, Sam's Club, Walgreen's, Wal-Mart sc
19	**PA 462, Market St (NB)**
18	**PA 124, Mt Rose Ave**
Gas	E: Exxon, Mobil, Rutter's
Food	E: Burger King, Denny's
Lodg	E: Budget Host Inn
Other	E: CVS, Kmart, Penn State Univ/York Campus
16B	**PA 74N, Queen St**
Gas	W: Exxon
Food	W: McDonald's, Subway, Taco Bell
Other	W: York College, CVS
16A	**PA 74S, Queen St, York**
Gas	E: Mobil
Food	E: Cracker Barrel, Pizza Hut, Ruby Tuesday
15	**US 83 N, S George St**
Med	W: + Hospital
Other	W: York College of PA
14	**PA 182, Leader Heights**
Gas	W: Exxon, Sunoco
Food	W: McDonald's
Lodg	W: Comfort Inn, Holiday Inn Express
Other	W: Indian Rock Campground▲, Ryan Auto & RV Parts
10	**PA 214, Loganville**
Food	W: Lee's Rest, Pizza
Lodg	W: Midway Motel
Other	W: PA State Hwy Patrol Post
8	**PA 216, Glen Rock**
Lodg	W: Rocky Ridge Motel
Other	E: Amish & Farmers Market

Page 406

◇ = Regular Gas Stations with Diesel   ▲ = RV Friendly Locations   ♥ = Pet Friendly Locations
RED PRINT SHOWS LARGE VEHICLE PARKING/ACCESS ON SITE OR NEARBY   BROWN PRINT SHOWS CAMPGROUNDS/RV PARKS

EXIT		PA / MD
4		PA 851, Shrewsbury
	FStop	E: Tom's Mobil, Tom's Cigarette Cellar #22/Crown
	Gas	W: Exxon◊
	Food	E: Cracker Barrel, Ruby Tuesday
		W: Arby's, McDonald's, Subway
	Lodg	E: Hampton Inn
	Other	E: Home Depot
		W: CVS, Grocery, Wal-Mart sc, Naylor Winery
	NOTE:	NB: NO Trucks Over 13' 6" Beyond Exit #4
(2)		PA Welcome Center (NB) (RR, Phone, Picnic, Info)

(EASTERN TIME ZONE)

⊙ PENNSYLVANIA
⊙ MARYLAND

(EASTERN TIME ZONE)
(I-83 begins/ends in MD on Fayette St, Ex #1)

	NOTE:	MM 38: Pennsylvania State Line
37		Freeland Rd, Parkton (SB)
36		MD 439, Old York Rd, Parkton, Maryland Line, Bel Air
	Other	W: to appr 5mi Morris Meadows Campground▲
(35)		Weigh Station (SB)
33		MD 45, York Rd, Parkton
	Gas	E: Exxon◊
31		Middletown Rd, Parkton, Wiseburg, Rayville
27		MD 137, Mt Carmel Rd, Parkton
	Gas	E: Exxon◊
	Other	E: US Post Office, Pharmacy, Gunpowder Falls State Park

EXIT		MARYLAND
24		Belfast Rd, Sparks Glencoe, to Butler, Sparks
20AB		Shawan Rd, Cockeysville, to Hunt Valley, Shawan
	Gas	E: BP, Exxon◊
	Food	E: Burger King, Carrabba's, Damon's, McDonald's, Outback Steakhouse, Quiznos, Wendy's
	Lodg	E: Courtyard, Econo Lodge, Embassy Suites, Hampton Inn, Marriott
	Other	E: Grocery, Wal-Mart, Mall, Baltimore Convention Center
		W: Oregon Ridge Park/Nature Center
18		Cockeysville Rd, Warren Rd (NB, Exit only)
	FStop	E: Southern States
	Gas	E: Exxon
	Lodg	E: Residence Inn
17		Padonia Rd, Lutherville Timonium
	Gas	E: BP◊, Hess
	Food	E: Applebee's, Bob Evans, Chili's, Romano's Macaroni Grill
	Lodg	E: Days Inn, Extended Stay America
16		Timonium Rd (SB)
	Gas	E: Sunoco
	Food	E: Steak & Ale
	Lodg	E: Extended Stay America, Holiday Inn
	Other	W: MD State Fairgrounds
16B		Timonium Rd West (NB)
16A		Timonium Rd East (NB)
(14)		Jct I-695N,
(13)		Jct I-695S, Glen Burnie, Towson
	Med	+ Hospital
	Other	MD State Hwy Patrol Post
12		Ruxton Rd, Towson (NB, Exit Only)
	Other	E: to Robert E Lee Park
10		Northern Pky, Baltimore (SB)
	Med	E: + Hospital

EXIT		MARYLAND
10B		Northern Pkwy W, Baltimore (NB)
10A		Northern Pkwy E, Baltimore (NB)
9AB		Cold Spring Lane, Baltimore (SB)
9B		Cold Spring Lane W (NB)
9A		Cold Spring Lane E (NB)
8		MD 25, Falls Rd (NB)
7B		28th St (fr SB, Left Exit)
	Med	E: + Hospital
7A		Druid Park Lake Dr (SB)
	Other	W: Druid Lake Park, to Baltimore Conservatory, Zoo
6A		US 1, North Ave, Mt Royal Ave (SB)
6B		US 1, North Ave, to W 28th St, to Druid Park Lake Dr (NB)
5		MD 2, St Paul St, Calvert St, Maryland Ave, Downtown (SB)
4		Guilford Ave (SB), Eager St (NB), MD 2, St Paul St, Mt Royal Ave, Downtown, Baltimore (SB)
3		Fallsway, Chase St, (NB) Guilford Ave, Madison St (SB)
2		N Holiday St, E Pleasant St (fr SB, Left Exit)
1		E Fayette St, Downtown
	Other	W: to National Aquarium, M&T Bank Stadium, to US 395

(I-83 begins/ends at Exit #70 on I-81)
(EASTERN TIME ZONE)

⊙ MARYLAND

Begin Northbound I-83 in Baltimore to Jct I-81 near Harrisburg, PA.

EXIT		OREGON
		Begin Eastbound I-84 from Portland, OR to Jct I-90 near Sturbridge, MA.

⊙ OREGON

(PACIFIC TIME ZONE)
(I-84 Begins/Ends on I-90, Ex #9 in MA)

1A		OR 99E, 12th Ave, Lloyd Blvd (WB)
	Food	N: Quiznos, Asst'd Café's & Restaurants
	Lodg	N: Courtyard, DoubleTree Hotel, La Quinta Inn♥, Inn at Conv Center, Residence Inn, Shilo Inn
		S: Dunes Motel, Executive Lodge
	Med	N: + Legacy Emanuel Hospital
	Other	N: Convention Center, Lloyd Center, Rose Garden Arena
		S: Office Depot
1B		33rd Ave, Lloyd Blvd (EB)
	Gas	N: 76, Shell◊
	Food	S: Pizza Hut, Wendy's
	Other	N: Grocery, RiteAid
		S: Auto Dealers

EXIT		OREGON
2		39th Ave (EB), Halsey St (WB)
	Gas	N: Chevron, Shell
	Food	N: Blackwell's Steak Grill, Burger King, McDonald's, Pagoda, Poor Richard's, Quiznos, Subway
	Lodg	N: Banfield Value Inn, Econo Lodge
	Med	S: + Providence Portland Hospital
3		Glisan St, 60th Ave (EB)
	Gas	S: KC's MiniMart
	Med	S: + Providence Portland Hospital
4		68th Ave, Halsey St (EB)
5		OR 213, 82nd Ave (EB ex, diff reacc)
	Gas	N: 7-11, Shell
		S: Chevron, Shell
	Food	N: DQ, Chinese
		S: Burgerville USA, Chinese Village, Elmer's, McDonald's, Pizza Hut, Subway, Taco Bell, Wendy's
	Lodg	N: Days Inn, Cabana Motel
		S: Comfort Inn, Microtel
(6)		Jct I-205S, Salem, Oregon City (EB)

EXIT		OREGON
7		Hasley St, Gateway District (EB)
	Gas	S: ArcoAmPm Chevron
	Food	S: Carl's Jr, Carrow's, Subway
(8)		I-205N, Seattle, Portland, Airport (EB, Exit only)
	Other	N: to Portland Int'l Airport ✈
(9)		102nd Ave, Portland (EB)
		I-205, S to Oregon City, Salem, N to Seattle (WB, Left exit)
10		122nd Ave (EB)
13		181st Ave, Gresham, Fairview
	Gas	N: Chevron
		S: 7-11, Circle K
	Food	S: Burger King, Francis Xavier's, IHOP, Jungs Dynasty, Little Caesars, McDonald's, Shari's, Wendy's
	Lodg	N: Hampton Inn
		S: Comfort Suites, Extended Stay America, Econo Lodge, Quality Inn, Sleep Inn, Sheraton, Super 8♥
	Other	S: ATMs, Auto Services, Safeway, Vet♥

◊ = Regular Gas Stations with Diesel   ▲ = RV Friendly Locations   ♥ = Pet Friendly Locations
RED PRINT SHOWS LARGE VEHICLE PARKING/ACCESS ON SITE OR NEARBY   BROWN PRINT SHOWS CAMPGROUNDS/RV PARKS

EXIT		OREGON
14		207th Ave, Fairview
	Gas	N: Shell◇
	Food	N: CJ's Café, Gin Sun Rest & Lounge
	Other	N: Portland Fairview RV Park▲, Rolling Hills RV Park▲, American Dream RV
16		238th Dr, Wood Village, Gresham
	Gas	N: ArcoAmPm◇
		S: Chevron
	Food	N: Jack in the Box, Chinese, Quiznos
	Lodg	N: Travelodge♥
		S: Best Western, McMenamins Edgefield
	Med	S: + Legacy Mt Hood Medical Center
	Other	N: Wal-Mart sc▲, Olinger Travel Homes/Camping World
		S: RV Center
17		Marine Dr, 257th Ave, Graham Rd, Frontage Rd, Troutdale, Portland
	TStop	S: Travel Center of America #183/Arco (Scales), Flying J Travel Plaza #5019/Conoco (Scales)
	Gas	S: Chevron
	Food	N: Wendy's
		S: Buckhorn/Subway/Popeyes/TA TC, Rest/BurgerKing/FJ TP, Arby's, McDonald's, Shari's, Taco Bell
	Lodg	N: Holiday Inn Express♥
		S: Best Value Inn/TA TC, Comfort Inn♥, Motel 6♥
	TServ	S: TA TC/Tires
	Other	N: Portland Troutdale Airport✈
		S: Laundry/WiFi/TA TC, Laundry/WiFi/RVDump/LP/FJ TP, Outlet Mall, to Mt Hood Comm College, Sandy Riverfront RV Resort▲
18		Lewis & Clark State Park
	Other	S: RR, Picnic, Trails, Beach, Boat Ramp, to appr 6mi Crown Point RV Park▲
22		Corbett Hill Rd, Corbett
	Food	S: Rest/Chinook Inn
	Lodg	S: Royal Chinook Inn
	Other	S: to Steep Grade Crown Point RV Park▲
(23)		Scenic View (WB)
25		Rooster Rock State Park (NO Trucks)
28		to Bridal Veil State Park (EB)
30		Benson State Park (EB)
31		Multnomah Falls (Left Exit, Both dir)
35		Columbia River Scenic Hwy Ainsworth State Park
	Other	S: RV/Camp▲, RVDump, Elec, Showers, RR, Playground, Walking/Hiking Trail, Picnic, Waterfall, Amphitheater

Personal Notes

EXIT		OREGON
37		Warrendale Rd, Tumalt Rd, Cascade Locks, Warrandale (WB)
40		Bonneville Dam
	Other	N: Bonneville Dam, Bonneville Fish Hatchery, Bonneville Lock & Dam
41		Eagle Creek Rec Area
44A		US 30E, Cascade Locks (EB) Bridge of the Gods to WA
	Gas	N: Chevron, Shell◇
	Lodg	N: Best Western, Bridge of the Gods Motel, Econo Lodge
	Other	N: Sternwheeler Columbia Gorge, Port of Cascade Locks & Marine Park, Sternwheeler RV Park▲
44B		US 30, Cascade Locks (WB)
	Other	N: Cascade Locks/Portland East KOA▲
(44.9)		Weigh Station (EB)

EXIT		OREGON
47		Herman Creek Rd, Forest Ln (WB)
(49)		Pull Off Area (EB)
51		Wyeth Rd, Herman Creek Rd, Cascade Locks, Wyeth
(54)		Weigh Station (WB)
(55)		Starvation Peak Trail Head (EB) (RR, Phones)
55		Starvation Creek State Park
56		Viento State Park
	Other	N: RV/Camp▲, Elec, Showers, Picnic, Beach Access, Hiking, Playground
(58)		Mitchell Pt Overlook (EB)
60		Service Rd, Morton Rd (WB exit, No re-entry)
(61)		Pull Out Area (WB)
62		US 30E, OR 35, Cascade Ave, Westcliff Dr, Hood River
	Gas	S: Chevron◇, Shell◇
	Food	N: Charburger Country, Red Panda
		S: McDonald's, Quiznos, Shari's, Subway, Starbucks, Taco Bell
	Lodg	N: Columbia Gorge Hotel, Vagabond Lodge♥
		S: Comfort Suites, Lone Pine Motel, Red Carpet Inn, Stonehenge Inn
	Med	S: + Hospital
	Other	S: ATMs, Laundromat, Grocery, Wal-Mart, Auto Dealers, to Hood River Airport✈
63		2nd St, Hood River
	Gas	N: 76d, Shell
	Food	S: Burger King, Chinese, Hood River Rest, Horse Feathers
	Lodg	S: Hood River Hotel, Riverview Lodge
	Med	S: + Hospital
	Other	S: to Hood River Airport✈, 818 Riverside Dr Hood River Waste Treatment Plant/RVDump
64		OR 35, Button Bridge Rd, US 30W, Hood River, to White Salmon, WA
	Gas	N: Chevron, Shell
		S: Exxon
	Food	N: McDonald's, Starbucks, Taco Time
	Lodg	S: Oak Street Hotel
	Other	N: OR State Hwy Patrol Post
(66)		Rest Area (WB) (RR, Picnic)

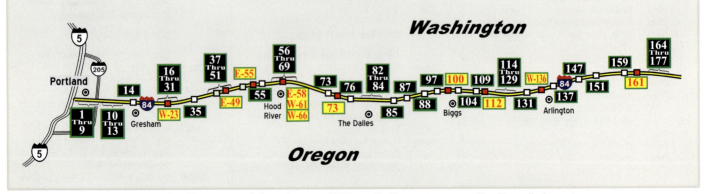

◇ = Regular Gas Stations with Diesel   ▲ = RV Friendly Locations   ♥ = Pet Friendly Locations
RED PRINT SHOWS LARGE VEHICLE PARKING/ACCESS ON SITE OR NEARBY   BROWN PRINT SHOWS CAMPGROUNDS/RV PARKS

EXIT	OREGON	EXIT	OREGON	EXIT	OREGON
69	US 30E, Mosier	109	US 30, John Day Dam Ln, Rufus	182	OR 207, Hermiston Hwy, Hermiston, Lexington
73	Memaloose State Park	FStop	S: Pacific Pride	TStop	N: Space Age Fuel Travel Center (Scales)
Other	N: Camp/RV▲, Elec, Showers, RR, RVDump	Gas	S: BP, Shell	Food	N: FastFood/Space Age TC
		Food	S: Bob's Texas T-Bone	Lodg	N: Comfort Inn
(73)	Rest Area (Both dir) (RR, Phone, Picnic, RVDump/EB)	Lodg	S: Dinty Motor Inn, Rufus Rocks Motel ♥, Tyee Motel	Med	N: + Hospital
76	Rowena River Rd, The Dalles, Rowena, Mayer State Park	Other	N: John Day Visitor Center S: Bob's Budget RV & Trailer Park▲, Rufus RV Park▲, Deschutes State Park▲, to appr 18mi Sherman Co Fairgrounds, Sherman Co RV Park▲	Other	N: Laundry/RVDump/LP/Space Age FC, appr 3mi Pioneer RV Park▲
82	Chenoweth Rd, to US 30, W 6th St Columbia River Discovery Center			(187)	Rest Area (Both dir) (RR, Phone, Picnic, Vend)
Gas	S: Shell◊, Astro◊, Exxon	(112)	Parking Area (Both dir)	188	US 395N, OR 32, Stanfield, Hermiston, Old Pendleton River Rd, Echo
Food	S: Arby's, Burger King, Cousins, Pietro's Pizza, Subway, Wendy's	114	John Day Dam, LePage Park Rd	TStop	N: Pilot Travel Center #390 (Scales)
Lodg	S: Country Cousins Inn, Motel 6 ♥, Oregon Trail Motel	Other	S: COE/LePage Park/RVDump	Gas	N: Chevron◊
Other	S: Columbia River Discovery Center	123	Quinton Canyon Rd, Phillippi Canyon, Lewis & Clark Trail	Food	N: Subway/McDonald's/Pilot TC, Denny's
83	US 30E, The Dalles (EB)	129	Blalock Canyon Rd, Arlington, Blalock, Lewis & Clark Trail	Lodg	N: appr 4-5 mi Best Western, Oak Tree Inn, Oxford Suites, Economy In
Gas	S: Chevron, Exxon, Shell◊	131	Woelpern Rd (EB, No re-entry)	Med	N: + Hospital
Food	S: Arby's, Burger King, DQ, Skipper's Seafood, McDonald's, Subway, Taco Bell	(136)	Scenic View (WB)	Other	N: Laundry/WiFi/RVPark▲/Pilot TC, to appr 6mi Hat Rock Campground▲, Stage Gulch RV Park▲, Pilot RV Park▲, Greyhound, Hermiston Muni Airport✈ S: Fort Henrietta RV Park▲
Lodg	S: Best Western, Days Inn, Quality Inn, Shilo Inn, Super 8	137	OR 13, Arlington, Condon		
Other	N: NAPA S: Albertson's, Kmart, RiteAid, Staples	Gas	S: 76, Shell◊		
84	2nd St, to US 30W, The Dalles (WB) (Access to Ex #83 Serv)	Food	S: Happy Canyon, Village Inn	193	Whitmore Rd, Stage Gulch Rd, OR 320, Echo, Lexington
		Lodg	S: Arlington Motel	198	McClintock-Lorenzen Rd
85	Riverfront Park Rd, The Dalles	Other	S: Grocery, Columbia River RV Park▲, Arlington RV & MH Park▲, Arlington Muni Airport✈	199	Yoakum Rd, Pendleton
N:	Riverfront Park Rd (RR, Phone, Picnic, Playground, Marina)	147	OR 74, Heppner Hwy, Arlington, to Ione, Heppner, Blue Mountain Scenic Byway	202	Barnhart Rd, Pendleton
Gas	S: 76◊, Chevron			207	US 30E, Pendleton Hwy, Pendleton
Food	S: Burgerville USA, Casa El Miridor, The Wagon Seafood & Steaks	151	Three Mile Canyon	Gas	N: Chevron◊, Shell◊
Lodg	S: Best Western	159	Tower Rd, Boardman Rd, Boardman	Food	N: DQ, Taco Bell
Med	S: + Hospital	Other	S: Boardman Airstrip✈, Boardman Bombing Range	Lodg	N: Longhorn Motel, Travelodge ♥, Vagabond Inn
Other	S: Auto Services & Repairs	(161)	Rest Area (Both dir) (RR, Phone, Picnic, Vend, Info/EB)	Other	N: Lookout RV Park▲, Brooke RV Park▲, Eastern OR Reg'l Airport✈
87	US 197, US 30W, The Dalles, Maupin, Dufur, Bend			209	US 395S, to US 30, OR 37, Pendleton, to Burns
Gas	N: 76, Chevron, Shell	164	N Main St, Boardman	Gas	N: ArcoAmPm, Safeway S: 76◊, Exxon
Food	S: Big Jim's, McDonald's	FStop	N: Main St Shell	Food	N: Jack in the Box, KFC, Taco Bell S: Arby's, Burger King, Denny's, Pizza, McDonald's, Rooster's, Subway, Wendy's
Lodg	N: Comfort Inn, Shilo Inn ♥	TStop	N: Devon Oil/Shell 76		
Other	N: OR State Hwy Patrol Post, Lone Pine RV Park▲, to Columbia Hills RV Village▲, to Wishbone Campground▲, to The Dalles Muni Airport✈	Gas	N: Chevron◊ S: Shell◊	Lodg	N: Oxford Suites, Travelodge ♥ S: Econo Lodge
		Food	N: C&D Drive In S: Nomad Rest	TServ	N: Cummins
		Lodg	N: Dodge City Inn, Riverview Motel S: Econo Lodge	Med	N: + Hospital
Other	S: to Dufur RV Park, appr 20 mi Wasco Co Fairgrounds▲, to Pine Hollow Lakeside Resort & RV Park▲	Other	N: Boardman RV Park & Marina▲ S: ATMs, Auto Services, Grocery	Other	N: ATMs, Grocery, RiteAid, Safeway, Wal-Mart sc, Camp Da-Kon-Ya▲ S: ATMs, Auto Dealers, Grocery, Kmart, Schwab Tire, Thompson RV Center, Heritage Station Museum/RVDump
88	to The Dalles Dam	165	Messner Rd, Port of Morrow		
Other	N: to Dalles Dam	FStop	S: Pacific Pride		
97	OR 206, Celilo Park, The Dalles, Celilo, Wasco	168	US 730, Columbia River Hwy, to Irrigon, Umatilla	210	OR 11, Oregon-Washington Hwy, Pendleton, Walla Walla
Other	N: Celilo Park S: Celilo Village▲, Deschutes River Rec Area▲	Other	N: to appr 8 mi Oasis RV Park▲	FStop	S: Pacific Pride
		171	CR 930, Patterson Ferry Rd, Frontage Rd, Irrigon	Gas	N: 76, Exxon S: 76◊, Shell
(100)	Scenic Area: Columbia River Gorge, Deschutes River	177	Umatilla Army Depot, Hermiston	Food	S: Kopper Kitchen, Shari's
104	US 97, Wasco, Biggs Junction, to Yakima, Bend	(179)	Jct I-82W, Umatilla, to Yakima, Kennewick	Lodg	S: Best Western, Holiday Inn Express ♥, Motel 6 ♥, Red Lion Hotel
TStop	S: Pilot Travel Center #195 (Scales), Grand Central Travel Stop	180	Westland Rd, Westland, Hermiston, to McNary Dam	Med	N: + Hospital
Gas	S: Chevron	FStop	S: Western Express/Shell	Other	N: Catalpa Tree RV Park▲, Wild Rose RV Park▲ S: Grocery, Mountain View RV Park▲, OR State Hwy Patrol Post
Food	S: McDonald's/Pilot TC, Rest/Grand Central TS, Dinty's Café, Jack's Fine Food, Linda's Rest	Food	S: FastFood/Western Express		
		TServ	N: Truck Body Trailer & Repair, Freightliner	213	US 30, Pendleton Hwy (WB) (Addtl Serv 3-5 mi N)
Lodg	S: Biggs Motel, Travelodge	Other	N: LP/Western Express		
Other	N: to Peach Beach RV Park▲, Maryhill State Park▲ S: WiFi/Pilot TC, Auto Repair			Other	N: Oregon Trail RV Park▲

◊= Regular Gas Stations with Diesel   ▲ = RV Friendly Locations   ♥ = Pet Friendly Locations

RED PRINT SHOWS LARGE VEHICLE PARKING/ACCESS ON SITE OR NEARBY   BROWN PRINT SHOWS CAMPGROUNDS/RV PARKS

Page 409

INTERSTATE 84 W/E

EXIT	OREGON
216	OR 331, to OR 11, Milton-Freewater, Walla Walla, Mission, Umatilla Indian Reservation
TStop	N: PacPride/Arrowhead Travel Plaza (Scales)
Food	N: Rest/Arrowhead TP
Lodg	N: Wildhorse Resort & Casino/RVPark▲
Other	N: WiFi/LP/Arrowhead TP, Wildhorse Golf Course
(220)	RunAway Truck Ramp (WB)
(221)	Scenic View (EB)
(223)	Scenic View (WB)
224	Poverty Hill Rd, Old Emigrant Rd, Umatilla Indian Reservation
(227)	Weigh Station (WB) Brake Inspection Area
228	Deadman Pass, Evergreen Ln Rest Area (Both dir) (RR, Phone, Picnic, Vend)
234	Old Emigrant Hill Scenic Frontage Rd, Pendleton, Meacham
Other	N: Emigrant Spring State Park▲
235	Emigrant Spring State Park (WB)
238	Beaver Creek Rd, Pendleton, Meacham, Kamela
243	Summit Rd, to Kamela
Other	N: Emily Summit State Park
248	Spring Creek Rd, to Kamela
Other	S: Spring Creek Campground▲
252	OR 244, Starkey, Hilgard
Other	S: Hilgard State Park▲
(253)	Rest Area (Both dir) (RR, Picnic)
256	Perry (EB)
257	Perry (WB)
(258)	Weigh Station (EB)
259	US 30E, LaGrande (EB)
Gas	S: Chevron, Exxon, Shell
Food	S: Smokehouse Rest, BurgerKing/Exxon
Lodg	S: Royal Motor Inn♥
261	OR 82, LaGrande, Elgin
FStop	S: PacPride/Buy Rite/Exxon
TStop	N: Gem Stop/Chevron
Gas	N: Shell S: 76♦, Chevron♦, Exxon♦
Food	N: Denny's, Pizza Hut, Subway S: DQ, Little Caesars, McDonald's, Taco Time, Skipper's, Wendy's

EXIT	OREGON
Lodg	N: Howard Johnson, LeGrande Inn S: Best Value Inn, Best Western, Super 8
TServ	N: Eagle Truck & Machine Co S: Trail West Truck Service Center
Med	S: + Grande Ronde Hospital
Other	N: OR State Hwy Patrol Post, Auto Dealers, Wal-Mart, Thunder RV, Island City Trailer Sales, La Grande Rendezvous RV Park▲ S: Albertson's, RiteAid, Safeway, E OR Univ, Curt's RV Service & Repair
265	US 30, OR 203, LaGrande, Union
TStop	S: Flying J Travel Plaza #10120(Scales)
Food	S: Rest/FastFood/FJ TP
Lodg	S: Royal Motor Inn♥
TServ	S: Freightliner
Other	N: appr 8mi Eagles Hot Lake RV Resort▲ S: Laundry/WiFi/FJ TP, East OR Univ

EXIT	OREGON
268	Foothill Rd, Union
Other	N: appr 8mi Eagles Hot Lake RV Resort▲
(269)	Rest Area (Both dir) (RR, Phone, Picnic, Vend, RVDump)
270	Ladd Canyon Rd (EB)
273	Brush Creek Rd, Ladd Creek
278	Clover Creek
283	Wolf Creek Rd
285	US 30E, Haines, OR 237, N Powder
FStop	N: North Powder Co-Op/Cenex
Food	N: Rest/Cenex
Lodg	N: Powder River Motel
Other	S: to Ski Area, Anthony Lakes
NOTE:	MM 287.5: 45th Parallel halfway between the North Pole & the Equator
(295)	Rest Area (Both dir) (RR, Phone, Picnic, Vend)
298	OR 203, Medical Springs, Haines
Other	N: Baker City Muni Airport✈
302	OR 86E, Richland, Baker City
Other	S: Oregon Trails West RV Park/Gas▲
304	OR 7, Baker City, Sumpter
FStop	N: Baker City Chevron
TStop	S: CFN/Baker AmBest Truck Corral/Sinclair (Scales), Jacksons Food Mart #83/Shell
Food	N: Burger King/Chevron S: CountryCafe/Baker TC, Blimpie/Jackson, McDonald's, Pizza Hut, Subway
Lodg	S: Motel/Baker TC, Always Welcome Inn, Best Western, Eldorado Inn, Rodeway Inn♥, Super 8, Western Motel
TServ	S: Baker TC/Tires
Med	S: + St Elizabeth's Hospital
Other	S: Laundry/RVDump/LP/Baker TC, Carwash/RVDump/LP/Jackson FM, Albertson's, RiteAid, Safeway, Mountain View Holiday Trav-L-RV Park▲
306	US 30W, Baker City
Gas	S: Gilly's Service Center/Chevron♦
Food	S: Burger Bob's Drive-In, Inland Café, Janet's Cook Shack
Lodg	S: Budget Inn, Baker City Motel & RV Park▲, OR Trail Motel, Western Motel
Other	S: OR State Hwy Patrol Post
313	Pleasant Valley (EB)
315	Pleasant Valley (WB)
317	Old Hwy 30, Pleasant Valley (WB)
319	Pleasant Valley

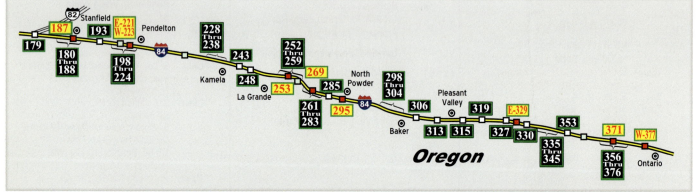

◆ = Regular Gas Stations with Diesel   ▲ = RV Friendly Locations   ♥ = Pet Friendly Locations
RED PRINT SHOWS LARGE VEHICLE PARKING/ACCESS ON SITE OR NEARBY   BROWN PRINT SHOWS CAMPGROUNDS/RV PARKS

EXIT	OREGON
327	Durkee
FStop	N: Oregon Trail Travel Center/Cenex
Food	N: Café/Cenex TS
Other	N: RVDump/Cenex TS
(329)	Pull Off Area (EB)
330	Plano Rd, Cement Plant Rd, Nelson
Other	S: Cement Plant
335	to Weatherby
N:	Rest Area (Both dir) (RR, Phone, Picnic, Vend)
338	Lookout Mountain
Other	N: OR Trail RV Park▲
340	Rye Valley
342	Lime (EB)
345	US 30 Bus, Huntington Hwy, Huntington, Lime
NOTE:	MM 351: PACIFIC/MOUNTAIN Time Zone
353	US 30, to Huntington, Farewell Bend
TStop	N: Farewell Bend Travel Plaza
Food	N: Deli/Farewell Bend TP
(354)	Weigh Station (EB)
356	OR 201N, to Weiser, ID
Other	N: Oasis RV Park & Campground▲, Catfish Junction RV Park▲, Snake River RV Park▲
362	Moores Hollow Rd
(371)	Rest Area (Both dir) (RR, Picnic)
371	Stanton Blvd
374	OR 201, US 30 Bus, to US 20, US 26, Ontario, Weiser
FStop	S: Pacific Pride
TStop	N: Love's Travel Stop #372
Gas	S: Shell◊
Food	N: FastFood/Love's TS
Lodg	S: Budget Inn
Med	S: + Hospital
Other	N: Ontario State Park/RVDump S: U-Haul, to Ontario Muni Airport✈, Lake Owl State Park▲, Country Campground▲
376A	US 30 Bus, to US 20, US 26, to Ontario, Burns
376B	to US 95, Payette
376	US 30, US 95, Idaho Ave, Ontario, Payette
TStop	S: Pilot Travel Center #232 (Scales)

EXIT	OR / ID
Gas	N: Chevron S: Shell◊
Food	N: Burger King, Country Kitchen, DQ, Denny's, McDonald's, China Buffet S: Arby's/TJCinn/Pilot TC, BBQ, Chinese, DJ's Rest, Sizzler, Skippers Seafood, Taco Bell, Wendy's, Winger's Diner
Lodg	N: Best Western, Colonial Motor Inn, Motel 6♥, Sleep Inn, Super 8 S: Economy Inn, Holiday Motor Inn, Oregon Trail Motel, Rodeway Inn
Med	S: + Hospital
Other	N: ATMs, Auto Dealers, Home Depot, Kmart, Staples, Wal-Mart sc▲, OR State Hwy Patrol Post S: Laundry/WiFi/RVDump/Pilot TC, Ontario Muni Airport✈, Auto Dealers, NAPA, Tires, Radio Shack, U-Haul, Museum
(377)	OR Welcome Center (WB) (RR, Phone, Picnic, Vend, Info, WiFi)
NOTE:	MM 378: Idaho State Line

(MOUNTAIN TIME ZONE)
⬆ OREGON
⬇ IDAHO
(MOUNTAIN TIME ZONE)

(1)	ID Welcome Center (EB) (RR, Phone, Picnic, Vend, Info, WiFi)
3	US 95, Fruitland, Payette
Gas	N: Shell◊
Food	N: A&W Addtl food 3.5mi
Other	N: Exit 3 RV Park▲, Hells Canyon Rec Area, Hollis RV Repair S: Neat Retreat RV Park▲
9	US 30 Bus, New Plymouth
13	Black Canyon Rd, Caldwell, Bliss
TStop	S: Stinker Station #45/Sinclair (Scales)
Food	S: Rest/FastFood/Stinker
Lodg	S: Motel/Stinker
Other	S: Laundry/Stinker
17	Oasis Rd, Caldwell, Sand Hollow
Gas	N: Sinclair
Food	N: Sandhollow Country Café
Lodg	S: Wild Rose Manor B&B
Other	N: Country Corners Campground & RV Park/RVDump▲
25	ID 44E, Caldwell, Middleton
Gas	N: 44 Quick Stop/Shell◊
26	US 20, US 26, Nyssa, Burns, Caldwell, Notus
Gas	S: Stinker/Sinclair
Other	N: Caldwell Campground & RV Park▲

EXIT	IDAHO
27	I-84 Bus, ID 19, Centennial Way, to US 95, Caldwell, Wilder
FStop	S: 122 Simplot Blvd: Pacific Pride
TStop	S: to approx 11mi 128 5th St/Wilder: Jackson Food Store #3/Shell (Scales)
Other	S: Laundry/RVDump/Jackson FS
28	10th Ave, Caldwell
Gas	N: Maverik Country Store S: Chevron
Food	S: Carl's Jr, DQ, Jack in the Box, Mr. V's, Pizza Hut, Wendy's
Lodg	N: I-84 Motor Inn S: Holiday Motel♥, Sundowner Motel♥
Med	S: + West Valley Medical Center
Other	N: Birds of Prey Harley Davidson S: CarWash
29	US 20E, US 26E, Franklin Rd, Caldwell, Boise, Garden City
TStop	N: Flying J Travel Plaza #5002/Conoco (Scales) S: Sage Travel Plaza/Sinclair
Food	N: CountryMarket/FastFood/FJ TP S: Rest/FastFood/Sage TP, Cattleman's Café, McDonald's, Perkins
Lodg	S: Best Western, La Quinta Inn♥
Med	S: + Hospital
Other	N: Laundry/WiFi/RVDump/LP/FJ TP, Ambassador RV Resort/RVDump, Caldwell Industrial Airport✈ S: Laundry/RVDump/LP/Sage TP, Auto Dealers, Albertson's, Best Buy, RiteAid, Tires, Wal-Mart sc, Les Schwab Tires, Albertson College, Fairgrounds/RVDump, Nelson's Out West RV's
33AB	ID 55S, Karcher Rd, Nampa (WB)
33	ID 55S, Karcher Rd, Midland Blvd, Nampa (EB)
Gas	S: Jackson FS, Maverik
Food	N: Starbucks S: Acapulco Grill, Applebee's, Arby's, Carl's Jr, IHOP, Jack in the Box, Jade Garden, Jalapeno Rest, Outback Steakhouse, Shari's, Taco Bell
Other	N: Best Buy, Costco, PetCo♥, Target S: ATMs, Auto Repairs & Services, Big O Tires, Big Lots, Dollar Tree, Kmart, Office Depot, Pharmacy, ShopKO, Staples, UPS Store, Freedom Boat & RV, Bob's RV Center, appr 7mi Decoy RV Park▲
35	ID 55S, Nampa Blvd, Nampa
TStop	S: CFN/Jackson Food Store #85/Shell
Food	S: FastFood/Jackson FS, Burger King, Blazen Burgers, Denny's, KFC, McDonald's, Pizza Hut

◊ = Regular Gas Stations with Diesel   ▲ = RV Friendly Locations   ♥ = Pet Friendly Locations

Page 411

Interstate 84 W/E

EXIT		IDAHO
	Lodg	S: Days Inn, Shilo Inn, Super 8
	Med	S: + Hospital
	TWash	S: Jackson FS
	Other	S: Laundry/WiFi/Jackson FS, ATM, Auto Service, Tires, Fred Meyer, Pharmacy, Walgreen's
36		Franklin Blvd, Nampa
	TStop	S: PacPr/Jackson Food Store #5/Shell (Scales)
	Gas	N: Maverik
		S: Chevron◊
	Food	N: Elmer's, Jack in the Box, Rest/Shilo Inn
		S: FastFood/Jackson FS
	Lodg	N: Shilo Inn
		S: Sleep Inn
	TWash	S: Action RV & Truck Wash, Jackson FS
	Med	S: + Hospital
	Other	N: Nelson Freeway RV's
		S: Laundry/RVDump/Jackson FS, Mason Creek RV Park/RVDump▲, ID RV Service & Repair, Seventh Heaven RV & Marine Superstore
38		I-84 Bus, ID 45S, Garrity Blvd, Nampa
	Gas	N: Chevron◊
		S: Phillips 66◊, Shell
	Food	N: Port of Subs, Subway
		S: McDonald's/66
	Lodg	N: Hampton Inn
		S: Holiday Inn Express
	Med	S: + Mercy Health Center
	Other	N: Auto Dealers, Sam's Club, Wal-Mart sc
		S: Garrity Blvd RV Park/RVDump▲, Earl's RV, RV Furniture Center, Nampa Muni Airport✈
44		1st St, Meridian Rd, ID 69S, Meridian, Kuna
	FStop	N: 234 W Franklin Pacific Pride
	Gas	N: Chevron◊, Sinclair
		S: Shell◊
	Food	N: Bolo's Pub, DQ, KFC, McDonald's, Pizza Hut, Quiznos, Shari's, Starbucks, Subway, Taco Bell, Tony Roma's, Wendy's
		S: JB's Family Rest, Pizza Hut
	Lodg	N: Best Western, Motel 6♥, Wyndham
		S: Mr. Sandman Motel
	TServ	N: Idaho Fleet Service
		S: Western States Truck Shop/CAT
	Other	N: ATMs, Auto Repairs, Banks, CarQuest, Grocery, Home Depot, Les Schwab Tires, Pharmacy, Sierra Trading Post, Meridian Speedway, Boise-Meridian RV Resort/RVDump▲
		S: U-Haul, Vet♥, Playground RV Park▲, Bodily RV Center/RVDump, Roaring Springs Waterpark, Boondocks Fun Center
46		ID 55N, Eagle Rd, McCall
	FStop	N: to 549 Partridge Pl appr 3mi Pacific Pride◊◊
		S: to 3291 E Pine CFN/Jackson Food Store #105
	Gas	N: Chevron◊◊, Shell◊
	Food	N: IHOP, McDonald's, Subway
		S: Durango's Mexican, NY Deli, Quiznos, Subway, TCBY
	Lodg	N: Holiday Inn Express
	Med	N: + St Luke's Meridian Medical Center
	Other	N: FedEx Kinko's, PetSmart♥, Office Depot, Pharmacy, Fiesta RV Park▲, to appr 7mi Hi-Valley RV Park▲
		S: High Desert Harley Davidson, Carwash/Jackson FS, UPS Store, US Post Office

EXIT		IDAHO
(49)		Jct I-184, W Boise (fr EB, Left Exit)
	Other	N: to 1st Ex Boise Town Square Mall, to Bogus Basin Mountain Resort, Ski Area
50A		W Overland Rd, Boise (EB)
	Gas	S: Phillips 66, Jackson FS
	Food	S: Black Angus, Burger King, CK Hawaiian BBQ, ChuckARama Buffet, Goodwood BBQ, Johnny Carino's Italian, McDonald's, Pollo Rey Mex Rest, On the Border, Starbucks
	Lodg	S: Ameritel Inn, Budget Host Inn, Hilton Garden Inn, Homewood Suites, Oxford Suites
	Other	S: CarWash, Lowe's, Wal-Mart sc
50B		S Cole Rd, Overland Rd (EB)
	Gas	S: Stinker/Shell, Maverik
	Food	S: Cracker Barrel, McGrath's Fish House
	Other	S: CarWash, Commercial Tire, Costco
50A		S Cole Rd, Overland Rd (WB)
	Gas	N: Jackson FS, Chevron
	Lodg	N: Plaza Suite, Residence Inn, Candlewood Suites
	Med	N: + St Alphonsus Hospital
	Other	N: to Boise Towne Square Mall, to appr 6mi On the River RV Park/RVDump▲, Riverpond Campground▲
50B		W Overland Rd, Cole Rd, Boise (WB)
	Gas	N: Chevron
	Food	N: Cobby's Sandwich Shop, Eddie's, McDonald's, Outback Steakhouse, Pizza Hut, Subway, Taco Bell
52		Orchard St, Boise (Access to Ex 50AB Serv N)
	FStop	N: to 3712 Chinden Blvd 3.5mi Pacific Pride◊◊
	Gas	N: Shell
	Food	N: Jack in the Box
53		Vista Ave, Boise Airport
	Gas	N: Shell, Sinclair
		S: Chevron
	Food	N: McDonald's, Pizza Hut
		S: Denny's, McDonald's, Kopper Kitchen, Pizza Hut
	Lodg	N: Cambria Suites, Extended Stay America, Fairfield Inn, Hampton Inn, Holiday Inn Express♥, Super 8
		S: Best Western, Comfort Inn, Holiday Inn, Inn America, Motel 6♥, Sleep Inn
	Other	N: ID State Hwy Patrol Post
		S: Boise Air Terminal/Gowen Field✈, Budget RAC, Rental Cars
54		US 20W, US 26W, Broadway Ave, Federal Way, Downtown Boise
	TStop	N: Flying J Travel Plaza #10380 (Scales)
		S: Travel Center of America #167/Tesoro (Scales)
	Gas	N: Chevron◊
	Food	N: Rest/FastFood/FJ TP
		S: Buckhorn/Subway/TacoBell/TA TC
	Lodg	S: Shilo Inn
	TServ	N: Cummins Intermountain, NW Equipment
		S: TA TC/Tires, Lake City International, Smith Detroit Diesel-Allison, Trebar Kenworth
	Med	N: + Hospital
	Other	N: Laundry/WiFi/RVDump/LP/FJ TP, NAPA, to Boise State Univ, Boise Zoo
		S: Laundry/WiFi/TA TC, Boise Air Terminal/Gowen Field✈, Mountain View RV Park/RVDump▲

EXIT		IDAHO
57		ID 21 Gowen Rd, Boise, Idaho City
	Gas	N: Albertson's
		S: Chevron, Shell
	Food	N: Jack in the Box, Perkins, Subway
		S: Burger King/Chevron, McDonald's
	Lodg	N: Best Western
	TServ	N: Boise Peterbilt, Cummins Rocky Mtn
	Other	N: Albertson's, Micron Technology, Simplot Sports Complex, to Lucky Peak State Park
		S: Boise VF Factory Outlet Mall, Jack's Tires & Oil, ID Ice World
59A		Eisenman Rd (EB)
59B		Federal Way (EB)
59		Memory Rd, Eisenman Rd, S Federal Way, Boise (WB) (Access to Ex #57 Serv)
(62)		Rest Area (Both dir) (RR, Phone, Picnic, Vend)
64		Kuna More Rd, Boise
(67)		Weigh Station (Both dir)
71		Orchard Access Rd, Boise, Mayfield, Orchard
	TStop	S: PacPride/Boise Stage Stop/Sinclair (Scales)
	Food	S: Rest/Boise SS
	Lodg	S: Motel/Boise SS
	TWash	S: Boise SS
	TServ	S: Boise SS/Tires
	Other	S: Laundry/CB/WiFi/RVDump/Boise SS, Ada Co Nat'l Guard Maneuver Area
74		Simco Rd
90		I-84 Bus, Frontage Rd, to ID 51, ID 67, Mountain Home (Access to Ex #95 Serv-3mi)
95		US 20E, Idaho Falls (EB), ID 51S, American Legion Blvd, Mountain Home, Elko
	FStop	S: Sunset C-Store/Sinclair
	TStop	N: Pilot Travel Center #350 (Scales)
	Gas	N: Chevron
		S: Mirastar
	Food	N: Arby's/TJCinn/PilotTC KFC, Jack in the Box, Subway
		S: Golden Crown Rest, Jade Palace Rest, McDonald's, Subway, Wendy's
	Lodg	N: Best Western, Hampton Inn, Sleep Inn
		S: Towne Center Motel♥
	Med	S: + Elmore Hospital
	Other	N: Laundry/WiFi/Pilot TC
		S: ATMs, Albertson's, Family Dollar, Wal-Mart sc, Golf Course, Mountain Home Muni Airport✈, Mountain Home RV Park▲, The Wagon Wheel RV Park▲, Mountain Home KOA/RVDump▲, Cottonwood RV Park▲, Mountain Home AFB
99		I-84 Bus, Bennett Rd, to ID 51, to ID 67, to Mountain Home (Access to Ex #95 Serv)
112		I-84 Bus, Hammett Hill Rd, to ID 78W, Glenns Ferry, Murphy
	Other	S: Cold Springs Winery, to Bruneau Dunes State Park

◊ = Regular Gas Stations with Diesel   ▲ = RV Friendly Locations   ♥ = Pet Friendly Locations
RED PRINT SHOWS LARGE VEHICLE PARKING/ACCESS ON SITE OR NEARBY   BROWN PRINT SHOWS CAMPGROUNDS/RV PARKS

EXIT	IDAHO	EXIT	IDAHO	EXIT	IDAHO
114	I-84 Bus, ID 30, to ID 78, Cold Springs Rd (WB)	Lodg	N: Hub City Inn	Other	S: Laundry/Travelers TP, Oregon Trail Campground▲ & Family Fun Center
120	I-84 Bus, N Bannock Ave, Glenns Ferry (EB) (Access to Ex #121 Serv)	Other	N: Intermountain Motor Homes & RV Park/RVDump▲, to 210 S Shohone St: City RVDump	188	Valley Rd, to Eden, Hazelton
Other	S: Trail Break RV Park▲,		S: RVDump/Wendell G&O	194	ID 25W, Ridgeway Rd, Hazelton, Eden
121	I-84 Bus, King Hill Loop, E 1st Ave, Glenns Ferry	165	ID 25E, Main St, Appleton Rd, to US 93, Jerome (Access to Ex #168 Serv)	TStop	S: R&E Greenwood Store/Sinclair
Gas	S: Sinclair	Gas	N: Valley Co-Op, Sinclair◇	Food	S: Café/Sinclair
Food	S: Oregon Trail Café, Café/Hanson's Motel, Pizza, Rest/Carmela Winery	Food	N: China Village, Café, Family Dinner	Other	S: Laundry/RVDump/Sinclair
Lodg	S: Hanson's Motel, Harvester Inn, Redford Motel	Lodg	N: Holiday Motel, Towles Motel	201	ID 25E, Kasota Rd, to Paul, Rupert
Other	S: Power Pop RV Stop▲, Carmela Winery, Glenns Ferry Muni Airport✈, Carmela RV Park▲, Three Island State Park▲	TServ	N: Centennial Truck Service, Fleet Tire Service	208	I-84 Bus, ID 27, Burley, Paul
		Med	N: + St Benedicts Hospital	FStop	S: Chevron, Sinclair (Both Chevron & Sinclair DAD/DAND)
		Other	N: Auto Services, ATMs	TStop	N: Hub Plaza/P66 (Scales)
125	Paradise Valley, Grave Rd, King Hill	168	ID 79N, Jerome	Gas	S: Shell◇
		FStop	N: Honker's Mini Mart/Sinclair (Scales)	Food	N: FastFood/Hub Plz
129	Parks Loop Rd, Gopher Knoll Rd, King Hill	Gas	N: Chevron, Mirastar, Shell		S: Arby's, Burger King, Jack in the Box, McDonald's, JB's Family Rest, Perkins, Wendy's
		Food	N: FastFood/Honkers, Jerome Café, McDonald's, Sonic, Wendy's/Shell	Lodg	N: Super 8
(133)	Rest Area (Both dir) (RR, Phone, Picnic, Vend)	Lodg	N: Best Western, Crest Motel		S: Best Western, Budget Motel, Fairfield Inn, Starlite Motel
		TServ	N: Kenworth	Med	S: + Hospital
137	I-84 Bus, US 26, to US 30, Pioneer Rd, Bliss (Access to Ex #141 Serv-1.5mi)	Other	N: Laundry/RVDump/LP/Honkers, Tires, Wal-Mart sc, Brockman's RV Sales	Other	N: Cassia Co Fairgrounds/RVDump
			S: ID RV & Marine		S: Auto Dealers, Auto Services, Kelly Tire, Kmart, Wal-Mart sc, Golf Course, to Snake River Rec Area
141	US 26E, Gooding, Snoshone (EB), US 30E, Buhl, Bliss (WB)	(171)	Rest Area (EB) (RR, Phone, Picnic, Vend)	211	I-84 Bus, US 30W, Burley (EB), ID 24, Rupert, Heyburn (WB)
TStop	S: Stinker Station #74/Sinclair, Roadrunner (EB: Access via Ex #137)	(171)	Weigh Station (EB)	FStop	N: Stinker Station #66/Sinclair
Gas	S: Ziggy's Express/66, Hagerman Shell	173	US 93, Jerome, Twin Falls, Sun Valley Wells, Missoula (S Serv are appr 5mi S in Twin Falls)	TStop	S: Love's Travel Stop #334 (Scales)
Food	S: Rest/Ziggy's, Larry & Mary's Café, Ox Bow Café, Riley Creek Rest, Skinny Pig, Snake River Grill	TStop	N: Flying J Travel Plaza #5116 (Scales)	Gas	N: Chevron
		Food	N: Rest/FastFood/FJ TP	Food	N: A&W, Café
Lodg	S: Amber Inn Motel, Y-Inn Motel, to appr 8mi Hagermann Valley Inn, Billingsley Creek Lodge	Lodg	N: Days Inn/FJ TP		S: Carl'sJr/Love's TS, Jill's
		TWash	N: Blue Beacon TW/FJ TP	Lodg	N: Tops Motel
			S: Wiley's Truck Wash	TWash	N: Truck Wash
Med	N: + Hospital	TServ	N: FJ TP/Tires	Med	N: + Hospital
Other	S: Laundry/Stinker, WiFi/Roadrunner, Hagerman RV Village▲	Med	S: + Magic Valley Memorial Hospital	Other	N: Country RV Village▲
		Other	N: Laundry/WiFi/LP/FJ TP, Twin Falls/Jerome KOA/RVDump▲		S: Laundry/WiFi/RVDump/Love's TS, to Burley Muni Airport✈, Heyburn Riverside RV Park/RVDump▲
147	2300 S, Hagerman, to Tuttle		S: appr 8.5mi South 93 RV Park▲, Bish's RV, College of Southern ID, Twin Falls/Sun Valley Reg'l Airport✈, Shoshone Falls Park	216	ID 25W, to Rupert (EB), ID 77S, to Declo (WB)
Other	S: High Adventure River Tours, Malad Gorge State Park			FStop	N: Conoco 66/Village of Trees
155	ID 46 Spur, Wendell, Hagerman (Access to Ex #157 Sev)	182	ID 50, Eden, to Hansen, Twin Falls, Eden	Gas	S: Pit Stop/Shell◇
Other	N: Intermountain Motor Homes & RV Park/RVDump▲, Bert Harbaugh Motors	TStop	S: PacPride/AmBest/Travelers Oasis Travel Plaza/Shell (Scales)	Other	N: Village of Trees RV Resort/RVDump▲, to Lake Walcott State Park▲
	S: Thousand Springs Resort▲, to Mineral Hot Springs & Campground▲	Gas	N: Sinclair/Anderson CG▲	(222)	Jct I-86, US 30E, to Pocatello
		Food	S: Rest/Blimpie/TacoBell/Travelers TP	228	ID 81, Yale Rd, to Declo, Malta
157	ID 46N, Idaho St, Wendell, Gooding	Lodg	S: Amber Inn	(229)	Rest Area (Both dir) (Next RA 97mi) (RR, Phone, Picnic, Vend)
FStop	S: Wendell Gas & Oil/Sinclair	TServ	S: Travelers TP/Tires/Towing	(229)	Weigh Stations (Both dir)
Food	N: Family Rest, Pizza, Subway	Other	N: Anderson Campground/RVDump▲, Gary's Freeway RV, Xtreme Motorsports & RV	237	Idahome Rd
	S: Farmhouse Rest				

◇ = Regular Gas Stations with Diesel   ▲ = RV Friendly Locations   ♥ = Pet Friendly Locations
RED PRINT SHOWS LARGE VEHICLE PARKING/ACCESS ON SITE OR NEARBY   BROWN PRINT SHOWS CAMPGROUNDS/RV PARKS

INTERSTATE 84 W/E

EXIT	ID / UT
245	Sublett Rd, Malta, Sublett
TStop	N: Mountain View Truck Stop/Sinclair
Food	N: Rest/Mtn View TS
254	Sweetzer Rd
263	Juniper Rd, Juniper
(269)	Rest Area (Both dir) (RR, Picnic)
NOTE:	MM 275: Utah State Line

(MOUNTAIN TIME ZONE)

IDAHO
UTAH
(MOUNTAIN TIME ZONE)

5	UT 30, Snowville, to Park Valley, to Elko, NV
7	Snowville
TStop	N: Flying J Travel Plaza #1139 (Scales)
Food	N: FastFood/Flying J TP, Mollie's Café, Ranch House Diner, Subway
Lodg	N: Outsiders Motel
Other	N: WiFi/RVDump/LP/FJ TP, Lottie Dell Campground & RV Park▲
12	Ranch Exit
16	Ranch Exit, Hansel Valley
17	Ranch Exit
20	Blue Creek
24	Valley
26	UT 83S, Howell, Thiokol
32	Ranch Exit
39	to I-15, Garland, Bothwell
Med	N: + Hospital
40	I-84 Bus, UT 102, Tremonton, Bothwell
FStop	N: Jim & Dave's Sinclair
TStop	N: RJ's Fuel Stop/Sinclair (Scales), CFN/Golden Spike Travel Plaza/Chevron
Food	N: BurgerKing/Quiznos/RJ's FS, Rest/Golden Spike TP, Denny's, McDonald's, Wendy's
Lodg	N: Western Inn
TWash	N: RJ's FS, Golden Spike TP
TServ	N: RJ's FS/Tires, Golden Spike TP/Tires, Transport Diesel Service
Med	N: + Hospital
Other	N: Laundry/RVDump/RJ's FS, Laundry/BarbSh/WiFi/RVDump/LP/Golden Spike TP, Interstate Auto & Truck Center, Jack's RV Sales
NOTE:	I-84 below runs with I-15. Exit #'s follow I-15.
(379/41)	Jct I-84W to Boise, Tremonton Jct I-15N, to Pocatello Jct I-15S, I-84E, to Salt Lake City
376	UT 13, N 5200 St W, Tremonton, to UT 102, Garland, Bear River (lodging N to UT 102W)
FStop	E: Exxon Travel Center
Gas	E: Conoco◆
Food	E: Arby's/Exxon TC, Crossroads Family Rest, JC's Country Diner, Subway

EXIT	UTAH
Lodg	E: Marble Motel, Sandman Motel W: Western Inn♥
Other	E: Co Fairgrounds
372	UT 240, Honeyville, to UT 13, UT 38, Bear River
Other	E: Crystal Hot Springs Campground▲
(370)	Rest Area (SB) (RR, Phone, Picnic, Vend)
365	900 North St, Brigham City (EB), UT 13, Corinne (WB)
Other	E: Brigham City Airport✈
363	Forest St, Brigham City
Other	E: Parson's Service Center, Auto & Truck Repair, Towing, U-Haul
362	US 91, to US 89, 1100 South St, Brigham City, Logan
FStop	E: Flying J Travel Plaza #1188 (Scales)
Gas	E: 7-11, Chevron, Sinclair, Mirastar
Food	E: Rest/FastFood/Flying J TP, Arby's, Aspen Grill, Burger King, KFC, McDonald's, Subway
Lodg	E: Crystal Inn, Galaxie Motel, Howard Johnson
TServ	E: Willard Auto & Diesel Service W: S&M Diesel Service
Med	E: + Brigham City Comm Hospital
Other	E: WiFi/LP/RVDump/FJ TP, Golden Spike RV Park▲, Walker Cinemas, Auto Dealers, Auto Zone, Checkers Auto, Wal-Mart sc, Eagle Mtn Golf Course, Logan State Univ
(363)	Perry Rest Area (NB) (RR, Phones, Picnic)

EXIT	UTAH
(361)	Port of Entry / Weigh Station (Both dir)
357	750N, UT 360, UT315, N Willard, Perry, Willard Bay
TStop	E: Flying J Travel Plaza #1125 (Scales)
Food	E: CountryMarket/FastFood/FJ TP
Other	E: Laundry/WiFi/RVDump/LP/FJ TP, Brigham City/Perry South KOA▲, Police Dept W: Willard Bay State Park▲
351	UT 126, to US 89, S Willard, Pleasant View, Willard Bay
Other	W: Willard Bay State Park▲
(349)	Emergency Pull Out (NB)
349	2700 N, UT 134, Ogden, Farr West, Pleasant View
Gas	E: 7-11, Chevron, Maverik, Phillips 66 W: Conoco◆
Food	E: Arby's, McDonald's, Melinas Mex Rest, Subway, Wendy's
Other	E: Auto Repair, Fort Carson Army Res Center W: Tips RV
346	Pioneer Rd, Ogden, Harrisville, Defense Depot
Gas	W: Excel Conv Store
TServ	W: Diesel Service
Other	E: Mulligan's Golf Course, Fort Carson Army Res Center
344	UT 39, 1200S, 12th St, Ogden
TStop	W: Pilot Travel Center #294 (Scales)
Gas	E: Chevron, Phillips 66, Shell◆
Food	E: Rest/BW, Jeremiah's, Hogi Yogi W: DQ/Subway/TacoBell/Pilot TC, CJ's Rest & Bakery
Lodg	E: Best Western W: Holiday Inn Express, Sleep Inn
TServ	W: General Diesel Services
Other	E: Steve's Car Care W: WiFi/Pilot TC
343	UT 104, 21st St, Wilson Lane
FStop	W: Super Stop Shell
TStop	E: Flying J Travel Plaza #5001/Conoco (Scales), Wilson Lane Chevron
Gas	W: Phillips 66
Food	E: Rest/FastFood/FJ TP, Arby's/Wilson Lane, Cactus Red's, McDonald's, Mi Rancho Rest, Rest/Comf Sts, Rest/HI W: FastFood/Texaco, Café/Super 8, Blimpie
Lodg	E: Flying J Inn/FJ TP, Big Z Motel, Best Rest Inn♥, Comfort Suites, Holiday Inn Express♥ W: Super 8♥
Tires	E: Flying J TP, Wilson Lane
TWash	E: Wilson Lane Service
TServ	E: Ogden Diesel Sales & Service
Other	E: Laundry/BarbSh/CB/WiFi/RV Dump/LP/FJ TP, RV Dump/Wilson Lane, Century MH & RV Park▲, Justus Bros RV & Marine W: Auto Repair, Diesel Services
342	UT 53, Pennsylvania Ave, 24th St, Ogden (NB)
FStop	E: Sinclair
Food	W: Sunrise Cafe
Other	E: Animal Hospital♥, Auto Repair, Fort Buenaventura State Park

◆ = Regular Gas Stations with Diesel ▲ = RV Friendly Locations ♥ = Pet Friendly Locations
RED PRINT SHOWS LARGE VEHICLE PARKING/ACCESS ON SITE OR NEARBY BROWN PRINT SHOWS CAMPGROUNDS/RV PARKS

EXIT	UTAH
341B	UT 79, 31st St, Ogden
Other	W: Ogden Hinckley Airport✈, U-Haul
341A	UT 79, 31st St, Hinckley, to UT 204, US 89, Ogden (Serv E to Wall St/UT204/US89)
Gas	E: 7-11
Food	E: Arby's, Golden Corral, Skippers
Lodg	E: Days Inn ♥
Med	E: + Hospital
Other	E: Newgate Mall, to Weber St Univ
(340)	Jct I-84E, to Cheyenne (SB, Left exit)
NOTE:	I-84 above runs with I-15. Exit #'s follow I-15.
81	UT 26, to I-15S, Riverdale
Gas	N: Conoco◆, Sinclair
Food	N: Applebee's, Carl's Jr, Chili's, La Salsa Mex Rest, IHOP, McDonald's
	S: McDonald's
Lodg	S: Motel 6 ♥
Other	N: ATMs, Auto Dealers, Circuit City, Home Depot, Harley Davidson, Lowe's,
Other	N: PetSmart ♥, Sam's Club, Target, Wal-Mart sc, Auto Services, Wilderness RV

EXIT	UTAH
85	Adams Ave Pkwy, Uintah, S Weber
Med	N: + Ogden Reg'l Medical Center
87A	US 89N, to I-15, UT 203, Ogden
87B	US 89S, to I-15, UT 193, Salt Lake City
87	US 89, Ogden, Salt Lake City (EB)
Gas	S: Shell, Chevron
Food	N: Wendy's, Village Inn
(91)	Rest Area (EB) (RR, Picnic)
92	UT 167, Mountain Green, to Huntsville (EB)
(94)	Rest Area (WB) (RR, Picnic)
96	to UT 167, Peterson, Mountain Green, Enterprise, Stoddard
Gas	S: Sinclair
Other	N: to Powder Mountain, Snow Basin, Nordic Valley Ski Areas

EXIT	UTAH
103	UT 66, Morgan
Gas	S: 7-11, Chevron
Food	S: Subway, Chicken Hut, Steph's Drive In, Spring Chicken Cafe
Other	S: Fairgrounds, East Canyon
106	Ranch Exit
108	Devils Slide, Taggert
111	Croydon
112	Henefer
115	Henefer, Echo
(120)	Jct I-80, W to Ogden, E to Cheyenne
	(I-84 Begins/Ends on I-80, Exit #168)
	(MOUNTAIN TIME ZONE)
⛽	**UTAH**
	Resume WB I-84 at Jct I-80, near Echo, UT to near I-5 in Portland, OR.

EXIT	PENNSYLVANIA
	Resume I-84EB from Jct I-81 near Dunsmore, PA to Jct I-90 near Sturbridge, MA.
⛽	**PENNSYLVANIA** (EASTERN TIME ZONE) (I-84 Begins/Ends on I-81, Exit #186/187)
(0)	Jct I-81, US 6W, to Wilkes-Barre, Binghamton, NY (WB) US 6E, Expressway, to Carbondale (WB, Exit only) Begin I-84 / I-380 EB, End WB
1	Tigue St, Dunmore
Gas	N: Shell
	S: Mobil
Food	S: Anna Marie's Rest
Lodg	S: Holiday Inn ♥
2	PA 435S, Scranton, to Elmhurst (EB, Left Exit only)
(4)	Jct I-380S, to Mt Pocono (fr WB, Left exit)

EXIT	PENNSYLVANIA
8	PA 247N, Line Rd, to PA 348, Lake Ariel, to Mount Cobb, Hamlin
NOTE:	NO Trucks over 10.5 Tons on PA 247
FStop	S: Joe's Kwik Mart/Mobil
Gas	N: Gulf◆
17	PA 191, Twin Rocks Rd, Sterling, to Newfoundland, Hamlin
TStop	N: Howe's 84 AmBest Auto Truck Plaza/Exxon (Scales)
Food	N: Rest/Howe's ATP
Lodg	N: Comfort Inn
TServ	N: Howe's ATP/Tires
Other	N: Laundry/Howe's ATP
	S: Spring Hill Airpark✈, PA State Hwy Patrol Post
20	PA 507, Greentown, Lake Wallenpaupack
TStop	N: Lakewood 84/Exxon
Food	N: Rest/Lakewood 84
Other	N: WiFi/Lakewood 84
(26)	Rest Area (Both dir) (RR, Phone, Picnic, Info)
(26)	Weigh Station (Both dir)

EXIT	PENNSYLVANIA
26	PA 390, Greentown, Tafton
TStop	N: Promised Land Fuel Stop/Exxon
Food	N: FastFood/Promised Land FS
Other	S: to Promised Land State Park
30	PA 402, Tafton to Porters Lake, Blooming Grove
NOTE:	PA 402S: 10 Ton Weight Limit
Other	N: PA State Hwy Patrol Post
34	PA 739, Dingman Tpk, Tafton, to Dingmans Ferry, Lords Valley
Gas	S: Sunoco◆
Food	S: McDonald's
46	US 6, to Milford (Addt'l Serv 3mi S in Milford)
Gas	S: Citgo◆, Hilltop Xtra Mart◆, Turkey Hill
Food	S: Big Willie's BBQ, Apple Valley Family Rest, Waterwheel Cafe
Lodg	S: Red Carpet Inn, to Milford Motel, Myer Motel, Cliff Park Inn, Mt Haven Resort to appr 11 mi Harmony Ridge Farm & Campground▲
53	US 6, US 209, Matamoras
NOTE:	US 209S: NO Trucks
N:	PA Welcome Center (WB)

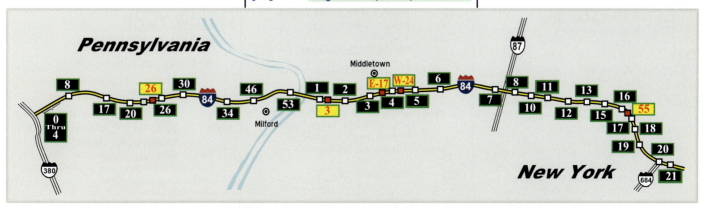

◆ = Regular Gas Stations with Diesel   ▲ = RV Friendly Locations   ♥ = Pet Friendly Locations
RED PRINT SHOWS LARGE VEHICLE PARKING/ACCESS ON SITE OR NEARBY   BROWN PRINT SHOWS CAMPGROUNDS/RV PARKS

Page 415

EXIT		PA / NY	EXIT		NEW YORK	EXIT		NY / CT
53		Rest Area (EB) (NO TRUCKS 7am-7pm) (RR, Phone, Picnic, Info)		Food	S: Chili's, Outback Steakhouse, Red Robin, TGI Friday	41/11		NY 9D, NY 52 Bus, Beacon, Wappingers Falls
	Gas	N: Shell, Turkey Hill, Exxon S: Mobil◊		Lodg	N: Howard Johnson, Super 8 S: Courtyard, Hampton Inn, Holiday Inn		Gas	N: Mobil◊
	Food	N: Applegrill, Little Caesars, Stewarts Family Rest, Taco Palace S: McDonald's, Little Caesars, Perkins, Subway, Wendy's, Westfall Family Rest		Med Other	N: + Orange Reg'l Medical Center N: ATMS, Auto Services, Best Buy, CVS, Borders, Circuit City, Firestone, Gander Mountain, Home Depot, Lowe's, PetCo♥, PetSmart♥, RiteAid, Sam's Club, Staples, Wal-Mart sc, Crystal Run Mall, U-Haul, Randall Airport✈		Med Other	N: + Castlepoint VA Hospital N: Dutchess Stadium
	Lodg	S: Best Western, Riverview Inn, Scottish Inn				44/12		NY 52E, Main St, Fishkill
	Other	N: AutoZone, TriState Campground▲ S: ATMs, Grocery, Home Depot, Kmart, Pharmacy, Lowe's, Staples, Wal-Mart sc, River Beach Campsites▲					Gas	N: Coastal, Valero S: Mobil, SunocoSam's Club◊,
							Food	S: I-84 Diner
							Other	N: UPS Store
	NOTE:	MM 54: New York State Line	(24)		Rest Area (WB) (RR, Phone, Picnic, NY St Police) Random DOT Inspections	46/13		US 9, S-Peekskill, N-Poughkeepsie
		(EASTERN TIME ZONE)					Gas	N: Citgo, Gulf, Mobil◊ S: Hess
ⓃPENNSYLVANIA Ⓢ NEW YORK (EASTERN TIME ZONE)			28/5		NY 208, Montgomery, to Walden, Maybrook		Food	N: Burger King, Charlie Brown Steakhouse, Cracker Barrel, Denny's, Pizza Hut, Ruby Tuesday, Starbucks, Taco Bell, Wendy's S: McDonald's, Pizza Hut, Subway
				TStop	S: Travel Center of America #210 (Scales)			
				Gas	N: Exxon, Mobil S: Hess◊		Lodg	N: Courtyard, Extended Stay America, Hampton Inn, Hilton Garden, Holiday Inn, Homestead Suites, Ramada Inn, Residence Inn, Sierra Suites
	NOTE:	NYS does NOT use Mile Marker Exits. Listed is MileMarker/Exit #.		Food	N: Burger King, Cascarino's, McDonald's S: Buckhorn/PizzaHut/TA TC, Subway			
				Lodg	S: Motel/TA TC, Super 8		TServ	HO Penn Machinery
.66/1		US 6, NJ 23, CR 15, to NY 97, Port Jervis, Sussex NJ		TServ	S: TA TC		Other	N: ATMs, Grocery, Pharmacy, Sam's Club, Wal-Mart sc, to Duchuss Co Airport✈ S: Home Depot
	Gas	N: Sunoco S: Citgo◊, CF, Mobil◊		Other	N: Grocery, Pharmacy, to Orange Co Airport✈, to Winding Hills Golf Club/ Campground▲ S: Laundry/WiFi/TA TC			
	Food	N: Arlene & Tom's, Baskin Robbins, Dunkin Donuts, Ponderosa S: DQ, McDonald's, Village Pizza				50/15		CR 27, Lime Kiln Rd, to NY 52, E Fishkill, Hopewell Junction
			33/5A		NY 747, International Blvd, Stewart Int'l Airport	52/16		Taconic State Pkwy, N to Albany, S to NY (NO Trucks)
	Lodg	N: Painted Aprons Motel, Shady Brook Motel S: Comfort Inn				(55)		Rest Area (Both dir) (RR, Phones) Random DOT Inspections
	Med	N: + Bon Secours Comm Hospital	34/6		NY 17K, Montgomery, Newburgh			
	Other	N: 84 Rayewood RV Center, Tri State Golf Carts, to Butler Home & RV S: Mall, to High Point State Park▲/NJ, Rockview Valley Campground▲/NJ, Cedar Ridge Campground▲/NJ, to appr 8.5 mi Pleasant Acres Farm Campground▲		TStop	N: Pilot Travel Center #394 (Scales)	59/17		CR 40, Ludingtonville Rd, to NY 52
				Gas	N: Mobil S: Exxon◊		Gas	S: Hess◊, Sunoco
				Food	N: Arby's/TJCinn/Pilot TC, Airport Diner, Deli, KFC		Food	S: Blimpie/Hess, Rest, Deli
				Lodg	N: Comfort Inn S: Courtyard	62/18		NY 311, Lake Carmel, Patterson
							Gas	S: BP
				Other	N: Laundry/WiFi/Pilot TC S: Stewart Int'l Airport✈	65/19		NY 312, to NY 22, Brewster, Carmel
(3)		Parking Area (Both dir)					Food	S: Applebee's, McDonald's, Wendy's
5/2		CR 35, Mountain Rd, to US 6, Port Jervis, Smith Corners	36/7A		NY 300S, to I-87, Albany, New York (Direct ThruWay Under Const thru '09)		Med Other	S: + Hospital N: NY State Police S: Home Depot
	Food	S: Greenville's Firehouse Deli		Gas	S: Citgo, Sunoco			
	Other	S: to appr 8.5 mi Pleasant Acres Farm Campground▲		Food	S: Applebee's, Burger King, Denny's, Café Int'l, China City, TGI Friday	(68/20)		I-684, US 6, US 202, NY 22, White Plains, New York City, NY 22, Paulin
15/3		US 6, NY 17M, Middletown, Goshen		Lodg	S: Clarion, Hampton Inn, Hilton Garden Inn, Holiday Inn, Howard Johnson, Ramada, Super 8		Gas	N: Mobil, Shell, Valero
	Gas	N: Citgo◊, Mobil, Shell S: 84 Quick Stop, Sunoco◊					Food	N: Burger King, McDonald's
	Food	N: Burger King, IHOP, McDonald's, NY Buffet, Perkins, Pizza Hut, Quiznos, Subway, Taco Bell, Wendy's		Other	S: ATMs, B&N, Greyhound, Home Depot, Lowe's, Target, Wal-Mart sc, Auto Dealers	69/21		US 6, US 202, NY 121, N Salem, Brewster, Pauling (WB)
							NOTE:	MM 71.5: Connecticut State Line
	Lodg	S: Days Inn	36/7B		NY 300N, Union Ave, to NY 32		NOTE:	NYS does NOT use Mile Marker Exits. Listed is MileMarker/Exit #.
	Med	N: + Orange Reg'l Medical Center		Gas	N: Exxon, Mobil			
	Other	N: to Randall Airport✈ S: Rudy's Towing, US Post Office		Food	N: McDonald's, Perkins, Taco Bell, Wendy's	(EASTERN TIME ZONE)		
(17)		Rest Area (EB) (RR, Phone, Picnic, NY St Police) Random DOT Inspections		Other	N: AutoZone, Newburgh Mall	ⓃNEW YORK Ⓢ CONNECTICUT (EASTERN TIME ZONE)		
			37/8		NY 52, S Plank Rd, to Walden			
				Gas	N: Citgo◊, Sunoco			
				Other	S: UPS Store			
19/4		NY 17 (FUTURE I-86), W-Binghamton, E-New York (Serv at 1st Ex on NY 17)	39/10		US 9W, NY 32, Newburgh			
				NOTE:	EB: Last FREE Exit Before TOLL		NOTE:	CT does NOT use Mile Marker Exits. Listed is MileMarker/Exit #.
	Gas	N: Getty, Mobil, Sunoco S: Citgo◊, Mobil		Gas	N: Citgo, Mobil, Shell S: Exxon◊, Sunoco◊			
	Food	N: Applebee's, Chuck E Cheese, Denny's, Friendly's, KFC, McDonald's, Olive Garden, Perkins, Red Lobster, Ruby Tuesday, Subway, Taco Bell, Wendy's		Food	N: Bagel World, Bruno Pizza, Burger King, McDonald's, Perkins, Pizza Hut S: Alexis Diner, Family Deli	.36/1		Saw Mill Rd, Danbury (WB, Exit only)
						.78/2		US 6, US 202, Mill Plain Rd, Old Ridgeberry Rd, Danbury (EB)
				Lodg	N: Budget Inn, Economy Inn		S:	CT Welcome Center (EB) (RR, Phone, Picnic, Info, RVDump)
				Med	S: + Hospital			
			(41)		TOLL Booth (EB)		S:	Weigh Station (EB)
							Gas	N: Exxon◊

◊ = Regular Gas Stations with Diesel ▲ = RV Friendly Locations ♥ = Pet Friendly Locations
RED PRINT SHOWS LARGE VEHICLE PARKING/ACCESS ON SITE OR NEARBY   BROWN PRINT SHOWS CAMPGROUNDS/RV PARKS

CONNECTICUT

EXIT		
	Food	N: Bambino Pizza, Desert Moon Mex Grill, Rosy Tomorrows, Starbucks
	Lodg	N: Comfort Suites, Hilton Garden Inn S: Sheraton ♥, Springhill Suites
	Other	N: Pharmacy, Staples
1/2A		US 6, US 202, Mill Plain Rd (WB)
1/2B		Old Ridgeberry Rd (WB)
3/3		US 7S, Park Ave, Airport, Norwalk (fr EB, Exit Only / fr WB, Left Exit)
	Food	S: Charley's Grilled Subs, Cosmos Brick Oven, Great Wraps, Kitchen Café, Uno Chicago Grill
	Other	S: CVS, Danbury Fair Mall, Danbury Muni Airport✈, to Wooster Mtn State Park
4/4		US 6W, US 202W, Lake Ave
	Gas	N: Shell◊, Xtra
	Food	N: Abe's Steak & Seafood House, Chuck's Steakhouse, Soup 2 Nutz S: Dunkin Donuts, McDonald's
	Lodg	N: Residence Inn♥ S: Ethan Allen Hotel♥, Maron Hotel♥, Super 8
	Other	N: CVS, Laundromat, Pharmacy, Staples S: Staples, UPS Store
5/5		CT 37, CT 39, CT 53, Main St, Downtown Danbury, Bethel
	Gas	N: Shell, Sunny Mart S: Mobil, Citgo
	Food	S: Taco Bell
	Lodg	N: Best Value Inn
	Med	S: + Danbury Hospital
	Other	N: to Squantz Pond State Park S: W CT State Univ, Costco, to Putnam Memorial State Park
6/6		CT 37, North St, New Fairfield (WB)
	Gas	N: Gulf, Texaco, Mobil S: BP
	Food	N: Burger King, McDonald's, Moon Star Chinese, Pizza S: KFC
	Med	N: + Hospital
	Other	N: CVS, Grocery, Pharmacy
7/7		US 7N, US 202E, New Milford, Brookfield (Both dir, Exit only) (fr EB, Left Exit) (Serv on Federal Rd)
	Lodg	S: Quality Inn
	Other	N: Home Depot, Staples, UPS Store, to appr 24mi Hemlock Hill Camp Resort▲ S: Auto Services, Tires
8/8		US 6E (EB), Newtown Rd, Bethel
	Gas	N: Gulf, Mobil◊ S: BP, Shell, Sunoco
	Food	N: Bertucci's Brick Oven Rest, Burger King, Chili's, Denny's, Friendly's, McDonald's, Outback Steakhouse, Taco Bell
	Lodg	S: Best Western, Courtyard, Hampton Inn, Holiday Inn, Howard Johnson, Microtel, Stony Hill Inn, Travel Inn, Wellesley Inn
	Other	S: ATMs, Auto Dealers, Auto Services, Banks, CVS, PetCo♥, Target, Tires, Wal-Mart, Dave's RV Center
11/9		CT 25, to US 6, Brookfield, Bridgeport, New Milford, Hawleyville Newtown (Acc Ex #8 Serv via US 6)
15/10		US 6W, Church Hill Rd, Newtown, Sandy Hook (WB, Exit Only) US 6W, Newton Business Dist (EB)
	NOTE:	Low Bridge on US 6-12'7'', Alt Use Ex# 9
	Gas	S: Mobil◊, Shell

EXIT		CONNECTICUT
	Food	N: Katherine's Kitchen, Subway S: Newtown Pizza Palace, Sandy Hook Family Diner
	Other	S: CVS, Grocery, Pharmacy, US Post Office, UPS Store
16/11		CT 34, Derby, New Haven
	Other	S: Vet♥
19/13		River Rd (EB)
20/14		CT 172, Main St, South Britain
	Gas	N: Mobil
	Food	N: Starbucks
	Other	N: CT State Hwy Patrol Post S: to Kettletown State Park▲
22/15		US 6E, CT 67, Southbury, Seymour, Ski Area, Oxford, Woodbury
	FStop	N: Hine Bros/Mobil
	Gas	N: Shell
	Food	N: Dunkin Donuts, McDonald's
	TServ	N: Hine Bros/Tires
	Other	N: Kmart, Grocery, Golf Courses
25/16		CT 188, Middlebury, Southford
	Gas	N: Mobil
	Lodg	N: Crowne Plaza
	Other	N: to Quassy Amusement Park S: Waterbury Oxford Airport✈
30/17		CT 63, CT 64, Middlebury, to Watertown, Naugatuck
	Gas	N: Mobil S: Mobil◊
	Food	N: Maggie McFly's Rest S: Maples Rest, Subway
31.5/18		Chase Pkwy (EB), W Main St, Highland Ave (WB)
	Gas	N: Exxon

EXIT		CONNECTICUT
	Med	N: + Waterbury Hospital
	Other	N: CVS, Naugatuck Valley Comm College
32/19		CT 8S, Naugatuck, Bridgeport (fr EB, Exit Only / fr WB, Left Exit)
32/20		CT 8N, Torrington (fr EB, Left Exit / fr WB, Exit Only)
	Gas	N: Shell
	Food	N: McDonald's
	Other	N: to Black Rock State Park▲, White Pines Campsites▲
33/21		Meadow St, Bank St (fr EB, Exit only)
	Gas	N: 7-11, Gulf, Hess S: Exxon
	Food	N: Diorio Rest, Subway
	Lodg	N: Courtyard
	Other	S: Home Depot, PetSmart♥, Pharmacy
33/22		Baldwin St (EB), Union St (WB), Downtown Waterbury
	Food	N: Arby's, Burger King, Chili's, McDonald's, Olive Garden, Ruby Tuesday, TGI Friday
	Lodg	N: Holiday Inn Express
	Med	N: + St Mary's Hospital
	Other	N: Auto Services, B&N, Sears, Tires, Walgreen's, Brass Mill Center Mall, to Wal-Mart (1mi-Wolcott St)
34/23		CT 69, Wolcott, Prospect (EB, Exit Only), Hamilton Ave (WB), Waterbury (Access to Ex #22 Serv)
35/24		Harpers Ferry Rd, Waterbury (WB)
	Gas	S: Texaco, DM, Getty
36/25		Harpers Ferry Rd (EB), E Main St, Scott Rd, Reidville Dr (WB)
	Gas	N: Exxon, Gulf◊ S: Mobil
	Food	N: China Buffet, Dunkin Donuts, Grinders, Subway, Taylors Family Rest S: Burger King, Friendly's, McDonald's, Nino's Rest
	Lodg	S: Super 8
	Other	S: CVS, BJ's, Grocery
36/25A		Austin Rd, Waterbury (EB)
	Lodg	N: CT Grand Hotel
	Other	N: Costco
38/26		CT 70, Waterbury Rd, Chesire, Waterbury, Prospect
(40/27)		I-691E, to Meriden, Middletown (EB)
41/28		CT 322, Meridien Waterbury Rd, Marion, Southington, Milldale
	TStop	S: Travel Center of America #154 (Scales)
	Gas	N: Sam's Food Store S: Mobil
	Food	S: CountryPride/TA TC, Applebee's, Burger King, Blimpie, China Gourmet, DQ, Dunkin Donuts, Grace's Rest, Milldale Diner
	Lodg	S: Days Inn
	TServ	S: TA TC/Tires
	Other	N: Hemlock Hill RV S: Laundry/BarbSh/WiFi/TA TC
(41/27)		Jct I-691E, to Meriden (WB)
(42)		Rest Area (EB) (RR, Phone, Picnic, RVDump)
42/29		CT 10, Milldale (WB, Left Exit) (Access to Exits #27 & 30 Serv)
43/30		W Main St, Marion Ave, Downtown Southington, Plantsville
	Gas	S: Getty, Mobil, Main St Food Mart

◊ = Regular Gas Stations with Diesel ▲ = RV Friendly Locations ♥ = Pet Friendly Locations

RED PRINT SHOWS LARGE VEHICLE PARKING/ACCESS ON SITE OR NEARBY BROWN PRINT SHOWS CAMPGROUNDS/RV PARKS

EXIT	CONNECTICUT
Food	S: Gene's Corner House Rest, Italian Rest, Pig Out BBQ, Pizza, Steve's Rest
Med	S: + Hospital
Other	N: Mt Southington Ski Area
44/31	**CT 229, West St, Bristol**
Gas	N: Mobil, Sunoco
	S: Citgo
Food	N: Dunkin Donuts/Mobil
Lodg	S: Residence Inn
46/32	**CT 10, Queen St, Southington**
Gas	N: Exxon, Shell
	S: Hess, Mobil, Sunoco
Food	N: Bertucci's Brick Oven, Burger King, Chili's, Denny's, McDonald's, KFC, Pizza Hut, Outback Steakhouse, Starbucks, Subway, Taco Bell
	S: El Sombrero, Friendly's, Little Caesars, Ponderosa, Subway, Wendy's
Lodg	N: Motel 6 ♥
	S: Howard Johnson Express, Holiday Inn Express, Traveler Inn
Med	N: + Hospital
Other	N: CVS, Grocery, PetCo ♥, Staples, Custom Camper
49/33	**CT 72W, to Bristol** (fr EB, Left Exit / fr WB, Exit Only)
Other	N: Redman's Trailer Sales, Crowley RV
49/34	**CT 372, Crooked St, Plainville**
Gas	N: Sunoco
Food	N: Applebee's, Friendly's, Long John Silver, McDonald's, Pizza, Starbucks, Wendy's
Lodg	N: Advance Motel, Hotel Plainville
Other	N: Lowe's, Grocery, PetSmart ♥, CT Dept of Motor Vehicles, Robertson Airport ✈
50/35	**CT 72E, to CT 9, New Britain, Middletown** (fr WB, Left Exit)
51/36	**Slater Rd** (fr EB, Left Exit)
53/37	**to US 6W (EB), Fienemann Rd**
Gas	N: Shell
Lodg	N: Marriott
	S: Extended Stay America
Other	N: Hertz RAC
54/38	**US 6W, Bristol (WB)**
54/39	**CT 4, Farmington** (fr EB, Left Exit / fr WB, Exit Only)
Med	N: + Univ of CT Health Center
55/39A	**CT 9S, Newington, New Britain** (Both dir, Exit only)
56/40	**CT 71, New Britain Ave, Corbins Corner**
Gas	S: Shell, Sunoco
Food	S: Joe's Grill, Olive Garden, Red Robin, Starbucks, Wendy's
Lodg	S: Courtyard
Other	S: Westfarms Mall, B&N, Borders, Best Buy, Office Depot, Target
57/41	**S Main St, Elmwood**
58/42	**Trout Brook Dr, Elmwood** (WB, Left Exit)
58/43	**Park Rd, W Hartford** (fr EB, Left exit)
Other	N: St Joseph College, U Conn Campus
59/44	**Prospect Ave (EB), Oakwood Ave**
Gas	N: Exxon, Shell

EXIT	CONNECTICUT
Food	N: Burger King, McDonald's
TServ	N: Toce Bros Tire
Other	N: Pharmacy
60/45	**Flatbush Ave** (WB, Left Exit)
60/46	**Sisson Ave, Downtown** (fr EB, Left Exit / fr WB, Exit only)
Other	N: U Conn Law School, Hartford College for Women, Hartford Seminary, Mark Twain House, Harriet B Stowe House
61/47	**Sigourney St** (WB, Exit Only)
Med	N: + St Francis Hospital
61/48A	**Asylum St, Downtown (EB)**
Other	S: Civic Center, Bus & Train Stations
61/48B	**Capital Ave** (EB, Exit Only)
61/48	**Asylum St, Downtown** (WB, Exit Only)
Med	S: + Hartford Hospital
Other	S: Bus & Train Stations, Trinity College
61/49	**Ann St, High St**
Other	S: Civic Center, Trumbull St
62/50	**Main St (EB), US 44W, to I-91S (WB)** (fr WB, Exit Only)
Other	S: Civic Center
Lodg	S: Marriott
(62/51)	**Jct I-91N, Springfield, Bradley Int'l Airport**
(62/52)	**Jct I-91S, New Haven** (EB, Exit Only)
62/53	**US 44E, Connecticut Blvd, E River Dr, East Hartford (EB)**
63/54	**CT 2W, Downtown Hartford** (fr WB, Left exit)
63/55	**CT 2E, Norwich, New London** (fr EB, Exit Only / fr WB, Left Exit)
63/56	**Governor St, E Hartford, Downtown E Hartford** (fr EB, Left exit)
64/57	**CT 15S, to I-91S, Charter Oak Br, NY City** (WB, Left Exit)
65/58	**Roberts St, Burnside Ave, Silver Lane, E Hartford**
Food	S: Hong Kong Buffet, Mr Steak
Lodg	N: Holiday Inn, Nantucket Island Resort, Wellesley Inn
Other	S: Goodwin College, Pratt & Whitney, Rentschler Field, Hartford Brainard Airport ✈
(66/59)	**Jct I-384E, to Providence** (EB, Exit only), **Spencer St, Silver Lane (WB)**
Other	S: to appr 4.5 mi Nickerson Park Family Campground▲
NOTE:	MM 67.42: Begin EB / End WB, Left Lane Truck Prohibition
67/60	**US 6, US 44, Middle Tpk West, Manchester, Burnside Ave (EB)**
Gas	S: Mobil
Med	S: + Hospital

EXIT	CONNECTICUT
(68/61)	**Jct I-291W, to Windsor, to Bradley Int'l Airport**
69/62	**Buckland St (EB), Middle Tpk, Buckland St (WB)**
Gas	N: Exxon ◇
	S: Mobil, Xtra
Food	N: Boston Market, Chili's, Friendly's, Hooters, Hops, KFC, Olive Garden, Taco Bell, Vinny T's
	S: Burger King, Carrabba's, Dunkin Donuts, Ground Round, McDonald's, Subway, Texas Roadhouse, Wendy's
Lodg	N: Fairfield Inn
Other	N: ATMs, Banks, Borders, Firestone, Home Depot, PetCo ♥, PetSmart ♥, Sam's Club, Buckland Hills Mall
	S: ATMs, Banks, Auto Services
71/63	**CT 30, CT 83, Deming St, Manchester, South Windsor**
Gas	N: Shell
	S: Getty, Xtra Mart, Shell, Sunoco
Food	N: Applebee's, McDonald's, Hometown Buffet, Outback Steakhouse, Panera Bread, Romano's Macaroni Grill, TGI Friday, Uno Chicago Grill
	S: Roy Rogers Rest, Shea's Amer Grill
Lodg	N: Courtyard, Residence Inn
	S: Best Value Inn, Super 8, Extended Stay America
Med	S: + Hospital
Other	N: Best Buy, B&N, Office Depot, Walgreen's, Wal-Mart
	S: Auto Dealers, Grocery, Pharmacy, Certified On Site RV Service
73/64	**CT 30, CT 83, Vernon, Bus Distr, Rockville**
Gas	N: Mobil, Sunoco
Food	N: Denny's, Damon's, McDonald's, Taco Bell
	S: Chuckwagon, Elmo's Sea Catch, George's Seafood & Prime Rib
Lodg	N: Holiday Inn Express
	S: Quality Inn
Other	N: ATMs, Advance Auto, CVS, Firestone, Goodyear, Grocery, Kmart, AdvanceAuto, Staples
75/65	**CT 30, CT 83, Vernon Center**
Gas	N: Mobil, Shell
Food	N: Bennigan's, Burger King, Denny's, KFC, Pizza Hut, Vernon Diner
Lodg	N: Comfort Inn, Howard Johnson ♥
Med	N: + Rockville Gen'l Hospital
Other	N: ATMs, CarQuest, Pharmacy, Grocery
76/66	**CT 85, Tunnel Rd, Vernon, Bolton**
77/67	**CT 31, Mile Hill Rd, Vernon, Rockville, Coventry**
Gas	N: Mobil, Shell
Food	N: Burger King, China Taste, McDonald's Outback Steakhouse
Med	N: + Hospital
Other	N: Grocery, Vernon Police Dept, to appr 7mi Del-Aire Camping Resort▲, to Stafford Speedway

Page 418   ◇ = Regular Gas Stations with Diesel   ▲ = RV Friendly Locations   ♥ = Pet Friendly Locations
RED PRINT SHOWS LARGE VEHICLE PARKING/ACCESS ON SITE OR NEARBY   BROWN PRINT SHOWS CAMPGROUNDS/RV PARKS

EXIT		CONNECTICUT
81/68		CT 195, Merrow Rd, Tolland, Mansfield
	FStop	N: Tolland Getty
	Gas	N: Mobil S: Citgo
	Food	N: Subway S: Capt Matt's Lobster House, Lee's Garden, Villa Italiana
	Lodg	N: Tolland Inn
84/69		CT 74, to US 44, Willington, Putnam (fr WB, Exit only)
	Other	N: to Del-Aire Campground▲ S: CT State Hwy Patrol Post, Brialee RV & Tent Park▲, to Charlie Brown Campground▲, appr 4.5 mi Nickerson Park Family Campground▲, Peppertree Camping▲, Moosemeadow Camping Resort▲
(85/69)		CT Welcome Center (EB) Rest Area (Both dir) (RR, Phones, Vend, RVDump)
85/70		CT 32, Stafford Springs (EB, Exit only), Willington, Willimantic
	Gas	S: Mobil, Sunoco
	Med	N: + Hospital
	Other	N: Wilderness Lake Campground & Resort▲, to appr 6.5 mi Mineral Springs Family Campground▲, appr 11mi Oak Haven Family Campground▲, appr 17mi Sunsetview Farm Camping Area▲, to Stafford Motor Speedway S: appr 17mi Waters Edge Campground▲
88/71		CT 320, Ruby Rd, Willington
	TStop	S: Travel Center of America #22/Shell (Scales)
	Food	S: CountryPride/BurgerKing/TA TC
	Lodg	S: Econo Lodge♥, Rodeway Inn♥
	TWash	S: TA TC
	TServ	S: TA TC/Tires
	Other	S: Laundry/WiFi/RVDump/TA TC
92/72		CT 89, Hillside Rd, Fish Pt Rd, Stafford Spgs, Ashford, Westford
	Lodg	N: Ashford Motel
	Other	N: Roaring Brook Co-Op Campground▲ S: to appr 7mi Brialee RV & Tent Park▲
93/73		CT 190, Buckley Hwy, Union, Stafford Springs
	Other	N: CT State Hwy Patrol Post, Roaring Brook Co-Op Campground▲, to Mineral Springs Family Campground▲, to Stafford Motor Speedway S: Bigelow Hollow State Park to appr 8mi Beaver Pines Campground▲

EXIT		CONNECTICUT
	Other	S: to Chamberlain Lake Campground▲
(95.5)		Weigh Station (WB)
97/74		CT 171, Holland Rd, Stafford Springs, Union, to Holland, MA
	FStop	S: Citgo
	Food	S: Traveler's Rest

NOTE: MM 98: Massachusetts State Line

NOTE: CT does NOT use Mile Marker Exits. Listed is Mile Marker / Exit #.

(EASTERN TIME ZONE)

ⓘ CONNECTICUT

EXIT		MASSACHUSETTS
		ⓘ MASSACHUSETTS (EASTERN TIME ZONE)
	NOTE:	MA does NOT use Mile Marker Exits. Listed is Exit # / Mile Marker.
(1)		Picnic Area (EB)
(3)		Weigh Station (WB)
1/2.5		MA 15, Mashapaug Rd, Haynes St, Sturbridge, Southbridge
	FStop	S: Mobil Mart
	TStop	S: Pilot Travel Center #222 (Scales)
	Gas	S: Shell◊
	Food	N: CountryKitchen/Pilot TC, Sbarro/RoyRogers/Mobil
	Lodg	S: Quality Inn/Pilot TC
	Med	S: + Hospital
	Other	S: Laundry/WiFi/Pilot TC, Outdoor World-Sturbridge Resort▲, Westville Lake Rec Area
(4)		Picnic Area (WB)
2/5		MA 131, Sturbridge
	Lodg	S: Days Inn, Historic Inn
	Other	S: Yogi Bear's Jellystone Park Camp Resort▲, to Southbridge Muni Airport✈
3AB/9		US 20, Main St, Charlton Rd, Sturbridge, Worcester
	TStop	S: PTP/New England Truck Stop
	Gas	N: Citgo, Mobil◊ S: Citgo
	Food	N: Burger King, McDonald's S: Rest/NE TS, Applebee's, Colonial House Family Rest, Charlie's, Cracker Barrel, Gracie's Roadside Café, Subway, Wendy's
	Lodg	N: Best Western, Carriage House Inn, Hampton Inn, Old Sturbridge Village Lodge, Super 8, Travelodge S: Comfort Inn, Public House Historic Inn & Resort, Rodeway Inn
	Other	S: ATMs, Grocery, Staples, Wal-Mart N: US Post Office

NOTE: MA does NOT use Mile Marker Exits. Listed is Exit # / Mile Marker.

(I-84 Begins/Ends on I-81, Ex #186 in PA)
(EASTERN TIME ZONE)

ⓘ MASSACHUSETTS

Begin Westbound I-84 from Jct I-90 near Sturbridge, MA to Jct I-81 in Dunmore, PA.

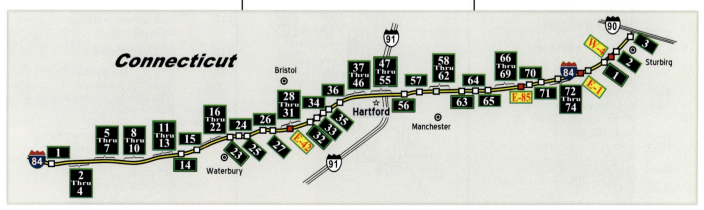

◊ = Regular Gas Stations with Diesel   ▲ = RV Friendly Locations   ♥ = Pet Friendly Locations
RED PRINT SHOWS LARGE VEHICLE PARKING/ACCESS ON SITE OR NEARBY   BROWN PRINT SHOWS CAMPGROUNDS/RV PARKS

INTERSTATE 85 S

EXIT	VIRGINIA
	Begin Southbound I-85 from Jct I-95 near Richmond to Jct I-65 in Montgomery, AL.

VIRGINIA
(EASTERN TIME ZONE)
(I-85 begins/ends on I-95, Exit #51)

Exit		
69		Washington St, Wythe St, Petersburg
(68)		Jct I-95, Crater Rd, Petersburg
65		Squirrel Level Rd, Petersburg
	Gas	W: BP◊
63AB		US 1, US 460 Bus, Petersburg
	TStop	W: Thrift Mart Truck Plaza/Exxon
	Gas	E: Chevron◊, Shell
		W: AmocoBP
	Food	E: Burger King, Waffle House
		W: Blimpie, Hardee's, McDonald's
	Lodg	E: Holiday Inn Express
	Med	W: + Central State Hospital
	Other	W: Laundry/Exxon, Auto Repairs
61		US 460 Bus, Airport St, Petersburg, to Blackstone
	FStop	E: East Coast Oil/Mapco Express #4064
	Gas	W: Shell◊
	Food	E: Subway/Mapco, Huddle House
	Other	E: to appr 4mi Camptown Campground▲
		W: Picture Lake Campground▲, Dinwiddie Co Airport✈
(55)		Dinwiddie Rest Area (Both dir) (RR, Phone, Picnic, Vend)
53		VA 703, Carson Rd, Dinwiddie
	Gas	W: Exxon◊
	Food	W: Rumorz Cafe
	Other	E: to appr 5mi Camptown Campground▲
48		VA 650, Hamilton Arms Rd, DeWitt
42		VA 40, McKenney Hwy, McKenney
	FStop	W: Citgo
	Gas	W: Exxon
	Lodg	W: Economy Inn
39		VA 712, Old Stage Rd, Warfield, to Rawlings
	FStop	W: Circle D Mart #108/Chevron
	Gas	W: Citgo◊
	Food	W: Nottoway Rest/Motel
	Lodg	W: Nottoway Motel
34		VA 630, Sturgeon Rd, Warfield
	Gas	W: Exxon◊
(32)		Alberta Rest Area (Both dir) (RR, Phone, Picnic, Vend)
28		US 1, VA 46, Alberta, Lawrenceville
27		VA 46, Alberta, to Blackstone, Lawrenceville (SB)
24		VA 644, Meredithville
(22)		Weigh station (Both dir)
15		US 1, South Hill, to Kenbridge (Acc to Ex #12 Serv via US 1W)
	Gas	W: Shell
	Food	W: Kahills Rest, Rumorz Cafe
12		US 58, VA 47, Atlantic St, South Hill, Norfolk
	FStop	E: Slip In Shell, appr 5mi S: Red Barn
		W: Citgo
	Gas	E: Racetrac
		W: Chevron◊, Exxon◊, Save U Time, Shell◊

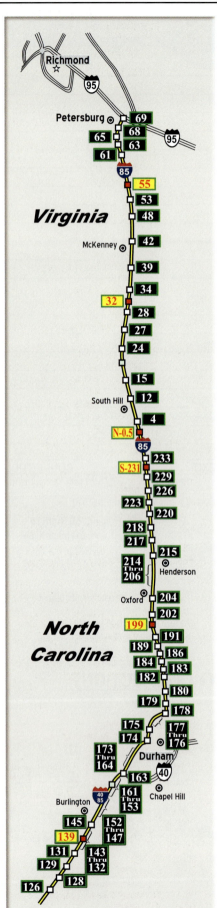

EXIT	VA / NC
	Food	E: Arby's, Arnold's Diner, Domino's, Nest Egg Café, Subway
		W: Brian's Steakhouse, Burger King, Cracker Barrel, Denny's, Hardee's, McDonald's, New China, Pizza Hut, Subway, Taco Bell, Wendy's
	Lodg	E: Hampton Inn, Holiday Inn Express, Super 8
		W: Best Value Inn, Comfort Inn♥
	Med	W: + Hospital
	Other	E: Dollar Tree, Wal-Mart, Mecklenburg Brunswick Reg'l Airport✈
		W: Auto Dealers, CVS, Family Dollar, Laundromat, Tires, Winn Dixie, Auto Repairs, Towing
4		VA 903, Bracey, Lake Gaston
	TStop	E: Simmons Travel Center/Exxon (Scales)
	Gas	W: Shell
	Food	E: JctRest/FastFood/Simmons TC
		W: Countryside Rest, Memphis Grill, Pizza Hut, Quiznos
	Lodg	W: Days Inn
	TServ	E: Simmons TC/Tires
	Other	E: Laundry/WiFi/Simmons TC
(.5)		VA Welcome Center (NB) (RR, Phones, Picnic, Vend)

(EASTERN TIME ZONE)

VIRGINIA
NORTH CAROLINA
(EASTERN TIME ZONE)

	NOTE:	MM 234: Virginia State Line
233		US 1, Norlina, Wise
	TStop	E: Wise Truck Stop/Citgo
	Food	E: Rest/Wise TS
	Lodg	E: Budget Inn
(231)		NC Welcome Center (SB) (RR, Phone, Picnic)
229		Oine Rd, to Norlina
226		Ridgeway Rd
223		Manson Rd
	Gas	E: BP◊
220		US 1, US 158, Fleming Town Rd, Henderson, Norlina, Middleburg
	TStop	W: Chex Truck Stop/Exxon (Scales)
	Gas	E: BP
	Food	W: Rest/Chex TS
	Lodg	W: Motel/Chex TS
	TWash	W: Chex TS
	TServ	W: Chex TS/Tires
	Other	W: Laundry/CB/WiFi/Chex TS, to Kerr Lake State Rec Area
218		US 1 ByPass, to Raleigh (SB ex, NB entr)
217		NC 1319, Henderson
215		US 1, US 158E ByPass, Parham Rd, Garnett St, Henderson (fr NB diff reacc, Re-enter Next Exit N)
	FStop	E: to 2101 Garnett Pacific Pride
	Gas	E: Citgo◊, Hess, Shell
	Food	E: 220 Seafood, Burger King, Subway
	Lodg	E: Ambassador Inn, Best Value Inn, Budget Host Inn, Comfort Inn, Howard Johnson, Scottish Inn
	Other	E: Goodyear, Grocery

◊= Regular Gas Stations with Diesel ▲ = RV Friendly Locations ♥ = Pet Friendly Locations
RED PRINT SHOWS LARGE VEHICLE PARKING/ACCESS ON SITE OR NEARBY   BROWN PRINT SHOWS CAMPGROUNDS/RV PARKS

I-85 N/S — NORTH CAROLINA

Exit 214 — NC 39, Andrews Ave, Henderson
- Gas: E: BP, Shell

Exit 213 — US 158, Dabney Dr, Henderson
- Gas: E: BP, Shell; W: Exxon, Shell
- Food: E: Bamboo Garden, Bojangles, Denny's, KFC, McDonald's, Subway, Wendy's; W: Golden Corral, McDonald's, Pizza Hut, Taco Bell
- Other: E: CVS, Family Dollar, Food Lion, Goodyear, Pharmacy, Radio Shack, Winn Dixie; W: Auto Dealers, Auto Services, Dollar Tree, Kmart, Lowe's, Staples, Tires, Wal-Mart sc

Exit 212 — NC 1128, Ruin Creek Rd, Henderson (Access to Ex #213 Serv)
- Gas: E: Shell◊; W: BP
- Food: E: Cracker Barrel, Mexican Rest; W: Gary's BBQ, Golden Corral
- Lodg: E: Days Inn, Hampton Inn; W: Holiday Inn Express, Jameson Inn
- Med: W: + Maria Parham Hospital

Exit 209 — NC 1126, Poplar Creek Rd

Exit 206 — US 158, Oxford, Roxboro
- Gas: W: Shell◊

Exit 204 — NC 96, Linden Ave, Oxford
- Gas: E: BP◊; W: Exxon, Shell, Trade/Hess◊
- Food: W: Burger King, KFC, McDonald's, Pizza Hut, Subway, Taco Bell, Wendy's
- Lodg: E: Kings Inn; W: Best Western, Econo Lodge
- Med: W: + Hospital
- Other: E: Auto Dealers; W: Dollar General, Family Dollar, Grocery, Pharmacy, Radio Shack, Wal-Mart

Exit 202 — US 15, Oxford, Clarksville
- Gas: W: Citgo
- Lodg: W: Crown Motel

(199) — Rest Area (Both dir) (RR, Phone, Picnic)

Exit 191 — NC 56, Butner, Creedmoor
- FStop: E: Trade Mart #27/WilcoHess; W: Rose Mart #2/Shell
- Gas: E: BP◊; W: Exxon◊
- Food: E: Bob's BBQ, Bojangles, Burger King, KFC, McDonald's, Pizza Hut, Taco Bell, Wendy's; W: Domino's, Hardee's
- Lodg: E: Comfort Inn, Econo Lodge♥; W: Holiday Inn Express, Ramada Ltd
- Other: E: Food Lion, Pharmacy

Exit 189 — NC 1103, Butner

Exit 186 — US 15N, Creedmoor (SB)

Exit 184AB — US 15, Creedmoor (NB)
- Other: E: Falls Lake State Rec Area▲

Exit 183 — Redwood Rd, Durham
- Gas: E: Days Inn
- Food: E: Redwood Cafe
- Lodg: E: Days Inn
- Other: E: Durham Skypark Airport✈

Exit 182 — Red Mill Rd, Durham
- Gas: E: Redmill Quick Stop/Exxon
- Food: E: Perky's Pizza

Exit 180 — Glenn School Rd
- Gas: W: William Bros Country Store/Heritage

Exit 179 — East Club Blvd
- Gas: E: C-Mart/Exxon

Exit 178 — US 70E, ByP, to Airport (NB)

Exit 177B — NC 55, Avondale Dr, Durham
- FStop: E: WilcoHess C-Store #191
- Gas: W: Amoco, BP, Shell
- Food: W: Arby's, Dunkin Donuts, Hong Kong Buffet, Hardee's, KFC, McDonald's, Pizza Hut

Exit 177C — NC 55N, Avondale Dr (NB)

Exit 177A — US 501 Bus, US 15 Bus, Roxboro St, Downtown Durham
- Gas: W: BP
- Lodg: W: Chesterfield Motel

Exit 176B — US 501N, Duke St, Roxboro

Exit 176A — Gregson St
- Gas: E: Shell, Texaco
- Food: E: BBQ n Stuff, Biscuitville, Burger King, Cajun Café, ChickFilA, Ruby Tuesday, Subway, Yamato Japanese
- Med: E: + Duke Univ Medical Center; W: + Durham Reg'l Hospital
- Other: E: Amtrak, Northgate Mall, to Duke Univ; W: Staples, Durham Co Stadium

Exit 175 — NC 157, Guess Rd, Durham
- Gas: E: Shell◊; W: AmocoBP◊, Kangaroo Express
- Food: E: Hog Heaven BBQ, Pizza Hut; W: Bojangles, Honey's Rest, IHOP, Rudino's Pizza & Grinders, Texas Roadhouse
- Lodg: E: Best Value Inn♥, Holiday Inn Express♥, Super 8; W: Red Roof Inn♥
- Other: W: CVS, Home Depot, Kroger, PetSmart♥

Exit 174A — Hillandale Rd
- Gas: W: BP◊
- Food: W: China King, Papa's Grill, Shoney's
- Lodg: W: Courtyard, Hampton Inn, Howard Johnson
- Other: W: Pharmacy, Winn Dixie, UPS Store

Exit 174B — US 15S ByPass, US 501S, Chapel Hill (SB exit, NB entr)

Exit 173 — US 15, US 501S, Cole Mill Rd, Durham (diff reaccess)
- Gas: E: BP, Exxon◊, Shell
- Food: E: Arby's, Bojangles, Burger King, Checkers, ChickFilA, Cracker Barrel, Dunkin Donuts, Galley Seafood, McDonald's, Subway, Taco Bell, Waffle House, Wendy's
- Lodge: E: Days Inn, Fairfield Inn, Hilton, Innkeeper
- Med: E: + Hospital
- Other: E: AutoZone, Kroger, Laundromat, Pharmacy

Exit 172 — NC 147S, to US 15S, US 501S (NB exit, SB entr)

Exit 170 — US 70, to NC 751, Duke University
- Food: E: Harbor Bay Seafood
- Other: W: Eno River State Park

Exit 165 — NC 86, Hillsborough, to Chapel Hill
- TStop: E: Express America Truck Stop (Scales)
- Gas: W: BP◊
- Food: E: Rest/Expr Amer TS, McDonald's, Papa John's, Subway; W: Heartland Steakhouse, Wendy's
- Other: E: Wal-Mart sc

Exit 164 — S Churton St, Hillsborough
- Gas: E: Citgo◊; W: Exxon◊, Shell
- Food: E: McDonald's; W: Burger King, Hardee's, KFC, Pizza Hut, Occoneechee Steakhouse, Waffle House, Wendy's
- Lodg: E: Holiday Inn Express; W: Microtel, Southern Country Inn
- Other: W: Auto Dealers, All Pro Auto Parts, Food Lion, Firestone, Goodyear, Sanchez Auto Care, Wagner Tire & Auto

NOTE: I-85 below runs with I-40. Exit #'s follow I-85.

(163) — Jct I-40E, to Raleigh

Exit 161 — to US 70E Conn, NC 86, Efland

Exit 160 — Mt Willing Rd, US 70E Conn, Efland
- Gas: W: BP◊, Exxon◊

(159) — Weigh Station (Both dir)

Exit 157 — Buckhorn Rd, Mebane
- TStop: E: Petro Stopping Center #29/Mobil (Scales)
- Gas: E: BP◊; W: Exxon, Mobil
- Food: E: IronSkillet/FastFood/Petro SC
- TServ: E: Petro SC/Tires
- Other: E: Laundry/BarbSh/CB/WiFi/Petro SC

Exit 154 — Mebane Oaks Rd, Mebane
- FStop: W: Arrowhead Shell
- Gas: E: Sheetz, Murphy; W: BP, Exxon◊
- Food: E: Quiznos; W: Bojangles, China Garden, La Fiesta, McDonald's, Roma's Pizza, Waffle House
- Lodg: W: Budget Inn
- Other: E: Wal-Mart sc, Tires; W: Winn Dixie

Exit 153 — NC 119, S 5th St, Mebane
- Gas: E: BP Pepsi Jct◊, Citgo; W: Tommy's Mini Mart/P66
- Food: E: Cracker Barrel, Hibachi Rest, KFC, Jersey Mike's Subs, Pizza Hut, Smithfield's Chicken & BBQ, Taco Bell; W: Burger King, Mex Rest, Subway
- Lodg: E: Hampton Inn, Holiday Inn Express
- Other: E: Lowe's; W: CVS, Food Lion, Vet♥

Exit 152 — NC 1981, Trollingwood Rd, Mebane
- FStop: E: Speedway
- TStop: E: Pilot Travel Center # 57 (Scales); W: Fuel City/Circle K Truck Stop #5364
- Food: E: McDonald's/Pilot TC; W: FastFood/Circle K TS
- TWash: E: Pilot TC
- Other: E: Laundry/WiFi/Pilot TC

Exit 150 — Jimmie Kerr Rd, Haw River, Graham
- TStop: W: Flying J Travel Plaza #5332/Conoco (Scales), WilcoHess Travel Plaza #165 (Scales)
- Food: W: Cookery/FastFood/FJ TP, DQ/Wendy's/WilcoHess TP
- Lodg: W: Days Inn
- TWash: W: Blue Beacon TW/FJ TP
- TServ: W: Speedco
- Other: W: Laundry/BarbSh/WiFi/RVDump/LP/FJ TP, Laundry/WilcoHess TP

Exit 148 — NC 54, E Harden St, Graham to Chapel Hill, Carrboro
- FStop: E: Kangaroo Express #3791
- Gas: E: BP◊, Quality Plus

◊ = Regular Gas Stations with Diesel ▲ = RV Friendly Locations ♥ = Pet Friendly Locations
RED PRINT SHOWS LARGE VEHICLE PARKING/ACCESS ON SITE OR NEARBY BROWN PRINT SHOWS CAMPGROUNDS/RV PARKS

EXIT		NORTH CAROLINA
	Food	E: Waffle House
	Lodg	E: Comfort Suites
		W: Embers Motor Lodge, Econo Lodge
147		NC 87, Main St, Graham, Pittsboro
	Gas	E: BP
		W: Exxon◊, Shell
	Food	E: Arbys, Burger King, Bojangles, Harbor House Seafood, Sagebrush Steakhouse, Subway, Wendy's
		W: Biscuitville, McDonald's, Taco Bell
	Lodg	E: Affordable Suites of America
	Med	W: + Hospital
	Other	E: Auto Dealers, Advance Auto, Food Lion, Goodyear, Laundromat, Winn Dixie
		W: CVS, Lowe's, Walgreen's, Graham Police Dept
145		NC 49, Maple Ave, Downtown Burlington, Liberty
	FStop	E: Interstate Shell
	Gas	E: BP◊
		W: BP, Hess
	Food	E: Captain D's
		W: Biscuitville, Bojangles, Burger King, China Inn, Hardee's, KFC, Waffle House
	Lodg	E: Econo Lodge, Microtel, Motel 6 ♥
		W: Days Inn, Holiday Inn, La Quinta Inn ♥, Quality Inn, Scottish Inn
	Other	E: Davis Harley Davidson, NC State Hwy Patrol Post
		W: Food Lion, Kmart, Pharmacy
143		NC 62, Alamance Rd, Downtown Burlington, Alamance
	Gas	E: Citgo
		W: Circle K, Exxon, Kangaroo Express
	Food	E: Bob Evans, Hardee's, Waffle House
		W: K&W Cafeteria, Libby Hill Seafood
	Lodg	W: Ramada Inn
	Other	E: JR Outlet, Burlington Muni Airport ✈
		W: Auto Dealers, Food Lion, Home Depot, Greyhound, Train Station
141		Huffman Mill Rd, Burlington
	Gas	E: BP, Kangaroo,
		W: Crown, Phillips 66◊
	Food	E: IHOP, Mayflower Seafood, Outback Steakhouse
		W: Applebee's, Arby's, Bojangles, Biscuitville, Burger King, Cracker Barrel, China Gate, Golden Corral, Hooters, Indian Rest, KFC, Krystal, McDonald's, O'Charley's, Panera, Ruby Tuesday, Rock-Ola Café, Starbucks, Steak 'n Shake, Subway, Taco Bell
	Lodg	E: Comfort Inn, Corporate Suites
		W: Best Western, Country Inn, Courtyard, Super 8
	Med	E: + Alamance Hospital
	Other	W: Auto Dealers, Food Lion, Kmart SC, Office Max, Wal-Mart sc, UPS Store, Burlington Square Mall, to Elon College
140		University Dr, Burlington, Elon
	Other	W: Best Buy, PetSmart ♥, Target, to Elon Univ
(139)		Rest Area (Both dir) (RR, Phone, Picnic, Vend)
138		NC 61, Whitsett, Gibsonville, Greensboro
	TStop	W: Travel Center of America #2/BP (Scales)
	Gas	W: Shell◊
	Food	W: CountryPr/Burger King/Popeye/TA TC
	Lodg	W: DaysInn/TA TC
	TWash	W: TA TC

EXIT		NORTH CAROLINA
	TServ	W: TA TC/Tires
	Other	W: Laundry/WiFi/TA TC, Hawley's Camping Center
135		Rock Creek Dairy Rd, Whitsett
	Gas	W: Citgo, Exxon
	Food	W: Bojangles, Jersey Mike's, McDonald's
	Other	W: CVS, Food Lion
132		Mt Hope Church Rd, McLeansville
	TStop	W: WilcoHess Travel Plaza #308
	Gas	E: Stop & Save/Citgo
		W: Shell
	Food	E: Subway, Pizza Corner
		W: Wendy's/WilcoHess TP
	Lodg	W: Hampton Inn
(131A)		Jct I-840, to US 70, Greensboro
(131)		Jct I-85N/I-40E (Left exit)
NOTE:		I-85 above runs with I-40. Exit #'s follow I-85.
129		Youngs Mill Rd, Greensboro
128		Alamance Church Rd
126B		US 421, Greensboro, Sanford
126A		US 421S, Sanford
126		US 421, Sanford, Greensboro
	FStop	S: The Pantry/Kangaroo Express #170
124		S Elm Eugene St, Greensboro
	Food	E: Cracker Barrel
122		US 220, Greensboro, Asheboro (Future I-73 South)
122B		US 220S, Asheboro, Greensboro

EXIT		NORTH CAROLINA
122C		US 220N, Asheboro, Greensboro
122A		Groometown Rd, to Grandover Parkway (SB)
(121)		Jct I-73N, US 421W to I-40W, Winston-Salem (SB)
(120B)		Jct I-73N, US 421W to I-40W, Winston-Salem (NB)
120A		I-85 Bus N, US 29N, US 79E, Greensboro (NB exit, SB entr)
119		Groometown Rd (NB)
	Gas	W: Phillips 66◊
118		I-85 Bus S, US 29S, US 70W, to High Point, Jamestown
	Lodg	W: Grandover Resort
113		NC 62, Liberty Rd, High Point, Archdale
	FStop	E: Moose Tracks/Citgo
	Gas	W: BP◊
	Lodg	W: Best Western
111		US 311, N Main St, Downtown High Point, to Archdale
	Gas	W: BP◊, Citgo, Exxon, Shell◊
	Food	E: Biscuitville, Bojangles, Hardee's, Little Caesar's, Subway, Wendy's
		W: Waffle House
	Lodg	E: Innkeeper
		W: Comfort Inn, Fairfield Inn, Hampton Inn, Holiday Inn Express
	Med	W: + Hospital
	Other	E: CVS, Dollar General, Food Lion
		W: Advance Auto, Firestone
108		Hopewell Church Rd, Trinity
106		Finch Farm Rd, Trinity, Thomasville
	FStop	E: Quik Shop-Gas Stop/Exxon
103		NC 109, Randolph St, Thomasville
	Gas	E: Citgo, Shell
		W: BP◊, Coastal, Crown, Hess
	Food	E: Arby's, Taco Bell
		W: Burger King, China Garden, Golden Corral, Hardee's, KFC, McDonald's, Pizza Hut, Subway, Waffle House
	Lodg	W: Country Hearth Inn, Howard Johnson, Quality Inn
	Other	E: CVS, Grocery, Kmart, Wal-Mart sc
		W: AutoZone, Advance Auto, Food Lion, Family Dollar, Tires, Walgreen's
102		Lake Rd, Thomasville
	Gas	W: Phillips 66, Shell◊
	Lodg	W: Days Inn, Microtel
	Med	W: + Hospital
(99)		Rest Area (Both dir) (RR, Phone, Picnic, Vend)
96		US 64, Lexington, Asheboro,
	Gas	E: Exxon
		W: Chevron◊
94		Old US 64, Raleigh Rd, Lexington
	Gas	E: Shell
91		NC 8, Cotton Grove Rd, Lexington
	Gas	E: BP◊, Citgo, Phillips 66, Shell◊
		W: Exxon◊, QM
	Food	E: McDonald's, Sonic, Subway, Wendy's
		W: Applebee's, Arby's, Burger King, Cracker Barrel, Hardee's, Taco Bell
	Lodg	E: Comfort Suites, Super 8
		W: Country Hearth Inn, Holiday Inn Express
	Med	W: + Lexington Memorial Hospital

◊ = Regular Gas Stations with Diesel ▲ = RV Friendly Locations ♥ = Pet Friendly Locations
RED PRINT SHOWS LARGE VEHICLE PARKING/ACCESS ON SITE OR NEARBY BROWN PRINT SHOWS CAMPGROUNDS/RV PARKS

INTERSTATE 85 N/S

NORTH CAROLINA

EXIT		
	Other	E: Food Lion, to appr 8mi **High Rock Lake Marina & Campground**▲ W: Grocery, **Wal-Mart**
88		NC 47E, Hargrave Rd, Linwood, High Rock Lake
	Gas	W: BP◊
87		I-85N Bus, US 52N, US 29N, US 70E, Lexington, Winston-Salem (NB Exit, SB entr)
86		NC 47, Belmont Rd, Linwood
	TStop	E: Bill's Truck Stop/66 (Scales)
	Food	E: Rest/Bill's TS
	TServ	E: Bill's TS/Tires
	Other	E: Laundry/Bills TS
85		Clark Rd, Linwood
83		NC 150E, to Spencer (NB ex, SB entr) US 29S, US 70W, NC 150W, Spencer Linwood (SB Left Exit, NB entr)
81		Long Ferry Rd, Salisbury, Spencer
	Gas	E: Exxon◊
79		Andrew St, Salisbury, Spencer
76B		US 52N, E Innes St, Salisbury
76A		US 52S, E Innes St, Salisbury
76		US 52, E Innes St, Salisbury
	Gas	E: BP, RaceTrac, Speedway W: Circle K◊, Exxon◊, Shell
	Food	E: Applebee's, IHOP, Little Caesar's, Lone Star Steakhouse, Shoney's W: Blue Bay Seafood, Bojangles, Burger King, Captain D's, ChickFilA, Hardee's, KFC, O'Charley's, Outback Steakhouse, Pizza Hut, Waffle House, Wendy's
	Lodg	E: Days Inn, Happy Traveler Inn, Sleep Inn, Studio Suites, Super 8 W: Budget Inn, Comfort Suites, Howard Johnson
	Med	E: + Hospital
	Other	E: CVS, Circuit City, Food Lion, Lowe's, Staples W: Auto Zone, Family Dollar, Firestone, Kmart, Goodyear, Office Depot, **Wal-Mart**
75		US 601N, Jake Alexander Blvd, Salisbury, Rowan
	FStop	W: WilcoHess C-Store #363
	Gas	E: BP, Exxon◊, Rushco, Shell◊
	Food	E: Arby's, Farmhouse Rest W: Burger King, Fire Mountain Grill, Ichiban, Jasmine's, McDonald's, Pizza Hut, Sagebrush Steakhouse, Subway, Waffle House, Wendy's
	Lodg	E: Ramada W: Best Western, Days Inn, Hampton Inn, Holiday Inn
	Other	W: Auto Dealers, **Wal-Mart**
74		Julian Rd, Salisbury
	Lodg	E: Affordable Suites of America
72		Peach Orchard Rd
71		Peeler Rd, Salisbury
	TStop	E: PTP/Derrick Travel Plaza/Shell (Scales) W: WilcoHess Travel Plaza #364 (Scales)
	Food	E: CW's Rest/Derrick TP W: Bojangles/Subway/TB/WilcoHess TP
	TWash	E: Derrick TP
	TServ	E: Derrick TP/Tires
	Other	E: Laundry/BarbSh/CB/WiFi/**LP**/Derrick TP

EXIT		
70		Webb Rd, Salisbury
	Other	E: Flea Market W: NC State Hwy Patrol Post
68		US 29, US 601S, NC 152, Rockwell Hwy, China Grove, Rockwell
63		Lane St, Kannapolis
	TStop	E: Pilot Travel Center #56 (Scales)
	Gas	W: Exxon◊
	Food	E: Subway/Pilot TC, Waffle House W: Hardee's, KFC
	Other	E: WiFi/Pilot TC
60		Dale Earnhardt Blvd, Copperfield Blvd, Kannapolis, Concord
	Gas	E: BP, Exxon◊, Kangaroo Express W: BP◊
	Food	E: Bojangles, Bob Evans, Cracker Barrel, Wendy's W: Johnny Carino's, Logan's Roadhouse, McDonald's, Ruby Tuesday, Subway
	Lodg	E: Hampton Inn, Sleep Inn W: Holiday Inn Express
	Med	E: + Hospital
	Other	W: Sam's Club, **Wal-Mart sc**
(59)		Rest Area (Both dir) (RR, Phone, Picnic, Vend)
58		US 29, US 601, Concord Pkwy, Cannon Blvd, Ridge Ave, US 29A, Kannapolis Hwy, Concord
	Gas	E: BP, Crown, Exxon, Shell◊, Wilco W: Phillips 66, Wilco Food Mart
	Food	E: Applebee's, Burger King, Captain D's, ChickFilA, Golden Corral, KFC, Little Caesars, McDonald's, Mexican Rest, O'Charley's, Pizza Hut, Subway, Shoney's, Starbucks, Taco Bell, Waffle House, Wendy's W: CiCi's, IHOP, Ryan's Grill
	Lodg	E: Best Value Inn, Colonial Inn, Holiday Inn Express, Rodeway Inn W: Comfort Inn, Econo Lodge, Fairfield Inn, Microtel, Mainstay Suites, Park Inn
	Med	E: + NE Medical Center
	Other	E: Auto Dealers, Auto Services, Food Lion, FedEx Kinko's, UPS Store, U-Haul, Carolina Mall, Mall 8, NC State Hwy Patrol Post, to Lowe's Motor Speedway W: Grocery, Home Depot, Pharmacy, Target, Vet♥, Greyhound, Family Adventures Fun Park
55		NC 73, Davidson Hwy, Concord, Huntersville
	Gas	E: Exxon◊, Shell W: 76◊, Phillips 66◊, Shell
	Food	E: McDonald's, Waffle House W: Huddle House
	Lodg	W: Days Inn
	Other	E: to Lowe's Motor Speedway
54		Kannapolis Pkwy, Geo Liles Pkwy
52		Poplar Tent Rd
	Gas	E: Shell◊ W: Exxon
	Other	E: to Lowe's Motor Speedway, Race Driving Schools, **Fleetwood RV Race Campground**▲ W: Concord Reg'l Airport✈
49		Concord Mills Blvd, Speedway Blvd
	Gas	E: BP, Shell◊ W: Citgo, Petro Express

◊ = Regular Gas Stations with Diesel   ▲ = RV Friendly Locations   ♥ = Pet Friendly Locations
RED PRINT SHOWS LARGE VEHICLE PARKING/ACCESS ON SITE OR NEARBY   BROWN PRINT SHOWS CAMPGROUNDS/RV PARKS

INTERSTATE 85 N/S

NORTH CAROLINA

EXIT		
	Food	E: Arby's, Bob Evans, Bojangles, BBQ, Carrabba's, Chuck E Cheese, **Cracker Barrel**, Hooters, KFC, McDonald's, Quaker Steak & Lube, Quiznos, Subway W: Alabama Grill, Applebee's, Panera Bread, Olive Garden, Red Lobster, Steak 'n Shake, Texas Roadhouse, TGI Friday
	Lodg	E: **Comfort Suites**, Hampton Inn, Holiday Inn Express, **Sleep Inn**, Springhill Suites, Suburban Extended Stay ♥, Wingate Inn W: Days Inn
	Other	E: Lowe's Motor Speedway, Driving Schools, **Fleetwood RV Race Campground/RVDump▲**, **Tom Johnson Camping Center** W: Discount Tire, PetCo ♥, Radio Shack, Concord Mills Mall, AMC Cinemas, Bass Pro Shop, Concord Reg'l Airport✈
(48)		Jct I-485, to US 29, Charlotte
46		Mallard Creek Church Rd (SB)
	Gas	E: Exxon, Wilco◊ W: Exxon, Petro Express
46B		Mallard Creek Church Rd (NB)
46A		Mallard Creek Church Rd, to US 29
45B		NC 24, WT Harris Blvd, Charlotte
45A		NC 24, WT Harris Blvd, Charlotte
45		NC 24, WT Harris Blvd, Charlotte
	Gas	E: Phillips 66◊, Sonic Mart
	Food	E: Applebee's, Bojangles, Burger King, Chili's, Hops, McDonald's, Max & Erma's, Shoney's, TGI Friday, Waffle House W: McDonald's, Romano's Macaroni Grill, Subway, Wendy's
	Lodg	E: Courtyard, Drury Inn, Extended Stay America, Hilton, Hampton Inn, Holiday Inn, Homewood Suites, Microtel, Residence Inn, Sleep Inn W: Springhill Suites, Towneplace Suites
	Med	E: + Hospital
	Other	E: Best Buy, Food Lion, Lowe's, Office Depot, Radio Shack, Sam's Club, **Walgreen's**, **Wal-Mart**, Mall, Univ of NC/Charlotte W: Food Lion, **Pharmacy**
43		City Blvd, to NC 24, US 29 (NB)
42		to US 29, NC 49 (NB exit, SB entr)
41		Sugar Creek Rd, Charlotte
	Gas	E: RaceTrac, Shell◊ W: 76, BP◊, Exxon◊
	Food	E: Bojangles, McDonald's, Taco Bell, Wendy's W: Shoney's, Waffle House
	Lodg	E: Best Value Inn, Brookwood Inn, Continental Inn, Econo Lodge, Economy Inn, Microtel, Motel 6 ♥, Red Roof Inn W: Comfort Inn, Country Hearth Inn, Days Inn, Ramada Inn, Rodeway Inn, Super 8
40		Graham St, Charlotte
	Gas	E: Exxon◊ W: Citgo
	Food	E: Hardee's, Hereford Barn Steakhouse
	Lodg	E: **Howard Johnson**
	TServ	E: **Adams Int'l Trucks**, **Peterbilt Carolina**, **Tar-Heel Ford Trucks**, **Volvo/GMC** W: **Freightliner**, **Mack Truck**
39		Statesville Ave, Charlotte
	TStop	E: **Pilot Travel Center #275** (Scales)

EXIT		
	Gas	W: Shell◊
	Food	E: **Subway/Pilot TC**
	Lodg	W: Knights Inn
	TServ	W: **Bradley's Truck Service**
	Other	E: WiFi/**Pilot TC**, CarQuest, Carwash
(38)		Jct I-77, US 21, N to Statesville, S to Columbia
	TServ	W: **Carolina Engine**
37		Beatties Ford Rd
	Gas	E: Phillips 66◊, Shell◊ W: BP
	Food	E: Burger King, KFC, McDonald's, Subway, Taco Bell W: McDonalds Cafeteria
	Lodg	W: Travelodge
	Other	E: **CVS**, Food Lion, Johnson C Smith Univ
36		NC 16, Brookshire Blvd, to US 74E, Downtown Charlotte
	Gas	E: BP◊ W: Exxon, RaceTrac, Speedway
	Food	W: Burger King, Jack in the Box
	Med	E: + Hospital
35		Glenwood Dr
	Gas	E: Circle K, Shell◊
	Lodg	E: Knights Inn
34		NC 27, Freedom Dr, Tuckaseegee Rd, Charlotte, Lincolnton
	Gas	E: BP◊, Circle K
	Food	E: Bojangles, Burger King, IHOP, Mayflower Seafood, McDonald's, Pizza Hut, Taco Bell, Wendy's
	Lodg	W: **Howard Johnson**, Ramada Inn
	Med	E: + Pro-Med Minor Emergency Center
33		US 521, Billy Graham Pkwy, to Charlotte Douglas Int'l Airport
	Gas	E: 76◊, Crown W: Exxon◊
	Food	E: Krystal, KFC/Taco Bell, Wendy's W: **Cracker Barrel**, Waffle House
	Lodg	E: Comfort Suites, **Days Inn**, Hawthorne Suites, Royal Inn, Sheraton, Springhill Suites W: Best Value Inn, Fairfield Inn, La Quinta Inn ♥, Hampton Inn, Microtel, Red Roof Inn ♥, Sheraton
	Other	E: to Airport✈, Coliseum Area, Farmers Market
32		Little Rock Rd, Charlotte
	FStop	W: **Sam's Mart**/Shell
	Gas	E: Exxon W: Crown, Exxon◊, Texaco
	Food	E: Waffle House W: Arby's, Hardee's, Shoney's, Subway
	Lodg	E: Courtyard, Fairfield Inn, Holiday Inn W: Best Western, Country Inn, Motel 6 ♥, Shoney's Inn, Wingate Inn
	Other	E: Tires, **Fieldridge Acres Campground▲** W: Food Lion, Family Dollar, **Pharmacy**
(30B)		Jct I-485N, to NC 27 (SB)
(30A)		Jct I-485S, to I-77S (SB)
(30)		Jct I-485, to I-77S, Pineville (NB)
29		Sam Wilson Rd
	Gas	W: BP, Handy Dandy/Shell
(28)		Weigh Station (Both dir)
27		NC 273, Park St, Beatty Dr, Belmont, Mount Holly
	Gas	E: Citgo, Exxon◊ W: BP

EXIT		
	Food	E: Arby's, Burger King, Captain's Cap, Pizza Hut, Sub Corral, Subway, Taco Bell, Waffle House, Wendy's
	Lodg	E: American Motel, Heritage Inn W: Holiday Inn Express
	Other	E: Food Lion, NAPA, Radio Shack, **Walgreen's** W: Belmont Abbey College
26		Belmont-Mt Holly Rd (SB), NC 7, McAdenville Rd (NB), Belmont
	Gas	E: BP, Citgo, Petro Express W: Circle K
	Food	E: Bojangles, Hardee's, McDonald's, Western Sizzlin
	Other	E: Laundromat, Grocery, **Pharmacy** W: **Quality RV Services & Rentals**, Belmont Abbey College
23		NC 7, Main St, Lowell, McAdenville
	Gas	W: Exxon, World
	Food	W: Hardee's, Hillbilly's BBQ & Steaks
22		S Main St, Lowell, Cramerton
	Gas	E: Petro Express
	Food	E: Applebee's, Burger King, Hooters, Long John Silver, Zaxby's
	Other	E: Auto Dealers, Sam's Club, U-Haul
21		Cox Rd, Gastonia, Ranlo
	Gas	E: Citgo◊, Petro Express W: Exxon, Shell, Petro Express
	Food	E: Arby's, Chili's, Don Pablo, Krispy Kreme, Longhorn Steakhouse, McDonald's, Ryan's Grill, Subway W: IHOP
	Lodg	E: Holiday Motel W: Villager Lodge, Super 8
	Med	W: + Gaston Memorial Hospital
	Other	E: Best Buy, Grocery, Home Depot, Harley Davidson Carolina, Lowe's, Sam's Club, **Wal-Mart**, Gaston Mall W: **Pharmacy**
20		NC 279, New Hope Rd, Dallas, Gastonia
	Gas	E: BP, Shell
	Food	E: Arby's, Burger King, Checkers, Little Caesars, McDonald's, Morrison's Cafeteria, Pizza Hut, Red Lobster, Sake, Shoney's, Taco Bell W: Bojangles, **Cracker Barrel**, KFC, Outback Steakhouse, Texas Roadhouse, Waffle House
	Lodg	E: Best Western, Holiday Inn Express, Ramada W: **Comfort Suites**, Courtyard, Fairfield Inn, Hampton Inn
	Med	W: + Gaston Memorial Hospital
	Other	E: Advance Auto, Firestone, Kmart, Laundromat, Office Depot, Target, Winn Dixie, UPS Store, Westfield Eastridge Mall W: Circuit City
19		NC 7, Ozark Ave, Long Ave, Gastonia
	Gas	E: Shell, World
	Other	E: Amtrak, Greyhound
17		US 321, N Chester St, Gastonia, to Lincolnton
	Gas	E: Exxon◊ W: Citgo◊, Petro Express◊ x2
	Food	W: McDonald's, Pancake House, Waffle House, Wendy's, Western Sizzlin
	Lodg	E: **Days Inn**, Villager Lodge W: Holiday Inn Express, Microtel, Motel 6 ♥
	TServ	W: **Freightliner**
	Other	W: to Gaston College

◊ = Regular Gas Stations with Diesel ▲ = RV Friendly Locations ♥ = Pet Friendly Locations
RED PRINT SHOWS LARGE VEHICLE PARKING/ACCESS ON SITE OR NEARBY BROWN PRINT SHOWS CAMPGROUNDS/RV PARKS

I-85 N/S

EXIT	NC / SC
14	**NC 274, Bessemer City Rd, East Bessemer City, W Gastonia**
FStop	W: Grab & Go/Citgo
Gas	E: Phillips 66
Food	E: Burger King, McDonald's, Subway
	W: Waffle House
Lodg	W: Affordable Suites of America, Express Inn
13	**Edgewood Rd, Bessemer City**
Gas	W: BP, Exxon◆
Lodg	W: Economy Inn
Other	W: Young RV
10B	**US 74W, Kings Mountain (NB)**
10A	**US 29, US 74E, Shelby (NB)**
10	**US 29N, US 74, Kings Mountain, Shelby (SB)**
8	**NC 161, York Rd, Kings Mountain**
Gas	E: Exxon
	W: BP
Food	W: Burger King, Hardee's, McDonald's, KFC, Taco Bell, Waffle House
Lodg	E: Holiday Inn Express
	W: Comfort Inn, Quality Inn
TServ	W: Sterling Equipment Co.
Med	W: + Hospital
(6)	**Rest Area (SB)**
	(RR, Phones, Picnic, Vend)
5	**Dixon School Rd, Kings Mountain**
TStop	E: AmBest/Kings Mountain Travel Center/Shell (Scales)
Gas	E: Citgo
Food	E: Rest/FastFood/Kings Mtn TC, 50's Diner
TServ	E: Kings Mtn TC/Tires
Other	E: Laundry/RVDump/Kings Mtn TC, Tobacco Outlet
4	**US 29S, NC 216 (SB Exit, NB entr)**
(2)	**NC Welcome Center (NB)**
	(RR, Phone, Picnic, Vend, Info, Weather)
2	**NC 216, Battleground Rd, Kings Mountain**
Gas	W: Chevron
Other	E: to Kings Mountain Nat'l Military Park
	(EASTERN TIME ZONE)

⬆ NORTH CAROLINA
⬇ SOUTH CAROLINA
(EASTERN TIME ZONE)

NOTE:	MM 106.5: North Carolina State Line
106	**US 29, E Blacksburg, Grover**
TStop	W: WilcoHess Travel Plaza #905 (Scales)
Gas	W: Exxon
Food	W: DQ/Wendy's/WilcoHess TP
Other	W: Laundry/WilcoHess TP, Budget RAC
104	**Rd 99, Blacksburg**
TStop	E: Mr Waffle #104 (Scales)
Food	E: Rest/Mr Waffle
TServ	E: Mr Waffle/Tires
Other	E: Laundry/CB/WiFi/Mr Waffle
	W: Fireworks
(103)	**SC Welcome Center (SB)**
	(RR, Phone, Picnic, Vend, Info)

EXIT	SOUTH CAROLINA
102	**SC 198, Mtn St, Blacksburg, Earl**
FStop	E: Gasland #8/BP
TStop	E: Flying J Travel Plaza #5510/Conoco (Scales)
Gas	W: Shell
Food	E: Hardee's
	W: Cookery/FastFood/FJ TP, McDonald's, Waffle House
Other	W: Laundry/BarbSh/WiFi/LP/FJ TP (RV Dump Closed)
100	**SC 5, Blacksburg Hwy, Blacksburg, to Rock Hill, Shelby**
TStop	W: Sharma Petroleum/Sunoco (Scales)
Gas	W: Shell◆
Food	W: Subway/Sharma
Other	E: to Kings Mountain State Park▲
98	**Frontage Rd, Blacksburg (NB)**
	(Exit Only / Re-access at Ex #100)
TStop	E: Broad River Truck Stop
Food	E: Rest/Broad River TS
Tserv	E: Broad River TS/Tires
96	**SC 18, Shelby Hwy, Shelby**
TStop	E: Kangaroo #3438
Gas	W: Sunoco
Food	E: Krystal/Kangaroo
Other	E: Laundry/Kangaroo
95	**Hampshire Dr, to SC 18, Limestone St (NB), Rd 82, Pleasant School Rd, Gaffney, Shelby (SB)**
FStop	E: Mini Mart Food Store #3406
TStop	E: Kangaroo Express, Mr Waffle Auto & Truck Plaza
	W: Norma's Truck Stop
Food	E: Mr Waffle, Auntie M's Cafe/Kang Exp, Dog House Café
	W: Rest/Norma's Truck Stop
Lodg	E: Gaffney Inn, Shamrock Motel
Med	E: + Upstate Carolina Medical Center
92	**SC 11, Floyd Baker Blvd, to SC 150, Gaffney, Boiling Springs, NC**
Gas	E: Citgo, Murphy, Petro Express
	W: Exxon, Texaco◆
Food	E: Applebee's, Blue Bay Seafood, Burger King, Bojangles, KFC, McDonald's, Pizza Hut, Ruby Tuesday, Ryan's Grill, Sagebrush Steakhouse, Sonic, Subway, Taco Bell, Wendy's, Western Sizzler
	W: Fatz Cafe, Waffle House
Lodg	E: Jameson Inn, Super 8
	W: Homestead Lodge♥, Quality Inn♥
Other	E: Grocery, Pharmacy, Wal-Mart sc, to Limestone College
90	**SC 105, SC 81, Hyatt St, Gaffney**
TStop	E: Pilot Travel Center #453 (Scales)
Gas	E: BP◆, Kangaroo Express
	W: Citgo, Gasland, Petro Express
Food	E: Arby's/TJCinn/Pilot TC, Bronco Mex Rest, Subway, Waffle House
	W: BurgerKing/Citgo, Cracker Barrel, La Fogata Mex Rest, Outback Steakhouse
Lodg	E: Red Roof Inn, Sleep Inn
	W: Hampton Inn
Other	E: Laundry/WiFi/RVDump/Pilot TC, Pinecone Campground▲
	W: Prime Outlets at Gaffney
(89)	**Rest Area (NB)**
	(RR, Phones, Picnic, Vend)
(88)	**Rest Area (SB)**
	(RR, Phones, Picnic, Vend)

EXIT	SOUTH CAROLINA
87	**Rd 39, Green River Rd, Macedonia Rd, Gaffney**
Other	E: Pinecone Campground▲
83	**SC 110, Horry Rd, Battleground Rd, Cowpens, Cowpens Battlefield**
TStop	W: Mr Waffle Auto Truck Plaza/Citgo (Scales)
Gas	E: HotSpot
Food	E: Red Rooster, Subway
	W: Rest/Mr Waffle ATP
TWash	W: Mr Waffle ATP
TServ	E: Horton's Truck Repair
	W: Mr Waffle ATP/Tires
Other	W: Laundry/Mr Waffle ATP, Cowpens Battlefield, Abbott Farms, Fireworks
82	**Frontage Rd (NB)**
80	**Rd 57, Gossett Rd (NB)**
78	**US 221, Chesnee Hwy, Chesnee, Spartanburg**
Gas	E: Shell◆
	W: Exxon◆, RaceTrac◆
Food	E: Blimpie/Shell, Hardee's
	W: Arby's, Bojangles, Burger King/Exxon, Hardee's, McDonald's, Southern BBQ, Subway, Wendy's, Waffle House
Lodg	E: Motel 6♥, Sun 'n Sand Motel
	W: Hampton Inn
Other	W: Advance Auto, Dollar General, Grocery, Spartanburg Harley Davidson
77	**I-85 Bus S, Spartanburg**
75	**SC 9, Spartanburg, Boiling Springs**
Gas	E: Exxon
	W: BP◆, Citgo, RaceTrac
Food	E: Denny's
	W: Burger King, Long John Silver, McDonald's, Pizza Hut, Steak & Ale, Waffle House, Zaxby's
Lodg	E: Best Western, Red Roof Inn
	W: Comfort Inn, Days Inn
Med	E: + Spartanburg Hospital
Other	E: Dollar General
	W: CVS, Grocery, Auto Service, US Post Office, Masters RV Center
72	**US 176, to I-585, Spartanburg, Inman, Downtown**
Gas	W: BP, RaceTrac
Other	E: to Univ of SC/Spartanburg
(70B)	**Jct I-26W, to Asheville**
Other	W: Cunningham RV Park▲
(70A)	**Jct I-26E, to Columbia**
(70)	**Jct I-26, W to Asheville, NC, E to Columbia**
69	**I-85 Bus N, to Spartanburg (NB Exit, SB entr)**
68	**SC 129, to Wellford, Greer (SB)**
66	**US 29, Greenville Hwy, Spartanburg, to Wellford, Lyman**
Other	W: to Flowermill RV Park▲, Creekside RV Park▲
63	**SC 290, E Main St, Duncan, Moore, Spartanburg**
FStop	E: Kangaroo Express #3414/Citgo
TStop	W: Pilot Travel Center #310 (Scales), Travel Center of America #25/BP (Scales)
Gas	E: Circle K, Exxon
	W: Shell

◆ = Regular Gas Stations with Diesel ▲ = RV Friendly Locations ♥ = Pet Friendly Locations
RED PRINT SHOWS LARGE VEHICLE PARKING/ACCESS ON SITE OR NEARBY BROWN PRINT SHOWS CAMPGROUNDS/RV PARKS

Page 425

INTERSTATE 85 N/S

EXIT	SOUTH CAROLINA
	Food E: Burger King, Denny's, Jack in the Box, Pizza Inn, Taco Bell, Waffle House W: Wendy's/Pilot TC, CountryPride/TA TC, Arby's, Bojangles, Hardee's, McDonald's, Waffle House, Wendy's
	Lodg E: Hampton Inn, Jameson Inn, Microtel W: Days Inn/TA TC, Days Inn, Holiday Inn Express, Quality Inn
	TServ W: TA TC/Tires
	Other W: Laundry/WiFi/Pilot TC, Laundry/CB/WiFi/TA TC, Sonny's RV
60	SC 101, Greer, Woodruff
	FStop E: Grand Foodstuff #2
	Gas E: BP, Citgo◊ W: Exxon
	Food E: Subway W: Burger King
	Other W: BMW Assembly Plant
58	Brockman McClimon Rd, to SC 101
	Other W: BMW Assembly Plant
57	Aviation Dr, Airport
	Other W: Greenville Spartanburg Int'l Airport✈
56	SC 14, Greer, Pelham
	FStop W: Sphinx #121
	Gas E: Shell◊ W: BP◊
	Other W: LP/Spinx, Outdoor RV & Marine World
54	Pelham Rd, Greenville
	Gas E: BP◊, Citgo◊ W: BP◊, Sphinx
	Food E: Burger King, Waffle House W: Applebee's, Ca Dreamin, ChickFilA, Hardee's, Jack in the Box, Joe's Crab Shack, Logan's Roadhouse, Mayflower Seafood, Max & Erma's, McDonald's, On the Border, Ruby Tuesday, Romano's Macaroni Grill, Starbucks, Tony Roma, Wendy's
	Lodg E: Best Western W: Comfort Suites, Courtyard, Extended Stay America, Fairfield Inn, Hampton Inn, Holiday Inn Express, MainStay Suites, Microtel, Residence Inn, Wingate Inn
	Other E: Harley Davidson W: CVS, FedEx Kinko's, Grocery, Goodyear, Radio Shack
(52)	Weigh Station (NB)
(51C)	Jct I-385N, Greenville, Downtown
(51B)	Jct I-385S, to Columbia
(51)	Jct I-385, SC 146, Woodruff Rd, Columbia, Greenville (Access to Ex #48 Serv)
	Gas E: Hess, Spinx W: BP, Kangaroo Express, RaceWay, Shell
	Food E: Bob Evans, Burger King, Chili's, Fatz Café, Fuddrucker's, IHOP, MiMi's Café, Monterey Mexican, Waffle House W: Carrabba's, Capri's Italian Rest, Cracker Barrel, Flat Rock Grille, Jack in the Box, K&W, McDonald's, MiMi's Café, Ruby Tuesday, Salsarita's, Subway, Sushi, TGI Friday, Waffle House
	Lodg E: Drury Inn♥, Hampton Inn♥, Staybridge Suites W: Crowne Plaza♥, Days Inn, Fairfield Inn, Holiday Inn Express, La Quinta Inn♥, Microtel, Towneplace Suites

EXIT	SOUTH CAROLINA
	Other E: ATMs, Auto Services, Best Buy, B&N, Discount Tire, Goodyear, Lowe's, Sam's Club, Staples, Wal-Mart sc, Frankie's Funpark W: ATMs, BJ's, Best Buy, Circuit City, Firestone, Home Depot, Lowe's, Office Max, PetSmart♥, Target, Haywood Mall
50	Woodruff Rd
48AB	US 276, Laurens Rd, Greenville, Mauldin, Laurens
48	US 276, Mauldin, Greeenville
	Gas W: BP, Exxon◊, Murphy
	Food E: Waffle House W: Arby's, Bojangles, Burger King, Happy China, Hooters, Jack in the Box, KFC, Melting Pot, Ryan's Grill, Roadhouse Grill, Subway, Taco Bell, Zaxby's
	Lodg E: Red Roof Inn W: Best Inn, Days Inn, Embassy Suites, Phoenix Inn, Sleep Inn
	Other E: Car Max W: Auto Dealers, Auto Zone, Advance Auto, Auto Repairs, Best Buy, CVS, Office Depot, PetSmart♥, UPS Store, Haywood Mall, Convention Center, Greenville Downtown Airport✈
47	Mauldin Rd
46	Mauldin Rd, SC 291, Pleasantburg Dr, US 25, Augusta Rd
46C	Mauldin Rd, to US 25, SC 291
	Gas W: Citgo, Shell, Spinx
	Food W: Jack in the Box, Subway
	Lodg W: Comfort Inn, InTowne Suites, Quality Inn
	Other E: to Greenville Muni Stadium W: Grocery W: Advance Auto, CVS, Grocery, Home Depot, Tires, to Greenville Tech
46B	SC 291, Pleasantburg Dr, to US 25
	Food E: Waffle House W: Burger King, Jack in the Box, Logan's
	Lodg W: Economy Inn, Travelers Inn
46A	Mauldin Rd, SC 291S, Augusta Rd, to Greenwood
	Gas E: Chevron, Spinx
	Lodg E: Holiday Inn, Motel 6♥, Southern Suites
	Other E: to Springwood RV Park▲, Donaldson Center Airport✈
44B	White Horse Rd, US 25
	FStop E: Spinx Travel Plaza #138
	Gas W: RaceTrac
	Food E: Subway/Spinx W: McDonald's, Waffle House
	TServ W: Cherokee Kenworth
	Med W: + Greenville Hospital, + Childrens Hospital
	Other E: to Springwood RV Park▲ W: Sun Coast RV, Wrecker
44A	Piedmont Hwy, SC 20 (SB Exit, NB entr)
	Other E: Auto Service, LC Diesel Service
44	US 25, White Horse Rd, SC 20, Piedmont Hwy, Greenville (NB)
(42)	Jct I-185 (TOLL), US 29N, Downtown Greenville, Columbia

◊ = Regular Gas Stations with Diesel   ▲ = RV Friendly Locations   ♥ = Pet Friendly Locations
RED PRINT SHOWS LARGE VEHICLE PARKING/ACCESS ON SITE OR NEARBY   BROWN PRINT SHOWS CAMPGROUNDS/RV PARKS

INTERSTATE 85

EXIT	SOUTH CAROLINA
40	**SC 153, SC 190, Piedmont, Easley**
Gas	E: Exxon
	W: Pantry, RaceTrac, Shell
Food	E: Waffle House
	W: Arby's, Burger King, Cracker Barrel, Hardee's, Huddle House, KFC, McDonald's, Pizza Hut, Subway
Lodg	W: Executive Inn, Super 8
Other	W: Grocery, Pharmacy
39	**SC 143, River Rd, to SC 153 (Access to Ex #40 Serv)**
Gas	W: Shell
Other	E: to Ivy Acres RV Park▲
35	**SC 86, Anderson Hwy, Piedmont**
TStop	E: Pilot Travel Center #63 (Scales)
Gas	W: BP◊
Food	E: McDonald's/Pilot TC
Other	E: WiFi/Pilot TC
34	**US 29, Anderson, Williamston (SB Left Exit, NB entr)**
32	**SC 8, Easley Hwy, Pelzer, Easley, Williamston, Belton**
Gas	E: Shell◊
27	**SC 81, Williamsburg Rd, Anderson**
TStop	W: Anderson Travel Center (Scales)
Gas	E: BP◊, Exxon
Food	E: Arby's, McDonald's, Waffle House
	W: Rest/Anderson TC
Lodg	E: Holiday Inn Express
Tires	E: Anderson TC
Other	E: Laundry/WiFi/Anderson TC
(24)	**Rest Area (SB) (RR, Phones, Picnic, Vend)**
21	**US 178, Liberty Hwy, Anderson, Liberty (Access to Ex #19 Serv)**
FStop	E: Liberty Crossroads/Shell
Food	E: Applebee's, O'Charley's, Ruby Tuesday
Lodg	E: La Quinta Inn♥, Quality Inn, Super 8
19A	**US 76W**
19B	**US 76E**
19	**US 76, Clemson Hwy, to SC 28, Pendleton, Anderson, Clemson, to Abbeville, Greenwood**
Gas	E: BP, Exxon◊
	W: RaceWay Trac
Food	E: Chili's, Fuddrucker's, Hardee's, Jack in The Box, O'Charley's, Olive Garden, Texas Roadhouse
	W: Cracker Barrel, Hooters, McDonald's, Outback Steakhouse, Waffle House, Wendy's
Lodg	E: Best Value Inn, Days Inn, La Quinta Inn♥, Mainstay Suites, Quality Inn
	W: Comfort Suites, Country Inn, Fairfield Inn, Hampton Inn, Holiday Inn Express, Jameson Inn
Other	E: Best Buy, Harley Davidson, Sam's Club, Target, Wal-Mart sc, Auto Dealers
	W: to Clemson Univ, to appr 20 mi Crooked Creek RV Park▲
(17)	**Rest Area (NB) (RR, Phone, Picnic, Vend)**
14	**SC 187, Williams Rd, Townville, Anderson, Pendleton, Clemson**
FStop	E: Fuel Club
Gas	W: AmocoBP
Food	E: Huddle House

EXIT	SC / GA
Lodg	W: Budget Inn
Other	E: Anderson/Lake Hartwell KOA▲
11	**SC 24, SC 243, Townville, Anderson, to Westminster**
FStop	E: Sunoco #2687
Gas	E: Exxon◊
	W: Shell
Food	E: Subway
	W: Circles Café
Other	W: to appr 15mi Crooked Creek RV Park▲
(9)	**Weigh Station (NB)**
4	**SC 243, Old Dobbins Bridge Rd, to SC 24, Fair Play**
Gas	E: Exxon
	W: Russell's Gen'l Store/Marathon
2	**SC 59, Fair Play Blvd, Fair Play**
1	**SC 11, Walhalla, Westminster (NB Exit and Entrance)**
(0)	**SC Welcome Center (NB) (RR, Phones, Picnic, Vend, Info)**

(EASTERN TIME ZONE)

⏶ SOUTH CAROLINA
⏷ GEORGIA

(EASTERN TIME ZONE)

NOTE: MM 179: South Carolina State Line

177	**GA 77S, Whitworth Rd, Lavonia, to Elberton, Hartwell**
Gas	E: BP◊
Other	E: to Hart State Park▲

EXIT	GEORGIA
(176)	**GA Welcome Center (SB) (RR, Phone, Picnic, Vend, RVDump)**
173	**GA 17, Jones St, Lavonia, Toccoa**
Gas	E: RaceTrac
	W: Exxon◊, Shell
Food	E: Hardee's, La Cabana, McDonald's, Subway, Taco Bell, Wendy's
	W: Arby's, Burger King, Pizza Hut, Shoney's, Waffle House, Zaxby's
Lodg	E: Best Western, Sleep Inn
	W: GuestHouse Inn, Super 8
Other	E: Dollar General, RiteAid
	W: Sunset Campground▲, to Tugaloo State Park▲
(171)	**Weigh Station (NB)**
(169)	**Weigh Station (SB)**
166	**GA 106, GA 145, Carnesville, Toccoa**
TStop	E: WilcoHess Travel Plaza #3001 (Scales)
	W: Echo Auto Truck Plaza (Scales)
Food	E: Wendy's/WilcoHess TP
	W: Rest/Echo ATP
TServ	W: Echo ATP/Tires
Other	E: Laundry/WilcoHess TP
164	**GA 320, Church Rd, Carnesville**
(160)	**Franklin Co Rest Area (NB) (RR, Phone, Picnic, Vend)**
160	**GA 51, Sandy Cross Rd, Carnesville, Homer, Royston, Elberton**
TStop	E: Shell Travel Plaza (Scales)
	W: Flying J Travel Plaza #5096 (Scales), Petro Stopping Center #60 (Scales)
Food	E: Chesters/Subway/Shell TP
	W: CountryMarket/FastFood/FJ TP, IronSkillet/PizzaHut/Petro SC
TWash	W: Blue Beacon TW/Petro SC
TServ	W: Petro SC/Tires
Other	E: Laundry/Shell TP, to Victoria Bryant State Park▲
	W: Laundry/WiFi/RVDump/LP/FJ TP, Laundry/BarbSh/CB/RVDump/Petro SC
154	**GA 63, Martin Bridge Rd, Commerce**
149	**US 441, GA 15, Commerce, Homer**
TStop	E: Travel Center of America #156/76 (Scales)
Gas	E: Chevron, Shell, Murphy
	W: RaceTrac◊, Sam's Food Mart
Food	E: Buckhorn/TA TC, Captain D's, Grand China, Outback Steakhouse, Sonny's BBQ, Shoney's, Taco Bell, Waffle House, Zaxby's
	W: Applebee's, Arby's, Burger King, Checkers, ChickFilA, Cracker Barrel, KFC, Denny's, La Hacienda, McDonald's, Pizza Hut, Ruby Tuesday, Ryan's Grill, Subway, Starbucks, Waffle House, Wendy's
Lodg	E: Admiral Benbow Inn, Days Inn, Hampton Inn, Red Roof Inn♥, Scottish Inn
	W: Best Western, Comfort Inn, Dollar Wise, Holiday Inn Express, Howard Johnson♥, Jameson Inn, Ramada, Super 8
TServ	E: TA TC/Tires
Med	E: + Hospital
Other	E: Laundry/WiFi/TA TC, Dollar Tree, Radio Shack, Wal-Mart sc, Tanger Outlet Mall 1, County Boys RV Park▲

◊ = Regular Gas Stations with Diesel   ▲ = RV Friendly Locations   ♥ = Pet Friendly Locations
RED PRINT SHOWS LARGE VEHICLE PARKING/ACCESS ON SITE OR NEARBY   BROWN PRINT SHOWS CAMPGROUNDS/RV PARKS

Interstate 85 N/S

EXIT		GEORGIA
	Other	W: Auto Dealers, Home Depot, Tanger Outlet Mall 2, Tires, Lightnin RV, The Pottery Campground▲, Atlanta Dragway
147		GA 98, Maysville Rd, Commerce, Maysville
	FStop	E: Fuel Mart #636
	TStop	E: Flying J Travel Plaza #5169 (Scales)
	Gas	E: Speedway W: Shell
	Food	E: Rest/FastFood/FJ TP
	Med	E: + Hospital
	Other	E: Laundry/WiFi/RVDump/LP/FJ TP
140		GA 82, Dry Pond Rd, Pendergrass
	Other	E: to Jackson Co Airport✈
137		US 129, GA 11, Pendergrass, Gainesville, Jefferson
	TStop	W: QT #737 (Scales)
	Gas	E: BP, Shell
	Food	E: Arby's, Hardee's, McDonald's, Waffle House, Zaxby's W: Deli/QT, Burger King, Waffle House
	Lodg	E: Comfort Inn
129		GA 53, Winder Hwy, Braselton, Hoschton, Lanier Raceway
	TStop	W: Pilot Travel Center #66 (Scales)
	Gas	E: BP, Shell◆
	Food	E: Subway/BP, Waffle House W: McDonald's/Pilot TC, Cracker Barrel
	Other	W: Laundry/WiFi/Pilot TC
126		GA 211, Winder Hwy, Hoschton, Braselton, Winder
	Gas	E: Shell◆ W: BP◆
120		CR 134, Hamilton Mill Pkwy, Hamilton Mill Rd, Buford
	Gas	E: BP, QT◆ W: Chevron, Shell◆
	Food	E: McDonald's, Starbucks, Subway, Wendy's, Zaxby's W: Huddle House/Shell
115AB		GA 20, Buford Dr NE, Buford
115		GA 20, Buford Dr NE, Buford, Lawrenceville
	Gas	E: QT W: BP, Chevron, QT◆
	Food	W: Arby's, Burger King, Chili's, ChickFilA, Chuck E Cheese, Longhorn Steakhouse, McDonald's, Moe's SW Grill, O'Charley's, Olive Garden, On the Border, Red Lobster, Romano's Macaroni Grill, Starbucks, Subway, TGI Friday, Waffle House
	Lodg	W: Country Inn, Hampton Inn, Springhill Suites, Wingate Inn
	Med	E: + Hospital
	Other	W: Best Buy, Borders, Circuit City, FedEx Kinko's, Firestone, Lowe's, Office Max, PetCo♥, PetSmart♥, Sam's Club, Staples, Target, Wal-Mart sc, UPS Store, Mall of GA, Southland Motorhome
(114)		Rest Area (SB) (RR, Phone, Picnic, Vend)
(113)		Jct I-985N, Gainesville, GA 365, Lanier Pkwy, Lake Lanier Islands, Buford Dam (NB)
(112)		Rest Area (NB) (RR, Phones, Picnic, Vend)

EXIT		GEORGIA
111		GA 317, Lawrenceville-Suwanee Rd, Suwanee, Lawrenceville
	FStop	W: FA Simms Oil #104/66
	Gas	E: BP W: Chevron, RaceTrac, Shell
	Food	E: Applebee's, Arby's, Blimpie, Burger King, ChickFilA, Cracker Barrel, Pizza Hut, Outback Steakhouse, Subway, Taco Bell, Waffle House, Wendy's W: CiCi's, Denny's, McDonald's, Waffle House
	Lodg	E: Comfort Inn, Fairfield Inn, Howard Johnson, Red Roof Inn♥, Sun Suites W: Best Western, Days Inn, Motel 6♥
	Other	E: CVS, Publix, UPS Store W: Office Depot, Wal-Mart sc
109		Old Peachtree Rd, Lawrenceville
	Gas	E: QT◆
	Food	E: McDonald's, Quiznos W: Waffle House
	Other	W: Home Depot
108		Sugarloaf Pkwy
	Food	W: ChickFilA, Roadhouse Grill
	Lodg	W: Hilton Garden Inn, Holiday Inn
	Other	W: Gwinnett Convention Center, Bass Pro Shop
107		GA 120, Duluth Hwy, to GA 316, Duluth, Lawrenceville
	Gas	E: Shell W: BP, Chevron, QT
	Food	E: Burger King, Carino's, Zaxby's W: McDonald's, Subway, China Gate
	Lodg	W: La Quinta Inn♥, Suburban Extended Stay

EXIT		GEORGIA
	Med	E: + Gwinett Medical Center
	Other	E: to Appalachee RV Center
106		GA 316E, Lawrenceville ByPass (NB, Exit only)
	Other	E: to Lightnin RV, Gwinett Co Airport/Briscoe Field✈
104		Pleasant Hill Rd, Duluth, Norcross
	Gas	E: Chevron, Circle K, Exxon, RaceTrac W: BP◆, Phillips 66, QT, Shell, Murphy
	Food	E: Burger King, ChickFilA, Carrabba's, Joe's Crab Shack, Romano's Macaroni Grill, Smoky Bones BBQ, Starbucks, Subway, TGI Friday, Waffle House, Wendy's W: Applebee's, Arby's, Burger King, Checkers, Chili's, Hooters, IHOP, KFC, Olive Garden, McDonald's, On the Border, Panda Express, Pizza Hut, Red Lobster, Ryan's Grill, Shoney's, Starbucks, Steak 'n Shake, Taco Bell, Waffle House, Wendy's
	Lodg	E: Candlewood Suites, Comfort Suites, Country Inn, Hampton Inn, Holiday Inn Express, Marriott, Residence Inn, Studio 6 W: Courtyard, Days Inn, Hyatt, Quality Inn, Wellesley Inn, Wingate Inn
	TServ	E: International Trucks
	Other	E: Best Buy, CVS, FedEx Kinko's, Goodyear, Home Depot, Kmart, Office Depot, Publix W: Auto Dealers, Auto Repairs, Banks, B&N, Circuit City, Firestone, Goodyear, Kroger, PetCo♥, PetSmart♥, Staples, Target, UPS Store, Venture Cinemas, Art City Art World, Gwinnett Place Mall, Sagon RV
103		CR 557, Steve Reynolds Blvd (NB) (Access to Ex #104 Serv)
	Gas	W: QT
	Food	W: Starbucks
	Lodg	E: Sun Suites W: InTown Suites
	Other	W: Circuit City, Target
102		GA 378, Beaver Ruin Rd, Norcross
	Gas	E: Shell◆ W: BP, QT
	Other	W: Casey's Mobile RV Repair
101		Indian Trail Rd, CR 560, Lilburn Rd, Norcross
	Gas	E: QT◆, Shell◆ W: BP◆, Chevron, Speed Mart
	Food	E: Blimpie, Krystal, McDonald's, Taco Bell, Shoney's, KFC, Waffle House W: Arby's, DQ, Little Caesars, Waffle House, Wendy's
	Lodg	E: GuestHouse Inn, Shoney's Inn, Suburban Lodge, Super 8 W: Red Roof Inn♥
	Other	E: Jones RV Park▲ W: CVS, Grocery, Lowe's, Outlet Mall
99		GA 140W, Jimmy Carter Blvd, Norcross, Doraville
	Gas	E: BP, Exxon, Phillips 66◆, Shell W: Chevron, Citgo, QT◆
	Food	E: Burger King, ChickFilA, Chili's, Cracker Barrel, Denny's, McDonald's, Long John Silver, Pizza Hut, Steak & Taco Bell, Wendy's W: Arby's, Hooters, Pappadeaux Seafood, Shoney's, Waffle House
	Lodg	E: Best Western, Comfort Inn, Courtyard, Motel 6♥, La Quinta Inn♥, Travelodge W: Country Inn, Drury Inn, Microtel

◆ = Regular Gas Stations with Diesel ▲ = RV Friendly Locations ♥ = Pet Friendly Locations
RED PRINT SHOWS LARGE VEHICLE PARKING/ACCESS ON SITE OR NEARBY BROWN PRINT SHOWS CAMPGROUNDS/RV PARKS

I-85 N/S — GEORGIA

EXIT		
	TServ	W: Peachstate Ford
	Med	E: + GA Family Medicine Center
	Other	E: Budget RAC, CVS, Firestone, Hertz RAC, Kmart, Office Depot, Walgreen's, U-Haul, UPS Store
		W: AutoZone, NTB, Tires
96		Pleasantdale Rd, Northcrest Rd, Northcrest Rd (NB)
	FStop	W: QT #707 (Scales)
	Gas	W: Exxon
	Food	E: Burger King
		W: Deli/QT, Waffle House
	Lodg	W: Howard Johnson, US Economy Lodge
(95B)		Jct I-285W, to Chattanooga, Birmingham (SB)
(95A)		Jct I-285E, to Macon, Augusta (SB)
(95)		Jct I-285, Atl ByP, E to Augusta, W to Chattanooga (NB)
94		Chamblee Tucker Rd, Atlanta, Chamblee, Tucker
	Gas	E: BP, Shell
		W: QT◆, Shell
	Food	E: Chinese
		W: DQ, Waffle House
	Lodg	E: Masters Inn
		W: Motel 6♥, Red Roof Inn♥
	Other	W: to Mercer Univ
93		Shallowford Rd, to Briarcliffe Rd, Doraville
	Gas	E: Shell
		W: Circle K, Shell◆
	Food	E: Waffle House, Blimpie/Shell
		W: Quality Inn, Chicken Plaza
	Lodg	E: Super 8
		W: Quality Inn
	Other	E: Laundromat, Publix, U-Haul
91		US 23, GA 155, Clairmont Rd, Decatur, to Airport
	Gas	E: Express, Chevron, Speedway
		W: Amoco, BP
	Food	E: IHOP, McDonald's, Popeye's
		W: Waffle House, Roadhouse Grill, Starbucks, Pizza
	Lodg	W: Clairmont Lodge, Days Inn, Marriott, Wingate Inn
	Other	E: CVS
		W: Laundromat, Grocery, Pharmacy, Kmart, Sam's Club, DeKalb-Peachtree Airport✈, Emory Univ
89		GA 42, N Druid Hills Rd
	Gas	E: Amoco, Crown, QT◆
		W: BP, Chevron◆, Exxon, Hess
	Food	E: Arby's, Burger King, McDonald's, Piccadilly, Taco Bell
		W: Pizza Hut, Waffle House
	Lodg	E: Courtyard, Homestead Suites
		W: Hampton Inn, Microtel, Radisson, Red Roof Inn♥
	Med	E: + Hospital
	Other	E: CVS, Target, to Oglethorpe Univ
88		to GA 400N, Cheshire Bridge Rd, Lenox Rd (SB)
	Gas	E: BP, Exxon, Shell, Spur
	Food	E: Waffle House, Sonny's BBQ
	Lodg	E: Baymont Inn
87		GA 400N, Harvey Mathis Pkwy, Cumming (NB)

EXIT		
86		GA 13S, Peachtree St (SB), GA 13N, Buford Hwy (NB)
	Gas	E: BP, Chevron
	Food	E: Denny's, Wendy's
	Lodg	E: Intown Suites, Piedmont Inn
		W: Ramada
	NOTE:	I-85 below runs with I-75. Exit #'s follow I-75.
(85/251)		Jct I-85N, to Greeneville, SC Jct I-75N to Marietta, Chattanooga, TN
84/ 250		17th St, 14th St, 10th St, to GA Tech (SB, Exit only)
250		10th St, 14th St, GA Tech (NB)
249D		US 78, US 278, North Ave (SB)
	Gas	E: BP
	Food	E: Checker's, Pizza Hut
		W: McDonald's
	Lodg	W: Comfort Inn, Holiday Inn Express
249D		US 29, US 19, Spring St, W Peachtree St, to US 78, US 278 (NB)
249C		Downtown Atlanta, Williams St, Georgia Dome (SB, Exit Only)
249B		Pine St, Peachtree St, Civic Center, (NB, Exit Only)
	Med	E: + Crawford Long Hospital
249A		Courtland St, GA St Univ (SB, Exit only)
	Other	W: GA State Univ
248D		J W Dobbs Ave, Edgewood Ave (SB)
248C		GA 10E, Freedom Pkwy, Carter Ctr, Andrew Young Int'l Blvd
248B		Edgewood Ave, Auburn Ave, Butler St, J W Dobbs Ave
248A		MLK Jr Dr, State Capitol (SB)
(247)		Jct I-20, E to Augusta, W to Birmingham
246		Fulton St, Central Ave, Downtown
	Gas	E: BP
	Lodg	E: Hampton Inn, Holiday Inn
	Other	E: Torner Field, Atlanta Zoo
		W: to Coliseum, GA State Univ
245		Abernathy Blvd, Capitol Ave (NB ex, SB ent)
	Lodg	E: Holiday Inn, Hampton Inn
	Other	E: Turner Field
		W: State Capitol
244		University Ave, Pryor St
	Gas	E: Chevron, Exxon
	TServ	E: Cummins South, Southern Freight
		W: Brown Transport, Ford Trucks, Freight Direct, Great Dane Trailers
243/ (242/ 77)		GA 166, Lankford Pkwy, East Point Jct I-85S, to Atlanta Airport, Montgomery
	NOTE:	I-85 above runs with I-75. Exit #'s follow I-75.

EXIT		
77		GA 166, Langford Pky, Lakewood Fwy (NB exit, SB entr) US 19, US 41, Metropolitan Pkwy, GA 3 (SB exit, NB entr)
76		Cleveland Ave, Atlanta
	Gas	E: BP, Citgo◆, Hess, Phillips 66
		W: Amoco, Texaco
	Food	E: Arby's, Burger King, Mrs Winners
		W: KFC, Church's
	Lodg	E: Days Inn, New American Inn
	Med	W: + Hospital
	Other	E: CVS, Kroger, to Atlanta Tech
75		Sylvan Rd, Central Ave, Hapeville
	Gas	E: Fina, Shell◆
	Food	E: ChickFilA, McDonald's, Waffle House
	Lodg	E: InTown Suites
		W: Mark Inn
	Other	E: Laundromat
74		Loop Rd (SB exit, NB entr) (Access to Ex #73 Serv)
	Lodg	E: Residence Inn
73		Virginia Ave (SB)
73B		Virginia Ave West (NB)
	Gas	W: Chevron, Shell
	Food	W: Arby's, BBQ Kitchen, KFC, Sandwich Factory, Steak & Ale, Waffle House
	Lodg	W: AmeriSuites, Crowne Plaza, DoubleTree, Econo Lodge, Fairfield Inn, Hampton Inn, Holiday Inn
73A		Virginia Ave East (NB)
	Gas	E: Citgo◆
	Food	E: Hardee's, IHOP, McDonald's, Pizza Hut, Ruby Tuesday, Waffle House, Wendy's
	Lodg	E: Courtyard, Hilton, Marriott, Red Roof Inn♥, Residence Inn, Sheraton
72		GA 6, Camp Creek Pkwy, Atlanta Airport, Air Cargo
	Gas	W: Amoco, Chevron, Shell
	Med	E: + Grady Medical Center
	Other	E: Hartsfield Jackson Atl Intl Airport✈
		W: Goodyear
71		GA 139, Riverdale Rd, Airport, Camp Creek Pkwy, Air Cargo
	Gas	E: QT
	Food	E: Ruby Tuesday, Rest/Hol Inn
		W: Rest/Westin
	Lodg	E: Courtyard, Fairfield Inn, Hampton Inn, Holiday Inn, Hyatt, La Quinta Inn♥, Microtel, Sheraton, Sleep Inn, Super 8, Wingate Inn
		W: Embassy Suites, Hilton Garden Inn, Marriott, Westin
(70)		Jct I-285, E to Macon, Augusta, W to Birmingham, Chattanooga (SB ex, NB entr)
69B		GA 279, Old National Hwy (NB)
	Gas	E: BP, Chevron×2, Citgo, Texaco
		W: Chevron, Conoco◆, Shell, Texaco
	Food	E: Burger King, Checkers, El Ranchero, Indian Rest, McDonald's, Taco Bell, Waffle House, Wendy's
		W: City Café Diner, Subway, Waffle House
	Lodg	E: Clarion, Comfort Inn, Days Inn, Howard Johnson, Motel 6♥, Quality Inn
		W: Econo Lodge, Hilton Garden Inn
	Other	E: Auto Repairs, Firestone, Grocery, Pharmacy, U-Haul
		W: Advance Auto, Auto Zone, Family Dollar, Kroger, Radio Shack, Target

◆ = Regular Gas Stations with Diesel ▲ = RV Friendly Locations ♥ = Pet Friendly Locations
RED PRINT SHOWS LARGE VEHICLE PARKING/ACCESS ON SITE OR NEARBY BROWN PRINT SHOWS CAMPGROUNDS/RV PARKS

Interstate 85 N/S

EXIT		GEORGIA
69A		GA 14 Spur, S Fulton Pkwy (NB, Left Exit)
69		GA 279, GA 14 Spur (SB)
(68)		Jct I-285, E to Macon, Tampa, FL N to Birmingham, Chattanooga, TN
66		Flat Shoals Rd, CR 1384, Union City (Access to Ex #64 Serv)
	FStop	W: Chevron Food Mart #122
	Food	W: Waffle House
	Lodg	W: Motel 6
64		GA 138, Jonesboro Rd, Union City, Jonesboro
	Gas	E: BP◊ W: Chevron, QT, Shell◊
	Food	E: Waffle House W: Arby's, Burger King, ChickFilA, Cracker Barrel, IHOP, Krystal, McDonald's Pizza Hut, Subway, Taco Bell, Waffle House, Wendy's
	Lodg	E: Econo Lodge, Ramada, Super 8 W: Baymont Inn, Best Western, Comfort Inn, Days Inn, Holiday Inn Express, Microtel, Red Roof Inn
	Other	E: Auto Dealers W: Auto Repairs, Big Lots, Carwash, Dollar Tree, Firestone, Goodyear, Grocery, Kroger, NTB, PepBoys, Wal-Mart sc, Shannon Mall
61		GA 74, Senoia Rd, Fairburn
	TStop	E: Greenway Fairburn Family Travel Center/BP (Scales) (DAND)
	Gas	E: Chevron◊, RaceTrac, Shell W: Citgo◊, Marathon, Pit Stop, Phillips 66◊
	Food	E: Rest/Fairburn TC, Chili's, Dunkin Donuts, McDonald's Subway, Wendy's, Waffle House, Zaxby's
	Lodg	E: Hampton Inn, Sleep Inn, Wingate Inn W: Efficiency Motel
	Other	E: Laundry/Fairburn TC, Carwash
56		Collinsworth Rd, CR 548, Palmetto, Tyrone
	Gas	E: BP, Marathon
	Food	E: Frank's Family Rest
	Other	W: South Oaks RV & MH Park▲, Pine Acres MH & RV Park▲
51		GA 154, McCollum-Sharpsburg Rd
	Gas	E: BP, Phillips 66 W: Shell
	Food	E: Blimpie, Hardee's W: Krystal, Waffle House
47		GA 34, Newnan, Peachtree City
	FStop	W: Lakeside Shell
	Gas	E: Chevron◊, HotSpot◊, QT, Shell◊ W: Exxon, Phillips 66, RaceTrac
	Food	E: Arby's, Applebee's, CiCi's, Cracker Barrel, Longhorn Steakhouse, McDonald's, Mama Lucia's, Moe's SW Grill, Panda Express, Pizza Inn, Ryan's Grill, Starbucks, Subway, Waffle House, Wendy's W: Burger King, Golden Corral, IHOP, Krystal, Waffle House, Zaxby's
	Lodg	E: Best Western, Country Inn, Hampton Inn, Jameson Inn, Springhill Suites W: Comfort Inn, Holiday Inn Express, La Quinta Inn, Motel 6
	Med	W: + Hospital

EXIT		GEORGIA
	Other	E: BJ's, Best Buy, Circuit City, Goodyear, Home Depot, Kaufmann Tires, Lowe's, Office Max, PetSmart, Target, Wal-Mart sc, Outlet Mall, Tourist Info W: Auto Dealers, BJ's, Office Depot, Publix, Tires Plus, Target, UPS Store, Univ of W GA/Newnan
(Future)		FUTURE 2010: Poplar Rd, to GA 26, GA 34, 154
	Med	W: (FUTURE)+ Piedmont Newnan Hosp
41		US 27A, US 29, GA 14, to GA 16, Newnan, Moreland
	TStop	E: Pilot Travel Center # 422 (Scales) W: Greenway Stores #612/BP (Scales)
	Gas	W: Phillips 66
	Food	E: Subway/Wendy's/Pilot TC W: McDonald's, Waffle House
	Lodg	W: Days Inn, Ramada, Rodeway Inn, Super 8
	TWash	E: Pilot TC
	Other	E: Laundry/WiFi/RVDump/Pilot TC, Newnan-Coweta Co Airport✈
35		US 29, GA 14, Grantville, Moreland
	Gas	W: Phillips 66◊
28		GA 54, GA 100, Hogansville
	FStop	W: Money Back #14/AmocoBP
	TStop	W: Hogansville 66 Truck Plaza (Scales), Love's Travel Stop #376 (Scales)
	Gas	E: Shell
	Food	E: Janie's Country Kitchen W: Rest/66 TP, Arby's/Love's TS, McDonald's, Rogers BBQ, Subway, Waffle House, Wendy's
	Lodg	W: Days Inn, Econo Lodge
	TWash	W: Baileys TW/66 TP
	Tires	W: 66 TP
	Other	W: Flat Creek Campground▲
(22)		Weigh Station (Both dir)
(21)		Jct I-185S, to Columbus, Ft Benning
18		GA 109, Greenville Rd, LaGrange, Greenville, Warm Springs
	Gas	E: Chevron◊ W: RaceTrac, Shell◊, BP◊, Spectrum◊
	Food	W: Applebee's, Burger King, Church's Chicken, Cracker Barrel, Hoofer's Rest, IHOP, Ryan's Grill, Subway, Waffle House, Wendy's, Zaxby's
	Lodg	W: AmeriHost Inn, Best Western, Holiday Inn Express, Jameson Inn, Quality Inn, Super 8
	Med	W: + Hospital
	Other	W: ATMs, Auto Dealers, Auto Repairs, Banks, Home Depot, Wal-Mart, LaGrange Mall, Hoofers RV Park▲
14		US 27, GA 1, LaGrange
	Gas	W: BP, Pure Food Mart
	Food	W: Church's Chicken
	Lodg	W: Hampton Inn
	Other	W: GA State Hwy Patrol Post
13		GA 219, Whitesville Rd, LaGrange
	FStop	W: Money Back #5/AmocoBP
	TStop	E: LaGrange Travel Center/Shell (Scales) W: Pilot Travel Center #69 (Scales)
	Food	E: Rest/LaGrange TC, Waffle House W: Subway/Pilot TC, McDonald's
	Lodg	E: Days Inn
	TServ	E: LaGrange TC/Tires
	Med	W: + West GA Medical Center

EXIT		GA / AL
	Other	E: Laundry/WiFi/LaGrange TC W: WiFi/Pilot TC, GA Tech, Callaway Airport✈
2		GA 18, West Point, Pine Mountain, Callaway Gardens
	Gas	E: Shell◊
	Food	E: KFC, Subway, Church's Chkicken
	Lodg	E: Travelodge
(1)		GA Welcome Center (NB) (RR, Phone, Picnic, Vend, Info)
		(EASTERN TIME ZONE)

○ **GEORGIA**
◎ **ALABAMA**

(EASTERN / CENTRAL TIME ZONE)

EXIT		
79		US 29, AL 15, Valley, Lanett
	Gas	E: BP◊ W: Jet Pep, QV, Phillips 66◊
	Food	E: Burger King, Captain D's, Hardee's, McDonald's, KFC, Krystal, Taco Bell, Waffle House, Wendy's
	Lodg	W: Days Inn, Econo Lodge
	Med	E: + Hospital
	Other	E: Dollar General, Dollar Tree, Pharmacy, Wal-Mart sc, to Valley View Airport✈ W: CVS, Kroger
(78)		AL Welcome Center (SB) (RR, Phone, Picnic, Vend, RVDump)
77		CR 208, Valley, Huguley
	TStop	E: Spectrum #40
	Food	E: Waffle King
	Lodg	E: Holiday Inn Express
	Med	E: + Hospital
NOTE:		MM 76: Eastern / Central Time Zone
70		CR 388, to Cusseta
	TStop	E: AmBest/Bridges Travel Plaza/Shell (Scales)
	Gas	E: BP
	Food	E: CountryPride/Subway/Bridges TP
	TWash	E: Bridges TP
	TServ	E: Bridges TP/Tires
	Other	E: Laundry/Bridges TP
66		Andrews Rd, to US 29, AL 15
64		US 29, AL 15N, Opelika
	Gas	E: BP W: Tiger Fuel◊
	Lodg	E: GuestHouse Int'l
62		US 280E, US 431, Opelika, Phenix City
	FStop	E: Spectrum #22/BP
	Gas	E: Chevron, Libert W: Jet Pep, Shell
	Food	E: Burger King, Denny's, McDonald's, Shoney's, Subway W: Cracker Barrel, Waffle House, Western Sizzlin'
	Lodg	E: Holiday Inn, Knights Inn, Red Carpet Inn, Travelodge W: Comfort Inn, Days Inn, Econo Lodge, Motel 6, Travelodge
	Other	E: Lakeside RV Park▲, Opelika RV Outlet W: Auto Dealers, Grocery, Outlet Mall, Flea Market, Harley Davidson
60		AL 51, AL 169, Opelika, Hurtsboro
	Gas	E: BP◊, RaceTrac W: Shell◊

◊ = Regular Gas Stations with Diesel   ▲ = RV Friendly Locations   ♥ = Pet Friendly Locations
RED PRINT SHOWS LARGE VEHICLE PARKING/ACCESS ON SITE OR NEARBY   BROWN PRINT SHOWS CAMPGROUNDS/RV PARKS

EXIT		ALABAMA
	Food	E: Hardee's W: Krystal, Wendy's
58		US 280W, AL 38W, Gateway Dr, Opelika
	Gas	W: BP, Chevron, Liberty
	Food	W: Arby's, ChickFilA, Golden Corral, Outback Steakhouse, Starbucks, Subway, Taco Bell
	Lodg	W: Best Western, Homestead Suites, Tiger Inn
	Med	W: + East AL Medical Center
	Other	W: Home Depot, Lowe's, Office Depot, Target
57		Glenn Ave, Auburn
	Gas	W: Exxon, QV
	Lodg	W: Hilton Garden Inn
	Other	W: Auburn Opelika Airport✈
51		US 29, AL 147, College St, Auburn
	Gas	E: BP◊ W: RaceWay, Exxon
	Food	W: Arby's, Krystal, McDonald's, Ruby Tuesday, Waffle House,
	Lodg	E: Best Western, Hampton Inn, Sleep Inn W: Comfort Inn, Econo Lodge, Microtel♥, Sleep Inn
	Other	E: Leisure Time Campground▲, Bar W RV Park▲, Chewacle State Park▲ W: Wal-Mart sc, to Auburn Univ
(44)		Rest Area (Both dir) (RR, Phone, Picnic, Vend, Sec247, RVDump)
42		AL 186E, to US 80, Wire Rd, Tuskegee, to Phenix City, Columbus
	TStop	W: PacPr/Torch 85 Truck Stop/AmocoBP
	Food	W: Rest/Torch 85 TS
	TWash	W: Torch 85 TS
	Tires	W: Torch 85 TS
38		AL 81, Tuskegee, Notasulga
	Other	E: to airport
32		AL 49N, Tuskegee, Franklin
	Gas	E: BP◊
	Med	E: + Hospital
	Other	E: to Tuskegee Univ
26		AL 229N, Franklin Rd, Tallassee
	Gas	E: Shell
22		to US 80, AL 138 to AL 8, Shorter
	TStop	E: Petro 2/Chevron (Scales) (DAND)
	Gas	E: Exxon◊
	Food	E: QuickSkillet/Petro2
	Lodg	E: Days Inn
	Other	E: Laundry/WiFi/Petro2, Wind Drift Travel Park▲, Macon Co Greyhound Park
16		AL 126, Cecil, Waugh, Mt Meigs
	FStop	E: Entec BP
	Food	E: Subway/BP
(13)		Future Exit-Montgomery Outer Lp
11		US 80, AL 110, Mitylene, Mt Meigs
	Gas	E: Exxon◊, Liberty◊ W: Chevron◊
	Food	E: Cracker Barrel, Waffle House
	Lodg	E: Best Western, Holiday Inn Express

EXIT		ALABAMA
9		AL 271, to US 231, to Taylor Rd, Auburn Univ at Montgomery
	Gas	W: Citgo◊
	Food	E: Applebee's, Arby's, Bonefish Grill, ChickFilA, Chili's, McDonald's, Moe's SW Grill, Ruby Tuesday, Starbucks, Subway, Wendy's, Whataburger
	Lodg	E: Hampton Inn
	Med	W: + Hospital
	Other	E: The Shoppes at Eastchase W: Southern Christian Univ, Auburn Univ/Montgomery, Golf Course
6		US 80, US 231, AL 21, Eastern Blvd, Wetumpka, Troy, Maxwell AFB
	Gas	E: Chevron, Exxon◊, Liberty, RaceWay, Texaco W: BP, Citgo, Liberty◊, Shell
	Food	E: Arby's, Carrabba's, ChickFilA, Cracker Barrel, Don Pablo, Golden Corral, KFC, McDonald's, O'Charley's, Olive Garden, Popeye's, Shogun, Smokey Bones BBQ, Starbucks, Taco Bell, Texas Roadhouse, Waffle House, Wendy's, Whataburger, Zaxby's W: Burger King, Lone Star Steakhouse, McDonald's, Outback Steakhouse, Waffle House
	Lodg	E: Best Inn, Comfort Inn, Country Inn, Courtyard, Extended Stay America, Fairfield Inn, Hampton Inn, Quality Inn, Residence Inn, Springhill Suites, Super 8 W: Best Western, Comfort Suites, Drury Inn, Econo Lodge♥, Motel 6
	Other	E: Home Depot, Lowe's, PetSmart♥, Radio Shack, Target, Wal-Mart sc W: Auto Dealers, Sam's Club, to Eastdale Mall, Faulkner Univ, Gunter AFB
4		Perry Hill Rd
	Gas	W: Chevron
	Food	W: Hardee's
	Lodg	W: Hilton Garden Inn, Homewood Suites
	Other	E: Grocery, Pharmacy
3		Ann St
	Gas	E: BP◊, Chevron W: Exxon, PaceCar, Murphy
	Food	E: Arby's, Captain D's, Dominos, Hardee's, KFC, Krystals, McDonald's, Taco Bell, Waffle House, Wendy's
	Lodg	E: Days Inn
	Other	E: Big 10 Tire W: Wal-Mart sc
2		Mulberry St (SB), Forest Ave (NB)
	Med	W: + Jackson Hospital
	Other	W: Huntingdon College
1		Union St (SB), Court St (NB), Downtown
	Gas	E: BP◊, Exxon
	Med	W: + Hospital
	Other	E: to AL State Univ W: Bank, to Troy State Univ, Crawford Stadium

(I-85 Begins/Ends on I-65, Exit #171)
(CENTRAL TIME ZONE)

ALABAMA

Begin NB I-85 from Jct I-65 in Montgomery, AL, to Jct I-95 near Richmond, VA.

◊ = Regular Gas Stations with Diesel   ▲ = RV Friendly Locations   ♥ = Pet Friendly Locations
RED PRINT SHOWS LARGE VEHICLE PARKING/ACCESS ON SITE OR NEARBY   BROWN PRINT SHOWS CAMPGROUNDS/RV PARKS

EXIT **IDAHO**

Begin Eastbound I-86 from Jct I-84 near Burley, ID to Jct I-15, Pocatello, ID.

🈁 IDAHO

(MOUNTAIN TIME ZONE)
(I-86 Begins/Ends on I-15, Ex #72)
(I-86 Begins/Ends on I-84, Ex #222)

Exit		
(1)		Jct I-84E, to Ogden (WB)
15		Raft River Rd, Yale Rd N, Albion, Raft River Area
(19)		Rest Area (EB) (RR, Phone, Picnic, Vend)
21		Barkdull Rd, Coldwater Rd, Osborn Lp, Coldwater Area, American Falls
28		Register Rd, Park Lane, Massacre Rocks State Park
	Other	N: to Massacre Rocks State Park/RVCamp/RVDump▲
(31)		Rest Area (WB) (RR, Phone, Picnic, Vend, Trails)
33		Rock Creek Rd, Neeley
36		I-86 Bus, American Falls, ID 37S, Rockland Hwy, Rockland
	Gas	N: Jackson Food Store/Shell◇
	Lodg	N: Falls Motel
	Med	N: + Harms Memorial Hospital
	Other	W: Indian Springs Swimming & RV Park▲
40		Lakeview Rd, I-86 Bus, American ID 39N, Aberdeen
	Gas	N: Phillips 66◇
	Food	N: Pizza Hut, Mexican Rest
	Lodg	N: American Motel
		S: Hillview Motel ♥
	Med	N: + Harms Memorial Hospital
	Other	N: NAPA, Les Schwab Tires, American Falls Airport✈, Amer Falls Police Dept, to Willow Bay Rec Area, American Falls Rec Area

EXIT **IDAHO**

44		Ramsey Rd, Boone Lane
49		Gas Plant Rd, Schaffer Lane, Rainbow Rd
	Other	Fort Hall Indian Reservation
52		Arbon Valley Hwy, Pocatello
	FStop	S: Bannock Peak Truck Stop/Sinclair
	Food	S: FastFood/Bannock TS
	Other	S: Sho-Ban Gaming Casino Outpost

EXIT **IDAHO**

56		Terminal Way, Pocatello Airport
	TStop	S: Jet Stop/Exxon (Scales)
	Food	S: FastFood/JetStop
	Other	N: Pocatello Reg'l Airport✈
		S: LP/Jet Stop
58		US 30E, Garrett Way, Pocatello (Access to Ex #61 Serv)
	FStop	E: Smoking Hot Deals/Sinclair
		W: Cowboy West Truck Stop
	Food	W: Shifters Café/Cowboy West TS
	Other	E: to ParkAway RV Center, Bish's RV Supercenter, Bob's Intermountain RV & Marina Sales
		W: LP/Cowboy W TS
61		US 91, Yellowstone Ave, Chubbuck, Pocatello
	FStop	N: Jackson Food Stop #30/Shell
		S: Flying J C Store
	Gas	N: Exxon
		S: Phillips 66◇
	Food	N: FastFood/Jackson FS, Artic Circle, Burger King, Johnny B Goode, Pizza Hut, Subway, Wendy's
		S: Del Taco, Denny's, IHOP, McDonald's, Red Lobster, Subway
	Lodg	N: Motel 6 ♥, Ramada
	TServ	S: Western States Equipment/CAT, Kenworth
	Other	N: ATMs, Banks, Family Dollar, Grocery, U-Haul, Budget RV Park▲, Crossroads RV Center▲, Intermountain Golf Cars
		S: RVDump/Jackson FS, ATMs, Banks, Home Depot, Kmart, Lowe's, PetCo♥, ShopKO, Staples, Starbucks, UPS Store, Wal-Mart sc, Walgreen's, Eagle Rock Harley Davidson, Pine Ridge Mall, Westwood Mall, Bish's RV Supercenter
(63AB)		Jct I-15, N to Idaho Falls, Butte; S to Salt Lake City (Serv at 1st Ex I-15S)

(I-86 Begins/Ends on I-84, Ex #222)
(I-86 Begins/Ends on I-15, Ex #72)

(MOUNTAIN TIME ZONE)

🎧 IDAHO

Begin Westbound I-86 from Jct I-15 near Pocatello, ID to Jct I-84 near Burley, ID.

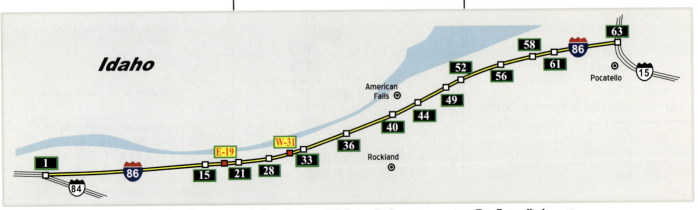

◇ = Regular Gas Stations with Diesel ▲ = RV Friendly Locations ♥ = Pet Friendly Locations
RED PRINT SHOWS LARGE VEHICLE PARKING/ACCESS ON SITE OR NEARBY   BROWN PRINT SHOWS CAMPGROUNDS/RV PARKS

INTERSTATE 86 E

EXIT	PA / NY	EXIT	NEW YORK	EXIT	NEW YORK
	Begin Eastbound I-86 from North East, PA to Jct I-87 near Highland Falls, NY.	20/10	to NY 430W (EB, Left Exit)	Food	N: McDonald's, Burger King
		Other	N: Wildwood Acres Campground▲	Other	N: LP/Seneca OneStop, Seneca-Iroquis Museum, Rail Museum, Casino
	PENNSYLVANIA (EASTERN TIME ZONE)	21/10	NY 430, Bemus Point (WB)	60/21	US 219N, Parkway Dr, Salamanca
	(I-86 Begins/Ends on I-90, Exit #37)	(24)	NY Welcome Center (EB) (RR, Phone, Picnic, Info)	(22)	PROPOSED NEW EXIT US 219N, Springville, Buffalo
	(I-86 Begins/Ends on I-87, Exit #16)	(24)	Weigh Station (EB)	69/23	US 219S, Limestone, Carrollton, Bradford, PA
(1A)	Jct I-90W, to Erie	26/11	Strunk Rd, Jamestown	TStop	N: M&M Allegany Jct Truck Stop
(1B)	Jct I-90E, to Buffalo	Lodg	S: Apple Inn	Food	N: Subway/Allegany TS
3	PA 89, North East, Wattsburg	28/12	NY 60, N Main St, Jamestown	(71)	Seneca Nation Allegany Res (WB)
Other	N: Lake Erie Speedway	TStop	S: Main Express Travel Plaza/Mobil	(73)	Rest Area (WB) (RR, Phone, Picnic, Info)
	S: Moon Meadows Campground▲, Creekside Campground▲	Gas	N: KwikFill◇	(73)	Weigh Station (WB)
	(EASTERN TIME ZONE)	Food	S: McDonald's/Main Express, Bob Evans	75/24	NY 417, W Five Mile Rd, Allegany
	PENNSYLVANIA	Lodg	S: Comfort Inn, Hampton Inn	Lodg	S: Country Inn & Suites, Allegany Motel, Lantern Motel
	NEW YORK (EASTERN TIME ZONE)	Other	N: Harley Davidson, Chautauqua Co Jamestown Airport✈	Other	S: St Bonaventure Univ
	NOTE: NYS does NOT use Mile Marker Exits. Listed is MileMarker / Exit #.		S: Airport✈, Jamestown Comm College, NY State Hwy Patrol Post	78/25	Buffalo St, Olean (Serv 2-3 mi S on Constitution Ave)
1/4	NY 426, N East Rd, to NY 430, Sherman, Findley Lake	31/13	NY 394, E Main St, Falconer	Gas	S: Citgo, KwikFill
Food	N: I-86 Express Rest	Gas	S: Mobil	Food	S: Applebee's, Burger King, Pizza Hut, Quiznos, Tim Horton's
	S: Curly Maple Rest, Country Kitchen	Food	S: Burger King	Lodg	S: Comfort Inn, Country Inn, Microtel
Lodg	N: Holiday Inn Express	Lodg	S: Budget Inn, Red Roof Inn♥	Other	S: Convention Center, BJ's, Home Depot, Wal-Mart
	S: Blue Heron Inn, Findley Lake Inn	36/14	US 62, Frewsburg Rd, Kennedy, Warren, PA	79/26	NY 16, N Union St Ext, Olean
Other	N: Family Affair Campground▲	Other	S: to Forest Haven Campground▲, Homestead Park Campground▲, Kinzua Lake Campground▲	Gas	S: Wilson Farms/Mobil
	S: Peek 'n Peak Resort & Conf Center▲, Peek 'n Peak Ski Resort, to French Creek R&R Campground▲, Paradise Bay Park Campground▲	(38)	Picnic Area (Phone) (WB)	Food	S: Burger King
10/6	NY 76, Osborne St, Sherman	38/15	School House Rd, Randolph	Lodg	S: Hampton Inn
Gas	N: Sherman Service Center, Sherman Country General	Other	S: Randolph Airport✈	Med	S: + Olean General Hospital
Food	N: Village Pizzeria	(39)	Picnic Area (Phone) (EB)	87/27	NY 16, NY 446, Hinsdale
Lodg	N: Sherman Hotel, Millers Angel Inn	40/16	W Main St, Randolph, Gowanda	Gas	S: Crosby Dairyland
16/7	CR 33, Panama-Stedman Rd, Panama	TStop	N: Wilson Farms #166/Mobil	Food	N: Burger King, Denny's Hut Family
18/8	NY 394, W Lake Rd, Ashville, to Mayville, Lakewood	Food	N: Rest/FastFood/Wilson Farms, R&M Rest	Other	N: Triple R Camping Resort & Trailer Sales▲, to Cattaraugus Co Olean Airport✈, Olean Munil Airport✈, to Emerald Acres Campground▲, Whispering Pine Campground▲
Gas	N: Hogan's Hut/Mobil◇	Other	N: WiFi/LP/Wilson Farms, Pope Haven Campground▲	92/28	NY 305, Genesee St, Cuba
Other	S: James Lakefront Camping▲	(45)	Seneca Nation Allegany Res (EB)	Gas	S: Exxon, Sunoco
20/9	NY 430E, E Lake Rd, Main St, Bemus Point (EB ex, WB entr)	46/17	NY 394, W Perimeter Rd, Randolph, Steamburg, Onoville	Food	N: Cruisers Cafe
Gas	N: Bridgeview One Stop/Mobil	TStop	S: M&M Diesel Mart		S: Fox's Pizza Den, McDonald's
Food	N: Gracie's on Main, Main St Pizzeria, Italian Fisherman	Food	N: HideAWay Rest	Lodg	N: Cuba Coachlight Motel
Lodg	N: Lenhart Hotel, Redwood Ranch Motel	Other	N: Highbank Campground▲		S: St James Hotel
			S: LP/M&M Diesel Mart	Other	N: Maple Lane Campground & RV Park▲
		48/18	NY 280, Salamanca, Allegany State Park, Quaker Run Area	99/29	NY 275, Friendship, Bolivar
		52/19	Allegany State Park Rd 2, Red House Area, Salamanca	Gas	S: Mobil
		57/20	NY 353, NY 417, Broad St, Salamanca	Food	S: Subway
		FStop	N: Seneca One Stop	(101)	Rest Area (EB) (RR, Phone, Picnic)

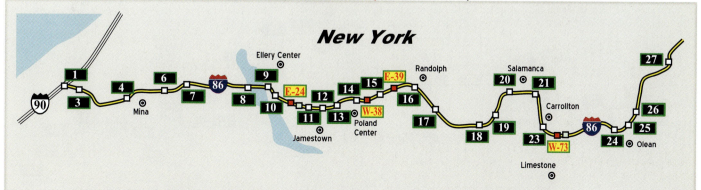

◇= Regular Gas Stations with Diesel   ▲= RV Friendly Locations   ♥= Pet Friendly Locations
RED PRINT SHOWS LARGE VEHICLE PARKING/ACCESS ON SITE OR NEARBY   BROWN PRINT SHOWS CAMPGROUNDS/RV PARKS

INTERSTATE 86

EXIT		NEW YORK
(101)		Weigh Station (EB)
105/30		NY 19, Belmont, Wellsville
	TStop	S: All American Plaza
	Food	S: Rest/All Amer Pl
	TWash	S: All Amer Pl
	Other	N: to appr 9mi Evergreen Trails Campground▲
		S: WiFi/LP/All Amer Pl, Riverside Park Campground▲
109/31		Clossek Ave, Angelica
	Gas	N: Citgo
	Food	N: Rest/American Hotel
	Lodg	N: Park Circle B&B, American Hotel
	Other	N: to McCarthy Ranch▲, Allegany Co Fairgrounds
117/32		CR 2, Karrdale Ave, West Almond
	NOTE:	MM 117.2: WB: Highest Elev on I-86 MM 117.3: EB: 2080'
124/33		CR 2, Karr Valley Rd, to NY 21, Almond, Andover
	Gas	S: Tops Market/Mobil
	Other	S: Lake Lodge Campground▲, Kanakadea Park Campgrounds▲
(125)		Scenic View (EB)
129/34		NY 36, Genesee St, Arkport, Hornell
	Food	N: Dunkin Donuts, McDonald's
		S: Angel's, Ruperts
	Lodg	S: Econo Lodge
	Other	N: Wal-Mart, to appr 7 mi Sun Valley Campsites▲, to Sugar Creek Glen Campground▲
		S: Kanakadea Park Campground▲
138/35		CR 70, Avoca, Howard
	Other	S: to Lake Demmon Rec Area
(146/36)		Jct I-390N, NY 15N, Rochester (fr WB, Left Exit)
	Other	N: to Tumble Hill Campground▲
146.5/37		NY 53, Bath, Kanona, Prattsburg
	TStop	S: Wilson Farms AmBest #167/Sunoco (Scales), Pilot Travel Center #322 (Scales)
	Food	S: Rest/Wilson Farms, Subway/Pilot TC
	TWash	S: Wilson Farms
	Other	N: to Wagon Wheel Campground▲
		S: Laundry/WiFi/LP/Wilson Farms, Laundry/WiFi/Pilot TC
(147)		Rest Area (WB) (RR, Phone, Picnic)
150/38		NY 54, W Washington St, Bath, Hammondsport
	Gas	N: KwikFill, Mobil
	Food	N: Arby's, Burger King, Chinese Buffet, Dunkin Donuts, McDonald's, Pizza Hut

EXIT		NEW YORK
	Lodg	N: Budget Inn, Days Inn
	Med	S: + US Veterans Medical Center
	Other	N: Advance Auto, Auto Repair, Grocery, Kmart, Hickory Hill Family Camping Resort▲, Campers Haven▲, NY State Police
		S: Wilkens RV Center
153/39		CR 11, Babcock Hollow Rd, to NY 415, Bath
	Other	N: to Sanford Lake
		S: Babcock Hollow Campground▲
157/40		NY 226, CR 12, Lamoka Ave, Savona
	Gas	N: Savona Arrow Mart/Mobil◆
	Food	N: Mom's Savona Diner, Subway/Mobil
(160)		Rest Area (EB) (RR, Phone, Picnic)
(101)		Weigh Station (EB)
161/41		CR 333, Campbell
	Gas	S: Sunoco
	Other	N: Campbell Camping
		S: to Cardinal Campground▲
165/42		CR 26, Meads Creek Rd, to NY 415, Painted Post, Coopers Plains
	Other	N: NY State Police
(167)		Picnic Area (Phone) (WB)
168/43		NY 415, Coopers-Bath Rd, Painted Post
	Gas	N: Pump n Pantry, Wilson Farms
		S: Sunoco
	Food	N: Burger King, Denny's, McDonald's, Pizza Hut
	Lodg	S: Hampton Inn
	Other	N: CarQuest, Pharmacy
169/44		US 15S, NY 417W, Painted Post, Future 99, Gang Mills, Williamsport
	Lodg	S: Best Western, Holiday Inn
170/45		NY 415, Coopers-Bath Rd, Riverside (WB ex, EB entr), NY 352, Denison Pkwy, Downtown Corning (EB ex, WB entr)
	Food	S: Bob Evans, Burger King, Ponderosa, Subway, Wendy's
	Lodg	S: Fairfield Inn
172/46		NY 414, Corning, Watkins Glen
	Gas	S: Citgo◆
	Food	S: Garcia's Mexican, Pizza Hut
	Lodg	S: Comfort Inn, Days Inn, Staybridge Suites♥, Radisson Hotel♥
	Other	N: Corning KOA▲, to appr 5mi Ferenbaugh Campsites▲
		S: Corning Museum of Glass, to Sunflower Acres Family Campground▲

EXIT		NEW YORK
175/47		NY 352, Gibson, Downtown
176.8/48		NY 352, East Corning
	Gas	S: Citgo
178/49		Olcott Rd, Canal St, Big Flats
	Other	N: Elmira/Corning Reg'l Airport✈
180/50		CR 63, Kahler Rd, Elmira
	Other	N: Elmira/Corning Reg'l Airport✈, Soaring Museum
181/51A		CR 35, Chambers Rd, Elmira
	Gas	N: Mobil◆, Sunoco◆
	Food	N: Chili's, McDonald's, Olive Garden, Outback Steakhouse, Red Lobster, Ruby Tuesday
		S: Applebee's, China Inn, Panera Bread, TGI Friday
	Lodg	N: Country Inn, Hilton Garden Inn
		S: Econo Lodge, Relax Inn
	Other	N: Firestone, Mall
		S: B&N, Best Buy, Grocery, Petco♥, Lowe's, Sam's Club, Staples, Wal-Mart
181/51B		Colonial Dr (WB, exit only) (Access to Ex #51 Serv)
182/52 A		Commerce Center Dr (EB) (Access to Ex #51 Serv)
52B		NY 14, CR 64, Elmira, Watkins Glen (EB)
52AB		NY 14, CR 64, Watkins Glen, Elmira (WB)
	Lodg	N: Holiday Inn, Howard Johnson
183.5/53		Horseheads
185/54		NY 13, to Ithaca, Horseheads, to Cayuga Lake
189/56		NY 352, Church St (EB), CR1, Water St (WB), Elmira, Jerusalem Hill
	Gas	S: Citgo, KwikFill
	Food	S: Hoss's Steak & Sea House, Pizza Hut, McDonald's
	Lodg	S: Holiday Inn
195/58		CR 2/8/60, Lowman, Wellsburg
	Other	S: Gardner Hill Campground▲
(199)		Rest Area (WB) (RR, Phone, Picnic)
200/59		NY 427, CR 3, CR 60, Wyncoop Creek Rd, Chemung, Wellsburg
	FStop	N: Dandy Mini Mart #10
203/59A		CR 56, White Wagon Rd, Waverly, Wilawana, PA

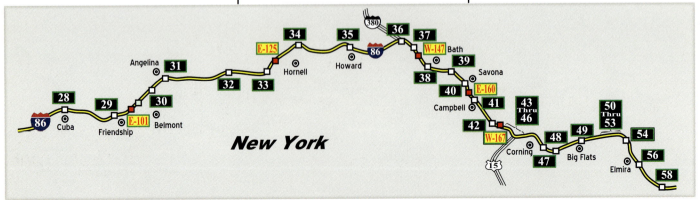

◆ = Regular Gas Stations with Diesel ▲ = RV Friendly Locations ♥ = Pet Friendly Locations
RED PRINT SHOWS LARGE VEHICLE PARKING/ACCESS ON SITE OR NEARBY BROWN PRINT SHOWS CAMPGROUNDS/RV PARKS

INTERSTATE 86 W/E

EXIT	NEW YORK
	NOTE: MM 204.2: State Border
205/60	US 220, to Waverly NY, Sayre, PA
Gas	S: Citgo, Mobil
Lodg	N: O'Brien's Inn
Other	S: Kmart, Grocery, RiteAid
	NOTE: MM 205.8: State Border
206/61	NY 34, PA 199, to Waverly NY, Sayre, PA
Gas	S: KwikFill, Citgo
Food	S: McDonald's
Lodg	S: Best Western
Other	S: Home Depot
	S: Joe's RV Center
(212)	Rest Area (EB) (RR, Phone, Picnic)
(212)	Weigh Station (EB)
215/62	NY 282, River Rd, Nichols
FStop	S: Dandy Mini Mart #14/Citgo
Other	S: RV Center
219/63	CR 509, Stanton Hill Rd, CR 502, River Rd, Nichols, Lounsberry
TStop	S: Lounsberry Truck Stop/Exxon
Food	S: Lounsberry TS
Other	S: WiFi/LP/Lounsberry TS
(221)	Rest Area (WB) (RR, Phone, Picnic)
(221)	Weigh Station (WB)
224/64	CR 503, Southside Dr (EB), NY 434, (WB), to NY 96, Owego, Ithaca
224/65	NY 17C, NY 434, Owego
Gas	N: Mobil◊
Food	N: Burger King, KFC, Subway, Wendy's
Lodg	N: Hampton Inn, Holiday Inn Express
Other	N: Grocery, Pharmacy
231/66	NY 434, Valley View Dr, NY 17C, Apalachin, Endicott, Campville
FStop	S: Express Mart #357/Mobil
Gas	S: KwikFill
Food	S: Blue Dolphin Diner, McDonald's
Lodg	S: Dolphin Inn, Quality Inn
TWash	S: Express Mart
Other	S: LP/Express Mart
237/67	NY 26, to NY 434, Endicott, Vestal (Serv S on NY 26 to NY 434)
Gas	S: Valero
Food	S: Burger King, McDonald's, Olive Garden, Red Lobster, Starbucks, Subway, Taco Bell, TGI Friday, Uno Pizza
Other	N: Tri-Cities Airport✈
	S: Advance Auto, Grocery, Lowe's, Sam's Club, Tires, Wal-Mart

EXIT	NEW YORK
238/68	CR 44, Old Vestal Rd (EB ex, WB entr) (NO Re-entry to NY 17)
240/69	NY 17C, E to Westover (EB ex, WB entr) W to Endwell (WB ex, EB entr)
241/70	NY 201S, Johnson City
Gas	N: Exxon, Hess, Valero
Food	N: Blimpie, Friendly's, Great China Buffet, Buffet, McDonald's, Pizza Hut, Ponderosa, Quiznos, Ruby Tuesday, Taco Bell
Lodg	N: Best Western, Hampton Inn
Other	N: Grocery, Gander Mountain, Mall
	S: Home Depot
243/71	CR 69, Airport Rd, Binghamton (EB) Airport Rd, Johnson City (WB)
Other	N: Binghamton Reg'l/Edwin Link Field✈
244/72	Mygatt St, Clinton St (WB, exit only), US 11, Front St (EB, exit only)
	NOTE: MM 244.5: EB: Kamikaze Curve ALERT
(245)	Jct I-81N, to I-88, Syracuse, Albany (EB, Left Exit) NY 17W, Owego, Elmira (WB, Left Exit)
	NOTE: I-81 below runs with NY 17. Exit #'s are I-81, Mile Marker / Exit #.
12/4	NY 7, Binghamton, Hillcrest
Gas	W: Express Mart, Mobil
Food	W: Subway
Lodg	W: Howard Johnson, Super 8
Other	W: ATM, CVS, Grocery
12/3	Broad Ave, Downtown (WB ex, EB entr)
Gas	W: Exxon
9/3	Colesville Rd, Industrial Park Binghamton (EB exit, WB entr)
TStop	W: NB: Access Via Ex #2: Travel Center of America #207 (Scales), Pilot Travel Center #170 (Scales)
Gas	W: Exxon
Food	W: Buckhorn/TA TC, Wendy's/Pilot TC, KFC, McDonald's
Lodg	W: Del Motel, Holiday Inn, Super 8, Wright Motel
Other	W: Laundry/WiFi/TA TC, Laundry/WiFi/ Pilot TC, CVS, Grocery
(7/75)	NY 17, New York, I-86E (SB, Left Exit) Jct I-81, US 11, Binghamton, Scranton, PA (WB)
	NOTE: I-81 above runs with NY 17. Exit #'s are I-81, Mile Marker / Exit #.
251/76	Haskins Rd, Johnson Rd, Foley Rd, Windsor

EXIT	NEW YORK
254/77	CR 47, Place Rd, North Rd, West Windsor
Gas	N: Mobil◊
256/78	CR 28, Dunbar Rd, Windsor, Occanum
258/79	NY 79, Main St (EB), CR 28, Old NY 17, Chapel St, (WB), Windsor
Gas	N: Xtra Mart, Sunoco◊
Food	N: Pizza Wings & Things, Subway
	S: Yesteryear's Diner
Other	N: Lakeside Campground▲
261/80	CR 225, State Line Rd (EB), CR 28, Old NY 17 (WB), Damascus
Gas	N: Mighty Mart 7/Exxon◊
Food	N: J&K Family Diner
Other	N: Forest Lake Campground▲
263/81	E Bosket Rd, CR 28, Windsor
269/82	NY 41, McClure, Sanford
Other	N: Kellystone Park
	S: Oquaga Lake State Park, Guestward Ho Family Campground▲
273/83	CR 28, Old NY 17, Deposit, Oquaga Lake
Other	S: to Oquaga Lake
275/84	NY 8, NY 10, Deposit, Walton
Gas	N: Citgo◊, Deposit Country Store
Food	N: Wendy's, Timbers
Lodg	N: Deposit Motel, Laurel Bank Motel
Other	N: NY State Hwy Patrol Post
85	Hale Eddy
86	Silver Lake Rd, Roods Creek Rd
87	NY 97, to PA 191, NY 268, Cadosia, Hancock, Calicoun
Gas	S: Getty, Mobil, Sunoco
Food	S: Circle E Diner, McDonald's, Subway
Lodg	S: Colonial Motel
87A	NY 268, Old State Rd, Cadosia, Hancock (WB ex, EB entr)
292/89	CR 17, Old State Rd, Hancock, Fishs Eddy
(294)	Rest Area (WB) (RR, Phone, Picnic) Weigh Station (WB)
296/90	NY 30, Old State Rd, Harvard Rd, East Branch, Downsville
Gas	N: Sunoco
Other	N: Oxbow Campsites▲, Beaver Del Hotel & Campsites▲, Del Valley Campground▲, to appr 9mi Peaceful Valley Campsite▲

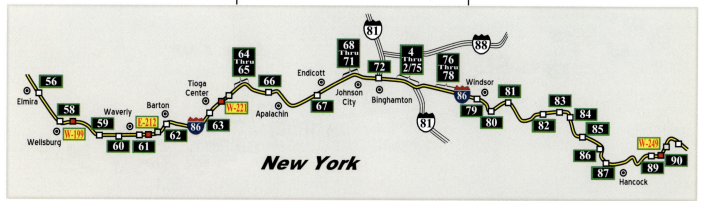

◊ = Regular Gas Stations with Diesel   ▲ = RV Friendly Locations   ♥ = Pet Friendly Locations

RED PRINT SHOWS LARGE VEHICLE PARKING/ACCESS ON SITE OR NEARBY   BROWN PRINT SHOWS CAMPGROUNDS/RV PARKS

Page 435

EXIT		NEW YORK
302/92		CR 17, Roscoe, Cooks Falls, Horton
	Gas	S: Sunoco◊
	Other	N: **Russell Brooks Campsites**▲
305/93		CR 17, Roscoe, Cooks Falls (WB exit, EB entr)
310/94		NY 206, Roscoe, Tennanah Lk (EB) Walton (WB), Oneonta, Lew Beach
	Gas	N: Exxon◊, Sunoco◊ S: Mobil
	Food	N: Roscoe Diner, 1910 Coffees Shop
	Lodg	N: Rockland House, Roscoe Motel, Tennanah Lake Motel
	Other	N: **Roscoe Campsites**▲, **Butternut Grove Campsites**▲, **Miller Hollow Campground**▲, **Beaverkill State Campgrounds**▲ S: **Twin Islands Campsites**▲
(313)		Rest Area (EB) (last rest area on I-86) (RR, Phone, Picnic, Vend)
(313)		Weigh Station (EB)
316/96		CR 178, White Roe Lake Rd, Livingston Manor, Lew Beach
318/97		CR 178, Livingston Manor, Morrston
321/98		CR 176, Parksville, Cooley
	Other	N: **Hunter Lake Campground**▲
324/99		Main St, to NY 52, to NY 55, Liberty
	Gas	S: Exxon, Sunoco
325/100A		NY 52, to NY 55, Liberty (WB ex, EB entr)
326/100		NY 52, Liberty, Loch Sheldrake
	Gas	N: Sunoco S: Citgo, Exxon◊, Mobil
	Food	N: Burger King, McDonald's, Taco Bell S: Dunkin Donuts
	Lodg	N: Best Inn, Days Inn S: Budget Inn, Lincoln Motel, Liberty Motel
	Other	N: **Neversink River Campground**▲, to appr 10 mi **Yogi Bear's Jellystone Park**▲ S: Auto Dealers, Grocery
327/101		Ferndale, Swan Lake
	Gas	S: Exxon
	Food	N: Manny's Steakhouse & Seafood S: Burger King, McDonald's, Wendy's
	Lodg	S: Days Inn
331/102		CR 174, to Harris-Bushville Rd, Monticello, Harris, Bushville
	Other	S: to **Swan Lake Campground**▲
333/103		Rapp Rd, Monticello (WB ex, EB entr)

EXIT		NEW YORK
335/104		NY 17B, Jefferson St, Monticello, Raceway
	Gas	S: Citgo, Exxon◊
	Food	S: Tilly's Diner
	Lodg	S: Best Western, Raceway Motel
	Other	S: to **Happy Days Campground**▲, **Swinging Bridge Lake Campground**▲, Raceway, Sullivan Co Int'l Airport✈
337/ 105AB		NY 42, Pleasant St, Monticello, to Kiamesha, Forestburg
	Gas	S: Citgo, Mobil, Stewarts, Valero
	Food	S: Burger King, Chinatown, Crown Fried Chicken, Pizza Hut, Wendy's
	Lodg	N: Rosemond Motel & **Campsites**▲ S: Econo Lodge, Ramada, Travel Inn
	Other	N: Wal-Mart sc, **Lazy G Campground**▲
339/106		Cimarron Rd, East Monticello (WB)
340/107		CR 173, CR 161, Heiden Rd, South Fallsburg, Monticello, Bridgeville
	Food	S: Mana Rest, Old Homestead Rest
341/108		CR 173, Holiday Mountain Trail, Monticello, Bridgeville (EB) (Access Services at Ex #109)
342/109		Katrina Falls Rd, Rock Hill Dr, to CR57/58, Rock Hill, Woodridge
	Gas	N: Exxon◊ S: Mobil
	Food	N: Rock Hill Diner, Land & Sea Rest
	Lodg	N: Rock Hill Lodge
	Other	N: **Hilltop Farm Campsites**▲, **Yogi Bear's Jellystone Camp**▲, **Mountaindale Campground**▲
343/110		Lake Louise Marie, Wanaksink Lake (EB), Fall Brook Rd, CR 172, Rock Hill, Lake Louise Marie, Wanaksink Lake, Wolf Lake (WB)
344/111		Wolf Lake Rd, Rock Hill (EB)
347/112		Masten Lake, Yankee Lake, Wurtsboro, Mountaindale
	Other	N: to **Catskill Mountain Ranch & Camping Club**▲
349/113		US 209, Wurtsboro, Ellenville
	Gas	N: Mobil◊, Stewarts
	Food	N: A&B Diner, Benny's Café, Danny's Village Inn, Subway S: Giovanni's Café
	Lodg	N: Days Inn ♥
	Other	N: **Berentsens Campground**▲ S: to appr 8mi **Oakland Valley Campground**▲, to **American Family Campground**▲

EXIT		NEW YORK
352/114		CR 171, Bloomingburg, Highview, Wurtsboro (WB, exit only) (Reacc next exits, No re-entry to NY17)
354/115		Burlingham Rd (WB ex, EB entr)
	Other	N: **Berentsens Campground**▲, **Rainbow Valley Campground**▲
354/116		NY 17K, Bloomingburg, Newburgh
	Gas	S: Citgo, Mobil
	Other	S: to **Korn's Campground**▲, **Rainbow Valley Campground**▲
357/118		CR 76, Bloomingburg Rd, Brown Rd, Middletown, Fair Oaks
	Gas	S: Exxon◊, Mobil
	Food	S: Fair Oaks Deli
	Lodg	N: Heritage Motel
359/119		NY 302, Middletown, Pine Bush
361/120		NY 211, Middletown, Montgomery
	Gas	N: Mobil, Sunoco S: Mobil
	Food	N: Olive Garden S: Arby's, Burger King, China Buffet, Denny's, KFC, Red Lobster, Taco Bell
	Lodg	N: Middletown Motel, Howard Johnson, Super 8
	Other	N: Best Buy, Grocery, Sam's Club, Wal-Mart S: AutoZone, Grocery, Home Depot, Kmart, Pharmacy, Staples, U-Haul
(362/121)		Jct I-84, E to Newburgh, W to Port Jervix
363/122		CR 67, Crystal Run Rd, E Main St
	Gas	N: Mobil S: Getty
	Food	N: TGI Friday, Outback Steakhouse
	Lodg	N: Hampton Inn, Holiday Inn, Marriott
	Other	S: Randall Airport✈, Fantasy Balloon Flights
365/122A		Fletcher St, Goshen
366/123		US 6W, NY 17M W, Middletown, Port Jervis, FUTURE I-86
369/124		NY 17A, to NY 207, Goshen, Florida
	Gas	N: Exxon, Mobil
	Food	N: Burger King, Goshen Diner, Pizza Hut
	Lodg	N: Comfort Inn, Goshen Inn
	Other	N: CVS S: **Black Bear Campground**▲
367.5/125		NY 17M E, South St, Future I-86
370/126		NY 94, Chester, Florida
	Gas	N: Shell, Sunoco
	Food	N: McDonald's, Wendy's
	Lodg	N: Holiday Inn Express

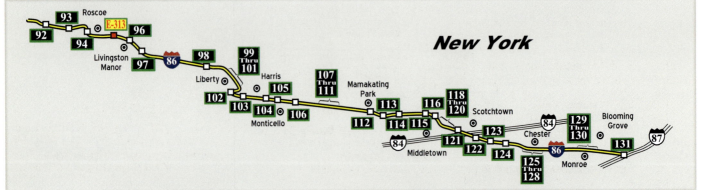

◊ = Regular Gas Stations with Diesel   ▲ = RV Friendly Locations   ♥ = Pet Friendly Locations
RED PRINT SHOWS LARGE VEHICLE PARKING/ACCESS ON SITE OR NEARBY   BROWN PRINT SHOWS CAMPGROUNDS/RV PARKS

INTERSTATE 86 W

EXIT		NEW YORK
	Other	N: Grocery, Pharmacy
		S: Black Bear Campground▲
372/127		Lehigh Ave, Chester, Greycourt Rd, Sugar Loaf, Warwick (WB ex, EB entr)
374/128		CR 51, Craigville Rd, Oxford Depot (WB Exit Only, NO Re-entry to NY 17)
375/129		Museum Village Rd, to Monroe (NO re-entry to NY 17)
376/130		NY 208, Monroe, Washingtonville
	Gas	N: Sunoco◆
		S: Mobil◆
	Food	S: Burger King, Pizza Hut
379/130A		US 6E, Bear Mountain, Future I-86, (EB exit, WB entr) (WB)
	Gas	S: Exxon, Mobil
	Food	S: Chili's, McDonald's, TGI Friday
	Other	N: Outlet Mall
		S: BJ's, Home Depot, Staples, Wal-Mart sc
379.6/131		NY 17S, NY 32, Newburgh, Suffern (EB), US 6E, NY 17S, NY 32, Harriman (WB)
(380)		Jct I-87, NY THRUWAY (TOLL), to Albany, New York (EB ex, WB entr), NY 17, Future I-86 (WB)
	NOTE:	NYS does NOT use Mile Marker Exits. Listed is Mile Marker / Exit #.

(I-86 Begins/Ends on I-87, Exit #16)
(EASTERN TIME ZONE)

⊙ NEW YORK

Begin I-86 at Jct I-87 to Jct I-90 near North East, PA.

INTERSTATE 87 S

EXIT		NEW YORK
		Begin Southbound I-87 from Champlain to NYC.

⊙ NEW YORK
(EASTERN TIME ZONE)
(I-87 Begins/Ends at the Canada Border)

NOTE: NYS does NOT use Mile Marker Exits. Listed is MileMarker / Exit #.

(333)		US/Canada Border, NY St Line US Customs/New York (SB), Canadian Customs/Quebec (NB)
333/43		US 9, Champlain
	TStop	W: Champlain Peterbilt (Scales)
	Food	W: FastFood/Peterbilt TS
	TWash	W: Peterbilt TS
	TServ	W: Peterbilt TS/Tires
	Other	E: World Duty Free
		W: Laundry/BarbSh/WiFi/LP/Peterbilt TS
331/42		US 11, Mooers, Rouses Point, Champlain
	FStop	W: Garceau Exxon
	TStop	W: Rte 11 Mobil, 11-87 Truck Plaza (Scales)
	Gas	E: Mobil
	Food	E: Peppercorn Family Rest, Chinese, Three Forks Pizza & Deli
		W: Rest/FastFood/11-87 TP, McDonald's, Subway
	TWash	W: 11-87 TP
	TServ	W: 11-87 TP/Tires
	Other	E: Grocery, Laundromat, Pharmacy
		W: WiFi/Garceau Exxon, Laundry/WiFi/ 11-87 TP
325/41		NY 191, CR 23, Chazy, Sciota
(319)		NY Welcome Center (SB) Rest Area (NB) (RR, Phone, Picnic, SB: Info, NY St Police
318/40		NY 456, Plattsburgh, Beekmantown, Point au Roche
	Gas	E: Mobil◆
	Food	E: Café/Stonehelm Motel
	Lodg	E: Stonehelm Motel
	Other	E: Monty's Bay Campsites▲
		W: Plattsburgh RV Park▲
314/39		NY 314, Moffitt Rd, Plattsburgh, Cumberland Head, Plattsburgh Bay
	Gas	E: Stewarts

EXIT		NEW YORK
	Food	E: Gus' Red Hots, McDonald's
	Lodg	E: Chateau Motel, Rip Van Winkle Motel, Super 8♥
	Other	E: Plattsburgh RV Park▲, Cumberland Bay State Park
		W: Shady Oaks RV Park▲
312/38		NY 22N, NY 374, Plattsburgh, to Tupper Lake, Sarnac Lake
	Gas	E: Mobil, Sunoco
	TServ	W: Plattsburgh Diesel Service
	Med	E: + Hospital
310/37		NY 3, Plattsburgh, Morrisonville, Saranac Lake
	Gas	E: Short Stop◆, Sunoco, Stewarts
		W: BP, Exxon, Mobil, Sunoco◆
	Food	E: Burger King, Domino's, IHOP, KFC, McDonald's, Papa John's, Pizza Hut, Quiznos, Subway, Wendy's
		W: Applebee's, Ponderosa, Red Lobster
	Lodg	E: Comfort Inn, Holiday Inn
		W: Baymont Inn, Best Western♥, Days Inn, Econo Lodge, Microtel, Quality Inn, Super 8
	Med	E: + Champlain Valley Hospital
	Other	E: Auto Dealers, Big Lots, Firestone, Grocery, Sam's Club, Wal-Mart sc, State Univ of NY, CarWash
		W: Auto Repair, Kmart, Grocery, Miidas, Wal-Mart sc, Lowe's, Clinton Co Airport✈, Twin Ells Campsites▲
308/36		NY 22, Plattsburgh Air Force Base, Lake Champlain Shore, Plattsburgh
	TStop	E: Exit 36 Truck Stop/Mobil (Scales)
	Gas	E: Citgo
	Tires	E: Exit 36 TS
	TServ	E: MA Jerry Co/International, Charlebois Truck Parts
		W: Phil's Auto & Truck Service
	Other	E: BarbSh/WiFi/LP/Exit 36 TS, Plattsburgh AFB
		W: NY State Police, to Northway Airport✈
(304)		NY Welcome Center (SB) Rest Area (NB) (RR, Phones, Picnic)
302/35		NY 442, Bear Swamp Rd, Peru, Valcour, Port Kent
	TStop	E: Chase's Mobil #2
	Gas	W: Wilson Farms, Mobil

EXIT		NEW YORK
	Food	E: Dunkin Donuts/Subway/Mobil
		W: Crickets, McDonald's
	TWash	E: Chase's
	Other	E: Amtrak, AuSable Point Campground▲ Iroquis RV Park & Campground▲, to appr 12mi AuSable Pines Campground & RV Sales▲
	NOTE:	MM 143: Begin SB Call Boxes, End NB
296/34		NY 9N, Keeseville, AuSable Chasm, AuSable Forks
	Gas	W: Sunoco◆
	Food	E: Mac's Diner, Pleasant Corner Rest
	Lodg	W: Shamrock Motel
	Other	E: Holiday Travel Park▲
		W: Lake Placid KOA, AuSable River Campsites▲, to appr 12mi AuSable Chasm Campground▲
292/33		US 9, NY 22, Keeseville, Willsboro, Essex-Ferry
	Gas	E: Mobil
	Lodg	E: Chesterfield Motel
281/32		CR 12, Stowersville Rd, Lewis, to Willsboro
	FStop	W: Pierce's Service Station
(280)		Picnic Area (NB, NO Trucks) Rest Area (SB) (RR, Phone, Picnic)
275/31		NY 9N, Westport, Elizabethtown
	Gas	E: Mobil
	Lodg	E: Hilltop Motel
	Med	W: + Hospital
	Other	E: NY State Police, to appr 7mi Barber Homestead Park▲
(270)		Rest Area (NB) (RR, Phone, Picnic)
262/30		US 9, NY 73, North Hudson, Keene, Keene Valley
	Other	W: Lake Placid KOA▲
(257)		Rest Area (Both dir) (RR, Phones, Picnic) NOTE: SB: Border Patrol
252/29		CR 2, Boreas Rd, North Hudson, Newcomb
	Other	E: Yogi Bear's Jellystone Park▲
		W: Blue Ridge Falls Campground▲

◆ = Regular Gas Stations with Diesel   ▲ = RV Friendly Locations   ♥ = Pet Friendly Locations
RED PRINT SHOWS LARGE VEHICLE PARKING/ACCESS ON SITE OR NEARBY   BROWN PRINT SHOWS CAMPGROUNDS/RV PARKS

EXIT		NEW YORK
240/28		NY 74E, Crown Point, Schroon Lake, Ticonderoga Ferry
	Gas	E: Sunoco◊, Stewarts
	Lodg	E: Starry Nite Cabins
	Other	E: On the River Campground▲, NY State Hwy Patrol Post, Medcalf Acres Riverfront Campground▲, Schroon Lake Airport✈
(239)		Rest Area (NB) (RR, Phones, Picnic)
239/27		US 9, Schroon Lake (NB, diff reacc)
	Gas	E: Stewarts
	Lodg	E: Elm Tree Cabins & Motel
237/26		US 9, Valley Farm Rd, Pottersville
235/26		US 9, Pottersville (NB)
	FStop	W: Pottersville Nice N Easy/Mobil
	Food	E: Café Andirondack, Hometown Deli W: Black Bear Diner
	Lodg	E: Lee's Corner Motel
	Other	E: Ideal Campground▲, Eagle Point Campsite▲ W: WiFi/Nice N Easy
231/25		NY 8, Chestertown, Hague, Brant Lake
	FStop	W: Riverside Nice N Easy #1501/Mobil, Buckman's Family Fuel
	Other	E: Rancho Pines Campground▲, Country Haven Campground▲, Riverside Pines Campground▲, Hidden Pond Campsite▲ W: WiFi/Nice N Easy
225/24		CR 11, Bolton Landing-Riverbank Rd, Bolton Landing, Warrensburg
	Other	E: Bakersfield East Campground▲, to Scenic View Campground▲, Ridin Hy Ranch Resort▲ W: Lake George Schroon Valley Resort▲, to Schroon River Campsites▲
(223)		Picnic Area (Phone) (SB)
(222)		Picnic Area (Phone) (NB)
217/23		CR 35, Diamond Point Rd, to US 9, to NY 28, Lake George, Warrensburg, Diamond Point
	FStop	W: Exit 23 Truck Stop/Citgo
	Gas	W: Mobil
	Food	W: McDonald's
	Lodg	W: Super 8, Seasons B&B, White House Lodge
	Other	E: to appr 6mi Schroon River Resort▲, W: WiFi/LP/Ex 23 TS, Warrensburg Travel Park▲, Queen Village Campground▲, Crazy Creek Campsite▲, Schroon River Campsite▲, to appr 14mi Daggett Lake Campsites▲, Glen-Hudson Campsite▲
213/22		US 9, NY 9N, Lake Shore Dr, Lake George Village, Diamond Point
	Gas	E: Citgo, Mobil
	Food	E: China Wok, Guiseppe's, Jasper's Steak & More, McDonald's, Pizza Hut, Luigi's, Subway, Taco Bell
	Lodg	E: Adirondack Oasis, Blue Moon Motel, Econo Lodge, Lake Motel, Quality Inn, Sundowner Motel, Travelodge
	Other	E: Mohawk Campground▲, Shoreline Cruises of Lake George, Ft William Henry Museum

EXIT		NEW YORK
211/21		NY 9N, to US 9, Lake George, Lake Luzerne
	Gas	E: Mobil, Stewarts W: Mobil◊
	Food	E: Barnsider BBQ, George's, Jasper's, Lake George Pancake House
	Lodg	E: Best Western, Comfort Inn, Harbor Motel, Holiday Inn, Howard Johnson, Lyn-Aire Motel, Ramada, Super 8, Studio Motel, Village Motor Inn W: King John's Manor Cabins, Lake George Luzerne Gardens Motel
	Other	E: Whippoorwill Campsites▲ W: to Alpine Lake RV Resort▲, to Juniper Woods Campground
207/20		US 9, NY 149, W Mountain Rd, Lake George, to Fort Ann, Whitehall, Queensbury
	Gas	E: Mobil, Shell, Sunoco◊
	Food	E: Log Jam Rest, Montcalm Rest
	Lodg	E: Days Inn, French Mtn Motel, Capri Village, Kay's Motel
	Other	E: Lake George Campsites▲, NY State Police, Great Escape Fun Park, Factory Outlet Stores W: Saugerties/Woodstock KOA▲, Brookside Campground/RVDump▲
205/19		US 9, NY 254, Aviation Rd, to US 209, Glens Falls, Hudson Falls, Queensbury
	Gas	E: Citgo, Hess W: Mobil, Stewarts
	Food	E: Burger King, China Buffet, Friendly's, KFC, McDonald's, Olive Garden, Pizza Hut, Ponderosa, Red Lobster, Taco Bell W: 7 Steers Western Grill
	Lodg	E: Econo Lodge, Sleep Inn W: Ramada Inn
	Other	E: Advance Auto, CVS, Firestone, Goodyear, Home Depot, Staples, Mall, Wal-Mart, Floyd Bennett Memorial Airport✈ W: NY State Police, to Rondout Valley Resort▲
203/18		CR 28, Main St, to NY 32, NY 299, NY 213, Corinth Rd, New Paltz, Glens Falls, Queensbury
	Gas	E: Hess◊, Mobil, Citgo W: Stewarts
	Food	E: Carl R's Café, Pizza Hut, Subway W: Lone Bull Pancake House, Nicky's Pizzeria, McDonald's
	Lodg	W: Best Inn, Super 8
	Med	E: + Hospital
	Other	E: CVS, U-Haul W: to appr 20mi So-Hi Campground▲, Sacandaga Campground▲
(201)		Rest Area (Both dir) (RR, Phones, Picnic)
199/17		US 9, Saratoga Rd, Gansvoort, South Glens Falls, Moreau St Park
	FStop	E: Moreau Xtra Mini Mart/Sunoco
	TStop	E: Nice N Easy/Mobil, KC Truck Stop/Getty
	Gas	E: Citgo
	Food	E: FastFood/Nice N Easy, Blimpie, Dunkin Donuts, Winslow's Diner
	Lodg	E: Landmark Motor Inn, Swiss American Motel, Town & Country Motel
	TServ	E: Nice N Easy

◊ = Regular Gas Stations with Diesel ▲ = RV Friendly Locations ♥ = Pet Friendly Locations
RED PRINT SHOWS LARGE VEHICLE PARKING/ACCESS ON SITE OR NEARBY BROWN PRINT SHOWS CAMPGROUNDS/RV PARKS

I-87 N/S — NEW YORK

EXIT		NEW YORK
	Other	E: BarbSh/WiFi/LP/Nice N Easy, Laundry/BarbSh/WiFi/LP/KC TS, American RV Campground▲ W: Moreau Lake State Park
193.2/16		CR 33, Ballard Rd, Wilton, Gurn Springs
	TStop	W: Wilton Travel Plaza/Sunoco
	Gas	W: Mobil, Stewarts
	Food	W: Rest/Wilton TP
	TServ	W: Wilton TP/Tires
	Other	E: Cold Brook Campsites▲, NY State Police W: Laundry/WiFi/LP/Wilton TP, Alpine Haus RV Center, to appr 7mi Saratoga Springs Resort▲, Fort Bink Campground▲
188.6/15		NY 50, NY 29, Saratoga Springs, Gansvoort, Schuylerville
	Gas	E: Hess◊, Mobil
	Food	E: Applebee's, Burger King, Denny's, Golden Corral, KFC, McDonald's, Ruby Tuesday, TGI Friday
	Lodg	E: Super 8 W: Residence Inn, Saratoga Motel
	Other	E: Best Buy, BJ's, Kmart, Grocery, Home Depot, Lowe's, Staples, Target, Wal-Mart sc, Wilton Mall W: to Alpine Lake RV Resort▲, to appr 8mi Saratoga RV Park▲
187.1/14		NY 9P, Y 29, Saratoga Springs, Saratoga Lake, Schuylerville
	Gas	E: Stewarts, Mobil W: Citgo
	Lodg	E: Longfellow Inn, Saratoga Springs Motel W: Holiday Inn, Malta Motor Court
	Other	E: Lee's RV Park▲
183/13		US 9, Ballston Spa, Saratoga Lake, Saratoga Springs
	Gas	W: Mobil, Stewarts
	Lodg	E: Post Road Lodge W: Coronet Motel, Hilton Garden Inn
	Other	E: Northway RV, Ballston Spa State Park
175/12		NY 67, Dunning St, Malta, Ballston Spa
	Gas	E: Mobil◊, Sunoco
	Food	E: Malta Diner, McDonald's, Subway
	Lodg	E: Fairfield Inn
	Other	E: CVS, Grocery
175/11		CR 80, Round Lake Rd, Curry Ave, Burnt Hill, Round Lake
	TStop	W: Exit 11 Truck Stop/Citgo
	Gas	W: Sunoco
	Food	W: FastFood/Ex 11 TS, Gran-Prix Grill
	Lodg	W: Gran-Prix Inn
	Other	W: WiFi/LP/Exit 11 TS
174.3/10		Ushers Rd, Ballston Lake, Jonesville
	Gas	E: Hess◊, Sunoco◊ W: Stewarts
(172.1)		Rest Area (NB) (RR, Phones, Picnic, Info, NY St Police)
(172.1)		Truck Inspection Station (NB)
171.4/9		NY 146 E/W, Clifton Park, Rexford, Halfmoon, Waterford
	Gas	E: Hess◊, USA W: Mobil, Sunoco◊

EXIT		NEW YORK
	Food	E: Burger King, Chili's, Cracker Barrel, Hardee's, Pizza Hut, Red Robin W: Applebee's, Denny's, Dunkin Donuts, Friendly's, McDonald's, Outback Steakhouse, TGI Friday, Wendy's
	Lodg	E: Comfort Inn W: Best Western, Hampton Inn
	Med	W: + Medi-Call
	Other	E: Grocery, Home Depot, Laundromat, Lowe's, Pharmacy W: AutoZone, CVS, Kmart, Mall, NY State Police, Freedom RV
169.9/8A		CR 91, Groom's Rd, Clifton Park, Waterford
	Other	E: Wal-Mart sc
168.4/8		Vischer Ferry Rd, Crescent Rd
	Gas	E: Hess◊ W: Coastal◊
	Food	E: McDonald's, Blimpie/Hess W: MrSub/Coastal
164/6+7		NY 2/7W, Troy, Schenectady (SB)
164.5/7		NY 7E, Troy (NB) (All Services E on US 9)
	Gas	E: Hess◊, Mobil
	Food	E: McDonald's, Subway
	Lodg	E: Hampton Inn, Holiday Inn Express
	Med	E: + Hospital
	Other	E: Auto Dealers, Auto Services, Grocery, Outlet Mall
163.9/6		NY 7W, NY 2, to US 9, Troy, Schenectady, Watervliet (NB)
	Gas	E: Mobil

EXIT		NEW YORK
	Gas	W: Mobil
	Food	E: Applebee's, Dakota's, Golden Wok, Ground Round, McDonald's, Panera W: Chuck E Cheese, Carrabba's, Friendly's
	Lodg	W: Clarion, Microtel, Super 8
	Other	E: Latham Circle Mall, CVS, Lowe's, Sam's Club, Staples, Wal-Mart W: Target, Albany Co Airport✈
162.3/4+5		NY 155, Albany Airport, Latham (SB)
161/5		NY 155, CR 153, Latham (NB)
	Lodg	E: Econo Lodge
161/4		Albany-Shaker Rd, Albany, Airport (E Serv on Wolf Rd)
	Gas	E: Hess◊, Mobil, Sunoco
	Food	E: Arby's, Denny's, Long John Silver, McDonald's, Olive Garden, Pizza Hut, Outback Steakhouse, Real Seafood, Romano's Macaroni Grill, Red Lobster
	Lodg	E: Best Western, Courtyard, Hampton Inn, Holiday Inn, Red Roof Inn
	Other	E: Auto Dealers, CVS, Firestone, Albany Airport✈
(160.3/3)		Future EXIT Albany Int'l Airport
159.3/2		NY 5, Central Ave, to Wolf Rd, Schenectady, Albany (Addt'l E Serv on Wolf Rd)
	Gas	E: Mobil, Sunoco W: Mobil, Exxon
	Food	E: Applebee's, Chili's, IHOP, Lone Star Steakhouse, Panchos Mexican, Starbucks, Wendy's W: Domino's, Delmonico's Italian Steak House, Garcia's, Red Lobster, Truman's
	Lodg	E: Days Inn, Econo Lodge, Park Inn W: Ambassador Motor Inn, Comfort Inn, Howard Johnson, Northway Inn, Super 8
	Other	E: BJ's, B&N, Firestone, Goodyear, Laundromat, Staples, Target, Mall
NOTE:		I-87 below runs with NY St Thruway (TOLL). Exit #'s are MM / Thruway.
(158.3/1)		Jct I-87S, Jct I-90, W to Buffalo, E to Albany, Boston, NY State Thruway (TOLL) (SB)
(158.1)		Washington Ave TOLL Plaza
NOTE:		SB Begin TOLL, NB End
(157/24)		Jct I-90E, to Albany, Jct I-87N, to Plattsburgh, Montreal (NB), I-87S to NYC (Thruway cont with I-90W)
(150/23)		Jct I-787, US 9W, Albany, Troy, Glenmont, Rensselaer
	FStop	W: Petro 9W
	TStop	E: (I-787, Ex 2NB/3SB) Riverside Travel Plaza (Scales), Big Main Truck Stop
	Gas	E: Mobil
	Food	E: Rest/FastFood/Riverside TP, Rest/Big Main TS, W: Applebee's, Dunkin Donuts, Johnny B's Diner, Wendy's
	Lodg	E: Comfort Inn, Days Inn W: Econo Lodge, Quality Inn, Stone Ends Motel
	TWash	E: Riverside TP
	TServ	E: Riverside TP/Tires
	Med	E: + Hospital

◊ = Regular Gas Stations with Diesel ▲ = RV Friendly Locations ♥ = Pet Friendly Locations
RED PRINT SHOWS LARGE VEHICLE PARKING/ACCESS ON SITE OR NEARBY BROWN PRINT SHOWS CAMPGROUNDS/RV PARKS

Page 439

EXIT	NEW YORK
Other	E: Laundry/BarbSh/WiFi/LP/Riverside TP, Laundry/BarbSh/WiFi/LP/Big Main TS, to Knickerbocker Arena, Times Union Center, Albany Airport
(148)	Picnic Area (Phone) (SB)
143.7/22	NY 144, NY 396, Selkirk
(143/21A)	to Jct I-90E, to Mass Tpk, Boston (to I-90W, Thruway-Cont on I-87N)
(136)	New Baltimore Service Area
FStop	Mobil
Food	Roy Rogers, TCBY, Mrs Fields, Starbucks
Other	LP
133.3/21B	US 9W, NY 81, Coxsackie, Ravena, New Baltimore, Athens
TStop	W: 21B Travel Plaza (Scales)
Gas	W: Sunoco
Food	W: Rest/21B TP
Lodg	W: Best Western
TWash	W: 21B TP
Other	W: Laundry/BarbSh/WiFi/LP/21B TP, Boat & RV Center
122.6/21	NY 23, Catskill, Cairo
Gas	E: Mobil, Sunoco◊
Food	E: Rest/Catskill Motor Lodge
Lodg	E: Catskill Motor Lodge
Other	E: Home Depot
(112)	Malden Service Area (NB) Picnic Area (Phone) (SB)
FStop	Mobil
Food	McDonald's, Carvel
110/20	NY 32, NY 212, Saugerties, Woodstock, Hunter, Tannersville
Gas	E: Mobil◊, Stewarts W: Hess◊, Sunoco◊
Food	E: McDonald's, Subway W: Blimpie/Hess, McDonald's, Land & Sea Grill & Steakhouse, Subway
Lodg	W: Comfort Inn, Howard Johnson
(108)	Picnic Area (NB)
(108)	Inspection Station (NB)
(107)	Ulster Service Area (SB)
FStop	Mobil
Food	Nathan's, TCBY, Roy Rogers, Mrs Field, Cinnabon
100.1/19	NY 28, Onteora Trail, to I-587, US 209, Kingston, Rhinecliff Bridge
Gas	E: Citgo◊, Mobil
Food	E: Gateway Diner W: Rest/Ramada Inn
Lodg	E: Holiday Inn, Super 8 W: Ramada Inn, Super Lodge
Other	E: Grocery, Walgreen's, Zoo, Bus Station
NOTE:	MM 19-21: Catskill Ski Region
84.8/18	NY 299, Main St, New Paltz, Poughkeepsie, Hyde Park
Gas	E: Citgo◊, Mobil W: Sunoco
Food	E: China Buffet, College Diner W: Burger King, McDonald's, Subway

EXIT	NEW YORK
Lodg	E: 87 Motel, Econo Lodge, Days Inn W: Super 8
Other	W: Grocery, Laundromat, Pharmacy
(75)	Plattekill Service Area (NB)
FStop	Mobil
Food	Nathan's, Big Boy, Cinnabon
(74.8)	Modena Service Area (SB)
FStop	Mobil
Food	Arby's, McDonald's, Carvel
68.9/17	NY 300, Union Ave, to I-84, NY 17K, Newburgh, Int'l Airport, Bear Mtn
Gas	E: Exxon, Mobil, Sunoco◊ W: Citgo◊
Food	E: Applebee's, Burger King, Denny's, Café Int'l, China City, McDonald's, Subway, Taco Bell
Lodg	E: Clarion, Holiday Inn, Hampton Inn, Ramada Inn, Super 8
Other	E: Auto Dealers, Auto Services, Grocery, Home Depot, Wal-Mart, Harley Davidson, Pharmacy, Mall, Greyhound W: Stewart Int'l Airport
(53.8)	Woodbury TOLL Plaza (NB)
NOTE:	NB Begin TOLL, SB End
54/16	US 6, NY 17, West Point, Harriman (Future I-86) Bear Mtn, Middletown, Monticello, Liberty, Monroe, Woodbury Outlets Blvd
Gas	W: Exxon◊
Other	W: Wal-Mart sc, Woodbury Outlet Mall, NY State Police
(41.8)	Sloatsburg Service Area (NB) Ramapo Service Area (SB)
FStop	Sunoco
Food	NB: Burger King, Sbarro, Dunkin Donuts SB: McDonald's, Carvel
40.1/15A	NY 17N, NY 59, (NB), NY 17 (SB) Sloatsburg, Hillburn, Suffern
(38.9/15)	Jct I-287S, to NJ 17S, New Jersey
NOTE:	I-87S & I-287 run together
35.4/14B	Airmont Rd, Suffern, Montebello
Gas	W: Exxon◊
Food	W: Airmont Diner, Applebee's, Friendly's, J & R Lobster & Seafood, Outback Steakhouse, Starbucks
Lodg	E: Holiday Inn, Inn at Gulfshores W: Wellesley Inn
Med	W: + Hospital
Other	W: Grocery, Walgreen's, Wal-Mart
(33.1)	Spring Valley TOLL Plaza (NB) (Truck TOLL Only)
32.3/14A	Garden State Pkwy, Spring Valley, to New Jersey (Passenger Cars Only)

◊ = Regular Gas Stations with Diesel ▲ = RV Friendly Locations ♥ = Pet Friendly Locations
RED PRINT SHOWS LARGE VEHICLE PARKING/ACCESS ON SITE OR NEARBY BROWN PRINT SHOWS CAMPGROUNDS/RV PARKS

EXIT		NEW YORK
31.6/14		NY 59, Grandview Ave (NB), NY 59, Pascack Rd (SB), Spring Valley, Nyack, Nanuet
	Gas	E: Shell◊ W: Citgo
	Food	E: Denny's, McDonald's, Subway W: Dunkin Donuts, Great China, IHOP, Red Lobster, Taco Bell
	Lodg	E: Fairfield Inn W: Days Inn, Nanuet Inn
	Other	E: Grocery, Mall, Target W: Grocery, Home Depot, Staples
29.7/13		Palisades Interstate Pkwy N/S, to Ft Lee, Pekskill, Bear Mtn, NJ (Passenger Cars Only)
27.5/12		NY 303, Vriesendael Rd, West Nyack, Palisades Center Dr
	Gas	W: Mobil
	Food	W: Grill 303, Outback Steakhouse, Panda Express, Romano's Macaroni Grill
	Lodg	W: Nyack Motor Lodge
	Other	W: Best Buy, B&N, BJ's, Home Depot, Staples, Target, Mall, Grocery, Pharmacy
26.2/11		Main St, High Ave, to US 9W, Highland Ave, NY 59, Nyack
	Gas	E: Mobil W: Shell◊
	Lodg	E: Best Western, Super 8
	Med	W: + Hospital
25.5/10		US 9W, Hillside Ave, Ft Lee, Nyack, S Nyack (NB)
(21.8)		Tappan Zee Bridge TOLL Plaza (SB)
21.6/9		US 9, Broadway, NY 119, Tarrytown White Plains Rd, Sleepy Hollow
	Gas	E: Hess, Shell W: Mobil
	Lodg	E: Marriott W: Hilton
20.1/8A		NY 119, Saw Mill Pkwy North, Elmsford (SB)
(20.1/8)		Jct I-287E, Cross Westchester Expy, to Saw Mill Pkwy, Rye, White Plains
	Other	to Saw Mill State Park, Taconic State Park
19.1/7A		Saw Mill River Pkwy, Yonkers, Bronx, Katonah (NO SB entry)
	Other	to Saw Mill State Park, Taconic State Park
16.6/7		NY 9A, Ardsley, Saw Mill River Rd, Dobbs Ferry, Ardsley (NB)
	Med	W: + Hospital
(15.8)		Ardsley Service Area (NB)
	FStop	Sunoco
	Food	Burger King, Popeye's, TCBY
(14.2)		Yonkers TOLL Plaza
13.6/6A		Corporate Dr, to Ridge Hill
	Other	W: Costco, Home Depot

EXIT		NEW YORK
12.7/6		Tuckahoe Rd E/W, Yonkers, Bronxville
	Gas	W: Gulf, Mobil
	Lodg	E: Tuckahoe Motor Inn W: Holiday Inn
11.5/5		NY 100N Central Park Ave, Yonkers
	Gas	E: Shell, Sunoco
10.9/4		Cross Country Pkwy (W/E NB), Mile Square Rd, Yonkers Ave (SB), Yonkers, Bronxville
	Gas	E: Getty W: Shell
	Other	E: Cross Country Mall W: to Yonkers Speedway
9.5/3		Mile Square Rd, Yonkers (NB)
9.2/2		Central Park Ave, to Yonkers Ave, Yonkers, Mt Vernon (NB)
	Other	E: Yonkers Raceway
8.8/1		Hall Place, McLean Ave
NOTE:		I-87 runs above with NY State Thruway (TOLL). Exit #'s are MM / Thruway.
8.8/14		McLean Ave (NB)
	Gas	E: Shell
8/13		West 233rd St
8/12		Mosholu Pkwy (NB)
7/11		Van Cortlandt Pk S
6/10		West 230th St
5/9		Fordham Rd, Bronx
	Med	E: + Hospital
	Other	E: Fordham Univ
5/8		West 179th St, Cedar Ave (NB)
(4/7)		Jct I-95, Cross Bronx Expy, Throgs Neck Bridge to New Haven CT, Geo Washington Bridge to Newark, NJ
3/6		E 161st St (SB)
	Other	E: to Yankee Stadium
2/5		W 155th St, E 153rd St, Macombs Dam Bridge
2/4		E 149th St (NB)
	Other	E: to Yankee Stadium
1/3		E 138th St, Grand Concourse, Madison Ave Bridge
1/2		Willis Ave, 3rd Ave Bridge
1/1		E 134th St, Brook Ave (SB)
	Gas	E: Hess
(0)		Jct I-278, Bruckner Expy, Triborough Bridge
NOTE:		NYS does NOT use Mile Marker Exits. Listed is MileMarker/Exit #.

(I-87 begins/ends on I-278, Exit #47, Bronx NY)

(EASTERN TIME ZONE)

NEW YORK

Begin Northbound I-87 from New York City to Champlain, NY.

◊ = Regular Gas Stations with Diesel ▲ = RV Friendly Locations ♥ = Pet Friendly Locations
RED PRINT SHOWS LARGE VEHICLE PARKING/ACCESS ON SITE OR NEARBY BROWN PRINT SHOWS CAMPGROUNDS/RV PARKS

INTERSTATE 88 E

EXIT	ILLINOIS
	Begin Eastbound I-88 from Jct I-80 near Rock Island, IL to Jct I-290, near Hillside, IL.

ILLINOIS
(CENTRAL TIME ZONE)
(I-88 Begins/Ends at Jct I-290 near Hillside)

Exit		
(0)		IL 5, IL 92, W to Moline, Rock Island, Sterling, Rock Falls (WB)
	Other	S: to Lundeen's Landing Campground▲
(1A)		Jct I-80E, to I-74, Peoria
(1B)		Jct I-80W, to Des Moines
2		Former IL 2
6		IL 92E, 38th Ave, Hillsdale, Joslin
	Other	S: 3mi Spirit in the Oaks Campground▲, Sunset Lake Campground▲, to Geneseo Campground▲
10		IL 2, Moline Rd, Hillsdale, Pt Byron
	TStop	S: Hillsdale Fast Break (Scales)
	Food	S: Mama J's/Hillsdale
	Other	N: to Camp Hauberg Campground▲
18		CR 13, Albany Rd, Erie, Albany
26		IL 78, Crosby Rd, Lyndon, to Morrison, Prophetstown
	Other	N: to Morrison Rockwood State Park▲
		S: to Prophetstown State Park▲
36		Como Rd, to Moline Rd, US 30, Rock Falls Rd, Sterling, Clinton
	Other	S: Crow Valley Campground▲
41		IL 40, IL 88, Hoover Rd, Rock Falls, Sterling (Use N Serv as Last Free Exit)
	Gas	N: Casey's, Marathon, Mobil, Shell◇
	Food	N: Arby's, Culver's, Hardee's, KFC, McDonald's, Red Apple Family Rest, Subway
	Lodg	N: All Seasons Motel, Country Inn, Holiday Inn♥, Super 8
	Med	N: + Hospital
	Other	N: Grocery, Goodyear, Walgreen's, Wal-Mart, Leisure Lake Campground▲
		S: Whiteside Co Airport✈
44		US 30, E Rock Falls Rd, Rock Falls
	NOTE:	LAST FREE EXIT
(53)		Dixon TOLL Plaza, Ronald Reagan Memorial Tollway
54		IL 26, Dixon
	TStop	N: DND Travel Plaza/BP (Scales)
	Food	N: Rest/FastFood/DND TP, Hardee's, Pizza Hut

Personal Notes

EXIT	ILLINOIS
Lodg	N: Comfort Inn♥, Quality Inn♥, Super 8♥
Med	N: + KSB Hospital
Other	N: Laundry/DND TP, Wal-Mart sc, to Dixon Muni Airport✈, to Ronald Reagan Birthplace, Lake LaDonna Family Campground▲, Hanson's Hideaway Campground▲, Grand Detour Islands Retreat▲
	S: to Pine View Campground▲, Green River Oaks Resort▲, Mendota Hills Resort▲, O'Connell's Jellystone Park
76	IL 251, Rochelle, Mendota
Gas	N: BP, Casey's, Shell, Stop n Go
Food	N: Blimpie/BP, TJ Cinn, Casey's Pizza
(78)	Jct I-39, US 51, S to Bloomington, Normal, N to Rockford
(91)	DeKalb TOLL Plaza

Exit		
92		Fairview Dr, to IL 23, IL 38, Annie Glidden Rd, DeKalb, Sycamore IL 251 (All Serv 3 mi N to IL 38/W Lincoln Hwy)
	Fstop	Stop n Go #527
	Other	N: DeKalb Taylor Muni Airport✈, to Sycamore RV Resort▲
(93)		DeKalb Oasis (Both dir)
	FStop	S: Mobil
	Food	S: McDonald's, Panda Express, Starbucks, Subway
	Other	S: WiFi
94		Peace Rd, to IL 23, IL 38, DeKalb, Taylor
	Other	N: DeKalb Taylor Muni Airport✈, N IL Univ, to Sycamore RV Resort▲
109		IL 47, Sugar Grove (EB ex, WB reacc)
114		IL 56W, to IL 30, to IL 47, Aurora, Sugar Grove (WB ex, EB reacc)
115		Orchard Rd, Aurora (Serv S to Galena Blvd)
	Gas	S: 7-11
	Food	S: Blackberry Café, Chili's, IHOP, KFC, McDonald's, Pizza Hut, Starbucks, Subway, Taco Bell
	Lodg	S: Hampton Inn
	Med	S: + Dreyer Medical Clinic
	Other	N: Auto Dealers
		S: CVS, Home Depot, Wal-Mart, Auto Repair, to Hide-A-Way-Lakes Camping & RV Park▲, to Blackberry Historical Farm Village
117		IL 31, IL 56, to IL 25, Aurora, Batavia
	Gas	N: Citgo◇, Marathon
		S: Mobil, Thorntons
	Food	S: Denny's, McDonald's, Popeye's
	Lodg	S: Baymont Inn, La Quinta Inn♥
	Med	S: + Indian Trail Medical Center
	Other	S: AutoZone, Walgreen's, U-Haul
(118)		Aurora TOLL Plaza
119		CR 77, Farnsworth Ave, to Kirk Rd
	Gas	S: Mobil◇, Phillips 66, Shell, Speedway
	Food	N: New Ser Family Rest, Papa Bear Family Rest
		S: McDonald's, Little Caesar, Subway, Taco Bell, Wok In
	Lodg	N: Fox Valley Inn, Motel 6♥
	Other	N: Outlet Stores
123		IL 59, Naperville, Warrenville
	Gas	S: Mobil◇
	Food	S: Cracker Barrel, Steak 'n Shake, Subway, Wendy's

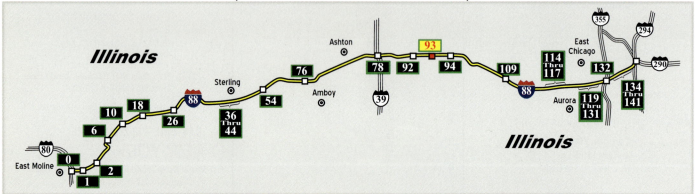

Page 442

◇ = Regular Gas Stations with Diesel   ▲ = RV Friendly Locations   ♥ = Pet Friendly Locations
RED PRINT SHOWS LARGE VEHICLE PARKING/ACCESS ON SITE OR NEARBY   BROWN PRINT SHOWS CAMPGROUNDS/RV PARKS

EXIT		ILLINOIS
	Lodg	N: Marriott S: Country Inn, Hawthorn Suites, Red Roof Inn♥, Sleep Inn, Townplace Suites
	Other	N: Odyssey Fun World
125		**Winfield Rd, Warrenville**
	Gas	N: BP S: BP, Phillips 66
	Food	N: Arby's, McDonald's S: Chipolte Mexican Grill, McDonald's, Max & Erma's, Red Robin
	Lodg	N: Residence Inn♥ S: Springhill Suites
	Other	N: Walgreen's S: Target
128		**CR 23, Naperville Rd, Naper Blvd, Naperville, Lisle, Wheaton**
	Gas	S: Mobil, Shell
	Food	S: Bob Evans, Chevy's, Fresh Mex, McDonald's, TGI Friday
	Lodg	N: Hilton, Marriott, Wyndham S: Best Western, Courtyard, Days Inn♥, Fairfield Inn, Holiday Inn Select, Hampton Inn
	Other	S: Mendota Hills Camping Resort▲
130		**IL 53, Lincoln Ave, Lisle** (Exit Both Dir, EB reaccess)
	Gas	N: BP
	Food	N: McDonald's
	Other	N: Wal-Mart

EXIT		ILLINOIS
(131)		I-355S, to US 34, Joliet (EB)
(132)		I-355S, to IL 56, NW Suburbs (WB)
134		**CR 9, Highland Ave, Downers Grove** (Exit Both Dir, EB reaccess)
	Food	N: CiCi's, Fuddrucker's, Hooters, Joe's Crab Shack, Kyoto, Olive Garden, Potbelly Sandwiches, Red Lobster, Ruby Tuesday, Starbucks, TGI Friday S: Elliot's Deli, Parker's Ocean Grill
	Lodg	N: Comfort Inn, Embassy Suites, Extended Stay America, Hampton Inn, Homestead Suites, Hyatt Place, Red Roof Inn♥, Residence Inn, Townplace Suites
	Med	S: + Good Samaritan Hospital
	Other	N: ATMs, Auto Services, Best Buy, FedEx Kinko's, Firestone, Office Max, PetSmart♥, Pharmacy, Target, Walgreen's, Yorktown Center Mall S: Pharmacy, UPS Store
(135.5)		Meyers Rd TOLL Plaza (EB)
136		**IL 15, Midwest Rd, Oakbrook (EB)**
	Gas	N: Shell, Costco
	Food	N: Denny's, McDonald's, Starbucks
	Lodg	N: Holiday Inn, La Quinta Inn♥
	Other	N: Costco, Home Depot, Walgreen's

EXIT		ILLINOIS
137		**IL 83S, Kingery Hwy (WB)**
	Lodg	N: Hilton Garden Inn, Hyatt, InTown Suites, La Quinta Inn♥, Marriott S: Residence Inn
	Other	N: FedEx Kinko's, Office Max, Oak Brook Center Mall
137		**Spring Rd, W 22nd St, to Cermak Rd to I-83N (WB)**
138		**IL 8N, Cermak Rd, to to IL 83N**
(138)		York Rd TOLL Plaza
(139)		I-294S, Tri-State Tollway, Indiana
(140.5)		I-294, Tri-State Tollway (TOLL), S to Indiana, N to O'Hare, Milwaukee I-290, W to Rockford, IL 38W
(141)		I-290, E to Chicago, Mannheim Rd, to US 12, US 20, US 45

(I-88 Begins/Ends at Jct I-80 near Hampton)

(CENTRAL TIME ZONE)

⊙ ILLINOIS

Begin Eastbound I-88 from Jct I-290 near Rock Island, IL to Jct I-80, near Hampton, IL

EXIT		NEW YORK
		Begin I-88 from Jct I-81 in Binghamton to Jct I-90 in Schenectady.

⊙ NEW YORK
(EASTERN TIME ZONE)
(I-88 Begins/Ends I-90, Exit# 25A)

NOTE: NYS does NOT use Mile Marker Exits. Listed is MileMarker/Exit #.

(0)		Jct I-81, to NY 17, N to Syracuse, S to Binghamton (WB), Jct I-88E, NY 7E (EB)
	Other	S: Hillcrest RV
1/1		NY 7W, to Binghamton (WB, no reacc)
2/2		NY 12A W, to Chenango Bridge
4/3		NY 369, Port Crane
	Gas	S: FasTrac◊, KwikFill
	Other	N: Chenango Valley State Park

EXIT		NEW YORK
8/4		**NY 7E, to NY 7B, Sanitaria Springs**
	FStop	S: Hess Express #32379
12/5		**Martin Hill Rd, to Belden**
	Gas	N: Exxon◊
	Other	N: Belden Hill Campground▲
15/6		**NY 79, to NY 7, Harpursville, Ninevah**
	TStop	S: Red Barrel #2
	Food	S: FastFood/Red Barrel
	Other	S: WiFi/LP/Red Barrel, to Forest Lake Campground▲, to appr 15 mi Lakeside Campground▲
23/7		**NY 41, to Afton**
	Gas	N: Mobil, Xtra
	Other	N: Echo Lake Resort Campground▲ S: to appr 6mi Kellystone Park Campground▲
29/8		**NY 206, Bainbridge, Masonville**
	FStop	N: Xtra Mart/Sunoco
	Gas	N: Mobil

EXIT		NEW YORK
	Food	N: TacoBell/XtraMart, Bob's Family Diner
	Other	N: Kmart, Riverside RV Park▲ S: to appr 5mi Oquaga Creek State Park▲
32/9		**NY 8, to NY 7, Sidney, Utica**
	Gas	N: Citgo◊, Hess◊, Mobil◊
	Food	N: Burger King, Gavin's Pizzeria & Steak House, Little Caesars, McDonald's, Pizza Hut, Subway
	Lodg	N: Super 8
	Med	N: + Hospital
	Other	N: ATMs, Bank, Auto Services, Grocery Kmart, US Post Office, Sidney Muni Airport✈, to appr 3mi Tall Pines Riverfront Campground▲
37/10		**NY 7, to Unadilla**
	Gas	N: Kwikfill
	Other	N: NY State Police
(39)		Rest Area (EB) (RR, Phone, Picnic)

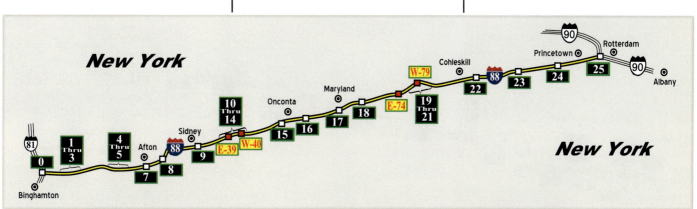

◊ = Regular Gas Stations with Diesel   ▲ = RV Friendly Locations   ♥ = Pet Friendly Locations

RED PRINT SHOWS LARGE VEHICLE PARKING/ACCESS ON SITE OR NEARBY   BROWN PRINT SHOWS CAMPGROUNDS/RV PARKS

W I-88

EXIT		NEW YORK
40/11		NY 357, Franklin, Unadilla, Delhi
	Other	S: appr 4mi Unadilla/I-88/Oneonta KOA▲
(40)		Rest Area (WB) (RR, Phone, Picnic)
46/12		NY 7, Otego
	TStop	S: Red Barrel #25/Mobil
	Food	S: FastFood/Red Barrel
	Other	S: WiFi/LP/Red Barrel
53/13		NY 7, NY 205, Oneonta
	Gas	N: Citgo, Hess, Mobil
	Food	N: Burger King, McDonald's, Ponderosa
	Lodg	N: Hampton Inn, Maple Terrace Motel, Oasis Motor Inn
	Other	N: Auto Dealers, Auto Services, Grocery, Pharmacy, to appr 16mi Meadow-Vale Campsites▲
55/14		NY 28E, Main St, Oneonta, Delhi (Access to Ex #15 Serv)
	Gas	N: Kwikfill, Stewarts, Sunoco
	Food	N: Deli
		S: Denny's, McDonald's, Taco Bell
	Lodge	N: Clarion, Oneonta Motel, Town House Motor Inn
	Other	N: ATMs, Banks, CVS, Dollar General, Grocery, Pharmacy, Harwick College, State Univ
56/15		NY 28, NY 23, Oneonta, Davenport
	FStop	S: Red Barrel #1/Citgo
	Gas	S: Hess, KwikFill, Mobil, BJ's
	Food	S: TacoBell/Red Barrel, Applebee's, Brookes BBQ, Denny's, McDonald's, Italian Rest, Neptune Diner, Quiznos, Subway, Wendy's
	Lodg	S: Budget Inn, Holiday Inn, Super 8
	TWash	S: Red Barrel
	Med	N: + Hospital
	Other	N: Pharmacy, to Soccer Hall of Fame S: WiFi/LP/Red Barrel, ATMs, Auto Services, Banks, BJ's, Borders, Grocery, Home Depot, Office Max, Wal-Mart sc, Southside Mall, Leatherstocking RV
58/16		NY 7, to Emmons
	Food	N: Arby's, Burger King, Farmhouse Rest, Pizza Hut
	Lodg	N: Rainbow Inn
61/17		NY 28N, to NY 7, Colliersville, Cooperstown
	Gas	N: Mobil◊
	Food	N: Homestead Rest
	Lodg	N: Best Western, Redwood Motel
	Other	N: to appr 14mi Hartwick Highlands Campground▲, to Baseball Hall of Fame

EXIT		NEW YORK
71/18		to Schenevus
	Gas	N: Citgo
(74)		Rest Area (EB) (RR, Phone, Picnic)
77/19		to NY 7, Worcester
	Gas	N: Stewarts, Sunoco◊
(79)		Rest Area (WB) (RR, Phone, Picnic)
88/20		NY 7S, NY 10, to Richmondville
	Gas	S: Sunoco, Mobil◊
	Lodg	S: Econo Lodge
	Other	S: Hi View Campground▲
90/21		NY 7, NY 10, to Cobleskill, Warnerville
	Gas	N: Mobil◊, Hess

EXIT		NEW YORK
	Food	N: Burger King, Pizza Hut
	Other	N: Wal-Mart sc, to State Univ of NY
95/22		NY 7, NY 145, Cobleskill, Middleburgh
	FStop	N: Hess Express
	Gas	N: Mobil
	Food	N: Arby's, Burger King, McDonald's, Subway, Taco Bell, Rest/Howe Caverns Motel
	Lodg	N: Best Western, Holiday Motel, Howe Caverns Motel
	Med	N: + Hospital
	Other	N: Twin Oaks Campground▲, Howe Caverns S: Happy Trails RV Parts & Service, NY State Police
100/23		NY 7, NY 30, NY 30A, to Schoharie, Central Bridge
	Gas	N: Mobil S: Mobil◊
	Food	S: Dunkin Donuts, McDonald's
	Lodg	S: Holiday Inn Express
	Other	N: Locust Park Campground▲, Hideaway Campground▲
112/24		US 20, NY 7, to Duanesburg
	Gas	N: Mobil S: Mobil, Stewarts
	Food	S: Duanesburg Diner
	Other	N: NY State Police
117/25		NY 7, to Rotterdam, Schenectady, to US 20, NY 70/107/52/103
	NOTE:	EB: Last FREE Exit
	TStop	S: Quick Way Food Store #47/Citgo
	Food	S: FriendlyCafe/DunkinDonut/QuickWay, Burger King, McDonald's, Midway Café, Topps Diner
	TWash	S: Quick Way FS
	Other	N: WiFi/LP/Quick Way FS, 3 mi Frosty Acres Campground▲ S: White RV Specialists
(117.5)		I-90, NY Thruway (TOLL), to Albany, Buffalo
NOTE:		NYS does NOT use Mile Marker Exits. Listed is MileMarker /Exit #.

(EASTERN TIME ZONE)
(I-88 Begins/Ends I-90, Exit# 25A)

NEW YORK

Begin I-88 from Jct I-90 in Schenectady to Jct I-81 in Binghamton.

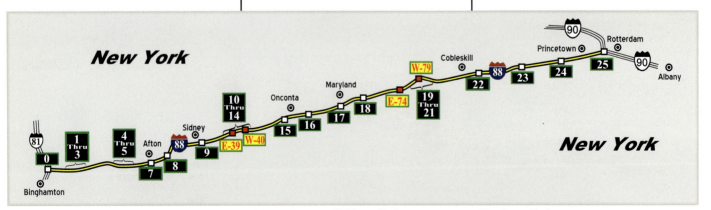

◊ = Regular Gas Stations with Diesel   ▲ = RV Friendly Locations   ♥ = Pet Friendly Locations
RED PRINT SHOWS LARGE VEHICLE PARKING/ACCESS ON SITE OR NEARBY   BROWN PRINT SHOWS CAMPGROUNDS/RV PARKS

INTERSTATE 89 S

VERMONT

Begin Southbound I-89 from Canada/VT border to Jct I-93 near Concord, NH.

ⓥ VERMONT
(EASTERN TIME ZONE)

EXIT	VERMONT
(130)	VT State Line, US / Canada Border
(129.5)	**Rest Area (SB)** (RR, Phone, Picnic, Vend)
129/22	US 7S, Swanton, Highgate Springs
Gas	E: Mobil◊
Other	E: AmEx Duty Free
NOTE:	MM 129: 45 degrees N Latitude: Mid Point between N Pole & Equator
123/21	VT 78, 1st St, to US 7, Swanton
TStop	E: Champlain Farms/Exxon W: Hometown Sunoco, Swanton Mobil Mart
Gas	W: Shell
Food	W: Big Wok, Dunkin Donuts, McDonald's
117/20	VT 207, to US 7, St Albans
Gas	W: Mobil, Shell◊
Food	W: Burger King, McDonald's, Pizza Hut
Other	W: Auto Dealers, Grocery, Laundromat, Staples
113/19	VT 104, to US 7, VT 36, St Albans
TStop	W: The Jolly Short Stop/Exxon (Scales)
Gas	W: Mobil, Shell
Food	W: FastFood/Jolley SS
Lodg	W: Econo Lodge
TWash	W: Jolley SS
TServ	W: Jolley SS/Tires
Med	W: + Hospital
Other	W: Laundry/WiFi/RVDump/Jolly SS, Amtrak, Auto Dealers, VT State Hwy Patrol Post
(111)	**Rest Area (Both dir)** (RR, Phones, Picnic, Vend, Info)
106/18	US 7, VT 104A, Georgia, Fairfax
FStop	E: Maplefields/Mobil
Gas	E: Shell
Other	E: Homestead Campground▲
97/17	US 2, US 7, Colchester, Lake Champlain Islands
Gas	E: Mobil, Shell◊
Other	W: to appr 4mi Lone Pine Campsites▲
(96)	Weigh Station (Both dir)
91/16	US 2, US 7, to VT 15, Roosevelt Hwy Colchester, Essex Jct, Winooski
FStop	W: Champlain Farms/Shell
Gas	E: Mobil W: Citgo
Food	E: Friendly's W: Burger King, McDonald's, Diner
Lodg	E: Hampton Inn W: Fairfield Inn, Motel 6
Other	W: to appr 4mi Lone Pine Campsites▲
90/15	VT 15, Winooski, Burlington (NB Exit, SB reaccess)
Gas	W: Mobil
Lodg	E: Days Inn

EXIT	VERMONT
Other	E: Burlington Int'l Airport✈, Ft Ethan Allen
88/14	US 2, Burlington
Gas	E: Exxon, Mobil, Shell◊ W: Exxon, Mobil
Food	E: Applebee's, Burger King, Dunkin Donuts, Friendly's, KFC, McDonald's, Outback Steakhouse, Quiznos
Lodg	E: Best Western, Clarion, Comfort Inn, Days Inn, Holiday Inn, University Inn W: Sheraton
Med	W: + Hospital
Other	E: B&N, Grocery, Pharmacy, Mall, Natural Foods Market, Burlington Int'l Airport✈ W: Advance Auto, Greyhound, Staples
(87/13)	Jct I-189, to US 7, Shelburn (All Services W to US 7N/S)
Other	W: Shelburne Camping Area▲
84/12	VT 2A, St George Rd, to US 2, Williston
Gas	E: Mobil, Sunoco◊
Food	W: Chili's, Friendly's, Ponderosa, Longhorn Steakhouse
Lodg	E: Fairfield Inn W: Marriott, Residence Inn
Other	E: ATMs, Bank, Best Buy, Circuit City, Grocery, Home Depot, Staples, Wal-Mart, VT State Hwy Patrol Post
(82)	**Rest Area (Both dir)** (RR, Phone, Picnic, Vend)
78/11	US 2, to VT 117, Richmond
Gas	W: Mobil◊
Food	E: Checkered Rest
Lodg	E: Checkered House Motel
(67)	Parking Area (SB)
(66)	Parking Area (NB)
63/10	VT 100, to US 2, Waterbury
Gas	E: Mobil◊, Exxon◊ W: Citgo
Lodg	E: Best Western
58/9	US 2, to VT 100B, Middlesex
Gas	W: Getty
Food	W: Rest/Camp Meade Motor Inn
Lodg	W: Camp Meade Motor Inn
Other	W: VT State Hwy Patrol Post
53/8	US 2, VT 12, Montpelier
Gas	E: CF, Exxon◊, Mobil, Sunoco
Food	E: Subway
Other	E: Grocery
50/7	to US 302, VT 62, Berlin Corners
FStop	E: Maplewood Ltd/Mobil
Food	E: Applebee's
Lodg	E: Comfort Inn
Med	E: + Hospital
Other	E: Auto Dealers, Grocery, Staples
46/6	VT 63, to VT 14, S Barre (Serv 4-5 mi in Barre)
Other	E: Limehurst Lake Campground▲
43/5	VT 64, to VT 12, VT 14, Northfield
(34)	**Rest Area (Both dir)** (RR, Phone)
(33)	Weigh Station (Both dir)
30/4	VT 66, Randolph
NOTE:	STEEP Grade on hill
Gas	W: Mobil
Food	W: McDonald's
Med	W: + Hospital
Other	E: Lake Champagne Campground▲

◊ = Regular Gas Stations with Diesel ▲ = RV Friendly Locations ♥ = Pet Friendly Locations

RED PRINT SHOWS LARGE VEHICLE PARKING/ACCESS ON SITE OR NEARBY BROWN PRINT SHOWS CAMPGROUNDS/RV PARKS

EXIT	VT / NH
22/3	VT 107, Main St, S Royalton, to Bethel, Rutland
Gas	E: Shell◊
	W: Citgo◊
Other	W: VT State Hwy Patrol Post, to approx 8mi White River Valley Campground▲
13/2	VT 132, to VT 14, Sharon
Gas	W: Citgo◊, Mobil
Food	W: Dixie's Kitchen
(9)	VT Welcome Center (NB) (RR, Phone, Vend) Weigh Station (Both dir)
3/1	US 4, Woodstock, Quechee
Gas	E: Shell◊
Lodg	E: Hampton Inn, Super 8
(1)	Jct I-91, N to St Johnsbury, S to Brattleboro

(EASTERN TIME ZONE)

○ **VERMONT**
○ **NEW HAMPSHIRE**

(EASTERN TIME ZONE)

NOTE: MM 61: Vermont State Line

60/20	NH 12A, Main St, W Lebanon, Claremont
Gas	E: Mobil, Sunoco
	W: Citgo◊
Food	E: KFC, Chili's, 99 Rest, Mex Rest, Subway, Weathervane Seafood Rest
	W: Applebee's, Burger King, Denny's, Friendly's, Japanese Rest, McDonald's, Pizza Hut, Weathervane Seafood, Wendy's
Lodg	W: Fireside Inn
Other	E: Grocery, Kmart, Pharmacy
	W: ATMs, Auto Services, Auto Zone, BJ's, Best Buy Borders, CVS, Grocery, Home Depot, Radio Shack, Staples, Wal-Mart, Lebanon Muni Airport✈
58/19	US 4, NH 10, Mechanic St, Lebanon, Hanover
Gas	E: Exxon◊, Shell
Food	E: Little Caesars, Blimpie/Shell
Other	E: Family Dollar, Laundry, Grocery, Radio Shack, Harley Davidson
	W: Lebanon Muni Airport✈
(57)	NH Welcome Center (SB) (RR, Phones, Picnic, Vend) Weigh Station (Both dir)
56/18	NH 120, Lebanon, Hanover
TStop	E: Exit 18 Truck Stop/Getty (Scales)
Gas	W: Citgo◊, Shell
Food	E: Rest/Exit 18 TS
Lodg	E: Days Inn, Residence Inn
TWash	E: Exit 18 TS
TServ	E: Exit 18 TS/Tires
Med	W: + Hospital
Other	E: Laundry/WiFi/LP/Exit 18 TS
54/17	US 4, NH 4A, Enfield, Canaan
Other	E: Mascoma Lake Campground▲
52/16	Eastman Hill Rd, Enfield
FStop	W: Exit 16 Mobil
TStop	E: Evans Exit 16 Truck Stop/Exxon
Food	E: Subway/Ex 16 TS
	W: Burger King/Ex 16 Mobil
Other	W: Whaleback Ski Area

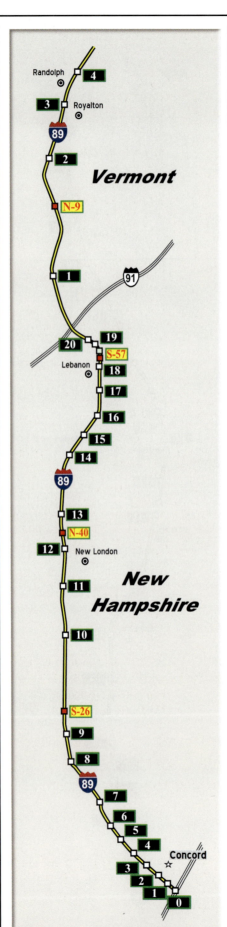

EXIT	NEW HAMPSHIRE
50/15	Smith Pond Rd, Enfield, Montcalm
48/14	N Grantham (SB exit, NB reaccess)
43/13	NH 10, Grantham, Croydon, Newport
Gas	E: General Store/Gulf
	W: Mobil
Other	W: to North Star Campground▲, Appr 13mi Crow's Nest Campground▲
(40)	Rest Area (NB) (RR, Phones, Picnic, Vend)
37/12A	Georges Mills Rd, Springfield Rd, Sunapee, Georges Mills
Other	W: Crow's Nest Campground▲
35/12	NH 11W, NH 114, Newport Rd, New London, Sunapee
Lodg	E: Maple Hill Farm Inn
Med	E: + Hospital
31/11	NH 11E, King Hill Rd, New London
27/10	Gile Pond Rd, to NH 114, Sutton
(26)	Rest Area (SB) (RR, Phones, Picnic, Vend)
20/9	NH 103, Main St, Warner, Bradford
Gas	E: Citgo, Exxon, Mobil◊
Food	E: Dunkin Donuts, McDonald's
Other	W: to appr 6mi Northstar Campground▲
17/8	NH 103, Warner (NB ex, SB reacc)
15/7	NH 103, Davisville, Contoocook
11/6	NH 127, Maple St, Contoocook
Other	E: Sandy Beach RV Resort▲
	W: appr 3mi Keyser Pond Campground▲, appr 6mi Mile Away Campground▲
9/5	US 202, NH 9, Hopkinton, Henniker (NB, Left Exit)
Other	W: appr 3mi Keyser Pond Campground▲, Appr 6mi Mile Away Campground▲, Appr 10mi Cold Springs Camp Resort▲, Appr 30mi Idle Times Campground▲
7/4	US 202, NH 9, to NH 103, Contoocook, Hopkinton (NB Ex, SB reacc)
4/3	Stickney Hill Rd, Concord (NB ex, SB reacc)
2/2	NH 13, Clinton St, Concord
Med	E: + Hospital
Other	W: Friendly Beaver Campground▲, to appr 6mi Cold Springs Camp Resort & RV Sales/Service/Rentals▲
1/1	Logging Hill Rd, South St, Bow
Gas	E: Mobil
Lodg	E: Hampton Inn
(0)	Jct I-93, N to Concord, S to Manchester

(I-89 Begins/Ends I-93, MM 36)

(EASTERN TIME ZONE)

○ **NEW HAMPSHIRE**

Begin Northbound I-89 near Concord, NH to Vermont / Canada border.

◊ = Regular Gas Stations with Diesel   ▲ = RV Friendly Locations   ♥ = Pet Friendly Locations
RED PRINT SHOWS LARGE VEHICLE PARKING/ACCESS ON SITE OR NEARBY   BROWN PRINT SHOWS CAMPGROUNDS/RV PARKS

EXIT		WASHINGTON
	Begin Eastbound I-90 from near Jct I-5 in Seattle, WA to near Jct I-93 in Boston MA.	
	WASHINGTON (PACIFIC TIME ZONE) (I-90 Begins/Ends on I-93, Ex #20 in Boston, MA) (I-90 Begins/Ends on I5, Ex #164)	
2A		4th Ave S (WB)
	Other	W: Qwest Field, Safeco Field, Amtrak
(2CB)		Jct I-5, S to Tacoma, Portland, OR; N to Everett, Vancouver, BC
3		Rainier Ave South, Seattle (EB)
	Gas	N: Shell◊
	Food	S: Burger King, McDonald's, Wendy's
	NOTE:	Tunnel, Mercer Island Floating Bridge, Tunnel
3A		Rainier Ave South (WB)
3B		Rainier Ave North (WB)
6		W Mercer Way (EB)
7		Island Crest Way (WB)
7A		77th Ave (EB)
7B		Island Crest Way (EB)
7AB		76th Ave, 80th Ave, Island Crest Way (EB)
	Gas	S: 76, Shell◊
	Food	S: McDonald's, Starbucks, Subway S: Islander Steakhouse
	Lodg	S: Travelodge
	Other	S: Auto Repair/Shell, Walgreen's
7C		80th Ave SE (fr WB, Left Exit)
8		East Mercer Way, Mercer Island
9		Bellevue Way
(10A)		Jct I-405, N to Everett, Vancouver, S to Renton, Tacoma (EB)
10B		SE 36th St, 128th Ave (EB)
(10)		Jct I-405, N to Everett, Vancouver, S to Renton, Tacoma (WB)
10C		Richards Rd, Factoria Blvd (EB)
11		Eastgate Way, 156th Ave, 150th Ave (WB)
	Gas	N: Shell S: 76, Shell◊
	Food	N: DQ, Lil John's, McDonald's, Starbucks S: Denny's, Pizza Hut, Outback Steakhouse

EXIT		WASHINGTON
	Lodg	N: Days Inn, Eastgate Motel, Embassy Suites S: Candlewood Suites, Homestead Suites
	Other	N: Safeway S: Albertson's, RiteAid
11A		150th Ave SE, SE 36th/35th St, Eastgate Way (EB)
11B		148th Ave SE (EB)
13		Lakemont Blvd, West Lake Sammamish Parkway, Bellevue, Issaquah, to Redmond
15		WA 900S, 17th Ave, Renton Rd, Issaquah Rd, Issaquah, to Renton
	Gas	N: ArcoAmPm, Costco S: Shell
	Food	N: IHOP, Red Robin S: Burger King, Cascade Garden, Jack in the Box, Denny's, McDonald's, Subway, Starbucks, Taco del Mar
	Lodg	N: Holiday Inn, Motel 6♥
	Other	N: ATMs, B&N, Costco, Lowe's, Grocery, Office Depot, PetSmart♥, Trader Joe's, to Lake Sammamish State Park/RVDump S: PetCo♥, RiteAid, Safeway, Target, Harley Davidson, Issaquah Highlands Camping▲
17		E Lake Sammamish Pkwy, Front St, Issaquah
	Gas	N: 76 S: ArcoAmPm, Chevron, Shell
	Food	N: McDonald's, Qdoba Mex, Starbucks S: Extreme Pizza, Front St Deli, Skippers
	Other	N: Albertson's, Home Depot, Walgreen's, Issaquah Village RV Park/RVDump▲ S: U-Haul, Auto Repair
18		Sunset Way, Highlands Dr
	Gas	S: Shell
	Food	S: Domino's, Shanghai Garden
	Lodg	S: Issaquah B&B
20		High Point Way, Issaquah
22		82nd St, High Pt Way, to WA 203, Preston Fall City Rd, Preston
	Gas	N: Chevron, Shell◊
	Food	N: Savannah's, Espresso Cafe
	Other	N: to Snoqualmie River RV Park & Campground▲ S: Blue Sky RV Park▲
25		Snoqualmie Pkwy, Snoqualmie WA 18W, Auburn, Federal Way
27		N Bend Way, Snoqualmie, to North Bend (EB)

EXIT		WASHINGTON
31		WA 202E, Bendigo Blvd, North Bend, Snoqualmie
	Gas	N: 76◊, Chevron, Shell◊
	Food	N: Arby's, DQ, McDonald's, Taco Time
	Lodg	N: North Bend Motel, Sunset Motel
	Other	N: Safeway, Factory Stores at North Bend, PL/Tinkham Campground▲, PL/Denny Creek Campground▲, WA State Hwy Patrol Post
32		436th Ave SE, North Bend, Tanner
	Food	S: Gordy's Steak & BBQ Smokehouse
34		468th Ave SE, North Bend
	FStop	N: Edgewick Shell & Deli
	TStop	N: Travel Center of America #176 (Scales)
	Food	N: Ken's/TA TC, Subway/Edgewick Shell
	Lodg	N: Edgewick Inn, Nor'west Motel & RV Park▲
	TServ	N: TA TC/Tires
	Other	N: WiFi/CB/TA TC, LP/Edgewick Shell
38A		Homestead Valley Rd, Olallie State Park (EB)
38B		Homestead Valley Rd, Fire Training Center (WB)
	Other	S: Olallie State Park
42		Tinkham Rd
45		Bandera Rd
47		Asahel Curtis Rd, North Bend, Asahel Curtis, Denny Creek
52		WA 906 W, Summit Rd, Snoqualmie Summit Rec Area (EB)
	NOTE:	MM 53: Snoqualmie Summit Elev 3022'
53		E Summit Rd, to WA 906, Snoqualmie Summit Rec Area
	Gas	S: Chevron
	Food	S: Family Pancake House
	Lodg	S: Best Western
54		WA 906, Hyak, Cle Elum
(56)		Parking Area (EB)
62		Kachess Lake Rd, Cle Elum, Stampede Pass, Kachess Lake
	Other	N: to Lake Kachess S: to Stampede Pass
63		Cabin Creek Rd
70		Railroad St, Lake Easton State Park, Easton
	Gas	N: Shell◊
	Food	N: Mtn High Hamburgers, Parkside Cafe
	Other	N: Silver Ridge Ranch Campground▲

◊ = Regular Gas Stations with Diesel ▲ = RV Friendly Locations ♥ = Pet Friendly Locations
RED PRINT SHOWS LARGE VEHICLE PARKING/ACCESS ON SITE OR NEARBY BROWN PRINT SHOWS CAMPGROUNDS/RV PARKS

EXIT		WASHINGTON
	Other	S: Lake Easton Resort▲, Lake Easton State Park/RVDump▲
71		Railroad St, Easton
	Gas	S: CB's Café & Grocery◆
74		Nelson Siding Rd
78		Golf Course Rd, Nelson
(80)		Weigh Station (Both dir)
80		Bullfrog Rd, to Roslyn
84		WA 903, 1st St W (EB), Cle Elum, Oakes Ave (WB)
	Gas	N: 76, Chevron◆, Conoco, Shell◆
	Food	N: Burger King, Caboose Bar & Grill, DQ, El Caporal, Los Cabos, Mama Vallone's Steakhouse, Yum Yang Chinese
	Lodg	N: Best Western, Hummingbird Inn, Stewart Lodge, Timber Lodge Motel
	Med	N: + Cle Elum Urgent Care Center
	Other	N: ATMs, Auto Services, Safeway, Beverly Campground▲, PL/Kachess Campground▲ S: Whispering Pines RV Center, Mountain River Trails Camping▲
85		WA 970, to US 97N, Wenatchee, WA 903, I-90 Bus, Cle Elum
	FStop	N: Willette's Shell Service, Storey Service
	Gas	N: Conoco
	Food	N: Rest/Willette's Shell, Cottage Café
	Lodg	N: Cascade Mountain Inn, Cle Elum Travelers Inn, Wind Blew Inn Motel
	Tires	N: Willette's Shell
	Other	N: LP/RVDump/Willette's Shell, Cle Elum Muni Airport✈, Trailer Corral RV Park▲ S: Eagle Valley Campground▲
(89)		Rest Area (Both dir) (RR, Phone, Picnic, Vend, WiFi, RVDump)
93		Elk Heights Rd
101		Thorp Hwy, Thorp
106		Cascade Way, I-90 Bus, Ellensburg, US 97N to Wenatchee
	TStop	N: Pilot Travel Center #389 (Scales)
	Gas	N: 76, Chevron, Conoco◆, Texaco
	Food	N: Subway/Pilot TC, Jack in the Box, DQ, Perkins S: Wild West Ranch
	Lodg	N: I-90 Inn Motel
	TWash	N: Cascade Truck & RV Wash
	Other	N: Laundry/WiFi/Pilot TC, Bowers Field Airport✈, Central WA Univ, Canopy Country RV, to Icicle River RV Park▲ S: Ellensburg KOA▲, WA State Hwy Patrol Post
109		Canyon Rd, Ellensburg
	TStop	S: Flying J Travel Plaza/Exxon (Scales)
	Gas	N: Big B Mini Mart, Chevron, Sun Mart, Toad's Express Mart◆
	Food	N: Arby's, Bar 14 Ranch House, Burger King, Fiesta Mex Rest. McDonald's, Pizza Hut, Quiznos, Skippers Seafood, Subway, Taco Bell, Windbreak Deli S: Saks/FJ TP
	Lodg	N: Best Western, Comfort Inn, Ellensburg Inn, Holiday Inn Express, Inn at Goose Creek, Super 8, Thunderbird Motel S: Best Inn
	Med	N: + to Kittitas Valley Comm Hospital

EXIT		WASHINGTON
	Other	N: ATMs, Bank, Auto Services, Grocery, Les Schwab Tire, Radio Shack, RiteAid, Vet♥ S: Laundry/WiFi/LP/FJ TP, R & R RV Park▲, to Riverview Campground▲
(110)		I-82E, US 97S, to Yakima, Tri Cities
115		Badger Pocket Rd, Kittitas
	FStop	N: Exit 115 Auto Truck Stop/Shell
	Food	N: FastFood/Ex 115 ATS
	Other	N: LP/Exit 115 ATS
(125)		Rest Area (Both dir) (RR, Phone, Picnic, WiFi)
136		Huntzinger Rd, Vantage, Gingko State Park
	Gas	N: Texaco◆
	Food	N: Golden Harvest, Ft Wanapum Inn
	Lodg	N: Vantage Riverstone Resort & RV Park▲
	Other	N: Ginkgo State Park▲
137		WA 26E, to Othello, Pullman, WA State Univ, to WA 243, to Tri Cities (Vista Viewpoints Ex #137E-Both dir)
NOTE:		Frontage Rd Access Ex #143-174
143		Silica Rd, Quincy
	Other	N: to the Gorge Amphitheatre, Wild Horse Campground▲
149		WA 281N, Quincy, Wenatchee, Royal Anne Ave, George
	FStop	S: 300 Washington Way PacPride/George Scales(Scales)
	Gas	S: Exxon
	Food	S: Martha's Inn Café, Rest/George Scales
	Other	N: to Crescent Bar Resort, Marina & Campground▲, Gorge Amphitheatre, Wild Horse Campground▲
151		WA 281N, Ephrata, WA 283N, George, Quincy, Wenatchee
	FStop	N: Midway Mini Mart/Shell
	Lodg	N: to Best Western, Travelodge
	Other	N: to Stars & Stripes RV Park▲, Oasis RV Park▲ & Golf, Ephrata Muni Airport✈
154		Adams Rd, Quincy
(161)		Rest Area (EB) (RR, Phone, Picnic, WiFi, RVDump)
(162)		Rest Area (WB) (RR, Phone, Picnic, WiFi, RVDump)
164		Dodson Rd, Road C, Ephrata
	Other	S: Sun Basin RV Park & Campground▲ to Potholes State Park▲, 16mi Mar Don Resort & Campground▲, Last Resort▲
169		Hiawatha Rd, Moses Lake
174		Westlake, Moses Lake State Park Pritchard Rd (EB), Hansen Rd (WB)
	Gas	S: Conoco◆
	Food	S: Burger Inn
	Other	N: Sun Crest Resort▲, Moses Lake State Park S: WA State Hwy Patrol Post
NOTE:		Frontage Rd Access Ex #174-143
175		Westshore Dr, West Lake Rd, Moses Lake State Park (WB)
176		I-90 Bus, Lakeshore Dr, Moses Lake
	Gas	N: Cenex, Exxon◆, Shell◆
	Food	N: Mex Rest, Perkins

EXIT		WASHINGTON
	Lodg	N: Best Western♥, Heritage Suites♥, Interstate Inn, Microtel, Super 8♥ S: Lakeshore Resort Motel
	Other	N: Golf Course, Big Sun Resort▲, Lakefront RV Park▲, Desert Oasis RV Park▲
NOTE:		Frontage Rd Access Ex #179-184
179		WA 17N, Moses Lakes, WA 17S, to US 395S, Othello, Kennewick
	TStop	N: Ernie's Truck Stop #9/Chevron (Scales)
	Gas	N: Conoco◆, Exxon, Shell◆
	Food	N: FastFood/Ernie's TS, Arby's, Burger King, Denny's, Shari's, Starbucks
	Lodg	N: Best Value Inn♥, Holiday Inn Express, Inn at Moses Lake, Shilo Inn, Travelodge
	Med	N: + Hospital
	Other	N: Laundry/Ernie's TS, Safeway, US Post Office, Pharmacy, TLC Mobile RV Repair, Sun Country RV, to Grant Co Fairgrounds, Grant Co Int'l Airport✈, Moses Lake Muni Airport✈, Cascade Campground▲, to Sun Lake State Park, R&R RV Park▲ S: I-90 RV, Willows Trailer Village▲, to 15mi Sage Hills Golf Club & RV Resort▲, 15miPotholes State Park▲, 14 mi Mar Don Resort & Campground▲, Last Resort▲
182		Road O, Moses Lake, to Wheeler
	Tstop	N: Flying J Travel Plaza
	Food	N: Rest/FastFood/FJ TP
	Other	N: Laundry/WiFi/FJ TP
184		Road Q, Raugust Rd, to Wheeler
NOTE:		Frontage Rd Access Ex #184-179
188		Rd U, Warden Rd, to Ruff, Warden
196		Deal Rd, Lind, Schrag
	Other	N: to Lincoln Recreation & RV Park▲
(198)		Rest Area (Both dir) (RR, Phone, Picnic, WiFi, WB: RVDump, Weather)
206		WA 21, to Odessa, Lind
215		Paha Packard Rd, Ritzville
220		W 1st Ave, Ritzville, US 395S, Kennewick, Pasco
	FStop	N: Vista 24hr Fuel Stop, Jake's Exxon
	Food	N: Jake's Café, Blue Bike Café, Whispering Palms Rest
	Lodg	N: Best Value Inn♥, Top Hat Motel, West Side Motel
	Other	N: Laundry/Vista Astro QM, Auto Repair, Les Schwab Tires, Ritzville Muni Airport✈, WA State Hwy Patrol Post
221		WA 261S, Ralston, Division St, Ritzville
	Gas	N: Chevron, Sun Mart, Shell◆
	Food	N: McDonald's, Perkins, Zip's
	Lodg	N: Best Western♥, La Quinta Inn♥
	Med	N: + E Adams Rural Hospital
	Other	N: ATMs, Golf Course, Ritzville City Park
226		Coker Rd, Schoessler Rd, Ritzville
231		Danekas Rd, to Tokio, Sprague
(231)		Weigh Station (Both dir)
	FStop	S: Templins Country Corner/Exxon◆
	Food	S: Templin's Corner Café
(242)		Rest Area (Both dir) (RR, Phone, Picnic, Info, Weather, RVDump)

◆ = Regular Gas Stations with Diesel ▲ = RV Friendly Locations ♥ = Pet Friendly Locations
RED PRINT SHOWS LARGE VEHICLE PARKING/ACCESS ON SITE OR NEARBY BROWN PRINT SHOWS CAMPGROUNDS/RV PARKS

EXIT	WASHINGTON
245	**WA 23, to WA 231, Sprague, to Harrington, Edwall, St John**
Gas	S: Chevron◇
Food	S: Viking Drive In
Lodg	S: Purple Sage Motel♥, Sprague Motel & RV Park▲
Other	S: Grocery, US Post Office, to Klink's Williams Lake Resort▲, appr 7mi Four Seasons Campground▲, Sprague Lake Resort▲
254	**Old State Hwy, Fishtrap Rd**
257	**WA 904E, to Tyler, Cheney, to East WA University**
264	**WA 902, Salnave Rd, Cheney, Medical Lake**
Other	N: to Dan's Landing▲, Ruby's Resort on Silver Lake▲, Silver Lake Camp▲, West Medical Lake Resort▲, Mallard Bay Resort▲ S: to Eastern WA Univ, 10mi Peaceful Pines Campground▲
270	**WA 904W, Four Lakes, Cheney**
Gas	S: Exxon
Other	N: to 7mi Peaceful Pines RV Park▲ S: to appr 15mi Klinks Williams Lake Resort▲
272	**WA 902W, Hayford Rd, Aero Rd, Spokane, to Medical Lake**
TStop	S: Petro Stopping Center (Scales)
Gas	N: Shell◇
Food	S: IronSkillet/Subway/Starbucks/Petro SC
Lodg	S: Super 8
TServ	S: Petro SC/Tires, Freightliner
Other	N: to Fairchild AFB, Overland Station RV Park▲ S: Laundry/BarbSh/WiFi/Petro SC, Ponderosa Falls RV Resort▲, Yogi Bear's Jellystone Park▲
276	**Grove Rd, Geiger Blvd, I-90 Bus**
TStop	N: Flying J Travel Plaza #106/Exxon (Scales)
Gas	S: Shell◇
Food	N: Saks/Subway/FJ TP, Denny's
Lodg	N: Airway Express Inn, Best Western
Other	N: WiFi/LP/FJ TP, Spokane Int'l Airport✈, WA State Hwy Patrol Post
277	**US 2W, Garden Springs Rd, to I-90 Bus, Spokane Int'l Airport (WB)**
Lodg	N: Cedar Village Motel, Days Inn, Hampton Inn, Holiday Inn, Motel 6♥, Ranch Motel, Travelodge
277A	**Abbott Rd, Garden Springs Rd, to US 90 Bus, Spokane Int'l Airport, US 2W (EB)**
277B	**US 2W, Wenatchee, Spokane Int'l Airport, to Fairchild AFB, Grand Coulee Dam (EB)**
279	**US 195S, to Pullman, Colfax, WA State University**
280	**Maple St, Walnut St, Downtown Spokane (EB)**
Food	S: Burger King, IHOP, Taco Bell
280A	**Maple St, Walnut St, Downtown (WB)**
Gas	N: Cenex, Conoco◇, Shell◇
Food	N: Perkins, Subway
Lodg	N: Tiki Lodge
Med	S: + Deaconess Medical Center

EXIT	WASHINGTON
Other	N: Grocery, NAPA
280B	**Howard St, Wall St, Lincoln St, 3rd Ave, Downtown (WB)**
Gas	N: Chevron, Conoco◇, Shell
Food	N: Burger King, Carl's Jr, Deli, IHOP, Molly's Family Rest, Jack in the Box, Spaghetti Factory, Taco Bell
Lodg	N: Trade Winds Motel, Davenport Hotel, Hotel Lusso, Montvale Hotel, Ramada, Rodeway Inn
Other	N: ATMs, CarWash, Grocery
281	**US 2E, US 395N, Division St, Downtown, Newport, Colville**
Gas	N: Citgo, Shell, Tesoro◇
Food	N: Arby's, Dick's Hamburgers, McDonald's, Jack in the Box, Perkins, Pizza Hut, Starbucks, Subway, Taco Time, Waffles Café
Lodg	N: Best Value Inn, Econo Lodge, Howard Johnson S: Quality Inn, Madison Inn
Med	S: + Sacred Heart Medical Center
Other	N: Amtrak, Divine's Auto Center & Towing, Firestone, Les Schwab Tire, U-Haul
282	**2nd Ave, Hamilton St (EB)**
Gas	N: Shell◇
Food	N: Something Else Deli, Shogun
Lodg	N: Budget Saver Motel, Shilo Inn
282A	**Hamilton St (WB)**
Other	N: to Wa State Univ/Spokane, Gonzaga Univ
282B	**2nd Ave, Trent Ave (WB)**
Other	N: Office Depot, Ray's Truck & MH Service
283A	**Altamont St**
Gas	N: Circle K/76
283B	**Thor St, Freya St**
Gas	N: Chevron, Conoco◇, Tesoro◇ S: Citgo, Shell
Food	N: Burger Basket, CJ's Pizza, Peking Garden, McDonald's, Calgary Steak House, Little Caesars
Lodg	N: Park Lane Motel & RV Park▲
Other	N: Kmart
285	**Sprague Ave, Spokane**
Gas	N: Shell, Costco S: Exxon
Food	N: Denny's, IHOP, Wendy's S: Mandarin House, Puerto Vallarta, Starbucks, Subway, Taco Bell, Zip's
Lodg	N: Maple Tree Motel & RV Park▲
Other	N: Costco, Kmart, Home Depot, Lowe's, Radio Shack S: Auto Dealers, Auto Services, Tires
286	**Broadway Ave, Spokane**
TStop	N: Flying J Travel Plaza/ Conoco (Scales)
Gas	S: 7-11, Tesoro
Food	N: Saks/FJ TP, Zip's
Lodg	N: Best Inn, Comfort Inn
TServ	N: FJ TP/Tires, International Trucks, Inland Truck Center, Les Schwab Tires, Northland Peterbilt, Western States CAT, Spokane Diesel, White/Volvo/GMC, Titan Truck, Goodyear
Other	N: WiFi/LP/FJ TP S: Airstream of Spokane, Johnson RV Repair
287	**Argonne Rd, Mullan Rd, Spokane Valley, to Millwood**
Gas	N: Exxon, Holiday, Albertson's S: Chevron, Exxon, 76◇

EXIT	WASHINGTON
Food	N: Burger King, Denny's, Dominos, Jack in the Box, Longhorn BBQ, McDonald's, Subway, Wendy's S: Casa De Oro, Godfather's Pizza, Little Caesar's, Perkins, Starbucks, Sub Shop
Lodg	N: Motel 6♥, Super 8 S: Quality Inn, Maple Tree Motel & RV Park▲, Park Lane Motel & RV Park▲
Other	N: Albertson's, Auto Services, Walgreen's S: RiteAid, Safeway, Trailers Inn RV Park▲
289	**WA 27, Pines Rd, Opportunity**
FStop	S: Divine's Shell
Gas	N: 7-11
Food	N: Matthew's Rest S: Applebee's, Brown Bag, Denny's, Jack in the Box, Jimmy Chang's, Quiznos
Lodg	S: Best Western
Med	S: + Valley Hospital & Medical Center
Other	S: RVDump/Divine's Shell, Walgreen's
291A	**Evergreen Rd**
Gas	S: Shell
Food	N: Arby's, Azteca, Black Angus, Boston's Gourmet Pizza, Flaming Wok, Ivar's Seafood's Bar, IHOP, McDonald's, Outback Steakhouse, TGI Friday, Wendy's
Lodge	N: Oxford Suites
Other	N: ATMs, Best Buy, Tires, Spokane Valley Mall, Sportsman's Warehouse
291B	**Sullivan Rd (EB), Indiana Ave (WB), Veradale**
Gas	N: Chevron, Shell S: 76, Shell◇, Tesoro
Food	N: Arby's, McDonald's, Tony Roma's, Red Robin S: DQ, Jack in the Box, KFC, McDonald's, Mongolian BBQ, Panda Express, Pizza Hut, Quiznos, Shari's Rest, Starbucks, Subway, Taco Bell, Wendy's
Lodg	N: La Quinta Inn♥, Residence Inn S: Comfort Inn
Other	N: Auto Services, B&N, Best Buy, Circuit City, Staples, Tires, Mobil RV Repair S: ATMs, Auto Services, Dollar Tree, Fred Meyer, Grocery, PetSmart♥, Target, Walgreen's, Wal-Mart sc
293	**Barker Rd, Green Acres, Spokane**
Gas	N: Conoco◇ S: Exxon◇, Shell◇
Food	N: Wendy's S: Subway/Exxon
Lodg	N: Alpine Motel & RV Park▲
Other	N: Spokane KOA▲ S: N Country RV & Boat
294	**Appleway Ave, I-90 Bus, Opportunity (WB)**
296	**Appleway Ave Liberty Lake Rd, Liberty Lakes, Otis Orchards**
Gas	N: Shell◇ S: Conoco, Chevron, Safeway
Food	S: Burger King, McDonald's, Pizza Hut, Starbucks, Subway, Taco Bell
Lodg	N: Best Western S: Comfort Inn
Other	N: Auto Dealers S: Albertson's, Home Depot, Safeway, Tires, RNR RV Center

◇ = Regular Gas Stations with Diesel   ▲ = RV Friendly Locations   ♥ = Pet Friendly Locations

RED PRINT SHOWS LARGE VEHICLE PARKING/ACCESS ON SITE OR NEARBY   BROWN PRINT SHOWS CAMPGROUNDS/RV PARKS

Page 449

EXIT	WA / ID	EXIT	IDAHO	EXIT	IDAHO
299	**Spokane Bridge Rd**	Food	N: La Cocina, Pizza Factory, Starbucks, Subway, Wendy's	Other	S: Albertson's, RiteAid, ShopKO, Staples, Blackwell Island RV Park▲, Wild Waters Water Park
N:	Port of Entry/Weigh Station (WB)		S: Capone's Pub & Grill, Denny's, Hot Rod Café, KFC, McDonald's, Rancho Veijo, Subway, Taco Bell	**13**	**4th St, 3rd St, to Government Way, Coeur d'Alene**
N:	WA Welcome Center (WB) (RR, Phones, Picnic, Info)	Lodg	S: Comfort Inn	Gas	N: Conoco◊
Gas	N: Shell, Gas n Go	TServ	S: Northern Diesel, Ross Point Truck Repair, Boat & RV Werkes		S: Exxon◊
	NOTE: MM 300: Idaho State Line	Other	N: Dollar Tree, Radio Shack, Wal-Mart sc, Coeur d'Alene RV Resort/RVDump▲	Food	N: Carl's Jr, DQ, Denny's, IHOP, KFC, Little Caesars, Taco John's, Wendy's
	(PACIFIC TIME ZONE)		S: Auto Services, U-Haul, McCall RV Resort▲		S: Subway
⊙	**WASHINGTON**	**(8)**	**ID Welcome Center (EB) Rest Area (WB) (RR, Phone, Picnic, Vend, Info)**	Lodg	N: Comfort Inn, Fairfield Inn
⊙	**IDAHO**			Other	N: NAPA, Radio Shack, Tire, Auto Services, Ericksons RV Sales/Service/Rentals
	(PACIFIC TIME ZONE)	**(9)**	**Weigh Station (EB)**		S: Wild Waters Water Park
2	**Pleasant View Rd, Post Falls, McGuire**	**11**	**Northwest Blvd, Coeur d'Alene**	**14**	**15th St, Coeur d'Alene**
TStop	N: Flying J Travel Plaza #5005/Conoco (Scales)	Gas	N: Texaco	Other	N: Coeur d'Alene Pkwy State Park
Gas	N: Shell		S: Exxon, Quik Stop◊	**15**	**I-90 Bus, 23rd St, Sherman Ave**
	S: Exxon◊	Food	N: Top of China Buffet II	TStop	S: Tesoro to Go
Food	N: Thad's/FJ TP, Burger King, McDonald's, Toro Veijo II		S: Deli, Joey's Smokin BBQ, Outback Steakhouse, Subway, Sunshine Trader	Gas	S: Cenex
	S: Cabin Rest, Jack in the Box, Zip's	Lodg	S: Days Inn♥, Garden Motel, Holiday Inn Express, Blvd Motel & RV Park/RVDump▲	Food	S: FastFood/Teroso, Down the Street, Moon Rest, Café, Zip's
Lodg	N: Howard Johnson Express	Other	N: Public Golf Course, Lowe's	Lodg	S: Cedar Motel & RV Park/RVDump▲, Budget Saver Motel, El Rancho Motel♥, Flamingo Motel, Holiday Motel, Japan House Suites, La Quinta Inn♥, Resort City Inn, Sandman Motel, State Motel
	S: Riverbend Inn, Sleep Inn		S: River Walk RV Park▲, to Blackwell Island RV Park▲, North ID College, to appr 25mi Coeur d'Alene Casino & Hotel		
TWash	N: Splash N Dash Truck & RV Wash	**12**	**US 95, N Lincoln Way, Lewiston, Sandpoint, Moscow**	Other	S: Laundry/RVDump/LP/Tesoro, NAPA
TServ	N: Post Falls Performance	Gas	N: Chevron, Exxon◊, Holiday◊, Shell◊, Costco, Safeway	**17**	**Mullan Trail Rd**
Other	N: Laundry/WiFi/RVDump/LP/FJ TP, Cabela's, U-Haul, Suntree RV Park/RVDump▲	Food	N: Applebee's, Arby's, Burger King, Chili's, Domino's Pizza, Dragon House Rest, Elmer's Rest, JB's Rest, McDonald's, Perkins, Pizza Hut, Red Lobster, Taco Bell	**22**	**ID 97S, Harrison, to St Maries**
	S: Post Falls Outlet Mall, Prime Outlet Mall, Greyhound Racetrack		S: Jack in the Box, Qdoba Mex Grill, Quiznos, Sub Shop, Shari's	Food	N: Wolf Lodge Steakhouse
5	**I-90 Bus, Spokane St, Post Falls**	Lodg	N: Best Western, Guest House Inn, La Quinta Inn♥, Motel 6♥, Shilo Inn, Super 8♥	Lodg	N: Wolf Lodge Inn
Gas	N: Shell◊, GasMart, 76◊			Other	S: Wolf Lodge RV Campground▲, Coeur d'Alene KOA/RVDump▲, appr 3mi PL/Beauty Creek Campground▲ appr 7mi Squaw Bay Resort & Marina/RVDump▲, to Lake Coeur d'Alene Rec Area
	S: Pacific Pride◊, Handy Mart	Med	N + Idaho Immediate Care Center		
Food	N: Golden Dragon, Hunters Steakhouse, Rob's Seafood & Burgers, Whitehouse Grill		S: + Kootenai Medical Center, + After Hours Urgent Care		
	S: Milltown Grill Rest	Other	N: RVDump/Holiday, ATMs, Banks, Auto Services, Costco, Dollar Tree, Enterprise RAC, Fred Meyer, Grocery, Office Depot, Kmart, Home Depot, Les Schwab Tires, Safeway, U-Haul, Walgreen's, Kootenai Co Fairgrounds, Coeur d'Alene Airport✈, to 15mi Silverwood Theme Park/RVPark▲, Bambi RV Park/RVDump▲, Magic Carpet RV Center, Tamarack RV Park▲, To Alpine Country Store & RV Park▲	**(24)**	**ChainUp (EB) / Removal Area (WB)**
Lodg	S: Red Lion Hotel♥			**28**	**Cedar Creek Rd, 4th of July Pass Rec Area (Turn off Lanes, Both dir) NOTE: Elev 3069'**
Other	N: Perfection Tire & Auto Repair/Les Schwab Tires, Seltice RV			Other	Ski & Snowmobile Area
	S: Pop's RV Service & Repair			**(32)**	**Weigh Station / ChainUp Area (WB)**
6	**I-90 Bus, Seltice Way (WB ex, EB entr)**			**34**	**ID 3S, Cataldo, Rose Lake, St Maries**
Gas	N: 7-11, HiCo Country Store			FStop	S: Junction Quick Stop/Conoco
Food	N: Caruso's Deli, Del Taco, La Cabana Mex Rest, Paul Bunyan Rest, Pizza Hut			Gas	S: Rose Lake General Store
	S: Arby's, Little Caesars			Food	S: Rose Lake Rest, Country Chef Café
Med	N: + North ID Medical Care Center, + After Hours Urgent Care Clinic, + NW Specialty Hospital			**39**	**Old Mission State Park**
				Other	S: Visitor Center/RR/Picnic
Other	N: ATMs, Auto Zone, Banks, Grocery, Vet♥, Walgreen's			**40**	**Latour Creek Rd, Cataldo**
	S: Grocery, Tires, Vet♥, McCall RV Resort▲			Other	S: Kahnderosa RV Campground/RVDump▲
7	**ID 41N, Rathdrum, Spirit Lake**				
Gas	N: Exxon◊, Murphy				
	S: Chevron				

◊ = Regular Gas Stations with Diesel   ▲ = RV Friendly Locations   ♥ = Pet Friendly Locations
RED PRINT SHOWS LARGE VEHICLE PARKING/ACCESS ON SITE OR NEARBY   BROWN PRINT SHOWS CAMPGROUNDS/RV PARKS

Interstate W 90 E

EXIT		IDAHO
43		Coeur d'Alene River Rd, Kingston
	Gas	S: Kingston Kwik Stop/Exxon
	Other	N: Country Lane RV Resort▲
		S: RVDump/Exxon, to appr 12mi BLM/ Bumblebee Campground▲
45		Division St, Pinehurst
	FStop	S: Carousel Gas & Tire
	Gas	S: Chevron◆, Conoco◆
	Other	S: By the Way RV Park▲, Pinehurst RV
48		Airport Rd, Murray, Smelterville
	TStop	N: Silver Valley Car & Truck Stop
	Food	N: Rest/Silver Valley CTS
	Lodg	N: Motel/Silver Valley CTS
	Other	N: RVDump/LP/Silver Valley CTS, Shoshone Co Airport✈
49		I-90 Bus, Bunker Ave, Kellogg
	Gas	N: Conoco◆
	Food	N: McDonald's, Subway, Sam's D/I
		S: Gondola Café/Silver Mountain
	Lodg	N: Silverhorn Motor Inn, Silver Ridge Mountain Lodge
		S: Baymont Inn
	Med	N: + Shoshone Medical Center
	Other	N: Silver Mountain Resort
		S: to New St City/RVDump
50		Hill St, Kellogg (EB)
	Gas	S: Conoco
	Lodg	N: Trail Motel
	Other	S: Silver Mountain Resort/Rec Area▲
51		Division St, Kellogg, Wardner
	Gas	N: Conoco◆
	Med	N: + Hospital
	Other	N: Auto Dealers
		S: Kellogg RV Center
54		Big Creek Rd, Elk Creek, Murray
	Other	N: Miners Memorial, Crystal Gold Mine
57		I-90 Bus, 3rd St, Wallace, Osburn
	Gas	S: Shell◆
	Other	S: Blue Anchor RV Park▲
60		Markwell Ave, Wallace, Silverton
	Lodg	S: Molly B'Damm Motel
61		I-90 Bus, Front St, Wallace
	Gas	S: Conoco◆, Exxon
	Food	S: Albi's Steakhouse, Brooks Rest, Deb's Café, Pizza Factory, Wallace Café, Silver Lantern D/I
	Lodg	S: Wallace Inn, Brooks Hotel, Stardust Hotel, Ryan Hotel
62		I-90 Bus, ID 4, Wallace, Burke
	Gas	S: Exxon
	Food	S: Jameson Rest/Saloon/Inn
	Med	S: + Hospital
64		Golconda
65		Grouse Creek Rd
66		Gold Creek
67		Lower Mill St
68		I-90 Bus, River St, Mullan (EB)
	Gas	N: Exxon◆
	Food	N: Mullan Cafe
69		I-90 Bus, Atlas Rd, Mullan
(70)		RunAWay Truck Ramp (WB)
(71)		RunAWay Truck Ramp (WB)
(72)		Scenic Area (EB)

EXIT		ID / MT
(73)		Scenic Area (WB)
	NOTE:	EB: TRUCK INFO Pacific / Mountain Time Zone Lookout Pass: Elev 4680'
	NOTE:	MM 73.88: Montana State Line (PACIFIC / MOUNTAIN TIME ZONE)
		⌒ IDAHO
		⌒ MONTANA (MOUNTAIN TIME ZONE)
(0)		Lookout Pass (Elev 4680)
	Other	Lookout Pass Ski & Recreation Area Rest/RVPark▲, Tourist Info, Ski Area
(5)		Lookout Pass Rest Area (Both dir) (RR, Picnic, ChainUp / Remove)
5		Taft Area, Saltese
10		Saltese Rd, Saltese, St Regis
	Lodg	N: Mangold Gen'l Store & Motel
(15)		Weigh Station (Both dir, Left Exit)
16		Haugan Rd, Haugan, St Regis
	FStop	N: Lincoln's Silver Dollar/Exxon
	Food	N: Rest/Silver Dollar Bar
	Lodg	N: Motel/Silver Dollar & RV Park▲
	Other	N: Casino/Silver Dollar
18		Thompson De Borgia Rd, De Borgia, Henderson
	Lodg	N: Pinecrest Motel, Black Diamond Guest Camp Ranch♥ & Resort▲

EXIT		MONTANA
22		Henderson Rd, St Regis
	Other	S: to appr 5mi BLM/Cabin City Campground▲
25		Drexel Rd, St Regis
26		Ward Creek Rd (EB only)
29		Fishing Access (WB ex & reacc)
30		Two Mile Rd, St Regis
33		MT 135, Old US 10, St Regis
	FStop	N: St Regis Travel Center/Conoco
	Gas	N: Exxon, Sinclair
	Food	N: Rest/St Regis TC, Frosty Drive In, OK Café & Casino
	Lodg	N: Little River Motel, Super 8 ♥
	Other	N: Campground St Regis/RVDump▲, St Regis Riding Stables Campground▲ Nugget RV Resort▲
37		Sloway Rd, Sloway Area
43		Southside Rd, Dry Creek Rd, Superior
47		River St, 4th Ave, to Diamond Rd, MT 257, Superior
	TStop	S: Town Pump #3800/Pilot #911/Exxon
	Gas	N: Conoco◆
	Food	N: Café, Rock 'n Rodeo Bar & Grill
		S: FastFood/Town Pump
	Lodg	N: Big Sky Motel, Hilltop Motel
	Med	N: + Mineral Community Hospital
	Other	N: Grocery, Pharmacy
		S: Casino/Laundry/TownPump
55		Lozeau Rd, Lozeau, Superior
(58)		Quartz Flats Rest Area (Both dir) (RR, Phone, Picnic)
61		Tarkio Rd, Alberton
66		Fish Creek Rd, Albertson
70		Old Hwy 10, Alberton, Cyr (WB exit, EB reaccess)
(72)		Parking Area (EB)
(73)		Parking Area (WB)
75		MT 507, Railroad St, Alberton
	Lodg	S: Ghost Rail Inn B&B, Rivers Edge Resort/ Motel/Rest/Casino/RV Park & Campground/RVDump▲
77		CR 507, Petty Creek Rd, Alberton (Acc Ex #75 W on Fred Thompson Rd)
82		Nine Mile Rd, Huson
85		Frontage Rd, Huson Rd, Huson
	Other	S: Larry's Six Mile Casino & Cafe
89		MT 263, Frenchtown, Huson
	Gas	S: Conoco◆
	Food	S: Alcan Bar & Café, Coffee Cup Rest, Eugene's Pizza, King Ranch Rest
	Other	S: Axmen Propane
(93)		Inspection Station (Both dir)
96		US 93N, I-90 Bus, MT 200W, Missoula, Kalispell
	TStop	N: PacPride/Muralt's AmBest Travel Plaza/ Conoco (Scales)
		S: Crossroads Travel Center/Sinclair
	Food	N: Muralts Cafe/Muralt's TP
		S: Rest/Crossroads TC

◆ = Regular Gas Stations with Diesel   ▲ = RV Friendly Locations   ♥ = Pet Friendly Locations
RED PRINT SHOWS LARGE VEHICLE PARKING/ACCESS ON SITE OR NEARBY   BROWN PRINT SHOWS CAMPGROUNDS/RV PARKS

Page 451

INTERSTATE 90 W/E

EXIT		MONTANA
	Lodg	N: DaysInn♥/Muralt's TP
		S: Redwood Lodge
	TWash	N: Muralt's TP
	TServ	N: Muralt's TP/Tires, Freightliner, Ford, GMC, Kenworth, Peterbilt, Volvo, Wabash, Utility & Thermo King, NW Truck & Trailer
		S: Transport Equipment, Missoula Truck & Auto Body
	Other	N: Laundry/BarbSh/WiFi/RVSvc/RVDump/LP/Muralts TP, Wye West Casino/Muralt's TP, Yogi Bear's Jellystone Park Camp Resort/RVDump▲, Jim & Mary's RV Park/RVDump▲, Outpost Campground/RVDump▲, to (approx 98 miles) EdgeWater RV Resort and Motel▲ (See AD Page 456)
		S: Laundry/WiFi/RVDump/LP/Crossroads TC, Missoula RV Repair, U-Haul, to Missoula Int'l Airport✈
99		Airway Blvd, Broadway St, Missoula (Access to Ex #101 Serv)
	Gas	S: Mobil◊
	Lodg	S: Wingate Inn
	TServ	S: Interstate Power Systems
	Other	S: Montana Harley Davidson, Missoula Int'l Airport✈
101		US 93, Grant Creek Rd, Reserve St, Missoula
	FStop	S: Harvest States Cenex
	TStop	S: Deano's Travel Plaza/Exxon
	Gas	N: Conoco◊
		S: Conoco
	Food	N: Cracker Barrel, Mac Kenzie River Pizza, Starbucks
		S: Rest/Deano's TP, 4 B's, Arby's, Fiesta En Jalisco, IHOP, Kadena's, McDonald's, Montana Club, Johnny Carino's, Java Junction, Quiznos, Taco Time
	Lodg	N: Best Western♥, C'Mon Inn
		S: America's Best Inn, Comfort Inn, Courtyard, Hampton Inn, Hilton Garden Inn, Microtel, Ruby's Inn, Super 8
	TServ	S: CAT, Cummins NW, Western Truck
	Med	S: + Community Medical Center
	Other	S: RVDump/Harvest St Cenex, RVDump/Casino/Deano's TP, Albertson's, Auto Dealers, Auto Services, ATM's, Banks, B&N, Best Buy, Costco, Firestone, Home Depot, Les Schwab Tires, PetSmart♥, REI, Staples, Target, Tire-Rama, Walgreen's, Wal-Mart sc, to Southgate Mall, Bob Wards, Golf Courses, Missoula KOA/RVDump▲, Bretz RV & Marine/RVDump, Gull Boats & RV, Rangitsch Bros RV, Silver Creek Casino, Jokers Wild Casino, Lucky Lil's Casino, Casinos, to appr 12mi Lolo Hot Springs RV Park▲
104		US 93S, Orange St, to Hamilton
	Gas	S: Conoco◊, Sinclair
	Food	S: Depot, Double Front Café, Pagoda Chinese, Starbucks, Subway, Taco John's
	Lodg	S: Days Inn, Holiday Inn, Inn on Broadway♥, Mountain Valley Inn, Orange St Inn, Red Lion Inn
	Med	S: + St Patrick Hospital
	Other	S: FedEx Kinko's, Greyhound, Pharmacy, Safeway, Tire-Rama, UPS Store, Whitefish KOA▲

EDGEWATER R.V. Resort & Motel
On Beautiful Flathead Lake
- 46 Full Hook Ups
- Pull Throughs
- Clean Restrooms
- Laundry & Cable TV
- 20 Room & Kitchenette Units
- Lake Dock & Swimming Access
- RV Rallies
- 7 Luxury Cabins

Lakeside, Montana
(406) 844-3644
1-800-424-3798
edgewaterrv.com
98 Miles N. On 93

EXIT		MONTANA
105		I-90 Bus, US 12, Van Buren St, Greenough Dr, Missoula
	Gas	S: Conoco◊, Exxon, Pacific Pride◊, Sinclair◊
	Food	S: Burger King, Finnegan's Family Rest, Little Caesars, McDonald's, Pizza Hut, Subway, Taco Bell
	Lodg	S: Campus Inn, Creekside Inn♥, DoubleTree Hotel, Family Inn, Holiday Inn Express, Ponderosa Lodge♥, Thunderbird Motel
	Other	S: ATMs, Albertson's, Auto Services, PetSmart♥, Pharmacy, Univ of MT
107		MT 200, Broadway St, E Missoula (Access to Ex #105 via S)
	TStop	N: Ole's Truck Stop/Conoco
	Gas	N: Sinclair
	Food	N: Rest/Ole's TS
	Lodg	N: Aspen Motel
109		MT 200E, Milltown, to Bonner, Great Falls
	TStop	N: Town Pump #8500/Pilot #905/Exxon (Scales)
	Food	N: Arby's/Subway/TownPump
	TServ	N: Boss Truck Shop
	Other	N: Laundry/BarbSh/Casino/WiFi/LP/TownPump
113		Turah Rd, Turah
	Other	S: Turah RV Park/RVDump▲
120		MT 210, Mullan Rd, Clinton
126		Rock Creek Rd, Clinton, Rock Creek Rec Area
	Gas	S: Rock Creek Lodge

EXIT		MONTANA
	Food	S: Rock Creek Lodge, Pioneer Rest, Ekstroms Stage Stn
	Lodg	S: Rock Creek Lodge, to 4mi Elkhorn Guest Ranch
	Other	S: Ekstroms Stage Station Campground/RVDump▲, Rock Creek Lodge RV/RVDump, to 12 mi PL/Grizzly Campground▲, appr 18 mi PL/Harry's Flat Campground▲, 15 mi PL/Dalles Campground▲
(128)		Parking Area (Both dir)
130		Beavertail Rd, Clinton
	Other	S: Beavertail Hill State Park▲
138		Drummond Frontage Rd, Clinton, Bearmouth Area
	Other	N: Chalet Bearmouth Motel/Restaurant/RV Park & Campground/RVDump▲
(143)		Bearmouth Rest Area (Both dir) (RR, Phone, Picnic)
(151)		Weigh Station (Both dir)
153		MT 1, US 10A, Frontage Rd, Drummond, to Philipsburg (EB exit, WB reaccess) (Acc to Ex #154)
	Other	N: to appr 6 mi Good Time Camping & RV Park▲
		S: to appr 25mi The Inn at Philipsburg/Motel/RV Park & Campground▲
154		MT 271, Front St, Drummond, Philipsburg (WB ex, EB reaccess)
	Gas	S: Conoco◊, Sinclair
	Food	S: Wagon Wheel Cafe
	Lodg	S: Sky Motel, Wagon Wheel Motel
162		Jens Rd, Gold Creek
166		Gold Creek Rd, Gold Creek
	Other	S: to Camp Mak-A-Dream
(167)		Gold Creek Rest Area (WB) (RR, Phone, Picnic)
(169)		Gold Creek Rest Area (EB) (RR, Phone, Picnic)
170		Phosphate Rd, Gold Creek
174		US 12E, Garrison, Helena (EB)
175		US 12E, Garrison, Helena (WB)
	Other	N: to Riverfront RV Park/RVDump▲
179		Beck Hill Rd, Garrison
184		I-90 Bus, Boulder Rd, Deer Lodge
	FStop	S: Town Pump #9150/Exxon
	TStop	S: I-90 Auto Truck Plaza/Conoco
	Gas	S: Cenex◊
	Food	S: Rest/I-90 ATP, 4 B's Rest, Broken Arrow Casino & Steakhouse, Coffee House, McDonald's, Outlaw Café, Scharf's Family Rest
	Lodg	S: Super 8♥, Scharf's Motor Inn, Western Big Sky Inn
	Other	N: Deer Lodge KOA▲
		S: Casino/TownPump, Casino/RVDump/I-90 ATP, Indian Creek Campground/RVDump▲, Auto Repairs, Les Scwab Tires, IGA, Safeway
187		I-80 Bus, Main St, Deer Lodge (Access to Ex #184 Serv)
	Other	N: Deer Lodge KOA/RVDump▲
		S: to Deer Lodge City & Co Airport✈
195		Racetrack Rd, Deer Lodge
197		MT 273, Galen Rd, Anaconda

◊ = Regular Gas Stations with Diesel   ▲ = RV Friendly Locations   ♥ = Pet Friendly Locations
RED PRINT SHOWS LARGE VEHICLE PARKING/ACCESS ON SITE OR NEARBY   BROWN PRINT SHOWS CAMPGROUNDS/RV PARKS

EXIT	MONTANA
201	MT 48, Anaconda, Warm Springs
Other	S: to Anaconda Airport✈, Big Sky RV Park & Campground▲, Willow Springs RV Park & Campground▲
208	MT 1, Anaconda (All Serv 3-5 mi S in Anaconda)
Med	S: + Hospital
(210)	Parking Area (WB)
211	Fairmont Rd, to MT 441, Butte, Gregson, Fairmont, Hot Springs
Other	S: to appr 2.5 mi Fairmont RV Park▲, Fairmont Hot Springs Resort & Golf Course
216	Ramsey Rd, Nissler Rd, Butte
NOTE:	I-90 below runs with I-15 for appr 8 mi. Exit #'s follow I-15.
(219/121)	Jct I-15S, to Dillon, Idaho Falls Jct I-90W to Missoula, I-15S to Idaho Falls, I-15N/I-90E to Butte
122	MT 276, Butte, Rocker
N:	Weigh Station (Both dir)
TStop	E: Flying J Travel Plaza #5130 (Scales) W: Town Pump Travel Plaza #5600/Pilot #908/Conoco
Food	E: Cookery/Arby's/FJ TP W: Arby's/Subway/McDonald's/Town Pump TP
Lodg	E: Rocker Inn W: Motel 6♥
TServ	E: Rocker Repair
Other	E: Casino/Laundry/WiFi/RVDump/LP/FJ TP W: Laundry/Casino/TownPump TP
(124)	Jct I-115, Butte City Center, Harrison Ave, Montana St (NB)
126	Montana St, Butte
Gas	E: Thriftway, Town Pump◊ W: Cenex, Kum & Go
Food	W: Jokers Wild Casino & Rest
Lodg	W: Budget Motel, Eddy's Motel
Med	W: + St James Healthcare
Other	W: Butte KOA/RVDump▲, Grocery
127B	I-15 Bus N, Harrison Ave, Butte (NB)
127A	I-15 Bus S, Harrison Ave, Butte (NB)
127	I-15 Bus, Harrison Ave, Butte (SB)
Gas	E: Conoco, Exxon, Sinclair, Town Pump W: Conoco, Town Pump
Food	E: 4 B's Rest, Arbys, Burger King, DQ, Godfather's, KFC, McDonald's, Perkins, Taco Bell, Wendy's W: Rest/Red Lion Hotel, Denny's, Hanging Five Family Rest, Papa John's, Papa Murphy's, Quiznos
Lodg	E: Best Western, Hampton Inn, Super 8 W: Comfort Inn, Days Inn, Holiday Inn Express, Red Lion Hotel
Other	E: Casinos, Auto Dealers, Grocery, Kmart, Wal-Mart sc, Our Lady of the Rockies, Butte Plaza Mall, Bert Mooney Airport✈, Rocky Mtn RV Sales & Srv, Al's RV Center W: RVDump/Town Pump, Casino, Grocery, Laundromat, NAPA, Animal Hospital♥
(129/227)	Jct I-90E to Billings, Jct I-15S/I-90W to Butte, N-Helena
NOTE:	I-90 above runs with I-15 for appr 8 mi. Exit #'s follow I-15.

Personal Notes

EXIT	MONTANA
(230)	ChainUp / Removal Area (Both dir)
233	Homestake, Continental Divide
(235)	Parking Area (Both dir)
(237)	Pull-Off (EB)
(238.5)	RunAWay Truck Ramp (EB)
(240.5)	ChainUp / Removal Area (Both dir)
241	Pipestone Rd, Whitehall
Other	S: Pipestone RV Park/RVDump▲
249	MT 55, MT 69, Whitehall
TStop	S: Town Pump Travel Plaza #8945/Exxon
Food	S: CountrySkillet/Subway/Lucky Lil's Casino/TownPump TP
Lodg	S: Super 8
Other	S: Laundry/LP/TownPump TP, Whitetail Creek RV Park▲
256	MT 69, MT 2, MT 359, Whitehall, Cardwell, Boulder
Gas	S: Corner Store/Conoco
Other	S: RVDump/Conoco, to Lewis & Clark Caverns State Park/RVDump▲, to Yellowstone Nat'l Park
267	Milligan Canyon Rd, Cardwell
274	US 287, Three Forks, Helena, Ennis
TStop	S: Town Pump Travel Plaza #350/Pilot #910/Exxon (Scales)
Gas	N: Conoco
Food	N: Cattlemen's Cafe S: Subway/TownPump TP
Lodg	N: Fort Three Forks Motel♥ & RV Park/HorseCorrals▲

EXIT	MONTANA
Other	S: Laundry/Casino/LP/WiFi/Town Pump, Three Forks KOA/RVDump▲
278	US 10, MT 2, Three Forks, Trident
Gas	S: 3 Forks Sinclair
Food	S: 3 Forks Café, D&L Country Diner, Stageline Pizza
Lodg	S: Broken Spur Motel
Other	N: to Missouri River Headwaters State Park S: 3 Forks Sinclair/RVDump, Marble's Laundry/RVDump, Golf, 3 Forks Airport✈
283	Buffalo Jump Rd, Three Forks, Logan
Other	S: to Madison Buffalo Jump State Park
288	MT 288, Manhattan, Amsterdam
Gas	N: Thriftway/Conoco◊
Food	N: Café on Broadway, Garden Cafe, Sir Scott's Oasis Steakhouse
Other	N: Manhattan RV Park/RVDump▲
298	MT 347, Amsterdam Rd, (EB) MT 291, MT 85, Jackrabbit Ln (WB) Belgrade, W Yellowstone
TStop	S: Flying J Travel Plaza/Conoco (Scales)
Gas	N: Cenex◊, Conoco, Exxon
Food	N: Burger King, McDonald's, Pizza Hut, Subway S: Rest/FJ TP
Lodg	S: Motel/FJ TP, Best Inn, Holiday Inn♥, La Quinta Inn♥, Super 8
Other	N: Albetson's, IGA, NAPA, Whalen Tire, Gallatin Field Airport✈ S: Laundry/WiFi/LP/FJ TP, to appr 8mi Bozeman KOA▲
305	MT 412, N 19th Ave, Bozeman
Gas	N: Exxon
Food	S: Arby's, Burger King, Denny's, Johnny Carino's, Perkins, Pizza Hut
Lodg	N: AmericInn S: C'Mon Inn, Wingate Inn
Other	S: Rest Area, Bozeman Ford Lincoln Mercury RV, ATMs, Bank, Costco, Home Depot, Lowe's, Target
306	I-90 Bus, US 10, US 191N, N 7th, Bozeman
Gas	N: Conoco, Sinclair S: Conoco◊, Exxon, Sinclair◊
Food	N: McDonald's S: Applebee's, Hardee's, Subway, Taco Bell, Wendy's
Lodg	N: Best Value Inn, Fairfield Inn, Microtel, Ramada S: Best Western♥, Comfort Inn♥, Days Inn♥, Hampton Inn, Hilton Garden Inn, Holiday Inn♥, Sunset Motel & Trailer Park▲
Other	N: C&T Mobile Home Repair, Whalen Tire S: RVDump/Conoco, ATMs, Banks, Big O Tires, Firestone, Grocery, IGA, Kmart, Pharmacy, Wal-Mart sc, U-Haul, to MT State Univ
309	US 191S, Main St, Bozeman
FStop	S: Town Pump #9110/Exxon Town Pump #8927/Exxon
Gas	S: Exxon, Sinclair
Food	S: 4 B's, Black Angus Steakhouse, Eastside Diner, Montana Ale Works
Lodg	S: Continental Motor Inn, Ranch House Motel, Western Heritage Inn
Med	S: + Hospital
Other	N: Sunrise Campground/RVDump▲

◊ = Regular Gas Stations with Diesel ▲ = RV Friendly Locations ♥ = Pet Friendly Locations
RED PRINT SHOWS LARGE VEHICLE PARKING/ACCESS ON SITE OR NEARBY BROWN PRINT SHOWS CAMPGROUNDS/RV PARKS

Page 453

EXIT		MONTANA
	Other	S: Jackpot Casino East, Lucky Dog Saloon
313		Bozeman Trail Rd, Bear Canyon Rd
	Other	S: Bear Canyon Campground/RVDump▲
316		Trail Creek Rd, Bozeman
(319)		ChainUp / Removal Area (Both dir)
319		Jackson Creek Rd
324		Ranch Access
330		I-90 Bus Loop, US 10, Livingston
	TStop	N: Yellowstone Truck Stop
	Food	N: Rest/Yellowstone TS
	TServ	N: Yellowstone TS/Tires
	Other	N: Laundry/RVDump/Yellowstone TS
333		US 89S, Park St, Livingston, to Yellowstone Park
	TStop	S: Town Pump #610/Conoco
	Gas	N: Conoco, Exxon, Sinclair S: Cenex, Exxon
	Food	N: Pizza Hut S: FastFood/TownPump, Hardee's, McDonald's, Subway
	Lodg	N: Best Western♥, Budget Host Motel, Econo Lodge♥, Travelodge♥ S: Comfort Inn, Super 8
	Med	N: + Hospital
	Other	N: Grocery, Pharmacy, Oasis RV Park▲ S: Laundry/CarWash/Casino/Town Pump, Albertson's, Pharmacy, Osen's RV Park & Campground/RVDump▲, Livingston/Paradise Valley KOA/RVDump▲, to Yellowstone
337		I-90 Bus, Livingston, Local Access
340		US 89N, White Sulphur Springs
343		MT 295, Mission Creek Rd
350		East End Access
352		Ranch Access
354		MT 563, Big Timber, Springdale
362		Frontage Rd, Big Timber, DeHart
367		I-90 Bus Lp, US 191, US 10, Big Timber, Harlowton
	TStop	N: WB: Acc Ex #370: Town Pump #922/Exxon
	Gas	N: Conoco
	Food	N: Country Skillet/FastFood/Town Pump
	Lodg	N: Super 8
	Other	N: Laundry/Town Pump S: Spring Creek Campground & Trout Ranch/RVDump▲

EXIT		MONTANA
384		Bridger Creek Rd, Greycliff
392		Division St, Reed Point
	Gas	N: Sinclair
	Other	N: US Post Office
396		Ranch Access
400		Springtime Rd, Columbus
408		MT 78, N 9th St, Columbus
	TStop	S: Town Pump #8924/Pilot #906/Exxon (Scales)
	Gas	S: Conoco
	Food	S: CountrySkillet/McDonald's/T Pump, Apple Village Café
	Lodg	S: Super 8/T Pump
	Med	S: + Hospital
	Other	S: Laundry/Casino/WiFi/RVDump/T Pump
(418)		Columbus Rest Area (Both dir) (RR, Phone, Picnic)
426		Old US 10, Park City
	TStop	S: Kum&Go #829/Cenex
	Food	S: Rest/FastFood/Kum&Go
	Other	S: Laundry/WiFi/LP/Kum&Go
433		I-90 Bus Lp, W Laurel (EB ex, Wb entr)
434		US 212, US 310, Laurel, Red Lodge
	FStop	N: Town Pump/Exxon
	Gas	N: Cenex◊, Conoco◊
	Food	N: Deli/T Pump, Burger King, Hardee's, Pizza Hut
	Lodg	N: Best Western, Howard Johnson, Russell Motel
	Other	N: Casino/CarWash/T Pump, RVDump/Cenex, IGA, Pharmacy, to Laurel Airport ✈
437		Frontage Rd, US 212, MT 2, Laurel
	TStop	S: Pelican Truck Plaza/Sinclair (Scales)
	Food	S: Rest/FastFood/Pelican TP
	Lodg	S: Motel/Pelican TS & RV Park▲
	Tires	S: Pelican TP
	Other	S: Laundry/Casino/RVDump/LP/Pelican TP
(439)		Weigh Station (Both dir)
443		Zoo Dr, to Shiloh Rd, Billings
	Gas	S: Cenex
	Other	N: Zoo S: I-90 Motors & RV, Beartooth Harley Davidson, Billings RV
446		I-90 Bus, Laurel Rd, Mullowney Ln, King Ave, Billings
	TStop	N: Sinclair West Parkway
	Gas	N: Conoco, Holiday◊ S: Conoco, Exxon
	Food	N: Rest/Sinclair, Burger King, Denny's, Fuddrucker's, Olive Garden, Outback Steakhouse, Perkins, Red Lobster

EXIT		MONTANA
	Food	S: Cracker Barrel
	Lodg	N: C'Mon Inn, Comfort Inn♥, Days Inn♥, Fairfield Inn, Quality Inn♥, Super 8 S: Best Western♥, Holiday Inn♥, Motel 6♥, Kelly Inn♥, Ramada Inn♥, Red Roof Inn♥
	TServ	N: Sinclair/Tires, Interstate Tire Rama, Tractor & Equipment Co, Kenworth
	Other	N: Laundry/Sinclair, RVDump/Holiday, Casino's, Costco, Best Buy, Albertson's, Home Depot, Lowe's, Mall, PetSmart♥, Office Depot, Target, Wal-Mart sc, Big Sky Campground/RVDump▲
447		Billings Blvd, Billings
	Gas	N: Conoco◊
	Food	N: McDonald's, 4 B's
	Lodg	N: Hampton Inn, Sleep Inn, Super 8♥
	Other	S: Billings KOA
450		MT 3, 27th St, Billings
	Gas	N: Conoco◊, Sinclair, Exxon
	Food	N: Pizza Hut, Denny's, Perkins
	Lodg	N: War Bonnet Inn, Howard Johnson♥
	Med	N: + Hospital
	Other	N: to Billings Logan Int'l Airport ✈ S: Billings KOA/RVDump▲, Yellowstone River Campground/RVDump▲
452		US 87N, Billings, to Lockwood, Roundup
	FStop	N: Town Pump/Conoco
	TStop	S: Kum&Go #824/Cenex
	Gas	N: Exxon◊, Cenex, Holiday◊
	Food	N: Arby's/TownPump, Elmer's, Peking Express, Subway, Taco Bell, Wendy's S: FastFood/Cenex
	Other	N: Casino/T Pump, Albertson's, CarQuest, Office Depot, Target, Wal-Mart sc, U-Haul, Fairgrounds, Metra RV Center S: Laundry/Kum&Go
455		Johnson Lane, Billings
	TStop	S: Flying J Travel Plaza #5490/Conoco (Scales)
	Gas	S: Exxon
	Food	S: Cookery/FastFood/FJ TP, Burger King, Subway
	TWash	S: Fly In Wash
	Other	S: Laundry/WiFi/RVDump/LP/FJ TP
(456A)		Jct I-94, Hardin, Sheridan
(456B)		Jct I-94E, Miles City, Bismarck (WB)
462		Pryor Creek Rd, Indian Creek Rd, Huntley
	Other	S: Crow Indian Reservation
469		Arrow Creek Rd
(476)		Hardin Rest Area (Both dir) (RR, Phone, Picnic)

Page 454

◊ = Regular Gas Stations with Diesel ▲ = RV Friendly Locations ♥ = Pet Friendly Locations
RED PRINT SHOWS LARGE VEHICLE PARKING/ACCESS ON SITE OR NEARBY BROWN PRINT SHOWS CAMPGROUNDS/RV PARKS

EXIT	MT / WY	EXIT	WYOMING	EXIT	WYOMING
478	CR 30, Fly Creek Rd, Hardin	Lodg	S: Foothills Motel & Campground▲	Other	N: Dalton's RV Center
484	Frontage Rd, Hardin, Toluca	Other	S: Lazy R Campground, to Bear Lodge Resort & Campground▲		S: Firestone, Grocery, Pharmacy, Walgreen's, Wal-Mart sc, Auto Service, Mall, Sheridan Jr College, Sheridan Co Airport✈, Sheridan RV Park▲, RVDump/Washington Park
495	I-90 Bus Lp, MT 47, MT 313, Hardin	14	WY 345, Acme Rd, Ranchester		
FStop	N: Interstate Texaco	(15)	Parking Area (WB)		
	S: Town Pump #1710/Exxon, Red Eagle Shell	16	WY 339, Sheridan, to Decker	(31)	Parking Area (EB)
TStop	S: Broadway/Flying J Fuel Stop/Conoco	20	I-90 Bus, US 87S, Main St, Sheridan	33	Meade Creek Rd, Big Horn, Story
Gas	S: Sinclair◊	S:	WY Port of Entry (WB)	37	Prairie Dog Creek Rd, Story
Food	N: Purple Cow	FStop	S: Red Eagle #17/Shell	(39)	Parking Area (WB)
	S: FastFood/Flying J FS, FastFood/TownPump, McDonald's	TStop	S: Common Cents Travel Plaza #210/Exxon	44	US 87N, Piney Creek Rd, Buffalo, to Story, Banner
Lodg	S: American Inn, Super 8, Lariat Motel	Gas	S: Conoco, Cenex, Kum&Go	Other	N: Fort Phil Kearney
Med	S: + Hospital	Food	S: Country Kitchen/CommonCents TP, Little Caesar's, McDonald's, Pizza Hut, Pablo's Rest, Subway, WY Rib & Chop House	47	Shell Creek Rd, Buffalo
Other	N: Hardin KOA/RVDump▲, Grand View Campground/RVDump▲, Sunset Village RV/RVDump			51	CR 39, Lake Ridge Rd, Buffalo, Monument Rd, to Lake Desmet
	S: WiFi/RVDump/LP/FJ FS, Casino/T Pump	Lodg	S: Super 8♥, Stage Stop Motel, Trails End Motel	Other	N: Lake Stop Resort/Motel/RVPark▲
497	I-90 Bus, MT 47, 3rd St, Hardin	TServ	S: Steve's Truck Service	53	Rock Creek Rd
Med	S: + Hospital	Other	N: Sheridan/Big Horn Mtns/KOA▲	56A	I-90 Bus, I-25 Bus, Main St, to Buffalo (EB ex, WB entr) (All Serv at 1st Exit, I-25S, x299)
Other	S: Crow Indian Res		S: Laundry/CommonCents TP, Safeway, Kmart		
503	Frontage Rd, Dunmore	23	WY 336, 5th St, Sheridan		
509	Crow Agency	N:	Rest Area (Both dir) (RR, Phone, Picnic, RVDump)	Other	S: Johnson Co Airport✈, Buffalo KOA▲, to appr 3.5mi Big Horn Mountain Campground▲
Gas	N: Conoco				
Food	N: Chester Fried Chicken	Gas	N: Rock Stop◊	(56B)	I-25S, Buffalo, Casper, Cheyenne (All Serv at 1st Exit S x299)
(509)	Weigh Station (Both dir)		S: Cenex, Holiday, Maverik, Shell		
510	US 212E, Garryowen	Food	N: Subway/Rock Stop	Other	S: Buffalo KOA▲, to Mountain View Motel & Campground▲, to Indian Campground▲
Gas	N: Exxon◊		S: Artic Circle, Bubba's BBQ, KFC, WY Rib & Chop House		
	S: Little Big Horn	Lodg	S: Alamo Motel, Best Western, Bramble Motel & RV Park▲, Motel 6♥, Sheridan Inn, Sundown Motel	NOTE:	EB: CHECK YOUR FUEL! No Services Between Exits #58 & #124.
Food	N: Crow's Nest Cafe				
Lodg	S: Little Big Horn Casino & Motel & Campground	Med	S: + Sheridan Memorial Hospital	58	I-90 Bus, US 16, US 87, Buffalo, Ucross, I-25
Med	N: + Hospital	Other	S: ATMs, Kmart, Pharmacy, Tires, Auto Services, Peter D's RV Park/RVDump▲, Summertime RV Service	TStop	S: Big Horn Travel Plaza, Kum&Go/Cenex
Other	S: Little Big Horn Battlefield Nat'l Mon			Gas	S: Shell◊, Sinclair
514	MT 451, Garryowen	370	US 191, I-90 Bus, Big Timber	Food	S: Rest/Big Horn TP, McDonald's, Pizza Hut, Subway
Gas	N: Conoco	Gas	N: Conoco, Exxon, Sinclair		
Other	S: 7th Ranch RV Camp/RVDump▲	Other	S: Spring Creek Campground & Trout Ranch/RVDump▲	Lodg	S: Best Value Inn♥, Best Western♥, Comfort Inn♥, Econo Lodge♥, Super 8♥, Wyoming/WYO Motel
530	US 87, MT 463, Lodge Grass				
Gas	S: Cenex◊	377	Frontage Rd, Greycliff		
544	MT 457, Wyola	Other	S: Big Timber KOA/RVDump▲	Med	S: + Family Medical Center
549	CR 382, MY 451, to Aberdeen	(381)	Greycliff Rest Area (Both dir) (RR, Phone, Picnic)	Other	S: RVDump/Cenex, Buffalo KOA, Big Horn Mountains Campground▲, Deer Park RV Park & Campground/RVDump, Indian Campground▲, Carousel Park
NOTE:	MM 558: Wyoming State Line				
	(MOUNTAIN TIME ZONE)	25	I-90 Bus, Brundage Ln, US 14E, Sheridan, Big Horn		
○ MONTANA		Gas	S: Conoco◊, Exxon◊, Holiday, Maverik	(59)	Parking Area (Both dir)
○ WYOMING		Food	S: Arby's, Burger King, Golden China, JB's Family Rest, Perkins, Prime Dining, Subway, Taco Bell, Wendy's	65	Red Hills Rd, Tipperary Rd
	(MOUNTAIN TIME ZONE)			(68)	Parking Area (Both dir)
1	CR 65, Barker Rd, Parkman	Lodg	N: Comfort Inn		
9	US 14W, Ranchester, Dayton		S: Days Inn♥, Holiday Inn♥, Mill Inn		
Gas	S: Big Country Oil				

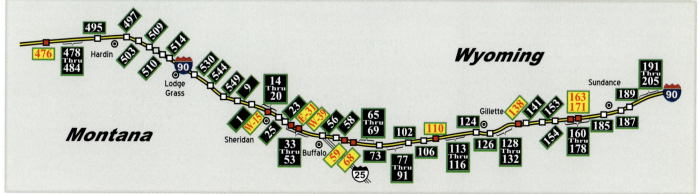

◊ = Regular Gas Stations with Diesel ▲ = RV Friendly Locations ♥ = Pet Friendly Locations
RED PRINT SHOWS LARGE VEHICLE PARKING/ACCESS ON SITE OR NEARBY BROWN PRINT SHOWS CAMPGROUNDS/RV PARKS

Interstate 90 W/E

EXIT		WYOMING
69		Dry Creek Rd, Buffalo
73		Crazy Woman Creek Rd
77		Schoonover Rd, Buffalo
82		Indian Creek Rd, Buffalo
88		Powder River Rd, Buffalo
	N:	Rest Area (Both dir) (RR, Phone, Picnic)
91		Dead Horse Creek Rd
102		Barber Creek Rd, Gillette
106		Barlow Rd, Kingsbury Rd
(110)		Parking Area (Both dir)
113		Wild Horse Creek Rd
116		Force Rd
124		I-90 Bus, Skyline Dr, to US 14, US 16W, WY 50, Gillette
	FStop	N: Shell Food Mart
	Gas	N: Conoco◊
		S: Cenex◊, Kum&Go◊
	Food	N: Long John Silver, Pizza Hut, Subway
	Lodg	N: Best Western♥, Budget Inn, Comfort Inn, Hampton Inn, Motel 6♥, Super 8♥
	Med	N: + Campbell Co Memorial Hospital
	Other	N: to PL/Green Tree's Crazy Woman Campground▲
	NOTE:	WB: CHECK YOUR FUEL! No Services Between Exits #124 & #58.
126		WY 59, Douglas Hwy, Gillette
	TStop	S: Flying J Travel Plaza
	Gas	N: Cenex◊, Conoco
		S: Exxon, Shell
	Food	N: McDonald's, Subway, Prime Rib Rest, Starbucks
		S: Cookery/FJ TP, Applebee's, Arby's, Bootlegger's Rest, Burger King, DQ, China Buffet, Golden Corral, KFC, Perkins, Pizza Hut, Quiznos, Starbucks, Taco Bell, Wendy's
	Lodg	N: Best Value Inn♥, Mustang Motel, Smart Choice Inn,
		S: Clarion♥, Days Inn, Fairfield Inn, Holiday Inn Express♥, Wingate Inn
	Other	N: Discount Tire, Grocery, Pharmacy, Radio Shack, Tires
		S: Laundry/WiFi/RVDump/LP/FJ TP, Albertson's, Advance Auto, Auto Dealers, Big O Tire, Goodyear, Home Depot, Kmart, Pharmacy, Wal-Mart sc
128		I-90 Bus, Gillette, US 14W, US 16W Port Of Entry
	Gas	N: Conoco, Kum&Go, Maverick◊
	Food	N: Hardee's, KFC, Mona's Café
	Lodg	N: Best Value Inn, Rolling Hills Motel, Motel 6♥, National 9 Motel, Quality Inn
	Other	N: AdvancedAuto, PL/Greentrees Crazy Woman Campground▲, East Side RV Center, to Gillette Campbell Co Airport✈
		S: High Plains Campground▲
129		Garner Lake Rd, Gillette
	Other	S: WY Marine & RV Repair
132		American Rd, Wyodak Rd
(138)		Parking Area (Both dir)
141		Adon Rd, Rozet

Personal Notes

EXIT		WYOMING
153		I-90 Bus, to US 14E, to US 16E, Moorcraft, Newcastle, Aglett
	N:	Rest Area (Both dir) (RR, Phone, Picnic, RVDump)
	Other	N: Devils Tower KOA▲
154		I-90 Bus, E Moorcroft, US 14E, Devils Tower, US 16E, Newcastle
	TStop	S: PTP/Coffee Cup Fuel Stop #5/Conoco
	Food	S: FastFood/CoffeeCup FS, Donna's Diner, Hub Café, Subway
	Lodg	S: Cozy Motel, Moorcourt Motel, WY Motel, Rangeland Court Motel & RV Park▲
160		Wind Creek Rd, Moorcroft
(163)		Parking Area (Both dir)
165		Pine Ridge Rd, Wagner Rd, to Pine Haven
	Other	N: to appr 9mi Keyhole State Park/RVDump▲
(171)		Parking Area (Both dir)
172		Inyan Kara Rd, Moorcroft
(177)		Parking Area (Both dir)
178		Coal Divide Rd, Beaver Creek Rd
185		I-90 Bus, to WY 116, Sundance, US 14W, Devils Tower Natl Mon
	Gas	S: Conoco
	Other	N: to Devils Tower KOA▲
187		WY 585, Sundance, Newcastle
	Gas	N: BP◊, Conoco◊
	Food	N: Flo's Place, Subway

EXIT		WY / SD
	Lodg	N: Best Western, Sundance Mountain Inn
189		I-90 Bus, US 14W, Sundance, Newcastle
	S:	WY Port of Entry / Weigh Station
	S:	Rest Area (Both dir) (RR, Phones, Info, Picnic, RVDump)
	TStop	N: Sundance BP Travel Center
	Food	N: Subway
	Lodg	N: Best Western♥
	Med	N: + Hospital
	Other	N: Laundry/Sundance TC
		S: Mountain View Campground▲
191		Moskee Rd, Sundance
199		WY 111, to Aladdin
205		CR 129, Sand Creek Rd, Beulah
	Gas	N: Stateline Station
	Food	N: Buffalo Jump Saloon & Steakhouse
	NOTE:	MM 207: South Dakota State Line

(MOUNTAIN TIME ZONE)

○ WYOMING
○ SOUTH DAKOTA

(MOUNTAIN TIME ZONE)

(1)		SD Welcome Center (EB) (RR, Phone, Picnic, Info, RVDump)
2		Shenk Ln, Spearfish
	Other	N: McNenny State Fish Hatchery
8		McGuigan Rd, W Spearfish
	Other	S: Spearfish KOA▲
10		I-90 Bus, US 85N, Spearfish, to Belle Fourche
	Gas	S: Valley Corner Gas/Casino
	Food	S: Burger King, Guadalajara Mexican, Golden Dragon, Subway, Wendy's
	Lodg	S: Days Inn♥
	Other	S: Auto Dealers, Grocery, Jos Field Dreams Campground▲, Spearfish KOA▲
12		E Jackson Blvd, Spearfish
	Gas	S: Mini Mart, Sinclair
	Food	S: Bay Leaf Café, Bell's Steakhouse, China Town, Country Kitchen, Domino's, Millstone Fam Rest, Pizza Ranch
	Lodg	S: Best Western♥, Travelodge♥
	Med	S: + Lookout Memorial Hospital
	Other	S: Black Hills State College, Spearfish Campground▲, Spearfish KOA▲
14		27th St, I-90 Bus, US 14A, Spearfish
	Gas	S: AmocoBP Speedy Mart
	Food	N: Applebee's
		S: PizzaRanch/HJE, Applebee's, KFC, Long John Silver, Perkins
	Lodg	N: Fairfield Inn, Holiday Inn♥, Quality Inn, Ramada
		S: All American Inn, Best Western, Super 8♥, Howard Johnson Express♥
	Other	N: Wal-Mart sc, Black Hills Airport✈, Centennial Campground▲
		S: Kmart, Northern Hills Cinema, Mountain View Campground▲, Chris's Camping & RV Park▲, Trout Haven Campground▲, High Plains Museum
17		US 85S, to Deadwood, Lead (All Serv 10-15mi S in Deadwood)
	Lodg	S: AmericInn/Rest/Casino, Best Western/Casino, ComfortInn/Casino, Historic Franklin Hotel,

Page 456

◊ = Regular Gas Stations with Diesel   ▲ = RV Friendly Locations   ♥ = Pet Friendly Locations
RED PRINT SHOWS LARGE VEHICLE PARKING/ACCESS ON SITE OR NEARBY   BROWN PRINT SHOWS CAMPGROUNDS/RV PARKS

EXIT		SOUTH DAKOTA
	Lodg	S: HamptonInn/FourAces Casino/Rest, HolidayInnExpress/Gold Dust Casino/Rest, Super 8
	Other	S: Deadwood KOA▲, Elkhorn Ridge RV Resort & Cabins▲, Hidden Valley Campground▲, Fish N Fry Campground▲, Deadwood Gulch Resort & Gaming▲, Whistler Gulch Campground▲
23		SD 34W, Laurel St, Whitewood
	Gas	S: April's Place◊, BP
	Food	S: Shea's Family Rest
	Lodg	S: Tony's Motel
	Other	N: RV Center
30		I-90 Bus, SD 34, Boulder Canyon Rd, US 14A, Sturgis, Deadwood
	Gas	N: BP, Cenex◊
		S: BJ's Country Store, Conoco◊
	Food	N: China Buffet, McDonald's, Pizza Hut, Subway
		S: Burger King, McDonald's, Subway
	Lodg	N: Days Inn♥, Canyon Inn, Holiday Inn Express, Motel 6♥
		S: Super 8♥
	Other	N: CarQuest, Laundromat, Grocery, Tires, Radio Shack, Iron Horse Campground▲, Glencoe Campground▲, Free Spirit Campground▲
		S: Deadwood KOA▲, Hidden Valley Campground▲, Fish N Fry Campground▲, Wild Bill's Campground▲, Fort Meade, to Recreational Springs Resort▲
32		I-90 Bus, SD 79N, Junction Ave, Sturgis, Fort Meade
	Gas	N: Conoco, BP, CommonCents
	Food	N: Subway/Conoco, Taco John's
	Lodg	N: Best Western♥, Lantern Motel, Star Lite Motel, South Pine Motel
	Med	N: + Fort Mead VA Medical Center
	Other	N: Casino/BW, Fort Meade, Big Rig RV Park▲, Glencoe Campground▲, Mt Rodney Luxury Coach Park/Mt Rodney's Downtown RV & Camping Park▲, Bob & Lea's Campground▲, Vanocker Campground▲
34		Old Stone Rd, Pleasant Valley Dr
	Other	S: Katmandu RV Park & Campground▲, No Name City RV Park & Cabins▲, Black Hills National Cemetary
37		Pleasant Valley Dr, Sturgis
	Other	N: Elkview Campground & Resort▲
		S: Bulldog Campground▲, Rush-No-More RV Park & Campground▲
(38)		Port of Entry / Weigh Station (EB)
40		214th St, Sturgis, Tilford
(42)		Rest Area (Both dir) (RR, Phone, Picnic, Info, RVDump/Wtr)
44		218th St, Bethlehem Rd, Piedmont
	Other	S: Bethlehem RV Park, Jack's RV
46		Piedmont Rd, Elk Creek Rd
	Gas	S: Conoco◊
	Food	N: Elk Creek Steakhouse
	Other	N: Covered Wagon Resort▲, Lazy JD RV Park▲, Elk Creek Resort & Lodge & Campground▲
48		Stagestop Rd, Blackhawk
	Gas	S: Sinclair
	Food	S: Classics Bar & Grill, Mike's Pizza
	Lodg	S: Ramada Inn♥, Super 8
	TServ	N: Northwest Peterbilt
	Med	S: + Piedmont Medical Center
	Other	S: Casino/Ramada Inn, Bethlehem Road RV Park▲
51		Foothills Blvd, I-90 Bus, SD 79, Black Hawk Rd, Blackhawk
	Other	N: Three Flags RV Park▲
55		Deadwood Ave, Rapid City
	TStop	S: Bosselman Travel Center/Pilot #918 Sinclair (Scales)
	Food	S: Rest/Pilot TC
	TWash	S: Superior TW/Pilot TC
	TServ	N: Butler CAT
		S: Pilot TC/Boss Truck Shop/Tires, West River International
	Other	N: Rushmore Mall, Harley Davidson, Lazy JD RV Park▲
		S: Laundry/BarbSh/RVDump/LP/Pilot TC, Golf Course
(57)		Jct I-190, US 16W, Rapid City, to Mt Rushmore
	Gas	S: Conoco
	Food	S: Hardee's, Little Caesars, McDonald
	Lodg	S: Alex Johnson♥, Days Inn, Holiday Inn♥, Howard Johnson Express, Radisson
	Other	S: Happy Holiday Resort & Campground▲, Hart Ranch Resort▲, Lazy JD RV Park▲, Lake Park Campground & Cottages▲, Lazy J RV Park & Campground▲, Mystery Mountain Resort▲
58		Haines Ave, Rapid City
	Gas	N: Conoco, Shell
		S: Mini Mart◊, Conoco
	Food	N: Applebee's, Chili's, Hardee's, IHOP, Red Lobster, Mall Food Court
		S: Taco John's, Wendy's
	Lodg	N: Best Value Inn♥
	Med	S: + Hospital
	Other	N: Rushmore Mall, Best Buy, Lowe's, Target, Tires +
		S: ShopKO
59		N La Crosse St, Rapid City
	Gas	N: BP, Phillips 66, Shell
		S: Cenex◊, Exxon, Murphy
	Food	N: Burger King, Denny's, Fuddruckers, Olive Garden, Outback Steakhouse, TGI Friday
		S: Chuck E Cheese, Golden Corral, McDonald's, Millstone Rest, Perkins, Red Lobster, Subway
	Lodg	N: Best Western♥, Country Inn, Econo Lodge♥, GrandStay Residential Suites, Holiday Inn Express♥, Quality Inn, Super 8♥
		S: AmericInn, Comfort Inn, Days Inn, Fair Value Inn, Foothills Inn♥, Grand Gateway Hotel, Hampton Inn, Microtel♥, Motel 6♥, Quality Inn♥, Ramada Inn♥
	Other	N: SD State Hwy Patrol Post, Mall, Tires
		S: Sam's Club, Target, Tires, Walgreen's, Wal-Mart sc
60		I-90 Bus, SD 79, North St, Rapid City, Mt Rushmore (fr WB, Left Exit)
	Food	S: Bonanza, Hong Kong Café, Great Wall, KFC, Long John Silver
	Lodg	S: Budget Inn, Comfort Inn, Four Seasons Motel, Gold Star Motel
	Med	S: + Hospital
	Other	S: Berry Patch Campground▲, Hart Ranch Resort▲
61		Elk Vale Rd, St Patrick St, Rapid City
	TStop	N: Flying J Travel Plaza/Conoco (Scales)
	Food	N: CountryMarket/FastFood/FJ TP
		S: Arby's, McDonald's
	TWash	N: FJ TP
	TServ	S: Hills Brake & Equipment
	Other	N: Laundry/BarbSh/WiFi/RVDump/LP/FJ TP, RV Center
		S: Lazy J RV Park & Campground▲, Rapid City KOA▲
63		Ellsworth AFB Comm'l Entrance, Box Elder, (EB exit, WB reacc)
67		Liberty Blvd, Ellsworth AFB, Main Main Entrance (WB)
67AB		Liberty Blvd (EB)
(69)		Parking Area (Both dir)
78		161st Ave, New Underwood
	Gas	S: Steve's General Store
	Food	S: Diamond Café

◊ = Regular Gas Stations with Diesel ▲ = RV Friendly Locations ♥ = Pet Friendly Locations

RED PRINT SHOWS LARGE VEHICLE PARKING/ACCESS ON SITE OR NEARBY BROWN PRINT SHOWS CAMPGROUNDS/RV PARKS

EXIT	SOUTH DAKOTA	EXIT	SOUTH DAKOTA	EXIT	SOUTH DAKOTA
Lodg	S: Jake's Motel	Food	N: Rest/Dakota Inn	220	NO Access
Other	S: Boondocks Campground▲		S: Happy Chef	(221)	Rest Area (WB)
84	CR 497, 167th Ave, Duncan Rd	Lodg	N: Dakota Inn		(RR, Phones, Picnic, Info, RVDump)
88	171st Ave (EB exit, WB reaccess)		S: Best Western, Budget Host, Downtowner Motor Inn, Super 8, Ponderosa Motel & RV Park▲	225	I-90 Bus, SD 16, Presho
90	173rd Ave, CR C492, Owanka			FStop	N: New Frontier Station/Conoco
99	Base Line Rd, Wasta	Other	S: Laundromat, to Pine Ridge Indian Res	Gas	N: Sinclair◊
Gas	N: BP◊	152	I-90 Bus, Kadoka, S Creek Rd	Food	N: Café/Frank's Hutch's Motel, Pizza
Food	N: Packard Café	TStop	N: Badlands Travel Stop/66	Lodg	N: Coachlight Inn, Hutch's Motel
Lodg	N: Redwood Motel	Food	N: Rest/Badlands TS	Other	N: New Frontier RV Park▲
Other	N: US Post Office, Sunrise RV Park & Campground▲	Lodg	N: Best Western	226	I-90 Bus, US 183S, Presho, Winner (Access Serv at Ex #225)
		Other	N: Laundry/Tires/Badlands TS		
(100)	Rest Area (Both dir) (RR, Phone, Picnic, Info, RVDump/Wtr)		S: Kadoka Campground▲	235	SD 273, I-90 Bus, Kennebec
		163	SD 63S, Belvidere	Gas	N: Conoco◊
101	CR T504, Jensen Rd	Gas	S: BP◊, Sinclair◊	Lodg	N: Budget Host Inn
107	168th Ave, Cedar Butte Rd	(165)	Rest Area (EB) (RR, Phone, Picnic, RVDump)	Other	N: Kennebec KOA▲
109	W 4th Ave, Wall			241	to Lyman
110	I-90 Bus, SD 240, Glenn St, Wall, Badlands Loop	(167)	Rest Area (WB) (RR, Phone, Picnic, RVDump)	248	SD 47N, Reliance
				Gas	N: BP◊, Cenex
Gas	N: BP◊, Exxon, Phillips 66	170	SD 63N, to Midland	251	SD 47N, Reliance, Gregory, Winner
Food	N: Cactus Café, DQ, Elkton House Rest, Subway	Gas	N: Shell	Other	N: to Golden Buffalo Casino
		Other	N: Belvidere East KOA▲	260	SD 50, Dougan Ave, Oacoma
Lodg	N: Best Western♥, Best Value Inn, Days Inn, Econo Lodge♥, Elk Motel, Homestead Motel, Kings Inn, Knights Inn, Motel 6♥, Sunshine Inn, Super 8, Wall Motel	172	to Cedar Butte	FStop	S: Oasis Pump & Pack/Conoco
		177	NO Access	Gas	N: BP◊, Shell◊
		183	Okaton	Food	N: Taco John's
		(188)	Parking Area (Both dir)	Lodg	N: Days Inn♥, Comfort Inn♥, Holiday Inn Express, Oasis Kelly Inn♥
		NOTE:	MM 190: Central / Mountain Time Zone	Other	N: Al's Oasis/Rest/Motel/River Ranch Resort/Campground▲, Familyland Camping▲, Hi & Dri Camping▲, Cedar Shore Resort▲
Other	N: NAPA, US Post Office, Pharmacy, Sleepy Hollow Campground▲, Arrow Campground▲, to Badlands Nat'l Park	191	Old US 16, Murdo		
		192	US 83, I-90 Bus, Murdo, White River	263	Main St, Chamberlain, Crow Creek Sioux Tribal Headquarters
		TStop	N: Triple H Truck Stop/Shell		
112	US 14E, to Phillip	Gas	N: BP◊, Phillips 66, Sinclair	Gas	N: Sinclair◊
116	239th St, Wall	Food	N: Rest/Triple H TS, KFC/P66, Murdo Drive In, Tee Pee	Food	N: Casey's Café, McDonald's, Pizza Hut, Subway, Taco John's
121	Big Foot Pass, CR C511, to US 14				
127	CS 23A, Big Foote Rd, Kadoka	Lodg	N: AmericInn, Best Western♥, Days Inn♥, Lee Motel, Super 8, Tee Pee Motel & RV Park▲	Lodg	N: Best Western♥, Riverview Inn, Super 8♥
(129.5)	Scenic View (EB)			Other	N: IGA
131	SD 240, Badlands Loop, CR 8, Badlands Interior, Kadoka		S: Country Inn	(264)	Rest Area (Both dir) (RR, Phone, Info, Picnic, View, RVDump)
		TServ	N: Triple H TS/Tires		
Gas	S: BP, Conoco	Other	N: Laundry/LP/Triple H TS, Grocery	265	I-90 Bus, SD 50, 344th Ave, Chamberlain
Other	S: Badland Circle 10/Motel/Rest/ Campground▲, to appr 9 mi Badlands Nat'l Park, to appr 15 mi Badlands/ White River KOA▲	(194)	Parking Area (Both dir)		
		201	CR N13, Draper	FStop	S: Vet's Whoa & Go/Conoco
		208	CR S10, Draper	Gas	N: BP
		212	US 83N, SD 53, Ft Pierre, Pierre	Other	S: Keiner's Kampground▲, Happy Camper Park▲
(138)	Scenic View (WB)	TStop	N: PTP/Coffee Cup Fuel Stop #8/66		
143	SD 73N, Kadoka, to Phillip	Food	N: Vivian Jct Rest	272	SD 50, Pukwana
Med	N: to + Hospital	214	US 83, SD 53, Vivian	284	SD 45N, Main St, Kimball
150	SD 73S, I-90 Bus, Kadoka	(218)	Rest Area (EB) (RR, Phones, Picnic, RVDump)	FStop	N: CBS Miller Oil/Corner Bottle Stop
FStop	S: Discount Fuel/Conoco			Tstop	N: Corner Pantry Café/66
Gas	S: BP			Gas	N: BP

South Dakota

Page 458

◊ = Regular Gas Stations with Diesel   ▲ = RV Friendly Locations   ♥ = Pet Friendly Locations
RED PRINT SHOWS LARGE VEHICLE PARKING/ACCESS ON SITE OR NEARBY   BROWN PRINT SHOWS CAMPGROUNDS/RV PARKS

INTERSTATE W 90 E

EXIT	SOUTH DAKOTA
Food	N: Diner/Corner Panty
Lodg	N: Super 8, Dakota Winds
Other	N: Parkway Campground▲
289	SD 45S, Kimball, to Platte
Other	S: to Snake Creek/Platte Creek Rec Area
(293)	Parking Area (Both dir)
296	CR 11, White Lake
Gas	S: Cenex, Shell
Lodg	N: White Lake Motel
(301)	Rest Area (Both dir) (RR, Phone, Picnic, RVDump)
308	I-90 Bus, SD 258, to Plankinton
Gas	N: Phillips 66◆
Food	N: Al's I-90 Café
Lodg	N: Super 8
310	US SD 281, Plankinton, to Stickney, Aberdeen
TStop	S: PTP/Coffee Cup Fuel Stop #4/Conoco
Food	S: FastFood/Coffee Cup FS
319	Mt Vernon
Gas	N: Cenex
325	Betts Rd, 403rd Ave
Other	S: Famil-E-Fun Campground▲
330	SD 37N, Mitchell, Corn Palace
N:	Weigh Station (Both dir)
TStop	N: West Haven Cenex
Gas	N: Shell◆
Food	N: AJ's, Country Kitchen, DQ, Happy Chef
Lodg	N: Holiday Inn, Motel 6♥
Med	N: + Hospital
Other	N: RV Center, RonDee's Campground▲, Mitchell KOA▲, to Mitchell Muni Airport✈ Lake Mitchell Campground▲ S: Dakota Campground▲, Jack'sRV
332	I-90 Bus, SD 37S, Mitchell
TStop	N: Cenex, I-90 Fuel Services/Pilot Travel Center #919 (Scales)
Gas	N: BP, Phillips 66 S: Highland Travel Plaza/Shell◆/Murphy
Food	N: Rest/Subway/Pilot TC/I-90 TC, Arby's, Bonanza Steak House, Burger King, Country Kitchen, Embers Rest, Hardee's, Kinders Rest, McDonald's, Perkins, Pizza Hut S: TacoBell/Godfathers/Highland TP, Quiznos
Lodg	N: AmericInn, Best Western, Comfort Inn, Days Inn, Super 8, Thunderbird Lodge S: Corn Palace Motel, Hampton Inn, Kelly Inn
TServ	N: Pilot TC/ I-90 TC/Tires
Med	N: + Hospital
Other	N: Laundry/Pilot/I-90 TC, Auto Services, Advance Auto, Corn Palace, Kmart, Pharmacy, R & R Campground▲, Rondees Campground▲, to Mitchell Muni Airport✈, Dakota Wesleyan Univ S: Cabela's/RVDump, Dollar Tree, Menard's, Radio Shack, Highland Mall, Wal-Mart sc
335	Riverside Rd
Other	N: Mitchell KOA▲
(337)	Parking Area (Both dir)
344	SD 262E, Fulton, Alexandria
Gas	S: Shell◆
350	SD 25, Emery, Farmer
Other	N: to home of Laura Ingalls Wilder
353	431st Ave, Spencer, Emery
Fstop	N: AmBest/Fuel Mart #645

EXIT	SOUTH DAKOTA
TStop	S: Travel Center of America/Amoco (Scales)
Food	S: FastFood/TA TC
Other	S: Laundry/WiFi/TA TC
357	Bridgewater, Canova
(362)	Rest Area (Both dir) (RR, Phone, Picnic, RVDump, SD Hwy Patrol)
364	US 81, Canistota, Salem, Yankton
368	445th Ave, Canistota
Other	S: RVFishing.com RV Park▲
374	451st Ave, to SD 38, Montrose (Serv 3-4 mi N in Montrose)
Other	S: Lake Vermillion Rec Area▲
379	SD 19, 456th Ave, Humboldt, to Madison
Gas	N: Mobil◆
Food	N: Cafe
387	SD 151, 463rd Ave, Hartford
FStop	N: Tammen Oil/66
Tires	66
390	SD 38, Sioux Falls, Buffalo Ridge, Hartford
Gas	S: Buffalo Ridge, Phillips 66
Food	S: Buffalo Ridge, Pizza Ranch
(396AB)	Jct I-29, S-Sioux City, N-Fargo
399	I-90 Bus, SD 115, Cliff Ave, Sioux Falls
FStop	S: Kum&Go #613/Cenex
TStop	N: Frontier Village Truck Stop/Sinclair (Scales) S: Pilot Travel Center #349 (Scales)
Gas	N: Phillips 66◆ S: Holiday◆
Food	N: Rest/Frontier Village TS S: Grandma's/Subway/Pilot TC, Burger King, McDonald's, Perkins, Taco John's
Lodg	S: Comfort Inn, Country Inn, Days Inn, Econo Lodge, Super 8
TWash	S: Blue Beacon TW/Pilot TC
TServ	S: Pilot TC/Tires, American Rim & Brake, Crossroads Trailer, Cummins Great Plains Diesel, Dakota White/GMC Volvo, Diesel Machinery, Graham Tire, International Dealer, Peterbilt Dealer, Sheehan Mack, Sioux Falls Kenworth, T&W Tires, Boss Truck Shop
Med	S: + Hospital
Other	N: Laundry/CB/Frontier Village TS, Sioux Falls KOA▲, Spaders RV S: Laundry/BarbSh/WiFi/Pilot TC
(400)	Jct I-229S, Sioux Falls, Sioux City
402	CR 121, S 478th Ave, EROS Data Center
Other	N: Yogi Bear's Jellystone Resort▲
406	SD 11, 482nd Ave, Brandon, Corson
FStop	S: PTP/Coffee Cup Fuel Stop #7/BP (Scales)
Gas	S: Sinclair
Food	S: Brandon Steakhouse, DQ, Domino's, McDonald's, Subway
Lodg	S: Holiday Inn Express
Other	S: Golf Courses, to Big Sioux State Rec Area
410	CR 105, 486th Ave, Valley Springs, Garretson
Other	N: Palisades State Park▲

EXIT	SD / MN
(412)	SD Welcome Center (WB) Port of Entry / Weigh Station (WB) Rest Area (EB) (RR, Phone, Picnic, RVDump/WB)
NOTE:	MM 412: Minnesota State Line
	(CENTRAL TIME ZONE)
	🎧 SOUTH DAKOTA
	⊙ MINNESOTA
	(CENTRAL TIME ZONE)
(0)	MN Welcome Center (EB) (RR, Phone, Picnic, Info, Vend)
1	MN 23, CR 17, Beaver Creek, Manley, Jasper, Pipestone
Other	N: Split Rock Creek State Park
3	CR 4, Beaver Creek (EB)
5	CR 6, Beaver Creek
Gas	N: Shell◆
12	US 75, S Kniss Ave, Luverne, to Pipestone, Rock Rapids
Gas	N: Casey's Gen'l Store, Cenex◆, FuelTime◆, Phillips 66◆, Shell◆
Food	N: Chit Chat Rest, China Inn, Pizza Hut, McDonald's, Subway, Taco John's S: Magnolia Lounge & Steakhouse
Lodg	N: Comfort Inn S: Super 8♥
Med	N: + Luverne Community Hospital
Other	N: Blue Mounds State Park▲, Auto Dealers, Split Rock Creek State Park S: Luverne Muni Airport✈
18	CR 3, Magnolia, Kanaranzi
(24)	Adrian Rest Area (EB) (RR, Phone, Picnic, Vend)
(25)	Adrian Rest Area (WB) (RR, Phone, Picnic, Vend)
26	MN 91, Adrian, to Lake Wilson, Ellsworth
Gas	S: Cenex◆
33	CR 13, Jones Ave, Rushmore
42	MN 266N, CR 25, Worthington, Reading, Wilmont
Lodg	S: Days Inn♥, Super 8♥
43	US 59, Humiston Ave, Worthington
FStop	S: Cenex AmPride Fuel Stop, Plaza 66/66
Gas	N: Conoco◆ S: BP, Casey's, Shell, Murphy
Food	S: Arby's, Country Kitchen, DQ, KFC, Ground Round, Perkins, McDonald's, Pizza Hut, Subway
Lodg	N: Travelodge♥ S: AmericInn, Budget Inn, Holiday Inn Express
Med	S: + Hospital
Other	N: Worthington Muni Airport✈ S: ATMs, Dollar Tree, Family Dollar, Grocery, ShopKO, Wal-Mart sc, Auto Dealers, Visitor Center, Pioneer Village, Northland Mall, Campbell Soup
45	MN 60, Worthington, Windom
S:	MN Welcome Center Rest Area
TStop	N: Blue Line Travel Center/BP (Scales) S: AmBest/Worthington Travel Plaza/Shell (Scales)

◆ = Regular Gas Stations with Diesel ▲ = RV Friendly Locations ♥ = Pet Friendly Locations
RED PRINT SHOWS LARGE VEHICLE PARKING/ACCESS ON SITE OR NEARBY. BROWN PRINT SHOWS CAMPGROUNDS/RV PARKS

EXIT		MINNESOTA	EXIT		MINNESOTA	EXIT		MINNESOTA
	Food	N: Rest/Blue Line TC S: McDonald's, King Wok Buffet		Lodg	S: Budget Inn, Comfort Inn ♥, Holiday Inn ♥, Super 8 ♥	(171)		Oakland Woods Rest Area (WB) (RR, Phone, Picnic, Vend, PlayArea)
	Lodg	S: Sunset Inn		Med	S: + Hospital	175		MN 105S, I-90 Bus E, CR 46, Oakland Ave, Austin
	Other	N: Laundry/RVDump/Blue Line TC S: Wheel Camping▲ & Marine Center		Other	S: CarQuest, Goodyear, Kmart, Fairmont Muni Airport✈		FStop	S: Apollo #3/Conoco
(46)		Weigh Station (EB)	107		MN 262N, CR 53, Granada, Imogene		Gas	S: BP
47		CR 53 (EB)		Other	S: Flying Goose Campground▲		Food	S: McDonald's
50		MN 264S, CR 1, Round Lake	113		CR 1, Blue Earth, Huntley, Gukeen		Lodg	N: Countryside Inn
57		CR 9, Round Lake, Oakabena	(119)		Rest Area (Both dir) (RR, Phone, Picnic, Vend, PlayArea)		Other	S: River Side Campground▲
64		MN 86, Lakefield	119		US 169, Blue Earth, Mankato	177		US 218N, 14th St NW, Blooming Prairie, Austin (WB: Use 218N for Owatonna)
	Gas	N: Standard Station, Mitch's Corner		FStop	S: Blue Earth Auto & Truck Stop/Sinclair		Gas	N: Holiday
	Food	N: Hilltop Café		Gas	S: Shell◊			S: Sinclair◊
	Lodg	N: Windmill Motel		Food	S: Country Kitchen, McDonald's, Pizza Hut, Subway		Food	N: Applebee's, Arby's, KFC, Quiznos S: Hardee's, Burger King, Subway
(69)		Clear Lake Rest Area (EB) (RR, Phones, Picnic, Vend)		Lodg	S: AmericInn, Budget Inn, Super 8		Lodg	S: Super 8 ♥
(72)		Des Moines Rest Area (WB) (RR, Phones, Picnic, Vend, PlayArea)		TServ	S: Blue Earth ATS/Tires		Other	N: Grocery, Kmart, Staples, Target, Mall
				Med	S: + Hospital	178A		Broadway St, Mapleview, CR 45, 4th St NW, Downtown
73		US 71, Jackson, Windom		Other	S: Wal-Mart, Fairbault Co Fairgrounds/RVDump		Gas	S: BP, Conoco◊, Sinclair
	TStop	N: Vets Whoa & Go Fuel Stop #2/Conoco	128		MN 254S, CR 17, Easton, Frost		Food	N: Perkins S: Burger King
	Gas	S: BP, Casey's General Store	134		MN 253S, CR 21, Bricelyn		Lodg	N: AmericInn, Days Inn ♥, Holiday Inn ♥
	Food	N: Burger King, Santee Crossing Family Rest S: China Buffet, DQ, Casey's C/O Pizza, Pizza Ranch, Subway	138		MN 22, Wells		Med	S: + Hospital
			146		MN 109W, CR 6, Alden, Wells		Other	S: Spam Museum, Visitor Center
	Lodg	N: Best Western ♥, Econo Lodge, Super 8 ♥ S: Budget Host Inn, Earth Inn		TStop	S: Petrol Pumper AmBest #73/BP	178B		6th St NE, Downtown Austin
				Gas	S: Cenex	179		11th Dr NE, 10th Pl, Austin
	Med	S: + Jackson Medical Center, + Jackson Clinic		Food	N: Café		TStop	N: Austin Auto Truck Plaza/Citgo (Scales)
	Other	N: Jackson KOA▲, Jackson Muni Airport✈, Auto Dealers, RVDump/BurgerKing S: Kilen Woods State Park	154		MN 13, to US 65, US 69, Albert Lea, Manchester		Food	N: Rest/Austin ATP
				FStop	N: Vets Whoa & Go/SuperAmerica		TWash	N: Austin ATP
80		CR 29, Alpha		Other	S: Spam Museum, Visitor Center		Other	N: Laundry/Austin ATP
87		MN 4, Main St, Sherburn	157		CR 22, Bridge Ave, Albert Lea, Bancroft	180A		I-90 Bus W, Oakland Place NE (WB)
	Gas	S: Cenex		FStop	S: Budget Mart #5119/Mobil	180B		US 218S, 21st St NE, Lyle
93		MN 263S, CR 27, Welcome		Gas	S: Conoco		Gas	S: Shell
	Gas	S: Cenex		Food	S: Applebee's, Arby's, McDonald's		Lodg	S: Austin Motel
	Food	S: Welcome Cafe		Lodg	S: AmericInn, Holiday Inn Express		Other	N: Jay C Hormel Nature Center S: Austin Muni Airport✈
	Other	S: Checkers Welcome Campground▲		Med	S: + Hospital	181		28th St NE
99		CR 39, 190th Ave, Fairmont		Other	S: Grocery, Harley Davidson, Pharmacy, Mall, Albert Lea Muni Airport✈		Other	S: Austin Muni Airport✈
102		I-90 Bus W, MN 15, State St, Fairmont (EB: Use MN 15 to MN 60E, Mankato)	(159AB)		Jct I-35, N-Twin Cities, Albert Lea, S to Des Moines	183		MN 56, 590th Ave, Brownsdale, Rose Creek
			(162)		Hayward Rest Area (EB) (RR, Phone, Picnic, Vend, PlayArea)		Gas	S: Cenex
	TStop	S: Whoa & Go/SuperAmerica, NuMart/Cenex	163		CR 26, Hayward (Serv 4-5mi S in Hayward)	187		CR 20, 630th Ave, Elkton
	Gas	S: Conoco◊, Phillips 66◊		Other	S: Myre Big Island State Park▲		Other	S: Beaver Trails Campground & RV Park▲
	Food	S: Happy Chef, McDonald's, Perkins, Pizza Hut, Subway	166		CR 46, Oakland Rd, Hayward	189		CR 13, 650th Ave, Elkton
				Other	N: to Albert Lea/Austin KOA▲	193		MN 16E, CR 7, Dexter, Preston, Grand Meadow
							TStop	S: Windmill Travel Center/66
							Food	S: Rest/Windmill TC
							Lodg	S: Budget Inn

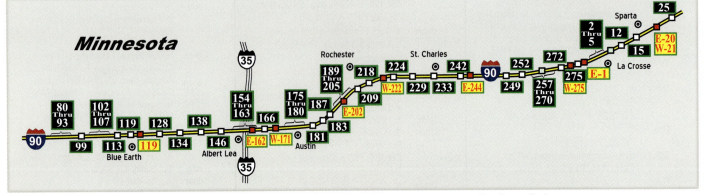

◊ = Regular Gas Stations with Diesel   ▲ = RV Friendly Locations   ♥ = Pet Friendly Locations
RED PRINT SHOWS LARGE VEHICLE PARKING/ACCESS ON SITE OR NEARBY   BROWN PRINT SHOWS CAMPGROUNDS/RV PARKS

MINNESOTA

EXIT	
(202)	**High Forest Rest Area (EB)** (RR, Phones, Picnic, Vend, PlayArea)
205	CR 6/8, Stewartville, High Forest
209A	US 63S, MN 30E, Stewartville (EB)
Gas	S: KwikTrip
Food	S: DQ
Lodg	S: AmericInn♥
209B	US 63N, MN 30W, Rochester, (EB) US 63, MN 30, Stewartville (WB)
Med	N: + Hospital (10mi N)
Other	N: Autumn Woods RV Park▲, Rochester Int'l Airport✈, Willow Creek RV Park & Campground▲
209	US 63N, MN 30W, Rochester (EB), US 63, MN 30, Stewartville (WB)
218	US 52, Chatfield (EB), Rochester (WB)
Gas	S: BP◆
Med	N: + Hospital (9mi N)
Other	N: Autumn Woods RV Park▲, Brookside RV Park▲ S: Rochester/Marion KOA▲
(222)	**Marion Rest Area (WB)** (RR, Phones, Picnic, Vend, PlayArea)
224	MN 42N, CR 7, Eyota, Elgin, Plainview
229	CR 10, Chatfield St, Dover
233	MN 74, Chatfield, St Charles
TStop	S: Amish Market Square Auto Truck Plaza/Texaco
Gas	N: KwikTrip
Food	N: Del's Café, Hometown Café, Pizza Factory, Subway S: Rest/Amish Market
Tires	S: Amish Mkt Sq ATP/Tires
Other	N: Whitewater State Park S: RVDump/LP/Amish Market
242	CR 29, Utica, Lewiston
(244)	**Enterprise Rest Area (EB)** (RR, Phone, Picnic, Vend, PlayArea)
249	MN 43S, Rushford
TServ	N: Peterbilt
252	MN 43N, Winona (All Serv 7 mi N in Winona)
Med	N: + Hospital (7mi N)
Other	N: to Pla-Moor Campground & Marina▲, to Great River Bluffs State Park, Winona Muni Airport✈
257	MN 76S, Houston, Ridgeway, Witoka
Other	S: Money Creek Haven Campground▲
(260)	Weigh Station (Both dir)
266	CR 12, CR 3, Dakota, Nodine
TStop	S: PTP/Truckers Inn/BP (Scales)
Food	S: Rest/FastFood/Truckers Inn
Lodg	S: Motel/Truckers Inn
TWash	S: Truckers Inn
TServ	S: Truckers Inn/Tires
Other	N: Great River Bluff State Park S: Laundry/Truckers Inn
NOTE:	EB: MM 268 thru MM 269 STEEP GRADE

MN / WI

EXIT	
269	to US 61N, US 14W, CR 12, Cr 101, Dakota (EB), I-90W Albert Lea, US 61N, US 14W, Winona (WB)
Other	N: Pla-Mor Campground & Marina▲
270	CR 12, Center St (EB), CR 101, River St (WB), to US 14/61, Dakota
272A	CR 12, Dresbach (EB)
272B	CR 12, Dresbach (EB)
272	CR 12, Dresbach (WB)
275	US 61S, US 14E, to MN 16, La Crescent, La Crosse (All Serv 4-5 mi S in La Crescent)
(275)	**MN Welcome Center (WB)** (RR, Phone, Picnic, Vend, Info)
NOTE:	MM 275: Wisconsin State Line

(CENTRAL TIME ZONE)

⊙ **MINNESOTA**
⊙ **WISCONSIN**

(CENTRAL TIME ZONE)

(1)	**WI Welcome Center (EB)** (RR, Phone, Picnic, Vend, Info)
2	CR B, French Island
Gas	N: Mobil◆ S: Citgo◆
Food	S: Adams Ribs & Steak House
Lodg	S: Days Inn
TServ	N: International
Other	N: La Crosse Muni Airport✈

WISCONSIN

EXIT	
3	WI 35N, Onalaska (EB), US 53S, WI 35, La Crosse, Onalaska (WB)
FStop	S: KwikTrip #767
Gas	S: Speedway◆
Food	S: Burger King, Country Kitchen, Embers KFC, McDonald's, North Country Steak Buffet, Pizza Hut, Subway
Lodg	N: Onalaska Inn S: Best Western, Exel Inn, Hampton Inn, Night Saver Inn, Roadstar Inn, Super 8
Med	S: + Hospital
Other	S: Univ of WI/La Crosse, Viterbo College
3A	US 53S, WI 35S, La Crosse (EB)
Other	S: Univ of WI/La Crosse, Viterbo College
3B	WI 35N, Onalaska (EB)
4	US 53N, WI 157, to WI 16, La Crosse, Onalaska, Midway, Holmen
Gas	S: Citgo, KwikTrip
Food	S: Applebee's, Bakers Square, Burger King, Famous Dave's BBQ, Hardee's, Hong Kong Buffet, McDonald's, Panera, Red Lobster, Subway, Taco Bell, Wendy's
Lodg	S: Comfort Inn, Days Inn
Med	S: + Hospital
Other	N: Harley Davidson S: Grocery, Goodyear, Kmart, Office Depot, Sam's Club, ShopKO, Valley View Mall
5	WI 16, Onalaska, W Salem (EB), WI 16, Onalaska, La Crosse (WB)
Gas	S: Holiday◆, KwikTrip◆
Food	N: Outback Steakhouse, Quiznos S: Applebee's, Carlos O'Kelly, Chuck E Cheese, Hong Kong Buffet, McDonald's, Olive Garden, Perkins, Subway, TGI Friday
Lodg	N: Baymont Inn, Hampton Inn, Microtel S: Holiday Inn Express
Med	S: + Hospital
Other	N: ATMs, Bank, Grocery, Home Depot, Wal-Mart sc, Grocery S: Best Buy, ShopKO, Mall
(10.6)	Weigh Station (EB)
12	CR C, Neshonoc Rd, West Salem
TStop	N: I-90 Cenex
Food	N: Rest/I-90 Cenex
Lodg	S: AmericInn
Tires	N: I-90 Cenex
Other	N: RV Center, Lakeside Camp Resort▲, Neshonoc Campground▲
15	WI 162, Bangor, Rockland
Gas	N: Spur
Other	N: Grocery
(20)	**Rest Area (EB)** (RR, Phone, Picnic, Vend)
(21)	**Rest Area (WB)** (RR, Phone, Picnic, Vend)
25	WI 27, to WI 71N, WI 21, Sparta, Rockland, Melvina
FStop	S: Cenex #27, Kwik Trip #318, Amish Cheese House Shell
Gas	N: Citgo S: Phillips 66
Food	N: Burger King, Country Kitchen, Happy Chef, Hardee's, McDonald's, Pizza Hut S: Burger King, KFC, Subway
Lodg	N: Country Inn, Super 8
Other	S: Wal-Mart sc

◆= Regular Gas Stations with Diesel ▲ = RV Friendly Locations ♥ = Pet Friendly Locations
RED PRINT SHOWS LARGE VEHICLE PARKING/ACCESS ON SITE OR NEARBY   BROWN PRINT SHOWS CAMPGROUNDS/RV PARKS

INTERSTATE 90 W/E

EXIT		WISCONSIN
28		WI 16, to WI 71S, Sparta
	FStop	N: Kwik Trip #317
	Gas	N: BP
	Other	N: Sparta Ft McCoy Airport✈
		N/S: Fort McCoy Military Res
41		WI 131, Superior Ave, Tomah
	Gas	N: Mobil◇, KwikTrip◇
	Food	N: Chinese, Cafe
	Lodg	N: Days Inn, Park Motel
	Med	N: + Hospital
	Other	N: Bloyer Field✈, Amtrak, WI State Hwy Patrol Post
43		US 12, WI 16, Tomah
	Gas	N: KwikTrip◇
	Med	N: + Hospital
	Other	N: Bloyer Field✈
	NOTE:	I-90 below runs with I-94 for 93 mi. Exit #'s follow I-90.
(45A)		Jct I-94W, Twin Cities (EB) (L exit)
(45B)		Jct I-90/94E, Wisconsin Dells, Madison (EB), I-90W La Crosse, I-94W St Paul (WB)
(47.5)		Weigh Station (WB)
48		CR PP, Tomah, Oakdale
	TStop	N: Road Ranger #209/Citgo (Scales)
		S: Love's Travel Stop # 345 (Scales)
	Food	N: Rest/Road Ranger
		S: Hardee's/Love's TS
	Other	N: Laundry/RoadRanger, Oakdale KOA▲
		S: WiFi/Love's TS
(51)		Weigh Station (EB)
55		CR C, CR H, US 12, WI 16, Camp Douglas, Volk Field
	TStop	S: Camp Douglas BP
	Gas	S: Mobil◇
	Food	S: Subway/Mobil
	Lodg	S: Walsh's K&K Motel, Travelers Rest
	TServ	S: CL Chase Truck Service
	Other	N: Mill Bluff State Park, Camp Williams Military Res
		S: Laundry/Camp Douglas BP
61		WI 80, CR A, New Lisbon, Necedah
	TStop	N: New Lisbon Travel Center/Citgo, The Bunk House/Mobil
	Food	N: Rest/Bunk House
	Lodg	N: Motel/Bunk House
	Other	N: Laundry/RVDump/New Lisbon TC, Laundry/RVDump/Bunk House, to Buckhorn State Park, Ken's Marina & Campground▲
		S: Mauston New Lisbon Union Airport✈

EXIT		WISCONSIN
69		WI 82, Mauston, Necedah
	TStop	N: Pilot Travel Center #164 (Scales) Citgo Travel Plaza
		S: Kwik Trip #775/BP (Scales)
	Gas	N: Shell
		S: Citgo◇
	Food	N: Wendy's, Pilot TC, FastFood/Citgo TP, Country Kitchen
		S: Rest/KwikTrip, McDonald's, Pizza Hut, Roman Castle Rest
	Lodg	N: Best Western, Country Inn, Super 8
		S: The Alaskan Motel
	Med	S: + Hospital
	Other	N: Laundry/WiFi/Pilot TC
		S: Laundry/RVDump/KT, Mauston New Lisbon Union Airport✈, Auto Dealers , Walgreen's, Wal-Mart
(74)		Rest Area (EB)
		(RR, Phone, Picnic, Vend)
(75)		Rest Area (WB)
		(RR, Phone, Picnic, Vend)
79		WI HH, Rock St, Lyndon Station
	TStop	S: Lyndon Station BP
	Food	S: FastFood/Lyndon Station
85		US 12, WI 16, Wisconsin Dells
	Lodg	S: Days End Motel
	TServ	S: Rocky Arbor Truck & Trailer Repair
	Other	N: Rocky Arbor State Park, Sherwood Forest Camping & RV Park▲
		S: Bass Lake Campground▲, Crockett Resort Camping & RV▲, Arrowhead Resort Campground▲, Dells Timberland Camping Resort▲, Wisconsin Dells KOA▲, Edge O'Dells Camping & RV Resort▲
87		WI 13N, Wisconsin Dells, to WI 23E, Briggsville
	FStop	N: Interstate BP
	Gas	N: Citgo◇, Mobil◇, Shell
	Food	N: Burger King, Country Kitchen, Pedros, Denny's, Perkins, Rococo's Pizza, Taco Bell, Wendy's
	Lodg	N: Best Western, Comfort Inn, Days Inn, Holiday Inn, Howard Johnson, Super 8
	Other	N: RVDump/Interstate BP, Amtrak, Christmas MountainVillage & Ski Area, American World Resort & RV Park▲, Sherwood Forest Camping & RV Park▲, Erickson's Tepee Park Campground▲, Wisconsin Dells KOA▲
89		WI 23, Lake Delton, Reedsburg
	Gas	N: Mobil◇
	Food	N: Howie's, Internet Cafe

EXIT		WISCONSIN
	Lodg	N: Country Squire Inn, Grand Marquis Inn, Hilton Garden Inn, Sandman Inn
	Other	S: Home Depot, Wal-Mart sc, Mirror Lake State Park, Country Roads RV Park▲
92		US 12, Baraboo, Lake Delton
	Gas	N: BP◇, Cenex◇, Citgo◇, Mobil◇, Sinclair
	Food	N: Cracker Barrel, Damon's, Denny's, McDonald's, Subway/Sinclair
	Lodg	N: AmericInn, Camelot Inn, Del Rancho, Grand Marquis Inn, Ramada Ltd
		S: Travelodge
	Med	S: + Hospital (7mi S)
	Other	N: WI Cheese Museum
		S: Wisconsin Opry, Baraboo Wisconsin Dells Airport✈, Fox Hill RV Park & Campground▲, Yogi Bear's Jellystone Park, Dell Boo Campground▲, Mirror Lake State Park
106		WI 33, Portage, Baraboo
	FStop	N: Lake Morgaune Mobil
	Gas	S: BP
	Lodg	S: Cascade Mountain Motel
	Med	N: + Hospital
	Other	M: Portage Muni Airport✈
		S: Cascade Mountain Ski Area, Sky High Camping Resort▲, Devil's Lake State Park
	NOTE:	I-90 continues EB with I-94 & I-39. Exit #'s follow I-90.
108A		WI 78S, to US 51N, Wausau, Merrimac
	TStop	S: Petro Stopping Center #53 (Scales)
	Gas	S: Phillips 66
	Food	S: Subway/Petro SC, Little Caesars
	Lodg	S: Comfort Suites, Days Inn
	TServ	S: Petro SC/Tires
	TWash	S: Blue Beacon TW/Petro SC
	Other	S: Laundry/WiFi/Petro SC, Devil's Lake State Park
(108B)		I-39N, Wausau, Merrimac, Portage
	Med	N: + Hospital
	Other	N: to WI Dells, Portage Muni Airport✈
(113)		Rest Area (Both dir)
		(RR, Phone, Picnic, Vend, RVDump)
115		CR CS/J, Poynette, Lake Wisconsin
	FStop	N: North Point Plaza/BP
	Food	N: McDonald's, Subway
119		WI 60, Arlington, Lodi
	Gas	S: Mobil◇
	Food	S: Rococo's Pizza
	Lodg	S: Best Western
	Other	S: Interstate RV Center

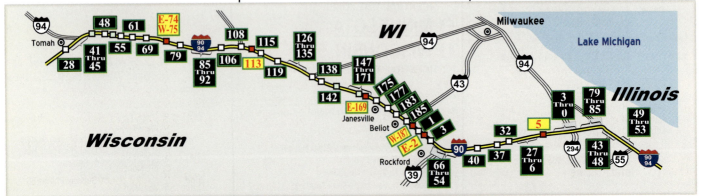

◇ = Regular Gas Stations with Diesel   ▲ = RV Friendly Locations   ♥ = Pet Friendly Locations
RED PRINT SHOWS LARGE VEHICLE PARKING/ACCESS ON SITE OR NEARBY   BROWN PRINT SHOWS CAMPGROUNDS/RV PARKS

INTERSTATE W 90 E

EXIT	WISCONSIN	EXIT	WISCONSIN	EXIT	WI / IL
126	CR V, De Forest, Dane	**147**	CR N, Cottage Grove, Stoughton	**183**	CR S, Shopiere Rd, Beloit
Gas	N: BP, Phillips 66◊	TStop	S: Road Ranger #136/Citgo	TStop	N: Rollette Oil #4/Citgo
	S: Citgo, Exxon◊	Gas	S: BP	Med	N: + Hospital
Food	N: Arby's, McDonald's, Subway	Food	S: FastFood/Road Ranger, BurgerKing/	Other	N: Turtle Creek Campground▲
Lodg	N: Holiday Inn Express		BP	**185A**	WI 81W, Milwaukee Rd, Beloit
131	WI 19, Waunakee,	Other	N: Grocery	FStop	S: Speedway #4293
	Sun Prairie	**(147.8)**	Weigh Station (WB)	TStop	S: Pilot Travel Center #289 (Scales)
Gas	N: Mobil, KwikTrip, Speedway	**156**	US 51N, Stoughton	Gas	S: BP, Exxon◊, Shell
Food	N: McDonald's, Taco Bell/Speedway	Lodg	S: Coachmen's Inn	Food	S: TacoBell/Pilot TC, Applebee's,
Lodg	N: Days Inn, Super 8	**160**	US 51S, WI 73, to WI 106,		Arby's, Country Kitchen, Hong Kong
	S: Country Inn Suites		Edgerton, Deerfield		Buffet, McDonald's, Perkins, Wendy's
TServ	N: Kenworth	TStop	S: Edgerton AmBest Oasis (Scales)	Lodg	S: Comfort Inn, Econo Lodge, Fairfield
TWash	N: Windsor Truck Wash	Food	S: Rest/Oasis		Inn, Holiday Inn Express, Super 8
Other	N: Walgreen's	TServ	S: Edgerton Oasis/Tires	Other	S: Auto Dealers, Staples, Tires +,
132	US 51, Madison, De Forest	Lodg	S: Towne Edge Motel		Wal-Mart sc
TStop	N: Hwy 51 Citgo, AmBest/Truckers	Other	N: Hickory Hills Campground▲	**(185B)**	Jct I-43N, to Milwaukee
	Inn #1/Shell (Scales)		S: Laundry/WiFi/LP/BP, Jana Airport✈	**(187)**	WI Welcome Center (WB)
	S: Travel Center of America #50/Mobil	**163**	WI 59, Edgerton, Milton, Newville		(RR, Phones, Picnic, Vend, Info)
	(Scales)	Gas	N: Mobil, Shell	NOTE:	I-90 runs above with I-39 WB to Ex #138.
Food	N: Rest/Hwy 51, Rest/Truckers Inn		S: BP		Exit #'s follow I-90.
	S: CountryPride/Subway/TacoBell/TA TC	Food	N: Burger King/Shell, McDonald's,	NOTE:	MM 188: Illinois State Line
TWash	N: Truckers Inn		Red Apple/Mobil		(CENTRAL TIME ZONE)
TServ	N: Truckers Inn/Tires, Peterbilt of WI,	Lodg	N: Comfort Inn		⊙ **WISCONSIN**
	Volvo/White/GMC/Freightliner	Other	N: Blackhawk Campground/Sales/Svc▲,		⊙ **ILLINOIS**
	S:TA TC/Tires, Brad Ragan Truck, Auto		Hidden Valley RV Resort &		
	& RV Tire Service		Campground▲, Lakeland Camping		(CENTRAL TIME ZONE)
Other	N: Laundry/Hwy 51, Laundry/BarbSh/		Resort▲, Lakeview Lodge &	NOTE:	I-90 below runs with I-39.
	CB/Truckers Inn		Campground▲		Exit #'s follow I-90.
	S: Laundry/WiFi/TA TC, WI RV World,	**(169)**	Rest Area (EB)	**1**	US 51N, IL 75W, S Beloit
	Camperland RV		(RR, Phone, Picnic, Vend)	TStop	S: Flying J Travel Plaza #5097 (Scales),
135A	US 151S, Washington Ave, Madison	**171A**	WI 26, Milton Ave, Janesville (EB)		Road Ranger Travel Center #205 (Scales)
Gas	S: BP, Shell, Sinclair	FStop	N: Mulligan's Truckstop/66	Food	S: Rest/FastFood/FL TP, Rest/Subway/
Food	S: Applebee's, Chili's, Country Kitchen,	TStop	S: Road Ranger #107/Citgo		RR TC
	Cracker Barrel, Denny's, Dunkin Donuts,	Food	N: Cracker Barrel	Lodg	S: Knights Inn, Ramada Inn
	Hardee's, IHOP, KFC, McDonald's, Mtn		S: Rest/Road Ranger	TServ	S: FJ TP
	Jack's Steakhouse, Olive Garden, Perkins,	Lodg	N: Best Western, Hampton Inn, Motel 6♥	Other	S: Laundry/WiFi/BarbSh/RVDump/LP/
	Ponderosa, Red Lobster, Tumbleweed	Other	N: Auto Dealers, Blackhawk		FJ TP, Auto Dealers, Auto Services,
	Grill, Steak 'n Shake, Wendy's		Campground▲		Pearl Lake RV Park & Campground
Lodg	S: Best Western, Comfort Inn, Fairfield	**171A**	WI 26N, Milton Ave, Janesville (WB)		Sales & Service▲, to Finnegan's RV
	Inn, Econo Lodge, Hampton Inn, Holiday	FStop	N: Mulligan's Truckstop/P66		Center
	Inn, Madison Suites, Microtel, Motel 6♥,	Food	N: Cracker Barrel	**(2)**	IL Welcome Center (EB)
	Residence Inn, Select Inn	Lodg	N: Best Western, Hampton Inn, Motel 6♥		(RR, Phone, Picnic, Vend, Info, RVDump)
Other	S: Best Buy, Kmart, Mall, WI State	Other	N: to Yogi Bear's Jellystone Park▲,	**(76)/3**	CR 9, Rockton Rd, Roscoe
	Hwy Patrol Post, Mall, Dane Co Reg'l		Pilgrim's Campground▲	TStop	N: Love's Travel Stop #322 (Scales)
	Airport✈	**171B**	US 14W, Janesville (EB)	Food	N: Hardee's/Love's TS
135B	US 151N, Washington Ave		US 14W, WI 26S (WB)	Other	N: Laundry/WiFi/RVDump/Love's TS
135C	High Crossing Blvd (WB)	Lodg	S: Oasis Motel, Ramada Inn, Super 8		S: Auto Museum
Lodg	N: Courtyard, Staybridge Suites	**171C**	US 14, Humes Rd, Janesville	NOTE:	I-90 runs below with Tollway
	S: East Town Suites, Microtel	TStop	N: Travel Center of America #71/Mobil		Exit #'s follow Tollway.
(138A)	I-94E, Milwaukee (EB, Left exit)		(Scales)	**(75.5)**	S Beloit TOLL Plaza
138B	WI 30W, Madison (WB, Left exit)	Food	N: Wendy's/TA TC	**69**	IL 173
NOTE:	I-90 runs with I-94 above for 93 mi.		S: Asia Buffet, Milwaukee Grill	**66**	CR 55, Riverside Blvd,
	Exit #'s follow I-90.	Lodg	N: Holiday Inn Express, Microtel		Rockford
NOTE:	I-90 runs below with I-39 to IL State		S: Ramada Inn, Super 8	FStop	S: Road Ranger Travel Center #211
	Line. Exit #'s follow I-90.	Other	N: Laundry/TA TC, Auto Dealers	Gas	S: BP, Phillips 66◊
142A	US 12W, US 18W	**175C**	WI 14E	Food	S: FastFood/RR TC, Arby's, Culver's, KFC,
Gas	S: Cenex, Shell	**175A**	US 14 Bus, Racine St		McDonald's, Subway, Wendy's
Food	S: Arby's, Denny's, Wendy's	Gas	S: BP	Lodg	S: Days Inn
Lodg	S: AmericInn, Days Inn, Holiday Inn	Food	S: Hardee's	Other	S: Auto Dealers, Auto Services, ATMs,
	Express, Quality Inn	Lodg	S: Lannon Stone Motel		Banks, Grocery
Med	S: + Hospital	**175B**	WI 11E, Janesville	**63**	US 20 Bus, E State St, Rockford
Other	S: to Univ of WI	TStop	N: J&R Quick Mart/BP	Gas	N: Phillips 66◊
142B	US 12E, US 18E	Food	N: Subway/QuickMart, Denny's		S: BP, Mobil◊
FStop	N: Wagner's Mobil	Lodg	N: Baymont Inn	Food	N: Cracker Barrel, Subway/Phillips 66
Food	N: McDonald's, Subway	**177**	WI 11W, WI 351, Avalon Rd,		
Lodg	N: Knights Inn, Motel 6♥, Ramada Inn,		Avalon, Janesville		
	Wingate Inn	Gas	S: BP, KwikTrip		
(145.5)	Weigh Station (EB)	Other	S: S WI Reg'l Airport✈		

◊ = Regular Gas Stations with Diesel ▲ = RV Friendly Locations ♥ = Pet Friendly Locations
RED PRINT SHOWS LARGE VEHICLE PARKING/ACCESS ON SITE OR NEARBY   BROWN PRINT SHOWS CAMPGROUNDS/RV PARKS

INTERSTATE 90 W/E

EXIT		ILLINOIS
	Food	S: Applebee's, Arby's, Burger King, Chili's, Country Kitchen, Denny's, Don Pablo, KFC, Hooters, IHOP, Lone Star Steakhouse, McDonald's, Machine Shed Rest, Olive Garden, Perkins, Ruby Tuesday, Steak n Shake, Tumbleweed Grill
	Lodg	N: Baymont Inn, Exel Inn
		S: Alpine Inn, Best Western, Candlewood Suites, Comfort Inn, Courtyard, Fairfield Inn, Hampton Inn, Holiday Inn Express, Quality Suites, Ramada Inn, Red Roof Inn, Residence Inn, Sleep Inn, Super 8
	Med	S: + St Anthony Medical Center
	Other	N: Greyhound, Museum
		S: Amtrak, Auto Services, Advance Auto, B&N, Best Buy, Borders, Circuit City, CompUSA, Discount Tire, Dollar Tree, Home Depot, Kmart, Lowe's, Office Depot, Pharmacy, ShopKO, Sam's Club, Target, Wal-Mart
(61/123)		Jct I-39S, US 51S, to US 20, Cherry Valley, to Rockford
		Jct I-90E, TOLL, to Chicago
	Other	S: Magic Waters Theme Park, to Blackhawk Valley Campground▲
	NOTE:	I-90 above runs with I-39 and Tollway. Exit #'s follow Tollway.
	NOTE:	I-90 below continues with Tollway. Exit #'s follow Tollway.
(55)		Belvidere TOLL Plaza (WB)
(54.5)		Belvidere Oasis (Both dir)
54		Belvidere-Genoa Rd, Belvidere, Sycamore
	Other	N: to Boone Co Fairgrounds, to appr 5 mi Holiday Acres Camping Resort▲
		S: to Sycamore RV Resort▲
(40)		TOLL Plaza (EB)
37		US 20, Grant Hwy, Hampshire, Elgin, Marengo
	TStop	N: Travel Center of America #44/BP (Scales), AmBest/Arrowhead Oasis (Scales), Road Ranger #235/Citgo (Scales)
	Food	N: CountryPride/BurgerKing/Popeye's/ TA TC, Rest/Arrowhead, Subway/RR, Wendy's
	Lodg	N: Super 8
	TWash	N: Arrowhead TW
	TServ	N: TA TC/Tires, Arrowhead/Tires
	Other	N: Laundry/WiFi/RVDump/TA TC, Laundry/CB/WiFi/Arrowhead, to appr 4mi Lehman's Lakeside RV Resort▲, Chicago Northwest KOA▲
32		IL 47, Woodstock (WB)
	Food	N: Culver's, Great Steak & Potato, Starbucks, Subway, Taco Bell
	Other	N: Prime Outlet Stores, Botts Welding & Truck Service, to appr 14 mi Will Oaks Campground▲
27		CR 34, Randall Rd, Elgin
	Food	N: Jimmy's Charhouse, Starbucks
	Lodg	N: Country Inn, Comfort Suites
	Med	S: + to Provena St Joseph Hospital
	Other	S: Train Station, Wal-Mart
(25)		TOLL Plaza
24		IL 31N, State St, Elgin
	Gas	N: Thornton's◊ BP

EXIT		ILLINOIS
	Food	N: Alexander's, Cracker Barrel, McDonald's, Quiznos, Wendy's
	Lodg	N: Hampton Inn, Marriott, Quality Inn, Super 8, Towneplace Suites
	Other	N: ATMs, Auto Services, Firestone, NTB, Spring Hill Mall, UPS Store
		S: Judson College
23		IL 25, Dundee Ave, Elgin
	Gas	S: Shell, Speedway◊
	Food	S: Arby's, Subway
	Lodg	N: Days Inn
	Med	S: + Hospital
21		Beverly Rd, Elgin (WB)
	Other	N: Sears Arena
19		IL 59, Sutton Rd, Barrington
	Lodg	N: Marriott
	Med	S: + Hospital
	Other	N: Cabela's
17		Barrington Rd, Schaumburg (WB)
	Gas	S: 7-11, BP, Shell
	Food	S: Chili's, IHOP, Lone Star Steakhouse, Max & Erma's, Romano's Macaroni Grill, Steak 'n Shake, TGI Friday
	Lodg	S: Baymont Inn, Candlewood Suites, Hampton Inn, Hilton Garden Inn, Hyatt Place, La Quinta Inn♥, Red Roof Inn♥
	Med	S: + St Alexius Medical Center
	Other	N: to Cabela's
		S: ATMs, Auto Services, Pharmacy, Sam's Club, Target, Tires
13		Roselle Rd, Schaumburg (WB)
	Food	N: Medieval Times Dinner Theatre
		S: Ho Luck Rest, Outback Steakhouse, Red Lobster, Super China Buffet

EXIT		ILLINOIS
	Lodg	N: Extended Stay America
		S: Country Inn, Holiday Inn, Homestead Suites, Wingate Inn
	Other	N: Harper College
		S: Auto Dealers
(11)		Jct I-290, IL 53, IL 58, Golf Rd, Rolling Meadows, Elk Grove
	Food	N: Ming's Chinese, Hong Kong Cafe
		S: Joe's Crab Shack, Olive Garden, Stir Crazy Café, Morton's
	Lodg	N: Holiday Inn, Radisson
		S: AmeriSuites, Hyatt, Residence Inn, Springhill Suites
	Other	S: Woodfield Mall, Costco, Sam's Club
9		Arlington Heights Rd, Golf Rd
	Gas	N: BP
		S: Shell
	Food	N: Applebee's, Arby's, Baja Fresh, Chili's, Denny's, Magnum's Steakhouse, Panda Express, Starbucks, Sushi Rest, Yanni's Greek Rest
	Lodg	N: AmeriSuites, Courtyard, DoubleTree, Extended Stay America, Holiday Inn Express, Motel 6♥, Red Roof Inn, Wingate Inn
		S: Sheraton Suites♥
	Med	N: + NW Medical Center
	Other	N: ATMs, Auto Services, Banks, Golf Courses, Firestone, NTB, Sam's Club, Wal-Mart, US Army Reserve Center
		S: Golf Courses, Tires
6		Elmhurst Rd, Des Plaines, Elk Grove Village, Mt Pleasant (WB)
	Gas	N: 7-11, Citgo, Mobil
		S: Amoco, BP, Marathon
	Food	S: Burger King, Dunkin Donuts, Lou's Pizzeria, McDonald's, Subway
	Lodg	N: Country Inn
		S: Comfort Inn, Days Inn, Excel Inn, Holiday Inn, Howard Johnson, InTowne Suites
	Other	N: Sam's Club
(5)		Des Plaines Oasis (Both dir)
	FStop	Mobil
	Food	McDonald's, Panda Express, Starbucks
	Other	CarWash
3		IL 72, Lee St, Higgins Rd (WB)
	Food	N: Cafe La Cave, Chili's, Chipolte Mex Grill, IHOP, Potbelly Sandwiches, Starbucks, Steak 'n Shake, Subway
		S: Elliots Deli, Harry Carey's Ital Steakhouse, Nick's Fish Market
	Lodg	N: Extended Stay America, Quality Inn, Radisson, Residence Inn, Wyndham
		S: Best Western, Holiday Inn Select, Holiday Inn Express, Travelodge
	Other	N: Allstate Arena
		S: Train Station, O'Hare Airport✈
(2)		TOLL Plaza
(1)		Jct I-294N, Tri State Tollway, to Wisconsin (WB)
		Jct I-294, I-190, Wisconsin, Indiana, O'Hare Airport (EB)
(.5)		TOLL Plaza Begin/End IL NW Tollway

◊ = Regular Gas Stations with Diesel   ▲ = RV Friendly Locations   ♥ = Pet Friendly Locations
RED PRINT SHOWS LARGE VEHICLE PARKING/ACCESS ON SITE OR NEARBY   BROWN PRINT SHOWS CAMPGROUNDS/RV PARKS

EXIT	ILLINOIS	EXIT	ILLINOIS	EXIT	IL / ID
(0)	US 190W, Chicago O'Hare, to I-294S, Tri State Tollway (WB) I-90E, Kennedy Expy, Chicago Lp (EB)	47A Gas Food Other	Western Ave, Fullerton Ave N: Citgo, Phillips 66 S: Marathon N: Dunkin Donuts, Popeye's, Subway N: Home Depot	58B Gas Med (59A)	63rd St (EB) N: Shell S: BP S: + Hospital Jct I-94E (EB)
NOTE:	I-90 above runs with Tollway. Exit #'s follow Tollway.	47B	Damen Ave	NOTE:	I-90 above runs with I-94. Exit #'s follow I-94.
NOTE:	I-90 below continues as Kennedy Expy. Exit #s follow Kennedy Expy.	48A Gas	Armitage Ave N: Mobil S: BP		Begin/End Chicago Skyway Toll Rd
79A Food Lodg Other	IL 171, Cumberland Ave S S: Deli, Subway, Triangle Cafe S: Clarion, Marriott S: Train Station, Greyhound Terminal	48B Gas Food	IL 64, North Ave, Ashland Ave N: BP S: BP, Shell S: Huddle House	6 Exit 5.5	State St, to I-94E (WB) St Lawrence Ave (WB) E 79th St (WB)
79B Gas Food Lodg Other	IL 72, Higgins Rd, Cumberland Ave N: Citgo, Mobil N: Chicago Hot Dog Factory, Denny's, Hooters, McDonald's, Porters Steak House, Outback Steakhouse, Starbucks N: AmeriSuites, Holiday Inn, Marriott N: Grocery, Walgreen's	49A Gas 49B 50A 50B	Division St S: BP, Shell Augusta Blvd, Milwaukee Ave Ogden Ave Ohio St	5 3 Exit Exit	Stony Island Ave, to IL 41 E 87th St (WB) Toll Plaza 92nd St (EB)
80	Canfield Rd (WB)	51A	Randolph St, Lake St (WB)	(2) Gas Food	Chicago Skyway Plaza AmocoBP McDonald's
81A Gas Food Med Other	IL 43, Harlem Ave S: BP, Shell S: Hansen's Fish Pier, Mr K's, Sally's Pancakes, Wendy's N: + Resurrecton Medical Center S: Train Station	51B 51C	Lake St, Randolph St (EB), Washington Blvd, Ohio St (WB) Madison, Washington Blvd (WB) Randolph, Washington (EB)	1 Gas Food	US 12, US 20, US 41, Indianapolis Blvd, 106th St, State Line Rd (EB) S: BP◊, Shell◊ S: Burger King, McDonald's
81B	Sayre Ave	51D	Washington, Madison St (EB) Monroe St, Madison St (WB)	(0)	Begin/End Chicago Skyway Toll Rd
82A	Nagle Ave	51E	Madison St, Monroe St (EB) Adams St, Monroe St (WB)	NOTE:	MM 103: Indiana State Line
82B	Bryn Mawr Ave (WB)	51F	Monroe St, Adams St (EB)		(CENTRAL TIME ZONE)
82C	Avondale Ave, Austin Ave (EB)	51G	Adams St, Jackson Blvd (EB)		ILLINOIS
83AB Gas Food Other	Foster Ave, Central Ave (WB) N: BP N: Checkers, Dunkin Donuts N: Walgreen's	51HI	Van Buren St, I-290, Congress Pkwy, West Suburbs		INDIANA (CENTRAL TIME ZONE)
84 Gas Food	Lawrence Ave N: BP S: Dunkin Donuts, McDonald's, Subway	52A Gas	Taylor St, Roosevelt Rd (EB) N: Shell S: Citgo	(0)	Begin IN TOLL EB, End WB
(85)	I-94W, Skokie, Chicago	52B	Roosevelt Rd, Taylor St (WB)	1 Gas Food Other	US 12, US 20, US 41, 106th St, 108th St, Indianapolis Blvd N: BP◊, Mobil, Shell◊ S: Burger King, KFC, McDonald's S: Amtrak
NOTE:	I-90 below runs with I-94. Exit #'s follow I-94.	52C Gas	18th St (EB) N: Shell	(1)	TOLL Plaza
43A	Wilson Ave (WB)	53	Cermak Rd, Archer Ave, I-55 (EB)	3	IN 912E, Cline Ave, Hammond, Gary
(43B)	Jct I-90W	53A	Archer Ave, I-55 (EB), Cermak Rd, S Canalport Ave (WB)	5 FStop Gas Food Lodg Other	US 41, Calumet Ave, Hammond N: IMK Truck Stop GasARoo S: Speedway #8305 N: Gas City S: Marathon S: Arby's, Dunkin Donuts, KFC, McDonald's, Taco Bell, White Castle S: AmericInn, Ramada Inn, Super 8 S: AutoZone, Walgreen's, Self-Serv Car/Truck Wash
43C	Montrose Ave	(53B)	Jct I-55, Stevenson Expy		
43D	Kostner Ave	(53C)	Jct I-55, St Louis, Lake Shore Dr		
44A Gas Other	IL 19, Keeler Ave N: BP, Shell N: Wrigley Field	54 Med	31st St N: + Hospital		
44B Gas	Pulaski Rd, Irving Park Rd N: BP, Mobil	55A	35th St		
45A	Addison St	55B	Pershing Rd		
45B Gas Food	Kimball Ave N: Marathon◊ S: Marathon, Mobil S: Dunkin Donuts, Subway, Wendy's	56A	43rd St	10 Other	IN 912, Cline Ave, Gary N: Gary Reg'l Airport✈, Trump IN Casino
		56B	47th St (EB)		
45C	Kedzie Ave, Belmont Ave	57A Food Other	51st St N: McDonald's N: Chicago District Police Hdqtrs	14A Med Other	Grant St, Buchanan St, Gary S: + Methodist Hospital N: US Steel
46A Gas Food Other	California Ave S: Mobil S: IHOP, Popeye's Chicken N: Laundromat	57B Gas Food	Garfield Blvd S: Mobil, Shell N: Checkers S: Wendy's	14B Other	IN 53, Broadway N: US Steel S: Greyhound Terminal, Train Station
46B	Diversey Ave	58A	59th St	(17)	Jct I-65, US 12, US 20, Dunes Hwy, to Indianapolis

INTERSTATE 90 W/E

INDIANA

EXIT		
	NOTE:	I-90 below runs with I-80EB. Runs separately WB. I-80 & I-94 run together WB.
(21)		Jct I-80W (IL TOLL), Jct I-94E, to Detroit, US 6W, IN 51, to Des Moines (Serv on IN 51)
	TStop	N: Road Ranger Travel Center #239/Citgo (Scales), Flying J Travel Plaza #5085 (Scales), Travel Center of America #219/BP (Scales), Dunes Center Truck Stop (Scales)
	Food	N: Subway/Road Ranger TC, Rest/FastFood/FJ TP, Buckhorn/Popeyes/Subway/TA TC, McDonald's, Ponderosa
	TWash	N: Road Ranger, FJ TP, TA TC
	TServ	N: FJ TP/Tires, TA TC/Tires, Dunes Center TS/Tires
	Other	N: Laundry/BarbSh/CB/WiFi/FJ TP, Laundry/WiFi/TA TC
(22)		George Ade Service Area (EB) John T McCutcheon Service Area (WB)
	FStop	BP #70512/#70511
	Food	Hardee's
23		600W, Portage, Port of Indiana
	Gas	N: Marathon, Shell S: AmocoBP, Marathon
	Food	S: Burger King, Dunkin Donuts, KFC, Jimmy John Subs, First Wok, McDonald's, Starbucks, Subway, Wendy's
	Lodg	N: Comfort Inn, Holiday Inn Express
	Other	N: Yogi Bear's Jellystone Park▲ S: Grocery, Walgreen's, US Post Office
(24)		Indiana TOLL Plaza
31		IN 49, Chesterton, Valparaiso
	Med	S: + Hospital
	Other	N: to appr 4mi Sand Creek RV Park▲
(38)		Truck Rest Area (Both dir)
39		US 421, Westville, Michigan City
49		IN 39, La Porte, Rolling Prairie (Addt'l services 4 mi S in La Porte)
	Lodg	N: Hampton Inn S: Best Value Inn, Cassidy Motel & RV Park▲
(56)		Knute Rockne Service Area (EB) Wilbur Shaw Service Area (WB)
	FStop	BP #70510/#70509
	Food	McDonald's, DQ
	Other	Phone, RVDump
	NOTE:	MM 62: Central / Eastern Time Zone
72		US 31, St Joseph Valley Pkwy, South Bend, to Plymouth, Niles
	FStop	N: Speedway #6674 (Scales)

EXIT		
	TStop	N: Pilot Travel Center #35 (Scales)
	Food	N: Subway/Pilot TC S: McDonald's, Ponderosa, Taco Bell
	Lodg	N: Super 8 S: Days Inn, Quality Inn
	TServ	S: Whiteford Kenworth
	Other	N: WiFi/Speedway, WiFi/Pilot TC S: Amtrak, Michiana Reg'l Transportation Center Airport✈, South Bend Reg'l Airport✈, IN State Hwy Patrol Post
77		IN 933, US 31 Bus, South Bend, to Notre Dame University
	Gas	N: Meijer◇, Mobil, Phillips 66 S: Marathon, Phillips 66◇
	Food	N: Arby's, Burger King, DQ, Damon's, Fazoli's, McDonald's, Papa John's, Pizza Hut, Ponderosa, Steak & Ale, Subway S: Bob Evans, Denny's, Perkins, Taco Bell, Wendy's
	Lodg	N: Comfort Suites, Days Inn, Hampton Inn, Motel 6♥, Ramada Inn, Super 8 S: Best Inn, Howard Johnson, Holiday Inn, Knights Inn, Inn at St. Mary's, Signature Inn, Wingate Inn
	Other	N: Auto Zone, NAPA, Radio Shack, Walgreen's S: to Notre Dame Univ
83		IN 331, Capital Ave, Granger, to Mishawaka
	Gas	N: BP◇, Citgo, Phillips 66◇ S: Meijer◇
	Food	N: Applebee's, Arby's, Olive Garden, Panda Express, Pizza Hut, Taco Bell, Wendy's S: Arby's, Burger King, Carrabba's, Chili's, Lone Star Steakhouse, McDonald's, Outback Steakhouse, Ryan's Grill, Steak 'n Shake, Subway, TGI Friday
	Lodg	N: Carlton Lodge, Fairfield Inn, Hampton Inn, Holiday Inn, Super 8 S: Best Western, Courtyard, Extended Stay America, Studio Plus
	Other	N: Best Buy, CVS, Kroger, Office Depot, Target, Walgreen's, Mall, South Bend KOA▲ S: Auto Dealers, B&N, Discount Tire, Lowe's, Sam's Club, Wal-Mart sc
(90)		George N Craig Service Area (EB) Henry F Schricker Service Area (WB)
	TStop	BP #70508/#70507
	Food	Arby's, Burger King, Pizza Hut, Starbucks
	Other	RVDump
92		IN 19, Cassopolis St, Elkhart
	Gas	N: 7-11, Phillips 66◇ S: Marathon◇, Shell, Speedway

EXIT		
	Food	N: Applebee's, Cracker Barrel, Perkins, Steak 'n Shake, Starbucks S: Arby's, Bob Evans, Burger King, KFC, Long John Silver, McDonald's, Olive Garden, Red Lobster, Ryan's Grill, Taco Bell, Texas Roadhouse, Wendy's
	Lodg	N: Best Western, Comfort Suites, Country Inn, Econo Lodge, Hampton Inn, Holiday Inn Express, Knights Inn, Quality Inn, Sleep Inn S: Budget Inn, Days Inn, Jameson Inn, Ramada, Red Roof Inn♥, Super 8
	Med	S: + Hospital
	Other	N: ATMs, Grocery, CVS, Kmart, RV Repair, Tiara RV Center, Elkhart Campground▲ S: ATMs, AutoZone, CarQuest, Dollar Tree, Walgreen's, Wal-Mart sc, Elkhart City Airport✈, Holiday World RV Center, Michiana RV, Cruise America, to Camping World/RVDump
96		Elkhart East
	Gas	S: 7-11, BP◇
	Food	S: McDonald's, Subway
101		IN 15, Bristol, to Goshen
	Gas	S: Speedway◇
107		US 131, IN 13, Constantine, Middlebury (Addt'l Serv 5 mi S in Middlebury)
	FStop	N: Marathon S: Snappy Food Mart/BP
	Lodg	N: Plaza Motel
	Other	S: Eby's Pines RV Park▲, Elkhart Co/Middlebury KOA▲, to Coachman RV Factory
(108)		Truck Rest Area
121		IN 9, Howe, Sturgis, LaGrange
	Food	N: Applebee's, Golden Corral, Wendy's
	Lodg	N: Hampton Inn, Travel Inn Motel, Comfort Inn, Knights Inn S: Holiday Inn, Super 8
	Med	N: + Hospital S: + Hospital
	Other	S: to Grand View Bend RV Park/RVDump
(126)		Gene Porter Service Area (EB) Ernie Pyle Service Area (EB)
	FStop	Mobil #70572
	Food	Hardee's
	Other	RVDump
(144)		Jct I-69, US 27, Fremont, Angola, Fort Wayne, Lansing
	TStop	N: Petro 2 #45/Mobil (Scales), Pilot Travel Center #29 (Scales), Pioneer Auto Truck Stop/Shell (At Exit #157 on I-69)

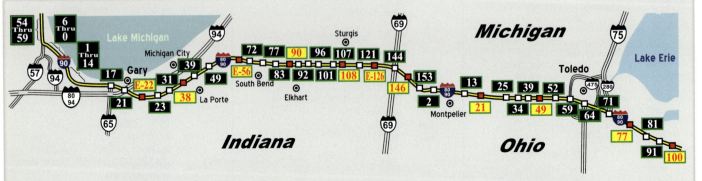

◇ = Regular Gas Stations with Diesel   ▲ = RV Friendly Locations   ♥ = Pet Friendly Locations
RED PRINT SHOWS LARGE VEHICLE PARKING/ACCESS ON SITE OR NEARBY   BROWN PRINT SHOWS CAMPGROUNDS/RV PARKS

Interstate 90 W/E

EXIT		IN / OH
	Gas	S: Marathon◊
	Food	N: Rest/FastFood/Petro2, Wendy's/Pilot TC
	Lodg	N: Redwood Lodge
		S: Hampton Inn, Holiday Inn Express, Super 8, Travelers Inn
	TServ	S: Cummins, Discover Volvo Trucks
	Other	N: Laundry/WiFi/LP/Petro2, Laundry/WiFi/Pilot TC
		S: Outlet Mall, U-Haul
(146)		**J R Riley Service Area (EB)**
		Booth Tarkington Service Area (EB)
	FStop	Mobil #70580
	Food	McDonald's
(153)		**Indiana TOLL Plaza**
	NOTE:	MM 157: Ohio State Line
		(EASTERN TIME ZONE)
⊙ **INDIANA**		
⊙ **OHIO**		
		(EASTERN TIME ZONE)
	NOTE:	I-90 runs below with I-80. Exit #'s follow I-80.
	NOTE:	EB: Begin TOLL, WB End
(2.7)		**TOLL Plaza Westgate**
2		**OH 49, Edon, Edgerton, to US 20, Allen MI**
	Gas	N: Mobil
	Food	N: Burger King, Subway
13		**OH 15, US 20 Alt, Holiday City, Montpelier, Bryan**
	FStop	S: Holiday City Stop N Go/Sunoco, Hutch's Karry Out/Marathon
	Food	S: Subway/Marathon, Country Fair Rest
	Lodg	S: Econo Lodge♥, Holiday Inn Express, Ramada Inn
	TServ	S: Hutch's Marathon/Tires
	Other	N: Lazy River Resort Campground▲, to appr 7 mi Loveberry's Funny Farm Campground▲
(21)		**Tiffin River Service Plaza (EB)**
		Indian Meadow Service Plaza (WB)
	TStop	Sunoco #7106/#7105
	Food	Hardee's
	Other	Picnic, RVDump/Overnite▲
25		**OH 66, Archbold-Fayette, Burlington**
	Lodg	S: to Sauder Heritage Inn
	Other	N: to Harrison Lake State Park▲
		S: to Hidden Valley Campground▲
34		**OH 108, Wauseon, Napoleon**
	TStop	S: Turnpike Shell
	Gas	S: Circle K, DM, Mobil
	Food	S: Subway/Shell, Burger King, Pizza Hut, McDonald's, Smith's Rest, Taco Bell, Wendy's
	Lodg	S: Arrowhead Motel♥, Best Western, Holiday Inn Express, Super 8
	TServ	S: Turnpike Shell, Wood Truck Service
	Med	S: + Hospital
	Other	N: Fulton Co Fairgrounds/RVDump▲, appr 5mi Sunny's Shady Rec Area▲, to appr 18mi Lake Hudson Rec Area▲
		S: ATMs, Auto Service, Family Dollar, Wal-Mart
39		**OH 109, Delta, Lyons**
	TStop	S: Country Corral/Citgo
	Food	S: Rest/Country Corral,

Personal Notes
_____

EXIT		OHIO
	Other	S: Delta Wings Airport✈, Maumee State Forest
(49)		**Fallen Timbers Service Plaza (EB)**
		Oak Openings Service Plaza (WB)
	TStop	Valero
	Food	Nathan's, Cinnabon, Pizza Uno, Great American Bagel
	Other	Picnic
52		**OH 2, Swanton, Toledo Airport**
	Lodg	S: Days Inn, Quality Inn
	Other	N: CFS Truck & Fleet Repair
		S: Grocery, Budget, U-Haul, Express Auto & Truck Service, Toledo Express Airport✈, RV Center, to Big Sandy Campground▲, Twin Acres Campground▲, Bluegrass Campground▲, Hidden Lake Campground▲, Betty's Country Campground▲
59		**US 20, Reynolds Rd, to I-475, to US 23, Maumee, Toledo**
	Gas	N: BP◊, Shell, Speedway◊
		S: Meijer◊, Speedway
	Food	N: Arby's, Bob Evans, Damon's, Dragon Buffet, Little Caesars, McDonald's, Olive Garden, Pizza Hut, Steak n Shake, Waffle House
		S: Fazoli's, Outback Steakhouse, Red Lobster, Taco Bell
	Lodg	N: Clarion, Econo Lodge, Holiday Inn, Motel 6♥, Quality Inn
		S: Baymont Inn, Courtyard, Country Inn, Comfort Inn, Days Inn, Econo Lodge, Fairfield Inn, Hampton Inn, Homewood Suites, Red Roof Inn♥, Super 8

EXIT		OHIO
	Med	N: + to Medical Univ of OH/Toledo
		S: + St Luke's Hospital
	Other	N: ATMs, Advance Auto, Banks, FedEx Kinko's, Grocery, Goodyear, Kmart, RiteAid, Walgreen's, Southwyck Mall, Auto & RV Repair, to Toledo Stadium
		S: Auto Dealers, UPS Store
(64)		**Jct I-75N, Perrysburg, Toledo**
	Other	to Bowling Green State Univ, Toledo Zoo, Fifth Third Field
(71)		**I-280, OH 420, Perrysburg, Stony Ridge, Toledo, to I-75N, Detroit**
	TStop	N: I-280/1B: Petro Stopping Center #17/ Mobil (Scales), Flying J Travel Plaza #5450/ Conoco (Scales)
		S: Travel Center of America #87/BP (Scales), Fuel Mart #641 (Scales), Pilot Travel Center #12 (Scales)
	Food	N: IronSkillet/PizzaHut/Petro SC, Cookery/ FastFood/FJ TP
		S: CountryPride/BurgerKing/TacoBell/ TA TC, Rest/Fuel Mart, McDonald's/Pilot TC, Wendy's
	Lodg	N: Motel/Petro SC, Howard Johnson, Crown Inn, Ramada Ltd, Stony Ridge Inn, Super 8, Vista Inn Express
	TWash	N: Blue Beacon TW/Petro SC
		S: Fuel Mart
	TServ	N: Petro SC/Tires
		S: TA TC/Tires, Fuel Mart/Tires, 795 Tire Service, Williams Detroit Diesel
	Other	N: Laundry/BarbSh/WiFi/Petro SC, Laundry BarbSh/WiFi/RVDump/LP/FJ TP, to Metcalf Field✈
		S: Laundry/WiFi/TA TC, Laundry/Fuel Mart, WiFi/Pilot TC, Toledo East/Stony Ridge KOA▲
(77)		**Wyandot Service Plaza (EB)**
		Blue Heron Service Plaza (WB)
	TStop	Valero
	Food	Hardee's, Gloria Jeans Coffees, Mancino's Italian Eatery
	Other	WiFi, Picnic Area, RVDump/OverNite▲
81		**OH 51, Elmore, Gibsonburg, Woodville**
	Other	S: Wooded Acres Campground▲, to Eagle Lake Camping Resort▲
91		**OH 53, Fremont, Port Clinton, to US 6, US 20, US 2, Sandusky**
	FStop	S: BP #137
	Lodg	N: Days Inn
		S: Comfort Inn, Fremont Turnpike Motel, Hampton Inn, Holiday Inn
	Med	S: + Hospital
	Other	N: to Lake Erie Islands, Rutherford B Hayes Presidential Center, to RV Dealer, Shade Acres Campground▲, Erie Islands Resort & Marina▲
		S: Wooded Acres Campground▲, RV Dealer, Fremont Airport✈, to Cactus Flats Campground▲
(100)		**Comm Perry Service Plaza (EB)**
		Erie Islands Service Plaza (WB)
	TStop	Valero
	Food	Burger King, Carvel, Cinnabon, Einstein Bros, Starbucks, Sbarro
	Other	WiFi, Picnic Area
110		**OH 4, Bellevue, Sandusky, Attica**
	Other	N: to Cedar Point, Lazy J RV Resort▲

◊ = Regular Gas Stations with Diesel   ▲ = RV Friendly Locations   ♥ = Pet Friendly Locations
RED PRINT SHOWS LARGE VEHICLE PARKING/ACCESS ON SITE OR NEARBY   BROWN PRINT SHOWS CAMPGROUNDS/RV PARKS

INTERSTATE 90 W/E

EXIT	OHIO
118	US 250, Sandusky, Norwalk, Milan
Gas	N: Marathon, Speedway
Food	N: McDonald's, Subway S: Homestead Rest
Lodg	N: Comfort Inn, Colonial Inn South & Milan Travel Park▲, Days Inn, Fairfield Inn, Great Wolf Lodge, Hampton Inn, Holiday Inn Express, Motel 6♥, Super 8
Other	N: Wal-Mart sc, to Cedar Point, Lake Erie S: OH State Hwy Patrol Post, to Milan Thomas Edison Museum, Wilcart RV, Pin Oak RV, Norwalk Raceway Park, S: to appr 10 mi Berlin Heights Holiday Park▲
135	Baumhart Rd, to OH 2, Amherst, Vermilion, Huron, Sandusky
Other	N: to Swift Hollow RV Resort▲, Neff Bros RV/RVDump S: to appr 8mi Berlin Heights Holiday Park▲
(139)	Vermilion Valley Service Plaza (EB) Middle Ridge Service Plaza (WB)
TStop	Valero
Food	Burger King, Great Steak, Manchu Wok, Panera, Popeye's, Starbucks, TCBY
Other	Picnic, WiFi, RVDump/OverNite▲
140	OH 58, Leavitt Rd, Amherst, Oberlin
Gas	N: Sunoco◊
Food	N: Subway/Sunoco
Other	S: to Lorain Co Reg'l Airport ✈
(142)	Jct I-90E, to OH 2, W Cleveland (EB)
Other	to Cleveland, Erie PA, Buffalo NY
NOTE:	I-90WB runs above with I-80/OH TPK. Exit #'s follow I-80.
145AB	OH 57, Lorain, Elyria, to I-80E, OH Tpk
145	OH 57, Lorain Blvd, Lorain, Elyria, to I-80E, OH Tpk
Gas	N: BP◊, Speedway, Shell S: Shell, Speedway
Food	N: Applebee's, Bob Evans, Country Kitchen, Denny's, Lone Star Steakhouse, Red Lobster, Smokey Bones BBQ, Subway, Wendy's
Lodg	N: Best Western, Comfort Inn, Country Suites, Econo Lodge, Holiday Inn S: Journey Inn, Super 8
Med	N: + Hospital
Other	N: Mall, Best Buy, Firestone, Goodyear, Lowe's, PetSmart♥, Staples, Wal-Mart S: Home Depot, OH State Hwy Patrol

EXIT	OHIO
148	OH 351, OH 254, Avon
Gas	S: BP, Speedway
Food	S: Arby's, Cracker Barrel, Burger King, McDonald's, Ruby Tuesday, Subway
Other	S: CVS, Dollar General, Dollar Tree, Gander Mountain, Grocery, Sam's Club, Tires, Lorain Co Comm College
151	OH 611, Colorado Ave, Avon, Sheffield
TStop	N: Pilot Travel Center #4 (Scales)
Gas	N: BP◊ S: BJ's
Food	N: Subway/Pilot TC, Dianna's Deli, McDonald's
Lodg	N: Fairfield Inn
Other	N: Lake Erie Harley Davidson, Avon RV Superstore S: BJ's
153	OH 83, Avon Belden Rd, Avon
Gas	N: BP, Circle K, Murphy's, Shell S: Speedway, Costco
Food	N: Burger King, McDonald's, Perkins S: Bob Evans, IHOP, Panera, Wendy's
Other	N: Best Buy, Wal-Mart S: CVS, Costco, Home Depot, Target
156	OH 113, Crocker Rd, Bassett Rd, Westlake, Bay Village
Gas	N: BP, Shell S: Marathon◊
Food	S: Applebee's, Bob Evans, Max & Erma's, McDonald's, Subway, Wendy's
Lodg	N: Extended Stay America, Holiday Inn, Marriott, Red Roof Inn♥, Residence Inn S: Hampton Inn
Med	S: + Hospital
Other	S: Mall, Cinema, CVS, Grocery, Kmart, UPS Store
159	OH 252, Columbia Rd, Westlake
Gas	N: Speedway S: BP
Food	N: Carrabba's, Dave & Buster's, Joe's Crab Shack, Outback Steakhouse, Tony Roma S: Houlihan's, McDonald's
Lodg	N: Courtyard, Super 8
Med	N: + Lakewood Medical Center
Other	S: CVS, Grocery, NTB, UPS Store
160	Clague Rd, Westlake, Rocky River (WB) (Access to Ex #159 Serv)
161	OH 2E, OH 254, Detroit Rd, Rocky River, Lakewood (EB)
162	Hilliard Blvd, Rocky River (WB)
Other	S: to Westgate Mall

EXIT	OHIO
164	McKinley Ave, Lakewood
165	Warren Rd, W 140th St, Bunts Rd, Lakewood (EB)
165A	Warren Rd, Cleveland (WB)
Med	N: + Hospital
165B	W 140th St, Bunts Rd (WB)
Gas	N: Marathon
166	W 117th St, Cleveland
Gas	N: BP, Shell
Other	N: Carwash, Home Depot
167	OH 10, Lorain Ave, West Blvd, Cleveland (EB)
167A	98th St, West Blvd (WB)
167B	OH 10, Lorain Ave (WB)
169	W 44th St, W 41st St
Med	N: + Hospital
170A	Wade Ave, US 42, W 25th St, OH 3, Scranton Rd, Cleveland (EB)
(170B)	Jct I-71S, I-176, Columbus (EB)
(170C)	I-490E, to I-77, South Akron (EB)
(170B)	Jct I-71S, to Columbus, to I-176, Parma, Zoo (WB)
171C	W 14th St, Abbey Ave (WB)
171	Abbey Ave, Fairfield Ave, W 14th (WB)
171A	US 422S, OH 14, Ontario Ave (EB)
171B	US 422N, OH 14, OH 8, OH 10 (EB)
Other	to Cleveland Browns Stadium, Convention Center, Jacobs Field
(172)	Jct I-77S, to Akron (WB)
(172A)	Jct I-77S, to Akron (EB)
172B	E 9th St, Central Ave (EB)
Med	S: + St Vincent Hospital
Other	N: Jacobs Field, Gund Arena
172C	E 22nd St, Central Ave, to Carnegie Ave West (EB)
Other	to Cuyahoga Comm College, to Cleveland State Univ
172D	Carnegie Ave E, to Euclid Ave, OH 20, Cleveland (EB)
173A	Prospect Ave E, to Euclid Ave, US 20 Jacobs Field, Gund Arena (WB)

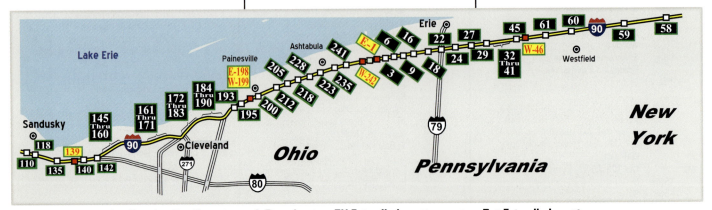

Page 468   ◊ = Regular Gas Stations with Diesel   ▲ = RV Friendly Locations   ♥ = Pet Friendly Locations
RED PRINT SHOWS LARGE VEHICLE PARKING/ACCESS ON SITE OR NEARBY   BROWN PRINT SHOWS CAMPGROUNDS/RV PARKS

EXIT		OHIO
173B		US 322, Chester Ave East (EB) E 24th St, Chester Ave (WB)
	Other	N: Cleveland St Univ, Playhouse Square
173C		Superior Ave, E 30th St (EB), E 26th St, US 6, St Clair Ave (WB)
174A		Lakeside Ave (EB)
174B		OH 2W, Lakewood (EB, SHARP Curve) OH 2W, Downtown Cleveland (WB)
	Other	N: Burke Lakefront Airport→, to The Flats, Rock & Roll Hall of Fame, Amtrak Station, Cleveland Browns Stadium, Convention Center, Port of Cleveland
175		E 55th St, Marginal Rd
176		E 72nd St
177		University Circle, Martin Luther King Dr (NO Trucks)
	Med	S: + Hospital
178		Eddy Rd, to Bratenahl
179		OH 283E, Lake Shore Blvd (EB)
180		E 140th St, E 152nd St (WB)
180A		E 140th St, Cleveland (EB)
180B		E 152nd St (EB)
181		E 156th St (WB) (NO Trucks)
182A		E 185th St, Cleveland (EB) Villaview Rd, Neff Rd (WB)
	FStop	S: Marathon Mart
	Gas	N: BP S: BP, Shell, Speedway
	Other	N: Home Depot
182B		E 200th St, Waterloo Rd (EB) Lakeland Blvd, E 200th St (WB)
	Gas	N: BP S: BP
	Med	N: + Hospital
	Other	N: Laundromat
183		Lakeland Blvd, E 222nd St
	Gas	N: Sunoco◆
184		OH 175, E 260th St, Babbitt Rd (WB)
184A		Babbitt Rd (EB)
184B		OH 175, E 260th St (EB)
	Gas	N: BP
	Other	S: Euclid Square Mall, Cuyahoga Co Airport→
185		OH 2E, Painesville (fr EB, Left exit)
186		US 20, Euclid Ave, Euclid, Wickliffe
	Gas	N: Sunoco S: Shell
	Food	N: Denny's, Joe's Crab Shack, McDonald's S: KFC, Pizza Hut, Sidewalk Café
	Lodg	N: Hampton Inn, Sheraton
	Other	S: CVS, Firestone, Kmart, Laundromat
187		OH 84, Bishop Rd, Wickliffe, to Willoughby Hills, Richmond Hts
	Gas	S: BP, Shell
	Food	S: Burger King, McDonald's, Subway
	Lodg	S: Holiday Inn
	Med	S: + Hospital
	Other	S: CVS, Grocery, Laundromat, Sam's Club, Cuyahoga Co Airport→, Bryant & Stratton College
(188)		Jct I-271S, to Akron, Columbus

EXIT		OHIO
189		OH 91, Sam Center Rd, Willoughby, Willoughby Hills
	Gas	N: BP◆, Shell
	Food	N: Bob Evans, Burger King, Cracker Barrel, Damon's, Eat 'n Park, Subway
	Lodg	N: Courtyard, Fairfield Inn, Travelodge
	Med	N: + Hospital
	Other	N: CVS, Walgreen's, to Classic Field
(190)		Jct I-271S, Akron, Columbus
193		OH 306, Broadmoor Rd, Mentor, Kirtland, Willoughby
	Gas	N: BP, Shell, Speedway S: Marathon
	Food	N: McDonald's, Ponderosa, Red Lobster S: Burger King, Roadhouse Grill
	Lodg	N: Comfort Inn, Motel 6♥, Super 8 S: Days Inn, Red Roof Inn♥, Travelodge
	Other	N: Lakeland Comm College, Holden Arboretum, Lake Farmpark
195		OH 615, Center St, Mentor, Kirtland Hills
(198)		Rest Area (EB) (RR, Phone, Picnic)
(199)		Rest Area (WB) (RR, Phone, Picnic)
200		OH 44, Painesville, Chardon
	Gas	S: BP◆, Sunoco◆
	Food	S: CK's Steakhouse, McDonald's, Waffle House
	Lodg	S: AmeriHost Inn, Quail Hollow Resort
	Med	N: + Hospital
	Other	S: OH State Hwy Patrol Post, Lake Erie College, Headlands Beach State Park
205		CR 227, Vrooman Rd, to OH 86 (NB: NO Trucks)
	Gas	S: BP◆
212		OH 528, River St, Madison Rd, Madison, Thompson
	Gas	N: Marathon◆
	Food	N: McDonald's, Potbelly Sandwiches
218		OH 534, Geneva, Geneva on the Lake
	TStop	N: Geneva Auto Truck Plaza #227/Kwik Fill (Scales)
	Gas	N: BP, Sunoco
	Food	N: Best Friends Rest, KFC, McDonald's, Lighthouse Grill, Pizza Hut, Wendy's
	Lodg	N: Howard Johnson
	TWash	N: Geneva Truck Wash
	Med	N: + Hospital
	Other	N: to appr 7mi Indian Creek Resort▲, Willow Lake Campground▲, Geneva State Park▲
223		OH 45, Austinburg, W to Warren, E to Ashtabula
	TStop	N: Flying J Travel Plaza /Shell (Scales) S: Pilot Travel Center #2 (Scales)
	Gas	S: BP
	Food	N: Rest/FastFood/Flying J TP S: FastFood/Pilot TC, Burger King, McDonald's
	Lodg	N: Best Value Inn, Comfort Inn, Holiday Inn Express, Sleep Inn, Travelodge S: Hampton Inn

EXIT		OH / PA
	TWash	S: Pilot TC
	Other	N: Laundry/BarbSh/WiFi/RVDump/LP/FJ TP, to Hide-A-Way Lakes Campground▲, to 10mi Indian Creek Resort▲ S: Laundry/Pilot TC, Grand River Academy, Kent State Univ
228		OH 11, Ashtabula, Youngstown, to OH 46, Jefferson
	Med	N: + Hospital
235		OH 84, OH 193, Kingsville
	FStop	N: Circle K #5564 S: Fuel Mart/Speedway
	TStop	S: Travel Center of America/BP (Scales)
	Gas	N: Grab & Go
	Food	S: Rest/FastFood/TA TC, Kay's Place
	Lodg	N: Dav-Ed Motel S: Kingsville Motel
	TServ	S: TA TC/Tires, Kingsville Towing/Recovery
	Other	N: Locust Lane Campground▲, Village Green Campground▲ S: Laundry/WiFi/TA TC
241		OH 7, Conneaut, Andover
	Food	N: Burger King, McDonald's S: Beef & Beer Rest
	Lodg	N: Days Inn
	Other	N: CVS, Grocery, Kmart, Evergreen Lake Park Campground▲ S: to Bayshore Family Camping▲
(242)		OH Welcome Center (WB) (RR, Phone, Picnic, Info) Weigh Station (WB)
NOTE:		MM 244: Pennsylvania State Line

(EASTERN TIME ZONE)

⊙ OHIO
⊙ PENNSYLVANIA

(EASTERN TIME ZONE)

EXIT		PA
(1)		PA Welcome Center (EB) (RR, Phone, Picnic, Vend, Info) Weigh Station (EB)
3		US 6N, Cherry Hill, W Springfield
	TStop	S: Stateline BP (Scales)
	Food	N: Blue Plate Rest S: Rest/Stateline BP
	Lodg	N: EJ's Motel, Sunset Motel
	TServ	S: Stateline BP/Tires
	Other	S: Laundry/Stateline BP, to Whispering Trails Campground▲
6		PA 215, Girard, Albion, E Springfield
	Gas	S: Sunoco
	Lodg	S: Miracle Motel
	Other	N: Pine Lane Campground▲, Erie Bluffs State Park, Virginia's Beach Lakefront Cottages & Camping▲
9		PA 18, Platea, Girard
	Gas	N: Gulf
	Lodg	S: Green Roof Inn
	TServ	N: Penn Detroit Diesel
	Other	N: PA State Hwy Patrol Post
16		PA 98, Avonia Rd, Fairview, Franklin Center
	Other	N: to Erie Int'l Airport→, Follys End Campground▲, Pine Lane Campground▲, Erie Bluffs State Park

◆ = Regular Gas Stations with Diesel   ▲ = RV Friendly Locations   ♥ = Pet Friendly Locations

RED PRINT SHOWS LARGE VEHICLE PARKING/ACCESS ON SITE OR NEARBY   BROWN PRINT SHOWS CAMPGROUNDS/RV PARKS

EXIT	PENNSYLVANIA
18	PA 832, Sterrettania Rd, McKean, Presque Isle State Park
Gas	N: Citgo, Shell◊
Food	N: Burger King
Lodg	S: Best Western
Other	N: Hills Family Campground▲, Sara's Campground on the Beach▲, Waldameer Amusement Park & Water World, Presque Isle State Park S: Erie KOA▲
(22A)	Jct I-79S, to Pittsburgh
(22B)	Jct I-79N, to Erie
24	US 19, Peach St, Waterford (Exit only)
Gas	N: Citgo◊, Kwik Fill S: Citgo, Exxon, Sunoco
Food	N: Applebee's, Burger King, Chuck E Cheese, Cracker Barrel, Damon's, Eat 'n Park, Golden Corral, Longhorn Steakhouse, McDonald's, Panera Bread, Ponderosa, Quaker Steak & Lube, Taco Bell, TGI Friday, Wendy's S: Bob Evans
Lodg	N: Courtyard, Motel 6♥ S: Comfort Inn, Country Inn, Econo Lodge, Hampton Inn, Holiday Inn, Microtel
Med	N: + St Vincent Health Center
Other	N: Best Buy, Circuit City, Grocery, Home Depot, Kmart, Lowe's, PetSmart♥, Sam's Club, Staples, Target, Wal-Mart Greyhound, Mill Creek Mall, Tinseltown S: Family First Sports Park, Sparrow Pond Family Campground & Rec Center▲, Boyer RV Center, Shorehaven Campground▲
27	PA 97, Perry Hwy, State St, Erie, Waterford
FStop	S: Holiday Shell Truck Stop
TStop	S: Pilot Travel Center #311 (Scales)
Gas	N: Citgo◊, Kwik Fill
Food	N: Arby's, Barbato's Italian, McDonald's S: FastFood/Shell, FastFood/Pilot TC
Lodg	N: Best Western, Days Inn♥, Red Roof Inn♥ S: Blue Spruce Motel, Quality Inn♥
Med	N: + Hamot Medical Center, + US Veterans Medical Center
Other	N: Amtrak, Erie Zoo, WW II Monument, U-Haul, Erie Veterans Memorial Stadium
29	PA 8, Wattsburg Rd, Parade St, Erie, to Hammett
Gas	N: Country Fair/Citgo S: Kwik Fill
Food	N: Wendy's S: Rest/Travelodge

EXIT	PA / NY
Lodg	S: Travelodge
TServ	S: Lake Erie Ford Trucks, Peterbilt, Tri-Star Truck Service, Cummins, Five Star International
Other	S: Mercyhurst College
32	PA 430, PA 290W, Station Rd, Erie, Wesleyville, Colt Station
Gas	N: Citgo
TServ	S: Beckwith CAT, Freightliner
Other	S: PA State Hwy Patrol Post, to Moon Meadows Campground▲, Creekside Campground▲
35	PA 531, Depot Rd, Erie, Harborcreek
TStop	N: Travel Center of America/BP (Scales)
Food	N: Rest/FastFood/TA TC
Lodg	N: Rodeway Inn♥/TA TC
TWash	N: Blue Beacon TW/TA TC
TServ	N: TA TC/Tires
Other	N: Laundry/WiFi/RVDump/TA TC S: to Moon Meadows Campground▲
(37)	Jct I-86 E, to Jamestown, NY
Other	S: to Creekside Campground▲
41	PA 89, North East
Gas	N: Shell
Food	N: New Harvest Rest & Pub
Lodg	N: Super 8, Vineyard B&B
Other	S: to Creekside Campground▲, Family Affair Campground▲, Campers Hill Campground▲
45	US 20, Buffalo Rd, State Line, North East
TStop	N: Kwik-Fill Auto Truck Plaza (Scales) S: Stateline BP, North East Truck Plaza (Scales)
Food	N: McDonald's, Jammin Vine S: Rest/NE TP, Subway/Stateline BP
Lodg	S: Red Carpet Inn
TServ	S: NE TP
Other	N: Heritage Wine Cellar
(46)	Weigh Station (WB)
(46)	PA Welcome Center (WB) (RR, Phone, Picnic, Vend, Info)
NOTE:	MM 47: New York State Line
	(EASTERN TIME ZONE)
⭕	**PENNSYLVANIA**
⭕	**NEW YORK**
NOTE:	NY does not use Mile Marker Exits. We have listed MM / Exit #.
495/61	NY 815, Shortman Rd, Ripley
TStop	N: Ripley State Line Truck Stop/Shell (Scales)

EXIT	NEW YORK
Food	N: Rest/Ripley SL TS
Lodg	N: Pines Motel
TServ	N: Ripley SL TS/Tires
Other	N: Laundry/LP/Ripley SL TS, Lakeshore RV Park▲
(494)	TOLL Plaza
485/60	NY 394, N Portage St, Westfield, to Mayville
Gas	N: Keystone◊
Lodg	S: Thruway Holiday Motel
Med	S: + Hospital
Other	N: Westfield/Lake Erie KOA▲, Blue Water Beach Campground▲, Lake Erie State Park S: to Camp Chautauqua▲, Webb's Lake Resort
468/59	NY 60, Bennett, Rd, Dunkirk, Fredonia
FStop	S: Wilson Farms Mobil
Gas	S: Kwik Fill◊, Citgo, Murphy
Food	S: Arby's, Bob Evans, China King, KFC, McDonald's, Perkins, Wendy's
Lodg	S: Best Western♥, Comfort Inn♥, Clarion♥, Days Inn♥
Med	S: + Hospital
Other	S: LP/Wilson Farms, Grocery, Home Depot, Kmart, NAPA, Wal-Mart sc, NY State Hwy Patrol Post, RiteAid
455/58	US 20, NY 5, Irving, Silver Creek
TStop	N: Seneca Hawk, Seneca One Stop, Native Pride Travel Center
Gas	S: Atlantic, Kwik Fill
Food	N: Rest/Seneca Hawk, Rest/Native Pride TC S: Burger King, Subway, Sunset Grill, Tim Horton's, Tom's Family Rest
TWash	N: Native Pride TC
Med	N: + Lake Shore Health Care Center
Other	N: WiFi/BarbSh/LP/Seneca Hawk, Seneca OS, WiFi/LP/Native Pride TC, Golf Course
(447)	Angola Service Plaza (Both dir)
FStop	Mobil
Food	Denny's, McDonald's
445/57A	Eden, Angola
(443)	Parking Area (Both dir)
436/57	NY 75, Camp Rd, Hamburg, Aurora
TStop	N: Exit 57 Truck Plaza (Scales)
Gas	S: Kwik-Fill◊, Mobil◊
Food	N: Rest/FastFood/Ex 57 TP, Bob Evans, Bozanna's, Denny's, McDonald's, Tim Horton's, Wendy's S: Arby's, Burger King, Camp Rd Diner, Pizza Hut, Subway

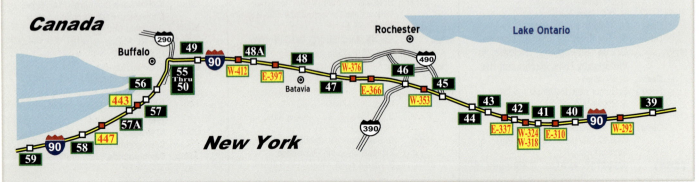

Page 470

◊ = Regular Gas Stations with Diesel   ▲ = RV Friendly Locations   ♥ = Pet Friendly Locations
RED PRINT SHOWS LARGE VEHICLE PARKING/ACCESS ON SITE OR NEARBY   BROWN PRINT SHOWS CAMPGROUNDS/RV PARKS

EXIT	NEW YORK
Lodg	N: Motel/Exit 57 TP, Days Inn ♥, Comfort Inn ♥, Red Roof Inn ♥, Tallyho Motel S: Holiday Inn
TWash	N: Exit 57 TP
TServ	N: Exit 57 TP/Tires
Other	N: WiFi/LP/Ex 57 TP, Auto Dealers, to Mall, Buffalo Speedway, Erie Co Fairgrounds, Ballard's Camping Center Sales/Service/Campground▲ S: Goodyear, Camping World RV Sales, To Hilbert College
432/56	**NY 179, Mile Strip Rd, Blasdell, Orchard Park**
Gas	N: Sunoco
Food	N: Family Rest, Burger King S: Applebee's, Chuck E Cheese, Outback Steaks, McDonald's, Olive Garden, Pizza Hut, Ruby Tuesday, TGI Friday, Wendy's
Lodg	N: Econo Lodge ♥
Other	S: Grocery, Home Depot, McKinley Mall, to Buffalo RV, Erie Comm College, Ralph Wilson Stadium
(430)	**TOLL Plaza**
429/55	**Ridge Rd, Orchard Park, Lackawanna (EB), US 219, Ridge Rd (WB)**
Food	S: Arby's, Denny's, Wendy's
TServ	N: Kenworth Truck of Upstate NY
Other	S: FedEx Kinko's, Grocery, Home Depot, Kmart
427/54	**NY16, NY400, W Seneca, E Aurora**
(426/53)	**Jct I-190, Downtown Buffalo, Niagra Falls (TOLL)**
425/52A	**William St**
423/52	**Walden Ave, Buffalo, Cheektowaga**
TStop	S: AmBest/Jim's Truck Plaza/Sunoco (Scales)
Food	N: Applebee's, Arby's, Bob Evan's, Famous Dave's BBQ, IHOP, McDonald's, Ruby Tuesday, Starbucks, Subway, TGI Friday, Tim Horton's, Wendy's S: Rest/Jim's TP, Alton's, Fuddrucker's, McDonald's, Olive Garden, Pizza Hut, Smokey Bones BBQ, Starbucks
Lodg	N: Hampton Inn, Residence Inn ♥ S: Sheraton, Millenium Airport Hotel
Med	N: + St Joseph Hospital
Other	N: Grocery, Goodyear, Office Depot, PetSmart ♥, Target, Wal-Mart S: Laundry/LP/Jim's TP, Best Buy, Kmart, Sam's Club, Walden Galleria Mall
422/51	**NY 33, Buffalo Niagara Int'l Airport**
Lodg	S: Best Western, Comfort Suites ♥, Days Inn, Holiday Inn ♥, Homewood Suites ♥, Quality Inn
Other	S: NY State Hwy Patrol Post
421/50A	**Cleveland Dr (EB)**
(420/50)	**Jct I-290, to Niagara Falls (EB-Last Free Exit)**
Other	N: to appr 9 mi Leisurewood Rec Comm & Campground▲
(420)	**TOLL Plaza**
417/49	**NY 78, Transit Rd, Buffalo, Depew, Lockport**
Gas	N: Mobil S: Kwik Fill, Mobil

EXIT	NEW YORK
Food	N: Arby's, Bennigan's, Chili's, Cracker Barrel, Don Pablo, Dunkin Donuts, McDonald's, Old Country Buffet, Perkins, Ponderosa, Pizza Hut, Protocol Rest, Red Lobster, Ruby Tuesday, Shogun, Subway, Starbucks, TGI Friday, Wendy's S: Bob Evans, Salvatores Ital Gardens
Lodg	N: Clarion, Econo Lodge, Fairfield Inn, Microtel, Ramada Inn ♥ S: Howard Johnson, Garden Place Hotel, Red Roof Inn ♥, Residence Inn ♥
Med	N: + Hospital
Other	N: ATMs, Auto Services, Auto Dealers, Banks, B&N, BJ's, Cinema, Dollar General, Fedex Kinko's, Firestone, Grocery, Home Depot, Kmart, Lowe's, Office Depot, Pharmacy, Radio Shack, Target, Tires, UPS Store, Wal-Mart sc, Eastern Hills Mall, to Erie Comm College, Epic Sports Center S: Greater Buffalo Int'l Airport ✈, All Seasons RV, to Samcoe RV
(412)	**Clarence Service Plaza (WB)**
FStop	Sunoco
Food	Burger King, Pizza Hut, Mrs Fields
402/48A	**NY 77, Allegheny Rd, Pembroke, Corfu, Medina, Akron, Six Flags Darien Lake, to NY 5, NY 33**
TStop	S: Flying J Travel Plaza #5049 (Scales), Travel Center of America (Scales)
Food	S: CountryMarket/FastFood/FJ TP, Rest/TA TC, Exit 48A Diner
TWash	S: TA TC
TServ	S: TA TC/Tires
Other	N: to appr 6mi Leisurewood Rec Comm & Campground▲ S: Laundry/BarbSh/WiFi/RVDump/LP/FJ TP, Laundry/WiFi/RVDump/TA TC, Darien Lake Theme Park & Camping Resort▲, to Skyline Camping Resort & RV Sales▲, to appr 4.5mi Sleepy Hollow Lake Resort Campground▲, to appr 6mi Darien Lake State Park▲
(397)	**Pembroke Service Plaza (EB)**
FStop	Sunoco
Food	Burger King, Popeye's, TCBY
390/48	**NY 98, Oak St, Batavia, Albion, Attica**
Gas	S: Citgo
Food	S: Aby's, Bob Evans, Denny's, Perkins
Lodg	N: Hampton Inn S: Best Western, Days Inn, Holiday Inn, Quality Inn, Ramada ♥, Super 8
Med	S: + Hospital
Other	N: Genesee Co Airport ✈, NY State Police S: AutoZone, Auto Dealers, Auto Repairs, CVS, Home Depot, Tires, Wal-Mart sc, Dwyer Stadium, to Lei-Ti Campground▲
(379/47)	**Jct I-490, to NY 19, Leroy, Rochester**
TStop	N: 490 Truck Stop/Coastal
Other	N: LP/490 TS S: to Lei-Ti Too Campground▲
(376)	**Ontario Service Plaza (WB)**
FStop	Mobil
Food	McDonald's, Ben & Jerry's
TServ	AJ Ulgiati Enterprises
(366)	**Scottsville Service Plaza (EB)**
FStop	Mobil
Food	Burger King, Dunkin Donuts, TCBY

EXIT	NEW YORK
(362/46)	**Jct I-390, Rochester, Corning Henrietta (Serv N on NY 253)**
TStop	N: Western Truck Stop/Citgo
Gas	N: Hess
Food	N: McDonald's, Wendy's
Lodg	N: Country Inn, Days Inn ♥, Fairfield Inn, Microtel, Red Roof Inn ♥, Super 8 ♥
TServ	N: Regional International
Other	N: WiFi/LP/Western TS
(353)	**Parking Area (EB)**
(351/45)	**Jct I-490, NY 96, Victor Rd, Victor, Fairport, Rochester**
Gas	S: Kwik Fill
Food	N: TGI Friday S: Burger King, Chili's, Denny's, Wendy's
Lodg	N: Hampton Inn S: Holiday Inn Express, Microtel, Royal Inn
Other	N: Eastview Mall S: Ballatyne RV & Marine, Bristol Woodlands
(350)	**Seneca Service Plaza (WB)**
FStop	Mobil
Food	Burger King, Sbarro, Mrs Fields
347/44	**NY 332, Rochester Rd, Victor, Canandaigua**
FStop	S: Wilson Farms #142/Mobil
Food	S: KFC, McDonald's, Subway
Lodg	S: Best Value Inn, Econo Lodge
Other	S: Canandaigua/Rochester KOA▲, NY State Police
340/43	**NY 21, Main St, Manchester, Palmyra**
Gas	S: Mobil ◊
Food	S: Steak-Out Rest, McDonald's
Lodg	S: Roadside Inn
(337)	**Clifton Spring Service Plaza (EB)**
FStop	Sunoco
Food	Roy Rogers, Sbarro, TCBY
327/42	**NY 14, to NY 318, Geneva, Lyons**
TStop	S: Wilson Farms AmBest #184/Mobil (Scales)
Food	S: Rest/Wilson Farms
Lodg	S: Relax Inn
Other	N: to appr 20mi Cherry Grove Campground▲ S: Laundry/LP/Wilson Farms
(324)	**Junius Ponds Service Plaza (WB)**
FStop	Sunoco
Food	Dunkin Donuts, Roy Rogers
(318)	**Parking Area (WB)**
317/41	**NY 414, Ridge Rd, Mound Rd, NY 318, Waterloo, Clyde**
FStop	S: Nice N Easy #21/Mobil
TStop	S: Petro Stopping Center #71 (Scales)
Food	S: IronSkillet/Subway/Petro SC, Country Diner
TWash	S: Petro SC
TServ	S: Petro SC/Tires
Other	S: Laundry/BarbSh/CB/WiFi/Petro SC, Waterloo Outlet Mall, to Hejamada Campground & RV Park▲
(310)	**Port Byron Service Plaza (EB)**
FStop	Mobil
Food	McDonald's, Ben & Jerry's
304/40	**NY 34, Weedsport, Auburn, Oswego**
FStop	S: Fast Track Market #210
TStop	S: The Pit Stop Auto Truck Plaza/Sunoco
Gas	S: Qwik Fill

◊ = Regular Gas Stations with Diesel   ▲ = RV Friendly Locations   ♥ = Pet Friendly Locations
RED PRINT SHOWS LARGE VEHICLE PARKING/ACCESS ON SITE OR NEARBY   BROWN PRINT SHOWS CAMPGROUNDS/RV PARKS

INTERSTATE 90 W/E

NEW YORK

EXIT		
	Food	S: Arby's, Arnold's Family Rest, Ashby's Fish & Grill, Old Erie Diner, Village Diner
	Lodg	S: Best Western, Days Inn, Microtel
	Other	N: Riverforest RV Park▲, Whitford Airport✈
		S: WiFi/LP/Pit Stop ATP, to Hejamada Campground & RV Park▲
(292)		Warners Service Plaza (WB)
	FStop	Mobil
	Food	McDonald's, Ben & Jerry's
(290/39)		Jct I-690, NY 690, Syracuse, Fulton, to Solvay, Baldwinsville, Onondaga Lake, State Fairgrounds
	Other	N: Camping World RV Center
286/38		NY 57, Liverpool, Syracuse, Fulton, Oswego
	Gas	N: Hess, KwikFill
		S: Mobil, Sunoco
	Food	N: Pier 57 Rest, Pizza Hut
		S: Burger King
	Lodg	N: Super 8
283/37		Electronics Pkwy, 7th St, Syracuse
	Gas	S: Hess, Mobil
	Food	S: Bob Evans, Denny's, Ground Round, McDonald's, Colorado Steaks
	Lodg	S: Days Inn, Hampton Inn, Quality Inn, Ramada Inn, Super 8
(283/36)		Jct I-81, N to Watertown, S to Binghamton Courtland, Syracuse, 1000 Islands, Syracuse Airport
	TStop	S: I-81, #25 Pilot Travel Center #380 (Scales)
	Food	S: FastFood/Pilot TC
	Other	N: Syracuse Hancock Int'l Airport✈, USMC Reserve Training Center
		S: WiFi/Pilot TC
(280)		DeWitt Service Plaza (EB)
	FStop	Sunoco
	Food	McDonald's, Ben & Jerry's
279/35		NY 298, Syracuse, East Syracuse
	Gas	S: Mobil, Kwik Fill
	Food	S: Denny's, McDonald's
	Lodg	S: Comfort Inn, Days Inn, Fairfield Inn, Embassy, Hampton Inn, Holiday Inn, Howard Johnson, Marriott, Microtel, Motel 6♥, Red Roof Inn♥, Super 8
(277/34A)		Jct I-481, Syracuse, Chittenango (EB) Syracuse, Oswego (WB)
(266)		Chittenango Service Plaza (WB)
	FStop	Sunoco
	Food	Dunkin Donuts, Sbarro, TCBY
262/34		NY 13, Canastota, Oneida (EB), Canastota, Chittenango (WB)
	FStop	S: Nice N Easy Sunoco
	Gas	S: Mobil◊

NEW YORK

EXIT		
	Food	S: Arby's, McDonald's
	Lodg	S: Days Inn♥
	Other	N: The Landing Campground▲, Verona Beach State Park▲, Boxing Hall of Fame
(256)		Parking Area (WB)
253/33		NY 365, Verona, Rome (EB), Verona, Oneida (WB)
	FStop	S: SavOn Diesel
	Gas	N: Citgo, Sunoco
	Lodg	N: Verona Motor Inn
		S: Super 8
	Med	S: + Hospital
	Other	N: Turning Stone Resort & Casino/RV Park▲, The Landing Campground▲
(250)		Parking Area (EB)
(244)		Oneida Service Plaza (EB)
	FStop	Sunoco
	Food	Burger King, Sbarro, TCBY
243/32		NY 233, Westmoreland, Rome
	Food	S: Carriage Motor Inn
	Lodg	S: Carriage Motor Inn
	Other	N: Oneida Co Airport✈, Griffiss AFB
(233/31)		Jct I-790, NY 8 NY 12, Utica, Rome, St Lawrence Seaway, 1000 Islands, Watertown, Norwich
	FStop	N: North Utica Citgo
	Gas	N: Fastrac
		S: Hess◊
	Food	N: Burger King, Subway
		S: Denny's, Friendly's, McDonald's, Pizza Hut, Taco Bell, Wendy's
	Lodg	S: Best Western♥, Radisson, Red Roof Inn♥, Super 8
	Other	N: ATMs, BJ's, Big Lots, Grocery, Lowe's, Laundromat, Pharmacy, Wal-Mart sc, West Canada Creek Campsites▲, Trail's End Campground▲
(227)		Schuyler Service Plaza (WB)
	FStop	Sunoco
	Food	McDonald's, Breyer's
	Other	NY State Police
220/30		NY 28, Herkimer, Mohawk
	Gas	N: Mobil◊, Fastrac◊
	Food	N: Applebee's, Burger King, Denny's, Friendly's, McDonald's, Tony's Pizzeria
	Lodg	N: Budget Motel, Herkimer Inn
	TServ	S: Eggers, Cary & Corrigan Tires
	Med	S: + Hospital
	Other	N: Auto Dealer, Auto Services, Goodyear, Kmart, RiteAid, Wal-Mart sc, West Canada Creek Campsites▲, to appr 7 mi Herkimer KOA▲
		S: Grocery, to Baseball Hall of Fame

NEW YORK

EXIT		
211/29A		NY 169, Front St, Little Falls, Dolgeville
	Lodg	N: Best Western♥
	Other	N: Crystal Grove Diamond Mine & Campground▲
(210)		Indian Castle Service Plaza (EB) Iroquois Service Plaza (WB)
	FStop	Sunoco
	Food	Roy Rogers, Bob's Big Boy, Mrs Fields Burger King, Dunkin Donuts, TCBY
194/29		NY 10, Canajoharie, Sharon Springs
	FStop	S: Betty Beaver Fuel Stop/Getty
	Gas	N: Stewarts
		S: Sunoco
	Food	S: McDonald's, Pizza Hut
	Lodg	S: Rodeway Inn♥
(184)		Parking Area (Both dir)
182/28		NY 30A, Fultonville, Fonda
	TStop	N: Betty Beaver Fuel Stop/Getty, Travel Center of America (Scales), AmBest/FultonvilleSuper Stop/Citgo (Scales)
	Food	N: Buckhorn/TA TC, Rest/Fultonville SS
	Lodg	N: Motel/TA TC, Motel/Fultonville SS
	TWash	N: Betty Beaver FS, Fultonville SS
	TServ	N: TA TC/Tires
	Med	N: + Hospital
	Other	N: Laundry/LP/Betty Beaver FS, Laundry/WiFi/CB/TA TC, Laundry/CB/WiFi/LP/Fultonville SS
174/27		NY 30, Amsterdam
	Gas	N: Mobil
	Food	N: Diner/Super 8 Motel
	Lodg	N: Super 8, Valley View Motor Inn
	Med	N: + Hospital
(172)		Mohawk Service Plaza (EB)
	FStop	Sunoco
	Food	McDonald's, Breyer's
(168)		Pattersonville Service Plaza (WB)
	FStop	Sunoco
	Food	Roy Rogers, Bob's Big Boy, TCBY
(162/26)		Jct I-890, NY 5, NY 5S, Scotia, Schenectady, Rotterdam
(159/25A)		Jct I-88S, Schenectady, Binghamton Cooperstown, Oneonta
(154/25)		Jct I-890, NY 7, 146, Schenectady
(153)		Guilderland Service Plaza (EB)
	FStop	Sunoco
	Food	McDonald's, Mr Sub, Ben & Jerry's
(148/24)		Jct I-87N, I-90E, Albany, Montreal (EB, Left Exit), I-90W, I-87S, New York, Buffalo, to US 20 (WB)

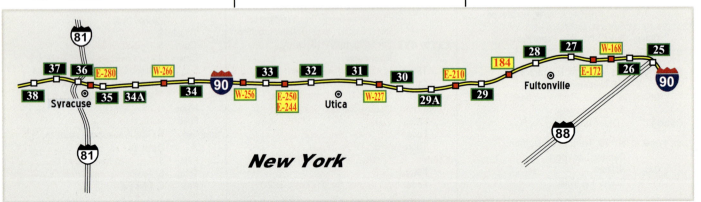

Page 472

◊ = Regular Gas Stations with Diesel   ▲ = RV Friendly Locations   ♥ = Pet Friendly Locations
RED PRINT SHOWS LARGE VEHICLE PARKING/ACCESS ON SITE OR NEARBY   BROWN PRINT SHOWS CAMPGROUNDS/RV PARKS

INTERSTATE 90 W/E

EXIT	NEW YORK		
(148)	TOLL Plaza		
02/1S	Western Ave, to US 20		
	NOTE:	WB: Last FREE Exit Before TOLL	
	Other	S:	ATMs, Restaurants, Best Buy, Home Depot, Sam's Club, Wal-Mart, Cross Gates Mall
(04/1N)	Jct I-87N, to Saratoga, Montreal, Albany Int'l Airport		
1/2	Fuller Rd, to NY 5, US 20, Western Ave, Univ of Albany		
2/3	State Offices, NYS Police Academy		
2/4	NY 85, Albany, to Slingerlands, Voorheesville		
3/5	Everett Rd, to NY 5, College of St Rose		
	Gas	S:	Hess
	Food	S:	Denny's, Friendly's, McDonald's, Pizza Hut, Subway, Taco Bell
	Lodg	S:	Clarion, Quality Inn
	Other	S:	AdvanceAuto, Auto Dealers, Auto Services, CVS, AutoZone, Home Depot
3/5A	Corporate Woods Blvd		
5/6	US 9, New Loudon Rd, Loudonville, Arbor Hill, Henry Johnson Blvd		
	Gas	N:	Stewarts
	Med	N:	+ Hospital
(6/6A)	Jct I-787, Albany, Troy, Watervliet, to NY 7, South Mall Expy		
	Other	S:	to Downtown Albany, Empire State Plaza
7/7	Washington Ave, Rensselaer (EB)		
7/8	NY 43, Sand Lake Rd, US 4, Broadway, Defreestville, Sand Lake		
	Other	N:	to Joseph L Bruno Stadium, Hudson Valley Comm College
10/9	US 4, E Greenbush Rd, Troy Rd, Troy, Greenbush, Glens Falls		
	Gas	N:	Mobil
		S:	Citgo, Stewarts
	Food	N:	Applebee's, McDonald's, Panera Bread, Starbucks, Subway
		S:	Cracker Barrel, Denny's, Wendy's
	Lodg	N:	Holiday Inn Express
		S:	Econo Lodge, Fairfield Inn
	Other	N:	ATMs, Grocery, Home Depot, Staples, PetSmart♥, Bank, Target, Wal-Mart sc
13/10	Miller Rd, E Greenbush		
	Gas	S:	Mobil◊, Stewarts
	Food	S:	Dunkin Donuts, Pizza Hut, Weather Vane Rest

EXIT	NY / MA		
14/11	US 9, US 20, E Greenbush, Nassau		
	Gas	N:	Citgo◊, Hess◊
		S:	Mobil
	Food	S:	Burger King
	Lodg	S:	Econo Lodge, Rodeway Inn
	Other	N:	NY State Police
(18)	Rest Area (WB) (RR, Phone, Picnic, Vend)		
20/12	US 9, Hudson		
	Gas	S:	Mobil◊, Xtra, Sunoco◊
	TStop	S:	Pilot Travel Center #146 (Scales)
	Food	S:	Subway/McDonald's/Pilot TC
	Other	S:	WiFi/Pilot TC
(B1)	TOLL Plaza		
(B6/B1)	Jct I-90W, US 9, Albany, Hudson (WB)		
B15/B2	NY 295, Taconic State Pkwy		
	Other	S:	Woodland Hills Campground▲
(B18)	TOLL Plaza		
B23/B3	NY 22, NY 10, Austerlitz, New Lebanon, W Stockbridge, Mass		
	FStop	N:	Canaan Super Stop/Citgo (Scales)
	Gas	S:	Sunoco◊
	Food	N:	Rest/Canaan SS
	Other	N:	Laundry/Canaan Super Stop
		S:	Camp Waubeeka Family Campground▲, Woodland Hills Campground▲
	NOTE:	MM 391: Massachusetts State Line	

⬆ NEW YORK
⬇ MASSACHUSETTS
(EASTERN TIME ZONE)

	NOTE:	MA does not use Mile Marker Exits. We have listed MM / Exit #.	
3/1	MA 41, Great Barrington Rd, West Stockbridge		
	Food	N:	Orient Express Rest
	Lodg	N:	Marble Inn, Pleasant Valley Motel
	TOLL Plaza (EB Begin Toll, WB End)		
(8)	Lee Travel Plaza (Both dir)		
	FStop	E/W:	Gulf
	Food	E:	McDonald's, D'Angelo's, Edy's Ice Cream Pretzels, Fresh City
		W:	McDonald's
	Other	E:	Visitor Info
11/2	US 20, Housatonic St, to MA 102, Lee, to Pittsfield, Adams		
	FStop	N:	Lee Shell

EXIT	MASSACHUSETTS		
	TStop	S:	Lee Travel Plaza
	Gas	N:	Citgo, Sunoco
		S:	Shell
	Food	N:	Burger King, McDonald's, Pizza Hut
	Lodg	N:	Best Western, Pilgrim Inn, Super 8, Sunset Motel
		S:	Inn at Lee Plaza, Best Value Inn♥
	Other	N:	Walker Island Family Campground▲
		S:	Outlet Stores, Camp Overflow▲, Prospect Mountain Campground & RV Park▲, Bonny Rigg Campground▲
(12)	Parking Area (Both dir)		
(29)	Blandford Travel Plaza (Both dir)		
	FStop	E/W:	Gulf
	Food	E:	McDonald's
		W:	McDonald's, Honey Dew, Pizza
	NOTE:	MM: 29: Steep Grade, Trucks use Right Lane, LOW Gear	
(35.5)	RunAWay Truck Ramp (EB)		
40/3	US 202, MA 10, Westfield, Southampton, Northampton		
	Gas	N:	Mobil
		S:	Shell
	Food	N:	New England Pizza
		S:	Dunkin Donuts, Friendly's, Napoli II Italian Rest, Subway, Wendy's
	Lodg	S:	Econo Lodge
	Med	S:	+ Noble Hospital
	Other	N:	Barnes Muni Airport✈, MA State Police Barracks, Walker Island Family Campground▲, Windy Acres Family Campground▲
		S:	Camp Overflow▲, Sodom Mountain Campground▲, Southwick Acres Campground▲, Bonny Rigg Campground▲
(41)	MA State Hwy Patrol Barracks (WB)		
(45/4)	Jct I-91, US 5, Hartford, Springfield, Holyoke (Serv on US 5)		
	Gas	S:	Mobil
	Food	N:	Dunkin Donuts
		S:	Piccadilly, Outback Steakhouse
	Lodg	N:	Welcome Inn
		S:	Best Western, Hampton Inn♥, Knights Inn♥, Quality Inn, Red Roof Inn♥, Springfield Inn, Super 8
	Med	N:	+ Providence Hospital
	Other	N:	Holyoke Mall, Univ of MA, Amherst, Holyoke Soldiers Home
		S:	Basketball Hall of Fame, Six Flags
49/5	MA 33, Memorial Dr, MA 141, Chicopee, Westover Field		
	Gas	N:	Sunoco, Stop & Shop

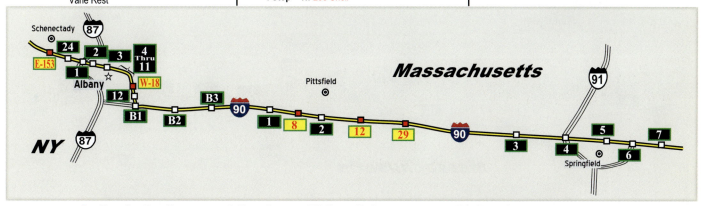

◊= Regular Gas Stations with Diesel   ▲ = RV Friendly Locations   ♥ = Pet Friendly Locations
RED PRINT SHOWS LARGE VEHICLE PARKING/ACCESS ON SITE OR NEARBY   BROWN PRINT SHOWS CAMPGROUNDS/RV PARKS

Interstate 90 W

EXIT	MASSACHUSETTS
Food	N: Applebee's, Arby's, Burger King, Dunkin Donuts, Denny's, Pizza Hut, Starbucks, Subway, Wendy's
Lodg	N: Days Inn ♥, Hampton Inn, Super 8 ♥
Other	N: BJ's, Grocery, Home Depot, Staples, Tires, Wal-Mart, Mall, U-Haul, Westover Air Force Base, Westover Metro Airport ✈
(51/6)	Jct I-291, Springfield, Hartford CT
TStop	S: AmBest/Pride Travel Center
Lodg	N: Motel 6 ♥, Ramada Inn
54/7	MA 21, Center St, Ludlow, Belchertown
Gas	N: Sunoco, Mobil
Food	N: Burger King, Friendly's, McDonald's, Joy's Country Kitchen, Subway
Lodg	S: Comfort Inn
Med	N: + Hospital
Other	N: CVS, Grocery
(56)	Ludlow Travel Plaza (Both dir)
FStop	E/W: Gulf
Food	E: McDonald's, Honey Dew
	W: Boston Market, Honey Dew
63/8	MA 32, Thorndike St, to US 20, Palmer, Amherst, Ware (Addt'l Serv on US 20S)
Gas	S: Citgo, Shell◊
Food	S: Dunkin Donuts, McDonald's, Subway
Med	N: + Hospital
Other	N: Pine Acres Family Camp Resort▲
	S: Grocery, CVS, Oak Haven Campground▲
(78/9)	Jct I-84, to US 20, EB - Hartford, Sturbridge, WB-Hartford, NY City (Serv on I-84S, Ex #3AB)
TStop	S: #3A New England Truck Stop (Scales)
	I-84, Ex #1: Pilot Travel Center #222 (Scales)
Food	S: Rest/NE TS, Cracker Barrel, Subway, Wendy's, Gracie's Roadside Cafe
Lodg	S: Motel/NE TS, Best Western ♥, Comfort Inn, Hampton Inn, Super 8 ♥
TServ	S: NE TS/Tires
Other	S: Laundry/NE TS, Southbridge Muni Airport ✈, MA State Police Barracks, Oak Haven Campground▲, Yogi Bear's Jellystone Park Resort▲, Sunset View Farm Camping Area▲, Quinebaug Cove Campground▲
(79)	MA State Police Barracks (EB)
(79)	TOLL Plaza
(80)	Charlton Travel Plaza (EB)
FStop	E: Gulf
Food	E: McDonald's, Auntie Anne's, Ben & Jerry's, Papa Gino's
Other	E: MA State Hwy Patrol, Visitor Info

EXIT	MASSACHUSETTS
(84)	Charlton Travel Plaza (WB)
FStop	W: Gulf
Food	W: McDonald's, Auntie Anne's, Ben & Jerry's, Papa Gino's
Other	W: Visitor Info
(87)	Weigh Station (EB)
(90/10)	Jct I-395S, I-290E, MA 12, Auburn, Worcester, New London
Gas	N/S: Shell
Food	N: Piccadilly's, Papa Gino's
	S: Applebee's, Friendly's, Golden Lion, Chuck's Steakhouse, Wendy's
Lodg	N: Comfort Inn, La Quinta Inn ♥,
	S: Ramada Inn
Med	S: + Hospital
Other	N: Auburn Reg'l Mall, Pine Acres Family Camping Resort▲
	S: CVS, MA State Police Barracks, Indian Ranch Resort▲, Lake Manchaug Camping▲
93/10A	US 20, to MA 146, MA 122A, Worcester, Providence
96/11	MA 122, Millbury, Worcester, to Providence, RI
TServ	N: Southworth Milton
	S: Dario Diesel Volvo Trucks
Med	N: + Hospital
(104)	Westborough Travel Plaza (WB)
FStop	W: Gulf
Food	W: Auntie Anne's, Ben & Jerry's, Boston Market, Dunkin Donuts
(106/11A)	Jct I-495, N to New Hampshire, S to Cape Cod, Maine
111/12	MA 9, Framingham, Marlborough
Gas	N: Circle K, Getty
Food	N: Subway, Ground Round
Lodg	N: Residence Inn ♥, Sheraton ♥
	S: Econo Lodge, Framingham Inn, Motel 6 ♥
Med	N: + Hospital
(115)	Framingham Travel Plaza (WB)
FStop	W: Gulf
Food	W: McDonald's, Boston Market, Auntie Anne's, Edy's Ice Cream, Honey Dew
117/13	MA 30, Framingham, Natick
Gas	S: Exxon, Mobil◊
Food	S: Burger King, Naked Fish, McDonald's
Lodg	S: Courtyard, Hampton Inn, Peabody Hotel, Red Roof Inn ♥, Travelodge
Med	S: + Hospital
Other	S: Mall, Home Depot, Target
(118)	Natick Travel Plaza (EB)
	NOTE: Last Travel Plaza on Mass Pike
FStop	E: Gulf

EXIT	MASSACHUSETTS
Food	E: McDonald's, Dunkin Donuts, Papa Gino's
(123/14)	Jct I-95, MA 128, MA 30, Portsmouth, Providence (WB)
(124)	TOLL Plaza (EB End TOLL, WB Begin)
(124/15)	Jct I-95, MA 128, MA 30, Weston Portsmouth, Providence (EB)
125/16	Washington St, West Newton (EB)
	NOTE: Last FREE Exit Before TOLL
Gas	S: Mobil
Other	S: Auto Services
126/17	Washington St, Newton, Watertown
131/18	Allston, Cambridge, Brighton (EB, Left exit) Cambridge St, Soldiers Field Rd, River St Bridge
131/19	Cambridge TOLL Plaza, Beacon Park
131/20	Allston, Brighton, Cambridge (EB)
(131)	TOLL Plaza
132/21	Massachusetts Ave (WB)
133/22	Dartmouth St, Prudential Center, Copley Square (WB)
133/22A	Clarendon St (WB)
133/23	Arlington St (WB)
133/23	Downtown Boston, South Station
(134/24)	Jct I-93N, Central Artery (Left exit)
(134/24C)	Jct I-93S, Quincy (Left exit) Haul Rd, Dorchester (WB)
25	South Boston Northern Ave, World Trade Ctr (WB) TOLL Plaza-Ted Williams Tunnel
138/26	Logan Int'l Airport Merge to 1A N, McClellan Hwy, East Boston

NOTE: MM 160: Massachusetts State Line

(I-90 Begins/Ends on I-5, Exit #164 in Seattle, WA)
(EASTERN TIME ZONE)

⊙ MASSACHUSETTS

Begin WB I-90 from Jct I-93 in Boston, MA to I-5 in Seattle, WA.

◊ = Regular Gas Stations with Diesel   ▲ = RV Friendly Locations   ♥ = Pet Friendly Locations
RED PRINT SHOWS LARGE VEHICLE PARKING/ACCESS ON SITE OR NEARBY   BROWN PRINT SHOWS CAMPGROUNDS/RV PARKS

INTERSTATE 91 S

VERMONT

EXIT	VERMONT
	Begin Southbound I-91 from Canada/VT border to Jct I-95 in New Haven, CT.
⊙	**VERMONT** (EASTERN TIME ZONE)
	NOTE: VT does not use Mile Marker Exits. We have listed MM/Exit #.
	NOTE: Rest Area Hours 7am-11pm
(178)	US/Canada Border, US Customs, VT State Line
177/29	to US 5, Caswell Ave, Derby Line
Gas	W: Derby Irving Mainway◊
Lodg	W: Derby Village Inn
Other	E: AmEx Duty Free
(176)	Latitude 45 degrees North, MidPoint between Equator & North Pole
(175)	VT Welcome Center (SB) (RR, Phone, Picnic, Vend, Info)
172/28	US 5, VT 105, Derby, Newport
FStop	E: Champlain Farms/Exxon, Short Stop #113/Mobil
Gas	E: Citgo, Gulf W: Gulf◊, Shell◊
Food	W: Craving Rest, McDonald's, Village Pizza, Roasters Café & Deli
Lodg	E: Border Motel W: Pepins Motel, Super 8, Top of the Hills Hotel
Med	W: + Hospital
Other	E: VT State Hwy Patrol Post W: RiteAid, Border Patrol, Elk Newport State Airport→
170/27	VT 191, to US 5, VT 105, Newport
Gas	W: Exxon/Carwash
Med	W: + Hospital
(166.5)	Parking Area (NB)
162/26	to US 5, VT 58, Orleans, Irasburg
Gas	E: Irving◊, Lanoues Serv Stn, Sunoco W: Royers Service Station
Food	E: Loon's Landing, Orleans Pizza Place, Just Good Food, Subway W: Martha's Diner
Other	E: to Will-O-Wood Campground▲
156/25	VT 16, Glover Rd, to US 5, Barton, Hardwick
Gas	E: Barton Irving Mainway◊, Barton One Stop Mini Mart/Mobil◊
Food	E: Village Coffee House
Lodg	E: Pinecrest Motor Court
Other	E: Belview Campground▲
(154)	Parking Area (NB)
(150.5)	Highest Elev on I-91 (1856')
(143)	Scenic View (NB)
(141)	Rest Area (SB) (RR, Phone, Picnic, Vend, Info)
140/24	VT 122, Gilman Rd, Lydonville, Wheelock, Sheffield (NB) VT 122, to VT 114, Burke, Lyndon Center, Lydonville (SB)
Gas	E: Nick's Mini Mart, Irving Mainway
Food	E: Asia Rest, Sweet Basil Café, Subway
Lodg	E: Lynburke Motel
Other	E: Lyndon State College

EXIT	VERMONT
137/23	US 5, Memorial Dr, to VT 114, Lyndonville, Lydon, Burke
Gas	E: Mobil
Food	E: Dunkin Donuts/Mobil, McDonald's
Lodg	E: Colonnade Inn W: Lyndon Motor Lodge
Other	N: White Caps Campground▲, Burke Mountain Ski Area, Lake Willoughby, Lyndon State College
133/22	Hospital Dr, to US 5, St Johnsbury NOTE: STEEP Grade-Trucks Low Gear
Gas	E: Citgo◊
Food	E: Pizza Hut, TacoBell/KFC
Med	E: + Hospital
131/21	to US 2, to US 5, St Johnsbury, Montpelier
Gas	E: Western Ave Station
Lodg	E: Fairbanks Inn
Other	E: to Moose River Campground▲, Rustic Haven Campground▲, Breezy Meadows Campground▲ W: Sugar Ridge RV Village & Campground▲
129/20	US 5, to US 2, St. Johnsbury, Passumpsic (Serv 2-3mi E in St Johnsbury)
Gas	E: Irving Mainway◊, Shell◊
Lodg	W: Comfort Inn
Other	E: VT State Hwy Patrol Post
(128/19)	Jct I-93S, to Littleton, New Hampshire, (Truck Route) to US 2
(122)	Scenic View (NB)
121/18	US 5, Barnet, Peecham NOTE: Steep Grade on exit ramp
Other	E: to Warner's Campground▲ W: to appr 5mi Harvey's Lake Cabins & Campground▲, Stillwater Campground▲
(115)	Parking Area (SB)
(113)	Parking Area (NB)
110/17	US 302, to US 5, Wells River, Barre, Woodsville, NH
TStop	W: P&H Truck Stop (Scales)
Food	E: Warners Gallery Rest W: Rest/P&H TS
Med	E: + Hospital
Other	E: to appr 10mi Crazy Horse Campground▲ W: Laundry/P&H TS, to Pleasant Valley Campground▲, Ricker Pond Campground▲
(107)	Parking Area (SB), Weigh Station (SB)
(100)	Rest Area (NB) (RR, Phone, Picnic, Vend, Info)
98/16	VT 25, Waits River Rd, to US 5, Bradford, Barre
Gas	E: Mobil◊
Food	E: Hungry Bear Rest
Lodg	E: Bradford Motel
Other	W: VT State Hwy Patrol Post
92/15	Lake Morey Rd, to US 5, Fairlee, to Oxford, NH
Gas	E: Citgo◊, Mobil, Shell◊
Food	E: Fairlee Diner, Pizza, Your Place
Lodg	E: Fairlee Motel W: Lake Morey Inn
Other	E: Jacobs Brook Campground▲

◊ = Regular Gas Stations with Diesel   ▲ = RV Friendly Locations   ♥ = Pet Friendly Locations
RED PRINT SHOWS LARGE VEHICLE PARKING/ACCESS ON SITE OR NEARBY   BROWN PRINT SHOWS CAMPGROUNDS/RV PARKS

Page 475

EXIT	VERMONT
84/14	VT 113, Main St, to US 5, Fairlee to Thetford
Other	E: Rest 'N Nest Campground▲
75/13	VT 10A, Main St, to US 5, Norwich, to Hanover, NH
Med	E: + Hospital
Other	E: to Dartmouth College
72/12	Bugbee St, to US 5, to US 4, White River Junction, Wilder
Gas	E: Gulf◊, Mobil
70/11	US 5, White River Junction
Gas	E: Exxon◊, Mobil, Sunoco W: Citgo, Shell
Food	E: Crossroads Café, John's Place, McDonald's, Mustard Seed Deli
Lodg	E: Comfort Inn, Pines Motel W: Best Western, Hampton Inn, Holiday Inn Express, Super 8
TServ	E: Gateway Ford Trucks
Other	E: US Post Office, Amtrak, Auto Dealers
69/10	Jct I-89, N to Barre, Montpelier, S to Airport, New Hampshire
(68)	Rest Area (Both dir) (RR, Phone, Picnic, Vend, Info)
(67)	US Customs Check Point / Weigh Station (SB)
61/9	US 5, VT 12, Hartland, Windsor
Med	E: + Hospital
51/8	VT 131, to US 5, VT 12, Ascutney, Windsor
Gas	E: Citgo◊, Mobil, Sunoco◊
Food	E: Red Barn Rest, Roadside Cafe
Med	E: + Hospital
Other	E: Running Bear Camping Area▲
42/7	US 5, VT 11, VT 106, Springfield
TStop	W: On the Run Mobil
Food	W: FastFood/Mobil, Paddock Seafood
Lodg	W: Holiday Inn Express
Med	W: + Hospital
Other	W: Laundry/Mobil, Tree Farm Campground▲
(39)	Parking Area (Both dir)
35/6	US 5, VT 103, Bellows Falls, Rockingham, Rutland
Gas	E: Shell W: Sunoco◊
Other	W: VT State Hwy Patrol Post
29/5	Westminster St Hwy, to US 5, to VT 12, Westminster, Walpole NH
(26)	Parking Area (SB)
(25)	Parking Area (NB)
(23)	Weigh Station (SB)
(22)	Parking Area (NB)
18/4	US 5, VT 4, Putney
Gas	W: Sunoco◊
Food	E: Rest/Putney Inn W: Curtis BBQ
Lodg	E: Putney Inn
Other	W: Brattleboro KOA▲
12/3	VT 9E, to US 5, Brattleboro, Keene, Chesterfield, NH
	NOTE: SB: Clearance 13'9", Ex #2 alternate
FStop	E: Citgo

EXIT	VERMONT/MA
Gas	E: Mobil, Sunoco
Food	E: Dunkin Donuts, McDonald's, Pizza Hut, Steak Out Rest
Lodg	E: Best Inn, Colonial Inn, Hampton Inn, Holiday Inn, Motel 6♥ Lamplighter Inn, Quality Inn, Super 8
Other	E: Auto Mall, Home Depot, Grocery, Staples, U-Haul, US Post Office W: Brattleboro KOA▲
9/2	VT 9W, Western Ave, Molly Stark Trail, to VT 30, Brattleboro
Gas	E: Sunoco W: Shell
Lodg	E: Crosby House, Tudor B&B W: West Village Motel
Other	W: VT State Hwy Patrol Post
8/1	US 5, Brattleboro, Vernon
Gas	E: Mobil, Shell◊
Food	E: Burger King, Adams Seafood, VT Inn Pizza, Subway/Shell
Lodg	E: Econo Lodge
Med	E: + Hospital
Other	E: Grocery, Walgreen's, Amtrak, to Ft Drummer State Park, Hinsdale Campground▲
(7)	VT Welcome Center (NB) (RR, Phone, Picnic, Vend, Info)
(2)	Parking Area (SB)
(1)	Parking Area (NB)

(EASTERN TIME ZONE)

⊖ **VERMONT**
⊖ **MASSACHUSETTS**

(EASTERN TIME ZONE)

NOTE: MA does not use Mile Marker Exits. We have listed MM/Exit #.

(55)	Begin SB/End NB Call Boxes
(54)	Parking Area (Both dir)
50/28	MA 10, Bernardston, Northfield
Gas	W: Sunoco
Food	E: Italian Rest
Lodg	E: Fox Inn W: Falls River Inn
Other	W: Travelers Woods of New England Campground▲
50/28A	MA 10N, Northfield (NB)
50/28B	MA 10S, Bernardston (NB)
Other	E: Travelers Woods of New England Campground▲
46/27	MA 2E, Boston, Greenfield (SB, Left exit)
Gas	E: Mobil, Sunoco
Food	E: Friendly's, McDonald's
Med	E: + Hospital
Other	E: CVS
43/26	MA 2W, MA 2A E, Mohawk Trail, Greenfield Center
Gas	E: Citgo◊, Mobil W: Exxon, Shell
Food	E: Applebee's, China Gourmet, Dunkin Donuts W: Friendly's, McDonald's, Pizza Hut

EXIT	MASSACHUSETTS
Lodg	E: Howard Johnson W: Candlelight Resort Inn, Marriott, Super 8
Med	E: + Hospital
Other	E: Auto Dealers, Mtn View Auto Repair W: BJ's, Home Depot, Grocery, Pharmacy, Staples, Auto Services, Peppermint Park Camping Resort▲, Country Aire Campground▲
(37)	Weigh Station (Both dir)
35/25	MA 116, Conway Rd, Deerfield, Conway (SB) (Difficult reaccess)
Gas	E: Mobil
Lodg	E: Red Roof Inn♥
Other	E: Yankee Candle Co
34/24	US 5, MA 10, Deerfield, Whately
FStop	W: Whately Truck Stop/Exxon
Gas	E: Mobil
Food	E: Sara's Café & Deli W: Rest/Whately TS
Lodg	E: Motel 6♥
Other	E: Yankee Candle Co
(34)	Parking Area (Both dir)
31/23	US 5, MA 10, Whately (SB)
30/22	US 5, MA 10, Whately (NB)
27/21	US 5, MA 10, Allen Rd, N King St, Northampton, Hatfield, Whately
Gas	W: Sunoco
Lodg	W: Country View Motel
Other	W: MA State Hwy Patrol Post
26/20	US 5, MA 9, MA 10, Hadley, Northampton (SB)
Gas	W: Citgo
Food	W: Burger King, Friendly's, McDonald's
Med	W: + Hospital
Other	W: Auto Dealers, CVS, Grocery, Laundromat
25/19	MA 9, Bridge St, Damon Rd, Northampton, Amherst
Gas	W: Citgo
Food	E: Websters Fish Hook Rest.
Lodg	W: Hampshire Inn
Med	W: + Hospital
23/18	US 5, Mt Tom Rd, Northampton, Easthampton
Gas	E: Mobil W: Shell
Food	W: Friendly's, McDonald's, Spaghetti Freddy's, Roberto's
Lodg	E: Clarion Hotel W: Best Western, Northampton Lodging
(18)	Scenic Area (Both dir)
16/17	MA 141, Easthampton, Holyoke Ctr
Gas	E: Citgo◊, Mobil◊
Food	E: Real China, Deli, Subway
Lodg	E: Super 8
Other	E: Walgreen's
16/17A	MA 141E, Holyoke Ctr (NB)
16/17B	MA 141W, Easthampton (NB)
14/16	US 202, Cherry St, Holyoke, S Hadley, Westfield
Food	E: Burger King, Denny's, McDonald's

Page 476   ◊= Regular Gas Stations with Diesel   ▲ = RV Friendly Locations   ♥ = Pet Friendly Locations
RED PRINT SHOWS LARGE VEHICLE PARKING/ACCESS ON SITE OR NEARBY   BROWN PRINT SHOWS CAMPGROUNDS/RV PARKS

I-91

EXIT		MASSACHUSETTS
	Lodg	E: Yankee Peddler Inn & Rest
12/15		Lower Westfield Rd, to US 5, Holyoke, Ingleside
	Gas	E: Shell
	Food	E: Cracker Barrel, Friendly's, JP's Rest, Ruby Tuesday, Surf n Turf, Wendy's
	Lodg	E: Holiday Inn
	Other	E: Holyoke Mall, Best Buy, Target
(11/14)		Jct I-90, MA Turnpike (TOLL), E to Boston, W to Albany, NY
9/13		US 5, S-Springfield, N-Riverdale St
	Gas	W: Mobil, Sunoco◇
	Food	E: Bickford's Family Rest, Chili's, Donut Dip, Empire Buffet, Longhorn Steakhouse, On the Border, Outback Steakhouse W: Burger King, Calamari's Seafood Grill, Friendly's, McDonald's, KFC, Old Country Buffet, Pizza Hut, Wendy's
	Lodg	E: Comfort Inn, Quality Inn♥, Red Roof Inn♥, Residence Inn W: Best Western, Econo Lodge, Elsie's Motel, Hampton Inn
	Other	E: Mall, Home Depot W: Auto Dealers, Costco, Grocery, Pharmacy
(9/12)		I-391N, Chicopee, Holyoke Ctr (fr NB, Right Two Lanes)
8/11		US 20W, W Springfield (SB)
	Gas	E: Mobil
	Med	E: + Hospital
8/10		Main St, Chicopee, Springfield (NB)
	Gas	E: Mobil
	Med	W: + Hospital
7/9		US 20W, MA 20A, W Springfield (NB) NOTE: Trucks Use US 20W to Springfield
(7/8)		Jct I-291E, US 20E, Boston (SB) I-291E, US 20E, to I-90 (NB) (Both dir: Use Right Two Lanes)
7/7		Columbus Ave, Springfield Ctr (SB)
6/6		Springfield Ctr (NB), Union St (SB)
	FStop	W: Pride◇
	Food	E: Various Rest
	Lodg	E: Marriott, Sheraton
	Med	E: + Hospital
	Other	E: Greyhound Station W: to Basketball Hall of Fame
5/5		Broad St (NB)
5/4		MA 83, Main St, Springfield E Longmeadow (SB)
	TStop	W: Broad St Truck Stop/Sunoco
	Gas	E: Mobil◇, Sunoco, Texaco
	Food	E: McDonald's, Wendy's
4/3		US 5N, to MA 57, Agawam (SB) Columbus Ave, W Springfield
	Gas	E: Pride, Sunoco
	Other	W: Southwick Acres Campground▲, Sodom Mountain Campground▲

EXIT		MA / CT
4/2		MA 83, Forest Park, to E Longmeadow (NB)
4/1		US 5S, Longmeadow (SB)
(0)		End SB/Begin NB Call Boxes

(EASTERN TIME ZONE)

⬇ **MASSACHUSETTS**
⬆ **CONNECTICUT**

(EASTERN TIME ZONE)

NOTE: CT does not use Mile Marker Exits. We have listed MM/Exit #.

EXIT		
58/49		US 5, Enfield St, Enfield, to Longmeadow MA
	Gas	E: Citgo, Mobil, Valero W: Gas & Service
	Food	E: Friendly's, McDonald's, Steve's Boston Seafood W: DQ, Cloverleaf Cafe
	Lodg	E: Crown Plaza Hotel, Marriott W: Cloverleaf Motel
56/48		CT 220, Elm St, Enfield, to Thompsonville (Acc to Ex #47 Serv)
	Gas	E: Mobil
	Food	E: Arby's, Burger King, Denny's, Dunkin Donuts, McDonald's, TGI Friday, Wendy
	Other	E: CVS, Grocery, Home Depot, Target, Asnuntuck Comm College, U-Haul
55/47		CT 190, Hazard Ave, Enfield, W to Suffield, E to Hazardville
	Gas	E: Citgo
	Food	E: Dunkin Donuts, Ground Round, KFC, McDonald's, Olive Garden, Pizza Hut, Red Lobster, Taco Bell
	Lodg	E: Motel 6♥, Red Roof Inn♥
	Other	E: AutoZone, B&N, CVS, Goodyear, Staples, Walgreen's, Mall, Stafford Speedway
53/46		US 5, King St, Enfield
	Gas	E: Mobil
	Lodg	W: Super 8
51/45		CT 140, Bridge St, Warehouse Pt, E Windsor, Ellington
	Gas	E: Shell W: Sunoco
	Food	E: Burger King, Cracker Barrel, Great Wall, Kowloon Rest, Sophia's W: Maine Fish Market & Rest
	Lodg	E: Comfort Inn W: Best Western, Ramada
	Other	E: Laundromat, Wal-Mart W: AmTrak
50/44		US 5S, Prospect Hill Rd, E Windsor
	Gas	E: Citgo, Mobil
	Food	E: Dunkin Donuts, Wendy's
	Lodg	E: Holiday Inn Express
	Other	E: Longview RV
49/42		CT 159, S Main St, Windsor Locks
	Gas	E: Citgo, Gulf
49/41		Center St (SB) (Exits with #39)
	Gas	W: Shell
	Lodg	W: Howard Johnson
48/40		Bradley Field Connector, to Bradley Int'l Airport
	Lodg	W: Sheraton, Baymont Inn, Days Inn, DoubleTree Inn, Fairfield Inn, Homewood Suites, Motel 6♥

EXIT		CONNECTICUT
	Other	W: Conn Air Nat'l Guard
47/39		Kennedy Rd, Center St (NB) (Exits with #41)
	Gas	E: Shell◇
46/38		CT 75, Poquonock Ave, Windsor
	Gas	E: Mobil◇
	Food	E: China Sea, Dunkin Donuts, McDonald's, Pizza Rama, Subway W: Rivercity Grille Rest.
	Lodg	W: Courtyard, Hilton Garden Inn
45/37		CT 305, Bloomfield Ave, Windsor
	Gas	E: Mobil◇
	Lodg	W: Residence Inn
	Other	E: Amtrak
44/36		CT 178, Park Ave, Bloomfield
43/35B		CR 218, Windsor, Bloomfield
	Gas	W: Shell
(43/35A)		I-291E, to Manchester
(43/35)		I-291, Windsor, CT 218, Bloomfield
41/34		CT 159, Windsor Ave (NB), North Main St (SB), Hartford
	Gas	E: Shell◇ W: Citgo◇
	Food	W: Ranch House, Lunch Box Cafe
	Lodg	W: Flamingo Inn
	Med	W: + Hospital
40/33		Jennings Rd, Hartford
	Gas	W: Exxon◇
	Food	W: Burger King, McDonald's, Quiznos, Subway
	Lodg	W: Marriott, Motel 6♥, Super 8
	Other	E: CT State Hwy Patrol Post
(39/32B)		Jct I-84W, Trumbull St, Waterbury (fr NB, Left exit)
(39/32A)		Jct I-84W, Trumbull St, Waterbury
38/31		State St (SB)
	Other	W: Various Dining & Lodging, Constitution Plaza, Greyhound Station, State Capitol
(38/30)		Jct I-84E, CT 2, East Hartford (SB) New London (fr SB, Left exit)
37/29A		Whitehead Hwy, Capitol Area (fr NB, Left exit)
	Other	W: State Capitol, CT Conv Center, Civic Center, Old State House
37/29		US 5, CT 15, to CT 2, I-84E, to E Hartford, Boston (NB)
37/27		Airport Rd (NB), Brainard Rd (SB)
	Gas	E: Shell◇ W: Mobil
	Food	E: Chowder Pot IV, McDonald's W: Airport Rd Café, Burger King, Dunkin Donuts, Wendy's
	Lodg	E: Days Inn
	TServ	E: Interstate Ford, Nutmeg International
	Other	E: Hartford-Brainard Airport✈ W: Oasis Truck Tire Center
36/28		CT 15S, Newington, Wethersfield, (NB), US 5S, CT 15, Berlin Tpk (SB)
35/27		Brainard Rd, Airport Rd (NB)
	Gas	E: Shell
	Food	E: Chowder Pot IV, McDonald's
	Lodg	E: Days Inn
	TServ	E: Interstate Ford, Nutmeg International
	Other	E: Hartford-Brainard Airport✈

◇ = Regular Gas Stations with Diesel   ▲ = RV Friendly Locations   ♥ = Pet Friendly Locations

RED PRINT SHOWS LARGE VEHICLE PARKING/ACCESS ON SITE OR NEARBY   BROWN PRINT SHOWS CAMPGROUNDS/RV PARKS

EXIT		CONNECTICUT
34/26		Mart St, Old Wethersfield (SB)
	Other	E: Motor Vehicle Dept
34/25		CT 3N, Glastonbury, Wethersfield (NB)
34/25		CT 3N, Glastonbury, CT 3S, Wethersfield
32/24		CT 99, Silas Deane Hwy, Rocky Hill, Wethersfield
	Gas	E: Mobil W: Mobil, Shell
	Food	E: Bickford's Family Rest, Dakota Rest, On the Border Rest W: Denny's, D'Angelo's, Ground Round, KFC, Hometown Buffet, McDonald's, Panda King, Red Lobster, Wendy's
	Lodg	E: Great Meadow Inn, Howard Johnson W: Best Western, Hampton Inn, Motel 6 ♥
	Other	W: CVS, Tru Value Hardware, Lowe's, AutoZone, Wal-Mart, Walgreen's
30/23		CT 3, West St, Rocky Hill
	Gas	E: Citgo, Mobil
	Food	E: Marriott W: D'Angelo's, Elizabeth's Rest.
	Lodg	E: Marriott
	Other	E: Dinosaur State Park
28/22		CT 9, N to New Britain, S to Middletown, Old Saybrook
	Other	S: Nelson's Family Campground ▲
27/21		CT 372, Berlin Rd, Cromwell, Berlin
	Gas	E: Sunoco W: Citgo, Mobil, Shell
	Food	E: Franco's Pizzeria, Diamond Trio, Friendly's, Wooster St Pizza Shop W: Blimpie's, Burger King, McDonald's, Subway
	Lodg	E: Comfort Inn, Crowne Plaza W: Courtyard, Holiday Inn, Super 8
	Other	W: Grocery, Wal-Mart, Longview RV
24/20		Country Club Rd, Middle St
(22)		Rest Area (NB) (RR, Phone, Picnic, Vend, RVDump)
(22)		Weigh Station (NB)
21/19		Baldwin Ave, Preston Ave (SB)
(20/18)		I-691W, to Meriden, Waterbury (SB) CT 66E, Middlefield, Middletown (NB)
19/17		CT 15S, W Cross Pkwy, E Main St, (NO Comm'l Vehicles) (SB), CT 15N, Berlin Tpk, to I-691, CT 66 (NB)
	Gas	W: BP
	Food	W: Great Wall Chinese
	Lodg	W: East End Hotel, Extended Stay America, Hampton Inn, Residence Inn
	Other	W: Powder Ridge Ski Area
18/16		E Main St, Shelton (NB)
	Gas	E: Mobil, Valero W: BP, Gulf, Sunoco
	Food	E: American Steakhouse, Little Caesar's Pizza, NY Pizza, Subway W: Burger King, KFC, Pizza Hut, McDonald's, Royal Guard Fish & Chips, Taco Bell

EXIT		CONNECTICUT
	Lodg	E: Candlewood Suites, Hampton Inn W: Days Inn, Howard Johnson
	Med	E: + Hospital
	Other	E: CVS, Grocery
16/15		CT 68, Barnes Rd, Wallingford, Yalesville, Durham
	Lodg	E: Marriott
(15)		Rest Area (SB) (RR, Phone, Picnic, Vend, RVDump)
14/14		CT 150, E Center St, Wallingford Woodhouse Ave
11/13		to US 5, Wallingford, North Haven (fr NB, Left Exit)
	Other	W: Wharton Brook State Park
9/12		US 5, Washington Ave
	Gas	E: Citgo, Shell, Valero W: Exxon
	Food	E: Boston Market, Burger King, China Buffet, Dunkin Donuts, Rustic Oak Steak, McDonald's, Subway, Wendy's W: Athena Diner, Roy Rogers
	Lodg	W: Holiday Inn
	Other	E: CVS, Walgreen's W: Grocery, Pharmacy
8/11		CT 22, New Haven (NB) (Access to Ex #12 Serv)
	Gas	E: Citgo
	Food	E: Hunan Rest
7/10		CT 40, Mt Carmel, Hamden (SB), Hamden, Cheshire (NB)
5/9		Montowese Ave, North Haven
	Gas	W: Sunoco
	Food	W: Sbarro, Subway
	Other	W: BJ's, Circuit City, Home Depot, Target
3/8		CT 17, CT 80, Middletown Ave
	Gas	E: 7-11, BP◊, Exxon, Shell W: Mobil
	Food	E: Burger King, Dunkin Donuts, KFC, McDonald's, Pizza Hut, Taco Bell
	Lodg	E: Days Inn
	Other	E: Lowe's, Wal-Mart
3/7		Ferry St, Fair Haven (SB)
2/6		US 5, Willow St, Blatchley Ave (fr NB, Left exit)
2/5		US 5, State St, Fair Haven (NB)
2/4		State St, Downtown (SB)
1/3		Trumbull St
1/2		Hamilton St (NB access fr I-95 only)
(0)		Jct I-95N, CT Tpk, New London (SB, Left exit)
0/1		CT 34W, Downtown, New Haven (SB)

NOTE: CT does not use Mile Marker Exits. We have listed MM/Exit #.

(I-91 Begins/Ends at Exit # 48, I-95)
(EASTERN TIME ZONE)

🎧 CONNECTICUT

Begin Northbound I-91 from Jct I-95 in New Haven, CT to Vermont/Canada border

Page 478 ◊ = Regular Gas Stations with Diesel ▲ = RV Friendly Locations ♥ = Pet Friendly Locations
RED PRINT SHOWS LARGE VEHICLE PARKING/ACCESS ON SITE OR NEARBY   BROWN PRINT SHOWS CAMPGROUNDS/RV PARKS

Interstate 93 S

EXIT	VT / NH

Begin Southbound I-93 from Jct I-91 near St Johnsbury, VT to Jct I-95 in Boston, MA.

⊙ VERMONT
(EASTERN TIME ZONE)
(I-93 begins/ends Exit #19, I-91 VT and/or I-95 Ex #12, Dedham, MA)

NOTE: VT does not use Mile Marker Exits. We have listed MM/Exit #.

(11/2/1) Jct I-91, N to St Johnsbury, S to White River Junction VT 18, to US 2, St. Johnsbury
- Lodg: N: Aime's Motel
- Other: N: Moose River Campground▲

(1) VT Welcome Center (NB) (RR, Phone, Picnic, Vend)

(EASTERN TIME ZONE)

⊙ VERMONT
⊙ NEW HAMPSHIRE
(EASTERN TIME ZONE)

NOTE: NH does not use Mile Marker Exits. We have listed MM/Exit #.

130.5/44 NH 18, NH 135, Littleton, Monroe, to Waterford, VT
- W: Rest Area (SB) (8a-8p) (RR, Phone, Picnic, Vend, Info, View)

126.2/43 NH 135, to NH 18, Dalton Rd, Littleto
- Med: S: + Little Regional Hospital
- Other: E: Crazy Horse Campground▲

124.6/42 US 302, NH 10, Dartmouth College Hwy, Littleton, Woodsville
- Gas: E: Citgo, Cumberland, Sunoco
  W: Mobil
- Food: E: Burger King, Cantina Di Gerardo, Clam Shell, Dunkin Donuts, McDonald's, Pizza Hut, Italian Oasis Rest, Subway
  W: 99 Rest & Pub, Applebee's, Asian Garden Rest
- Lodg: E: Country Squire Motel, Littleton Motel, Maple Leaf Motel, Thayers Inn
  W: Econo Lodge ♥, Hampton Inn
- Other: E: Grocery, Laundromat, Pharmacy
  W: Auto Dealers, Grocery, Staple, Tires, Wal-Mart, Littleton/Lisbon KOA▲, Mink Brook Family Campground▲

122.6/41 to US 302, NH 18, NH 116, Gilmantor Hill Rd, Littleton, Whitefield
- Gas: E: Irving◊
- Food: E: Rest/Eastgate Motor Inn
- Lodg: E: Eastgate Motor Inn

121/40 US 302, NH 10E, NH 18, NH 116, Bethlehem, Twin Mountain
- Gas: E: Exxon
- Lodg: E: Pinewood Motel
- Other: E: Snowy Mountain Campground▲, Apple Hill Campground/RVDump▲, Tarry Ho Campground & Cottages▲, Twin Mountain Airport✈

119.4/39 NH 18, NH 116, Bethlehem (SB) N Franconia, Sugar Hill

116.8/38 Wallace Hill Rd, Easton Rd, to NH 18, NH 116, NH 117, NH 142, Franconia, Sugar Hill, Lisbon
- Gas: W: Mobil

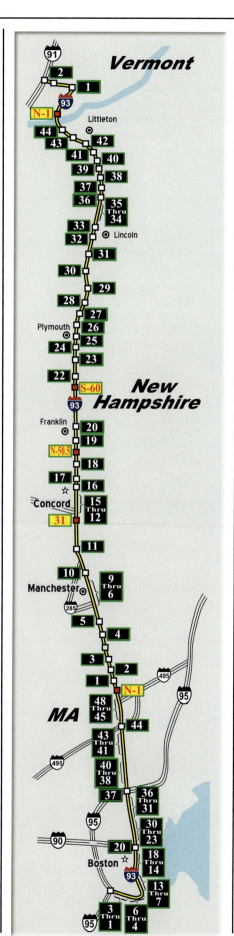

EXIT	NEW HAMPSHIRE

- Food: W: Franconia Café, Franconia Seafood & Dairy Bar, Subway
- Lodg: E: Red Coach Inn
  W: Cannon Mtn Motor Lodge, Gale River Motel, Hillwinds Motel,
- Other: W: Grocery, US Post Office, Fransted Family Campground▲, Cannon Mtn Ski Area, Franconia Airport✈

115.6/37 NH 142, Forest Hill Rd, to NH 18, Franconia, Bethlehem (NB)
- Gas: W: Mobil
- Food: W: Above the Notch, Franconia Village House Rest
- Lodg: W: Cannon Mtn View Lodge
- Other: W: Fransted Family Campground▲, to Franconia Notch State Park

113.2/36 NH 141, Butterhill Rd, to US 3N, to S Franconia, Twin Mtn (SB), NH 141(NB)

112.6/35 US 3N, Twin Mtn, Lancaster (NB)
- Other: E: to Rogers Campground & Motel▲, Beaver Trails Campground▲, Twin Mtn KOA▲, Twin Mtn Motor Court & RV Park▲, Tarry Ho Campground & Cottages▲, Beech Hill Campground▲

NOTE: I-93 interrupted below MM 103-112 for Franconia Notch Parkway. Two Lanes NB, Single Lane SB.

111/34C NH 18, Echo Lake Beach, Peabody Slopes, Cannon Mountain

110/34B Cannon Mountain Tramway
Cannon Mtn Ski Area, Old Man of the Mountains Museum, NE Ski Museum, Cannon RV Park▲

109 Trailhead Pkg (SB), Boise Rock, Old Man Historic Site (NB)
NO Trucks, Picnic Area, Scenic Overlook

108 Lafayette Place Campground (SB) Trailhead Parking (NB/SB)
Single Lane NB, Two Lanes SB

107 The Basin
Scenic View, Picnic

106/34A US 3, The Flume Gorge, Park Info Center

NOTE: I-93 interrupted above MM 103-112 for Franconia Notch Parkway.

102.4/33 US 3, Daniel Webster Hwy, N Woodstock, N Lincoln
- Gas: E: Irving◊
- Food: E: Notch View Country Kitchen, Longhorn Palace
  W: Eagle Cliff
- Lodg: E: Drummer Boy Motor Inn, Mount Coolidge Motel, Red Doors Motel
  W: Cozy Cabins, Mount Liberty Motel
- Other: W: Smitty's Auto Repair, Country Bumpkins Campground▲, Clarks Trading Post
  N: Whales Tale Water Park, Indian Head Viewing

100.6/32 NH 112, Kancamagus Hwy, N Woodstock, Lincoln
- Gas: E: Citgo, Mobil
  W: Mobil

◊ = Regular Gas Stations with Diesel ▲ = RV Friendly Locations ♥ = Pet Friendly Locations
RED PRINT SHOWS LARGE VEHICLE PARKING/ACCESS ON SITE OR NEARBY BROWN PRINT SHOWS CAMPGROUNDS/RV PARKS

EXIT	NEW HAMPSHIRE
Food	E: Dunkin Donuts, Emperor Chinese, Earl of Sandwich, Flapjack's, Seven Seas Rest, McDonald's, White Mtn Bagel Co
Lodg	E: Comfort Suites, Mill House Inn W: Carriage Motel, Woodstock Inn
Other	E: Loon Mtn Ski Resort W: Grocery, Maple Haven Resort▲, Lost River Valley Campground▲, White Mountains Motorsports Park
97.3/31	to NH 175, Tripoli Rd, N Woodstock
Other	W: Woodstock KOA▲
94.8/30	US 3, Daniel Webster Hwy, Woodstock, Thornton
88.6/29	US 3, Daniel Webster Hwy, Campton, Thornton
Lodg	W: Gilcrest Motel
Other	E: Pemi River Campground▲, Clear Stream Natural Campground▲
86.8/28	NH 49, to NH 175, Campton Village Rd, Waterville Valley, Campton
Gas	E: Citgo, Mobil W: Citgo
Food	E: Campton Pizza W: Sunset Grill
Lodg	W: Inn
Other	W: Convention Center, Tourist Info, Branch Brook Campground▲
83.6/27	Blair Rd, to US3, W Campton
Lodg	E: Super 8
81/26	US 3, NH 25, NH 3A, Plymouth, Rumney
Gas	W: to Mobil, Kwik Stop
Food	W: McDonald's
Lodg	W: Best Inn, Pilgrim Motel
Med	W: + Hospital
Other	W: to Jacobs Brook Campground▲, Newfound RV Park▲, Plymouth State Univ, Tenney Mountain Ski Area, Plymouth Muni Airport ✈
80.2/25	NH 175A, Bridge St, Holderness Rd, Plymouth
Gas	W: Irving◇
Food	W: Ashland Mtn View Deli, Fosters Steakhouse, Main St Station, Plymouth Bagels, Tom Bros Pizza
Lodg	W: Comman Man Inn & Spa
Med	W: + Hospital
Other	W: Plymouth State Univ
76/77	CAUTION Dangerous Crosswinds
75.3/24	US 3, NH 25, Ashland, Holderness, Squam Lake Region, Science Ctr
Gas	E: Irving Mainway, Mobil◇
Food	E: Burger King, Subway
Lodg	E: Comfort Inn
Other	E: Museum, Ames Brook Campground▲, Mountain View Family Campground▲, The Inn at Bethel Woods Campground▲
69.2/23	NH 104, NH 132, New Hampton, Meredith, Bristol
Gas	E: Kwik Stop, Irving◇
Food	E: Dunkin Donuts, Rossi's, Subway
Other	E: Twin Tamarack Family Camping▲, Clearwater Campground▲, Bear's Pine Woods Campground▲, to US 3, Lake Winnipisaukee Region W: Ragged Mtn Ski Area, Ruggles Mine, Yogi Bear's Jellystone Campground▲, Davidson's Country Campground▲, Newfound RV Park▲

EXIT	NEW HAMPSHIRE
61/22	NH 127, New Hampton Rd, Sanbornton, W Franklin
Med	W: + Franklin Reg'l Hospital
(60)	Rest Area (SB) (RR, Phone, Picnic, Vend, Info)
57/20	US 3, NH 11, NH 132, NH 140, Franklin, Laconia, Tilton
Gas	E: Exxon◇, Irving◇, Mobil
Food	E: Applebee's, Burger King, Dunkin Donuts, KFC, Kalliopes Rest, McDonald's, Tilt'n Diner, Wendy's
Lodg	E: Super 8
Other	E: BJ's, Home Depot, Staples, Outlet Mall W: Auto Dealers, Wal-Mart, to Thousand Acres Family Campground▲
54.8/19	NH 132, Park St, Tilton, Northfield, Franklin (NB)
Gas	W: Exxon
Med	W: + Hospital
Other	W: NH Veterans Home
(50.5)	Rest Area (NB) (RR, Phone, Picnic, Vend, Info)
48/18	West Rd, to NH 132, Centerbury, Boscawen
Gas	E: Mobil
Other	E: Shaker Village Historic Site
44.5/17	US 4W, Holt Rd, to US 3, NH 132, Penacook, Boscawen (NB)
17E	to NH 132 (SB)
17W	US 4W, to US 3, Penacook, Boscawen (SB)
Other	W: Veterans Cemetery
40/16	NH 132, Mountain Rd, Portsmouth St, East Concord
Gas	E: Mobil◇, Complete Car Care
39/15B	US 202W, to US 3, N Main St
Gas	E: Citgo, Hess
Food	E: Family Buffet W: Friendly's
Lodg	W: Courtyard
Med	W: + Hospital
Other	W: Convention Center
(39/15A)	I-393E, US 4E, US 202E, Main St, Concord, to Loudon, Portsmouth
Other	to NH Tech Inst, Planetarium, Speedway
39/14	NH 9, Loudon Rd, State Offices
FStop	E: Loudon Rd Shell
Gas	E: Mobil, Sunoco W: Citgo, Exxon◇, Hess
Food	E: Boston Market, Pizzeria Uno, Family Buffet, Olive Garden, Panera Bread, Outback Steakhouse, Ruby Tuesday
Lodg	W: Holiday Inn
Med	W: + Hospital
Other	E: Grocery, Pharmacy, US Post Office, U-Haul, AutoZone, Wal-Mart sc, Advance Auto, Everett Area, NH Air Nat'l Guard W: Cinema 93 Video, State Library, Capitol, Museum of NH History
38/13	US 3, Manchester St, Downtown
FStop	E: Fred's Kwik Stop & Deli/Sunoco
Gas	E: Mobil◇ W: Hess

◇ = Regular Gas Stations with Diesel ▲ = RV Friendly Locations ♥ = Pet Friendly Locations
RED PRINT SHOWS LARGE VEHICLE PARKING/ACCESS ON SITE OR NEARBY BROWN PRINT SHOWS CAMPGROUNDS/RV PARKS

 **I-93 S**

EXIT	NEW HAMPSHIRE
Food	E: Cityside Grill, Dunkin Donuts W: D'Angelo's, Hawaiian Isle II, KFC, McDonald's
Lodg	W: Best Western, Comfort Inn, Fairfield Inn
TServ	W: Yankee GMC Trucks, Kenworth, Concord Tire & Auto Service
Other	E: RV Center W: NAPA, Firestone,
37/12N	**NH 3A N, S Main St, Concord**
Gas	E: Exxon, Irving W: Mobil
Food	E: Subway W: Pizza
Lodg	E: Days Inn W: Hampton Inn
Med	W: + Hospital
Other	E: Auto Dealers
37/12S	**NH 3A S, to I-89, to Bow Junction**
TStop	E: Bow Jct Irving Mainway
Gas	E: Citgo◇
Food	E: Subway/Irving
Other	E: Laundry/WiFi/Irving
(36)	**TOLL Begins/Ends**
(36)	**Jct I-89N, to Lebanon, White River Junction, VT, to US 202, NH 9W, Bow, Keene, Claremont**
(31)	**Rest Area (Both dir)** **(RR, Phone, Picnic, Vend, Info)** **(NH Liquor Store)**
29/11	**TOLL Plaza, Hackett Hill Rd, to NH 3A, Bow, Hooksett**
TStop	E: Mr Mike's Travel Plaza/Citgo
Food	E: Rest/Mr Mike's TP
Other	E: Laundry/Mr Mike's TP
(29)	**TOLL Begins/Ends**
(26)	**Jct I-293S, Everett Tpk, Manchester, Nashua, Airport** (fr SB, Left 2 Lanes, Left exit), **Jct I-93S, Salem, Boston** (fr SB, Right 2 Lanes)
26/10	**NH 3A, W River Rd, Hooksett** NOTE: NB: Last FREE Exit before TOLL
FStop	E: Irving Mainway #1511
Gas	W: Exxon, Mobil
Food	E: Wendy's
Other	E: UNH Manchester, NH Tech College W: BJ's, Home Depot, Staples, Target
24/9	**US 3, NH 28, N to Hooksett, S to Manchester**
Gas	E: Exxon, Mobil W: Manchester Market & Gas, Sunoco
Food	E: Chantilly's Rest, Pizza Hut W: D'Angelo Grilled Sandwiches, KFC, La Carreta, Luisa's Italian Pizzeria, Shogun, Shorty's Mexican Road House
Other	E: Twin Oaks Campground▲, Big Bear State Park & Campground▲, Southern NH Univ
22/8	**Bridge Rd, Wellington Rd, to NH 28A, Manchester**
Med	W: + US Veterans Medical Center
Other	W: Civic Arena
21/7	**NH 101E, Seacost, Portsmouth** (fr SB, Left Exit/ fr NB, Exit Only)

EXIT	NEW HAMPSHIRE
21/6	**Candia Rd (NB), Hanover St (SB), Candia, Manchester**
FStop	W: Kwik Stop Mobil
Gas	W: Citgo◇, Shell
Food	E: Wendy's
Med	W: + Hospital
19	**Jct I-293N, NH 101W, to Manchester, Bedford, Airport** (fr NB, Left exit / fr SB, Exit only)
Other	W: Gas, Food, Lodge, Airport, Malls
15/5	**NH 28, N Londonderry**
FStop	E: RMZ Truckstop/Sunoco
Gas	E: 7-11 W: Exxon◇
Food	E: Poor Boys Family Dining, Burger King, Applebee's, Dunkin Donuts W: Honey Dew, TD's Deli
Lodg	W: Sleep Inn
Other	E: Wal-Mart, Grocery, LBP Towing & Auto Repair W: Manchester Airport✈, Stonyfield Farm
12/4	**NH 102, Nashua Rd, Derry, to Londonderry**
FStop	E: Freedom Fuel & Food/Citgo
Gas	E: Mobil, Sunoco◇, Shell W: Exxon◇, Getty, Hess, Shell◇
Food	E: Cracker Barrel, Derry Pizza, Dunkin Donuts W: Ginger Garden Chinese, McDonald's, Jerome's Deli, Papa Gino's, Wendy's
Med	E: + Hospital
Other	W: Cinema 8, Grocery, K-Mart, Home Depot, Walgreen's, Hudson Speedway
(7)	**Weigh Station (Both dir)**
6/3	**NH 111, Indian Rock Rd, Windham, N Salem, Canobie Lake, Hudson**
Gas	E: Mobil, Oasis Gas & MiniMart W: Sunoco
Food	E: Windham House of Pizza, McDonald's W: Dunkin Donuts, Subway
Other	E: Canobie Lake Park, Searles Castle
3/2	**Pelham Rd, to NH 38, NH 97, Salem**
Gas	W: Mobil
Food	E: Pudgy's Pizza W: A&A Rest, Margarita's, Loafer's
Lodg	E: Red Roof Inn♥ W: Holiday Inn, Fairfield Inn
Other	E: Canobie Lake Park
2/1	**Rockingham Park Blvd, to NH 28, NH 38, Salem**
FStop	E: Rockingham Fuel/Citgo
Gas	E: 7-11, Exxon, Getty
Food	E: Bickford's Family Rest, Burger King, Chili's, Denny's, Friendly's, McDonald's, Papa Gino's, 99 Rest & Pub
Lodg	E: Park View Inn
Other	E: AMC 20, B&N, Best Buy, Home Depot, Grocery, K-Mart, Staples, Target, Walgreen's, Rockingham Park Racetrack, Mall
(1)	**NH Welcome Center (NB)** **(RR, Phone, Picnic, Vend, Info)**

NOTE: NH does not use Mile Marker Exits. We have listed MM/Exit #.

(EASTERN TIME ZONE)

◯ NEW HAMPSHIRE

EXIT	MASSACHUSETTS
◯	**MASSACHUSETTS** (EASTERN TIME ZONE)
NOTE:	MA does not use Mile Marker Exits. We have listed MM/Exit #.
NOTE:	MM 47: Begin / End Call Boxes
45.8/48	**MA 213E, Methuen, Haverhill**
45.2/47	**MA 213, Pelham St, Pelham, Methuen**
Gas	E: Sunoco W: Getty
Food	E: McDonald's, Outback Steakhouse W: Rest/Days Inn, Fireside Restaurant, Julie's II Roast Beef & Seafood
Lodg	W: Days Inn, Guest Towers Inn
43.9/46	**MA 110, MA 113, Lawrence, Dracut**
Gas	E: Getty W: Citgo
Food	E: Burger King, McDonald's, Pizza Hut W: Dunkin Donuts, Pizza
Lodg	W: Motel 110
Med	E: + Hospital
42.7/45	**River Rd, Andover, S Lawrence**
Gas	W: Mobil
Lodg	E: Courtyard, Hawthorne Suites, Wyndham W: Residence Inn, Springhill Suites
(41/44BA)	**Jct I-495, S to Lawrence, N to Lowell**
39.6/43	**MA 133, Lowell St, Andover**
Gas	E: Mobil
Food	E: Dunkin Donuts/Mobil
Lodg	E: Ramada
38/42	**Dascomb Rd, Andover, Tewksbury**
35/41	**MA 125, Ballardvale St, Wilmington, Andover, N Andover**
Other	E: to Camp Forty Acres Campground▲
34.1/40	**MA 62, Wilmington, N Reading**
33/39	**Concord St, Wilmington**
31.4/38	**MA 129, Lowell St, Wilmington**
Gas	W: Mobil
29.7/37C	**Commerce Way, Atlantic Ave**
(29/37BA)	**Jct I-95, S-Waltham, N-Peabody** (Serv at 1st Exit S on I-95)
27.5/36	**Montvale Ave, Woburn, Stoneham**
FStop	W: Bob's Fuel Stop/Citgo
Gas	E: Mobil W: 7-11, Exxon, Mobil, Shell
Food	E: Kyoto Japanese Rest W: Bickford's Family Rest, Dunkin Donuts, Friendly's, McDonald's, Wendy's
Lodg	E: Courtyard W: Best Western, Comfort Inn

◇ = Regular Gas Stations with Diesel   ▲ = RV Friendly Locations   ♥ = Pet Friendly Locations

RED PRINT SHOWS LARGE VEHICLE PARKING/ACCESS ON SITE OR NEARBY   BROWN PRINT SHOWS CAMPGROUNDS/RV PARKS

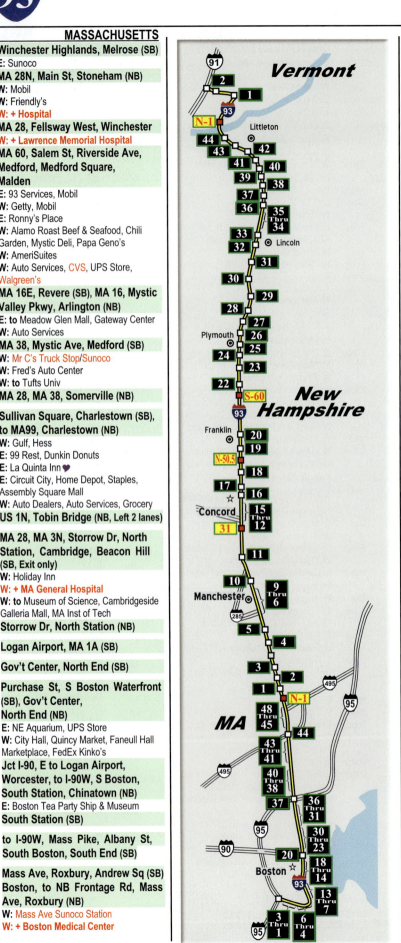

EXIT	MASSACHUSETTS
26.4/35	Winchester Highlands, Melrose (SB)
Gas	E: Sunoco
25.8/34	MA 28N, Main St, Stoneham (NB)
Gas	W: Mobil
Food	W: Friendly's
Med	W: + Hospital
23.5/33	MA 28, Fellsway West, Winchester
Med	W: + Lawrence Memorial Hospital
22.8/32	MA 60, Salem St, Riverside Ave, Medford, Medford Square, Malden
Gas	E: 93 Services, Mobil
	W: Getty, Mobil
Food	E: Ronny's Place
	W: Alamo Roast Beef & Seafood, Chili Garden, Mystic Deli, Papa Geno's
Lodg	W: AmeriSuites
Other	W: Auto Services, CVS, UPS Store, Walgreen's
22/31	MA 16E, Revere (SB), MA 16, Mystic Valley Pkwy, Arlington (NB)
Other	E: to Meadow Glen Mall, Gateway Center
	W: Auto Services
22/30	MA 38, Mystic Ave, Medford (SB)
FStop	W: Mr C's Truck Stop/Sunoco
Gas	W: Fred's Auto Center
Other	W: to Tufts Univ
20.6/29	MA 28, MA 38, Somerville (NB)
20.2/28	Sullivan Square, Charlestown (SB), to MA99, Charlestown (NB)
Gas	W: Gulf, Hess
Food	E: 99 Rest, Dunkin Donuts
Lodg	E: La Quinta Inn ♥
Other	E: Circuit City, Home Depot, Staples, Assembly Square Mall
	W: Auto Dealers, Auto Services, Grocery
18.9/27	US 1N, Tobin Bridge (NB, Left 2 lanes)
19/26	MA 28, MA 3N, Storrow Dr, North Station, Cambridge, Beacon Hill (SB, Exit only)
Lodg	W: Holiday Inn
Med	W: + MA General Hospital
Other	W: to Museum of Science, Cambridgeside Galleria Mall, MA Inst of Tech
18.5/26	Storrow Dr, North Station (NB)
18/24B	Logan Airport, MA 1A (SB)
18/24A	Gov't Center, North End (SB)
17.5/23	Purchase St, S Boston Waterfront (SB), Gov't Center, North End (NB)
Other	E: NE Aquarium, UPS Store
	W: City Hall, Quincy Market, Faneuil Hall Marketplace, FedEx Kinko's
(16.4/20)	Jct I-90, E to Logan Airport, Worcester, to I-90W, S Boston, South Station, Chinatown (NB)
Other	E: Boston Tea Party Ship & Museum
20A	South Station (SB)
20B	to I-90W, Mass Pike, Albany St, South Boston, South End (SB)
15.9/18	Mass Ave, Roxbury, Andrew Sq (SB) Boston, to NB Frontage Rd, Mass Ave, Roxbury (NB)
FStop	W: Mass Ave Sunoco Station
Med	W: + Boston Medical Center

EXIT	MASSACHUSETTS
15.5/16	Southampton St, Andrew Square (NB)
Gas	W: Shell
Lodg	W: Holiday Inn Express
Other	W: Home Depot
14.7/15	Columbia Rd, JFK Library, Edward Everett Square
Gas	W: Shell
13.2/14	Morrissey Blvd, JFK Library (NB)
13/13	Freeport St, Dorchester (NB)
Gas	W: 7-11
Other	W: CVS
12.1/12	MA 3A S, Neponset, Quincy (SB)
Gas	E: Shell
	W: 7-11, Exxon, Shell
Food	W: Arby's, Boston Market, Ground Round
Lodg	E: Best Western
Other	W: Auto Zone, Auto Dealers, Auto Service, CVS, Staples, Walgreen's
11.3/11B	to MA 203, Granite Ave, Ashmont (SB)
11.3/11A	Granite Ave, E Milton (SB)
11.3/11	to MA 203, Granite Ave, Ashmont (NB)
10.4/10	Squantum St, Milton (SB)
9.7/9	Bryant Ave, W Quincy (SB) Adam St, Milton, N Quincy (NB)
Gas	W: Mobil, Shell
8.4/8	Furnace Brook Pkwy, Quincy
Med	E: + Hospital
7.4/7	MA 3S, Braintree, Cape Cod (SB) I-93S, US 1S, to I-95, Dedham, Providence (SB) (Rt 2 lanes)
7.2/7	MA 3S, Cape Cod, I-93N, US 1, Boston (NB) (Rt 2 lanes)
6.7/6	MA 37, W Quincy, Braintree
Gas	E: Mobil
	W: Sunoco
Food	E: D'Angelo's, Pizza, TGI Friday
Lodg	E: Sheraton
	W: Extended Stay, Hampton Inn, Holiday Inn Express
Other	W: Auto Services, Mall
4.5/5BA	MA 28, N-Milton, S-Randolph
Gas	W: Shell, Sunoco, Texaco
Food	W: D'Angelo's, Dunkin Donuts, IHOP
Lodg	W: Holiday Inn
3.8/4	MA 24S, Brocktown, New Bedford (fr SB, Left exit)
3/3	Houghtons Pond, Ponkapoag Trail
2/2BA	MA 138, N-Milton, S-Stoughton
Gas	E: Mobil, Sunoco, Shell
(0/1)	I-95N, US 1S, Portsmouth, NH I-95S, Providence RI

NOTE: MA does not use Mile Marker Exits. We have listed MM/Exit #.

(EASTERN TIME ZONE)

🎧 MASSACHUSETTS

Begin Northbound I-93 from Jct I-95 south of Dedham, MA to Jct I-91 near St Johnsbury, VT.

Page 482 ◊ = Regular Gas Stations with Diesel ▲ = RV Friendly Locations ♥ = Pet Friendly Locations
RED PRINT SHOWS LARGE VEHICLE PARKING/ACCESS ON SITE OR NEARBY   BROWN PRINT SHOWS CAMPGROUNDS/RV PARKS

EXIT	MONTANA	EXIT	MONTANA	EXIT	MONTANA
	Begin Eastbound I-94 from Jct I-90 in Billings, MT to I-69 in Pt Huron, MI.	95	18th Ave, Forsyth	Med	N: + Hospital
		Food	N: Hong Kong Rest	Other	N: Terry's RV Oasis▲
	MONTANA (MOUNTAIN TIME ZONE) (I-94 Begins/Ends on I-90, Ex #456)	Med	N: + Hospital		S: Terry Airport✈
		Other	N: Forsyth Auto Repair, Art's Tires & Service, Gamble Repair	185	MT 340, Terry, Fallon
			S: Wagon Wheel Campground▲	192	Bad Route Rd, Glendive
(0)	Jct I-90, W-Billings, E-Sheridan	(99)	Weigh Station (Both dir)		Rest Area (Both dir) (RR, Phone, Picnic, Info)
6	MT 522, Pryor Creek Rd, Huntley	103	MT 447, MT 446, Rosebud Creek Rd, Rosebud		Weigh Station (Both dir)
Gas	N: Express Way	106	Butte Creek Rd, Rosebud	198	CR 260, Cracker Box Rd, Glendive
Food	N: Ernie's Bakery & Deli, Pryor Creek Café & Grill, Sam's Cafe	(113)	Rest Area (WB) (4/15-11/15) (RR, Phone, Picnic, RVDump)	204	Whoopup Creek Rd, Glendive
Lodg	N: Yellowstone Inn & Cabins	(114)	Rest Area (EB) (4/15-11/15) (RR, Phone, Picnic, RVDump)	206	Pleasant View Rd, Glendive
14	S 16th Rd, Ballantine, Worden			210	I-94 Bus, MT 200S, Glendive, Circle
Gas	N: Tiger Town	117	Graveyard Creek Rd, Rosebud, Hathaway	Gas	S: Cenex
Food	S: Longbranch Cafe Casino	126	Moon Creek Rd, Miles City	Food	S: McDonald's
23	S 31st St, US 312, Pompeys Pillar	128	Local Access	211	MT 200S, Circle (WB, diff WB reacc)
36	Reed Creek Rd, Waco, Custer	135	I-94 Bus, Miles City, Jordan	213	MT 16, Glendive, Sidney
(38.2)	Rest Area (EB) (RR, Phone, Picnic) (Open 4/15-11/15)	Other	N: Temp Dir: to Miles City KOA/RVDump▲	TStop	S: Trail Star Truck Stop/Sinclair
(41.3)	Rest Area (WB) (RR, Phone, Picnic) (Open 4/15-11/15)	138	MT 59, S Haynes Ave, Miles City, US 312, to Broadus	Gas	N: Exxon◇
					S: Conoco◇
47	MT 310, 5th St, Custer	TStop	N: Kum&Go #820/Cenex, Town Pump #8300/Pilot #907/Exxon	Food	S: Rest/Trail Star TS, McDonald's, Pizza Hut, Subway
Gas	S: Conoco◇	Gas	N: Conoco	Lodg	S: Budget Host Inn, Parkwood Motel
Food	S: D&L Café, Junction City Saloon	Food	N: Rest/Deli/DQ/McDonald's/Town Pump/Pilot TC, 4 B's Family Rest, Blimpie, Gallaghers Family Rest, Hardee's, KFC, Pizza Hut, Subway, Wendy's	Other	N: MT State Hwy Patrol Post
Lodg	S: D&L Motel				S: Laundry/Trail Star TS, Grocery, Kmart, Green Valley Campground/RVDump▲
Other	S: Conv Store		S: Hunan Chinese	215	I-94 Bus, N Merrill Ave, Glendive
49	MT 47, Custer, Hardin	Lodg	N: Best Western, Budget Inn, Econo Lodge♥, Motel 6♥	Gas	N: Conoco
Other	S: Ft Custer Rest & Bar, Grandview Campground▲, Little BigHorn Battlefield		S: Comfort Inn, GuestHouse Inn, Holiday Inn Express, Super 8		S: Exxon◇, Holiday, Sinclair◇
53	Tullock Rd, Bighorn, Hysham	Other	N: Laundry/RVDump/Kum&Go, Laundry/CarWash/WiFi/Casino/TP Pilot, Auto Dealers, ATMs, Albertson's, Grocery, Kmart, Pharmacy, Wal-Mart sc	Food	N: CC's Family Café, Rustic Inn
63	Ranch Access, Bighorn				S: Hardee's
(65)	Rest Area (Both dir) (RR, Phone, Picnic)			Lodg	N: Comfort Inn, Days Inn, Super 8
					S: Best Western, Glendive Budget Motel
67	US 10, US 312, MT 311, Bighorn, Hysham	141	I-94 Bus, US 12E, Miles City, Baker	Med	S: + Hospital
		Other	N: Use #135: Miles City KOA/RVDump▲, Big Sky Camp & RV Park/RVDump▲	Other	N: Glendive Campground/RVDump▲, to Makoshika State Park▲
72	MT 384, Sarpy Creek Rd, Bighorn	148	Valley Dr E, Ismay	224	Griffith Creek, Frontage Rd
82	Reservation Creek Rd, Forsyth	159	Frontage Rd, Diamond Ring, Ismay	231	Hodges Rd
87	MT 39, Forsyth, to Colstrip	169	Powder River Rd, Terry	236	Ranch Access
93	US 12W, Forsyth, Roundup	176	MT 253, Airport Rd, Terry	(240)	Weigh Station (Both dir)
FStop	N: Town Pump #8932/Exxon	Gas	N: Cenex, Conoco◇	241	I-94 Bus, MT 261, Wibaux, Baker (EB, NO EB reaccess)
Gas	N: Kum&Go/Cenex	Food	N: Diner, Roy Rogers Saloon, Terry's Landing	Gas	S: Amsler Conv Store◇
Food	N: Big Sky Café, DQ, Fitzgerald's, Top That Eatery	Lodg	N: Diamond Motel, Kempton Hotel	Lodg	S: Beaver Creek Inn, Super 8
Lodg	N: Best Western, Montana Inn, Rails Inn Motel, Restwell Motel			242	I-94 Bus, MT 7, to MT 261, Wibaux, Baker (WB)
Med	N: + Rosebud Health Care Center				Rest Area (RR, Phone, Picnic)
Other	N: Lucky Lil's Casino, Buff's Bar & Casino, Tom's Casino				

◇ = Regular Gas Stations with Diesel   ▲ = RV Friendly Locations   ♥ = Pet Friendly Locations
RED PRINT SHOWS LARGE VEHICLE PARKING/ACCESS ON SITE OR NEARBY   BROWN PRINT SHOWS CAMPGROUNDS/RV PARKS

Page 483

EXIT	MT / ND
248	Carlyle Rd, Wibaux
	NOTE: MM 250: North Dakota State Line
	(MOUNTAIN TIME ZONE)
	◐ **MONTANA**
	◑ **NORTH DAKOTA**
	(MOUNTAIN TIME ZONE)
(1)	Weigh Station (Both dir)
1	ND 16, 1st Ave NW, Beach
FStop	S: Interstate Cenex
TStop	S: Flying J Travel Plaza #5004 (Scales)
Food	S: Rest/FastFood/FJ TP, Backyard Rest, Crazy Charlie's, DQ, La Playa
Lodg	N: Outpost Motel
	S: Buckboard Inn
TServ	S: Walz Truck Repair Service, W Dakota Truck Repair/Auto/Towing/Tires/RV
Other	S: Laundry/WiFi/LP/FJ TP, Beach Field ✈
7	Home on the Range
10	Sentinel Butte, Camp Hump Lake
(13)	Rest Area (EB) (RR, Phone, Picnic)
(15)	Rest Area (WB) (RR, Phone, Picnic)
18	Buffalo Gap, Sentinel Butte
(21)	Scenic View (EB)
23	W River Rd, Medora (WB)
24	Historic Medora, T Roosevelt National Park/South Unit
27	Historic Medora (EB)
32	T Roosevelt Nat'l Park, Painted Canyon Visitor Area
N:	Rest Area (Both dir) (RR, Phone, Picnic)
36	Fryburg
42	US 85, Belfield, Grassy Butte, Williston
TStop	S: Super Pumper #22/Tesoro
Gas	S: Interstate Conoco◊
Food	S: DQ, Trapper's Kettle Rest & Pizzeria
Lodg	S: Trapper's Inn ♥ & RV Park▲
Other	S: Laundry/Tesoro, NAPA
51	CMC 4511, Belfield, South Heart

EXIT	NORTH DAKOTA
59	I-94 Bus, 30th Ave W, City Center, Dickinson (Access to Ex #61 Serv)
Gas	S: Conoco
Lodg	S: Oasis Motel, Queen City Motel
Other	S: Camp on the Heart Campground▲
61	ND 22, 3rd Ave W, Dickinson, Kill Deer
FStop	N: The General Store/Cenex
Gas	N: Simonson's Station Store◊
	S: Amoco, Cenex◊, Conoco, Holiday◊
Food	N: Applebee's, Arby's, Bonanza Steak House, Burger King, El Sombrero Mex Rest, Happy Joe's Pizza, Skipper's Seafood, Taco Bell, Wendy's
	S: China Doll Chinese, Country Kitchen, Domino's, KFC, Pizza Hut, McDonald's, Perkins, Subway
Lodg	N: AmericInn, Comfort Inn, Days Inn, Holiday Inn Express
	S: Best Western, Budget Inn, Quality Inn, Super 8, Travel Host Motel
Med	S: + St Joseph's Hospital
Other	N: LP/Gen'l Store, ATMs, Albertson's, Auto Services, Goodyear, Kmart, NAPA Pharmacy, Laundromat, Tires, True Value Hardware, Wal-Mart sc, Prairie Hills Mall, UPS Store, North Park Campground▲
	S: Auto Repair/Conoco, Auto Dealers, Tires, Dickinson State Univ, ND State Hwy Patrol Post
64	I-94 Bus, Dickinson (Access to Ex #61 Serv)
TStop	S: Tiger Discount Truck Stop/Tesoro
Food	S: FastFood/Tiger Disc TS, Dakota Diner
TServ	S: George's Tire Shop, NW Tire, Schmidt Repair
Other	S: Laundry/Tiger TS
(69)	Rest Area (Both dir) (RR, Phone, Picnic)
72	CMC 4531, Gladstone, Lefor
78	94 R Ave SW, Gladstone, Taylor
84	ND 8, Richardton, Mott
FStop	N: Cenex C-Store
Food	N: Wrangler Cafe
Med	N: + Richardton Memorial Hospital
90	CMC 4510, Richardton, Antelope
(94)	Rest Area (Both dir) (RR, Phone, Picnic)
97	CR 90, Hebron
Gas	N: Farmers
Food	N: Wagon Wheel Cafe
Lodg	N: Brick City Motel

EXIT	NORTH DAKOTA
102	CR 139, Hebron, Glen Ullin, Lake Tschida (Serv S 3-4 mi in Glen Ullin)
Gas	S: Crossroads Express
Lodg	S: M&M Motel
Other	S: Glen Ullin Muni Airport✈, Glen Ullin Memorial Park Campground▲
108	CR 88, 65th Ave, Glen Ullin (Serv 3-4 mi S in Glen Ullin)
110	ND 49, Glen Ullin, Beulah
113	Glen Ullin, Geck Township
117	CR 87, New Salem, Dengate
(119)	Rest Area (Both dir) (RR, Phone, Picnic)
120	New Salem, Blue Grass, Ullin
123	CR 86, New Salem, Almont
127	ND 31, New Salem, Hannover
FStop	S: U-Serve/Cenex
Food	S: Sunset Inn Café
Lodg	S: Sunset Inn, Sunset Motel
Other	S: Grocery, Laundromat, Pharmacy, Golf Course
134	CR 84, New Salem, to Judson, Sweet Briar Lake
(135)	Scenic View (WB)
140	33rd Ave, Mandan, Crown Butte, Crown Butte Dam
NOTE:	MM 143: Mountain / Central Time Zone
147	I-94 Bus, ND 25, to ND 6, Mandan
TStop	S: PTP/Freeway 147 Truck Stop/Sinclair (Scales)
Food	S: Rest/Freeway 147 TS
Other	S: Laundry/RVDump/LP/Frwy 147 TS
(151)	Scenic View (EB)
152	ND 6, Sunset Dr, Mandan
Gas	N: Conoco
	S: Tesoro
Food	S: Fried's Family Rest, Los Amigos
Lodg	N: Best Western, Ridge Motel ♥
Med	S: + Hospital
Other	N: Casino/Ridge Motel
153	Mandan Ave, Mandan
Gas	S: Cenex, StaMart◊, Tesoro
Food	S: Burger King, Dakota Farms Family Rest, Hardee's, McDonald's, Pizza Hut, Subway, Taco Johns', Wendy's
Lodg	S: N Country Inn, TP Motel
Other	S: ATMs, Auto Dealers, Auto Services, Goodyear, Grocery, Golf Course, Tires, Old Town Tavern 72 Casino

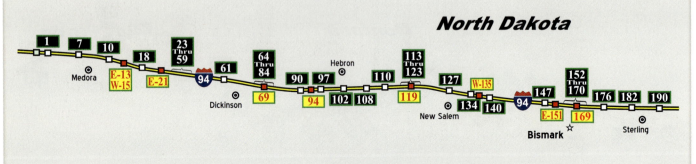

Page 484

◊ = Regular Gas Stations with Diesel   ▲ = RV Friendly Locations   ♥ = Pet Friendly Locations
RED PRINT SHOWS LARGE VEHICLE PARKING/ACCESS ON SITE OR NEARBY   BROWN PRINT SHOWS CAMPGROUNDS/RV PARKS

EXIT	NORTH DAKOTA
155	I-94 Bus, to ND 6 (WB, Left exit) (Access to Serv at Ex #153)
Other	S: Corral Sales RV Superstore, to Ft Lincoln State Park▲
(156)	I-194, ND 810, W Bismarck Expy, NC 1804, W Bismarck, E Mandan
Other	S: to Kirkwood Mall, Bismarck Muni Airport✈
157	Divide Ave, Tyler Pkwy, Bismarck
Gas	N: Conoco◊
	S: Cenex◊
Food	N: Cracker Barrel, McDonald's, Quiznos, Texas Roadhouse, Wendy's
Other	N: Best Buy, Lowe's
	S: Grocery, Pharmacy, Bismarck State College, RVDump/Cenex
159	US 83N, ND 1804, State St, Bismarck, Minot, Willton
Gas	N: Gas Plus, Best Stop◊, Sinclair◊
	S: Conoco◊, StaMart
Food	N: Applebee's, Arby's, Burger King, China Star, KFC, McDonald's, Mex Rest, Perkins, Red Lobster, Royal Fork Buffet, Taco Bell
	S: DQ, Hardee's, Pizza Hut, Starbucks, Subway, Taco Bell, Wendy's
Lodg	N: Comfort Inn, Country Inn, Fairfield Inn, Motel 6♥
	S: Best Western, Days Inn, Kelly Inn, Select Inn♥, Super 8
Med	S: + Hospital
Other	N: Grocery, Home Depot, Kmart, Tires, Pharmacy, Wal-Mart sc, U-Haul, Gateway Mall
	S: to Kirkwood Mall
161	N Bismarck Expy, Centennial Rd
FStop	N: Cenex C-Store
TStop	S: StaMart Travel Center #15/Tesoro (Scales)
Food	S: Rest/StaMart TC, McDonald's
Lodg	S: Ramada Ltd
TServ	S: Butler CAT Engine Service, Johnson Trailer Sales, Trucks of Bismarck
Other	N: LP/RVDump/Cenex, Bismarck KOA▲
	S: Laundry/RVDump/StaMart TC, Capital RV Center, Tires
(169)	Rest Area (Both dir) (RR, Phones, Picnic, Vend)
170	158th St NE, Menoken
Other	S: A Prairie Breeze RV Park▲
176	236th St NE, Sterling, McKenzie
182	US 83S, ND 14, Sterling, Wing
TStop	S: Tops Truck Stop/Cenex
Food	S: Rest/Tops TS, Darnell's Cafe
Lodg	S: Tops Motel
Other	S: Laundry/Tops TS

EXIT	NORTH DAKOTA
190	405th St NE, Driscoll
195	20th Ave SE, Steele, Long Lake
200	ND 3, Mitchell Ave N, Steele, to Dawson, Tuttle
TStop	S: PTP/Coffee Cup Fuel Stop #2/Conoco
Gas	S: Cenex
Food	S: FastFood/Coffee Cup, Lone Steer Rest
Lodg	S: Lone Steer Motel, Casino & RV Park▲, OK Motel & Campground▲
205	30th Ave SE, Steele, Robinson
208	ND 3S, Lake Ave, Dawson, Napolean
Food	S: Dawson Cafe
214	39th Ave SE, Tappen
Gas	S: Marlin's Standard
217	42nd Ave SE, Tappen, Pettibone
(221)	Rest Area (EB) (RR, Phone, Picnic, Vend, RVDump)
221	CR 39, CR 70, Medina, Crystal Springs
(224)	Rest Area (WB) (RR, Phone, Picnic, Vend, RVDump)
228	ND 30S, CR 39, Medina, Streeter
230	1st Ave S, 55th Ave SE, Medina
Gas	N: Cenex◊
Food	N: Coffee Cup Café, Medina Cafe
Lodg	N: Medina's Cozy Corners Motel, North Country Lodge/Motel
233	CR 68, 58th Ave SE, Medina, to Halfway Lake
238	CR 67, 5th Ave, Euclid Ave, Cleveland, to Windsor, Gackle
242	67 1/2 Ave SE, Cleveland, Windsor
245	70th Ave SE, Cleveland, Oswego
248	CR 65, 74th Ave SE, Jamestown, Lippert Township
251	CMC 4728, Jamestown, Eldridge
(254)	Rest Area (Both dir) (RR, Phone, Picnic, Vend)
256	US 52, US 281, Truck, 81st Ave SE, Jamestown, Woodbury
Other	S: Jamestown Campground▲
257	I-94 Bus, 17th St SW, to US 52, US 281, Jamestown (EB, Left Exit)

EXIT	NORTH DAKOTA
258	US 281, US 52, Jamestown, Edgly
FStop	N: Interstate Sinclair
TStop	S: Super Pumper #26/Conoco
Gas	N: BP
Food	N: Arby's, DQ, Depot, Hardee's, McDonald's, Pizza Ranch, Taco Bell
	S: Subway/SuperPumper, Applebee's, Burger King, Embers Rest. Little Caesar's, Perkins, Paradiso Mex Rest, Super Buffet
Lodg	N: Buffalo Motel, Comfort Inn, Days Inn, Gladstone Inn & Suites♥, Holiday Inn Express, Jamestown Motel, Ranch House Motel
	S: Best Western, Quality Inn♥, Super 8
TServ	N: James River Diesel Service
Med	N: + Jamestown Hospital
Other	N: Auto Repair, Auto Dealers, Firestone, Jamestown Mall, Civic Center, ND Sports Hall of Fame, Museum, Jamestown College Jamestown Reg'l Airport✈, Jamestown Speedway, Stutsman Co Fairgrounds, Frontier Fort Campground▲, to appr 7mi Lakeside Marina & Campground▲
	S: Kmart, Wal-Mart, Cinemas, Buffalo Mall, Dale's Motorsports, Countryside RV, Uncle Bob's Trailers
260	I-94 Bus, 14th St, to US 52, US 281, Jamestown
TStop	N: Jamestown Truck Plaza/BP (Scales)
Gas	N: Stop 'n Go
Food	N: Rest/Jamestown TP
Lodg	N: Budget Lodge, Star Lite Motel♥
TWash	N: Jamestown TP
TServ	N: Jamestown TP/Tires
Med	S: + ND State Hospital
Other	N: Laundry/Jamestown TP, Buffalo Museum, Golf Course, Stutsman Harley Davidson
262	Frey Rd, Jamestown, Bloom
Other	N: to Jamestown College, Jamestown Reg'l Airport✈
269	CR 62, Jamestown, Spiritwood
272	97th Ave SE, Sanborn, to Urbana
276	CR 7, 101st Ave SE, Eckelson
Other	S: Prairie Haven Campground▲/Gas
281	CR 11, 106th Ave SE, Sanborn, to Litchville
283	ND 1N, Valley City, Rogers
288	ND 1S, 113th Ave SE, CR 22N, Valley City, to Oakes
290	I-94 Bus, US 52, Main St, CR 19, Valley City (Access to Ex #292 Serv)
Gas	N: Cenex, Tesoro◊

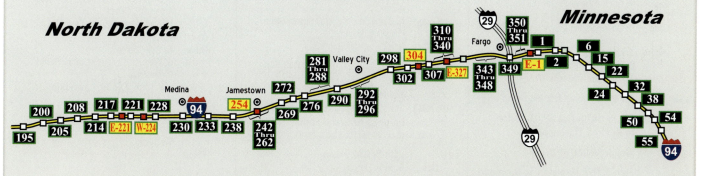

◊ = Regular Gas Stations with Diesel   ▲ = RV Friendly Locations   ♥ = Pet Friendly Locations

RED PRINT SHOWS LARGE VEHICLE PARKING/ACCESS ON SITE OR NEARBY   BROWN PRINT SHOWS CAMPGROUNDS/RV PARKS

EXIT		NORTH DAKOTA
	Food	N: Burger King, Kenny's Rest, Pizza Hut, Subway
	Lodg	N: Bel-Air Motel, Valley City Motel S: Flickertail Inn
	Med	N: + Hospital
	Other	N: LP/Dakota Plains Co-Op
292		CR 21, 8th Ave SW, Valley City, to Kathryn
	TStop	N: John's I-94 Tesoro
	Food	N: Sabir's Dining & Lounge
	Lodg	N: AmericInn, Super 8, Wagon Wheel Inn & RV Park▲
	TServ	N: Berger Auto & Diesel Repair
	Med	N: + Mercy Hospital
	Other	N: to Barnes Co Muni Airport✈, Auto Dealers, to appr 14mi COE/Lake Ashtabula▲ S: Public Golf Course
294		I-94 Bus, US 52 Bus, Valley City (Access to Ex #292 Serv)
	Med	N: + Hospital
	Other	N: Wagon Wheel Inn & RV Park▲
296		CR 27, 121st St SE, Valley City, Peak
298		Cuba
302		ND 32, Oriska, Fingal
(304)		Rest Area (Both dir, Left exit) (RR, Phone, Picnic, Vend)
307		CR 1, 132nd Ave SE, Tower City
	TStop	N: Tower Fuel Stop/Mobil
	Food	N: Rest/Tower FS, Tower View Café
	Lodg	N: Tower Motel & Campground▲
	TWash	N: Tower FS
	TServ	N: Tower FS/Tires
	Other	N: Laundry/RVDump/Tower FS
310		36th St SE, 135th Ave SE, Tower City, Hill Township
314		ND 38, 139th Ave SE, Tower City, to Buffalo, Alice
317		CR 3, 142nd Ave SE, Wheatland, Ayr
320		CR 7, 145th Ave SE, to Embden
322		147th Ave SE, to Absaraka
324		CR 5, 149th Ave SE, Wheatland, to Chaffee
(327)		Truck Parking Area (EB)
328		153rd Ave SE, Casselton, to Lynchburg, Everest
331		ND 18, Casselton, Leonard
	Gas	N: Gordy's Travel Plaza◆, Cenex
	Food	N: Gordy's Café, Subway
	Lodg	N: Governors Inn & Conf Center/Rest/ RVPark▲
	Other	N: NAPA S: Casselton Reg'l Airport✈
(337)		Truck Parking Area (WB)
338		CR 11, Meridian Rd, Mapleton
340		CR 15, 165th Ave SE, Mapleton, to Kindred, Davenport
(342)		Weigh Station (Both dir)
342		38th St NW, Mapleton, to Raymond

Personal Notes

EXIT		NORTH DAKOTA
343		I-94 Bus, US 10, W Fargo
	TStop	N: West Fargo Truck Stop
	Food	N: FastFood/W Fargo TS, Speedway Rest
	Lodg	N: Hi-10 Motel, Sunset Motel, Days Inn, Super 8
	Other	N: LP/W Fargo TS, Adventure RV Sales, Fargo Harley Davidson
346AB		Sheyenne St, West Fargo (WB)
346		CR 17, Sheyenne St, West Fargo to Horace (EB)
	Gas	N: Sooper Stop, Stop N Go S: RJ's Conoco◆
348		45th St SW, Fargo
	TStop	N: Petro Stopping Center #61/Mobil (Scales)
	Gas	N: BP, Cenex
	Food	N: IronSkillet/FastFood/Petro SC, Bennigan's, Carino's, McDonald's, Qdoba Mex Rest, Mongolian Grill, Mexican Grill, Olive Garden, Quiznos, Subway, Wendy's S: Applebee's, Culver's Rest, KFC, Pizza Hut
	Lodg	N: C'Mon Inn, Mainstay Suites, Sleep Inn, Wingate Inn
	TWash	N: Blue Beacon/Petro SC
	TServ	N: Petro SC/Tires
	Other	N: Laundry/RVDump/LP/Petro SC, Home Depot, NAPA, Sam's Club, Target, Wal-Mart sc
(349AB)		Jct I-29, US 81, S to Sioux Falls, Fargo, N to Grand Forks (Serv at 1st Ex S on I-29, Ex #62)
350		25th St SW, Fargo
	Gas	S: BP◆, Holiday

EXIT		ND / MN
351		US 81 Bus, S University Dr, Downtown Fargo
	Gas	N: Conoco, Loaf n Jug, Stop N Go S: Phillips 66◆, Stop-N-Go
	Food	N: Duane's House of Pizza, Great Harvest Bread Co, Pizza Hut, Starbucks, Taco Bell S: Burger King, Denny's, Domino's, KFC, McDonald's, N American Steak Buffet, Randy's Diner, Subway, Taco Bell
	Lodg	N: Dakota Day Inn S: Expressway Inn, Rodeway Inn
	Med	N: + Dakota Medical Center
	Other	N: Greyhound, AutoZone, Pharmacy S: Kmart, Blue Wolf Casino
	NOTE:	MM 352: Minnesota State Line

(CENTRAL TIME ZONE)

ⓄNORTH DAKOTA
ⓄMINNESOTA

(CENTRAL TIME ZONE)

1A		US 75, S 8th St, Moorhead
	Gas	N: Phillips 66, Brady's Service Ctr S: Bud's Amoco & Service Ctr, Casey's Gen'l Store
	Food	N: Burger King, Little Caesar's, Qdoba Mex Grill, Starbucks, Village Inn S: Hardee's, Snap Dragon, Speak Easy Rest & Lounge, Subway
	Lodg	N: Courtyard S: AmericInn, Grand Inn♥, Super 8
	Other	N: CarWash/Repairs/Towing/Brady's, MN State Univ/Moorhead, MSU Planetarium, Moorhead Center Mall
1B		20th St (EB exit, WB reaccess)
	Gas	S: Stop N Go
	Other	N: MN State & Tech College
(1)		MN Welcome Center (EB) (RR, Phones, Picnic, Vend, Info)
2		I-94 Bus, US 52, Main Ave, to US 10, Moorhead
	Gas	N: Holiday Station Store◆
	Food	N: Bennigan's, China Buffet, Perkins
	Lodg	N: Guest House Motel
	Other	N: Larry's RV, Moorhead/Fargo KOA▲, to US10: Kmart, Target, Wal-Mart
(5)		Weigh Station (EB)
6		MN 336, CR 11, to US 10, Glyndon, to Sabin, Dilworth
	Other	N: to Buffalo River State Park▲
15		MN 10, Barnesville, Downer, Sabin
22		MN 9, CR 55, Barnesville
	Gas	S: Barnesville Gen'l Store, Barnesville AmocoBP, Cenex◆
24		MN 34, Barnesville, Detroit Lakes
	Gas	S: Cenex◆
	Other	N: Golf Course S: Wagner City Park Campground/ RVDump▲
32		MN 108E, CR 30, Lawndale, Pelican Rapids
	Other	S: to Maplewood State Park▲
38		US 52, CR 11, MN 88, Center St, Rothsay
	TStop	S: Rothsay Truck Stop/Tesoro

Page 486   ◆ = Regular Gas Stations with Diesel   ▲ = RV Friendly Locations   ♥ = Pet Friendly Locations
RED PRINT SHOWS LARGE VEHICLE PARKING/ACCESS ON SITE OR NEARBY   BROWN PRINT SHOWS CAMPGROUNDS/RV PARKS

INTERSTATE 94 W E — MINNESOTA

EXIT		MINNESOTA
	Food	S: Rest/Rothsay TS
	Lodg	S: Comfort Zone Inn
	TServ	S: Neuleib Repair Shop, Rothsay Truck & Trailer Repair
	Other	S: LP/Rothsay TS
50		US 59N, CR 88, Fergus Falls, Elizabeth, Pelican Rapids
	FStop	N: Interstate Fuel & Food
	Food	N: Rest/Interstate F&F
	Other	N: RVDump/LP/Interstate F&F
54		MN 210W, W Lincoln Ave, Fergus Falls, Breckenridge
	TStop	N: Kum & Go #107
	Gas	N: Amoco, Casey's, Holiday Station
	Food	N: Applebee's, Burger King, Hardee's, KFC, McDonald's, Mabel Murphy's, Pizza Hut, Perkins, Pizza Ranch, Subway
	Lodg	N: AmericInn♥, Best Western, Comfort Inn♥, Days Inn♥, Motel 7, Super 8
	Med	N: + Fergus Falls State Hospital
	Other	N: RVDump/Holiday, Auto Services, Auto Dealers, Grocery, Home Depot, Kmart, NAPA, Radio Shack, Target, Tires Plus, Westridge Mall, Wal-Mart, MN State & Tech College
		S: Fergus Falls Muni Airport✈
55		CR 1, Wendell Rd, Fergus Falls
57		MN 210E, CR 25, Fergus Falls
	Other	N: to Swan Lake Resort Campground▲
(60)		Rest Area (EB) (RR, Phone, Picnic, Vend)
61		US 59S, CR 82, Fergus Falls, to Elbow Lake
	TStop	N: Big Chief Truck Stop/Citgo
	Food	N: Rest/Big Chief TS
	Other	N: WiFi/Big Chief TS, to Swan Lake Resort & Campground▲
		S: River N Woods Campground▲
67		CR 35, Dalton
	Other	N: Big Island Campsite▲
(69)		Rest Area (WB) (RR, Phone, Picnic, Vend)
77		MN 78N, CR 10, Barrett, Ashby
	Other	N: Ashby Resort & Campground▲, Prairie Cove Campground & RV Park▲
82		MN 79W, CR 41, Evansville, Elbow Lake
	Other	S: Tipsinah Mounds Campground▲
90		CR 7, Brandon
97		MN 114, CR 40, Alexandria, Garfield, Lowry
	Other	N: Alexandria Oak Park▲
(100)		Rest Area (EB) (RR, Phones, Picnic, Vend)
100		MN 27, Alexandria
	Other	N: Steinbring Motorcoach & Service
103		MN 29, MN 27, Alexandria, Glenwood
	FStop	N: B&H Self Serve
	Gas	N: Citgo, Holiday Station Store
	Food	N: Burger King, Country Kitchen, Culver's, Hardee's, KFC, McDonald's, Perkins, Taco Bell, Wendy's
		S: Rudy's Red Eye Grill
	Lodg	N: AmericInn, Days Inn♥, Ramada Ltd♥, Super 8♥
		S: Country Inn♥, Holiday Inn♥
	TServ	S: Steussy's Diesel Service
	Med	N: + Douglas Co Hospital, + Midway Medical Clinic
	Other	N: RVDump/Holiday, Kmart, Pharmacy, Target, Wal-Mart sc, Chandler Field, Jiffy Lube, Midas, Sun Valley Resort & Campground▲, Steinbring Motorcoach & Service
		S: Alexandria RV
(105)		Rest Area (WB) (RR, Phones, Picnic, Vend)
114		MN 127, CR 3, Osakis, Westport
	Other	N: to Sportmens Motel & RV Park▲, Midway Beach Resort & Campground▲, Head of the Lakes Resort▲
119		CR 46, CR 91, 137th Ave, West Union, Sauk Centre
124		CR 72, Beltline Rd, Sinclair Lewis Ave, Sauk Centre (EB exit, no reacc)
127		US 71, MN 28, Sauk Centre, Glenwood, Willmar
	TStop	N: Holiday Super Stop
		S: Truckers Inn #6/BP (Scales)
	Gas	N: Casey's Gen'l Store, Super America
	Food	N: DQ, Hardee's, Pizza Hut, McDonald's
		S: Rest/Truckers Inn
	Lodg	N: AmericInn♥, Best Value♥, Super 8♥
	TWash	S: Truckers Inn
	TServ	S: Truckers Inn/Tires, St Cloud Truck Sales
	Med	N: + St Michael's Hospital
	Other	N: Auto Repairs, Tires, Head of the Lakes Resort▲
		S: Laundry/Truckers Inn, Sauk Centre Muni Airport✈, Midwest RV Service
131		MN 4S, Meire Grove, Paynesville
135		MN 13, S 2nd Ave E, Melrose
	Gas	N: Mobil◆, Tesoro◆
		S: Conoco◆
	Food	N: Burger King, Subway
		S: DQ
	Lodg	S: Super 8♥
	Med	N: + Melrose Hospital
	Other	N: ATMs, Grocery, NAPA, Auto Repairs & Towing/Mobil, Sauk River City Park/RVDump
		S: Grocery
137		MN 237, CR 65, New Munich
140		MN 11, 1st Ave S, Freeport
	Gas	N: Conoco◆
	Food	N: Pioneer Supper Club, Charlie's Café
	Lodg	N: Pioneer Inn
	Other	N: US Post Office
147		MN 238N, MN 10, 8th St S, Albany
	Gas	N: Holiday Station◆, QuikMart, Shell
	Food	N: DQ, Hillcrest Family Rest
		S: KFC, Subway
	Lodg	N: Country Inn
	Med	N: + Albany Medical Center
	Other	N: RVDump/Holiday, CarWash, IGA, Laundromat
(152)		Rest Area (Both dir) (RR, Phone, Picnic, Vend)
153		CR 9, Avon Ave S, Avon
	Gas	N: Avon QuikMart◆, Avon Shell◆
	Food	N: Neighbors BBQ & Smokehouse
	Lodg	N: AmericInn
	Other	N: Grocery, US Post Office
		S: to El Rancho Manana Campground▲
156		CR 159, 135th Ave N, Avon, St John's University
158		CR 75, St Joseph, St. Cloud, Waite Park (EB, Left Exit, No reacc)
	Other	N: to St Cloud Campground & RV Park▲
160		CR 2, St. Joseph, Cold Springs
164		MN 23, Waite Park, St Cloud, Rockville (Serv 3-4 mi N in Waite Park)
167AB		MN 15, St. Cloud, Kimball (EB), MN 15, to US 10W, to MN 371N, St Cloud, Kimball, Brainerd (WB) (Serv 4 mi N in St Cloud)
	Med	N: + Hospital
	Other	N: to St Cloud Campground & RV Park/RVDump▲
171		CR 75, CR 7, St Cloud, St Augusta
	TStop	N: Pilot Travel Center #134 (Scales)
	Gas	N: Cenex
		S: Holiday Station

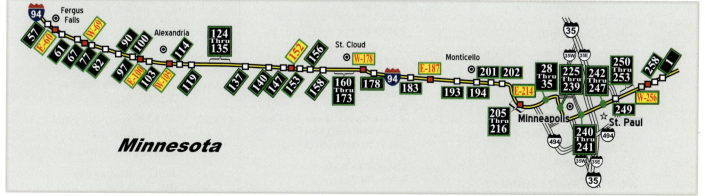

Minnesota

◆ = Regular Gas Stations with Diesel   ▲ = RV Friendly Locations   ♥ = Pet Friendly Locations
RED PRINT SHOWS LARGE VEHICLE PARKING/ACCESS ON SITE OR NEARBY   BROWN PRINT SHOWS CAMPGROUNDS/RV PARKS

EXIT	MINNESOTA
	Food N: FastFood/Pilot TC, FastFood/Cenex
	Lodg N: AmericInn, Holiday Inn Express
	TServ N: Casey's Truck Repair, Joe's Auto & Truck Repair, Heartland Tire & Service
	Other N: WiFi/RVDump/Pilot TC
	S: RVDump/Holiday, Pleaseland RV Center/RVDump
173	CR 75, Opportunity Dr
(178)	Fuller Lake Rest Area (WB) (RR, Phone, Picnic, Vend)
178	MN 24, Clearwater, Annandale
	TStop N: Petro 2/Clearwater Travel Plaza/Citgo (Scales)
	Gas N: Holiday Station◊
	Food N: Rest/FastFood/Petro2/Clw TP, Burger King, DQ, Subway
	Lodg N: Best Western, Budget Inn
	TServ N: Petro2/Clw TP
	Other N: Laundry/RVDump/LP/Petro2/Clw TP, Grocery, St Cloud/Clearwater/I-94 KOA▲, to St Cloud Campground & RV Park▲, Leaders Clear Lake Airport✈
	S: Clearwater Auto Parts, A-J Acres Campground/RVDump▲
183	CR 8, Elder Ave NW, Hasty, Clearwater, Silver Creek
	TStop S: AmBest/Olsen's Truck Stop (Scales)
	Food S: Pump House Rest&Deli/Olson's TS
	TServ S: Petrol Pumper/Tires
	Other N: Miesner RV Services, Northern RV & Boat
	S: Laundry/WiFi/Petrol Pumper, Olson's Campground▲, Lake Maria State Park
(187)	Enfield Rest Area (EB) (RR, Phone, Picnic, Vend)
193	MN 25, Pine St, Monticello, Buffalo
	FStop S: Tom Thumb/BP
	Gas N: Holiday Station Store◊, Marathon, Kwik Stop, Conoco◊
	S: Super America◊
	Food N: Burger King, DQ, KFC, Mex Rest, Perkins, Taco Bell
	S: Applebee's, Arby's, McDonald's, Pizza Factory, Subway
	Lodg N: AmericInn, Rand House B&B
	S: Best Western, Days Inn, Select Inn
	TServ S: Hoglund Bus Co Sales & Service
	Med N: + Big Lake Hospital
	Other N: Auto Value Parts Store, Grocery, Home Depot, Kmart, Pharmacy, Target, River Terrace Park▲, Monticello RV Center, to Big Lake RV
	S: LP/TomThumb, Checker Auto Parts, Auto Dealers, Wal-Mart sc, Pilots Cove Airport✈, Lake Maria State Park
194	Fenning Ave NE, Monticello (Access to Ex #193 Serv)
201	MN 19, La Beaux Ave, Albertville, St Michael (EB) (Access to Ex #202 Serv)
202	MN 37, 60th St NE, Albertville
	FStop S: Pat's Shell
	Gas N: Conoco◊
	S: Amoco, Casey's Gen'l Store, Mobil
	Food N: Burger King, Subway
	S: Hot Stuff Pizza/Pat's
	Other N: Albertville Premium Outlets
	S: Dale's Auto Repair & Towing

EXIT	MINNESOTA
205	MN 241, CR 36, 42nd St SE, 45th St NE, St Michael
	FStop S: to Super America #4554
207	MN 101, CR 81, Main St, Rogers, Elk River, to US 169N
	TStop N: Travel Center of America #190/Citgo (Scales)
	Gas N: Super America◊
	S: Amoco, Holiday Station Store
	Food N: Fulton'sRest/TA TC, Arby's, Applebee's, Burger King, Culver's, Rest, Denny's, Dominos, McDonald's, Subway, Taco Bell, Wendy's
	S: Black Bear Lodge & Saloon, Country Kitchen, DQ, Embers Rest, Guadalajara Mex Rest, Subway
	Lodg N: Super 8
	S: AmericInn
	TServ N: TA TC/Tires, Goodyear, MN Trailer Sales
	S: Campbell Diesel Service, Glen's Truck Center, Boyer Trucks
	Other N: Laundry/WiFi/RVDump/TA TC, ATMs, Grocery,Lube & CarWash, Target, Tires +, UPS Store, Cabela's/RVDump, Camping World
	S: Grocery
(212)	FUTURE Exit, MN 610E
213	CR 30, 97th Ave N, 93rd Ave N, Osseo, Maple Grove
	Gas N: Maple Square Fuel & Wash, Phillips 66, Super America◊
	S: Holiday
	Food S: Culver's Rest, McDonald's, Quiznos
	Other S: Goodyear, Sam's Club, Target, Tires, Wal-Mart sc, Minneapolis NW KOA▲
(214)	Elm Creek Rest Area (EB) (RR, Phones, Picnic, Vend)
215	CR 109, Weaver Lake Rd, Maple Grove, Osseo
	Gas N: Super America◊, Citgo
	Food N: Bakers Square, Burger King, DQ, Cattle Co Steakhouse, Don Pablo, HOPS Grill, Joe's Crab Shack, KFC, McDonald's, Little Caesars, Pizza Hut, Starbucks, Subway, Taco Bell, Wendy's
	S: Applebee's, Fuddrucker's
	Lodg N: Hampton Inn, Staybridge Suites
	Other N: ATMs, Banks, B&N, Best Buy, Borders, FedEx Kinko's, Gander Mountain, Grocery, Goodyear, Kmart, Tires Plus, Walgreen's, Mall, US Post Office, Modern RV
(216)	Jct I-94E, I-694E, I-494S (EB), I-94W, US 52 (WB)
	I-694: to Twin Cities N ByPass, Eau Claire
	I-94: to Downtown
	I-494: to Minn-St Paul Int'l Airport✈, Mall of America
	NOTE: I-94 runs below with I-694. Exit #'s follow I-694.
28	MN 61, Hemlock Lane, Maple Grove, to Osseo (Acc N to Ex 15 Serv)
	Gas S: BP
	Food N: Arby's, Chuck E Cheese, Don Pablo, Famous Dave's BBQ, Olive Garden, Red Lobster, Starbucks, Subway
	S: Perkins
	Lodg N: Holiday Inn, Hampton Inn
	S: Select Inn, Travelodge

EXIT	MINNESOTA
	Other N: ATMs, Best Buy, Grocery, Tires
29AB	US 169, to Osseo, Hopkins
30	Boone Ave, Minneapolis
	Food N: Rest/Northland Inn
	Lodg N: Northland Inn Hotel, Sleep Inn
	Other S: Home Depot
31	MN 81, MN 8, Lakeland Ave, Downtown Minneapolis
	Gas N: Shell, SuperAmerica◊
	Food N: DQ, Wendy's
	Lodg N: Ramada Inn
	S: Best Value Inn, Budget Host Inn, Super 8
	Other S: Crystal Airport✈
33	CR 152, Brooklyn Blvd
	Gas N: Mobil, Shell
	S: BP
	Other S: Grocery, Walgreen's
34	Shingle Creek Pkwy, to MN 100
	Gas N: Mobil
	Food N: Cracker Barrel, Denny's, Olive Garden, TGI Friday
	S: Boston Market, Indian Rest, Panera Bread, Pizza Hut
	Lodg N: AmericInn, Baymont Inn, Comfort Inn, Super 8
	S: Inn on the Farm
	Other S: Target, Best Buy, Tires
35A	Dupont Ave, MN 100, Robbinsdale
(35B)	Jct I-94E, Downtown Minneapolis
(225/35C)	I-694E, MN 252N, to MN 610 (WB)
	NOTE: I-94 runs above with I-694. Exit #'s follow I-694.
226	53rd Ave N, 49th Ave N
	Food S: DQ, Pizza
	Lodg S: Camden Motel
	Other S: Grocery
228	Dowling Ave N, Minneapolis
229	26th Ave N, CR 81, CR 66, Broadway Ave, Plymouth Ave (EB), CR 152, N Washington Ave (WB)
	Gas N: Holiday
	Food S: Subway, Taco Bell, Wendy's
	Other S: Grocery, Target, Walgreen's
230	W Broadway, N Plymouth, 4th St N, US 52, MN 55W, W Suburbs (EB) CR 40, Glenwood Ave, MN 55 (WB)
	NOTE: EB: HAZMAT Vehicles Prohibited thru Tunnel. MUST Use Exit #231A.
(231A)	Jct I-394, US 12W, Downtown Lyndale Ave, Hennepin Ave (EB), I-394, US 12W (WB)
231B	Hennepin Ave, Lyndale Ave (WB)
	NOTE: WB: HAZMAT Vehicles Prohibited thru Tunnel. MUST Use Exit #231B.
(233B)	Jct I-35W S, to S Suburbs, Albert Lea (EB, Left exit)
(233C)	Jct I-35W N, to NE Suburbs, Duluth (EB, Left exit)
233A	11th St, Downtown (WB)
234A	MN 55E, Hiawatha Ave
	Other S: to Minn St Paul Int'l Airport✈

◊ = Regular Gas Stations with Diesel ▲ = RV Friendly Locations ♥ = Pet Friendly Locations
RED PRINT SHOWS LARGE VEHICLE PARKING/ACCESS ON SITE OR NEARBY   BROWN PRINT SHOWS CAMPGROUNDS/RV PARKS

Interstate 94 W/E

EXIT	MINNESOTA
(233C)	Jct I-35W S, Albert Lea (WB, Left exit)
234B	5th St, Downtown (WB, diff reaccess)
234C	CR 152, Cedar Ave (WB)
235A	25th Ave, Riverside Ave
235B	Huron Blvd, University of MN
Med	N: + Hospital
Other	N: Univ of MN
236	MN 280, to I-35W N, University Ave
Med	N: + St Paul Veterans Center
237	Vandalia St, Cretin Ave N
FStop	N: Pro Stop Fuel (N to Cleveland Ave)
TServ	N: Kenworth
Other	N: AmTrak
238	MN 51, Snelling Ave, St Paul
Gas	S: Citgo
Food	N: Applebee's, Best Steak House, McDonald's, Perkins
Other	N: to Zoo, State Fairgrounds
239A	Hamline Ave (WB, No reaccess)
Food	N: Hardee's
Lodg	N: Sheraton
Med	N: + Hospital
Other	N: Grocery, Target
239B	CR 51, Lexington Pkwy, St Paul
Gas	N: BP, Super America
Food	N: Best Steak House, DQ, Hardee's, KFC, Pizza Hut, White Castle
Med	N: + Hospital
240	CR 53, Dale St
Other	S: St Paul College
241A	CR 56, 12th St, Marion St, Kellogg Blvd, to (EB) I-35E, State Capitol
Other	N: State Capitol, Vietnam Memorial
241B	5th St, 10th St W, St Paul (EB)
(241C)	Jct I-35E S, to Albert Lea (WB) NOTE: NO Trucks over 9000# GVW
(242B)	Jct I-35E N, US 10W (EB, Left exit)
242A	12th St, State Capitol (WB)
Med	N: + Regions Hospital S: + St Joseph's Hospital
(242B)	Jct I-35E N, US 10W (WB)
242C	7th Ave, MN 5 (EB, Exit only)
242D	US 52S, MN 3, 6th St, Downtown St Paul (fr WB, Left exit)
243	US 61, Mounds Blvd, Kellogg Blvd (fr EB, Left Exit, diff reacc)
Other	N: Metropolitan State Univ S: St Paul Downtown Holman Field
244	US 10E, US 61S, Hastings, Prescott
245	R 65, White Bear Ave, St Paul
Gas	N: Super America S: BP
Food	N: Embers, Hardee's, Pizza Hut, Subway S: Arby's, Bakers Square, Burger King, Davanni's Pizza, Ground Round, KFC, McDonald's, Perkins, Taco Bell
Lodg	N: Excel Inn, Travelodge
Other	S: Auto Dealer, Firestone, Target, Pharmacy
246A	Ruth St (EB, No reacc)
246BC	CR 68, McKnight Rd
Lodg	S: Holiday Inn
Other	N: 3M, Petland♥

Personal Notes

EXIT	MINNESOTA
247	MN 120, Century Ave, St Paul
Gas	S: Super America
Food	N: Denny's, Toby's Rest S: McDonald's
Lodg	N: Super 8 S: Country Inn
(249AB)	Jct I-694, Jct I-494
I-494S:	to Mall of America, Minn St Paul Intl Airport✈
I-694N:	to Twin Cities North ByPass, St Cloud
250	CR 13, Radio Dr, Inwood Ave, Lake Elmo, Woodbury
Gas	S: Holiday Station Store
Food	S: Blimpie, Don Pablo, India Palace, Machine Shed, Quiznos, Starbucks, Sushi Tango, Taco Bell, TGI Friday, Wendy's
Lodg	N: Hilton Garden Inn, Wildwood Lodge
Med	S: + Health Partners Clinic
Other	N: Auto Repairs, Best Buy, Lake Elmo Reg'l Park▲ S: ATMs, Animal Hospital♥, Auto Service, Borders, Circuit City, CompUSA, Home Depot, Grocery, Office Max, PetSmart♥, Tires Plus
251	CR 19, Woodbury Dr, Keats Ave
Gas	S: Kwik Trip, Super America◆
Food	S: Applebee's, Arby's, Burger King, Chili's, Chipotle Mex Grill, Outback Steakhouse, Food Court/Horizon Outlet Ctr
Lodg	S: Extended Stay America, Holiday Inn Express
Other	N: Lake Elmo Reg'l Park▲ S: Auto Repairs, Gander Mountain, Horizon Outlet Center, Sam's Club, Tires, Wal-Mart, to St Paul East RV Park▲

EXIT	MN / WI
253	MN 95S, CR 15, Manning Ave, Lake Elmo, St Paul, Hastings
Other	N: Lake Elmo Airport✈ S: to Afton State Park▲, St Croix Bluff's Reg'l Park▲
(254)	Weigh Station (WB)
(256)	MN Welcome Center (WB) (RR, Phones, Vend, Picnic, Info)
258	MN 95N, CR 18, St Croix Trail, Lakeland, Afton, Stillwater
Other	S: Afton State Park, Afton Alps Ski Area
NOTE:	MM 259: Wisconsin State Line

(CENTRAL TIME ZONE)
⬆ MINNESOTA
⬇ WISCONSIN
(CENTRAL TIME ZONE)

1	WI 35N, 2nd St S, Hudson
Gas	N: Auto Stop Gas, Freedom Valu Ctr◆, Holiday Station Store, Mike's Standard
Food	N: Corby's, DQ, Dragon Pearl, Subway
Lodg	N: Dibbo Hotel, Grapevine Inn B&B, Phipps Inn S: Best Western, Comfort Inn♥, Super 8
Med	N: + Hudson Hospital
Other	N: Rick's Auto Service, to Willow River State Park▲ S: Hudson Cinema 9, Kmart
2	CR F, Carmichael Rd, Hudson
S:	WI Welcome Center (EB) Hudson Rest Area (WB) (RR, Phone, Picnic, Vend, Info)
Gas	N: BP, Holiday S: Kwik Trip, Freedom Valu◆
Food	N: Applebee's, Cousins Subs, KFC S: Arby's, Burger King, Country Kitchen, Denny's, Kingdom Buffet, McDonald's, Taco Bell, Wendy's
Lodg	N: Best Value Inn♥, Royal Inn S: Best Western, Comfort Inn♥, Fairfield Inn, Holiday Inn Express
Med	S: + Hudson Memorial Hospital
Other	N: Auto Dealers, Grocery, Pharmacy, Target S: Auto Dealers, Checker Auto Parts, Grocery, Home Depot, Kmart, Pharmacy, Tires Plus, Wal-Mart
3	WI 35S, Hudson, River Falls
Lodg	S: Stageline Inn
Other	S: to Univ of WI/River Falls
4	US 12, CR U, 60th St, Hudson, Burkhardt, Somerset
TStop	N: Travel Center of America #192/Mobil (Scales)
Gas	N: Mr Convenience/Citgo◆
Food	N: Rest/TA TC, Jr Ranch Bar & Grill
Lodg	N: Best Value Inn
TServ	N: TA TC/Tires
Other	N: Laundry/WiFi/TA TC, to Willow River State Park▲, Float Rite Park
(8)	Weigh Station (EB)
10	WI 65, Roberts, River Falls, New Richmond,
Other	N: to Rivers Edge Tubing, Camping, Rest S: to Univ of WI/River Falls

◆ = Regular Gas Stations with Diesel   ▲ = RV Friendly Locations   ♥ = Pet Friendly Locations

RED PRINT SHOWS LARGE VEHICLE PARKING/ACCESS ON SITE OR NEARBY   BROWN PRINT SHOWS CAMPGROUNDS/RV PARKS

Interstate 94 W/E

EXIT	WISCONSIN
16	CR T, Baldwin, Hammonds
Gas	N: AmocoBP
Lodg	N: Hammond Hotel
19	US 63, Baldwin, Ellsworth
TStop	S: Ray's Super Truck Stop/Citgo
Gas	N: Freedom Valu◆, Kwik Trip #747/BP◆
Food	N: A&W, DQ, Hardee's, McDonald's, Subway/KT
	S: Rest/Ray's SS, Coachman Supper Club
Lodg	N: AmericInn
	S: Super 8
Med	N: + Baldwin Area Medical Center
Other	S: LP/Ray's Super TS
24	CR B, Woodville, Spring Valley
Gas	N: Stop-A-Sec/Mobil
Food	N: Woodville Cafe
Lodg	N: Woodville Motel
28	WI 128, Wilson, Glenwood City, Spring Valley, Elmwood
TStop	S: Kwik Trip #603/BP
Food	S: Rest/KT
32	CR Q, to Knapp
41	WI 25, N Broadway St, to US 12, Menomonie, Barron, Wheeler (WB)
Gas	N: Cenex
	S: Holiday Station Store, SA/Speedway◆
Food	N: Applebee's, China Buffet, Old 400 Depot Café, Quiznos
	S: Arby's, Country Kitchen, Green Mill Rest, KFC, Kernel Rest, McDonald's, Perkins, Pizza Hut, Taco Bell, Wendy's
Lodg	S: AmericInn, Country Inn♥, Motel 6♥, Super 8♥
Other	N: Auto Repair Dollar Tree, Grocery, Radio Shack, Wal-Mart sc, to Skyport Airport✈, Twin Springs Resort Campground▲
	S: Auto Repair, Advance Auto, Auto Dealers, Grocery, Kmart, O'Reilly Auto Parts, Walgreen's
(43)	Menomonie Rest Area (Both dir) (RR, Phone, Picnic, Vend, Info, Weather)
45	CR B, Menomonie
TStop	N: Exit 45 Auto Truck Plaza/Cenex (Scales)
	S: Kwik Trip #674/BP (Scales)
Food	N: Rest/Ex 45 ATP
	S: Subway/KT, Country Kitchen
Lodg	S: Comfort Inn
TServ	S: Kenworth, International
Other	N: LP/Ex 45 ATP
	S: Laundry/KT, Aok RV Sales & Service, Menomonie Muni Airport/Score Field✈, Univ of WI

EXIT	WISCONSIN
(48.3)	Weigh Station (WB)
52	US 12, WI 29, WI 40, Elk Mound, Chippewa Falls, Colfax, Green Bay
59	Partridge Rd, CR EE, to US 12, WI 312E, Eau Claire, Elk Mound
TStop	N: Mega Express #1/BP, Holiday Station Store #16 (Scales)
Food	N: Burger King/Mega Expr, Subway/Holiday Anderson's Grill & Bar, Embers Rest, McDonald's, Peppermill Rest
Lodg	N: AmericInn♥, Days Inn, Super 8
TServ	N: Peterbilt, Eau Claire Diesel Service, Badger Truck Refrigeration, River States Truck & Trailer
	S: Eau Claire Truck & Trailer, Fabco Engine Systems
Med	N: + Hospital
Other	N: LP/Mega Express, Interstate Auto & Towing, Golf Course, U-Haul, Chippewa Valley Reg'l Airport✈
65	WI 37, WI 85, to US 12, Eau Claire, Mondovi (Addt'l serv N to US 12)
Gas	N: Exxon
Food	N: Arby's, A&W, China Buffet, Green Mill Rest/Hol Inn, Godfather's Pizza, Hardee's, McDonald's, Red Lobster, Taco Bell, Wendy's
Lodg	N: Best Western♥, Comfort Inn♥, Days Inn♥, Hampton Inn, Highlander Inn, Holiday Inn, Super 8
Med	N: + Sacred Heart Hospital
Other	N: Univ of WI/Eau Claire, to Ferry St: Eau Claire Wastewater Plant/RVDump
	S: Tires
68	WI 93, to US 53, US 12, Eau Claire, to Eleva, Altoona
Gas	N: BP, Holiday Station, KwikTrip
Food	N: Burger King, DQ, Quiznos, Red Robin
Lodg	N: Econo Lodge♥
Other	N: Auto Dealers, Goodyear, to Oakwood Mall/Cinema
	S: Auto Dealers, US RV Supercenter
70AB	US 53, S Hastings Way, Eau Claire, Chippewa Falls, Altoona
Gas	N: Conoco◆, Handy Mart, Holiday, KwikTrip
Food	N: Applebee's, Buffalo Wild Wings, Fazoli's, McDonald's, Olive Garden, Panera Bread, Starbucks, TGI Friday, Timber Lodge Steakhouse
Lodg	N: Country Inn♥, Grand Stay Residential Suites, Heartland Inn♥

EXIT	WISCONSIN
Other	N: ATMs, Banks, Auto Services, Best Buy, Borders, Gander Mountain, Grocery, Office Depot, PetCo♥, Pharmacy, Sam's Club, Target, Tires, Wal-Mart sc, Oakwood Mall, Cinema, 50/50 Factory Outlet
81	CR HH, to US 53, to CR KK, Strum, Foster, Fall Creek, Augusta
88	US 10, 10th St, to US 53, to CR R, Osseo, Fairchild, Strum, Augusta
FStop	N: Direct Travel Center/Mobil
	S: SA/Speedway #4523
TStop	N: AmBest/Golden Express Travel Plaza (Scales)
Gas	S: Kwik Trip
Food	N: ElderberryRest/Golden Express TP, DQ, Hardee's
	S: Hardee's, McDonald's, Moe's Diner, Subway, Taco John's
Lodg	N: Ten Seven Inn, Super 8
	S: Red Carpet Inn♥
TServ	N: Golden Express TP/Tires
Med	S: + Osseo Area Medical Center
Other	N: Laundry/Golden Express TP, Stoney Creek RV Resort & Campground▲
98	WI 121, CR FF, Hixton, Northfield, Alma Center, Pigeon Falls
Gas	S: Farmers Co-Op/Cenex◆
Food	N: York's Last Resort
	S: Jackie's Inn Bar & Grill
105	WI 95, CR FF, Hixton, Alma Center, Taylor
TStop	S: Hixton Travel Plaza
Gas	S: Cenex◆, Citgo
Food	S: Rest/Hixton TP, Hixton Café
Lodg	N: Motel 95 & Campground▲
Other	N: Hixton/Alma Center KOA▲
	S: Laundry/LP/Hixton TP
115	US 12, WI 27, Black River Falls, Merrillan, Melrose
Gas	S: I-94 Mobil Express, Holiday◆
Food	S: Hardee's, KFC, Sunrise Inn Family Rest, Subway
Lodg	N: River Crest Resort
	S: E & F Motel
Med	S: + Black River Memorial Hospital
Other	S: Goods Times RV, Auto & Trailer
116	WI 54, Main St, to WI 27, Black River Falls, Wisconsin Rapids
FStop	N: Black River Crossing Oasis/BP
TStop	S: Kwik Trip #648, Flying J Travel Plaza #5010 (Scales)
Food	N: Perkins, Subway, Taco John's
	S: Rest/FJ TP, Burger King, McDonald's, Oriental Kitchen

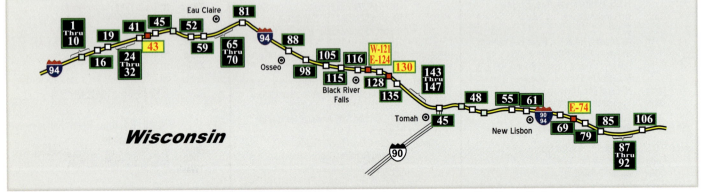

◆ = Regular Gas Stations with Diesel   ▲ = RV Friendly Locations   ♥ = Pet Friendly Locations
RED PRINT SHOWS LARGE VEHICLE PARKING/ACCESS ON SITE OR NEARBY   BROWN PRINT SHOWS CAMPGROUNDS/RV PARKS

EXIT		WISCONSIN
	Lodg	N: Best Western ♥, Holiday Inn, Majestic Pines Hotel & Casino, Super 8
		S: Days Inn
	TWash	S: FJ TP
	TServ	S: FJ TP/Tires
	Med	S: + Black River Falls Hospital
	Other	N: RVDump/LP/Blk River Oasis Crossing, Parkland Village Campground▲
		S: Laundry/KT, Laundry/WiFi/RVDump/ LP/FJ TP, Wal-Mart sc, Hwy 54 Towing & Repair, Black River Falls Area Airport✈
(121)		Black River Falls Rest Area (WB) (RR, Phone, Picnic, Vend, Info, Weather)
(124)		Millston Rest Area (EB) (RR, Phone, Picnic, Vend, Info, Weather)
128		CR O, Mill St, Black River Falls, Millston, Warrens
(130)		Rest Area (Both dir) (RR, Phones, Picnic, Vend)
135		CR EW, Warrens
	Gas	N: Citgo
	Other	N: Jellystone Park Camp Resort▲
143		US 12, N Superior Ave, Tomah (EB) WI 21, Eaton Ave, Necedah (WB)
	TStop	S: Kwik Trip #796/BP (Scales)
	Gas	N: Mobil◊
		S: Mobil, Shell◊, Murphy's◊
	Food	N: Long John Silver, Perkins, Rest/Spr8
		S: Rest/KT, Culver's, Ground Round, KFC, McDonald's, Subway, Taco Bell
	Lodg	N: AmericInn, Holiday Inn ♥, Microtel, Super 8 ♥
		S: Motel/KT, Cranberry Country Lodge ♥, Comfort Inn, Econo Lodge ♥
	Med	S: + Tomah Memorial Hospital, + VA Hospital
	Other	N: Humbird Cheese Mart, Whispering Pines Campground▲
		S: Laundry/WiFi/RVDump/KwikTrip, Advance Auto, Dollar Tree, U-Haul, Wal-Mart sc, to Ft McCoy Military Res
145		Industrial Ave
	NOTE:	I-94 runs with I-90 below for 93 mi. Exit #'s follow I-90.
(147)		Jct I-90W, to La Crosse I-90/94E, Wisconsin Dells, Madison
(45A)		Jct I-94W, Twin Cities (EB Left exit)
(45B)		Jct I-90/94E, Wisconsin Dells, Madison (EB), I-90W La Crosse, I-94W St Paul (WB)
(47.5)		Weigh Station (WB)
48		CR PP, Tomah, Oakdale
	TStop	N: Road Ranger #209/Citgo (Scales)
	Food	N: Rest/Road Ranger
	Other	N: Laundry/RoadRanger, Oakdale KOA▲
(51)		Weigh Station (EB)
55		CR C, CR H, US 12, WI 16, Camp Douglas, Volk Field
	TStop	S: Camp Douglas BP
	Gas	S: Mobil◊
	Food	S: Subway/Mobil
	Lodg	S: Walsh's K&K Motel, Travelers Rest
	TServ	S: CL Chase Truck Service

EXIT		WISCONSIN
	Other	N: Mill Bluff State Park, Camp Williams Military Res
		S: Laundry/Camp Douglas BP
61		WI 80, CR A, New Lisbon, Necedah
	TStop	N: New Lisbon Travel Center/Citgo, The Bunk House/Mobil
	Food	N: Rest/Bunk House
	Lodg	N: Motel/Bunk House
	Other	N: Laundry/RVDump/New Lisbon TC, Laundry/RVDump/Bunk House, to Buckhorn State Park, Ken's Marina & Campground▲
		S: Mauston New Lisbon Union Airport✈
69		WI 82, Mauston, Necedah
	TStop	N: Pilot Travel Center #164 (Scales) Citgo Travel Plaza
		S: Kwik Trip #775/BP (Scales)
	Gas	N: Shell
		S: Citgo◊
	Food	N: Wendy's, Pilot TC, FastFood/Citgo TP, Country Kitchen
		S: Rest/KwikTrip, McDonald's, Pizza Hut, Roman Castle Rest
	Lodg	N: Best Western, Country Inn, Super 8
		S: The Alaskan Motel
	Med	S: + Hospital
	Other	N: Laundry/WiFi/Pilot TC
		S: Laundry/RVDump/KT, Mauston New Lisbon Union Airport✈, Auto Dealers, Walgreen's, Wal-Mart
(74)		Rest Area (EB) (RR, Phone, Picnic, Vend)
(75)		Rest Area (WB) (RR, Phone, Picnic, Vend)

EXIT		WISCONSIN
79		WI HH, Rock St, Lyndon Station
	TStop	S: Lyndon Station BP
	Food	S: FastFood/Lyndon Station
85		US 12, WI 16, Wisconsin Dells
	Lodg	S: Days End Motel
	TServ	S: Rocky Arbor Truck & Trailer Repair
	Other	N: Rocky Arbor State Park, Sherwood Forest Camping & RV Park▲
		S: Bass Lake Campground▲, Crockett Resort Camping & RV▲, Arrowhead Resort Campground▲, Dells Timberland Camping Resort▲, Wisconsin Dells KOA▲, Edge O'Dells Camping & RV Resort▲
87		WI 13N, Wisconsin Dells, to WI 23E, Briggsville
	FStop	N: Interstate BP
	Gas	N: Citgo◊, Mobil◊, Shell
	Food	N: Burger King, Country Kitchen, Pedros, Denny's, Perkins, Rococo's Pizza, Taco Bell, Wendy's
	Lodg	N: Best Western, Comfort Inn, Days Inn, Holiday Inn, Howard Johnson, Super 8
	Other	N: RVDump/Interstate BP, Amtrak, Christmas Mountain Village & Ski Area, American World Resort & RV Park▲, Sherwood Forest Camping & RV Park▲, Erickson's Tepee Park Campground▲, Wisconsin Dells KOA▲
89		WI 23, Lake Delton, Reedsburg
	Gas	N: Mobil◊
	Food	N: Howie's, Internet Cafe
	Lodg	N: Country Squire Inn, Grand Marquis Inn, Hilton Garden Inn, Sandman Inn
	Other	S: Home Depot, Wal-Mart sc, Mirror Lake State Park, Country Roads RV Park▲
92		US 12, Baraboo, Lake Delton
	Gas	N: BP◊, Cenex◊, Citgo◊, Mobil◊, Sinclair
	Food	N: Cracker Barrel, Damon's, Denny's, McDonald's, Subway/Sinclair
	Lodg	N: AmericInn, Camelot Inn, Del Rancho, Grand Marquis Inn, Ramada Ltd
		S: Travelodge
	Med	S: + Hospital (7mi S)
	Other	N: WI Cheese Museum
		S: Wisconsin Opry, Baraboo Wisconsin Dells Airport✈, Fox Hill RV Park & Campground▲, Yogi Bear's Jellystone Park, Dell Boo Campground▲, Mirror Lake State Park
106		WI 33, Portage, Baraboo
	FStop	N: Lake Morgaune Mobil
	Gas	S: BP
	Lodg	S: Cascade Mountain Motel
	Med	N: + Hospital
	Other	M: Portage Muni Airport✈
		S: Cascade Mountain Ski Area, Sky High Camping Resort▲, Devil's Lake State Park
	NOTE:	I-94 continues EB with I-90 & I-39. Exit #'s follow I-90.
108A		WI 78S, to US 51N, Wausau, Merrimac
	TStop	S: Petro Stopping Center #53 (Scales)
	Gas	S: Phillips 66
	Food	S: Subway/Petro SC, Little Caesars
	Lodg	S: Comfort Suites, Days Inn
	TWash	S: Blue Beacon TW/Petro SC

◊ = Regular Gas Stations with Diesel   ▲ = RV Friendly Locations   ♥ = Pet Friendly Locations

RED PRINT SHOWS LARGE VEHICLE PARKING/ACCESS ON SITE OR NEARBY   BROWN PRINT SHOWS CAMPGROUNDS/RV PARKS

Page 491

INTERSTATE 94 W-E

EXIT	WISCONSIN
TServ	S: Petro SC/Tires
Other	N: Laundry/WiFi/Petro SC, Devil's Lake State Park
(108B)	Jct I-39N, to Wausau, Merrimac, Portage
Med	N: + Hospital
Other	N: to WI Dells, Portage Muni Airport →
(113)	Rest Area (Both dir) (RR, Phone, Picnic, Vend, RVDump)
115	CR CS/J, Poynette, Lake Wisconsin
FStop	N: North Point Plaza/BP
Food	N: McDonald's, Subway
119	WI 60, Arlington, Lodi
Gas	S: Mobil◇
Food	S: Rococo's Pizza
Lodg	S: Best Western
Other	S: Interstate RV Center
126	CR V, De Forest, Dane
Gas	N: BP, Phillips 66◇
	S: Citgo, Exxon◇
Food	N: Arby's, Burger King, Culver's Rest, McDonald's, Subway
Lodg	N: Holiday Inn Express
131	WI 19, Waunakee, Sun Prairie
Gas	N: Mobil, KwikTrip, Speedway◇
Food	N: McDonald's, Taco Bell/Speedway
Lodg	N: Days Inn, Super 8
	S: Country Inn Suites
TWash	N: Windsor Truck Wash
TServ	N: Kenworth
Other	N: Walgreen's
132	US 51, Madison, De Forest
TStop	N: Hwy 51 Citgo, PTP/Truckers Inn #1/Shell (Scales)
	S: Travel Center of America #50/Mobil (Scales)
Food	N: Rest/Hwy 51, Rest/Truckers Inn
	S: CountryPride/Subway/TacoBell/TA TC
TWash	N: Truckers Inn
TServ	N: Truckers Inn/Tires, Peterbilt of WI, Volvo/White/GMC/Freightliner
	S: TA TC/Tires, Brad Ragan Truck, Auto & RV Tire Service
Other	N: Laundry/Hwy 51, Laundry/BarbSh CB/Truckers Inn
	S: Laundry/WiFi/TA TC, WI RV World, Camperland RV
135A	US 151S, Washington Ave, Madison
Gas	S: BP, Shell, Sinclair
Food	S: Applebee's, Chili's, Country Kitchen, Cracker Barrel, Denny's, Dunkin Donuts, Hardee's, IHOP, KFC, McDonald's, Mtn Jack's Steakhouse, Olive Garden, Perkins, Ponderosa, Red Lobster, Tumbleweed Grill, Steak 'n Shake, Wendy's

EXIT	WISCONSIN
Lodg	S: Best Western, Comfort Inn, Fairfield Inn, Econo Lodge, Hampton Inn, Holiday Inn, Madison Suites, Microtel, Motel 6♥, Residence Inn, Select Inn
Other	S: Best Buy, Kmart, Mall, WI State Hwy Patrol Post, Dane Co Reg'l Airport →
135B	US 151N, Washington Ave
135C	High Crossing Blvd (WB)
Lodg	N: Courtyard, Staybridge Suites
	S: East Town Suites, Microtel
(138A)	Jct I-94E, Milwaukee (EB, Left exit)
138B/240	WI 30W, to Madison (WB, Left exit)
NOTE:	I-94 runs with I-90 above for 93 mi. Exit #'s follow I-90.
244	CR N, Sun Prairie, Cottage Grove, Sun Prairie
Gas	S: Stop 'n Go
Food	S: Blimpie, Black Bear Inn, McDonald's, Papa Jimmy's Pizzeria, Village Inn
Lodg	S: Shortstop Inn
Other	N: Madison KOA▲
250	WI 73, Deerfield, Marshall
259	WI 89, CR V, CR G, Lake Mills, Marshall, Waterloo
FStop	S: Kwip Trip #306
TStop	N: Lake Oasis Travel Plaza/Citgo (Scales)
Gas	S: BP◇, Roman's Quick Stop/Mobil
Food	N: Rest/Lake Oasis TP
	S: McDonald's, Pizza Pit, Subway
Lodg	N: Rodeway Inn
	S: Bade's Resort, Fargo Mansion Inn B&B, Pyramid Motel
TWash	N: Lake Oasis TP
TServ	N: Lake Oasis TP/Tires
Other	N: Laundry/Lake Oasis TP
	S: to Pilgrims Campground▲
(261)	Lake Mills Rest Area (EB) (next RA 86 mi) (RR, Phone, Picnic, Vend, Info, Weather)
(263)	Johnson Creek Rest Area (WB) (RR, Phone, Picnic, Vend, Info, Weather)
267	N Watertown St, WI 26, Frontage St, Johnson Creek, Watertown
TStop	N: Pine Cone Travel Plaza/Shell (Scales)
Gas	N: BP◇
	S: Citgo
Food	N: Rest/Pine Cone TP, Arby's, 2 Loons Café, McDonald's,
	S: A&W, Culver's, KFC/Citgo, Subway
Lodg	N: Comfort Inn, Days Inn♥
TServ	N: J & L Tire

EXIT	WISCONSIN
Med	N: + Watertown Memorial Hospital
Other	N: Laundry/Pine Cone TP, Goodyear, Watertown Muni Airport →
	S: to Fort Atkinson, Ft Atkinson Muni Airport →
275	CR F, CR B, Oconomowoc, Concord Sullivan, Ixonia
Gas	N: Concord Gen'l Store/BP◇
AServ	S: Gesell's Auto Service
277	Willow Glen Rd, to CR B, to CR Dr (EB exit, WB reaccess)
282	WI 67, Summit Ave, to CR B, CR Dr, Oconomowoc, Dousman
Gas	N: Mobil, SA/Speedway
Lodg	N: Hilton Garden Inn, Olympia Resort & Spa
Med	N: + Hospital
Other	N: Kmart, Pharmacy, Target
283	CR P, N Sawyer Rd (WB, Exit only)
285	CR C, Genesee St, Delafield
Gas	N: Mobil
Food	N: Andrews Rest, Loaf & Jug Rest
Lodg	N: Delafield Hotel♥
287	WI 83, Delafield, Hartland, Wales
Gas	S: BP
Food	N: Applebee's, Hardee's, McDonald's, Perkins, Starbucks
	S: Burger King, DQ, Subway
Lodg	N: Country Pride Inn, Holiday Inn Express
	S: La Quinta Inn♥
Other	N: Golf Course, Golf Course, Best Buy, Walgreen's
	S: Grocery, Home Depot, Pharmacy, PetCo♥, Target, Tires Plus, Wal-Mart
290	CR SS, Prospect Ave, Pewaukee
291	CR G, Meadowbrook Rd, Pewaukee
Gas	S: BP
Food	N: Rest/Country Inn
Lodg	N: Country Inn
293AB	CR T, Waukesha, Pewakee (EB)
Gas	S: Mobil
Food	S: Denny's, Hardee's, McDonald's, Mr Wok, Peking House, Rocky Rococo, Taco Amigo, Wendy's
Lodg	N: Country Inn
	S: Best Western
TServ	S: Peterbilt of WI
Other	N: GE Medical Systems
	S: ATM's, Firestone, Grocery, Office Depot, Radio Shack, Walgreen's, Waukesha Co Fairgrounds, Waukesha Co Airport →
293	CR T, Grandview Blvd, Waukesha Pewaukee (WB)

◇ = Regular Gas Stations with Diesel   ▲ = RV Friendly Locations   ♥ = Pet Friendly Locations
RED PRINT SHOWS LARGE VEHICLE PARKING/ACCESS ON SITE OR NEARBY   BROWN PRINT SHOWS CAMPGROUNDS/RV PARKS

W 94 E — WISCONSIN

EXIT	WISCONSIN
293C	WI 16, Waukesha, Pewaukee, Oconomowoc (WB)
Other	N: GE Medical Systems, to UPS Store
294	CR J S, WI 164N, Pewaukee Rd, Pewaukee, Waukesha
Gas	N: Mobil
Food	N: WI Machine Shed Rest S: Taste of Italy
Lodg	N: Comfort Suites
TServ	S: Peterbilt of WI
295	WI F, WI 164, CR F, Waukesha, Sussex
FStop	N: Kwik Trip #396 S: Hopson Oil/66
Med	N: + Aurora Health Center S: + Hospital
297	US 18, WI 164S, CR JJ, Barker Rd, Waukesha, Blue Mound Rd, Barker
Gas	N: BP, Mobil
Food	N: Applebee's, Burger King, Chuck E Cheese, KFC, McDonald's, Meltin Pot, Olive Garden, Perkins, Starbucks, Subway, Tony Roma's, Zorba's Greek, Wendy's S: Arby's, Cousin's, Famous Dave's BBQ, McDonald's, Taco Bell, Dunkin Donuts
Lodg	N: Baymont Inn, Comfort Inn, Fairfield Inn, Motel 6 ♥ S: Holiday Inn, Select Inn, Super 8
Other	N: ATMs, Advance Auto, Best Buy, CompUSA, Grocery, Kmart S: WI State Hwy Patrol, Auto Dealers, Firestone, Home Depot, Sam's Club, Target, Tires Plus, Walgreen's
301AB	Moorland Rd, Brookfield (EB)
Gas	N: BP, Mobil S: Mobil
Food	N: Fuddrucker's, McDonald's, Pizza Uno, Rocky Rococo, Wong's Wok S: Outback Steakhouse
Lodg	N: Courtyard, Marriott, Sheraton S: Country Inn, Embassy Suites, Midway Hotel, Residence Inn
Other	N: B&N, Circuit City, Firestone, Goodyear, Office Depot, PetCo ♥, Walgreen's, Mall S: Walgreen's
301A	Moorland Rd S, New Berlin (WB)
301B	Moorland Rd N, Brookfield (WB)
304AB	WI 100, S 108th St, Milwaukee (EB)
Gas	N: Citgo, Shell◊ S: Phillips 66, Speedway◊
Food	N: McDonald's, Pizza Hut, Qdoba Mex Rest, Starbucks, Taco Bell S: Dunkin Donuts, Steakhouse 100, Wendy's
Lodg	N: Best Western, Exel Inn, Westwood Inn
TServ	S: Central WhiteGMC
Other	N: to Milwaukee Co Zoo, Oceans of Fun S: Auto Dealers, Auto Services, U-Haul
304B	WI 100N, Milwaukee (WB)
304A	WI 100S, Milwaukee (WB)
305B	US 45N, Fond du Lac, Appleton
(305A)	Jct I-894E, US 45S, to Chicago
306	WI 181, 84th St, Milwaukee
Med	N: + Hospital
Other	S: Pettit National Ice Center, WI State Fairgrounds▲ /RVDump
307A	68th St, 70th St

Personal Notes

EXIT	WISCONSIN
307B	Hawley Rd, Milwaukee
308A	VA Center, Milwaukee County Stadium, Mitchell Blvd (Left exit)
308B	Miller Park Way
Other	Milwaukee Co Stadium, Miller Park
308C	US 41N, Lisbon Ave, Milwaukee
Other	N: to Washington Park Zoo
309A	35th St, Milwaukee
Gas	N: SA/Speedway
309B	26th St, St. Paul Ave (EB) 25th St, 2nd St, Clybourn St (WB)
Other	N: Pabst Mansion, Marquette Univ
Med	N: + Aurora Sinai Medical Center, + Milwaukee Hospital
Other	N: Marquette Univ
NOTE:	I-94 below runs with I-43. Exit numbers follow I-94.
310A	13th St, N Ember Lane (EB)
(310B)	Jct I-43N, to Green Bay
(310C)	Jct I-794E, Downtown Milwaukee
311	WI 59, National Ave, 6th St
312A	Lapham Blvd, Mitchell St (EB)
312B	Becher St, Lincoln Ave (EB)
312AB	Becher St, Mitchell St, Lapham Blvd, Greenfield Ave (WB)
314A	Holt Ave (EB)
314B	Howard Ave (EB)

EXIT	WISCONSIN
314AB	Howard Ave, Holt Ave (WB)
(316)	I-43, I-894 (EB) I-894W, I-43S, I-894 ByPass, Beloit (WB, Left exit)
NOTE:	I-94 above runs below with I-43. Exit numbers follow I-94.
317	Layton Ave, Milwaukee
Gas	E: Clark
Food	E: Prime Quarter Steakhouse W: Big City Pizza, Howard Johnson
Lodg	E: Holiday Inn W: Howard Johnson
318	WI 119, Airport, Mitchell Field
Other	E: Amtrak, Gen'l Mitchell Int'l Airport✈
319	College Ave, CR ZZ, Milwaukee
Gas	E: SA Speedway, Shell W: BP, Citgo
Food	E: McDonald's, Perkins W: Boy Blue French Cuisine
Lodg	E: Country Inn, Econo Lodge, Exel Inn, Hampton Inn, Ramada Inn, Red Roof Inn ♥
Other	E: Penske W: Grocery, Laundromat
320	CR BB, Rawson Ave, Oak Creek, Milwaukee
Gas	E: BP, Mobil
Food	E: Burger King
Lodg	E: La Quinta Inn ♥ W: Park Motel
Other	E: Cinema
322	WI 100, Ryan Rd, Oak Creek
TStop	W: Flying J Travel Plaza #5124 (Scales), Pilot Travel Center #40 (Scales)
Gas	W: Shell◊
Food	E: McDonald's, Perkins, Wendy's W: CountryMarket/FastFood/FJ TP, Subway/Pilot TC, Arby's, Country Kitchen, Starbucks
Lodg	W: Travelers Motel, Sunrise Motel, Value Inn
TWash	W: Blue Beacon TW/Pilot TC
TServ	E: Cummins Truck Service W: Freightliner, Kenworth
Other	W: Laundry/WiFi/RVDump/LP/FJ TP, WiFi/Pilot TC
325	US 41N, 27th St, Oak Creek, Franklin, Racine (WB ex, EB entr)
326	Seven Mile Rd, Caledonia
Gas	E: BP W: Mobil
Lodg	E: Hi View Motel, Seven Mile Motel
Other	E: Yogi Bear's Jellystone Park▲
327	CR G, Caledonia
Other	W: U-Haul
(327.3)	Weigh Station (EB)
329	CR K, Northwestern Ave, Racine, Thompsonville, Franksville
TStop	E: Pilot Travel Center #324 (Scales)
Gas	N: Mobil, Phillips 66
Food	E: Arby's/TJCinn/Pilot TC
Lodg	E: Days Inn
TServ	W: D&D Truck Repair, Racine Truck Sales & Equipment
Other	E: Laundry/WiFi/Pilot TC, Greyhound Racetrack W: to Happy Acres Kampground▲

◊ = Regular Gas Stations with Diesel   ▲ = RV Friendly Locations   ♥ = Pet Friendly Locations
RED PRINT SHOWS LARGE VEHICLE PARKING/ACCESS ON SITE OR NEARBY   BROWN PRINT SHOWS CAMPGROUNDS/RV PARKS

EXIT	WISCONSIN	EXIT	ILLINOIS	EXIT	ILLINOIS
333	WI 20, Washington Ave, Sturtevant, Racine, Waterford		**ILLINOIS** (CENTRAL TIME ZONE)	**29**	US 41, to Waukegan, Tri State Tollway (WB)
FStop	E: I-94/20 Shell Plaza, Kwik Trip #686	**1A**	CR 19, CR A1, Russell Rd, Zion	**30AB**	IL 68, Dundee Rd, Northbrook (WB, difficult reaccess)
TStop	W: Citgo Auto Truck Plaza, Petro Stopping Center #68/Mobil (Scales)	TStop	W: Travel Center of America #30 (Scales), Toor's Car & Truck Plaza/Citgo (Scales)	**31**	Tower Rd, Frontage Rd, Winnetka (EB)
Food	E: CousinsSubs/I-94/20 Shell, Burger King, McDonald's	Food	W: CountryPride/PizzaHut/TA TC, Rest/Toor's CTP	Other	S: Auto Dealers
	W: Wendy's/Citgo ATP, IronSkillet/Petro SC, Black Bear Bar & Grill, Culver's, Subway	TWash	W: TA TC	**33AB**	Willow Rd, Winnetka
		TServ	W: TA TC/Tires, Peterbilt	Gas	S: Shell
Lodg	E: Paul's Motel, Holiday Inn Express, Ramada Ltd	Other	W: Laundry/WiFi/RVDump/TA TC	Food	S: Starbucks
	W: Best Western, Comfort Inn	**1B**	US 41S, to Waukegan	**34A**	US 41S, Skokie Rd, Wilmette (EB)
TServ	W: Petro SC/Tires, Pomp's Tire Service, Lakeside International	Other	E: Sky Harbor RV Center	**34BC**	E Lake Ave, Wilmette (WB)
Other	W: Laundry/WiFi/Citgo ATP, Laundry/WiFi/RVDump/Petro SC	NOTE:	Begin EB / End WB TriState Tollway, Edens Expy Spur	Gas	N: BP S: BP, Shell
335	WI 11, Durand Ave, Sturtevant, to Racine, Burlington	**76**	IL 173, Rosecrans Rd, Wadsworth	Food	N: Panda Express, Starbucks
Gas	N: Kwik Trip	**(73.5)**	TOLL Plaza	**35**	Old Orchard Rd, Skokie
Lodg	S: Travelers Inn Motel & Campground▲	**70**	IL 132, Grand Ave, Gurnee, Waukegan	Gas	N: BP, Shell
Other	N: Amtrak Stations S: Sylvania Airport✈			Lodg	S: Hampton Inn
337	CR KR, 1st St, County Line Rd	Gas	E: Speedway◊ W: Mobil, Shell	Med	N: + Hospital
Other	E: to Sanders Park, Great Lakes Dragway	Food	E: Burger King, Cracker Barrel, IHOP, Joe's Crab Shack, McDonald's, Olive Garden, Outback Steakhouse, Subway	**37AB**	IL 58, Dempster St, Skokie
339	CR E, 12th St, Somers, Sturtevant			**39AB**	Touhy Ave, Skokie
FStop	N: Toor Petro/Marathon			Gas	N: BP◊, Shell S: Citgo, Mobil, Shell
340	WI 142, CR S, Burlington Rd, Kenosha, Burlington		W: Applebee's, Boston Market, Chili's, Denny's, Lone Star Steakhouse, Max & Erma's, McDonald's, Pizza Hut, Starbucks, Steak 'n Shake, TGI Friday, Taco Bell, Wendy's, White Castle	Food	S: Dunkin Donuts, Jack's, McDonald's
Gas	N: Mobil◊			Lodg	N: Radisson
Food	N: Wispride Cheese S: Mars Cheese Castle, Star Bar			Other	S: Auto Services
Lodg	S: Easter Day Motel	Lodg	E: Baymont Inn, Comfort Suites, Country Inn, Hampton Inn, La Quinta Inn♥	**41C**	IL 50, Cicero Ave, to US 41, to I-90, Lincolnwood (WB)
342	WI 158, Kenosha		W: Fairfield Inn, Holiday Inn	**41AB**	US 14, Caldwell Ave, Peterson Ave, Chicago
TServ	S: Kenosha Truck & Equipment	Other	E: to Six Flags W: Grocery, Home Depot, Pharmacy, Sam's Club, Target, Wal-Mart, Outlet Mall	**41C**	IL 50S, to I-90W (EB)
Other	N: Kenosha Reg'l Airport✈			**42**	W Foster Ave (WB)
344	WI 50, 75th St, Kenosha, Bristol, Salem, Lake Geneva			**43A**	Wilson Ave (WB)
Gas	N: Shell◊, Citgo◊ S: BP, Speedway	**68**	IL 21, Milwaukee Ave, Gurnee, Libertyville, Graysflack (EB)	**(43B)**	Jct I-90W (WB)
Food	N: Noodles & Co, Quiznos, Pizza Hut, Starbucks, Wendy's	Med	S: + Hospital	**43C**	Montrose Ave
	S: Arby's, Brat Stop, Chef's Table, Cracker Barrel, Denny's, KFC, Long John Silver, McDonald's, Perkins, Taco Bell, Wendy's	Other	S: to Six Flags	**43D**	Kostner Ave
		67	IL 120, Belvidere Rd, Gurnee (WB)	**44A**	IL 19, Keeler Ave
		64	IL 137, Buckley Rd, Lake Bluff	Gas	N: BP, Shell
		Med	E: + VA Medical Center	Other	N: Wrigley Field
Lodg	N: Baymont Inn, La Quinta Inn♥, Super 8	**62**	IL 176, Rockland Rd, Park Ave, Libertyville, Lake Bluff (WB)	**44B**	Pulaski Rd, Irving Park Rd
	S: Best Western, Comfort Suites, Days Inn, Value Inn♥	**(60)**	Lake Forest Oasis (Both dir)	Gas	N: BP, Mobil
Other	N: Best Buy, Gander Mountain, Walgreen's	FStop	Mobil	**45A**	Addison St (EB)
	S: Outlet Mall, Shopping	Food	Wendy's	**45B**	Kimball Ave
345	CR C, Wilmot Rd, Pleasant Prairie	**59**	IL 60, Townline Rd, Lake Forest	Gas	N: Marathon◊ S: Gas Depot, Marathon, Mobil
FStop	S: Kenosha Truck Stop/P66	**57**	IL 22, Half Day Rd, Deerfield	Food	S: Dunkin Donuts, Pizza Hut, Subway, Wendy's
E:	WI Welcome Center (WB) Kenosha Rest Area (EB) (RR, Phone, Picnic, Vend, Weather, WiFi)	**54**	Deerfield Rd, Deerfield (WB)	Other	S: Grocery, Walgreen's
		(53.5)	TOLL Plaza	**45C**	Kedzie Ave, Belmont Ave
347	WI 165, CR Q, 104th St, Lakeview Pkwy, Pleasant Prairie	**(53)**	Jct I-294S, to O'Hare Int'l Airport	**46A**	California Ave
		50	IL 43, Waukegan Rd, Northbrook (EB)	Gas	S: Mobil
Gas	N: BP◊	Gas	S: Amoco, Shell	Food	S: IHOP, Popeye's Chicken
Food	N: McDonald's	Food	N: Baha Fresh, Boston Market, China Palace, Hunan Garden, Kegon Japanese S: KFC	Other	N: Laundromat
Lodg	N: Radisson			**46B**	Diversey Ave
Other	N: Factory Outlet Center	Lodg	N: Red Roof Inn♥	**47A**	Western Ave, Fullerton Ave
(349.8)	Weigh Station (WB)	TServ	S: CVS Truck & Auto Repair	Gas	N: Citgo, Phillips 66, Costco S: Marathon
NOTE:	MM 350: Illinois State Line	Other	N: Best Buy, Home Depot	Food	N: Burger King, Dunkin Donuts, Popeye's, Subway
	(CENTRAL TIME ZONE)	NOTE:	Begin WB / End EB TriState Tollway, Edens Expy Spur	Other	N: Costco, Home Depot, Target
	WISCONSIN			**47B**	Damen Ave (WB)

◊ = Regular Gas Stations with Diesel   ▲ = RV Friendly Locations   ♥ = Pet Friendly Locations
RED PRINT SHOWS LARGE VEHICLE PARKING/ACCESS ON SITE OR NEARBY   BROWN PRINT SHOWS CAMPGROUNDS/RV PARKS

EXIT		ILLINOIS
48A	Armitage Ave	
Gas	N: Mobil	
	S: BP	
Other	S: Best Buy	
48B	IL 64, North Ave	
Gas	N: BP	
	S: Gas Depot, Shell	
Food	S: Huddle House	
Other	N: Home Depot	
49A	Division St	
Gas	S: BP, Shell	
49B	Augusta Blvd, Milwaukee Ave	
50A	Ogden Ave	
50B	Ohio St	
Gas	S: Marathon	
51A	Randolph St, Lake St (WB)	
51B	Lake St, Randolph St (EB), Washington Blvd, Randolph St (WB)	
51C	Madison, Washington Blvd (WB) Randolph, Washington (EB)	
51D	Washington, Madison St (EB)	
51E	Madison St, Monroe St (EB) Adams St, Monroe St (WB)	
Other	S: Walgreen's	
51F	Monroe St, Adams St (EB)	
51G	Adams St, Jackson Blvd (EB)	
51HI	Van Buren St, I-290, Congress Pkwy, West Suburbs	
52A	Taylor St, Roosevelt Rd (EB)	
Gas	N: Shell	
	S: Citgo	
52B	Roosevelt Rd, Taylor St (WB)	
52C	18th St (EB)	
Gas	N: Shell	
53	W Cermak Rd, S Archer Ave (EB)	
53A	Archer Ave, I-55 (EB), Cermak Rd, S Canalport Ave (WB)	
(53B)	Jct I-55 S, Stevenson Pkwy	
(53C)	Jct I-55, Lake Shore Dr, Downtown	
54	31st St	
Med	N: + Hospital	
55A	35th St	
55B	Pershing Rd	
56A	43rd St	
Gas	S: Citgo	

EXIT		ILLINOIS
56B	47th St (EB)	
57A	51st St	
Food	N: McDonald's	
Other	N: Chicage District Police Hdqtrs	
57B	Garfield Blvd	
Gas	S: Mobil, Shell	
Food	N: Checkers	
	S: Wendy's	
58A	59th St	
58B	63rd St (EB)	
Gas	N: Shell	
	S: BP	
Med	S: + Hospital	
(59A)	Jct I-94E, I-90E, to Indiana (EB)	
NOTE:	I-94 runs with I-90 above. Exit #'s follow I-94.	
59B	69th St	
59C	71st St	
Gas	N: BP	
Food	S: McDonald's	
60A	75th St (EB)	
Gas	N: Mobil, Shell	
Food	S: KFC, Popeye's	
60B	76th St	
Gas	N: BP, Mobil, Shell	
Other	N: Walgreen's	
60C	79th St	
Gas	N: Shell	
	S: Citgo	
61A	83rd St (EB)	
Gas	N: Shell	
Other	N: IL State Hwy Patrol Post	
61B	87th St	
Gas	N: BP, Shell	
Food	N: Burger King, McDonald's	
Other	S: Grocery, Pharmacy, Home Depot	
62	US 12, US 20, 95th St	
Gas	N: Shell	
	S: BP	
(63)	Jct I-57S, to Memphis	
65	95th St, 103rd St, Stony Island Ave	
66A	111th St	
Gas	S: Shell	
Other	S: Wentworth Tire Center, Firestone	
66B	115th St	
68AB	130th St	
69	Beaubien Woods	
70AB	Dolton Ave, Dolton	

EXIT		ILLINOIS
71AB	Sibley Blvd, IL 83	
Gas	N: Mobil	
	S: BP, Shell	
Food	N: McDonald's, Popeye's, Subway	
	S: Arby's, Dunkin Donuts, Long John Silver's, KFC, Ponderosa, Red Lobster, Wendy's, White Castle	
Lodg	N: Baymont Inn	
Other	N: Grocery, Pharmacy	
	S: Grocery, Kmart	
73AB	US 6, 159th St, S Holland	
TStop	N: AmBest Truck-O-Mat (Scales)	
Gas	S: Marathon	
Food	N: Fuddruckers, Outback Steakhouse	
	S: Little Caesars Pizza, McDonald's, Subway	
Lodg	S: Cherry Lane Motel, Dutch Motel	
TWash	N: TruckOMat	
NOTE:	I-94 runs below with I-80 for 3 mi. Exit #'s follow I-80.	
74A/160A	IL 394S, to Danville	
(74B/160B)	Jct I-80W, Jct I-294 (TOLL) Jct I-94, W to Chicago	
161	US 6, IL 83, Torrence Ave	
FStop	S: Park Service/Mobil	
Gas	N: BP	
	S: Gas City	
Food	N: Arby's, Bob Evans, Chili's, Hooters, IHOP, Olive Garden, On the Border, Wendy's	
	S: Al's Hamburgers, Café Borgia, DQ, Dunkin Donuts, Golden Crown, Pappy's Gyros, McDonald's	
Lodg	N: Best Western, Comfort Suites, Days Inn, Extended Stay America, Fairfield Inn, Holiday Inn, Red Roof Inn♥, Sleep Inn, Super 8	
	S: Pioneer Motel	
Med	N: + Ingalls Urgent Aid Walk-In Clinic	
Other	N: Auto Dealers, Auto Services, Best Buy, Firestone, Grocery, Kmart, Home Depot, Radio Shack	
	S: Walgreen's, Sam's Club	
NOTE:	I-94 runs above with I-80 for 3 mi. Exit #'s follow I-80.	
NOTE:	MM 77: Indiana State Line	

(CENTRAL TIME ZONE)

ILLINOIS

◊ = Regular Gas Stations with Diesel ▲ = RV Friendly Locations ♥ = Pet Friendly Locations
RED PRINT SHOWS LARGE VEHICLE PARKING/ACCESS ON SITE OR NEARBY   BROWN PRINT SHOWS CAMPGROUNDS/RV PARKS

Page 495

INTERSTATE 94 W E

EXIT — INDIANA

🅞 INDIANA
(CENTRAL TIME ZONE)

NOTE: I-94 runs with I-80 below. Exit #'s follow I-94.

1 — US 41N, Calumet Ave, Hamilton
- Gas: N: BP◊, Gas City◊
  S: BP, Gas City, Marathon, Shell
- Food: N: Dunkin Donuts, Subway/BP
  S: Arby's, Burger King, Starbucks, Taco Bell, Wendy's
- Other: N: ATM, Firestone, Laundromat, Walgreen's
  S: CVS, Grocery

2AB — US 41S, IN 152N, Indianapolis Blvd, Hamilton, Hammond
- TStop: S: Pilot Travel Center #31 (Scales)
- Gas: N: SavAStop, Shell
  S: Thorntons
- Food: N: Arby's, Domino's, Dunkin Donuts
  S: Subway/Pilot TC, Burger King, Little Caesar's, Taco Bell
- Lodg: S: Ameri Host Inn
- Med: N: + Hospital
  S: + Hospital
- Other: N: to Purdue Univ/Calumet
  S: WiFi/Pilot TC, Cabela's, Dollar General, Grocery, Kmart

3AB — Kennedy Ave, Hammond
- Gas: N: Clark, Speedway
  S: Citgo, Speedway
- Food: N: Burger King, Dominos, McDonald's
  S: Cracker Barrel, Subway, Wendy's
- Lodg: S: Courtyard, Fairfield Inn, Residence Inn
- Other: N: Walgreen's, NAPA

5AB — IN 912, Cline Ave, Gary, Hammond
- Gas: S: BP, Clark, Shell, Speedway
- Food: S: Arby's, Bob Evans, Burger King, DQ, McDonald's, Pizza Hut, White Castle
- Lodg: S: Best Western, Motel 6 ♥

6 — Burr St, Gary
- TStop: N: Travel Center of America #10/BP(Scales) Pilot Travel Center #271 (Scales)
- Gas: N: BP
  S: Shell◊
- Food: N: CountryPride/Chester/PizzaHut/Taco Bell/TA TC, Subway/Pilot TC
- TWash: N: Pilot TC
- TServ: N: TA TC/Tires
- Other: N: Laundry/CB/WiFi/TA TC, WiFi/Pilot TC

9AB — Grant St, Gary, Chicago
- TStop: S: Flying J Travel Plaza #5024 (Scales) AmBest/Steel City Truck Plaza (Scales)
- Food: N: Chicago Hot Dogs
  S: Cookery/FastFood/FJ TP, Rest, FastFood/Steel City TP, Burger King, DQ, KFC, McDonald's, Subway
- TWash: S: FJ TP
- TServ: S: FJ TP/Tires
- Other: N: Laundromat, Walgreen's
  S: Laundry/WiFi/RVDump/LP/FJ TP, ATMs, AutoZone, Firestone, Grocery, Outlet Mall

10AB — IN 53, Broadway, Gary
- Gas: N: Citgo, Marathon
  S: BP, Citgo
- Food: N: Broadway BBQ
  S: DQ, Rally's

(11) — Jct I-65S, Indianapolis (EB)

EXIT — INDIANA

(12A) — Jct I-65S, to Indianapolis (WB)

(12B) — Jct I-65N, to Gary, IN

13 — Central Ave (EB, No re-entry)

15A — US 6E, IN 51S, to US 20, Lake Station
- TStop: S: Road Ranger Travel Center #240/Citgo (Scales)
- Gas: S: Mobil◊, Shell
- Food: S: Subway/RoadRanger, Burger King, DQ, Papa John's, Long John Silver, Wendy's
- Other: S: Walgreen's

15B — US 6W, IN 51N, Ripley St, Melton Rd, Central Ave, Gary, Lake Station
- TStop: N: Road Ranger Travel Center #239/Citgo (Scales), Flying J Travel Plaza #5085 (Scales), Travel Center of America #219/BP (Scales), Dunes Center Truck Stop (Scales)
- Food: N: Subway/Road Ranger TC, Cookery/FastFood/FJ TP, Buckhorn/Popeyes/Subway/TA TC, McDonald's, Ponderosa
- TWash: N: Road Ranger, FJ TP, TA TC
- TServ: N: FJ TP/Tires, TA TC/Tires, Dunes Center TS/Tires
- Other: N: Laundry/BarbSh/CB/WiFi/FJ TP, Laundry/WiFi/TA TC

(16/21) — Jct I-90, Jct I-80, US 6, IN 51

NOTE: I-94 runs with I-80 above. Exit #'s follow I-94.

19 — IN 249, Crisman Rd, Portage, Port of Indiana
- Gas: S: Shell, Citgo
- Food: S: Andy's, Burger King, Denny's, Cactus Carlos, KFC, Subway
- Lodg: S: Days Inn, Dollar Inn, Hampton Inn, Inn, Ramada Inn, Super 8, Travel Inn
- TServ: N: Great Lakes Peterbilt GMC

22AB — US 20, Melton Rd, Chesterton, Porter, Burns Harbor
- FStop: N: Steel City Express (Scales)
- TStop: N: Travel Center of America / Mobil (Scales)
  S: Pilot Travel Center #445 (Scales)
- Food: N: FastFood/Steel City, Rest/Subway/TA TC
  S: McDonald's/Subway/Pilot TC
- TWash: N: Blue Beacon TW/TA TC
- TServ: N: TA TC/Tires
- Other: N: Laundry/CB/WiFi/TA TC
  S: Laundry/RVDump/Pilot TC, Auto Dealers, Camp-Land RV Center

26AB — IN 49, Chesterton, Porter
- Gas: S: BP, Speedway
- Food: S: Applebee's, Burger King, Dunkin Donuts, KFC, Little Caesars, Long John Silver, McDonald's, Pizza Hut, Quiznos, Subway, Taco Bell, Wendy's
- Lodg: S: Econo Lodge, Super 8
- Other: N: to Indian Dunes State Park
  S: Grocery, Kmart, Walgreen's

(29) — Weigh Station (Both dir)

34AB — US 421, Franklin St, Michigan City, Westville
- TStop: S: Steel City (Scales)
- Gas: S: BP◊, Citgo◊, Mobil◊, Shell, Speedway◊
- Food: N: Applebee's, Arby's, Bob Evans, Burger King, Chili's, Culver's Rest, Denny's, Damon's, IHOP, KFC, McDonald's, Pizza Hut, Popeye's, Quiznos, Red Lobster,

EXIT — IN / MI

- Food: N: Ryan's Grill, Starbucks, Steak 'n Shake, Subway, Taco Bell, Wendy's
- Lodg: N: Comfort Inn, Days Inn, Holiday Inn, Knights Inn, Red Roof Inn, Super 8
- Med: N: + Hospital
- Other: N: Auto Dealers, AutoZone, Auto Service, Dollar Tree, Grocery, Lowe's, Radio Shack, Wal-Mart
  S: Auto Dealers, Harley Davidson

40AB — US 20, US 35, Michigan City, South Bend, La Porte
- FStop: S: Speedway
- Med: N: + Hospital
- Other: N: Michigan City Muni Airport ✈

(42) — IN Welcome Center (WB)
(RR, Phone, Picnic, Vend)

NOTE: MM 46: Michigan State Line

(CENTRAL TIME ZONE)

🎧 INDIANA
🅞 MICHIGAN
(EASTERN TIME ZONE)

(1) — MI Welcome Center (EB)
(RR, Phone, Picnic, Vend, Info, WiFi)

1 — MI 239, La Porte Rd, New Buffalo
- TStop: S: Plaza One Truck Stop (Scales)
- Gas: N: Shell
  S: Speedway
- Food: N: Dominics Ital Rest, McDonald's, Quiznos, Wheel Inn Rest
  S: Arby's, Wendy's, Zeke's
- Lodg: N: Best Western, Holiday Inn Express
  S: Obrien Inn
- Other: N: CarWash/Shell, AmTrak, Rogers Wrecker Service, Tire & Auto Services, Golf course
  S: Four Winds Casino Resort

(2) — Weigh Station (Both dir)

4AB — US 12, E-Niles, W-New Buffalo Pulaski Hwy, S Red Arrow Hwy
- TStop: N: J & J 12&60 Truck Stop
- Food: N: Rest/J&J TS, Pizza Hut, Redamak's Tavern
- Lodg: N: Harbor Grand Hotel, New Buffalo All Suites Inn, White Rabbit Inn B&B
- Other: N: MI State Hwy Patrol Post
  S: U-Haul, Dale's Auto Service, M&N Towing Service

6 — Union Pier Rd, Union Pier
- Other: E: Bob-A-Ron Campground & RV Sales▲

12 — Sawyer Rd, Sawyer
- TStop: N: Dunes Auto Truck Plaza/Citgo (Scales)
  S: Travel Center of America #116/Amoco (Scales)
- Food: N: FastFood/Dunes ATP
  S: CountryPride/BKing/PizzaHut/Popeyes/TacoBell/TA TC
- Lodg: S: Super 8
- TWash: N: Dunes TW
- TServ: S: TA TC/Tires
- Other: N: Kamp Across from the Dunes▲
  S: Laundry/WiFi/TA TC

16 — MI 12N, Red Arrow Hwy, Bridgman
- TStop: N: USA Travel Center/Marathon (Scales)
  S: Bridgman Travel Center (Scales)
- Gas: N: Bridgman Amoco◊
  S: Speedway

◊ = Regular Gas Stations with Diesel   ▲ = RV Friendly Locations   ♥ = Pet Friendly Locations

RED PRINT SHOWS LARGE VEHICLE PARKING/ACCESS ON SITE OR NEARBY   BROWN PRINT SHOWS CAMPGROUNDS/RV PARKS

EXIT		MICHIGAN
	Food	N: A&W/Amoco S: McDonald's, Pizza Pizza Hut, Subway
	Lodg	S: Bridgman Inn
	Other	N: Kamp Across from the Dunes RV Park▲, Warren Dunes State Park, Weko Beach Campground▲
22		Grand Mere Rd, John Beers Rd, Stevensville
	Gas	S: P&R Shell, H&S Gas & Food Mart
	Other	N: Grand Mere State Park
23		I-94 Bus E, Red Arrow Hwy, Stevensville, St Joseph, Benton Harbor
	Gas	N: Admiral Station, Central Station Food Mart, Lakeshore Shell Food Mart◊, Marathon◊
	Food	N: Bob's Big Boy, Burger King, Cracker Barrel, Culver's, DQ, Long John Silver, McDonald's, Papa John's, Popeye's, Subway, Tony's Family Rest S: Cajun Deli, Schuler's Rest.
	Lodg	N: Baymont Inn♥, Candlewood Suites♥, Comfort Suites, Park Inn♥, Ray's Motel S: Hampton Inn♥
	Other	N: Walgreen's
27		US 33, MI 63, St Joseph, Niles
	Gas	N: I-94 AmocoBP
	Food	N: Dino's Family Rest, Qdoba Mex Grill, McDonald's, Taco Bell, Wendy's
	Lodg	N: Econo Lodge
	Other	S: Goodyear, Wingfoot Comm'l Tire
28		US 31S, MI 139, Fair Ave, Nickerson Ave, Scottsdale Rd, Benton Harbor
	TStop	N: Speedway #8718
	Gas	N: Citgo◊, Quik Shop, Marathon
	Food	N: Burger King, Country Kitchen, DQ, KFC, Little Caesar's, Pizza Hut, Subway, Taco Bell, Wendy's
	Lodg	N: Howard Johnson♥, Rodeway Inn♥ S: Lake Breeze Hotel
	Med	N: + Lakeland Hospital
	Other	S: AutoZone, Big Lots, Dollar Tree, Office Depot, RiteAid, Target, Tires, MI State Hwy Patrol Post
29		Pipestone Rd, Benton Harbor
	FStop	S: Pri Mar Fuel Center #10/Mobil
	Gas	N: Meijer◊, Total
	Food	N: Applebee's, Burger King, China Buffet, Denny's, El Rodeo Mex Rest, Great Steak & Potato, Hacienda Mex Rest, IHOP, McDonald's, Jimmy's Family Buffet, Pizza Hut, Red Lobster, Sophia's House of Pancakes, Steak 'n Shake, Subway, Texas Corral S: Bob Evans

EXIT		MICHIGAN
	Lodg	N: Best Western♥, Courtyard, Motel 6♥, Red Roof Inn♥ S: Comfort Suites, Holiday Inn Express
	Med	N: + Urgent Care Medical Walk-In
	Other	N: Best Buy, Dollar Tree, Grocery, Home Depot, Goodyear, Kmart, Lowe's, Radio Shack, Meijer, PetSmart♥, Staples, Tires, Walgreen's, Mall, Wal-Mart sc
30		US 31, Napier Ave, Benton Harbor
	TStop	N: Flying J Travel Plaza #5121 (Scales)
	Gas	N: Shell
	Food	N: FastFood/FJ TP
	Lodg	N: Super 8
	TWash	N: Blue Beacon TW/FJ TP
	TServ	N: FJ TP/Tires
	Other	N: Laundry/WiFi/LP/FJ TP, Discount Tire, Tires, Orchard Mall, Animal Care Center♥ S: Lake Michigan College
33		I-94 Bus, E Main St, Downtown St Joseph, Bar Harbor (WB)
	Other	N: Benton Harbor Airport✈
(34)		I-196N, US 31N, South Haven, Holland, Grand Rapids
	Other	N: to Coloma/St Joseph KOA▲, Dune Lake Campground▲
(36)		Rest Area (EB) (RR, Phone, Picnic, Vend, Info)
39		Friday Rd, Church St, Columa, Millburg, Deer Forest
	Gas	N: Speedway, Randy's Svc Ctr/Towing S: BP◊
	Food	N: McDonald's, Pizza Hut
	Other	N: Krenek RV Super Center
41		MI 140, Watervliet Rd, Watervliet
	Gas	N: Dave's AmocoBP S: Pri Mart Quik Shop
	Food	N: Taco Bell S: Burger King, Waffle House
	Other	N: to Covert/South Haven KOA▲, Paw Paw River Campground▲
(42)		Rest Area (WB) (RR, Phones, Picnic, Vend, Info)
46		CR 687, 64th St, Hartford
	Gas	N: Hartford Shell◊
	Food	N: McDonald's S: Patio Donut Shop
	Other	S: Thousand Adventures Travel Inn Resort▲
52		CR 365, 52nd St, Lawrence
	Gas	N: Lawrence Self Serve, Village Marathon
	Food	N: Waffle House
	Other	S: to Oak Shores Campground▲, Timber Trails RV Park▲

EXIT		MICHIGAN
56		MI 51, CR 671, Paw Paw, to Decatur, Dowagiac
	TStop	S: Paw Paw Fuel Stop (Scales)
	Gas	S: Lawson's M51 Service◊
60		MI 40, Paw Paw, Lawton
	Gas	N: AmocoBP, Speedway
	Food	N: Arby's, Big Boy, Burger King, Chicken Coop, McDonald's, Pizza Hut, Taco Bell, Wendy's
	Lodg	N: Comfort Inn♥, Econo Lodge, Super 8♥
	Med	N: + Lakeview Community Hospital
	Other	N: Pharmacy, UPS Store, US Post Office, St Julian Winery, Warner Winery
66		CR 652, 24th St, Main St, Mattawan
	FStop	N: Speedway #6604 (Scales)
	Gas	S: Shell
	Food	N: Subway/Speedway, Mancino's Italian
	Other	N: Family Dollar
72		9th St, Kalamazoo, Oshtemo
	FStop	N: Short Stop Citgo
	Gas	N: Speedway◊
	Food	N: Arby's, Burger King, Culver's, McDonald's, Taco Bell, Wendy's S: Burger King, Cracker Barrel
	Lodg	N: Hampton Inn S: Fairfield Inn
(73)		Rest Area (EB) (RR, Phone)
74AB		US 131N, I-94 Bus, to Kalamazoo, Grand Rapids, Three Rivers (EB)
	Other	N: to W MI Univ
74B		US 131N, Grand Rapids (WB, Exit only)
74A		US 131S, Three Rivers
75		Oakland Dr, Portage, Kalamazoo
76A		Westnedge Ave S, Portage
	Gas	S: Shell
	Food	S: Applebee's, Bob Evans, Burger King, Carrabba's, Chili's, Chuck E Cheese, Chinese Buffet, Fazoli's, KFC, Logan's Roadhouse, Mountain Jack's, McDonald's, Olive Garden, Panera Bread, Peking Palace, Qdoba Mex Rest, Red Lobster, Red Robin, Subway, Taco Bell, Wendy's
	Lodg	S: Holiday Motel
	Other	S: ATMs, Auto Services, Banks, Southland Mall, Crossroads Mall, B&N, Best Buy, Circuit City, Firestone, Grocery, Home Depot, Kmart, Radio Shack, Target, World Market, Walgreen's

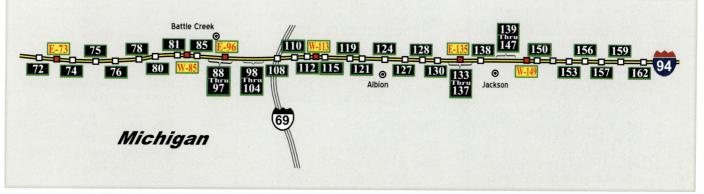

◊ = Regular Gas Stations with Diesel ▲ = RV Friendly Locations ♥ = Pet Friendly Locations

RED PRINT SHOWS LARGE VEHICLE PARKING/ACCESS ON SITE OR NEARBY   BROWN PRINT SHOWS CAMPGROUNDS/RV PARKS

Page 497

INTERSTATE 94 W/E — MICHIGAN

EXIT		
76B	**Westnedge Ave N, Kalamazoo**	
FStop	N: Speedway #3561	
Gas	N: Admiral, Speedway, Meijer◇	
Food	N: Arby's, Bennigan's, Hooters, IHOP, Papa John's, Pappy's Mexican, Outback Steakhouse, Mancino's Italian, Steak 'n Shake, Subway, Taco Bell	
Lodg	N: Quality Inn	
Other	N: Discount Tire, Gander Mountain, Goodyear, Lowe's, Office Depot, RiteAid	
78	**Portage Rd, Kilgore Rd, Portage**	
Gas	N: Circle K	
	S: Mobil, Shell, Marathon	
Food	N: Cottage Inn Pizza, Hungry Howie's Pizza, Subway, Taco Bob's, Uncle Ernie's Pancake House	
	S: McDonald's, Pizza King, Gum Ho Chinese, Taco Bell	
Lodg	N: Hampton Inn, Residence Inn♥	
	S: Airport Inn, Country Inn, Lee's Inn♥	
Other	S: Sam's Club, Kalamazoo/Battle Creek Int'l Airport✈, Aviation History Museum	
80	**Sprinkle Rd, Cork St, Kalamazoo**	
Gas	N: Citgo◇, Speedway◇	
	S: BP◇, Speedway◇, Shell	
Food	N: Arby's, Burger King, Denny's, Chicken Coop, Perkins, Taco Bell	
	S: McDonald's, Subway, Wendy's	
Lodg	N: Best Western♥, Clarion Hotel♥, Fairfield Inn, Holiday Inn Express, Red Roof Inn♥	
	S: Comfort Inn, Days Inn, Econo Lodge, Motel 6♥	
TServ	N: GMC/Volvo Trucks	
	S: Mi CAT	
81	**I-94 Bus Loop (WB)** (Serv 1st Ex & Acc to Ex #80 N Serv)	
Other	N: Kalamazoo Co Fairgrounds▲	
(85)	**Rest Area (WB)** (RR, Phone, Picnic, Vend)	
85	**35th St S, Augusta, Galesburg**	
Gas	N: Shell◇	
Food	N: FastFood/Shell, McDonald's	
Other	N: Galesburg Speedway, to Shady Bend Campground▲	
	S: to Timber Lake Campground & Riding Stables▲, Peterson & Sons Winery	
88	**E Michigan Ave, 40th St S, Galesburg, Climax, Augusta**	
Other	N: Galesburg Speedway, Fort Custer Training Center, Ft Custer St Rec Area	
92	**I-94 Bus, Climax & Battle Creek Rd to MI 37, MI 96, Battle Creek**	
TStop	N: Arlene's Truck Stop/Citgo	
Gas:	N: Shell	
Food	N: Rest/Arlene's TS	
TServ	N: Glen's Tire Center	
95	**Helmer Rd, Battle Creek, Springfield**	
Gas	N: Ps Food Mart/Citgo	
Other	N: MI State Hwy Patrol, WK Kellogg Airport✈	
(96)	**Rest Area (EB)** (RR, Phone, Picnic, Vend)	
97	**Capital Ave, 5 Mile Rd, B Dr N, Beckley Rd, Battle Creek**	
Gas	N: BP, Clark	
	S: Citgo, Shell	
Food	N: Arby's, Lakeview Family Rest, Lone Star Steakhouse, McDonald's, Red Lobster	
Food	S: Applebee's, Bob Evans, Burger King, Cracker Barrel, Denny's, Don Pablo, Old Country Buffet, Pancake House, Subway, Taco Bell, Wendy's	
Lodg	N: Comfort Inn, Knights Inn♥, Ramada Inn♥	
	S: Battle Creek Inn, Baymont Inn♥, Best Western, Days Inn♥, Fairfield Inn, Hampton Inn, Motel 6♥, Ramada, Super 8♥	
Other	S: Lakeview Square Mall, Firestone, Goodyear, Kmart, Lowe's, Target, UPS Store, Mahrle's Harley Davidson	
98A	**MI 66S, to Sturgis**	
Gas	S: Citgo◇, Meijer◇	
Food	S: Chili's, McDonald's, Steak 'n Shake, Ruby Tuesday, Taco Bell	
Lodg	S: Super 8	
Other	S: Best Buy, Discount Tire, Grocery, Lowe's, Sam's Club, Staples, Walgreen's, Wal-Mart sc, to Camper Village▲	
(98B)	**Jct I-194N, MI 66, to Battle Creek**	
100	**Beadle Lake Rd, Battle Creek**	
FStop	S: Jim Hazel's Fuel Stop	
Food	N: Moonraker Rest	
103	**Jct I-94 Bus, MI 96, Battle Creek** (WB exit, EB entr)	
104	**to MI 96, 11 Mile Rd, Michigan Ave**	
FStop	S: Pilot Travel Center #17, Interstate Truck & Car Stop	
TStop	S: Te-Khi AmBest Travel Plaza/Sunoco (Scales)	
Food	S: Rest/Te-Khi TP	
Lodg	S: Quality Inn	
TWash	S: Te-Khi TS	
TServ	S: Te-Khi TS	
Other	S: Laundry/WiFi/Te-Khi TP, WiFi/Pilot TC	
(108)	**Jct I-69, I-94 Bus, N to Lansing, S to Ft Wayne**	
Other	S: Tri Lake Trails Campground▲	
110	**17 Mile Rd, Old 27, Marshall**	
FStop	S: Brewer Park Ps Food Mart	
TStop	N: Pioneer Auto Truck Stop/Shell	
Food	N: Rest/Subway/Pioneer ATS, Country Kitchen	
Lodg	S: Hampton Inn, Holiday Inn Express	
Med	S: + Hospital	
Other	S: MI Sheriff	
112	**I-94 Bus, Partello Rd, Marshall**	
TStop	S: Love's Travel Stop #336 (Scales)	
Food	S: Hardee's/Love's TS	
Other	S: WiFi/RVDump/Love's TS	
(113)	**Rest Area (WB)** (RR, Phone, Picnic, Vend, Info)	
115	**22 1/2 Mile Rd**	
TStop	N: PTP/One Fifteen Truck Stop	
Food	N: Rest/115 TS	
119	**MI 199, 26 Mile Rd, Albion**	
121	**I-94 Bus, 28 Mile Rd, Albion**	
Gas	N: Mobil	
	S: Speedway◇	
Food	N: Arby's	
	S: Burger King, McDonald's, Pete's Place, Pizza Hut	
Lodg	N: Best Western♥	
	S: Super 9 Inn♥	
Med	S: + Trillium Hospital	
Other	S: Auto Dealers, Auto Zone, Dollar General, Family Dollar, Pharmacy, Radio Shack	
124	**MI 99, I-94 Bus, Eaton Rapids, Albion, Parma, Springport**	
127	**N Concord Rd, Parma, Concord**	
128	**Michigan Ave, Parma**	
TStop	N: Parma Travel Center/BP (Scales)	
Gas	N: Petro Shop◇	
Food	N: Burger King	
Lodg	S: Hilltop Farm	
Other	N: Laundry/Parma TC	
130	**N Parma Rd, Parma**	
TStop	S: Parma Citgo Truck Stop/Citgo	
Rest	S: Rest/Parma TS	
133	**Dearing Rd, Parma, Spring Arbor**	
(135)	**Rest Area (EB)** (RR, Phone, Picnic, Vend, Info)	
136	**I-94 Bus, MI 60, Jackson, Spring Arbor**	
137	**Airport Rd, Jackson**	
Gas	N: 7-11, Shell, Meijer◇	
	S: BP, Sam's	
Food	N: Denny's, McDonald's, Subway	
	S: Cracker Barrel, Olive Garden	
Other	N: Laundromat	
	S: Kmart, Sam's Club, Jackson Co Airport✈	
138	**US 127N, MI 50, Lansing, Jackson**	
Gas	S: Marathon, Shell, Total	
Food	N: Red Lobster	
	S: Bob Evans, Ground Round, KFC, Long John Silver, McDonald's, Pizza Hut, Old Country Buffet, Outback Steakhouse, Pizza Hut	
Lodg	N: Comfort Inn, Fairfield Inn, Holiday Inn, Super 8	
	S: Best Motel, Motel 6♥	
Other	S: Best Buy, Circuit City, Home Depot, Lowe's, Pharmacy, Target, Walgreen's	
139	**MI 106, Cooper St, Jackson**	
Gas	S: Citgo, Marathon	
Food	S: Jackson Café, Subway	
Med	S: + Hospital	
Other	N: MI State Hwy Patrol Post	
	S: Amtrak Station	
141	**Elm Rd, Jackson**	
142	**US 127S, Jackson, to Hudson**	
144	**I-94 Bus, Ann Arbor Rd** (WB exit, EB entr)	
145	**Ann Arbor Rd, Sargent Rd, Jackson**	
TStop	S: 145 Auto Truck Plaza/Mobil (Scales)	
Food	S: Rest/145 TP, McDonald's, Wendy's	
Lodg	S: Cascade Motel, Michigan Motel	
TServ	S: 145 TP/Tires	
Other	S: to Hideaway Campground▲	
147	**Race Rd, Grass Lake**	
Other	N: to Waterloo State Rec Area, Robin Hood of Sherwood Forest Campground▲, The Oaks Campground▲	
	S: Grass Lake Resort▲, Greenwood Acres Family Campground▲, to MI Int'l Speedway	
(149)	**Rest Area (WB)** (RR, Phone, Picnic, Vend, Info)	
150	**Mt Hope Rd, Grass Lake**	
Gas	S: Grass Lake Mini Mart, Mobil	
Food	S: Subway	

Page 498

◇ = Regular Gas Stations with Diesel   ▲ = RV Friendly Locations   ♥ = Pet Friendly Locations
RED PRINT SHOWS LARGE VEHICLE PARKING/ACCESS ON SITE OR NEARBY   BROWN PRINT SHOWS CAMPGROUNDS/RV PARKS

EXIT	MICHIGAN
Other	N: Waterloo State Rec Area, to Robin Hood of Sherwood Forest, Portage Lake Family Campground▲ S: Apple Creek Resorts-Grass Lake
(151)	Weigh Station (Both dir)
153	Clear Lake Rd, Grass Lake, Waterloo
Gas	N: Clear Lake Oil/Marathon◊
156	Kalmbach Rd, Grass Lake
Other	N: Waterloo State Rec Area
157	Old 12, Pierce Rd, Chelsea
159	MI 52, Main St, Chelsea, Manchester
Gas	N: Chelsea AmocoBP◊, Mobil◊
Food	N: Big Boy, McDonald's, Schumm's, Taco Bell, Wendy's
Lodg	N: Comfort Inn, Holiday Inn Express
Med	N: + Chelsea Community Hospital
Other	N: RVDump/Mobil, Auto Service/Amoco, CVS, Lloyd Bridges Traveland RV▲
162	Old 12, Fletcher Rd, Jackson Rd, Chelsea, Dexter
FStop	S: Chelsea Plaza/Clark
Food	S: Subway/Chelsea Plaza
167	Baker Rd, Dexter
TStop	N: Pilot Travel Center #21 (Scales) S: Pilot Travel Center #296 (Scales), Travel Center of America #89/BP (Scales)
FStop	S: Wolverine Truck Stop
Food	N: Subway/Pilot TC S: Arby's/TJCinn/Pilot TC, CountryPride/TC
TWash	S: Blue Beacon TW/TA TC
TServ	S: TA TC/Tires
Other	N: WiFi/Pilot TC, Hell Creek Ranch Campground▲ S: Laundry/WiFi/TA TC
(168)	Rest Area (EB) (Next RA 87 mi) (RR, Phone, Picnic, Vend, Info)
169	Zeeb Rd, Ann Arbor
Gas	N: AmocoBP◊ S: Citgo◊, Mobil
Food	N: Baxter's Deli, German Rest, McDonald's S: Arby's, Pizza Hut, Subway, Taco Bell, Wendy's
Other	S: Lowe's, Harley Davidson
171	MI 14, Plymouth, to Ann Arbor, Flint (EB, Left Exit)
172	I-94 Bus, Jackson Rd (EB), Jackson Ave (WB), to Ann Arbor
Gas	N: AmocoBP, Marathon, Shell S: Sunoco
Food	N: DQ, KFC, Panda House, Knight's Steakhouse

EXIT	MICHIGAN
Food	S: Michigan Inn, Webers
Lodg	S: Best Western, Garden Point Inn, Weber's Inn
Med	S: + Hospital
Other	N: Kroger, Kmart, Staples, Tires, Mall
175	Ann Arbor Saline Rd, Ann Arbor
Gas	N: BP, Marathon, Shell
Food	N: Applebee's, Lone Star Steakhouse, Old Country Buffet, Panera, Subway S: McDonald's, Joe's Crab Shack, Outback Steakhouse
Lodg	N: Candlewood Hotel
Other	N: Mall, Office Depot S: Best Buy, Grocery, Target
177	State St, Ann Arbor
Gas	N: BP, Mobil, Shell S: Citgo, Total
Food	N: Bennigan's, Max & Erma's, Olive Garden, Romano's Macaroni Grill S: McDonald's, Taco Bell
Lodg	N: Courtyard, Fairfield Inn, Hampton Inn, Holiday Inn, Holiday Inn Express, Red Roof Inn ♥, Residence Inn, Sheraton S: Motel 6 ♥
Other	N: to Univ of MI, Grocery, Mall S: Ann Arbor Municipal Airport✈
180AB	US 23, I-94 Bus, S to Toledo, N to Flint (EB)
180B	US 23N, to Flint (WB)
Other	N: to Univ of MI
180A	US 23S, S to Toledo (WB)
Gas	N: Meijer◊, Speedway S: Shell
Food	N: Burger King, Taco Bell S: McDonald's, Subway
Other	N: Grocery, Wal-Mart
181	US 12W, Michigan Ave (EB)
181B	Michigan Ave East (WB)
181A	US 12W, Michigan Ave, Saline (WB)
183	US 12 Bus, Huron St, Ypsilanti
Gas	N: Marathon◊
Food	S: McDonald's
Lodg	S: Marriott
Med	N: + Hospital
Other	N: Ford Motor Co, Eastern MI Univ S: MI State Hwy Patrol Post
185	US 12E, Michigan Ave, Ypsilanti (EB Exit, WB entr)
Other	Willow Run Airport✈, GM Plant
186	Williard Rd, Willow Run Airport (WB Exit, EB Entr)
Other	Willow Run Airport✈, GM Plant

EXIT	MICHIGAN
187	Rawsonville Rd, Belleville
Gas	S: Mobil◊, Speedway◊
Food	S: Burger King, Denny's, Hardee's, KFC, Little Caesars, Lone Star Steakhouse, Pizza Hut, Wendy's
Other	S: Kmart, RiteAid, Detroit/Greenfield KOA▲
190	Belleville Rd, Belleville
Gas	N: Amoco, Marathon, Meijer◊ S: Shell
Food	N: Applebee's, Cracker Barrel, McDonald's, Taco Bell, Wendy's S: Burger King, China City, China King, Domino's, Subway
Lodg	N: Hampton Inn, Holiday Inn, Red Roof Inn ♥ S: Super 8
Other	N: CVS, U-Haul, Camping World, Walt Michaels RV Center/RVDump, Wal-Mart, Wayne Co Fairgrounds S: Laundromat, US Post Office
192	Haggerty Rd, Belleville
Gas	N: Mobil
(194A)	Jct I-275S, to Toledo (EB)
(194B)	Jct I-275N, to Livonia, Novi (EB)
(194)	Jct I-275, N-Livonia, S-Toledo (WB)
196	Wayne Rd, Wayne, Romulus
Gas	N: Citgo, Shell S: Mobil, Total
Food	N: McDonald's S: Burger King
197	Vining Rd, Romulus
198	Merriman Rd, Middle Belt Rd, Detroit Metro Wayne Co Airport
FStop	N: M& J Petro
Gas	N: Speedway S: Metro Gas
Food	N: American Grill, Bob's Big Boy, Bob Evans, Beirut Rest, Fortune Chinese, Leonardo's Pizzeria & Rest, McDonald's, Merriman St Grill, Subway S: Denny's, McDonald's, Wendy's
Lodg	N: Baymont Inn, Best Western, Comfort Inn, Clarion, Courtyard, Crown Plaza, Doubletree Hotel, Extended Stay America, Hampton Inn, Hilton Suites, Motel 6 ♥, Quality Inn, Relax Inn S: Days Inn, Howard Johnson, Super 8
199	Middle Belt Rd, Romulus (Acc to Serv at Ex #198)
200	Ecorse Rd, Taylor
TStop	N: Madco Truck Plaza/Marathon (Scales)
Food	N: Rest/Madco TP

◊ = Regular Gas Stations with Diesel   ▲ = RV Friendly Locations   ♥ = Pet Friendly Locations

RED PRINT SHOWS LARGE VEHICLE PARKING/ACCESS ON SITE OR NEARBY   BROWN PRINT SHOWS CAMPGROUNDS/RV PARKS

INTERSTATE 94 W/E — MICHIGAN

EXIT		Description
	TWash	N: Madco TP
	TServ	N: Madco TP/Tires
	Other	N: Laundry/Madco TP
202A		US 24N, Telegraph Rd, Dearborn Hts
	Gas	N: Shell
	Food	N: Pizza Hut, Taco Bell, Wendy's
	Lodg	N: Casa Bianca Motel
	Other	N: Grocery, Walgreen's, to Henry Ford Museum & Greenfield Village
202B		US 24S, Telegraph Rd, Taylor
	FStop	S: Metro Truck Plaza/BP
	Gas	S: Citgo, Marathon◆, Mobil, Shell
	Food	S: Burger King, Pizza Hut, Red Lobster
	Lodg	S: Quality Inn
	TServ	S: Metro TP/Tires
	Med	S: + Oakwood Heritage Hospital
	Other	S: Laundry/Metro TP, CVS, Wal-Mart
204		MI 39, Southfield Freeway, Pelham Rd, Allen Park, Dearborn
206A		Oakwood Blvd S, Allen Park (WB)
206B		Oakwood Blvd N, Allen Park (WB)
206		Oakwood Blvd, Allen Park (EB)
	Gas	N: Marathon
		S: BP, Mobil
	Food	S: Burger King, Pizza Hut, Subway
	Lodg	S: Best Western, Holiday Inn Express
	TServ	S: Belle Tire
	Med	N: + Oakwood Hospital
208		Greenfield Rd, Schaefer Rd
	FStop	S: to Fuel Mart of America
209		Rotunda Dr, Dearborn (WB ex, EB entr)
210A		US 12, Michigan Ave, Wyoming Ave, Dearborn
	FStop	S: MAH Fuel & Auto Service, MI & WY Food Shop/BP
	TStop	S: Wyoming Fuel Plaza/Truck City
	Food	S: Drake's Iron Skillet, WY Lunch
	TWash	S: MAH
	TServ	S: MAH
210B		MI 153, Ford, Rd, Addison St (WB Exit, EB entr)
	Gas	N: Mobil
211A		Lonyo St (WB exit, EB entr)
211B		Central Ave, Cecil Ave (WB exit, EB entr)
212		Livernois Ave (WB)
212A		Livernois Ave, Detroit (EB)
	FStop	S: I-94 & Livernois Marathon
212B		Warren Ave (EB)
213A		W Grand Blvd, Warren Ave (EB, Left exit)
(213B)		Jct I-96, Lansing, Ambassador Bridge to Canada
214		Linwood Ave, Grand River Ave (WB)
214A		Linwood Ave, Grand River Ave (EB)
214B		Trumbull Ave (EB exit, WB entr)
215		MI 10, Downtown Detroit (EB)
215A		MI 10S, Downtown, Tunnel to Canada
215B		MI 10N, Lodge Freeway
215C		MI 1, Woodward Ave, John R St
(216A)		Jct I-75, N to Flint, S to Toledo, Chrysler Frwy, Tunnel to Canada
216B		Russell St (EB, Exit only)
217		Chene St, E Grand Blvd, Mount Elliot Ave (WB)
217A		Chene St, E Grand Blvd (EB)
217B		Mount Elliott Ave (EB)
218		MI 53, Van Dyke Ave
	Gas	N: AmocoBP, Mobil
219		MI 3, Gratiot Ave
	Gas	N: Marathon
		S: BP
	Food	N: McDonald's, KFC
220A		French Rd (EB)
220B		Conner Ave, City Airport
	Gas	N: BP, Kwik Fill
	Lodg	N: Travel Inn
222A		Outer Dr, Chalmers Ave
	Gas	N: AmocoBP◆, Marathon
	Food	N: Little Caesar's, White Castle
222B		Harper Ave (EB exit, WB entr)
223		Cadieux Ave
	Gas	S: Amoco, Shell, Sunoco
	Food	S: McDonald's, Taco Bell, Wendy's
224A		Moross Rd
	Gas	S: Shell
224B		Allard Ave, Eastwood Ave
225		MI 102, 8 Mile Rd, Vernier Rd
227		9 Mile Rd, St Clair Shores
	Gas	N: Mobil, Speedway, Sunoco
		S: Mobil
	Food	N: Mama Rosa's, McDonald's, Taco Bell, Wendy's
	Lodg	S: Shore Point Motor Lodge
	Other	N: CVS, Grocery, US Post Office
228		10 Mile Rd
	Gas	N: Amoco, Shell
	Food	N: Eastwind, Jet's Pizza
(229)		Jct I-696W, to 11 Mile Rd
	Gas	N: BP
		S: BP, DM, Speedway
230		12 Mile Rd, St Clair Shores
	Gas	N: Marathon, Citgo
		S: Marathon
	Food	N: Burger King, Buffet World, Outback
	Other	N: CVS, Mall, Wal-Mart
231		MI 3, Gratiot Ave (EB, Left exit) (EB exit, WB entr)
	Gas	N: Shell, Speedway
	Food	N: Applebee's, Arby's, Big Boy, Chuck E Cheese, Denny's, Mountain Jack's, Pizza Hut, Texas Roadhouse
	Lodg	N: Best Western, Days Inn, Knights Inn, Super 8
	Other	N: Discount Tire, Firestone, Sam's Club, Target, Mall, U-Haul
232		Little Mack Ave, Roseville
	Gas	N: Sunoco
		S: AmocoBP, Meijer◆, Speedway◆
	Food	N: Bob Evans, Famous Dave's BBQ
		S: Dunkin Donuts, Cracker Barrel, IHOP
	Lodg	N: Comfort Inn, Microtel, Holiday Inn Microtel, Red Roof Inn♥, Super 8
	Lodg	S: Baymont Inn
	Other	S: Sam's Club
		S: Home Depot, Kmart
234A		Harper Ave S, Clinton Twp
234B		Harper Ave N, Clinton Twp
234		Harper Ave, Clinton Twp
	Gas	N: Amoco, Citgo, Sunoco◆
		S: Mobil
	Food	N: Pizza, Subway
		S: Little Caesar's, Subway
235		Shook Rd (WB exit, EB entr)
236		16 Mile Rd, Metropolitan Pkwy
	Food	S: McDonald's, Subway
	Med	S: + Hospital
237		N River Rd, Mt Clemens
	FStop	N: North River AmocoBP
	Gas	N: Mobil◆
	Food	N: McDonald's
	Lodg	N: Comfort Inn
	Other	N: RV Center
240A		Rosso Hwy E, to MI 59, Utica (EB)
240B		Rosso Hwy W, to MI 59, Utica (EB)
240		Rosso Hwy, to MI 59, Utica
	Gas	N: 7-11, BP, Marathon, Speedway
	Food	N: Arby's, Bob Evan's, McDonald's, O'Charley's, Tim Horton
	Lodg	N: Best Western
	Other	N: Wal-Mart
241		21 Mile Rd, Selfridge (Access to Ex #240 Serv)
	FStop	N: M&M Gas & Grocery/Citgo
	Gas	N: Marathon
	Food	N: Quiznos, Subway
	Other	N: CVS
243		23 Mile Rd, MI 29, to MI 3, MI 59, New Baltimore, Utica
	FStop	S: Speedway #2314
	Gas	N: Marathon, Meijer◆, Shell◆, Sunoco
		S: Marathon◆
	Food	N: Applebee's, Arby's, McDonald's, Outback Steakhouse, Starbucks, Steak 'n Shake, Texas Roadhouse, White Castle, Wendy's
		S: Big Boy, Taco Bell
	Lodg	N: Chesterfield Motel
	Other	N: Discount Tire, Home Depot, Lowe's, Kmart, Staples, Walgreen's, Target, MI CAT, Roseville RV Center
247		MI 19, Washington St, New Haven Rd, New Baltimore, New Haven (EB exit, WB entr)
	FStop	N: New Haven Citgo
	Food	N: NobleRomansPizza/NH Citgo, New Haven Coney Island, AM Donut
248		26 Mile Rd, New Haven, Marine City
	Gas	N: BP
		S: 7-11, Mobil
	Food	N: McDonald's
(250)		Rest Area (WB) (Next RA 62 mi) (RR, Phone, Picnic, Vend)
(255)		Rest Area (EB) (RR, Phone, Picnic, Vend)
257		Division Rd, Adair, Casco, St Clair
	FStop	S: 257 BP
	Other	S: MI State Hwy Patrol Post

◆ = Regular Gas Stations with Diesel   ▲ = RV Friendly Locations   ♥ = Pet Friendly Locations
RED PRINT SHOWS LARGE VEHICLE PARKING/ACCESS ON SITE OR NEARBY   BROWN PRINT SHOWS CAMPGROUNDS/RV PARKS

W 94 — MICHIGAN

EXIT		
262		Wadhams Rd, St Clair
	FStop	S: Road Hawk Travel Center/Marathon (Scales)
	Other	N: St Clair Thousand Trails▲, to Port Huron KOA▲
		S: Laundry/Road Hawk TC
266		I-94 Bus, MI 25, Gratiot Rd, Smiths Creek, Marysville
	FStop	S: Sunrise/Amoco Express
	Gas	S: Shell, Plum's Conv Store
	Food	S: Burger King, Big Boy, KFC, Little Caesar's, McDonald's, Taco Bell
	Lodg	S: Days Inn, Microtel, Super 8
	Med	S: + Hospital
	Other	N: St Clair Co Int'l Airport✈
		S: CVS, AutoZone
269		Range Rd, Dove St, Port Huron
	Gas	N: Speedway◆
	Food	N: Burger King
	Lodg	N: AmeriHost
NOTE:		I-94 runs with I-69 below. Exit #'s follow I-94.
(271)		Jct I-69W, to Flint
		Jct I-69E, to Pt Huron
274		Water St, Lapeer Ave, Pt Huron
	N:	MI Welcome Center (WB) (RR, Phone, Picnic, Vend, Info)
	FStop	S: ByLo Speedy Q #6
	Gas	S: Speedway◆
	Food	N: Cracker Barrel
		S: Bob Evans
	Lodg	N: Best Western, Ramada Inn
		S: Comfort Inn, Fairfield Inn, Hampton Inn, Knights Inn
	Other	N: Lake Port State Park
275		I-69 Bus, MI 25, Pine Grove Ave, Port Huron, Toll Bridge to Canada (EB, Left exit)
	Gas	S: BP, Clark, Shell, Speedway
	Food	S: McDonald's, Wendy's, White Castle
	Lodg	S: Best Western, Days Inn, Holiday Inn
	Other	S: CanAm Duty Free, Pharmacy
		(I-94 begins/ends on MI 25) (EASTERN TIME ZONE)

⊙ MICHIGAN

Interstate 95 S — MAINE

Begin Southbound I-95 from Canada / Maine border to Miami, FL.

⊙ MAINE (EASTERN TIME ZONE)

EXIT		
(306)		US/Canada Border, US Customs, ME State Line
305		Airport Rd, to US 2, Military St, Houlton (Last US Exit)
	Other	E: Houlton Int'l Airport✈, AmEx Duty Free
302		US 1, North St, Houlton, Downtown, Presque Isle
	W:	ME Welcome Center (SB) Rest Area (NB) (RR, Phone, Picnic, Info)
	FStop	W: Doc's Place
	TStop	W: FJ TP/Travelers Irving Big Stop (Scales)
	Gas	E: Irving Mainway◆
	Food	E: Burger King, KFC, McDonald's, Pizza Hut, Tangs Chinese
		W: BigStopRest/Irving Big Stop, Governor Rest & Bakery, Tim Horton's, Subway
	Lodg	E: Scottish Inns
		W: Ivey's Motor Lodge, Stardust Motel
	TServ	W: Irving Big Stop/Tires, Hogan Tire
	Med	E: + Houlton Reg'l Hospital
	Other	E: Houlton Tire, Grocery, Pharmacy, VIP Auto Center, to Houlton Int'l Airport✈, to Greenland Cove Campground▲
		W: Auto Dealers, Wal-Mart, ME State Hwy Patrol Post, My Brothers Place Campground▲
291		US 2, Silver Ridge Rd, Oakfield, Smyrna Mills, New Limerick
286		Oakfield Rd, to US 2, ME 212, ME 11, Oakfield, Smyrna Mills
	Gas	W: Irving Mainway◆, Valero◆
	Food	W: Crossroads Café, A Place to Eat
	Other	W: to appr 4mi Birch Point Campground & Cottages▲
276		ME 159, to US 2, Island Falls, Patten
	Gas	E: Citgo
	Other	E: to appr 4mi Birch Point Campground & Cottages▲
		W: to Baxter State Park, Matagamon Wilderness
264		Main St, ME 158, ME 11, Sherman
	TStop	W: Irving Big Stop
	Gas	E: Mobil
	Food	W: Rest/Irving BS
	Lodg	W: Katahdin Valley Motel
	Other	E: to Barnett's Cabins & Camping▲
		W: LP/Irving
259		Casey Rd, Pond Rd, to US 2, ME 11 Benedicta, Sherman (NB ex, SB reacc)
(252)		Scenic View Mt Katahdin (NB) (May-Oct) (RR, Phone, Picnic)
244		ME 157, Medway Rd, Medway, Millinocket, Mattawamkeag
	TStop	W: Irving Big Stop
	Food	W: Rest/Irivng BS, Gram's Place
	Lodg	W: Gateway Inn
	Other	W: to Baxter State Park, Pine Grove Campground & Cottages▲, Katahdin Shadows Campground▲, Hidden Springs Campground▲, Big Moose Inn Cabins & Campground▲
(243)		Rest Area (Both dir) (RR, Phone, Picnic, Vend)
227		to ME 16, US 2, Penobscot Valley Ave, Lincoln (All Serv in Lincoln)
	Gas	E: Doc's Place, Irving Conv
	Food	E: McDonald's, China Light, Taco Bell, Subway, Mill St Diner, Steak & Stuff
	Lodg	E: Briarwood Motor Inn, Thomas Motel
	Med	E: + Penobscot Valley Hospital
	Other	E: Lincoln Reg'l Airport✈, to Sleeping Bear Camping▲
217		ME 155, ME 6, Howland, LaGrange Enfield, Milo
	Gas	E: Citgo, Irving
	Food	E: Little Peter's Seafood
	Other	E: Lakeside Campground & Cabins▲
199		ME 6, Old Town, to Alton, LaGrange, Milo (NB ex, SB reacc)
(198)		Weigh Station (Both dir)
197		ME 43, Old Town, Hudson, Milford
	Gas	E: Exxon, Mike's Car Service
	Food	E: Wendy's
	Other	E: DeWitt Field Airport✈, Grocery, to Greenwood Acres Campground▲
193		Stillwater Ave, Old Town, Orono
	Gas	E: Citgo◆, Irving, Mobil◆
	Food	E: Burger King, China Garden, Governor Rest, KFC, McDonald's, Subway
	Lodg	E: Best Western
	Other	E: Dollar Tree, Grocery, Univ of ME/Orono
		W: Pushaw Lake Campground▲
191		Kelly Rd, Orono, Veazie
	Other	E: Univ of ME/Orono
187		Hogan Rd, Bangor, Veazie
	Gas	E: Exxon, Mobil, Sam's Club
		W: Exxon◆, Irving, Doc's Place
	Food	E: Denny's
		W: Applebee's, Arby's, Bugaboo Creek Steakhouse, Burger King, Chili's, KFC, McDonald's, Olive Garden, Pizza Hut, Quiznos, Red Lobster, Smokey Bones BBQ, Starbucks, Wendy's, 99 Rest
	Lodg	W: Bangor Motor Inn, Comfort Inn♥, Country Inn, Days Inn, Hampton Inn
	TServ	E: Bangor Peterbilt
	Med	E: + Hospital
	Other	E: Auto Dealers, Sam's Club
		W: Bangor Mall, Cinema 1-8, Advance Auto, Best Buy, CarWash, Circuit City, Goodyear, Home Depot, Office Depot, Staples, Target, UPS Store, Wal-Mart
186		Stillwater Ave, Bangor (Access to Ex #187)
185		ME 15, Broadway, Bangor, Brewer
	Gas	E: Irving
		W: Mobil, Exxon
	Food	E: Tri-City Pizza
		W: China Light, Friendly's, Pizza Hut, Governor's, McDonald's, KFC
	Med	E: + Hospital
	Other	W: Firestone, Grocery, RiteAid

◆ = Regular Gas Stations with Diesel ▲ = RV Friendly Locations ♥ = Pet Friendly Locations
RED PRINT SHOWS LARGE VEHICLE PARKING/ACCESS ON SITE OR NEARBY BROWN PRINT SHOWS CAMPGROUNDS/RV PARKS

EXIT	MAINE
184	ME 222, Union St, Ohio St, Airport
Gas	E: Citgo, Exxon
	W: Exxon, Mobil◆
Food	W: Burger King, McDonald's, Wendy's
Lodg	W: Sheraton
Other	E: Holden Family Campground▲
	W: Staples, Bangor Int'l Airport✈, Paul Bunyan Campground▲, to appr 5mi Pleasant Hill RV Park & Campground▲
183	US 2, US 2A, ME 100, Hammond St
Gas	E: Exxon, Gulf
Food	E: Subway, Papa Gambino's Pizza & Subs
Other	W: Bangor Int'l Airport✈
182B	to US 2W, ME 100W, Hermon
Gas	W: Irving◆, Mobil◆
Food	W: Barnaby's, Dunkin Donuts, Ground Round, Jason's NY Style Pizza
Lodg	W: Days Inn, Econo Lodge, Fairfield Inn, Holiday Inn, Motel 6♥, Ramada, Super 8
Other	W: Movie City 8, Gopher Ridge RV Park▲, Webb's RV Center, Bangor Int'l Airport✈
(182A)	Jct I-395S, ME 15, to US 1A, ME 9, Bangor, Brewer
Other	E: Brewer Airport✈, Downtown, USS ME Monument, WW II Memorial, to Red Barn Campground▲
180	Coldbrook Rd, Hampden, Hermon
TStop	W: Dysart's Service/Citgo (Scales)
Gas	E: Dysart Conv Store
Food	W: Rest/Dysart's
Lodg	W: Best Western♥
TWash	W: Dysart's
TServ	W: Dysart's
Other	W: Laundry/RVDump/Dysart's, Pumpkin Patch RV Resort▲, to Wheeler Stream Camping Area▲
(178)	Rest Area (SB) (RR, Phone, Picnic, Vend, Info)
(176)	Rest Area (NB) (RR, Phone, Picnic, Vend, Info)
174	ME 69, Hampden Rd, Carmel Rd N, Carmel, Winterport
Gas	E: Citgo◆
Other	W: Shady Acres RV & Campground▲
167	to ME 69, ME 143, Lakins Rd, Etna, Dixmont
Other	W: Ring Hill Airport✈, Stetson Shores Campground▲
161	ME 7, Moosehead Trail, to US 2, ME 100, E Newport, Plymouth
159	Ridge Rd, to US 2, ME 100, Newport, Dexter, Plymouth (SB)
Other	W: Sebasticook Lake Campground▲, Christie's Campground▲
157	ME 11, ME 100, Ox Bow Rd, to US 2, ME 7, Newport, Dexter
TStop	W: FJ TP/Irving Big Stop
Gas	W: Citgo, Mobil◆
Food	E: Burger King, Dunkin Donuts
	W: Rest/Irving BS, House of Pizza, Pat's Pizza, Front Porch Rest BBQ & Grill, Sawyers Dairy Bar, Subway
Lodg	W: Pray's Motel
Med	E: + Hospital
Other	W: LP/Irving, Auto Dealers, Carquest, Grocery, Pharmacy, Radio Shack, Wal-Mart sc,

EXIT	MAINE
Other	W: to Moose Mtn, Sugarloaf Ski Area, Skowhegan/Canaan KOA▲, Palmyra RV Resort/Palmyra Golf▲
150	Weeks Rd, Somerset Ave, to ME 11/100/152, Pittsfield, Palmyra, Hartland, Burnham
Gas	E: Mobil
Food	E: Subway
Lodg	E: Pittsfield Motor Inn
Med	E: + Hospital
Other	E: Auto Services, Family Dollar, Grocery, RiteAid, Pittsfield Muni Airport✈
(145)	Rest Area (Both dir) (RR, Phone, Picnic, Vend)
138	Hinckley Rd, Baker St, Clinton
Gas	W: Citgo◆
133	US 201, Main St, Fairfield, Skowhegan, Quebec City
TStop	W: FJ TP/Irving 201 Big Stop (Scales)
Food	W: Rest/Irving BS
TServ	W: Irving BS/Tires
Other	W: Laundry/LP/Irving BS, Skowhegan/Canaan KOA▲
132	ME 139, Western Ave, Fairfield
TStop	W: Pilot Travel Center #203 (Scales)
Food	W: Subway/Pilot TC
Other	W: Laundry/WiFi/Pilot TC
130	ME 104, Main St, Waterville
Gas	E: Mobil
Food	E: Arby's, McDonald's, Ruby Tuesday, Starbucks, Subway, Wendy's
Lodg	E: Best Western, Comfort Inn, Holiday Inn
Med	E: + ME Gen'l Medical Center
Other	E: Auto Dealers, Square Cinema, Grocery, Home Depot, Pharmacy, Radio Shack, Staples, Wal-Mart sc, to Colby College
127	ME 11, ME 137, Kennedy Memorial Dr, Waterville
Gas	E: Citgo, Irving◆, Mobil
	W: Exxon◆, Valero
Food	E: Applebee's, Angelo's, Burger King, McDonald's, Papa John's, Pizza Hut, Quiznos, Subway, Weathervane Seafood
	W: China Express
Lodg	E: Budget Host, Econo Lodge, Hampton Inn
Med	E: + Inland Hospital
Other	E: Auto Dealers, Cinema, Grocery, RiteAid, Wal-Mart, Countryside Camping▲, to appr 10mi Green Valley Campground▲ Waterville Robert Lefleur Airport✈
	W: Mid-Maine Marine & RV
120	Lyons Rd, Sidney, Augusta
(117)	Rest Area (Both dir) (RR, Phone, Picnic, Vend)
113	ME 3, to ME 104, Augusta
112	ME 8, ME 11, ME 27, N to Belgrade, S to Augusta (SB)
Gas	E: Citgo, Getty
	W: Irving◆
Food	E: Denny's, Ground Round, Longhorn Steakhouse, Olive Garden, Red Robin, Ruby Tuesday
	W: Taco Bell, Wendy's, 99 Rest
Lodg	E: Holiday Inn
	W: Comfort Inn

◆ = Regular Gas Stations with Diesel ▲ = RV Friendly Locations ♥ = Pet Friendly Locations
RED PRINT SHOWS LARGE VEHICLE PARKING/ACCESS ON SITE OR NEARBY   BROWN PRINT SHOWS CAMPGROUNDS/RV PARKS

I-95 MAINE

EXIT		
	Other	E: ATMs, Banks, B&N, Circuit City, Grocery, Home Depot, Sam's Club, Staples, **Wal-Mart sc**, Civic Center, Univ of ME/Augusta
112A		ME 11, ME 27, S-Augusta (NB)
112B		ME 11, ME 27, N-Belgrade (NB)
109		US 202, ME 11/17/100, E to Augusta, W to Winthrop (NB)
	Gas	E: Irving◊, Shell
		W: Exxon, Getty, Valero
	Food	E: Applebee's, Arby's, Burger King, DQ, KFC, McDonald's, Oyster Bar & Grill, Subway, Wendy's
		W: Ponderosa, Tea House Chinese
	Lodg	E: Best Western
		W: Best Inn, Econo Lodge, Motel 6♥, **Super 8**
	Other	E: Auto Services, Dollar Tree, Grocery, Kmart, Tires, Augusta State Airport✈
		W: Grocery, ME Comm'l Tire, PetCo♥, Auto Dealers, Auto Services, **Scott's Recreation**
109B		US 202, ME 11/17/100, W to Winthrop (SB)
109A		US 202, ME 11/17/100, E to Augusta (SB)
NOTE:		I-95 below runs with ME Tpk
(103)		Jct I-495S, Maine Tpk, to Litchfield, Gardiner
102		ME 9, ME 126, Lewiston Rd, Gardiner, to Sabbatus
(100)		Gardiner TOLL Plaza
(97)		**Litchfield Service Plaza (NB)**
	FStop	Mobil
	Food	Burger King
86		ME 9, Middle Rd, Sabattus, to Richmond, Lisbon
(83)		**Lewiston Service Plaza (SB)**
	FStop	Mobil
	Food	Burger King
80		ME 196, Lisbon St, Lisbon, Lewiston
	Gas	W: Getty, Mobil, Shell
	Food	W: KFC, Lisbon Donuts, Carribou Café, Governor's Rest, Little Caesar's
	Lodg	W: Motel 6♥, Ramada Inn, Super 8
	Med	W: + St Mary's Regional Med Center, + Central ME Medical Center
	Other	W: Flagship Cinema, Pharmacy, UPS Store
75		to US 202, ME 4, ME 100, Kittyhawk Ave, Auburn
	FStop	E: FJ TP/Irving Mainway #1475
	Food	E: Rest/Auburn Inn
	Lodg	E: Auburn Inn, Sleepytime Motel
	TServ	W: Freightliner
	Other	W: Auburn Lewiston Muni Airport✈
(67)		New Gloucester TOLL Plaza
63		US 202, ME 115, ME 26, ME 100, Gray, New Gloucester
	Gas	E: Mobil, Oil
		W: Gary's
	Food	E: Subway, McDonald's, China Gray
	Other	W: to 26N: Sunday River Ski Resort, Mt Abram Ski Area

Personal Notes

EXIT		MAINE
(58)		**Cumberland Service Plaza** (Hours 6a-10p)
	FStop	Mobil
	Food	Burger King, TCBY
53		ME 26, ME 100, Falmouth, Portland
	Gas	E: Irving◊
52		Falmouth Spur, to I-295, US 1 Falmouth, Freeport
48		Larrabee Rd, Riverside St, to ME 25, US 302, Westbrook, Portland
	FStop	W: Mobil
	Gas	E: Citgo, BJ's
		W: Exxon, Shell
	Food	E: Applebee's, Burger King, Subway
		W: Denny's, KFC, McDonald's, Panda Garden, Ruby Tuesday, Tim Horton's, Valle's Steakhouse, Wendy's
	Lodg	E: Ramada Inn, Rodeway Inn
		W: Howard Johnson, Motel 6♥, Holiday Inn, Super 8, Travelodge
	TServ	W: Freightliner
	Other	E: BJ's, Grocery, Lowe's, Auto Dealers, **Wal-Mart**
		W: Auto Dealers, Auto Service, Grocery, Home Depot, Pharmacy, Tires
47		Rand Rd, Westbrook Arterial, to MI 25, Portland
46		Jetport Rd, to ME 9, ME 22, Congress St, Portland (Access to Ex #45 Serv)
	Other	W: Auto & Truck Service, Commercial Tires

EXIT		MAINE
45		to ME Mall Rd, Payne Rd, to US 1, ME 9, I-295, S Portland
	Gas	E: Gulf, Mobil, Shell
	Food	E: Bugaboo Creek Steakhouse, Chili's, Friendly's, IHOP, Old Country Buffet, Olive Garden, Outback Steakhouse, Panda Express, Panera Bread, Romano Macaroni Grill, Ruby Tuesday, Starbucks, TGI Friday, Tim Horton, Weathervane Seafood
		W: Applebee's, Starbucks
	Lodg	E: Comfort Inn, Courtyard, Days Inn, Econo Lodge, Fairfield Inn, Hampton Inn, Hilton Garden Inn, Residence Inn, Sheraton Towneplace Suites
		W: Holiday Inn Express, Marriott
	Other	E: ATMs, AAA, Banks, Best Buy, Borders, Circuit City, Grocery, Office Depot, PetCo♥, Staples, Sam's Club, Tires, **Wal-Mart**, ME Mall, Portland Int'l Jetport✈, to **Kenworth**
44		to ME 114, Jct I-295N, S Portland, Downtown (NB) (Acc to Ex #45 Serv)
42		Haigais Pkwy, to US 1, Scarborough
	Lodg	E: Millbrook Motel, Oak Leaf Motel, Moosehead Motel, Shady Pine Motel
	Other	E: NE Truck Tires, Scarborough Downs Racetrack
		W: Beech Ridge Motor Speedway
(36)		Jct I-195E, Saco, Old Orchard Beach
	Lodg	E: Hampton Inn
	Other	E: to **Saco/Old Orchard Beach KOA**▲
32		ME 111, Biddiford
	FStop	E: Irving
	Food	E: Ruby Tuesday, Subway, Wendy's
		W: Applebee's
	Lodg	E: Best Value Inn, Biddiford Motel
	Med	E: + Hospital
	Other	E: AutoZone, Grocery, **Wal-Mart sc**, Biddiford Muni Airport✈
		W: Best Buy, Home Depot, Lowe's, PetSmart♥, Staples, Target
25		ME 35, Kennebunk, to US 1
	Lodg	E: Turnpike Motel
		W: Lodge at Kennebunk
	TServ	E: Freightliner
(24)		**Kennebunk Service Area (Both dir)**
	FStop	Mobil
	Food	Burger King, Popeye's, TCBY
		Burger King, Sbarro, TCBY
19		ME 109, ME 9, Wells, Sanford
	Other	W: Amtrak
(7)		York Toll Plaza
NOTE:		Begin NB/End SB TOLL
NOTE:		I-95 above runs with ME Tpk
7		to US 1, ME 91, Yorks, Ogunquit (Last Free Exit NB)
	Gas	E: Irving◊, Mobil◊, Shell
	Food	E: Greenleaves Chinese, Mandarin Inn, Ruby's Grill, Safina's Italian Rest.
	Lodg	E: York Commons Inn, Mic Macmotel
	Other	E: Auto Dealers, Grocery
	Med	E: + York Hospital
(6)		Weigh Station (NB)
(3)		Weigh Station (SB)
(3)		**ME Welcome Center (NB)** (RR, Phone, Picnic, Vend, Info)

◊ = Regular Gas Stations with Diesel ▲ = RV Friendly Locations ♥ = Pet Friendly Locations
RED PRINT SHOWS LARGE VEHICLE PARKING/ACCESS ON SITE OR NEARBY BROWN PRINT SHOWS CAMPGROUNDS/RV PARKS

Page 503

INTERSTATE 95 N/S

EXIT		ME / NH
3		to US 1N, ME 236, Coastal Route, Kittery (NB)
2		ME 236, Kittery (NB)
	TStop	E: Howell's Travel Stop/Irving (Scales)
	Food	E: Rest/Howell's TS
1		Dennot Rd, to ME 103 (NB ex, SB reacc)
	Gas	E: Citgo, Sunoco
	Food	E: Sue's Seafood, Warren's Lobster House
	Lodg	E: Days Inn, Blue Roof Motel, NorEaster Motel, Inn at Portsmouth Harbor
	Other	E: to Portsmouth Naval Base

(EASTERN TIME ZONE)

⋂ MAINE
⋃ NEW HAMPSHIRE
(EASTERN TIME ZONE)

NOTE: Listings show Mile Marker / Exit #

17/7		Market St, Woodbury Ave, Portsmouth Bus Distr, Waterfront Historic Sites
	Food	W: Applebee's, Bickford's Family Rest, Ruby Tuesday, Wendy's
	Lodg	W: Courtyard, Hampton Inn, Homewood Suites
	Other	W: BJ's, Grocery, Pep Boys, Home Depot
15/6		Woodbury Ave, Portsmouth (NB)
	Gas	E: Shell
	Lodg	E: Anchorage Inn, Best Inn, Holiday Inn
14/5		Spaulding Tpk, US 4, NH 16, Newington, Dover (SB) NH Tpk, US 1 ByP, (NB, Exit only) I-95N, to Maine (NB, Left 3 lanes)
	FStop	E: O'Brien's #2/Citgo (US 1 ByP)
	TStop	E: Hanscom's Truck Stop (US 1 ByP)
(14)		Begin/End TOLL Road
13/4		Spaulding Tpk, US 4, NH 16, NH Lakes, Newington, Dover (NB, Left exit)
12/3A		Grafton Rd, Pease Int'l Tradeport Airport, Trailways (SB)
12/3B		NH 33, Greenland Rd, Portsmouth
	NOTE:	SB: Last Exit Before TOLL
12/3		NH 33, Greenland Rd, Portsmouth
	FStop	W: Exit 3 Truck Stop/Sunoco
	TStop	W: Travel Center of America (Scales) (SB: Access via Exit #3B)
	Food	W: Buckhorn/TA TC
	Other	E: Shel-Al Campground▲ W: Laundry/WiFi/TA TC
(6)		Hampton TOLL Plaza
6/2		NH 101, Hampton, Exeter
	Other	E: to US 1/1A, Hampton Beach W: to Manchester, Epping
(1)		Begin/End TOLL Road
1/1		NH 107, to US 1, Seabrook
	FStop	E: Seabrook One Stop/Sunoco
	Gas	E: Getty W: Citgo

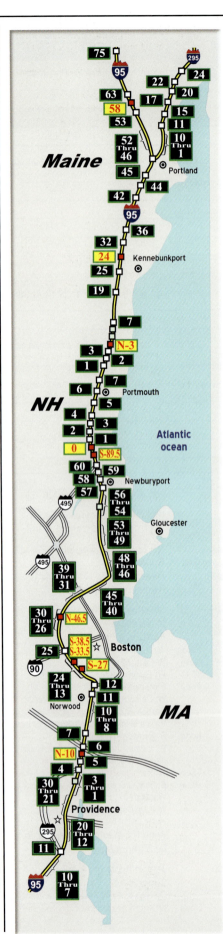

EXIT		NH / MA
	Food	E: Applebee's, Burger King, Dunkin Donuts, McDonald's, Rock in Lobster, Steak & Seafood, Subway, Wendy's W: Capt K's Seafood, Master MacGrath's
	Lodg	E: Hampshire Inn W: Best Western
	Other	E: AutoZone, CVS, Home Depot, Lowe's, Grocery, Laundromat, Staples, Tires, Wal-Mart W: Sam's Club, Greyhound Park, Green Gate Campground▲, Exeter Elms Family Campground▲
(0)		NH Welcome Center (NB) (RR, Phone, Picnic, Info)

(EASTERN TIME ZONE)

⋂ NEW HAMPSHIRE
⋃ MASSACHUSETTS
(EASTERN TIME ZONE)

NOTE: Listings show Mile Marker / Exit #

(89.5)		MA Welcome Center (SB) (RR, Phone, Picnic, Vend, Info)
89.5/60		Main St, MA 286, US 1, Beaches, Salisbury
	Gas	W: Pump & Pantry
	Food	E: Lena's Seafood
	Lodg	W: Johnson's Motel
	Other	E: Black Bear Family Campground▲, Rusnik Campground▲
(88.8/59)		I-495S, Worcester (SB, rt 2 lanes)
87.2/58		MA 110, to I-495S, W-Amesbury, E-Salisbury (SB)
	Gas	E: Sunoco◊ W: Irving, Mobil
	Food	E: China Buffet, Crossroads Pizza, Dunkin Donuts, Frankie's Roast Beef, Sylvan St Grill, Winners Circle W: Burger King, McDonald's, Papa Gino's
	Lodg	W: Fairfield Inn
	Other	E: Pines Camping Area▲, Beach Rose RV Park▲, Auto Dealers, U-Haul, Penske W: Pharmacy, Auto Dealers
58A		MA 110E, to Salisbury (NB)
87.4/58B		MA 110W, to I-495 (NB)
85.7/57		MA 113, Storey Ave, Newburyport W Newbury
	Gas	E: Mobil, Shell, Sunoco
	Food	E: Dunkin Donuts, Friendly's, McDonalds, Jade Chinese, Papa Gino's
	Med	E: + Hospital
	Other	E: Kmart, Walgreen's, Grocery
82.6/56		Scotland Rd, South St, Byfield, Newbury, W Newbury
	Other	E: MA State Hwy Patrol
80.9/55		Central St, Byfield, Newbury
	Gas	E: Prime Energy
	Food	E: Village Diner
(79)		Weigh Station (Both dir)
77/54		MA 133, Main St, W-Georgetown, E-Rowley (SB)
77.1/54A		MA 133, Main St, E-Rowley (NB)
77.3/54B		MA 133W, to Georgetown (NB)

◊ = Regular Gas Stations with Diesel ▲ = RV Friendly Locations ♥ = Pet Friendly Locations
RED PRINT SHOWS LARGE VEHICLE PARKING/ACCESS ON SITE OR NEARBY BROWN PRINT SHOWS CAMPGROUNDS/RV PARKS

EXIT	MASSACHUSETTS
75.4/53	MA 97, Boxford, Topsfield
72.9/52	Topsfield Rd, Boxford, Topsfield
71.2/51	Endicott Rd, Topsham, Middleton
68.6/50	US 1, Topsfield, to MA 62, Danvers
Gas	E: Exxon, Mobil
Food	W: Quiznos, Subway, Supino's Italian
Lodg	W: Sheraton
Other	E: Beverly Muni Airport✈
	W: CVS, Staples
67.9/49	MA 62, Danvers, Middletown (NB)
66.5/48	Centre St, Danvers (SB)
Food	W: Italian Rest
Lodg	W: Comfort Inn, Extended Stay America, Village Green
66.3/47AB	MA 114, S-Peabody, N-Middleton (NB)
Gas	E: Exxon◆, Shell, Sunoco
Food	E: Friendly's, Papa Gino's
	W: Chili's, McDonald's
Lodg	W: Motel 6♥, Residence Inn
Other	E: Lowe's, Wal-Mart
	W: Auto Dealers, Home Depot
65.1/46	US 1S, Boston
Gas	W: Gulf, Shell, Sunoco
Food	W: Burger King, Seawitch Seafood
Lodg	W: Mario's Motor Inn, Sir John Motel
65/45	MA 128N, Gloucester, Peabody
65/44AB	US 1, MA 129, Peabody, Boston, Everett
FStop	W: Best Auto Truck Stop
Gas	E: Shell
	W: Shell
Food	W: Rest/Best ATS, Bennigan's, Bickford's Family Rest, Carrabba's, Wendy's
Lodg	W: Holiday Inn
Med	E: + Hospital
Other	E: MA State Hwy Patrol Post
63/43	Walnut St, Lynnfield, Saugus
62/42	Salem St, Audubon Rd, Wakefield
Gas	E: Mobil, Sunoco
Lodg	W: Sheraton
60/41	Main St, Vernon St, Lynnfield, Wakefield
59/40	MA 129, Wakefield, N Reading
Gas	E: Exxon
Other	W: Camp Curtis Guild Natl Guard Res
58/39	North Ave, Wakefield, Reading
Gas	E: Exxon
	W: Shell
Lodg	E: Best Western
Med	E: + Hospital
57/38AB	MA 28, Main St, Reading
Gas	E: Gulf, Shell, Hess◆
	W: Exxon, Mobil, Shell
Food	E: Baja Fresh, Bickford's Family Rest, Dunkin Donuts, Ground Round, 99 Rest, Subway
	W: McDonald's
Med	E: + Hospital
Other	E: CVS, Grocery
(56/37AB)	Jct I-93, S-Boston, N-Manchester
55/36	Washington St, Woburn, Winchester
Gas	E: Getty
	W: Mobil, Shell

EXIT	MASSACHUSETTS
Food	E: Dunkin Donuts, Far East, Nick's Oasis
	W: D'Angelo's, McDonald's, 99 Rest
Lodg	E: Crowne Plaza
	W: Comfort Inn, Fairfield Inn, Hampton Inn, Red Roof Inn♥
Other	E: BJ's, Staples, Auto Dealers
	W: CVS, Lowe's, Hogan Tire, Office Depot, Mall, US Post Office
54/35	MA 38, Main St, Wilmington, Woburn
FStop	W: Jimmy's Garage/Mobil
Food	W: Baldwin's, Applebee's
Lodg	E: Ramada
	W: Sierra Suites
Other	W: Grocery
53/34	Winn St, Burlington, Woburn
52/33AB	US 3S, MA 3A N, Cambridge St, Winchester, Burlington
Gas	W: Citgo, Hess
Food	E: Chuck E Cheese Pizza, Papa Razzi's, Outback Steakhouse, Bickford's Family Rest
Lodg	W: Marriott
Med	W: + Hospital
Other	E: CVS
51/32BA	Middlesex Tpk, to US 3, Burlington, Arlington
Gas	E: Mobil, Shell
Food	E: Burger King, Charlie's, McDonald's
	W: Boston Market, Chili's, Romano Macaroni Grill
Lodg	E: Sheraton, Staybridge Suites
	W: Howard Johnson, Homestead Village
Med	W: + Hospital
Other	E: Circuit City
	W: Mall, Staples
32A	US 3N, Lowell, Nashua, NH (SB)
32B	Middlesex Tunrpike (NB)
48/31AB	MA 4, MA 225, Hanscom AFB, Lexington, Carlisle, Bedford
Gas	E: Mobil, Shell
	W: Shell, Exxon
Food	E: Starbucks
	W: McDonald's
Lodg	W: Holiday Inn Express, Quality Inn
Other	W: Hanscom Field, Hanscom AFB
47/30AB	MA 2A, Concord, E Lexington
Gas	E: Shell
Lodg	W: Sheraton
Other	W: Minute Man Nat'l Historic Park, Hanscom AFB
(46.5)	Service Area (NB)
FStop	Mobil
Food	McDonald's
46/29AB	MA 2E, Cambridge Tpk, Lexington
45/28AB	Trapelo Rd, Belmont, Lincoln
Gas	E: Exxon◆, Mobil◆, Shell
Food	E: Burger King, Friendly's, McDonald's
44/27AB	Totten Pond Rd, Winter St, Waltham
Gas	E: Shell
Food	E: Best Western, Home Suites Hotel, Hilton Garden Inn
Lodg	E: Best Western, Courtyard, Hometree Suites, Homestead Studio, Sheraton
	W: Doubletree, Marriott
Other	W: Costco, Home Depot

EXIT	MASSACHUSETTS
43/26	US 20, Weston St, Boston Post Rd, to MA 117, Waltham, Weston
Gas	E: Sunoco
	W: Mobil
Med	E: + Hospital
(42/25)	Jct I-90, MA Tpk/TOLL
41/24	MA 30, South Ave, Weston, Newton, Wayland, Waltham
Gas	E: Mobil
Lodg	E: Marriott
Med	E: + Hospital
40/23	to Recreation Rd, to MA Tpk, to MA 30 (NB)
39/22AB	Grove St
Lodg	E: Holiday Inn Express
Other	E: Greyhound
(38.5)	Service Area (SB)
FStop	Mobil
Food	McDonald's
38/21AB	MA 16, Washington St, Newton, Lower Falls, Wellesley
Med	E: + Hospital
36/20AB	MA 9, Worcester St, Wellesley Hills Boston, Brookline
35/19AB	Highland Ave, Newton, Highlands
Gas	E: Gulf, Hess
	W: Shell
Food	E: Ground Round, McDonald's, Mighty Subs
	W: IHOP, Bickford's Family Rest
Lodg	E: Sheraton
Other	E: PetCo♥, Staples
34/18	Great Plain Ave, W Roxbury
(33.5)	Parking Area (SB)
33/17	MA 135, Needham, Wellesley
31/16AB	MA 109, High St, Dedham, Westwood
29/15AB	US 1, to MA 128, MA 1A, Dedham
Gas	W: Shell◆
Food	E: Bickford's Family Rest, Chili's, Joe's Grill, Panera Bread, TGI Friday
	W: Dunkin Donuts, Burger King
Lodg	E: Comfort Inn, Holiday Inn, Residence Inn
	W: Budget Inn
Med	E: + Walk-In Medical Center
Other	E: Grocery, BJ's, Costco, Best Buy
28/14	East St, Canton St, Westwood
Lodg	E: Hilton
TServ	E: Cummins, Kenworth
(27)	Rest Area (SB)
	(RR, Phone, Picnic)
26.5/13	Railway Station, University Ave
Other	W: Amtrak
(26/12)	Jct I-93N, Braintree, Boston
NOTE:	Begin SB/End NB Motorist Call Boxes
23/11AB	Neponset St, Norwood, Canton
Gas	E: Citgo, Sunoco
	W: Gulf
Med	W: + Hospital
Other	W: Norwood Memorial Airport✈
20/10	Coney St, to US 1, to MA 27, Sharon, Walpole (fr SB, diff reaccess/Serv W on US 1)
Gas	W: Shell

◆ = Regular Gas Stations with Diesel   ▲ = RV Friendly Locations   ♥ = Pet Friendly Locations

RED PRINT SHOWS LARGE VEHICLE PARKING/ACCESS ON SITE OR NEARBY   BROWN PRINT SHOWS CAMPGROUNDS/RV PARKS

Page 505

Interstate 95 N/S

EXIT		MA / RI
	Food	W: IHOP, McDonald's, Pizza Hut, Taco Bell, 99 Rest
	Lodg	W: Best Western
	Other	W: Mall, CVS, Home Depot, Staples, Auto Services, Walgreen's
19/9		US 1, to MA 27, Walpole (SB to Gillette Stadium)
	Gas	W: Exxon, Mobil, Shell
	Food	W: Bickford's Family Rest
	Lodg	W: Holiday Inn Express
	Other	W: Wal-Mart, Grocery
16.6/8		S Main S, Sharon, Mechanic St, Foxboro
13/7AB		MA 140, S-Mansfield, N-Foxboro
	Gas	W: Mobil
	Food	E: 99 Rest, Piccadilly
	Lodg	E: Comfort Inn, Courtyard, Holiday Inn, Red Roof Inn ♥, Residence Inn
	Other	E: Foxborough Business Center
(11/6AB)		Jct I-495, N to Worcester, S to Cape Cod
	Other	N: to Gillette Stadium, to US 1 Normandy Farms Family Camping Resort▲, to Circle CG Farm Campground▲
(10)		MA Welcome Center (NB) (RR, Phone, Picnic, Vend, Info) (Parking Area) (SB)
6.9/5		to MA 152, Attleboro
	Gas	W: Gulf◊
	Food	W: Wendy's
	Med	E: + Hospital
	Other	W: Laundromat, Grocery, Pharmacy
(5.9/4)		Jct I-295, to Woonsocket, Warwick
4.2/3AB		MA 123, Norton, Attleboro
	Gas	E: Shell◊
	Med	E: + Hospital
(3)		Weigh Station (Both dir) Picnic Area (NB)
1.5/2B		US 1A N, to US 1, Attleboro
1/2A		US 1A S, Pawtucket RI (NB), Newport Ave (SB), Attleboro
	Gas	E: Mobil, Shell, Sunoco
	Food	E: McDonald's, Olive Garden
	Other	E: Grocery, Home Depot, Kmart
.2/1		US 1 S, Broadway, Pawtucket (SB)
	Gas	W: Gulf, Sunoco
	Food	W: Burger King, Taco Bell
	Lodg	E: Days Inn

(EASTERN TIME ZONE)

⌂ MASSACHUSETTS
⌂ RHODE ISLAND
(EASTERN TIME ZONE)

NOTE: Exits list Mile Marker / Exit #.
NOTE: MM 43: Massachusetts State Line

43/30		East St, Central Falls, Roosevelt Ave, Pawtucket
	Food	E: Dunkin Donuts, Subway
	Other	E: Greyhound
43/29		US 1, Broadway, Cottage St (NB), US 1, to RI 114, Pawtucket (SB)
42/28		RI 114, Water St, School St (NB)
	Gas	E: Sunoco

Personal Notes

EXIT		RHODE ISLAND
42/27		Pearl St, Garden St, to US 1, Downtown Pawtucket (NB), US 1, George St, to RI 15, Providence, Pawtucket (SB)
	Gas	W: Shell, Sunoco◊
	Food	W: Burger King, Dunkin Donuts
	Lodg	W: Comfort Inn
	Med	W: + Hospital
41/26		RI 122, Main St, Pawtucket, Downtown (NB)
40/25AB		RI 126, Foch St, to US 1,N Main St, Smithfield Ave (NB)
40/25		RI 126, Foch St, to US 1,N Main St, Smithfield Ave, Providence (SB)
	Gas	E: Hess, Shell W: Gulf◊ Valero
	Med	E: + Hospital
	Other	E: CVS, Grocery
39/24		Branch Ave, Providence
	Gas	W: Mobil
39/23		RI 146, US 44, Woonsocket, Downtown, State Offices (NB), Charles St, to RI 146N (SB)
38/22ABC		US 6W, RI 10, Downtown Providence to Hartford, CT
22A:		US 6W, ME 10, Hartford Ct Univ of RI-Providence, Amtrak
22C:		Providence Place Civic Center, Mall
37/21		Washington St, Franklin St, Broadway (NB), Atwells Ave (SB)
	Lodg	E: Holiday Inn

EXIT		RHODE ISLAND
	Other	E: Civic/Convention Center W: Auto & Tire Services
(37/20)		Jct I-195, US 6E, East Providence, Cape Cod
36/19		Eddy St, to RI 1A, Allens Ave (SB)
	Med	W: + Hospital
35/18		US 1A, Thurbers Ave, Providence
	Gas	W: Shell
	Food	W: Burger King
	Med	W: + Hospital
34/17		US 1, Elmwood Ave (NB)
	Other	E: Roger Williams Park & Zoo
34/16		RI 10, to US 1, to RI 2/12, Cranston
	Other	E: Roger Williams Park & Zoo
32/15		Jefferson Blvd, Warwick, Cranston
	Gas	E: Getty◊, Mobil
	Food	E: Bickford's Family Rest, Bugaboo Creek Steakhouse, Dunkin Donuts, Shogun Steak & Seafood
	Lodg	E: Courtyard, La Quinta Inn ♥, Motel 6 ♥
	Other	E: U-Haul W: Coastal International Trucks, Colony RV Dealer, Budget RAC
31/14AB		RI 37, to RI 2, Cranston, to US 1, Jefferson Blvd, Warwick
	Gas	W: Shell, Sunoco
	Food	W: Burger King
	Other	E: Lincoln Ave Auto & Truck Service
30/13		Airport Connector Rd, to US 1, to TF Green State Airport, Warwick
	Gas	E: Exxon, Mobil
	Food	E: Capelli's Italian Rest, Dave's Bar & Grill, Great House Chinese, Legal Seafood
	Lodg	E: Best Western, Comfort Inn, Hampton Inn, Hilton Garden Inn, Holiday Inn Express, Homewood Suites ♥, Homestead Hotel ♥, Radisson, Residence Inn ♥, Sheraton
	Other	E: TF Green Int'l Airport ✈
(28/12B)		Jct I-295N, RI 113, to RI 2 (SB)
28/12A		RI 113E, East Ave, Warwick (SB)
28/12		RI 113E, East Ave, to RI 5, Warwick (NB)
	Gas	E: Sunoco, Shell◊
	Food	E: Ocean Express Seafood, Remington's
	Lodg	E: Crowne Plaza
	Other	E: Lowe's W: Wal-Mart, Warwick Mall
28/11		I-295N, Woonsocket (NB, Left exit)
10AB		Rte 117, E to Warwick, W to West Warwick (SB)
27/10		RI 117, Centerville Rd, Warwick (NB)
	Med	W: + Hospital
	Other	E: Park & Ride
25/9		RI 4S, E Greenwich, N Kingstown (SB, Left exit)
8AB		RI 2, Quaker Lane, S to RI 4, E Greenwich, N to West Warwick (NB)
8		RI 2, Quaker Ln, W Warwick (SB)
	Gas	E: Shell◊ W: Sunoco◊
	Food	E: Dunkin Donuts, McDonald's, Outback Steakhouse, Ruby Tuesday W: 99 Rest, Applebee's, Denny's, Papa Gino's, TGI Friday, Wendy's

◊ = Regular Gas Stations with Diesel   ▲ = RV Friendly Locations   ♥ = Pet Friendly Locations
RED PRINT SHOWS LARGE VEHICLE PARKING/ACCESS ON SITE OR NEARBY   BROWN PRINT SHOWS CAMPGROUNDS/RV PARKS

EXIT		RHODE ISLAND
	Lodg	E: Extended Stay America
		W: Comfort Suites, Marriott, Open Gate Motel, Springhill Suites
	Med	W: + Hospital
	Other	E: Walgreen's
		W: Auto Dealers, Best Buy, Mall, Grocery, Lowe's, Sam's Club, **Arlington RV SuperCenter**/RVDump, Camping▲
21/7		New London Tpike, W Greenwich, Coventry, West Warwick
	Gas	E: Ray's Service/Mobil◊
	Food	W: Applebee's, Cracker Barrel, Denny's, Quiznos, Wendy's
	Lodg	W: Hampton Inn, Wingate Inn
	Other	E: Auto repairs/Mobil, BJ's, Home Depot, **Wal-Mart sc**
20/6A		Hopkins Hill Rd
	Other	W: Park & Ride, Technology Park
18/6		RI 3, Nooseneck Hill Rd, Division Rd W Greenwich, to Coventry
	Gas	E: Shell◊, Sunoco◊
	Food	W: Dunkin Donuts, Mark's Grill, Pizza, Tim Horton's
	Lodg	E: Best Western, Super 8
15/5AB		RI 102, Victory Hwy, W Greenwich, S to N Kingstown, Exeter, N-Foster, West Greenwich
	TStop	W: PTP/RI's Only 24 Hr A/T Plaza (Scales)
	Food	W: FastFood/RI's ATP
	Lodg	W: Classic Motor Lodge
	TServ	W: RI's ATP
	Other	E: Wawaloam Campground▲
		W: Laundry/CB/WiFi/RI ATP, to appr 7mi **Oak Embers Campground▲**
(10)		Weigh Station **Picnic Area (SB)**
9/4		RI 3, to RI 165, Wyoming, Arcadia, Exeter (NB)
	Other	W: Arcadia State Park, to appr 8mi **Oak Embers Campground▲**
7/3AB		RI 138, E-Kingstown Rd, to US 1, Kingston, Newport, W-to RI 3, Wyoming, Hope Valley
	Gas	W: Exxon, Hess, Mobil, Valero
	Food	E: McDonald's, Tim Horton's, Wendy's
		W: Bickford's, Pizza
	Lodg	E: Cookie Jar B&B
		W: Stagecoach House, Sun Valley Inn
	Other	E: Grocery, Pharmacy, Richmond Airport✈, Univ of RI
		W: CVS, RI State Hwy Patrol, **Whispering Pines Campground▲**
(6)		RI Welcome Center (NB) (RR, Phone, Picnic, Vend, Info) (Closed daily 2a-5a)
4/2		Woodville Alton Rd, Hope Valley, Hopkinton, Alton
	Other	W: Whispering Pines Campground▲
1/1		RI 3, Main St, Ashaway, Hopkinton, Westerly
	Med	E: + Hospital
	Other	E: Holly Tree Camper Park▲, Frontier Family Camper Park▲, to Misquamicut State Park, Burlingame State Park, to Timber Creek RV Resort▲
NOTE:		MM 0: Begin NB / End SB Call Boxes Listings show Mile Marker/ Exit #.

🎧 RHODE ISLAND

EXIT		CONNECTICUT
		CONNECTICUT (EASTERN TIME ZONE)
NOTE:		Exits show Mile Marker / Exit #
NOTE:		MM 112: Rhode Island State line
111/93		CT 216, Clark Falls Rd, Clark Falls, N Stonington, to CT 184, Ashaway, RI
	FStop	W: Spicer Plus Food & Fuel/Mobil
	TStop	W: R&R Truck Stop/Republic Auto & Truck Plaza (Scales)
	Gas	E: Shell
	Food	W: Rest/R&R TS, McDonald's, Tim Horton's
	Lodg	W: Budget Inn, Stardust Motel
	TServ	W: Republic ATP
	Other	E: to Frontier Family Camper Park▲
109/92		CT 49, Pendleton Hill Rd, to CT 2, N Stonington, Pawcatuck (SB)
	Other	E: to Worden Pond Family Campground▲
		W: Highland Orchards Resort Park/ RV Dealer▲
(108)		CT Welcome Center (SB) (RR, Phone, Picnic, Vend, Info, RVDump)
108/92		CT 49, Pendleton Hill Rd, to CT 2, Pawcatuck, N Stonington (NB)
	Food	W: Rest/Cedar Park, Rest/Randall's
	Lodg	W: Cedar Park Inn, Randall's
104/91		Taugwonk Rd, CT 234, Pequot Tr, Stonington, Borough
	Med	E: + Hospital
102/90		CT 27, Whitehall Ave, Mystic
	Gas	E: Mobil
		W: Mobil, Shell◊
	Food	E: Bickford's Family Rest, Friendly's, McDonald's, Quiznos, Starbucks
		W: Ashby's, Ground Round, Pizza Grille, Subway/DunkinDonuts/Shell
	Lodg	E: AmeriSuites, Econo Lodge, Howard Johnson, Hilton, Holiday Inn
		W: Best Western, Comfort Inn, Days Inn, Residence Inn
	Other	E: Factory Outlet Mall, Mystic Seaport, Mystic Aquarium, Cinema, Amtrak
		W: Auto Dealers, Seaport Campground▲
(101)		Scenic Overlook (NB, NO Trucks)
100/89		Allyn St, Mystic St, Mystic, to US 1
98/88		CT 117, North Rd, Groton, Noank, Groton Point, Downtown Groton
	Lodg	W: Hampton Inn, Marriott
	Med	S: + Emergency Medical Center
	Other	E: to Groton New London Airport✈, **Bluff Point State Park, Haley Farm State Park**
97/87		CT 349, Clarence B Sharp Hwy, to US 1, Industrial Area (SB, Left exit)
	Lodg	E: Econo Lodge, Quality Inn
	Other	E: Groton New London Airport✈
96/86		US 1, CT 12, CT 184, Groton (NB, Left exit)
	Gas	W: Hess, Shell◊
	Food	E: Applebee's, 99 Rest
		W: Flanagan's, Dunkin Donuts, IHOP, KFC, Marcie's Pancake House/Rest, NY Family Pizza, Russell's Ribs, Rosie's Diner, Taco Bell
	Lodg	E: Hampton Inn, Knights Inn, Quality Inn

◊ = Regular Gas Stations with Diesel ▲ = RV Friendly Locations ♥ = Pet Friendly Locations

RED PRINT SHOWS LARGE VEHICLE PARKING/ACCESS ON SITE OR NEARBY BROWN PRINT SHOWS CAMPGROUNDS/RV PARKS

Page 507

EXIT	CONNECTICUT
Lodg	W: Best Way Inn, Best Western, Clarion, Groton Inn, Super 8
Other	W: Grocery, Wal-Mart, New London Naval Sub Base, USS Nautilus, WW II Sub Museum
95/85	Bridge St, to US 1N, Thames St, Downtown Groton (NB exit, NO NB reaccess)
Gas	E: Quick Stop Deli
Food	E: Boomer's Café, Norm's Diner
Lodg	E: Quality Inn
94/84	CT 32, Downtown New London (SB)
94/83	US 1, CT 32, New London (SB), Briggs St, Huntington St, CT 32 (NB)
Other	E: Ferries to Block Island, Fishers Island
	W: Malls, US Coast Guard Academy
92/82A	Frontage Rd, Coleman St, Briggs St, to US 1, CT 32, CT 85
Gas	E: Mobil
	W: Sunoco
Food	E: Dunkin Donuts, Pizza Hut
	W: American Steakhouse, Chili's, Golden Wok, Panda Buffet, Outback Steakhouse
Lodg	W: Red Roof Inn ♥
Other	E: Auto Services, Staples, Tires
92/82	CT 85, Broad St, to I-395, Waterford
Gas	W: Mobil
Food	E: Real Italian Pizzeria
	W: Burger King, Charley's, D'Angelo's, Olive Garden, Panda Express, Ruby Tuesday, Subway, Wendy's
Lodg	W: Fairfield Suites, Holiday Inn
Med	E: + Hospital
Other	W: Crystal Mall, Best Buy, PetCo ♥, Target, Home Depot, Salem Farms Campground▲
(90)	Weigh Station (Both dir)
90/81	Cross Rd, Waterford
Gas	W: BJ's
Food	W: McDonald's, Rock & Roll Pizza House
Lodg	W: Rodeway Inn ♥
Other	W: BJ's, Grocery, Lowe's, Wal-Mart sc
88/80	Parkway N, Oil Mill Rd (SB) (Access to Ex #81 Services)
(86/76)	Jct I-395N, CT Tpk, to Norwich, Plainfield (SB, Left exit) I-95N, New London, Providence (SB, Rt 2 lanes)
395N:	Foxwood Resort & Casino, Mohegun Sun Casino
88/75	US 1, Boston Post Rd, E Lyme, Waterford, Flanders
Lodg	E: Blue Anchor Motel
Med	E: + Hospital
87/74	CT 161, Flanders Rd, East Lyme, Flanders, Niantic
Gas	E: Citgo, Mobil, Sunoco◊, Texaco
	W: Shell
Food	E: Burger King, Bickford's Family Rest, Dunkin Donuts
	W: Flanders Pizza, King Garden Chinese, Flanders Fish Market & Rest, Flanders House Café, McDonald's, Wendy's
Lodg	E: Best Value Inn, Best Western, Days Inn, Motel 6 ♥, Sleep Inn
Other	E: Auto Services, Park & Ride
	W: Grocery, Pharmacy, Aces High RV Park▲, to Island Campground & Cottages▲

EXIT	CONNECTICUT
86/73	Society Rd, Niantic
84/72	Rocky Neck Connector to CT 156, Rocky Neck State Park
Food	E: Pier IV Café
Lodg	E: Rocky Neck Motor Inn
Other	E: Rocky Neck SP/Public Beach/Camp▲
84/71	Four Mile River Rd, Old Lyme
Other	E: to CT 156, Rocky Neck State Park▲
	W: to US 1, Stone Ranch Military Res.
79/70	US 1, Lyme St, Old Lyme (SB), CT 156, Neck Rd, to US 1, Old Lyme (NB) (use Halls Rd (w) to reaccess NB/SB)
Gas	W: All Pro Automotive/Irving, Shell◊
Food	W: Rest/Old Lyme Inn, Chinese Rest
Lodg	W: Old Lyme Inn
Other	W: Repairs/Tires All Pro Automotive, Grocery, Pharmacy, Salem Farms Campground▲
78/69	CT 9N, Essex Rd, Old Saybrook, to CT 154, Essex, Hartford
Food	E: Rest/CI, Dunkin Donuts, Saybrook Fish House
Lodg	E: Comfort Inn ♥
77/68	US 1S, Old Saybrook (SB, exit only)
Gas	E: Citgo, Mobil
Food	E: Italian Rest, Frankie's Rest
Lodg	W: Liberty Inn
Other	E: Auto Dealers
	W: Auto Dealers
76/67	CT 154, Middlesex Tpke, to US 1, Old Saybrook (NB ex, SB reacc)
Gas	E: Gulf, Mobil, Sunoco
Food	E: Andriana's Seafood Rest, Emilio's, Pat's Kountry Kitchen, Pizza Works
Lodg	E: Old Saybrook Motor Lodge
Other	E: Amtrak
76/67	Elm St, Old Saybrook (SB, NB reacc)
74/66	CT 166, Spencer Plain Rd, to US 1, CT 153, Old Saybrook
Gas	E: Citgo◊
Food	E: Angus Steakhouse, Aleia's Italian Rest, Dunkin Donuts, Gateway Indian Rest, Nishiki Japanese
Lodg	E: Super 8, Days Inn, Saybrook Motor Inn, Heritage Motor Inn, Knights Inn
(74)	CT Welcome Center (NB) (RR, Phone, Picnic, Vend, Info) CT State Hwy Patrol, Phones (SB)
73/65	CT 153, Essex Rd, Westbrook, to CT 166, US 1
Gas	E: Exxon
Food	E: Andy's Steak & Seafood, Denny's, Subway
Lodg	E: Westbrook Inn B&B, Angels Watch Inn, Waters Edge Resort & Spa
	W: Welcome Inn
Other	E: Tanger Factory Outlets
71/64	CT 145, Horse Hill Rd, Clinton
69/63	CT 81, High St, Killingworth Tpk, Clinton, Killingworth
Gas	E: Shell, Citgo◊, Shell◊
Food	E: Friendly's, McDonald's, Wendy's
Lodg	E: Comfort Inn, Marriott
Other	E: CVS, to Griswold Airport✈
	W: Clinton Crossing Outlet Mall, Park & Ride

EXIT	CONNECTICUT
66/62	Hammonaset Conn, Duck Hole Rd, Hammonaset State Park, Madison
Other	E: State Park/Public Beach/Camping▲, Griswold Airport✈
	W: Riverdale Farm Campground▲, Keith's RV & Trailer Repair
(65)	Madison Service Area (Both dir)
FStop	Mobil
Food	McDonald's
65/61	CT 79, Durham Rd, Madison (Gas/Food/Lodg E to US 1)
64/60	Mungertown Rd, Madison (SB, No reacc) (Food & Lodg E to US 1)
61/59	Goose Lane, to US 1, Guilford
Gas	E: Mobil, Shell◊
Food	E: Dunkin Donuts, Ichiban Japanese Steakhouse, McDonald's, Rio Grande Steakhouse, Wendy's
Lodg	E: Comfort Inn, Tower Inn
60/58	CT 77, Church St, Guilford
Gas	E: Getty, Mobil
Food	E: Friendly's, Subway
59/57	US 1, Boston Post Rd, Guilford
Food	E: Quattro's Italian
	W: Anthony's, Roadhouse Grille
Lodg	E: Frenchmans Reef Beach
	W: Guilford Suites Hotel
56/56	Leetes Island Rd, Branford, to US 1, CT 139, Stony Creek, New Haven
FStop	W: Leetes Island Fuel/Berkshire Farms
TStop	W: Travel Center of America #171 (Scales)
Gas	W: Mobil
Food	W: CountryPride/PizzaHut/Popeyes/TA TC, Dunkin Donuts, Friendly's, USS Chowder Pot, Starbucks, Subway
Lodg	E: Advanced Motel
	W: Ramada Inn
TServ	W: Freightliner of Southern CT
Med	W: + Coastline Medical Emer Center
Other	E: Grocery, Pharmacy
	W: Laundry/WiFi/TA TC
55/55	US 1, E Main St, Branford
Gas	E: Mobil, Sunoco, Thornton's
	W: Citgo, Exxon◊, Mobil◊
Food	E: Dunkin Donuts, Lynn's Deli, Marco Pizzeria, Shoreline Buffet, McDonald's
	W: Gourmet Wok, Parthenon Diner, Margarita's Mexican, Salerno Pizza
Lodg	E: Economy Inn, Holiday Inn Express, Motel 6
	W: Days Inn ♥
Other	E: Walgreen's
53/54	Cedar St, CT 740, Branford
Gas	E: A&M Service Stn, Mobil
Food	E: Branford Townhouse Diner & Rest, Fortune Village Chinese, La Luna
	W: Lion City Chinese
Lodg	E: By the Sea Inn & Spa
Other	E: Auto Dealers, Staples
(52)	Branford Service Area (Both dir)
FStop	Mobil
Food	McDonald's
Other	ATM, Gift Shop
52/53	Branford Connector to US 1, CT 142, CT 146, Short Beach (NB, NO reaccess
50/52	CT 100, N High St, East Haven (SB)
Gas	E: Citgo
Food	E: Subway
Other	E: to Tweed New Haven Airport✈

◊ = Regular Gas Stations with Diesel   ▲ = RV Friendly Locations   ♥ = Pet Friendly Locations
RED PRINT SHOWS LARGE VEHICLE PARKING/ACCESS ON SITE OR NEARBY   BROWN PRINT SHOWS CAMPGROUNDS/RV PARKS

I-95 S — CONNECTICUT

EXIT		
50/51		**US 1, Frontage Rd, East Haven**
	Gas	E: Hess, Sunoco W: Gulf, Mobil, Shell
	Food	E: Boston Market, Chili's, Friendly's, McDonald's W: Dunkin Donuts, Wendy's
	Lodg	E: Quality Inn ♥
	Other	E: Auto Services, to Tweed New Haven Airport ✈ W: Radio Shack
49/50		**Woodward Ave, Lighthouse Pt (NB)**
	Other	E: to Tweed New Haven Airport ✈, US Naval/Marine Reserve, Ft Nathan Hale
49/49		**Stiles St, to US 1, New Haven (NB)**
(47/48)		**Jct I-91N, to Hartford, Yale Univ** (SB exit only, NB left exit)
47/47		**CT 34, Downtown New Haven** (fr NB, Left exit)
47/46		**Long Wharf Dr, Sargent Dr**
	Gas	E: Shell W: Mobil ◆
	Food	E: Rusty Scrupper Rest W: Brazi's Rest
	Lodg	W: Fairfield Inn, Residence Inn
	Med	E: + Hospital
	Other	W: Amtrak, Greyhound Station
46/45		**CT 10, Grasso Blvd (SB)**
46/44		**CT 122, Kimberley Ave, to CT 10**
45/43		**Campbell Ave, Downtown** (NB, NO Trks) **CT 122, First Ave (SB)**
	Med	W: + Veterans Hospital
	Other	W: Univ of New Haven
44/42		**CT 162, Saw Mill Rd, West Haven**
	Gas	E: Mobil W: Shell, 7-11
	Food	E: Billy's Café, Pizza Hut, Great Wall W: American Steakhouse, El Gallo, D'Angelo's, Dunkin Donuts, Friendly
	Lodge	E: Econo Lodge W: Best Western
	Other	W: Staples
42/41		**Marsh Hill Rd, Orange**
	Food	W: Outback Steakhouse
	Lodg	W: Courtyard
(41)		**Milford Service Area (Both dir)**
	FStop	Mobil
	Food	McDonald's
	Other	ATM, Gift Shop
41/40		**Old Gate Lane (NB), Woodmont Rd (SB), to US 1, Milford**
	TStop	E: Secondi Truck Stop/Citgo (Scales), Pilot Travel Center #255 (Scales)
	Gas	E: Shell W: Mobil
	Food	E: Wendy's/Pilot TC, Bennigan's, Cracker Barrel, Dunkin Donuts, D'Angelo's, Duchess Family Rest W: to US 1: Chili's, Boston Market, Taco Bell
	Lodg	E: Best Value Inn, Comfort Inn, Milford Inn, Mayflower Motel
	TWash	E: Blue Beacon TW/Pilot TC
	TServ	E: Mayflower Kenworth
	Other	E: Laundry/WiFi/Pilot TC, Laundry/Secondi TS

EXIT		CONNECTICUT
39AB		**US 1, Boston Post Rd, Milford**
	Gas	E: Gulf ◆ W: Mobil
	Food	E: Athenian Diner, Friendly's, Hooters, Pizzeria Uno W: Burger King, Chili's, Dunkin Donuts, KFC, Little Caesars, Miami Subs, Panda Express, McDonald's, Steak & Sword Rest, Subway, Taco Bell, Wendy's
	Lodg	E: CT Tpk Motel, Howard Johnson, Super 8
	Med	E: + Milford Hospital
	Other	E: Tires, Walgreen's W: Mall, US Post Office, Grocery, Auto Dealers, Pharmacy
39/38		**Milford Pkwy, to Merritt Pkwy, CT 15, Wilbur Cross Pkwy** (NO Comm'l Vehicles/Trucks)
38/37		**High St, Milford (NB, no NB reacc)**
37/36		**Plains Rd, Milford, Stratford**
	Gas	E: Exxon
	Lodg	E: Hampton Inn
	Med	E: + Hospital
36/35		**School House Rd, Bic Dr, Milford to US 1**
	Gas	E: Citgo
	Food	E: Subway, Wendy's
	Lodg	E: Fairfield Inn W: Marriott, Red Roof Inn ♥, Springhill Suites
	Other	E: Auto Dealers
35/34		**US 1, Bridgeport Ave, Milford**
	Gas	E: Gulf, Shell

EXIT		CONNECTICUT
	Food	E: Belair Seafood, Denny's, Gourmet Buffet, Dunkin Donuts, McDonald's, Taco Bell
	Lodg	E: Devon Motel, Liberty Rock Motel
34/33		**Ferry Blvd, to US 1, CT 110, Devon Stratford (NB, no NB reaccess)**
	Gas	E: Shell, Sunoco
	Food	W: Ponderosa, Villa Pizza
	Other	E: Laundromat, Staples, Walgreen's W: Home Depot, Wal-Mart sc
33/32		**W Broad St, Stratford**
	Gas	E: BP W: Gulf
	Food	W: Dunkin Donuts, Italian Rest
32/31		**Honeyspot Rd (NB), South Ave (SB)**
	Gas	E: Gulf ◆ W: Citgo ◆
	Food	E: New Honeyspot Diner
	Lodg	E: Camelot Motel, Honeyspot Motor Lodge
31/30		**CT 113, Lordship Blvd (NB), Surf Ave (SB), Stratford**
	Gas	E: Shell W: Sunoco
	Lodg	E: Ramada Inn
	Other	E: to Sikorsky Memorial Airport ✈
30/29		**CT 130, CT Ave, Stratford Ave, Seaview Ave, Bridgeport**
	Med	W: + Hospital
30/28		**Ann St, Pembroke St, Main St, Waterview Ave, Bridgeport**
	Gas	E: BP
	Food	E: La Familia Rest
29/27		**Lafayette Blvd, Downtown (SB)**
	Other	W: Greyhound Station, Amtrak
29/27A		**CT 25, CT 8, Trumbull, Waterbury**
27		**Frontage Rd, Lafayette St (NB)**
	Other	E: Port Jefferson Ferry W: Amtrak, Greyhound
28/26		**Wordin Ave, Bridgeport**
28/25		**CT 130, Fairfield Ave (SB), State St, Commerce Dr (NB)**
	Gas	E: Getty W: Gulf
27/24		**Chambers St, to US 1, (SB), Kings Hwy (NB) Black Rock Turnpike**
	Food	E: Black Rock Oyster Bar & Grill, Antonio's Rest, D'Angelo Deli
	Lodg	E: Bridgeport Motor Inn
26/23		**US 1, Kings Hwy, Fairfield**
	Gas	E: Sunoco ◆
	Other	E: Home Depot
25/22		**CT 135, N Benson Rd (SB)**
(25)		**Fairfield Service Area (Both dir)**
	FStop	NB/SB: Mobil
	Food	NB: McDonald's SB: McDonald's, Hebrew Nat'l Hot Dogs, Hot Subs
	Other	ATM, Gift Shop
24/21		**Mill Plain Rd, Fairfield**
	Gas	E: Mobil
24/20		**Bronson Rd, Southport (SB, NB reacc)**
23/19		**US 1, Post Rd, Southport (SB) Center St, Old Post Rd (NB)**
	Gas	W: Shell

◆ = Regular Gas Stations with Diesel   ▲ = RV Friendly Locations   ♥ = Pet Friendly Locations

RED PRINT SHOWS LARGE VEHICLE PARKING/ACCESS ON SITE OR NEARBY   BROWN PRINT SHOWS CAMPGROUNDS/RV PARKS

Interstate 95 N/S

EXIT	CONNECTICUT
21/18	Sherwood Island State Park
Gas	W: Mobil
Other	E: Sherwood Island State Park, Beach
	W: CT State Hwy Patrol Post
18/17	CT 33, CT 136, Saugatuck Ave, Westport
17/16	East Ave, Norwalk
Gas	E: Mobil, Shell◇
Food	E: East Side Cafe, Penny's Diner
16/15	US 7, Norwalk, Danbury
Gas	E: Shell, Sunoco
	W: Getty
Med	W: + Norwalk Hospital
Other	W: Norwalk Police Dept
15/14	Fairfield Ave, Norwalk (NB)
	US 1, Connecticut Ave, Norwalk (SB)
Gas	W: BP◇, Coastal
Food	W: China King, Pizza Hut, Silver Star Diner
Med	W: + Norwalk Hospital
Other	E: CT State Hwy Patrol
	W: Circuit City, Firestone, Grocery, Laundromat
13/13	US 1, Boston Post Rd, Darien
Gas	W: Mobil, Shell
Food	W: Burger King, Dunkin Donuts, Driftwood Diner, IHOP, McDonald's, Pasta Fare, Wendy's
Lodg	W: Doubletree Hotel, Marriott
Other	W: ATMs, Costco, Grocery, Home Depot, Pharmacy, Staples, Tires, Norwalk Comm College
(12)	Darien Service Area (NB)
FStop	Mobil
Food	McDonald's, Hebrew Nat'l, Hot Subs
Other	ATM, Gift Shop
	CT Welcome Center
12/12	CT 136, Tokeneke Rd, Rowayton (NB)
11/11	US 1, Boston Post Rd, Darien
Gas	E: BP
	W: Exxon
Food	W: Rest/Howard Johnson
Lodg	W: Howard Johnson
10/10	Noroton Ave, Darien
Gas	W: Getty, Mobil, Shell
(9)	Darien Service Area (SB)
FStop	Mobil
Food	McDonald's
Other	ATM, Gift Shop
9/9	US 1, CT 106, Seaside Ave, Stamford, Glenbrook
Gas	W: Gulf
Food	W: McDonald's, Stamford Pizza
Lodg	E: Stamford Motor Inn
8/8	Elm St (SB), Atlantic St (NB)
Gas	W: Exxon, Sunoco
Food	E: Mandarin Rest, Sam's Place
Lodg	W: Budget Inn, Holiday Inn
Other	E: Greyhound, Amtrak, U-Haul
7/7	CT 137N, Greenwich Ave (NB), Atlantic St (SB), Stamford
Lodg	E: Westin Hotel
7/6	Harvard Ave (NB), West Ave (SB)
Gas	E: Exxon
	W: Shell
Food	E: Vincent's Steakhouse
	W: Boston Market, Subway, Taco Bell
Lodg	E: Fairfield Inn
	W: Super 8

EXIT	CT / NY
Med	W: + Hospital
Other	W: Firestone
6/5	US 1, E Putnam Ave, Riverside
Gas	W: Shell
Food	W: Hunan Café, McDonald's, Taco Bell
Lodg	W: Howard Johnson, Hyatt
Other	W: Grocery, Staples, Pharmacy, US Post Office
4/4	Indian Field Rd, Greenwich
3/3	Steamboat Rd, Arch St, Greenwich
Gas	W: Mobil, Shell
Food	E: Atlantis, Manero's
Lodg	E: Greenwich Harbor Inn
Med	W: + Hospital
Other	E: Bruce Museum
(2)	Weigh Station (NB)
1/2	Delavan Ave, Byram Shore Rd, Greenwich
NOTE:	Listings show Mile Marker / Exit #.

(EASTERN TIME ZONE)

⋂ **CONNECTICUT**
⋃ **NEW YORK**

(EASTERN TIME ZONE)

22	Midland Ave, Port Chester, Rye
Gas	W: BP, Shell
Med	W: + Hospital
Other	W: Grocery, Home Depot, Staples
(21)	Jct I-287W, US 1N, Tappan Zee, Port Chester, White Plains
20	US 1S, Rye, Port Chester (NB)
19	Playland Pkwy, Rye, Harrison
18B	Mamaroneck Ave, White Plains
18A	Fenimore Rd, Mamaroneck
17	Chatsworth Ave, Larchmont (NB)
(7)	New Rochelle TOLL Plaza (NB)
16	North Ave, Cedar St, New Rochelle (Last exit before NB TOLL)
Food	E: McDonald's, Taco Bell
Lodg	E: Ramada
Med	E: + Hospital
15	US 1, New Rochelle, The Pelhams
Gas	E: Getty, PitStop
	W: Scot
Food	E: Thruway Diner
Other	E: ATMs, CVS, Costco, Home Depot
14	Hutchinson River Pkwy S, Whitestone Br (fr SB, NO Trks) (SB exit, NB entr)
13	Conner St, Baychester Ave
Gas	E: Gulf◇
	W: BP
Food	W: McDonald's
Lodg	E: Econo Lodge
	W: Holiday Motel
TServ	E: Frank's Truck & Auto, Mack
Other	E: Car Wash
12	Baychester Ave (fr NB, Left exit) (NB exit, SB entr)

EXIT	NY / NJ
11	Bartow Ave, Co-op City Blvd
Gas	E: Mobil, Shell
	W: BP, Shell, Sunoco
Food	E: Applebee's, Burger King, Checker's, McDonald's, Red Lobster
Other	E: ATMs, Kmart, Staples
	W: ATMs, Grocery, Home Depot
10	Gun Hill Rd (NB, Left exit, SB entr)
9	Hutchinson River Pkwy N
8C	Pelham Pkwy West
8B	Orchard Beach, City Island
8A	Westchester Ave (SB ex, NB entr)
7C	Country Club Rd, Pelham Bay Park (NB exit, NB entr)
7B	E Tremont Ave (SB ex, NB entr)
(7A)	Jct I-695 (SB), to I-295S, Throgs Neck Bridge (SB exit, NB entr)
(12)	Jct I-295S, Throgs Neck Bridge (NB exit, SB entr)
(11)	Jct I-278W, Bruckner Expressway, Triboro Bridge (SB exit, NB entr)
(10)	Jct I-678S, Bruckner Blvd, Whitestone Bridge
5B	Castle Hill Ave (NB exit, SB entr)
5A/8	White Plains Rd, Westchester Ave
4B	Rosedale Ave, Bronx River Pkwy
(4A)	Jct I-895S, Sheridan Expwy (NB exit, SB entr)
3	Third Ave (SB ex, NB entr)
2B	US 1N, Webster Ave (NB)
2A	Jerome Ave, to I-87
(1C)	Jct I-87, Deegan Expwy, Amsterdam Ave, Albany, Queens (SB)
(3NS)	Jct I-87, Deegan Expwy, Amsterdam Ave, Albany, Queens (NB)
2	Harlem River Dr, Amsterdam Ave, to FDR Dr, Manhattan (NB exit, SB entr)
1	US 9, NY 9A, W 178th St, W 181st St, Henry Hudson Pkwy, George Washington Bridge (TOLL)

(EASTERN TIME ZONE)

⋂ **NEW YORK**
⋃ **NEW JERSEY**

(EASTERN TIME ZONE)

NOTE:	Listings show Mile Marker / Exit #.
123/74	Palisades Pkwy (SB)
73AB	NJ 67, Center Ave, Lemoine Ave
122/72	US 9 W, to Palisades Int'l Pkwy (SB) US 1S, US 9S, US 46, Ft Lee (NB)
121/71	Broad Ave, Leonia, Englewood

◇ = Regular Gas Stations with Diesel   ▲ = RV Friendly Locations   ♥ = Pet Friendly Locations
RED PRINT SHOWS LARGE VEHICLE PARKING/ACCESS ON SITE OR NEARBY   BROWN PRINT SHOWS CAMPGROUNDS/RV PARKS

EXIT	NEW JERSEY
120/70	CR 12, Degraw Ave, Teaneck
(119/69)	Jct I-80W, to Paterson (SB)
118/68	US 46, Challenger Blvd
NOTE:	I-95 runs with NJ Tpk below.
117/18	US 46E, Ft Lee, Hackensack
(115)	**Vince Lombardi Service Area (NB)**
FStop	Shell
Food	Bob's Big Boy, Roy Rogers
116/16E,17	NY 3, Lincoln Tunnel, Secaucus
(114)	TOLL Plaza
113/16W	NY 3, Secaucus, Rutherford
Gas	E: Hess, Shell
(112)	**Alexander Hamilton Service Area (SB)**
FStop	Sunoco
Food	Roy Rogers
(109/15W)	Jct I-280, Newark, Harrison
107/15E	US 1, US 9, Newark, Jersey City
(105/14)	I-78W, US 1, US 9, Holland Tunnel, Newark Airport
102/13A	Newark Airport, Elizabeth Seaport
(100/13)	I-278, Elizabeth, Staten Island
96/12	Carteret, Rahway
(93)	**Grover Cleveland Serv Area (NB)** **Thomas Edison Serv Area (SB)**
FStop	Sunoco
Food	Bob's Big Boy, Roy Rogers, Starbucks, TCBY
91/11	US 9, Garden State Pkwy, Woodbury Shore Points
(88/10)	I-287, NJ 440, Metchuen, Percy Amboy, Outerbridge Crossing
83/9	US 11, US 1, NJ 18, New Brunswick, East Brunswick
Gas	E: Hess◊
Food	E: Grand Buffet, On the Border
	W: Bennigan's, Denny's, Fuddruckers
Lodg	E: Days Inn, Motel 6
	W: Holiday Inn Express, Sheraton
(79)	**Joyce Kilmer Service Area (NB)**
FStop	Sunoco
Food	Burger King, Starbucks
74/8A	Cranbury, Jamesburg
(72)	**Molly Pritcher Service Area (SB)**
FStop	Sunoco
Food	Bob's Big Boy, Nathan's, Roy Rogers, Starbucks, TCBY
67/8	NJ 33, Hightstown, Freehold
Gas	E: Exxon◊
Food	E: Diners
Lodg	E: Hampton Inn, Holiday Inn, Quality Inn
Other	E: Grocery Store
(60/7A)	Jct I-95/195, W-Trenton, E-Neptune
NOTE:	I-95 runs with NJ Tpk above.
NOTE:	I-95 below runs with I-195. Exit #'s follow I-195.
6	Edgebrook Rd
5AB	US 130

EXIT	NJ / PA
3AB	Yardville Hamilton Square Rd
2	Lakeside Blvd, Arena Dr, Broad St
1AB	US 206
NOTE:	I-95 above runs with I-195. Exit #'s follow I-195.
NOTE:	I-95 below runs with I-295. Exit #'s follow I-295.
(60B)	Jct I-95N/I-295N
61AB	Arena Dr, NJ 620
62	Old Olden Ave (SB, reacc NB only)
63AB	Nottingham Way, NJ 33
64	E State St
65AB	Sloan Ave
67AB	US 1, to Trenton, New Brunswick
Gas	E: Shell
	W: BP◊, Mobil◊
Food	W: Applebee's, Charlie Brown's Steakhouse, Chili's, Denny's, Hooters, Joe's Crab Shack, Olive Garden, Pizza Hut, Red Lobster, TGI Friday, Wendy's
Lodg	E: Howard Johnson
	W: AmeriSuites, Extended Stay, Red Roof Inn ♥
Other	E: Auto Dealers
	W: Best Buy, Firestone, Grocery, Lowe's, Kmart, Home Depot, Mall, NTB, Staples, **Wal-Mart**
NOTE:	I-95 above runs with I-295. Exit #'s follow I-295. I-95 runs for next 10 exits around Trenton.
NOTE:	I-95S continues below. Exit #'s follow I-95.
8B	Princeton, Trenton
8A	CR 546, Franklin Corner Rd, Trenton
7AB	US 206, Lawrenceville Rd, Trenton
5AB	Federal City Rd (SB)
4	NJ 31, Pennington Rd, Pennington
Gas	E: Exxon
	W: Mobil
3AB	CR 611, Scotch Rd, Trenton
Other	E: Mercer Co Airport ✈
2	CR 579, Bear Tavern Rd, Trenton
Gas	E: Exxon, Mobil
	W: BP
1	NJ 29, River Rd, Trenton
Other	W: NJ State Hwy Patrol Post
(EASTERN TIME ZONE)	

⬆ NEW JERSEY
⬇ PENNSYLVANIA
(EASTERN TIME ZONE)

NOTE:	MM 51: New Jersey State Line
(51)	**PA Welcome Center (SB)** (RR, Phone, Picnic, Vend)
(51)	Weigh Station (SB)

◊ = Regular Gas Stations with Diesel ▲ = RV Friendly Locations ♥ = Pet Friendly Locations
RED PRINT SHOWS LARGE VEHICLE PARKING/ACCESS ON SITE OR NEARBY BROWN PRINT SHOWS CAMPGROUNDS/RV PARKS

INTERSTATE 95 N/S

EXIT	PENNSYLVANIA
51BA	Taylorsville Rd, Morrisville W-New Hope, E-Yardley (SB)
51	Taylorsville Rd, Morrisville
Other	W: Washington Crossing Hist Park
49	PA 332, Newtown Yardley Rd
Lodg	W: Hampton Inn
Med	W: + Hospital
Other	W: to Tyler State Park
46AB	US 1, N-Morrisville, S-Langhorne
Other	W: to I-276, PA Tpk
44	US 1 Bus, PA 413, Langhorne, Penndel, Levittown
Gas	E: Shell◊ W: Mobil◊
Food	E: Chuck E Cheese, Classic Steaks & Hoagies, Dunkin Donuts, Friendly's, Panera Bread, Ruby Tuesday, Wendy's W: Denny's, McDonald's
Med	E: + Hospital
Other	E: Auto Dealers, Grocery, Kmart, Lowe's, Mall, Sam's Club, Pharmacy, Harley Davidson W: U-Haul
40	to PA 413, to PA Tpk, to US 13
37	PA 132, Street Rd, Bensalem, to PA Turnpike, to US 1
FStop	W: Jai Sunoco
Gas	W: BP, Shell
Food	W: Burger King, Denny's, IHOP, KFC
Other	E: Neshaminy State Park W: Firestone, Radio Shack, Philadelphia Park Race Track
35	PA 63W, Woodhaven Rd, to US 13, to US 1, to NE Philadelphia Airport
Gas	W: Mobil, Exxon, Sunoco
Food	W: Arby's, KFC, McDonald's, Perkins, Pizza Hut, Taco Bell, Wendy's
Lodg	W: Hampton Inn
Med	W: + Hospital
Other	E: Park & Ride, Amtrak W: CompUSA, Grocery, Home Depot, Mall, NTB, Wal-Mart
32	Academy Rd, Linden Ave
Med	W: + Hospital
30	PA 73, Cottman Ave, Rhawn St
27	Bridge St, Harbison Ave (SB), Lefevre St, Aramingo Ave (NB)
Gas	W: Getty
Med	W: + Hospital
Other	W: Pharmacy
26	Aramingo Ave, Betsy Ross Bridge, to NJ 90
25	Allegheny Ave, Castor Ave
Gas	W: Getty, WaWa
Med	W: + Hospital
23	Girard Ave, Lehigh Ave.
Gas	W: Exxon, Shell
Food	W: Pizza Hut, Dunkin Donuts, Ruby Tuesday
Med	W: + Hospital
(22)	to I-676, US 30, Central Philadelphia
20	Columbus Blvd, Washington Ave
Gas	E: BP, Mobil, Sunoco
Food	E: Burger King, Boston Market, Chuck E Cheese, Hooters, McDonald's
Other	E: Auto Services, Grocery, Home Depot, Staples, Target, Wal-Mart

EXIT	PENNSYLVANIA
(19)	Jct I-76E, Walt Whitman Bridge (All services W to Oregon Ave)
17	PA 611N, Broad St, Pattison Ave
Med	W: + Hospital
Other	W: to Naval Shipyard, to Stadium
15	Enterprise Ave, Island Ave (SB)
14	Bartram Ave, Essington Ave (SB)
13	PA 291W, to I-76W, Valley Forge (fr NB, Exit Only)
Gas	E: Exxon◊
Lodg	E: Hilton, Residence Inn, Westin Hotel
12B	Cargo City (SB)
12A	to PA 291, Phila Int'l Airport (SB)
Lodg	W: Courtyard, Embassy, Fairfield Inn
12	Philadelphia Int'l Airport (NB)
Lodg	W: Courtyard, Embassy Suites
10	PA 291E, Bartram Ave, Cargo City (NB)
Food	E: Hunan Garden
Lodg	E: Econo Lodge, Renaissance Hotel W: Courtyard, Extended Stay America, Fairfield Inn, Hampton Inn, Microtel
9AB	PA 420, Wanamaker Ave, Essington, S-Essington, N-Prospect Park
Gas	E: Coastal, Sunoco◊, Valero◊
Food	E: Denny's, Shoney's
Lodg	E: Comfort Inn, Econo Lodge, Evergreen Hotel, Holiday Inn, Motel 6♥, Red Roof Inn♥
Other	E: John Heinz Nat'l Wildlife Refuge, Westinghouse

EXIT	PA / DE
8	Ridley Park, Chester Waterfront
(7)	Jct I-476N, to Plymouth Meeting
6	to PA 320, to PA 352, Edgemont Ave, Providence Ave, Chester
Lodg	W: Days Inn, Howard Johnson
Med	W: + Hospital
Other	W: Widener Univ, Radio Shack, Wal-Mart
5	Kerlin St (NB)
4	US 322E, to NJ, Bridgeport
3B	Highland Ave (SB)
3A	US 322W, West Chester (SB)
TServ	W: Watkins Motor Trucks
3	Highland Ave (NB)
2	PA 452, Market St, to US 322W
Gas	W: Exxon, Getty
Food	W: McDonald's
1	Chichester Ave, Marcus Hook
(1)	Weigh Station (NB)
(1)	PA Welcome Center (NB) (RR, Phone, Picnic, Info)

⋂ PENNSYLVANIA
⋃ DELAWARE
(Eastern Time Zone)

NOTE: MM 23: Pennsylvania State Line
NOTE: Exits show Mile Marker / Exit #.
NOTE: MM 23: Begin SB/End NB Call Boxes

(22/11)	Jct I-495S, DE 92, Naamans Rd, Claymont, Port of Wilmington
Gas	E: WaWa W: Gulf◊
Food	E: China Star, Wendy's
Lodg	W: Holiday Inn
Other	E: Goodyear, Grocery W: Home Depot, Pharmacy, Radio Shack
21/10	Harvey Rd, Claymont (No NB reacc)
19/9	DE 3, Marsh Rd, Wilmington
Other	E: Bellevue State Park, DE State Hwy Patrol Post
17/8AB	US 202, DE 202, Concord Pike, Wilmington, West Chester
16/7B	DE 52, Delaware Ave, N Jackson St, W 10th St (SB)
16/7A	DE 52, Delaware Ave, N Adams St, W 11th St (SB)
15/7	DE 52, Delaware Ave (NB)
Lodg	E: Courtyard, Sheraton
14/6	N Jackson St, to DE 48, to DE 4 (SB), DE 4, Maryland Ave, to DE 48, MLK Blvd, Lancaster Ave (NB) Downtown Wilmington
Food	E: Joe's Crab Shack, Lee's Chinese
Other	E: Greyhound, Amtrak
(12/5D)	Jct I-495, Port of Wilmington, Philadelphia
(10.6/5C)	Jct I-295, NJ Tpk, DE Memorial Br

Page 512

◊ = Regular Gas Stations with Diesel   ▲ = RV Friendly Locations   ♥ = Pet Friendly Locations
RED PRINT SHOWS LARGE VEHICLE PARKING/ACCESS ON SITE OR NEARBY   BROWN PRINT SHOWS CAMPGROUNDS/RV PARKS

EXIT	DE / MD
11/5B	**DE 141N, Newport**
10/5A	**DE 141, US 202S, to US 13, New Castle, Newport**
Lodg	E: Radisson
Other	E: New Castle Co Airport ✈
8/4B	**DE 58, DE 7N, Churchmans Rd, Newark, Stanton, Wilmington**
Food	W: Chili's, Applebee's, Longhorn Steak House, Ruby Tuesday
Lodg	W: Courtyard, Country Suites, Days Inn, Fairfield Inn, Hilton, Red Roof Inn ♥
Med	W: + Christiana Hospital
Other	E: Circuit City, Costco, Mall W: DE Park Racetrack
7.6/4A	**DE 1, DE 7S, Newark, New Castle**
Food	E: Food Court/Mall, Ruby Tuesday
Med	W: + Christiana Hospital
Other	E: Christiana Mall W: DE Park Racetrack
7/3	**DE 273, Christiana Rd, Newark, W to Newark, E to Dover (SB)**
6.6/3B	**DE 273, Christiana Rd, Newark, W to Newark (NB)**
Gas	E: Exxon◆
Food	E: Bob Evans, Chinese Rest, Wendy's W: Denny's
Lodg	W: Best Western, Hawthorne Suites, Residence Inn
6.3/3A	**DE 273, Christiana Rd, Newark, E to Dover (NB)**
Gas	W: Shell, Getty
Food	W: Denny's, Pizza Hut, Rest/Hol Inn
Lodg	W: Comfort Inn, Hampton Inn, Holiday Inn
(5)	**Service Area (Both dir, Left exit)**
FStop	Exxon, Sunoco
Food	Big Boy, Roy Rogers, Sbarro, Taco Bell, TCBY
2/1AB	**DE 896, S College Ave, N-Newark, S-Middletown, to US 301**
Gas	W: Exxon, Mobil, Shell◆
Food	W: Boston Market, Diner, Dunkin Donuts, Friendly's, McDonald's
Lodg	W: Howard Johnson, Quality Inn
Other	W: Univ of DE-Campus & Stadium
(0/1)	**DE Tpk TOLL Plaza** DE State Hwy Patrol
NOTE:	MM 1: Begin NB/End SB Call Boxes
NOTE:	Exits show Mile Marker / Exit #.

(EASTERN TIME ZONE)

⊖ DELAWARE
⊖ MARYLAND
(EASTERN TIME ZONE)

NOTE:	MM 110: Delaware State Line
109AB	**MD 279, Elkton Rd, to MD 213, Elkton, Newark, DE**
TStop	E: Petro Stopping Center #51 (Scales) W: Travel Center of America #19/Mobil (Scales)
Gas	E: Shell◆
Food	E: IronSkillet/Petro SC, Cracker Barrel, KFC, McDonald's, Waffle House W: CountryPride/Subway/TA TC

EXIT	MARYLAND
Lodg	E: Days Inn, Elkton Lodge, Hampton Inn, Hawthorn Suites, Knights Inn ♥, Motel 6 ♥
Tires	E: Petro SC
TWash	E: Blue Beacon TW
TServ	W: TA TC
Med	E: + Union Hospital of Cecil Co
Other	E: Laundry/Petro SC W: Laundry/WiFi/CB/Med/RVDump/TA TC, to Univ of DE
100	**MD 272, North East Rd, North East**
TStop	E: Flying J Travel Plaza (Scales)
Gas	W: Mobil
Food	E: Rest/FastFood/FJ TP, McDonald's
Lodg	E: Crystal Inn/FJ TP
Other	E: Laundry/WiFi/RVDump/LP/FJ TP, MD State Hwy Patrol W: Cecil Comm College, Zoo
(97)	**Chesapeake House Service Area (Both dir, Left exit)**
FStop	Exxon, Sunoco
Food	Burger King, Popeye's, Pizza Hut, Starbucks
93	**MD 222, MD 275, Perrylawn Dr, Perryville, Port Deposit**
TStop	E: Pilot Travel Center #290 (Scales)
Gas	E: Exxon◆
Food	E: Subway/Pilot TC, DQ, Denny's, KFC
Lodg	E: Comfort Inn
Other	E: WiFi/Pilot TC, Prime Outlets Mall W: MD State Hwy Patrol Post
(93)	**Weigh Station (SB)**
(93)	**TOLL Booth (NB)**
89	**MD 155, Level Rd, Havre de Grace** NOTE: NB: Last exit BEFORE TOLL
Med	E: + Hospital
Other	W: to Susquehanna State Park
85	**MD 22, Aberdeen Throughway, Churchville Rd, Aberdeen**
Gas	E: 7-11, Amoco, Crown◆, Shell◆
Food	E: Applebee's, Appleby's, Bob Evans, Burger King, Fast Eddie's Pit Beef, Golden Corral, KFC, Little Caesar's, McDonald's, Olive Tree Rest, Pizza Hut, Subway, Taco Bell, Wendy's
Lodg	E: Clarion Hotel ♥, Days Inn ♥, Holiday Inn, La Quinta Inn ♥, Red Roof Inn ♥, Super 8 ♥, Travelodge W: Courtyard, Residence Inn
Other	E: Dollar Tree, Dollar General, Grocery, Kmart, Pharmacy, Radiio Shack, Target W: Ripken Stadium
(82)	**MD House Service Area (Both dir, Left exit)**
FStop	Exxon, Sunoco
Food	Big Boy, Roy Rogers, Sbarro, TCBY
80	**MD 543, Creswell Rd, Bel Air, Riverside, Churchville**
Gas	E: 7-11, BP, Crown◆, Mobil◆
Food	E: Bliss Coffee & Wine Bar, Burger King, China Moon Chinese Rest, Cracker Barrel, Riverside Pizza, Ruby Tuesday, Waffle House
Lodg	E: Country Inn, Extended Stay America, Springhill Suites, Wingate Inn
Other	E: to appr 4mi Bar Harbor RV Park▲
77AB	**MD 24, Emmorton Rd, Abingdon, Edgewood, Bel Air**
Gas	E: Exxon◆, Shell W: Exxon◆, WaWa

◆ = Regular Gas Stations with Diesel   ▲ = RV Friendly Locations   ♥ = Pet Friendly Locations
RED PRINT SHOWS LARGE VEHICLE PARKING/ACCESS ON SITE OR NEARBY   BROWN PRINT SHOWS CAMPGROUNDS/RV PARKS

Page 513

INTERSTATE 95 N/S

EXIT		MARYLAND
	Food	E: Burger King, Country Kitchen, Denny's, Vitale's Rest, Waffle House, Rest/BW
		W: KFC, McDonald's
	Lodg	E: Best Western ♥, Comfort Inn, Days Inn, Hampton Inn, Holiday Inn Express, La Quinta Inn ♥, Ramada Inn, Sleep Inn
	Med	W: + Hospital
	Other	E: BJ's, Grocery, Pharmacy, Petco ♥, Target, Wal-Mart
74		MD 152, Mountain Rd, Joppa, Joppatowne, Fallston
	Gas	E: Citgo◊, Exxon◊
	Food	E: IHOP, McDonald's, Wendy's, Addt'l Food S to US 40
	Lodg	E: Super 8 ♥
	Med	E: + Hospital
	Other	E: Days RV Center
67AB		MD 43, White Marsh Blvd, to US 40, MD 7, to US 1, I-695, White Marsh
	FStop	E: S&E Truck Stop, White Marsh Truck Stop (MD 43E to US 40N)
	Gas	E: BP◊, Crown, Shell, Sunoco
		W: 7-11, Exxon◊
	Food	E: Burger King
		W: Chili's, China Wok, ChickFilA, Don Pablo, Fuddruckers, Lin's China Buffet, McDonald's, Olive Garden, Philip's Seafood Grill, Red Lobster, Ruby Tuesday, Starbucks, Taco Bell, TGI Friday
	Lodg	W: Fairfield Inn, Hilton Garden Inn, Hampton Inn, Residence Inn
	Other	E: Best Buy, Target, to Gunpowder Falls State Park
		W: ATMs, Auto Services, B&N, Grocery, FedEx Kinkos, Staples, Tires, White Marsh Mall
(64AB)		Jct I-695 Beltway, W to Towson, E to Essex (NB, B-WB-Left exit, SB-EB-Left exit)
(62)		Jct I-895S, Harbor Tunnel (SB)
61		US 40, Pulaski Hwy, Rosedale (NB)
	Other	E: Park & Ridge, Industrial Park
		W: MD Truck Tire Serv
60		Moravia Rd, to US 40, I-8895 (NB)
	Gas	E: Citgo◊
59		MD 150, Eastern Ave, Baltimore
	Gas	E: Sunoco
		W: AmocoBP◊, Exxon, Hess
	Food	E: Glass Grill, Ice Cream Factory
		W: Broadway Diner, China East, Dunkin Donuts, Subway, Wendy's
	Med	W: + John Hopkins Bayview Med Ctr
	Other	E: to Eastpoint Mall
		W: Home Depot, Kimmel Tire & Auto Center, US Post Office
58		Dundalk Ave (NB)
	Gas	E: Citgo, Mobil
57		O'Donnell St (SB), Interstate Ave (NB)
	FStop	E: Midway Truck Stop
	TStop	E: Travel Center of America #216 (Scales)
	Food	E: Buckhorn/Subway/TA TC, KFC, McDonald's, Sbarro
	Lodg	E: Best Western
	TWash	E: Baltimore Truck Wash
	TServ	E: TA TC/Tires
	Other	E: Laundry/WiFi/CB/TA TC
(56)		Ft McHenry Tunnel TOLL Plaza
56		Keith Ave, Baltimore

EXIT		MARYLAND
55		McComas St, Key Hwy NOTE: NB: Last Exit Before TOLL-No Serv
	Other	W: Ft McHenry Nat'l Monument
54		MD 2, Hanover St
(53)		Jct I-395N, Downtown, Oriole Pk
52		MD 295, Baltimore-Washington Pkwy, Russell St, BWI Int'l Airport
51		Washington Blvd
50		Caton Ave (NB), Desoto Rd (SB), to Wilkens Ave, US 1, US 1A
	Gas	E: Hess◊, Shell
	Food	E: Caton House, McDonald's
	Lodg	E: Holiday Inn Express
	Med	E: + Hospital
(49AB)		I-695, W-Towson, E-Glen Burnie (W to I-70, I-83, E to I-97)
(47AB)		I-195, o tMD 166, Catonsville (I-195 to BWI Airport)
(46)		I-895N, Harbor Tunnel Thrwy (NB)
43		MD 100, Elkridge, Glen Burnie
	Gas	E: Citgo◊, Exxon
	Food	E: Wendy's
	Lodg	E: Best Western, Red Roof Inn
41AB		MD 175, Waterloo Rd, to US 1, Elkridge, Columbia, Jessup
	TStop	E: Travel Center of America #151 (Scales)
	Gas	E: Exxon◊, Shell
		W: Crown

EXIT		MARYLAND
	Food	E: CountryPride/Subway/TA TC, Burger King, McDonald's
		W: Bob Evans, Olive Garden, TGI Friday
	Lodg	E: Knights Inn/TA TC, Holiday Inn, Fairfield Inn, Red Roof Inn ♥, Super 8
		W: Homewood Suites
	TServ	E: TA TC/Tires
	Med	W: + Hospital
	Other	E: Laundry/WiFi/CB/TA TC, MD State Hwy Patrol Post
		W: to John Hopkins Univ
38AB		MD 32, Patuxent Fwy, to US 1, Jessup, Ft Meade, Columbia (All Serv at 1st Exit E to US 1)
(37)		MD Welcome Center (NB) Rest Area (SB) (RR, Phone, Picnic, Vend, Info, RVDump)
35AB		MD 216, Scaggsville Rd, Laurel (All Serv at 1st Exit E to US 1)
33AB		MD 198, Sandy Spring Rd, Laurel (Addt'l Serv E to US 1)
	Gas	E: Exxon
		W: Exxon, Shell
	Food	E: Domino's
		W: Blimpie, Outback Steakhouse
	Lodg	W: Holiday Inn
	Med	E: + Laurel Regional Hospital
29AB		MD 212, Powder Mill Rd, Beltsville, Calverton
	Gas	E: 7-11 appr 1mi
		W: Exxon◊
	Food	W: Baskin Robbins, Danny's, Flagship Deli, KFC, McDonald's, Sunrise Cafe, Sun Spot Café, T & J's Rest, Wendy's, Rest/Sheraton
	Lodg	W: Fairfield Inn, Sheraton ♥
	Other	E: Cherry Hill Park/RVDump▲ (See AD on this page), El Monte RV Rentals & Sales
		W: CVS, Grocery
(27)		Jct I-495, Washington ByPass, to Silver Spring
NOTE:		I-95 runs with I-495E below around Washington, DC. Exit #'s follow I-495.
25AB		Cherry Hill Rd, US 1, Baltimore Blvd, Laurel, College Park
	Gas	E: 7-11, Amoco, Exxon◊, Shell
		W: Shell
	Food	E: Arby's, Austin Steak House, Burger King, Danny's, McDonald's, Starbucks, Wendy's
		W: College Park Diner, Dunkin Donuts, Hard Times Cafe, IHOP, Kebab Rest, Pizza, Starbucks
	Lodg	E: Holiday Inn
		W: Econo Lodge, Hampton Inn, Days Inn, Ramada Inn, Super 8
	Other	E: Cherry Hill Park▲ (SEE AD PG X), RiteAid, Tires, Queenstown RV & Marine Service
		W: Grocery, Home Depot, Pharmacy, Auto Services & Tires, Queenstown RV & Marine Sales, College Park Airport✈, to Univ of MD/College Pk
24		Greenbelt Station Rd (SB)
	Other	W: Auto Dealers
23		MD 201, Kenilworth Ave, Greenbelt
	Gas	W: Shell
	Food	E: Rest/Marriott, Starbucks
		W: Boston Market, Checker's, Popeye's, Starbucks, TGI Friday

RV Campground Open All Year

CHERRY HILL PARK
A Monumental Experience

800-801-6449
301-937-7116
9800 Cherry Hill Road
College Park, MD 20740
www.cherryhillpark.com

◊ = Regular Gas Stations with Diesel   ▲ = RV Friendly Locations   ♥ = Pet Friendly Locations
RED PRINT SHOWS LARGE VEHICLE PARKING/ACCESS ON SITE OR NEARBY   BROWN PRINT SHOWS CAMPGROUNDS/RV PARKS

INTERSTATE 95 N/S

EXIT		MARYLAND
	Lodg	E: Marriott
		W: Courtyard, Residence Inn
	Other	W: CVS, Grocery, Pharmacy, Staples, Target, Tires, Beltway Plaza Mall
22		MD 295, Baltimore Washington Pkwy, Greenbelt
22AB		MD 295, Baltimore Washington Pkwy, Greenbelt
	Food	E: Starbucks
	Lodg	E: Holiday Inn, Days Inn, Howard Johnson
	Other	E: to Nasa Goddard Space Flight Ctr
20AB		MD 450, Annapolis Rd, Lanham
	Gas	E: Mobil
		W: 7-11, Chevron, Shell, Sunoco
	Food	E: McDonald's, Jerry's, Pizza Hut, Red Lobster, Rest/DI, Rest/BW
		W: Chesapeake Bay Seafood House, KFC, Popeye's, Wendy's
	Lodg	E: Best Western, Days Inn, Red Roof Inn ♥
		W: Ramada Inn
	Med	W: + Hospital
	Other	W: CVS, Grocery, Office Depot, Radio Shack, Safeway, Staples, Tires, Auto Dealers, Auto Services
19AB		US 50, Annapolis, Washington
17AB		MD 202, Landover Rd, Hyattsville, Bladensburg, Upper Marlboro
	Food	E: Outback Steakhouse, Ruby Tuesday
		W: China Restaurant, IHOP
	Lodg	E: Holiday Inn
	Other	W: Sam's Club
15AB		MD 214, Central Ave, Upper Marlboro
	FStop	W: Crown, Exxon
	Gas	W: Shell
	Food	E: Rest/Hampton Inn
		W: Jerry's, McDonald's, Pizza Hut, Wendy's
	Lodg	E: Hampton Inn, Extended Stay America
		W: Days Inn, Motel 6 ♥
	Other	E: FedEx Center, to Six Flags
		W: U-Haul, Goodyear, Home Depot, Staples
13		Ritchie Marlboro Rd, Upper Marlboro
11AB		MD 4, Pennsylvania Ave, Upper Marlboro, Washington
	Gas	W: Exxon, Sunoco
	Food	W: Applebee's, Arby's, IHOP, Pizza Hut, Starbucks, Taco Bell, Wendy's
	Other	W: CVS, MD Hwy Patrol Post
9		Forestville Rd, Suitland Pkwy, to PA Ave (SB), MD 337, Allentown Rd, Andrews Air Force Base (NB)
	Gas	E: Crown, Shell
	Food	E: Checker's, McDonald's, Popeye's
	Lodg	E: Holiday Inn Express, Ramada Inn, Super 8
	Med	E: + Hospital
	Other	E: U-Haul, Andrews AFB
7AB		MD 5, Branch Ave, Temple Hills, Waldorf, Silver Hill
	Gas	E: Exxon, Sunoco
		W: Shell ◊
	Lodg	W: Days Inn, Econo Lodge
	Med	W: + Hospital

Personal Notes

EXIT		MD / VA
4AB		MD 414, St Barnabas Rd, Oxon Hill, Marlow Heights
	Gas	E: Citgo, Exxon
		W: Exxon ◊, Shell
	Food	E: Bojangles, Burger King, McDonald's, KFC, Outback Steakhouse, Wendy's
		W: McDonald's
	Lodg	E: Red Roof Inn ♥
	Other	E: Grocery, Home Depot, Staples
3AB		MD 210, Indian Head Hwy, Oxon Hill, Forest Heights
	Gas	E: Mobil, Shell
		W: 7-11, BP ◊, Crown, Shell
	Food	E: Danny's, Pizza Hut, Taco Bell
		W: CiCi's, McDonald's, Wendy's
	Lodg	E: Best Western, Park Inn
	Other	E: Advance Auto
		W: Safeway
(2AB)		Jct I-295N, to Washington

NOTE: I-95 runs with I-495E above around Washington, DC. Exit #'s follow I-495.

(EASTERN TIME ZONE)

⚭ MARYLAND
⚮ VIRGINIA

(EASTERN TIME ZONE)

NOTE: MM 178: Maryland State Line

177CBA		US 1, Richmond Hwy, GW Mem'l Hwy, Fort Belvoir, to Alexandria
	Gas	W: Exxon, Hess, Shell

EXIT		VIRGINIA
	Food	E: Diner, Domino's, Great American Steak Buffet, Western Sizzlin', Rest/RRI
	Lodg	E: Hampton Inn, Red Roof Inn ♥, Travelers Inn, Statesman Motel
	Other	E: Auto Dealers
		W: Amtrak
	NOTE:	SB: Expect construction near X176, Telegraph Rd, thru 2012.
176AB		VA 241, Telegraph Rd, Alexandria
	Gas	E: Exxon, Hess ◊
	Lodg	W: Courtyard, Holiday Inn
	NOTE:	NB: Expect construction near X176, Telegraph Rd, thru 2012.
174		Eisenhower Ave, Alexandria
173		VA 613, Van Dorn St, Alexandria, to Franconia
	Gas	W: Exxon, Shell
	Food	W: Dunkin Donuts, Jerry's, McDonald's, Papa John's, Red Lobster
	Lodg	E: Comfort Inn
	Other	W: Grocery, NTB, Radio Shack
(170B)		Jct I-395N, to Washington
(170A)		Jct I-495N, to Rockville
	NOTE:	I-95 runs above with I-495 around Washington, DC. Exit #'s follow I-95.
169		VA 644, Old Keene Mill Rd, Franconia Rd, Springfield (SB) Franconia-Springfield Pky (NB)
	Gas	E: Mobil
		W: Mobil, Shell
	Food	E: Bennigan's, Bertucci's, Sbarro
		W: Bob Evans, Chesapeake Bay Seafood, Chili's, KFC, Long John Silver, McDonald's, Outback Steakhouse, Pizza Hut, Popeye's, Subway
	Lodg	E: Best Western, Courtyard, Days Inn, Hampton Inn, Hilton
		W: Holiday Inn Express, Red Roof Inn ♥, Townplace Suites
	Med	E: + Hospital
	Other	E: Springfield Mall, B&N, Circuit City, Firestone
		W: CVS, Grocery, Kmart, Radio Shack, Auto Dealers, Auto Services
169A		VA 644, Franconia Rd (SB)
169B		VA 644, Old Keene Mill Rd, Loisdale Rd, Spring Mall Rd (SB)
167		VA 617, Backlick Rd, Fullerton Rd (SB, diff reacc)
166AB		VA 7100, VA 617, Fairfax Co Pky, Springfield, Ft. Belvoir, Newington
	Gas	E: Exxon ◊
		W: Exxon
	Lodg	E: Hunter Motel
	Other	E: Davison Airfield ✈, Fort Belvoir Mil Res
		W: Costco, Fort Belvoir Military Res
163		VA 643, Lorton Rd, Lorton
	Gas	E: Shell
		W: Shell
	Food	W: Burger King, Gunston Wok
	Lodg	W: Best Western, Comfort Inn
	Other	E: Amtrak, Davison Airfield ✈, Fort Belvoir Military Res

◊ = Regular Gas Stations with Diesel ▲ = RV Friendly Locations ♥ = Pet Friendly Locations
RED PRINT SHOWS LARGE VEHICLE PARKING/ACCESS ON SITE OR NEARBY   BROWN PRINT SHOWS CAMPGROUNDS/RV PARKS

INTERSTATE 95 N/S

VIRGINIA

EXIT	
161	**US 1, Richmond Hwy, Loran, Woodbridge (SB Left ex, No NB reacc)**
Gas	E: Crown, Exxon, Shell
Food	E: Denny's, McDonald's, Taco Bell
Lodg	E: Econo Lodge, Hampton Inn, Inn of VA, Quality Inn
Other	E: Amtrak
160AB	**VA 123N, Gordon Blvd, Woodbridge, Occoquan, Lake Ridge**
Gas	E: Mobil W: Exxon◆, Mobil, Shell
Food	E: Subway W: KFC, McDonald's
Lodg	E: Econo Lodge, Hampton Inn, Quality Inn
Other	E: Grocery, Amtrak, Diamond Labs
158AB	**VA 3000, VA 639, Prince William Pky, Horner Rd, Woodbridge**
Gas	W: 7-11, Exxon, Shell, Sunoco, WaWa
Food	W: ChickFilA, IHOP, Red Lobster, Romano Macaroni Grill, Starbucks, Subway, Taco Bell, Wendy's
Lodg	W: Courtyard, Country Inn, Fairfield Inn, Holiday Inn Express, Residence Inn, Sleep Inn, WyteStone Suites
Other	W: FedEx Kinko's, PetSmart♥, Sam's Club, Wal-Mart, to BJ's
156	**Optiz Blvd, to VA 784 (SB), VA 784, Dale Blvd, Woodbridge (NB)**
Gas	E: Exxon, WaWa W: Chevron, Exxon, Mobil, Shell
Food	E: McDonald's, Taco Bell W: Burger King, Bob Evans, Chesapeake Bay Seafood House, Chli's, Dunkin Donuts, Jerry's Subs & Pizza, Lone Star Steak House, McDonald's, Olive Garden, Pizza Hut, Outback Steakhouse, Ruby Tuesday, Sakura Japanese Steak & Seafood, Starbucks
Lodg	W: Best Western, Days Inn
Med	E: + Potomac Hospital
Other	E: Auto Dealers, Grocery, N Va Comm College W: CVS, Circuit City, Costco, Firestone, Kmart, Staples, U-Haul, Potomac Mills Outlet Mall, Dale City Animal Hospital♥
(155)	**Dale City CAR Rest Area (Both dir)** NOTE: CAR ONLY Rest Area (RR, Phone, Picnic, Vend)
(154)	**Dale City TRUCK Rest Area (Both dir)** NOTE: Trucks ONLY Rest Area (RR, Phone, Picnic, Vend)
(154)	**Weigh Station (Both dir)**
152AB	**VA 234, Dumfries Rd, Dumfries**
Gas	E: BP◆, Shell◆ W: 7-11, Exxon, Shell
Food	E: Golden Corral, KFC, McDonald's, Subway, Taco Bell W: Cracker Barrel, Starbucks, Waffle House
Lodg	E: Super 8, Sleep Inn W: Days Inn, Econo Lodge, Hampton Inn, Holiday Inn Express
Other	E: Wal-Mart W: to appr 2.5mi: Prince William Trailer Village/RVDump▲
150AB	**VA 619, Joplin Rd, Triangle**
Gas	E: Exxon, Shell◆
Food	E: Burger King, Dent's Seafood, McDonald's, Wendy's

EXIT	
Lodg	E: Best Value Inn, Ramada Inn, US Inn
Other	E: Quantico US Marine Corps Res W: Quantico Nat'l Cemetery, Prince William Forest Park
148	**Russell Rd, US Marine Corps Base, Quantico**
Lodg	E: Crossroads Inn, Spring Lake Motel
143AB	**VA 610, Garrisonville Rd, US 1, Jefferson Davis Hwy, Stafford**
Gas	E: BP, Exxon, Shell W: Amoco◆, Citgo◆, WaWa
Food	E: Carlos O'Kelly's, DQ, Imperial Gardens, Little Caesars, KFC, King St Blues, McDonald's, Pizza Hut, Ruby Tuesday, Shoney's, Subway, Taco Bell, VA BBQ W: Applebee's, Burger King, Bob Evans, ChickFilA, Dunkin Donuts, Golden Corral, Hardee's, McDonald's, Kobe Japanese, Popeye's, Starbucks, Taco Bell, Wendy's
Lodg	E: Days Inn, Hampton Inn, Towneplace Suites W: Comfort Inn, Country Inn, Holiday Inn Express, Super 8, Wingate Inn
Other	E: Big Lots, Grocery, Laundromat, Radio Shack, Pharmacy, Tires, Aquia Pines Camp Resort▲ W: AutoZone, Best Buy, CVS, Grocery, Home Depot, Lowe's, Staples, Target, Wal-Mart
140	**VA 630, Courthouse Rd, Stafford**
Gas	E: Texaco◆ W: BP◆, Shell◆
Food	E: McDonald's
136	**VA 627, to US 1**
Gas	E: Chevron
Other	E: Centreport RV Sales & Service W: Stafford Reg'l Airport✈
133B	**US 17W, Warrenton Rd (SB)**
133A	**US 17E, Warrenton Rd (SB)**
133	**US 17, US 17 Bus, Warrenton Rd, Fredericksburg, Falmouth (NB)**
FStop	W: East Coast Oil/Mapco Express #4050
TStop	W: Servicetown Truck Plaza (Scales)
Gas	E: Exxon◆, Mobil◆, RaceWay W: Chevron, Shell◆
Food	E: Arby's, Burger & Kabob Place, Tex-Mex Grill, Paradise Diner, Taco Mexico & More, Rest/H J W: Servicetown Diner/TP, Hardee's, McDonald's, Outback Steakhouse, Perkins, Pizza Hut, Ponderosa, Popeye's, Sam's Pizza, Subway, Taco Bell, Waffle House, Wendy's, Rest/Qual Inn
Lodg	E: Motel 6♥, Howard Johnson W: Best Inn, Comfort Suites, Days Inn♥, Holiday Inn♥, Quality Inn♥, Sleep Inn, Super 8, Wingate Hotel, Travelodge
TWash	W: Blue Beacon TW
TServ	W: Road Runners Truck & Tire Services, ABC Truck & Tire Repair
Other	E: Auto & Tire Service W: Grocery, CVS, Auto Service, Bowling
(131)	**Fredericksburg Welcome Ctr (SB)** (RR, Phone, Picnic, Vend)
130AB	**VA 3, Plank Rd, Fredericksburg, Culpepper**
Gas	E: BP◆, WaWa W: 7-11, Crown, Exxon◆, Shell, Sheetz, WaWa

EXIT	
Food	E: Arby's, Bob Evans, Carlos O'Kelly's, CiCi's, Friendly's, Hardee's, Hunan Inn, Lone Star Steakhouse, KFC, Popeye's, Shoney's, Tops China Buffet, Wendy's W: Applebee's, Boston Market, Burger King, Carrabba's, Cracker Barrel, Chili's, Denny's, Fuddrucker's, IHOP, Joe's Crab Shack, McDonald's, O'Charley's, Outback Steakhouse, Olive Garden, Panera, Pizza Hut, Popeye's, Red, Hot & Blue, Red Lobster, Ruby Tuesday, Santa Fe Grill, Starbucks, Taco Bell, TGI Friday, Waffle House, Wendy's
Lodg	E: Best Western♥, Hampton Inn♥, Quality Inn W: Best Western♥, Holiday Inn Select, Hilton Garden Inn, Ramada Inn, Super 8
Med	E: + Hospital
Other	E: Home Depot, Pep Boys, Radio Shack, Staples, to Univ of Mary/WA W: Spotsylvania Mall, BJ's, Best Buy, Circuit City, FedEx Kinkos, Grocery, Kmart, Lowe's, NTB, Office Depot, Target, Wal-Mart sc, US Post Office
126AB	**US 1, US 17S, Fredericksburg (NB)**
126	**US 1, US 17S, Fredericksburg (SB)**
FStop	W: RaceWay Fuel Stop
Gas	E: BP, Citgo, Exxon, Mobil, Shell◆ W: Exxon, WalMart
Food	E: Arby's, Denny's, Friendly's, Garden Terrace Rest, Golden Corral, Hooters, McDonald's, Pancho Villa Mex Rest, Pizza Hut, Ruby Tuesday, Subway, Waffle House, Vital Felice Italian Rest, Wendy's W: Applebee's, Bob Evans, Burger King, ChickFilA, Cracker Barrel, Chili's, KFC, Golden Corral, Longhorn Steakhouse, McDonald's, Wendy's
Lodg	E: Days Inn♥, Econo Lodge♥, Fairfield Inn, Hampton Inn, Ramada Inn, TownePlace Suites♥ W: Comfort Inn, Sleep Inn, Wytestone Suites
Other	E: Auto Dealers, Auto Services, CVS, Goodyear, Radio Shack, Tires, UPS Store, Vet/Animal Hospital♥, Safford RV, Fredericksburg/WA DC S KOA▲ W: FedEx Kinkos, Wal-Mart sc, Massaponax Factory Outlet Center, Vet/Animal Hospital♥
118	**VA 606, Mudd Tavern Rd, Woodford, Thornburg**
Gas	E: BP, Shell◆ W: Citgo◆, Exxon, Shell, Valero
Food	W: Burger King, McDonald's
Lodg	E: Quality Inn W: Holiday Inn Express
Other	E: Fredericksburg KOA▲
110	**VA 639, Ladysmith Rd, Ruther Glen**
Gas	E: Shell◆ W: Citgo◆, Exxon◆
(107)	**Ladysmith Rest Area (Both dir)** (RR, Phone, Picnic, Vend)
104	**VA 207, Rogers Clark Blvd, Ruther Glen, Carmel Church, Bowling Green**
TStop	E: Mr Fuel #2 (Scales), Petro Stopping Center #56/Shell (Scales), Pilot Travel Center #291 (Scales) W: Flying J Travel Plaza #5033 (Scales)

◆= Regular Gas Stations with Diesel   ▲ = RV Friendly Locations   ♥ = Pet Friendly Locations
RED PRINT SHOWS LARGE VEHICLE PARKING/ACCESS ON SITE OR NEARBY   BROWN PRINT SHOWS CAMPGROUNDS/RV PARKS

EXIT		VIRGINIA	EXIT		VIRGINIA	EXIT		VIRGINIA
	Gas	E: BP◊, Exxon◊	(84AB)		I-295, to I-64, Glen Allen, Norfolk, Williamsburg, Charlottesville		Food	E: Imperial Seafood House
		W: Exxon◊						W: Applebee's, Burger King, Captain D's, Cracker Barrel, Denny's, Hardee's, Hooters, McDonald's, Pizza Hut, O'Charley's, Starbucks, Taco Bell, Waffle House, Western Sizzlin'
	Food	E: Rest/Petro SC, Subway/DQ/Pilot TC, McDonald's	83AB		VA 73, Parham Rd, Richmond			
				Gas	W: 7-11, Exxon, Shell◊			
		W: Rest/FastFood/FJ TP, Waffle House		Food	W: Denny's, Hardee's, KFC, Little Caesar's, McDonald's, Subway, Taco Bell, Waffle House, Wendy's			
	Lodg	E: Howard Johnson♥, Super 8					Lodg	E: Comfort Inn, Courtyard, Hampton Inn, Holiday Inn Express, Homewood Suites, Quality Inn
		W: Comfort Inn, Days Inn, Red Roof Inn♥, Quality Inn, Travelodge♥		Lodg	W: Econo Lodge, GuestHouse Inn, Holiday Inn, Quality Inn, Sleep Inn			
	TWash	E: Blue Beacon TW/Petro SC		Med	W: + Hospital			W: Clarion, Country Inn, Days Inn, Fairfield Inn, Super 8
	TServ	E: Petro SC/Tires, Speedco		Other	W: CVS, Food Lion, Kroger, Lowe's, Wal-Mart sc		TServ	E: VA Truck Center
	Other	E: Laundry/WiFi/Petro SC, Laundry/Pilot TC	82		US 301, VA 2, Chamberlayne Ave		Med	E: + Hospital
		W: Laundry/BarbSh/WiFi/RVDump/LP/FJ TP, US Post Office		Gas	E: Mobil◊		Other	W: CVS, Kmart, Lowe's, RiteAid, Winn Dixie, Targe, John Tyler Comm College, Pocahontas State Park▲
				Food	E: McDonald's, Rest/RRI			
98		VA 30, Kings Dominion Blvd, Doswell		Lodg	E: Red Roof Inn♥, Super 8, Travelodge♥	58		VA 746, Ruffin Mill Rd (NB), VA 620, Woods Edge Rd, Colonial Heights, Walthall, Richmond
	TStop	E: Doswell All American Travel Plaza/Texaco (Scales)	81		US 1N, Brook Rd, Wilmer Ave (NB)			
			80		Westbrook Ave, VA 161, Hermitage Rd (NB, no NB reaccess)			
	Gas	E: 7-11, Exxon					TStop	E: Pilot Travel Center #384 (Scales)
	Food	E: Rest/All Amer TP, Burger King, Denny's, Subway	(79)		Jct I-64W, I-195S, Charlottesville		Gas	E: Shell, WaWa
								W: Chevron◊
	Lodg	E: Best Western, Econo Lodge/Doswell AA TP	78		N Blvd (SB), Hermitage Rd (NB)		Food	E: Wendy's/Pilot TC
				Gas	W: Citgo◊			W: Subway, Rest/Interstate Inn
	TWash	E: All American TP		Food	E: Double T's Café		Lodg	E: Chester Inn
	TServ	E: All American TP/Tires			W: Bill's VA BBQ, Rest/Days Inn			W: Interstate Inn, Days Inn
	Other	E: Laundry/RVDump/All Amer TP, Paramount's Kings Dominion Fun Park/Campground▲, All American CG▲		Lodg	E: Holiday Inn		TWash	E: Pilot TC
					W: Comfort Inn, Days Inn, Prestige Inn		Other	E: Laundry/Pilot TC
				TServ	W: Dolan International	54		VA 144, Conduit Ave, Temple Ave, Colonial Heights, Hopewell
		W: #1 Towing/Repair		Med	W: + Hospital			
92AB		VA 54, Courthouse Rd, Ashland (NB)	76B		Lehigh St, Gilmer St, to US 1, US 301, Belvidere St (SB)		Gas	E: BP, Citgo, Crown, Exxon, Shell
								W: Shell
92		VA 54, Courthouse Rd, Ashland (SB)		Lodg	E: Quality Inn		Food	E: Arby's, Great Steak & Fry, Golden Corral, La Carreta, Old Country Buffet, Outback Steakhouse, Red Lobster, Taco Bell, Sagebrush Steakhouse, Wendy's
	FStop	W: Mapco Express #4068	76A		Chamberlayne Ave, Richmond (NB)			
	TStop	W: Travel Center of America (Scales)	(75)		Jct I-64E, Williamsburg, Norfolk N 3rd St (SB), N 7th St (NB)			
	Gas	E: Mobil						W: Hardee's, McDonald's, Subway
		W: Citgo, Exxon, Shell◊	74C		US 33, US 250, Broad St (SB) US 360, N 17th St (NB)		Lodg	E: Comfort Inn, Hampton Inn, Hilton Garden Inn
	Food	W: Rest/TA TC, Arby's, Burger King, Cracker Barrel, KFC, McDonald's, Pizza Hut, Perkins, Ponderosa, Ruby Tuesday, Taco Bell, Wendy's						
			74B		Franklin St, to US 60 (SB)		Other	E: Mall, Home Depot, Kmart, Sam's Club, Staples, Target, Wal-Mart
			(74A)		Jct I-195N, Downtown Exprwy			W: U-Haul, to VA State Univ
	Lodg	W: Budget Inn, Comfort Inn, Days Inn♥, Econo Lodge♥, Hampton Inn, Howard Johnson♥, Microtel, Quality Inn, Sleep Inn, Super 8♥	73		Maury St, Commerce Rd	53		Southpark Blvd, Colonial Heights (Access to Ex #54 Serv)
			69		VA 161, Commerce Rd, Richmond			
				Gas	W: Exxon◊, Shell◊	52AB		US 301, E Bank St, Washington St, Wythe St (SB), US 301, Bank St, Petersburg (NB)
	TServ	W: TA TC/Tires		Food	W: Hardee's, McDonald's			
	Other	W: Laundry/WiFi/CB/TA TC, CVS, Food Lion, Amtrak, U-Haul		Lodg	W: Holiday Inn, Red Roof Inn♥		Gas	E: Citgo, Crown, Shell◊
				TServ	W: VA Truck Center			W: Shell
89		VA 802, Lewistown Rd, Ashland		Other	E: Port of Richmond		Lodg	E: Best Value Inn, Econo Lodge, Holiday Inn, Howard Johnson, Star Motel
	TStop	E: Travel Center of America #142 (Scales)	67AB		VA 895E (TOLL), to I-295, VA 150, to US 60, to US 360			
	Gas	E: Shell						W: Quality Inn, Ramada Inn
	Food	E: CountryPride/PizzaHut/TA TC	64		VA 613, Willis Rd, Richmond	(51)		Jct I-85S, Durham, Atlanta
	Lodg	W: Cadillac Motel		Gas	E: Exxon, Shell	50ABCD		US 460, County Dr, Petersburg (NB)
	TServ	E: TA TC/Tires			W: 7-11, Mobil◊, Shell◊		Lodg	E: American Inn, CA Inn, Rodeway Inn Knights Inn, Flagship Inn Super 8, Travelodge, Howard Johnson, Star Motel, Royal Inn
	Other	E: Laundry/WiFi/CB/TA TC, Hanover Co Muni Airport✈, Americamps Richmond North▲		Food	E: Arby's, Waffle House			
					W: Burger King, McDonald's			
		W: Kosmo Village Campground▲, Auto Dealers, RV Center		Lodg	E: Best Value Inn, Econo Lodge, Ramada Inn			W: Quality Inn, Ramada Inn
					W: Country Inn, Sleep Inn, Super 8, VIP Inn		Other	E: Petersburg Nat'l Battlefield
86		VA 656, Sliding Hill Rd, Ashland, Atlee, Elmont						W: Greyhound
	Gas	E: BP, Sheetz		TServ	E: Kenworth	50		US 301, US 460, S Crater Rd (SB) to US 460, County Dr, Petersburg US 301, Wythe, Washington (NB)
		W: 7-11, Mobil, Shell◊		Other	E: Hayden's RV Center			
	Food	W: Applebee's, Burger King, Chili's, ChickFilA, McDonald's, O'Charley's, Panera Bread, Red Robin, Ruby Tuesday, Shoney's, Sbarro, Subway, Wendy's			W: Flea Market			
			62		VA 288, to Powhite Pkwy		Gas	E: 7-11, BP
			61AB		VA 10, W Hundred Rd, Chester, Chesterfield, Hopewell		Lodg	E: Flagship Inn, Knights Inn
							Med	W: + Hospital
	Lodg	W: Best Western, Springhill Suites		Gas	E: RaceTrac	48AB		Wagner Rd, Petersburg
	Other	W: Mall, Circuit City, Firestone, Goodyear, Target, Walgreen's			W: 7-11◊, Crown, Exxon◊, Shell		Gas	E: Exxon
								W: Chevron◊, Exxon, Shell◊

◊ = Regular Gas Stations with Diesel   ▲ = RV Friendly Locations   ♥ = Pet Friendly Locations

RED PRINT SHOWS LARGE VEHICLE PARKING/ACCESS ON SITE OR NEARBY   BROWN PRINT SHOWS CAMPGROUNDS/RV PARKS

EXIT		VIRGINIA
	Food	E: McDonald's
		W: Hardee's, KFC, McDonald's, Pizza Hut, Ponderosa, Subway, Taco Bell
	Other	W: Auto Dealers, Auto Services, US Post Office
47		VA 629, Rives Rd, Petersburg
	Gas	W: Citgo, Shell
	Lodg	W: Heritage Motor Lodge
(46)		Jct I-295N, to Washington (fr SB, Left exit)
45		US 301, S Crater Rd, Petersburg
	Gas	E: Shell◊
		W: Exxon
	Food	W: Rest/BW, Rest/Days Inn, Rest/Qual Inn
	Lodg	E: Hampton Inn
		W: Best Western♥, Comfort Inn, Days Inn♥, Holiday Inn Express, Quality Inn
41		US 301, VA 35, VA 156, Courtland
	FStop	E: US Gas/Chevron
	Food	E: Nino's Rest
		W: Rest/Rose Garden Inn
	Lodg	E: Econo Lodge
		W: Rose Garden Inn, Travelodge
	Other	E: Petersburg KOA▲
(40)		Weigh Station (Both dir)
37		VA 623, Carson
	Gas	W: BP◊, Shell
(37)		Carson Rest Area (NB) (RR, Phone, Picnic, Vend, Playground)
33		VA 602, St John Church Rd, Cabin Point Rd, S 301, Stony Creek
	TStop	W: AmBest/Davis Travel Center/Exxon (Scales)
	Gas	W: Chevron◊
	Food	W: Denny's/Starbucks/Subway/Davis TC, Burger King
	Lodg	W: Hampton Inn♥, Sleep Inn♥
	TServ	W: Davis TC/Tires
	Other	W: Laundry/Davis TC
31		VA 40, US 301, Stony Creek, Waverly
	FStop	W: Carter's One Stop/Shell
	Food	W: Carter's Rest, Stony Creek BBQ
	Other	W: Carters Car & Truck Repair, Tires
24		VA 645, Owen Rd, Jarratt
20		VA 631, Jarratt Rd, Jarratt
	Gas	W: Exxon◊, Shell◊
17		US 301, Jarratt
	Food	E: China Star/Reste Motel
	Lodg	E: Knights Inn, Reste Motel
	Other	E: Yogi Bear's Jellystone Camp Resort▲
13		VA 614, Otterdam Rd, Emporia
	TStop	E: Emporia Travel Plaza/Shell
	Lodg	E: Dixie Motel
	Other	E: RVDump/Shell
12		US 301 (NB)
11AB		US 58, Emporia, S Hill, Norfolk
	TStop	W: Sadler Travel Plaza/Shell (Scales)
	Gas	E: BP◊, Exxon, Shell
		W: Citgo, Exxon
	Food	E: Burger King, Cracker Barrel, Hardee's, KFC, Long John Silver, McDonald's, Pizza Hut
		W: Rest/Sadler TP, Bojangles

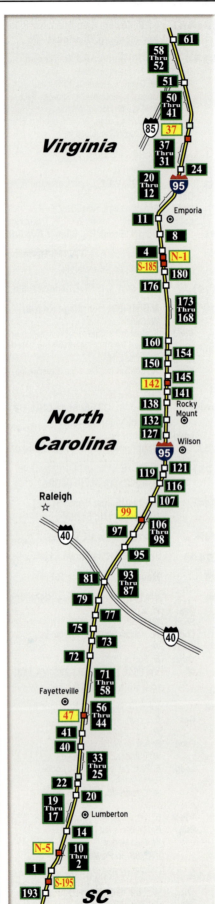

EXIT		VA / NC
	Lodg	E: Best Value Inn♥, Holiday Inn Express, Fairfield Inn, Marriott, US Inn
		W: Best Western♥, Days Inn♥, Hampton Inn♥, Holiday Inn Express, Quality Inn, Sleep Inn
	TServ	W: Sadler TP/Tires
	Med	E: + Hospital
	Other	E: Auto Services, CVS, Food Lion, Radio Shack, Wal-Mart sc
		W: Laundry/RVDump/Sadler TP
8		US 301, Skippers Rd, Emporia
	TStop	E: Simmons Travel Center #2/AmocoBP (Scales)
	Gas	E: Citgo
	Food	E: Rest/Red Carpet Inn, Rest/Simmons TC, Denny's
	Lodg	E: Comfort Inn♥, Red Carpet Inn♥
	TServ	E: Simmons TC/Tires
	Other	E: Laundry/Simmons TC
4		VA 629, Moores Ferry Rd, Skippers
	TStop	E: Love's Travel Stop #317 (Scales)
	Food	E: McDonald's/Love's TS
	Lodg	W: Econo Inn
	Other	E: WiFi/RVDump/Love's TS
		W: Cattail Creek RV Park▲
(1)		VA Welcome Center (NB) (NO TRUCKS) (RR, Phone, Picnic, Vend, Info, Playground)

(EASTERN TIME ZONE)

⋂ VIRGINIA
⋃ NORTH CAROLINA

(EASTERN TIME ZONE)

	NOTE:	MM 181: Virginia State Line
(181)		NC Welcome Center (SB) (RR, Phone, Picnic, Vend)
180		NC 48, Pleasant Hill Rd, Pleasant Hill, Gaston, Lake Gaston
	TStop	W: Pilot Travel Center #58 (Scales)
	Food	W: Subway/Pilot TC
	Other	W: WiFi/Pilot TC
176		NC 46, Garysburg, Gaston
	Gas	E: Texaco
		W: Shell
	Food	E: Stuckey's/Texaco
		W: Rest/Comfort Inn
	Lodg	W: Comfort Inn
173		US 158, Weldon, Roanoke Rapids
	Gas	E: Shell, BP◊, Texaco◊
		W: BP◊, Exxon, RaceTrac, WalMart
	Food	E: Ralph's BBQ, Trigger's Steakhouse, Waffle House
		W: Burger King, Cracker Barrel, Little Caesars, Hardee's, KFC, McDonald's, Pizza Hut, Ryan's Grill, Shoney's, Subway, Taco Bell, Wendy's
	Lodg	E: Days Inn, Interstate Inn
		W: Comfort Inn, Hampton Inn, Jameson Inn, Motel 6♥, Sleep Inn
	Med	E: + Hospital
	Other	E: Interstate Inn Campground▲
		W: Auto Dealers, Auto Zone, ATMs, Dollar General, Firestone, Food Lion, Wal-Mart sc
171		NC 125, Roanoke Rapids
	Lodg	W: Holiday Inn Express
	Other	W: NC State Hwy Patrol

◊ = Regular Gas Stations with Diesel ▲ = RV Friendly Locations ♥ = Pet Friendly Locations
RED PRINT SHOWS LARGE VEHICLE PARKING/ACCESS ON SITE OR NEARBY   BROWN PRINT SHOWS CAMPGROUNDS/RV PARKS

Page 518

INTERSTATE 95 S

EXIT	NORTH CAROLINA
168	NC 903, Roanoke Rapids, Halifax
Gas	E: Exxon◆, Shell◆
Food	E: Hardee's
160	NC 561, Enfield, Louisburg
Gas	E: Exxon
	W: Citgo◆
Food	W: Rest/Citgo
154	NC 481, Enfield
Gas	E: Mobil
Other	W: Enfield/Rocky Mt KOA▲
(151)	Weigh Station (Both dir)
150	NC 33, Whitakers
Gas	W: BP
Food	W: DQ/Stuckey's/BP
145	NC 48, NC 4, to US 301, Battleboro
Gas	E: AmocoBP◆, Exxon, Shell◆
Food	E: Denny's, Hardee's, Shoney's, Waffle House, Wendy's, Rest/DI
Lodg	E: Comfort Inn, Days Inn, Deluxe Inn, Howard Johnson, Quality Inn, Super 8, Travelodge
(142)	Rest Area (Both dir) (RR, Phone, Picnic, Vend)
141	NC 43, Dortches Blvd, Main St, Rocky Mount, Red Oak
Gas	E: Exxon◆
	W: BP◆
Food	W: Rest/Holiday Inn
Lodg	W: Econo Lodge, Holiday Inn
138	US 64, Nashville, Rocky Mount
Food	E: Cracker Barrel
Med	E: + Hospital
132	Mountain Rd, to NC 58, Nashville
Gas	E: Citgo◆
127	NC 97, Bailey, Airport, Stanhope
Gas	E: BP◆
Food	E: Cracker Barrel, Denny's
Other	E: Rocky Mt Wilson Airport ✈
121	US 264 A, Wilson, Greenville
FStop	E: Kangaroo Express
Gas	E: BP, Citgo, Shell
Food	E: Blimpie, Bojangles, Hardee's, Long John Silver, KFC, McDonald's, Subway, Waffle House
	W: Burger King, Cracker Barrel, McDonald's
Lodg	E: Comfort Inn
	W: Hampton Inn, Holiday Inn, Jameson Inn, Microtel, Sleep Inn
Med	E: + Hospital
Other	E: Lowe's, Kmart, Staples, Wal-Mart sc
119AB	US 264, to US 117, US 301
116	NC 42, Wilson, Rock Ridge
Gas	E: Shell◆
	W: BP◆
Other	W: Rock Ridge Campground▲
107	US 301, Kenly
FStop	E: Kangaroo Express/BP
TStop	E: Flying J Travel Plaza (Scales)
Gas	E: Exxon◆, Shell
Food	E: Rest/Flying J TP, Burger King, McDonald's, Pizza, Subway, Waffle House, Wendy's
Lodg	E: Budget Inn, Deluxe Inn, Econo Lodge
Other	E: Laundry/WiFi/Flying J TP, Family Dollar, Food Lion

EXIT	NORTH CAROLINA
106	Truck Stop Rd, Kenly
TStop	E: Flying J Travel Plaza (Scales)
	W: Travel Center of America (Scales), WilcoHess Travel Plaza #218 (Scales)
Food	E: CountryMarket/FJ TP
	W: CountryPride/TA TC, Hardee's, Waffle House, FastFood/WilcoHess TP
Lodg	W: Days Inn, Super 8
TWash	W: Blue Beacon TW/TA TC, Speedco
TServ	W: TA TC/Tires, Speedco
Other	E: Laundry/WiFi/FJ TP
	W: Laundry/WiFi/TA TC
105	Bagley Rd, Selma
TStop	E: Big Boy's Truck Stop/Citgo (Scales)
Food	E: Bob's Big Boy/Big Boys TS
TServ	E: Big Boy's TS/Tires
102	Main St, Selma, Micro
Gas	E: BP
	W: Phillips 66
Food	W: Wayne's Rest
101	NC 2137, Pittman Rd, Selma
(99)	Rest Area (Both dir) (RR, Phone, Picnic, Vend)
98	Anderson St, Selma
Other	E: Rvacation Campground▲
97	US 70, Selma, Pine Level
FStop	E: M&N Truck Stop/Citgo
Gas	E: Discount Gas◆
	W: BP◆, Exxon, Shell
Food	E: Denny's, Subway
	W: Bojangles, Denny's, Golden Corral, Hardee's, KFC, Pizza Hut, McDonald's, Shoney's, Waffle House

EXIT	NORTH CAROLINA
Lodg	E: Holiday Inn Express
	W: Comfort Inn, Days Inn, Regency Inn, Masters Economy Inn
TServ	W: I-95 Truck Center
Med	W: + Hospital
Other	E: Food Lion, Pharmacy, J&R Outlets
95	US 70 Bus, E Market St, Smithfield
FStop	W: Speedway
Gas	W: Shell
Food	E: Rest/HJ, Rest/Village Motor Lodge, Rest/Log Cabin Motel
	W: Bob Evans, Burger King, Waffle House Cracker Barrel, CiCi's, Outback Steakhouse, Ruby Tuesday, Smithfield BBQ, Zaxby's
Lodg	E: Howard Johnson, Village Motor Lodge, Log Cabin Motel
	W: Jameson Inn, Super 8
Other	W: Factory Outlet Stores
93	Brogden Rd, Smithfield
Gas	W: BP◆, Shell
TServ	E: Smithfield Diesel Repair
90	US 701, NC 96, to US 301, Four Oaks
Gas	E: BP◆, Citgo◆
	W: Phillips 66
Lodg	E: Travelers Inn
	W: Four Oaks Motel
Other	E: Smithfield KOA▲, Holiday Trav-L-Park▲
	W: NC State Hwy Patrol Post
87	Keen Rd (SB), Hockaday Rd, Main St, Brewer Rd (NB), Four Oaks
(81AB)	Jct I-40, W-Raleigh, E-Wilmington
79	NC 50, NC 242, Main St, Benson
Gas	E: Mobil, BP◆, Citgo, Phillips 66
	W: Coastal, Exxon
Food	E: Benson's BBQ, Frank's Pizza, Waffle House
	W: Burger King, KFC, McDonald's, Pizza Hut, Subway
Lodg	E: Dutch Inn
	W: Days Inn
Other	E: Food Lion
	W: Grocery, Pharmacy
77	Chapel Rd, Denning Rd, Parker Rd, Dunn, Hodges
TStop	E: Pilot Travel Center #55 (Scales)
Food	E: Subway/Pilot TC
TServ	E: Rai Truck Repair Shop, Peterbilt
75	Jonesboro Rd, Dunn
TStop	W: Sadler Travel Plaza/Shell (Scales)
Food	W: Rest/Sadler TP, Milestone Diner, Quiznos
TServ	W: Sadler TP/Tires, Peterbilt of Dunn
Other	W: Sadler TP
73	US 421, NC 55, Dunn, Clinton
Gas	W: Exxon◆, Chevron
Food	E: Cracker Barrel, Wendy's
	W: Bojangles, Burger King, KFC, Sagebrush Steakhouse, Triangle Waffle
Lodg	W: Comfort Inn, Econo Lodge, Holiday Inn Express, Jameson Inn, Ramada Inn
Med	W: + Hospital
Other	E: Auto Dealers, Grocery
	W: Grocery, Campbell Univ
72	Pope Rd, Poole Rd, Dunn
Gas	E: BP
	W: BP
Food	E: Rest/Best Western
	W: Brass Lantern Steakhouse

◆ = Regular Gas Stations with Diesel ▲ = RV Friendly Locations ♥ = Pet Friendly Locations
RED PRINT SHOWS LARGE VEHICLE PARKING/ACCESS ON SITE OR NEARBY BROWN PRINT SHOWS CAMPGROUNDS/RV PARKS

EXIT	NORTH CAROLINA		EXIT	NORTH CAROLINA		EXIT	NC / SC
	Lodg	E: Comfort Inn, Royal Inn W: Budget Inn, Express Inn	(24)	Weigh Station (Both dir)		Food	E: Pedro's Diner, Sombrero Rest W: Waffle House
71		Long Branch Rd, Dunn	22		US 301, Fayetteville Rd, Lumberton	Lodg	E: Budget Inn, South of the Border Motel W: Days Inn, Holiday Inn Express
	TStop	E: Kangaroo/Citgo		FStop	W: Sun-Do	Other	E: Camp Pedro▲
	Food	E: Hardee's/Kangaroo		TStop	W: Minuteman #24		
70		NC 1811, Bud Hawkins Rd, Dunn		Gas	E: Exxon, Xpress Depot W: Mobil, Pure	(EASTERN TIME ZONE)	
	Lodg	E: Relax Inn		Food	E: Burger King, Denny's, Hardee's, Outback Steakhouse, Ryan's Grill, Smithfield BBQ, Waffle House, Rest/HI W: Rest/Minuteman	⬆NORTH CAROLINA ⬇SOUTH CAROLINA	
65		NC 82, Godwin Falcon Rd, Godwin					
61		Wade Stedman Rd, Wade				(EASTERN TIME ZONE)	
	FStop	E: Citgo W: Lucky 7 Truck Stop/BP		Lodg	E: Best Western, Comfort Suites, Holiday Inn, Hampton Inn, Super 8	NOTE:	MM 198: North Carolina State Line
	Food	E: Dixie Boy, DQ W: Subway/Lucky 7		Other	E: Grocery, Goodyear, Lowe's, Office Depot, Wal-Mart sc, NC State Hwy Patrol Post	(195)	SC Welcome Center (SB) (RR, Phone, Picnic, Vend, Info)
	Other	E: Fayetteville/Wade KOA▲				193	SC 9, SC 57, Dillon, Bennettsville, Little Rock, to N Myrtle Beach
58		US 13, to US 401, Fayetteville, Newton Grove	20		NC 211, Roberts Ave, to NC 41, Lumberton, Red Springs	Gas	E: BP, Mobil, Speedway◆, Sunoco W: BP
	Food	E: Rest/Days Inn		Gas	E: Citgo, Exxon◆, Liberty◆ W: Exxon, Shell◆	Food	E: Burger King, Golden Corral, Huddle House, Shoney's, Waffle House, Wendy's
	Lodg	E: Days Inn		Food	E: Arby's, Bojangles, Burger King, CiCi's, Hardee's, KFC, Little Caesars, McDonald's, Shoney's, Subway, Taco Bell, Waffle House, Wendy's, Western Sizzlin, Rest/Ramada, Rest/Quality Inn W: Cracker Barrel	Lodg	E: Best Value Inn ♥, Comfort Inn, Days Inn ♥, Hampton Inn, Knights Inn, Ramada Ltd W: Econo Lodge ♥, Super 8 ♥
56		I-95S Bus, to US 301, Fayetteville, Hope AFB, Fort Bragg (SB)					
55		NC 1832, Murphy Rd, Fayetteville, Eastover					
	Gas	W: Apco, Kangaroo				TServ	W: Cottingham Trailer Service
	Lodg	W: Budget Inn		Lodg	E: Deluxe Inn, Quality Inn, Ramada Ltd W: Comfort Inn, Country Suites, Days Inn, Econo Lodge	Med	E: + Mcleod Medical Center
52AB		NC 24, Fayetteville, Clinton				Other	W: Dillon Co Airport✈, Bass Lake RV Campground▲, Trailer Service
49		NC 53, NC 210, Fayetteville		Med	E: + Hospital	190	SC 34, Dillon, Bingham
	Gas	E: BP◆, Exxon, Kangaroo, Shell W: Exxon◆, Shell◆		Other	E: CVS, Food Lion, Kmart	Tstop	W: Love's Travel Stop #371
	Food	E: Burger King, Denny's, McDonald's, Pizza Hut, Waffle House W: Cracker Barrel, Ruby Tuesday, Shoney's	19		Carthage Rd, Lumberton	Gas	E: BP
				Gas	E: BP◆ W: Exxon◆, Texaco	Food	E: Stuckey's/DQ W: Arby's/Love's TS
				Food	E: Rest/Red Carpet Inn W: Sullivan's	Other	W: WiFi/Love's TS
	Lodg	E: Days Inn, Deluxe Inn, Motel 6 ♥, Quality Inn		Lodg	E: Red Carpet Inn, Travelers Inn W: Knights Inn, Motel 6 ♥	181B	SC 38W, SC 917, Bennettsville
						181A	SC 38E, SC 917, Marion
	Lodg	W: Best Western, Comfort Inn, Hampton Inn, Econo Lodge, Fairfield Inn, Holiday Inn, Innkeeper I-95, Red Roof Inn ♥, Sheraton, Sleep Inn, Super 8	17		NC 72, NC 711, Caton Rd, Lumberton, Pembroke	181	SC 38, SC 917, Latta, Marion, to Myrtle Beach
				Gas	E: BP◆, Citgo, Exxon, Mobil◆, Shell◆	TStop	E: Flying J Travel Plaza/Conoco (Scales) W: WilcoHess Travel Plaza #938 (Scales)
				Food	E: Burger King, Hardee's, McDonald's, Waffle House, Huddle House/Exxon	Gas	E: BP, Shell W: Kangaroo
	TServ	W: Smith International Truck Center		Lodg	E: Southern Inn, Budget Inn, Economy Inn, Super 8	Food	E: Cookery/FJ TP, McDonald's/Shell, Subway/BP W: Wendy's/WilcoHess TP
(47)		Rest Area (Both dir) (RR, Phone, Picnic, Vend)		TServ	E: Smith International Truck Center	Lodg	W: Best Westerm
46AB		NC 87, Fayetteville, Elizabethtown		Other	E: Auto Services, Food Lion, Pharmacy	Other	E: Laundry/WiFi/RVDump/LP/FJ TP, Green's Tire Service W: Laundry/WiFi/WilcoHess TP, Auto & Truck Repairs
	Med	W: + Hospital	(14)		I-74, US 74, Lumberton, to Maxton, Laurinburg		
44		NC 2341, Claude Lee Rd, Snow Hill Rd, Fayetteville		Gas	W: BP◆		
	Other	W: Lazy Acres Campground▲, to Fayetteville Reg'l Airport✈		Food	W: Rest/Exit 14 Inn	(171)	Pee Dee Rest Area (Both dir) (RR, Phones, Picnic, Vend)
				Lodg	W: Exit 14 Inn		
41		NC 59, Chickenfoot Rd, Hope Mills, Fayetteville		Other	W: Sleepy Bear's Family Campground▲ to NC Battleship Memorial	170	SC 327, Florence, Marion, to Myrtle Beach
	Gas	E: Kangaroo W: BP◆	10		US 301S, Chicken Rd, Fairmont, Lumberton	TStop	E: Pilot Travel Center #62 (Scales)
						Gas	E: BP
	Other	W: Spring Valley RV Park▲, Hawley's Camping Center	7		Raynham Rd, Fairmont, McDonald, Raynham	Food	E: Wendy's/Pilot TC, Waffle & Egg, McDonald's
40		Jct I-95 Bus, to US 301, Fayetteville, Fort Bragg, Hope AFB (NB)				Lodg	E: Holiday Inn Express
			(5)		NC Welcome Center (NB) (RR, Phone, Picnic, Vend)	Other	E: Laundry/WiFi/RVDump/Pilot TC, Johnson's Trailer Park▲, to Myrtle Beach
33		US 301, to NC 71, St Pauls					
	Gas	E: BP◆	2		NC 130, to NC 904, Rowland, Fairmont		
31		NC 20, St Pauls, Raeford, Pinehurst				169	TV Rd, Florence, Quinby
	TStop	E: Poco Shop/Shell	1AB		US 301, US 501, Rowland, Dillon, South of the Border (SB)	TStop	W: Petro Stopping Center #58/Exxon (Scales)
	Gas	E: BP, Citgo, Mobil W: Exxon◆					
	Food	E: Rest/Poco Shop, Burger King, Hardee's, Huddle House, McDonald's	1		US 301, US 501, Rowland, Dillon, Laurinburg, South of the Border	Gas	W: BP
						Food	W: IronSkillet/PizzaHut/Petro SC
	Lodg	E: Days Inn		FStop	W: Border Shell	Lodg	W: Best Value Inn ♥, Rodeway Inn
	TServ	E: Central Carolina Trucks		Gas	E: Amoco, Exxon, Shell		
25		US 301, Lumberton					
	FStop	E: BP					

Page 520
◆ = Regular Gas Stations with Diesel ▲ = RV Friendly Locations ♥ = Pet Friendly Locations
RED PRINT SHOWS LARGE VEHICLE PARKING/ACCESS ON SITE OR NEARBY   BROWN PRINT SHOWS CAMPGROUNDS/RV PARKS

INTERSTATE 95 N/S

SOUTH CAROLINA

EXIT		SOUTH CAROLINA
	TWash	W: Blue Beacon TW/Petro SC
	TServ	E: Cummins, Peterbilt of Florence, Stone Truck Center
		W: Petro SC/Tires, K&L Chrome Shop
	Other	E: Florence KOA▲
		W: Laundry/WiFi/RVDump/Petro SC
164		US 52, W Lucas St, Florence, Darlington, Darlington Int'l Raceway
	TStop	W: Travel Center of America/BP (Scales), Pilot Travel Center #337 (Scales)
	Gas	E: Exxon◊, Raceway
		W: Hess◊
	Food	E: Cracker Barrel, Denny's, Hardee's, Kobe Japanese, McDonald's, Perkins, Ruby Tuesday, Waffle House, Wendy's
		W: Popeye's/TA TC, Subway/TacoBell/Pilot TC, Arby's, Bojangles, Burger King, KFC, McDonald's, Pizza Hut, Quincy's Steakhouse, Shoney's
	Lodg	E: Best Western, Comfort Inn, Hampton Inn, Holiday Inn♥, Motel 6♥, Super 8♥
		W: Comfort Inn♥, Days Inn♥, Guest House Int'l, Microtel, Ramada Inn♥, Shoney's Inn, Sleep Inn, Suburban Hotel♥, Thunderbird Inn♥, Wingate Inn
	Med	W: + McLeod Reg'l Medical Center
	Other	E: Laundry/WiFi/TA TC, Auto Dealer, Auto Services, Towing
		W: ATMs, Auto Services, Florence Darlington Tech College, Pee Dee Farmers Market, to Darlington Int'l Raceway
(160B)		Jct I-20W, to Columbia
(160A)		Jct I-20 Bus E, US 76, to Florence
	Gas	E: Shell◊, Scotchman
	Food	E: Arby's, Burger King, ChickFilA, Huddle House, IHOP, Pizza Hut, Outback Steakhouse, Red Lobster, Ruby Tuesday, Shoney's, Waffle House, Western Sizzlin
	Lodg	E: Courtyard, Fairfield Inn, Hampton Inn, Hilton Garden Inn, Red Roof Inn♥, Springhill Suites
	Other	E: Civic Center, Auto Services, Best Buy, CVS, Dollar Tree, Lowe's, Sam's Club, Target, Wal-Mart, Mall
157		US 76, Florence, Timmonsville
	Gas	E: AmocoBP◊, Exxon◊, Kangaroo◊, Phillips 66
		W: Sunoco
	Food	E: McDonald's, Las Palmas Family Mex Rest, Swamp Fox Diner, Waffle House
		W: Carol's, Magnolia Dining Room
	Lodg	E: Days Inn♥, Howard Johnson, Swamp Fox Inn, Travelodge
		W: Econo Lodge, Ramada at Young's Plantation
	Med	W: + Hospital
	Other	E: Food Lion
		W: Swamp Fox Campground▲
153		Honda Way, Timmonsville
	Other	W: Honda Plant
150		SC 403, Timmonsville, Sardis
	FStop	E: Sardis Auto Truck Plaza/BP
	Gas	W: Exxon◊
	Food	E: Rest/Sardis ATP
	Lodg	E: Budget Inn
	Other	W: Lake Honeydew Campground▲

EXIT		SOUTH CAROLINA
146		SC 341, Lynchburg Hwy, Lynchburg, Lake City, Olanta
	Gas	E: Exxon◊
	Lodg	E: Relax Inn
141		SC 53, SC 58, Lynchburg, Shiloh
	FStop	E: Mary O's Exxon
	Gas	W: Shell
	Other	E: RV Center
(139)		Shiloh Rest Area (Both dir) (RR, Phone, Picnic, Vend)
135		US 378, Clarence Coker Hwy, Lynchburg, Turbeville, Sumter
	Gas	E: BP, Citgo◊
		W: Exxon
	Food	E: Rest/Days Inn
	TServ	E: Truck Service Inc
	Lodg	E: Comfort Inn, Days Inn
	Other	W: to Dabbs Airport ✈
132		SC 527, Gable, Sardinia, Bishopville
122		SC 521, Alcolu, Sumter, Manning
	Gas	W: Exxon◊
119		SC 261, Paxville Hwy, Manning, Paxville
	TStop	E: Travel Center of America/BP (Scales)
	Gas	E: Shell
		W: Exxon
	Food	E: Rest/FastFood/TA TC, Huddle House, Subway, Waffle House, Wendy's
		W: Burger King
	Lodg	E: Best Western, Holiday Inn Express
		W: Super 8
	TWash	E: Mid Eastern TW
	TServ	E: TA TC/Tires
	Med	E: + Hospital
	Other	E: Laundry/WiFi/CB/RVDump/TA TC, CVS, Food Lion, Goodyear, Wal-Mart, Campers Paradise Campground▲
115		US 301, Alex Harvin Hwy, Manning, Summerton
	FStop	W: Moore's Food Store/Shell
	Gas	E: Exxon◊
	Food	E: Rest/Travelers Inn
		W: Rest/Days Inn
	Lodg	E: Carolina Inn, Travelers Inn
		W: Days Inn, Econo Lodge, Sunset Inn
108		SC 102, Buff Blvd, Summerton
	Gas	E: Citgo, Shell
		W: BP
	Food	E: Stuckey's/DQ/Citgo
		W: Summerton Motel, Family Folks
	Lodg	W: Knights Inn, Summerton Motel
102		US 15, US 301N, Rd 400, N Santee, St Paul, Summerton
	NOTE:	US 15/US 301 exits NB, joins SB
	Gas	E: BP
		W: Shell◊
	Food	E: Howard Johnson
	Lodg	E: Howard Johnson
	Other	E: Santee Lakes Campground▲
		W: Santee State Park
(99)		SC Welcome Center (SB) Santee Rest Area (NB) (RR, Phone, Picnic, Vend, Info)
98		SC 6, Santee, Eutawville
	Gas	E: BP, Chevron, Mobil
		W: BP◊, Exxon, Hess◊, Horizon◊, Shell

◊ = Regular Gas Stations with Diesel ▲ = RV Friendly Locations ♥ = Pet Friendly Locations
RED PRINT SHOWS LARGE VEHICLE PARKING/ACCESS ON SITE OR NEARBY BROWN PRINT SHOWS CAMPGROUNDS/RV PARKS

Page 521

EXIT	SOUTH CAROLINA	EXIT	SOUTH CAROLINA	EXIT	SC / GA
	Food E: Georgio's House of Pizza, Huddle House, Jake's Steaks, KFC, Shoney's, Subway, Western Steer W: Burger King, Cracker Barrel, Denny's Hardee's, McDonald's, Waffle House Lodg E: Best Western, Days Inn, Hampton Inn♥, Ramada Inn, Travelodge W: Baymont Inn, Clark's Inn & Rest, Country Inn, Economy Inn, Holiday Inn, Quality Inn Other E: Dollar General, Grocery, Golf Course, Lake Marion Resort▲ W: ATMs, Auto Services, CarQuest, Family Dollar, Food Lion, Grocery, NAPA, Pharmacy, Laundromat, US Post Office, Golf Course, Santee State Park		Lodg E: Carolina Lodge, Sleep Inn, Southern Inn W: Microtel, Super 8♥ Med E: + Hospital Other E: AutoZone, CVS, Food Lion, Grocery W: Wal-Mart sc		Gas W: Chevron, Kangaroo Food E: Rest/Joker Joe's TS, Huddle House, Wendy's, McDonald's/Shell W: Pizza Hut, Waffle House Lodg W: Motel 6♥ Tires E: Joker Joe's TS Other E: Laundry/Joker Joe's TS, Hardeeville RV-Thomas Parks & Sites▲
53			SC 63, to US 17, Sniders Hwy, Walterboro, Varnville, Hampton	5	US 17, US 321, Hardeeville, Savannah
		FStop Gas	E: Angler's Mini Mart/Citgo E: BP, Exxon, Shell W: El Cheapo	FStop Gas	W: Speedway, Sunoco #2656 E: Exxon, Shell W: BP◆, Citgo, Chevron
		Food	E: Burger King, Glass House Seafood Rest, KFC, McDonald's, Ruby Tuesday, Waffle House W: Cracker Barrel, Shoney's	Food	E: KFC, Waffle House W: Burger King, KFC, McDonald's, Shoney's, Subway, Wendy's
		Lodg	E: Best Western♥, Comfort Inn, Howard Johnson Express♥, Econo Lodge, Ramada Inn♥ W: Days Inn, Deluxe Inn, Hampton Inn, Holiday Inn Express	Lodg	E: Days Inn, Economy Inn♥, Sleep Inn W: Comfort Inn, Deluxe Inn, Holiday Inn, Hampton Inn, Howard Johnson♥, Knights Inn♥, Quality Inn♥, Scottish Inn, Super 8
97	US 301S, to Orangeburg (SB exit, NB entr)				
	NOTE: US 301 joins NB, leaves SB	Other	W: Green Acres Family Campground▲	Other	E: Hardeeville RV-Thomas Parks & Sites
93	US 15, Bass Dr, Holly Hill, Santee	(47)	Hendersonville Rest Area (Both dir) (RR, Phone, Picnic, Vend)	(4.3)	SC Welcome Center (NB) (RR, Phone, Picnic, Vend, Info)
	NOTE: US 15 joins NB, leaves SB	42	US 21, Lowcountry Hwy, Walterboro, Orangeburg, Yemassee, Beaufort, Pt Royal	(3)	Weigh Station (Both dir)
90	US 176, Old State Rd, Holly Hill				(EASTERN TIME ZONE)
(86)	Jct I-26, E-Charleston, W-Columbia	38	SC 68, Yemassee, Hampton, Beaufort, Port Royal		**◯ SOUTH CAROLINA**
(86A)	Jct I-26, E to Charleston				**◯ GEORGIA**
(86B)	Jct I-26, W-Orangeburg, Columbia				(EASTERN TIME ZONE)
82	US 178, St George, to Harleyville, Bowman	TStop Gas	W: Simco Travel Plaza (Scales) E: Chevron W: BP, Exxon, Shell		NOTE: MM 113: South Carolina State Line
	TStop E: WilcoHess Travel Plaza #930 (Scales) Gas E: BP W: Shell◆	Food Lodg	W: Rest/Simco TP, J's Rest, Subway W: Motel/Simco TP, Palmetto Lodge, Super 8	(111)	GA Welcome Center (SB) (RR, Phone, Picnic, Vend, Info, RVDump)
	Food E: Wendy's/DQ/WilcoHess TP, Pizza Inn, Blimpie, Church Fried Chicken Lodg E: Peach Tree Inn♥ Other E: Laundry/RVDump/WilcoHess, TP Billy's Towing & Tires W: Truck & Trailer Repair, Tires	TServ	W: Simco TP/Tires	109	GA 21, Augusta Rd, Port Wentworth, Savannah, Rincon (Addt'l Serv E on GA 21)
		33	US 17N, Beaufort, Charleston, Point South NOTE: US 17 exits NB, joins SB	FStop TStop Gas	W: Circle K #5352/76 E: Pilot Travel Center #71 (Scales) E: Enmark◆ W: Shell
77	US 78, St George, Branchville	Gas Food Lodg	E: BP◆, Exxon, Shell E: Denny's, McDonald's, Waffle House E: Best Western, Days Inn, Hampton Inn, Holiday Inn Express, Knights Inn	Food	E: McDonald's/Subway/Pilot TC, Waffle House W: Quiznos/Circle K, Sea Grill Rest, Wendy's, Zaxby's
	FStop W: Rainbow Gas Garden #8/Shell Gas E: Exxon W: BP, Shell◆	Other	E: Visitor Info, Point South KOA▲, The Oaks RV Resort▲	Lodg	E: Country Inn, Hampton Inn, Wingate Inn W: Comfort Suites, Days Inn, Holiday Inn Express, Quality Inn, Ramada Ltd, Savannah Inn♥, Sleep Inn, Super 8♥
	Food E: Hardee's, McDonald's, Western Sizzlin', Waffle House W: Huddle House, Taco Bell	28	SC 462, Coosawhatchie, Hilton Head Island	Tires TServ	E: Pilot TC E: Kenworth of Savannah, Peterbilt of Savannah, Roberts WhiteGMC, Stuart's Alignment
	Lodg E: Best Value Inn, Comfort Inn & RV Park▲, Econo Lodge, Quality Inn W: Best Western, Days Inn, Southern Inn, Super 8	FStop Gas Other	W: Tiger Express #11/Exxon W: Chevron W: Auto & Truck Tires	Other	E: Laundry/WiFi/Pilot TC W: to appr 3 mi Whispering Pines RV Park▲, appr 5mi Greenpeace RV Park▲
	Other E: CVS, Food Lion, US Post Office	22	US 17S, Ridgeland NOTE: US 17 exits SB, joins NB	106	Jimmy Deloach Pky, Port Wentworth
68	SC 61, Augusta Hwy, Walterboro, Canadys, Bamberg	Gas Lodg	W: Sunoco W: Plantation Inn	104	Airways Ave, Pooler Pky, Savannah Savannah Hilton Head Intl Airport
	TStop E: PTP/Circle C Truck Plaza/Shell (Scales) Gas E: BP, El Cheapo◆ Food E: Subway/Circle C TS TServ E: Circle C TS/Tires, InFingers Auto & Diesel Other E: Laundry/CB/RVDump/LP/Circle C TS, to Colleton State Park▲, Shuman's RV Trailer Park▲	21	SC 336, Main St, Ridgeland, Hilton Head Island	Gas	E: BP, Shell◆ W: Shell, Murphy
		Gas	W: BP◆, Chevron◆, Citgo, Exxon, Shell◆	Food	E: Starbucks, Waffle House, Rest/Fairfield Inn, Rest/Sheraton
		Food	W: Burger King, Huddle House, KFC, Subway, Waffle House		
		Lodg	W: Comfort Inn♥, Carolina Lodge, Days Inn		
62	SC 34, McLeod Rd, Walterboro	Other	E: RV Mega Store W: Family Dollar, Food Lion, Pharmacy		
57	SC 64, Bells Hwy, Walterboro, Lodge	18	RD 13, Ridgeland, Switzerland		
	FStop E: Rhoades Way/Mobil	(18)	TRUCK Only Parking Area		
	Gas E: BP◆, Citgo, Shell, Speedway W: BP	8	US 278, Hardeeville, Hilton Head, Bluffton, Sun City		
	Food E: Arby's, Burger King, Huddle House, McDonald's, Longhorn Steakhouse, Olde House Café, Waffle House, Wendy's	TStop Gas	E: Joker Joe's Truck Stop/BP (Scales) E: BP, Mobil		

Page 522   ◆ = Regular Gas Stations with Diesel   ▲ = RV Friendly Locations   ♥ = Pet Friendly Locations
RED PRINT SHOWS LARGE VEHICLE PARKING/ACCESS ON SITE OR NEARBY   BROWN PRINT SHOWS CAMPGROUNDS/RV PARKS

INTERSTATE 95 N/S — GEORGIA

EXIT		GEORGIA
	Food	W: Arby's, Cheddar's Cafe, ChickFilA, Ruby Tuesday, Zaxby's, Subway/Shell, McDonald's/WalMart
	Lodg	E: Cambria Suites, Fairfield Inn, Four Points by Sheraton, Hawthorn Suites ♥, Hilton Garden Inn, Springhill Suites, Staybridge Suites ♥, TownePlace Suites W: Red Roof Inn ♥
	Other	E: to Sav-HH Int'l Airport ✈ W: Home Depot, Wal-Mart sc
102		US 80, GA 26, Louisville Hwy, Pooler, Garden City, Tybee Beach, Ft Pulaski Nat'l Monument
	FStop	E: Amit Food Mart #4/Shell W: Gate #209
	Gas	E: Enmark ◊ W: BP
	Food	E: Cracker Barrel, Huddle House, Taco Bell, Krystal, McDonald's, Waffle House W: Burger King, Hardee's, Mex Rest, Spanky's Pizza, Subway, Wendy's
	Lodg	E: Best Western, Microtel, Travelodge W: Comfort Inn, Econo Lodge, Jameson Inn, Holiday Inn, Quality Inn, Ramada Ltd
	Other	E: ATMs, Grocery, Museum, Tires, Camping World W: ATMs, Auto Services, Pooler Tire & Auto Center, Tires
(99)		Jct I-16, E-Savannah, W-Macon
(99A)		Jct I-16, E to Savannah
(99B)		Jct I-16, W to Macon
94		GA 204, Bacon Hwy, Savannah, Pembroke
	FStop	E: El Cheapo #41/Shell
	Gas	E: AmocoBP ◊, Exxon, Murphy W: Chevron ◊, Shell
	Food	E: Applebee's, Cracker Barrel, Denny's, Hardee's, Houlihan's, McDonald's, Perkins, Ruby Tuesday, Shellhouse Rest, Shoney's, Sonic, Waffle House W: El Potro Mex Rest, Hooter's, Huddle House, Subway
	Lodg	E: Best Western, Best Value Inn, Clarion Inn, Comfort Suites, Fairfield Inn, Holiday Inn Express, Hampton Inn, Howard Johnson, La Quinta Inn ♥, Quality Inn ♥, Red Roof Inn ♥, Ramada Inn, Sleep Inn, Springhill Suites, Wingate Hotel W: Clean Stay, Econo Lodge, Microtel, Travelodge
	Med	E: + Hospital
	Other	E: Wal-Mart sc, Bass Pro Shop, CarWash, Keller's Flea Market/RVPkg/RVDump, Savannah Festival Factory Outlet Stores, Savannah Mall Biltmore Gardens RV Park▲, to Waterway RV Park▲ W: Bass Pro Shop, Savannah Harley Davidson, to appr 3mi Savannah Oaks RV Resort▲
90		GA 144, Old Clyde Rd, Fort Stewart, Richmond Hill
	TStop	W: Love's Travel Stop #338 (Scales)
	Gas	E: Chevron, Exxon, Shell ◊
	Food	E: Little Caesars, Frank's BBQ W: McDonald's/Love's TS
	TServ	W: Roberts White/GMC, International

EXIT		GEORGIA
	Other	E: to Waterway RV Park▲, Ft McAllister State Park, Ft Stewart Military Res W: WiFi/RVDump/Love's TS, Dick Gores RV World
87		US 17, Coastal Hwy, GA 25, Richmond Hill
	TStop	W: Travel Center of America (Scales), El Cheapo #4/Shell
	Gas	E: Chevron ◊, Citgo, RaceTrac W: BP, Exxon ◊, Speedway ◊
	Food	E: Arby's, Denny's, Huddle House, McDonald's, Subway, Waffle House W: Rest/LongJohnSilver/PizzaHut/Popeyes/TA TC, McDonald's
	Lodg	E: Days Inn, Scottish Inn, Travelodge W: Best Western, Comfort Inn, Econo Lodge, Hampton Inn, Holiday Inn, Knights Inn, Motel 6
	TWash	W: TA TC
	TServ	W: TA TC/Tires
	Other	W: Laundry/WiFi/TA TC, Savannah South KOA▲
76		US 84, GA 38, Sunbury Rd, Midway, Hinesville, Sunbury, Fort Stewart
	TStop	W: El Cheapo #50 (Scales)
	Gas	W: BP ◊
	Food	W: Huddle House, Holton Seafood Rest
	Lodg	W: appr 10 mi
	Med	W: + Hospital
	Other	W: Martin's Glebe Campground▲
67		US 17, Coastal Hwy, Riceboro, to South Newport
	Gas	E: BP, Chevron ◊, Citgo, El Cheapo W: BP

EXIT		GEORGIA
	Food	E: McDonald's, Subway/Chevron
	Other	W: Riverfront RV Park▲
58		GA 57, GA 99, Ridge Rd, Wiregrass Trail, Townsend, Eulonia
	Gas	E: BP ◊, Citgo W: Chevron ◊, Shell
	Food	W: Huddle House
	Lodg	W: Days Inn, Knights Inn, Ramada
	Other	W: McIntosh Lake Campground▲, Lake Harmony RV Park▲
(55)		Weigh Station (Both dir)
49		GA 251, Bus I-95N, Briardam Rd, Darien
	FStop	W: El Cheapo #54 (Scales)
	Gas	E: BP ◊, Chevron W: BP, Mobil ◊, Shell ◊
	Food	E: McDonald's, Waffle House W: Subs/El Cheapo, Burger King, Huddle House, Ruby Tuesday, Wendy's, Pizza Hut/Taco Bell, BBQ
	Lodg	E: Ft King George Motel W: Comfort Inn, Hampton Inn, Quality Inn, Super 8
	Other	E: Tall Pines Campground▲, Darien Inland Harbor RV Park▲ W: Preferred Outlets at Darien, Interstate Truck Repair
42		GA 99, Bus I-95S, Grant Ferry Rd, Darien
(40)		Rest Area (SB) (RR, Phone, Picnic, Vend, Info, WiFi, RVDump)
38		to US 17, GA Spur 25, Brunswick, N Golden Isles Pkwy
	Gas	E: Chevron ◊, Conoco, RaceTrac W: BP, Shell ◊
	Food	E: Applebee's, Captain D's Seafood, Millhouse Steak House, Ruby Tuesday W: China Town, Denny's, Huddle House, Mex Rest, Starbucks, Waffle House
	Lodg	E: Country Inn, Fairfield Inn, Holiday Inn, Jameson Inn, Microtel, St James Suites W: Courtyard, Econo Lodge, Quality Inn, Guest Cottage & Suites
	Med	E: + Applecare Minor Emergency Treatment Center, + Glynco Immed Care Center
	Other	E: ATMs, Glynco Jetport ✈ W: Grocery, Golden Isles Harley Davidson, Rainbow CarWash, Golden Isles Vacation Park▲, Blythe Island Regional Campground▲
36		US 25, US 341, Brunswick, Jesup
	Gas	E: Chevron ◊, Exxon ◊, RaceWay W: BP, El Cheapo ◊, Mobil ◊, Sunoco
	Food	E: Burger King, Cracker Barrel, IHOP, KFC, Krystal, McDonald's, Pizza Hut, Quiznos, Shoney's, Starbucks, Taco Bell, Waffle House, Wendy's, Subway/Chevron W: Allen's BBQ, Beef O'Brady's, Capt Joe's Seafood, Denny's, Huddle House, Sonny's BBQ, Subway, Waffle House
	Lodg	E: Baymont Inn ♥, Days Inn, Hampton Inn, Knights Inn, Red Roof Inn ♥, Travelodge W: Best Western, Clarion Inn ♥, Comfort Inn, Clean Stay USA, Motel 6 ♥, Rodeway Inn, Sleep Inn, Super 8

◊ = Regular Gas Stations with Diesel ▲ = RV Friendly Locations ♥ = Pet Friendly Locations
RED PRINT SHOWS LARGE VEHICLE PARKING/ACCESS ON SITE OR NEARBY   BROWN PRINT SHOWS CAMPGROUNDS/RV PARKS

INTERSTATE 95 N/S

EXIT	GEORGIA
Other	E: Newcastle RV Center W: ATMs, Auto Services, Advance Auto, Banks, CVS, Dollar General, Family Dollar, Fred's, Pharmacy, Winn Dixie, Express Lube, CarWash, Laundromat, Police Dept, Suncoast RV Center, GA State Hwy Patrol Post
36A	US 25S, US 341S, Brunswick
36B	US 25N, US 341N, Jesup
29	US 17, US 82, GA 520, S Ga Pkwy, to GA 303, Brunswick
TStop	E: Pilot Travel Center #379 (Scales), El Cheapo #53/Shell (Scales) W: Flying J Travel Plaza/Conoco (Scales)
Gas	E: Citgo◊, Flash Foods/Exxon◊, P66 W: GOASIS #702/TA TC, Mobil◊, Sunoco
Food	E: Rest/Steak'nShake/Subway/Pilot TC, FastFood/El Cheapo, Church's Chicken, Huddle House, McDonald's, Krystal W: CountryMkt/FastFood/FJ TP, Burger King/PlanetSmoothie/SeattlesBestCoffee/Subway/GOASIS TC, Waffle House
Lodg	W: Days Inn, GuestHouse Inn, Microtel, Super 8
TWash	E: Blue Beacon TW/Pilot TC
TServ	E: Speedco W: TA TC/Tires, Glenn Diesel & RV Service Angels CB & Chrome Shop
Other	W: Laundry/WiFi/TA TC, Laundry/WiFi/RVDump/LP/FJ TP, Vet♥, Golden Isles RV Park▲, to appr 3mi Blythe Island Reg'l Park▲, appr 12 mi Golden Isles Speedway
26	Dover Bluff Rd, CR 145, Waverly
Gas	E: Mobil◊
Other	E: Ocean Breeze Campground▲
14	GA 25 Spur, Woodbine
TStop	W: Sunshine Travel Center (Scales)
Food	W: Rest/Sunshine TC
Other	W: Laundry/Sunshine TC
7	Harrietts Bluff Rd, CR 141, Woodbine
FStop	E: Flash Foods #195/Exxon
Gas	E: Shell W: BP◊
Food	E: Huddle House, Jack's Famous BBQ, Subway
Tires	E: A&D Tire Shop, Flash Foods
Other	E: Raintree RV Park▲
6	Colerain Rd, Kingsland, Laurel Island Pkwy, CR 90
TStop	E: AmBest/Cisco Travel Plaza #1/BP (Scales), Cone Auto Truck Plaza #201
Food	E: Arby's/Cisco TP, FastFood/Cone ATP
Other	E: Laurel Oaks Animal Hospital♥
3	GA 40, Kingsland St, Mary's Rd, Kingsland, St Mary's
TStop	W: Petro 2 (Scales)
Gas	E: BP◊, Chevron, El Cheapo, Mobil, Shell W: Exxon◊, RaceWay
Food	E: Applebee's, Burger King, ChickFilA, McDonald's, KFC, Pizza Hut, Ponderosa, Subway, Sonny's BBQ, Taco Bell, Waffle House, Wendy's, Zaxby's W: Church's/Quiznos/Petro 2, Cracker Barrel, Shoney's, Waffle House

EXIT	GA / FL
Lodg	E: Comfort Suites, Country Inn, Hampton Inn, Holiday Inn Express, Magnolia Inn, Sleep Inn, Super 8 W: Clean Stay USA, Days Inn, Econo Lodge, Jameson Inn, Ramada Inn, Scottish Inn
TServ	W: Petro 2/Tires
Med	E: + Hospital
Other	E: Auto Dealers, CVS, Grocery, Kmart, Publix, Vet♥, Winn Dixie, to Wal-Mart sc, to Crooked River State▲, Park A Big Wheel RV Park▲ W: Laundry/Petro2, Henry B's Mobile RV Repair
1	St Mary's Rd, CR 61, Kingsland, St Mary's
	GA Welcome Center (NB) (RR, Phone, Picnic, Vend, Info)
TStop	E: AmBest/Cisco Travel Plaza #2 (Scales) W: WilcoHess Travel Plaza #3060 (Scales)
Gas	E: Shell◊ W: BP◊
Food	E: DQ/LJSilver/MrsWinners/PizzaHut/Cisco TP W: Wendy's/WilcoHess TP
TServ	E: Cisco TP/Tires
Other	E: Laundry/RVDump/Cisco TP W: Jacksonville North/Kingsland KOA▲, Country Oaks RV Park & Campground▲

(EASTERN TIME ZONE)

⦿ GEORGIA
⦿ FLORIDA

(EASTERN TIME ZONE)
(I-95 begins/ends on US 1 in Miami)

NOTE:	MM 382: Georgia State Line
NOTE:	Begin SB/End NB Motorist Call Boxes
(381)	Inspection Station (Both dir)
380	US 17, Yulee, Hilliard
Gas	W: BP, Shell
Other	E: Hance's First in FL RV Park▲, Osprey RV Park▲ W: Bow & Arrow Campground▲
(378)	FL Welcome Center (SB) (RR, Phone, Picnic, Vend, Sec24/7)
(376)	Weigh Station (Both dir)
373	FL 200, FL A1A, Yulee, Callahan, Amelia, Amelia Island
Gas	E: Flash Foods/Exxon W: BP, Citgo, Sunoco
Food	E: Burger King, KFC/PizzaHut, McDonald's, Subway Wendy's, Krystal/Flash Foods, on US 17 Jinwright Seafood Rest W: Waffle House, Subway/Citgo
Lodg	E: Comfort Inn, Holiday Inn Express
Tserv	E: CAT Truck Service
Other	E: Lofton Creek Campground▲
366	Pecan Park Rd, Jacksonville
FStop	E: Baine Truck Stop (S on N Main St)
Other	W: Jacksonville Intl Airport✈, Pecan Park RV Resort▲, Pecan Park, Flea Market, RV Having Fun Yet

◊ = Regular Gas Stations with Diesel   ▲ = RV Friendly Locations   ♥ = Pet Friendly Locations
RED PRINT SHOWS LARGE VEHICLE PARKING/ACCESS ON SITE OR NEARBY   BROWN PRINT SHOWS CAMPGROUNDS/RV PARKS

EXIT		FLORIDA
363		Duval Rd, Int'l Airport (SB)
	Gas	E: Chevron x2, Mobil, Sunoco
		W: BP, Flash Foods, Island Food Store, Kangaroo Express, Shell◊
	Food	E: Arby's, Cracker Barrel, Chili's, Dunkin Donuts/Sunoco, Five Guys Famous Burgers, Green Papaya Rest, Wasabi Japanese Rest, Starbucks
		W: Denny's, Longhorn Steakhouse, Mill House Rest, Panera, Ruby Tuesday, Subway, Waffle House, Wendy's, Zaxby's
	Lodg	E: Red Roof Inn ♥
		W: Best Western, Comfort Suites, Country Hearth Inn ♥, Courtyard, Days Inn, Econo Lodge ♥, Hampton Inn ♥, Hilton Garden Inn, Holiday Inn ♥, Jacksonville Plaza Hotel & Suites, Ramada ♥, Travelodge ♥, Wingate Inn
	Other	E: Lowe's, PetSmart ♥, Wal-Mart sc
		W: Cinema, Mall, Jacksonville Int'l Airport✈, U-Haul, Dick Gore's RV World, Camping Time RV/
363A		Duval Rd E, Jacksonville (NB)
363B		Duval Rd W, Airport (NB)
	Other	W: Jacksonville Int'l Airport✈, Dick Gore's RV World
(362B)		Jct I-295S, Jacksonville, Beaches
362A		FL 9A, Blount Island
	Other	E: Anheuser Busch Brewery
360		FL 104, Dunn Ave, Busch Dr
	FStop	E: Gate #1143
	Gas	W: BP, Chevron, Exxon, Hess, Shell
	Food	E: Applebee's, Hardee's, Waffle House
		W: Arby's, Bono's BBQ, Burger King, CiCi's, KFC, Krystal, McDonald's, New Century Buffet, Popeye's, Quincy's, Shoney's, Sonny's BBQ, Taco Bell, Wendy's
	Lodg	E: Executive Inn, ValuePlace
		W: Best Western, Best Value Inn, La Quinta Inn ♥, Motel 6 ♥
	Med	W: + St Vincent's Family Med Center
	Other	E: Sam's Club, Anheuser Busch Brewery, Bowling
		W: ATMs, Auto Services, Big Lots, Family Dollar, Jiffy Lube, Pep Boys, Publix, Radio Shack, Tires Plus, Walgreen's, Winn Dixie
358B		Broward Rd, Jacksonville
	Lodg	W: Best USA Inn
358A		FL 105, Zoo Pky, to US 17
	Other	E: Zoo, to Little Talbot Island St Park
357		FL 111, Edgewood Ave
	Gas	E: BP, Shell
356B		FL 115, Lem Turner Rd (NB)
356A		FL 117, Norwood Ave (NB)
356		FL 117 Norwood Ave, FL 115, Lem Turner Rd (SB)
	Gas	W: BP, Hess, Shell
	Food	E: Hardee's
		W: Crab Hut, Krystal, Golden Egg Roll
	Med	W: + St Vincent's Family Med Center
	Other	W: Grocery, Walgreen's
355		FL 122, Golfair Blvd, Jacksonville
	Gas	E: BP, Shell
		W: Chevron, RaceTrac
	Other	E: Greyhound Station

EXIT		FLORIDA
354B		US 1N, MLK Jr Pky W
354A		US 1S, MLK Jr Pky E
	TServ	W: Cummins Southeastern
	Med	E: + University Medical Center
353D		FL 114, W 8th St
	Food	E: McDonald's
	Med	E: + University Medical Center
353C		US 23N, Kings Rd
353B		US 90 Alt, Union St, US 17N, US 23S FL 139S, Downtown
	Other	E: to Alltel Stadium
NOTE:		SB: Ongoing construction thru 2011
353A		Church St, Monroe St, Forsyth St (SB)
352C		Monroe St (NB)
352B		Forsyth St (NB)
352A		Myrtle Ave
351D		Stockton St (SB)
351C		Margaret St (SB)
(351B)		Jct I-10W, to Lake City, Tallahassee (fr NB, Left Exit)
NOTE:		NB: Ongoing construction thru 2011
351A		Park St (NB exit, SB entr)
350B		FL 13, San Marco Blvd (SB ex, NB ent
350A		US 1N, Prudential Dr, Riverside Ave, FL 13, Main St, US 90W, FL 5N, FL 10W (NB)
349		US 90E, Jacksonville Beaches (SB exit, NB entr)
348		US 1S, Philips Hwy (SB ex, NB ent)
	Lodg	W: City Center Hotel, Scottish Inn
347		US 1 Alt, FL 126, Emerson St
	Gas	E: Shell
		W: AmocoBP◊, Gate, Hess
	Food	E: Subway
		W: McDonald's, Taco Bell
	Lodg	W: Emerson Inn, Howard Johnson ♥, Villager Lodge
	Other	E: Auto Services, Family Dollar, Grocery, Walgreen's
346AB		FL 109, University Blvd (SB) (NB access via Exit #345)
	Gas	E: BP, Hess, Shell
		W: RaceTrac, BP
	Food	E: Huddle House, Kosher Kitchen, DQ, Krystal, Subway, Hungry Howie's Pizza & Subs, Shoney's
		W: Burger King, IHOP, Taco Bell, Ryan's Grill, Waffle House
	Lodg	W: Days Inn ♥, Comfort Lodge, Red Carpet Inn, Ramada Inn ♥, Super 8
	TServ	W: Detroit Diesel Truck Service
	Med	E: + Physician Care Center
		W: + Jacksonville Gen'l Hospital
	Other	E: CVS, Firestone, Firestone, Goodyear, Winn Dixie, Pharmacy
		W: Auto Services, U-Haul, Vet
345		Bowden Rd, to FL 109, University Blvd (NB ex, SB entr)
	Gas	E: Chevron, Gate◊, Hess◊, Kangaroo Express

EXIT		FLORIDA
	Food	E: Bono Pit BBQ, Blimpie/Pizza/Hess. Larry's Giant Subs, Schnitzel House
	Lodg	E: Ramada
	Other	E: CVS, FedEx Kinkos
344		FL 202, J Turner Butler Blvd, Jacksonville Beaches
	Gas	W: BP◊, Kwik Trip, Shell
	Food	E: Rest/Marriott
		W: Applebee's, Cracker Barrel, Hardee's, McDonald's, Sonic, Starbucks, Waffle House
	Lodg	E: Best Western ♥, Candlewood Suites, Econo Lodge ♥, Howard Johnson ♥, Marriott
		W: Courtyard, Extended Stay America ♥, Fairfield Inn, Jameson Inn, La Quinta Inn ♥, Microtel ♥, Red Roof Inn ♥, Wingate Inn
	Med	E: + St Luke's Hospital, + Mayo Clinic
	Other	E: Pharmacy
341		FL 152, Baymeadows Rd
	Gas	E: BP, Shell, Gate, Lil Champ
		W: Exxon◊, Kangaroo, Shell
	Food	E: Applebee's, Arby's, Chili's, Hardee's, Quincy's Steak House, Roadhouse Grill, Subway, Waffle House
		W: Bulls BBQ, Burger King, Denny's, Hardee's, IHOP, McDonald's, Pizza Hut, Red Lobster, Steak & Ale, Wendy's
	Lodg	E: AmeriSuites, Fairfield Inn, Embassy Suites, Holiday Inn ♥, Homestead Inn ♥
		W: Best Inn ♥, Comfort Inn, Homewood Suites ♥, La Quinta Inn ♥, Motel 6 ♥, Quality Inn ♥, Residence Inn ♥, Studio 6 ♥
	Other	E: FedEx Kinkos, Food Lion, Publix, Tires
		W: Goodyear, Office Depot, Harley Davidson
340		FL 115, Southside Blvd (NB)
	Gas	E: Kangaroo Express
	Food	E: Longhorn Steakhouse, Sierra Grill
	Lodg	E: Marriott
	Other	E: CompUSA, Home Depot, Target
339		US 1, FL 5, Phillips Hwy
	Gas	E: BP, Chevron, RaceTrac
		W: BP◊
	Food	E: Arby's, Burger King, McDonald's, Olive Garden, Ruby Tuesday, Taco Bell, Waffle House
	TServ	E: Perkins Engine Parts & Service
	Other	E: Auto Dealers, Best Buy, Mall
(337)		Jct I-295N, Orange Park, Beaches
335		St Augustine Rd
	Gas	W: Shell
	Food	W: Applebee's, Brooklyn Pizza, Chili's, McDonald's, Panera Bread
	Med	E: + Baptist Medical Center
(331)		Rest Area (Both dir) (RR, Phone, Picnic, Sec24/7)
329		CR 210, Jacksonville, Green Cove Springs
	TStop	E: Travel Center of America #126/Shell (Scales), Pilot Travel Center #91 (Scales)
	Gas	E: Speedway, Sunoco
		W: Amoco◊, Mobil, Kangaroo Express
	Food	E: T&CRest/NobleRomansPizza/TA TC, McDonald's/Pilot TC, Waffle House
	TServ	E: TA TC/Tires
	Other	E: Laundry/TA TC, Laundry/WiFi/Pilot TC, St Augustine KOA▲
		W: CVS, Grocery

◊ = Regular Gas Stations with Diesel ▲ = RV Friendly Locations ♥ = Pet Friendly Locations
RED PRINT SHOWS LARGE VEHICLE PARKING/ACCESS ON SITE OR NEARBY BROWN PRINT SHOWS CAMPGROUNDS/RV PARKS

INTERSTATE 95 N/S

EXIT	FLORIDA
323	**International Golf Pkwy, St Augustine**
Gas	E: BP◆, Shell
Food	E: Subway/Shell
Lodg	E: Comfort Suites
318	**FL 16, St Augustine**
Gas	E: BP, Gate◆, Kangaroo, Shell W: Exxon
Food	E: Burger King, DQ, McDonald's, Huddle House, Subway, Waffle House W: Cracker Barrel, Denny's, KFC, IHOP, Ruby Tuesday, Shoney's, Sonny's BBQ, Taco Bell, Wendy's
Lodg	E: Country Inn, Econo Lodge, Holiday Inn Express W: Best Western ♥, Comfort Inn, Days Inn, Hampton Inn, Ramada Inn ♥, Super 8 ♥, Scottish Inn
Other	E: Belz Outlet Mall, Prime Outlets, Camping Time RV/Camping World W: St Augustine Outlet Center, Stage Coach RV Park▲
311	**FL 207, St Augustine**
Gas	E: BP◆, Chevron, Hess◆, Indian River Fruit W: Mobil◆, Texaco
Lodg	W: Comfort Inn, Sleep Inn, Super 8 ♥
Med	E: + Hospital
Other	E: Indian Forest RV Park▲, St John's RV Park▲, St Augustine Beach KOA▲, Flea Market
305	**FL 206, St Augustine, to Hastings, Crescent Beach, Marineland**
TStop	E: Flying J Travel Plaza (Scales)
Food	E: CountryMarket/FastFood/FJ TP
TServ	W: Continental Truck Repair
Other	E: Laundry/WiFi/RVDump/LP/FJ TP, Gore RV Center, Ocean Grove RV Sales
(303)	**Rest Area (SB)** (RR, Phone, Picnic, Vend, Sec24/7)
(302)	**Rest Area (NB)** (RR, Phone, Picnic, Vend, Sec24/7)
298	**US 1, FL 5, St Augustine, Hastings**
Gas	E: BP◆, Citgo, Indian River Fruit, Shell W: Mobil◆, Hess, Sunrise
Food	W: Waffle House
289	**Palm Coast Pkwy, to FL A1A (TOLL)**
Gas	E: Exxon◆, BP, RaceTrac, Shell W: Shell, Kangaroo Express x2
Food	E: Cracker Barrel, Denny's, McDonald's, KFC, Pizza Hut, Wendy's W: Bob Evans, China King, Dunkin Donuts, Firehouse Subs, Papa John's, Perkins, Pizza Hut, Ruby Tuesday, Sonny's BBQ, Steak 'n Shake, Subway, Taco Bell
Lodg	E: Hampton Inn, Microtel, Sleep Inn
Other	E: ATMs, Advance Auto, Auto Services, CVS, Publix, Radio Shack, Staples, Walgreen's, to A1A: addt'l services and Campgrounds/RV Parks▲ W: Home Depot, PetSmart ♥, Pharmacy, Tires, Wal-Mart sc, Winn Dixie, Walgreen's
(286)	**Weigh Station (Both dir)**
284	**FL 100, Moody Blvd, Palm Coast, Bunnell, Flagler Beach**
Gas	E: BP, Chevron◆, Hess◆, Shell W: BP◆
Food	E: Burger King, Denny's, Domino's, KFC, McDonald's, Popeye's, Subway, Wendy's, Woody's BBQ

EXIT	FLORIDA
Food	W: Hijacker's Rest
Lodg	E: Holiday Inn Express
Med	W: + Hospital
Other	E: ATMs, Bowling, Dollar General, Winn Dixie, to A1A: addt'l services and Campgrounds/RV Parks▲ W: Auto Dealers, Flagler Co Airport✈
278	**Old Dixie Hwy, Bunnell, Tomaka State Park**
Gas	E: 7-11 W: BP◆
Lodg	W: Country Hearth Inn
Other	E: Publix, Bulow Creek State Park, Bulow RV Resort Campground▲ W: Holiday Trav-L-Park Co-op▲
273	**US 1, FL 5, Ormond Beach**
TStop	E: Valero Truck Stop (Scales), Mobil #8 W: Love's Travel Stop #316 (Scales)
Gas	E: Chevron, RaceTrac W: Exxon
Food	E: Denny's, McDonald's, Saddle Jack's Bar & Grill, Waffle House, BBQ W: Arby's/TJCinn/Love's TS, Burger King/Exxon, DQ, Houligan's, Pig Stand
Lodg	E: Comfort Inn ♥, Destination Daytona Hotel & Suites W: Best Value Inn ♥, Days Inn ♥, Econo Lodge, Super 8 ♥, Scottish Inn ♥
TServ	E: Valero TS/Tires
Med	E: + Ormond Memorial Hospital
Other	E: RVDump/Valero TS, to Ormond Beach Muni Airport✈, Giant Recreation World, Harris Village & RV Park▲ W: WiFi/RVDump/Love's TS, Harley Davidson, RV Center, Encore Superpark RV Park▲
268	**FL 40, W Granada Blvd, Ormond Beach**
Gas	E: Shell, Chevron W: 7-11, BP, Hess, Mobil◆
Food	E: Applebee's, Boston Market, Chili's, ChickFilA, Denny's, McDonald's, Steak 'n Shake, Starbucks, Subway, Waffle House, Wendy's W: Cracker Barrel
Lodg	E: America's Best Value Inn, Ivanhoe Beach Resort, Sleep Inn W: Hampton Inn, Jameson Inn ♥
Med	E: + Ormond Memorial Hospital
Other	E: ATMs, Lowe's, Publix, Regal Cinemas, Wal-Mart sc, Tomaka State Park W: Walgreen's
265	**LPGA Blvd, Holly Hill, Ormond Beach, Daytona Beach**
Gas	E: 7-11, Shell◆
261B	**US 92W, DeLand (SB)**
261A	**US 92E, Daytona Beach (SB)**
Other	E: Daytona Int'l Speedway, Daytona Beach Int'l Airport✈
261	**US 92, International Speedway Blvd, E-Daytona Beach, W-DeLand (NB)**
Gas	E: 7-11, BP, Citgo, Chevron, Hess◆, Mobil, RaceWay, Shell◆ W: BP, Exxon, Sunoco
Food	E: Bob Evans, Burger King, Carrabba's, Chili's, Cracker Barrel, Hooters, Hops, KFC, Krystal, Longhorn Steakhouse, Logan's Roadhouse, Olive Garden, Red Lobster, Ruby Tuesday, Shoney's,

EXIT	FLORIDA
Food	E: Starbucks, Subway, Taco Bell, Waffle House, Wendy's W: Denny's, IHOP, McDonald's
Lodg	E: America's Best Value Inn, Castaways Beach Resort, Hampton Inn, Holiday Inn Express, La Quinta Inn ♥, Ramada Inn, Travelodge W: Days Inn, Super 8
Med	E: + Hospital
Other	E: Volusia Mall, AMC 8, B&N, Best Buy, Circuit City, Home Depot, Pep Boys, PetCo ♥, Staples, Target, IMAX, Walgreen's, International RV Park & Campground▲, Daytona Beach Int'l Airport✈, Daytona Int'l Speedway, Racetrack RV▲ W: Flea Market, Cycle World, Town & Country RV Park ♥, Crazy Horse Camping▲
(260B)	**Jct I-4W, to Orlando**
260A	**FL 400E, to South Daytona**
Gas	E: Chevron
Food	E: Red Carpet Inn
256	**FL 421, Taylor Rd, Port Orange**
Gas	E: Citgo◆, Shell W: 7-11, Hess, Shell
Food	E: Bob Evans, ChickFilA, Denny's, Dustin's BBQ, Papa John's, Quiznos, Spruce Creek Pizza W: Subway, McDonald's, Wendy's
Lodg	E: Days Inn, Dream Inn of DB, Hampton Inn, Holiday Inn
Other	E: Lowe's, Target, Walgreen's, Wal-Mart sc, Daytona Beach Campground▲, Nova Family Campground▲, Orange Isles Campground▲ W: Publix
249B	**FL 44W, DeLand (SB)**
249A	**FL 44E, New Smyrna Beach (SB)**
249	**FL 44, DeLand, New Smyrna Beach**
Gas	E: Shell W: Chevron◆
Food	E: Burger King, Denny's, McDonald's
Med	E: + Hospital
Other	E: Publix, Harley Davidson, New Smyrna Beach Muni Airport✈
244	**FL 442, Indian River Blvd, Edgewater, Oak Hill**
Gas	E: Chevron◆ W: Exxon◆
Other	E: Massey Ranch Airpark✈
231	**CR 5A, Stuckway Rd, to US 1, Mims, Scottsmoor, Oak Hill**
FStop	E: Sugar Creek Stuckey's/BP
Food	E: Stuckey's/BP
Other	W: Crystal Lake RV Park▲
(227)	**Rest Area (SB)** (RR, Phone, Picnic, Vend, Sec24/7)
(225)	**Rest Area (NB)** (RR, Phone, Picnic, Vend, Sec24/7)
223	**FL 46, W Main St, Mims, Sanford**
Gas	W: BP, Shell
Food	E: McDonald's
Other	E: Willow Lakes Campground▲ W: Titusville/Kennedy Space Center KOA▲, Seasons RV Camp▲

◆ = Regular Gas Stations with Diesel ▲ = RV Friendly Locations ♥ = Pet Friendly Locations

RED PRINT SHOWS LARGE VEHICLE PARKING/ACCESS ON SITE OR NEARBY BROWN PRINT SHOWS CAMPGROUNDS/RV PARKS

EXIT		FLORIDA
220		FL 406, Garden St, Titusville
	Gas	E: Shell◊, BP◊
		W: Chevron◊
	Food	E: McDonald's, Subway, Wendy's
	Lodg	E: Days Inn, Travelodge
	Med	E: + Hospital
	Other	E: Dollar General, Publix, Tires Plus, Walgreen's, Arthur Dunn Airpark✈
215		FL 50, Cheney Hwy, Titusville, to Orlando
	FStop	E: Space Shuttle Fuel/Sunoco
	Gas	E: BP◊, Circle K, Mobil◊, Shell◊, Murphy
	Food	E: Burger King, Denny's, Durango's, KFC/PizzaHut/BP, McDonald's, Sonny's BBQ, Waffle House, Wendy's
		W: Cracker Barrel, IHOP
	Lodg	E: Best Western, Comfort Inn♥, Holiday Inn, Ramada♥
		W: Days Inn, Hampton Inn
	Other	E: Lowe's, Staples, Wal-Mart sc, Space Coast Visitor's Center
		W: Great Outdoors RV Nature & Golf Resort▲, St John's National Wildlife Refuge
212		FL 407, Challenger Memorial Pkwy, to FL 528W (TOLL) (SB ex, NB entr)
	Other	E: to Space Coast Reg'l Airport✈, John F Kennedy Space Center
(209)		Parking Area (Both dir)
208		Port St John Rd, Cocoa
205		FL 528 (TOLL), Beachline Expy, to Cape Canaveral, City Point
202		FL 524, Cocoa
	Gas	E: Shell◊
		W: BP◊
	Lodg	E: Days Inn, Ramada Inn, Super 8
201		FL 520, Cocoa, Orlando
	FStop	E: Sunshine Food Store/BP
	TStop	E: Pilot Travel Center #88 (Scales)
	Gas	E: Chevron
		W: Shell
	Food	E: Subway/Pilot TC, IHOP, Olive Garden, Waffle House
		W: McDonald's
	Med	E: + Hospital
	Lodg	E: Best Western, Budget Inn
		W: Holiday Inn Express
	Other	E: WiFi/Pilot TC
		W: Forest Village RV Park▲, Sun Coast RV Center
195		FL 519, Fiske Blvd, Rockledge
	Gas	E: 7-11, Shell◊
	Med	E: + Hospital
	Other	E: Lowe's, Rockledge Airpark✈, Space Coast RV Resort▲
191		FL 509, Wickham Rd, Melbourne, Satellite Beach, Patrick AFB
	Gas	E: 7-11, Hess◊
		W: Chevron◊, Murphy
	Food	E: Bob Evans, Denny's, McDonald's, Perkins, Wendy's
		W: Burger King, Chili's, Cracker Barrel, Longhorn Steakhouse, Mimi's Café, Starbucks, Subway
	Lodg	E: Comfort Inn
		W: Baymont Inn, La Quinta Inn♥

Personal Notes
_____

EXIT		FLORIDA
	Other	E: Pharmacy, to Patrick AFB
		W: ATMs, Petco♥, Target, Wal-Mart sc
183		FL 518, Eau Gallie Blvd, Melbourne, Indian Harbor Beach
	Gas	E: 7-11, BP, Chevron◊, RaceTrac
	Other	E: to Melbourne Int'l Airport✈
		W: Flea Market
180		US 192, FL 500, W Melbourne
	Gas	E: 7-11, BP◊, Circle K, Mobil◊, Sam's
		W: Shell
	Food	E: Denny's, IHOP, Shoney's, Steak 'n Shake, Waffle House
	Lodg	E: Best Value Inn, Courtyard, Days Inn, Holiday Inn, Hampton Inn, Howard Johnson, Super 8, Travelodge, York Inn
	Med	E: + Hospital
	Other	E: Sam's Club, Target, Melbourne Int'l Airport✈
176		CR 516, Palm Bay Rd, Palm Bay
	Gas	E: 7-11, BP◊, Chevron, Murphy
		W: 7-11, Shell
	Food	E: Applebee's, Bob Evans, Denny's, Cracker Barrel, Dunkin Donuts, Golden Corral, Starbucks, Taco Bell, Wendy's
	Lodg	E: Jameson Inn, Ramada Inn
	TServ	E: Ringhaver Power Systems
	Other	E: Albertson's, BJ's, Wal-Mart sc
		W: Walgreen's, Publix, USAF Annex
173		FL 514, Palm Bay, Malabar
	FStop	W: Sunoco #2573
	Gas	E: Shell◊
		W: BP◊, Hess, Shell, Sunoco

EXIT		FLORIDA
	Food	W: Arby's, Burger King, Dunkin Donuts, IHOP, McDonald's, Sonny's BBQ, Subway, Taco Bell, Texas Roadhouse, Waffle House, Wendy's, Woody's BBQ
	Lodg	W: Motel 6♥
	Med	E: + PCA Family Medical Center, + Palm Bay Community Hospital
	Other	E: Firestone, Truck/RV Repair
		W: ATMs, Advance Auto, Big Lots, CVS, Dollar General, Goodyear, Home Depot, Publix, Tires, Walgreen's, Wal-Mart sc
(169)		Rest Area (SB) (RR, Phone, Picnic, Vend, Sec24/7)
(168)		Rest Area (NB) (RR, Phone, Picnic, Vend, Sec24/7)
NOTE:		Begin NB/End SB Call Boxes
156		CR 512, Fellsmere Rd, 95th St
	Gas	E: BP◊, Chevron, Mobil◊
	Food	E: McDonald's, Subway
	Med	E: + Hospital
	Other	E: Encore RV Park▲, Sebastian Muni Airport✈
147		FL 60, Osceola Blvd, Vero Beach, Lake Wales
	FStop	E: Hill Mart
	TStop	E: Gator Truck Stop, Travel Center of America #197/Amoco (Scales)
	Gas	E: 7-11, Hess◊, Mobil◊, Speedway
		W: Shell◊
	Food	E: Rest/TA TC, Waffle House, Wendy's
		W: Cracker Barrel, McDonald's, Steak 'n Shake
	Lodg	E: Howard Johnson, Best Western
		W: Country Inn, Holiday Inn Express, Hampton Inn
	TServ	E: TA TC/Tires
	Med	E: + Hospital
	Other	E: Laundry/WiFi/TA TC, NAPA, to Vero Beach Muni Airport✈
		W: Prime Outlets
138		FL 614, Indrio Rd, Fort Pierce
	Other	E: St Lucie Co Int'l Airport✈
(133)		Rest Area (Both dir) (RR, Phone, Picnic, Vend, Sec24/7)
131AB		FL 68, Orange Ave, Ft Pierce
	TStop	W: Flying J Travel Plaza #5063 (Scales)
	Gas	E: Valero
	Food	W: CountryMarket/FastFood/FJ TP
	Twash	W: Blue Beacon TW/FJ TP
	Other	W: Laundry/BarbSh/WiFi/RVDump/LP/FJ TP
129		FL 70, Okeechobee Rd, Ft Pierce
	FStop	W: Falcon Citgo Truck Stop
	TStop	W: Pilot Travel Center #327 (Scales), Pilot Travel Center #90 (Scales)
	Gas	E: Hess◊, RaceTrac, Sunoco◊, Murphy
		W: Chevron, Exxon, Shell◊
	Food	E: Applebee's, Golden Corral, Waffle House
	Food	W: McDonald's/Pilot TC90, Arby's/TJCinn/Pilot TC327, Burger King, KFC, Cracker Barrel, Denny's, McDonald's, Red Lobster, Shoney's, Waffle House, Wendy's
	Lodg	W: Crossroads Inn, Days Inn♥, Hampton Inn, Motel 6♥, Quality Inn, Sleep Inn
	Tires	E: Elpex Truck Tire Center

◊ = Regular Gas Stations with Diesel   ▲ = RV Friendly Locations   ♥ = Pet Friendly Locations
RED PRINT SHOWS LARGE VEHICLE PARKING/ACCESS ON SITE OR NEARBY   BROWN PRINT SHOWS CAMPGROUNDS/RV PARKS

Page 527

INTERSTATE 95 N/S — FLORIDA

EXIT		FLORIDA
	TWash	W: Wild Wash Truck Wash
	TServ	W: Crossroads USA Truck Repair, K&R Truck, RV & Bus Repair
	Med	E: + Hospital
	Other	E: Orange Blossom Mall, Dollar Tree, Firestone, Goodyear, Home Depot, Radio Shack, Wal-Mart sc▲ W: Laundry/WiFi/Pilot TC 90, Laundry/WiFi/Pilot TC 327, Grand Prix Amusement Park, to FL TPK
126		CR 712, Midway Rd, Ft Pierce (All serv 3-5 mi E in Ft Pierce)
121		St Lucie West Blvd, Port St Lucie
	Gas	E: 7-11, Chevron, Shell◇, Murphy W: Mobil
	Food	E: Bob Evans, Burger King, Chili's, McDonald's, Outback Steakhouse, Ruby Tuesday, Wendy's
	Lodg	E: Hampton Inn, Spring Hill Suites
	Other	E: Publix, Walgreen's, Wal-Mart sc
118		Gatlin Blvd, Port St Lucie
	FStop	E: BP
	Gas	E: Chevron◇, Shell◇
	Food	E: Burger King, Dunkin Donuts, Subway
	Other	E: LP/BP
	NOTE:	SB: New In Motion Weigh Station Scheduled for 6/09 Northern Martin Co
110		FL 714, Martin Hwy, Stuart, Palm City
(107)		Rest Area (SB) (RR, Phone, Picnic, Vend, Sec24/7)
(106)		Rest Area (NB) (RR, Phone, Picnic, Vend, Sec24/7)
102		CR 713, High Meadows Rd, Stuart, Palm City
101		FL 76, Kanner Hwy, Stuart
	Gas	E: Chevron, Sunoco◇ W: Shell
	Food	E: Cracker Barrel, McDonald's, Wendy's W: Stuckey's/DQ
	Med	E: + Hospital
	Other	E: Ronny's RV Ranch▲
96		CR 708, SE Bridge Rd, Hobe Sound
	Other	E: to Jonathan Dickinson State Park
	NOTE:	NB: New In Motion Weigh Station Scheduled for 6/09 Northern Martin Co
87		FL 706, Indiantown Rd, Jupiter, Okeechobee
	FStop	E: Circle K Fuel Stop
	Gas	E: Chevron, Mobil, Hess, Shell, Mobil W: Mobil◇
	Food	E: Applebee's, Burger King, Dunkin Donuts, IHOP, KFC, Little Caesars, McDonald's, Subway, Taco Bell
	Lodg	E: Fairfield Inn, Wellesley Inn
	Med	E: + Hospital
	Other	E: ATMs, Advance Auto, Auto Services, Home Depot, Laundromat, Publix, Wal-Mart, Winn Dixie W: Tourist Info Center, West Jupiter Camping Resort▲
87B		FL 706, Indiantown Rd, Jupiter, Okeechobee
87A		FL 706, Indiantown Rd, Jupiter, Okeechobee

EXIT		FLORIDA
83		Donald Ross Rd, Jupiter
	Lodg	E: Donald Ross Inn
	Med	E: + Hospital
	Other	E: to Juno Beach RV Park▲
79C		Military Trail S, FL 786, PGA Blvd (SB)
79AB		FL 786, PGA Blvd, Palm Beach (SB)
	Gas	E: Sunoco W: Chevron, Hess, Shell◇
	Food	E: China Wok, Durango's Steak House W: Blvd Rest, Outback Steakhouse, Rest/Hol Inn
	Lodg	E: Marriott, Palm Beach Gardens W: Doubletree Hotel, Embassy Suites, Holiday Inn
	Med	E: + Hospital
	Other	E: Cinema 6, Palm Beach Gardens RV Park▲ W: Publix
79B		FL 786W, PGA Blvd (NB)
79A		FL 786E, PGA Blvd (NB)
77		CR 850, CR 809A, Northlake Blvd
	Gas	E: Hess, Shell◇ W: Chevron, Mobil◇, Hess, Shell
	Food	E: Arby's, Applebee's, Checker's, McDonald's, Taco Bell, Wendy's W: Subway, Pizza Hut, Wendy's
	Med	E: + Hospital, + Northlake Medical
	Other	W: CVS, Grocery, Laundromat, Publix, Radio Shack, Winn Dixie
76		FL 708, Blue Heron Blvd
	Gas	E: BP◇, Shell◇ W: Mobil, RaceTrac, Texaco
	Food	E: Wendy's W: Burger King, Denny's, McDonald's
	Lodg	E: Villager Lodge W: Motel 6♥, Super 8
	TServ	E: Kenworth Truck Service, Mack Trucks
74		CR 702, 45th St, W Palm Beach
	Gas	W: RaceTrac, Mobil
	Food	E: Burger King, IHOP, Subway W: Cracker Barrel, Pizza Hut, Wendy's
	Lodg	E: Days Inn, Knights Inn W: Courtyard, Residence Inn, Red Roof Inn♥
	Med	E: + Glenbeigh Hospital
	Other	E: Walgreen's W: Goodyear
71		Palm Beach Lakes Blvd
	Gas	E: BP, Mobil
	Food	E: McDonald's, Wendy's W: Carrabbas, Hooter's, Olive Garden, Piccadilly, Durango's Steakhouse, Red Lobster, Sweet Tomatoes
	Lodg	E: Best Western W: Comfort Inn, Wellesley Inn
	Med	E: + Hospital
	Other	E: Palm Beach Mall, Palm Beach Co Visitor's Center, Best Buy, Firestone, Pharmacy, Target W: Walgreen's
70AB		FL 704, Okeechobee Blvd, Downtwn West Palm Beach
	Gas	E: Exxon W: Chevron, Hess, Shell
	Food	W: Subway, McDonald's, Waffle House

◇ = Regular Gas Stations with Diesel   ▲ = RV Friendly Locations   ♥ = Pet Friendly Locations

RED PRINT SHOWS LARGE VEHICLE PARKING/ACCESS ON SITE OR NEARBY   BROWN PRINT SHOWS CAMPGROUNDS/RV PARKS

I-95 S — FLORIDA

EXIT		FLORIDA
69		**Belvedere Rd, Palm Beach Int'l Airport (NB)**
	Gas	E: Fina, Exxon
		W: Shell
	Food	E: McDonald's, Lucky Star Chinese
		W: Denny's, IHOP, Phillip's Seafood, Shoney's, Wendy's
	Lodg	W: Crowne Plaza, Hampton Inn, Holiday Inn
	Med	E: + Hospital
	Other	E: Winn Dixie
		W: Palm Beach Int'l Airport ✈
69B		**Palm Beach Int'l Airport (SB)**
69A		**Belvedere Rd (SB)**
68		**US 98, FL 80, Southern Blvd**
	Gas	E: Chevron, Mobill, Texaco
	Food	E: Grand China, Soprano's Pizza
	Lodg	W: Hilton
	Med	E: + Hospital
	Other	E: Publix, Pharmacy
		W: W Palm Beach/Lion Country Safari KOA ▲
66		**FL 882, Forest Hill Blvd**
	Other	E: Palm Beach Zoo
64		**10th Ave N, Lake Worth**
	Gas	W: Citgo, Shell ◆
63		**6th Ave S, Lake Worth**
	Med	W: + Hospital
61		**CR 812, Lantana Rd**
	Gas	E: Shell, Costco
	Food	E: Dunkin Donuts, KFC, McDonald's, Subway
	Lodg	E: Motel 6 ♥
	Med	W: + Hospital
	Other	E: CVS, Costco, Dollar General, Laundromat, Publix, Pharmacy, FL State Hwy Patrol Post
		W: Palm Beach Co Park Airport ✈
60		**Hypoluxo Rd, Lake Worth**
	FStop	W: High Ridge Marathon
	Gas	E: Mobil, Shell ◆
		W: Hess
	Food	E: Shoney's, Taco Bell, Wendy's, Denny's
	Lodg	E: Comfort Inn, Super 8, Best Western
	Other	E: U-Haul, Sam's Club, Tires
59		**Gateway Blvd, NW 22nd Ave**
	Gas	E: Shell ◆
		W: Mobil ◆
	Food	W: Carrabbas, Chili's, McDonald's
	Lodg	W: Hampton Inn
	Other	W: Publix, Target
57		**FL 804, Boynton Beach Blvd**
	Gas	W: 7-11, Mobil, Shell ◆
	Food	W: Wendy's, Waffle House, Subway, TGI Friday
	Lodg	E: Holiday Inn Express
	Other	W: ATMs, Auto Services, Publix, Office Depot, Wal-Mart sc
56		**FL 792, Woolbright Rd**
	Gas	E: Shell
		W: RaceTrac
	Food	E: McDonald's
		W: Cracker Barrel, Subway
	Med	E: + Boynton Beach Medical Center
	Other	W: Home Depot, Lowe's, Staples
52B		**FL 806W, Atlantic Ave (SB)**
52A		**FL 806E, Atlantic Ave (SB)**

EXIT		FLORIDA
52		**FL 806, Atlantic Ave, Delray Beach**
	Gas	E: BP
		W: Chevron, Shell, Mobil
	Food	W: Burger King, McDonald's, Sandwich Man, Moe's Seafood
	Lodg	W: Ramada
	Other	W: Amtrak, Publix, Walgreen's
51		**CR 782, Linton Blvd, Delray Beach**
	Gas	E: Exxon
		W: Chevron, Shell
	Food	E: Outback Steakhouse, McDonald's, DQ
		W: Palace, Grass Roots Café, The Grille
	Lodg	W: Hampton Inn, Springhill Suites
50		**Congress Ave, Boca Raton**
	Food	W: Denny's
	Lodg	W: Hilton, Homestead, Residence Inn
48B		**FL 794W, Yamato Rd (NB)**
48A		**FL 794E, Yamato Rd (NB)**
48		**FL 794, Yamato Rd (SB)**
	Gas	E: Chevron
		W: Mobil
	Food	W: Café 777, BT Food, McDonald's, Park Place Food, Starbucks, Subway
	Lodg	W: Embassy, Springhill Suites
45		**FL 808, Glades Rd, Boca Raton**
	Gas	E: Shell
		W: BP, DX Trading
	Food	E: PF Chang's
		W: Chipolte Mex Grill, Houston Rest, Moe's SW Grill, Quiznos, Romano's Macaroni Grill, Starbucks

EXIT		FLORIDA
	Lodg	E: Fairfield Inn
		W: Holiday Inn, Residence Inn, Marriott
	Med	E: + Hospital
	Other	E: B&N, Circuit City, Whole Foods, Boca Raton Airport ✈
44		**FL 798, Palmetto Park Rd**
	Gas	E: Exxon
	Food	E: BBQ, Denny's, Pizza Time, Subway
	Med	E: + Hospital
	Other	E: Publix
42		**FL 810E, Hillsboro Blvd (SB)**
42B		**FL 810W, Hillsboro Blvd, Deerfield Beach (NB)**
	Gas	W: Chevron, Mobil ◆
	Food	W: Boston Market, Pizza Hut, Denny's
	Lodg	W: Days Inn, Villager Inn, Wellesley Inn
	Other	W: Walgreen's, Home Depot, CVS
42A		**FL 810E, Hillsboro Blvd (NB)**
	Gas	E: BP, Shell ◆
	Food	E: Popeye's, McDonald's, Pasta Café, Wendy's
	Lodg	E: Comfort Inn, Starwood Hotel, La Quinta Inn ♥
41		**FL 869 (TOLL), SW 10th St, to I-75**
	Gas	E: Mobil ◆
	Food	E: Cracker Barrel
		W: Wok & Roll, Quiznos
	Lodg	E: Extended Stay America
		W: Quality Inn, Comfort Suites
39		**FL 834, NW 36th, Sample Rd**
	Gas	E: BP, Hess, Mobil, Shell ◆
		W: Mobil ◆
	Food	E: Port Hole, Four Corners, Hops Rest
		W: Arby's, China Express, IHOP, McDonald's, Miami Subs, Subway
	Med	E: + Mini Medical Center, + North Broward Medical Center
	Other	E: Highland Pines RV Resort Park ▲
		W: CVS, Family Dollar, Winn Dixie, Harley Davidson
38B		**Copans Rd W, Pompano Beach (SB)**
38A		**Copans Rd W (SB)**
38		**Copans Rd, NW 24th (NB)**
	Gas	E: 7-11, BP
	Food	E: McDonald's
	Other	E: Wal-Mart, Pompano Beach Airpark ✈
		W: Home Depot, Harley Davidson
36B		**FL 814W, Atlantic Blvd (SB)**
36A		**FL 814E, Atlantic Blvd (SB)**
36		**FL 814, Atlantic Blvd, Pompano Beach (NB)**
	FStop	E: Hardy Bros Marathon
	Gas	E: RaceTrac, Texaco
		W: Mobil ◆, Shell ◆, Murphy
	Food	E: Burger King, Golden Corral, KFC, McDonald's, Taco Bell
	Med	E: + Hospital
	Other	E: CVS, Winn Dixie, Harness Racetrack
		W: ATMs, Dollar Tree, Radio Shack, Wal-Mart sc
33AB		**FL 840, Cypress Creek Rd (NB)**
33		**FL 840, Cypress Creek Rd (SB)**
	Gas	E: BP, Hess
		W: Hess, Shell

◆ = Regular Gas Stations with Diesel   ▲ = RV Friendly Locations   ♥ = Pet Friendly Locations
RED PRINT SHOWS LARGE VEHICLE PARKING/ACCESS ON SITE OR NEARBY   BROWN PRINT SHOWS CAMPGROUNDS/RV PARKS

EXIT		FLORIDA
	Food	E: Duffy's Diner, Boston Bagel W: Arby's, Burger King, Chili's, Hooters, Longhorn Steakhouse, McDonald's, Steak & Ale, Miami Subs, Cypress Café, Wendy's
	Lodg	E: Extended Stay America, Hampton Inn, Westin W: La Quinta Inn♥, Marriott, Sheraton
	Med	E: + North Ridge Gen'l Hospital
	Other	W: Auto Services, Office Depot
32		FL 870, Commercial Blvd
	Gas	W: BP, Circle K, Mobil, Coastal
	Food	W: Miami Subs, Sonny's BBQ, KFC, McDonald's, Waffle House
	Lodg	W: Best Western, Holiday Inn, Red Roof Inn♥, Travelodge
	Other	W: Ft Lauderdale Executive Airport✈
31B		FL 816W, Oakland Park Blvd (NB)
31A		FL 816E, Oakland Park Blvd (NB)
31		FL 816, Oakland Park Blvd (SB) Fort Lauderdale
	Gas	E: Chevron, Amoco, Mobil W: BP◇, Hess, Shell
	Food	E: Checker's, Denny's, Miami Subs, Burger King, McDonald's, Wendy's W: KFC, Burger King, IHOP, Dunkin Donuts
	Lodg	E: Roman Motel W: Days Inn
	Med	W: + PCA Family Medical Center
	Other	E: Laundromat, Lowe's W: Walgreen's, Home Depot, US Post Office/Shell, RV Park▲
29AB		FL 838, Sunrise Blvd (NB)
29		FL 838, Sunrise Blvd (SB)
	Gas	E: Hess, Mobil W: Exxon, Shell
	Food	E: Burger King, Popeye's Chicken W: Church's Chicken, McDonald's
	Med	W: + Hospital
	Other	W: Laundromat, Walgreen's
27		FL 842, Broward Blvd, Downtown Fort Lauderdale
	Gas	E: BP W: Shell
	Lodg	E: Days Inn
(26D)		Jct I-595W (SB)
(26C)		Jct I-595E, to Airport (SB)
	Other	E: Ft Lauderdale/Hollywood Int'l Airport✈
26		FL 736, Davie Blvd
	Gas	W: BP, Hess, Mobil
	Food	W: Subway, Wendy's
25		FL 84, SW 24th St, Marina Mile Rd
	FStop	E: 84 Shell
	Gas	E: Texaco, Twin Mini Shop, Mobil
	Food	E: McDonald's, Barbell's Grill, Lil Red W: Christopher's Ice Cream
	Lodg	E: Best Western, Hampton Inn, Motel 6♥, Sky Motel, Budget Inn W: Red Carpet Inn, Ramada
	Other	W: Yacht Heaven Park & Marina▲
(24)		Jct I-595, FL 862, to Tpk, I-75, Fort Lauderdale Int'l Airport, Port Everglades (NB)
23		FL 818, Griffin Rd, Dania Beach
	Gas	W: BP, Citgo◇
	Food	E: Garden Cafe, Rest/Sheraton W: Rest/Bass Pro Shop

EXIT		FLORIDA
	Lodg	E: Hilton♥, Sheraton W: Courtyard, Homewood Suites
	Other	E: Ft Lauderdale Int'l Airport✈ W: Bass Pro Shop, North Coast RV Park & Marina▲
22		FL 848, Stirling Rd, Dania Beach
	Gas	E: Mobil W: Circle K
	Food	E: Burger King, McDonald's, Taco Bell, Sweet Tomatoes, TGI Friday, Wendy's W: Dunkin Donuts, Subway
	Lodg	E: Comfort Inn, Hampton Inn, Springhill Suites
	Other	E: B&N, Big Lots, BJ's, Home Depot, Boomers of Dania, RaceARama, Atlantis W: CVS, Walgreen's, Pep Boys, Tires, to Hollywood Indian Reservation
21		FL 822, Sheridan St, Hollywood
	Gas	E: BP, Cumberland Farms, Citgo, Mobil W: Shell
	Food	E: TGI Friday, Sweet Tomatoes W: Denny's
	Lodg	E: La Quinta Inn♥ W: Days Inn, Holiday Inn
	Other	E: Oakwood 18 Cinemas
20		FL 820, Hollywood Blvd
	Gas	E: Gascom, Shell W: BP, Chevron, Mobil
	Food	E: Miami Subs, IHOP, McDonald's W: Boston Market, McDonald's, Subway, Quizno's, Starbucks, Taco Bell
	Lodg	E: Howard Johnson Express
	Med	W: + Hospital
	Other	W: Publix, Target, Walgreen's, Hollywood Mall, Hollywood Police Dept
19		FL 824, Pembroke Rd, Hollywood
	Gas	E: Shell, Mobil W: Sunoco◇
18		FL 858, Hallandale Beach Blvd
	Gas	E: 7-11, BP, Exxon W: BP, RaceTrac, Speedway
	Food	E: Burger King, Denny's, Wendy's, Dunkin Donuts, KFC, Little Caesars, Long John Silver, McDonald's, Smokehouse BBQ, Subway W: Park Food Court
	Lodg	E: Ramada, Best Western
	Med	W: + PCA Family Medical Center
	Other	E: Walgreen's, Winn Dixie, Holiday RV Park▲
16		Ives Dairy Rd, NE 203rd St, Miami
	Gas	W: 7-11, BP
	Food	W: Subway
	Med	E: + Hospital
	Other	W: to Dolphin Stadium
14		FL 860, Miami Gardens Dr, North Miami Beach
	Gas	W: BP, Chevron, Marathon◇
	Other	W: Walgreen's
12		US 441S, FL 826, FL Tpk, FL 9N (SB exit, NB entr)
12C		US 441N, FL 7 (NB exit, SB entr)
	Gas	E: Citgo, Hess, Valero
	Lodg	E: Days Inn, Holiday Inn
	Med	E: + Hospital
12B		FL 826E, N Miami Beach (NB) (SB Access via Exit #12)
12A		FL 826W, FL Tpk (NB) (SB Access via Exit #12)

Page 530

◇ = Regular Gas Stations with Diesel   ▲ = RV Friendly Locations   ♥ = Pet Friendly Locations
RED PRINT SHOWS LARGE VEHICLE PARKING/ACCESS ON SITE OR NEARBY   BROWN PRINT SHOWS CAMPGROUNDS/RV PARKS

N I-95

EXIT		FLORIDA
11		NW 151st St (NB exit, SB entr)
	Gas	W: Twin Service Station, Sunoco
	Food	W: McDonald's
10B		FL 916, Opa Locka Blvd
	Gas	W: BP, Chevron, Liberty, Mobil
	Food	W: Subway, Pizza Hut
	Lodg	W: Motel 7, Uptown Arms Motel
10A		NW 125th St, N Miami, Bal Harbour
	Gas	W: Shell
	Food	W: Arnold's Castle, Wendy's
	Other	W: Grocery
9		FL 924, NW 119th St (NB ex, SB entr)
	Gas	E: Mobil, BP
	Food	W: KFC, Sub Center, BBQ Barn
	Lodg	W: Bay Thrift Lodge
	Other	W: Familly Dollar, Winn Dixie, Walgreen's
8B		FL 932, NW 103rd St, Miami
	Gas	W: Exxon, Shell, Chevron, Mobil
	Food	W: Carmen's, Dunkin Donuts
	Other	W: Grocery
8A		NW 95th St
	Gas	BP, Mobil, Shell
	Food	W: Burger King, McDonald's
	Lodg	W: Days Inn

EXIT		FLORIDA
	Med	W: + N Shore Medical Center
	Other	W: Walgreen's
7		FL 934, NW 79th St, NW 81st St
	Gas	E: Chevron
		W: Exxon, Shell
	Food	W: Ma's Rest
	Lodg	W: City Inn
6B		NW 69th St (SB exit, NB entr)
6A		FL 944, NW 62nd St, NW 54th St, Dr Martin Luther King Jr Blvd
	Gas	W: Shell
	Food	W: McDonald's, Subway
	Other	W: Winn Dixie, Walgreen's
(4B)		Jct I-195, FL 112W (TOLL) (NB)
	Other	W: to Miami Int'l Airport ✈
(4A)		Jct I-195E, Miami Beach (NB)
(4)		Jct I-195E, FL 112 (TOLL), Miami Beach, Miami Int'l Airport (SB)
3B		NW 8th St, Port of Miami, Orange Bowl (SB exit, NB entr)

EXIT		FLORIDA
3A		FL 836W, Miami Int'l Airport (fr NB, Left exit)
(2D)		Jct I-395, NW 8th St, Orange Bowl (SB Left exit)
	Other	E: to American Airlines Arena
2C		Miami Ave (SB, Left exit)
2B		NW 2nd St (NB)
	Other	E: Miami Art Museum
2A		US 1, to S Miami Ave
1B		SW 8th St, SW 7th St
1A		SW 25th Rd, SW 26th Rd, Rickenbacker Causeway (SB)

(I-95 begins/ends on US 1 in Miami, FL)
(EASTERN TIME ZONE)

○ **FLORIDA**
Begin Northbound I-95 from Miami, FL to Maine/Canada border.

I-96 E

EXIT		MICHIGAN
		Begin Eastbound I-96 from Muskegon, MI to Detroit, MI.
○ **MICHIGAN**		
(EASTERN TIME ZONE)		
1		US 31 Bus N, Downtown Muskegon, to Ludington, Grand Haven
	Gas	N: Citgo◊
	Food	N: Applebee's, Arby's, McDonald's, Old Country Buffet, Ruby Tuesday, Wendy's
	Lodg	N: Alpine Motel, Bel-Aire Motel, Comfort Inn
	Med	N: + Hospital
	Other	N: ATMs, Lowe's, Sam's Club, Wal-Mart sc, All Seasons RV Center
		S: Airport ✈, Racetrack
1A		US 31S, Airline Rd, to Ludington, Grand Haven, (WB access Hile Rd)
1B		US 31N, to Ludington, Grand Haven
1C		E Hile Rd, Muskegon (EB only)

EXIT		MICHIGAN
4		Airline Rd (NB), 3rd Ave (SB)
	Gas	N: Wesco◊
		S: Speedway◊, Shell, Wesco
	Food	S: McDonald's, Subway
	Other	S: Fruitport Foods, Pleasure Island Water Park
5		Fruitport Rd, Fruitport (WB exit, EB entr)
(8)		Rest Area (WB) (RR, Phone, Picnic, Vend)
9		M 104, Spring Lake, Grand Haven, Spring Lake (WB ex, EB entr)
10		CR B 31, 112th Ave, Nunica
	Gas	S: Nunica EZ Mart
	Other	S: Campers Paradise▲, Conestoga Grand River Campground▲
16		CR B 35, 68th Ave, Coopersville, Eastmanville
	FStop	N: Speedway
	Gas	N: BP◊, Shell◊

EXIT		MICHIGAN
	Food	N: Arby's, Dunkin Donuts, Hardee's, McDonald's, Pizza Hut/Taco Bell
	Lodg	N: AmeriHost
	Other	N: Grocery, Pharmacy, Fun 'n Sun RV Center
		S: River Pines Campground▲
19		48th St, Coopersville, Lamont
	Food	S: Sam's Joint
	Other	N: Prime Time RV Sales & Service
23		16th Ave, Marne
	Gas	N: Shell
	Other	N: Fairgrounds
24		M 11, 8th Ave, 4 Mile Rd, Grand Rapids, Walker, Grandville (EB)
	Gas	S: Marathon◊
	Lodg	S: Wayside Motel
25		8th Ave, 4 Mile Rd (WB) (Access to Exit #24 Serv)
(25)		Rest Area (EB) (RR, Phone, Picnic, Vend)
27		Fruit Ridge Ave, Grand Rapids
	Gas	N: Citgo◊

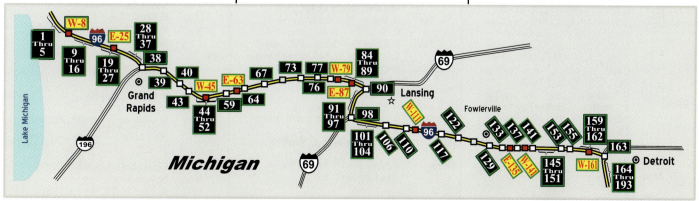

◊ = Regular Gas Stations with Diesel   ▲ = RV Friendly Locations   ♥ = Pet Friendly Locations
RED PRINT SHOWS LARGE VEHICLE PARKING/ACCESS ON SITE OR NEARBY   BROWN PRINT SHOWS CAMPGROUNDS/RV PARKS

Page 531

INTERSTATE 96 W/E — MICHIGAN

EXIT		Services
	S:	BP
28		**Walker Ave, Grand Rapids**
	Gas	S: Meijer◇
	Food	S: Bob Evans, McDonald's
	Lodg	S: AmeriHost, Baymont Inn
30AB		**M 37N, Alpine Ave, 3 Mile Rd, Grand Rapids, Newaygo**
	FStop	S: Speedway #8766
	Gas	N: 7-11, BP, Marathon, Shell
		S: Admiral◇, Meijer◇
	Food	N: Applebee's, Bennigan's, Blimpie, Cracker Barrel, Damon's, IHOP, Little Caesar's, Logan's Steakhouse, Olive Garden, Outback Steakhouse, Perkins, Steak 'n Shake, Subway, Taco Bell, TGI Friday
		S: Burger King, KFC, Long John Silver, McDonald's, Ponderosa, Wendy's
	Lodg	N: Hampton Inn, Holiday Inn, Springhill Suites
		S: Motel 6♥
	Other	N: ATMs, Auto Services, Best Buy, Circuit City, Discount Tire, Pep Boys, Sam's Club, Target, Wal-Mart
		S: Home Depot, Goodyear, U-Haul
31AB		**US 131, S-Kalamazoo, N-Cadillac**
33		**M 44 Connector, Plainfield Ave**
	Gas	N: Meijer◇, Speedway, BP
	Food	N: Arby's, Burger King, KFC, Pizza Hut, Subway, Taco Bell, Wendy's
		S: Denny's
	Lodg	N: Grand Inn, Lazy T Motel
	Med	N: + Family Physicians Urgent Care
	Other	N: Auto Dealers, AutoZone, Big Lots, Discount Tire, Goodyear, NAPA, NTB, U-Haul, Walgreen's
36		**Leonard St NE, Grand Rapids**
(37)		**Jct I-196, Downtown Grand Rapids, Holland (WB, Left Exit)**
	TServ	S: Michigan CAT
38		**M 37S, M 44, E Beltline Ave, M 21, Grand Rapids, Flint**
	Med	S: + Hospital
39		**M 21, E Fulton St, to Flint (EB)**
40AB		**Cascade Rd, Grand Rapids**
	Gas	N: 7-11, BP, Marathon◇
		S: Shell, Speedway◇
	Food	N: Subway
	Lodg	S: Harley Hotel
	Med	S: + Hospital
43AB		**M 11, 28th St, Kent Co Airport, Grand Rapids, Cascade**
	Gas	N: Marathon◇, Meijer◇
		S: BP, Shell, Speedway
	Food	N: Brann's Steakhouse, Burger King, Romano's Macaroni Grill, Panera Bread, Sundance Grill, Shanghai Garden
		S: Arby's, Bob Evans, Chili's, Denny's, Dunkin Donuts, Hooters, IHOP, Olive Garden, McDonald's, Perkins, Rio Bravo, Red Lobster, Subway, Wendy's
	Lodg	N: Baymont Inn, Country Inn, Days Inn
		S: Comfort Inn, Extended Stay America, Exel Inn, Hampton Inn, Hilton, Motel 6♥, Quality Inn, Red Roof Inn♥
	Other	N: Wal-Mart
		S: B&N, CarQuest, Circuit City, Costco, Home Depot, Target, Sam's Club, U-Haul
44		**36th St**
	Other	S: Gerald Ford Int'l Airport✈

EXIT		Services
(45)		**Rest Area (WB)** (RR, Phone, Picnic, Vend, Info)
46		**M 6, to Holland**
52		**M 50, Alden Nash Ave, Lowell**
	Gas	S: Marathon◇
59		**Nash Hwy, Clarksville**
(63)		**Rest Area (EB)** (RR, Phone, Picnic, Vend)
64		**Jordan Lake Rd, Lake Odessa**
	Other	N: Ionia State Rec Area
		S: I-96 Speedway
67		**M 66, Ionia, Battle Creek**
	TStop	N: Pilot Travel Center #23 (Scales)
	Gas	N: Meijer◇
	Food	N: Subway/Pilot TC
	Lodg	N: Midway Motel, Super 8
	Med	N: + Hospital
	Other	N: Ionia Co Airport✈, MI State Hwy Patrol Post
(69)		**Weigh Station (Both dir)**
73		**Grand River Ave, Portland Rd, Portland, Lyons, Muir**
76		**Kent Rd, Portland**
	Gas	N: Marathon◇
77		**I-196 Bus, Grand River Ave, Portland**
	TStop	N: Speedway #2319
	Gas	N: BP, Marathon◇, Speedway◇
	Food	N: Arby's, Burger King, McDonald's, Subway
	Other	N: Best Western
(79)		**Rest Area (WB)** (RR, Phone, Picnic, Vend, Info)
84		**Grange Rd, Eagle**
86		**M 100, Wright Rd, Eagle, Grand Ledge, Potterville**
	TStop	S: Pohl Oil/Mobil
	Food	S: McDonald's/Mobil
(87)		**Rest Area (EB)** (RR, Phone, Picnic, Vend)
(89)		**Jct I-69N, US 27N, to Flint (EB)**
90		**I-196 Bus, Grand River Ave, Lansing**
	TStop	N: Flying J Travel Plaza (Scales)
	Food	N: Rest/FastFood/FJ TP
	Other	N: Laundry/WiFi/RVDump/LP/FIJ TP, Capital City Airport✈
(91)		**Jct I-69N, US 27N, to Flint (WB)**
93AB		**I-69 Bus, M 43, Saginaw Hwy, Lansing, Grand Ledge**
	Gas	N: Meijer◇, Shell, Speedway◇
		S: BP
	Food	N: Burger King, Denny's, McDonald's
		S: Bob Evans, Cracker Barrel, Subway
	Lodg	N: Best Western, Fairfield Inn, Hampton Inn, Holiday Inn, Motel 6♥, Quality Inn, Red Roof Inn♥
	Med	N: + Hospital
	Other	S: Discount Tire, Lowe's, Auto Dealers, Wal-Mart
(95)		**Jct I-496, Downtown Lansing**
(97)		**Jct I-69, US 27, S to Ft Wayne, N to Lansing**

EXIT		Services
98AB		**Lansing Rd, Lansing**
	TStop	S: AmBest/Windmill Truck Stop/Citgo (Scales)
	Food	S: Rest/Windmill TS
	Lodg	S: Motel/Windmill TS
	TWash	S: Windmill TS
	TServ	N: General White/GMC
		S: Windmill TS
	Other	S: Laundry/Windmill TS
101		**M 99, MLK Jr Blvd, Eaton Rapids Rd, Lansing, Eaton Rapids**
	FStop	S: Super Stop Express/Sunoco
	Gas	S: Speedway
	Food	S: McDonald's, Wendy's
	Other	S: CarQuest, Kroger, Lowe's, NAPA
104		**I-96 Bus, Cedar St, Pennsylvania Ave, Lansing, to Holt**
	Gas	N: Meijer◇, Shell, Speedway
		S: Speedway
	Food	N: Arby's, Blimpie, Bob Evans, Burger King, Denny's, Dunkin Donuts, Long John Silver, Hooters, KFC, Pizza Hut, Taco Bell, Wendy's
		S: Flapjack's Rest, LA Chicken & Ribs, McDonald's, Ponderosa
	Lodg	N: Best Western, Days Inn, Motel 6♥, Super 8
		S: Holiday Inn, Howard Johnson
	Med	N: + Hospital
		S: + Ready Care Walk-In Clinic
	Other	N: Grocery, Sam's Club, Target
		S: Kroger, Lowe's, NAPA
(106AB)		**Jct I-496W, US 127, to Jackson, Lansing**
110		**Okemos Rd, Okemos, Mason**
	Gas	N: 7-11, BP, Marathon, Mobil
	Food	N: Arby's, Burger King, Big John Steak Onion, Cracker Barrel, Dunkin Donuts, McDonald's, Subway
	Lodg	N: Comfort Inn, Fairfield Inn, Holiday Inn
(111)		**Rest Area (WB)** (RR, Phone, Picnic, Vend)
117AB		**N Williamston Rd, Williamston**
	Gas	N: Marathon
		S: Sunoco◇
122		**M 43W, M 52, Webberville, Stockbridge**
	FStop	N: Mobil
	Food	N: West Side Deli, McDonald's
(126)		**Weigh Station (Both dir)**
129		**Fowlerville Rd, Fowlerville**
	Gas	N: BP, Shell◇
		S: Mobil
	Food	N: Big Boy, Fowlerville Farms, Subway, McDonald's, Taco Bell, Wendy's
	Lodg	N: Best Western
	Med	N: McAuley-McPherson Walk-in Clinic
133		**I-96 Bus, M 59, Highland Rd, Howell, Highland**
	Gas	N: Sunoco◇
	Food	N: Arby's, McDonald's
	Lodg	N: AmeriHost
	Other	N: Livingston Co Airport✈, MI Sheriff
(135)		**Rest Area (EB)** (RR, Phone, Picnic, Vend)
137		**CR D 19, Pinckney Rd, Howell**
	Gas	N: Mobil, Shell◇, Speedway
	Food	N: Time Out Grill, Five Star Pizza

◇ = Regular Gas Stations with Diesel   ▲ = RV Friendly Locations   ♥ = Pet Friendly Locations

RED PRINT SHOWS LARGE VEHICLE PARKING/ACCESS ON SITE OR NEARBY   BROWN PRINT SHOWS CAMPGROUNDS/RV PARKS

W 96 INTERSTATE

MICHIGAN

EXIT		
	Food	S: Benny's Grill, Country Kitchen
	Lodg	N: Kensington Inn, Quality Inn
		S: Best Western
	Med	N: + Hospital
(141)		**Rest Area (WB)** (RR, Phone, Picnic, Vend)
141		I-96 Bus, Grand River Ave, Howell
	Gas	N: Sunoco◊, Shell
	Food	N: Applebee's, Bob Evans, McDonald's
		S: Arby's, Taco Bell, Wendy's
	Lodg	N: Grand View Inn
145		Grand River Ave, Brighton
	Gas	N: BP, Shell
		S: Clark◊, Meijer◊
	Food	N: Arby's, Cracker Barrel, Outback Steak House, Pizza Hut
		S: Burger King, Dunkin Donuts, KFC, McDonald's, Ponderosa, Taco Bell
	Lodg	N: Courtyard
		S: Holiday Inn Express
	Med	S: + McAuley-McPherson Walk-In Clinic
	Other	S: Mall, Best Buy, Home Depot, Kmart, Staples, Target, Pharmacy, to Brighton Ski Area
147		Spencer Rd, Brighton
148AB		US 23, N-Flint, S-Ann Arbor
150		Pleasant Valley Rd, Brighton (WB Exit, EB reaccess)
	Other	S: Island Lake State Rec Area
151		Kensington Rd, Brighton
	Other	N: Kensington Metropark
		S: Island Lake State Rec Area
153		Grand River Rd (EB), Kent Lake Rd, Huron River Pky, Milford
	Gas	S: Mobil
	Other	N: Kensington Metropark
		S: Island Lake State Rec Area
155		Milford Rd, Milford, Hudson
	Gas	S: BP, Mobil, Sunoco
	Food	S: Applebee's, Chili's, Subway, Tim Horton's, Wendy's
	Other	S: Discount Tire, Lowe's, Wal-Mart sc
155AB		Milford Rd, Milford, Hudson
159		Wixom Rd, Wixom
	Gas	S: Mobil, Shell, Meijer◊
	Food	S: Arby's, McDonald's, Taco Bell
	Lodg	N: Baymont Inn
	Other	N: Ford Wixom Assembly Plant, Proud Lake State Rec Area
160		12 Mile Rd, Beck Rd, Novi
	Med	N: + Hospital
	Other	S: Grocery, Home Depot, Staples
(161)		**Rest Area (WB)** (RR, Phone, Picnic, Vend)
162		Novi Rd, Novi, Walled Lake
	Gas	N: BP
		S: Mobil, Sunoco
	Food	N: Carrabba's, Great Steak & Potato, McDonald's, Pizza Hut, Red Lobster
		S: Bob Evans, Hardee's, Olive Garden, TGI Friday, Wendy's
	Lodg	N: DoubleTree Hotel, Sheraton
		S: Courtyard, Wyndham
	Med	N: + Hospital

EXIT		
	Other	N: Mall, Circuit City, Kmart, Kroger, Pharmacy
		S: Discount Tire, Shopping
NOTE:		I-96 runs below with I-275 for 10 mi. Exit #'s follow I-96.
(163)		Jct I-696, M 5, Grand River Ave (EB)
164		M 5N, 12 Mile Rd (EB)
165		M 5N, 12 Mile Rd (WB)
167		8 Mile Rd, Northville
	Gas	S: Speedway, Meijer◊
	Food	S: Chili's, McDonald's, Kyoto Japanese Steakhouse, Taco Bell
	Lodg	S: Hampton Inn, Ramada, Sheraton
	Med	S: + Hospital
	Other	S: Best Buy, Costco, Home Depot, Grocery, Target
169AB		7 Mile Rd, Livonia
	Food	N: Lone Star Steakhouse, Rest/Embassy Suites
		S: Cooker, Romano's Macaroni Grill
	Lodg	N: Embassy Suites
		S: AmeriSuites
170		6 Mile Rd, Livonia
	Gas	S: AmocoBP, Mobil
	Food	N: Denison's, Max & Erma's, Red Robin, The Ground Round
		S: McDonald's
	Lodg	N: Best Western, Courtyard, Holiday Inn, Marriott, Quality Inn
		S: Fairfield Inn, Residence Inn
	Other	N: Mall
		S: CVS, Office Depot
(172)		Jct I-275S, to Toledo, M 14 W, Ann Arbor
NOTE:		I-96 runs above with I-275 for 10 mi. Exit #'s follow I-96.
173		Newburgh Rd, Levan Rd (EB) Schoolcraft Rd
	Other	S: GM Chassis Plant, Ford Livonia Plant
173A		Newburgh Rd, Livonia (WB) Schoolcraft Rd
173B		Levan Rd (WB)
	Med	N: + Hospital
174		Farmington Rd, Livonia
	Gas	N: Mobil◊
		S: Amoco
	Food	N: Looney Baker Café
		S: KFC, Mason's Grill
	Other	N: Ford Athletic Field
175		Merriman Rd, Livonia
	Gas	N: Mobil
		S: Sunoco
	Food	S: Mountain Jack's Steakhouse
	Other	S: Commerce Center
176		Middlebelt Rd, Livonia
	Gas	S: Meijer◊
	Food	N: Bob Evans, IHOP, Olive Garden
		S: Boss Hogg's BBQ, Mesquite Junction Steakhouse, Logan's Roadhouse
	Lodg	N: Comfort Inn, Super 8
	Other	S: Ford Parts Depot, GM-Cadillac Div,. GM Inland Div, Costco, Home Depot, Wal-Mart

EXIT		
177		Inkster Rd, Livonia, Redford
	Food	N: Panda Rest, Subway
	Other	N: 7-11
		S: Jerusalem Food Market
178		Beech Daily Rd, Redford
	Gas	N: Citgo
179		US 24, Telegraph Rd, Redford, to Dearborn, Pontiac
	Gas	S: BP, Marathon◊
	Food	N: Arby's, Taco Bell, White Castle
	Lodg	N: Tel 96 Inn
	Other	N: Family Dollar, Goodyear
		S: Detroit Diesel
180		Outer Dr West, I-96 Express
NOTE:		EB: No exits til Exit #185
182		Evergreen Rd, Jeffries Rd, Glendale St (EB), Detroit
183		M 39, Southfield Freeway
NOTE:		Begin/End I-96 Express Lanes
184		Greenfield Rd, Detroit
185		M 5, Grand River Ave, Schaefer Hwy, Detroit
	Gas	N: BP, Mobil, Shell
		S: Sunoco
	Food	N: McDonald's
	Other	N: CVS, Police Dept.
186A		Wyoming St, Detroit
186B		M 8, Davison Ave, I-96 Express
NOTE:		WB: no exits til Exit #182
187		M 5, Grand River Ave (EB)
188		Jeffries Frwy, Livernois Ave Joy Rd (access fr EB)
	Gas	N: Mobil, Shell
	Food	N: Burger King, KFC, McDonald's, Wendy's, Young's BBQ
188A		Jeffries Frwy, Livernois Ave Joy Rd (access fr EB)
188B		Joy Rd, Grand River Ave (WB)
	Food	N: Famous Pizza, Popeye's Chicken
189		W Grand Blvd, Tireman Ave
	Gas	N: BP, Mobil
(190A)		Jct I-94 (EB)
190B		Warren Ave, Detroit
	Gas	N: Citgo
		S: Marathon
	Food	N: Green's BBQ
191		MLK Blvd, to US 12, Michigan Ave
(193)		Jct I-75, N-Flint, S-Toledo, OH, to Porter St, Ambassador Br to Canada to M 10, John C Lodge Frwy
	Other	to Downtown Detroit, Civic Center

(EASTERN TIME ZONE)

🅗 MICHIGAN

Begin Westbound I-96 from Detroit, MI to Muskegon, MI.

◊ = Regular Gas Stations with Diesel   ▲ = RV Friendly Locations   ♥ = Pet Friendly Locations
RED PRINT SHOWS LARGE VEHICLE PARKING/ACCESS ON SITE OR NEARBY   BROWN PRINT SHOWS CAMPGROUNDS/RV PARKS

INTERSTATE 97

EXIT	MARYLAND
	I-97 from Jct I-695 near Pumphrey, MD to Jct US 301/50 near Annapolis, MD

ⓤ MARYLAND

Exit	Description
(17)	Jct I-895N, Harbor Tunnel
(17B)	Jct I-695E, Essex, Towson
(17A)	Jct I-695W, Baltimore
(17)	Jct I-695, Key Bridge, Baltimore, Towson, Dundalk (NB exit, SB entr)
16	MD 648, Baltimore Annapolis Rd, Glen Burnie, Ferndale (SB)
Gas	E: BP W: Mobil, Amoco
Food	E: KFC, McDonald's, Wendy's, Deven's Deli, China King, Pizza Choice, Willie's, Heritage Rest
Other	E: Grocery, Banks
15A	MD 176, Dorsey Rd (NB)
15B	MD 162, Aviation Blvd (NB)
15	MD 176, Dorsey Rd (SB) MD 162, Aviation Blvd (SB)
Gas	E: BP

Exit	MARYLAND
Other	W: to BWI Int'l Airport✈, Banks, **Police Dept**
Food	Serv E on Baltimore Annapolis Blvd KFC, McDonald's, Subway, Wendy's
Lodg	Serv 3 miles east in Glen Burnie
14A	MD 100E, Columbia, Ellicott City, Gibson Island (SB)
14B	MD 100W, Columbia, Ellicott City, Gibson Island (SB)
14	MD 100, Columbia, Ellicott City, Gibson Island
13	MD 174, Quarterfield Rd
Gas	E: 7-11, Exxon W: Shell◆
Food	E: Pizza, China Wok, Bayou Bay Cafe
12	MD 3 Bus N, Crain Hwy, New Cut Rd, Glen Burnie (Serv E on Veterans Hwy)
Gas	Amoco, Crown, Exxon, WaWa
Food	Burger King, KFC, Taco Bell, Pizza Hut, Popeye's, Wendy'ssd
Other	Banks, Goodyear, Target, **Wal-Mart**, **Walgreen's**
10A	Benfield Blvd E, Veterans Hwy (SB)
10B	Benfield Blvd W, Veterans Hwy

Exit	MARYLAND
10	Benfield Blvd, Veterans Hwy, Millersville, Severna Park
Gas	E: Exxon◆, Citco
Food	E: Deli, Hella's Seafood
Other	W: **Washington DC/Capitol KOA**▲ **Police Dept**
7	MD 32W, MD 3S, Laurel, Bowie, Columbia, Odenton
Food	Shoeless Joe, Bull's Eye Sport and Pub
Lodg	Freestate Lodging
Other	**Elm Truck Maintenance**
5	MD 178, Generals Hwy, Crownsville (SB Exit, NB entr) (Serv E on Generals Hwy)
Gas	Texaco, Citco, Amoco
Food	Sonny's Real Pit BBQ, SK Pizza And Subs, Trifles Rest
Med	E: + Hospital
1	US 301, US 50, Annapolis, Bay Bridge, Washington, Richmond (Serv E off of US 301)(SB exit, NB entr) (SB exit, NB entr)
(0)	MD 665, Aris T Allen Blvd, Riva Rd (SB exit, NB entr)

ⓤ MARYLAND

INTERSTATE 99 S

EXIT	PENNSYLVANIA
	Begin Southbound I-99 from US 220 in Tyrone to Jct I-70/76 in Bedford

ⓤ PENNSYLVANIA
(EASTERN TIME ZONE)

Exit	Description
(EXIT)	FUTURE Jct I-80W
83	PA 550, Zion Rd, Zion, Bellafonte (Addtl Serv 2 mi west in Bellefonte)
Food	Spectators Sport Bar
81	PA 26S, to PA 64, Pleasant Gap
80	Harrison Rd, Bellafonte (NB, no reacc)
NOTE:	Enter SB/Exit NB State Corr Institute at Rockview Property EMER STOP ONLY
78B	PA 150N, Bellafonte
78A	PA 150S
Other	Rockview State Corr Institution
NOTE:	Enter NB/Exit SB State Corr Institute at Rockview Property EMER STOP ONLY
76	Shiloh Rd
74	Park Ave, Innovation Park, Penn St Univ, State College (SB)
Other	W: University Park Airport✈
73	US 322E, Penn State Univ, State College (NB), State College, Lewistown (SB)
Gas	Sheetz

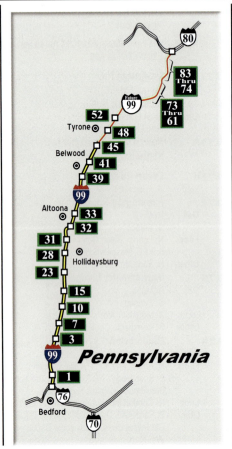

Exit	PENNSYLVANIA
Food	DQ, Red Lobster
Other	Grocery, **Wal-Mart**
71	Toftrees, Woodycrest
70	Valley Vista Dr, State College
69	US 322E Bus, Atherton St (exit only)
62	US 322W, Phillipsburg
61	Port Matilda
52	PA 350, US 220S Bus, Bald Eagle
Gas	W: BP
Food	W: Subway
48	PA 453, Tyrone, to PA 550
Gas	W: Sheetz◆, Amoco
Food	W: Burger King, Mario's Pizza Palace, TCBY, Subway, Frozen Cow, Joybean, Italian Pizza
Med	W: + Hospital
Other	Grocery, Banks
45	Tipton, Grazierville
Gas	W: Exxon
Food	W: Pizza Hut
Med	W: + Hospital
Other	W: DelGrosso's Amusement Park, Auto Dealers
41	PA 865N, Bellwood
Gas	W: Sheetz◆, Martin Gen'l Store◆
Other	W: DelGrosso's Amusement Park

Page 534

◆ = Regular Gas Stations with Diesel   ▲ = RV Friendly Locations   ♥ = Pet Friendly Locations
RED PRINT SHOWS LARGE VEHICLE PARKING/ACCESS ON SITE OR NEARBY   BROWN PRINT SHOWS CAMPGROUNDS/RV PARKS

EXIT		PENNSYLVANIA
39		PA 764S, Bellwood, Pinecroft
	Gas	W: Choice, Sheetz
	Lodg	W: Cedar Grove Motel
	Other	W: Oak Spring Winery
33		17th St, Altoona
	Gas	W: Sheetz
	Other	W: U-Haul, Lowe's, Penn State-Altoona, Central Business District, Museum
32		to PA 36, Frankstown Rd, Altoona
	Gas	W: Sheetz, Exxon, Rabit, GFF Oil
	Food	W: Dunkin Donuts, McDonald's, Olive Garden, Perkins, Pizza Hut, Red Lobster, Subway, Wendy's, Woody's
	Lodg	W: Days Inn, Econo Lodge, Holiday Inn, Super 8
	Med	W: + Hospital
	Other	E: Canoe Creek State Park
		W: CVS, NAPA, AutoZone, Radio Shack, Blair Co Stadium, Logan Valley Mall
31		US 220 Bus, Plank Rd, Altoona
	Gas	W: BP
	Food	E: Friendly's, Outback Steakhouse, Ruby Tuesday, TGI Friday
		W: Applebee's, Arby's, Cracker Barrel, Denny's, KFC, Ponderosa, Ruby Tuesday, Taco Bell, TGI Friday, Subway/BP
	Lodg	E: Comfort Inn, Courtyard, Ramada Inn

EXIT		PENNSYLVANIA
	Lodg	W: Hampton Inn, Motel 6♥
	Other	E: Wal-Mart, Circuit City, Firestone, Sam's Club, Target, Blair Co Convention Center, Wright's Orchard Station Campground▲
		W: ATMs, Advance Auto, Dollar General, Grocery, Kmart, Pharmacy, Staples, Logan Valley Mall
28		to US 22, Ebensburg, Hollidaysburg, to PA 764, Duncansville
	Other	E: PA State Hwy Patrol Post
23		PA 36, PA 164, Roaring Spring, Portage, to US 22E
	Gas	E: Exxon, Mobil◇, Sheetz
	Food	E: Pizza/Exxon, Blimpie/Mobil, Lynn's
	Lodg	E: Haven Rest Motel
	Med	E: + Hospital
	Other	E: Altoona-Blair Co Airport✈, to Heritage Cove Resort▲
15		US 220N Bus, Claysburg, King
	Gas	W: Sheetz
	Food	W: Burger King, Wendy's
	Other	W: Blue Knob Valley Airport✈
10		Sarah Furnance Rd, Osterburg, Imler
	Other	W: Blue Knob State Park▲
7		PA 869, Osterburg, St Clairsville

EXIT		PENNSYLVANIA
3		PA 56, Quaker Valley Rd, US 220S Bus, Bedford, Johnstown, Cessna
	Gas	RG's BP◇
	Food	Apple Bin Rest
	Other	E: Bedford Co Airport✈, PA State Hwy Patrol Post
(1)		Jct I-70/76, PA Tpk, US 220, Pittsburgh, Harrisburg
	Gas	E: BP, Sheetz, Amoco, Sunoco
	Food	E: Denny's, Pizza Hut, Wendy's Long John Silver, China Inn, McDonald's, Ed's Steak House, Best Way Pizza, Donut Connections
	Lodg	E: Best Western, Hampton Inn, Super 8, Quality Inn, Travelodge, Econo Lodge, Janey's Lynn Motel, Jean Bonnet B & B
	Other	E: Bedford Airport✈, Friendship Village Campground and RV Resort▲

(EASTERN TIME ZONE)

⊙ PENNSYLVANIA

Begin I-99 Northbound from Jct I-70/76 in Bedford to US 220 in Tyrone

EXIT		CALIFORNIA
		Begin Eastbound I-105 near Imperial Hwy to I-605N.

⊙ CALIFORNIA

1		Imperial Hwy E, Inglewood (Addt'l Serv N on Century Blvd)
	Food	Goody's Rest, Mexican Rest, Thai Rest, Cutting Board Snack Bar
	Lodg	Twin Towers Motel
	Other	LAX Int'l Airport✈
(2)		Jct 405
3		Prairie Ave, Hawthorne Blvd
	Gas	Shell, Arco, Chevron
	Food	Italian Rest, Jack in the Box
	Lodg	Howard Johnson, La Mirage Inn, Del Aire Inn, Jade Tree Motel, Holly Park Motel, Star Motel
	Other	Grocery, Casinos (N on Century Blvd)
5		Crenshaw Blvd, Hawthorne
	Gas	Mobil
	Food	China Spoon, China Express, New China Buffet, Subway, Thai Chinese Express
	Lodg	Marriott, Dream Inn, Palm Inn Motel, Kings Motel, Diamond Inn, Casa Belle Motel, Tourist Lodge
	Med	S: + Robert Kennedy Medical Center
	Other	Auto Repair, Hawthorne Muni Airport✈
7A		Vermont Ave
	Gas	Arco, Mobil, Shell, Mini Mart
	Food	Caesar Rest, LA Fried Chicken, Chinese & American Rest, Mom's BBQ
	Lodg	Vegas Motel, Magic Carpet Motor Inn, Paradise Inn, Western Motel
	Other	Auto Repairs
(7B)		Jct I-110

EXIT		CALIFORNIA
9		Central Ave (Serv N on Imperial Hwy)
	Gas	Shell
	Other	Magic Johnson Rec Center
10		Wilington Ave
	Food	China Gate
	Lodg	Crown Motel
12		Long Beach Blvd
	Food	Chinese Rest, El Paraiso Rest
	Lodg	World Motel, Travelodge, Lynnwood Hotel, Mission Motel, Rainbow Inn, Rocky Motel, Flaming Motel
	Other	Lynwood City Park
(13)		Jct I-710

EXIT		CALIFORNIA
14		Garfield Ave, Paramont
	Gas	Garfield Gas, Mobil, Shell
	Food	Dragon Lee Rest, Mexican Rest
16		Lakewood Blvd
	Gas	Mobil, Shell
	Food	Great China Rest, Little Caesar's Pizza
	Lodg	Colonial Motel, American Inn Motel
17		Belleflower Blvd (Other Serv N on Imperial Hwy)
	Other	Thompson Park, Boeing Defense & Space Group
(18AB)		Jct I-605

⊙ CALIFORNIA

Begin WB I-105 near I-605N to Imperial Hwy

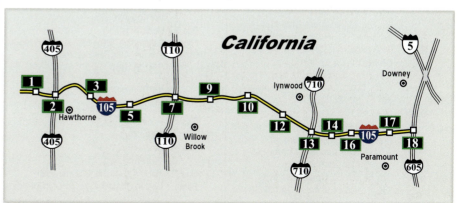

◇ = Regular Gas Stations with Diesel ▲ = RV Friendly Locations ♥ = Pet Friendly Locations
RED PRINT SHOWS LARGE VEHICLE PARKING/ACCESS ON SITE OR NEARBY BROWN PRINT SHOWS CAMPGROUNDS/RV PARKS

EXIT	CALIFORNIA
	Begin Southbound I-110 from Jct I-10 in Los Angeles to CA 47

ⓘ CALIFORNIA

Exit	Description
(0)	NB End / SB Begin CA 110 Fwy, California Blvd, to CA 134, I-210 (NB, Left Exit)
31B	Fair Oaks Ave, S Pasadena
Food	Baskin Robbins, El Pollo Loco, Starbucks
Other	ATMs, Banks, Theatre
31A	Orange Grove Ave
Gas	ArcoAmPm
30B	Bridewell St (NB)
30A	York Blvd, Pasadena Ave (NB)
30	York Blvd, Pasadena Ave (SB)
29	Ave 60
28B	Via Marisol
Gas	Snack Shop
Food	Big Burger, El Pollo Loco
28A	Ave 52 (Services W to Figueroa St)
27	Ave 43, Figueroa St, Los Angeles (Auto Serv/Gas/Groc W to Figueroa St)
(26B)	Figueroa St (NB, Left Exit), Jct I-5, N to Sacramento, S to Santa Ana (SB)
(26A)	Jct I-5, N to Sacramento (NB, Left Exit), Ave 26 (SB)
25	Solano Ave, Academy Rd
24D	Stadium Way, Dodger Stadium (SB)
24C	Hill St, Civic Center (SB, Left exit)
24B	Hill St, Stadium Way, Dodger Stadium (NB), Sunset Blvd, Figueroa St (SB)
Gas	Chevron
Food	Full House Seafood, Golden City
Lodg	Best Western, Royal Pagoda Motel
Other	ATMs, Banks, Grocery, Pavilion
24A	US 101, N to Hollywood, S to I-5S, I-10E, Santa Ana, San Bernardino
23C	3rd St
23B	4th St, 3rd St, 6th St, Downtown
Other	ATMs, Auto Services, Banks, LA Chamber of Commerce, Museums, Theatres, Visitor & Conv Bureau, Wells Fargo Center I & II, World Trade Center LA
23A	6th St (NB), Wilshire Blvd (SB)
Food	Pacific Grill, Starbucks, Cafe Wilshire
Lodg	Wilshire Grand Hotel, City Center, Motel De Ville
Med	W: + Good Samaritan Hospital
Other	ATMs, Banks, LA Visitor & Conv Bureau
22B	8th St, 9th St (SB)
Other	Avis RAC
22A	Olympic Blvd (SB) (Rest/Lodging E to Figuaro St)
Other	ATMs, Banks, CarWash, Museum, LA Conv Center, Staples Center
22	9th St, 6th St, Downtown (NB)
NOTE:	NB continue as CA 110, SB start

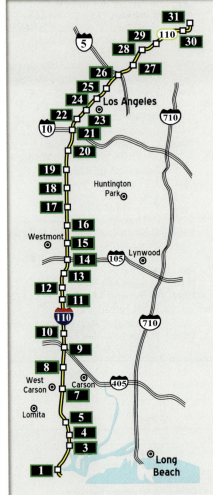

EXIT	CALIFORNIA
(21)	Jct I-10, W to Santa Monica, E to San Bernardino
20C	Adams Blvd
Gas	Mobil
Food	Popeye's, Quiznos, Taco Bell, 2-4-1 Pizza
Other	Banks, Grocery, Midas
20B	Exposition Blvd
Gas	Chevron
Food	Sizzler
Lodg	Radisson
Other	LA Expo Park
20A	MLK Jr Blvd
Gas	Chevron
Food	La Pizza Loca, McDonald's, Subway
19B	Vernon Ave (SB)
Gas	Mobil, Shell
Food	Burger King, China Express, JackintheBox
Other	Grocery, Auto Services, Ralph's
19A	51st St (SB)
19	Vernon Ave (NB)
18B	Slauson Ave, Los Angeles
Gas	Mobil
18A	Gage Ave
Gas	ArcoAmPm, Valero
17	Florence Ave
Gas	Mobil, ArcoAmPm, Chevron, Shell
Food	Golden Ox, Jack in the Box, McDonald's

EXIT	CALIFORNIA
16	Manchester Ave
Gas	ArcoAmPm, Circle K
Food	El Pollo Loco, McDonald's, Church's, Chinatown Express, Jack in the Box, Popeye's
Other	Banks, Grocery, PepBoys, Ralph's
15	Century Blvd (SB)
Gas	ArcoAmPm, Shell
(14B)	Jct I-105W, Imperial Hwy, Century Blvd, to El Segundo
(14A)	Jct I-105E, to Norwalk
13	El Segundo Blvd, Gardena
Food	Ceasars Rest, La Perla Tacos, Taco Bell
12	Rosecrans Ave
FStop	333 E Rosecrans: Gardena Truck Stop
Gas	ArcoAmPm, Chevron, Mobil, Valero
Food	Jack in the Box, Long John Silver, Subway
11	Redondo Beach Blvd
Gas	76, Mobil
Med	W: + Memorial Hospital of Gardenia
10B	CA 91W, Artesia Blvd, Redondo Beach (NB)
10A	CA 91E, Anaheim, Riverside (NB)
10	CA 91, E - Anaheim, Riverside, W - Artesia Blvd, Redondo Bch (SB)
Food	Jack in the Box, McDonald's, Taco Bell
Other	Albertson's, Sam's Club
(9)	Jct I-405, San Diego Fwy, N to Santa Monica, S to Long Beach, 190th St (SB)
8	Torrance Blvd, Del Amo Blvd
Gas	Mobil, Shell◆
Food	Burger King, Starbucks
7B	Carson St (SB)
Gas	76, Mobil, Shell
Food	In 'n Out Burger, JackintheBox, Starbucks
Med	W: + LA Co Harbor UCLA Med Center
7A	223rd St
7	Carson St (NB)
5	Sepulveda Blvd
Gas	ArcoAmPm, Mobil
Food	Burger King, Carl's Jr, McDonald's, Popeye's, Starbucks, Taco Bell
Other	Albertson's, Home Depot, Staples, Target, RiteAid, Von's, ATMs, Banks
4	CA 1, Pacific Coast Hwy
Gas	Chevron, Mobil, Shell, PCH Quick Corner
Food	Alberta's Mex, Denny's, Jack in the Box
Lodg	Best Western, Islander Motel, W Coast Inn
Med	W: + Hospital
3B	Anaheim St, Wilmington
Gas	ArcoAmPm
Food	Boston Cream, Golden Kitchen
3A	C St, Harry Bridges Blvd
Gas	Shell◆
1B	Channel St, John S Gibson Blvd, Gaffey St, San Pedro
Gas	ArcoAmPm, Chevron
(1A)	CA 47, Vincent Thomas Bridge, Terminal Island

ⓘ CALIFORNIA

Begin Northbound I-110 from CA 47 to Jct I-10 in Los Angeles

◆ = Regular Gas Stations with Diesel ▲ = RV Friendly Locations ♥ = Pet Friendly Locations
RED PRINT SHOWS LARGE VEHICLE PARKING/ACCESS ON SITE OR NEARBY   BROWN PRINT SHOWS CAMPGROUNDS/RV PARKS

EXIT	KANSAS
	Begin Southbound I-135 from I-70 near Salina to Jct I-35, South of Wichita, KS.

⛽ KANSAS
(I-135 Begins/Ends on I-70, Ex #250)

EXIT		KANSAS
(95AB)		Jct I-70, E-Kansas City, W-Denver, US 40, US 81, Topeka
93		KS 140, State Rd
92		Crawford St
	Gas	BP◊, Citgo, Shell, Phillips 66◊
	Food	E: Blimpie, Braum's, Subway, Taco Bell, Western Sizzlin
	Lodg	E: Best Western, Comfort Inn, Fairfield Inn, Holiday Inn, Super 8
		W: Red Coach Inn
	Other	E: Grocery, Walgreen's
90		Magnolia Rd
	Gas	Phillips 66◊, Shell, Conoco
	Food	E: Burger King, Carlos O'Kelly's, Chili's, Golden Corral, Hong Kong Buffet, IHOP, McDonald's, Sonic, Subway
	Lodg	E: Country Inn
	Other	E: Mall, Grocery, Advance Auto, Auto Dealers
89		Schilling Rd
	Gas	Shell◊, Casey's
	Food	E: Applebee's, Burger King, Fazoli's, Pizza Hut, Red Lobster, Sonic, Tuscon's
	Lodg	Candlewood Suites, Country Inn, Hampton Inn
		W: Baymont Inn
	Other	E: Grocery, Lowe's, Sam's Club, Target, Wal-Mart sc
88		9th St, Schilling Rd
86		KS 141, Harrington, Smolan
82		KS 4, Salun Rd
78		Bus 81, KS 4, Lindsborg, Roxbury
	Gas	E: Shell
	Food	E: DQ/Stuckey's
72		Bus 81, Lindsborg, Roxbury
(68)		Rest Area (Both dir, Left exit) (RR, Phone, Picnic, RVDump)
65		Pawnee Rd
60		US 56, Bus 81, McPherson, Marion
	Gas	W: Conoco◊, Phillips 66
	Food	W: Applebee's, Arby's, Braum's, KFC, McDonald's, Perkins, Pizza Hut, Subway Taco Tico
	Lodg	W: Best Value Inn, Best Western, Days Inn, Red Coach Inn, Super 8
	Med	W: + Hospital
	Other	W: Wal-Mart sc, AutoZone
58		KS 61, Hutchinson, McPherson
54		Elyria
48		KS 260, Moundridge
	Other	Spring Lake RV Resort▲
46		KS 260, Moundridge
40		Lincoln Blvd, Hesston
	Gas	W: Cenex◊, Save-A-Trip
	Food	W: Pizza Hut, Sonic, Subway
	Lodg	AmericInn, Hesston Inn
	Other	W: Cottonwood Grove Campground▲

EXIT		KANSAS
34		KS 15, N Newton, Abilene
	Food	W: Subway
33		US 50E, Peabody, Emporia (NB)
32		Broadway Ave
31		1st St
	Gas	E: AmPride, Conoco◊, Shamrock, Shell
	Food	E: Applebee's, Pancake House, KFC

EXIT		KANSAS
	Lodg	Days Inn, Super 8, Best Western
	Other	E: Auto Dealers
30		US 50, KS 15, Newton, Hutchinson
	Gas	W: Phillips 66◊
	Med	W: + Hospital
	Other	W: AutoZone, Grocery, Wal-Mart sc, to Spring Lake RV Resort▲
28		SE 36th St, Newton
	Food	W: Burger King, Taco Bell
	Other	W: Newton Outlet Mall
25		KS 196, White Water, El Dorado
(23)		Rest Area (Both dir) (RR, Phone, Picnic, Vend, RVDump)
22		125th St, Sedgewick
19		101st St
	Other	Wagons HO RV Park▲
17		KS Coliseum, Valley Ctr, 85th St
	Other	E: Kansas Coliseum
16		77th St
	Other	E: Wichita Greyhound Park
14		61st St, Kechi
	Gas	QT◊, Coastal, Phillips 66◊
	Food	E: Applebee's, Cracker Barrel, Taco Bell
		W: KFC, McDonald's
	Lodg	E: Comfort Inn
		W: Super 8
13		53rd St
	Gas	Phillips 66
	Food	Country Kitchen
	Lodg	Best Western, Days Inn
(11AB)		Jct I-235W, KS 254, Hutchinson
10AB		KS 96E, 29th St
9		21st St, Wichita State Univ
8		13th St
7B		8th St, 9th St
7A		Central Ave
6C		1st St, 2nd St
6AB		US 54, US 400, Kellogg Ave
5B		Wichita
5A		Lincoln St
	Gas	W: QT
4		Harry St
	Gas	QT, BP
	Food	E: Denny's, McDonald's, Wendy's
3B		Pawnee St
3A		KS 15, SE Blvd
2		Hydraulic Ave
	Gas	E: QT
	Food	E: McDonald's, Subway
(1C)		Jct I-235N
1AB		47th St, US 81S
	Gas	Coastal, Conoco, Phillips 66
	Food	W: Applebee's, Burger King, KFC, Long John Silver, McDonald's, Subway
	Lodg	E: Comfort Inn, Days Inn, Holiday Inn Express
		W: Best Western, Red Carpet Inn
	Other	W: Grocery, Kmart, O'Reilly's

⛽ KANSAS
Begin NB I-135 from Jct I-35 near Wichita to Jct I-70 near Salina, KS.

◊ = Regular Gas Stations with Diesel ▲ = RV Friendly Locations ♥ = Pet Friendly Locations
RED PRINT SHOWS LARGE VEHICLE PARKING/ACCESS ON SITE OR NEARBY BROWN PRINT SHOWS CAMPGROUNDS/RV PARKS

Page 537

EXIT	MICHIGAN
	Begin I-196 on I-94 at Benton Harbor to I-96 in E Grand Rapids

MICHIGAN
(I-196 Begins/Ends on I-94, Ex #34)

(0)		Jct I-94, E - Detroit, W - Chicago
1		Red Arrow Hwy
	Other	N: Ross Field Airport ✈
4		Riverside, to Coloma
	Gas	S: Marathon◇
	Other	S: Coloma/St Joseph KOA▲
7		MI 63, to Benton Harbor
13		to Covert
	Other	N: Van Buren State Park, CAMP▲
18		MI 140, MI 43, to Watervliet
	Gas	N: Shell◇, Speedway
	Food	N: Ma's Coffeepot Rest, Burger King, McDonald's, Pizza Hut
	Lodg	N: Budget Lodge
	Other	N: Auto Dealers
20		Rd A-2, Phoenix Rd
	Gas	N: BP, Marathon◇ S: BP
	Food	N: Arby's, Taco Bell S: McDonald's, Wendy's
	Lodg	N: Southaven Motel S: Hampton Inn, Holiday Inn Express
	Med	N + Hospital
	Other	N: AutoZone, MI State Hwy Patrol Post S: Wal-Mart sc
22		N Shore Dr
	Other	N: to Kal Haven Trail State Park
(25)		Rest Area (EB) (RR, Phone, Picnic, Vend)
26		109th Ave, to Pullman
30		Rd A-2, Glenn, Ganges
34		MI 89, to Fennville
	Gas	S: Shell
36		Rd A-2, Ganges
	Gas	N: Shell
	Lodg	N: AmericInn
41		Rd A-2, Douglas, Saugatuck
	Gas	N: Marathon◇, Shell◇
	Food	N: Burger King
	Lodg	N: AmericInn, Holiday Inn Express
	Other	N: Saugatuck State Park, Saugatuck RV Resort▲
(43)		Rest Area (WB) (RR, Phone, Picnic, Vend)
44		US 31N, to Holland (EB)
	Med	N: + Hospital
	Other	N: to Oak Grove Campground▲ Resort▲, Drew's Country Camping
49		MI 40, to Allegan
	TStop	S: Tulip City Marathon
	Gas	N: BP◇
	Food	N: McDonald's/BP
52		16th St, Adams St
	Gas	N: Meijer◇, Speedway S: Mobil◇

EXIT	MICHIGAN
	Food	N: Wendy's S: Burger King
	Lodg	N: Best Inn, Econo Lodge
	Med	N: + Hospital
55		Byron Rd, Zeeland
	Gas	N: 7-11
	Food	N: McDonald's
	Med	N: + Hospital
	Other	N: Dutch Treat Camping & Rec▲
(58)		Rest Area (EB) (RR, Phone, Picnic, Vend)
62		32nd Ave, to Hudsonville
	Gas	N: BP◇ S: Mobil◇
	Food	N: Arby's, McDonald's, Village Seafood & Grill S: Subway
	Lodg	N: Super 8 S: AmeriHost Inn
64		MI 6E, to Lansing
67		44th St
	Gas	N: Mobil◇
	Food	N: Burger King, Cracker Barrel, Steak 'n Shake
	Lodg	N: Comfort Suites
	Other	N: Wal-Mart S: Discount Tire, Gander Mountain, Lowes
69AB		Chicago Dr
	Gas	N: Meijer◇ S: BP, Speedway
	Food	N: KFC, McDonald's, Perkins, Subway S: Arby's, Pizza Hut, Wendy's
	Lodg	S: Best Western, Holiday Inn Express
	Other	N: AutoZone, Target, Grocery
70AB		MI 11, Grandville, Walker (WB, Left exit)
	Gas	S: BP◇, Shell, Speedway
	Food	S: Arby's, Logan's Roadhouse
	Lodg	S: Lands Inn Hotel
72		Jct I-196 Bus, Chicago Dr E (EB)
	Other	E: to GM Delphi Plant, Reynolds Metal Factory
73		Market Ave, Grand Rapids
	Other	N: to Vanandel Arena
75		MI 45W, Lake Michigan Dr
	Other	N: to Grand Valley St Univ
76		MI 45E, Lane Ave
	Gas	S: BP
	Other	S: Gerald R Ford Museum, John Ball Park & Zoo
77AB		US 131, S-Kalamazoo, N-Cadillac
77C		Ottawa Dr
	Other	S: Gerald Ford Museum
78		College Ave
	Gas	S: Dairy Mart, Marathon
	Food	S: McDonald's
	Med	S: + Hospital
79		Fuller Ave
	Other	N: Sheriff's Dept

MICHIGAN

Begin I-196 on I-96 in E Grand Rapids to I-94, Ex #34 in Benton Harbor.

◇ = Regular Gas Stations with Diesel   ▲ = RV Friendly Locations   ♥ = Pet Friendly Locations
RED PRINT SHOWS LARGE VEHICLE PARKING/ACCESS ON SITE OR NEARBY   BROWN PRINT SHOWS CAMPGROUNDS/RV PARKS

INTERSTATE 275

EXIT	FLORIDA
	Begin I-275 on I-75 in Tampa to I-75 in St Petersburg

FLORIDA

53 Bearss Ave
- Gas: Citgo, BP, RaceTrac, Shell
- Food: Burger King, McDonald's, Perkins, Subway, Wendy's
- Lodg: Quality Inn
- Other: Albertson's, Pharmacy

52 Fletcher Ave
- Gas: RaceTrac, BP, Citgo
- Lodg: Days Inn, Super 8

51 FL 582, Fowler Ave
- Gas: Citgo, Shell
- Food: Burger King, Denny's, McDonald's, Ponderosa, Subway, Waffle House
- Lodg: Howard Johnson, Quality Inn, Motel 6 ♥

50 FL 580, Busch Blvd
- Gas: Chevron, Exxon, Marathon, Shell
- Food: Burger King, KFC, Wendy's
- Lodg: Comfort Inn
- Other: Busch Gardens, Wal-Mart, Home Depot

49 Bird Ave (NB)
- Gas: Shell
- Food: KFC, Wendy's

48 Sligh Ave
- Gas: BP, Marathon
- Other: Zoo

47AB US 92, to US 41S, Hillsborough Ave
- Gas: Citgo, Valero, BP
- Food: Burger King, Wendy's

46B FL 574, MLK Blvd
- Gas: BP, Chevron, Marathon
- Food: McDonald's
- Med: W: + Hospital
- Other: Grocery

46A Floribraska Ave

(45B) Jct I-4E, to Orlando, I-75

45A Jefferson St

44 Ashley Dr, Tampa St

42 Howard Ave, Armenia Ave
- Gas: Citgo, BP, Shell

41C Himes Ave (SB)
- Other: Raymond James Stadium

41AB US 92, Dale Mabry Ave
- Gas: BP, Exxon, Mobil, Shell
- Food: Carrabba's, Krystal, Ruby Tuesday, Village Inn, Bennigan's, Chili's, Denny's, Longhorn Steakhouse, KFC, Sweet Tomatos, Waffle House
- Lodg: Courtyard, Days Inn, Westin Suites
- Other: to MacDill AFB, Best Buy, Home Depot, Grocery, Wal-Mart

40B Lois Ave
- Gas: Shell
- Lodg: DoubleTree Hotel, Sheraton

40A FL 587, Westshore Blvd
- Gas: Citgo, Shell
- Food: Steak & Ale, Waffle House, Durango
- Lodg: Embassy Suites, Best Western, Marriott, SpringHill Suites

39AB FL 60W
- Food: Outback Steakhouse
- Lodg: Clarion Hotel
- Other: to Airport ✈

EXIT	FLORIDA

32 FL 687S, 4th St N, to US 92

31B FL 688W, Ulmerton Rd, to Largo, Seminole, Beaches, Airport (Gas, Food, Lodg on FL 688W)

31A 9th ST N, MLK St (SB, Left exit)

30 FL 686, Roosevelt Blvd

28 FL 694W, Gandy Blvd, Indian Shores
- Other: Roberts M/H & RV Resort▲, Greyhound Racetrack

28AB 54th Ave N, St Petersburg
- Gas: Citgo, Racetrac
- Food: Cracker Barrel, Waffle House
- Lodg: Days Inn, Ramada Inn

25 38th Ave N, to Beaches
- Gas: Citgo
- Food: Burger King, McDonald's

24 22nd Ave N
- Gas: 7-11, Racetrac
- Other: Home Depot, Lowe's

23B FL 595, 5th Ave N
- Med: E: + Hospital

(23A) I-375, Downtown St Petersburg
- Other: The Pier

(22) Jct I-175E, to Tropicana Field, Downtown St Petersburg

21 28th St S, Downtown

20 31st Ave (NB)

19 22nd Ave S, Gulfport
- Gas: Citgo

18 26th Ave S (NB)

17 FL 682W, 54th Ave S, Pinellas Bayway, St Pete Beach
- Gas: 7-11, Sunoco
- Food: Bob Evans, Taco Bell, Wendy's
- Lodg: Bayway Inn
- Other: Pharmacy, Grocery, to Beaches

16 Pinellas Pt Dr, Skyway Lane

(16) TOLL Plaza (SB)

(13) N Sunshine Skyway Fishing Pier
- W: Rest Area (Both dir) (RR, Phone, Picnic, Vend)

(7) S Sunshine Skyway Fishing Pier
- E: Rest Area (Both dir) (RR, Phone, Picnic, Vend)

(6) TOLL Plaza (NB)

5 US 19, to Palmetto, Bradenton

2 US 41, Palmetto, Bradenton

(0) I-275 Begins / Ends on I-75

FLORIDA

Begin I-275 on I-75 in near Bradenton to I-75 in Tampa

◆ = Regular Gas Stations with Diesel   ▲ = RV Friendly Locations   ♥ = Pet Friendly Locations

RED PRINT SHOWS LARGE VEHICLE PARKING/ACCESS ON SITE OR NEARBY   BROWN PRINT SHOWS CAMPGROUNDS/RV PARKS

Page 539

EXIT	MICHIGAN
	Begin I-275 on I-96 near Detroit to I-75, near Monroe, MI

MICHIGAN

NOTE: I-275 runs below with I-96 for 10 mi. Exit #'s follow I-96.

Exit	Description
(163)	Jct I-696, M 5, Grand River Ave (EB)
164	M 5N, 12 Mile Rd (EB)
165	M 5N, 12 Mile Rd (WB)
167	8 Mile Rd, Baseline Rd, Northville
Gas	S: Speedway, Meijer◊, Costco
Food	S: Benihana, Big Boy, Chili's, McDonald's, Kyoto Japanese Steakhouse, On the Border, Taco Bell
Lodg	S: Hampton Inn, Hilton, Ramada, Sheraton
Med	S: + Hospital
Other	S: Best Buy, Costco, Firestone, Home Depot, Grocery, Target
169A	7 Mile Rd West, Livonia
169B	7 Mile Rd East, Livonia
169AB	7 Mile Rd, Livonia
Food	N: Lone Star Steakhouse, Rest/Embassy Suites
	S: Cooker, Romano's Macaroni Grill
Lodg	N: Embassy Suites
	S: AmeriSuites
Other	S: Home Depot
170	6 Mile Rd, Livonia
Gas	S: AmocoBP, Mobil
Food	N: Denison's, Max & Erma's, Red Robin, The Ground Round
	S: Applebee's, McDonald's, Ital Rest
Lodg	N: Best Western, Courtyard, Holiday Inn, Marriott, Quality Inn
	S: Fairfield Inn, Residence Inn
Other	N: Mall
	S: CVS, Office Depot
(172/29)	Jct I-275S, to Toledo, M 14 W Jct I-96E, to Detroit, M 14W, to Ann Arbor

NOTE: I-275 abobe runs with I-96 for 10 mi. Exit #'s follow I-96.

EXIT	MICHIGAN
28	Ann Arbor Rd, Plymouth
Gas	BP, Shell
Food	Denny's, Dunkin Donuts, Bennigan's Burger King, Steak & Ale
Lodg	Days Inn, Red Roof Inn♥, Quality Inn

EXIT	MICHIGAN
25	M 153, Ford Rd, Garden City, Westland, Canton
Gas	BP, Shell, Speedway, Sunoco◊
Food	Arby's, Bob Evans, Chili's, Chuck E Cheese, Dunkin Donuts, KFC, Little Caesars, Olive Garden, Outback Steak House, Tim Hortons, Wendy's, White Castle
Lodg	Baymont Inn, Extended Stay America, Fairfield Inn, Motel 6♥
Other	Discount Tire, Kmart, Target
(23)	Rest Area (NB) (RR, Phone, Picnic, Info)
22	US 12, Michigan Ave, to Wayne, Ypsilanti, Dearborn, Canton
Gas	BP, Mobil◊, Shell, Speedway, Marathon◊
Food	McDonald's, Subway, Wendy's
Lodg	Days Inn, Holiday Inn Express, Super 8
20	Ecorse Rd, to Romulus
Gas	Mobil◊
Food	Burger King/Mobil
Other	Willow Run Airport
(17)	Jct I-94, E-Detroit, W-Ann Arbor, (W to Detroit Metro Airport)
15	Eureka Rd, to Detroit Metro Airport
13	Sibley Rd, New Boston
11A	S Huron Rd East (SB)
11B	S Huron Rd West (SB)
11	S Huron Rd
Gas	Sunoco◊
Food	Burger King/Sunoco
8	Will Carleton Rd, to Flat Rock
5	Carleton, S Rockwood
(4)	Rest Area (SB) (RR, Phone, Picnic)
2	US 24, to Telegraph Rd
Gas	Marathon◊
(0/20)	Jct I-75, Detroit, Toledo, Ohio

MICHIGAN

 E

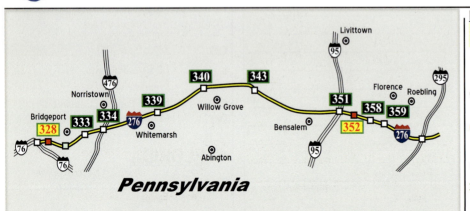

EXIT	PENNSYLVANIA
	Begin Eastbound I-276 from Jct I-76 in Philadelphia, PA to NJ Tpk /NJ State Line

PENNSYLVANIA
(EASTERN TIME ZONE)

Exit	Description
(326)	Jct I-76E, to US 202, Valley Forge, Philadelphia
(328)	King of Prussia Service Plaza (WB)
FStop	Sunoco
Food	Breyer's, Hot Dog City, McDonald's
(330)	PA State Hwy Patrol Post (EB)
333	Germantown Pike, to I-476S, Norristown
Gas	N: Mobil

Page 540 ◊ = Regular Gas Stations with Diesel   ▲ = RV Friendly Locations   ♥ = Pet Friendly Locations
RED PRINT SHOWS LARGE VEHICLE PARKING/ACCESS ON SITE OR NEARBY   BROWN PRINT SHOWS CAMPGROUNDS/RV PARKS

EXIT		PENNSYLVANIA
	S:	Circle K
Lodg	N:	Springhill Suites
Med	N:	+ Hospital
Other	N:	Mall
(334)		Jct I-476N, Allentown (EB), Jct I-476, Philadelphia, Chester, Allentown (WB)
339		PA 309, Ft Washington, Philadelphia, Ambler
Gas	N:	Circle K, Mobil
Lodg	N:	Best Western, Holiday Inn
Other	N:	Montgomery Mall, Ft Washington Expo Center, Temple Univ/Ambler Campus
340		Virginia Dr, Ft Washington (WB) (EZ Pass only, NO Trucks)
343		PA 611, Willow Grove, Doylestown, Jenkintown
Gas	N:	Mobil
	S:	7-11, Hess, Mobil, Shell

EXIT		PENNSYLVANIA
Food	S:	Bennigan's, Friendly's, McDonald's
Lodg	S:	Hampton Inn
Other	S:	ATMs, Auto Services, Best Buy, Staples, Peddlers Village, Penn's Purchase Factory Outlets, Penn State Univ/Abington Campus, Willow Grove Park
351		US 1, to I-95, Philadelphia, Trenton
Gas	S:	AmocoBP, Exxon, Sunoco
Food	N:	Bob Evans, Ruby Tuesday
Lodg	N:	Hampton Inn, Holiday Inn
	S:	Comfort Inn, Howard Johnson, Knights Inn
Other	S:	ATMs, Banks, Target, Neshaminy Mall, Oxford Valley Mall, Franklin Mills, Sesame Place, Philadelphia Park Racetrack
(352)		N Neshaminy Service Plaza (WB)
FStop		Sunoco
Food		Burger King, Nathan's Express, Starbucks
(353)		FUTURE: Phila Park Slip Ramp (EB) (E-Z Pass only)

EXIT		PENNSYLVANIA
(355)		FUTURE: PA TPK/I-95/I-195 Interchange
358		US 13, Delaware Valley, Bristol, Levittown
Fstop	S:	Lukoil
Gas	N:	WaWa
	S:	Getty, Mobil
Food	S:	Burger King, Italian Rest, McDonald's
Lodg	N:	Days Inn, Ramada Inn
Other	S:	LP/Lukoil
(359)		Delaware River Bridge, NJ Tpk, to NY City, NY; Wilmington, DE
NOTE:		TOLL Plaza (End EB, Begin WB) (EB End, WB Begin Call Box for 34 mi)

(EASTERN TIME ZONE)

PENNSYLVANIA
Begin Westbound I-276 from NJ / PA Border to Jct I-76 near King of Prussia, PA.

EXIT		GEORGIA
		Begin I-285 ByPass around Atlanta, GA from Jct I-85, South of Atlanta.

GEORGIA

1		Washington Rd, Atlanta
Gas		BP, Chevron, Texaco ◊
Food		Sunny Garden Family Buffet
Lodg		Mark Inn, Regency Inn
2		Camp Creek Pkwy, Atlanta Airport
Gas		BP, BP, Exxon, Shell, Texaco
Food		Checkers, McDonald's, Carino's, Chick-Fil-A, Jason's Deli, Longhorn Steak House, Panda Express, Red Lobster, Ruby Tuesday, Wendy's
Lodg		Clarion, Comfort Inn
Other		BJ's, Circuit City, Lowe's, PetSmart♥, Staples, Target, Walgreen's, Convention Center, Hartfield Jackson Atlanta Int'l Airport✈
5AB		GA 166W, Lakewood Freeway, GA 154S, Campbellton Rd
Gas		BP, Citgo◊, Conoco, Raceway, Shell ◊
Food		Burger King, Checkers, IHOP, KFC, Pizza Hut, Mrs Winner's, Starbucks, Taco Bell, Wendy's
Other		Greenbriar Mall, CVS, Goodyear, Kmart, Firestone, Family Dollar, Kroger, AutoZone, Vet♥, to Fort McPherson
7		Cascade Rd, Atlanta
Gas		BP, Chevron, Marathon, Phillips 66, Shell
Food		Applebee's, KFC, McDonald's, Pizza Hut, Starbucks, Subway, Wendy's
Med	W:	+ Hospital
Other		Home Depot, Publix, Kroger, Tires Plus
9		GA 139, ML King Jr Dr, Atlanta
Gas		Amoco, Phillips 66, Chevron, Shell
Food		McDonald's, Mrs Winner's
Other		Grocery, to Fulton Co Airport Brown Field✈
(10A)		Jct I-20, E-Atlanta (SB, Left exit)

EXIT		GEORGIA
(10B)		Jct I-20, W-Birmingham (NB, Left exit)
Other		to Six Flags
12		US 78, US 278, Bankhead Hwy
TStop	E:	Petro Stopping Center #22 (Scales)

EXIT		GEORGIA
Gas		BP, Citgo◊
Food	E:	Rest/Petro SC, McDonald's, Mrs Winner's
TWash	E:	Blue Beacon TW/Petro SC

◊ = Regular Gas Stations with Diesel   ▲ = RV Friendly Locations   ♥ = Pet Friendly Locations
RED PRINT SHOWS LARGE VEHICLE PARKING/ACCESS ON SITE OR NEARBY   BROWN PRINT SHOWS CAMPGROUNDS/RV PARKS

Interstate 285 — GEORGIA

EXIT	Services
	TServ: E: Petro SC, Quick Fleet Tire Sales
	Other: to Fulton Co Airport Brown Field ✈
13	**GA 70, Bolton Rd** (NB, No reacc)
15	**GA 280, S Cobb Dr, Smyrna**
	Gas: BP◊, Exxon, RaceTrac, Shell
	Food: Arby's, IHOP, Krystal, Mrs Winner's, McDonald's, Subway, Taco Bell, Waffle House
	Lodg: AmeriHost, Comfort Inn, Knights Inn, Microtel
	TServ: Kenworth
	Med: W: + Hospital
	Other: U-Haul
16	**S Atlanta Rd, Smyrna**
	TStop: S: Pilot Travel Center #344 (Scales)
	Gas: Shell◊, Exxon, Texaco
	Food: Waffle House; S: Wendy's/Pilot TC
	Lodg: Holiday Inn Express
	Other: S: RV Center
18	**Paces Ferry Rd SE, Atlanta, Vinings**
	Gas: BP, Chevron, QT, Shell
	Food: Blimpie, Mrs Winner's, Subway
	Lodg: Fairfield Inn, La Quinta Inn ♥, Hampton Inn, Wyndham
	Other: Publix, Pharmacy, Home Depot, Goodyear
19	**US 41, GA 3, Cobb Pkwy SE, to Dobbins AFB**
	Gas: BP, Chevron, Citgo, Shell
	Food: Arby's, Carrabba's, Denny's, Hardee's, McDonald's, Olive Garden, Red Lobster, Steak 'n Shake, Waffle House
	Lodg: Hilton, Holiday Inn, Hampton Inn, Red Roof Inn ♥, Sheraton, Wingate Inn
	Other: Auto Dealers, Mall, Target, Cobb Galleria Center
(20)	**Jct I-75, S to Atlanta, N to Chattanooga**
	Other: N: to Brookwood RV Resort▲
22	**New Northside Dr, Powers Ferry Rd**
	Gas: Shell, BP, Chevron
	Food: Bennigan's, Blimpie, McDonald's, Sideline Grill, Waffle House, Wendy's
	Lodg: Crowne Plaza, Hawthorne Inn
	Other: CVS
24	**Riverside Dr**
25	**US 19S, Roswell Rd, Sandy Springs**
	Gas: Chevron, Citgo, BP, Phillips 66, Shell◊
	Food: Burger King, Checkers, El Toro Mexican, IHOP, KFC, McDonald's, Pizza Hut, Ruth Chris Steak House, TGI Friday
	Lodg: Comfort Inn, Days Inn, Country Hearth Inn, Hampton Inn, Homestead Suites
	Med: S: + St Joseph's Hospital of Atlanta
	Other: Kmart, Firestone, NAPA, Office Depot, Auto Services, Tires Plus
26	**Glenridge Dr, Peachtree Dunwoody Rd** (EB exit, WB reacc)
27	**US 19N, GA 400** (SB, Toll Rd)
28	**Peachtree-Dunwoody Rd, Glenridge Dr.** (WB exit, EB reaccess)
	Food: Burger King, McDonald's
	Med: + Hospital
	Other: Pharmacy, Publix, Mall
29	**Ashford-Dunwoody Rd**
	Gas: Amoco, Exxon, Chevron, Conoco
	Food: Applebee's, Burger King, Mrs Winner's, Subway
	Lodg: Fairfield Inn, Holiday Inn, Hilton Garden, Marriott, Residence Inn
	Other: Best Buy, Goodyear, Home Depot, Mall, Kroger, Firestone, Oglethorpe Univ
30	**Chamblee-Dunwoody Rd, N Shallowford Rd, N Peachtree Rd**
	Gas: BP, Exxon, Mobil, Phillips 66, Shell
	Food: Burger King, KFC, Mrs Winner's, Taco Bell, Wendy's, Waffle House
	Lodg: Holiday Inn
31AB	**GA 141, Peachtree Industrial Blvd, Chamblee**
	Food: Piccadilly Cafeteria, Red Lobster, Waffle House, Wendy's
	Other: Auto Dealers, CVS
32	**US 23, Beauford Hwy, Doraville**
	Gas: Amoco, Phillips 66◊
	Food: Arby's, Burger King, McDonald's, KFC, Mrs Winner's, Subway, Taco Bell
	Lodg: Comfort Inn
	Other: Firestone, Goodyear, Kmart, Target
(33)	**Jct I-85, N-Greenville, S-Atlanta**
34	**Chamblee-Tucker Rd**
	Gas: Chevron, Citgo, Phillips 66, Shell
	Food: Arby's, Mrs Winner's, KFC, Taco Bell, Lone Star Steakhouse, Waffle House
	Lodg: Days Inn
	Other: Pharmacy, Big Lots, Dollar Tree, Kroger
37	**GA 236, LaVista Rd, Tucker**
	Gas: BP◊, Chevron, Circle K, Shell, Texaco
	Food: Black Eyed Pea, Blimpie's, Checkers, Dunkin Donuts, Fuddrucker's, IHOP, Panera Bread, Piccadilly, Pizza Hut, Olive Garden, Red Lobster, Taco Bell, Steak & Ale, Waffle House
	Lodg: Comfort Suites, Country Inn, Days Inn, Fairfield Inn, Marriott, Masters Inn, Radisson, Ramada Inn, Starwood Hotel, Wyndham
	Other: Best Buy, Kroger, Pharmacy, Publix, Firestone, Office Depot, Target, Mall
38	**US 29, Lawrenceville Hwy**
	Gas: Amoco, Phillips 66, Shell, USA
	Food: Waffle House
	Lodg: Knights Inn, Masters Inn, Super 8
	Med: W: + Hospital
39AB	**US 78, GA 410, W to Decatur, E to Athens, to Stone Mountain**
	Other: E: to Stone Mountain Park▲
40	**E Ponce de Leon, Church St, Clarkston**
	Gas: Chevron, Shell◊, Texaco
	Food: Waffle House
41	**GA 10, Memorial Dr, Avondale Estates**
	Gas: Citgo, QT, Mobil, Shell◊
	Food: Applebee's, Arby's, Burger King, KFC, Hardee's, Waffle House, Wendy's
	Lodg: Savannah Suites, Comfort Inn
	Other: Auto Zone, Big 10 Tire, Firestone, Office Depot, U-Haul
43	**US 278, Covington Hwy.**
	Gas: BP, Chevron, Citgo◊, QT, Shell◊
	Food: Blimpie, Checkers, Hardee's, KFC, Mrs Winner's, Waffle House, Wendy's
	Lodg: Best Inn
44	**GA 260, Glenwood Rd, Decatur**
	Gas: Citgo, Shell
	Food: Burger King, Mrs Winner's
	Lodg: Glenwood Inn, Super 8
(46AB)	**Jct I-20, E-Atlanta, W-Augusta**
48	**GA 155, Flat Shoals Rd, Candler Rd.**
	Gas: Circle K, Marathon, QT, Shell◊
	Food: Arby's, Checkers, DQ, KFC, Pizza Hut, McDonald's, Taco Bell, Waffle King
	Lodg: Gulf American Inn, Econo Lodge, Ramada Inn
51	**Bouldercrest Rd, Atlanta**
	TStop: Pilot Travel Center #331 (Scales)
	Gas: Chevron
	Food: Wendy's/WiFi/Pilot TC, KFC
	Lodg: Knights Inn
(52)	**Jct I-675S, to Macon**
53	**US 23, GA 42, Conley, Ft Gillem**
	FStop: BP Food Shop; Citgo Food Mart
	TStop: Conoco Fuel Stop; Travel Center of America (Scales)
	Food: Rest/FastFood/TA TC, Popeye's, Wendy's
	Lodg: Econo Lodge
	TServ: TA TC /Tires
	Other: Laundry/WiFi/CB/TA TC
55	**GA 54, Jonesboro Rd (EB); US 19, US 41, Forest Park (WB)**
	Gas: AmocoBP, Citgo◊, RaceTrac, Shell◊
	Food: Arby's, McDonald's, Waffle House
	Lodg: Super 8
	Other: Home Depot, Atlanta Expo Center
(58)	**Jct I-75, N to Atlanta, S to Macon to US 19, US 41, Forest Park (EB)** (Serv on US 19S)
	Gas: BP, Chevron
	Food: Subway, Waffle House, Wendy's
	Lodg: Home Lodge, Sunset Lodge
59	**Clark Howell Hwy**
	Other: Atlanta Int'l Airport ✈, Air Cargo
60	**GA 139, Riverdale Rd, Atlanta**
	Gas: BP, Exxon, QT, Speedway, Shell◊
	Food: Burger King, Checker's, McDonald's, Waffle House, Wendy's
	Lodg: Best Western, Country Suites, Days Inn, Motel 6 ♥, Ramada, Microtel
	Other: Auto Services, Dollar General, Grocery, U-Haul
(61)	**Jct I-85, N-Atlanta, S-Montgomery** (Access All Serv 1st I-85N, Exit #71)
62	**GA 14, to GA 279, Old National Hwy**
	Gas: BP, Chevron, Exxon, Shell
	Food: Burger King, Checkers, KFC, Krystal, Longhorn Steakhouse, McDonald's, Mrs Winner's, Red Lobster, Taco Bell, Waffle House, Wendy's
	Lodg: Comfort Inn, Clarion, Days Inn, Fairfield Inn, La Quinta Inn ♥, Howard Johnson Express, Motel 6, Radisson, Red Roof Inn ♥
	Other: U-Haul, Auto Zone, Auto Repairs, Family Dollar, NAPA

⛽ GEORGIA

Begin I-285 Bypass around Atlanta from near Jct I-85, South of Atlanta, GA.

◊ = Regular Gas Stations with Diesel   ▲ = RV Friendly Locations   ♥ = Pet Friendly Locations
RED PRINT SHOWS LARGE VEHICLE PARKING/ACCESS ON SITE OR NEARBY   BROWN PRINT SHOWS CAMPGROUNDS/RV PARKS

INTERSTATE 294

ILLINOIS

EXIT	ILLINOIS
	Begin I-294 ByPass around Chicago.

⛽ ILLINOIS
(I-294 begins/ends on I-94)

NOTE: I-294 runs below with I-80 for 5 mi. Exit #'s follow I-80.

Exit	Description
(160B)	Jct I-80E / I-94E, to Indiana

NOTE: TOLL begins WB, Ends EB

Exit	Description
(160A)	Jct I-94W, to Chicago, IL 394S, to Danville (SB ex, NB entr)
(159)	**Lincoln Oasis**
FStop	Mobil
Food	Burger King
157	IL 1, Halsted St, 800W
156	Dixie Hwy (SB ex, NB entr)
(155/5)	Jct I-80W, to I-57, to Iowa; Jct I-294N, Tri State Toll Plaza

NOTE: I-294 runs above with I-80 for 5 mi. Exit #'s follow I-80

Exit	Description
(6)	163rd St TOLL Plaza
6	US 6, 159th St, Harvey
Gas	BP, Mobil, Shell, Clark, Marathon
Food	Burger King, Popeye's, Taco Bell
Lodg	Holiday Inn Express
Other	Auto Zone, Firestone, Grocery, Radio Shack, Walgreen's, U-Haul
12	IL 50, Cicero Ave, IL 83, Islip
Gas	BP, Gas City◇
Food	Boston Market, IHOP, Pizza Hut, Popeye's, Quiznos, Starbucks
Lodg	Baymont Inn, Hampton Inn
Other	Pep Boys, Best Buy
18	US 12, US 20, 95th St, 76th Ave, Hickory Hill, Oaklawn
Gas	7-11, Shell, Speedway
Food	Arby's, Denny's, Wendy's
Lodg	Exel Inn
Med	+ Hospital
Other	Walgreen's
(20)	83rd St TOLL Plaza (NB) 82nd St TOLL Plaza (SB)
21	US 12, US 20, US 45, LaGrange Rd, Il 171, Archer Ave (SB entr only)
22	75th St, Willow Springs Rd, La Grange
(23)	Jct I-55, to Chicago, St Louis
24	Wolf Rd (NB ex, SB entr)
(25)	**Hinsdale Oasis (Both dir)**
Gas	Mobil◇
28	US 34, Ogden Ave
Gas	BP, Shell
Food	Dunkin Donuts, McDonald's, Starbucks
Med	+ Hospital

Exit	ILLINOIS
(29)	Jct I-88W, Ronald Reagan Memorial Tollway, to Aurora (NB exit, SB entr)
29.5	Cermak Rd, 22nd St (SB, no reacc)
(30)	Cermak Rd TOLL Plaza
31	IL 38, Roosevelt Rd (NB ex, SB entr) (diff NB reaccess)
(32)	Jct I-290E, to Chicago
(34)	Jct I-290W, to US 20, IL 64, Rockford
(38)	**O'Hare Oasis (Both dir)**
Gas	Mobil◇
Food	Burger King
39	IL 19W, Irving Park Rd (SB ex, NB ent)
Gas	BP, Marathon
Food	Dunkin Donuts, McDonald's, Subway, Wendy's
Lodg	Comfort Suites, Candlewood Suites, Hampton Inn, Howard Johnson, Sheraton
(39)	Irving Park TOLL Plaza (SB)
(40)	Jct I-190W, River Rd, Des Plaines

Exit	ILLINOIS
(41)	Jct I-90, Rockford, Chicago
(42)	Touhy Ave TOLL Plaza (NB)
42	Touhy Ave (NB ex, SB entr)
44	US 14, Dempster St (NB, No reacc)
Med	E: + Hospital
45	IL 58, Golf Rd (SB ex, NB entr)
Gas	Citgo◇, Shell
Other	CVS, Best Buy, Target
49	Willow Rd
Gas	BP
Food	Burger King, Denny's, McDonald's, TGI Friday
Lodg	Courtyard, Doubletree Hotel, Fairfield Inn, Motel 6 ♥
(50.5-53)	Jct I-94E, Chicago
54	Lake Cook Rd (NB, no reaccess)

(I-294 begins/ends on I-94)

⛽ ILLINOIS

Begin I-294 ByPass around Chicago.

◇ = Regular Gas Stations with Diesel ▲ = RV Friendly Locations ♥ = Pet Friendly Locations

RED PRINT SHOWS LARGE VEHICLE PARKING/ACCESS ON SITE OR NEARBY BROWN PRINT SHOWS CAMPGROUNDS/RV PARKS

EXIT	MA / RI
	Begin Southbound I-295 at Jct I-95 near Attleboro, MA to Jct I-95 near Warwick, RI

⭘ MASSACHUSETTS
(Exit listings show MileMarker / Exit #)
(EASTERN TIME ZONE)
(I-295 begins/ends on I-95, Exit #4)

(3/2AB)		I-95, S-Providence, N-Boston
	Other	S to I-93, MA 128, Gillette Stadium
1.5/1AB		US 1, S-Pawtucket, N-Attleboro

⭕ MASSACHUSETTS
⭘ RHODE ISLAND
(Exit listings show MileMarker / Exit #)

23/11		RI 114, Diamond Hill Rd, Cumberland
	Gas	Shell
	Food	Dunkin Donuts, J's Deli
	Other	CVS, Diamond Hill State Park
21/10		RI 122, Mendon Rd, Cumberland
	Gas	Gulf
	Food	Burger King, McDonald's, Subway
	Other	CVS, Grocery
(20)		Weigh Station (Both dir)
19/9AB		RI 146, S-Lincoln, N-Woonsocket
	Other	E: N Central State Airport ✈
16/8AB		RI 7, S to N Providence, N to Smithfield
	Gas	7-11
	Other	E: N Central State Airport ✈

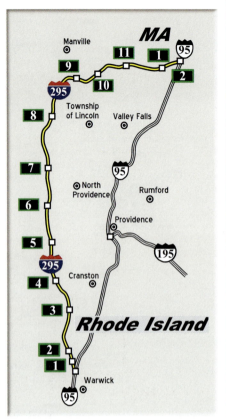

EXIT	RHODE ISLAND
13/7AB	US 44, E-Centerville, W-Greenville
Gas	Valero, Exxon, Mobil, Shell
Food	Applebee's, Burger King, Chili's, KFC, McDonald's, Pizza Hut, Subway
Med	E: + Hospital
Other	NAPA, CVS, Home Depot, Target
10/6ABC	US 6, US 6A, Johnston, Providence
Gas	7-11, Mobil, Shell
Food	Burger King, KFC, Wendy's
Lodg	HiWay Motel, Bel-Air Motor Inn
Other	Auto Dealers, AutoZone, CVS
8/5	RI Resource Recovery Indust Park
7/4	RI 14, Plainfield Pike, Johnston
4/3B	RI 37W, to RI 51, Phenix Ave
4/3A	RI 37E, to RI 2, Cranston
Other	E to TF Green State Airport ✈, RI Nat'l Guard
1/2	RI 2, Warwick, Cranston
Gas	Exxon, Mobil, Shell
Food	Chili's, Chuck E Cheese, Dunkin Donuts, Lone Star Steakhouse, McDonald's, Taco Bell, Subway, Wendy's
Other	Mall, Sam's Club, Wal-Mart, NAPA
0/1	RI 113, East Ave, to I-95N

⭕ RHODE ISLAND
(I-295 Begins/Ends on I-95, Exit #11)

EXIT	DE / NJ

⭘ DELAWARE
(I-295 begins/ends on I-95)

(14.5)		TOLL Plaza
14		DE 9, New Castle Ave, New Castle, to Wilmington
	Gas	BP, Citgo
	Food	McDonald's
	Lodg	Days Inn, Motel 6 ♥
	Other	Grocery, Harley Davidson, Pharmacy
13		Landers Lane (NB) US 13N, to Wilmington US 13S, US 40W, US 301S, New Castle, Dover, Baltimore, Norfolk
	Gas	BP, Exxon, Hess, Shell
	Food	Burger King, Denny's, Dunkin Donuts, IHOP, McDonald's, Taco Bell
	Lodg	Quality Inn
	Other	Grocery, Pep Boys
(12)		Jct I-95, I-495, Port of Wilmington, Philadelphia
		(I-295 begins/ends on I-95)

⭕ DELAWARE
⭘ NEW JERSEY
Begin Southbound I-295 from Jct I-95 to Jct I-195.

(1)		I-295N

EXIT	NEW JERSEY
1A	NJ 49, Canal St, Pennsville (NB)
1B	NJ 49, US 130, N Broadway (SB)
1C	N Hook Rd, I-295
2A	US 40W, to Delaware Bridge (NB)
2B	US 40E, Hawks Bridge Rd, NJ 14 to NJ Tpk, Penns Grove (NB)
TStop	Pilot Travel Center (Scales), Turnpike Mobil, Route 40 Truck Stop
Food	Subway/WiFi/Pilot TC
Lodg	Comfort Inn, Econolodge, Holiday Inn Express, Quality Inn, Wellesley Inn
2C	Hawks Bridge Rd, NJ 140, to US 130, Penns Grove, Deepwater (SB)
TStop	Flying J Travel Plaza (Scales)
Food	Rest/FastFood/Flying J TP
Med	+ Hospital
Other	Laundry/WiFi/RVDump/LP/FJ TP
(3)	Rest Area (NB) (RR, Phones, Picnic, Vend)
(4)	Weigh Station (NB)

EXIT	NEW JERSEY
4	NJ 48, Harding Hwy, Penns Grove, Woodstown
Other	Four Seasons Campground ▲
7	CR 643, Straughns Mill Rd, Pedricktown, Auburn
TStop	E: 295 Auto/Truck Plaza (Scales)
10	CR 620, Center Square Rd, Swedesboro
Gas	Exxon
Food	Applebee's, McDonald's, Subway
Lodg	Hampton Inn, Holiday Inn
Other	Supplies/Service
11	US 322, Swedesboro, Mullica Hill, Bridgeport
13	US 130S, to US 322W, Bridgeport
14	CR 684, Repaupo Station Rd, Repaupo
15	CR 607, Gibbstown, Harrisonville
16A	CR 653, Swedesboro, Paulsboro
16B	CR 551, Gibbstown, Mickleton
17	CR 680, Gibbstown, Mickleton
Gas	Mobil
Food	Burger King, Little Caesar's

Page 544

♦ = Regular Gas Stations with Diesel   ▲ = RV Friendly Locations   ♥ = Pet Friendly Locations
RED PRINT SHOWS LARGE VEHICLE PARKING/ACCESS ON SITE OR NEARBY   BROWN PRINT SHOWS CAMPGROUNDS/RV PARKS

EXIT	NEW JERSEY
Lodg	Ramada Inn
Other	Laundromat, Grocery, Pharmacy
18	Timberlane Rd, Clarksboro (NB)
Other	Timberlane Campground▲
18AB	CR 678, CR 667, Paulsboro, Mount Royal, Clarksboro
TStop	Travel Center of America/Exxon (Scales)
Food	Rest/TA TC, Wendy's, McDonald's
TServ	TA TC
Other	Laundry/WiFi/TA TC
19	CR 656, Mantua Grove Rd, Mantua, Paulsboro
20	Mid Atlantic Pky, to CR 643, NJ 44, Thorofare, Nat'l Park
21	NJ 44, Crown Pt Rd (SB), CR 640, Delaware St, Thorofare (NB)
Lodg	Highway Motel, Red Bank Inn
22	CR 644, Red Bank Ave, Thorofare, Redbank, Woodbury
Gas	Mobil
23	US 130N, Academy Ave, Westville, Gloucester, Woodbury
Lodg	Budget Motel
24A	NJ 45, Gateway Blvd, Westville (NB)
24B	CR 551, Broadway St, Westville (SB)
25AB	NJ 47, Delsea Dr, Westville (SB)
(26)	Jct I-76, NJ 42, to I-676, Bellmawr, Camden, Philadelphia
8	NJ 168, Black Horse Pike, to NJ Tpk, Bellmawr, Mt Ephraim
Gas	BP, Coastal, Exxon, Shell, Valero
Food	Burger King, Dunkin Donuts, Wendy's, McDonald's, Subway, Taco Bell
Lodg	Bellmawr Motel, Comfort Inn, Holiday Inn, Howard Johnson, Budget Inn
Other	Walgreen's, CVS, AutoZone
29AB	US 30, Copley Rd, Barrington, Berlin, Collingswood
Gas	BP, Exxon
Food	Dunkin Donuts, KFC, Subway
Med	E: + Hospital
Other	Home Depot, KMart, AutoZone
30	CR 669, Warwick Rd, Lawnside (SB)
31	Woodcrest Station
32	CR 561, Berlin Rd, Cherry Hill, Haddonfield, Voorhees
Gas	Shell
Food	Burger King
Med	E: + Hospital
34AB	NJ 70, Marlton Pike, Cherry Hill
Gas	BP, Exxon, Mobil, Shell
Food	Burger King, Denny's, Friendly's, Old Country Buffet, McDonald's, Steak & Ale
Lodg	Clarion, Extended Stay America, Marriott, Residence Inn
Med	W: + Hospital
36AB	NJ 73, Mt Laurel, Berlin, Tacony Bridge, to NJ Tpk
Gas	E: Exxon, Mobil W: Citgo, Exxon, Shell
Food	E: Bob Evans, Denny's, McDonald's W: Burger King, Dunkin Donuts, KFC, Pizza Hut, Ponderosa, Wendy's

EXIT	NEW JERSEY
Lodg	E: Comfort Inn, Econo Lodge, Fairfield Inn, Radisson, Red Roof Inn♥, Super 8 W: Motel 6♥, Bel-Air Motel, Quality Inn, Rodeway Inn, Track & Turf Motel
Other	Home Depot, Grocery, Firestone, Mall, Pep Boys, Lowe's, Pharmacy
40AB	NJ 38, Mt Holly, Moorestown
Gas	Exxon, Mobil
Food	Dunkin Donuts
Med	+ Hospital
Other	Target, U-Haul
43	CR 636, Creek Rd, Mt Laurel, Rancocas Woods, Delran
Gas	Exxon
45AB	CR 626, Rancocas Rd, Mt. Holly, Willingboro
Gas	Mobil
Med	+ Hospital
Other	E: Rancocas State Park
47AB	CR 541, Burlington-Mt Holly Rd, Burlington, Mt Holly
Gas	Exxon, Mobil, Hess
Food	Applebee's, Burger King, Chuck E Cheese, Cracker Barrel, McDonald's, Taco Bell, TGI Friday, Wendy's
Lodg	Best Western, Econo Lodge, Holiday Inn, Hampton Inn, Howard Johnson
Med	W: + Hospital
Other	Wal-Mart, AutoZone, Grocery, Mall
(50)	Rest Area (Both dir) (RR, Phone, Picnic, Vend)
52AB	CR 656, Florence Columbus Rd, Bordentown, Columbus, Florence

EXIT	NEW JERSEY
56	Rising Sun Rd, to US 206, to NJ Tpk, Fort Dix, McGuire AFB (NB)
TStop	Petro Stopping Center (Scales)
Food	IronSkillet/Petro SC
Other	Tires/TServ/Twash/Petro SC
57/AB	US 130, US 206, Bordentown
Gas	Mobil, Shell
Food	McDonald's, Rosario's Pizza
Lodg	Best Western, Comfort Inn, Days Inn, Ramada
Other	W: NJ State Hwy Patrol Post
(58)	Scenic Overlook (Both dir)
(60AB)	Jct I-195, to I-95, W to Trenton, E to Neptune
61AB	CR 620, Arena Dr, Trenton
62	Olden Ave (fr SB, no reaccess)
63AB	NJ 33W, Rd 535, Mercerville, Trenton
Gas	Mobil, Exxon
Food	Applebee's, McDonald's, Pizza Hut
64	NJ 535N, to NJ 33E (SB)
65AB	CR 649, Sloan Ave, Trenton
Gas	Exxon
Food	Burger King, Subway, Taco Bell
Other	CVS, Grocery
67AB	US 1, Brunswick Pike, Trenton (I-295 becomes I-95)

⊙ NEW JERSEY

Begin Southbound I-295 from Jct I-195 to Jct I-95.

◆ = Regular Gas Stations with Diesel   ▲ = RV Friendly Locations   ♥ = Pet Friendly Locations
RED PRINT SHOWS LARGE VEHICLE PARKING/ACCESS ON SITE OR NEARBY   BROWN PRINT SHOWS CAMPGROUNDS/RV PARKS

INTERSTATE 295

MAINE

EXIT — Begin Southbound I-295 at Jct I-95 near Gardiner, ME to Jct I-95 near Portland, ME

MAINE
(Exit listings show Mile Marker/Exit #)
(EASTERN TIME ZONE)
(I-295 begins/ends on I-95, Exit #102)

Exit	Description
51	ME 9, ME 126, Gardiner, to ME Tpk, I-95S
49	US 201, Gardiner
Other	KOA▲
43	ME 197, Richmond, Litchfield
37	ME 125, ME 138, Bowdoinham
Other	E: to Merrymeeting Field Airport✈
31AB	ME 196, New Lewiston Rd, Topsham S-Brunswick, N-Lisbon, Lewiston
Gas	Irving, J&S Oil Xpress Stop
Food	Arby's, Pasta Conn, Subway, Wendy's
28	to US 1, Coastal Rte, Brunswick, Bath (Serv E to US 1)
Med	+ Hospital
Other	to Brunswick Naval Air Station
24	US 1, Freeport (NB)
22	ME 125, ME 136, Freeport, Durham (Serv E to US 1)
Other	W: Blueberry Pond Campground▲, Cedar Haven Campground▲, Freeport/Durham KOA▲
20	Desert Rd, Freeport, to US 1 (Serv E to US 1)
Other	E: to Recompence Shore Campground▲ Flying Point Campground▲ W: Desert of Maine▲
17	US 1, Yarmouth, Freeport **Visitor Info Center/Rest Area** (NB: next Rest Area 80 mi)
Gas	Big Apple Food Store, Yarmouth Clipper Mart
15	US 1, Yarmouth, Cumberland (SB) (Serv W to US 1)
11	US 1, Yarmouth, Cumberland (NB) Falmouth Spur (SB)
10	Bucknam Rd, Falmouth, Cumberland (Serv E to US 1)
9	US 1N (NB), US 1S, ME 26N, Baxter Blvd (SB), Portland
8	ME 26 N, Washington Ave (NB), ME 26 S, Washington Ave (SB)
Other	Andover College
7	US 1A, Franklin Arterial, Portland
6B	US 1N, US 302W, ME 100N
6A	US 1, ME 100S, Univ of S ME
5AB	ME 22, Congress St
4	US 1N, Portland, Waterfront (NB) US 1S, S Portland (SB)
3	ME 9, Westbrook St, Airport (SB)
Other	to Portland Int'l Jetport✈
2	to US 1S, Scarborough (SB)
Other	to Portland Int'l Jetport✈
1	to US 1, S Portland (NB), to ME Tpk, Maine Mall Rd (SB) (Serv W/N to Maine Mall Rd)
(44)	I-295N, Portland, Downtown

(I-295 begins/ends on I-95, Exit #44)

MAINE

FLORIDA

EXIT — Begin I-295 from Jct I-95, Exit #362AB around Jacksonville to Jct I-95, Exit #337

FLORIDA
(I-295 begins/ends on I-95, Exit #362B)

Exit	Description
(35AB)	Jct I-95, S-Jacksonville, N-Savannah
33	CR 110, Duval Rd
Other	W: Jacksonville Int'l Airport✈
32	FL 115, Lem Turner Rd
Food	E: McDonald's, Subway, Wendy's
Other	E: Home Depot, Wal-Mart W: Flamingo Lake RV Resort▲
30	FL 104, Dunn Ave
Gas	Gate, Shell
Food	McDonald's
Other	Big Tree RV Park▲
28AB	US 1, US 23, Jacksonville
Gas	BP, Chevron, Gate, RaceTrac
Other	Amtrak
25	Pritchard Rd
Gas	W: Kangaroo
Food	W: Subway
22	Commonwealth Ave
Gas	Kangaroo, Sprint
Food	Burger King, Hardee's, Waffle House, Wendy's
Lodg	Holiday Inn
TServ	Kenworth, Freightliner, Cummins
Other	Grocery, Dogtrack
(21AB)	Jct I-10, W to Tallahassee, E to Jacksonville
19	FL 228, Normandy Blvd
Gas	BP, Shell, RaceTrac
Food	Golden Corral, McDonald's, Pizza Hut, Popeye's, Subway, Wendy's
Other	Walgreen's, Food Lion W: FL State Hwy Patrol Post
17	FL 208, Wilson Blvd
Gas	BP, Hess
16	FL 134, 103rd St, Cecil Field
Gas	BP, Exxon, Gate, Hess, Shell
Food	Arby's, Burger King, IHOP, McDonald's, Pizza Hut, Popeye's, Wendy's
Lodg	Hospitality Inn
Other	Wal-Mart, Goodyear, Walgreen's, U-Haul
12	FL 21, Blanding Blvd
Gas	BP, Chevron, Kangaroo, RaceTrac
Food	Burger King, Chili's, McDonald's, Denny's, Longhorn Steakhouse, Olive Garden, Steak & Ale, Taco Bell
Lodg	Economy Inn, Hampton, Inn, La Quinta Inn ♥, Motel 6 ♥, Red Roof Inn ♥
Other	Publix, Target, Home Depot, Walgreen's,
10	US 17, FL 15, Orange Park
Gas	BP, RaceTrac, Shell
Food	Cracker Barrel, Krystal, Long John Silver, McDonald's, Pizza Hut, Waffle House
Lodg	Comfort Inn, Days Inn, Econo Lodge, Holiday Inn, Quality Inn
Other	E: Jacksonville Naval Air Station, MIL/Jay RV Park▲
5/AB	FL 13, San Jose Blvd
Gas	Exxon, Shell, BP
Food	Applebee's, Arby's, Bob Evans, Chili's, Golden Corral, Hardee's, Pizza Hut
Lodg	Baymont Inn, Ramada Inn
Other	Albertson's, NAPA, Publix, Target, Walgreen's, U-Haul, Wal-Mart
3	Old St Augustine Rd
Gas	BP, Gate, Shell, Kangaroo
Food	Burger King, Denny's, McDonald's, Pizza Hut, Taco Bell
Lodg	Holiday Inn
Other	Lowe's, Walgreen's, Publix, MIL/Pelican Roost RV Park▲
(0)	I-95, N-Jacksonville, S-St Augustine

(I-295 begins/ends on I-95, Exit #337)

FLORIDA

Page 546
◆= Regular Gas Stations with Diesel   ▲ = RV Friendly Locations   ♥= Pet Friendly Locations
RED PRINT SHOWS LARGE VEHICLE PARKING/ACCESS ON SITE OR NEARBY   BROWN PRINT SHOWS CAMPGROUNDS/RV PARKS

EXIT	VIRGINIA
	Begin I-295 from Jct I-64 near Glen Allen to Jct I-95 near Petersburg, VA

⤓ VIRGINIA
(I-295 begins/ends on I-64, Exit #177)

Exit	Description
(53AB)	Jct I-64, E-Richmond, to US 250, W-Charlottesville
51AB	Nuckols Rd, Glen Allen
Gas	BP, Exxon
Other	CVS
49AB	US 33, Glen Allen, Richmond
45AB	Woodman Rd, Glen Allen
(43)	US 1, Brook Rd, Glen Allen (EB) I-95, N-Washington, S-Richmond (WB) (All Serv on US 1)
41AB	US 301, VA 2, Mechanicsville
Gas	BP, Exxon, Shell
Food	McDonald's, Burger King, Subway
38AB	Meadowbridge Rd, Pole Green Rd, Mechanicsville
Gas	BP, Citgo
37AB	US 360, Mechanicsville
Gas	7-11, BP, Crown, Shell
Food	Applebee's, Arby's, Cracker Barrel, IHOP, McDonald's, Outback Steakhouse, Taco Bell, Waffle House, Wendy's
Lodg	Hampton Inn, Holiday Inn
Other	NAPA, BJ's, Wal-Mart, Home Depot, Target, Grocery
34AB	VA 615, Creighton Rd, Mechanicsville

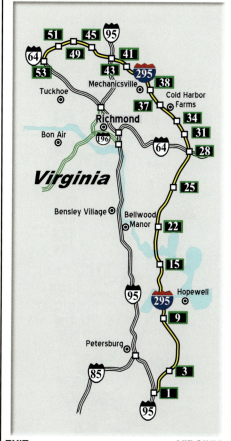

EXIT	VIRGINIA
31AB	VA 156, N Airport Dr, Highland Springs
(28AB)	Jct I-64, US 60, VA 156, Sandston (SB)
Other	W: Richmond Int'l Airport

Exit	Description
28	US 60, VA 156, Sandston (NB)
Other	W: Richmond Int'l Airport
25	VA 895, (TOLL), to Richmond
22AB	VA 5, New Market Rd, Richmond
Gas	BP, Exxon
15AB	VA 10, Chester, Hopewell
FStop	S: Mapco
Gas	BP, Exxon, Citgo
Food	Burger King, Cracker Barrel, Denny's, McDonald's, Waffle House, Wendy's
Lodg	AmeriSuites, Hampton Inn, Holiday Inn
Med	E: + Hospital
9AB	VA 36, Oaklawn Blvd, Hopewell
Gas	Chevron, BP, Shell, Exxon
Food	Burger King, Denny's, McDonald's, Pizza Hut, Shoney's, Subway, Taco Bell, Waffle House, Wendy's, Western Sizzlin
Lodg	Candlewood Suites, Econo Lodge, Fairfield Inn, Hampton Inn, Holiday Inn Express, InnKeeper
Other	W: Ft Lee Military Res, Food Lion, U-Haul
3AB	US 460, County Dr, Petersburg, to Norfolk
FStop	E: Mapco
Gas	Exxon
Food	Hardee's, McDonald's, Subway
Other	W: Petersburg Nat'l Battlefield, Ft Lee Military Res
(1)	Jct I-95, N to Petersburg, S to Emporium

(I-295 begins/ends on I-95, Exit #46)

⤒ VIRGINIA
Begin I-295 from Jct I-95 near Petersburg to Jct I-64 near Glen Allen, VA

EXIT	OREGON

⤓ OREGON
Begin I-405 from Jct I-5, Exit #305B to Jct I-5, Exit #299B

Exit	Description
(3)	Jct I-5N, to Seattle (NB ex, SB entr) Kerby Ave (NB exit, SB entr) US 30E, The Dalles (NB ex, SB entr) US 30W, St Helens
2B	Everett St
2A	Burnside St, Couch St (SB ex, NB ent) Salmon St, PGE Park (NB ex, SB ent)
1D	12th Ave (NB ex, SB entr) US 26W, Beaverton
1C	US 26E, 6th Ave

Exit	OREGON
1B	4th Ave (NB exit, SB entr) Jct I-5N, to I-84E, The Dalles, Seattle (SB exit, NB entr)
1A	Naito Pkwy (NB ex, SB entr)

Exit	OREGON
(0)	Jct I-5, S to Salem (SB ex, NB entr)

⤒ OREGON

◆ = Regular Gas Stations with Diesel   ▲ = RV Friendly Locations   ♥ = Pet Friendly Locations
RED PRINT SHOWS LARGE VEHICLE PARKING/ACCESS ON SITE OR NEARBY   BROWN PRINT SHOWS CAMPGROUNDS/RV PARKS

INTERSTATE 405

EXIT	WASHINGTON
	Begin I-405 from Jct I-5 near Lynnwood to Jct I-5 near Seattle, WA

WASHINGTON
(I-405 begins/ends on I-5, Exit #177)

Exit		
(30)		Jct I-5, N to Canada, S to Seattle
26		WA 527, Bothel, Mill Creek
	Gas	7-11, Chevron, Shell
	Food	Applebee's, Arby's, Bonefish Grill, Burger King, Denny's, Jack in the Box, Outback Steakhouse, Qdoba Mex Rest, Starbucks, Taco Bell, Tully's Coffee
	Lodg	Comfort Inn, Extended Stay America
	Other	Albertson's, Pharmacy
24		NE 195th St, Beardslee Blvd
	Gas	Shell◊
	Lodg	Residence Inn, Wyndham Garden Hotel
23B		WA 522W, Bothell
23A		WA 522E, to WA 202, Woodinville, Monroe
22		NE 160th St, Bothell
	Gas	Chevron, Shell◊
21		NE 132nd
(NEW)		NE 128th
20		NE 124th St, Kirkland (SB)
	Gas	Kirkland Gas Mart/Arco, 76◊, Shell
	Food	Burger King, Denny's, Hunan Wok, Old Country Buffet, McDonald's, Pizza Hut, Starbucks, Taco Time, Wendy's
	Lodg	Courtyard
	Other	Park & Ride, Auto Dealers, Auto Services, CompUSA, Discount Tire, Firestone, Grocery, RiteAid
20B		NE 124th St, Totem Lake Blvd (NB)
	Gas	Shell
	Food	Cowboy Steakhouse, Denny's, Pizza Hut
	Lodg	Comfort Inn, Motel 6♥, Silver Cloud Inn
	Med	E: + Hospital
	Other	Mall, Grocery, Firestone
20A		NE 116th St, Kirkland (NB ex, SB ent)
	Food	Jack in the Box, Little Italy, Shari's, Taco Bell, Subway, Rest/BI
	Lodg	Baymont Inn
18		WA 908, Kirkland, Redmond
	Gas	Circle K, Chevron, Shell◊
	Food	Burger King, Garlic Jim's, McDonald's, Outback Steakhouse, Starbucks, Subway, TGI Friday, Wendy's
	Other	Auto Dealers, Auto Services, Costco, Tires, Walgreen's, U-Haul
17		NE 70th Pl, NE 72nd Pl
14AB		WA 520, Seattle, Redmond
13B		NE 12th St, NE 8th St, NE 4th St, Main St, Bellevue
	Gas	Arco, Chevron◊, Shell◊
	Food	Burger King, Denny's, Hunan Garden, Starbucks

Exit		
	Lodg	DoubleTree Hotel, Extended Stay America, Pacific Guest Suites
	Other	Auto Dealers, Best Buy, Home Depot, Whole Food Market
(NEW)		NE 6th St, HOV access only
13A		NE 4th St, Main St
	Lodg	Best Western, Doubletree Hotel, Hilton
12		SE 8th St, 116th Ave NE, Bellevue
(11)		Jct I-90, E to Spokane, W to Seattle
10		Coal Creek Parkway, Bellevue, Factoria, Newport
		(Gas/Food/Lodg E to Factoria Blvd)
	Other	E: Mall, Grocery, RiteAid, Target
9		112th Ave SE, Lake Washington Blvd Bellevue, Newcastle
7		NE 44th St, Renton
	Food	Denny's, Teriyaki Wok, McDonald's
	Lodg	Econo Lodge, Travelers Inn
6		NE 30th St, Renton
	Gas	7-11, Shell
5		WA 900E, NE Park Dr, Sunset Blvd
4		WA 900, Sunset Blvd NE (SB), WA 169S, WA 900W, Renton (NB)
(NEW)		WA 515, Talbot Rd, Renton
2B		WA 167N, Rainier Ave
2A		WA 167S, Rainier Ave
2		WA 167, Rainier Ave, Renton, Kent, Auburn
	Gas	ArcoAmPm, Chevron, Shell
	Food	Arby's, Applebee's, Burger King, Denny's, IHOP, Jack in the Box, McDonald's, Panda Express, Pizza Hut, Popeye;s, Qdoba Mex Rest, Taco Bell, Wendy's
	Med	E: + Hospital
	Other	Walgreen's, Wal-Mart, Auto Dealers
1		WA 181S, Seattle, Tukwila
	Gas	Chevron◊, Shell, 76◊
	Food	Burger King, Jack in the Box, McDonald's, Starbucks, Taco Bell, Wendy's
	Lodg	Best Western, Comfort Inn, Courtyard, Embassy Suites, Hampton Inn, Harrah's Hotel & Casino
	Other	B&N, Circuit City, Firestone, Lowe's, Office Depot, Target

(I-405 begins/ends on I-5, Exit #154)

WASHINGTON
Begin I-405 from Jct I-5 near Seattle to Jct I-5 near Lynnwood, WA.

◊ = Regular Gas Stations with Diesel ▲ = RV Friendly Locations ♥ = Pet Friendly Locations
RED PRINT SHOWS LARGE VEHICLE PARKING/ACCESS ON SITE OR NEARBY   BROWN PRINT SHOWS CAMPGROUNDS/RV PARKS

Page 548

INTERSTATE 405 S

CALIFORNIA

Begin I-405 from Jct I-5 near Irvine to Jct I-5 near Granada Falls

EXIT	CALIFORNIA
(73)	Jct I-5N, to Sacramento
72	Rinaldi St, Mission Hills
Gas	E: ArcoAmPm
	W: Shell
Food	E: Arby's, Subway
Lodg	W: Granada Motel
Med	E: + Hospital
71B	San Fernando Mission Blvd
71A	CA 118, Simi Valley
71	CA 118W, Ronald Reagan Frwy, Granada Hills, Simi Valley (SB)
70	Devonshire St, Granada Hills
Gas	E: Mobil, Shell
Food	E: Holiday Burger
Other	E: Grocery, Pharmacy
69	Nordhoff St
Gas	E: 7-11, Mobil
Lodg	E: Hillcrest Inn, Tahiti Inn, Vacation Inn
68	Roscoe Blvd, to Panorama City
Gas	E: 76, Exxon
	W: Shell
Food	E: Burger King, Carl's, Denny's, Jack in the Box, McDonald's, Tyler Tx BBQ
Lodg	E: Holiday Inn, Hiway Host Motor Inn, Panorama Motel, Travel Inn
	W: Motel 6 ♥
66B	Sherman Way W (NB)
66A	Sherman Way E (NB)
66	Sherman Way, Van Nuys, Reseda
Gas	E: 76, Chevron, Mobil
	W: Mobil
Food	E: Sizzling Wok
Lodg	E: Hyland Motel
Med	W: + Hospital
65	Victory Blvd, Van Nuys
Gas	E: Mobil
	W: El Pollo Loco, Jack in the Box
64	Burbank Blvd, Encino
Gas	E: Shell
Food	E: Denny's
Lodg	E: Best Western, Carriage Inn, Starlight Cottage
63B	US 101, Ventura Frwy, Ventura, Sherman Oaks, Los Angeles
63A	Valley Vista Blvd, Ventura Blvd, Sepulveda Blvd
Gas	E: Mobil
	W: Chevron
Food	E: Denny's
	W: McDonald's
Lodg	W: Heritage Motel, Radisson
Other	E: Mall
61	Mulholland Dr, Skirball Center Dr
59	Getty Center Dr
57B	Morago Dr (NB exit & entr)
57A	Sunset Blvd
57	Sunset Blvd (SB)
Gas	E: Chevron, Shell
Other	E: to UCLA

EXIT	CALIFORNIA
56	Waterford St (CLOSED), Montana Ave (NB exit only)
55C	Wilshire Blvd West (SB)
55B	Wilshire Blvd East (SB)
55B	Wilshire Blvd (NB)
55A	CA 2, Santa Monica Blvd
Gas	E: Exxon, Mobil
	W: 7-11, Shell
Food	E: Jack in the Box
54	Olympic Blvd, Pico Blvd (SB)
Gas	E: 7-11
Food	E: Subway
(53)	Jct I-10, Santa Monica Fwy (SB)
(53B)	Jct I-10, Santa Monica Freeway
53A	National Blvd (NB ex, SB entr)
52	Venice Blvd, Washington Blvd
Gas	E: Shell, Mobil
51	Culver Blvd, Washington Blvd, Culver City
50B	CA 90W, Slauson Ave, Marina Del Ray
Gas	E: 76
	W: ArcoAmPm
Food	W: Denny's
Other	W: Albertson's
50A	Jefferson Blvd (SB)
Other	W: to LAX Airport ✈
49B	Sepulveda Blvd, Slauson Ave
49A	Howard Hughes Pkwy, Sepulveda Blvd (NB)
49	Howard Hughes Pkwy, Centinela Ave, Speulveda Blvd (SB)
Gas	E: Mobil
	W: Chevron
Lodg	E: Ramada Inn, Sheraton
	W: Extended Stay America
Other	E: Mall
	W: Pharmacy, Mall
48	La Tijera Blvd
Gas	W: 76, Chevron
Food	E: El Pollo Loco, McDonald's, KFC
47	CA 42, Manchester Ave, Florence Ave, La Cienega Blvd, Inglewood
Gas	E: Chevron
	W: 76, Shell
Food	E: Carl Jr's
	W: Arby's, Jack in the Box
Lodg	E: Best Western
	W: Days Inn
Other	W: Kmart
46	Century Blvd, LAX Airport, Imperial Hwy, Rental Car Return
Gas	E: 76
	W: Chevron, Circle K
Food	E: Burger King, Subway
	W: Carl Jr, Denny's, McDonald's
Lodg	E: Best Western, Comfort Inn, Motel 6 ♥
	W: Hampton Inn, Holiday Inn, Hilton, Travelodge, Westin
45B	Imperial Hwy (NB)
(45A)	Jct I-105 (NB)
(45)	Jct I-105, El Segundo, Norwalk (SB)
Gas	E: Mobil, Shell

◊ = Regular Gas Stations with Diesel ▲ = RV Friendly Locations ♥ = Pet Friendly Locations
RED PRINT SHOWS LARGE VEHICLE PARKING/ACCESS ON SITE OR NEARBY BROWN PRINT SHOWS CAMPGROUNDS/RV PARKS

Page 549

INTERSTATE N 405 S

EXIT		CALIFORNIA
	Food	E: El Pollo Loco, Jack in the Box, McDonald's
44		**El Segundo Blvd, to El Segundo**
	Gas	E: ArcoAmPm, Chevron
	Food	E: Burger King, Jack in the Box W: Denny's
	Lodg	W: Ramada Inn
43B		**Rosecrans Ave W (SB)**
43A		**Rosecrans Ave E (SB)**
43		**Rosecrans Ave, Manhattan Beach**
	Gas	E: Mobil, Shell W: ArcoAmPm, Shell
	Food	E: El Pollo Loco, Pizza Hut, Subway W: McDonald's
	Other	E: Albertson's, Home Depot, Best Buy W: Costco
42B		**Inglewood Ave**
	Gas	E: ArcoAmPm W: Mobil, Shell
	Food	E: Denny's, Del Taco
42A		**CA 107, Hawthorne Blvd, Lawndale**
	Gas	W: Mobil, ArcoAmPm
	Food	E: Jack in the Box, McDonald's W: Subway, Taco Bell
	Lodg	E: Best Western, Days Inn
40B		**Redondo Beach Blvd, Hermosa Beach (SB ex, NB entr)**
	Gas	E: ArcoAmPm
	Food	E: Chuck E Cheese W: Boston Market
	Other	W: U-Haul, Grocery, Pharmacy
40A		**CA 91E, Artesia Blvd, to Torrance**
	Gas	E: 76, Chevron
40		**CA 91E, Artesia Blvd, Redondo Bch, Prairie Ave, Hermosa Beach (NB)**
39		**Crenshaw Blvd, to Torrance**
	Gas	E: Shell, Mobil, Chevron W: Mobil, Shell
	Food	E: Burger King, Denny's W: Subway
38B		**Western Ave, to Torrance**
	Gas	E: Chevron, Mobil W: Mobil
	Food	E: Denny's, Wendy's
	Lodg	W: Courtyard
38A		**Normandie Ave, to Gardena**
	Gas	W: Shell
	Food	W: Carl Jr, Subway, Taco Bell
	Lodg	W: Extended Stay America
37B		**Vermont Ave (SB ex, NB entr)**
	Lodg	W: Holiday Inn
	Other	W: CA State Hwy Patrol Post
(37A)		**Jct I-110, Harbor Freeway**
(37)		**Jct I-110, Harbor Fwy, S to San Pedro, N to Los Angeles (NB)**
36		**Main St (NB ex, SB entr)**
(36)		**Weigh Station (Both dir)**
35		**Avalon Blvd, to Carson**
	Gas	E: Chevron, Mobil, Shell W: Mobil, Shell
	Food	E: Denny's, Jack in the Box, Subway, McDonald's, Tony Roma W: IHOP
	Lodg	E: Quality Inn
	Other	E: Mall, Firestone

EXIT		CALIFORNIA
34		**Carson St, Avalon Blvd, to Carson**
	Gas	W: Mobil
	Food	W: Carl Jr, IHOP, Jack in the Box, Subway
	Lodg	E: Comfort Inn W: Hilton
33B		**Wilmington Ave**
	Gas	E: Chevron W: Shell
33A		**Alameda St, CA 47**
32D		**Santa Fe Ave, Hughes Way (SB)**
	Gas	W: Chevron, Shell
32C		**Hughes Way, Santa Fe Ave**
(32C)		**Jct I-710N, Long Beach Fwy (SB)**
(32B)		**Jct I-710S, to Long Beach (NB)**
(32A)		**Jct I-710N, to Pasadena (NB)**
(32)		**Jct I-710, Long Beach, Pasadena**
32A		**Pacific Ave (SB ex, NB entr)**
30B		**Long Beach Blvd**
	Gas	E: 76 W: Mobil
	Med	W: + Hospital
30A		**Atlantic Ave, Long Beach**
	Gas	E: Chevron, Shell
	Food	E: Arby's, Denny's, Jack in the Box
	Med	W: + Hospital
29C		**Orange Ave**
29B		**Cherry Ave N, Spring St**
	Gas	E: Mobil
29A		**Spring St, Cherry Ave S**
29		**Spring St, Cherry Ave, Signal Hill**
27		**CA 19, Lakewood Blvd, Long Beach Airport, Long Beach**
	Gas	W: Chevron, Shell
	Lodg	E: Marriott W: Holiday Inn, Residence Inn
	Med	W: + Hospital
26B		**Bellflower Blvd, Long Beach (NB)**
	Gas	E: Chevron W: 76, Mobil
	Food	W: Burger King, Carl Jr, McDonald's, KFC, Wendy's
	Med	W: + Hospital
	Other	E: Kmart, Lowe's W: Pharmacy, Target
26A		**Woodruff Ave (NB)**
26		**Bellflower Blvd (SB)**
25		**Palo Verde Ave, Long Beach**
	Gas	W: 76
24B		**Studebaker Rd (SB ex, NB entr)**
(24A)		**Jct I-605N (SB)**
(24)		**Jct I-605N (NB)**
23		**CA 22W, 7th St, to Long Beach**
22		**Seal Beach Blvd, Los Alamitos Blvd**
	Gas	E: Chevron, Mobil
	Food	E: Carl Jr, KFC
	Other	E: Target, Albertson's, Grocery, Caribbean Casino

EXIT		CALIFORNIA
21		**CA 22E, Garden Grove Fwy, Valley View St, Garden Grove**
	Gas	E: Mobil, Shell
	Other	E: Grocery, Pharmacy
19		**Westminster Ave, Springdale St**
	Gas	E: 76, ArcoAmPm, Chevron W: Chevron, Shell
	Food	E: Carl Jr, KFC, McDonald's W: Pizza Hut, Subway
	Lodg	E: Motel 6 ♥, Travelodge W: Best Western, Days Inn
	Other	E: Albertson's, Home Depot
18		**Bolsa Ave, Golden West St**
	Gas	W: 76, Mobil, Shell
	Food	W: IHOP, Jack in the Box
	Other	W: Mall
16		**CA 39, Beach Blvd, Westminster, Huntington Beach**
	Gas	E: Shell W: 76, Mobil
	Food	E: Jack in the Box W: Arby's, Burger King, Jack in the Box, Popeye's
	Lodg	W: Holiday Inn
	Med	E: + Hospital
	Other	E: Kmart W: Target
15B		**Magnolia St, Warner Ave (SB)**
15A		**Warner Ave (SB ex, NB entr)**
15		**Magnolia St, Warner Ave (NB)**
	Gas	E: Shell W: Chevron, Mobil
	Lodg	W: Ramada Inn
	Other	W: Grocery, Pharmacy
14		**Brookhurst St, Fountain Valley**
	Gas	E: ArcoAmPm, Chevron W: Chevron, Shell
	Lodg	E: Courtyard, Residence Inn
12		**Euclid St, Newhope St**
11B		**Harbor Blvd, Costa Mesa (SB)**
	Gas	W: Chevron, Mobil, Shell
	Food	W: Burger King, Denny's, El Pollo Loco, IHOP, Jack in the Box, Subway
	Lodg	W: Motel 6 ♥, Super 8
	Other	W: Auto Dealers, Target, Albertson's
11A		**Fairview Rd, Costa Mesa (SB)**
	Gas	E: Shell W: Chevron, Mobil
	Food	W: Jack in the Box
11		**South Coast Dr, Fairview Rd, Harbor Blvd, Costa Mesa (NB)**
10		**CA 73, to CA 55S, Corona del Mar, Newport Beach (SB)**
9B		**Bristol St, Costa Mesa**
	Gas	E: Chevron, Shell W: 7-11, Shell, Chevron
	Food	E: Jack in the Box, McDonald's W: El Pollo Loco, McDonald's, Subway
	Lodg	E: Holiday Inn, Marriott, Westin W: DoubleTree Hotel, Holiday Inn
	Other	W: Mall, Target, Goodyear, Grocery, Pharmacy
9A		**CA 55, Costa Mesa Frwy, Riverside, Newport Beach**

◆ = Regular Gas Stations with Diesel ▲ = RV Friendly Locations ♥ = Pet Friendly Locations
RED PRINT SHOWS LARGE VEHICLE PARKING/ACCESS ON SITE OR NEARBY   BROWN PRINT SHOWS CAMPGROUNDS/RV PARKS

EXIT		CALIFORNIA	EXIT		CALIFORNIA	EXIT		CALIFORNIA
8		MacArthur Blvd		Food	W: Subway	2		CA 133S, to Laguna Beach
	Gas	W: Chevron	4		Jeffrey Rd, University Dr	1C		Irvine Center Dr, Irvine (SB)
	Food	E: Carl Jr, McDonald's		Gas	E: Chevron	1B		Baker Pkwy, Irvine
		W: IHOP			W: Mobil	1A		Lake Forest Dr, Irvine
	Lodg	E: Embassy Suites, Holiday Inn		Food	E: El Pollo Loco, McDonald's, Taco Bell	1		Irvine Center Dr, Irvine (NB)
		W: Hilton, Marriott			W: IHOP			
	Other	W: John Wayne Airport ✈		Med	W: + Hospital	⏏ **CALIFORNIA**		
7		Jamboree Rd, Irvine		Other	E: Grocery, Pharmacy, Irvine Valley College, Concordia Univ	Begin I-405 from I-5 near to Irvine, CA		
	Lodg	E: Courtyard, Residence Inn	3		Sand Canyon Ave, Shady Canyon Dr	I-5 near Granada Hills Irvine, CA.		
		W: Marriott		Med	E: + Hospital			
5		Culver Dr, Irvine						
	Gas	W: Chevron, Shell						

EXIT		ALABAMA		EXIT		ALABAMA
⏏ **ALABAMA**				10		AL 150, Waverly, Hoover, Bessemer
(I-459 begins/ends on I-59, Exit #137)					Gas	N: Chevron
(33AB)		Jct I-59, N to Gadsden, S to Birmingham				S: Crown, Exxon, Shell
					Other	S: Walgreen's, Grocery
32		US 11, Trussville		6		AL 52, Helena, Bessemer
	Gas	E: Chevron, RaceTrac, Shell			Gas	N: BP
		W: BP				S: Exxon, Shell
	Food	E: Arby's, Chili's, McDonald's, Waffle House			Food	N: Arby's, McDonald's, Pizza Hut, Taco Bell, Waffle House, Wendy's
	Lodg	E: Hampton Inn			Lodg	N: Sleep Inn
	Other	E: Home Depot, Target			Other	N: CVS, Grocery
31		Derby Parkway		1		AL 18, Bessemer, McCalla
(29)		Jct I-20, E to Atlanta, W to Birmingham			Gas	N: Shell
						S: BP
27		Grants Mill Rd			Food	N: McDonald's, Subway
23		Liberty Parkway			Other	N: Grocery
19		US 280, Mountain Brook, Childersburg				S: to Tannehill State Park
	Gas	N: Chevron		(0)		I-459N Jct I-20E, I-59N, to Birmingham, Meridian
		S: Exxon				
	Food	S: Burger King, McDonald's		⏏ **ALABAMA**		
	Lodg	S: Drury Inn, Fairfield Inn, Hilton, Hampton Inn, Holiday Inn Express		(I-459 begins/ends on I-20/59, Exit #106)		
17		Action Rd				
	Gas	N: Shell				
	Food	N: Krystal, McDonald's				
(15AB)		Jct I-65, N to Birmingham, S to Montgomery				
13AB		US 31, Galleria Rd, Hoover, Pelham				
	Gas	N: Chevron, Shell				
		S: Crown, Shell				
	Food	N: McDonald's, Shoney's, Subway				
		S: Burger King, CiCi's, Grady's, Olive Garden, Piccadilly's, Taco Bell				
	Lodg	N: Comfort Inn, Days Inn, Hampton Inn, Holiday Inn				
		S: AmeriSuites, Courtyard				
	Other	N: Auto Dealers				
		S: Mall, Wal-Mart, Kmart				

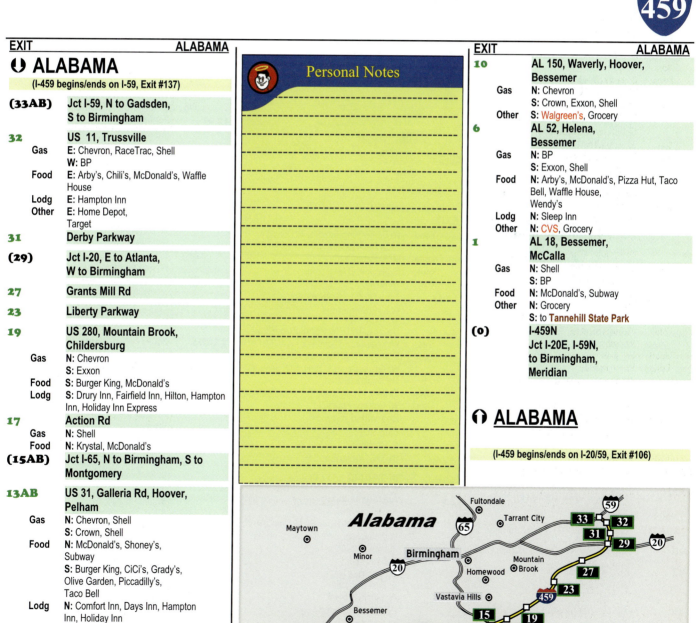

◇ = Regular Gas Stations with Diesel   ▲ = RV Friendly Locations   ♥ = Pet Friendly Locations
RED PRINT SHOWS LARGE VEHICLE PARKING/ACCESS ON SITE OR NEARBY   BROWN PRINT SHOWS CAMPGROUNDS/RV PARKS

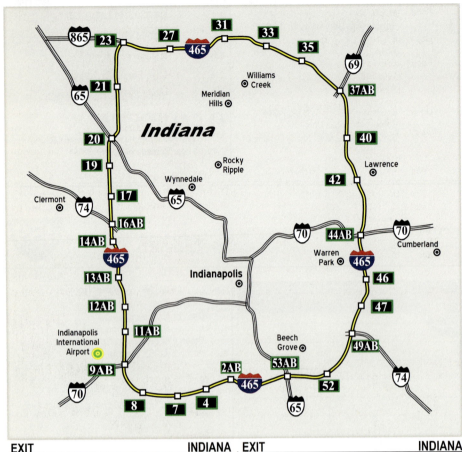

EXIT		INDIANA
31		US 31, Meridian St
	Gas	S: Shell
	Food	S: McDonald's
	Lodg	N: Residence Inn, Wyndham Garden Inn
27		US 421N, Michigan Rd
	Gas	S: BP, Shell, Sunoco
	Food	N: DQ, McDonald's
		S: Arby's, Black-Eyed Pea, Bob Evans, China Buffet, Cracker Barrel, Denny's, IHOP, Max & Erma's, Olive Garden, Outback Steakhouse, Red Lobster, Shoney's, Subway
	Lodg	S: Best Western, Comfort Inn, Drury Inn, Embassy Suites, Holiday Inn, Miicrotel, Quality Inn, Residence Inn
	Other	S: CVS, Kmart, Lowe's, Wal-Mart
(25)		Jct I-865W, to I-65N
23		86th St
	Gas	E: Shell, Speedway
	Food	E: Arby's, Burger King
	Lodg	E: MainStay Suites
	Med	E: + Hospital
21		71st St
	Gas	E: Amoco, Marathon
	Food	E: Galahad's Café, McDonald's, Subway
	Lodg	E: Hampton Inn, Courtyard
(20)		Jct I-65, N to Chicago, S to Indianapolis
19		56th St (NB)
	Gas	E: Speedway
17		38th St, Indianapolis
	Gas	E: BP, Marathon, Shell
	Food	E: China Chef, DQ, Dunkin Donuts, Pizza Hut, Subway
		W: Burger King, Chili's, Cracker Barrel, Don Pablo's, McDonald's, Taco Bell
	Lodg	E: Days Inn
		W: Signature Inn
	Other	E: Coin Laundry, Home Depot, Kmart, Kroger, Pharmacy
NOTE:		I-465 runs above with I-74 for 20 mi. Exit #'s follow I-465
(16B)		Jct I-74W, to Peoria, IL
16A		US 136, Crawfordsville Rd, Speedway, Clermont
	Gas	N: Big Foot, Shell, Thornton's
	Food	N: Burger King, Denny's, Hardee's, KFC, Long John Silvers, Taco Bell, Wendy's, White Castle
	Lodg	N: Dollar Inn, Motel 6 ♥, Red Roof Inn ♥, Super 8
	Other	N: Kroger, Firestone, Goodyear
		S: Raceview Family Campground ▲
14AB		10th St
	Gas	N: Shell, Marathon
		S: BP, Shell, Speedway
	Food	N: Pizza Hut, Wendy's
		S: Arby's, Hardee's, McDonald's
	Other	S: Grocery, CVS
13AB		US 36E, Danville, Rockville Rd
	Gas	N: Citgo
		S: Speedway
	Food	N: Burger King
		S: Bob Evans
	Lodg	N: Comfort Inn, Wingate Inn
		S: Best Western
	Other	N: Sam's Club

EXIT		INDIANA
		Begin I-465 ByPass around Indianapolis, IN from Jct I-65, Exit #108
		INDIANA
(53AB)		Jct I-65, N to Indianapolis, S to Louisville, KY
52		Emerson Ave, Beech Grove
	Gas	N: Shell, Speedway
		S: Shell, Speedway
	Food	N: Burger King, Domino's, KFC, Taco Bell, Subway, Wendy's
		S: Arby's, Hardee's, Hunan House, Pizza Hut, McDonald's, Ponderosa, Subway, Waffle House, White Castle
	Lodg	N: Motel 6 ♥
		S: Holiday Inn, Red Roof Inn ♥, Super 8
	Med	N: + Hospital
	Other	N: CVS
		S: Kmart, Walgreen's, AutoZone
NOTE:		I-465 runs below with I-74 for 20 mi. Exit #'s follow I-465
(49AB)		Jct I-74E, US 421S, to Cincinnati
48		Shadeland Ave, to US 52 (NB)
47		US 52, Brooksville Rd, New Palestine
	Gas	E: Shell
46		US 40, Washington St, Greenfield
	Gas	E: Marathon
		W: Thornton's
	Food	E: Arby's, China Buffet, Olive Garden, Old Country Buffet, Perkins, Subway

EXIT		INDIANA
	Food	W: Burger King, Fazoli's, McDonald's, Pizza Hut, Wendy's
	Lodg	W: Signature Inn
	Other	E: Pharmacy, Target
		W: Kmart
(44)		Jct I-70, E to Columbus, W to Indianapolis
42		US 36E, IN 67N, Pendleton Pike
	Gas	W: Speedway, Thornton's
	Food	E: Burger King, Hardee's, Pizza Hut
		W: Arby's, Denny's, Long John Silver's, McDonald's, Subway
	Lodg	E: Days Inn, Sheraton
	Other	W: Grocery, Kmart
40		Shadeland Ave, 56th St
	Gas	E: Marathon
37A		IN 37S, Indianapolis
37B		IN 37N, I-69, to Ft Wayne
35		Allisonville Rd
	Gas	Speedway, Shell
	Food	E: Applebee's, Hardee's, McDonald's
		W: Bob Evans, Little Caesars, Perkins, Subway, White Castle
	Lodg	E: Courtyard
		W: Signature Inn
	Other	E: Best Buy, Mall
		W: Kmart, Kroger
33		IN 431, Keystone Ave
	Gas	N: BP, Shell
	Food	N: Arby's, Bob Evans, Burger King, Steak & Ale, Subway
	Lodg	N: Motel 6 ♥

◊ = Regular Gas Stations with Diesel   ▲ = RV Friendly Locations   ♥ = Pet Friendly Locations
RED PRINT SHOWS LARGE VEHICLE PARKING/ACCESS ON SITE OR NEARBY   BROWN PRINT SHOWS CAMPGROUNDS/RV PARKS

INTERSTATE 465

EXIT	INDIANA
12AB	US 40E, Washington St, Plainfield
Gas	BP, Phillips 66, Shell, Thornton's
Food	N: Burger King, McDonald's, Taco Bell, White Castle
	S: Arby's, Burger King, Dunkin Donuts, Fazoli's, Hardee's, Long John Silvers, Omelet Shop, Pizza Hut, Steak n Shake, Subway, Wendy's
Lodg	S: Dollar Inn, Skylark Motel
Other	N: Laundry, AutoZone, Walgreen's, Kroger, U-Haul
	S: Goodyear, Kmart, Target
11AB	Airport Expressway, Indianapolis Int'l Airport
Gas	S: BP
Food	S: Burger King
Lodg	N: Baymont Inn, Extended Stay America, Days Inn, Motel 6 ♥
	S: Holiday Inn, Hilton, Ramada Inn
(9AB)	Jct I-70, E to Indianapolis, W to Terre Haute

EXIT	INDIANA
8	IN 67S, Kentucky Ave, Mooresville Rd
Gas	S: BP, Speedway, Shell
Food	S: Hardee's, KFC, Denny's
Med	N: + Hospital
7	Mann Rd
Med	N: + Hospital
4	IN 37, Harding St, Martinsville, Bloomington
TStop	N: Mrr Fuel (Scales), Pilot Travel Center
	S: Flying J Travel Plaza (Scales)
Gas	S: Marathon
Food	N: Subway/Pilot TC, Omelet Shop
	S: Rest/FastFood/FJ TP, Hardee's, McDonald's, Waffle & Steak
Lodg	N: Dollar Inn, Super 8
	S: Knights Inn
TWash	S: FJ TP
TServ	S: FJ TP, Stoop's Freightliner
Other	S: Laundry/BarbSh/RVDump/LP/FJ TP, to Indy Lakes Campground▲, Lake Haven Retreat RV Campground▲

EXIT	INDIANA
2AB	US 31, IN 37, Indianapolis, East St
Gas	BP, Shell, Sunoco
Food	N: Arby's, Burger King, DQ, Dutch Oven, Golden Wok, Hardee's, KFC, Long John Silver, McDonald's, Steak 'n Shake, Papa John's, Pizza Hut, Rally's, Old Country Buffet, Steak & Ale, Taco Bell, White Castle
	S: Applebee's, Bob Evans, Denny's, Red Lobster, Wendy's
Lodg	S: Comfort Inn, Days Inn, Holiday Inn Express, Quality Inn, Red Roof Inn ♥
Other	N: AutoZone, AutoWerks, CVS, Kroger, Firestone, Goodyear, Target, U-Haul
(53AB)	Jct I-65, N to Indianapolis, S to Louisville

◯ **INDIANA**

Begin I-465 ByPass around Indianapolis, IN from Jct I-65, Exit #108

INTERSTATE 476

EXIT	PENNSYLVANIA
	Begin I-476 near Jct I-81 near Clarks Summit to Jct I-95 near Woodlyn, PA

◯ **PENNSYLVANIA**

(I-476 begins/ends on I-81, Exit #194)

EXIT	PENNSYLVANIA
131	US 6, US 11, Clarks Summit
Lodg	W: Days Inn, Ramada, Summit Inn
122	Keyser Ave, Old Forge, Taylor
(121)	TOLL Plaza
115	PA 315, to I-81, Pittston
TStop	W: Pilot Travel Center (Scales)
Gas	W: Mobil
Food	W: Wendy's/Pilot TC, Arby's, McDonald's, Perkins
Lodg	W: Howard Johnson, Knights Inn
(112)	TOLL Plaza
105	PA 115, Bear Creek Bld, Wilkes Barre, Bear Creek
Gas	E: Mobil, Shell
(103)	Parking Area (SB)
(100)	Parking Area (Both dir)
(97)	Parking Area (Both dir)
95	PA 940, to I-80, Lake Harmony, to Pocono, Hazelton
Gas	W: BP, Shell, WaWa
Food	W: Arby's, McDonald's
Lodg	W: Comfort Inn, Days Inn, Ramada
Other	E: Hickory Run State Park
(90)	Parking Area (SB)
(86)	Hickory Run Service Plaza (Both dir)
Gas	Sunoco
Food	McDonald's
74	US 209, Mahoning Valley
Gas	E: Shell
(71)	Lehigh Tunnel
56	US 22, to I-78, Allentown

EXIT	PENNSYLVANIA
(56)	Allentown Service Plaza (Both dir)
Gas	Sunoco
Food	Nathan's, Pizza Hut, TCBY

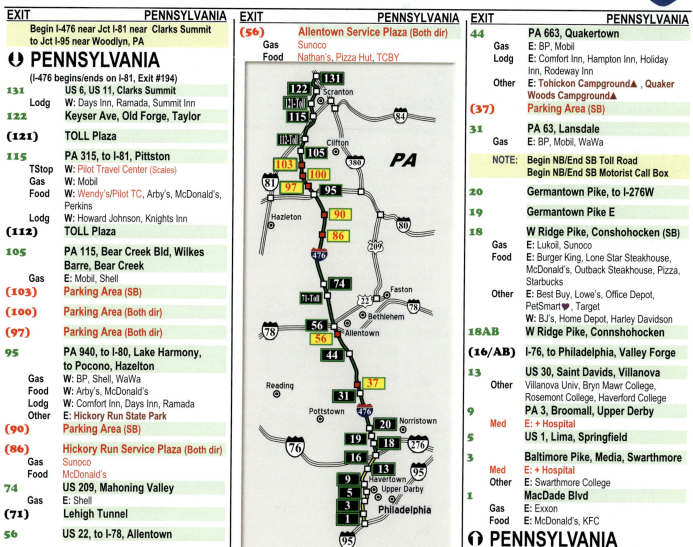

EXIT	PENNSYLVANIA
44	PA 663, Quakertown
Gas	E: BP, Mobil
Lodg	E: Comfort Inn, Hampton Inn, Holiday Inn, Rodeway Inn
Other	E: Tohickon Campground▲, Quaker Woods Campground▲
(37)	Parking Area (SB)
31	PA 63, Lansdale
Gas	E: BP, Mobil, WaWa
NOTE:	Begin NB/End SB Toll Road Begin NB/End SB Motorist Call Box
20	Germantown Pike, to I-276W
19	Germantown Pike E
18	W Ridge Pike, Conshohocken (SB)
Gas	E: Lukoil, Sunoco
Food	E: Burger King, Lone Star Steakhouse, McDonald's, Outback Steakhouse, Pizza, Starbucks
Other	E: Best Buy, Lowe's, Office Depot, PetSmart ♥, Target
	W: BJ's, Home Depot, Harley Davidson
18AB	W Ridge Pike, Connshohocken
(16/AB)	I-76, to Philadelphia, Valley Forge
13	US 30, Saint Davids, Villanova
Other	Villanova Univ, Bryn Mawr College, Rosemont College, Haverford College
9	PA 3, Broomall, Upper Derby
Med	E: + Hospital
5	US 1, Lima, Springfield
3	Baltimore Pike, Media, Swarthmore
Med	E: + Hospital
Other	E: Swarthmore College
1	MacDade Blvd
Gas	E: Exxon
Food	E: McDonald's, KFC

◯ **PENNSYLVANIA**

◆ = Regular Gas Stations with Diesel   ▲ = RV Friendly Locations   ♥ = Pet Friendly Locations

RED PRINT SHOWS LARGE VEHICLE PARKING/ACCESS ON SITE OR NEARBY   BROWN PRINT SHOWS CAMPGROUNDS/RV PARKS

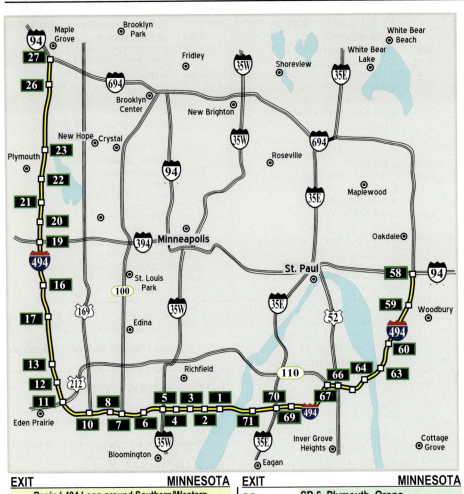

EXIT		MINNESOTA
	Food	Outback Steakhouse
	Lodg	Extended Stay America
	Other	Banks, Auto/Tire Service, Enterprise RAC, Home Depot
11C		TH 5 West, Eden Prairie
11		US 212
11A		US 212W, Prairie Center Dr (WB)
	Gas	Phillips 66, Mobil
	Food	Subway, Roly Poly, Fuddrucker's, KFC, Bakers Ribs, Starbucks, Caribou Cafe, Little Tokyo, Wendy's, McDonald's, Boston Market, Applebee's, Taco Bell, Cafe Oasis
	Lodg	Hampton Inn, Residence Inn, America's Suites, Courtyard, Fairfield Inn, Hyatt, Springhill Suites, TownePlace Suites, Best Western, Homestead Studio Suites
	Other	ATMs, Bank, Cinema, Costco, Eden Prairie Mall, Grocery, Office Depot, **Wal-Mart**
11B		US 212 E, Flying Cloud Dr, N to I-35W, I-35E
10		US 169, N - Hopkins, S - Shakopee
10A		US 169 N, to Hopkins
10B		US 169 S, to Shakopee
8		CR 28, E Bush Lake Rd (Clockwise ex, counterclockwise entr) (Access to Exit #7B Services)
7B		CR 34, Normandale Blvd
	Gas	Citgo, Langs 1 Stop◊, Holiday Station Store
	Food	Caribou Coffee, Burger King, Cafe in the Park, DQ, Subway, TGI Friday, Chili's, Moon Rise Cafe, Majors Sports Cafe, Tony Roma's, Classic Market, Olive Garden, Ryan's Grill
	Lodg	Country Inn, Crowne Plaza, Days Inn, La Quinta Inn♥, Hilton Garden Inn, Sheraton, Staybridge Suites
	Other	ATMs, Banks, Golf Course
7A		TH 100, St Louis Park (Access to Exit #7B Services)
6B		CR 17, France Ave, Minneapolis
	Gas	Bobby & Stevens Mobil, BP, Sinclair
	Food	McDonald's, Romano's Macaroni Grill, Fuddrucker's, Denny's, Joe Sensers Grill, Northland Cafe, Olive Garden
	Lodg	Residence Inn, Park Plaza, Le Bourget Suites, Hampton Inn, Embassy Suites
	Med	N: + Fairview Southdale Hospital
	Other	ATMs, Circuit City, CompUSA, Grocery, Office Depot, Southdale Shopping Center
6A		CR 32, Penn Ave (diff EB reaccess)
	Food	Applebee's, Starbucks, Steak & Ale, Atlantic Buffet, KFC, Red Lobster, Subway, Wendy's
	Other	Southtown Center, Best Buy, Grocery, Jiffy Lube, Pharmacy, Target, ATMs, Auto Dealers, Auto Services, Banks, Walgreen's, Cardinal Stritch Univ
(5)		Jct I-35W, N to Minneapolis, S to Albert Lea
(5A)		Jct I-35W N, to Minneapolis
(5B)		Jct I-35W S, to Albert Lea
4B		Lyndale Ave
NOTE:		Lyndale Ave Interchange closed for reconstruction-to be opened NOV 2009

EXIT		MINNESOTA
		Begin I-494 Loop around Southern/Western portion of metro Minneapolis-St Paul, MN.
		◯ MINNESOTA (CENTRAL TIME ZONE)
(0)		Jct I-94E, I-694 (Clockwise ex, counterclockwise entr)
(27)		Jct I-94W, to St Cloud (NB)
26		CR 10, Bass Lake Rd, Osseo
	Gas	Freedom Value, Sinclair, BP
	Food	McDonald's, Subway
	Lodg	Extended Stay America, Hilton Garden Inn
23		CR 9, Rockford Rd, Minneapolis
	Gas	BP, Holiday Station Store, Freedom Value, PDQ
	Food	Chili's, Bakers Square, Caribou Coffee, DQ, Starbucks x2, Subway, TGI Friday
	Other	Auto Service, ATMs, Grocery, PetSmart♥, Radio Shack, Target, Walgreen's, Zylla Gallery, to Plymouth Creek Center
22		TH 55, Minneapolis, to Buffalo, Rockford
	Gas	Holiday Station Store◊ x2
	Food	McDonald's, Green Meal Rest, Starbucks, Arby's, Burger King, Chinese, Perkins, Rest/Comf Inn, Rest/Radisson
	Lodg	Best Western♥, Radisson Hotel, Red Roof Inn♥, Residence Inn♥, Comfort Inn, Days Inn, Holiday Inn
	Other	ATMs, Banks, Cinema 12, Goodyear, Tires Plus, Plymouth Ice Center

EXIT		MINNESOTA
21		CR 6, Plymouth, Orono
	Gas	BP, Kwik Trip
	Other	Discount Tire, Home Depot
20		Carlson Pkwy, Plymouth
	Gas	Holiday Station Store◊
	Food	Einstein Bros, Subway, Woody's Grill
	Lodg	Country Inn & Suites
(19)		Jct I-394E, US 12, Minneapolis, Wayzata
	Food	Applebee's, Bakers Square, Big Bowl, Origami West, Wendy's, Pizza
	Lodg	Country Inn, Radisson
	Other	Best Buy, Circuit City, FedEx Kinkos, Office Max, Pharmacy, Target, Tires Plus
(19A)		Jct I-394E, US 12E, to Minneapolis
(19B)		Jct I-394E, US 12W, to Wayzata
17		Minnetonka Blvd, CR 5, CR 16
	Gas	Glenn's 1 Stop, Benny's Feed n Fuel
	Other	Minnetonka Police Dept
16		TH 7, Minnetonka
	Food	Famous Dave's BBQ, McDonald's, Perkins, General Store Cafe, Subway, Taco Bell
16A		TH 7 East
16B		TH 7 West
13		TH 62, CR 62 (Services Avail E to Shady Oak Rd)
12		CR 39, Valley View Rd (SB) (Counterclockwise ex, clockwise entr)
	Gas	Mobil

Page 554 ◊ = Regular Gas Stations with Diesel ▲ = RV Friendly Locations ♥ = Pet Friendly Locations
RED PRINT SHOWS LARGE VEHICLE PARKING/ACCESS ON SITE OR NEARBY BROWN PRINT SHOWS CAMPGROUNDS/RV PARKS

Interstate 494

EXIT	MINNESOTA
4A	**Nicollet Ave, CR 52**
Gas	Super America◆, Holiday Station Store
Food	Burger King, Johnny Angels, McDonald's
Lodg	Candlewood Suites, Baymont Inn
Other	Auto Services, Best Buy, Radio Shack, Home Depot, PetSmart♥, Sam's Club, Vet♥
3	**12th Ave, Portland Ave, CR 35**
Gas	Sinclair, Phillips 66, BP
Food	Arby's, Denny's, Hong Kong Rest, New Century Buffet, McDonald's, Outback Steakhouse, Subway, Shell's Cafe
Lodg	AmericInn, Courtyard, Holiday Inn Express, Grand Lodge, Microtel, Quality Inn, Residence Inn, Travelodge
Other	Walgreen's, Wal-Mart
2CB	**TH 77, Cedar Ave, N to Minneapolis, E S to Eagan**
Other	S: Mall of America
2B	**TH 77 N, to Minneapolis**
2C	**TH 77 S, to Eagan**
Other	S: Mall of America
2A	**24th Ave, CR 1**
Other	S: Mall of America
1B	**34th Ave, HHH Terminal (EB)**
Lodg	Embassy Suites, Hilton, Holiday Inn
1A	**TH 5 E, Main Terminal, St Paul, Fort Snelling**
1AB	**TH 5E, Main Terminal, 34th Ave, HHH Terminal, St Paul (WB)**
71	**CR 31, Pilot Knob Rd**
Lodg	Courtyard, Fairfield Inn, Best Western, Crowne Plaza
(70)	**Jct I-35E, N - St Paul, S - Albert Lea**
69	**TH 149, Dodd Rd, to TH 55**
Food	Caribou Coffee, McDonald's, Subway
Lodg	Budget Host Inn, Country Inn

EXIT	MINNESOTA
67	**TH 110, to MN 3, Robert St (WB) MN 3, Robert St (EB)**
Gas	BP, Mobil, Holiday Station Store
Food	Arby's, Bakers Square, Burger King, Chuck E Cheese, Chipolte Mex Grill, KFC, Old Country Buffet, Pizza Hut, Taco Bell, Timber Lodge Steakhouse, White Castle
Other	ATMs, Auto Services, Auto Dealers, Best Buy, Grocery, Target, Tires Plus, Wal-Mart
66	**US 52, St Paul, Rochester**
Gas	Super America
Food	Applebee's, Major Sports Cafe, Old World Pizza, Outback Steakhouse, Quiznos
Lodg	Country Inn, Microtel
65	**5th Ave, 7th Ave**
NOTE:	EB: Reconstruction/Upgrade Work on Exit #'s 64B - 60 thru 2010. Expect closures, delays, etc.
64B	**TH 156, CR 56, Concord St**
Gas	Conoco◆
Lodg	Best Western, S St Paul Hotel
TServ	Peterbilt, Independent Diesel Repair
Other	Auto Services, Goodyear, MN State Hwy Patrol Post, Wakota Arena, S to South St Paul Muni Airport✈
64A	**Hardman Ave, Stockyard Rd**
TStop	Stockmen's Truck Stop (Scales)
Food	Rest/Stockmen's TS
Other	Laundry/WiFi/Stockmen's TS
63C	**Maxwell Ave, CR 38**
63	**US 10, US 61, Bailey Rd, Hastings, Downtown St Paul**
Gas	BP, Super America
Food	Burger King, North Pole Rest, Pig in a Blanket, Subway
Lodg	Boyd's Motel, Extended Stay
Other	ATMs, Auto Services, Banks

EXIT	MINNESOTA
63A	**US 10W, US 61N, Bailey Rd, Military Rd, St Paul, Hastings (SB)**
63B	**US 10E, US 61S, Bailey Rd, St Paul, Hastings (SB)**
60	**Lake Rd**
Gas	Super America◆
Lodg	Country Inn
Med	W: + Health East Woodwinds Hospital
NOTE:	WB: Reconstruction/Upgrade work on Exit #'s 60 - 64B thru 2010. Expect closures, delays, etc.
59	**Valley Creek Rd, CR 16**
Gas	BP, Super America◆, PDQ
Food	Applebee's, Broadway Pizza, Chipolte Mex Grill, Cold Stone Creamery, DQ, Old Country Buffet, Perkins, Starbucks, Burger King, Pizza Hut, McDonald's, Subway
Lodg	Red Roof Inn, Hampton Inn
Other	ATMs, Banks, Best Buy, Goodyear, Grocery, Target, Walgreen's, Tires
58C	**Tamarack Rd** (Services E 2mi to MN 13)
(58)	**Jct I-94, W to St Paul, E to Madison**
(58A)	**Jct I-94W, to St Paul**
(58B)	**Jct I-94E, to Madison**
(0)	**Jct I-694 N, End I-494** (Counterclockwise ex, clockwise entr)
	(CENTRAL TIME ZONE)
⊙	**MINNESOTA**
	Begin I-494 Loop around Southern / Western portion of metro Minneapolis-St Paul, MN.

Interstate 526

EXIT	SOUTH CAROLINA
	Begin I-526 Loop around Charleston South Carolina
⊙	**SOUTH CAROLINA** (EASTERN TIME ZONE)
(0)	**Jct US 17**
11AB	**Paul Cantrell Blvd, Ashley River Rd**
Gas	APlus, Jensen's Discount Gas, Hess
Food	Chick-Fil-A, McDonald's, Baskin Robbins
Lodg	Captain D's, O'Charley's, Burger King
Med	W: + Hospital
Other	Auto Service, Banks, ATM's, Grocery
14	**Leeds Ave**
15	**Dorchester Rd**
Gas	Citgo, Sunoco
Food	Burger King, Huddle House, Checkers
Lodg	Airport Inn
Other	Diesel Service
16AB	**International Blvd**
Gas	BP, Murphy

EXIT	SOUTH CAROLINA
Food	Wendy's, Starbucks, Quiznos Sub, Palm Tree Grill, Sportz Cafe, Indigo
Lodg	Embassy Suites, Homeplace Suites, Holiday Inn, Hilton Garden Inn
Other	North Charleston Coliseum
(17AB)	**Jct I-26**
18AB	**US 52, US 78**
Gas	Hess, Kangaroo X2, Exxon
Food	Popeyes, McDonald's, KFC, Oriental Cuisine
Lodg	Catalina Motel, Economy Inn, Extended Stay America
Other	Auto Service, Amtrak
19	**N Rhett Rd**
Gas	The Pantry
Food	Bagel Nation, Mcguiness Doe
20	**Virginia Ave**
Other	Banks, ATM's
23AB	**Clements Ferry Rd, Cainhoy Rd**

EXIT	SOUTH CAROLINA
24	**Island Park Dr**
Gas	Citgo
Food	Soda Water Grill, Moo-Na Lisa's Gourmet Ice Cream, Lana's Mexican Rest, Orlando Bros Pizza, Soda Water Grill
Lodg	Hampton Inn-Charleston
28	**Long Point Rd**
Gas	Blue Water, Rew's Run-In
Food	Starbucks, Wendy's, Brixx Wood Fired Pizza, Sunray's Dogs and Deli, Waffle House
29	**US 701, US 17**
Gas	Hess, The Loop Marts, Sunoco
Food	Applebee's, Subway, Dunkin' Donuts, Ye Olde Fashioned Ice Cream, Gullah Cuisine Lowcountry Rest
30	**Jct I-526 Bus, US 17 S**
⊙	**SOUTH CAROLINA**
	Begin I-526 Loop around Charleston South Carolina

◆ = Regular Gas Stations with Diesel   ▲ = RV Friendly Locations   ♥ = Pet Friendly Locations

RED PRINT SHOWS LARGE VEHICLE PARKING/ACCESS ON SITE OR NEARBY   BROWN PRINT SHOWS CAMPGROUNDS/RV PARKS

EXIT		CALIFORNIA
Begin I-605 ByPass around LA from Jct I-210 near Baldwin Park to Jct I-405, Seal Beach, CA		
⟳ CALIFORNIA		
(I-605 begins/ends on I-210)		
(28)		Jct I-210
26		Arrow Hwy, Live Oak Ave
	Other	E: Santa Fe Dam Rec Area
24		Lower Azusa Rd, LA St
23		Ramona Blvd, Baldwin Park
(22)		Jct I-10, E - San Bernardino, W - LA
21		Valley Blvd, La Puente
19		CA 60, Pomona Fwy, Whittier
	Gas	E: Chevron
	Food	E: McDonald's
18		Peck Rd
	Gas	E: Shell
	Other	E: Freightliner, Ford
17		Beverley Blvd W, Rose Hills Rd
16		Beverley Blvd East
15		Whittier Blvd
	Gas	E: 7-11, Shell
	Other	W: Auto Dealers
14B		Norwalk Blvd, Washington Blvd E
14A		Washington Blvd W
13		Slauson Ave
	Gas	E: ArcoAmPm, Mobil
	Food	E: Denny's
	Lodg	E: Motel 6 ♥
	Med	E: + Hospital
12		Telegraph Rd
	Other	E: CA State Hwy Patrol Post

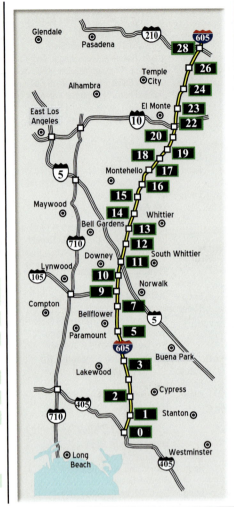

EXIT		CALIFORNIA
(11)		Jct I-5
10		Firestone Blvd
	Gas	E: 76, Shell
		W: 76, Chevron
	Food	E: KFC, McDonald's, Taco Bell
	Lodg	E: Best Western
9A		Rosecrans Ave
7B		Alondra Blvd
	Gas	E: Chevron
	Lodg	E: Motel 6 ♥
5		CA 91
5B		South St, Cerritos
	Gas	W: 76, Shell
	Other	E: Mall
		W: Auto Dealers
5A		Del Amo Blvd
3		Carson St
	Gas	E: ArcoAmPm, Shell
		W: Chevron, Mobil
	Food	E: Jack in the Box, KFC, McDonald's
		W: Denny's, El Pollo Loco, TGI Friday
	Lodg	E: Lakewood Inn
		W: Tradewinds Motel
	Other	W: Lowe's, Sam's Club, Wal-Mart
2B		Spring St
2A		Willow St
1D		Katella Ave, Los Alamitos
	Med	E: + Hospital
	Other	E: Los Alamitos Armed Forces Res Center
(0)		Jct I-405
(I-605 begins/ends on I-405)		
⟳ CALIFORNIA		
Begin I-605 ByPass around LA from Jct I-405 near Seal Beach to Jct I-210, Baldwin Park, CA		

EXIT		TENNESSEE
Begin I-640 ByPass around Knoxville		
⟳ TENNESSEE		
(0)		Jct I-40E, to Asheville, Jct 25W
8		Washington Pike, Millertown Pike, Mall Road North, Knoxville
	Gas	N: Exxon, Conoco
		S: Shell

EXIT		TENNESSEE
	Food	N: Applebee's, Burger King, Cracker Barrel, KFC, McDonald's, Taco Bell, Texas Roadhouse, Wendy's
	Other	N: Sam's Club, Wal-Mart, Mall
		S: Food Lion, Home Depot, Lowe's
6		US 441, Broadway
	Gas	N: BP, Chevron, Phillips 66, Pilot
	Food	N: Arby's, CiCi's, Long John Silver, Subway, Taco Bell

EXIT		TENNESSEE
		S: Buddy's BBQ, Shoney's
	Lodg	N: Best Western
	Other	N: Auto Zone, CVS, Kroger, Walgreen's
		S: CVS, Kmart, Walgreen's
(3)		Jct I-75N, to Lexington, KY Jct I-275S, to Knoxville
3A		US 25W N, Clinton Hwy (EB)
3B		US 25W N, Gap Rd (WB)
1AB		TN 62, Western Ave, Knoxville
	Gas	N: Shell, RaceTrac
		S: BP
	Food	N: KFC, Long John Silver, Shoney's, McDonald's, Ruby Tuesday
	Other	N: CVS, Kroger
(0)		Jct I-40, E - Asheville, W - Nashville, Jct I-75S, to Chattanooga
(I-640 begins/ends on I-40, Exit #385)		
⟳ TENNESSEE		
Begin I-640 ByPass around Knoxville		

Page 556

◆ = Regular Gas Stations with Diesel ▲ = RV Friendly Locations ♥ = Pet Friendly Locations
RED PRINT SHOWS LARGE VEHICLE PARKING/ACCESS ON SITE OR NEARBY BROWN PRINT SHOWS CAMPGROUNDS/RV PARKS

INTERSTATE 680 S

EXIT	CALIFORNIA
	Begin Southbound I-680 from Jct I-80 near Cordelia to Jct I-280 in San Jose, CA.

CALIFORNIA
(PACIFIC TIME ZONE)

Exit	Road / Services
(71B)	Jct I-80W, to Oakland
(71A)	Jct I-80E, to Sacramento
70	Green Valley Rd, Cordelia
Other	Costco, Long's, Safeway
68	Gold Hill Rd, Fairfield
Gas	Tower Mart◆
65	Marshview Rd
63	Parish Rd, Benicia
61	Lake Herman Rd
Gas	ArcoAmPm◆, Gas City, Shell◆
Food	JackintheBox/Arco, Carl'sJr/Shell, Pot Belly Deli
60	Industrial Park (SB)
Other	Auto Services
58B	Bayshore Rd, Industrial (NB)
(58A)	Jct I-780, Benicia (NB, Left Exit)
(58)	Jct I-780, Benicia (SB)
56	Marina Vista, Martinez
54	Pacheco Blvd (Both dir), Arthur Rd (SB)
Gas	7-11, 76, Shell◆
Food	Big Burger
53	CA 4, E to Concord, W to Richmond
52	Concord Ave (Both dir), Burnett Ave (NB), Concord
Gas	76, Chevron, Grand Gasoline, Shell
Food	Burger King, McDonald's, Round Table Pizza, Starbucks, Taco Bell, Wendy's
Lodg	Crowne Plaza, Holiday Inn
Other	ATMs, Banks, Grocery, Jiffy Lube
51	Willow Pass Rd, Taylor Blvd
Food	Baja Fresh, Benihana, Buffet City, Burger King, Cactus Cafe, Cinnabon, Denny's, Fuddruckers, Marie Callanders, McDonald Red Lobster, Sizzler, Starbucks, Subway
Lodg	Hilton, Residence Inn
Other	ATMs, Auto Services, Banks, Circuit City, CompUSA, Firestone, Office Depot, Trader Joe's, Sun Valley Mall, Willow Shopping Center
50	CA 242, Concord (NB)
49	Monument Blvd, Gregory Ln, Pleasant Hill (SB)
Gas	Chevron, Valero
Food	Boston Market, Fatburger, Jack in the Box, L & L Hawaiian BBQ, McDonald's, NY Pizza, Plaza Cafe, Starbucks, Taco Bell
Lodg	Extended Stay America, Courtyard, Summerfield Suites, Sun Valley Inn
Other	ATMs, Auto Services, Banks, Best Buy, Grocery
49B	Monument Blvd (NB)
49A	Contra Costa Blvd (NB)

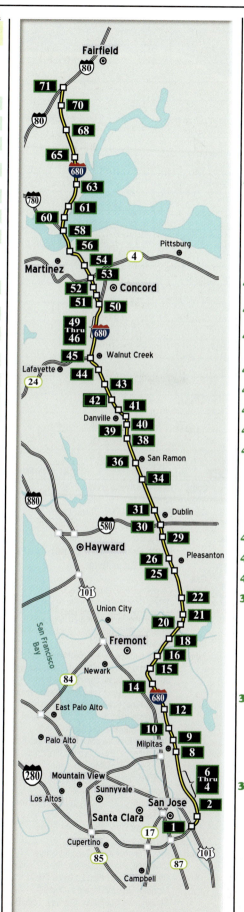

Exit	Road / Services
48	Treat Blvd, Geary Rd, Walnut Creek
Gas	7-11, Chevron, Chevron, Shell◆
Food	Subway, Black Angus Steakhouse, Burger King, Cactus Cafe, Curry House, Quiznos, Starbucks, Sweet Tomatoes, Wendy's
Lodg	Embassy Suites, Extended Stay America, Courtyard, Holiday Inn, Renaissance
Other	ATMs, Banks, Best Buy, Grocery, Staples, Walgreen's
47	North Main St, Walnut Creek
Gas	Chevron, Shell, 76◆
Food	Fuddrucker's, Foster Freeze, Jack in the Box, Plaza Deli, Starbucks, Taco Bell
Lodg	Marriott, Motel 6, Walnut Creek Motel
Other	Auto Dealers, Auto Services, ATM, Target
46B	Ygnacio Valley Rd
Gas	Chevron, USA
46A	CA 24W, to Lafayette, Oakland
Gas	USA
45	South Main St, Walnut Creek (SB)
45B	Olympic Blvd (NB)
45A	South Main St (NB)
44	Rudgear Rd (NB)
43	Livorna Rd
42B	Stone Valley Rd W, Alamo
Gas	Chevron, Shell◆
Food	Asian House Rest, Bagel Street Cafe, High Tech Burrito, Round Table Pizza, Starbucks, Subway, Taco Bell
Other	Safeway, Alamo Plaza Shopping Center
42A	Stone Valley Rd E, Alamo
41	El Pintado Rd, Danville (SB)
40	El Cerro Blvd
39	Diablo Rd, Danville
Gas	76, Chevron, 76
Food	Amber Bistro, Burger King, Christy's Donuts, Panda Express, Pizza Hut, Quiznos, Starbucks, Taco Bell, Uptown Cafe
Other	ATMs, Albertson's, Banks, Jiffy Lube, Museum, Pharmacy
38	Sycamore Valley Rd
Gas	Shell, 76, Valero, All Town Station
Food	Bagel Street Cafe, Cold Stone Creamery, Denny's, High Tech Burrito, Luna Loca Mexican Rest, Patrick Davis Rest
Lodg	Best Western
Other	ATMs, Banks, Grocery
36	Crow Canyon Rd, San Ramon
Gas	Shell, 76, Chevron, Shell, Valero
Food	Burger King, Carl's Jr, Chili's, Boston Market, Chipotle Mex Grill, In 'n Out Burgers, McDonald's, NY Pizza, Rice Garden, Starbucks, Taco Bell, TGI Friday
Lodg	Extended Stay America, Sierra Suites
Other	Albertson's, ATMs, Auto Services, Pharmacy, RiteAid, Long's, Safeway

◆ = Regular Gas Stations with Diesel   ▲ = RV Friendly Locations   ♥ = Pet Friendly Locations
RED PRINT SHOWS LARGE VEHICLE PARKING/ACCESS ON SITE OR NEARBY   BROWN PRINT SHOWS CAMPGROUNDS/RV PARKS

Page 557

N 680 INTERSTATE

EXIT		CALIFORNIA
34		**Bollinger Canyon Rd**
	Gas	Chevron, Valero
	Food	Subway, Applebee's, Chevy's Mex Rest, Baja Fresh, Cactus Cafe, Rice Garden
	Lodg	Marriott, Residence Inn, Courtyard, Homestead Studio Suites
	Other	Banks, Grocery, Target, Whole Foods
31		**Alcosta Blvd, Dublin**
	Gas	76, Chevron, Shell
	Food	Chuck E Cheese, DQ, Lumpia House, McDonald's, Mountain Mike's Pizza, Pizza Palace, Starbucks, Subway, Taco Bell
	Other	ATMs, Albertson's, Pharmacy, Walgreen's
(30B)		**Jct I-580W, to Oakland**
(30A)		**Jct I-580E, to Tracy**
29		**Stoneridge Dr, Pleasanton**
	Food	Black Angus Steakhouse, Planet Fresh Burrito, Plaza Market & Deli, Starbucks, Taco Bell. Togos
	Lodg	Crowne Plaza, Hilton, Wyndham
	Other	ATMs, Banks, Stoneridge Shopping Center
26		**Bernal Ave, Pleasanton**
	Gas	Shell
	Food	Jack in the Box/Shell, Lindo's Mex Rest
25		**Sunol Blvd (Both dir), Castlewood Dr (SB)**
22		**Sunol (SB)**
21		**CA 84, Calaveras Rd, Dumbarton Bridge, Sunol**
21B		**CA 84E, Livermore (NB)**
21A		**CA 84W, Calaveras Rd, Sunol (NB)**
20		**Andrade Rd (Both dir), Sheridan Rd (SB), Sunol**
	Gas	Sunol Super Stop
(18)		**Weigh Station (NB)**
18		**Vargas Rd (SB)**
18B		**Sheridan Rd (NB)**
18A		**Vargas Rd (NB)**
16		**CA 238N, Mission Blvd, Hayward**
	Gas	Shell, Fig Tree Gas
	Food	McDonald's
	Lodg	Lord Bradley's Inn
15		**Washington Blvd (Both dir), Irvington District (NB)**
	Gas	Quick Stop
	Food	Chinese Rest, Covent Gardens, Mission Pizza
	Other	Grocery
14		**Durham Rd, to Auto Mall Pkwy, Fremont**
	Gas	76, Shell
	Food	Subway, Jack in the Box/Shell, Starbucks
	Other	Home Depot
12		**Mission Blvd, to I-880, Warm Springs District**
	Gas	76, Valero
	Food	Baskin Robbins, Burger King, Carl's Jr, Denny's, Donut House, Jack in the Box, Jamba Juice, KFC, L & L Hawaiian BBQ, Little Caesars, Starbucks, Subway, Taco Bell, Wok City Diner, Zorba's Deli, Z Pizza

EXIT		CALIFORNIA
	Lodg	Days Inn, Econo Lodge, Extended Stay America, Motel 6, Quality Inn
	Other	Albertson's, ATMs, Banks, Long's, Pharmacy, Safeway, Walgreen's
10		**Scott Creek Rd (Both dir), Warm Springs District (NB)**
9		**Jacklin Rd, Milpitas**
	Gas	Shell
	Food	Chez Christina, Little Table
	Other	ATMs, Grocery, Save Dollar Store
8		**CA 237W, Calaveras Blvd, Central Milpitas**
	Gas	76, Shell, Shell
	Food	El Torito Mexican Grill, Giorgio's, Pizza, McDonald's, Red Lobster, Sizzler, Subway, Sushi Maru, Sushi Lovers Japanese Cuisine, Luu New Tung Kee Noodle House, Burger King, Chili's, Lee's Sandwiches, 909 Restaurant, Flames Coffee Shop of Milpitas, Round Table Pizza
	Lodg	Days Inn, Embassy Suites, Extended Stay America, Executive Inn, Park Inn
	Other	Auto Services, ATMs, Albertson's, FedEx Kinko's, Grocery, Library, Long's, Pharmacy, Staples, Target, Tires, Walgreen's, UPS Store, Vet♥, El Monte RV Rentals & Sales
6		**Landess Ave, Montague Expy**
	Gas	76, ArcoAmPm, Chevron's
	Food	Arby's, Burger King, Coconut Grove, Cinnabon, Dave & Buster's, Fresh Choice Rest, Jack in the Box, La Salsa Fresh Mexican Grill, McDonald's, Outback Steakhouse, Starbucks, Subway, Taco Bell, Togos

EXIT		CALIFORNIA
	Lodg	Marriott, TownePlace Suites, Sleep Inn, Sheraton
	Other	ATMs, Banks, Albertson's, Dollar Plus, Firestone, Home Depot, Pharmacy, RiteAid, Target, Walgreen's, Great Mall of the Bay Area, Home Depot, Radio Shack, Vet♥
5		**Capitol Ave, Hostetter Rd (SB)**
	Gas	Shell, Valero
	Food	Carl's Jr, KFC, Popeye's, Saiko Sushi Rest, Chinese Rest, Quiznos, Starbucks
	Other	ATMs, Auto Services, Banks, Costco, Midas, Wal-Mart SC
5B		**Capitol Ave (NB)**
5A		**Hostetter Rd (NB)**
4		**Bereyessa Rd**
	Gas	ArcoAmPm, USA, Valero
	Food	Bay Leaf Cuisine of India, Denny's, Jade China Chinese Rest, Lee's Sandwiches, McDonald's, Round Table Pizza, Rose Gardens Chinese Rest, Starbucks, Taco Bell
	Other	Albertson's, Auto Zone, ATMs, Banks, Century Berryessa 10 Cinema, Home Depot, Long's, Pharmacy, Safeway, Target, UPS Store, San Jose Flea Market
2B		**McKee Rd, San Jose**
	Gas	76, Chevron, Shell, World Gas
	Food	Burger King, Pizza Hut, Quiznos, Sizzler, Starbucks, Togos, Baskin-Robbins, McDonald's, Winchells
	Med	W: + Regional Medical Center of San Jose
	Other	Albertson's, Auto Services, Grocery, Pharmacy, Radio Shack, Target, Tires, Towing, U-Haul, Walgreen's
2A		**CA 130, Alum Rock Ave, San Jose**
	Gas	Shell◆, 76, Exxon
	Food	Carl's Jr, KFC, La Costa, Subway
	Med	W: + Santa Clara Valley Medical Center
	Other	ATMs, Auto Services, Banks, CarQuest Auto Parts, Calderon New & Used Tires, CarWash/Shell, Penske Truck Rental, Towing, US Post Office, Pharmacy, Vet♥, United Rentals/LP, Cruise America Motor home Rental & Sales
1D		**Capitol Expressway (SB)**
	Other	S to Reid-Hillview Airport of Santa Clara County✈
1C		**King Rd (SB), Capitol Expy (NB)**
	Gas	76, 7-11, Shell
	Food	Jack in the Box, Taco Bell
	Med	E: + First Health Medical Clinic of San Jose/Urgent Care
		W: + Foothills Family Medical Clinic
	Other	Capital CarWash, Golf Course, Radio Shack, Walgreen's
1B		**US 101, S - Los Angeles, N - San Francisco (SB), Jackson Ave (NB)**
(1A)		**Jct I-280 (SB, Left Exit), King Rd (NB)**
	Other	Calderon Gas/LP, U-Haul, Towing

(PACIFIC TIME ZONE)

🎧 CALIFORNIA

Begin Southbound I-680 from Jct I-280 near San Jose to Jct I-80 near Cordelia, CA.

◆ = Regular Gas Stations with Diesel   ▲ = RV Friendly Locations   ♥ = Pet Friendly Locations
RED PRINT SHOWS LARGE VEHICLE PARKING/ACCESS ON SITE OR NEARBY   BROWN PRINT SHOWS CAMPGROUNDS/RV PARKS

INTERSTATE 694

EXIT	MINNESOTA
	Begin I-694 Loop around Northern/Eastern portion of metro Minneapolis-St Paul, MN.

MINNESOTA (CENTRAL TIME ZONE)

Exit	Description
(0)	Jct I-494S, Eden Prairie (counterclockwise ex, clockwise entr)
NOTE	I-694 below runs with I-94 for 8 mi. Exit #'s follow I-694.
(27)	Jct I-94W, to St Cloud
28	CR 61, Hemlock Lane
Gas	Citgo, BP
Food	Arby's, Chuck E Cheese, Famous Dave's BBQ, Hops Grill, Joe's Crab Shack, Old Country Buffet, Olive Garden, Potbelly's, Qdoba Mex Rest, Red Lobster, Starbucks, Perkins
Lodg	Courtyard, Hampton Inn, Holiday Inn, Staybridge Suites, Select Inn
Other	Best Buy, Grocery, Lowe's, Tires
29	US 169, N - Osseo, S - Hopkins
29A	US 169S, to Hopkins
29B	US 169N, to Osseo
30	Boone Ave
Other	Discount Tire, Home Depot
31	CR 81
Gas	Super America
Food	Wendy's
Lodg	Ramada Inn
Other	S to Crystal Airport
33	CR 152, Brooklyn Blvd
Gas	Shell, Super America, BP
Food	Subway, Arby's, Embers Rest, Taco Bell
Other	Grocery, Walgreen's
34	to TH 100, Shingle Creek Pkwy
Food	Denny's, Olive Garden, TGI Friday, Perkins
Lodg	AmericInn, Comfort Inn, Country Inn, Days Inn, Extended Stay America, La Quinta Inn♥, Motel 6, Super 8
Other	Best Buy, Target, Tires, Auto Services
35A	TH 100S, Brookdale (counterclockwise ex, clockwise entr)
(35B)	Jct I-94E, Downtown Minneapolis
NOTE	I-694 above runs with I-94 for 8 mi. Exit #'s follow I-694.
35C	TH 252N, to TH 610
Gas	Holiday Station Store, Super America
36	East River Rd, CR 1
37	TH 47, University Ave, to Anoka, Coon Rapids
Gas	Holiday Station Store, SuperAmerica, Shell
Food	Burger King, McDonald's, Pizza
Other	Auto Service, Grocery, Home Depot, PetSmart♥, Walgreen's
38	TH 65, Central Ave, NE Minneapolis, Cambridge
Gas	Holiday Station Store♦, Super America
Food	Subway, Applebee's, Arby's, Denny's, McDonald's, Papa John's, Wendy's
Lodg	Starlite Motel
Other	Auto Services, Discount Tire, Radio Shack, Target
39	CR 44, Silver Lake Rd
Gas	BP, Sinclair
Food	McDonald's, Culver's, Wendy's

Exit	MINNESOTA
40	CR 45, Long Lake Rd, 10th St NW
(41)	Jct I-35W, N to Duluth, S to Downtown Minneapolis
(41A)	Jct I-35W S, to Minneapolis
(41B)	Jct I-35W N, to Duluth
42B	US 10W, to Anoka (counterclockwise ex, clockwise entr)
42A	TH 51, Snelling Ave, Hamline Ave (Left exit)
Gas	Shell
Food	McDonald's
Lodg	Country Inn, Holiday Inn
43A	CR 51, Lexington Ave
Gas	BP♦, Exxon, Sinclair
Food	Burger King, Perkins, Subway, Wendy's
Lodg	Hampton Inn, Hilton Garden Inn, Holiday Inn, Super 8
Other	Auto Services, Grocery, Target
43B	CR 52, Victoria St
45	TH 49, Rice St
Gas	Marathon♦x2, Phillips 66
Food	Subway, Taco Bell, Burger King,
(46)	Jct I-35E S, US 10E, to St Paul
(47)	Jct I-35E, N to Duluth
48	US 61, White Bear Lake
Food	Chili's, McDonald's, Olive Garden
Lodg	Best Western
50	CR 65, White Bear Ave
Gas	Gas4Less, Super America, BP, Shell

Exit	MINNESOTA
Food	Arby's, Applebee's, Bakers Square, Burger King, Caribou Coffee, Chili's, Denny's, IHOP, Old Country Buffet, Perkins, Red Lobster, TGI Friday, Taco Bell, Wendy's
Lodg	Best Western
Other	Auto Services, Best Buy, Circuit City, Goodyear, Petco♥, Maplewood Mall
51	TH 120, Century Ave
Gas	BP, Conoco, Super America♦, Kelly's Corner
Food	Starbucks, Taco Bell
52A	TH 36W, N St Paul, Stillwater
Gas	BP♦
Food	Burger King, DQ, Pizza,
52B	TH 36E, N St Paul, Stillwater
55	TH 5, 34th St N, Stillwater
Gas	Holiday Station Store♦
57	10th St N, CR 10
Gas	Holiday Station Store
Food	Burger King, KFC
Other	Grocery, Mall, Petco♥
(58)	Jct I-94, US 12, St Paul, Madison
(58A)	Jct I-94W, US 12, to St Paul
(58B)	Jct I-94E, US 12, to Madison
(0)	Jct I-494S, End I-694 (clockwise ex, counterclockwise entr)

MINNESOTA

Begin I-694 Loop around Northern/Eastern portion of metro Minneapolis-St Paul, MN.

♦ = Regular Gas Stations with Diesel ▲ = RV Friendly Locations ♥ = Pet Friendly Locations
RED PRINT SHOWS LARGE VEHICLE PARKING/ACCESS ON SITE OR NEARBY BROWN PRINT SHOWS CAMPGROUNDS/RV PARKS

Page 559

INTERSTATE 710

EXIT		CALIFORNIA
		Begin I-710 ByPass around Los Angeles

ⓄCALIFORNIA

23		Valley Blvd, Alhambra
	Gas	ArcoAmPm
	Other	Cal State Univ LA
(22B)		Jct I-10E, San Bernardino Fwy, to San Bernardino (SB)
(22A)		Jct I-10W, San Bernardino Fwy, to Los Angeles (SB)
(22)		Jct I-10, San Bernardino Fwy, to Los Angeles, San Bernardino, Pasadena (NB)
21		Ramona Blvd (NB ex, SB entr)
	Other	Golf Course
20C		Cesar Chavez Ave
	Gas	Star Mart, Shell
	Food	Domino's, Gallo's Grill, Channel Cafe Jack in the Box, Pizza
	Med	W: + Santa Marta Hospital
	Other	Grocery, Cinema, E LA Comm College
20B		3rd St (NB), CA 60, Pomona Fwy, to Pomona, Los Angeles (SB)
	Gas	Shell
	Food	El Pollo Loco, Porky's
	Other	Grocery
20A		CA 60, Pomona Fwy, to Pomona, Los Angeles (NB), 3rd St (SB)
19		Whittier Blvd, Olympic Blvd (SB)
	Gas	Shell
	Food	McDonald's
18B		Whittier Blvd, Olympic Blvd (NB)
(18A)		Jct I-5N, Santa Ana Fwy, to Los Angeles (NB Left exit, SB entr)
(18)		Jct I-5S, to Santa Ana (SB Left exit, NB entr)
17C		Washington Blvd, Commerce (NB)
17B		Atlantic Blvd S (NB) Washington Blvd, Commerce (SB)
	TStop	4560 E Washington: CFN/Commerce Truck Stop (Scales)
17A		Atlantic Blvd N, Bandini Blvd E (NB) Atlantic Blvd, Bandini Blvd (SB)
	FStop	2mi W 3152 Bandini: CFN/Bandini Truck Terminal
	TStop	2mi W 3308 Bandini: West Coast Petroleum
	Food	FastFood/WC Petro
	TWash	WC Petro
	TServ	WC Petro/Tires
15		Florence Ave, CA 42, Bell Gardens
	FStop	on Gage Ave: Webb Truck Service/Chevron
	Gas	Mobil
	Food	El Pollo Loco, IHOP, Jim's Grill, KFC, Little Caesars, Subway, Taco Bell
	Lodg	Ramada Inn
	Other	Grocery, RiteAid, Ralph's, Bicycle Club Casino, Florence Village MH & RV Park▲
13		Firestone Blvd, Cudahy
	FStop	CA 42W to 8330 Atlantic N: Cudahy Fuel Stop
	Gas	ArcoAmPm
	Food	Burger King, Denny's, McDonald's, Panda Express, Starbucks
	Lodg	GuestHouse Inn

EXIT		CALIFORNIA
	Med	E: + to Downey Reg'l Medical Center
	Other	Auto Dealers, Grocery, Radio Shack, Sam's Club, Target
12		Imperial Hwy, CA 90, Lynwood (NB)
	Gas	Shell◆, Chevron◆, Shell, 76
	Food	Church's Chicken, Chinese Cook Rest, El Pollo Loco, McDonald's, Subway/Shell, Long John Silver, Panda Express, Subway, Starbucks, Taco Bell/Pizza Hut
	Lodg	Cozy Motel
	Med	W: + to St Francis Medical Center
	Other	Auto Repair, Auto Zone, Radio Shack, Tires, Walgreen's
12B		Imperial Hwy W, Lynwood (SB)
12A		Imperial Hwy E, Lynwood (SB)
11B		MLK Jr Blvd (SB exit & entr)
(11A)		Jct I-105, Century Fwy, Norwalk, El Segundo (SB)
(11)		Jct I-105, Century Fwy, Norwalk, El Segundo (NB)
10		Rosecrans Ave
	FStop	E to 7201: PacPr/Cool Fuel Center
	Med	E: + to Kaiser Foundation Hospital
9B		Alondra Blvd W, Compton (SB)
9A		Alondra Blvd E, Compton (SB)
	Med	E: + to Suburban Medical Center

EXIT		CALIFORNIA
9		Alondra Blvd, Compton (NB)
	Other	Home Depot, Compton Comm College
8B		CA 91W (NB), CA 91E, Riverside (SB)
8A		CA 91E, Riverside, Artesia Blvd (NB) CA 91W (SB)
7B		Long Beach Blvd N (SB)
	FStop	6230 LB Blvd: Freeway Fuel
7A		Long Beach Blvd S (SB)
7		Long Beach Blvd (NB)
	Gas	Mobil, ArcoAmPm
	Food	Jack in the Box, Taco Bell
	Lodg	Days Inn
6B		Del Amo Blvd West (NB)
6A		Del Amo Blvd East (NB)
6		Del Amo Blvd (SB)
(4)		Jct I-405, San Diego Fwy, N to Carson, S to CA 22, Seal Beach
4		Wardlow Rd (SB exit, NB entr)
	Other	E to Long Beach Airport ✈
3B		Willow St West
	Gas	Chevron, Conoco
	Food	KFC, Popeye's
	Other	Auto Services, Ralph's
3A		Willow St East
	Gas	Chevron
	Med	E: + Pacific Hospital of Long Beach, + Long Beach Memorial Medical Ctr
	Other	Walgreen's
2		CA 1, Pacific Coast Hwy
	FStop	3 blks E to 1603 W PCH: Express C & T/Chevron 1mi W 2130 PCH: Harbor Truck Stop 4 blks E 1670 W PCH: Long Beach Travel Center
	Gas	ArcoAmPm, Shell, Valero◆, 76, Mini Mart, Shell
	Food	Jack in the Box, McDonald's, Tom's Burgers, Winchells
	Lodg	Sea Breeze Motel
1D		Anaheim St (SB)
1C		Shoreline Dr, Pico Ave, Downtown Long Beach, Aquarium, Piers B-E (SB Left exit, NB entr)
1B		Pico Ave, Piers F thru J (SB)
	FStop	Port Petroleum
1A		Harbor Scenic Dr (SB), Piers F - J, S & T, Queen Mary (SB exit, NB entr)
1		Anaheim St (NB)
	FStop	E on Cowles: Speedy Fuel
	Gas	Valero, 76, Shell
	Food	Hong Kong Express, Golden Star, Jack in the Box, Larry's Pizza King, McDonald's
	Lodg	El Capitan Motor Inn, La Mirage Inn, Poolside Inn, Tower Motel, Travel King Motel, Eagle Motel, Highland Motel, Seabreeze Motel
	Med	E: + St Mary Medical Center
(0)		Port of Long Beach, Piers A - J

ⓄCALIFORNIA
Begin I-710 ByPass around Los Angeles

◆ = Regular Gas Stations with Diesel   ▲ = RV Friendly Locations   ♥ = Pet Friendly Locations
RED PRINT SHOWS LARGE VEHICLE PARKING/ACCESS ON SITE OR NEARBY   BROWN PRINT SHOWS CAMPGROUNDS/RV PARKS